BLACKSTO

PRO
R

BLACKSTONE'S GUIDE TO THE

CIVIL PROCEDURE RULES

Second Edition

Editor-in-Chief

Charles Plant, Solicitor, Partner Herbert Smith

Editor

His Honour Judge William Rose

Authors

Julie Brannan, Jane Ching, Derek French,
Peter Jones, Michael Napier,
Craig Osborne, Stuart Sime

BLACKSTONE PRESS LIMITED

First published in Great Britain 1999 by Blackstone Press Limited,
Aldine Place, London W12 8AA. Telephone (020) 8740 2277
www.blackstonepress.com

First edition March 1999
Second edition September 1999

© Blackstone Press Limited, 1999

ISBN: 1 85431 991 4

British Library cataloguing in Publication Data
A CIP catalogue record for this book is available from the British Library

Typeset by Style Photosetting Limited, Mayfield, East Sussex
Printed by Ashford Colour Press, Gosport, Hampshire

All rights reserved. No part of this book may be reproduced or transmitted in any form or by any means, electronic or mechanical, including photo-copying, recording, or any information storage or retrieval system without prior permission from the publisher.

INTRODUCTION TO THE SECOND EDITION

Since the first edition of this guide was published a substantial number of amendments have been made to the Civil Procedure Rules 1998 (CPR), and about 30 new practice directions have been introduced. Further, the number of new forms to supplement the CPR has been increased, and a number of specialist forms have been introduced, particularly for cases in the Admiralty and Commercial Courts, and in the Technology and Construction Court (the new term for the Official Referees' Department). A number of cases have also been reported dealing with aspects of the new Rules. In one of these, *Nascimento* v *Kerrigan* (1999) *The Times*, 23 June 1999, a provision from the new PD Court of Appeal (Civil Division) survived a challenge based on an argument that it was *ultra vires*. However, the controversial provision in CPR, r. 48.7(3), allowing the court to require the disclosure of documents otherwise protected by legal professional privilege in a wasted costs application was declared *ultra vires* (and contrary to arts 6 and 8 of the European Convention on Human Rights for good measure) by Toulson J in *General Mediterranean Holdings SA* v *Patel* [1999] 3 All ER 673.

This Introduction will highlight these developments. In the first section it will give a commentary on how the recent changes affect the text in the first part of this book, chapter by chapter. The second section will consider new topics that were not covered in any of the chapters in the first edition of this guide.

Many of the amendments that have been published since March 1999 are to correct minor drafting errors, and they will not be mentioned in this Introduction.

In this second edition of the guide, all the appendices have been updated, and contain the full text of the CPR, practice directions and protocols as at 1 August 1999. A number of court guides have been published, either in final or draft form. These include the Chancery Guide and the Commercial Court Guide. These are substantial documents: the Commercial Court Guide comprises 183 pages. Accordingly they have not been included in this book. Large numbers of these specialist guides were distributed to the profession by the Court Service in March through to May 1999. The Chancery Division Practice Directions, which appear in the Chancery Guide, are included in appendix 3 of this book.

INTRODUCTION TO THE SECOND EDITION

DEVELOPMENTS AFFECTING CHAPTERS 1 TO 25

The headings and their numbers correspond to the headings in the main text of the book.

CHAPTER 1   THE NEW LANDSCAPE

1.5   The overriding objective

Not surprisingly, many if not most of the procedural cases decided since 26 April 1999 have made reference to the overriding objective of dealing with cases justly. The following discussion will concentrate on cases where the overriding objective played a central part in the decision.

1.5.1   Dealing with cases justly

In addition to the specific matters set out in CPR, r. 1.1, the main concept in the overriding objective means that the primary concern of the court is to do justice. Shutting a litigant out through a technical breach of the rules will not often be consistent with this, because the primary purpose of the civil courts is to decide cases on their merits, not to reject them for procedural default. An example of this is *Jones* v *Telford and Wrekin District Council* (1999) *The Times*, 29 July 1999, where service had been delayed beyond the period of validity because the claimant's solicitors had problems in obtaining psychiatric reports for service with the particulars of claim. The Court of Appeal upheld an extension of time largely because there were no previous authorities dealing with this situation, the Master of the Rolls commenting that the court must not lose sight of the fact that its primary concern was doing justice. Another example is *Chilton* v *Surrey County Council* (24 June 1999 unreported), where the Court of Appeal indicated that dealing with a claim justly involved dealing with the real claim, and allowed the claimant to rely on a revised statement of past and future loss and expense quantifying the claim at about £400,000 rather than the original statement, which indicated a claim value of about £5,000.

1.5.2   Equal footing

Ensuring parties are on an equal footing was relied upon in *Maltez* v *Lewis* (1999) *The Times*, 4 May 1999, in an application designed to prevent the other side from briefing leading counsel for the trial. Neuberger J dismissed the application. Although the CPR confer wide new powers on the courts, they do not extend to depriving a litigant of the right to instruct lawyers of his choice. However, in cases where one of the parties is in a dominant financial position, the court could seek to achieve a level playing field by, for example, ordering that party to prepare the trial bundles. Further, the courts were used to ensuring that trials were fair in cases where one side was more expertly represented than the other.

In *McPhilemy* v *Times Newspapers Ltd* (1999) *The Times*, 26 May 1999, the Master of the Rolls said that if a party wanted the court to restrain the activities of another party with the object of achieving greater equality, the party making the application had to demonstrate they were themselves conducting the proceedings with a desire to limit expense so far as practical. However, the powers of the court to restrain excess did not extend to preventing a party from putting forward allegations which were central to their case. That said, it was open to the court to attempt to control how those allegations were litigated with a view to limiting costs.

1.5.3 Dealing with cases expeditiously and fairly

In *Cadogan Properties Ltd* v *Mount Eden Land Ltd* (29 June 1999 unreported) the court at first instance had made an order for substituted service in circumstances where there were no grounds for doing so. That order was set aside on appeal, with the result that proceedings had not been served and the period of validity had expired. The Court of Appeal relied on CPR, r. 1.1(2)(d), and the need to deal with cases fairly and expeditiously, and also on the need for proportionality (r. 1.1(2)(c)), to justify making an order extending the validity of the originating process. The defendant was aware of the proceedings, and suffered no significant prejudice by the course adopted by the court.

1.5.4 Allotting an appropriate share of the court's resources

In *Stephenson (SBJ) Ltd* v *Mandy* (1999) *The Times*, 21 July 1999 the defendant appealed against an interim order restraining him from breaching a restrictive covenant in his contract of employment. The appeal came before the Court of Appeal on 30 June, and the trial had been fixed for 20 July. Given the short period before the start and the fact that the claimant had given the usual undertaking in damages, the court decided that considering the merits of the appeal would not be in accordance with the overriding objective. Expense would not be saved by hearing the appeal, and given the short time to trial, hearing the appeal would not be a good use of the court's resources. An appeal was also dismissed (with costs on the indemnity basis) in *Adoko* v *Jemal* (1999) *The Times*, 8 July 1999, in very different circumstances, on the ground of allotting to it no more than an appropriate share of the court's resources. In this case the appellant had failed to correct the notice of appeal despite a warning from the respondent that it was seriously defective, and had failed to comply with the directions relating to appeal bundles. The Court of Appeal spent over an hour trying to sort out the mess, and then decided it was inappropriate that any further share of the court's resources should be allocated to the appeal.

1.5.5 Cooperating

In *Chilton* v *Surrey County Council* (24 June 1999 unreported), referred to above at paragraph 1.5.1, the Court of Appeal took against the defendant partly because it seemed to be attempting to take tactical advantage of a mistake by the claimant's solicitors in overlooking to serve the revised statement of past and future loss and expense rather than cooperating with the claimant's solicitors to put matters right.

CHAPTER 2 SCOPE OF THE NEW RULES, TRANSITIONAL PROVISIONS, INTERPRETATION AND RE-ENACTED PROVISIONS

2.1 Scope of the Civil Procedure Rules 1998

The table in CPR, r. 2.1, has been amended to add adoption proceedings under the Adoption Act 1976, s. 66, to the list of civil proceedings to which the CPR do not apply. This is consistent with the fact that family proceedings are also outside the scope of the CPR.

2.2 Transitional Provisions

In *Biguzzi v Rank Leisure plc* (26 July 1999 unreported) the Court of Appeal, dealing with an application to strike out a case for wholesale disregard of the rules, said that under the transitional provisions of the CPR a court could not ignore the fact that until 26 April 1999 the parties had been acting under the old rules, but it was not constrained to reach the same decision as would have been made previously. This approach is underlined by PD 51, para. 14, which provides in effect that the courts will now apply CPR tests on applications heard on or after 26 April 1999. A tougher attitude was expressed by a differently constituted Court of Appeal on the same issue in *Shikari v Malik* (1999) *The Times*, 20 May 1999, where Henry LJ said that litigants who commenced actions before 26 April 1999 could not count on what had been tolerated in the past being tolerated in the future. In a different field, it was decided in *Bajwa v British Airways* (1999) *The Times*, 1 July 1999, predictably, that payments in under the old system are to be treated in the same way as Part 36 payments under the new system.

2.3 Interpretation of the CPR: a procedural code?

Biguzzi v Rank Leisure plc (26 July 1999 unreported) deals with interpretation of the CPR. The Court of Appeal agreed with the judge that the pre-CPR cases on abuse of process in the form of wholesale disregard of court rules (such as *Arbuthnot Latham Bank Ltd v Trafalgar Holdings Ltd* [1998] 1 WLR 1426) are not binding or persuasive authorities on the exercise of the court's discretion under the CPR. The Court of Appeal said the position under the CPR was fundamentally different from under the old system. It pointed out that under r. 1.1 the CPR are a 'new procedural code', and now compliance with court orders would be regarded as more serious than under the previous system. Sometimes, however, a different approach is necessary. In *Harrison v Bloom Camillin* (12 May 1999 unreported) Neuberger J said that although the court had to be careful in relying on old cases, in the context of the application he was dealing with (to set aside a witness summons) some regard was to be paid to the authorities under the old rules.

2.4.5.5 Service outside the jurisdiction

PD RSC ord. 11 supplements the preserved provisions of RSC ord. 11 to be found in sch. 1 to the CPR. Where a claim form is served outside the jurisdiction under the Brussels or Lugano Conventions on a defendant in a European territory of a contracting State (or in Scotland or Northern Ireland), the defendant must acknowledge service within 21 days of service (RSC, ord. 11, r. 1A(2) in CPR, sch. 1). The period is 31 days for defendants in non-European territories of contracting States (r. 1A(3)). Where proceedings are served on a defendant outside the jurisdiction who resides outside the territories of contracting States to the Brussels or Lugano Conventions (where permission to serve has been obtained, or where arts 16 or 17 of the Conventions apply and the defendant is not in the territory of a contracting State), the period for acknowledging service is set out in the table at the end of PD RSC ord. 11. The periods for acknowledging service or filing an admission in the response pack included with a claim form served outside the jurisdiction have to be amended accordingly (PD RSC ord. 11, para. 1.2). After service of the claim form the defence must be served within the number of days set out in the table, but a defendant who has acknowledged service, is given an extra 14 days to file the defence (para. 8.2). Where application notices or orders have to be served out of the jurisdiction, the period for responding to service is seven days less than the periods set out in the table (para. 10.2). Apart from pre-action applications and orders made in undefended cases this latter provision should have a limited application, as CPR, r. 6.5(2), provides that all parties must give an address for service within the jurisdiction.

Where proceedings are to be served outside the jurisdiction without permission, the claim form must include a certificate that the courts of England and Wales have jurisdiction under the Civil Jurisdiction and Judgments Act 1982 and that there are no other pending proceedings between the parties. Precedents for this certificate are given in paras 1.5 to 1.7 of PD RSC ord. 11. Where proceedings are served out of the jurisdiction under art 16 or 17 of either Convention the particulars of claim must be served with, or be included in, the claim form (para. 1.3). Paragraph 3 deals with translations where the defendant is to be served in a country where English is not an official language, and provides that in addition to the claim form and particulars of claim, translations are also required for the forms in the response pack.

CHAPTER 4 PRE-ACTION PROTOCOLS

4.4 Personal Injury Claims Protocol

Paragraph 3.2 of the Pre-action Protocol for Personal Injury Claims has been amended to require claimants to include the name and address of the hospital where the claimant was treated in road traffic accidents, and the claimant's hospital reference number. This information is used in relation to hospital treatment claims under the Highways Act 1980. Paragraph 3.4 has also been amended. It now says that details of the claimant's National Insurance number and date of birth (for the benefits recoupment certificate) should not be included in the letter of claim, but should be sent to the defendant's insurer once the insurer has responded to the letter of claim.

4.4.1 Experts

PD 29, para. 5.5(2), has been toned down to take into account the instruction of experts pursuant to pre-action protocols. The earlier version said that in multi-track cases a party who obtained an expert's report before obtaining a direction about it did so at his own risk as to costs. That remains the same, except there is now a proviso to the effect that this does not apply where the expert evidence is obtained in compliance with a pre-action protocol.

4.6 Future protocols

A new para. 5.4 of PD Protocols says that as and when new protocols are introduced, further PDs will be made specifying the date from which compliance or non-compliance will be taken into account by the court. At the time of writing a professional negligence protocol was being pilot tested, a debt recovery protocol is about to be published, and several protocols are in the process of development.

CHAPTER 5 EARLY STAGES OF A CLAIM

5.2 Allocation of cases to different levels of the judiciary

A new PD 2B sets out the new scheme dealing with how hearings are allocated between the different levels of the judiciary.

The High Court Applications for injunctions, orders for specific performance, freezing orders, search orders, and orders authorising entry on to land to recover, inspect or sample property, must be made to a judge. As before the CPR came into effect, masters and district judges may grant ordinary injunctions in terms agreed by the parties, or connected to charging orders and receivership by way of equitable execution (PD 2B, para. 2.3). Examinations made under freezing orders will usually be conducted by a master (para. 8). Other situations which have to be dealt with by a judge rather than a master or district judge include applications relating to the liberty of a subject, and most applications relating to judicial review (PD 2B, para. 3.1). Paragraph 5.1 contains a list of Chancery applications that should be dealt with by a judge rather than a master or district judge.

Cases will continue to be assigned to individual masters (para. 7.1), although from time to time hearings may be dealt with by other masters or deputies as the circumstances may require. There is no restriction on masters and district judges trying Part 8 claims, but other cases on the multi-track may be tried by a master or district judge only with the consent of the parties (para. 4.1). Hearings to assess damages may be dealt with by masters and district judges without limit (para. 4.2).

County courts Trial jurisdiction of district judges is increased so that they can deal with all small claims and fast track cases, effectively raising their trial jurisdiction to £15,000 (PD 2B, para. 11.1). District judges may also hear cases seeking the recovery of land, the assessment of damages, and Part 8 claims allocated to the multi-track. Injunction and committal applications may only be heard by a district judge if the claim has been allocated to the fast or small claims tracks, or if the financial value is below £15,000 (in cases that have not been allocated at the time of the application), or if the terms have been agreed by the parties, or if the injunction is connected to a charging order or receivership order by way of equitable execution. A district judge may hear any other proceedings with the consent of the parties and the permission of the designated civil judge.

5.5.2 Joinder

PD 5, para. 3, provides that any new party joined to proceedings is entitled to require the party who joined him to supply copies of all the statements of case, written evidence and documents appended or exhibited to those documents. The documents must be served within 48 hours of any written request, and must be supplied without charge.

5.6 Addition and substitution of parties

Although the wording of CPR, r. 19.1, is different from the old Rules of the Supreme Court, ord. 15, r. 6, it is almost certain that there has been no change in the practice regarding adding parties (see *Re Blenheim Leisure (Restaurants) Ltd* (1999) *The Times*, 13 August 1999, per Aldous LJ).

5.7 Special kinds of litigant

A new para. 7 has been added to PD 3 to deal with applications made by vexatious litigants for permission to begin or continue civil proceedings after a 'civil proceedings order' or 'all proceedings order' has been made under the Supreme Court Act 1981, s. 42. There are detailed requirements as to the evidence required in support of such an application, which is dealt with by a High Court judge (PD 2B, para. 3.1(f)).

5.7.3 Children and patients

PD 21 has been amended by the addition of a new para. 2.4A. This provides that a litigation friend acting for a patient is not required to serve any medical evidence dealing with the question whether the party is a patient when the certificate of suitability is served on the person with whom the patient is residing or in whose care he is.

In applications for the court's approval of a settlement on behalf of a person under disability, a new para. 6.3 of PD 21 provides that, except in very clear cases, an opinion on the merits of the settlement or compromise given by counsel or a solicitor acting for the person under disability should be supplied to the court. Unless the instructions are sufficiently set out in the opinion, a copy of the instructions should also be provided to the court. PD 21, para. 1.8, provides that hearings to approve settlements of parties under disability will take place in private unless the court directs otherwise. Buckley J referred to this paragraph in *Beatham* v *Carlisle Hospitals NHS Trust* (1999) *The Times*, 20 May 1999, and then turned it on its head by saying that although the submissions in such applications should normally be heard in private, if the judge decided to approve the settlement, the actual approval would normally be given in open court. He also referred to the public and press being given access to the particulars of claim and defence once approval was given. This is not the general practice in most courts around the country, which generally deal with the entirety of such applications in private. Although the hearing is in private, the order made will usually be considered a public document (*Forbes* v *Smith* (1997) *The Times*, 14 January 1998). The report of *Beatham* v *Carlisle Hospitals NHS Trust* in *The Times* seems to indicate that it is simply a statement of the learned judge's own practice.

5.8.3 Issuing a claim form

The practice direction referred to at 5.8.3 in the main text has now been made (PD 7C) dealing with claims issued in the county court production centre at Northampton. A code of practice will provide for the forms of magnetic media that may be used when delivering data to the centre. Claims that may be issued at the production centre are restricted to claims for specified sums up to £100,000 brought against no more than two defendants, none of whom is to be served out of the jurisdiction, where the claimant is not assisted by legal aid, and where none of the parties is a child or patient. The centre can deal with such cases through service, entry of default judgment and judgment on admissions, and to the registration of judgment and issuing warrants of execution. It can also handle defences, but when this happens it will send a notice to the claimant requiring a reply within 28 days stating whether the claimant wishes the claim to proceed. If no such notification is given, the claim will be stayed, otherwise it will be transferred to the defendant's home court for track allocation and subsequent steps (PD 7C, para. 5.2).

5.8.5 Application to extend time for serving a claim form

As mentioned above (1.5.3), in *Cadogan Properties Ltd* v *Mount Eden Land Ltd* (29 June 1999 unreported) the court at first instance had made an order for substituted service in circumstances where there were no grounds for doing so. That order was set aside on appeal, and the Court of Appeal also said that purported service under the earlier order was a nullity rather than a mere irregularity as it was combined with service outside the jurisdiction (in Guernsey) without first seeking permission. The result was that proceedings had not been served and the period of validity had expired as the Court of Appeal hearing was 11 months after proceedings were issued. The Court of Appeal relied on CPR, r. 1.1(2)(d), and the need to deal with cases fairly and expeditiously, and also on the need for proportionality (r. 1.1(2)(c)), to justify making an order extending the validity of the originating process. The defendant was aware of the proceedings and suffered no significant prejudice by the course adopted by the court.

Under the old rules, the key concept on an application relating to the renewal of process was whether there was a 'good reason' for an extension. In *Jones* v *Telford and Wrekin District Council* (1999) *The Times*, 29 July 1999, service had been delayed beyond the period of validity because the claimant's solicitors had problems in obtaining psychiatric reports for service with the particulars of claim. In an act of supreme generosity the Court of Appeal upheld an extension of time largely because there were no previous authorities dealing with this situation. However, Lord Woolf MR immediately went on to say that if the situation were to occur again it would not amount to a proper reason for not serving proceedings in time.

5.8.6 Claims for the recovery of taxes

A short practice direction, PD 7D, lays down the procedure in claims by the Inland Revenue for the recovery of taxes. In these cases, once a defence is filed the court will fix a date for the hearing without going through the usual track allocation procedure. Normally the claim will be disposed of at the first hearing. Only exceptionally will such cases proceed any further. If they do, the court will give case management directions and may allocate the claim to a track.

5.17 Part 8 procedure

PD 8B lays down a number of rules regulating how to commence claims and appeals under the various preserved provisions in the schedules to the CPR, which form to use as the claim form, and the procedure to be followed. The practice direction is divided into three sections (A, B and C), each of which contains a lengthy list of various types of claims or appeals to which it relates.

Section A covers 46 types of High Court claim, including various claims relating to charging orders, reciprocal enforcement, applications for warrants to arrest witnesses under RSC ord. 79, r. 11(1) in CPR, sch. 1, applications under various statutes, and summary proceedings for possession of land under RSC, ord. 113 in CPR, sch. 1. All these claims are brought using the Part 8 procedure, with such amendments as may be necessary to comply with the rules governing the particular type of application.

Section B covers 50 types of High Court and county court claims. Examples include applications to the High Court for orders to state a case (RSC, ord. 56, r. 8(1) in CPR, sch. 1); a number of specialised appeals and applications to the High Court; various specialised applications pursuant to statute to the county courts, including applications under various provisions of the landlord and tenant legislation and the Consumer Credit Act 1974. For most of these claims the general Part 8 claim form should be used, but the Table setting out the types of applications to which section B applies also gives details of some specialised claim forms that should be used. For example, a claim for summary possession under CCR, ord. 24, r. 1(1) in CPR, sch. 2, must be brought using form N312, and an application for a new tenancy under the Landlord and Tenant Act 1954, s. 24, must be brought using form N397. In section B claims for the recovery of land and similar claims, county court proceedings must be started in the court serving the district where the land is situated (PD 8B, para. B.7). In section B claims, the court will fix a date for the hearing when the claim form is issued (para. B.9), and the claim form must be served at least 21 days before the hearing (para. B.10). The defendant is not required to acknowledge service (para. B.12). At the hearing the court may either dispose of the claim or give case management directions (para. B.13). If a defence has been filed, the court may allocate the case to a track.

Section C contains a list of 14 High Court appeals governed by various provisions of the RSC. These include appeals to the Court of Appeal (RSC, ord. 59, r. 3 in CPR, sch. 1), as well as a number of appeals under specialised statutes. Section C appeals are brought by notice of appeal, and the detailed procedures are laid down in the relevant provisions of CPR, sch. 1 and any specialised practice directions, particularly PD Court of Appeal (Civil Division).

CHAPTER 6   CLAIM FORMS AND PARTICULARS OF CLAIM

6.3.1   Heading

PD 7 has been amended by adding a new para. 4 and subsequent paragraphs have been renumbered. The title of every statement of case must state the number of the proceedings, the court and Division, the full names of all parties (multiple parties being numbered (1), (2) etc.), and whether they are claimants, defendants etc.

6.4.4   Points of law, witnesses and documents

PD 16 has been amended by deleting the former para. 10.3, which was unnecessary as it duplicated para. 16.3. Paragraph 16.3, which remains, says the parties may refer in their statements of case to any point of law, may name witnesses, and attach or serve with their statements of case copies of documents necessary to the claim or defence. Paragraph 9.3, which says that copies of contracts relied upon should be served with the particulars of claim, remains. The same is also true in personal injuries cases regarding medical reports and schedules of past and future expenses and losses (paras 4.2 and 4.3), which must be served with the particulars of claim. Paragraphs 14.1(3) and 14.2 continue to say that any medical report relied upon by the defendant (if available) should be attached to the defence, together with a counter-schedule.

In *McPhilemy* v *Times Newspapers Ltd* (1999) *The Times*, 26 May 1999, the Court of Appeal considered the role of statements of case (which they continued to refer to as 'pleadings'), in the context of defamation actions. Nevertheless, the decision is relevant to pleadings generally. Lord Woolf MR stated that the need for extensive pleadings, including particulars should be reduced by the requirement for the exchange of witness statements. Therefore, in the majority of cases, identification of the documents upon which a party relies, together with copies of that party's witness statements, will make obvious the detail of the nature of the case the other side has to meet. No more than a concise statement of the facts on which a party relies is required. However, statements of case are still required to mark out the parameters of the case that is being advanced by each party, and are crucial to identifying the issues and the extent of the dispute.

6.7 Signature on statements of case

Statements of case and other documents drafted by a legal representative must be signed. Documents drafted by counsel must bear counsel's signature, and those drafted by a solicitor must be signed in the name of the firm (PD 5, paragraph 2.1).

6.8 Form of statements of case etc.

PD 5, para. 2.2, contains a number of requirements for documents that need to be filed at court. They must be on A4 paper, and have a margin at least 3.5 cm wide. They should normally be typed, have pages numbered consecutively, be divided into numbered paragraphs, state numbers in figures, be securely bound, and have marginal references to any documents referred to that have already been filed. Filed documents will be date stamped, and the details will be entered into the court records (PD 5, paras 5.1–5.3). Once filed there are restrictions on removal from the court office without the permission of the court (paras 5.4 and 5.5).

CHAPTER 8 ADDITIONAL CLAIMS AND FURTHER STEPS IN THE CLAIM

8.7 Obtaining further information

In *McPhilemy* v *Times Newspapers Ltd* (1999) *The Times*, 26 May 1999, the Court of Appeal said that all that is required in statements of case, even in complex libel claims, is a concise statement of the facts on which the parties are relying. The need for extensive pleadings and requests for further information has been reduced by the requirement for the exchange of witness statements, and contests over the technicalities of pleading are to be discouraged.

8.8 Amendments to statements of case

An amendment sought at a late stage in an attempt to save a claim that would otherwise have been struck out as disclosing no reasonable claim was refused in accordance with the overriding objective in *Christofi* v *Barclays Bank plc* (unreported 28 June 1999), Court of Appeal. It is not clear how late the application was made, but it may have been during the appeal hearing itself. On the other hand, amendments were allowed in accordance with the overriding objective in *Finley* v *Connell Associates* (9 June 1999 unreported).

CHAPTER 9   APPLICATIONS AND INTERIM ORDERS

9.5.6   Hearings by telephone

Paragraphs 6.1 to 6.3 of PD 23 revise the former provisions dealing with telephone hearings for interim applications. Telephone hearings will not normally be ordered unless all the parties consent. It is no longer an absolute requirement that all parties should be legally represented. If any party is acting in person, the court may still order an application to be dealt with by telephone provided the litigant(s) in person is attended by a responsible person who knows the litigant and can confirm that person's identity to the court (para. 6.3(1)(a)). A 'responsible person' may be a barrister, solicitor, legal executive, doctor, clergyman, police officer or someone of similar status.

9.7.2.5   Exhibits to affidavits and witness statements

There is a new para. 15.4 to PD 32, which says that where on account of their bulk the service of exhibits on other parties would be difficult or impracticable, directions should be sought dealing with arrangements for bringing the exhibits to the attention of the other parties and as to their custody pending trial. PD 32, para. 18.5, has been amended to make it clear that the new para. 15.4 also applies to witness statements.

9.9   General powers regarding interim relief and orders

PD 25C says that at any stage of proceedings, on application by a party or on its own motion, the court may make an order directing accounts to be taken or inquiries to be made. The new PD 40 deals with the practice on taking such accounts and conducting such inquiries. When making such an order the court may also at the same time or later give directions as to how the account is to be taken or the inquiry conducted (PD 40, para. 1.1). Among the directions that may be made are the following:

   (a)   that the relevant books of account shall be evidence of their contents, subject to the parties having the right to make objections (para. 1.2);
   (b)   that an accounting party must make out his account and verify it by exhibiting it to an affidavit or witness statement (para. 2(1)); and
   (c)   that, if appropriate, and at any stage in the proceedings, the parties must serve points of claim and points of defence (para. 5).

A party alleging that an account drawn by an accounting party is inaccurate (or making similar allegations) must give written notice of the objections to the accounting party (para. 3.1). These objections must give full particulars, specify the grounds on which it is alleged the account is inaccurate, and be verified by a statement of truth (or exhibited to an affidavit or witness statement).

Section 2 of PD 40 makes provision for the application of RSC, ord. 44 in CPR, sch. 1 (which deals with proceedings under Chancery Division judgments and orders) to judgments and orders made in the county courts.

9.13 Summary judgment

In CPR, r. 24.3(2), which deals with cases excluded from summary judgment as against defendants, the category relating to claims for possession of residential property has been clarified to make it clear that this relates to tenants and persons holding over who are protected by the Rent Act 1977 or the Housing Act 1988. A further category has been added, relating to contentious probate proceedings.

CHAPTER 10 INTERIM INJUNCTIONS, FREEZING INJUNCTIONS AND SEARCH ORDERS

A new r. 25.11 of the CPR provides that if the court has granted an interim injunction, and the claim is struck out for non-payment of the fees payable at allocation or listing, the interim injunction will lapse 14 days after the claim is struck out. However, if within that 14-day period the claimant applies to reinstate the claim, the injunction will remain in force until the hearing of that application (unless the court otherwise orders).

10.2.4 The order and related matters

The new form of penal notice to be inserted in injunction orders etc. is, by PD 40B, para. 9.1;

If you the within-named [   ] do not comply with this order you may be held to be in contempt of court and imprisoned or fined, or [in the case of a company or corporation] your assets may be seized.

CHAPTER 11 CASE MANAGEMENT

11.3 Transfer to appropriate court

Paragraph 10.2(10) of PD 26 has been replaced. The former provision said that a feeder court could as an exceptional measure retain a multi-track case rather than transferring it to a civil trial centre. The new provision says that a feeder court may retain a multi-track case where it is envisaged there may need to be more than one case management conference and the parties or their legal advisers are located inconveniently far from the designated civil trial centre. The situation is under review, and it is possible that more case management of multi-track cases will be undertaken by feeder courts once the initial impact of the CPR has been assessed.

11.4 Allocation

On filing an allocation questionnaire the claimant is required to pay a fee of £80. The fee is also payable where the court dispenses with the need to file allocation questionnaires. In these cases the fee is payable within 14 days of the dispatch of the notice of allocation to a track. In cases which are automatically allocated to a track, the fee is payable within 28 days of the filing of the last defence. In claims proceeding only on a counterclaim the fee is payable by the defendant. No fee is payable in Part 8 claims. Rule 3.7 of the CPR provides that claims will be struck out automatically if allocation or listing fees are not paid after due warning, which the court gives by sending the claimant a form N173. A new PD 3B says that if a claim is struck out, the court will send the defendant a notice which will explain the effect of r. 25.11, which provides that any interim injunction will cease having any effect after 14 days unless the claimant applies to reinstate the claim.

PD 26 now contains a note reminding practitioners that PD 43, para. 4.5(1), requires parties in claims outside the financial scope of the small claims track to file and serve estimates of their costs at the same time as they file their allocation questionnaires.

An explanatory note has been added to PD 26, paragraph 7.4, to the effect that if, in relation to a claim with a value above the small claims limit of £5,000, the defendant makes an admission before allocation reducing the amount in dispute below £5,000, the normal track for the claim will be the small claims track. Where such an admission is made, it may be in the interests of the claimant to apply for judgment on the admission under CPR Part 14 in order to recover costs, although even in such an application recovery of costs will be discretionary (see CPR r. 44.5(3)).

11.8 Sanctions

The Court of Appeal in *Biguzzi* v *Rank Leisure plc* (26 July 1999 unreported), in affirming a decision to strike out for wholesale disregard of the court's rules, commented that striking out would not always be the correct approach. Under the CPR the court has much wider powers than before which it could use to deal with cases fairly without resorting to Draconian remedies such as striking out. These include making orders for indemnity costs, for paying money into court, and awarding interest at higher or lower rates. By a proper exercise of case management powers it should be possible for the courts to ensure parties do not disregard timetables, whilst producing a just result. In *Chilton* v *Surrey County Council* (24 June 1999 unreported) the Court of Appeal was dealing with a case where a substantially revised (and increased!) statement of past and future loss and expense was served 12 days before trial. The fact that the real value of the claim was substantially greater than the figures stated in the original schedule of loss and damage was revealed many months previously when an employment expert's report was disclosed, and the revised statement had not been served through a mistake by the claimant's solicitors, who believed it had already been served. The Court of Appeal disapproved of the defendant's tactics, but also commented that if the revised statement was to be excluded it was for the defendant to point to details of any prejudice it might suffer if permission for late service was to be granted.

Failure to comply with an unless order was considered in *Newton* v *Dorset Travel Service Ltd* (5 May 1999 unreported). The defendants had sought additional time for serving their psychiatric evidence in a personal injuries claim, and an order had been made to the effect that unless they served their report by Friday, 29 January 1999 they would be debarred from calling psychiatric evidence. There were delays in obtaining their report, which disclosed a marked disagreement with the claimant's expert evidence, and it was sent by fax to the claimant's solicitors first thing on Monday 1 February. The judge refused them a one-day extension, saying the rules had to be obeyed. Although the defendant's solicitors should have pushed their expert for the report, they had not deliberately flouted the order, the extension sought was minimal, and the recognised need to enforce orders with vigour had to be tempered by proportionality. It was held that an extension should have been granted. On the other hand, if a

INTRODUCTION TO THE SECOND EDITION

party holds on to a report for some time, and then serves it at the last minute, permission to adduce the report may well be refused. In *Baron* v *Lovell* (27 July 1999 unreported) the defendant obtained a medical report (which did not differ very greatly from that produced for the claimant) in February 1999, but did not disclose it until June 1999, on the day the trial was fixed for hearing in August 1999. The defendant was in substantial breach of the direction on disclosure of medical evidence. The Court of Appeal held that in the circumstances, particularly the narrow difference between the two sides' medical evidence, the defendant had been correctly refused permission to rely on any medical evidence. *O'Hara* v *Rye* (12 February 1999 unreported) was a case under the old system, but the judgment of the Court of Appeal makes express reference to the impact of the CPR. Points that emerge from the case include stressing the importance, when a directions timetable becomes impossible to adhere to, of disclosing all material difficulties to the court so that the court can give directions that are realistic, and where an unless order gives a bias to a case which is inappropriate, the court is entitled to exercise its discretion by refusing to strike out.

11.8.1 Non-compliance with directions

PD 40B, para. 8.2, lays down formulae for drafting unless orders. These are in the following forms (to be adapted as necessary):

(a) 'Unless the claimant serves his list of documents by 4.00 p.m. on Friday, 22 January 1999 his claim will be struck out and judgment entered for the defendant.' This is the preferred form.

(b) 'Unless the claimant serves his list of documents within 14 days of service of this order . . .'. This should be used where the defaulting party did not attend the hearing where the order was made.

CHAPTER 12 SMALL CLAIMS

PD 27, para. 3.2, has been amended to take account of the Lay Representatives (Right of Audience) Order 1999 (SI 1999/1225). Generally, a lay representative will be unable to represent a party where the client does not attend the hearing, and lay representation is not permitted at any stage after judgment or on any appeal brought against any decision by the district judge in the proceedings. However, the court does have a general discretion to allow lay representation in these generally excluded circumstances.

There has been an amendment to the CPR, r. 27.14(2), to provide that the fixed costs payable even in a small claims track case are those which are payable under Part 45, or would be payable under Part 45 if that Part applied to the case. This change was necessary because the fixed costs rules in Part 45 apply only to claims for specified sums of money and to claims for the delivery of goods (r. 45.1(2)). Part 45 does not apply, for example, to unspecified money claims (most damages claims), and the plain intention is that the same fixed costs should be recoverable in all types of small claims track cases.

CHAPTER 14 MULTI-TRACK

14.6 Listing questionnaires

PD 28 now contains a note after para. 6.1(4) reminding practitioners that PD 43, para. 4.5(2), says that costs estimates must be filed and served at the same time as listing questionnaires are filed.

A fee of £200 must be paid by the claimant on filing the listing questionnaire in a fast track case. In a multi-track case the listing fee is £300. If listing questionnaires are dispensed with, the fee is payable within 14 days of dispatch of the notice of the trial date or period. In cases which are proceeding on a counterclaim alone the fee is payable by the defendant. The listing fee is refundable if the party who paid it gives written notice to the court at least seven days before the trial (or before the trial date has been fixed) that the claim has been settled or discontinued.

CHAPTER 15 DISCLOSURE

15.8.2 Documents referred to in statements of case etc.

A new para. 7 has been added to PD 31 on disclosure of documents. The new paragraph makes reference to PD 35 for provisions dealing with applications to inspect documents mentioned in experts' reports. Rule 31.14(3) of the CPR says that a party may inspect a document referred to in an expert's report, but that this right to inspect is subject to r. 35.10(4). By r. 35.10(3) the substance of an expert's instructions must be referred to in the expert's report. It is then provided by r. 35.10(4) that those instructions are not privileged, but the court will not order disclosure of letters of instruction unless there are reasonable grounds to believe the expert's statement of instructions is inaccurate or incomplete. These rules are confirmed by PD 35, para. 3.

15.10.4 Restriction on use of an inadvertently disclosed privileged document

Breeze v *John Stacey and Sons Ltd* (1999) *The Times*, 8 July 1999, confirms the point made in the first edition of this work that the CPR do not affect the principles applied in cases of inadvertent disclosure of privileged documents.

CHAPTER 16 EVIDENCE, INCLUDING WITNESS STATEMENTS

16.2 Court's power to control evidence

In *Grobbelaar* v *Sun Newspapers Ltd* (1999) *The Times*, 12 August 1999, the Court of Appeal decided that r. 32.1 of the CPR means what it says and gives the court a discretion to exclude otherwise admissible evidence, provided doing so accords with the overriding objective. In particular, in a civil trial by jury, the judge has a discretion to exclude potentially prejudicial evidence.

16.6 Form of witness statements

Paragraph 17.1 of PD 32 has been amended to say that the heading of witness statements must follow the requirements in PD 7, para. 4 (see note 6.8 above), and indicating that multiple parties may be identified in the heading in the form 'AB (and others)'. The reference in PD 32, para. 19.1(1), to the margins in witness statements needing to be 3.5 cm should be read as meaning at least 3.5 cm (see the new PD 5, para. 2.2(1)).

16.8 Late service of witness statements

In *Cowland* v *District Judges of the West London County Court* (20 July 1999 unreported) the claimants were occupiers of premises, and alleged that their goods, which were taken by the county court bailiffs pursuant to a judgment against a third party, were sold at an undervalue. The key issue on liability was whether the original judgment creditor had given notice to the court before the sale that the goods did not belong to the original judgment debtor. On the morning of the trial the claimant sought to introduce evidence from the original judgment creditor's solicitor on the question whether he had given notice to the court. It was plain that this evidence went to the heart of the main issue, and was likely to be highly persuasive if not conclusive on the issue. The trial judge refused permission. An appeal was allowed. The solicitor was not and had not been retained by either party to the present proceedings, and there was no property in a witness. It had therefore been open to both sides to seek his testimony, and the reality was that both sides were at fault in not seeking his evidence earlier. Excluding his evidence prevented the claimants from adducing evidence crucial to their case, thus preventing justice from being done. The Court of Appeal said the defendants had not been prejudiced in any way, despite referring to the fact that if they knew of the evidence it was possible they could have protected themselves by making a Part 36 payment. This did not generate material prejudice, because it could be guarded against by an appropriate costs order.

Mealey Horgan plc v *Horgan* (1999) *The Times*, 6 July 1999, dealt with the more usual situation of one party serving its witness statements slightly late (in this case two weeks later than that required by directions as extended, and six weeks before trial). Buckley J said that making an order depriving the defaulting party of its evidence would be out of proportion to the default. Such a response would be appropriate only if there had been deliberate flouting of court orders, or inexcusable delay which would otherwise result in the adjournment of the trial.

On the other hand, permission to serve the statement of one witness late was refused in *Coore* v *Chief Constable of Leicestershire* (10 May 1999 unreported). However, although there are comments that the case was based on the exercise of the discretion to allow late service, the main reason given is to the effect that the witness did not address the essential issue in the case.

CHAPTER 17 HEARSAY AND NON-VERBAL EVIDENCE

Exceptions where there is no need to serve a hearsay notice in order to comply with the Civil Evidence Act 1995, s. 2, have been expanded to include an affidavit or witness statement which is to be used at trial but which does not contain hearsay evidence (CPR, r. 33.3(aa)). The new PD 33 deals with transitional provisions for claims commenced before 31 January 1997, the commencement date for the Civil Evidence Act 1995, and to take into account s. 16(3A) of the Act. By PD 33, paras 2 and 3, the 1995 Act will in general apply even to claims commenced before 31 January 1997, but the old law and practice as set out in the Civil Evidence Act 1968 and the old rules will apply to claims in which directions or orders were given as to the evidence to be given at the trial, or where the trial or hearing began before 26 April 1999. It is unclear from para. 3 whether the date of 26 April 1999 refers only to the beginning of the trial or hearing or to both that and the date when directions or orders as to evidence have been made. However, it is almost certainly intended that the

INTRODUCTION TO THE SECOND EDITION

old law should apply to directions and orders made before 31 January 1997.

CHAPTER 18 DEPOSITIONS AND COURT ATTENDANCE BY WITNESS

18.3.3 Examination out of the jurisdiction — Letters of request

Rule 34.13(4) of the CPR has been amended, and now says it is the country where the witness is located that may grant permission for an examination to be conducted by a person appointed by the High Court. The earlier version of the rule limited the approval to the country to which the letter of request was sent. PD 34, para. 5.2, has also been amended, and now says an application for an order for the issue of a letter of request should always be made under the procedure in Part 23 (issue of an application notice supported by written evidence). The earlier version said that applications for letters of request made before proceedings were commenced had to be brought by issuing a Part 8 claim (and the old sub-paras 1.4(3) and (4) have accordingly been deleted from PD 8). There is a new para. 5.6, which deals with applications to vary or discharge orders for letters of request if made without notice. Paragraphs 6.1 to 6.8 of PD 34 have been redrafted, again to ensure that all applications to give effect to requests made by foreign courts for the examination of witnesses living in England or Wales are made using the Part 23 procedure (rather than the procedure under Part 8). A new PD 34B deals with calculating the fees and the recoverable expenses of examiners of the court.

CHAPTER 19   EXPERTS AND ASSESSORS

19.1 Introduction

PD 16, para. 4.3, provides that a claimant bringing a claim for personal injuries who is relying on the evidence of a medical practitioner must serve with (or attach to) the particulars of claim a report from the expert about the alleged personal injuries. There are often time problems in complying with this requirement. An example is *Knight* v *Sage Group plc* (28 April 1999 unreported). By the time proceedings had to be served the claimant had a general practitioner's report, but did not have satisfactory evidence from a consultant psychiatrist. She therefore served her proceedings with just the general practitioner's report. The defendant applied to strike out the claim on the ground that the medical report did not comply with the rules. The Court of Appeal held that the report served was no more than a preliminary report, and did not come within the definition of a 'medical report' required by the CPR. However, the court went on to say that the report was capable of satisfying the requirements of the CPR at least for the initial stages of the proceedings. The court made an order requiring the claimant to file and serve further medical evidence within three months.

19.2 Duties of experts and the court's power to restrict expert evidence

In *Stevens* v *Gullis* (27 July 1999 unreported) one of the experts refused to sign a joint memorandum after a without prejudice meeting and generally seemed not to understand his duties to the court, despite having been provided with a copy of PD 35. The Court of Appeal held that the judge had been right to control the evidence by ruling that the expert could not give expert evidence, and the Court of Appeal held that the expert should not be allowed to give factual evidence either. Remarkably, the effect of the decision was to deprive the party instructing the expert of its expert evidence.

19.7 Single joint expert

Knight v *Sage Group plc* (28 April 1999 unreported) was a substantial personal injuries case, which was clearly suitable for the multi-track . The court declined to make an order in the early stages of the proceedings for the joint instruction of a single expert given objections from the defendant. However, the Court of Appeal commented that on any future hearing for directions the judge would want to know whether the defendant was in fact complying with the requirement to cooperate.

CHAPTER 20   OFFERS TO SETTLE

20.5.3.3 Service

There is a small change to CPR, r. 36.6(3). Previously it said the court would serve a Part 36 payment notice unless the offeror informed the court he *had served* the notice. The new version says the exception applies where the offeror informs the court he will serve the notice, making clear that service takes place after the money is paid into court.

20.7.2 Failure to beat a Part 36 offer

Rule 36.20(1)(b) of the CPR has been corrected to make it clear that the provision (which deals with the costs consequences of failing to obtain a more advantageous judgment than the terms of the offer) is referring to a defendant's Part 36 offer. By omitting the word 'defendant's' it had been suggested that the original draft of r. 36.20(1)(b) extended also to the effect on a claimant of failing to achieve a result better than the claimant's own Part 36 offer.

Bajwa v *British Airways plc* (1999) *The Times*, 1 July 1999 was a personal injuries claim where the defendant paid into court the sum of £2,500 at a time when the CRU certificate was in the sum of £2,573.34. It was held that the effective payment in was these two sums added together, £5,073.34. At trial the claimant recovered £4,874.43. An appeal against the CRU certificate resulted in the recoupable benefits being reduced to £142.80. The defendant therefore had to pay £142.80 to the Secretary of State and £4,731.63 to the claimant. However, the important figures for costs purposes were the judgment (£4,874.43), which was less than the effective payment in (£5,073.34). The correct order on costs was that the claimant should recover her costs to the last date for accepting the payment in, but had to pay the defendant's costs thereafter.

CHAPTER 21   CHANGE OF SOLICITOR

PD 42 supplements CPR, Part 42, on giving notice of change of solicitor and related matters. PD 42, para. 1.3, provides that a solicitor appointed to represent a party only as an advocate is not to be regarded as acting for that party within the meaning of Part 42. The new form N434 should be used for giving notice of any change.

CHAPTER 23   TRIAL

23.2.2   Multi-track listing

There is a new practice direction dealing with fixing trial dates and windows in High Court multi-track claims. It excludes Admiralty, Commercial and TCC claims. Trial windows are supposed to be up to a week, but the demands on the Royal Courts of Justice are such that this cannot be adhered to. Consequently, the court may:

(a) direct that the trial is not to begin earlier than a specified date; and/or
(b) direct that the trial date be within a specified period; and/or
(c) specify the trial date or window.

If either option (a) or (b) is used, the court will also direct the parties to attend upon the listing officer to fix the trial date or window. The claimant (unless another party agrees to do it) must within the next seven days of a date directed by the court for the purpose take out an appointment with the listing officer and give notice of the appointment to the other parties. At the listing hearing the trial will be fixed in accordance with the main direction.

23.2.4   Availability of experts and listing

Two important concepts are that trials should be listed as soon as practicable, and once fixed should not be adjourned unless absolutely necessary. A party that wants to change experts in the run-up to trial, or to instruct an expert for the first time shortly before trial, is obliged to instruct experts who will report in sufficient time and be available for the trial. In *Rollinson v Kimberley Clark Ltd* (15 June 1999 unreported) an expert instructed about six months before trial was unable to attend trial. On an application made about three months before trial the judge refused to break the fixture, and her decision was upheld by the Court of Appeal. A decision of great practical importance is *Matthews v Tarmac Bricks and Tiles Ltd* (1999) *The Times*, 1 July 1999. There had been some difficulty in fixing the trial, and the court convened a listing hearing which was attended by a young member of the Bar on behalf of the defendant. Counsel had been provided with a list of unavailable dates, which included 15 July. The judge asked why the defendant's two experts were unavailable on 15 July, to which counsel replied she had no instructions. The judge then said: 'I can do two things. I can fix 15 July or I can adjourn this matter so that you can make phone calls and then I'll fix 15 July. Which would you prefer?' Given the judge was going to fix the trial for 15 July anyway, Counsel replied 'You might as well fix 15 July'. On being informed of the result the defendant's solicitors then wrote to the court saying they would like permission to appeal, but did not tell the court why their experts were unavailable. The judge refused permission, and did not list the matter for a hearing. In fact one expert was booked to be on holiday, and the other was due to appear as a witness in another trial. The Master of the Rolls said it was not enough simply to tell the court dates experts could not attend, but that reasons had to be given as well. Even if the actual reasons had been given, it did not follow that the court would not have still listed the case for 15 July. The two courts could have consulted together to produce trial timetables to allow the double-booked expert to attend both trials. An effort should have been made with the other doctor to change his holiday plans: doctors holding themselves out as practising in the medico-legal field had to be prepared to arrange their affairs to meet the commitments of the courts where that was practical. The case clearly underlines the importance of having someone familiar with the case and fully briefed attend at case management hearings (see CPR, r. 29.3(2)). The Master of the Rolls in this case was expressly concerned to stamp out the causes of delays in personal injuries cases, which is plainly desirable. However, expecting busy consultants to break their summer holiday plans seems to be pushing things too far: July may be regarded as a working month by the legal profession, but for almost everyone else in society it is at the peak of the holiday season. Also, coordinating trial timetables between different courts is often easier in theory than practice. It may be that the Master of the Rolls went as far as he did because of the history in this case of difficulties in fixing the trial, and the decision should not be seen as always applicable in other cases.

23.4 Statements of issues

Guidance was given in *St Albans Court Ltd* v *Daldorch Estates Ltd* (1999) *The Times*, 24 May 1999, on including case summaries in cases of any size, and identifying essential reading for the judge in the skeleton argument. Counsel will not always be permitted to take the judge through the documents at the start of the trial.

23.7.2 Open court or in private

A new para. 1.4A has been added to PD 39 to the effect that in deciding whether to hold a hearing in public or private the judge must have regard to art. 6(1) of the European Convention on Human Rights. This requires, with certain exceptions, that generally court hearings must be in public. The list of hearings which are normally held in private set out in para. 1.5 has been extended to include applications under the Variation of Trusts Act 1958 where there are no facts in dispute.

23.7.3 Trial location

There has been a slight amendment to PD 29, para. 10.1, which now says that multi-track trials will normally take place at a civil trial centre, but they may be held elsewhere if that is appropriate given the needs of the parties and the availability of court resources.

23.7.4 Sittings

There is also a new PD 39B, which deals with the sittings of the High Court and Court of Appeal, and with vacation arrangements for the High Court (vacation arrangements for the Court of Appeal are dealt with in the Court of Appeal Practice Direction). The four sittings are:

Michaelmas: from 1 October to 21 December.
Hilary: from 11 January to the Wednesday before Easter Sunday.
Easter: from the second Tuesday after Easter Sunday to the Friday before the spring holiday at the end of May.
Trinity: from the second Tuesday after the spring holiday to 31 July.

Where a claim proceeding in London needs to be heard immediately or promptly during a vacation, an application should be made for the claim to be heard in vacation (PD 39B, para. 3.1(2)). For proceedings in the

Queen's Bench Division, para. 3.5 lists 10 types of application which may be listed for hearing before a master during August without first seeking permission. They include applications for extensions of time, setting aside judgment and approval of settlements. Likewise, Queen's Bench Division appeals to the judge during August will generally be limited to the 10 listed types of hearing. Applications to the judge in the Queen's Bench Division during August should be restricted to matters of real urgency (para. 3.3(2)). During September all types of applications and appeals may be made in the Queen's Bench Division, but a September hearing date may not be obtainable. Where it is important to have a Queen's Bench Division application or appeal heard in August or September it is wise to include a request with the papers to have the application marked 'fit for August' or 'fit for vacation' (see para. 3.3(3)).

In the Chancery Division masters deal with all types of application throughout the summer, with deputies dealing with much of the work during this period (para. 3.4). For High Court district registry cases circuit arrangements may be made for sittings in vacation (para. 3.2).

23.8.1 Representation of companies at hearings

Paragraphs 5.2 to 5.5 of PD 39 are new. They deal with the representation of companies and corporations at hearings by employees (which is of some importance following the abolition of the rule that companies have to act by solicitors in the High Court). Rule 39.6 of the CPR provides that a company or corporation may appear at a hearing through a duly authorised employee provided the court gives permission. PD 39, para. 5.3, says that permission should usually be given unless there is some particular and sufficient reason why it should be withheld. Permission should generally be sought on an occasion prior to the hearing, but may be granted at the hearing itself. Permission may be sought informally. Like all representatives, the employee's status has to be included in the written statement of representatives pursuant to PD 39, para. 5.1. In this case the statement must include the full name and registered number of the company or corporation, the employee's position within the company, and details of the board or other authorisation for the employee to act for the company.

23.8.2 Transcripts

Paragraphs 6.3 to 6.5 of PD 39 are also new, and deal with obtaining transcripts of proceedings on payment of authorised charges.

23.8.3 Mortgage possession claims

Regarding claims by mortgagees against individuals for possession of land, where the hearing is listed to be held in private (as will be normal), a new para. 1.15 of PD 39 provides that any fact which needs to be proved by the evidence of witnesses may be proved by evidence in writing.

23.8.4 Submissions of no case to answer

In *Mullan* v *Birmingham City Council* (1999) *The Times*, 29 July 1999, the learned deputy High Court judge felt his new case management powers under the CPR were sufficiently wide to allow him to rule on a submission of no case to answer without putting the defendant to its election whether to call any evidence. The old authorities, such as *Alexander* v *Rayson* [1936] 1 KB 169, were to the effect that generally the defendant should be required to elect whether to make the submission or to call evidence. There were several reasons, such as the difficulties created when trials continued after unsuccessful submissions of no case, and the need to have a complete retrial if a successful submission were to be overturned on appeal. It is hard to see why the practical reasons for the earlier practice have been overtaken by the new rules.

23.9 Drawing up judgment after trial

Most of CPR, Part 40, deals with technical points on drawing up and entering judgments and orders. A new PD 40B supplements these provisions. Rule 40.3(1) of the CPR provides that generally orders and judgments will be drawn up by the court, but the court may order a party to do so, and of course consent orders will be drawn by the parties. Where the court orders a party to draw up an order, this must be done within seven days (r. 40.3(3)). Paragraphs 1.1 to 1.5 of PD 40B supplement these provisions dealing with variations such as orders to be drawn up by a party subject to checking by a court, and orders to be drawn up by the court in terms to be agreed by the parties.

23.9.1 Procedure

Paragraphs 5 and 6 of PD 40B deal respectively with technical requirements where final judgment is given in cases where social security benefits recoupment applies, and where interim payments have been made. Paragraph 10 deals with judgments in foreign currency, and para. 12 with judgments by instalments. Paragraph 14 gives examples of forms that can be used for judgments, and lays down certain matters to be included in the preamble of a judgment, such as the questions put to a jury and their findings, any orders made during the trial regarding the use of evidence, and the findings of the judge in respect of each head of damage in a personal injury case.

23.9.2.4 Provisional damages

PD 41 lays down a model form of provisional damages judgment. This includes the filing of a case file of documents to be preserved until the expiry of the period (or any extension) during which the claimant is entitled to apply for further damages if the specified disease develops or the specified deterioration is suffered. The documents that will usually be included in the case file are the judgment, the statements of case, a transcript of the judge's oral judgment, all medical reports relied upon, and a transcript of the claimant's own evidence in so far as the judge regards it as necessary (PD 41, para. 3.2). The PD also deals with entering consent orders for provisional damages (para. 4, which is similar to the existing practice) and default judgments (which can only be entered with the court's permission, with the master or district judge having to decide whether the case is an appropriate one for a provisional damages award: para. 5).

23.9.2.5 Structured settlements

PD 40C lays down the procedure to be followed where a structured settlement is used following the compromise of a claim or after trial. If the matter follows the compromise of the claim an application needs to be made under Part 23 for the entry of a consent order, which may be combined with seeking the court's approval if the claimant is a child or patient. The application should be accompanied by a draft order. Annexed to the practice direction are sample orders. The practice direction recognises at para. 1.6 that it will usually be important to get an early hearing date as the annuity rate applicable to the structure may be open only for a limited time. If the claimant is not a child or patient, a consent order may be made without a hearing (para. 1.5).

23.9.2.6 Tomlin orders

Consent judgments and orders must be expressed as being 'by consent' (CPR, r. 40.6(7)(b)) and signed by the legal representatives for each party (or by the litigants in person where this is allowed). PD 40B, para. 3.4, provides that the signatures of the legal representatives may be those of the solicitors or counsel acting for the parties. By para. 3.5 where a consent order is in the form of a stay of proceedings on agreed terms recorded in a schedule (a Tomlin order), any direction for the payment of money out of court or for the payment and assessment of costs must be contained in the body of the order and not the schedule. The reason is that these two forms of direction require action on the part of the court, and must therefore be included in the public part of the order and not concealed in the schedule. If the amount of costs has been agreed this can be included in the schedule.

23.9.3 Correction of errors and appeals

Paragraphs 4.1 to 4.5 of PD 40B deal with applications to correct errors in judgments and orders. If the error is obvious, the court may deal with the application without notice. Opposed applications will normally be listed before the judge who gave the judgment or made the order.

CHAPTER 24   COSTS

24.7.1 Summary assessment

Where a substantial dispute arises on the sum claimed in a successful party's statement of costs, it would be appropriate to refer the matter for a detailed assessment (*R* v *Cardiff County Council* (11 June 1999 unreported), where there were disputes about the hourly rate and whether it infringed the indemnity principle).

24.7.3 Discretion

A new sub-para. 4.4(2) has been inserted into PD 44 so as to provide that the general rule that the court will make a summary assessment of costs after hearings that take less than a day does not apply to a mortgagee's costs in a mortgage possession claim. Instead, the principles explained in *Gomba Holdings (UK) Ltd* v *Minories Finance Ltd (No. 2)* [1993] Ch 171 continue to apply, so that the court will give effect to a contractual right of a mortgagee to indemnity-basis costs in respect of both litigation and non-litigation costs, and for those costs to be recovered or retained out of the mortgaged property. Such costs will be subject to a detailed assessment, if not agreed.

24.12 Wasted costs orders

In *General Mediterranean Holdings SA* v *Patel* [1999] 3 All ER 673 it was held that CPR, r. 48.7(3), which purported to give the court power on a wasted costs application to order the disclosure of privileged documents, is *ultra vires*. *Fahani* v *Merc Property Ltd* (1999) *The Times*, 19 May 1999, emphasised the point that wasted costs applications should be summary in nature. If a wasted costs hearing will be longer than the substantive hearing, the proportionality concept will be infringed.

CHAPTER 25 APPEALS

On 19 April 1999 a very detailed PD Court of Appeal (Civil Division) was released. It consolidates, with some amendments, all the principal practice directions governing appeals to the Court of Appeal. It covers the procedure for seeking permission to appeal and the test that is applied to such applications (paras 2.1 to 2.19). Paragraph 2.19.1 provides that where there has already been one unsuccessful appeal against a decision being challenged, permission to appeal further to the Court of Appeal should only be granted if the case raises a point of principle or practice or if there is some other compelling reason why the case should be considered by the Court of Appeal. This provision has been considered in a number of cases. In one, *Nascimento* v *Kerrigan* (1999) *The Times*, 23 June 1999, it survived a challenge based on an argument that it was *ultra vires*. In another, *Piglowski* v *Piglowski*, (1999) *The Times*, 25 June 1999, Lord Hoffmann in the House of Lords referred to the expense of repeated appeals and the need to maintain a sense of proportionality in the appeals process, which would be assisted by the operation of para. 2.19.1.

Paragraph 3 is a greatly expanded section dealing with skeleton arguments. Paragraph 4 deals with case management of appeals, including the role of supervising Lords Justices and their power to give directions concerning the progress of appeals on their own initiative. Paragraph 5 deals with the procedure on appeals to the Court of Appeal, including the contents of notices of appeal (para. 5.3), lists of appeals (which are set out in annex F of the direction), setting down of appeals, respondents' notices, time estimates and appeal bundles. Paragraph 6 deals with listing, hear-by dates and fixtures. Paragraph 7 contains guidance on various matters relating to documents, particularly points that are common sources of problems in appeals. Paragraph 8 deals with the procedure when there are litigants in person, and para. 9 deals with handing down of judgments. Paragraph 10 covers matters such as citing authorities and Hansard, renewal of application for permission to apply in judicial review cases, dismissal of appeals by consent, allowing appeals by consent, structured settlements and some other miscellaneous matters. Paragraph 11 deals with ADR arrangements; para. 12 deals with supplying documents from the Civil Appeals Office files; para. 13 with hearings in private; and para. 14 gives guidance for seeking references to the European Court of Justice. Various forms (and other information) are included in the annexes to the practice direction. These include the forms for notices of appeal and for permission to appeal.

There are two shorter recent Court of Appeal practice directions. Practice Note (Court of Appeal: Assessment of Costs) [1999] 1 WLR 871 deals with summary assessment of appeal costs, and says that the Court of Appeal will identify appeals which may be suitable for the summary assessment of costs, and will notify the parties accordingly. It will only be in those appeal cases that the parties will need to file statements of costs. Practice Note (Court of Appeal: Disposal of Bundles) [1999] 3 All ER 384 deals with disposal of appeal papers after appeals and applications for permission to appeal. Generally papers should be collected at the end of the hearing, but, to avoid original papers being destroyed, the appeal bundles should only contain copies.

25.5 High Court appeals from masters and district judges

PD RSC ord. 58 confirms that appeals from interim orders made by masters and district judges in the High Court continue to be made to the judge sitting in private, and appeals from decisions after trial by consent by a master or district judge are to the Court of Appeal.

NEW TOPICS

COURT OFFICES

PD 2 deals with matters such as the hours when court offices are open for business.

FORMS

CPR, r. 4(1), provides that the forms set out in a practice direction shall be used as appropriate. The forms may be varied as required by the circumstances of the case, but guidance notes and information for the recipient must always be included. As can be seen at Appendix 3 of this edition of this Guide, almost 100 forms have now been released for use with the main provisions of the CPR. Since the previous edition, a new PD 4 has been published, which also:

    (a) points out that a number of specialist forms have been published with other CPR practice directions, particularly those governing specialist courts;
    (b) lists 78 old prescribed forms from Appendix A to the old Rules of the Supreme Court 1965 which continue in use;
    (c) lists 105 old Queen's Bench Division practice forms, which continue in use;
    (d) lists 34 old Chancery Division practice forms, which continue in use; and
    (e) lists 234 county court forms, which continue in use.

CONTENTIOUS PROBATE PROCEEDINGS

PD 49 contains detailed provisions for dealing with contentious probate claims. It covers claims in respect of any contentious matter arising in connection with an application for the grant or revocation of probate or letters of administration, and includes claims for orders pronouncing for or against the validity of alleged wills. High Court contentious probate proceedings are issued in the Chancery Division or one of the Chancery district registries. Every person who may be affected by the claim, such as beneficiaries and those entitled on intestacy, must either be parties or given notice of the proceedings (PD 49, para. 2.5). Every person who is or claims to be entitled to administer the estate must be a party (para. 2.7). On a claim form being issued the court will send a notice to the Leeds District Probate Registry requesting that all testamentary scripts (wills, draft wills etc.) and any other relevant documents in any registry be sent to the court office where the claim is proceeding (para. 2.3). If the claim seeks the revocation of a grant of probate or letters of administration, the grant or letters of administration must be lodged in court (para. 3). Defendants should acknowledge service within 14 days of service of the claim form. This is unlike the main CPR, under which acknowledging service is required after service of the claim form rather than after service of the particulars of claim. Particulars of claim may be served with the claim form, or may be left until after the defendants acknowledge service (para. 7.1). PD 49 contains further provisions dealing with filing of affidavits or witness statements describing testamentary scripts each party has knowledge of (para. 5) and subsequent stages in the proceedings. It is not possible to obtain a default judgment on the defendants failing to acknowledge service in contentious probate claims. Instead, all the claimant can do (apart from discontinuing) is to apply for trial.

APPLICATIONS UNDER THE COMPANIES ACT 1985

The former Rules of the Supreme Court 1965, ord. 102, is replaced by the new PD 49B. The old ord. 102 contained detailed rules governing when proceedings pursuant to various provisions of the Companies Act 1985 had to be brought by originating summons, originating notice of motion, or petition. Under PD 49B the general rule is that all proceedings pursuant to the 1985 Act have to be brought using the Part 8 procedure (PD 49B, para. 2(1)). Exceptions are:

(a) unfair prejudice petitions, which are governed by their own procedure under the Companies (Unfair Prejudice Applications) Proceedings Rules 1986 (SI 1986/2000) and have to be brought by petition; and

(b) a list of 12 types of application under the 1985 Act, which, by PD 49B, para. 4(1), have to be brought by petition.

All High Court applications under the 1985 Act have to be brought in the Chancery Division (PD 49B, para. 3). They are allocated to the multi-track (para. 9), and the provisions in the CPR relating to allocation questionnaires and track allocation do not apply.

Interim applications in the Companies Court should be stated to be made to 'the Companies Judge' (CDPD 3, para. B(iii)).

TECHNOLOGY AND CONSTRUCTION COURT

The Technology and Construction Court (TCC) is the new name for the Official Referees' Department. PD 49C sets out the practice relating to TCC claims. There is unlikely to be any dramatic change in the types of claim that are suitable for the TCC, which will continue to deal with technically complex matters, with a particular emphasis on construction cases. TCC claims may be dealt with in county courts which are also High Court district registries, and also the Central London County Court (PD 49C, para. 2.3), but a great proportion of TCC claims will be conducted in the TCC on Fetter Lane in central London.

Claims intended for the TCC should be marked with the words 'Technology and Construction Court' in the top right corner under the entry for the court (whether the Queen's Bench Division or county court). Once issued, the claim will be assigned to a named TCC judge who will have primary responsibility for the case management of the claim (para. 2.4). All TCC claims are allocated to the multi-track (para. 4.1). For claims issued in the TCC, the claimant must apply for directions within 14 days of the defendant filing an acknowledgment of service or a defence (whichever is the earlier) (para. 4.2). Applications for directions in claims that come into the TCC by transfer must be made within 14 days of the date of the order making the transfer. The first directions hearing will be a case

INTRODUCTION TO THE SECOND EDITION

management conference. All parties are required to complete, exchange and file case management questionnaires and case management directions forms no later than 4 p.m. two days before the case management conference (para. 5.3). At this hearing the judge will usually fix dates for a pre-trial review and also for the trial. The trial will usually be conducted by the assigned judge.

COMMERCIAL COURT

PD 49D replaces the old Rules of the Supreme Court 1965, ord. 72, for commercial claims proceeding in the Commercial Court of the Queen's Bench Division. Claim forms should be marked with the words 'Queen's Bench Division, Commercial Court' in the top right of the form. All claims in the commercial list are allocated to the multi-track (PD 49D, para. 6.1), and generally all applications in these cases are dealt with by a judge (rather than a master or district judge, para. 2.2). The detailed practice governing claims proceeding in the Commercial Court is set out in the new edition of the Commercial Court Guide, and the practice set out in the Guide should be followed, subject to the provisions of PD 49D and any orders made in individual cases (para. 9.5). The new Commercial Court Guide is at present in a draft form, but contains very detailed provisions for the conduct of commercial cases.

PATENTS

PD 49E replaces the old Rules of the Supreme Court 1965, ord. 104, and related provisions of the Rules of the Supreme Court and the County Court Rules for patents cases. Patents cases are dealt with either in the Chancery Division or the Patents County Court. Claim forms should be marked 'Patents Court' (PD 49E para. 2.2). Every claim in the Patents Court will be allocated to the multi-track (PD 49E, para. 2.4). Applications for directions must be made within 14 days of the defendant filing an acknowledgment of service or a defence, or within 14 days of transfer.

ADMIRALTY CLAIMS

PD 49F replaces the old Rules of the Supreme Court 1965, ord. 75. It preserves claims *in rem* and claims *in personam*. There are special admiralty forms, including admiralty claim forms. There are special rules on service of a claim form *in rem* (see PD 49F, para. 2.2), including fixing it on the outside of the property proceeded against in a position where it might reasonably be expected to be seen. Initially, a claim form *in rem* is valid for 12 months for service (para. 2.1(6)). Acknowledgments of service must be filed in claims *in personam* within 14 days of service of the claim form irrespective of whether the claim form is served with the particulars of claim (para. 3.3). Paragraph 4 deals with filing of preliminary acts in collision cases, and there are detailed provisions dealing with matters such as the arrest and release of property in claims *in rem* (para. 6); sale by the court (para. 8); and limitation claims (para. 9). The practice in the Commercial Court Guide will be followed in admiralty claims, subject to the provisions of PD 49F and any orders made in individual cases (para. 16.1). Paragraph 17 repeats in substance the special provision for issuing admiralty claim forms at times when the court office is closed by sending the draft claim form to the court by fax.

ARBITRATION ACT CLAIMS

PD 49G replaces the old Rules of the Supreme Court 1965, ord. 73, and deals with claims under the Arbitration Act 1996, proceedings to determine whether there is a valid arbitration agreement and related arbitration matters. There is a special arbitration claim form (form N8A). Arbitration claims may be commenced in the Admiralty and Commercial Registry, a district registry where there is a Mercantile Court, or in the Business List at the Central London County Court (PD 49G, para. 5.3). There are special rules relating to service (see paras 7 and 8). The Applicant must file affidavit or witness statement evidence in support of the claim, which has to be served with the arbitration claim form (para. 9.1). There is a special acknowledgment of service form (N15A). Paragraph 13 sets out a number of automatic directions that apply unless the court otherwise directs. These govern the time limits for respondents to serve their written evidence, and for the applicant to serve written evidence in response. They also deal with applying for a date to be fixed, time estimates and lodging compete sets of the documents to be used at the hearing, chronologies and skeleton arguments. Arbitration claims are not subject to the usual rules on track allocation, but instead the court may make such orders and directions as it thinks are most likely to secure the just, expeditious and economical disposal of the claim (para. 14.1).

SALE OF LAND BY ORDER OF THE COURT

PD RSC ord. 31 says that applications for orders for the sale of land under RSC, ord. 31, r. 1 in CPR, sch. 1 and applications under the Law of Property Act 1925, s. 50, for the sale of land free from incumbrances (subject to payment into court to provide for the incumbrance and costs and expenses), are to be made using the CPR, Part 23, procedure. PD RSC ord. 31 also deals with parties seeking permission to bid for land to be sold under a direction of the court, and referring matters to conveyancing counsel of the court.

COMMITTAL APPLICATIONS

The main provisions governing applications for orders to commit to prison for contempt of court are to be found in RSC, ord. 52 in CPR, sch. 1, for High Court and Court of Appeal matters, and in CCR, ord. 29 in CPR, sch. 2, for county court matters. PD RSC ord. 52 supplements both orders.

Applications for committal to a divisional court require permission (RSC, ord. 52, r. 2 in CPR, sch. 1), and permission in these case must be granted before making an application for committal (PD RSC ord. 52, para. 2.3). If a committal application is made in existing proceedings (which means before final judgment), it is commenced by issuing an application notice in those proceedings (para. 2.2). Otherwise it is commenced by issuing a Part 8 claim form (para. 2.1). Personal service is required (paras 2.5(1) and 2.6(1)). The Part 8 claim form or application notice must set out in full the grounds on which the committal is sought, and should identify, separately and numerically, each alleged act of contempt (paras 2.5(2) and 2.6(2)). The evidence in support must be by affidavit (para. 3.1). When the claim form or application notice is issued the applicant must obtain from the court a date for the hearing of the committal application (para. 4.1), which must, unless the court orders otherwise, be not less than 14 clear days after service. The hearing date will be inserted in the claim form or application notice, or must be included in a notice attached to the relevant document. On the hearing date the court may proceed to deal with it forthwith if it is ready to be heard. Otherwise it will give case management directions with a view to holding the committal hearing at a later date (para. 4.4). Committal hearings are generally held in public (para. 9) and are dealt with by a judge (para. 11). Certain provisions of the CPR, such as joint instruction of a single expert, and seeking further information from the respondent, do not apply to committal proceedings (paras 6 and 7).

JUDICIAL REVIEW

PD RSC ord. 53 supplements the provisions of RSC, ord. 53 in CPR, sch. 1, on judicial review. It largely leaves matters as they were before 26 April 1999. RSC, ord. 53, r. 5(2A), provides that applications for judicial review must be made by issuing a claim form, and PD RSC ord. 53, para. 3.1, says the claim form must be in the old form 86 duly modified. The statement in support required by RSC, ord. 53, r. 6(1) in CPR, sch. 1, continues to be form 86A (PD RSC ord. 53, para. 4.1), which must be attached to form 86 and served with it. Written evidence under RSC, ord. 53, rr. 5(6), 6 and 11 in CPR, sch. 1, may be given either by affidavit or witness statement (PD RSC ord. 53, para. 5.1). All documents apart from orders must be prepared and served by the parties (para. 6). The operation of the Crown Office List continues to be governed by Practice Direction (Crown Office List) [1987] 1 WLR 232 (PD RSC ord. 53, para. 7.1). Eight other old practice directions dealing with judicial review matters continue in force by virtue of PD RSC ord. 53, para. 8.

HABEAS CORPUS

PD RSC ord. 54 deals with habeas corpus applications in much the same way as PD RSC ord. 53 deals with judicial review. It preserves seven old practice directions which continue in operation (PD RSC ord. 54, para. 7.1). The operation of the Crown Office List continues to be governed by Practice Direction (Crown Office List) [1987] 1 WLR 232 (PD RSC ord. 54, para. 6.1). The old forms of writ (forms 89, 91 and 92) continue in use (RSC, ord. 54, r. 10 in CPR, sch. 1) as do (slightly modified) versions of forms 87, 88 and 90 (see PD RSC, ord. 54, paras 3.1, 4.1 and 5.1).

INSOLVENCY PROCEEDINGS

There is a new Insolvency Practice Direction which replaces the old Chancery Division practice direction dealing with winding up of companies and individual bankruptcy and all other old practice notes and practice directions dealing with insolvency matters.

Part 2 of the new Insolvency PD deals with compulsory winding up. It repeats the stress put on the need to advertise in accordance with the Insolvency Rules 1986 (SI 1986/1925), r. 4.11(2)(b), and the relaxation for filing the certificate of compliance in High Court petitions by 4.30 p.m. on the Friday before the petition day. This part also deals with correcting

INTRODUCTION TO THE SECOND EDITION

errors in petitions after winding-up orders have been made (para. 4); the distribution of business between the judge, registrar and court manager (para. 5); drawing up of orders (usually by the court: para. 6); the rescission of winding-up orders, and the procedure on applying to restrain the presentation of winding-up petitions (which are to be brought by issuing an originating application under the Insolvency Rules 1986: para. 8).

Part 3 of the Insolvency PD contains detailed provisions relating to individual bankruptcy. Paragraph 9 deals with the distribution of business and states that certain matters shall be heard in public, such as public examinations of debtors, opposed applications for discharge, opposed applications for permission to be a director, and all matters and applications heard by a judge (subject to orders to the contrary). Paragraph 10 deals with service abroad of statutory demands. Paragraph 11 deals with substituted service of statutory demands and bankruptcy petitions, and also lays down a standard form of advertisement to be used by way of substituted service of a statutory demand. Applications to set aside statutory demands are dealt with in para. 12. Applications for these orders are made on form 6.4 (from the Insolvency Rules 1986) supported by written evidence on form 6.5 exhibiting a copy of the statutory demand. The application should be made within 18 days of service of the statutory demand: any late application will need to be combined with an application for an extension of time, and the evidence in support needs to state the reasons for failing to make the application in time. Standard paragraphs for the evidence in support of a late application are set out in para. 12.5. As to the merits of an application to set aside, para. 12.3 restates the approach where the demand is based on a judgment or order (normally the application is adjourned to await the result of an application to set aside the judgment) and para. 12.4 restates the approach where the debtor relies on a counterclaim or disputes the debt (the statutory demand will normally be set aside if there is a genuine triable issue).

Paragraph 13 deals with the form of written evidence proving service of statutory demands in individual bankruptcy. Paragraph 14 deals with applications to extend hearing dates. Paragraph 15 contains a number of provisions as to the form of bankruptcy petitions (such as there being no requirement to date, sign or witness the petition; that only the debtor's name need be mentioned in the title; and if based on a statutory demand only the debt claimed in the demand may be included in the petition); the payment of the official receiver's deposit; and the certificate made on the day of the hearing that inquiries have been made and the debt is still due and owing. Paragraph 16 deals with the procedure on making consent orders and orders in respect of individual voluntary arrangements without attendance. Paragraph 16.8 draws attention to PD 44, para. 4.4(3), which says that consent orders to be entered without attendance should include an agreed figure for costs, or should provide that there be no order for costs. If costs cannot be agreed, the parties may be required to attend (but the costs of the attendance may well be disallowed).

Paragraph 17 contains detailed provisions dealing with the procedure on making appeals from county court circuit judges and district judges, and also from High Court registrars, to the single judge of the High Court under the Insolvency Act 1986, s. 375(2), and the Insolvency Rules 1986, r. 7.48(2).

COMPANY DIRECTORS DISQUALIFICATION

There is a new PD Directors Disqualification Proceedings, which replaces all old practice directions covering applications under the Company Directors Disqualification Act 1986 (CDDA). Disqualification proceedings are applications for disqualification orders under various provisions of the CDDA. They are commenced by issuing a special version of the Part 8 claim form (set out in an annex to the PD), which includes an endorsement stating the maximum disqualification periods allowed by the CDDA. All claim forms, affidavits and other documents used in disqualification proceedings must be entitled in the name of the company and in the matter of the CDDA (para. 5.1). Service is effected by the parties (para. 7.1). Defendants are required to acknowledge service within 14 days of service of the claim form (para. 8.3). Evidence is given by affidavit (except that the official receiver may continue to use written reports) (para. 9.1). The evidence in support must be filed when the claim is issued, and must be served with the claim form (para. 9.3). Defendants have 28 days from service to serve and file their evidence in opposition (para. 9.4). Claimants are permitted to serve and file further evidence in reply within 14 days from receiving the defendant's evidence (para. 9.6). All disqualification proceedings are allocated to the multi-track (para. 2.1). Not less than eight weeks from the date of issue of the claim form the claim will be given a first hearing before the registrar, who may determine the case or give directions and adjourn it (paras 10.1 and 10.3). Paragraph 11 deals with case management and para. 12 with trial preparation (bundles, skeletons etc.). Paragraph 13 deals with the summary *Re Carecraft Construction Co. Ltd* [1994] 1 WLR 172 procedure. Paragraphs 14 to 19 deal with miscellaneous matters. Paragraphs 20 to 23 deal with the procedure on applications for permission to act as a director once a disqualification order has been made. Paragraphs 24 to 26 deal with interim applications in disqualification proceedings. These are made in accordance with CPR, Part 23, except that the application notice must have the same title as the claim form, and service is the responsibility of the parties.

WELSH LANGUAGE

When all parties and witnesses consent the court may conduct the whole of a hearing in Welsh on an ad hoc basis (PD Welsh Language, para. 1.2). In any case where it is possible that the Welsh language may be used by any of the parties or witnesses, or if any of the documents may be in Welsh, the court must be informed in advance so that appropriate arrangements can be made (para. 1.3). This possibility should be included in the allocation questionnaire (para. 2.1). Wherever practicable the court will attempt to list such cases before a Welsh-speaking judge, and at a court with simultaneous translation facilities (para. 4).

DEVOLUTION ISSUES

'Devolution issues' are, in general terms, questions as to whether devolved bodies under the Government of Wales Act 1998, the Northern Ireland Act 1998 or the Scotland Act 1998, have acted, or are proposing to act, within their powers, or whether they have failed to comply with duties imposed on them. There is a detailed practice direction, PD Devolution

INTRODUCTION TO THE SECOND EDITION

Issues, which deals with how devolution issues should be dealt with, and also with Crown Office applications in Wales.

CHANCERY DIVISION PRACTICE DIRECTIONS

Section C of the Chancery Guide sets out the current Chancery Division Practice Directions (CDPDs). They broadly adopt the content of the old Chancery Division Practice Directions. The new CDPDs deal with the following matters:

CDPD 1   Appeals

There are sections on appeals in contempt of court applications, on dismissal of appeals by consent, and appeals from Chancery masters.

CDPD 2   Hearings by Chancery judges out of London

There are Chancery district registries in Birmingham, Bristol, Cardiff, Leeds, Liverpool, Manchester, Newcastle upon Tyne and Preston. This CDPD deals with trials outside London, making applications (formerly motions) out of London, making applications out of hours and by telephone, agreed interim orders, and local listing arrangements.

CDPD 3   Judge's applications

This is the new term for applying by motion. Motions days are now application days, and the motions judge is now the applications judge. An application notice must be used instead of a motion, and it should usually state that it is to be heard by 'the Chancery Applications Judge'. The CDPD 3 goes on to deal with adjournments of judge's applications and the arrangements for the order of hearing these applications.

CDPD 4   Landlord and tenant

Claims seeking the grant of new business tenancies under the Landlord and Tenant Act 1954 are covered by this CDPD, and there are no substantial changes from the previous practice.

CDPD 5   Listing

The three main Chancery Division lists have been renamed as the trial list (for trials to be heard with witnesses), the interim hearings list (for interim applications and appeals from masters), and the general list (for all other matters). There continues to be a warned list which will be published on Fridays showing the cases liable to be heard in the following week. CDPD 5 also deals with time estimates, unassigned cases, appeals from masters, and listing of bankruptcy applications and appeals, companies applications and petitions, judge's applications, adjourning judge's applications, applications by order, short service, short applications and summary judgment, as well as revenue appeals and hearings in claims for the variation of trusts.

CDPD 6   Masters

CDPD 6 deals with assignment of cases to Chancery masters and with oral applications without notice to Chancery masters.

CDPD 7   Mortgages and possession orders

CDPD 7 deals with mortgages and possession orders with no real change from the previous practice.

INTRODUCTION TO THE SECOND EDITION

CDPD 8   Orders

CDPD 8 deals with drawing up Chancery orders. There are some minor changes to reflect provisions in the CPR. Interestingly the term 'Tomlin order' is expressly retained.

CDPD 9   Probate

No substantial changes.

CDPD 10   Sale

CDPD 10 deals with estate agents' and auctioneers' charges in relation to properties sold pursuant to Chancery Division orders. There are no substantial changes.

CDPD 11   Title of proceedings

This has been simplified so there is only one exception to the rule that the title should only contain the names of the parties to the proceedings. The exception relates to the administration of estates and probate claims, which should be entitled 'In the estate of AB deceased'. As before, if proceedings are under an Act of Parliament the Act need not be mentioned in the title, but should be referred to in the body of the claim form.

CDPD 12   Trusts

This is largely unchanged, and deals with applications under the Administration of Justice Act 1985, s. 48; applications after the disability of trustees; lodgements of funds under the Trustee Act 1925, s. 63; making available originals of documents at hearings; property in Scotland; the variation of trusts; and estates of deceased Lloyd's names.

ABUSE OF PROCESS

A number of recent cases have dealt with whether a claim which is inconsistent with an earlier claim or evidence given by the claimant in earlier proceedings (such as an affidavit used in an application to discharge a freezing injunction) should be struck out as an abuse of process. It is clear from cases such as *Bradford and Bingley Building Society* v *Seddon* (1999) *The Times*, 30 March 1999, that there are two main elements:

(a)   that the second claim is one that could have been brought in the first claim, or is in conflict with an earlier claim or evidence; and

(b)   an additional element, such as a collateral attack on the earlier decision, or dishonesty, election, or unjust harassment.

It was commented in the *Bradford and Bingley* case that abuse of process cases of this nature will perhaps be less frequent under the new rules given the requirement that the claimant must sign a statement of truth in relation to the second claim, which might be difficult given an earlier, inconsistent, claim.

PREFACE TO THE FIRST EDITION

Litigation practitioners are confronted on all sides by a period of profound change. The publication of Lord Woolf's *Access to Justice: Final Report* in July 1996 has led to the most fundamental reform of the ethos and procedure of civil justice this century, and the Civil Procedure Rules 1998, their accompanying practice directions, pre-action protocols and court forms, which will be in use from 26 April 1999, will need to be thoroughly assimilated and applied by the legal profession.

The Civil Procedure Rules 1998 introduce a significant culture change. Whilst the civil justice system will continue to be essentially adversarial in character, the ability of the parties to control the pace and direction of proceedings is now constrained. Litigation practitioners will have to abandon hitherto well-established tactics, learn new tactics and recognise that the new culture will also impose additional professional burdens, which might not always coincide with the best interests of their clients.

In this new landscape it is essential that practitioners should gain a complete understanding of the entire range of the procedural reforms and the manner in which they interact. Each topic cannot be studied in isolation. The full extent of the change in culture and the consequent need for the legal professions to adapt quickly to meet the challenges will only be apparent from a detailed study of all the components in the reforms.

The new Civil Procedure Rules are one element in wider reforms of the civil justice system. Conditional fee arrangements are now available in almost all civil proceedings, and in limited circumstances contingency arrangements are permitted. The practitioner must understand the relationship between these new funding arrangements and the Civil Procedure Rules, and we have included a chapter specifically on this point.

By various means the court will now exercise greater control over the legal costs incurred in proceedings and the ability of the successful party to recover costs. Practitioners must provide economy and efficiency. Early identification of the issues, which lies at the heart of the reforms, will require a level of professionalism and a depth of resources not always displayed. The procedural reforms and the Access to Justice Bill currently progressing through Parliament will inevitably accelerate the blurring of traditional boundaries between the two sides of the legal profession.

Although those with access to the Internet have been able to see some of the draft rules and practice directions for several months, the process of continual (and often substantial) revision has meant that the final version was not released until the end of January 1999; amendments to practice directions are still being made at the time of publication; the all important practice directions on costs did not appear until late February; only two pre-action protocols have so far been published; and much more awaits in the pipeline. Thus, although the general principles behind the new reforms have been known for some time, the profession has had little time to prepare for the details of the new procedure, which will be rigorously applied from inception.

PREFACE TO THE FIRST EDITION

Blackstone's Guide to the Civil Procedure Rules is the precursor to the full *Blackstone's Civil Practice*, which will be published in January 2000, and annually thereafter. The guide has been written with the specific objective of assisting the legal profession to come to terms with the spirit and form of the new procedural code as easily as possible. The guide provides helpful, comprehensive, and above all *practical* commentary, designed to enable the busy practitioner to know, in the shortest possible time, what he or she is required to do. We have included:

- the entire Civil Procedure Rules, including the schedules of re-enacted provisions of the RSC and CCR (see appendix 1);
- all practice directions (see appendix 1);
- pre-action protocols so far published (see appendix 2);
- the forms published so far (see appendix 3).

To achieve a practical book for the busy practitioner, we have deliberately omitted discussion of a purely academic nature. Nevertheless, we have not hesitated to point out areas of potential difficulty or ambiguity. Nor have we laboured overmuch on the past — save where a comparison was felt necessary to assist in understanding the new rules. The commentary has been written with input from the perspectives of the judiciary, both sides of the legal profession and the academic world. The book has been prepared using material available to the authors up to 1 March 1999.

This project would never have come to fruition without the foresight and enthusiasm of its publishers. I should like to thank Alistair MacQueen, Heather Saward and Jeremy Stein of Blackstone Press for their encouragement, unfailing good humour and their unswerving support for this project, and their confidence in those who have created a book which, I hope, will help everyone involved in civil litigation at a time of tremendous change.

Charles Plant
Editor-in-Chief
March 1999

CONTENTS

Introduction to the Second Edition		v
Preface to the First Edition		xxxix
Table of cases		xlvii
Table of statutes		li
Table of rules, practice directions and protocols		lv
Abbreviations		lxxiv

1 The new landscape — 1

1.1	Introduction	1
1.2	Outline of the reforms	2
1.3	A fundamentally new approach to interpretation	3
1.4	Principles underlying the reforms	3
1.5	The overriding objective	5
1.6	Implications of the overriding objective and the new landscape	6
1.7	The role of the client	7
1.8	The role of the court — principles of case management	8
1.9	The role of the professional adviser — overall responsibility and professional conduct issues	9
1.10	Tactics in the new landscape	11

2 Scope of the new rules, transitional provisions, interpretation and re-enacted provisions — 13

2.1	Scope of the Civil Procedure Rules 1998	13
2.2	Transitional provisions	14
2.3	Interpretation of the CPR: a procedural code?	18
2.4	Re-enacted provisions of the old rules	21

3 Conditional fees and the new rules — 31

3.1	Introduction	31
3.2	Conditional fees in context	32
3.3	Proportionality, transparency and certainty	34
3.4	Assessment of conditional fee agreement costs	35
3.5	Special issues relating to conditional fees under the CPR	38
3.6	Extension of conditional fees to new areas of work	41
3.7	Access to Justice Bill 1999	42

4 Pre-action protocols — 44

4.1	Introduction	44
4.2	Protocols so far	45
4.3	Consequences of failure to comply with protocols	45
4.4	Personal Injury Claims Protocol	47
4.5	Transitional provisions	49
4.6	Future protocols	49

5 The early stages of a claim — 51

5.1	Introduction	52
5.2	Allocation of business between the High Court and the county courts	53

5.3	Transfer	55
5.4	Proceedings started in the wrong court	57
5.5	Parties	57
5.6	Addition and substitution of parties	59
5.7	Special kinds of party	61
5.8	Starting proceedings	64
5.9	Service	68
5.10	Step-by-step guide to issue and service	75
5.11	Responding to the particulars of claim	76
5.12	Admissions	76
5.13	Acknowledging service	78
5.14	Judgment in default	79
5.15	Setting aside a default judgment	82
5.16	Disputing the court's jurisdiction	84
5.17	Part 8 procedure	85

6 Claim forms and particulars of claim — 88

6.1	Introduction	88
6.2	Terminology	89
6.3	Contents of a claim form	90
6.4	Particulars of claim	93
6.5	Statement of truth	96
6.6	Contents of a Part 8 claim form	98

7 Defending a claim — 99

7.1	Introduction	99
7.2	When a defence is required	99
7.3	Period for filing a defence	100
7.4	Extending the time for service of a defence	101
7.5	Stay of claim where no action taken	101
7.6	Contents of a defence — general matters	101
7.7	Contents of a defence — specific matters	102
7.8	Set-offs	103

8 Additional claims and further steps in the claim — 104

8.1	Counterclaims	105
8.2	Reply	106
8.3	Subsequent statements of case	106
8.4	Defence to counterclaim	107
8.5	Special procedure where the defence claims that money claimed has been paid	107
8.6	Part 20 claims	107
8.7	Obtaining further information	112
8.8	Amendments to statements of case	116

9 Applications and interim orders — 119

9.1	Introduction	120
9.2	To which court should an application be made?	121
9.3	Stage when interim remedies should be sought or considered	121
9.4	Applications without notice	123
9.5	Applications with notice	124
9.6	Orders made on the court's own initiative	128
9.7	Evidence in support	128

9.8	Drawing up interim orders	134
9.9	General powers regarding interim relief and orders	135
9.10	Pre-action inspection and inspection against non-parties	136
9.11	Interim payments	136
9.12	Striking out	140
9.13	Summary judgment	141

10 Interim injunctions, freezing injunctions and search orders   145

10.1	Introduction	145
10.2	Pre-issue applications for interim injunctions	146
10.3	Applications for interim injunctions during the course of proceedings	150
10.4	Evidence in support of an application	152
10.5	Freezing injunctions	153
10.6	Search orders	153
10.7	Criteria for obtaining an injunction	155

11 Case management   160

11.1	Introduction	160
11.2	Procedural judges	161
11.3	Transfer to appropriate court	161
11.4	Allocation	162
11.5	Stay to allow for settlement	168
11.6	Assessment of damages cases	169
11.7	Subsequent case management	170
11.8	Sanctions	173

12 Small claims   178

12.1	Introduction	178
12.2	The small claims jurisdiction — venue and level	179
12.3	Pre-allocation procedures: the possibility of summary judgment	180
12.4	The small claims track	180
12.5	Distinctive features of the small claims track	181
12.6	Restriction on application of rules	181
12.7	Procedure after allocation to the small claims track	182
12.8	Conduct of the final hearing	184
12.9	Appeals	188
12.10	Costs	189

13 Fast track   191

13.1	Introduction	191
13.2	Directions	193
13.3	Varying the directions timetable	198
13.4	Listing for trial	199
13.5	Trial	202
13.6	Costs	203

14 Multi-track   204

14.1	Introduction	204
14.2	Case management stages in multi-track cases	205
14.3	Directions on allocation	207

14.4	Case management conferences	209
14.5	Fixing the date for trial	211
14.6	Listing questionnaires	211
14.7	Pre-trial review	212
14.8	Directions given at other hearings	214
14.9	Variation of case management timetable	215
14.10	Non-compliance with case management timetable	216

15 Disclosure   217

15.1	Introduction	217
15.2	Basic principles	219
15.3	Standard disclosure	219
15.4	Documents	221
15.5	Procedure for standard disclosure	222
15.6	Continuing duty of disclosure	224
15.7	Specific disclosure or inspection	224
15.8	Inspection and copying	225
15.9	Pre-action and non-party disclosure	226
15.10	Claim to withhold inspection or disclosure	229
15.11	Consequences of failure to disclose	231
15.12	Subsequent use of disclosed documents	231

16 Evidence, including witness statements   233

16.1	Introduction	233
16.2	Court's power to control evidence	233
16.3	Written or oral evidence	234
16.4	Evidence by video link or other means	234
16.5	Requirement to serve witness statements for use at trial	235
16.6	Form of witness statements	235
16.7	Witness summaries	236
16.8	Consequence of failure to serve witness statement or summary	236
16.9	Use at trial of witness statements	237
16.10	Sanction for false statements	239
16.11	Evidence in proceedings other than at trial	239
16.12	Use of witness statements for other purposes	240
16.13	Affidavit evidence	241
16.14	Notice to admit facts	241
16.15	Admission or proof of disclosed documents	242
16.16	Questions of foreign law	242
16.17	Evidence of consent of trustee to act	242

17 Hearsay and non-verbal evidence   243

17.1	Introduction	243
17.2	Hearsay	243
17.3	Use of plans, photographs and models as evidence	245

18 Depositions and court attendance by witnesses   247

18.1	Introduction	247
18.2	Witness summonses	247
18.3	Evidence by deposition	249

19 Experts and assessors — 252

19.1	Introduction	252
19.2	Duties of experts and the court's power to restrict expert evidence	253
19.3	Directions about experts	254
19.4	What if a party has instructed his own expert?	254
19.5	Written reports	255
19.6	Written questions to experts	255
19.7	Single joint expert	256
19.8	Direction to provide information	258
19.9	Contents of an expert's report	258
19.10	Use by other parties of disclosed expert's report	259
19.11	Discussions between experts	260
19.12	Consequences of failure to disclose expert's report	261
19.13	Expert's right to ask court for directions	261
19.14	Assessors	261

20 Offers to settle — 263

20.1	Introduction	264
20.2	When to use Part 36 offers and payments	264
20.3	Pre-action offer	265
20.4	Defendant's Part 36 offer	267
20.5	Defendant's Part 36 payment	271
20.6	Claimant's Part 36 offer	275
20.7	Failure to beat a Part 36 payment or offer	277
20.8	Non-disclosure	279
20.9	Court intervention	280
20.10	Costs consequences when both claimant and defendant have made an offer	281
20.11	What should be the response to an unacceptable offer or payment?	282

21 Change of solicitor — 285

21.1	Introduction	285
21.2	Presumed continuation	286
21.3	Notice of change	286
21.4	Revocation or discharge of legal aid	286
21.5	Coming off the record	286
21.6	Removal of solicitor on application of another party	287

22 Discontinuance — 288

22.1	Introduction	288
22.2	Distinction between discontinuing and abandoning	288
22.3	What may be discontinued	289
22.4	Permission to discontinue	289
22.5	Procedure for discontinuing	289
22.6	Setting aside notice of discontinuance	290
22.7	Effect of discontinuance	290
22.8	Subsequent proceedings	290

23 Trial — 291

23.1	Introduction	291
23.2	Listing	292
23.3	Trial timetables	293
23.4	Statement of issues	294
23.5	Trial bundles	295
23.6	Disposal without an oral hearing	296
23.7	Mode of trial	297
23.8	Conduct of trial	298
23.9	Drawing up judgment after trial	299
23.10	Non-attendance	300
23.11	Register of county court judgments	300
23.12	Interest on judgment debts	301

24 Costs — 302

24.1	Introduction	303
24.2	General principles	304
24.3	Costs orders	305
24.4	Rights to costs	309
24.5	Costs orders against non-parties	310
24.6	Fast track costs	310
24.7	Method of quantification of costs	312
24.8	Basis of quantification	313
24.9	Procedure for detailed assessment of costs	314
24.10	Conditional fee agreements	320
24.11	Litigants in person	321
24.12	Wasted costs orders	321

25 Appeals — 323

25.1	Introduction	323
25.2	County court appeals from district judges	324
25.3	County court rehearings	324
25.4	County court appeals from the judge	324
25.5	High Court appeals from masters and district judges	325
25.6	High Court appeals from judges	325
25.7	Appeals to the Court of Appeal	327
25.8	Judicial review	329
25.9	Appeals to the High Court from tribunals	330
25.10	Appeals to the High Court by case stated	330
25.11	Divisional Court proceedings	330
25.12	Appeals to the Court of Appeal from the Restrictive Practices Court	330
25.13	Appeals from tribunals to the Court of Appeal by way of case stated	330
25.14	References to the European Court	331
25.15	Variation of directions	331

Appendix 1	**Civil Procedure Rules 1998 and practice directions**	333
Appendix 2	**Pre-action protocols**	1193
Appendix 3	**Forms**	1223
Appendix 4	**Civil Procedure Act 1997**	1344
Appendix 5	**Fees orders**	1351
Index		1383

TABLE OF CASES

Aiden Shipping Co. Ltd v Interbulk Ltd [1986] AC 965	310
Alexander v Rayson [1936] 1 KB 169	xxv
Allen v Gulf Oil Refining Ltd [1981] AC 1001	192
Alpine Bulk Transport Co. Inc. v Saudi Eagle Shipping Co. Inc. [1986] 2 Lloyd's Rep 221	20, 83, 143, 188
American Cyanamid Co. v Ethicon Ltd [1975] AC 396	155
Anton Piller KG v Manufacturing Processes Ltd [1976] Ch 55	154
Apple Corp Ltd v Apple Computer Inc. [1992] 1 CMLR 969	232
Arbuthnot Latham Bank Ltd v Trafalgar Holdings Ltd [1998] 1 WLR 1426	vii
B v B [1978] Fam 181	222
Bajwa v British Airways plc (1999) The Times, 1 July 1999	viii, xxii
Baron v Lovell (27 July 1999 unreported)	xvii
Beatham v Carlisle Hospitals NHS Trust (1999) The Times, 20 May 1999	xi
Beoco Ltd v Alfa Laval Co. Ltd [1995] QB 137	304
Biguzzi v Rank Leisure plc (26 July 1999 unreported)	viii, xvii
Blenheim Leisure (Restaurants) Ltd, Re (1999) The Times, 13 August 1999	xi
Booker McConnell plc v Plascow [1985] RPC 425	154
Bradford and Bingley Building Society v Seddon (1999) The Times, 30 March 1999	xxxviii
Breeze v John Stacey and Sons Ltd (1999) The Times, 8 July 1999	xix
Brinks Ltd v Abu-Saleh (No. 1) [1995] 1 WLR 1478	142
British and Commonwealth Holdings plc v Quadrex Holdings Inc. [1989] QB 842	138
Cadogan Properties Ltd v Mount Eden Land Ltd (29 June 1999 unreported)	vii, xii
Carecraft Construction Co. Ltd, Re [1994] 1 WLR 172	xxxvi
Carter (R.G.) Ltd v Clarke [1990] 1 WLR 578	192
Chilton v Surrey County Council (24 June 1999 unreported)	vi, vii
Chilton v Saga Holidays plc [1986] 1 All ER 841	186
Christofi v Barclays Bank plc (unreported 28 June 1999)	xv
Co-operative Insurance Society Ltd v Argyll Stores (Holdings) Ltd [1998] AC 1	157
Compagnie Financiere et Commerciale du Pacifique v Peruvian Guano Co. (1882) 11 QBD 55	218
Company, re a (No. 004055 of 1991) [1991] 1 WLR 1003	310
Coore v Chief Constable of Leicestershire (10 May 1999 unreported)	xx
Cowland v District Judges of the West London County Court (20 July 1999 unreported)	xix
Creehouse Ltd, Re [1983] 1 WLR 77	287
Day v Royal Automobile Club Motoring Services Ltd (1998) The Times, 24 November 1998	143
Debtor, re a (No. 1 of 1987) [1989] 1 WLR 271	20
Derby v Weldon (No. 2) (1988) The Times, 20 October 1988	232
Dunning v United Liverpool Hospitals' Board of Governors [1973] 1 WLR 586	122
Elgindata Ltd (No. 2), Re [1992] 1 WLR 1207	304
Ernst and Young v Butte Mining plc [1996] 1 WLR 1605	290
Fahani v Merc Property Ltd (1999) The Times, 19 May 1999	xxviii

TABLE OF CASES

Faircharm Investments Ltd v Citibank International plc (1998) The Times, 20 February 1998 — 82
Fakih Brothers v A.P. Moller (Copenhagen) Ltd [1994] 1 Lloyd's Rep 103 — 290
Filmlab Systems International Ltd v Pennington [1995] 1 WLR 673 — 321
Financial Services Authority v Millward (27 May 1999 unreported) — 426, 433
Finley v Connell Associates (9 June 1999 unreported) — xv
Forbes v Smith (1997) The Times, 14 January 1998 — xi
Forward v West Sussex County Council [1995] 1 WLR 1469 — 73

Garcin v Amerindo Investment Advisors Ltd [1991] 1 WLR 1140 — 234
Gardner v Southwark London Borough Council (No. 2) [1996] 1 WLR 561 — 141
General Mediterranean Holdings SA v Patel [1999] 3 All ER 673 — v, xxvii
Gomba Holdings (UK) Ltd v Minories Finance Ltd (No. 2) [1993] Ch 171 — xxvii
Grobbelaar v Sun Newspapers Ltd (1999) The Times, 12 August 1999 — xix
Gupta v Klito (1989) The Times, 23 November 1989 — 304

Hadmor Productions Ltd v Hamilton [1983] 1 AC 191 — 19, 326
Harrison v Bloom Camillin (12 May 1999 unreported) — viii
Hodgson v Imperial Tobacco Ltd [1998] 1 WLR 1056 — 39
Hytec Information Systems Ltd v Coventry City Council [1997] 1 WLR 1666 — 175

Jones v Telford and Wrekin District Council (1999) The Times, 29 July 1999 — vi, xii

Ketteman v Hansel Properties Ltd [1987] AC 189 — 60
Khanna v Lovell White Durrant [1995] 1 WLR 121 — 228, 229, 248
Kirkup v British Rail Engineering Ltd [1983] 1 WLR 1165 — 235, 258
Kleinwort Benson Ltd v Barbrak Ltd [1987] AC 597 — 67, 68
Knight v Sage Group plc (28 April 1999 unreported) — xxi, xxii

Ladd v Marshall [1954] 1 WLR 1489 — 22
Liddell v Middleton [1996] PIQR P36 — 253
Lock International plc v Beswick [1989] 1 WLR 1268 — 157
Lonrho Ltd v Shell Petroleum Co. Ltd [1980] 1 WLR 627 — 222

Maltez v Lewis (1999) The Times, 4 May 1999 — vi
Mareva Compania Naviera SA v International Bulk Carriers SA [1980] 1 All ER 213 — 153
Matthews v Tarmac Bricks and Tiles Ltd (1999) The Times, 1 July 1999 — xxiii
McFarlane v E.E Caledonia Ltd (No. 2) [1995] 1 WLR 366 — 310
McPhilemy v Times Newspapers Ltd (1999) The Times, 26 May 1999 — vi, xiv
Mealey Horgan plc v Horgan (1999) The Times, 6 July 1999 — xx
Mullan v Birmingham City Council (1999) The Times, 29 July 1999 — xxv

Nascimento v Kerrigan (1999) The Times, 23 June 1999 — v, xxviii
National Westminster Bank plc v Daniel [1993] 1 WLR 1453 — 130
Natural Resources Inc. v Origin Clothing Ltd [1995] FSR 280 — 142
Newton v Dorset Travel Service Ltd (5 May 1999 unreported) — xvii
Norwich Pharmacal Co. v Commissioners of Customs and Excise [1974] AC 133 — 122, 229

O'Hara v Rye (12 February 1999 unreported) — xviii

Piglowski v Piglowski, (1999) The Times, 25 June 1999 — xxviii
Plenty v Gladwin (1986) 67 ALR 26 — 287

TABLE OF CASES

Practice Direction (Order 14: Return Date) [1970] 1 WLR 258	143
R v Cardiff County Council (11 June 1999 unreported)	xxvii
Rasu Maritima SA v Perusahaan Pertambangan Minyak Dan Gas Bumi Negara [1978] QB 644	157
Restick v Crickmore [1994] 1 WLR 420	57
Ricci Burns Ltd v Toole [1989] 1 WLR 993	138
Richard Roberts Holdings v Douglas Smith Stimson Partnership (No. 3) (1990) 47 BLR 113	260
Riddick v Thames Board Mills Ltd [1977] QB 881	232
Ridehalgh v Horsefield [1994] Ch 205	321
Rockwell Machine Tool Co. Ltd v E.P. Barrus (Concessionaires) Ltd [1968] 1 WLR 693	221
Rollinson v Kimberley Clark Ltd (15 June 1999 unreported)	xxiii
Shaw v Smith (1886) 18 QBD 193	287
Shearson Lehman Brothers Inc. v Maclaine Watson and Co. Ltd [1987] 1 WLR 480	138
Shikari v Malik (1999) The Times, 20 May 1999	viii
Shocked v Goldschmidt [1998] 1 All ER 372	128, 188, 300
Singh v Christie (1993) The Times, 11 November 1993	232
Singh v Observer Ltd [1989] 2 All ER 751	310
Sir Lindsay Parkinson and Co. Ltd v Triplan Ltd [1973] QB 609	22
Smith v Braintree District Council [1990] 2 AC 215	21
St Albans Court Ltd v Daldorch Estates Ltd (1999) The Times, 24 May 1999	xxiv
Stephenson (SBJ) Ltd v Mandy (1999) The Times, 21 July 1999	vii
Stevens v Gullis (27 July 1999 unreported)	xxi
Stringman v McArdle [1994] 1 WLR 1653	137
Symphony Group plc v Hodgson [1994] QB 179	310
Tecnion Investments Ltd, Re [1985] BCLC 434	222
Thai Trading Co. v Taylor [1998] QB 781	42
Thompson v Brown [1981] 1 WLR 744	20
Thomson v Pheney (1832) 1 Dowl Pr Cas 441	70
Underwood, Son and Piper v Lewis [1894] 2 QB 306	286
Waddon v Whitecroft Scovell Ltd [1988] 1 WLR 309	67

TABLE OF STATUTES

Access to Health Records Act 1990 308
Access to Justice Bill 1999   7, 9, 31–2, 34, 39
  cl.27   32
  cl.29   33, 36
  cl.29(1)   42
  cl.30   43
  Part III   42
Access to Neighbouring Land Act 1992   30
Administration of Justice Act 1960   30, 326
Administration of Justice Act 1985
  s.48   xxxviii, 30
  s.50   30
Adoption Act 1976
  s.66   vii
Agricultural Holdings Act 1986   29
Agriculture (Miscellaneous Provisions) Act 1954
  s.6   30
Arbitration Act 1996   xxxiii
  Part I   326

Bills of Sale Act 1878   30
Bills of Sale Act 1882   30

Charities Act 1993   30
Children Act 1989
  s.25   327
Civil Evidence Act 1968   xx, 95
Civil Evidence Act 1972   242
Civil Evidence Act 1995   xx, 132, 235, 243
  s.1   243
  s.1(1)   296
  s.2   xx, 237, 238, 239, 243, 244
  s.2(4)   238, 296
  s.3   245
  s.4(2)   244
  s.5(2)   245
  s.9   246
  s.16(3A)   xx
Civil Jurisdiction and Judgments Act 1982   ix, 74, 82, 95
Civil Procedure Act 1997   1344–50
  s.7   153, 155, 229
  s.7(3)-(5)   154
  s.8   226
  sch.1
    para.4   210, 322

Companies Act 1985   xxxi, 14
  s.459   24
  s.694A   72
  s.695   72
  s.725   72
  s.726(1)   297
Companies Act 1989   14
Company Directors Disqualification Act 1986   xxxvi
Consumer Credit Act 1974   xiii, 30, 54, 80, 297
  s.141   94
County Courts Act 1984
  s.14   25, 29
  s.23   54
  s.38   155
  s.40(1)   57
  s.40(2)   56
  s.41(1)   56
  s.42(1)   57
  s.42(2)   56
  s.49   26
  s.52   122, 135, 136, 226
  s.53   135, 136, 226
  s.63   261
  s.66   297
  s.73   300
  s.73A   300
  s.74   301
  s.76   25
  s.92   25, 29
  s.124   25, 29
Courts and Legal Services Act 1990
  s.27   9
  s.58   32, 33, 36, 42
  s.58(2)   42
  s.58(2)(a)-(b)   42
  s.58A   42
  s.58A(4)   42
  s.58A(6)   42
Criminal Justice (International Cooperation) Act 1990   30

Deeds of Arrangement Act 1914
  s.7   24, 30
Drug Trafficking Act 1994   30

Evidence (Proceedings in Other Jurisdictions) Act 1975   251

Family Law Reform Act 1969   30
Fatal Accidents Act 1976   137, 281

TABLE OF STATUTES

Foreign Limitation Periods Act 1984 118

Government of Wales Act 1998 xxxvi

Highways Act 1980 ix
Housing Act 1988 xvi, 30
Housing Act 1996 25, 30
Human Rights Act 1998 184, 185

Industrial and Provident Societies Act 1967 30
Inheritance (Provision for Family and Dependants) Act 1975 23, 30, 297
Insolvency Act 1986
  s.9(1) 24
  s.124(1) 24
  s.264(1) 24
  s.375(2) xxxv
Interpretation Act 1978
  s.7 72

Judgments Act 1838
  s.17 301, 310

Landlord and Tenant Act 1927 29, 30
Landlord and Tenant Act 1954 xxxvii, 29, 30
  s.24 xiii
  s.38 85
Landlord and Tenant Act 1985 29
Landlord and Tenant Act 1987 29, 30
Late Payment of Commercial Debts (Interest) Act 1998 301
  s.3(1) 301
Law of Property Act 1925
  s.21 30
  s.25 30
  s.50 xxxiii
Law Reform (Miscellaneous Provisions) Act 1934 281
Leasehold Reform Act 1976 30
Legal Aid Act 1988
  s.17 279, 297
Legitimacy Act 1976 30
Limitation Act 1980 65, 118, 140
  s.33 60
Local Government Finance Act 1982 30

Mental Health Act 1983 61, 62, 63
  Part VII 13, 61, 62
  s.139 122

Merchant Shipping Act 1995 29
Mines (Working Facilities and Support) Act 1966 30

Northern Ireland Act 1998 xxxvi

Pensions Appeal Tribunals Act 1943 30
Prosecution of Offences Act 1985 249
Protection from Harassment Act 1997 297
  s.3(5)(a) 129
Public Trustee Act 1906 30

Race Relations Act 1976 30
Rent Act 1977 xvi
Representation of the People Act 1983 29, 30
Road Traffic Act 1988
  s.57 272
  s.151 138
  s.157 274
Road Traffic Act 1991 25, 30

Scotland Act 1998 xxxvi
Sex Discrimination Act 1975 30
Social Security Administration Act 1992 30
Social Security (Recovery of Benefits) Act 1997 139
  s.6 92
  s.8 272
  sch.2 272
Solicitors Act 1974 30
  Part III 318
  s.65(2) 286
Supreme Court Act 1981
  s.18 325–6
  s.33 122, 135, 136, 226
  s.34 135, 136, 226
  s.37 21, 155
  s.42 xi, 30
  s.49(2) 58
  s.51 304
  s.51(6) 321
  s.51(8)-(9) 57
  s.69 297
  s.70 261
  sch.1
    para.1 54
    para.2(a)-(b) 54
Supreme Court of Judicature Act 1875 1

Torts (Interference with Goods) Act 1977
  s.4 135

TABLE OF STATUTES

Town and Country Planning Act 1990 30
Tribunals and Inquiries Act 1971 30
Tribunals and Inquiries Act 1992 30
Trustee Act 1925
  s.63 xxxviii

Variation of Trusts Act 1958 xxiv, 30

European legislation
European Convention on Human Rights and Fundamental Freedoms 185
  art.6 v
  art.6(1) xxiv
  art.8 v

TABLE OF RULES, PRACTICE DIRECTIONS AND PROTOCOLS

Page numbers in bold refer to text of the rules

Chancery Division Practice Directions xxxvii, **1175–91**
  CDPD 1 xxxvii
  CDPD 2 xxxvii
  CDPD 3 xxxvii
    para.B(iii) xxxi
  CDPD 4 xxxvii
  CDPD 5 xxxvii
  CDPD 6 xxxvii
  CDPD 7 xxxvii
  CDPD 8 xxxvii
  CDPD 9 xxxvii
  CDPD 10 xxxvii
  CDPD 11 xxxvii
  CDPD 12 xxxvii
Civil Legal Aid (General) Regulations 1989 (SI 1989/339)
  reg.83 286
  reg.127 297
Civil Procedure (Amendment) Rules 1999 (SI 1999/1008) 333
Civil Procedure (Modification of Enactments) Order 1998 (SI 1998/2940) 226
Civil Procedure Rules 1998 (SI 1998/3132) and supplementary practice directions
  Part 1 14, 256, **351**
  r.1.1 vi, viii, 3, 32, 97
  r.1.1(1) 2, 5, 14, 18, 22
  r.1.1(2) 3, 160, 178, 303
  r.1.1(2)(a) 218
  r.1.1(2)(b) 150, 218
  r.1.1(2)(c) vii, xii, 38, 191, 218
  r.1.1(2)(c)(ii) 3
  r.1.1(2)(c)(iv) 279
  r.1.1(2)(d) vii, xii, 67, 123
  r.1.1(2)(e) 3, 151
  r.1.2 2, 3, 6, 18, 19, 155, 218, 279
  r.1.3 2, 7, 9, 98, 198
  r.1.4(1) 8, 160
  r.1.4(1)(h) 120
  r.1.4(2) 8
  r.1.4(2)(a) 173, 199, 305
  r.1.4(2)(b) 305
  r.1.4(2)(c) 142, 144, 295, 305
  r.1.4(2)(d) 295
  r.1.4(2)(e) 169

Civil Procedure Rules 1998 – *continued*
  r.1.4(2)(f) 168, 265
  r.1.4(2)(i) 120, 151
  r.1.4(2)(j) 127, 296
  r.1.4(2)(k) 127
  Part 2 **352–5**
  r.2.1 vii
  r.2.1(1) 13
  r.2.1(2) 13, 24
  r.2.3(1) 55, 57, 68, 84, 88, 90, 96, 99
  r.2.4 161
  r.2.6(1)-(2) 65
  r.2.6(3) 133
  r.2.7 121
  r.2.8 74, 125
  r.2.8(2)-(4) 75
  r.2.9 74, 75, 175
  r.2.9(1) 136
  r.2.9(1)(b) 75
  r.2.10 74, 75
  r.2.11 174
  PD 2 xxx, **356–7**
  PD 2B x, **358–61**
    para.2.3 x
    para.3.1 x
    para.3.1(f) xi
    para.4.1 x
    para.4.2 x
    para.5.1 x
    para.7.1 x
    para.8 x
    para.11.1 x
  Part 3 **362–5**
  r.3.1 175
  r.3.1(1) 212
  r.3.1(2) 59, 135
  r.3.1(2)(a) 101, 175, 199, 216
  r.3.1(2)(d) 127
  r.3.1(2)(e) 109, 295
  r.3.1(2)(i)-(j) 295
  r.3.1(2)(l) 295
  r.3.1(2)(m) 128
  r.3.1(3) 83, 136
  r.3.1(4) 45
  r.3.1(5) 45, 47, 265
  r.3.3 57
  r.3.3(1)-(2) 128

Civil Procedure Rules 1998 –
continued
r.3.3(3)   128, 210
r.3.3(5)(a)   126
r.3.3(5)(b)   126, 128
r.3.3(6)   126, 128
r.3.4   140, 173
r.3.4(1)   140
r.3.4(2)   140, 141
r.3.4(2)(a)-(b)   140
r.3.4(2)(c)   141, 173
r.3.4(4)-(5)   141
r.3.5   176
r.3.7   xvi, 163, 173, 196, 213
r.3.8   47, 176, 216
r.3.9   47, 176
r.3.9(1)(e)   45, 47
r.3.10   175
r.3.10(2)   175
r.3.17(2)-(3)   228
PD 3   **366–8**
  para.1.5   140
  para.2-para.3   141
  para.4.1   140
  para.4.2   141
  para.5.2   140
  para.7   xi
PD 3B   xvi, **369**
Part 4   **370**
  r.4(1)   xxx
PD 4   **371–85**
Part 5   **386**
PD 5   **387–91**
  para.2.1   xiv
  para.2.2   xiv
  para.2.2(1)   xix
  para.3   x
  para.5.1–para.5.5   xiv
Part 6   285, **392–8**
  r.6.2   70, 72, 76
  r.6.2(2)   72
  r.6.3   125, 134
  r.6.3(1)   69
  r.6.3(1)(b)   69
  r.6.3(2)   69, 75
  r.6.3(3)   69
  r.6.4   70
  r.6.4(2)   71
  r.6.4(3)   70
  r.6.4(4)   70, 73
  r.6.4(5)   72
  r.6.5   70
  r.6.5(1)   70
  r.6.5(2)   ix, 102, 285
  r.6.5(3)   285
  r.6.5(4)   70
  r.6.5(5)   55, 71, 285
  r.6.5(6)   71, 72, 73

Civil Procedure Rules 1998 –
continued
r.6.6   62
r.6.6(1)   63
r.6.7   75, 125
r.6.7(1)   73
r.6.7(2)   66
r.6.8(1)   73
r.6.8(3)   74
r.6.9   74
r.6.10   76
r.6.11   69, 75
r.6.13(2)   71
r.6.14   69
r.6.14(1)   75
r.6.14(2)(a)   76
r.6.14(2)(b)   69
r.6.16(4)   100
PD 6   **399–403**
  para.2-para.3   70, 71
  para.4.2   72
  para.6.1-para.6.2   73
  para.7   285
  para.8.1   69, 75, 125
  para.8.2   69, 75
  para.9.1   74
Part 7   64, **404–5**
  r.7.2(1)-(2)   65
  r.7.3   58
  r.7.4(1)   65, 93
  r.7.4(2)   65
  r.7.4(3)   65, 69
  r.7.5   65
  r.7.6   66, 67, 68
  r.7.6(1)   67
  r.7.6(3)   67
  r.7.6(4)   123
  r.7.6(4)(a)-(b)   66
  r.7.8   86
  r.7.8(1)   65, 75, 76, 77, 78
  r.7.8(2)(b)   78
PD 7 How to Start Proceedings
    406–9
  para.1   53
  para.2.1   92
  para.2.2-para.2.4   53
  para.2.5-para.2.6   54
  para.2.9   53, 54
  para.3   91
  para.3.5   74
  para.3.8-para.3.9   92
  para.4   xiii, xix
  para.4.1-para.4.2   65
  para.4.4   65
  para.4.5   64
  para.7.2   66
PD 7B Consumer Credit Act
    Claims   **410–14**

TABLE OF RULES, PRACTICE DIRECTIONS AND PROTOCOLS

Civil Procedure Rules 1998 –
continued
  para.4 54
  para.9.1 95
PD 7C xi, **415–17**
  para.5.2 xi
PD 7D xii, **418**
Part 8 64, 78, 85, 88, **419–21**
  r.8.1(2) 85
  r.8.1(3) 85, 87
  r.8.1(5) 79, 86
  r.8.2 98
  r.8.3(1) 78, 86
  r.8.3(3) 86
  r.8.3(3)(b) 86
  r.8.3(4) 86
  r.8.4 79, 86
  r.8.5 87
  r.8.5(1) 65, 98
  r.8.5(2) 66, 98
  r.8.5(3)-(6) 86
  r.8.6(2)-(3) 85
  r.8.8(1) 86
  r.8.9 86
  r.8.9(c) 86, 162
PD 8 **422–3**
  para.1.1-para.1.2 85
  para.1.4 85
  para.1.4(3) xxi
  para.1.4(4) xxi
  para.1.6 85
  para.3.2 86
  para.3.6 86
  para.5.2 98
PD 8B xii, **424–33**
  section A xii
  section B xiii
    para.B.7 xxiii
    para.B.9 xxiii
    para.B.10 xxiii
    para.B.12 xxiii
    para.B.13 xxiii
  section C xxiii
Part 9 **434**
Part 10 **435**
  r.10.1(3) 78
  r.10.3(1) 78
  r.10.3(2) 86
  r.10.3(2)(a)-(b) 79
  r.10.5 86
  r.10.5(a)-(b) 79
PD 10 **436**
  para.4.3-para.4.5 79
  para.5.3-para.5.4 79
Part 11 74, 84, 86, 100, **437**
  r.11(2) 84
  r.11(3) 78, 84
  r.11(4)(a)-(b) 84

Civil Procedure Rules 1998 –
continued
  r.11(5)(b) 84
  r.11(6)-(8) 84
  r.11(9) 84, 100
Part 12 69, 79, 86, 98, 100, 105,
    110, 111, **438–41**
  r.12.2-r.12.3 80
  r.12.4 80
  r.12.4(1) 79
  r.12.4(3) 81
  r.12.5 81
  r.12.5(3) 81
  r.12.6(1)-(2) 81
  r.12.7 81, 219
  r.12.7(2)(b) 162
  r.12.8(1)-(3) 82
  r.12.9(1)(b) 81
  r.12.10 80, 81
  r.12.11(1) 80, 82
  r.12.11(2) 82
  r.12.11(4) 82
PD 12 **442–4**
  para.1.1-para.1.2 80
  para.2.3 81
  para.4 82
  para.4.1 80
  para.4.2(1)-(2) 82
  para.5.1 82
Part 13 **445–6**
  r.13.2 83
  r.13.3(1) 83
  r.13.3(1)(a) 83
  r.13.3(2) 83
  r.13.4(1) 84
  r.13.4(3) 84
  r.13.5 83
  r.13.6 81
Part 14 xvii, 101, **447–51**
  r.14.1(1)-(2) 76, 110
  r.14.2 77
  r.14.3 110
  r.14.3(1) 76
  r.14.4 77
  r.14.4(2) 76, 77
  r.14.4(3)-(6) 77
  r.14.5 55, 77, 179
  r.14.6 77, 78
  r.14.7 77
  r.14.8 162, 219
  r.14.9 77
  r.14.9(4)-(5) 77
  r.14.10 77
  r.14.10(4) 77
PD 14 **452–3**
  para.2.1 77
Part 15 105, **454–5**
  r.15.2 99

TABLE OF RULES, PRACTICE DIRECTIONS AND PROTOCOLS

Civil Procedure Rules 1998 – *continued*
  r.15.3   100
  r.15.4   100
  r.15.4(1)(a)-(b)   100
  r.15.4(2)   107
  r.15.4(2)(a)   100
  r.15.5   101
  r.15.5(2)   101
  r.15.6   100
  r.15.8   106
  r.15.9   90, 106
  r.15.10   179
  r.15.10(1)-(4)   107
  r.15.11   101
  PD 15   456
    para.3.1   105
  Part 16   457–9
    r.16.2(1)(a)-(c)   91
    r.16.2(1)(d)   93
    r.16.2(3)-(4)   90
    r.16.2(5)   91
    r.16.3   91, 102
    r.16.3(2)   91
    r.16.3(2)(b)   92
    r.16.3(3)-(6)   92
    r.16.3(7)   91
    r.16.4(1)(a)-(b)   93
    r.16.4(1)(c)-(e)   94
    r.16.4(2)   93
    r.16.4(2)(a)-(b)   94
    r.16.5   102
    r.16.5(1)   101
    r.16.5(2)   99, 101
    r.16.5(3)   101
    r.16.5(4)-(8)   102
    r.16.6   103
    r.16.7(1)   106
    r.16.8   93
  PD 16   460–5
    para.3.1   65, 93
    para.3.6(2)   94
    para.3.8   93
    para.4-para.8   95
    para.4.2   xiv
    para.4.3   xiv, xxi
    para.9.2   94, 95
    para.9.3   xiii
    para.9.3-para.9.6   94
    para.10.1   95
    para.10.2   94
    para.10.3   xiii, 89, 95
    para.11.1   92
    para.12.2   101, 106
    para.13.2   99
    para.14.1   102
    para.14.1(1)(c)   103
    para.14.1(2)   102

Civil Procedure Rules 1998 – *continued*
    para.14.1(3)   xiv, 102
    para.14.2   xiv
    para.14.2(1)   103
    para.15   103
    para.16.1-para.16.2   103
    para.16.3   xii
  Part 17   466–7
    r.17.1(1)   116, 117
    r.17.1(2)(a)   116, 118
    r.17.1(2)(b)   116
    r.17.2   118
    r.17.2(1)-(2)   116
    r.17.3(1)-(2)   117
    r.17.4   117, 118
    r.17.4(1)-(4)   118
  PD 17   468
    para.1.1-para.1.2   116
    para.1.3-para.1.5   117
    para.2.1(1)   117
    para.2.1(2)   116
    para.2.2   116, 117
    para.2.3-para.2.4   117
  Part 18   102, 112, 141, 182, 235, 469
    r.18.1   88
    r.18.1(1)(a)-(b)   114
    r.18.1(2)-(3)   114
    r.18.2   116
  PD 18   470–1
    para.1.1   112
    para.1.2   113
    para.1.3   112
    para.1.4-para.1.5   113
    para.1.6   113
    para.1.6(1)   113
    para.1.6(2)   113, 114
    para.2.1   114
    para.2.2(1)   114
    para.2.3   115
    para.2.3(1)(c)   113
    para.2.3(2)   115
    para.2.4   115
    para.3   113, 114
    para.4.1(a)-(b)   115
    para.4.2(1)   115
    para.5.2   114
    para.5.3   114
    para.5.3(1)   114
    para.5.4-para.5.8   114
  Part 19   118, 472–3
    r.19.1   x, 117
    r.19.1(2)-(3)   59
    r.19.1(4)   60
    r.19.2   58
    r.19.3   59
    r.19.3(2)   60

TABLE OF RULES, PRACTICE DIRECTIONS AND PROTOCOLS

Civil Procedure Rules 1998 – *continued*
  r.19.3(3)   59
  r.19.4   60, 117
  r.19.4(4)   60
PD 19   **474–5**
  para.1.2   60
  para.1.3-para.1.4   59
  para.2.1-para.2.2   59
  para.2.3(1)-(3)   60
  para.3.2(1)-(2)   60
  para.3.3   60
  para.4-para.5   60
Part 20   64, 84, 88, 90, 103, 105, 107, 123, 163, 168, 265, **476–9**
  r.20.2(1)   105
  r.20.2(2)   108
  r.20.3   268
  r.20.3(1)   105, 272, 276
  r.20.3(2)   105
  r.20.3(3)   110
  r.20.4(1)   105
  r.20.4(2)(a)   105
  r.20.4(2)(b)   105, 108
  r.20.4(3)   105
  r.20.5   219
  r.20.5(1)   105, 108
  r.20.5(2)-(3)   105
  r.20.6   108, 112
  r.20.7(1)   108, 109, 112
  r.20.7(3)   108
  r.20.7(3)(a)   108
  r.20.7(4)   109
  r.20.7(5)   108, 123
  r.20.8   112
  r.20.8(1)   105, 108
  r.20.8(1)(b)   108
  r.20.8(2)   108
  r.20.8(3)   105, 110
  r.20.9   109, 112
  r.20.10   110, 112
  r.20.11   110, 111, 112
  r.20.11(1)(a)   110
  r.20.11(2)(a)-(b)   111
  r.20.11(3)   111
  r.20.11(3)(b)   111
  r.20.11(4)-(5)   111
  r.20.12   112
  r.20.12(1)-(2)   108, 110
  r.20.13   107, 219
  r.20.13(1)-(2)   110
PD 20   **480–1**
  para.1.1-para.1.2   108
  para.2.1   108
  para.2.2-para.2.3   109
  para.3   105
  para.4.1-para.4.2   106, 110
  para.5.1-para.5.2   110

Civil Procedure Rules 1998 – *continued*
  para.5.3-para.5.4   111
  para.6.1   105
  para.6.2   107
  para.7.1   109
  para.7.2   105, 109
  para.7.3-para.7.5   109
Part 21   39, **482–5**
  r.21.1(2)(a)-(b)   61
  r.21.2   61
  r.21.2(3)-(5)   62
  r.21.3(2)   61, 82
  r.21.3(3)-(4)   61
  r.21.4(3)   61
  r.21.5   62
  r.21.5(6)   62
  r.21.6   62, 82
  r.21.6(2)   62
  r.21.7   62
  r.21.8(2)-(3)   63
  r.21.9(1)   62
  r.21.9(2)   63
  r.21.10   271
  r.21.10(2)   267
  r.21.11-r.21.12   64
PD 21   **486–91**
  para.1.3   61
  para.1.5   61
  para.1.5(2)   62
  para.1.8   xi
  para.2.1   61
  para.2.3(2)   62
  para.2.4A   xi
  para.3.4   62
  para.3.4(4)   63
  para.4   62
  para.5.3   63
  para.5.7-para.5.8   63
  para.6.3   xi
  para.7-para.12   64
Part 22   **492–3**
  r.22.1(1)   106
  r.22.1(1)(a)   96, 98, 106, 110, 113, 114
  r.22.1(3)   129
  r.22.1(4)   96, 129
  r.22.1(5)   97
  r.22.1(6)   96
  r.22.1(6)(a)(i)-(ii)   96
  r.22.2(1)-(2)   98
  r.22.3   236
  r.22.4   98
PD 22   **494–5**
  para.1.5   96
  para.2.1   96, 129
  para.2.3   96
  para.3.4-para.3.6   96

Civil Procedure Rules 1998 –
continued
  para.3.7   10, 96
  para.3.8   10, 97
  para.3.9   96
  para.3.10   10, 96
  para.4.2–para.4.3   98
  Part 23   xxi, xxvi, xxxiii, xxxvi, 16,
    22, 57, 59, 62, 74, 80, 81, 82,
    84, 114, 145, 281, 330, **496–8**
  r.23.1   57
  r.23.2(1)-(3)   121, 150
  r.23.2(4)   53, 121, 147
  r.23.2(5)   121, 150
  r.23.3(1)   124, 147
  r.23.3(2)(b)   147
  r.23.4(1)   123, 124, 228
  r.23.4(2)   123
  r.23.6   124, 147
  r.23.7   147
  r.23.7(1)   125
  r.23.7(3)   125, 129
  r.23.7(5)   125, 129
  r.23.8   66, 126, 147
  r.23.8(a)   125
  r.23.9   67, 149, 152
  r.23.9(2)-(3)   124
  r.23.10   67, 149, 152
  r.23.11(1)   128
  PD 23   **499–502**
    para.1   121
    para.2.1   124, 147
    para.2.3   66, 125
    para.2.7   120, 121, 148, 150
    para.2.8   120, 150
    para.2.9   128, 151
    para.2.10   124, 212
    para.4.2   124
    para.5   146
    para.6   127
    para.6.1   151
    para.6.1–para.6.3   xv
    para.6.3(1)(a)   xv
    para.7   151
    para.8   128
    para.9.1   129
    para.9.4   153
    para.10.2   126
    para.12   128
    para.13.2   305–6
  Part 24   20, 100, 101, 240, **503–4**
    r.24.2   144
    r.24.2(a)   180
    r.24.3(1)   142
    r.24.3(2)   xvi, 142
    r.24.4(1)   123, 141
    r.24.4(2)   100, 142
    r.24.4(3)   142, 143

Civil Procedure Rules 1998 –
continued
    r.24.5(1)-(3)   143
    r.24.6   219
  PD 24   **505–7**
    para.2(5)   143
    para.4.3   143, 144
    para.5   144
    para.5.1–para.5.2   144
    para.7   143
    para.10   144
  Part 25   181, 240, **508–12**
    r.25.1   145
    r.25.1(1)   135, 145
    r.25.1(1)(a)   145
    r.25.1(1)(c)   135
    r.25.1(1)(f)   145, 153
    r.25.1(1)(g)   153
    r.25.1(1)(h)   145, 153
    r.25.1(1)(k)   136
    r.25.1(1)(n)   136
    r.25.1(2)   153
    r.25.1(3)   122
    r.25.1(4)   145
    r.25.2(1)   145, 146
    r.25.2(1)(b)   123
    r.25.2(2)   122, 146, 150
    r.25.2(2)(b)   122, 148, 152
    r.25.2(2)(c)   142, 150
    r.25.2(3)   122, 136, 148, 290
    r.25.2(4)   122, 136
    r.25.3(1)   147
    r.25.3(2)   121, 124, 128, 140,
      142, 147, 152
    r.25.3(3)   124, 152
    r.25.5   136
    r.25.6(1)   123, 137
    r.25.6(2)-(5)   137
    r.25.6(7)   139
    r.25.7   137
    r.25.7(1)   137
    r.25.7(1)(c)-(d)   138
    r.25.7(2)   138
    r.25.7(3)-(5)   139
    r.25.8   139
    r.25.8(2)   299
    r.25.9   139
    r.25.11   xvi
  PD 25 Interim Injunctions   129,
    145, 153, **513–29**
    para.1   121
    para.1.1–para.1.4   146
    para.2.1   147
    para.2.3   150
    para.2.4   147
    para.3.1   153, 154
    para.3.2–para.3.4   152
    para.4.2   148

Civil Procedure Rules 1998 – *continued*
  para.4.3(1)-(3) 151
  para.4.4(2)-(3) 149
  para.4.5(1) 148
  para.4.5(5) 148
  para.5.1(1) 149
  para.5.1(2)-(3) 149
  para.5.1(4) 147
  para.5.1(5) 148
  para.5.2-para.5.3 149
  para.7.1.-para.7.2 154
  para.7.3 154
  para.7.3(1)-(2) 154
  para.7.4-para.7.5 154, 155
  para.8.1-para.8.2 154
  para.8.5 155
PD 25B Interim Payments 299, **530–1**
  para.2.1 137
  para.3 139
  para.4.1-para.4.4 139
  para.5 139
PD 25C Accounts and Inquiries xv, **532**
Part 26 86, 105, **533–6**
  r.26.2(1) 55, 179
  r.26.2(3)-(5) 55
  r.26.3 179
  r.26.3(1)-(2) 163
  r.26.3(6) 106
  r.26.4(2) 169, 179
  r.26.4(3)-(5) 169
  r.26.5 219
  r.26.5(1) 162
  r.26.5(2) 162, 169
  r.26.5(3) 164, 207
  r.26.5(4)-(5) 164
  r.26.6(1) 166, 180
  r.26.6(1)(a) 165
  r.26.6(1)(b) 92, 165
  r.26.6(2) 165, 166, 180
  r.26.6(3) 165, 166
  r.26.6(4) 166
  r.26.6(5) 166, 194
  r.26.6(5)(a) 92
  r.26.6(6) 167
  r.26.7(2) 167
  r.26.7(3) 165
  r.26.7(4) 165, 181
  r.26.8 165, 167
  r.26.8(1) 167
  r.26.8(2) 165
  r.26.9-r.26.10 168
PD 26 xvii, **537–45**
  para.2.2 123, 168
  para.2.2(2) 163, 207
  para.2.3 163

Civil Procedure Rules 1998 – *continued*
  para.2.4 152, 163
  para.2.5(1) 164
  para.2.5(2)(b) 164
  para.3.1(1) 169
  para.4.2(2) 164
  para.5.3(1) 123, 142
  para.5.4 142
  para.6.5 164
  para.6.6(2)-(3) 164
  para.7.4 xvii, 165
  para.7.4(2) 144
  para.7.5 167
  para.7.7 167
  para.8.1(1)(d) 165
  para.8.1(2)(b)-(c) 166
  para.9.1(3)(b)-(c) 166
  para.10.2(1)-(2) 55
  para.10.2(5)-(6) 55
  para.10.2(8) 55
  para.10.2(10) xvi
  para.10.2(11) 55
  para.11.1(2) 168, 331
  para.11.2 168
  para.12.1(1)-(2) 169
  para.12.2(2) 170
  para.12.3 170
  para.12.5(2) 170
  para.12.8(1)-(2) 170
  para.12.8(4) 170
  para.12.10 170
Part 27 309, **546–50**
  r.27.2 181
  r.27.2(1) 146, 265
  r.27.3 181
  r.27.4(1) 182
  r.27.4(1)(a) 182
  r.27.4(1)(b)-(c) 183
  r.27.4(1)(d) 184
  r.27.4 182, 184
  r.27.5 165, 189
  r.27.6 183, 184
  r.27.6(4) 184
  r.27.7 183
  r.27.8 185, 292
  r.27.9(1) 186, 187
  r.27.9(2)-(4) 187
  r.27.10 184, 186, 187
  r.27.11(1)-(3) 187
  r.27.11(4) 188
  r.27.12 189, 324
  r.27.12(1)-(2) 188
  r.27.13 188
  r.27.14 303, 309
  r.27.14(2) xviii, 189
  r.27.14(2)(d) 190
  r.27.14(3) 189

TABLE OF RULES, PRACTICE DIRECTIONS AND PROTOCOLS

Civil Procedure Rules 1998 – *continued*
r.27.14(5)   165, 166, 190
r.27.15   168, 190, 309
PD 27   184, **551–6**
  para.3.2   xviii, 185
  para.4.2-para.4.3   185
  para.5.3-para.5.5   186
  para.5.7   186
  para.7.2   189
  para.7.3   189
  para.7.3(2)   165
  para.8   188
  para.8.7   189
  para.8.10   189
  appendix A   182, 183
Part 28   254, **557–8**
  r.28.2   219
  r.28.2(1)   193
  r.28.2(2)   193, 197
  r.28.2(3)-(4)   197
  r.28.2(5)   203
  r.28.3   193, 219
  r.28.3(2)   194, 221
  r.28.4   173
  r.28.4(1)-(2)   198
  r.28.5(2)   196
  r.28.6   293
  r.28.6(1)   199, 294
  r.28.6(1)(b)   201
  r.28.6(2)   202
  r.28.7   294
PD 28   199, 295, **559–66**
  para.2.3   193
  para.2.5   120, 193
  para.2.8   193
  para.3   194, 198
  para.3.3   193
  para.3.6-para.3.8   254
  para.3.9   254
  para.3.9(4)   195
  para.3.11   193
  para.3.12   194, 195
  para.3.13   197
  para.4.2(1)   199
  para.4.2(2)   128, 175, 199, 294
  para.4.3(2)   331
  para.4.5(1)   198
  para.5   174, 175
  para.5.1   174, 237
  para.5.2   174
  para.5.4   174, 237
  para.5.4(4)   199
  para.5.4(6)   199
  para.6.1(4)   xviii
  para.6.3   201
  para.6.5   201
  para.7.2(1)   201

Civil Procedure Rules 1998 – *continued*
  para.7.2(4)   201
  para.8.1-para.8.2   298
  para.8.3   202, 294
  para.8.5   203
  para.8.6   202
Part 29   254, **567–8**
  r.29.2   219, 221
  r.29.2(1)   207
  r.29.2(2)   211, 212, 293
  r.29.2(3)   212
  r.29.3(2)   xxiv, 11, 210
  r.29.5   173
  r.29.5(1)   215
  r.29.6   212
  r.29.6(1)   212
  r.29.6(3)   213
  r.29.7   214
  r.29.8   293
  r.29.8(c)(ii)   293
  r.29.8(i)   294
  r.29.9   294
PD 29   **569–75**
  para.2   53, 56, 205
  para.2.4-para.2.5   56
  para.3.1   205
  para.3.2(2)   205
  para.3.4   214, 215
  para.3.5   120, 205, 214
  para.3.6   151, 215, 216
  para.3.7   210
  para.3.8   123, 215
  para.3.10   161, 205
  para.4.3   207
  para.4.6   207, 208
  para.4.7   208, 254
  para.4.10   208
  para.4.10-para.4.13   254
  para.4.12   209
  para.4.12(2)   210
  para.4.13   209
  para.5.1   210
  para.5.2(3)   210
  para.5.3-para.5.4   211
  para.5.5(2)   ix
  para.5.6   210, 211, 295
  para.5.7   295
  para.5.8   123, 212
  para.5.9   211
  para.6.2   123, 215
  para.6.2(2)   128, 175, 208
  para.6.3   216
  para.6.5(1)-(2)   215
  para.6.6(2)   294
  para.7   174, 175
  para.7.1   174, 216, 237
  para.7.2   174, 216

TABLE OF RULES, PRACTICE DIRECTIONS AND PROTOCOLS

Civil Procedure Rules 1998 –
continued
  para.7.4   174
  para.8.1(2)-(3)   212
  para.8.1(5)   213
  para.8.3(1)-(2)   213
  para.9.3   214
  para.10.1   xxiv, 214, 298
  para.10.2   298
  para.10.3   294
Part 30   55, **576–7**
  r.30.2   56
  r.30.2(1)   56
  r.30.2(1)(b)   56
  r.30.2(2)-(3)   57
  r.30.2(4)-(5)   56
  r.30.2(6)-(7)   57
  r.30.3(1)   56
  r.30.3(2)   56, 57
  r.30.4(1)-(2)   57
  r.30.5   57
  r.30.5(1)   57
  r.30.6   57
PD 30   **578**
  para.4.1   57
Part 31   23, 181, 218, 242, **579–84**
  r.31.1   218
  r.31.2   219
  r.31.3   219
  r.31.3(2)   219, 221, 223, 224, 229, 230
  r.31.4   221
  r.31.5   219
  r.31.5(1)   219
  r.31.5(3)   221
  r.31.6   219
  r.31.6(b)-(c)   220, 221
  r.31.7   220, 224
  r.31.7(2)   220
  r.31.7(3)   220, 223
  r.31.8   219
  r.31.8(1)-(2)   222
  r.31.9   222
  r.31.9(1)   222
  r.31.10   222
  r.31.10(2)   222
  r.31.10(3)   223, 225
  r.31.10(4)   222
  r.31.10(5)   223
  r.31.10(6)   7, 223
  r.31.10(7)   223
  r.31.10(8)   224
  r.31.11   224
  r.31.12   121, 219, 224, 225
  r.31.13   224
  r.31.14   225
  r.31.14(3)   xix
  r.31.15(a)-(c)   225

Civil Procedure Rules 1998 –
continued
  r.31.16   226, 228, 229
  r.31.16(3)(a)-(d)   226
  r.31.16(4)   227
  r.31.16(4)(a)   226
  r.31.16(5)   227
  r.31.17   226, 228, 229
  r.31.17(4)-(5)   228
  r.31.18   229
  r.31.19(1)-(2)   229
  r.31.19(3)   230
  r.31.19(4)   222, 230
  r.31.19(6)   230
  r.31.19(8)   230
  r.31.20   231
  r.31.21   231
  r.31.22(1)   231, 232
  r.31.22(1)(a)   232
  r.31.22(2)-(3)   232
PD 31   **585–7**
  para.1.4   221, 224
  para.2   220
  para.3   222
  para.3.1   222
  para.3.2   223
  para.3.3   224
  para.4   222
  para.4.2   223
  para.4.2(2)   220, 223
  para.4.3   223
  para.4.4   221
  para.4.5-para.4.6   223
  para.5.2-para.5.4   225
  para.6.1   230
  para.7   xix
Part 32   173, 181, 243, **588–91**
  r.32.1   xix, 166, 181, 233, 234, 238
  r.32.1(1)(a)-(c)   295
  r.32.1(2)   233, 234
  r.32.2   234
  r.32.2(1)   129
  r.32.3   234
  r.32.4   236
  r.32.4(1)-(2)   235
  r.32.5   238
  r.32.5(1)   237, 238
  r.32.5(2)   234, 235, 298
  r.32.5(3)   236, 238, 298
  r.32.5(4)   194, 238, 298
  r.32.5(5)   238, 239, 259
  r.32.6   66, 239, 245
  r.32.6(1)   100, 129
  r.32.6(2)   98, 100, 240
  r.32.6(2)(a)-(b)   129
  r.32.7   245
  r.32.7(1)   239

TABLE OF RULES, PRACTICE DIRECTIONS AND PROTOCOLS

Civil Procedure Rules 1998 – *continued*
r.32.7(2) 240
r.32.9 236
r.32.9(1) 194, 236
r.32.9(2) 236
r.32.9(4) 236
r.32.10 237
r.32.11 239, 298
r.32.12 240
r.32.13(1)-(2) 240
r.32.13(4) 241
r.32.14(1) 89, 97, 239
r.32.14(2) 97, 239
r.32.14(2)(b) 97
r.32.15 239, 241
r.32.15(1) 241
r.32.15(2) 66, 129, 153
r.32.16 130, 241
r.32.17-r.32.18 241
r.32.19 242
r.32.19(1) 242
r.32.19(2) 242
PD 32 129, 134, 173, 241, **592–8**
  para.1.4 239
  para.1.4(2) 153
  para.1.6 239
  para.1.7 129
  para.2-para.16 130
  para.4.2 132
  para.5 133
  para.6.1 133
  para.6.1(7) 132
  para.6.2 132
  para.8.1 133
  para.9 133
  para.10.1 133
  para.13.1-para.13.2 133
  para.14 133
  para.15 133
  para.15.3 134
  para.15.4 xv
  para.17.1 xix
  para.17–1-para.22.2 235
  para.18.3 100
  para.18.5 xv
  para.19.1(1) xix
  para.25 173
  para.25.1 134, 236, 241
Part 33 181, 243, **599–601**
  r.33.1 243
  r.33.2 243
  r.33.2(2) 238, 244
  r.33.2(3)-(4) 244
  r.33.3 244
  r.33.3(a) 132
  r.33.3(aa) xx

Civil Procedure Rules 1998 – *continued*
r.33.4-r.33.5 245
r.33.6 245, 246, 296
r.33.6(3) 246
r.33.6(6)-(8) 246
r.33.7-r.33.8 242
PD 33 **602**
  para.2 xx
  para.3 xx
Part 34 **603–6**
  r.34.1-r.34.7 247
  r.34.2(1)-(5) 247
  r.34.3(1)-(2) 248
  r.34.3(4) 248
  r.34.4 248
  r.34.5(1)-(3) 249
  r.34.6(1)-(2) 249
  r.34.7 249
  r.34.8 247, 249, 250
  r.34.9 247, 250
  r.34.10 247
  r.34.11-r.34.12 247, 250
  r.34.13-r.34.15 247, 251
  r.34.13(4) xxi
PD 34 **607–11**
  para.1.2 247
  para.2.4 249
  para.3.3 249
  para.4.2-para.6.6 249
  para.4.12 250
  para.5.2 xxi
  para.5.6 xxi
  para.6.1-para.6.8 xxi
PD 34B xxi, **612–13**
Part 35 95, 181, 253, 254, **614–17**
  r.35.1 181, 253
  r.35.3 181, 253, 257, 261
  r.35.4 253, 259, 261
  r.35.5 255
  r.35.5(2) 195
  r.35.6 195, 255, 256, 260
  r.35.6(1)-(3) 255
  r.35.6(4) 255, 256
  r.35.7 194, 255, 256, 257
  r.35.7(3) 256
  r.35.8 181, 257
  r.35.8(3) 257
  r.35.8(4)(a) 257
  r.35.8(5) 257
  r.35.9 258
  r.35.10(2) 258
  r.35.10(3) xix, 258, 259
  r.35.10(4) xix, 225, 258
  r.35.11 259
  r.35.12 195, 254, 260
  r.35.12(2)-(5) 260
  r.35.13 173, 261

Civil Procedure Rules 1998 –
continued
  r.35.14 261
  r.35.14(1) 261
  r.35.14(3) 261
  r.35.15 261
  r.35.15(3)-(7) 262
 PD 35 xix, xxii, 253, 258, **618–19**
  para.1.1 258
  para.1.3-para.1.4 258
  para.1.6 258
  para.3 xix
  para.4.1 195
  para.5 257
 Part 36 33, 41, 182, 190, 264, 293, 309, **620–7**
  r.36.1(2) 265
  r.36.2(1) 264, 267
  r.36.2(4) 268, 276
  r.36.2(5) 265
  r.36.3(1) 267, 272
  r.36.3(2) 272
  r.36.4 268, 272
  r.36.4(3) 269
  r.36.4(3)(a)-(b) 273
  r.36.5(1) 268
  r.36.5(2) 268, 276
  r.36.5(3)(a)-(c) 268
  r.36.5(4)-(7) 268
  r.36.5(8) 269, 281
  r.36.6(1) 272
  r.36.6(2) 274
  r.36.6(2)(a)-(c) 273
  r.36.6(2)(d) 272, 273
  r.36.6(3) xxii, 274
  r.36.6(4) 274
  r.36.6(5) 269, 281
  r.36.7 272
  r.36.7(2)-(3) 274
  r.36.7(5) 275, 281
  r.36.7(6) 275, 280
  r.36.7(11) 275
  r.36.8(1) 276
  r.36.8(2) 274
  r.36.8(3) 269, 271, 276, 277
  r.36.8(4) 274
  r.36.8(5) 269, 276
  r.36.9 267
  r.36.9(1) 281
  r.36.9(3) 281
  r.36.10 264, 265–6, 267, 276, 280
  r.36.10(1) 266
  r.36.10(2)(a) 266
  r.36.10(2)(b) 266, 267
  r.36.10(2)(c) 266
  r.36.10(4) 266
  r.36.11 274

Civil Procedure Rules 1998 –
continued
  r.36.11(1) 269, 277
  r.36.11(2) 269, 280
  r.36.11(2)(a)(ii) 270
  r.36.11(2)(b)(ii) 270
  r.36.11(3) 270
  r.36.12(2) 280
  r.36.13 310
  r.36.13(1) 269, 275
  r.36.13(2) 270, 271, 276
  r.36.13(3) 270, 271, 275, 277
  r.36.13(4) 269
  r.36.14 266, 267
  r.36.15 275, 279, 281
  r.36.15(1) 269, 276
  r.36.15(2) 275, 276
  r.36.15(3) 270, 271, 275, 276
  r.36.16 265, 274
  r.36.17 271, 275
  r.36.17(2)-(3) 280
  r.36.17(4) 271
  r.36.17(4)(a)-(b) 280
  r.36.18 278
  r.36.18(1) 271, 275, 280
  r.36.18(2) 269, 280
  r.36.18(3) 275, 280
  r.36.19(1) 267
  r.36.19(3) 279
  r.36.20 268, 272, 277, 278, 280, 284
  r.36.20(1)(b) xxii
  r.36.20(5) 282
  r.36.21 275, 280
  r.36.21(1) 278
  r.36.21(2) 46, 278, 279
  r.36.21(3) 278, 279
  r.36.21(4) 279
  r.36.21(5) 278, 279, 284
  r.36.22(1)-(2) 268, 273
  r.36.23 273
  r.36.23(2) 274
  r.36.23(4) 273
 PD 36 277, **628–32**
  para.2.3 276
  para.3.1 272
  para.3.4 281
  para.4.1 272
  para.4.1(1)(a)-(b) 272
  para.5.1 268, 272
  para.5.1(2) 268, 272
  para.5.2 268
  para.5.3 272
  para.5.4-para.5.5 268, 272
  para.5.6 272
  para.6.1 281
  para.7.4(2) 269
  para.7.6 269, 274, 276

TABLE OF RULES, PRACTICE DIRECTIONS AND PROTOCOLS

Civil Procedure Rules 1998 – *continued*
  para.7.7 269, 276
  para.7.8 281
  para.7.9 280, 281
  para.7.10-para.7.11 275
  para.8.1-para.8.4 274
  para.10.1 272
  para.10.2 274
  para.10.3 272
  para.11.1 269, 274, 276
  para.11.2 272, 274
Part 37 **633–4**
  r.37.3 272
PD 37 **635–6**
Part 38 **637–8**
  r.38.1(1)-(2) 289
  r.38.2(1) 289
  r.38.2(2)(a)-(c) 289
  r.38.2(3) 289
  r.38.3(2)-(3) 289
  r.38.3(4) 290
  r.38.4-r.38.5 290
  r.38.6(1)-(3) 290
  r.38.7-r.38.8 290
Part 39 182, **639–40**
  r.39.2 124, 127, 151, 182
  r.39.2(1) 297
  r.39.2(2) 185
  r.39.2(3) 185
  r.39.2(3)(a) 124
  r.39.2(3)(e) 124
  r.39.3(1)-(5) 300
  r.39.4 201, 294
  r.39.5(2) 295
  r.39.6 xxv, 61
PD 39 **641–4**
  para.1.4A xxiv
  para.1.5 xxiv, 297
  para.1.12 297
  para.1.15 xxv
  para.3 295
  para.3.3 295
  para.3.9 296
  para.3.10 295
  para.4.1 293
  para.5 298
  para.5.1 xxv
  para.5.2 xxv
  para.5.3 xxv
  para.5.4 xxv
  para.5.5 xxv
  para.6.1 299, 325
  para.6.3 xxv
  para.6.4 xxv
  para.6.5 xxv
  para.7 298
PD 39B xxiv, **645–6**

Civil Procedure Rules 1998 – *continued*
  para.3.1(2) xxiv
  para.3.2 xxv
  para.3.3(2) xxv
  para.3.3(3) xxv
  para.3.4 xxv
  para.3.5 xxv
Part 40 xxvi, **647–50**
  r.40.1(b) 299
  r.40.2(1) 134
  r.40.2(2) 134, 299
  r.40.3 299
  r.40.3(1) xxvi
  r.40.3(1)(c) 134
  r.40.3(3) xxvi, 134
  r.40.4(1)-(2) 134
  r.40.5 7, 134
  r.40.6(2)(b) 125
  r.40.6(3) 125
  r.40.6(7) 126
  r.40.6(7)(b) xxvii
  r.40.7 134
  r.40.7(1) 299
  r.40.8 301
  r.40.11 299
  r.40.12(1) 300
  r.40.13(2)-(3) 299
  r.40.14 299
PD 40 xv, **651–2**
  para.1.1 xv
  para.1.2 xv
  para.2(1) xv
  para.3.1 xv
  para.5 xv
  section 2 xv
PD 40B xxvi, **653–7**
  para.1.1–para.1.5 xxvi
  para.3.4 xxvii
  para.3.5 xxvii
  paras4.1 to 4.5 xxvii
  para.5 xxvi
  para.6 xxvi
  para.8.2 xviii
  para.9.1 xvi
  para.10 xxvi
  para.12 xxvi
  para.14 xxvi
PD 40C xxvi, **658–60**
  para.1.5 xxvii
  para.1.6 xxvii
Part 41 **661**
  r.41.2(2) 299
  r.41.3(6) 300
PD 41 xxvi, **662–4**
  para.3.2 xxvi
  para.4 xxvi
  para.5 xxvi

Civil Procedure Rules 1998 –
continued
  Part 42   xxii, 285, **665–6**
    r.42.1   286
    r.42.2   286
    r.42.2(5)   286
    r.42.2(6)   286
    r.42.2(6)(b)   286
    r.42.3   287
    r.42.3(2)-(3)   287
    r.42.4   287
    r.42.4(1)   287
    r.42.4(3)   287
  PD 42   xxii, **667–8**
    para.1.3   xxii
  Part 43   **669**
    r.43.2(1)   312
    r.43.2(2)(iii)   304
  Part 43 to Part 48   17
  PD Costs Practice Direction about Costs — Introduction   **670**
  PD 43   **671–6**
    para.2.1   315
    para.2.2   316
    para.2.5(9)   318
    para.2.8   316
    para.2.10   316
    para.2.13   317
    para.2.15   316
    para.2.16   318
    para.4.5(1)   xvii, 162
    para.4.5(2)   xvii, 196
    para.4.5(3)   196
  Part 44   254, **677–81**
    r.44.2   7, 309
    r.44.3   41, 241
    r.44.3(1)   304
    r.44.3(2)   304
    r.44.3(2)(a)   277
    r.44.3(4)   7, 46, 265, 266, 304
    r.44.3(5)   7, 46, 242, 265, 304
    r.44.3(5)(a)   266
    r.44.3(5)(b)   242
    r.44.3(6)-(7)   305
    r.44.3(8)   313
    r.44.4   40
    r.44.4(2)   313
    r.44.4(3)-(4)   314
    r.44.5(3)   xvii, 17, 318
    r.44.7   312
    r.44.9(1)-(2)   308
    r.44.10   312
    r.44.11   189
    r.44.12   310
    r.44.13(1)   305
    r.44.13(2)   309
    r.44.13(3)-(4)   308
    r.44.14   320

Civil Procedure Rules 1998 –
continued
  PD 44   **682–6**
    para.1.1   309
    para.2.3-para.2.4   306
    para.3.1   313
    para.3.2-para.3.3   314
    para.4.2   307
    para.4.3–para.4.10   203
    para.4.4   127, 202
    para.4.4(2)   xxvii, 127, 307
    para.4.4(3)   xxxv, 126
    para.4.5   127
    para.4.6   202
    para.4.8   127
    para.4.10   127, 202
    para.5.1(2)   309
    para.6.2-para.6.3   309
    para.7.1-para.7.2   320
  Part 45   xviii, 307, **687–9**
    r.45.1(2)   xviii
    r.45.4   81
  PD 45   307, **690**
    para.2.1   308
  Part 46   34, 311, **691–3**
    r.46.2   311
    r.46.2(3)-(4)   311
    r.46.2(6)   311
    r.46.3(2)-(4)   312
    r.46.3(6)   311
    r.46.3(7)-(8)   312
  PD 46   **694**
  Part 47   18, **695–702**
    r.47.1   313
    r.47.4   314
    r.47.4(2)   315
    r.47.4(3)   314
    r.47.6(2)   315
    r.47.7   315
    r.47.8   319
    r.47.9   317
    r.47.9(3)-(4)   317
    r.47.11   317
    r.47.11(2)   317
    r.47.12   317
    r.47.12(5)   317
    r.47.13   317
    r.47.14   317
    r.47.14(7)   318
    r.47.15   319
    r.47.16(2)-(3)   319
    r.47.16(5)   319
    r.47.17   318
    r.47.17(1)-(2)   315
    r.47.18   318
    r.47.19   319
    r.47.21(1)   319
    r.47.22(1)-(3)   320

lxvii

Civil Procedure Rules 1998 –
continued
  r.47.23 319
  r.47.24-r.47.25 320
  r.47.26(1) 320
  r.47.26(3) 320
  PD 47 **703–14**
    para.1.1(1) 313
    para.1.1(4) 313
    para.1.4 314
    para.1.5(3) 315
    para.2.2 315
    para.2.5 315
    para.2.7 315
    para.2.11(2) 319
    para.3.8-para.3.11 317
    para.4.13 315
    para.5.5 319
    para.6.3 315
    para.7.1 318
    para.7.4-para.7.6 319
    para.8.3 320
    para.8.6 320
    para.8.10 320
  Part 48 **715–18**
    r.48.1 308
    r.48.1(2) 227, 228
    r.48.1(3) 47, 227, 228, 308
    r.48.2 36, 310
    r.48.3 267
    r.48.4 314
    r.48.5 267, 271, 313
    r.48.5(2) 63
    r.48.6 321
    r.48.7 321
    r.48.7(3) v, xxvii, 322
    r.48.8 314
    r.48.8(1)(b) 36
    r.48.8(2) 36
    r.48.9 35, 36, 42
    r.48.9(2) 36
    r.48.9(3) 320
    r.48.9(4) 36
    r.48.9(5) 36, 37, 38, 39
    r.48.9(6) 39
    r.48.10(2)-(4) 318
  PD 48 17, 35, 39, **719–24**
    para.1.2 313
    para.1.6 321
    para.2.2-para.2.3 321
    para.2.4 322
    para.2.5 321
    para.2.6 322
    para.2.9-para.2.36 318
    para.2.13 35, 38
    para.2.14 35, 37
    para.2.15 35, 36
    para.2.16 35, 37

Civil Procedure Rules 1998 –
continued
    para.2.18 318
    para.2.23 318
    para.3.2(2)(c) 17
    para.3.3 17
    para.3.5 17
    para.3.7(3)-(4) 18
  Part 49 14, 64, 80, **725**
    r.49(2) 56
  PD 49 xxx, xxxii, **726–31**
    para.2.3 xxx
    para.2.5 xxx
    para.2.7 xxx
    para.3 xxx
    para.5 xxxi
    para.7.1 xxxi
  PD 49B xxxi, **732–5**
    para.2(1) xxxi
    para.3 xxxi
    para.4(1) xxxi
    para.9 xxxi
  PD 49C xxxi, **736–50**
    para.2.3 xxxi
    para.2.4 xxxi
    para.4.1 xxxi
    para.4.2 xxxi
    para.5.3 xxxii
  PD 49D xxxii, **751–3**
    para.2.2 xxxii
    para.6.1 xxxii
    para.9.5 xxxii
  PD 49E xxxii, **754–65**
    para.2.2 xxxii
    para.2.4 xxxii
  PD 49F xxxii, **766–97**
    para.2.1(6) xxxii
    para.2.2 xxxii
    para.3.3 xxxii
    para.6 xxxii
    para.9 xxxii
    para.16.1 xxxii
    para.17 xxxii
  PD 49G xxxiii, **798–810**
    para.5.3 xxxiii
    para.7 xxxiii
    para.8 xxxiii
    para.9.1 xxxiii
    para.13 xxxiii
    para.14.1 xxx
  PD 49H **811–15**
  Part 50 21, **816**
    r.50(2) 22
  Part 51 **817**
  PD 51 14, **818–21**
    para.1(1) 14
    para.2 14
    para.4-para.5 15

Civil Procedure Rules 1998 –
continued
  para.7 15
  para.7(2)-(4) 15
  para.8 15
  para.8(2)-(3) 15
  para.9 16
  para.10 14
  para.12 14
  para.13 16
  para.14 viii
  para.14(1) 14
  para.14(2) 17
  para.14(4)-(5) 16
  para.15(1)-(2) 14, 17
  para.15(3) 17
  para.16(3)-(4) 15
  para.16(6) 15
  para.17-para.18 17
  para.19 15
Glossary **822–3**
sch.1 21
  RSC
    ord.10 **824**
      r.4 25, 74
    ord.11 viii, 25–6, 74, **824–30**
      r.1(3) 26
      r.1A 26, 79
      r.1A(2) viii
      r.1A(3) viii
      r.1B 26
      r.4(2) 22
    PD ord. 11 viii, **965–72**
      para.1.2 ix
      para.1.3 ix
      paras1.5 to 1.7 ix
      para.3 ix
      para.8.2 ix
      para.10.2 ix
    ord.15 **830–4**
      r.6A 26
      r.7(1) 26
      r.9 26
      r.11 26
      r.12 26
      r.12A 26
      r.12A(8)(c) 23
      r.13 26
      r.13A 26
      r.14-r.17 26
    ord.17 27, **834–7**
    ord.23 27, **838**
      r.A1 27
    ord.30 29, **838–40**
    ord.31 29, **840–1**
      r.1 xxxiii
    PD ord. 31 xxxiii, **973**
    ord.44 xv, 28, **841–4**

Civil Procedure Rules 1998 –
continued
    ord.45 28, **844–8**
    ord.46 28, **848–50**
    ord.47 28, **850–2**
    ord.48 28, **852–3**
    ord.49 28, **853–5**
    ord.50 29, **855–9**
    ord.51 **859**
    ord.52 xxxiii, 28, **860–2**
      r.2 xxxiii
    PD ord. 52 xxxiii, **974–6**
      para.2.1 xxxiii
      para.2.2 xxxiii
      para.2.3 xxxiii
      para.2.5(1) xxxiii
      para.2.5(2) xxxiii
      para.2.6(1) xxxiii
      para.2.6(2) xxxiii
      para.3.1 xxxiii
      para.4.1 xxxiv
      para.4.4 xxxiv
      para.6 xxxiv
      para.7 xxxiv
      para.9 xxxiv
      para.11 xxxiv
    ord.53 xxxiv, 28, 329, **862–6**
      r.4(1) 329
      r.5(2A) xxxiv, 28, 330
      r.5(6) xxxiv
      r.6 xxxiv
      r.6(1) xxxiv
      r.11 xxxiv
    PD ord. 53 xxxiv, **977–8**
      para.3.1 xxxiv
      para.4.1 xxxiv
      para.5.1 xxxiv
      para.6 xxxiv
      para.7.1 xxxiv
      para.8 xxxiv
    ord.54 28, **866–8**
      r.10 xxxiv
    PD ord. 54 xxxiv, **979–80**
      para.3.1 xxxiv
      para.4.1 xxxiv
      para.5.1 xxxiv
      para.6.1 xxxiv
      para.7.1 xxxiv
    ord.55 330, **868–70**
      r.3(1) 330
    ord.55 to ord.61 29
    ord.56 330, **870–3**
      r.8(1) xiii, 330
      r.10(1) 330
    ord.57 330, **873–4**
      r.2(1) 330
    ord.58 325, **874–5**
      r.1(2) 325

TABLE OF RULES, PRACTICE DIRECTIONS AND PROTOCOLS

Civil Procedure Rules 1998 –
continued
    r.2 325
    r.3(2) 325
  PD ord. 58 xxix, **981**
    ord.59 324, **875–84**
      r.1B(2) 329
      r.3 xiii
      r.6(1)(c) 329
      r.9 329
      r.19 324, 326
      r.19(4) 325
    ord.60 330, **884–5**
      r.1 330
      r.3(1) 330
    ord.61 330, **885–6**
      r.2(2) 330
      r.3(A1) 330
      r.3(A2) 330
      r.3(1)(a) 331
    ord.62
      appendix 3 29, 307, 308, **886–8**
    ord.64 **888**
      r.4 28
    ord.69 29, **888–9**
    ord.70 29, **889–91**
    ord.71 29, **891–901**
    ord.74 29, **901**
    ord.77 27, **901–5**
      r.4 74
      r.4(3)-(5) 27
      r.7 142
    ord.79 **906–7**
      r.8-r.11 28
      r.11(1) xii
    ord.81 26, **907–10**
      r.1 61
      r.9 27
    ord.82 27, **910–12**
    ord.85 27, **912–13**
    ord.87 27, **913–15**
    ord.88 27, 80, **915–18**
    ord.91 27, **918–20**
    ord.92 27, **921–2**
    ord.93 30, **922–6**
      r.16(3) 24
    ord.94 30, **926–33**
      r.4(1) 24
      r.6(5) 24
    ord.95 30, **933–4**
    ord.96 30, **934–6**
    ord.97 30, **936–40**
    ord.98 30, **940–1**
    ord.99 30, **941–2**
      r.A1 23
    ord.101 30, **942–3**
    ord.106 30, 318, **943–6**

Civil Procedure Rules 1998 –
continued
    ord.108 30, **946–7**
    ord.109 30, **947–8**
    ord.110 30, **948–9**
    ord.111 30, **949–50**
    ord.112 xiii, 30, **950**
    ord.113 xiii, 27, **950–2**
    ord.114 28, 331, **952–3**
      r.2(2) 331
      r.6 331
    ord.115 30, **953–61**
    ord. 116 **961–4**
  sch.2 21
  CCR
    ord.1 25, **982**
    ord.3
      r.6 25, **982–3**
      r.6(6)-(11) 25
    ord.4 **983**
      r.3 25, 54
    ord.5 **983–6**
      r.5-r.8 26
      r.9 26, 61
      r.10 26
      r.12-r.14 26
    ord.6 **986–9**
      r.3 27
      r.5 27
      r.5A 27
      r.6 27
    ord.7 **989–90**
      r.15 25, 74
      r.15A 25, 74
    ord.13 **990**
      r.1(10)-(11) 29, 324
    ord.16 **990**
      r.7 27
    ord.18
      r.15 28
    ord.19 **990–1**
      r.15 331
    ord.22 **991–3**
      r.8 28
      r.10-r.11 28
      r.13 28
    ord.24 27, 80, **993–7**
      r.1(1) xiii
    ord.25 28, **998–1003**
      r.9 26
    ord.26 28, **1003–7**
    ord.27 28, **1007–15**
      r.5(1) 25
    ord.28 28, **1015–18**
    ord.29 xxxiii, 28, **1018–20**
    ord.30 28, **1020–2**
    ord.31 29, **1022–4**
    ord.33 24, 27, **1024–7**

TABLE OF RULES, PRACTICE DIRECTIONS AND PROTOCOLS

Civil Procedure Rules 1998 – *continued*
    ord.34   25, 29, **1027–8**
    ord.35   29, **1028–30**
    ord.37   **1030–1**
        r.1   29, 324
        r.6   29, 324
        r.8   29
    ord.38   **1031–4**
        r.8   29
        appendix B   29, 307, 308, **1031–4**
    ord.39   29, **1034–8**
    ord.42   27, **1038–41**
        r.5(5)   142
        r.7   74
        r.8   27
        r.12(2)   23
    ord.43   29, **1041–5**
    ord.44   29, **1046–7**
    ord.45   29, **1047–8**
    ord.46   30, **1048–9**
    ord.47   30, **1049**
    ord.48B   30, **1049–53**
        r.2   25
    ord. 48D   **1053–4**
    ord.49   30, **1054–70**
        r.6   25
        r.6A   25
        r.6B   25
Code of Conduct of the Bar of England and Wales
    para.202   9
Companies (Unfair Prejudice Applications) Proceedings Rules 1986 (SI 1986/2000)   xxxi
Conditional Fee Agreements Order 1995 (SI 1995/1674)   32
Conditional Fee Agreements Order 1998 (SI 1998/1860)   33, 41
Conditional Fee Agreements Regulations 1995 (SI 1995/1675)   32, 34, 39
    reg.4(2)(d)   35
Costs in Criminal Cases (General) Regulations 1986 (SI 1986/1335)   249
Costs Information Code   34
    para.4(j)   34
County Court Fees Order 1999 (SI 1999/689)   **1363–74**
County Court Rules 1981 (SI 1981/1687)   2, 20, 21, 99
    ord.2
        r.8   65
    ord.8   26
    ord.13
        r.1(10)-(11)   324

County Court Rules 1981 – *continued*
    r.7   135
    r.8   27
    r.12   137
    ord.17
        r.11   288
    ord.37
        r.2   128
    ord.48   23
    ord.48C   22
    ord.49   22
    ord.50
        r.5   285
        r.9   27
County Courts Jurisdiction Order 1981 (SI 1981/1123)   54

Family Proceedings Fees Order 1999 (SI 1999/690)   **1375–82**

Guide to the Professional Conduct of Solicitors
    Principle 21.07   9
    Principle 21.11   40

High Court and County Courts Jurisdiction Order 1991 (SI 1991/724)   53
    art.6   54
    art.9   53

Insolvency Rules 1986 (SI 1986/1925)   xxxv
    r.4.11(2)(b)   xxxiv
    r.7.2-r.7.3   24
    r.7.48(2)   xxxv

Jurisdiction Order *see* High Court and County Courts Jurisdiction Order 1991 (SI 1991/724)

Late Payment of Commercial Debts (Interest) Act 1998 (Commencement No.1) Order 1998 (1998/2479)   301
Lay Representatives (Right of audience) Order 1999 (SI 1999/1225)   xviii

Non-contentious Probate Fees Order 1999 (SI 1999/688)   **1360–2**

Practice Direction, Chancery and Queen's Bench Divisions Excluding the Admiralty and Commercial Courts, and the Technology and Construction Court — the Fixing of Trial Dates and Windows in the Multi-track   xxiii, **1192**

Practice Direction (Civil Litigation:
  Procedure) [1999] 1 WLR 1124
  333
Practice Direction (Costs: Summary
  Assessment) [1999] 1 WLR 420
  35, 38, 127
Practice Direction (Court of Appeal:
  Leave to Appeal and Skeleton
  Arguments) [1999] 1 WLR 2
  326, 328, 329
  para.8   328, 329
  para.9   328
  para.15 328
  para.16 19
  para.18-para.19   328
  para.27 328
  para.30 328
  para.32-para.34   329
  para.38 328
Practice Direction (Crown Office
  List) [1987] 1 WLR 232   xxxiv
Practice Direction — Devolution
  Issues (and Crown Office
  Applications in Wales)   xxxvi,
  1151–63 (English),   **1164–74**
  (Welsh)
Practice Direction — Directors
  Disqualification Proceedings
  xxxvi, **1124–46**
  para.2.1   xxxvi
  para.5.1   xxxvi
  para.7.1   xxxvi
  para.8.3   xxxvi
  para.9.1   xxxvi
  para.9.3   xxxvi
  para.9.4   xxxvi
  para.10.1   xxxvi
  para.10.3   xxxvi
  para.11   xxxvi
  para.12   xxxvi
  para.13   xxxvi
  paras 14–19   xxxvi
  paras 20–3   xxxvi
  paras 24–6   xxxvi
Practice Direction (ECJ References:
  Procedure) [1999] 1 WLR 260
  331
Practice Direction for the Court of
  Appeal (Civil Division)
  v, xiii, xxiv, xxviii, **1071–1111**
  paras 2.1 to 2.19   xxviii
  para.2.19.1   xxviii
  para.3   xxviii
  para.4   xxviii
  para.5   xxviii
  para.5.3   xxviii
  para.6   xxviii
  para.7   xxviii

Practice Direction for the Court of
  Appeal (Civil Division) –
  continued
  para.8   xxviii
  para.9   xxviii
  para.10   xxviii
  para.11   xxviii
  para.12   xxviii
  para.13   xxviii
  para.14   xxviii
  annex F   xxviii
Practice Direction — Insolvency
  Proceedings   xxxiv, **1112–23**
  part.2   xxxiv
  para.4   xxxv
  para.5   xxxv
  para.6   xxxv
  para.8   xxxv
  part.3   xxxv
  para.9   xxxv
  para.10   xxxv
  para.11   xxxv
  para.12   xxxv
  para.12.3   xxxv
  para.12.4   xxxv
  para.12.5   xxxv
  para.13   xxxv
  para.14   xxxv
  para.15   xxxv
  para.16   xxxv
  para.16.8   xxxv
  para.17   xxxv
Practice Direction (Interlocutory
  Injunctions: Forms) [1996]
  1 WLR 1551   149
Practice Direction (Order 14: Return
  Date) [1970] 1 WLR 258
  143
Practice Direction Protocols   46,
  1194–5
  para.2.3   45, 176, 304
  para.2.4   46, 177
  para.4   46
  para.5.1   49
  para.5.4   ix
Practice Direction Relating to the Use
  of the Welsh Language in Cases
  in the Civil Courts in
  Wales   **1147–8** (English),
  1149–50 (Welsh)
  para.1.2   xxxvi
  para.1.3   xxxvi
  para.2.1   xxxvi
  para.4   xxxvi
Practice Note (Court of Appeal:
  Assessment of Costs) [1999] 1
  WLR 871   xxviii

TABLE OF RULES, PRACTICE DIRECTIONS AND PROTOCOLS

Practice Note (Court of Appeal: Disposal of Bundles) [1999] 3 All ER 384   xxviii
Pre-action Protocol for Personal Injury Claims   ix, 45, 46, 47, **1196–1205**
 para.2.2-para.2.4   48
 para.2.8   49
 para.2.11   48
 para.3.2   ix
 para.3.4   ix
 para.3.14-para.3.18   48
Pre-action Protocol for the Resolution of Clinical Disputes   45, 46, **1206–22**

Register of County Court Judgments Regulations 1985 (SI 1985/1807)   300
Rules of the Supreme Court 1965 (SI 1965/1776)   1, 2, 20, 21, 99
 ord.5
  r.6(2)   61
 ord.11   25–6
  r.4(2)   22
 ord.14   20, 100
 ord.14A   141
 ord.15
  r.6   x
 ord.18
  r.7(1)   93
 ord.23   297
 ord.24
  r.10   225
  r.14A   232
 ord.29
  r.2   135
  r.2A   135
  r.11   137
  r.11(1)(c)   138
  r.11(2)   138
  r.12   137
  r.12(1)(c)   138
  r.15   139
  r.17   139
 ord.35
  r.2   128

Rules of the Supreme Court 1965 – *continued*
 ord.38
  r.3   234
  r.28   234
  r.38   260
 ord.43   136
 ord.58
  r.4   327
  r.4(3)   327
  r.6   325, 326
 ord.59   327
  r.1A   327
  r.1B   327
  r.2C   327
  r.4(1)   327
  r.14(2)   327
 ord.62
  r.3(3)   304
  r.15A   39
  appendix 2
   para.1   318
 ord.65
  r.2   70
  r.7   27
  r.9-r.10   27
 ord.67   285
 ord.72   xxxii
 ord.73   xxxiii
 ord.75   xxxii
 ord.80   39
 ord.86   143
 ord.93 to ord.112   22
 ord.99   23
 ord.102   xxxi
 ord.104   xxxii
 ord.115   22
 appendix A   xxx

Social Security (Recovery of Benefits) Regulations 1997 (SI 1997/2205)   139
Solicitors' Practice Rules 1990   8
Supreme Court Fees Order 1999 (SI 1999/687)   **1352–9**

ABBREVIATIONS

CCR	County Court Rules 1981 (SI 1981/1687) as amended, or as re-enacted in CPR, sch. 2
CDPD	Chancery Division Practice Direction
CPR	Civil Procedure Rules 1998 (SI 1998/3132)
CRU	Compensation Recovery Unit
Final Report	Lord Woolf, *Access to Justice. Final Report* (London: HMSO, 1996)
Interim Report	Lord Woolf, *Access to Justice. Interim Report* (London: Lord Chancellor's Department, 1995)
ord.	order
para.	paragraph
paras	paragraphs
PD *n*	practice direction supplementing CPR, Part *n* (the Part number is followed by an abbreviated title where it is necessary to distinguish between two or more practice directions supplementing the same Part)
PD Protocols	Practice Direction Protocols
r.	rule
rr.	rules
RSC	Rules of the Supreme Court 1965 (SI 1965/1776) as amended, or as re-enacted in CPR, sch. 1
s.	section
sch.	schedule
ss.	sections
TCC	Technology and Construction Court

CHAPTER 1   THE NEW LANDSCAPE

CONTENTS

1.1	Introduction	1
1.2	Outline of the reforms	2
1.3	A fundamentally new approach to interpretation	3
1.4	Principles underlying the reforms	3
1.5	The overriding objective	5
1.6	Implications of the overriding objective and the new landscape	6
1.7	The role of the client	7
1.8	The role of the court — principles of case management	8
1.9	The role of the professional adviser — overall responsibility and professional conduct issues	9
1.9.1	The solicitor	9
1.9.2	The barrister	9
1.9.3	The overriding objective	10
1.9.4	Statements of truth	10
1.9.5	Stays for purposes of settlement	10
1.9.6	Confidentiality and the overriding objective	11
1.9.7	Advice to clients	11
1.10	Tactics in the new landscape	11

1.1 INTRODUCTION

On 28 March 1994 Lord Woolf was appointed by the then Lord Chancellor, Lord Mackay of Clashfern, to review the rules and procedures of the civil courts in England and Wales. The aims of the review were:

(a) to improve access to justice and reduce the cost of litigation;
(b) to reduce the complexity of the rules and modernise terminology;
(c) to remove unnecessary distinctions of practice and procedure.

The result of Lord Woolf's review, and much subsequent work, has been the promulgation of the Civil Procedure Rules 1998 (CPR), which will come into effect on 26 April 1999, and which embody the most radical reform of civil litigation since 1875. The CPR are supplemented by practice directions (PDs). All the rules and practice directions are printed in appendix 1 to this guide. The previous Rules of the Supreme Court 1965 (RSC) were an extensively revised version of rules set out in sch. 1 to the Supreme Court of Judicature Act 1875, which were themselves in part distilled from pre-existing procedures. However successful they may have been in 1875, or even 1965, the subsequent growth and increase in complexity of litigation have ensured that the RSC became cumbersome, slow and expensive to operate. Although many of the new rules incorporate concepts and practice from the old, the overall effect is fundamentally to revise not merely the procedure by which a civil case now comes before the courts, but the principles and ethos of civil litigation generally.

CHAPTER 1 THE NEW LANDSCAPE

1.2 OUTLINE OF THE REFORMS

The principal reforms made by the CPR are as follows:

(a) The Rules of the Supreme Court 1965 (RSC) and County Court Rules 1981 (CCR) are revoked with effect from 26 April 1999 and are replaced by the CPR.

(b) Rules governing some specialist jurisdictions and procedures continue in force but are adapted to fit in with the new procedures in the CPR.

(c) The CPR are a new procedural code with the 'overriding objective' of enabling the court to deal with cases justly (CPR, r. 1.1(1)). The new rules require the court to give effect to this overriding objective when exercising any power under the rules, or when interpreting any rule (r. 1.2). They also require the parties to litigation to help the court to further that overriding objective (r. 1.3). As a result previous authorities must be applied with considerable caution when interpreting the new rules.

(d) The principles on which justice is to be administered are now to include financial considerations. In particular, the court must ensure that it deals with a case in a way that is both proportionate to the amount of money involved and gives the case an appropriate share of the court's resources, bearing in mind the requirements of other cases.

(e) There are changes in the way in which litigation is to be funded.

(f) Proceedings in both the Supreme Court and the county courts will be governed by a unified set of rules, the CPR, supplemented by practice directions.

(g) Procedural requirements and documentation are standardised, and more modern terminology is introduced.

(h) Protocols are being established specifying what is to be done before beginning proceedings in certain common types of claim.

(i) There is an underlying desire to change the culture of civil litigation, to make the process less adversarial, and encourage and require greater cooperation between parties in the preparation of cases for trial.

(j) There is a new system of judicial case management for all cases, which effectively removes control of the timescale and cost of litigation from the parties, identifying the relevant issues at an early stage, and controlling the extent to which a party can inflate the costs of the litigation, including a curtailment on the rights of parties to require others to disclose documents.

(k) Proceedings are to be allocated by the court to the small claims track, the fast track or the multi-track, depending on the complexity of the matters to be tried, and the amount in issue. These tracks have different timetables and pre-trial procedures.

(l) There is an overall emphasis on reducing the role of tactics and procedural requirements, and encouraging the identification and speedy trial of relevant issues only.

The reforms have aroused controversy, as was only to be expected. In particular, for the first time, the overriding objective of dealing with cases justly is defined in terms that include expense and resources, which has caused concern to purists who consider that the principle of justice implies and requires that it should be done without regard to the cost at which it is achieved. However, it is quite clear that the cost of achieving justice in cases both in the county courts and the High Court can exceed or be out of all proportion to the amount in issue between the parties, and thus on occasion litigation has been conducted as much with a view to recovering costs as with resolving the issues. A principal objective of many of the reforms is to reduce, and if possible eliminate, wasteful litigation.

Rule 1.1(2) provides that dealing with a case justly includes dealing with it in ways which are proportionate to the importance of the case (r. 1.1(2)(c)(ii)) and allotting to it an appropriate share of the court's resources, while taking into account the need to allot resources to other cases (r. 1.1(2)(e)). It is not clear how the importance of the case is to be assessed. It appears to require consideration of factors other than the amount of money involved and the complexity of the case, which are mentioned separately. Presumably there must be an objective standard — are not all cases important to the parties involved? The court resources to be considered will presumably include not merely available finance but the availability of judiciary or judicial time to deal with a matter. There is, of course, room for reservations about justice being defined to include a reference to the ability of the state to provide sufficient resources for a case to be tried, and it might be thought that 'expedient determination' may be a more appropriate way of defining the overriding objective of the CPR. But no radical reform of civil procedure could attract uniform approval, and the time for debate is past. It is clear that many long-standing and well-founded criticisms of the previous procedure have been addressed, and that a swift adoption of the principles behind them by all involved will be the best means of ensuring that the objectives of *Access to Justice* are met.

1.3 A FUNDAMENTALLY NEW APPROACH TO INTERPRETATION

The civil procedure reforms comprise not merely new rules, but an entirely new procedural code (CPR, r. 1.1), which must be interpreted and applied so as to give effect to the overriding objective of enabling the court to deal with cases justly (r. 1.2). As a result, courts will now adopt a totally different approach to the application of discretion and interpretation of the rules.

The old 'quasi-statutory' approach to interpretation, based upon fine distinctions of language, will no longer be followed. It is for this reason that the drafting of the new rules may seem noticeably less precise than hitherto. This may well offend many purists, but the requirement to give effect to the overriding objective when interpreting the meaning of any rule or exercising any discretion given by the rules, renders such precision of less importance than would traditionally be required.

1.4 PRINCIPLES UNDERLYING THE REFORMS

In June 1995 Lord Woolf issued his *Interim Report*. He identified a range of defects in the civil justice system, concluding that the system was:

(a)   too expensive, in that the costs often exceed the value of the claim;
(b)   too slow in bringing cases to a conclusion;
(c)   too unequal, in that there was a lack of equality between the powerful wealthy litigant and the under-resourced litigant;

(d) too uncertain, causing difficulties in estimating cost and duration;
(e) too fragmented in the way in which the system was organised.

Fundamentally Lord Woolf concluded that the system was excessively adversarial, leading to cases being managed by the parties and not the courts and to the rules of court all too often being ignored by the parties, and not enforced by the courts. To redress these problems he identified a number of principles which he considered the civil justice system should meet in order to ensure access to justice. The new system should:

(a) be just in the results it delivers;
(b) be fair in the way it treats litigants;
(c) offer appropriate procedures at a reasonable cost;
(d) deal with cases with reasonable speed;
(e) be understandable to those who use it;
(f) provide as much certainty as the nature of the particular case allows;
(g) be effective, by adequate resourcing and organisation.

In his *Interim Report*, Lord Woolf proposed a system under which the courts would be responsible for the management of cases, and where litigants would be obliged to cooperate and assist in such management. Parties would no longer be allowed to dictate the timetable or progress of the case. The second stage of his inquiry then concentrated on particular areas of litigation where he considered the civil justice system was failing most conspicuously to meet the needs of litigants. The *Final Report* of July 1996 was accompanied by a draft of the new rules to apply to civil litigation in both the High Court and the county courts. These rules have now been promulgated as the Civil Procedure Rules 1998, and they come into effect on 26 April 1999. They are supplemented by practice directions coming into force on the same day.

The original principles postulated by Lord Woolf have been further developed into an ethos which underlies the Civil Procedure Rules:

(a) *Litigation should be avoided wherever possible.* Steps should be taken to encourage alternative dispute resolution (ADR), and pre-litigation protocols should be formulated, initially in relation to medical negligence and personal injury cases, but later in other fields, with the objective of enabling parties to obtain relevant information at an early stage, and to promote settlement of the dispute (see chapter 4). With the same objective, additional powers should be given to the court in relation to pre-litigation disclosure (see chapter 15). Before commencing litigation, both parties should be able to make offers to settle the whole or part of the dispute, with the potential sanction of a special regime of costs, and higher rates of interest, should the offer not be accepted and no additional benefit gained in the litigation (see chapter 20).

(b) *Litigation should be less adversarial and more cooperative.* The parties are required to exhibit openness and cooperation, from the outset, in the expeditious resolution of their dispute. This requirement will be supported by pre-litigation protocols, the encouragement of ADR, and a system of judicial case management which will rigorously scrutinise the conduct, cost, and progress of litigation.

(c) *Litigation should be less complex.* The Civil Procedure Rules will apply to both the High Court and the county courts, and all proceedings will be commenced in the same way (see chapter 5). Pleadings (now to be called 'statements of case') must clearly set out the facts alleged, the grounds on which the remedy is sought, and any relevant points of law. As such, the real issues between the parties should be identified at an early stage, and with greater precision. Greater control will be exercised over discovery, which will be considerably limited in many cases. The fresh approach to this part of the litigation process has probably contributed to it being given the new name of 'disclosure'. Special procedures will be put in place to deal with multi-party actions expeditiously and fairly.

(d) *The timescale of litigation should be shorter, and more certain.* The system of judicial case management will mean that parties no longer have control of the timetable of litigation. The court will establish and monitor a timetable for the progress of all cases to trial. Departures from this timetable will be the exception rather than the rule. For example, in non-complex litigation involving between £5,000 and £15,000 (which will be allocated to a 'fast track' procedure), and for any other litigation which the parties agree (with the consent of the court) should be so allocated, there will be fixed timetables of no more than 30 weeks between commencement of litigation and trial. Strict sanctions will be applied to parties who do not comply with the procedures or timetables.

(e) *The cost of litigation should be more affordable, more predictable and more proportionate to the value, or to the complexity, of individual cases.* Parties of limited financial means must be able to conduct litigation on a more equal footing. New procedures and judicial case management will make it more difficult for a better-off party to be able to gain a tactical advantage over opponents by expending money on his case. In fast-track cases, costs will eventually be on a fixed scale, and limited to an overall amount. The new approach will be supported by more effective sanctions, including orders for costs to be paid forthwith.

(f) *There should be clear lines of judicial and administrative responsibility for the civil justice system.*

(g) *The structure of the courts and the deployment of judges should be designed and allocated to meet the needs of litigants.* The more complex cases (assigned to the multi-track) will be heard at civil trial centres which have the required resources, including specialist judges. The courts will have access to the technology needed to monitor the progress of litigation, and litigants will be able to communicate with the courts electronically and through conference facilities. Trials will take place on the date assigned. The required technology will not be fully available at the outset, but will be phased in as soon as resources allow.

(h) *Judges should be deployed effectively so that they can manage litigation in accordance with the new rules and protocols.* Judges will be given the training they need to manage cases, and will have administrative and technical support to achieve this aim. Cases will be dealt with by the most appropriate part of the civil justice system. All judges will have received training in the new rules and procedures before 26 April 1999. The distinctions between the county courts and the High Court, and between individual divisions of the High Court will become of less significance.

1.5 THE OVERRIDING OBJECTIVE

The new ethos is now encapsulated in CPR, r. 1.1(1), which provides:

These Rules are a new procedural code with the overriding objective of enabling the court to deal with cases justly.

By r. 1.1(2):

Dealing with a case justly includes, so far as is practicable—
    (a) ensuring that the parties are on an equal footing;
    (b) saving expense;
    (c) dealing with the case in ways which are proportionate—
        (i) to the amount of money involved;
        (ii) to the importance of the case;
        (iii) to the complexity of the issues; and
        (iv) to the financial position of each party;
    (d) ensuring that it is dealt with expeditiously and fairly; and
    (e) allotting to it an appropriate share of the court's resources while taking into account the need to allot resources to other cases.

1.6 IMPLICATIONS OF THE OVERRIDING OBJECTIVE AND THE NEW LANDSCAPE

Two central and interrelated themes emerge from the new landscape — the need for greater judicial control over proceedings (and the consequent reduction in control by the parties themselves), and the introduction of procedures which will demand the early identification of the real issues in the case. These new procedures can be expected to have profound implications for litigation practitioners. For example:

    (a) The active management of the more complex and substantial cases assigned to the multi-track (see chapter 14) will require practitioners to investigate the facts, research the legal principles and identify the issues in greater depth and at an earlier stage, than under the old rules. A defendant's case must be set out fully, rather than being hidden behind a series of simple denials. At case management conferences the judge can ask searching questions about a party's case, with the objective of narrowing the issues to be tried, and may eliminate minor issues which are of little or no relevance to the substance of the dispute.

    (b) In cases assigned to the fast track (see chapter 13) litigation will have to be conducted with greater financial control, and within strict budgets. For many practitioners, this will be a novel experience. Improved access to the justice system should generate more cases which will have to be handled over a shorter period. This should not create problems for the efficient practitioner with appropriate resources, who will be able to respond to these various challenges. Those without the appropriate efficiency and legal ability will find their shortcomings exposed.

In all cases, litigation practitioners will have to adapt to the imposition of a more rigorous timetable, and a regime of real sanctions on default. It is expected that the steps which have been taken to make litigation less complex and less expensive (for example, the simplification of the 'pleadings' process) will encourage solicitors to play an increasing part in both written and oral advocacy. There may thus be an increasing overlap between the two branches of the legal profession and, to take one example, it is difficult to see how, in other than the most exceptional cases, the presence of both barrister and solicitor at a case management conference could be warranted. As a result, it seems clear that there will be little or no room in the new landscape for the solicitor who cannot identify the issues and argue them before the judge at the case management conference. The professional implications of this development may be considerable — if the simplification of procedures and the automatic presence of solicitors at case management conferences leads to solicitors expanding their role in the conduct of proceedings, the inevitable next step is that they will, in increasing numbers, conduct cases through to trial — a situation which was encouraged by the Lord Chancellor in the Access to Justice Bill, which proposes that, subject to appropriate training regulations, solicitors should obtain automatic rights of audience in all courts.

1.7 THE ROLE OF THE CLIENT

Rule 1.3 of the CPR provides that:

> The parties are required to help the court to further the overriding objective.

The involvement and cooperation of the client in the litigation process was a recurring theme in Lord Woolf's *Final Report*, which contained proposals that:

(a) Unreasonable failure by a party to comply with a pre-action protocol should be taken into account by the court, for example, in the allocation of costs.

(b) In multi-track cases, the lay client should attend the case management conference and the pre-trial review.

(c) If sanctions were imposed, leading to a costs or wasted costs order being made against a party, copies of such orders should be sent to the party personally, as well as to the party's legal advisers.

(d) Statements of case should contain a declaration by or on behalf of the party, of belief in the accuracy and truth of the matters put forward;

(e) The client should be involved in certifying compliance with disclosure obligations.

As will be seen in subsequent chapters, these proposals have largely been carried through to the CPR. All statements of case have to be verified by a statement of truth, declaring the belief of the party that the contents are true and accurate (see chapter 6). A party giving disclosure is required to make a statement setting out the extent of the search which has been made to locate documents which he is required to disclose, and certifying that he understands his duty to disclose and that to the best of his knowledge he has complied with that duty (CPR, r. 31.10(6)). The court may order that a judgment or order be served on a party in person as well as any solicitor acting for the party (r. 40.5). A solicitor is under a duty to notify a client against whom a costs order is made, if the client was not present when the costs order was made (r. 44.2). When deciding what order to make in respect of costs, the court should have regard not only to which party succeeded, but also to the conduct of the parties, including the manner in which a claim was pursued or defended, and whether a claim was exaggerated (r. 44.3(4)). Additionally, the conduct of the parties before, as well as during, the proceedings, and efforts made, if any, before or during the proceedings to resolve the dispute, are factors to be taken into account in deciding the amount of costs (r. 44.3(5)).

Closer client involvement in the proceedings will also be accomplished by another route. In his *Final Report*, Lord Woolf suggested that all clients or funders of litigation should impose eight requirements on their solicitors, that they should:

(a) prevent major litigation strategies without instructions;
(b) eliminate unnecessary research and detail;
(c) control the hiring and use of barristers and experts;
(d) forbid interlocutory/discovery activities without prior approval;
(e) prevent convening of meetings, when telephone calls will suffice;
(f) control the level of manning;
(g) agree the level and method of charging;
(h) emphasise that the case belongs to the client.

All the above are matters which should ordinarily be included in the contract of retainer of solicitors and, particularly with regard to charging structures, are to an extent already covered by the Solicitors' Practice Rules 1990 and The Law Society Costs Information Code currently awaiting approval from the Lord Chancellor. Thus the overall effect should be to ensure that tighter control of proceedings by the courts will be accompanied by greater client involvement in the litigation process.

1.8 THE ROLE OF THE COURT — PRINCIPLES OF CASE MANAGEMENT

The court itself is under a duty to further the overriding objective, by 'actively managing cases' (CPR, r. 1.4(1)). This drastically alters the role of the court away from merely adjudicating on whatever cases the parties choose to present. It propels the judge into the arena to ensure not merely that the litigation progresses smoothly, but also that every aspect of the dispute is considered in terms of time and expense before allowing it to continue, and to assist the parties, if possible, in settling the dispute or seeking other means of resolving it. Rule 1.4(2) sets out some (but not all) of the ways in which the court may actively manage cases namely:

(a) encouraging the parties to cooperate with each other in the conduct of the proceedings;
(b) identifying the issues at an early stage;
(c) deciding promptly which issues need full investigation and trial and accordingly disposing summarily of the others;
(d) deciding the order in which issues are to be resolved;
(e) encouraging the parties to use an alternative dispute resolution procedure if the court considers that appropriate, and facilitating the use of such procedure;
(f) helping the parties to settle the whole or part of the case;
(g) fixing timetables or otherwise controlling the progress of the case;
(h) considering whether the likely benefits of taking a particular step justify the cost of taking it;
(i) dealing with as many aspects of the case as it can on the same occasion;
(j) dealing with the case without the parties needing to attend at court;
(k) making use of technology; and
(l) giving directions to ensure that the trial of a case proceeds quickly and efficiently.

This expansion of the role of the court in the litigation process will have considerable implications not only for the parties but also for their legal advisers.

1.9 THE ROLE OF THE PROFESSIONAL ADVISER — OVERALL RESPONSIBILITY AND PROFESSIONAL CONDUCT ISSUES

In case management the court will become involved in matters which were hitherto regarded as the almost exclusive province of the parties and their legal advisers. This does not mean that legal advisers are absolved from the duty and responsibility to give their clients proper advice about how litigation should be conducted, or whether it should be conducted at all — indeed it is arguable that the fact that the court will actively inquire into such matters makes it all the more important that they have already been efficiently and conscientiously approached by professional advisers.

Specific areas of professional conduct will be considered in context in the following chapters. However, the very nature of the expectation that the parties (and thus their representatives) will help the court to further the overriding objective, expressed in CPR, r. 1.3, raises certain matters of potential difficulty.

1.9.1 The solicitor

Principle 21.07 of the Guide to the Professional Conduct of Solicitors is:

> Solicitors who act in litigation, whilst under a duty to do their best for their client, must never deceive or mislead the court.

If a solicitor is instructed by a client to conduct a case without regard to the overriding objective of the CPR (such as a well-heeled client instructing his solicitor to incur disproportionate expenditure when acting against a client of limited means), the solicitor must warn the client of the potential sanctions in costs that may be incurred as a result. As CPR, r. 1.3, *requires* parties to help the court to further the overriding objective, the question arises whether the solicitor would be in breach of principle 21.07 by carrying out the client's instructions and would thus be forced to withdraw. At present the situation appears to be unclear, and open to interpretation. However, it is likely that the Law Society will review the relevant provision of the Guide in the light of the CPR. The Access to Justice Bill, currently being considered by Parliament, proposes to insert a new provision in the Courts and Legal Services Act 1990, s. 27 (rights of audience), that any person exercising a right of audience before any court has 'a duty to the court to act in the interests of justice' and that the duty 'shall override' any other obligation with which it is inconsistent (other than an obligation under the criminal law). Any doubt about the relative importance of a solicitor's duties to court and to client is therefore likely to be removed shortly.

1.9.2 The barrister

A barrister must 'assist the court in the administration of justice and must not deceive or knowingly or recklessly mislead the court' (Code of Conduct of the Bar of England and Wales, para. 202). The positive manner in which this obligation is expressed may sit more easily beside the overriding objective of the CPR than the obligation of solicitors under principle 21.07 of their code, but may, as a result, make it more likely for a barrister to feel professionally embarrassed when faced with instructions to do some act which may be contrary to the requirement in CPR, r. 1.3.

1.9.3 The overriding objective

Whatever may be the position in relation to the rules of conduct, one thing is clear — legal representatives must ensure that, from the outset, clients are made aware of the requirement that they (and therefore their representatives) will support the overriding objective. For some time, lawyers have been pro-active in advising clients on their obligations with respect to discovery, and it is clear that such advice must now encompass a far wider range of activities by the client.

1.9.4 Statements of truth

An unguarded practitioner may be vulnerable to allegations of misconduct in relation to the statements of truth which are required by the CPR to accompany all statements of case (see 6.5). Even before the new rules come into force there was a strong body of opinion that practitioners should, wherever possible, avoid signing statements of truth. However, there are doubtless going to be circumstances, for example, where instructed by an insurer to defend an accident claim, where the lawyer will be under pressure to sign the statement of truth — for example, to verify an assertive defence — in far from ideal conditions. It may not have been possible fully to investigate the case or to meet the defendant face to face. Whenever a statement of truth is signed by a legal representative on behalf of a client, the statement of truth is that of the client's belief (PD 22, para. 3.7), although it must be signed by the legal representative personally, and not in the name of his or her firm or employer (PD 22, para. 3.10). The representative must state the capacity in which he signs and the name of his firm where appropriate (PD 22, para. 3.7). If this is done, the contents of the statement of truth and the consequences of signing it are deemed, by virtue of the signature, to have been explained to the claimant (PD 22, para. 3.8), who thereafter takes responsibility for any default. Additionally, the signature of the legal representative will be taken by the court as meaning that he is duly authorised to make the statement of truth on the client's behalf. A legal adviser should never sign a statement of truth without being duly authorised to do so, and should never sign one without fully explaining the consequences to the client and receiving from the client an express assurance in respect of the contents of the case so verified. These precautions must be taken in order to avoid allegations of professional misconduct, in addition to any other sanctions which may be applied.

1.9.5 Stays for purposes of settlement

There is cause for concern that the provisions relating to stays for settlement will be abused, so as to 'buy time' in the proceedings, and that legal advisers could be accused of professional misconduct as a result. Given that litigation (and trial) is considered to be a last resort, and that the court has powers to stay proceedings whilst the parties try to settle the case by ADR or otherwise, it is arguable that there is a positive professional duty on a legal representative to enter the settlement arena bona fide in an attempt to reach agreement. There is little assistance to be gained from the current codes of conduct on this point. If, for example, the court has directed a stay of its own motion, or on the application of one of the parties and the other party then expressly instructs his representative *not* to settle for less than the full value of the claim, could that representative be

CHAPTER 1   THE NEW LANDSCAPE

accused of misconduct for failing to enter settlement negotiations in good faith? It is submitted that, short of deceitful conduct, it is unlikely that this would be the case, and that in any event, given that such negotiations will take place without prejudice and will be evidentially privileged, it is difficult to see how any such allegations could be substantiated without breaching the confidentiality of the process.

1.9.6   Confidentiality and the overriding objective

Conflict may occur between the overriding objective and the duty of a practitioner not to disclose confidential information. For example, CPR, r. 29.3(2), provides for a representative to attend a case management conference 'with sufficient authority to deal with any issues that are likely to arise'. A representative who attends a conference without his or her client, and without authority to act on the client's behalf, and who seeks an adjournment in order to obtain instructions will not be likely to be well received. During the case management conference, it is possible that the court may seek information, the disclosure of which would involve a waiver of privilege. The court may well ask about the costs expended to date, the relative financial standing of the parties (one of the issues to be taken into account in meeting the overriding objective), and details of the funding arrangements for the litigation. It is doubtful that the court would have power to *order* a representative to disclose privileged information, but it is conceivable that it may invoke its wide powers to stay proceedings until information is disclosed, in order to assist in meeting the overriding objective.

Although many of these issues still remain to be decided, there are traps for the unwary practitioner who discloses confidential information in the course of proceedings in breach of professional duties to a client. If the client is not to attend the case management conference, specific authority will be required to disclose the categories of information which are likely to be sought.

1.9.7   Advice to clients

The extent of the reforms introduced by the CPR may take even a legally sophisticated client by surprise. It is therefore important that every client should be advised at an early stage, not only about the general duties to promote the overriding objective, but also other matters, including:

(a)   the wide-ranging costs and interest sanctions available to the court (see 11.8);
(b)   the client's duty in relation to a statement of truth (see 6.5.3);
(c)   the client's duties of search in relation to disclosure of documents (see 15.3);
(d)   the duties of the expert to the court (see 19.2);
(e)   the potential loss of privilege in correspondence between solicitor and client in relation to a wasted costs application (see 24.12).

1.10   TACTICS IN THE NEW LANDSCAPE

It is probable that tactical considerations will and should play a less important part in the litigation process than hitherto — the excessive use of tactics being one of the criticisms which led to the civil procedure reforms and the new ethos of *Access to Justice*. It is clear that the tactical use of statements of case and disclosure will be heavily circumscribed under the new regime. Having said that, although there is little doubt that the emphasis will be on identification of the significant issues between the parties, and their just and expedient resolution, the new procedures do raise some tactical considerations that did not exist before, such as use by claimants of offers to settle.

For all that it is intended that litigation should be less adversarial and more cooperative, the adversarial culture does encourage settlement of disputes (albeit at times for the wrong reasons). Following the reforms, the civil justice system will continue to be essentially adversarial in nature, as the ethos of *Access to Justice* is not to undermine the adversarial approach itself, but simply to eliminate its excesses. The effect of the new procedures will be that the legal profession will continue to perform its traditional adversarial role, but in a managed environment governed by the courts, and by rules which will require the parties to focus their efforts on the key issues.

In the past, lax control of proceedings, and the late identification of issues, often resulted in the bulk of legal costs being incurred relatively late in the litigation cycle, so that the parties would be under the greatest pressure to settle before the heaviest costs were incurred. The new procedure will require the parties to incur signficant legal costs much earlier in the proceedings and this front-loading of work will result in the front-loading of costs. This could be regarded as a disincentive to settle. The English rule that costs generally follow the event has contributed greatly to a high rate of settlements achieved, as the party who risks losing and bearing both his and his opponent's costs has a real incentive to settle. However, in fast track cases, where costs will now follow the event only to a limited extent (because the court's power to award trial costs is limited: see 13.6) the party who risks losing may decide to take his chance at trial, if his costs exposure on failure is limited in amount.

The new Civil Procedure Rules have also to be seen in the context of other developments in the civil justice system, such as the extension of conditional fees. A defendant to a multi-track case, being pursued on a conditional-fee basis, may want to employ every available device to make the claimant's side incur substantial legal fees, hoping that this will put pressure on the claimant's lawyers (who will be funding the litigation) to settle the case. A defendant who behaved in this way might be kept under control by an application of the proportionality principle in CPR, r.1(3), and, as discussed above, the court may impose a costs sanction on a party whose conduct of litigation has been unreasonable. It remains to be seen whether the judicial control of proceedings will be sufficiently stringent to enforce proportionality and apply sanctions, in circumstances where cost-inflating tactics have been used.

CHAPTER 2 SCOPE OF THE NEW RULES, TRANSITIONAL PROVISIONS, INTERPRETATION AND RE-ENACTED PROVISIONS

CONTENTS

2.1	Scope of the Civil Procedure Rules 1998	13
2.2	Transitional provisions	14
2.2.1	Claims issued but not served before 26 April 1999 and claims where pleadings have not closed by 26 April 1999	15
2.2.2	Default judgments, and judgments on admissions in the county court	15
2.2.3	Claims where directions or discovery have commenced but have not yet been completed at 26 April 1999	16
2.2.4	Orders made in existing proceedings before 26 April 1999	16
2.2.5	Issuing and renewing proceedings on or after 26 April 1999	16
2.2.6	Making applications in existing proceedings on or after 26 April 1999	16
2.2.7	Applying the new rules	17
2.2.8	Agreeing to apply the CPR	17
2.2.9	Costs	17
2.3	The interpretation of the CPR: A procedural code?	18
2.3.1	A procedural code	18
2.3.2	Purposive interpretation	18
2.3.3	Relationship between the rules and case law	19
2.3.4	Relevance of old case law	20
2.4	Re-enacted provisions of the old rules	21
2.4.1	Introduction	21
2.4.2	Differences between the High Court and county courts	23
2.4.3	Drafting deficiencies	23
2.4.4	Types of originating process	23
2.4.5	Preserved rules of general application	25
2.4.6	Proceedings pursuant to statute	29

2.1 SCOPE OF THE CIVIL PROCEDURE RULES 1998

The general rule is that the Civil Procedure Rules 1998 (CPR) apply to all claims commenced on or after 26 April 1999 in any county court, in the High Court, or in the Civil Division of the Court of Appeal (CPR, r. 2.1(1)). The exceptions to the general rule, as provided by r. 2.1(2), are:

(a) insolvency proceedings;
(b) family proceedings;
(c) non-contentious or common form probate proceedings;
(d) proceedings when the High Court is acting as a Prize Court; and
(e) proceedings under Part VII of the Mental Health Act 1983.

The CPR apply to claims being conducted in specialist lists, but subject to the provisions of practice directions governing the procedure to be adopted in the specialist courts. The types of claim for which there are special practice directions are listed in CPR, Part 49. They are: admiralty proceedings; arbitrations; commercial and mercantile actions; Patents Court business and specified intellectual property claims; proceedings before the Technology and Construction Court (the new name for the Official Referees' Department); applications under the Companies Acts 1985 and 1989; and contentious probate proceedings.

Although the CPR are described as 'a new procedural code' (r. 1.1(1)), some areas of procedure at present remain largely unaffected, for the CPR have re-enacted substantial sections of the old RSC and CCR, albeit with modifications to ensure that they comply with the general scheme of the CPR and employ the new terminology. The provisions of the old rules which have been re-enacted are discussed in 2.4.

2.2 TRANSITIONAL PROVISIONS

Transitional arrangements are set out in PD 51. This defines 'existing proceedings' as proceedings issued before 26 April 1999 (para. 1(1)). Three principles underpin the transitional provisions:

(a) The overriding objective (CPR, Part 1) will apply to all proceedings, including existing proceedings, as from 26 April 1999 (PD 51, para. 12).
(b) Existing proceedings which are not defended will be disposed of under the CCR or RSC, as appropriate (PD 51, para. 2).
(c) The CPR will be applied to existing proceedings which are defended, as far as is practicable (PD 51, para. 2).

This means that:

(i) Proceedings started before 26 April 1999 will continue under the old rules where the parties are taking steps which do not involve the court, such as serving pleadings or complying with an existing order for directions. But steps taken on or after 26 April 1999 involving the court must be taken in accordance with the new rules. Thus, all applications made in existing proceedings on or after after 26 April 1999 must be made in accordance with the CPR (see further 2.2.6) (PD 51, para. 14(1)).
(ii) Steps taken under the old rules, whether before 26 April 1999, or on or after that date but in accordance with the transitional provisions, will remain valid, and parties will not normally be required to repeat steps already taken under the old rules (PD 51, para. 10).
(iii) When proceedings issued before 26 April 1999 first come before a judge, district judge or master on a date after 25 April 1999, the court will at that stage decide the extent to which the CPR will apply to the case. This applies whether the matter has come before the judge at a hearing or on paper. The general presumption will be that the CPR will apply to the proceedings from then on, but the judge has a general discretion to decide on the extent to which the new rules will apply, and may direct that certain provisions of the CPR shall not apply to the case (PD 51, para. 15(1) and (2)). At the same time as giving a direction on the extent to which the CPR will apply to the case, the judge may also give case management directions and may allocate the case to a case management track.

(iv) Claims in which there has been no court hearing 'between 26 April 1999 and 25 April 2000' will automatically be stayed. (It is clear that it was intended to make this period inclusive of the start and end dates.) Any party may apply for the stay to be lifted. The implication is that if the court lifts the stay, it will do so on terms that the case will continue under the CPR (PD 51, para. 19). The automatic stay will not apply to cases which have been given a fixed trial date which is after 25 April 2000, in personal injury cases where the case has been adjourned to determine prognosis, or in trust administration proceedings.

How these principles will impact on a particular claim depends upon the stage it has reached by 26 April 1999.

2.2.1 Claims issued but not served before 26 April 1999 and claims where pleadings have not closed by 26 April 1999

In these cases the action will proceed to close of pleadings under the old rules. Thereafter, the court will serve an allocation questionnaire and the case will proceed under the CPR. The detailed provisions are as follows:

(a) For a claim issued before 26 April 1999 but not served by that date, the plaintiff should proceed to serve the old type of originating process, effecting service under the old rules, and the defendant should respond in accordance with the old rules (PD 51, paras 4 and 5). Proceedings on such claims, and also on those served before 26 April 1999 in which exchange of pleadings is not complete by 26 April 1999, will then progress to close of pleadings under the old rules (PD 51, para. 4). PD 51, para. 16(6), explains how to calculate the date upon which pleadings are deemed to close.

(b) If the defence is filed at court on or after 26 April 1999, the court will then normally serve an allocation questionnaire (see 11.4). Thereafter the claim will proceed under the CPR (PD 51, para. 16(3)).

(c) However, there is no obligation to file a pleading before close of pleadings in existing proceedings where there was no obligation to do so under the old rules. Where pleadings have not been filed at court earlier, the claimant must do so within 14 days of the close of pleadings. The court will then normally serve an allocation questionnaire and the claim will then proceed under the CPR (PD 51, para. 16(4)).

2.2.2 Default judgments, and judgments on admissions in the county court

A party who wishes to enter judgment in default in existing proceedings should do so under the old rules. Likewise, a party in a county court action who wishes to enter judgment on an admission should do so under the old rules (PD 51, paras 7 and 8). In both types of proceedings, if judgment is entered on liability only in an unliquidated claim, at the hearing to assess damages the court will give directions bringing the claim under the CPR (PD 51, paras 7(2) and 8(2)).

However, applications for leave to enter default judgment or judgment on an admission, and applications to set aside a default judgment, must be made under the new rules even in existing proceedings. The rationale for this appears to be that both these steps will involve a court hearing (PD 51, paras 7(3) and (4) and 8(3)).

2.2.3 Claims where directions or discovery have commenced but have not yet been completed at 26 April 1999

The position is set out in table 2.1.

Stage of the action reached by 26 April 1999	Application of old or new rules
Timetable for automatic directions begun — High Court	Continue under old rules until directions are completed. If a hearing takes place, the court may apply CPR.
Timetable for automatic directions begun, or notice in form N450 sent by court to parties — county court	Continue under old rules until directions are completed. If a hearing takes place, the court may apply CPR. Note that automatic striking-out provisions if hearing not requested within 15 months of close of pleadings will not apply.
Order for directions — High Court or county court	Order will continue to have effect (even if inconsistent with CPR). Parties should continue to follow it.
Timetable for automatic discovery begun — High Court	Continue under old rules until discovery complete. If a hearing takes place (e.g., for specific discovery) court may apply CPR.

Table 2.1 Transitional rules in cases with pending directions and discovery

2.2.4 Orders made in existing proceedings before 26 April 1999

These remain in force, even where they are inconsistent with the CPR (PD 51, para. 9).

2.2.5 Issuing and renewing proceedings on or after 26 April 1999

On and after 26 April 1999, the court will only issue claim forms (see 5.8) and other types of originating process permitted by the CPR. A request to issue an old form of originating process will be returned unissued. Applications to extend the period of validity of originating process issued before 26 April 1999 must be made under CPR, Part 23, but the court will decide whether to allow the application under the old law (PD 51, para. 13).

2.2.6 Making applications in existing proceedings on or after 26 April 1999

2.2.6.1 Procedure On and after 26 April 1999, parties to existing proceedings must use the new procedure under CPR, Part 23, on any application to court. The new forms for the application notice and evidence in support must be used, and the new rules of service will apply (PD 51, para. 14(4)).

Where pleadings had not previously been filed at court (principally this will affect proceedings in the Queen's Bench Division), the applicant must file them with the application notice (PD 51, para. 14(5)).

2.2.6.2 Substance of the application Other than in applications to extend the period of validity of old originating process (see 2.2.5) (and save in relation to costs — see 2.2.9), all applications made on and after 26 April 1999 will be decided under the new rules, not the old (PD 51, para. 14(2)). This will normally be the case even where the application was made before 26 April 1999 but is not listed for hearing until on or after that date (PD 51, para. 15.3).

2.2.7 Applying the new rules

When existing proceedings first come before a judge (whether at a hearing or on paper) on or after 26 April 1999, he will give directions on how the CPR are to apply to the claim. He may also give case management directions (PD 51, para. 15(1)). According to PD 51, para. 15(2), 'The general presumption will be that the CPR will apply to the proceedings from then on unless the judge directs or this practice direction provides otherwise'.

2.2.8 Agreeing to apply the CPR

Parties may agree in writing that the CPR will apply to any proceedings from the date of the agreement. All parties must agree, and the claimant must file a copy of the agreement at court. The agreement is irrevocable and the agreement must be for the rules to apply in their entirety (PD 51, para. 17).

2.2.9 Costs

On and after 26 April 1999 costs will be quantified under the new assessment procedure, rather than the old-style taxation. But the court will normally apply old principles to costs incurred before 26 April 1999, and will apply the new principles only to costs for work undertaken on or after that date. Thus, the presumption is that no costs for work undertaken before 26 April 1999 will be disallowed if they would have been allowed under the old rules (PD 51, para. 18). Work undertaken on or after 26 April 1999 will generally be assessed in accordance with CPR, Parts 43 to 48.

This means that CPR, r. 44.5(3), which gives the court a discretion to take into account the conduct of all the parties (and efforts made to try and resolve the dispute) in deciding to allow costs, will not be used to disallow costs for work undertaken before 26 April 1999.

Further transitional provisions dealing with costs are to be found in PD 48. These provide for the following:

(a) County court costs orders made before 26 April 1999 allowing costs on scale 1 or the lower scale (the old scales are not carried forward into the CPR) shall be dealt with in assessments after 25 April 1999 with the same limitations as applied in taxations before 26 April 1999 (PD 48, para. 3.3).

(b) In cases where a bill has been provisionally taxed before 26 April 1999, but the receiving party is unwilling to accept the result of the provisional taxation, the previous rules apply on the question of who can request a hearing and the time limits for doing so, but the CPR will apply on any subsequent hearing in the case (PD 48, paras. 3.2(2)(c) and 3.5).

(c) In cases where taxation proceedings were commenced and assigned to a taxing master or district judge before 26 April 1999 and were still pending on 26 April 1999, the hearing will be conducted in accordance with the CPR. However, PD 48, para. 3.7(3), preserves the right to carry in objections or to apply for a reconsideration to the same costs judge (the new name for taxing masters) or district judge who conducted the detailed assessment (the new term for a taxation hearing). This preservation of the old rights to object in this category of pending taxations may be regarded as somewhat anomalous, and can be removed in individual cases under PD 48, para. 3.7(4), if the court sends all the parties to the taxation a notice at least 28 days before the hearing that their rights of appeal will be governed by CPR Part 47 (which basically provides that parties wishing to challenge decisions made in hearings to assess costs need permission to appeal, see 24.9.11).

2.3 THE INTERPRETATION OF THE CPR: A PROCEDURAL CODE?

Rule 1.1(1) of the CPR describes the rules as 'a new procedural code with the overriding objective of enabling the court to deal with cases justly'.

Rule 1.2 goes on to state that the court must seek to give effect to the overriding objective when it:

(a) exercises any power given to it by the Rules; or
(b) interprets any rule.

These provisions give rise to a number of questions about how the courts will interpret the CPR from 26 April 1999. To what extent do the CPR constitute a completely fresh start to questions of procedure and practice? Are the CPR intended to be a self-contained procedural code? What effect does the overriding objective have on the way the rules should be interpreted? To what extent can the interpretation of the rules and the exercise of the court's discretion be limited by case law? To what extent can case law on the old rules be used to clarify the meaning of the new rules or the nature of the court's discretion?

2.3.1. A procedural code

Rule 1.1(1) specifically refers to the CPR as being a 'procedural' code. However, there is a clear distinction between procedure (or how the court system operates) and practice (the principles applied when dealing with procedural problems). Rule 1.1(1) does not say, perhaps deliberately, that the CPR are to be regarded as being a new codification of the practice to be adopted by the courts when making procedural decisions.

2.3.2 Purposive interpretation

Lord Woolf himself made clear in the *Final Report* how the overriding objective must be used to interpret the rules. At paras 10–11 of ch. 20 he stated:

> Every word in the rules should have a purpose, but every word cannot sensibly be given a minutely exact meaning. Civil procedure involves more judgment and knowledge than the rules can directly express. In this respect, rules of court are not like an instruction manual for operating a piece of machinery. Ultimately their purpose is to guide the

court and the litigants towards the just resolution of the case. Although the rules can offer detailed directions for the technical steps to be taken, the effectiveness of those steps depends upon the spirit in which they are carried out. That in turn depends on an understanding of the fundamental purpose of the rules and of the underlying system of procedure.

In order to identify that purpose at the outset, I have placed at the very beginning of the rules a statement of their overriding objective.

In other words, interpretation is to be purposive rather than a matter of close analysis of the meaning of individual words without taking into account their context.

2.3.3 Relationship between the rules and case law

The rules must be interpreted, and the court must exercise powers given to it by the rules, in such a way as to further the overriding objective (CPR, r. 1.2). The implication of this is that the court must use the rules to obtain a just result in the particular case before it. But this requirement to give effect to the overriding objective and to do justice in each individual case is at odds with a strict system of case law precedent.

It is only to be expected that there will be a series of Court of Appeal decisions following implementation of the CPR clarifying the meaning of the rules and the way the court should exercise its discretion. To what extent can these decisions restrict the court's discretion in the light of its duty to further the overriding objective?

Lord Woolf commented in the *Final Report*, ch. 14, para. 5, that:

> . . . judges exercising appellate functions will have a significant part to play in giving effect to the new system of case management . . . by laying down principles to be followed in exercising the new powers of case management.

But in the very next sentence he went on to say:

> It should be borne in mind, however, that management decisions are pre-eminently matters of discretion with which an appeal court would seldom interfere.

This comment is a reflection of the long-standing principle that an appellate court (principally the Court of Appeal) will only interfere with questions of discretion if it is satisfied that the judge below was wrong (Practice Note (Court of Appeal: Procedure) [1999] 1 All ER 186, para. 16). Guidelines on the question of whether a discretionary decision may be reconsidered on appeal were given in *Hadmor Productions Ltd* v *Hamilton* [1983] 1 AC 191. In that case Lord Diplock identified errors such as misunderstandings of the law or of the evidence, or decisions which were so aberrant that no reasonable judge acting judicially could have made them, or changes in circumstances since the first decision or new evidence coming to light, as constituting grounds for interfering with discretionary decisions.

Clearly, under the new system the appellate courts are not going to be any more willing to interfere with discretionary decisions on matters of practice than they were under the old.

An important practical point is the extent to which the courts should look at unreported first-instance procedural decisions handed down on or after

26 April 1999 and similar decisions reported in the legal periodicals. Often such reports are very short they are often misleading when compared with the full transcripts, and there is also a worrying tendency for cases which are in fact contrary to the rules to be the subject of such reports. It is an established principle that any decision below the Court of Appeal cannot be anything more than guidance. Further, even Court of Appeal decisions, if unreported, should be treated with some caution, as often they remain unreported because they turn on special considerations which can be misleading. Lord Diplock in *Thompson* v *Brown* [1981] 1 WLR 744, referring to one such case, commented that '. . . the law reporters, in my opinion, exercised a wise discretion in consigning it to the limbo of unreported cases'. The danger in citing such cases, especially when they are at first instance, is that they can distract the court away from applying the overriding objective and the spirit and intention of the CPR in general and the provisions that directly apply to a case. On the other hand, they can on occasions provide valuable guidance on how a discretion should be exercised, and may promote consistency between the approach of courts around the country. It is to be hoped that at some stage authoritative guidance will be given on the use of such case law.

It may be that the obligation to give effect to the overriding objective, coupled with the reluctance of appeal courts to interfere with the discretion of the lower court, means that case law may operate as guidance only rather than binding authority.

2.3.4 Relevance of old case law

In certain key areas the CPR clearly introduce new principles. For example, in order to resist a summary judgment application under Part 24, the respondent must show that he has a claim or defence (as the case may be) with a reasonable prospect of success. It is clear that old cases on what might constitute a triable issue on the facts for the purpose of RSC, ord. 14, will be of no application.

But many of the new rules are couched in similar language to the old CCR and RSC. In the above example, the words 'reasonable prospect of success' are those which (following *Alpine Bulk Transport Co. Inc.* v *Saudi Eagle Shipping Co. Inc.* [1986] 2 Lloyd's Rep 221) were used by the court in deciding whether to set aside a default judgment which had been entered regularly. Can cases on setting aside judgment under the old rules, then, be used to shed light on the test for entering summary judgment under the CPR? The answer appears to be no.

The reference to the CPR being a 'new procedural code' means that the court will not be bound to follow old authorities and may be unwilling to have old cases cited. However, where the new and old rules have similar or identical wording, and where it can be shown that the operation of old authorities is consistent with the requirement to further the overriding objective as it applies in the particular case, the court may be prepared to take them into account or at least be persuaded by arguments based on existing principles. In the early days following implementation of the CPR, the pragmatic approach must be to invite the court to do so, whilst recognising that it is not bound to do so.

The position is probably not very different from that relating to the new insolvency legislation in 1986. In *Re a Debtor (No. 1 of 1987)* [1989] 1 WLR 271 Nicholls LJ said:

CHAPTER 2   SCOPE OF THE NEW RULES ETC

I do not think that on [the question arising in the appeal] the new bankruptcy code simply incorporates and adopts the same approach as the old code. The new code has made many changes in the law of bankruptcy, and the court's task, with regard to the new code, must be to construe the new statutory provisions in accordance with the ordinary cannons of construction, unfettered by previous authorities.

Similar comments were made by Lord Jauncey of Tullichettle in *Smith* v *Braintree District Council* [1990] 2 AC 215. However, there are areas where pre-1986 authorities are resorted to in the insolvency field, and, as already mentioned, likewise it is clear that a number of provisions in the CPR are modelled very closely on the old rules.

Further, as mentioned at 2.3.1, there is a distinction between matters of procedure and matters of practice. Quite a few areas of practice have developed in the way they have to reflect the substantive law (such as the 'cheque rule' and the rules relating to set-offs in summary judgment applications) or statutory provisions (such as the Supreme Court Act 1981, s. 37, on injunctions) which have not been changed by the introduction of the CPR. It is difficult to see why the practice in such areas should change without change to the underlying law or statutory provisions.

There are also many places where the rules do not make any reference at all to well-established principles derived from or set out in case law. One example is that neither the CPR nor the practice directions state explicitly the requirement to make full and frank disclosure on an application made without notice to the respondent. It must be unlikely, however, that the requirement has disappeared. Certainly, in this case, the operation of the overriding objective would suggest that the obligation must still apply. The position may be that where the CPR do not address an issue at all, old case law on the point survives (see further 2.4.1).

2.4   RE-ENACTED PROVISIONS OF THE OLD RULES

2.4.1   Introduction

Although the CPR are being introduced with the intention of providing a unified procedural code for civil proceedings, substantial sections of the old RSC and CCR have been retained. These provisions continue in force by virtue of Part 50 of the CPR, and are set out in sch. 1 (the re-enacted provisions of the RSC) and sch. 2 (the re-enacted provisions of the CCR). The re-enacted provisions have been modified, mainly to ensure that they comply with the general scheme of the CPR. They therefore refer to claim forms rather than writs or other originating process. A recurring change in the schedules is that applications pursuant to statute or the old rules which previously had to be made by originating summons or originating application are now to be made by issuing a claim form. Although the modified rules do not say this, it will almost always be appropriate to use a Part 8 claim form for these types of proceedings.

There are several other frequently recurring modifications. The rules as set out in the schedules tend to refer to written evidence (or more usually, to witness statements or affidavits) rather than to affidavits, and to witnesses rather than deponents. References to applications in these retained provisions have been reworded so as to be consistent with the rules in CPR,

Part 23. References to interlocutory applications are therefore modified so as to refer to application notices, and *ex parte* applications are now called applications made without notice being served on any other party. Obtaining the court's leave is now referred to as obtaining the court's permission. Applications heard in chambers are now said to be held in private, and hearings in open court are referred to as being held in public. Changes of this nature appear throughout the schedules, and will not be discussed further in this chapter.

The rules re-enacted in the schedules are of two general types. First, a number of general procedural rules are retained, such as the rules on service outside the jurisdiction, enforcement of judgments, and appeals. Secondly, there are various orders from the old rules dealing with the civil courts' special jurisdiction under a number of statutes, which appeared mainly in CCR, ord. 48C and 49, and RSC, ord. 93 to 112 and 115.

Rule 50(2) of the CPR provides that the CPR apply in relation to the proceedings to which the schedules apply, subject to the provisions in the schedules and the relevant practice directions. This means that the overriding objective applies to applications under these re-enacted provisions from the old rules. An unanswered question is the extent to which the principles developed by the courts in applications under these provisions will remain valid on and after 26 April 1999. The courts may be tempted into saying that as r. 1.1(1) of the CPR says that the CPR are a new procedural code, there must be a completely new start, and that must be so in applications under the provisions in the schedules as much as when the courts are considering the main provisions in the CPR.

It might be thought that it is rather unlikely that the new rules have simply swept away such well-entrenched concepts as the doctrine of *forum non conveniens*, the rule in *Ladd v Marshall* [1954] 1 WLR 1489, and the principles in *Sir Lindsay Parkinson and Co. Ltd v Triplan Ltd* [1973] QB 609, which apply to matters which arise under rules re-enacted in the schedules to the CPR. That these, and other similar concepts, have not disappeared is supported by the fact that often the wording of the old rules on which the old principles were based has been retained unaltered. For example, RSC, ord. 11, r. 4(2), still provides that permission to serve outside the jurisdiction in non-Brussels or Lugano Convention cases will not be permitted 'unless it shall be made sufficiently to appear to the court that the case is a proper one for service out of the jurisdiction', which is as clear an indication as is possible that the doctrine of *forum non conveniens* will continue to apply in such cases under the new system.

It is possible that the courts will say that the established concepts in their old form have gone, but will then go on to apply the new ethos and the overriding objective in ways that produce results that resemble the results that would have been achieved if the old principles had been applied. Alternatively (and perhaps this is the most likely of the possibilities) the courts may be rather more tolerant of reference being made to the old cases and principles where the governing rules are to be found preserved in one of the schedules to the CPR than when acting under the main provisions of the CPR. If the courts do adopt this approach, they will also have to bear in mind the overriding objective, and may have to modify the old principles from time to time as a result.

It may also be questioned whether it is desirable to look at the old rules to discern the meaning of the re-enacted rules. For example, RSC, ord. 15, r. 12A(8)(c) in CPR, sch. 1, refers to the court's power in certain circumstances in derivative actions to give directions for the 'cross-examination of witnesses'. This could be taken as being a reference to directions regarding witnesses at trial. Cross-referencing to the old rule makes it absolutely clear that this phrase is simply updated terminology for cross-examining the deponents of affidavits (who, under the new system, could be people who have signed witness statements).

2.4.2 Differences between the High Court and county courts

The CPR were intended to introduce a unified set of rules to apply equally in the High Court and county courts. This has been achieved so far as the main provisions of the CPR are concerned. It has also been achieved in places in the schedules to the CPR. For example, under the old system there were detailed differences in the rules applicable to claims brought under the Inheritance (Provision for Family and Dependants) Act 1975 between RSC, ord. 99 and CCR, ord. 48. These differences have been swept away by the simple device of not re-enacting CCR, ord. 48 and inserting a new r. A1 into RSC, ord. 99, in CPR, sch. 1, saying that ord. 99 applies to proceedings both in the High Court and the county court. Rather unfortunately this device has not been used in a number of other areas. Consequently there remain detailed differences between the High Court and county court rules in quite a few areas which can only be identified by comparing the two schedules.

2.4.3 Drafting deficiencies

Work on the schedules to make them consistent with the main CPR has been a little rushed, and there are plenty of drafting problems that will need to be tidied up at some stage. In a number of places some thought has been given to making consequential amendments and deletions from the old rules. For many of the rules amendments are limited to making the most obvious terminology changes, leaving some less obvious concepts from the old rules *in situ* despite the fact that they might be redundant or otherwise inconsistent with the new system. For example, CCR, ord. 42, r. 12(2) in CPR, sch. 2, deals with the procedure when the Crown may be ordered to verify a list of documents by affidavit. The rule has been changed so that the reference to discovery now says 'disclosure', and the reference to verification by affidavit now refers to verification by 'witness statement or affidavit'. However, the whole paragraph is redundant because under CPR, Part 31, verification of a list by affidavit has disappeared, and has been replaced by the almost universal use of disclosure statements.

2.4.4 Types of originating process

In the *Final Report* Lord Woolf said (ch. 12, paras 1–3):

> In my interim report I argued that the complexity of the present rules of court could be seen as an obstacle to access to justice. A prime example of that complexity is the fact that there are four different ways of starting proceedings in the High Court, and another four in the county courts: the writ, originating summons, originating motion and petition in the High Court; and the summons, originating application, petition and

notice of appeal in the county courts. Within those categories there can be further variations: there are three types of forms of originating summons, and a number of different forms of summons. . . .

Needless complexity is introduced into the system at the outset.

I therefore propose that all proceedings should be begun by means of a claim. There should be a single claim form which could be used for every case. I regard this as an important step towards achieving simplicity in civil litigation.

Achieving this seems to have proved impossible. Early drafts of the CPR did provide for a single all-purpose claim form for commencing proceedings. However, as refinements were made, and detailed provisions included based on the old rules, various different forms for commencing proceedings have been introduced or borrowed from the old rules. The result is that on and after 26 April 1999 there will be about 11 ways of commencing claims. These are by:

(a) Claim form, the main method under the CPR.

(b) Part 8 claim, which was introduced very late in the drafting process, and is intended as a replacement for the old originating summons and originating application.

(c) Part 20 claim. This is the successor to the old third-party notice, and shares some of the indicia of an originating process in that it has to be issued, issue stops time running for limitation purposes, and it has a life of its own which is not entirely dependent on the underlying claim.

(d) Originating applications under the Insolvency Rules 1986 (SI 1986/1925) (see Insolvency Rules 1986, rr. 7.2 and 7.3). Insolvency proceedings are outside the scope of the CPR (see CPR, r. 2.1(2)). As mentioned in paragraph (e) below, the main types of insolvency proceedings are commenced by petition. However, other applications under the insolvency legislation which are not made in pending proceedings must be brought by originating application.

(e) Some proceedings are required by statute to be by petition, and these statutory requirements have not been altered. For example applications for administration orders, winding-up orders and bankruptcy orders must be by petition (Insolvency Act 1986, ss. 9(1), 124(1) and 264(1)) as must an application for relief of unfairly prejudicial conduct of a company's affairs (Companies Act 1985, s. 459).

(f) Notice of appeal. Many applications to the High Court under provisions retained in CPR, sch. 1, are commenced by notice of appeal, which is often (by comparing the equivalent provisions from the old rules) the direct successor to the old notice of originating motion (see, for example, RSC, ord. 94, r. 6(5) in CPR, sch. 1).

(g) Case stated. Several kinds of application to the High Court have to be brought by way of case stated. Proceedings under the Commons Registration Act 1965, s. 18, are an example (see RSC, ord. 93, r. 16(3) in CPR, sch. 1).

(h) Some cases can be brought very informally simply by making an application by witness statement or affidavit, an example being applications under the Deeds of Arrangement Act, 1914, s. 7 (see RSC, ord. 94, r. 4(1) in CPR, sch. 1).

(i) Interpleader notice. This type of process will only be used in certain circumstances in county court interpleader proceedings (see CCR, ord. 33 in CPR, sch. 2), and is not used in the High Court.

(j) Summons in respect of alleged offences contrary to the County Courts Act 1984, ss. 14, 92 and 124 (see CCR, ord. 34 in CPR, sch. 2), which is a procedure more of a criminal nature than civil.

(k) Filing a request, such as under the rules for enforcing parking penalties under the Road Traffic Act 1991 in CCR, ord. 48B, r. 2 in CPR, sch. 2.

In addition, there will be special prescribed forms for commencing certain types of proceedings, such as proceedings to recover possession of dwelling houses let under assured tenancies and assured shorthold tenancies under the Housing Act 1988 if the conditions in CCR, ord. 49, r. 6 and 6A respectively in CPR, sch. 2, are satisfied, and for Housing Act 1996 injunctions under CCR, ord. 49, r. 6B in CPR, sch. 2.

2.4.5 Preserved rules of general application

This section identifies provisions from the old RSC and CCR which have been preserved through being included in the schedules to the CPR.

2.4.5.1 Application of RSC to county court proceedings Rule 6 of CCR, ord. 1 in CPR, sch. 2, provides that where by virtue of 'these rules' (which presumably has to be read as the CCR provisions in CPR, sch. 2) or the County Courts Act 1984, s. 76, any provision of the RSC is applied in relation to proceedings in a county court, the provision takes effect subject to necessary modifications so that references to masters are to be read as references to district judges etc.

2.4.5.2 Commencement Rule 6 of CCR, ord. 3 in CPR, sch. 2, lays down the procedure on appealing under statutory authority to the county court from any order, decision or award of any tribunal or person.

2.4.5.3 Venue Rule 3 of CCR, ord. 4 in CPR, sch. 2, provides that claims to recover land etc. must be brought in the court for the district where the land is situated.

2.4.5.4 Service Paragraphs (6) to (11) of CCR, ord. 3, r. 6 in CPR, sch. 2, lay down rules for service in relation to appeals from tribunals etc. These service rules are of slightly wider application, because they are also borrowed by a number of other specialised rules preserved in sch. 2, such as in CCR, ord. 27, r. 5(1) in CPR, sch. 2, in relation to attachment of earnings orders. These service rules provide that unless the party otherwise requests, service will be effected by the court by first-class post to the other side's address for service, with service being deemed to take effect unless the contrary is shown on the seventh (not second as under the CPR) day after posting. Service may instead be effected by the party by personal service, and the rules also make provision for documents returned undelivered.

Rule 4 of RSC, ord. 10 CPR, sch. 1, allows claim forms in certain circumstances which claim possession of land to be served by affixing a copy to some conspicuous part of the land. In the county court, the rather similar CCR, ord. 7, r. 15 is also re-enacted in CPR, sch. 2, as is CCR, ord. 7, r. 15A, which requires claimants in mortgage possession cases to serve notice of the proceedings to the occupiers.

2.4.5.5 Service outside the jurisdiction The whole of RSC, ord. 11 is re-enacted in CPR, sch. 1 subject to some detailed changes, such as the replacement of r. 1(3) with rr. 1A and 1B, which deal with the time allowed for acknowledging service or filing a defence. The periods are the same (mainly 21 days for EU countries, with periods for other countries set out in a practice direction, which had not been published at the time of writing). There are no changes of substance, except that a new r. 10 provides that the order also applies to county court proceedings, thereby replacing the old CCR, ord. 8.

2.4.5.6 *Causes of action and parties* The following rules are retained:

(a) RSC, ord. 15, r. 6A in CPR, sch. 1, and CCR, ord. 5, r. 8 in CPR, sch. 2, on proceedings against estates;
(b) RSC, ord. 15, r. 7(1) in CPR, sch. 1, which provides that if a cause of action survives after death or bankruptcy, any pending claim does not abate, and the similar CCR, ord. 5, r. 14 in CPR, sch. 2, which deals with the bankruptcy of the claimant by reference to the County Courts Act 1984, s. 49;
(c) RSC, ord. 15, r. 9 in CPR, sch. 1, and CCR, ord. 5, r. 12 in CPR, sch. 2, on failure to proceed after the death of a party;
(d) RSC, ord. 15, r. 11 in CPR, sch. 1, on relator proceedings;
(e) RSC, ord. 15, r. 12 in CPR, sch. 1 and CCR, ord. 5, r. 5 in CPR, sch. 2, on representative proceedings;
(f) RSC, ord. 15, r. 12A in CPR, sch. 1, on derivative claims in company law;
(g) RSC, ord. 15, r. 13 in CPR, sch. 1, and CCR, ord. 5, r. 6 in CPR, sch. 2, on representation of interested persons who cannot be ascertained in proceedings concerning the estates of deceased persons, trust property and what used to be called construction summonses (which will now be dealt with under CPR, Part 8);
(h) RSC, ord. 15, r. 13A in CPR, sch. 1, on giving notice to persons who may be affected by claims relating to the estates of deceased persons and trust property;
(i) RSC, ord. 15, r. 14 in CPR, sch. 1, on representation of beneficiaries by trustees;
(j) RSC, ord. 15, r. 15 in CPR, sch. 1, and CCR, ord. 5, r. 7 in CPR, sch. 2, on representation of deceased persons in litigation;
(k) RSC, ord. 15, r. 16 in CPR, sch. 1, providing that no claim is open to objection on the ground that it merely seeks a declaratory judgment;
(l) RSC, ord. 15, r. 17 in CPR, sch. 1, giving the court power to give conduct of any claim to such person as it thinks fit; and
(m) CCR, ord. 5, r. 13 in CPR, sch. 2, dealing with claims to money in court where there are changes after judgment through death, assignment or otherwise.

2.4.5.7 *Partnerships* For the High Court, the whole of RSC, ord. 81 is re-enacted in CPR, sch. 1. In the county courts, the similar but different rules in CCR, ord. 5, r. 9 and ord. 25, r. 9 are re-enacted in CPR, sch. 2. The result is that different rules apply in cases involving partnerships depending on whether the claim is started in the High Court or a county court.

2.4.5.8 *Sole traders* Rule 10 of CCR, ord. 5 in CPR, sch. 2, allows county court proceedings against a sole trader to be brought in the

CHAPTER 2 SCOPE OF THE NEW RULES ETC

defendant's trading name. The broadly equivalent RSC, ord. 81, r. 9, is also preserved for High Court proceedings in CPR, sch. 1.

2.4.5.9 Crown proceedings RSC, ord. 77 has been re-enacted in CPR, sch. 1 and CCR, ord. 42 in CPR, sch. 2. The biggest change is to CCR, ord. 42, r. 8, which has been expanded to bar orders being made against the Crown by a county court (there is no High Court equivalent) of its own initiative requiring the Crown to file or serve any statement of case or to give any particulars for defining the issues (this should say 'further information' rather than 'particulars') with a sanction in default, or from ordering some questions or issues to be tried before the others. Paragraphs (3) to (5) of RSC, ord. 77, r. 4 in CPR, sch. 1, incorporate rules from the old RSC, ord. 65, rr. 7, 9 and 10 (service after 4pm, default in acknowledgment of service and the ban on service on Sundays) which have not been preserved for other litigants. There are several differences between the High Court and county court orders, and it is difficult to see the justification for having different rules for the two courts.

2.4.5.10 Statements of case The detailed requirements for statements of case (pleadings) in claims for the recovery of land, mortgage claims and the additional requirements for mortgage claims in respect of dwelling houses, and for hire-purchase cases, are preserved (CCR, ord. 6, rr. 3, 5, 5A, and 6 respectively in CPR, sch. 2). Similarly, the detailed rules for High Court defamation cases in RSC, ord. 82 are also preserved in CPR, sch. 1.

2.4.5.11 Interpleader For the High Court, the whole of RSC, ord. 17 has been re-enacted in CPR, sch. 1. The rather different treatment of the subject in the county court by CCR, ord. 16, r. 7, and CCR, ord. 33, has also been re-enacted in CPR, which leads to a very unsatisfactory difference between the two courts.

2.4.5.12 Summary possession proceedings The whole of RSC, ord. 113 has been re-enacted in CPR, sch. 1 and CCR, ord. 24 has been re-enacted in full in CPR, sch. 2. The minor procedural differences in ordinary summary possession cases (such as the need to provide the county court with stakes and transparent envelopes) remain. Interim possession orders remain in the sole province of the county courts.

2.4.5.13 Certain types of Chancery proceedings The following rules relating to certain types of Chancery Division work have been re-enacted in CPR, sch. 1:

(a) RSC, ord. 85 on administration and similar claims;
(b) RSC, ord. 87 on debenture holders' claims;
(c) RSC, ord. 88 on mortgage claims;
(d) RSC, ord. 91 on revenue proceedings; and
(e) RSC, ord. 92, on the lodgment and investment of funds in court.

2.4.5.14 Security for costs The High Court rules in RSC, ord. 23 have been re-enacted in CPR, sch. 1, and by a new r. A1 have been made to apply also in the county courts, replacing the old CCR, ord. 13, r. 8, and ord. 50, r. 9. It will therefore be possible in future to make an application in the county court for security for costs against nominal claimants and claimants who do not state their addresses, or change them to avoid having to pay the costs of the litigation.

CHAPTER 2 SCOPE OF THE NEW RULES ETC

2.4.5.15 *Reference to European Court* RSC, ord. 114 and the slightly different CCR, ord. 18, r. 15, have both been re-enacted, in CPR, sch. 1 and sch. 2 respectively. They are discussed at 25.14.

2.4.5.16 *Applications for judicial review* RSC, ord. 53 in CPR, sch. 1, is more or less unchanged, except that judicial review applications are now commenced by issuing a claim form (RSC, ord. 53, r. 5(2A)). Forms 86A and 86B will continue in use.

2.4.5.17 *Habeas corpus* RSC, ord. 54 in CPR, sch. 1, which deals with applications for the writ of *habeas corpus ad subjiciendum*, is more or less unchanged.

2.4.5.18 *Criminal proceedings* The rules in RSC, ord. 79, rr. 8 to 11 in CPR, sch. 1, on estreatment of recognisances, bail, issuing witness summonses and applications for warrants of arrest are re-enacted with no substantive changes.

2.4.5.19 *Divisional Court vacation business* Rule 4 of RSC, ord. 64 in CPR, sch. 1, allows urgent Divisional Court business during the vacation to be brought before a single judge.

2.4.5.20 *Judgments and orders* The following provisions have been re-enacted with no substantive changes:

   (a) CCR, ord. 22, r. 8 in CPR, sch. 2, on obtaining a certificate of judgment;

   (b) CCR, ord. 22, r. 10 in CPR, sch. 2, on applying to vary the date or rate of payment;

   (c) CCR, ord. 22, r. 11 in CPR, sch. 2, on setting-off cross-judgments;

   (d) CCR, ord. 22, r. 13 in CPR, sch. 2, on filing in the county court orders of the High Court and Court of Appeal after appeals; and

   (e) The whole of RSC, ord. 44 in CPR, sch. 1, on proceedings under judgments and orders in the Chancery Division.

2.4.5.21 *Enforcement* The whole enforcement system remains unchanged, though there is a continuing review. Accordingly, the following orders are to be found in the schedules to the CPR:

   (a) RSC, ord. 45 in CPR, sch. 1, High Court general provisions on enforcement;

   (b) CCR, ord. 25 in CPR, sch. 2, county court general provisions on enforcement;

   (c) RSC, ord. 46 in CPR, sch. 1, general provisions relating to enforcement by execution;

   (d) RSC, ord. 47 in CPR, sch. 1, on writs of *fieri facias*;

   (e) CCR, ord. 26 in CPR, sch. 2, on warrants of execution, delivery and possession;

   (f) RSC, ord. 48 in CPR, sch. 1, on the oral examination of judgment debtors in the High Court;

   (g) CCR, ord. 27 in CPR, sch. 2, on attachment of earnings;

   (h) CCR, ord. 28 in CPR, sch. 2, on judgment summonses;

   (i) RSC, ord. 52 in CPR, sch. 1, on committal in the High Court;

   (j) CCR, ord. 29 in CPR, sch. 2, on committal for breach of orders and undertakings in the county court;

   (k) RSC, ord. 49 in CPR, sch. 1, and CCR, ord. 30 in CPR, sch. 2, on garnishee proceedings;

CHAPTER 2   SCOPE OF THE NEW RULES ETC

(l)   RSC, ord. 50 in CPR, sch. 1, and CCR, ord. 31 in CPR, sch. 2, on charging orders;
(m) RSC, ord. 30 in CPR, sch. 1, on receivers and RSC, ord. 51 in CPR, sch. 1, on receivers by way of equitable execution; and
(n)   CCR, ord. 39 in CPR, sch. 2, on administration orders.

2.4.5.22   Conveyancing counsel   Order 31 of the RSC in CPR, sch. 1, deals with sales of land by order of the court, and with the reference of conveyancing matters to conveyancing counsel.

2.4.5.23   Appeals   The rules on appeals contained in CCR, ord. 13, r. 1(10) and (11) in CPR, sch. 2; CCR, ord. 37, rr. 1, 6 and 8 in CPR, sch. 2; and RSC Orders 55 to 61 in CPR, sch. 1, are largely unaltered. This subject is considered in more detail in chapter 25.

2.4.5.24   Fixed costs   Parts of the rules on fixed costs in RSC, ord. 62, appendix 3, and CCR, ord. 38, r. 8 and appendix B, are re-enacted in CPR, sch. 1 and sch. 2 respectively.

2.4.5.25   International aspects   The following orders have been re-enacted:

(a)   RSC, ord. 69 in CPR, sch. 1, on service of foreign process;
(b)   RSC, ord. 70 in CPR, sch. 1, dealing with obtaining evidence for foreign courts by deposition etc.; and
(c)   RSC, ord. 71 in CPR, sch. 1, and CCR, ord. 35, sch. 2, which deal with reciprocal enforcement of judgments.

2.4.6   Proceedings pursuant to statute

Most of the provisions in the old rules laying down procedures for applications pursuant to specialised statutes have been preserved. These provisions tend to deal with questions such as which court and/or which High Court Division should be used for these cases and the nature of the originating process required. Detailed requirements for the evidence in support are sometimes provided for. Broadly, applications which previously had to be brought by action, originating application or originating summons must now be brought by claim form. Applications which previously were brought by originating notice of motion (High Court) or notice of appeal (county court) are in future to be brought by notice of appeal, although sometimes the modified rules lay down that a claim form must be used. For the most part, where under the old rules evidence had to be given by affidavit, now there is a choice between using affidavits and witness statements. There are very few significant drafting changes to these rules other than updating the language to be consistent with the CPR.

The procedural rules of this nature that have been re-enacted are:

(a)   RSC, ord. 74 in CPR, sch. 1, on applications and appeals under the Merchant Shipping Act 1995;
(b)   CCR, ord. 34 in CPR, sch. 2, on penal and disciplinary powers under the County Courts Act 1984, ss. 14, 92 and 124;
(c)   CCR, ord. 43 in CPR, sch. 2, on county court proceedings under the Landlord and Tenant Acts 1927, 1954, 1985 and 1987;
(d)   CCR, ord. 44 in CPR, sch. 2, on applications under the Agricultural Holdings Act 1986;
(e)   CCR, ord. 45 in CPR, sch. 2, on applications and appeals under the Representation of the People Act 1983;

(f) CCR, ord. 46 in CPR, sch. 2, on applications under the Legitimacy Act 1976;

(g) CCR, ord. 47, r. 5 in CPR, sch. 2, on county court directions for blood tests under the Family Law Reform Act 1969;

(h) CCR, ord. 48B in CPR, sch. 2, on enforcement of parking penalties under the Road Traffic Act 1991;

(i) CCR, ord. 49 in CPR, sch. 2, dealing with claims and applications under a number of statutes, including the Access to Neighbouring Land Act 1992, the Consumer Credit Act 1974, the Housing Act 1988, the Housing Act 1996, the Town and Country Planning Act 1990, the Leasehold Reform Act 1976, the Sex Discrimination Act 1975 and the Race Relations Act 1976;

(j) RSC, ord. 93 in CPR, sch. 1, dealing with applications and appeals to the Chancery Division of the High Court under a range of statutes, such as the Public Trustee Act 1906, the Variation of Trusts Act 1958, the Law of Property Act 1925, ss. 21 and 25, and the Administration of Justice Act 1985, ss. 48 and 50;

(k) RSC, ord. 94 in CPR, sch. 1, dealing with applications and appeals to the Queen's Bench Division of the High Court under a range of statutes, such as the Deeds of Arrangement Act 1914, s. 7, the Representation of the People Acts, the Agriculture (Miscellaneous Provisions) Act 1954, s. 6, the Tribunals and Inquiries Acts 1971 and 1992 and for vexatious litigant orders under the Supreme Court Act 1981, s. 42;

(l) RSC, ord. 95 in CPR, sch. 1, dealing with applications under the Bills of Sale Acts 1878 and 1882 and the Industrial and Provident Societies Act 1967;

(m) RSC, ord. 96 in CPR, sch. 1, dealing with applications under the Mines (Working Facilities and Support) Act 1966;

(n) RSC, ord. 97 in CPR, sch. 1, dealing with High Court proceedings under the Landlord and Tenant Acts 1927, 1954 and 1987;

(o) RSC, ord. 98 in CPR, sch. 1, dealing with applications and appeals under the Local Government Finance Act 1982;

(p) RSC, ord. 99 in CPR, sch. 1, dealing with High Court and county court applications under the Inheritance (Provision for Family and Dependants) Act 1975;

(q) RSC, ord. 101 in CPR, sch. 1, dealing with applications and appeals under the Pensions Appeal Tribunals Act 1943;

(r) RSC, ord. 106 in CPR, sch. 1, dealing with the High Court's jurisdiction under the Solicitors Act 1974;

(s) RSC, ord. 108 in CPR, sch. 1, dealing with proceedings relating to charities under the Charities Act 1993;

(t) RSC, ord. 109 in CPR, sch. 1, dealing with applications and appeals under the Administration of Justice Act 1960;

(u) RSC, ord. 110 in CPR, sch. 1, dealing with injunctions to prevent environmental harm under the Town and Country Planning Act 1990 and related legislation;

(v) RSC, ord. 111 in CPR, sch. 1, dealing with appeals and references under the Social Security Administration Act 1992;

(w) RSC, ord. 112 in CPR, sch. 1, dealing with High Court directions for blood tests under the Family Law Reform Act 1969; and

(x) RSC, ord. 115 in CPR, sch. 1, dealing with confiscation and forfeiture orders under the Drug Trafficking Act 1994 and the Criminal Justice (International Cooperation) Act 1990.

CHAPTER 3 CONDITIONAL FEES AND THE NEW RULES

CONTENTS

3.1	Introduction	31
3.2	Conditional fees in context	32
3.3	Proportionality, transparency and certainty	34
3.4	Assessment of conditional fee agreement costs	35
3.4.1	Assessment of base costs	36
3.4.2	Assessment of the percentage increase (success fee)	36
3.5	Special issues relating to conditional fees under the CPR	38
3.5.1	Applying proportionality to conditional fee agreements	38
3.5.2	Interim costs	38
3.5.3	Children and patients	39
3.5.4	The fast track	39
3.5.5	Experts and conditional fees	40
3.5.6	Pre-action protocols and conditional fees	40
3.5.7	'Offers to settle' and conditional fees	41
3.5.8	The multi-track and conditional fees	41
3.6	Extension of conditional fees to new areas of work	41
3.7	Access to Justice Bill 1999	42

3.1 INTRODUCTION

In the debate on the second reading of the Access to Justice Bill in the House of Lords on 14 December 1998 Lord Woolf said:

> Another small reform which is included in the Bill is one to which I attach importance; namely, the question of conditional fees. At present, conditional fees are providing a means of obtaining access to justice in a small range of cases, which was not available before their introduction. Conditional fees are not a panacea; someone has to pay the uplift involved in using conditional fees. Someone also has to meet the insurance premiums involved.
>
> One of the problems faced by those who bring proceedings within the area now covered by conditional fees is that, all too often, defendants — and by 'defendants' I want to make it clear that I am really referring to insurers — do not dispose of those cases as early as they should. As a result, considerable distress is caused to members of the public who often have to wait substantial periods of time before their litigation is concluded. In many cases the latter is concluded on the day that the case is listed before a court when, for the first time, a sensible offer is made.
>
> The proposal that those who have to resort to a conditional fee in order to have the benefit of legal representation should be able to recover the uplift and also the insurance premium must surely be a just and sensible suggestion. It is my belief that it would help to bring about a change in the culture which we would like to see; namely, that when claims are put forward they are disposed of much more rapidly, much more sensibly and, indeed, much more appropriately than they are now.

CHAPTER 3 CONDITIONAL FEES AND THE NEW RULES

Lord Woolf sees a clear connection between the CPR and conditional fees when they emerge in their amended form after the enactment of the Access to Justice Bill in the latter part of 1999. But a tension exists between the 'payment by results' culture of conditional fees and the overriding objective (CPR, r. 1.1) the effect of which is that litigation should be the last resort.

The Lord Chancellor, Lord Irvine of Lairg also sees a link between the CPR and the costs of litigation. In his foreword to the Stationery Office's loose-leaf edition of the CPR he said:

> Managing cases in a proportionate way will exert a strong downward pressure on costs.

So another tension exists between the culture of litigation as the last resort and the basic premise of conditional fees that the success fee — the 'reward' for winning — is calculated as a percentage of costs chargeable by the solicitor (and barrister). 'Strong downward pressure' means lower costs and therefore lower success fees. So the aim to reduce costs, one of the cornerstones of Lord Woolf's *Access to Justice* reforms from which the CPR have emerged, could actually impede the development of conditional fees casting a cloud over government plans for conditional fees to plug the gap caused by the proposed removal of legal aid for all civil money claims.

3.2 CONDITIONAL FEES IN CONTEXT

Conditional fees must be seen in the context of the 'pick and mix' variety of costs options that are now becoming available for litigation funding.

No longer can it be assumed that one form of funding may be the correct or only method to adopt during the lifetime of a case. Increasingly, solicitors and barristers will need to adopt flexible attitudes towards litigation funding arrangements, being prepared to move from one form of funding to another, depending upon the nature of the case, stage of litigation and the insurance cover. At different stages a case can be funded by legal aid, legal expense insurance (before or after the event) or one of the two varieties of conditional fees that are set out in cl. 27 of the Access to Justice Bill. These options will be examined more closely below but practitioners must be alert to the need for flexibility in funding civil cases both at the outset and throughout the case, particularly where a conditional fee agreement is used.

Section 58 of the Courts and Legal Services Act 1990 is the enabling provision for the Conditional Fee Agreements Order 1995 (SI 1995/1674) which introduced conditional fees in July 1995 in three areas of 'specified proceedings':

(a) proceedings for personal injuries or death;
(b) insolvency proceedings;
(c) human rights proceedings in Strasbourg under the European Convention on Human Rights.

Simultaneously the Conditional Fee Agreements Regulations 1995 (SI 1995/1675) set out the regulatory framework for solicitors to follow when entering into a conditional fee agreement with a client.

Since July 1995 the conditional fee learning curve has been steep. The key to making conditional fees work was provided by the 'After the Event'

CHAPTER 3 CONDITIONAL FEES AND THE NEW RULES

insurance policy to cover costs ordered against an unsuccessful claimant, which the Law Society endorsed. The policy is available only to firms of solicitors that belong to the Law Society's Accident Line scheme, membership of which is dependent upon at least one member of the firm being a member of the personal injury panel. Guidance to practitioners trying to grapple with this new method of funding was also provided by M. Napier and F. Bawdon, *Conditional Fees — A Survival Guide* (London: Law Society, 1995), to which readers should refer for more detailed information on conditional fees generally. A second edition will be published in late 1999.

In September 1997, two years after the introduction of conditional fees, the Policy Studies Institute published the first research into the subject in its report *The Price of Success — Lawyers, Clients and Conditional Fees* (by Stella Yarrow). Based on a survey of 197 conditional fee agreements during their first 15 months, the results gave solicitors a good conduct report in their dealings with clients. The Law Society's plain English model agreement with safeguard clauses for consumers had been universally used and its recommended 25 per cent cap to answer criticism that damages could be absorbed by lawyers' fees had become 'virtually standard'.

However, the report was more cautious about the ability of solicitors to assess the right level of success fee to match the prospects of winning or losing a case. Another core finding was that in 99 per cent of the cases studied (all personal injury) an after the event insurance policy had been taken out with Abbey Legal Protection under the Accident Line Protect scheme. It was too early for the research to contain outcome studies of completed conditional fee cases but further research is being done.

But the 'so far so good' diagnosis in the Policy Studies Institute report was catapulted into a new dimension when, in November 1997, the Lord Chancellor, Lord Irvine of Lairg, announced that the apparent success of conditional fees would be the peg for the withdrawal of legal aid for civil money claims. Simultaneously he forged an important link between conditional fees and the CPR in the title of the government's consultation paper, *Access to Justice with Conditional Fees* (March 1998).

In July 1998 the Conditional Fee Agreements Order 1998 (SI 1998/1860) extended conditional fees to all areas of civil litigation (excluding family). However, just as in personal injury, the take-up of conditional fees in new areas such as commercial litigation largely depends on the availability of affordable after the event insurance. Insurers are cautious about new risks and look for stability. In the still immature market of conditional fees, insurers will have to weigh up whether the new CPR will make conditional fees more or less attractive than before. The trend in the CPR towards proportionality and certainty of costs may give insurers some comfort, but they are unlikely to come rushing forward as they wait to see how the new rules will work out, such as the new 'offer to settle' procedure (CPR, Part 36; see chapter 20).

Any assessment of the relationship between conditional fees and the CPR must be measured against the backdrop of cl. 29 of the Access to Justice Bill, which proposes to amend s. 58 of the Courts and Legal Services Act 1990. Allowing for the hiatus period of a few months between the implementation of the CPR on 26 April 1999 and the enactment of the

Access to Justice Bill later in the same year, the remainder of this chapter examines how conditional fees will be affected by the CPR.

3.3 PROPORTIONALITY, TRANSPARENCY AND CERTAINTY

The tripartite theme of proportionality, transparency and certainty in the CPR has a direct impact on the operation of conditional fees. The court's attention to proportionality between costs and damages under the CPR echoes the legitimate concern that in a conditional fee agreement the level of the success fee must not absorb a disproportionate amount of the client's damages — which is why the Law Society's model agreement adopts a 25 per cent cap.

The drive toward transparency of costs information, another theme of the CPR, also echoes the Conditional Fee Agreements Regulations 1995 that the client must receive full information about the costs implications of a conditional fee agreement. An explanation to the client of the level of the success fee and how it is calculated inevitably involves discussion about the likely outcome of the case and about the economic equation of damages, costs and success fee that must be accurately balanced before deciding whether making a claim is 'worth the candle'.

Allied to the transparency theme is the new Costs Information Code which the Law Society Council adopted in December 1998. Assuming that the Code is approved by the Lord Chancellor later this year it will say in para. 4(j):

Client's ability to pay and source of funding
I. The solicitor should discuss with the client how, when and by whom any costs are to be met and consider—
    A. Whether the client may be eligible and should apply for legal aid (including advice and assistance);
    B. Whether the client's liability for their own costs may be covered by insurance;
    C. Whether the client's liability for another party's costs may be covered by pre-purchased insurance and, if not, whether it would be advisable for the client's liability for another party's costs to be covered by after the event insurance (including in every case where a conditional fee or contingency fee arrangement is proposed); and
    D. Whether the client's liability for costs (including the costs of another party) may be covered by another person e.g. an employer or trade union.

If proportionality leads to transparency, so transparency that provides information about costs will lead to greater certainty. The elusive certainty factor is a key feature of a conditional fee agreement. Thus the aim of the CPR to promote certainty in the procedural process should help foster certainty of understanding between lawyers and clients about costs.

In conditional fee cases the certainty factor will largely be influenced by the track to which the case is allocated. In the fast track the costs of trial (but not the costs of preparation) are fixed (CPR, Part 46). When handling a conditional fee case, particularly at the stage of assessing the costs/damages/success fee equation, it will be important for the solicitors to have in mind the areas of costs which are fixed by the CPR and those which are not.

CHAPTER 3 CONDITIONAL FEES AND THE NEW RULES

The probable approach to the costs of interim proceedings on the fast track and multi-track is indicated by the Practice Direction (Costs: Summary Assessment) [1999] 1 WLR 420 1999 (coming into force on 1 March 1999). The practice direction says that unless there is good reason not to do so the court should assess costs at the end of an interlocutory hearing that does not exceed one day. The practice direction includes guideline hourly rates which are included only to relate to summary assessment of costs. These rates are not a scale and do not prevail over local knowledge or local rates that have been agreed for the relevant area of the country between the local Law Society and the designated civil judge and/or district judge.

3.4 ASSESSMENT OF CONDITIONAL FEE AGREEMENT COSTS

The main references to conditional fees in the CPR are in r. 48.9 and PD 48, which are concerned with assessment by the court of conditional fee agreement costs. For the procedure on assessment of costs generally see 24.9.

Rule 48.9 is essentially a plain English redraft of the 1995 amendments to the RSC and CCR setting out the new arrangements necessary for assessment (taxation) if the client wishes to challenge the fees of the solicitor or barrister employed under a conditional fee agreement.

In a successful conditional fee case the solicitor will calculate his or her fees (referred to in the model agreement as 'basic costs') and the barrister's fees at the rates set out in the conditional fee agreement with the client. The solicitor will seek to recover 100 per cent of the basic costs plus the barrister's fees and disbursements from the unsuccessful paying party. The solicitor may in addition recover from the client:

(a) any shortfall in the solicitor's basic costs plus counsel's fees and disbursements recovered from the paying party;
(b) the agreed success fee (which cannot be more than 100 per cent) calculated as a percentage of the basic costs (and as a separate percentage of the barrister's fees) subject to the 25 per cent cap if the Law Society model agreement is used.

When a client receives from the solicitor a bill calculated on the above basis the client is entitled to challenge:

(a) the shortfall in full recovery of the solicitor's basic costs and the barrister's fees,
(b) the solicitor's and barrister's success fees.

The procedure to facilitate such a challenge by the client is set out in CPR, r. 48.9, and is further explained in PD 48, paras 2.13 to 2.16.

In order to comply with the Conditional Fee Agreements Regulations 1995, reg. 4(2)(d), a conditional fee agreement must include 'The circumstances in which the client may seek taxation of the fees and expenses of the legal representative and the procedure for so doing'. This requirement is covered in the Law Society's model agreement and would need to be included in any other conditional fee agreement if it is to be lawful and enforceable in order to recover costs.

CHAPTER 3 CONDITIONAL FEES AND THE NEW RULES

Somewhat confusingly CPR, r. 48.9(2), uses the term 'base costs', which are different from the similar sounding 'basic costs' used in the model agreement to describe the solicitor's costs excluding the success fee. In effect 'base costs' in r. 48.9(2) means the solicitor's 'basic costs' plus counsel's fees, both calculated at the rates set out in the conditional fee agreements.

3.4.1 Assessment of base costs

Rule 48.9(4) of the CPR provides that an application by the client for assessment of the base costs of a conditional fee agreement is to proceed on the same basis as the assessment of solicitor and client costs, which is explained in more detail in r. 48.8(1)(b). Rule 48.8(2) then provides that base costs are to be assessed on the indemnity basis, in which costs are presumed:

(a) to have been reasonably incurred if they were incurred with the express or implied approval of the client;
(b) to be reasonable in amount if their amount was expressly or impliedly approved by the client;
(c) to have been unreasonably incurred if:
    (i) they are of an unusual nature or amount and
    (ii) the solicitor did not tell the client that as a result he might not recover all of them from the other party.

Rule 48.9(4) also emphasises that the detailed assessment of base costs under r. 48.2 is to take place 'as if the solicitor and his client had not entered into a conditional fee agreement'. This must be right because the level of the success fee is of no relevance to the assessment of the base costs which are calculated by reference to the solicitor's hourly rates and the barrister's fees set out in the conditional fee agreement.

3.4.2 Assessment of the percentage increase (success fee)

Further confusion exists because at least four different terms are used to describe the central feature of a conditional fee agreement:

(a) Rule 48.9 of the CPR refers to the 'percentage increase'.
(b) The Law Society's model agreement refers to the 'success fee'.
(c) The barrister's conditional fee agreement (sometimes) refers to 'uplift',
(d) Clause 29 of the Access to Justice Bill, introducing a new s. 58 of the Courts and Legal Services Act 1990, refers to 'enhanced fee'.

Rule 48.9(5) of the CPR provides the framework for assessment of the percentage increase and refers to the 'relevant factors' to be taken into account on an assessment where the client is seeking a reduction in the percentage increase. The relevant factors are set out in PD 48, para. 2.15:

(a) the risk that the circumstances in which the fees or expenses would be payable might not occur;
(b) the disadvantages relating to the absence of payment on account;
(c) whether the amount which might be payable under the conditional fee agreement is limited to a certain proportion of any damages recovered by the client;
(d) whether there is a conditional fee agreement between the solicitor and counsel;
(e) the solicitor's liability for any disbursements.

CHAPTER 3   CONDITIONAL FEES AND THE NEW RULES

These are all fairly obvious factors but, as so often happens with the relatively new concept of conditional fees, they unveil more questions to which there are no easy answers, not least because there are no reports of an assessment hearing dealing with a client's challenge to the base or percentage costs of a conditional fee agreement, let alone a review on appeal.

Rule 48.9(5) of the CPR, echoed in PD 48, para. 2.16, provides that when the court is assessing the percentage increase the costs judge should do so 'having regard to all relevant factors as they reasonably appeared to the solicitor or counsel when the conditional fee agreement was entered into'. The wisdom of hindsight is therefore not permitted.

However, at the hearing the parties and the court will need to consider carefully the conditional fee agreement, which may contain many provisions that are highly relevant. Many of these are covered in *Conditional Fees — A Survival Guide*, referred to at 3.2. They include:

(a) the criteria that apply to 'risk assessment' (the prospects of success);
(b) the formula for calculation of the success fee (*Conditional fees — A Survival Guide* includes a 'ready reckoner');
(c) the level of financial subsidy by the solicitor (e.g., disbursements);
(d) the 'lightning factor' (the need to allow for the risk of losing the 'dead cert' case that contrary to evidence and expectations 'goes wrong' at trial — every litigator has had this experience);
(e) the impact of the cap on the actual amount of success fee recoverable.

So that the solicitor and barrister whose costs are being challenged know what is in issue, PD 48, para. 2.14, makes it clear that the client who wishes to challenge the percentage increase must set out in writing:

(a) the reasons why the percentage increase should be reduced; and
(b) what the percentage increase should be.

No doubt in setting out these arguments the client will ask the court to consider the relevant factors by reference to his or her individual case. But the solicitors and counsel may ask the court to consider the level of their success fees on a wider front. From a business point of view the solicitor may wish to take into account the economics of conducting a litigation practice of numerous conditional fee cases on the no win no fee (payment by results) basis. The principle behind this is that the success fees from the winning cases should cover the lost fees (and possibly disbursements) in the losing cases. There may well be arguments that the client's case should not be viewed in isolation but that wider economic considerations apply. The 'ready reckoner' in *Conditional Fees — A Survival Guide* (based on the mathematical laws of probability) takes the win–lose equation into account but the solicitor may increase the success fee to reflect any additional financial cross-subsidy that applies particularly where handling a large volume of cases on the conditional fee basis.

In the absence of any authority on the approach that the court should take when assessing the percentage increase, it is reasonable to suppose that it will readily accept the fundamental principle that winners must pay for losers. However, if the solicitor or barrister wishes to justify the level of the percentage increase by reference not only to the individual case but also to the wider considerations of conducting a litigation practice on conditional fees, the court is likely to require supporting data.

A policy of applying a blanket success fee to all cases regardless of their individual merits is likely to be scrutinised very closely by the court. The importance of maintaining careful records of the ingredients of the success fee when it was agreed with the client cannot be overemphasised. Only by producing such evidence could the solicitor or barrister begin to explain to the court that, for example, the witness whose evidence dramatically strengthened the prospects of success had emerged only after the 90 per cent success fee had been set to reflect the risks of what initially appeared to be a very difficult case. It is at this point that the costs judge is not permitted to use 'hindsight', but must weigh up the calculation of the success fee as if he were a fly on the wall at the time it was agreed between the solicitor and client.

It is no surprise that the concept of proportionality underpins the assessment of the percentage increase, as it is an important element of the overriding objective (r. 1.1(2)(c)). Rule 48.9(5) says that the court may reduce the percentage increase 'where it considers it to be disproportionate'. PD 48, para. 2.13, says, 'Where the court is to assess the percentage increase, proportionality is relevant'.

3.5 SPECIAL ISSUES RELATING TO CONDITIONAL FEES UNDER THE CPR

3.5.1 Applying proportionality to conditional fee agreements

A novel feature of proportionality in assessing the success fee in a conditional fee case is the risk that if the case is lost, the solicitor and counsel will receive no fees at all. Proportionality means maintaining a balance between damage and costs. This assumes some payment of costs at the end of the case. But in a conditional fee case there may be no payment of costs at all. Even so in a conditional fee case the proportionality of damages to costs should be no different from any other case as long as the success fee is ignored, because it only applies if the case is won.

3.5.2 Interim costs

Another special difficulty in a conditional fee case is the Practice Direction (Costs: Summary Assessment) [1999] 1 WLR 420, on summary assessment of costs for interlocutory hearings of less than one day (see 3.3). If costs are awarded against the claimant in a conditional fee case where the client is on a no win no fee arrangement, it is unclear who will be expected to pay the assessed costs of an interim application, particularly if they are ordered to be paid in full or in part (as the rules provide) within 14 days. If the client has the benefit of after the event insurance which covers orders of interim costs (as the Law Society's Accident Line Protect policy does) there may still be a problem about interim payment of the costs so ordered. Moreover, where an impecunious client has no insurance cover (or cover is not available) there will be no funds to pay costs awarded at an interim stage. Further, the solicitor who has agreed to receive no fee for losing will not have agreed to pay costs (interim or otherwise) if the case is lost. The only sensible answer to these practical difficulties must be that in a conditional fee case a summary assessment of costs order should not be enforceable until the outcome of the case is known.

It should also be made clear that a solicitor who acts for a client without insurance is not under any extra risk of being made to pay costs personally if the case is lost. The threat of a successful defendant seeking to recover costs against the solicitor or barrister in a conditional fee case because of 'maintenance' or 'champerty' has been removed by the Court of Appeal in *Hodgson* v *Imperial Tobacco Ltd* [1998] 1 WLR 1056. This protection depends on the agreement complying with the Conditional Fee Agreements Regulations 1995. If it does not do so then, as the Access to Justice Bill confirms, it would be unlawful and unenforceable, because it would amount to a contingency fee which is still contrary to public policy. The decision in *Hodgson* does not protect a solicitor or barrister against an application for a 'wasted costs' order.

3.5.3 Children and patients

A glaring omission from the statutory and regulatory framework that established conditional fees in 1995 was the lack of attention to the special provisions required for conditional fee cases conducted on behalf of children or patients. Part 21 of the CPR sets out the new basis for court approval of an award of damages to a child or patient. Under the old RSC, ord. 80, at the settlement approval or award of damages to a child or patient the court was also required to approve costs. This caused a problem in conditional fee cases. The solicitor who had entered into a conditional fee agreement with the litigation friend of a child or patient was vulnerable to the court disapproving the level of the success fee at the approval stage without the in built protection of the conditional fee taxation procedure under the old RSC, ord. 62, r. 15A (for the new assessment procedure see 3.4). This anomaly has been corrected by r. 48.9(6) of the CPR which provides that precisely the same procedure applies to the assessment of the percentage increase under r. 48.9(5) in a conditional fee case on behalf of a child or patient as it would on behalf of any other claimant. At the approval stage the court would presumably pay attention to the 'relevant factors' (and proportionality) set out in PD 48 (see 3.4).

3.5.4 The fast track

Lord Woolf in his *Final Report*, ch. 2, para. 27, said:

> The whole concept of the fast track is intended to increase access to justice by removing the uncertainty over excessive cost which deters people from litigating. Conditional fee agreements combined with after the event insurance contribute to the same objective. The two must work together to improve access rather than reduce it. It will be clear, however, from the preceding discussion, that conditional fees do not answer the case for a more economical level of costs. Indeed, they could, taken by themselves, shore up an uneconomic level of costs. An acceptable level of costs can best be achieved by ensuring that the costs regime provides a realistic and fair reward for litigating such cases and that solicitors generally accept this regime of fixed limited costs for solicitor and own client costs.

The proportionality regime of the new rules is at its most patent in the fast track. Already there are fixed costs for trial. Whether fixed costs for preparation will also be imposed depends on the outcome of further work by the Lord Chancellor's Department following previous research showing that in personal injury cases at least it was not possible to set fixed fees for preparation with any degree of certainty that would be consistent with fairness.

Nevertheless, there is pressure from the judiciary to move toward fixed costs where possible. This poses a problem for conditional fees in the fast track. Especially where the margins are low, there is a delicate relationship between:

(a) damages recovered for the client;
(b) costs recovered from the paying party;
(c) the success fee due from the client;
(d) the cap on the success fee; and
(e) any shortfall of costs not recovered from the paying party.

In assessing the economic equation of whether the claim is 'worth the candle', in any fast track case on a conditional fee agreement the solicitor, barrister and client will need to consider this relationship with special care, particularly if fixed fees apply for preparation as well as trial. As for the solicitor and own client element of costs (referred to at the end of Lord Woolf's quote) the solicitor's entitlement to charge this will be preserved by a late amendment which is expected to be made to CPR, r. 44.4.

3.5.5 Experts and conditional fees

There is much controversy and some confusion over suggestions that the advent of conditional fees has made it legitimate for solicitors to instruct an expert on a no win no fee basis. This is not allowed. It is not permissible to enter into an agreement with an expert witness at the time of giving instructions that the expert will agree not to charge a fee if the case is lost. Any such arrangement is prohibited by the rules of professional conduct. Principle 21.11 of the *Guide to the Professional Conduct of Solicitors*, 7th ed., says:

> A solicitor must not make or offer to make payments to a witness contingent upon the nature of the evidence given or upon the outcome of a case.

It is, though, permissible to make a deferred fee arrangement by which the expert (particularly one who does a lot of work for a firm of solicitors) agrees not to render a fee until the end of the case when, if it is lost, he may decide to waive the fee. Provided there is no antecedent agreement that the expert will not charge if the case is lost the deferred arrangement does not breach the professional conduct rules.

3.5.6 Pre-action protocols and conditional fees

Pre-action protocols are an integral part of the CPR. They are currently limited to personal injury and clinical negligence, both areas of practice where conditional fees have been piloted (mainly in personal injury) since their introduction in 1995. Although there is no major link between conditional fees and the protocols one comment is appropriate. Protocols are designed to promote openness and settlement. This is likely to be of benefit to the client and solicitor running a case on a conditional fee. When risk assessing a conditional fee case for the purposes of calculating the

CHAPTER 3 CONDITIONAL FEES AND THE NEW RULES

success fee, the solicitor should bear in mind that (in theory at least) if a pre-action protocol is in place, settlement may be more likely and more speedy.

3.5.7 'Offers to settle' and conditional fees

The same considerations apply to offers to settle (CPR, Part 36) as to pre-action protocols (see 3.5.6). The innovative procedure of the offer to settle is designed to promote settlement. The fact that such a device now exists could influence the risk assessment exercise for calculating the success fee.

3.5.8 The multi-track and conditional fees

Moving towards certainty of costs may be helpful to the solicitor and client when they sit down to agree the success fee in a conditional fee case. Whereas the fast track promotes certainty of procedure and some certainty for costs at trial (see 3.5.4), this does not apply to the multi-track. Here the emphasis is on the discretion of the case managing judge to adopt flexibility (which may mean uncertainty) of approach during the case. Flexible attitudes may mean that costs are increased or decreased compared with original expectations. This impinges on the costs estimates on which the conditional fee arrangement will have been based (as well as on the estimates that solicitors are being encouraged to provide to the client and the court as the case proceeds). At the conclusion of the case the court has a wide discretion to award costs. This has always existed but r. 44.3 of the CPR spells out a wider discretion that takes into account a number of factors including the conduct of the parties, the level of success and the costs consequences of payments in and offers to settle. The message is that in conditional fee cases in the multi-track solicitors should make allowance for the court's wider discretion to assess costs with the added uncertainties which that may introduce to the risk assessment process.

3.6 EXTENSION OF CONDITIONAL FEES TO NEW AREAS OF WORK

If the CPR introduce some areas of uncharted territory for conditional fees, so the Conditional Fee Agreements Order 1998 (SI 1998/1860) has opened up even more areas of exploration by extending conditional fees to all civil matters excluding matrimonial. Some pioneer litigators are already beginning to feel their way in these new areas at the same time as they will be getting used to the CPR. Some idea of the areas of civil litigation to which conditional fees now extend is as follows:

Since July 1995
Personal injury (including clinical negligence)
Insolvency
Human rights

Since 30 July 1998
Defamation
Commercial — contract, construction, debt
Intellectual property
Contentious probate
Landlord and tenant (housing)
Professional negligence
Civil liberty
Employment

3.7 ACCESS TO JUSTICE BILL 1999

At the time of going to press the Access to Justice Bill is still proceeding through Parliament. Part III of the Bill, entitled 'Funding' begins with cl. 29, which sets out the new statutory framework for conditional fee agreements.

Clause 29(1) replaces s. 58 of the Courts and Legal Services Act 1990 (the enabling legislation for conditional fees) with new ss. 58 and 58A.

The new s. 58(2) introduces the concept of two different types of conditional fee agreement. Although both amount to an agreement which depends on the 'payment by results' method it is confusing that the same term, 'conditional fee agreement', is used for two quite different types of agreement. They are as follows:

(a) Section 58(2)(a) may be described in shorthand as 'less if you lose'. This fee arrangement stems from the landmark case of *Thai Trading Co.* v *Taylor* [1998] QB 781, in which the Court of Appeal approved a fee arrangement by which the lawyer can agree to charge the client no more than normal fees if the case is won, but will receive a discounted fee (or even nothing) if the case is lost. In the past this type of fee agreement has been loosely described as 'speccing'. The current jargon for it is a '*Thai Trading*' or 'discounted' fee agreement.

(b) Section 58(2)(b) may be described in shorthand as 'more if you win'. This is the now familiar conditional fee agreement that provides for a success fee (which in s. 58(2)(b) is called an 'enhanced' fee) if the case is won, but no fees for the solicitor or barrister if the case is lost.

There is clear room for confusion if the term 'conditional fee agreement' can mean either of two different types of fee arrangement. Rule 48.9 of the CPR on assessment of the base and percentage fee (see 3.4) refers to conditional fees under the existing provisions of the Courts and Legal Services Act 1990, s. 58. It therefore relates only to the enhanced 'more if you win' arrangement. If the assessment provisions of r. 48.9 are to be extended to apply to the '*Thai Trading*' type of 'less if you lose' conditional fee agreement an amendment may be necessary to make this clear.

There are three other important provisions of the Bill in respect of conditional fees.

The proposed new s. 58A(4) of the Courts and Legal Services Act 1990 makes it clear that the 'proceedings' to which conditional fees can relate 'includes any sort of proceedings for resolving disputes (and not just proceedings in a court)'. Conditional fees can therefore be used very widely both within and outside the CPR, including arbitration.

The proposed new s. 58(A)(6) sets out the controversial reform that the unsuccessful party should pay the success fee that would otherwise be deducted from the client's damages. Comments earlier in this chapter about the economic equation of a conditional fee agreement and the operation of the 25 per cent cap need to be considered in the light of this

CHAPTER 3 CONDITIONAL FEES AND THE NEW RULES

fundamental change, which means, in theory at least, that successful claimants would receive 100 per cent of their damages without any deduction for the success fee. (It should be remembered that there is nothing to prevent a defendant's solicitor or barrister acting on a conditional fee basis, for example, where there is a counterclaim).

Clause 30 of the Access to Justice Bill provides for the unsuccessful party to pay the insurance premium paid by the successful party. This is intended to refer only to the costs of an after the event insurance policy, although it seems possible that as drafted the Bill does not exclude with any clarity the cost of a before the event policy. It is to be hoped that this will be made clear before it concludes its parliamentary passage.

If these provisions of the Access to Justice Bill are enacted (as seems likely), new rules and practice directions will be needed to make these procedures workable. Complex questions remain. At what stage of the case should notice of the existence of a conditional fee agreement be given to the other party (and/or the court)? At what stage should the level of the success fee be disclosed? At what stage can the success fee be challenged by the other party?

If these provisions of the Access to Justice Bill are enacted (as seems likely), detailed consequential amendments will be necessary to Part 48.9 of the CPR and to PD 48 to accommodate these statutory extensions to the arrangements for conditional fee agreements.

CHAPTER 4 PRE-ACTION PROTOCOLS

CONTENTS

4.1	Introduction	44
4.2	Protocols so far	45
4.3	Consequences of failure to comply with protocols	45
4.3.1	The spirit of the protocols applies generally	46
4.3.2	Costs generally	46
4.3.3	Pre-action disclosure	47
4.3.4	Other sanctions generally	47
4.4	Personal Injury Claims Protocol	47
4.4.1	Experts	48
4.4.2	Application to the small claims track	49
4.4.3	Expiry of the limitation period	49
4.5	Transitional provisions	49
4.6	Future protocols	49

4.1 INTRODUCTION

In ch 10, of his *Final Report* (p. 107) Lord Woolf identified the importance of pre-action protocols. These were intended 'to build on and increase the benefits of early, but well-informed settlements which genuinely satisfy both parties'. The purposes of pre-action protocols were said to be:

(a) to focus the attention of litigants on the desirability of resolving disputes without litigation;
(b) to enable them to obtain the information they reasonably need in order to enter into an appropriate settlement;
(c) to make an appropriate offer (of a kind which can have costs consequences if litigation ensues); and
(d) if a pre-action settlement is not achievable, to lay the ground for expeditious conduct of proceedings.

The approach was that disputes should where possible be resolved without litigation, but that if litigation is unavoidable, pre-action protocols would make both parties well informed at the outset of the litigation. The *Final Report* pointed out that delay before the start of proceedings is just as undesirable and can be just as expensive as delay in the course of litigation and that there is little point in offering a fast track timetable of 30 weeks to a claimant who has spent two or three years in fruitless negotiations before bringing the case to court at all. What was needed was:

> a system which enables the parties to a dispute to embark on meaningful negotiation as soon as the possibility of litigation is identified, and ensures that as early as possible they have the relevant information to define their claims and make realistic offers to settle.

The mechanism for achieving that is to be pre-action protocols, but Lord Woolf's report goes on to stress that the objectives can only be achieved if the court itself takes more account of pre-litigation activity. Protocols are intended to make it easier for parties to obtain the information they need by the use of standard forms and questionnaires and this is assisted by the wider powers for the courts to order pre-action disclosure (which is no longer to be confined to personal injury and death claims, see 15.9).

The *Final Report* indicated that progress was being made on protocols in some areas of litigation and instanced housing disrepair claims, medical negligence litigation and personal injury cases. It also referred to 'a group of construction industry professionals' working to produce guidelines to lead to the resolution of disputes through arbitration.

It was firmly suggested that protocols would be more effective if their contents were agreed on behalf of those likely to be frequent users of the procedures, for example, in a personal injury context, representatives of plaintiffs (such as the Association of Personal Injury Lawyers) and of the insurance industry.

The report concluded with recommendations for pre-action protocols to be incorporated into relevant practice guides. Most importantly it was suggested that:

> Unreasonable failure by either party to comply with the relevant protocol should be taken into account by the court, for example in the allocation of costs or in considering any application for an extension of the timetable.

4.2 PROTOCOLS SO FAR

At the time of writing the hopes for a number of protocols have not been borne out. At present there are only two fully formulated in existence, the Pre-action Protocol for Personal Injury Claims and the Pre-action Protocol for the Resolution of Clinical Disputes. Copies of those protocols with their introductions appear in appendix 2. They are akin to statements of best practice in both these fields and have the object of encouraging contact between the parties at the earliest opportunity, exchange of information, pre-action investigation and putting the parties in a position to settle cases fairly and early. They are clearly written and it is unnecessary to give a detailed commentary on them in this chapter. But there are some problems with the interpretation of the Personal Injury Claims Protocol and they are discussed in 4.4.

4.3 CONSEQUENCES OF FAILURE TO COMPLY WITH PROTOCOLS

It is important to consider what the court's attitude will be to the protocols. PD Protocols has been issued applicable to the two protocols already approved and any others that may subsequently come into existence. The practice direction sets out the objectives. It then goes on to consider the crucial issue of compliance with the protocols and notes that the court will expect all parties to have complied in substance with the terms of an approved protocol and that the court will take into account compliance and non-compliance when giving directions for the management of proceedings under CPR, rr. 3.1(4) and (5) and 3.9(1)(e), and when making orders for costs. In particular, PD Protocols, para. 2.3, provides that if in the opinion of the court non-compliance with the protocol has led to the commencement of proceedings which might otherwise not have been needed or has led to costs being incurred in the proceedings that might not have been incurred, the orders the court may make include:

(a) an order that the party at fault pay the costs of the proceedings or part of them;

(b) an order that the party at fault pay those costs on an indemnity basis;

(c) if the party at fault is a claimant in whose favour an order for the payment of damages or some specified sum is subsequently made, an order depriving that party of interest on such sum and for such period as may be specified or awarding interest at a lower rate;

(d) if the party at fault is a defendant, an order awarding interest on any damages awarded to the plaintiff at a higher rate, not exceeding 10 per cent above base rate (see also CPR, r. 36.21(2)), than the rate at which interest would otherwise have been awarded.

PD Protocols goes on to give examples of culpable failure to comply with a pre-action protocol, which in the case of a claimant includes not having provided sufficient information or not having followed the procedures required; and in the case of a defendant, not making a preliminary response to the letter of claim in time (21 days under the Personal Injury Claims Protocol, 14 days under the Clinical Negligence Protocol); or not making a full response within three months of the letter of claim or not disclosing documents.

Where there has been non-compliance with the protocol, PD Protocols, para. 2.4, says that the court will exercise its powers with the object of placing the innocent party in no worse a position than he would have been in if the protocol had been complied with. The question of sanctions is further discussed in 4.3.4.

4.3.1 The spirit of the protocols applies generally

The general importance of the new spirit of cooperation underpinning the protocols is further stressed by PD Protocols, para. 4, which provides that the court will expect the parties, *even in cases not covered by any approved protocol*, to act reasonably in exchanging information and documents and generally to try to avoid the necessity for the start of proceedings. Thus unless genuine urgency can be demonstrated, a claimant will be expected to have attempted to resolve matters with the defendant and failing that, to have obtained and exchanged information about the claim. Thus commencing proceedings, unless there is great urgency, without at least a letter before action, is likely to be frowned on.

The above cannot be taken too far in every case, of course. The majority of all litigation is in fact nothing more than debt collecting and where a debtor fails to respond to reasonable correspondence, including reminders and final reminders, it is not suggested that anything more than a last letter before action is required, but every case will turn on its own facts.

4.3.2 Costs generally

By CPR, r. 44.3(4), in deciding what order to make about costs, the court is to have regard to all the circumstances including the conduct of all the parties. Rule 44.3(5) then says:

The conduct of the parties includes—

CHAPTER 4 PRE-ACTION PROTOCOLS

(a) conduct before, as well as during, the proceedings and in particular the extent to which the parties followed any relevant pre-action protocol.

This applies both in relation to orders made during the case and at the conclusion.

4.3.3 Pre-action disclosure

Where a party applies for pre-action disclosure the usual principle is that the court will award the costs of the application and of complying with any order made against the party applying. By CPR, r. 48.1(3), the court may make a different order having regard to all the circumstances, including the extent to which it was reasonable for the person against whom the order was sought to oppose the application and in particular whether the parties to the application have complied with any relevant pre-action protocol.

A potential party, therefore (and in the nature of things this is more likely to be the defendant), who refuses a reasonable application for documents or simply drags his heels in failing to comply with the protocol, thus prompting the application, may well be ordered to pay the costs of it.

4.3.4 Other sanctions generally

By CPR, r. 3.8, where a party has failed to comply with a rule, practice direction or court order, the court may impose a sanction which will take effect unless the party in default applies for and obtains relief from that sanction. When deciding whether to grant relief, under r. 3.9, the court will have regard to a number of factors, but in particular: 'the extent to which the party in default has complied with other rules, practice directions, court orders and any relevant pre-action protocol' (r. 3.9(1)(e)).

Thus, failure to abide by a protocol can lead to a sanction immediately, but even if no sanction is imposed, the failure can be taken into account generally when considering the party's conduct in the litigation at later stages.

The sanctions that might be imposed include the following:

(a) if the claimant is in default, a stay of proceedings to allow the defendant to collect its information and, so to speak, 'catch up';
(b) costs (which can be ordered to be paid forthwith);
(c) an order refusing permission to call evidence from an expert who has been instructed by one or other party without compliance with the protocols;
(d) under r. 3.1(5) the court may order a party to pay a sum of money into court if that party has without good reason failed to comply with a rule, practice direction or relevant pre-action protocol. This seems to be a general sanction. If applied against a plaintiff it could in effect amount to having to give security for costs or for the costs of some future stage, such as the joint instruction of an expert. A defendant might be ordered to pay the whole amount of the claim or some part of it into court.

4.4 PERSONAL INJURY CLAIMS PROTOCOL

The notes of guidance at the beginning of the Pre-action Protocol for Personal Injury Claims say that the protocol is intended for claims which include a claim for compensation of less than £15,000 for personal injury resulting from road traffic, tripping or slipping accidents or accidents at work. The protocol is intended for claims which are likely to be allocated to the fast track (paras 2.2 and 2.3). This is because time in such cases will be of the essence once proceedings are issued. The notes of guidance do acknowledge that some flexibility in the timescale of the protocol may be necessary. Paragraph 2.4 goes on to note, however, that the approach advocated by the protocol may well be appropriate to some higher value claims and suggests that the spirit, if not the letter, of the protocol should still be followed for claims which would end up on the multi-track.

The protocol applies to the entirety of claims which include a claim of less than £15,000 for personal injury. This may cause difficulties, for example, where the personal injury element of a claim is modest and may be easily resolved, but there are expensive vehicle repairs. In that situation the claimant may wish to move very swiftly to have the vehicle examined and repaired, if repairable, or scrapped and replaced if not. Despite the terms of the protocol relating to instruction of experts, it is suggested that it would be considered reasonable for a claimant to give the defendant's insurers very much less notice of his intentions in relation to the vehicle and to insist that they have it inspected, if they wish to do so, very much more swiftly than the timescale in the protocol might indicate. A claimant should not be put in the position of wondering whether a defendant's dilatory insurer will or will not accept his own assessment of the vehicle and garage estimates, especially when a defendant may well mount arguments about the length of the period of alternative vehicle hire. Common sense will have to allow for some variations of the timetables in the protocol about such matters.

4.4.1 Experts

There are some apparent discrepancies in the Pre-action Protocol for Personal Injury Claims which leads to an overall impression of vagueness. Paragraph 2.11 of the notes of guidance, whilst acknowledging the need for joint selection of experts, says that 'The protocol promotes the practice of the claimant obtaining a medical report, disclosing it to the defendant who then asks questions and/or agrees to it and does not obtain his own report'. In fact the wording of the protocol suggests at para. 3.14, quite properly, that before *any party* instructs an expert, he should give the other party a list of the names of one or more experts in the relevant speciality whom he considers suitable to instruct, and that is surely the proper procedure.

A frequently encountered objection is that the plaintiff may have needed treatment and may choose to go for his medical report to the specialist who has treated him. It is suggested that this should not happen in future under the protocol. Although there are advantages to the claimant in using the doctor who has actually treated him, the court may well conclude that the expert is less objective, both because he will have established a relationship with his patient and because he will naturally conclude that, being the treating doctor, his own views on prognosis etc. are unchallengeable. It is therefore suggested that the procedure for joint instruction of experts canvassed in paras 3.14 to 3.18 is preferable so that a mutually acceptable expert can be instructed.

A claimant who goes ahead and instructs his own expert unilaterally, may well find that, in imposing the spirit of the protocol, the court will subsequently refuse permission to call that expert and insist that an expert be jointly instructed. This will leave the claimant to bear the irrecoverable costs of the first expert, whatever the outcome of the case. Of course the court will approach this with common sense and, for example, a district judge may invite a defendant to specify exactly why there is an objection to an expert and whether his position cannot be protected by delivering questions to the expert so that progress can be made and costs saved. It must still be the case, however, that a claimant who ignores the provisions for joint instruction of an expert will run the costs risks referred to above.

4.4.2 Application to the small claims track

For a case to be allocated to the small claims track the personal injury element must be less than £1,000. It is suggested that although the spirit of the protocol ought to be honoured to the point of giving some reasonable opportunity to compromise the claim, where there is a limited fixed costs regime the court would not be too prescriptive in criticising the actions of a claimant's lawyer who simply wished to get on with the case as economically as possible once it was clear that liability would not be accepted. It is suggested that only the most flagrant disregard of the spirit of cooperation provided for in the protocols would be likely to lead to a costs sanction and a finding of unreasonableness on the small claims track.

4.4.3 Expiry of the limitation period

If solicitors are first instructed very late in the limitation period for a claim covered by the Pre-action Protocol for Personal Injury Claims then, as indicated at para. 2.8 of the Notes of Guidance, the solicitors should give as much notice of intention to issue proceedings as is practicable and the parties should consider whether the court might be invited to extend time for service of the claimant's supporting documents and the service of any defence or, alternatively, to stay the proceedings while the recommended steps in the protocol are followed.

4.5 TRANSITIONAL PROVISIONS

In principle a court dealing with proceedings commenced after 26 April 1999 will expect relevant protocols to have been honoured. PD Protocols, para. 5.1, indicates that compliance or non-compliance, as the case may be, with relevant protocols will be taken into account by the court in dealing with any proceedings commenced after 26 April 1999, but will not be taken into account by the court in dealing with proceedings started before that date. However, where parties to proceedings commenced after 26 April 1999 did not have time since the publication of the protocols in January 1999 to comply with them, their failure to have done so will not be treated as non-compliance.

The profession, therefore, will be given a short period of grace, although as three months will have elapsed from publication of the protocols to the coming into force of the CPR, practitioners may well be in difficulty in demonstrating, in respect of proceedings commenced after 26 April 1999 that they 'have not had time' since January 1999 to comply with the applicable provisions.

4.6 FUTURE PROTOCOLS

There would seem to be no reason why protocols cannot be developed in due course for other classes of claim, particularly construction disputes.

CHAPTER 4 PRE-ACTION PROTOCOLS

Other kinds of case also suggest themselves, including holiday disappointment cases and housing disrepair claims, as well as possibly the more common kinds of mainstream contractual disputes, for example, between the public utilities and their customers, though as many cases of these kinds will be on the small claims track and will have unrepresented parties, protocols for them may not be so useful as in personal injury claims, clinical disputes and construction disputes.

CHAPTER 5 THE EARLY STAGES OF A CLAIM

CONTENTS

5.2	Introduction	52
5.2	Allocation of business between the High Court and the county courts	53
5.2.1	General rule	53
5.2.2	Claims which may not be brought in a county court	53
5.2.3	Claims which must be brought in a particular county court	54
5.2.4	Claims which must be brought in the Queen's Bench Division of the High Court	54
5.2.5	Chancery business	54
5.3	Transfer	55
5.3.1	Automatic transfer	55
5.3.2	Transfer upon application by a party or by the court acting on its own initiative	55
5.4	Proceedings started in the wrong court	57
5.5	Parties	57
5.5.1	Description	57
5.5.2	Joinder	58
5.6	Addition and substitution of parties	59
5.6.1	Principles	59
5.6.2	Procedure	59
5.6.3	Transfer of interest or liability	60
5.6.4	Addition of a party after limitation period	60
5.7	Special kinds of party	61
5.7.1	Partnerships	61
5.7.2	Companies	61
5.7.3	Children and patients	61
5.7.4	Estate of a deceased individual	64
5.8	Starting proceedings	64
5.8.1	Introduction	64
5.8.2	Standard procedure and Part 8 procedure	64
5.8.3	Issuing a claim form	65
5.8.4	Date for service of claim form and particulars of claim	65
5.8.5	Application to extend time for serving a claim form	66
5.9	Service	68
5.9.1	Introduction	68
5.9.2	Filing documents	68
5.9.3	Who may serve documents?	68
5.9.4	Service of a claim form and other documents by the court	69
5.9.5	Service of a claim form and other documents by a party	69
5.9.6	Methods by which documents may be served	70
5.9.7	Personal service	70
5.9.8	Address for service	70
5.9.9	Service by DX, by fax or by other electronic method	71
5.9.10	Service on registered companies	72

CHAPTER 5   THE EARLY STAGES OF A CLAIM

5.9.11	Service on a partnership	72
5.9.12	Service on a corporation other than a registered company	73
5.9.13	Service on a child or a patient	73
5.9.14	Deemed dates of service	73
5.9.15	Service by an alternative method	73
5.9.16	Power of court to dispense with service	74
5.9.17	Objecting to defective service of a claim form	74
5.9.18	Service out of the jurisdiction	74
5.9.19	Service on the Crown and service in proceedings for the recovery of land and mortgage possession actions	74
5.9.20	Computing time	74
5.10	Step-by-step guide to issue and service	75
5.10.1	Where service of the claim form is to be effected by the court	75
5.10.2	Where service of the claim form is to be effected by the claimant	75
5.11	Responding to the particulars of claim	76
5.12	Admissions	76
5.12.1	General rule	76
5.12.2	Admission of money claims within 14 days of service of the particulars of claim	76
5.13	Acknowledging service	78
5.13.1	Time for filing the acknowledgment	78
5.13.2	Contents of the form of acknowledgment	79
5.14	Judgment in default	79
5.14.1	Conditions for entering judgment in default	80
5.14.2	Request for default judgment	80
5.14.3	Application for default judgment	81
5.14.4	Two or more defendants	82
5.15	Setting aside a default judgment	82
5.15.1	Principle upon which a default judgment will be set aside	82
5.15.2	Duty of claimant to set aside a default judgment	83
5.15.3	Procedure	84
5.15.4	Default judgments on a Part 20 claim	84
5.16	Disputing the court's jurisdiction	84
5.17	Part 8 Procedure	85
5.17.1	When the procedure is used	85
5.17.2	Acknowledgment	86
5.17.3	Consequences of failing to file an acknowledgment of service	86
5.17.4	Subsequent procedure	86

5.1   INTRODUCTION

This chapter considers first how the CPR divide business between the High Court and the county courts (see 5.2). It goes on to address the rules governing transfer of claims between and within the courts (see 5.3 and 5.4).

The chapter then considers the various provisions in the CPR relating to parties: first general provisions, including adding and joining a party to a claim (5.5 and 5.6), then provisions relating to special kinds of party (5.7).

CHAPTER 5   THE EARLY STAGES OF A CLAIM

The CPR introduce a new method of starting proceedings, the claim form, and almost entirely abolishes the old forms of originating process. The new method of starting proceedings is considered in 5.8 to 5.10. Ways in which a defendant may respond to a claim are considered in 5.11 to 5.13.

A claimant may apply for default judgment (5.14), which, if granted, may be subsequently set aside (5.15). The defendant may dispute the court's jurisdiction (5.16).

5.2   ALLOCATION OF BUSINESS BETWEEN THE HIGH COURT AND THE COUNTY COURTS

5.2.1   General rule

Since the entry into force in July 1991 of the High Court and County Courts Jurisdiction Order 1991 (SI 1991/724) ('the Jurisdiction Order'), the High Court and the county courts have had concurrent jurisdiction over most claims, including over all claims in contract and tort. Under the CPR the general position is that, where both the High Court and the county courts have jurisdiction to deal with a claim, the claimant may start proceedings in the High Court or any county court (PD 7 How to Start Proceedings, para. 1). However:

(a)   A money claim may be issued in the High Court only where the claimant expects to recover £15,000 or more (para. 2.1). The term 'money claim' would include both claims for a debt or liquidated demand and claims for damages. However, a claim worth less than £50,000 issued in the Central Office or Chancery Chambers of the Royal Courts of Justice (other than one in any of the specialist lists listed in CPR, r. 49(2)) will generally be transferred to a county court, unless it is suitable for trial in the Royal Courts of Justice (see 11.4.7.6) or is required by statute to be tried in the High Court (PD 29, para. 2).

(b)   A claim for personal injuries must not be commenced in the High Court unless the claimant expects to recover £50,000 or more (PD 7 How to Start Proceedings, para. 2.2).

(c)   A claim must be issued in the High Court or in a county court where an enactment requires it (para. 2.3).

(d)   Subject to (a) and (b) above, a claim should be started in the High Court if the claimant believes it should be tried by a High Court judge because of the financial value of the claim, its complexity or its importance to the general public (para. 2.4).

The value of the claim is determined under the provisions of art. 9 of the Jurisdiction Order.

Applications made before a claim has started should be made to the court where it is likely that the claim to which the application relates will be issued, unless there is good reason to make the application to a different court (CPR, r. 23.2(4)). There is no explanation in the rules of what is meant by 'good reason'.

5.2.2   Claims which may not be brought in a county court

The following claims may not be issued in (or transferred to) a county court:

(a)   a claim for libel or slander (PD 7 How to Start Proceedings, para. 2.9);

CHAPTER 5 THE EARLY STAGES OF A CLAIM

(b) a claim in which the title to any toll, fair, market or franchise is in question (para. 2.9);

(c) applications concerning the decisions of local authority auditors (Jurisdiction Order, art. 6).

5.2.3 Claims which must be brought in a particular county court

Claims under the Consumer Credit Act 1974 may only be brought in a county court, normally the county court where the debtor resides or carries on business (PD 7 Consumer Credit Act Claims, para. 4).

Claims for the recovery of land and mortgage possession actions must be brought in the county court for the district in which the land is situated (CCR, ord. 4, r. 3 in CPR, sch. 2).

5.2.4 Claims which must be brought in the Queen's Bench Division of the High Court

The following claims must be issued in the Queen's Bench Division of the High Court:

(a) applications for a writ of habeas corpus (PD 7 How to Start Proceedings, para. 2.6; Supreme Court Act 1981, sch. 1, para. 2(a));

(b) applications for judicial review (PD 7 How to Start Proceedings, para. 2.6; Supreme Court Act 1981, sch. 1, para. 2(b)).

5.2.5 Chancery business

Claims involving Chancery business may be dealt with either in the High Court or in a county court (PD 7 How to Start Proceedings, para. 2.5). The claim form must be marked 'Chancery Division' in the top right-hand corner, if issued in the High Court, and 'Chancery Business' if issued in the county court (ibid.). The county court's jurisdiction over equity claims is limited to £30,000 (County Courts Act 1984, s. 23; County Courts Jurisdiction Order 1981).

PD 7 How to Start Proceedings, para 2.5, defines 'Chancery business' as including any of the matters specified in the Supreme Court Act 1981, sch. 1, para 1. Those matters are:

(a) the sale, exchange or partition of land, or the raising of charges on land;
(b) the redemption or foreclosure of mortgages;
(c) the execution of trusts;
(d) the administration of the estates of deceased persons;
(e) bankruptcy;
(f) the dissolution of partnerships or the taking of partnership or other accounts;
(g) the rectification, setting aside or cancellation of deeds or other instruments in writing;
(h) probate business, other than non-contentious or common form business;
(i) patents, trade marks, registered designs, copyright or design right;
(j) the appointment of a guardian of a minor's estate,
(k) all causes and matters involving the exercise of the High Court's jurisdiction under the enactments relating to companies.

CHAPTER 5   THE EARLY STAGES OF A CLAIM

5.3   TRANSFER

5.3.1   Automatic transfer

A claim may be issued in any court which has jurisdiction to hear it. However, a claim for a specified sum of money against a defendant who is an individual will be transferred to the individual's home court, if not started there, when the defendant files a defence (CPR, r. 26.2(1) and (3)). Where there is more than one defendant who is an individual, and they have different home courts, the claim will be transferred to the home court of the individual defendant whose defence is filed first (r. 26.2(5)).
The 'defendant's home court' is defined by r. 2.3(1) to mean:

   (a)   if the claim is proceeding in a county court, the county court for the district in which the defendant's address for service, as shown on the defence, is situated; and
   (b)   if the claim is proceeding in the High Court, the district registry for the district in which the defendant's address for service, as shown on the defence, is situated or, if there is no such district registry, the Royal Courts of Justice.

By virtue of r. 6.5(5), the address for service of a defendant who is represented by a solicitor will be the business address of the solicitor, not the defendant's personal address. The solicitor's address should be stated on the defence and will determine which court is the defendant's home court.

Where the claim is for a specified sum and either the defendant claims that the money has been paid or a partial admission has been made under r. 14.5, automatic transfer will not happen on the filing of the defence. Rather, the claim will be retained at the issuing court unless and until the claimant has been notified of the defence and files notice at court that he wishes the claim to proceed (r. 26.2(4)).

Automatic transfer will not happen where the case is in a specialist list (r. 26.2(2)). Specialist proceedings under Part 49 not issued in a civil trial centre will be transferred there automatically for allocation and case management (PD 26, para. 10.2(2)).

Claims allocated to the multi-track will be normally be dealt with in a civil trial centre (PD 26, para. 10.2(1)). Where a district judge in a court which is not a civil trial centre considers a case suitable for allocation to the multi-track, he will normally allocate the claim to the track, give case management directions and then transfer the claim to a civil trial centre (para 10.2(5)), though he may transfer the claim to a civil trial centre for allocation and directions there (para. 10.2(8)). Where the district judge is in doubt about allocation, he may hold a hearing (para. 10.2(6)).

A designated civil judge may transfer a claim to a civil trial centre at any stage of the action, and regardless of the track to which it has been allocated (para. 10.2(11)). Although the practice direction does not say so, the implication must be that this power would be used only exceptionally.

5.3.2   Transfer upon application by a party or by the court acting on its own initiative

Part 30 of the CPR enables:

CHAPTER 5 THE EARLY STAGES OF A CLAIM

(a) the High Court to transfer proceedings or any part of proceedings (for example, a counterclaim or any application made in proceedings) from the Royal Courts of Justice to a district registry, or vice versa, or from one district registry to another (r. 30.2(4));

(b) a county court to transfer proceedings or any part of proceedings (for example, a counterclaim or any application made in proceedings) to another county court (r. 30.2(1)).

Power to transfer cases between the High Court and the county courts is conferred by the County Courts Act 1984, ss. 40(2), 41(1) and 42(2).

The factors which will govern the court's decision to order transfer are, by CPR, r. 30.3(1), those set out in r. 30.3(2). They are:

(a) the financial value of the claim and the amount in dispute, if different;

(b) whether it would be more convenient or fair for hearings (including the trial) to be held in some other court;

(c) the availability of a judge specialising in the type of claim in question;

(d) whether the facts, legal issues, remedies or procedures involved are simple or complex;

(e) the importance of the claim to the public in general;

(f) the facilities available at the court where the claim is being dealt with and whether they may be inadequate because of any disabilities of a party or potential witness.

The power to transfer may be exercised either upon application by a party or by the court acting under its own initiative (see below).

A claim worth less than £50,000, issued in the Central Office or Chancery Chambers of the Royal Courts of Justice (other than one in any of the specialist lists listed in r. 49(2)) will generally be transferred to a county court, unless it is suitable for trial in the Royal Courts of Justice (see 11.4.7.6) or is required by statute to be tried in the High Court (PD 29, para. 2). The decision to transfer a claim worth less than £50,000 out of the Royal Courts of Justice may be made at any stage of the proceedings, but should be made as soon as possible (PD 29, para. 2.4). It will usually be convenient to hear an application to strike out or for summary judgment or for an interim remedy before making the decision (para. 2.5). The decision should be taken at the latest before the date for filing listing questionnaires (para. 2.4).

5.3.2.1 Additional rules about transfer between county courts
A county court may make an order transferring a claim to another county court where it considers that proceedings for the detailed assessment of costs or for the enforcement of a judgment or order could more conveniently or fairly be taken in that other county court (CPR, r. 30.2(1)(b)). The criteria in r. 30.3(2) do not apply to this kind of transfer.

5.3.2.2 Additional rules about transfer within the High Court
A district registry may make an order transferring a claim to another district registry where it considers that proceedings for the detailed assessment of costs could more conveniently or fairly be taken in that other district registry (CPR, r. 30.2(5)). The criteria in r. 30.3(2) do not apply to this kind of transfer.

CHAPTER 5 THE EARLY STAGES OF A CLAIM

The High Court also has power to transfer a claim between divisions and in or out of specialist lists (r. 30.5(1) and (2)) and the criteria in r. 30.3(2) do not apply.

5.3.2.3 Power to specify where hearing should be held As an alternative to an order for transfer the court has power to order trial or some other hearing to be held at a particular court without ordering transfer of the proceedings to that court (CPR, r. 30.6).

5.3.2.4 Procedure An application for transfer should be made to the court where the claim is proceeding (CPR, r. 30.2(3) and (6)) (or to the judge in charge of the specialist list in the case of applications under r. 30.5). The application should be made in accordance with the general rules about applications for court orders set out in Part 23 (see chapter 9).

The court has the power to make an order for transfer on its own initiative. Where it decides to proceed on its own initiative, it must follow the procedure set out in r. 3.3 (see 9.6).

Once it has made an order for transfer, the court from which the claim is to be transferred must give notice of the transfer to the receiving court (PD 30, para. 4.1) and to the parties (CPR, r. 30.4(1)). Transfer does not affect any order made earlier (r. 30.4(2)). PD 30 sets out details of the procedure for appealing against orders for transfer.

5.4 PROCEEDINGS STARTED IN THE WRONG COURT

Proceedings started in the 'wrong' county court may, by CPR, r. 30.2(2), be:

(a) transferred to the county court in which they ought to have been started;
(b) continued in the county court in which they have been started (subject to any statutory requirement preventing this: r. 30.2(7)); or
(c) struck out.

If proceedings have been started in the High Court which should have been started in the county court and vice versa, the claim will normally be transferred to the correct court and the claimant will normally be required to pay the costs of transfer, though the claim may be struck out (County Courts Act 1984, ss. 40(1) and 42(1)). In *Restick* v *Crickmore* [1994] 1 WLR 420 the Court of Appeal held that striking out is inappropriate for bona fide mistakes.

A claimant who issued a claim in the High Court which should have been started in a county court may, in addition, have any award of costs reduced by up to 25 per cent (Supreme Court Act 1981, s. 51(8) and (9)).

5.5 PARTIES

5.5.1 Description

The CPR change the name for the party who makes a claim. No longer is that party called the plaintiff. The new term is 'claimant' (r. 2.3(1)). The party against whom proceedings are brought remains the 'defendant' (ibid.). Parties to applications may also be referred to as 'applicant' and 'respondent' (r. 23.1).

The form of words to be used in describing different types of parties in the headings of statements of case and other court documents is set out in table 5.1.

Class of party	Form of words
An individual	All known forenames and surname: e.g., John Richard Brown
A child under 18	Jane Mary Brown (a child by Joe Bloggs her litigation friend)
A child under 18 who is conducting proceedings on his or her own behalf	Jane Mary Brown (a child)
An individual who is a patient within the meaning of the Mental Health Act 1983	Jane Mary Brown (by Joe Bloggs her litigation friend)
An individual who is trading under another name	John Smith, trading as Smith's Groceries
An individual who is suing or being sued in a representative capacity	Jane Mary Brown, as the representative of Hilda Marion Brown (deceased)
An individual who is suing or being sued in the name of a club or other unincorporated organisation	Jane Mary Brown, suing/sued on behalf of the Northtown Under 16 Football Club
A firm	Brown & Co. (a firm)
A corporation (other than a company)	The full name of the corporation
A company, whether registered in England and Wales, or an overseas company	The full name of the company

Table 5.1 Names of parties

5.5.2 Joinder

Section 49(2) of the Supreme Court Act 1981 requires the court to exercise its discretion to ensure that:

> as far as possible, all matters in dispute between the parties are completely and finally determined, and all multiplicity of legal proceedings with respect to any of those matters is avoided.

This is reflected in the CPR, which state that a single claim form may be used to start all claims which can be conveniently disposed of in the same proceedings (r. 7.3). All persons jointly entitled to a remedy must be joined as joint claimants, unless a person refuses to be joined as claimant, in which case that person must be joined as defendant (r. 19.2).

It is likely that the court will consider the constitution of an action, and make appropriate orders of its own initiative, as part of its duty to manage a case. The case management powers given to the court expressly include

CHAPTER 5   THE EARLY STAGES OF A CLAIM

the power to direct that part of a claim be dealt with separately, power to consolidate, and power to try two or more claims on the same occasion (r. 3.1(2)).

No guidance is provided about which claims it might be considered convenient to dispose of in the same action. But the court will take into account the overriding objective in coming to its decision, in particular the objectives of saving expense and of ensuring that cases are dealt with expeditiously and fairly. Thus claims involving common questions of law or fact between the same parties, or different causes of action involving the same parties, should, as previously, be included within a single claim.

5.6   ADDITION AND SUBSTITUTION OF PARTIES

5.6.1   Principles

The court is given a wide discretion under the CPR to order that a person be added or removed as a party to the claim where it is 'desirable' to do so, provided that (in the case of adding a party) the limitation period has not yet expired. This power may be exercised upon application by a party, or by a person who wishes to become a party, or by the court acting on its own initiative.

The court is empowered by r. 19.1(2) to add a party where it is desirable:

   (a)   to enable it to resolve all the matters in dispute in the proceedings; or
   (b)   to resolve a matter between an existing party and a proposed new party, which is connected with an issue in the claim.

A person may not be added as a claimant without his written consent, which must be filed at court (r. 19.3(3)). Any order made by the court joining a new claimant will not take effect unless and until his signed, written consent has been filed (PD 19, para. 2.2).

The court may remove a party where it is not desirable for him to remain a party to the claim (CPR, r. 19.1(3)).

5.6.2   Procedure

A party may be added or removed only with the permission of the court. Thus where an existing party, or the proposed new party, wishes to change the parties to a claim, an application for permission to do so must be made under CPR Part 23 (r. 19.3).

5.6.2.1   The application   The application must be made on notice (save in the case of a transfer of interest or liability — see 5.6.3) and must, in the case of an application to add a party, be supported by evidence setting out the proposed new party's interest in or connection with the claim (PD 19, paras 1.3 and 1.4). The rules contain no requirement for evidence to be submitted in support of an application to remove a party. The party applying for the amendment will usually be ordered to pay the costs of the application and any additional costs arising from the amendment.

Where the party to be added is a claimant, a copy of the proposed amended claim form and particulars of claim and the signed written consent of the new party must be filed with the application notice (PD 19, para. 2.1).

5.6.2.2 The hearing
Where all parties (and the proposed new party) agree the change, the application may be dealt with without a hearing (PD 19, para. 1.2).

5.6.2.3 The order and consequential directions
Where the court makes an order adding parties it will normally also make consequential directions. These will normally include orders that:

(a) the claimant or the party who made the application file and serve the amended claim form and particulars of claim within 14 days (PD 19, paras 2.3(3) and 3.2(1));

(b) the new party be served with a copy of the existing statements of case (and documents referred to in them) (para. 2.3(2));

(c) any new defendant be served with the usual response pack (forms for admitting, defending and acknowledging the claim) (para. 3.2(3)); and

(d) a copy of the order be served on the parties, and on any other person affected by it (paras 2.3(1) and 3.2(2)).

A new defendant does not become a party to the proceedings until the amended claim form is served on him (para. 3.3). Thus it is this step (not the making of the application) which will interrupt the running of the limitation period against that person (giving effect to the decision in *Ketteman v Hansel Properties Ltd* [1987] AC 189).

When a party is removed, the claimant must file in court an amended claim form and particulars of claim, and a copy of the order must be served on every party and on any other person affected (para. 4).

5.6.3 Transfer of interest or liability

Where an existing party's interest or liability has passed to another person, the court may order that person to be substituted as a party to a claim where it is desirable to do so, to enable the court to resolve the matters in dispute in the proceedings (CPR, r. 19.1(4)).

An application for such an order may be made without notice but must be supported by evidence (r. 19.3(2)) showing the stage the claim has reached and setting out details of the transfer of interest or liability (PD 19, para. 5).

5.6.4 Addition of a party after limitation period

Rule 19.4 of the CPR restricts the power of the court to add a new party after the expiry of a statutory limitation period. In claims other than for personal injury the court may do so only where the limitation period had not expired when the claim was issued, and:

(a) the order is sought to correct a mistake; or

(b) the claim cannot properly be continued against the original party without the addition or substitution of the new party; or

(c) the original party has died or been made bankrupt and his interest or liability has passed to the new party.

But r. 19.4(4) gives the court an additional power to make an order adding a new party to a personal injury case or to a claim under the fatal accidents legislation after the expiry of the limitation period:

(a) where it has exercised its discretion under s. 33 of the Limitation Act 1980 to override the usual three-year limitation period; or

(b) where it directs that this issue should be decided at trial.

CHAPTER 5   THE EARLY STAGES OF A CLAIM

5.7 SPECIAL KINDS OF PARTY

5.7.1 Partnerships

A partnership carrying on business within the jurisdiction may sue and be sued in the firm name as under the old rules (RSC, ord. 81, r. 1 in CPR, sch. 1; CCR, ord. 5, r. 9 in CPR, sch. 2).

5.7.2 Companies

A significant change introduced by the CPR is the removal of the requirement previously in RSC, ord. 5, r. 6(2), that a company or other body corporate cannot begin or carry on High Court proceedings except by a solicitor. The Rules go on to permit a company to be represented at trial by an employee who has been authorised to do so, provided the court gives its permission (r. 39.6).

5.7.3 Children and patients

The CPR contain special provisions governing proceedings involving children and patients. 'Children' are persons under 18 (r. 21.1(2)(a)). 'Patients' are persons who are incapable of managing and administering their own affairs, by reason of mental disorder within the meaning of the Mental Health Act 1983 (r. 21.1(2)(b)).

5.7.3.1 Litigation friends   Both patients and children (subject in the latter case to any order by the court to the contrary — see 5.7.3.4) must have a litigation friend to conduct proceedings on their behalf (CPR, r. 21.2). The title to the action should read 'AB (by CD his litigation friend)' or, in the case of a child, 'AB (a child by CD his litigation friend)' (PD 21, paras 1.3 and 1.5).

A claimant who sues a child or patient who has no litigation friend may take no step in an action other than issuing and serving the claim form. Thereafter the claimant must make an application for the appointment of a litigation friend before pursuing the claim any further (CPR, r. 21.3(2)). If a party to proceedings becomes a patient, no further step in the action may be taken until he or she has a litigation friend (r. 21.3(3)). Any step taken before the appointment of the litigation friend has no effect, subject to any order by the court to the contrary (r. 21.3(4)).

5.7.3.2 Who may be a litigation friend?   A litigation friend may be:

   (a)   a person authorised under Part VII of the Mental Health Act 1983 to conduct legal proceedings in the name of a patient; or
   (b)   a person who can fairly and competently conduct proceedings on behalf of the child or patient and who has no adverse interest in the claim.

A litigation friend who acts for a claimant must also undertake to pay any costs which the claimant may be ordered to pay (subject to any right he or she may have to be repaid from the assets of the child or patient) (CPR, r. 21.4(3)).

PD 21, para. 2.1, places the litigation friend under a duty to conduct the proceedings fairly and competently, and to take all decisions and steps in the action for the benefit of the child or patient.

In practice, a child's litigation friend will normally be a parent, guardian or other relative who can comply with these requirements. A patient's litigation friend may be a receiver appointed under the Mental Health Act 1983 or the person with whom the patient lives or who is caring for the patient. Alternatively, in either case the litigation friend can be the Official Solicitor.

5.7.3.3 How is a litigation friend appointed? There are two methods whereby a litigation friend may be appointed.

First, a person may become a litigation friend without a court order, under CPR, r. 21.5, by filing either:

(a) in the case of a patient, his or her authorisation to act under Part VII of the Mental Health Act 1983; or

(b) in the case of a child or a patient without such authorisation, a certificate of suitability. The details of what the certificate must state are set out in PD 21, para. 2.3(2).

These documents must be filed when proceedings are first issued (where the litigation friend acts on behalf of the claimant) or when the litigation friend first takes a step in the proceedings (where he acts on behalf of the defendant). A copy of the certificate of suitability must also be served on every person on whom the claim form must be served under CPR, r. 6.6 (r. 21.5(6)).

Alternatively, a litigation friend may be appointed by court order under r. 21.6. An application for an order under this rule may be made by any person who wishes to be appointed litigation friend or by any party to the action (r. 21.6(2)). The application should be made under the Part 23 procedure. It must, by PD 21, para. 3.4, be supported by evidence that the litigation friend:

(a) consents to act;
(b) can conduct proceedings fairly and competently;
(c) has no adverse interest to the child or patient; and
(d) in the case of a claimant, undertakes to pay any costs order against the child or patient (subject to any right to be repaid from the assets of the child or patient).

5.7.3.4 When may a child conduct proceedings without a litigation friend? In the case of a child (but not a patient) the court has a discretion to make an order permitting the child to conduct proceedings without a litigation friend (CPR, r. 21.2(3)). The order may be made on application by the child, on notice to the litigation friend if the child already has one (r. 21.2(4)). Where the child has no litigation friend, the application may be made without notice. Having made such an order the court can nevertheless appoint a litigation friend subsequently if it appears to be desirable to do so (r. 21.2(5)).

Where a child is conducting proceedings on his own behalf, the action should be headed 'AB (a child)' (PD 21, para. 1.5(2)).

5.7.3.5 Terminating the appointment of a litigation friend The court may substitute or remove a litigation friend (CPR, r. 21.7). Application for such an order should be made under the Part 23 procedure, and should be supported by evidence (PD 21, para. 4).

When a child reaches 18, the appointment of his or her litigation friend ceases (CPR, r. 21.9(1)). No application to court to terminate the appointment is necessary. Either the child or the friend may serve a notice that the

CHAPTER 5   THE EARLY STAGES OF A CLAIM

appointment has ceased. The heading in the action then becomes: 'AB (formerly a child but now of full age)' (PD 21, para. 5.3).

In the case of a patient who recovers, however, an application to court must be made in order to terminate the appointment (CPR, r. 21.9(2)). The application must be supported by medical evidence that the patient is capable of managing and administering his or her own affairs (PD 21, para. 5.7). The patient must file in court a notice that the litigation friend's appointment has ceased, giving an address for service and stating whether he intends to continue to pursue or defend the proceedings (para. 5.8). Any order made must be served on other parties to the proceedings (para. 5.8).

5.7.3.6 Service of a document on a child or patient   Where proceedings are begun against a child, the claim form must be served on one of his or her parents or guardians, or, if there is none, on the person with whom the child resides or in whose care the child is (CPR, r. 6.6(1)). In the case of a patient, the claim form must be served on the person authorised under the Mental Health Act 1983 to conduct proceedings on the patient's behalf, or where there is no person so authorised, the person with whom the patient resides or in whose care the patient is (CPR, r. 6.6(1)).

An application for the appointment or removal of a litigation friend under rr. 21.6 and 21.7 must be served on the same people and also the litigation friend himself (if different) (r. 21.8(3)).

An application for the appointment of a litigation friend in the case of a patient must be served on the patient himself (r. 21.8(2)).

Once proceedings have been commenced with a litigation friend acting on behalf of the child or patient, any document which would otherwise be served on the child or patient should be served on his or her litigation friend (r. 6.6(1)).

These rules are subject to any order to the contrary made by the court. Where a document has been served on some other person, the court may make an order that service should stand.

5.7.3.7 Liability for costs   A litigation friend who acts on behalf of a claimant must undertake to pay any costs which the child or patient may be ordered to pay, subject to any right to be repaid from the assets of the child or the patient (PD 21, para. 3.4(4); see 5.7.3.3). The CPR make no express reference to the liability for costs of a litigation friend who acts for a defendant. It seems likely, therefore, that the old position where he or she would be liable only for costs incurred as a result of personal negligence or misconduct remains.

By virtue of CPR, r. 48.5(2), where money is ordered or agreed to be paid to or by a child or patient, or on his or her behalf, the court will generally order a detailed assessment of the costs payable by the child or patient to his or her solicitor. The assessment must include an assessment of any costs payable to the child or patient. The only amount then payable will be the amount which the court certifies.

5.7.3.8 Investment of funds   Any moneys recovered on behalf of a patient or child may be dealt with only as directed by the court (CPR,

r. 21.11). The court has power to appoint a guardian of a child's estate (r. 21.12). Paragraphs 7 to 12 of PD 21 set out details concerning how moneys recovered for a child or patient should be applied.

5.7.4 Estate of a deceased individual

Where it is sought to start proceedings against the estate of a deceased individual before there has been a grant of probate or letters of administration, the claim should be issued against 'the personal representatives of AB deceased' (PD 7 How to Start Proceedings, para. 4.5). The practice direction goes on to advise that the claimant should, before the time limit for service of the claim expires, apply for the appointment of an administrator.

5.8 STARTING PROCEEDINGS

5.8.1 Introduction

The *Final Report* commented that 'A prime example of [the complexity of the old rules] is the fact that there are four different ways of starting proceedings in the High Court, and another four in the county courts' (ch. 12, para. 1). In order to further the aim of achieving simplicity in civil proceedings, Lord Woolf recommended that there should be a single claim form which could be used for every case (ch. 12, para. 3).

The dramatic simplification called for by Lord Woolf has not been fully achieved (see 2.4.4), but the CPR have made it possible for one prescribed form to be used to start a very large proportion of proceedings.

Under the CPR, the standard method by which a claimant starts a claim, whether in the High Court or in a county court, is by presenting a suitable number of copies of a completed claim form to the court office, where officials will stamp on it (or the covering letter if it is presented by post) the date of receipt, assign it a claim number, create a case management file and then issue the claim form for service on the defendant(s).

An issued claim form must be served on the defendant, and, unless they are given on the claim form, particulars of claim must also be served (see 5.8.4, 5.8.5 and 5.9). There is detailed discussion of the contents of the claim form and of particulars of claim in 6.3 and 6.4.

After a claim has been started, parties to the proceedings other than the claimant may add their own claims and counterclaims, which in the CPR are called Part 20 claims: they are discussed in chapter 8.

5.8.2 Standard procedure and Part 8 procedure

Part 7 of the CPR sets out the standard CPR procedure for starting proceedings by claim form, and most of this chapter is concerned with that procedure. There is also an alternative procedure for claims in Part 8 of the CPR (see 5.17).

Different starting procedures may be prescribed in practice directions or separate rules applying to the specialist proceedings listed in Part 49. As explained in 2.4.4 a remarkable number of other methods of starting particular types of proceeding survive in the schedules to the CPR.

CHAPTER 5   THE EARLY STAGES OF A CLAIM

5.8.3   Issuing a claim form

Proceedings under the CPR are started when the court issues a claim form at the request of the claimant (r. 7.2(1)).

In order to have a claim form issued, the claimant must take or send to court one copy of the completed claim form for the court, and one for each defendant. The court will issue the claim form by affixing the court seal (r. 2.6(1)), which it may do by hand or by printing a facsimile of the seal on the document, electronically or otherwise (r. 2.6(2)). Of course, the claimant should make a copy of the claim form for his own use. The notes for claimant accompanying form N1 mention the claimant's own copy but are ambiguous about whether it should be submitted to the court for sealing. However, the existence of forms (N205A, N205B, N205C) by which the court gives notice of issue of a claim suggests that this is not required.

For the purposes of the Limitation Act 1980 and other statutes a claim is 'brought' when received by the court office (PD 7, para. 4.1). The court records this date either on the court copy of the claim form or on the letter which enclosed it (PD 7, para. 4.2). For the purposes of the CPR, proceedings are started when the claim form is issued by the court (r. 7.2(1)). The date of issue is entered on the form by the court (r. 7.2(2)). PD 7, para. 4.4, enjoins claimants for whom the date of receipt is crucial to make their own arrangements for recording it.

Two varieties of claim form have been devised. Most claimants will use form N1 (see appendix 3), but a claimant using the Part 8 procedure (see 5.8.2) will use form N208 (also in appendix 3). Chapter 6 deals in detail with the contents of these forms.

If the Part 8 procedure is being used, any written evidence on which the claimant intends to rely must be filed with the claim form (CPR, r. 8.5(1)).

Certain claim forms and other related matters will be issued from a production centre, in accordance with a practice direction which has not yet been published, but will presumably continue the arrangements referred to in the old CCR, ord. 2, r. 8, for the production centre in Northampton, which deals with the bulk issue of debt recovery claims by, for example, credit card companies and public utilities.

5.8.4   Date for service of claim form and particulars of claim

Once issued, a claim form must be served on the defendant within four months after issue, or six months, where it is to be served out of the jurisdiction (CPR, r. 7.5). Where particulars of claim are not contained in or served with the claim form, they must be served within 14 days after serving the claim form (r. 7.4(1)) and no later than the latest time for serving the claim form (r. 7.4(2)). If particulars of claim are served separately from the claim form, a copy of the particulars must be filed within seven days of service on the defendant together with a certificate of service (r. 7.4(3)). If practicable the particulars of claim should be set out in the claim form (PD 16, para. 3.1). With the particulars of claim there must be served forms for admitting and for defending the claim and for acknowledging service (CPR, r. 7.8(1)). The collection of forms for the defendant's use is known as a 'response pack'. Where the Part 8 procedure is being used r. 7.8(1) does not apply, but the claim form must be accompanied by a form for acknowledging service. Any written evidence on which a claimant using the Part 8 procedure intends to rely must be served on the defendant with the claim form (r. 8.5(2)).

'Month' means calendar month (r. 2.10). Thus a claim form issued on 26 August 1999 must be served within the jurisdiction on or before 25 December 1999.

There is no restriction on the day on which any document, including a claim form, may be served. However, if a document other than a claim form is served after 5 p.m. on a business day, or at any time on a Saturday, Sunday or a bank holiday, it is treated as having been served on the next business day (r. 6.7(2)).

Thus in the example above, the claim form will be validly served on Christmas Day. But particulars of claim (not included in the claim form) served on 25 December 1999 would be treated as being served on the next business day, and would not have been served in time.

Deemed dates for service of the claim form and other documents are dealt with in 5.9.14.

Where a claimant has issued but not yet served the claim form, the defendant can serve a notice under r. 7.7 requiring him either to do so, or to discontinue the claim by a date which is at least 14 days after the date of service of the notice. If the claimant fails to comply, the defendant may apply to court for an order dismissing the claim.

5.8.5 Application to extend time for serving a claim form

If it is not possible to serve a claim form or particulars of claim within the time limit set out in 5.8.4, the claimant can apply under CPR, r. 7.6, for an extension.

5.8.5.1 Procedure An application for extending time for serving a claim form should be made using the Part 23 procedure. It may be made without notice to other parties (CPR, r. 7.6(4)(b)). Indeed it normally would be made without notice, as the defendant whom it is sought to serve is not yet on the record.

The application must be supported by evidence (r. 7.6(4)(a)). The evidence will either be set out in the notice of application (which must then be verified by a statement of truth) or be in the form of a witness statement (r. 32.6). Alternatively, evidence may be in affidavit form, although any additional cost of producing the evidence in this form may not be recovered from any other party without a court order (r. 32.15(2)).

PD 7 How to Start Proceedings, para. 7.2, says that the evidence should include the following details:

    (a)   all the circumstances relied on;
    (b)   the date of issue of the claim;
    (c)   the expiry date of any extension already granted under r. 7.6; and
    (d)   a full explanation of why the claim form has not been served.

An applicant who wishes to have the application dealt with without a hearing should request this in his application notice (PD 23, para. 2.3). The court has the power to dispense with a hearing where it does not consider a hearing appropriate (CPR, r. 23.8). It is likely that where the

CHAPTER 5 THE EARLY STAGES OF A CLAIM

claimant has established a case for granting an extension in his evidence the court will be prepared to proceed on this basis.

There is no limit on the length of any extension, or on the number of extensions which a court may grant. It will be for the applicant to justify the length of extension sought. Bearing in mind the court's duty as part of the overriding objective to ensure that cases are dealt with expeditiously it is unlikely that the court will be prepared to grant long or multiple extensions in the absence of good reason (see below).

Where an order is made without notice to the defendant, a copy of the order, the application notice and any evidence in support must be served on the defendant (r. 23.9), who has seven days from the date of service to apply to the court for the order to be varied or set aside (r. 23.10).

5.8.5.2 Grounds on which the court will grant an extension The CPR are silent on the test to be applied in deciding whether to allow an extension.

Under the old rules the discretion to extend the period of validity of a writ was exercised with caution. In *Kleinwort Benson Ltd* v *Barbrak Ltd* [1987] AC 597 the House of Lords held that:

(a) the power to extend the validity of a writ should only be exercised for good reason;
(b) what was good reason depended on all the circumstances of the case; and
(c) where there were matters which could potentially constitute good reason for granting an extension, the court had a discretion. In exercising the discretion, the court should take account of the balance of hardship between the parties. The most significant factor was the question of limitation.

'Good reason' included difficulties in effecting service, particularly where the defendant was evading service, and the agreement by the defendant not to object to an application to extend the period of validity of a writ. Problems in obtaining legal aid, where these were due to delays on the part of the legal aid authorities, were good reason but not where due to the failure of the plaintiff or his solicitor to make a prompt application (*Waddon* v *Whitecroft Scovell Ltd* [1988] 1 WLR 309).

'Good reason' did not include either the fact that negotiations were under way between the parties or problems in obtaining evidence.

Whether the court will apply these authorities to cases under CPR, r. 7.6, remains to be seen. However, in coming to its decision, the court will take into account its duties under the overriding objective to ensure that cases are dealt with expeditiously (r. 1.1(2)(d)).

5.8.5.3 Applications made after the usual period of service has expired The general rule is that an application to extend the time for service of a claim form should be made within the usual period of service (or that period as already extended by the court) (CPR, r. 7.6(1)). The CPR permit the making of an application after the expiry of this time limit. But then the court may only grant an extension where (r. 7.6(3)):

(a) the court has been unable to serve the claim form, or
(b) the claimant has taken all reasonable steps to serve the claim form but has been unable to do so, and

CHAPTER 5   THE EARLY STAGES OF A CLAIM

(c) in either case the claimant has acted promptly in making the application.

Under the old rules, in addition to showing a good reason why a writ should be renewed, the plaintiff also had to give a satisfactory explanation for the failure to apply for renewal before the writ had expired (*Kleinwort Benson Ltd v Barbrak Ltd* [1987] AC 597). It is not clear whether these principles will apply to applications made under r. 7.6. However, until clarification from the courts, it would be prudent to address these additional matters in the evidence in support of any such application.

5.9 SERVICE

5.9.1 Introduction

The *Final Report* recommended that there should be no restriction on the methods by which a document could be served, provided that the method used either put the recipient in a position to ascertain its contents or was reasonably likely to enable him to do so within any relevant time period (ch. 12, para. 25). However, comments made in the course of the consultation process on the new rules encouraged the rule committee to opt in favour of certainty rather than flexibility. The CPR therefore still prescribe methods for effecting service. However, the forms of service allowed under the CPR are far wider than was formerly permissible. Further, the old distinction between the rules of service of originating process and the rules of ordinary service no longer applies. Thus, in addition to personal service and service by post, all documents (including claim forms) may now be served by document exchange, by fax and by e-mail.

5.9.2 Filing documents

The CPR distinguish between serving a document (the procedure whereby a document is brought to the attention of another party) and filing a document, the procedure whereby the court receives a copy of a document. 'Filing' is defined in the CPR as: 'delivering [a document], by post or otherwise, to the court office' (r. 2.3(1)). It is not clear whether this means that a document can be filed at court by fax, document exchange or e-mail.

The CPR make clear which documents must be filed, and when. The detailed requirements are addressed at relevant points in this guide. But a copy of most formal documents generated in the course of a claim must be filed at court. All statements of case must be filed, and witness statements and experts' reports may be ordered to be filed. The purpose of the requirement is clear: it is only by having access to information about the case as it progresses that the court is able to exercise its case management powers.

The remainder of 5.9 deals with the provisions relating to service of documents, including service of the claim form.

5.9.3 Who may serve documents?

Regardless of whether a claim is proceeding in the High Court or a county court, service of any document which the court has issued or prepared may be effected either by the court or the party on whose behalf the document is to be served, at the option of the party concerned, unless otherwise required by a court order or a practice direction (CPR, r. 6.3(1)).

The option of court service extends to more than just the claim form: the court may also serve application notices and court orders.

5.9.4 Service of a claim form and other documents by the court

Where a party prepares any document (including the claim form) which it wishes to be served by the court, a copy of the document, together with a copy for each party to be served must be filed at court (CPR, r. 6.3(3)).

The court will then decide which method of service to use (r. 6.3(2)). The method will normally be first-class post (PD 6, para. 8.1).

Where the court serves a claim form (but not other documents), the court will notify the claimant that the claim form has been served in the notice of issue, which will also indicate the deemed date of service (CPR, r. 6.14). The court must also notify the claimant when it has been unable to effect service. It does this by sending him a notice of non-service indicating what method was attempted (r. 6.11).

The CPR do not require the court to give notice of service in the case of documents other than the claim form. But the court must notify the party concerned when service has not been effected, by a notice of non-service (r. 6.11).

Where a party receives a notice of non-service, the court is under no further obligation to effect service. It is up to the party to try to effect service (PD 6, para. 8.2).

5.9.5 Service of a claim form and other documents by a party

It is up to the party concerned to decide whether to have the court serve documents. It is likely that many practitioners will prefer to continue to serve documents themselves, in order to retain control over the process, particularly where service is being effected shortly before the expiry of a deadline.

A party intending to effect service itself must notify the court of that intention when the document concerned is filed at court (CPR, r. 6.3(1)(b)).

A claimant who effects service of a claim form, must file a certificate of service within seven days of service stating that the document has not been returned undelivered and giving the details set out in the table in r. 6.10, which is reproduced in table 5.2. Until the claimant does this he may not obtain judgment in default under Part 12 (r. 6.14(2)(b)).

If the particulars of claim are served by the claimant separately from the claim form, a certificate of that service must be filed with the particulars (r. 7.4(3)).

Method of service	Details to be certified
Post	Date of posting
Personal	Date of personal service
Document exchange	Date of delivery to the document exchange

Method of service	Details to be certified
Delivery of document to or leaving it at a permitted place	Date when the document was delivered or left at the permitted place
Fax	Date and time of transmission
Other electronic means	Date of transmission and the means used
Alternative method permitted by the court	As required by the court

Table 5.2 Contents of certificate of service

5.9.6 Methods by which documents may be served

The methods of service prescribed in CPR, r. 6.2, are:

(a) personal service in accordance with r. 6.4 (see 5.9.7);
(b) first-class post;
(c) leaving the document at a place specified in r. 6.5 (see 5.9.8);
(d) through a document exchange in accordance with PD 6, para. 2;
(e) by fax or other electronic means in accordance with PD 6, para. 3.

Any of these methods can be used to serve claim forms as well as any other document generated in the course of the proceedings.

PD 6 includes guidelines for service on members of HM Forces and the US Air Force.

5.9.7 Personal service

A document may be served personally on the person to be served, unless a solicitor has been authorised to accept service on that person's behalf (CPR, r. 6.4). For service on a party's solicitor see 5.9.8.

A document is served personally on an individual by leaving it with that individual (r. 6.4(3)). This wording mirrors that in RSC, ord. 65, r. 2. It therefore seems likely that (as previously) where the person to be served is uncooperative, service would be effective if he was informed of what the document was and it was left as nearly as possible in his possession or control (*Thomson v Pheney* (1832) 1 Dowl Pr Cas 441).

Personal service on a registered company or other corporation is effected by leaving a document with a person holding a senior position (director, treasurer, secretary, chief executive, manager or other officer) within the company (CPR, r. 6.4(4); PD 6, para. 6.2).

For personal service on a registered company, a partnership and a corporation, see 5.9.10, 5.9.11 and 5.9.12 respectively.

5.9.8 Address for service

A party must give an address for service within the jurisdiction where all documents to be served by any method other than personal service must be served (CPR, r. 6.5(1) and (4)).

The address for service of a party who is represented by a solicitor is the business address of the solicitor. All documents, with the exception of the

CHAPTER 5 THE EARLY STAGES OF A CLAIM

claim form should be served at that address (r. 6.5(5)). The claim form, on the other hand, may only be served on the defendant's solicitor if the solicitor is authorised to accept service on the defendant's behalf, and has notified the claimant that he or she is so authorised (rr. 6.13(2) and 6.4(2)).

Where no solicitor is acting for the party to be served, and no address for service is given, the rules contain a table showing the place where documents must be served (r. 6.5(6)). This is reproduced in table 5.3.

Nature of party to be served	*Place of service*
Individual	• Usual or last known residence.
Proprietor of a business	• Usual or last known residence; or • Place of business or last known place of business.
Individual who is suing or being sued in the name of a firm	• Usual or last known residence; or • Principal or last known place of business of the firm.
Corporation incorporated in England and Wales other than a company	• Principal office of the corporation; • Any place within the jurisdiction where the corporation carries on its activities and which has a real connection with the claim.
Company registered in England and Wales	• Principal office of the company; or • Any place of business of the company within the jurisdiction which has a real connection with the claim.
Any other company or corporation	• Any place within the jurisdiction where the corporation carries on its activities. • Any place of business of the company within the jurisdiction.

Table 5.3 Service when there is no address for service

5.9.9 Service by DX, by fax or by other electronic method

Where it is sought to effect service by one of these methods the detailed requirements of PD 6, paras 2 and 3, must be complied with. Broadly, the scheme is as follows:

(a) In the case of service by DX, service is permitted where the party's address for service, or its headed notepaper includes a DX address, provided it has not specifically indicated that it would not accept service by DX.

(b) Service by fax or e-mail may only be effected where the party, or its legal representative, has indicated in writing willingness to accept service by the method being used. It is not mandatory to send by post a hard copy of a document served by fax or e-mail. But where the other party claims not to have received the document by fax or e-mail, the court may take account of the fact that a hard copy was not sent.

It remains to be seen whether litigants or their legal representatives will avail themselves of these methods of service often. It is likely in the early days following implementation of the CPR, at least, that parties will continue to effect service by traditional methods.

5.9.10 Service on registered companies

The address for service of a company shown in the table in CPR, r. 6.5(6), is not its registered office, but either its principal office or any place within the jurisdiction which has a real connection with the claim.

A company may still be served at its registered office, however, under s. 725 of the Companies Act 1985, as an alternative to service by the methods specified under CPR, r. 6.2(2). Section 725 provides that: 'A document may be served on a company by leaving it at, or sending it by post to, the company's registered office'. Where the document is sent by post, it may be sent either by first or second-class post. The deemed date of service is two working days after posting if sent by first-class post and four working days after posting if sent by second-class post (Interpretation Act 1978, s. 7).

Likewise, overseas companies having a place of business or a branch office in Great Britain can be served either by any of the methods provided for in CPR, r. 6.2, or, as an alternative, under the provisions of ss. 694A and 695 of the Companies Act 1985 (CPR, r. 6.2(2)). Such companies are required to provide to the registrar of companies the names and addresses of persons resident in Great Britain authorised to accept service of process on the company's behalf. Service will be effective if addressed to any such person and left at or delivered by post to the address given. Where the document is sent by post, it may be sent either by first or second-class post. The deemed date of service is two working days after posting if sent by first-class post and four working days after posting if sent by second-class post (Interpretation Act 1978, s. 7).

5.9.11 Service on a partnership

A document is served personally on a partnership by leaving it with any of the partners, or with a person having, at the time of service, management of the partnership business, at the firm's principal place of business (CPR, r. 6.4(5)). If it is left with a person at the partnership's principal or last known place of business, the person served must also be served with a notice informing him whether he is being served as a partner, as a person having control or management of the partnership business, or both (PD 6, para. 4.2).

Service on a partnership which has not given an address for service should be effected by sending the document to be served either to the usual or last known residential address of a partner, or to the principal or last known place of business of the firm (CPR, r. 6.5(6)).

5.9.12 Service on a corporation other than a registered company

Personal service on a corporation other than a registered company is effected by leaving the document to be served with any of the following: a director, the treasurer, secretary, chief executive, manager or other officer of the corporation, the mayor, chairman, president, town clerk or similar officer (CPR, r. 6.4(4); PD 6, paras 6.1 and 6.2).

Service when the corporation has not given an address for service is effected by sending the document to either the principal place of business of the corporation or any place within the jurisdiction where the corporation carries on business and which has a real connection with the claim (CPR, r. 6.5(6)).

5.9.13 Service on a child or a patient

For the rules about service on a child or a patient see 5.7.3.6.

5.9.14 Deemed dates of service

Rule 6.7(1) of the CPR sets out a table showing deemed dates of service for service by first-class post, by delivering a document to or leaving it at the place of service, through a document exchange, and by fax or by other electronic method. This is reproduced in table 5.4.

Method of Service	*Deemed day of service*
First-class post	The second day after it was posted.
Document exchange	The second day after it was left at the document exchange.
Delivering the document to or leaving it at a permitted address	The day after it was delivered to or left at the permitted address.
Fax	• If it is transmitted on a business day before 4 p.m., on that day; or • in any other case, on the business day after the day on which it is transmitted.
Other electronic method	The second day after the day on which it is transmitted.

Table 5.4 Deemed days of service

It is submitted that, as under the old rules, these deemed dates create no more than a presumption of service, which either party can rebut by adducing evidence that service was not effected at all or was effected on some other date (*Forward* v *West Sussex County Council* [1995] 1 WLR 1469).

There are no dates for deemed service where service is effected personally: personal service will take effect immediately.

5.9.15 Service by an alternative method

The court may authorise service by an alternative method 'where there is a good reason' to do so (CPR, r. 6.8(1)). This is the equivalent to the rules in the RSC and CCR on substituted service. There is no guidance in the CPR about what 'good reason' means.

CHAPTER 5   THE EARLY STAGES OF A CLAIM

Under the old rules, an order could be made where there was evidence that the defendant was evading service or could not easily be found. The applicant normally also had to show that service in the manner sought would be effective to bring the existence of proceedings to the defendant's attention. Substituted service would not be ordered where one of the prescribed methods of service would be effective, nor simply because it had been impractical to serve the writ in time (*Paragon Group Ltd* v *Burnell* [1991] Ch 498).

An application for an order permitting service by an alternative method should be made using the Part 23 procedure. The application may be made without notice to other parties. It must be supported by evidence showing why the order is sought and what steps have been taken to serve by permitted means (PD 6, para. 9.1).

Where the court makes an order permitting alternative service, it will specify the method of service and the date of deemed service (CPR, r. 6.8(3)).

5.9.16   Power of court to dispense with service

The court may dispense with service of a document 'if it is appropriate to do so'. An application for an order to dispense with service may be made without notice (CPR, r. 6.9).

5.9.17   Objecting to defective service of a claim form

A defendant objecting to defective service of a claim form should make an application under CPR, Part 11 (see 5.16).

5.9.18   Service out of the jurisdiction

Service out of the jurisdiction continues to be governed by RSC, ord. 11, in CPR, sch. 1, both as to the claimant's entitlement to serve out of the jurisdiction and also the manner in which service should be effected.

Where the claim is being served out of the jurisdiction without leave under the Civil Jurisdiction and Judgments Act 1982, the claim form (and the particulars of claim, if separate) must contain a statement that the court has power under the Act to deal with the claim and that no proceedings based on the same claim are pending between the parties in Scotland, Northern Ireland or another Convention territory (PD 7 How to Start Proceedings, para. 3.5).

5.9.19   Service on the Crown and service in proceedings for the recovery of land and mortgage possession actions

Service in these cases also continues to be governed by re-enacted rules from the RSC and CCR (for service on the Crown: RSC, ord. 77, r. 4 in CPR, sch. 1, and CCR, ord. 42, r. 7 in CPR, sch. 2; and for service in proceedings for the recovery of land and mortgage possession actions: RSC, ord. 10, r. 4 in CPR, sch. 1, and CCR, ord. 7, rr. 15 and 15A in CPR, sch. 2).

5.9.20   Computing time

CPR, rr. 2.8 to 2.10, set out the rules for computing any time limit contained in the CPR, any practice direction or any judgment or order of the court. They are as follows:

CHAPTER 5 THE EARLY STAGES OF A CLAIM

(a) Any period expressed as a number of days is to be computed as clear days (r. 2.8(2) and (3)). For example, if an order requires service to be effected at least three days before a hearing on Friday 20 October, the last date for service is Monday 16 October.

(b) Where a period is five days or less, it excludes any Saturday, Sunday, bank holiday, Christmas Day or Good Friday which falls within it (r. 2.8(4)). For example, if an order requires service to be effected at least three days before a hearing on Monday 20 October, the last date for service is Tuesday 14 October.

(c) Where time is expressed as 'a month', it means a calendar month (r. 2.10).

Rule 2.9 encourages the court to express time limits in calendar dates wherever practicable to do so, rather than a number of days from the date of the order (i.e., 'on or before 20 October 2000', rather than 'no later than 14 days after the date of this order'. The court will also wherever practicable specify the time of day by which an act must be done (r. 2.9(1)(b)).

5.10 STEP-BY-STEP GUIDE TO ISSUE AND SERVICE

5.10.1 Where service of the claim form is to be effected by the court

Where the court is to effect service the procedure is as follows:

(a) The claimant sends or takes to court one copy of the claim form for the court and a copy for each defendant to be served, together with the issue fee. (For the claimant's copy of the claim form see 5.8.3.)

(b) The court issues the claim by entering the issue date on the claim form, affixing the court seal to the claim form and allocating a number to the claim. It creates a case management file and files on it its copy of the claim form.

(c) The court serves the claim form. It is for the court to decide which method of service to choose, although the method will normally be by first-class post (CPR, r. 6.3(2); PD 6, para. 8.1).

(d) Where particulars of claim are contained in the claim form or are to be served with it, court staff will add to the documents for service forms for admitting and for defending the claim and for acknowledging service (CPR, r. 7.8(1)). Where the particulars of claim are to be served later, these documents do not accompany the claim form.

(e) The court will send the claimant a notice of issue (form N205A, N205B or N205C), which will include the date when the claim form is deemed to be served under CPR, r. 6.7 (r. 6.14(1)).

(f) Where the court attempts to serve the claim form and is unable to do so the court must send a notice of non-service to the claimant stating the method attempted (r. 6.11).

(g) A claimant who receives a notice of non-service should take steps to effect service of the claim form himself. The court is under no further duty to effect service (PD 6, para. 8.2).

5.10.2 Where service of the claim form is to be effected by the claimant

Where the claimant is to effect service the procedure is as follows:

(a) The claimant sends or takes to court one copy of the claim form for the court and a copy for each defendant to be served, together with the issue fee. (For the claimant's own copy of the claim form see 5.8.3.)

(b) The court issues the claim by entering the issue date on the claim form, affixing the court seal to the claim form and allocating a number to the claim. It creates a case management file and files on it its copy of the claim form.

(c) The claimant's copy of the claim form and the copies for service on the defendants will be returned. The court will also send the claimant a notice of issue (form N205A, N205B or N205C).

(d) The claimant will effect service, in one of the ways specified in CPR, r. 6.2. Where particulars of claim are contained in the claim form or are to be served with it, the claimant must add to the documents for service forms for acknowledging service, for admitting and for defending the claim (r. 7.8(1)). Where the particulars of claim are to be served later, these documents do not accompany the claim form.

(e) The claimant must file a certificate of service within seven days of service of the claim form stating that the claim form has not been returned undelivered and giving the other details set out in r. 6.10 (r. 6.14(2)(a)).

5.11 RESPONDING TO THE PARTICULARS OF CLAIM

Until the claimant serves particulars of claim on the defendant, the defendant need take no step in the action. On receipt of the particulars of claim, the defendant has three choices.

(a) If he wishes to admit the claim, he should file a form of admission (see 5.12).

(b) If he wishes to contest the claim, he should file a defence within 14 days of service of the particulars of claim (see chapter 6).

(c) If he wishes to contest the claim but needs more than 14 days to prepare his defence or if he wishes to contest the jurisdiction of the courts, he should file an acknowledgment of service (see 5.13).

5.12 ADMISSIONS

5.12.1 General rule

Any party may admit the truth of the whole or any part of another party's case at any stage of the proceedings (CPR, r. 14.1(1)) by giving notice in writing, such as in a statement of case or by letter (r. 14.1(2)). Where a defendant makes an admission, the claimant is then entitled to apply for judgment (r. 14.3(1)). The court will enter such judgment as it appears that the applicant is entitled to on the admission (r.14.3(2)).

5.12.2 Admission of money claims within 14 days of service of the particulars of claim

In money claims (whether for a specified sum or not), the CPR contain an additional procedure for the admission of the claim at an early stage. The rules are aimed primarily at individual defendants in debt claims. They provide a mechanism whereby the rate and time by which the admitted claim is to be paid can be agreed between the parties or fixed by the court.

The rules are divided into four different categories:

CHAPTER 5 THE EARLY STAGES OF A CLAIM

(a) admission of the whole of a claim for a specified sum (r. 14.4);
(b) admission of part of a claim for a specified sum (r.14.5);
(c) admission of liability to pay the whole of a claim for an unspecified amount of money (r. 14.6); and
(d) admission of liability to pay the whole of a claim for an unspecified amount of money, where the defendant offers a sum in satisfaction of the claim (r. 14.7).

Any such admission by the defendant must be made within 14 days of service of the claim form, or, where the claim form states that particulars of claim will follow, within 14 days after service of the particulars of claim (r. 14.2).

When particulars of claim are served on a defendant, the response pack will include a series of forms for responding to the claim. These will include forms for making an admission (r. 7.8(1); PD 14, para. 2.1). The defendant will need to choose the correct form for making his admission from the pack.

5.12.2.1 *The defendant admits the whole of a claim for a specified sum (CPR, r. 14.4)* Here the defendant has three choices:

(a) If he is able, he may simply pay the sum claimed in full (together with interest, and the amount of fixed costs and issue fee endorsed on the claim form) direct to the claimant in full within 14 days after service.

(b) Alternatively, the defendant may ask the claimant for time to pay, or ask to pay by instalments (r. 14.9), by sending form N9A to the claimant having completed the details sought about his means (r. 14.4(2)). Where the claimant accepts the defendant's proposals, the claimant may obtain judgment by filing request form N225 (r. 14.9(4)). The court will then enter judgment for payment at the time and rate specified in the defendant's request (r. 14.9(5)). If the claimant does not accept the defendant's proposals, he should still file request form N225, but give notice that he does not accept the proposals (r. 14.10). The court will then decide the time and rate at which payment should be made (r. 14.10(4)).

(c) The defendant may simply admit the claim without seeking time to pay. In this case, the claimant may obtain judgment by filing a request for judgment in form N225 (r. 14.4(3)). He may specify the date by which the judgment should be paid or the times and rates at which it is to be paid by instalments (r. 14.4(4)). Judgment will then be entered by the court in the terms specified by the claimant (r. 14.4(5) and (6)).

5.12.2.2 *The defendant admits only part of a claim for a specified sum (CPR, r. 14.5)* Here he should complete forms N9A and N9B and return them to the court within 14 days after service. The claimant then has the choice of accepting the partial admission and entering judgment, or refusing the admission altogether, in which case the claim will continue as a defended claim.

On receipt of the defendant's admission, the court will serve notice on the claimant requiring him to notify the court within 14 days whether he wishes to accept the defendant's offer, reject it, or accept the amount of the offer but reject the proposals for payment. If the claimant does not reply within 14 days, the claim will be stayed until he does so.

The defendant may or may not have asked for time to pay. Where the claimant has accepted the partial admission in principle, the procedure in

5.12.2.1(b) and (c) then applies in relation to proposals for payment (except that form N225A is used instead of N225).

5.12.2.3 The defendant admits liability on a claim for an unspecified sum (CPR, r. 14.6) In this case, he should complete form N9C and return it to the court within 14 days after service. This form is then sent by the court to the claimant, who may request the court to enter judgment on liability, with damages to be assessed. The court will then enter judgment and give directions for the assessment of damages.

If the claimant does not file a request for judgment within 14 days after service of the admission on him, the claim is stayed until he files the request.

5.12.2.4 The defendant admits liability for an unspecified sum and offers an amount of money to satisfy the claim Here, he should complete form N9C and send it to the court. The court will forward it to the claimant. The claimant may then either accept the admission and enter judgment, or refuse the admission altogether, in which case the claim will continue as a defended claim. The claimant must notify the court of his intention within 14 days of being served with a notice requesting him to do so. If he does not reply within 14 days, the claim will be stayed until he does so.

The defendant may or may not have asked for time to pay. Where the claimant has accepted the admission in principle, the procedure in 5.12.2.1(b) and (c) then applies in relation to proposals for payment.

5.13 ACKNOWLEDGING SERVICE

When particulars of claim are served on the defendant, the response pack will include a form for acknowledging service of the claim (CPR, r. 7.8 (1)). It is part of form N9.

Except in the case of Part 8 claims (see below), even where the defendant wishes to contest the claim, he is under no obligation to file an acknowledgment. He may, if he wishes, proceed immediately to file and serve a defence.

A defendant may, by r. 10.1(3), file an acknowledgment in any case where:

(a) he is unable to file a defence within 14 days after service of the particulars of claim; or
(b) he wishes to dispute the court's jurisdiction.

In the latter case, filing an acknowledgment will not constitute a submission to the jurisdiction (r. 11(3)) (see further 5.16 on disputing the court's jurisdiction).

If the claim has been brought under the Part 8 procedure (in which case the claim form must state that Part 8 applies), the claim form is accompanied only by a form of acknowledgment of service (r. 7.8(2)(b)). The defendant must then file an acknowledgment within 14 days after service of the claim form (r. 8.3(1)). See further 5.17.

5.13.1 Time for filing the acknowledgment

Where the defendant wishes to file an acknowledgment, by CPR, r. 10.3(1), he must do so:

CHAPTER 5 THE EARLY STAGES OF A CLAIM

(a) within 14 days after service of the particulars of claim, where the particulars of claim are served after the claim form; or

(b) within 14 days after service of the claim form, where the particulars of claim are served on or with the claim form.

These deadlines are extended where the claim form has been served out of the jurisdiction: in these circumstances the time limits set out in RSC, ord. 11, r. 1A in CPR, sch. 1, apply (CPR, r. 10.3(2)(a)).

Where the court makes an order for an alternative form of service under r. 6.16, the deadline for filing the acknowledgment will be that specified in the order (r. 10.3(2)(b)).

5.13.2 Contents of the form of acknowledgment

The form of acknowledgment of service (form N9) requires the defendant:

(a) to indicate his intention to defend all or part of the claim; and
(b) to state whether he intends to contest the jurisdiction.

The defendant must give his full name if different from the name given on the claim form. He must also give an address for service in the jurisdiction. Where he is legally represented, and his solicitor has signed the acknowledgment, the solicitor's address will be the defendant's address for service (CPR, r. 10.5(b)).

The acknowledgment must be signed either by the defendant or by his legal representative (r. 10.5(a)). In the case of a company or other corporation, the acknowledgment must be signed by a person in a senior position. Persons who fall into this category are listed in PD 10, para. 4.3. Where the defendant is a partnership, the acknowledgment may be signed by any partner or a person having control or management of the partnership business (PD 10, para. 4.4). Children and patients may sign an acknowledgment only through their litigation friend or their solicitor, unless the court orders to the contrary (PD 10, para. 4.5).

The same form may be used for two or more defendants, if they are represented by the same solicitor (PD 10, para. 5.3).

An acknowledgment of service may be amended or withdrawn only with permission of the court (PD 10, para. 5.4).

5.14 JUDGMENT IN DEFAULT

Failure to file an acknowledgment or a defence within the time limits laid down in the CPR may result under CPR, Part 12, in the claimant entering judgment in default, that is, judgment without a trial of the claim.

If the Part 8 procedure is being used, Part 12 does not apply (r. 8.1(5)), but a defendant who fails to file an acknowledgment will be unable to take any active part in the hearing without leave of the court (r. 8.4).

There are two mechanisms under the CPR for entering default judgment. Which applies, depends on the nature of the claim.

(a) A simple request-for-judgment procedure under Part 12 is available in money claims (r. 12.4(1)). A money claim will include both claims for specified sums and for unquantified damages. Here, judgment is entered over the counter on filing a request for default judgment, without any consideration of the merits of the claim (see 5.14.2).

CHAPTER 5 THE EARLY STAGES OF A CLAIM

(b) In a claim for a remedy other than a money claim, in a claim only for costs (other than fixed costs) and in certain other cases set out in r. 12.10, an application for judgment must be made using the Part 23 procedure (see chapter 9). On any application for the entry of a default judgment there will be a hearing and the court will give 'such judgment as it appears to the court that the claimant is entitled to on his statement of case' (r. 12.11(1)). In this procedure, then, the court will consider the merits of the claim (see 5.14.3).

In practice, this regime is not as different to the regime under the RSC and CCR as it at first appears: the cases where an application must be made correspond broadly to the cases under the old rules where default judgment could not be entered without leave. In the overwhelming majority of cases under the CPR, default judgment will be entered simply upon filing a request in the appropriate form.

5.14.1 Conditions for entering judgment in default

Judgment in default may be entered in appropriate cases on most types of claim. By CPR, r. 12.2, and PD 12, para. 1.2, judgment in default may not be entered:

(a) on a claim where the Part 8 procedure has been used;
(b) on a claim for 'delivery of goods' (i.e., delivery up of goods) subject to an agreement regulated by the Consumer Credit Act 1974;
(c) on a mortgage claim to which RSC, ord. 88 in CPR, sch. 1, or CCR, ord. 24 in CPR, sch. 2, applies;
(d) in the case of the specialist proceedings listed in CPR, Part 49 (such as admiralty claims or arbitration proceedings), where special provision is made in relevant practice directions about obtaining a default judgment.

In all cases (i.e., whether the claimant is proceeding by way of request or application for default judgment), in order to enter judgment in default, the court is required by CPR, r. 12.3, and PD 12, para. 4.1, to be satisfied that:

(a) the particulars of claim have been served (a certificate of service on the court file will be sufficient evidence);
(b) either the defendant has not filed an acknowledgment of service or has not filed a defence, and, in either case, time for doing so has expired;
(c) the defendant has not satisfied the claim;
(d) the defendant has not filed or served an admission together with a request for time to pay; and
(e) the defendant has not made an application for summary judgment which has not been disposed of.

For the purpose of (b) above, the filing of any document purporting to be a defence will prevent the claimant obtaining judgment in default (PD 12, para. 1.1).

5.14.2 Request for default judgment

By CPR, r. 12.4, a claimant may obtain judgment in default by filing a form requesting judgment to be entered where the claim is for:

(a) a specified sum of money (save where the claim is only for costs other than fixed costs);

(b) an amount of money to be decided by the court;
(c) delivery of goods where the claim form gives the defendant the alternative of paying their value; or
(d) any combination of these remedies.

Where a claimant has included a claim or claims for a remedy other than money in his claim form, he may proceed with the request for judgment procedure provided he abandons the additional claims in his request form (r. 12.4(3)). However, where he does so and default judgment is entered only to be later set aside, the abandoned claim will be restored when judgment is set aside (r. 13.6).

5.14.2.1 *Claim for specified sum* Here, the claimant files a request for judgment in form N205A or N255.

Judgment will be entered for the amount sought in the claim form, plus fixed costs (set out in the table at CPR, r. 45.4). However, where the claimant wishes to give the defendant time to pay or to permit the defendant to pay in instalments, he may set out the rate and times of payment acceptable in the request for judgment form. Judgment will then be entered on this basis (r. 12.5).

By r. 12.6(1) default judgment will include interest on claims for specified sums which has accrued due up to the date on which the default judgment was entered, provided that:

(a) full particulars of interest were pleaded in the particulars of claim;
(b) on a claim for statutory interest, the rate sought is no higher than that payable on judgment debts; and
(c) the request for judgment sets out a calculation of the interest claimed between the date to which interest has been calculated in the claim form, and the date of the request for judgment.

Otherwise, judgment will be entered for interest to be decided by the court (r. 12.6(2)).

5.14.2.2 *Claim for unspecified sum* Here the claimant files form N225B or N227 and judgment will be for an amount to be decided by the court, plus costs (CPR, r. 12.5(3)).

In any case where the court enters judgment for:

(a) an amount to be decided by the court,
(b) the value of goods to be decided by the court, or
(c) interest to be decided by the court,

it will also give any directions it considers appropriate and may allocate the case to a judge for hearing (r. 12.7). The directions will address issues such as the calling of witnesses, expert evidence, disclosure and the production of documents and other evidence necessary to enable the court to decide the question of quantum.

5.14.3 Application for default judgment

5.14.3.1 *Claims where application for judgment in default must be made* The CPR, rr. 12.9(1)(b) and 12.10, and PD 12, para. 2.3, specify certain types of claim on which default judgment may only be obtained by making an application under Part 23. They include claims for costs (other than fixed costs), claims where service has been effected out of the jurisdiction without leave under the Civil Jurisdiction and Judgments Act 1982, claims against the Crown, claims by one spouse against the other in tort and claims against children and patients.

A claimant who has served a claim form and particulars of claim on a child or a patient cannot apply immediately for summary judgment, because r. 21.3(2) of the CPR forbids any step being taken in the proceedings until a litigation friend has been appointed for the defendant. Therefore, the appropriate procedure is to apply for the appointment of a litigation friend under r. 21.6, before applying for default judgment (PD 12, para. 4.2(1)).

5.14.3.2 Application procedure under CPR, Part 23 A notice of application must be filed in accordance with the procedure in CPR, Part 23. Notice of the application must be given to the defendant in all cases, except claims served under the Civil Jurisdiction and Judgments Act 1982 and claims against a State where the defendant has failed to file an acknowledgment (CPR, r. 12.11(4) and (5); PD 12, para. 5.1).

Evidence in support of an application for default judgment must deal with the matters set out in PD 12, para. 4. But evidence in support of the application need not be served on a defendant who has failed to file an acknowledgment of service (CPR, r. 12.11(2)).

There will be a hearing and judgment will be entered for what it appears to the court that the claimant is entitled to on the statement of case (r. 12.11(1)). In other words, the court will consider the merits of the claim, albeit only as they appear on the particulars of claim.

On an application for default judgment to be entered against a child or a patient, the applicant must produce evidence which satisfies the court that he is entitled to the judgment claimed (PD 12, para. 4.2(2)).

5.14.4 Two or more defendants

If there are two or more defendants, the claimant may obtain a judgment on request against one defendant and proceed with his claim against any other defendants (CPR, r. 12.8(1)). However, where a claimant applies for default judgment against some defendants and not others, the court will only enter default judgment where the claim can be dealt with separately from the claim against other defendants (r. 12.8(2)).

Having obtained the default judgment, a claimant may enforce it against only some defendants, save where it is for the possession of land or delivery of goods. Here, the defendant may enforce only where he has obtained judgment against all defendants, or where the court gives its permission (r.12.8(3)).

5.15 SETTING ASIDE A DEFAULT JUDGMENT

A defendant against whom judgment in default has been entered may apply for it to be varied or set aside.

5.15.1 Principles upon which a default judgment will be set aside

Broadly, the rules remain as they were under the RSC and CCR before the right to have an irregular judgment set aside was restricted by the Court of Appeal's decision in *Faircharm Investments Ltd* v *Citibank*

International plc (1998) *The Times*, 20 February 1998. In other words, a judgment which has been entered wrongly (as defined in the CPR) must be set aside by the court. In other cases, the court has a discretion to set the judgment aside and it will normally require the defendant to show a real prospect of successfully defending the claim before it will do so.

5.15.1.1 Where the default judgment was entered wrongly The court must set aside any judgment entered wrongly (CPR, r. 13.2). The phrase 'entered wrongly' is defined precisely in r.13.2. It is limited to the following cases:

(a) time for acknowledging service, or for filing a defence (as the case may be) had not expired by the time the default judgment was entered;

(b) there was a summary judgment application by the defendant pending when the default judgment was entered; or

(c) the defendant had satisfied the whole claim or filed an admission and a request for time to pay at the time the default judgment was entered.

5.15.1.2 Where the default judgment was not entered wrongly In any other case, the court has a discretion to set aside a default judgment. It may exercise its discretion if (CPR, r. 13.3(1)):

(a) the defendant has a real prospect of successfully defending the claim; or

(b) it appears to the court that there is some other good reason why:

(i) the judgment should be set aside or varied; or
(ii) the defendant should be allowed to defend the claim.

In considering whether to set aside or vary a judgment entered under Part 12, the matters to which the court must have regard include whether the person seeking to set aside the judgment made an application to do so promptly (r. 13.3(2)).

The wording of r.13.3(1)(a) mirrors the test established in *Alpine Bulk Transport Co. Inc.* v *Saudi Eagle Shipping Co. Inc.* [1986] 2 Lloyd's Rep 221, that the defendant must have a case with a reasonable prospect of success, and that it is not enough to show a merely arguable defence.

Under the old rules, although in theory the court's jurisdiction was not limited, in practice it was an almost inflexible rule that a defence on the merits had to be shown. The defendant's explanation for allowing judgment in default to be entered was a secondary consideration. It remains to be seen whether the reference in the new rules to 'some other good reason' will allow the court a wider discretion than before.

In any case where the court sets aside a default judgment, it may attach conditions, such as the payment of money into court (r. 3.1(3)).

5.15.2 Duty of claimant to set aside a default judgment

The CPR impose a duty on a claimant to apply to set aside his own default judgment on discovering that it has been entered wrongly.

A claimant who serves the claim form, enters judgment, but subsequently has good reason to believe that the claim form did not reach the defendant before judgment was entered, must file a request for the judgment to be set aside or apply for directions. The claimant may take no step to enforce the judgment in the meantime (CPR, r. 13.5).

CHAPTER 5   THE EARLY STAGES OF A CLAIM

5.15.3   Procedure

The defendant will apply for judgment in default to be varied or set aside under the Part 23 procedure (see chapter 9). An application to set aside a default judgment which has not been entered wrongly must be supported by evidence (CPR, r. 13.4(3)).

Where the claim is for a specified sum of money, has not been started in a specialist list and the judgment is entered against an individual in a court which is not the defendant's home court (defined in r. 2.3(1)), the court will automatically transfer the application there (r. 13.4(1)).

5.15.4   Default judgments on a Part 20 claim

There are special rules which apply in relation to entering judgment in default on a Part 20 claim. These are dealt with in 8.6.7.

5.16   DISPUTING THE COURT'S JURISDICTION

Part 11 of the CPR makes provision for the defendant to challenge the jurisdiction of the English courts.

The procedure is as follows:

(a) The defendant should file an acknowledgment of service within the usual time limit (i.e., within 14 days after service of the claim form, or of the particulars of claim if served later) stating his intention to contest the jurisdiction (r. 11(2)).

(b) Then, within the time limited for filing a defence (i.e., within 28 days after service of the particulars of claim), the defendant should make an application for the order sought, using the Part 23 procedure (r. 11(4)(a)). Failure to make the application within this time limit will be taken as a submission to the jurisdiction (r. 11(5)(b)). The application must be supported by evidence (r. 11(4)(b)). No defence need be served before the hearing of the application (r. 11(9)).

(c) Neither acknowledging service nor making the application will affect any right the defendant might have to contest the jurisdiction of the court (r. 11(3)). Although the CPR do not address the point explicitly, it is to be assumed that a defendant who took any other step in the action would be taken to have submitted to the jurisdiction of the English courts.

(d) The court may make a declaration that it has no jurisdiction over the claim, or that it will not exercise its jurisdiction. The order may also (r. 11(6)):

   (i)   set aside the claim form;
   (ii) set aside service of the claim form;
   (iii) discharge any order made before the claim was commenced or the claim form served;
   (iv) stay the proceedings.

(e) Where the court does not make any such declaration, the acknowledgment already filed by the defendant will cease to have effect and the defendant should complete and file another form within 14 days or such period as the court may order. This acknowledgment will be treated as a submission to the jurisdiction (r. 11(7) and (8)).

CHAPTER 5   THE EARLY STAGES OF A CLAIM

5.17   PART 8 PROCEDURE

5.17.1   When the procedure is used

The Part 8 procedure is intended for cases where the nature of the relief or remedy sought, or the lack of factual dispute, would make the standard procedure unnecessarily combersome. It will doubtless be used in many instances where formerly the originating summons procedure would have been the appropriate method of commencing an action, although the Part 8 procedure will not be limited to these.

A claimant may use the Part 8 procedure where he seeks the court's decision on a question which is unlikely to involve a substantial dispute of fact, or where a rule or practice direction permits use of the procedure to be made (CPR, r. 8.1(2) and (6)(a); PD 8, paras 1.1 and 1.2). PD 8, para. 1.4, lists the following types of claim for which the Part 8 procedure may be used:

(a) a claim by or against a child or patient which has been settled before proceedings have been commenced, and where the sole purpose of the claim is to obtain the court's approval to the settlement;

(b) a claim for provisional damages which has been settled before proceedings have been commenced, and where the sole purpose of the claim is to obtain a consent judgment;

(c) an application to take a deposition abroad, made other than in existing proceedings; or to take a deposition in England and Wales for use before courts abroad;

(d) a claim for summary possession of property against named or unnamed trespassers or squatters, where there is unlikely to be a substantial dispute of fact.

If the court considers that the use of the procedure is inappropriate, or the defendant takes objection and the court agrees, the matter can be ordered to proceed in the normal manner, and the court may give appropriate directions (CPR, r. 8.1(3); PD 8, para. 1.6)

It is envisaged that the majority of cases using this procedure will be dealt with on written evidence, although the court may permit or require a party to give oral evidence at the hearing (CPR, r. 8.6(2)), and may give directions requiring the attendance for cross-examination of a witness who has given written evidence (r. 8.6(3)). Thus it appears that oral evidence cannot be given without the permission of the court.

Any party can apply to the court to give directions immediately upon the issue of the Part 8 claim form. The court is also able to give such directions of its own initiative. Such directions are most likely to be sought by consent where the application is being made for the approval of a child or patient settlement, or where provisional damages have been agreed, subject to the court's consent. Such directions may often include the immediate fixing of a hearing date, even in claims such as for mortgage possession where there may be a dispute, but where a hearing date could conveniently be given. Alternatively, certain applications, such as under the Landlord and Tenant Act 1954, s. 38, do not require a hearing. Otherwise, the court will normally give directions once the acknowledgment of service has been filed, or the date for doing so has passed. The court may convene a directions hearing before giving directions. The case will be treated as being allocated to the multi-track, and therefore Part 26 of the CPR (preliminary case management) will not apply (r. 8.9(c)).

5.17.2 Acknowledgment

Due to the nature of the procedure, a defendant to a Part 8 claim is not required to file a defence, neither can the claimant obtain judgment by request on an admission, or in default under CPR, Part 12. As a result the claimant need not serve the defendant with a form for admitting the claim, or for defending it, under r. 7.8 (r. 8.9).

If the defendant does not object to the use of the Part 8 procedure, he must file an acknowledgment of service either in form N210 or in an informal document such as a letter (PD 8, para. 3.2), not more than 14 days after service of the claim form (unless r. 10.3(2) (see 5.13.1) applies: r. 8.3(3)(a)) and must serve it on the claimant and any other party (r. 8.3(1)). The acknowledgment of service must state whether the defendant contests the claim, and, should he seek a different remedy from that set out in the claim form, say what that remedy is (r. 8.3(2)). The acknowledgment of service should, by r. 8.3(3)(b), comply with r. 10.5.

The defendant must file any written evidence on which he may wish to rely at the same time as he files his acknowledgment of service, and serve it on the other parties (r. 8.5(3) and (4)).

If the defendant wishes to object to the use of the Part 8 procedure (for example, because he contends that there is a substantial dispute of fact, or that the use of the procedure is not required or permitted by a rule or practice direction), he must file an acknowledgment of service as if he did not object to the procedure, but state in it his reasons for objecting to the use of the procedure and verify any matters of evidence included in such objections, by a statement of truth (r. 8.8(1); PD 8, para. 3.6).

An application to the court under Part 11 disputing jurisdiction in respect of a Part 8 claim must be made within 14 days from the filing of an acknowledgment of service (r. 8.3(4)).

5.17.3 Consequences of failing to file an acknowledgment of service

If the defendant to a Part 8 claim fails to file an acknowledgment of service within the appropriate time, he may attend the hearing of the claim, but may not take part in the hearing unless the court gives permission (CPR, r. 8.4). Clearly, the likelihood of such permission being granted will depend on the reasons for the failure, and the speed with which the claimant and the court were notified of the wish to be heard.

Due to the nature of the proceedings, however, the claimant may not obtain default judgment under Part 12 (r. 8.1(5)).

5.17.4 Subsequent procedure

If the defendant to a Part 8 claim does file evidence, the claimant may file further written evidence in reply within 14 days of service of such evidence on him, and must serve a copy of the further evidence on the other parties (CPR, r. 8.5(5) and (6)).

The court will give directions after the filing of the acknowledgment of service (or the time for doing so has expired), unless such directions have

CHAPTER 5 THE EARLY STAGES OF A CLAIM

already been given (see 5.8.2). Such directions may be that the claim continue as if the claimant had not used the Part 8 procedure. This may either be as a result of objections taken by the Defendant (should the court be of the view that they have merit), or of the court's own volition (r. 8.1(3)).

No written evidence may be relied upon at the hearing of the claim unless it had been served in accordance with r. 8.5 (at the time of the claim, acknowledgment of service or in reply 14 days thereafter), unless the court gives permission. Oral evidence may also be given with permission, which would normally be obtained at the time that the court gave directions.

CHAPTER 6 CLAIM FORMS AND PARTICULARS OF CLAIM

CONTENTS

6.1	Introduction	88
6.2	Terminology	89
6.3	Contents of a claim form	90
6.3.1	Heading	90
6.3.2	Brief details of claim	91
6.3.3	Remedy sought	91
6.3.4	Statement of value	91
6.3.5	Foreign currency claim	92
6.3.6	Other matters to be set out in the claim form	93
6.3.7	Power to dispense with statements of case	93
6.3.8	Statement of truth	93
6.4	Particulars of claim	93
6.4.1	Requirement	93
6.4.2	Content	93
6.4.3	Special rules for certain types of claim	95
6.4.4	Points of law, witnesses and documents	95
6.5	Statement of truth	96
6.5.1	Requirements	96
6.5.2	Who may sign a statement of truth	96
6.5.3	Liability for a statement of truth	96
6.5.4	Consequences of failure to verify a statement of case	98
6.6	Contents of a Part 8 claim form	98

6.1 INTRODUCTION

This chapter will examine and discuss what has to be included (and omitted) from the documents by which cases are started and defended.

The term 'pleadings' has now been abolished, and replaced by the more modern (if somewhat inelegant) 'statements of case'. This expression is generic: it applies to all documentation in which a party formally sets out its case, not merely documents in or by which proceedings are actually commenced. According to CPR, r. 2.3(1):

'statement of case'—
  (a) means a claim form, particulars of claim where these are not included in a claim form, defence, Part 20 claim, or reply to defence; and
  (b) includes any further information given in relation to them voluntarily or by court order under rule 18.1.

One of the most significant achievements of the CPR has been to rationalise the means by which proceedings are started. In general, all claimants will start their actions in the same way, using a claim form, although there is a separate Part 8 procedure, with its own claim form, for use in situations where there is no substantial dispute of fact, and where

CHAPTER 6   CLAIM FORMS AND PARTICULARS OF CLAIM

the claimant is asking the court to resolve a specific question or series of questions, or seeking a specific remedy premised on a particular legal basis. (For other forms of originating process in particular types of claim see 2.4.4.)

The general principles of pleading appear to remain substantially unaltered by the CPR, although there is now considerably greater scope for setting out details of facts and law supporting a claim than existed hitherto. Some of the more radical proposals contained in the original draft rules (for example a restriction on starting proceedings in the Royal Courts of Justice in London unless the requirements to be included in a 'London certificate' in the claim form were met; or the inclusion in the particulars of claim or a short summary of evidence of proposed witnesses) have been dropped in the final version. However, a significant departure from previous pleading practice is the new option of including in the particulars of claim any point of law on which the claim is based, together with the names of proposed witnesses, and/or copies of relevant documents (PD 16, para. 10.3). How this enlargement of previous procedure will affect the art of pleading remains to be seen.

One considerable departure from previous practice is the requirement for all statements of case to be verified by a 'statement of truth' in default of which any party on whom they are served may apply to the court for an order that such statement be served within a specified period or the offending document struck out (see 6.5). A person making a false statement in a statement of case (or a witness statement, or an application containing a statement of truth) without an honest belief in its truth, is guilty of a contempt of court (CPR, r. 32.14(1)). Thus there is now a degree of consanguinity between statements of case, witness statements and affidavits, and it would not perhaps be surprising were there to be further blurring between such documentation in the fullness of time.

Pleadings used under the old rules had been much criticised for being over-stylised and complex, with much use of anachronistic language and obscure terminology. The growth and availability of precedents of pleading often led to formalistic drafting in which the objectives of the pleadings process were at best obscured, and at worst often ignored altogether. Additionally, pleadings have been increasingly drafted with tactical considerations in mind, which it may well be felt is inconsistent with the avowed principles of *Access to Justice*. The Woolf report took pains to criticise the system by which time and expense have in the past been taken up in interlocutory proceedings concerning the pleading process, and the avowed aim of the CPR is to ensure that matters progress on their merits, and not on technicalities.

It is to be hoped that the new rules may not so much require a fundamental readjustment of approach to legal drafting, but a refocusing on the original aims and purposes of the pleadings process — these being the concise and clear identification of the subject matter of the action, the issues in the case, and the parties' respective positions in respect of those issues.

6.2   TERMINOLOGY

There has been an overall simplification (or at least modernisation) of terminology to be used under CPR, which is summarised in table 6.1.

CHAPTER 6   CLAIM FORMS AND PARTICULARS OF CLAIM

Table 6.1   Changes in terminology

Old terminology	New terminology
pleadings	statements of case*
action	claim
summons	claim form
writ	claim form
particulars/statement of claim	particulars of claim
plaintiff	claimant
defendant	defendant
defence	defence
reply	reply
rejoinder/rebutter/surrejoinder/surrebutter	(abolished)†
counterclaim	Part 20 claim‡
third party proceedings	Part 20 claim
admitting/denying/not admitting	admitting/denying/not admitting
amendment	amendment

* Statements of case comprise claim form, particulars of claim (where not included in the claim form), defence (including defence to counterclaim), Part 20 claims, reply to defence (CPR, r. 2.3(1)).
† No statement of case may be filed after a reply without the permission of the court (r. 15.9), and no title has been provided for such documentation should permission be granted.
‡ Although the term 'counterclaim' is still referred to in the rules to distinguish it from a claim against a person not already a party to the action.

6.3   CONTENTS OF A CLAIM FORM

Form N1 (see appendix 3) is the form to be used to start any proceedings under the CPR which are to be started by claim form, other than a Part 8 claim.

6.3.1   Heading

On page 1 of form N1 there must be stated:

(a) The court in which the claimant wishes to issue the claim. In High Court claims the division and district registry should be specified.

(b) The parties, who should be described as in table 5.1. If the claimant is claiming in a representative capacity, the claim form must state what that capacity is (CPR, r. 16.2(3)). If the defendant is sued in a representative capacity, the claim form must state what that capacity is (r. 16.2(4)).

(c) The addresses of all parties, as specified in table 5.3. The claimant's address goes under the heading 'Claimant' on page 1. The defendant's name and address go in the space provided at the foot of the page. A separate claim form must be prepared for each defendant, giving that defendant's name and address in this box. If the claimant's address for service is different from the address on page 1, it should be entered on page 2 in the box headed 'Clamant's or claimant's solicitor's address'.

6.3.2 Brief details of claim

Every claim form must contain a concise statement of the nature of the claim (CPR, r. 16.2(a)). This should be inserted in page 1 of form N1 under the heading 'Brief details of claim'. It is suggested that save in the most straightforward cases where the particulars of claim will be included in the claim form, this will be no more than what in the past would have been generally endorsed on a writ, e.g.:

> The plaintiff's claim is for damages for personal injury caused by the defendant's negligence when driving a motor car along Oxford Street, London W1 on 1 July 1999.

More precise details of the allegations and issues will be contained in the particulars of claim, and from a drafting standpoint, it would perhaps not be amiss to state that in the brief details.

6.3.3 Remedy sought

Every claim form must specify the remedy which the claimant seeks (CPR, r. 16.2(1)(b)). There is no separate heading for this statement in form N1 and it would be appropriate to place it at the end of the brief details of claim.

An important departure from previous practice is that a failure to specify a particular remedy will not limit any power of the court to grant such a remedy if the claimant is entitled to it (r. 16.2(5)). Thus it should no longer be possible for a defendant to rely on a technical but unmeritorious defence that a particular remedy has not been pleaded, in order to escape liability. Notwithstanding this, it is suggested that it would clearly be bad practice not to set out all remedies that are being claimed against the defendant.

6.3.4 Statement of value

Where the claimant is making a claim for money, the claim form must contain a statement of value (CPR, r. 16.2(1)(c)). The term 'claim for money' would include both a claim for a debt or liquidated demand and a claim for damages.

The clear objective of this rule is not merely to ensure precision and avoid ambiguity, but also to enable the court to allocate the case to the appropriate jurisdiction and track. A statement of value on a claim form does not, however, limit the power of the court to give judgment for the amount to which it considers the claimant to be entitled (r. 16.3(7)).

By r. 16.2(1)(c), a statement of value must be in accordance with r. 16.3, and there are additional requirements in PD 7 How to Start Proceedings, para. 3. On form N1 there is a space headed 'Value' on page 1. By r. 16.3(2) a statement of value must specify:

(a) the amount of money being claimed;
(b) that the claimant expects to recover not more than £5,000, or between £5,000 and £15,000, or more than £15,000 (these are the basic delineations between cases on the small claims track, the fast track and the multi-track); or
(c) that he cannot say how much he expects to recover.

If the claim is one for personal injuries, the claimant must state whether the amount that he expects to recover as general damages for pain, suffering and loss of amenity is not more than £1,000 or more than £1,000 (CPR, r. 16.3(3); PD 7 How to Start Proceedings, para. 3.8).

This declaration is in addition to the overall expected value of the claim required by CPR, r. 16.3(2)(b), as it relates solely to the general damages aspect of the claim value. This may be important if the overall value of the claim is less than £5,000, in which event it would normally fall to be tried on the small claims track, but where the general damages aspect of the case is expected to be over £1,000, which would lift it into the fast track, by virtue of r. 26.6(5)(a).

If the claim includes a claim by a tenant of residential premises against his landlord seeking an order requiring the landlord to carry out repairs or other work to the premises, the claimant must state whether the amount expected to be recovered as damages in respect of those repairs or other work is not more than £1,000 or more than £1,000; and whether or not the claimant expects to recover more than £1,000 in respect of any claim for damages (CPR, r. 16.3(4); PD 7 How to Start a Claim, para. 3.9). This will determine whether the claim can be allocated to the small claims track (see CPR, r. 26.6(1)(b)).

If the claim form is to be issued in the High Court, the claim form must explain why it is being filed there, by stating (r. 16.3(5)):

    (a) that the claimant expects to recover more than £15,000 (or else the claim must be commenced in the county court (PD 7 How to Start a Claim, para. 2.1));
    (b) that some other enactment provides that the claim may be commenced only in the High Court (stating the relevant enactment);
    (c) if the claim is one for personal injuries, that the claimant expects to recover £50,000 or more; or
    (d) that the claim needs to be in one of the specialist High Court lists, stating which list.

The way in which the financial details are to be entered in the claim form is detailed in the notes for claimant on form N1.

6.3.4.1 Computation of values
In calculating how much it is expected to recover, the following matters should be disregarded (CPR, r. 16.3(6)):

    (a) interest;
    (b) costs;
    (c) any potential finding of contributory negligence;
    (d) any potential counterclaim or defence of set-off;
    (e) any potential payments that the defendant may have to make, out of any award to the claimant, to the Secretary of State for Social Security under the Social Security (Recovery of Benefits) Act 1997, s. 6.

6.3.5 Foreign currency claim

Where a claim is for a sum of money expressed in a foreign currency, the claim form should expressly state (PD 16, para. 11.1):

    (a) that the claim is for payment in a specified foreign currency;
    (b) why it is for payment in that currency;

CHAPTER 6   CLAIM FORMS AND PARTICULARS OF CLAIM

   (c)   the sterling equivalent of the sum at the date of the claim; and
   (d)   the source of the exchange rate used in calculating the sterling equivalent.

6.3.6   Other matters to be set out in the claim form

The claim form must contain such other matters as may be set out in a practice direction (CPR, r. 16.2(1)(d)). Such matters are dealt with in context in the course of this chapter.

6.3.7   Power to dispense with statements of case

If a claim form has been properly issued and served on a defendant, the court has the power under CPR, r. 16.8, to order that the claim will then continue without any statements of case having to be filed. This will presumably be reserved for cases of considerable urgency where the matter can be dealt with expeditiously without formal disclosure of the respective parties' cases, or matters where the issue is extremely simple, and where the service of statements of case would only add to the delay and expense of the proceedings.

6.3.8   Statement of truth

A claim form must be verified by a statement of truth (see 6.5).

6.4   PARTICULARS OF CLAIM

6.4.1   Requirement

Particulars of claim must be contained in a claim form, served with it or served after it (CPR, r. 7.4(1); see 5.8.4 for rules on service). If practicable the particulars of claim should be set out in the claim form (PD 16, para. 3.1). Page 2 of form N1 has a space headed 'Particulars of claim'.

6.4.2   Content

Where the particulars of claim are served separately from the claim form, they must state (PD 16, para. 3.8):

   (a)   the name of the court in which the claim is proceeding;
   (b)   the claim number;
   (c)   the title of the proceedings; and
   (d)   the claimant's address for service.

Particulars of claim must include:

   (a)   a concise statement of the facts on which the claimant relies (CPR, r. 16.4(1)(a)). This rule appears to make no radical change to previous practice. The word 'facts', it is submitted, equates to the concept of 'material particulars' in previous pleading practice, and the new rules should not be read or interpreted as suggesting that the particulars of claim should contain evidence. This distinction between material facts (relevant), and the evidence by which those facts are to be proved (irrelevant), was contained in the old RSC, ord. 18, r. 7(1), and still remains good practice.
   (b)   Details of any interest claimed (CPR, r. 16.4(1)(b) and (2)). This rule is not dissimilar to present practice. A claimant who is seeking interest must state whether it is being claimed under the terms of a contract, or under a specified enactment, or for some other (defined) reason

CHAPTER 6 CLAIM FORMS AND PARTICULARS OF CLAIM

(r. 16.4(2)(a)). If the claim is for a specified sum of money, the particulars of claim should state the percentage rate claimed, the date from which interest is claimed, the date to which it is calculated (being not later than the date of issue of the claim form), the amount claimed up until that date, and the daily rate of interest accruing after that date (r. 16.4(2)(b)). Thus, on a specified sum, a claim for interest 'pursuant to statute' or 'at such rate and for such period as the court shall deem fit' will not comply with the rule.

(c) Where appropriate a statement to the effect that aggravated or exemplary damages (or both) are being claimed; together with the grounds on which they are claimed (r. 16.4(1)(c)). This rule requires the claimant to give details of the grounds on which such additional damages are claimed, and not merely the fact that they are claimed. It may well now be necessary to give more details of such grounds than would hitherto have been the case.

(d) Where appropriate, a statement to the effect that provisional damages are being claimed, together with the grounds on which they are claimed (r. 16.4(1)(d)).

(e) Where a claim is brought to enforce a right to recover possession of goods, a statement showing the value of the goods (PD 16, para. 9.2).

(f) Where a claim is based upon a written agreement, a copy of the contract or contractual documents attached to or served with the particulars of claim; together with relevant parts of the contract or documents incorporating any general conditions of sale (PD 16, para. 9.3). The original documents should be available at the hearing.

(g) Where a claim is based upon an oral agreement, the contractual words including by whom, to whom, when and where they were spoken (PD 16, para. 9.4).

(h) Where a claim is based upon an agreement by conduct, particulars of the conduct relied on, stating by whom, when and where the acts constituting the conduct were done (PD 16, para. 9.5).

(i) In a claim issued in the High Court relating to a Consumer Credit Act 1974 agreement, a statement that the action is not one to which s. 141 of the Act applies (PD 16, para. 9.6).

(j) Any other matters required by specific rules or practice direction to be included in respect of certain types of claim (CPR, r. 16.4(1)(e); PD 16, para. 3.6(2)).

Additionally, the following specific matters are required by PD 16, para. 10.2, to be set out in particulars of claim, if the claimant wishes to rely on them:

(a) any allegation of fraud;
(b) the fact of any illegality;
(c) details of any misrepresentation;
(d) details of all breaches of trust;
(e) notice or knowledge of a fact;
(f) details of unsoundness of mind or undue influence;
(g) details of wilful default;
(h) any facts relating to mitigation of loss or damage.

It has always been good drafting practice to deal with these matters so as to ensure that the relevant issues are exposed at the earliest possible moment.

CHAPTER 6   CLAIM FORMS AND PARTICULARS OF CLAIM

6.4.3   Special rules for certain types of claim

For special requirements in:

(a) personal injury claims, see PD 16, para. 4;
(b) fatal accident claims, see PD 16, para. 5;
(c) claims for the recovery of land, see PD 16, para. 6;
(d) mortgage claims, see PD 16, para. 7;
(e) hire-purchase claims, see PD 16, para. 7;
(f) defamation claims, see PD 16, para. 8;
(g) claims made for an injunction or declaration in respect of land or its possession, see PD 7, para. 9.1;
(h) claims for recovery of goods, see PD 16, para. 9.2;
(i) cases concerning the Civil Jurisdiction and Judgments Act 1982, see 5.9.19;
(j) cases where a claimant wishes to rely on the Civil Evidence Act 1968 on a conviction of an offence, or a finding of adultery or paternity, see PD 16, para. 10.1.

6.4.4   Points of law, witnesses and documents

PD 16, para. 10.3, states that particulars of claim may include:

(a) a reference to any point of law on which the claim is based;
(b) the name of any witness whom the claimant wishes to call; and
(c) (by way of service or attachment) a copy of any document which the claimant considers is necessary to his claim (including any expert's report to be filed in accordance with Part 35).

It is interesting that there is no reference to this option in the guidance notes on drafting particulars of claim which are given to claimants on form N1A.

PD 16, para. 10.3 represents a fundamental and radical departure from previous pleading practice, where a strict distinction has always been maintained between material particulars on the one hand, and evidence on the other. Even the adoption of the mandatory exchange of witness statements in recent years has not fundamentally altered this concept, as such exchange is ordinarily amongst the last of the procedural steps to take place before trial, and well after the the close of pleadings. The original draft rules of July 1996 provided for the optional inclusion of a synopsis of the evidence of a proposed witness to be included in the particulars of claim, but that has been dropped. It could, it is suggested, have led to duplication of material, as well as an increased (and judicially unwelcome) opportunity for parties to highlight any discrepancies between the version given in the particulars of claim and that given in the witness statement. However, even as matters presently stand, it seems that, at least until the climate of litigation changes in line with the overriding objective (which requires the erosion of long-held attitudes to litigation), the scope for tactical manoeuvring afforded by this direction may be considerable — and it may not perhaps be too long before one party attempts (successfully or not will be another matter!) to take the point that its case is to be preferred as a result of having been more expeditious in the declaration of its evidence than the other. Thus, although optional, the ability to include matters of law and evidence in the particulars of claim may well provoke a reassessment of the tactical manner in which a case is to be presented,

CHAPTER 6   CLAIM FORMS AND PARTICULARS OF CLAIM

which may not altogether be consistent with the aims and objectives of the new rules.

6.5 STATEMENT OF TRUTH

6.5.1 Requirements

Both a claim form and, if separate, particulars of claim are statements of case (CPR, r. 2.3(1)). Rule 22.1(1)(a) requires every statement of case to be verified by a statement of truth, that is, a statement that the party putting forward the document believes the facts stated in the document are true (r. 22.1(4)). The basic format of a statement of truth is (PD 22, para. 2.1):

> I believe that the facts stated in this [name of document being verified] are true.

It is possible for the legal representative of a party to make a statement of truth verifying a document put forward by that party (r. 22.1(6)), and then the basic format of the statement is:

> The [claimant/defendant] believes that the facts stated in this [name of document being verified] are true.

There is a pro forma statement of truth on form N1 for use when the particulars of claim are included in the statement of claim.

A statement of truth may be contained in the document it verifies, or it may be in a separate document served subsequently (PD 22, para. 1.5). If it is in a separate document, the formalities set out in PD 22, para. 2.3, must be observed.

6.5.2 Who may sign a statement of truth

A statement of truth verifying a document put forward by a party must be signed by the party or his or her litigation friend (CPR, r. 22.1(6)(a)(i)). Alternatively it can be signed by the party's legal representative (r. 22.1(6)(a)(ii)), provided the capacity in which the representative signs and the name of his or her firm are stated (PD 22, para. 3.7). A statement of truth signed by a legal representative will refer to the client's belief and not the representative's but must be signed in the representative's own name and not that of his or her firm or employer (PD 22, para. 3.10). The individual who signs a statement of truth must print his or her full name clearly beneath the signature (PD 22, para. 3.9).

In the case of a company or other corporation, the statement of truth must be signed by one of the senior personnel listed in PD 22, para. 3.5, giving his or her position in the organisation (director, treasurer, secretary etc.) (PD 22, para. 3.4).

When the claimant is a partnership, the statement of truth may be signed by any of the partners or a person having the control or management of the partnership business (PD 22, para. 3.6). It is not thought that there is any significance in the difference between the word 'must' used in PD 22, para. 3.4, and 'may' used in para. 3.6.

6.5.3 Liability for a statement of truth

A person who makes a false statement in a document verified by a statement of truth, or who causes such a statement to be made, without an honest belief in its truth, is guilty of contempt of court (CPR, r. 32.14(1)), although proceedings for such contempt can only be brought by the Attorney-General or with the permission of the court (r. 32.14(2)).

The belief stated in a statement of truth (and the consequent responsibility for making a false statement) is that of the party putting forward the document, save in the case where a party is conducting proceedings with the aid of a litigation friend, in which event the statement of belief is that of the litigation friend (r. 22.1(5)).

When a statement of truth verifying a document is signed by a legal adviser of the party putting forward the document, its contents and the consequences of signing it are deemed, by virtue of the signature, to have been explained to the claimant, and the signature will be taken by the court as meaning that the client has authorised the representative to sign (PD 22, para. 3.8).

The effect of this rule is to rest the responsibility for the contents of the document squarely on the shoulders of the person putting foward the facts. It is no longer sufficient for a legal representative to put forward matters in the belief (however genuine) that what his client has told him is the truth — it is now incumbent on him to ensure that he has received direct instructions to that effect. This is particularly important in view of the explanation deemed to have been made to the client by PD 22, para 3.8, which, if not actually given, could well lead to an allegation of professional misconduct (see 1.9.4). Provided that such instructions have been given, the legal representative signing a statement should not incur personal liability in respect of any default, unless he is aware that the contents are false, notwithstanding his instructions to the contrary.

A consequence of this new rule is to equate the status of a statement of case in many ways with that of an affidavit (and indeed with a witness statement). All now effectively contain declarations which render a party liable to proceedings for contempt of court should statements be proved to have been made without honest belief in their truth, although the precise means by which a party becomes so liable varies according to the nature of the document. It is perhaps difficult to see how the requirement to verify the contents of a statement of case is going to prove much of a disincentive to a groundless (or even dishonest) claim or defence. It seems unlikely that a client would inform his legal adviser that the substance of his statement of case is false, and in such an event it would presumably not be signed by the adviser in any event. It is also difficult to envisage a situation serious enough to warrant proceedings for contempt where the court's powers to punish contemnors will have to be predicated solely upon the fact that the claimant or defendant is proved not to have had an honest belief in the truth of his statement of case. We no longer live in an age in which the threat of one's soul being consigned to perdition provides a compelling sanction against making false declarations, and the court's willingness or desire to investigate the honesty of a belief in order to impose criminal sanctions once it has resolved a civil dispute must surely be open to doubt. The permission of the court, under CPR, r. 32.14(2)(b), will presumably be applied for by the other party, which procedure could be open to tactical abuse and/or a desire to inflict additional retribution on the losing side. It does not seem that any of the above would be consistent with the overriding objectives of saving expense, ensuring expedition and fairness, and appropriate allocation of resources (r. 1.1), let alone the requirement that the parties will help the courts to further the overriding objective (r. 1.3).

There is one important practical consequence of the verification of a statement of case, by a statement of truth. By r. 32.6(2), at hearings other than the trial, a party may rely on the matters set out in his statement of case in support of his application, provided that it is verified by a statement of truth. Thus the contents of the statement of case can have evidential value in such circumstances.

6.5.4 Consequence of failure to verify a statement of case

If a statement of case is not verified by a statement of truth, it will remain effective unless struck out, but the party putting it forward may not rely on it as evidence of any of the matters set out in it (CPR, r. 22.2(1)). The omission simply means that the statement of case cannot be used for the purpose of supporting an application under r. 32.6(2).

Where a statement of case remains unverified, any party may apply either:

(a) under r. 22.4 for an order that the statement be verified within such period as the court may specify, or be struck out in default (PD 22, para. 4.2); or

(b) under r. 22.2(2) for an order that the statement be struck out.

The cost of such an application will normally be ordered to be paid by the defaulting party in any event, and forthwith (PD 22, para. 4.3). It is probable that the majority of such applications will be as a result of oversight on the part of the party putting forward the document, rather than as a result of any deliberate intention to avoid the rule.

6.6 CONTENTS OF A PART 8 CLAIM FORM

Form N208 (see appendix 3) is the claim form to be used to start a Part 8 claim. It is required by CPR, r. 8.2, to state:

(a) that the Part 8 procedure applies;
(b) the question which the claimant wants the court to decide; or the remedy being sought and the legal basis for the claim to that remedy;
(c) any enactment under which the claim is being brought;
(d) any representative capacity in which the claimant is bringing the action;
(e) any representative capacity in which the defendant is being sued.

Because of the nature of the procedure, it would not normally be appropriate for a Part 8 claim form to contain particulars of claim. Instead, the claimant may rely on the matters set out in the claim form as evidence, if (as it is required to be by r. 22.1(1)(a)) it is verified by a statement of truth (see 6.5). Additionally, the claimant must file any written evidence on which he intends to rely when he files his claim form, and this must be served on the defendant together with the claim form (r. 8.5(1) and (2)). Such evidence can be contained in the claim form itself, but will normally be in the form of a witness statement or an affidavit (PD 8, para. 5.2), which must be verified by a statement of truth.

Due to the nature of the procedure, the defendant is not required to file a defence, neither can the claimant obtain judgment by request on an admission, or in default under CPR Part 12.

CHAPTER 7   DEFENDING A CLAIM

CONTENTS

7.1	Introduction	99
7.2	When a defence is required	99
7.3	Period for filing a defence	100
7.4	Extending the time for service of a defence	101
7.5	Stay of claim where no action taken	101
7.6	Contents of a defence — general matters	101
7.7	Contents of a defence — specific matters	102
7.7.1	Defendant in representative capacity	102
7.7.2	Address for service	102
7.7.3	Personal injury claim	102
7.7.4	Limitation defence	103
7.7.5	Defamation	103
7.7.6	Tender	103
7.8	Set-offs	103

7.1 INTRODUCTION

The principal rules concerning the drafting of the defence can be found in CPR, Parts 15 and 16, and their associated practice directions.

The matters discussed below do not apply where the claimant uses the Part 8 procedure, and apply with limited effect to specialist claims. They do however apply to cases where a defence is drafted to a counterclaim.

The defence is now classified as a 'statement of case' by CPR, r. 2.3(1), and not a 'pleading' and the new terminology may initially lead to some confusion with the old 'statement of claim'. With certain exceptions which will be discussed below, there is no radical departure from the principles of pleading that applied under the old RSC and CCR. However, the matters which led to the criticism of the pleadings process, and need for reform (discussed in 6.1) applied as much to the defence as the claim. In particular it appeared often to be forgotten that it was (and is) as incumbent upon a defendant to state full particulars of his case, as it was and is for the plaintiff/claimant. Too often in the past, defences concentrated point by point on the allegations set out in the claim, stating whether they were admitted, denied or not admitted, but then wholly neglected to aver the defendant's own case on the issues. The requirement on a defendant to state his own case on an allegation or issue is now expressly stated in CPR, r. 16.5(2).

A defence must be verified by a statement of truth (see 6.5). The form of statement is (PD 16, para. 13.2):

> [I believe] [the defendant believes] that the facts stated in the defence are true.

7.2 WHEN A DEFENCE IS REQUIRED

A defendant who wishes to defend all or part of a claim must file a defence (CPR, r. 15.2). If a defence is not filed, default judgment (see 5.14) may

CHAPTER 7 DEFENDING A CLAIM

be entered if allowed by Part 12 (r. 15.3). A copy of the defence must be served on every other party (r. 15.6).

7.3 PERIOD FOR FILING A DEFENCE

The general rule is that a defence must be filed within 14 days after service of the particulars of claim (CPR, r. 15.4(1)(a)). Therefore, no defence need be filed where a claim form is served which does not include, and is not accompanied by, particulars of claim (which can be served within 14 days thereafter: see 5.8.4). As the particulars of claim can be contained within the body of the claim form (as opposed to served with it, or at a later date) care should therefore be taken to ensure whether the claim form contains the full particulars of claim, or merely the basic information required.

The defendant is allowed to extend this time limit by 14 days. To gain this extension the defendant must file an acknowledgment of service under Part 10 (see 5.13). If this is done, the time for filing a defence is extended to 28 days after service of the particulars of the claim (r. 15.4(1)(b)).

There are different periods for filing a defence where the claim form is served out of the jurisdiction (see r. 15.4(2)(a)); and in a case where a claim form is served on the agent of a principal who is overseas the court will, under r. 6.16(4), specify the period for responding.

There are two further exceptions to the above rules:

(a) Where the defendant makes an application disputing the jurisdiction of the court under Part 11 (see 5.16), the defence need not be filed before the hearing of the application (r. 11(9)).

(b) Where the claimant applies for summary judgment under Part 24 (see 9.13) before the defendant has filed a defence, the defendant need not file a defence before the summary judgment hearing (r. 24.4(2)).

The words of r. 15.4 do not appear to prohibit the filing of a defence should the defendant wish. Under RSC, ord. 14, where an application for summary judgment was made, the defendant was then unable to file his defence, and time for such service was suspended until the application had been heard. The summons was defended on affidavit, and it would of course be an unwise defendant who did not exhibit a copy of his defence to his affidavit. Under CPR, Part 24, however, the defendant would appear to have a choice:

(a) His response may be supported by evidence, defined in r. 32.6(1) (in the absence of any direction to the contrary by the court, a practice direction or any other enactment) as a witness statement. By PD 32, para. 18.3, a witness statement may contain an exhibit, produced according to the procedures laid down in that direction. Presumably therefore a draft defence could be produced as such an exhibit.

(b) Alternatively, under r. 32.6(2), a party may rely on his statement of case in hearings other than the trial, provided that it is verified by a statement of truth. Thus it appears, should the defendant wish to file his defence, he may do so, and then rely on it in addition to any witness statement he may wish to file.

In practice, it is suggested that the simplest procedure will be for the draft defence to be exhibited to the witness statement.

7.4 EXTENDING THE TIME FOR SERVICE OF A DEFENCE

The defendant and the claimant may, under CPR, r. 15.5, agree that the period for filing a defence shall be extended by up to 28 days. Where this is done, the defendant must notify the court in writing (r. 15.5(2)). Thus there is now a strict limit to the degree of 'slippage' which the parties may, by consent, allow. This is consistent with the principles of *Access to Justice* in that whereas there is an acknowledgment that the time limits set out in the rules may have to be extended, the principle of judicially led case management now precludes the parties from agreeing further (or even open-ended) extensions of time. Any party wishing a further extension of time (whether by consent or otherwise) will now have to make an application to the court under r. 3.1(2)(a).

7.5 STAY OF CLAIM WHERE NO ACTION TAKEN

Where at least six months have expired since the end of the period for filing a defence, and no defendant has served or filed any admission, defence or counterclaim, and the claimant has not entered or applied for default judgment under CPR Part 12, or summary judgment under Part 24, the claim shall be stayed, although any party can apply for such stay to be lifted (r. 15.11).

7.6 CONTENTS OF A DEFENCE — GENERAL MATTERS

As has previously been the case, a defence to a claim must say which of the allegations in the particulars of claim are admitted, which are denied and which allegations the defendant is unable to admit or deny, but requires the claimant to prove (CPR, r. 16.5(1)). The recommendation in the July 1996 *Final Report* that there be a fourth category in which a defendant could 'doubt' an allegation has (perhaps fortunately) been dropped from the final version of the rules. Every allegation made in a claim should be dealt with in the defence (PD 16, para. 12.2).

It may be useful to restate the established principles behind the three possible responses to an allegation in particulars of claim, and their consequences so far as the claimant is concerned.

If an allegation is *admitted*, the claimant is absolved from any obligation to bring any further evidence in support of that allegation. This is apart from any other consequences that may flow from the admission made. Where the defendant wishes to admit the truth of all or part of the other party's case, he may adopt the admissions procedure set out in Part 14 (see 5.12).

Where an allegation is *denied*, this normally implies that the defendant intends to put up a positive case to the contrary. Indeed, r. 16.5(2) specifically provides that where the defendant denies an allegation, he must state his reasons for doing so; and if he intends to put forward a different version of events from that given by the claimant, he must state his own version. This essentially restates what always was required under the old rules of pleading, even though often omitted. However, if a defendant fails to answer a specific allegation, he shall nevertheless be taken to require that allegation to be proved, provided that in his defence, he has set out the nature of his case in relation to the issue to which that allegation is relevant (r. 16.5(3)). In such an event, it will presumably be open to the claimant to apply to the court that the defendant give further information under Part 18, or for the court to order it of its own volition. But if the defendant totally fails to deal with an allegation, he shall be taken to have admitted it (r. 16.5(5)), unless it is an allegation relating to a money claim, in which case he shall be taken to require that any allegation relating to the amount of money claimed by proved, unless he expressly admits the allegation (r. 16.5(4)).

Where (apart from costs and interest) the only claim against a defendant is for a specified sum of money, and a defence is filed stating that the sum has been paid to the claimant, a special procedure will then apply.

7.7 CONTENTS OF A DEFENCE — SPECIFIC MATTERS

A claim form is required by CPR, r. 16.3, to contain a statement of value (see 6.3.4). If this statement is disputed, the defendant must state why he disputes it, and if he can, give his own statement of the value of the claim (r. 16.5(6)).

7.7.1 Defendant in representative capacity

If a defendant is defending in a representative capacity, he must state that fact in his defence, and also say what that capacity is (CPR, r. 16.5(7)).

7.7.2 Address for service

Rule 16.5(8) of the CPR requires a defence to contain an address for service, within the jurisdiction (r. 6.5(2)), to which documents can be sent to the defendant, if no acknowledgment of service has been filed.

7.7.3 Personal injury claim

Where a defended claim is one in respect of personal injury, and the claimant has attached a medical report in respect of his alleged injuries, PD 16, para. 14.1, provides that the defendant should state whether he:

(a) agrees with the medical report; or
(b) disputes it (in which event he should state his reasons for doing so (PD 16, para. 14.1(2)), and, where he has obtained his own medical report on which he intends to rely, attach it to his defence (para. 14.1(3)); or
(c) neither agrees nor disputes it, but has no knowledge of the matters contained in the medical report.

It is submitted that 'should' in PD 16, para. 14.1, has the same mandatory force as 'must' in CPR, r. 16.5, and that no technical distinction should be drawn between the two.

Thus, for the first time, there is an obligation on a defendant who disputes medical evidence served with the particulars of claim to attach his own medical report to his defence, when it has been obtained by the time the defence is drafted. There is, interestingly, no mandatory requirement to attach a medical report to a defence *whenever* the claimant's report is in dispute, but only where the defendant has already obtained his own medical report at the time of drafting the defence. However, it may well be difficult to dispute the claimant's report (particularly when reasons have to be given) save on grounds obtained as a result of a defence medical report, which is frequently not predicated upon a defence medical examination of the claimant, but upon an examination of medical records. If a defence medical report is not attached to a defence when detailed reasons for dispute are given, it would almost certainly prompt the claimant to question the basis for the response and apply for disclosure of the report. If the defendant has not had the opportunity to obtain his own expert evidence by the time the defence is drafted, it is likely that he would then have to state that he had 'no knowledge of the matters contained in the [claimant's] medical report', under PD 16, para 14.1(1)(c).

Additionally, where in a personal injuries case, the claimant has included a schedule of past and future expenses and losses, the defendant must include in or attach to his defence a counter-schedule stating which items are agreed, in dispute, or neither agreed nor disputed, because of lack of knowledge (PD 16, para. 14.2(1)). Where items are disputed, alternative figures where appropriate, should be supplied (PD 16, para. 14.2(1)).

7.7.4 Limitation defence

A defendant who relies on the expiry of any limitation period, must give in his defence details of the date on which it is alleged the relevant limitation period expired (PD 16, para. 16.1).

7.7.5 Defamation

For particular rules in cases of defamation etc., see PD 16, para. 15.

7.7.6 Tender

For particular rules where the defence is one of tender see PD 16, para. 16.2.

7.8 SET-OFFS

Where a defendant wishes to rely wholly or in part on a defence of set-off, he may, by CPR, r. 16.6, include this in the defence, whether or not it will also form the subject of a counterclaim under Part 20. Interestingly, the rule does not *require* this to be done, but as set-off was almost invariably pleaded in the defence under the old rules, there seems no reason why that practice should not continue.

CHAPTER 8 ADDITIONAL CLAIMS AND FURTHER STEPS IN THE CLAIM

CONTENTS

8.1	Counterclaims	105
8.1.1	General and procedural requirements	105
8.1.2	Contents of a counterclaim	105
8.2	Reply	106
8.2.1	General and procedural requirements	106
8.2.2	Contents of a reply	106
8.3	Subsequent statements of case	106
8.4	Defence to counterclaim	107
8.4.1	General and procedural requirements	107
8.4.2	Contents of defence to counterclaim	107
8.5	Special procedure where the defence claims that money claimed has been paid	107
8.6	Part 20 claims	107
8.6.1	Is permission required?	108
8.6.2	Procedure for filing a Part 20 claim when permission is not required	108
8.6.3	Procedure for filing a Part 20 claim when permission is required	108
8.6.4	Relevant considerations in applications on a Part 20 claim	109
8.6.5	Contents of a Part 20 claim	109
8.6.6	Procedure and case management after filing	110
8.6.7	Default judgment in Part 20 claims	111
8.6.8	Defendant's claim against a co-defendant for contribution or indemnity	112
8.7	Obtaining further information	112
8.7.1	Principle	112
8.7.2	Making the request	112
8.7.3	Form and contents of the request	113
8.7.4	Applications to the court when there is no or insufficient response	114
8.7.5	Response ordered by the court	114
8.7.6	Form and contents of the response	114
8.7.7	Objections to responding	115
8.7.8	Restrictions on the use of further information	116
8.8	Amendments to statements of case	116
8.8.1	When permission is not required	116
8.8.2	When permission is required	116
8.8.3	Format of an amended statement of case	117
8.8.4	Amendments after a relevant limitation period has expired	118

CHAPTER 8   ADDITIONAL CLAIMS AND FURTHER STEPS IN THE CLAIM

8.1   COUNTERCLAIMS

8.1.1   General and procedural requirements

The rules governing counterclaims are contained in CPR, Part 20 and its associated practice direction. For claims against co-defendants and other parties (which are also covered by Part 20) see 8.6.

Any claim other than a claim by a claimant against a defendant, is classed as a 'Part 20 Claim' (r. 20.2(1)), and thus a counterclaim by a defendant (whether against the claimant or against the claimant and some other person) falls within this class.

A defendant may make a counterclaim against a claimant by filing particulars of the counterclaim (r. 20.4(1)). As in previous practice, the defence and counterclaim should normally form one document with the counterclaim following on from the defence (PD 15, para. 3.1; PD 20, para. 6.1). Provided that it is filed with the defence, the court's permission is not required to make a counterclaim (CPR, r. 20.4(2)(a)). However, if for some reason, the defendant wishes to file a counterclaim after service of his defence, the permission of the court will have to be obtained (r. 20.4(2)(b)), and the procedure and conditions laid down in Part 20 and PD 20 will have to be followed. A defendant who wishes to counterclaim against a person other than the claimant must apply to the court for an order adding that person as a defendant to the counterclaim (r. 20.5(1)). An application for such an order may be made without notice, unless the court directs otherwise (r. 20.5(2)), and if the order is made, the court will at the same time give directions for the management of the case (r. 20.5(3)).

Where the permission of the court to make a counterclaim is not required, the counterclaim should also be served on every other party when a copy of the defence is served (r. 20.8(1)). Where the permission of the court is required, the court will give directions as to service (r. 20.8(3)).

The manner in which a counterclaim against both the claimant and another party should be headed is set out in PD 20, para. 7.2.

Save where CPR, Part 20, states to the contrary, the CPR apply to Part 20 claims as if they were claims (r. 20.3(1)). In particular, as PD 20, para. 3, points out, the provisions relating to failure to respond will apply as much to a counterclaim as they do to a claim. Part 15 of the CPR applies to a defence to counterclaim. Thus it is, for example, open to a defendant to obtain judgment in default of a defence to a counterclaim, subject to the conditions and procedure laid down in Part 12. However, a claimant wishing to defend a counterclaim need not file an acknowledgment of service (r. 20.4(3), and various consequential rules pertaining to time limits, statements of value for the purposes of issue in the High Court, and preliminary case management under Part 26 also do not apply (see r. 20.3(2) for details).

8.1.2   Contents of a counterclaim

As a counterclaim is treated as if it were a claim, for the purposes of the CPR, it should be set out in the same format, and with the same particularity as particulars of claim.

CHAPTER 8 ADDITIONAL CLAIMS AND FURTHER STEPS IN THE CLAIM

The contents of a counterclaim must be verified by a statement of truth (see 6.5; CPR, r. 22.1(1)(a); PD 20, para. 4.1). The form of statement is (PD 20, para. 4.2):

[I believe] [the defendant believes] that the facts stated in this counterclaim are true.

8.2 REPLY

8.2.1 General and procedural requirements

Although a claimant may file a reply to a defence, he does not have to do so, and failure to file a reply must not be taken as an admission of any of the matters raised in the defence (CPR, r. 16.7(1)). If a reply is filed, but fails to deal with a matter raised in the defence, the claimant shall nevertheless be taken to require that matter to be proved. Thus, strictly speaking, it should no longer be necessary for the reply to commence with a statement joining issue with the defendant upon all matters not specifically admitted in the defence (the old 'general traverse'), as there is now an implied joinder of issue. Where, however, the defence includes a counterclaim to which it is intended to file a defence, it is suggested that a formal reply should also be filed in the conventional manner, joining issue with the defendant on his defence and counterclaim, although the rules do not specifically provide for, or require this to be done.

When a claimant intends to file a reply, this must be done when he files his allocation questionnaire under r. 26.3(6), and the reply must be served on the other parties at the same time as it is filed (r. 15.8).

8.2.2 Contents of a reply

Conventionally, a reply may respond to any matters raised in the defence which were not, and which should not have been, dealt with in the particulars of claim, and exists solely for the purpose of dealing disjunctively with matters which could not properly have been dealt with in the particulars of claim, but which require a response once they have been raised in the defence. It has always been a cardinal principle of pleading (which has certainly not been altered by the CPR) that a claim should not anticipate a potential defence (popularly known as 'jumping the stile'). Once, however, a defence has been raised which requires a response so that the issues between the parties can be defined, a reply becomes necessary for the purpose of setting out the claimant's case on that point. The reply is, however, neither an opportunity to restate the claim, nor is it a 'defence to the defence'.

Where the defence takes issue with a fact set out in the particulars of claim, and the claimant accepts that the pleaded fact is incorrect, the proper course should be for the claimant to seek to amend his statement of case accordingly (see 8.8), and not to deal with the matter in a reply (PD 16, para. 12.2). Thus where, for example, the particulars of claim contain an error as to the quantity of goods ordered, and the correct quantity is set out in the defence, the error should be corrected by way of amendment, rather than reply.

A reply must be verified by a statement of truth (see 6.5; CPR, r. 22.1(a)).

8.3 SUBSEQUENT STATEMENTS OF CASE

A party may not file or serve any statement of case beyond a reply, without the permission of the court (CPR, r. 15.9). Such permission should rarely

CHAPTER 8   ADDITIONAL CLAIMS AND FURTHER STEPS IN THE CLAIM

be required, and presumably will rarely be granted. Under the previous rules, leave had to be granted to file a rejoinder, surrejoinder, rebutter or surrebutter, and such instances were so rare as to have almost fallen into disuse. Save in the most exceptional cases the supposed need for additional pleadings normally evidenced a failure to plead the case properly in the first place, which could be resolved either by amendment or by request for further and better particulars. The same holds equally if not even more true under the CPR.

8.4   DEFENCE TO COUNTERCLAIM

8.4.1   General and procedural requirements

Where a claimant files a reply and defence to a counterclaim, these should normally form one document with the reply following on from the defence (CPR, r. 15.4(2); PD 20, para. 6.2).

Where a defence is filed to a counterclaim or other Part 20 claim, the court must consider the future conduct of the proceedings and give appropriate directions, in the course of which it must ensure that both the main claim and the Part 20 claim are managed together, so far as this is practicable (CPR, r. 20.13).

8.4.2   Contents of defence to counterclaim

A defence to a counterclaim is governed by the same rules as a defence to a claim (see chapter 7), and must be verified by a statement of truth (see 6.5).

8.5   SPECIAL PROCEDURE WHERE THE DEFENCE CLAIMS THAT MONEY CLAIMED HAS BEEN PAID

Where (apart from a claim for costs and interest) the only claim against a defendant is for a specified sum of money (i.e., a liquidated sum, using old parlance) and the defendant states in his defence that he has paid that sum to the claimant, the court will then send a notice (form N236) to the claimant requiring him to state in writing (by completing the form and returning it to the court) whether he wishes the proceedings to continue (CPR, r. 15.10(1)). If he fails to respond to the notice within 28 days after it has been served on him, the claim shall be stayed (r. 15.10(3)), although any party may thereafter apply to have the stay lifted (r. 15.10(4)). If the claimant does wish the proceedings to continue, he must serve a copy of his response to the notice on the defendant (r. 15.10(2)). The CPR do not require the claimant to respond to the court's notice accepting that the sum has actually been paid, and that the case should be withdrawn, but this option is provided in form N236. The position of a defendant who, having at all times maintained that the sum had been paid, is forced to go to the expense of filing a defence, after which the claimant concedes the point, seems presently to be unclear.

8.6   PART 20 CLAIMS

This section considers claims made by a defendant, either against a co-defendant seeking a contribution or indemnity, or against a third party. Together with counterclaims (which are discussed in 8.1), these are

CHAPTER 8 ADDITIONAL CLAIMS AND FURTHER STEPS IN THE CLAIM

generically to be known as 'Part 20 claims', and a party making such a claim is to be known as a 'Part 20 claimant' (CPR, r. 20.2(2)). Part 20 also applies to third parties wishing to make a claim either against a fourth party, or against a person already a party to an action. For reasons of clarity, this part of the chapter should be read as including such persons, without them being specifically mentioned.

8.6.1 Is permission required?

The permission of the court is not required in order to bring a Part 20 claim, save in the three following circumstances (PD 20, para. 1.1):

   (a) where a defendant wishes to counterclaim against a claimant after having already filed his defence (CPR, r. 20.4(2)(b); see 8.1);
   (b) where a defendant wishes to counterclaim against a person other than the claimant (r. 20.5(1); see 8.1);
   (c) where a defendant wishes to make a claim (whether for a contribution or indemnity or otherwise) against a person who is not a co-defendant, and where the claim is not a counterclaim, and where such claim is not issued before or at the same time as he files his defence (CPR, r. 20.7(1) and (3)).

It follows that the permission of the court to make a Part 20 claim is not required:

   (a) where a defendant wishes to counterclaim against the claimant at the same time that he files his defence (see 8.1);
   (b) where a defendant who has filed an acknowledgment of service or a defence wishes to make a claim against a co-defendant for a contribution or an indemnity (r. 20.6; see 8.6.8);
   (c) where a defendant wishes to make any claim against a third party before or at the same time as he files his defence (r. 20.7(3)(a)). The expression 'defendant' in r. 20.7(3) clearly applies to a third (or fourth) party wishing to make a further claim against a person not already a party — as they would, of course, be 'defendants' to the claim made against them.

8.6.2 Procedure for filing a Part 20 claim, when permission is not required

The claim and particulars must be served on the person against whom it is made within 14 days after the date on which the Part 20 claimant files his defence (CPR, r. 20.8(1)(b)). There is no express provision that copies must also be served on every other party, which apparently only has to be done, under r. 20.12(2), when a Part 20 claim is served on a person who is not already a party (r. 20.12(2) refers to 'the Part 20 claim form', referring to the form which is the subject of r. 20.12(1)). Rule 20.8(1) does not apply to a defendant's claim against a co-defendant for contribution or indemnity, for which see 8.6.8 (r. 20.8(2)).

8.6.3 Procedure for filing a Part 20 claim when permission is required

A party may apply to make a Part 20 claim without notice unless the court directs otherwise (CPR, r. 20.7(5)). The application notice should be filed together with a copy of the proposed claim (PD 20, para. 1.2), and the evidence in support should set out (PD 20, para. 2.1):

CHAPTER 8 ADDITIONAL CLAIMS AND FURTHER STEPS IN THE CLAIM

(a) the stage which the action has reached;
(b) the nature of the claim to be made by the Part 20 claimant, or details of the question or issue which needs to be decided;
(c) a summary of the facts on which the Part 20 is based; and
(d) the name and address of the Part 20 defendant.

Where there has been delay which has caused or contributed to the need to apply for permission an explanation of the delay should be given in evidence (PD 20, para. 2.2).

Additionally, where possible, the evidence should include a timetable of the action to date (PD 20, para. 2.3).

8.6.4 Relevant considerations in applications on a Part 20 claim

When considering whether or not to give permission for the filing of a Part 20 claim, the court clearly has the power either to grant the application, dismiss it, or, under CPR, r. 3.1(2)(e), require the claim to be dealt with separately from the claim by the claimant against the defendant. Apart from the question of whether or not it would be proper to allow the claim to be filed on its merits, or when there has been any delay, the court may also, by r. 20.9 have regard to:

(a) the connection between the Part 20 claim and the claim made by the claimant against the defendant;
(b) whether the Part 20 claimant is seeking substantially the same remedy which some other party is claiming from him;
(c) whether the Part 20 claimant wants the court to decide any question connected with the subject matter of the proceedings not only between existing parties, but between existing parties and a third party; or against an existing party in some different capacity in which he may stand, as well as in the capacity in which he is already a party.

Essentially, therefore, the establishment of some factual, legal or personal connection between the Part 20 claim and the original claim will be helpful in ensuring the success of the application.

8.6.5 Contents of a Part 20 claim

A Part 20 claim must contain particulars, or particulars must be served with the claim (CPR, r. 20.7(4)). Rule 20.7 does not apply to a defendant's claim against a co-defendant for contribution or indemnity, for which see 8.6.8 (r. 20.7(1)). The title of a Part 20 claim should contain the full name of each party, and their status in the proceedings (e.g., 'defendant', 'Part 20 claimant/defendant') (PD 20, para. 7.1; there are further examples of headings in paras 7.2 and 7.3). A helpful provision is that where the full name of a party is lengthy, it must appear in the title, but can thereafter appear in the body of the claim by an abbreviation, such as initials or a recognised shortened name (PD 20, para. 7.4; see also para. 7.5 for abbreviations where a party has more than one status in the action).

It has always been conventional practice to draft a third-party notice in the personal rather than impersonal voice thus:

> At all material times you held yourself out as being competent in the manufacture of . . .

rather than:

At all material times the Third Party held itself out to be competent in the manufacture of . . .

PD 20 clearly contemplates the continuation of this practice and allows for abbreviations in order to assist clarity. This is perhaps no momentous change, but merely reflects what has always been established practice with competent pleaders.

A Part 20 claim should be verified by a statement of truth (see 6.5; CPR, r. 22.1(1)(a); PD 20, para. 4.1). The form of statement is (PD 20, para. 4.2):

[I believe] [the Part 20 claimant believes] that the facts stated in this Part 20 claim are true.

8.6.6 Procedure and case management after filing

Though it applies to counterclaims (see 8.1.1), CPR, Part 12 (obtaining of judgment in default of a defence), does not apply to other Part 20 claims (r. 20.3(3)). Instead, the procedure where no acknowledgment of service or defence is filed to a Part 20 claim is set out in r. 20.11 (which does not apply to a defendant's claim against a co-defendant for contribution or indemnity: r. 20.11(1)(a)).

Part 14 (admissions) also does not apply (r. 20.3(3)), save for the provisions relating to the ability to admit in writing the truth of another party's case (under r. 14.1(1) and (2)), so that the other party can obtain judgment under r. 14.3.

Where the court gives permission to make a Part 20 claim it will at the same time give directions as to its service (r. 20.8(3)).

Once a Part 20 claim is served on a person, he either becomes a party if he is not one already, or if he is already a party but the Part 20 claim is served on him for the purpose of requiring the court to decide a question against him in a further capacity, he also becomes a party in such further capacity (r. 20.10).

If a Part 20 claim form is served on a person who is not already a party, r. 20.12(1) requires it to be accompanied by:

(a) a form for defending the claim;
(b) a form for admitting the claim;
(c) a form for acknowledging service;
(d) a copy of every statement of case which has already been served in the proceedings; and
(e) such other documents as the court may direct.

A copy of the Part 20 claim form must also be served on every existing party (r. 20.12(2)).

Where a defence is filed to a Part 20 claim, the court must consider the future conduct of the proceedings and give appropriate directions (r. 20.13(1)). In order to do so, the court will arrange a hearing to consider case management of the Part 20 claim, and will give notice of the hearing to each party likely to be affected by any order made at the hearing (PD 20, paras 5.1 and 5.2). When giving directions, the court must ensure that, so far as practicable, the Part 20 and the main claims are managed together (CPR, r. 20.13(2)). A Part 20 claim which is unsuitable for hearing with the main claim may be filtered out at an earlier stage if it requires the court's permission before it can be made (see 8.6.4). However, if the leave of the court was not required, the question of the best means by which the two matters should be heard, will be decided at this stage.

At the hearing, the court may (PD 20, para. 5.3):

(a) treat the matter as a summary judgment hearing (whether on the application of the Part 20 claimant, defendant, or of its own volition);

(b) order that the Part 20 proceedings be dismissed (presumably as an outcome of (a) above);

(c) give directions as to the manner in which any matter set out in or arising from the Part 20 claim should be dealt with, and as to the part, if any, that the Part 20 defendant will take at the trial of the claim, and the extent to which he is to be bound by any judgment or decision to be made in the claim.

Any of the above orders can be made either before or after any judgment in the claim has been entered by the claimant or the defendant (PD 20, para. 5.4).

8.6.7 Default judgment in Part 20 claims

Where no acknowledgment of service or defence is filed in respect of a Part 20 claim, the procedure is governed by CPR, r. 20.11. The provisions for judgment in default under Part 12 are not applicable, because a default judgment in a 'third-party' Part 20 claim may depend on the success or otherwise of the principal claim against the Part 20 claimant.

A failure to file acknowledgment of service or defence will be deemed to be an admission of the Part 20 claim, and, to the extent that it is relevant, the Part 20 defendant will be bound by any judgment or decision in the main proceedings (r. 20.11(2)(a)). This is similar to the old third-party procedure. The consequences of default are set out in the notes for defendant which will be sent with the Part 20 claim.

If a default judgment under Part 12 is given against a defendant who has himself made a Part 20 claim, then, if no acknowledgment of service or defence has been filed by the Part 20 defendant, the Part 20 claimant may, in turn, obtain judgment in respect of the Part 20 claim, by filing a request in the relevant practice form (r. 20.11(2)(b)). This may be done without the court's permission, provided that the defendant has satisfied the default judgment against himself, and does not wish to obtain judgment against the Part 20 defendant for any other remedy than a contribution or indemnity (r. 20.11(3)). However, if he has not satisfied the judgment against himself, or if he wishes to obtain judgment for some other remedy than a contribution or indemnity, the permission of the court has to be obtained, on an application which can be made without notice, unless the court otherwise directs (r. 20.11(4)). Such a judgment can be set aside or varied by the court at any time (r. 20.11(5)). The rule requiring prior payment (unless the court's permission is obtained) is presumably to ensure that a defendant does not profit by a default judgment against him, by keeping the proceeds of a default judgment against the third party, and failing to pass it on to the claimant. Rule 20.11(3)(b) does not appear to preclude the obtaining of a default judgment against a Part 20 defendant where a claim has been made against him for a remedy in addition to that of a contribution or indemnity, provided that it is not intended to pursue that part of the claim — the rule uses the words 'he wishes to obtain judgment for any remedy' rather than 'the claim is for any remedy'.

8.6.8 Defendant's claim against a co-defendant for contribution or indemnity

Rule 20.6 of the CPR allows a defendant who has filed an acknowledgment of service or a defence to make a Part 20 claim against a co-defendant for contribution or indemnity by:

(a) filing a notice containing a statement of the nature and grounds of the claim; and

(b) serving that notice on the co-defendant against whom the claim is to be made.

The permission of the court is not required, even if the claim is made after filing a defence (r. 20.7(1)).

Rules 20.7 to 20.12 are either irrelevant to or are expressed not to apply to a defendant's claim against a co-defendant for contribution or indemnity. There is apparently no provision for any form of judgment in default of defence. The co-defendant against whom the claim is made will presumably remain a party to the main action (unless he fails to file a defence to that action, in which event judgment in default will presumably be obtained in the main action), and thus all issues will be heard together.

8.7 OBTAINING FURTHER INFORMATION

8.7.1 Principle

The distinction between the old 'request for further and better particulars' and 'interrogatories' now appears to have been abolished, and CPR, Part 18 (further information), contains a new procedure. Formerly the distinction between the two was that the request for F & BP was part of the pleadings process, and was (at least technically) limited to matters which should have been disclosed in the first place, so that a proper answer to the pleading could be made. Although the process had no application to the discovery of evidence, being limited merely to material particulars, the tactical potential of the medium to cause embarrassment to the other side and reveal weaknesses in their case was such that the line was frequently overstepped. Interrogatories, on the other hand, were technically part of the discovery process and were answered on affidavit. Occasionally a creature of fashion, and, when well drafted, a devastating means of exposing shortcomings in the other side's argument, they nevertheless were not used in the vast majority of cases.

8.7.2 Making the request

The new procedure for obtaining further information is much simplified. Essentially, a party should not make an application to the court for an order under CPR, Part 18, without serving a written request on the party from whom the information or clarification is sought, giving a reasonable time to respond, but setting a date by which the response should be served (PD 18, para. 1.1). That request should be made, as far as possible, in a single comprehensive document, and not piecemeal (para. 1.3), and should be concise, and strictly confined to matters which are reasonably necessary and proportionate to enable the party requesting the information to prepare his own case or to understand the case he has to meet (para. 1.2). The requirement of proportionality is of course to ensure compliance with the overriding objective in Part 1, and provides the recipient with a new ground for refusing to give further information (although, it is suggested, not clarification) even though the request might otherwise be legitimate.

8.7.3 Form and contents of the request

There is no requirement that the request should be in a particular form. If the text is brief, and the reply likely to be so as well, it may be made by letter (PD 18, para. 1.4). However, the requirement that such a letter should expressly state that it contains a request made under CPR, Part 18, and in particular that it should deal with no matters other than the request (PD 18, para. 1.5), and is required to contain the same formalities as a request made in a separate document (para. 1.6), tends perhaps to blur the distinction between the two formats to the extent that there seems little advantage in making the request other than by way of a formal separate document.

Whether made by letter or in a separate document, the request must (PD 18, para. 1.6(1)):

(a) be headed with the name of the court and the title and number of the claim;
(b) state in its heading that it is a request made under Part 18;
(c) identify the party making the request and the party to whom the request is made (referred to in the practice direction as the 'first party' and the 'second party');
(d) set out in a separate numbered paragraph, each request for information or clarification;
(e) identify any document referred to in the request, and (if relevant) the paragraph or words to which the request relates;
(f) state the date by which the response is expected.

Thus there is now no distinction between the manner in which what were formerly either requests for further and better particulars, or interrogatories, are made or responded to.

A further advantage of making the request by way of separate document rather than by letter is that, if convenient, it may be prepared with the number paragraphs set out on the left-hand half of each sheet, leaving room for the response to appear on the same document on the right. Thus the entire request and response would appear on the same document. If the request is prepared in this manner, an extra copy should be served for the use of the recipient (PD 18, para. 1.6(2)). It may well be, however, that, save in straightforward cases, limitations of space, and word-processing difficulties may make it easier for the 'second party' to adopt the alternative response procedure, where the text of the request is repeated, followed by the response (PD 18, para. 2.3(1)(c)) (as was formerly the case when responding to a request for further and better particulars).

The request need not, of course, contain a statement of truth, although the response must be so verified (see 6.5; CPR, r. 22.1(1)(a); PD 18, para. 3).

8.7.4 Applications to the court when there is no or insufficient response

If a party makes no response to a request (in whole or in part) or it is considered that such response as is made is inadequate, an application can be made to the court in the manner laid down in CPR, Part 23 (see chapter 9). The application notice should set out, or have attached to it, the text of the order sought, and in particular should specify the matter or matters in respect of which the clarification or information is sought (PD 18, para. 5.2). In practice, it would presumably be helpful to set out or attach the request (or that part of it that is said still to be unanswered) in the format in which it was originally sent to the 'second party'. If no request had originally been sent to the 'second party', an explanation for this should be set out in the application notice (PD 18, para. 5.3(1)), as should any response made by the 'second party' to any request that had been made (PD 18, para. 5.3).

If a request had been served, and no response received, the party making the application need not serve the application notice on the second party, and the court may deal with the application without a hearing, provided that at least 14 days have passed since the request was served, and the time stated in it for a response has expired (PD 18, para. 5.5). In all other cases, the application notice must be served on the second party and on all other parties to the claim (PD 18, para. 5.6).

Both parties to the application (or just the first party if an application notice is not served) should consider whether evidence in support of or in opposition to the application is required (PD 18, para. 5.4).

8.7.5 Response ordered by the court

Subject to any rule of law to the contrary (CPR, r. 18.1(2)), the court may at any time order a party to clarify any matter which is in dispute in the proceedings (r. 18.1(1)(a)), or give additional information in relation to any such matter (r. 18.1(1)(b)). The 'clarification' appears to correspond to what were formerly further and better particulars, the 'additional information' to interrogatories.

Where an order is made, the party required to provide the clarification or information must file his response and serve it on the other parties within the time specified (r. 18.1(3)). The order itself must be served on all parties to the claim (PD 18, para. 5.7), regardless of whether or not notice of the application was originally given. The order may also make a summary assessment of costs (PD 18, para. 5.8).

8.7.6 Form and contents of the response

The response must be in writing and must be dated and signed by the second party or his legal representative (PD 18, para. 2.1). It must be verified by a statement of truth (see 6.5; CPR, r. 22.1(1)(a); PD 18, para. 3). Where the request is made by letter, the response may be in like form, or in a formal reply (PD 18, para. 2.2(1)), but if the response is made in a letter it should identify itself as a response, and deal with no matters other than the response (PD 18, para. 2.2(2)). To this extent the format of the letter will be similar to that containing the original request.

If the original request was prepared in the form set out in PD 18, para. 1.6(2) (so that the response could be made on the same form as the

CHAPTER 8 ADDITIONAL CLAIMS AND FURTHER STEPS IN THE CLAIM

request), the second party may choose whether to use it, or to reply in a separate document. If he uses the original form, no additional formalities are required (save for the date, signature and verification). However, if the response is made in a formal document, it must (PD 18, para. 2.3(1)):

(a) be headed with the name of the court and the title and number of the claim;
(b) in its heading, identify itself as a response to the request;
(c) repeat the text of each separate paragraph of the request and set out under each paragraph the response to it;
(d) refer to and have attached to it, a copy of any document not already in the possession of the first party, which forms part of the response.

A second or supplementary response must identify itself as such in its heading (PD 18, para. 2.3(2)).

It seems clear from the practice direction, that where the original request is made in a formal document, the response should not be by way of letter.

The response must be served on all parties (in addition to the first party), and a copy should be filed with the court together with a copy of the request (PD 18, para. 2.4).

8.7.7 Objections to responding

The second party appears to be allowed four principal grounds on which to object to part or all of a request:

(a) that it is a request for information or clarification that is unnecessary, irrelevant or improper;
(b) that he is unable to provide the information or clarification requested;
(c) that insufficient time has been given to him to formulate a reply;
(d) that the request can only be complied with at an expense which is disproportionate to the claim.

In the event of an objection being taken on the basis of one or more of (a) to (c) above, the second party must inform the first party promptly, and in any event within the time stipulated in the request (PD 18, para. 4.1(a)). Such information may be by letter, or by way of a formal response in a separate document, but in either event must be accompanied by reasons for the objection, and, where relevant, a date by which he expects to be able to comply with the request (PD 18, para. 4.1(b)). Presumably, there is no reason why such objection(s) could not be taken in the course of a response that does answer other requests, although this is not specifically dealt with in the practice direction.

Where the objection is one of disproportionate expense, it seems that it will not be sufficient for the second party to adopt the above course. Instead, he must serve a reply, and explain in it briefly why he has taken the view (PD 18, para. 4.1(b)).

Once the second party has indicated his objection(s) in the appropriate format, there is no need for him to make any application to the court of the request (PD 18, para. 4.2(1)). Upon receipt of the response or objection, it will be for the first party to decide whether or not to make an application to the court for an order that the information be provided.

8.7.8 Restrictions on the use of further information

Whether or not further information is given voluntarily or following an order of the court, the court may direct that such information must not be used for any purpose except for that of the proceedings in which it is given (CPR, r. 18.2).

8.8 AMENDMENTS TO STATEMENTS OF CASE

The CPR continue to provide for a system whereby a party can amend his statement of case, although there are now additional restrictions on the degree and extent to which this can be done.

8.8.1 When permission is not required

A party may amend his statement of case at any time before it has been served on any other party (r. 17.1(1)), and in such an event, the permission of the court is not required. However, such an amendment can subsequently be disallowed by the court (r. 17.2(1)) on the application, within 14 days of service of the amendment, by the party on whom it is served (r. 17.2(2)). The rules do not presently state any specific matters that the court will take into consideration when deciding whether or not to grant such an application, but it is almost certain that the overriding objective and general principles of case management will be applied.

If a statement of case has been served, an amendment can be made without permission of the court, provided the written consent of all the other parties has been obtained (r. 17.1(2)(a)). Note that it will not be sufficient under this rule, simply to obtain the consent of the party to whom the statement of case has been directed.

Where an amended statement of case is filed without need for the permission of the court, it should be endorsed in the following manner (PD 17, para. 2.1(2)):

> Amended [particulars of claim/defence (or as may be)] under CPR, [rule 17.1(1) or 17.1(2)(a)] dated . . .

For the format of an amended statement of case, see 8.8.3.

8.8.2 Where permission is required

Where a statement of case has been served, and the written consent of all the other parties has not been obtained, or is not forthcoming, a party may apply to the court for permission to make an amendment (CPR, r. 17.1(2)(b)). The applicant should file with the court the application notice and a copy of the statement of case with the proposed amendments (PD 17, para. 1.2). Interestingly, although by PD 17, para. 2.2, the statement of case in its amended form need not show the original text (see 8.8.3), it is hard to see how the court will be assisted in making a decision on an application to amend, if the original text is not shown in the copy to be filed with the application.

The application may be dealt with at a hearing, or, where all parties consent, without a hearing (i.e., on written submissions) (PD 17, para. 1.1). If permission to amend is given, the court may (not must) give directions as to amendments to be made to any other statement of case,

CHAPTER 8   ADDITIONAL CLAIMS AND FURTHER STEPS IN THE CLAIM

and service of any amendments (CPR, r. 17.3(1)). Thus provision can (and it is suggested normally will) be made by the court for the service of any amendments that will have to be made by other parties consequent upon the service of the amended statement of case on them. In any event, the amended statement of case should be filed by the applicant within 14 days of the date of the order, unless the court directs otherwise (PD 17, para. 1.3). A copy of the amended statement of case and the order should be served on every party to the proceedings unless the court directs otherwise (PD 17, para. 1.5). The court's power to give permission is subject to the rules on change of parties, both before and after the end of a relevant limitation period, set out in CPR, rr. 19.1 and 19.4, and to r. 17.4 dealing with amendments after the expiry of a relevant limitation period (r. 17.3(2)).

Where an amended statement of case is filed with the permission of the court, it should be endorsed in the following manner (PD 17, para. 2.1(1)):

Amended [particulars of claim/defence (or as may be)] by order of [Master . . . /District Judge . . . or as may be] dated . . .

8.8.3   Format of an amended statement of case

The amended form of the statement of case need not show the original text, unless the court thinks that it is desirable for it to do so, in which event it may direct that the amendments should be shown either by coloured amendments (either manuscript or computer-generated) or by use of a numerical code in a monochrome computer-generated document (PD 17, para. 2.2). (Many word processing packages include the facility to print an amended text automatically showing corrections and deletions.) Where colour is used, the deleted text should be struck through in colour, and any replacement text should be inserted or underlined in the same colour (PD 17, para. 2.3). The order for successive amendments is, as has always been the case: red for the first amendment, green for the second, violet for the third, and yellow for the fourth (PD 17, para. 2.4).

If the substance of the statement of case is changed by reason of the amendment, the statement of case should be re-verified by a statement of truth (PD 17, para. 1.4).

Presumably the court will normally direct whether the original text should be shown together with the amendment at the time that it gives the permission for the amendment to be made. However, if no such permission is required, such a direction would have to be given after service. The principal purpose of displaying the original text has always been to enable the parties and the court to see the degree and extent to which a party has departed from its original stated case. Obviously, if the amendment is comparatively minor, and has been undertaken under CPR, r. 17.1(1), the case for showing the original text is far less persuasive. In cases where it is wished to amend a statement of case after it has been served, there seems no reason why, as a precondition of giving written consent, the other party should not require the amendment to display the original text as well, failing which the 'amending party' will have to apply to the court, which may well be persuaded by the opposing party to order that the original text be shown.

8.8.4 Amendments after a relevant limitation period has expired

Provision is made in CPR, r. 17.4, for the problem which can arise when a party wishes to amend his statement of case after a period of limitation has expired. The rule is expressed to apply where a party applies to amend his statement of case under Part 17, and a period of limitation has expired under the Limitation Act 1980, the Foreign Limitation Periods Act 1984 or other statutory provision (CPR, r. 17.4(1)). The rule appears to remain silent on a situation in which no application is made because a party is entitled to amend without permission. Clearly, if the statement of case has been served, it is unlikely that the other party will give written permission under r. 17.1(2)(a), and an application would have to be made to the court. But if proceedings had been filed immediately before the expiry of the limitation period, but had not been served, and it was wished to amend them before service, no application would ordinarily be made to the court. Of course, the court may disallow the amendment on an application under r. 17.2, but it is suggested that r. 17.4 implies that such an amendment should only be made upon application to the court.

If the effect of a proposed amendment will be to add or substitute a new claim, after a limitation period has expired, the court may allow it, but only if the new claim arises out of the same, or substantially the same facts as a claim in respect of which the party wishing to amend has already claimed a remedy in the proceedings (r. 17.4(2)).

A proposed amendment to correct a mistake in the name of a party, once a limitation period has expired, may be allowed, but only where the mistake was genuine, and not one which would cause reasonable doubt as to the identity of the party in question (r. 17.4(3)). Thus is seems that the correction of a 'slip', where there was never any mistake as to the identity, but merely the name, of the party in question, will be allowed, but not an amendment where the original name caused ambiguity as to the identity of a party, which the amendment hoped to correct.

An amendment may be allowed after the expiry of a relevant limitation period to alter the capacity in which a party claims, if that capacity was one which that party had when the proceedings started, or has since acquired (r. 17.4(4)).

For the rules relating to addition and substitution of parties after the end of a relevant limitation period, and generally, see CPR, Part 19, and 5.6.

CHAPTER 9   APPLICATIONS AND INTERIM ORDERS

CONTENTS

9.1	Introduction	120
9.2	To which court should an application be made?	121
9.3	Stage when interim remedies should be sought or considered	121
9.3.1	Pre-action interim remedies	122
9.3.2	Obligation to apply early	123
9.4	Applications without notice	123
9.5	Applications with notice	124
9.5.1	Documentation	124
9.5.2	Service	125
9.5.3	Consent orders	125
9.5.4	Disposal without a hearing	126
9.5.5	Summary determination of interim costs	126
9.5.6	Hearings by telephone	127
9.5.7	Court hearing	127
9.5.8	Non-attendance	128
9.6	Orders made on the court's own initiative	128
9.7	Evidence in support	128
9.7.1	Form of witness statements	130
9.7.2	Form of affidavit evidence	130
9.8	Drawing up interim orders	134
9.9	General powers regarding interim relief and orders	135
9.10	Pre-action inspection and inspection against non-parties	136
9.11	Interim payments	136
9.11.1	Time for applying	137
9.11.2	Procedure	137
9.11.3	Grounds	137
9.11.4	Additional condition in personal injuries cases	138
9.11.5	Standard of proof	138
9.11.6	Multiple defendants	138
9.11.7	Amount to be ordered	139
9.11.8	Non-disclosure	139
9.11.9	Adjustment	139
9.12	Striking out	140
9.13	Summary judgment	141
9.13.1	Time at which the application may be made	141
9.13.2	Excluded proceedings	142
9.13.3	Effect in application is made before filing the defence	142
9.13.4	Procedure	142
9.13.5	Specific performance, rescission and forfeiture in property cases	143
9.13.6	Principles	143
9.13.7	Orders available	144
9.13.8	Directions on summary judgment hearing	144

CHAPTER 9 APPLICATIONS AND INTERIM ORDERS

9.1 INTRODUCTION

The first part of this chapter (9.2 to 9.8) deals with the new system for making interim (the new word for interlocutory) orders, including the new rules on how to make interim applications and the form of evidence required to support such applications. It also considers orders made and hearings convened by the court of its own initiative. The second part of the chapter considers how the new rules deal with some specific types of interim application, namely:

(a) pre-action inspection and inspection against non-parties (see 9.10);
(b) interim payments (see 9.11);
(c) striking out (see 9.12); and
(d) summary judgment (see 9.13).

Chapter 10 deals with interim injunctions and also 'freezing injunctions' (*Marevas*) and 'search orders' (*Anton Piller* orders). Applications for disclosure orders, such as specific dislosure and pre-action dislosure, are dealt with in chapter 15 on disclosure (the new word for discovery). Various other types of application are considered elsewhere, such as applications for 'alternative service' (formerly substituted service) and setting aside default judgments in chapter 5, and applications to amend and for 'further information' (a combination of interrogatories and requests for further and better particulars), in chapter 8.

Under the new system there should be a reduced need for making interim applications because of the increased involvement of the judiciary in case management. One of the criticisms made about the way litigation has been conducted in recent times is that too many unnecessary interlocutory applications are made, and it is also said that many interlocutory applications result in significant overall delays and increased costs. Under the CPR, part of the obligation placed on the courts in furthering the overriding objective is to consider whether the likely benefits of taking a particular step will justify the cost of taking it (r. 1.4(2)(h)). The court is also required to deal with as many aspects of the case as is practicable on the same occasion (r. 1.4(2)(i)).

As will be seen in chapters 11, 13 and 14, in fast track and multi-track cases the procedural judge will scrutinise defended actions shortly after defences are filed, and there will be further judicial consideration of the case at the listing for trial stage. A party seeking a particular order can ask the court to consider it during the scrutiny process.

Whenever the parties are notified that an interim hearing, such as a case management conference or listing hearing, has been fixed, they must consider and make any application which it may be appropriate for the court to deal with at the hearing (PD 23, para. 2.8; PD 28, para. 2.5 (fast track cases); PD 29, para. 3.5 (multi-track cases)).

Consequently, most interim orders ought to be made as part of the regular case management system. Further, there is a general obligation to make all interim applications as soon as it becomes apparent they are necessary or desirable (PD 23, para. 2.7).

There are several interesting innovations in the new rules. These include the court making orders on its own initiative, and holding hearings by telephone or other direct means of communication. Another development is that the ordinary rule under the new system is that interim hearings will be in public, although there are a significant number of exceptions.

A distinction needs to be drawn between applications for directions and applications for what are now called 'interim remedies'. A somewhat more formal approach is taken with applications for interim remedies, which should in almost all cases be supported by written evidence (see r. 25.3(2)). The distinction is between:

(a) case management matters, such as standard disclosure of documents, exchange of factual and expert evidence, and trial directions, and
(b) applications for specific remedies, such as specific disclosure (this is the new term for specific discovery, now dealt with by r. 31.12), interim injunctions, interim payments and striking out.

9.2 TO WHICH COURT SHOULD AN APPLICATION BE MADE?

In general an application in relation to a claim must be made to the court where the claim is presently being dealt with. This will be the court where the proceedings were commenced (CPR, r. 23.2(1)), unless:

(a) the claim has been transferred (r. 23.2(2));
(b) the claim has been listed for trial at another court, in which event the application should be made to the trial court (r. 23.2(3)); or
(c) the application is made after judgment, in which event the application may need to be made to the court dealing with enforcement (r. 23.2(5)).

An application for a pre-action remedy (such as for an injunction, freezing order or search order), should be made to the court where the substantive proceedings are likely to be brought, unless there is a good reason for applying to another court (r. 23.2(4)).

Rule 2.7 gives the court a general power to deal with a case at any place that it considers appropriate. This power may be used in courts with shared listing arrangements, or where a court with congested lists arranges to release some cases to another court to reduce listing delays.

Unless otherwise provided for by an act, rule or practice direction, interim applications can be dealt with by judges, masters and district judges (r. 2.4). The most significant exceptions are freezing orders and search orders, which are dealt with by High Court judges, and ordinary interim injunctions, which are generally dealt with by a judge who would have jurisdiction to try the action (see PD 25 Interim Injunctions, para. 1). As was the case under the old rules, masters and district judges will be able to grant interim injunctions by consent, in connection with charging orders and receivers and in aid of execution. Apart from injunctions, most applications will continue to be dealt with by masters and district judges, but they may refer particular applications up to be dealt with by a judge (PD 23, para. 1).

9.3 STAGE WHEN INTERIM REMEDIES SHOULD BE SOUGHT OR CONSIDERED

The basic rules are that interim applications should be made as early as possible (PD 23, para. 2.7), but after the party making the application has

CHAPTER 9   APPLICATIONS AND INTERIM ORDERS

come on to the court record. For claimants this means after proceedings are issued, and for defendants it means after they have acknowledged service or filed their defence (CPR, r. 25.2(2)).

9.3.1   Pre-action interim remedies

A claimant may exceptionally make an application for an interim order before the commencement of proceedings (see CPR, r. 25.2(2)(b)) if either:

(a) the matter is urgent; or
(b) it is otherwise desirable to grant the interim remedy before the claim is brought, in the interests of justice.

The courts may thus entertain pre-commencement applications for urgent interlocutory injunctions (such as in some libel cases where publication is threatened within hours of the applicant finding out about the matter) and some applications for freezing injunctions and search orders.

If a pre-action interim remedy is granted, the court may give directions requiring a claim to be commenced (r. 25.2(3)). Early drafts of this provision used the word 'must' rather than 'may', but made exceptions for pre-action disclosure and inspection under the Supreme Court Act 1981, s. 33, and the County Courts Act 1984, s. 52. The final version of r. 25.2(4) preserves a distinction between s. 33 and s. 52 orders and other types of pre-action orders. The reason for the distinction is that pre-action disclosure or inspection orders may result in the claimant deciding not to bring substantive proceedings at all, as recognised in *Dunning* v *United Liverpool Hospitals' Board of Governors* [1973] 1 WLR 586, and it would not make sense to require the claimant to bring a substantive claim in such circumstances. The same can be said for *Norwich Pharmacal* orders (which although similar to the pre-action applications are not the same, see below), which may not result in the true wrongdoer being identified. Otherwise it is to be expected that normally directions for bringing substantive proceedings will be made in other types of pre-action order.

Superficially similar to pre-action applications are applications for leave to bring certain proceedings under the Mental Health Act 1983, s. 139, and *Norwich Pharmacal* applications. The Mental Health Act 1983, s. 139, provides that no civil proceedings shall be brought against any person in any court in respect of any act purporting to have been done under the 1983 Act without the leave of the High Court. *Norwich Pharmacal* orders may, as in *Norwich Pharmacal Co.* v *Commissioners of Customs and Excise* [1974] AC 133, be sought against innocent facilitators who have been, as described by Lord Reid, 'mixed up' in some civil wrongdoing, requiring them to identitify the wrongdoers. The CPR do not specifically make provision for *Norwich Pharmacal* orders (neither did the RSC or CCR), which are made under the court's inherent jurisdiction. However, r. 25.1(3) of the CPR provides that the fact that a particular kind of interim remedy is not specifically listed does not affect any power that the court may have to grant that remedy. Although these two types of application are similar to true pre-action orders, they have the significant difference that the court's jurisdiction is invoked by issuing a self-contained originating process limited to preparing for later separate, substantive proceedings, whereas other pre-action applications are a part of a main action, and are not intended to have any separate existence. These two types of application should ordinarily be brought using the Part 8 procedure.

CHAPTER 9   APPLICATIONS AND INTERIM ORDERS

9.3.2   Obligation to apply early

This stems from the overriding objective, which includes ensuring cases are dealt with expeditiously (CPR, r. 1.1(2)(d)).

Parties should normally notify the court of any intention to apply for interim remedies when they file their allocation questionnaires (see PD 26, para. 2.2).

In multi-track cases the appropriate time to consider most forms of interim relief, if possible, is the first case management conference. A party that wishes to invite the court to make directions or orders of types not usually dealt with on case management conferences and which are likely to be opposed, is required by PD 29, para. 5.8, to issue and serve an application returnable at the same time as that set for the case management conference (with a time estimate if it is clear the time originally allowed for the case management conference will be insufficient, so a fresh date can be fixed). Paragraph 3.8 expressly says that applications in multi-track cases must be made as early as possible so as to minimise the need to change the directions timetable, and an application to vary a directions timetable laid down by the court (perhaps on its own initiative) must ordinarily be made within 14 days of service of the directions (para. 6.2).

There are some express restrictions in the CPR about when some types of application can be made. Examples include summary judgment, which can be applied for only after the defendant has acknowledged service or entered a defence, and interim payments, where a similar restriction applies (rr. 24.4(1) and 25.6(1)). Nevertheless, summary judgment (and striking-out) applications should normally be made on or before filing of allocation questionnaires (see PD 26, para. 5.3(1)).

Of course the need for an interim remedy may not become apparent until some later stage. Rule 25.2(1)(b) of the CPR of the CPR provides that applications can be made even after final judgment has been given. Where it becomes necessary to make an application shortly before trial, it should be dealt with on the pre-trial review if there will be one (under the new system there is a pre-trial review about eight to 10 weeks before the trial in some multi-track cases, see 14.7). If this is not possible, another option is to make the application at the start of the trial itself.

9.4   APPLICATIONS WITHOUT NOTICE

Applications without notice are what used to be called *ex parte* applications. The general rule, as hitherto, is that all applications must be made on notice to the other parties (CPR, r. 23.4(1)). Exceptions to this rule are only allowed where permitted by a provision in the CPR, a practice direction, or a court order (CPR, r. 23.4(2)). For example, applications to extend the time for serving a claim form (renewal of process) are permitted without notice (r. 7.6(4)), as are applications for leave to issue Part 20 claims (third-party notices etc.) after filing of the defence (r. 20.7(5)). These are both examples of applications where the opposite party will not be on the court record when the application is made. Other situations where applications may be made without giving notice to the other parties are:

(a)   Where the application arises in urgent circumstances, so there is no practical possibility of giving the required minimum of three clear days'

CHAPTER 9 APPLICATIONS AND INTERIM ORDERS

notice to the other side. In cases of this sort, informal notification should be given to the other parties unless the circumstances require secrecy (PD 23, para. 4.2).

(b) Where a party decides to make an application at a hearing that has already been fixed, but there is insufficient time to serve an application notice. In cases of this sort the applicant should inform the other parties and the court (preferably in writing) as soon as possible of the nature of the application, the reason for it, and then make the application orally at the hearing (PD 23, para. 2.10).

(c) Where the application depends on secrecy for its efficacy, such as most applications for freezing injunctions and search orders.

Like applications on notice, applications without notice should normally be made by filing an application notice (CPR, r. 23.3(1)) in form N244, which must state the order being sought and the reasons for seeking the order (r. 23.6). The application notice must also be signed, and include the title of the claim, its reference number and the full name of the applicant. If the applicant is not already a party, the notice should also give the applicant's address for service. If the applicant wants a hearing, that too must be stated (PD 23, para. 2.1). The application should normally be supported by evidence, which should set out the evidence in support of the relief sought, and must state the reasons why notice was not given (CPR, r. 25.3(3)).

By virtue of r. 39.2, which applies to all types of hearings, including interim hearings and trials, applications without notice will in general be heard in public. However, it is reasonably likely that one of the exceptions may apply, such as publicity defeating the object of the application (such as in applications for freezing injunctions and search orders), or the application being made without notice and it being unjust to the respondent for there to be a public hearing (r. 39.2(3)(a) and (e)).

Where an application is made without notice to the respondent, r. 23.9(2) provides that the order made on the application must be served on the respondent together (unless the court orders otherwise) with the application notice and any evidence in support. The order must, by virtue of r. 23.9(3), contain a statement to the effect that the respondent has a right to apply to set aside or vary the order within seven clear days of it being served. Applications to set aside or vary are normally made back to the judge who made the original order.

9.5 APPLICATIONS WITH NOTICE

9.5.1 Documentation

The general rule is that applications must be made on notice (see CPR, r. 23.4(1)), and should normally be made by filing an application notice stating the order being sought and the reasons for seeking it (r. 23.3(1) and r. 23.6). The application notice must be signed, and include the title of the claim, its reference number and the full name of the applicant. If the applicant is not already a party, the notice should also give the applicant's address for service. If the applicant wants a hearing, that too must be stated (PD 23, para. 2.1). The application should normally be supported by written evidence setting out the facts justifying the relief sought (r. 25.3(2)). The notice must be filed at court, and served as soon as

CHAPTER 9   APPLICATIONS AND INTERIM ORDERS

possible thereafter (r. 23.7(1)). The standard form of application notice is form N244 (see appendix 3).

On receipt of the application notice the court may either notify the parties of the time and date of the hearing, or may notify them that it proposes to consider the application without a hearing (PD 23, para. 2.3).

9.5.2   Service

Unless the applicant notifies the court to the contrary, the normal rule is that the court will serve the application notice and documents in support by first-class post (CPR, rr. 6.3 and 23.7(3); PD 6, para. 8.1). Alternatively, the applicant may notify the court that he wishes to effect service himself. When the court is to effect service, the applicant must file with the court copies of the evidence in support for service on the respondents and a copy of any draft order prepared on behalf of the applicant. There is no requirement to refile or reserve documents which have already been filed or served at an earlier stage (r. 23.7(5)).

Service must be effected as soon as possible after the application is issued, and in any event not less than three clear days before it is to be heard (r. 23.7(1)). Under the general rules on computing time in r. 2.8, the three clear days exclude the date of effective service and the date of the hearing, and, because the period is less than five days, also exclude weekends, bank holidays, Christmas Day and Good Friday.

Take for example a hearing which is listed for Wednesday 19 May 1999. Assume the solicitor for the applicant decides to serve the application and evidence in support by document exchange. The three clear days before the hearing are Friday 14, Monday 17 and Tuesday 18 May 1999. The documents must arrive on Thursday 13 May, and, given the provision in r. 6.7 that documents transmitted by document exchange are deemed to be served on the second day after being left at the exchange, the latest the documents could be left at the exchange would be Tuesday 11 May 1999.

9.5.3   Consent orders

Consent orders are divided into those which can be entered on a purely administrative basis, without seeking the approval of a judicial officer, and those that need approval. The court may deal with an application without a hearing if the parties agree on the terms of the order sought (CPR, r. 23.8(a)).

9.5.3.1   Administrative consent orders   Administrative entry of consent orders is only permitted where none of the parties is a litigant in person (CPR, r. 40.6(2)(b)). By r. 40.6(3) only the following types of orders may be entered by this process:

(a)   judgments and orders for the payment of money;
(b)   judgments and orders for the delivery up of goods with or without the option of paying the value of the goods or an agreed value;
(c)   orders for the dismissal of the whole or part of proceedings;
(d)   Tomlin orders (for the stay of proceedings on agreed terms, which are usually set out in a schedule to the order) and other stays on agreed terms disposing of the proceedings;
(e)   orders for the stay of enforcement of a judgment, either unconditionally or on condition that the money due under the judgment be paid by specified instalments;

CHAPTER 9   APPLICATIONS AND INTERIM ORDERS

(f) orders setting aside unsatisfied default judgments;
(g) orders for the payment out of money paid into court;
(h) orders for the discharge from liability of any party; and
(i) orders for the payment, assessment or waiver of costs.

9.5.3.2 *Approved consent orders*   Where proposed orders or directions are agreed between the parties, and either one or more of them is a litigant in person, or any of the orders or directions fall outside the list set out at 9.5.3.1, the proposed order has to be submitted to the court for scrutiny. The procedural judge has a discretion to allow or refuse agreed orders and directions. The court will be particularly concerned to ensure that orders and directions that may have been agreed between the parties are consistent with the overriding objective and with the case management structure for the case. The parties may agree terms for interim orders at or shortly before a hearing, and submit them to the court for approval. As hitherto the court will usually expect the agreed terms to be reduced into writing before being submitted to the court, which is often done in a fairly informal manner. If there is time it may be possible to draw up a formal Tomlin order or other suitable order for approval by the court.

9.5.3.3 *Costs*   Where the parties agree to an order by consent in an interim application, they should also agree a figure for costs to be inserted in the consent order, or agree that there should be no order for costs (PD 44, para. 4.4(3)). If they cannot agree on the figure for costs, they will need to attend on the appointment. If this happens, no costs will be allowed for the attendance unless good reason can be shown for the failure to agree the figure for the costs.

9.5.3.4 *Drawing up consent orders*   A consent order must be drawn up in the terms that have been agreed, must be expressed to be 'by consent', and must be signed by the legal representatives of all parties (or, if approved by the court, any litigant in person) affected by the order (CPR, r. 40.6(7)). Letters sent to the court by the parties signifying their consent to a draft order are sufficient (PD 23, para. 10.2). The order is then filed with the court, which will arrange for it to be sealed, entered in the court records, and sent out to the parties.

9.5.4   Disposal without a hearing

Rule 23.8 of the CPR provides that the court may deal with an interim application without a hearing if either:

(a) the parties agree that the court should dispose of the application without a hearing (the applicant's view on whether there should be a hearing should be stated in the application notice); or
(b) the court does not consider that a hearing would be appropriate.

A party dissatisfied with any order or direction made without a hearing is able to apply to have it set aside, varied or stayed (r. 3.3(5)(a)). Such an application must be made within seven days after service of the order, and the right to make such an application must be stated in the order (r. 3.3(5)(b) and (6)).

9.5.5   Summary determination of interim costs

Where an interim application is disposed of in less than a day (which will cover the vast majority of such applications), and provided none of the parties is assisted by legal aid or is a person under a disability, the court may well make a summary assessment of the costs of the application immediately after making its order (PD 44, para. 4.4). To assist the judge in assessing costs the parties are required by PD 44, para. 4.5, to file and serve not less than 24 hours before the interim hearing signed statements of their costs for the interim hearing in costs form 1 setting out:

(a) the number of hours claimed;
(b) the hourly rate claimed;
(c) the amount and nature of disbursements;
(d) the solicitor's costs for attending or appearing at the hearing;
(e) counsel's fees; and
(f) VAT on the above.

Any failure to file or serve a statement of costs, without reasonable excuse, will be taken into account in deciding the costs order to be made on the application. The pre-CPR Practice Direction (Costs: Summary Assessment) [1999] 1 WLR 420, said that a failure to comply might be taken as indicating that the party in default would not be seeking an order for costs.

Immediate summary assessment of costs will only be appropriate where the court decides to order costs in any event. Where the interim costs are to be in the case (the new term for 'in the cause'), assessment of the costs will almost certainly be left to the conclusion of the case (PD 44, para. 4.4(2)). In cases where costs are awarded in any event, the court should make a summary assessment there and then, but may decide to give directions for a further hearing to deal with the costs (PD 44, para. 4.8). Summary assessment will be unnecessary in cases where the parties have agreed the amount of costs (PD 44, para. 4.10).

9.5.6 Hearings by telephone

Active case management in accordance with the overriding objective includes dealing with cases without the parties needing to attend court, and by making use of technology (CPR, r. 1.4(2)(j) and (k)). Both may be achieved by dealing with some applications by telephone conference calls, which is specifically provided for by r. 3.1(2)(d). The rule enables the court to hold a hearing by telephone or any other method of direct oral communication, so other means of electronic communication may be used as technology develops.

Telephone hearings will only be held if all parties consent, and if all the parties are legally represented. If the court decides to hold a telephone hearing, it will allocate a time and give suitable directions. The applicant will be responsible for ensuring all the legal representatives are put on line in order (applicant followed by respondents), then the judge, and also for ensuring that the conference is tape-recorded by the the telephone service provider. PD 23, para. 6, contains detailed provisions for setting up and paying for telephone hearings.

9.5.7 Court hearing

As discussed at 9.4 above, the general rule is that interim hearings will be in public (CPR, r.39.2). As previously mentioned, there are exceptions, including it being impracticable to accommodate the public (which would be the case regarding the rooms used by many district judges).

At the hearing the applicant should bring a draft order, unless the application is particularly simple. If the order is unusually long or complex the draft should be supplied on disk with a hard copy (PD 23, para. 12). In addition to dealing with the specific application that has been made, the court may wish to review the conduct of the case as a whole and give any necessary case management directions. The parties will therefore have to be prepared for this and be able to answer any questions the court may ask (PD 23, para. 2.9). The procedural judge will keep, either by way of a note or a tape recording, brief details of all proceedings, including a short statement of the decision taken at each hearing (PD 23, para. 8).

9.5.8 Non-attendance

The court may proceed in the absence of any party to an application (CPR, r. 23.11(1)). When this happens the court has a general discretion to relist the application, which is likely to be exercised as hitherto, taking into account matters which include the reasons for the absence, the interests of justice, any undue delay since the missed hearing, and in certain cases the merits of the absent party's case or application (see RSC, ord. 35, r. 2; CCR, ord. 37, r. 2; and cases such as *Shocked* v *Goldschmidt* [1998] 1 All ER 372).

9.6 ORDERS MADE ON THE COURT'S OWN INITIATIVE

As part of the new ethos of active case management, the courts are now encouraged to exercise their powers on their own initiative where this is appropriate, and to this end r. 3.3(1) of the CPR gives the court the power to make orders of its own initiative. This power is intended to be exercised for the purpose of managing the case and furthering the overriding objective (see r. 3.1(2)(m)). Orders made in this way must, by virtue of r. 3.3(5)(b) and (6), include a statement that parties who are affected may apply within seven days (or such other period as the court may specify) after service for the order to be set aside, varied or stayed. Failing to make an application to vary or set aside is likely to result in the court assuming the orders or directions made were correct in the circumstances then existing (PD 28, para. 4.2(2), for fast track cases; PD 29, para. 6.2(2), for multi-track cases).

There is a related power enabling the court to make orders on its own initiative after giving the parties an opportunity of making representations on the matter. Where the court proposes to make such an order it will specify a time within which the representations must be made (r. 3.3(2)).

The court has power to fix a hearing for the purpose of deciding whether to make any order it might propose to make of its own initiative. For example, in order to reduce the issues in a case it might convene a summary judgment hearing. Unless some other period is specified in the rules regarding notice, any application convened by the court must be notified to parties likely to be affected by the proposed order at least three clear days in advance (CPR, r. 3.3(3)).

9.7 EVIDENCE IN SUPPORT

The general rule is that applications for interim remedies must be supported by evidence (CPR, r. 25.3(2)). There is no need for the CPR to say anything about the need for evidence in support of specific types of

CHAPTER 9 APPLICATIONS AND INTERIM ORDERS

application, as the need for evidence follows from the general rule. As mentioned in 9.1, there is a distinction between applications for interim remedies, which are covered by the general rule, and case management directions, for which there is no need for evidence. Some judgment is required from lawyers when deciding whether they need evidence for their applications. PD 23, para. 9.1, specifically mentions that, as a practical matter, the court will often need to be satisfied by evidence of the facts that are relied on in support of or for opposing an application. Sometimes the matter will be put beyond doubt if the court gives directions for filing evidence when it fixes a hearing. Four options are available to the applicant regarding the format of the evidence to be used in support of an interim application. They are:

(a) To provide sufficiently full factual information in support of the application in the body of the application notice itself (CPR, rr. 22.1(3) and 32.6(2)(b)), and include a statement of truth in the notice. This is a signed statement that the applicant believes any facts stated in the application are true (r. 22.1(4) and (6); PD 22, para. 2.1).

(b) To rely on the facts stated in a statement of case filed in the proceedings, provided it contains a statement of truth (CPR, r. 32.6(2)(a)). This will usually have been previously served and filed, and if so there is no need to reserve or refile (r. 23.7(5)).

(c) To rely on witness statements, each with statements of truth signed by the witnesses (rr. 22.1(4) and 32.6(1)). These must be served with the application (r. 23.7(3)). The witness statements used may be ones drafted specifically for the interim application, or it may be possible to rely on the main witness statements that have been disclosed on the substantive issues in the case. The general rule is that any fact that needs to be proved at any hearing other than the trial should be proved by the evidence of witnesses in writing (r. 32.2(1)), and it is further provided by r. 32.6(1) that at hearings other than the trial evidence is to be by witness statement unless the court, a practice direction or any other enactment requires otherwise. Consequently, evidence by witness statement is expected to be the primary means of adducing evidence at interim hearings.

(d) To rely on affidavit evidence. Rule 32.15(2) allows a witness to give evidence by affidavit at any hearing other than a trial if he chooses to do so; this also allows the use of affirmations, see PD 32, para. 1.7. However, using affidavits may result in the loss of the additional costs over and above the cost of using ordinary witness statements. There are situations where affidavit evidence is required either by specific court order, or by virtue of a practice direction or other enactment. Affidavits are required, for example, in applications under the Protection from Harassment Act 1997, s. 3(5)(a); certain applications relating to confiscation and forfeiture in connection with criminal proceedings; and under the environmental control legislation. PD 32 and PD 25 Interim Injunctions require affidavit evidence in support of applications for search orders, freezing injunctions, orders to require an occupier to permit another to enter land, and applications for contempt of court. Affidavits are not to be used in applications for other types of interim injunction unless specifically ordered by the court.

Unless the form the evidence in support has to take is prescribed, a party making an interim application may choose the method of adducing evidence in support from the above options. This allows flexibility, and should assist in ensuring applications are prepared in a cost-efficient manner. Form N244 requires the applicant to indicate which type of evidence will be relied on by ticking an appropriate box. It may on occasion be appropriate to use a combination of these methods. It may be important to place the background facts of the case before the court (which could be done by use of the statement of case), and also facts relevant solely to the application in hand (which could be adduced by a specifically drawn-up witness statement or affidavit). Form N244 militates against this by allowing only one of the boxes to be ticked.

Another consideration is the degree to which the courts will give the same weight to the new forms of adducing evidence as they have previously given to affidavits used in interlocutory proceedings. It has always been the case that, unless deponents are called for cross-examination, on an interlocutory application evidence adduced by affidavit will usually be accepted as correct for the purposes of the application. Cases such as *National Westminster Bank plc v Daniel* [1993] 1 WLR 1453 established that the court would only go behind an affidavit if its contents were incredible. If courts show any greater readiness in going behind the other forms of evidence now allowed by the CPR, it may be that affidavits will continue to be used more widely than might have been hoped.

9.7.1 Form of witness statements

This is considered in detail at 16.6.

9.7.2 Form of affidavit evidence

Rule 32.16 of the CPR provides that affidavits must be in the form set out in the appropriate practice direction, which is PD 32, paras 2 to 16. Although the new prescribed form is broadly similar to that used in the past, there are some technical refinements, which will be traps for the unwary. Figure 9.1 is an example of an affidavit in the new form.

Figure 9.1 Affidavit in new form seeking to set aside a judgment in default and transfer of action

---

Sworn on behalf of the defendant
Deponent: G. Fielding
1st affidavit of deponent
Exhibits: GF 1 to GF 3
Sworn: 24.6.1999

IN THE HIGH COURT OF JUSTICE
QUEEN'S BENCH DIVISION
BETWEEN:

1999 B No. 6590

BETTER CAR PARTS LIMITED   Claimant

and

DAVID KEVIN REDFERN
(and others)   Defendants

I, GERALD FIELDING, Car Salesman, of 30 Beresford Road, London, N23 8GD, STATE ON OATH as follows:

1. I am the second defendant, and a partner in the firm of Beresford Motors, which I run in partnership with the first and

third defendants. I have full knowledge of the facts of this case and I am duly authorised to make this affidavit by each of the other defendants. I make this affidavit in support of our application to set aside a default judgment entered on 19 May 1999. In so far as the contents of this affidavit are within my personal knowledge they are true otherwise they are true to the best of my knowledge, information and belief.

2. The defendants have a trading account with the claimant, and we have been regularly purchasing goods and supplies from it for the purposes of our car repairing business. Our arrangement with the claimant was that our orders from the claimant would be individually invoiced by the claimant, which would provide us with periodic statements. We would make monthly payments to the claimant, usually within 2 weeks of receipt of the claimant's monthly statement.

3. When the claim form and particulars of claim in this action were received by the defendants at the end of April 1999 we had recently cleared our account with the claimant by making a payment of £11,256.88 in respect of the account to 28 February 1999. As at the date this claim was issued payment in respect of the March 1999 account had not become due, so nothing was owed to the claimant as at the date this claim was commenced.

4. There is now shown to me marked 'GF 1' a bundle containing relevant documentation. At pages 1 to 5 are the claimant's trading account statements with our firm for the months of January through to May 1999. Page 2 is the February 1999 statement, which it will be seen was in the sum of £11,256.88. The March 1999 account at page 3 was in the sum of £15,255.17. The amount claimed in this action is the total of these two accounts, £26,512.05. At page 6 of 'GF 1' is the partnership's bank statement for March 1999, which confirms the payment of £11,256.88 on 26 March 1999.   GF 1

5. As soon as I received the court papers in this action I raised the matter with Mrs Sarah Goodman, the finance director of the claimant. A true copy of my letter to her dated 30 April 1999 is at page 1 of the bundle of correspondence now shown to me marked 'GF 2'. Her reply, at page 2, says she will look into the matter. Nevertheless, judgment was entered on 19 May 1999.   GF 2

6. For the reasons set out above, I ask that this judgment be set aside on the merits. There is now shown to me marked 'GF 3' a draft defence which the defendants intend to file if judgment is set aside, and I confirm the truth of the contents of the draft defence.   GF 3

7. If judgment is set aside and the case allowed to continue, I respectfully ask that the action be transferred to the Edmonton County Court, the local court of the defendants.

Sworn at
on
before me,
[Name and qualification of person taking the affidavit]

This affidavit is filed on behalf of the defendants.

9.7.2.1 Corner markings At the top right-hand corner of the first page *and* the backsheet there must appear the following details:

(a) The party on whose behalf it is filed.
(b) The initials and surname of the deponent.
(c) The number of the affidavit (or affirmation) in relation to that deponent.
(d) The identifying initials and numbers of the exhibits referred to in this affidavit. If the affidavit is not the first one by this deponent, the numbering of the exhibits must run consecutively from one affidavit to the next, and not start again with each affidavit.
(e) The date it is sworn (or affirmed).

9.7.2.2 Heading An affidavit or affirmation should be headed with the name and number of the proceedings, and the court (and division) where they are proceeding. It is sufficient to identify the parties with the phrase, 'Between A.B. (and others) claimants/applicants and C.D. (and others) defendants/respondents'.

9.7.2.3 Commencement There is a new form of commencement, which should read: 'I [full name] of [address, which can still be a business address if sworn in the deponent's professional business or occupational capacity] state on oath:'. For affirmations the commencement should read: 'I [full name] of [address] do solemnly and sincerely affirm:'.

9.7.2.4 Body of affidavit An affidavit must, if practicable, be in the deponent's own words. It should be expressed in the first person. The opening paragraph (alternatively, the commencement) should give details of the deponent's occupation or description, and if relevant state the position he holds and the name of his employer, and should also state if he is a party in the proceedings, or employed by a party. It is usually convenient to follow the chronological sequence of events. Each paragraph should, so far as possible, be confined to a distinct portion of the subject (PD 32, para. 6.2). Since the Civil Evidence Act 1995 has been in force it has been no objection that some of the evidence in an affidavit might be hearsay, but where it is, the deponent should identify it as a matter based on information or belief, and give the source of that information or belief (PD 32, para. 4.2). Further, there is no need to serve hearsay notices in relation to hearings other than trials (CPR, r. 33.3(a)). All numbers, including dates, should be expressed in figures.

A rather unnecessary refinement to be found in PD 32, para. 6.1(7), is that affidavits now have to 'give in the margin the reference to any document or documents mentioned'. It is not entirely clear whether this is intended to mean the original reference of the document (if any), or, rather more probably, the exhibit mark of the document. At present this information is given in professionally drafted affidavits in the text, and it is difficult to see why a marginal note, making typesetting more complicated, should be mandatory (the practice direction uses the word 'must' for this requirement).

9.7.2.5 Exhibits For the numbering of exhibits see 9.7.2.1. In the body of the affidavit exhibits must be introduced with the words 'there is now shown to me marked "[deponent's initials and exhibit number]"' followed by a description of the exhibit. Exhibits must be kept separate from the affidavit. They should have a frontsheet having the same markings in the top right corner and heading as the affidavit. Where it contains several documents the front sheet should list them out with their dates, and/or a statement of the nature of the documents exhibited (such as so many original letters and so many copy letters). The frontsheet needs to bear the correct exhibit mark and a declaration of the person before whom the affidavit is sworn. Documents of a similar nature, such as correspondence, should be gathered together into a single exhibit, and arranged chronologically with the earliest document on top, and with each page numbered consecutively at the bottom centre. It is permissible to use copy documents in exhibits, provided the originals are available at the hearing should they be needed (PD 32, para. 13.1). Illegible pages should be followed with a typed version with an 'a' number.

Exhibits other than documents should be clearly marked with the appropriate exhibit number in such a manner that the mark cannot become detached from the exhibit. Small items may be placed in a container, with the container being appropriately marked (PD 32, para. 14).

A common mistake is to exhibit court documents. This is unnecessary as sealed copies of these documents prove themselves (CPR, r. 2.6(3), a point specifically made by PD 32, para. 13.2).

9.7.2.6 Jurat A jurat is a statement at the end of an affidavit which authenticates it. The jurat must follow on from the body of the affidavit and must not appear on a separate page. After giving the oath the affidavit has to be signed by all deponents (exceptionally an affidavit may be sworn by more than one person), and be completed by the person taking the affidavit, who must insert his or her full address, signature and printed name and qualification under the signature (PD 32, para. 5).

The person taking the affidavit has to be duly qualified (solicitors, commissioners for oaths, magistrates, certain court officials and judges, and others authorised by statute, such as barristers), and independent of the parties and their representatives (PD 32, para. 9).

In an affirmation, the word 'sworn' in the jurat is replaced by the word 'affirmed'.

9.7.2.7 Alterations Alterations need to be initialled by both the deponent and the person taking the affidavit (PD 32, para. 8.1).

9.7.2.8 Printing and binding In a departure from the previous practice, affidavits should now be typed on one side of the paper only (PD 32, para. 6.1). The pages should be numbered consecutively, and the text should be in numbered paragraphs. They must be produced on durable quality A4 paper with a 3.5 cm margin. They should, if possible, be securely bound in a manner that will not hamper filing. Otherwise, each page must be endorsed with the case number and bear the initials of the deponent and the person taking the affidavit.

Exhibits must not be stapled, but should be securely fastened in a way that does not hinder the reading of the documents they contain (PD 32, para. 15).

9.7.2.9 Filing If the court directs that an affidavit is to be filed, filing should be at the court (or division of the court) in which the case is proceeding (PD 32, para. 10.1).

9.7.2.10 Failure to comply with the practice direction If the form of an affidavit, affirmation or exhibit fails to comply with PD 32, the court may refuse to admit it as evidence and refuse to allow the costs arising out of its preparation (PD 32, para. 25.1). Permission to use a defective affidavit or affirmation may be obtained from a judge of the court. There must be severe doubts whether some of the more exacting requirements of the practice direction comply with the overriding objective of the CPR, and whether an objection raised to the form of an opponent's affidavit (such as a margin which is slightly too narrow, or putting references to exhibited documents in the text as opposed to the margin) would itself be in breach of the parties' duties to further the overriding objective.

9.7.2.11 Use of voluminous affidavits and exhibits Voluminous affidavits and exhibits are generally deprecated, and have been for some time. However, there are cases where voluminous evidence on interim applications is inevitable. In such cases the affidavits and exhibits to be used should be put into separate bundles, with the pages numbered consecutively throughout (PD 32, para. 15.3).

9.8 DRAWING UP INTERIM ORDERS

Rules 40.2(2) and 40.3(1)(c) of the CPR provide that all interim orders have to be drawn up and sealed by the court, unless it dispenses with the need to do so. Normally the court will take responsibility for drawing up, but:

(a) the court may order a party to draw up an order; or
(b) a party may, with the permission of the court, agree to draw up an order; or
(c) the court may direct a party to draw up the order subject to checking by the court before it is sealed; or
(d) the court may direct the parties to file an agreed statement of the terms of the order before the court itself draws up the order; or
(e) the order may be entered administratively by consent, in which event the parties will submit a drawn-up version of their agreement for entry.

A party required to draw up a judgment is allowed seven days to file the relevant document, together with sufficient copies for all relevant parties, failing which any other party may draw it up and file it for sealing (rr. 40.3(3) and 40.4(1)).

Every judgment (apart from judgments on admissions, default judgments and consent judgments) must state the name and judicial title of the judge who made it (r. 40.2(1)).

Once an order has been drawn up the court will serve sealed copies on the applicant and respondent, and also on any other person the court may order to be served (r. 40.4(2)). (Service will not be by the court if one of the exceptions set out in r. 6.3 applies.) The court is given a specific power by r. 40.5 to order service on a litigant as well as the litigant's solicitor.

Judgments and orders normally take effect from the day they are given or made, not from the time they are drawn up, sealed or served (r. 40.7). However, a court making an order is given the power to specify some later date from which it shall take effect.

CHAPTER 9   APPLICATIONS AND INTERIM ORDERS

9.9   GENERAL POWERS REGARDING INTERIM RELIEF AND ORDERS

Rule 3.1(2) of the CPR sets out a non-exhaustive list of orders that may be made for the purpose of managing cases, and r. 25.1(1) sets out a non-exhaustive list of interim remedies that may be granted by the court. The r. 3.1(2) list includes orders:

(a)   extending or shortening time for compliance with rules, orders and practice directions;
(b)   adjourning or bringing forward hearing dates;
(c)   requiring a party or a legal representative to attend court;
(d)   directing part of proceedings, such as a counterclaim, to be dealt with as separate proceedings;
(e)   dealing with part of a case as a preliminary issue;
(f)   staying all or part of the proceedings generally or to a specified date or event;
(g)   consolidating two or more actions, or trying two or more actions on the same occasion;
(h)   deciding the order in which issues are to be tried; and
(i)   excluding an issue from consideration.

The r. 25.1(1) list of interim remedies includes:

(a)   Interim injunctions (see chapter 10).
(b)   Interim declarations (introduced for the first time).
(c)   Freezing injunctions (*Marevas*), including ancillary disclosure orders (see chapter 10).
(d)   Search orders (*Anton Pillers*) (see chapter 10).
(e)   Orders for the detention, custody, preservation, inspection, taking samples or sale of relevant property, carrying out of experiments on relevant property, or for the payment of income from relevant property. The order may include authority to enter land in the possession of a party to the proceedings for one of these purposes. 'Relevant property' means property which is the subject of a claim, or in relation to which any question may arise in a claim. The powers set out in r. 25.1(1)(c) are basically the same as those formerly contained in RSC, ord. 29, r. 2 (which had effect also in the county courts by virtue of CCR, ord. 13, r. 7).
(f)   Orders for interim delivery up of goods pursuant to the Torts (Interference with Goods) Act 1977, s. 4. This is basically the same as the former RSC, ord. 29, r. 2A (which had effect also in the county courts by virtue of CCR, ord. 13, r. 7).
(g)   Orders for pre-action disclosure and inspection pursuant to the Supreme Court Act 1981, s. 33, or the County Courts Act 1984, s. 52. So far as these provisions relate to disclosure of documents, see 15.9. In so far as they relate to inspection of property, see 9.10.
(h)   Disclosure or inspection orders against non-parties pursuant to the Supreme Court Act 1981, s. 34, or the County Courts Act 1984, s. 53. So far as these provisions relate to disclosure of documents, see 15.9. In so far as they relate to inspection of property, see 9.10.
(i)   Orders for interim payments, see 9.11.
(j)   An order that a specified fund be paid into court or otherwise secured.
(k)   An order permitting a party seeking to recover personal property to pay money into court pending the outcome of the case, and directing that

if he does, the property shall be given to him (which is new, and provides a useful means of recovering disputed property while protecting the defendant by means of the security provided by the payment into court).

(l) An order directing a party to prepare and file accounts relating to the dispute (see CPR, r. 25.1(1)(n), which has substantially less detail than RSC, ord. 43).

Where an order imposes a time limit for doing any act, the date for compliance must be expressed as a calendar date, and must include the time of day by which the act must be done (CPR, r. 2.9(1)). Orders may be made subject to conditions, and may, at the court's discretion, specify the consequences of failing to comply (r. 3.1(3)).

9.10 PRE-ACTION INSPECTION AND INSPECTION AGAINST NON-PARTIES

The jurisdiction to make orders for inspection of things which will be relevant to forthcoming proceedings is given by the Supreme Court Act 1981, ss. 33 and 34, and the County Courts Act 1984, ss. 52 and 53. The procedure on applications under these provisions as laid down by CPR, r. 25.5, requires the evidence in support to show, if practicable by reference to any statement of case prepared in relation to the proceedings or anticipated proceedings, that the property to be inspected:

(a) is, or may become, the subject matter of the proceedings; or
(b) is relevant to the issues that will arise in relation to the proceedings.

A copy of the application notice and a copy of the evidence in support must be served on the person against whom the order is sought, and, in relation to applications against non-parties, on every party to the proceedings other than the applicant. If the order is made, the court will probably decide against giving directions requiring a claim to be commenced (see r. 25.2(3) and (4)). One significant change introduced by the new rules is that pre-action inspection is now made by a simple pre-action application, rather than by a separate, preliminary, action, as was the case under the old rules.

9.11 INTERIM PAYMENTS

An order for interim payment is defined in CPR, r. 25.1(1)(k), as an order for payment by a defendant on account of any damages, debt or other sum (except costs) which the court may hold the defendant liable to pay. The purpose behind this procedure is to alleviate the hardship that may otherwise be suffered by claimants who may have to wait substantial periods of time before they recover any damages in respect of wrongs they may have suffered. In addition to providing resources to the claimant, sometimes making an interim payment will enable the claimant to pay for treatment, or to save assets which would otherwise be lost, or to have an asset repaired earlier than might otherwise be the case, and may thereby reduce the amount of the claim. Further, making an early interim payment will reduce the defendant's liability to pay interest.

Cases on the small-claims track are unlikely to be large enough to justify the expense of applications for interim payments, and small-claims and fast-track cases, unless delayed, are likely to proceed to final hearing so

CHAPTER 9 APPLICATIONS AND INTERIM ORDERS

quickly that there will be little point in making an application, unless the hearing results in a judgment for damages to be assessed. Most applications for interim payments are therefore likely to be made in multi-track cases (or cases likely to be allocated to the multi-track when track allocation is considered).

9.11.1 Time for applying

An application for an order for an interim payment cannot be made until the period for filing an acknowledgement of service has expired (CPR, r. 25.6(1)). However, voluntary interim payments may be made at any time, including the period before proceedings are issued. It is possible to make several applications for interim payments during the life of an action (r. 25.6(2)).

9.11.2 Procedure

Applications for interim payments are made on notice, and must be served at least 14 clear days before the hearing of the application. Rather unnecessarily, it is specifically stated as a requirement by CPR, r. 25.6(3), that applications for interim payments must be supported by evidence which must be served with the application. PD 25 Interim Payments, para. 2.1, provides that the evidence in support should set out all relevant matters including:

(a) the amount sought by way of interim payment;
(b) what the money will be used for (which under the old system was regarded as irrelevant by virtue of the decision in *Stringman* v *McArdle* [1994] 1 WLR 1653);
(c) the likely amount of money that will be awarded;
(d) the reasons for believing the relevant ground (see 9.11.3 below) is satisfied;
(e) in a personal injuries claim, details of special damages and past and future loss; and
(f) in a claim under the Fatal Accidents Act 1976, details of the persons on whose behalf the claim is made and the nature of the claim.

All relevant documents in support should be exhibited. In personal injuries claims these will include the medical reports.

Respondents wishing to rely on witness statements (or affidavits) in reply must file and serve their evidence at least seven clear days before the hearing. If the applicant wants to respond to the respondent's evidence, any further evidence must be filed and served at least three clear days before the return day (r. 25.6(4) and (5)).

9.11.3 Grounds

The conditions set out in CPR, r. 25.7, which must be satisfied before an interim payment order can be made, are similar to those provided under the old rules (RSC, ord. 29, rr. 11 and 12, which also applied in the county court by virtue of CCR, ord. 13, r. 12). However, there is now a single rule which coalesces the old distinction between damages cases and claims for sums other than damages. Under CPR, r. 25.7(1), an interim payment may only be ordered if:

(a) the defendant has admitted liability to pay damages or some other sum of money to the claimant; or

(b) the claimant has obtained judgment against the defendant for damages or some other sum (other than costs) to be assessed; or

(c) the court is satisfied that, if the claim went to trial, the claimant would obtain judgment against the defendant from whom the interim payment is sought for a substantial sum of money (other than costs); or

(d) the claimant is seeking possession of land, and the court is satisfied that if the case went to trial the defendant would be held liable to pay the claimant a sum of money for use and occupation of the land while the claim is pending.

9.11.4 Additional condition in personal injuries cases

Rule 25.7(2) of the CPR lays down an additional requirement in applications for interim payments in personal injuries cases, which is similar to that made in the old rules in RSC, ord. 29, r. 11(2), that, in effect, the defendant must have the means to pay. This requirement will be satisfied under the new rules if either:

(a) the defendant is insured in respect of the claim; or

(b) the defendant's liability will be met by an insurer under the Road Traffic Act 1988, s. 151, or by an insurer under the Motor Insurers' Bureau Agreement; or

(c) the defendant is a public body.

Sub-paragraph (b) is in the same form as the 1996 amendment to the old rules allowing interim payments in Motor Insurers' Bureau cases. Sub-paragraphs (a) and (c) are the same as before, but there is no equivalent under the new rule for the old provision allowing an interim payment order to be made against a defendant whose means and resources were such as to enable him to make the interim payment.

9.11.5 Standard of proof

On an application under sub-paragraphs (c) or (d) of CPR, r. 25.7(1), as set out in 9.11.3, the court has to be satisfied on the balance of probabilities that the claimant 'would' obtain judgment. This wording is identical to that used in the old rules (RSC, ord. 29, rr. 11(1)(c) and 12(1)(c)), and it ought to be the case, despite the new approach to interpretation, that the same principles will apply regarding the standard of proof on these two grounds. If so, the claimant has to show he will win on the balance of probabilities, but at the upper end of the scale, the burden being a high one. Being likely to succeed at trial is not enough. The leading authorities under the old rules establishing these principles were *Shearson Lehman Brothers Inc.* v *Maclaine Watson and Co. Ltd* [1987] 1 WLR 480 and *British and Commonwealth Holdings plc* v *Quadrex Holdings Inc.* [1989] QB 842.

9.11.6 Multiple defendants

9.11.6.1 Non-personal injuries cases The wording of the new ground (c) in CPR, r. 25.7(1) (see 9.11.3), confirms the position as stated in *Ricci Burns Ltd* v *Toole* [1989] 1 WLR 993 as regards non-personal injuries cases. This is that it is not enough for the claimant to establish to the required standard that the claim will succeed, unless the claimant also establishes to that standard that the claim will succeed against the defendant who is being asked to make the interim payment. This is often very difficult where there is more than one defendant, and in cases where

CHAPTER 9 APPLICATIONS AND INTERIM ORDERS

it is clear the claimant will win, but unclear which of two defendants who blame each other will lose, no interim payment can be ordered.

9.11.6.2 *Personal injuries cases* The operation of the rule discussed in 9.11.6.1 is mitigated in personal injuries cases by CPR, r. 25.7(3), which provides that in these cases an interim payment order may be made against any defendant provided the court is satisfied the claimant will obtain judgment for substantial damages against at least one of the defendants, and that the resources requirement discussed in 9.11.4 is fulfilled in relation to each of the defendants. If it later transpires that the wrong decision was made, it should be possible, if all the defendants are (for example) insured, to adjust the position after final determination of the case.

9.11.7 Amount to be ordered

The court is not permitted to order an interim payment of more than a reasonable proportion of the likely amount of any final judgment, taking into account any contributory negligence and any relevant set-off or counterclaim (CPR, r. 25.7(4) and (5)). This is the same test as before, when judges took very different views of what a 'reasonable proportion' of the final award might be.

In personal injuries claims the defendant will need to obtain a certificate of recoverable benefits from the Secretary of State under the Social Security (Recovery of Benefits) Act 1997. A copy of the certificate should be filed at the hearing, and any order made must set out the amount by which the payment to be made to the claimant has been reduced in accordance with the Act and the Social Security (Recovery of Benefits) Regulations 1997 (PD 25 Interim Payments, paras 4.1 to 4.4).

Rule 25.6(7) of the CPR allows an interim payment order to require payment by instalments. Where this happens, the order should set out the total amount of the interim payment, the amount of each instalment, the number of instalments and the dates they are to be paid, and to whom the payments should be made (PD 25 Interim Payments, para. 3).

9.11.8 Non-disclosure

As under the old system (see RSC, ord. 29, r. 15), the fact that a defendant has made an interim payment must not be disclosed to the trial judge until all questions of liability and quantum have been determined (CPR, r. 25.9), unless the defendant agrees.

9.11.9 Adjustment

The court retains its powers to order all or part of an interim payment to be repaid, to vary or discharge an interim payment order, and to order a co-defendant to reimburse a defendant who has made an interim payment (provided the defendant who made the interim payment has claimed a contribution, indemnity or other remedy against the co-defendant being ordered to reimburse) (CPR, r. 25.8; the old power was in RSC, ord. 29, r. 17). Interest may, as under the old rules, be ordered in favour of the defendant on any overpaid interim payment. These powers are usually exercised, if at all, at trial. PD 25 Interim Payments, para. 5, contains detailed rules on recording the effect of interim payments and any order for adjustment on the final award for damages.

9.12 STRIKING OUT

Rule 3.4 of the CPR, which is the new rule dealing with striking out, has been shorn of the old phraseology dealing with pleadings which are frivolous, vexatious or embarrassing, but retains the concepts of striking out on the basis of there being no reasonable cause of action or defence, and on the ground that a statement of case is an abuse of process. The redundant concepts are replaced by a provision authorising striking out if a statement of case is likely to obstruct the just disposal of the proceedings, and to some extent reintroduced through the back door by PD 3, para. 1.5, which states that a claim may be regarded as an abuse of process or otherwise likely to obstruct just disposal of the proceedings if it is vexatious, scurrilous or obviously ill-founded. The new rule further provides for striking out for failing to comply with the CPR, a practice direction or court order. Paragraph (1) of the rule says that the rule applies to parts of a statement of case as well as attacks on a whole statement of case. Paragraph (2) provides:

> The court may strike out a statement of case if it appears to the court—
> (a) that the statement of case discloses no reasonable grounds for bringing or defending the claim;
> (b) that the statement of case is an abuse of the court's process or is otherwise likely to obstruct the just disposal of the proceedings; or
> (c) that there has been a failure to comply with a rule, practice direction or court order.

All or part of a statement of case may be struck out on grounds (a) or (b) at any time, or an application made by the parties or by the court on its own initiative (PD 3, para. 4.1).

As under the old rules, applications under sub-para. (a) are limited to alleging that the statement of case under attack fails on its face to disclose a claim or defence which is sustainable as a matter of law. When considering an application it will be assumed that the facts alleged are true, and it is not permissible to undermine the claim or defence with evidence in support. Although this is the plain intention, the rule does not say that evidence is not receivable on such an application, and in fact r. 25.3(2) provides that all applications must be supported by evidence unless the court otherwise orders, and PD 3, para. 5.2, merely says that 'many applications' under CPR, r. 3.4(2), can be made without evidence, but applicants should consider whether evidence in support should be filed and served.

Rule 3.4(2)(b) is more wide ranging than r. 3.4(2)(a), and includes applications based on allegations that claims are time-barred under the Limitation Act 1980, that the claimant might be seeking to go behind a previous judgment or that the whole or part of a statement of case is covered by *res judicata* or issue estoppel, and generally that a litigant is misusing the court's process for an illegitimate purpose.

A number of examples are given by PD 3. A claim may be struck out if it sets out no facts indicating what the claim is about (such as a claim simply saying it is for 'Money owed £5,000'), or if it is incoherent and makes no sense, or if the facts it states, even if true, do not disclose a legally recognisable claim against the defendant. A defence may be struck out if it consists of a bare denial or otherwise fails to set out a coherent statement of facts, or if the facts it sets out, even if true, do not amount in law to a defence to the claim. Many institutional defendants at present are in the habit of filing eight-line defences making blanket denials without stating any positive case. These defences ought to be a thing of the past.

Paragraphs 2 and 3 of PD 3 deal with situations where court officials see, when asked to issue claims or on receipt of defences, that the contents of the relevant document fail to meet these standards. The official may decide to consult the judge, who may on his own initiative make an order staying the proceedings or striking out the claim or defence. The judge may or may not give the party a hearing before making such an order, or may make an order under Part 18 requiring additional information about the defective statement of case with a sanction in default. An order can also be made that the document is to be retained by the court and not served until any stay imposed is lifted.

If a striking-out order is made, the judge may enter such judgment as the other party may appear entitled to (PD 3, para. 4.2).

Rule 3.4(2)(c) is an essential tool in support of the court's case management powers, and provides the teeth the court needs to ensure its orders and directions are not ignored. This is considered further in 11.8.

Rule 3.4(5) makes it plain that r. 3.4(2) does not inhibit the court's power to strike out a statement of case under any of the other provisions of the CPR, such as when giving summary judgment under Part 24. Endorsing the rule laid down in *Gardner v Southwark London Borough Council (No. 2)* [1996] 1 WLR 561, r. 3.4(4) provides that where a claim is struck out and the claimant is ordered to pay the defendant's costs, if the claimant commences a second action (within the limitation period) arising out of substantially the same facts as those forming the basis of the struck-out claim, the defendant may apply for a stay of the second action until the costs of the first action have been paid.

9.13 SUMMARY JUDGMENT

In the *Final Report*, p. 123, summary judgment was seen as being capable of performing the important function of stopping weak cases from dragging on, and reducing complexity and costs by eliminating issues as the case proceeds. The procedure as formulated in the CPR, like the procedure under the old rules, provides a means of entering a speedy judgment in cases where the other side put up a spurious defence, but there are some significant changes. The main ones are:

(a) The procedure is now also available to a defendant, and supplements the power to strike out, operating as a broad replacement for the old RSC, ord. 14A.
(b) The procedure may be invoked by the court of its own initiative.
(c) The main test is now whether the claim or defence has a real prospect of success, which should make it rather easier to obtain summary judgment than under the old system, where the defendant merely had to show a triable issue.

9.13.1 Time at which the application may be made

A claimant may only apply for summary judgment after the defendant has filed either an acknowledgment of service or a defence (r. 24.4(1)). If the defendant fails to do either of these within the time limited by the CPR, the claimant may enter a default judgment, either with or without the court's permission, depending on the nature of the claim. By analogy with r. 25.2(2)(c), a defendant likewise can only apply for summary judgment after either filing an acknowledgment of service or a defence.

It is normally appropriate to make the application early on in the litigation process, if possible very shortly after the acknowledgment or defence, because if the other side have no realistic prospects of success, entering summary judgment early prevents unnecessary costs being incurred. Under the old Rules there was nothing to prevent a late application for summary judgment (see, for example, *Brinks Ltd v Abu-Saleh (No. 1)* [1995] 1 WLR 1478), but as a practical matter the judge dealing with a late application might well have felt there was a lack of conviction on the part of the applicant if the application was significantly delayed. Under the CPR the application should be made before or when the applicant files the allocation questionnaire (PD 26, para. 5.3(1)).

9.13.2 Excluded proceedings

Compared to the position under the old rules, the list of proceedings excluded from applications for summary judgment has been greatly reduced. Under CPR, r. 24.3(2), the only excluded proceedings where the application is brought by the claimant are residential possession proceedings (whether brought against a tenant, mortgagee or a person holding over at the end of a tenancy) and admiralty claims *in rem*. In applications *against* claimants there are no excluded types of proceedings (r. 24.3(1)).

Summary judgment is not available against the Crown, whether it is acting as a claimant or a defendant (RSC, ord. 77, r. 7 in CPR, sch. 1; CCR, ord. 42, r. 5(5) in CPR, sch. 2).

9.13.3 Effect if application is made before filing the defence

If the application is made after filing an acknowledgment of service but before filing of the defence, there is no need to file a defence before the hearing (CPR, r. 24.4(2)). At that stage the court will give directions, which will include providing a date for filing the defence. The permissive wording of the rule confirms *Natural Resources Inc.* v *Origin Clothing Ltd* [1995] FSR 280, in which it was held that there is nothing to prevent a defendant from serving a defence in the period before the hearing if the defendant chooses to do so.

9.13.4 Procedure

The general rules on making interim applications (see 9.2 and 9.5 to 9.8) apply on making an application for summary judgment, with certain refinements. The application is made by application notice, which must be supported by evidence (CPR, r. 25.3(2)). The rules specifically mention that the court may fix a summary judgment hearing of its own initiative (r. 24.4(3)), and doing so may further the overriding objective, which includes deciding promptly which issues need full investigation and trial, and accordingly disposing summarily of the others (r. 1.4(2)(c)). If the court is minded to make use of this power, it is most likely to do so on the initial scrutiny at the track allocation stage shortly after filing of the defence. If the court uses the power it will not allocate the case to a track, but instead it will fix a hearing, giving the parties 14 days' notice and informing them of the issues it proposes to decide (PD 26, para. 5.4).

CHAPTER 9 APPLICATIONS AND INTERIM ORDERS

The obligation to give notice at least 14 clear days before the date fixed for the hearing of the issues which it is proposed the court will decide at the hearing extends to applications for summary judgment made by the parties (CPR, r. 24.4(3)).

The respondent must file and serve any evidence in reply at least seven clear days before the hearing (r. 24.5(1)). The application notice must inform the respondent of this time limit (PD 24, para. 2(5)). Under the old system this time limit was just three days before the hearing (Practice Direction (Order 14: Return Date) [1970] 1 WLR 258). If the applicant wishes to respond to the respondent's evidence, the further evidence must be served and filed at least three clear days before the hearing of the application (CPR, r. 24.5(2)).

In cases where the hearing is fixed by the court on its own initiative, all parties must file and serve their evidence at least seven clear days before the return day, and if they want to respond to their opponents' evidence, that must be done at least three clear days before the return day (r. 24.5(3)).

9.13.5 Specific performance, rescission and forfeiture in property cases

A similar speedy process for obtaining summary judgment to that formerly provided by RSC, ord. 86 is laid down by PD 24, para. 7, for specific performance and similar claims arising out of mortgage and tenancy agreements. Summary judgment in these cases can be sought at any time after the claim is served, rather than having to wait until after acknowledgment or defence, and the application can be made even in the absence of particulars of claim. The application notice, evidence in support and a draft order must be served no less than four clear days before the hearing.

9.13.6 Principles

The main change is that the respondent can no longer avoid having judgment entered by merely pointing to a triable issue, but now he has to show a case with real prospects of success. This means that the well-known 'shadowy' defence, which under the old rules would have resulted in conditional leave to defend, will now no doubt be regarded as one that does not have a 'real prospect of success' so that summary judgment will be entered under the new rules. The 'real prospect of success' formula is taken from the *Supreme Court Practice's* note on the effect of the decision in *Alpine Bulk Transport Co. Inc.* v *Saudi Eagle Shipping Co. Inc.* [1986] 2 Lloyd's Rep 221 regarding the test to be applied on an application to set aside a judgment in default. The note was criticised as a misstatement of the *Saudi Eagle* decision by the Court of Appeal in *Day* v *Royal Automobile Club Motoring Services Ltd* (1998) *The Times*, 24 November 1998, the test laid down in the *Saudi Eagle* being whether the defence has merits to which the court should pay heed. However, as the discredited test has now been adopted by the CPR, which have the force of a statutory instrument, this is the test which ought to be applied. Strangely, PD 24, para. 4.3, introduces an element of doubt. This paragraph is dealing with the situation in the grey area between cases where judgment should be entered and those where summary judgment applications should be dismissed, and says that conditional orders (for which, see 9.13.7) should be made where it appears to be possible but improbable that the respondent will succeed.

This formulation could be interpreted as reducing the burden on the respondent below what might otherwise be understood by the phrase 'real prospects of success'.

Apart from the change in the standard of proof, it may be that the other principles that have developed in summary judgment cases, such as the 'cheque' rule, and the effect of cross-claims and set-offs, will continue in effect. However, it is clear that the intention is that the CPR will make a fresh start. PD 24, para. 5, even has a note saying that the court will no longer follow the former practice of granting leave to defend, whether conditional or unconditional. However, the change in approach should not sweep away substantive rules of law, and the practices relating to cheque actions and set-offs are based on underlying statutory substantive law, which cannot have been changed by the new procedural system.

9.13.7 Orders available

PD 24, para. 5.1, purports to set out the range of orders available on a summary judgment application, as follows:

(a) judgment on the claim;
(b) striking out or dismissal of the claim;
(c) dismissal of the application; and
(d) a conditional order.

A conditional order is similar to the old conditional leave to defend. It is appropriate for cases in the grey area between granting judgment and dismissing the application (PD 24, para. 4.3). It is an order either to pay a sum of money into court or to take a specified step in the action, with a provision that the claim will be dismissed or a statement of case will be struck out if the respondent does not comply (PD 24, para. 5.2).

The way in which PD 24, para. 5, is worded makes it appear that the court cannot make a 'split' order (as it could under the old rules) where the defendant has a defence to only part of the claim. In such a case the most natural order is to grant judgment for the part of the claim against which there is no defence, and to grant unconditional leave to defend for the balance. This seems to be expressly negatived as a possibility by the note to para. 5. However, r. 24.2 of the CPR expressly says that summary judgment may be entered on the whole of the case *or on a particular issue*. Further, active case management includes, according to r. 1.4((2)(c), deciding which issues need full investigation with the others being disposed of summarily, and PD 26, para. 7.4(2), which deals with the financial value of claims for track allocation purposes, says sums in respect of items forming part of a claim for which, for example, summary judgment has been entered, are not in dispute. It is clear, therefore, that despite the implication from PD 24, para. 5, summary judgment can be entered for part of a claim in an appropriate case.

9.13.8 Directions on summary judgment hearing

If a summary judgment application is dismissed or otherwise fails finally to dispose of the action, the court will give case management directions as to the future conduct of the case (PD 24, para. 10).

CHAPTER 10 INTERIM INJUNCTIONS, FREEZING INJUNCTIONS AND SEARCH ORDERS

CONTENTS

10.1	Introduction	145
10.2	Pre-issue applications for interim injunctions	146
10.2.1	Urgency or desirability of applying before issue	146
10.2.2	Procedure	147
10.2.3	Pre-action injunction hearings	148
10.2.4	The order and related matters	148
10.2.5	Service of pre-action interim injunction	149
10.3	Applications for interim injunctions during the course or proceedings	150
10.3.1	Time for applying	150
10.3.2	Procedure	150
10.3.3	Hearing of interim injunction applications in pending proceedings	151
10.3.4	The order and related matters	152
10.3.5	Service of an order obtained without notice	152
10.4	Evidence in support of an application	152
10.5	Freezing injunctions	153
10.6	Search orders	153
10.7	Criteria for obtaining an interim injunction	155
10.7.1	Cost and proportionality	157
10.7.2	Cooperation and ADR	158
10.7.3	Delay in this case and others	158

10.1 INTRODUCTION

The court is authorised by CPR, r. 25.1(1), to grant interim remedies. Fourteen kinds of interim remedies are listed in r. 25.1(1), but this chapter will concentrate on interim injunctions (which used to be called interlocutory injunctions) (r. 25.1(1)(a)), freezing injunctions (which used to be called *Mareva* orders) (r. 25.1(1)(f)) and search orders (which used to be called *Anton Piller* orders) (r. 25.1(1)(h)). The rules on interim remedies are in CPR, Part 25. The procedure for making applications to the court for interim orders is set out in CPR, Part 23, and this chapter should be read in conjunction with chapter 9. The three kinds of interim remedy dealt with in this chapter are the subject of a substantial practice direction accompanying Part 25 (PD 25 Interim Injunctions).

An order for an interim remedy may be made at any time, including before proceedings are started (i.e., before a claim form is issued) and after judgment has been given (CPR, r. 25.2(1)), and an interim remedy may be granted whether or not there has been a claim for a final remedy of the same kind (r. 25.1(4)). But the CPR contemplate that the kinds of interim remedies discussed in this chapter will be applied for in the course of proceedings or in contemplation of proceedings which the applicant undertakes to commence.

CHAPTER 10   INTERIM INJUNCTIONS ETC

When exercising its power to grant an interim remedy, as when exercising any power given to it by the CPR, the court must seek to give effect to the overriding objective (r. 1.2).

After a claim has been allocated to the small claims track the only interim remedy that may be applied for is an interim injunction (r. 27.2(1)).

Paragraphs 1.1 to 1.4 of PD 25 Interim Injunctions lay down rules regulating the status of the judges who may grant different types of interim orders. The effect of the rules is set out in table 10.1.

Type of order	Can be obtained from
Search order	High Court judge and any other judge 'duly authorised'
Freezing injunction	High Court judge and any other judge 'duly authorised'
Interim injunction in a High Court case	Master or district judge if by consent, related to charging orders and appointment of receivers or in aid of execution of judgment. Otherwise any judge with jurisdiction to try the action
Interim injunction in a county court case	Any judge with jurisdiction to try the action
Variation of interim injunction	A master or district judge by consent (otherwise a judge)

Table 10.1   Power to grant interim orders

10.2   PRE-ISSUE APPLICATIONS FOR INTERIM INJUNCTIONS

10.2.1   Urgency or desirability of applying before issue

Rule 25.2(1) of the CPR empowers the court to grant an interim injunction before a claim form has been issued. An application for an interim injunction at that stage must be made under Part 23 (PD 23, para. 5). By CPR, r. 25.2(2), an interim injunction can be obtained prior to issue of proceedings provided:

   (a)   no rule or practice direction prohibits the granting of the order;
   (b)   the matter is urgent or it is otherwise desirable to make the order in the interests of justice;
   (c)   in the less common circumstance in which the applicant is an intended defendant, the defendant has obtained the court's permission to make the application. The defendant cannot without this permission apply for an interim remedy prior to the filing of an acknowledgment of service or defence (which can only happen after issue). It seems that the defendant could apply for permission and for the injunction in the same application and at the same hearing.

For discussion of the substantive criteria for obtaining an injunction see 10.7.

10.2.2 Procedure

The application itself will normally be in a written application notice (CPR, r. 23.3(1)), the general requirement for which is that it should set out the order sought and why the order is being sought (r. 23.6). Form N244 should usually be used for the application notice. It must be completed to include the title of the proposed action, the full name of the applicant, and, as the applicant is not yet a party, the application notice must state his address for service, and it should contain a request for a hearing or ask that the application be dealt with without a hearing (PD 23, para. 2.1). It will be very rare for injunctions to be sought without hearings. Dispensing with a hearing is only permissible if the parties agree to the terms of the order sought, or if the parties agree that the court should dispose of the application without a hearing, or if the court does not consider a hearing would be appropriate (CPR, r. 23.8). None of these is very likely in the case of pre-action injunctions. PD 25 Interim Injunctions, para. 2.1, provides that an application notice for an interim injunction should:

(a) state the order sought, and
(b) give the date, time and place of the hearing.

Many pre-action applications for injunctions are made in cases of real urgency. Drafting and issuing an application notice may delay matters to the detriment of the applicant, and the court may in such cases exercise its power in CPR, r. 23.3(2)(b), to dispense with the requirement for an application notice. If the court dispenses with the application notice, it will usually only do so for the purposes of the initial hearing. PD 25 Interim Injunctions, para. 5.1(4), provides that in these circumstances the court will, unless it orders otherwise, require an undertaking from the applicant to file an application notice and pay the appropriate fee on the same or the next working day.

An application for an interim remedy must be supported by evidence, unless the court orders otherwise (CPR, r. 25.3(2)). The evidence required is discussed fully in 10.4.

The application should be made in the court in which the substantive proceedings are likely to be be issued unless 'there is good reason to make the application to a different court' (CPR, r. 23.2(4)).

Especially where the terms of the injunction sought are complex, it will continue to be good practice to attach a draft of the order to the application notice and to provide it on computer disk in WordPerfect 5.1 (PD 25 Interim Injunctions, para. 2.4).

If the court is to serve the application on the respondent, a suitable number of copies of the application notice and evidence in support must be filed with the court. Unless the court orders otherwise, or an application without service of an application notice can be justified, the application notice should be served as soon as practicable and in any event at least three clear days before the hearing (CPR, r. 23.7). Obviously, if three days' notice can be given of an application for an interim injunction, there will be time to issue proceedings. Pre-action applications will therefore always be made without full notice to the respondent. This can only be justified if there are 'good reasons for not giving notice' (r. 25.3(1)). It is likely that urgency and/or the need for secrecy will be accepted as good reasons.

Although PD 23, para. 2.7, says that 'Every application should be made as soon as it becomes apparent that it is necessary or desirable', para. 2.8 adds that 'Applications should wherever possible be made so that they can be considered at any other hearing for which a date has already been fixed or for which a date is about to be fixed'. This simply adds to the applicant's burden in demonstrating that the matter is so urgent that a pre-action application is justified under CPR, r. 25.2(2)(b).

10.2.3 Pre-action injunction hearings

As mentioned in 10.2.2, pre-action interim injunction applications will almost always be considered at a hearing but without full (or any) notice to the respondent. Such applications will almost certainly be of an urgent nature. If they arise during or shortly before the ordinary times when the court is sitting, the hearing will take place in court as soon as the circumstances permit. This means that generally such applications are heard before other matters that are listed, either as soon as the court sits in the morning or immediately after lunch. The necessary arrangements must be made with the court staff, who will invariably do all they can to ensure urgent applications are dealt with at the first available opportunity. Solicitors should therefore contact the court by telephone as soon as they know they will need to make an urgent application, so as to allow the court time to make the necessary arrangements. Sometimes urgent applications arise during the course of the morning or afternoon in circumstances where it is not possible to wait to the beginning of the next session. If the case is sufficiently urgent the court will invariably interrupt whatever it is doing at a convenient moment so that it can hear the urgent application.

On other occasions the need for a pre-action interim injunction arises at a time when it is not possible to wait until the next occasion when the court will be sitting. If the application is of extreme urgency it may be dealt with by telephone (PD 25 Interim Injunctions, para. 4.2). If the problem has arisen during business hours, but in circumstances where it will not be possible to go before a judge before the close of business, initially it is necessary to telephone the court (either the High Court on 0171 936 6000 or the appropriate county court) asking to be put in touch with a High Court judge of the appropriate division or county court judge available to deal with an emergency application (PD 25 Interim Injunctions, para. 4.5(1)).

If the problem has arisen outside office hours, the applicant should telephone either the High Court (on the same number as above) asking to be put in touch with the clerk to the appropriate duty judge (or the appropriate area circuit judge where known), or should telephone the urgent court business officer of the appropriate circuit, who will contact the local duty judge.

If the facilities are available, a draft of the order sought will usually be required to be sent by fax to the duty judge who will be dealing with the application.

Telephone hearings are only available if the applicant is acting by solicitors or counsel (PD 25 Interim Injunctions, para. 4.5(5)).

10.2.4 The order and related matters

If the order is granted, the court may give directions requiring a claim to be commenced (CPR, r. 25.2(3)). PD 25 Interim Injunctions, para. 5.1(5), gives effect to this by providing that an order made before issue of

CHAPTER 10 INTERIM INJUNCTIONS ETC

the claim form will, unless the court orders otherwise, include 'an undertaking to issue and pay the appropriate fee on the same or next working day' or contain directions for the commencement of the claim.

The order 'must set out clearly what the respondent must do or not do' (PD 25 Interim Injunctions, para. 5.3).

It is also prescribed that there will be an undertaking in damages 'unless the court orders otherwise' (PD 25 Interim Injunctions, para. 5.1(1)). The practice direction gives no guidance on the circumstances in which no undertaking will be required, and it is likely that the court will continue the existing practice of not requiring one if:

(a) the applicant is legally aided, or
(b) the applicant is a public authority enforcing the general law.

However, since in dealing with the application the court must also apply the overriding objective, there may be other circumstances in which an undertaking will not be required: for example, where the applicant is in a weaker financial position than the respondent.

According to PD 25 Interim Injunctions, para. 4.4(3), the order should include in the title, after the names of the applicant and respondent, the words 'the claimant and defendant in an intended action'. In fact the last of these words should be 'claim' rather than 'action'. As the application will invariably have been made without notice to the respondent, the order must, by PD 25 Interim Injunctions, para. 5.1(2) and (3), include, unless the court orders otherwise:

(a) an undertaking by the applicant to the court to serve the respondent with the application notice, evidence in support and any order made, as soon as practicable; and
(b) a return date for a further hearing at which the other party can be present.

Where the order is made in the presence of all relevant parties (or at least at a hearing of which they have had notice but which they did not attend) it may be expressed to last 'until trial or further order' (PD 25 Interim Injunctions, para. 5.2). This will not, of course, apply to most pre-action injunctions.

No example of an interim injunction is provided in PD 25 Interim Injunctions. Until new forms are laid down, the form of injunction before issue laid down by Practice Direction (Interlocutory Injunctions: Forms) [1996] 1 WLR 1551 should be used with necessary changes to accord with the CPR, at least in High Court cases.

10.2.5 Service of pre-action interim injunction

Generally, pre-action applications for interim injunctions will be made without notice to the respondent. Therefore, r. 23.9 of the CPR applies. This requires a copy of the application notice and any evidence in support to be served with the injunction order on all parties and persons against whom the order was sought or made. The order must also contain a statement of the right to apply under r. 23.10 to set aside or vary the order within seven days after it is served.

Where possible the claim form should be served with the injunction order (PD 25 Interim Injunctions, para. 4.4(2)).

10.3 APPLICATIONS FOR INTERIM INJUNCTIONS DURING THE COURSE OF PROCEEDINGS

10.3.1 Time for applying

An application for an interim injunction in proceedings must be made after the claim form commencing the proceedings is issued if applying before issue is prevented by the conditions laid down in CPR, r. 25.2(2) (see 10.2.1). This will be the case where a pre-action application is prohibited by a rule or practice direction, or the matter is not urgent and it is not desirable to grant an injunction before issue in the interests of justice, or the applicant is an intended defendant and the court refuses permission. As mentioned in 10.2.2, paras 2.7 and 2.8 of PD 23 say that any application in proceedings should be made as soon as it becomes apparent that it is necessary or desirable, but should preferably be made at a hearing for which a date has already been, or is about to be, fixed. In many cases this means that the right time to apply for an interim injunction will be at the allocation stage, but an earlier, separate hearing would be justified if delay would make it more difficult to preserve the status quo.

If the applicant is a defendant who has yet to file either an acknowledgment or a defence, the applicant must obtain the court's permission to make the application (CPR, r. 25.2(2)(c)).

For a discussion of substantive criteria see 10.7.

10.3.2 Procedure

Procedure will be as described in 10.2.2 for pre-action applications except that:

(a) The application notice need not give the applicant's address for service.

(b) The application will be made:

(i) to the court in which the substantive proceedings were stated (CPR, r. 23.2(1)), or
(ii) to the court in which the proceedings were subsequently transferred (r. 23.2(2)), or
(iii) if a date has been fixed for trial, to the court where the trial is to take place (r. 23.2(3)), or
(iv) if after enforcement proceedings have been started, to the court dealing with enforcement 'unless any rule or practice direction provides otherwise' (r. 23.2(5)).

Where the court is to serve, sufficient copies of the application notice and evidence in support should be provided for the court and each respondent (PD 25 Interim Injunctions, para. 2.3). Service should be effected as soon as possible, and in any event not less than three clear days before the hearing.

Although PD 23, para. 2.8, provides that 'Applications should wherever possible be made so that they can be considered at any other hearing for which a date has already been fixed or for which a date is about to be fixed', clearly an application for an injunction, even where both parties are to appear at the hearing will very often be of sufficient urgency to make it inappropriate to wait to make it until, say, the case management conference. Given the requirement to save expense (CPR, r. 1.1(2)(b)) and to

CHAPTER 10 INTERIM INJUNCTIONS ETC

allot to the case an appropriate share of the court's resources, while taking into account the need to allot resources to other cases (r. 1.1(2)(e)), an applicant should expect to be called on to justify the need for a separate hearing.

Respondents to applications made on notice are not under any specific duty under the rules to disclose their evidence in reply in advance of the hearings. However, deliberately holding back evidence in reply to the last minute will be a clear breach of the overriding objective. If the minimum of three clear days' notice was given by the applicant, it might be difficult or impossible for a respondent to compile and serve evidence in reply, which is why the CPR require the applicant to serve the application notice and evidence in support as soon as practicable after issue. The greater the notice given to the respondent, the greater is the effective obligation on the respondent to serve its evidence in advance of the hearing. The rules seek to avoid multiple hearings (CPR, r. 1.4(2)(i); PD 29, para. 3.6), and although the court may be prepared to give directions as to the service of evidence on the first hearing (as was commonly the case under the old system), it may well impose sanctions if it considers the need to give directions was caused by the default of either party.

10.3.3 Hearing of interim injunction applications in pending proceedings

Normally the hearing of an application for an interim injunction will be listed in the usual way for disposal in public (see CPR, r. 39.2). There are exceptional circumstances in which the hearing will be in private, such as where the hearing involves confidential information, the interests of children or patients, or where it would be unjust to proceed in public because the respondent has not been given due notice.

If the application is of an urgent nature justifying giving less than the usual three clear days' notice, unless secrecy is essential, the applicant should give the respondents informal notice (PD 25 Interim Injunctions, para. 4.3(3)), which should be explained in the evidence in support. If the urgency justifies making the application without first issuing an application notice, a draft order (at least) should be provided at the hearing. Normally the court will direct that an application notice and evidence in support must be filed with the court on the same or the next working day (PD 25 Interim Injunctions, para. 4.3(2)). If possible, even in the case of urgent applications, the application notice, evidence in support and draft order should be filed with the court at least two hours before it is intended to go before the judge (PD 25 Interim Injunctions, para 4.3(1)).

In cases of extreme urgency, the court may interrupt its list, or conduct the hearing by telephone with the duty judge, in the same way as extremely urgent pre-action applications (see 10.2.3).

Where there is to be a hearing, then with consent of all parties (and provided no party is acting in person), the court can order the hearing to be dealt with by telephone (PD 23, para. 6.1) or by video conference (PD 23, para. 7).

Both parties should be prepared to deal with the future case management of the action. PD 23, para. 2.9, warns them that: '. . . at any hearing the court may wish to review the conduct of the case as a whole and give any necessary case management directions. They should be ready to assist the court in doing so and to answer questions the court may ask for this purpose.' Indeed if the application takes place before allocation, the court may deal with allocation at the hearing (PD 26, para. 2.4).

10.3.4 The order and related matters

This will be as described in 10.2.4 in relation to pre-action applications except, of course, that no undertaking or direction to commence proceedings will be necessary and the order will not be in an intended action.

10.3.5 Service of an order obtained without notice

When an interim injunction is obtained in the course of proceedings without notice to the respondent, CPR, r. 23.9 and 23.10, apply as they do to pre-action injunctions (see 10.2.5).

10.4 EVIDENCE IN SUPPORT OF AN APPLICATION

An application for an interim injunction must be supported by evidence unless the court orders otherwise (CPR, r. 25.3(2)). The evidence must cover the substantive issues and also, if the application is without notice, why notice has not been given (r. 25.3(3) and PD 25 Interim Injunctions, para. 3.4). If the application is made before the issue of a claim form, the evidence should also address the urgency of the application or why it is 'desirable . . . in the interests of justice' to make the order (CPR, r. 25.2(2)(b)). The evidence should also address why making the order is consistent with the overriding objective.

PD 25 Interim Injunctions, para. 3.2, states that unless the court or an Act requires evidence by affidavit, evidence is to be:

(a) by witness statement;
(b) set out in the application, provided it is verified by a statement of truth; or
(c) set out in a statement of case, provided it is verified by a statement of truth.

The provision whereby a statement of case can be relied on as evidence is more likely to be of use where an application for an interim injunction is made during the course of proceedings.

PD 25 Interim Injunctions, para. 3.3, provides that 'The evidence must set out the facts on which the applicant relies for the claim being made against the respondent, including all material facts of which the court should be made aware'. This provision is not restricted to applications without notice. It appears to import at least some of the concepts of the previous duty of full and frank disclosure in relation to *ex parte* applications. The extent to which there is any duty, in any applications on full notice, to make reasonable inquiries remains obscure. Further, the 'material facts of which the court should be made aware' are likely to be more wide-ranging in an application made without notice than one made with the required three clear days' notice. Nevertheless, this paragraph of the practice direction is clearly intended to make parties address adverse facts in their evidence, even where the application is on notice and the respondent has a clear ability to file evidence and make representations at the hearing.

CHAPTER 10 INTERIM INJUNCTIONS ETC

Where the application is on notice the respondent may, of course, file evidence in opposition (PD 23, para. 9.4). PD 25 Interim Injunctions gives no guidance as to the form of this evidence. In particular there is no requirement that such evidence should be in the form of an affidavit. The financial risk may be small, but where there is unnecessary use of an affidavit, the additional costs of doing so will generally be irrecoverable (CPR, r. 32.15(2)).

10.5 FREEZING INJUNCTIONS

A freezing injunction is defined in CPR, r. 25.1(1)(f), as an order:

    (i) restraining a party from removing from the jursidiction assets located there; or

    (ii) restraining a party from dealing with any assets whether located within the jurisdiction or not.

Freezing injunctions used to be known as *Mareva* injunctions (from *Mareva Compania Naviera SA* v *International Bulk Carriers SA* [1980] 1 All ER 213).

Two examples of freezing injunction orders are given in the annex to PD 25 Interim Injunctions. The first example deals only with assets within the jurisdiction; the second is a worldwide freezing injunction. Apart from using the new terminology of the CPR, there are no significant changes from the previous approved precedents.

The procedures for applying for a freezing injunction are the same as for an interim injunction, discussed in 10.2 to 10.4, except that the application must be supported by affidavit evidence (PD 25 Interim Injunctions, para. 3.1; PD 32, para. 1.4(2)).

Freezing injunctions rely on secrecy for their effectiveness, so they will continue to be applied for without notice to the respondents. They often arise in urgent circumstances, so they will commonly be applied for before proceedings are issued. They are often combined with ancillary orders. Typical ancillary orders relate to identifying the location of assets, and it is expressly provided in CPR, r. 25.1(1)(g), that the court has power to make orders directing a party to provide information about the location of relevant property or assets, or to provide information about relevant property or assets which are or may be the subject of an application for a freezing injunction. 'Relevant property' is defined by r. 25.1(2) as meaning property, including land, which is the subject of a claim or as to which any question may arise on a claim.

Although it is possible that the courts will decide the CPR have made a completely fresh start, it is far more probable that the courts will continue to apply the established principles when considering whether to grant freezing orders, on what terms, and whether to discharge or vary their terms. The model forms of order in PD 25, Interim Injunctions, are to a great extent based on principles derived from the reported cases on *Mareva* injunctions, so it would be extremely surprising if there is to be any substantial change in the practice relating to granting these orders.

10.6 SEARCH ORDERS

A search order is defined in CPR, r. 25.1(1)(h), as an order under the Civil Procedure Act 1997, s. 7. That section empowers the court to make an order for the purpose of securing, in the case of any existing or proposed proceedings in the court:

CHAPTER 10 INTERIM INJUNCTIONS ETC

(a) the preservation of evidence which is or may be relevant, or
(b) the preservation of property which is or may be the subject matter of the proceedings or as to which any question arises or may arise in the proceedings.

Subsections (3) to (5) of s. 7 state various provisions which may be included in a search order:

(3) Such an order may direct any person to permit any person described in the order, or secure that any person so described is permitted—
  (a) to enter premises in England and Wales, and
  (b) while on the premises, to take in accordance with the terms of the order any of the following steps.
(4) Those steps are—
  (a) to carry out a search for or inspection of anything described in the order, and
  (b) to make or obtain a copy, photograph, sample or other record of anything so described.
(5) The order may also direct the person concerned—
  (a) to provide any person described in the order, or secure that any person so described is provided, with any information or article described in the order, and
  (b) to allow any person described in the order, or secure that any person so described is allowed, to retain for safe keeping anything described in the order.

Search orders used to be known as *Anton Piller* orders (from *Anton Piller KG* v *Manufacturing Processes Ltd* [1976] Ch 55).

Because of considerable public and judicial disquiet about the way in which *Anton Piller* orders used to be executed there have been in force for some time various safeguards for respondents including a rule of practice that an *Anton Piller* order must be executed by a supervising solicitor who is experienced in the operation of such orders and is independent of the solicitors acting for the applicant for the order. This system is continued under PD 25 Interim Injunctions, paras 7.1 to 7.5, 8.1 and 8.2. As before, the supervising solicitor must not be an employee or member of the applicant's firm of solicitors (para. 8.1). The court can dispense with the need for a supervising solicitor, by making an order to that effect (para. 8.2). The reasons for the dispensation must be set out in the order.

The formal procedures for applying for a search order are the same as for an interim injunction, discussed in 10.2 to 10.4, with the following additions:

(a) The application must be supported by affidavit evidence (PD 25 Interim Injunctions, para. 3.1).
(b) The affidavit must state the name and experience of the supervising solicitor, his or her firm name and its address, plus the address of the premises to be searched and whether it is a private or business address (para. 7.3(1)).
(c) The affidavit must disclose 'very fully' the reason why the order is sought, 'including the probability that relevant material would disappear if the order were not made' (para. 7.3(2)). It is questionable whether this is any different from the criterion of a 'real possibility' that evidence would be destroyed (*Booker McConnell plc* v *Plascow* [1985] RPC 425 per Dillon LJ), which was used as a test for granting *Anton Piller* orders. Otherwise,

CHAPTER 10   INTERIM INJUNCTIONS ETC

as with freezing injunctions (see 10.5), it is probable that the same principles will be applied in deciding whether to grant search orders as applied previously on applications for *Anton Piller* orders.

(d) Applications in intellectual property cases should be made in the Chancery Division of the High Court (PD 25 Interim Injunctions, para. 8.5).

An example of a search order is set out in the annex to PD 25 Interim Injunctions. There are some minor changes from the previous approved precedent:

(a) The order must be served within the usual working hours 'unless the court has ordered otherwise'.

(b) The fact that the privilege against self-incrimination is not available in all cases is made clearer to the respondent.

(c) It is explicit that during any hiatus whilst legal advice and/or an application to discharge is being made the respondent must not 'disturb or move anything'.

(d) It is made explicit in the order (and in slightly different words in PD 25 Interim Injunctions, para. 7.4) that the circumstances in which it is obligatory to include a woman in the search team are where 'the premises are likely to be occupied by an unaccompanied woman and the supervising solicitor is a man'.

PD 25 Interim Injunctions, para. 7.5, requires the supervising solicitor who carries out a search order to provide a report on carrying it out to the applicant's solicitors, who will then file a copy with the court and serve one on the respondent. The undertaking in the standard order, however, provides for the supervising solicitor to provide the report to the applicant's solicitors and to the 'judge who made the order'. In practice it would be as well for the applicant's solicitors to liaise closely with the supervising solicitor to ensure that one of them sends the appropriate copy to the court.

10.7   CRITERIA FOR OBTAINING AN INTERIM INJUNCTION

The CPR do not reproduce the criteria for granting an interlocutory injunction set out in *American Cyanamid Co.* v *Ethicon Ltd* [1975] AC 396. Nor do they reproduce the criteria on which applications for *Mareva* injunctions and *Anton Piller* orders were assessed in the past. All three types of injunction are based on statutory provisions allowing the courts to grant injunctions where it is 'just and convenient' (Supreme Court Act 1981, s. 37; County Courts Act 1984, s. 38; Civil Procedure Act 1997, s. 7). Detailed guidelines on how this jurisdiction should be exercised have always been based on case law.

The general criterion established by the CPR for the grant of an interim remedy is that it will give effect to the overriding objective (r. 1.2). Is it possible to subsume the existing criteria for injunctions within the overriding objective? Even if the existing guidelines continue alongside the overriding objective, does this mean that there are now additional requirements that must be satisfied in order to obtain an interim injunction, freezing injunction or search order? Clearly if the latter is the case, the evidence tendered in support of the application must satisfy these additional requirements.

Set out side by side, as in table 10.2, it can be seen that there are several areas in which the criteria are consistent with each other.

CHAPTER 10 INTERIM INJUNCTIONS ETC

American Cyanamid criteria for an interlocutory injunction	Criteria for a Mareva	Criteria for an Anton Piller	Overriding objective
A serious question to be tried.	A cause of action justiciable in England and Wales.	An extremely strong prima facie case on the merits.	Ensuring the parties are on an equal footing.
Damages an inadequate remedy for the claimant's interim loss pending trial.	A good arguable case on the merits.	Very serious damage to the claimant.	Saving expense.
Claimant's cross-undertaking in damages provides adequate protection for the defendant.	Defendant has assets within the jurisdiction.	Clear evidence of possession and of a real possibility of removal or destruction. (PD 25 Interim Injunctions refers to 'the probability' that material will disappear.)	Dealing with the case in ways which are proportionate: • to the amount of money involved; • to the importance of the case; • to the complexity of the issues; • to the parties' financial position.
Balance of convenience in favour of granting the injunction.	Real risk of removal or disposal.	Harm caused by execution of order on respondent not excessive.	Ensuring that it is dealt with expeditiously and fairly.
			Alloting to it an appropriate share of the court's resources, while taking into account the need to allot resources to other cases.
			Furthering the overriding objective by actively managing cases: • identifying the issues at an early stage; • deciding promptly which issues need full investigation and trial and accordingly disposing summarily of the others; • encouraging the parties to use an alternative dispute resolution procedure; • encouraging the parties to cooperate with each other; • helping the parties to settle the whole or part of a case; • deciding the order in which issues are to be raised; • fixing timetables or otherwise controlling the progress of a case; • considering whether the likely benefits of taking a particular step will justify the costs of taking it; • dealing with as many aspects of the case as is practicable on the same occasion; • dealing with the case without the parties needing to attend at court; • making appropriate use of technology; • giving directions to ensure that the trial of a case proceeds quickly and efficiently.

Table 10.2 Comparison between existing criteria and the overriding objective

CHAPTER 10 INTERIM INJUNCTIONS ETC

The balance of convenience aspects of the existing criteria are consistent with the drive of the overriding objective towards ensuring the parties are on an equal footing. Criteria involving the inadequacy or otherwise of damages as an alternative remedy are not dissimilar to the requirement to deal with the case in ways which are proportionate to the importance of the case (at least to the parties) and to the parties' financial position. Criteria involving the strength of the case may be related to the importance of the case and the complexity of the issues (although a strong case may very well be a simple one). The court may be increasingly inclined to adjudicate summarily on a peripheral issue rather than grant an injunction intended to preserve the issue to trial.

Even the emphasis in the previous criteria on granting injunctive relief only where there are substantial merits in the substantive cases is reflected to a large extent in the requirement of 'deciding promptly which issues need full investigation and trial and accordingly disposing summarily of the others'.

There are perhaps three major areas to which the overriding objective seems to add emphasis in this context:

(a) costs and proportionality;
(b) cooperation and ADR; and
(c) delay in this case and in others caused by injunction proceedings.

In the light of the general tenor of the Woolf reforms, none of these should be surprising.

10.7.1 Cost and proportionality

There are numerous references to costs and proportionality in connection with the overriding objective:

(a) ensuring the parties are on an equal footing;
(b) saving expense;
(c) dealing with the case in ways which are proportionate:
   (i) to the amount of money involved,
   (ii) to the importance of the case,
   (iii) to the complexity of the issues,
   (iv) to the parties' financial position;

(d) considering whether the likely benefits of taking a particular step will justify the costs of taking it.

To some extent proportionality was considered in relation to injunctions even under the old system. So, for example, a *Mareva* would not be ordered if the assets frozen would amount to no more than 'a drop in the ocean' when compared to the value of the claim (*Rasu Maritima SA* v *Perusahaan Pertambangan Minyak Dan Gas Bumi Negara* [1978] QB 644). The court would also before April 1999 consider the realistic benefits of granting an injunction (although perhaps not explictly in comparison with costs) when considering an application for a mandatory injunction. For a recent exposition of the principles, see *Co-operative Insurance Society Ltd* v *Argyll Stores (Holdings) Ltd* [1998] AC 1). In relation to *Anton Piller* orders, Hoffmann J in *Lock International plc* v *Beswick* [1989] 1 WLR 1268 said at p. 1281, '. . . there must be *proportionality* between the perceived threat to the plaintiff's rights and the remedy granted'.

Measuring the balance of convenience of each party in granting or refusing the injunction is a means of addressing whether or not the parties are, or will be after the grant of the injunction, on an equal footing as far as possible or relevant.

What the overriding objective seems to have added is, if anything, a positive obligation on the part of the applicant to demonstrate that the costs of granting an injunction (and, if relevant, the granting of it pre-action and/or without notice) are justified. This will be of particular relevance where the application is for a search order, the costs of execution of which will be particularly high.

10.7.2 Cooperation and ADR

There are numerous references in CPR, Part 1, to the emphasis on cooperation and resolution short of trial:

(a) encouraging the parties to use an alternative dispute resolution procedure;
(b) encouraging the parties to cooperate with each other;
(c) helping the parties to settle the whole or part of a case.

The injunction as a concept is noticeably at odds with this ethos: an *Anton Piller* order has never been a noticeably cooperative operation. The previous procedure in this field perhaps encouraged a shoot first, talk afterwards approach: get the injunction first, then talk about replacing it with an undertaking. This is perhaps inevitable when such an order can only be made against a respondent who is unlikely to abide by any order made on notice.

If the application is of an ugent nature and made without notice, and the claimant can justify not notifying the respondent of the application, similar arguments should, it is suggested, also justify not inviting the respondent to resolve the same issue by consent. However, after the grant of such an injunction, the court will no doubt encourage the parties to resolve the issue, by undertaking or otherwise, between themselves.

10.7.3 Delay in this case and others

It is a central tenet of the reforms that a case should be resolved fairly, but quickly:

(a) ensuring that it is dealt with expeditiously;
(b) allotting to it an appropriate share of the court's resources, while taking into account the need to allot resources to other cases;
(c) dealing with as many aspects of the case as is practicable on the same occasion;
(d) dealing with the case without the parties needing to attend at court;
(e) making appropriate use of technology.

In exercise of these criteria, applications can and will be made by telephone and even by e-mail. It is a presumption that interim applications, rather than being made piecemeal, will be 'saved up' to the next scheduled hearing. Where an application is made for an injunction, then, one can expect to have to justify why interim injunctive relief is more satisfactory than, say, proceeding to a speedy trial by imposing a directions timetable with a limited period before a fixed trial date. The same applies to summary disposal of the issue on which the injunction is based. The court will seek to ensure that the parties' focus on the injunction and its consequences (for example, where there is a search order) does not detract from the efficient and speedy progress towards full resolution. In an appropriate case the court might achieve this by refusing to grant the injunction at all.

The additional factor that any given case should only be allocated an appropriate share of the court's resources ('Why should I spend all day on your injunction hearing if it holds up the cases behind you?') should also be addressed by both parties. This should be the case not only in deciding whether to apply for an injunction at all, but in preparing and presenting the arguments as concisely and efficiently as possible. Ill-thought-out and unnecessary applications will be dismissed on this ground, or run the risk of sanctions being imposed.

CHAPTER 11　CASE MANAGEMENT

CONTENTS

11.1	Introduction	160
11.2	Procedural judges	161
11.3	Transfer to appropriate court	161
11.4	Allocation	162
11.4.1	Time when track allocation is decided	162
11.4.2	Allocation questionnaires	162
11.4.3	Extra information	163
11.4.4	Failure to file an allocation questionnaire	164
11.4.5	Further information	164
11.4.6	Allocation hearing	164
11.4.7	Allocation rules	164
11.5	Stay to allow for settlement	168
11.6	Assessment of damages cases	169
11.6.1	Disposal hearings	170
11.6.2	Assessment directions	170
11.6.3	Hearing to assess damages	170
11.7	Subsequent case management	170
11.8	Sanctions	173

11.1　INTRODUCTION

Judicial case management of civil litigation is one of the central planks of the new rules. The *Final Report* stressed the idea that ultimate responsibility for the control of litigation should move from the litigants and their advisers to the court. Under the new rules, the legal profession is intended to perform its traditional adversarial role in a managed environment governed by the courts. One of the purposes behind the CPR is to require the parties to focus their efforts on the key issues rather than allowing every issue to be pursued regardless of expense and time. Case management is seen as the means by which the judiciary will ensure this happens.

In exercising their powers to manage cases, the courts will be seeking to secure the overriding objective of the CPR of ensuring that cases are dealt with justly. Rule 1.1(2) provides that dealing with cases justly includes ensuring they are dealt with expeditiously and fairly, allotting to them an appropriate share of the court's resources, and ensuring they are dealt with proportionately bearing in mind factors such as the importance and complexities of the issues and the monetary value of the claim.

The *Final Report*, ch. 1, para. 4, envisaged there would be active case management by the courts, with procedural judges identifying the issues in the case, summarily disposing of some issues and deciding the order in which other issues are to be resolved, fixing timetables for the procedural steps in preparing cases for trial, and limiting evidence, particularly documentary and expert evidence. These ideas are put into effect by r. 1.4(1), which provides that the court must further the overriding objective by actively managing cases. The rule goes on to list 12 methods that may be used to achieve this, a number of which adopt the ideas listed at the beginning of this paragraph. It is intended that procedural judges will be far more willing to intervene during the early stages of proceedings than they have been in the past so as to ensure that the issues are narrowed, that cases are prepared economically and speedily, and disposed of fairly and without undue delay or expense.

To assist with this process defended actions will be assigned to one of three 'tracks'. The smallest and simplest cases will be assigned to the 'small claims track', which will be similar to the old small claims arbitration system. Cases with a monetary value in the range of £5,000 to £15,000 will usually be allocated to the 'fast track' with standard directions and tight timetables of up to 30 weeks for completion of the interlocutory stages before trial. Larger and more important cases will be assigned to the 'multi-track'. Cases on the multi-track will have widely differing values and complexity, and the courts will be given a great deal of flexibility in the way they can manage these cases commensurate with the particular features of each case. Multi-track cases will be dealt with mainly at civil trial centres, to which they will be transferred at an early stage as necessary.

To ensure that case management is proportionate the *Final Report* envisaged there will be hands-on judicial intervention only in cases which will require and repay it. Basic management, with a fixed timetable and standard procedure, will be used wherever possible, on the multi-track as well as on the fast track. Keeping case management proportionate may, however, prove quite difficult, particularly on the multi-track. The new rules envisage directions being given by consent and without hearings (see 9.5.3 and 9.5.4). They also give the courts powers to hold four types of procedural hearing (allocation hearings, case management conferences, pre-trial reviews, and listing hearings) which, unless kept under control, could result in substantial increases in the use of court resources and expense to the parties. The overall result should be that the majority of defended cases will proceed between the filing of a defence and trial with directions in a more or less standard form, but tailored to the needs of the particular case, without the need for the parties to attend court for a directions hearing, with case management hearings restricted to the more difficult and important cases. Whether this will occur in practice remains to be seen.

11.2 PROCEDURAL JUDGES

Case management decisions will generally be dealt with by masters for cases proceeding in the Royal Courts of Justice, and by district judges in High Court district registry and county court cases. Technically, the governing rule (CPR, r. 2.4) in fact gives the courts a great deal of flexibility, allowing performance by any judicial officer whether a district judge, master or judge, subject to any specific contrary provision in any enactment, rule or practice direction. However, PD 29, para. 3.10, says that masters will in general perform case management functions in the Royal Courts of Justice, district judges in district registry matters, and either district judges or circuit judges in county court cases.

11.3 TRANSFER TO APPROPRIATE COURT

Subject to the rules relating to commencing proceedings in the High Court, a claimant has a free choice of which court to use when commencing proceedings (see 5.2). The first case management intervention may be to transfer the case to a more appropriate court. This is considered in 5.3.

11.4 ALLOCATION

Every defended claim has to be allocated to one of the three tracks by an order by a procedural judge. To assist the court the parties are usually required to file allocation questionnaires shortly after defences are filed providing the court with additional information about the progress that has been made to date in seeking a resolution with the other parties and in preparing the evidence for trial, and also with information relevant to the likely length of the trial and about costs. In cases outside the financial scope of the small claims track the parties are required to give a breakdown of their estimated costs using the standard statements of costs form (see appendix 3), which must be filed and served with their allocation questionnaires (PD 43, para. 4.5(1)).

11.4.1 Time when track allocation is decided

The usual position is that the procedural judge will decide which track to allocate a case to when every defendant has filed an allocation questionnaire, or when the period for filing allocation questionnaires has expired, whichever is the sooner (CPR, r. 26.5(1)). Although the rule only mentions questionnaires filed by defendants, it is to be expected that the court will wait for the claimant's questionnaire if the specified period has not expired. There are some additional provisions dealing with track allocation in special cases, as follows:

(a) In cases where there is a stay for settlement (see 11.5), allocation is dealt with at the end of the period of the stay (r. 26.5(2)).

(b) In cases which are automatically transferred, allocation decisions are taken after the transfer takes place and are made by a procedural judge of the destination court.

(c) In cases which could be allocated either to the fast or the multi-track, allocation decisions are usually taken in the court where the proceedings are commenced, but occasionally they will be transferred to the appropriate civil trial centre for allocation and directions.

(d) Where a claimant enters a default judgment for an amount of money to be decided by the court (what used to be described as 'damages to be assessed') or for the value of goods or the amount of interest to be decided by the court, the case will not be 'defended' in that a defence will not have been filed. These cases therefore are not governed by the standard track allocation provisions. Instead, when judgment is entered the court will give any necessary directions and will, if appropriate, allocate the case to one of the three tracks (r. 12.7(2)(b)). These cases are considered further in 11.6.

(e) When judgment is entered for damages to be decided on an admission by the defendant in a claim for money that has not been specified, then, as in (d), the court will give any necessary directions and, if appropriate, allocate the case to one of the three tracks (r. 14.8). These cases are also considered in 11.6.

(f) Part 8 claims (which are broadly equivalent to the old originating summons) are treated as allocated to the multi-track (r. 8.9(c)).

11.4.2 Allocation questionnaires

When a defendant files a defence (or, in the case of multiple defendants, when they have all filed defences or the time limited for doing so has

CHAPTER 11   CASE MANAGEMENT

expired), the court will serve allocation questionnaires in form N150 (see appendix 3) on each party, or will make a direction dispensing with the need for questionnaires (CPR, r. 26.3(1) and (2)). Questionnaires may be dispensed with if there has already been an application, such as for summary judgment, which has been treated as an allocation hearing (PD 26, para. 2.4). The obligation of serving allocation questionnaires rests with the court where proceedings were commenced, even in actions that are automatically transferred to the defendant's home court.

The form will state the date by which it must be filed, which should be at least 14 days after the date it is deemed to have been served on the party in question. A fee is payable by the claimant when the questionnaire is filed. If the court dispenses with the need to file allocation questionnaires, the same fee is still payable. If the fee is not paid, the court will send a notice to pay the fee, using form N173. If the notice to pay is not complied with, the claim will be struck out (CPR, r. 3.7).

The questionnaire asks whether the relevant pre-action protocol (if any) was complied with. It also asks whether a stay is sought for settlement (see 11.5), about possible transfer to another court, for the party's view on the appropriate track for the case, for details about expert and factual witnesses, and for details of any contemplated applications. This is obviously an important document, and care in completing it will assist the court in deciding whether to transfer the case to a more appropriate venue, on the appropriate track for the case, on the nature of any directions that may be appropriate, and whether a case management conference will be required if the case is allocated to the multi-track.

The parties are encouraged to consult one another and cooperate in completing their allocation questionnaires, and also in deciding on any additional information, which may include suggested directions (see 11.4.3), they may send to the court with their questionnaires (PD 26, para. 2.3). However, they should not allow consultation to delay filing of their questionnaires.

11.4.3   Extra information

Parties may file additional information with their allocation questionnaires if this will assist the court in making its decisions regarding track allocation and case management. However, such additional information should only be filed if all the parties have agreed the information is correct and that it should be put before the court, or if the party intending to file the information confirms that copies have been delivered to all the other parties (PD 26, para. 2.2(2)). Information and matters that might assist the court include:

(a)   whether any of the parties intends to apply for summary judgment or some other order that might dispose of the case or reduce the amount in dispute or the issues to be decided;
(b)   whether any of the parties intends to make a Part 20 claim or to apply to add another party;
(c)   information about the steps taken and intended to be taken regarding preparing the evidence for trial; and
(d)   suggested case management directions for the case.

11.4.4 Failure to file an allocation questionnaire

If a party fails to file an allocation questionnaire, the court may give any direction it considers appropriate (CPR, r. 26.5(5)). The court's response will depend to quite an extent on whether the other parties have filed their questionnaires. If they have, the party in default can hardly complain if allocation and directions decisions are made based entirely on the information given by the other parties. If the court decides it does not have enough information, it will list the matter for an allocation hearing (PD 26, para. 2.5(2)(b)), and will almost certainly order the costs of the hearing to be paid by the party in default on the indemnity basis, usually with a summary assessment of those costs and an order for them to be paid forthwith or within a stated period (PD 26, para. 6.6(2)). If all the parties are in default, the file will be referred to the judge, who will usually order that unless allocation questionnaires are filed within three days from service of the order, the claim and any counterclaim will be struck out (PD 26, para. 2.5(1)).

11.4.5 Further information

The documents filed by the parties may not be sufficiently informative for the court to decide on the appropriate track for the case. In such cases, r. 26.5(3) of the CPR provides that the court may order a party to provide further information about its case. Usually any such order will stipulate that it must be complied with within 14 days (PD 26, para. 4.2(2)). The standard notice of allocation or listing hearing form (N153, see appendix 3) incorporates a section for the court to set out the further information it requires from the parties. How the court may deal with cases where inadequate information is given is considered further at 14.3.2.

11.4.6 Allocation hearing

The court may hold an allocation hearing if it thinks it is necessary (CPR, r. 26.5(4)). Alternatively, the court may treat any other interlocutory hearing as an allocation hearing, the most likely candidates being applications for summary judgment and interim injunctions. Given the rules set out at 11.4.7, and the use of the word 'necessary' in this rule, it is to be expected that allocation hearings will be rather exceptional. At such a hearing the procedural judge will consider which track will be most suitable for the case, bearing in mind its financial value and the other factors set out at 11.4.7.5, and give suitable case management directions. Consequently, a person attending for a party should, if possible, be the person responsible for the case. In any event, the representative must be familiar with the case, be able to provide the court with the information it is likely to require, and have sufficient authority to deal with any issues that are likely to arise (PD 26, para. 6.5).

If an allocation hearing is listed because of one of the parties being in default of the requirement to file an allocation questionnaire, and that party fails to attend the hearing, the court will usually make an order specifying the steps which that party is required to take, and providing that unless those steps are taken within stated periods of time his statement of case will be struck out (PD 26, para. 6.6(3)).

11.4.7 Allocation rules

The primary rules for track allocation are based on the financial value of the claim. This is the monetary value of the claim disregarding any amount not in dispute, any claim for interest or costs, and also disregarding any allegation of contributory negligence (CPR, r. 26.8(2)). It is for the court to assess the financial value of the claim, though it will take into account the way in which the claim is formulated in the particulars of claim and any information given in the allocation questionnaire. Any sum for which the defendant does not admit liability is in dispute, but the court will not regard the following as in dispute (PD 26, para. 7.4):

(a) sums for which summary judgment on a part of a claim has been entered;

(b) any distinct items in the claim for which the defendant has admitted liability; and

(c) any distinct items in the claim which have been agreed between the parties.

Generally claims will be allocated in accordance with their financial value, but may be allocated to another track if the procedural judge decides that the claim can be dealt with more justly on another track, taking into account a number of factors set out in CPR, r. 26.8 (see 11.4.7.5). However, a claim will not be allocated to a lower track than its financial value would indicate was appropriate, unless all the parties consent to the lower track allocation (r. 26.7(3)).

11.4.7.1 Small claims track The small claims track is intended to provide a proportionate procedure for the most straightforward types of cases, such as consumer disputes, small accident claims, disputes about the ownership of goods, and landlord and tenant cases other than claims for possession. This is the normal track for defended claims with a value not exceeding £5,000 (CPR, r. 26.6(3)). Allocation to this track is by judicial order. (This is unlike the former small claims 'arbitration', to which there was automatic allocation.) Although most claims under £5,000 will end up in the small claims track, the following types of claim will not normally be allocated there even if they have a value under £5,000:

(a) personal injuries cases where the value of the claim for pain, suffering and loss of amenity exceeds £1,000 (r. 26.6(1)(a) and (2));

(b) claims by tenants of residential premises seeking orders that their landlords should carry out repairs or other works to the premises where the value of the claim exceeds £1,000 (r. 26.6(1)(b));

(c) claims by residential tenants seeking damages against their landlords for harassment or unlawful eviction (r. 26.7(4)); and

(d) Claims involving a disputed allegation of dishonesty (PD 26, para. 8.1(1)(d)).

Even if the claim is worth less than £5,000 there may be other reasons why it should not be allocated to the small claims track. One relates to expert evidence, which is not allowed in small claims track cases, either by calling an expert at the hearing or simply relying on an expert's report, unless the court gives permission (CPR, r. 27.5). Although permission may be granted, there are also severe restrictions on the costs recoverable for expert evidence in small claims track cases, including a limit of £200 for experts' fees (PD 27, para. 7.3(2)), which may make it unjust for a small case which requires expert evidence to be allocated to this track.

If the claim is worth more than £5,000, the parties may consent to it being allocated to the small claims track (CPR, rr. 26.7(3) and 27.14(5)). However, the court retains control, and may refuse to allocate the case in

CHAPTER 11   CASE MANAGEMENT

accordance with the parties' wishes if it feels the case is not suitable for the small claims track (PD 26, para. 8.1(2)(b)). For example, it is unlikely to agree to a case being allocated to the small claims track if the hearing is likely to take more than a day (PD 26, para. 8.1(2)(c)). If the court agrees with the parties and allocates the case to the small claims track, the case is treated for the purposes of costs as a fast track case, except that trial costs are in the discretion of the court (CPR, r. 27.14(5)).

11.4.7.2   Fast track   The fast track is the normal track for cases broadly falling into the £5,000 to £15,000 bracket, and which can be disposed of by a trial which will not exceed a day. There are therefore two factors for deciding whether the fast track is the normal track for defended cases that are not allocated to the small claims track. The first factor, financial value (CPR, r. 26.6(1)–(4)), is to the effect that the following cases will normally be allocated to the fast track:

(a)   personal injuries cases with a financial value between £5,000 and £15,000;

(b)   personal injuries cases with an overall value under £5,000, but where the damages for pain, suffering and loss of amenity are likely to exceed £1,000;

(c)   claims by residential tenants for orders requiring their landlords to carry out repairs or other work to the premises where the financial value of the claim is between £1,000 and £15,000;

(d)   claims by residential tenants for damages against their landlords for harassment or unlawful eviction where the financial value of the claim does not exceed £15,000; and

(e)   other categories of cases, where the financial value of the claim is between £5,000 and £15,000.

The second factor, disposal at trial (r. 26.6(5)), is to the effect that cases falling within the normal limits for allocation to the fast track must also be likely to be disposed of by a trial lasting no more than a day, and with oral expert evidence limited to experts in no more than two expert fields and to one expert per field of expertise. However, the possibility that the trial might last longer than a day (which in this context means five hours) is not necessarily a conclusive reason for allocating a case to the multi-track (PD 26, para. 9.1(3)(c)). The assessment of likely trial length and the nature of the expert evidence necessary usually has to be made in the early stages of the proceedings, although it can arise again on a subsequent application to reallocate the case. It remains to be seen to what extent the courts will force claims into the fast track and force the parties into a limited one-day trial. The court has power under CPR, r. 32.1, to give directions limiting the issues on which it wishes to be addressed, and on the evidence that may be adduced at trial on those issues, despite the fact that doing so may result in the exclusion of material that would otherwise be admissible under the law of evidence (see chapter 16), and may take this into consideration when allocating (PD 26, para. 9.1(3)(b)). The court therefore does have the power to limit the duration of a trial if it so chooses, although it should only do so in accordance with the overriding objective. This requires that cases must be dealt with justly and fairly, so use of the court's power to limit evidence should not be so intrusive that it prevents either or both parties from proving their cases at trial. However, the result is that procedural judges are likely to feel that cases could be

CHAPTER 11 CASE MANAGEMENT

dealt with within the one-day limit under the new system which might have taken more than a day in the old system.

11.4.7.3 Multi-track The multi-track is the normal track for claims not falling for allocation to either the small claims or fast track (CPR, r. 26.6(6)). Typically these will be cases involving claims exceeding £15,000, and cases worth less than that sum where the trial is likely to exceed a day.

11.4.7.4 Claims with no monetary value A claim with no financial value will be allocated to the track which the procedural judge considers to be most suitable to enable it to be dealt with justly, taking into account the factors discussed at 11.4.7.5 (CPR, r. 26.7(2)). In these cases the importance of careful completion of the allocation questionnaire cannot be over-emphasised.

11.4.7.5 Discretionary factors In addition to the financial value of the claim (if it has one), when deciding which track to allocate it to the court is required to have regard to the following factors (CPR, r. 26.8):

(a) The nature of the remedy sought.
(b) The likely complexity of the facts, law or evidence.
(c) The number of parties or likely parties.
(d) The value of any counterclaim or other Part 20 claim (third-party claims etc.) and the complexity of any matters relating to those claims. In these cases the court will not aggregate the sums claimed in the claim, counterclaim and so on, but will generally simply look at the value of the largest of the cross-claims (PD 26, para. 7.7).
(e) The amount of oral evidence which may be required.
(f) The importance of the claim to persons who are not parties to the proceedings.
(g) The views expressed by the parties. These views will be regarded as important, but the court will not be bound by any agreement or common view expressed by the parties (PD 26, para. 7.5).
(h) The circumstances of the parties.

The *Final Report*, ch. 2, paras 15 and 16, envisaged that the following types of cases would be allocated to the multi-track even if the amount at stake was within the normal financial value for allocation to the fast track:

(a) cases involving issues of public importance;
(b) test cases;
(c) medical negligence cases (clinical disputes); and
(d) cases where there is a right to trial by jury, including deceit cases.

It is to be expected that the discretion given by CPR, r. 26.8(1), will be exercised to ensure such cases are allocated to the multi-track. The *Final Report* also commented on professional negligence cases in general and building cases that might fall within the financial parameters of the fast track, and pointed out that these vary considerably in complexity, and should be allocated to the most suitable track depending on the complexity of each case.

11.4.7.6 Trial in the Royal Courts of Justice A related question is whether a multi-track case should be managed and tried in the Royal Courts of Justice as opposed to another civil trial centre. The idea is that only the most important cases justify use of the resources of the Royal

CHAPTER 11 CASE MANAGEMENT

Courts of Justice. Thus, in general cases with an estimated value of less than £50,000 will be transferred out of the Royal Courts of Justice to a county court (PD 29, para. 2.2). Exceptions are:

(a) cases which are required by an enactment to be tried in the High Court;
(b) cases falling within any of the specialist lists;
(c) professional negligence claims;
(d) Fatal Accident Act claims;
(e) fraud and undue influence claims;
(f) defamation claims;
(g) claims for malicious prosecution and false imprisonment;
(h) claims against the police; and
(i) contentious probate claims.

11.4.7.7 Notice of allocation After the court has decided on the track to which a case is to be allocated, it will send a notice of allocation to the parties, together with copies of all relevant allocation questionnaires and further information provided by the other parties (CPR, r. 26.9). Several forms of notice of allocation have been devised for different circumstances (see appendix 3). There are four different forms for cases allocated to the small claims track (N157 to N160), one for the fast track (N154) and one for the multi-track (N155). Each has a space for allocation directions and for the judge's reasons for the allocation.

11.4.7.8 Changing tracks The court may make a subsequent order reallocating a claim to a different track (CPR, r. 26.10). Where a claim was initially allocated to the small claims track, and is later reallocated to another track, the small claims costs restrictions cease to apply from the date of reallocation (r. 27.15).

A party who is dissatisfied with an allocation decision may challenge the decision either by appealing up to the next higher court or by making an application back to the judge who made the initial decision. Applications should be used where the decision was made without a hearing of which he was given due notice or if there has been a material change of circumstances. If the party was present, represented or given due notice of the hearing where the decision was made, the only appropriate route is by way of appeal (PD 26, paras 11.1(2) and 11.2).

If a Part 20 claim is issued, it may be necessary to redetermine the most suitable track for the proceedings. Mere issue of a Part 20 claim will not have this effect, but where a defence to a Part 20 claim has been filed the proceedings will be reconsidered by the procedural judge to determine whether the claim should remain on its existing track (particularly in cases on the small claims and fast tracks), and whether there needs to be any adjustment to the timetable. At the same time the procedural judge will consider whether the Part 20 claim should be dealt with separately from the main action.

11.5 STAY TO ALLOW FOR SETTLEMENT

One of the court's case management functions is to help the parties to settle the whole or part of the case (CPR, r. 1.4(2)(f)), and another is to encourage the parties to use alternative dispute resolution procedures if appropriate, and to facilitate the use of such procedures (r. 1.4(2)(e)). It is with these objectives in mind that the new rules provide for a new procedure for the court ordering a stay of proceedings to allow for settlement of the case.

The allocation questionnaire allows a party to include a request for the proceedings to be stayed while the parties try to settle the case. If all the parties make such a request, or if the court on its own initiative considers that such a stay would be appropriate, a direction will be made staying the proceedings for one month (r. 26.4(2)). The court has power to extend the stay for such specified period as it thinks appropriate (r. 26.4(3)), which it will generally exercise on receipt of a letter from either party confirming that the extension is sought with the agreement of all the parties and giving a reasonable explanation of the steps being taken and the identity of the mediator or expert assisting with the process (PD 26, para. 3.1(1)). Extensions will not usually exceed four weeks at a time unless there are clear reasons to justify a longer time. During the period of such a stay the claimant is under a duty to inform the court if a settlement is reached (CPR, r. 26.4(4)). If, by the end of the defined period of the stay, the claimant has not told the court that the case has been settled, the court will give such directions for the management of the case as it considers appropriate, including allocating it to an appropriate track (rr. 26.4(5) and 26.5(2)). The periods of stays under these rules are carefully restricted so as to prevent the procedure being used to secure protracted 'authorised' delays after proceedings are commenced, under the guise of attempting to settle.

11.6 ASSESSMENT OF DAMAGES CASES

Cases where judgment is entered for damages to be assessed (or 'decided') do not fall into the usual pattern of 'defended' cases. The orders being considered here are described as 'relevant orders' by PD 26, para. 12.1(1), in which 'relevant order' is defined as meaning any order or judgment which requires the amount of money that has to be paid to be decided by the court. This includes orders that require:

(a) the assessment of damages;
(b) the assessment of interest;
(c) the taking of an account;
(d) the making of an inquiry as to any sum due; or
(e) the assessment of costs payable under a contract (other than a contract between a solicitor and client for legal services).

According to PD 26, para. 12.1(2), relevant orders may be made on entry of judgment in default, on entry of judgment on an admission, on the striking out of a statement of case, on a summary judgment application, on the determination of a preliminary issue or on a split trial as to liability, or even by consent or at trial.

Once a relevant order is made the court will either list the matter for a disposal hearing, or will give directions, or will stay the action while the parties try to settle the case using ADR or other means. Stays for settlement are dealt with in the same way as described in 11.5.

11.6.1 Disposal hearings

At a disposal hearing the court will either give directions or decide the amount payable (PD 26, para. 12.8(1)). If the relevant order was made by entry of default judgment without a hearing, and generally if the relevant order was entered after an admission, the court will deal with the matter by way of a disposal hearing. Disposal hearings may also be used where the claim has not been allocated to a track and the amount payable is not genuinely disputed on substantial grounds.

If the case is listed for a disposal hearing and the claim is worth less than £5,000, the court will usually allocate it to the small claims track (for costs purposes) and decide the amount payable there and then (PD 26, para. 12.8(2)). This provision effectively removes one of the loopholes in the old rules that an assessment of damages after judgment in default in a claim below what would have been the small claims threshold nevertheless attracted scale 1 costs because it had never formally been referred to small claims arbitration. Under the CPR if the financial value of a claim is more than £5,000, the court may still determine the amount payable at the disposal hearing, but in these cases the ordinary costs rules will apply. In cases determined at disposal hearings evidence may, unless the court otherwise directs, be adduced under r. 32.6 (see PD 26, para. 12.8(4)). This means that reliance may be placed on the matters set out in the particulars of claim (provided it is verified by a statement of truth) or by witness statement. The evidence relied upon must be served on the defendant at least three clear days before the disposal hearing.

11.6.2 Assessment directions

If a relevant order is made by consent, the parties should file agreed directions with the draft consent order which they should invite the court to give (PD 26, para. 12.5(2)). For other relevant orders, other than those dealt with by stays for settlement or by way of a disposal hearing, the court will give directions, which may include allocating or reallocating the case to a case management track, directing that allocation questionnaires be filed within a stated period of time, and directing that the case be listed for a hearing or a further hearing. Allocating a case to the fast track or multi-track after a relevant order has been made should only happen if the amount payable is genuinely disputed on grounds that appear to be substantial (PD 26, para. 12.3).

11.6.3 Hearing to assess damages

Generally, hearings to assess damages will be listed before masters and district judges irrespective of the amount in issue (PD 26, para. 12.10), but the court may give directions specifying the level or type of judge who is to deal with the case (PD 26, para. 12.2(2)).

11.7 SUBSEQUENT CASE MANAGEMENT

The following three chapters deal in more detail with the further progress of cases on each of the three case management tracks following allocation. Figure 11.1 shows the routes which cases may take from either a defence being filed or a 'relevant order' being made up to the decision to allocate the case to a case management track. Figure 11.2 shows in broad terms what happens to cases on the three case management tracks from the time they are allocated to a track until trial.

CHAPTER 11 CASE MANAGEMENT

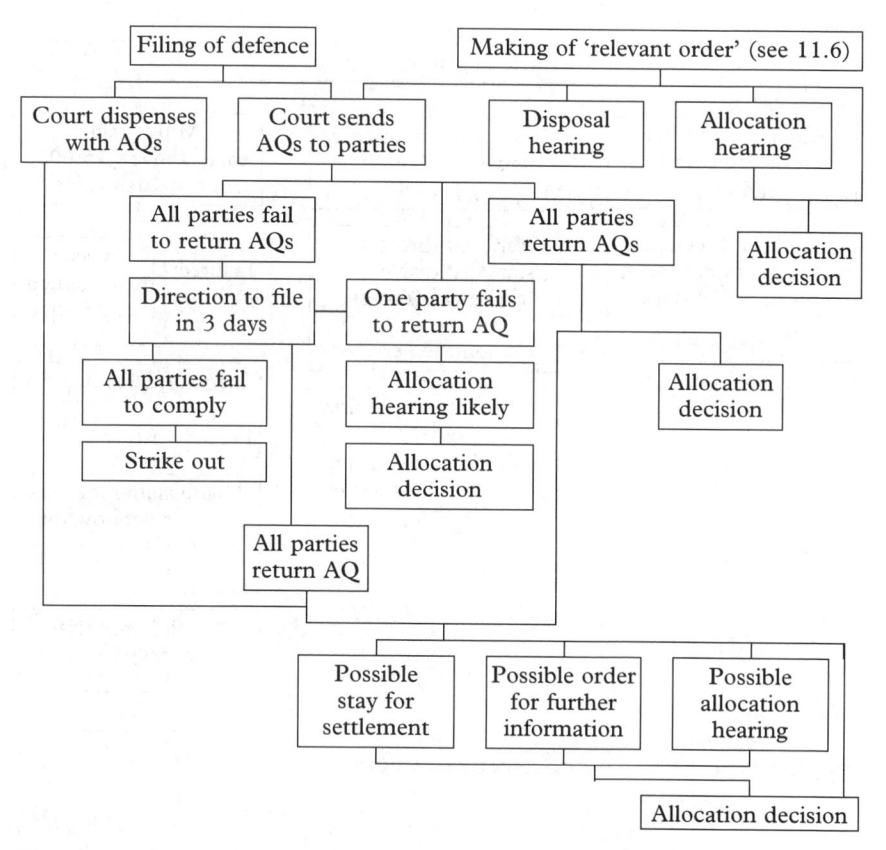

Figure 11.1 Routes to making track allocation decision

AQ = Allocation questionnaire

CHAPTER 11 CASE MANAGEMENT

```
                    ┌─────────────────────────────┐
                    │  Track allocation decision  │
                    └─────────────────────────────┘
        ┌──────────────────────┼──────────────────────┐
┌───────────────────┐ ┌───────────────────┐ ┌───────────────────┐
│ Small claims track:│ │ Fast track: most cases│ │    Multi-track:    │
│  most cases up to  │ │  between £5,000 and │ │ cases above £15,000,│
│       £5,000       │ │       £15,000       │ │  Part 8 Claims etc.│
└───────────────────┘ └───────────────────┘ └───────────────────┘
```

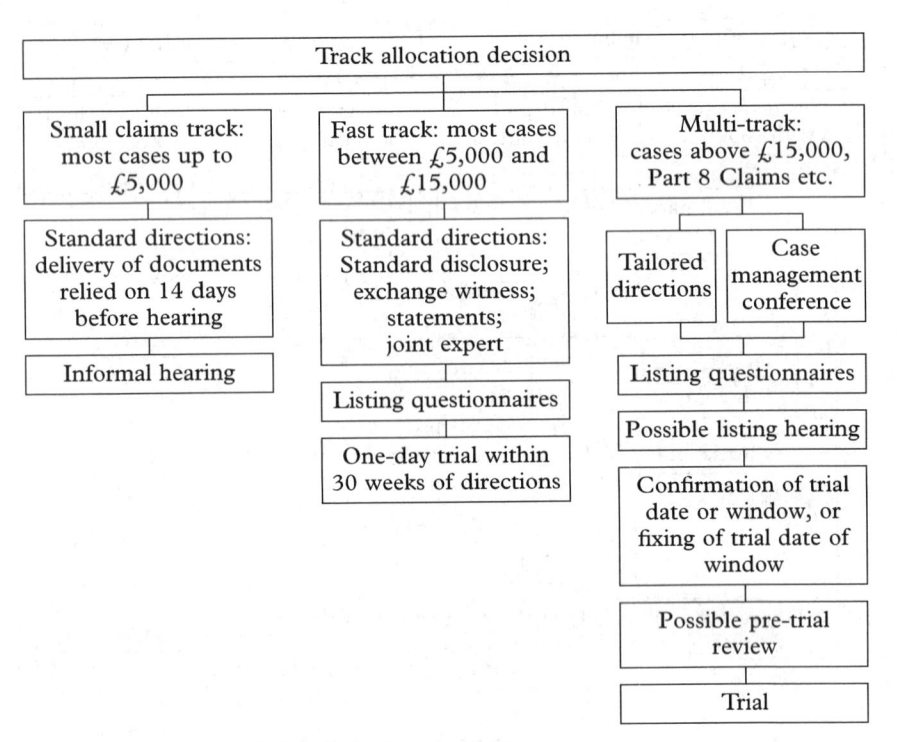

Figure 11.2 The case management tracks

Small claims track:
- Standard directions: delivery of documents relied on 14 days before hearing
- Informal hearing

Fast track:
- Standard directions: Standard disclosure; exchange witness; statements; joint expert
- Listing questionnaires
- One-day trial within 30 weeks of directions

Multi-track:
- Tailored directions | Case management conference
- Listing questionnaires
- Possible listing hearing
- Confirmation of trial date or window, or fixing of trial date of window
- Possible pre-trial review
- Trial

11.8 SANCTIONS

So that the court can ensure that its case management directions and orders are complied with, and to retain control over the conduct of litigation, it needs to be armed with suitable coercive powers. These are provided in the CPR in the form of sanctions. The most draconian sanction that may be imposed is striking out. Rule 3.4(2)(c) provides that the court may strike out a statement of case if it appears that there has been a failure to comply with a rule, practice direction or court order. Striking out the whole of a party's statement of case ought to be reserved for the most serious, or repeated, breaches or defaults. In less serious cases of default or breach the court may be prepared to impose a sanction which, in a phrase used in some of the recent cases under the old rules, 'fits the crime'. Rule 3.4 itself states that the power to strike out may be exercised over the whole or just a part of a statement of case. For example, a party may be in default of an order to provide further information on a single issue in a case where several issues are raised. A suitable sanction in such circumstances may be striking out the part of the statement of case dealing with that issue.

As alternatives to striking out, the court may impose costs sanctions, including ordering a party to pay certain costs forthwith. It may also debar a party in default from adducing evidence in a particular form or from particular witnesses. Alternatively, the court may impose sanctions that limit or deprive a party, if successful, of interest on any money claim, or which increase the amount of interest payable by the party in default.

There are various provisions in the CPR and practice directions that impose certain types of sanction in default of due compliance. For example, r. 35.13 of the CPR provides that a party who fails to disclose an expert's report may not use the report at the trial or call the expert to give evidence orally, unless the court gives permission. A more severe sanction is imposed by r. 3.7, which provides for the striking out of claims for non-payment of allocation and listing fees after the time set by a notice of non-payment. An example from the practice directions is PD 32, para. 25, which provides that if an affidavit, witness statement or exhibit does not comply with the requirements of CPR, Part 32, or PD 32, the court may refuse to admit it as evidence and may refuse to allow the costs arising from its preparation. This last example differs from the previous two in that it provides for a sanction which the court may choose to impose, whereas the other two provide for sanctions which apply unless the court grants relief.

11.8.1 Non-compliance with directions

It is to be expected that from time to time one or other of the parties to proceedings will be unable to keep to the directions timetable imposed by the court. This will not generally be a problem provided the parties cooperate and can still keep to the directions relating to the 'key' dates governing case management conferences, pre-trial reviews, filing listing questionnaires and trial (CPR, rr. 28.4 and 29.5). If the non-compliance is through events outside the control of the defaulting party or is otherwise not deliberate, normally it would be expected that the parties would cooperate in compliance with r. 1.4(2)(a) and resolve the difficulty by agreeing a new timetable that preserved the 'key' dates. The time specified by any provision of the CPR or by the court for doing any act may be varied by the written agreement of the parties, unless there is an express prohibition on variation in the rules (r. 2.11). If non-compliance cannot be resolved without, say, impinging on one of the 'key' dates, or if the other side insist on compliance, the matter is likely to come before the court.

In a departure from the position under the old rules, an 'innocent' party faced with an opponent who has not complied with the court's directions is not permitted either:

(a) to sit back and wait for the other side's default to get worse by the additional passage of time; or

(b) to make an immediate application for an order.

Instead, the correct procedure is that laid down in PD 28, para. 5 (for fast track cases) and PD 29, para. 7 (which is in identical terms and applies in multi-track cases). The innocent party should first write to the defaulting party referring to the default and warn the defaulting party of his intention to apply for an order if the default is not rectified within a short reasonable period (PD 28, para. 5.2; PD 29, para. 7.2). This will usually be seven or 14 days. If there is continued default, the innocent party may apply for an order to enforce compliance or for a sanction to be imposed or both (PD 28, para. 5.1; PD 29, para. 7.1). Any application for such an order must be made without delay (PD 28, para. 5.2; PD 29, para. 7.2). If the innocent party does delay in making the application, the court may take the delay into account when it decides whether to make an order imposing a sanction or whether to grant relief from a sanction imposed by the rules or any practice direction.

11.8.2 Court's approach on breach of orders or directions

The general approach that will be adopted where there has been a breach of case management directions is set out in PD 28, para. 5.4 (fast track) and PD 29, para. 7.4 (multi-track). It is to be expected that a similar approach will be taken where the breach is of a practice direction or provision in the CPR. According to PD 28 and PD 29:

(a) The court will not allow a failure to comply with directions to lead to the postponement of the trial unless the circumstances of the case are exceptional.

(b) If practicable to do so, the court will exercise its powers in a manner that enables the case to come on for trial on the date or within the period previously set.

(c) In particular the court will assess what steps each party should take to prepare the case for trial, direct that those steps are taken in the shortest possible time and impose a sanction for non-compliance. Such a sanction may, for example, deprive a party of the right to raise or contest an issue or to rely on evidence to which the direction relates.

(d) Where it appears that one or more issues are or can be made ready for trial at the time fixed while others cannot, the court may direct that the trial will proceed on the issues that are or will then be ready, and order that no costs will be allowed for any later trial of the remaining issues or that those costs will be paid by the party in default.

(e) Where the court has no option but to postpone the trial, it will do so for the shortest possible time and will give directions for the taking of the necessary steps in the meantime as rapidly as possible.

CHAPTER 11 CASE MANAGEMENT

(f) Litigants and lawyers must be in no doubt that the court will regard the postponement of a trial as an order of last resort. The court may exercise its power to require a party as well as his legal representative to attend court at a hearing where such an order is to be sought.

In this connection, PD 28, para. 4.2(2), and PD 29, para. 6.2(2), are relevant, as they provide that the court will assume for the purposes of any later application that a party who did not appeal and who made no application to vary within 14 days of service of any order containing directions was content that they were correct in the circumstances then existing.

As mentioned at 11.8.1, the court may seek to achieve the aims set out in PD 28, para. 5, and PD 29, para. 7, by making an order against the defaulting party which may be combined with a sanction. It is to be expected that the courts will be far more ready to impose sanctions than they were under the old system. It was an accepted principle under the old system that 'unless' orders were not made on the first default of a party, but were a last resort to ensure compliance (see *Hytec Information Systems Ltd* v *Coventry City Council* [1997] 1 WLR 1666). Such an approach will often be unworkable in the new system, particularly in cases on the fast track. In these cases there will be a very limited time between any breach and the date or window fixed for the trial, and there simply will not be time for an order without sanctions to be made if trial dates are not to be lost. Consequently, courts are going to be very much more willing to make orders with sanctions, even on a first breach by a defaulting party.

11.8.3 Avoiding sanctions being imposed

The court has a general power to extend and abridge time (CPR, r. 3.1(2)(a)). A party who is unable to comply with an order or direction in time (or who is already in breach) and who has not been able to agree an extension with the other side may make an application asking the court to extend time for compliance. The discretion given to the court by r. 3.1 is unfettered other than by the general requirement to give effect to the overriding objective.

On other occasions, a default may arise through the defective performance of the requirements of a rule, practice direction or court order. For example, it may be that the wrong form was used, or that it was sent to the wrong address (but still came to the attention of the other side), or that the document used was not completed correctly. These are errors of procedure. By r. 3.10 such errors do not invalidate the step purportedly taken, unless the court so orders. The court may make an order invalidating a step if it was so badly defective that the other side were misled, or where the defects are so great that it would not be right to regard the purported performance as performance at all. Further, by r. 3.10(2) the court may make an order to remedy any error of procedure. A defaulting party should consider seeking such an order where there is an objection made regarding defective performance.

11.8.4 Form of order with sanctions

Like all other orders, orders with sanctions must specify the time within which the step under consideration must be taken by reference to a calendar date and a specific time (CPR, r. 2.9). The sanction part of the order may take the form of an 'unless' provision. This is to the effect that if the terms of the order are breached, the other party may file a request for judgment to be entered and costs (r. 3.5). Such an order may read:

> Unless by 4.00 p.m. on Friday 4 June 1999 the defendant do file and serve a list of documents giving standard disclosure, the defence shall be struck out and judgment entered for the claimant for damages to be decided by the court.

11.8.5 Non-compliance with order imposing a sanction

If a party fails to comply with a rule, practice direction or court order imposing any sanction, the sanction will take effect unless the defaulting party applies for and obtains relief from the sanction (CPR, r. 3.8). The rule goes on to provide that extensions cannot be agreed between the parties.

11.8.6 Relief from sanctions

A party in breach of a rule, practice direction or order imposing a sanction for non-compliance may apply for relief from the sanction (CPR, r. 3.8). This is done by issuing an application notice, which must be supported by evidence. On such an application r. 3.9 provides that the court will consider all the circumstances, and then sets out a list of the following nine factors which will be considered:

(a) the interests of the administration of justice;
(b) whether the application for relief has been made promptly;
(c) whether the failure to comply was intentional;
(d) whether there is a good explanation for the failure;
(e) the extent to which the party in default has complied with other rules, practice directions, court orders and any relevant pre-action protocol;
(f) whether the failure to comply was caused by the party or his legal representative;
(g) whether the trial date or the likely trial date can still be met if relief is granted;
(h) the effect which any failure to comply had on each party; and
(i) the effect which the granting of relief would have on each party.

11.8.7 Non-compliance with applicable pre-action protocols

If, in the opinion of the court, non-compliance with a pre-action protocol that applies to a case leads to the commencement of proceedings which might otherwise not have needed to be commenced, or leads to costs being incurred in the proceedings that might otherwise not have been incurred, PD Protocols, para. 2.3, provides that the orders the court may make include:

(a) an order that the party at fault pay the costs of the proceedings, or part of those costs, of the other party or parties;
(b) an order that the party at fault pay those costs on an indemnity basis;
(c) if the party at fault is a claimant in whose favour an order for the payment of damages or some specified sum is subsequently made, an order depriving that party of interest on such sum and in respect of such period as may be specified, and/or awarding interest at a lower rate than that at which interest would otherwise have been awarded;

(d) if the party at fault is a defendant and an order for the payment of damages or some specified sum is subsequently made in favour of the claimant, an order awarding interest on such sum and in respect of such period as may be specified at a higher rate, not exceeding 10 per cent above base rate, than the rate at which interest would otherwise have been awarded.

Paragraph 2.4 of the same PD provides that the court will exercise its powers under para. 2.3 with the object of placing the innocent party in no worse a position than he would have been in if the protocol had been complied with.

CHAPTER 12   SMALL CLAIMS

CONTENTS

12.1	Introduction	178
12.2	The small claims jurisdiction — venue and level	179
12.3	Pre-allocation procedures: the possibility of summary judgment	180
12.4	The small claims track	180
12.4.1	A specific exception	181
12.4.2	Power to grant a final remedy	181
12.5	Distinctive features of the small claims track	181
12.6	Restriction on application of rules	181
12.7	Procedure after allocation to the small claims track	182
12.7.1	Option 1: standard directions and fixed final hearing date	182
12.7.2	Option 2: special directions and further directions	183
12.7.3	Option 3: special directions and fixed final hearing date	183
12.7.4	Option 4: preliminary hearing	184
12.7.5	Option 5: proceeding without a hearing	184
12.8	Conduct of the final hearing	184
12.8.1	Representation	185
12.8.2	Public hearing	185
12.8.3	Method of proceeding	185
12.8.4	Recording evidence and giving reasons	186
12.8.5	Non-attendance of the parties at the final hearing	186
12.8.6	Setting judgment aside and rehearing	187
12.8.7	If judgment is set aside	188
12.9	Appeals	188
12.9.1	Rights of appeal	188
12.9.2	Procedure on appeal	189
12.10	Costs	189
12.10.1	Costs before allocation to the small claims track	189
12.10.2	Costs after allocation	189
12.10.3	Unreasonable behaviour	190
12.10.4	Reallocation from the small claims track	190
12.10.5	Costs in exceptional cases	190
12.10.6	Allocation of assessments of damages and disposals	190

12.1   INTRODUCTION

An important objective of the CPR, according to r. 1.1(2), is that the court should seek to deal with a case in ways which save expense and are proportionate:

(a) to the amount of money involved;
(b) to the importance of the case;
(c) to the complexity of the issues; and
(d) to the parties' financial position.

To carry out this objective a separate regime is set up for the 'small claims track', which to some extent mirrors the previous provisions relating to county court arbitrations. The term 'small claims' is unfortunate given that the upper limit of the financial jurisdiction represents a sum which many would consider a very large claim indeed and it may be that this name will be changed in due course.

12.2 THE SMALL CLAIMS JURISDICTION — VENUE AND LEVEL

When a claim is commenced and a defence is filed the first matter to be dealt with will be whether it should stay in the same court where it was issued (see 5.3). Under CPR, r. 26.2(1), if the defendant is an individual and the claim is for a specified amount of money and was not commenced in the defendant's home court, the court will transfer the proceedings to the defendant's home court or, if there are two or more defendants, to the home court of the first defendant to file a defence. In two kinds of case the claimant will be asked whether he wishes to proceed. These are where the defence is that the money claimed has been paid (r. 15.10) and where the defendant admits part of a claim for a specified amount of money (r. 14.5).

The phrase 'specified amount of money' is not the same as the old term 'liquidated sum'. Under the CPR it is apparently open to a claimant, and clearly this is only likely to be done by litigants in person, to state the amount of money he thinks the claim is worth, even where it is in essence a claim for unliquidated damages, such as in a personal injuries or holiday disappointment claim. The advantage of doing so is that if the defendant takes no action, the claimant can then obtain judgment in default for the amount of the claim and there will be no judicial investigation of quantum. If the defendant then applies successfully to set aside the judgment, quantum will of course remain at large when the proceedings continue. The disadvantage of claiming a specified sum of money rather than, as in the old formula, damages limited to some upper figure, is that on the filing of a defence the case will be transferred to the defendant's home court. If the claim is not for a specified amount of money, the case will remain in the court of issue. The court anyway has a discretionary power to transfer proceedings to another county court, district registry, division or list if it considers it appropriate to do so before allocating a claim to a track (r. 26.3).

If no issue of transfer arises, the court will serve allocation questionnaires (see 11.4), which must be returned by the date specified on them.

When completing the allocation questionnnaire a party may request the proceedings to be stayed whilst the parties try to settle the case by alternative dispute resolution or other means (see 11.5). In modest claims this is unlikely to involve a formal alternative dispute resolution procedure, though it may include such things as participation in an arbitration system within a given industry (as in the case of holiday claims). It may merely amount to an indication of a desire to negotiate. If all parties request a stay or the court of its own initiative considers that such a stay would be appropriate, the court will direct that the proceedings are stayed for one month or for such longer period as it considers appropriate (r. 26.4(2)). If the claim is in fact settled, the claimant must tell the court. If he does not notify the court that the claim is settled then the court will give such directions as to the management of the case as are appropriate. At the expiry of whatever period is allowed the court will give further directions about the case.

The court will then proceed to allocate the claim to a track when every defendant has filed his allocation questionnnaire or the period for filing questionnaires has expired. For this purpose the court may order a party to provide further information about his case. There is no 'automatic allocation' to the small claims track. It is always a positive judicial decision.

12.3 PRE-ALLOCATION PROCEDURES: THE POSSIBILITY OF SUMMARY JUDGMENT

It is not inevitable that a claim for £5,000 or less will be allocated to the small claims track at all. It may end before allocation. It is open to a claimant, immediately upon receiving an acknowledgment of service or defence, to apply for summary judgment. There are two reasons why this may well prove to be a means of disposing of a fair proportion of small claims. The first is the increase in jurisdiction to £5,000 which means that there are likely to be more heavyweight disputes within the system. The second is the change in the test which a defendant is required to satisfy before he can defeat a summary judgment application, from the former test of 'arguable issue' to the rather more demanding *Saudi Eagle* test, provided by the words 'no real prospect of successfully defending the claim' (CPR, r. 24.2(a)). A defendant may also apply for summary judgment against a claimant to dispose of a hopeless claim on the same test. Where one or other party successfully takes this early initiative, the case will be disposed of there and then with the consequence that it will never have been allocated to any track. In that situation the successful party can apply for costs in the ordinary way and is not subject to the rule providing for only modest fixed costs on small claims, which is discussed below. Where a case does end early by summary judgment, the court will undoubtedly undertake a summary assessment of costs there and then.

12.4 THE SMALL CLAIMS TRACK

By CPR, r. 26.6(1), the small claims track is the normal track for:

(a) Any claim which has a financial value of not more than £5,000.
(b) Any claim for personal injuries where:

(i) the financial value of the whole claim is not more than £5,000; and
(ii) the financial value of any claim for damages for personal injuries is not more than £1,000.

By r. 26.6(2) the phrase 'damages for personal injuries' is defined to include only damages claimed for pain and suffering and loss of amenity. Thus special damages in any form, even loss of earnings, are not taken into account in fixing the value of a personal injury claim below £1,000. Thus if there is a minor injury, say to the finger of a professional musician which incapacitates him for a short period, causing him to lose a lucrative booking, if the general damages would be under £1,000, the special damages aspect will not bring the claim outside the small claims limit, unless the whole claim would then exceed £5,000.

(c) Any claim which includes a claim by a tenant of residential premises against his landlord where:

(i) the tenant is seeking an order requiring the landlord to carry out repairs or other work to the premises (whether or not he also seeks some other remedy);

(ii) the cost of the repairs or other work to the premises is estimated to be not more than £1,000; and

(iii) the financial value of any other claim for damages is not more than £1,000.

The drafting of the rule on housing disrepair claims has been troublesome. It would seem that for such a claim to be allocated to the small claims track there is now an artificial limit of £2,000 to the whole claim, given that the cost of repairs must be under £1,000 and there is a similar limit on any other general damages claim.

12.4.1 A specific exception

The small claims track is *not* the normal track for a claim which includes a claim by a tenant of residential premises against his landlord for damages for harassment or unlawful eviction (CPR, r. 26.7(4)).

12.4.2 Power to grant a final remedy

There is no restriction on the nature of remedies which can be granted on the small claims track (CPR, r. 27.3). Thus injunctions, possession, restitution, specific performance and the like are available to the same extent as on the other tracks, though jurisdiction to grant freezing (*Mareva*) injunctions and search (*Anton Piller*) orders is restricted to the High Court.

12.5 DISTINCTIVE FEATURES OF THE SMALL CLAIMS TRACK

The important differences between small claims and the other tracks are:

(a) Some rules and procedures have no application on the small claims track (see 12.6).
(b) The procedures after allocation are different (see 12.7).
(c) The procedure at the hearing is different (see 12.8).
(d) There is a restriction on appeals (see 12.9).
(e) Costs provisions are different (see 12.10).

12.6 RESTRICTION ON APPLICATION OF RULES

Rule 27.2 of the CPR provides that on the small claims track the following parts of the CPR do not apply:

(a) Part 25 (interim remedies) except as it relates to interim injunctions;
(b) Part 31 (disclosure and inspection);
(c) Part 32 (evidence) except r. 32.1, which gives the court a general power to control evidence;
(d) Part 33 (miscellaneous rules about evidence);
(e) Part 35 (experts and assessors) except r. 35.1, which restricts the use of expert evidence, r. 35.3, which sets out the expert's overriding duty to the court and r. 35.8 (use of a single joint expert);

(f) Part 18 (request for further information);
(g) Part 36 (offers to settle and payments into court); and
(h) Part 39 (hearings) except r. 39.2, which is the general rule that hearings are to be in public.

In principle the other parts of the CPR apply to small claims except to the extent that any rule limits such application.

12.7 PROCEDURE AFTER ALLOCATION TO THE SMALL CLAIMS TRACK

Under r. 27.4 of the CPR once a case has been allocated to the small claims track the court will give standard directions in one of several forms depending on the type of case. These forms of directions are set out in PD 27, appendix A, and the relevant one will be sent out by the court as an official court form. There is a variety of alternative ways in which a case may proceed on the small claims track under CPR, r. 27.4(1).

12.7.1 Option 1: standard directions and fixed final hearing date

The court may simply give standard directions and fix a date for the final hearing (CPR, r. 27.4(1)(a)).

The form of standard directions differs depending on the type of case. If no other form of directions is specified then the basic standard directions (PD 27, appendix A, form A) are simply directions for service of copies of any documents on which a party intends to rely no later than 14 days before the hearing; for the original documents to be brought to the hearing; for notice of the hearing date and duration; and an instruction to the parties to inform the court immediately if the case is settled by agreement.

District judges' experience of the previous small claims jurisdiction will usually enable them to give a reasonable estimate of the length of hearing for routine cases. Experience of small claims shows a very high rate of late settlement or simply 'no show' by the parties even for consumer disputes which hitherto appear to have been litigated with enthusiasm, or even personal animosity between the parties. This feature has enabled the courts in the past generally to adopt 'back-to-back' small claims case listings, so that, for example, two or more district judges are jointly listed to hear many hours' worth of cases whose litigants are all instructed to attend court at 10.00 a.m. or 2.00 p.m. Experience shows that it is usually safe for the court to list twice or even three times the number of cases that could in fact be properly dealt with if all were tried. There is no reason in principle why that should be less a feature of the new regime, although there are two new aspects. The first is that the increase in the value of the small claims jurisdiction will mean that there are more cases where the litigants most certainly will appear and take longer to present their cases because the amounts involved are more significant. The second is that the standard directions for certain types of cases (see below) to exchange witness statements and for the claimant to prepare other documents for use by the court ought to assist in identifying the issues and resolving them more swiftly. Having said that it must be acknowledged that litigants in person, even well-educated ones, often have difficulty drafting witness statements and differentiating between relevant and irrelevant facts. Moreover in the end, without a series of preliminary appointments it may be difficult to extract a full detailed witness statement from unintelligent litigants and the court will have to rely on, as previously, extracting information through questioning by the district judge at the hearing.

The other standard directions in PD 27, appendix A, show different features for road traffic cases; building disputes, vehicle repairs and similar claims; claims for return of deposit or in respect of damage by tenants; and holiday and wedding cases. These are adapted to the peculiarities of the respective type of case, and generally impose a certain level of formality of procedure on the parties which will assist in clarifying the issues and shortening the hearing.

The court has a general power under CPR, r. 27.7, to add to, vary or revoke directions.

12.7.2 Option 2: special directions and further directions

Instead of using the standard directions in PD 27, appendix A, the court can give 'special directions' and consider what further directions are to be given no later than 28 days after giving special directions (CPR, r. 27.4(1)(c)).

Examples of special directions are shown in PD 27, appendix A, form F. A commonly encountered example where such directions are useful in practice is where both the claimant's statement of case and the defence are wholly inadequate to convey to the court just what the issues are. For example, the claimant may simply refer to an unpaid invoice for a large sum; and the defendant may simply deny any liability at all. The court is then presented with two short documents which might not even indicate the types of goods or materials supplied and the reason why payment is disputed. Often such cases are between parties who have had a continuing contractual relationship, e.g., builders' merchant and builder, where large sums of money have been paid over the years but internal accounting procedures have not always been very satisfactory at allocating payments to invoices and some long-running discrepancy is now being sued for and challenged. To resolve this kind of case almost always requires a preliminary appointment but it is useful to send out directions with a debarring provision to require the parties intially to go to some effort to clarify matters for the court.

Special directions will usually be appropriate where the issues need to be clarified in some way, particularly by the disclosure of documents between the parties and to the court. After further documents setting out the parties' positions, their legal entitlement (and sometimes whether the correct parties have been involved hitherto) the court may be in a position to decide how to proceed, which will be either for listing, giving yet further directions, or perhaps calling the parties before it for a preliminary hearing under CPR, r. 27.6 (see 12.7.4).

12.7.3 Option 3: special directions and fixed final hearing date

The court may give special directions and fix a date for the final hearing (CPR, r. 27.4(1)(b)). This will be appropriate where there is some issue which can be clarified which falls outside the usual run of standard directions, but it seems unlikely that a further hearing or supplementary directions will be necessary.

12.7.4 Option 4: preliminary hearing

The court may fix a date for a preliminary hearing (CPR, r. 27.4(1)(d)).

Rule 27.6 provides that the court may hold a preliminary hearing for the consideration of a small claim only in one of three situations:

(a) Where the court considers that special directions under r. 27.4 are needed to ensure a fair hearing, and it appears necessary for a party to attend court to ensure that he understands what he must do to comply with the special directions. This will presumably involve circumstances in which the court considers (possibly from the content of the documents received) that it may be necessary to have the parties before the court to ensure that they understand what is necessary to do in order that the case may be properly and efficiently progressed. Alternatively, it may be that special directions need to be considered, and that it would be inappropriate for the district judge to make them without hearing the parties.

(b) To enable the court to dispose of the claim on the basis that one of the parties has no real prospect of success. This may become apparent from the documents, for example, where in an action on a dishonoured cheque, the defence makes some complaint about the quality of the goods supplied; or where the claimant is attempting to base his case on a cause of action not known to English law; or where the reality of the situation is simply that the defendant does not have the means to pay. The overriding objective will clearly be served by the matter being disposed of during a short appointment at a preliminary stage.

(c) To enable the court to strike out a statement of case, or where part of a statement of case discloses no reasonable grounds for bringing or defending the claim. This provision follows on from the one before. Clearly, if the failure to disclose a cause of action or defence is due to sloppy drafting, an opportunity should be given to correct this, but if on examination it is clear that the case is hopeless, the court will exercise its power in much the same way as at (b) above.

By r. 27.6(4), the court may treat a preliminary hearing as the final hearing of the claim if all parties agree. It is unlikely that this will commonly apply unless the point is a very short one, as it would otherwise mean that the preliminary appointment could take the same time as the substantive hearing.

After the preliminary hearing, the court will fix the date of the final hearing and inform the parties of the amount of time allowed, together with any other appropriate directions.

12.7.5 Option 5: proceeding without a hearing

The court may, *if all parties agree*, deal with a small claim without a hearing (CPR, r. 27.10). The penultimate draft of the rule provided a power for the court to impose this on the parties whether or not they agreed. The change in mind was no doubt prompted by the view that refusing to give a public hearing to a case would infringe the right to such a hearing enshrined in the Human Rights Act 1998, which is due to come into force some time in the year 2000.

12.8 CONDUCT OF THE FINAL HEARING

The final hearing of a small claim will normally be before a district judge, but there is a provision in PD 27 that it may be before a circuit judge. It is suggested that this would be highly unlikely, not least because it makes for extreme difficulty in the question of appeals.

12.8.1 Representation

Under PD 27, para. 3.2, the parties may present their own case at the hearing or it may be presented by a lawyer (i.e., barrister, solicitor or legal executive employed by a solicitor: para. 3.1) or by a lay representative. A lay representative may only appear if the party is present or if he is that party's employee or if the court gives permission. Any officer or employee may represent a corporate party.

12.8.2 Public hearing

The hearing will be in public. However, the judge may decide to hold it in private if:

(a) the parties agree, or
(b) a ground mentioned in CPR, r. 39.2(3), applies.

Under r. 39.2(3) the court is entitled to take into account a variety of factors in directing that a hearing or any part of it is to be in private, including the fact that publicity would defeat the object of the hearing; that there are matters of national security (unlikely in a small claims context!); that publicity would damage confidentiality of information including information relating to personal financial matters (a provision which arguably may often apply in small claims cases); or where the court considers it to be necessary in the interests of justice.

PD 27 goes on to say at para. 4.2 that a hearing that takes place at the court will generally be in the judge's room, but it may take place in a courtroom.

CPR, r. 39.2(2), qualifying in relation to trials generally the rule that a hearing must be in public, says that, 'the requirement for a hearing to be in public does not require the court to make special arrangements for accommodating members of the public'. This would seem to be a heroic attempt to get round the requirement for a public trial in the European Convention on Human Rights and Fundamental Freedoms, incorporated into UK law by the Human Rights Act 1998 with effect from some time in the year 2000. Such is the number of small claims hearings that it is suggested they will in almost all cases be conducted in chambers by district judges because open court accommodation is simply not available.

12.8.3 Method of proceeding

Rule 27.8 of the CPR allows the court to adopt any method of proceeding at a small claims hearing that it considers to be fair, and to limit cross-examination. PD 27, para. 4.3, provides that the judge may in particular:

(a) ask questions of any witnesses himself before allowing any other person to do so,
(b) ask questions of all or any of the witnesses himself before allowing any other person to ask questions of any witnesses,
(c) refuse to allow cross-examination of any witness until all the witnesses have given evidence-in-chief,
(d) limit cross-examination of a witness to a fixed time or to a particular subject or issue or both.

It will therefore be up to the district judge hearing the case to decide how he proposes to proceed and it is suggested that he is likely to proceed very much as under the previous jurisdiction. So that justice has the appearance, as well as the substance, of fairness it may be helpful for the court to follow the previous protocol on county court arbitrations. That protocol described the way in which a district judge might wish to introduce the proceedings, explaining the order of events to unrepresented parties, and explaining that it will be for him to decide whether, e.g., cross-examination by the parties themselves is needed or whether he feels that he can get at the truth bettter by himself asking the questions. If both parties are legally represented, matters may proceed more efficiently with some degree of formality so that events mirror an open court trial, e.g., opening speeches, formal evidence given in chief (although in such cases provision for witness statements to stand as evidence-in-chief may be useful), cross-examination and re-examination, and closing speeches. With unrepresented litigants, the district judge will assess the situation and the parties and decide what he needs to hear in order both to do justice and to ensure that the parties feel that within reason they have had their say. Although a district judge may control cross-examination by the parties, it is suggested that it is not appropriate to forbid cross-examination entirely (*Chilton* v *Saga Holidays plc* [1986] 1 All ER 841).

12.8.4 Recording evidence and giving reasons

By PD 27, para. 5, the judge may direct that all or any part of the proceedings will be tape-recorded and a party may thereafter obtain a transcript on payment of the proper charges. The fact that a party has fees exemption generally does not mean that he can obtain a transcript without charge, since such charges are not made by the Court Service directly.

By para. 5.3 the judge will make a note of the central points of the oral evidence, unless it is tape-recorded. By paras 5.4 and 5.5 he will make a note of the central reasons for his judgment, unless it is given orally and tape-recorded by the court; the judge is expressly permitted to give his reasons 'as briefly and simply as the nature of the case allows' and he will normally do so orally at the hearing, but he may give them later, either in writing or at a hearing fixed for him to do so.

Where the judge decides the case without a hearing under CPR, r. 27.10, or a party who has given notice under r. 27.9(1) does not attend the hearing, the judge will prepare a note of his reasons and the court will send a copy to each party.

By PD 27, para. 5.7, a party is entitled to a copy of any note made by the judge under paras 5.3 or 5.4.

It therefore follows that the judge must make some form of record of the salient points of evidence and the reasons for his decision. This would always have represented the best practice, but the position is now formalised and the rights of the parties to obtain copies of the judge's notes are made clearer.

12.8.5 Non-attendance of the parties at the final hearing

If a party who does not attend a final hearing has given the court written notice at least seven days before the date that he will not attend and has requested the court to decide the claim in his absence, the court will take into account his statement of case and other documents he has filed (CPR, r. 27.9(1)). If a *claimant* does not either attend or give that notice then the court *may* strike out the claim (r. 27.9(2)).

It will be appreciated that the word 'may' gives the court a discretion and thus a party who has misunderstood the requirement to give seven days' notice and perhaps sends in a fax on the morning of the hearing, requesting the court to deal with the case on the basis of his written statements, will no doubt be given some indulgence. If the opposing party can demonstrate any prejudice caused by the lack of notice of the other party's non-appearance, an adjournment may be permitted. This may be, for example, because the party who is present needed to cross-examine the absent party about some feature of his case which would have demonstrated, e.g., the falseness of a particular piece of evidence, or that a certain document was not authentic. There may well also be a class of case where one party needs the other to attend in order to establish quantum, e.g., claims by former employees to commission payments based on sales. Generally speaking, a party who attends is likely to do better than a party who does not attend.

If a *defendant* does not attend a hearing or give the notice referred to and the claimant does attend or give the notice referred to, the court may decide the claim on the basis of the evidence of the claimant only (r. 27.9(3)).

If *neither party* attends or gives notice, the court may strike out the claim and any defence and counterclaim (r. 27.9(4)).

Nothing in these provisions affects the general power of the court to adjourn a hearing for good reason, e.g., where a party who wishes to attend cannot do so for reasons such as illness.

12.8.6 Setting judgment aside and rehearing

A party who was neither present nor represented at the hearing of the claim, and who did not give written notice to the court under CPR, r. 27.9(1), may apply for an order that a judgment shall be set aside and the claim reheard (r. 27.11(1)).

To do this, application must be made not more than 14 days after the day on which notice of the judgment was served on that party (r. 27.11(2)). The court may then, by r. 27.11(3), grant an application *only* if the applicant:

(a) had a good reason for not attending or being represented at the hearing or giving written notice to the court under r. 27.9(1); and
(b) has a reasonable prospect of success at the hearing.

A party may not apply to set judgment aside under this rule if the court dealt with the claim without a hearing under r. 27.10 (i.e., by order of the court with the consent of the parties dispensing with the hearing.)

This provides a twofold test for someone who did not appear at the hearing (an extremely common feature of the previous arbitration jurisdiction) and who seeks to reopen the case. The court will first require the application to be made within 14 days of the party in question receiving notice; the application to set aside will itself be on notice to the other party; and the party applying will have to show a good reason for not having attended, been represented or having given written notice to proceed in his absence.

It will be for the court to decide what form of proof is required, but the burden is clearly on the applicant. The court may continue to be sceptical of alleged postal failures, sudden unspecific illnesses, urgent commitments at work and the like. The principles to be applied were listed by Leggatt LJ in *Shocked v Goldschmidt* [1998] 1 All ER 372. A party who was deliberately absent from court without a proper reason has no right to have a rehearing, however strong that party's case may be.

If the court concludes that there is good reason then there is still an obligation on the party applying to show a reasonable prospect of success which will obviously go beyond consideration of whatever documents have been filed or provided hitherto and may lead to the court asking for an affidavit, further documentary proof or as the case may warrant. It is suggested that the test of 'a reasonable prospect of success' is more stringent than the test of 'an arguable defence', such as would suffice to prevent summary judgment. It is suggested that this is rather more akin to the test established in *Alpine Bulk Transport Co. Inc. v Saudi Eagle Shipping Co. Inc.* [1986] 2 Lloyd's Rep 221, for applications to set aside a regular default judgment.

12.8.7 If judgment is set aside

By CPR, r. 27.11(4), if judgment is set aside, the court must fix a new hearing date and the hearing may take place immediately after the hearing of the application to set aside the judgment and may be dealt with by the judge who set aside the judgment.

It is suggested that, unless the claim is a very simple one or a considerable time has been allocated to the application to set aside, most courts are likely to approach the matter in two stages as has been the previous practice. The courts will probably be reluctant to allocate to an application to set aside a judgment as long a time as was allocated to the original hearing, because experience shows that a proportion of people who apply to set aside judgments obtained against them in their absence do not attend on the application to set aside either!

12.9 APPEALS

12.9.1 Rights of appeal

There is a limited right of appeal against the decision of the court on a small claims hearing. There is a right of appeal only on the grounds that there was a serious irregularity affecting the proceedings or the court made a mistake of law (CPR, r. 27.12(1)).

PD 27, para. 8 provides that an appeal will be dealt with by a circuit judge. Notice of appeal must be filed no later than 14 days after the day on which notice of the order was served on the appealing party and must set out the grounds, including particulars of the serious irregularity or mistake of law alleged (CPR, r. 27.13). The notice will be put before the circuit judge as soon as possible after it is filed and he will decide how to deal with the appeal. The court will serve a copy of the notice on all other parties.

The circuit judge may either:

   (a) dismiss the appeal without a hearing if no sufficient ground is shown in the notice of appeal; or
   (b) order that the appeal is to be listed for hearing.

12.9.2 Procedure on appeal

If the appeal is to proceed, the circuit judge will give any necessary directions about the filing of any evidence concerning allegation of serious irregularity and about the supply to the parties of copies of any documents, including any notes made by the district judge who heard the case (PD 27, para. 8.7).

If the circuit judge at the hearing allows the appeal, he will if possible dispose of the case at the same time without ordering the claim to be reheard and may do so without hearing further evidence (PD 27, para. 8.10).

On appeal the court may make any order it considers appropriate (CPR, r. 27.12(2)).

12.10 COSTS

12.10.1 Costs before allocation to the small claims track

There are special costs rules in relation to costs incurred before a claim is allocated to the small claims track. CPR, r. 44.11, provides that the costs regime to be applied is that relevant at the time in question and thus if a case has been on some other track before being reallocated to the small claims track, the relevant provision will be the provision on that original track.

12.10.2 Costs after allocation

After a claim has been allocated to the small claims track there are considerable restrictions on *inter partes* costs orders. In principle (CPR, r. 27.14(2)) the court may not order a party to pay a sum to another party in respect of that other party's costs except:

(a) the fixed costs payable under Part 45 attributable to issuing the claim;

(b) in proceedings which include a claim for an injunction or specific performance, an amount for legal advice and assistance relating to that claim, not exceeding £260.00 (PD 27, para. 7.2);

(c) costs assessed by the summary procedure in relation to an appeal under CPR, r. 27.12; and

(d) such further costs as the court may assess by the summary procedure and order to be paid by a party who has behaved unreasonably.

The court may also (r. 27.14(3)) order a party to pay all or part of any court fees paid by another party; expenses which a party or witness has reasonably incurred in travel and subsistence for a hearing; any loss of earnings, up to £50 per day (PD 27, pra. 7.3), for attending a hearing; an expert's fees, up to £200 per expert (PD 27, para. 7.3). By virtue of CPR, r. 27.5, no expert may give evidence, whether written or oral, at a hearing without the permission of the court.

This is a significant restriction on *inter partes* costs, though it echoes the restrictions in the previous rules. The costs to be awarded will be decidedly modest and will be a serious disincentive to employing a lawyer for parties who do not have the benefit of legal expenses insurance guaranteeing them such representation, as remains common in road traffic accident claims.

12.10.3 Unreasonable behaviour

The court will no doubt in due course develop its own jurisprudence as to what is intended by 'behaved unreasonably' in CPR, r. 27.14(2)(d), but this will inevitably involve the court exercising a wide discretion. Cases dealing with the word 'unreasonably' in the previous county court rule, of which there are many reported, mainly in *Current Law*, tended to show that an objective test should be applied. The following may be considered to be unreasonable: making a claim which the court has found to be wholly false (although the court should be wary of coming to the conclusion that a claim is wholly false merely because it has in the end preferred one party's evidence to another); failure to inform of non-attendance of a witness; deliberate delay in dealing with an undeniable claim so as to force a party to issue proceedings; filing a spurious defence and then not attending the final hearing; paying the claim in full just before the final hearing; making unnecessary procedural applications. A material factor may be that the rules on payments into court and offers to settle have no application in small claims proceedings. It remains to be seen whether the court will develop a way of giving effect to Part 36 offers despite this, by treating them as relevant to reasonableness.

When the court concludes that a party has behaved unreasonably, the court must assess the costs by the summary procedure. It will thus be important for a party who anticipates being able successfully to press a claim for costs to have completed, and be able to justify, the 'statement of costs' form which is to be used on summary assessments of costs, indicating the status of the fee earner, and time claimed for attendances, correspondence, documents and so on.

12.10.4 Reallocation from the small claims track

If a case is reallocated from the small claims track to another track, the costs provisions cease to apply after the claim has been reallocated and the fast track or multi-track rules will thereafter apply (CPR, r. 27.15).

12.10.5 Costs in exceptional cases

If the parties have consented to a claim being allocated to the small claims track from some other track, even though the financial value of the claim exceeds the limit for the small claims track, then for costs purposes the claim is to be treated as if it were proceeding on the fast track, except that trial costs are in the discretion of the court and shall not exceed the amount set out for the value of the claim if it were a fast track case (CPR, r. 27.14(5)).

12.10.6 Allocation of assessments of damages and disposals

Cases may come into the small claims track on issues of quantum only after liability has been determined elsewhere, whether by trial of a preliminary issue, judgment in default or summary judgment. Where such cases are referred to the small claims track, the limitation on costs in respect of the small claims hearing will apply, although costs of earlier stages will be based on the sums available on the track concerned. In principle it is likely that at the conclusion of any hearing, after which proceedings are to be transferred to the small claims track, the court will already have undertaken a summary assessment of costs of the proceedings hitherto.

CHAPTER 13   FAST TRACK

CONTENTS

13.1	Introduction	191
13.2	Directions	193
13.2.1	Disclosure	193
13.2.2	Witness statements	194
13.2.3	Expert evidence	194
13.2.4	Questions to experts	195
13.2.5	Further statements of case	196
13.2.6	Requests for further information	196
13.2.7	Filing listing questionnaires	196
13.2.8	Fixing the date for trial	196
13.2.9	The overall standard timetable	197
13.2.10	Agreed directions	198
13.3	Varying the directions timetable	198
13.4	Listing for trial	199
13.4.1	Confirmation of expert directions	201
13.4.2	Trial timetable	201
13.4.3	Trial bundles	201
13.4.4	Case summary	201
13.4.5	Confirmation of trial date	202
13.4.6	Summary assessment of fast track costs	202
13.5	Trial	202
13.6	Costs	203

13.1   INTRODUCTION

The fast track is intended to cover the majority of defended actions within the £5,000 to £15,000 monetary band. It will also deal with non-monetary claims such as injunctions, declarations and claims for specific performance which are unsuitable for the small claims track and do not require the more complex treatment of the multi-track. The fast track provides a 'no-frills' procedure with cases being progressed to trial within a short timescale after the filing of defences. Rule 1.1(2)(c) of the CPR provides that part of the overriding objective is that cases should be dealt with proportionately, and it is this idea that underlies the whole concept of having a fast track with limited costs recoverable from the unsuccessful party (*Final Report*, ch. 2, para. 19). The intention is to increase access to justice by removing the uncertainty faced by many litigants under the old system over the excessive cost of litigating, and by replacing it with a means of obtaining justice speedily and with a degree of certainty over how much the legal costs are likely to be.

When claims are allocated to the fast track, directions will be given setting out the timetable to be followed, with a fixed trial date or trial period no more than 30 weeks later. It is intended that the timetable will be sufficient for the parties to undertake the work necessary for preparing the case for trial, but sufficiently tight to discourage elaboration. By imposing a strict timetable for preparing fast track cases for trial it is intended that there will be little scope for any party to undertake extra work so as to gain a tactical advantage over the other side, and no reward so far as costs are concerned for doing so (*Final Report*, ch. 2, para. 30). The *Final Report* also made the point that it will be particularly important in fast track cases for the court to provide protection against oppressive or unreasonable behaviour, and in particular against a powerful opponent driving up the costs so as to overwhelm a weaker litigant. Use of the power to impose sanctions (see 11.8) will discourage such conduct.

Under the new system the court will be expected to enforce the timetable it sets so as to ensure it is not simply ignored by those conducting litigation, and to ensure fast track cases really do proceed to a speedy resolution by trial if they are not settled beforehand. It is for this reason that, as will be seen in this chapter, although some scope is given for the parties to alter some of the dates in the timetable set by the court, changing the date of the trial is only a matter of last resort. To ensure the timetable is not invalidated by listing difficulties the *Final Report* also envisaged that any applications that might be needed in the period between allocation to the fast track and trial would be dealt with speedily, in a matter of days rather than weeks, and with applications wherever possible being dealt with on paper rather than requiring hearings (*Final Report*, ch. 2, paras 33 and 34).

Under the new regime the full range of interlocutory applications are available in fast track cases (*Final Report*, ch. 3, para. 21). How this is compatible with having a speedy process with limited time to trial remains to be seen. It was notorious under the old system that intended short cuts, such as applications for summary judgment and trials of preliminary issues, had a habit of turning out to be time-consuming and expensive detours. Trenchant comments to this effect were made by Lord Donaldson of Lymington MR in *R.G. Carter Ltd* v *Clarke* [1990] 1 WLR 578, a summary judgment case, and by Lord Roskill in *Allen* v *Gulf Oil Refining Ltd* [1981] AC 1001, a preliminary issue case.

Once a case is allocated to the fast track and directions are given there will be no more than seven months in which to prepare the case for trial. Claimants will therefore be well advised to ensure that their cases are in an advanced state of preparation before they issue proceedings, to make sure they do not fall behind schedule once the timetable starts running. They should ensure they have available for disclosure all disclosable documents, both on liability and quantum. They should also have identified and if necessary traced all material witnesses, and preferably have reduced into writing at least draft statements for each witness. They should also have made some progress regarding obtaining any expert evidence that might be necessary. It is to be expected that in most fast track cases the court will direct that there should be joint instruction of experts. Prospective claimants will therefore be well advised to have identified possible experts to be instructed, and to seek agreement with their prospective defendants for the joint instruction of agreed experts. Anything less than this will be storing up trouble for later on.

Defendants are in a similar, and sometimes more precarious, position. They too will easily find themselves in time difficulties later on unless they have completed at least some of the necessary preparation before the claim is issued. Full compliance with any relevant pre-action protocol will at least put them in a reasonably advanced state of preparedness. They should have available for disclosure at least their documentation on liability, and have draft statements from material witnesses. They should also be in the process of seeking agreement on the joint instruction of experts. Like claimants, failing to have these matters in hand will mean there will be little time to get the case ready before the trial arrives.

13.2 DIRECTIONS

When it allocates a case to the fast track, the court will at the same time give case management directions and set a timetable for the steps to be taken from that point through to trial (CPR, r. 28.2(1)). The directions given will be designed to ensure the issues are identified and the necessary evidence is prepared and disclosed (PD 28, para. 3.3). Usually the court will give directions of its own initiative without a hearing, and will take into account the respective statements of case, the allocation questionnaires, and any further information provided by the parties. Occasionally it may hold a directions hearing, such as when it is proposing to make an unusual order, such as to appoint an assessor (see PD 28, para. 3.11). It is the duty of the parties to ask for all directions that might be needed on any hearing that may be fixed (PD 28, para. 2.5). If any direction or order is required that has not been provided for, it is the duty of the parties to make an application as soon as possible so as to avoid undue interference with the overall timetable (PD 28, para. 2.8). If a directions hearing becomes necessary because of the default of any of the parties the court will usually impose a sanction (PD 28, para. 2.3).

Typically, by CPR, rr. 28.2(2) and 28.3, the matters to be dealt with in directions given on allocation to the fast track will include:

(a) disclosure of documents;
(b) service of witness statements;
(c) expert evidence; and
(d) fixing a date for the trial, or a period in which the trial is to take place.

Standard directions to be used in fast track cases are set out in the appendix to PD 28. It will be seen that they include matters, such as orders for the provision of further information, which are not included in the basic list. This is because the directions given will be tailored by the procedural judge to the circumstances of each individual case. The time periods for taking the various steps will again be tailored to the requirements of each individual case, but a few indications of the probable times allowed for different steps will be given in the following paragraphs. It will be noted that the rules contemplate that further directions may be given at the listing stage, which will be usually about eight weeks before trial, and directions at that stage are considered in more detail at 13.4.1 to 13.4.5.

13.2.1 Disclosure

Disclosure is the new name for discovery, and is discussed fully in chapter 15. If there is a pre-action protocol governing the case, disclosure in some form should have taken place before proceedings were issued. Information

CHAPTER 13 FAST TRACK

about this should have been given with the allocation questionnaire. Based on the respective statements of case and these questionnaires, the procedural judge may direct the parties to give standard disclosure as one of the directions made at this stage, or may direct that no disclosure need take place, or may specify the documents or classes of documents which the parties must disclose (CPR, r. 28.3(2); PD 28, para. 3). The standard directions will provide for disclosure to be given by service of lists of documents, which must be delivered by a specified calendar date. It is also possible for disclosure to be given more informally without a list and with or without a disclosure statement. Disclosure is likely to be ordered for 28 days after service of the notice of allocation (PD 28, para. 3.12).

13.2.2 Witness statements

The exchange of witness statements is considered further in chapter 16. Standard directions will usually provide for simultaneous exchange by a specified calendar date of statements from all the factual witnesses on whose evidence each party intends to rely. Exchange is likely to be required between seven and 10 weeks from the notice of allocation (compare the *Final Report*, ch. 3, para. 14 and PD 28, para. 3.12). The *Final Report* raised the possibility of using witness summaries rather than witness statements in fast track cases, but the CPR require the exchange of witness statements, with witness summaries being used where witness statements cannot be obtained for practical reasons (r. 32.9(1)). In order to keep costs down the *Final Report* indicated that it expected witness statements in fast track cases to be reasonably brief and factual (*Final Report*, ch. 3, para. 26), but there is nothing overt to this effect in the CPR or the practice directions. In fact r. 32.5(4) points firmly in the direction of full witness statements, as witnesses will only be allowed to amplify their statements if there is 'good reason' not to confine them to their disclosed witness statements.

13.2.3 Expert evidence

The *Final Report* stressed the need to limit the use of experts on fast track cases in order to achieve the goal of proportionate cost (*Final Report*, ch. 3, para. 25). The *Final Report* envisaged there would be no oral expert evidence at fast track trials, with the parties being encouraged to use a single expert and the court being empowered to order a single expert to be appointed. These proposals have not been entirely carried forward into the new rules. Part of the reason is that the fast track has been expanded from the proposal in the *Final Report*, which envisaged it covering cases from £3,000 to £10,000, to the present range of £5,000 to £15,000. It has also been expanded from a restriction in the *Final Report* to cases that could be disposed of in three hours to the current restriction to cases that can be disposed of in a single day. There will therefore be cases of somewhat greater importance and complexity on the fast track under the rules as they now stand than had been envisaged at the time of the *Final Report*.

Under the new rules cases will not normally be on the fast track unless oral expert evidence at trial is limited to one expert per party in each expert field, and to two fields of expertise (CPR, r. 26.6(5)). One of the new powers available to the court is that of directing that the evidence on particular issues may be given by a single expert jointly instructed by the opposing parties (r. 35.7). In order to keep down costs and to reduce the

CHAPTER 13 FAST TRACK

length of fast track trials, it will be usual for the court to make directions for the joint instruction of a single expert unless there is good reason for doing something else (PD 28, para. 3.9(4)). In addition, in fast track cases the court will not direct an expert to attend at trial unless it is necessary to do so in the interests of justice (r. 35.5(2)).

If, before issuing proceedings, the parties have instructed their own experts (perhaps because the claim is not governed by a pre-action protocol or because one side has failed to cooperate in jointly instructing experts), or if the court decides not to make a joint expert direction, the likelihood is that the experts will give conflicting evidence on the matters they deal with. When this happens, the court has a power under r. 35.12 to direct a discussion between the experts with a view to producing an agreed statement of the issues on which they agree and the areas on which they are in disagreement. This rule has been deliberately altered from the old phrase ('direct a meeting of experts') to make it plain that what used to be called 'without prejudice meetings of experts' can take place on the telephone or by other means of communication. If the experts cannot reach agreement, the interests of justice are likely to be served only by allowing both parties to call their experts at the trial so the areas of disagreement can be adjudicated upon by the judge. In such cases it may not be possible to deal with the case in a single day, and the court may need to consider reallocating the case to the multi-track.

Normally expert evidence should be prepared and/or exchanged about 14 weeks after the notice of allocation (PD 28, para. 3.12). The standard fast track directions have several different options regarding expert evidence, as alternatives to the joint instruction of experts. Options provided within the standard directions are:

(a) Sequential service of experts' reports. Normally it will be the claimant who will serve first.

(b) Simultaneous exchange of reports on some issues, with sequential service on the others.

(c) Holding of a discussion between experts in cases where the other side's reports cannot be agreed within a short time (usually 14 days) after service. This form of direction provides for a specified calendar date by which the discussion must take place, and the filing of a joint statement of the agreed issues and those in dispute (with reasons for the lack of agreement) by another specified date (which will often be close to the date for filing listing questionnaires).

(d) That expert evidence is not necessary and no party has permission to call or rely on expert evidence at the trial.

(e) That the parties may rely on experts' reports at trial, but cannot call oral expert evidence.

(f) That the parties may rely on experts' reports, and the court will reconsider whether there is any need for experts to be called when the claim is listed for trial.

13.2.4 Questions to experts

The standard directions also make provision pursuant to the power given by CPR, r. 35.6, for written questions to be put to the other side's experts for the purpose of clarifying their reports. Questions should be sent, if at all, within 28 days of receipt of the expert's report (PD 35, para. 4.1).

Questions can be sent direct to the expert, but copies should be sent to the other side's solicitors. No time is laid down for the answers (although this may be done by a specific court order), but 28 days would seem to be reasonable. Sensible questions can only be asked if the party (or more commonly its solicitor) is guided by its own expert. If its own expert knows the answers, there will be little point in asking the questions in the first place, so it must be sensible to clear the written questions with the party's own experts first. It will clearly take a little time for a party to receive the other side's expert reports, consider them, decide if it is a case where written questions should be put, contact its own expert and take its expert's advice about the written questions to be put, to formulate the questions, and then serve them. Experts are often busy consultants and professionals with many calls on their time, so periods of 28 days for questions and answers may be rather tight in many cases.

13.2.5 Further statements of case

When giving directions the procedural judge may also direct that a party must file a further statement of case, such as a reply or defence to counterclaim. The direction will provide a specified calendar date for doing so.

13.2.6 Requests for further information

Requests for further information are considered in more detail at 8.7. Standard directions provide for two possible times for service of such requests (with either, both or neither being directed in any particular case):

(a) Within a short, specified, time after directions are given, where the request is based on the other side's statement of case. The direction will also specify the date by which the request must be dealt with. A response time of about 14 days is likely.

(b) After disclosure or exchange of witness statements. The direction will lay down a limited time after disclosure or service of the statement within which the request must be served, and a limited time within which it must be dealt with. Strangely, the time for the response will be set before the request has been drafted.

13.2.7 Filing listing questionnaires

Standard fast track directions will provide for all parties to file completed listing questionnaires no later than specific dates set out in the directions, unless the court considers the claim can be listed for trial without the need for these questionnaires. When they are used, listing questionnaires must be returned within the time specified by the court, which will be no later than eight weeks before the trial date or the beginning of the trial period (r. 28.5(2)). At the same time each party must file an estimate of costs in the standard statement of costs form (see appendix 3). The statement of costs must be divided into parts showing the costs already incurred and an estimate of the future costs to trial (PD 43, para. 4.5(2), (3)). A listing fee is payable whether or not listing questionnaires are used. The fee is payable by the claimant. If the fee is not paid, the court will send a notice to pay in form N173, and failing payment within the time stated in the notice, the claim will be struck out (r. 3.7).

13.2.8 Fixing the date for trial

Although the new rules include provision for automatic striking out for non-payment of the fees payable at the allocation and listing stages (see

CHAPTER 13 FAST TRACK

11.4.2 and 13.2.7), automatic striking out in county court cases for failing to request a hearing date has gone. In its place, for fast track cases, there will be a strict timetable, usually of about 30 weeks, during which the case must be prepared and tried. When giving directions the court will fix the trial date or a period, not exceeding three weeks, within which the trial is to take place, and which will be specified in the notice of allocation (CPR, r. 28.2(2) to (4)). The equivalent rule for multi-track cases provides for fixed trial dates or a period of a single week during which the trial will start (r. 29.8(c)(ii)). Regarding the date for trial, r. 28.2(4) provides that the 'standard' period between the giving of directions and the trial will be not more than 30 weeks. It is therefore open for procedural judges to lay down even tighter timetables, which may happen if the court decides that some or all of the usual steps can be omitted, or if it is informed that a pre-trial protocol has been complied with or that the steps it was contemplating have already been taken (PD 28, para. 3.13). There is also scope, if the procedural judge can be persuaded that it is necessary, for the timetable to be longer than the standard period. Factors such as those mentioned at 13.3 may influence the court when considering a longer timetable in an individual case.

13.2.9 The overall standard timetable

Table 13.1 charts the progress of a fast track case from issue, through allocation to the fast track, up to trial. The case illustrated takes 39 weeks, or about nine months, from issue to trial. The various stages will vary from case to case (such as where there is a stay for negotiation or if the claimant effects service rather than the court), and as mentioned in 13.2.8, even the 30-week period between directions and trial may be considerably reduced in some cases. It will be obvious that the parties will have to be in a high state of preparedness before proceedings are issued in all but the very simplest of cases if they are to have any real prospect of adhering to such tight timetables without being forced on the mercy of the courts.

Week	Step in the proceedings	Time limit
1	Issue of proceedings	Usual limitation period
	Service by court (takes effect on second day after posting)	Four months from issue (six months if outside the jurisdiction)
3	Acknowledgement of service or filing of defence	14 days after deemed service of the particulars of claim
(Say) 5	Service of allocation questionnaires (may be dispensed with)	Not before all defendants have filed defences, or expiry of time for filing defences
(Say 5)	Possible transfer to defendant's home court	On filing defence
7	Return of allocation questionnaires and service and filing of statements of costs	Not less than 14 days after service of the questionnaire
(Say 9)	Allocation decision and directions given by the procedural judge	After return of questionnaires
13	Disclosure of documents	Usually 4 weeks after allocation
19	Exchange of witness statements	Usually 10 weeks after allocation

Week	Step in the proceedings	Time limit
19	Service of hearsay notices	With exchanged witness statements
23	Experts' reports	Usually 14 weeks after allocation
29	Service of listing questionnaires (may be dispensed with)	Usually 20 weeks after allocation
31	Return of listing questionnaires and service and filing of statements of costs	Usually 22 weeks after allocation
(Say) 33	Any directions arising out of the listing questionnaires	Optional
(33)	Hearing if listing questionnaires not returned	Only if parties in default
36	Confirmation of trial date	Three weeks before trial
38	Lodging trial bundle	Three to seven days before trial
39	Service and filing of statements of costs	Not less than 24 hours before the hearing
39	Trial	30 weeks after allocation

Table 13.1   Progress of fast track case to trial

13.2.10 Agreed directions

The parties are encouraged to seek to agree suitable directions to be submitted to the court with their allocation questionnaires. If this is done, the court will at least take them into account when giving directions, and if they are suitable, will simply approve them. To be approved the directions should essentially follow the above rules (see PD 28, para. 3), which means they must deal with disclosure, witness statements and expert evidence, lay down a timetable by calendar dates, and provide for a trial or trial period no more than 30 weeks after the start of the timetable.

13.3   VARYING THE DIRECTIONS TIMETABLE

A party that wishes to vary the date fixed by the court's directions for returning listing questionnaires or for the trial must apply to the court (CPR, r. 28.4(1)). Any other date set by the court cannot be varied by the parties if the variation would make it necessary to vary the dates for either filing listing questionnaires or trial (r. 28.4(2)). The effect of these rules is that it is quite permissible for the parties to agree to the variation of the other directions for service of lists of documents, witness statements and experts' reports without troubling the court, provided the two key dates (filing listing questionnaires and trial) are not affected by slippage elsewhere. If the parties agree to a variation which does not impinge on any of the key dates, they can act on their agreement without having to file anything at court (PD 28, para. 4.5(1)).

One of the innovations brought in by the CPR is that the parties are expected to help the court to further the overriding objective (r. 1.3), and the court is expected to encourage the parties to cooperate with each other in the conduct of proceedings (r. 1.4(2)(a)). If a party falls a little behind on the timetable, one would expect that, even if the other side are in a position to comply at the right time, they would assist by agreeing to a slight revision to the timetable, rather than insisting on strict compliance. The court has a general power to extend and abridge the time for compliance with any rule, practice direction or court order, even if the application is made after the time for compliance has elapsed (r. 3.1(2)(a)).

A party that disagrees with the directions timetable laid down should either appeal or apply to the court for it to reconsider its directions. Orders and directions made at hearings attended by a party or his representative or regarding which the party was given due notice should be appealed against, but it is only necessary to make an application in relation to directions made of the court's own initiative. Any appeal or application must be made as soon as possible (PD 28, para. 4.2(1)). The court will assume for the purposes of any later application that a party who did not appeal and who made no application to vary any directions given within 14 days, was content that they were correct in the circumstances then existing (PD 28, para. 4.2(2)). Obviously, parties should not feel forced into making speculative applications in relation to directions that are based on future events (such as requests for further information and questions to experts), and it is to be hoped that applications to extend these (and some of the other) time limits will be dealt with realistically when the need arises.

PD 28, para. 5.4(6), makes it very clear that variations involving loss of the trial date will be considered matters of last resort. However, even the *Final Report* recognised there will be cases where it will become necessary to vary the timetabled date for trial. Examples include cases where there are significant problems with the evidence, where there is a change of solicitor, where proceedings are issued at the very end of the limitation period, and in personal injuries cases where the prognosis is uncertain (*Final Report*, ch. 3, para. 19). If there is no option but to postpone the trial, the postponement will be for the shortest possible time, and the court will give directions for taking the necessary steps outstanding as rapidly as possible. In some of these cases the best course may be to have split trials of liability and quantum, or to proceed only on the issues that are ready (PD 28, para. 5.4(4)). Where this happens the court may disallow the costs of the remaining issues, or order them to be paid by the party in default in any event.

13.4 LISTING FOR TRIAL

On receipt of the listing questionnaires, under CPR, r. 28.6(1), the court will:

(a) Fix the date for the trial (or, if it has already done so, confirm the date).

(b) Give any further directions for the trial as may seem necessary, including setting a trial timetable. Standard directions for this stage are also set out in the appendix to PD 28 (see figure 13.1).

(c) Specify any further steps that need to be taken before trial.

Expert evidence

The parties have permission to rely at the trial on expert evidence as follows:

   The claimant:
     Oral evidence—
     Written evidence—
   The defendant
     Oral evidence—
     Written evidence—

Trial timetable

The time allowed for the trial is

[The timetable for the trial may be agreed by the parties, subject to the approval of the trial judge.]

[The timetable for the trial (subject to the approval of the trial judge) will be that   ]

[The evidence-in-chief for each party will be contained in witness statements and reports, the time allowed for cross-examination by the defendant is limited to   and the time allowed for cross-examination by the claimant is limited to   ].

[The time allowed for the claimant's evidence is   .

The time allowed for the defendant's evidence is   ]

The time allowed for the submissions on behalf of each party is   .

The remainder of the time allowed for the trial (being   ) is reserved for the judge to consider and give the judgment and to deal with costs.]

Trial bundle etc.

The claimant shall lodge at the court at least 7 days before the hearing an indexed bundle of documents contained in a ring binder and with each page clearly numbered.

[A case summary (which should not exceed 250 words) outlining the matters still in issue, and referring where appropriate to the relevant documents shall be included in the bundle for the assistance of the judge in reading the papers before the trial.]

[The parties shall seek to agree the contents of the trial bundle and the case summary.]

Settlement

Each party must inform the court immediately if the claim is settled whether or not it is then possible to file a draft consent order to give effect to their agreement.

Figure 13.1 Standard directions following the filing of listing questionnaires

If none of the listing questionnaires is returned within the stated time, the court will normally make an order that if no listing questionnaires are filed within three days from service of the order, the claim and any counterclaim will be struck out. If only some of the parties are in default, the court will give listing directions based on the questionnaires that are returned (PD 28, para. 6.5). Notice of a listing hearing will be in form N153.

The parties should seek to agree directions at the listing stage, and they may submit a proposed order (PD 28, para. 7.2(1)). Usually listing directions will be made by the court without a hearing, but it may decide to hold a listing hearing, giving the parties three clear days' notice (para. 6.3).

13.4.1 Confirmation of expert directions

Directions given at the listing stage will confirm or make provision for the permission granted to the parties regarding reliance on written experts' reports and calling expert witnesses at trial. The direction will specify the experts by name, and say whether they can be called or whether only their reports can be relied upon. Oral evidence from experts will only be allowed if the court believes it is necessary in the interests of justice (PD 28, para. 7.2(4)).

13.4.2 Trial timetable

The court may, if it considers it appropriate to do so, in consultation with the parties, set a timetable for the trial. Setting a timetable is discretionary (CPR, r. 28.6(1)(b)), but if the court decides to set one, it must consult with the parties (r. 39.4). The timetable contemplated is not the same as the directions timetable, but will define how much time the court will allow at trial for the various stages of the trial itself. A suitable direction may limit the time to be spent by each party in calling its evidence and in addressing the court in closing submissions. More sophisticated timetables will define how much time will be allowed for each witness, or even for cross-examination and re-examination.

13.4.3 Trial bundles

Standard listing directions will provide that an indexed, paginated bundle of documents contained in a ring binder must be lodged with the court not more than seven days or less than three days before the trial. Slightly inconsistently, the standard direction in the appendix to PD 28 provides that trial bundles must be lodged at least seven days before trial. The parties must seek to agree the contents of the trial bundle a reasonable time in advance, which in practical terms means no later than 14 days before the trial. For further details on the contents of trial bundles see 23.5. Responsibility for lodging the bundle is that of the claimant. Lodging the bundle at court is required so that the trial judge can read the case papers in advance of the trial. Judges are likely to take a very dim view if the bundle is not lodged in time. Identical bundles will be needed for each of the parties, with an additional bundle for the witness box.

13.4.4 Case summary

Standard listing directions give the procedural judge the option of directing that a case summary should be included in the trial bundle. This document is intended to be non-partisan, and to be agreed if possible. It should be no more than 250 words, and should outline the matters in issue, referring where appropriate to the relevant documents in the trial bundle. Again, responsibility for this rests with the claimant and, if possible, it should be agreed with the other side.

13.4.5 Confirmation of trial date

The court will give the parties at least three weeks' notice of the date of the trial unless, in exceptional circumstances, the court directs that shorter notice will be given (CPR, r. 28.6(2)).

13.4.6 Summary assessment of fast track costs

The general rule is that at the end of a fast track trial, and provided none of the parties is assisted by legal aid or is a person under a disability, the court will make a summary assessment of the costs of the whole claim immediately after giving judgment (PD 44, para. 4.4). To assist the judge in assessing costs the parties are required to file and serve not less than 24 hours before the trial signed statements of their costs for the interim hearing in costs form 1 (see appendix 3). These must set out:

(a) the number of hours claimed;
(b) the hourly rate claimed;
(c) the amount and nature of disbursements;
(d) the solicitor's costs for attending or appearing at the hearing;
(e) counsel's fees; and
(f) VAT on the above.

Any failure to file or serve a statement of costs, without reasonable excuse, will be taken into account in deciding the costs order to be made regarding the claim, the trial, and/or any detailed assessment hearing that might become necessary as a result of that failure (PD 44, para. 4.6). Summary assessment will be unnecessary in cases where the parties have agreed the amount of costs (PD 44, para. 4.10).

Parties should try to ensure that their costs statements filed pursuant to PD 44, para. 4.4, are realistic. If a party who is ordered to pay costs has inflated his own statement, it may well be that the court and the other side will use it against him. Underpricing one's own costs may assist in attacking one's opponent's costs if one loses, but will be counter-productive if one is awarded costs.

If no costs statement is filed or served, the court may well take this as an indication that no costs are being sought from the other side.

13.5 TRIAL

Trials will usually take place in the county court where they are proceeding, but may take place in a civil trial centre or any other court if it is appropriate because of listing difficulties, the needs of the parties or for other reasons. The judge will generally have read the trial bundle and may well dispense with opening speeches. Unless the trial judge otherwise directs, the trial will be conducted in accordance with any order previously made (see 13.4.2). This means that the judge is free to set a trial timetable (PD 28, para. 8.3). Given the time constraints and the need for proportionality, it is likely that the trial judge will order witness statements to stand as the evidence-in-chief and otherwise control the evidence to be presented. If a trial is not concluded on the day it is listed, the judge will normally sit on the following day to complete it (PD 28, para. 8.6).

13.6 COSTS

At one stage it was proposed that fast track cases would be subject to fixed *inter partes* costs, with the amounts fixed at very low levels. For the time being the existing costs system will continue to apply to fast track cases, with the exception of trial costs. CPR, r. 28.2(5), provides that the court's power to award trial costs is limited in accordance with Part 46, which sets fixed amounts for the costs of trial depending on the amount recovered, with a small uplift if counsel is attended by a solicitor, see 24.6.) However, normally there should be no detailed assessment (taxation) of costs in fast track cases (see 13.4.6). The usual practice will be for the costs to be assessed summarily by the trial judge at the conclusion of the trial (PD 28, para. 8.5 and PD 44, paras 4.3–4.10).

CHAPTER 14   MULTI-TRACK

CONTENTS

14.1	Introduction	204
14.2	Case management stages in multi-track cases	205
14.3	Directions on allocation	207
14.3.1	Making an informed decision regarding directions	207
14.3.2	Inadequate information	207
14.3.3	Avoiding the need for a directions hearing	208
14.4	Case management conferences	209
14.4.1	Listing of case management conferences	210
14.4.2	Attendance at case management conferences	210
14.4.3	Business at case management conferences	210
14.4.4	Case summary	211
14.4.5	Usual directions	211
14.4.6	Unusual directions	211
14.5	Fixing the date for trial	212
14.6	Listing questionnaires	212
14.6.1	Purpose	213
14.6.2	Exchange of questionnaires	213
14.6.3	Failure to file listing questionnaires	213
14.6.4	Listing hearings	213
14.7	Pre-trial review	213
14.7.1	Notice of pre-trial review	214
14.7.2	Attendance	214
14.7.3	Pre-trial review directions	214
14.7.4	Agreed pre-trial review directions	214
14.8	Directions given at other hearings	214
14.9	Variation of case management timetable	215
14.9.1	Variation by agreement	215
14.9.2	Consensual variation of 'key dates'	215
14.9.3	Variation by court	215
14.9.4	Objecting to directions made without prior notice	215
14.9.5	Objecting to directions made after due notice	216
14.10	Non-compliance with case management timetable	216

14.1   INTRODUCTION

A vast range of cases will be dealt with on the multi-track, from simple contractual disputes involving little more than £15,000, to complex commercial cases involving difficult issues of fact and law with values of several million pounds, to cases where perhaps no money is at stake but which raise points of real public importance. Case management on the multi-track is intended to reflect this. Simpler cases should be given standard directions without the need for hearings, and the parties will be expected to comply with those directions without complicating or delaying matters. At the other end of the scale, the courts will adopt a far more active approach, possibly with several directions hearings in the form of case management conferences and pre-trial reviews. The courts are expected to adopt a flexible approach to ensure each case receives the right amount of case management input from the court (PD 29, para. 3.2(2)).

The result may be that straightforward multi-track cases are given tight timetables from defence to trial that are similar to those on the fast track. In such cases, the comments made in 13.1 about the need to be well prepared before commencing proceedings apply with equal force, the main difference being on costs. Even in complex multi-track cases it will be important for case preparation to be reasonably advanced before issue, because under the new system there is a great deal of 'front loading', and the procedural judge will want to be assisted by the parties in identifying the issues and the evidence required at the first case management conference.

Cases on the multi-track will generally be dealt with either in the Royal Courts of Justice or at another civil trial centre (see PD 29, paras 2 and 3.1). The procedural judge may need to order a transfer on first consideration or at an allocation hearing (see 5.3). Case management will generally be dealt with by a master in the Royal Courts of Justice, in a district registry by a district judge, and in a county court by either a district or a circuit judge (PD 29, para. 3.10). It is the duty of the parties at all hearings to consider whether any directions should be made, as this can avoid the need for additional case management hearings later on (PD 29, para. 3.5).

14.2 CASE MANAGEMENT STAGES IN MULTI-TRACK CASES

Allocation decisions are made after filing of the defence and return of allocation questionnaires (see 11.4.1). Once a case is allocated to the multi-track the court will give directions and hold such procedural hearings as may be appropriate in order to progress the case to trial or resolution by other means. Figure 14.1 illustrates the main stages in the progress of a multi-track case to trial.

CHAPTER 14 MULTI-TRACK

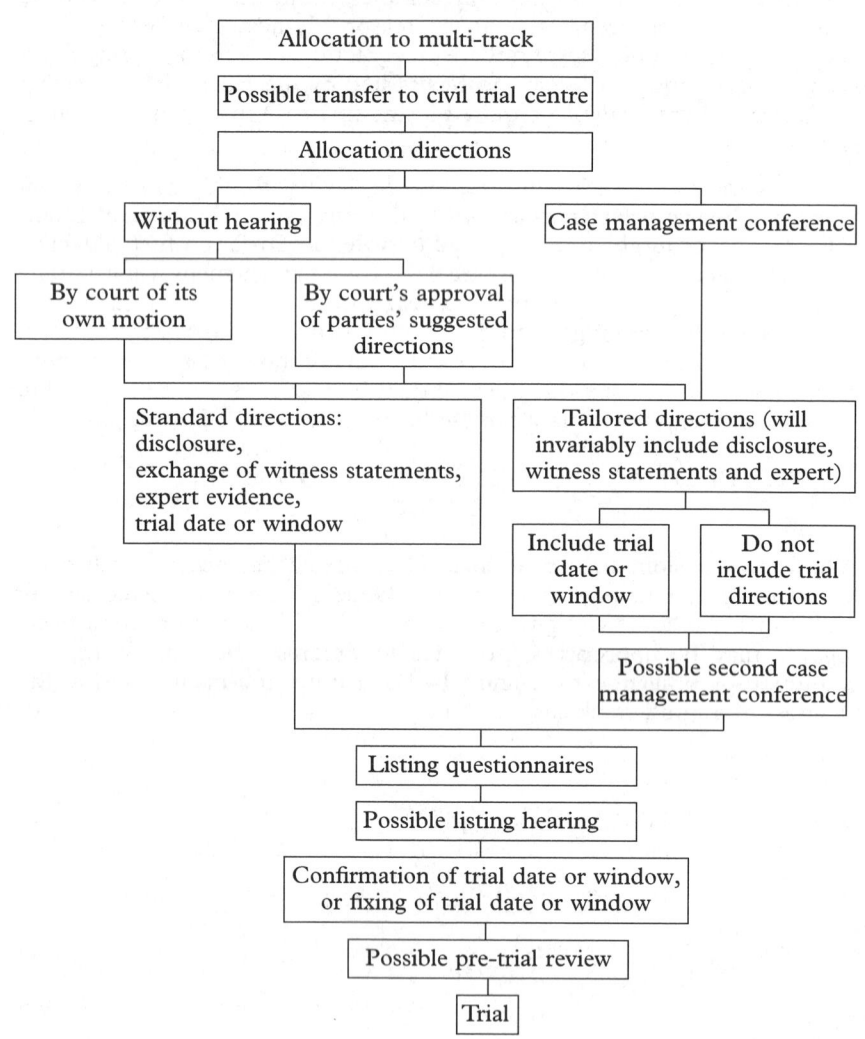

Figure 14.1 The multi-track

14.3 DIRECTIONS ON ALLOCATION

At the same time as a case is allocated to the multi-track the procedural judge will decide whether to give directions or to fix a case management conference or pre-trial review (or both a case management conference and a pre-trial review and such other directions as are thought fit: CPR, r. 29.2(1)). The procedural judge will therefore take a view as to the complexity of the case, and the amount of work required to get it ready for trial, and decide whether or not it is necessary to call the parties in before the court for a procedural hearing.

The court will seek to tailor its directions to the needs of the case, and the steps the parties have already taken to prepare it for trial. It will also take into account the extent to which the parties have complied with any pre-action protocol (see chapter 4). The court's concern will be to ensure the issues between the parties are identified, and that the evidence required for the trial is prepared and disclosed (PD 29, para. 4.3).

14.3.1 Making an informed decision regarding directions

It is important that the court should be informed of the progress made by the parties in gathering the necessary evidence and in identifying the real issues in the case. It is in the interests of the parties to make sure that they provide all necessary information to the court. This will ensure the directions given are realistic and suitable for the case, and prevent the court feeling the need to ask for further information and perhaps imposing sanctions. The information the court will act on may be gathered from:

(a) the claim form;
(b) the particulars of claim (if provided in addition to the claim form);
(c) the defence;
(d) any documents (such as witness statements and experts' reports) filed with the particulars of claim or defence;
(e) the completed allocation questionnaires and costs statements;
(f) any further documents filed with the allocation questionnaires, provided these are agreed between the parties, or have been served on the other parties, with a statement to that effect (PD 26, para. 2.2(2));
(g) any further information that the parties may be required to produce on an order by the court to clarify the matters in dispute or to give additional information; and
(h) any proposed directions, particularly where they have been agreed between the parties (PD 29, para. 4.6).

14.3.2 Inadequate information

It is expected that there will be cases allocated to the multi-track where the parties provide little or no information other than that contained in their statements of case. In such cases the court could call a case management conference, and it could order one or more of the parties to provide further information about their cases pursuant to CPR, r. 26.5(3). An order for further information at the allocation stage will be made in form N156 (see appendix 3). The order will set out the nature of the information and documentation required, and provide that copies must be sent to the court and other parties by a specified time. A note on form N156 warns that if an allocation hearing becomes necessary through a failure to provide the information ordered, the defaulting party may be ordered to pay the costs of that hearing.

However, it is perhaps more likely that it will simply impose directions giving a tight timetable for trial (PD 29, para. 4.10). Doing so will put enormous pressure on the parties. They will either have to comply, or will find themselves in considerable difficulty unless they apply promptly for tailored directions. This is because the court will assume for the purposes of any later application (in the absence of any appeal or application within 14 days to vary) that the parties were content that the directions were correct in the circumstances then existing (PD 29, para. 6.2(2)).

The general approach in these cases where there is inadequate information is for directions along the following lines to be made by the court of its own initiative:

(a) filing and service of any further information required to clarify either party's case;
(b) standard disclosure (for further details on which, see chapter 15) between the parties;
(c) simultaneous exchange of witness statements;
(d) for the appointment of a single expert unless there is good reason for not doing so;
(e) simultaneous exchange of experts' reports in cases or on issues where single expert directions have not been given (unless expert evidence is required on both liability and quantum, in which event the direction may be for simultaneous exchange on the liability issues, but sequential exchange on quantum issues);
(f) if experts' reports are not agreed, that there be a discussion between the experts for the purpose of identifying the expert evidence issues, and, if possible, reaching agreement between the experts, and the preparation of a statement setting out the issues on which they are agreed and a summary of their reasons on the issues where they disagree;
(g) listing a case management conference after the final date in the above directions; and
(h) specifying a trial period.

14.3.3 Avoiding the need for a directions hearing

If the parties in a multi-track case agree proposals for the management of the case and the court considers that the proposals are suitable, the court may simply approve them without the need for a directions hearing (PD 29, paras 4.6 and 4.7). This is encouraged by the new rules, as it obviously saves costs and court time. In order to obtain the court's approval the agreed directions must:

(a) if appropriate, include a direction regarding the filing of a reply;
(b) if appropriate, provide for amending any statement of case;
(c) include provision about the disclosure of documents;
(d) include provision about both factual and expert evidence (the provision about expert evidence may be to the effect that no expert evidence is required);
(e) if appropriate, include dates for service of requests for further information and/or questions to experts, and when they should be answered;
(f) include a date or a period when it is proposed the trial will take place; and
(g) if appropriate, a date for a case management conference.

It will be seen that only items (c), (d) and (f) are obligatory in all cases, although the others will frequently arise in practice. Proposed agreed directions must lay down a timetable by reference to calendar dates. The court will scrutinise the timetable carefully, with particular attention to the proposals for the trial and case management conference, and will be astute to ensure these are no later than is reasonably necessary.

The provision in any agreed directions relating to disclosure may:

(a) limit disclosure to standard disclosure, or less than that; and/or
(b) direct that disclosure will take place by the supply of copy documents without a list of documents, but if so, it must say either that the parties must serve a disclosure statement with the copies, or that they have agreed to disclose in this way without a disclosure statement.

The provision regarding factual and expert evidence should, if appropriate, deal with:

(a) whether the evidence should be disclosed simultaneously or sequentially;
(b) the use of a single expert; and
(c) without prejudice discussions between the experts if a single expert is not going to be instructed.

The court is free to reject directions that have been agreed between the parties, but will take them into account when making its own directions (either without a hearing or on a case management conference).

14.4 CASE MANAGEMENT CONFERENCES

Case management conferences are an integral part of the new system of active case management by the courts. They are not simply directions hearings, but are intended to ensure that the real issues between the parties are identified. Side issues will be dispensed with either by agreement between the parties with due encouragement from the judge, or by means of summary judgment or striking-out determinations at an early stage. Case management conferences may be held immediately after a case is allocated to the multi-track or at any time thereafter through to the listing stage. They can be used as the vehicle for laying down directions at the allocation stage, or may be used later in order to assess how the case is progressing when the initial directions on allocation should have been completed. Normally the court has a discretion whether to call a case management conference. However, where it is contemplated that an order may be made either for the evidence on a particular issue to be given by a single expert, or that an assessor should be appointed, PD 29, para. 4.13, provides that a case management conference must be held unless the parties have consented to the order in writing.

Case management conferences will also be called in cases where the court feels it cannot properly give directions on its own initiative, and where no agreed directions have been filed which it feels can be approved (PD 29, para. 4.12).

The *Final Report* at ch. 1, para. 6, envisaged that case management conferences would result in fewer cases going to final trial. By encouraging the parties to settle their dispute or resolve it outside the court system, and by forcing the parties into identifying the real issues at an early stage, it was hoped that case management conferences would be a means of using court time to save more time. They are intended to involve a more focused and directed use of time than was expended under the old system in directions hearings.

14.4.1 Listing of case management conferences

There is a commitment towards having case management conferences listed as promptly as possible (PD 29, para. 4.12(2)). The minimum period of notice the court will give to the parties of the date for the case management conference is three clear days (CPR, r. 3.3(3); PD 29, para. 3.7).

14.4.2 Attendance at case management conferences

If a case management conference is to be attended by a legal representative on behalf of a party, the representative must be someone familiar with the case (CPR, r. 29.3(2)). It will no longer be acceptable to send a trainee with a two-page briefing note on such a hearing. Instead it will have to be the fee-earner concerned, or someone (possibly counsel) who is fully familiar with the file, the issues and the proposed evidence, who must attend. They must be able to field the questions that are likely to be asked at the hearing, and have the authority to agree and/or make representations on the matters reasonably to be expected to arise. Where the inability of the person attending to deal with the case leads to the adjournment of the hearing, it will be normal for a wasted costs order to be made (PD 29, para. 5.2(3)) . Unless a specific direction is made by the court, the former idea of having the parties attend as well has been dropped.

14.4.3 Business at case management conferences

At a case management conference the court will, as stated by PD 29, para. 5.1:

(a) make a thorough review of the steps the parties have taken to date in preparing the case for trial;
(b) consider the extent to which they have complied with any previous orders and directions;
(c) decide on the directions needed to progress the action in accordance with the overriding objective;
(d) ensure that reasonable agreements are made between the parties about the matters in issue and the future conduct of the action; and
(e) record all such agreements.

To assist the court the legal representatives for all parties should ensure that all documents (and in particular witness statements and experts' reports) that the court is likely to ask to see are brought to court. They should also consider whether the parties themselves should attend, and consider in advance what orders and directions may be appropriate (PD 29, para. 5.6). If the witness statements and experts' reports have not been exchanged at the time of the case management conference, there is an as yet unresolved issue regarding legal professional privilege should the court ask to see these documents. Although the Civil Procedure Act 1997, sch. 1, para. 4, provides that the CPR may modify the rules of evidence for the purposes of civil proceedings, it is difficult to see that the practice direction can have the effect of abrogating the privilege. It should follow that the only reports and statements that can legitimately be called for are those that have been disclosed or that may be voluntarily disclosed at the hearing (see 1.9.6).

14.4.4 Case summary

An additional matter the parties are required by PD 29, para. 5.6, to consider is whether the court may be assisted by a written case summary. This should be a short document not exceeding 500 words which is designed to assist the court in understanding and dealing with the issues raised in the case. It should give a brief chronology of the claim, and state the factual issues that are agreed and those in dispute, and the nature of the evidence needed to decide them. Responsibility for preparing the document rests with the claimant, and if possible it should be agreed by the other parties.

14.4.5 Usual directions

In all cases the court will set a timetable at the case management conference for the steps it decides are necessary for preparing the case for trial (PD 29, paras 5.3 and 5.4). Typically the court will consider giving directions on the following matters:

(a) Whether the claimant has made clear the claim that is being made and the amount being claimed, and whether the defence is no more than a bare denial or is otherwise unclear. Orders for amendment and/or for further information may be appropriate if the statements of case are insufficiently clear for the other side to understand the case that has to be met.

(b) The scope of disclosure of documents required.

(c) The nature of the expert evidence required, and how and when it should be obtained. The court will not give permission for the use of expert evidence unless it can identify each expert by name or field of expertise, and say whether each expert's evidence should be given orally or by use of a report. Further matters that may be considered are whether the evidence on a particular issue should be given by a single expert, or that an assessor should be appointed, and whether there should be discussions between the experts.

(d) Disclosure of witness statements and summaries.

(e) Whether further information should be provided on matters other than statements of case, such as witness statements.

(f) Arrangements for questions that may be put to experts.

(g) Whether it would be just and save costs to have split trials on liability and quantum, or whether there should be a trial of one or more preliminary issues.

(h) Whether there should be another case management conference or a pre-trial review.

(i) Whether it is possible to fix a date for the trial, or to give a trial window. The court will be anxious to comply with the rule that the trial should be fixed as soon as practicable (CPR, r. 29.2(2)).

(j) Whether the trial should be heard by a High Court judge, or by a specialist judge. If so, the court will also consider transferring the case to the appropriate court (PD 29, para. 5.9).

14.4.6 Unusual directions

It is the duty of the parties to ensure that all interim matters are dealt with on the case management conference. If they want an order dealing with a matter that is not normally dealt with on a case management conference, such as an order for an interim payment or for specific disclosure, and they know the application is likely to be opposed, they should issue and serve an application notice in time for it to be heard at the case management conference. If the time allowed for the case management conference is insufficient to deal also with the contested application, they must inform the court at once so a fresh date can be fixed. Failure to take these steps may result in a costs sanction (PD 29, para. 5.8). Note also PD 23, para. 2.10, which provides that where a party decides to make an application at a hearing that has already been fixed, but there is insufficient time to serve an application notice, it may be sufficient simply to give such written notice as is possible, and to make the application orally at the original hearing.

Other directions from those provided for by CPR, r. 3.1(1), that may be considered in appropriate cases include:

(a) directing that part of the proceedings, such as a counterclaim, be dealt with as separate proceedings;
(b) staying the whole or part of the proceedings either generally or until a specified date or event;
(c) consolidating proceedings;
(d) trying two or more actions at the same time;
(e) deciding the order in which issues are to be tried; and
(f) excluding an issue from consideration.

14.5 FIXING THE DATE FOR TRIAL

The court will fix the trial date or the period in which the trial is to take place as soon as practicable (CPR, r. 29.2(2)). This may be possible when it gives allocation directions, but in complex cases (and also, perhaps, badly prepared cases and cases where the facts are developing, such as many personal injuries claims) this may have to be delayed, perhaps for a considerable period of time. Where fixing the trial date is postponed, it may be revisited either at a later case management conference, or on the application of the parties, or after further scrutiny by the court.

When the court fixes the date for trial (or lays down a trial period or window), it will give written notice to the parties, and will also specify a date by which the parties must file listing questionnaires (r. 29.2(3)). The court may alternatively make an order for an early trial on a fixed date and dispense with listing questionnaires (PD 29, para. 8.1(2)), or may simply list the case for trial when it reconsiders the case at the time when listing questionnaires would be sent out, dispensing with the need for questionnaires at that stage (r. 29.6(1)).

14.6 LISTING QUESTIONNAIRES

Listing questionnaires in form N170 will (unless dispensed with) be sent out to the parties by the court for completion and return by the date specified in the directions given when the court fixed the date or period for trial (CPR, r. 29.6). The specified date should be not less than eight weeks before the trial date or window (PD 29, para. 8.1(3)). The forms should be served by the court at least 14 days before they must be returned. Each party is under an obligation to return a completed questionnaire before the specified date together with costs statements, and the claimant is required to pay the listing fee. There is a possible sanction of automatic striking out for non-payment within the time specified by the court in a notice to pay (form N173; CPR, r. 3.7). The fee is payable even if questionnaires are dispensed with.

14.6.1 Purpose

A listing questionnaire is used to check that earlier orders and directions have been complied with, and to provide up-to-date information to assist the court with deciding when to hold the trial and how long it will take, and in making trial timetable directions. Once all the questionnaires have been received, or the time limit has expired, the file will be placed before the procedural judge, who will make directions for trial along the same lines as those set out in 14.7.3 or direct that there should be a listing hearing or pre-trial review.

14.6.2 Exchange of questionnaires

The CPR do not require the parties to exchange copies of their listing questionnaires, but doing so may avoid the parties giving conflicting or incomplete information to the court (PD 29, para. 8.1(5)). Getting this right may avoid the court considering that there is a need for a listing hearing or pre-trial review.

14.6.3 Failure to file listing questionnaires

If no one returns a listing questionnaire by the specified date, the court will usually make an order that the parties must do so within three days of service of the order, failing which the claim and any counterclaim will be struck out (PD 29, para. 8.3(1)). Where only some of the parties file listing questionnaires, the court will fix a listing hearing. It will also fix a listing hearing if any of the questionnaires do not provide the necessary information, or if the court considers that such a hearing is necessary to decide what further directions should be given to complete the preparations for trial (r. 29.6(3)).

14.6.4 Listing hearings

Listing hearings serve a similar purpose to pre-trial reviews, and concentrate on making the decisions relevant to fixing the date of the trial. They are fixed for dates as early as possible, and the parties are given at least three clear days' notice of the date. Even if a listing hearing is fixed because some of the parties did not file their questionnaires, the court will normally fix or confirm the trial date and make orders about the steps to prepare the case for trial (PD 29, para. 8.3(2)). The court is likely to make further directions similar to those set out in 14.7.3.

14.7 PRE-TRIAL REVIEW

If a pre-trial review is listed, it is likely to take place about eight to 10 weeks before trial. Lord Woolf intended that a pre-trial review would settle a statement of the issues to be tried, and set a programme and budget for the trial (*Final Report*, ch. 5, para. 26). The costs aspect has not been carried forward into the new rules. The pre-trial review gives the court a further opportunity to check that the parties have complied with earlier orders and directions, and may help in promoting settlement. They are not held in all cases, but only in those that merit the additional hearing. The intention is that they should be conducted by the eventual trial judge.

14.7.1 Notice of pre-trial review

A pre-trial review may be required by earlier directions made by the court of its own initiative or on a case management conference. The court may make the decision to hold a pre-trial review, or may actually fix the pre-trial review at a later stage, in which event it will give the parties at least seven clear days' notice of the hearing (CPR, r. 29.7).

14.7.2 Attendance

The same rules about a fully informed representative being present apply to pre-trial reviews as apply to case management conferences (see 14.4.2).

14.7.3 Pre-trial review directions

The court will not readily go behind earlier directions, and will apply the same principles as are applied generally when the parties fail to comply with case management directions (PD 29, para. 9.3).

Perhaps the most important task on a pre-trial review is to determine the timetable for the trial itself. This can lay down time limits for examination and cross-examination of witnesses, and for speeches. Doing this is intended to force advocates to focus their preparation, and to produce better managed trials. Other matters to be dealt with are:

(a) Evidence, particularly expert evidence. At this stage there should have been full disclosure and perhaps also discussions between the experts. It may be possible to make more rigorous directions about which experts really do need to be called at the trial, and which experts (or which parts of the expert evidence) can be taken from the experts' reports.
(b) A time estimate for the trial.
(c) Preparation of trial bundles.
(d) Fixing a trial date or week.
(e) Fixing the place of trial. This will normally be the court where the case is being managed, but it may be transferred depending on the convenience of the parties and the availability of court resources (PD 29, para. 10.1).

14.7.4 Agreed pre-trial review directions

The parties are required to seek to agree the directions to be made on the pre-trial review, and may file an agreed order. The court may then make an order in the terms agreed, or make some other order, or reject the proposals and continue with the pre-trial review.

14.8 DIRECTIONS GIVEN AT OTHER HEARINGS

The court is not restricted to making case management directions on the occasions described above, but can do so on any occasion on which the case comes before the court (PD 29, para. 3.4). In fact, whenever there is a hearing it is the duty of the parties to consider whether any directions should be made, and to make any appropriate application on that occasion (PD 29, para. 3.5). Further, the court may hold an ad hoc directions hearing on three clear days' notice whenever it appears necessary to do so. This can include situations where progress is delayed because one or other of the parties is in default of directions previously made (PD 29, para. 3.6). It can also occur because a party needs a direction not already in place, perhaps because a need to amend, or to ask for further information, has arisen since the last case management hearing. In such cases the application must be made as soon as possible so as to minimise the disruption to the original timetable (PD 29, para. 3.8).

14.9 VARIATION OF CASE MANAGEMENT TIMETABLE

As mentioned earlier, the court will assume for the purposes of any later application that the parties were content that any case management directions given were correct in the circumstances then existing in the absence of any appeal or application to vary made within 14 days. It is also regarded as essential that any party wanting to vary the timetable should take steps to do so as soon as possible (PD 29, para. 6.2). A delay in making an essential application to vary the timetable may well have the effect of losing all the time used before the application is eventually heard, which is not going to be looked upon favourably given the objective of dealing with cases expeditiously.

14.9.1 Variation by agreement

Case management directions fall into two categories:

(a) Those that can only be varied on an order being made the court on an application by a party seeking a variation (r. 29.5(1)). These 'key dates' are:

    (i) dates fixed for holding a case management conference;
    (ii) dates fixed for holding a pre-trial review;
    (iii) dates specified for the return of listing questionnaires; and
    (iv) dates fixed for trial (including a trial window).

(b) All other types of case management direction. These may be varied by the parties by consent, provided the variation does not affect any of the 'key dates' in category (a) above. There is no need to file anything with the court when a variation is agreed that does not affect any of the 'key dates' (PD 29, para. 6.5(1)).

14.9.2 Consensual variation of 'key dates'

If the parties agree to a variation of the case management timetable as laid down by the court, they must apply for an order by consent, file a draft of the order sought, and also file an agreed statement of the reasons why the variation is sought (PD 29, para. 6.5(2)). If the procedural judge is satisfied with the stated reasons, an order will be made without a hearing, either in the terms agreed or as thought fit by the procedural judge. Otherwise, the application will be listed for hearing, at which the parties will need to justify their position.

14.9.3 Variation by court

The court has power to vary previous directions of its own initiative (PD 29, para. 3.4).

14.9.4 Objecting to directions made without prior notice

This section deals with directions made:

(a) by the court of its own motion; and

(b) in circumstances where a party can establish it did not receive notice of the hearing where the directions were made.

A party who is dissatisfied with the directions given in such circumstances must apply for the court to reconsider its decision, and the application will normally be heard by the same judge as gave the original directions (PD 29, para. 6.3). The court will give the parties at least three clear days' notice of the hearing to reconsider the directions. At the hearing the court may confirm the original directions, or may make such different order as it thinks just.

14.9.5 Objecting to directions made after due notice

These can be varied only by mounting an appeal. The procedure for appealing is considered in chapter 25.

14.10 NON-COMPLIANCE WITH CASE MANAGEMENT TIMETABLE

Non-compliance with directions raises the area of sanctions, which is dealt with more fully in 11.8. At this point it should be noted that:

(a) The innocent party is allowed to apply for an order that the defaulting party must comply with the directions in place and/or for a sanction to be imposed. However, there is an obligation to write first to the defaulting party giving warning of the proposed application, and to make the application without delay (PD 29, paras 7.1 and 7.2).

(b) The defaulting party may apply for an order to remedy the failure under CPR, r. 3.9 (assuming it is an 'error of procedure'), and/or to extend the time for complying with the direction under r. 3.1(2)(a) and/or for relief from any sanction imposed under r. 3.8.

(c) If the court holds a hearing to give directions because of the default of a party or its legal representatives, it will usually impose a sanction (PD 29, para. 3.6).

CHAPTER 15 DISCLOSURE

CONTENTS

15.1	Introduction	217
15.2	Basic principles	219
15.3	Standard disclosure	219
15.3.1	Requirements of standard disclosure	219
15.3.2	Reasonable search	220
15.3.3	Inspection considered disproportionate	221
15.3.4	Limitation of standard disclosure	221
15.3.5	Duties of solicitors	221
15.4	Documents	221
15.4.1	What is a 'document'?	221
15.4.2	Documents in the party's control	222
15.4.3	Disclosure of copies	222
15.5	Procedure for standard disclosure	222
15.6	Continuing duty of disclosure	224
15.7	Specific disclosure or inspection	224
15.8	Inspection and copying	225
15.8.1	Inspection and copying of documents	225
15.8.2	Documents referred to in statements of case etc.	225
15.9	Pre-action and non-party disclosure	226
15.9.1	Test for granting an order for pre-action disclosure	226
15.9.2	Form of order for pre-action disclosure	227
15.9.3	Costs of pre-action disclosure	227
15.9.4	Non-party disclosure	228
15.9.5	Form of order for non-party disclosure	228
15.9.6	Costs of non-party disclosure applications	228
15.9.7	Objections to pre-action and non-party disclosure	228
15.9.8	Saving for other powers to order pre-action and non-party disclosure	229
15.10	Claim to withhold inspection or disclosure	229
15.10.1	Public interest immunity	229
15.10.2	Private privilege	230
15.10.3	Disproportionality	230
15.10.4	Restriction on use of an inadvertently disclosed privileged document	231
15.11	Consequences of failure to disclose	231
15.12	Subsequent use of disclosed documents	231

15.1 INTRODUCTION

At p. 137 of his *Final Report* Lord Woolf indicated his belief that one of the two major generators of unnecessary cost in civil litigation was uncontrolled discovery, and said that no one has seriously challenged that contention. As a result of that, at p. 105, he proposed attempting to curb disclosure of documents as an area of procedural activity and expressed the need 'to find a halfway house between a system with little or no disclosure and the present, unlimited obligation of disclosure'. Lord Woolf stressed

CHAPTER 15 DISCLOSURE

that what was required was a more proportionate but workable system, not one which is theoretically impeccable but unaffordable.

The CPR do not use the term 'discovery'. Instead Part 31 deals with 'disclosure and inspection of documents'. Part 31 applies to all claims except those on the small claims track (r. 31.1).

One reason why discovery became uncontrolled under the old rules was that it was the rules themselves which imposed an obligation to give disclosure of documents relating to any matter in question between the parties. In the new regime of active case management, the CPR require the court to take control of disclosure and inspection of documents, which is now to occur only when ordered by the court. The CPR then indicate that normally the court's requirements are to be limited. Under Part 31, disclosure is normally to be limited to standard disclosure (see 15.3), which itself may be limited or dispensed with (see 15.3.4). On the small claims track, disclosure is required only when ordered by the court in special directions (see chapter 12).

In exercising its power to order disclosure, as when exercising any power under the rules, the court must seek to give effect to the overriding objective (r. 1.2; see chapter 1). The aspect of the overriding objective which disclosure and inspection promote is r. 1.1(2)(a):

Dealing with a case justly includes, so far as is practicable—
   (a) ensuring that the parties are on an equal footing.

Disclosure and inspection ensure that all parties have access to the same evidence relating to their claim, even if they differ on how it is to be interpreted. But the CPR provisions on disclosure and inspection are inbued with the spirit of r. 1.1(2)(b) and (c):

Dealing with a case justly includes, so far as is practicable—
. . .
   (b) saving expense;
   (c) dealing with the case in ways which are proportionate—
     (i) to the amount of money involved;
     (ii) to the importance of the case;
     (iii) to the complexity of the issues; and
     (iv) to the financial position of each party.

Discovery became disproportionate under the old system because the courts had given such a wide interpretation of the phrase 'documents relating to any matter in question between the parties' in the rule specifying what documents had to be disclosed. In *Compagnie Financiere et Commerciale du Pacifique* v *Peruvian Guano Co.* (1882) 11 QBD 55 Brett LJ said:

. . . every document relates to the matters in question in the action, which not only would be evidence upon any issue, but also which, it is reasonable to suppose, contains information which *may* — not which *must* — either directly or indirectly enable the party [seeking discovery] either to advance his own case or to damage the case of his adversary . . . a document can properly be said to contain information which may enable the party [seeking discovery] either to advance his own case or to damage the case of his adversary, if it is a document which may fairly lead him to a train of inquiry, which may have either of these two consequences.

These words, from a time before photocopiers, and innocuous in themselves, have been the foundation for the excessive discovery and inspection prevalent in some kinds of litigation in recent years. They have been much criticised as contributing more to the increase of the cost of commercial litigation in particular than almost any other factor. It is the approach based on this case which has been overturned by the CPR, under which both disclosure and inspection will be expected to be proportionate to the issues and the objectives to be achieved.

15.2 BASIC PRINCIPLES

When ordered by the court to do so, a party must disclose documents as required by the order. A party discloses a document by stating that the document exists or has existed (CPR, r. 31.2). A party's duty to disclose documents is limited to documents which are or have been in that party's control, as defined in r. 31.8 (see 15.4.2). A party to whom a document has been disclosed has a right, under r. 31.3, to inspect that document, except where:

(a) the document is no longer in the control of the party who disclosed it; or
(b) the party disclosing the document has a right or a duty to withhold inspection of it; or
(c) where r. 31.3(2) applies.

Rule 31.3(2) is a provision permitting a party to refuse to permit inspection of documents where he considers it would be disproportionate to the issues in the case to do so. This is more fully discussed in 15.10.3.

The court's order to give disclosure will be an order to give only 'standard disclosure' (see 15.3), unless the court directs otherwise (r. 31.5). There is also a power in r. 31.12 to order specific disclosure (see 15.7).

Disclosure may be ordered by the court at the following times and under the following rules:

(a) Rule 12.7 when default judgment is obtained.
(b) Rule 14.8 when certain judgments on admissions are given.
(c) Rule 20.5 when a defendant applies to counterclaim against a person not already a party.
(d) Rule 20.13 when a defence is filed which contains a counterclaim.
(e) Rule 24.6 after deciding a summary judgment application
(f) Rule 26.5 after the end of a period of stay of proceedings for the purpose of enabling alternative dispute resolution to take place.
(g) Rules 28.2 and 28.3 upon allocation of a case to the fast track
(h) Rule 29.2 upon allocation to the multi-track.
(i) At a case management conference or upon any other interim application.

15.3 STANDARD DISCLOSURE

By CPR, r. 31.5(1), a court order requiring a party to give disclosure is an order to give standard disclosure, unless the court directs otherwise.

15.3.1 Requirements of standard disclosure

By r. 31.6 standard disclosure requires a party to disclose *only*:

(a) the documents on which he relies; and
(b) the documents which:
  (i) adversely affect his own case;
  (ii) adversely affect another party's case; or
  (iii) support another party's case; and

(c) the documents which he is required to disclose by a relevant practice direction.

No practice directions relevant to r. 31.6(c) had been issued at the time of writing.

15.3.2 Reasonable search

Rule 31.7 requires a party ordered to give standard disclosure to 'make a reasonable search for documents falling within r. 31.6(b) and (c)' (adverse material and documents specifically required by a practice direction). The effect of this, reinforced by PD 31, para. 2, is to apply the principle of proportionality to searching for the purposes of standard disclosure. The factors relevant in deciding what kind of search would be reasonable include (r. 31.7(2)):

(a) the number of documents involved;
(b) the nature and complexity of the proceedings;
(c) the ease and expense of retrieval of any particular document; and
(d) the significance of any document which is likely to be located during the search.

This list is not exhaustive.

A party who has not searched for a category or class of document on the grounds that to do so would be unreasonable must state this in his disclosure statement (see (15.5) and identify the category or class of document (r. 31.7(3)). PD 31, para. 2, interprets 'category or class of document' in CPR, r. 31.7(3), to mean a category or class defined by the searcher (such as documents before a particular date, or documents that are not in particular locations), not one of the categories defined in r. 31.6(b) or (c). This suggests that proportionality cannot be used as an excuse for not searching, for example, for any document that adversely affects the searcher's case. In the prescribed form of disclosure statement in PD 31, annex, and form N265 the statement required by r. 31.7(3) is turned into a description of the boundaries of a search:

I did not search for documents—
 1. pre-dating ——
 2. located elsewhere than ——
 3. in categories other than ——

In the disclosure statement the disclosing party should draw attention to any particular limitations which were adopted for proportionality reasons and give the reasons why the limitations were adopted (PD 31, para. 4.2(2)).

The searcher must search for the documents required by CPR, r. 31.6(b) and (c), but may make a policy decision not to search in places where the cost of searching could not be justified by the small chance of finding anything disclosable.

15.3.3 Inspection considered disproportionate

A disclosing party who has found documents within r. 31.6(b) (adverse documents) is not required to permit inspection of them if he considers that it would be disproportionate to the issues in the case to permit inspection of them (r. 31.3(2)). This is considered in 15.10.3. A description of the category or class of documents for which inspection is refused on this ground must be given in the disclosure statement (see 15.5).

15.3.4 Limitation of standard disclosure

Standard disclosure may be dispensed with or limited by the court under r. 31.5(2) or, under r. 31.5(3), by written agreement, between the parties, which should be lodged with the court (PD 31, para. 1.4). Rule 28.3(2) of the CPR provides that on the fast track the court may decide not to direct standard disclosure, but may direct that no disclosure takes place or specify the documents or classes of documents which the parties must disclose. This is likely to occur if, for example, whether in pursuance of the pre-action protocols or otherwise, there has already been substantial or total disclosure at some earlier stage. On the multi-track r. 29.2 deals with case management generally.

The court when exercising its case management powers, and having scrutinised the documents before it, may decide to limit standard disclosure to what it perceives to be the relevant issues. For example, where the pleaded facts make it clear that the whole litigation turns on whether a written contract was or was not subsequently varied by agreement between the parties, the court may limit disclosure, e.g., 'to the issue as to whether or not the contract dated 25 February 1999 was varied in the course of correspondence between the parties, between 15 April and 7 May 1999'.

15.3.5 Duties of solicitors

PD 31, para. 4.4, requires the legal representative of a disclosing party to endeavour to ensure that the individual making the disclosure statement (see 15.5) understands the duty of disclosure under Part 31. It is submitted that the requirement in r. 31.6(b) to disclose adverse documents is a concise restatement of the previous requirement to give honest discovery. It follows that under the CPR solicitors will have the same duty as they did under the old system to give clients full and early advice that it is necessary to preserve documents that may have to be disclosed (*Rockwell Machine Tool Co. Ltd* v *E.P. Barrus (Concessionaires) Ltd* [1968] 1 WLR 693). Solicitors may well be under a further duty under the CPR to advise clients to make an early and thorough search for documents that may have to be disclosed.

15.4 DOCUMENTS

15.4.1 What is a 'document'?

Rule 31.4 of the CPR defines 'document' as 'anything in which information of any description is recorded', and a copy, in relation to a document, is defined as 'anything onto which information recorded in the document has been copied, by whatever means and whether directly or indirectly'. Thus 'document', as under the previous law, is not confined to paper and includes disks, audio cassettes, video cassettes, computer programs, and the like.

15.4.2 Documents in the party's control

By r. 31.8(1) of the CPR a party's duty to disclose documents is limited to documents which are now or have been previously within the party's control. Rule 31.8(2) says that a document is or was in a party's control if:

(a) it is or was in his physical possession;
(b) he has or has had a right to possession of it; or
(c) he has or has had a right to inspect or take copies of it.

This does not seem to be any different from the 'possession, custody or power' criterion for giving discovery under the old rules. Therefore, as under the old rules, it may be possible to require the controller of a company to disclose the company's documents in a claim to which the controller but not the company is a party (*B v B* [1978] Fam 181; *Lonrho Ltd v Shell Petroleum Co. Ltd* [1980] 1 WLR 627; *Re Tecnion Investments Ltd* [1985] BCLC 434).

Disclosure is the process of revealing the existence of documents, whether or not the disclosing party has access to them at present. A disclosing party who has parted with the only copy of a document must nonetheless disclose it, because it may be open to the opposing party to apply to the court to obtain inspection of the document wherever it is now or to force the disclosing party to seek to recover it or copies of it.

15.4.3 Disclosure of copies

By CPR, r. 31.9, a copy of a document must be treated as a separate document, and therefore separately disclosed, if it contains a modification, obliteration or other marking or feature:

(a) on which 'a party' (which clearly means the disclosing party) intends to rely; or
(b) which adversely affects the disclosing party's own case or supports another party's case.

So if, for example, several copies of a memorandum have been produced and some have been returned to the originator with other people's comments on them, and those comments are within (a) or (b) above, the copies must be disclosed. Otherwise it is not necessary to disclose the existence of copies of disclosed documents (r. 31.9(1)).

15.5 PROCEDURE FOR STANDARD DISCLOSURE

The procedure for standard disclosure is specified in CPR, r. 31.10, and PD 31, paras 3 and 4. When standard disclosure has been ordered, each party must make a list of documents it is disclosing, using form N265 (see appendix 3), and serve it on every other party (CPR, r. 31.10(2); PD 31, para. 3.1). On form N265, as required by CPR, rr. 31.10(4) and 31.19(4), the list is in three parts:

(a) Documents presently in the disclosing party's control which the controlling party does not object to being inspected.
(b) Documents presently in the disclosing party's control which the controlling party objects to being inspected, giving the reason for the

objection. PD 31, para. 4.5, says that the disclosing party must state in writing that he has a right or duty to withhold a document or part of a document from inspection and the grounds on which he claims that right or duty, and para. 4.6 says that this should normally be stated in the disclosure statement (see below), but form N265 is not laid out in that way.

(c) Documents that have been in the disclosing party's control but are no longer, saying when each was last in the party's control and where each is now.

Rule 31.10(3) of the CPR says that the list must identify the documents in a convenient order and manner and as concisely as possible. PD 31, para. 3.2, advises that this must normally be done by listing the documents in date order, numbering them consecutively and giving each a concise description, such as, 'letter, claimant to defendant'. Paragraph 3.2 goes on to suggest that if there is a large number of documents falling into a particular category, the disclosing party may list the documents as a category rather than individually, e.g., '50 bank statements relating to account number —— at —— Bank between 1990 and 1994'.

There must also be a 'disclosure statement' (r. 31.10(5)). This is a statement made by the party disclosing the documents which (r. 31.10(6)):

(a) sets out the extent of the search that has been made to locate documents which he is required to disclose;
(b) certifies that he understands the duty to disclose documents; and
(c) certifies that to the best of his knowledge he has carried out that duty.

In addition:

(a) PD 31, para. 4.2, says that a disclosure statement should expressly state that the disclosing party believes the extent of the search to have been reasonable in all the circumstances.
(b) Rule 31.7(3) of the CPR requires a party who has not searched for a category or class of document on the grounds that to do so would be unreasonable (see 15.3) to state this in the disclosure statement and identify the category or class of document not searched for.
(c) Rule 31.3(2) requires a party who considers that it would be disproportionate to the issues in the case to permit inspection of a category or class of documents to state that fact in the disclosure statement.
(d) Rule 31.10(7) provides that if the party making the disclosure is not an individual, the statement must identify the person who is making it and explain why he or she is considered an appropriate person to make it. PD 31, para. 4.3 requires in addition the name and address of the person making the statement and the office or position he or she holds in the disclosing party.
(e) In setting out the extent of the search the disclosing party should draw attention to any particular limitations which were adopted for proportionality reasons (see 15.3) and give the reasons why the limitations were adopted (PD 31, para. 4.2(2)).

The disclosure statement on the front of form N265 deals with these matters, but it departs from PD 31 by describing the search as having been reasonable 'and proportionate', does not mention the address of a person signing on behalf of a firm or company, and does not provide space for item (e). The prescribed form of statement in PD 31, annex, omits items (c), (d) and (e).

A disclosure statement must be signed by the party making the disclosure (or his or her litigation friend), not by a solicitor. Nevertheless, as the disclosure statement states that the party is making disclosure in accordance with the rules, the party will be wise to seek guidance from a solicitor on what has to be done to comply. There is no formulaic advice on what kind of search for adverse material would be reasonable, to comply with r. 31.7, since the essence of the question is: What is reasonable in the circumstances of the claim? So the extent of searching required must be discussed with the client at all stages of planning the litigation, as issues and evidential requirements are clarified. In order to make and justify decisions on reasonableness of search where large numbers of documents are involved, the client must provide a realistic measurement of the quantity, and estimate of the cost of searching; and the lawyer must assess the legal significance of what might be turned up if the search were extended. These factors must be set against the value of the claim.

The parties may agree in writing to disclose documents without making a formal list and without making a disclosure statement (r. 31.10(8)). Any such written agreement should be lodged with the court (PD 31, para. 1.4).

The parties may agree in writing or the court may direct that disclosure or inspection or both shall take place in stages (CPR, r. 31.13). A written agreement by the parties should be lodged with the court (PD 31, para. 1.4).

15.6 CONTINUING DUTY OF DISCLOSURE

The duty of disclosure continues until the proceedings are concluded and if documents come to a party's notice at any time during the proceedings that party must immediately notify all other parties (CPR, r. 31.11). PD 31, para. 3.3 says that this should be done by a 'supplemental list', presumably in form N265. This further reinforces the suggestion made above that the duty of honest disclosure is precisely parallel to that under the previous rule.

15.7 SPECIFIC DISCLOSURE OR INSPECTION

The court may, under CPR, r. 31.12, make an order for specific disclosure ordering a party to do one or more of the following, namely:

(a) disclose documents or classes of documents specified in the order;
(b) carry out a search to the extent stated in the order;
(c) disclose any documents located as a result of that search.

Also under r. 31.12 the court may make an order for specific inspection, which is an order that a party permit inspection of a document, named in the order, which the party sought to exclude from inspection under r. 31.3(2) (permission to inspect would be disproportionate to the issues in the case, see 15.3 and 15.10.3).

Any application for an order under this paragraph must be made by application notice, specifying the order that the applicant intends to ask the court to make, and must be supported by evidence (PD 31, para. 5.2). The rules do not provide what this evidence should contain, but it is suggested that, as in the case where previously an application for specific discovery was made, it should explain the nature of the dispute, the stage reached in the proceedings, and the factors which lead the applicant to conclude that the documents sought exist, are disclosable and are within the control of the opposing party.

PD 31, para. 5.3, says that 'the grounds on which the order is sought' may be set out in the application notice itself or in the evidence filed in support. Paragraph 5.4 goes on to make the rather insubstantial statement that:

> . . . if the court concludes that the party from whom specific disclosure is sought has failed adequately to comply with the obligations imposed by an order for disclosure (whether by failing to make a sufficient search for documents or otherwise) the court will usually make such order as is necessary to ensure that those obligations are properly complied with.

Rule 31.12 of the CPR does not say in what form compliance with an order for specific disclosure must be undertaken. Form N265 (which is expressed to be for standard rather than specific disclosure) could be adapted, but it is likely that the court will want more formality and require the party against whom the order is made to file evidence or certify in some form whether the documents exist and the extent of any search made.

15.8 INSPECTION AND COPYING

15.8.1 Inspection and copying of documents

A party who has a right to inspect a document must give the party who disclosed the document written notice of his wish to inspect it (CPR, r. 31.15(a)) and must be permitted to inspect it not more than seven days after the date of receipt of that notice (r. 31.15(b)). A party may instead of physical inspection request a copy of the document and if he also undertakes to pay reasonable copying costs, the party who disclosed the document must supply him with a copy no later than seven days after the date of receipt of the request (r. 31.15(c)).

15.8.2 Documents referred to in statements of case etc.

Quite apart from the right to inspect documents disclosed by either standard or specific disclosure, a party may, by CPR, r. 31.14, inspect a document mentioned in a statement of case, a witness statement, a witness summary, an affidavit, or (subject to r. 35.10(4)), an expert's report.

This provision mirrors the previous RSC, ord. 24, r.10. If a document is of sufficient relevance to have been referred to in any of the kinds of document mentioned in r. 31.14 above then clearly it ought to be shown to the opposite party. An expert's report must state the substance of all material instructions (r. 35.10(3)). Rule 35.10(4) provides that the instructions themselves are not privileged against disclosure but the court will not order disclosure of any specific document or permit any questioning in court other than by the party who instructed the expert, unless it is satisfied that there are reasonable grounds to consider that the statement of material instructions is inaccurate or incomplete.

15.9 PRE-ACTION AND NON-PARTY DISCLOSURE

Rule 31.16 of the CPR governs the procedure for applying for disclosure of documents before proceedings have started. Rule 31.17 deals with applications after proceedings have started for disclosure by a person who is not a party to the proceedings. These applications are made under the Supreme Court Act 1981, ss. 33 and 34, and the County Courts Act 1984, ss. 52 and 53. Those provisions were at first applied only to proceedings in respect of personal injury and wrongful death. It was recommended in the *Final Report* that this restriction should no longer apply. The Civil Procedure Act 1997, s. 8, empowers the Lord Chancellor by order to amend those sections so as to extend the provision to circumstances where other claims may be made or generally. In fact the Civil Procedure (Modification of Enactments) Order 1998 (SI 1998/2940) amends the statutes to enable orders for pre-action and non-party disclosure to be made in any type of case. This amendment comes into force at the same time as the CPR, i.e., 26 April 1999.

15.9.1 Test for granting an order for pre-action disclosure

An application for pre-action disclosure must be supported by evidence and may only be made where the applicant and respondent are likely to be parties to proceedings (the same proceedings) and, if proceedings had started, the respondent's duty by way of standard disclosure would extend to the document or class of document of which the applicant now seeks disclosure (CPR, r. 31.16(3)(a), (b) and (c)).

In addition, the court may only make an order if disclosure before proceedings have started is 'desirable in order to dispose fairly of the anticipated proceedings; assist the dispute to be resolved without proceedings; or save costs' (r. 31.16(3)(d)).

This is a more rigorously defined test than that under the preceding rules. It must be shown not merely that the document might eventually be disclosable should the litigation start, but that disclosing it now will further one of the purposes set out in r. 31.16(3)(d), for example, where it will demonstrate whether or not in essence the claimant is likely to have a case at all. It is submitted that pre-action disclosure ought to be seen as exceptional and if the document will not further one of the r. 31.16(3)(d) purposes, the court is likely to rule that the claimant should be left to decide whether or not to issue proceedings on the basis of the information presently before him and then seek ordinary disclosure in the course of those proceedings.

The celebratedly contentious term 'fishing expedition' will no doubt continue to feature largely in applications for pre-action disclosure, especially now that they are no longer restricted to personal injury cases and so will be available in all manner of commercial disputes. An order for pre-action disclosure must specify the documents or classes of documents to be disclosed (r. 31.16(4)(a)) and it is suggested that a general application for 'standard disclosure' will fail. All applications will turn on their own facts, and the extent to which commercial litigators will wish to make use of this provision remains to be seen, but the courts will certainly not countenance any attempt to use the provision oppressively, speculatively or so as to become routine, as a means of advancing the stage at which disclosure should be given. In this connection regard must be had to the usual costs provision described below.

15.9.2 Form of order for pre-action disclosure

An order for pre-action disclosure will specify the documents or classes of documents which the respondent must disclose, and require the respondent to specify any of those documents which are no longer in his control, or in respect of which he claims a right or duty to withhold inspection (CPR, r. 31.16(4)). It may require the respondent to indicate what has happened to any documents no longer in his control, and it may specify the time and place for disclosure and inspection (r. 31.16(5)).

15.9.3 Costs of pre-action disclosure

In the nature of things pre-action disclosure is more likely to be undertaken by a potential claimant than a potential defendant, though there will be exceptional circumstances where a person who has been notified of a potential claim against him seeks to take the initiative in getting documents which go to the heart of the action which had not been voluntarily disclosed in advance by the claimant.

Under CPR, r. 48.1(2), the general rule is that the court will award the person against whom the order for pre-action disclosure is sought his costs of the application and of complying with any order made on the application.

Such costs will inevitably be determined by summary assessment although it may not be possible to have the summary assessment immediately after the application, for example, where the respondent does not know to what lengths he may have to go to search for and provide copies of the documents of which he is now required to permit inspection.

That is the prima facie rule, but regard must also be had to r. 48.1(3) which provides that the court may make a different order, having regard to all the circumstances including:

   (a)   the extent to which it was reasonable for the person against whom the order was sought to oppose the application; and
   (b)   whether the parties to the application have complied with any relevant pre-action protocol.

The court will therefore have regard to the general duty of cooperation between the parties and the overall reasonableness of the parties' conduct. In personal injury, and particularly in clinical negligence cases, deliberate non-cooperation or non-response which provokes an application for pre-action disclosure may well lead to costs being ordered on some other basis entirely, and even against the respondent. In personal injury litigation particularly, the duties enjoined on the parties by the protocols may mean that any application which is successful is likely in itself to demonstrate unreasonableness on the part of the respondent, and costs orders against the respondent may well become the norm. In other forms of litigation where the uses of this provision are as yet unexplored, it will be for the courts to decide on a consistent approach in the light of the fact that whilst no pre-action protocols at present exist, the parties are in every case exhorted to have regard to the spirit of them in pre-action cooperation.

15.9.4 Non-party disclosure

An application for an order requiring disclosure by a person who is not a party to the proceedings in which the application is made must be supported by evidence (CPR, r. 3.17(2)) and may only lead to an order where the documents of which disclosure is sought are likely to support the case of the applicant or adversely affect the case of another party and disclosure is 'necessary in order to dispose fairly of the claim or to save costs' (r. 3.17(3)).

The rules in Part 31 do not mention whether the application should be served on the non-party, but by virtue of r. 23.4(1) the general rule is that a copy of any application notice must be served on each respondent unless some rule, practice direction or court order permits otherwise. There is no apparent rule applicable here and therefore in principle the notice application should be served on the non-party, together with the evidence in support.

It may be argued that it is not necessary for the applicant to see the document in advance of trial and that a witness summons for the person in possession of the document to attend the trial will suffice. However, few documents will be so simple that they can be adequately dealt with and digested, by both parties, on the morning of the hearing and without them appearing in the trial bundle for pre-trial reading.

The ability to make an order for non-party disclosure in all kinds of proceedings will avoid the need for devices of the kind used in *Khanna* v *Lovell White Durrant* [1995] 1 WLR 121 where the court invented the concept of 'production appointments' for witnesses to attend under subpoena to bring documents to a hearing before the trial, so that they could be photocopied.

15.9.5 Form of order for non-party disclosure

An order for non-party disclosure will specify the documents or classes of documents which the respondent must disclose, and require the respondent to specify any of those documents which are no longer in his control, or in respect of which he claims a right or duty to withhold inspection (CPR, r. 31.17(4)). It may require the respondent to indicate what has happened to any documents no longer in his control, and it may specify the time and place for disclosure and inspection (r. 31.17(5)).

15.9.6 Costs of non-party disclosure applications

As with the costs of pre-action disclosure (see 15.9.3), by r. 48.1(2) and (3) there is a presumption that the court will award the non-party the costs of the application and of complying with any order made on the application. There is a saving provision allowing the court to make some different order to reflect the reasonableness of the non-party's opposition to the application.

15.9.7 Objections to pre-action and non-party disclosure

Nothing in the provisions in CPR, rr. 31.16 and 31.17, relating to pre-action or non-party disclosure prevents the party from whom disclosure is sought claiming to withhold inspection of the document on the basis of privilege, or, for example, that the documents could only be discovered after a search which would in the circumstances be unreasonable. The court will then have to consider the merits of those objections in the same way as in the case of disclosure generally (see 15.10).

15.9.8 Saving for other powers to order pre-action and non-party disclosure

Rule 31.18 of the CPR provides that rr. 31.16 and 31.17 do not limit any other power which the court may have to order pre-action and non-party disclosure. This preserves the practice in *Khanna* v *Lovell White Durrant* [1995] 1 WLR 121 (see 15.9.4), should that be thought preferable to the more routine form of application now envisaged. It also preserves the basis of the so called *Norwich Pharmacal* jurisdiction, pursuant to the case of *Norwich Pharmacal Co.* v *Commissioners of Customs and Excise* [1974] AC 133, under which discovery may be ordered against a defendant who, through no fault of his own and whether voluntarily or not 'has got mixed up in the tortious acts of others so as to facilitate their wrongdoing', and so comes under a duty to assist the person who has been wronged by giving him full information and disclosing the identity of the wrongdoers. Similarly the powers to order disclosure in advance of action by search orders under the Civil Procedure Act 1997, s. 7 (see 10.6), are unaffected by rr. 31.16 and 31.17.

15.10 CLAIM TO WITHHOLD INSPECTION OR DISCLOSURE

A person holding a document which a party seeks to inspect may dispute aspects of disclosure or inspection on a number of bases, namely:

(a) there may be factual disputes about the disclosability or existence of the document;
(b) there may be factual disputes about whether the document is or has ever been under the party's control;
(c) there may be a claim to withhold disclosure on the basis of public interest immunity (see 15.10.1);
(d) there may be a claim to withhold inspection on the basis of private privilege, i.e., professional legal privilege, litigation privilege, or the privilege against self-incrimination (see 15.10.2);
(e) there may be a claim by a person under CPR, r. 31.3(2), that it would be 'disproportionate' to the issues in the case to permit inspection of documents (see 15.10.3).

Nothing further need be said about factual disputes about the existence of documents or their disclosability.

15.10.1 Public interest immunity

A person may apply without notice for an order permitting him to withhold disclosure of a document on the ground that disclosure would damage the public interest (CPR, r. 31.19(1)). Use of the word 'person' rather than 'party' in r. 31.19(1) indicates that it is open to non-parties who have received an application for non-party disclosure to make applications.

Unless the court otherwise orders an order of the court under r. 31.19(1) must not be served on any other person or be open to inspection by any other person (r. 31.19(2)).

This provides a procedure for claiming public interest immunity. It will involve the court in a weighing exercise, especially where evidence and submissions are from one party only. Under r. 31.19(6) the court may require the persons seeking to withhold disclosure to produce the document to the court and it may invite any person, whether or not a party, to make representations. Where appropriate, therefore, the court can convert the without-notice procedure into an application on notice. Rule 31.19(8) expressly declares that nothing in Part 31 affects any rule of law permitting or requiring a document to be withheld from disclosure or inspection on the ground of public interest.

15.10.2 Private privilege

Under r. 31.19(3) a person who wishes to claim that he has a right or a duty to withhold inspection of a document or part of a document must state in writing that he has such a right and the grounds on which he claims that right or duty. That claim must be in the list in which the document is disclosed, or, if there has been no list, in a formal notice to the person wishing to inspect the document (r. 31.19(4)). A party may then apply to the court to decide whether a claim made under r. 31.19(3) should be upheld. In other words a party may take the initiative to claim privilege in his own documents and seek an order of the court to that effect; or the opposing party from whom disclosure is withheld may make that application. It is suggested in PD 31, para. 6.1, that a claim to withhold inspection of a document does not require an application to the court and that therefore, generally speaking, it is the party who wishes to challenge that claim who must apply to the court. Although this is applicable in the case of disputes about private privilege, in the case of public interest immunity the r. 31.19(1) procedure referred to above is likely to be the usual course. In disputes about private privilege the court may require the person seeking to withhold inspection of a document to produce it to the court and it may invite any person, whether or not a party, to make representations (r. 31.19(6)).

15.10.3 Disproportionality

Under r. 31.3(2) of the CPR, where a party considers that it would be disproportionate to the issues in the case to permit inspection of documents within a category or class of document, he is not required to permit inspection of documents, but must state in his disclosure statement that inspection of those documents will not be permitted on the grounds that to do so would be disproportionate.

This is a wholly new basis for withholding inspection of a document whose existence and disclosability appear to be admitted. The concept of proportionality is an important one in considering the CPR purposively. It imports considerations not merely of technical relevance to the litigation, but of how expensive or time-consuming the carrying out of inspection is likely to be. Given that by this time the party having the documents will have presumably found them and identified them so that any search is likely to have been successful, this would seem to focus the court's attention on the cost of carrying out inspection and therefore presumably on the fact that inspection would need, e.g., to be in some distant place, or that the time to be taken in view of the number of documents would be excessive, or the like.

This is a very difficult concept because, the disclosing party having concluded that the documents fall within the proper bounds of standard disclosure, on what basis is the court to determine that the costs of the opposite party inspecting them will be disproportionate? If the disclosing party has done its job properly under the rules and searched for and sifted the documents to determine disclosability, the cost of physical inspection of the documents would seem likely to be only a small proportion of the cost of finding and identifying them in the first place. If the documents were not sufficiently relevant, they need not have been disclosed at all. The test will presumably focus on how peripheral to the litigation the documents are and the cost of inspecting them, although on the face of it one might think that whether or not to incur the cost should initially be a matter for the inspecting party, no further costs to the disclosing party being involved, save those of permitting the inspecting party access to the documents. Early guidance from the higher courts on the concept of 'proportionality' in this context is likely to be forthcoming.

15.10.4 Restriction on use of an inadvertently disclosed privileged document

Rule 31.20 of the CPR provides that where a person inadvertently allows a privileged document to be inspected, the party who has inspected the document may use it or its contents only with the consent of the court.

The rule itself sets out no new principle and there is no reason to suppose that any change in the law is contemplated.

15.11 CONSEQUENCES OF FAILURE TO DISCLOSE

A party may not rely on any document which he fails to disclose or in respect of which he fails to permit inspection unless the court permits (CPR, r. 31.21).

It is difficult to see why a court should grant any latitude to a party who, having failed to disclose and allow inspection of a document as required by the court's order, then seeks to use the document at trial. The key issue will of course be prejudice to the other party, though, given the obvious default of the party seeking to introduce the document, the court may not be inclined to enquire too nicely into this matter. The rule will permit the court some residual discretion which may perhaps be more liberally exercised in the case of accidental non-disclosure, especially by unrepresented parties. Solicitors will need to protect themselves by writing comprehensively to clients about the nature of the duty of disclosure in order to protect themselves from potential wasted costs orders.

15.12 SUBSEQUENT USE OF DISCLOSED DOCUMENTS

By r. 31.22(1) of the CPR a party to whom a document has been disclosed may use it only for the purpose of the proceedings in which it is disclosed except where:

(a) the document has been read to or by the court, or referred to, at a hearing which has been held in public; or
(b) the court gives permission; or
(c) the party who disclosed the document and the person to whom the document belongs agree.

The court may make an order restricting or prohibiting the use of a document which has been disclosed, even where the document has been read to or by the court, or referred to, at a public hearing (r. 31.22(2)). An application for such an order may be made by a party or by any person to whom the document belongs (r. 31.22(3)).

This preserves the principle that, as one is required to complete disclosure with absolute honesty and thus confidential documents may be disclosed, it is right that a party should have the protection of ensuring that they are used only for the current litigation. Thus the rule which evolved from *Riddick* v *Thames Board Mills Ltd* [1977] QB 881 is preserved so that a document disclosed in proceedings may not be used, for example, for unrelated commercial purposes or as the basis on which to found another claim. Indeed, misuse of such documents will constitute a serious contempt of court. That restriction disappears in the circumstances indicated in r. 31.22(1), although the reference 'or referred to' in r. 31.22(1)(a) may cause some difficulty. Is it enough for the protection granted by the rule to be lost merely because some witness, however briefly, mentions the document in question in evidence, or must the document play some significant part in the case? The wording of r. 31.22(2) and (3) would seem to be neutral on who has the onus of satisfying the court that despite the document having been referred to or read in court, it should not be used in other proceedings. In the previously relevant rule (RSC, ord. 24, r. 14A) the restriction was lifted where 'the document has been read to or by the court or referred to in open court unless the court for special reasons has otherwise ordered'. These words led to some difficulty so that it was unclear how fleeting a reference would suffice, and 12 years after that rule came into effect there was still very little case law to explain it. It would seem that a person wishing to restrict the use of a document which has been read to the court will have to discharge the onus of showing why that should be (see *Singh* v *Christie* (1993) *The Times*, 11 November 1993). The phrase 'read to or by the court' has been interpreted as including being made available to the judge with the reading list before the trial starts (*Derby* v *Weldon (No. 2)* (1988) *The Times*, 20 October 1988).

An order may in any event be made by the court permitting a party to use a document for other purposes in its general discretion. One example in previous case law is *Apple Corp Ltd* v *Apple Computer Inc.* [1992] 1 CMLR 969 where documents, which had been disclosed in English proceedings, were required for the purposes of parallel proceedings before the European Commission, which constituted a cogent reason why the documents were permitted to be used outside the English proceedings.

CHAPTER 16 EVIDENCE, INCLUDING WITNESS STATEMENTS

CONTENTS

16.1	Introduction	233
16.2	Court's power to control evidence	233
16.3	Written or oral evidence	234
16.4	Evidence by video link or other means	234
16.5	Requirement to serve witness statements for use at trial	235
16.6	Form of witness statements	235
16.7	Witness summaries	236
16.8	Consequence of failure to serve witness statement or summary	236
16.9	Use at trial of witness statements	237
16.9.1	Evidence outside the witness statement	238
16.9.2	Use by another party	238
16.9.3	Cross-examination on the witness statement	239
16.10	Sanction for false statements	239
16.11	Evidence in proceedings other than at trial	239
16.11.1	Order for cross-examination	239
16.11.2	Use of statement of case or application notice	240
16.12	Use of witness statements for other purposes	240
16.12.1	Availability of witness statements for inspection	240
16.13	Affidavit evidence	241
16.14	Notice to admit facts	241
16.15	Admission or proof of disclosed documents	242
16.16	Question of foreign law	242
16.17	Evidence of consent of trustee to act	242

16.1 INTRODUCTION

Parts 32 to 35 of the CPR deal comprehensively with the subject of evidence both at trial and in the pre-trial stages. They are aimed at fulfilling the underlying objectives of the CPR by requiring pre-trial disclosure of the evidence that is to be used by parties and by setting out how that disclosure is to be achieved.

16.2 COURT'S POWER TO CONTROL EVIDENCE

It is provided in CPR, r. 32.1, that the court may control the evidence to be used in proceedings by giving directions about:

(a) the issues on which it requires evidence;
(b) the nature of the evidence which it requires to decide those issues; and
(c) the way in which the evidence is to be placed before the court.

Very importantly, under r. 32.1(2): 'The court may use its power under this rule to exclude evidence that would otherwise be admissible'.

CHAPTER 16 EVIDENCE, INCLUDING WITNESS STATEMENTS

These provisions really take to its zenith the principle of court control. They allow the court to override the wishes of the parties as to how they would conduct their case, whether on liability, quantum, or remedies sought, and to impose the court's own robust view of what evidence would be appropriate to allow the parties fairly to demonstrate their cases. The provisions allow the court to specify the order in which it will deal with the issues and to restrict the ways in which evidence about those issues can be given, e.g., whether as oral, written, hearsay or other evidence.

Rule 32.1 is the dominant rule which will enable the court to restrict the number of witnesses, lay or expert. Most importantly the provision that the court may exclude evidence which would otherwise be admissible is an extraordinary extension of the court's powers, because evidence is only ever admissible if it is relevant, and r. 32.1(2) enables the court to impose its own view of what is 'relevant' on the parties. This power may be used at a pre-trial stage or at the start of or during the trial itself. It will be a strong-minded procedural judge who, in the face of objection by either or both parties, decides to restrict the evidence substantially in advance of trial, although the power will be commonly used to aid the identification of preliminary issues under other rules (e.g., in split trials of liability and quantum). It is suggested that this power will be more commonly used during a trial by a judge who has the full trial bundles and considers that some of the evidence intended to be adduced would not assist him, whether because it is peripheral, irrelevant or repetitive.

16.3 WRITTEN OR ORAL EVIDENCE

Rule 32.2 of the CPR provides that generally any fact which needs to be proved is to be proved at trial by oral evidence in public, and at any other hearing by evidence in writing. This is subject to any provision to the contrary in the CPR or any order of the court.

Accordingly, evidence at trial is to be given orally, as under the old rules. This is subject to r. 32.5(2), which provides that generally speaking a witness statement will stand as evidence-in-chief unless the court orders otherwise. The witness must nonetheless attend and be available for cross-examination, and this will satisfy the requirement for 'oral evidence given in public'.

At pre-trial hearings of whatever kind written evidence is to be the norm. This reflects the previous position under which oral evidence at chambers hearings was highly exceptional and required leave of the master or district judge. In an appropriate case oral evidence in chambers may be permitted on application.

16.4 EVIDENCE BY VIDEO LINK OR OTHER MEANS

Rule 32.3 of the CPR provides that the court may allow a witness to give evidence through a video link or by other means. This takes advantage of new technology which had been usefully permitted in a number of cases previously, notwithstanding that there was no clear rule adverting to it. Rules such as RSC, ord. 38, rr. 3 and 28, were stretched in the case of *Garcin* v *Amerindo Investment Advisors Ltd* [1991] 1 WLR 1140 to accommodate video link evidence. To facilitate more frequent use of this possibility video conferencing equipment has been available for some time, e.g., in the studio operated by the Bar Council, and there was a previous video conferencing protocol. Taken together with the provisions of the Civil Evidence Act 1995 it provides a power for the court to overcome technical objections of whatever kind about means and manner of giving evidence and would, for example, permit evidence by telephone or any other means of communications providing the overriding consideration of fairness and convenience is satisfied.

16.5 REQUIREMENT TO SERVE WITNESS STATEMENTS FOR USE AT TRIAL

Rule 32.4(1) of the CPR defines 'witness statement' as a statement signed by a person which contains the evidence which that person would be allowed to give orally.

The court will, at the time when case management directions are given, order the parties to serve witness statements of the evidence on which they intend to rely on trial and stipulate a time for doing so, by reference to a calendar date (r. 32.4(2)). The court may give directions about the order in which witness statements are to be served and whether or not the witness statements are to be filed in court.

The principles underlying these provisions are familiar. Witness statements must be restricted to material issues but, as hitherto, difficulty will be caused to any party who has not drafted a witness statement sufficiently fully and widely to encompass everything which the party might have wished the witness to say in chief. It will remain necessary therefore, to some extent, to anticipate what might be contained in an opposing party's witness statement. As, by virtue of r. 32.5(2), the witness statement will stand as evidence-in-chief, it will be necessary to do more than set out the bare skeleton of what the witness might have wished to say. A witness who does not set out his or her account of events fully in the statement runs the risk of it standing alone as evidence-in-chief and of not being able to amplify it if the cross-examiner is sufficiently skilful to ask questions only for the purpose of challenging the version in writing, leaving it open for his own witnesses to provide a fuller and more compelling account if their witness statements have been drafted more expansively.

The court will give directions about the order in which witness statements are to be served and the normal principle will be that they should be served simultaneously, unless there is some reason why sequential service might be appropriate. In the past sequential service has been ordered where, for example, one party might not know fully what case has to be met until it is set out in the opponent's witness statement, which might occur where requests for further information under CPR, Part 18, have been unsuccessful. One party may be ordered to serve witness statements first, or at least the witness statement of the claimant. Such circumstances may arise in cases such as *Kirkup* v *British Rail Engineering Ltd* [1983] 1 WLR 1165, where, in an industrial deafness case, the defendant could not truly identify some of the issues until the plaintiff's statement was served.

16.6 FORM OF WITNESS STATEMENTS

Paragraphs 17.1 to 22.2 of PD 32 set out in detail how witness statements are to be laid out. If a witness statement does not comply with CPR, Part

CHAPTER 16 EVIDENCE, INCLUDING WITNESS STATEMENTS

32, or with PD 32, the court may refuse to admit it as evidence and may refuse to allow the costs arising from its preparation (PD 32, para. 25.1). A witness statement must be verified by a statement of truth and if it is not the court may direct that it shall not be admissible as evidence (CPR, r. 22.3).

16.7 WITNESS SUMMARIES

A party who is required to serve a witness statement for use at trial, but is unable to obtain one, can apply without notice for permission to serve a 'witness summary' instead (CPR, r. 32.9(1)).

A witness summary is a summary of the evidence if known, which would otherwise be included in a witness statement, or of the matters about which the party serving the summary will question the witness (r. 32.9(2)).

Rule 32.9 deals with the situation where the witness's whereabouts are known so that he or she can effectively be called at trial, but the witness has been uncooperative, or where the witness is untraceable. Clearly it is tactically undesirable to call a witness, especially one whose evidence is central to the party's case if the witness has been uncooperative, to the point of refusing to give a witness statement. This position commonly arises in cases between former employees and employers, whether personal injury or other, where people still working for the employer could give useful evidence for the claimant, but are inhibited by their unwillingness to compromise their prospects by appearing to side with the former employee. Although the risks are obvious, the only way of getting the evidence to trial is likely to be a witness summons and it will be necessary to attempt to serve a summary of what the witness would say. Clearly it will often be impossible to give much detail, although there will be circumstances in which the evidence is available virtually in its full form, e.g., where a witness has initially given a verbal statement but declined to sign the written version. Rule 32.9 provides a 'without notice' procedure by which the court, acting on evidence itself in witness statement form from the party, will be asked to make an order permitting the use of a witness summary. If satisfactory evidence is put forward, there is no reason why the court should decline to make the order sought. The only consideration would be whether the procedure is in some way an abuse of process, e.g., where the witness is peripheral and there is an attempt to embarrass by calling someone such as a senior employee in an organisation for tactical or publicity purposes, even though he knows nothing personally of the matters in question.

Unless the court orders otherwise a witness summary must include the name and address of the intended witness and must be served within the period in which a statement would have had to be served (r. 32.9(4)). So far as practicable, the other rules of Part 32 will then apply, e.g., r. 32.5(3) (the power to amplify witness statements), and r. 32.9(1) (the form of witness statements).

16.8 CONSEQUENCE OF FAILURE TO SERVE WITNESS STATEMENT OR SUMMARY

The operation of CPR, r. 32.4, requires teeth more than almost any other provision of the CPR if it is to be effective in achieving early mutual

CHAPTER 16 EVIDENCE, INCLUDING WITNESS STATEMENTS

disclosure of the parties' full cases with the object of encouraging compromise and avoiding trial, or alternatively of making the trial efficient. Rule 32.10 is briefly expressed and simply provides that if a witness statement or summary for use at trial is not served within the time specified by the court then the witness may not be called to give oral evidence unless the court permits.

It is probable that, in order to show that the rules have teeth, the court will be very sparing in the use of its discretion to permit a party to call witnesses where the evidence was not disclosed, either at all, or at the right time. Thus late applications for permission to call witnesses may be unsuccessful. It will remain to be seen to what extent the court will really be prepared to see substantial injustice done in a case where the fault is entirely that of the legal advisers in failing adequately to identify the issues so as to collect evidence properly and serve it at the right time. The issue of prejudice to an opposing party will be relevant, but is unlikely to be conclusive. Litigants may therefore be left to their remedies against their advisers where there has been such failure, whether as a consequence of honest oversight, tactical misjudgment or simple incompetence.

The practice directions relevant to case management indicate some procedures in relation to sanctions, e.g., PD 28, para. 5.4, which provides that on the fast track postponing the trial will be an option of last resort. It is of course open to a party who has not been served with any witness statements to apply for an order to enforce compliance or for a sanction to be imposed, or both (PD 28, para. 5.1). There are similar provisions for failure to comply with case management directions, including service of witness statements in PD 29, para. 7.1.

If, after the final date for serving witness statements a party discovers that it has material evidence which has not been served, it will need to apply immediately under r. 32.10 for permission to call it and it would be extremely risky to make that application only at trial. An attempt to serve it, even without permission, should be made at the earliest moment so as to minimise prejudice to the opponent. The court's discretion is more likely to be used in respect of witnesses who have only recently been traced or identified where reasonable competence has been shown hitherto. Early guidance from the Court of Appeal on the way in which the competing interests of efficiency in the conduct of litigation and the overriding concerns of injustice caused by refusal to permit a party to call an obviously material witness will be welcome.

16.9 USE AT TRIAL OF WITNESS STATEMENTS

A party who has served a witness statement and who wishes to rely at trial on the evidence of the witness must nonetheless call the witness to give oral evidence unless the court orders otherwise or the statement is put in as hearsay evidence (CPR, r. 32.5(1)).

A party who does not wish to call a witness who has provided a witness statement may put the statement in as hearsay evidence at trial. The notice required by the Civil Evidence Act 1995, s. 2, should be served. CPR, r. 32.5(1), empowers the court to order that a witness who has given a witness statement need not attend the trial to give oral testimony and that the witness statement can be used, but it is difficult to see why the court should do this if no notice has been given under the Civil Evidence Act 1995, s. 2. The parties will know whether they wish to rely on the facts set out in the statement and will either call the witness to comply with r. 32.5 or alternatively have served a Civil Evidence Act notice under CPR, r. 33.2(2). Presumably r. 32.5(1) is to govern matters at trial where, for one or other reason, a witness is found to be unavailable or does not appear. The rule will supplement the provisions in the Civil Evidence Act 1995, although by virtue of s. 2(4) of that Act failure to serve notice does not affect the *admissibility* of the statement in any way. The court may, however, take the failure to comply with the requirement to give notice into account in considering the exercise of its powers with respect to the course of proceedings and costs, i.e., it may adjourn the proceedings so that the witness can be called at the cost of the party in question, or may treat it as a matter adversely affecting the weight to be given to the evidence of the absent witness.

16.9.1 Evidence outside the witness statement

A witness may with the permission of the court amplify his or her witness statement or give evidence in relation to new matters which have arisen since the witness statement was served on the other parties (CPR, r. 32.5(3)). This will, however, require the permission of the court which, it must be anticipated, will be given so long as the court considers the issues material and that no prejudice is caused. The court has a very general and wide-ranging power to control evidence under r. 32.1. If a new matter has arisen, or the deficiencies of the original witness statement have been perceived some time in advance of trial, it may well be better to seek permission to serve supplementary witness statements rather than relying on the discretion of the trial judge to permit a witness in evidence-in-chief to go outside his witness statement. Rule 32.5(3) does not restrict the way in which a party not calling the witness shall treat him and cross-examiners may be expected to be permitted to range freely outside the witness statement. It would be a foolish cross-examiner who allowed a witness to bring in evidence matters favourable to the case of the party calling him which he had not already set out in his witness statement, and which the party calling the witness had not been able to introduce under r. 32.5(3).

The court must anyway consider that there is good reason not to confine the evidence of the witness to the contents of his witness statement if it is to give permission to go beyond that statement in chief (r. 32.5(4)). The onus will clearly be on the party in default to satisfy the court that there is such good reason. It will remain to be seen whether the court will find there is good reason arising out of the incompetence with which the witness statement was drafted if it failed to deal sufficiently or at all with some material matter. The court will have to balance the factor of surprise and prejudice with other factors, such as the importance of the evidence, whether the default was due to honest oversight or whether new material has recently arisen.

16.9.2 Use by another party

If a party who has served a witness statement does not call the witness or put the witness statement in as hearsay evidence, any other party may put in the witness statement as hearsay evidence (r. 32.5(5)). If at trial, and for the first time, it became clear that the opposing party did not intend to call the witness whose statement had been served, the court would clearly be entitled to use its discretion to permit the statement to be used by the opponent, notwithstanding the failure to serve a Civil Evidence Act 1995, s. 2, notice. Rule 32.5(5) is the very converse of the previous rule under which an opposing party could not use a witness statement which had been served where the witness was not to be called.

16.9.3 Cross-examination on the witness statement

A witness who is called to give evidence at trial may be cross-examined on his witness statement whether or not the statement or any part of it was referred to during the witness's evidence-in-chief (CPR, r. 32.11).

16.10 SANCTION FOR FALSE STATEMENTS

By CPR, r. 32.14(1), a person who makes or causes to be made a false statement in a document verified by a statement of truth without an honest belief in its truth is guilty of contempt of court. Proceedings for a contempt of court of this kind may only be brought by the Attorney-General or by someone who has the permission of the court (r. 32.14(2)).

Rule 32.14 creates an offence in relation to false evidence, thus avoiding the need to bring it within the scope of more nebulous crimes such as attempts to pervert the course of justice. False evidence on oath, whether by affidavit or in the course of the trial, will of course amount to perjury as before.

16.11 EVIDENCE IN PROCEEDINGS OTHER THAN AT TRIAL

Rule 32.6 of the CPR deals with hearings other than the trial, such as interim applications or hearings relating to enforcement of judgment. The general rule will be that evidence at such hearings is to be by witness statement, unless the court or any practice direction or enactment requires otherwise. Oral evidence will therefore remain highly exceptional as previously. In such proceedings a party can rely on matters set out in his statement of case or his application if verified by a statement of truth.

Evidence must be provided by affidavit rather than witness statement in the following circumstances (PD 32, para. 1.4):

   (a) where sworn evidence is required by any enactment, statutory instrument, rule, order or practice direction;
   (b) in any application for a search order, a freezing injunction, or an order requiring an occupier to permit another to enter his land; and
   (c) in any application for an order against anyone for alleged contempt of court.

The court may give a direction under CPR, r. 32.15, that evidence shall be given by affidavit instead of or in addition to a witness statement or statement of case, either on its own initiative or after any party has applied to the court for such a direction (PD 32, para. 1.6).

16.11.1 Order for cross-examination

Where at a hearing other than the trial, evidence is to be given in writing, any party may apply to the court for permission to cross-examine the person giving the evidence (CPR, r. 32.7(1)), and if the court gives permission, but the person does not attend as required, his evidence may not be used unless the court permits (r. 32.7(2)).

A separate application to the court to call for the attendance of witnesses at pre-trial hearings is therefore required. It is probable that in the interests of economy such applications will rarely be made, and even more rarely succeed. The court will have to be sure that in order to do justice on some interim issue it is necessary for there to be a relatively thorough investigation of evidence, although the court will of course have the power to restrict the issue narrowly and to restrict what evidence it will hear likewise under r. 32.1. To call evidence at interim applications is usually self-defeating. For example, under the provisions relating to summary judgment (Part 24) or interim payments (Part 25), it will generally demonstrate to the court too high a degree of doubt for the applicant to succeed if, to establish his case, he needs permission to cross-examine the defendant. Conversely, it may well be a useful tactic for a defendant opposing such applications to seek an order for cross-examination of the plaintiff, but in the interests of efficient case management, it seems unlikely that the court will permit this in other than exceptional cases.

16.11.2 Use of statement of case or application notice

By virtue of r. 32.6(2) at hearings other than the trial a party may in support of his application rely on the matters set out in his statement of case or his application notice if the statement of case or application notice is verified by a statement of truth. This avoids the need to file formal witness statements verifying a statement of case or an application which would merely duplicate their contents.

16.12 USE OF WITNESS STATEMENTS FOR OTHER PURPOSES

By CPR, r. 32.12, a witness statement may be used only for the purpose of the proceedings in which it is served unless;

(a) the witness gives consent in writing to some other use of it;
(b) the court gives permission for some other use; or
(c) the witness statement has been put in evidence at a hearing held in public. Thus, witness statements only used in chambers proceedings may not be used generally outside the litigation by the opposing party or anyone else into whose hands they fall without the consent of the witness or the permission of the court.

16.12.1 Availability of witness statements for inspection

A corollary of the previous rule is that witness statements are available for inspection where they stand as evidence-in-chief unless the court otherwise directs during the course of the trial (CPR, r. 32.13(1)). Any person may ask for a direction that a witness statement should not be open to inspection (r. 32.13 (2)). This will include the witness himself where, e.g., the subject matter has some sensitivity and nothing said during the trial, whether in other evidence, submissions or cross-examination, has brought the matters out into the open, so that the witness may reasonably ask that the contents of his statement remain confidential. There is, however, a strong presumption against withholding inspection unless, by r. 32.13(2), the court is satisfied that the statement should be withheld from inspection because of:

CHAPTER 16   EVIDENCE, INCLUDING WITNESS STATEMENTS

(a)   the interests of justice;
(b)   the public interest;
(c)   the nature of expert medical evidence in the statement;
(d)   the nature of confidential information (including information relating to personal financial matters) in the statement; or
(e)   the need to protect the interests of any child or patient.

Moreover the court has the power to exclude from inspection words or passages in the statement whilst permitting the rest to remain open (r. 32.13(4)).

16.13   AFFIDAVIT EVIDENCE

Affidavit evidence must be given instead of or in addition to a witness statement when required by the court, or by a provision contained in any other rule, practice direction or other enactment (CPR, r. 32.15(1)). A witness is permitted to give evidence by affidavit if he chooses to do so at any hearing other than a trial (r. 32.15(2)), in which case the rules relating to the filing and service of the affidavit apply as if it were a witness statement. Affidavits are required by r. 32.16 to comply with requirements set out in PD 32.

Affidavits made outside the jurisdiction may be made in accordance with CPR, Part 32 or the law of the place where the affidavit is made (CPR, r. 32.17). Where evidence is not specifically required to be by affidavit the party putting forward the affidavit may not recover any additional costs of making it from any other party unless the court orders otherwise (r. 32.15).

The provisions of PD 32 describing the form of affidavits almost entirely echo RSC, ord. 41, and the practice directions under it. If an affidavit does not comply with CPR, Part 32, or PD 32, the court may refuse to admit it as evidence and refuse to allow the costs arising from its preparation (PD 32, para. 25.1)

16.14   NOTICE TO ADMIT FACTS

By CPR, r. 32.18, a party may serve notice on another party requiring the other party to admit facts or the part of the case of the serving party specified in the notice. Notice must be served no later than 21 days before the trial.

If the notice attracts an admission, that admission may only be used in the proceedings in question and by the party who served the notice. Admissions made in pursuance of the notice to admit may be amended or withdrawn on such terms as the court thinks just. This preserves previous practice. Where a party is able to identify a severable fact or series of facts which he thinks he can prove irrespective of the outcome of the litigation as a whole, he may attempt to obtain an admission by this procedure. If a fact is admitted then the cost of proving it is saved. If the fact is not admitted, but the person tendering the notice succeeds in proving it at trial, whatever the outcome otherwise, then he should have the costs of proving it. No specific rule now states this, but the generality of r. 44.3 and in particular the discretion which the court has and the matters to which it must have regard, including the conduct of the parties and the reasonableness of the party in raising, pursuing or contesting a particular allegation or issue (r. 44.3(5)(b)) shows that the costs outcome will be the same as previously.

16.15 ADMISSION OR PROOF OF DISCLOSED DOCUMENTS

A party to whom any document is disclosed under CPR, Part 31 (see chapter 15), is deemed to have admitted its authenticity, unless he serves a notice that he wishes the document to be proved at trial (r. 32.19(1)). By r. 32.19(2) a notice requiring a disclosed document to be proved at trial must be served:

(a) by the latest date for serving witness statements; or
(b) within seven days of disclosure of the document,

whichever is later.

There are likely to be costs consequences, under r. 44.3(5), of unnecessarily requiring proof of a disclosed document.

Incidentally the title of r. 32.19 does not accurately summarise the content of the rule.

16.16 QUESTION OF FOREIGN LAW

A party intending to put in evidence a finding on a question of foreign law by virtue of the Civil Evidence Act 1972, s. 4(2), must give notice to the other parties of his intentions not later than the latest date for serving witness statements or otherwise not less than 21 days before the hearing and must specify the question on which the finding was made and enclose a copy of the document where it is recorded or reported (CPR, r. 33.7).

16.17 EVIDENCE OF CONSENT OF TRUSTEE TO ACT

A document purporting to contain the written consent of a person to act as trustee and to bear his signature verified by some other person is evidence of such consent, that is, no further formal proof is required (CPR, r. 33.8).

CHAPTER 17 HEARSAY AND NON-VERBAL EVIDENCE

CONTENTS

17.1	Introduction	243
17.2	Hearsay	243
17.2.1	Definition of 'hearsay'	243
17.2.2	Notice of intention to rely on hearsay evidence	243
17.2.3	Circumstances in which notice of intention to rely on hearsay evidence is not required	244
17.2.4	Cross-examination on hearsay evidence	245
17.2.5	Attacking the credibility of absent witnesses	245
17.3	Use of plans, photographs and models as evidence	245
17.3.1	Opportunity to inspect	246

17.1 INTRODUCTION

Part 33 of the CPR is chiefly concerned with the provisions which give effect to the Civil Evidence Act 1995 so as to tie in with Part 32. The Civil Evidence Act 1995 came into force in February 1997 and provides that all hearsay is admissible and that the court has no discretion to refuse to permit it, although what weight is to be attached to the evidence remains a matter for the court.

17.2 HEARSAY

17.2.1 Definition of 'hearsay'

Rule 33.1 of the CPR repeats the meaning of the term 'hearsay' given in s. 1 of the Civil Evidence Act 1995, that is:

(a) 'hearsay' means a statement made, otherwise than by a person while giving oral evidence in proceedings, which is tendered as evidence of the matter stated; and

(b) references to hearsay include hearsay of whatever degree.

Where a statement, whether oral or in writing, is tendered to prove the truth of what is stated out of court, it will be hearsay. A statement tendered for some other purpose, for example, simply to show that the words spoken were uttered at all, so as to found a defamation case, or to show that a document contains an entry that has been tampered with or forged, is not hearsay.

17.2.2 Notice of intention to rely on hearsay evidence

A party who intends to rely on hearsay evidence at trial is required by the Civil Evidence Act 1995, s. 2, to notify the other parties. Rule 33.2 of the CPR provides that serving a witness statement on the other parties in accordance with the court's order is sufficient notice for this purpose if:

(a) the hearsay evidence is to be given by a witness in the course of giving oral evidence, or

(b) it is contained in a witness statement of a person who is not being called to give oral evidence.

A party who intends to put in evidence a witness statement containing hearsay evidence without calling the maker must, when serving the witness statement, inform the other parties that the witness is not being called to give oral evidence and give the reason why the witness will not be called (r. 33.2(2)).

The decision whether to put in hearsay evidence in the form of a witness statement or orally must be taken before the witness statements are served and the 1995 Act must be complied with by giving notice of the intention at that time. If hearsay is contained in a witness statement of a person who is not being called to give oral evidence then the reason why the witness is not to be called may be taken into account by the court when assessing what weight to attach to the evidence by virtue of s. 4(2) of the 1995 Act, which provides:

Regard may be had, in particular, to the following—
(a) whether it would have been reasonable and practicable for the party by whom the evidence was adduced to have produced the maker of the original statement as a witness; . . .
(f) whether the circumstances in which the evidence is adduced as hearsay are such as to suggest an attempt to prevent proper evaluation of its weight.

In all other cases where a party intends to rely on hearsay evidence at trial, the party must comply with s. 2 of the 1995 Act by serving a notice under CPR, r. 33.2(3), on the other parties which:

(a) identifies the hearsay evidence;
(b) states that the party serving the notice proposes to rely on the hearsay evidence at trial; and
(c) gives a reason why the witness will not be called.

This notice must be served no later than the latest date for serving witness statements and, if the hearsay evidence is to be in a document, a copy must be supplied to any party that asks for one (r. 33.2(4)). This rule applies where the hearsay evidence in question is not in the form of a witness statement at all, but is, for example, a set of business documents, accounts or the like.

17.2.3 Circumstances in which notice of intention to rely on hearsay evidence is not required

The rules discussed in 17.2.2 apply in the case of evidence at trial, but CPR, r. 33.3, declares that the duty to give notice of intention to adduce hearsay evidence does not apply:

(a) to evidence at hearings other than trials (i.e., interim applications);
(b) to a statement which a party to a probate action wishes to put in evidence and which is alleged to have been made by a person whose estate is the subject of the proceedings; or
(c) where the requirement is excluded by any practice direction.

In each of these situations therefore no notice of intention to rely on hearsay evidence is required. Since there is in interim proceedings a strong presumption against oral evidence, it will be obvious to the recipient of any evidence in written form which is served that the party serving the evidence does not intend to call the maker, indeed the permission of the court would be necessary to do so (see CPR 32.6 and 32.7).

17.2.4 Cross-examination on hearsay evidence

By CPR, r. 33.4, where a party proposes to rely on hearsay and does not propose to call the person who made the original statement to give oral evidence the court may on the application of any other party permit that party to call the maker of the statement to be cross-examined on the contents of the statement. An application for permission must be made not more than 14 days after the day on which a notice of intention to rely on the hearsay evidence was served on the applicant.

This rule is made under the provisions of the Civil Evidence Act 1995, s. 3, and provides an opportunity for a person confronted with a hearsay notice who wishes to challenge the evidence to obtain the permission of the court to call the maker of the statement in question for cross-examination. It means that in effect it will be pointless to serve a hearsay notice about controversial evidence unless there is good reason for the maker's unavailability to attend the trial and thus that attempts not to call apparently important witnesses for tactical reasons are likely to fail since there will then simply be an application to the court for leave to call them. It is difficult to see on what grounds the court could refuse such an application. If the evidence was sufficiently material to be used at all, and the witness is available, then one ought to have the right to test it in cross-examination.

17.2.5 Attacking the credibility of absent witnesses

By CPR, r. 33.5, where a party proposes to rely on hearsay and does not propose to call the person who made the original statement and another party wishes to call evidence to attack the credibility of that person, the party who so wishes must give notice of his intention, to the party who proposes to give the hearsay statement in evidence, not more than 14 days after the day on which a hearsay notice relating to the hearsay evidence was served on him.

This provision is made under the Civil Evidence Act 1995, s. 5(2). Thus if one is confronted with a hearsay notice from one's opponent, and the maker of the statement being put in as hearsay is either not available at all to be brought to trial (e.g., because he lives abroad and will not return, is dead or cannot be traced) or alternatively the party receiving the notice decides not to have the witness called for cross-examination, but rather to attack his credibility at trial, e.g., by the production of a prior inconsistent statement, evidence of bad character, evidence of bias, or as the case may be, then the party intending to mount such attack must give notice as described in the rule. This then at least provides a last opportunity for the party putting in the hearsay to decide whether to make further attempts to get the witness there, if that is possible, to give oral evidence so as to face the assault on his credibility.

17.3 USE OF PLANS, PHOTOGRAPHS AND MODELS AS EVIDENCE

Rule 33.6 of the CPR applies to evidence other than evidence contained in a witness statement, affidavit or expert's report or evidence to be given

CHAPTER 17 HEARSAY AND NON-VERBAL EVIDENCE

orally at trial. The rule gives plans, photographs and models as examples of such evidence. The rule also applies to documents to be received under the Civil Evidence Act 1995, s. 9 (that is, documents that form part of the records of a business or public authority, which may generally be received in evidence without further proof of authenticity).

Rule 33.6(3) provides that such evidence shall not be receivable at trial unless the party intending to put it in evidence has given notice to the other parties. Where that evidence is to be given then notice must be given no later than the latest date for serving witness statements, unless there are not to be witness statements at all or the party intends to put in the evidence solely in order to disprove an allegation made in a witness statement, in which case the notice must be given at least 21 days before the hearing.

If the evidence is not free-standing, but forms part of expert evidence (e.g., plans or photographs attached to an expert's report), the party proposing to adduce the evidence must give notice of it when the expert's report is served on the other party (r. 33.6(6)). In any event, such documents should be served with or annexed to the expert's report at the time of serving it.

By r. 33.6(7) if the evidence is being produced to the court for any reason other than as part of factual or expert evidence then notice must be given at least 21 days before the hearing. This would apply where, e.g., the plan, photograph etc. to be produced is proof of something other than its contents, e.g., it is produced to prove that the plan was drawn at all and by whom, or to provide real evidence of forgery or tampering.

17.3.1 Opportunity to inspect

A party who has given notice of intention to put in evidence under CPR, r. 33.6, must, by r. 33.6(8), give every other party an opportunity to inspect the evidence in question and to agree to its admission without further proof.

Consequently, the procedure for adducing photographs, plans etc. and the other documents referred to in r. 33.6 requires proper notice to be given to one's opponent. That opponent is then to have the opportunity of 'agreeing' the evidence, i.e., accepting it as both authentic and true, for example, that a plan does accurately record the relevant dimensions and show the proper layout. If the document cannot be 'agreed' then competing plans etc. from each side must be put in and the court must decide which to prefer, which may involve a view of the place in question.

CHAPTER 18   DEPOSITIONS AND COURT ATTENDANCE BY WITNESSES

CONTENTS

18.1	Introduction	247
18.2	Witness summonses	247
18.2.1	Issue of a witness summons	248
18.2.2	Witness summons in aid of inferior court or of tribunal	248
18.2.3	Time for serving a witness summons	249
18.2.4	Service of a witness summons	249
18.2.5	Right of witness to travelling expenses and compensation for loss of time	249
18.3	Evidence by deposition	249
18.3.1	Use of deposition of the hearing	250
18.3.2	Restriction on subsequent use of deposition taken for the purpose of any hearing except for trial	250
18.3.3	Examination out of the jurisdiction — letters of request	251
18.3.4	Fees and expenses of examiner and appointment by the court	251

18.1   INTRODUCTION

Part 34 of the CPR deals with the procedure for ensuring that a witness attends court to testify or produce a document. This is dealt with in rr. 34.1 to 34.7 and it is these which will be overwhelmingly the most important aspects. Rules 34.8 to 34.15 deal with evidence by depositions and will be only briefly examined.

18.2   WITNESS SUMMONSES

A witness summons is defined as a document issued by the court requiring a witness to attend court to give evidence or produce a document to the court (CPR, r. 34.2(1)). It must be in form N20 (r. 34.2(2)) and there must be a separate one for each witness (r. 34.2(3)). Two copies of the witness summons should be filed with the court for sealing, one of which will be retained on the court file (PD 34, para. 1.2). By CPR, r. 34.2(4), a witness summons may require a witness to produce documents to the court either:

(a)   on the date fixed for a hearing; or
(b)   on such date as the court may direct.

The documents that a person can be required to produce before a hearing are only those documents which that person could be required to produce at the hearing (r. 34.2(5)).

The rule is self-explanatory in so far as it relates to requiring witnesses to attend the trial to give evidence orally or to produce documents. The scope of r. 34.2(4) may be viewed as an alternative to non-party discovery, which is now available against witnesses in any form of proceedings and not, as previously, limited to personal injury and wrongful death cases. It provides a re-statement of the device arrived at by the court in *Khanna* v *Lovell White Durrant* [1995] 1 WLR 121, in which the court invented the concept of a 'production appointment' for witnesses to attend under summons to bring documents to some hearing earlier than the trial where, for example, the documents were needed by one or other party to prepare the case properly for trial and production on the morning of the trial itself would have been insufficient.

18.2.1 Issue of a witness summons

A witness summons is issued on the date entered on the summons by the court (CPR, r.34.3(1)). It must be issued by:

(a) the court where the case is proceeding; or
(b) the court where the hearing in question will be held.

The procedure is, as under the old rules, an *ex parte* procedure in which the party wishing to issue the witness summons simply attends at the court with the summons in form N20 and the court will seal it for service. If the witness summons is for a trial, there is no requirement to obtain the permission of the court. But there are three sets of circumstances where permission must be obtained (r. 34.3(2)) and they are where a party wishes:

(a) to have a summons issued less than seven days before the date of the trial;

(b) to have a summons issued for a witness to attend court to give evidence or to produce documents on any date except the date fixed for the trial; or

(c) to have a summons issued for a witness to attend court to give evidence or to produce documents at any hearing except the trial.

The circumstances in which permission of the court is required are where the witness summons is to be issued very late before a trial; where a witness summons is required for attendance at an interim hearing and where documents are to be produced in those circumstances. The procedure for applying for permission is by application without notice to a district judge or master. On the face of it there is no requirement to produce evidence in written form and it will be enough to indicate orally at the hearing of an application what the purpose of calling the witness is.

Under r. 33.3(4) the court may set aside or vary a witness summons issued under the rule. This may be on the application of a party or of the witness himself where, for example, he may claim that he has no connection with the action, no knowledge of the action and is being summoned for ulterior purposes, such as to cause disruption or embarrassment. This sometimes happens where a party, usually unrepresented, attempts to serve a witness summons on the chairman of a large plc, a government minister or the like.

18.2.2 Witness summons in aid of inferior court or of tribunal

Rule 34.4 of the CPR provides that in relation to proceedings before any court or tribunal which does not have power to issue a witness summons the High Court or a county court may issue a witness summons in aid of that inferior court or tribunal. This is clearly a discretionary power and the court will bear in mind the reasons why the inferior court or tribunal was originally constituted without the power to summon witnesses. PD 34 indicates that a witness summons may be set aside by the court which issued it and an application to set aside the summons will be heard:

(a) in the High Court by a master or district judge;
(b) in a county court by a district judge.

By para. 2.4 of PD 34 there must usually be at least two days' notice by the applicant to the party who issued the witness summons of the application to set aside, which will normally be dealt with at a hearing.

18.2.3 Time for serving a witness summons

The general rule is that a witness summons is binding if it is served at least seven days before the date on which the witness is required to attend before the court (CPR, r. 34.5(1)). The court has power under r. 34.5(2) to direct that a witness summons shall be binding though served less than seven days before the date in question. Once served the witness summons is binding until the conclusion of the hearing in question (r. 34.5(3)).

18.2.4 Service of a witness summons

A witness summons is to be served by the court unless the party on whose behalf it is issued indicates in writing when he asks the court to issue the summons that he wishes to serve it himself (CPR, r. 34.6(1)). If the court is to serve the witness summons, the party on whose behalf it is issued must, by r. 34.6(2), deposit in the court office the money to be paid or offered to the witness under r. 34.7 (see 18.2.5).

In principle, then, the court will undertake service of the summons and this will presumably be by post or by county court bailiff. Solicitors requiring the greater speed and certainty of professional service are likely to wish to undertake this themselves, as under the old rules.

18.2.5 Right of witness to travelling expenses and compensation for loss of time

By r. 34.7 of the CPR, at the time of service of a witness summons the witness must be offered or paid a sum reasonably sufficient to cover his expenses in travelling to and from the court and such sum by way of compensation for loss of time as may be specified in the relevant practice direction. PD 34, para. 3.3, indicates that the sum referred to is to be based on the sums payable to witnesses attending the Crown Court. These are fixed pursuant to the Prosecution of Offences Act 1985 and the Costs in Criminal Cases (General) Regulations 1986 (SI 1986/1335).

18.3 EVIDENCE BY DEPOSITION

Rule 34.8 of the CPR provides that a party may apply for an order for a person to be examined before the hearing takes place in which case that person is referred to as a 'deponent' and the evidence is referred to as a deposition. Further detailed provisions appear in PD 34, paras 4.2 to 6.6. An order under this rule shall be for a deponent to be examined before either a judge, an examiner of the court or such other person as the court appoints. The order may also require the production of any document which the court considers is necessary for the purposes of the examination.

A party who obtains an order for examination of a deponent before an examiner of the court must, according to PD 34, para. 4.2:

CHAPTER 18 DEPOSITIONS AND COURT ATTENDANCE BY WITNESSES

(a) apply to the Foreign Process Section of the Masters' Secretary's Department at the Royal Courts of Justice for the allocation of an examiner;
(b) when allocated, provide the examiner with copies of all documents in the proceedings necessary to inform the examiner of the issues; and
(c) pay the deponent a sum to cover his travelling expenses to and from the examination and compensation for his loss of time.

By CPR, r. 34.9, the examination, subject to any directions contained in the order for examination, must be conducted in the same way as if the witness were giving evidence at a trial. In other words all parties are in principle present and have the right to ask questions under the usual rules of evidence. All the evidence given must be recorded in full in writing by the examiner or a shorthand writer (and may also be recorded on audiotape or videotape) and a copy of the deposition sent to the person who obtained the order for the examination of the witness and to the court where the case is proceeding. The party who obtained the order must then send each of the other parties a copy of the deposition which he receives from the examiner.

A witness's attendance at examination may be enforced under r. 34.10, in that if he fails to attend or refuses to be sworn or to answer lawful questions, a certificate of that failure or refusal signed by the examiner must be filed by the party requiring the deposition and thereupon that party may apply to the court for an order requiring that person to attend, be sworn or answer any question or produce any document. The court may thereupon order the person against whom an order is made to pay any costs resulting from his failure or refusal and in addition that person may be proceeded against for contempt of court.

PD 34, para 4.12 requires that a deposition must:

(a) be signed by the examiner;
(b) have any amendments to it initialled by the examiner and the deponent;
(c) be endorsed by the examiner with a statement of the time occupied by the examination and a record of any refusal by the deponent to sign the deposition and of his reasons for not doing so;
(d) be sent by the examiner to the court where the proceedings are taking place for filing on the court file.

18.3.1 Use of deposition of the hearing

Under CPR, r. 34.11, once a deposition has been obtained under r. 34.8 it may be given in evidence at a hearing unless the court otherwise orders. Notice of intention to adduce it must be given by the party wishing to do so to every other party at least 21 days before the date fixed for the hearing and the court may require a deponent to attend the hearing and give evidence orally.

18.3.2 Restriction on subsequent use of deposition taken for the purpose of any hearing except for trial

Rule 34.12 of the CPR provides that where the court orders a party to be examined about his or any other assets for the purpose of any hearing except the trial, the deposition may be used only for the purposes of the proceedings in which the order was made. It may, however, be used for some other purpose:

(a) by the party who was examined;
(b) if the party who was examined agrees; or
(c) if the court gives permission.

This rule is limited to depositions concerning a party's assets and thus to the outcome of procedures concerning enforcement of judgment, freezing injunctions (previously *Mareva* injunctions) and the like.

18.3.3 Examination out of the jurisdiction — letters of request

Rule 34.13 of the CPR sets out the procedure for obtaining examination of a person out of the jurisdiction and for issuing a letter of request to the judicial authority of the country in which the proposed deponent is to arrange for the examination. The Evidence (Proceedings in Other Jurisdictions) Act 1975 applies to these depositions. There are detailed practical requirements set out in paras 5.1 to 6.6 of PD 34.

18.3.4 Fees and expenses of examiner and appointment by the court

Rules 34.14 and 34.15 of the CPR make provision for fees of an examiner (on the basis that this is not to be a member of the full-time judiciary) and describe the procedure whereby the Lord Chancellor may appoint persons to be examiners of the court.

CHAPTER 19 EXPERTS AND ASSESSORS

CONTENTS

19.1	Introduction	252
19.2	Duties of experts and the court's power to restrict expert evidence	253
19.3	Directions about experts	254
19.4	What if a party has already instructed his own expert?	254
19.5	Written reports	255
19.6	Written questions to experts	255
19.7	Single joint expert	256
19.7.1	Instructions to a single joint expert	257
19.8	Direction to provide information	258
19.9	Contents of an expert's report	258
19.10	Use by other parties of disclosed expert's report	259
19.11	Discussion between experts	260
19.12	Consequences of failure to disclose expert's report	261
19.13	Expert's right to ask court for directions	261
19.14	Assessors	261

19.1 INTRODUCTION

At p. 137 of his *Final Report* Lord Woolf stated baldly:

> It was a basic contention of my interim report that two of the major generators of unnecessary cost in civil litigation were uncontrolled discovery and expert evidence. No one has seriously challenged that contention.
>
> A large litigation support industry, generating a multi-million-pound fee income, has grown up among professions such as accountants, architects and others, and new professions have developed such as accident reconstruction and care experts. This goes against all principles of proportionality and access to justice. In my view, its most damaging effect is that it has created an ethos of what is acceptable which has in turn filtered down to smaller cases. Many potential litigants do not even start litigation because of the advice they are given about cost, and in my view this is as great a social ill as the actual cost of pursuing litigation.

In a further 60 detailed and trenchant paragraphs Lord Woolf discussed the perceived problems of cost and lack of impartiality of experts, concluding with seven recommendations, which were in short:

(a) That as a general principle single experts should be used wherever the case concerns a substantially established area of knowledge and it is not necessary for the court directly to sample a range of opinions.

(b) Parties and procedural judges should always consider whether a single expert would be sufficient.

(c) Where opposing experts are appointed they should adopt a cooperative approach including if possible joint investigation and a single report.

CHAPTER 19   EXPERTS AND ASSESSORS

(d) Expert evidence should not be admissible unless all written instructions, including letters subsequent upon the original instructions, are included as an annexe to the expert's report.

(e) The court should have a wide power to order that an examination or test should be carried out and a report submitted to the court.

(f) Meetings between experts advising opposing parties (which Lord Woolf wanted to encourage) should normally be held in private.

(g) Training courses and published materials should provide expert witnesses with a basic understanding of the legal system and their role within it, focusing on the expert's duty to the court.

In the light of these recommendations Part 35 of the CPR, and the consequent directions on fast track and multi-track cases and PD 35 have been formulated.

19.2   DUTIES OF EXPERTS AND THE COURT'S POWER TO RESTRICT EXPERT EVIDENCE

Part 35 of the CPR commences with three provisions to which the other rules in Part 35 are subject. These are:

(a) Rule 35.1, which provides that expert evidence shall be restricted to that which is reasonably required to resolve the proceedings.

(b) Rule 35.3, which provides that it is the duty of an expert (that is, one who has been instructed to give or prepare evidence for the purpose of court proceedings) to help the court on the matters within his expertise and that that duty overrides any obligation to the person from whom he has received instructions, or by whom he is paid.

(c) Rule 35.4, which provides that:

(1) No party may call an expert or put in evidence an expert's report without the court's permission.

(2) When a party applies for permission under this rule he must identify—

(a) the field in which he wishes to rely on expert evidence; and

(b) where practicable, the expert in that field on whose evidence he wishes to rely.

(3) If permission is granted under this rule it shall be in relation only to the expert named or the field identified under paragraph (2).

(4) The court may limit the amount of the expert's fees and expenses that the party who wishes to rely on the expert may recover from any other party.

It will therefore first be the task of the court to decide whether it needs expert evidence at all. Under general principles of evidence, expert evidence is only admissible where the court needs it because the matters in question fall outside the court's experience. Even before the Woolf reforms the Court of Appeal had often expressed itself strongly about the unnecessary proliferation of experts, e.g., in *Liddell* v *Middleton* [1996] PIQR P36, where the court deplored the fact that a road accident reconstruction specialist had been permitted to comment on the evidence of witnesses of fact.

Rule 35.4 therefore permits the court at the time of giving directions about expert evidence to identify the expert from whom such evidence will be

CHAPTER 19 EXPERTS AND ASSESSORS

received and to specify an upper limit on the expert's fees, quite apart from the general powers which the court would have to restrict them on an *inter partes* basis at the time of the detailed assessment of costs under Part 44.

19.3 DIRECTIONS ABOUT EXPERTS

The stages at which the court may be required to give directions about expert evidence may arise by virtue of the practice directions under Part 35 (expert evidence) and Parts 28 (fast track) and 29 (multi-track).

The issue of experts will first come up in the context of directions on allocation. Where a case is allocated to the fast track, directions will be given tailored to the needs of the case and in the light of the steps that the parties have already taken to prepare the case and in particular the extent to which any pre-action protocol has been observed. It is possible for the parties to obtain the court's approval under PD 28, para. 3.6, for agreed directions, which may include directions for the use of a single joint expert or, if that has not been agreed, the exchange and agreement of other expert evidence and without prejudice meetings of experts. The court may decline to approve what the parties put forward as agreed directions and the court may thereupon order an allocation hearing to give further and different directions. These matters are dealt with in PD 28, paras 3.7 to 3.9. If experts' reports are to be exchanged, in general, they will be exchanged within 14 weeks of the directions order.

On the multi-track agreed directions may be approved upon allocation under PD 29, para. 4.7, and they should include provisions for experts' reports. The court has specific powers under PD 29, paras 4.10 to 4.13 in respect of expert evidence, including the power to direct:

    (a) a single joint expert on any appropriate issue, unless there is good reason not to do so (thus indicating that it will be for the parties to establish to the court's satisfaction that a single expert will not suffice);
    (b) to direct disclosure of experts' reports by way of simultaneous exchange on issues where a single joint expert is not directed;
    (c) if experts' reports are not agreed, to direct a discussion between experts for the purposes set out in CPR, r. 35.12 (see 19.11);
    (d) if it appears that expert evidence will be required on both liability and quantum, the court may direct the exchange of reports on liability simultaneously, but that those relating to the amount of damages be exchanged sequentially.

Unless the parties have consented in writing to the proposed order, these matters must be dealt with at the case management conference.

19.4 WHAT IF A PARTY HAS ALREADY INSTRUCTED HIS OWN EXPERT?

In principle, a party who instructs his own expert without attempting to agree a single joint expert with his opponent will be at risk as to costs. The pre-action protocols, where they are relevant, generally presuppose a jointly instructed expert (although the provisions are not without some ambiguity — see 4.4). Even in actions where the protocols do not strictly apply, the parties are required to observe the spirit of them. Instructing one's own expert may lead to the following problems:

(a) the court may not give permission for the expert's report to be used, so that the party concerned loses the costs of instructing him;

(b) the opposing party may attempt to insist upon a jointly instructed expert so that again the costs of the first expert are wasted;

(c) if the first party wishes to attempt to persuade the opponent to use his expert's report as the only report in the case, he will obviously have to disclose it at an earlier stage than that at which disclosure might have been ordered by the court and the opponent might still not agree to its use.

As against that, there may sometimes be powerful considerations where one party will wish to obtain an expert's report of his own including:

(a) in technical cases, it may not be until an expert's report has been obtained that a claimant can be sure that he has a case at all;

(b) there may be such lengthy waiting lists to get a report from the chosen expert that the claimant needs to initiate these procedures as soon as he instructs solicitors;

(c) in straightforward cases and given that he will disclose the letter of instructions, if the expert he has instructed is well-known and accepted as reputable by the opponent, time may be saved and the report may be accepted, perhaps subject to further questions being put by the opponent under CPR, r. 35.6 (see 19.6).

In general, however, it is undoubtedly better to approach one's opponent in an attempt to agree a jointly instructed expert, whether specifically under the protocols where they apply or in the spirit of them where they do not.

19.5 WRITTEN REPORTS

By CPR, r. 35.5, expert evidence is to be given in a written report unless the court directs otherwise. In particular, if a claim is on the fast track, the court will not direct an expert to attend a hearing unless it is necessary to do so in the interests of justice.

There is thus a strong presumption in favour of expert evidence being given in written form with the consequent saving of witness fees. On the fast track the presumption is that the order will debar oral evidence. For rules on the contents of experts' reports see 19.9.

19.6 WRITTEN QUESTIONS TO EXPERTS

By CPR, r. 35.6(1), a party may put written questions to an expert instructed by another party on that expert's report. If a single joint expert is instructed under r. 35.7 (see below), either party may put written questions to that expert about his report.

Such questions may be put once only; must be put within 28 days of service of the expert's report; and must be for the purpose only of clarification of the report, unless in any case the court gives permission or the other party agrees (r. 35.6(2)). Thereafter an expert's answers to those questions shall be treated as part of the expert's report (r. 35.6(3)).

By r. 35.6(4), if an expert who has received questions put under r. 35.6(1) does not answer, the court may make one or both of the following orders in relation to the party who instructed the expert, namely:

(a) that the party may not rely on the evidence of that expert;
(b) that the party may not recover the fees and expenses of that expert from any other party.

Rule 35.6 provides a general procedure to replace cross-examination when an expert's evidence will be in written form only. The practice will now be that where an expert's report is received from an opponent, there is the opportunity to raise, as it were, interrogatories upon the expert's report by way of putting questions, requiring comment on supplementary material, or putting opposing viewpoints. There is a 28-day prima facie time limit for undertaking this procedure and therefore litigators will have to be alert to the need to act promptly. Although experienced litigators will no doubt be able to formulate many questions themselves, it is probably the case that in substantial litigation a party will want to confer with his own expert upon the text of the opponent's report and obtain assistance in drafting technical questions. It may be indeed in some litigation that counsel's assistance will be required in drafting the questions where the opposition to aspects of the expert's report is of substance or may even be determinative of the litigation.

The sanctions for failure to reply set out in r. 35.6(4) are not exhaustive. Clearly the most aggressive approach would be an application that the evidence of the expert who has failed to respond should be disallowed entirely and it may well be that that order will be made unless some reason for non-reply can be shown. If that order is not made then it will of course be open to the trial judge to disregard the evidence in so far as the expert has not responded to legitimate questions and if there is an opposing report to prefer that report. In any application for sanctions in respect of non-reply to questions, the appropriateness of the questions themselves may be investigated, so that questions which are designed to score points, harass, are unreasonable, or are clearly outside the expert's area of expertise or even on areas on which expert evidence is not required, such as simple disputes of fact, may be, so to speak, 'disallowed' in that the court may decline to direct that the expert who is failing to reply should have his report disregarded. In all these applications the aspects of the overriding objective set out in CPR, Part 1, must always be borne in mind: the court will always seek solutions which are proportionate in time and cost to the issues and which should reflect an attitude of cooperation between the lawyers.

19.7 SINGLE JOINT EXPERT

Where two or more parties wish to submit expert evidence on a particular issue, the court may direct that the evidence is to be given by one expert only (CPR, r. 35.7). In that case the parties wishing to submit the expert evidence, the 'instructing parties', should attempt to agree who the expert should be, reflecting the attitude of cooperation enjoined by Part 1. If they cannot do so, by r. 35.7(3) the court may:

(a) select the expert from a list prepared or identified by the instructing parties; or
(b) direct that the expert be selected in such other manner as the court may direct.

Where the court has directed that the evidence on a particular issue is to be given by one expert only, but there are a number of disciplines relevant to that issue, a leading expert in the dominant discipline should be identified as the single expert. That expert should prepare the general part of the report and be responsible for annexing or incorporating the contents of any reports from experts in other disciplines (PD 35, para. 5).

The good sense and simplicity of this procedure are obvious. It is to be hoped that in most litigation, applications to the court to appoint an expert will prove unnecessary, and the court is likely to be critical of parties who decline to cooperate, to the point of imposing costs sanctions. Given the attitude of impartiality and objective assistance to the court, which is enjoined upon the expert by r. 35.3, there should be few cases in which solicitors cannot agree upon an expert.

There may continue to be objections to a given expert, e.g., because in the past he has been viewed as something of a 'defendant's man' or because he has been exclusively instructed by one or other firm of solicitors. Experts in those categories may find their forensic practice diminishing.

Disputes may well focus in future on questions of location and availability, especially in spheres of expertise where historically experts have had very substantial waiting lists. Likewise if the plaintiffs' and defendants' solicitors are several hundred miles apart, one may have no knowledge of the competence of an expert suggested by the other. Solicitors are entitled at least to be in a position to formulate some views about the acceptability and competence of a given expert and if they are unable to obtain any information about an expert, it may be that they will legitimately be able to resist inclusion of that expert on a list from which selection is to be made.

19.7.1 Instructions to a single joint expert

By CPR, r. 35.8, where the court gives directions under r. 35.7 for a single joint expert to be used, each instructing party may give instructions to the expert but must at the same time send a copy of the instructions to the other instructing parties.

The court may give directions about the payment of the expert's fees and expenses and any inspection, examination or experiments which the expert wishes to carry out (r. 35.8(3)).

In other words the court may arbitrate on identifying the questions and issues on which the expert is to give advice where that involves inspection, examination or experiments, either in the interests of limiting costs, accelerating the procedure, or identifying what is reasonable in the circumstances of the case.

The court may, under r. 35.8(4)(a), before an expert is instructed, limit the amount that can be paid by way of fees and expenses to the expert and direct that the instructing parties pay that amount into court. Unless the court otherwise directs the instructing parties are jointly and severally liable for the payment of the expert's fees and expenses, even if the court has not directed them to be paid into court (r. 35.8(5)).

By this means the court will ensure that the expert's fees are known fully in advance to both parties and therefore that they can proceed with certainty and bear in mind also the likely costs. No doubt a procedure will be developed whereby experts will initially be asked to confirm that they will be available and are willing to be instructed and invited to indicate the likely level of their fees. This may not, however, cover a situation where complications occur and/or where an expert considers that additional specialist advice, possibly in a different field, will be required.

19.8 DIRECTION TO PROVIDE INFORMATION

Where a party has access to information which is not reasonably available to the other party, the court may, under CPR, r. 35.9, direct the party who has access to the information:

(a) to prepare and file a document recording the information; and
(b) to serve a copy of that document on the other party.

This power supplements the court's other powers and may assist in ensuring openness between the parties. One can envisage a variety of cases where it is essential that information is made available so that an expert can be adequately instructed and both parties proceed in the light rather than the dark. An example from litigation under the previous rules is *Kirkup v British Rail Engineering Ltd* [1983] 1 WLR 1165, where, in an industrial deafness case arising from many years before, the defendant's expert would simply not have known what he was to examine about until he had had some information from the plaintiff of what the plaintiff had been subjected to and over what period. There will be many other cases where one or other party has an apparent monopoly of vital information which ought to be conveyed to the other party. This may involve provision of witness statements, or perhaps the raw material on which the expert needs to base his opinion, such as books of accounts, business documents, technical data and the like.

19.9 CONTENTS OF AN EXPERT'S REPORT

Rule 35.10 of the CPR specifies what an expert's report must contain. It provides in particular that the report must comply with the requirements set out in PD 35, which is self-explanatory.

An expert's report should be addressed to the court and not to the party from whom the expert has received his instructions (PD 35, para. 1.1). At the end of the report there must be a statement that the expert understands his duty to the court and has complied with that duty (CPR, r. 35.10(2)) and the report must be verified by a statement of truth (PD 35, para. 1.3) using the following words (PD 35, para. 1.4):

> I believe that the facts I have stated in this report are true and that the opinions I have expressed are correct.

PD 35 also provides that an expert's report should comply with the requirements of any approved expert's protocol which may be published (para. 1.6). There are none at the time of writing.

The report must state the substance of all material instructions, whether written or oral, on the basis of which the report was written (CPR, r. 35.10(3)). The instructions will not be privileged against disclosure, but (r. 35.10(4)) the court will not, in relation to those instructions:

CHAPTER 19 EXPERTS AND ASSESSORS

(a) order disclosure of any specific document; or

(b) permit any questioning in court other than by the party who instructed the expert, unless it is satisfied that there are reasonable grounds to consider the statement of instructions given under r. 35.10(3) to be inaccurate or incomplete.

If in the latter case the court is so satisfied, it will allow cross-examination where it appears to be in the interests of justice to do so. Although it may have been the intention by those who drafted the rule for it to refer to cross-examination of the expert only, it is not in fact so limited. It could be argued that if it is to be permitted at all, cross-examination could be directed at the party on whose behalf the expert was instructed if it is said, for example, that matters in the instructions are inaccurate or inconsistent with the party's own version contained in his witness statement or oral evidence. This is a potentially awkward incursion into the law of privilege and may provide a middle ground between documents that are privileged and those that are not. Since the substance of instructions must be disclosed, it can be argued that privilege is waived anyway and that the halfway status of the document gives adequate protection to the instructing solicitor who may have, for example, included material in the letter of instructions which he would not otherwise have wished to put before the court. The letter of instructions will therefore have to be drafted in a very careful way in order not to contain or refer to material which a party is entitled to withhold from disclosure.

19.10 USE BY OTHER PARTIES OF DISCLOSED EXPERT'S REPORT

By CPR, r. 35.11, where a party has disclosed an expert's report, any party may use that expert's report as evidence at the trial. Thus where both parties have been permitted to use competing experts and one party has disclosed its expert's report, but later decides not to rely on it at trial, the opposing party may do so.

This echoes the corresponding provision about witness statements in r. 32.5(5). Nothing in the rule, however, compels a party to disclose an expert's report that it does not intend to use. One might therefore think that this does give a party an opportunity, after receiving an unfavourable report from its expert, to instruct another for a second opinion. However, r. 35.4 provides that where an application is made for the court's permission to use an expert's report, the application must identify 'where practicable' the expert to be selected, and indicates that if permission is granted, the order granting permission will name the expert. This rule indicates that the court's prior approval should be sought before instructing an expert. Accordingly, it may happen that one party will be aware that the other has instructed an expert on whose report he does not intend to rely, and that information may well provide a tactical advantage. Although nothing in terms prevents a party from obtaining its own report from an expert before seeking the court's approval, there is a serious risk of a costs penalty being imposed on a party adopting this course if, for example, a court insisted on a jointly instructed expert or for any reason disapproved the expert already chosen when considering whether to grant permission under r. 35.4.

19.11 DISCUSSION BETWEEN EXPERTS

Rule 35.12 of the CPR provides that the court may at any stage direct a discussion between experts for the purpose of requiring them:

(a) to identify the issues in the proceedings; and
(b) where possible, to reach agreement on issues.

The court may specify the issues which the experts must discuss (r. 35.12(2)) and may direct that, following a discussion, they must prepare a statement for the court showing the issues on which they agree and those on which they disagree and a summary of their reasons for disagreeing (r. 35.12(3)).

The contents of the discussion between the experts must not be referred to at the trial unless the parties agree (r. 35.12(4)).

Where experts reach agreement on an issue during the discussions, the agreement does not bind the parties, unless the parties expressly agree to be bound by it (r. 35.12(5)).

Rule 35.12 repeats the essence of the previous RSC, ord. 38, r. 38. In essence the court may direct, whether or not the parties request it, a 'without prejudice' meeting of experts, although the use of the word 'discussion' in the rule expressly provides for the communication to be indirect, for example, by telephone, should this be more practical, expedient and less expensive. Unless there are exceptional circumstances, this will only be appropriate on the multi-track where a court has already accepted that it is inappropriate to proceed with one single jointly instructed expert. It is commonly said that meetings of experts in most fields are better where there has been no mutual disclosure of their evidence, so that they do not have to appear to withdraw from positions already taken up. But in the new climate an order for this further expensive step is perhaps unlikely, unless there is already a clear indication that the experts have disagreed. Moreover, in many cases before this step is taken the parties may wish to attempt to move towards agreement by delivering written questions to the opposing expert under r. 35.6. It is clear that the outcome of the discussions are to be, in effect, without prejudice, because of the provision that the contents of the discussion may not be referred to at trial, nor is any agreement between the experts binding on the parties unless the parties expressly agree.

The new rule does not entirely clarify the difficulties caused by the case of *Richard Roberts Holdings* v *Douglas Smith Stimson Partnership (No. 3)* (1990) 47 BLR 113, in which it was held that where experts meet and agree a joint statement, the order that they should do so could not confer upon them an authority to bind the parties instructing them and their joint statement would not automatically be an 'open' statement. In practice, however, an expert would have great difficulty in giving evidence contrary to the view expressed at such a meeting. It is implicit in the present provision that a party should not be unwilling to cooperate and its expert not excessively hesitant in participating for fear of binding the party concerned with some unwelcome concession, real or apparent. That is the purpose behind the provision that the outcome of these discussions is not to bind the party concerned. If it were not the case, one would in effect be having compulsory arbitration by a panel of experts.

CHAPTER 19 EXPERTS AND ASSESSORS

19.12 CONSEQUENCES OF FAILURE TO DISCLOSE EXPERT'S REPORT

Rule 35.13 of the CPR provides that a party who fails to disclose an expert's report may not use the report at the trial or call the expert to give evidence orally, unless the court gives permission.

This rule to an extent states the obvious, given that r. 35.4 provides a general power for the court to restrict expert evidence. It is difficult to conceive of circumstances in which the court would permit oral or written evidence from an expert at trial which had not previously been disclosed, unless perhaps in a case where remarkable latitude was being given to an unrepresented litigant, the point was simple and could be dealt with without surprise or prejudice by the opponent and the costs of adjourning would be substantial.

19.13 EXPERT'S RIGHT TO ASK COURT FOR DIRECTIONS

Under CPR, r. 35.3, an expert's duty is to assist the court rather than to assist the party instructing him. Since it is to be assumed that experts will be made fully aware of their obligations, r. 35.14 provides a channel whereby experts may communicate directly with the court to ensure they are not subsequently subject to any criticism for having in some way misunderstood the issues or reported too widely or narrowly on the important questions.

Rule 35.14(1) provides that an expert may file a written request for directions to assist him in carrying out his function as an expert and indeed may do so without giving notice to any party. This may be dealt with on paper without notice to the parties or, exceptionally, may be listed for a hearing with or without the attendance of the parties. When it gives directions the court may also direct that a party be served with a copy of the directions and a copy of the request for directions (r. 35.14(3)).

Rule 35.14 therefore envisages a situation where the expert has been unable to obtain clarification of his instructions from one or other party, and perhaps for fear of wishing to appear partial in approaching the parties seeks the court's assistance directly. It is difficult to envisage a situation where an acknowledged expert would not appreciate the matters on which he needs to report and if the case is of that level of difficulty, it is suggested that the court ought to list a hearing so that the parties can attend to make representations on what directions should be given to the expert. Rule 35.14(3) is somewhat strange in providing that the court may direct that 'a party' be served with a copy of the directions and a copy of the request for directions, which would seem to indicate that the court has the power to serve these on only one of the parties, whereas one would imagine that for justice to be served, all parties ought to receive those documents.

19.14 ASSESSORS

Rule 35.15 of the CPR relates to the appointment of one or more persons as assessors under the Supreme Court Act 1981, s. 70, or the County Courts Act 1984, s. 63. An assessor is an expert who assists the court in dealing with a matter within his expertise and who generally sits with the

CHAPTER 19 EXPERTS AND ASSESSORS

judge. A common example from previous practice was the appointment of assessors by a High Court judge when hearing disputed appeals concerning costs.

By CPR, r. 35.15(3), an assessor is to take such part in the proceedings as the court may direct and in particular the court may direct the assessor to prepare a report for the court and direct the assessor to attend the whole or any part of the trial to advise the court on any matter. If a report is prepared before the trial has begun, the court must send a copy to each of the parties and the parties may use it at trial (r. 35.15(4)).

The remuneration to be paid to an assessor is to be determined by the court and forms part of the cost of the proceedings (r. 35.15(5)), and the court may order any party to deposit in the court office a specified sum in respect of the assessor's fees (r. 35.15(6)), except in cases where the remuneration of the assessor is to be paid out of money provided by Parliament (r. 35.15(7)).

CHAPTER 20   OFFERS TO SETTLE

CONTENTS

20.1	Introduction	264
20.2	When to use Part 36 offers and payments	264
20.3	Pre-action offer	265
20.3.1	Informal offers	265
20.3.2	Formal pre-action offer under r. 36.10	265
20.3.3	Contents of the offer	266
20.3.4	Pre-action offer accepted after issue	266
20.3.5	Pre-action offer not accepted	266
20.3.6	Offer accepted before issue	267
20.3.7	Relationship between r. 36.10 and the rest of Part 36	267
20.4	Defendant's Part 36 offer	267
20.4.1	Introduction	267
20.4.2	Notice	268
20.4.3	Acceptance	269
20.4.4	Acceptance where there are multiple defendants	271
20.4.5	Rejection	271
20.5	Defendant's Part 36 payment	271
20.5.1	Introduction	271
20.5.2	Mixed claims	272
20.5.3	Making a Part 36 payment	272
20.5.4	Acceptance	274
20.5.5	Acceptance where there are multiple defendants	275
20.5.6	Acceptance of a combined payment and offer	275
20.5.7	Acceptance after a defence of tender before claim	275
20.6	Claimant's Part 36 offer	275
20.6.1	Introduction	275
20.6.2	Notice	276
20.6.3	Acceptance	276
20.6.4	Rejection	277
20.7	Failure to beat a Part 36 payment or offer	277
20.7.1	Failure to beat a Part 36 payment	277
20.7.2	Failure to beat a Part 36 offer	278
20.7.3	Failure to beat a claimant's Part 36 offer	278
20.8	Non-disclosure	279
20.9	Court intervention	280
20.9.1	Permission	280
20.9.2	Order to pay money out of court	280
20.9.3	Order for costs	280
20.9.4	Withdrawal or reduction	281
20.9.5	Clarification	281
20.9.6	Other orders	281
20.10	Costs consequences when both claimant and defendant have made an offer	281
20.11	What should be the response to an unacceptable offer or payment?	282

CHAPTER 20 OFFERS TO SETTLE

20.1 INTRODUCTION

In his *Final Report*, Lord Woolf said that he felt that negotiated settlements were even more important than he had done when formulating his *Interim Report*. The CPR encourage parties to settle by providing financial incentives.

The provisions for making and accepting offers to settle set out in the CPR are intended to extend to all parties in all fast track and multi-track cases a more flexible version of the previous system of payments into court and *Calderbank* letters. The ability of the claimant to put the defendant at risk of financial penalties is a significant alteration to the balance of power in litigation. It also raises a number of questions about the relationship between claimants' and defendants' offers which are explored more fully at the end of this chapter: if you don't like the payment in, do you simply reject it and invite the defendant to increase it, or do you make an offer to settle of your own?

The use of offers to settle which, if not accepted, may lead to adverse consequences in costs (and, for a defendant, in increased interest) is governed by Part 36 of the CPR.

20.2 WHEN TO USE PART 36 OFFERS AND PAYMENTS

When a litigant wishes to make an offer to settle having costs or other financial consequences if not accepted by the other side, the basic scheme of CPR, Part 36, is as follows:

(a) Before proceedings are issued, the litigant should make an offer under r. 36.10 (see 20.3).

(b) After issue, offers in non-monetary claims should be made by way of Part 36 offers. These are broadly equivalent to the former *Calderbank* offers, but the procedure has been developed in a number of respects. See 20.4.

(c) After issue, if the claim is for money, the defendant must make a Part 36 payment, unless it is a personal injuries case and the defendant is awaiting the certificate of recoverable benefit. If the certificate is awaited, a Part 36 offer may be made, but must be replaced by a Part 36 payment within seven days of receipt of the certificate. A Part 36 payment is the equivalent to the previous payment into court. See 20.5.

(d) After issue, a defendant who wishes to offer to settle the whole of a claim seeking money together with non-monetary relief must make a Part 36 payment in respect of the money claim and a Part 36 offer in respect of the non-monetary relief, and must refer to the Part 36 offer in the Part 36 payment notice. See 20.5.2.

(e) When proceedings are being appealed after trial, Part 36 payments and offers are the approved methods as discussed at (b) to (d) above.

(f) A claimant wishing to put proposals to the defendants may make a claimant's Part 36 offer. This is another derivative from what used to be called *Calderbank* offers. See 20.6.

Definitions appear in r. 36.2(1):

> An offer made in accordance with the requirements of this Part is called—
> (a) if made by way of a payment into court, 'a Part 36 payment';
> (b) otherwise 'a Part 36 offer'.

Although Part 36 does not actually say a claimant cannot make a Part 36 payment (and note that either party can be required to pay money into court by way of sanction under r. 3.1(5)), Part 36 contains no mechanism by which a claimant could do so, except as a defendant to a counterclaim or other Part 20 claim. It is difficult to envisage circumstances that would justify a claimant paying money into court.

Part 36 does not apply to cases on the small claims track (r. 27.2(1)). Where a Part 36 offer or payment has been made in a case subsequently allocated to the small claims track, there are no costs consequences unless the court orders otherwise (r. 36.2(5)).

Part 36 has no relevance as such to offers made with the aim of disposing of interim applications. Such offers may nevertheless have costs consequences if refused, by virtue of r. 44.3(4) and (5).

Lord Woolf considered it important that his new regime should apply, not simply to offers in respect of all or part of the case made during the course of proceedings, but also to offers made before the issue of proceedings (r. 36.10)). This is entirely consistent with the tenor of the CPR, of the onus placed on the court of 'helping the parties to settle the whole or part of the case' (r. 1.4(2)(f)), of the pre-action protocols and of the allocation questionnaire's demand that the parties consider a month's stay to attempt settlement at an early stage of the proceedings.

20.3 PRE-ACTION OFFER

20.3.1 Informal offers

There is nothing in the CPR preventing the normal to and fro of pre-issue negotiations, so often bolstered only by the threat of issue. Rule 36.1(2) provides:

> Nothing in this part prevents a party making an offer to settle in whatever way he chooses, but if that offer is not made in accordance with this Part, it will only have the consequences specified in this Part if the court so orders.

This is presumably not intended actually to prohibit offers made otherwise than under Part 36 which coincidentally have identical consequences. For example, an offer made 'without prejudice' by a potential defendant to pay a certain sum of money plus costs to date of acceptance should not be incapable of acceptance on a purely contractual basis without a court order just because the offer as to costs is identical to the costs consequences set out in r. 36.16. The rule is directed at the penalising effects of a failure to accept a Part 36 offer or payment.

20.3.2 Formal pre-action offer under r. 36.10

Pre-action protocols should enable parties to make well informed judgments about the prospects of success at trial in the pre-issue period. In that context it makes sense to be able to offer the parties the same incentives to settle that are available after the issue of proceedings — the particular incentive here being the ability to throw the risk of paying the costs of (or additional interest on the costs of) the entire proceedings on one's opponent.

By r. 36.10(1), if, before proceedings are begun, a person makes an offer to settle which complies with r. 36.10, the court will take that offer into account when making any order as to costs. Clearly r. 36.10(1) only comes into operation if the offer is not taken up, proceedings ensue, and the court goes on to make an order as to costs.

20.3.3 Contents of the offer

In order to comply with CPR, r. 36.10, a pre-action offer must satisfy the following conditions:

(a) The offer must be expressed to be open for at least 21 days after the date it was made (r. 36.10(2)(a)). There is no obligation on a claimant making such an offer to hold off issuing a claim form for 21 days. If issue intervenes during the 21-day period, the court's permission will be required to accept the offer (r. 36.10(4)). On that application, although r. 36.10(4) does not specifically state that the court will make a costs order, presumably it will, normally that the claimant receives its costs (by analogy with r. 36.14) but if the court considers issue of proceedings to be premature, this may be reflected in the costs order made (see r. 44.3(4) and (5)(a)).

(b) If made by a prospective defendant, the offer must include an offer to pay the claimant's costs up to a date 21 days after the date the offer was made (r. 36.10(2)(b)). There is no equivalent provision in relation to an offer made by a claimant.

(c) The offer must comply with the remainder of Part 36 (r. 36.10(2)(c)). Since much of Part 36 deals with the consequences of offers rather than the offer itself, this appears to be a reference to the contents of and way in which the offer is made.

(d) If the offer is made by a defendant in a money claim, a Part 36 payment (see 20.5) must be made within 14 days of being served with a claim form and that payment must be not less than the amount offered pre-action.

20.3.4 Pre-action offer accepted after issue

If an offer complying with CPR, r. 36.10, is accepted after issue, even if still within the initial 21-day period, the permission of the court will be required to accept it (r. 36.10(4)). Since it is a defendant's offer, which must, by r. 36.10(2)(b), specifically incorporate an offer to pay the claimant's costs, it is likely that the court will normally make an order to the same effect, but disallowing costs from issue.

20.3.5 Pre-action offer not accepted

If an offer complying with CPR, r. 36.10, is not accepted and the claim proceeds to trial, the court will 'take that offer into account when making any order as to costs' (r. 36.10(1)).

It is suggested that the practice of the courts will be to extend the costs and penalising interest consequences set out in Part 36 for post-issue offers to pre-action offers (but taking as a start date for the penalty the date 21 days from the pre-action offer or the date of issue, whichever is the later). Otherwise there is little or no incentive to use r. 36.10 and little certainty in advising a client of the effect of failing to accept the offer. If practice in relation to pre-issue offers differs from that applying to post-issue offers, an offer made the day after issue might have an entirely different effect to an offer made the day before. In this context one should remember that a defendant may well be unaware, until served, of the date of issue, which could have been at least four months beforehand.

20.3.6 Offer accepted before issue

If an offer complying with CPR, r. 36.10, is made by a defendant, it must incorporate an offer to pay the claimant's costs (r. 36.10(2)(b)). It follows that on a simple contractual basis, if accepted, the defendant will pay the amount of the offer (if a money claim) and the claimant's costs. Although not specifically stated, it must be presumed that the court has jurisdiction under r. 48.3 to assess the amount of those costs if they are disputed. A pre-action offer which incorporates an offer of only a specific amount of money towards the claimant's costs would fall outside r. 36.10 and consequently outside Part 36.

There is no equivalent provision that a claimant's pre-action offer should include provision for costs. If the offer is post-issue the position is clear: the claimant receives costs to the date of acceptance (r. 36.14). There is a risk, given the lack of express reference to provision for costs being included in claimants' pre-issue offers, that a claimant's offer including costs will be held to be outside the ambit of r. 36.10. The consequence of including provision for costs then would seem to be that:

(a) if the offer is accepted, the claimant gains the benefit of receiving costs;
(b) if the offer is not accepted but is more generous than the eventual award, the court may not make a penalising order against the defendant.

If either of the prospective parties is a child or patient, then (whether the settlement derived from a pre-issue offer under r. 36.10 or not) court approval must in any event be sought by issuing proceedings under Part 8 solely for that purpose (r. 21.10(2)). Costs may also need to be assessed under r. 48.5.

20.3.7 Relationship between r. 36.10 and the rest of Part 36

Rule 36.10 of the CPR is expressed in terms of a pre-action offer complying with Part 36 rather than applying the provisions of Part 36 to the offer. Rule 36.10 also operates from the perspective of an offer that remains unaccepted, resulting in the issue of proceedings ending in trial. If proceedings are never issued then it is difficult to see what jurisdiction the court has to make any order in relation to a r. 36.10 offer. However, it could be argued that, as r. 36.10 is in Part 36, an offer complying with the provisions of r. 36.10 is, by r. 36.2(1), a Part 36 offer, because it is 'made in accordance with the requirements of this Part'. It could then be argued that other provisions of Part 36, such as the clarification procedure in r. 36.9, apply to a r. 36.10 offer, even if no proceedings are commenced.

20.4 DEFENDANT'S PART 36 OFFER

20.4.1 Introduction

A defendant can make a Part 36 offer to settle the whole or part of a claim on terms 'without prejudice except as to costs' (CPR, r. 36.19(1)). However, a defendant's offer to settle a money claim must, by r. 36.3(1), be made by way of a Part 36 payment (see 20.5), so defendants' Part 36 offers will normally be concerned with matters such as willingness to accept an injunction or an offer to accept a proportion of liability (which is specifically mentioned in r. 36.5(4)). The incentive for a defendant to make a Part 36 offer is that if it is refused and, at trial, the claimant fails to obtain a judgment which is more advantageous than the offer, then the court will order the claimant to pay the defendant's costs incurred since the latest date on which the offer could have been accepted without the court's permission, unless this would be unjust (r. 36.20).

'Defendant' here includes a claimant in relation to a counterclaim and a third party in relation to a third-party claim (r. 20.3).

The making of a defendant's offer pre-action is discussed in 20.3. A defendant's Part 36 offer can be made at any stage after commencement of proceedings (r. 36.2(4)). The offer can relate to the whole claim, to any part of it or to any issue (r. 36.5(2)).

A defendant to a claim which has both money and non-money parts, who is making money and non-money offers as a proposal to settle the whole claim, must make both a Part 36 offer and a Part 36 payment, specifying that acceptance of the payment will constitute acceptance of the offer as well (r. 36.4; see 20.5).

20.4.2 Notice

In order to comply with CPR, Part 36, an offer must:

(a) Be in writing (CPR, r. 36.5(1)).
(b) State that it is a Part 36 offer (PD 36, para. 5.1).
(c) State whether it applies to the whole of the proceedings or to part of them or to a particular issue (and identify any such part or issue) (PD 36, para. 5.2; CPR, r. 36.5(3)(a)).
(d) State whether it takes into account any counterclaim (PD 36, para. 5.2; CPR, r. 36.5(3)(b)).
(e) In a money claim only — if not inclusive of interest, state whether interest is offered in addition and if so the amount, rate and period (PD 36, para. 5.4; CPR, r. 36.5(3)(c) and 36.22(2)). If interest is not mentioned, the offer is assumed to be inclusive of interest to the last date when the offer could be accepted without the court's permission (r. 36.22(1)). This will be relevant where a certificate of recoverable benefit is awaited. A draft of the Rules stated that if interest was not offered, the notice had to explain why not but this does not appear in the final version.
(f) Be signed by the claimant or by the claimant's legal representative (PD 36, para. 5.1(2)). If the claimant is a company or other corporation, the offer can, by PD 36, para. 5.5, be signed by one of the senior personnel listed in para. 5.6, giving his or her position in the organisation (director, treasurer, secretary etc.).

The offer can be made 'by reference to an interim payment' (CPR, r. 36.5(5)).

If the offer is made 21 days or more before the trial, it must, by r. 36.5(6):

(a) State that the offer is open for 21 days from the date is it made.
(b) State that after 21 days it can only be accepted if:

(i) the parties agree the liability for costs; or
(ii) permission of the court is obtained.

CHAPTER 20 OFFERS TO SETTLE

If the offer is made less than 21 days before the trial, it must, by r. 36.5(7) state that it can only be accepted if:

(a) the parties agree the liability for costs; or
(b) permission of the court is obtained.

In a mixed claim, the notice must in addition cross-refer to the Part 36 payment made in respect of the monetary part (r. 36.4(3)).

A defendant's Part 36 offer is effective when received by the claimant (r. 36.8(1)) as is an improvement to the offer (r. 36.8(3)). If the claimant is legally represented, the offer must be served on the legal representative (CPR, para. 11.1). Withdrawal of a defendant's offer does not require the permission of the court (r. 36.5(8)), although on withdrawal the costs consequences are lost. In a money claim where the defendant must make a payment into court, withdrawal does require consent (r. 36.6(5)).

20.4.3 Acceptance

If the claimant accepts a defendant's Part 36 offer, a notice of acceptance must be sent to the defendant and filed with the court (PD 36, para. 7.6). The notice must state the claim number and title of the proceedings, identify the defendant's written offer, and be signed by the claimant or by the claimant's legal representative (PD 36, para. 7.7). If the defendant is legally represented, the acceptance must be served on the legal representative (PD 36, para. 11.1). Acceptance is effective on receipt of the notice of acceptance by the defendant (CPR, r. 36.8(5)).

The consequences of acceptance of a Part 36 offer depend on whether the offer related to the whole of the claim, whether the offer was made less than 21 days before trial (and if so whether the parties have agreed costs), whether it was accepted within 21 days of being made, whether either party is under disability and whether the offer was made by some of a number of joint defendants. In a straightforward situation where the defendant's offer covers the whole claim, is made more than 21 days before trial, and is accepted within 21 days of the offer being made, the consequences are that:

(a) the whole claim is stayed (r. 36.15(1));
(b) no permission is required from the court (r. 36.11(1)); and
(c) the claimant will be entitled to his costs of the proceedings up to the date of serving notice of the acceptance (r. 36.13(1)) which are payable on the standard basis (r. 36.13(4)).

The various consequences in different situations are set out in table 20.1.

For acceptance of a combined payment and offer see 20.5.6.

If the trial has started, permission will be required for an acceptance unless the parties agree costs (r. 36.11(2)). Once the trial has commenced permission, if required, is sought from the trial judge (see PD 36, para. 7.4(2)). Such an application has practical difficulties, because if permission is refused the trial judge may feel obliged to retire from the case as he should not normally be informed of the existence of a Part 36 offer or payment (see 20.8). However, if permission is granted, the court must also deal with the entire costs of the proceedings (CPR, r. 36.18(2)).

CHAPTER 20 OFFERS TO SETTLE

Type of offer	Time of acceptance	Permission to accept	Effect on action	Costs
Whole claim	Within 21 days	Not required	Stayed	Defendant pays claimant's costs on standard basis
Whole claim and counterclaim	Within 21 days	Not required	Stayed	Defendant pays claimant's costs of claim and counterclaim on standard basis (r. 36.13(3))
Whole claim	Outside 21 days	Not required if parties agree costs	Stayed	As agreed between parties (r. 36.11(2)(b)(ii))
Whole claim	Outside 21 days	Required if parties do not agree costs	Stayed if permission granted	Court will make an order as to costs (r. 36.11(3))
Whole claim, offer less than 21 days before trial	Within 21 days	Not required if parties agree costs	Stayed	As agreed between parties (r. 36.11(2)(a)(ii))
Whole claim, offer less than 21 days before trial	Within 21 days	Required if parties do not agree costs	Stayed if permission granted	Court will make an order as to costs (r. 36.11(3))
Part of claim	Within 21 days	Not required	Relevant part stayed	Costs decided by court unless costs agreed (r. 36.15(3))
Part of claim, but claimant abandons the rest	Within 21 days	Not required	Stayed	Defendant pays claimant's costs on standard basis (r. 36.13(2))

CHAPTER 20   OFFERS TO SETTLE

Type of offer	Time of acceptance	Permission to accept	Effect on action	Costs
Either party under disability	Within 21 days	Required (rr. 36.18(1) and 21.10)	Stayed if permission granted	If money payable, costs will be assessed under r. 48.5

Table 20.1   Effect of acceptance of Part 36 offer

It is specifically provided that the claimant's costs include any costs attributable to the counterclaim if the defendant's offer was phrased so as to take this into account (r. 36.13(3)). Where the offer relates only to part of the claim, r. 36.15(3) contains the general provision that the relevant part only will be stayed and 'unless the parties have agreed costs, the liability for costs shall be decided by the court'. However, under r. 36.13(2) if:

(a) the offer is by a defendant; and
(b) as to part only of the claim; and
(c) the claimant abandons the remainder of the claim,

the claimant will obtain his costs up to the date of acceptance in the normal way (including the costs of the counterclaim if the offer took it into account).

20.4.4   Acceptance where there are multiple defendants

Under CPR, r. 36.17, where an offer is made by one or more (but not all) of multiple defendants then:

(a) If the defendants are sued jointly or in the alternative, the offer can be accepted provided that the claimant abandons his claim against the non-offering defendants and those defendants give written consent to the acceptance of the offer.

(b) If the claims against each of the defendants are distinct, the claimant may accept the offer as against the defendant or defendants who made it and continue against the remaining defendants.

Otherwise the claimant must apply to court for a costs order (but not apparently for permission to accept the offer should the distinction be relevant (r. 36.17(4)).

20.4.5   Rejection

There is no requirement in the CPR to notify a defendant of non-acceptance of the defendant's Part 36 offer, although obviously this will often be done, if only in the hopes of an improved offer. The defendant can make an improvement to the offer (r. 36.8(3)) and the improved offer takes effect from when it is received by the defendant. The advantages and disadvantages of seeking an improved offer, and the other options available, are discussed in 20.11.

20.5   DEFENDANT'S PART 36 PAYMENT

20.5.1   Introduction

A defendant's offer to settle a money claim (or the money part of a mixed money and non-money claim) must be accompanied by payment to the court of the amount offered in settlement. There seems to be a drafting error in PD 36, para. 3.1, which refers to CPR, r. 36.3(1), and says an offer to settle a claim for a 'specified sum' must be made by a Part 36 payment, whereas r. 36.3(1) in fact says that a Part 36 payment must be used for a 'money claim'.

If a payment is made in accordance with CPR, Part 36 (and so is a Part 36 payment), but the offer is refused and, at trial, the claimant fails to better the payment, then the court will order the claimant to pay the defendant's costs incurred since the latest date on which the offer could have been accepted without the court's permission, unless this would be unjust (r. 36.20).

'Defendant' here includes a claimant in relation to a counterclaim and a third party in relation to a third-party claim (r. 20.3(1)). Where the defence is one of tender before claim the defendant is required to pay the sum alleged to have been tendered into court under separate provisions of r. 37.3 (and the defendant may choose to treat this payment as a Part 36 payment).

A defendant's Part 36 payment may only be made after commencement of proceedings (but at any stage thereafter) (r. 36.3(2)). The payment can relate to the whole claim or any part of it or to any issue (r. 36.6(1)).

A Part 36 payment may take into account an interim payment (r. 36.6(2)(d)) and can be made in a claim for provisional damages (r. 36.7).

20.5.2 Mixed claims

If the claim is partly a money claim and partly a non-money claim, and the defendant wants to offer to settle the whole claim by payment coupled with an offer in respect of the non-money claim, both a Part 36 payment and a Part 36 offer must be made under CPR, r. 36.4, and the Part 36 payment will be made on the basis that acceptance of it will constitute acceptance of the Part 36 offer as well.

20.5.3 Making a Part 36 payment

20.5.3.1 Material to be filed in court To make a Part 36 payment in an action which is proceeding in the county court or a district registry the defendant must file:

(a) the Part 36 payment notice (PD 36, para. 4.1(1)(a)) (see 20.5.3.2);
(b) a cheque for the payment made payable to Her Majesty's Paymaster General (PD 36, para. 4.1(1)(b));
(c) (if relevant) a certificate of recoverable benefits (PD 36, para. 10.1);
(d) (if relevant) notice of a payment to a hospital in a road traffic case made under the Road Traffic Act 1988, s. 57 (PD 36, para. 11.2, requires such a notice to be given to the court and to all other parties: if available it seems sensible to file it at the same time as the other documents).

If the action is proceeding in the Royal Courts of Justice the defendant must add Court Funds Office form 100 and a sealed copy of the claim form. The cheque is made payable to the Accountant General of the Supreme Court (PD 36, para. 4.1).

20.5.3.2 Part 36 payment notice
A defendant making a Part 36 payment must file a Part 36 payment notice.

Unlike a Part 36 offer, a Part 36 payment notice is not required to set out details of the dates and mechanisms for its acceptance. A Part 36 payment notice must:

(a) State the amount of the payment (CPR, r. 36.6(2)(a)).
(b) State that the payment into court is a Part 36 payment (PD 36, para. 5.1).
(c) State whether it applies to the whole of the proceedings or to part of them or to a particular issue (which part or issue must be identified) (PD 36, para. 5.3; CPR, r. 36.6(2)(b)).
(d) State whether it takes into account any counterclaim (PD 36, para. 5.3; CPR, r. 36.6(2)(c)).
(e) If an interim payment has been made, state that this has been taken into account (PD 36, para. 5.3; CPR, r. 36.6(2)(d)).
(f) If not inclusive of interest, state whether interest is offered in addition and if so the amount, rate and period (PD 36, para. 5.4; CPR, rr. 36.6(2)(e) and 36.22(2)). If interest is not mentioned, the offer is assumed to be inclusive of interest to the last date it could be accepted without the court's permission (r. 36.22(1)).
(g) Be signed by the defendant or by the defendant's legal representative (PD 36, para. 5.1(2)). If the defendant is a company or other corporation, the notice can, by PD 36, para. 5.5, be signed by one of the senior personnel listed in para. 5.6, giving his or her position in the organisation (director, treasurer, secretary etc.).

A defendant to a claim which has both money and non-money parts, who is making money and non-money offers as a proposal to settle the whole claim, must, in the Part 36 payment notice, identify the document which sets out the non-money Part 36 offer (CPR, r. 36.4(3)(a)) and state that acceptance of the Part 36 payment will constitute acceptance of the Part 36 offer as well (r. 36.4(3)(b)). It is suggested that the Part 36 payment notice should also expressly state that the Part 36 offer and Part 36 payment together relate to the whole claim.

Where deduction of social security benefits is relevant, a Part 36 payment notice must include the following statement prescribed by r. 36.23 and PD 36, para. 10.3:

1 [the total amount represented by the Part 36 payment (the gross compensation)].
2 The defendant has reduced this sum by £[   ], in accordance with section 8 of and Schedule 2 to the Social Security (Recovery of Benefits) Act 1997, which was calculated as follows:
Name of benefit   Amount

3 The amount paid in, being the sum of £[   ] is the net amount after the deduction of the amount of benefit.

For the purpose of calculating whether the payment in has been beaten, the payment in is treated as being of the gross sum (CPR, r. 36.23(4)). If the defendant has applied for but is yet to receive the certificate, provided a Part 36 payment is made within seven days of receipt of the certificate, the defendant can make an offer of settlement taking effect as a Part 36 payment backdated to the date of the offer (r. 36.23(2); PD 36, para. 10.2).

If the claim is for provisional damages, the Part 36 payment notice must state whether or not the defendant is offering to agree to an award of provisional damages (CPR, r. 36.7(2)). If so agreeing, the notice must, by r. 36.7(3), also state:

    (a)   that the payment in is made on the assumption that the claimant will not develop a named disease or deterioration;

    (b)   that the offer of provisional damages is conditional on the claimant making any claim for further damages within a limited period; and

    (c)   what that period is.

20.5.3.3 Service   Under CPR, r. 36.6(2) and (3), a Part 36 payment notice is filed by the defendant with the court and is then served by the court on the claimant, unless the defendant notifies the court on making the payment in that the notice has been served by the defendant. If the claimant is legally represented, the Part 36 payment notice must be served on the legal representative (PD 36, para. 11.1). If the defendant serves the notice, a certificate of service must be filed with the court (CPR, r. 36.6(4)). Rule 36.6(3) contemplates that the defendant may serve the notice on the claimant before paying the money into court. This may be significant as, for the purpose of calculating time for acceptance (and so for assessing penalties), a Part 36 payment is 'made' when the claimant is served with the payment notice (r. 36.8(2)).

Where relevant, notice of any payment under the Road Traffic Act 1988, s. 157, must also be served on all other parties, apparently by the defendant rather than by the court (PD 36, para. 11.2).

Although a certificate of recoverable benefits is to be filed under PD 36, the practice direction does not require notice to be given to the claimant or to other parties to the action although the relevant details will appear in the payment notice sent to the claimant. The best practice is to serve a copy of the certificate with the payment notice.

The defendant can increase the payment subsequently, increases being effective when 'notice of the increase' is received by the claimant (r. 36.8(4)).

20.5.4 Acceptance

If a Part 36 payment is accepted without the need for any approval or court permission, then a notice of acceptance must be sent to the defendant and filed with the court (PD 36, para. 7.6). If the defendant is legally represented, the acceptance must be served on the legal representative (PD 36, para. 11.1). A request for payment (form N243) giving addresses and bank details (CPR, r. 36.16 and PD 36, paras 8.1 to 8.5) should also be sent by the claimant to the court (together with a copy of Court Funds Office form 201 if the claim is in the Royal Courts of Justice).

A Part 36 payment can be accepted without the court's permission under the same time limits as a defendant's offer in a non-money claim (CPR, r. 36.11; see 20.4.3). Unless the parties have agreed otherwise, interest accruing up to the date of acceptance goes to the defendant and interest

CHAPTER 20 OFFERS TO SETTLE

accruing thereafter to the claimant (PD 36, para. 7.10). If either party is a child or patient, payment out of court requires a court order (CPR, r. 36.18(1)).

Where the court's permission is not required, r. 36.13(1) states that the claimant will be entitled to costs up to the date of giving notice of acceptance, to be assessed on the standard basis if not agreed (r. 36.13(4)). It is specifically provided that this includes including any costs attributable to the counterclaim if the defendant's payment notice was phrased so as to take this into account (r. 36.13(3)).

On acceptance, the claim will be stayed under r. 36.15 as with a Part 36 offer. If the Part 36 payment related only to part of the claim then only that part will be stayed and costs will be resolved by the court (r. 36.15(3)). As with a defendant's Part 36 offer, a part payment in can be accepted as resolving the entire claim if the claimant abandons the remainder of the claim (r. 36.13(2)).

A claimant who accepts a Part 36 payment in respect of a claim for provisional damages must, within seven days of acceptance, apply for an award of provisional damages (r. 36.7(5)) and cannot obtain payment out of money in court until this application has been disposed of (r. 36.7(6)).

20.5.5 Acceptance where there are multiple defendants

Under CPR, r. 36.17, the position is identical to that described in 20.4.4 in relation to acceptance of a defendant's Part 36 offer.

20.5.6 Acceptance of a combined payment and offer

If the claim is partly a money claim and partly a non-money claim, and the Part 36 payment notice has identified a contemporaneous Part 36 offer, and stated that acceptance of the Part 36 payment will constitute acceptance of the offer as well, then acceptance of either the offer or the payment will be deemed to be acceptance of the offer to settle the whole claim (CPR, r. 36.4(4); PD 36, para. 7.11).

20.5.7 Acceptance after a defence of tender before claim

In these circumstances, an order of the court is required before payment out can be made (CPR, r. 36.18(3)).

20.6 CLAIMANT'S PART 36 OFFER

20.6.1 Introduction

Part 36 of the CPR provides a procedure by which a claimant may offer to settle all or part of the claim 'without prejudice save as to costs'. If the offer complies with the provisions of Part 36 (and so is 'a Part 36 offer') and is refused but at trial the claimant is awarded more than was offered, the court may, under r. 36.21, impose three penalties on the defendant:

(a) It may order interest at up to 10 per cent above base rate to be paid on some or all of the award for some or all of the period starting with the latest date on which the defendant could have accepted the offer without needing the court's permission.

(b) It may order the defendant to pay the claimant's costs from that date on the idemnity basis.

CHAPTER 20   OFFERS TO SETTLE

(c) It may order interest to be paid on those costs at up to 10 per cent above base rate.

'Claimant' here includes a defendant in relation to a counterclaim and in relation to a third-party claim (CPR, r. 20.3(1)).

A claimant's Part 36 offer can be made at any stage after commencement of proceedings (r. 36.2(4)). Although the offer can relate to the whole claim, to any part of it or to any issue (r. 36.5(2)), it seems likely that there will be two main forms of claimant's offer:

(a) the offer to settle a money claim for a particular sum less than that in fact claimed; and

(b) the offer to accept a particular proportion of contributory negligence.

Part 36 offers do not have to be financial (PD 36, para. 2.3). There is nothing to suggest that a claimant's offer to accept, say, an injunction against the defendant in particular terms, would not fall under Part 36.

20.6.2   Notice

A claimant's Part 36 offer must be in writing and must comply with the requirements set out in 20.4.2.

A Part 36 offer is effective when received by the defendant (CPR, r. 36.8(1)) as is an improvement to the offer (r. 36.8(3)). If the defendant is legally represented, the offer must be served on the legal representative (PD 36, para. 11.1).

20.6.3   Acceptance

If the defendant accepts a claimant's Part 36 offer, a notice of acceptance must be sent to the claimant and filed with the court (PD 36, para. 7.6). The notice must contain the claim number and title of the proceedings, identify the claimant's offer to which it is a response and be signed by the defendant or by the defendant's legal representative (PD 36, para. 7.7). Acceptance is effective on receipt of the notice of acceptance by the claimant (CPR, r. 36.8(5)). If the claimant is legally represented, the acceptance must be served on the legal representative (PD 36, para. 11.1). Where the offer and acceptance are pre-issue, although r. 36.10 only applies Part 36 to the offer and not to the acceptance, it would seem sensible to accept in the same format as far as possible.

On acceptance, if the offer relates to the whole claim, the action will be stayed on the terms of the offer with liberty to apply by either party to enforce the terms of the offer (r. 36.15(1) and (2)).

Where an accepted Part 36 offer is in relation to only part of the claim, then under r. 36.15(3) the claim is stayed as to that part and, unless costs are agreed between the parties, the court will resolve liability for costs. Consequently, although the court's permission may not be required to accept the offer, an application may have to be made for a costs order.

In the rules governing acceptance of a claimant's Part 36 offer there is no equivalent of the following two provisions which apply to acceptance of a defendant's offer (see 20.4.3):

(a) r. 36.13(2), which provides for the claimant to accept the defendant's offer relating to part only of the claim and abandon the rest of it (this is irrelevant to a claimant's offer, as it is not within the defendant's power to abandon any part of the claimant's claim);

(b) r. 36.13(3), which provides that costs includes the costs of any counterclaim if the offer was expressed to take a counterclaim into account.

20.6.4 Rejection

There is no requirement in the CPR to notify a claimant of non-acceptance of the claimant's Part 36 offer, although obviously this will often be done, if only in the hopes of an improved offer. Although PD 36 does not make specific provision for improvements to offers, CPR, r. 36.8(3), prescribes that an improvement to an offer is effective on receipt of its details by the offeree. It would seem safest to notify by the same form of notice, suitably adapted, as required for the original offer. The defendant may wish to consider whether there is any tactical or other advantage in inviting the claimant to improve the offer as opposed to making a defendant's Part 36 offer. This is discussed in more detail in 20.8.

20.7 FAILURE TO BEAT A PART 36 PAYMENT OR OFFER

Once an effective Part 36 payment or offer has been made, the issue at trial is whether the offeree is able to recover more (whether in money or non-monetary terms) than the amount or terms paid in or offered. Achieving an identical result to the offer or payment is a failure to beat it. The normal result on a failure to beat a Part 36 offer or payment is that the offeree must pay the costs of the proceedings from the latest date on which the offer or payment could have been accepted without the court's permission. This will be 21 days after the offer or payment was made (CPR, r. 36.11(1)). The reason is that the offeree has achieved nothing by continuing the proceedings beyond that date, and should pay the costs which the offeror has incurred by being required to go through the remaining stages of the litigation. The costs incurred before the latest date for acceptance will be determined under the usual principles regarding costs, which usually means that the overall winner in the litigation recovers these costs from the losing party (r. 44.3(2)(a)).

However, imposing the traditional costs sanction referred to in the previous paragraph will not achieve anything in the case of a claimant's Part 36 offer, because, if it was effective and if the defendant is adjudged liable in a greater sum than the claimant's offer, in the normal course of events the defendant will be paying the whole costs of the claim (albeit on the standard basis) in any event. Alternative financial consequences are therefore provided for claimants' Part 36 offers.

20.7.1 Failure to beat a Part 36 payment

Rule 36.20 of the CPR sets out the costs consequences if 'at the trial a claimant . . . fails to better a Part 36 payment', namely that the claimant will pay the defendant's costs from the latest date for acceptance of the payment without permission of the court, unless it is unjust to do so. If the payment could never be accepted without the permission of the court, it seems that this provision cannot apply, although it is of course entirely within the general discretion of the court as to costs to make an order to the same effect.

20.7.2 Failure to beat a Part 36 offer

Under CPR, r. 36.20, if 'at trial a claimant . . . fails to obtain a judgment which is more advantageous than a [defendant's] Part 36 offer', the claimant will pay the defendant's costs from the date for acceptance of the offer, unless it is unjust to do so. No specific criteria by which the court will assess whether or not it is unjust are provided. It is not unreasonable to suggest that the court will, however, consider similar factors to those listed in r. 36.21(5) (see 20.7.3, where the potential difficulty in a non-monetary claim in establishing what a 'more advantageous' judgment is and the position where a costs-paying party is in receipt of legal aid are discussed).

So, for example, if the defendant's offer (in a negligence case) was to accept 75 per cent liability (and 25 per cent contributory negligence), the claimant has beaten the offer if a judgment awards a degree of contributory negligence of less than 25 per cent.

20.7.3 Failure to beat a claimant's Part 36 offer

Rule 36.21(1) of the CPR sets out the costs consequences if 'at trial— (a) a defendant is held liable for more; or (b) the judgment against a defendant is more advantageous to the claimant', than the terms of the claimant's offer. The first limb is straightforward and of obvious application in money claims. The second limb is more difficult and offers considerable scope for argument about whether or not, for instance, the injunction actually awarded is more or less advantageous to the claimant than the injunction the claimant offered to accept.

The CPR have abandoned Lord Woolf's original scheme for tapering interest (*Final Report*, ch. 11). Rule 36.21(2) provides that where a defendant has not 'beaten' the claimant's offer, the court 'may' order:

> interest on the whole or part of any sum of money (excluding interest) awarded to the claimant at a rate not exceeding 10% above base rate for some or all of the period starting with the latest date on which the defendant could have accepted the offer without needing the permission of the court.

There are circumstances where a claimant's Part 36 offer cannot be accepted at all without the permission of the court (as, for example, under r. 36.18, where either party is a child or patient). Where this is the case it is suggested that r. 36.21(2) cannot apply, because there is no latest date on which the offer could have been accepted without the court's permission and consequently no start date from which the penalty can run. In advising a client, however, it would be dangerous to assume that this is necessarily the way in which the court will interpret the provision (especially perhaps in the case of a child claimant).

Under r. 36.21(3) where a defendant has not beaten the claimant's offer the court 'may also order':

(a) that the claimant is entitled to costs on an indemnity basis from the latest date on which the defendant could have accepted the offer without needing the permission of the court; and
(b) interest on 'those costs' (i.e., only if indemnity costs are ordered) at a maximum of 10 per cent above base rate.

Again, it would appear that if there are circumstances where the defendant can never accept without the court's permission, the provision does not apply.

CHAPTER 20 OFFERS TO SETTLE

It is suggested that the word 'also' in r. 36.21(3) should be read as 'in addition or alternatively' rather than simply as 'in addition'. If read simply as 'in addition' (i.e., that r. 36.21(3) is entirely dependent on higher interest on damages having been awarded under r. 36.21(2)), the rule has no or little application to non-monetary claims, as there is no 'sum of money . . . awarded' to which r. 36.21(2) can apply.

Despite the use in both paras (2) and (3) of r. 36.21 of the words 'the court *may* order' (emphasis added), r. 36.21(4) then provides that the orders referred to in paras (2) and (3) (implying both the interest penalty and the costs penalty rather than just one or the other) *will* be made unless the court 'considers it unjust to do so'. It is unlikely that the claimant will be interested in dislodging this presumption, so it will be for the defendant to persuade the court that the orders should not be made (or should be limited in some way).

In deciding whether it would be unjust to make the penalty orders the court is directed in r. 36.21(5) to:

take into account all the circumstances of the case including—
    (a) the terms of any Part 36 offer;
    (b) the stage in the proceedings when any Part 36 offer or Part 36 payment was made;
    (c) the information available to the parties at the time when the Part 36 offer or Part 36 payment was made; and
    (d) the conduct of the parties with regard to the giving or refusing to give information for the purposes of enabling the offer or payment into court to be made or evaluated.

As when exercising any power under the CPR, the court must seek to give effect to the overriding objective (r. 1.2).

The Legal Aid Act 1988, s. 17, protects the legally aided defendant only against orders for costs and not against orders for higher interest on damages. A legally aided claimant has no such difficulty as his or her penalty for failing to beat a defendant's offer is in costs alone. However, the legal aid position must fall within 'all the circumstances of the case' in r. 36.21(5) as well as being a factor relevant to the financial circumstances of the parties under r. 1.1(2)(c)(iv).

The defendant's legal advisers must not only evaluate the offer carefully, they must also advise the defendant clearly on the effects of not accepting it.

20.8 NON-DISCLOSURE

Rule 36.19(2) of the CPR provides that the fact that a Part 36 payment has been made must 'not be communicated to the trial judge' until both liability and quantum have been decided, unless, by r. 36.19(3):

    (a) the defence is one of tender before claim; or
    (b) proceedings have already been stayed under r. 36.15 after acceptance of a Part 36 offer or payment; or
    (c) liability has been determined before and separately from quantum, and the fact of the Part 36 payment may be relevant to costs on liability.

The effect of failure to accept the defendant's Part 36 payment will then depend on the result at trial.

CHAPTER 20 OFFERS TO SETTLE

20.9 COURT INTERVENTION

20.9.1 Permission

The court's permission is required:

(a) For acceptance after proceedings have begun of a pre-action offer to which r. 36.10, applies.

(b) For a claimant to accept a defendant's Part 36 offer or payment made less than 21 days before the start of the trial, if the parties do not agree liability for costs (r. 36.11(2)).

(c) For a claimant to accept a defendant's Part 36 offer or payment after the time limit for acceptance has expired, if the parties do not agree liability for costs (r. 36.11(2)).

(d) For a defendant to accept a claimant's Part 36 offer made less than 21 days before the start of the trial, if the parties do not agree liability for costs (r. 36.12(2)).

(e) For a defendant to accept a claimant's Part 36 offer after the time limit for acceptance has expired, if the parties do not agree liability for costs (r. 36.12(2)).

(f) For payment out of any sum in court where an offer is made by some but not all of multiple defendants and the claimant does not fall within r. 36.17(2) or (3) (r. 36.17(4)(a)).

(g) For acceptance of a Part 36 offer or payment where either party is a child or a patient (r. 36.18(1)).

PD 36 refers to obtaining the court's permission (paras 7.2 to 7.5) or approval (para. 7.8), in both cases by an application under Part 23. It must be assumed that 'approval' in para. 7.8 means 'permission'. If granted, the order will include a direction for payment out of any money in court and interest (para. 7.9) and an order for costs (para. 7.5).

20.9.2 Order to pay money out of court

An order to pay money out of court is required:

(a) Where a defendant's offer is to settle a claim for provisional damges (CPR, r. 36.7(6)).

(b) Where an offer is made by some but not all of multiple defendants and the claimant does not fall within r. 36.17(2) or (3) (r. 36.17(4)(a)).

(c) Where the claimant has required permission to accept a Part 36 payment after the beginning of the trial (r. 36.18(2)).

(d) Where there has been a defence of tender before claim (r. 36.18(3)).

Applications are to be made under Part 23 and, if granted, the order will include a direction for payment out of any money in court and interest (PD 36, para. 7.9).

20.9.3 Order for costs

An order for costs will be made:

(a) Where an offer is made by some but not all of multiple defendants and the claimant does not fall within CPR, r. 36.17(2) or (3) (r. 36.17(4)(b)).

(b) Where the claimant has required permission to accept a Part 36 payment after the beginning of the trial (r. 36.18(2)).

(c) Where either party fails to 'beat' an offer or payment and penalties are imposed (rr. 36.20 and 36.21).

20.9.4 Withdrawal or reduction

Withdrawal or reduction of money paid into court requires the permission of the court (CPR, r. 36.6(5)). By PD 36, para. 3.4, such an application must be made in accordance with CPR, Part 23, by issuing an application notice supported by evidence. The reasons for seeking the order must be given in the evidence. Traditionally these orders were only made if there was 'good reason', and the formulation in PD 36, para. 3.4, seems to reflect this. The courts were reluctant to find good reason for allowing payments in to be withdrawn or reduced, but would do so if there was a change of circumstances or a change in the law affecting the amount of damages likely to be awarded, or if fresh facts came to light having a bearing on the likely level of damages.

No permission is required if a Part 36 offer (including a claimant's Part 36 offer) is withdrawn or replaced by a less generous offer. However, withdrawing a Part 36 offer results in the costs and other financial consequences being lost (CPR, r. 36.5(8)).

20.9.5 Clarification

Within seven days of receipt of a Part 36 offer, the offeree may make a written request for clarification of it (CPR, r. 36.9(1)). If there is no response to this request or if the clarification offered is inadequate, the offeree may, unless the trial has already begun, apply to court for an order that the offer be clarified (r. 36.9(2); PD 36, para. 6.1). This application should be made in accordance with the provisions of CPR, Part 23. The application notice (which can be relied on as evidence at the hearing if verified by a statement of truth) must set out the respects in which the offer requires clarification. Any order made in response to such an application will specify the date on which the offer is to be treated as having been made (r. 36.9(3)). If clarification is necessary before the offeree can properly consider the offer, this date is likely to be the date of the order, rather than the date on which the offer was received. This pushes back the date from which the penalising orders against the offeree, if made (and the availability of information to the offeree is a factor in that decision), will start to run. It is consequently in the offeror's interest to avoid clarification proceedings.

20.9.6 Other orders

Court orders are required:

(a) Where the claimant applies for provisional damages after accepting a defendant's offer to settle a claim for provisional damages (r. 36.7(5))).

(b) Where proceedings have been stayed after acceptance and the terms of the stay are to be enforced (r. 36.15).

(c) Where the money in court is to be apportioned between Fatal Accidents Act 1976 and/or Law Reform (Miscellaneous Provisions) Act 1934 claimants (PD 36, para. 7.8). There is a specific provision that this application is to be made under CPR, Part 23, and, if granted, the order will include a direction for payment out of any money in court and interest (PD 36, paras 7.8 and 7.9).

20.10 COSTS CONSEQUENCES WHEN BOTH CLAIMANT AND DEFENDANT HAVE MADE AN OFFER

There is nothing in the CPR which specifically governs the position when both parties have used Part 36. An example is probably the

CHAPTER 20 OFFERS TO SETTLE

most instructive method of exploring the question. To simplify the following discussion, interest will be disregarded.

Example

Claimant offers to accept £10,000. Defendant pays £5,000 into court. Neither offer is accepted.

If the trial judge awards:

(a) £4,000, the claimant has failed to better the defendant's payment and pays the defendant's costs from time for acceptance of payment in, unless it is unjust. The defendant has not been held liable for more than the claimant's offer so no unusual costs consequences arise (presumably the order will be that the defendant pays the claimant's costs on the standard basis until time for acceptance of payment in and the claimant pays the defendant's thereafter).

(b) £5,000, the result is the same as in (a).

(c) £8,000, the claimant has bettered the defendant's payment. The defendant has not been held liable for more than the claimant's offer so no unusual costs consequences arise. Subject to the court's discretion, the defendant will pay costs on the standard basis.

(d) £10,000, the result is the same as in (c).

(e) £12,000, the claimant has bettered the defendant's payment so no unusual costs consequences arise. The defendant has been held 'liable for more' than the claimant's offer and will pay additional interest on damages, indemnity costs and additional interest on them from time for acceptance of offer, subject to r. 36.20(5), which lists a number of factors to be taken into account, including the stage at which the defendant's payment in was made and the information available when the defendant's payment in was made as well as the existence of the claimant's offer.

20.11 WHAT SHOULD BE THE RESPONSE TO AN UNACCEPTABLE OFFER OR PAYMENT?

Now that the opportunity to make a payment into court has been extended to both parties, there is a potential dilemma if one's opponent's offer or payment is unacceptable. It is possible, of course, to invite the opponent to improve the offer. An alternative is to make an offer of one's own under Part 36. The question is ultimately whether, by careful use of Part 36, one can reduce the risk to one's own client of rejecting the Part 36 offer and obtaining a worse result at trial.

As in 20.10 examples are probably the best way of exploring this area and interest is ignored for simplicity.

Example

Claimant makes a Part 36 offer of £12,000. Defendant considers claim to be worth £10,000 at most. The timing of the offer and any counter-offer, which could of course also have a significant effect on rejection, is ignored for the purpose of this example, as is the fact that if the claimant improved the offer to £10,000, the defendant would no doubt accept it.

CHAPTER 20 OFFERS TO SETTLE

Result at trial	C's Part 36 offer of £12,000 only	C improves offer to £11,000 at D's instigation	C improves offer to £10,000 at D's instigation	C's offer remains at £12,000 but D pays in £10,000
D wins on liability	D gets costs	D gets costs	D gets costs	D gets costs
C obtains some damages up to £10,000	D has not been held liable for more than the offer. No unusual costs/interest consequences — D pays damages and costs	D has not been held liable for more than the offer. No unusual costs/interest consequences — D pays damages and costs	D has not been held liable for more than the offer. No unusual costs/interest consequences — D pays damages and costs	C has failed to better D's payment in. D pays costs to the payment in and C pays costs thereafter. D has not been held liable for more than C's offer so no unusual costs/interest consequences, D pays damages
C obtains damages of £10,001 to £11,000		D has been held liable for more than the offer. Penalties apply — D pays damages and costs plus higher interest and indemnity costs	D has been held liable for more than the offer. Penalties apply — D pays damages and costs plus higher interest and indemnity costs	C has bettered D's payment in — no unusual costs consequences. D has not been held liable for more than C's offer. No unusual costs/interest consequences — D pays damages and costs
C obtains damages of £11,001 to £11,999	D has not been held liable for more than the offer. No unusual costs/interest consequences — D pays damages and costs	D has been held liable for more than the offer. Penalties apply — D pays damages and costs plus higher interest and indemnity costs		
C obtains damages of £12,000				
C obtains damages exceeding £12,000	D has been held liable for more than the offer. Penalties apply — D pays damages and costs plus higher interest and indemnity costs			C has bettered D's payment in — no unusual costs consequences. D has been held liable for more than the offer. Penalties apply — D pays damages and costs plus higher interest and indemnity costs

Table 20.2 Consequences of offers and counter-offers

Table 20.2 shows the possibilities. If only the claimant has made an offer, the claimant places the defendant on risk if the defendant has undervalued the claim, the claimant (assuming r. 36.20 does not operate to this effect) taking on no risk other than that of losing the trial. The better the claimant's estimate of the risk and the earlier the offer is made, the greater the period for which the defendant is at risk of paying interest of 10 per cent above base rate, indemnity costs and penalty interest on those costs. The saving for the defendant is then either to accept the offer (comparing overcompensating the claimant by accepting an offer that is too high with the amount of additional costs and interest payable if the offer is not accepted) or to exploit r. 36.21(5).

If, on the other hand, the defendant makes a payment into court, risk is placed on the claimant if the claimant has overvalued the claim and a degree of bargaining power is placed in the hands of the defendant. Further, it would appear that the existence of offers by both parties can be a factor in operating r. 36.21(5) in the defendant's favour.

CHAPTER 21   CHANGE OF SOLICITOR

CONTENTS

21.1	Introduction	285
21.2	Presumed continuation	286
21.3	Notice of change	286
21.4	Revocation or discharge of legal aid	286
21.5	Coming off the record	286
21.6	Removal of solicitor on application of another party	287

21.1 INTRODUCTION

A retainer to conduct litigation is generally regarded as an entire contract, with the effect that a solicitor, once retained, must see the litigation to its conclusion. However, the retainer is subject to an implied term that the solicitor may withdraw if there is good cause and provided reasonable notice is given to the client, and the client may terminate the retainer at any time. When a party decides to change solicitors, or to retain a solicitor having previously acted in person, or to start acting in person having previously employed a solicitor, the other parties and the court need to be informed so that future correspondence and court applications, orders and other documents can be sent to the correct address.

Part 6 of the CPR contains general rules on service of documents. Although there are several refinements, some of the basic rules on where litigation documents should be served are:

(a)   Under CPR, r. 6.5(2), each party to litigation must provide an address for service within the jurisdiction.

(b)   Rule 6.5(5) provides that where a solicitor is acting for a party, that party's address for service for all purposes other than service of the claim form is the business address of the solicitor.

(c)   The address for service of a party who is acting in person is usually his residential address or that of his place of business (r. 6.5(3)).

(d)   Any change of address of a party or of a party's solicitor (without changing the identity of the person acting for that party) must be notified in writing to the court and to other parties as soon as the change take place (PD 6, para. 7).

(e)   In recent times the practice has been that if one solicitor acts for a number of parties in an action, it is sufficient to serve on that solicitor a single copy of any documents that need to be served.

The claim form will identify whether the claimant is acting by a solicitor or in person, and the defence or defence and counterclaim form will similarly identify whether the defendant is acting in person or by a solicitor. Part 42 of the CPR contains rules dealing with giving notice of changes relating to representation by solicitors. It is similar in effect to the former provisions in CCR, ord. 50, r. 5, and RSC, ord. 67, but takes a middle course between the simplicity of the old county court rule and the more detailed provisions in RSC, ord. 67.

21.2 PRESUMED CONTINUATION

Once a solicitor is on the court record as acting for a party, by CPR, rr. 42.1 and 42.2(5), that solicitor will be considered to be continuing to act for that party until due notice is given or an order is made in accordance with the CPR, Part 42.

21.3 NOTICE OF CHANGE

By CPR, r. 42.2, notice of change, stating the change and the new address for service, must be filed at court and served on all other parties whenever:

(a) a party who has been acting by a solicitor wants to change his solicitor;
(b) a party who has been acting in person appoints a solicitor to act on his behalf, or
(c) a party who has been acting by a solicitor intends to act in future as a litigant in person.

In the circumstances set out in (a) and (c) above the notice of change must also be served on the former solicitor. The copy of the notice filed at court must state that it has also been served on the other parties, and, if appropriate, the former solicitor. The form of notice of change of solicitor is form N434.

21.4 REVOCATION OR DISCHARGE OF LEGAL AID

Regulation 83 of the Civil Legal Aid (General) Regulations 1989 provides that the retainer of any solicitor acting on behalf of an assisted person determines forthwith upon receipt of a notice of revocation or discharge of a legal aid certificate. As soon as the retainer of a solicitor is ended under reg. 83, the solicitor is required by CPR, r. 42.2(6), to cease to act for the assisted person. If the assisted person wishes to continue the action after the discharge or revocation of the legal aid certificate, he or she must, by r. 42.2(6)(b):

(a) appoint a new solicitor and file and serve notice of change on the court and the other parties; or
(b) if the intention is to act in person, provide an address for service within the jurisdiction. The rule simply says the litigant must 'give' an address for service, without providing who it must be given to. Presumably it must be given to the court and the other parties.

21.5 COMING OFF THE RECORD

Once retained, a solicitor may withdraw only for good cause and upon giving reasonable notice to the client. There may be good cause to withdraw (see *Underwood, Son and Piper* v *Lewis* [1894] 2 QB 306) where the client fails to give instructions, acts unreasonably, or fails or refuses to pay a reasonable sum on account of the past and future costs of the litigation within a reasonable time of a request for payment (Solicitors Act 1974, s. 65(2)). A solicitor who withdraws in the absence of good cause is in breach of the contract of retainer, and as it is an entire contract, will be unable to recover any fees from the client.

CHAPTER 21 CHANGE OF SOLICITOR

When a solicitor ceases to act for a client, whether or not there is a breach of contract as between the solicitor and client, the change has to be entered in the court records by one means or another. In most cases this will be done by the client or any new solicitor retained by the client giving notice of change as discussed in 21.3. If this does not happen, the former solicitor will in practical terms be obliged to come off the record. To do this he will have to apply for an order under CPR, r. 42.3. It is reasonably clear from *Plenty* v *Gladwin* (1986) 67 ALR 26 (High Court of Australia) that such an application has nothing to do with whether or not the solicitor was right to withdraw, but is simply a matter of ensuring that the court's record accords with the reality of whether the solicitor is continuing to act for the client. Unless there are special circumstances to the contrary, orders to come off the record are generally made as a matter of course when it is shown that the solicitor is no longer acting for the party, and that no notice of change has been given.

An application under r. 42.3 is made by application notice, which must be served on the client unless the court directs otherwise, and must be supported by evidence, usually by witness statement (see r. 42.3(2) and Part 23). The application and evidence must not be served on the other parties as it will often contain information which is confidential between the solicitor and client (*Re Creehouse Ltd* [1983] 1 WLR 77).

If an order is made under r. 42.3 that a solicitor has ceased to act, the order must be served on all parties to the proceedings, and if the order is not served by the court, the server must also file a certificate of service in form N215 (r. 42.3(3)).

21.6 REMOVAL OF SOLICITOR ON APPLICATION OF ANOTHER PARTY

Where a solicitor has died, become bankrupt, ceased to practise or gone missing, the court and other parties should be informed and the client's address for service duly altered. Although this is not expressly provided by the CPR, ceasing practice covers a multitude of circumstances, including retirement, changing professions, and also being struck off the roll of solicitors, failing to take out a practising certificate and being suspended from practising.

Normally the client will appoint a new solicitor who will serve and file the appropriate notice of change. However, if no notice of change is served, the position can be regularised on the application of any other party under CPR, r. 42.4, for an order declaring that the solicitor has ceased acting for the relevant party. Under the RSC the phrase 'any other party', which appeared in a number of contexts in the old rules and also appears in the CPR, r. 42.4(1), was interpreted in *Shaw* v *Smith* (1886) 18 QBD 193 as limited to opposite parties, with the result that a co-defendant was not included. There is no prospect of this restrictive interpretation being carried forward into the CPR. The result is that an application under r. 42.4 may be made by any party other than the party whose solicitor is no longer available.

An application notice seeking a declaration under r. 42.4 must be given to the client whose solicitor is unavailable, unless the court otherwise directs. If the declaration is made, a copy of the order must be served on all the other parties, and if the order is not served by the court, the server must also file a certificate of service (r. 42.4(3)).

CHAPTER 22 DISCONTINUANCE

CONTENTS

22.1	Introduction	288
22.2	Distinction between discontinuing and abandoning	288
22.3	What may be discontinued	289
22.4	Permission to discontinue	289
22.5	Procedure for discontinuing	289
22.6	Setting aside notice of discontinuance	290
22.7	Effect of discontinuance	290
22.8	Subsequent proceedings	290

22.1 INTRODUCTION

From time to time a claimant may think better of having commenced proceedings, and will want to pull out of them without incurring all the costs of litigating to trial. It may be, for example, that after seeing the evidence available to the defendant it will be clear that the claim has limited prospects of success. A claimant in this situation may be able to negotiate a compromise with the defendant, who may agree terms which are not too onerous on the claimant. Under the old system a plaintiff could simply allow the case to go to sleep. In the county court this might result in the claim being struck out automatically under CCR, ord. 17, r. 11, after which the defendant would be entitled to apply for an order against the plaintiff for payment of the costs of the action. In the High Court such a case might simply die a natural death, with no one taking any further steps. In both the High Court and county courts, cases drifting in this way could be brought to an end by the defendant applying for 'unless' orders and/or for dismissal for want of prosecution. What in fact happened would depend on the steps, if any, taken by the defendant. Under the old system the plaintiff had the further alternative of seeking to discontinue, either the whole action or just a part. Doing so produced a definite end to the action (or part), but was visited by a costs sanction in that the plaintiff would be liable to pay the defendant's costs of the action.

Under the new system it is rather more difficult to allow a case simply to go to sleep, given the active case management regime now in place. In most situations, a claimant who decides not to proceed should therefore now either seek to come to an accommodation with the defendant, or should discontinue. Any other course will almost certainly result in increased costs liabilities, particularly if there is a contested hearing.

A claimant who wishes to discontinue proceedings under the new system must file a notice of discontinuance. As before, the general rule is that once a claim is discontinued, the claimant has to pay the defendant's costs of the claim.

22.2 DISTINCTION BETWEEN DISCONTINUING AND ABANDONING

Discontinuance as a concept is restricted to causes of action. If a single cause of action gives rise to more than one remedy (or more than one head of damages), some of the remedies or heads of damage may be abandoned without producing a formal discontinuance (CPR, r. 38.1(2)). A claimant abandoning some of the relief claimed simply has to comply with the rules on amendment (see 8.8). The result is that if some of the relief claimed is abandoned, the claimant will almost certainly have to pay the costs of and arising from the amendments to the statements of case, but will incur no wider liability in relation to the costs of the action.

22.3 WHAT MAY BE DISCONTINUED

A claimant may discontinue:

(a) the whole claim (CPR, r. 38.1(1)); or
(b) part of the claim (i.e., some of the causes of action pleaded: r. 38.1(1)); and
(c) against all of the defendants (r. 38.2(3)); or
(d) against some of the defendants (r. 38.2(3)).

22.4 PERMISSION TO DISCONTINUE

Generally, a claimant has the right to discontinue without seeking permission first (CPR, r. 38.2(1)). However, in some cases permission is required. These are:

(a) If an interim injunction has been granted in relation to the claim being discontinued, permission has to be sought from the court (r. 38.2(2)(a)).

(b) If any party has given an undertaking to the court in relation to the claim being discontinued, permission has to be sought from the court (r. 38.2(2)(a));

(c) If the claimant has received an interim payment (whether by agreement or pursuant to a court order) in relation to the claim being discontinued, permission must be sought from the court or consent must be given in writing by the defendant (r. 38.2(2)(b)).

(d) Where there is more than one claimant, the claimant wishing to discontinue must either obtain permission to discontinue from the court, or must obtain consent in writing from all the other claimants (r. 38.2(2)(c)).

If consent is required, the signed consent(s) must be obtained before the claimant files the notice of discontinuance. If the court's permission has to be sought, a separate application for permission must be issued, and the claimant is only allowed to file the notice of discontinuance after the order granting permission is made.

22.5 PROCEDURE FOR DISCONTINUING

A claimant discontinues all or part of the claim by filing a notice of discontinuance (form N279) with the court, and serving a copy on all other parties. Regarding contents:

(a) The notice of discontinuance that is filed at court must state that copies have been served on all other parties (CPR, r. 38.3(2)).

(b) In cases where the consent of another party is required, all copies of the notice of discontinuance must have copies of the consent annexed (r. 38.3(3)).

(c) In cases where there is more than one defendant, the notice of discontinuance must identify the defendants against whom the claim is being discontinued (r. 38.3(4)).

22.6 SETTING ASIDE NOTICE OF DISCONTINUANCE

A defendant may apply for an order setting aside a notice of discontinuance served without consent or permission, provided the application is made within 28 days of the notice (CPR, r. 38.4). A notice of discontinuance was set aside in *Fakih Brothers* v *A.P. Moller (Copenhagen) Ltd* [1994] 1 Lloyd's Rep 103, where a notice of discontinuance was served to avoid the imposition of an onerous term in a consent order, and in *Ernst and Young* v *Butte Mining plc* [1996] 1 WLR 1605, where the notice of discontinuance was served in order to pre-empt the effective service of a counterclaim.

22.7 EFFECT OF DISCONTINUANCE

Notice of discontinuance takes effect, and brings the proceedings to an end, as against each defendant on the date it is served upon him. This of course is subject to any right to apply to set aside the notice, and does not affect the court's power to deal with costs (CPR, r. 38.5).

The position on costs after a discontinuance is much the same as at present, with the claimant being liable for the defendant's costs up to the date of service of the notice of discontinuance (r. 38.6(1)). However, there are no costs consequences regarding discontinued small claims track cases (r. 38.6(3)).

If only part of the claim is discontinued, the claimant's liability is limited to the costs of the part of the claim that has been discontinued. Usually the claimant does not have to pay the defendant's costs following a partial discontinuance until the conclusion of the action. However, the court may in its discretion order these costs to be paid immediately, either after they have been agreed between the parties or after they have been assessed by the court (r. 38.6(2)). Where the claimant is required to pay the costs of the discontinued part of the claim straight away, the liability to do so arises 21 days after the relevant costs are agreed or assessed by the court. Failure to pay gives grounds for the court imposing a stay on the remainder of the proceedings until the costs are paid (r. 38.8).

22.8 SUBSEQUENT PROCEEDINGS

A claimant who discontinues after a defence has been filed is not allowed to commence new proceedings against the same defendant arising out of the same or substantially the same facts as the original action, unless the court first gives permission for the second action to be issued (CPR, r. 38.7). If permission is granted, the court will normally give directions regarding issuing the substantive second action (r. 25.2(3)).

CHAPTER 23 TRIAL

CONTENTS

23.1	Introduction	291
23.2	Listing	292
23.2.1	Fast track listing	292
23.2.2	Multi-track listing	293
23.2.3	Settlement before trial	293
23.3	Trial timetables	293
23.4	Statement of issues	294
23.5	Trial bundles	295
23.6	Disposal without an oral hearing	296
23.7	Mode of trial	297
23.7.1	Trial by jury	297
23.7.2	Open court or in private	297
23.7.3	Trial location	298
23.8	Conduct of the trial	298
23.9	Drawing up judgment after trial	299
23.9.1	Procedure	299
23.9.2	Special forms of judgment	299
23.9.3	Correction of errors and appeals	300
23.10	Non-attendance	300
23.11	Register of county court judgments	300
23.12	Interest on judgment debts	301

23.1 INTRODUCTION

Although trials are the focus of almost every part of civil procedure, they have always been very expensive. Most parties therefore make concentrated efforts at some stage to reach agreement with their opponents in order to avoid trial, and in practice, under the old system, just a tiny proportion of cases actually went to trial. Whether this will remain the case under the CPR remains to be seen. A significant part of the reforms is the encouragement of pre-action negotiations on an informed basis through compliance with pre-action protocols. If this part of the reforms operates as intended, fewer actions should be brought under the new system. However, for those cases that are brought, the essential steps in preparing for trial will have to be completed far sooner after commencing proceedings than under the old system. Under the new system fast track and many multi-track cases will be given trial dates at an early stage in the proceedings, with trials being held perhaps six to 12 months after issue, depending on the directions made in each case. It may well be that many litigants, once they have issued proceedings and incurred most of the costs of preparing for trial, will be less willing to settle in the run-up to the trial than under the old system. Other reforms should restrict the length of trials, reduce the expert evidence required, limit the recoverable costs of trial and generally reduce the expense of the trial itself. These reforms are likely to reduce the incentive to settle in order to save cost. The result may well be that there will be a substantial increase in the number of cases that are actually tried.

The move to a system of judicial case management has led to a number of procedural reforms. These include:

(a) Holding pre-trial reviews in selected multi-track cases a few weeks before trial. These will usually be heard by the trial judge, and one of their main purposes is to decide how to conduct the trial in the most efficient manner.

(b) Setting of trial timetables in advance, limiting the amount of time allowed for speeches and questioning of witnesses.

(c) A greater emphasis on written preparation.

(d) The use of Fridays as preparation days in long trials (although this is not set out anywhere in the CPR or practice directions, and is likely to be a matter for individual courts and judges).

Small claims track cases will be determined by district judges in much the same way as arbitrations were under the previous system. Hearings will be informal, and the rules of evidence will not be applied strictly (CPR, r. 27.8). Further details can be found in chapter 12. This chapter will be limited to a consideration of trials in fast track and multi-track cases.

23.2 LISTING

The present system of fixtures, running and warned lists is to be replaced by a system of fixed trial dates and trial windows.

23.2.1 Fast track listing

A trial date or a period in which the trial is to take place will be given in fast track cases as part of the standard directions at the track allocation stage (see 13.2, especially 13.2.8). If a trial period is given, it should not exceed three weeks. The trial date or period should not be more than 30 weeks from the date of the directions. The trial date or period will be confirmed or altered at the listing stage, which is fixed as one of the standard fast track directions, and is usually about eight weeks before trial see 13.2 and 13.4).

In his *Final Report*, ch. 3, para. 28, Lord Woolf said in relation to fast track listing: 'I attach great importance to trial dates being honoured and I know that the Court Service is already working towards developing an effective listing system to meet the needs of the fast track'. The report went on to explain the difficulties and delays that are likely if all cases are given fixed dates, which stem largely from the fact that most cases settle, and the probability that when this happens the courts will not be in use for a substantial part of the working week. It also identified a number of well-known problems in the present listing system. These include the Court Service being unable to find a judge or court for some trials when they are listed; urgent applications being listed immediately before trials, resulting in trials being delayed or adjourned; the practice of the courts deliberately 'overbooking' in the hope that most of the cases booked for one particular day will settle; and 'block listing' a number of cases for the same time in circumstances where it is almost inevitable that the parties and witnesses in some of the cases blocked together will have to wait in court for a substantial time before their cases are reached. All these problems, if they persist, will have a substantial impact on fast track cases. These cases are intended to be tried within a single day, and have restrictions on the costs recoverable, both of which may be rendered meaningless if listing shortcomings result in adjournments and part-heard trials.

As recognised by the *Final Report*, ch. 3, para. 31, ensuring fast track cases are tried as intended by the new system will involve changes in the working practices of everyone involved. Practitioners are under an obligation to provide accurate information in their listing questionnaires to enable hearing times to be calculated on a realistic basis. District judges will need to make realistic assessments of hearing times based on the information on the court files. Listing officers will need to make provision for hearing urgent matters in ways that do not interfere with fast track trials, and must provide specific staggered times for hearings rather than block lists.

23.2.2 Multi-track listing

The key obligation in the CPR regarding fixing multi-track cases for trial is in r. 29.2(2), which provides that the court must fix the trial date or period in which the trial will take place as soon as practicable. Given the wide variety of cases on the multi-track this will vary considerably from case to case. For some cases the trial date or period may be given in the directions made at the track allocation stage. In other cases it may not be possible until a considerable time later, perhaps in a case management conference or pre-trial review. Like fast track cases, there is a listing questionnaire procedure in multi-track cases (see 14.6). Directions for filing these questionnaires will be made at some stage in the directions process, normally with a view to the questionnaires being filed about 10 weeks before the intended trial. The trial date will be confirmed or altered at that stage.

As multi-track trials may sometimes stretch over several days or weeks, minor delays due to urgent applications being listed first are not so likely to have such an impact as in fast track cases, so the concerns noted in 23.2.1, although still important, are not so fundamental.

It is interesting to note that if the court gives a trial period in a multi-track case instead of a fixture, the period should be just one week (r. 29.8(c)(ii)), rather than the possible three-week period for fast track cases.

23.2.3 Settlement before trial

If an action is settled, whether by agreement or acceptance of a Part 36 offer, or is discontinued, in the period between the giving of a trial date or window and the commencement of the trial, it is the duty of the parties to notify the listing officer for the trial court immediately (PD 39, para. 4.1). If an order is drawn up giving effect to a settlement or discontinuance, a copy of the order should be lodged with the listing officer.

23.3 TRIAL TIMETABLES

The court must, in consultation with the parties, set a timetable for the trial, unless it considers that it would be inappropriate to do so (CPR, rr. 28.6 and 29.8). In multi-track cases, if there is a pre-trial review, that is the occasion when the court must set the trial timetable. In other cases on the fast or multi-tracks, the court sets the timetable either at a listing hearing (which is rarely required) or when (or shortly after) it lists the case for trial (rr. 28.6(1) and 29.8(i)). Pre-trial reviews are appropriate in only some multi-track cases, so trial timetables are most likely to be set when the court lists the case for trial. Thus, for most cases trial timetables will be set by the court of its own initiative without a hearing, but after consulting with the parties (r. 39.4). If no trial timetable is laid down before trial, the trial judge may lay down a timetable at the start of the trial (PD 28, para. 8.3, for fast track cases; PD 29, para. 10.3, for cases on the multi-track).

Parties will need to make sure that any views they might have regarding the trial timetable are notified to the court at the same time as they file their listing questionnaires. Among the matters to be considered are:

(a) whether an opening speech is required on behalf of the claimant, and if so, how long will be required for this;
(b) how much time will be required in chief to elucidate or expand upon the witness statements relied upon on behalf of the client;
(c) which of the other side's witnesses it will be necessary to cross-examine, and which of their witnesses' evidence can be agreed, whether in whole or in part (and if the latter, which parts);
(d) how much of the expert evidence can be agreed, and how many of the experts need to be called to give oral evidence at the trial;
(e) how long each of the closing speeches will require.

Other factors will include whether the trial should be limited to certain specified issues, the order in which witnesses should be called and the length of time required for delivery of judgment and arguments about costs and any other outstanding matters.

It is important that the trial timetable laid down is realistic, because, unless the trial judge makes an order to the contrary, the trial will follow the pattern laid down in the timetable (rr. 28.7 and 29.9). Any party disagreeing with trial timetable directions should appeal against them or apply for them to be varied within 14 days of them being served. If an application is not made until after that 14 days, the court will assume that the party was content that the directions were correct in the circumstances then existing (PD 28, para. 4.2(2) (fast tract); PD 29, para. 6.6(2) (multi-track)).

One of the objects in setting trial timetables is to limit the length of trials. The time given will therefore usually be restrictive. Advocates will consequently be forced to give even more careful consideration to the questions they want to put to the various witnesses, as time in court will be at a premium. The *Final Report* recognised that more time will be required for preparation, which is why recommendation 50 was that there would be no sittings on Fridays.

23.4 STATEMENT OF ISSUES

One of the matters to be considered on a pre-trial review (if one is held) is the preparation of a statement of the issues to be tried (*Final Report*, ch. 5, para. 26). In complex cases this document will assist in focusing on the matters that need to be dealt with. The court may decide to use some of its more far-reaching case management powers to ensure that the trial is focused on what the court regards as the real issues in the case, rather than what the parties may want to keep in issue if they can. The court, for example, has power:

(a) to decide which issues need full investigation at trial, and to dispose of the others summarily (such as by fixing a summary judgment hearing of its own initiative: CPR, r. 1.4(2)(c));
(b) to direct that part of the proceedings be dealt with separately (r. 3.1(2)(e));
(c) to order the trial of preliminary issues, or the split trial of liability and quantum or other issues (r. 3.1(2)(i) and (l))
(d) to decide the order in which issues are to be resolved or tried (rr. 1.4(2)(d) and 3.1(2)(j));
(e) to give directions on the issues on which it requires evidence (r. 32.1(1)(a));
(f) to give directions on the nature of the evidence it requires to decide the issues it identifies (r. 32.1(1)(b)); and
(g) to direct how the evidence is to be placed before the court (r. 32.1(1)(c)).

In multi-track cases, PD 29, paras 5.6 and 5.7, provide that the parties are required to consider, before the court holds a case management conference, whether a case summary will be helpful. This is not quite the same thing as a statement of issues, but is a document designed to assist the court in understanding the issues and questions in the case. A case summary should be no more than 500 words, should set out a brief chronology, must state the issues of fact which are agreed and in dispute, and should set out the evidence required to decide the disputed issues.

23.5 TRIAL BUNDLES

All the documents likely to be referred to at trial should be placed into paginated trial bundles for use by the judge, witnesses and parties. Directions regarding the preparation and lodging of trial bundles will commonly be included with the directions made at the listing stage, but the rules require a bundle to be lodged not more than seven and not less than three days before the trial (CPR, r. 39.5(2)). Standard fast track directions as set out in the appendix to PD 28 provide, slightly inconsistently, that in fast track cases trial bundles must be lodged at court at least seven days before trial. If there is a trial window, presumably these periods are to be calculated from the start of the window. Although there is no duty to do so in the rules, a defendant should, as a matter of practicality, notify the solicitor for the claimant about 14 days before the start of the trial of the documents it wants to be included in the trial bundles. The claimant will need to compile identical bundles also for each of the parties and another one for use by the witnesses at the trial (PD 39, para. 3.10). The originals of the documents in the bundle should be available for production at the hearing (PD 39, para. 3.3).

Detailed rules governing the format of trial bundles, which differ in a number of respects from the existing rules, are to be found in PD 39, para. 3. These are that:

(a) The bundles should contain copies of:

(i) the claim form and all statements of case;
(ii) a case summary and/or chronology where appropriate;
(iii) all requests for further information and the answers;
(iv) all witness statements and summaries to be relied upon;
(v) any hearsay notices;
(vi) any notices of intention to rely on plans, photographs etc. under CPR, r. 33.6;
(vii) all experts' reports and responses to questions to those experts;
(viii) any order giving trial directions; and
(ix) any other necessary documents. This last category will include all the relevant contemporaneous documentation and documentary evidence, as well as relevant correspondence.

(b) The bundles should be continuously paginated throughout, and indexed with a description of each document with its page number.
(c) If any of the documents is illegible, it should be followed by a typed transcript with a suitable cross-reference.
(d) Where the bundle exceeds 100 pages, numbered dividers should be used between groups of documents.
(e) If the documentation is particularly voluminous, a separate core bundle should be compiled containing the most important documents with cross-references to where the documents it contains can be found in the main bundles.
(f) The bundles should normally be contained in ring or lever arch files. If more than one file is needed, they should be in different colours or should be clearly marked by distinguishing letters, and obviously the same coding should be used for each set of the bundles. It is sometimes convenient to have a separate file containing the expert evidence.

The contents of the bundles should be agreed where possible (PD 39, para. 3.9). The parties should also, if possible, agree which of the documents in the bundles are authentic, and which of the documents are to be treated as evidence of the facts they state even if hearsay notices have not been served. The last point seems to contain a misunderstanding of the Civil Evidence Act 1995, which provides in s. 1(1) that in civil proceedings evidence will not be excluded on the ground that it is hearsay, and by s. 2(4) that any failure to serve a hearsay notice (even if required) does not affect admissibility, but only goes to the questions of costs and weight.

Where it is not possible to agree the contents of the bundles, a summary of the points on which the parties are unable to agree should be included.

23.6 DISPOSAL WITHOUT AN ORAL HEARING

The *Final Report*, recommendation 49, was that suitable cases should be determined on the statements of case without the need for an oral hearing, where this would save time and costs. Rule 1.4(2)(j) of the CPR implements this by providing that active case management includes a power to deal with cases without the parties needing to attend at court. It is expected that this power will be used most often in cases raising straightforward points of construction or law, where the facts are agreed or not in dispute and where the parties agree to this type of determination.

23.7 MODE OF TRIAL

23.7.1 Trial by jury

There are statutory rights in the County Courts Act 1984, s. 66, and the Supreme Court Act 1981, s. 69, to trial by jury in some cases, so the circumstances in which juries will be used are unchanged by the CPR. The right to trial by jury will therefore continue for actions in deceit, libel, slander, malicious prosecution and false imprisonment. The exceptions relating to cases involving prolonged examination of documents or accounts, or scientific or local investigations which cannot conveniently be made by a jury, also continue. Under the old system the correct time to request a jury was the summons for directions. Under the new system this will be at the allocation questionnaire stage or case management conference.

23.7.2 Open court or in private

The general rule in CPR, r. 39.2(1), is that trials will be conducted in public, but there are exceptions. These include cases involving national security or confidential information, or where a private hearing is necessary to protect the interests of a child or mental patient. There is also a general power to hold hearings in private where it is necessary in the interests of justice. A number of specific types of proceedings which will be conducted in private are set out in PD 39, para. 1.5, broadly as follows:

(a) mortgage possession claims against individuals;
(b) repossession claims for non-payment of rent in respect of dwelling houses;
(c) most hearings relating to the enforcement and execution of judgments, including applications to suspend warrants, applications to vary or suspend payment of judgment debts by instalments, applications for charging orders, garnishee orders, attachment of earnings, administration orders, the appointment of receivers, and the oral examination of judgment debtors;
(d) the determination of an assisted person's liability for costs under the Legal Aid Act 1988, s. 17, and the Civil Legal Aid (General) Regulations 1989, reg. 127;
(e) applications for security for costs under the Companies Act 1985, s. 726(1) (nothing is said about similar applications under the preserved RSC, ord. 23);
(f) proceedings under the Consumer Credit Act 1974;
(g) proceedings under the Inheritance (Provision for Family and Dependants) Act 1975;
(h) proceedings under the Protection from Harassment Act 1997; and
(i) hearings which involve the interests of a child or patient.

Where a hearing is to proceed in private a sign to that effect will be placed on the door to the court or room where the hearing is taking place. After a hearing in private the order drawn up will be clearly marked in the title 'Before [name of judge] sitting in private'. Anyone other than a party will not be allowed to obtain a copy of the judgment or the order except with the leave of the judge who decided the matter (PD 39, para. 1.12). On the other hand, if the hearing was in public anyone can obtain copies of the judgment and order after paying the appropriate fee.

23.7.3 Trial location

Normally a trial will take place at the court where the case has been proceeding, but it may be transferred to another court for trial if this is appropriate having regard to the convenience of the parties and the availability of court resources (PD 28, para. 8.1, for the fast track; PD 29, para. 10.1, for cases on the multi-track). Multi-track cases will generally have been transferred to civil trial centres when allocated to the multi-track (if commenced in a feeder court).

23.8 CONDUCT OF THE TRIAL

Before a trial the court should be provided with a written statement of the name and address of each advocate, his or her qualification as an advocate, and the party for which he or she acts (PD 39, para. 5). It is unclear whether this will continue to be done, as at present, by advocates completing a slip provided by the court immediately before the hearing.

The trial judge will generally have read the papers in the trial bundle before the trial. Usually if that has been done, an opening speech may be dispensed with (PD 28, para. 8.2, for the fast track; PD 29, para. 10.2, for cases on the multi-track). The trial will then follow the timetable previously laid down, or laid down by the trial judge at the start, or will follow the traditional sequence of events.

As before the CPR, witness statements of witnesses called at trial will stand as the evidence-in-chief unless the court otherwise orders (CPR, r. 32.5(2)). Under the old rules, witnesses could amplify their evidence by agreement between the parties or to deal with the new matters arising since exchange, but otherwise only with the leave of the court. Under r. 32.5(3) and (4), however, witnesses will be confined to their exchanged statements unless the court grants permission, which it will grant only if it considers there is good reason to allow the witness:

(a) to amplify the witness statement; and/or
(b) to give evidence on new matters which have arisen since the statement was served.

What will be regarded as a sufficiently 'good reason' to allow supplementary questions remains to be seen. There is a fear that different judges will take different views. Witness statements drafted in a deliberately concise way in accordance with the ethos of the *Final Report* (see ch. 12, paras 54 to 59 on avoiding elaborate over-drafting) may fall into the trap (which was also mentioned in the *Final Report* at ch. 12, para. 55) of encountering a trial judge who refuses to allow the witness to depart from or amplify the witness statement.

Witnesses who are called at trial may be cross-examined on their witness statements, whether or not their statements are referred to in chief (CPR, r. 32.11).

Exhibits which are handed in and proved during the course of the trial will be recorded in an exhibit list and kept in the custody of the court until the conclusion of the trial, unless the judge directs otherwise (PD 39, para. 7). At the conclusion of the trial the parties have the responsibility for taking away and preserving the exhibits pending any possible appeal.

Further discussion on how the new rules impact on the law of evidence can be found in chapters 16 to 19.

The time limits imposed by trial timetables may have the practical effect of forcing advocates to make even greater use of skeleton arguments, so as to ensure they are able to cover the required ground within the time limited by the court.

The court will always record judgments given at trial, both in the High Court and county courts. Often the evidence will also be recorded (PD 39, para. 6.1). Unofficial tape-recording is a contempt of court.

23.9 DRAWING UP JUDGMENT AFTER TRIAL

23.9.1 Procedure

Normally the judgment after a trial will be drawn up by the court (CPR, r. 40.3), although the court may order a party to draw it up, or a party may agree to do so with the court's permission. If drawn up by a party, sufficient copies must be filed for service on all parties, and the draft will be checked by the court before it is sealed. Once it is sealed, it will be served by the court on all the parties (rr. 40.2(2) and 40.4(1)(b)).

Although there is likely to be a delay between judgment being pronounced and being sealed and served, r. 40.7(1) provides that judgment takes effect from the day it is given. A judgment for the payment of money (including costs) must be complied with within 14 days of the judgment, unless the court specifies some other date for compliance (r. 40.11). It may, for example, instead of requiring immediate payment, impose an order for payment by instalments.

23.9.2 Special forms of judgment

23.9.2.1 Counterclaims The court has power to give separate judgments when dealing with cases where there are claims and counterclaims. It also has power, as at present, to order a set-off between the two claims, and simply enter judgment for the balance (CPR, r. 40.13(2)). Where it does so, it retains power to make separate costs orders in respect of the claims and counterclaims (r. 40.13(3)).

23.9.2.2 Part owners in relation to claims for the detention of goods In a claim by a person who is one of several people with interests in goods which are the subject of proceedings for wrongful interference and which is not based on a right to possession, any judgment can only be for damages unless all other part owners give written authority to the claimant to represent them (CPR, r. 40.14).

23.9.2.3 Interim payments Detailed rules for the form of judgments given in cases where there have been interim payments are laid down in PD 25 Interim Payments. In a preamble to the judgment in such a case there should be set out the total amount awarded and the amounts and dates of all interim payments. The total amount awarded should then be reduced by the total amount of the interim payments, with judgment being given for the balance. If the interim payments exceed the amount awarded at trial, by virtue of CPR, r. 25.8(2), the judgment should set out any orders made for repayment, reimbursement, variation or discharge, and any award of interest on the overpaid interim payments.

23.9.2.4 Provisional damages In personal injuries cases where provisional damages are awarded, r. 41.2(2) of the CPR provides that the order making the award:

(a) must specify the disease or type of deterioration in respect of which an application may be made for further damages at a future date;
(b) must specify the period within which that application may be made; and
(c) may be made in respect of more than one disease or type of deterioration, and may, in respect of each disease or type of deterioration, specify a different period for applying for further damages.

The periods for applying for further damages may be extended. If the deterioration occurs, the claimant must give 28 days' notice of his intention to ask for further damages. Within 21 days of the expiry of the 28 days' notice the claimant has to apply to the court for directions. Otherwise, the rules relating to applying for interim payments (described at 9.11) apply on the application for further damages (r. 41.3(6)).

23.9.3 Correction of errors and appeals

As under the old rules, the court has power under the CPR to correct any accidental slip or omission in any judgment (r. 40.12(1)). Any alleged substantive error can be corrected only on appeal (see chapter 25).

23.10 NON-ATTENDANCE

A trial may proceed despite the non-attendance of any of the parties, and the court may simply strike out that party's claim or defence (CPR, r. 39.3(1)). In provisions similar to the old rules on non-attendance, the court has a power to restore proceedings (or any part of proceedings) that have been struck out due to non-attendance (r. 39.3(2)), and may set aside any judgment entered in such circumstances (r. 39.3(3)). Applications to set aside or restore must be supported by evidence (r. 39.3(4)). In place of the general discretion to set aside given by the old rules, r. 39.3(5) now provides that orders to restore or set aside may only be granted if the applicant:

(a) acted promptly when he found out that the court had exercised its power to strike out or enter judgment or otherwise make an order against him; and
(b) had a good excuse for not attending; and
(c) has a reasonable prospect of success at a reconvened trial.

These conditions are cumulative. They are similar to those enunciated by the Court of Appeal in *Shocked* v *Goldschmidt* [1998] 1 All ER 372 for the equivalent applications under the old rules. The predominant requirement according to *Shocked* is the reason for not attending. The new rule does not on its face indicate the relative weighting of the three factors, which is presumably left to the discretion of the court.

23.11 REGISTER OF COUNTY COURT JUDGMENTS

The register of county court judgments operated by Registry Trust Ltd has statutory force under the County Courts Act 1984, ss. 73 and 73A, and the Register of County Court Judgments Regulations 1985 (SI 1985/1807) outside the CCR, so will continue in operation in the same form as before.

23.12 INTEREST ON JUDGMENT DEBTS

The authority for claiming interest on judgment debts derives from statutory provisions which operate outside the rules of court. The Judgments Act 1838, s. 17, and the County Courts Act 1984, s. 74, are the general provisions, which allow simple interest, currently at 8 per cent per annum, on all High Court money judgments and county court money judgments of £5,000 and more. In addition a county court judgment for any amount of money carries interest at 8 per cent if it is in respect of a debt which is a qualifying debt for the purposes of the Late Payment of Commercial Debts (Interest) Act 1998. A debt is a qualifying debt for the purposes of that Act if it was created by virtue of an obligation under a contract to which the Act applies (s. 3(1) of the Act). The Act is being brought into force in stages between 1 November 1998 and 1 November 2002. In the first phase it applies to commercial contracts for the supply of goods and services where the supplier is a small business and the purchaser is a large business or a United Kingdom public authority, as defined in the Late Payment of Commercial Debts (Interest) Act 1998 (Commencement No. 1) Order 1998 (SI 1998/2479).

Under CPR, r. 40.8, interest on costs now runs from the date the judgment is given. Under the old rules it ran from the date the judgment was entered. After a claim is automatically struck out for non-payment of the fees payable at the allocation or listing stages, or after acceptance of a payment in or an offer to settle, or after a claim is discontinued, interest on costs runs from the date of the event giving rise to the entitlement to the costs (i.e., the date of striking out, acceptance, or service of the notice of discontinuance) (r. 40.8).

CHAPTER 24 COSTS

CONTENTS

24.1	Introduction	303
24.2	General principles	304
24.3	Costs order	305
24.3.1	Range of possible costs orders	305
24.3.2	Interim costs orders	305
24.3.3	Fixed costs on judgments etc.	307
24.3.4	Costs of pre-commencement disclosure and disclosure against non-parties	308
24.3.5	Costs after transfer	308
24.3.6	Costs before track allocation	308
24.3.7	Reallocation from the small claims track	309
24.3.8	Costs after an appeal	309
24.3.9	Notifying client	309
24.4	Rights to costs	309
24.4.1	Payments in and offers to settle	309
24.4.2	Discontinuance	310
24.5	Costs orders against non-parties	310
24.6	Fast track costs	310
24.7	Method of quantification of costs	312
24.7.1	Summary assessment	312
24.7.2	Detailed assessment	312
24.7.3	Discretion	313
24.8	Basis of quantification	313
24.8.1	Standard basis	313
24.8.2	Indemnity basis	314
24.8.3	Choice of basis	314
24.9	Procedure for detailed assessment of costs	314
24.9.1	Appropriate office	314
24.9.2	Commencement of detailed assessment proceedings	315
24.9.3	Bill of costs	315
24.9.4	Points of dispute	316
24.9.5	Default costs certificate	317
24.9.6	Reply	317
24.9.7	Assessment hearing	317
24.9.8	Assessment procedure between solicitor and own client under the Solicitors Act 1974, Part III	318
24.9.9	Costs of assessment	318
24.9.10	Failure to adhere to time limits	319
24.9.11	Interim costs certificate	319
24.9.12	Final costs certificate	319
24.9.13	Appeals against assessment decisions	319
24.9.14	Misconduct	320
24.10	Conditional fee agreements	320
24.11	Litigants in person	321
24.12	Wasted costs orders	321

CHAPTER 24 COSTS

24.1 INTRODUCTION

One of the main aims of the new reforms is to provide a system of civil justice which is more affordable. Allied to this is the goal of making the costs of litigation more predictable, so that clients will have a far clearer idea of the likely cost of proceedings they might become involved in at as early a stage as possible. These objectives are seen as being achievable by a combination of measures. These are:

(a) Increasing the number of cases dealt with as small claims by raising the basic threshold to £5,000. As under the old system, costs recoverable from the losing party will be limited to the court fees paid by the successful party, a nominal fixed sum to cover the claimant's solicitor's costs of issuing the claim, and limited witness expenses and experts' fees (CPR, r. 27.14). Costs in small claims track cases are dealt with in chapter 12.

(b) Imposing a limited costs regime on fast track cases. Details of the new scheme for fast track costs have not yet been decided, and for the time being most of the existing costs system will continue in operation. There are some changes that will have immediate effect. One is that at the end of any fast track trial the usual position will be that the trial judge will simply make a summary assessment of the winner's costs of the action there and then. Another is that there will be a system of limited fixed trial costs, which will depend on the value of the claim. An outline of the latest proposals for fast track costs is given at 24.6 below.

(c) Increasing the level of judicial case management of cases, with the aim of focusing case preparation on the real issues in the case, and ensuring litigation progresses to trial without undue delay.

(d) Requiring the parties' solicitors to provide costs estimates at the allocation and listing stages.

(e) Widening the categories of cases which may be funded under conditional fee agreements. Litigants who take advantage of conditional fee arrangements will know that, provided they keep to the agreement they reach with their solicitors, they will not have to pay anything towards their own lawyers' costs. By taking out insurance they may also be able to obtain protection against having to pay the costs of the other side.

These measures, taken together, are intended to increase the possibilities of obtaining access to justice through the civil courts for middle-income members of society. It was notorious that the old system gave a good service to people on low incomes who would often be able to make use of legal aid, and for the reasonably rich, who could pay the costs of litigation and could often offset the expense against their tax liabilities, whereas people between these extremes could ill afford their own lawyers' fees, let alone having to pay their opponent's costs as well if they lost.

The effect of judicial case management is a pervasive feature of the CPR, and is a recurring theme throughout this Guide. The overriding objective requires the courts to deal with cases in ways that will save expense and which are proportionate to the nature of the case (CPR, r. 1.1(2)). The impact of the extension of conditional fee arrangements is considered in chapter 3, together with the related issues raised by the reduced future availability of legal aid in civil proceedings. The rules on costs in the CPR cover not only the costs recoverable between the parties (usually on the basis that the winner recovers its costs from the loser), but also the costs of proceedings before arbitrators, umpires, tribunals and other statutory bodies, and cases where the costs between a solicitor and his or her client may be assessed by the court (r. 43.2(2)(iii)). This chapter will consider the specific rules relating to costs in the CPR, it will then discuss fast track costs, and then look at the new system for quantifying costs in multi-track cases.

24.2 GENERAL PRINCIPLES

The two main principles when it comes to deciding which party should pay the costs of an application or of the whole proceedings are unchanged, namely:

(a) the costs payable by one party to another are in the discretion of the court (Supreme Court Act 1981, s. 51 and CPR, r. 44.3(1)); and

(b) the general rule, as now stated in r. 44.3(2), is that the unsuccessful party will be ordered to pay the costs of the successful party ('costs follow the event' in the old terminology).

The second of these rules is prefaced by the phrase 'If the court decides to make an order about costs', which is very similar to the phrase used in the equivalent rule in the RSC (which is ord. 62, r. 3(3), 'If the court in the exercise of its discretion sees fit to make any order as to the costs of any proceedings'). Case law under the old system (*Gupta v Klito* (1989) *The Times*, 23 November 1989) established that a successful party in normal circumstances was entitled to have an order for costs against the loser, with limited exceptions, such as cases where a successful plaintiff recovered no more than nominal damages, or where the successful party acted improperly or unreasonably (*Re Elgindata Ltd (No. 2)* [1992] 1 WLR 1207) or where the issue on which a party succeeded was raised for the first time by amendment at a very late stage (*Beoco Ltd v Alfa Laval Co. Ltd* [1995] QB 137). This general approach is unlikely to alter under the new system.

In exercising its discretion on costs the court is required to have regard to all the circumstances, and in particular to the following matters (CPR, r. 44.3(4) and (5)):

(a) the extent to which the parties followed any applicable pre-action protocol;

(b) the extent to which it was reasonable for the parties to raise, pursue or contest each of the allegations or issues;

(c) the manner in which the parties pursued or defended the action or particular allegations or issues;

(d) whether the successful party exaggerated the value of the claim;

(e) whether a party was only partly successful; and

(f) any payment into court or admissible offer to settle.

The first of these factors is one of the methods by which pre-action protocols will be enforced, albeit indirectly (others include a less tolerant attitude on applications by defaulting parties for more time and for relief from sanctions and the interest sanctions discussed at 11.8.7). PD Protocols, para. 2.3, provides that if the court concludes that non-compliance with a pre-action protocol led to the commencement of proceedings which otherwise might not have been commenced, or to costs being incurred which might have been avoided, the court may order the defaulting party to pay all or part of those costs, or to pay those costs on an indemnity basis. Factors (b) and (e) indicate there will be a greater willingness than under the old system to take into account the extent to which the overall winner was in fact successful on the various issues, heads of claim etc. raised in the case, when dealing with costs. This is intended to support the aspects of the overriding objective relating to identifying the real issues in the case, and only pursuing those issues to trial (see CPR, r. 1.4(2)(b) and (c)). The third factor, which covers unreasonable conduct, has always been relevant on costs, but could also be used against parties who fail to conduct litigation in accordance with the new ethos, such as those who are unreasonably uncooperative (see r. 1.4(2)(a)). Exaggeration of the value of a claim (factor (d)) will obviously be relevant where the claim is inflated for the purpose of bringing it in the High Court or to have the case allocated to a higher track than it deserves. It could also be used in cases where exaggeration of the claim makes it difficult for the defendant to assess its true value for the purposes of making an offer to settle or a payment into court.

24.3 COSTS ORDERS

24.3.1 Range of possible costs orders

Under CPR, r. 44.3(6), there are seven possible variations from the main rule that the unsuccessful party should pay the whole of the successful party's costs. These variations are:

(a) that a party must pay only a proportion of another party's costs;
(b) that a party must pay a specified amount in respect of the other side's costs;
(c) that a party must pay costs from or until a certain day only;
(d) that a party must pay costs incurred before proceedings have begun;
(e) that a party must pay costs relating only to certain steps taken in the proceedings, although an order of this type can only be made if an order in either of the forms set out at (a) or (c) would not be just (r. 44.3(7));
(f) that a party must pay costs relating only to a certain distinct part of the proceedings;
(g) that a party must pay interest on costs from or until a certain date, including a date before judgment.

When compared with the current position, all these variations appear to be restrictive in nature, assuming that a decision has been made that a winning party should recover its costs from the loser. They would seem appropriate, therefore, to mark the court's displeasure at some conduct on the part of the winning party, or to reflect a partial rather than a full win. However, they are all given a positive wording, which would seem to point to a need, in particular, to get a specific order for pre-commencement costs to make sure that these are included in the costs recoverable from the losing party.

24.3.2 Interim costs orders

If an order makes no reference to costs, none are payable in respect of the proceedings to which the order relates (CPR, r. 44.13(1); PD 23, para. 13.2). Detailed provisions dealing with interim costs orders are made in PD 44. Paragraph 2.3 provides that the court may make an order about costs at any stage in a case, and in particular it may make interim costs orders when it deals with interim applications. Paragraph 2.4 sets out in tabular form the meanings of commonly used interim costs orders, see table 24.1.

Table 24.1 The meanings of common interim costs orders

Term	Effect
Costs Costs in any event	The party in whose favour the order is made is entitled to the costs in respect of the part of the proceedings to which the order relates whatever other costs orders are made in the proceedings.
Costs in the case Costs in the application	The party in whose favour the court makes an order for costs at the end of the proceedings is entitled to his costs of the part of the proceedings to which the order relates.
Costs reserved	The decision about costs is deferred to a later occasion, but if no later order is made the costs will be costs in the case.
Claimant's/defendant's costs in the case/application	If the party in whose favour the costs order is made is awarded costs at the end of the proceedings, that party is entitled to his costs of the part of the proceedings to which the order relates. If any other party is awarded costs at the end of the proceedings, the party in whose favour the costs order is made is not liable to pay the costs of any other party in respect of the part of the proceedings to which the order relates.

Costs thrown away	Where, for example, a judgment or order is set aside, the party in whose favour the costs order is made is entitled to the costs which have been incurred as a consequence.
	This includes the costs of—
	    (a) preparing for and attending any hearing at which the judgment or order which has been set aside was made;
	    (b) preparing for and attending any hearing to set aside the judgment or order in question;
	    (c) preparing for and attending any hearing at which the court orders the proceedings or the part in question to be adjourned;
	    (d) any steps taken to enforce a judgment or order which has subsequently been set aside.

Costs of and caused by	Where, for example, the court makes this order on an application to amend a statement of case, the party in whose favour the costs order is made is entitled to the costs of preparing for and attending the application and the costs of any consequential amendment to his own statement of case.

Term	Effect
Costs here and below	The party in whose favour the costs order is made is entitled not only to his costs of the proceedings in which the court makes the order but also to his costs of the proceedings in any lower court. In the case of an appeal from a Divisional Court the party is not entitled to any costs incurred in any court below the Divisional Court.
No order as to costs Each party to pay his own costs	Each party is to bear his own costs of the proceedings to which the order relates whatever costs order the court makes at the end of the proceedings.

24.3.2.1 Summary assessment of interim costs The costs of interim hearings likely to last less than a day will often be dealt with by way of summary assessment there and then. This was considered at 9.5.5, where it was pointed out that the parties are required to file and serve statements of their costs not less than 24 hours before the hearing. Summary assessment is not possible if any of the parties is assisted by legal aid, or is acting under a disability. Nor is summary assessment normally appropriate where the interim costs are treated as costs in the case (see PD 44, para. 4.4(2)), or, presumably if the costs are reserved.

24.3.2.2 Detailed assessment of interim costs Orders for costs will be treated as requiring detailed assessment (the new term for taxation) unless the order specifies the sum to be paid or states that fixed costs are to be paid (PD 44, para. 4.2). Detailed assessments generally take place after the proceedings are concluded.

24.3.3 Fixed costs on judgments etc.

Part 45 of the CPR, supplemented by PD 45, RSC, ord. 62, appendix 3 in CPR, sch. 1, and CCR, ord. 38, appendix B in CPR, sch. 2, lays down the new system for calculating the amount of fixed costs on entering default judgments, judgment on admissions, summary judgment, the striking out of a defence as disclosing no reasonable grounds for defending, where a defendant pays the claim within 14 days after service and on issuing default costs certificates. Where the fixed costs provisions apply, the claimant is entitled to recover, in addition to the substantive remedy, the court fee paid on issue plus the fixed costs set out in the tables in CPR, Part 45, RSC, ord. 62, appendix 3, or CCR, ord. 38, appendix B, as appropriate.

Table 1 in CPR, Part 45, sets out the fixed commencement costs in money claims and claims for the delivery of goods, which are the equivalent of the old 14-day costs payable if the defendant simply pays the claim in the 14 days after service of process.

Table 2 in CPR, Part 45, sets out the fixed costs for entering judgment recoverable on entering default, summary judgments etc. in money claims and claims for the delivery of goods

Table 3 in CPR, Part 45, sets out miscellaneous allowances for cases where personal service has been effected by the claimant's solicitor, where defendants have been served by alternative methods, and where defendants have been served outside the jurisdiction.

RSC, ord. 62, appendix 3 in CPR, sch. 1, sets out the fixed costs in cases in the High Court for:

(a) entering judgment in claims for possession of land and additional costs for service; and

(b) taking certain enforcement proceedings.

CCR, ord. 38, appendix B in CPR, sch. 2, sets out fixed costs in county court cases for:

(a) money claims;

(b) claims for the recovery of land (with or without a claim for money); and

(c) claims for the recovery of goods including goods supplied under hire-purchase agreements.

The fixed costs included in CCR, ord. 38, appendix B, include fixed costs to be entered on the claim form in respect of solicitors' charges, the costs on entering judgment in actions for the delivery of goods and possession of land suspended on payment of arrears of rent, and for miscellaneous enforcement proceedings.

PD 45, para. 2.1 provides for fixed costs of £80 plus the appropriate court fee to be included in default costs certificates (for which, see 24.9.5).

24.3.4 Costs of pre-commencement disclosure and disclosure against non-parties

Applications for pre-commencement disclosure and for orders against persons who are not parties for disclosure of documents were considered at 15.9. The general rule is that the court must award the costs of the application to the person against whom the order is sought (CPR, r. 48.1). The practice has been to add the costs of the application as a head of damages in the case of pre-commencement disclosure. This may no longer be necessary as under the new system the pre-commencement application is made in the same action as the main claim, whereas under the old system the application formed a separate action commenced by its own originating process. In the case of disclosure against a non-party the costs will be part of the costs of the action, and should be dealt with by a specific costs order between the parties. The court retains a discretion to make a different costs order in a particular case, having regard to all the circumstances, including the extent to which it may have been reasonable for the respondent to have opposed the disclosure application (r. 48.1(3)). This may be the case where the respondent has failed to honour its obligations under the Access to Health Records Act 1990 (which applies to most medical records compiled since 1 November 1991) or under any applicable pre-action protocol (which will potentially apply to many applications for pre-commencement disclosure against likely defendants).

24.3.5 Costs after transfer

Subject to any order that may have been made by the original court, once a case is transferred the new court will deal with all questions as to costs, including the costs incurred before the transfer (CPR, r. 44.13(3)(4)).

24.3.6 Costs before track allocation

The special rules relating to costs in cases on the small claims track and fast track do not apply until a claim is allocated to one of these tracks (CPR, r. 44.9(1) and (2)). Once a claim is allocated to either of these tracks the special rules relating to that track will apply to work done before as well as after allocation, with the exception that any costs orders made before a claim is allocated to one of these two tracks are not affected by any subsequent allocation (PD 44, para. 5.1(2)). This means, for example, that the usual costs order against the defendant made on a successful application to set aside a default judgment would be unaffected by a subsequent decision to allocate the case (say) to the small claims track. A 'costs reserved' order, such as on an application without notice, however, would lapse if the case is allocated to the small claims track before any substantive decision was made about the reserved costs.

24.3.7 Reallocation from the small claims track

Before making an order to reallocate a claim from the small claims track to another track, the court must decide whether any party is to pay costs to any other party down to the date of the reallocation order (PD 44, para. 6.2). Such costs must be those payable under CPR, Part 27, which in effect means that they are limited to fixed costs and any further costs which may be ordered for unreasonable behaviour (r. 27.14). If a costs order is made on reallocation, the court should make an immediate summary assessment of those costs (PD 44, para. 6.3). Fast track or multi-track costs rules will apply from the date of reallocation (CPR, r. 27.15).

24.3.8 Costs after an appeal

A court dealing with a case on appeal can make orders relating to the costs of the proceedings giving rise to the appeal as well as the appeal itself (CPR, r. 44.13(2)). If an appeal is successful, the appeal court may order the losing party to pay the costs 'here and below', or may make different orders relating to the proceedings at the two levels, or may leave the costs order of the court below undisturbed while making whatever order may be appropriate for the costs of the appeal.

24.3.9 Notifying client

Where a costs order is made against a legally represented client who is not present in court when the order is made, the solicitor representing the client is under a duty to inform the client of the costs liability within seven days of the order being made (CPR, r. 44.2). The 'client' may be an insurer or trade union or other body which has instructed the solicitor (PD 44, para. 1.1). At the same time as informing the client about the order, the solicitor should explain why it was made. The July 1998 draft CPR additionally provided that a solicitor who failed to notify the client within the seven-day period was personally liable to indemnify the client for the costs in question, unless the court directed otherwise. This was apparently felt to be too draconian a penalty for merely failing to send a letter, and could have given rise to unnecessary disputes over when and whether letters were sent or received. However, the court has the power to order the solicitor to produce evidence that reasonable steps were taken to comply with the duty to notify the client (PD 44, para. 1.3).

24.4 RIGHTS TO COSTS

24.4.1 Payments in and offers to settle

A party who accepts an offer to settle or payment into court under CPR, Part 36, is given a right to recover the costs of the proceedings on the standard basis if not agreed up to the date of giving notice of acceptance (r. 36.13). If the offer or payment in took into account any counterclaim made by the defendant the costs recoverable on acceptance will include the costs attributable to the counterclaim. Interest on the costs, which is payable under the Judgments Act 1838, s. 17, runs from the date of the notice of acceptance (CPR, r. 44.12).

24.4.2 Discontinuance

Interest on costs payable after a claim is discontinued runs from the date of the notice of discontinuance (CPR, r. 44.12).

24.5 COSTS ORDERS AGAINST NON-PARTIES

It was held by the House of Lords in *Aiden Shipping Co. Ltd* v *Interbulk Ltd* [1986] AC 965 that the discretion given to the courts on costs was wide enough to allow a costs order to be made against a person who was not a party to the proceedings in which the order is made. Such orders are exceptional, and are only made where they accord with reason and justice. They may be made against an outsider who is funding the litigation for one party (*Singh* v *Observer Ltd* [1989] 2 All ER 751, but doubted in *Symphony Group plc* v *Hodgson* [1994] QB 179), or against directors who improperly cause costs to be incurred in proceedings involving their company (*Re a Company (No. 004055 of 1991)* [1991] 1 WLR 1003), or an outsider guilty of infringing the rule against maintenance or champerty (*McFarlane* v *E.E Caledonia Ltd (No. 2)* [1995] 1 WLR 366). In *Aiden Shipping* itself an order was made against a party to one claim to pay the costs of a closely related claim even though the two claims had not been consolidated. Balcombe LJ in *Symphony Group plc* v *Hodgson* laid down a number of guidelines for courts dealing with applications for costs orders against non-parties. The person against whom the costs order would be sought ought to be joined as a party if there was a substantive cause of action against that person; an early warning ought to be given to the person against whom the costs order would be sought of the possibility that this would happen; the procedure on the application should be summary, normally conducted by the trial judge, and the strict rules of evidence would not apply. The new costs rules in CPR, r. 48.2, for the first time lay down a statutory framework for the procedure to be followed on these applications. In future the person against whom the order will be sought must be added as a party (even though, apparently, there may be no substantive cause of action against that person), and must be given a reasonable opportunity to attend the hearing to give reasons why the court should not make the order.

24.6 FAST TRACK COSTS

Part of the scheme of the Woolf proposals was that there should be restricted costs recoverable in fast track cases. The *Final Report* contemplated that the restriction would take the form of bands of fixed profit costs depending on the value of the claim. It was hoped that by having fixed costs in fast track cases there would be a degree of certainty about a party's exposure on costs if a case was unsuccessful. It was also hoped that such a system would keep costs down and under control in relatively small cases (albeit those worth more than the small claims threshold). However, it has not proved possible to approve a workable scheme in time for introduction on 26 April 1999, and the eventual form of the restriction on costs recoverable in fast track cases has not yet been decided. Nevertheless, it is almost certain that special restrictive rules on costs will be made for fast track cases in the relatively near future.

Several different ways of dealing with fast track costs have been considered over the period during which the Woolf proposals have been developed. A consultation paper published in June 1998 under the title *Justice at the Right Price* provided perhaps the most likely scheme. It suggests that fast track costs will in fact be assessed (whether summarily or by detailed assessment, the new terms describing assessed and taxed costs), but be subject to a 'cap' related to the amount at stake. Under such a system solicitors would never 'win' on some cases so as to provide a fund for subsidising other cases (as would have happened in the scheme suggested in the *Final Report*), but will have to justify their fees in all cases, and may find their fees arbitrarily cut down by the cap in individual cases in which they have done a lot of work. A refinement of this proposed scheme would provide a cap of £2,500 for solicitors' profit costs and counsel's fees (but excluding experts' fees and other disbursements) for the work done up to trial in cases worth up to £5,000. In cases worth between £5,000 and £15,000 the cap would be at 50 per cent of the value of the claim. In cases with no direct monetary value, such as claims for injunctions, the cap would be £7,500 for profit costs and counsels' fees. In addition, if the case proceeded to trial an additional fixed trial fee would be allowed. There would be no discretion to alter the fixed trial fee.

The last point has in fact been incorporated into the final version of the CPR by Part 46, which strongly suggests that the rest of the scheme will be adopted in due course. Rule 46.2 provides that advocates' trial fees in fast track cases will be:

Value of claim up to £3,000	£350
Value of claim between £3,000 and £10,000	£500
Claims for non-money remedies	£500
Value of claim over £10,000	£750
Additional fee for solicitor attending trial with counsel	£250

For a successful claimant the value of the claim is the amount of the judgment excluding interest, costs and any reduction for contributory negligence, whereas for a successful defendant it is the amount the claimant specified on the claim form (or the maximum amount that could have been recovered on the pleaded case) (r. 46.2(3)). If there is a counterclaim and both parties succeed, the relevant amount is the difference between the value of the two claims (r. 46.3(6)). If there is a counterclaim with a greater value than the claim, and the claimant succeeds on the claim and defeats the counterclaim, the relevant amount is the value of the counterclaim (r. 46.2(6)). There are detailed rules dealing with cases where there are several claimants or several defendants, including whether more than one party can be awarded fast track trial costs, which are set out in r. 46.4. For claims for non-monetary remedies the court has a discretion to make some other order, see r. 46.2(4).

The additional allowance for a solicitor attending with counsel is provided by r. 46.3. The allowance of £250 is slightly more than the £150 suggested in the consultation paper, although the figures for counsel's fast track trial fees are the same as in the paper. The solicitor's attendance fee will only be payable if the court awards fast track trial costs and if the court considers that it was necessary for a legal representative to attend to assist counsel (r. 46.3(2)).

If a fast track claim settles before the start of the trial, costs may be allowed in respect of the advocate preparing for trial, but the amount allowed cannot be more than the above figures (r. 44.10). In deciding the amount to be allowed for the abortive preparation, the court will take into account when the claim settled and when the court was notified of that fact.

If there are split trials, such as on liability and quantum, it is possible to be awarded a second tranche of fast track trial costs, but the second award should not exceed two thirds of the amount payable under the first award, subject to a minimum award of £350 (r. 46.3(3) and (4)).

A successful party may, by r. 46.3(7), be awarded less than the above fixed fast track trial costs for unreasonable or improper behaviour during the trial, and the losing party may be ordered to pay an additional amount if it is guilty of behaving improperly during the trial (r. 46.3(8)).

24.7 METHOD OF QUANTIFICATION OF COSTS

Rule 44.7 of the CPR provides that when the court makes a costs order it may either:

(a) take a summary assessment of the costs; or
(b) order a detailed assessment by a costs officer.

A 'costs officer' is defined by CPR, r. 43.2(1), to mean a costs judge (which in turn means a taxing master of the Supreme Court), a district judge or an authorised court officer (i.e., a civil servant in a district registry, the Principal Registry of the Family Division, the Supreme Court Costs Office or a county court who is authorised by the Lord Chancellor to assess costs).

24.7.1 Summary assessment

Summary assessment is the same thing as assessing costs in the old terminology, and involves the court determining the amount payable by way of costs there and then, usually on a relatively rough and ready basis. As mentioned in 9.5.5, 13.4.6 and 24.3.2.1, the parties in short interim applications and fast track trials (which are the most likely candidates for summary assessment) are required to provide analyses of their costs in the form of costs statements 24 hours before the relevant hearings. Courts sometimes develop conventional figures for summarily assessed costs for certain types of proceeding, such as the costs awarded for straightforward landlord and tenant possession proceedings. The courts tend to err on the side of caution when summarily assessing the amount of costs to be paid, but it has been known for the amount summarily assessed to be relatively large. The court can call for whatever evidence is available at the time in deciding on the figure to allow, such as looking at counsel's brief to see the brief fee, as well as looking at the costs statements and hearing the advocates on the work involved in the matter.

24.7.2 Detailed assessment

Under the new terminology a 'detailed assessment' means the same thing as a 'taxation' of costs under the old system. Unlike summary assessment, a detailed assessment is not generally conducted until the conclusion of the proceedings (CPR, r. 47.1). Proceedings are concluded when the court has finally determined the matters in issue in the claim, whether or not there is an appeal (PD 47, para. 1.1(1)). However, the court retains a power to order an assessment at an earlier stage. An order may be made allowing detailed assessment proceedings to be commenced if there is no realistic prospect of the claim continuing (PD 47, para. 1.1(4)). The court also has a power to make an order for an amount to be paid on account of costs which will be assessed at some later stage (CPR, r. 44.3(8)).

24.7.3 Discretion

Generally the court has a discretion to decide whether to make a summary assessment or to order a detailed assessment if the costs cannot be agreed. However, where money is claimed by or ordered or agreed to be paid to or for the benefit of a child or patient the court in general must order a detailed assessment of the costs payable by the claimant to his solicitor (CPR, r. 48.5). Exceptions to this general rule are set out in PD 48, para. 1.2, and include cases where another party has agreed to pay a specified sum towards the costs of the person under disability, and the solicitor has waived the right to any further costs. Detailed assessment is the most likely approach with multi-track cases and interim applications lasting more than a day.

24.8 BASIS OF QUANTIFICATION

Costs may be quantified (taxed) either on the standard or the indemnity basis. Under the old system there was a twofold test to be applied when deciding whether to allow costs on either basis. Costs would only be recoverable if, first, they were reasonably incurred and secondly, to the extent that they were reasonable in amount. These concepts were approached from opposite directions under the two different bases, with doubts resolved in favour of the paying party on the standard basis, and in favour of the receiving party under the indemnity basis. Under the new system it will still be necessary to consider both whether individual items of costs should have been incurred, and whether they should be allowed in full or reduced. However, to tie in with the overriding objective, on an assessment on the standard basis the court is now required to consider not only concepts of reasonableness, but also of proportionality.

24.8.1 Standard basis

On an assessment on the standard basis, consequently, r. 44.4(2) of the CPR provides that the court will:

(a) only allow costs which are proportionate to the matters in issue; and

(b) resolve any doubt which it may have about whether costs were reasonably incurred or reasonable and proportionate in amount in favour of the paying party.

In applying the test of proportionality on a standard basis assessment, PD 44, para. 3.1, says that the relationship between the total costs incurred and the financial value of the claim is not always a reliable guide, and still less can the court simply apply a fixed percentage to the value of the claim and say that any costs above that percentage have to be disproportionate.

PD 44, para. 3.2, makes the point that some costs inevitably have to be incurred, or are otherwise necessary, for the successful conduct of a case. It also says that even in smaller cases solicitors are not required to work at uneconomic rates. Consequently, in small cases legal costs may legitimately even equal or exceed the amount in dispute. Further, PD 44, para. 3.3, says the court should be wary of using the length of the eventual hearing as an accurate guide to the time properly spent by the parties' legal representatives in preparing for the hearing. It is often the case that careful preparation reduces the time taken by hearings in court.

24.8.2 Indemnity basis

On an assessment on the indemnity basis there is no reference to proportionality, and as before any doubts on whether costs were reasonably incurred or were reasonable in amount is resolved in favour of the receiving party (r. 44.4(3)).

24.8.3 Choice of basis

Costs orders should identify the intended basis of quantification. Unless the phrase 'indemnity basis' is used, quantification will be on the standard basis (CPR, r. 44.4(4)). As under the old system, the usual rule in contentious litigation is that costs are payable on the standard basis. Also, as under the old system, parties who act in the capacity of trustee, personal representative or mortgagee are in general entitled to costs on the indemnity basis, but the court may order otherwise if the party has acted otherwise than for the benefit of the fund (r. 48.4).

Assessments between solicitor and own client (other than in legal aid cases and where there is a conditional fee agreement) are by virtue of r. 48.8 dealt with on the indemnity basis, but subject to the following presumptions:

    (a) that costs were reasonably incurred if they were incurred with the express or implied approval of the client;

    (b) that costs were reasonable in amount if the amount was expressly or impliedly approved by the client; and

    (c) that costs were unreasonably incurred if they are unusual in nature or amount and the solicitor did not tell the client that for that reason they might not be recoverable from the other side.

24.9 PROCEDURE FOR DETAILED ASSESSMENT OF COSTS

24.9.1 Appropriate office

All applications and requests in detailed assessment proceedings must be made to or filed at the 'appropriate office' (CPR, r. 47.4). In High Court cases this is usually the Supreme Court Costs Office (the new name for the Supreme Court Taxing Office). If the court dealing with the case when the judgment or order was made or when the event occurred which gave rise to the right to assessment, or to which the case has subsequently been transferred, is the Principal Registry of the Family Division or a district registry or a county court then that registry or court is the appropriate office (PD 47, para. 1.4). County courts can specify another county court as the appropriate office for the assessment of costs (CPR, r. 47.4(3)). Any court can direct that the Supreme Court Costs Office is to be the appropriate office (CPR, r. 47.4(2)), but should only do so having regard to the size of the bill of costs, its difficulty, length of hearing and costs to the parties (PD 47, para. 1.5(3)).

24.9.2 Commencement of detailed assessment proceedings

Detailed assessment proceedings must be commenced within three months of the judgment, order, award or other determination giving rise to the right to costs (CPR, r. 47.7). The period may be extended or shortened by agreement between the parties (PD 47, para. 2.7). A similar three-month period is laid down in respect of cases terminated by discontinuance, dismissal and acceptance of Part 36 offers and payments (CPR, r. 47.7). This is done by serving on the paying party a notice of commencement (form N252 see appendix 3) together with a copy of the bill of costs (r. 47.6(1)). The receiving party is also required to serve copies of counsel's fee notes and experts' fee invoices, written evidence for all disbursements exceeding £250, and a statement giving the name and address for service of any person upon whom the receiving party intends to serve the notice of commencement (PD 47, para. 2.2). The persons referred to in the previous sentence are known as 'relevant persons', who are defined by PD 47, para. 2.5, as persons who took part in the proceedings and who are directly liable to pay the costs under a costs order, and also persons who have given notice that they have a financial interest in the outcome of the assessment and any other person the court may direct to be treated as a relevant person. Relevant persons must also be served with the notice of commencement and with the bill of costs (CPR, r. 47.6(2)). These additional persons are thereafter regarded as being parties to the assessment proceedings.

In cases where the costs to be assessed are payable out of the legal aid fund, the assessment is commenced by filing a request for a detailed assessment of legal aid costs (in costs form 8, see appendix 3), which must be served on the assisted person (r. 47.17(1)). Again, this must be done within three months from the date when the right to detailed assessment arose (r. 47.17(2)). In legal aid assessments, in addition to the documents referred to in the previous paragraph, the request for a detailed assessment must, by PD 47, para. 6.3, be accompanied by the legal aid certificates, amendments and authorities, and any certificate of discharge or revocation, and also the relevant papers in support of the bill described in PD 47, para. 4.13, and names and addresses of any person with financial interests in the assessment, and of the assisted person if he wishes to attend.

24.9.3 Bill of costs

Costs form 2 (see appendix 3) is a model form of bill of costs. PD 43, para. 2.1, provides that a bill of costs may consist of such of the following sections as may be appropriate:

(a) a title page;
(b) background information;
(c) items of costs claimed under the following headings:

    (i) attendances on the court and on counsel up to the date of the notice of commencement;
    (ii) attendances on and communications with the receiving party;

(iii) attendances on and communications with witnesses including expert witnesses;

(iv) attendances to inspect any property or place for the purposes of the proceedings;

(v) searches and enquiries made at offices of public records, the Companies Registry and similar searches and enquiries;

(vi) attendances on and communications with other persons;

(vii) communications with the court and with counsel;

(viii) work done in connection with arithmetical calculations of compensation and/or interest;

(ix) work done on documents: preparing and considering documentation relevant to the proceedings, including time spent on pre-action protocols and on collating documents;

(x) work done in connection with mediation, ADR and negotiations with a view to settlement if not already covered in the heads listed above;

(xi) attendances on and communications with London and other agents and work done by them;

(xii) other work done which was of or incidental to the proceedings and which is not already covered in the heads listed above.

(d) a summary showing the total costs claimed on each page of the bill;
(e) schedules of time spent on non-routine attendances; and
(f) appropriate certificates as set out in costs form 4.

The bill may be divided into two or more parts to distinguish between times when the receiving party was acting in person and by different firms of solicitors, and between times before and during the continuance of legal aid (PD 43, para. 2.2).

Each item in the bill must be consecutively numbered (PD 43, para. 2.8). The bill should be organised into five columns, headed 'Item', 'Amount claimed', 'VAT', with the last two left blank, but headed 'Amount allowed' and 'VAT' (PD 43, para. 2.10). Routine letters (those which by reason of their simplicity should not be regarded as letters of substance) and routine telephone calls (which cannot properly amount to an attendance) will in general be allowed on a unit basis of 6 minutes each, the charge being calculated by reference to the appropriate hourly rate. The unit charge for letters out will include perusing and considering the relevant letters in, and no separate charge should be made for incoming letters. E-mails received and sent will not normally be allowed, but the court has a discretion to allow the actual time spent on preparing them provided the time is recorded. A sum in relation to e-mail may also be allowed if otherwise the number of communications will have been substantially greater than the number claimed. Local travelling expenses incurred by solicitors (normally within 10 miles of the court) will not be allowed. The cost of postage, couriers, outgoing telephone calls, fax and telex messages will in general not be allowed unless unusually heavy. Nor will the cost of making copies normally be allowed, unless the documents to be copied were unusually numerous. Agency charges as between a principal solicitor and his agent will be dealt with normally on the basis that the charges form part of the principal solicitor's charges (PD 43, para. 2.15).

24.9.4 Points of dispute

In a detailed assessment of costs the paying party and others served with the notice of commencement may dispute any item in the bill by serving all the other parties with points of dispute. Points of dispute should be short and to the point, and should follow as closely as possible costs form 6 (PD 47, para. 2.13). They must:

    (a)   identify each item in the bill of costs which is disputed;
    (b)   in each case state concisely the nature and grounds of the dispute;
    (c)   where practicable suggest a figure to be allowed for each item in respect of which a reduction is sought; and
    (d)   be signed by the party serving them or his solicitor.

Copies of the points of dispute should also be served on other persons appearing on the statement of persons the receiving party intended to serve with the notice of commencement. These must be served within 21 days after service of the notice of commencement (see CPR, r. 47.9).

24.9.5 Default costs certificate

If the paying party fails to serve points of dispute within the permitted time, the receiving party may, on filing a request (form N254), obtain a default costs certificate (CPR, rr. 47.9(4) and 47.11), which means that all the costs in the bill are allowed. A default certificate includes an order to pay the relevant costs (r. 47.11(2); see forms N255 and N255HC). The right to a default certificate is lost if the receiving party delays making the request until after the paying party serves points of dispute, albeit late. A party who serves points of dispute late will not be heard on the assessment hearing, unless the court so permits (r. 47.9(3)). There is a power to set aside a default costs certificate on the ground of there being good reason to do so. The court will also be concerned to see a draft of the proposed points of dispute and will take into account whether the application to set aside was made promptly (r. 47.12; PD 47, paras 3.8 to 3.11).

24.9.6 Reply

The receiving party has the right, but is not obliged, to serve a reply to any points of dispute. Any reply should be served on the party who served the points of dispute within 21 days after service (CPR, r. 47.13).

24.9.7 Assessment hearing

Once points of dispute have been served the receiving party must, within three months of the expiry of the period for commencing the detailed assessment proceedings, file a request for an assessment hearing (CPR, r. 47.14). If the receiving party fails to do so the paying party may apply under r. 47.14(3) for an order that the receiving party must file the request within a specified period, and the court may direct that if there is a breach of that direction, the receiving party will lose all or part of the costs that would otherwise have been recoverable. There will be cases where the receiving party fails to request an assessment hearing within the three month period, the paying party makes no application requiring a request, and the receiving party then makes a late request for the assessment hearing. In these cases, if the court is minded to impose a sanction to mark the delay in making the request it will normally be restricted to disallowing interest (r. 47.12(5)).

In legal aid cases, unless the assisted party wishes to attend, the court will provisionally assess the costs without a hearing unless it considers a hearing is necessary. If a bill is provisionally assessed, the solicitor has 14 days after it is returned to request an assessment hearing. In cases where the assisted party wants to attend, the solicitor will certify to this effect, and the court will fix the assessment hearing (r. 47.17).

Unless the court otherwise permits, only matters raised in the points of dispute may be raised at the hearing (r. 47.14(7), which is a slightly tougher attitude than under the old rules).

In deciding whether costs were reasonably incurred or were reasonable and proportionate in amount, the court is to have regard to all the circumstances. Under the old system the court was assisted in this task by what were called the 'seven pillars', such as the complexity of the item or the action, and the difficulty or novelty of the questions involved. The 'seven pillars' were set out in RSC, ord. 62, appendix 2, para. 1. In the CPR, r. 44.5(3) provides for eight matters to be taken into account. They echo the former position, but have been expanded to include the conduct of the parties before as well as during the proceedings (and thus take into account compliance, or otherwise, with any applicable pre-action protocol) and their efforts to resolve the dispute. The new matters to be taken into account omit the old third pillar, which required the court to have regard to the number and importance of the documents prepared or perused. However, time spent on documentation can still be charged for as is plain from PD 43, para. 2.5(9), which includes the time spent on preparing, considering and collating documents.

24.9.8 Assessment procedure between solicitor and own client under the Solicitors Act 1974, Part III

Applications for orders under the Solicitors Act 1974, Part III, are to be made by Part 8 claim form (PD 48, para. 2.18). The provisions of RSC, ord. 106 in CPR, sch. 1, continue to apply.

Within 28 days of an order made under the Solicitors Act 1974, Part III, for the assessment of costs payable to a solicitor by his or her client, the solicitor must serve the client with a breakdown of the costs (CPR, r. 48.10(2)). The client must serve points of dispute within 14 days of service of the breakdown, and the solicitor may serve a reply within 14 days thereafter (r. 48.10(3) and (4)). When points of dispute have been served, and in any event no later than three months from the date of the original order, either party may file a request for a hearing date. The provisions relating to default costs certificates do not apply to Solicitors Act assessments (PD 48, para. 2.23). Further detailed provisions for these cases can be found in PD 48, paras 2.9 to 2.36.

24.9.9 Costs of assessment

By PD 43, para. 2.16 a claim can be made for the reasonable costs of preparing and checking the bill of costs. Generally, by virtue of CPR, r. 47.18, the receiving party is also entitled to his costs of the assessment proceedings. Normally these will be assessed summarily and added to the bill of costs (PD 47, para. 7.1). However, the court may make some other order as to the costs of the assessment having regard to all the circumstances, including:

(a) the conduct of all the parties;
(b) the amount, if any, by which the bill of costs is reduced; and
(c) whether it was reasonable for particular items to appear in the bill, or for particular objections to have been taken.

Provided neither the receiving nor the paying party is assisted by legal aid, the paying party may make a *Calderbank* offer in writing to settle the costs in dispute expressed to be 'without prejudice save as to the costs of the detailed assessment proceedings'. The amount of the offer must not be communicated to the costs officer until the question of the costs of the assessment is to be decided, and at that stage it may be taken into account in deciding who should pay the costs of the assessment proceedings (CPR, r. 47.19). Normally, if the *Calderbank* offer equals or exceeds the amount allowed, the receiving party should pay the paying party's costs of the assessment proceedings, at least from the date of service of the offer.

Normally offers to settle should, if made by the paying party, be made within 14 days of service of the notice of commencement, and if made by the receiving party, within 14 days of service of the points of dispute (PD 47, para. 7.4). Offers made at a later stage will be given less weight when it comes to costs.

When an offer is accepted, an application may be made for a certificate in agreed terms, or the bill may be withdrawn (PD 47, para. 7.5).

Where the receiving party is an assisted person, an offer to settle will not have any costs consequences unless the court so orders (PD 47, para. 7.6).

24.9.10 Failure to adhere to time limits

If a receiving party fails to commence assessment proceedings, or to request an assessment hearing, in time, the paying party may apply in writing under CPR, r. 47.8, for an order requiring the receiving party to do this within such time as the court may specify. The application must be served at least seven days before the hearing (PD 47, para. 2.11(2)). The order may be made in the form of an unless order, the sanction for further breach being the disallowance of the costs.

24.9.11 Interim costs certificate

The court has a power to issue interim costs certificates in such sums as it considers appropriate (CPR, r. 47.15). The court may order the costs covered by such a certificate to be paid into court.

24.9.12 Final costs certificate

Within 14 days after the end of the detailed assessment hearing the receiving party must complete the bill and return it to the court (CPR, r. 47.16(2)) together with receipted fee notes and accounts (PD 47, para. 5.5). Once the completed bill is filed at the court, a final costs certificate, which includes an order to pay the costs to which it relates, will be served by the court on all the parties to the assessment proceedings (r. 47.16(3) and (5)).

24.9.13 Appeals against assessment decisions

An appeal against a decision in detailed assessment proceedings may not be launched until the appellant has obtained written reasons for the decision (CPR, r. 47.21(1)). Reasons are sought by filing a request, which the receiving party should file with the completed bill (i.e., within 14 days of the detailed assessment hearing). A paying party has only seven days after the end of the detailed assessment hearing (r. 47.23) to file a request for reasons. A request must identify clearly the particular parts of the decision for which reasons are sought (PD 47, para. 8.3). The court may direct that written reasons are unnecessary, for example, if the decision to be appealed is of a case management nature rather than a decision on the substance of the assessment proceedings (PD 47, para. 8.6). Permission to appeal must be obtained, unless the appeal is against a decision of an authorised court officer, or against a decision of a costs judge or district judge to impose a sanction for misconduct or a wasted costs order (CPR, r. 47.24). Permission to appeal must be sought from the costs judge or district judge who made the decision under appeal, or from a High Court or circuit judge (depending on whether the case is in the High Court or a county court). Permission to appeal must be sought within 14 days of receiving the reasons for the initial detailed assessment. A request for permission may be made by a letter setting out the basis upon which permission is sought (PD 47, para. 8.10).

An appeal is brought by filing a notice of appeal. The notice of appeal must be filed within 14 days after service of the court officer's reasons, or within 14 days of receiving permission to appeal (as appropriate), see CPR, r. 47.25. On the appeal the court may appoint assessors (r. 47.26(3)). On the appeal the court will rehear the proceedings, and make any order and give such directions as it considers appropriate (r. 47.26(1)).

Where the initial decision is that of an authorised officer, the initial appeal is to a costs judge or district judge. A further appeal then lies to a High Court judge or circuit judge depending on whether the matter is in the High Court or county court (r. 47.22(1) and (2)). Where the appeal is from the decision of a costs judge or district judge any appeal lies to a High Court or circuit judge depending on which court dealt with the original detailed assessment (r. 47.22(3)).

24.9.14 Misconduct

Rule 44.14 of the CPR deals with cases where there has been a failure to conduct detailed assessment proceedings in accordance with the rules, and where the court finds that the conduct of a party or a legal representative before or during the proceedings was unreasonable or improper. The latter includes steps calculated to prevent or inhibit the court from furthering the overriding objective (PD 44, para. 7.2). In any of these cases the court has a power to disallow all or part of the costs being assessed, or to order the party or legal representative in default to pay any other party's costs incurred because of the misconduct. Before making such an order the court must give the party or legal representative a reasonable opportunity to attend a hearing and give reasons why the proposed order should not be made (PD 44, para. 7.1).

24.10 CONDITIONAL FEE AGREEMENTS

A client who retains a solicitor under a conditional fee agreement may apply to the court for it to assess the base costs (i.e., the costs other than the percentage increase) or the percentage increase (i.e., the percentage increase pursuant to the conditional fee agreement either between the solicitor and client or between the solicitor and counsel, and otherwise sometimes known as the success fee) or both (CPR, r. 48.9(3)). Base costs are assessed on the indemnity basis as if there was no conditional fee agreement. The percentage increase may be reduced if the court considers it disproportionate, having regard to all the relevant factors as they appeared to the solicitor or counsel when the conditional fee agreement was entered into. See further 3.4.

24.11 LITIGANTS IN PERSON

A litigant in person who recovers costs may have his or her costs quantified either by summary or detailed assessment in the court's discretion. When quantifying these costs, r. 48.6 of the CPR provides that the litigant will not recover more than two thirds of the costs and all the disbursements which would have been allowed if the litigant had been represented by a legal representative. In quantifying the costs for time spent on the litigation, the litigant in person will be allowed his or her financial loss for doing the work on the case. A litigant who cannot establish any such loss will be allowed an amount in respect of time spent reasonably doing the work and at a rate of £9.25 per hour (PD 48, para. 1.6). A litigant in person is not entitled to a witness allowance for his or her own attendance at court.

24.12 WASTED COSTS ORDERS

The Supreme Court Act 1981, s. 51(6), provides that legal representatives may be ordered to pay personally any wasted costs. 'Wasted costs' are defined as those resulting from any improper, unreasonable or negligent act or omission on the part of a legal representative, or which, in the light of any such act or omission, the court considers it unreasonable for the party to pay. Detailed guidance on such applications was given in *Ridehalgh* v *Horsefield* [1994] Ch 205. According to *Filmlab Systems International Ltd* v *Pennington* [1995] 1 WLR 673 wasted costs applications were to be made after the end of the proceedings. They were to be conducted in a summary manner, with the lawyer having been given adequate notice of the allegations said to justify the order being made. One of the drawbacks of the procedure was that the lawyers involved were often unable to make use of documents protected by legal professional privilege to justify their actions, the privilege belonging to their clients rather than to themselves, and it being a matter for the client whether to waive privilege. The court was therefore often unable to draw adverse inferences because it did not have the material to do so.

Specific procedural rules for these applications are included in the costs rules by CPR, r. 48.7. Wasted costs orders can be made on an application by a party made under Part 23, or by the court on its own initiative (PD 48, para. 2.2). On an application by a party, the legal representative against whom the order is sought must be given written notice, at least three days before the hearing, of what he or she is alleged to have done or failed to do and of the costs sought (PD 48, para. 2.3). The court is required to give the legal representative a reasonable opportunity to attend a hearing to give reasons why the order should not be made. This is the same as the current practice of initially making an order to show cause why a wasted costs order should not be made. The court will give directions to ensure that the issues are dealt with in a way that is fair and as simple and summary as the circumstances permit (PD 48, para. 2.5). The court may also direct that notice be given to the legal representative's client. It is also provided that for the purposes of such applications the court may direct that privileged documents are to be disclosed to the court and, if the court so directs, to the other party to the application for the order (CPR, r. 48.7(3)). This obviously cuts across legal professional privilege, but that is permissible because the Civil Procedure Act 1997, sch. 1, para. 4, provides that the CPR may modify the rules of evidence as they apply to proceedings in any court within the scope of the rules. Wasted costs applications will generally be considered in two stages (PD 48, para. 2.6):

(a) At the first stage the applicant has to adduce evidence which, if unanswered, would be likely to lead to a wasted costs order, and the court must be satisfied that the wasted costs application appears to be justified having regard to the likely costs involved.

(b) At the second stage the court will give the legal representative an opportunity of putting forward his or her case, and will make a wasted costs order only if (PD 48, para. 2.4):

(i) the legal representative has acted improperly, unreasonably or negligently;

(ii) the legal representative's conduct has caused another party to incur unnecessary costs; and

(iii) it is just in all the circumstances to order the legal representative to compensate that party for the whole or part of those costs.

If the court makes an order, it must specify the amount to be paid or disallowed.

CHAPTER 25   APPEALS

CONTENTS

25.1	Introduction	323
25.2	County court appeals from district judges	324
25.2.1	Interim orders	324
25.2.2	Final orders	324
25.3	County court rehearings	324
25.4	County court appeals from the judge	324
25.5	High court appeals from masters and district judges	325
25.5.1	Masters' interim orders	325
25.5.2	Masters' final orders	325
25.6	High Court appeals from judges	325
25.6.1	High Court judges' interim orders	325
25.6.2	High Court judges' final orders	327
25.7	Appeals to the Court of Appeal	327
25.7.1	Time for appealing	327
25.7.2	Permission to appeal	327
25.7.3	Respondent's notice	329
25.7.4	Skeletons for the main appeal	329
25.7.5	The 'Document List'	329
25.7.6	Other provisions	329
25.8	Judicial review	329
25.9	Appeals to the High Court from tribunals	330
25.10	Appeals to the High Court by case stated	330
25.11	Divisional Court proceedings	330
25.12	Appeals to the Court of Appeal from the Restrictive Practices Court	330
25.13	Appeals from tribunals to the Court of Appeal by way of case stated	330
25.14	References to the European Court	331
25.15	Variation of directions	331

25.1   INTRODUCTION

The major change in relation to civil appeals brought about by the Woolf reforms was the introduction as from 1 January 1999 of a need to obtain permission to appeal to the Court of Appeal for all but three types of appeal. There is a question mark on whether the new rules intend to abolish interlocutory appeals to the Court of Appeal, a point of fundamental importance which is considered at 25.6.1. Otherwise, although there are detailed changes, sch. 1 and sch. 2 to the CPR simply re-enact the old provisions from the RSC and CCR using the same order and rule numbering. There are several terminological changes, the main ones being:

(a) hearings in open court are referred to as hearings in public;
(b) hearings in chambers are referred to as hearings in private;
(c) *ex parte* hearings are referred to as hearings without notice;
(d) leave to appeal is now called permission to appeal;

(e) references to affidavit evidence are changed sometimes to references to written evidence, but sometimes the revised provisions simply provide for evidence by witness statement or affidavit;

(f) references to interlocutory procedures use the CPR terminology (such as disclosure and requests for further information), and references to old rules have had to be changed to references to the equivalent provisions in the CPR; and

(g) references to paperwork are changed to refer to the new forms, so that notices of motion, summonses etc. become claim forms, application notices and sometimes notices of appeal.

25.2 COUNTY COURT APPEALS FROM DISTRICT JUDGES

25.2.1 Interim orders

Regarding appeals from interim orders made by county court district judges, the old rules in CCR, ord. 13, r. 1(10) and (11), are reproduced in CPR, sch. 2, with inconsequential changes. The result is that an appeal may be made as of right and by way of rehearing to the circuit judge. The notice of appeal must be filed and served on the other side within five days after the order under appeal. The appeal will usually be dealt with in private.

25.2.2 Final orders

Regarding appeals from final orders made by county court district judges, CCR, ord. 37, r. 6, is re-enacted without any significant change in CPR, sch. 2. There is a right to appeal to the judge, but the appellant has to show grounds for the appeal. Notice of appeal must be served within 14 days of the order under appeal.

Regarding small claims track cases, the CPR restrict appeals in the same way as the old rules relating to small claims. By r. 27.12 an appeal may only be brought if there was a serious irregularity affecting the proceedings or if the court made a mistake of law. The court is permitted to dismiss an appeal under Part 27 without a hearing.

25.3 COUNTY COURT REHEARINGS

The county court power in CCR, ord. 37, r. 1, to order a rehearing where there is no error is retained unchanged in CPR, sch. 2. An application for such a rehearing is made by a notice stating the grounds of the application, which must be served within 14 days of the trial. Rehearings take place before the same judge as dealt with the original trial.

25.4 COUNTY COURT APPEALS FROM THE JUDGE

Appeals from county court judges are made to the Court of Appeal. Order 59 of the RSC is re-enacted almost unchanged in CPR, sch. 1. The most obvious change is that virtually all appeals to the Court of Appeal now require permission, so there is no longer any substance in the distinction between final and interlocutory orders or between judgments above and below £5,000: generally all appeals from the county court to the Court of Appeal require permission. There are a number of changes to RSC, ord. 59, r. 19, but they are mainly consequential on the general requirement for permission to appeal. However, r. 19(4) (which imposed a duty on the appellant to apply for a signed note of the proceedings in the county court) has been deleted, presumably to take into account the general tape recording of county court judgments and the more prevalent tape recording of the evidence in county court cases (see PD 39, para. 6.1).

25.5 HIGH COURT APPEALS FROM MASTERS AND DISTRICT JUDGES

25.5.1 Masters' interim orders

Appeals from interim orders made by masters and High Court district judges will continue to be governed by RSC, ord. 58, which is re-enacted with a number of minor changes in CPR, sch. 1. The appeal continues to be to the judge, who is now described as the judge sitting in private, which hardly has the same ring as the old appeal to the judge in chambers. The old notice to attend before the judge (RSC, ord. 58, r. 1(2)) is now called a notice of appeal. The appeal continues to be as of right and by way of rehearing. Notice of appeal in Royal Courts of Justice matters must be issued within five days of the judgment or order, served within five days of issue, and there must be at least two clear days between service and the hearing of the appeal. In district registry matters the notice of appeal must be issued within seven days of the judgment or order under appeal, and must be served at least three clear days before the hearing (RSC, ord. 58, r. 3(2) in CPR, sch. 1).

25.5.2 Masters' final orders

Appeals from final orders and assessments of damages by masters and High Court district judges must be made to the Court of Appeal (RSC, ord. 58, r. 2 in CPR, sch. 1). This is the same as before, except for the general requirement that permission is required for appeals to the Court of Appeal.

25.6 HIGH COURT APPEALS FROM JUDGES

25.6.1 High Court judges' interim orders

It is almost certain that interim orders made by High Court judges will continue to be capable of being appealed to the Court of Appeal. This follows from the Supreme Court Act 1981, s. 18, and the court's inherent jurisdiction. The doubt arises from the fact that the old RSC, ord. 58, r. 6, which provided that an appeal would lie to the Court of Appeal from any judgment, order or decision of a judge in chambers, has not been reproduced anywhere in the CPR. It could be thought that this has the rather startling result that interlocutory appeals from the High Court to the Court of Appeal have been abolished. Under the old rules there was no direct equivalent of RSC, ord. 58, r. 6, for appeals from final orders made by High Court judges, and none was needed because the right to appeal from the High Court to the Court of Appeal is part of the inherent jurisdiction of the superior civil courts. The Supreme Court Act 1981, s. 18, provides:

18. Restrictions on appeals to Court of Appeal
(1) No appeal shall lie to the Court of Appeal—

CHAPTER 25 APPEALS

(a) except as provided by the Administration of Justice Act 1960, from any judgment of the High Court in any criminal cause or matter;

(b) from any order of the High Court or any other court or tribunal allowing an extension of time for appealing from a judgment or order;

(c) from any order, judgment or decision of the High Court or any other court or tribunal which, by virtue of any provision (however expressed) of this or any other Act, is final;

(d) from a decree absolute of divorce or nullity of marriage, by a party who, having had time and opportunity to appeal from the decree nisi on which that decree was founded, has not appealed from the decree nisi;

(dd) from a divorce order;

[(e), (f) repealed]

(g) except as provided by Part I of the Arbitration Act 1996, from any decision of the High Court under that Act;

[(h) repealed]

(1A) In any such class of case as may be prescribed by rules of court, an appeal shall lie to the Court of Appeal only with the leave of the Court of Appeal or such court or tribunal as may be specified by the rules in relation to that class.

(1B) Any enactment which authorises leave to appeal to the Court of Appeal being given by a single judge, or by a court consisting of two judges, shall have effect subject to any provision which—

(a) is made by rules of court; and

(b) in such classes of case as may be prescribed by the rules, requires leave to be granted by such greater number of judges (not exceeding three) as may be so specified.

[(2) Repealed]

Section 18(1A) does not affect the position, because all it provides is that if there is going to be a restriction on the right to appeal in the form of a requirement of seeking leave, that requirement has to be laid down by the rules of court. It is not saying that appeals to the Court of Appeal may only be made in classes of case prescribed by rules of court. Consequently, the revocation of RSC, ord. 58, r. 6, does not affect the position that appeals can be made to the Court of Appeal from interim orders and judgments made by High Court judges. Indeed such a position would be preposterous given that appeals from interim orders made by county court judges are preserved by RSC, ord. 59, r. 19 in CPR, sch. 2, and would fly in the face of various provisions in the recent Practice Direction (Court of Appeal: Leave to Appeal and Skeleton Arguments) [1999] 1 WLR 2 which assume a continuing jurisdiction over interlocutory appeals from the High Court.

Appeals from the judge sitting in private to the Court of Appeal follow the old practice. This will be considered in more detail at 25.7.

The Practice Direction (Court of Appeal: Leave to Appeal and Skeleton Arguments) makes a number of points about interlocutory appeals:

(a) The Court of Appeal will not interfere with the exercise of discretion of a judge unless it is satisfied that the judge below was wrong (*Hadmor Productions Ltd* v *Hamilton* [1983] 1 AC 191). The burden on an appellant is a heavy one. It will therefore be rare to obtain permission to appeal, although it is recognised that permission may be granted if the case raises a point of general principle.

CHAPTER 25   APPEALS

(b) There will be cases where the point under appeal is of insufficient significance to justify the costs of the appeal in accordance with the overriding objective.
(c) The procedural consequences of an appeal, including the possible loss of the trial date, may outweigh the desirability of launching an appeal against an interim order.
(d) It may be more convenient to determine the point at or after the trial.

25.6.2   High Court judges' final orders

Appeals from final judgments and orders of High Court judges remain governed by RSC, ord. 58 in CPR, sch. 1. The changes to the general provisions in RSC, ord. 59 are considered in 25.7. Judges of the Technology and Construction Court (the old official referees) are treated in the same way (RSC, ord. 58, r. 4 in CPR, sch. 1).

25.7   APPEALS TO THE COURT OF APPEAL

25.7.1   Time for appealing

The rules remain much the same as before, but with minor changes. Notice of appeal must be served not later than four weeks after the date on which the judgment or order below was sealed or otherwise perfected (RSC, ord. 59, r. 4(1) in CPR, sch. 1), or, in the case of an appeal from the county court, from the date on which the court gave its decision. In most cases permission to appeal will be required. Provided an application for permission is made within the four-week period, the notice of appeal may alternatively be served within seven days from the date permission is granted (RSC, ord. 58, r. 4(3)). A new provision is RSC, ord. 59, r. 2C in CPR, sch. 1, which provides that any date set by the court or ord. 59 for doing any act may not be varied by the parties. Consequently, permission to appeal out of time can only be granted by the Court of Appeal (for which, see RSC, ord. 59, r. 14(2)).

25.7.2   Permission to appeal

Amendments to RSC, ord. 59, r. 1B, and the repeal of r. 1A mean that permission to appeal is always required, except for an appeal against:

(a) the making of a committal order;
(b) a refusal to grant habeas corpus; or
(c) a secure accommodation order made under the Children Act 1989, s. 25.

The basic test is the same as it always has been. Permission to appeal is granted unless the appeal has no realistic prospect of success. A fanciful prospect is not enough. There will also be some cases where permission to appeal will be given almost regardless of the prospects if there is an issue which ought to be considered by the Court of Appeal in the public interest. An example is where authority binding on the Court of Appeal may call for reconsideration. Permission may be granted on a point of law if there is a real prospect that the Court of Appeal will differ from the judge below and the point materially affects the outcome. An appeal on the ground that there was no evidence to support a finding of fact is an appeal on a point of law. An appeal on the basis that there was little evidence for a finding of fact will not succeed. Appeals on findings of fact rarely succeed. However, if the challenge is to the inferences to be drawn from the primary facts, there may be scope for a successful appeal. There may also be prospects of success if the judge did not receive any particular benefit from having seen the witnesses.

Practice Direction (Court of Appeal: Leave to Appeal and Skeleton Arguments) [1999] 1 WLR 2 states at para. 8 that the court below is often in the best position to decide whether a case is suitable for an appeal. Where the parties are present when judgment is delivered in a court of first instance, it should be routine for the judge to ask whether either party wants permission to appeal and to deal with the matter there and then. At present judges tend to raise this by the cryptic remark, 'Is there anything else?' If the court of first instance is in any doubt whether an appeal would have a real prospect of success or involves a point of general principle, the safe course is to refuse permission to appeal, leaving the decision to the Court of Appeal if the party decides to take the matter further. It is particularly important for the judge to give reasons for granting or refusing permission to appeal in cases involving considering many witnesses and/or documents, because in such cases the Court of Appeal is at some disadvantage in assessing whether an appeal would be appropriate (para. 15). Paragraph 9 points out that the advantages enjoyed by the judge of first instance are lost if the application for permission is listed before a different judge, and says the Court of Appeal will be sympathetic in cases where it is impracticable to apply for permission from the court below.

Paragraphs 18 and 19 of Practice Direction (Court of Appeal: Leave to Appeal and Skeleton Arguments) state that permission to appeal may be limited to one or more points, and may be made conditional on, for example, a special order as to costs. If limited permission is granted, the court should expressly refuse permission on the other issues. If an appellant later wishes to raise other points, written notice to this effect must be given to all other parties and the court within 28 days of permission being granted. A respondent wishing to challenge the appellant's right to raise the additional matters must inform the appellant within 14 days after receiving the notice, and the appellant is then required within the next 14 days to apply for permission to raise the additional points. The parties file short written submissions on the matter, and the court will usually decide whether the additional matters can be raised before the hearing of the appeal.

Applications for leave to appeal must be accompanied by skeleton arguments: (Practice Direction (Court of Appeal: Leave to Appeal and Skeleton Arguments), para. 27). Where dates are significant, a chronology must be filed at the same time (para. 30). If the application for leave is listed for an oral hearing with both sides in attendance, the respondent must lodge and serve its skeleton argument within 14 days of receipt of the applicant's bundle.

If the single Lord Justice is minded to refuse leave on the papers, reasons will be sent to the applicant's solicitors (or the applicant if acting in person). A letter will accompany the reasons giving information about the right to seek an oral hearing, together with the single Lord Justice's decision as to whether such a hearing should be listed before one or two Lords Justices (Practice Direction (Court of Appeal: Leave to Appeal and Skeleton Arguments) para. 38).

25.7.3 Respondent's notice

A new RSC, ord. 59, r. 1B(2), in CPR, sch. 1, provides that a respondent to an appeal who wishes to serve a respondent's notice contending that the decision of the court below should be varied, either in any event or in the event of the appeal being allowed in whole or in part, must first obtain permission to cross-appeal. There will, however, be no need to obtain permission to serve a respondent's notice merely contending that the decision of the court below should be affirmed on grounds other than those relied upon by the court below. The other change brought about by the new form of RSC, ord. 59 as it appears in CPR, sch. 1 is that the old r. 6(1)(c) has been deleted. This provided that a cross-appeal that the decision of the court below was wrong in whole or in part was to be included in a respondent's notice. Under the new system such a contention is an appeal in its own right that requires leave, and the normal time limits apply.

25.7.4 Skeletons for the main appeal

If the single Lord Justice, on consideration of the papers, grants permission to appeal, he may give directions as to the maximum time to be allowed to each party for oral argument on the appeal and as to the lodging and service of skeleton arguments for the substantive appeal (Practice Direction (Court of Appeal: Procedure) [1995] 1 WLR 1191, para. 8). In this circumstance, or when leave is granted after an opposed hearing, the parties may in fact rely on their skeleton arguments from the leave application, or may prepare fresh skeletons for the main appeal (Practice Direction (Court of Appeal: Leave to Appeal and Skeleton Arguments) [1999] 1 WLR 2, para. 32). Four copies of an appellant's skeleton must be included with the appeal bundles. Four copies of a respondent's skeleton must be lodged within 21 days of being served with the appeal bundle, or, if earlier, not later than 14 days before the appeal hearing (see paras 33 and 34). No supplementary skeleton arguments will be allowed unless there are good reasons for granting permission.

25.7.5 The 'Document List'

The revised RSC, ord. 59 as it appears in CPR, sch. 1, calls the old List of Forthcoming Appeals the 'Document List' (see RSC, ord. 59, r. 9 in CPR, sch. 1). Within 14 days of first appearing in this list the appellant is required to file the appeal bundles. The former version of r. 9 provided a detailed statement of the documents that had to be included. This will now be stated in a practice direction.

25.7.6 Other provisions

The other detailed provisions of RSC, ord. 59, relating to appeals to the Court of Appeal basically continue as they were before the CPR, subject to various terminology changes.

25.8 JUDICIAL REVIEW

RSC, ord. 53, is re-enacted in CPR, sch. 1, with minor changes. Applications must still be made promptly and in any event within three months from the date grounds first arose (RSC, ord. 53, r. 4(1)). The main change, apart from terminology and consequential changes, is that an application for judicial review must now be made by issuing a claim form (RSC, ord. 53, r. 5(2A)). Forms 86A and 86B will continue in use.

25.9 APPEALS TO THE HIGH COURT FROM TRIBUNALS

RSC, ord. 55 survives in CPR, sch. 1, almost unchanged. The only significant change is that instead of issuing a notice of motion to bring an appeal an appellant will issue a notice of appeal (RSC, ord. 55, r. 3(1) in CPR, sch. 1).

25.10 APPEALS TO THE HIGH COURT BY CASE STATED

RSC, ord. 56, appears in CPR, sch. 1, almost unchanged. The main changes are:

(a) applications for orders directing a Minister, tribunal or other person to state a case will now be brought by issuing a claim form rather than the old originating motion (RSC, ord. 56, r. 8(1) in CPR, sch. 1); and

(b) the substantive proceedings for the determination by the High Court of a case stated or a question of law referred by way of case stated must now be begun by issuing a claim form, which again replaces the old originating motion (RSC, ord. 56, r. 10(1) in CPR, sch. 1).

25.11 DIVISIONAL COURT PROCEEDINGS

RSC, ord. 57, remains almost unchanged in CPR, sch. 1. Instead of using a notice of motion, however, under the new system applications are made by issuing a claim form (RSC, ord. 57, r. 2(1) in CPR, sch. 1).

25.12 APPEALS TO THE COURT OF APPEAL FROM THE RESTRICTIVE PRACTICES COURT

These appeals are governed by RSC, ord. 60, which remains largely unchanged in its new form in CPR, sch. 1. Instead of using a notice of motion these appeals will now use a notice of appeal (RSC, ord. 60, r. 1 in CPR, sch. 1). The other small change is that in ord. 60, r. 3(1) in CPR, sch. 1, the time when the appellant must file the judgment constituting the case and copies of the notice is enlarged from two days after service of the notice of appeal to seven days after service.

25.13 APPEALS FROM TRIBUNALS TO THE COURT OF APPEAL BY WAY OF CASE STATED

These appeals are governed by RSC, ord. 61, which is re-enacted in substantially the same form in CPR, sch. 1. Under the old rules an application to require a tribunal other than the Lands Tribunal to state a case was made by notice of motion. Under the new system the application is by ordinary application notice under CPR, Part 23 (see RSC, ord. 61, r. 2(2) in CPR, sch. 1). RSC, ord. 61 in CPR, sch. 1, has new r. 3(A1) and (A2), which provide that an application for permission to appeal to the Court of Appeal from any tribunal to which ord. 61 applies may be combined with an application to the tribunal to state a case, and an application for permission to appeal may not be made to the Court of

Appeal until the tribunal has stated a case. These changes stem from the extension of the requirement for permission to appeal to the Court of Appeal. If permission to appeal is granted, the appeal is brought now by notice of appeal (RSC, ord. 61, r. 3(1)(a) in CPR, sch. 1).

25.14 REFERENCES TO THE EUROPEAN COURT

The old rules governing the procedure on making a reference to the Court of Justice of the European Communities are basically re-enacted in CPR, sch. 1 (RSC, ord. 114, for High Court proceedings), and sch. 2 (CCR, ord. 19, r. 15, for county court proceedings). The provisions in the schedules are based on the old provisions in the RSC and CCR, and no attempt has been made to harmonise the slight differences between the old rules. Consequently, an appeal from a High Court order to make a reference must be brought within 14 days (RSC, ord. 114, r. 6 in CPR, sch. 1), but an equivalent appeal from the county court does not have a special rule, so the time for a county court appeal is 28 days. Only the High Court rules make provision for an application for a reference being made before the trial or hearing, and the only change of substance is to this rule, which now provides that such an application must be made by claim form (RSC, ord. 114, r. 2(2) in CPR, sch. 1). Most references will be made at trial or on appeal after trial.

A recent Practice Direction (ECJ References: Procedure) [1999] 1 WLR 260 contains a reminder that before making a reference close attention should be given to the *Guidance of the European Court of Justice on References by National Courts for Preliminary Rulings*, which is reproduced in a schedule to the practice direction. It is the responsibility of the court, not the parties, to settle the terms of the reference, which must identify the question being referred as clearly, succinctly and simply as the nature of the case permits. A reference should, in a single document:

(a) identify the parties and summarise the nature and history of the proceedings;
(b) summarise the salient facts, indicating whether these have been proved, admitted or assumed;
(c) make reference to rules of national law relevant to the dispute;
(d) summarise the contentions of the parties so far as relevant;
(e) explain why a ruling of the European Court is sought, identifying the EC provisions whose effect is in issue; and
(f) formulate, without avoidable complexity, the questions to which answers are requested.

25.15 VARIATION OF DIRECTIONS

Under the new system various decisions, such as allocation to a case management track, and directions, will be taken without conducting a hearing. In these cases a party dissatisfied with the decision can usually simply apply back to the judge asking for the decision to be reconsidered, rather than needing to appeal. A party should appeal if the decision was made at a hearing at which he was present or represented, or of which he had due notice (see, for example, PD 26, para. 11.1(2); PD 28, para. 4.3(2)). Otherwise, a simple application to reconsider is the appropriate way ahead.

APPENDIX 1
CIVIL PROCEDURE RULES 1998 AND PRACTICE DIRECTIONS

This appendix contains the text of the Civil Procedure Rules 1998 (SI 1998/3132) as amended by the Civil Procedure (Amendment) Rules 1999 (SI 1999/1008), with the text of all supplementing practice directions. Each practice direction has been placed after the Part of the CPR which it supplements. Appendix 1 includes all the practice directions which were brought into force by the Lord Chief Justice, the Master of the Rolls and the Vice-Chancellor in Practice Direction (Civil Litigation: Procedure) [1999] 1 WLR 1124, apart from the Practice Direction — Protocols, which is in appendix 2. The text of the practice directions incorporates all amendments made up to 1 August 1999.

To clarify the headings, we have inserted 'CPR' at the beginning of the heading of each Part of the CPR, and 'PD' and the relevant Part number at the beginning of the heading of each practice direction.

CONTENTS

CPR PART 1	**OVERRIDING OBJECTIVE**	351
Rule 1.1	The overriding objective	351
Rule 1.2	Application by the court of the overriding objective	351
Rule 1.3	Duty of the parties	351
Rule 1.4	Court's duty to manage cases	351
CPR PART 2	**APPLICATION AND INTERPRETATION OF THE RULES**	352
Rule 2.1	Application of the Rules	352
Rule 2.2	The glossary	352
Rule 2.3	Interpretation	352
Rule 2.4	Power of judge, Master or district judge to perform functions of the court	353
Rule 2.5	Court staff	353
Rule 2.6	Court documents to be sealed	353
Rule 2.7	Court's discretion as to where it deals with cases	354
Rule 2.8	Time	354
Rule 2.9	Dates for compliance to be calendar dates and to include time of day	354
Rule 2.10	Meaning of 'month' in judgments, etc.	355
Rule 2.11	Time limits may be varied by parties	355
PD 2	**PRACTICE DIRECTION — COURT OFFICES**	356
PD 2B	**PRACTICE DIRECTION — ALLOCATION OF CASES TO LEVELS OF JUDICIARY**	358
CPR PART 3	**THE COURT'S CASE MANAGEMENT POWERS**	362
Rule 3.1	The court's general powers of management	362
Rule 3.2	Court officer's power to refer to a judge	363
Rule 3.3	Court's power to make order of its own initiative	363
Rule 3.4	Power to strike out a statement of case	363
Rule 3.5	Judgment without trial after striking out	364
Rule 3.6	Setting aside judgment entered after striking out	364

CONTENTS OF APPENDIX 1

Rule 3.7	Sanctions for non-payment of certain fees	364
Rule 3.8	Sanctions have effect unless defaulting party obtains relief	365
Rule 3.9	Relief from sanctions	365
Rule 3.10	General power of the court to rectify matters where there has been an error of procedure	365

PD 3 PRACTICE DIRECTION — STRIKING OUT A STATEMENT OF CASE 366

PD 3B PRACTICE DIRECTION — SANCTIONS FOR NON-PAYMENT OF FEES 369

CPR PART 4 FORMS 370
Rule 4	Forms	370

PD 4 PRACTICE DIRECTION — FORMS 371

CPR PART 5 COURT DOCUMENTS 386
Rule 5.1	Scope of this Part	386
Rule 5.2	Preparation of documents	386
Rule 5.3	Signature of documents by mechanical means	386
Rule 5.4	Supply of documents from court records	386

PD 5 PRACTICE DIRECTION — COURT DOCUMENTS 387

CPR PART 6 SERVICE OF DOCUMENTS 392
	I General rules about service	392
Rule 6.1	Part 6 rules about service apply generally	392
Rule 6.2	Methods of service — general	392
Rule 6.3	Who is to serve	392
Rule 6.4	Personal service	393
Rule 6.5	Address for service	393
Rule 6.6	Service of documents on children and patients	395
Rule 6.7	Deemed service	396
Rule 6.8	Service by an alternative method	396
Rule 6.9	Power of court to dispense with service	396
Rule 6.10	Certificate of service	397
Rule 6.11	Notice of non-service	397
	II Special provisions about service of the claim form	397
Rule 6.12	General rules about service subject to special rules about service of claim form	397
Rule 6.13	Service of claim form by the court — defendant's address for service	397
Rule 6.14	Certificate of service relating to the claim form	397
Rule 6.15	Service of claim form by contractually agreed method	397
Rule 6.16	Service of claim form on agent of principal who is overseas	398

PD 6 PRACTICE DIRECTION — SERVICE 399

CPR PART 7 HOW TO START PROCEEDINGS — THE CLAIM FORM 404
Rule 7.1	Where to start proceedings	404
Rule 7.2	How to start proceedings	404
Rule 7.3	Right to use one claim form to start two or more claims	404
Rule 7.4	Particulars of claim	404
Rule 7.5	Service of a claim form	404
Rule 7.6	Extension of time for serving a claim form	404
Rule 7.7	Application by defendant for service of a claim form	405
Rule 7.8	Form for defence etc. must be served with particulars of claim	405

Rule 7.9	Fixed date and other claims	405
Rule 7.10	Production Centre for claims	405

PD 7 PRACTICE DIRECTION — HOW TO START PROCEEDINGS — THE CLAIM FORM   406

PD 7B PRACTICE DIRECTION — CONSUMER CREDIT ACT CLAIM   410

PD 7C PRACTICE DIRECTION — PRODUCTION CENTRE   415

PD 7D PRACTICE DIRECTION — CLAIMS FOR THE RECOVERY OF TAXES   418

CPR PART 8 ALTERNATIVE PROCEDURE FOR CLAIMS   419

Rule 8.1	Types of claim in which Part 8 procedure may be followed	419
Rule 8.2	Contents of the claim form	419
Rule 8.3	Acknowledgment of service	419
Rule 8.4	Consequence of not filing an acknowledgment of service	420
Rule 8.5	Filing and serving written evidence	420
Rule 8.6	Evidence — general	420
Rule 8.7	Part 20 claims	420
Rule 8.8	Procedure where defendant objects to use of Part 8 procedure	420
Rule 8.9	Modifications to the general rules	421

PD 8 PRACTICE DIRECTION — ALTERNATIVE PROCEDURE FOR CLAIMS   422

PD 8B PRACTICE DIRECTION — PART 8   424

CPR PART 9 RESPONDING TO PARTICULARS OF CLAIM — GENERAL   434

Rule 9.1	Scope of this Part	434
Rule 9.2	Defence, admission or acknowledgment of service	434

CPR PART 10 ACKNOWLEDGMENT OF SERVICE   435

Rule 10.1	Acknowledgment of service	435
Rule 10.2	Consequence of not filing an acknowledgment of service	435
Rule 10.3	The period for filing an acknowledgment of service	435
Rule 10.4	Notice to claimant that defendant has filed an acknowledgment of service	435
Rule 10.5	Contents of acknowledgment of service	435

PD 10 PRACTICE DIRECTION — ACKNOWLEDGMENT OF SERVICE   436

CPR PART 11 DISPUTING THE COURT'S JURISDICTION   437

Rule 11	Procedure for disputing the court's jurisdiction	437

CPR PART 12 DEFAULT JUDGMENT   438

Rule 12.1	Meaning of 'default judgment'	438
Rule 12.2	Claims in which default judgment may not be obtained	438
Rule 12.3	Conditions to be satisfied	438
Rule 12.4	Procedure for obtaining default judgment	439
Rule 12.5	Nature of judgment where default judgment obtained by filing a request	439
Rule 12.6	Interest	439
Rule 12.7	Procedure for deciding an amount or value	440
Rule 12.8	Claim against more than one defendant	440
Rule 12.9	Procedure for obtaining default judgment for costs only	440
Rule 12.10	Default judgment obtained by making an application	440
Rule 12.11	Supplementary provisions where applications for default judgment are made	441

CONTENTS OF APPENDIX 1

PD 12	**PRACTICE DIRECTION — DEFAULT JUDGMENT**	442
CPR PART 13	**SETTING ASIDE OR VARYING DEFAULT JUDGMENT**	445
Rule 13.1	Scope of this Part	445
Rule 13.2	Cases where the court must set aside judgment entered under Part 12	445
Rule 13.3	Cases where the court may set aside or vary judgment entered under Part 12	445
Rule 13.4	Application to set aside or vary judgment — procedure	445
Rule 13.5	Claimant's duty to apply to set aside judgment	446
Rule 13.6	Abandoned claim restored where default judgment set aside	446
CPR PART 14	**ADMISSIONS**	447
Rule 14.1	Making an admission	447
Rule 14.2	Period for making an admission	447
Rule 14.3	Admission by notice in writing — application for judgment	448
Rule 14.4	Admission of whole of claim for specified amount of money	448
Rule 14.5	Admission of part of claim for specified amount of money	448
Rule 14.6	Admission of liability to pay whole of claim for unspecified amount of money	449
Rule 14.7	Admission of liability to pay claim for unspecified amount of money where defendant offers a sum in satisfaction of the claim	449
Rule 14.8	Allocation of claims in relation to outstanding matters	450
Rule 14.9	Request for time to pay	450
Rule 14.10	Determination of rate of payment	450
Rule 14.11	Determination of rate of payment by court officer	450
Rule 14.12	Determination of rate of payment by judge	451
Rule 14.13	Right of re-determination	451
Rule 14.14	Interest	451
PD 14	**PRACTICE DIRECTION — ADMISSIONS**	452
CPR PART 15	**DEFENCE AND REPLY**	454
Rule 15.1	Part not to apply where claimant uses Part 8 procedure	454
Rule 15.2	Filing a defence	454
Rule 15.3	Consequence of not filing a defence	454
Rule 15.4	The period for filing a defence	454
Rule 15.5	Agreement extending the period for filing a defence	454
Rule 15.6	Service of copy of defence	454
Rule 15.7	Making a counterclaim	455
Rule 15.8	Reply to defence	455
Rule 15.9	No statement of case after a reply to be filed without court's permission	455
Rule 15.10	Claimant's notice where defence is that money claimed has been paid	455
Rule 15.11	Claim stayed if it is not defended or admitted	455
PD 15	**PRACTICE DIRECTION — DEFENCE AND REPLY**	456
CPR PART 16	**STATEMENTS OF CASE**	457
Rule 16.1	Part not to apply where claimant uses Part 8 procedure	457
Rule 16.2	Contents of the claim form	457
Rule 16.3	Statement of value to be included in the claim form	457
Rule 16.4	Contents of the particulars of claim	458
Rule 16.5	Contents of defence	458
Rule 16.6	Defence of set-off	459
Rule 16.7	Reply to defence	459
Rule 16.8	Court's power to dispense with statements of case	459
PD 16	**PRACTICE DIRECTION — STATEMENTS OF CASE**	460

CONTENTS OF APPENDIX 1

CPR PART 17	**AMENDMENTS TO STATEMENTS OF CASE**	**466**
Rule 17.1	Amendments to statements of case	466
Rule 17.2	Power of court to disallow amendments made without permission	466
Rule 17.3	Amendments to statements of case with the permission of the court	466
Rule 17.4	Amendments to statements of case after the end of a relevant limitation period	466
PD 17	**PRACTICE DIRECTION — AMENDMENTS TO STATEMENTS OF CASE**	**468**
CPR PART 18	**FURTHER INFORMATION**	**469**
Rule 18.1	Obtaining further information	469
Rule 18.2	Restriction on the use of further information	469
PD 18	**PRACTICE DIRECTION — FURTHER INFORMATION**	**470**
CPR PART 19	**ADDITION AND SUBSTITUTION OF PARTIES**	**472**
Rule 19.1	Change of parties — general	472
Rule 19.2	Provisions applicable where two or more persons are jointly entitled to a remedy	472
Rule 19.3	Procedure for adding and substituting parties	472
Rule 19.4	Special provisions about adding or substituting parties after the end of a relevant limitation period	473
PD 19	**PRACTICE DIRECTION — ADDITION AND SUBSTITUTION OF PARTIES**	**474**
CPR PART 20	**COUNTERCLAIMS AND OTHER ADDITIONAL CLAIMS**	**476**
Rule 20.1	Purpose of Part 20	476
Rule 20.2	Meaning of 'Part 20 claim'	476
Rule 20.3	Part 20 claim to be treated as a claim for the purposes of the Rules	476
Rule 20.4	Defendant's counterclaim against the claimant	476
Rule 20.5	Counterclaim against a person other than the claimant	477
Rule 20.6	Defendant's claim for contribution or indemnity from co-defendant	477
Rule 20.7	Procedure for making any other Part 20 claim	477
Rule 20.8	Service of a Part 20 claim form	477
Rule 20.9	Matters relevant to question of whether a Part 20 claim should be separate from main claim	477
Rule 20.10	Effect of service of a Part 20 claim	478
Rule 20.11	Special provisions relating to default judgment on a Part 20 claim other than a counterclaim or a contribution or indemnity notice	478
Rule 20.12	Procedural steps on service of a Part 20 claim form on a non-party	478
Rule 20.13	Case management where there is a defence to a Part 20 claim form	479
PD 20	**PRACTICE DIRECTION — COUNTERCLAIMS AND OTHER PART 20 CLAIMS**	**480**
CPR PART 21	**CHILDREN AND PATIENTS**	**482**
Rule 21.1	Scope of this Part	482
Rule 21.2	Requirement for litigation friend in proceedings by or against children and patients	482
Rule 21.3	Stage of proceedings at which a litigation friend becomes necessary	482

CONTENTS OF APPENDIX 1

Rule 21.4	Who may be a litigation friend without a court order	483
Rule 21.5	How a person becomes a litigation friend without a court order	483
Rule 21.6	How a person becomes a litigation friend by court order	483
Rule 21.7	Court's power to change litigation friend and to prevent person acting as litigation friend	484
Rule 21.8	Appointment of litigation friend by court order — supplementary	484
Rule 21.9	Procedure where appointment of litigation friend ceases	484
Rule 21.10	Compromise etc. by or on behalf of child or patient	485
Rule 21.11	Control of money recovered by or on behalf of child or patient	485
Rule 21.12	Appointment of guardian of child's estate	485
PD 21	**PRACTICE DIRECTION — CHILDREN AND PATIENTS**	**486**
CPR PART 22	**STATEMENTS OF TRUTH**	**492**
Rule 22.1	Documents to be verified by a statement of truth	492
Rule 22.2	Failure to verify a statement of case	492
Rule 22.3	Failure to verify a witness statement	492
Rule 22.4	Power of the court to require a document to be verified	493
PD 22	**PRACTICE DIRECTION — STATEMENTS OF TRUTH**	**494**
CPR PART 23	**GENERAL RULES ABOUT APPLICATIONS FOR COURT ORDERS**	**496**
Rule 23.1	Meaning of 'application notice' and 'respondent'	496
Rule 23.2	Where to make an application	496
Rule 23.3	Application notice to be filed	496
Rule 23.4	Notice of an application	496
Rule 23.5	Time when an application is made	496
Rule 23.6	What an application notice must include	497
Rule 23.7	Service of a copy of an application notice	497
Rule 23.8	Applications which may be dealt with without a hearing	497
Rule 23.9	Service of application where application made without notice	497
Rule 23.10	Application to set aside or vary order made without notice	497
Rule 23.11	Power of the court to proceed in the absence of a party	498
PD 23	**PRACTICE DIRECTION — APPLICATIONS**	**499**
CPR PART 24	**SUMMARY JUDGMENT**	**503**
Rule 24.1	Scope of this Part	503
Rule 24.2	Grounds for summary judgment	503
Rule 24.3	Types of proceedings in which summary judgment is available	503
Rule 24.4	Procedure	503
Rule 24.5	Evidence for the purposes of a summary judgment hearing	504
Rule 24.6	Court's powers when it determines a summary judgment application	504
PD 24	**PRACTICE DIRECTION — THE SUMMARY DISPOSAL OF CLAIMS**	**505**
CPR PART 25	**INTERIM REMEDIES**	**508**
Rule 25.1	Orders for interim remedies	508
Rule 25.2	Time when an order for an interim remedy may be made	509
Rule 25.3	How to apply for an interim remedy	509
Rule 25.4	Application for an interim remedy where there is no related claim	509
Rule 25.5	Inspection of property before commencement or against a non-party	510

CONTENTS OF APPENDIX 1

Rule 25.6	Interim payments — general procedure	510
Rule 25.7	Interim payments — conditions to be satisfied and matters to be taken into account	510
Rule 25.8	Powers of court where it has made an order for interim payment	510
Rule 25.9	Restriction on disclosure of an interim payment	511
Rule 25.10	Interim injunction to cease if claim stayed	511
Rule 25.11	Interim injunction to cease after 14 days if claim struck out	511

PD 25 PRACTICE DIRECTION — INTERIM INJUNCTIONS 513

PD 25B PRACTICE DIRECTION — INTERIM PAYMENTS 530

PD 25C PRACTICE DIRECTION — ACCOUNTS AND INQUIRIES 532

CPR PART 26 CASE MANAGEMENT — PRELIMINARY STAGE 533

Rule 26.1	Scope of this Part	533
Rule 26.2	Automatic transfer	533
Rule 26.3	Allocation questionnaire	534
Rule 26.4	Stay to allow for settlement of the case	534
Rule 26.5	Allocation	534
Rule 26.6	Scope of each track	535
Rule 26.7	General rule for allocation	535
Rule 26.8	Matters relevant to allocation to a track	536
Rule 26.9	Notice of allocation	536
Rule 26.10	Re-allocation	536

PD 26 PRACTICE DIRECTION — CASE MANAGEMENT — PRELIMINARY STAGE: ALLOCATION AND RE-ALLOCATION 537

CPR PART 27 THE SMALL CLAIMS TRACK 546

Rule 27.1	Scope of this Part	546
Rule 27.2	Extent to which other Parts apply	546
Rule 27.3	Court's power to grant a final remedy	547
Rule 27.4	Preparation for the hearing	547
Rule 27.5	Experts	547
Rule 27.6	Preliminary hearing	547
Rule 27.7	Power of court to add to, vary or revoke directions	548
Rule 27.8	Conduct of the hearing	548
Rule 27.9	Non-attendance of parties at a final hearing	548
Rule 27.10	Disposal without a hearing	548
Rule 27.11	Setting judgment aside and re-hearing	548
Rule 27.12	Right of appeal under Part 27	549
Rule 27.13	Procedure for making an appeal	549
Rule 27.14	Costs on the small claims track	549
Rule 27.15	Claim re-allocated from the small claims track to another track	550

PD 27 PRACTICE DIRECTION — SMALL CLAIMS TRACK 551

CPR PART 28 THE FAST TRACK 557

Rule 28.1	Scope of this Part	557
Rule 28.2	General provisions	557
Rule 28.3	Directions	557
Rule 28.4	Variation of case management timetable	557
Rule 28.5	Listing questionnaire	557
Rule 28.6	Fixing or confirming the trial date and giving directions	558
Rule 28.7	Conduct of trial	558

PD 28 PRACTICE DIRECTION — THE FAST TRACK 559

CONTENTS OF APPENDIX 1

CPR PART 29	**THE MULTI-TRACK**	**567**
Rule 29.1	Scope of this Part	567
Rule 29.2	Case management	567
Rule 29.3	Case management conference and pre-trial review	567
Rule 29.4	Steps taken by the parties	567
Rule 29.5	Variation of case management timetable	567
Rule 29.6	Listing questionnaire	568
Rule 29.7	Pre-trial review	568
Rule 29.8	Setting a trial timetable and fixing or confirming the trial date or week	568
Rule 29.9	Conduct of the trial	568
PD 29	**PRACTICE DIRECTION — THE MULTI-TRACK**	**569**
CPR PART 30	**TRANSFER**	**576**
Rule 30.1	Scope of this Part	576
Rule 30.2	Transfer between county courts and within the High Court	576
Rule 30.3	Criteria for a transfer order	577
Rule 30.4	Procedure	577
Rule 30.5	Transfer between Divisions and to and from a specialist list	577
Rule 30.6	Power to specify place where hearings are to be held	577
Rule 30.7	Transfer of control of money in court	577
Rule 30.8	Certiorari or prohibition	577
PD 30	**PRACTICE DIRECTION — TRANSFER**	**578**
CPR PART 31	**DISCLOSURE AND INSPECTION OF DOCUMENTS**	**579**
Rule 31.1	Scope of this Part	579
Rule 31.2	Meaning of disclosure	579
Rule 31.3	Right of inspection of a disclosed document	579
Rule 31.4	Meaning of document	580
Rule 31.5	Disclosure limited to standard disclosure	580
Rule 31.6	Standard disclosure — what documents are to be disclosed	580
Rule 31.7	Duty of search	580
Rule 31.8	Duty of disclosure limited to documents which are or have been in a party's control	580
Rule 31.9	Disclosure of copies	580
Rule 31.10	Procedure for standard disclosure	581
Rule 31.11	Duty of disclosure continues during proceedings	581
Rule 31.12	Specific disclosure or inspection	581
Rule 31.13	Disclosure in stages	581
Rule 31.14	Documents referred to in statements of case etc.	581
Rule 31.15	Inspection and copying of documents	582
Rule 31.16	Disclosure before proceedings start	582
Rule 31.17	Orders for disclosure against a person not a party	582
Rule 31.18	Rules not to limit other powers of the court to order disclosure	583
Rule 31.19	Claim to withhold inspection or disclosure of a document	583
Rule 31.20	Restriction on use of a privileged document inspection of which has been inadvertently allowed	583
Rule 31.21	Consequence of failure to disclose documents or permit inspection	583
Rule 31.22	Subsequent use of disclosed documents	583
PD 31	**PRACTICE DIRECTION — DISCLOSURE AND INSPECTION**	**585**
CPR PART 32	**EVIDENCE**	**588**
Rule 32.1	Power of court to control evidence	588
Rule 32.2	Evidence of witnesses — general rule	588

CONTENTS OF APPENDIX 1

Rule 32.3	Evidence by video link or other means	588
Rule 32.4	Requirement to serve witness statements for use at trial	588
Rule 32.5	Use at trial of witness statements which have been served	589
Rule 32.6	Evidence in proceedings other than at trial	589
Rule 32.7	Order for cross-examination	589
Rule 32.8	Form of witness statement	589
Rule 32.9	Witness summaries	589
Rule 32.10	Consequence of failure to serve witness statement or summary	590
Rule 32.11	Cross-examination on a witness statement	590
Rule 32.12	Use of witness statements for other purposes	590
Rule 32.13	Availability of witness statements for inspection	590
Rule 32.14	False statements	590
Rule 32.15	Affidavit evidence	590
Rule 32.16	Form of affidavit	591
Rule 32.17	Affidavit made outside the jurisdiction	591
Rule 32.18	Notice to admit facts	591
Rule 32.19	Notice to admit or produce documents	591

PD 32 PRACTICE DIRECTION — WRITTEN EVIDENCE 592

CPR PART 33 MISCELLANEOUS RULES ABOUT EVIDENCE 599

Rule 33.1	Introductory	599
Rule 33.2	Notice of intention to rely on hearsay evidence	599
Rule 33.3	Circumstances in which notice of intention to rely on hearsay evidence is not required	599
Rule 33.4	Power to call witness for cross-examination on hearsay evidence	600
Rule 33.5	Credibility	600
Rule 33.6	Use of plans, photographs and models as evidence	600
Rule 33.7	Evidence of finding on question of foreign law	600
Rule 33.8	Evidence of consent of trustee to act	601

PD 33 PRACTICE DIRECTION — CIVIL EVIDENCE ACT 1995 602

CPR PART 34 DEPOSITIONS AND COURT ATTENDANCE BY WITNESSES 603

Rule 34.1	Scope of this Part	603
Rule 34.2	Witness summonses	603
Rule 34.3	Issue of a witness summons	603
Rule 34.4	Witness summons in aid of inferior court or of tribunal	604
Rule 34.5	Time for serving a witness summons	604
Rule 34.6	Who is to serve a witness summons	604
Rule 34.7	Right of witness to travelling expenses and compensation for loss of time	604
Rule 34.8	Evidence by deposition	604
Rule 34.9	Conduct of examination	605
Rule 34.10	Enforcing attendance of witness	605
Rule 34.11	Use of deposition at a hearing	605
Rule 34.12	Restrictions on subsequent use of deposition taken for the purpose of any hearing except the trial	605
Rule 34.13	Where a person to be examined is out of the jurisdiction — letter of request	606
Rule 34.14	Fees and expenses of examiner of the court	606
Rule 34.15	Examiners of the court	606

PD 34 PRACTICE DIRECTION — DEPOSITIONS AND COURT ATTENDANCE BY WITNESSES 607

PD 34B PRACTICE DIRECTION — FEES FOR EXAMINERS OF THE COURT 612

CONTENTS OF APPENDIX 1

CPR PART 35   EXPERTS AND ASSESSORS — 614
Rule 35.1   Duty to restrict expert evidence — 614
Rule 35.2   Interpretation — 614
Rule 35.3   Experts — overriding duty to the court — 614
Rule 35.4   Court's power to restrict expert evidence — 614
Rule 35.5   General requirement for expert evidence to be given in written report — 614
Rule 35.6   Written questions to experts — 614
Rule 35.7   Court's power to direct that evidence is to be given by a single joint expert — 615
Rule 35.8   Instructions to a single joint expert — 615
Rule 35.9   Power of court to direct party to provide information — 615
Rule 35.10   Contents of report — 615
Rule 35.11   Use by one party of expert's report disclosed by another — 616
Rule 35.12   Discussions between experts — 616
Rule 35.13   Consequence of failure to disclose expert's report — 616
Rule 35.14   Expert's right to ask court for directions — 616
Rule 35.15   Assessors — 616

PD 35   PRACTICE DIRECTION — EXPERTS AND ASSESSORS — 618

CPR PART 36   OFFERS TO SETTLE AND PAYMENTS INTO COURT — 620
Rule 36.1   Scope of this Part — 620
Rule 36.2   Part 36 offers and Part 36 payments — general provisions — 620
Rule 36.3   A defendant's offer to settle a money claim requires a Part 36 payment — 621
Rule 36.4   Defendant's offer to settle the whole of a claim which includes both a money claim and a non-money claim — 621
Rule 36.5   Form and content of a Part 36 offer — 621
Rule 36.6   Notice of a Part 36 payment — 622
Rule 36.7   Offer to settle a claim for provisional damages — 622
Rule 36.8   Time when a Part 36 offer or a Part 36 payment is made and accepted — 623
Rule 36.9   Clarification of a Part 36 offer or a Part 36 payment notice — 623
Rule 36.10   Court to take into account offer to settle made before commencement of proceedings — 623
Rule 36.11   Time for acceptance of a defendant's Part 36 offer or Part 36 payment — 623
Rule 36.12   Time for acceptance of a claimant's Part 36 offer — 624
Rule 36.13   Costs consequences of acceptance of a defendant's Part 36 offer or Part 36 payment — 624
Rule 36.14   Costs consequences of acceptance of a claimant's Part 36 offer — 624
Rule 36.15   The effect of acceptance of a Part 36 offer or a Part 36 payment — 624
Rule 36.16   Payment out of a sum in court on the acceptance of a Part 36 payment — 625
Rule 36.17   Acceptance of a Part 36 offer or a Part 36 payment made by one or more, but not all, defendants — 625
Rule 36.18   Other cases where a court order is required to enable acceptance of a Part 36 offer or a Part 36 payment — 625
Rule 36.19   Restriction on disclosure of a Part 36 offer or a Part 36 payment — 626
Rule 36.20   Costs consequences where a claimant fails to do better than a Part 36 offer or a Part 36 payment — 626
Rule 36.21   Costs and other consequences where claimant does better than he proposed in his Part 36 offer — 626
Rule 36.22   Interest — 627
Rule 36.23   Deduction of benefits — 627

CONTENTS OF APPENDIX 1

PD 36 PRACTICE DIRECTION — OFFERS TO SETTLE AND PAYMENTS INTO COURT		**628**
CPR PART 37 MISCELLANEOUS PROVISIONS ABOUT PAYMENTS INTO COURT		**633**
Rule 37.1	Money paid into court under a court order — general	633
Rule 37.2	Money paid into court may be treated as a Part 36 payment	633
Rule 37.3	Money paid into court where defendant wishes to rely on defence of tender before claim	633
Rule 37.4	Proceedings under Fatal Accidents Act 1976 and Law Reform (Miscellaneous Provisions) Act 1934 — apportionment by court	633
PD 37 PRACTICE DIRECTION — MISCELLANEOUS PROVISIONS ABOUT PAYMENTS INTO COURT		**635**
CPR PART 38 DISCONTINUANCE		**637**
Rule 38.1	Scope of this Part	637
Rule 38.2	Right to discontinue claim	637
Rule 38.3	Procedure for discontinuing	637
Rule 38.4	Right to apply to have notice of discontinuance set aside	638
Rule 38.5	When discontinuance takes effect where permission of the court is not needed	638
Rule 38.6	Liability for costs	638
Rule 38.7	Discontinuance and subsequent proceedings	638
Rule 38.8	Stay of remainder of partly discontinued proceedings where costs not paid	638
CPR PART 39 MISCELLANEOUS PROVISIONS RELATING TO HEARINGS		**639**
Rule 39.1	Interpretation	639
Rule 39.2	General rule — hearing to be in public	639
Rule 39.3	Failure to attend the trial	639
Rule 39.4	Timetable for trial	640
Rule 39.5	Trial bundles	640
Rule 39.6	Representation at trial of companies or other corporations	640
Rule 39.7	Impounded documents	640
PD 39 PRACTICE DIRECTION — MISCELLANEOUS PROVISIONS RELATING TO HEARINGS		**641**
PD 39B PRACTICE DIRECTION — COURT SITTINGS		**645**
CPR PART 40 JUDGMENTS AND ORDERS		**647**
Rule 40.1	Scope of this Part	647
Rule 40.2	Standard requirements	647
Rule 40.3	Drawing up and filing of judgments and orders	647
Rule 40.4	Service of judgments and orders	648
Rule 40.5	Power to require judgment or order to be served on a party as well as his solicitor	648
Rule 40.6	Consent judgments and orders	648
Rule 40.7	When judgment or order takes effect	649
Rule 40.8	Time from which interest begins to run	649
Rule 40.9	Who may apply to set aside or vary a judgment or order	649
Rule 40.10	Judgment against a State in default of acknowledgment of service	649
Rule 40.11	Time for complying with a judgment or order	649
Rule 40.12	Correction of errors in judgments and orders	649
Rule 40.13	Cases where court gives judgment both on claim and counterclaim	649
Rule 40.14	Judgment in favour of certain part owners relating to the detention of goods	650

CONTENTS OF APPENDIX 1

PD 40 PRACTICE DIRECTION — ACCOUNTS, INQUIRIES ETC. 651

PD 40B PRACTICE DIRECTION — JUDGMENTS AND ORDERS 653

PD 40C PRACTICE DIRECTION — STRUCTURED SETTLEMENTS 658

CPR PART 41 PROVISIONAL DAMAGES 661
Rule 41.1 Application and definitions 661
Rule 41.2 Order for an award of provisional damages 661
Rule 41.3 Application for further damages 661

PD 41 PRACTICE DIRECTION — PROVISIONAL DAMAGES 662

CPR PART 42 CHANGE OF SOLICITOR 665
Rule 42.1 Solicitor acting for a party 665
Rule 42.2 Change of solicitor — duty to give notice 665
Rule 42.3 Order that a solicitor has ceased to act 665
Rule 42.4 Removal of solicitor who has ceased to act on application of another party 666

PD 42 PRACTICE DIRECTION — CHANGE OF SOLICITOR 667

CPR PART 43 SCOPE OF COSTS RULES AND DEFINITIONS 669
Rule 43.1 Scope of this Part 669
Rule 43.2 Definitions and application 669
Rule 43.3 Meaning of summary assessment 669
Rule 43.4 Meaning of detailed assessment 669

PD COSTS PRACTICE DIRECTION ABOUT COSTS — INTRODUCTION 670
Schedule of cost forms 670

PD 43 PRACTICE DIRECTION — SCOPE OF COSTS RULES AND DEFINITIONS 671

CPR PART 44 GENERAL RULES ABOUT COSTS 677
Rule 44.1 Scope of this Part 677
Rule 44.2 Solicitor's duty to notify client 677
Rule 44.3 Court's discretion and circumstances to be taken into account when exercising its discretion as to costs 677
Rule 44.4 Basis of assessment 678
Rule 44.5 Factors to be taken into account in deciding the amount of costs 679
Rule 44.6 Fixed costs 679
Rule 44.7 Procedure for assessing costs 679
Rule 44.8 Time for complying with an order for costs 679
Rule 44.9 Costs on the small claims track and fast track 679
Rule 44.10 Limitation on amount court may allow where a claim allocated to the fast track settles before trial 680
Rule 44.11 Costs following allocation and re-allocation 680
Rule 44.12 Cases where costs orders deemed to have been made 680
Rule 44.13 Special situations 680
Rule 44.14 Court's powers in relation to misconduct 681

PD 44 PRACTICE DIRECTION — GENERAL RULES ABOUT COSTS 682

CPR PART 45 FIXED COSTS 687
Rule 45.1 Scope of this Part 687
Rule 45.2 Amount of fixed commencement costs 687
Rule 45.3 When defendant only liable for fixed commencement costs 688
Rule 45.4 Costs on entry of judgment 688
Rule 45.5 Miscellaneous fixed costs 689

CONTENTS OF APPENDIX 1

PD 45	**PRACTICE DIRECTION — FIXED COSTS**	**690**
CPR PART 46	**FAST TRACK TRIAL COSTS**	**691**
Rule 46.1	Scope of this Part	691
Rule 46.2	Amount of fast track trial costs	691
Rule 46.3	Power to award more or less than the amount of fast track trial costs	692
Rule 46.4	Fast track trial costs where there is more than one claimant or defendant	693
PD 46	**PRACTICE DIRECTION — FAST TRACK TRIAL COSTS**	**694**
CPR PART 47	**PROCEDURE FOR DETAILED ASSESSMENT OF COSTS AND DEFAULT PROVISIONS**	**695**
	I General rules about detailed assessment	**696**
Rule 47.1	Time when detailed assessment may be carried out	646
Rule 47.2	No stay of detailed assessment where there is an appeal	696
Rule 47.3	Powers of an authorised court officer	696
Rule 47.4	Venue for detailed assessment proceedings	696
	II Costs payable by one party to another — commencement of detailed assessment proceedings	**696**
Rule 47.5	Application of this section	696
Rule 47.6	Commencement of detailed assessment proceedings	696
Rule 47.7	Period for commencing detailed assessment proceedings	697
Rule 47.8	Sanction for delay in commencing detailed assessment proceedings	697
Rule 47.9	Points of dispute and consequence of not serving	698
Rule 47.10	Procedure where costs are agreed	698
	III Costs payable by one party to another — default provisions	**698**
Rule 47.11	Default costs certificate	698
Rule 47.12	Setting aside default costs certificate	698
	IV Costs payable by one party to another — procedure where points of dispute are served	**699**
Rule 47.13	Optional reply	699
Rule 47.14	Detailed assessment hearing	699
	V Interim costs certificate and final costs certificate	**700**
Rule 47.15	Power to issue an interim certificate	700
Rule 47.16	Final costs certificate	700
	VI Detailed assessment procedure for costs of an assisted person where costs are payable out of the legal aid fund	**700**
Rule 47.17	Detailed assessment procedure for costs of an assisted person where costs are payable out of the legal aid fund	700
	VII Costs of detailed assessment proceedings	**700**
Rule 47.18	Liability for costs of detailed assessment proceedings	700
Rule 47.19	Offers to settle without prejudice save as to costs of the detailed assessment proceedings	701
	VIII Appeal against decisions in detailed assessment proceedings	**701**
Rule 47.20	Right to appeal	701
Rule 47.21	Preliminary requirements for bringing an appeal	701
Rule 47.22	Court to hear appeal	701
Rule 47.23	Duty to seek reasons	702
Rule 47.24	Obtaining the court's permission to appeal	702
Rule 47.25	Appeal procedure	702
Rule 47.26	Powers of the court on appeal	702

CONTENTS OF APPENDIX 1

PD 47 PRACTICE DIRECTION — PROCEDURE FOR DETAILED ASSESSMENT OF COSTS AND DEFAULT PROVISIONS   703

CPR PART 48 COSTS — SPECIAL CASES   715
    I Costs payable by or to particular persons   715
Rule 48.1   Pre-commencement disclosure and orders for disclosure against a person who is not a party   715
Rule 48.2   Costs orders in favour of or against non-parties   715
Rule 48.3   Amount of costs where costs are payable pursuant to a contract   716
Rule 48.4   Limitations on court's power to award costs in favour of trustee or personal representative   716
Rule 48.5   Costs where money is payable by or to a child or patient   716
Rule 48.6   Litigants in person   716

    II Costs relating to solicitors and other legal representatives   717
Rule 48.7   Personal liability of legal representative for costs — wasted costs orders   717
Rule 48.8   Basis of detailed assessment of solicitor and client costs   717
Rule 48.9   Conditional fees   718
Rule 48.10   Assessment procedure   718

PD 48 PRACTICE DIRECTION — COSTS — SPECIAL CASES   719

CPR PART 49 SPECIALIST PROCEEDINGS   725
Rule 49   Specialist proceedings   725

PD 49 PRACTICE DIRECTION — CONTENTIOUS PROBATE PROCEEDINGS   726

PD 49B PRACTICE DIRECTION — APPLICATIONS UNDER THE COMPANIES ACT 1985 AND THE INSURANCE COMPANIES ACT 1982   732

PD 49C PRACTICE DIRECTION — TECHNOLOGY AND CONSTRUCTION COURT   736

PD 49D PRACTICE DIRECTION — COMMERCIAL COURT   751

PD 49E PRACTICE DIRECTION — PATENTS ETC.   754

PD 49F PRACTICE DIRECTION — ADMIRALTY   766

PD 49G PRACTICE DIRECTION — ARBITRATIONS   798

PD 49H PRACTICE DIRECTION — MERCANTILE COURTS AND BUSINESS LISTS   811

CPR PART 50 APPLICATION OF THE SCHEDULES   816
Rule 50   Application of the Schedules   816

CPR PART 51 TRANSITIONAL ARRANGEMENTS   817
Rule 51   Transitional Arrangements   817

PD 51 PRACTICE DIRECTION — TRANSITIONAL ARRANGEMENTS   818

GLOSSARY   822

CPR SCHEDULE 1

RSC ORDERS
Order 10   Service of originating process: general provisions   824
Order 11   Service of process, etc., out of the jurisdiction   824
Order 15   Causes of action, counterclaims and parties   830
Order 17   Interpleader   834

CONTENTS OF APPENDIX 1

Order 23	Security for costs	838
Order 30	Receivers	838
Order 31	Sales, etc., of land by order of court: conveyancing counsel of the court	840
Order 44	Proceedings under judgments and orders: Chancery Division	841
Order 45	Enforcement of judgments and orders: general	844
Order 46	Writs of execution: general	848
Order 47	Writs of fieri facias	850
Order 48	Examination of judgment debtor, etc.	852
Order 49	Garnishee proceedings	853
Order 50	Charging orders, stop orders, etc.	855
Order 51	Receivers: equitable execution	859
Order 52	Committal	860
Order 53	Applications for judicial review	862
Order 54	Applications for writ of habeas corpus	866
Order 55	Appeals to High Court from court, tribunal or person: general	868
Order 56	Appeals, etc., to High Court by case stated: general	870
Order 57	Divisional Court proceedings, etc.: supplementary provisions	873
Order 58	Appeals from masters, registrars, referees and judges	874
Order 59	Appeals to the Court of Appeal	875
Order 60	Appeals to Court of Appeal from the Restrictive Practices Court	884
Order 61	Appeals from tribunals to Court of Appeal by case stated	885
Order 62	Costs	886
Order 64	Sittings, vacations and office hours	888
Order 69	Service of foreign process	888
Order 70	Obtaining evidence for foreign courts, etc.	889
Order 71	Reciprocal enforcement of judgments and enforcement of European Community judgments and recommendations etc. under the Merchant Shipping (Liner Conferences) Act 1982	891
Order 74	Applications and appeals under the Merchant Shipping Act 1995	901
Order 77	Proceedings by and against the Crown	901
Order 79	Criminal proceedings	906
Order 81	Partners	907
Order 82	Defamation claims	910
Order 85	Administration and similar actions	912
Order 87	Debenture holders' claims: receiver's register	913
Order 88	Mortgage claims	915
Order 91	Revenue proceedings	918
Order 92	Lodgment, investment, etc., of funds in court: Chancery Division	921
Order 93	Applications and appeals to High Court under various Acts: Chancery Division	922
Order 94	Applications and appeals to High Court under various Acts: Queen's Bench Division	926
Order 95	Bills of Sale Acts 1878 and 1882 and the Industrial and Provident Societies Act 1967	933
Order 96	The Mines (Working Facilities and Support) Act 1966, etc.	934
Order 97	The Landlord and Tenant Acts 1927, 1954 and 1987	936
Order 98	Local Government Finance Act 1982, Part III	940
Order 99	Inheritance (Provision for Family and Dependants) Act 1975	941

CONTENTS OF APPENDIX 1

Order 101	The Pensions Appeal Tribunals Act 1943	942
Order 106	Proceedings relating to solicitors: the Solicitors Act 1974	943
Order 108	Proceedings relating to charities: the Charities Act 1993	946
Order 109	The Administration of Justice Act 1960	947
Order 110	Environmental control proceedings	948
Order 111	The Social Security Administration Act 1992	949
Order 112	Applications for use of blood tests in determining paternity	950
Order 113	Summary proceedings for possession of land	950
Order 114	References to the European Court	952
Order 115	Confiscation and forfeiture in connection with criminal proceedings	953
Order 116	The Criminal Procedure and Investigations Act 1996	961

PD RSC ORD. 11 PRACTICE DIRECTION — SERVICE OUT OF THE JURISDICTION 965

PD RSC ORD. 31 PRACTICE DIRECTION — SALE, ETC. OF LAND BY ORDER OF COURT: CONVEYANCING COUNSEL OF THE COURT 973

PD RSC ORD. 52 PRACTICE DIRECTION — COMMITTAL APPLICATIONS 974

PD RSC ORD. 53 PRACTICE DIRECTION — SCHEDULE 1, ORDER 53 (APPLICATION FOR JUDICIAL REVIEW) 977

PD RSC ORD. 54 PRACTICE DIRECTION — SCHEDULE 1, ORDER 54 (APPLICATION FOR WRIT OF HABEAS CORPUS) 979

PD RSC ORD. 58 PRACTICE DIRECTION — APPEALS FROM MASTERS ETC. 981

CPR SCHEDULE 2

CCR ORDERS

Order 1	Citation, application and interpretation	982
Order 3	Commencement of proceedings	982
Order 4	Venue for bringing proceedings	983
Order 5	Causes of action and parties	983
Order 6	Particulars of claim	986
Order 7	Service of documents	989
Order 13	Applications and orders in the course of proceedings	990
Order 16	Transfer of proceedings	990
Order 19	Reference to European Court	990
Order 22	Judgments and orders	991
Order 24	Summary proceedings for the recovery of land	993
Order 25	Enforcement of judgments and orders: general	998
Order 26	Warrants of execution, delivery and possession	1003
Order 27	Attachment of earnings	1007
Order 28	Judgment summonses	1015
Order 29	Committal for breach of order or undertaking	1018
Order 30	Garnishee proceedings	1020
Order 31	Charging orders	1022
Order 33	Interpleader proceedings	1024
Order 34	Penal and disciplinary provisions	1027
Order 35	Enforcement of county court judgments outside England and Wales	1028
Order 37	Rehearing, setting aside and appeal from district judge	1030
Order 38	Costs	1031

CONTENTS OF APPENDIX 1

Order 39	Administration orders	1034
Order 42	Proceedings by and against the Crown	1038
Order 43	The Landlord and Tenant Acts 1927, 1954, 1985 and 1987	1041
Order 44	The Agricultural Holdings Act 1986	1046
Order 45	The Representation of the People Act 1983	1047
Order 46	The Legitimacy Act 1976	1048
Order 47	Domestic and matrimonial proceedings	1049
Order 48B	Enforcement of parking penalties under the Road Traffic Act 1991	1049
Order 48D	Enforcement of fixed penalties under the Road Traffic (Vehicle Emissions) (Fixed Penalty) Regulations 1997	1053
Order 49	Miscellaneous statutes	1054

PRACTICE DIRECTION FOR THE COURT OF APPEAL (CIVIL DIVISION) — 1071

PRACTICE DIRECTION — INSOLVENCY PROCEEDINGS — 1112

PRACTICE DIRECTION — DIRECTORS DISQUALIFICATION PROCEEDINGS — 1124

PRACTICE DIRECTION RELATING TO THE USE OF THE WELSH LANGUAGE IN CASES IN THE CIVIL COURTS IN WALES — 1147

CYFARWYDDIADAU YMARFER AR DDEFNYDDIO'R IAITH GYMRAEG MEWN ACHOSION YN Y LLYSOEDD SIFIL YNG NGHYMRU — 1149

PRACTICE DIRECTION — DEVOLUTION ISSUES (AND CROWN OFFICE APPLICATIONS IN WALES) — 1151

CYFARWYDDYD YMARFER — MATERION YN YMWNEUD Â DATGANOLI (A CHEISIADAU SWYDDFA'R GORON YNG NGHYMRU) — 1164

CHANCERY DIVISION PRACTICE DIRECTIONS — 1175

PRACTICE DIRECTION, CHANCERY AND QUEEN'S BENCH DIVISIONS EXCLUDING THE ADMIRALTY AND COMMERCIAL COURTS, AND THE TECHNOLOGY AND CONSTRUCTION COURT — THE FIXING OF TRIAL DATES AND WINDOWS IN THE MULTI-TRACK — 1192

CIVIL PROCEDURE RULES 1998

The Civil Procedure Rule Committee, having power under section 2 of the Civil Procedure Act 1997 to make rules of court under section 1 of that Act, make the following rules which may be cited as the Civil Procedure Rules 1998—

CPR PART 1 OVERRIDING OBJECTIVE

CONTENTS OF THIS PART
The overriding objective	Rule 1.1
Application by the court of the overriding objective	Rule 1.2
Duty of the parties	Rule 1.3
Court's duty to manage cases	Rule 1.4

1.1 THE OVERRIDING OBJECTIVE
(1) These Rules are a new procedural code with the overriding objective of enabling the court to deal with cases justly.
(2) Dealing with a case justly includes, so far as is practicable—
  (a) ensuring that the parties are on an equal footing;
  (b) saving expense;
  (c) dealing with the case in ways which are proportionate—
    (i) to the amount of money involved;
    (ii) to the importance of the case;
    (iii) to the complexity of the issues; and
    (iv) to the financial position of each party;
  (d) ensuring that it is dealt with expeditiously and fairly; and
  (e) allotting to it an appropriate share of the court's resources, while taking into account the need to allot resources to other cases.

1.2 APPLICATION BY THE COURT OF THE OVERRIDING OBJECTIVE
The court must seek to give effect to the overriding objective when it—
  (a) exercises any power given to it by the Rules; or
  (b) interprets any rule.

1.3 DUTY OF THE PARTIES
The parties are required to help the court to further the overriding objective.

1.4 COURT'S DUTY TO MANAGE CASES
(1) The court must further the overriding objective by actively managing cases.
(2) Active case management includes—
  (a) encouraging the parties to co-operate with each other in the conduct of the proceedings;
  (b) identifying the issues at an early stage;
  (c) deciding promptly which issues need full investigation and trial and accordingly disposing summarily of the others;
  (d) deciding the order in which issues are to be resolved;
  (e) encouraging the parties to use an alternative dispute resolution[GL] procedure if the court considers that appropriate and facilitating the use of such procedure;
  (f) helping the parties to settle the whole or part of the case;
  (g) fixing timetables or otherwise controlling the progress of the case;
  (h) considering whether the likely benefits of taking a particular step justify the cost of taking it;
  (i) dealing with as many aspects of the case as it can on the same occasion;
  (j) dealing with the case without the parties needing to attend at court;
  (k) making use of technology; and
  (l) giving directions to ensure that the trial of a case proceeds quickly and efficiently.

CPR PART 2 APPLICATION AND INTERPRETATION OF THE RULES

CONTENTS OF THIS PART
Application of the Rules	Rule 2.1
The glossary	Rule 2.2
Interpretation	Rule 2.3
Power of judge, Master or district judge to perform functions of the court	Rule 2.4
Court staff	Rule 2.5
Court documents to be sealed	Rule 2.6
Court's discretion as to where it deals with cases	Rule 2.7
Time	Rule 2.8
Dates for compliance to be calendar dates and to include time of day	Rule 2.9
Meaning of 'month' in judgments, etc.	Rule 2.10
Time limits may be varied by parties	Rule 2.11

2.1 APPLICATION OF THE RULES
   (1) Subject to paragraph (2), these Rules apply to all proceedings in—
      (a) county courts;
      (b) the High Court; and
      (c) the Civil Division of the Court of Appeal.
   (2) These Rules do not apply to proceedings of the kinds specified in the first column of the following table (proceedings for which rules may be made under the enactments specified in the second column) except to the extent that they are applied to those proceedings by another enactment—

PROCEEDINGS	ENACTMENTS
1. Insolvency proceedings	Insolvency Act 1986, ss. 411 and 412
2. Non-contentious or common form probate proceedings	Supreme Court Act 1981, s. 127
3. Proceedings in the High Court when acting as a Prize Court	Prize Courts Act 1894, s. 3
4. Proceedings before the judge within the meaning of Part VII of the Mental Health Act 1983	Mental Health Act 1983, s. 106
5. Family proceedings	Matrimonial and Family Proceedings Act 1984, s. 40
6. Adoption proceedings	Adoption Act 1976, s. 66

2.2 THE GLOSSARY
   (1) The glossary at the end of these Rules is a guide to the meaning of certain legal expressions used in the Rules, but is not to be taken as giving those expressions any meaning in the Rules which they do not have in the law generally.
   (2) Subject to paragraph (3), words in these Rules which are included in the glossary are followed by '(GL)'.
   (3) The words 'counterclaim', 'damages', 'practice form' and 'service', which appear frequently in the Rules, are included in the glossary but are not followed by '(GL)'.

2.3 INTERPRETATION
   (1) In these Rules—
   'child' has the meaning given by rule 21.1(2);

CPR PART 2 APPLICATION AND INTERPRETATION OF THE RULES

'claim for personal injuries' means proceedings in which there is a claim for damages in respect of personal injuries to the claimant or any other person or in respect of a person's death, and 'personal injuries' includes any disease and any impairment of a person's physical or mental condition;

'claimant' means a person who makes a claim;

'CCR' is to be interpreted in accordance with Part 50;

'court officer' means a member of the court staff;

'defendant' means a person against whom a claim is made;

'defendant's home court' means—

    (a) if the claim is proceeding in a county court, the county court for the district in which the defendant's address for service, as shown on the defence, is situated; and

    (b) if the claim is proceeding in the High Court, the district registry for the district in which the defendant's address for service, as shown on the defence, is situated or, if there is no such district registry, the Royal Courts of Justice;

(Rule 6.5 provides for a party to give an address for service)

'filing', in relation to a document, means delivering it, by post or otherwise, to the court office;

'judge' means, unless the context otherwise requires, a judge, Master or district judge or a person authorised to act as such;

'jurisdiction' means, unless the context requires otherwise, England and Wales and any part of the territorial waters of the United Kingdom adjoining England and Wales;

'legal representative' means a barrister or a solicitor, solicitor's employee or other authorised litigator (as defined in the Courts and Legal Services Act 1990) who has been instructed to act for a party in relation to a claim.

'litigation friend' has the meaning given by Part 21;

'patient' has the meaning given by rule 21.1(2);

'RSC' is to be interpreted in accordance with Part 50;

'statement of case'—

    (a) means a claim form, particulars of claim where these are not included in a claim form, defence, Part 20 claim, or reply to defence; and

    (b) includes any further information given in relation to them voluntarily or by court order under rule 18.1;

'statement of value' is to be interpreted in accordance with rule 16.3;

'summary judgment' is to be interpreted in accordance with Part 24.

(2) A reference to a 'specialist list' is a reference to a list[GL] that has been designated as such by a relevant practice direction.

(3) Where the context requires, a reference to 'the court' means a reference to a particular county court, a district registry, or the Royal Courts of Justice.

2.4 POWER OF JUDGE, MASTER OR DISTRICT JUDGE TO PERFORM FUNCTIONS OF THE COURT

Where these Rules provide for the court to perform any act then, except where an enactment, rule or practice direction provides otherwise, that act may be performed—

    (a) in relation to proceedings in the High Court, by any judge, Master or district judge of that Court; and

    (b) in relation to proceedings in a county court, by any judge or district judge.

2.5 COURT STAFF

(1) Where these Rules require or permit the court to perform an act of a formal or administrative character, that act may be performed by a court officer.

(2) A requirement that a court officer carry out any act at the request of a party is subject to the payment of any fee required by a fees order for the carrying out of that act.

(Rule 3.2 allows a court officer to refer to a judge before taking any step)

2.6 COURT DOCUMENTS TO BE SEALED

(1) The court must seal[GL] the following documents on issue—

    (a) the claim form; and

CPR PART 2   APPLICATION AND INTERPRETATION OF THE RULES

    (b) any other document which a rule or practice direction requires it to seal.
  (2) The court may place the seal$^{(GL)}$ on the document—
    (a) by hand; or
    (b) by printing a facsimile of the seal on the document whether electronically or otherwise.
  (3) A document purporting to bear the court's seal$^{(GL)}$ shall be admissible in evidence without further proof.

2.7 COURT'S DISCRETION AS TO WHERE IT DEALS WITH CASES
The court may deal with a case at any place that it considers appropriate.

2.8 TIME
  (1) This rule shows how to calculate any period of time for doing any act which is specified—
    (a) by these Rules;
    (b) by a practice direction; or
    (c) by a judgment or order of the court.
  (2) A period of time expressed as a number of days shall be computed as clear days.
  (3) In this rule 'clear days' means that in computing the number of days—
    (a) the day on which the period begins; and
    (b) if the end of the period is defined by reference to an event, the day on which that event occurs
are not included.
Examples
    (i) Notice of an application must be served at least 3 days before the hearing.
       An application is to be heard on Friday 20 October.
       The last date for service is Monday 16 October.
    (ii) The court is to fix a date for a hearing.
       The hearing must be at least 28 days after the date of notice.
       If the court gives notice of the date of the hearing on 1 October, the earliest date for the hearing is 30 October.
    (iii) Particulars of claim must be served within 14 days of service of the claim form.
       The claim form is served on 2 October.
       The last day for service of the particulars of claim is 16 October.
  (4) Where the specified period—
    (a) is 5 days or less; and
    (b) includes—
       (i) a Saturday or Sunday; or
       (ii) a Bank Holiday, Christmas Day or Good Friday,
that day does not count.
Example
       Notice of an application must be served at least 3 days before the hearing.
       An application is to be heard on Monday 20 October.
       The last date for service is Tuesday 14 October.
  (5) When the period specified—
    (a) by these Rules or a practice direction; or
    (b) by any judgment or court order,
for doing any act at the court office ends on a day on which the office is closed, that act shall be in time if done on the next day on which the court office is open.

2.9 DATES FOR COMPLIANCE TO BE CALENDAR DATES AND TO INCLUDE TIME OF DAY
  (1) Where the court gives a judgment, order or direction which imposes a time limit for doing any act, the last date for compliance must, wherever practicable—
    (a) be expressed as a calendar date; and
    (b) include the time of day by which the act must be done.

CPR PART 2 APPLICATION AND INTERPRETATION OF THE RULES

(2) Where the date by which an act must be done is inserted in any document, the date must, wherever practicable, be expressed as a calendar date.

2.10 MEANING OF 'MONTH' IN JUDGMENTS, ETC.
Where 'month' occurs in any judgment, order, direction or other document, it means a calendar month.

2.11 TIME LIMITS MAY BE VARIED BY PARTIES
Unless these Rules or a practice direction provide otherwise or the court orders otherwise, the time specified by a rule or by the court for a person to do any act may be varied by the written agreement of the parties.

(Rules 3.8 (sanctions have effect unless defaulting party obtains relief), 28.4 (variation of case management timetable — fast track); 29.5 (variation of case management timetable — multi-track) provide for time limits that cannot be varied by agreement between the parties)

PD 2 PRACTICE DIRECTION — COURT OFFICES

This practice direction supplements CPR Part 2

CENTRAL OFFICE OF THE HIGH COURT AT THE ROYAL COURTS OF JUSTICE
1 The Central Office shall be divided into such departments, and the business performed in the Central Office shall be distributed among the departments in such manner, as is set out in the Queen's Bench Division Guide.

BUSINESS IN THE OFFICES OF THE SUPREME COURT
2.1 (1) The offices of the Supreme Court shall be open on every day of the year except
    (a) Saturdays and Sundays,
    (b) Good Friday and the day after Easter Monday,
    (c) Christmas Day and, if that day is a Friday or Saturday, then 28th December,
    (d) Bank Holidays in England and Wales under the Banking and Financial Dealings Act 1971, and
    (e) such other days as the Lord Chancellor, with the concurrence of the Lord Chief Justice, the Master of the Rolls, the President of the Family Division and the Vice-Chancellor ('the Heads of Division') may direct.
    (2) The hours during which the offices of the Supreme Court shall be open to the public shall be as follows:
    (a) at the Principal Probate Registry at First Avenue House, 42–49 High Holborn, London WC1V 6HA, from 10 a.m. to 4.30 p.m,
    (b) at the Supreme Court offices at the Royal Courts of Justice (including the Construction & Technology Court Registry in St. Dunstan's House, 133–137 Fetter Lane, London EC4A 1HD), from 10 a.m. to 4.30 p.m., except during the month of August in every year, when the hours shall be from 10 a.m. to 2.30 p.m.,
    (c) such other hours as the Lord Chancellor, with the concurrence of the Heads of Division, may from time to time direct.
    (3) Every District Registry shall be open on the days and during the hours that the Lord Chancellor from time to time directs and, in the absence of any such directions, shall be open on the same days and during the same hours as the county court offices of which it forms part are open.
2.2 One of the Masters of the Queen's Bench Division (the 'Practice Master') shall be present at the Central Office on every day on which the office is open for the purpose of superintending the business performed there and giving any directions which may be required on questions of practice and procedure.

COUNTY COURTS
3.1 Every County Court shall have an office or, if the Lord Chancellor so directs, two or more offices, situated at such place or places as he may direct, for the transaction of the business of the court.
3.2 (1) Every County Court office, or if a court has two or more offices at least one of those offices, shall be open on every day of the year except—
    (a) Saturdays and Sundays,
    (b) the day before Good Friday from noon onwards and Good Friday,
    (c) the Tuesday after the Spring bank holiday,
    (d) Christmas Day and, if that day is a Friday or Saturday, then the 28th December,
    (e) bank holidays and
    (f) such other days as the Lord Chancellor may direct.
    (2) In this paragraph 'bank holiday' means a bank holiday in England and Wales under the Banking and Financial Dealings Act 1971 and 'Spring holiday'

means the bank holiday on the last Monday in May or any day appointed instead of that day under section 1(2) of that Act.

3.3 Subject to paragraph 3.2(1)(b), the hours during which any court office is open to the public shall be from 10 am. to 4 p.m. or such other hours as the Lord Chancellor may from time to time direct.

PD 2B PRACTICE DIRECTION — ALLOCATION OF CASES TO LEVELS OF JUDICIARY

1.1 Rule 2.4 provides that Judges, Masters and District Judges may exercise any function of the court except where an enactment, rule or practice direction provides otherwise. This Practice Direction sets out the matters over which Masters and District Judges do not have jurisdiction or which they may deal with only on certain conditions. It does not affect jurisdiction conferred by other enactments. Reference should also be made to other relevant Practice Directions (e.g. Part 24, paragraph 3 and Part 26, paragraphs 12.1–10). References to Circuit Judges include Recorders and Assistant Recorders and references to Masters and District Judges include Deputies.

1.2 Wherever a Master or District Judge has jurisdiction, he may refer the matter to a Judge instead of dealing with it himself.

THE HIGH COURT

Injunctions

2.1 Search orders (rule 25.1(1)(h)), freezing orders (rule 25.1(1)(f)), an ancillary order under rule 25.1(1)(g) and orders authorising a person to enter land to recover, inspect or sample property (rule 25.1(1)(d)) may only be made by a Judge.

2.2 Except where paragraphs 2.3 and 2.4 apply, injunctions and orders relating to injunctions, including orders for specific performance where these involve an injunction, must be made by a Judge.

2.3 A Master or a District Judge may only make an injunction
   (a) in terms agreed by the parties;
   (b) in connection with or ancillary to a charging order;
   (c) in connection with or ancillary to an order appointing a receiver by way of equitable execution; or
   (d) in proceedings under RSC Order 77 rule 16 (order restraining person from receiving sum due from the Crown).

2.4 A Master or District Judge may make an order varying or discharging an injunction or undertaking given to the court if all parties to the proceedings have consented to the variation or discharge.

Other pre-trial orders and interim remedies

3.1 A Master or District Judge may not make orders or grant interim remedies:
   (a) relating to the liberty of the subject;
   (b) relating to criminal proceedings or matters except procedural applications in appeals to the High Court (including appeals by case stated) under any enactment;
   (c) relating to proceedings for judicial review, except applications under RSC Order 53 rule 8 (interlocutory applications);
   (d) relating to appeals from Masters or District Judges;
   (e) in appeals against a costs assessment under Parts 43–48, except:
      (i) on an appeal under rule 47.22 against the decision of an authorised court officer; or
      (ii) on an application for the grant of permission where rule 47.24 requires this;
   (f) in applications under section 42 of the Supreme Court Act 1981 by a person subject to a Civil or a Criminal or an All Proceedings Order (vexatious litigant) for permission to start or continue proceedings.

3.2 This Practice Direction is not concerned with family proceedings. It is also not concerned with proceedings in the Family Division except to the extent that such proceedings can be dealt with in the Chancery Division or the Family

Division e.g. proceedings under the Inheritance (Provision for Family and Dependants) Act 1975 or under section 14 of the Trusts of Land and Appointment of Trustees Act 1996. District Judges (including District Judges of the Principal Registry of the Family Division) have jurisdiction to hear such proceedings, subject to any Direction given by the President of the Family Division.

Trials and assessments of damages
4.1 A Master or District Judge may, subject to any Practice Direction, try a case which is treated as being allocated to the multi-track because it is proceeding under Part 8 (see rule 8.9(c)). He may try a case which has been allocated to the multi-track under Part 26 only with the consent of the parties. Restrictions on the trial jurisdiction of Masters and District Judges do not prevent them from hearing applications for summary judgment or, if the parties consent, for the determination of a preliminary issue.
4.2 A Master or a District Judge may assess the damages or sum due to a party under a judgment without limit as to the amount.

Chancery proceedings
5.1 In proceedings in the Chancery Division, a Master or a District Judge may not deal with the following without the consent of the Vice-Chancellor:
  (a) approving compromises (other than applications under the Inheritance (Provision for Family and Dependants) Act 1975) (i) on behalf of a person under disability where that person's interest in a fund, or if there is no fund, the maximum amount of the claim, exceeds £100,000 and (ii) on behalf of absent, unborn and unascertained persons;
  (b) making declarations, except in plain cases;
  (c) making final orders under section 1(1) of the Variation of Trusts Act 1958, except for the removal of protective trusts where the interest of the principal beneficiary has not failed or determined;
  (d) where the proceedings are brought by a Part 8 claim form in accordance with paragraph A.1(2) or (3) of the Part 8B Practice Direction (statutory or other requirement to use originating summons), determining any question of law or as to the construction of a document which is raised by the claim form;
  (e) giving permission to executors, administrators and trustees to bring or defend proceedings or to continue the prosecution or defence of proceedings, and granting an indemnity for costs out of the trust estate, except in plain cases;
  (f) granting an indemnity for costs out of the assets of a company on the application of minority shareholders bringing a derivative action, except in plain cases;
  (g) making an order for rectification, except for rectification of the register under the Land Registration Act 1925 in plain cases;
  (h) making orders to vacate entries in the register under the Land Charges Act 1972, except in plain cases;
  (i) making final orders on applications under section 19 of the Leasehold Reform Act 1967, section 48 of the Administration of Justice Act 1985 and sections 21 and 25 of the Law of Property Act 1969;
  (j) making final orders under the Landlord and Tenant Acts 1927 and 1954, except (i) by consent, (ii) orders for interim rents under section 24A of the 1954 Act and (iii) on applications to authorise agreements under section 38(4) of the 1954 Act;
  (k) making orders in proceedings in the Patents Court except (i) by consent, (ii) to extend time, (iii) on applications for permission to serve out of the jurisdiction and (iv) on applications for security for costs.
5.2 A Master or District Judge may only give directions for early trial after consulting the Judge in charge of the relevant list.
5.3 Where a winding-up order has been made against a company, any proceedings against the company by or on behalf of debenture holders may be dealt with, at the Royal Courts of Justice, by a Registrar and, in a District Registry with insolvency jurisdiction, by a District Judge.

Group or Multi-party claims
6.1 In group or multi-party claims the Lord Chief Justice and/or the Vice-Chancellor may give directions that all pre-trial applications in the group, or multi-party act claims must be made to and heard by a designated High Court Judge, Circuit Judge, Master or District Judge.

6.2 A party seeking a direction under paragraph 6.1 must apply to the Senior Master, the Chief Master or the appropriate Designated Civil Judge for the matter to be referred to the Lord Chief Justice and/or the Vice-Chancellor for such a direction. Any judge may on his own initiative refer a case for such a direction to be made.

6.3 When a direction has been made under paragraph 6.1, all pre-trial applications must be made in accordance with it.

Assignment of claims to masters and transfer between masters
7.1 The Senior Master, and the Chief Master will make arrangements for proceedings to be assigned to individual Masters. They may vary such arrangements generally or in particular cases, for example, by transferring a case from a Master to whom it had been assigned to another Master.

7.2 The fact that a case has been assigned to a particular Master does not prevent another Master from dealing with that case if circumstances require, whether at the request of the assigned Master or otherwise.

Freezing orders: cross-examination of deponents about assets
8 Where the court has made a freezing order under rule 25.1(f) and has ordered a person to make a witness statement or affidavit about his assets and to be cross-examined on its contents, unless the Judge directs otherwise, the cross-examination will take place before a Master or a District Judge, or if the Master or District Judge directs, before an examiner of the Court.

COUNTY COURTS

Injunctions and committal
9.1 Injunctions which a county court has jurisdiction to make may only be made by a Circuit Judge, except:—

(a) where the injunction is to be made in proceedings which a District Judge otherwise has jurisdiction to hear (see paragraph 11. 1 below);

(b) where the injunction is sought in a money claim which has not yet been allocated to a track, where the amount claimed does not exceed the fast track financial limit;

(c) in the circumstances provided by paragraph 2.3.

9.2 A District Judge may make orders varying or discharging injunctions in the circumstances provided by paragraph 2.4.

9.3 A District Judge may not make an order committing a person to prison except where an enactment authorises this: see section 23 of the Attachment of Earnings Act 1971, sections 14 and 18 of the County Courts Act 1984, sections 152–157 of the Housing Act 1996, section 3 of the Protection from Harassment Act 1997, and the relevant rules.

Other pre-trial orders and interim remedies
10.1 In addition to the restrictions on jurisdiction mentioned at paragraphs 9.1–3, paragraph 3(d) and (e) above applies.

Trials and assessments of damages
11.1 A District Judge has jurisdiction to hear the following:—

(a) any claim which has been allocated to the small claims track or fast track or which is treated as being allocated to the multi-track under rule 8.9(c) and Table 2 of the Practice Direction to Part 8, except proceedings under:—

    (i) CCR Order 43 rules 4, 6 and 18 (certain applications under the Landlord and Tenant Acts 1927 and 1954);

    (ii) CCR Order 43, rule 20 (Landlord and Tenant Act 1987);

    (iii) CCR Order 44, (Agricultural Holdings Act 1986);

(iv) CCR Order 46, rule 1 (Legitimacy Act 1976);
(v) CCR Order 49, rule 5 (Fair Trading Act 1973);
(vi) CCR Order 49, rule 10 (Local Government and Finance Act 1982);
(vii) CCR Order 49, rule 12 (Mental Health Act 1983);

(b) proceedings for the recovery of land;

(c) the assessment of damages or other sum due to a party under a judgment without any financial limit;

(d) with the consent of the parties and the permission of the Designated Civil Judge in respect of that case, any other proceedings.

11.2 A case allocated to the small claims track may only be assigned to a Circuit Judge to hear with his consent.

Freezing orders: cross-examination of deponents about assets

12 To the extent that a county court has power to make a freezing order, paragraph 8 applies as appropriate.

Distribution of business between circuit judge and district judge

13 Where both the Circuit Judge and the District Judge have jurisdiction in respect of any proceedings, the exercise of jurisdiction by the District Judge is subject to any arrangements made by the Designated Civil Judge for the proper distribution of business between Circuit Judges and District Judges.

14.1 In District Registries of the High Court and in the county court, the Designated Civil Judge may make arrangements for proceedings to be assigned to individual District Judges. He may vary such arrangements generally or in particular cases.

14.2 The fact that a case has been assigned to a particular District Judge does not prevent another District Judge from dealing with the case if the circumstances require.

CPR PART 3   THE COURT'S CASE MANAGEMENT POWERS

CONTENTS OF THIS PART

The court's general powers of management	Rule 3.1
Court officer's power to refer to a judge	Rule 3.2
Court's power to make order of its own initiative	Rule 3.3
Power to strike out a statement of case	Rule 3.4
Judgment without trial after striking out	Rule 3.5
Setting aside judgment entered after striking out	Rule 3.6
Sanctions for non-payment of certain fees	Rule 3.7
Sanctions have effect unless defaulting party obtains relief	Rule 3.8
Relief from sanctions	Rule 3.9
General power of the court to rectify matters where there has been an error of procedure	Rule 3.10

3.1   THE COURT'S GENERAL POWERS OF MANAGEMENT

(1)   The list of powers in this rule is in addition to any powers given to the court by any other rule or practice direction or by any other enactment or any powers it may otherwise have.

(2)   Except where these Rules provide otherwise, the court may—

   (a)   extend or shorten the time for compliance with any rule, practice direction or court order (even if an application for extension is made after the time for compliance has expired);

   (b)   adjourn or bring forward a hearing;

   (c)   require a party or a party's legal representative to attend the court;

   (d)   hold a hearing and receive evidence by telephone or by using any other method of direct oral communication;

   (e)   direct that part of any proceedings (such as a counterclaim) be dealt with as separate proceedings;

   (f)   stay$^{(GL)}$ the whole or part of any proceedings or judgment either generally or until a specified date or event;

   (g)   consolidate proceedings;

   (h)   try two or more claims on the same occasion;

   (i)   direct a separate trial of any issue;

   (j)   decide the order in which issues are to be tried;

   (k)   exclude an issue from consideration;

   (l)   dismiss or give judgment on a claim after a decision on a preliminary issue;

   (m)   take any other step or make any other order for the purpose of managing the case and furthering the overriding objective.

(3)   When the court makes an order, it may—

   (a)   make it subject to conditions, including a condition to pay a sum of money into court; and

   (b)   specify the consequence of failure to comply with the order or a condition.

(4)   Where the court gives directions it may take into account whether or not a party has complied with any relevant pre-action protocol$^{(GL)}$.

(5)   The court may order a party to pay a sum of money into court if that party has, without good reason, failed to comply with a rule, practice direction or a relevant pre-action protocol.

(6)   When exercising its power under paragraph (5) the court must have regard to—

   (a)   the amount in dispute; and

(b) the costs which the parties have incurred or which they may incur.

(6A) Where a party pays money into court following an order under paragraph (3) or (5), the money shall be security for any sum payable by that party to any other party in the proceedings, subject to the right of a defendant under rule 37.2 to treat all or part of any money paid into court as a Part 36 payment.
(Rule 36.2 explains what is meant by a Part 36 payment).

(7) A power of the court under these Rules to make an order includes a power to vary or revoke the order.

3.2 COURT OFFICER'S POWER TO REFER TO A JUDGE

Where a step is to be taken by a court officer—
    (a) the court officer may consult a judge before taking that step;
    (b) the step may be taken by a judge instead of the court officer.

3.3 COURT'S POWER TO MAKE ORDER OF ITS OWN INITIATIVE

(1) Except where a rule or some other enactment provides otherwise, the court may exercise its powers on an application or of its own initiative.
(Part 23 sets out the procedure for making an application)

(2) Where the court proposes to make an order of its own initiative—
    (a) it may give any person likely to be affected by the order an opportunity to make representations; and
    (b) where it does so it must specify the time by and the manner in which the representations must be made.

(3) Where the court proposes—
    (a) to make an order of its own initiative; and
    (b) to hold a hearing to decide whether to make the order,
it must give each party likely to be affected by the order at least 3 days' notice of the hearing.

(4) The court may make an order of its own initiative, without hearing the parties or giving them an opportunity to make representations.

(5) Where the court has made an order under paragraph (4)—
    (a) a party affected by the order may apply to have it set aside varied or stayed[GL]; and
    (b) the order must contain a statement of the right to make such an application.

(6) An application under paragraph (5)(a) must be made—
    (a) within such period as may be specified by the court; or
    (b) if the court does not specify a period, not more than 7 days after the date on which the order was served on the party making the application.

3.4 POWER TO STRIKE OUT A STATEMENT OF CASE

(1) In this rule and rule 3.5, reference to a statement of case includes reference to part of a statement of case.

(2) The court may strike out[GL] a statement of case if it appears to the court—
    (a) that the statement of case discloses no reasonable grounds for bringing or defending the claim;
    (b) that the statement of case is an abuse of the court's process or is otherwise likely to obstruct the just disposal of the proceedings; or
    (c) that there has been a failure to comply with a rule, practice direction or court order.

(3) When the court strikes out a statement of case it may make any consequential order it considers appropriate.

(4) Where—
    (a) the court has struck out a claimant's statement of case;
    (b) the claimant has been ordered to pay costs to the defendant; and
    (c) before the claimant pays those costs, he starts another claim against the same defendant, arising out of facts which are the same or substantially the same as those relating to the claim in which the statement of case was struck out,
the court may, on the application of the defendant, stay[GL] that other claim until the costs of the first claim have been paid.

CPR PART 3 THE COURT'S CASE MANAGEMENT POWERS

(5) Paragraph (2) does not limit any other power of the court to strike out[GL] a statement of case.

3.5 JUDGMENT WITHOUT TRIAL AFTER STRIKING OUT
(1) This rule applies where—
 (a) the court makes an order which includes a term that the statement of case of a party shall be struck out if the party does not comply with the order; and
 (b) the party against whom the order was made does not comply with it.
(2) A party may obtain judgment with costs by filing a request for judgment if—
 (a) the order referred to in paragraph (1)(a) relates to the whole of a statement of case; and
 (b) where the party wishing to obtain judgment is the claimant, the claim is for—
  (i) a specified amount of money;
  (ii) an amount of money to be decided by the court;
  (iii) delivery of goods where the claim form gives the defendant the alternative of paying their value; or
  (iv) any combination of these remedies.
(3) The request must state that the right to enter judgment has arisen because the court's order has not been complied with.
(4) A party must make an application in accordance with Part 23 if he wishes to obtain judgment under this rule in a case to which paragraph (2) does not apply.

3.6 SETTING ASIDE JUDGMENT ENTERED AFTER STRIKING OUT
(1) A party against whom the court has entered judgment under rule 3.5 may apply to the court to set the judgment aside.
(2) An application under paragraph (1) must be made not more than 14 days after the judgment has been served on the party making the application.
(3) If the right to enter judgment had not arisen at the time when judgment was entered, the court must set aside[GL] the judgment.
(4) If the application to set aside[GL] is made for any other reason, rule 3.9 (relief from sanctions) shall apply.

3.7 SANCTIONS FOR NON-PAYMENT OF CERTAIN FEES
(1) This rule applies where—
 (a) an allocation questionnaire or a listing questionnaire is filed without payment of the fee specified by the relevant Fees Order; or
 (b) the court dispenses with the need for an allocation questionnaire or a listing questionnaire or both; or
 (c) these Rules do not require an allocation questionnaire or a listing questionnaire to be filed in relation to the claim in question.
(Rule 26.3 provides for the court to dispense with the need for an allocation questionnaire and rules 28.5 and 29.6 provide for the court to dispense with the need for a listing questionnaire)
(2) The court will serve a notice on the claimant requiring payment of the fee which the relevant Fees Order specifies as being due—
 (a) on the filing of the allocation questionnaire or the listing questionnaire; or
 (b) in the circumstances where the claimant is not required to file an allocation questionnaire or a listing questionnaire,
if, at the time the fee is due, the claimant has not paid the fee or made an application for exemption from or remission of the fee.
(3) The notice will specify the date by which the claimant must pay the fee.
(4) If the claimant does not—
 (a) pay the fee; or
 (b) make an application for an exemption from or remission of the fee,
by the date specified in the notice—
  (i) the claim shall be struck out; and
  (ii) the claimant shall be liable for the costs which the defendant has incurred unless the court orders otherwise.

(Rule 44.12 provides for the basis of assessment where a right to costs arises under this rule)

(5) Where an application for exemption from or remission of a fee is refused, the court will serve notice on the claimant requiring payment of the fee by the date specified in the notice.

(6) If the claimant does not pay the fee by the date specified in the notice—
    (a) the claim shall be struck out; and
    (b) the claimant shall be liable for the costs which the defendant has incurred unless the court orders otherwise.

(7) If—
    (a) a claimant applies under rule 3.9 (relief from sanctions) to have the claim reinstated; and
    (b) the court grants relief under that rule,
the relief shall be conditional on the claimant—
    (i) paying the fee; or
    (ii) filing evidence of exemption from payment or remission of the fee,
within 2 days of the date of the order.

3.8 SANCTIONS HAVE EFFECT UNLESS DEFAULTING PARTY OBTAINS RELIEF

(1) Where a party has failed to comply with a rule, practice direction or court order, any sanction for failure to comply imposed by the rule, practice direction or court order has effect unless the party in default applies for and obtains relief from the sanction.
(Rule 3.9 sets out the circumstances which the court may consider on an application to grant relief from a sanction)

(2) Mere the sanction is the payment of costs, the party in default may only obtain relief by appealing against the order for costs.

(3) Where a rule, practice direction or court order—
    (a) requires a party to do something within a specified time, and
    (b) specifies the consequence of failure to comply,
the time for doing the act in question may not be extended by agreement between the parties.

3.9 RELIEF FROM SANCTIONS

(1) On an application for relief from any sanction imposed for a failure to comply with any rule, practice direction or court order the court will consider all the circumstances including—
    (a) the interests of the administration of justice;
    (b) whether the application for relief has been made promptly;
    (c) whether the failure to comply was intentional;
    (d) whether there is a good explanation for the failure;
    (e) the extent to which the party in default has complied with other rules, practice directions, court orders and any relevant preaction protocol[GL];
    (f) whether the failure to comply was caused by the party or his legal representative;
    (g) whether the trial date or the likely trial date can still be met if relief is granted;
    (h) the effect which the failure to comply had on each party; and
    (i) the effect which the granting of relief would have on each party.

(2) An application for relief must be supported by evidence.

3.10 GENERAL POWER OF THE COURT TO RECTIFY MATTERS WHERE THERE HAS BEEN AN ERROR OF PROCEDURE

Where there has been an error of procedure such as a failure to comply with a rule or practice direction—
    (a) the error does not invalidate any step taken in the proceedings unless the court so orders; and
    (b) the court may make an order to remedy the error.

PD 3 PRACTICE DIRECTION — STRIKING OUT A STATEMENT OF CASE

This practice direction supplements CPR rule 3.4.

INTRODUCTORY

1.1 Rule 1.4(2)(c) includes as an example of active case management the summary disposal of issues which do not need full investigation at trial.

1.2 The rules give the court two distinct powers which may be used to achieve this. Rule 3.4 enables the court to strike out the whole or part of a statement of case which discloses no reasonable grounds for bringing or defending a claim (rule 3.4(2)(a)), or which is an abuse of the process of the court or otherwise likely to obstruct the just disposal of the proceedings (rule 3.4(2)(b)). Rule 24.2 enables the court to give summary judgment against a claimant or defendant where that party has no real prospect of succeeding on his claim or defence. Both those powers may be exercised on an application by a party or on the court's own initiative.

1.3 This practice direction sets out the procedure a party should follow if he wishes to make an application for an order under rule 3.4.

1.4 The following are examples of cases where the court may conclude that particulars of claim (whether contained in a claim form or filed separately) fall within rule 3.4(2)(a):

(1) those which set out no facts indicating what the claim is about, for example 'Money owed £5000',

(2) those which are incoherent and make no sense,

(3) those which contain a coherent set of facts but those facts, even if true, do not disclose any legally recognisable claim against the defendant.

1.5 A claim may fall within rule 3.4(2)(b) where it is vexatious, scurrilous or obviously ill-founded.

1.6 A defence may fall within rule 3.4(2)(a) where:

(1) it consists of a bare denial or otherwise sets out no coherent statement of facts, or

(2) the facts it sets out, while coherent, would not even if true amount in law to a defence to the claim.

1.7 A party may believe he can show without a trial that an opponent's case has no real prospect of success on the facts, or that the case is bound to succeed or fail, as the case may be, because of a point of law (including the construction of a document). In such a case the party concerned may make an application under rule 3.4 or Part 24 (or both) as he thinks appropriate.

1.8 The examples set out above are intended only as illustrations.

CLAIMS WHICH APPEAR TO FALL WITHIN RULE 3.4(2)(a) OR (b)

2.1 If a court officer is asked to issue a claim form which he believes may fall within rule 3.4(2)(a) or (b) he should issue it, but may then consult a judge (under rule 3.2) before returning the claim form to the claimant or taking any other step to serve the defendant. The judge may on his own initiative make an immediate order designed to ensure that the claim is disposed of or (as the case may be) proceeds in a way that accords with the rules.

2.3 The judge may allow the claimant a hearing before deciding whether to make such an order.

2.4 Orders the judge may make include:

(1) an order that the claim be stayed until further order,

(2) an order that the claim form be retained by the court and not served until the stay is lifted,

(3) an order that no application by the claimant to lift the stay be heard unless he files such further documents (for example a witness statement or an amended claim form or particulars of claim) as may be specified in the order.

PD 3 PRACTICE DIRECTION — STRIKING OUT A STATEMENT OF CASE

2.5 Where the judge makes any such order or, subsequently, an order lifting the stay he may give directions about the service on the defendant of the order and any other documents on the court file.

2.6 The fact that a judge allows a claim referred to him by a court officer to proceed does not prejudice the right of any party to apply for any order against the claimant.

DEFENCES WHICH APPEAR TO FALL WITHIN RULE 3.4(2)(a) OR (b).

3.1 A court officer may similarly consult a judge about any document filed which purports to be a defence and which he believes may fall within rule 3.4(2)(a) or (b).

3.2 If the judge decides that the document falls within rule 3.4(2)(a) or (b) he may on his own initiative make an order striking it out. Where he does so he may extend the time for the defendant to file a proper defence.

3.3 The judge may allow the defendant a hearing before deciding whether to make such an order.

3.4 Alternatively the judge may make an order under rule 18.1 requiring the defendant within a stated time to clarify his defence or to give additional information about it. The order may provide that the defence will be struck out if the defendant does not comply.

3.5 The fact that a judge does not strike out a defence on his own initiative does not prejudice the right of the claimant to apply for any order against the defendant.

GENERAL PROVISIONS

4.1 The court may exercise its powers under rule 3.4(2)(a) or (b) on application or on its own initiative at any time.

4.2 Where a judge at a hearing strikes out all or part of a party's statement of case he may enter such judgment for the other party as that party appears entitled to.

APPLICATIONS FOR ORDERS UNDER RULE 3.4(2)

5.1 Attention is drawn to Part 23 (General Rules about Applications) and to the practice direction that supplements it. The practice direction requires all applications to be made as soon as possible and before allocation if possible.

5.2 While many applications under rule 3.4(2) can be made without evidence in support, the applicant should consider whether facts need to be proved and, if so, whether evidence in support should be filed and served.

APPLICATIONS FOR SUMMARY JUDGMENT

6.1 Applications for summary judgment may be made under Part 24. Attention is drawn to that Part and to the practice direction that supplements it.

VEXATIOUS LITIGANTS

7.1 This Practice Direction applies where a 'civil proceedings order' or an 'all proceedings order' (as respectively defined under section 42(1A) of the Supreme Court Act, 1981) is in force against a person ('the litigant').

7.2 An application by the litigant for permission to begin or continue, or to make any application in, any civil proceedings shall be made by application notice issued in the High Court and signed by the litigant.

7.3 The application notice must state:
 (1) the title and reference number of the proceedings in which the civil proceedings order or the all proceedings order, as the case may be, was made,
 (2) the full name of the litigant and his address,
 (3) the order the applicant is seeking, and
 (4) briefly, why the applicant is seeking the order.

7.4 The application notice must be filed together with any written evidence on which the litigant relies in support of his application.

7.5 Either in the application notice or in written evidence filed in support of the application, the previous occasions on which the litigant made an application for permission under section 42(1A) of the said Act must be listed.

7.6 The application notice, together with any written evidence, will be placed before a High Court judge who may:
(1) without a hearing make an order dismissing the application or granting the permission sought, or
(2) give direction for further written evidence to be supplied by the litigant before an order is made on the application, or
(3) give directions for a hearing of the application.

7.7 Directions given under paragraph 6(3) may include an order that the application notice be served on the Attorney General and on any person against whom the litigant desires to bring the proceedings for which permission is being sought.

7.8 Any order made under paragraphs 6 or 7 will be served on the litigant at the address given in the application notice. CPR Part 6 will apply.

7.9 A person may apply to set aside the grant of permission if:
(1) the permission allowed the litigant to bring or continue proceedings against that person or to make any application against him, and
(2) the permission was granted other than at a hearing of which that person was given notice under paragraph 7.

7.10 Any application under paragraph 9 must be made in accordance with CPR Part 23.

PD 3B   PRACTICE DIRECTION — SANCTIONS FOR NON-PAYMENT OF FEES

This practice direction supplements CPR rule 3.7

1. If a claim is struck out under rule 3.7, the court will send notice that it has been struck out to the defendant.

2. The notice will also explain the effect of rule 25.11. This provides that any interim injunction will cease to have effect 14 days after the date the claim is struck out under rule 3.7. Paragraph (2) provides that if the claimant applies to reinstate the claim before the interim injunction ceases to have effect, the injunction will continue until the hearing of the application unless the court orders otherwise. If the claimant makes such an application, the defendant will be given notice in the ordinary way under rule 23.4.

CPR PART 4 FORMS

4—(1) The forms set out in a practice direction shall be used in the cases to which they apply.

(2) A form may be varied by the court or a party if the variation is required by the circumstances of a particular case.

(3) A form must not be varied so as to leave out any information or guidance which the form gives to the recipient.

(4) Where these Rules require a form to be sent by the court or by a party for another party to use, it must be sent without any variation except such as is required by the circumstances of the particular case.

(5) Where the court or a party produces a form shown in a practice direction with the words 'Royal Arms', the form must include a replica of the Royal Arms at the head of the first page.

PD 4 PRACTICE DIRECTIONS — FORMS

This practice direction supplements CPR Part 4

SCOPE OF THIS PRACTICE DIRECTION
1.1 This practice direction lists the forms to be used in civil proceedings on or after 26th April 1999, when the civil procedure rules (CPR) come into force.
1.2 The forms may be modified as the circumstances require, provided that all essential information, especially information or guidance which the form gives to the recipient, is included.
1.3 This practice direction contains 3 tables—
- Table 1 lists forms required by CPR parts 1–48 and therefore applicable in both the High Court and county court
- Table 2 lists High Court forms in use before 26th April 1999 that will remain in use on or after that date (see paragraph 4 below)
- Table 3 lists county court forms in use before 26th April 1999 that will remain in use on or after that date (see paragraph 5 below)

OTHER FORMS:
2.1 Other forms may be authorised by practice directions supplementing Part 49 (specialist proceedings). For example the forms relating to Admiralty proceedings are authorised by, and annexed to, the Admiralty practice direction.

Table 1
'N' Forms

Contents
3.1 This table lists the 'N' forms that are referred to and required to be used by Practice Directions supplementing particular Parts of the CPR. A Practice Direction and its paragraphs are abbreviated by reference to the Part of the CPR which it supplements and the relevant paragraph of the Practice Direction, for example, Pt 34 PD 1.2.

No.	Title
N1	Part 7 (general) claim form (Pt 7 PD 3.1)
N1CPC	Claim Production Centre ('CPC') claim form (rule 7.10)
N1A	Notes for claimant
N1C	Notes for defendant
N1(FD)	Notes for defendant (Consumer Credit Act cases)
N9	Acknowledgment of service/response pack (Pt 10 PD 2)
N9 CPC	CPC acknowledgment of service/response pack (Pt 10 PD 2)
N9A	Admission and statement of means (specified amount) (Pt 14 PD 2.1)
N9B	Defence and counterclaim (specified amount) (Pt 15 PD 1.3)
N9C	Admission and statement of means (unspecified amount and non money claims) (Pt 14 PD 2.1)
N9D	Defence and counterclaim (unspecified amount and non money claims) (Pt 15 PD 1.3)
N10	Notice that acknowledgment of service has been filed (rule 10.4)
N17	Judgment for claimant (amount to be decided by court) (rules 12.5(3), 14.6(7) and 14.7(10))
N20	Witness summons (Pt 34 PD 1.2)
N21	Order for Examination of Deponent before the hearing (Pt 34 PD 4.1)
N24	Blank form of order or judgment
N30	Judgment for claimant (default HC) (rule 12.5(2))

No.	Title
N30	Judgment for claimant (default CC) (rule 12.5(2))
N30(1)	Judgment for claimant (acceptance HC) (Pt 14 PD 4.2)
N30(1)	Judgment for claimant (acceptance CC) (Pt 14 PD 4.2)
N30(2)	Judgment for claimant (after determination HC) (Pt 14 PD 10 (4))
N30(2)	Judgment for claimant (after determination CC) (Pt 14 PD 10 (4))
N30(3)	Judgment for claimant (after re-determination HC) (rule 14.13)
N30(3)	Judgment for claimant (after re-determination CC) (rule 14.13)
N32	Judgment for return of goods
N32(1)	HP/CCA Judgment for delivery of goods
N32(2)	HP/CCA Judgment for delivery of goods (suspended)
N32(3)	HP/CCA Judgment for delivery of goods
N32(4)	Variation order (return of goods)
N32(5)	HP/CCA Order for balance of purchase price
N33	Judgment for delivery of goods
N34	Judgment for claimant (after amount decided by court HC)
N34	Judgment for claimant (after amount decided by court CC)
N150	Allocation questionnaire (Pt 26 PD 2.1)
N150A	Master/DJ's directions on allocation
N151	Allocation Questionnaire (amount to be decided by court)
N151A	Master/DJ's directions on allocation
N152	Notice that [defence] [counterclaim] has been filed (Pt 26 PD 2.5)
N153	Notice of allocation or listing hearing (Pt 26 PD 6.2)
N154	Notice of allocation to fast track (Pt 26 PD 4.2 and 9)
N155	Notice of allocation to multi-track (Pt 26 PD 4.2 and 10)
N156	Order for further information (for allocation) (Pt 26 PD 4.2(2))
N157	Notice of allocation to small claims track (Pt 26 PD 4.2 and 8)
N158	Notice of allocation to small claims track (preliminary hearing) (Pt 26 PD 4.2 and 8)
N159	Notice of allocation to small claims track (no hearing) (Pt 26 PD 4.2 and 8)
N160	Notice of allocation to small claims track (with parties' consent) (Pt 26 PD 4.2 and 8)
N170	Listing questionnaire (Pt 26 PD 6.1 and Pt 28 PD 8.1)
N171	Notice of date for return of listing questionnaire (Pt 26 PD 6.1 and Pt 28 PD 8.1)
N172	Notice of trial date
N173	Notice of non-payment of fee (rule 3.7)
N205A	Notice of issue (specified amount)
N205B	Notice of issue (unspecified amount)
N205C	Notice of issue (non-money claim)
N208	Part 8 claim form (Pt 8 PD 2.2)
N208A	Part 8 notes for claimant
N208C	Part 8 notes for defendant
N209	Part 8 notice of issue
N210	Part 8 acknowledgment of service (Pt 8 PD 3.2)
N211	Part 20 claim form (rule 20.7)
N211A	Part 20 notes for claimant
N211C	Part 20 notes for defendant
N212	Part 20 notice of issue
N213	Part 20 acknowledgment of service (rule 20.12)
N215	Certificate of service (rule 6.10)
N216	Notice of non-service (rule 6.11)
N217	Order for substituted service (rule 6.8)
N218	Notice of service on a partner (Pt 6 PD 4.2)
N225	Request for judgment and reply to admission (specified amount) (Pt 12 PD 3)

No.	Title
N225A	Notice of part admission (specified amount) (rule 14.5)
N226	Notice of admission (unspecified amount) (rule 14.7)
N227	Request for judgment by default (amount to be decided by the court) (rule 12.5)
N228	Notice of admission (return of goods) (Pt 7 PD Consumer Credit Act 8.5)
N235	Certificate of suitability of litigation friend (Pt 21 PD 2.3)
N236	Notice of defence that amount claimed has been paid (rule 15.10)
N242A	Notice of payment into court (in settlement) (rule 36.6(2))
N242B	Notice of payment into court (by order)
N243	Notice of acceptance of payment into court (Pt 36 PD 7.7)
N244	Application notice (Pt 23 PD 2.1)
N244A	Notice of hearing of application (Pt 23 PD 2.2)
N252	Notice of commencement of assessment (Pt 47 PD 2.3)
N253	Notice of amount allowed on provisional assessment (Pt 47 PD 6.5)
N254	Request for default costs certificate (Pt 47 PD 3.1)
N255	Default costs certificate HC (Pt 47 PD 3.3)
N255	Default costs certificate CC (Pt 47 PD 3.3)
N256	Final costs certificate HC (Pt 47 PD 5.11)
N256	Final costs certificate CC (Pt 47 PD 5.11)
N257	Interim costs certificate (Pt 47 PD 5.11)
N258	Request for assessment hearing (Pt 47 PD 4.3)
N259	Notice of appeal against a detailed assessment (Pt 47 PD 8.16)
N265	List of documents (Pt 31 PD 3.1)
N266	Notice to admit facts/admission of facts (rule 32.18)
N268	Notice to prove documents at trial (rule 32.19)
N271	Notice of transfer of proceedings (rule 30)
N279	Notice of discontinuance (rule 38.3)
N292	Order on settlement on behalf of child or patient (Pt 21 PD 11.3)
N294	Claimant's application for a variation order
N367	Notice of hearing to consider why fine should not be imposed (rule 34.10)
N434	Notice of change of solicitor (rule 42.2)

Table 2
Practice Forms

Contents:

4.1 This table lists the Practice Forms that may be used under this Practice Direction. It contains forms that were previously:
- Prescribed Forms contained in Appendix A to the Rules of the Supreme Court 1965
- Queen's Bench Masters' Practice Forms
- Chancery Masters' Practice Forms

4.2 The former prescribed forms are shown as 'No 00'. The former practice forms where they are appropriate for use in either the Chancery or Queen's Bench Division (or where no specific form is available for use in the county court, in that court also) are prefixed 'PF' followed by the number. Where the form is used mainly in the Chancery or Queen's Bench Division, the suffix CH or QB follows the form number.

4.3 Where a rule permits, a party intending to use a witness statement as an alternative to an affidavit should amend any form in this Table to be used in connection with that rule so that 'witness statement' replaces 'affidavit' wherever it appears in the form.

4.4 The forms in this list are reproduced in an Appendix to the Chancery and Queen's Bench Guides, and in practitioners' textbooks.

PD 4 PRACTICE DIRECTIONS — FORMS

No.	Title
No 8A	Arbitration application/claim form
No 15	Acknowledgment of service on non-party
No 15A	Acknowledgment of service of arbitration application
No 32	Order for examination within jurisdiction of witness before trial (rule 34.8)
No 33	Application for issue of letter of request to judicial authority out of jurisdiction (Pt 34 PD 5.2)
No 34	Order for issue of letter of request to judicial authority out of jurisdiction (Pt 34 PD 5.1)
No 35	Letter of request for examination of witness out of jurisdiction (Pt 34 PD 5.3(1))
No 37	Order for appointment of examiner to take evidence of witness out of jurisdiction (rule 34.13(4))
No 41	Default judgment in claim relating to detention of goods
No 42	Default judgment in claim for possession of land
No 42A	Order for possession (sched.1 - RSC O.113)
No 44	Judgment under Part 24
No 45	Judgment after trial before judge without jury (Pt 40 PD 14)
No 46	Judgment after trial before judge with jury (Pt 40 PD 14)
No 47	Judgment after trial before a master/Technology & Construction Court judge (Pt 40 PD 14)
No 48	Judgment after decision of preliminary issue
No 49	Judgment against personal representatives (Pt 40 PD 14)
No 50	Judgment for defendant's costs on discontinuance
No 51	Judgment for costs after acceptance of money paid into court
No 52	Notice of [claim] [proceedings]
No 52A	Notice of judgment or order to an interested party
No 53	Writ of fieri facias (sched.1 - RSC O.46 and 47)
No 54	Writ of fieri facias on order for costs (sched.1-RSC O.46 and 47)
No 55	Notice of seizure (sched.1 - RSC O.45)
No 56	Writ of fieri facias after levy of part (sched.1-RSC O.45)
No 57	Writ, of fieri facias against personal representatives (sched.1-RSC O.45)
No 58	Writ of fieri facias de bonis ecclesiasticis (sched.1-RSC 45)
No 59	Writ of sequestrari de bonis ecclesiasticis (sched.1-RSC O.45)
No 62	Writ of fieri facias to enforce Northern Irish or Scottish judgment (sched.1-RSC O.45)
No 63	Writ of fieri facias to enforce foreign registered judgment (sched.1-RSC O.45)
No 64	Writ of delivery: delivery of goods, damages and costs (sched.1-RSC O.45)
No 65	Writ of delivery: delivery of goods or value, damages and costs (sched.1-RSC O.45)
No 66	Writ of possession (sched. 1 - RSC ord. 45)
No 66A	Writ of possession (sched. 1 - RSC ord. 113)
No 67	Writ of sequestration (sched. 1 -RSC ord. 45)
No 68	Writ of restitution (sched. 1 - RSC ord. 46)
No 69	Writ of assistance (sched. 1 - RSC ord. 46)
No 71	Notice of renewal of writ of execution (sched. 1 - RSC O.46)
No 72	Garnishee order to show cause (sched. 1 - RSC ord. 49 r. 1)
No 73	Garnishee order absolute: garnishee owes more than judgment debt (sched. 1 - RSC O.49 r. 1)
No 74	Garnishee order absolute: garnishee owes less than judgment debt (sched. 1 - RSC ord. 49 r. 1)
No 75	Charging order: notice to show cause (sched. 1 - RSC 0.50 r. 1)
No 76	Charging order absolute (sched. 1 - RSC ord. 50 r. 3)

PD 4 PRACTICE DIRECTIONS — FORMS

No.	Title
No 79	Stop order on capital and income of funds in court (sched. 1 - RSC ord. 50 r.10)
No 80	Affidavit and notice under RSC ord. 50, scheduled to Part 50 CPR
No 81	Order on claim to restrain transfer of stock (sch. 1 RSC ord. 50)
No 82	Application for appointment of a receiver (sched. 1 - RSC ord. 51 r. 3)
No 83	Order directing application for appointment of receiver and granting injunction meanwhile (sched. 1 - RSC ord. 51 r. 3)
No 84	Order for appointment of receiver by way of equitable execution (s. 37 of Supreme Court Act and sched. 1 - RSC ord. 51)
No 85	Order of committal (sched. 1 - RSC ord. 52)
No 86	Claim form for judicial review (sched. 1 RSC ord. 53 r. 5(2A))
No 86A	Application for permission to apply for judicial review (sched. 1 - RSC ord. 53 r. 3)
No 86B	Renewal application for permission to apply for judicial review (sched. 1 - RSC ord. 53 r. 3)
No 87	Claim form for writ of habeas corpus ad subjiciendum
No 88	Notice of adjourned application for writ of habeas corpus
No 89	Writ of habeas corpus ad subjiciendum
No 90	Notice to be served with writ of habeas corpus ad subjiciendum
No 91	Writ of habeas corpus ad testificandum
No 92	Writ of habeas corpus ad respondendum
No 93	Order under the Evidence (Proceedings in Other Jurisdictions) Act 1975
No 94	Order for production of documents in marine insurance action (Pt 49D PD 7.1)
No 95	Certificate of order against the Crown (sched. 1 - RSC ord. 77 r. 15)
No 96	Certificate of order for costs against the Crown (sched. 1 - RSC ord. 77 r. 15)
No 97	Claim form to grant bail (criminal proceedings) (sched. 1 - RSC ord. 79 r. 9)
No 97A	Claim form to vary arrangements for bail (criminal proceedings) (sched. 1 - RSC ord. 79 r. 9)
No 98	Order to release prisoner on bail (sched. 1 - RSC ord. 79 r. 9)
No 98A	Order varying arrangements for bail (sched. 1 - RSC ord. 79 r. 9)
No 99	Order of Court of Appeal to admit prisoner to bail (sched. 1 - RSC ord. 59 r. 20)
No 100	Notice of sureties for bail
No 101	Witness summons — Crown Court
No 103	Witness summons — Crown Court
No 104	Attachment of earnings order (Attachment of Earnings Act 1971)
No 105	Notice under s. 10(2) of the Attachment of Earnings Act 1971
No 108	Application for reference to the European Court (sched. 1 - RSC ord. 114 r. 20)
No 109	Order for reference to the European Court (sched. 1 - RSC ord. 14 r. 2)
No 110	Certificate under s. 12 of the Civil Jurisdiction and Judgments Act, 1982 (sched. 1 - RSC ord. 71 r. 36(3))
No 111	Certificate of money provisions contained in a judgment for registration under Schedule 6 to the Civil Jurisdiction, and Judgments Act 1982 (sched. 1 - RSC ord. 71 r. 37(3))
No. 112	Certificate of non-money provisions contained in a judgment under Schedule 7 to the Civil Jurisdiction and Judgments Act 1982 (sched. 1 - RSC ord. 71 r. 38(2))
PF 1	Application for time (rule 3.1(2)(a))

PD 4 PRACTICE DIRECTIONS — FORMS

No.	Title
PF 2	Order for time (rule 3.1(2)(a))
PF 3	Application for an extension of time for serving a claim form (rule 7.6(1))
PF 4	Order for an extension of time for serving a claim form (rule 7.6(1))
PF 5	Order as to service in claim for possession where premises empty (sched. 1 RSC ord. 10 r. 4)
PF 6	Order for service out of the jurisdiction (rule 6A.4)
PF 7 QB	Request for service of document abroad (rule 6A.11)
PF 8	Application for judgment for possession
PF 9	Order for possession
PF 11	Application for Part 24 judgment (whole claim)
PF 12	Application for Part 24 judgment (one or some of several claims)
PF 13	Order under Part 14 (No 1)
PF 14	Order under Part 14 (No 2)
PF 15	Order under Part 14 (for assessment of solicitor's bill of costs) (Part 48)
PF 20	Application for Part 20 directions
PF 21	Order for Part 20 directions
PF 23 QB	Notice of claim to goods taken in execution (sched. 1 - RSC ord. 17)
PF 24 QB	Notice by claimant of admission or dispute of title of interpleaderclaimant (sched. 1 - RSC ord. 17)
PF 25 QB	Interpleader application by defendant (sched. 1 - RSC ord. 17)
PF 26 QB	Interpleader application by sheriff (sched. 1 - RSC ord. 17)
PF 27 QB	Evidence in support of interpleader application (sched. 1 - RSC ord. 17)
PF 28 QB	Interpleader order (1) claim barred where Sheriff interpleads (sched. 1 - RSC ord. 17)
PF 29 QB	Interpleader order (1a) Sheriff to withdraw (sched. 1 - RSC ord. 17)
PF 30 QB	Interpleader order (2) interclaimant substituted as defendant (sched. 1 - RSC ord. 17)
PF 31 QB	Interpleader order (3) trial of issue (sched. 1 - RSC ord. 17)
PF 32 QB	Interpleader order (4) conditional order for Sheriff to withdraw and trial of issue (sch. 1 - RSC ord. 17)
PF 34 QB	Interpleader order (6) summary disposal (sched. 1 - RSC ord. 17)
PF 43	Application for security for costs
PF 44	Order for security for costs
PF 48	Court record available for use before and at hearing
PF 49	Request to parties to state convenient dates for hearing
PF 50	Application for directions (Part 29)
PF 52	Order for directions following an application or otherwise (Part 29)
PF 53	Order for trial of an issue
PF 56	Request for further information or clarification with provision for response (Pt 18 PD 1.6(2))
PF 57	Application for further information or clarification (Pt 18 PD 5)
PF 58	Order for further information or clarification (rule 18.1)
PF 63	Interim order for receiver in pending claim (sched. 1 - RSC ord. 30)
PF 67	Evidence in support of application to make order of House of Lords an order of the High Court (Pt 40B PD 13.2)
PF 68	Order making an order of the House of Lords an order of the High Court (Pt 40B PD 13.3)
PF 72	List of exhibits
PF 74	Order for trial by Master

No.	Title
PF 78 QB	Solicitor's undertaking as to expenses (re letter of request) (rule 6A.11 and Pt 34 PD 5.3(5))
PF 79	Default judgment for possession of land, damages and costs (Part 12)
PF 83	Judgment (non-attendance of party) (rule 39.3)
PF 84	Judgment as a consequence of failure to comply with an order or condition (rules 3.1(3) and 3.5)
PF 86	Praecipe for writ of fieri facias (sched. 1 - RSC ord. 46 and 47)
PF 87	Praecipe for writ of sequestration (sched. 1 - RSC ord. 46)
PF 88	Praecipe for writ of possession (sched. 1 - RSC ord. 45)
PF 89	Praecipe for writ of possession and fieri facias combined (sched. 1 RSC ord. 45)
PF 90	Praecipe for writ of delivery (sched. 1 - RSC ord. 45)
PF 91	Evidence in support of application to enforce judgment for possession (sched. 1 - RSC ord. 45)
PF 97 QB	Order for sale by Sheriff by private contract (sched. 1 - RSC ord. 47)
PF 98	Evidence in support of application for order for examination of judgment debtor or officer (sched. 1 - RSC ord. 48)
PF 99	Order for oral examination of judgment debtor or officer (sched. 1 RSC ord. 48)
PF 100	Evidence in support of garnishee order (sched. 1 - RSC ord. 49)
PF 101	Evidence in support of charging order (sched. 1 - RSC ord. 49)
PF 103	Warrant of committal (general) (sched. 1 - RSC ord. 52)
PF 104	Warrant of committal (in face of court) (sched. 1 - RSC ord. 52)
PF 105	Warrant of committal (failure of witness to attend) (sched. 1 - RSC ord. 52)
PF110	Notice of appeal to judge from Master or district judge (sched. 1 - RSC ord. 58)
PF 113	Evidence in support of application for service by an alternative method (Pt 6 PD 9.1)
PF 114	Order for service by an alternative method (rule 6.8)
PF 130	Form of advertisement
PF 141	Evidence of personal service
PF 147	Application for order declaring solicitor ceased to act (death etc.) (rule 42.4)
PF 148	Order declaring solicitor has ceased to act (rule 42.4)
PF 149	Application by solicitor that he has ceased to act (rule 42.3)
PF 150	Order that solicitor has ceased to act (rule 42.3)
PF 152 QB	Evidence in support of application for examination of witness under the Evidence (Proceedings in Other Jurisdictions) Act 1975
PF 153 QB	Certificate witness under the Evidence (Proceedings in Other Jurisdictions) Act 1975 (sched. 1 - RSC ord. 70)
PF 154 QB	Order for registration of foreign judgment under the Foreign Judgments (Reciprocal Enforcement) Act 1933 (sched. 1 - RSC ord. 71)
PF 155 QB	Certificates under s. 10 of the Foreign, Judgments (Reciprocal Enforcement) Act 1933 (sched. 1 - RSC ord. 71)
PF 156 QB	Evidence in support of application for registration of a Community judgment (sched. 1 - RSC ord. 71)
PF 157 QB	Order for registration of a Community judgment (sched. 1 - RSC ord. 71)
PF 158 QB	Notice of registration of a Community judgment (sched. 1 - RSC 0.71)
PF 159 QB	Evidence in support of application for registration of a judgment of another Contracting State (sched. 1 - RSC ord. 71)

PD 4 PRACTICE DIRECTIONS — FORMS

No.	Title
PF 160 QB	Order for registration of a judgment of another Contracting State under s. 4 of the Civil Jurisdiction and Judgments Act 1982 (sched. 1 - RSC ord. 71)
PF 161 QB	Notice of registration of a judgment of another Contracting State (sched. 1 - RSC ord. 71)
PF 163 QB	Evidence in support of application for certified copy of a judgment for enforcement in another Contracting State (sched. 1 - RSC ord. 71)
PF 164 QB	Evidence in support of application for certificate as to money provisions of a judgment of the High Court for registration elsewhere in the United Kingdom (sched. 1 - RSC ord. 71)
PF 165 QB	Evidence in support of application for registration of a judgment of a court in another part of the United Kingdom containing non-money provisions (sched. 1- RSC ord. 71)
PF 166 QB	Certificate as to finality etc. of arbitration award for enforcement abroad (Arbitration Act 1996, s.58)
PF 167 QB	Order to stay proceedings under s. 9 of the Arbitration Act 1996
PF 168	Order to transfer claim to county court (County Courts Act 1984)
PF 170	Application for child or patient's settlement in personal injury or fatal accident claims Pt 21 PD 6 and 7)
PR 72 QB	Application in respect of funds in court or to be brought into court (Pt 21 PD 8)
PF 177	Order for written statement as to partners in firm (sched. 1 - RSC ord. 81 r. 2)
PF 179 QB	Evidence in support of an application for registration of a bill of sale (sched. 1 RSC ord. 95)
PF 180 QB	Evidence in support of an application for registration of an absolute bill of sale, settlement and deed of gift (sched. 1 - RSC ord. 95)
PF 181 QB	Evidence in support of an application for re-registration of a bill of sale (sched. 1 - RSC ord. 95)
PF 182 QB	Order for extension of time to register or re-register a bill of sale (sched. 1 - RSC ord. 95)
PF183 QB	Evidence in support of an application for permission to enter a memorandum of satisfaction on a bill of sale (sched. 1 - RSC ord. 95)
PF 184 QB	Claim form for entry of satisfaction on a registered bill of sale (sched. 1 - RSC ord. 95)
PF 185 QB	Order for entry of satisfaction on a registered bill of sale (sched. 1 - RSC ord. 95)
PF 186 QB	Evidence in support of application for registration of assignment of book debts (sched. 1 - RSC ord. 95)
PF 187	Application for solicitor's charging order (sched. 1 - RSC ord. 106 r. 2)
PF 188	Charging order: solicitor's costs (sched. 1 - RSC ord. 106 r. 2)
PF 197	Application for order for transfer from the Royal Courts of Justice to a district registry or vice versa or from one district registry to another (rule 30.2(4))
PF 198	Order under PF 197
PF 200	Notice of proposed order to transfer to county court, or strike out (s. 40(1) and (8) of the County Courts Act 1984)
PF 201	Notice of hearing to decide whether to order transfer to county court or strike out
PF 202	Notice of proposed order to transfer to county court (s. 40(2) of the County Courts Act 1984)
PF 203	Notice of objection to proposed transfer to county court (s. 40(2) of the County Courts Act 1984)

PD 4 PRACTICE DIRECTIONS — FORMS

No.	Title
PF 205	Evidence in support of application for permission to execute for earlier costs of enforcement under s. 15(3) and (4) of the Courts and Legal Services Act 1990
PF 5 CH	Order for possession on mortgaged property
PF 6 CH	Certificate on application for leave to issue execution on suspended order for possession where defendant in default of acknowledgement of service
PF 7 CH	Inquiry for persons entitled to the property of an intestate dying on or after 1 January 1926
PF 8CH	Summons after master's findings on kin enquiry for *Re Benjamin* order giving leave to distribute estate upon footing
PF 9 CH	*Re Benjamin* order giving leave to distribute estate upon footing
PF 10 CH	Judgment in beneficiaries' administration action where deceased died on or after 1 January 1926
PF 11 CH	Judgment in creditors' administration action where deceased died on or after 1 January 1926
PF 12 CH	Advertisement for creditors
PR 13 CH	Advertisement for claimants other than creditors
PF 14 CH	Affidavit verifying list of creditors' claims
PF 15 CH	List of claims sent in pursuant to advertisement by persons claiming to be creditors
PF 16 CH	List of claims by persons claiming to be creditors other than those sent in pursuant to advertisement
PF 17 CH	List of sums of money which may be due in respect of which no claim has been received
PF 18 CH	Notice to creditor to prove claim
PF 19 CH	Notice to creditor or other claimant to produce documents
PF 20 CH	Notice to creditor of allowance of claim
PF 21 CH	Notice to creditor of disallowance of claim
PF 22 CH	Order for administration: beneficiaries' action reconstituted as creditors' claims
PF 23 CH	Affidavit verifying list of claims other than creditors' claims
PF 24 CH	List of claims not being creditors' claims sent in pursuant to advertisement
PF 25 CH	List of claims not being creditors' claims other than those sent in pursuant to advertisement
PF 26 CH	Notice to claimant other than a creditor to prove claim
PF 27 CH	Affidavit verifying accounts and answering usual enquiries in administration action
PF 28 CH	Executor's (or administrator's account)
PF 29 CH	Master's order stating the results of proceedings before him on the usual accounts and inquiries in an administration action
PF 30 CH	Security of receiver or administrator
PF 31 CH	Consent to act as trustee
PF 32 CH	Affidavit in support of application for appointment of new next friend of minor plaintiff
PF 33 CH	Order for cross-examination of deponents on their affidavits
PF 34 CH	Order in inquiry as to title in proceedings to enforce charging order where the defendant's title is not disclosed
PF 35 CH	Subpoena to bring in a script
PF 36 CH	Order appointing administrator
PF 37 CH	Affidavit of testamentary scripts
PF 38 CH	Order approving compromise in probate action

Table 3

Contents

5.1 This table lists county court forms in use before 26 April 1999 that will continue to be used, on or after that date.

5.2 Where a rule permits, a party intending to use a witness statement as an alternative to an affidavit should amend any form in this Table to be used in connection with that rule so that 'witness statement' replaces 'affidavit' wherever it appears in the form.

No.	Title
N5	Summons for possession of property
N5A	Application for accelerated possession (assured tenancies) s. 8 of the Housing Act 1988
N5B	Application for accelerated possession (assured tenancies) s. 21 of the Housing Act 1988
N6	Possession summons (forfeiture and right of re-entry)
N8	Notice to respondent when a matter will be heard
N8(1)	Notice to respondent when a matter will be heard under Order 24
N8(2)	Notice to respondent in application under section 53
N8(4)	Notice to respondent in application under Section 17/18 of the Leasehold Reform Act 1967
N11	Form of reply — possession summons
N11A	Form of reply to application for accelerated possession (assured tenancies) s. 8 of the Housing Act 1988
N11(B)	Acknowledgment of service Business List actions
N118	Form of reply to application for accelerated possession (assured tenancies) s. 21 of the Housing Act 1988
N11M	Form of reply (mortgaged property)
N11R	Form of reply (rented property)
N16	General form of injunction
N16(1)	General form of injunction (formal parts only)
N16A	General form of application for injunction
N26	Order for possession (rented property)
N26A	Order that claimant have possession (assured tenancies)
N27	Judgment for claimant in action of forfeiture for non-payment of rent
N27(1)	Judgment for claimant — forfeiture for non-payment of rent where order refused under Rent Acts
N27(2)	Judgment for claimant — for non-payment of rent where order suspended under Rent Acts
N28	Order for possession (possession suspended) (rented property)
N29	Order for possession (mortgaged property)
N31	Order for possession of mortgaged property suspended under s. 36 of the Administration of Justice Act 1970
N35	Variation order
N35A	Variation order (determination)
N36	Order for possession under Order 24
N37	Oral examination of judgment debtor
N38	Oral examination (person other than judgment debtor)
N39	Order for defendant's attendance at an adjourned hearing of an oral examination
N40	Warrant of committal (oral examination)
N41	Order suspending judgment or order, and/or warrant of execution/committal
N41A	Order suspending warrant (determination)
N42	Warrant of execution

PD 4 PRACTICE DIRECTIONS — FORMS

No.	Title
N46	Warrant of delivery and execution for damages and costs
N48	Warrant of delivery, where, if goods are not returned, levy is to be made for their value
N49	Warrant for possession of land
N50	Warrant of restitution (Order 26 rule 17)
N51	Warrant of restitution (Order 24, rule 6(1))
N52	Warrant of possession under Order 24
N53	Warrant of execution or committal to district judge of foreign court
N55	Notice of application for attachment of earnings order
N55A	Notice of application for attachment of earnings order (maintenance)
N56	Form for replying to an attachment of earnings application (statement of means)
N58	Order for defendant's attendance at an adjourned hearing of an attachment of earnings application (maintenance)
N59	Warrant of committal under s. 23(1) of the Attachment of Earnings Act 1971
N60	Attachment of earnings order (judgment debt)
N61	Order for production of statement of means
N61A	Order to employer for production of statement of earnings
N62	Summons for offence under Attachment of Earnings act 1971
N63	Notice to show cause section 23 of the Attachment of Earnings Act 1971
N64	Suspended attachment of earnings order
N64A	Suspended attachment of earnings order (maintenance)
N65A	Attachment of earnings arrears order
N65	Attachment of earnings order (priority maintenance)
N66	Consolidated attachment of earnings order
N66A	Notice of application for consolidated attachment of earnings order
N67	Judgment summons under the Debtors Act 1869
N68	Certificate of service (judgment summons)
N69	Order for debtor's attendance at an adjourned hearing of judgment summons
N70	Order of commitment under s. 110 of the County Courts Act 1984
N71	Order revoking an order of commitment under s. 110 of the County Courts Act 1984
N72	Notice to defendant where a committal order made but directed to be suspended under Debtors Act 1869
N73	New order on judgment summons
N74	Warrant of committal on a judgment summons under the Debtors Act 1869
N75	Indorsement on a warrant of committal sent to a foreign court
N76	Certificate to be endorsed on duplicate warrant of committal issued for re-arrest of debtor
N77	Notice as to consequences of disobedience to court order
N78	Notice to show good reason why an order for your committal to prison should not be made (Family proceedings only)
N79	Committal of other order, upon proof of disobedience of a court order or breach of undertaking
N80	Warrant for committal to prison
N81	Notice to solicitor to show cause why an undertaking should not be enforced by committal to prison
N82	Order for committal for failure by solicitor to carry out undertaking
N83	Order for discharge from custody under warrant of committal
N84	Garnishee order to show cause
N85	Garnishee order absolute

PD 4 PRACTICE DIRECTIONS — FORMS

No.	Title
N86	Charging order nisi
N87	Charging order absolute
N88	Interpleader summons to execution creditor
N88(1)	Interpleader summons to claimant claiming goods or rent under an execution
N89	Interpleader summons to persons making adverse claims to debt
N90	Summons for assaulting an officer of the court or rescuing goods
N91	Order of commitment and/or imposing a fine for assaulting an officer of the court or rescuing goods
N92	Request for administration order
N93	List of creditors furnished under the [Attachment of Earnings Act] 1971
N94	Administration order
N95	Order revoking an administration order
N95A	Order suspending or varying an administration order
N110	Power of arrest attached to injunction under s. 2 of the Domestic Violence and Matrimonial Proceedings Act 1976
N110A	Antisocial behaviour injunction — power of arrest s. 152/153 Housing Act 1996
N112	Order for Arrest under s. 110 of the County Courts Act 1984
N112A	Power of arrest, s. 23 of the Attachment of Earnings Act 1971
N117	General form of undertaking
N118	Notice to defendant where committal order made but directed to be suspended
N119	Particulars of claim for possession (rented property)
N120	Particulars of claim for possession (mortgaged property)
N130	Application for possession including application for interim possession order
N131	Notice of application for interim possession order
N132	Affidavit of service of notice of application for interim possession order
N133	Affidavit to occupier to oppose the making of an interim possession order
N134	Interim possession order
N135	Affidavit of service of interim possession order
N136	Order for possession
N138	Injunction order
N139	Application for warrant of arrest
N140	Warrant of arrest
N206	Notice of issue of fixed date claim
N206A	Notice of issue of application (assured tenancies)
N207	Plaint note (adoption freeing for adoption)
N200	Petition — Note old number was N208
N201	Request for entry of appeal — Note old number was N209
N202	Order for party to sue or defend on behalf of others having the same interest — Note old number was N210
N203	Notice to persons on whose behalf party has obtained leave to sue or defend — Note old number was N211
N204	Notice to person against whom party has obtained leave to sue or defend on behalf of others — Note old number was N212
N220	Request for service of possession summons on defendant's representative
N220(1)	Notice to representative of defendant in action for recovery of land
N224	Request for service out of England and Wales through the court
N229	Notice of admission in possession action

PD 4 PRACTICE DIRECTIONS — FORMS

No.	Title
N245	Application for suspension of a warrant and/or variation of an instalment order
N246	Claimant's reply to defendant's application to vary instalment order
N246A	Claimant's reply to defendant's application to suspend warrant of execution
N270	Notes for guidance (application for administration order)
N276	Notice of hearing of interpleader proceedings transferred from High Court
N277	Notice of pre-trial review of interpleader proceedings transferred from the High Court
N280	Order of reference of proceedings or questions for inquiry and report
N285	General form of affidavit
N288	Order to produce prisoner
N289	Judgment for defendant
N291	Judgment for defendant in action for recovery of land
N293	Certificate of judgment or order
N293A	Combined certificate of judgment and request for writ of fieri facias
N295	Order for sale of land
N296	Notice of judgment or order to party directed to be served with notice
N297	Order for accounts and inquiries in creditors' administration action
N298	Order for administration
N299	Order for foreclosure nisi of legal mortgage of land
N300	Order for sale in action by equitable mortgagee
N302	Judgment in action for specific performance (vendor's action, title accepted)
N303	Order for dissolution of partnership
N304	Notice to parties to attend upon taking accounts
N305	Notice to creditor to prove his claim
N306	Notice to creditor of determination of claim
N307	District Judge's order (accounts and inquiries)
N309	Order for foreclosure absolute
N310	Partnership order on further consideration
N311	Administrative action order on further consideration
N312	Claim form for possession under Order 24
N313	Endorsement on certificate of judgment (transfer)
N316	Request for oral examination
N317	Bailiff's report
N317A	Bailiff's report to the claimant
N319	Notice of execution of warrant of committal
N320	Request for return of, or to, warrant
N322	Order for recovery of money awarded by tribunal
N322A	Application for an order to recover money awarded to a tribunal or other body
N322H	Request to register a High Court judgment or order for enforcement
N323	Request for warrant of execution
N324	Request for warrant of goods
N325	Request for warrant for possession of land
N326	Notice of issue of warrant of execution
N327	Notice of issue of warrant of execution to enforce a judgment or order
N328	Notice of transfer of proceedings to the High Court
N329	Notes for guidance on completion of N.79

No.	Title
N330	Notice of sale or payment under execution in respect of a judgment for a sum exceeding £500
N331	Notice of withdrawal from possession or payment of moneys on notice of receiving or winding-up order
N332	Inventory of goods removed
N333	Notice of time when and where goods will be sold
N335	Request to hold walking possession and authority to re-enter
N336	Request and result of search in the attachment of earnings index
N337	Request for attachment of earnings order
N338	Request for statement of earnings
N339	Discharge of attachment of earnings order
N340	Notice as to payment under attachment of earnings order made by the High Court
N341	Notice of intention to vary attachment of earnings order under s. 10(2) of the Attachment of Earnings Act 1971
N342	Request for judgment summons
N343	Notice of result of hearing of a judgment summons issued on a judgment or order of the High Court
N344	Request for warrant of committal on judgment summons
N345	Certificate of payment under the Debtors Act 1869
N349	Affidavit in support of application for garnishee order
N353	Order appointing receiver of real and personal property
N354	Order appointing receiver of partnership
N355	Interim order for appointment of receiver
N356	Order for appointment of receiver by way of equitable execution
N358	Notice of claim to goods taken in execution
N359	Notice to claimant to goods taken in execution to make deposit or give security
N360	Affidavit in support of interpleader summons other than an execution
N361	Notice of application for relief in pending action
N362	Order on interpleader summons under an execution where the claim is not established
N363	Order on interpleader summons under an execution where the claim is established
N364	Order on interpleader summons (other than execution) where there is an action
N365	Order on interpleader summons (other than execution) where there is no action
N366	Summons for neglect to levy execution
N368	Order fining a witness for non-attendance
N370	Order of commitment or imposing a fine for insult or misbehaviour
N372	Order for rehearing
N373	Notice of application for an administration order
N374	Notice of intention to review an administration order
N374A	Notice of intention to revoke an administration order
N375	Notice of further creditors' claim
N376	Notice of hearing administration order (by direction of the court)
N377	Notice of dividend
N388	Notice to probate registry to produce documents
N390	Notice that a claim has been entered against the Crown
N391	Crown Proceedings Act 1947 affidavit in support of application directing payment by Crown to judgment creditor
N392	Crown Proceedings Act 1947 notice of application for order directing payment by the Crown to the judgment creditor

No.	Title
N394	Claim form for determining the right to compensation for improvement (Landlord and Tenant Act 1927)
N395	Claim form for certificate or determination of question other than compensation (Landlord and Tenant Act 1927)
N396	Claim form for statutory tenancy under Part I of the Landlord and Tenant Act 1954
N397	Claim form for new tenancy under Part II of the Landlord and Tenant Act 1954
N398	Order on application for certificate as to improvement (Landlord and Tenant Act 1927)
N399	Final order (Landlord and Tenant Act 1927)
N400	Answer to claim form for new tenancy under Part II of the Landlord and Tenant Act 1954
N401	Order on application for a new tenancy under Part II of the Landlord and Tenant Act 1954
N402	Order substituting date in landlord's notice or tenant's request
N403	Application for certificate of ground for refusing new tenancy
N404	Certificate of ground for refusing new tenancy
N404(1)	Order authorising agreement excluding act
N405	Notice of proceedings
N425	Notice to repair
N426	Notice of proceedings
N432	Affidavit on payment into court under section 63 of the Trustee Act 1925
N436	Order for sale of land under charging order
N437	District Judge's report
N438	Notice to charge holder under Matrimonial Homes Act 1983
N440	Notice of application for time order by debtor or hirer — Consumer Credit Act 1974
N441	Notification of request for certificate of satisfaction or cancellation
N441A	Certificate of satisfaction or cancellation of judgment debt
N444	Details of sale under a warrant of execution
N445	Request for re-issue of warrant
N446	Request for re-issue of post-judgment process (other than warrant)
N447	Notice to claimant of date fixed for adjourned hearing
N448	Request to defendant for employment details, attachment of earnings
N449	Notice to employer, failure to make deductions under attachment of earnings order

CPR PART 5   COURT DOCUMENTS

CONTENTS OF THIS PART
Scope of this Part Rule 5.1
Preparation of documents Rule 5.2
Signature of documents by mechanical means Rule 5.3
Supply of documents from court records Rule 5.4

5.1 SCOPE OF THIS PART
This part contains general provisions about—
- (a) documents used in court proceedings; and
- (b) the obligations of a court officer in relation to those documents.

5.2 PREPARATION OF DOCUMENTS
(1) Where under these Rules, a document is to be prepared by the court, the document may be prepared by the party whose document it is, unless—
- (a) a court officer otherwise directs; or
- (b) it is a document to which—
  - (i) CCR Order 25, rule 5(3) (reissue of enforcement proceedings);
  - (ii) CCR Order 25, rule 8(9) (reissue of warrant where condition upon which warrant was suspended has not been complied with); or
  - (iii) CCR Order 28, rule 11(1) (issue of warrant of committal), applies.

(2) Nothing in this rule shall require a court officer to accept a document which is illegible, has not been duly authorised, or is unsatisfactory for some other similar reason.

5.3 SIGNATURE OF DOCUMENTS BY MECHANICAL MEANS
Where any of these Rules or any practice direction requires a document to be signed, that requirement shall be satisfied if the signature is printed by computer or other mechanical means.

5.4 SUPPLY OF DOCUMENTS FROM COURT RECORDS
(1) Any party to proceedings may be supplied from the records of the court with a copy of any document relating to those proceedings (including documents filed before the claim was commenced), provided that the party seeking the document—
- (a) pays any prescribed fee; and
- (b) files a written request for the document.

(2) Any other person who pays the prescribed fee may, during office hours, search for, inspect and take a copy of the following documents, namely—
- (a) a claim form which has been served;
- (b) any judgment or order given or made in public;
- (c) any other document if the court gives permission.

(3) An application for permission under paragraph (2)(c) may be made without notice.

(4) This rule does not apply in relation to any proceedings in respect of which a practice direction makes different provision.

PD 5 PRACTICE DIRECTION — COURT DOCUMENTS

This practice direction supplements CPR Part 5

SIGNATURE OF DOCUMENTS BY MECHANICAL MEANS

1   Where, under rule 5.3, a replica signature is printed electronically or by other mechanical means on any document, the name of the person whose signature is printed must also be printed so that the person may be identified. This paragraph does not apply to claim forms issued through the Claims Production Centre.

FORM OF DOCUMENTS

2.1   Statements of case and other documents drafted by a legal representative should bear his/her signature and if they are drafted by a legal representative as a member or employee of a firm they should be signed in the name of the firm.

2.2   Every document prepared by a party for filing or use at the Court must

(1)   Unless the nature of the document renders it impracticable, be on A4 paper of durable quality having a margin, not less than 3.5 centimetres wide,

(2)   be fully legible and should normally be typed,

(3)   where possible be bound securely in a manner which would not hamper filing or otherwise each page should be endorsed with the case number,

(4)   have the pages numbered consecutively,

(5)   be divided into numbered paragraphs,

(6)   have all numbers, including dates, expressed as figures, and

(7)   give in the margin the reference of every document mentioned that has already been filed.

2.3   A document which is a copy produced by a colour photostat machine or other similar device may be filed at the court office provided that the coloured date seal of the Court is not reproduced on the copy.

SUPPLY OF DOCUMENTS TO NEW PARTIES

3.1   Where a party is joined to existing proceedings, the party joined shall be entitled to require the party joining him to supply, without charge, copies of all statements of case, written evidence and any documents appended or exhibited to them which have been served in the proceedings by or upon the joining party which relate to any issues between the joining party and the party joined, and copies of all orders made in those proceedings. The documents must be supplied within 48 hours after a written request for them is received.

3.2   If the party joined is not supplied with copies of the documents requested under paragraph 3.1 within 48 hours, he may apply under Part 23 for an order that they be supplied.

3.3   The party by whom a copy is supplied under paragraph 3.1 or, if he is acting by a solicitor, his solicitor, shall be responsible for it being a true copy.

SUPPLY OF DOCUMENTS FROM COURT RECORDS

4.1   Where a person makes a search for the documents mentioned in CPR rule 5.4(2), that search may be conducted by means of a computer, if the court office has a computer with the appropriate search facility.

4.2   When the document searched for under CPR rule 5.4(2) is identified and upon payment of the prescribed fee, the document will be produced for inspection by a member of the Court staff.

4.3   If, in the course of a computer search, the computer identifies documents held on the Court file, other than those which the person searching is entitled to inspect, that person may not, without the Court's permission, inspect, take a copy or make any note of, or relating to, those documents.

4.4   An application for inspection of a document under CPR rule 5.4(2)(c), even if made without notice, must be made under CPR Part 23 and the application

PD 5 PRACTICE DIRECTION — COURT DOCUMENTS

notice must identify the document in respect of which permission is sought and the grounds relied upon.

4.5 CPR rules 5.4(2) and 5.4(3) do not apply to proceedings in a county court. (it is intended that these rules will be applied to county courts once the facilities for a computer search have been installed.)

DOCUMENTS FOR FILING AT COURT

5.1 The date on which a document was filed at court must be recorded on the document. This may be done by a seal or a receipt stamp.

5.2 Particulars of the date of delivery at a court office of any document for filing and the title of the proceedings in which the document is filed shall be entered in court records, on the court file or on a computer kept in the court office for the purpose. Except where a document has been delivered at the court office through the post, the time of delivery should also be recorded.

5.3 Where the Court orders any document to be lodged in Court, the document must, unless otherwise directed, be deposited in the office of that Court.

5.4 A document filed, lodged or held in any court office shall not be taken out of that office without the permission of the Court unless the document is to be sent to the office of another court (for example under CPR Part 30 (Transfer)), except in accordance with CPR rule 39.7 (impounded documents) or in accordance with paragraph 5.5 below.

5.5 (1) Where a document filed, lodged or held in a court office is required to be produced to any Court, Tribunal or arbitrator, the document may be produced by sending it by registered post (together with a Certificate as in paragraph 5.5(8)(b)) to the Court, Tribunal or arbitrator in accordance with the provisions of this paragraph.

(2) Any Court, Tribunal or arbitrator or any party requiring any document filed, lodged or held in any court office to be produced must apply to that court office by sending a completed request (as in paragraph 5.5 (8)(a)), stamped with the prescribed fee.

(3) On receipt of the request the court officer will submit the same to a Master in the Royal Courts of Justice or to a District Judge elsewhere, who may direct that the request be complied with. Before giving a direction the Master or District Judge may require to be satisfied that the request is made in good faith and that the document is required to be produced for the reasons stated. The Master or District Judge giving the direction may also direct that, before the document is sent, an official copy of it is made and filed in the court office at the expense of the party requiring the document to be produced.

(4) On the direction of the Master or District Judge the court officer shall send the document by registered post addressed to the Court, Tribunal or arbitrator, with:

(a) an envelope stamped and addressed for use in returning the document to the court office from which it was sent;

(b) a Certificate as in paragraph 5.5(8)(b);

(c) a covering letter describing the document, stating at whose request and for what purpose it is sent, referring to this paragraph of the Practice Direction and containing a request that the document be returned to the court office from which it was sent in the enclosed envelope as soon as the Court or Tribunal no longer requires it.

(5) It shall be the duty of the Court, Tribunal or arbitrator to whom the document was sent to keep it in safe custody, and to return it by registered post to the court office from which it was sent, as soon as the Court, Tribunal or arbitrator no longer requires it.

(6) In each court office a record shall be kept of each document sent and the date on which it was sent and the Court, Tribunal or arbitrator to whom it was sent and the date of its return. It shall be the duty of the court officer who has signed the certificate referred to in para 5.5(8)(b) below to ensure that the document is returned within a reasonable time and to make inquiries and report to the Master or District Judge who has given the direction under paragraph (3)

above if the document is not returned, so that steps may be taken to secure its return.

(7) Notwithstanding the preceding paragraphs, the Master or District Judge may direct a court officer to attend the Court, Tribunal or arbitrator for the purpose of producing the document.

(8) (a) I,   of   , an officer of the   Court/Tribunal at   /an arbitrator of   /the Claimant/Defendant/Solicitor for the Claimant/Defendant *[describing the Applicant so as to show that he is a proper person to make the request]* in the case of   v.   [19 No.] REQUEST that the following document [or documents] be produced to the Court/Tribunal/arbitrator on the day of 19 [and following days] and I request that the said document [or documents] be sent by registered post to the proper officer of the Court/Tribunal/arbitrator for production to that Court/Tribunal/arbitrator on that day.
(Signed).
Dated the day of 1999/2

(b) I, A.B., an officer of the   Court   of   certify that the document sent herewith for production to the Court/Tribunal/arbitrator on the   day of   1999/2   in the case of   v.   and marked 'A.B.' is the document requested on the   day of   1999/2   and I FURTHER CERTIFY that the said document has been filed in and is produced from the custody of the Court.
(Signed)
Dated the day of 1999/2

ENROLMENT OF DEEDS AND OTHER DOCUMENTS

6.1 (1) Any deed or document which by virtue of any enactment is required or authorised to be enrolled in the Supreme Court may be enrolled in the Central Office of the High Court.

(2) Attention is drawn to the Enrolment of Deeds (Change of Name) Regulations 1994 which are reproduced in the Appendix to this Practice Direction.
6.2 The following paragraph of the Practice Direction describes the practice to be followed in any case in which a child's name is to be changed and to which the 1994 Regulations apply.

6.3 (1) Where a person has by any order of the High Court, County Court or Family Proceedings Court been given parental responsibility for a child and applies to the Central Office, Filing Department, for the enrolment of a Deed Poll to change the surname (family name) of a child who is under the age of 18 years (unless a child who is or has been married), the application must be supported by the production of the consent in writing of every other person having parental responsibility.

(2) In the absence of that consent, the application will be adjourned generally unless and until permission is given in the proceedings, in which the said order was made, to change the surname of the child and the permission is produced to the Central Office.

(3) Where an application is made to the Central Office by a person who has not been given parental responsibility for a child by any order of the High Court, County Court or Family Proceedings Court for the enrolment of a Deed Poll to change the surname of the child who is under the age of 18 years (unless the child is or has been married), permission of the Court to enrol the Deed will be granted if the consent in writing of every person having parental responsibility is produced or if the person (or, if more than one, persons) having parental responsibility is dead or overseas or despite the exercise of reasonable diligence it has not been possible to find him or her for other good reason.

(4) In cases of doubt the Senior Master or, in his absence, the Practice Master will refer the matter to the Master of the Rolls.

(5) In the absence of any of the conditions specified above the Senior Master or the Master of the Rolls, as the case may be, may refer the matter to the Official Solicitor for investigation and report.

APPENDIX

Regulations made by the Master of the Rolls, Sir Thomas Bingham MR on March 3, 1994 (SI 1994/604) under s. 133(1) of the Supreme Court Act 1981.

1 (1) These regulations may be cited as the Enrolment of Deeds (Change of Name) Regulations 1994 and shall come into force on 1 April, 1994.

(2) These Regulations shall govern the enrolment in the Central Office of the Supreme Court of deeds evidencing change of name (referred to in these Regulations as 'deeds poll').

2 (1) A person seeking to enrol a deed poll ('the applicant') must be a Commonwealth citizen as defined by section 37(1) of the British Nationality Act 1981.

(2) If the applicant is a British citizen, a British Dependent Territories citizen or a British Overseas citizen, he must be described as such in the deed poll, which must also specify the section of the British Nationality Act under which the relevant citizenship was acquired.

(3) In any other case, the applicant must be described as a Commonwealth citizen.

(4) The applicant must be described in the deed poll as single, married, widowed or divorced,

3 (1) As proof of the citizenship named in the deed poll, the applicant must produce
   (a) a certificate of birth; or
   (b) a certificate of citizenship by registration or naturalisation or otherwise; or
   (c) some other document evidencing such citizenship.

(2) In addition to the documents set out in paragraph (1), an applicant who is married must
   (a) produce his certificate of marriage; and
   (b) show that the notice of his intention to apply for the enrolment of the deed poll had been given to his spouse by delivery or by post to his spouse's last known address; and
   (c) show that he has obtained the consent of his spouse to the proposed change of name or that there is good reason why such consent should be dispensed with,

4 (1) The deed poll and the documents referred to in regulation 3 must be exhibited to a statutory declaration by a Commonwealth citizen who is a householder in the United Kingdom and who must declare that he is such in the statutory declaration.

(2) The statutory declaration must state the period, which should ordinarily not be less than 10 years, during which the householder has known the applicant and must identify the applicant as the person referred to in the documents exhibited to the statutory declaration.

(3) Where the period mentioned in paragraph (2) is stated to be less than 10 years, the Master of the Rolls, may, in his absolute discretion decide whether to permit the deed poll to be enrolled and may require the applicant to provide more information before so deciding.

5 If the applicant is resident outside the United Kingdom, he must provide evidence that such residence is not intended to be permanent and the applicant may be required to produce a certificate by a solicitor or as to the nature and probable duration of such residence,

6 The applicant must sign the deed poll in both his old and new names.

7 Upon enrolment the deed poll shall be advertised in the London Gazette by the clerk in charge for the time being of the Filing and Record Department at the Central Office of the Supreme Court.

8 (1) Subject to the following provisions of this regulation, these Regulations shall apply in relation to a deed poll evidencing the change of name of a child as if the child were the applicant.

(2) Paragraphs (3) to (8) shall not apply to a child who has attained the age of 16, is female and is married.

(3) If the child is under the age of 16, the deed poll must be executed by a person having parental responsibility for him,

(4) If the child has attained the age of 16, the deed poll must, except in the case of a person mentioned in paragraph (2 be executed by a person having parental responsibility for the child and be endorsed with the child's consent signed in both his old and new names and duly witnessed.

(5) The application for enrolment must be supported
   (a) by an affidavit showing that the change of name is for the benefit of the child, and
      (i) that the application is submitted by all persons having parental responsibility for the child; or
      (ii) that it is submitted by one person having parental responsibility for the child with the consent of every other person; or
      (iii) that it is submitted by one person having parental responsibility for the child without the consent of every other such person, or by some other person whose name and capacity are given, for reasons set out in the affidavit; and
   (b) by such other evidence, if any, as the Master of the Rolls may require in the particular circumstances of the case.

(6) Regulation 4(2) shall not apply but the statutory declaration mentioned in regulation 4(1) shall state how long the householder has known the deponent under paragraph (5)(a) and the child respectively.

(7) Regulation 6 shall not apply to a child who has not attained the age of 16.

(8) In this regulation 'parental responsibility' has the meaning given in section 3 of the Children Act 1989,

9 The Enrolment of Deeds (Change of Name) Regulations 1983 and the Enrolment of Deeds (Change of Name) (Amendment) Regulations 1990 are hereby revoked.

CPR PART 6   SERVICE OF DOCUMENTS

CONTENTS OF THIS PART
I   GENERAL RULES ABOUT SERVICE

Part 6 rules about service apply generally	Rule 6.1
Methods of service — general	Rule 6.2
Who is to serve	Rule 6.3
Personal service	Rule 6.4
Address for service	Rule 6.5
Service of documents on children and patients	Rule 6.6
Deemed service	Rule 6.7
Service by an alternative method	Rule 6.8
Power of court to dispense with service	Rule 6.9
Certificate of service	Rule 6.10
Notice of non-service	Rule 6.11

II   SPECIAL PROVISIONS ABOUT SERVICE OF THE CLAIM FORM

General rules about service subject to special rules about service of claim form	Rule 6.12
Service of claim form by the court — defendant's address for service	Rule 6.13
Certificate of service relating to the claim form	Rule 6.14
Service of claim form by contractually agreed method	Rule 6.15
Service of claim form on agent of principal who is overseas	Rule 6.16

I   GENERAL RULES ABOUT SERVICE

6.1   PART 6 RULES ABOUT SERVICE APPLY GENERALLY
The rules in this Part apply to the service of documents, except where—
   (a)   any other enactment, a rule in another Part, or a practice direction makes a different provision; or
   (b)   the court orders otherwise.

6.2   METHODS OF SERVICE — GENERAL
   (1)   A document may be served by any of the following methods—
      (a)   personal service, in accordance with rule 6.4;
      (b)   first class post;
      (c)   leaving the document at a place specified in rule 6.5;
      (d)   through a document exchange in accordance with the relevant practice direction; or
      (e)   by fax or other means of electronic communication in accordance with the relevant practice direction.
(Rule 6.8 provides for the court to permit service by an alternative method)
   (2)   A company may be served by any method permitted under this Part as an alternative to the methods of service set out in—
      (a)   section 725 of the Companies Act 1985 (service by leaving a document at or posting it to an authorised place);
      (b)   section 695 of that Act (service on overseas companies); and
      (c)   section 694A of that Act (service of documents on companies incorporated outside the UK and Gibraltar and having a branch in Great Britain).

6.3   WHO IS TO SERVE
   (1)   The court will serve a document which it has issued or prepared except where—
      (a)   a rule provides that a party must serve the document in question;
      (b)   the party on whose behalf the document is to be served notifies the court that he wishes to serve it himself;
      (c)   a practice direction provides otherwise;

(d) the court orders otherwise; or
(e) the court has failed to serve and has sent a notice of non-service to the party on whose behalf the document is to be served in accordance with rule 6.11.
(2) Where the court is to serve a document, it is for the court to decide which of the methods of service specified in rule 6.2 is to be used.
(3) Where a party prepares a document which is to be served by the court, that party must file a copy for the court, and for each party to be served.

6.4 PERSONAL SERVICE
(1) A document to be served may be served personally, except as provided in paragraph (2).
(2) Where a solicitor—
    (a) is authorised to accept service on behalf of a party; and
    (b) has notified the party serving the document in writing that he is so authorised,
a document must be served on the solicitor, unless personal service is required by an enactment, rule, practice direction or court order.
(3) A document is served personally on an individual by leaving it with that individual.
(4) A document is served personally on a company or other corporation by leaving it with a person holding a senior position within the company or corporation.
(The service practice direction sets out the meaning of 'senior position')
(5) A document is served personally on a partnership where partners are being sued in the name of their firm by leaving it with—
    (a) a partner; or
    (b) a person who, at the time of service, has the control or management of the partnership business at its principal place of business.

6.5 ADDRESS FOR SERVICE
(1) Except as provided by RSC Order 11 (service out of the jurisdiction) a document must be served within the jurisdiction.
('jurisdiction' is defined in rule 2.3)
(2) A party must give an address for service within the jurisdiction.
(3) Where a party—
    (a) does not give the business address of his solicitor as his address for service; and
    (b) resides or carries on business within the jurisdiction,
he must give his residence or place of business as his address for service.
(4) Any document to be served—
    (a) by first class post;
    (b) by leaving it at the place of service;
    (c) through a document exchange; or
    (d) by fax or by other means of electronic communication,
must be sent or transmitted to, or left at, the address for service given by the party to be served.
(5) Where—
    (a) a solicitor is acting for the party to be served; and
    (b) the document to be served is not the claim form;
the party's address for service is the business address of his solicitor.
(Rule 6.13 specifies when the business address of a defendant's solicitor may be the defendant's address for service in relation to the claim form)
(6) Where—
    (a) no solicitor is acting for the party to be served; and
    (b) the party has not given an address for service,
the document must be sent or transmitted to, or left at, the place shown in the following table.
(Rule 6.2(2) sets out the statutory methods of service on a company)

CPR PART 6   SERVICE OF DOCUMENTS

NATURE OF PARTY TO BE SERVED	PLACE OF SERVICE
Individual	• Usual or last known residence.
Proprietor of a business	• Usual or last known residence; or • Place of business or last known place of business.
Individual who is suing or being sued in the name of a firm	• Usual or last known residence; or • Principal or last known place of business of the firm.
Corporation incorporated in England and Wales other than a company	• Principal office of the corporation; or • Any place within the jurisdiction where the corporation carries on its activities and which has a real connection with the claim.
Company registered in England and Wales	• Principal office of the company; or • Any place of business of the company within the jurisdiction which has a real connection with the claim.
Any other company or corporation	• Any place within the jurisdiction where the corporation carries on its activities; or • Any place of business of the company within the jurisdiction.

(7)   This rule does not apply where an order made by the court under rule 6.8 (service by an alternative method) specifies where the document in question may be served.

6.6 SERVICE OF DOCUMENTS ON CHILDREN AND PATIENTS

(1) The following table shows the person on whom a document must be served if it is a document which would otherwise be served on a child or a patient—

TYPE OF DOCUMENT	NATURE OF PARTY	PERSON TO BE SERVED
Claim form	Child who is not also a patient	• One of the child's parents or guardians; or • If there is no parent or guardian, the person with whom the child resides or in whose care the child is.
Claim form	Patient	• The person authorised under Part VII of the Mental Health Act 1983 to conduct the proceedings in the name of the patient or on his behalf; or • If there is no person so authorised, the person with whom the patient resides or in whose care the patient is.
Application for an order appointing a litigation friend, where a child or patient has no litigation friend	Child or patient	See rule 21.8.
Any other document	Child or patient	The litigation friend who is conducting proceedings on behalf of the child or patient.

(2) The court may make an order permitting a document to be served on the child or patient, or on some person other than the person specified in the table in this rule.

(3) An application for an order under paragraph (2) may be made without notice.

(4) The court may order that, although a document has been served on someone other than the person specified in the table, the document is to be treated as if it had been properly served.

(5) This rule does not apply where the court has made an order under rule 21.2(3) allowing a child to conduct proceedings without a litigation friend.

(Part 21 contains rules about the appointment of a litigation friend)

6.7 DEEMED SERVICE

(1) A document which is served in accordance with these rules or any relevant practice direction shall be deemed to be served on the day shown in the following table—

METHOD OF SERVICE	DEEMED DAY OF SERVICE
First class post	The second day after it was posted.
Document exchange	The second day after it was left at the document exchange.
Delivering the document to or leaving it at a permitted address	The day after it was delivered to or left at the permitted address.
Fax	• If it is transmitted on a business day before 4 p.m., on that day; or • In any other case, on the business day after the day on which it is transmitted.
Other electronic method	The second day after the day on which it is transmitted.

(2) If a document (other than a claim form) is served after 5 p.m. on a business day, or at any time on a Saturday, Sunday or a bank holiday, the document shall be treated as having been served on the next business day.

(3) In this rule—

'business day' means any day except Saturday, Sunday or a bank holiday; and

'bank holiday' includes Christmas Day and Good Friday.

6.8 SERVICE BY AN ALTERNATIVE METHOD

(1) Where it appears to the court that there is a good reason to authorise service by a method not permitted by these Rules, the court may make an order permitting service by an alternative method.

(2) An application for an order permitting service by an alternative method—
  (a) must be supported by evidence; and
  (b) may be made without notice.

(3) An order permitting service by an alternative method must specify—
  (a) the method of service; and
  (b) the date when the document will be deemed to be served.

6.9 POWER OF COURT TO DISPENSE WITH SERVICE

(1) The court may dispense with service of a document.

(2) An application for an order to dispense with service may be made without notice.

6.10 CERTIFICATE OF SERVICE

Where a rule, practice direction or court order requires a certificate of service, the certificate must state—
- (a) that the document has not been returned undelivered; and
- (b) the details set out in the following table—

METHOD OF SERVICE	DETAILS TO BE CERTIFIED
Post	Date of posting
Personal	Date of personal service
Document exchange	Date of delivery to the document exchange
Delivery of document to or leaving it at a permitted place	Date when the document was delivered to or left at the permitted place
Fax	Date and time of transmission
Other electronic means	Date of transmission and the means used
Alternative method permitted by the court	As required by the court

6.11 NOTICE OF NON-SERVICE

Where—
- (a) a document is to be served by the court; and
- (b) the court is unable to serve it,

the court must send a notice of non-service stating the method attempted to the party who requested service.

II SPECIAL PROVISIONS ABOUT SERVICE OF THE CLAIM FORM

6.12 GENERAL RULES ABOUT SERVICE SUBJECT TO SPECIAL RULES ABOUT SERVICE OF CLAIM FORM

The general rules about service are subject to the special rules about service contained in rules 6.13 to 6.16.

6.13 SERVICE OF CLAIM FORM BY THE COURT — DEFENDANT'S ADDRESS FOR SERVICE

(1) Where a claim form is to be served by the court, the claim form must include the defendant's address for service.

(2) For the purposes of paragraph (1), the defendant's address for service may be the business address of the defendant's solicitor if he is authorised to accept service on the defendant's behalf but not otherwise.

(Rule 6.5 contains general provisions about the address for service)

6.14 CERTIFICATE OF SERVICE RELATING TO THE CLAIM FORM

(1) Where a claim form is served by the court, the court must send the claimant a notice which will include the date when the claim form is deemed to be served under rule 6.7.

(2) Where the claim form is served by the claimant—
- (a) he must file a certificate of service within 7 days of service of the claim form; and
- (b) he may not obtain judgment in default under Part 12 unless he has filed the certificate of service.

(Rule 6.10 specifies what a certificate of service must show)

6.15 SERVICE OF CLAIM FORM BY CONTRACTUALLY AGREED METHOD

(1) Where—
- (a) a contract contains a term providing that, in the event of a claim being issued in relation to the contract, the claim form may be served by a method specified in the contract; and

(b) a claim form containing only a claim in respect of that contract is issued, the claim form shall, subject to paragraph (2), be deemed to be served on the defendant if it is served by a method specified in the contract.

(2) Where the claim form is served out of the jurisdiction in accordance with the contract, it shall not be deemed to be served on the defendant unless—

(a) permission to serve it out of the jurisdiction has been granted under RSC Order 11, r. 1(1); or

(b) it may be served without permission under RSC Order 11, r. 1(2).

6.16 SERVICE OF CLAIM FORM ON AGENT OF PRINCIPAL WHO IS OVERSEAS

(1) Where—

(a) the defendant is overseas; and

(b) the conditions specified in paragraph (2) are satisfied,

the court may, on an application only, permit a claim form relating to a contract to be served on a defendant's agent.

(2) The court may not make an order under this rule unless it is satisfied that—

(a) the contract to which the claim relates was entered into within the jurisdiction with or through the defendant's agent; and

(b) at the time of the application either the agent's authority has not been terminated or he is still in business relations with his principal.

(3) An application under this rule—

(a) must be supported by evidence; and

(b) may be made without notice.

(4) An order under this rule must state a period within which the defendant must respond to the particulars of claim.

(Rule 9.2 sets out how a defendant may respond to particulars of claim)

(5) The power conferred by this rule is additional to the power conferred by rule 6.8 (service by an alternative method).

(6) Where the court makes an order under this rule, the claimant must send to the defendant copies of—

(a) the order; and

(b) the claim form.

PD 6 PRACTICE DIRECTION — SERVICE

This practice direction supplements CPR Part 6

METHODS OF SERVICE
1.1 The various methods of service are set out in rule 6.2.
1.2 The following provisions apply to the specific methods of service referred to.

SERVICE BY NON-ELECTRONIC MEANS
Service by document exchange
2.1 Service by document exchange (DX) may take place only where:
  (1) the party's address for service[1] includes a numbered box at a DX, or
  (2) the writing paper of the party who is to be served or of his legal representative[2] sets out the DX box number, and
  (3) the party or his legal representative has not indicated in writing that they are unwilling to accept service by DX.
2.2 Service by DX is effected, unless the contrary is proved, by leaving the document addressed to the numbered box:
  (1) at the DX of the party who is to be served, or
  (2) at a DX which sends documents to that party's DX every business day.

SERVICE BY ELECTRONIC MEANS
Service by facsimile
3.1 Subject to the provisions of paragraph 3.2 below, where a document is to be served by facsimile (fax):
  (1) the party who is to be served or his legal representative must previously have indicated in writing to the party serving—
    (a) that he is willing to accept service by fax, and
    (b) the fax number to which it should be sent.
  (2) if the party on whom the document is to be served is acting by a legal representative, the fax must be sent to the legal representative's business address, and
  (3) a fax number
    (a) provided in writing expressly for the purpose of accepting service where the party to be served is acting in person, or
    (b) set out on the writing paper of the legal representative of the party who is to be served, or
    (c) set out on a statement of case or a response to a claim filed with the court,
shall be taken as sufficient written indication for the purposes of paragraph 3.1(1).
3.2 A legal representative's business address must be within the jurisdiction and is the physical location of his office. Where an electronic address or identification is given in conjunction with the business address, the electronic address will be deemed to be at the business address.
3.3 Service by other electronic means may take place only where:
  (1) the party serving the document and the party on whom it is to be served are both acting by legal representative,
  (2) the document is served at the legal representative's business address, and
  (3) the legal representative who is to be served has previously expressly indicated in writing to the party serving his willingness to accept service by this means and has provided
    (a) his e-mail address, or
    (b) other electronic identification such as an ISDN or other telephonic link number.

---

[1] See rule 6.5.
[2] See rule 2.3 for the definition of legal representative.

3.4 Where a document is served by fax or other electronic means, the party serving the document is not required in addition to send a copy by post or document exchange, but if he does not do so and the document is proved not to have been received then the court may, on any application arising out of that non-receipt, take account of the fact that a hard copy was not sent.

SERVICE ON CERTAIN INDIVIDUALS
Personal service on partners

4.1 Where partners are sued in the name of a partnership, service should be in accordance with rule 6.4(5) and the table set out in rule 6.5(5) where it refers to an 'individual who is suing or being sued in the name of a firm'.

4.2 A claim form or particulars of claim which are served by leaving them with a person at the principal or last known place of business of the partnership, must at the same time have served with them a notice as to whether that person is being served:
　(1)　as a partner,
　(2)　as a person having control or management of the partnership business, or
　(3)　as both.

Service on members of H.M. Forces and United States Air Force

5 The Lord Chancellor's Office issued a memorandum on 26 July 1979 as to service on members of H.M. Forces and guidance notes as to service on members of the United States Air Force. The provisions annexed to this practice direction are derived from that memorandum and guidance notes.

SERVICE GENERALLY
Personal service on a company or other corporation

6.1 Personal service on a registered company or corporation in accordance with rule 6.4(4) service is effected by leaving a document with 'a person holding a senior position'.

6.2 Each of the following persons is a person holding a senior position:
　(1)　in respect of a registered company or corporation, a director, the treasurer, secretary, chief executive, manager or other officer of the company or corporation, and
　(2)　in respect of a corporation which is not a registered company, in addition to those persons set out in (1), the mayor, chairman, president, town clerk or similar officer of the corporation.

CHANGE OF ADDRESS

7 A party or his legal representative who changes his address for service shall give notice in writing of the change as soon as it has taken place to the court and every other party.

Service by the court

8.1 Where the court effects service of a document in accordance with rule 6.3(1) and (2), the method will normally be by first class post.

8.2 Where a party receives a notice of non-service of a document by the court, he should take steps to effect service of the document himself as the court is under no further duty to effect service.

CONTENT OF EVIDENCE
The following applications relating to service require evidence in support

9.1 An application for an order for service by an alternative method[3] should be supported by evidence stating:
　(1)　the reason an order for an alternative method of service is sought, and
　(2)　what steps have been taken to serve by other permitted means.

9.2 An application for service of a claim form relating to a contract on the agent of a principal who is overseas should be supported by evidence setting out:
　(1)　full details of the contract and that it was entered into within the jurisdiction with or through an agent who is either an individual residing or carrying on business within the jurisdiction, or a registered company or corporation having a registered office or a place of business within the jurisdiction,

---

[3] See rule 6.8.

(2) that the principal for whom the agent is acting was, at the time the contract was entered into and is at the time of making the application, neither an individual, registered company or corporation as described in (1) above, and

(3) why service out of the jurisdiction cannot be effected.

ANNEX
SERVICE ON MEMBERS OF H.M. FORCES

1. The following information is for litigants and legal representatives who wish to serve legal documents in civil proceedings in the courts of England and Wales on parties to the proceedings who are (or who, at the material time, were) regular members of Her Majesty's Forces.

2. The proceedings may take place in the county court or the High Court, and the documents to be served may be both originating claims, interim applications and pre-action applications. Proceedings for divorce or maintenance and proceedings in the Family Courts generally are subject to special rules as to service which are explained in a practice direction issued by the Senior District Judge of the Principal Registry on 26 June 1979.

3. In these instructions, the person wishing to effect service is referred to as the 'claimant' and the person to be served is referred to as the 'serviceman'; the expression 'overseas' means outside the United Kingdom.

ENQUIRIES AS TO ADDRESS

4. As a first step, the claimant's legal representative will need to find out where the serviceman is serving, if he does not already know. For this purpose he should write to the appropriate officer of the Ministry of Defence as specified in paragraph 10 below.

5. The letter of enquiry should in every case show that the writer is a legal representative and that the enquiry is made solely with a view to the service of legal documents in civil proceedings.

6. In all cases the letter should give the full name, service number, rank or rating, and Ship, Arm or Trade, Regiment or Corps and Unit or as much of this information as is available. Failure to quote the service number and the rank or rating may result either in failure to identify the serviceman or in considerable delay.

7. The letter should contain an undertaking by the legal representative that, if the address is given, it will be used solely for the purpose of issuing and serving documents in the proceedings and that so far as is possible the legal representative will disclose the address only to the court and not to his client or to any other person or body. A legal representative in the service of a public authority or private company should undertake that the address will be used solely for the purpose of issuing and serving documents in the proceedings and that the address will not be disclosed so far as is possible to any other part of his employing organisation or to any other person but only to the court. Normally on receipt of the required information and undertaking the appropriate office will give the service address.

8. If the legal representative does not give the undertaking, the only information he will receive will be whether the serviceman is at that time serving in England or Wales, Scotland, Northern Ireland or overseas.

9. It should be noted that a serviceman's address which ends with a British Forces Post Office address and reference (BFPO) will nearly always indicate that he is serving overseas.

10. The letter of enquiry should be addressed as follows:
    (a) *Royal Navy Officers*
        The Naval Secretary
        Room 161
        Victory Building
        HM Naval Base
        Portsmouth Hants PO1 3LS

RN Ratings
Commodore Naval Drafting
Centurion Building
Grange Road
Gosport
Hants PO13 9XA

RN Medical and Dental Officers
The Medical Director General
(Naval)
Room 114 Victory Building
HM Naval Base
Portsmouth
Hants PO1 3LS

Officers of Queen Alexandra's Royal Naval Nursing Service
The Matron-in-Chief
QARNNS
Room 129
Victory Building
HM Naval Base
Portsmouth
Hants PO1 3LS

Naval Chaplains
Director General Naval
Chaplaincy Service
Room 201
Victory Building
HM Naval Base
Portsmouth
Hants PO1 3LS

(b) *Royal Marine Officers and Ranks*
Personnel section
West Battery
Whale Island
Portsmouth
Hants PO2 8DX

RM Ranks HQRM
(DRORM)
West Battery
Whale Island
Portsmouth
Hants PO2 8DX

(c) *Army Officers and Other Ranks*
Ministry of Defence
Army Personnel Centre
Secretariat, Public Enquiries
RM CD424
Kentigern House
65 Brown Street
Glasgow G2 8EH

(d) *Royal Air Force Officers and Other Ranks*
Personnel Management Agency (RAF)
Building 248
RAF Innsworth
Gloucester GL3 1EZ

ASSISTANCE IN SERVING DOCUMENTS ON SERVICEMEN

11. Once the claimant's legal representative has learnt the serviceman's address he may use that address as the address for service by post, in cases where this method of service is allowed by the Civil Procedure Rules. There are, however, some situations in which service of the proceedings, whether in the High Court or in the county court, has to be effected personally; in these cases an appointment will have to be sought, through the Commanding Officer of the Unit, Establishment or Ship concerned, for the purpose of effecting service. The procedure for obtaining an appointment is described below, and it applies whether personal service is to be effected by the claimant's legal representative or his agent or by a court bailiff, or, in the case of proceedings served overseas (with the leave of the court) through the British Consul or the foreign judicial authority.

12. The procedure for obtaining an appointment to effect personal service is by application to the Commanding Officer of the Unit, Establishment or Ship in which the serviceman is serving. The Commanding Officer may grant permission for the document server to enter the Unit, Establishment or Ship but if this is not appropriate he may offer arrangements for the serviceman to attend at a place in the vicinity of the Unit, Establishment or Ship in order that he may be served. If suitable arrangements cannot be made the legal representative will have evidence that personal service is impracticable, which may be useful in an application for service by an alternative method.

GENERAL

13. Subject to the procedure outlined in paragraphs 11 and 12, there are no special arrangements to assist in the service of process when a serviceman is outside the United Kingdom. The appropriate office will however give an approximate date when the serviceman is likely to return to the United Kingdom.

14. It sometimes happens that a serviceman has left the service by the time that the enquiry is made. If the claimant's legal representative confirms that the proceedings result from an occurrence when the serviceman was in the Forces and he gives the undertaking referred to in paragraph 7, the last known private address after discharge will normally be provided. In no other case however will the Department disclose the private address of a member of H.M. Forces.

SERVICE ON MEMBERS OF UNITED STATES AIR FORCE

15. In addition to the information contained in the memorandum of 26 July 1979, the Lord Chancellor's Office, some doubts having been expressed as to the correct procedure to be followed by persons having civil claims against members of the United States Air Force in this country, issued the following notes for guidance with the approval of the appropriate United States authorities:

16. Instructions have been issued by the U.S. authorities to the commanding officers of all their units in this country that every facility is to be given for the service of documents in civil proceedings on members of the U.S. Air Force. The proper course to be followed by a creditor or other person having a claim against a member of the U.S. Air Force is for him to communicate with the commanding officer or, where the unit concerned has a legal officer, with the legal officer of the defendant's unit requesting him to provide facilities for the service of documents on the defendant. It is not possible for the U.S. authorities to act as arbitrators when a civil claim is made against a member of their forces. It is, therefore, essential that the claim should either be admitted by the defendant or judgment should be obtained on it, whether in the High Court or a county court. If a claim has been admitted or judgment has been obtained and the claimant has failed to obtain satisfaction within a reasonable period, his proper course is then to write to: Office of the Staff Judge Advocate, Headquarters, Third Air Force, R.A.F. Mildenhall, Suffolk, enclosing a copy of the defendant's written admission of the claim or, as the case may be, a copy of the judgment. Steps will then be taken by the Staff Judge Advocate to ensure that the matter is brought to the defendant's attention with a view to prompt satisfaction of the claim.

CPR PART 7   HOW TO START PROCEEDINGS — THE CLAIM FORM

CONTENTS OF THIS PART
Where to start proceedings	Rule 7.1
How to start proceedings	Rule 7.2
Right to use one claim form to start two or more claims	Rule 7.3
Particulars of claim	Rule 7.4
Service of a claim form	Rule 7.5
Extension of time for serving a claim form	Rule 7.6
Application by defendant for service of a claim form	Rule 7.7
Form for defence etc. must be served with particulars of claim	Rule 7.8
Fixed date and other claims	Rule 7.9
Production Centre for claims	Rule 7.10

7.1   WHERE TO START PROCEEDINGS
Restrictions on where proceedings may be started are set out in the relevant practice direction.

7.2   HOW TO START PROCEEDINGS
(1) Proceedings are started when the court issues a claim form at the request of the claimant.
(2) A claim form is issued on the date entered on the form by the court.
(A person who seeks a remedy from the court before proceedings are started or in relation to proceedings which are taking place, or will take place, in another jurisdiction must make an application under Part 23)
(Part 16 sets out what the claim form must include)

7.3   RIGHT TO USE ONE CLAIM FORM TO START TWO OR MORE CLAIMS
A claimant may use a single claim form to start all claims which can be conveniently disposed of in the same proceedings.

7.4   PARTICULARS OF CLAIM
(1) Particulars of claim must—
    (a) be contained in or served with the claim form; or
    (b) subject to paragraph (2) be served on the defendant by the claimant within 14 days after service of the claim form.
(2) Particulars of claim must be served on the defendant no later than the latest time for serving a claim form.
(Rule 7.5 sets out the latest time for serving a claim form)
(3) Where the claimant serves particulars of claim separately from the claim form in accordance with paragraph (1)(b), he must, within 7 days of service on the defendant, file a copy of the particulars together with a certificate of service.
(Part 16 sets out what the particulars of claim must include)
(Part 22 requires particulars of claim to be verified by a statement of truth)
(Rule 6.10 makes provision for a certificate of service)

7.5   SERVICE OF A CLAIM FORM
(1) After a claim form has been issued, it must be served on the defendant.
(2) The general rule is that a claim form must be served within 4 months after the date of issue.
(3) The period for service is 6 months where the claim form is to be served out of the jurisdiction.

7.6   EXTENSION OF TIME FOR SERVING A CLAIM FORM
(1) The claimant may apply for an order extending the period within which the claim form may be served.

CPR PART 7 HOW TO START PROCEEDINGS — THE CLAIM FORM

(2) The general rule is that an application to extend the time for service must be made—
    (a) within the period for serving the claim form specified by rule 7.5; or
    (b) where an order has been made under this rule, within the period for service specified by that order.
(3) If the claimant applies for an order to extend the time for service of the claim form after the end of the period specified by rule 7.5 or by an order made under this rule, the court may make such an order only if—
    (a) the court has been unable to serve the claim form; or
    (b) the claimant has taken all reasonable steps to serve the claim form but has been unable to do so; and
    (c) in either case, the claimant has acted promptly in making the application.
(4) An application for an order extending the time for service—
    (a) must be supported by evidence; and
    (b) may be made without notice.

7.7 APPLICATION BY DEFENDANT FOR SERVICE OF CLAIM FORM
(1) Where a claim form has been issued against a defendant, but has not yet been served on him, the defendant may serve a notice on the claimant requiring him to serve the claim form or discontinue the claim within a period specified in the notice.
(2) The period specified in a notice served under paragraph (1) must be at least 14 days after service of the notice.
(3) If the claimant fails to comply with the notice, the court may, on the application of the defendant—
    (a) dismiss the claim; or
    (b) make any other order it thinks just.

7.8 FORM FOR DEFENCE ETC. MUST BE SERVED WITH PARTICULARS OF CLAIM
(1) When particulars of claim are served on a defendant, whether they are contained in the claim form, served with it or served subsequently, they must be accompanied by—
    (a) a form for defending the claim;
    (b) a form for admitting the claim; and
    (c) a form for acknowledging service.
(2) Where the claimant is using the procedure set out in Part 8 (alternative procedure for claims)—
    (a) paragraph (1) does not apply; and
    (b) a form for acknowledging service must accompany the claim form.

7.9 FIXED DATE AND OTHER CLAIMS
A practice direction—
    (a) may set out the circumstances in which the court may give a fixed date for a hearing when it issues a claim;
    (b) may list claims in respect of which there is a specific claim form for use and set out the claim form in question; and
    (c) may disapply or modify these Rules as appropriate in relation to the claims referred to in paragraphs (a) and (b).

7.10 PRODUCTION CENTRE FOR CLAIMS
(1) There shall be a Production Centre for the issue of claim forms and other related matters.
(2) The relevant practice direction makes provision for—
    (a) which claimants may use the Production Centre;
    (b) the type of claims which the Production Centre may issue;
    (c) the functions which are to be discharged by the Production Centre;
    (d) the place where the Production Centre is to be located; and
    (e) other related matters.
(3) The relevant practice direction may disapply or modify these Rules as appropriate in relation to claims issued by the Production Centre.

PD 7 PRACTICE DIRECTION — HOW TO START PROCEEDINGS — THE CLAIM FORM

This practice direction supplements CPR Part 7

GENERAL

1 Subject to the following provisions of this practice direction, proceedings which both the High Court and the county courts have jurisdiction to deal with may be started in the High Court or in a county court.

WHERE TO START PROCEEDINGS

2.1 Proceedings (whether for damages or for a specified sum) may not be started in the High Court unless the value of the claim is more than £15,000.

2.2 Proceedings which include a claim for damages in respect of personal injuries must not be started in the High Court unless the value of the claim is £50,000 or more (paragraph 9 of the High Court and County Courts Jurisdiction Order 1991 (S.I. 1991/724 as amended) describes how the value of a claim is to be determined).

2.3 A claim must be issued in the High Court or a county court if an enactment so requires.

2.4 Subject to paragraphs 2.1 and 2.2 above, a claim should be started in the High Court if by reason of:

(1) the financial value of the claim and the amount in dispute, and/or

(2) the complexity of the facts, legal issues, remedies or procedures involved, and/or

(3) the importance of the outcome of the claim to the public in general,

the claimant believes that the claim ought to be dealt with by a High Court judge.

(CPR Part 30 and the practice direction supplementing Part 30 contain provisions relating to the transfer to the county court of proceedings started in the High Court and vice versa.)

2.5 A claim relating to Chancery business (which includes any of the matters specified in paragraph 1 of Schedule 1 to the Supreme Court Act 1981) may, subject to any enactment, rule or practice direction, be dealt with in the High Court or in a county court. The claim form should, if issued in the High Court, be marked in the top right hand corner 'Chancery Division' and, if issued in the county court, be marked 'Chancery Business'.

(For the equity jurisdiction of county courts, see section 23 of the County Courts Act 1984.)

2.6 A claim relating to any of the matters specified in sub-paragraphs (a) and (b) of paragraph 2 of Schedule 1 to the Supreme Court Act 1981 must be dealt with in the High Court and will be assigned to the Queen's Bench Division.

2.7 Practice directions which supplement CPR Part 49 (Specialist Proceedings) will contain provisions relating to the commencement and conduct of the specialist proceedings listed in that Part.

2.8 A claim in the High Court for which a jury trial is directed will, if not already being dealt with in the Queen's Bench Division, be transferred to that Division.

2.9 The following proceedings may not be started in a county court unless the parties have agreed otherwise in writing:

(1) a claim for damages or other remedy for libel or slander, and

(2) a claim in which the title to any toll, fair, market or franchise is in question.

THE CLAIM FORM

3.1 A claimant must use practice form N1 or practice form N208 (the Part 8 claim form) to start a claim (but see paragraphs 3.2 and 3.4 below).

3.2   Rule 7.9 deals with fixed date claims and rule 7.10 deals with the Production Centre for the issue of claims; there are separate practice directions supplementing rules 7.9 and 7.10.

3.3   If a claimant wishes his claim to proceed under Part 8, or if the claim is required to proceed under Part 8, the claim form should so state. Otherwise the claim will proceed under Part 7. But note that in respect of claims in specialist proceedings (listed in CPR Part 49) and claims brought under the RSC or CCR set out in the Schedule to the CPR (see CPR Part 50) the CPR will apply only to the extent that they are not inconsistent with the rules and practice directions that expressly apply to those claims.

3.4   To commence specialist proceedings (listed in CPR Part 49) it may be necessary to use the practice form approved for that purpose by the practice direction relating to the specialist proceedings in question. Reference should be made to that practice direction.

3.5   Where a claim which is to be served out of the jurisdiction is one which the court has power to deal with under the Civil Jurisdiction and Judgments Act 1982, the claim form and, when they are contained in a separate document, the particulars of claim should be endorsed with a statement that the court has power under that Act to deal with the claim and that no proceedings based on the same claim are pending between the parties in Scotland, Northern Ireland or another Convention territory[1].

3.6   If a claim for damages or for an unspecified sum is started in the High Court, the claim form must:

   (1)   state that the claimant expects to recover more than £15,000 (or £50,000 or more if the claim is for personal injuries) or

   (2)   state that some enactment provides that the claim may only be commenced in the High Court and specify that enactment or

   (3)   state that the claim is to be in one of the specialist High Court lists (see CPR Part 49) and specify that list.

3.7   If the contents of a claim form commencing specialist proceedings complies with the requirements of the specialist list in question the claim form will also satisfy paragraph 3.6 above.

3.8   If a claim for damages for personal injuries is started in the county court, the claim form must state whether or not the claimant expects to recover more than £1000 in respect of pain, suffering and loss of amenity.

3.9   If a claim for housing disrepair which includes a claim for an order requiring repairs or other work to be carried out by the landlord is started in the county court, the claim form must state:

   (1)   whether or not the cost of the repairs or other work is estimated to be more than £1000, and

   (2)   whether or not the claimant expects to recover more than £1000 in respect of any claim for damages[2].

If either of the amounts mentioned in (1) and (2) is more than £1000, the small claims track will not be the normal track for that claim.

TITLE OF PROCEEDINGS

4.1   The claim form and every other statement of case, must be headed with the title of the proceedings. The title should state:

   (1)   the number of proceedings,
   (2)   the court or division in which they are proceeding,
   (3)   the full name of each party,
   (4)   his status in the proceedings (i.e. claimant/defendant).

4.2   Where there is more than one claimant and/or more than one defendant, the parties should be described in the title as follows:

---

[1] Convention territory' means the territory or territories of any Contracting State as defined by s. 1(3) of the Civil Jurisdiction and Judgments Act 1982, to which the Brussels Convention or Lugano Convention apply.

[2] See rules 16.3(4) and 26.6.

PD 7 PRACTICE DIRECTION — HOW TO START PROCEEDINGS

    (1) AB
    (2) CD
    (3) EF   Claimants
           and
    (1) GH
    (2) IJ
    (3) KL   Defendants

START OF PROCEEDINGS

5.1 Proceedings are started when the court issues a claim form at the request of the claimant (see rule 7.2) but where the claim form as issued was received in the court office on a date earlier than the date on which it was issued by the court, the claim is 'brought' for the purposes of the Limitation Act 1980 and any other relevant statute on that earlier date.

5.2 The date on which the claim form was received by the court will be recorded by a date stamp either on the claim form held on the court file or on the letter that accompanied the claim form when it was received by the court.

5.3 An enquiry as to the date on which the claim form was received by the court should be directed to a court officer.

5.4 Parties proposing to start a claim which is approaching the expiry of the limitation period should recognise the potential importance of establishing the date the claim form was received by the court and should themselves make arrangements to record the date.

5.5 Where it is sought to start proceedings against the estate of a deceased defendant where probate or letters of administration have not been granted, the claimant should issue the claim against 'the personal representatives of A.B. deceased'. The claimant should then, before the expiry of the period for service of the claim form, apply to the court for the appointment of a person to represent the estate of the deceased.

PARTICULARS OF CLAIM

6.1 Where the claimant does not include the particulars of claim in the claim form, particulars of claim may be served separately:
    (1) either at the same time as the claim form, or
    (2) within 14 days after service of the claim form[4] provided that the service of the particulars of claim is not later than 4 months from the date of issue of the claim form[5] (or 6 months where the claim form is to be served out of the jurisdiction[6]).

6.2 If the particulars of claim are not included in or have not been served with the claim form, the claim form must contain a statement that particulars of claim will follow[7].

(These paragraphs do not apply where the Part 8 procedure is being used. For information on matters to be included in the claim form or the particulars of claim, see Part 16 (statements of case) and the practice direction which supplements it.)

STATEMENT OF TRUTH

7.1 Part 22 requires the claim form and, where they are not included in the claim form, the particulars of claim, to be verified by a statement of truth.

7.2 The form of the statement of truth is as follows:

'[I believe] [the claimant believes] that the facts stated in [this claim form] [these particulars of claim] are true.'

7.3 Attention is drawn to rule 32.14 which sets out the consequences of verifying a statement of case containing a false statement without an honest belief in its truth.

---

[4] See rule 7.4(1)(b). [The text issued by the Lord Chancellor's Department, which is followed here, does not have a footnote 3.]
[5] See rules 7.4(2) and 7.5(2).
[6] See rule 7.5(3).
[7] See rule 16.2(2).

PD 7 PRACTICE DIRECTION — HOW TO START PROCEEDINGS

(For information regarding statements of truth see Part 22 and the practice direction which supplements it.)

EXTENSION OF TIME

8.1 An application under rule 7.6 (for an extension of time for serving a claim form under rule 7.6(1)) must be made in accordance with Part 23 and supported by evidence.

8.2 The evidence should state:
   (1) all the circumstances relied on,
   (2) the date of issue of the claim,
   (3) the expiry date of any rule 7.6 extension, and
   (4) a full explanation as to why the claim has not been served.

(For information regarding (1) written evidence see Part 32 and the practice direction which supplements it and (2) service of the claim form see Part 6 and the practice direction which supplements it.)

PD 7B PRACTICE DIRECTION — CONSUMER CREDIT ACT CLAIM

This practice direction supplements CPR rule 7.9

1.1 In this practice direction 'the Act' means the Consumer Credit Act 1974, a section referred to by number means the section with that number in the Act, and expressions which are defined in the Act have the same meaning in this practice direction as they have in the Act.

1.2 'Consumer Credit Act procedure' means the procedure set out in this practice direction.

WHEN TO USE THE CONSUMER CREDIT ACT PROCEDURE

2.1 A claimant must use the Consumer Credit Act procedure where he makes a claim under a provision of the Act to which paragraph 3 of this practice direction applies.

2.2 Where a claimant is using the Consumer Credit Act procedure the CPR are modified to the extent that they are inconsistent with the procedure set out in this practice direction.

2.3 The court may at any stage order the claim to continue as if the claimant had not used the Consumer Credit Act procedure, and if it does so the court may give any directions it considers appropriate.

2.4 This practice direction also sets out matters which must be included in the particulars of claim in certain types of claim, and restrictions on where certain types of claim may be started.

THE PROVISIONS OF THE ACT

3.1 Subject to paragraph 3.2 and 3.3 this practice direction applies to claims made under the following provisions of the Act:

(1) section 141 (claim by the creditor to enforce regulated agreement relating to goods etc),

(2) section 129 (claim by debtor or hirer for a time order),

(3) section 90 (creditor's claim for an order for recovery of protected goods),

(4) section 92(1) (creditor's or owner's claim to enter premises to take possession of goods),

(5) section 139(a) (debtor's claim for a credit agreement to be reopened as extortionate), and

(6) creditor's or owner's claim for a court order to enforce a regulated agreement relating to goods or money where the court order is required by—

   (a) section 65(1) (improperly-executed agreement),

   (b) section 86(2) of the Act (death of debtor or hirer where agreement is partly secured or unsecured),

   (c) section 111(2) (default notice etc not served on surety),

   (d) section 124(1) or (2) (taking of a negotiable instrument in breach of terms of section 123), or

   (e) section 105(7)(a) or (b) (security not expressed in writing, or improperly executed).

3.2 This practice direction does not apply to any claim made under the provisions listed in paragraph 3.1 above if that claim relates to the recovery of land.

(Provisions governing the procedure for such claims can be found in CPR Schedule 2, CCR Order 49, r. 4 and related rules about the matters to be included in the particulars of claim can be found in CPR Schedule 2, CCR Order 6.)

3.3 This practice direction also does not apply to a claim made by the creditor under section 141 of the Act to enforce a regulated agreement where the agreement relates only to money. Such a claim must be started by the issue of a Part 7 claim form.

PD 7B PRACTICE DIRECTION — CONSUMER CREDIT ACT CLAIM

RESTRICTIONS ON WHERE TO START SOME CONSUMER CREDIT ACT CLAIMS

4.1 Where the claim includes a claim to recover goods to which a regulated hire purchase agreement or conditional sale agreements relates, it may only be started in the county court for the district in which the debtor, or one of the debtors:
    (1) resides or carries on business, or
    (2) resided or carried on business at the date when the defendant last made a payment under the agreement.

4.2 In any other claim to recover goods, the claim may only be started in the court for the district:
    (1) in which the defendant, or one of the defendants, resides or carries on business, or
    (2) in which the goods are situated.

4.3 A claim of a debtor or hirer for an order under section 129(1)(b) of the Act (a time order) may only be started in the court where the claimant resides or carries on business.

(Costs rule 45.1(2)(b) allows the claimant to recover fixed costs in certain circumstances where such a claim is made.)

(Paragraph 7 sets out the matters the claimant must include in his particulars of claim where he is using the Consumer Credit Act procedure.)

THE CONSUMER CREDIT ACT PROCEDURE

5.1 In the types of claim to which paragraph 3 applies the court will fix a hearing date on the issue of the claim form.

5.2 The particulars of claim must be served with the claim form.

5.3 Where a claimant is using the Consumer Credit Act procedure, the defendant to the claim is not required to:
    (1) serve an acknowledgment of service, or
    (2) file a defence, although he may choose to do so.

5.4 Where a defendant intends to defend a claim, his defence should be filed within 14 days of service of the particulars of claim. If the defendant fails to file a defence within this period, but later relies on it, the court may take such a failure into account as a factor when deciding what order to make about costs.

5.5 Part 12 (default judgment) does not apply where the claimant is using the Consumer Credit Act procedure.

5.6 Each party must be given at least 28 days' notice of the hearing date.

5.7 Where the claimant serves the claim form, he must serve notice of the hearing date at the same time, unless the hearing date is specified in the claim form.

POWERS OF THE COURT AT THE HEARING

6.1 On the hearing date the court may dispose of the claim.

6.2 If the court does not dispose of the claim on the hearing date:
    (1) if the defendant has filed a defence, the court will:
        (a) allocate the claim to a track and give directions about the management of the case, or
        (b) give directions to enable it to allocate the claim to a track,
    (2) if the defendant has not filed a defence, the court may make any order or give any direction it considers appropriate.

6.3 Rule 26.5(3) to (5) and rules 26.6 to 26.10 apply to the allocation of a claim under paragraph 6.2.

MATTERS WHICH MUST BE INCLUDED IN THE PARTICULARS OF CLAIM

7.1 Where the Consumer Credit Act procedure is used, the claimant must state in his particulars of claim that the claim is a Consumer Credit Act claim.

7.2 A claimant making a claim for the delivery of goods to enforce a hire purchase agreement or conditional sale agreement which is:
    (1) a regulated agreement for the recovery of goods, and

PD 7B PRACTICE DIRECTION — CONSUMER CREDIT ACT CLAIM

(2) let to a person other than a company or other corporation, must also state (in this order) in his particulars of claim:
  (a) the date of the agreement,
  (b) the parties to the agreement,
  (c) the number or other identification of the agreement (with enough information to allow the debtor to identify the agreement),
  (d) where the claimant was not one of the original parties to the agreement, the means by which the rights and duties of the creditor passed to him,
  (e) the place where the agreement was signed by the defendant (if known),
  (f) the goods claimed,
  (g) the total price of the goods,
  (h) the paid up sum,
  (i) the unpaid balance of the total price,
  (j) whether a default notice or a notice under section 76(1) or section 88(1) of the Act has been served on the defendant, and, if it has, the date and the method of service,
  (k) the date on which the right to demand delivery of the goods accrued,
  (l) the amount (if any) claimed as an alternative to the delivery of goods, and
  (m) the amount (if any) claimed in addition to—
    (i) the delivery of the goods, or
    (ii) any claim under sub paragraph (l) above with the grounds of each such claim.

7.3 A claimant who is a debtor or hirer making a claim for an order under section 129(1)(b) of the Act (a time order) must state (in the following order) in his particulars of claim:
  (1) the date of the agreement,
  (2) the parties to the agreement,
  (3) the number or other means of identifying the agreement,
  (4) details of any sureties,
  (5) if the defendant is not one of the original parties to the agreement then the name of the original party to the agreement,
  (6) the names and addresses of the persons intended to be served with the claim form,
  (7) the place where the claimant signed the agreement,
  (8) details of the notice served by the creditor or owner giving rise to the claim for the time order,
  (9) the total unpaid balance the claimant admits is due under the agreement, and—
    (a) the amount of any arrears (if known), and
    (b) the amount and frequency of the payments specified in the agreement,
  (10) the claimant's proposals for payments of any arrears and of future instalments together with details of his means;
  (11) where the claim relates to a breach of the agreement other than for the payment of money the claimant's proposals for remedying it.

7.4 (1) This paragraph applies where a claimant is required to obtain a court order to enforce a regulated agreement by:
  (a) section 65(1) (improperly-executed agreement),
  (b) section 105(7)(a) or (b) (security not expressed in writing, or improperly-executed),
  (c) section 111(2) (default notice etc. not served on surety),
  (d) section 124(1) or (2) (taking of a negotiable instrument in breach of terms of section 123), or
  (e) section 86(2) of the Act (death of debtor or hirer where agreement is partly secured or unsecured).

(2) The claimant must state in his particulars of claim what the circumstances are that require him to obtain a court order for enforcement.

PD 7B PRACTICE DIRECTION — CONSUMER CREDIT ACT CLAIM

ADMISSION OF CERTAIN CLAIMS FOR RECOVERY OF GOODS UNDER REGULATED AGREEMENTS

8.1 In a claim to recover goods to which section 90(1)[1] applies:

(1) the defendant may admit the claim, and

(2) offer terms on which a return order should be suspended under section 135(1)(b).

8.2 He may do so by filing a request in practice form N9C.

8.3 He should do so within the period for making an admission specified in rule 14.2(b). If the defendant fails to file his request within this period, and later makes such a request, the court may take the failure into account as a factor when deciding what order to make about costs.

8.4 On receipt of the admission, the court will serve a copy on the claimant.

8.5 The claimant may obtain judgment by filing a request in practice form N228.

8.6 On receipt of the request for judgment, the court will enter judgment in the terms of the defendant's admission and offer and for costs.

8.7 If:

(1) the claimant does not accept the defendant's admission and offer, and

(2) the defendant does not appear on the hearing date fixed when the claim form was issued,

the court may treat the defendant's admission and offer as evidence of the facts stated in it for the purposes of sections 129(2)(a)[2] and 135(2)[3].

ADDITIONAL REQUIREMENTS ABOUT PARTIES TO THE PROCEEDINGS

9.1 The court may dispense with the requirement in section 141(5) (all parties to a regulated agreement and any surety to be parties to any proceedings) in any claim relating to the regulated agreement, if:

(1) the claim form has not been served on the debtor or the surety, and

(2) the claimant either before or at the hearing makes an application (which may be made without notice) for the court to make such an order.

9.2 In a claim relating to a regulated agreement where—

(1) the claimant was not one of the original parties to the agreement, and

(2) the former creditor's rights and duties under the agreement have passed to him by—

(a) operation of law, or

(b) assignment,

the requirement of section 141(5) (all parties to a regulated agreement and any surety to be parties to any proceedings) does not apply to the former creditor, unless the court otherwise orders.

9.3 Where a claimant who is a creditor or owner makes a claim for a court order under section 86(2) (death of debtor or hirer where agreement is partly

---

[1] Section 90(1) provides that:

'At any time when—

(a) the debtor is in breach of a regulated hire-purchase or a regulated conditional sale agreement relating to goods, and

(b) the debtor has paid to the creditor one-third or more of the total price of the goods, and

(c) the property in the goods remains in the creditor, the creditor is not entitled to recover possession of the goods from the debtor except on an order of the court.'

[2] Section 129(2) provides that—

'A time order shall provide for one or both of the following, as the court considers just—

(a) the payment by the debtor or hirer or any surety of any sum owed under a regulated agreement or a security by such instalments, payable at such times, as the court, having regard to the means of the debtor or hirer and any surety, considers reasonable;

(b) the remedying by the debtor or hirer of any breach of a regulated agreement (other than non-payment of money) within such period as the court may specify.'

[3] Section 135(2) provides that—

'The court shall not suspend the operation of a term [in an order relating to a regulated agreement] requiring the delivery up of goods by any person unless satisfied that the goods are in his possession or control.'

PD 7B PRACTICE DIRECTION — CONSUMER CREDIT ACT CLAIM

secured or unsecured) the personal representatives of the deceased debtor or hirer must be parties to the proceedings in which the order is sought, unless no grant of representation has been made to the estate.

9.4 Where no grant of representation has been made to the estate of the deceased debtor or hirer, the claimant must make an application in accordance with Part 23 for directions about which persons (if any) are to be made parties to the claim as being affected or likely to be affected by the enforcement of the agreement.

9.5 The claimant's application under paragraph 9.4:
(a) may be made without notice, and
(b) should be made before the claim form is issued.

NOTICE TO BE GIVEN TO RE-OPEN A CONSUMER CREDIT AGREEMENT

10.1 Where a debtor or any surety intends to apply for a consumer credit agreement to be reopened after a claim on or relating to the agreement has already begun, and:
(1) section 139(1)(b)[4]; or
(2) section 139(1)(c),

applies, the debtor or surety must serve written notice of his intention on the court and every other party to the proceedings within 14 days of the service of the claim form on him.

10.2 If the debtor or surety (as the case may be) serves a notice under paragraph 10.1 he will be treated as having filed a defence for the purposes of the Consumer Credit Act procedure.

---

[4] Section 139(1) provides that—
(1) A credit agreement may, if the court thinks just, be reopened on the ground that the credit bargain is extortionate:
(a) on an application for the purpose made by the debtor or any surety to the High Court, county court or sheriff court; or
(b) at the instance of the debtor or a surety in any proceedings to which the debtor and creditor are parties, being proceedings to enforce the credit agreement, any security relating to it or any linked transaction; or
(c) at the instance of the debtor or a surety in other proceedings in any court where the amount paid or payable under the credit agreement is relevant.

PD 7C PRACTICE DIRECTION — PRODUCTION CENTRE

This practice direction supplements CPR rule 7.10

GENERAL

1.1 In this Practice Direction

'the Centre' means the Production Centre.

'Centre user' means a person who is for the time being permitted to issue claims through the Centre, and includes a solicitor acting for such a person.

'officer' means the officer in charge of the Centre or another officer of the Centre acting on his behalf.

'national creditor code' means the number or reference allotted to a Centre user by the officer.

'Code of Practice' means any code of practice which may at any time be issued by the Court Service relating to the discharge by the Centre of its functions and the way in which a Centre user is to conduct business with the Centre.

'data' means any information which is required to be given to the court or which is to be contained in any document to be sent to the court or to any party.

1.2 For any purpose connected with the exercise of its functions, the Centre will be treated as part of the office of the court whose name appears on the claim form to which the functions relate, or in whose name the claim form is requested to be issued and, the officer will be treated as an officer of that court.

1.3 (1) The functions of the Centre include the provision of a facility which, through the use of information technology, enables a Centre user to have claim forms issued and served, whether or not those claim forms are to be treated as issued in the Northampton County Court or in another county court.

(2) If a Centre user issues claim forms in the name of Northampton County Court, the functions of the Centre also include:

(a) the handling of defences and admissions,

(b) the entry of judgment in default, on admission, on acceptance, or on determination,

(c) the registration of judgments,

(d) the issue of warrants of execution,

(e) the transfer to the defendant's home court of any case which is to continue following the filing of a defence or where a hearing is required before judgment, and

(f) the transfer to the defendant's home court, in the circumstances to which CCR Order 25 rule 2 (transfer for enforcement) applies, of any case for an oral examination or where enforcement of a judgment (other than by warrant of execution) is to follow.

1.4 (1) Where the officer is to take any step, any rule or Practice Direction which requires a document to be filed before he does so will be treated as complied with if the data which that document would contain is delivered to the Centre in computer readable form in accordance with the Code of Practice.

(2) Data relating to more than one case may be included in a single document or delivery of data.

(3) CPR Rule 6.3(3) (copies of documents to be served by court) does not apply to any document which is to be produced by electronic means from data supplied by a Centre user.

(4) Paragraph 10.3 of the practice direction supplementing CPR Part 16 (statements of case), which requires documentation to be attached to the particulars of contract claims, does not apply to claims to be issued by the Centre.

(5) The practice direction supplementing CPR Part 22 (statements of truth) is modified as follows:

(a) a single statement of truth may accompany each batch of requests to issue claim forms and may be in electronic form,

(b) the form of such a statement should be as follows: 'I believe that the facts stated in the attached claim forms are true.', and

(c) the signature of the appropriate person (as to which see section 3 of the practice direction supplementing CPR Part 22) may be in electronic form.

CLAIMS WHICH MAY NOT BE ISSUED THROUGH THE CENTRE

2.1 The Centre will not issue any claim form which is to be issued in the High Court.

2.2 The Centre will only issue a claim form if the claim is for a specified sum of money less than £100,000.

2.3 The Centre will not issue any of the following types of claim:

(1) a claim against more than two defendants,

(2) a claim against two defendants where a different sum is claimed against each of them,

(3) a claim where particulars of claim separate from the claim form are required,

(4) a claim against the Crown,

(5) a claim for an amount in a foreign currency,

(6) a claim where either party is known to be a child or patient within Part 21 of the Civil Procedure Rules,

(7) a claim where the claimant is a legally assisted person within the meaning of the Legal Aid Act 1988,

(8) a claim where the defendant's address for service as it appears on the claim form is not in England or Wales.

(9) a claim which is to be issued under Part 8 of the Civil Procedure Rules.

CENTRE USERS

3.1 Only a Centre user may issue or conduct claims through the Centre.

3.2 The officer may permit any person to be a Centre user.

3.3 The officer may withdraw the permission for any person to be a Centre user.

3.4 A Centre user must comply with the provisions of the Code of Practice in his dealings with the Centre.

3.5 The officer will allot a national creditor code to each Centre user.

THE CODE OF PRACTICE

4.1 The Code of Practice will contain provisions designed to ensure that the Centre can discharge its functions efficiently, and it may in particular provide for:

(1) the forms of magnetic media that may be used,

(2) the circumstances in which data may or must be supplied in magnetic form,

(3) the circumstances in which data may or must be supplied in a document and the form that such a document must take,

(4) how often data may be supplied,

(5) the numbering of cases and data relating to cases,

(6) data to be given to the Centre by the Centre user about cases which have been settled or paid or are otherwise not proceeding, and

(7) accounting arrangements and the method of payment of fees.

4.2 The Court Service may change the Code of Practice from time to time.

OTHER MODIFICATIONS TO THE CIVIL PROCEDURE RULES

Powers of the officer to make orders

5.1 The officer may make the following orders:

(1) an order to set aside a default judgment where, after that judgment has been entered, the claim form in the case is returned by the Post Office as undelivered,

(2) an order to set aside a judgment on application by a Centre user,

PD 7C PRACTICE DIRECTION — PRODUCTION CENTRE

(3) an order to transfer the case, in the circumstances to which CCR Order 25 rule 2 applies (transfer for enforcement or oral examination), of any case to another county court on the application of a Centre user.

Procedure on the filing of a defence

5.2 (1) This paragraph applies where a Centre user has issued a claim in the Northampton County Court and the defendant has filed a defence to the claim or to part of the claim.

(2) On the filing of the defence the officer will serve a notice on the Centre user requiring the Centre user to notify him within 28 days whether he wishes the claim to proceed.

(3) If the Centre user does not notify the officer within the time specified in the notice that he wishes the claim to proceed the claim will be stayed, and the officer will notify the parties accordingly.

(4) The proceedings will not be transferred to the defendant's home court under CPR rule 26,2, and no allocation questionnaires will be served under CPR rule 26.3(3) until the Centre user notifies the officer that he wishes the claim to continue.

PD 7D PRACTICE DIRECTION — CLAIMS FOR THE RECOVERY OF TAXES

This practice direction supplements CPR rule 7.9

SCOPE

1.1 This practice direction applies to claims by the Inland Revenue for the recovery of:
 (a) Income Tax,
 (b) Corporation Tax,
 (c) Capital Gains Tax,
 (d) Interest, penalties and surcharges on Income Tax, Corporation Tax or Capital Gains Tax which by virtue of section 69 of the Taxes Management Act 1970 are to be treated as if they are taxes due and payable,
 (e) National Insurance Contributions and interest, penalties and surcharges thereon.

PROCEDURE

2.1 If a defence is filed, the court will fix a date for the hearing.

2.2 Part 26 (Case management — preliminary stage) apart from CPR rule 26.2 (automatic transfer) does not apply to claims to which this practice direction applies.

AT THE HEARING

3.1 On the hearing date the court may dispose of the claim.

(Section 70 of the Taxes Management Act 1970 and section 118 of the Social Security Administration Act 1992 provide that a certificate of an officer of the Commissioners of Inland Revenue is sufficient evidence that a sum mentioned in such a certificate is unpaid and due to the Crown.)

3.2 But exceptionally, if the court does not dispose of the claim on the hearing date it may give case management directions, which may, if the defendant has filed a defence, include allocating the case.

CPR PART 8 ALTERNATIVE PROCEDURE FOR CLAIMS

CONTENTS OF THIS PART
Types of claim in which Part 8 procedure may be followed	Rule 8.1
Contents of the claim form	Rule 8.2
Acknowledgment of service	Rule 8.3
Consequence of not filing an acknowledgment of service	Rule 8.4
Filing and serving written evidence	Rule 8.5
Evidence — general	Rule 8.6
Part 20 claims	Rule 8.7
Procedure where defendant objects to use of Part 8 procedure	Rule 8.8
Modifications to the general rules	Rule 8.9

8.1 TYPES OF CLAIM IN WHICH PART 8 PROCEDURE MAY BE FOLLOWED

(1) The Part 8 procedure is the procedure set out in this Part.

(2) A claimant may use the Part 8 procedure where—

(a) he seeks the court's decision on a question which is unlikely to involve a substantial dispute of fact; or

(b) paragraph (6) applies.

(3) The court may at any stage order the claim to continue as if the claimant had not used the Part 8 procedure and, if it does so, the court may give any directions it considers appropriate.

(4) Paragraph (2) does not apply if a practice direction provides that the Part 8 procedure may not be used in relation to the type of claim in question.

(5) Where the claimant uses the Part 8 procedure he may not obtain default judgment under Part 12.

(6) A rule or practice direction may, in relation to a specified type of proceedings—

(a) require or permit the use of the Part 8 procedure; and

(b) disapply or modify any of the rules set out in this Part as they apply to those proceedings.

(Rule 8.9 provides for other modifications to the general rules where the Part 8 procedure is being used)

8.2 CONTENTS OF THE CLAIM FORM

Where the claimant uses the Part 8 procedure the claim form must state—

(a) that this Part applies;

(b) (i) the question which the claimant wants the court to decide; or

(ii) the remedy which the claimant is seeking and the legal basis for the claim to that remedy;

(c) if the claim is being made under an enactment, what that enactment is;

(d) if the claimant is claiming in a representative capacity, what that capacity is; and

(e) if the defendant is sued in a representative capacity, what that capacity is.

(Part 22 provides for the claim form to be verified by a statement of truth)

(Rule 7.5 provides for service of the claim form)

8.3 ACKNOWLEDGMENT OF SERVICE

(1) The defendant must—

(a) file an acknowledgment of service in the relevant practice form not more than 14 days after service of the claim form; and

(b) serve the acknowledgment of service on the claimant and any other party.

(2) The acknowledgment of service must state—

(a) whether the defendant contests the claim; and

CPR PART 8 ALTERNATIVE PROCEDURE FOR CLAIMS

(b) if the defendant seeks a different remedy from that set out in the claim form, what that remedy is.

(3) The following rules of Part 10 (acknowledgment of service) apply—
   (a) rule 10.3(2) (exceptions to the period for filing an acknowledgment of service); and
   (b) rule 10.5 (contents of acknowledgment of service).

(4) Part 11 (disputing the court's jurisdiction) applies subject to the modification that in rule 11(4)(a) and (5)(b) (time limit for application disputing court's jurisdiction) references to the period for filing a defence are treated as if they were references to a period of 14 days from the filing of an acknowledgment of service.

8.4 CONSEQUENCE OF NOT FILING AN ACKNOWLEDGMENT OF SERVICE

(1) This rule applies where—
   (a) the defendant has failed to file an acknowledgment of service; and
   (b) the time period for doing so has expired.

(2) The defendant may attend the hearing of the claim but may not take part in the hearing unless the court gives permission.

8.5 FILING AND SERVING WRITTEN EVIDENCE

(1) The claimant must file any written evidence on which he intends to rely when he files his claim form.

(2) The claimant's evidence must be served on the defendant with the claim form.

(3) A defendant who wishes to rely on written evidence must file it when he files his acknowledgment of service.

(4) If he does so, he must also, at the same time, serve a copy of his evidence on the other parties.

(5) The claimant may, within 14 days of service of the defendant's evidence on him, file further written evidence in reply.

(6) If he does so, he must also, within the same time limit, serve a copy of his evidence on the other parties.

(7) The claimant may rely on the matters set out in his claim form as evidence under this rule if the claim form is verified by a statement of truth.

8.6 EVIDENCE — GENERAL

(1) No written evidence may be relied on at the hearing of the claim unless—
   (a) it has been served in accordance with rule 8.5; or
   (b) the court gives permission.

(2) The court may require or permit a party to give oral evidence at the hearing.

(3) The court may give directions requiring the attendance for cross-examination[GL] of a witness who has given written evidence.

(Rule 32.1 contains a general power for the court to control evidence)

8.7 PART 20 CLAIMS

Where the Part 8 procedure is used, Part 20 (counterclaims and other additional claims) applies except that a party may not make a Part 20 claim (as defined by rule 20.2) without the court's permission.

8.8 PROCEDURE WHERE DEFENDANT OBJECTS TO USE OF THE PART 8 PROCEDURE

(1) Where the defendant contends that the Part 8 procedure should not be used because—
   (a) there is a substantial dispute of fact; and
   (b) the use of the Part 8 procedure is not required or permitted by a rule or practice direction,

he must state his reasons when he files his acknowledgment of service.

(Rule 8.5 requires a defendant who wishes to rely on written evidence to file it when he files his acknowledgment of service)

CPR PART 8 ALTERNATIVE PROCEDURE FOR CLAIMS

(2) When the court receives the acknowledgment of service and any written evidence it will give directions as to the future management of the case.

(Rule 8.1(3) allows the court to make an order that the claim continue as if the claimant had not used the Part 8 procedure)

8.9 MODIFICATIONS TO THE GENERAL RULES

Where the Part 8 procedure is followed—

(a) provision is made in this Part for the matters which must be stated in the claim form and the defendant is not required to file a defence and therefore—

    (i) Part 16 (statements of case) does not apply;

    (ii) Part 15 (defence and reply) does not apply;

    (iii) any time limit in these Rules which prevents the parties from taking a step before a defence is filed does not apply;

    (iv) the requirement under rule 7.8 to serve on the defendant a form for defending the claim does not apply;

(b) the claimant may not obtain judgment by request on an admission and therefore—

    (i) rules 14.4 to 14.7 do not apply; and

    (ii) the requirement under rule 7.8 to serve on the defendant a form for admitting the claim does not apply; and

(c) the claim shall be treated as allocated to the multi-track and therefore Part 26 does not apply.

PD 8 PRACTICE DIRECTION — ALTERNATIVE PROCEDURE FOR CLAIMS

This practice direction supplements CPR Part 8

TYPES OF CLAIM IN WHICH PART 8 PROCEDURE MAY BE USED

1.1 A claimant may use the Part 8 procedure where he seeks the court's decision on a question which is unlikely to involve a substantial dispute of fact.

1.2 A claimant may also use the Part 8 procedure if a practice direction permits or requires its use for the type of proceedings in question.

1.3 The practice directions referred to in paragraph 1.2 above may in some respects modify or disapply the Part 8 procedure and, where that is so, it is those practice directions that must be complied with.

1.4 The types of claim for which the Part 8 procedure may be used include:

(1) a claim by or against a child or patient which has been settled before the commencement of proceedings and the sole purpose of the claim is to obtain the approval of the court to the settlement,

(2) a claim for provisional damages which has been settled before the commencement of proceedings and the sole purpose of the claim is to obtain a consent judgment, and

(3) provided there is unlikely to be a substantial dispute of fact, a claim for a summary order for possession against named or unnamed defendants occupying land or premises without the licence or consent of the person claiming possession.

1.5 Where it appears to a court officer that a claimant is using the Part 8. procedure inappropriately, he may refer the claim to a judge for the judge to consider the point.

1.6 The court may at any stage order the claim to continue as if the claimant had not used the Part 8 procedure and, if it does so, the court will allocate the claim to a track and give such directions as it considers appropriate[1].

ISSUING THE CLAIM

2.1 Part 7 and the practice direction which supplements it contain a number of rules and directions applicable to all claims, including those to which Part 8 applies. Those rules and directions should be applied where appropriate.

2.2 Where a claimant uses the Part 8 procedure, the claim form (practice form N208) should be used and must state the matters set out in rule 8.2 and, if paragraphs 1.2 or 1.3 apply, must comply with the requirements of the practice direction in question. In particular, the claim form must state that Part 8 applies; a Part 8 claim form means a claim form which so states.

RESPONDING TO THE CLAIM

3.1 The provisions of Part 15 (defence and reply) do not apply where the claim form is a Part 8 claim form.

3.2 Where a defendant who wishes to respond to a Part 8 claim form is required to file an acknowledgment of service, that acknowledgment of service should be in practice form N210[3] but can, alternatively, be given in an informal document such as a letter.

3.3 Rule 8.3 sets out provisions relating to an acknowledgment of service of a Part 8 claim form.

3.4 Rule 8.4 sets out the consequence of failing to file an acknowledgment of service.

3.5 The provisions of Part 12 (obtaining default judgment) do not apply where the claim form is a Part 8 claim form.

---

[1] Rule 8.1(3).
[3] Rule 8.3(1)(a). [Following an amendment to the practice direction there is now no footnote 2.]

PD 8 PRACTICE DIRECTION — ALTERNATIVE PROCEDURE FOR CLAIMS

3.6 Where a defendant believes that the Part 8 procedure should not be used because there is a substantial dispute of fact or, as the case may be, because its use is not authorised by any rule or practice direction, he must state his reasons in writing when he files his acknowledgment of service[4]. If the statement of reasons includes matters of evidence it should be verified by a statement of truth.

MANAGING THE CLAIM

4.1 The court may give directions immediately a Part 8 claim form is issued either on the application of a party or on its own initiative. The directions may include fixing a hearing date where:

(1) there is no dispute, such as in child and patient settlements, or

(2) where there may be a dispute, such as in claims for mortgage possession or appointment of trustees, but a hearing date could conveniently be given.

4.2 Where the court does not fix a hearing date when the claim form is issued, it will give directions for the disposal of the claim as soon as practicable after the defendant has acknowledged service of the claim form or, as the case may be, after the period for acknowledging service has expired.

4.3 Certain applications, such as a consent application under section 38 of the Landlord and Tenant Act 1954, may not require a hearing.

4.4 The court may convene a directions hearing before giving directions.

EVIDENCE

5.1 A claimant wishing to rely on written evidence should file it when his Part 8 claim form is issued[5] (unless the evidence is contained in the claim form itself).

5.2 Evidence will normally be in the form of a witness statement or an affidavit but a claimant may rely on the matters set out in his claim form provided that it has been verified by a statement of truth.

(For information about (1) statements of truth see Part 22 and the practice direction that supplements it, and (2) written evidence see Part 32 and the practice direction that supplements it.)

5.3 A defendant wishing to rely on written evidence, should file it with his acknowledgment of service[6].

5.4 Rule 8.5 sets out the times and provisions for filing and serving written evidence.

5.5 A party may apply to the court for an extension of time to serve and file evidence under Rule 8.5 or for permission to serve and file additional evidence under Rule 8.6(1).

(For information about applications see Part 23 and the practice direction that supplements it.)

5.6 (1) The parties may, subject to the following provisions, agree in writing on an extension of time for serving and filing evidence under Rule 8.5(3) or Rule 8.5(5).

(2) An agreement extending time for a defendant to file evidence under Rule 8.5(3)—

(a) must be filed by the defendant at the same time as he files his acknowledgment of service; and

(b) must not extend time by more than 14 days after the defendant files his acknowledgment of service.

(3) An agreement extending time for a claimant to file evidence in reply under Rule 8.5(5) must not extend time to more than 28 days after service of the defendant's evidence on the claimant.

---

[4] Rule 8.8(1).
[5] Rule 8.5.
[6] Rule 8.5(3).

PD 8B   PRACTICE DIRECTION — PART 8

This practice direction supplements CPR Part 8, and Schedule 1 and Schedule 2 to the CPR

TERMINOLOGY

1.1 In this practice direction 'Schedule rules' means provisions contained in the Schedules to the CPR, which were previously contained in the Rules of the Supreme Court (1965) or the County Court Rules (1981).

CONTENTS OF THIS PRACTICE DIRECTION

2.1 This practice direction explains:
  (1) how to start the claims referred to in Sections A and B;
  (2) which form to use as the claim form;
  (3) the procedure which those claims will follow; and
  (4) how to start the appeals referred to in Section C.

(Further guidance about Forms other than claim forms can be found the practice direction supplementing Part 4.)

(Forms to be used when making applications under Schedule 1, RSC. O. 53 for judicial review and under Schedule RSC. O. 54 for writs of habeas corpus are forms 86 and 87 (modified as necessary). Reference should be made to the relevant existing Crown Office practice directions for further guidance on procedure).

HOW TO USE THIS PRACTICE DIRECTION

3.1 This Practice direction is divided into three sections — Section A, Section B and Section C. Only one section will be relevant to how to make a particular claim or appeal.

3.2 If the claim is described in paragraph A. 1 — use section A.

3.3 If the claim is described in paragraph B. 1 — use section B.

3.4 If the appeal is described in paragraph C.1 — use section C.

SECTION A

APPLICATION

A.1 Section A applies if:
  (1) the claim is listed in Table 1 below;
  (2) an Act provides that a claim or application in the High Court is to be brought by originating summons; or
  (3) before 26 April 1999, a claim or application in the High Court would have been brought by originating summons, and is not listed in Section C, and no other method for bringing the claim or application on and after 26 April 1999 is specified in a Schedule rule or practice direction.

A.2 (1) The claimant must use the Part 8 procedure unless an Act, Schedule rule, or practice direction, makes any additional or contrary provision.

(2) Where such additional or contrary provision is made the claimant must comply with it and modify the Part 8 procedure accordingly.

CLAIM FORM

A.3 The claimant must use the Part 8 claim form.

Table 1

RSC O. 11, r. 8A	Service of process etc., out of the jurisdiction: Applications for interim remedy under section 25(1) of the Civil Jurisdiction and Judgments Act 1982
RSC O. 17, r. 3(1)	Interpleader (Mode of application)
RSC O. 50, r. 9A	Charging orders, Stop orders etc., Enforcement of charging order by sale

Table 1

RSC O. 50, r. 10(2)	Charging orders, Stop orders etc., Funds in court: Stop order
RSC O. 50, r. 14(4)	Charging orders, Stop orders etc., Withdrawal etc. of Stop Notice
RSC O. 50, r. 15(2)	Charging orders, Stop orders etc., Order prohibiting transfer, etc., of securities
RSC O. 71, r. 2(1)	Reciprocal Enforcement of Judgments and Enforcement of European Community Judgments and Recommendations etc. under the Merchant Shipping (Liner Conferences) Act 1982 (I Reciprocal Enforcement: the Administration of Justice Act 1920 and the Foreign Judgments (Reciprocal Enforcement) Act 1933 — Application for registration)
RSC O. 71, r. 38	Reciprocal Enforcement of Judgments and Enforcement of European Community Judgments and Recommendations etc. under the Merchant Shipping (Liner Conferences) Act 1982 (III Reciprocal Enforcement: the Civil Jurisdiction and Judgments Act 1982 — Enforcement of United Kingdom Judgments in other Parts of the United Kingdom: Non-money Provisions)
RSC O. 71, r. 41	Reciprocal Enforcement of Judgments and Enforcement of European Community Judgments and Recommendations etc. under the Merchant Shipping (Liner Conferences) Act 1982 (IV Enforcement of Recommendations etc. under the Merchant Shipping (Liner Conferences) Act 1982 — Application for registration)
RSC O. 77, r. 11	Proceedings by and against the Crown (Interpleader: Application for order against Crown)
RSC O. 77, r. 16(2)	Proceedings by and against the Crown (Attachment of debts, etc.)
RSC O. 77, r. 17(1)	Proceedings by and against the Crown (Proceedings relating to postal packets)
RSC O. 77, r. 18(1)	Proceedings by and against the Crown (Applications under sections 17 and 29 of Crown Proceedings Act)
RSC O. 79, r. 8(2)	Criminal Proceedings (Estreat of recognizances)
RSC O. 79, r. 9(2)	Criminal Proceedings (Bail)
RSC O. 79, r. 10(2)	Criminal Proceedings (issue of witness summons, etc.)
RSC O. 79, r. 11(1)	Criminal Proceedings (Application for warrant to arrest witness)
RSC O. 81, r. 10(1)	Partners (Applications for orders charging partner's interest in partnership property)
RSC O. 82, r. 8(2)	Defamation claims (Fulfilment of offer of amends under section 4 of the Defamation Act 1952)
RSC O. 88, r. 3	Mortgage claims (Commencement of claim)[1]
RSC O. 92, r. 5(2)	Lodgment, Investment etc. of Funds in Court: Chancery Division (Applications with respect to funds in court)
RSC O. 93, r. 5(2)	Applications and Appeals to High Court under Various Acts: Chancery Division (Applications under section 2(3) of the Public Order Act 1936)
RSC O. 93, r. 6(2)	Applications and Appeals to High Court under Various Acts: Chancery Division (Application under the Variation of Trusts Act 1958)

---

[1] This type of claim may also be brought by the Part I procedure in Section 8.

PD 8B   PRACTICE DIRECTION — PART 8

Table 1

RSC O. 93, r. 18(2)	Applications and Appeals to High Court under Various Acts: Chancery Division (Proceedings under section 86 of the Civil Aviation Act 1982)
RSC O. 93, r. 20(2)	Applications and Appeals to High Court under Various Acts: Chancery Division (Proceedings under section 50 of the Administration of Justice Act 1985)
RSC O. 93, r. 21	Applications and Appeals to High Court under Various Acts: Chancery Division (Proceedings under section 48 of the Administration of Justice Act 1985)
RSC O. 93, r. 23(2)[*]	Applications and Appeals to High Court under Various Acts: Chancery Division (Proceedings under the Banking Act 1987)
RSC O. 94, r. 5	Applications and Appeals to High Court under Various Acts: Queen's Bench Division (Exercise of jurisdiction under Representation of the People Acts)
RSC O. 95, r. 2(1)(b)	Bills of Sale Acts 1878 and 1882 and the Industrial and Provident Societies Act 1967 (Entry of satisfaction)
RSC O. 95, r. 3	Bills of Sale Acts 1878 and 1882 and the Industrial and Provident Societies Act 1967 (Restraining removal on sale of goods seized)
RSC O. 96, r. 1	The Mines (Working Facilities and Support) Act 1966 etc. (Assignment to Chancery Division)
RSC O. 96, r. 3	The Mines (Working Facilities and Support) Act 1966 etc. (Issue of claim form)
RSC O. 97, r. 2	The Landlord and Tenant Acts 1927, 1954 and 1987 (Assignment of proceedings to Chancery Division etc.)
RSC O. 97, r. 5	The Landlord and Tenant Acts 1927, 1954 and 1987 (Proceedings under Part 1 of the Act of 1927)
RSC O. 97, r. 6(1)	The Landlord and Tenant Acts 1927, 1954 and 1987 (Application for new tenancy under section 24 of the Act of 1954)
RSC O. 97, r. 6A(1)	The Landlord and Tenant Acts 1927, 1954 and 1987 (Application to authorise agreement)
RSC O. 97, r. 9A(1)(b)	The Landlord and Tenant Acts 1927, 1954 and 1987 r. 9A(1)(b) (Application to determine interim rent)
RSC O. 97, r. 14	The Landlord and Tenant Acts 1927, 1954 and 1987 (Application under section 19 of the Act of 1987)
RSC O. 97, r. 15(3)	The Landlord and Tenant Acts 1927, 1954 and 1987 (Application for order under section 24 of the Act of 1987)
RSC O. 97, r. 16(3)	The Landlord and Tenant Acts 1927, 1954 and 1987 (Application for acquisition order under section 29 of the Act of 1987)
RSC O. 99, r. 3(1)	Inheritance (Provision for Family and Dependants) Act 1975 (Application for Financial Provision) (High Court and County Court cases)
RSC O. 106, r. 3(2)	Proceedings Relating to Solicitors: The Solicitors Act 1974 (Power to order solicitor to deliver cash account etc.)
RSC O. 106, r. 6(2)	Proceedings Relating to Solicitors: The Solicitors Act 1974 (Applications under schedule 1 to the Act)
RSC O. 106, r. 8(1)	Proceedings Relating to Solicitors: The Solicitors Act 1974 (interim order restricting payment out of banking account)

[* The reference should be to r. 23(2)(a) (*Financial Services Authority* v *Millward* (27 May 1999 unreported).]

Table 1

RSC O. 109 r. 1(3)	Administration Act 1960 (Applications under Act)
RSC O. 113, r. 1	Summary proceedings for possession of land (Proceedings to be brought by claim form)

SECTION B

APPLICATION

B.1 Section B applies if the claim:
 (1) is listed in Table 2;
 (2) in the county court is for, or includes a claim for:
  (a) the recovery of possession of land; or
  (b) for damages for harassment under Section 3 of the Protection from Harassment Act 1997
 (3) would have been brought before 26 April 1999:
  (a) in the High Court, by originating motion and is not listed in Section C;
  (b) in the county court:
   (i) by originating application; or
   (ii) by petition, and
no other procedure is prescribed in an Act, a Schedule rule or a practice direction.

Table 2

Schedule Rule		Claim Form
RSC O. 56, r. 8(1)	Appeals, etc., to High Court by Case Stated: General (Application for order to state a case)	
RSC O. 56, r. 10(1)	Appeals, etc., to High Court by Case Stated: General (Proceedings for determination of case)	
RSC O. 71, r. 24[2]	Reciprocal Enforcement of Judgments and Enforcement of European Community Judgments and Recommendations etc., under the Merchant Shipping (Liner Conferences) Act 1982, II Enforcement of European Community Judgments. (Application for enforcement of Euratom inspection order)	
RSC O. 77, r. 8(2)[3]	Proceedings by and against the Crown (Summary applications to the court in certain revenue matters)	
RSC O. 93, r. 19(1)	Applications and Appeals to High Court under Various Acts: (Proceedings under section 85(7) of the Fair Trading Act 1973 and the Control of Misleading Advertisements Regulations 1988)	
RSC O. 93, r. 22(3)	Applications and Appeals to High Court under Various Acts: Chancery Division (Proceedings under the Financial Services Act 1986) (Applications by claim form)	

[2] This type of claim may also be brought by the Part 8 procedure.
[3] These types of claim may also be brought by the Part 8 procedure.

Schedule Rule	Claim Form
RSC O. 94, r. 1(2)	Applications and Appeals to High Court under Various Acts: Queen's Bench Division (Jurisdiction of High Court to Quash Certain Orders, Schemes etc.)
RSC O. 94, r. 7(2)	Applications and Appeals to High Court under Various Acts: Queen's Bench Division (Reference of Question of Law by Agricultural Land Tribunal)
RSC O. 94, r. 11(4)	Applications and Appeals to High Court under Various Acts: Queen's Bench Division (Case stated by Mental Health Review Tribunal)
RSC O. 94, r. 12(5)(c)	Applications and Appeals to High Court r. 12(5)(c) under Various Acts: Queen's Bench Division Applications for permission under section 289(6) of the Town and Country Planning Act 1990 and section 65(5) of the Planning (Listed Buildings and Conservation Areas) Act 1990
RSC O. 94, r. 13(5)	Applications and Appeals to High Court under Various Acts: Queen's Bench Division Proceedings under sections 289 and 290 of the Town and Country Planning Act 1990 and under section 65 of the Planning (Listed Buildings and Conservation Areas) Act 1990
RSC O. 94, r. 14(2)	Applications and Appeals to High Court under Various Acts: Queen's Bench Division Applications under section 13 of the Coroners Act 1988
RSC O. 94, r. 15(2)	Applications and Appeals to High Court under Various Acts: Queen's Bench Division Applications under section 42 of the Supreme Court Act 1981
RSC O. 98, r. 2(1)	Local Government Finance Act 1982, Part III (Application by auditor for declaration)
RSC O. 109, r. 2(4)	Administration of Justice Act 1960 (Appeals under section 13 of Act)
RSC O. 114, r. 2(2)	References to the European Court (Making of order)
RSC O. 115, r. 2B(1)	Confiscation and Forfeiture in Connection with Criminal Proceedings (I. Drug Trafficking Act 1994 and Criminal Justice (International Co-operation) Act 1990 — Application for confiscation order)

PD 8B PRACTICE DIRECTION — PART 8

Schedule Rule		Claim Form
RSC O. 115, r. 3(1)	Confiscation and Forfeiture in Connection with Criminal Proceedings (I. Drug Trafficking Act 1994 and Criminal Justice (International Co-operation) Act 1990 — Application for restraint order or charging order)	
RSC O. 115, r. 7(1)	Confiscation and Forfeiture in Connection with Criminal Proceedings (I. Drug Trafficking Act 1994 and Criminal Justice (International Co-operation) Act 1990 — Realisation of property)	
RSC O. 115, r. 26(1)	Confiscation and Forfeiture in Connection with Criminal Proceedings (III. Prevention of Terrorism (Temporary Provisions) Act 1989 — Application for restraint order)	
RSC O. 116, r. 5(1)	The Criminal Procedure and Investigations Act 1996 (Application under section 54(3)).	
CCR O. 24, r. 1(1)	Summary proceedings for the recovery of land (Part I — Land: proceedings to be by claim form)	N312
CCR O. 24, r. 10(2)(a)	Summary proceedings for the recovery of land — (Part II Interim possession orders — issue of the applications)	N130
CCR O. 31, r. 4(1)	Charging orders (Enforcement of charging order by sale)	
CCR O. 43, r. 2(1)	The Landlord and Tenant Acts 1927, 1954, 1985 and 1987 (Commencement of proceedings and answer)	
CCR O. 43, r. 4(1)	The Landlord and Tenant Acts 1927, 1954, 1985 and 1987 (Proceedings under Part I of the Act of 1927)	N394 N395 N396
CCR O. 43, r. 6(1)	The Landlord and Tenant Acts 1927, 1954, 1985 and 1987 (Application for a new tenancy under section 24 of the Act of 1954)	N397
CCR O. 43, r. 16	The Landlord and Tenant Acts 1927, 1954, 1985 and 1987 (Application under section 12(2) of the Act of 1985)	
CCR O. 43, r. 18(1)	The Landlord and Tenant Acts 1927, 1954, 1985 and 1987 (Application for order under section 24 of the Act of 1987)	
CCR O. 43, r. 19(1)	The Landlord and Tenant Acts 1927, 1954, 1985 and 1987 (Application for acquisition order under section 29 of the Act of 1987)	

Schedule Rule		Claim Form
CCR O. 43, r. 20(1)	The Landlord and Tenant Acts 1927, 1954, 1985 and 1987 (Application for order under section 38 or 40 of the Act of 1987)	
CCR O. 44, r. 1(1)	The Agricultural Holdings Act 1986 (Special case stated by arbitrator)	
CCR O. 44, r. 3(1)	The Agricultural Holdings Act 1986 (Removal of arbitrator or setting aside award)	
CCR O. 45, r. 1(1)	The Representation of the People Act 1983 (Application for detailed assessment of returning officer's account)	N408
CCR O. 46, r. 1(1)	The Legitimacy Act 1976 (Manner of application)	
CCR O. 49, r. 1(2)	Miscellaneous Statutes: (Access to Neighbouring Land Act 1992)	
CCR O. 49, r. 4(5)	Miscellaneous Statutes: (Consumer Credit Act 1974 — claim relating to land (Application under section 129(1)(b)))	
CCR O. 49, r. 4(9)	Miscellaneous Statutes: (Consumer Credit Act 1974 — claim relating to land (Application for enforcement order))	
CCR O. 49, r. 4(14)	Miscellaneous Statutes: (Consumer Credit Act 1974 — claim relating to land (Application under section 139(1)(a) for a credit agreement to be reopened))	
CCR O. 49, r. 4(15)	Miscellaneous Statutes: (Consumer Credit Act 1974 — claim relating to land (proceedings as are mentioned in section 139(1)(b) or (c)))	
CCR O. 49, r. 5(1)	Miscellaneous Statutes: Fair Trading Act 1973 (Proceedings under section 35, 38 or 40)	
CCR O. 49, r. 6(5)	Miscellaneous Statutes: Housing Act 1988: assured tenancies (application for accelerated possession)	N5A
CCR O. 49, r. 6A(5)	Miscellaneous Statutes: Housing Act 1988: assured shorthold tenancies (application for accelerated possession)	N5B
CCR O. 49, r. 6B(1)	Miscellaneous Statutes: Housing Act 1996: Injunctions and Powers of Arrest (Application for injunction under section 152)	N16A
CCR O. 49, r. 7(2)	Miscellaneous Statutes: Injunctions to Prevent Environmental Harm: Town and Country Planning Act 1990 etc. (Application for injunction)	
CCR O. 49, r. 9(3)	Miscellaneous Statutes: Leasehold Reform, Housing and Urban Development Act 1993	

Schedule Rule		Claim Form
CCR O. 49, r. 10(3)	Miscellaneous Statutes: Local Government Finance Act 1982	
CCR O. 49, r. 12(2)	Miscellaneous Statutes: Mental Health Act 1983 (Application)	
CCR O. 49, r. 13(1)	Miscellaneous Statutes: Mobile Homes Act 1983 (Applications and questions)	
CCR O. 49, r. 15(1)	Miscellaneous Statutes: Post Office Act 1969 (Application under section 30(5))	

SPECIAL PROVISIONS TAKE PRECEDENCE

B.2 The claimant must first comply with any special provision set out in the Schedule rules, practice direction or any Act relating to the claim.
(In Schedule 2, CCR O.6 makes special provisions about particulars of claim and CCR O.7 makes special provision for service, for certain types of claim.)

B.3 Special provisions contained in Schedule rules or an Act may set out:
   (1) where the claim may be started;
   (2) the contents of the claim form;
   (3) whether a hearing is required;
   (4) the nature of evidence required in support of the claim, and when it must be filed or served;
   (5) the method of service of the claim form and evidence;
   (6) persons on whom service must or may be effected;
   (7) the form and content of Notices, and when they must or may be filed, and on whom served;
   (8) the form and content of any affidavit, answer, or reply and when they must or may be filed or served;
   (9) persons who may apply to be joined as parties to the claim;
   (10) minimum periods of notice before the hearing date.

B.4 Where a Schedule rule makes special provision for the contents of particulars of claim, those particulars must be attached to the claim form and served with it.

B.5 Subject to any special or contrary provision in an Act or Schedule rule, the claimant must use the procedure set out in the remainder of this section.

RESTRICTIONS ON WHERE TO START THE CLAIM

B.6 Where the claimant is bringing a claim In a county court that claim may only be started
   (1) in the county court for the district in which:
      (a) the defendants or one of the defendants lives or carries on business; or
      (b) the subject matter of the claim is situated; or
   (2) if there is no defendant named in the claim form, in the county court for the district in which the claimant or one of the claimants lives or carries on business.

B.7 Where the claimant is making a claim in the county court for:
   (1) the recovery of land;
   (2) the foreclosure or redemption of any mortgage;
   (3) enforcing any charge or lien on land;
   (4) the recovery of moneys secured by a mortgage or charge on land,
the claim must be started in the court for the district in which the land, or any part of it, is situated.

CLAIM FORM

B.8 This paragraph sets out which Form is to be used as the claim form:
   (1) where a claim form number is listed against a particular claim in Table 2, the claimant must use that numbered form as the claim form;

(2) where the claimant intends to make a claim in the county court which is for, or includes, the recovery of possession of land, the claimant must use the claim form numbered in the practice direction supplementing Part 4 (Forms), and
(3) in every other claim, the claimant must use the Part 8 claim form.

COURT WILL FIX A DATE

B.9 When the court issues the claim form it will:
(1) fix a date for the hearing; and
(2) prepare a notice of the hearing date for each party.

SERVICE OF THE CLAIM FORM

B.10 The claim form must be served not less than 21 days before the hearing date.

B.11 Where the claimant serves the claim form, he must serve notice of the hearing date at the same time, unless the hearing date is specified in the claim form. (CPR Rule 3.1(2) (a) and (b) provide for the court to extend or shorten the time for compliance with any rule or practice direction, and to adjourn or bring forward a hearing)

DEFENDANT IS NOT REQUIRED TO RESPOND

B.12 The defendant is not required to serve an acknowledgment of service.

AT THE HEARING

B.13 The court may on the hearing date:
(1) proceed to hear the case and dispose of the claim; or
(2) give case management directions.

B.14 Case management directions given under paragraph B.13 will, if the defendant has filed a defence, include the allocation of a case to a track, or directions to enable the case to be allocated.

B.15 CPR rule 26.5(3) to (5) and CPR rules 26.6 to 26.10 apply to the allocation of a claim under paragraph B.14.

SECTION C

C.1 Section C applies if the appeal is listed in Table 3.
C.2 The Schedule rules provide:
(1) that the appeal must be stated by Notice of Appeal; and
(2) the procedure the appeal should follow.

(Further information on the procedure to be followed, and the form of the Notice of Appeal for Appeals to the Court of Appeal can be found in the Practice Direction for the Court of Appeal (Civil Division)).

Table 3

Schedule Rule	Claim Form
RSC O. 55, r. 3(1)	Appeals, etc., to High Court from Court, Tribunal or person: general (Bringing of Appeal)
RSC O. 59, r. 3(1)	Appeals to the Court of Appeal
RSC O. 60, r. 1	Appeals to the Court of Appeal from Restrictive Practices Court
RSC O. 61, r. 3(1)	Appeals from Tribunals to Court of Appeal by Case Stated. (Proceedings on case stated)
RSC O. 91, r. 2(2)	Revenue proceedings (Appeal under section 222 of the Inheritance Tax Act 1984)
RSC O. 93, r. 11(3)	Applications and Appeals to High Court under various Acts: Chancery Division (Appeal under section 17 of the Industrial Assurance Act)

Schedule Rule		Claim Form
RSC O. 93, r. 12(1)	Applications and Appeals to High Court under various Acts: Chancery Division (Appeals, etc., affecting Industrial and Provident Societies, etc.)	
RSC O. 93, [r. 23(2)(b)*]	Applications and Appeals to High Court under various Acts: Chancery Division Appeal (Proceedings under the [Banking Act 1987*] — appeals under section 31(1))	
RSC O. 94, r. 10	Applications and Appeals to High Court under various Acts: Queen's Bench Division (Tribunals and Enquiries Act 1971: Appeal from Minister of Transport)	
RSC O. 94, r. 10A(2)	Applications and Appeals to High Court under various Acts: Queen's Bench Division (Consumer Credit Act 1974: Appeal from Secretary of State)	
RSC O. 101, r. 4(1)	The Pensions Appeal Tribunals Act 1943 (Appeal)	
RSC O. 106, r. 12(1)	Proceedings relating to Solicitors: The Solicitors Act 1974 (Title, service etc., of Notice of Appeal)	
RSC O. 108, r. 5(2)	Proceedings relating to Charities: The Charities Act 1993 (Appeal against order, etc., of Commissioners)	
RSC O. 111, r. 4(3)	Social Security Administration Act 1992 (Reference of question of law)	

[* The references in the text issued by the Lord Chancellor's Department to r. 22(2)(b) and the Banking Appeal Act 1987 are clearly erroneous (*Financial Services Authority* v *Millward* (27 May 1999 unreported)).]

CPR PART 9 RESPONDING TO PARTICULARS OF CLAIM — GENERAL

CONTENTS OF THIS PART
Scope of this Part — Rule 9.1
Defence, admission or acknowledgment of service — Rule 9.2

9.1 SCOPE OF THIS PART
(1) This Part sets out how a defendant may respond to particulars of claim.
(2) Where the defendant receives a claim form which states that particulars of claim are to follow, he need not respond to the claim until the particulars of claim have been served on him.

9.2 DEFENCE, ADMISSION OR ACKNOWLEDGMENT OF SERVICE
When particulars of claim are served on a defendant, the defendant may—
    (a) file or serve an admission in accordance with Part 14;
    (b) file a defence in accordance with Part 15,
    (or do both, if he admits only part of the claim); or
    (c) file an acknowledgment of service in accordance with Part 10.

CPR PART 10 ACKNOWLEDGMENT OF SERVICE

CONTENTS OF THIS PART
Acknowledgment of service	Rule 10.1
Consequence of not filing an acknowledgment of service	Rule 10.2
The period for filing an acknowledgment of service	Rule 10.3
Notice to claimant that defendant has filed an acknowledgment of service	Rule 10.4
Contents of acknowledgment of service	Rule 10.5

10.1 ACKNOWLEDGMENT OF SERVICE
(1) This Part deals with the procedure for filing an acknowledgment of service.

(2) Where the claimant uses the procedure set out in Part 8 (alternative procedure for claims) this Part applies subject to the modifications set out in rule 8.3.

(3) A defendant may file an acknowledgment of service if—
   (a) he is unable to file a defence within the period specified in rule 15.4; or
   (b) he wishes to dispute the court's jurisdiction.

(Part 11 sets out the procedure for disputing the court's jurisdiction)

10.2 CONSEQUENCE OF NOT FILING AN ACKNOWLEDGMENT OF SERVICE
If—
   (a) a defendant fails to file an acknowledgment of service within the period specified in rule 10.3; and
   (b) does not within that period file a defence in accordance with Part 15 or serve or file an admission in accordance with Part 14,
the claimant may obtain default judgment if Part 12 allows it.

10.3 THE PERIOD FOR FILING AN ACKNOWLEDGMENT OF SERVICE
(1) The general rule is that the period for filing an acknowledgment of service is—
   (a) where the defendant is served with a claim form which states that particulars of claim are to follow, 14 days after service of the particulars of claim; and
   (b) in any other case, 14 days after service of the claim form.

(2) The general rule is subject to the following rules—
   (a) RSC Order 11, r. 1A (which specifies how the period for filing an acknowledgment of service is calculated where the claim form is served out of the jurisdiction); and
   (b) rule 6.16(4) (which requires the court to specify the period for responding to the particulars of claim when it makes an order under that rule).

10.4 NOTICE TO CLAIMANT THAT DEFENDANT HAS FILED AN ACKNOWLEDGMENT OF SERVICE
On receipt of an acknowledgment of service, the court must notify the claimant in writing.

10.5 CONTENTS OF ACKNOWLEDGMENT OF SERVICE
An acknowledgment of service must—
   (a) be signed by the defendant or his legal representative; and
   (b) include the defendant's address for service.

(Rule 6.5 provides that an address for service must be within the jurisdiction)
(*RSC Order 81, in Schedule 1, makes special provision in relation to the acknowledgment of service in a claim against a firm*).
(*The Contentious Probate Proceedings Practice Direction provides that a defendant who wishes to defend a contentious probate claim must file an acknowledgment of service*).

PD 10 PRACTICE DIRECTION — ACKNOWLEDGMENT OF SERVICE

This practice direction supplements CPR Part 10

RESPONDING TO THE CLAIM
1.1 Part 9 sets out how a defendant may respond to a claim.
1.2 Part 10 sets out the provisions for acknowledging service (but see rule 8.3 for information about acknowledging service of a claim under the Part 8 procedure).

THE FORM OF ACKNOWLEDGMENT OF SERVICE
2 A defendant who wishes to acknowledge service of a claim should do so by using form N9.

ADDRESS FOR SERVICE
3.1 The defendant must include in his acknowledgment of service an address for the service of documents[1].
3.2 Where the defendant is represented by a legal representative[2] and the legal representative has signed the acknowledgment of service form, the address must be the legal representative's business address; otherwise the address for service that is given should be as set out in rule 6.5 and the practice direction which supplements Part 6.

SIGNING THE ACKNOWLEDGMENT OF SERVICE
4.1 An acknowledgment of service must be signed by the defendant or by his legal representative.
4.2 Where the defendant is a company or other corporation, a person holding a senior position in the company or corporation may sign the acknowledgment of service on the defendant's behalf, but must state the position he holds.
4.3 Each of the following persons is a person holding a senior position:
   (1) in respect of a registered company or corporation, a director, the treasurer, secretary, chief executive, manager or other officer of the company or corporation, and
   (2) in respect of a corporation which is not a registered company, in addition to those persons set out in (1), the mayor, chairman, president, town clerk or similar officer of the corporation.
4.4 Where the defendant is a partnership, the acknowledgment of service may be signed by:
   (1) any of the partners, or
   (2) a person having the control or management of the partnership business.
4.5 Children and patients may acknowledge service only by their litigation friend or his legal representative unless the court otherwise orders[3].

GENERAL
5.1 The defendant's name should be set out in full on the acknowledgment of service.
5.2 Where the defendant's name has been incorrectly set out in the claim form, it should be correctly set out on the acknowledgment of service followed by the words 'described as' and the incorrect name.
5.3 If two or more defendants to a claim acknowledge service of a claim through the same legal representative at the same time, only one acknowledgment of service need be used.
5.4 An acknowledgment of service may be amended or withdrawn only with the permission of the court.
5.5 An application for permission under paragraph 5.4 must be made in accordance with Part 23 and supported by evidence.

---

[1] See rule 6.5.
[2] See rule 2.3 for the definition of legal representative.
[3] See Part 21.

CPR PART 11 DISPUTING THE COURT'S JURISDICTION

CONTENTS OF THIS PART
Procedure for disputing the court's jurisdiction.   Rule 11

11 PROCEDURE FOR DISPUTING THE COURT'S JURISDICTION

(1) A defendant who wishes to—
   (a) dispute the court's jurisdiction to try the claim; or
   (b) argue that the court should not exercise its jurisdiction,
may apply to the court for an order declaring that it has no such jurisdiction or should not exercise any jurisdiction which it may have.

(2) A defendant who wishes to make such an application must first file an acknowledgment of service in accordance with Part 10.

(3) A defendant who files an acknowledgment of service does not, by doing so, lose any right that he may have to dispute the court's jurisdiction.

(4) An application under this rule must—
   (a) be made within the period for filing a defence; and
   (b) be supported by evidence.

(Rule 15.4 sets out the period for filing a defence)

(5) If the defendant—
   (a) files an acknowledgment of service; and
   (b) does not make such an application within the period for filing a defence,
he is to be treated as having accepted that the court has jurisdiction to try the claim.

(6) An order containing a declaration that the court has no jurisdiction or will not exercise its jurisdiction may also make further provision including—
   (a) setting aside the claim form;
   (b) setting aside service of the claim form;
   (c) discharging any order made before the claim was commenced or before the claim form was served; and
   (d) staying$^{(GL)}$ the proceedings.

(7) If on an application under this rule the court does not make a declaration—
   (a) the acknowledgment of service shall cease to have effect; and
   (b) the defendant may file a further acknowledgment of service within 14 days or such other period as the court may direct.

(8) If the defendant files a further acknowledgment of service in accordance with paragraph (7)(b) he shall be treated as having accepted that the court has jurisdiction to try the claim.

(9) Where a defendant makes an application under this rule he need not file a defence before the hearing of the application.

(10) Where the claimant uses the procedure set out in Part 8 (alternative procedure for claims) this Part applies subject to the modifications set out in rule 8.3.

CPR PART 12   DEFAULT JUDGMENT

CONTENTS OF THIS PART

Meaning of 'default judgment'	Rule 12.1
Claims in which default judgment may not be obtained	Rule 12.2
Conditions to be satisfied	Rule 12.3
Procedure for obtaining default judgment	Rule 12.4
Nature of judgment where default judgment obtained by filing a request	Rule 12.5
Interest	Rule 12.6
Procedure for deciding an amount or value	Rule 12.7
Claim against more than one defendant	Rule 12.8
Procedure for obtaining default judgment for costs only	Rule 12.9
Default judgment obtained by making an application	Rule 12.10
Supplementary provisions where applications for default judgment are made	Rule 12.11

12.1   MEANING OF 'DEFAULT JUDGMENT'
12.1   In these Rules, 'default judgment' means judgment without trial where a defendant—
  (a)   has failed to file an acknowledgment of service; or
  (b)   has failed to file a defence.
(Part 10 contains provisions about filing an acknowledgment of service and Part 15 contains provisions about filing a defence)

12.2   CLAIMS IN WHICH DEFAULT JUDGMENT MAY NOT BE OBTAINED
A claimant may not obtain a default judgment—
  (a)   on a claim for delivery of goods subject to an agreement regulated by the Consumer Credit Act 1974;
  (b)   where he uses the procedure set out in Part 8 (alternative procedure for claims); or
  (c)   in any other case where a practice direction provides that the claimant may not obtain default judgment.

12.3   CONDITIONS TO BE SATISFIED
  (1)   The claimant may obtain judgment in default of an acknowledgment of service only if—
    (a)   the defendant has not filed an acknowledgment of service or a defence to the claim (or any part of the claim); and
    (b)   the relevant time for doing so has expired.
  (2)   The claimant may obtain judgment in default of defence only if—
    (a)   the defendant has filed an acknowledgment of service but has not filed a defence; and
    (b)   the relevant time for doing so has expired.
(Rules 10.3 and 15.4 deal respectively with the period for filing an acknowledgment of service and the period for filing a defence)
  (3)   The claimant may not obtain a default judgment if—
    (a)   the defendant has applied for summary judgment under Part 24, and that application has not been disposed of;
    (b)   the defendant has satisfied the whole claim (including any claim for costs) on which the claimant is seeking judgment; or
    (c)   (i)   the claimant is seeking judgment on a claim for money; and
      (ii)   the defendant has filed or served on the claimant an admission under rule 14.4 or 14.7 (admission of liability to pay all of the money claimed) together with a request for time to pay.

CPR PART 12   DEFAULT JUDGMENT

(Part 14 sets out the procedure where a defendant admits a money claim and asks for time to pay)

(Rule 6.14 provides that, where the claim form is served by the claimant, he may not obtain default judgment unless he has filed a certificate of service)

12.4   PROCEDURE FOR OBTAINING DEFAULT JUDGMENT

(1) Subject to paragraph (2), a claimant may obtain a default judgment by filing a request in the relevant practice form where the claim is for—
    (a)   a specified amount of money;
    (b)   an amount of money to be decided by the court;
    (c)   delivery of goods where the claim form gives the defendant the alternative of paying their value; or
    (d)   any combination of these remedies.

(2) The claimant must make an application in accordance with Part 23 if he wishes to obtain a default judgment—
    (a)   on a claim which consists of or includes a claim for any other remedy; or
    (b)   where rule 12.9 or rule 12.10 so provides.

(3) Where a claimant—
    (a)   claims any other remedy in his claim form in addition to those specified in paragraph (1); but
    (b)   abandons that claim in his request for judgment,
he may still obtain a default judgment by filing a request under paragraph (1).

12.5   NATURE OF JUDGMENT WHERE DEFAULT JUDGMENT OBTAINED BY FILING A REQUEST

(1) Where the claim is for a specified sum of money, the claimant may specify in a request filed under rule 12.4(1)—
    (a)   the date by which the whole of the judgment debt is to be paid; or
    (b)   the times and rate at which it is to be paid by instalments.

(2) Except where paragraph (4) applies, a default judgment on a claim for a specified amount of money obtained on the filing of a request, will be judgment for the amount of the claim (less any payments made) and costs—
    (a)   to be paid by the date or at the rate specified in the request for judgment; or
    (b)   if none is specified, immediately.

(Interest may be included in a default judgment obtained by filing a request if the conditions set out in Rule 12.6 are satisfied)

(Rule 45.4 provides for fixed costs on the entry of a default judgment)

(3) Where the claim is for an unspecified amount of money a default judgment obtained on the filing of a request will be for an amount to be decided by the court and costs.

(4) Where the claim is for delivery of goods and the claim form gives the defendant the alternative of paying their value, a default judgment obtained on the filing of a request will be judgment requiring the defendant to—
    (a)   deliver the goods or (if he does not do so) pay the value of the goods as decided by the court (less any payments made); and
    (b)   pay costs.

(Rule 12.7 sets out the procedure for deciding the amount of a judgment or the value of the goods)

(5) The claimant's right to enter judgment requiring the defendant to deliver goods is subject to rule 40.14 (judgment in favour of certain part owners relating to the detention of goods).

12.6   INTEREST

(1) A default judgment on a claim for a specified amount of money obtained on the filing of a request may include the amount of interest claimed to the date of judgment if—
    (a)   the particulars of claim include the details required by rule 16.4;
    (b)   where interest is claimed under section 35A of the Supreme Court Act 1981 or section 69 of the County Courts Act 1984, the rate is no higher than the

CPR PART 12 DEFAULT JUDGMENT

rate of interest payable on judgment debts at the date when the claim form was issued; and

(c) the claimant's request for judgment includes a calculation of the interest claimed for the period from the date up to which interest was stated to be calculated in the claim form to the date of the request for judgment.

(2) In any case where paragraph (1) does not apply, judgment will be for an amount of interest to be decided by the court.

(Rule 12.7 sets out the procedure for deciding the amount of interest)

12.7 PROCEDURE FOR DECIDING AN AMOUNT OR VALUE

(1) This rule applies where the claimant obtains a default judgment on the filing of a request under rule 12.4(1) and judgment is for—
   (a) an amount of money to be decided by the court;
   (b) the value of goods to be decided by the court; or
   (c) an amount of interest to be decided by the court.

(2) Where the court enters judgment it will—
   (a) give any directions it considers appropriate; and
   (b) if it considers it appropriate, allocate the case.

12.8 CLAIM AGAINST MORE THAN ONE DEFENDANT

(1) A claimant may obtain a default judgment on request under this Part on a claim for money or a claim for delivery of goods against one of two or more defendants, and proceed with his claim against the other defendants.

(2) Where a claimant applies for a default judgment against one of two or more defendants—
   (a) if the claim can be dealt with separately from the claim against the other defendants—
      (i) the court may enter a default judgment against that defendant; and
      (ii) the claimant may continue the proceedings against the other defendants;
   (b) if the claim cannot be dealt with separately from the claim against the other defendants—
      (i) the court will not enter default judgment against that defendant; and
      (ii) the court must deal with the application at the same time as it disposes of the claim against the other defendants.

(3) A claimant may not enforce against one of two or more defendants any judgment obtained under this Part for possession of land or for delivery of goods unless—
   (a) he has obtained a judgment for possession or delivery (whether or not obtained under this Part) against all the defendants to the claim; or
   (b) the court gives permission.

12.9 PROCEDURE FOR OBTAINING A DEFAULT JUDGMENT FOR COSTS ONLY

(1) Where a claimant wishes to obtain a default judgment for costs only—
   (a) if the claim is for fixed costs, he may obtain it by filing a request in the relevant practice form;
   (b) if the claim is for any other type of costs, he must make an application in accordance with Part 23.

(2) Where an application is made under this rule for costs only, judgment shall be for an amount to be decided by the court.

(Part 45 sets out when a claimant is entitled to fixed costs)

12.10 DEFAULT JUDGMENT OBTAINED BY MAKING AN APPLICATION

The claimant must make an application in accordance with Part 23 where—
   (a) the claim is—
      (i) a claim against a child or patient;
      (ii) a claim in tort by one spouse against the other; or
      (iii) a claim against the Crown.

(b) he wishes to obtain a default judgment where the defendant has failed to file an acknowledgment of service—
 (i) against a defendant who has been served with the claim out of the jurisdiction under RSC Order 11, r. 1(2)(a) (service without leave under the Civil Jurisdiction and Judgments Act 1982);
 (ii) against a defendant domiciled in Scotland or Northern Ireland or in any other Convention territory;
 (iii) against a State;
 (iv) against a diplomatic agent who enjoys immunity from civil jurisdiction by virtue of the Diplomatic Privileges Act 1964; or
 (v) against persons or organisations who enjoy immunity from civil jurisdiction pursuant to the provisions of the International Organisations Acts 1968 and 1981.

12.11 SUPPLEMENTARY PROVISIONS WHERE APPLICATIONS FOR DEFAULT JUDGMENT ARE MADE
 (1) Where the claimant makes an application for a default judgment, judgment shall be such judgment as it appears to the court that the claimant is entitled to on his statement of case.
 (2) Any evidence relied on by the claimant in support of his application need not be served on a party who has failed to file an acknowledgment of service.
 (3) An application for a default judgment on a claim against a child or patient or a claim in tort between spouses must be supported by evidence.
 (4) An application for a default judgment may be made without notice if—
 (a) the claim was served in accordance with the Civil Jurisdiction and Judgments Act 1982;
 (b) the defendant has failed to file an acknowledgment of service; and
 (c) notice does not need to be given under any other provision of these Rules.
 (5) Where an application is made against a State for a default judgment where the defendant has failed to file an acknowledgment of service—
 (a) the application may be made without notice, but the court hearing the application may direct that a copy of the application notice be served on the State;
 (b) if the court—
 (i) grants the application; or
 (ii) directs that a copy of the application notice be served on the State, the judgment or application notice (and the evidence in support) may be served out of the jurisdiction without any further order;
 (c) where paragraph (5)(b) permits a judgment or an application notice to be served out of the jurisdiction, the procedure for serving the judgment or the application notice is the same as for serving a claim form under RSC Order 11 except where an alternative method of service has been agreed under section 12(6) of the State Immunity Act 1978.
(Rule 23.1 defines 'application notice')
 (6) For the purposes of this rule and rule 12.10—
 (a) 'domicile' is to be determined in accordance with the provisions of sections 41 to 46 of the Civil Jurisdiction and Judgments Act 1982;
 (b) 'Convention territory' means the territory or territories of any Contracting State, as defined by section 1(3) of the Civil Jurisdiction and Judgments Act 1982, to which the Brussels Conventions or Lugano Convention apply;
 (c) 'State' has the meaning given by section 14 of the State Immunity Act 1978; and
 (d) 'Diplomatic agent' has the meaning given by Article 1(e) of Schedule 1 to the Diplomatic Privileges Act 1964.

PD 12 PRACTICE DIRECTION — DEFAULT JUDGMENT

This practice direction supplements CPR Part 12

DEFAULT JUDGMENT

1.1 A default judgment is judgment without a trial where a defendant has failed to file either:

    (1) an acknowledgment of service, or
    (2) a defence.

For this purpose a defence includes any document purporting to be a defence. (See Part 10 and the practice direction which supplements it for information about the acknowledgment of service, and Parts 15 and 16 and the practice directions which supplement them for information about the defence and what it should contain.)

1.2 A claimant may not obtain a default judgment under Part 12 (notwithstanding that no acknowledgment of service or defence has been filed) if:

    (1) the procedure set out in Part 8 (Alternative Procedure for Claims) is being used, or
    (2) the claim is for delivery of goods subject to an agreement regulated by the Consumer Credit Act 1974, or
    (3) the claim is one to which RSC Order 88 (Schedule 1 to the CPR) (mortgage claims) applies, or
    (4) the claim is made in proceedings in respect of which, under CPR Part 49 and practice directions supplemental to that Part, either there is no requirement for an acknowledgement of service or a defence to be filed or special provision is made about the obtaining of a default judgment.

1.3 Examples of proceedings where default judgment under Part 12 cannot be obtained are:

    (1) admiralty proceedings;
    (2) arbitration proceedings;
    (3) contentious probate proceedings;
    (4) claims for provisional damages.

OBTAINING DEFAULT JUDGMENT

2.1 Rules 12.4(1) and 12.9(1) describe the claims in respect of which a default judgment may be obtained by filing a request in the appropriate practice form.

2.2 A default judgment on:

    (1) the claims referred to in rules 12.9(1)(b) and 12.10, and
    (2) claims other than those described in rule 12.4(1),

can only be obtained if an application for default judgment is made and cannot be obtained by filing a request.

2.3 The following are some of the types of claim which require an application for a default judgment:

    (1) against children and patients[1],
    (2) for costs (other than fixed costs) only[2],
    (3) by one spouse against the other[3] on a claim in tort[4],
    (4) for delivery up of goods where the defendant will not be allowed the alternative of paying their value,
    (5) against the Crown, and

---

[1] See rule 12.10(a)(i).
[2] See rule 12.9(b).
[3] See rule 12.10(a)(ii).
[4] Tort may be defined as an act or a failure to do an act which causes harm or damage to another person and which gives the other person a right to claim compensation without having to rely on a contract with the person who caused the harm or damage.

(6) against persons or organisations who enjoy immunity from civil jurisdiction under the provisions of the International Organisations Acts 1968 and 1981.

DEFAULT JUDGMENT BY REQUEST

3 Requests for default judgment;

(1) in respect of a claim for a specified amount of money or for the delivery of goods where the defendant will be given the alternative of paying a specified sum representing their value, or for fixed costs only, must be in Form N205A or N225, and

(2) in respect of a claim where an amount of money (including an amount representing the value of goods) is to be decided by the court, must be in Form N205B or N227.

EVIDENCE

4.1 Both on a request and on an application for default judgment the court must be satisfied that:

(1) the particulars of claim have been served on the defendant (a certificate of service on the court file will be sufficient evidence),

(2) either the defendant has not filed an acknowledgment of service or has not filed a defence and that in either case the relevant period for doing so has expired,

(3) the defendant has not satisfied the claim, and

(4) the defendant has not returned an admission to the claimant under rule 14.4 or filed an admission with the court under rule 14.6.

4.2 On an application against a child or patient[5]:

(1) a litigation friend[6] to act on behalf of the child or patient must be appointed by the court before judgment can be obtained, and

(2) the claimant must satisfy the court by evidence that he is entitled to the judgment claimed.

4.3 On an application where the defendant was served with the claim either:

(1) outside the jurisdiction[7] without leave under the Civil Jurisdiction and Judgments Act 1982, or

(2) within the jurisdiction but when domiciled[8] in Scotland or Northern Ireland or in any other Convention territory[9],

and the defendant has not acknowledged service, the evidence must establish that:

(1) the claim is one that the court has power to hear and decide,

(2) no other court has exclusive jurisdiction under the Act to hear and decide the claim, and

(3) the claim has been properly served in accordance with Article 20 of Schedule 1, 3C or 4 of the Act.

4.4 On an application against a State[10] the evidence must:

(1) set out the grounds of the application,

(2) establish the facts proving that the State is excepted from the immunity conferred by section 1 of the State Immunity Act 1978,

(3) establish that the claim was sent through the Foreign and Commonwealth Office to the Ministry of Foreign Affairs of the State (unless the State agreed to a different form of service), and

(4) establish that the time for acknowledging service, which is extended to two months by section 12(2) of the Act, has expired.

(See rule 40.8 for when default judgment against a State takes effect.)

4.5 Evidence in support of an application referred to in paragraphs 4.3 and 4.4 above must be by affidavit.

---

[5] As defined in rule 21.1(2).
[6] As defined in the practice direction which supplements Part 21.
[7] As defined in rule 2.3.
[8] As determined in accordance with the provisions of ss. 41 to 46 of the Civil Jurisdictions and Judgments Act 1982.
[9] Means the territory of a Contracting State as defined in s. 1(3) of the Civil Jurisdiction and Judgments Act 1982.
[10] As defined in s.14 of the State Immunity Act 1978.

PD 12 PRACTICE DIRECTION — DEFAULT JUDGMENT

4.6 On an application for judgment for delivery up of goods where the defendant will not be given the alternative of paying their value, the evidence must identify the goods and state where the claimant believes the goods to be situated and why their specific delivery up is sought.

GENERAL

5.1 On all applications to which this practice direction applies, other than those referred to in paragraphs 4.3 and 4.4 above[11], notice should be given in accordance with Part 23.

5.2 Where default judgment is given on a claim for a sum of money expressed in a foreign currency, the judgment should be for the amount of the foreign currency with the addition of 'or the Sterling equivalent at the time of payment'.

---

[11] See rule 12.11(4) and (5).

CPR PART 13   SETTING ASIDE OR VARYING DEFAULT JUDGMENT

CONTENTS OF THIS PART
Scope of this Part   Rule 13.1
Cases where the court must set aside judgment entered under Part 12   Rule 13.2
Cases where the court may set aside or vary judgment entered
   under Part 12   Rule 13.3
Application to set aside or vary judgment — procedure   Rule 13.4
Claimant's duty to apply to set aside judgment   Rule 13.5
Abandoned claim restored where default judgment set aside   Rule 13.6

13.1   SCOPE OF THIS PART
The rules in this Part set out the procedure for setting aside or varying judgment entered under Part 12 (default judgment).
(CCR Order 22, r. 10 sets out the procedure for varying the rate at which a judgment debt must be paid)

13.2   CASES WHERE THE COURT MUST SET ASIDE JUDGMENT ENTERED UNDER PART 12
13.2   The court must set aside[GL] a judgment entered under Part 12 if judgment was wrongly entered because—
   (a) in the case of a judgment in default of an acknowledgment of service, any of the conditions in rule 12.3(1) and 12.3(3) was not satisfied;
   (b) in the case of a judgment in default of a defence, any of the conditions in rule 12.3(2) and 12.3(3) was not satisfied; or
   (c) the whole of the claim was satisfied before judgment was entered.

13.3   CASES WHERE THE COURT MAY SET ASIDE OR VARY JUDGMENT ENTERED UNDER PART 12
   (1) In any other case, the court may set aside[GL] or vary a judgment entered under Part 12 if—
      (a) the defendant has a real prospect of successfully defending the claim; or
      (b) it appears to the court that there is some other good reason why—
         (i) the judgment should be set aside or varied; or
         (ii) the defendant should be allowed to defend the claim.
   (2) In considering whether to set aside[GL] or vary a judgment entered under Part 12, the matters to which the court must have regard include whether the person seeking to set aside the judgment made an application to do so promptly.
(Rule 3.1(3) provides that the court may attach conditions when it makes an order)

13.4   APPLICATION TO SET ASIDE OR VARY JUDGMENT — PROCEDURE
   (1) Where—
      (a) the claim is for a specified amount of money;
      (b) the judgment was obtained in a court which is not the defendant's home court;
      (c) the claim has not been transferred to another defendant's home court under rule 14.12 (admission — determination of rate of payment by judge) or rule 26.2 (automatic transfer); and
      (d) the defendant is an individual
the court will transfer an application by a defendant under this Part to set aside[GL] or vary judgment to the defendant's home court.
   (1A) In this rule, 'defendant's home court' has the meaning given to it by rule 2.3, except that reference to the defendant's address for service shall be a reference

CPR PART 13   SETTING ASIDE OR VARYING DEFAULT JUDGMENT

to that address shown on the last of the following documents to be filed at court giving an address for service for the defendant—
(a)   the application to set aside$^{(GL)}$;
(b)   any acknowledgment of service; and
(c)   the claim form.
(2)   Paragraph (1) does not apply where the claim was commenced in a specialist list.
(3)   An application under rule 13.3 (cases where the court may set aside$^{(GL)}$ or vary judgment) must be supported by evidence.

13.5   CLAIMANT'S DUTY TO APPLY TO SET ASIDE JUDGMENT
(1)   This rule applies where—
(a)   the claimant has purported to serve particulars of claim; and
(b)   the claimant has entered judgment under Part 12 against the defendant to whom the particulars of claim were sent.
(2)   If a claimant who has entered judgment subsequently has good reason to believe that the particulars of claim did not reach the defendant before the claimant entered judgment, he must—
(a)   file a request for the judgment to beset aside$^{(GL)}$; or
(b)   apply to the court for directions.
(3)   The claimant may take no further step in the proceedings for the enforcement of the judgment until the judgment has been set aside$^{(GL)}$ or the court has disposed of the application for directions.

13.6   ABANDONED CLAIM RESTORED WHERE DEFAULT JUDGMENT SET ASIDE
Where—
(a)   the claimant claimed a remedy in addition to one specified in rule 12.4(1) (claims in respect of which the claimant may obtain default judgment by filing a request);
(b)   the claimant abandoned his claim for that remedy in order to obtain default judgment on request in accordance with rule 12.4(3); and
(c)   that default judgment is set aside$^{(GL)}$ under this Part,
the abandoned claim is restored when the default judgment is set aside.

CPR PART 14 ADMISSIONS

CONTENTS OF THIS PART

Making an admission	Rule 14.1
Period for making an admission	Rule 14.2
Admission by notice in writing — application for judgment	Rule 14.3
Admission of whole of claim for specified amount of money	Rule 14.4
Admission of part of claim for specified amount of money	Rule 14.5
Admission of liability to pay whole of claim for unspecified amount of money	Rule 14.6
Admission of liability to pay claim for unspecified amount of money where defendant offers a sum in satisfaction of the claim	Rule 14.7
Allocation of claims in relation to outstanding matters	Rule 14.8
Request for time to pay	Rule 14.9
Determination of rate of payment	Rule 14.10
Determination of rate of payment by court officer	Rule 14.11
Determination of rate of payment by judge	Rule 14.12
Right of re-determination	Rule 14.13
Interest	Rule 14.14

14.1 MAKING AN ADMISSION

(1) A party may admit the truth of the whole or any part of another party's case.

(2) He may do this by giving notice in writing (such as in a statement of case or by letter).

(3) Where the only remedy which the claimant is seeking is the payment of money, the defendant may also make an admission in accordance with—

    (a) rule 14.4 (admission of whole claim for specified amount of money);

    (b) rule 14.5 (admission of part of claim for specified amount of money);

    (c) rule 14.6 (admission of liability to pay whole of claim for unspecified amount of money); or

    (d) rule 14.7 (admission of liability to pay claim for unspecified amount of money where defendant offers a sum in satisfaction of the claim).

(4) Where the defendant makes an admission as mentioned in paragraph (3), the claimant has a right to enter judgment except where—

    (a) the defendant is a child or patient; or

    (b) the claimant is a child or patient and the admission is made under rule 14.5 or 14.7.

(Rule 21.10 provides that, where a claim is made by or on behalf of a child or patient or against a child or patient, no settlement, compromise or payment shall be valid, so far as it relates to that person's claim, without the approval of the court)

(5) The court may allow a party to amend or withdraw an admission.

(Rule 3.1(3) provides that the court may attach conditions when it makes an order)

14.2 PERIOD FOR MAKING AN ADMISSION

(1) The period for returning an admission under rule 14.4 or for filing it under rules 14.5, 14.6 or 14.7 is—

    (a) where the defendant is served with a claim form which states that particulars of claim will follow, 14 days after service of the particulars; and

    (b) in any other case, 14 days after service of the claim form.

(2) Paragraph (1) is subject to the following rules—

    (a) RSC Order 11, r. 1A (which specifies how the period for filing or returning an admission is calculated where the claim form is served out of the jurisdiction); and

    (b) rule 6.16(4) (which requires the court to specify the period for responding to the particulars of claim when it makes an order under that rule).

(3) A defendant may return an admission under rule 14.4 or file it under rules 14.5, 14.6 or 14.7 after the end of the period for returning or filing it specified in paragraph (1) if the claimant has not obtained default judgment under Part 12.

(4) If he does so, this Part shall apply as if he had made the admission within that period.

14.3 ADMISSION BY NOTICE IN WRITING — APPLICATION FOR JUDGMENT

(1) Where a party makes an admission under rule 14.1(2) (admission by notice in writing), any other party may apply for judgment on the admission.

(2) Judgment shall be such judgment as it appears to the court that the applicant is entitled to on the admission.

14.4 ADMISSION OF WHOLE OF CLAIM FOR SPECIFIED AMOUNT OF MONEY

(1) This rule applies where—
 (a) the only remedy which the claimant is seeking is the payment of a specified amount of money; and
 (b) the defendant admits the whole of the claim.

(2) The defendant may admit the claim by returning to the claimant an admission in the relevant practice form.

(3) The claimant may obtain judgment by filing a request in the relevant practice form and, if he does so—
 (a) if the defendant has not requested time to pay, the procedure in paragraphs (4) to (6) will apply;
 (b) if the defendant has requested time to pay, the procedure in rule 14.9 will apply.

(4) The claimant may specify in his request for judgment—
 (a) the date by which the whole of the judgment debt is to be paid; or
 (b) the times and rate at which it is to be paid by instalments.

(5) On receipt of the request for judgment the court will enter judgment.

(6) Judgment will be for the amount of the claim (less any payments made) and costs—
 (a) to be paid by the date or at the rate specified in the request for judgment; or
 (b) if none is specified, immediately.

(Rule 14.14 deals with the circumstances in which judgment under this rule may include interest)

14.5 ADMISSION OF PART OF A CLAIM FOR A SPECIFIED AMOUNT OF MONEY

(1) This rule applies where—
 (a) the only remedy which the claimant is seeking is the payment of a specified amount of money; and
 (b) the defendant admits part of the claim.

(2) The defendant may admit part of the claim by filing an admission in the relevant practice form.

(3) On receipt of the admission, the court will serve a notice on the claimant requiring him to return the notice stating that—
 (a) he accepts the amount admitted in satisfaction of the claim;
 (b) he does not accept the amount admitted by the defendant and wishes the proceedings to continue; or
 (c) if the defendant has requested time to pay, he accepts the amount admitted in satisfaction of the claim, but not the defendant's proposals as to payment.

(4) The claimant must—
 (a) file the notice; and
 (b) serve a copy on the defendant,
within 14 days after it is served on him.

(5) If the claimant does not file the notice within 14 days after it is served on him, the claim is stayed$^{(GL)}$ until he files the notice.

CPR PART 14 ADMISSIONS

(6) If the claimant accepts the amount admitted in satisfaction of the claim, he may obtain judgment by filing a request in the relevant practice form and, if he does so—

    (a) if the defendant has not requested time to pay, the procedure in paragraphs (7) to (9) will apply;

    (b) if the defendant has requested time to pay, the procedure in rule 14.9 will apply.

(7) The claimant may specify in his request for judgment—

    (a) the date by which the whole of the judgment debt is to be paid; or

    (b) the time and rate at which it is to be paid by instalments.

(8) On receipt of the request for judgment, the court will enter judgment.

(9) Judgment will be for the amount admitted (less any payments made) and costs—

    (a) to be paid by the date or at the rate specified in the request for judgment; or

    (b) if none is specified, immediately.

(If the claimant files notice under paragraph (3) that he wishes the proceedings to continue, the procedure which then follows is set out in Part 26)

14.6 ADMISSION OF LIABILITY TO PAY WHOLE OF CLAIM FOR UNSPECIFIED AMOUNT OF MONEY

(1) This rule applies where—

    (a) the only remedy which the claimant is seeking is the payment of money;

    (b) the amount of the claim is not specified; and

    (c) the defendant admits liability but does not offer to pay a specified amount of money in satisfaction of the claim.

(2) The defendant may admit the claim by filing an admission in the relevant practice form.

(3) On receipt of the admission, the court will serve a copy on the claimant.

(4) The claimant may obtain judgment by filing a request in the relevant practice form.

(5) If the claimant does not file a request for judgment within 14 days after service of the admission on him, the claim is stayed $^{(GL)}$ until he files the request.

(6) On receipt of the request for judgment the court will enter judgment.

(7) Judgment will be for an amount to be decided by the court and costs.

14.7 ADMISSION OF LIABILITY TO PAY CLAIM FOR UNSPECIFIED AMOUNT OF MONEY WHERE DEFENDANT OFFERS A SUM IN SATISFACTION OF THE CLAIM

(1) This rule applies where—

    (a) the only remedy which the claimant is seeking is the payment of money;

    (b) the amount of the claim is not specified; and

    (c) the defendant—

        (i) admits liability; and

        (ii) offers to pay a specified amount of money in satisfaction of the claim.

(2) The defendant may admit the claim by filing an admission in the relevant practice form.

(3) On receipt of the admission, the court will serve a notice on the claimant requiring him to return the notice stating whether or not he accepts the amount in satisfaction of the claim.

(4) If the claimant does not file the notice within 14 days after it is served on him, the claim is stayed$^{(GL)}$ until he files the notice.

(5) If the claimant accepts the offer he may obtain judgment by filing a request in the relevant practice form and if he does so—

    (a) if the defendant has not requested time to pay, the procedure in paragraphs (6) to (8) will apply;

    (b) if the defendant has requested time to pay, the procedure in rule 14.9 will apply.

(6) The claimant may specify in his request for judgment—

CPR PART 14 ADMISSIONS

    (a) the date by which the whole of the judgment debt is to be paid; or
    (b) the times and rate at which it is to be paid by instalments.
  (7) On receipt of the request for judgment, the court will enter judgment.
  (8) Judgment will be for the amount offered by the defendant (less any payments made) and costs—
    (a) to be paid on the date or at the rate specified in the request for judgment; or
    (b) if none is specified, immediately.
  (9) If the claimant does not accept the amount offered by the defendant, he may obtain judgment by filing a request in the relevant practice form.
  (10) Judgment under paragraph (9) will be for an amount to be decided by the court and costs.

14.8 ALLOCATION OF CLAIMS IN RELATION TO OUTSTANDING MATTERS

Where the court enters judgment under rule 14.6 or 14.7 for an amount to be decided by the court it will—
    (a) give any directions it considers appropriate; and
    (b) if it considers it appropriate, allocate the case.

14.9 REQUEST FOR TIME TO PAY

  (1) A defendant who makes an admission under rules 14.4, 14.5 or 14.7 (admission relating to a claim for a specified amount of money or offering to pay a specified amount of money) may make a request for time to pay.
  (2) A request for time to pay is a proposal about the date of payment or a proposal to pay by instalments at the times and rate specified in the request.
  (3) The defendant's request for time to pay must be served or filed (as the case may be) with his admission.
  (4) If the claimant accepts the defendant's request, he may obtain judgment by filing a request in the relevant practice form.
  (5) On receipt of the request for judgment, the court will enter judgment.
  (6) Judgment will be—
    (a) where rule 14.4 applies, for the amount of the claim (less any payments made) and costs;
    (b) where rule 14.5 applies, for the amount admitted (less any payments made) and costs; or
    (c) where rule 14.7 applies, for the amount offered by the defendant (less any payments made) and costs; and
(in all cases) will be for payment at the time and rate specified in the defendant's request for time to pay.
(Rule 14.10 sets out the procedure to be followed if the claimant does not accept the defendant's request for time to pay)

14.10 DETERMINATION OF RATE OF PAYMENT

  (1) This rule applies where the defendant makes a request for time to pay under rule 14.9.
  (2) If the claimant does not accept the defendant's proposals for payment, he must file a notice in the relevant practice form.
  (3) Where the defendant's admission was served direct on the claimant, a copy of the admission and the request for time to pay must be filed with the claimant's notice.
  (4) When the court receives the claimant's notice, it will enter judgment for the amount admitted (less any payments made) to be paid at the time and rate of payment determined by the court.

14.11 DETERMINATION OF RATE OF PAYMENT BY COURT OFFICER

  (1) A court officer may exercise the powers of the court under rule 14.10(4) where the amount outstanding (including costs) is not more than £50,000.
  (2) Where a court officer is to determine the time and rate of payment, he must do so without a hearing.

14.12 DETERMINATION OF RATE OF PAYMENT BY JUDGE

(1) Where a judge is to determine the time and rate of payment, he may do so without a hearing.

(2) Where a judge is to determine the time and rate of payment at a hearing, the proceedings must be transferred automatically to the defendant's home court if—

 (a) the only claim is for a specified amount of money;
 (b) the defendant is an individual;
 (c) the claim has not been transferred to another defendant's home court under rule 13.4 (application to set aside$^{(GL)}$ or vary default judgment — procedure) or rule 26.2 (automatic transfer);
 (d) the claim was not started in the defendant's home court; and
 (e) the claim was not started in a specialist list.

(Rule 2.3 explains which court is a defendant's home court)

(3) If there is to be a hearing to determine the time and rate of payment, the court must give each party at least 7 days' notice of the hearing.

14.13 RIGHT OF RE-DETERMINATION

(1) Where—
 (a) a court officer has determined the time and rate of payment under rule 14.11; or
 (b) a judge has determined the time and rate of payment under rule 14.12 without a hearing,
either party may apply for the decision to be re-determined by a judge.

(2) An application for re-determination must be made within 14 days after service of the determination on the applicant.

(3) Where an application for re-determination is made, the proceedings must be transferred to the defendant's home court if—

 (a) the only claim (apart from a claim for interest or costs) is for a specified amount of money;
 (b) the defendant is an individual;
 (c) the claim has not been transferred to another defendant's home court under rule 13.4 (application to set aside$^{(GL)}$ or vary default judgment — procedure) or rule 26.2 (automatic transfer);
 (d) the claim was not started in the defendant's home court; and
 (e) the claim was not started in a specialist list.

(Rule 2.3 explains which court is a defendant's home court)

14.14 INTEREST

(1) Judgment under rule 14.4 (admission of whole of claim for specified amount of money) shall include the amount of interest claimed to the date of judgment if—

 (a) the particulars of claim include the details required by rule 16.4;
 (b) where interest is claimed under section 35A of the Supreme Court Act 1981 or section 69 of the County Courts Act 1984, the rate is no higher than the rate of interest payable on judgment debts at the date when the claim form was issued; and
 (c) the claimant's request for judgment includes a calculation of the interest claimed for the period from the date up to which interest was stated to be calculated in the claim form to the date of the request for judgment.

(2) In any case where judgment is entered under rule 14.4 and the conditions in paragraph (1) are not satisfied judgment shall be for an amount of interest to be decided by the court.

(3) Where judgment is entered for an amount of interest to be decided by the court, the court will give directions for the management of the case.

PD 14 PRACTICE DIRECTION — ADMISSIONS

This practice direction supplements CPR Part 14

ADMISSIONS GENERALLY

1.1 Rules 14.1 and 14.2 deal with the manner in which a defendant may make an admission of a claim or part of a claim.

1.2 Rules 14.3, 14.4, 14.5, 14.6 and 14.7 set out how judgment may be obtained on a written admission.

FORMS

2.1 When particulars of claim are served on a defendant the forms for responding to the claim that will accompany them will include a form[1] for making an admission.

2.2 If the defendant is requesting time to pay he should complete as fully as possible the statement of means contained in the admission form, or otherwise give in writing the same details of his means as could have been given in the admission form.

RETURNING OR FILING THE ADMISSION

3.1 If the defendant wishes to make an admission in respect of the whole of a claim for a specified amount of money, the admission form or other written notice of the admission should be completed and returned to the claimant within 14 days of service of the particulars of claim[2].

3.2 If the defendant wishes to make an admission in respect of a part of a claim for a specified amount of money, or in respect of a claim for an unspecified amount of money, the admission form or other written notice of admission should be completed and filed with the court within 14 days of service of the particulars of claim[3].

3.3 The defendant may also file a defence under rule 15.2.

REQUEST FOR TIME TO PAY

4.1 A defendant who makes an admission in respect of a claim for a specified sum of money or offers to pay a sum of money in respect of a claim for an unspecified sum may, in the admission form, make a request for time to pay[4].

4.2 If the claimant accepts the defendant's request, he may obtain judgment by filing a request for judgment contained in Form N225A[5]; the court will then enter judgment for payment at the time and rate specified in the defendant's request[6].

4.3 If the claimant does not accept the request for time to pay, he should file notice to that effect by completing Form N225A; the court will then enter judgment for the amount of the admission (less any payments made) at a time and rate of payment decided by the court (see rule 14.10).

DETERMINING THE RATE OF PAYMENT

5.1 In deciding the time and rate of payment the court will take into account:
    (1) the defendant's statement of means set out in the admission form or in any other written notice of the admission filed,
    (2) the claimant's objections to the defendant's request set out in the claimant's notice[7], and
    (3) any other relevant factors.

---

[1] Practice forms N9A (specified amount) or N9C (unspecified amount).
[2] Rules 14.2 and 14.4.
[3] Rules 14.2, 14.5, 14.6 and 14.7.
[4] Rule 14.9.
[5] Rule 14.9(4).
[6] Rule 14.9(5) and (6).
[7] Practice form N225A.

5.2 The time and rate of payment may be decided:
   (1) by a judge with or without a hearing, or
   (2) by a court officer without a hearing provided that—
      (a) the only claim is for a specified sum of money, and
      (b) the amount outstanding is not more than £50,000 (including costs).

5.3 Where a decision has been made without a hearing whether by a court officer or by a judge, either party may apply for the decision to be re-determined by a judge[8].

5.4 If the decision was made by a court officer the re-determination may take place without a hearing, unless a hearing is requested in the application notice.

5.5 If the decision was made by a judge the re-determination must be made at a hearing unless the parties otherwise agree.

5.6 Rule 14.13(2) describes how to apply for a re-determination.

VARYING THE RATE OF PAYMENT

6.1 Either party may, on account of a change in circumstances since the date of the decision (or re-determination as the case may be) apply to vary the time and rate of payment of instalments still remaining unpaid.

6.2 An application to vary under paragraph 6.1 above should be made in accordance with Part 23.

---

[8] Rule 14.13(1).

CPR PART 15   DEFENCE AND REPLY

CONTENTS OF THIS PART

Part not to apply where claimant uses Part 8 procedure	Rule 15.1
Filing a defence	Rule 15.2
Consequence of not filing a defence	Rule 15.3
The period for filing a defence	Rule 15.4
Agreement extending the period for filing a defence	Rule 15.5
Service of copy of defence	Rule 15.6
Making a counterclaim	Rule 15.7
Reply to defence	Rule 15.8
No statement of case after a reply to be filed without court's permission	Rule 15.9
Claimant's notice where defence is that money claimed has been paid	Rule 15.10
Claim stayed if it is not defended or admitted	Rule 15.11

15.1   PART NOT TO APPLY WHERE CLAIMANT USES PART 8 PROCEDURE

This Part does not apply where the claimant uses the procedure set out in Part 8 (alternative procedure for claims).

15.2   FILING A DEFENCE

A defendant who wishes to defend all or part of a claim must file a defence.
(Part 14 contains further provisions which apply where the defendant admits a claim)

15.3   CONSEQUENCE OF NOT FILING A DEFENCE

If a defendant fails to file a defence, the claimant may obtain default judgment if Part 12 allows it.

15.4   THE PERIOD FOR FILING A DEFENCE

(1) The general rule is that the period for filing a defence is—
   (a) 14 days after service of the particulars of claim; or
   (b) if the defendant files an acknowledgment of service under Part 10, 28 days after service of the particulars of claim.
(Rule 7.4 provides for the particulars of claim to be contained in or served with the claim form or served within 14 days of service of the claim form)
(2) The general rule is subject to the following rules—
   (a) RSC Order 11, r. 1B (which specifies how the period for filing a defence is calculated where the claim form is served out of the jurisdiction);
   (b) rule 11 (which provides that, where the defendant makes an application disputing the court's jurisdiction, he need not file a defence before the hearing);
   (c) rule 24.4(2) (which provides that, if the claimant applies for summary judgment before the defendant has filed a defence, the defendant need not file a defence before the summary judgment hearing); and
   (d) rule 6.16(4) (which requires the court to specify the period for responding to the particulars of claim when it makes an order under that rule).

15.5   AGREEMENT EXTENDING THE PERIOD FOR FILING A DEFENCE

(1) The defendant and the claimant may agree that the period for filing a defence specified in rule 15.4 shall be extended by up to 28 days.
(2) Where the defendant and the claimant agree to extend the period for filing a defence, the defendant must notify the court in writing.

15.6   SERVICE OF COPY OF DEFENCE

A copy of the defence must be served on every other party.

CPR PART 15   DEFENCE AND REPLY

(Part 16 sets out what a defence must contain)

15.7 MAKING A COUNTERCLAIM
Part 20 applies to a defendant who wishes to make a counterclaim.

15.8 REPLY TO DEFENCE
If a claimant files a reply to the defence, he must—
    (a) file his reply when he files his allocation questionnaire; and
    (b) serve his reply on the other parties at the same time as he files it.
(Rule 26.3(6) requires the parties to file allocation questionnaires and specifies the period for doing so)
(Part 22 requires a reply to be verified by a statement of truth)

15.9 NO STATEMENT OF CASE AFTER A REPLY TO BE FILED WITHOUT COURT'S PERMISSION
A party may not file or serve any statement of case after a reply without the permission of the court.

15.10 CLAIMANT'S NOTICE WHERE DEFENCE IS THAT MONEY CLAIMED HAS BEEN PAID
(1) Where—
    (a) the only claim (apart from a claim for costs and interest) is for a specified amount of money; and
    (b) the defendant states in his defence that he has paid to the claimant the amount claimed,
the court will send notice to the claimant requiring him to state in writing whether he wishes the proceedings to continue.

(2) When the claimant responds, he must serve a copy of his response on the defendant.

(3) If the claimant fails to respond under this rule within 28 days after service of the court's notice on him the claim shall be stayed[GL].

(4) Where a claim is stayed under this rule any party may apply for the stay[GL] to be lifted.

(If the claimant files notice under this rule that he wishes the proceedings to continue, the procedure which then follows is set out in Part 26)

15.11 CLAIM STAYED IF IT IS NOT DEFENDED OR ADMITTED
(1) Where—
    (a) at least 6 months have expired since the end of the period for filing a defence specified in rule 15.4;
    (b) no defendant has served or filed an admission or filed a defence or counterclaim; and
    (c) the claimant has not entered or applied for judgment under Part 12 (default judgment), or Part 24 (summary judgment),
the claim shall be stayed[GL].

(2) Where a claim is stayed[GL] under this rule any party may apply for the stay to be lifted.

PD 15 PRACTICE DIRECTION — DEFENCE AND REPLY

This practice direction supplements CPR Part 15

DEFENDING THE CLAIM

1.1 The provisions of Part 15 do not apply to claims in respect of which the Part 8 procedure is being used.

1.2 In relation to specialist proceedings (see CPR Part 49) in respect of which special provisions for defence and reply are made by the rules and practice directions applicable to those claims, the provisions of Part 15 apply only to the extent that they are not inconsistent with those rules and practice directions.

1.3 Form N9B (specified amount) or N9D (unspecified amount or non-money claims) may be used for the purpose of defence and is included in the response pack served on the defendant with the particulars of claim.

1.4 Attention is drawn to rule 15.3 which sets out a possible consequence of not filing a defence.

(Part 16 (statements of case) and the practice direction which supplements it contain rules and directions about the contents of a defence.)

STATEMENT OF TRUTH

2.1 Part 22 requires a defence to be verified by a statement of truth.

2.2 The form of the statement of truth is as follows:

'[I believe] [the defendant believes] that the facts stated in this defence are true.'

2.3 Attention is drawn to rule 32.14 which sets out the consequences of verifying a statement of case containing a false statement without an honest belief in its truth.

(For information about statements of truth see Part 22 and the practice direction which supplements it.)

GENERAL

3.1 Where a defendant to a claim serves a counterclaim under Part 20, the defence and counterclaim should normally form one document with the counterclaim following on from the defence.

3.2 Where a claimant serves a reply and a defence to counterclaim, the reply and defence to counterclaim should normally form one document with the defence to counterclaim following on from the reply.

3.3 Where a claim has been stayed under rules 15.10(3) or 15.11(1) any party may apply for the stay to be lifted[1].

3.4 The application should be made in accordance with Part 23 and should give the reason for the applicant's delay in proceeding with or responding to the claim.

---

[1] Rules 15.10(4) and 15.11(2).

CPR PART 16   STATEMENTS OF CASE

CONTENTS OF THIS PART
Part not to apply where claimant uses Part 8 procedure	Rule 16.1
Contents of the claim form	Rule 16.2
Statement of value to be included in the claim form	Rule 16.3
Contents of the particulars of claim	Rule 16.4
Contents of defence	Rule 16.5
Defence of set-off	Rule 16.6
Reply to defence	Rule 16.7
Court's power to dispense with statements of case	Rule 16.8

16.1   PART NOT TO APPLY WHERE CLAIMANT USES PART 8 PROCEDURE
This Part does not apply where the claimant uses the procedure set out in Part 8 (alternative procedure for claims).

16.2   CONTENTS OF THE CLAIM FORM
   (1)   The claim form must—
      (a)   contain a concise statement of the nature of the claim;
      (b)   specify the remedy which the claimant seeks;
      (c)   where the claimant is making a claim for money, contain a statement of value in accordance with rule 16.3; and
      (d)   contain such other matters as may be set out in a practice direction.
   (2)   If the particulars of claim specified in rule 16.4 are not contained in, or are not served with the claim form, the claimant must state on the claim form that the particulars of claim will follow.
   (3)   If the claimant is claiming in a representative capacity, the claim form must state what that capacity is.
   (4)   If the defendant is sued in a representative capacity, the claim form must state what that capacity is.
   (5)   The court may grant any remedy to which the claimant is entitled even if that remedy is not specified in the claim form.
(Part 22 requires a claim form to be verified by a statement of truth)

16.3   STATEMENT OF VALUE TO BE INCLUDED IN THE CLAIM FORM
   (1)   This rule applies where the claimant is making a claim for money.
   (2)   The claimant must, in the claim form, state—
     (a)   the amount of money which he is claiming;
     (b)   that he expects to recover—
        (i)   not more than £5,000;
       (ii)   more than £5,000 but not more than £15,000; or
      (iii)   more than £15,000; or
     (b)   that he cannot say how much he expects to recover.
   (3)   In a claim for personal injuries, the claimant must also state in the claim form whether the amount which he expects to recover as general damages for pain, suffering and loss of amenity is—
     (a)   not more than £1,000; or
     (b)   more than £1,000.
   (4)   In a claim which includes a claim by a tenant of residential premises against his landlord where the tenant is seeking an order requiring the landlord to carry out repairs or other work to the premises, the claimant must also state in the claim form—
     (a)   whether the estimated costs of those repairs or other work is—
        (i)   not more than £1,000; or
       (ii)   more than £1,000; and
     (b)   whether the financial value of any other claim for damages is—

(i) not more than £1,000; or
(ii) more than £1,000.

(5) If the claim form is to be issued in the High Court it must, where this rule applies—
   (a) state that the claimant expects to recover more than £15,000;
   (b) state that some other enactment provides that the claim may be commenced only in the High Court and specify that enactment;
   (c) if the claim is a claim for personal injuries state that the claimant expects to recover £50,000 or more; or
   (d) state that the claim is to be in one of the specialist High Court lists and state which list.

(6) When calculating how much he expects to recover, the claimant must disregard any possibility—
   (a) that he may recover—
      (i) interest;
      (ii) costs;
   (b) that the court may make a finding of contributory negligence against him;
   (c) that the defendant may make a counterclaim or that the defence may include a set-off; or
   (d) that the defendant may be liable to pay an amount of money which the court awards to the claimant to the Secretary of State for Social Security under section 6 of the Social Security (Recovery of Benefits) Act 1997.

(7) The statement of value in the claim form does not limit the power of the court to give judgment for the amount which it finds the claimant is entitled to.

16.4 CONTENTS OF THE PARTICULARS OF CLAIM

(1) Particulars of claim must include—
   (a) a concise statement of the facts on which the claimant relies;
   (b) if the claimant is seeking interest, a statement to that effect and the details set out in paragraph (2);
   (c) if the claimant is seeking aggravated damages[GL] or exemplary damages[GL], a statement to that effect and his grounds for claiming them;
   (d) if the claimant is seeking provisional damages, a statement to that effect and his grounds for claiming them; and
   (e) such other matters as may be set out in a practice direction.

(2) If the claimant is seeking interest he must—
   (a) state whether he is doing so—
      (i) under the terms of a contract;
      (ii) under an enactment and if so which; or
      (iii) on some other basis and if so what that basis is; and
   (b) if the claim is for a specified amount of money, state—
      (i) the percentage rate at which interest is claimed;
      (ii) the date from which it is claimed;
      (iii) the date to which it is calculated, which must not be later than the date on which the claim form is issued;
      (iv) the total amount of interest claimed to the date of calculation; and
      (v) the daily rate at which interest accrues after that date.

(Part 22 requires particulars of claim to be verified by a statement of truth)

16.5 CONTENTS OF DEFENCE

(1) In his defence, the defendant must state—
   (a) which of the allegations in the particulars of claim he denies;
   (b) which allegations he is unable to admit or deny, but which he requires the claimant to prove; and
   (c) which allegations he admits.

(2) Where the defendant denies an allegation—
   (a) he must state his reasons for doing so; and
   (b) if he intends to put forward a different version of events from that given by the claimant, he must state his own version.

CPR PART 16 STATEMENTS OF CASE

(3) A defendant who—
  (a) fails to deal with an allegation; but
  (b) has set out in his defence the nature of his case in relation to the issue to which that allegation is relevant, shall be taken to require that allegation to be proved.

(4) Where the claim includes a money claim, a defendant shall be taken to require that any allegation relating to the amount of money claimed be proved unless he expressly admits the allegation.

(5) Subject to paragraphs (3) and (4), a defendant who fails to deal with an allegation shall be taken to admit that allegation.

(6) If the defendant disputes the claimant's statement of value under rule 16.3 he must—
  (a) state why he disputes it; and
  (b) if he is able, give his own statement of the value of the claim.

(7) If the defendant is defending in a representative capacity, he must state what that capacity is.

(8) If the defendant has not filed an acknowledgment of service under Part 10, he must give an address for service.

(Part 22 requires a defence to be verified by a statement of truth)

(Rule 6.5 provides that an address for service must be within the jurisdiction)

16.6 DEFENCE OF SET-OFF

Where a defendant—
  (a) contends he is entitled to money from the claimant; and
  (b) relies on this as a defence to the whole or part of the claim,
the contention may be included in the defence and set off against the claim, whether or not it is also a Part 20 claim.

16.7 REPLY TO DEFENCE

(1) A claimant who does not file a reply to the defence shall not be taken to admit the matters raised in the defence.

(2) A claimant who—
  (a) files a reply to a defence; but
  (b) fails to deal with a matter raised in the defence,
shall be taken to require that matter to be proved.

(Part 22 requires a reply to be verified by a statement of truth)

16.8 COURT'S POWER TO DISPENSE WITH STATEMENTS OF CASE

If a claim form has been—
  (a) issued in accordance with rule 7.2; and
  (b) served in accordance with rule 7.5,
the court may make an order that the claim will continue without any other statement of case.

PD 16 PRACTICE DIRECTION — STATEMENTS OF CASE

This practice direction supplements CPR Part 16

GENERAL

1.1 The provisions of Part 16 do not apply to claims in respect of which the Part 8 procedure is being used.

1.2 In relation to specialist proceedings (see CPR Part 49) in respect of which special provisions for statements of case are made by the rules and practice directions applicable to those claims, the provisions of Part 16 and of this practice direction apply only to the extent that they are not inconsistent with those rules and practice directions.

THE CLAIM FORM

2 Rule 16.2 refers to matters which the claim form must contain. Where the claim is for money, the claim form must also contain the statement of value referred to in rule 16.3.

(For information about how and where a claim may be started see Part 7 and the practice direction which supplements it.)

PARTICULARS OF CLAIM

3.1 If practicable, the particulars of claim should be set out in the claim form.

3.2 Where the claimant does not include the particulars of claim in the claim form, particulars of claim may be served separately:

(1) either at the same time as the claim form, or

(2) within 14 days after service of the claim form[1] provided that the service of the particulars of claim is not later than 4 months from the date of issue of the claim form[2] (or 6 months where the claim form is to be served out of the jurisdiction[3]).

3.3 If the particulars of claim are not included in or have not been served with the claim form, the claim form must also contain a statement that particulars of claim will follow[4].

3.4 Particulars of claim which are not included in the claim form must be verified by a statement of truth, the form of which is as follows:

'[I believe] [the claimant believes] that the facts stated in these particulars of claim are true.'

3.5 Attention is drawn to rule 32.14 which sets out the consequences of verifying a statement of case containing a false statement without an honest belief in its truth.

3.6 The full particulars of claim must include:

(1) the matters set out in rule 16.4, and

(2) where appropriate, the matters set out in practice directions relating to specific types of claims.

3.7 Attention is drawn to the provisions of rule 16.4(2) in respect of a claim for interest.

3.8 Particulars of claim served separately from the claim form must also contain:

(1) the name of the court in which the claim is proceeding,
(2) the claim number,
(3) the title of the proceedings, and
(4) the claimant's address for service.

---

[1] See rule 7.4(1)(b).
[2] See rules 7.4(2) and 7.5(2).
[3] See rule 7.5(3).
[4] See rule 16.2(2).

MATTERS WHICH MUST BE INCLUDED IN THE PARTICULARS OF CLAIM IN CERTAIN TYPES OF CLAIM

Personal injury claims

4.1 The particulars of claim must contain:
   (1) the claimant's date of birth, and
   (2) brief details of the claimant's personal injuries.

4.2 The claimant must attach to his particulars of claim a schedule of details of any past and future expenses and losses which he claims.

4.3 Where the claimant is relying on the evidence of a medical practitioner the claimant must attach to or serve with his particulars of claim a report from a medical practitioner about the personal injuries which he alleges in his claim.

4.4 In a provisional damages claim the claimant must state in his particulars of claim:
   (1) that he is seeking an award of provisional damages under either section 32A of the Supreme Court Act 1981 or section 51 of the County Courts Act 1984,
   (2) that there is a chance that at some future time the claimant will develop some serious disease or suffer some serious deterioration in his physical or mental condition, and
   (3) specify the disease or type of deterioration in respect of which an application may be made at a future date.

(Part 41 and the practice direction which supplements it contain information about awards for provisional damages.)

Fatal accident claims

5.1 In a fatal accident claim the claimant must state in his particulars of claim:
   (1) that it is brought under the Fatal Accidents Act 1976,
   (2) the dependents on whose behalf the claim is made,
   (3) the date of birth of each dependent, and
   (4) details of the nature of the dependency claim.

5.2 A fatal accident claim may include a claim for damages for bereavement.

5.3 In a fatal accident claim the claimant may also bring a claim under the Law Reform (Miscellaneous Provisions) Act 1934 on behalf of the estate of the deceased.

(For information on apportionment under the Law Reform (Miscellaneous Provisions) Act 1934 and the Fatal Accidents Act 1976 or between dependants see Part 37 and the practice direction which supplements it.)

Recovery of land

6 In a claim for recovery of land the particulars of claim must:
   (1) identify the land sought to be recovered,
   (2) state whether the claim relates to residential premises,
   (3) if the claim relates to residential premises, and the tenancy is one which otherwise would be a protected tenancy within the meaning of the Rent Act 1977, state whether the rateable value of the premises on every day specified by section 4(2) of the Rent Act 1977 in relation to the premises exceeds the sum so specified or whether the rent for the time being payable in respect of the premises exceeds the sum specified in section 4(4)(b) of the Act,
   (4) where the claim relates to residential premises and is for non-payment of rent, state—
      (a) the amount due at the start of the proceedings,
      (b) details of all payments which have been missed,
      (c) details of any history of late or under-payment,
      (d) any previous steps taken to recover the arrears of rent with full details of any court proceedings, and
      (e) any relevant information about the defendant's circumstances, in particular whether any payments are made on his behalf directly to the claimant under the Social Security Contributions and Benefits Act 1992,
   (5) give details about the agreement or tenancy, if any, under which the land was held, stating when it determined and the amount of money payable by way of rent or licence fee,

PD 16 PRACTICE DIRECTION — STATEMENTS OF CASE

(6) in a case to which section 138 of the County Courts Act 1984 applies (forfeiture for non-payment of rent), state the daily rate at which the rent in arrear is to be calculated,

(7) state the ground on which possession is claimed whether statutory or otherwise, and

(8) in a case where the claimant knows of any person entitled to claim relief against forfeiture as underlessee (including a mortgagee) under section 146(4) of the Law of Property Act 1925 (or in accordance with section 38 of the Supreme Court Act 1981), give the name and address of that person.

(See also further rules about recovery of land in RSC Orders 88 and 113 (Schedule 1 to the CPR) and CCR Orders 6 and 24 (Schedule 2 to the CPR).

Hire purchase claims

7.1 Where the claim is for the delivery of goods let under a hire-purchase agreement or conditional sale agreement to a person other than a company or other corporation, the claimant must state in the particulars of claim:

(1) the date of the agreement,
(2) the parties to the agreement,
(3) the number or other identification of the agreement,
(4) where the claimant was not one of the original parties to the agreement, the means by which the rights and duties of the creditor passed to him,
(5) whether the agreement is a regulated agreement, and if it is not a regulated agreement, the reason why,
(6) the place where the agreement was signed by the defendant,
(7) the goods claimed,
(8) the total price of the goods,
(9) the paid-up sum,
(10) the unpaid balance of the total price,
(11) whether a default notice or a notice under section 76(1) or 98(1) of the Consumer Credit Act 1974 has been served on the defendant, and if it has, the date and method of service,
(12) the date when the right to demand delivery of the goods accrued,
(13) the amount (if any) claimed as an alternative to the delivery of goods, and
(14) the amount (if any) claimed in addition to—
  (a) the delivery of the goods, or
  (b) any claim under (13) above,
with the grounds of each claim.

(If the agreement is a regulated agreement the procedure set out in the practice direction relating to Consumer Credit Act claims (which supplements Part 7) should be used.)

7.2 Where the claim is not for the delivery of goods, the claimant must state in his particulars of claim:

(1) the matters set out in paragraph 8.1(1) to (6) above,
(2) the goods let under the agreement,
(3) the amount of the total price,
(4) the paid-up sum,
(5) the amount (if any) claimed as being due and unpaid in respect of any instalment or instalments of the total price, and
(6) the nature and amount of any other claim and how it arises.

Defamation

8.1 If the claim form starting a claim:

(1) for libel does not include or have served with it the full particulars of claim, at least sufficient detail must be given of the publications which are the subject of the claim to enable them to be identified, and

(2) for slander does not include or have served with it the full particulars of claim, at least sufficient detail must be given of the words complained of, including to whom they were spoken and when, to enable them to be identified.

8.2 Where in a claim for libel or slander the claimant alleges that the words or matters complained of were used in a defamatory sense other than their ordinary meaning, the particulars of claim must describe that defamatory sense.

8.3 Where a defendant to a claim for libel or slander alleges that the words complained of are true, or are fair comment on a matter of public interest, or similar, the claimant must serve a reply specifically admitting or denying the allegation and giving the facts on which he relies, unless they are set out elsewhere.

8.4 In a claim for libel or slander the claimant need not set out specific details of malice in his particulars of claim. However, if the defendant contends that any of the words or matters:

(1) are fair comment on a matter of public interest, or

(2) were published on a privileged occasion,

and the claimant intends to allege that the defendant acted with express malice, the claimant must serve a reply giving details of the facts or matters relied on.

8.5 A claimant must give full details of the facts and matters on which he relies in support of his claim for damages and of any conduct of the defendant which the claimant alleges has increased the loss suffered (and see rule 16.4(1)(c) in respect of aggravated or exemplary damages).

8.6 In a claim for slander the precise words used and the names of the persons to whom they were spoken must be set out in the particulars of claim.

8.7 RSC Order 82 (Schedule 1 to the CPR) contains additional requirements relating to defamation claims.

OTHER MATTERS TO BE INCLUDED IN PARTICULARS OF CLAIM

9.1 Where a claim is made for an injunction or declaration in respect of or relating to any land or the possession, occupation, use or enjoyment of any land the particulars of claim must:

(1) state whether or not the injunction or declaration relates to residential premises, and

(2) identify the land (by reference to a plan where necessary).

9.2 Where a claim is brought to enforce a right to recover possession of goods the particulars of claim must contain a statement showing the value of the goods.

9.3 Where a claim is based upon a written agreement:

(1) a copy of the contract or documents constituting the agreement should be attached to or served with the particulars of claim and the original(s) should be available at the hearing, and

(2) any general conditions of sale incorporated in the contract should also be attached (but where the contract is or the documents constituting the agreement are bulky this practice direction is complied with by attaching or serving only the relevant parts of the contract or documents).

9.4 Where a claim is based upon an oral agreement, the particulars of claim should set out the contractual words used and state by whom, to whom, when and where they were spoken.

9.5 Where a claim is based upon an agreement by conduct, the particulars of claim must specify the conduct relied on and state by whom, when and where the acts constituting the conduct were done.

9.6 In a claim issued in the High Court relating to a Consumer Credit Agreement, the particulars of claim must contain a statement that the action is not one to which section 141 of the Consumer Credit Act 1974 applies.

MATTERS WHICH MUST BE SPECIFICALLY SET OUT IN THE PARTICULARS OF CLAIM IF RELIED ON

10.1 A claimant who wishes to rely on evidence:

(1) under section 11 of the Civil Evidence Act 1968 of a conviction of an offence, or

(2) under section 12 of the above-mentioned Act of a finding or adjudication of adultery or paternity,

must include in his particulars of claim a statement to that effect and give the following details:

(1) the type of conviction, finding or adjudication and its date,
(2) the court or Court-Martial which made the conviction, finding or adjudication, and
(3) the issue in the claim to which it relates.

10.2 The claimant must specifically set out the following matters in his particulars of claim where he wishes to rely on them in support of his claim:
(1) any allegation of fraud,
(2) the fact of any illegality,
(3) details of any misrepresentation,
(4) details of all breaches of trust,
(5) notice or knowledge of a fact,
(6) details of unsoundness of mind or undue influence,
(7) details of wilful default, and
(8) any facts relating to mitigation of loss or damage.

10.3 A claimant may:
(1) refer in his particulars of claim to any point of law on which his claim is based,
(2) give in his particulars of claim the name of any witness whom he proposes to call, and
(3) attach to or serve with the particulars of claim a copy of any document which he considers is necessary to his claim (including any expert's report to be filed in accordance with Part 35).

GENERAL

11.1 Where a claim is for a sum of money expressed in a foreign currency it must expressly state:
(1) that the claim is for payment in a specified foreign currency,
(2) why it is for payment in that currency,
(3) the Sterling equivalent of the sum at the date of the claim, and
(4) the source of the exchange rate relied on to calculate the Sterling equivalent.

11.2 A subsequent statement of case must not contradict or be inconsistent with an earlier one; for example a reply to a defence must not bring in a new claim. Where new matters have come to light the appropriate course may be to seek the court's permission to amend the statement of case.

THE DEFENCE

General

12.1 Rule 16.5 deals with the contents of the defence.
12.2 A defendant should deal with every allegation in accordance with rule 16.5(1) and (2).
12.3 Rule 16.5(3), (4) and (5) sets out the consequences of not dealing with an allegation.

Statement of truth

13.1 Part 22 requires a defence to be verified by a statement of truth.
13.2 The form of the statement of truth is as follows:
'[I believe] [the defendant believes] that the facts stated in the defence are true.'
13.3 Attention is drawn to rule 32.14 which sets out the consequences of verifying a statement of case containing a false statement without an honest belief in its truth.

MATTERS WHICH MUST BE INCLUDED IN THE DEFENCE

Personal injury claims

14.1 Where the claim is for personal injuries and the claimant has attached a medical report in respect of his alleged injuries, the defendant should:
(1) state in his defence whether he—
   (a) agrees,

(b) disputes, or
(c) neither agrees nor disputes but has no knowledge of,
the matters contained in the medical report,
(2) where he disputes any part of the medical report, give in his defence his reasons for doing so, and
(3) where he has obtained his own medical report on which he intends to rely, attach it to his defence.

14.2 Where the claim is for personal injuries and the claimant has included a schedule of past and future expenses and losses, the defendant should include in or attach to his defence a counter-schedule stating:
(1) which of those items he—
 (a) agrees,
 (b) disputes, or
 (c) neither agrees nor disputes but has no knowledge of, and
(2) where any items are disputed, supplying alternative figures where appropriate.

Defamation

15 Where in a claim for libel or slander a defendant alleges that the words complained of are true or are fair comment on a matter of public interest he must give specific details in support of that allegation. RSC Order 82 (Schedule 1 to the CPR) contains requirements relating to defamation claims.

Other matters

16.1 The defendant must give details of the expiry of any relevant limitation period relied on.

16.2 Rule 37.3 and paragraph 2 of the practice direction which supplements Part 37 contains information about a defence of tender.

16.3 A party may:
(1) refer in his statement of case to any point of law on which his claim or defence, as the case may be, is based,
(2) give in his statement of case the name of any witness he proposes to call, and
(3) attach to or serve with this statement of case a copy of any document which he considers is necessary to his claim or defence, as the case may be (including any expert's report to be filed in accordance with Part 35).

CPR PART 17   AMENDMENTS TO STATEMENTS OF CASE

CONTENTS OF THIS PART

Amendments to statements of case	Rule 17.1
Power of court to disallow amendments made without permission	Rule 17.2
Amendments to statements of case with the permission of the court	Rule 17.3
Amendments to statements of case after the end of a relevant limitation period	Rule 17.4

17.1 AMENDMENTS TO STATEMENTS OF CASE

(1) A party may amend his statement of case at any time before it has been served on any other party.

(2) If his statement of case has been served, a party may amend it only—
 (a) with the written consent of all the other parties; or
 (b) with the permission of the court.

(Part 19 also applies where the amendment relates to the addition, substitution or removal of a party)

(Part 22 requires amendments to a statement of case to be verified by a statement of truth unless the court orders otherwise)

17.2 POWER OF COURT TO DISALLOW AMENDMENTS MADE WITHOUT PERMISSION

(1) If a party has amended his statement of case where permission of the court was not required, the court may disallow the amendment.

(2) A party may apply to the court for an order under paragraph (1) within 14 days of service of a copy of the amended statement of case on him.

17.3 AMENDMENTS TO STATEMENTS OF CASE WITH THE PERMISSION OF THE COURT

(1) Where the court gives permission for a party to amend his statement of case, it may give directions as to—
 (a) amendments to be made to any other statement of case; and
 (b) service of any amended statement of case.

(2) The power of the court to give permission under this rule is subject to—
 (a) rule 19.1 (change of parties — general);
 (b) rule 19.4 (special provisions about adding or substituting parties after the end of a relevant limitation period$^{(GL)}$); and
 (c) rule 17.4 (amendments of statement of case after the end of a relevant limitation period).

17.4 AMENDMENTS TO STATEMENTS OF CASE AFTER THE END OF A RELEVANT LIMITATION PERIOD

(1) This rule applies where—
 (a) a party applies to amend his statement of case in one of the ways mentioned in this rule; and
 (b) a period of limitation has expired under—
  (i) the Limitation Act 1980;
  (ii) the Foreign Limitation Periods Act 1984;
  (iii) section 190 of the Merchant Shipping Act 1995; or
  (iv) any other statutory provision.

(2) The court may allow an amendment whose effect will be to add or substitute a new claim, but only if the new claim arises out of the same facts or substantially the same facts as a claim in respect of which the party applying for permission has already claimed a remedy in the proceedings.

CPR PART 17 AMENDMENTS TO STATEMENTS OF CASE

(3) The court may allow an amendment to correct a mistake as to the name of a party, but only where the mistake was genuine and not one which would cause reasonable doubt as to the identity of the party in question.

(4) The court may allow an amendment to alter the capacity in which a party claims if the new capacity is one which that party had when the proceedings started or has since acquired.

(Rule 19.4 specifies the circumstances in which the court may allow a new party to be added or substituted after the end of a relevant limitation period[GL])

PD 17 PRACTICE DIRECTION — AMENDMENTS TO STATEMENTS OF CASE

This practice direction supplements CPR Part 17

A party applying for an amendment will usually be responsible for the costs of and arising from the amendment.

APPLICATIONS TO AMEND WHERE THE PERMISSION OF THE COURT IS REQUIRED

1.1 The application may be dealt with at a hearing or, if rule 23.8 applies, without a hearing.

1.2 When making an application to amend a statement of case, the applicant should file with the court:

(1) the application notice, and
(2) a copy of the statement of case with the proposed amendments.

1.3 Where permission to amend has been given, the applicant should within 14 days of the date of the order, or within such other period as the court may direct, file with the court the amended statement of case.

1.4 If the substance of the statement of case is changed by reason of the amendment, the statement of case should be re-verified by a statement of truth[1].

1.5 A copy of the order and the amended statement of case should be served on every party to the proceedings, unless the court orders otherwise.

GENERAL

2.1 The amended statement of case and the court copy of it should be endorsed as follows:

(1) where the court's permission was required:

'Amended [Particulars of Claim *or as may be*] by Order of [Master ....] [District Judge .... *or as may be*] dated ....'

(2) Where the court's permission was not required:

'Amended [Particulars of Claim *or as may be*] under CPR [rule 17.1(1) or (2)(a)] dated ....'

2.2 The statement of case in its amended form need not show the original text. However, where the court thinks it desirable for both the original text and the amendments to be shown, the court may direct that the amendments should be shown either:

(1) by coloured amendments, either manuscript or computer generated, or
(2) by use of a numerical code in a monochrome computer generated document.

2.3 Where colour is used, the text to be deleted should be struck through in colour and any text replacing it should be inserted or underlined in the same colour.

2.4 The order of colours to be used for successive amendments is; (1) red, (2) green, (3) violet and (4) yellow.

(For information about changes to parties see Part 19 and the practice direction which supplements it.)

---

[1] See Part 22 for information about the statement of truth.

CPR PART 18   FURTHER INFORMATION

CONTENTS OF THIS PART
Obtaining further information   Rule 18.1
Restriction on the use of further information   Rule 18.2

18.1 OBTAINING FURTHER INFORMATION

(1) The court may at any time order a party to—
   (a) clarify any matter which is in dispute in the proceedings; or
   (b) give additional information in relation to any such matter, whether or not the matter is contained or referred to in a statement of case.

(2) Paragraph (1) is subject to any rule of law to the contrary.

(3) Where the court makes an order under paragraph (1), the party against whom it is made must—
   (a) file his response; and
   (b) serve it on the other parties,
within the time specified by the court.
(Part 22 requires a response to be verified by a statement of truth)

18.2 RESTRICTION ON THE USE OF FURTHER INFORMATION

The court may direct that information provided by a party to another party (whether given voluntarily or following an order made under rule 18.1) must not be used for any purpose except for that of the proceedings in which it is given.

PD 18 PRACTICE DIRECTION — FURTHER INFORMATION

This practice direction supplements CPR Part 18

Attention is also drawn to Part 22 (Statements of Truth).

PRELIMINARY REQUEST FOR FURTHER INFORMATION OR CLARIFICATION

1.1 Before making an application to the court for an order under Part 18, the party seeking clarification or information (the first party) should first serve on the party from whom it is sought (the second party) a written request for that clarification or information (a Request) stating a date by which the response to the Request should be served. The date must allow the second party a reasonable time to respond.

1.2 A Request should be concise and strictly confined to matters which are reasonably necessary and proportionate to enable the first party to prepare his own case or to understand the case he has to meet.

1.3 Requests must be made as far as possible in a single comprehensive document and not piecemeal.

1.4 A Request may be made by letter if the text of the Request is brief and the reply is likely to be brief; otherwise the Request should be made in a separate document.

1.5 If a Request is made in a letter, the letter should, in order to distinguish it from any other that might routinely be written in the course of a case,

(1) state that it contains a Request made under Part 18, and
(2) deal with no matters other than the Request.

1.6 (1) A Request (whether made by letter or in a separate document) must—

(a) be headed with the name of the court and the title and number of the claim,

(b) in its heading state that it is a Request made under Part 18, identify the first party and the second party and state the date on which it is made,

(c) set out in a separate numbered paragraph each request for information or clarification,

(d) where a Request relates to a document, identify that document and (if relevant) the paragraph or words to which it relates,

(e) state the date by which the first party expects a response to the Request,

(2) (a) A Request which is not in the form of a letter may, if convenient, be prepared in such a way that the response may be given on the same document.

(b) To do this the numbered paragraphs of the Request should appear on the left hand half of each sheet so that the paragraphs of the response may then appear on the right.

(c) Where a Request is prepared in this form an extra copy should be served for the use of the second party.

RESPONDING TO A REQUEST

2.1 A response to a Request must be in writing, dated and signed by the second party or his legal representative.

2.2 (1) Where the Request is made in a letter the second party may give his response in a letter or in a formal reply.

(2) Such a letter should identify itself as a response to the Request and deal with no other matters than the response.

2.3 (1) Unless the Request is in the format described in paragraph 1.6(2) and the second party uses the document supplied for the purpose, a response must:

PD 18 PRACTICE DIRECTION — FURTHER INFORMATION

(a) be headed with the name of the court and the title and number of the claim,
(b) in its heading identify itself as a response to that Request,
(c) repeat the text of each separate paragraph of the Request and set out under each paragraph the response to it,
(d) refer to and have attached to it a copy of any document not already in the possession of the first party which forms part of the response.

(2) A second or supplementary response to a Request must identify itself as such in its heading.

2.4 The second party must when he serves his response on the first party serve on every other party and file with the court a copy of the Request and of his response.

STATEMENTS OF TRUTH

3 Attention is drawn to Part 22 and to the definition of a statement of case in Part 2 of the rules; a response should be verified by a statement of truth.

GENERAL MATTERS

4.1 (1) If the second party objects to complying with the Request or part of it or is unable to do so at all or within the time stated in the Request he must inform the first party promptly and in any event within that time.

(2) He may do so in a letter or in a separate document (a formal response), but in either case he must give reasons and, where relevant, give a date by which he expects to be able to comply.

4.2 (1) There is no need for a second party to apply to the court if he objects to a Request or is unable to comply with it at all or within the stated time. He need only comply with paragraph 4.1(1) above.

(2) Where a second party considers that a Request can only be complied with at disproportionate expense and objects to comply for that reason he should say so in his reply and explain briefly why he has taken that view.

APPLICATIONS FOR ORDERS UNDER PART 18

5.1 Attention is drawn to Part 23 (Applications) and to the Practice Direction which supplements that Part.

5.2 An application notice for an order under Part 18 should set out or have attached to it the text of the order sought and in particular should specify the matter or matters in respect of which the clarification or information is sought.

5.3 (1) If a Request under paragraph 1 for the information or clarification has not been made, the application notice should, in addition, explain why not.

(2) If a Request for clarification or information has been made, the application notice or the evidence in support should describe the response, if any.

5.4 Both the first party and the second party should consider whether evidence in support of or in opposition to the application is required.

5.5 (1) Where the second party has made no response to a Request served on him, the first party need not serve the application notice on the second party, and the court may deal with the application without a hearing.

(2) Sub-paragraph (1) above only applies if at least 14 days have passed since the Request was served and the time stated in it for a response has expired.

5.6 Unless paragraph 5.5 applies the application notice must be served on the second party and on all other parties to the claim.

5.7 An order made under Part 18 must be served on all parties to the claim.

5.8 Costs:

(1) Attention is drawn to the Costs Practice Direction and in particular the court's power to make a summary assessment of costs.

(2) Attention is also drawn to rule 43.5(5) which provides that if an order does not mention costs no party is entitled to costs relating to that order.

CPR PART 19 ADDITION AND SUBSTITUTION OF PARTIES

CONTENTS OF THIS PART
Change of parties — general ..... Rule 19.1
Provisions applicable where two or more persons are jointly entitled to a remedy ..... Rule 19.2
Procedure for adding and substituting parties ..... Rule 19.3
Special provisions about adding or substituting parties after the end of a relevant limitation period ..... Rule 19.4

19.1 CHANGE OF PARTIES — GENERAL

(1) This rule applies where a party is to be added or substituted except where the case falls within rule 19.4 (special provisions about changing parties after the end of a relevant limitation period$^{(GL)}$).

(2) The court may order a person to be added as a new party if—
   (a) it is desirable to add the new party so that the court can resolve all the matters in dispute in the proceedings; or
   (b) there is an issue involving the new party and an existing party which is connected to the matters in dispute in the proceedings, and it is desirable to add the new party so that the court can resolve that issue.

(3) The court may order any person to cease to be a party if it is not desirable for that person to be a party to the proceedings.

(4) The court may order a new party to be substituted for an existing one if—
   (a) the existing party's interest or liability has passed to the new party; and
   (b) it is desirable to substitute the new party so that the court can resolve the matters in dispute in the proceedings.

19.2 PROVISIONS APPLICABLE WHERE TWO OR MORE PERSONS ARE JOINTLY ENTITLED TO A REMEDY

(1) Where a claimant claims a remedy to which some other person is jointly entitled with him, all persons jointly entitled to the remedy must be parties unless the court orders otherwise.

(2) If any person does not agree to be a claimant, he must be made a defendant, unless the court orders otherwise.

(3) This rule does not apply in probate proceedings.

19.3 PROCEDURE FOR ADDING AND SUBSTITUTING PARTIES

(1) An application for permission to remove, add or substitute a party may be made by—
   (a) an existing party; or
   (b) a person who wishes to become a party.

(2) An application for an order under rule 19.1(4) (substitution of new party where existing party's interest or liability has passed)—
   (a) may be made without notice; and
   (b) must be supported by evidence.

(3) Nobody may be added or substituted as a claimant unless—
   (a) he has given his consent in writing; and
   (b) that consent has been filed with the court.

(4) An order for the removal, addition or substitution of a party must be served on—
   (a) all parties to the proceedings; and
   (b) any other person affected by the order.

(5) When the court makes an order for the removal, addition or substitution of a party, it may give consequential directions about—
   (a) filing and serving the claim form on any new defendant;

CPR PART 19 ADDITION AND SUBSTITUTION OF PARTIES

(b) serving relevant documents on the new party; and
(c) the management of the proceedings.

19.4 SPECIAL PROVISIONS ABOUT ADDING OR SUBSTITUTING PARTIES AFTER THE END OF A RELEVANT LIMITATION PERIOD

(1) This rule applies to a change of parties after the end of a period of limitation under—
 (a) the Limitation Act 1980;
 (b) the Foreign Limitation Periods Act 1984;
 (c) section 190 of the Merchant Shipping Act 1995; or
 (d) any other statutory provision.

(2) The court may add or substitute a party only if—
 (a) the relevant limitation period$^{(GL)}$ was current when the proceedings were started; and
 (b) the addition or substitution is necessary.

(3) The addition or substitution of a party is necessary only if the court is satisfied that—
 (a) the new party is to be substituted for a party who was named in the claim form in mistake for the new party;
 (b) the claim cannot properly be carried on by or against the original party unless the new party is added or substituted as claimant or defendant; or
 (c) the original party has died or had a bankruptcy order made against him and his interest or liability has passed to the new party.

(4) In addition, in a claim for personal injuries the court may add or substitute a party where it directs that—
 (a) (i) section 11 (special time limit for claims for personal injuries); or
  (ii) section 12 (special time limit for claims under fatal accidents legislation),
 of the Limitation Act 1980 shall not apply to the claim by or against the new party; or
 (b) the issue of whether those sections apply shall be determined at trial.

(Rule 17.4 deals with other changes after the end of a relevant limitation period$^{(GL)}$)

PD 19 PRACTICE DIRECTION — ADDITION AND SUBSTITUTION OF PARTIES

This practice direction supplements CPR Part 19

A party applying for an amendment will usually be responsible for the costs of and arising from the amendment.

CHANGES OF PARTIES

General

1.1 Parties may be removed, added or substituted in existing proceedings either on the court's own initiative or on the application of either an existing party or a person who wishes to become a party.

1.2 The application may be dealt with without a hearing where all the existing parties and the proposed new party are in agreement.

1.3 The application to add or substitute a new party should be supported by evidence setting out the proposed new party's interest in or connection with the claim.

1.4 The application notice should be filed in accordance with rule 23.3 and, unless the application is made under rule 19.1(4)[1], be served in accordance with rule 23.4.

1.5 An order giving permission to amend will, unless the court orders otherwise, be drawn up. It will be served by the court unless the parties wish to serve it or the court orders them to do so.

Addition or substitution of claimant

2.1 Where an application is made to the court to add or to substitute a new party to the proceedings as claimant, the party applying must file:
　(1) the application notice,
　(2) the proposed amended claim form and particulars of claim, and
　(3) the signed, written consent of the new claimant to be so added or substituted.

2.2 Where the court makes an order adding or substituting a party as claimant but the signed, written consent of the new claimant has not been filed:
　(1) the order, and
　(2) the addition or substitution of the new party as claimant,
will not take effect until the signed, written consent of the new claimant is filed.

2.3 Where the court has made an order adding or substituting a new claimant, the court may direct:
　(1) a copy of the order to be served on every party to the proceedings and any other person affected by the order,
　(2) copies of the statements of case and of documents referred to in any statement of case to be served on the new party,
　(3) the party who made the application to file within 14 days an amended claim form and particulars of claim.

Addition or substitution of defendant

3.1 The Civil Procedure Rules apply to a new defendant who has been added or substituted as they apply to any other defendant (see in particular the provisions of Parts 9, 10, 11 and 15).

3.2 Where the court has made an order adding or substituting a defendant whether on its own initiative or on an application, the court may direct:
　(1) the claimant to file with the court within 14 days (or as ordered) an amended claim form and particulars of claim for the court file,
　(2) a copy of the order to be served on all parties to the proceedings and any other person affected by it,

---

[1] See rule 19.3(2)(a).

(3) the amended claim form and particulars of claim, forms for admitting, defending and acknowledging the claim and copies of the statements of case and any other documents referred to in any statement of case to be served on the new defendant.

(4) unless the court orders otherwise, the amended claim form and particulars of claim to be served on any other defendants.

3.3 A new defendant does not become a party to the proceedings until the amended claim form has been served on him[2].

Removal of party

4 Where the court makes an order for the removal of a party from the proceedings:

(1) the claimant must file with the court an amended claim form and particulars of claim, and

(2) a copy of the order must be served on every party to the proceedings and on any other person affected by the order.

Transfer of interest or liability

5.1 Where the interest or liability of an existing party has passed to some other person, application should be made to the court to add or substitute that person[3].

5.2 The application must be supported by evidence showing the stage the proceedings have reached and what change has occurred to cause the transfer of interest or liability.

(For information about making amendments generally, see the practice direction supplementing Part 17.)

---

[2] *Ketteman* v *Hansel Properties Ltd* [1987] AC 189, HL.
[3] See rule 19.1(4).

CPR PART 20 COUNTERCLAIMS AND OTHER ADDITIONAL CLAIMS

CONTENTS OF THIS PART

Purpose of Part 20	Rule 20.1
Meaning of 'Part 20 claim'	Rule 20.2
Part 20 claim to be treated as a claim for the purposes of the Rules	Rule 20.3
Defendant's counterclaim against the claimant	Rule 20.4
Counterclaim against a person other than the claimant	Rule 20.5
Defendant's claim for contribution or indemnity from co-defendant	Rule 20.6
Procedure for making any other Part 20 claim	Rule 20.7
Service of a Part 20 claim form	Rule 20.8
Matters relevant to question of whether a Part 20 claim should be separate from main claim	Rule 20.9
Effect of service of a Part 20 claim	Rule 20.10
Special provisions relating to default judgment on a Part 20 claim other than a counterclaim or a contribution or indemnity notice	Rule 20.11
Procedural steps on service of a Part 20 claim form on a non-party	Rule 20.12
Case management where there is a defence to a Part 20 claim form	Rule 20.13

20.1 PURPOSE OF PART 20

The purpose of Part 20 is to enable Part 20 claims to be managed in the most convenient and effective manner.

20.2 MEANING OF 'PART 20 CLAIM'

(1) A Part 20 claim is any claim other than a claim by a claimant against a defendant and includes—

(a) a counterclaim by a defendant against the claimant or against the claimant and some other person;

(b) a claim by a defendant against any person (whether or not already a party) for contribution[GL] or indemnity[GL] or some other remedy; and

(c) where a Part 20 claim has been made against a person who is not already a party, any claim made by that person against any other person (whether or not already a party).

(2) In this Part 'Part 20 claimant' means a person who makes a Part 20 claim.

20.3 PART 20 CLAIM TO BE TREATED AS A CLAIM FOR THE PURPOSES OF THE RULES

(1) A Part 20 claim shall be treated as if it were a claim for the purposes of these Rules, except as provided by this Part.

(2) The following rules do not apply to Part 20 claims—

(a) rules 7.5 and 7.6 (time within which a claim form may be served);

(b) rule 16.3(5) (statement of value where claim to be issued in the High Court); and

(c) Part 26 (case management — preliminary stage).

(3) The following rules do not apply to Part 20 claims except where the Part 20 claim is a counterclaim—

(a) Part 12 (default judgment); and

(b) Part 14 (admissions) except rules 14.1(1) and (2) (which provide that a party may admit in writing the truth of another party's case) and 14.3 (admission by notice in writing — application for judgment).

(Rule 20.11 makes special provision for default judgment on a Part 20 claim)

20.4 DEFENDANT'S COUNTERCLAIM AGAINST THE CLAIMANT

(1) A defendant may make a counterclaim against a claimant by filing particulars of the counterclaim.

(2) A defendant may make a counterclaim against a claimant—

CPR PART 20 COUNTERCLAIMS AND OTHER ADDITIONAL CLAIMS

(a) without the court's permission if he files it with his defence; or
(b) at any other time with the court's permission.
(Part 15 makes provision for a defence to a claim and applies to a defence to a counterclaim by virtue of rule 20.3)
(3) Part 10 (acknowledgment of service) does not apply to a claimant who wishes to defend a counterclaim.

20.5 COUNTERCLAIM AGAINST A PERSON OTHER THAN THE CLAIMANT
(1) A defendant who wishes to counterclaim against a person other than the claimant must apply to the court for an order that that person be added as defendant to the counterclaim.
(2) An application for an order under paragraph (1) may be made without notice unless the court directs otherwise.
(3) Where the court makes an order under paragraph (1), it will give directions as to the management of the case.

20.6 DEFENDANT'S CLAIM FOR CONTRIBUTION OR INDEMNITY FROM CO-DEFENDANT
A defendant who has filed an acknowledgment of service or a defence may make a Part 20 claim for contribution$^{(GL)}$ or indemnity$^{(GL)}$ against another defendant by—
(a) filing a notice containing a statement of the nature and grounds of his claim; and
(b) serving that notice on the other defendant.

20.7 PROCEDURE FOR MAKING ANY OTHER PART 20 CLAIM
(1) This rule applies to any Part 20 claim except—
(a) a counterclaim; and
(b) a claim for contribution$^{(GL)}$ or indemnity$^{(GL)}$ made in accordance with rule 20.6.
(2) A Part 20 claim is made when the court issues a Part 20 claim form.
(3) A defendant may make a Part 20 claim—
(a) without the court's permission if the Part 20 claim is issued before or at the same time as he files his defence;
(b) at any other time with the court's permission.
(Rule 15.4 sets out the period for filing a defence)
(4) Particulars of a Part 20 claim must be contained in or served with the Part 20 claim.
(5) An application for permission to make a Part 20 claim may be made without notice, unless the court directs otherwise.

20.8 SERVICE OF A PART 20 CLAIM FORM
(1) Where a Part 20 claim may be made without the court's permission, the Part 20 claim form must—
(a) in the case of a counterclaim, be served on every other party when a copy of the defence is served;
(b) in the case of any other Part 20 claim, be served on the person against whom it is made within 14 days after the date on which the party making the Part 20 claim files his defence.
(2) Paragraph (1) does not apply to a claim for contribution$^{(GL)}$ or indemnity$^{(GL)}$ made in accordance with rule 20.6.
(3) Where the court gives permission to make a Part 20 claim it will at the same time give directions as to the service of the Part 20 claim.

20.9 MATTERS RELEVANT TO QUESTION OF WHETHER A PART 20 CLAIM SHOULD BE SEPARATE FROM MAIN CLAIM
(1) This rule applies where the court is considering whether to—
(a) permit a Part 20 claim to be made;
(b) dismiss a Part 20 claim; or

CPR PART 20 COUNTERCLAIMS AND OTHER ADDITIONAL CLAIMS

(c) require a Part 20 claim to be dealt with separately from the claim by the claimant against the defendant.

(Rule 3.1(2)(e) and (j) deal respectively with the court's power to order that part of proceedings be dealt with as separate proceedings and to decide the order in which issues are to be tried)

(2) The matters to which the court may have regard include—
 (a) the connection between the Part 20 claim and the claim made by the claimant against the defendant;
 (b) whether the Part 20 claimant is seeking substantially the same remedy which some other party is claiming from him; and
 (c) whether the Part 20 claimant wants the court to decide any question connected with the subject matter of the proceedings—
  (i) not only between existing parties but also between existing parties and a person not already a party; or
  (ii) against an existing party not only in a capacity in which he is already a party but also in some further capacity.

20.10 EFFECT OF SERVICE OF A PART 20 CLAIM

(1) A person on whom a Part 20 claim is served becomes a party to the proceedings if he is not a party already.

(2) When a Part 20 claim is served on an existing party for the purpose of requiring the court to decide a question against that party in a further capacity, that party also becomes a party in the further capacity specified in the Part 20 claim.

20.11 SPECIAL PROVISIONS RELATING TO DEFAULT JUDGMENT ON A PART 20 CLAIM OTHER THAN A COUNTERCLAIM OR A CONTRIBUTION OR INDEMNITY NOTICE

(1) This rule applies if—
 (a) the Part 20 claim is not—
  (i) a counterclaim; or
  (ii) a claim by a defendant for contribution[GL] or indemnity[GL] against another defendant under rule 20.6; and
 (b) the party against whom a Part 20 claim is made fails to file an acknowledgment of service or defence in respect of the Part 20 claim.

(2) The party against whom the Part 20 claim is made—
 (a) is deemed to admit the Part 20 claim, and is bound by any judgment or decision in the main proceedings in so far as it is relevant to any matter arising in the Part 20 claim;
 (b) subject to paragraph (3), if default judgment under Part 12 is given against the Part 20 claimant, the Part 20 claimant may obtain judgment in respect of the Part 20 claim by filing a request in the relevant practice form.

(3) A Part 20 claimant may not enter judgment under paragraph (2)(b) without the court's permission if—
 (a) he has not satisfied the default judgment which has been given against him; or
 (b) he wishes to obtain judgment for any remedy other than a contribution[GL] or indemnity[GL].

(4) An application for the court's permission under paragraph (3) may be made without notice unless the court directs otherwise.

(5) The court may at any time set aside[GL] or vary a judgment entered under paragraph (2)(b).

20.12 PROCEDURAL STEPS ON SERVICE OF A PART 20 CLAIM FORM ON A NON-PARTY

(1) Where a Part 20 claim form is served on a person who is not already a party it must be accompanied by—
 (a) a form for defending the claim;
 (b) a form for admitting the claim;
 (c) a form for acknowledging service; and
 (d) a copy of—

CPR PART 20 COUNTERCLAIMS AND OTHER ADDITIONAL CLAIMS

(i) every statement of case which has already been served in the proceedings; and

(ii) such other documents as the court may direct.

(2) A copy of the Part 20 claim form must be served on every existing party.

20.13 CASE MANAGEMENT WHERE THERE IS A DEFENCE TO A PART 20 CLAIM FORM

(1) Where a defence is filed to a Part 20 claim the court must consider the future conduct of the proceedings and give appropriate directions.

(2) In giving directions under paragraph (1) the court must ensure that, so far as practicable, the Part 20 claim and the main claim are managed together.

PD 20 PRACTICE DIRECTION — COUNTERCLAIMS AND OTHER PART 20 CLAIMS

This practice direction supplements CPR Part 20

A Part 20 claim is any claim other than the claim by the claimant against the defendant.

CASES WHERE COURT'S PERMISSION TO MAKE A PART 20 CLAIM IS REQUIRED

1.1 Rules 20.4(2)(b), 20.5(1) and 20.7(3)(b) set out the circumstances in which the court's permission will be needed for making a Part 20 claim.

1.2 Where an application is made for permission to make a Part 20 claim the application notice should be filed together with a copy of the proposed Part 20 claim.

APPLICATIONS FOR PERMISSION TO ISSUE A PART 20 CLAIM

2.1 An application for permission to make a Part 20 claim must be supported by evidence stating:
   (1) the stage which the action has reached,
   (2) the nature of the claim to be made by the Part 20 claimant or details of the question or issue which needs to be decided,
   (3) a summary of the facts on which the Part 20 claim is based, and
   (4) the name and address of the proposed Part 20 defendant.

(For further information regarding evidence see the practice direction which supplements Part 32.)

2.2 Where delay has been a factor contributing to the need to apply for permission to make a Part 20 claim an explanation of the delay should be given in evidence.

2.3 Where possible the applicant should provide a timetable of the action to date.

2.4 Rules 20.5(2) and 20.7(5) allow applications to be made to the court without notice unless the court otherwise directs.

GENERAL

3 The Civil Procedure Rules apply generally to Part 20 claims as if they were claims[1]. Parties should be aware that the provisions relating to failure to respond will apply.

STATEMENT OF TRUTH

4.1 The contents of a Part 20 claim should be verified by a statement of truth. Part 22 requires a statement of case to be verified by a statement of truth.

4.2 The form of the statement of truth should be as follows:

'[I believe] [the [Part 20 claimant]* believes] that the facts stated in this statement of case are true'

*(For the purpose of this practice direction the Part 20 claimant means any party making a Part 20 claim.)

4.3 Attention is drawn to rule 32.14 which sets out the consequences of verifying a statement of case containing a false statement without an honest belief in its truth.

(For information regarding statements of truth see Part 22 and the practice direction which supplements it.)

CASE MANAGEMENT WHERE THERE IS A PART 20 DEFENCE

5.1 Where the Part 20 defendant files a defence, other than to a counterclaim, the court will arrange a hearing to consider case management of the Part 20 claim.

5.2 The court will give notice of the hearing to each party likely to be affected by any order made at the hearing.

---

[1] Rule 20.3 but note the exceptions set out in rule 20.3(2) and (3).

5.3 At the hearing the court may:
(1) treat the hearing as a summary judgment hearing,
(2) order that the Part 20 proceedings be dismissed,
(3) give directions about the way any claim, question or issue set out in or arising from the Part 20 claim should be dealt with,
(4) give directions as to the part, if any, the Part 20 defendant will take at the trial of the claim,
(5) give directions about the extent to which the Part 20 defendant is to be bound by any judgment or decision to be made in the claim.

5.4 The court may make any of the orders in 5.3(1) to (5) either before or after any judgment in the claim has been entered by the claimant against the defendant.

FORM OF COUNTERCLAIM

6.1 Where a defendant to a claim serves a counterclaim under this Part, the defence and counterclaim should normally form one document with the counterclaim following on from the defence.

6.2 Where a claimant serves a reply and a defence to counterclaim, the reply and the defence to counterclaim should normally form one document with the defence to counterclaim following on from the reply.

TITLES OF PROCEEDINGS WHERE THERE ARE PART 20 CLAIMS

7.1 The title of every Part 20 claim should contain:
(1) the full name of each party, and
(2) his status in the proceedings (e.g. claimant, defendant, Part 20 claimant, Part 20 defendant etc.). For example:

    AB Claimant
    CD Defendant/Part 20 Claimant
    EF Part 20 Defendant

7.2 Where a defendant makes a counterclaim not only against the claimant but also against a non-party the title should show this as follows:

    AB Claimant/Part 20 Defendant
    CD Defendant/Part 20 Claimant
         and
    XY Part 20 Defendant

7.3 Where there is more than one Part 20 claim, the parties to the first Part 20 claim should be described as 'Part 20 Claimant (1st claim)' and 'Part 20 Defendant (1st claim)', the parties to the second Part 20 claim should be described as 'Part 20 Claimant (2nd claim)' and 'Part 20 Defendant (2nd claim)', and so on. For example:

    AB Claimant and Part 20 Defendant (2nd claim)
    CD Defendant and Part 20 Claimant (1st claim)
    EF Part 20 Defendant (1st claim) and Part 20 Claimant (2nd claim)
    GH Part 20 Defendant (2nd claim)

7.4 Where the full name of a party is lengthy it must appear in the title but thereafter in the statement of case it may be identified by an abbreviation such as initials or a recognised shortened name.

7.5 Where a party to proceedings has more than one status, e.g. Claimant and Part 20 Defendant (2nd claim) or Part 20 Defendant (1st claim) and Part 20 Claimant (2nd claim), the combined status must appear in the title but thereafter it may be convenient to refer to the party by name, e.g. Mr Smith or, if paragraph 7.4 applies, by initials or a shortened name.

7.6 Paragraph 4 of the practice direction supplementing Part 7 contains further directions regarding the title to proceedings.

CPR PART 21 CHILDREN AND PATIENTS

CONTENTS OF THIS PART

Scope of this Part	Rule 21.1
Requirement for litigation friend in proceedings by or against children and patients	Rule 21.2
Stage of proceedings at which a litigation friend becomes necessary	Rule 21.3
Who may be a litigation friend without a court order	Rule 21.4
How a person becomes a litigation friend without a court order	Rule 21.5
How a person becomes a litigation friend by court order	Rule 21.6
Court's power to change litigation friend and to prevent person acting as litigation friend	Rule 21.7
Appointment of litigation friend by court order — supplementary	Rule 21.8
Procedure where appointment of litigation friend ceases	Rule 21.9
Compromise etc. by or on behalf of child or patient	Rule 21.10
Control of money recovered by or on behalf of child or patient	Rule 21.11
Appointment of guardian of child's estate	Rule 21.12

21.1 SCOPE OF THIS PART

(1) This Part—
    (a) contains special provisions which apply in proceedings involving children and patients; and
    (b) sets out how a person becomes a litigation friend.

(2) In this Part—
    (a) 'child' means a person under 18; and
    (b) 'patient' means a person who by reason of mental disorder within the meaning of the Mental Health Act 1983 is incapable of managing and administering his own affairs.

(Rule 6.6 contains provisions about the service of documents on children and patients)

(Rule 48.5 deals with costs where money is payable by or to a child or patient)

21.2 REQUIREMENT FOR LITIGATION FRIEND IN PROCEEDINGS BY OR AGAINST CHILDREN AND PATIENTS

(1) A patient must have a litigation friend to conduct proceedings on his behalf.

(2) A child must have a litigation friend to conduct proceedings on his behalf unless the court makes an order under paragraph (3).

(3) The court may make an order permitting the child to conduct proceedings without a litigation friend.

(4) An application for an order under paragraph (3)—
    (a) may be made by the child;
    (b) if the child already has a litigation friend, must be made on notice to the litigation friend; and
    (c) if the child has no litigation friend, may be made without notice.

(5) Where—
    (a) the court has made an order under paragraph (3); and
    (b) it subsequently appears to the court that it is desirable for a litigation friend to conduct the proceedings on behalf of the child,
the court may appoint a person to be the child's litigation friend.

21.3 STAGE OF PROCEEDINGS AT WHICH A LITIGATION FRIEND BECOMES NECESSARY

(1) This rule does not apply where the court has made an order under rule 21.2(3).

(2) A person may not, without the permission of the court—
    (a) make an application against a child or patient before proceedings have started; or

CPR PART 21 CHILDREN AND PATIENTS

    (b)   take any step in proceedings except—
        (i)   issuing and serving a claim form; or
        (ii)   applying for the appointment of a litigation friend under rule 21.6,
until the child or patient has a litigation friend.

    (3)   If a party becomes a patient during proceedings, no party may take any step in the proceedings without the permission of the court until the patient has a litigation friend.

    (4)   Any step taken before a child or patient has a litigation friend shall be of no effect unless the court otherwise orders.

21.4 WHO MAY BE A LITIGATION FRIEND WITHOUT A COURT ORDER

    (1)   This rule does not apply if the court has appointed a person to be a litigation friend.

    (2)   A person authorised under Part VII of the Mental Health Act 1983 to conduct legal proceedings in the name of a patient or on his behalf is entitled to be the litigation friend of the patient in any proceedings to which his authority extends.

    (3)   If nobody has been appointed by the court or, in the case of a patient, authorised under Part VII, a person may act as a litigation friend if he—
    (a)   can fairly and competently conduct proceedings on behalf of the child or patient;
    (b)   has no interest adverse to that of the child or patient; and
    (c)   where the child or patient is a claimant, undertakes to pay any costs which the child or patient may be ordered to pay in relation to the proceedings, subject to any right he may have to be repaid from the assets of the child or patient.

21.5 HOW A PERSON BECOMES A LITIGATION FRIEND WITHOUT A COURT ORDER

    (1)   If the court has not appointed a litigation friend, a person who wishes to act as a litigation friend must follow the procedure set out in this rule.

    (2)   A person authorised under Part VII of the Mental Health Act 1983 must file an official copy$^{(GL)}$ of the order or other document which constitutes his authorisation to act.

    (3)   Any other person must file a certificate of suitability stating that he satisfies the conditions specified in rule 21.4(3).

    (4)   A person who is to act as a litigation friend for a claimant must file—
    (a)   the authorisation; or
    (b)   the certificate of suitability,
at the time when the claim is made.

    (5)   A person who is to act as a litigation friend for a defendant must file—
    (a)   the authorisation; or
    (b)   the certificate of suitability,
at the time when he first takes a step in the proceedings on behalf of the defendant.

    (6)   The litigation friend must—
    (a)   serve the certificate of suitability on every person on whom, in accordance with rule 6.6 (service on parent, guardian etc.), the claim form should be served; and
    (b)   file a certificate of service when he files the certificate of suitability.
(Rule 6.10 sets out the details to be contained in a certificate of service)

21.6 HOW A PERSON BECOMES A LITIGATION FRIEND BY COURT ORDER

    (1)   The court may make an order appointing a litigation friend.

    (2)   An application for an order appointing a litigation friend may be made by—
    (a)   a person who wishes to be the litigation friend; or
    (b)   a party.

    (3)   Where—
    (a)   a person makes a claim against a child or patient;
    (b)   the child or patient has no litigation friend;

(c) the court has not made an order under rule 21.2(3) (order that a child can act without a litigation friend); and
    (d) either—
        (i) someone who is not entitled to be a litigation friend files a defence; or
        (ii) the claimant wishes to take some step in the proceedings,
the claimant must apply to the court for an order appointing a litigation friend for the child or patient.
    (4) An application for an order appointing a litigation friend must be supported by evidence.
    (5) The court may not appoint a litigation friend under this rule unless it is satisfied that the person to be appointed complies with the conditions specified in rule 21.4(3).

21.7 COURT'S POWER TO CHANGE LITIGATION FRIEND AND TO PREVENT PERSON ACTING AS LITIGATION FRIEND
    (1) The court may—
        (a) direct that a person may not act as a litigation friend;
        (b) terminate a litigation friend's appointment;
        (c) appoint a new litigation friend in substitution for an existing one.
    (2) An application for an order under paragraph (1) must be supported by evidence.
    (3) The court may not appoint a litigation friend under this rule unless it is satisfied that the person to be appointed complies with the conditions specified in rule 21.4(3).

21.8 APPOINTMENT OF LITIGATION FRIEND BY COURT ORDER — SUPPLEMENTARY
    (1) An application for an order under rule 21.6 or 21.7 must be served on every person on whom, in accordance with rule 6.6 (service on parent, guardian etc.), the claim form should be served.
    (2) Where an application for an order under rule 21.6 is in respect of a patient, the application must also be served on the patient unless the court orders otherwise.
    (3) An application for an order under rule 21.7 must also be served on—
        (a) the person who is the litigation friend, or who is purporting to act as the litigation friend, when the application is made; and
        (b) the person who it is proposed should be the litigation friend, if he is not the applicant.
    (4) On an application for an order under rule 21.6 or 21.7, the court may appoint the person proposed or any other person who complies with the conditions specified in rule 21.4(3).

21.9 PROCEDURE WHERE APPOINTMENT OF LITIGATION FRIEND CEASES
    (1) When a child who is not a patient reaches the age of 18, a litigation friend's appointment ceases.
    (2) When a party ceases to be a patient, the litigation friend's appointment continues until it is ended by a court order.
    (3) An application for an order under paragraph (2) may be made by—
        (a) the former patient;
        (b) the litigation friend; or
        (c) a party.
    (4) The child or patient in respect of whom the appointment to act has ceased must serve notice on the other parties—
        (a) stating that the appointment of his litigation friend to act has ceased;
        (b) giving his address for service; and
        (c) stating whether or not he intends to carry on the proceedings.
    (5) If he does not do so within 28 days after the day on which the appointment of the litigation friend ceases the court may, on application, strike out[GL] any claim or defence brought by him.

(6) The liability of a litigation friend for costs continues until—
(a) the person in respect of whom his appointment to act has ceased serves the notice referred to in paragraph (4); or
(b) the litigation friend serves notice on the parties that his appointment to act has ceased.

21.10 COMPROMISE ETC. BY OR ON BEHALF OF CHILD OR PATIENT
(1) Where a claim is made—
(a) by or on behalf of a child or patient; or
(b) against a child or patient,
no settlement, compromise or payment and no acceptance of money paid into court shall be valid, so far as it relates to the claim by, on behalf of or against the child or patient, without the approval of the court.
(2) Where—
(a) before proceedings in which a claim is made by or on behalf of, or against a child or patient (whether alone or with any other person) are begun, an agreement is reached for the settlement of the claim; and
(b) the sole purpose of proceedings on that claim is to obtain the approval of the court to a settlement or compromise of the claim,
the claim must—
(i) be made using the procedure set out in Part 8 (alternative procedure for claims); and
(ii) include a request to the court for approval of the settlement or compromise.
(Rule 48.5 contains provisions about costs where money is payable to a child or patient)

21.11 CONTROL OF MONEY RECOVERED BY OR ON BEHALF OF CHILD OR PATIENT
(1) Where in any proceedings—
(a) money is recovered by or on behalf of or for the benefit of a child or patient; or
(b) money paid into court is accepted by or on behalf of a child or patient,
the money shall be dealt with in accordance with directions given by the court under this rule and not otherwise.
(2) Directions given under this rule may provide that the money shall be wholly or partly paid into court and invested or otherwise dealt with.

21.12 APPOINTMENT OF GUARDIAN OF CHILD'S ESTATE
(1) The court may appoint the Official Solicitor to be a guardian of a child's estate where—
(a) money is paid into court on behalf of the child in accordance with directions given under rule 21.11 (control of money received by a child or patient);
(b) the Criminal Injuries Compensation Board or the Criminal Injuries Compensation Authority notifies the court that it has made or intends to make an award to the child;
(c) a court or tribunal outside England and Wales notifies the court that it has ordered or intends to order that money be paid to the child;
(d) the child is absolutely entitled to the proceeds of a pension fund; or
(e) in any other case, such an appointment seems desirable to the court.
(2) The court may not appoint the Official Solicitor under this rule unless—
(a) the persons with parental responsibility (within the meaning of section 3 of the Children Act 1989) agree; or
(b) the court considers that their agreement can be dispensed with.
(3) The Official Solicitor's appointment may continue only until the child reaches 18.

PD 21 PRACTICE DIRECTION — CHILDREN AND PATIENTS

This practice direction supplements CPR Part 21

GENERAL

1.1 In this practice direction 'child' means a person under 18 years old and 'patient' means a person who by reason of mental disorder within the meaning of the Mental Health Act 1983 is incapable of managing and administering his own affairs[1].

1.2 A patient must bring or defend proceedings by a litigation friend (see paragraph 2 below for the definition of a litigation friend).

1.3 In the proceedings referred to in paragraph 1.2 above the patient should be referred to in the title as 'A.B. (by C.D. his litigation friend)'.

1.4 A child must bring or defend proceedings by a litigation friend unless the court has made an order permitting the child to do so on his own behalf[2].

1.5 Where:

(1) the child has a litigation friend, the child should be referred to in the title to proceedings as 'A.B. (a child by C.D. his litigation friend)', and

(2) the child is conducting proceedings on his own behalf, the child should be referred to in the title as 'A.B. (a child)'.

1.6 The approval of the court must be obtained if a settlement of a claim by or against a child or patient is to be valid[3]. A settlement includes an agreement on a sum to be apportioned to a dependent child under the Fatal Accidents Act 1976.

1.7 The approval of the court must also be obtained before making a voluntary interim payment to a child or patient.

1.8 A hearing of an application under Part 21 will take place in private unless the court directs otherwise.

THE LITIGATION FRIEND

2.1 It is the duty of a litigation friend fairly and competently to conduct proceedings on behalf of a child or patient. He must have no interest in the proceedings adverse to that of the child or patient and all steps and decisions he takes in the proceedings must be taken for the benefit of the child or patient.

2.2 A person may become a litigation friend:

(1) of a child—
    (a) without a court order under the provisions of rule 21.5, or
    (b) by a court order under rule 21.6, and

(2) of a patient
    (a) by authorisation under Part VII of the Mental Health Act 1983, or
    (b) by a court order under rule 21.6.

2.3 In order to become a litigation friend without a court order the person who wishes to act as litigation friend must:

(1) if he wishes to act on behalf of a patient, file an official copy of the order or other document which constitutes the authorisation referred to in paragraph 2.2(2)(a) above, or

(2) if he wishes to act on behalf of a child, or on behalf of a patient without the authorisation referred to in (1) above, file a certificate of suitability[4]—

    (a) stating that he consents to act,
    (b) stating that he knows or believes that the [claimant] [defendant] is a [child] [patient],
    (c) in the case of a patient, stating the grounds of his belief and if his belief is based upon medical opinion attaching any relevant document to the certificate,

---

[1] See rule 21.1(2).
[2] See rule 21.2(3).
[3] See rule 21.10.
[4] See rule 21.5(3).

(d) stating that he can fairly and competently conduct proceedings on behalf of the child or patient and has no interest adverse to that of the child or patient,

(e) where the child or patient is a claimant, undertaking to pay any costs which the child or patient may be ordered to pay in relation to the proceedings, subject to any right he may have to be repaid from the assets of the child or patient, and

(f) which he has signed in verification of its contents.

2.4 The litigation friend must serve a certificate of suitability[5]:

(1) in the case of a child (who is not also a patient) on one of the child's parents or guardians or if there is no parent or guardian, on the person with whom the child resides or in whose care the child is, and

(2) in the case of a patient on the person authorised under Part VII of the Mental Health Act 1983 to conduct proceedings on behalf of the patient or if there is no person so authorised, on the person with whom the patient resides or in whose care the patient is.

2.4A The litigation friend is not required to serve the documents referred to in paragraph 2.3(2)(c) when he serves a certificate of suitability on the person to be served under paragraph 2.4.

2.5 The litigation friend must file either the certificate of suitability together with a certificate of service[6] of it, or the authorisation referred to in paragraph 2.31(1) above:

(1) where the litigation friend is acting on behalf of a claimant, when the claim form is issued, and

(2) where the litigation friend is acting on behalf of a defendant, when he first takes a step in the action.

APPLICATION FOR A COURT ORDER APPOINTING A LITIGATION FRIEND

3.1 Rule 21.6 sets out who may apply for an order appointing a litigation friend.

3.2 An application should be made in accordance with Part 23 and must be supported by evidence[7].

3.3 The application notice must be served:

(1) on the persons referred to in paragraph 2.4 above, and

(2) where the application is in respect of a patient, on the patient unless the court orders otherwise.

3.4 The evidence in support must satisfy the court that the proposed litigation friend:

(1) consents to act,

(2) can fairly and competently conduct proceedings on behalf of the child or patient,

(3) has no interest adverse to that of the child or patient, and

(4) where the child or patient is a claimant, undertakes to pay any costs which the child or patient may be ordered to pay in relation to the proceedings, subject to any right he may have to be repaid from the assets of the child or patient.

3.5 Where a claimant wishes to take a step in proceedings against a child or patient who does not have a litigation friend he must apply to the court for an order appointing a litigation friend.

3.6 The proposed litigation friend must satisfy the conditions in paragraph 3.4(1), (2) and (3) above and may be one of the persons referred to in paragraph 2.4 above where appropriate, or otherwise may be the Official Solicitor. Where it is sought to appoint the Official Solicitor, provision should be made for payment of his charges.

---

[5] See rule 21.5(6) and rule 6.9 (service).
[6] See rule 6.10 for the certificate of service.
[7] See rule 21.6(4).

CHANGE OF LITIGATION FRIEND AND PREVENTION OF PERSON ACTING AS LITIGATION FRIEND

4.1 Rule 21.7(1) states that the court may:
 (1) direct that a person may not act as a litigation friend,
 (2) terminate a litigation friend's appointment,
 (3) substitute a new litigation friend for an existing one.

4.2 Where an application is made for an order under rule 21.7(1), the application notice must set out the reasons for seeking it. The application must be supported by evidence.

4.3 If the order sought is the substitution of a new litigation friend for an existing one, the evidence must satisfy the court of the matters set out in paragraph 3.4 above.

4.4 The application notice must be served:
 (1) on the persons referred to in paragraph 2.4 above, and
 (2) on the litigation friend or person purporting to act as litigation friend.

PROCEDURE WHERE THE NEED FOR A LITIGATION FRIEND HAS COME TO AN END

5.1 Rule 21.9 deals with the situation where the need for a litigation friend comes to an end during the proceedings because either:
 (1) a child who is not also a patient reaches the age of 18 (full age) during the proceedings, or
 (2) a patient ceases to be a patient (recovers).

5.2 A child on reaching full age must serve on the other parties to the proceedings and file with the court a notice:
 (1) stating that he has reached full age,
 (2) stating that his litigation friend's appointment has ceased[8],
 (3) giving an address for service[9], and
 (4) stating whether or not he intends to carry on with or continue to defend the proceedings.

5.3 If the notice states that the child intends to carry on with or continue to defend the proceedings he shall subsequently be described in the proceedings as:
 'A.B. (formerly a child but now of full age)'

5.4 Whether or not a child having reached full age serves a notice in accordance with rule 21.9(4)(a) and paragraph 5.2(2) above, a litigation friend may at any time after the child has reached full age serve a notice on the other parties that his appointment has ceased.

5.5 The liability of a litigation friend for costs continues until a notice that his appointment to act has ceased is served on the other parties[10].

5.6 Where a patient recovers, an application under rule 21.9(3) must be made for an order under rule 21.9(2) that the litigation friend's appointment has ceased.

5.7 The application must be supported by the following evidence:
 (1) a medical report indicating that the patient has recovered and that he is capable of managing and administering his property and affairs,
 (2) where the patient's affairs were under the control of the Court of Protection, a copy of the order or notice discharging the receiver, and
 (3) if the application is made by the patient, a statement whether or not he intends to carry on with or continue to defend the proceedings.

5.8 An order under rule 21.9(2) must be served on the other parties to the proceedings. The patient must file with the court a notice;
 (1) stating that his litigation friend's appointment has ceased,
 (2) giving an address for service[11], and
 (3) stating whether or not he intends to carry on with or continue to defend the proceedings.

---

[8] Rule 21.9(4)(a).
[9] See rule 6.5.
[10] Rule 21.9(6).
[11] See rule 6.5.

PD 21 PRACTICE DIRECTION — CHILDREN AND PATIENTS

SETTLEMENT OR COMPROMISE BY OR ON BEHALF OF A CHILD OR PATIENT

6.1 Where a claim by or on behalf of a child or patient has been dealt with by agreement prior to the start of proceedings and only the approval of the court to the agreement is sought, the claim:

(1) must be made using the Part 8 procedure,
(2) must include a request for approval of the settlement or compromise, and
(3) in addition to the details of the claim, must set out the terms of the settlement or compromise or have attached to it a draft consent order in practice form N292.

6.2 In order to approve the settlement or compromise, the information concerning the claim that the court will require will include:

(1) whether and to what extent the defendant admits liability,
(2) the age and occupation (if any) of the child or patient,
(3) the litigation friend's approval of the proposed settlement or compromise, and
(4) in a personal injury case arising from an accident—
   (a) the circumstances of the accident,
   (b) any medical reports,
   (c) where appropriate, a schedule of any past and future expenses and losses claimed and any other relevant information relating to personal injury as set out in the practice direction which supplements Part 16 (statements of case), and
   (d) where considerations of liability are raised—
     (i) any evidence or police reports in any criminal proceedings or in an inquest, and
     (ii) details of any prosecution brought.

6.3 (1) An opinion on the merits of the settlement or compromise given by counsel or solicitor acting for the child or patient should, except in very clear cases, be obtained.

(2) A copy of the opinion and, unless the instructions on which it was given are sufficiently set out in it, a copy of the instructions, must also be supplied to the court.

6.4 Applications for the approval of a settlement or compromise will normally be heard by a Master or district judge.

(For information about structured settlements see the practice direction on structured settlements supplementing Part 40 (judgments and orders))

(For information about provisional damages claims see Part 41 and the practice direction which supplements it)

APPORTIONMENT UNDER THE FATAL ACCIDENTS ACT 1976

7.1 A judgment on or settlement in respect of a claim under the Fatal Accidents Act 1976 must be apportioned between the persons by or on whose behalf the claim has been brought.

7.2 Where a claim is brought on behalf of a dependent child or children, the money apportioned to any child must be invested on his behalf in accordance with rules 21.10 and 21.11 and paragraphs 8 and 9 below.

7.3 In order to approve an apportionment of money to a dependent child, the court will require the following information;

(1) the matters set out in paragraph 6.2(1),(2) above, and
(2) in respect of the deceased
   (a) where death was caused by an accident, the matters set out in paragraph 6.2(3)(a),(b) and (c) above, and
   (b) his future loss of earnings, and
(3) the extent and nature of the dependency.

CONTROL OF MONEY RECOVERED BY OR ON BEHALF OF A CHILD OR PATIENT

8.1 Money recovered or paid into court on behalf of or for the benefit of a child or patient shall be dealt with in accordance with directions of the court under rule 21.11.

8.2 The court:
　(1)　may direct the money to be paid into the High Court for investment,
　(2)　may also direct that certain sums be paid direct to the child or patient, his litigation friend or his legal representative[12] for the immediate benefit of the child or patient or for expenses incurred on his behalf, and
　(3)　may direct the applications in respect of the investment of the money be transferred to a local district registry.
　8.3　The Master or district judge will consider the general aims to be achieved for the money in court (the fund) by investment and will give directions as to the type of investment.
　8.4　Where a child is also a patient, and likely to remain so on reaching full age, his fund should be administered as a patient's fund.
　8.5　Where a child or patient is legally aided the fund will be subject to a first charge under s. 16 of the Legal Aid Act 1988 (the legal aid charge) and an order for the investment of money on the child or patient's behalf must contain a direction to that effect.

GUARDIAN'S ACCOUNTS
　9　Paragraph 8 of the practice direction supplementing Part 40 (Judgments and Orders) deals with the approval of the accounts of a guardian of assets of a child.

INVESTMENT ON BEHALF OF A CHILD
　10.1　At the hearing of the application for the approval of the agreement the litigation friend or his legal representative should provide a CFO form 320 (request for investment) for completion by the Master or district judge.
　10.2　On receipt of that form in the Court Funds Office the investment managers of the Public Trust Office will make the appropriate investment.
　10.3　Where an award of damages for a child is made at trial the trial judge may direct:
　(1)　the money to be paid into court and placed in the special investment account, and
　(2)　the litigation friend to make an application to a Master or district judge for further investment directions.
　10.4　If the money to be invested is very small the court may order it to be paid direct to the litigation friend to be put into a building society account (or similar) for the child's use.
　10.5　If the money is invested in court it must be paid out to the child when he reaches full age.

INVESTMENT ON BEHALF OF A PATIENT
　11.1　The Court of Protection is responsible for protecting the property of patients and is given extensive powers to do so under the Mental Health Act 1983. Fees are charged for the administration of funds by the Court of Protection and these should be provided for in any settlement.
　11.2　Where the sum to be administered is:
　(1)　over £30,000, the order approving the settlement will contain a direction to the litigation friend to apply to the Court of Protection for the appointment of a receiver, after which the fund will be transferred to the Court of Protection,
　(2)　under £20,000, it may be retained in court and invested in the same way as the fund of a child, or
　(3)　in intermediate cases the advice of the Master of the Court of Protection should be sought.
　11.3　A form of order transferring the fund to the Court of Protection is set out in practice form N292.
　11.4　In order for the Court Funds Office to release a fund which is subject to the legal aid charge to the Court of Protection the litigation friend or his legal representative should provide the appropriate area office of the Legal Aid Board with an undertaking in respect of a sum to cover their costs, following which the

---
[12] See rule 2.3 for a definition of legal representative.

area office will advise the Court Funds Office in writing of that sum, enabling them to transfer the balance to the Court of Protection on receipt of a CFO form 200 payment schedule authorised by the court.

11.5 The CFO form 200 should be completed and presented to the court where the settlement or trial took place for authorisation, subject to paragraphs 11.6 and 11.7 below.

11.6 Where the settlement took place in the Royal Courts of Justice the CFO form 200 should be completed and presented for authorisation:

    (1)   on behalf of a child, in the Masters' Secretary's Office, Room E214, and

    (2)   on behalf of a patient, in the Action Department, Room E15.

11.7 Where the trial took place in the Royal Courts of Justice the CFO form 200 is completed and authorised by the court officer.

PAYMENT OUT OF FUNDS IN COURT

12.1 Applications to a Master or district judge;

    (1)   for payment out of money from the fund for the benefit of the child, or

    (2)   to vary an investment strategy,

may be dealt with without a hearing unless the court directs otherwise.

12.2 When the child reaches full age, his fund in court:

    (1)   where it is a sum of money will be paid out to him, and

    (2)   where it is in the form of investments other than money (for example shares or unit trusts), will be transferred into his name.

12.3 An application for payment out of funds being administered by the Court of Protection must be made to the Court of Protection.

(For further information on payments into and out of court see the practice directions supplementing Parts 36 and 37.)

CPR PART 22   STATEMENTS OF TRUTH

CONTENTS OF THIS PART
Documents to be verified by a statement of truth   Rule 22.1
Failure to verify a statement of case   Rule 22.2
Failure to verify a witness statement   Rule 22.3
Power of the court to require a document to be verified   Rule 22.4

22.1   DOCUMENTS TO BE VERIFIED BY A STATEMENT OF TRUTH
   (1)   The following documents must be verified by a statement of truth—
      (a)   a statement of case;
      (b)   a response complying with an order under rule 18.1 to provide further information; and
      (c)   a witness statement.
   (2)   Where a statement of case is amended, the amendments must be verified by a statement of truth unless the court orders otherwise.
   (Part 17 provides for amendments to statements of case)
   (3)   If an applicant wishes to rely on matters set out in his application notice as evidence, the application notice must be verified by a statement of truth.
   (4)   Subject to paragraph (5), a statement of truth is a statement that—
      (a)   the party putting forward the document; or
      (b)   in the case of a witness statement, the maker of the witness statement, believes the facts stated in the document are true.
   (5)   If a party is conducting proceedings with a litigation friend, the statement of truth in—
      (a)   a statement of case;
      (b)   a response; or
      (c)   an application notice,
is a statement that the litigation friend believes the facts stated in the document being verified are true.
   (6)   The statement of truth must be signed by—
      (a)   in the case of a statement of case, a response or an application—
         (i)   the party or litigation friend; or
         (ii)   the legal representative on behalf of the party or litigation friend; and
      (b)   in the case of a witness statement, the maker of the statement.
   (7)   A statement of truth which is not contained in the document which it verifies, must clearly identify that document.
   (8)   A statement of truth in a statement of case may be made by—
      (a)   a person who is not a party; or
      (b)   by two parties jointly,
where this is permitted by a relevant practice direction.

22.2   FAILURE TO VERIFY A STATEMENT OF CASE
   (1)   If a party fails to verify his statement of case by a statement of truth—
      (a)   the statement of case shall remain effective unless struck out; but
      (b)   the party may not rely on the statement of case as evidence of any of the matters set out in it.
   (2)   The court may strike out(GL) a statement of case which is not verified by a statement of truth.
   (3)   Any party may apply for an order under paragraph (2).

22.3   FAILURE TO VERIFY A WITNESS STATEMENT
If the maker of a witness statement fails to verify the witness statement by a statement of truth the court may direct that it shall not be admissible as evidence.

CPR PART 22 STATEMENTS OF TRUTH

22.4 POWER OF THE COURT TO REQUIRE A DOCUMENT TO BE VERIFIED

(1) The court may order a person who has failed to verify a document in accordance with rule 22.1 to verify the document.

(2) Any party may apply for an order under paragraph (1).

PD 22 PRACTICE DIRECTION — STATEMENTS OF TRUTH

This practice direction supplements CPR Part 22

DOCUMENTS TO BE VERIFIED BY A STATEMENT OF TRUTH

1.1 Rule 22.1(1) sets out the documents which must be verified by a statement of truth. The documents include:

    (1) a statement of case,

    (2) a response complying with an order under rule 18.1 to provide further information, and

    (3) a witness statement.

1.2 If an applicant wishes to rely on matters set out in his application notice as evidence, the application notice must be verified by a statement of truth[1].

1.3 An expert's report should also be verified by a statement of truth. For the form of the statement of truth verifying an expert's report (which differs from that set out below) see the practice direction which supplements Part 35.

1.4 In addition, a notice of objections to an account being taken by the court should be verified by a statement of truth unless verified by an affidavit or a witness statement[2].

1.5 The statement of truth may be contained in the document it verifies or it may be in a separate document served subsequently, in which case it must identify the document to which it relates.

FORM OF THE STATEMENT OF TRUTH

2.1 The form of the statement of truth verifying a statement of case, a response, an application notice or a notice of objections should be as follows:

'[I believe] [the (*claimant or as may be*) believes] that the facts stated in this [*name document being verified*] are true.'

2.2 The form of the statement of truth verifying a witness statement should be as follows:

'I believe that the facts stated in this witness statement are true.'

2.3 Where the statement of truth is contained in a separate document, the document containing the statement of truth must be headed with the title of the proceedings and the claim number. The document being verified should be identified in the statement of truth as follows:

    (1) claim form: 'the claim form issued on [*date*]',

    (2) particulars of claim: 'the particulars of claim issued on [*date*]',

    (3) statement of case: 'the [*defence or as may be*] served on the [*name of party*] on [*date*]',

    (4) application notice: 'the application notice issued on [*date*] for [*set out the remedy sought*]',

    (5) witness statement: 'the witness statement filed on [*date*] or served on [*party*] on [*date*]'.

WHO MAY SIGN THE STATEMENT OF TRUTH

3.1 In a statement of case, a response or an application notice, the statement of truth must be signed by:

    (1) the party or his litigation friend[3], or

    (2) the legal representative[4] of the party or litigation friend.

---

[1] See rule 22.1(3).

[2] See the Accounts and Inquiries practice direction supplementing Part 40 (judgments and orders).

[3] See Part 21 (children and patients).

[4] See rule 2.3 for the definition of legal representative.

3.2 A statement of truth verifying a witness statement must be signed by the witness.

3.3 A statement of truth verifying a notice of objections to an account must be signed by the objecting party or his legal representative.

3.4 Where a document is to be verified on behalf of a company or other corporation, subject to paragraph 3.7 below, the statement of truth must be signed by a person holding a senior position[5] in the company or corporation. That person must state the office or position he holds.

3.5 Each of the following persons is a person holding a senior position:

(1) in respect of a registered company or corporation, a director, the treasurer, secretary, chief executive, manager or other officer of the company or corporation, and

(2) in respect of a corporation which is not a registered company, in addition to those persons set out in (1), the mayor, chairman, president or town clerk or other similar officer of the corporation.

3.6 Where the document is to be verified on behalf of a partnership, those who may sign the statement of truth are:

(1) any of the partners, or

(2) a person having the control or management of the partnership business.

3.7 Where a party is legally represented, the legal representative may sign the statement of truth on his behalf. The statement signed by the legal representative will refer to the client's belief, not his own. In signing he must state the capacity in which he signs and the name of his firm where appropriate.

3.8 Where a legal representative has signed a statement of truth, his signature will be taken by the court as his statement:

(1) that the client on whose behalf he has signed had authorised him to do so,

(2) that before signing he had explained to the client that in signing the statement of truth he would be confirming the client's belief that the facts stated in the document were true, and

(3) that before signing he had informed the client of the possible consequences to the client if it should subsequently appear that the client did not have an honest belief in the truth of those facts (see rule 32.14).

3.9 The individual who signs a statement of truth must print his full name clearly beneath his signature.

3.10 A legal representative who signs a statement of truth must sign in his own name and not that of his firm or employer.

CONSEQUENCES OF FAILURE TO VERIFY

4.1 If a statement of case is not verified by a statement of truth, the statement of case will remain effective unless it is struck out[6], but a party may not rely on the contents of a statement of case as evidence until it has been verified by a statement of truth.

4.2 Any party may apply to the court for an order that unless within such period as the court may specify the statement of case is verified by the service of a statement of truth, the statement of case will be struck out.

4.3 The usual order for the costs of an application referred to in paragraph 4.2 will be that the costs be paid by the party who had failed to verify in any event and forthwith.

PENALTY

5 Attention is drawn to rule 32.14 which sets out the consequences of verifying a statement of case containing a false statement without an honest belief in its truth.

---

[5] See rule 6.4(4).
[6] See rule 22.2(1).

CPR PART 23 GENERAL RULES ABOUT APPLICATIONS FOR COURT ORDERS

CONTENTS OF THIS PART

Meaning of 'application notice' and 'respondent'	Rule 23.1
Where to make an application	Rule 23.2
Application notice to be filed	Rule 23.3
Notice of an application	Rule 23.4
Time when an application is made	Rule 23.5
What an application notice must include	Rule 23.6
Service of a copy of an application notice	Rule 23.7
Applications which may be dealt with without a hearing	Rule 23.8
Service of application where application made without notice	Rule 23.9
Application to set aside or vary order made without notice	Rule 23.10
Power of the court to proceed in the absence of a party	Rule 23.11

23.1 MEANING OF 'APPLICATION NOTICE' AND 'RESPONDENT'
In this Part—
'application notice' means a document in which the applicant states his intention to seek a court order; and
'respondent' means—
  (a) the person against whom the order is sought; and
  (b) such other person as the court may direct.

23.2 WHERE TO MAKE AN APPLICATION
(1) The general rule is that an application must be made to the court where the claim was started.
(2) If a claim has been transferred to another court since it was started, an application must be made to the court to which the claim has been transferred.
(3) If the parties have been notified of a fixed date for the trial, an application must be made to the court where the trial is to take place.
(4) If an application is made before a claim has been started, it must be made to the court where it is likely that the claim to which the application relates will be started unless there is good reason to make the application to a different court.
(5) If an application is made after proceedings to enforce judgment have begun, it must be made to any court which is dealing with the enforcement of the judgment unless any rule or practice direction provides otherwise.

23.3 APPLICATION NOTICE TO BE FILED
(1) The general rule is that an applicant must file an application notice.
(2) An applicant may make an application without filing an application notice if—
  (a) this is permitted by a rule or practice direction; or
  (b) the court dispenses with the requirement for an application notice.

23.4 NOTICE OF AN APPLICATION
(1) The general rule is that a copy of the application notice must be served on each respondent.
(2) An application may be made without serving a copy of the application notice if this is permitted by—
  (a) a rule;
  (b) a practice direction; or
  (c) a court order.
(Rule 23.7 deals with service of a copy of the application notice)

23.5 TIME WHEN AN APPLICATION IS MADE
Where an application must be made within a specified time, it is so made if the application notice is received by the court within that time.

CPR PART 23 GENERAL RULES ABOUT APPLICATIONS FOR COURT ORDERS

23.6 WHAT AN APPLICATION NOTICE MUST INCLUDE
An application notice must state—
  (a) what order the applicant is seeking; and
  (b) briefly, why the applicant is seeking the order.
(Part 22 requires an application notice to be verified by a statement of truth if the applicant wishes to rely on matters set out in his application notice as evidence)

23.7 SERVICE OF A COPY OF AN APPLICATION NOTICE
  (1) A copy of the application notice—
    (a) must be served as soon as practicable after it is filed; and
    (b) except where another time limit is specified in these Rules or a practice direction, must in any event be served at least 3 days before the court is to deal with the application.
  (2) If a copy of the application notice is to be served by the court, the applicant must, when he files the application notice, file a copy of any written evidence in support.
  (3) When a copy of an application notice is served it must be accompanied by—
    (a) a copy of any written evidence in support; and
    (b) a copy of any draft order which the applicant has attached to his application.
  (4) If—
    (a) an application notice is served; but
    (b) the period of notice is shorter than the period required by these Rules or a practice direction,
the court may direct that, in the circumstances of the case, sufficient notice has been given and hear the application.
  (5) This rule does not require written evidence—
    (a) to be filed if it has already been filed; or
    (b) to be served on a party on whom it has already been served.
(Part 6 contains the general rules about service of documents including who must serve a copy of the application notice)

23.8 APPLICATIONS WHICH MAY BE DEALT WITH WITHOUT A HEARING
The court may deal with an application without a hearing if—
  (a) the parties agree as to the terms of the order sought;
  (b) the parties agree that the court should dispose of the application without a hearing, or
  (c) the court does not consider that a hearing would be appropriate.

23.9 SERVICE OF APPLICATION WHERE APPLICATION MADE WITHOUT NOTICE
  (1) This rule applies where the court has disposed of an application which it permitted to be made without service of a copy of the application notice.
  (2) Where the court makes an order, whether granting or dismissing the application, a copy of the application notice and any evidence in support must, unless the court orders otherwise, be served with the order on any party or other person—
    (a) against whom the order was made; and
    (b) against whom the order was sought.
  (3) The order must contain a statement of the right to make an application to set aside$^{(GL)}$ or vary the order under rule 23.10.

23.10 APPLICATION TO SET ASIDE OR VARY ORDER MADE WITHOUT NOTICE
  (1) A person served with an order made on an application but on whom a copy of the application notice was not served may apply to the court for the order to be set aside$^{(GL)}$ or varied.
  (2) An application under this rule must be made within 7 days after the date on which the order was served on the person making the application.

23.11 POWER OF THE COURT TO PROCEED IN THE ABSENCE OF A PARTY

(1) Where the applicant or any respondent fails to attend the hearing of an application, the court may proceed in his absence.

(2) Where—

(a) the applicant or any respondent fails to attend the hearing of an application; and

(b) the court makes an order at the hearing,

the court may, on application or of its own initiative, re-list the application.

(Part 40 deals with service of orders)

PD 23 PRACTICE DIRECTION — APPLICATIONS

This practice direction supplements CPR Part 23

REFERENCE TO A JUDGE

1 A Master or district judge may refer to a judge any matter which he thinks should properly be decided by a judge, and the judge may either dispose of the matter or refer it back to the Master or district judge.

APPLICATION NOTICES

2.1 An application notice must, in addition to the matters set out in rule 23.6, be signed and include:
 (1) the title of the claim,
 (2) the reference number of the claim,
 (3) the full name of the applicant,
 (4) where the applicant is not already a party, his address for service, and
 (5) either a request for a hearing or a request that the application be dealt with without a hearing.
(Practice Form N244 may be used.)

2.2 On receipt of an application notice containing a request for a hearing the court will notify the applicant of the time and date for the hearing of the application.

2.3 On receipt of an application notice containing a request that the application be dealt with without a hearing, the application notice will be sent to a Master or district judge so that he may decide whether the application is suitable for consideration without a hearing.

2.4 Where the Master or district judge agrees that the application is suitable for consideration without a hearing, the court will so inform the applicant and the respondent and may give directions for the filing of evidence. (Rules 23.9 and 23.10 enable a party to apply for an order made without a hearing to be set aside or varied.)

2.5 Where the Master or district judge does not agree that the application is suitable for consideration without a hearing, the court will notify the applicant and the respondent of the time, date and place for the hearing of the application and may at the same time give directions as to the filing of evidence.

2.6 If the application is intended to be made to a judge, the application notice should so state. In that case, paragraphs 2.3, 2.4 and 2.5 will apply as though references to the Master or district judge were references to a judge.

2.7 Every application should be made as soon as it becomes apparent that it is necessary or desirable to make it.

2.8 Applications should wherever possible be made so that they can be considered at any other hearing for which a date has already been fixed or for which a date is about to be fixed. This is particularly so in relation to case management conferences, allocation and listing hearings and pre-trial reviews fixed by the court.

2.9 The parties must anticipate that at any hearing the court may wish to review the conduct of the case as a whole and give any necessary case management directions. They should be ready to assist the court in doing so and to answer questions the court may ask for this purpose.

2.10 Where a date for a hearing has been fixed and a party wishes to make an application at that hearing but he does not have sufficient time to serve an application notice he should inform the other party and the court (if possible in writing) as soon as he can of the nature of the application and the reason for it. He should then make the application orally at the hearing.

APPLICATIONS WITHOUT SERVICE OF APPLICATION NOTICE

3 An application may be made without serving an application notice only:
 (1) where there is exceptional urgency,

(2) where the overriding objective is best furthered by doing so,
(3) by consent of all parties,
(4) with the permission of the court,
(5) where paragraph 2.10 above applies, or
(6) where a court order, rule or practice direction permits.

GIVING NOTICE OF AN APPLICATION

4.1 Unless the court otherwise directs or paragraph 3 of this practice direction applies the application notice must be served as soon as practicable after it has been issued and, if there is to be a hearing, at least 3 clear days before the hearing date (rule 23.7(1)(b)).

4.2 Where an application notice should be served but there is not sufficient time to do so, informal notification of the application should be given unless the circumstances of the application require secrecy.

PRE-ACTION APPLICATIONS

5 All applications made before a claim is commenced should be made under Part 23 of the Civil Procedure Rules. Attention is drawn in particular to rule 23.2(4).

TELEPHONE HEARINGS

6.1 The court may order that an application or part of an application be dealt with by a telephone hearing.

6.2 An order under 6.1 will not normally be made unless every party entitled to be given notice of the application and to be heard at the hearing has consented to the order.

6.3 (1) Where a party entitled to be heard at the hearing of the application is acting in person, the court—

(a) may not make an order under 6.1 except on condition that arrangements will be made for the party acting in person to be attended at the telephone hearing by a responsible person to whom the party acting in person is known and who can confirm to the court the identity of the party; and

(b) may not give effect to an order under 6.1 unless the party acting in person is accompanied by a responsible person who at the commencement of the hearing confirms to the court the identity of the party.

(2) The 'responsible person' may be a barrister, solicitor, legal executive, doctor, clergyman, police officer, prison officer or other person of comparable status.

(3) If the court makes an order under 6.1 it will give any directions necessary for the telephone hearing.

6.4 No representative of a party to an application being heard by telephone may attend the judge in person while the application is being heard unless the other party to the application has agreed that he may do so.

6.5 If an application is to be heard by telephone the following directions will apply, subject to any direction to the contrary:

(1) The applicant's legal representative must arrange the telephone conference by the British Telecom conference call 'call out' system or by some other comparable system for precisely the time fixed by the court.

(2) He must tell the operator the telephone numbers of all those participating in the conference call and the sequence in which they are to be called.

(3) It is the responsibility of the applicant's legal representative to ascertain from all the other parties whether they have instructed counsel and, if so the identity of counsel, and whether the legal representative and counsel will be on the same or different telephone numbers.

(4) The sequence in which they are to be called will be:
(a) the applicant's legal representative and (if on a different number) his counsel,
(b) the legal representative (and counsel) for all other parties, and
(c) the judge.

PD 23 PRACTICE DIRECTION — APPLICATIONS

(5) The applicant's legal representative must arrange for the conference to be recorded on tape by the telecommunications provider whose system is being used and must send the tape to the court.

(6) Each speaker is to remain on the line after being called by the operator setting up the conference call. The call may be 2 or 3 minutes before the time fixed for the application.

(7) When the judge has been connected the applicant's legal representative (or his counsel) will introduce the parties in the usual way.

(8) If the use of a 'speakerphone' by any party causes the judge or any other party any difficulty in hearing what is said the judge may require that party to use a hand held telephone.

(9) The telephone charges debited to the account of the party initiating the conference call will be treated as part of the costs of the application.

VIDEO CONFERENCING

7 Where the parties to a matter wish to use video conferencing facilities, and those facilities are available in the relevant court, they should apply to the Master or district judge for directions.

NOTE OF PROCEEDINGS

8 The procedural judge should keep, either by way of a note or a tape recording, brief details of all proceedings before him, including the dates of the proceedings and a short statement of the decision taken at each hearing.

EVIDENCE

9.1 The requirement for evidence in certain types of applications is set out in some of the rules and practice directions. Where there is no specific requirement to provide evidence it should be borne in mind that, as a practical matter, the court will often need to be satisfied by evidence of the facts that are relied on in support of or for opposing the application.

9.2 The court may give directions for the filing of evidence in support of or opposing a particular application. The court may also give directions for the filing of evidence in relation to any hearing that it fixes on its own initiative. The directions may specify the form that evidence is to take and when it is to be served.

9.3 Where it is intended to rely on evidence which is not contained in the application itself, the evidence, if it has not already been served, should be served with the application.

9.4 Where a respondent to an application wishes to rely on evidence which has not yet been served he should serve it as soon as possible and in any event in accordance with any directions the court may have given.

9.5 If it is necessary for the applicant to serve any evidence in reply it should be served as soon as possible and in any event in accordance with any directions the court may have given.

9.6 Evidence must be filed with the court as well as served on the parties. Exhibits should not be filed unless the court otherwise directs.

9.7 The contents of an application notice may be used as evidence (otherwise than at trial) provided the contents have been verified by a statement of truth[1].

CONSENT ORDERS

10.1 Rule 40.6 sets out the circumstances where an agreed judgment or order may be entered and sealed.

10.2 Where all parties affected by an order have written to the court consenting to the making of the order a draft of which has been filed with the court, the court will treat the draft as having been signed in accordance with rule 40.6(7).

10.3 Where a consent order must be made by a judge (i.e. rule 40.6(2) does not apply) the order must be drawn so that the judge's name and judicial title can be inserted.

10.4 The parties to an application for a consent order must ensure that they provide the court with any material it needs to be satisfied that it is appropriate to

---

[1] See Part 22.

make the order. Subject to any rule or practice direction a letter will generally be acceptable for this purpose.

10.5 Where a judgment or order has been agreed in respect of an application or claim where a hearing date has been fixed, the parties must inform the court immediately. (Note that parties are reminded that under rules 28.4 and 29.5 the case management timetable cannot be varied by written agreement of the parties.)

OTHER APPLICATIONS CONSIDERED WITHOUT A HEARING

11.1 Where rule 23.8(b) applies the parties should so inform the court in writing and each should confirm that all evidence and other material on which he relies has been disclosed to the other parties to the application.

11.2 Where rule 23.8(c) applies the court will treat the application as if it were proposing to make an order on its own initiative.

MISCELLANEOUS

12 Except in the most simple application the applicant should bring to any hearing a draft of the order sought. If the case is proceeding in the Royal Courts of Justice and the order is unusually long or complex it should also be supplied on disk for use by the court office [the current word processing system to be used is WordPerfect 5.1].

COSTS

13.1 Attention is drawn to the costs practice direction and, in particular, to the court's power to make a summary assessment of costs.

13.2 Attention is also drawn to rule 44.13(i) which provides that if an order makes no mention of costs, none are payable in respect of the proceedings to which it relates.

CPR PART 24 SUMMARY JUDGMENT

CONTENTS OF THIS PART
Scope of this Part — Rule 24.1
Grounds for summary judgment — Rule 24.2
Types of proceedings in which summary judgment is available — Rule 24.3
Procedure — Rule 24.4
Evidence for the purposes of a summary judgment hearing — Rule 24.5
Court's powers when it determines a summary judgment application — Rule 24.6

24.1 SCOPE OF THIS PART
This Part sets out a procedure by which the court may decide a claim or a particular issue without a trial.

24.2 GROUNDS FOR SUMMARY JUDGMENT
The court may give summary judgment against a claimant or defendant on the whole of a claim or on a particular issue if—
  (a) it considers that—
    (i) that claimant has no real prospect of succeeding on the claim or issue; or
    (ii) that defendant has no real prospect of successfully defending the claim or issue; and
  (b) there is no other reason why the case or issue should be disposed of at a trial.
(Rule 3.4 makes provision for the court to strike out(GL) a statement of case or part of a statement of case if it appears that it discloses no reasonable grounds for bringing or defending a claim)

24.3 TYPES OF PROCEEDINGS IN WHICH SUMMARY JUDGMENT IS AVAILABLE
(1) The court may give summary judgment against a claimant in any type of proceedings.
(2) The court may give summary judgment against a defendant in any type of proceedings except—
  (a) proceedings for possession of residential premises against—
    (i) a mortgagor; or
    (ii) a tenant or person holding over after the end of his tenancy, whose occupancy is protected within the meaning of the Rent Act 1977, or the Housing Act 1988; and
  (b) proceedings for an admiralty claim in rem; and
  (c) contentious probate proceedings.

24.4 PROCEDURE
(1) A claimant may not apply for summary judgment until the defendant against whom the application is made has filed—
  (a) an acknowledgement of service; or
  (b) a defence,
unless—
  (i) the court gives permission; or
  (ii) a practice direction provides otherwise.
(Rule 10.3 sets out the period for filing an acknowledgment of service and rule 15.4 the period for filing a defence)
(2) If a claimant applies for summary judgment before a defendant against whom the application is made has filed a defence, that defendant need not file a defence before the hearing.
(3) Where a summary judgment hearing is fixed, the respondent (or the parties where the hearing is fixed of the court's own initiative) must be given at least 14 days' notice of—

CPR PART 24 SUMMARY JUDGMENT

(a) the date fixed for the hearing; and
(b) the issues which it is proposed that the court will decide at the hearing.
(Part 23 contains the general rules about how to make an application)
(Rule 3.3 applies where the court exercises its powers of its own initiative)

24.5 EVIDENCE FOR THE PURPOSES OF A SUMMARY JUDGMENT HEARING

(1) If the respondent to an application for summary judgment wishes to rely on written evidence at the hearing, he must—
    (a) file the written evidence; and
    (b) serve copies on every other party to the application,
at least 7 days before the summary judgment hearing.

(2) If the applicant wishes to rely on written evidence in reply, he must—
    (a) file the written evidence; and
    (b) serve a copy on the respondent,
at least 3 days before the summary judgment hearing.

(3) Where a summary judgment hearing is fixed by the court of its own initiative—
    (a) any party who wishes to rely on written evidence at the hearing must—
        (i) file the written evidence; and
        (ii) unless the court orders otherwise, serve copies on every other party to the proceedings,
at least 7 days before the date of the hearing;
    (b) any party who wishes to rely on written evidence at the hearing in reply to any other party's written evidence must—
        (i) file the written evidence in reply; and
        (ii) unless the court orders otherwise serve copies on every other party to the proceedings, at least 3 days before the date of the hearing.

(4) This rule does not require written evidence—
    (a) to be filed if it has already been filed; or
    (b) to be served on a party on whom it has already been served.

24.6 COURT'S POWERS WHEN IT DETERMINES A SUMMARY JUDGMENT APPLICATION

When the court determines a summary judgment application it may—
    (a) give directions as to the filing and service of a defence;
    (b) give further directions about the management of the case.
(Rule 3.1(3) provides that the court may attach conditions when it makes an order)

PD 24 PRACTICE DIRECTION — THE SUMMARY DISPOSAL OF CLAIMS

This practice direction supplements CPR Part 24

APPLICATIONS FOR SUMMARY JUDGMENT UNDER PART 24

1.1 Attention is drawn to Part 24 itself and to:
Part 3, in particular rule 3.1(3) and (5),
Part 22,
Part 23, in particular rule 23.6,
Part 32, in particular rule 32.6(2).

1.2 In this paragraph, where the context so admits, the word 'claim' includes:
   (1) a part of a claim, and
   (2) an issue on which the claim in whole or part depends.

1.3 An application for summary judgment under rule 24.2 may be based on:
   (1) a point of law (including a question of construction of a document),
   (2) the evidence which can reasonably be expected to be available at trial or the lack of it, or
   (3) a combination of these.

1.4 Rule 24.4(1) deals with the stage in the proceedings at which an application under Part 24 can be made (but see paragraph 7.1 below).

PROCEDURE FOR MAKING AN APPLICATION

2 (1) Attention is drawn to rules 24.4(3) and 23.6.

(2) The application notice must include a statement that it is an application for summary judgment made under Part 24.

(3) The application notice or the evidence contained or referred to in it or served with it must—
   (a) identify concisely any point of law or provision in a document on which the applicant relies, and/or
   (b) state that it is made because the applicant believes that on the evidence the respondent has no real prospect of succeeding on the claim or issue or (as the case may be) of successfully defending the claim or issue to which the application relates,
and in either case state that the applicant knows of no other reason why the disposal of the claim or issue should await trial.

(4) Unless the application notice itself contains all the evidence (if any) on which the applicant relies, the application notice should identify the written evidence on which the applicant relies. This does not affect the applicant's right to file further evidence under rule 24.5(2).

(5) The application notice should draw the attention of the respondent to rule 24.5(1).

THE HEARING

4 (1) The hearing of the application will normally take place before a Master or a district judge.

(2) The Master or district judge may direct that the application be heard by a High Court Judge (if the case is in the High Court) or a circuit judge (if the case is in a county court).

THE COURT'S APPROACH

4.1 Where a claimant applies for judgment on his claim, the court will give that judgment if:
   (1) the claimant has shown a case which, if unanswered, would entitle him to that judgment, and
   (2) the defendant has not shown any reason why the claim should be dealt with at trial.

PD 24 PRACTICE DIRECTION — THE SUMMARY DISPOSAL OF CLAIMS

4.2 Where a defendant applies for judgment in his favour on the claimant's claim, the court will give that judgment if either:
   (1) the claimant has failed to show a case which, if unanswered, would entitle him to judgment, or
   (2) the defendant has shown that the claim would be bound to be dismissed at trial.

4.3 Where it appears to the court possible that a claim or defence may succeed but improbable that it will do so, the court may make a conditional order, as described below.

ORDERS THE COURT MAY MAKE

5.1 The orders the court may make on an application under Part 24 include:
   (1) judgment on the claim,
   (2) the striking out or dismissal of the claim,
   (3) the dismissal of the application,
   (4) a conditional order.

5.2 A conditional order is an order which requires a party:
   (1) to pay a sum of money into court, or
   (2) to take a specified step in relation to his claim or defence, as the case may be,
and provides that that party's claim will be dismissed or his statement of case will be struck out if he does not comply.

(Note — the court will not follow its former practice of granting leave to a defendant to defend a claim, whether conditionally or unconditionally.)

ACCOUNTS AND INQUIRIES

6 If a remedy sought by a claimant in his claim form includes, or necessarily involves, taking an account or making an inquiry, an application can be made under Part 24 by any party to the proceedings for an order directing any necessary accounts or inquiries to be taken or made.

(This paragraph replaces RSC Order 43, rule 1, but applies to county court proceedings as well as to High Court proceedings. The Accounts practice direction supplementing Part 40 contains further provisions as to orders for accounts and inquiries.)

SPECIFIC PERFORMANCE

7.1 (1) If a remedy sought by a claimant in his claim form includes a claim—
      (a) for specific performance of an agreement (whether in writing or not) for the sale, purchase, exchange, mortgage or charge of any property, or for the grant or assignment of a lease or tenancy of any property, with or without an alternative claim for damages, or
      (b) for rescission of such an agreement, or
      (c) for the forfeiture or return of any deposit made under such an agreement,
the claimant may apply under Part 24 for judgment.

7.1 (2) The claimant may do so at any time after the claim form has been served, whether or not the defendant has acknowledged service of the claim form, whether or not the time for acknowledging service has expired and whether or not any particulars of claim have been served.

7.2 The application notice by which an application under paragraph 7.1 is made must have attached to it the text of the order sought by the claimant.

7.3 The application notice and a copy of every affidavit or witness statement in support and of any exhibit referred to therein must be served on the defendant not less than 4 days before the hearing of the application. (Note — the 4 days replaces for these applications the 7 days specified in rule 24.5.)

(This paragraph replaces RSC Order 86, rules 1 and 2, but applies to county court proceedings as well as to High Court proceedings.)

SETTING ASIDE ORDER FOR SUMMARY JUDGMENT

8.1 If an order for summary judgment is made against a respondent who does not appear at the hearing of the application, the respondent may apply for the order to be set aside or varied (see also rule 23.11).

8.2 On the hearing of an application under paragraph 8.1 the court may make such order as it thinks just.

COSTS

9.1 Attention is drawn to Part 44 (fixed costs).

9.2 Attention is drawn to the Costs Practice Direction and in particular to the court's power to make a summary assessment of costs.

9.3 Attention is also drawn to rule 43.5(5) which provides that if an order does not mention costs no party is entitled to costs relating to that order.

CASE MANAGEMENT

10 Where the court dismisses the application or makes an order that does not completely dispose of the claim, the court will give case management directions as to the future conduct of the case.

CPR PART 25   INTERIM REMEDIES

CONTENTS OF THIS PART
Orders for interim remedies   Rule 25.1
Time when an order for an interim remedy may be made   Rule 25.2
How to apply for an interim remedy   Rule 25.3
Application for an interim remedy where there is no related claim   Rule 25.4
Inspection of property before commencement or against a non-party   Rule 25.5
Interim payments — general procedure   Rule 25.6
Interim payments — conditions to be satisfied and matters to be taken
    into account   Rule 25.7
Powers of court where it has made an order for interim payment   Rule 25.8
Restriction on disclosure of an interim payment   Rule 25.9
Interim injunction to cease if claim stayed   Rule 25.10
Interim injunction to cease after [14*] days if claim struck out   Rule 25.11

25.1   ORDERS FOR INTERIM REMEDIES
 (1) The court may grant the following interim remedies—
     (a)   an interim injunction$^{(GL)}$;
     (b)   an interim declaration;
     (c)   an order—
         (i)   for the detention, custody or preservation of relevant property;
         (ii)   for the inspection of relevant property;
         (iii) for the taking of a sample of relevant property;
         (iv)   for the carrying out of an experiment on or with relevant property;
         (v)   for the sale of relevant property which is of a perishable nature or which for any other good reason it is desirable to sell quickly; and
         (vi)   for the payment of income from relevant property until a claim is decided;
     (d)   an order authorising a person to enter any land or building in the possession of a party to the proceedings for the purposes of carrying out an order under sub-paragraph (c);
     (e)   an order under section 4 of the Torts (Interference with Goods) Act 1977 to deliver up goods;
     (f)   an order (referred to as a 'freezing injunction$^{(GL)}$')—
         (i)   restraining a party from removing from the jurisdiction assets located there; or
         (ii)   restraining a party from dealing with any assets whether located within the jurisdiction or not;
     (g)   an order directing a party to provide information about the location of relevant property or assets or to provide information about relevant property or assets which are or may be the subject of an application for a freezing injunction$^{(GL)}$;
     (h)   an order (referred to as a 'search order') under section 7 of the Civil Procedure Act 1997 (order requiring a party to admit another party to premises for the purpose of preserving evidence etc.);
     (i)   an order under section 33 of the Supreme Court Act 1981 or section 52 of the County Courts Act 1984 (order for disclosure of documents or inspection of property before a claim has been made);
     (j)   an order under section 34 of the Supreme Court Act 1981 or section 53 of the County Courts Act 1984 (order in certain proceedings for disclosure of documents or inspection of property against a non-party);
     (k)   an order (referred to as an order for interim payment) under rule 25.6 for payment by a defendant on account of any damages, debt or other sum (except costs) which the court may hold the defendant liable to pay;

---

* In SI 1999/1008 this figure is mistakenly given as 24.

(l) an order for a specified fund to be paid into court or otherwise secured, where there is a dispute over a party's right to the fund;

(m) an order permitting a party seeking to recover personal property to pay money into court pending the outcome of the proceedings and directing that, if he does so, the property shall be given up to him; and

(n) an order directing a party to prepare and file accounts relating to the dispute.

(Rule 34.2 provides for the court to issue a witness summons requiring a witness to produce documents to the court at the hearing or on such date as the court may direct)

(2) In paragraph (1)(c) and (g), 'relevant property' means property (including land) which is the subject of a claim or as to which any question may arise on a claim.

(3) The fact that a particular kind of interim remedy is not listed in paragraph (1) does not affect any power that the court may have to grant that remedy.

(4) The court may grant an interim remedy whether or not there has been a claim for a final remedy of that kind.

25.2 TIME WHEN AN ORDER FOR AN INTERIM REMEDY MAY BE MADE

(1) An order for an interim remedy may be made at any time, including—

(a) before proceedings are started; and

(b) after judgment has been given.

(Rule 7.2 provides that proceedings are started when the court issues a claim form)

(2) However—

(a) paragraph (1) is subject to any rule, practice direction or other enactment which provides otherwise;

(b) the court may grant an interim remedy before a claim has been made only if—

(i) the matter is urgent; or

(ii) it is otherwise desirable to do so in the interests of justice; and

(c) unless the court otherwise orders, a defendant may not apply for any of the orders listed in rule 25.1(1) before he has filed either an acknowledgment of service or a defence.

(Part 10 provides for filing an acknowledgment of service and Part 15 for filing a defence)

(3) Where the court grants an interim remedy before a claim has been commenced, it may give directions requiring a claim to be commenced.

(4) In particular, the court need not direct that a claim be commenced where the application is made under section 33 of the Supreme Court Act 1981 or section 52 of the County Courts Act 1984 (order for disclosure, inspection etc. before commencement of a claim).

25.3 HOW TO APPLY FOR AN INTERIM REMEDY

(1) The court may grant an interim remedy on an application made without notice if it appears to the court that there are good reasons for not giving notice.

(2) An application for an interim remedy must be supported by evidence, unless the court orders otherwise.

(3) If the applicant makes an application without giving notice, the evidence in support of the application must state the reasons why notice has not been given.

(Part 3 lists general powers of the court)

(Part 23 contains general rules about making an application)

25.4 APPLICATION FOR AN INTERIM REMEDY WHERE THERE IS NO RELATED CLAIM

(1) This rule applies where a party wishes to apply for an interim remedy but—

(a) the remedy is sought in relation to proceedings which are taking place, or will take place, outside the jurisdiction; or

(b) the application is made under section 33 of the Supreme Court Act 1981 or section 52 of the County Courts Act 1984 (order for disclosure, inspection etc. before commencement) before a claim has been commenced.

CPR PART 25 INTERIM REMEDIES

(2) An application under this rule must be made in accordance with the general rules about applications contained in Part 23.

(The following provisions are also relevant—
- Rule 25.5 (inspection of property before commencement or against a non-party)
- Rule 31.16 (orders for disclosure of documents before proceedings start)
- Rule 31.17 (orders for disclosure of documents against a person not a party))

25.5 INSPECTION OF PROPERTY BEFORE COMMENCEMENT OR AGAINST A NON-PARTY

(1) This rule applies where a person makes an application under—
   (a) section 33(1) of the Supreme Court Act 1981 or section 52(1) of the County Courts Act 1984 (inspection etc. of property before commencement);
   (b) section 34(3) of the Supreme Court Act 1981 or section 53(3) of the County Courts Act 1984 (inspection etc. of property against a non-party).

(2) The evidence in support of such an application must show, if practicable by reference to any statement of case prepared in relation to the proceedings or anticipated proceedings, that the property—
   (a) is or may become the subject matter of such proceedings; or
   (b) is relevant to the issues that will arise in relation to such proceedings.

(3) A copy of the application notice and a copy of the evidence in support must be served on—
   (a) the person against whom the order is sought; and
   (b) in relation to an application under section 34(3) of the Supreme Court Act 1981 or section 53(3) of the County Courts Act 1984, every party to the proceedings other than the applicant.

25.6 INTERIM PAYMENTS — GENERAL PROCEDURE

(1) The claimant may not apply for an order for an interim payment before the end of the period for filing an acknowledgment of service applicable to the defendant against whom the application is made.
(Rule 10.3 sets out the period for filing an acknowledgment of service)
(Rule 25.1(1)(k) defines an interim payment)

(2) The claimant may make more than one application for an order for an interim payment.

(3) A copy of an application notice for an order for an interim payment must—
   (a) be served at least 14 days before the hearing of the application; and
   (b) be supported by evidence.

(4) If the respondent to an application for an order for an interim payment wishes to rely on written evidence at the hearing, he must—
   (a) file the written evidence; and
   (b) serve copies on every other party to the application,
at least 7 days before the hearing of the application.

(5) If the applicant wishes to rely on written evidence in reply, he must—
   (a) file the written evidence; and
   (b) serve a copy on the respondent,
at least 3 days before the hearing of the application.

(6) This rule does not require written evidence—
   (a) to be filed if it has already been filed; or
   (b) to be served on a party on whom it has already been served.

(7) The court may order an interim payment in one sum or in instalments.
(Part 23 contains general rules about applications)

25.7 INTERIM PAYMENTS — CONDITIONS TO BE SATISFIED AND MATTERS TO BE TAKEN INTO ACCOUNT

(1) The court may make an order for an interim payment only if—
   (a) the defendant against whom the order is sought has admitted liability to pay damages or some other sum of money to the claimant;

(b) the claimant has obtained judgment against that defendant for damages to be assessed or for a sum of money (other than costs) to be assessed;

(c) except where paragraph (3) applies, it is satisfied that, if the claim went to trial, the claimant would obtain judgment for a substantial amount of money (other than costs) against the defendant from whom he is seeking an order for an interim payment; or

(d) the following conditions are satisfied—

   (i) the claimant is seeking an order for possession of land (whether or not any other order is also sought); and

   (ii) the court is satisfied that, if the case went to trial, the defendant would be held liable (even if the claim for possession fails) to pay the claimant a sum of money for the defendant's occupation and use of the land while the claim for possession was pending.

(2) In addition, in a claim for personal injuries the court may make an order for an interim payment of damages only if—

   (a) the defendant is insured in respect of the claim;

   (b) the defendant's liability will be met by—

      (i) an insurer under section 151 of the Road Traffic Act 1988; or

      (ii) an insurer acting under the Motor Insurers Bureau Agreement, or the Motor Insurers Bureau where it is acting itself; or

   (c) the defendant is a public body.

(3) In a claim for personal injuries where there are two or more defendants, the court may make an order for the interim payment of damages against any defendant if—

   (a) it is satisfied that, if the claim went to trial, the claimant would obtain judgment for substantial damages against at least one of the defendants (even if the court has not yet determined which of them is liable); and

   (b) paragraph (2) is satisfied in relation to each of the defendants.

(4) The court must not order an interim payment of more than a reasonable proportion of the likely amount of the final judgment.

(5) The court must take into account—

   (a) contributory negligence; and

   (b) any relevant set-off or counterclaim.

25.8 POWERS OF COURT WHERE IT HAS MADE AN ORDER FOR INTERIM PAYMENT

(1) Where a defendant has been ordered to make an interim payment, or has in fact made an interim payment (whether voluntarily or under an order), the court may make an order to adjust the interim payment.

(2) The court may in particular—

   (a) order all or part of the interim payment to be repaid;

   (b) vary or discharge the order for the interim payment;

   (c) order a defendant to reimburse, either wholly or partly, another defendant who has made an interim payment.

(3) The court may make an order under paragraph (2)(c) only if—

   (a) the defendant to be reimbursed made the interim payment in relation to a claim in respect of which he has made a claim against the other defendant for a contribution$^{(GL)}$, indemnity$^{(GL)}$ or other remedy; and

   (b) where the claim or part to which the interim payment relates has not been discontinued or disposed of, the circumstances are such that the court could make an order for interim payment under rule 25.7.

(4) The court may make an order under this rule without an application by any party if it makes the order when it disposes of the claim or any part of it.

(5) Where—

   (a) a defendant has made an interim payment; and

   (b) the amount of the payment is more than his total liability under the final judgment or order,

the court may award him interest on the overpaid amount from the date when he made the interim payment.

25.9 RESTRICTION ON DISCLOSURE OF AN INTERIM PAYMENT

The fact that a defendant has made an interim payment, whether voluntarily or by court order, shall not be disclosed to the trial judge until all questions of liability and the amount of money to be awarded have been decided unless the defendant agrees.

25.10 INTERIM INJUNCTION TO CEASE IF CLAIM IS STAYED

If—
   (a) the court has granted an interim injunction$^{(GL)}$; and
   (b) the claim is stayed$^{(GL)}$ other than by agreement between the parties,
the interim injunction$^{(GL)}$ shall be set aside$^{(GL)}$ unless the court orders that it should continue to have effect even though the claim is stayed.

25.11 INTERIM INJUNCTION TO CEASE AFTER 14 DAYS IF CLAIM STRUCK OUT

  (1) If—
   (a) the court has granted an interim injunction$^{(GL)}$; and
   (b) the claim is struck out under rule 3.7 (sanction for non-payment of certain fees),
the interim injunction shall cease to have effect 14 days after the date that the claim is struck out unless paragraph (2) applies.

  (2) If the claimant applies to reinstate the claim before the interim injunction ceases to have effect under paragraph (1), the injunction shall continue until the hearing of the application unless the court orders otherwise.

PD 25 PRACTICE DIRECTION — INTERIM INJUNCTIONS

This practice direction supplements CPR Part 25

JURISDICTION

1.1 High Court Judges and any other Judge duly authorised may grant 'search orders'[1] and 'freezing injunctions'[2].

1.2 In a case in the High Court, Masters and district judges have the power to grant injunctions:
   (1) by consent,
   (2) in connection with charging orders and appointments of receivers,
   (3) in aid of execution of judgments.

1.3 In any other case any judge who has jurisdiction to conduct the trial of the action has the power to grant an injunction in that action.

1.4 A Master or district judge has the power to vary or discharge an injunction granted by any Judge with the consent of all the parties.

MAKING AN APPLICATION

2.1 The application notice must state:
   (1) the order sought, and
   (2) the date, time and place of the hearing.

2.2 The application notice and evidence in support must be served as soon as practicable after issue and in any event not less than 3 days before the court is due to hear the application[3].

2.3 Where the court is to serve, sufficient copies of the application notice and evidence in support for the court and for each respondent should be filed for issue and service.

2.4 Whenever possible a draft of the order sought should be filed with the application notice and a disk containing the draft should also be available to the court. This will enable the court officer to arrange for any amendments to be incorporated and for the speedy preparation and sealing of the order. The current word processing system to be used is WordPerfect 5.1.

EVIDENCE

3.1 Applications for search orders and freezing injunctions must be supported by affidavit evidence.

3.2 Applications for other interim injunctions must be supported by evidence set out in either:
   (1) a witness statement, or
   (2) a statement of case provided that it is verified by a statement of truth,[4] or
   (3) the application provided that it is verified by a statement of truth,
unless the court, an Act, a rule or a practice direction requires evidence by affidavit.

3.3 The evidence must set out the facts on which the applicant relies for the claim being made against the respondent, including all material facts of which the court should be made aware.

3.4 Where an application is made without notice to the respondent, the evidence must also set out why notice was not given.
(See Part 32 and the practice direction that supplements it for information about evidence.)

URGENT APPLICATIONS AND APPLICATIONS WITHOUT NOTICE

4.1 These fall into two categories:

---

[1] Rule 25.1(1)(g).
[2] Rule 25.1(1)(f).
[3] Rule 23.7(1) and (2) and see rule 23.7(4) (short service).
[4] See Part 22.

PD 25 PRACTICE DIRECTION — INTERIM INJUNCTIONS

(1) applications where a claim form has already been issued, and
(2) applications where a claim form has not yet been issued,
and, in both cases, where notice of the application has not been given to the respondent.

4.2 These applications are normally dealt with at a court hearing but cases of extreme urgency may be dealt with by telephone.

4.3 Applications dealt with at a court hearing after issue of a claim form:

(1) the application notice, evidence in support and a draft order (as in 2.4 above) should be filed with the court 2 hours before the hearing wherever possible,

(2) if an application is made before the application notice has been issued, a draft order (as in 2.4 above) should be provided at the hearing, and the application notice and evidence in support must be filed with the court on the same or next working day or as ordered by the court, and

(3) except in cases where secrecy is essential, the applicant should take steps to notify the respondent informally of the application.

4.4 Applications made before the issue of a claim form:

(1) in addition to the provisions set out at 4.3 above, unless the court orders otherwise, either the applicant must undertake to the court to issue a claim form immediately or the court will give directions for the commencement of the claim[5],

(2) where possible the claim form should be served with the order for the injunction,

(3) an order made before the issue of a claim form should state in the title after the names of the applicant and respondent 'the Claimant and Defendant in an Intended Action'.

4.5 Applications made by telephone:

(1) where it is not possible to arrange a hearing, application can be made between 10.00 a.m. and 5.00 p.m. weekdays by telephoning the Royal Courts of Justice on 0171 936 6000 and asking to be put in contact with a High Court Judge of the appropriate Division available to deal with an emergency application in a High Court matter. The appropriate district registry may also be contacted by telephone. In county court proceedings, the appropriate county court should be contacted,

(2) where an application is made outside those hours the applicant should either—

(a) telephone the Royal Courts of Justice on 0171 936 6000 where he will be put in contact with the clerk to the appropriate duty judge in the High Court (or the appropriate area Circuit Judge where known), or

(b) the Urgent Court Business Officer of the appropriate Circuit who will contact the local duty judge.

(3) where the facility is available it is likely that the judge will require a draft order to be faxed to him,

(4) the application notice and evidence in support must be filed with the court on the same or next working day or as ordered, together with two copies of the order for sealing,

(5) injunctions will be heard by telephone only where the applicant is acting by counsel or solicitors.

ORDERS FOR INJUNCTIONS

5.1 Any order for an injunction, unless the court orders otherwise, must contain:

(1) an undertaking by the applicant to the court to pay any damages which the respondent(s) (or any other party served with or notified of the order) sustain which the court considers the applicant should pay,

(2) if made without notice to any other party, an undertaking by the applicant to the court to serve on the respondent the application notice, evidence in support and any order made as soon as practicable,

(3) if made without notice to any other party, a return date for a further hearing at which the other party can be present,

---

[5] Rule 25.2(3).

(4) if made before filing the application notice, an undertaking to file and pay the appropriate fee on the same or next working day, and

(5) if made before issue of a claim form—

(a) an undertaking to issue and pay the appropriate fee on the same or next working day, or

(b) directions for the commencement of the claim.

5.2 An order for an injunction made in the presence of all parties to be bound by it or made at a hearing of which they have had notice, may state that it is effective until trial or further order.

5.3 Any order for an injunction must set out clearly what the respondent must do or not do.

FREEZING INJUNCTIONS

Orders to restrain disposal of assets worldwide and within England and Wales

6 Examples of Freezing Injunctions are annexed to this practice direction.

SEARCH ORDERS

Orders for the preservation of evidence and property

7.1 The following provisions apply to search orders in addition to those listed above.

The Supervising Solicitor

7.2 The Supervising Solicitor must be experienced in the operation of search orders. A Supervising Solicitor may be contacted either through the Law Society or, for the London area, through the London Solicitors Litigation Association.

7.3 Evidence:

(1) the affidavit must state the name, firm and its address, and experience of the Supervising Solicitor, also the address of the premises and whether it is a private or business address, and

(2) the affidavit must disclose very fully the reason the order is sought, including the probability that relevant material would disappear if the order were not made.

7.4 Service:

(1) the order must be served personally by the Supervising Solicitor, unless the court otherwise orders, and must be accompanied by the evidence in support and any documents capable of being copied,

(2) confidential exhibits need not be served but they must be made available for inspection by the respondent in the presence of the applicant's solicitors while the order is carried out and afterwards be retained by the respondent's solicitors on their undertaking not to permit the respondent—

(a) to see them or copies of them except in their presence, and

(b) to make or take away any note or record of them,

(3) the Supervising Solicitor may be accompanied only by the persons mentioned in the order,

(4) the Supervising Solicitor must explain the terms and effect of the order to the respondent in every day language and advise him of his right to—

(a) legal advice, and

(b) apply to vary or discharge the order,

(5) where the Supervising Solicitor is a man and the respondent is likely to be an unaccompanied woman, at least one other person named in the order must be a woman and must accompany the Supervising Solicitor, and

(6) the order may only be served between 9.30 a.m. and 5.30 p.m. Monday to Friday unless the court otherwise orders.

7.5 Search and custody of materials:

(1) no material shall be removed unless clearly covered by the terms of the order,

(2) the premises must not be searched and no items shall be removed from them except in the presence of the respondent or a person who appears to be a responsible employee of the respondent,

PD 25   PRACTICE DIRECTION — INTERIM INJUNCTIONS

(3)   where copies of documents are sought, the documents should be retained for no more than 2 days before return to the owner,

(4)   where material in dispute is removed pending trial, the applicant's solicitors should place it in the custody of the respondent's solicitors on their undertaking to retain it in safekeeping and to produce it to the court when required,

(5)   in appropriate cases the applicant should insure the material retained in the respondent's solicitors' custody,

(6)   the Supervising Solicitor must make a list of all material removed from the premises and supply a copy of the list to the respondent,

(7)   no material shall be removed from the premises until the respondent has had reasonable time to check the list,

(8)   if any of the listed items exists only in computer readable form, the respondent must immediately give the applicant's solicitors effective access to the computers, with all necessary passwords, to enable them to be searched, and cause the listed items to be printed out,

(9)   the applicant must take all reasonable steps to ensure that no damage is done to any computer or data,

(10)   the applicant and his representatives may not themselves search the respondent's computers unless they have sufficient expertise to do so without damaging the respondent's system,

(11)   the Supervising Solicitor shall provide a report on the carrying out of the order to the applicant's solicitors,

(12)   as soon as the report is received the applicant's solicitors shall—
   (a)   serve a copy of it on the respondent, and
   (b)   file a copy of it with the court, and

(13)   where the Supervising Solicitor is satisfied that full compliance with paragraph 7.5(7) and (8) above is impracticable, he may permit the search to proceed and items to be removed without compliance with the impracticable requirements.

GENERAL

8.1   The Supervising Solicitor must not be an employee or member of the applicant's firm of solicitors.

8.2   If the court orders that the order need not be served by the Supervising Solicitor, the reason for so ordering must be set out in the order.

8.3   The search order must not be carried out at the same time as a police search warrant.

8.4   There is no privilege against self incrimination in Intellectual Property cases (see the Supreme Court Act 1981, section 72) therefore in those cases, paragraph (4) of the Respondent's Entitlements and any other references to incrimination in the Search Order, should be removed.

8.5   Applications in intellectual property cases should be made in the Chancery Division.

8.6   An example of a Search Order is annexed to this Practice Direction.

PD 25   PRACTICE DIRECTION — INTERIM INJUNCTIONS

Annex

Freezing Injunction   **IN THE [HIGH COURT OF JUSTICE]**

Order to restrain assets in   **[CHANCERY DIVISION]**
England and Wales

                                 [Strand, London WC2A 2LL]

Before The Honourable Mr Justice [**]**

                                 Claim No.

                                 Dated

Applicant

                                 Seal

Respondent

Name, address and reference of Respondent

PENAL NOTICE

IF YOU THE WITHIN NAMED [   ] DISOBEY THIS ORDER YOU MAY BE HELD TO BE IN CONTEMPT OF COURT AND LIABLE TO IMPRISONMENT OR FINED OR YOUR ASSETS SEIZED

IMPORTANT

NOTICE TO THE RESPONDENT
You should read the terms of the Order and the Guidance Notes very carefully. You are advised to consult a Solicitor as soon as possible.

This Order prohibits you, the Respondent, from dealing with your assets up to the amount stated in the Order, but subject to any exceptions set out at the end of the Order. You have a right to ask the Court to vary or discharge this Order.

If you disobey this Order you may be found guilty of Contempt of Court and may be sent to prison or fined. In the case of a Corporate Respondent, it may be fined, its Directors may be sent to prison or fined or its assets may be seized.

THE ORDER
An application was made today [*date*] by [Counsel] [Solicitors] [*or as may be*] for the Applicant to Mr Justice [   ] who heard the application. The Judge read the affidavits listed in Schedule A and accepted the undertakings set out in Schedule B at the end of this Order. As a result of the application IT IS ORDERED that until [[   ] ('the return date')] [or further Order of the Court]:—

   1   The Respondent must not remove from England and Wales or in any way dispose of or deal with or diminish the value of any of his assets which are in

PD 25 PRACTICE DIRECTION — INTERIM INJUNCTIONS

England and Wales whether in his own name or not and whether solely or jointly owned up to the value of £   .
This prohibition includes the following assets in particular:—
    (a)   the property known as [*title/address*] or the net sale money after payment of any mortgages if it has been sold;
    (b)   the property and assets of the Respondent's business known as (or carried on at [*address*]) or the sale money if any of them have been sold; and
    (c)   any money in the account numbered [*a/c number*] at [*title/address*].

2   If the total unincumbered value of the Respondent's assets in England and Wales exceeds £   , the Respondent may remove any of those assets from England and Wales or may dispose of or deal with them so long as the total unincumbered value of his assets still in England and Wales remains above £   .

3   Exceptions to this Order:—
    (1)   This Order does not prohibit the Respondent from spending £   a week towards his ordinary living expenses [and £   a week towards his ordinary and proper business expenses] and also £   a week [*or a reasonable sum*] on legal advice and representation. But before spending any money the Respondent must tell the Applicant's legal representatives[7] where the money is to come from.
    [(2)   This Order does not prohibit the Respondent from dealing with or disposing of any of his assets in the ordinary and proper course of business.]
    (3)   The Respondent may agree with the Applicant's legal representatives that the above spending limits should be increased or that this Order should be varied in any other respect, but any agreement must be in writing.
    (4)   The Respondent may cause this Order to cease to have effect if the Respondent provides security by paying the sum of £   into Court or makes provision for security in that sum by another method agreed with the Applicant's legal representatives.

4   The Respondent must:—
    (1)   Inform the Applicant in writing at once of all his assets in England and Wales and whether in his own name or not and whether solely or jointly owned, giving the value, location and details of all such assets.
[The Respondent may be entitled to refuse to provide some or all of this information on the grounds that it may incriminate him. *This sentence may be inserted in cases not covered by the Theft Act 1968, s. 31.*]
    (2)   Confirm the information in an affidavit which must be served on the Applicant's legal representatives within [   ] days after this Order has been served on the Respondent.
[5   *Where an Order for service by an alternative means or service out of the jurisdiction has been made—*
    (1)   The Applicant may issue and serve a Claim Form on the Respondent at [*address*] by [*method of service*].
    (2)   If the Respondent wishes to defend the Claim where the Claim Form states that Particulars of Claim are to follow he must complete and return the Acknowledgement of Service within [   ] days of being served with the Claim Form. Where the Particulars of Claim are served with the Claim Form, and the Respondent wishes to defend part or all of the Claim he must complete and return an Acknowledgement of Service within [   ] days of being served with the Claim Form or a Defence within [   ] days.]

GUIDANCE NOTES

EFFECT OF THIS ORDER

(1) A respondent who is an individual who is ordered not to do something must not do it himself or in any other way. He must not do it through others acting on his behalf or on his instructions or with his encouragement.

---

[7] For the definition of legal representative see the glossary in Part 2. [The text issued by the Lord Chancellor's Department which is followed here does not have a footnote 6.]

(2) A respondent which is a corporation and which is ordered not to do something must not do it itself or by its directors, officers, employees or agents or in any other way.

VARIATION OR DISCHARGE OF THIS ORDER
The Respondent (or anyone notified of this Order) may apply to the court at any time to vary or discharge this Order (or so much of it as affects that person), but anyone wishing to do so must first inform the Applicant's legal representatives.

PARTIES OTHER THAN THE APPLICANT AND RESPONDENT
(1) Effect of this Order:
It is a Contempt of Court for any person notified of this Order knowingly to assist in or permit a breach of this Order. Any person doing so may be sent to prison, fined or have his assets seized.
(2) Set off by banks:
This injunction does not prevent any bank from exercising any right of set off it may have in respect of any facility which it gave to the respondent before it was notified of this Order.
(3) Withdrawals by the Respondent:
No bank need enquire as to the application or proposed application of any money withdrawn by the Respondent if the withdrawal appears to be permitted by this Order.

INTERPRETATION OF THIS ORDER
(1) In this Order, where there is more than one Respondent (unless otherwise stated), references to 'the Respondent' means both or all of them.
(2) A requirement to serve on 'the Respondent' means on each of them. However, the Order is effective against any Respondent on whom it is served.
(3) An Order requiring 'the Respondent' to do or not to do anything applies to all Respondents.

COMMUNICATIONS WITH THE COURT
All communications to the Court about this Order should be sent, where the Order is made in the Chancery Division, to [Room TM 510], Royal Courts of Justice, Strand, London WC2A 2LL quoting the case number. The telephone number is 0171 936 [6827]; and where the order is made in the Queen's Bench Division, to Room W11 (0171 936 6009). The offices are open between 10 a.m. and 4.30 p.m. Monday to Friday.

SCHEDULE A

AFFIDAVITS
The Applicant relied on the following affidavits:
[name]   [number of affidavit]   [date sworn]   [filed on behalf of]
(1)
(2)

SCHEDULE B

UNDERTAKINGS GIVEN TO THE COURT BY THE APPLICANT
(1) If the Court later finds that this Order has caused loss to the Respondent, and decides that the Respondent should be compensated for that loss, the Applicant will comply with any Order the Court may make.
(2) The Applicant will on or before [date] cause a written guarantee in the sum of £   to be issued from a bank having a place of business within England or Wales, such guarantee being in respect of any Order the Court may make pursuant to paragraph (1) above. The Applicant will further, forthwith upon issue of the guarantee, cause a copy of it to be served on the Respondent.
(3) As soon as practicable the Applicant will [issue and serve on the Respondent a Claim Form in the form of the draft produced to the Court] [serve on the Respondent the Claim Form] claiming the appropriate relief, together with this Order.

PD 25 PRACTICE DIRECTION — INTERIM INJUNCTIONS

(4) The Applicant will cause an affidavit to be sworn and filed [substantially in the terms of the draft affidavit produced to the Court] [confirming the substance of what was said to the Court by the Applicant's Counsel/Solicitors].

[(5) *Where a return date has been given* — As soon as practicable the Applicant will serve on the Respondent an Application for the return date together with a copy of the affidavits and exhibits containing the evidence relied on by the Applicant.]

(6) Anyone notified of this Order will be given a copy of it by the Applicant's legal representatives.

(7) The Applicant will pay the reasonable costs of anyone other than the Respondent which have been incurred as a result of this Order including the costs of ascertaining whether that person holds any of the Respondent's assets and if the Court later finds that this Order has caused such person loss, and decides that such person should be compensated for that loss, the Applicant will comply with any Order the Court may make.

(8) If for any reason this Order ceases to have effect (including in particular where the Respondent provides security as provided for above or the Applicant does not provide a bank guarantee as provided for above), the Applicant will forthwith take all reasonable steps to inform, in writing, any person or company to whom he has given notice of this Order, or who he has reasonable grounds for supposing may act upon this Order, that it has ceased to have effect.

NAME AND ADDRESS OF APPLICANT'S LEGAL REPRESENTATIVES
The Applicant's Legal Representatives are:—
   [Name, address, reference, fax and telephone numbers both in and out of office hours.]

Freezing Injunction   IN THE [HIGH COURT OF JUSTICE]

Order to restrain assets worldwide   [CHANCERY DIVISION]

            [Strand, London WC2A 2LL]

Before The Honourable Mr Justice [   ]

Claim No.

Dated

Applicant

Seal

Respondent

Name, address and reference of Respondent

PENAL NOTICE

IF YOU THE WITHIN NAMED [   ] DISOBEY THIS ORDER YOU MAY BE HELD TO BE IN CONTEMPT OF COURT AND LIABLE TO IMPRISONMENT OR FINED OR YOUR ASSETS SEIZED

PD 25 PRACTICE DIRECTION — INTERIM INJUNCTIONS

IMPORTANT

NOTICE TO THE RESPONDENT
You should read the terms of the Order and the Guidance Notes very carefully. You are advised to consult a Solicitor as soon as possible.

This Order prohibits you, the Respondent, from dealing with your assets up to the amount stated in the Order, but subject to any exceptions set out at the end of the Order. You have a right to ask the Court to vary or discharge this Order.

If you disobey this Order you may be found guilty of Contempt of Court and may be sent to prison or fined. In the case of a Corporate Respondent, it may be fined, its Directors may be sent to prison or fined or its assets may be seized.

THE ORDER
An application was made today [date] by [Counsel] [Solicitors] [or as may be] for the Applicant to Mr Justice [   ] who heard the application. The Judge read the affidavits listed in Schedule A and accepted the undertakings set out in Schedule B at the end of this Order. As a result of the application IT IS ORDERED that until [[   ] ('the return date')] [further Order of the Court]:—

1 The Respondent must not:—
   (1) remove from England and Wales or in any way dispose of or deal with or diminish the value of any of his assets which are in England and Wales whether in his own name or not and whether solely or jointly owned up to the value of £   , or
   (2) in any way dispose of or deal with or diminish the value of any of his assets whether they are in or outside England or Wales whether in his own name or not and whether solely or jointly owned up to the same value. This prohibition includes the following assets in particular:—
      (a) the property known as [title/address] or the net sale money after payment of any mortgages if it has been sold;
      (b) the property and assets of the Respondent's business known as (or carried on at [address]) or the sale money if any of them have been sold; and
      (c) any money in the account numbered [a/c number] at [title/address].

2 (1) If the total unincumbered value of the Respondent's assets in England and Wales exceeds £   , the Respondent may remove any of those assets from England and Wales or may dispose of or deal with them so long as the total unincumbered value of his assets still in England and Wales remains above £   .
   (2) If the total unincumbered value of the Respondent's assets in England and Wales does not exceed £   , the Respondent must not remove any of those assets from England and Wales and must not dispose of or deal with any of them, but if he has other assets outside England and Wales the Respondent may dispose of or deal with those assets so long as the total unincumbered value of all his assets whether in or outside England and Wales remains above £   .

3 Exceptions to this Order:—
   (1) This Order does not prohibit the Respondent from spending £   a week towards his ordinary living expenses [and £   a week towards his ordinary and proper business expenses] and also £   a week [or a reasonable sum] on legal advice and representation. But before spending any money the Respondent must tell the Applicant's legal representatives where the money is to come from.
   [(2) This Order does not prohibit the Respondent from dealing with or disposing of any of his assets in the ordinary and proper course of business.]
   (3) The Respondent may agree with the Applicant's legal representatives that the above spending limits should be increased or that this Order should be varied in any other respect, but any agreement must be in writing.
   (4) The Respondent may cause this Order to cease to have effect if the Respondent provides security by paying the sum of £   into Court or makes provision for security in that sum by another method agreed with the Applicant's legal representatives.

4 The Respondent must:—

(1) Inform the Applicant in writing at once of all his assets whether in or outside England and Wales and whether in his own name or not and whether solely or jointly owned, giving the value, location and details of all such assets.

[The Respondent may be entitled to refuse to provide some or all of this information on the grounds that it may incriminate him. *This sentence may be inserted in cases not covered by the Theft Act 1968, s. 31.*]

(2) Confirm the information in an affidavit which must be served on the Applicant's legal representatives within [   ] days after this Order has been served on the Respondent.

[5 *Where an Order for service by an alternative means or service out of the jurisdiction has been made—*

(1) The Applicant may issue and serve a Claim Form on the Respondent at [*address*] by [*method of service*]

(2) If the Respondent wishes to defend the Claim he must complete and return the Notice of Intention to Defend within [   ] days of being served with the Claim Form.]

GUIDANCE NOTES

EFFECT OF THIS ORDER

(1) A Respondent who is an individual who is ordered not to do something must not do it himself or in any other way. He must not do it through others acting on his behalf or on his instructions or with his encouragement.

(2) A Respondent which is a corporation and which is ordered not to do something must not do it itself or by its directors, officers, employees or agents or in any other way.

VARIATION OR DISCHARGE OF THIS ORDER

The Respondent (or anyone notified of this Order) may apply to the Court at any time to vary or discharge this Order (or so much of it as affects that person), but anyone wishing to do so must first inform the Applicant's legal representatives.

PARTIES OTHER THAN THE APPLICANT AND RESPONDENT

(1) Effect of this Order:—

It is a Contempt of Court for any person notified of this Order knowingly to assist in or permit a breach of this Order. Any person doing so may be sent to prison, fined or have his assets seized.

(2) Effect of this Order outside England and Wales:—

The terms of this Order do not affect or concern anyone outside the jurisdiction of this Court until it is declared enforceable by or is enforced by a Court in the relevant country and then they are to affect him only to the extent they have been declared enforceable or have been enforced UNLESS the person is:

  (i) a person to whom this Order is addressed or an officer or an agent appointed by power of attorney of that person; or

  (ii) a person who is subject to the jurisdiction of this Court and (a) has been given written notice of this Order at his residence or place of business within the jurisdiction of this Court and (b) is able to prevent acts or omissions outside the jurisdiction of this Court which constitute or assist in a breach of the terms of this Order.

(3) Set off by Banks:—

This injunction does not prevent any bank from exercising any right of set off it may have in respect of any facility which it gave to the Respondent before it was notified of this Order.

(4) Withdrawals by the Respondent:—

No bank need enquire as to the application or proposed application of any money withdrawn by the Respondent if the withdrawal appears to be permitted by this Order.

INTERPRETATION OF THIS ORDER

(1) In this Order, where there is more than one Respondent (unless otherwise stated), references to 'the Respondent' means both or all of them.

PD 25 PRACTICE DIRECTION — INTERIM INJUNCTIONS

(2) A requirement to serve on 'the Respondent' means on each of them. However, the Order is effective against any Respondent on whom it is served.

(3) An Order requiring 'the Respondent' to do or not to do anything applies to all Respondents.

COMMUNICATIONS WITH THE COURT
All communications to the Court about this Order should be sent, where the Order is made in the Chancery Division, to [Room TM 510], Royal Courts of Justice, Strand, London WC2A 2LL quoting the case number. The telephone number is 0171 936 [6827]; and where the order is made in the Queen's Bench Division, to Room W11 (0171 936 6009). The offices are open between 10 a.m. and 4.30 p.m. Monday to Friday.

SCHEDULE A

AFFIDAVITS
The Applicant relied on the following affidavits:
[*name*]   [*number of affidavit*]   [*date sworn*]   [*filed on behalf of*]
  (1)
  (2)

SCHEDULE B

UNDERTAKINGS GIVEN TO THE COURT BY THE APPLICANT

(1) If the Court later finds that this Order has caused loss to the Respondent, and decides that the Respondent should be compensated for that loss, the Applicant will comply with any Order the Court may make.

(2) The Applicant will on or before [*date*] cause a written guarantee in the sum of £   to be issued from a bank having a place of business within England or Wales, such guarantee being in respect of any Order the Court may make pursuant to paragraph (1) above. The Applicant will further, forthwith upon issue of the guarantee, cause a copy of it to be served on the Respondent.

[(3) As soon as practicable the Applicant will [issue and serve on the Respondent a Claim Form in the form of the draft produced to the Court] [serve on the Respondent the Claim Form] claiming the appropriate relief, together with this Order.]

(4) The Applicant will cause an affidavit to be sworn and filed [substantially in the terms of the draft affidavit produced to the Court] [confirming the substance of what was said to the Court by the Applicant's Counsel/Solicitors].

[(5) *Where a return date has been given* — As soon as practicable the Applicant will serve on the Respondent an application for the return date together with a copy of the affidavits and exhibits containing the evidence relied on by the Applicant.]

(6) Anyone notified of this Order will be given a copy of it by the Applicant's legal representatives.

(7) The Applicant will pay the reasonable costs of anyone other than the Respondent which have been incurred as a result of this Order including the costs of ascertaining whether that person holds any of the Respondent's assets and if the Court later finds that this Order has caused such person loss, and decides that such person should be compensated for that loss, the Applicant will comply with any Order the Court may make.

(8) If for any reason this Order ceases to have effect (including in particular where the Respondent provides security as provided for above or the Applicant does not provide a bank guarantee as provided for above), the Applicant will forthwith take all reasonable steps to inform, in writing, any person or company to whom he has given notice of this Order, or who he has reasonable grounds for supposing may act upon this Order, that it has ceased to have effect.

[(9) The Applicant will not without the leave of the Court begin proceedings against the Respondent in any other jurisdiction or use information obtained as a result of an Order of the Court in this jurisdiction for the purpose of civil or criminal proceedings in any other jurisdiction.]

[(10) The Applicant will not without the leave of the Court seek to enforce this Order in any country outside England and Wales [or seek an Order of a similar nature including Orders conferring a charge or other security against the Respondent or the Respondent's assets].]

NAME AND ADDRESS OF APPLICANT'S LEGAL REPRESENTATIVES
The Applicant's Legal Representatives are:—
[Name, address, reference, fax and telephone numbers both in and out of office hours.]

Search Order   IN THE [HIGH COURT OF JUSTICE]

Order to preserve evidence   [CHANCERY DIVISION]
and property
          [Strand, London WC2A 2LL]

Before The Honourable Mr Justice [   ]

Claim No.

Dated

Applicant

Seal

Respondent

Name, address and reference of Respondent

PENAL NOTICE

IF YOU THE WITHIN NAMED [   ] DISOBEY THIS ORDER YOU MAY BE HELD TO BE IN CONTEMPT OF COURT AND LIABLE TO IMPRISONMENT OR FINED OR YOUR ASSETS SEIZED

IMPORTANT

NOTICE TO THE RESPONDENT
You should read the terms of the Order and the Guidance Notes very carefully. You are advised to consult a Solicitor as soon as possible.

This Order orders you, the Respondent, to allow the persons mentioned in the Order to enter the premises described in the Order and to search for, examine and remove or copy the articles specified in the Order. The persons so named will have no right to enter the premises or, having entered, to remain at the premises, unless you give your consent to their doing so. If, however, you withhold your consent you will be in breach of this Order and may be held to be in Contempt of Court.

The Order also requires you to hand over any of such articles which are under your control and to provide information to the Applicant's Solicitors, and prohibits you from doing certain acts.

If you, the Respondent, disobey this Order you may be found guilty of contempt of Court and may be sent to prison or fined. In the case of a Corporate

Respondent, it may be fined, its Directors may be sent to prison or fined or its assets may be seized.

THE ORDER

AN APPLICATION was made today [*date*] by [Counsel] [Solicitors] for the Applicant to Mr Justice [   ] who heard the application. The Judge read the affidavits listed in Schedule F at the end of this Order and accepted the undertakings by the Applicant, the Applicant's Solicitors and the Supervising Solicitor set forth in the Schedules at the end of this Order. As a result of the application IT IS ORDERED that until [[   ] ('the return date')] [or further Order of the Court]:—

1 (1) The Respondent must allow Mr/Mrs/Miss [   ] ('the Supervising Solicitor'), together with Mr [   ] a Solicitor of the Supreme Court, and a partner in the firm of [   ] the Applicant's Solicitors and up to [   ] other persons being [*their capacity*] accompanying them, to enter the premises mentioned in Schedule A to this Order and any other premises of the Respondent disclosed under paragraph 4(1) below and any vehicles under the Respondent's control on or around the premises so that they can search for, inspect, photograph or photocopy, and deliver into the safekeeping of the Applicant's Solicitors all the documents and articles which are listed in Schedule B to this Order ('the listed items') or which Mr [   ] believes to be listed items.

(2) The Respondent must allow those persons to remain on the premises until the search is complete, and to re-enter the premises on the same or the following day in order to complete the search.

2 (1) No item may be removed from the premises until a list of the items to be removed has been prepared, and a copy of the list has been supplied to the person served with the Order, and he has been given a reasonable opportunity to check the list.

(2) The premises must not be searched, and items must not be removed from them, except in the presence of the Respondent or a person appearing to be a responsible employee of the Respondent or in control of the premises.

(3) If the Supervising Solicitor is satisfied that full compliance with paragraph 2(1) or (2) above is impracticable, he may permit the search to proceed and items to be removed without compliance with the impracticable requirements.

3 (1) The Respondent must immediately hand over to the Applicant's Solicitors any of the listed items which are in his possession or under his control save for any computer or hard disk integral to any computer.

(2) If any of the listed items exists only in computer readable form, the Respondent must immediately give the Applicant's Solicitors effective access to the computers, with all necessary passwords, to enable them to be searched, and cause the listed items to be printed out. A print-out of the items must be given to the Applicant's Solicitors or displayed on the computer screen so that they can be read and copied. All reasonable steps shall be taken by the Applicant to ensure that no damage is done to any computer or data. The Applicant and his representatives may not themselves search the Respondent's computers unless they have sufficient expertise to do so without damaging the Respondent's system.

4 (1) The Respondent must immediately inform the Applicant's Solicitors:—
    (a) where all the listed items are; and
    (b) so far as he is aware—
        (i) the name and address of everyone who has supplied him, or offered to supply him, with listed items,
        (ii) the name and address of everyone to whom he has supplied, or offered to supply, listed items, and
        (iii) full details of the dates and quantities of every such supply and offer.

(2) Within [   ] days after being served with this Order the Respondent must swear an affidavit setting out the above information.

5 (1) Except for the purpose of obtaining legal advice, the Respondent or anyone else with knowledge of this Order must not directly or indirectly inform

anyone of these proceedings or of the contents of this Order, or warn anyone that proceedings have been or may be brought against him by the Applicant until [[   ] the return date] [or further Order of the Court].

(2) The Respondent must not destroy, tamper with, cancel or part with possession, power, custody or control of the listed items otherwise than in accordance with the terms of this Order.

(3) [Insert any negative injunctions.]

[6 Insert any further order.]

GUIDANCE NOTES

EFFECT OF THIS ORDER

(1) A Respondent who is an individual who is ordered not to do something must not do it himself or in any other way. He must not do it through others acting on his behalf or on his instructions or with his encouragement.

(2) A Respondent which is a corporation and which is ordered not to do something must not do it itself or by its directors, officers, employees or agents or in any other way.

(3) This Order must be complied with either by the Respondent himself or by an employee of the Respondent or other person appearing to be in control of the premises and having authority to permit the premises to be entered and the search to proceed.

(4) This Order requires the Respondent or his employee or other person appearing to be in control of the premises and having that authority to permit entry to the premises immediately the Order is served upon him, except as stated in paragraph 6 below.

RESPONDENT'S ENTITLEMENTS

(1) Before you the Respondent or the person appearing to be in control of the premises allow anybody onto the premises to carry out this Order you are entitled to have the solicitor who serves you with this Order explain to you what it means in everyday language.

(2) You are entitled to insist that there is nobody [or nobody except Mr   ] present who could gain commercially from anything he might read or see on your premises.

(3) You are entitled to refuse to permit entry before 9.30 a.m. or after 5.30 p.m. or at all on Saturday and Sunday unless the Court has ordered otherwise.

(4) Except in certain cases, you may be entitled to refuse to permit disclosure of any documents which may incriminate you ('incriminating documents') or to answer any questions if to do so may incriminate you. It may be prudent to take advice, because if you so refuse, your refusal may be taken into account by the Court at a later stage.

(5) You are entitled to refuse to permit disclosure of any documents passing between you and your Solicitors or Patent or Trade Mark Agents for the purpose of obtaining advice ('privileged documents').

(6) You are entitled to seek legal advice, and to ask the Court to vary or discharge this Order, provided you do so at once, and provided you do not disturb or move anything in the interim and that meanwhile you permit the Supervising Solicitor (who is a Solicitor acting independently of the Applicant) to enter, but not start to search.

(7) Before permitting entry to the premises by any person other than the Supervising Solicitor, you (or any other person appearing to be in control of the premises) may gather together any documents you believe may be [incriminating or] privileged and hand them to the Supervising Solicitor for the Supervising Solicitor to assess whether they are [incriminating or] privileged as claimed. If the Supervising Solicitor concludes that any of the documents may be [incriminating or] privileged documents or if there is any doubt as to their status the Supervising Solicitor shall exclude them from the search and shall retain the documents of doubtful status in his possession pending further order of the Court. While this is being done, you may refuse entry to the premises by any other person, and may

PD 25 PRACTICE DIRECTION — INTERIM INJUNCTIONS

refuse to permit the search to begin, for a short time (not to exceed two hours, unless the Supervising Solicitor agrees to a longer period). If you wish to take legal advice and gather documents as permitted, you must first inform the Supervising Solicitor and keep him informed of the steps being taken.

RESTRICTIONS ON SERVICE
Paragraph 1 of the Order is subject to the following restrictions:—
    (1) This Order may only be served between 9.30 a.m. and 5.30 p.m. on a weekday unless the Court has ordered otherwise.
    (2) This Order may not be carried out at the same time as a police search warrant.
    (3) This Order must be served by the Supervising Solicitor, and paragraph 1 of the Order must be carried out in his presence and under his supervision. Where the premises are likely to be occupied by an unaccompanied woman and the Supervising Solicitor is a man, at least one of the persons accompanying him as provided by paragraph 1 of the Order shall be a woman.
    (4) This Order does not require the person served with the Order to allow anyone [or anyone except Mr   ] to enter the premises who in the view of the Supervising Solicitor could gain commercially from anything he might read or see on the premises if the person served with the Order objects.

VARIATION OR DISCHARGE OF THIS ORDER
The Respondent (or anyone notified of this Order) may apply to the Court at any time to vary or discharge this Order (or so much of it as affects that person), but anyone wishing to do so must first inform the Applicant's Solicitors.

INTERPRETATION OF THIS ORDER
    (1) In this Order, where there is more than one Respondent, references to 'the Respondent' means both or all of them.
    (2) A requirement to serve on 'the Respondent' means on each of them. However, the Order is effective against any Respondent on whom it is served.
    (3) An Order requiring 'the Respondent' to do or not to do anything applies to all Respondents.
    (4) Any other requirement that something shall be done to or in the presence of 'the Respondent' means to or in the presence of any one of them or in the case of a firm or company a director or a person appearing to the Supervising Solicitor to be a responsible employee.

COMMUNICATIONS WITH THE COURT
All communications to the Court about this Order should be sent, where the Order is made in the Chancery Division, to [Room TM 510], Royal Courts of Justice, Strand, London WC2A 2LL quoting the case number. The telephone number is 0171 936 [6827]; and where the order is made in the Queen's Bench Division, to Room W11 (0171 936 6009). The offices are open between 10 a.m. and 4.30 p.m. Monday to Friday.

SCHEDULE A
The premises

SCHEDULE B
The listed items

SCHEDULE C

UNDERTAKINGS GIVEN TO THE COURT BY THE APPLICANT
    (1) If the Court later finds that this Order or carrying it out has caused loss to the Respondent, and decides that the Respondent should be compensated for that loss, the Applicant will comply with any Order the Court may make. Further, if the carrying out of this Order has been in breach of the terms of this Order or otherwise in a manner inconsistent with the Applicant's Solicitors' duties as Officers of the Court the Applicant will comply with any order for damages the Court may make.

[(2) As soon as practicable to issue a Claim Form [in the form of the draft produced to the Court] [claiming appropriate relief.]]

[(3) To [swear and file an affidavit] [cause an affidavit to be sworn and filed] [substantially in the terms of the draft produced to the Court] [confirming the substance of what was said to the Court by the Applicant's Counsel/Solicitors].]

(4) To serve on the Respondent at the same time as this Order is served upon him:

    (i) the Claim Form, or if not issued, the draft produced to the Court,

    (ii) an Application for hearing on [*date*],

    (iii) copies of the affidavits [or draft affidavits] and exhibits capable of being copied containing the evidence relied on by the Applicant [Copies of the confidential exhibits need not be served, but they must be made available for inspection by or on behalf of the Respondent in the presence of the Applicant's Solicitors while the Order is carried out. Afterwards they must be provided to a Solicitor representing the Respondent who gives a written undertaking not to permit the Respondent to see them or copies of them except in his presence and not to permit the Respondent to make or take away any note or record of the exhibits], and

    (iv) a note of any allegation of fact made orally to the Judge where such allegation is not contained in the affidavits or draft affidavits read by the Judge.

(5) To serve on the Respondent a copy of the Supervising Solicitor's report on the carrying out of this Order as soon as it is received.

(6) Not, without the leave of the Court, to use any information or documents obtained as a result of carrying out this Order nor to inform anyone else of these proceedings except for the purposes of these proceedings (including adding further Respondents) or commencing civil proceedings in relation to the same or related subject matter to these proceedings until after the return date.

[(7) To maintain pending further order the sum of £   in an account controlled by the Applicant's Solicitors.]

[(8) To insure the items removed from the premises.]

SCHEDULE D

UNDERTAKINGS GIVEN BY THE APPLICANT'S SOLICITORS

(1) To answer at once to the best of their ability any question whether a particular item is a listed item.

(2) To return the originals of all documents obtained as a result of this Order (except original documents which belong to the Applicant) as soon as possible and in any event within two working days of their removal.

(3) While ownership of any item obtained as a result of this Order is in dispute, to deliver the article into the keeping of Solicitors acting for the Respondent within two working days from receiving a written undertaking by them to retain the article in safe keeping and to produce it to the Court when required.

(4) To retain in their own safe keeping all other items obtained as a result of this Order until the Court directs otherwise.

SCHEDULE E

UNDERTAKINGS GIVEN BY THE SUPERVISING SOLICITOR

(1) To offer to explain to the person served with the Order its meaning and effect fairly and in everyday language, and to inform him of his right to seek legal advice (such advice to include an explanation that the Respondent may be entitled to avail himself of [the privilege against self-incrimination or] [legal professional privilege]) and apply to vary or discharge the Order as mentioned in the Respondent's Entitlements above.

(2) To make and provide to the Applicant's Solicitors and to the Judge who made this Order (for the purposes of the Court file) a written report on the carrying out of the Order.

SCHEDULE F

AFFIDAVITS
The Applicant relied on the following affidavits:—
[*name*]　　　　　　　[*number of affidavit*]　[*date sworn*]　　[*filed on behalf of*]

NAME AND ADDRESS OF APPLICANT'S SOLICITORS
The Applicant's Solicitors are:—
[Name, address, reference, fax and telephone numbers both in and out of office hours.]

PD 25B PRACTICE DIRECTION — INTERIM PAYMENTS

This practice direction supplements CPR Part 25

GENERAL

1.1 Rule 25.7 sets out the conditions to be satisfied and matters to be taken into account before the court will make an order for an interim payment.

1.2 The permission of the court must be obtained before making a voluntary interim payment in respect of a claim by a child or patient.

EVIDENCE

2.1 An application for an interim payment of damages must be supported by evidence dealing with the following:
  (1) the sum of money sought by way of an interim payment,
  (2) the items or matters in respect of which the interim payment is sought,
  (3) the sum of money for which final judgment is likely to be given,
  (4) the reasons for believing that the conditions set out in rule 25.7 are satisfied,
  (5) any other relevant matters,
  (6) in claims for personal injuries, details of special damages and past and future loss, and
  (7) in a claim under the Fatal Accidents Act 1976, details of the person(s) on whose behalf the claim is made and the nature of the claim.

2.2 Any documents in support of the application should be exhibited, including, in personal injuries claims, the medical report(s).

2.3 If a respondent to an application for an interim payment wishes to rely on written evidence at the hearing he must comply with the provisions of rule 25.6(4).

2.4 If the applicant wishes to rely on written evidence in reply he must comply with the provisions of rule 25.6(5).

INSTALMENTS

3 Where an interim payment is to be paid in instalments the order should set out:
  (1) the total amount of the payment,
  (2) the amount of each instalment,
  (3) the number of instalments and the date on which each is to be paid, and
  (4) to whom the payment should be made.

COMPENSATION RECOVERY PAYMENTS

4.1 Where in a claim for personal injuries there is an application for an interim payment of damages:
  (1) which is other than by consent,
  (2) which fails under the heads of damage set out in column 1 of Schedule 2 of the Social Security (Recovery of Benefits) Act 1997 in respect of recoverable benefits received by the claimant set out in column 2 of that Schedule, and
  (3) where the defendant is liable to pay recoverable benefits to the Secretary of State,
the defendant should obtain from the Secretary of State a certificate of recoverable benefits.

4.2 A copy of the certificate should be filed at the hearing of the application for an interim payment.

4.3 The order will set out the amount by which the payment to be made to the claimant has been reduced according to the Act and the Social Security (Recovery of Benefits) Regulations 1997.

4.4 The payment made to the claimant will be the net amount but the interim payment for the purposes of paragraph 5 below will be the gross amount.

ADJUSTMENT OF FINAL JUDGMENT FIGURE

5.1 In this paragraph 'judgment' means:
   (1) any order to pay a sum of money,
   (2) a final award of damages,
   (3) an assessment of damages.

5.2 In a final judgment where an interim payment has previously been made which is less than the total amount awarded by the judge, the order should set out in a preamble:
   (1) the total amount awarded by the judge, and
   (2) the amounts and dates of the interim payment(s).

5.3 The total amount awarded by the judge should then be reduced by the total amount of any interim payments, and an order made for entry of judgment and payment of the balance.

5.4 In a final judgment where an interim payment has previously been made which is more than the total amount awarded by the judge, the order should set out in a preamble:
   (1) the total amount awarded by the judge, and
   (2) the amounts and dates of the interim payment(s).

5.5 An order should then be made for repayment, reimbursement, variation or discharge under rule 25.8(2) and for interest on an overpayment under rule 25.8(5).

5.6 A practice direction supplementing Part 40 provides further information concerning adjustment of the final judgment sum.

PD 25C PRACTICE DIRECTION — ACCOUNTS AND INQUIRIES

This practice direction supplements CPR Part 25

An application for an order for accounts and inquiries may also be made under Part 24 (summary judgment). Reference should be made to paragraph 6 of the practice direction that supplements that Part.

1. The remedies that the court may grant under Part 25 include orders directing accounts to be taken and inquiries to be made.

2. The court may, on application or on its own initiative, at any stage in the proceedings, whether before or after judgment, make an order directing any necessary accounts to be taken or inquiries to be made.

3. Every direction for an account to be taken or an inquiry to be made shall be numbered in the order so that, as far as possible, each distinct account and inquiry is given its own number.

(This practice direction replaces RSC Order 43, rule 2 and applies to county court proceedings as well as to High Court proceedings.)

(The accounts and inquiries practice direction supplementing Part 40 contains provisions regarding the taking of an account or conduct of an inquiry after the order for the account or inquiry has been made.)

CPR PART 26 CASE MANAGEMENT — PRELIMINARY STAGE

CONTENTS OF THIS PART

Scope of this Part	Rule 26.1
Automatic transfer	Rule 26.2
Allocation questionnaire	Rule 26.3
Stay to allow for settlement of the case	Rule 26.4
Allocation	Rule 26.5
Scope of each track	Rule 26.6
General rule for allocation	Rule 26.7
Matters relevant to allocation to a track	Rule 26.8
Notice of allocation	Rule 26.9
Re-allocation	Rule 26.10

26.1 SCOPE OF THIS PART
   (1) This Part provides for—
      (a) the automatic transfer of some defended cases between courts; and
      (b) the allocation of defended cases to case management tracks.
   (2) There are three tracks—
      (a) the small claims track;
      (b) the fast track; and
      (c) the multi-track.
(Rule 26.6 sets out the normal scope of each track. Part 27 makes provision for the small claims track. Part 28 makes provision for the fast track. Part 29 makes provision for the multi-track)

26.2 AUTOMATIC TRANSFER
   (1) This rule applies to proceedings where—
      (a) the claim is for a specified amount of money;
      (b) the claim was commenced in a court which is not the defendant's home court;
      (c) the claim has not been transferred to another defendant's home court under rule 13.4 (application to set aside[GL] or vary default judgment — procedure) or rule 14.12 (admission — determination of rate of payment by judge); and
      (d) the defendant is an individual.
   (2) This rule does not apply where the claim was commenced in a specialist list[GL].
   (3) Where this rule applies, the court will transfer the proceedings to the defendant's home court when a defence is filed, unless paragraph (4) applies.
(Rule 2.3 defines 'defendant's home court')
   (4) Where the claimant notifies the court under rule 15.10 or rule 14.5 that he wishes the proceedings to continue, the court will transfer the proceedings to the defendant's home court when it receives that notification from the claimant.
(Rule 15.10 deals with a claimant's notice where the defence is that money claimed has been paid)
(Rule 14.5 sets out the procedure where the defendant admits part of a claim for a specified amount of money)
   (5) Where—
      (a) the claim is against two or more defendants with different home courts; and
      (b) the defendant whose defence is filed first is an individual,
proceedings are to be transferred under this rule to the home court of that defendant.
   (6) The time when a claim is automatically transferred under this rule may be varied by a practice direction in respect of claims issued by the Production Centre.
(Rule 7.10 makes provision for the Production Centre)

26.3 ALLOCATION QUESTIONNAIRE

(1) When a defendant files a defence the court will serve an allocation questionnaire on each party unless—

   (a) rule 15.10 or rule 14.5 applies; or
   (b) the court dispenses with the need for a questionnaire.

(2) Where there are two or more defendants and at least one of them files a defence, the court will serve the allocation questionnaire under paragraph (1)—

   (a) when all the defendants have filed a defence; or
   (b) when the period for the filing of the last defence has expired, whichever is the sooner.

(Rule 15.4 specifies the period for filing a defence)

(3) Where proceedings are automatically transferred to the defendant's home court under rule 26.2, the court in which the proceedings have been commenced will serve an allocation questionnaire before the proceedings are transferred.

(4) Where—

   (a) rule 15.10 or rule 14.5 applies; and
   (b) the proceedings are not automatically transferred to the defendant's home court under rule 26.2,

the court will serve an allocation questionnaire on each party when the claimant files a notice indicating that he wishes the proceedings to continue.

(5) The court may, on the application of the claimant, serve an allocation questionnaire earlier than it would otherwise serve it under this rule.

(6) Each party must file the completed allocation questionnaire no later than the date specified in it, which shall be at least 14 days after the date when it is deemed to be served on the party in question.

(7) The time when the court serves an allocation questionnaire under this rule may be varied by a practice direction in respect of claims issued by the Production Centre.

(Rule 7.10 makes provision for the Production Centre)
(Rule 6.7 specifies when a document is deemed to be served)

26.4 STAY TO ALLOW FOR SETTLEMENT OF THE CASE

(1) A party may, when filing the completed allocation questionnaire, make a written request for the proceedings to be stayed(GL) while the parties try to settle the case by alternative dispute resolution(GL) or other means.

(2) Where—

   (a) all parties request a stay(GL) under paragraph (1); or
   (b) the court, of its own initiative, considers that such a stay would be appropriate,

the court will direct that the proceedings be stayed for one month.

(3) The court may extend the stay(GL) until such date or for such specified period as it considers appropriate.

(4) Where the court stays(GL) the proceedings under this rule, the claimant must tell the court if a settlement is reached.

(5) If the claimant does not tell the court by the end of the period of the stay(GL) that a settlement has been reached, the court will give such directions as to the management of the case as it considers appropriate.

26.5 ALLOCATION

(1) The court will allocate the claim to a track—

   (a) when every defendant has filed an allocation questionnaire, or
   (b) when the period for filing the allocation questionnaires has expired,

whichever is the sooner, unless it has—

   (i) stayed(GL) the proceedings under rule 26.4; or
   (ii) dispensed with the need for allocation questionnaires.

(Rules 12.7 and 14.8 provide for the court to allocate a claim to a track where the claimant obtains default judgment on request or judgment on admission for an amount to be decided by the court)

CPR PART 26 CASE MANAGEMENT — PRELIMINARY STAGE

(2) If the court has stayed^(GL) the proceedings under rule 26.4, it will allocate the claim to a track at the end of the period of the stay.

(3) Before deciding the track to which to allocate proceedings or deciding whether to give directions for an allocation hearing to be fixed, the court may order a party to provide further information about his case.

(4) The court may hold an allocation hearing if it thinks it is necessary.

(5) If a party fails to file an allocation questionnaire, the court may give any direction it considers appropriate.

26.6 SCOPE OF EACH TRACK

(1) The small claims track is the normal track for—
  (a) any claim for personal injuries where—
    (i) the financial value of the claim is not more than £5,000; and
    (ii) the financial value of any claim for damages for personal injuries is not more than £1,000;
  (b) any claim which includes a claim by a tenant of residential premises against his landlord where—
    (i) the tenant is seeking an order requiring the landlord to carry out repairs or other work to the premises (whether or not the tenant is also seeking some other remedy);
    (ii) the cost of the repairs or other work to the premises is estimated to be not more than £1,000; and
    (iii) the financial value of any other claim for damages is not more than £1,000.

(Rule 2.3 defines 'claim for personal injuries' as proceedings in which there is a claim for damages in respect of personal injuries to the claimant or any other person or in respect of a person's death)

(2) For the purposes of paragraph (1) 'damages for personal injuries' means damages claimed as compensation for pain, suffering and loss of amenity and does not include any other damages which are claimed.

(3) Subject to paragraph (1), the small claims track is the normal track for any claim which has a financial value of not more than £5,000.

(Rule 26.7(4) provides that the court will not allocate to the small claims track certain claims in respect of harassment or unlawful eviction)

(4) Subject to paragraph (5), the fast track is the normal track for any claim—
  (a) for which the small claims track is not the normal track; and
  (b) which has a financial value of not more than £15,000.

(5) The fast track is the normal track for the claims referred to in paragraph (4) only if the court considers that—
  (a) the trial is likely to last for no longer than one day; and
  (b) oral expert evidence at trial will be limited to—
    (i) one expert per party in relation to any expert field; and
    (ii) expert evidence in two expert fields.

(6) The multi-track is the normal track for any claim for which the small claims track or the fast track is not the normal track.

26.7 GENERAL RULE FOR ALLOCATION

(1) In considering whether to allocate a claim to the normal track for that claim under rule 26.6, the court will have regard to the matters mentioned in rule 26.8(1).

(2) The court will allocate a claim which has no financial value to the track which it considers most suitable having regard to the matters mentioned in rule 26.8(1).

(3) The court will not allocate proceedings to a track if the financial value of any claim in those proceedings, assessed by the court under rule 26.8, exceeds the limit for that track unless all the parties consent to the allocation of the claim to that track.

(4) The court will not allocate a claim to the small claims track, if it includes a claim by a tenant of residential premises against his landlord for a remedy in respect of harassment or unlawful eviction.

26.8 MATTERS RELEVANT TO ALLOCATION TO A TRACK

(1) When deciding the track for a claim, the matters to which the court shall have regard include—
  (a) the financial value, if any, of the claim;
  (b) the nature of the remedy sought;
  (c) the likely complexity of the facts, law or evidence;
  (d) the number of parties or likely parties;
  (e) the value of any counterclaim or other Part 20 claim and the complexity of any matters relating to it;
  (f) the amount of oral evidence which may be required;
  (g) the importance of the claim to persons who are not parties to the proceedings;
  (h) the views expressed by the parties; and
  (i) the circumstances of the parties.

(2) It is for the court to assess the financial value of a claim and in doing so it will disregard—
  (a) any amount not in dispute;
  (b) any claim for interest;
  (c) costs; and
  (d) any contributory negligence.

(3) Where—
  (a) two or more claimants have started a claim against the same defendant using the same claim form; and
  (b) each claimant has a claim against the defendant separate from the other claimants,
the court will consider the claim of each claimant separately when it assesses financial value under paragraph (1).

26.9 NOTICE OF ALLOCATION

(1) When it has allocated a claim to a track, the court will serve notice of allocation on every party.

(2) When the court serves notice of allocation on a party, it will also serve—
  (a) a copy of the allocation questionnaires filed by the other parties; and
  (b) a copy of any further information provided by another party about his case (whether by order or not).

(Rule 26.5 provides that the court may, before allocating proceedings, order a party to provide further information about his case)

26.10 RE-ALLOCATION

The court may subsequently re-allocate a claim to a different track.

PD 26 PRACTICE DIRECTION — CASE MANAGEMENT — PRELIMINARY STAGE: ALLOCATION AND RE-ALLOCATION

This practice direction supplements CPR Part 26

REMINDERS OF IMPORTANT RULE PROVISIONS OTHER THAN PARTS 26–29
Attention is drawn in particular to the following provisions of the Civil Procedure Rules:
Part 1 The Overriding Objective (defined in Rule 1.1).
The duty of the court to further that objective by actively managing cases (set out in Rule 1.4).
The requirement that the parties help the court to further that objective (set out in Rule 1.3).
Part 3 The court's case management powers (which may be exercised on application or on its own initiative) and the sanctions which it may impose.
Part 24 The court's power to grant summary judgment.
Parts 32–35 Evidence, especially the court's power to control evidence.
Attention is also drawn to the practice directions which supplement those Parts and Parts 27–29, and to those which relate to the various specialist jurisdictions.

THE ALLOCATION QUESTIONNAIRE

Form
2.1 The allocation questionnaire referred to in Part 26 will be in Form N150.
Attention is drawn to the Costs Practice Direction [PD 43], paragraph 4.5(1) which requires an estimate of costs to be filed and served when an allocation questionnaire is filed

Provision of extra information
2.2 (1) This paragraph sets out what a party should do when he files his allocation questionnaire if he wishes to give the court information about matters which he believes may affect its decision about allocation or case management.
(2) The general rule is that the court will not take such information into account unless the document containing it either:
  (a) confirms that all parties have agreed that the information is correct and that it should be put before the court, or
  (b) confirms that the party who has sent the document to the court has delivered a copy to all the other parties.
(3) The following are examples of information which will be likely to help the court:
  (a) a party's intention to apply for summary judgment or some other order that may dispose of the case or reduce the amount in dispute or the number of issues remaining to be decided,
  (b) a party's intention to issue a Part 20 claim or to add another party,
  (c) the steps the parties have taken in the preparation of evidence (in particular expert evidence), the steps they intend to take and whether those steps are to be taken in co-operation with any other party,
  (d) the directions the party believes will be appropriate to be given for the management of the case,
  (e) about any particular facts that may affect the timetable the court will set,
  (f) any facts which may make it desirable for the court to fix an allocation hearing or a hearing at which case management directions will be given.

Consultation

2.3 (1) The parties should consult one another and co-operate in completing the allocation questionnaires and giving other information to the court.

(2) They should try to agree the case management directions which they will invite the court to make. Further details appear in the practice directions which supplement Parts 28 and 29.

(3) The process of consultation must not delay the filing of the allocation questionnaires.

Hearings before allocation

2.4 Where a court hearing takes place (for example on an application for an interim injunction or for summary judgment under Part 24) before the claim is allocated to a track, the court may at that hearing:

(1) dispense with the need for the parties to file allocation questionnaires, treat the hearing as an allocation hearing, make an order for allocation and give directions for case management, or

(2) fix a date for allocation questionnaires to be filed and give other directions.

Consequences of failure to file an allocation questionnaire

2.5 (1) If no party files an allocation questionnaire within the time specified by Form N152:

(a) the file will be referred to a judge for his directions,

(b) the judge will usually order that unless an allocation questionnaire is filed within 3 days from service of that order the claim and any counterclaim will be struck out, but he may make a different order.

(2) Where a party files an allocation questionnaire but another party does not, the court may:

(a) allocate the claim to a track if it considers that it has enough information to do so, or

(b) order that an allocation hearing is listed and that all or any parties must attend.

STAY TO ALLOW FOR SETTLEMENT OF THE CASE

Procedure for the parties to apply to extend the stay

3.1 (1) (a) The court will generally accept a letter from any party or from the solicitor for any party as an application to extend the stay under rule 26.4.

(b) The letter should—

(i) confirm that the application is made with the agreement of all parties, and

(ii) explain the steps being taken and identify any mediator or expert assisting with the process.

(2) (a) An order extending the stay must be made by a judge.

(b) The extension will generally be for no more than 4 weeks unless clear reasons are given to justify a longer time.

(3) More than one extension of the stay may be granted.

3.2 Position at the end of the stay if no settlement is reached

(1) At the end of the stay the file will be referred to a judge for his directions.

(2) He will consider whether to allocate the claim to a track and what other directions to give, or may require any party to give further information or fix an allocation hearing.

3.3 Any party may apply for a stay to be lifted.

Position where settlement is reached during a stay

3.4 Where the whole of the proceedings are settled during a stay, the taking of any of the following steps will be treated as an application for the stay to be lifted:

(1) an application for a consent order (in any form) to give effect to the settlement,

(2) an application for the approval of a settlement where a party is a person under a disability,

(3) giving notice of acceptance of money paid into court in satisfaction of the claim or applying for money in court to be paid out.

ALLOCATION, RE-ALLOCATION AND CASE MANAGEMENT

The court's general approach

4.1 The Civil Procedure Rules lay down the overriding objective, the powers and duties of the court and the factors to which it must have regard in exercising them. The court will expect to exercise its powers as far as possible in cooperation with the parties and their legal representatives so as to deal with the case justly in accordance with that objective.

Allocation to track

4.2 (1) In most cases the court will expect to have enough information from the statements of case and allocation questionnaires to be able to allocate the claim to a track and to give case management directions.

(2) If the court does not have enough information to allocate the claim it will generally make an order under rule 26.5(3) requiring one or more parties to provide further information within 14 days.

(3) Where there has been no allocation hearing the notice of allocation will be in Forms N154 (fast track), N155 (multi-track) or N157–160 (small claims).

(4) (a) The general rule is that the court will give brief reasons for its allocation decision, and these will be set out in the notice of allocation.

(b) The general rule does not apply where all the allocation questionnaires which have been filed have expressed the wish for the claim to be allocated to the track to which the court has allocated it.

(5) Paragraph 6 of this practice direction deals with allocation hearings and Paragraph 7 deals with allocation principles.

(6) Paragraph 11 of this practice direction deals with re-allocation.

4.3 The practice directions supplementing Parts 27, 28 and 29 contain further information about the giving of case management directions at the allocation stage.

SUMMARY JUDGMENT OR OTHER EARLY TERMINATION

5.1 Part of the court's duty of active case management is the summary disposal of issues which do not need full investigation and trial (rule 1.4(2)(c)).

5.2 The court's powers to make orders to dispose of issues in that way include:

(a) under rule 3.4, striking out a statement of case, or part of a statement of case, and

(b) under Part 24, giving summary judgment where a claimant or a defendant has no reasonable prospect of success.

The court may use these powers on an application or on its own initiative. The practice direction 'Summary Disposal of Claims' contains further information.

5.3 (1) A party intending to make such an application should do so before or when filing his allocation questionnaire.

(2) Where a party makes an application for such an order before a claim has been allocated to a track the court will not normally allocate the claim before the hearing of the application.

(3) Where a party files an allocation questionnaire stating that he intends to make such an application but has not done so, the judge will usually direct that an allocation hearing is listed.

(4) The application may be heard at that allocation hearing if the application notice has been issued and served in sufficient time.

5.4 (1) This paragraph applies where the court proposes to make such an order of its own initiative.

(2) The court will not allocate the claim to a track but instead it will either:

(a) fix a hearing, giving the parties at least 14 days notice of the date of the hearing and of the issues which it is proposed that the court will decide, or

(b) make an order directing a party to take the steps described in the order within a stated time and specifying the consequence of not taking those steps.

5.5 Where the court decides at the hearing of an application or a hearing fixed under paragraph 5.4(2)(a) that the claim (or part of the claim) is to continue it may:

(1) treat that hearing as an allocation hearing, allocate the claim and give case management directions, or

(2) give other directions.

ALLOCATION HEARINGS

General principle

6.1 The court will only hold an allocation hearing on its own initiative if it considers that it is necessary to do so.

Procedure

6.2 Where the court orders an allocation hearing to take place:

(1) it will give the parties at least 7 days notice of the hearing in Form N153, and

(2) Form N153 will give a brief explanation of the decision to order the hearing.

6.3 Power to treat another hearing as an allocation hearing
Where the court may treat another hearing as an allocation hearing it does not need to give notice to any party that it proposes to do so.

6.4 The notice of allocation after an allocation hearing will be in Forms N154, N155 or N157.

Representation

6.5 A legal representative who attends an allocation hearing should, if possible, be the person responsible for the case and must in any event be familiar with the case, be able to provide the court with the information it is likely to need to take its decisions about allocation and case management, and have sufficient authority to deal with any issues that are likely to arise.

Sanctions

6.6 (1) This paragraph sets out the sanctions that the court will usually impose for default in connection with the allocation procedure, but the court may make a different order.

(2) (a) Where an allocation hearing takes place because a party has failed to file an allocation questionnaire or to provide further information which the court has ordered, the court will usually order that party to pay on the indemnity basis the costs of any other party who has attended the hearing, summarily assess the amount of those costs, and order them to be paid forthwith or within a stated period.

(b) The court may order that if the party does not pay those costs within the time stated his statement of case will be struck out.

(3) Where a party whose default has led to a fixing of an allocation hearing is still in default and does not attend the hearing the court will usually make an order specifying the steps he is required to take and providing that unless he takes them within a stated time his statement of case will be struck out.

ALLOCATION PRINCIPLES

Rules 26.6, 26.7 and 26.8

7.1 (1) Rule 26.6 sets out the scope of each track,

(2) Rule 26.7 states the general rule for allocation, and

(3) Rule 26.8 sets out the matters relevant to allocation to a track.

Objective of this paragraph

7.2 The object of this paragraph is to explain what will be the court's general approach to some of the matters set out in rule 26.8.

'the financial value of the claim'

7.3 (1) Rule 26.8(2) provides that it is for the court to assess the financial value of a claim.

(2) Where the court believes that the amount the claimant is seeking exceeds what he may reasonably be expected to recover it may make an order under rule 26.5(3) directing the claimant to justify the amount.

'any amount not in dispute'

7.4 In deciding, for the purposes of rule 26.8(2), whether an amount is in dispute the court will apply the following general principles:
    (1) Any amount for which the defendant does not admit liability is in dispute,
    (2) Any sum in respect of an item forming part of the claim for which judgment has been entered (for example a summary judgment) is not in dispute,
    (3) Any specific sum claimed as a distinct item and which the defendant admits he is liable to pay is not in dispute,
    (4) Any sum offered by the defendant which has been accepted by the claimant in satisfaction of any item which forms a distinct part of the claim is not in dispute.

It follows from these provisions that if, in relation to a claim the value of which is above the small claims track limit of £5,000, the defendant makes, before allocation, an admission that reduces the amount in dispute to a figure below £5,000 (see CPR Part 14), the normal track for the claim will be the small claims track. As to recovery of pre-allocation costs, the claimant can, before allocation, apply for judgment with costs on the amount of the claim that has been admitted (see CPR rule 14.3 but see also paragraph 5.1(3) of the Costs Directions relating to CPR Part 44 under which the court has a discretion to allow pre-allocation costs).

'the views expressed by the parties'

7.5 The court will treat these views as an important factor, but the allocation decision is one for the court, to be taken in the light of all the circumstances, and the court will not be bound by any agreement or common view of the parties.

'the circumstances of the parties'

7.6 See paragraph 8.

'the value of any counterclaim or other Part 20 claim'

7.7 Where the case involves more than one money claim (for example where there is a Part 20 claim or there is more than one claimant each making separate claims) the court will not generally aggregate the claims. Instead it will generally regard the largest of them as determining the financial value of the claims.

THE SMALL CLAIMS TRACK — ALLOCATION AND CASE MANAGEMENT

Allocation

8.1 (1) (a) The small claims track is intended to provide a proportionate procedure by which most straightforward claims with a financial value of not more than £5,000 can be decided, without the need for substantial pre-hearing preparation and the formalities of a traditional trial, and without incurring large legal costs. (Rule 26.6 provides for a lower financial value in certain types of case.)

    (b) The procedure laid down in Part 27 for the preparation of the case and the conduct of the hearing are designed to make it possible for a litigant to conduct his own case without legal representation if he wishes.

    (c) Cases generally suitable for the small claims track will include consumer disputes, accident claims, disputes about the ownership of goods and most disputes between a landlord and tenant other than those for possession.

    (d) A case involving a disputed allegation of dishonesty will not usually be suitable for the small claims track.

    (2) Rule 26.7(3) and rule 27.14(5)

    (a) These rules allow the parties to consent to the allocation to the small claims track of a claim the value of which is above the limits mentioned in rule 26.6(2) and, in that event, the rules make provision about costs.

    (b) The court will not allocate such a claim to the small claims track, notwithstanding that the parties have consented to the allocation, unless it is satisfied that it is suitable for that track.

PD 26 PRACTICE DIRECTION — CASE MANAGEMENT

(c) The court will not normally allow more than one day for the hearing of such a claim.

(d) The court will give case management directions to ensure that the case is dealt with in as short a time as possible. These may include directions of a kind that are not usually given in small claim cases, for example, for Scott Schedules.

Case management

8.2 (1) Directions for case management of claims allocated to the small claims track will generally be given by the court on allocation.

(2) Rule 27.4 contains further provisions about directions and the practice direction supplementing Part 27 sets out the standard directions which the court will usually give.

THE FAST TRACK

Allocation

9.1 (1) Where the court is to decide whether to allocate to the fast track or the multi-track a claim for which the normal track is the fast track, it will allocate the claim to the fast track unless it believes that it cannot be dealt with justly on that track.

(2) The court will, in particular, take into account the limits likely to be placed on disclosure, the extent to which expert evidence may be necessary and whether the trial is likely to last more than a day.

(3) (a) When it is considering the likely length of the trial the court will regard a day as being a period of 5 hours, and will consider whether that is likely to be sufficient time for the case to be heard.

(b) The court will also take into account the case management directions (including the fixing of a trial timetable) that are likely to be given and the court's powers to control evidence and to limit cross-examination.

(c) The possibility that a trial might last longer than one day is not necessarily a conclusive reason for the court to allocate or to re-allocate a claim to the multi-track.

(d) A claim may be allocated to the fast track or ordered to remain on that track although there is to be a split trial.

(e) Where the case involves a counterclaim or other Part 20 claim that will be tried with the claim and as a result the trial will last more than a day, the court may not allocate it to the fast track.

Case management

9.2 (1) Directions for the case management of claims which have been allocated to the fast track will be given at the allocation stage or at the listing stage (in either case with or without a hearing) or at both, and if necessary at other times. The trial judge may, at or before the trial, give directions for its conduct.

(2) The practice direction supplementing Part 28 contains further provisions and contains standard directions which the court may give.

THE MULTI-TRACK

10.1 The following paragraphs do not apply to a claim which is being dealt with at the Royal Courts of Justice.

Venue for allocation and case management

10.2 (1) The case management of a claim which is allocated to the multi-track will normally be dealt with at a Civil Trial Centre.

(2) In the case of a claim to which Part 49 (specialist proceedings) applies, case management must be dealt with at a Civil Trial Centre. Sub-paragraphs (4) to (10) do not apply to such a claim. The claim will be allocated to the multi-track irrespective of its value, and must be transferred to a Civil Trial Centre for allocation and case management if not already there.

(3) Where a claim is issued in or automatically transferred to a Civil Trial Centre it will be allocated and managed at that court.

(4) The following *sub-paragraphs* apply to a claim which is issued in or automatically transferred to a court which is not a Civil Trial Centre. Such a court is referred to as a 'feeder court'.

(5) Where a judge sitting at a feeder court decides, on the basis of the allocation questionnaires and any other documents filed by the parties, that the claim should be dealt with on the multi-track he will normally make an order:
    (a)   allocating the claim to that track,
    (b)   giving case management directions, and
    (c)   transferring the claim to a Civil Trial Centre.

(6) If he decides that an allocation hearing or some pre-allocation hearing is to take place (for example to strike out a statement of case under Part 3 of the Rules) that hearing will take place at the feeder court.

(7) If, before allocation, a hearing takes place at a feeder court and in exercising his powers under paragraph 2.4(1) above the judge allocates the claim to the multi-track, he will also normally make an order transferring the claim to a Civil Trial Centre.

(8) A judge sitting at a feeder court may, rather than making an allocation order himself, transfer the claim to a Civil Trial Centre for the decision about allocation to be taken there.

(9) When, following an order for transfer, the file is received at the Civil Trial Centre, a judge sitting at that Centre will consider it and give any further directions that appear necessary or desirable.

(10) Where there is reason to believe that more than one case management conference may be needed and the parties or their legal advisers are located inconveniently far from the Civil Trial Centre, a judge sitting at a feeder court may, with the agreement of the Designated Civil Judge and notwithstanding the allocation of the case to the multi-track, decide that in the particular circumstances of the case it should not be transferred to a Civil Trial Centre, but should be case managed for the time being at the feeder court.

(11) A Designated Civil Judge may at any time make an order transferring a claim from a feeder court to a Civil Trial Centre and he may do so irrespective of the track, if any, to which it has been allocated.

(12) No order will be made by a feeder court fixing a date for a hearing at a Civil Trial Centre unless that date has been given or confirmed by a judge or listing officer of that Centre.

Case management
10.3 Part 29 of the Rules and the practice direction supplementing that Part set out the procedure to be adopted.

RE-ALLOCATION OF CLAIMS AND THE VARIATION OF DIRECTIONS

11.1 (1) Where a party is dissatisfied with an order made allocating the claim to a track he may appeal or apply to the court to re-allocate the claim.

(2) He should appeal if the order was made at a hearing at which he was present or represented, or of which he was given due notice.

(3) In any other case he should apply to the court to re-allocate the claim.

11.2 Where there has been a change in the circumstances since an order was made allocating the claim to a track the court may re-allocate the claim. It may do so on application or on its own initiative.

The practice directions supplementing Parts 28 and 29 contain provisions about the variation of case management directions.

ALLOCATION AND CASE MANAGEMENT OF ASSESSMENTS OF DAMAGES AND ALLIED PROCEEDINGS

Scope
12.1 (1) In the following paragraphs a 'relevant order' means an order or judgment of the court which requires the amount of money to be paid by one party to another to be decided by the court.

(2) A relevant order may have been obtained:

(a) by a judgment in default under Part 12,
(b) by a judgment on an admission under Part 14,
(c) on the striking out of a statement of case under Part 3,
(d) on a summary judgment application under Part 24,
(e) on the determination of a preliminary issue or on a trial as to liability, or
(f) at trial.

(3) A relevant order includes an order for an amount of damages or interest to be decided by the court, an order for the taking of an account or the making of an inquiry as to any sum due, and any similar order.

(4) A relevant order does not include an order for the assessment of costs except where the court has made an order for the assessment of costs payable under a contract other than a contract between a solicitor and client for legal services.

Directions

12.2 (1) Directions which may be given under the following paragraphs may include:
(a) a direction allocating or re-allocating the claim,
(b) a direction that allocation questionnaires be filed by a specified date,
(c) a direction that a date be fixed for a hearing or a further hearing,
(d) an order that the claim be stayed while the parties try to settle the case by alternative dispute resolution or other means.

(2) Directions may specify the level or type of judge before whom a hearing or a further hearing will take place and the nature and purpose of that hearing.

Allocation

12.3 Where a claim has not been allocated to a track at the time a relevant order is made, the court will not normally consider it to be appropriate to allocate it to a track (other than the small claims track) unless the amount payable appears to be genuinely disputed on grounds which appear to be substantial. It may instead direct that a disposal hearing (referred to in paragraph 12.8) be listed.

Orders and judgments made at hearings

12.4 Where a relevant order is made by a judge at a hearing, the judge should at the same time give such directions as the information about the case available to him enables him to give.

Orders made by consent without a hearing

12.5 (1) Where a relevant order is made by consent without a hearing a judge will give directions.

(2) The parties should where possible file with the draft consent order agreed directions which they invite the court to give.

Judgments entered on admissions without a hearing

12.6 (1) Where a relevant order is a judgment entered without a hearing under Part 14 the court will give directions.

(2) The court may in particular direct that a disposal hearing be listed.

Judgments entered in default

12.7 (1) This paragraph applies where the relevant order is a judgment entered under Part 12 without a hearing.

(2) On the entry of the judgment the court will list a disposal hearing.

Disposal hearings

12.8 (1) At a disposal hearing the court may give directions or decide the amount payable in accordance with this sub-paragraph.

(2) If the financial value of the claim (determined in accordance with Part 26) is such that the claim would, if defended, be allocated to the small claims track, the court will normally allocate it to that track and may treat the disposal hearing as a final hearing in accordance with Part 27.

PD 26 PRACTICE DIRECTION — CASE MANAGEMENT

(3) If the court does not give directions and does not allocate the claim to the small claims track, it may nonetheless order that the amount payable is to be decided there and then without allocating the claim to another track.

(4) Rule 32.6 applies to evidence at a disposal hearing unless the court otherwise directs.

(5) The court will not exercise its powers under sub-paragraph 12.8(3) unless any written evidence on which the claimant relies has been served on the defendant at least 3 days before the disposal hearing.

Costs

12.9 (1) Attention is drawn to the costs practice directions and in particular to the court's power to make a summary assessment of costs.

(2) Attention is drawn to rule 44.13(1) which provides that if an order makes no mention of costs, none are payable in respect of the proceedings to which it relates.

(3) Attention is drawn to rule 27.14 (special rules about costs in cases allocated to the small claims track).

(4) Attention is drawn to Part 45 (fixed trial costs in cases which have been allocated to the fast track). Part 45 will not apply to a case dealt with at a disposal hearing whatever the financial value of the claim. So the costs of a disposal hearing will be in the discretion of the court.

Jurisdiction of Masters and district judges

12.10 Unless the court otherwise directs, a Master or a district judge may decide the amount payable under a relevant order irrespective of the financial value of the claim and of the track to which the claim may have been allocated.

CPR PART 27   THE SMALL CLAIMS TRACK

CONTENTS OF THIS PART
Scope of this Part	Rule 27.1
Extent to which other Parts apply	Rule 27.2
Court's power to grant a final remedy	Rule 27.3
Preparation for the hearing	Rule 27.4
Experts	Rule 27.5
Preliminary hearing	Rule 27.6
Power of court to add to, vary or revoke directions	Rule 27.7
Conduct of the hearing	Rule 27.8
Non-attendance of parties at a final hearing	Rule 27.9
Disposal without a hearing	Rule 27.10
Setting judgment aside and re-hearing	Rule 27.11
Right of appeal under Part 27	Rule 27.12
Procedure for making an appeal	Rule 27.13
Costs on the small claims track	Rule 27.14
Claim re-allocated from the small claims track to another track	Rule 27.15

27.1 SCOPE OF THIS PART
(1) This Part—
  (a) sets out the special procedure for dealing with claims which have been allocated to the small claims track under Part 26; and
  (b) limits the amount of costs that can be recovered in respect of a claim which has been allocated to the small claims track.
(Rule 27.14 deals with costs on the small claims track)
  (2) A claim being dealt with under this Part is called a small claim.
(Rule 26.6 provides for the scope of the small claims track. A claim for a remedy for harassment or unlawful eviction relating, in either case, to residential premises shall not be allocated to the small claims track whatever the financial value of the claim. Otherwise, the small claims track will be the normal track for—
- any claim which has a financial value of not more than £5,000 subject to the special provisions about claims for personal injuries and housing disrepair claims;
- any claim for personal injuries which has a financial value of not more than £5,000 where the claim for damages for personal injuries is not more than £1,000; and
- any claim which includes a claim by a tenant of residential premises against his landlord for repairs or other work to the premises where the estimated cost of the repairs or other work is not more than £1,000 and the financial value of any other claim for damages in respect of those repairs or other work is not more than £1,000)

27.2 EXTENT TO WHICH OTHER PARTS APPLY
(1) The following Parts of these Rules do not apply to small claims—
  (a) Part 25 (interim remedies) except as it relates to interim injunctions$^{(GL)}$;
  (b) Part 31 (disclosure and inspection);
  (c) Part 32 (evidence) except rule 32.1 (power of court to control evidence);
  (d) Part 33 (miscellaneous rules about evidence);
  (e) Part 35 (experts and assessors) except rules 35.1 (duty to restrict expert evidence), 35.3 (experts — overriding duty to the court) and 35.8 (instructions to a single joint expert);
  (f) Part 18 (further information);
  (g) Part 36 (offers to settle and payments into court); and
  (h) Part 39 (hearings) except rule 39.2 (general rule — hearing to be in public).

CPR PART 27 THE SMALL CLAIMS TRACK

(2) The other Parts of these Rules apply to small claims except to the extent that a rule limits such application.

27.3 COURTS POWER TO GRANT A FINAL REMEDY
The court may grant any final remedy in relation to a small claim which it could grant if the proceedings were on the fast track or the multi-track.

27.4 PREPARATION FOR THE HEARING
(1) After allocation the court will—
  (a) give standard directions and fix a date for the final hearing;
  (b) give special directions and fix a date for the final hearing;
  (c) give special directions and direct that the court will consider what further directions are to be given no later than 28 days after the date the special directions were given;
  (d) fix a date for a preliminary hearing under rule 27.6; or
  (e) give notice that it proposes to deal with the claim without a hearing under rule 27.10 and invite the parties to notify the court by a specified date if they agree the proposal.
(2) The court will—
  (a) give the parties at least 21 days' notice of the date fixed for the final hearing, unless the parties agree to accept less notice; and
  (b) inform them of the amount of time allowed for the final hearing.
(3) In this rule—
  (a) 'standard directions' means—
    (i) a direction that each party shall, at least 14 days before the date fixed for the final hearing, file and serve on every other party copies of all documents (including any expert's report) on which he intends to rely at the hearing; and
    (ii) any other standard directions set out in the relevant practice direction; and
  (b) 'special directions' means directions given in addition to or instead of the standard directions.

27.5 EXPERTS
No expert may give evidence, whether written or oral, at a hearing without the permission of the court.
(Rule 27.14(3)(d) provides for the payment of an expert's fees)

27.6 PRELIMINARY HEARING
(1) The court may hold a preliminary hearing for the consideration of the claim, but only—
  (a) where—
    (i) it considers that special directions, as defined in rule 27.4, are needed to ensure a fair hearing; and
    (ii) it appears necessary for a party to attend at court to ensure that he understands what he must do to comply with the special directions; or
  (b) to enable it to dispose of the claim on the basis that one or other of the parties has no real prospect of success at a final hearing; or
  (c) to enable it to strike out^(GL) a statement of case or part of a statement of case on the basis that the statement of case, or the part to be struck out, discloses no reasonable grounds for bringing or defending the claim.
(2) When considering whether or not to hold a preliminary hearing, the court must have regard to the desirability of limiting the expense to the parties of attending court.
(3) Where the court decides to hold a preliminary hearing, it will give the parties at least 14 days' notice of the date of the hearing.
(4) The court may treat the preliminary hearing as the final hearing of the claim if all the parties agree.
(5) At or after the preliminary hearing the court will—
  (a) fix the date of the final hearing (if it has not been fixed already) and give the parties at least 21 days' notice of the date fixed unless the parties agree to accept less notice;

CPR PART 27 THE SMALL CLAIMS TRACK

(b) inform them of the amount of time allowed for the final hearing; and
(c) give any appropriate directions.

27.7 POWER OF COURT TO ADD TO, VARY OR REVOKE DIRECTIONS
The court may add to, vary or revoke directions.

27.8 CONDUCT OF THE HEARING
(1) The court may adopt any method of proceeding at a hearing that it considers to be fair.
(2) Hearings will be informal.
(3) The strict rules of evidence do not apply.
(4) The court need not take evidence on oath.
(5) The court may limit cross-examination$^{(GL)}$.
(6) The court must give reasons for its decision.

27.9 NON-ATTENDANCE OF PARTIES AT A FINAL HEARING
(1) If a party who does not attend a final hearing—
   (a) has given the court written notice at least 7 days before the date of the hearing that he will not attend; and
   (b) has, in that notice, requested the court to decide the claim in his absence,
the court will take into account that party's statement of case and any other documents he has filed when it decides the claim.
(2) If a claimant does not—
   (a) attend the hearing; and
   (b) give the notice referred to in paragraph (1),
the court may strike out$^{(GL)}$ the claim.
(3) If—
   (a) a defendant does not—
      (i) attend the hearing; or
      (ii) give the notice referred to in paragraph (1); and
   (b) the claimant either—
      (i) does attend the hearing; or
      (ii) gives the notice referred to in paragraph (1),
the court may decide the claim on the basis of the evidence of the claimant alone.
(4) If neither party attends or gives the notice referred to in paragraph (1), the court may strike out$^{(GL)}$ the claim and any defence and counterclaim.

27.10 DISPOSAL WITHOUT A HEARING
The court may, if all parties agree, deal with the claim without a hearing.

27.11 SETTING JUDGMENT ASIDE AND RE-HEARING
(1) A party—
   (a) who was neither present nor represented at the hearing of the claim; and
   (b) who has not given written notice to the court under rule 27.9(1),
may apply for an order that a judgment under this Part shall be set aside$^{(GL)}$ and the claim re-heard.
(2) A party who applies for an order setting aside a judgment under this rule must make the application not more than 14 days after the day on which notice of the judgment was served on him.
(3) The court may grant an application under paragraph (2) only if the applicant—
   (a) had a good reason for not attending or being represented at the hearing or giving written notice to the court under rule 27.9(1); and
   (b) has a reasonable prospect of success at the hearing.
(4) If a judgment is set aside$^{(GL)}$—
   (a) the court must fix a new hearing for the claim; and
   (b) the hearing may take place immediately after the hearing of the application to set the judgment aside and may be dealt with by the judge who set aside$^{(GL)}$ the judgment.
(5) A party may not apply to set aside$^{(GL)}$ a judgment under this rule if the court dealt with the claim without a hearing under rule 27.10.

CPR PART 27 THE SMALL CLAIMS TRACK

27.12 RIGHT OF APPEAL UNDER PART 27

(1) A party may appeal against an order under this Part only on the grounds that—
  (a) there was serious irregularity affecting the proceedings; or
  (b) the court made a mistake of law.
(2) On an appeal the court may make any order it considers appropriate.
(3) The court may dismiss an appeal without a hearing.
(4) This rule does not limit any right of appeal arising under any Act.

27.13 PROCEDURE FOR MAKING AN APPEAL

(1) A party who wishes to appeal must file a notice of appeal not more than 14 days after the day on which notice of the order was served on him.
(2) Notice of appeal—
  (a) must be filed at the court which made the order; and
  (b) must set out the grounds for the appeal with particulars of the serious irregularity or mistake of law alleged.

27.14 COSTS ON THE SMALL CLAIMS TRACK

(1) This rule applies to any case which has been allocated to the small claims track unless paragraph (5) applies.
(Rules 44.9 and 44.11 make provision in relation to orders for costs made before a claim has been allocated to the small claims track)
(2) The court may not order a party to pay a sum to another party in respect of that other party's costs except—
  (a) the fixed costs attributable to issuing the claim which—
    (i) are payable under Part 45; or
    (ii) would be payable under Part 45 if that Part applied to the claim;
  (b) in proceedings which included a claim for an injunction[GL] or an order for specific performance a sum not exceeding the amount specified in the relevant practice direction for legal advice and assistance relating to that claim;
  (c) costs assessed by the summary procedure in relation to an appeal under rule 27.12; and
  (d) such further costs as the court may assess by the summary procedure and order to be paid by a party who has behaved unreasonably.
(3) The court may also order a party to pay all or part of—
  (a) any court fees paid by another party;
  (b) expenses which a party or witness has reasonably incurred in travelling to and from a hearing or in staying away from home for the purposes of attending a hearing;
  (c) a sum not exceeding the amount specified in the relevant practice direction for any loss of earnings by a party or witness due to attending a hearing or to staying away from home for the purpose of attending a hearing; and
  (d) a sum not exceeding the amount specified in the relevant practice direction for an expert's fees.
(4) The limits on costs imposed by this rule also apply to any fee or reward for acting on behalf of a party to the proceedings charged by a person exercising a right of audience by virtue of an order under section 11 of the Courts and Legal Services Act 1990 (a lay representative).
(5) Where—
  (a) the financial value of a claim exceeds the limit for the small claims track; but
  (b) the claim has been allocated to the small claims track in accordance with rule 26.7(3),
the claim shall be treated, for the purposes of costs, as if it were proceeding on the fast track except that trial costs shall be in the discretion of the court and shall not exceed the amount set out for the value of the claim in rule 46.2 (amount of fast track trial costs).
(Rule 26.7(3) allows the parties to consent to a claim being allocated to a track where the financial value of the claim exceeds the limit for that track)

27.15 CLAIM RE-ALLOCATED FROM THE SMALL CLAIMS TRACK TO ANOTHER TRACK

Where a claim is allocated to the small claims track and subsequently re-allocated to another track, rule 27.14 (costs on the small claims track) will cease to apply after the claim has been re-allocated and the fast track or multi-track costs rules will apply from the date of re-allocation.

PD 27 PRACTICE DIRECTION — SMALL CLAIMS TRACK

This practice direction supplements CPR Part 27

JUDGES

1 The functions of the court described in Part 27 which are to be carried out by a judge will generally be carried out by a district judge but may be carried out by a Circuit Judge.

CASE MANAGEMENT DIRECTIONS

2.1 Rule 27.4 explains how directions will be given, and rule 27.6 contains provisions about the holding of a preliminary hearing and the court's powers at such a hearing.

2.2 Appendix A sets out the Standard Directions which the court may give.

REPRESENTATION AT A HEARING

3.1 In this paragraph:

(1) a lawyer means a barrister, a solicitor or a legal executive employed by a solicitor, and

(2) a lay representative means any other person.

3.2 (1) A party may present his own case at a hearing or a lawyer or lay representative may present it for him.

(2) The Lay Representatives (Right of Audience) Order 1999 provides that a lay representative may not exercise any right of audience:—

(a) where his client does not attend the hearing;

(b) at any stage after judgment; or

(c) on any appeal brought against any decision made by the district judge in the proceedings.

(3) However the court, exercising its general discretion to hear anybody, may hear a lay representative even in circumstances excluded by the Order.

(4) Any of its officers or employees may represent a corporate party.

SMALL CLAIM HEARING

4.1 (1) The general rule is that a small claim hearing will be in public.

(2) The judge may decide to hold it in private if:

(a) the parties agree, or

(b) a ground mentioned in rule 39.2(3) applies.

(3) A hearing or part of a hearing which takes place other than at the court, for example at the home or business premises of a party, will not be in public.

4.2 A hearing that takes place at the court will generally be in the judge's room but it may take place in a courtroom.

4.3 Rule 27.8 allows the court to adopt any method of proceeding that it considers to be fair and to limit cross-examination. The judge may in particular:

(1) ask questions of any witness himself before allowing any other person to do so,

(2) ask questions of all or any of the witnesses himself before allowing any other person to ask questions of any witnesses,

(3) refuse to allow cross-examination of any witness until all the witnesses have given evidence in chief,

(4) limit cross-examination of a witness to a fixed time or to a particular subject or issue, or both.

RECORDING EVIDENCE AND THE GIVING OF REASONS

5.1 The judge may direct that all or any part of the proceedings will be tape recorded by the court. A party may obtain a transcript of such a recording on payment of the proper transcriber's charges.

5.2 Attention is drawn to section 9 of the Contempt of Court Act 1981 (which deals with the unauthorised use of tape recorders in court) and to the Practice Direction ([1981] 1 WLR 1526) which relates to it.

5.3 The judge will make a note of the central points of the oral evidence unless it is tape recorded by the court.

5.4 The judge will make a note of the central reasons for his judgment unless it is given orally and tape recorded by the court.

5.5 (1) The judge may give his reasons as briefly and simply as the nature of the case allows.

(2) He will normally do so orally at the hearing, but he may give them later either in writing or at a hearing fixed for him to do so.

5.6 Where the judge decides the case without a hearing under rule 27.10 or a party who has given notice under rule 27.9(1) does not attend the hearing, the judge will prepare a note of his reasons and the court will send a copy to each party.

5.7 A party is entitled to a copy of any note made by the judge under sub-paragraphs 5.3 or 5.4.

5.8 Nothing in this practice direction affects the duty of a judge at the request of a party to make a note of the matters referred to in section 80 of the County Courts Act 1984.

NON-ATTENDANCE OF A PARTY AT A HEARING

6.1 Attention is drawn to rule 27.9 (which enables a party to give notice that he will not attend a final hearing and sets out the effect of his giving such notice and of not doing so), and to paragraph 3 above.

6.2 Nothing in those provisions affects the general power of the court to adjourn a hearing, for example where a party who wishes to attend a hearing on the date fixed cannot do so for a good reason.

COSTS

7.1 Attention is drawn to Rule 27.14 which contains provisions about the costs which may be ordered to be paid by one party to another.

7.2 The amount which a party may be ordered to pay under rule 27.14(2)(b) (for legal advice and assistance in claims including an injunction or specific performance) is a sum not exceeding £260.

7.3 The amounts which a party may be ordered to pay under rule 27.14(3)(c) (loss of earnings) and (d) (experts' fees) are:

(1) for the loss of earnings of each party or witness due to attending a hearing or staying away from home for the purpose of attending a hearing, a sum not exceeding £50 per day for each person, and

(2) for expert's fees, a sum not exceeding £200 for each expert.

(As to recovery of pre-allocation costs in a case in which an admission by the defendant has reduced the amount in dispute to a figure below £5,000, reference should be made to paragraph 7.4 of the Practice Direction supplementing CPR Part 26 and to paragraph 5.1(3) of the Costs Directions relating to CPR Part 44.)

APPEALS FROM DECISIONS OF DISTRICT JUDGES

8.1 An appeal from a decision of a district judge under Part 27 will be dealt with by a Circuit Judge.

8.2 Attention is drawn to rule 27.12 and 13 and in particular to the limited grounds of appeal and the time limits for giving notice of appeal.

8.3 A notice of appeal must set out particulars of the serious irregularity or mistake of law relied on.

8.4 When a notice of appeal is filed it will be put before a Circuit Judge as soon as possible after it is filed and he will decide how to deal with the appeal.

8.5 The court will serve a copy of the notice on all other parties.

8.6 The Circuit Judge may either:

(1) dismiss the appeal without a hearing if no sufficient ground is shown in the notice of appeal, or

(2) order that the appeal is to be listed for hearing.

8.7 The Circuit Judge will give any necessary directions:
(1) about the filing of any evidence concerning any allegation of serious irregularity, and
(2) about the supply to the parties of copies of any document (including any note made by the judge who heard the case) which he has taken or may have taken into account in dealing with the appeal.

8.8 Where the Circuit Judge dismisses the appeal without a hearing his order will contain brief reasons for his decision.

8.9 Where the Circuit Judge directs that the appeal is to be listed for hearing the court will give at least seven days notice of the hearing to all parties.

8.10 If the appeal is allowed, the Circuit Judge will if possible dispose of the case at the same time without ordering the claim to be reheard. He may do so without hearing further evidence.

Appendix A

FORM A — THE STANDARD DIRECTIONS
(for use where the district judge specifies no other directions)

THE COURT DIRECTS

1 Each party shall deliver to every other party and to the court office copies of all documents (including any experts' report) on which he intends to rely at the hearing no later than [   ] [14 days before the hearing].

2 The original documents shall be brought to the hearing.

3 [Notice of hearing date and time allowed.]

4 The court must be informed immediately if the case is settled by agreement before the hearing date.

FORM B — STANDARD DIRECTIONS FOR USE IN CLAIMS ARISING OUT OF ROAD ACCIDENTS

THE COURT DIRECTS

1 Each party shall deliver to every other party and to the court office copies of all documents on which he intends to rely at the hearing. These may include:
- experts' reports (including medical reports where damages for personal injury are claimed),
- witness statements,
- invoices and estimates for repairs,
- documents which relate to other losses, such as loss of earnings,
- sketch plans and photographs.

2 The copies shall be delivered no later than [   ] [14 days before the hearing].

3 The original documents shall be brought to the hearing.

4 Before the date of the hearing the parties shall try to agree the cost of the repairs and any other losses claimed subject to the court's decision about whose fault the accident was.

5 Signed statements setting out the evidence of all witnesses on whom each party intends to rely shall be prepared and copies included in the documents mentioned in paragraph 1. This includes the evidence of the parties themselves and of any other witness, whether or not he is going to come to court to give evidence.

6 The parties should note that:
(a) In deciding the case the court will find it very helpful to have a sketch plan and photographs of the place where the accident happened.
(b) The court may decide not to take into account a document or the evidence of a witness if no copy of that document or no copy of a statement or report by that witness has been supplied to the other parties.

7 [Notice of hearing date and time allowed.]

8 The court must be informed immediately if the case is settled by agreement before the hearing date.

PD 27 PRACTICE DIRECTION — SMALL CLAIMS TRACK

FORM C — STANDARD DIRECTIONS FOR USE IN CLAIMS ARISING OUT OF BUILDING DISPUTES, VEHICLE REPAIRS AND SIMILAR CONTRACTUAL CLAIMS

THE COURT DIRECTS

1 Each party shall deliver to every other party and to the court office copies of all documents on which he intends to rely at the hearing. These may include:
- the contract,
- witness statements,
- experts' reports,
- photographs,
- invoices for work done or goods supplied,
- estimates for work to be done.

2 The copies shall be delivered no later than [   ] [14 days before the hearing].

3 The original documents shall be brought to the hearing.

4 [The   shall deliver to the   and to the court office [no later than   ] [with his copy documents] a list showing all items of work which he complains about and why, and the amount claimed for putting each item right.]

5 [The   shall deliver to the   and to the court office [no later than   ] [with his copy documents] a breakdown of the amount he is claiming showing all work done and materials supplied.]

6 Before the date of the hearing the parties shall try to agree about the nature and cost of any remedial work required, subject to the court's decision about any other issue in the case.

7 [Signed statements setting out the evidence of all witnesses on whom each party intends to rely shall be prepared and included in the documents mentioned in paragraph 1. This includes the evidence of the parties themselves and of any other witness, whether or not he is going to come to court to give evidence.]

8 The parties should note that:
   (a) in deciding the case the judge may find it helpful to have photographs showing the work in question,
   (b) the judge may decide not to take into account a document or the evidence of a witness if no copy of that document or no copy of a statement or report by that witness has been supplied to the other parties.

9 [Notice of hearing date and time allowed.]

10 The court must be informed immediately if the case is settled by agreement before the hearing date.

FORM D — TENANTS' CLAIMS FOR THE RETURN OF DEPOSITS/LANDLORDS CLAIMS FOR DAMAGE CAUSED

THE COURT DIRECTS

1 Each party shall deliver to every other party and to the court office copies of all documents on which he intends to rely at the hearing. These may include:
- the tenancy agreement and any inventory,
- the rent book or other evidence of rent and other payments made by the   to the   ,
- photographs,
- witness statements,
- invoices or estimates for work and goods.

2 The copies shall be delivered no later than [   ] [14 days before the hearing].

3 The original documents shall be brought to the hearing.

4 The   shall deliver with his copy documents a list showing each item of loss or damage for which he claims the   ought to pay, and the amount he claims for the replacement or repair.

PD 27 PRACTICE DIRECTION — SMALL CLAIMS TRACK

5   The parties shall before the hearing date try to agree about the nature and cost of any repairs and replacements needed, subject to the court's decision about any other issue in the case.

6   [Signed statements setting out the evidence of all witnesses on whom each party intends to rely shall be prepared and included in the documents mentioned in paragraph 1. This includes the evidence of the parties themselves and of any other witness whether or not he is going to come to court to give evidence.]

7   The parties should note that:

   (a)   in deciding the case the judge may find it helpful to have photographs showing the condition of the property,

   (b)   the judge may decide not to take into account a document or the evidence of a witness if no copy of that document or no copy of a statement or report by that witness has been supplied to the other parties.

8   [Notice of hearing date and time allowed.]

9   The court must be informed immediately if the case is settled by agreement before the hearing date.

FORM E — HOLIDAY AND WEDDING CLAIMS

THE COURT DIRECTS

1   Each party shall deliver to every other party and to the court office copies of all documents on which he intends to rely at the hearing. These may include:

- any written contract, brochure or booking form,
- photographs,
- documents showing payments made,
- witness statements,
- letters.

2   The copies shall be delivered no later than [   ] [14 days before the hearing].

3   The original documents shall be brought to the hearing.

4   Signed statements setting out the evidence of all witnesses on whom each party intends to rely shall be prepared and copies included in the documents mentioned in paragraph 1. This includes the evidence of the parties themselves and of any other witness, whether or not he is going to come to court to give evidence.

5   If either party intends to show a video as evidence he must:

   (a)   contact the court at once to make arrangements for him to do so, because the court may not have the necessary equipment, and

   (b)   provide the other party with a copy of the video or the opportunity to see it (if he asks) at least 2 weeks before the hearing.

6   The parties should note that the court may decide not to take into account a document or the evidence of a witness or a video if these directions have not been complied with.

7   [Notice of hearing date and time allowed.]

8   The court must be told immediately if the case is settled by agreement before the hearing date.

PD 27 PRACTICE DIRECTION — SMALL CLAIMS TRACK

FORM F — SOME SPECIAL DIRECTIONS

The   must clarify his case.
He must do this by delivering to the court office and to the
no later than
[a list of   ]
[details of   ]
[   ]

The   shall allow the   to inspect   by appointment within
days of receiving a request to do so.

The hearing will not take place at the court but at   .

The   must bring to court at the hearing the   .

Signed statements setting out the evidence of all witnesses on whom each party intends to rely shall be prepared and copies included in the documents mentioned in paragraph 1. This includes the evidence of the parties themselves and of any other witness, whether or not he is going to come to court to give evidence.

The court may decide not to take into account a document [or video] or the evidence of a witness if these directions have not been complied with.

If he does not [do so] [   ] his [Claim] [Defence] [and Counterclaim] and will be struck out and [(specify consequence)].

It appears to the court that expert evidence is necessary on the issue of
[   ]
and that that evidence should be given by a single expert
[   ]
to be instructed by the parties jointly. If the parties cannot agree about who to choose and what arrangements to make about paying his fee, either party may apply to the court for further directions.

If either party intends to show a video as evidence he must

   (a) contact the court at once to make arrangements for him to do so, because the court may not have the necessary equipment, and

   (b) provide the other party with a copy of the video or the opportunity to see it at least [   ] before the hearing.

CPR PART 28   THE FAST TRACK

CONTENTS OF THIS PART
Scope of this Part   Rule 28.1
General provisions   Rule 28.2
Directions   Rule 28.3
Variation of case management timetable   Rule 28.4
Listing questionnaire   Rule 28.5
Fixing or confirming the trial date and giving directions   Rule 28.6
Conduct of trial   Rule 28.7

28.1   SCOPE OF THIS PART
This Part contains general provisions about management of cases allocated to the fast track and applies only to cases allocated to that track.
(Part 27 sets out the procedure for claims allocated to the small claims track)
(Part 29 sets out the procedure for claims allocated to the multi-track)

28.2   GENERAL PROVISIONS
(1) When it allocates a case to the fast track, the court will give directions for the management of the case and set a timetable for the steps to be taken between the giving of the directions and the trial.
(2) When it gives directions, the court will—
   (a) fix the trial date; or
   (b) fix a period, not exceeding 3 weeks, within which the trial is to take place.
(3) The trial date or trial period will be specified in the notice of allocation.
(4) The standard period between the giving of directions and the trial will be not more than 30 weeks.
(5) The court's power to award trial costs is limited in accordance with Part 46.

28.3   DIRECTIONS
(1) The matters to be dealt with by directions under rule 28.2(1) include—
   (a) disclosure of documents;
   (b) service of witness statements; and
   (c) expert evidence.
(2) If the court decides not to direct standard disclosure, it may—
   (a) direct that no disclosure take place; or
   (b) specify the documents or the classes of documents which the parties must disclose.
(Rule 31.6 explains what is meant by standard disclosure)
(Rule 26.6(5) deals with limitations in relation to expert evidence and the likely length of trial in fast track cases)

28.4   VARIATION OF CASE MANAGEMENT TIMETABLE
(1) A party must apply to the court if he wishes to vary the date which the court has fixed for—
   (a) the return of a listing questionnaire under rule 28.5;
   (b) the trial; or
   (c) the trial period.
(2) Any date set by the court or these Rules for doing any act may not be varied by the parties if the variation would make it necessary to vary any of the dates mentioned in paragraph (1).
(Rule 2.11 allows the parties to vary a date by written agreement except where the rules provide otherwise or the court orders otherwise)

28.5   LISTING QUESTIONNAIRE
(1) The court will send the parties a listing questionnaire for completion and return by the date specified in the notice of allocation unless it considers that the claim can be listed for trial without the need for a listing questionnaire.

(2) The date specified for filing a listing questionnaire will not be more than 8 weeks before the trial date or the beginning of the trial period.

(3) If—

    (a) a party fails to file the completed questionnaire by the date specified;

    (b) a party has failed to give all the information requested by the listing questionnaire; or

    (c) the court considers that a hearing is necessary to enable it to decide what directions to give in order to complete preparation of the case for trial,

the court may fix a listing hearing or give such other directions as it thinks appropriate.

28.6 FIXING OR CONFIRMING THE TRIAL DATE AND GIVING DIRECTIONS

(1) As soon as practicable after the date specified for filing a completed listing questionnaire the court will—

    (a) fix the date for the trial (or, if it has already done so, confirm that date);

    (b) give any directions for the trial, including a trial timetable, which it considers appropriate; and

    (c) specify any further steps that need to be taken before trial.

(2) The court will give the parties at least 3 weeks' notice of the date of the trial unless, in exceptional circumstances, the court directs that shorter notice will be given.

28.7 CONDUCT OF TRIAL

Unless the trial judge otherwise directs, the trial will be conducted in accordance with any order previously made.

PD 28 PRACTICE DIRECTION — THE FAST TRACK

This practice direction supplements CPR Part 28

GENERAL
1.1 Attention is drawn in particular to the following Parts of the Civil Procedure Rules:
Part 1   The overriding objective
Part 3   The court's case management powers
Part 26   Case management — preliminary stage
Part 31   Disclosure and inspection of documents
Parts 32-34   Evidence
Part 35   Experts and assessors
and to the practice directions which relate to those Parts.
1.2 Attention is also drawn to:
Rule 26.6(5) — which makes provision about limitations on expert evidence and the length of trial in fast track cases.
Part 46 — Fast Track Trial Costs

CASE MANAGEMENT
2.1 Case management of cases allocated to the fast track will generally be by directions given at two stages in the case:
   (1) at allocation to the track, and
   (2) on the filing of listing questionnaires.
2.2 The court will seek whenever possible to give directions at those stages only and to do so without the need for a hearing to take place. It will expect to do so with the co-operation of the parties.
2.3 The court will however hold a hearing to give directions whenever it appears necessary or desirable to do so, and where this happens because of the default of a party or his legal representative it will usually impose a sanction.
2.4 The court may give directions at any hearing on the application of a party or on its own initiative.
2.5 When any hearing has been fixed it is the duty of the parties to consider what directions the court should be asked to give and to make any application that may be appropriate to be dealt with at that hearing.
2.6 When the court fixes a hearing to give directions it will give the parties at least 3 days' notice of the hearing.
2.7 Appendix A contains forms of directions. When making an order the court will as far as possible base its order on those forms. Agreed directions which the parties file and invite the court to make should also be based on those forms.
2.8 Where a party needs to apply for a direction of a kind not included in the case management timetable which has been set (for example to amend his statement of case or for further information to be given by another party) he must do so as soon as possible so as to minimise the need to change that timetable.
2.9 Courts will make arrangements to ensure that applications and other hearings are listed promptly to avoid delay in the conduct of cases.

DIRECTIONS ON ALLOCATION
3.1 Attention is drawn to the court's duty under rule 28.2(2) to set a case management timetable and to fix a trial date or a trial period, and to the matters which are to be dealt with by directions under Rule 28.3(1).
3.2 The court will seek to tailor its directions to the needs of the case and the steps of which it is aware that the parties have already taken to prepare the case. In particular it will have regard to the extent to which any pre-action protocol has or (as the case may be) has not been complied with.

PD 28 PRACTICE DIRECTION — THE FAST TRACK

3.3 At this stage the court's first concern will be to ensure that the issues between the parties be identified and that the necessary evidence is prepared and disclosed.

3.4 The court may have regard to any document filed by a party with his allocation questionnaire containing further information provided that the document states either that its contents have been agreed with every other party or that it has been served on every other party and when it was served.

3.5 If:

(1) the parties have filed agreed directions for the management of the case, and

(2) the court considers that the proposals are suitable,

it may approve them and give directions in the terms proposed.

3.6 (1) To obtain the court's approval the agreed directions must:

(a) set out a timetable by reference to calendar dates for the taking of steps for the preparation of the case,

(b) include a date or a period (the trial period) when it is proposed that the trial will take place,

(c) include provision about disclosure of documents, and

(d) include provision about both factual and expert evidence.

(2) The latest proposed date for the trial or the end of the trial period must be not later than 30 weeks from the date the directions order is made.

(3) The trial period must not be longer than 3 weeks.

(4) The provision in (1)(c) above may:

(a) limit disclosure to standard disclosure between all parties or to less than that, and/or

(b) direct that disclosure will take place by the supply of copy documents without a list, but it must in that case either direct that the parties must serve a disclosure statement with the copies or record that they have agreed to disclose in that way without such a statement.

(5) The provision in (1)(d) may be to the effect that no expert evidence is required.

3.7 Directions agreed by the parties should also where appropriate contain provisions about:

(1) the filing of any reply or amended statement of case that may be required,

(2) dates for the service of requests for further information under the practice direction supplementing Part 18 and questions to experts under rule 35.6 and when they are to be dealt with,

(3) the disclosure of evidence,

(4) the use of a single joint expert, or in cases where the use of a single expert has not been agreed the exchange and agreement of expert evidence (including whether exchange is to be simultaneous or sequential) and without prejudice discussions of the experts.

3.8 If the court does not approve the agreed directions filed by the parties but decides that it will give directions on its own initiative without a hearing, it will take them into account in deciding what directions to give.

3.9 Where the court is to give directions on its own initiative and it is not aware of any steps taken by the parties other than the service of statements of case, its general approach will be:

(1) to give directions for the filing and service of any further information required to clarify either party's case,

(2) to direct standard disclosure between the parties,

(3) to direct the disclosure of witness statements by way of simultaneous exchange,

(4) to give directions for a single joint expert unless there is good reason not to do so,

(5) in cases where directions for a single expert are not given:

(a) to direct disclosure of experts' reports by way of simultaneous exchange, and

(b) if experts' reports are not agreed, to direct a discussion between the experts for the purpose set out in rule 35.12(1) and the preparation of a report under rule 35.12(3).

3.10 (1) If it appears to the court that the claim is one which will be allocated to the fast track but that it cannot properly give directions on its own initiative or approve agreed directions that have been filed, the court may either:

    (a) allocate the claim to the fast track, fix a trial date or trial period and direct that a case management hearing is to be listed and give directions at that hearing, or

    (b) direct that an allocation hearing is to be listed and give directions at that hearing.

(2) In either case the hearing will be listed as promptly as possible.

3.11 Where the court is proposing on its own initiative to make an order under rule 35.15 (which gives the court power to appoint an assessor), the court must, unless the parties have consented in writing to the order, list a directions hearing.

3.12 The table set out below contains a typical timetable the court may give for the preparation of the case.

Disclosure	4 weeks
Exchange of witness statements	10 weeks
Exchange of experts' reports	14 weeks
Sending of listing questionnaires by the court	20 weeks
Filing of completed listing questionnaires	22 weeks
Hearing	30 weeks

These periods will run from the date of the notice of allocation.

3.13 (1) Where it considers that some or all of the steps in that timetable are not necessary the court may omit them and direct an earlier trial.

(2) This may happen where the court is informed that a pre-action protocol has been complied with or that steps which it would otherwise order to be taken have already been taken.

(3) It may also happen where an application (for example for summary judgment or for an injunction) has been heard before allocation and little or no further preparation is required. In such a case the court may dispense with the need for a listing questionnaire.

VARIATION OF DIRECTIONS

4.1 This paragraph deals with the procedure to be adopted:

    (1) where a party is dissatisfied with a direction given by the court,

    (2) where the parties agree about changes they wish made to the directions given, or

    (3) where a party wishes to apply to vary a direction.

4.2 (1) It is essential that any party who wishes to have a direction varied takes steps to do so as soon as possible.

(2) The court will assume for the purposes of any later application that a party who did not appeal and who made no application to vary within 14 days of service of the order containing the directions was content that they were correct in the circumstances then existing.

4.3 (1) Where a party is dissatisfied with a direction given or other order made by the court he may appeal or apply to the court for it to reconsider its decision.

(2) He should appeal if the direction was given or the order was made at a hearing at which he was present or represented, or of which he had due notice.

(3) In any other case he should apply to the court to reconsider its decision.

(4) If an application is made for the court to reconsider its decision:

    (a) it will usually be heard by the judge who gave the directions or another judge of the same level,

    (b) the court will give all parties at least 3 days' notice of the hearing, and

    (c) the court may confirm its decision or make a different order.

4.4 Where there has been a change in the circumstances since the order was made the court may set aside or vary any direction it has given. It may do so on application or on its own initiative.

PD 28 PRACTICE DIRECTION — THE FAST TRACK

4.5 Where the parties agree about changes to be made to the directions given:
 (1) If rule 2.11 (variation by agreement of a date set by the court for doing any act other than those stated in the note to that rule) or rule 31.5, 31.10(8) or 31.13 (agreements about disclosure) applied the parties need not file the written agreement.
 (2) (a) In any other case the parties must apply for an order by consent.
 (b) The parties must file a draft of the order sought and an agreed statement of the reasons why the variation is sought.
 (c) The court may make an order in the agreed terms or in other terms without a hearing, but it may direct that a hearing is to be listed.

FAILURE TO COMPLY WITH CASE MANAGEMENT DIRECTIONS

5.1 Where a party has failed to comply with a direction given by the court any other party may apply for an order to enforce compliance or for a sanction to be imposed or both of these.

5.2 The party entitled to apply for such an order must do so without delay but should first warn the other party of his intention to do so.

5.3 The court may take any such delay into account when it decides whether to make an order imposing a sanction or whether to grant relief from a sanction imposed by the rules or any practice direction.

5.4 (1) The court will not allow a failure to comply with directions to lead to the postponement of the trial unless the circumstances of the case are exceptional.
 (2) If it is practicable to do so the court will exercise its powers in a manner that enables the case to come on for trial on the date or within the period previously set.
 (3) In particular the court will assess what steps each party should take to prepare the case for trial, direct that those steps are taken in the shortest possible time and impose a sanction for non-compliance. Such a sanction may, for example, deprive a party of the right to raise or contest an issue or to rely on evidence to which the direction relates.
 (4) Where it appears that one or more issues are or can be made ready for trial at the time fixed while others cannot, the court may direct that the trial will proceed on the issues which are or will then be ready, and order that no costs will be allowed for any later trial of the remaining issues or that those costs will be paid by the party in default.
 (5) Where the court has no option but to postpone the trial it will do so for the shortest possible time and will give directions for the taking of the necessary steps in the meantime as rapidly as possible.
 (6) Litigants and lawyers must be in no doubt that the court will regard the postponement of a trial as an order of last resort. The court may exercise its power to require a party as well as his legal representative to attend court at a hearing where such an order is to be sought.

LISTING QUESTIONNAIRES AND LISTING

6.1 (1) The listing questionnaire will be in Form N170.
 (2) Unless it has dispensed with listing questionnaires, the court will send Forms N170 and N171 (Notice of date for return of the listing questionnaire) to each party no later than 2 weeks before the date specified in the notice of allocation or in any later direction of the court for the return of the completed questionnaires.
 (3) When all the listing questionnaires have been filed or when the time for filing them has expired the file will be placed before a judge for his directions.
 (4) Although the Rules do not require the parties to exchange copies of the questionnaires before they are filed they are encouraged to do so to avoid the court being given conflicting or incomplete information.
 Attention is drawn to the Costs Practice Direction [PD 43], paragraph 4.5(2), which requires a costs estimate to be filed and served at the same time as the listing questionnaire is filed.

6.2 Attention is drawn to rule 28.6(1) (which sets out the court's duty at the listing questionnaire stage) and to rule 28.5(3) (which sets out circumstances in which the court may decide to hold a listing hearing).

6.3 Where the judge decides to hold a listing hearing the court will fix a date which is as early as possible and the parties will be given at least 3 days' notice of the date.

The notice of a listing hearing will be in Form N153.

6.4 The court's general approach will be as set out in the following paragraphs. The court may however decide to make other orders, and in particular the court will take into account the steps, if any, which the parties have taken to prepare the case for trial.

6.5 (1) Where no party files a listing questionnaire the court will normally make an order that if no listing questionnaire is filed by any party within 3 days from service of the order the claim and any counterclaim will be struck out.

(2) Where a party files a listing questionnaire but another party does not do so, the court normally will give listing directions. These will usually fix or confirm the trial date and provide for steps to be taken to prepare the case for trial.

DIRECTIONS THE COURT WILL GIVE ON LISTING

7.1 Directions the court must give:

(1) The court must confirm or fix the trial date, specify the place of trial and give a time estimate. The trial date must be fixed and the case listed on the footing that the hearing will end on the same calendar day as that on which it commenced.

(2) The court will serve a notice of hearing on the parties at least 3 weeks before the hearing unless they agree to accept shorter notice or the court authorises shorter service under rule 28.6(2), and

(3) The notice of hearing will be in Form N172.

7.2 Other directions:

(1) The parties should seek to agree directions and may file the proposed order. The court may make an order in those terms or it may make a different order.

(2) Agreed directions should include provision about:
   (a) evidence,
   (b) a trial timetable and time estimate,
   (c) the preparation of a trial bundle,
   (d) any other matter needed to prepare the case for trial.

(3) The court will include such of these provisions as are appropriate in any order that it may make, whether or not the parties have filed agreed directions.

(4) (a) A direction giving permission to use expert evidence will say whether it gives permission for oral evidence or reports or both and will name the experts concerned.

(b) The court will not make a direction giving permission for an expert to give oral evidence unless it believes it is necessary in the interests of justice to do so.

(c) Where no 'without prejudice' meeting or other discussion between experts has taken place the court may grant that permission conditionally on such a discussion taking place and a report being filed before the trial.

7.3 The principles set out in paragraph 4 of this practice direction about the variation of directions apply also to directions given at this stage.

THE TRIAL

8.1 The trial will normally take place at the court where the case is being managed, but it may be at another court if it is appropriate having regard to the needs of the parties and the availability of court resources.

8.2 The judge will generally have read the papers in the trial bundle and may dispense with an opening address.

8.3 The judge may confirm or vary any timetable given previously, or if none has been given set his own.

8.4 Attention is drawn to the provisions in Part 32 and the following parts of the Rules about evidence, and in particular—

(1) to rule 32.1 (court's power to control evidence and to restrict cross-examination), and

(2) to rule 32.5(2) (witness statements to stand as evidence in chief).

8.5 At the conclusion of the trial the judge will normally summarily assess the costs of the claim in accordance with rule 44.7 and Part 46 (fast track trial costs). Attention is drawn to the steps the practice directions about costs require the parties to take.

8.6 Where a trial is not finished on the day for which it is listed the judge will normally sit on the next court day to complete it.

APPENDIX
FAST TRACK STANDARD DIRECTIONS

FURTHER STATEMENTS OF CASE
The   must file a   and serve a copy on   no later than   .

REQUESTS FOR FURTHER INFORMATION
Any request for clarification or further information based on another party's statement of case shall be served no later than   .
[Any such request shall be dealt with no later than   ].

DISCLOSURE OF DOCUMENTS
[No disclosure of documents is required].
[[Each party] [The   ]
shall give [to the   ]
[to every other party] standard disclosure of documents
[relating to   ]
by serving copies together with a disclosure statement no later than   ].
[Disclosure shall take place as follows:
[Each party shall give standard discovery to every other party by list]
[Disclosure is limited to [standard] [disclosure by the   to the   ]
[of documents relating to damage]
[the following documents   ]
[The latest date for delivery of the lists is   ]
[The latest date for service of any request to inspect or for a copy of a document is   ]].

WITNESSES OF FACT
Each party shall serve on every other party the witness statements of all witnesses of fact on whom he intends to rely.
There shall be simultaneous exchange of such statements no later than   .

EXPERT EVIDENCE
[No expert evidence being necessary, no party has permission to call or rely on expert evidence].
[On it appearing to the court that expert evidence is necessary on the issue of
[   ]
and that that evidence should be given by the report of a single expert instructed jointly by the parties, the   shall no later than   inform the court whether or not such an expert has been instructed].
[The expert evidence on the issue of
shall be   limited to a single expert jointly instructed by the parties.
If the parties cannot agree by   who that expert is to be and about the payment of his fees either party may apply for further directions.
Unless the parties agree in writing or the court orders otherwise, the fees and expenses of such an expert shall be paid to him [by the parties equally]
[   ] and be limited to £   .
[The report of the expert shall be filed at the court no later than   ].
[No party shall be entitled to recover by way of costs from any other party more than £   for the fees or   expenses of an expert].

The parties shall exchange reports setting out the substance of any expert evidence on which they intend to rely.
[The exchange shall take place simultaneously no later than   ].
[The   shall serve his report(s) no later than the   and the   shall serve his reports no later than the   ].
[The exchange of reports relating to [causation] [   ] shall take place simultaneously no later than   .
The   shall serve his report(s) relating to [damage] [   ] no later than   and the   shall serve his reports relating to it no later than   ].
Reports shall be agreed if possible no later than [days after service] [ ].
[If the reports are not agreed within that time there shall be a without prejudice discussion between the relevant experts no later than   to identify the   issues between them and to reach agreement if possible.
The experts shall prepare for the court a statement of the issues on which they agree and on which they disagree with a summary of their reasons, and that statement shall be filed with the court [no later than   ] [with] [no later than the date for filing] [the listing questionnaire].
[Each party has permission to use [   ] as expert witness(es) to give [oral] evidence [in the form of a   report] at the trial in the field of   provided that the substance of the evidence to be given has been disclosed as above and has not been agreed].
[Each party has permission to use in evidence   experts' report(s) [and the court will consider when the claim is listed for trial whether expert oral evidence will be allowed].]

QUESTIONS TO EXPERTS
The time for service on another party of any question addressed to an expert instructed by that party is not later than   days after service of that expert's report.
Any such question shall be answered within   days of service.

REQUESTS FOR INFORMATION ETC.
Each party shall serve any request for clarification or further information based on any document disclosed or statement served by another party no later than   days after disclosure or service.
Any such request shall be dealt with within   days of service.

DOCUMENTS TO BE FILED WITH LISTING QUESTIONNAIRES
The parties must file with their listing questionnaires copies of [their experts' reports] [witness statements] [replies to requests for further information]

DATES FOR FILING LISTING QUESTIONNAIRES AND THE TRIAL
Each party must file a completed listing questionnaire no later than   .
The trial of this case will take place [on   ][on a date to be fixed between   and   ].

DIRECTIONS FOLLOWING FILING OF LISTING QUESTIONNAIRE

Expert evidence
The parties have permission to rely at the trial on expert evidence as follows:
        The claimant: Oral evidence—
                           Written evidence—
        The defendant: Oral evidence—
                           Written evidence—

Trial timetable
The time allowed for the trial is
[The timetable for the trial may be agreed by the parties, subject to the approval of the trial judge].
[The timetable for the trial (subject to the approval of the trial judge) will be that   ].
[The evidence in chief for each party will be contained in witness statements and reports, the time allowed for cross-examination by the defendant is limited to   and the time allowed for cross-examination by the claimant is limited to   ].
[The time allowed for the claimant's evidence is   . The time allowed for the defendant's evidence is   ].
The time allowed for the submissions on behalf of each party is   .
The remainder of the time allowed for the trial (being   ) is reserved for the judge to consider and give the judgment and to deal with costs].

Trial bundle etc.
The claimant shall lodge an indexed bundle of documents contained in a ring binder and with each page clearly numbered at the court not more than 7 days and not less than 3 days before the start of the trial.
[A case summary (which should not exceed 250 words) outlining the matters still in issue, and referring where appropriate to the relevant documents shall be included in the bundle for the assistance of the judge in reading the papers before the trial].
[The parties shall seek to agree the contents of the trial bundle and the case summary].

Settlement
Each party must inform the court immediately if the claim is settled whether or not it is then possible to file a draft consent order to give effect to their agreement.

CPR PART 29 THE MULTI-TRACK

CONTENTS OF THIS PART
Scope of this Part   Rule 29.1
Case management   Rule 29.2
Case management conference and pre-trial review   Rule 29.3
Steps taken by the parties   Rule 29.4
Variation of case management timetable   Rule 29.5
Listing questionnaire   Rule 29.6
Pre-trial review   Rule 29.7
Setting a trial timetable and fixing or confirming the trial date or week Rule 29.8
Conduct of the trial   Rule 29.9

29.1 SCOPE OF THIS PART
This Part contains general provisions about management of cases allocated to the multi-track and applies only to cases allocated to that track.
(Part 27 sets out the procedure for claims allocated to the small claims track)
(Part 28 sets out the procedure for claims allocated to the fast track)

29.2 CASE MANAGEMENT
(1) When it allocates a case to the multi-track, the court will—
    (a) give directions for the management of the case and set a timetable for the steps to be taken between the giving of directions and the trial; or
    (b) fix—
        (i) a case management conference; or
        (ii) a pre-trial review,
or both, and give such other directions relating to the management of the case as it sees fit.
(2) The court will fix the trial date or the period in which the trial is to take place as soon as practicable.
(3) When the court fixes the trial date or the trial period under paragraph (2), it will—
    (a) give notice to the parties of the date or period; and
    (b) specify the date by which the parties must file a listing questionnaire.

29.3 CASE MANAGEMENT CONFERENCE AND PRE-TRIAL REVIEW
(1) The court may fix—
    (a) a case management conference; or
    (b) a pre-trial review,
at any time after the claim has been allocated.
(2) If a party has a legal representative, a representative—
    (a) familiar with the case; and
    (b) with sufficient authority to deal with any issues that are likely to arise,
must attend case management conferences and pre-trial reviews.
(Rule 3.1(2)(c) provides that the court may require a party to attend the court)

29.4 STEPS TAKEN BY THE PARTIES
If—
    (a) the parties agree proposals for the management of the proceedings (including a proposed trial date or period in which the trial is to take place); and
    (b) the court considers that the proposals are suitable,
it may approve them without a hearing and give directions in the terms proposed.

29.5 VARIATION OF CASE MANAGEMENT TIMETABLE
(1) A party must apply to the court if he wishes to vary the date which the court has fixed for—
    (a) a case management conference;

(b) a pre-trial review;
(c) the return of a listing questionnaire under rule 29.6;
(d) the trial; or
(e) the trial period.

(2) Any date set by the court or these Rules for doing any act may not be varied by the parties if the variation would make it necessary to vary any of the dates mentioned in paragraph (1).

(Rule 2.11 allows the parties to vary a date by written agreement except where the rules provide otherwise or the court orders otherwise)

29.6 LISTING QUESTIONNAIRE

(1) The court will send the parties a listing questionnaire for completion and return by the date specified in directions given under rule 29.2(3) unless it considers that the claim can be listed for trial without the need for a listing questionnaire.

(2) Each party must file the completed listing questionnaire by the date specified by the court.

(3) If—
(a) a party fails to file the completed questionnaire by the date specified;
(b) a party has failed to give all the information requested by the listing questionnaire; or
(c) the court considers that a hearing is necessary to enable it to decide what directions to give in order to complete preparation of the case for trial,
the court may fix a date for a listing hearing or give such other directions as it thinks appropriate.

29.7 PRE-TRIAL REVIEW

If, on receipt of the parties' listing questionnaires, the court decides—
(a) to hold a pre-trial review; or
(b) to cancel a pre-trial review which has already been fixed,
it will serve notice of its decision at least 7 days before the date fixed for the hearing or, as the case may be, the cancelled hearing.

29.8 SETTING A TRIAL TIMETABLE AND FIXING OR CONFIRMING THE TRIAL DATE OR WEEK

As soon as practicable after—
(a) each party has filed a completed listing questionnaire;
(b) the court has held a listing hearing under rule 29.6(3); or
(c) the court has held a pre-trial review under rule 29.7,
the court will—
(i) set a timetable for the trial unless a timetable has already been fixed, or the court considers that it would be inappropriate to do so;
(ii) fix the date for the trial or the week within which the trial is to begin (or, if it has already done so, confirm that date); and
(iii) notify the parties of the trial timetable (where one is fixed under this rule) and the date or trial period.

29.9 CONDUCT OF TRIAL

Unless the trial judge otherwise directs, the trial will be conducted in accordance with any order previously made.

PD 29 PRACTICE DIRECTION — THE MULTI-TRACK

This practice direction supplements CPR Part 29

GENERAL

1.1 Attention is drawn in particular to the following Parts of the Civil Procedure Rules:

Part 1	The overriding objective
Part 3	The court's case management powers
Part 26	Case management — preliminary stage
Part 31	Disclosure and inspection of documents
Parts 32 to 34	Evidence
Part 35	Experts and assessors

and to the practice directions which relate to those Parts.

1.2 Attention is also drawn to Part 49 of the Rules (Specialist Jurisdictions) and to the practice directions which apply to those jurisdictions.

CASE MANAGEMENT IN THE ROYAL COURTS OF JUSTICE

2.1 This part of the practice direction applies to claims begun by claim form issued in the Central Office or Chancery Chambers in the Royal Courts of Justice.

2.2 A claim with an estimated value of less than £50,000 will generally, unless:
   (a) it is required by an enactment to be tried in the High Court,
   (b) it falls within a specialist list (as defined in CPR Part 49), or
   (c) it fails within one of the categories specified in 2.6 below or is otherwise within the criteria of article 7(5) of the High Court and County Courts Jurisdiction Order 1991,
be transferred to a county court.

2.3 Paragraph 2.2 is without prejudice to the power of the court in accordance with Part 30 to transfer to a county court a claim with an estimated value that exceeds £50,000.

2.4 The decision to transfer may be made at any stage in the proceedings but should, subject to paragraph 2.5, be made as soon as possible and in any event not later than the date for the filing of listing questionnaires.

2.5 If an application is made under rule 3.4 (striking out) or under Part 24 (summary judgment) or under Part 25 (interim remedies), it will usually be convenient for the application to be dealt with before a decision to transfer is taken.

2.6 Each party should state in his allocation questionnaire whether he considers the claim should be managed and tried at the Royal Courts of Justice and, if so, why. Claims suitable for trial in the Royal Courts of Justice include:
   (1) professional negligence claims,
   (2) Fatal Accident Act claims,
   (3) fraud or undue influence claims,
   (4) defamation claims,
   (5) claims for malicious prosecution or false imprisonment,
   (6) claims against the police,
   (7) contentious probate claims.

Such claims may fall within the criteria of article 7(5) of the High Court and County Courts Jurisdiction Order 1991.

2.7 Attention is drawn to the practice direction on transfer (Part 30).

CASE MANAGEMENT — GENERAL PROVISIONS

3.1 (1) Case management of a claim which is proceeding at the Royal Courts of Justice will be undertaken there.

(2) (a) Case management of any other claim which has been allocated to the multi-track will normally be undertaken at a Civil Trial Centre.

PD 29 PRACTICE DIRECTION — THE MULTI-TRACK

(b) The practice direction supplementing Part 26 provides for what will happen in the case of a claim which is issued in or transferred to a court which is not a Civil Trial Centre.

3.2 The hallmarks of the multi-track are:

(1) the ability of the court to deal with cases of widely differing values and complexity, and

(2) the flexibility given to the court in the way it will manage a case in a way appropriate to its particular needs.

3.3 (1) On allocating a claim to the multi-track the court may give directions without a hearing, including fixing a trial date or a period in which the trial will take place,

(2) Alternatively, whether or not it fixes a trial date or period, it may either—

(a) give directions for certain steps to be taken and fix a date for a case management conference or a pre-trial review to take place after they have been taken, or

(b) fix a date for a case management conference.

(3) Attention is drawn to rule 29.20 which requires the court to fix a trial date or period as soon as practicable.

3.4 The court may give or vary directions at any hearing which may take place on the application of a party or of its own initiative.

3.5 When any hearing has been fixed it is the duty of the parties to consider what directions the court should be asked to give and to make any application that may be appropriate to be dealt with then.

3.6 The court will hold a hearing to give directions whenever it appears necessary or desirable to do so, and where this happens because of the default of a party or his legal representative it will usually impose a sanction.

3.7 When the court fixes a hearing to give directions it will give the parties at least 3 days' notice of the hearing unless rule 29.7 applies (7 days notice to be given in the case of a pre-trial review).

3.8 Where a party needs to apply for a direction of a kind not included in the case management timetable which has been set (for example to amend his statement of case or for further information to be given by another party) he must do so as soon as possible so as to minimise the need to change that timetable.

3.9 Courts will make arrangements to ensure that applications and other hearings are listed promptly to avoid delay in the conduct of cases.

3.10 (1) Case management will generally be dealt with by:

(a) a Master in cases proceeding in the Royal Courts of Justice,

(b) a district judge in cases proceeding in a District Registry of the High Court, and

(c) a district judge or a Circuit Judge in cases proceeding in a county court.

(2) A Master or a district judge may consult and seek the directions of a judge of a higher level about any aspect of case management.

(3) A member of the court staff who is dealing with the listing of a hearing may seek the directions of any judge about any aspect of that listing.

DIRECTIONS ON ALLOCATION

4.1 Attention is drawn to the court's duties under Rule 29.2.

4.2 The court will seek to tailor its directions to the needs of the case and the steps which the parties have already taken to prepare the case of which it is aware. In particular it will have regard to the extent to which any pre-action protocol has or (as the case may be) has not been complied with.

4.3 At this stage the court's first concern will be to ensure that the issues between the parties are identified and that the necessary evidence is prepared and disclosed.

4.4 The court may have regard to any document filed by a party with his allocation questionnaire containing further information, provided that the document states either that its contents has been agreed with every other party or that it has been served on every other party, and when it was served.

PD 29 PRACTICE DIRECTION — THE MULTI-TRACK

4.5 On the allocation of a claim to the multi-track the court will consider whether it is desirable or necessary to hold a case management conference straight away, or whether it is appropriate instead to give directions on its own initiative.

4.6 The parties and their advisers are encouraged to try to agree directions and to take advantage of rule 29.4 which provides that if:

(1) the parties agree proposals for the management of the proceedings (including a proposed trial date or period in which the trial is to take place), and

(2) the court considers that the proposals are suitable,

it may approve them without a hearing and give directions in the terms proposed.

4.7 (1) To obtain the court's approval the agreed directions must—

(a) set out a timetable by reference to calendar dates for the taking of steps for the preparation of the case,

(b) include a date or a period (the trial period) when it is proposed that the trial will take place,

(c) include provision about disclosure of documents, and

(d) include provision about both factual and expert evidence.

(2) The court will scrutinise the timetable carefully and in particular will be concerned to see that any proposed date or period for the trial and (if provided for) for a case management conference is no later than is reasonably necessary.

(3) The provision in (1)(c) above may—

(a) limit disclosure to standard disclosure or less than that, and/or

(b) direct that disclosure will take place by the supply of copy documents without a list, but it must in that case say either that the parties must serve a disclosure statement with the copies or that they have agreed to disclose in that way without such a statement.

(4) The provision in (1)(d) about expert evidence may be to the effect that none is required.

4.8 Directions agreed by the parties should also where appropriate contain provisions about:

(1) the filing of any reply or amended statement of case that may be required,

(2) dates for the service of requests for further information under the practice direction supplementing Part 18 and of questions to experts under rule 35.6 and by when they are to be dealt with,

(3) the disclosure of evidence,

(4) the use of a single joint expert, or in cases where it is not agreed, the exchange of expert evidence (including whether exchange is to be simultaneous or sequential) and without prejudice discussions between experts.

4.9 If the court does not approve the agreed directions filed by the parties but decides that it will give directions of its own initiative without fixing a case management conference, it will take them into account in deciding what directions to give.

4.10 Where the court is to give directions on its own initiative without holding a case management conference and it is not aware of any steps taken by the parties other than the exchange of statements of case, its general approach will be:

(1) to give directions for the filing and service of any further information required to clarify either party's case,

(2) to direct standard disclosure between the parties,

(3) to direct the disclosure of witness statements by way of simultaneous exchange,

(4) to give directions for a single joint expert on any appropriate issue unless there is a good reason not to do so,

(5) unless paragraph 4.11 (below) applies, to direct disclosure of experts' reports by way of simultaneous exchange on those issues where a single joint expert is not directed,

(6) if experts' reports are not agreed, to direct a discussion between experts for the purpose set out in rule 35.12(1) and the preparation of a statement under rule 35.12(3),

(7) to list a case management conference to take place after the date for compliance with those directions, and

(8) to specify a trial period.

4.11 If it appears that expert evidence will be required both on issues of liability and on the amount of damages, the court may direct that the exchange of those reports that relate to liability will be exchanged simultaneously but that those relating to the amount of damages will be exchanged sequentially.

4.12 (1) If it appears to the court that it cannot properly give directions on its own initiative and no agreed directions have been filed which it can approve, the court will direct a case management conference to be listed.

(2) The conference will be listed as promptly as possible.

4.13 Where the court is proposing on its own initiative to make an order under rule 35.7 (which gives the court power to direct that evidence on a particular issue is to be given by a single expert) or under rule 35.15 (which gives the court power to appoint an assessor), the court must, unless the parties have consented in writing to the order, list a case management conference.

CASE MANAGEMENT CONFERENCES

5.1 The court will at any case management conference:

(1) review the steps which the parties have taken in the preparation of the case, and in particular their compliance with any directions that the court may have given,

(2) decide and give directions about the steps which are to be taken to secure the progress of the claim in accordance with the overriding objective, and

(3) ensure as far as it can that all agreements that can be reached between the parties about the matters in issue and the conduct of the claim are made and recorded.

5.2 (1) Rule 29.3(2) provides that where a party has a legal representative, a representative familiar with the case and with sufficient authority to deal with any issues that are likely to arise must attend case management conferences and pre-trial reviews.

(2) That person should be someone who is personally involved in the conduct of the case, and who has the authority and information to deal with any matter which may reasonably be expected to be dealt with at such a hearing, including the fixing of the timetable, the identification of issues and matters of evidence.

(3) Where the inadequacy of the person attending or of his instructions leads to the adjournment of a hearing, the court will expect to make a wasted costs order.

5.3 The topics the court will consider at a case management conference are likely to include:

(1) whether the claimant has made clear the claim he is bringing, in particular the amount he is claiming, so that the other party can understand the case he has to meet,

(2) whether any amendments are required to the claim, a statement of case or any other document,

(3) what disclosure of documents, if any, is necessary,

(4) what expert evidence is reasonably required in accordance with rule 35.1 and how and when that evidence should be obtained and disclosed,

(5) what factual evidence should be disclosed,

(6) what arrangements should be made about the giving of clarification or further information and the putting of questions to experts, and

(7) whether it will be just and will save costs to order a split trial or the trial of one or more preliminary issues.

5.4 In all cases the court will set a timetable for the steps it decides are necessary to be taken. These steps may include the holding of a case management conference or a pre-trial review, and the court will be alert to perform its duty to fix a trial date or period as soon as it can.

5.5 (1) The court will not at this stage give permission to use expert evidence unless it can identify each expert by name or field in its order and say whether his evidence is to be given orally or by the use of his report.

PD 29   PRACTICE DIRECTION — THE MULTI-TRACK

(2) A party who obtains expert evidence before obtaining a direction about it does so at his own risk as to costs, except where he obtained the evidence in compliance with a pre-action protocol.

5.6 To assist the court, the parties and their legal advisers should:

(1) ensure that all documents that the court is likely to ask to see (including witness statements and experts' reports) are brought to the hearing,

(2) consider whether the parties should attend,

(3) consider whether a case summary will be useful, and

(4) consider what orders each wishes to be made and give notice of them to the other parties.

5.7 (1) A case summary:

(a) should be designed to assist the court to understand and deal with the questions before it,

(b) should set out a brief chronology of the claim, the issues of fact which are agreed or in dispute and the evidence needed to decide them,

(c) should not normally exceed 500 words in length, and

(d) should be prepared by the claimant and agreed with the other parties if possible.

5.8 (1) Where a party wishes to obtain an order not routinely made at a case management conference and believes that his application will be opposed, he should issue and serve the application in time for it to be heard at the case management conference.

(2) If the time allowed for the case management conference is likely to be insufficient for the application to be heard he should inform the court at once so that a fresh date can be fixed.

(3) A costs sanction may be imposed on a party who fails to comply with subparagraph (1) or (2).

5.9 At a case management conference the court may also consider whether the case ought to be tried by a High Court judge or by a judge who specialises in that type of claim and how that question will be decided. In that case the claim may need to be transferred to another court.

VARIATION OF DIRECTIONS

6.1 This paragraph deals with the procedure to be adopted:

(1) where a party is dissatisfied with a direction given by the court,

(2) where the parties have agreed about changes they wish made to the directions given, or

(3) where a party wishes to apply to vary a direction.

6.2 (1) It is essential that any party who wishes to have a direction varied takes steps to do so as soon as possible.

(2) The court will assume for the purposes of any later application that a party who did not appeal, and who made no application to vary within 14 days of service of the order containing the directions, was content that they were correct in the circumstances then existing.

6.3 (1) Where a party is dissatisfied with a direction given or other order made by the court he may appeal or apply to the court for it to reconsider its decision.

(2) Unless paragraph 6.4 applies, a party should appeal if the direction was given or the order was made at a hearing at which he was present, or of which he had due notice.

(3) In any other case he should apply to the court to reconsider its decision.

(4) If an application is made for the court to reconsider its decision:

(a) it will usually be heard by the judge who gave the directions or another judge of the same level,

(b) the court will give all parties at least 3 days' notice of the hearing, and

(c) the court may confirm its directions or make a different order.

6.4 Where there has been a change in the circumstances since the order was made the court may set aside or vary a direction it has given. It may do so on application or on its own initiative.

6.5 Where the parties agree about changes they wish made to the directions given:

(1) If rule 2.11 (variation by agreement of a date set by the court for doing any act other than those stated in the note to that rule) or rule 31.5, 31.10(8) or 31.13 (agreements about disclosure) applies the parties need not file the written agreement.

(2) (a) In any other case the parties must apply for an order by consent.

(b) The parties must file a draft of the order sought and an agreed statement of the reasons why the variation is sought.

(c) The court may make an order in the agreed terms or in other terms without a hearing, but it may direct that a hearing is to be listed.

FAILURE TO COMPLY WITH CASE MANAGEMENT DIRECTIONS

7.1 Where a party fails to comply with a direction given by the court any other party may apply for an order that he must do so or for a sanction to be imposed or both of these.

7.2 The party entitled to apply for such an order must do so without delay but should first warn the other party of his intention to do so.

7.3 The court may take any such delay into account when it decides whether to make an order imposing a sanction or to grant relief from a sanction imposed by the rules or any other practice direction.

7.4 (1) The court will not allow a failure to comply with directions to lead to the postponement of the trial unless the circumstances are exceptional.

(2) If it is practical to do so the court will exercise its powers in a manner that enables the case to come on for trial on the date or within the period previously set.

(3) In particular the court will assess what steps each party should take to prepare the case for trial, direct that those steps are taken in the shortest possible time and impose a sanction for non-compliance. Such a sanction may, for example, deprive a party of the right to raise or contest an issue or to rely on evidence to which the direction relates.

(4) Where it appears that one or more issues are or can be made ready for trial at the time fixed while others cannot, the court may direct that the trial will proceed on the issues which are then ready, and direct that no costs will be allowed for any later trial of the remaining issues or that those costs will be paid by the party in default.

(5) Where the court has no option but to postpone the trial it will do so for the shortest possible time and will give directions for the taking of the necessary steps in the meantime as rapidly as possible.

(6) Litigants and lawyers must be in no doubt that the court will regard the postponement of a trial as an order of last resort. Where it appears inevitable the court may exercise its power to require a party as well as his legal representative to attend court at the hearing where such an order is to be sought.

(7) The court will not postpone any other hearing without a very good reason, and for that purpose the failure of a party to comply on time with directions previously given will not be treated as a good reason.

LISTING QUESTIONNAIRES AND LISTING

8.1 (1) The listing questionnaire will be in Form N170.

(2) Unless it dispenses with listing questionnaires and orders an early trial on a fixed date, the court will specify the date for filing completed listing questionnaires when it fixes the trial date or trial period under rule 29.2(2).

(3) The date for filing the completed listing questionnaires will be not later than 8 weeks before the trial date or the start of the trial period.

(4) The court will serve the listing questionnaires on the parties at least 14 days before that date.

(5) Although the rules do not require the parties to exchange copies of the questionnaires before they are filed they are encouraged to do so to avoid the court being given conflicting or incomplete information.

(6) The file will be placed before a judge for his directions when all the questionnaires have been filed or when the time for filing them has expired.

8.2   The court's general approach will be as set out in the following paragraphs. The court may however decide to make other orders, and in particular the court will take into account the steps, if any, of which it is aware which the parties have taken to prepare the case for trial.

8.3   (1) Where no party files a listing questionnaire the court will normally make an order that if no listing questionnaire is filed by any party within 3 days from service of the order, the claim and any counterclaim will be struck out.

(2) Where a party files a listing questionnaire but another party (the defaulting party) does not do so, the court will fix a listing hearing. Whether or not the defaulting party attends the hearing, the court will normally fix or confirm the trial date and make other orders about the steps to be taken to prepare the case for trial.

8.4   Where the court decides to hold a listing hearing the court will fix a date which is as early as possible and the parties will be given at least 3 days' notice of the date.

8.5   Where the court decides to hold a pre-trial review (whether or not this is in addition to a listing hearing) the court will give the parties at least 7 days' notice of the date.

DIRECTIONS THE COURT WILL GIVE ON LISTING

Directions the court must give

9.1   The court must fix the trial date or week, give a time estimate and fix the place of trial.

Other directions

9.2   (1) The parties should seek to agree directions and may file an agreed order. The court may make an order in those terms or it may make a different order.

(2) Agreed directions should include provision about:
   (a) evidence especially expert evidence,
   (b) a trial timetable and time estimate,
   (c) the preparation of a trial bundle, and
   (d) any other matter needed to prepare the case for trial.

(3) The court will include such of these provisions as are appropriate in any order that it may make, whether or not the parties have filed agreed directions.

(4) Unless a direction doing so has been given before, a direction giving permission to use expert evidence will say whether it gives permission to use oral evidence or reports or both and will name the experts concerned.

9.3   The principles set out in paragraph 6 of this practice direction about variation of directions applies equally to directions given at this stage.

THE TRIAL

10.1   The trial will normally take place at a Civil Trial Centre but it may be at another court if it is appropriate having regard to the needs of the parties and the availability of court resources.

10.2   The judge will generally have read the papers in the trial bundle and may dispense with an opening address.

10.3   The judge may confirm or vary any timetable given previously, or if none has been given set his own.

10.4   Attention is drawn to the provisions in Part 32 and the following parts of the Rules about evidence, and in particular:

(1) to rule 32.1 (court's power to control evidence and to restrict cross-examination), and

(2) to rule 32.5(2) statements and reports to stand as evidence in chief.

10.5   In an appropriate case the judge may summarily assess costs in accordance with rule 44.7. Attention is drawn to the practice directions about costs and the steps the parties are required to take.

10.6   Once the trial of a multi-track claim has begun, the judge will normally sit on consecutive court days until it has been concluded.

CPR PART 30 TRANSFER

CONTENTS OF THIS PART
Scope of this Part	Rule 30.1
Transfer between county courts and within the High Court	Rule 30.2
Criteria for a transfer order	Rule 30.3
Procedure	Rule 30.4
Transfer between Divisions and to and from a specialist list	Rule 30.5
Power to specify place where hearings are to be held	Rule 30.6
Transfer of control of money in court	Rule 30.7
Certiorari or prohibition	Rule 30.8

30.1 SCOPE OF THIS PART
This Part deals with the transfer of proceedings between county courts, between the High Court and the county courts and within the High Court.
(Rule 26.2 provides for automatic transfer in certain cases)

30.2 TRANSFER BETWEEN COUNTY COURTS AND WITHIN THE HIGH COURT
(1) A county court may order proceedings before that court, or any part of them (such as a counterclaim or an application made in the proceedings), to be transferred to another county court if it is satisfied that—
    (a) an order should be made having regard to the criteria in rule 30.3; or
    (b) proceedings for—
        (i) the detailed assessment of costs; or
        (ii) the enforcement of a judgment or order, could be more conveniently or fairly taken in that other county court.

(2) If proceedings have been started in the wrong county court, a judge of the county court may order that the proceedings—
    (a) be transferred to the county court in which they ought to have been started;
    (b) continue in the county court in which they have been started; or
    (c) be struck out.

(3) An application for an order under paragraph (1) or (2) must be made to the county court where the claim is proceeding.

(4) The High Court may, having regard to the criteria in rule 30.3, order proceedings in the Royal Courts of Justice or a district registry, or any part of such proceedings (such as a counterclaim or an application made in the proceedings), to be transferred—
    (a) from the Royal Courts of Justice to a district registry; or
    (b) from a district registry to the Royal Courts of Justice or to another district registry.

(5) A district registry may order proceedings before it for the detailed assessment of costs to be transferred to another district registry if it is satisfied that the proceedings could be more conveniently or fairly taken in that other district registry.

(6) An application for an order under paragraph (4) or (5) must, if the claim is proceeding in a district registry, be made to that registry.

(7) Where some enactment, other than these Rules, requires proceedings to be started in a particular county court, neither paragraphs (1) nor (2) give the court power to order proceedings to be transferred to a county court which is not the court in which they should have been started or to order them to continue in the wrong court.

(8) Probate proceedings may only be transferred under paragraph (4) to the Chancery Division at the Royal Courts of Justice or to one of the Chancery district registries.

30.3 CRITERIA FOR A TRANSFER ORDER

(1) Paragraph (2) sets out the matters to which the court must have regard when considering whether to make an order under—
   (a) section 40(2), 41(1) or 42(2) of the County Courts Act 1984 (transfer between the High Court and a county court);
   (b) rule 30.2(1) (transfer between county courts); or
   (c) rule 30.2(4) (transfer between the Royal Courts of Justice and the district registries).

(2) The matters to which the court must have regard include—
   (a) the financial value of the claim and the amount in dispute, if different;
   (b) whether it would be more convenient or fair for hearings (including the trial) to be held in some other court;
   (c) the availability of a judge specialising in the type of claim in question;
   (d) whether the facts, legal issues, remedies or procedures involved are simple or complex;
   (e) the importance of the outcome of the claim to the public in general;
   (f) the facilities available at the court where the claim is being dealt with and whether they may be inadequate because of any disabilities of a party or potential witness.

30.4 PROCEDURE

(1) Where the court orders proceedings to be transferred, the court from which they are to be transferred must give notice of the transfer to all the parties.

(2) An order made before the transfer of the proceedings shall not be affected by the order to transfer.

30.5 TRANSFER BETWEEN DIVISIONS AND TO AND FROM A SPECIALIST LIST

(1) The High Court may order proceedings in any Division of the High Court to be transferred to another Division.

(2) The court may order proceedings to be transferred to or from a specialist list.

(3) An application for the transfer of proceedings to or from a specialist list must be made to a judge dealing with claims in that list.

30.6 POWER TO SPECIFY PLACE WHERE HEARINGS ARE TO BE HELD

The court may specify the place (for instance, a particular county court) where the trial or some other hearing in any proceedings is to be held and may do so without ordering the proceedings to be transferred.

30.7 TRANSFER OF CONTROL OF MONEY IN COURT

The court may order that control of any money held by it under rule 21.11 (control of money recovered by or on behalf of a child or patient) be transferred to another court if that court would be more convenient.

30.8 CERTIORARI OR PROHIBITION

A party obtaining from the High Court, on an application made without notice, an order giving permission to make an application for—
   (a) an order of certiorari to remove proceedings from a county court; or
   (b) an order of prohibition to any county court,
must immediately serve a copy of the order on the other parties and on the court officer of the county court.

(Other rules about transfer can be found in Schedule 2 in the following CCR — O.25 (transfer of proceedings for enforcement); O.30 (transfer of garnishee proceedings))

PD 30 PRACTICE DIRECTION — TRANSFER

This practice direction supplements CPR Part 30

VALUE OF A CASE AND TRANSFER

1   In addition to the criteria set out in Rule 30.3(2) attention is drawn to the financial limits set out in the High Court and County Courts Jurisdiction Order 1991, as amended.

2   Attention is also drawn to paragraph 2 of the Practice Direction on Part 29 (the multi-track).

DATE OF TRANSFER

3   Where the court orders proceedings to be transferred, the order will take effect from the date it is made by the court.

PROCEDURE ON TRANSFER

4.1   Where an order for transfer has been made the transferring court will immediately send notice of the transfer to the receiving court. The notice will contain:

(1)   the name of the case, and

(2)   the number of the case.

4.2   At the same time as the transferring court notifies the receiving court it will also notify the parties of the transfer under rule 30.4(1).

PROCEDURE FOR AN APPEAL AGAINST ORDER OF TRANSFER

5.1   An appeal against an order that proceedings be transferred:

(1)   where either the transferring court or the receiving court is the High Court, and the order was made by a Master or district judge, should be made in the High Court,

(2)   where the order was made in proceedings in the High Court by a High Court judge, should be made in the Court of Appeal,

(3)   where both the transferring and receiving courts are county courts, and the order was made by a district judge, should be made in the receiving court,

(4)   where the order was made in county court proceedings by a circuit judge, should be made in the Court of Appeal.

5.2   Where paragraph 5.1(3) applies, the receiving court may, if it is convenient to the parties, remit the appeal to the transferring court to be dealt with there.

5.3   An appeal made under 5.1(1) or 5.1(3) above must be begun by the issue of an application notice in accordance with Part 23 of the Rules and the practice direction which supplements Part 23.

5.4   An appeal made under 5.1(2) or 5.1(4) above must be begun by the issue of a notice of appeal in accordance with the provisions of RSC Order 59 (see Part 50 and Schedule 1 to the Rules).

APPLICATIONS TO SET ASIDE

6.1   Where a party may apply to set aside an order for transfer (e.g. under rule 23.10) the application should be made to the court which made the order.

6.2   Such application should be made in accordance with Part 23 of the Rules and the practice direction which supplements it.

CPR PART 31 DISCLOSURE AND INSPECTION OF DOCUMENTS

CONTENTS OF THIS PART
Scope of this Part	Rule 31.1
Meaning of disclosure	Rule 31.2
Right of inspection of a disclosed document	Rule 31.3
Meaning of document	Rule 31.4
Disclosure limited to standard disclosure	Rule 31.5
Standard disclosure — what documents are to be disclosed	Rule 31.6
Duty of search	Rule 31.7
Duty of disclosure limited to documents which are or have been in a party's control	Rule 31.8
Disclosure of copies	Rule 31.9
Procedure for standard disclosure	Rule 31.10
Duty of disclosure continues during proceedings	Rule 31.11
Specific disclosure or inspection	Rule 31.12
Disclosure in stages	Rule 31.13
Documents referred to in statements of case etc.	Rule 31.14
Inspection and copying of documents	Rule 31.15
Disclosure before proceedings start	Rule 31.16
Orders for disclosure against a person not a party	Rule 31.17
Rules not to limit other powers of the court to order disclosure	Rule 31.18
Claim to withhold inspection or disclosure of a document	Rule 31.19
Restriction on use of a privileged document inspection of which has been inadvertently allowed	Rule 31.20
Consequence of failure to disclose documents or permit inspection	Rule 31.21
Subsequent use of disclosed documents	Rule 31.22

31.1 SCOPE OF THIS PART
(1) This Part sets out rules about the disclosure and inspection of documents.
(2) This Part applies to all claims except a claim on the small claims track.

31.2 MEANING OF DISCLOSURE
A party discloses a document by stating that the document exists or has existed.

31.3 RIGHT OF INSPECTION OF A DISCLOSED DOCUMENT
(1) A party to whom a document has been disclosed has a right to inspect that document except where—
    (a) the document is no longer in the control of the party who disclosed it;
    (b) the party disclosing the document has a right or a duty to withhold inspection of it; or
    (c) paragraph (2) applies.
(Rule 31.8 sets out when a document is in the control of a party)
(Rule 31.19 sets out the procedure for claiming a right or duty to withhold inspection)
(2) Where a party considers that it would be disproportionate to the issues in the case to permit inspection of documents within a category or class of document disclosed under rule 31.6(b)—
    (a) he is not required to permit inspection of documents within that category or class; but
    (b) he must state in his disclosure statement that inspection of those documents will not be permitted on the grounds that to do so would be disproportionate.
(Rule 31.6 provides for standard disclosure)
(Rule 31.10 makes provision for a disclosure statement)

CPR PART 31 DISCLOSURE AND INSPECTION OF DOCUMENTS

(Rule 31.12 provides for a party to apply for an order for specific inspection of documents)

31.4 MEANING OF DOCUMENT
In this Part—
'document' means anything in which information of any description is recorded; and
'copy', in relation to a document, means anything onto which information recorded in the document has been copied, by whatever means and whether directly or indirectly.

31.5 DISCLOSURE LIMITED TO STANDARD DISCLOSURE
(1) An order to give disclosure is an order to give standard disclosure unless the court directs otherwise.
(2) The court may dispense with or limit standard disclosure.
(3) The parties may agree in writing to dispense with or to limit standard disclosure.
(The court may make an order requiring standard disclosure under rule 28.3 which deals with directions in relation to cases on the fast track and under rule 29.2 which deals with case management in relation to cases on the multi-track)

31.6 STANDARD DISCLOSURE — WHAT DOCUMENTS ARE TO BE DISCLOSED
Standard disclosure requires a party to disclose only—
    (a) the documents on which he relies; and
    (b) the documents which—
        (i) adversely affect his own case;
        (ii) adversely affect another party's case; or
        (iii) support another party's case; and
    (c) the documents which he is required to disclose by a relevant practice direction.

31.7 DUTY OF SEARCH
(1) When giving standard disclosure, a party is required to make a reasonable search for documents falling within rule 31.6(b) or (c).
(2) The factors relevant in deciding the reasonableness of a search include the following—
    (a) the number of documents involved;
    (b) the nature and complexity of the proceedings;
    (c) the ease and expense of retrieval of any particular document; and
    (d) the significance of any document which is likely to be located during the search.
(3) Where a party has not searched for a category or class of document on the grounds that to do so would be unreasonable, he must state this in his disclosure statement and identify the category or class of document.
(Rule 31.10 makes provision for a disclosure statement)

31.8 DUTY OF DISCLOSURE LIMITED TO DOCUMENTS WHICH ARE OR HAVE BEEN IN A PARTY'S CONTROL
(1) A party's duty to disclose documents is limited to documents which are or have been in his control.
(2) For this purpose a party has or has had a document in his control if—
    (a) it is or was in his physical possession;
    (b) he has or has had a right to possession of it; or
    (c) he has or has had a right to inspect or take copies of it.

31.9 DISCLOSURE OF COPIES
(1) A party need not disclose more than one copy of a document.
(2) A copy of a document that contains a modification, obliteration or other marking or feature—
    (a) on which a party intends to rely; or

CPR PART 31 DISCLOSURE AND INSPECTION OF DOCUMENTS

(b) which adversely affects his own case or another party's case or supports another party's case;
shall be treated as a separate document.
(Rule 31.4 sets out the meaning of a copy of a document)

31.10 PROCEDURE FOR STANDARD DISCLOSURE
(1) The procedure for standard disclosure is as follows.
(2) Each party must make and serve on every other party, a list of documents in the relevant practice form.
(3) The list must identify the documents in a convenient order and manner and as concisely as possible.
(4) The list must indicate—
   (a) those documents in respect of which the party claims a right or duty to withhold inspection; and
   (b) (i) those documents which are no longer in the party's control; and
       (ii) what has happened to those documents.
(Rule 31.19(3) and (4) require a statement in the list of documents relating to any documents inspection of which a person claims he has a right or duty to withhold)
(5) The list must include a disclosure statement.
(6) A disclosure statement is a statement made by the party disclosing the documents—
   (a) setting out the extent of the search that has been made to locate documents which he is required to disclose;
   (b) certifying that he understands the duty to disclose documents; and
   (c) certifying that to the best of his knowledge he has carried out that duty.
(7) Where the party making the disclosure statement is a company, firm, association or other organisation, the statement must also—
   (a) identify the person making the statement; and
   (b) explain why he is considered an appropriate person to make the statement.
(8) The parties may agree in writing—
   (a) to disclose documents without making a list; and
   (b) to disclose documents without the disclosing party making a disclosure statement.
(9) A disclosure statement may be made by a person who is not a party where this is permitted by a relevant practice direction.

31.11 DUTY OF DISCLOSURE CONTINUES DURING PROCEEDINGS
(1) Any duty of disclosure continues until the proceedings are concluded.
(2) If documents to which that duty extends come to a party's notice at any time during the proceedings, he must immediately notify every other party.

31.12 SPECIFIC DISCLOSURE OR INSPECTION
(1) The court may make an order for specific disclosure or specific inspection.
(2) An order for specific disclosure is an order that a party must do one or more of the following things—
   (a) disclose documents or classes of documents specified in the order;
   (b) carry out a search to the extent stated in the order;
   (c) disclose any documents located as a result of that search.
(3) An order for specific inspection is an order that a party permit inspection of a document referred to in rule 31.3(2).
(Rule 31.3(2) allows a party to state in his disclosure statement that he will not permit inspection of a document on the grounds that it would be disproportionate to do so)

31.13 DISCLOSURE IN STAGES
The parties may agree in writing, or the court may direct, that disclosure or inspection or both shall take place in stages.

31.14 DOCUMENTS REFERRED TO IN STATEMENTS OF CASE ETC.
A party may inspect a document mentioned in—

CPR PART 31 DISCLOSURE AND INSPECTION OF DOCUMENTS

    (a)   a statement of case;
    (b)   a witness statement;
    (c)   a witness summary;
    (d)   an affidavit[GL]; or
    (e)   subject to rule 35.10(4), an expert's report.
(Rule 35.10(4) makes provision in relation to instructions referred to in an expert's report)

31.15 INSPECTION AND COPYING OF DOCUMENTS

Where a party has a right to inspect a document—
    (a)   that party must give the party who disclosed the document written notice of his wish to inspect it;
    (b)   the party who disclosed the document must permit inspection not more than 7 days after the date on which he received the notice; and
    (c)   that party may request a copy of the document and, if he also undertakes to pay reasonable copying costs, the party who disclosed the document must supply him with a copy not more than 7 days after the date on which he received the request.
(Rule[s] 31.3 and 31.14 deal with the right of a party to inspect a document)

31.16 DISCLOSURE BEFORE PROCEEDINGS START

(1) This rule applies where an application is made to the court under any Act for disclosure before proceedings have started.
(2) The application must be supported by evidence.
(3) The court may make an order under this rule only where—
    (a)   the respondent is likely to be a party to subsequent proceedings;
    (b)   the applicant is also likely to be a party to those proceedings;
    (c)   if proceedings had started, the respondent's duty by way of standard disclosure, set out in rule 31.6, would extend to the documents or classes of documents of which the applicant seeks disclosure; and
    (d)   disclosure before proceedings have started is desirable in order to—
        (i)   dispose fairly of the anticipated proceedings;
        (ii)   assist the dispute to be resolved without proceedings; or
        (iii)   save costs.
(4) An order under this rule must—
    (a)   specify the documents or the classes of documents which the respondent must disclose; and
    (b)   require him, when making disclosure, to specify any of those documents—
        (i)   which are no longer in his control; or
        (ii)   in respect of which he claims a right or duty to withhold inspection.
(5) Such an order may—
    (a)   require the respondent to indicate what has happened to any documents which are no longer in his control; and
    (b)   specify the time and place for disclosure and inspection.

31.17 ORDERS FOR DISCLOSURE AGAINST A PERSON NOT A PARTY

(1) This rule applies where an application is made to the court under any Act for disclosure by a person who is not a party to the proceedings.
(2) The application must be supported by evidence.
(3) The court may make an order under this rule only where—
    (a)   the documents of which disclosure is sought are likely to support the case of the applicant or adversely affect the case of one of the other parties to the proceedings; and
    (b)   disclosure is necessary in order to dispose fairly of the claim or to save costs.
(4) An order under this rule must—
    (a)   specify the documents or the classes of documents which the respondent must disclose; and
    (b)   require the respondent, when making disclosure, to specify any of those documents—

CPR PART 31 DISCLOSURE AND INSPECTION OF DOCUMENTS

(i) which are no longer in his control; or
(ii) in respect of which he claims a right or duty to withhold inspection.
(5) Such an order may—
(a) require the respondent to indicate what has happened to any documents which are no longer in his control; and
(b) specify the time and place for disclosure and inspection.

31.18 RULES NOT TO LIMIT OTHER POWERS OF THE COURT TO ORDER DISCLOSURE

Rules 31.16 and 31.17 do not limit any other power which the court may have to order—
(a) disclosure before proceedings have started; and
(b) disclosure against a person who is not a party to proceedings.

31.19 CLAIM TO WITHHOLD INSPECTION OR DISCLOSURE OF A DOCUMENT

(1) A person may apply, without notice, for an order permitting him to withhold disclosure of a document on the ground that disclosure would damage the public interest.
(2) Unless the court orders otherwise, an order of the court under paragraph (1)—
(a) must not be served on any other person; and
(b) must not be open to inspection by any person.
(3) A person who wishes to claim that he has a right or a duty to withhold inspection of a document, or part of a document, must state in writing—
(a) that he has such a right or duty; and
(b) the grounds on which he claims that right or duty.
(4) The statement referred to in paragraph (3) must be made—
(a) in the list in which the document is disclosed; or
(b) if there is no list, to the person wishing to inspect the document.
(5) A party may apply to the court to decide whether a claim made under paragraph (3) should be upheld.
(6) For the purpose of deciding an application under paragraph (1) (application to withhold disclosure) or paragraph (3) (claim to withhold inspection) the court may—
(a) require the person seeking to withhold disclosure or inspection of a document to produce that document to the court; and
(b) invite any person, whether or not a party, to make representations.
(7) An application under paragraph (1) or paragraph (5) must be supported by evidence.
(8) This Part does not affect any rule of law which permits or requires a document to be withheld from disclosure or inspection on the ground that its disclosure or inspection would damage the public interest.

31.20 RESTRICTION ON USE OF A PRIVILEGED DOCUMENT INSPECTION OF WHICH HAS BEEN INADVERTENTLY ALLOWED

Where a party inadvertently allows a privileged document to be inspected, the party who has inspected the document may use it or its contents only with the permission of the court.

31.21 CONSEQUENCE OF FAILURE TO DISCLOSE DOCUMENTS OR PERMIT INSPECTION

A party may not rely on any document which he fails to disclose or in respect of which he fails to permit inspection unless the court gives permission.

31.22 SUBSEQUENT USE OF DISCLOSED DOCUMENTS

(1) A party to whom a document has been disclosed may use the document only for the purpose of the proceedings in which it is disclosed, except where—
(a) the document has been read to or by the court, or referred to, at a hearing which has been held in public;

CPR PART 31 DISCLOSURE AND INSPECTION OF DOCUMENTS

    (b) the court gives permission; or
    (c) the party who disclosed the document and the person to whom the document belongs agree.

    (2) The court may make an order restricting or prohibiting the use of a document which has been disclosed, even where the document has been read to or by the court, or referred to, at a hearing which has been held in public.

    (3) An application for such an order may be made—
    (a) by a party; or
    (b) by any person to whom the document belongs.

PD 31 PRACTICE DIRECTION — DISCLOSURE AND INSPECTION

This practice direction supplements CPR Part 31

GENERAL

1.1 The normal order for disclosure will be an order that the parties give standard disclosure.

1.2 In order to give standard disclosure the disclosing party must make a reasonable search for documents falling within the paragraphs of rule 31.6.

1.3 Having made the search the disclosing party must (unless rule 31.10(8) applies) make a list of the documents of whose existence the party is aware that fall within those paragraphs and which are or have been in the party's control (see rule 31.8).

1.4 The obligations imposed by an order for standard disclosure may be dispensed with or limited either by the court or by written agreement between the parties. Any such written agreement should be lodged with the court.

THE SEARCH

2 The extent of the search which must be made will depend upon the circumstances of the case including, in particular, the factors referred to in rule 31.7(2). The parties should bear in mind the overriding principle of proportionality (see rule 1.1(2)(c)). It may, for example, be reasonable to decide not to search for documents coming into existence before some particular date, or to limit the search to documents in some particular place or places, or to documents falling into particular categories.

THE LIST

3.1 The list should be in Form N265.

3.2 In order to comply with rule 31.10(3) it will normally be necessary to list the documents in date order, to number them consecutively and to give each a concise description (e.g. letter, claimant to defendant). Where there is a large number of documents all failing into a particular category the disclosing party may list those documents as a category rather than individually e.g. 50 bank statements relating to account number _at _ Bank, _ 19_ to _19_; or, 35 letters passing between _ and _ between _ 19_ and _ 19_.

3.3 The obligations imposed by an order for disclosure will continue until the proceedings come to an end. If, after a list of documents has been prepared and served, the existence of further documents to which the order applies comes to the attention of the disclosing party, the party must prepare and serve a supplemental list.

DISCLOSURE STATEMENT

4.1 A list of documents must (unless rule 31.10(8)(b) applies) contain a disclosure statement complying with rule 31.10. The form of disclosure statement is set out in the Annex to this practice direction.

4.2 The disclosure statement should:

(1) expressly state that the disclosing party believes the extent of the search to have been reasonable in all the circumstances, and

(2) in setting out the extent of the search (see rule 31.10(6)) draw attention to any particular limitations on the extent of the search which were adopted for proportionality reasons and give the reasons why the limitations were adopted, e.g. the difficulty or expense that a search not subject to those limitations would have entailed or the marginal relevance of categories of documents omitted from the search.

4.3 Where rule 31.10(7) applies, the details given in the disclosure statement about the person making the statement must include his name and address and the office or position he holds in the disclosing party.

4.4 If the disclosing party has a legal representative acting for him, the legal representative must endeavour to ensure that the person making the disclosure statement (whether the disclosing party or, in a case to which rule 31.10(7) applies, some other person) understands the duty of disclosure under rule 31.

4.5 If the disclosing party wishes to claim that he has a right or duty to withhold a document, or part of a document, in his list of documents from inspection (see rule 31.19(3)), he must state in writing:
  (1) that he has such a right or duty, and
  (2) the grounds on which he claims that right or duty.

4.6 The statement referred to in paragraph 4.5 above should normally be included in the disclosure statement and must identify the document, or part of a document, to which the claim relates.

SPECIFIC DISCLOSURE

5.1 If a party believes that the disclosure of documents given by a disclosing party is inadequate he may make an application for an order for specific disclosure (see rule 31.12).

5.2 The application notice must specify the order that the applicant intends to ask the court to make and must be supported by evidence (see rule 31.12(2) which describes the orders the court may make).

5.3 The grounds on which the order is sought may be set out in the application notice itself but if not there set out must be set out in the evidence filed in support of the application.

5.4 In deciding whether or not to make an order for specific disclosure the court will take into account all the circumstances of the case and, in particular, the overriding objective described in Part 1. But if the court concludes that the party from whom specific disclosure is sought has failed adequately to comply with the obligations imposed by an order for disclosure (whether by failing to make a sufficient search for documents or otherwise) the court will usually make such order as is necessary to ensure that those obligations are properly complied with.

CLAIMS TO WITHHOLD DISCLOSURE OR INSPECTION OF A DOCUMENT

6.1 A claim to withhold inspection of a document, or part of a document, disclosed in a list of documents does not require an application to the court. Where such a claim has been made, a party who wishes to challenge it must apply to the court (see rule 31.19(5)).

6.2 Rule 31.19(1) and (6) provide a procedure enabling a party to apply for an order permitting disclosure of the existence of a document to be withheld.

INSPECTION OF DOCUMENTS MENTIONED IN EXPERT'S REPORT (RULE 31.4(e))

7 Reference should be made to the practice direction supplementing Part 35 (Experts and Assessors) for provisions dealing with applications to inspect these documents.

ANNEX
DISCLOSURE STATEMENT

I, the above named claimant [or defendant] [if party making disclosure is a company, firm or other organisation identify here who the person making the disclosure statement is and why he is the appropriate person to make it] state that I have carried out a reasonable and proportionate search to locate all the documents which I am required to disclose under the order made by the court on   day of   . I did not search:
  (1) for documents predating .... ,
  (2) for documents located elsewhere than .... ,
  (3) for documents in categories other than ....

I certify that I understand the duty of disclosure and to the best of my knowledge I have carried out that duty. I certify that the list above is a complete list of all documents which are or have been in my control and which I am obliged under the said order to disclose.

CPR PART 32 EVIDENCE

CONTENTS OF THIS PART
Power of court to control evidence	Rule 32.1
Evidence of witnesses — general rule	Rule 32.2
Evidence by video link or other means	Rule 32.3
Requirement to serve witness statements for use at trial	Rule 32.4
Use at trial of witness statements which have been served	Rule 32.5
Evidence in proceedings other than at trial	Rule 32.6
Order for cross-examination	Rule 32.7
Form of witness statement	Rule 32.8
Witness summaries	Rule 32.9
Consequence of failure to serve witness statement or summary	Rule 32.10
Cross-examination on a witness statement	Rule 32.11
Use of witness statements for other purposes	Rule 32.12
Availability of witness statements for inspection	Rule 32.13
False statements	Rule 32.14
Affidavit evidence	Rule 32.15
Form of affidavit	Rule 32.16
Affidavit made outside the jurisdiction	Rule 32.17
Notice to admit facts	Rule 32.18
Notice to admit or produce documents	Rule 32.19

32.1 POWER OF COURT TO CONTROL EVIDENCE
   (1) The court may control the evidence by giving directions as to—
      (a) the issues on which it requires evidence;
      (b) the nature of the evidence which it requires to decide those issues; and
      (c) the way in which the evidence is to be placed before the court.
   (2) The court may use its power under this rule to exclude evidence that would otherwise be admissible.
   (3) The court may limit cross-examination[GL].

32.2 EVIDENCE OF WITNESSES — GENERAL RULE
   (1) The general rule is that any fact which needs to be proved by the evidence of witnesses is to be proved—
      (a) at trial, by their oral evidence given in public; and
      (b) at any other hearing, by their evidence in writing.
   (2) This is subject—
      (a) to any provision to the contrary contained in these Rules or elsewhere; or
      (b) to any order of the court.

32.3 EVIDENCE BY VIDEO LINK OR OTHER MEANS
The court may allow a witness to give evidence through a video link or by other means.

32.4 REQUIREMENT TO SERVE WITNESS STATEMENTS FOR USE AT TRIAL
   (1) A witness statement is a written statement signed by a person which contains the evidence which that person would be allowed to give orally.
   (2) The court will order a party to serve on the other parties any witness statement of the oral evidence which the party serving the statement intends to rely on in relation to any issues of fact to be decided at the trial.
   (3) The court may give directions as to—
      (a) the order in which witness statements are to be served; and
      (b) whether or not the witness statements are to be filed.

CPR PART 32 EVIDENCE

32.5 USE AT TRIAL OF WITNESS STATEMENTS WHICH HAVE BEEN SERVED
(1) If—
   (a) a party has served a witness statement; and
   (b) he wishes to rely at trial on the evidence of the witness who made the statement,
he must call the witness to give oral evidence unless the court orders otherwise or he puts the statement in as hearsay evidence.
(Part 33 contains provisions about hearsay evidence)
(2) Where a witness is called to give oral evidence under paragraph (1), his witness statement shall stand as his evidence in chief$^{(GL)}$ unless the court orders otherwise.
(3) A witness giving oral evidence at trial may with the permission of the court—
   (a) amplify his witness statement; and
   (b) give evidence in relation to new matters which have arisen since the witness statement was served on the other parties.
(4) The court will give permission under paragraph (3) only if it considers that there is good reason not to confine the evidence of the witness to the contents of his witness statement.
(5) If a party who has served a witness statement does not—
   (a) call the witness to give evidence at trial; or
   (b) put the witness statement in as hearsay evidence,
any other party may put the witness statement in as hearsay evidence.

32.6 EVIDENCE IN PROCEEDINGS OTHER THAN AT TRIAL
(1) Subject to paragraph (2), the general rule is that evidence at hearings other than the trial is to be by witness statement unless the court, a practice direction or any other enactment requires otherwise.
(2) At hearings other than the trial, a party may, in support of his application, rely on the matters set out in—
   (a) his statement of case; or
   (b) his application notice,
if the statement of case or application notice is verified by a statement of truth.

32.7 ORDER FOR CROSS-EXAMINATION
(1) Where, at a hearing other than the trial, evidence is given in writing, any party may apply to the court for permission to cross-examine the person giving the evidence.
(2) If the court gives permission under paragraph (1) but the person in question does not attend as required by the order, his evidence may not be used unless the court gives permission.

32.8 FORM OF WITNESS STATEMENT
A witness statement must comply with the requirements set out in the relevant practice direction.
(Part 22 requires a witness statement to be verified by a statement of truth)

32.9 WITNESS SUMMARIES
(1) A party who—
   (a) is required to serve a witness statement for use at trial; but
   (b) is unable to obtain one,
may apply, without notice, for permission to serve a witness summary instead.
(2) A witness summary is a summary of—
   (a) the evidence, if known, which would otherwise be included in a witness statement; or
   (b) if the evidence is not known, the matters about which the party serving the witness summary proposes to question the witness.
(3) Unless the court orders otherwise, a witness summary must include the name and address of the intended witness.

(4) Unless the court orders otherwise, a witness summary must be served within the period in which a witness statement would have had to be served.

(5) Where a party serves a witness summary, so far as practicable rules 32.4 (requirement to serve witness statements for use at trial), 32.5(3) (amplifying witness statements), and 32.8 (form of witness statement) shall apply to the summary.

32.10 CONSEQUENCE OF FAILURE TO SERVE WITNESS STATEMENT OR SUMMARY

If a witness statement or a witness summary for use at trial is not served in respect of an intended witness within the time specified by the court, then the witness may not be called to give oral evidence unless the court gives permission.

32.11 CROSS-EXAMINATION ON A WITNESS STATEMENT

Where a witness is called to give evidence at trial, he may be cross-examined on his witness statement whether or not the statement or any part of it was referred to during the witness's evidence in chief[GL].

32.12 USE OF WITNESS STATEMENTS FOR OTHER PURPOSES

(1) Except as provided by this rule, a witness statement may be used only for the purpose of the proceedings in which it is served.

(2) Paragraph (1) does not apply if and to the extent that—
   (a) the witness gives consent in writing to some other use of it;
   (b) the court gives permission for some other use; or
   (c) the witness statement has been put in evidence at a hearing held in public.

32.13 AVAILABILITY OF WITNESS STATEMENTS FOR INSPECTION

(1) A witness statement which stands as evidence in chief[GL] is open to inspection unless the court otherwise directs during the course of the trial.

(2) Any person may ask for a direction that a witness statement is not open to inspection.

(3) The court will not make a direction under paragraph (2) unless it is satisfied that a witness statement should not be open to inspection because of—
   (a) the interests of justice;
   (b) the public interest;
   (c) the nature of any expert medical evidence in the statement;
   (d) the nature of any confidential information (including information relating to personal financial matters) in the statement; or
   (e) the need to protect the interests of any child or patient.

(4) The court may exclude from inspection words or passages in the statement.

32.14 FALSE STATEMENTS

(1) Proceedings for contempt of court may be brought against a person if he makes, or causes to be made, a false statement in a document verified by a statement of truth without an honest belief in its truth.
(Part 22 makes provision for a statement of truth)

(2) Proceedings under this rule may be brought only—
   (a) by the Attorney General; or
   (b) with the permission of the court.

32.15 AFFIDAVIT EVIDENCE

(1) Evidence must be given by affidavit[GL] instead of or in addition to a witness statement if this is required by the court, a provision contained in any other rule, a practice direction or any other enactment.

(2) Nothing in these Rules prevents a witness giving evidence by affidavit[GL] at a hearing other than the trial if he chooses to do so in a case where paragraph (1) does not apply, but the party putting forward the affidavit[GL] may not recover the additional cost of making it from any other party unless the court orders otherwise.

32.16 FORM OF AFFIDAVIT

An affidavit$^{(GL)}$ must comply with the requirements set out in the relevant practice direction.

32.17 AFFIDAVIT MADE OUTSIDE THE JURISDICTION

A person may make an affidavit$^{(GL)}$ outside the jurisdiction in accordance with—
- (a) this Part; or
- (b) the law of the place where he makes the affidavit$^{(GL)}$.

32.18 NOTICE TO ADMIT FACTS

(1) A party may serve notice on another party requiring him to admit the facts, or the part of the case of the serving party, specified in the notice.

(2) A notice to admit facts must be served no later than 21 days before the trial.

(3) Where the other party makes any admission in response to the notice, the admission may be used against him only—
- (a) in the proceedings in which the notice to admit is served; and
- (b) by the party who served the notice.

(4) The court may allow a party to amend or withdraw any admission made by him on such terms as it thinks just.

32.19 NOTICE TO ADMIT OR PRODUCE DOCUMENTS

(1) A party shall be deemed to admit the authenticity of a document disclosed to him under Part 31 (disclosure and inspection of documents) unless he serves notice that he wishes the document to be proved at trial.

(2) A notice to prove a document must be served—
- (a) by the latest date for serving witness statements; or
- (b) within 7 days of disclosure of the document,

whichever is later.

PD 32 PRACTICE DIRECTION — WRITTEN EVIDENCE

This practice direction supplements CPR Part 32

EVIDENCE IN GENERAL

1.1 Rule 32.2 sets out how evidence is to be given and facts are to be proved.

1.2 Evidence at a hearing other than the trial should normally be given by witness statement[1] (see paragraph 17 onwards). However a witness may give evidence by affidavit if he wishes to do so[2] (and see paragraph 1.4 below).

1.3 Statements of case (see paragraph 26 onwards) and application notices[3] may also be used as evidence provided that their contents have been verified by a statement of truth[4].
(For information regarding evidence by deposition see Part 34 and the practice direction which supplements it.)

1.4 Affidavits must be used as evidence in the following instances:

(1) where sworn evidence is required by an enactment[5], Statutory Instrument, rule[6], order or practice direction,

(2) in any application for a search order, a freezing injunction, or an order requiring an occupier to permit another to enter his land, and

(3) in any application for an order against anyone for alleged contempt of court.

1.5 If a party believes that sworn evidence is required by a court in another jurisdiction for any purpose connected with the proceedings, he may apply to the court for a direction that evidence shall be given only by affidavit on any pre-trial applications.

1.6 The court may give a direction under rule 32.15 that evidence shall be given by affidavit instead of or in addition to a witness statement or statement of case:

(1) on its own initiative, or

(2) after any party has applied to the court for such a direction.

1.7 An affidavit, where referred to in the Civil Procedure Rules or a practice direction, also means an affirmation unless the context requires otherwise.

AFFIDAVITS

Deponent

2 A deponent is a person who gives evidence by affidavit or affirmation.

Heading

3.1 The affidavit should be headed with the title of the proceedings (see paragraph 4 of the practice direction supplementing Part 7 and paragraph 7 of the practice direction supplementing Part 20); where the proceedings are between several parties with the same status it is sufficient to identify the parties as follows:

Number:
A.B. (and others)   Claimants/Applicants
C.D. (and others)   Defendants/Respondents
(as appropriate)

3.2 At the top right hand corner of the first page (and on the backsheet) there should be clearly written:

---

[1] See rule 32.6(1).
[2] See rule 32.15(2).
[3] See Part 23 for information about making an application.
[4] Rule 32.6(2) and see Part 22 for information about the statement of truth.
[5] See, e.g., s. 3(5)(a) of the Protection from Harassment Act 1997.
[6] See, e.g., RSC, ord. 115, rr. 2B, 14 and others (Confiscation and Forfeiture in Connection with Criminal Proceedings) and RSC, ord. 110, r. 3 (Environmental Control Proceedings — injunctions '*in rem*' against unknown Defendant).

(1) the party on whose behalf it is made,
(2) the initials and surname of the deponent,
(3) the number of the affidavit in relation to that deponent,
(4) the identifying initials and number of each exhibit referred to, and
(5) the date sworn.

Body of affidavit
4.1 The affidavit must, if practicable, be in the deponent's own words, the affidavit should be expressed in the first person and the deponent should:
   (1) commence 'I (*full name*) of (*address*) state on oath ......',
   (2) if giving evidence in his professional, business or other occupational capacity, give the address at which he works in (1) above, the position he holds and the name of his firm or employer,
   (3) give his occupation or, if he has none, his description, and
   (4) state if he is a party to the proceedings or employed by a party to the proceedings, if it be the case.
4.2 An affidavit must indicate:
   (1) which of the statements in it are made from the deponent's own knowledge and which are matters of information or belief, and
   (2) the source for any matters of information or belief.
4.3 Where a deponent:
   (1) refers to an exhibit or exhibits, he should state 'there is now shown to me marked ". . ." the (*description of exhibit*)', and
   (2) makes more than one affidavit (to which there are exhibits) in the same proceedings, the numbering of the exhibits should run consecutively throughout and not start again with each affidavit.

Jurat
5.1 The jurat of an affidavit is a statement set out at the end of the document which authenticates the affidavit.
5.2 It must:
   (1) be signed by all deponents,
   (2) be completed and signed by the person before whom the affidavit was sworn whose name and qualification must be printed beneath his signature,
   (3) contain the full address of the person before whom the affidavit was sworn, and
   (4) follow immediately on from the text and not be put on a separate page.

Format of affidavits
6.1 An affidavit should:
   (1) be produced on durable quality A4 paper with a 3.5cm margin,
   (2) be fully legible and should normally be typed on one side of the paper only,
   (3) where possible, be bound securely in a manner which would not hamper filing, or otherwise each page should be endorsed with the case number and should bear the initials of the deponent and of the person before whom it was sworn,
   (4) have the pages numbered consecutively as a separate document (or as one of several documents contained in a file),
   (5) be divided into numbered paragraphs,
   (6) have all numbers, including dates, expressed in figures, and
   (7) give in the margin the reference to any document or documents mentioned.
6.2 It is usually convenient for an affidavit to follow the chronological sequence of events or matters dealt with; each paragraph of an affidavit should as far as possible be confined to a distinct portion of the subject.

Inability of deponent to read or sign affidavit
7.1 Where an affidavit is sworn by a person who is unable to read or sign it, the person before whom the affidavit is sworn must certify in the jurat that:
   (1) he read the affidavit to the deponent,

(2) the deponent appeared to understand it, and
(3) the deponent signed or made his mark, in his presence.

7.2 If that certificate is not included in the jurat, the affidavit may not be used in evidence unless the court is satisfied that it was read to the deponent and that he appeared to understand it. Two versions of the form of jurat with the certificate are set out at Annex 1 to this practice direction.

Alterations to affidavits

8.1 Any alteration to an affidavit must be initialled by both the deponent and the person before whom the affidavit was sworn.

8.2 An affidavit which contains an alteration that has not been initialled may be filed or used in evidence only with the permission of the court.

Who may administer oaths and take affidavits

9.1 Only the following may administer oaths and take affidavits:
 (1) Commissioners for oaths[7],
 (2) Practising solicitors[8],
 (3) other persons specified by statute[9],
 (4) certain officials of the Supreme Court[10],
 (5) a circuit judge or district judge[11],
 (6) any justice of the peace[12], and
 (7) certain officials of any county court appointed by the judge of that court for the purpose[13].

9.2 An affidavit must be sworn before a person independent of the parties or their representatives.

Filing of Affidavits

10.1 If the court directs that an affidavit is to be filed[14], it must be filed in the court or Division, or Office or Registry of the court or Division where the action in which it was or is to be used, is proceeding or will proceed.

10.2 Where an affidavit is in a foreign language:
 (1) the party wishing to rely on it—
  (a) must have it translated, and
  (b) must file the foreign language affidavit with the court, and
 (2) the translator must make and file with the court an affidavit verifying the translation and exhibiting both the translation and a copy of the foreign language affidavit.

EXHIBITS

Manner of exhibiting documents

11.1 A document used in conjunction with an affidavit should be:
 (1) produced to and verified by the deponent, and remain separate from the affidavit, and
 (2) identified by a declaration of the person before whom the affidavit was sworn.

11.2 The declaration should be headed with the name of the proceedings in the same way as the affidavit.

11.3 The first page of each exhibit should be marked:
 (1) as in paragraph 3.2 above, and
 (2) with the exhibit mark referred to in the affidavit.

---

[7] Commissioners for Oaths Acts 1889 and 1891.
[8] Section 81 of the Solicitors Act 1974.
[9] Section 65 of the Administration of Justice Act 1985, s. 113 of the Courts and Legal Services Act 1990 and the Commissioners for Oaths (Prescribed Bodies) Regulations 1994 and 1995.
[10] Section 2 of the Commissioners for Oaths Act 1889.
[11] Section 58 of the County Courts Act 1984.
[12] Section 58 as above.
[13] Section 58 as above.
[14] Rules 32.1(3) and 32.4(3)(b).

Letters

12.1 Copies of individual letters should be collected together and exhibited in a bundle or bundles. They should be arranged in chronological order with the earliest at the top, and firmly secured.

12.2 When a bundle of correspondence is exhibited, the exhibit should have a front page attached stating that the bundle consists of original letters and copies. They should be arranged and secured as above and numbered consecutively.

Other documents

13.1 Photocopies instead of original documents may be exhibited provided the originals are made available for inspection by the other parties before the hearing and by the judge at the hearing.

13.2 Court documents must not be exhibited (official copies of such documents prove themselves).

13.3 Where an exhibit contains more than one document, a front page should be attached setting out a list of the documents contained in the exhibit; the list should contain the dates of the documents.

Exhibits other than documents

14.1 Items other than documents should be clearly marked with an exhibit number or letter in such a manner that the mark cannot become detached from the exhibit.

14.2 Small items may be placed in a container and the container appropriately marked.

General provisions

15.1 Where an exhibit contains more than one document:

(1) the bundle should not be stapled but should be securely fastened in a way that does not hinder the reading of the documents, and

(2) the pages should be numbered consecutively at bottom centre.

15.2 Every page of an exhibit should be clearly legible; typed copies of illegible documents should be included, paginated with 'a' numbers.

15.3 Where affidavits and exhibits have become numerous, they should be put into separate bundles and the pages numbered consecutively throughout.

15.4 Where on account of their bulk the service of exhibits or copies of exhibits on the other parties would be difficult or impracticable, the directions of the court should be sought as to arrangements for bringing the exhibits to the attention of the other parties and as to their custody pending trial.

Affirmations

16 All provisions in this or any other practice direction relating to affidavits apply to affirmations with the following exceptions:

(1) the deponent should commence 'I (*name*) of (*address*) do solemnly and sincerely affirm ....', and

(2) in the jurat the word 'sworn' is replaced by the word 'affirmed'.

WITNESS STATEMENTS

Heading

17.1 The witness statement should be headed with the title of the proceedings (see paragraph 4 of the practice direction supplementing Part 7 and paragraph 7 of the practice direction supplementing Part 20); where the proceedings are between several parties with the same status it is sufficient to identify the parties as follows:

	Number:
A.B. (and others)	Claimants/Applicants
C.D. (and others)	Defendants/Respondents
	(as appropriate)

17.2 At the top right hand corner of the first page there should be clearly written:

(1) the party on whose behalf it is made,

(2) the initials and surname of the witness,
(3) the number of the statement in relation to that witness,
(4) the identifying initials and number of each exhibit referred to, and
(5) the date the statement was made.

Body of witness statement

18.1 The witness statement must, if practicable, be in the intended witness's own words, the statement should be expressed in the first person and should also state:
(1) the full name of the witness,
(2) his place of residence or, if he is making the statement in his professional, business or other occupational capacity, the address at which he works, the position he holds and the name of his firm or employer,
(3) his occupation, or if he has none, his description, and
(4) the fact that he is a party to the proceedings or is the employee of such a party if it be the case.

18.2 A witness statement must indicate:
(1) which of the statements in it are made from the witness's own knowledge and which are matters of information or belief, and
(2) the source for any matters of information or belief.

18.3 An exhibit used in conjunction with a witness statement should be verified and identified by the witness and remain separate from the witness statement.

18.4 Where a witness refers to an exhibit or exhibits, he should state 'I refer to the (*description of exhibit*) marked ". . .'".

18.5 The provisions of paragraphs 11.3 to 15.4 (exhibits) apply similarly to witness statements as they do to affidavits.

18.6 Where a witness makes more than one witness statement to which there are exhibits, in the same proceedings, the numbering of the exhibits should run consecutively throughout and not start again with each witness statement.

Format of witness statement

19.1 A witness statement should:
(1) be produced on durable quality A4 paper with a 3.5cm margin,
(2) be fully legible and should normally be typed on one side of the paper only,
(3) where possible, be bound securely in a manner which would not hamper filing, or otherwise each page should be endorsed with the case number and should bear the initials of the witness,
(4) have the pages numbered consecutively as a separate statement (or as one of several statements contained in a file),
(5) be divided into numbered paragraphs,
(6) have all numbers, including dates, expressed in figures, and
(7) give in the margin the reference to any document or documents mentioned.

19.2 It is usually convenient for a witness statement to follow the chronological sequence of the events or matters dealt with, each paragraph of a witness statement should as far as possible be confined to a distinct portion of the subject.

Statement of truth

20.1 A witness statement is the equivalent of the oral evidence which that witness would, if called, give in evidence; it must include a statement by the intended witness that he believes the facts in it are true[15].

20.2 To verify a witness statement the statement of truth is as follows:

'I believe that the facts stated in this witness statement are true'

20.3 Attention is drawn to rule 32.14 which sets out the consequences of verifying a witness statement containing a false statement without an honest belief in its truth.

Inability of witness to read or sign statement

21.1 Where a witness statement is made by a person who is unable to read or sign the witness statement, it must contain a certificate made by an authorised person.

---

[15] See Part 22 for information about the statement of truth.

21.2 An authorised person is a person able to administer oaths and take affidavits but need not be independent of the parties or their representatives.

21.3 The authorised person must certify:

(1) that the witness statement has been read to the witness,

(2) that the witness appeared to understand it and approved its content as accurate,

(3) that the declaration of truth has been read to the witness,

(4) that the witness appeared to understand the declaration and the consequences of making a false witness statement, and

(5) that the witness signed or made his mark in the presence of the authorised person.

21.4 The form of the certificate is set out at Annex 2 to this practice direction.

Alterations to witness statements

22.1 Any alteration to a witness statement must be initialled by the person making the statement or by the authorised person where appropriate (see paragraph 21).

22.2 A witness statement which contains an alteration that has not been initialled may be used in evidence only with the permission of the court.

Filing of witness statements

23.1 If the court directs that a witness statement is to be filed[16], it must be filed in the court or Division, or Office or Registry of the court or Division where the action in which it was or is to be used, is proceeding or will proceed.

23.2 Where the court has directed that a witness statement in a foreign language is to be filed:

(1) the party wishing to rely on it must—

(a) have it translated, and

(b) file the foreign language witness statement with the court, and

(2) the translator must make and file with the court an affidavit verifying the translation and exhibiting both the translation and a copy of the foreign language witness statement.

Certificate of court officer

24.1 Where the court has ordered that a witness statement is not to be open to inspection by the public[17] or that words or passages in the statement are not to be open to inspection[18] the court officer will so certify on the statement and make any deletions directed by the court under rule 32.13(4).

Defects in affidavits, witness statements and exhibits

25.1 Where:

(1) an affidavit,

(2) a witness statement, or

(3) an exhibit to either an affidavit or a witness statement

does not comply with Part 32 or this practice direction in relation to its form, the court may refuse to admit it as evidence and may refuse to allow the costs arising from its preparation.

25.2 Permission to file a defective affidavit or witness statement or to use a defective exhibit may be obtained from a judge[19] in the court where the case is proceeding.

STATEMENTS OF CASE

26.1 A statement of case may be used as evidence in an interim application provided it is verified by a statement of truth[20].

26.2 To verify a statement of case the statement of truth should be set out as follows:

---

[16] Rule 32.4(3)(b).
[17] Rule 32.13(2).
[18] Rule 32.13(4).
[19] Rule 2.3(1); definition of judge.
[20] See rule 32.6(2)(a).

'[I believe] [the (*party on whose behalf the statement of case is being signed*) believes] that the facts stated in the statement of case are true'.

26.3 Attention is drawn to rule 32.14 which sets out the consequences of verifying a witness statement containing a false statement without an honest belief in its truth.

(For information regarding statements of truth see Part 22 and the practice direction which supplements it.)

(Practice directions supplementing Parts 7, 9 and 17 provide further information concerning statements of case.)

ANNEX 1

CERTIFICATE TO BE USED WHERE A DEPONENT TO AN AFFIDAVIT IS UNABLE TO READ OR SIGN IT

Sworn at ...... this ...... day of ...... Before me, I having first read over the contents of this affidavit to the deponent [*if there are exhibits, add* 'and explained the nature and effect of the exhibits referred to in it'] who appeared to understand it and approved its content as accurate, and made his mark on the affidavit in my presence.

Or, (after, *Before me*) the witness to the mark of the deponent having been first sworn that he had read over etc. (*as above*) and that he saw him make his mark on the affidavit. (*Witness must sign*).

CERTIFICATE TO BE USED WHERE A DEPONENT TO AN AFFIRMATION IS UNABLE TO READ OR SIGN IT

Affirmed at ...... this ...... day of ...... Before me, I having first read over the contents of this affirmation to the deponent [*if there are exhibits, add* 'and explained the nature and effect of the exhibits referred to in it'] who appeared to understand it and approved its content as accurate, and made his mark on the affirmation in my presence.

Or, (after, *Before me*) the witness to the mark of the deponent having been first sworn that he had read over etc. (*as above*) and that he saw him make his mark on the affirmation. (*Witness must sign*).

ANNEX 2

CERTIFICATE TO BE USED WHERE A WITNESS IS UNABLE TO READ OR SIGN A WITNESS STATEMENT

I certify that I [*name and address of authorised person*] have read over the contents of this witness statement and the declaration of truth to the witness [*if there are exhibits, add* 'and explained the nature and effect of the exhibits referred to in it'] who appeared to understand (a) the statement and approved its content as accurate and (b) the declaration of truth and the consequences of making a false witness statement, and made his mark in my presence.

CPR PART 33 MISCELLANEOUS RULES ABOUT EVIDENCE

CONTENTS OF THIS PART
Introductory	Rule 33.1
Notice of intention to rely on hearsay evidence	Rule 33.2
Circumstances in which notice of intention to rely on hearsay evidence is not required	Rule 33.3
Power to call witness for cross-examination on hearsay evidence	Rule 33.4
Credibility	Rule 33.5
Use of plans, photographs and models as evidence	Rule 33.6
Evidence of finding on question of foreign law	Rule 33.7
Evidence of consent of trustee to act	Rule 33.8

33.1 INTRODUCTORY
In this Part—
    (a) 'hearsay' means a statement made, otherwise than by a person while giving oral evidence in proceedings, which is tendered as evidence of the matters stated; and
    (b) references to hearsay include hearsay of whatever degree.

33.2 NOTICE OF INTENTION TO RELY ON HEARSAY EVIDENCE
    (1) Where a party intends to rely on hearsay evidence at trial and either—
    (a) that evidence is to be given by a witness giving oral evidence; or
    (b) that evidence is contained in a witness statement of a person who is not being called to give oral evidence;
that party complies with section 2(1)(a) of the Civil Evidence Act 1995 by serving a witness statement on the other parties in accordance with the court's order.
    (2) Where paragraph (1)(b) applies, the party intending to rely on the hearsay evidence must, when he serves the witness statement—
    (a) inform the other parties that the witness is not being called to give oral evidence; and
    (b) give the reason why the witness will not be called.
    (3) In all other cases where a party intends to rely on hearsay evidence at trial, that party complies with section 2(1)(a) of the Civil Evidence Act 1995 by serving a notice on the other parties which—
    (a) identifies the hearsay evidence;
    (b) states that the party serving the notice proposes to rely on the hearsay evidence at trial; and
    (c) gives the reason why the witness will not be called.
    (4) The party proposing to rely on the hearsay evidence must—
    (a) serve the notice no later than the latest date for serving witness statements; and
    (b) if the hearsay evidence is to be in a document, supply a copy to any party who requests him to do so.

33.3 CIRCUMSTANCES IN WHICH NOTICE OF INTENTION TO RELY ON HEARSAY EVIDENCE IS NOT REQUIRED
Section 2(1) of the Civil Evidence Act 1995 (duty to give notice of intention to rely on hearsay evidence) does not apply—
    (a) to evidence at hearings other than trials;
    (aa) to an affidavit or witness statement which is to be used at trial but which does not contain hearsay evidence;
    (b) to a statement which a party to a probate action wishes to put in evidence and which is alleged to have been made by the person whose estate is the subject of the proceedings; or
    (c) where the requirement is excluded by a practice direction.

33.4 POWER TO CALL WITNESS FOR CROSS-EXAMINATION ON HEARSAY EVIDENCE

(1) Where a party—
   (a) proposes to rely on hearsay evidence; and
   (b) does not propose to call the person who made the original statement to give oral evidence,

the court may, on the application of any other party, permit that party to call the maker of the statement to be cross-examined on the contents of the statement.

(2) An application for permission to cross-examine under this rule must be made not more than 14 days after the day on which a notice of intention to rely on the hearsay evidence was served on the applicant.

33.5 CREDIBILITY

(1) Where a party—
   (a) proposes to rely on hearsay evidence; but
   (b) does not propose to call the person who made the original statement to give oral evidence; and
   (c) another party wishes to call evidence to attack the credibility of the person who made the statement,

the party who so wishes must give notice of his intention to the party who proposes to give the hearsay statement in evidence.

(2) A party must give notice under paragraph (1) not more than 14 days after the day on which a hearsay notice relating to the hearsay evidence was served on him.

33.6 USE OF PLANS, PHOTOGRAPHS AND MODELS AS EVIDENCE

(1) This rule applies to evidence (such as a plan, photograph or model) which is not—
   (a) contained in a witness statement, affidavit$^{(GL)}$ or expert's report;
   (b) to be given orally at trial; or
   (c) evidence of which prior notice must be given under rule 33.2.

(2) This rule includes documents which may be received in evidence without further proof under section 9 of the Civil Evidence Act 1995.

(3) Unless the court orders otherwise the evidence shall not be receivable at a trial unless the party intending to put it in evidence has given notice to the other parties in accordance with this rule.

(4) Where the party intends to use the evidence as evidence of any fact then, except where paragraph (6) applies, he must give notice not later than the latest date for serving witness statements.

(5) He must give notice at least 21 days before the hearing at which he proposes to put in the evidence, if—
   (a) there are not to be witness statements; or
   (b) he intends to put in the evidence solely in order to disprove an allegation made in a witness statement.

(6) Where the evidence forms part of expert evidence, he must give notice when the expert's report is served on the other party.

(7) Where the evidence is being produced to the court for any reason other than as part of factual or expert evidence, he must give notice at least 21 days before the hearing at which he proposes to put in the evidence.

(8) Where a party has given notice that he intends to put in the evidence, he must give every other party an opportunity to inspect it and to agree to its admission without further proof.

33.7 EVIDENCE OF FINDING ON QUESTION OF FOREIGN LAW

(1) This rule sets out the procedure which must be followed by a party who intends to put in evidence a finding on a question of foreign law by virtue of section 4(2) of the Civil Evidence Act 1972.

(2) He must give any other party notice of his intention.

(3) He must give the notice—
   (a) if there are to be witness statements, not later than the latest date for serving them; or

(b) otherwise, not less than 21 days before the hearing at which he proposes to put the finding in evidence.
  (4) The notice must—
    (a) specify the question on which the finding was made; and
    (b) enclose a copy of a document where it is reported or recorded.

33.8 EVIDENCE OF CONSENT OF TRUSTEE TO ACT

A document purporting to contain the written consent of a person to act as trustee and to bear his signature verified by some other person is evidence of such consent.

PD 33 PRACTICE DIRECTION — CIVIL EVIDENCE ACT 1995

This practice direction supplements CPR Part 33

1. Section 16(3A) of the Civil Evidence Act 1995 (as amended) provides that transitional provisions for the application of the provisions of the Civil Evidence Act 1995 to proceedings begun before 31st January 1997 may be made by practice direction.

2. Except as provided for by paragraph 3, the provisions of the Civil Evidence Act 1995 apply to claims commenced before 31st January 1997.

3. The provisions of the Civil Evidence Act 1995 do not apply to claims—

(a) in which directions have been given, or orders have been made, as to the evidence to be given at the trial or hearing; or

(b) where the trial or hearing began before 26th April 1999.

CPR PART 34 DEPOSITIONS AND COURT ATTENDANCE BY WITNESSES

CONTENTS OF THIS PART
Scope of this Part	Rule 34.1
Witness summonses	Rule 34.2
Issue of a witness summons	Rule 34.3
Witness summons in aid of inferior court or of tribunal	Rule 34.4
Time for serving a witness summons	Rule 34.5
Who is to serve a witness summons	Rule 34.6
Right of witness to travelling expenses and compensation for loss of time	Rule 34.7
Evidence by deposition	Rule 34.8
Conduct of examination	Rule 34.9
Enforcing attendance of witness	Rule 34.10
Use of deposition at a hearing	Rule 34.11
Restrictions on subsequent use of deposition taken for the purpose of any hearing except the trial	Rule 34.12
Where a person to be examined is out of the jurisdiction — letter of request	Rule 34.13
Fees and expenses of examiner [of the court*]	Rule 34.14
Examiners of the court	Rule 34.15

34.1 SCOPE OF THIS PART
 (1) This Part provides—
  (a) for the circumstances in which a person may be required to attend court to give evidence or to produce a document; and
  (b) for a party to obtain evidence before a hearing to be used at the hearing.
 (2) In this Part, reference to a hearing includes a reference to the trial.

34.2 WITNESS SUMMONSES
 (1) A witness summons is a document issued by the court requiring a witness to—
  (a) attend court to give evidence; or
  (b) produce documents to the court.
 (2) A witness summons must be in the relevant practice form.
 (3) There must be a separate witness summons for each witness.
 (4) A witness summons may require a witness to produce documents to the court either—
  (a) on the date fixed for a hearing; or
  (b) on such date as the court may direct.
 (5) The only documents that a summons under this rule can require a person to produce before a hearing are documents which that person could be required to produce at the hearing.

34.3 ISSUE OF A WITNESS SUMMONS
 (1) A witness summons is issued on the date entered on the summons by the court.
 (2) A party must obtain permission from the court where he wishes to—
  (a) have a summons issued less than 7 days before the date of the trial;
  (b) have a summons issued for a witness to attend court to give evidence or to produce documents on any date except the date fixed for the trial; or
  (c) have a summons issued for a witness to attend court to give evidence or to produce documents at any hearing except the trial.
 (3) A witness summons must be issued by—

---

* By oversight these words were not added to the contents list in SI 1998/3132 when r. 34.14 was amended by SI 1999/1008.

(a) the court where the case is proceeding; or
(b) the court where the hearing in question will be held.

(4) The court may set aside$^{(GL)}$ or vary a witness summons issued under this rule.

34.4 WITNESS SUMMONS IN AID OF INFERIOR COURT OR OF TRIBUNAL

(1) The court may issue a witness summons in aid of an inferior court or of a tribunal.

(2) The court which issued the witness summons under this rule may set it aside.

(3) In this rule, 'inferior court or tribunal' means any court or tribunal that does not have power to issue a witness summons in relation to proceedings before it.

34.5 TIME FOR SERVING A WITNESS SUMMONS

(1) The general rule is that a witness summons is binding if it is served at least 7 days before the date on which the witness is required to attend before the court or tribunal.

(2) The court may direct that a witness summons shall be binding although it will be served less than 7 days before the date on which the witness is required to attend before the court or tribunal.

(3) A witness summons which is—
   (a) served in accordance with this rule; and
   (b) requires the witness to attend court to give evidence,
is binding until the conclusion of the hearing at which the attendance of the witness is required.

34.6 WHO IS TO SERVE A WITNESS SUMMONS

(1) A witness summons is to be served by the court unless the party on whose behalf it is issued indicates in writing, when he asks the court to issue the summons, that he wishes to serve it himself.

(2) Where the court is to serve the witness summons, the party on whose behalf it is issued must deposit, in the court office, the money to be paid or offered to the witness under rule 34.7.

34.7 RIGHT OF WITNESS TO TRAVELLING EXPENSES AND COMPENSATION FOR LOSS OF TIME

At the time of service of a witness summons the witness must be offered or paid—
   (a) a sum reasonably sufficient to cover his expenses in travelling to and from the court; and
   (b) such sum by way of compensation for loss of time as may be specified in the relevant practice direction.

34.8 EVIDENCE BY DEPOSITION

(1) A party may apply for an order for a person to be examined before the hearing takes place.

(2) A person from whom evidence is to be obtained following an order under this rule is referred to as a 'deponent' and the evidence is referred to as a 'deposition'.

(3) An order under this rule shall be for a deponent to be examined on oath before—
   (a) a judge;
   (b) an examiner of the court; or
   (c) such other person as the court appoints.
(Rule 34.15 makes provision for the appointment of examiners of the court)

(4) The order may require the production of any document which the court considers is necessary for the purposes of the examination.

(5) The order must state the date, time and place of the examination.

(6) At the time of service of the order the deponent must be offered or paid—

CPR PART 34   DEPOSITIONS AND COURT ATTENDANCE BY WITNESSES

(a) a sum reasonably sufficient to cover his expenses in travelling to and from the place of examination; and

(b) such sum by way of compensation for loss of time as may be specified in the relevant practice direction.

(7) Where the court makes an order for a deposition to be taken, it may also order the party who obtained the order to serve a witness statement or witness summary in relation to the evidence to be given by the person to be examined.

(Part 32 contains the general rules about witness statements and witness summaries)

34.9   CONDUCT OF EXAMINATION

(1) Subject to any directions contained in the order for examination, the examination must be conducted in the same way as if the witness were giving evidence at a trial.

(2) If all the parties are present, the examiner may conduct the examination of a person not named in the order for examination if all the parties and the person to be examined consent.

(3) The examiner may conduct the examination in private if he considers it appropriate to do so.

(4) The examiner must ensure that the evidence given by the witness is recorded in full.

(5) The examiner must send a copy of the deposition—

(a) to the person who obtained the order for the examination of the witness; and

(b) to the court where the case is proceeding.

(6) The party who obtained the order must send each of the other parties a copy of the deposition which he receives from the examiner.

34.10   ENFORCING ATTENDANCE OF WITNESS

(1) If a person served with an order to attend before an examiner—

(a) fails to attend; or

(b) refuses to be sworn for the purpose of the examination or to answer any lawful question or produce any document at the examination,

a certificate of his failure or refusal, signed by the examiner, must be filed by the party requiring the deposition.

(2) On the certificate being filed, the party requiring the deposition may apply to the court for an order requiring that person to attend or to be sworn or to answer any question or produce any document, as the case may be.

(3) An application for an order under this rule may be made without notice.

(4) The court may order the person against whom an order is made under this rule to pay any costs resulting from his failure or refusal.

34.11   USE OF DEPOSITION AT A HEARING

(1) A deposition ordered under rule 34.8 may be given in evidence at a hearing unless the court orders otherwise.

(2) A party intending to put in evidence a deposition at a hearing must serve notice of his intention to do so on every other party.

(3) He must serve the notice at least 21 days before the day fixed for the hearing.

(4) The court may require a deponent to attend the hearing and give evidence orally.

(5) Where a deposition is given in evidence at trial, it shall be treated as if it were a witness statement for the purposes of rule 32.13 (availability of witness statements for inspection).

34.12   RESTRICTIONS ON SUBSEQUENT USE OF DEPOSITION TAKEN FOR THE PURPOSE OF ANY HEARING EXCEPT THE TRIAL

(1) Where the court orders a party to be examined about his or any other assets for the purpose of any hearing except the trial, the deposition may be used only for the purpose of the proceedings in which the order was made.

(2) However, it may be used for some other purpose—
   (a) by the party who was examined;
   (b) if the party who was examined agrees; or
   (c) if the court gives permission.

34.13 WHERE A PERSON TO BE EXAMINED IS OUT OF THE JURISDICTION — LETTER OF REQUEST

(1) Where a party wishes to take a deposition from a person outside the jurisdiction, the High Court may order the issue of a letter of request to the judicial authorities of the country in which the proposed deponent is.

(2) A letter of request is a request to a judicial authority to take the evidence of that person, or arrange for it to be taken.

(3) The High Court may make an order under this rule in relation to county court proceedings.

(4) If the government of a country allows a person appointed by the High Court to examine a person in that country, the High Court may make an order appointing a special examiner for that purpose.

(5) A person may be examined under this rule on oath or affirmation or in accordance with any procedure permitted in the country in which the examination is to take place.

(6) If the High Court makes an order for the issue of a letter of request, the party who sought the order must file—
   (a) the following documents and, except where paragraph (7) applies, a translation of them—
      (i) a draft letter of request;
      (ii) a statement of the issues relevant to the proceedings;
      (iii) a list of questions or the subject matter of questions to be put to the person to be examined; and
   (b) an undertaking to be responsible for the Secretary of State's expenses.

(7) There is no need to file a translation if—
   (a) English is one of the official languages of the country where the examination is to take place; or
   (b) a practice direction has specified that country as a country where no translation is necessary.

34.14 FEES AND EXPENSES OF EXAMINER OF THE COURT

(1) An examiner of the court may charge a fee for the examination.

(2) He need not send the deposition to the court unless the fee is paid.

(3) The examiner's fees and expenses must be paid by the party who obtained the order for examination.

(4) If the fees and expenses due to an examiner are not paid within a reasonable time, he may report that fact to the court.

(5) The court may order the party who obtained the order for examination to deposit in the court office a specified sum in respect of the examiner's fees and, where it does so, the examiner will not be asked to act until the sum has been deposited.

(6) An order under this rule does not affect any decision as to the party who is ultimately to bear the costs of the examination.

34.15 EXAMINERS OF THE COURT

(1) The Lord Chancellor shall appoint persons to be examiners of the court.

(2) The persons appointed shall be barristers or solicitor-advocates who have been practising for a period of not less than three years.

(3) The Lord Chancellor may revoke an appointment at any time.

(Other relevant rules can be found in Schedule 1, in the following RSC—
O.70 (obtaining evidence for foreign court); O.79 (issue of witness summons in relation to criminal proceedings in the High Court))

PD 34 PRACTICE DIRECTION — DEPOSITIONS AND COURT ATTENDANCE BY WITNESSES

This practice direction supplements CPR Part 34.

WITNESS SUMMONSES

Issue of witness summons
1.1 A witness summons may require a witness to:
 (1) attend court to give evidence,
 (2) produce documents to the court, or
 (3) both,
on either a date fixed for the hearing or such date as the court may direct[1].
1.2 Two copies of the witness summons[2] should be filed with the court for sealing, one of which will be retained on the court file.
1.3 A mistake in the name or address of a person named in a witness summons may be corrected if the summons has not been served.
1.4 The corrected summons must be re-sealed by the court and marked 'Amended and Re-Sealed'.

Witness summons issued in aid of an inferior court or tribunal
2.1 A witness summons may be issued in the High Court or a county court in aid of a court or tribunal which does not have the power to issue a witness summons in relation to the proceedings before it[3].
2.2 A witness summons referred to in paragraph 2.1 may be set aside by the court which issued it[4].
2.3 An application to set aside a witness summons referred to in paragraph 2.1 will be heard:
 (1) in the High Court by a Master at the Royal Courts of Justice or by a district judge in a District Registry, and
 (2) in a county court by a district judge.
2.4 Unless the court otherwise directs, the applicant must give at least 2 days' notice to the party who issued the witness summons of the application, which will normally be dealt with at a hearing.

Travelling expenses and compensation for loss of time
3.1 When a witness is served with a witness summons he must be offered a sum to cover his travelling expenses to and from the court and compensation for his loss of time[5].
3.2 If the witness summons is to be served by the court, the party issuing the summons must deposit with the court:
 (1) a sum sufficient to pay for the witness's expenses in travelling to the court and in returning to his home or place of work, and
 (2) a sum in respect of the period during which earnings or benefit are lost, or such lesser sum as it may be proved that the witness will lose as a result of his attendance at court in answer to the witness summons.
3.3 The sum referred to in 3.2(2) is to be based on the sums payable to witnesses attending the Crown Court[6].

---

[1] Rule 34.2(4).
[2] in Practice form N20.
[3] Rule 34.4(1).
[4] Rule 34.4(2).
[5] Rule 34.7.
[6] Fixed pursuant to the Prosecution of Offences Act 1985 and the Costs in Criminal Cases (General) Regulations 1986.

PD 34 PRACTICE DIRECTION — DEPOSITIONS ETC.

3.4 Where the party issuing the witness summons wishes to serve it himself[7], he must:

(1) notify the court in writing that he wishes to do so, and

(2) at the time of service offer the witness the sums mentioned in paragraph 3.2 above.

DEPOSITIONS

To be taken in England and Wales for use as evidence in proceedings in courts in England and Wales

4.1 A party may apply for an order for a person to be examined on oath before:

(1) a judge,

(2) an examiner of the court, or

(3) such other person as the court may appoint[8].

4.2 The party who obtains an order for the examination of a deponent[9] before an examiner of the court[10] must:

(1) apply to the Foreign Process Section of the Masters' Secretary's Department at the Royal Courts of Justice for the allocation of an examiner,

(2) when allocated, provide the examiner with copies of all documents in the proceedings necessary to inform the examiner of the issues, and

(3) pay the deponent a sum to cover his travelling expenses to and from the examination and compensation for his loss of time[11].

4.3 In ensuring that the deponent's evidence is recorded in full, the court or the examiner may permit it to be recorded on audiotape or videotape, but the deposition[12] must always be recorded in writing by him or by a competent shorthand writer or stenographer.

4.4 If the deposition is not recorded word for word, it must contain, as nearly as may be, the statement of the deponent; the examiner may record word for word any particular questions and answers which appear to him to have special importance.

4.5 If a deponent objects to answering any question or where any objection is taken to any question, the examiner must:

(1) record in the deposition or a document attached to it—

(a) the question,

(b) the nature of and grounds for the objection, and

(c) any answer given, and

(2) give his opinion as to the validity of the objection and must record it in the deposition or a document attached to it.

The court will decide as to the validity of the objection and any question of costs arising from it.

4.6 Documents and exhibits must:

(1) have an identifying number or letter marked on them by the examiner, and

(2) be preserved by the party or his legal representative[13] who obtained the order for the examination, or as the court or the examiner may direct.

4.7 The examiner may put any question to the deponent as to:

(1) the meaning of any of his answers, or

(2) any matter arising in the course of the examination.

4.8 Where a deponent:

(1) fails to attend the examination, or

(2) refuses to:

(a) be sworn, or

---

[7] Rule 34.6(1).
[8] Rule 34.8(3).
[9] See rule 34.8(2) for explanation of 'deponent' and 'deposition'.
[10] For the appointment of examiners of the court see rule 34.15.
[11] Rule 34.8(6).
[12] See rule 34.8(2) for explanation of 'deponent' and 'deposition'.
[13] For the definition of legal representative see rule 2.3.

PD 34 PRACTICE DIRECTION — DEPOSITIONS ETC.

    (b) answer any lawful question, or
    (c) produce any document,
the examiner will sign a certificate[14] of such failure or refusal and may include in his certificate any comment as to the conduct of the deponent or of any person attending the examination.

4.9 The party who obtained the order for the examination must file the certificate with the court and may apply for an order that the deponent attend for examination or as may be[15]. The application may be made without notice[16].

4.10 The court will make such order on the application as it thinks fit including an order for the deponent to pay any costs resulting from his failure or refusal[17].

4.11 A deponent who wilfully refuses to obey an order made against him under Part 34 may be proceeded against for contempt of court.

4.12 A deposition must:
    (1) be signed by the examiner,
    (2) have any amendments to it initialled by the examiner and the deponent,
    (3) be endorsed by the examiner with—
        (a) a statement of the time occupied by the examination, and
        (b) a record of any refusal by the deponent to sign the deposition and of his reasons for not doing so, and
    (4) be sent by the examiner to the court where the proceedings are taking place for filing on the court file.

4.13 Rule 34.14 deals with the fees and expenses of an examiner.

Depositions to be taken abroad for use as evidence in proceedings before courts in England and Wales

5.1 Where a party wishes to take a deposition from a person outside the jurisdiction, the High Court may order the issue of a letter of request to the judicial authorities of the country in which the proposed deponent is[18].

5.2 An application for an order referred to in paragraph 5.1 should be made by application notice in accordance with Part 23.

5.3 The documents which a party applying for an order for the issue of a letter of request must file with his application notice are set out in rule 34.13(6). They are as follows:
    (1) a draft letter of request is set out in Annex A to this practice direction,
    (2) a statement of the issues relevant to the proceedings,
    (3) a list of questions or the subject matter of questions to be put to the proposed deponent,
    (4) a translation of the documents in (1), (2) and (3) above unless the proposed deponent is in a country—
        (a) of which English is one of the official languages, or
        (b) listed at Annex B to this practice direction, unless the particular circumstances of the case require a translation,
    (5) an undertaking to be responsible for the expenses of the Secretary of State, and
    (6) a draft order.

5.4 The above documents should be filed with the Masters' Secretary in Room E214, Royal Courts of Justice, Strand, London WC2A 2LL.

5.5 The application will be dealt with by the Senior Master of the Queen's Bench Division of the High Court who will, if appropriate, sign the letter of request.

5.6 Attention is drawn to the provisions of rule 23.10 (application to vary or discharge an order made without notice).

5.7 If parties are in doubt as to whether a translation under paragraph 5.3(4) above is required, they should seek guidance from the Foreign Process Section of the Masters' Secretary's Department.

---

[14] Rule 34.10.
[15] Rule 34.10(2) and (3).
[16] Rule 34.10(3).
[17] Rule 34.10(4).
[18] Rule 34.13(1).

PD 34 PRACTICE DIRECTION — DEPOSITIONS ETC.

5.8 A special examiner appointed under rule 34.13(4) may be the British Consul or the Consul-General or his deputy in the country where the evidence is to be taken if:

(1) there is in respect of that country a Civil Procedure Convention providing for the taking of evidence in that country for the assistance of proceedings in the High Court or other court in this country, or

(2) with the consent of the Secretary of State.

5.9 The provisions of paragraphs 4.1 to 4.12 above apply to the depositions referred to in this paragraph.

Depositions to be taken in England and Wales for use as evidence in proceedings before courts abroad pursuant to letters of request

6.1 RSC Order 70, in Schedule 1, relates to obtaining evidence for foreign courts and should be read in conjunction with this part of the practice direction.

6.2 The Evidence (Proceedings in Other Jurisdictions) Act 1975 applies to these depositions.

6.3 Where a letter of request is received:

(1) by the Secretary of State and forwarded to the Senior Master on the basis that the request should be dealt with without the attendance of any party (or their agent) to the foreign proceedings, and

(2) by the Senior Master under a Civil Procedure Convention where no person has been named to make the necessary application,

the Senior Master will send the request to the Treasury Solicitor who will, with the consent of the Treasury, make an application to give effect to the request.

6.4 The Treasury Solicitor will arrange for the examination to take place at a specified time and place before an examiner of the court or such other person as the court may appoint.

6.5 The application should be made by the issue of a claim form under the Part 8 procedure and should be supported by evidence containing the following:

(1) the letter of request,

(2) a statement of the issues relevant to the proceedings,

(3) a list of questions or the subject matter of questions to be put to the proposed deponent,

(4) a translation of the documents in (1), (2) and (3) above if necessary, and

(5) a draft order.

6.6 The provisions of paragraphs 4.2 to 4.12 apply to the depositions referred to in this paragraph, except that the examiner must send the deposition to the Senior Master.

(For further information about evidence see Part 32 and the practice direction which supplements it.)

ANNEX A

DRAFT LETTER OF REQUEST

To the Competent Judicial Authority of
in the   of

I [name] Senior Master of the Queen's Bench Division of the Supreme Court of England and Wales respectfully request the assistance of your court with regard to the following matters.

1. A claim is now pending in the   Division of the High Court of Justice in England and Wales entitled as follows
[*set out full title and claim number*]
in which [*name*] of [*address*] is the claimant and [*name*] of [*address*] is the defendant.

2. The names and addresses of the representatives or agents of [*set out names and addresses of representatives of the parties*].

3. The claim by the claimant is for:—

   (a) [*set out the nature of the claim*]
   (b) [*the relief sought, and*]

PD 34   PRACTICE DIRECTION — DEPOSITIONS ETC.

(c) [*a summary of the facts.*]

4. It is necessary for the purposes of justice and for the due determination of the matters in dispute between the parties that you cause the following witnesses, who are resident within your jurisdiction, to be examined. The names and addresses of the witnesses are as follows:—

5. The witnesses should be examined on oath or if that is not possible within your laws or is impossible of performance by reason of the internal practice and procedure of your court or by reason of practical difficulties, they should be examined in accordance with whatever procedure your laws provide for in these matters.

6. Either/
The witnesses should be examined in accordance with the list of questions annexed hereto.
Or/
The witnesses should be examined regarding [*set out full details of evidence sought*]
N.B. Where the witness is required to produce documents, these should be clearly identified.

7. I would ask that you cause me, or the agents of the parties (if appointed), to be informed of the date and place where the examination is to take place.

8. Finally, I request that you will cause the evidence of the said witnesses to be reduced into writing and all documents produced on such examinations to be duly marked for identification and that you will further be pleased to authenticate such examinations by the seal of your court or in such other way as is in accordance with your procedure and return the written evidence and documents produced to me addressed as follows:—

Senior Master of the Queen's Bench Division
Royal Courts of Justice
Strand
London WC2A 2LL
England

ANNEX B

Countries where the translation referred to in paragraph 5.3(4) above should not be required:
Australia
Canada (other than Quebec)
Holland
New Zealand
The United States of America

PD 34B PRACTICE DIRECTION — FEES FOR EXAMINERS OF THE COURT

This practice direction supplements CPR Part 34

SCOPE

1.1 This practice direction sets out—

(1) how to calculate the fees an examiner of the court ('an examiner') may charge; and

(2) the expenses he may recover.

(CPR Rule 34.8(3)(b) provides that the court may make an order for evidence to be obtained by the examination of a witness before an examiner of the court).

1.2 The party who obtained the order for the examination must pay the fees and expenses of the examiner.

(CPR rule 34.14 permits an examiner to charge a fee for the examination and contains other provisions about his fees and expenses, and rule 34.15 provides who may be appointed as an examiner of the court).

THE EXAMINATION FEE

2.1 An examiner may charge an hourly rate for each hour (or part of an hour) that he is engaged in examining the witness.

2.2 The hourly rate is to be calculated by reference to the formula set out in paragraph 3.

2.3 The examination fee will be the hourly rate multiplied by the number of hours the examination has taken. For example—

Examination fee = hourly rate × number of hours.

HOW TO CALCULATE THE HOURLY RATE — THE FORMULA

3.1 Divide the amount of the minimum annual salary of a post within Group 7 of the judicial salary structure as designated by the Review Body on Senior Salaries[1], by 220 to give 'x'; and then divide 'x' by 6 to give **the hourly rate**. For example:

$$\frac{\text{minimum annual salary}}{220} = x$$

$$\frac{x}{6} = \text{hourly rate}$$

SINGLE FEE CHARGEABLE ON MAKING THE APPOINTMENT FOR EXAMINATION

4.1 An examiner of court is also entitled to charge a single fee of twice the hourly rate (calculated in accordance with paragraph 3 above) as 'the appointment fee' when the appointment for the examination is made.

4.2 The examiner is entitled to retain the appointment fee where the witness fails to attend on the date and time arranged.

4.3 Where the examiner fails to attend on the date and time arranged he may not charge a further appointment fee for arranging a subsequent appointment.

(The examiner need not send the deposition to the court until his fees are paid — see CPR rule 34.14 (2)).

EXAMINERS' EXPENSES

5.1 The examiner of court is also entitled to recover the following expenses—

1) all reasonable travelling expenses;

(2) any other expenses reasonably incurred; and

---

[1] The Report of the Review Body on Senior Salaries is published annually by the Stationery Office.

PD 34B PRACTICE DIRECTION — FEES FOR EXAMINERS OF THE COURT

(3) subject to paragraph 5,2, any reasonable charge for the room where the examination takes place.

5.2 No expenses may be recovered under sub-paragraph (3) above if the examination takes place at the examiner's usual business address.

(If the examiner's fees and expenses are not paid within a reasonable time he may report the fact to the court, see CPR Rule 34.14 (4) and (5)).

CPR PART 35 EXPERTS AND ASSESSORS

CONTENTS OF THIS PART
Duty to restrict expert evidence	Rule 35.1
Interpretation	Rule 35.2
Experts — overriding duty to the court	Rule 35.3
Court's power to restrict expert evidence	Rule 35.4
General requirement for expert evidence to be given in written report	Rule 35.5
Written questions to experts	Rule 35.6
Court's power to direct that evidence is to be given by a single joint expert	Rule 35.7
Instructions to a single joint expert	Rule 35.8
Power of court to direct party to provide information	Rule 35.9
Contents of report	Rule 35.10
Use by one party of expert's report disclosed by another	Rule 35.11
Discussions between experts	Rule 35.12
Consequence of failure to disclose expert's report	Rule 35.13
Expert's right to ask court for directions	Rule 35.14
Assessors	Rule 35.15

35.1 DUTY TO RESTRICT EXPERT EVIDENCE
Expert evidence shall be restricted to that which is reasonably required to resolve the proceedings.

35.2 INTERPRETATION
A reference to an 'expert' in this Part is a reference to an expert who has been instructed to give or prepare evidence for the purpose of court proceedings.

35.3 EXPERTS — OVERRIDING DUTY TO THE COURT
(1) It is the duty of an expert to help the court on the matters within his expertise.
(2) This duty overrides any obligation to the person from whom he has received instructions or by whom he is paid.

35.4 COURT'S POWER TO RESTRICT EXPERT EVIDENCE
(1) No party may call an expert or put in evidence an expert's report without the court's permission.
(2) When a party applies for permission under this rule he must identify—
 (a) the field in which he wishes to rely on expert evidence; and
 (b) where practicable the expert in that field on whose evidence he wishes to rely.
(3) If permission is granted under this rule it shall be in relation only to the expert named or the field identified under paragraph (2).
(4) The court may limit the amount of the expert's fees and expenses that the party who wishes to rely on the expert may recover from any other party.

35.5 GENERAL REQUIREMENT FOR EXPERT EVIDENCE TO BE GIVEN IN A WRITTEN REPORT
(1) Expert evidence is to be given in a written report unless the court directs otherwise.
(2) If a claim is on the fast track, the court will not direct an expert to attend a hearing unless it is necessary to do so in the interests of justice.

35.6 WRITTEN QUESTIONS TO EXPERTS
(1) A party may put to—
 (a) an expert instructed by another party; or
 (b) a single joint expert appointed under rule 35.7,
written questions about his report.

(2) Written questions under paragraph (1)—
  (a) may be put once only;
  (b) must be put within 28 days of service of the expert's report; and
  (c) must be for the purpose only of clarification of the report,
unless in any case—
    (i) the court gives permission; or
    (ii) the other party agrees.
(3) An expert's answers to questions put in accordance with paragraph (1) shall be treated as part of the expert's report.
(4) Where—
  (a) a party has put a written question to an expert instructed by another party in accordance with this rule; and
  (b) the expert does not answer that question,
the court may make one or both of the following orders in relation to the party who instructed the expert—
    (i) that the party may not rely on the evidence of that expert; or
    (ii) that the party may not recover the fees and expenses of that expert from any other party.

35.7 COURT'S POWER TO DIRECT THAT EVIDENCE IS TO BE GIVEN BY A SINGLE JOINT EXPERT

(1) Where two or more parties wish to submit expert evidence on a particular issue, the court may direct that the evidence on that issue is to given by one expert only.
(2) The parties wishing to submit the expert evidence are called 'the instructing parties'.
(3) Where the instructing parties cannot agree who should be the expert, the court may—
  (a) select the expert from a list prepared or identified by the instructing parties; or
  (b) direct that the expert be selected in such other manner as the court may direct.

35.8 INSTRUCTIONS TO A SINGLE JOINT EXPERT

(1) Where the court gives a direction under rule 35.7 for a single joint expert to be used, each instructing party may give instructions to the expert.
(2) When an instructing party gives instructions to the expert he must, at the same time, send a copy of the instructions to the other instructing parties.
(3) The court may give directions about—
  (a) the payment of the expert's fees and expenses; and
  (b) any inspection, examination or experiments which the expert wishes to carry out.
(4) The court may, before an expert is instructed—
  (a) limit the amount that can be paid by way of fees and expenses to the expert; and
  (b) direct that the instructing parties pay that amount into court.
(5) Unless the court otherwise directs, the instructing parties are jointly and severally liable[GL] for the payment of the expert's fees and expenses.

35.9 POWER OF COURT TO DIRECT A PARTY TO PROVIDE INFORMATION

Where a party has access to information which is not reasonably available to the other party, the court may direct the party who has access to the information to—
  (a) prepare and file a document recording the information; and
  (b) serve a copy of that document on the other party.

35.10 CONTENTS OF REPORT

(1) An expert's report must comply with the requirements set out in the relevant practice direction.
(2) At the end of an expert's report there must be a statement that—

CPR PART 35 EXPERTS AND ASSESSORS

    (a)   the expert understands his duty to the court; and
    (b)   he has complied with that duty.
   (3)   The expert's report must state the substance of all material instructions, whether written or oral, on the basis of which the report was written.
   (4)   The instructions referred to in paragraph (3) shall not be privileged[GL] against disclosure but the court will not, in relation to those instructions—
    (a)   order disclosure of any specific document; or
    (b)   permit any questioning in court, other than by the party who instructed the expert,
unless it is satisfied that there are reasonable grounds to consider the statement of instructions given under paragraph (3) to be inaccurate or incomplete.

35.11 USE BY ONE PARTY OF EXPERT'S REPORT DISCLOSED BY ANOTHER
Where a party has disclosed an expert's report, any party may use that expert's report as evidence at the trial.

35.12 DISCUSSIONS BETWEEN EXPERTS
   (1)   The court may, at any stage, direct a discussion between experts for the purpose of requiring the experts to—
    (a)   identify the issues in the proceedings; and
    (b)   where possible, reach agreement on an issue.
   (2)   The court may specify the issues which the experts must discuss.
   (3)   The court may direct that following a discussion between the experts they must prepare a statement for the court showing—
    (a)   those issues on which they agree; and
    (b)   those issues on which they disagree and a summary of their reasons for disagreeing.
   (4)   The content of the discussion between the experts shall not be referred to at the trial unless the parties agree.
   (5)   Where experts reach agreement on an issue during their discussions, the agreement shall not bind the parties unless the parties expressly agree to be bound by the agreement.

35.13 CONSEQUENCE OF FAILURE TO DISCLOSE EXPERT'S REPORT
A party who fails to disclose an expert's report may not use the report at the trial or call the expert to give evidence orally unless the court gives permission.

35.14 EXPERT'S RIGHT TO ASK COURT FOR DIRECTIONS
   (1)   An expert may file a written request for directions to assist him in carrying out his function as an expert.
   (2)   An expert may request directions under paragraph (1) without giving notice to any party.
   (3)   The court, when it gives directions, may also direct that a party be served with—
    (a)   a copy of the directions; and
    (b)   a copy of the request for directions.

35.15 ASSESSORS
   (1)   This rule applies where the court appoints one or more persons (an 'assessor') under section 70 of the Supreme Court Act 1981 or section 63 of the County Courts Act 1984.
   (2)   The assessor shall assist the court in dealing with a matter in which the assessor has skill and experience.
   (3)   An assessor shall take such part in the proceedings as the court may direct and in particular the court may—
    (a)   direct the assessor to prepare a report for the court on any matter at issue in the proceedings; and
    (b)   direct the assessor to attend the whole or any part of the trial to advise the court on any such matter.

(4) If the assessor prepares a report for the court before the trial has begun—
   (a) the court will send a copy to each of the parties; and
   (b) the parties may use it at trial.

(5) The remuneration to be paid to the assessor for his services shall be determined by the court and shall form part of the costs of the proceedings.

(6) The court may order any party to deposit in the court office a specified sum in respect of the assessor's fees and, where it does so, the assessor will not be asked to act until the sum has been deposited.

(7) Paragraphs (5) and (6) do not apply where the remuneration of the assessor is to be paid out of money provided by Parliament.

PD 35 PRACTICE DIRECTION — EXPERTS AND ASSESSORS

This practice direction supplements CPR Part 35

Part 35 is intended to limit the use of oral expert evidence to that which is reasonably required. In addition, where possible, matters requiring expert evidence should be dealt with by a single expert. Permission of the court is always required either to call an expert or to put an expert's report in evidence.

FORM AND CONTENT OF EXPERT'S REPORTS

1.1 An expert's report should be addressed to the court and not to the party from whom the expert has received his instructions.

1.2 An expert's report must:

(1) give details of the expert's qualifications,

(2) give details of any literature or other material which the expert has relied on in making the report,

(3) say who carried out any test or experiment which the expert has used for the report and whether or not the test or experiment has been carried out under the expert's supervision,

(4) give the qualifications of the person who carried out any such test or experiment, and

(5) where there is a range of opinion on the matters dealt with in the report—
 (i) summarise the range of opinion, and
 (ii) give reasons for his own opinion,

(6) contain a summary of the conclusions reached,

(7) contain a statement that the expert understands his duty to the court and has complied with that duty (rule 35.10(2)), and

(8) contain a statement setting out the substance of all material instructions (whether written or oral). The statement should summarise the facts and instructions given to the expert which are material to the opinions expressed in the report or upon which those opinions are based (rule 35.10(3)).

1.3 An expert's report must be verified by a statement of truth as well as containing the statements required in paragraph 1.2(7) and (8) above.

1.4 The form of the statement of truth is as follows:

'I believe that the facts I have stated in this report are true and that the opinions I have expressed are correct.'

1.5 Attention is drawn to rule 32.14 which sets out the consequences of verifying a document containing a false statement without an honest belief in its truth.

(For information about statements of truth, see Part 22 and the practice direction which supplements it.)

1.6 In addition, an expert's report should comply with the requirements of any approved expert's protocol.

INFORMATION

2 Under Part 35.9 the court may direct a party with access to information which is not reasonably available to another party to serve on that other party a document which records the information. The document served must include sufficient details of all the facts, tests, experiments and assumptions which underlie any part of the information to enable the party on whom it is served to make, or to obtain, a proper interpretation of the information and an assessment of its significance.

INSTRUCTIONS

3 The instructions referred to in paragraph 1.2(8) will not be protected by privilege (see rule 35.10(4)). But cross-examination of the expert on the contents

of his instructions will not be allowed unless the court permits it (or unless the party who gave the instructions consents to it). Before it gives permission the court must be satisfied that there are reasonable grounds to consider that the statement in the report of the substance of the instructions is inaccurate or incomplete. If the court is so satisfied, it will allow the cross-examination where it appears to be in the interests of justice to do so.

QUESTIONS TO EXPERTS

4.1 Questions asked for the purpose of clarifying the expert's report (see rule 35.6) should be put, in writing, to the expert not later than 28 days after receipt of the expert's report (see paragraphs 1.2 to 1.5 above as to verification).

4.2 Where a party sends a written question or questions direct to an expert and the other party is represented by solicitors, a copy of the questions should, at the same time, be sent to those solicitors.

SINGLE EXPERT

5 Where the court has directed that the evidence on a particular issue is to be given by one expert only (rule 35.7) but there are a number of disciplines relevant to that issue, a leading expert in the dominant discipline should be identified as the single expert. He should prepare the general part of the report and be responsible for annexing or incorporating the contents of any reports from experts in other disciplines.

ASSESSORS

6.1 An assessor may be appointed to assist the court under rule 35.15. Not less than 21 days before making any such appointment, the court will notify each party in writing of the name of the proposed assessor, of the matter in respect of which the assistance of the assessor will be sought and of the qualifications of the assessor to give that assistance.

6.2 Where any person has been proposed for appointment as an assessor, objection to him, either personally or in respect of his qualification, may be taken by any party.

6.3 Any such objection must be made in writing and filed with the court within 7 days of receipt of the notification referred to in paragraph 6.1 and will be taken into account by the court in deciding whether or not to make the appointment (section 63(5) of the County Courts Act 1984).

6.4 Copies of any report prepared by the assessor will be sent to each of the parties but the assessor will not give oral evidence or be open to cross-examination or questioning.

CPR PART 36 OFFERS TO SETTLE AND PAYMENTS INTO COURT

CONTENTS OF THIS PART

Scope of this Part	Rule 36.1
Part 36 offers and Part 36 payments — general provisions	Rule 36.2
A defendant's offer to settle a money claim requires a Part 36 payment	Rule 36.3
Defendant's offer to settle the whole of a claim which includes both a money claim and a non-money claim	Rule 36.4
Form and content of a Part 36 offer	Rule 36.5
Notice of a Part 36 payment	Rule 36.6
Offer to settle a claim for provisional damages	Rule 36.7
Time when a Part 36 offer or a Part 36 payment is made and accepted	Rule 36.8
Clarification of a Part 36 offer or a Part 36 payment notice	Rule 36.9
Court to take into account offer to settle made before commencement of proceedings	Rule 36.10
Time for acceptance of a defendant's Part 36 offer or Part 36 payment	Rule 36.11
Time for acceptance of a claimant's Part 36 offer	Rule 36.12
Costs consequences of acceptance of a defendant's Part 36 offer or Part 36 payment	Rule 36.13
Costs consequences of acceptance of a claimant's Part 36 offer	Rule 36.14
The effect of acceptance of a Part 36 offer or a Part 36 payment	Rule 36.15
Payment out of a sum in court on the acceptance of a Part 36 payment	Rule 36.16
Acceptance of a Part 36 offer or a Part 36 payment made by one or more, but not all, defendants	Rule 36.17
Other cases where a court order is required to enable acceptance of a Part 36 offer or a Part 36 payment	Rule 36.18
Restriction on disclosure of a Part 36 offer or a Part 36 payment	Rule 36.19
Costs consequences where claimant fails to do better than a Part 36 offer or a Part 36 payment	Rule 36.20
Costs and other consequences where claimant does better than he proposed in his Part 36 offer	Rule 36.21
Interest	Rule 36.22
Deduction of benefits	Rule 36.23

36.1 SCOPE OF THIS PART

(1) This Part contains rules about—
    (a) offers to settle and payments into court; and
    (b) the consequences where an offer to settle or payment into court is made in accordance with this Part.

(2) Nothing in this Part prevents a party making an offer to settle in whatever way he chooses, but if that offer is not made in accordance with this Part, it will only have the consequences specified in this Part if the court so orders.

(Part 36 applies to Part 20 claims by virtue of rule 20.3)

36.2 PART 36 OFFERS AND PART 36 PAYMENTS — GENERAL PROVISIONS

(1) An offer made in accordance with the requirements of this Part is called—
    (a) if made by way of a payment into court, 'a Part 36 payment';
    (b) otherwise 'a Part 36 offer'.

(Rule 36.3 sets out when an offer has to be made by way of a payment into court)

(2) The party who makes an offer is the 'offeror'.

CPR PART 36 OFFERS TO SETTLE AND PAYMENTS INTO COURT

(3) The party to whom an offer is made is the 'offeree'.
(4) A Part 36 offer or a Part 36 payment—
   (a) may be made at any time after proceedings have started; and
   (b) may be made in appeal proceedings.
(5) A Part 36 offer or a Part 36 payment shall not have the consequences set out in this Part while the claim is being dealt with on the small claims track unless the court orders otherwise.
(Part 26 deals with allocation to the small claims track)
(Rule 27.2 provides that Part 36 does not apply to small claims)

36.3 A DEFENDANT'S OFFER TO SETTLE A MONEY CLAIM REQUIRES A PART 36 PAYMENT

(1) Subject to rules 36.5(5) and 36.23, an offer by a defendant to settle a money claim will not have the consequences set out in this Part unless it is made by way of a Part 36 payment.
(2) A Part 36 payment may only be made after proceedings have started.
(Rule 36.5(5) permits a Part 36 offer to be made by reference to an interim payment)
(Rule 36.10 makes provision for an offer to settle a money claim before the commencement of proceedings)
(Rule 36.23 makes provision for where benefit is recoverable under the Social Security (Recovery of Benefit) Act 1997)

36.4 DEFENDANT'S OFFER TO SETTLE THE WHOLE OF A CLAIM WHICH INCLUDES BOTH A MONEY CLAIM AND A NON-MONEY CLAIM

(1) This rule applies where a defendant to a claim which includes both a money claim and a non-money claim wishes—
   (a) to make an offer to settle the whole claim which will have the consequences set out in this Part; and
   (b) to make a money offer in respect of the money claim and a non-money offer in respect of the non-money claim.
(2) The defendant must—
   (a) make a Part 36 payment in relation to the money claim; and
   (b) make a Part 36 offer in relation to the non-money claim.
(3) The Part 36 payment notice must—
   (a) identify the document which sets out the terms of the Part 36 offer; and
   (b) state that if the claimant gives notice of acceptance of the Part 36 payment he will be treated as also accepting the Part 36 offer.
(Rule 36.6 makes provision for a Part 36 payment notice)
(4) If the claimant gives notice of acceptance of the Part 36 payment, he shall also be taken as giving notice of acceptance of the Part 36 offer in relation to the non-money claim.

36.5 FORM AND CONTENT OF A PART 36 OFFER

(1) A Part 36 offer must be in writing.
(2) A Part 36 offer may relate to the whole claim or to part of it or to any issue that arises in it.
(3) A Part 36 offer must—
   (a) state whether it relates to the whole of the claim or to part of it or to an issue that arises in it and if so to which part or issue;
   (b) state whether it takes into account any counterclaim; and
   (c) if it is expressed not to be inclusive of interest, give the details relating to interest set out in rule 36.22(2).
(4) A defendant may make a Part 36 offer limited to accepting liability up to a specified proportion.
(5) A Part 36 offer may be made by reference to an interim payment.
(Part 25 contains provisions relating to interim payments)
(6) A Part 36 offer made not less than 21 days before the start of the trial must—

CPR PART 36   OFFERS TO SETTLE AND PAYMENTS INTO COURT

(a) be expressed to remain open for acceptance for 21 days from the date it is made; and
(b) provide that after 21 days the offeree may only accept it if—
   (i)   the parties agree the liability for costs; or
   (ii) the court gives permission.
(7) A Part 36 offer made less than 21 days before the start of the trial must state that the offeree may only accept it if—
(a) the parties agree the liability for costs; or
(b) the court gives permission.
(Rule 36.8 makes provision for when a Part 36 offer is treated as being made)
(8) If a Part 36 offer is withdrawn it will not have the consequences set out in this Part.

36.6   NOTICE OF A PART 36 PAYMENT
(1) A Part 36 payment may relate to the whole claim or part of it or to an issue that arises in it.
(2) A defendant who makes a Part 36 payment must file with the court a notice ('Part 36 payment notice') which—
(a) states the amount of the payment;
(b) states whether the payment relates to the whole claim or to part of it or to any issue that arises in it and if so to which part or issue;
(c) states whether it takes into account any counterclaim;
(d) if an interim payment has been made, states that the defendant has taken into account the interim payment; and
(e) if it is expressed not to be inclusive of interest, gives the details relating to interest set out in rule 36.22(2).
(Rule 25.6 makes provision for an interim payment)
(Rule 36.4 provides for further information to be included where a defendant wishes to settle the whole of a claim which includes a money claim and a non-money claim)
(Rule 36.23 makes provision for extra information to be included in the payment notice in a case where benefit is recoverable under the Social Security (Recovery of Benefit) Act 1997)
(3) The court will serve the Part 36 payment notice on the offeree unless the offeror informs the court, when the money is paid into court, that the offeror will serve the notice.
(4) Where the offeror serves the Part 36 payment notice he must file a certificate of service.
(Rule 6.10 specifies what must be contained in a certificate of service)
(5) A Part 36 payment may be withdrawn only with the permission of the court.

36.7   OFFER TO SETTLE A CLAIM FOR PROVISIONAL DAMAGES
(1) A defendant may make a Part 36 payment in respect of a claim which includes a claim for provisional damages.
(2) Where he does so, the Part 36 payment notice must specify whether or not the defendant is offering to agree to the making of an award of provisional damages.
(3) Where the defendant is offering to agree to the making of an award of provisional damages the payment notice must also state—
(a) that the sum paid into court is in satisfaction of the claim for damages on the assumption that the injured person will not develop the disease or suffer the type of deterioration specified in the notice;
(b) that the offer is subject to the condition that the claimant must make any claim for further damages within a limited period; and
(c) what that period is.
(4) Where a Part 36 payment is—
(a) made in accordance with paragraph (3); and
(b) accepted within the relevant period in rule 36.11,
the Part 36 payment will have the consequences set out in rule 36.13, unless the court orders otherwise.

CPR PART 36   OFFERS TO SETTLE AND PAYMENTS INTO COURT

(5) If the claimant accepts the Part 36 payment he must, within 7 days of doing so, apply to the court for an order for an award of provisional damages under rule 41.2.
(Rule 41.2 provides for an order for an award of provisional damages)
(6) The money in court may not be paid out until the court has disposed of the application made in accordance with paragraph (5).

36.8 TIME WHEN A PART 36 OFFER OR A PART 36 PAYMENT IS MADE AND ACCEPTED
(1) A Part 36 offer is made when received by the offeree.
(2) A Part 36 payment is made when written notice of the payment into court is served on the offeree.
(3) An improvement to a Part 36 offer will be effective when its details are received by the offeree.
(4) An increase in a Part 36 payment will be effective when notice of the increase is served on the offeree.
(5) A Part 36 offer or Part 36 payment is accepted when notice of its acceptance is received by the offeror.

36.9 CLARIFICATION OF A PART 36 OFFER OR A PART 36 PAYMENT NOTICE
(1) The offeree may, within 7 days of a Part 36 offer or payment being made, request the offeror to clarify the offer or payment notice.
(2) If the offeror does not give the clarification requested under paragraph (1) within 7 days of receiving the request, the offeree may, unless the trial has started, apply for an order that he does so.
(3) If the court makes an order under paragraph (2), it must specify the date when the Part 36 offer or Part 36 payment is to be treated as having been made.

36.10 COURT TO TAKE INTO ACCOUNT OFFER TO SETTLE MADE BEFORE COMMENCEMENT OF PROCEEDINGS
(1) If a person makes an offer to settle before proceedings are begun which complies with the provisions of this rule, the court will take that offer into account when making any order as to costs.
(2) The offer must—
  (a) be expressed to be open for at least 21 days after the date it was made;
  (b) if made by a person who would be a defendant were proceedings commenced, include an offer to pay the costs of the offeree incurred up to the date 21 days after the date it was made; and
  (c) otherwise comply with this Part.
(3) If the offeror is a defendant to a money claim—
  (a) he must make a Part 36 payment within 14 days of service of the claim form; and
  (b) the amount of the payment must be not less than the sum offered before proceedings began.
(4) An offeree may not, after proceedings have begun, accept—
  (a) an offer made under paragraph (2); or
  (b) a Part 36 payment made under paragraph (3),
without the permission of the court.
(5) An offer under this rule is made when it is received by the offeree.

36.11 TIME FOR ACCEPTANCE OF A DEFENDANT'S PART 36 OFFER OR PART 36 PAYMENT
(1) A claimant may accept a Part 36 offer or a Part 36 payment made not less than 21 days before the start of the trial without needing the court's permission if he gives the defendant written notice of acceptance not later than 21 days after the offer or payment was made.
(Rule 36.13 sets out the costs consequences of accepting a defendant's offer or payment without needing the permission of the court)
(2) If—

CPR PART 36 OFFERS TO SETTLE AND PAYMENTS INTO COURT

    (a) a defendant's Part 36 offer or Part 36 payment is made less than 21 days before the start of the trial; or
    (b) the claimant does not accept it within the period specified in paragraph (1)—
        (i) if the parties agree the liability for costs, the claimant may accept the offer or payment without needing the permission of the court;
        (ii) if the parties do not agree the liability for costs the claimant may only accept the offer or payment with the permission of the court.
    (3) Where the permission of the court is needed under paragraph (2) the court will, if it gives permission, make an order as to costs.

36.12 TIME FOR ACCEPTANCE OF A CLAIMANT'S PART 36 OFFER
    (1) A defendant may accept a Part 36 offer made not less than 21 days before the start of the trial without needing the court's permission if he gives the claimant written notice of acceptance not later than 21 days after the offer was made.
(Rule 36.14 sets out the costs consequences of accepting a claimant's offer without needing the permission of the court)
    (2) If—
    (a) a claimant's Part 36 offer is made less than 21 days before the start of the trial; or
    (b) the defendant does not accept it within the period specified in paragraph (1)—
        (i) if the parties agree the liability for costs, the defendant may accept the offer without needing the permission of the court;
        (ii) if the parties do not agree the liability for costs the defendant may only accept the offer with the permission of the court.
    (3) Where the permission of the court is needed under paragraph (2) the court will, if it gives permission, make an order as to costs.

36.13 COSTS CONSEQUENCES OF ACCEPTANCE OF A DEFENDANT'S PART 36 OFFER OR PART 36 PAYMENT
    (1) Where a Part 36 offer or a Part 36 payment is accepted without needing the permission of the court the claimant will be entitled to his costs of the proceedings up to the date of serving notice of acceptance.
    (2) Where—
    (a) a Part 36 offer or a Part 36 payment relates to part only of the claim; and
    (b) at the time of serving notice of acceptance the claimant abandons the balance of the claim,
the claimant will be entitled to his costs of the proceedings up to the date of serving notice of acceptance, unless the court orders otherwise.
    (3) The claimant's costs include any costs attributable to the defendant's counterclaim if the Part 36 offer or the Part 36 payment notice states that it takes into account the counterclaim.
    (4) Costs under this rule will be payable on the standard basis if not agreed.

36.14 COSTS CONSEQUENCES OF ACCEPTANCE OF A CLAIMANT'S PART 36 OFFER
Where a claimant's Part 36 offer is accepted without needing the permission of the court the claimant will be entitled to his costs of the proceedings up to the date upon which the defendant serves notice of acceptance.

36.15 THE EFFECT OF ACCEPTANCE OF A PART 36 OFFER OR A PART 36 PAYMENT
    (1) If a Part 36 offer or Part 36 payment relates to the whole claim and is accepted, the claim will be stayed$^{(GL)}$.
    (2) In the case of acceptance of a Part 36 offer which relates to the whole claim—
    (a) the stay$^{(GL)}$ will be upon the terms of the offer; and
    (b) either party may apply to enforce those terms without the need for a new claim.

CPR PART 36 OFFERS TO SETTLE AND PAYMENTS INTO COURT

(3) If a Part 36 offer or a Part 36 payment which relates to part only of the claim is accepted—
 (a) the claim will be stayed$^{(GL)}$ as to that part; and
 (b) unless the parties have agreed costs, the liability for costs shall be decided by the court.

(4) If the approval of the court is required before a settlement can be binding, any stay$^{(GL)}$ which would otherwise arise on the acceptance of a Part 36 offer or a Part 36 payment will take effect only when that approval has been given.

(5) Any stay$^{(GL)}$ arising under this rule will not affect the power of the court—
 (a) to enforce the terms of a Part 36 offer;
 (b) to deal with any question of costs (including interest on costs) relating to the proceedings;
 (c) to order payment out of court of any sum paid into court.

(6) Where—
 (a) a Part 36 offer has been accepted; and
 (b) a party alleges that—
  (i) the other party has not honoured the terms of the offer; and
  (ii) he is therefore entitled to a remedy for breach of contract,
the party may claim the remedy by applying to the court without the need to start a new claim unless the court orders otherwise.

36.16 PAYMENT OUT OF A SUM IN COURT ON THE ACCEPTANCE OF A PART 36 PAYMENT

Where a Part 36 payment is accepted the claimant obtains payment out of the sum in court by making a request for payment in the practice form.

36.17 ACCEPTANCE OF A PART 36 OFFER OR A PART 36 PAYMENT MADE BY ONE OR MORE, BUT NOT ALL, DEFENDANTS

(1) This rule applies where the claimant wishes to accept a Part 36 offer or a Part 36 payment made by one or more, but not all, of a number of defendants.

(2) If the defendants are sued jointly or in the alternative, the claimant may accept the offer or payment without needing the permission of the court in accordance with rule 36.11(1) if—
 (a) he discontinues his claim against those defendants who have not made the offer or payment; and
 (b) those defendants give written consent to the acceptance of the offer or payment.

(3) If the claimant alleges that the defendants have a several liability$^{(GL)}$ to him the claimant may—
 (a) accept the offeror payment in accordance with rule 36.11(1); and
 (b) continue with his claims against the other defendants if he is entitled to do so.

(4) In all other cases the claimant must apply to the court for—
 (a) an order permitting a payment out to him of any sum in court; and
 (b) such order as to costs as the court considers appropriate.

36.18 OTHER CASES WHERE A COURT ORDER IS REQUIRED TO ENABLE ACCEPTANCE OF A PART 36 OFFER OR A PART 36 PAYMENT

(1) Where a Part 36 offer or a Part 36 payment is made in proceedings to which rule 21.10 applies—
 (a) the offer or payment may be accepted only with the permission of the court; and
 (b) no payment out of any sum in court shall be made without a court order.
(Rule 21.10 deals with compromise etc. by or on behalf of a child or patient)

(2) Where the court gives a claimant permission to accept a Part 36 offer or payment after the trial has started—
 (a) any money in court may be paid out only with a court order; and
 (b) the court must, in the order, deal with the whole costs of the proceedings.

CPR PART 36   OFFERS TO SETTLE AND PAYMENTS INTO COURT

(3) Where a claimant accepts a Part 36 payment after a defence of tender before claim$^{(GL)}$ has been put forward by the defendant, the money in court may be paid out only after an order of the court.
(Rule 37.3 requires a defendant who wishes to rely on a defence of tender before claim (GL) to make a payment into court)

36.19 RESTRICTION ON DISCLOSURE OF A PART 36 OFFER OR A PART 36 PAYMENT

(1) A Part 36 offer will be treated as 'without prejudice$^{(GL)}$ except as to costs'.

(2) The fact that a Part 36 payment has been made shall not be communicated to the trial judge until all questions of liability and the amount of money to be awarded have been decided.

(3) Paragraph (2) does not apply—
   (a) where the defence of tender before claim$^{(GL)}$ has been raised;
   (b) where the proceedings have been stayed$^{(GL)}$ under rule 36.15 following acceptance of a Part 36 offer or Part 36 payment; or
   (c) where—
      (i) the issue of liability has been determined before any assessment of the money claimed; and
      (ii) the fact that there has or has not been a Part 36 payment may be relevant to the question of the costs of the issue of liability.

36.20 COSTS CONSEQUENCES WHERE CLAIMANT FAILS TO DO BETTER THAN A PART 36 OFFER OR A PART 36 PAYMENT

(1) This rule applies where at trial a claimant—
   (a) fails to better a Part 36 payment; or
   (b) fails to obtain a judgment which is more advantageous than a defendant's Part 36 offer.

(2) Unless it considers it unjust to do so, the court will order the claimant to pay any costs incurred by the defendant after the latest date on which the payment or offer could have been accepted without needing the permission of the court.
(Rule 36.11 sets out the time for acceptance of a defendant's Part 36 offer or Part 36 payment)

36.21 COSTS AND OTHER CONSEQUENCES WHERE CLAIMANT DOES BETTER THAN HE PROPOSED IN HIS PART 36 OFFER

(1) This rule applies where at trial—
   (a) a defendant is held liable for more; or
   (b) the judgment against a defendant is more advantageous to the claimant, than the proposals contained in a claimant's Part 36 offer.

(2) The court may order interest on the whole or part of any sum of money (excluding interest) awarded to the claimant at a rate not exceeding 10% above base rate$^{(GL)}$ for some or all of the period starting with the latest date on which the defendant could have accepted the offer without needing the permission of the court.

(3) The court may also order that the claimant is entitled to—
   (a) his costs on the indemnity basis from the latest date when the defendant could have accepted the offer without needing the permission of the court; and
   (b) interest on those costs at a rate not exceeding 10% above base rate$^{(GL)}$.

(4) Where this rule applies, the court will make the orders referred to in paragraphs (2) and (3) unless it considers it unjust to do so.
(Rule 36.12 sets out the latest date when the defendant could have accepted the offer)

(5) In considering whether it would be unjust to make the orders referred to in paragraphs (2) and (3) above, the court will take into account all the circumstances of the case including—
   (a) the terms of any Part 36 offer;
   (b) the stage in the proceedings when any Part 36 offer or Part 36 payment was made;

CPR PART 36   OFFERS TO SETTLE AND PAYMENTS INTO COURT

(c) the information available to the parties at the time when the Part 36 offer or Part 36 payment was made; and

(d) the conduct of the parties with regard to the giving or refusing to give information for the purposes of enabling the offer or payment into court to be made or evaluated.

(6) The power of the court under this rule is in addition to any other power it may have to award interest.

36.22   INTEREST

(1) Unless—

(a) a claimant's Part 36 offer which offers to accept a sum of money; or

(b) a Part 36 payment notice,

indicates to the contrary, any such offer or payment will be treated as inclusive of all interest until the last date on which it could be accepted without needing the permission of the court.

(2) Where a claimant's Part 36 offer or Part 36 payment notice is expressed not to be inclusive of interest, the offer or notice must state—

(a) whether interest is offered; and

(b) if so, the amount offered, the rate or rates offered and the period or periods for which it is offered.

36.23   DEDUCTION OF BENEFITS

(1) This rule applies where a payment to a claimant following acceptance of a Part 36 offer or Part 36 payment into court would be a compensation payment as defined in section 1 of the Social Security (Recovery of Benefits) Act 1997.

(2) A defendant to a money claim may make an offer to settle the claim which will have the consequences set out in this Part, without making a Part 36 payment if—

(a) at the time he makes the offer he has applied for, but not received, a certificate of recoverable benefit; and

(b) he makes a Part 36 payment not more than 7 days after he receives the certificate.

(Section 1 of the 1997 Act defines 'recoverable benefit')

(3) A Part 36 payment notice must state—

(a) the amount of gross compensation;

(b) the name and amount of any benefit by which that gross amount is reduced in accordance with section 8 and Schedule 2 to the 1997 Act; and

(c) that the sum paid in is the net amount after deduction of the amount of benefit.

(4) For the purposes of rule 36.20, a claimant fails to better a Part 36 payment if he fails to obtain judgment for more than the gross sum specified in the Part 36 payment notice.

(5) Where—

(a) a Part 36 payment has been made; and

(b) application is made for the money remaining in court to be paid out,

the court may treat the money in court as being reduced by a sum equivalent to any further recoverable benefits paid to the claimant since the date of payment into court and may direct payment out accordingly.

PD 36 PRACTICE DIRECTION — OFFERS TO SETTLE AND PAYMENTS INTO COURT

This practice direction supplements CPR Part 36

PART 36 OFFERS AND PART 36 PAYMENTS

1.1 A written offer to settle a claim[1] or part of a claim or any issue that arises in it made in accordance with the provisions of Part 36 is called:
 (1) if made by way of a payment into court, a Part 36 payment[2], or
 (2) if made otherwise, a Part 36 offer[3].
1.2 A Part 36 offer or Part 36 payment has the costs and other consequences set out in rules 36.13, 36.14, 36.20 and 36.21.
1.3 An offer to settle which is not made in accordance with Part 36 will only have the consequences specified in that Part if the court so orders and will be given such weight on any issue as to costs as the court thinks appropriate[4].

PARTIES AND PART 36 OFFERS

2.1 A Part 36 offer, subject to paragraph 3 below, may be made by any party.
2.2 The party making an offer is the 'offeror' and the party to whom it is made is the 'offeree'.
2.3 A Part 36 offer may consist of a proposal to settle for a specified sum or for some other remedy.
2.4 A Part 36 offer is made when received by the offeree[5].
2.5 An improvement to a Part 36 offer is effective when its details are received by the offeree[6].

PARTIES AND PART 36 PAYMENTS

3.1 An offer to settle for a specified sum made by a defendant[7] must, in order to comply with Part 36, be made by way of a Part 36 payment into court[8].
3.2 A Part 36 payment is made when the Part 36 payment notice is served on the claimant[9].
3.3 An increase to a Part 36 payment will be effective when notice of the increase is served on the claimant[10].
(For service of the Part 36 payment notice see rule 36.6(3) and (4).)
3.4 A defendant who wishes to withdraw or reduce a Part 36 payment must obtain the court's permission to do so.
3.5 Permission may be obtained by making an application in accordance with Part 23 stating the reasons giving rise to the wish to withdraw or reduce the Part 36 payment.

MAKING A PART 36 PAYMENT

4.1 To make a Part 36 payment the defendant must file the following documents:
 (1) where that court is a county court or a district registry—
  (a) the Part 36 payment notice, and
  (b) the payment, usually a cheque made payable to Her Majesty's Paymaster General,
with the court, and

---

[1] Includes Part 20 claims.
[2] See rule 36.2(1)(a).
[3] See rule 36.2(1)(b).
[4] See rule 36.1(2).
[5] See rule 36.8(1).
[6] See rule 36.8(3).
[7] Includes a respondent to a claim or issue.
[8] See rule 36.3(1).
[9] See rule 36.8(2).
[10] See rule 36.8(4).

PD 36 PRACTICE DIRECTION — OFFERS TO SETTLE ETC.

(2) where that court is the Royal Courts of Justice—
   (a) the Part 36 payment notice with the court, and
   (b) the payment, usually a cheque made payable to the Accountant General of the Supreme Court, and
   (c) a sealed copy of the Claim Form,
   (d) the Court Funds Office form 100 with the Court Funds Office.

PART 36 OFFERS AND PART 36 PAYMENTS — GENERAL PROVISIONS

5.1 A Part 36 offer or a Part 36 payment notice must:
   (1) state that it is a Part 36 offer or that the payment into court is a Part 36 payment, and
   (2) be signed by the offeror or his legal representative[13].

5.2 The contents of a Part 36 offer must also comply with the requirements of rule 36.5(3), (5) and (6).

5.3 The contents of a Part 36 payment notice must comply with rule 36.6(2) and, if rule 36.23 applies, with rule 36.23(3).

5.4 A Part 36 offer or Part 36 payment will be taken to include interest unless it is expressly stated in the offer or the payment notice that interest is not included, in which case the details set out in rule 36.22(2) must be given.

5.5 Where a Part 36 offer is made by a company or other corporation, a person holding a senior position in the company or corporation may sign the offer on the offeror's behalf, but must state the position he holds.

5.6 Each of the following persons is a person holding a senior position:
   (1) in respect of a registered company or corporation, a director, the treasurer, secretary, chief executive, manager or other officer of the company or corporation, and
   (2) in respect of a corporation which is not a registered company, in addition to those persons set out in (1), the mayor, chairman, president, town clerk or similar officer of the corporation.

CLARIFICATION OF PART 36 OFFER OR PAYMENT

6.1 An offeree may apply to the court for an order requiring the offeror to clarify the terms of a Part 36 offer or Part 36 payment notice (a clarification order) where the offeror has failed to comply within 7 days with a request for clarification[14].

6.2 An application for a clarification order should be made in accordance with Part 23.

6.3 The application notice should state the respects in which the terms of the Part 36 offer or Part 36 payment notice, as the case may be, are said to need clarification.

ACCEPTANCE OF A PART 36 OFFER OR PAYMENT

7.1 The times for accepting a Part 36 offer or a Part 36 payment are set out in rules 36.11 and 36.12.

7.2 The general rule is that a Part 36 offer or Part 36 payment made more than 21 days before the start of the trial may be accepted within 21 days after it was made without the permission of the court. The costs consequences set out in rules 36.13 and 36.14 will then come into effect.

7.3 A Part 36 offer or Part 36 payment made less than 21 days before the start of the trial cannot be accepted without the permission of the court unless the parties agree what the costs consequences of acceptance will be.

7.4 The permission of the court may be sought:
   (1) before the start of the trial, by making an application in accordance with Part 23, and

---

[13] For the definition of legal representative see rule 2.3. [Footnotes 11 and 12 were referred to in a paragraph in an earlier draft that has been deleted. In the text issued by the Lord Chancellor's Department, which is followed here, subsequent footnotes have not been renumbered to take account of that deletion.]

[14] See rule 36.9(1) and (2).

PD 36 PRACTICE DIRECTION — OFFERS TO SETTLE ETC.

(2) after the start of the trial, by making an application to the trial judge.

7.5 If the court gives permission it will make an order dealing with costs and may order that, in the circumstances, the costs consequences set out in rules 36.13 and 36.14 will apply.

7.6 Where a Part 36 offer or Part 36 payment is accepted in accordance with rule 36.11(1) or rule 36.12(1) the notice of acceptance must be sent to the offeror and filed with the court.

7.7 The notice of acceptance:
    (1) must set out—
        (a) the claim number, and
        (b) the title of the proceedings,
    (2) must identify the Part 36 offer or Part 36 payment notice to which it relates, and
    (3) must be signed by the offeree or his legal representative (see paragraphs 6.5 and 6.6 above).

7.8 Where:
    (1) the court's approval, or
    (2) an order for payment of money out of court, or
    (3) an order apportioning money in court—
        (a) between the Fatal Accidents Act 1976 and the Law Reform (Miscellaneous Provisions) Act 1934, or
        (b) between the persons entitled to it under the Fatal Accidents Act 1976,
is required for acceptance of a Part 36 offer or Part 36 payment, application for the approval or the order should be made in accordance with Part 23.

7.9 The court will include in any order made under paragraph 7.8 above a direction for;
    (1) the payment out of the money in court, and
    (2) the payment of interest.

7.10 Unless the parties have agreed otherwise:
    (1) interest accruing up to the date of acceptance will be paid to the offeror, and
    (2) interest accruing as from the date of acceptance until payment out will be paid to the offeree.

7.11 A claimant may not accept a Part 36 payment which is part of a defendant's offer to settle the whole of a claim consisting of both a money and a non-money claim unless at the same time he accepts the offer to settle the whole of the claim. Therefore:
    (1) if a claimant accepts a Part 36 payment which is part of a defendant's offer to settle the whole of the claim, or
    (2) if a claimant accepts a Part 36 offer which is part of a defendant's offer to settle the whole of the claim,
the claimant will be deemed to have accepted the offer to settle the whole of the claim[15].

(See paragraph 8 below for the method of obtaining money out of court.)

PAYMENT OUT OF COURT

8.1 To obtain money out of court following acceptance of a Part 36 payment, the claimant should file a request for payment with the court[16].

8.2 The request for payment should contain the following details:
    (1) where the party receiving the payment—
        (a) is legally represented—
            (i) the name, business address and reference of the legal representative, and
            (ii) the name of the bank and the sort code number, the title of the account and the account number where the payment is to be transmitted, and
    (2) where the party is acting in person—

---

[15] See rule 36.4.
[16] In practice form N243.

PD 36 PRACTICE DIRECTION — OFFERS TO SETTLE ETC.

    (a) his name and address, and
    (b) his bank account details as in (ii) above.

8.3 Where the request for payment is made to the Royal Courts of Justice, the claimant should also complete Court Funds Office form 201 and file it in the Court Funds Office.

8.4 Subject to paragraph 9.5(1) and (2), if a party does not wish the payment to be transmitted into his bank account or if he does not have a bank account, he may send a written request to the Accountant-General for the payment to be made to him by cheque.

8.5 Where a party seeking payment out of court has provided the necessary information, the payment:

    (1) where a party is legally represented, must be made to the legal representative,

    (2) if the party is not legally represented but is, or has been, in receipt of legal aid in respect of the proceedings and a notice to that effect has been filed, should be made to the Legal Aid Board by direction of the court,

    (3) where a person entitled to money in court dies without having made a will and the court is satisfied—

        (a) that no grant of administration of his estate has been made, and

        (b) that the assets of his estate, including the money in court, do not exceed in value the amount specified in any order in force under section 6 of the Administration of Estates (Small Payments) Act 1965,

may be ordered to be made to the person appearing to have the prior right to a grant of administration of the estate of the deceased, e.g. a widower, widow, child, father, mother, brother or sister of the deceased.

FOREIGN CURRENCY

9.1 Money may be paid into court in a foreign currency:

    (1) where it is a Part 36 payment and the claim is in a foreign currency, or

    (2) under a court order.

9.2 The court may direct that the money be placed in an interest bearing account in the currency of the claim or any other currency.

9.3 Where a Part 36 payment is made in a foreign currency and has not been accepted within 21 days, the defendant may apply for an order that the money be placed in an interest bearing account.

9.4 The application should be made in accordance with Part 23 and should state:

    (1) that the payment has not been accepted in accordance with rule 36.11, and

    (2) the type of currency on which interest is to accrue.

COMPENSATION RECOVERY

10.1 Where a defendant makes a Part 36 payment in respect of a claim for a sum or part of a sum:

    (1) which fails under the heads of damage set out in column 1 of Schedule 2 of the Social Security (Recovery of Benefits) Act 1997 in respect of recoverable benefits received by the claimant as set out in column 2 of that Schedule, and

    (2) where the defendant is liable to pay recoverable benefits to the Secretary of State,

the defendant should obtain from the Secretary of State a certificate of recoverable benefits and file the certificate with the Part 36 payment notice.

10.2 If a defendant wishes to offer to settle a claim where he has applied for but not yet received a certificate of recoverable benefits, he may, provided that he makes a Part 36 payment not more than 7 days after he has received the certificate, make a Part 36 offer which will have the costs and other consequences set out in rules 36.13 and 36.20.

10.3 The Part 36 payment notice should state in addition to the requirements set out in rule 36.6(2):

    (1) the total amount represented by the Part 36 payment (the gross compensation),

(2) that the defendant has reduced this sum by £   , in accordance with section 8 of and Schedule 2 to the Social Security (Recovery of Benefits) Act 1997, which was calculated as follows:

Name of benefit   Amount

and

(3) that the amount paid in, being the sum of £   is the net amount after the deduction of the amount of benefit.

10.4 On acceptance of a Part 36 payment to which this paragraph relates, a claimant will receive the sum in court which will be net of the recoverable benefits.

10.5 In establishing at trial whether a claimant has bettered or obtained a judgment more advantageous than a Part 36 payment to which this paragraph relates, the court will base its decision on the gross sum specified in the Part 36 payment notice.

GENERAL

11.1 Where a party on whom a Part 36 offer, a Part 36 payment notice or a notice of acceptance is to be served is legally represented, the Part 36 offer, Part 36 payment notice and notice of acceptance must be served on the legal representative.

11.2 In a claim arising out of an accident involving a motor vehicle on a road or in a public place:

(1) where the damages claimed include a sum for hospital expenses, and

(2) the defendant or his insurer pays that sum to the hospital under section 157 of the Road Traffic Act 1988,

the defendant must give notice of that payment to the court and all the other parties to the proceedings.

11.3 Money paid into court:

(1) as a Part 36 payment which is not accepted by the claimant, or

(2) under a court order,

will be placed after 21 days in a basic account[17] (subject to paragraph 11.4 below) for interest to accrue.

11.4 Where money referred to in paragraph 11.3 above is paid in in respect of a child or patient it will be placed in a special investment account[18] for interest to accrue.

(A practice direction supplementing Part 21 contains information about the investment of money in court in respect of a child or patient.)

(Practice directions supplementing Part 40 contain information about adjustment of the judgment sum in respect of recoverable benefits, and about structured settlements.)

(A practice direction supplementing Part 41 contains information about provisional damages awards.)

---

[17] See rule 26 of the Court Funds Office Rules 1987.
[18] See rule 26 as above.

CPR PART 37   MISCELLANEOUS PROVISIONS ABOUT PAYMENTS INTO COURT

CONTENTS OF THIS PART

Money paid into court under a court order — general	Rule 37.1
Money paid into court may be treated as a Part 36 payment	Rule 37.2
Money paid into court where defendant wishes to rely on defence of tender before claim	Rule 37.3
Proceedings under Fatal Accidents Act 1976 and Law Reform (Miscellaneous Provisions) Act 1934 — apportionment by court	Rule 37.4

37.1 MONEY PAID INTO COURT UNDER A COURT ORDER — GENERAL

(1) When a party makes a payment into court under a court order, the court will give notice of the payment to every other party.

(2) Money paid into court under a court order may not be paid out without the court's permission except where—

   (a) the defendant treats the money as a Part 36 payment under rule 37.2; and

   (b) the claimant accepts the Part 36 payment without needing the permission of the court.

(Rule 36.11 sets out when the claimant can accept a Part 36 payment without needing the permission of the court)

37.2 MONEY PAID INTO COURT MAY BE TREATED AS A PART 36 PAYMENT

(1) Where a defendant makes a payment into court following an order made under rule 3.1(3) or 3.1(5) he may choose to treat the whole or any part of the money paid into court as a Part 36 payment. 37

(Rule 36.2 defines a Part 36 payment)

(2) To do this he must file a Part 36 payment notice.

(Rule 36.6 sets out what a Part 36 payment notice must contain and provides for the court to serve it on the other parties)

(3) If he does so Part 36 applies to the money as if he had paid it into court as a Part 36 payment.

37.3 MONEY PAID INTO COURT WHERE DEFENDANT WISHES TO RELY ON DEFENCE OF TENDER BEFORE CLAIM

(1) Where a defendant wishes to rely on a defence of tender before claim[GL] he must make a payment into court of the amount he says was tendered.

(2) If the defendant does not make a payment in accordance with paragraph (1) the defence of tender before claim[GL] will not be available to him until he does so.

(3) Where the defendant makes such payment into court—

   (a) he may choose to treat the whole or any part of the money paid into court as a Part 36 payment; and

   (b) if he does so, he must file a Part 36 payment notice.

37.4 PROCEEDINGS UNDER FATAL ACCIDENTS ACT 1976 AND LAW REFORM (MISCELLANEOUS PROVISIONS) ACT 1934 — APPORTIONMENT BY COURT

(1) Where—

   (a) a claim includes claims arising under—

      (i) the Fatal Accidents Act 1976; and

      (ii) the Law Reform (Miscellaneous Provisions) Act 1934;

   (b) a single sum of money is paid into court in satisfaction of those claims; and

(c) the money is accepted,

the court shall apportion the money between the different claims.

(2) The court shall apportion money under paragraph (1)—

(a) when it gives directions under rule 21.11 (control of money received by a child or patient); or

(b) if rule 21.11 does not apply, when it gives permission for the money to be paid out of court.

(3) Where, in an action in which a claim under the Fatal Accidents Act 1976 is made by or on behalf of more than one person—

(a) a sum in respect of damages is ordered or agreed to be paid in satisfaction of the claim; or

(b) a sum of money is accepted in satisfaction of the claim,

the court shall apportion it between the persons entitled to it unless it has already been apportioned by the court, a jury, or agreement between the parties.

PD 37 PRACTICE DIRECTION — MISCELLANEOUS PROVISIONS ABOUT PAYMENTS INTO COURT

This practice direction supplements CPR Part 37

For information about payments into and out of court in relation to offers to settle see Part 36 and the practice direction which supplements it.

PAYMENTS INTO COURT UNDER AN ORDER

1.1 Where money is paid into court under an order, the party making the payment should:
   (1) lodge his payment, and
   (2) file a copy of the order directing payment into court.

1.2 Where the order is made in a county court or district registry the payment will usually be made by cheque payable to Her Majesty's Paymaster General.

1.3 Where the order is made in the Royal Courts of Justice, the payment will usually be made by cheque payable to the Accountant-General of the Supreme Court, and should be:
   (1) accompanied by
      (a) a completed Court Funds Office form 100 or 101, and
      (b) a sealed copy of the order, and
   (2) lodged in the Court Funds Office.

A copy of the Court Funds Office receipt should be filed in the appropriate court office in the Royal Courts of Justice.

DEFENCE OF TENDER

2.1 A defendant paying a sum of money into court in support of a defence of tender[1] should do so when filing his defence and should at the same time complete and file:
   (1) a notice of payment into court, and
   (2) where the defence is filed in the Royal Courts of Justice, Court Funds Office form 100.

2.2 A defence of tender will not be available to a defendant until he has complied with paragraph 2.1.

GENERAL

3.1 Where money is paid into court:
   (1) under an order permitting a defendant to defend or to continue to defend under rule 37.2(1), or
   (2) in support of a defence of tender under rule 37.3,
the party making the payment may, if a defendant, choose to treat the whole or any part of the money as a Part 36 payment[2].

3.2 In order to do so the defendant must file a Part 36 payment notice in accordance with rule 36.6 (see also paragraph 6 of the practice direction which supplements Part 36).

3.3 Rule 37.4 deals with the apportionment of money paid into court in respect of claims arising under:
   (1) the Fatal Accidents Act 1976, and
   (2) the Law Reform (Miscellaneous Provisions) Act 1934.

(See also paragraph 8.8 of the practice direction supplementing Part 36.)

PAYMENT OUT OF COURT

4.1 Except where money which has been paid into court is treated as a Part 36 payment and can be accepted by the claimant without needing the court's permission, the court's permission is required to take the money out of court.

---

[1] Rule 37.3.
[2] Rules 37.2(2) and 37.3(3).

PD37 PRACTICE DIRECTION — PAYMENTS INTO COURT

4.2 Permission may be obtained by making an application in accordance with Part 23. The application notice must state the grounds on which the order for payment out is sought. Evidence of any facts on which the applicant relies may also be necessary.

4.3 To obtain the money out of court the applicant must comply with the provisions of paragraph 9 of the practice direction supplementing Part 36 where they apply.

FOREIGN CURRENCY

5 For information on payments into court made in a foreign currency, see paragraph 9 of the practice direction supplementing Part 36.

CPR PART 38   DISCONTINUANCE

CONTENTS OF THIS PART

Scope of this Part	Rule 38.1
Right to discontinue claim	Rule 38.2
Procedure for discontinuing	Rule 38.3
Right to apply to have notice of discontinuance set aside	Rule 38.4
When discontinuance takes effect where permission of the court is not needed	Rule 38.5
Liability for costs	Rule 38.6
Discontinuance and subsequent proceedings	Rule 38.7
Stay of remainder of partly discontinued proceedings where costs not paid	Rule 38.8

38.1   SCOPE OF THIS PART

(1) The rules in this Part set out the procedure by which a claimant may discontinue all or part of a claim.

(2) A claimant who—

(a) claims more than one remedy; and

(b) subsequently abandons his claim to one or more of the remedies but continues with his claim for the other remedies,

is not treated as discontinuing all or part of a claim for the purposes of this Part.

(The procedure for amending a statement of case, set out in Part 17, applies where a claimant abandons a claim for a particular remedy but wishes to continue with his claim for other remedies)

38.2   RIGHT TO DISCONTINUE CLAIM

(1) A claimant may discontinue all or part of a claim at any time.

(2) However—

(a) a claimant must obtain the permission of the court if he wishes to discontinue all or part of a claim in relation to which—

(i) the court has granted an interim injunction$^{(GL)}$; or

(ii) any party has given an undertaking to the court;

(b) where the claimant has received an interim payment in relation to a claim (whether voluntarily or pursuant to an order under Part 25), he may discontinue that claim only if—

(i) the defendant who made the interim payment consents in writing; or

(ii) the court gives permission;

(c) where there is more than one claimant, a claimant may not discontinue unless—

(i) every other claimant consents in writing; or

(ii) the court gives permission.

(3) Where there is more than one defendant, the claimant may discontinue all or part of a claim against all or any of the defendants.

38.3   PROCEDURE FOR DISCONTINUING

(1) To discontinue a claim or part of a claim, a claimant must—

(a) file a notice of discontinuance; and

(b) serve a copy of it on every other party to the proceedings.

(2) The claimant must state in the notice of discontinuance which he files that he has served notice of discontinuance on every other party to the proceedings.

(3) Where the claimant needs the consent of some other party, a copy of the necessary consent must be attached to the notice of discontinuance.

(4) Where there is more than one defendant, the notice of discontinuance must specify against which defendants the claim is discontinued.

CPR PART 38 DISCONTINUANCE

38.4 RIGHT TO APPLY TO HAVE NOTICE OF DISCONTINUANCE SET ASIDE

(1) Where the claimant discontinues under rule 38.2(1) the defendant may apply to have the notice of discontinuance set aside[GL].

(2) The defendant may not make an application under this rule more than 28 days after the date when the notice of discontinuance was served on him.

38.5 WHEN DISCONTINUANCE TAKES EFFECT WHERE PERMISSION OF THE COURT IS NOT NEEDED

(1) Discontinuance against any defendant takes effect on the date when notice of discontinuance is served on him under rule 38.3(1).

(2) Subject to rule 38.4, the proceedings are brought to an end as against him on that date.

(3) However, this does not affect proceedings to deal with any question of costs.

38.6 LIABILITY FOR COSTS

(1) Unless the court orders otherwise, a claimant who discontinues is liable for the costs which a defendant against whom he discontinues incurred on or before the date on which notice of discontinuance was served on him.

(2) If proceedings are only partly discontinued—

   (a) the claimant is liable under paragraph (1) for costs relating only to the part of the proceedings which he is discontinuing; and

   (b) unless the court orders otherwise, the costs which the claimant is liable to pay must not be assessed until the conclusion of the rest of the proceedings.

(3) This rule does not apply to claims allocated to the small claims track.

(Rule 44.12 provides for the basis of assessment where right to costs arises on discontinuance)

38.7 DISCONTINUANCE AND SUBSEQUENT PROCEEDINGS

A claimant who discontinues a claim needs the permission of the court to make another claim against the same defendant if—

   (a) he discontinued the claim after the defendant filed a defence; and

   (b) the other claim arises out of facts which are the same or substantially the same as those relating to the discontinued claim.

38.8 STAY OF REMAINDER OF PARTLY DISCONTINUED PROCEEDINGS WHERE COSTS NOT PAID

(1) This rule applies where—

   (a) proceedings are partly discontinued;

   (b) a claimant is liable to pay costs under rule 38.6; and

   (c) the claimant fails to pay those costs within 21 days of—

      (i) the date on which the parties agreed the sum payable by the claimant; or

      (ii) the date on which the court ordered the costs to be paid.

(2) Where this rule applies, the court may stay[GL] the remainder of the proceedings until the claimant pays the whole of the costs which he is liable to pay under rule 38.6.

CPR PART 39 MISCELLANEOUS PROVISIONS RELATING TO HEARINGS

CONTENTS OF THIS PART
Interpretation	Rule 39.1
General rule — hearing to be in public	Rule 39.2
Failure to attend the trial	Rule 39.3
Timetable for trial	Rule 39.4
Trial bundles	Rule 39.5
Representation at trial of companies or other corporations	Rule 39.6
Impounded documents	Rule 39.7

39.1 INTERPRETATION
In this Part, reference to a hearing includes a reference to the trial.

39.2 GENERAL RULE — HEARING TO BE IN PUBLIC
(1) The general rule is that a hearing is to be in public.

(2) The requirement for a hearing to be in public does not require the court to make special arrangements for accommodating members of the public.

(3) A hearing, or any part of it, may be in private if—
   (a) publicity would defeat the object of the hearing;
   (b) it involves matters relating to national security;
   (c) it involves confidential information (including information relating to personal financial matters) and publicity would damage that confidentiality;
   (d) a private hearing is necessary to protect the interests of any child or patient;
   (e) it is a hearing of an application made without notice and it would be unjust to any respondent for there to be a public hearing;
   (f) it involves uncontentious matters arising in the administration of trusts or in the administration of a deceased person's estate; or
   (g) the court considers this to be necessary, in the interests of justice.

(4) The court may order that the identity of any party or witness must not be disclosed if it considers non-disclosure necessary in order to protect the interests of that party or witness.

(RSC Order 52, in Schedule 1, provides that a committal hearing may be in private)

39.3 FAILURE TO ATTEND THE TRIAL
(1) The court may proceed with a trial in the absence of a party but—
   (a) if no party attends the trial, it may strike out[GL] the whole of the proceedings;
   (b) if the claimant does not attend, it may strike out his claim and any defence to counterclaim; and
   (c) if a defendant does not attend, it may strike out his defence or counterclaim (or both).

(2) Where the court strikes out proceedings, or any part of them, under this rule, it may subsequently restore the proceedings, or that part.

(3) Where a party does not attend and the court gives judgment or makes an order against him, the party who failed to attend may apply for the judgment or order to be set aside[GL].

(4) An application under paragraph (2) or paragraph (3) for an order to restore proceedings must be supported by evidence.

(5) Where an application is made under paragraph (2) or (3) by a party who failed to attend the trial, the court may grant the application only if the applicant—
   (a) acted promptly when he found out that the court had exercised its power to strike out[GL] or to enter judgment or make an order against him;

(b) had a good reason for not attending the trial; and
(c) has a reasonable prospect of success at the trial.

39.4 TIMETABLE FOR TRIAL

When the court sets a timetable for a trial in accordance with rule 28.6 (fixing or confirming the trial date and giving directions — fast track) or rule 29.8 (setting a trial timetable and fixing or confirming the trial date or week — multi-track) it will do so in consultation with the parties.

39.5 TRIAL BUNDLES

(1) Unless the court orders otherwise, the claimant must file a trial bundle containing documents required by—
(a) a relevant practice direction; and
(b) any court order.

(2) The claimant must file the trial bundle not more than 7 days and not less than 3 days before the start of the trial.

39.6 REPRESENTATION AT TRIAL OF COMPANIES OR OTHER CORPORATIONS

A company or other corporation may be represented at trial by an employee if—
(a) the employee has been authorised by the company or corporation to appear at trial on its behalf; and
(b) the court gives permission.

39.7 IMPOUNDED DOCUMENTS

(1) Documents impounded by order of the court must not be released from the custody of the court except in compliance—
(a) with a court order; or
(b) with a written request made by a Law Officer or the Director of Public Prosecutions.

(2) A document released from the custody of the court under paragraph (1)(b) must be released into the custody of the person who requested it.

(3) Documents impounded by order of the court, while in the custody of the court, may not be inspected except by a person authorised to do so by a court order.

PD 39 PRACTICE DIRECTION — MISCELLANEOUS PROVISIONS RELATING TO HEARINGS

This practice direction supplements CPR Part 39

HEARINGS

1.1 In Part 39, reference to a hearing includes reference to the trial[1].

1.2 The general rule is that a hearing is to be in public[2].

1.3 Rule 39.2(3) sets out the type of proceedings which may be dealt with in private.

1.4 The decision as to whether to hold a hearing in public or in private must be made by the judge conducting the hearing having regard to any representations which may have been made to him.

1.4A The judge should also have regard to Article 6(1) of the European Convention on Human Rights. This requires that, in general, court hearings are to be held in public, but the press and public may be excluded in the circumstances specified in that Article. Article 6(1) will usually be relevant, for example, where a party applies for a hearing which would normally be held in public to be held in private as well as where a hearing would normally be held in private. The judge may need to consider whether the case is within any of the exceptions permitted by Article 6(1).

1.5 The hearings set out below shall in the first instance be listed by the court as hearings in private under rule 39.2(3)(c), namely:

(1) a claim by a mortgagee against one or more individuals for an order for possession of land,

(2) a claim by a landlord against one or more tenants or former tenants for the repossession of a dwelling house based on the non-payment of rent,

(3) an application to suspend a warrant of execution or a warrant of possession or to stay execution where the court is being invited to consider the ability of a party to make payments to another party,

(4) a redetermination under rule 14.13 or an application to vary or suspend the payment of a judgment debt by instalments,

(5) an application for a charging order (including an application to enforce a charging order), garnishee order, attachment of earnings order, administration order, or the appointment of a receiver,

(6) an oral examination,

(7) the determination of an assisted person's liability for costs under regulation 127 of the Civil Legal Aid (General) Regulations 1989,

(8) an application for security for costs under section 726(1) of the Companies Act 1985, and

(9) proceedings brought under the Consumer Credit Act 1974, the Inheritance (Provision for Family and Dependants) Act 1975 or the Protection from Harassment Act 1997,

(10) an application by a trustee or personal representative for directions as to bringing or defending legal proceedings, and

(11) an application under the Variation of Trusts Act 1958 where there are no facts in dispute.

1.6 Rule 39.2(3)(d) states that a hearing may be in private where it involves the interests of a child or patient. This includes the approval of a compromise or settlement on behalf of a child or patient or an application for the payment of money out of court to such a person.

1.7 Attention is drawn to paragraph 5.1 of the practice direction which supplements Part 27 (relating to the hearing of claims in the small claims track),

---

[1] Rule 39.1.
[2] Rule 39.2(1).

which provides that the judge may decide to hold a small claim hearing in private if the parties agree or if a ground mentioned in rule 39.2(3) applies. A hearing of a small claim in premises other than the court will not be a hearing in public.

1.8 Nothing in this practice direction prevents a judge ordering that a hearing taking place in public shall continue in private, or vice-versa.

1.9 If the court or judge's room in which the proceedings are taking place has a sign on the door indicating that the proceedings are private, members of the public who are not parties to the proceedings will not be admitted unless the court permits.

1.10 Where there is no such sign on the door of the court or judge's room, members of the public will be admitted where practicable. The judge may, if he thinks it appropriate, adjourn the proceedings to a larger room or court.

1.11 When a hearing takes place in public, members of the public may obtain a transcript of any judgment given or a copy of any order made, subject to payment of the appropriate fee.

1.12 When a judgment is given or an order is made in private, if any member of the public who is not a party to the proceedings seeks a transcript of the judgment or a copy of the order, he must seek the leave of the judge who gave the judgment or made the order.

1.13 A judgment or order given or made in private, when drawn up, must have clearly marked in the title:

'Before [*title and name of judge*] sitting in Private'

1.14 References to hearings being in public or private or in a judge's room contained in the Civil Procedure Rules (including the Rules of the Supreme Court and the County Court Rules scheduled to Part 50) and the practice directions which supplement them do not restrict any existing rights of audience or confer any new rights of audience in respect of applications or proceedings which under the rules previously in force would have been heard in court or in chambers respectively.

FAILURE TO ATTEND THE TRIAL

2.1 Rule 39.3 sets out the consequences of a party's failure to attend the trial.

2.2 The court may proceed with a trial in the absence of a party[3]. In the absence of:

(1) the defendant, the claimant may—

    (a) prove his claim at trial and obtain judgment on his claim and for costs, and

    (b) seek the striking out of any counterclaim,

(2) the claimant, the defendant may—

    (a) prove any counterclaim at trial and obtain judgment on his counterclaim and for costs, and

    (b) seek the striking out of the claim, or

(3) both parties, the court may strike out the whole of the proceedings.

2.3 Where the court has struck out proceedings, or any part of them, on the failure of a party to attend, that party may apply in accordance with Part 23 for the proceedings, or that part of them, to be restored and for any judgment given against that party to be set aside[4].

2.4 The application referred to in paragraph 2.3 above must be supported by evidence giving reasons for the failure to attend court and stating when the applicant found out about the order against him.

BUNDLES OF DOCUMENTS FOR HEARINGS OR TRIAL

3.1 Unless the court orders otherwise, the claimant must file the trial bundle not more than 7 days and not less than 3 days before the start of the trial.

3.2 Unless the court orders otherwise, the trial bundle should include a copy of:

(1) the claim form and all statements of case,

(2) a case summary and/or chronology where appropriate,

---

[3] Rule 39.3(1).
[4] Rule 39.3(2) and (3).

(3) requests for further information and responses to the requests,
(4) all witness statements to be relied on as evidence,
(5) any witness summaries,
(6) any notices of intention to rely on hearsay evidence under rule [33.2*],
(7) any notices of intention to rely on evidence (such as a plan, photograph etc.) under rule 33.6 which is not—
   (a) contained in a witness statement, affidavit or expert's report,
   (b) being given orally at trial,
   (c) hearsay evidence under rule 33.2,
(8) any medical reports and responses to them,
(9) any experts' reports and responses to them,
(10) any order giving directions as to the conduct of the trial, and
(11) any other necessary documents.

3.3 The originals of the documents contained in the trial bundle, together with copies of any other court orders should be available at the trial.

3.4 The preparation and production of the trial bundle, even where it is delegated to another person, is the responsibility of the legal representative[5] who has conduct of the claim on behalf of the claimant.

3.5 The trial bundle should be paginated (continuously) throughout, and indexed with a description of each document and the page number. Where the total number of pages is more than 100, numbered dividers should be placed at intervals between groups of documents.

3.6 The bundle should normally be contained in a ring binder or lever arch file. Where more than one bundle is supplied, they should be clearly distinguishable, for example, by different colours or letters. If there are numerous bundles, a core bundle should be prepared containing the core documents essential to the proceedings, with references to the supplementary documents in the other bundles.

3.7 For convenience, experts' reports may be contained in a separate bundle and cross referenced in the main bundle.

3.8 If a document to be included in the trial bundle is illegible, a typed copy should be included in the bundle next to it, suitably cross-referenced.

3.9 The contents of the trial bundle should be agreed where possible. The parties should also agree where possible:
   (1) that the documents contained in the bundle are authentic even if not disclosed under Part 31, and
   (2) that documents in the bundle may be treated as evidence of the facts stated in them even if a notice under the Civil Evidence Act 1995 has not been served.

Where it is not possible to agree the contents of the bundle, a summary of the points on which the parties are unable to agree should be included.

3.10 The party filing the trial bundle should supply identical bundles to all the parties to the proceedings and for the use of the witnesses.

SETTLEMENT OR DISCONTINUANCE AFTER THE TRIAL DATE IS FIXED

4.1 Where:
   (1) an offer to settle a claim is accepted,
   (2) or a settlement is reached, or
   (3) a claim is discontinued,
which disposes of the whole of a claim for which a date or 'window' has been fixed for the trial, the parties must ensure that the listing officer for the trial court is notified immediately.

4.2 If an order is drawn up giving effect to the settlement or discontinuance, a copy of the sealed order should be filed with the listing officer.

REPRESENTATION AT HEARINGS

5.1 At any hearing, a written statement containing the following information should be provided for the court:

---

[5] For the definition of legal representative see rule 2.3.
* The text issued by the Lord Chancellor's Department refers, mistakenly, to rule 32.2.

(1) the name and address of each advocate,
(2) his qualification or entitlement to act as an advocate, and
(3) the party for whom he so acts.

5.2 Where a party is a company or other corporation and is to be represented at a hearing by an employee the written statement should contain the following additional information:

(1) The full name of the company or corporation as stated in its certificate of registration.

(2) The registered number of the company or corporation.

(3) The position or office in the company or corporation held by the representative.

(4) The date on which and manner in which the representative was authorised to act for the company or corporation, e.g. _____ 19 _____ : written authority from managing director; or _____ 19 _____ : Board resolution dated _____ 19 _____ .

5.3 Rule 39.6 is intended to enable a company or other corporation to represent itself as a litigant in person. Permission under rule 39.6(b) should therefore be given by the court unless there is some particular and sufficient reason why it should be withheld.

5.4 Permission under rule 39.6(b) should be obtained in advance of the hearing from, preferably, the judge who is to hear the case, but may, if it is for any reason impracticable or inconvenient to do so, be obtained from any judge by whom the case could be heard.

5.5 The permission may be obtained informally and without notice to the other parties. The judge who gives the permission should record in writing that he has done so and supply a copy to the company or corporation in question and to any other party who asks for one.

RECORDING OF PROCEEDINGS

6.1 At any hearing, whether in the High Court or a county court, the judgment (and any summing up given by the judge) will be recorded unless the judge directs otherwise. Oral evidence will normally be recorded also.

6.2 No party or member of the public may use unofficial recording equipment in any court or judge's room without the permission of the court. To do so without permission constitutes a contempt of court[6].

6.3 Any party or person may require a transcript or transcripts of the recording of any trial or hearing to be supplied to him, upon payment of the charges authorised by any scheme in force for the making of the recording or the transcript.

6.4 Where the person requiring the transcript or transcripts is not a party to the proceedings and the trial or hearing or any part of it was held in private under CPR rule 39.2, paragraph 6.3 does not apply unless the court so orders.

6.5 Attention is drawn to paragraph 7.9 of the Court of Appeal (Civil Division) Practice Direction which deals with the provision of transcripts for use in the Court of Appeal at public expense.

EXHIBITS AT TRIAL

7 Exhibits which are handed in and proved during the course of the trial should be recorded on an exhibit list and kept in the custody of the court until the conclusion of the trial, unless the judge directs otherwise. At the conclusion of the trial it is the parties' responsibility to obtain the return of those exhibits which they handed in and to preserve them for the period in which any appeal may take place.

---

[6] Section 9 of the Contempt of Court Act 1981.

PD 39B PRACTICE DIRECTION — COURT SITTINGS

This practice direction supplements CPR Part 39

COURT SITTINGS

1.1 (1) The sittings of the Court of Appeal and of the High Court shall be four in every year, that is to say
    (a) the Michaelmas sittings which shall begin on 1st October and end on 21st December;
    (b) the Hilary sittings which shall begin on 11th January and end on the Wednesday before Easter Sunday;
    (c) the Easter sittings which shall begin on the second Tuesday after Easter Sunday and end on the Friday before the spring holiday; and
    (d) the Trinity sittings which shall begin on the second Tuesday after the spring holiday and end on 31st July.
    (2) In the above paragraph 'spring holiday' means the bank holiday falling on the last Monday in May or any day appointed instead of that day under section 1(2) of the Banking and Financial Dealings Act 1971.

VACATIONS

The Court of Appeal

2 Attention is drawn to paragraph 11.2 of the Court of Appeal (Civil Division) Practice Direction which deals with the sittings of the Court of Appeal during vacations.

The High Court

3.1 (1) One or more judges of each Division of the High Court shall sit in vacation on such days as the senior judge of that Division may from time to time direct, to hear such cases, claims, matters or applications as require to be immediately or promptly heard and to hear other cases, claims, matters or applications if the senior judge of that Division determines that sittings are necessary for that purpose.
    (2) Any party to a claim or matter may at any time apply to the Court for an order that such claim or matter be heard in vacation and, if the Court is satisfied that the claim or matter requires to be immediately or promptly heard, it may make an order accordingly and fix a date for the hearing.
    (3) Any judge of the High Court may hear such other cases, claims, matters or applications in vacation as the Court may direct.

3.2 The directions in paragraph 3.1 shall not apply in relation to the trial or hearing of cases, claims, matters or applications outside the Royal Courts of Justice but the senior Presiding Judge of each Circuit, with the concurrence of the Senior Presiding Judge, and the Vice-Chancellor of the County Palatine of Lancaster and the Chancery Supervising Judge for Birmingham, Bristol and Cardiff, with the concurrence of the Vice-Chancellor, may make such arrangements for vacation sittings in the courts for which they are respectively responsible as they think desirable.

3.3 (1) Subject to the discretion of the Judge, any appeal and any application normally made to a Judge may be made in the month of September.
    (2) In the month of August, save with the permission of a Judge or under arrangements for vacation sittings in courts outside the Royal Courts of Justice, appeals to a Judge will be limited to the matters set out in paragraph 3.5 below, and only applications of real urgency will be dealt with, for example urgent applications in respect of injunctions or for possession under RSC Order 113 (Schedule 1 to the CPR).
    (3) It is desirable, where this is practical, that applications or appeals are submitted to a Master, District Judge or Judge prior to the hearing of the

application or appeal so that they can be marked 'fit for August' or 'fit for vacation.' If they are so marked, then normally the Judge will be prepared to hear the application or appeal in August, if marked 'fit for August' or in September if marked 'fit for vacation'. A request to have the papers so marked should normally be made in writing, shortly setting out the nature of the application or appeal and the reasons why it should be dealt with in August or in September, as the case may be.

Chancery Masters

3.4 There is no distinction between term time and vacation so far as business before the Chancery Masters is concerned. The Masters will deal with all types of business throughout the year, and when a Master is on holiday his list will normally be taken by a Deputy Master.

Queen's Bench Masters

3.5 (1) An application notice may, without permission, be issued returnable before a Master in the month of August for any of the following purposes:

to set aside a claim form or particulars of claim, or service of a claim form or particulars of claim;
to set aside judgment; for stay of execution;
for any order by consent;
for judgment or permission to enter judgment;
for approval of settlements or for interim payment;
for relief from forfeiture; for charging order; for garnishee order;
for appointment or discharge of a receiver;
for relief by way of sheriff's interpleader;
for transfer to a county court or for trial by Master;
for time where time is running in the month of August;

(2) In any case of urgency any other type of application notice (that is other than those for the purposes in (1) above), may, with the permission of a Master be issued returnable before a Master during the month of August.

CPR PART 40 JUDGMENTS AND ORDERS

CONTENTS OF THIS PART

Scope of this Part	Rule 40.1
Standard requirements	Rule 40.2
Drawing up and filing of judgments and orders	Rule 40.3
Service of judgments and orders	Rule 40.4
Power to require judgment or order to be served on a party as well as his solicitor	Rule 40.5
Consent judgments and orders	Rule 40.6
When judgment or order takes effect	Rule 40.7
Time from which interest begins to run	Rule 40.8
Who may apply to set aside or vary a judgment or order	Rule 40.9
Judgment against a State in default of acknowledgment of service	Rule 40.10
Time for complying with a judgment or order	Rule 40.11
Correction of errors in judgments and orders	Rule 40.12
Cases where court gives judgment both on claim and counterclaim	Rule 40.13
Judgment in favour of certain part owners relating to the detention of goods	Rule 40.14

40.1 SCOPE OF THIS PART

This Part sets out rules about judgments and orders which apply except where any other of these Rules makes a different provision in relation to the judgment or order in question.

40.2 STANDARD REQUIREMENTS

(1) Every judgment or order must state the name and judicial title of the person who made it, unless it is—

(a) default judgment entered under rule 12.4(1) (entry of default judgment where judgment is entered by a court officer) or a default costs certificate obtained under rule 47.11;

(b) judgment entered under rule 14.4, 14.5, 14.6, 14.7 and 14.9 (entry of judgment on admission where judgment is entered by a court officer); or

(c) a consent order under rule 40.6(2) (consent orders made by court officers).

(2) Every judgment or order must—

(a) bear the date on which it is given or made; and

(b) be sealed(GL) by the court.

40.3 DRAWING UP AND FILING OF JUDGMENTS AND ORDERS

(1) Every judgment or order will be drawn up by the court unless—

(a) the court orders a party to draw it up;

(b) a party, with the permission of the court, agrees to draw it up;

(c) the court dispenses with the need to draw it up; or

(d) it is a consent order under rule 40.6.

(2) The court may direct that—

(a) a judgment or an order drawn up by a party must be checked by the court before it is sealed(GL); or

(b) before a judgment or an order is drawn up by the court, the parties must file an agreed statement of its terms.

(3) Where a judgment or an order is to be drawn up by a party—

(a) he must file it no later than 7 days after the date on which the court ordered or permitted him to draw it up so that it can be sealed(GL) by the court; and

(b) if he fails to file it within that period, any other party may draw it up and file it.

CPR PART 40 JUDGMENTS AND ORDERS

40.4 SERVICE OF JUDGMENTS AND ORDERS
(1) Where a judgment or an order has been drawn up by a party and is to be served by the court—
  (a) the party who drew it up must file a copy to be retained at court and sufficient copies for service on him and on the other parties; and
  (b) once it has been sealed$^{(GL)}$, the court must serve a copy of it on each party to the proceedings.
(2) Unless the court directs otherwise, any order made otherwise than at trial must be served on—
  (a) the applicant and the respondent; and
  (b) any other person on whom the court orders it to be served.
(Rule 6.3 specifies who must serve judgments and orders)
(RSC Order 44 in Schedule 1 contains rules about the service of notice of certain judgments)

40.5 POWER TO REQUIRE JUDGMENT OR ORDER TO BE SERVED ON A PARTY AS WELL AS HIS SOLICITOR
Where the party on whom a judgment or order is to be served is acting by a solicitor, the court may order the judgment or order to be served on the party as well as on his solicitor.

40.6 CONSENT JUDGMENTS AND ORDERS
(1) This rule applies where all the parties agree the terms in which a judgment should be given or an order should be made.
(2) A court officer may enter and seal$^{(GL)}$ an agreed judgment or order if—
  (a) the judgment or order is listed in paragraph (3);
  (b) none of the parties is a litigant in person; and
  (c) the approval of the court is not required by these Rules, a practice direction or any enactment before an agreed order can be made.
(3) The judgments and orders referred to in paragraph (2) are—
  (a) a judgment or order for—
    (i) the payment of an amount of money (including a judgment or order for damages or the value of goods to be decided by the court); or
    (ii) the delivery up of goods with or without the option of paying the value of the goods or the agreed value.
  (b) an order for—
    (i) the dismissal of any proceedings, wholly or in part;
    (ii) the stay$^{(GL)}$ of proceedings on agreed terms, disposing of the proceedings, whether those terms are recorded in a schedule to the order or elsewhere;
    (iii) the stay$^{(GL)}$ of enforcement of a judgment, either unconditionally or on condition that the money due under the judgment is paid by instalments specified in the order;
    (iv) the setting aside under Part 13 of a default judgment which has not been satisfied;
    (v) the payment out of money which has been paid into court;
    (vi) the discharge from liability of any party;
    (vii) the payment, assessment or waiver of costs, or such other provision for costs as may be agreed.
(4) Rule 40.3 (drawing up and filing of judgments and orders) applies to judgments and orders entered and sealed$^{(GL)}$ by a court officer under paragraph (2) as it applies to other judgments and orders.
(5) Where paragraph (2) does not apply, any party may apply for a judgment or order in the terms agreed.
(6) The court may deal with an application under paragraph (5) without a hearing.
(7) Where this rule applies—
  (a) the order which is agreed by the parties must be drawn up in the terms agreed;
  (b) it must be expressed as being 'By Consent';

CPR PART 40 JUDGMENTS AND ORDERS

(c) it must be signed by the legal representative acting for each of the parties to whom the order relates or, where paragraph (5) applies, by the party if he is a litigant in person.

40.7 WHEN JUDGMENT OR ORDER TAKES EFFECT
(1) A judgment or order takes effect from the day when it is given or made, or such later date as the court may specify.
(2) This rule applies to all judgments and orders except those to which rule 40.10 (judgment against a State) applies.

40.8 TIME FROM WHICH INTEREST BEGINS TO RUN
(1) Where interest is payable on a judgment pursuant to section 17 of the judgments Act 1838 or section 74 of the County Courts Act 1984, the interest shall begin to run from the date that judgment is given unless—
  (a) a rule in another Part or a practice direction makes different provision; or
  (b) the court orders otherwise.
(2) The court may order that interest shall begin to run from a date before the date that judgment is given.

40.9 WHO MAY APPLY TO SET ASIDE OR VARY A JUDGMENT OR ORDER
A person who is not a party but who is directly affected by a judgment or order may apply to have the judgment or order set aside or varied.

40.10 JUDGMENT AGAINST A STATE IN DEFAULT OF ACKNOWLEDGMENT OF SERVICE
(1) Where the claimant obtains default judgment under Part 12 on a claim against a State where the defendant has failed to file an acknowledgment of service, the judgment does not take effect until 2 months after service on the State of—
  (a) a copy of the judgment; and
  (b) a copy of the evidence in support of the application for permission to enter default judgment (unless the evidence has already been served on the State in accordance with an order made under Part 12).
(2) In this rule, 'State' has the meaning given by section 14 of the State Immunity Act 1978(49).

40.11 TIME FOR COMPLYING WITH A JUDGMENT OR ORDER
A party must comply with a judgment or order for the payment of an amount of money (including costs) within 14 days of the date of the judgment or order, unless—
  (a) the judgment or order specifies a different date for compliance (including specifying payment by instalments);
  (b) any of these Rules specifies a different date for compliance; or
  (c) the court has stayed the proceedings or judgment.
(Parts 12 and 14 specify different dates for complying with certain default judgments and judgments on admissions)

40.12 CORRECTION OF ERRORS IN JUDGMENTS AND ORDERS
(1) The court may at any time correct an accidental slip or omission in a judgment or order.
(2) A party may apply for a correction without notice.

40.13 CASES WHERE COURT GIVES JUDGMENT BOTH ON CLAIM AND COUNTERCLAIM
(1) This rule applies where the court gives judgment for specified amounts both for the claimant on his claim and against the claimant on a counterclaim.
(2) If there is a balance in favour of one of the parties, it may order the party whose judgment is for the lesser amount to pay the balance.
(3) In a case to which this rule applies, the court may make a separate order as to costs against each party.

40.14 JUDGMENT IN FAVOUR OF CERTAIN PART OWNERS RELATING TO THE DETENTION OF GOODS

(1) In this rule 'part owner' means one of two or more persons who have an interest in the same goods.

(2) Where—
  (a) a part owner makes a claim relating to the detention of the goods; and
  (b) the claim is not based on a right to possession,

any judgment or order given or made in respect of the claim is to be for the payment of damages only, unless the claimant had the written authority of every other part owner of the goods to make the claim on his behalf as well as for himself.

(3) This rule applies notwithstanding anything in subsection (3) of section 3 of the Torts (Interference with Goods) Act 1977, but does not affect the remedies and jurisdiction mentioned in subsection (8) of that section.

PD 40 PRACTICE DIRECTION — ACCOUNTS, INQUIRIES ETC.

This practice direction supplements CPR Part 40

Section 1 contains provisions as to taking accounts and conducting inquiries under a judgment or order. Section 2 contains provisions formerly in CCR Order 23.

As to obtaining an interim or summary order for accounts or inquiries, attention is drawn to the Accounts & Inquiries Practice Direction that supplements CPR Part 25 and to paragraph 6 of the Summary Judgment Practice Direction that supplements CPR Part 24.

SECTION 1
ACCOUNTS AND INQUIRIES: GENERAL

1.1 Where the court orders any account to be taken or any inquiry to be made, it may, by the same or a subsequent order, give directions as to the manner in which the account is to be taken and verified or the inquiry is to be conducted.

1.2 In particular, the court may direct that in taking an account, the relevant books of account shall be evidence of their contents but that any party may take such objections to the contents as he may think fit.

1.3 Any party may apply to the court in accordance with CPR Part 23 for directions as to the taking of an account or the conduct of an inquiry or for the variation of directions already made.

1.4 Every direction for the taking of an account or the making of an inquiry shall be numbered in the order so that, as far as possible, each distinct account and inquiry is given its own separate number.

VERIFYING THE ACCOUNT

2. Subject to any order to the contrary:

(1) the accounting party must make out his account and verify it by an affidavit or witness statement to which the account is exhibited,

(2) the accounting party must file the account with the court and at the same time notify the other parties that he has done so and of the filing of any affidavit or witness statement verifying or supporting the account.

OBJECTIONS

3.1 Any party who wishes to contend:

(a) that an accounting party has received more than the amount shown by the account to have been received, or

(b) that the accounting party should be treated as having received more than he has actually received, or

(c) that any item in the account is erroneous in respect of amount, or

(d) that in any other respect the account is inaccurate,

must, unless the court directs otherwise, give written notice to the accounting party of his objections.

3.2 The written notice referred to in paragraph 3.1 must, so far as the objecting party is able to do so:

(a) state the amount by which it is contended that the account understates the amount received by the accounting party,

(b) state the amount which it is contended that the accounting party should be treated as having received in addition to the amount he actually received,

(c) specify the respects in which it is contended that the account is inaccurate, and

(d) in each case, give the grounds on which the contention is made.

3.3 The contents of the written notice must, unless the notice contains a statement of truth, be verified by either an affidavit or a witness statement to which the notice is an exhibit.

PD 40 PRACTICE DIRECTION — ACCOUNTS, INQUIRIES ETC.

(Part 22 and the Practice Direction that supplements it contain provisions about statements of truth).

ALLOWANCES

4. In taking any account ail just allowances shall be made without any express direction to that effect.

MANAGEMENT OF PROCEEDINGS

5. The court may at any stage in the taking of an account or in the course of an inquiry direct a hearing in order to resolve an issue that has arisen and for that purpose may order that points of claim and points of defence be served and give any necessary directions.

DELAY

6.1 If it appears to the court that there is undue delay in the taking of any account or the progress of any inquiry the court may require the accounting party or the party with the conduct of the inquiry, as the case may be, to explain the delay and may then make such order for the management of the proceedings (including a stay) and for costs as the circumstances may require.

6.2 The directions the court may give under paragraph 6.1 include a direction that the Official Solicitor take over the conduct of the proceedings and directions providing for the payment of the Official Solicitor's costs.

DISTRIBUTION

7. Where some of the persons entitled to share in a fund are known but there is, or is likely to be, difficulty or delay in ascertaining other persons so entitled, the court may direct, or allow, immediate payment of their shares to the known persons without reserving any part of those shares to meet the subsequent costs of ascertaining the other persons.

GUARDIAN'S ACCOUNTS

8. The accounts of a person appointed guardian of the property of a child (defined in CPR 21.1(2)) must be verified and approved in such manner as the court may direct.

SECTION 2

APPLICATION OF RSC ORDER 44 TO COUNTY COURT PROCEEDINGS

9.1 The provision of rules 1 to 10 of RSC 44 (see Part 50 and Schedule 1 to the CPR) relating to proceedings under a judgment or order in the Chancery Division shall apply to proceedings under a judgment or order made in a County Court:
    (a) in proceedings for:
        (i) the administration of the estate of a deceased person; or
        (ii) the execution of a trust; or
        (iii) the sale of any property; or
    (b) in any other proceedings in the exercise of its equity jurisdiction.

9.2 Where a judgment or order directs an account to be taken or an inquiry to be made and does not otherwise provide, the account shall be taken or the inquiry made by a Master or district judge (if the proceedings are in the High Court) or a district judge (if the proceedings are in the county court).

10. The court shall give to every creditor or other person whose claim or any part of whose claim has been allowed or disallowed, and who did not attend when the claim was disposed of, a notice informing him of that fact.

11. Rule 11 of RSC 44 (Schedule 1 to the CPR) shall apply to proceedings in a county court as if references to 'the Master' were references to a district judge.

12. An appeal shall lie to the judge from any order made by a district judge under rules 1 to 10 of RSC Order 44 (including an order giving directions as to the further conduct of the proceedings) and the provisions about an appeal in rule 12 of RSC 44 shall apply.

PD 40B PRACTICE DIRECTION — JUDGMENTS AND ORDERS

This practice direction supplements CPR Part 40

DRAWING UP AND FILING OF JUDGMENTS AND ORDERS
1.1 Rule 40.2 sets out the standard requirements for judgments and orders and rule 40.3 deals with how judgments and orders should be drawn up.
1.2 A party who has been ordered or given permission to draw up an order must file it for sealing within 7 days of being ordered or permitted to do so[1]. If he fails to do so, any other party may draw it up and file it[2].
1.3 If the court directs that a judgment or order which is being drawn up by a party must be checked by the court before it is sealed, the party responsible must file the draft within 7 days of the date the order was made with a request that the draft be checked before it is sealed.
1.4 If the court directs the parties to file an agreed statement of terms of an order which the court is to draw up[3], the parties must do so no later than 7 days from the date the order was made, unless the court directs otherwise.
1.5 If the court requires the terms of an order which is being drawn up by the court to be agreed by the parties the court may direct:
   (1) a copy of the draft order to be sent to all parties for their agreement to be endorsed on it and returned to the court before the order is sealed, or
   (2) a copy of the draft order together with notice of an appointment to attend before the court to agree the terms of the order.

PREPARATION OF DEEDS OR DOCUMENTS UNDER AN ORDER
2.1 Where a judgment or order directs any deed or document to be prepared, executed or signed, the order will state:
   (1) the person who is to prepare the deed or document, and
   (2) if the deed or document is to be approved, the person who is to approve it.
2.2 If the parties are unable to agree the form of the deed or document, any party may apply in accordance with Part 23 for the form of the deed or document to be settled.
2.3 In such case the judge may:
   (1) settle the deed or document himself, or
   (2) refer it to
      (a) a master, or
      (b) a district Judge, or
      (c) a conveyancing counsel of the Supreme Court to settle.
(See also the Sale of Land practice direction supplementing RSC Order 31 scheduled to the CPR at Part 50)

CONSENT ORDERS
3.1 Rule 40.6(3) sets out the types of consent judgments and orders which may be entered and sealed by a court officer. The court officer may do so in those cases provided that:
   (1) none of the parties is a litigant in person, and
   (2) the approval of the court is not required by the Rules, a practice direction or any enactment.[4]

---

1 rule 40.3(3)(a)
2 rule 40.3(3)(b)
3 rule 40.3(2)(b)
4 Rule 40.6(2)

PD 40B   PRACTICE DIRECTION — JUDGMENTS AND ORDERS

3.2   If a consent order filed for sealing appears to be unclear or incorrect the court officer may refer it to a judge for consideration[5].

3.3   Where a consent judgment or order does not come within the provisions of rule 40.6(2):

(1)   an application notice requesting a judgment or order in the agreed terms should be filed with the draft judgment or order to be entered or sealed, and

(2)   the draft judgment or order must be drawn so that the judge's name and judicial title can be inserted.

3.4   A consent judgment or order must:

(1)   be drawn up in the terms agreed,
(2)   bear on it the words 'By Consent', and
(3)   be signed by
   (a)   solicitors or counsel acting for each of the parties to the order, or
   (b)   where a party is a litigant in person, the litigant[6].

3.5   Where the parties draw up a consent order in the form of a stay of proceedings on agreed terms, disposing of the proceedings[7], and where the terms are recorded in a schedule to the order, any direction for:

(1)   payment of money out of court, or
(2)   payment and assessment of costs

should be contained in the body of the order and not in the schedule.

CORRECTION OF ERRORS IN JUDGMENTS AND ORDERS

4.1   Where a judgment or order contains an accidental slip or omission a party may apply for it to be corrected[8].

4.2   The application notice (which may be an informal document such as a letter) should describe the error and set out the correction required. An application may be dealt with without a hearing:

(1)   where the applicant so requests,
(2)   with the consent of the parties, or
(3)   where the court does not consider that a hearing would be appropriate.

4.3   The judge may deal with the application without notice if the slip or omission is obvious or may direct notice of the application to be given to the other party or parties.

4.4   If the application is opposed it should, if practicable, be listed for hearing before the judge who gave the judgment or made the order.

4.5   The court has an inherent power to vary its own orders to make the meaning and intention of the court clear.

ADJUSTMENT OF FINAL JUDGMENT FIGURE IN RESPECT OF COMPENSATION RECOVERY PAYMENTS

5.1   In a final judgment[9] where some or all of the damages awarded:

(2)   fall under the heads of damage set out in column 1 of Schedule 2 to the Social Security (Recovery of Benefits) Act 1997 in respect of recoverable benefits received by the claimant set out in column 2 of that Schedule and

(3)   where the defendant has paid to the Secretary of State the recoverable benefits in accordance with the certificate of recoverable benefits,

there should be stated in a preamble to the judgment or order the amount awarded under each head of damage and the amount by which it has been reduced in accordance with section 8 and Schedule 2 to the Social Security (Recovery of Benefits) Act 1997.

5.2   The judgment or order should then provide for entry of judgment and payment of the balance.

---

5 Rule 3.2
6 Rule 40.6(7)
7 Rule 40.6(3)(b)(ii)
8 Rule 40.10
9 in this paragraph final 'judgment' includes any order to pay a sum of money, a final award of damages and an assessment of damages.

ADJUSTMENT OF FINAL JUDGMENT FIGURE IN RESPECT OF AN INTERIM PAYMENT

6.1 In a final judgment[10] where an interim payment has previously been made which is less than the total amount awarded by the judge, the judgment or order should set out in a preamble:

(1) the total amount awarded by the judge, and
(2) the amount and date of the interim payment(s).

6.2 The total amount awarded by the judge should then be reduced by the total amount of any interim payments, and the judgment or order should then provide for entry of judgment and payment of the balance.

6.3 In a final judgment where an interim payment has previously been made which is more than the total amount awarded by the judge, the judgment or order should set out in a preamble:

(1) the total amount awarded by the judge, and
(2) the amount and date of the interim payment(s).

6.4 An order should then be made for repayment, reimbursement, variation or discharge under rule 25.8(2) and for interest on an overpayment under rule 25.8(5).

STATEMENT AS TO SERVICE OF A CLAIM FORM

7.1 Where a party to proceedings which have gone to trial requires a statement to be included in the judgment as to where, and by what means the claim form issued in those proceedings was served, application should made to the trial judge when judgment is given.

7.2 If the judge so orders, the statement will be included in a preamble to the judgment as entered.

ORDERS REQUIRING AN ACT TO BE DONE

8.1 An order which requires an act to be done (other than a judgment or order for the payment of an amount of money) must specify the time within which the act should be done.

8.2 The consequences of failure to do an act within the time specified may be set out in the order. In this case the wording of the following examples suitably adapted must be used:

(1) Unless the [claimant] [defendant] serves his list of documents by 4.00pm on Friday, January 22, 1999 his [claim] [defence] will be struck out and judgment entered for the [defendant] [claimant], or

(2) Unless the [claimant] [defendant] serves his list of documents within 14 days of service of this order his [claim] [defence] will be struck out and judgment entered for the [defendant] [claimant].

Example (1) should be used wherever possible.

NON-COMPLIANCE WITH A JUDGMENT OR ORDER

9.1 An order which restrains a party from doing an act or requires an act to be done should, if disobedience is to be dealt with by an application to bring contempt of court proceedings, have the penal notice endorsed on it as follows:

'If you the within-named [   ] do not comply with this order you may be held to be in contempt of court and imprisoned or fined, or

[in the case of a company or corporation] your assets may be seized.'

9.2 The provisions of paragraph 8.1 above also apply to an order which contains an undertaking by a party to do or not do an act, subject to paragraph 8.3 below.

9.3 The court has the power to decline to:

(1) accept an undertaking, and
(2) deal with disobedience in respect of an undertaking by contempt of court proceedings,

unless the party giving the undertaking has made a signed statement to the effect that he understands the terms of his undertaking and the consequences of failure to comply with it.

---

10 as in Note 9 above.

PD 40B PRACTICE DIRECTION — JUDGMENTS AND ORDERS

9.4 The statement may be endorsed on the [court copy of the] order containing the undertaking or may be filed in a separate document such as a letter.

FOREIGN CURRENCY

10. Where judgment is ordered to be entered in a foreign currency, the order should be in the following form:

'It is ordered that the defendant pay the claimant (*state the sum in the foreign currency*) or the Sterling equivalent at the time of payment.'

COSTS

11.1 Attention is drawn to the costs practice direction and, in particular, to the court's power to make a summary assessment of costs.

11.2 Attention is also drawn to costs rule 43.5(5) which provides that if an order makes no mention of costs, none are payable in respect of the proceedings to which it relates.

JUDGMENTS PAID BY INSTALMENTS

12. Where a judgment is to be paid by instalments, the judgment should set out:
   (1) the total amount of the judgment,
   (2) the amount of each instalment,
   (3) the number of instalments and the date on which each is to be paid, and
   (4) to whom the instalments should be paid.

ORDER TO MAKE AN ORDER OF THE HOUSE OF LORDS AN ORDER OF THE HIGH COURT

13.1 Application may be made in accordance with Part 23 for an order to make an order of the House of Lords an order of the High Court. The application should be made to the procedural judge of the Division, District Registry or court in which the proceedings are taking place and may be made without notice unless the court directs otherwise.

13.2 The application must be supported by the following evidence:
   (1) details of the order which was the subject of the appeal to the House of Lords,
   (2) details of the order of the House of Lords, with a copy annexed, and
   (3) a copy annexed of the certificate of the Clerk of Parliaments of the assessment of the costs of the appeal to the House of Lords in the sum of £ ....

13.3 The order to make an order of the House of Lords an order of the High Court should be in form no PF68.

EXAMPLES OF FORMS OF TRIAL JUDGMENT

14.1 The following general forms may be used:
   (1) judgment after trial before judge without jury — form No. 45,
   (2) judgment after trial before judge with jury — form No. 46,
   (3) judgment after trial before a Master or district judge — form No. 47,
   (4) judgment after trial before a judge of the Technology and Construction court — form No. 47 but with any necessary modifications.

14.2 A trial judgment should, in addition to the matters set out in paragraphs 5, 6 and 7 above, have the following matters set out in a preamble:
   (1) the questions put to a jury and their answers to those questions,
   (2) the findings of a jury and whether unanimous or by a majority,
   (3) any order made during the course of the trial concerning the use of evidence,
   (4) any matters that were agreed between the parties prior to or during the course of the trial in respect of
      (a) liability,
      (b) contribution,
      (c) the amount of the damages or part of the damages, and
   (5) the findings of the judge in respect of each head of damage in a personal injury case.

PD 40B PRACTICE DIRECTION — JUDGMENTS AND ORDERS

14.3 Form No. 49 should be used for a trial judgment against an Estate.

The forms referred to in this practice direction are listed in the practice direction which supplements Part 4 (Forms).

FOR INFORMATION ABOUT

(1) Orders for provisional damages: see Part 41 and the practice direction which supplements it.

(2) Orders in respect of children and patients: see Part 22 and the practice direction which supplements it.

(3) Orders containing directions for payment of money out of court: see Parts 36 and 37 and the practice directions which supplement them.

(4) Structured settlement orders: see the separate practice direction supplementing Part 40.

(5) Taking accounts and conducting inquiries under a judgment or order: see the separate practice direction supplementing Part 40.

PD 40C PRACTICE DIRECTION — STRUCTURED SETTLEMENTS

This practice direction supplements CPR Part 40

STRUCTURED SETTLEMENTS:

1.1 A structured settlement is a means of paying a sum awarded to or accepted by a claimant by way of instalments for the remainder of the claimant's life. The payments are either funded by an annuity from an insurance company or, where the party paying is a government body, by payments direct from that body.

1.2 The agreed sum which purchases the annuity or provides for payments (including any sum to be retained as capital for contingencies) is based on the sum offered or awarded on a conventional basis, less an amount representing the tax benefits obtained by the structure.

1.3 This type of order may be used both on settlement of a claim and after trial where the judge has found in favour of the claimant. In the latter case the claimant or his legal representative should ask the judge:

   (1) not to provide for entry of judgment,
   (2) to state the total amount to which the judge has found the claimant to be entitled, and
   (3) for an adjournment to enable advice to be sought as to the formulation of a structured settlement based on that amount.

1.4 Where a claim settles before trial, an application should be made in accordance with CPR Part 23 for the consent order embodying the structured settlement to be made, and for the approval of the structured settlement where the claimant is a child or patient[1].

1.5 If the claimant is not a child or patient, the consent order may be made without a hearing.

1.6 Where a hearing is required and as the annuity rate applicable to the structure may only remain available for a short time, the claimant's legal representative on issue of his application notice, should immediately seek an early date for the hearing.

1.7 At such a hearing the court will require the following documents and evidence to be filed not later than midday on the day before the hearing is to take place:

   (1) Counsel's or the legal representative's opinion of the value of the claim on the basis of a conventional award (unless approval on that basis has already been given or the judge has stated the amount as in paragraph 1.3(2) above),
   (2) a report of forensic accountants setting out the effect of a structured settlement bearing in mind the claimant's life expectancy and the anticipated cost of future care,
   (3) a draft of the proposed structure agreement,
   (4) sufficient information to satisfy the court that:
      (a) enough of the agreed sum is retained as a contingency fund for anticipated future needs, and
      (b) the structured settlement is secure and the annuities are payable by established insurers,
   (5) details of any assets available to the claimant other than the agreed sum which is the subject of the application, and
   (6) where the claimant is a patient, the approval or consent of the Court of Protection.

1.8 To obtain the approval of the Court of Protection the claimant's legal representative should lodge the documents and information set out in paragraph 1.7(1) to (5) above together with a copy of the claim form and any statements of

---

[1] for the definition of child or patient see Part 21.

case filed in the proceedings in the Enquiries and Acceptances Branch of the Public Trust Office, Stewart House, 24 Kingsway, London WC2B 6JH by midday on the fourth day before the hearing.

1.9 If an application for the appointment of a receiver by the Court of Protection has not already been made:
  (1) two copies of the application seeking his appointment (form CP1),
  (2) a certificate of family and property (form CP5), and
  (3) a medical certificate (form CP3)

should be lodged at the same time as the documents and information mentioned in paragraph 1.8 above. Forms CP1, 3 and 5 may be obtained from the address set out in paragraph 1.8.

1.10 Wherever possible a draft order should also be filed at the same time as the documents in paragraph 1.7 above.

1.11 Examples of structured settlement orders are set out in an Annex to this practice direction which may be adapted for use after trial or as the individual circumstances require. It should be noted that the reference in the second paragraph of the Part 2 — structured settlement order to the 'defendant's insurers' means the Life Insurer providing the annuity on behalf of the defendant.

1.12 Where it is necessary to obtain immediate payment out of money in court upon the order being made, the claimant's legal representatives should:
  (1) contact the officer in charge of funds in court at the Court Funds Office at least 2 days before the hearing, and arrange for a cheque for the appropriate sum made payable to the insurers or government body to be ready for collection,
  (2) notify the court office the day before the hearing so that the court is aware of the urgency, and
  (3) bring to the hearing a completed Court Funds Office form 200 for authentication by the court upon the order being made.

ANNEX

PART 1 STRUCTURED SETTLEMENT ORDER
(Order to settle for conventional sum and for an adjournment to seek advice on the formulation of a structured settlement)

Title of Claim

UPON HEARING (Counsel/solicitor) for the claimant and (Counsel/solicitor) for the defendant

AND UPON the defendant by (Counsel/solicitor) having undertaken to keep open an offer of £.................... in full and final settlement of the claim and the claimant having undertaken to limit the claim to £ ....

AND UPON the claimant's solicitors undertaking to instruct appropriate advisers to advise upon a structured settlement and to use their best endeavours promptly to make proposals to the defendant's solicitors as to the most equitable formulation of a structured settlement and after to seek (further directions/ approval) from the court if necessary

IT IS ORDERED that this claim is adjourned with permission to both parties to apply in respect of the further hearing relating to further directions providing for a structured settlement as undertaken by the claimant's solicitors and that these proceedings be reserved to the (trial judge) unless otherwise ordered

AND IT IS ORDERED that the costs of these proceedings together with the costs relating to any proposal for a structured settlement be (as ordered).

PART 2 STRUCTURED SETTLEMENT ORDER
(Order giving effect to and approval of a structured settlement)

Title of Claim

UPON HEARING (Counsel/solicitor) for the claimant and (Counsel/solicitor for the defendant

PD 40C   PRACTICE DIRECTION — STRUCTURED SETTLEMENTS

AND the claimant and defendant having agreed to the terms set forth in the Schedule to this order in which the claimant accepts the sum of £ .... (*overall sum*) in satisfaction of the claim of which the sum of £ .... is to be used by the [defendant's insurers for the purchase of an annuity] [defendant for the provision of the appropriate payments]

AND UPON the Judge having approved the terms of the draft minute of order, the agreement and the schedule to this order

AND UPON the claimant and the insurer (name) undertaking to execute the agreement this day

BY CONSENT

IT IS ORDERED

(1)   that of the sum of £............... (*total sum in court*) now in court standing to the credit of this claim the sum of £............... be paid out to (*insurers/payee*) on behalf of the defendant for the purchase of an annuity as specified in the payment schedule to this order

(2)   (*other relevant orders*)

( )   that all further proceedings in this claim be stayed except for the purpose of carrying the terms into effect

( )   that the parties have permission to apply to carry the terms into effect

SCHEDULE

(*Attach draft agreement and set out any other terms of the settlement*)

CPR PART 41 PROVISIONAL DAMAGES

CONTENTS OF THIS PART
Application and definitions — Rule 41.1
Order for an award of provisional damages — Rule 41.2
Application for further damages — Rule 41.3

41.1 APPLICATION AND DEFINITIONS

(1) This Part applies to proceedings to which SCA s. 32A or CCA s. 51 applies.

(2) In this Part—
   (a) 'SCA s. 32A' means section 32A of the Supreme Court Act 1981;
   (b) 'CCA s. 51' means section 51 of the County Courts Act 1984; and
   (c) 'award of provisional damages' means an award of damages for personal injuries under which
      (i) damages are assessed on the assumption referred to in SCA s. 32A or CCA s. 51 that the injured person will not develop the disease or suffer the deterioration; and
      (ii) the injured person is entitled to apply for further damages at a future date if he develops the disease or suffers the deterioration.

41.2 ORDER FOR AN AWARD OF PROVISIONAL DAMAGES

(1) The court may make an order for an award of provisional damages if—
   (a) the particulars of claim include a claim for provisional damages; and
   (b) the court is satisfied that SCA s. 32A or CCA s. 51 applies.

(Rule 16.4(1)(d) sets out what must be included in the particulars of claim where the claimant is claiming provisional damages)

(2) An order for an award of provisional damages—
   (a) must specify the disease or type of deterioration in respect of which an application may be made at a future date;
   (b) must specify the period within which such an application may be made; and
   (c) may be made in respect of more than one disease or type of deterioration and may, in respect of each disease or type of deterioration, specify a different period within which a subsequent application may be made.

(3) The claimant may make more than one application to extend the period specified under paragraph (2)(b) or (2)(c).

41.3 APPLICATION FOR FURTHER DAMAGES

(1) The claimant may not make an application for further damages after the end of the period specified under rule 41.2(2), or such period as extended by the court.

(2) Only one application for further damages may be made in respect of each disease or type of deterioration specified in the award of provisional damages.

(3) The claimant must give at least 28 days' written notice to the defendant of his intention to apply for further damages.

(4) If the claimant knows—
   (a) that the defendant is insured in respect of the claim; and
   (b) the identity of the defendant's insurers,
he must also give at least 28 days' written notice to the insurers.

(5) Within 21 days after the end of the 28 day notice period referred to in paragraphs (3) and (4), the claimant must apply for directions.

(6) The rules in Part 25 about the making of an interim payment apply where an application is made under this rule.

PD 41 PRACTICE DIRECTION — PROVISIONAL DAMAGES

This practice direction supplements CPR Part 41

CLAIMS FOR PROVISIONAL DAMAGES

1.1 CPR Part 16 and the practice direction which supplements it set out information which must be included in the particulars of claim if a claim for provisional damages is made.

JUDGMENT FOR AN AWARD OF PROVISIONAL DAMAGES

2.1 When giving judgment at trial the judge will:

(1) specify the disease or type of deterioration, or diseases or types of deterioration, which

(a) for the purpose of the award of immediate damages it has been assumed will not occur, and

(b) will entitle the claimant to further damages if it or they do occur at a future date,

(2) give an award of immediate damages,

(3) specify the period or periods within which an application for further damages may be made in respect of each disease or type of deterioration, and

(4) direct what documents are to be filed and preserved as the case file in support of any application for further damages.

2.2 The claimant may make an application or applications to extend the periods referred to in paragraph 2.1(3) above[1].

2.3 A period specified under paragraph 2.1(3) may be expressed as being for the duration of the life of the claimant.

2.4 The documents to be preserved as the case file ('the case file documents') referred to in paragraph 2.1(4) will be set out in a schedule to the judgment as entered.

2.5 Causation of any further damages within the scope of the order shall be determined when any application for further damages is made.

2.6 A form for a provisional damages judgment is set out in the Annex to this practice direction.

THE CASE FILE

3.1 The case file documents must be preserved until the expiry of the period or periods specified or of any extension of them.

3.2 The case file documents will normally include:

(1) the judgment as entered,

(2) the statements of case,

(3) a transcript of the judge's oral judgment,

(4) all medical reports relied on, and

(5) a transcript of any parts of the claimant's own evidence which the judge considers necessary.

3.3 The associate/court clerk will:

(1) ensure that the case file documents are provided by the parties where necessary and filed on the court file,

(2) endorse the court file

(a) to the effect that it contains the case file documents, and

(b) with the period during which the case file documents must be preserved, and

(3) preserve the case file documents in the court office where the proceedings took place.

3.4 Any subsequent order:

---

[1] See CPR rule 41.2(3).

PD 41 PRACTICE DIRECTION — PROVISIONAL DAMAGES

(1) extending the period within which an application for further damages may be made, or

(2) of the Court of Appeal discharging or varying the provisions of the original judgment or of any subsequent order under sub-paragraph (1) above, will become one of the case file documents and must be preserved accordingly and any variation of the period within which an application for further damages may be made should be endorsed on the court file containing the case file documents.

3.5 On an application to extend the periods referred to in paragraph 2.1(3) above a current medical report should be filed.

3.6 Legal representatives are reminded that it is their duty to preserve their own case file.

CONSENT ORDERS

4.1 An application to give effect to a consent order for provisional damages should be made in accordance with CPR Part 23. If the claimant Is a child or patient[2] the approval of the court must also be sought and the application for approval will normally be dealt with at a hearing.

4.2 The order should be in the form of a consent judgment and should contain;

(1) the matters set out in paragraph 2.1(1) to (3) above, and

(2) a direction as to the documents to be preserved as the case file documents, which will normally be

    (a) the consent judgment,

    (b) any statements of case,

    (c) an agreed statement of facts, and

    (d) any agreed medical report(s).

4.3 The claimant or his legal representative must lodge the case file documents in the court office where the proceedings are taking place for inclusion in the court file. The court file should be endorsed as in paragraph 3.3(2) above, and the case file documents preserved as in paragraph 13(3) above.

DEFAULT JUDGMENT

5.1 Where a defendant:

(1) fails to file an acknowledgment of service in accordance with CPR Part 10, and

(2) fails to file a defence in accordance with CPR Part 15,

within the time specified for doing so, the claimant may not, unless he abandons his claim for provisional damages, enter judgment in default but should make an application in accordance with CPR Part 23 for directions.

5.2 The Master or district judge will normally direct the following issues to be decided:

(1) whether the claim is an appropriate one for an award of provisional damages and if so, on what terms, and

(2) the amount of immediate damages.

5.3 If the judge makes an award of provisional damages, the provisions of paragraph 3 above apply.

ANNEX

EXAMPLE OF AN AWARD OF PROVISIONAL DAMAGES AFTER TRIAL

Title of proceedings

THIS CLAIM having been tried before [*title and name of judge*] without a jury at [the Royal Courts of Justice *or as may be*] and [*title and name of judge*] having ordered that judgment as set out below be entered for the claimant

IT IS ORDERED:

(1) that the defendant pay the claimant by way of immediate damages the sum of £............... (being (i) £............... for special damages and £............... [agreed

---

[2] see CPR Part 21 for the definitions of child and patient.

interest] [interest at the rate of .... from .... to .... (ii) £............... for general damages and £............... [agreed interest] [interest at the rate of 2% from .... to ....] and (iii) £............... for loss of future earnings and/or earning capacity) on the assumption that the claimant would not at a future date as a result of the act or omission giving rise to the claim develop the following disease/type of deterioration namely [*set out disease or type of deterioration*]

(2) that if the claimant at a further date does develop that [disease] [type of deterioration] he should be entitled to apply for further damages provided that the application is made on or before [*set out period*]

(3) that the documents set out in the schedule to this order be filed on the court file and preserved as the case file until the expiry of the period set out in paragraph (2) above or of any extension of that period which has been ordered

(4) (costs)

SCHEDULE
(*list documents referred to in paragraph (3)*)

CPR PART 42   CHANGE OF SOLICITOR

CONTENTS OF THIS PART
Solicitor acting for a party   Rule 42.1
Change of solicitor — duty to give notice   Rule 42.2
Order that a solicitor has ceased to act   Rule 42.3
Removal of solicitor who has ceased to act on application of
another party   Rule 42.4

42.1   SOLICITOR ACTING FOR A PARTY
Where the address for service of a party is the business address of his solicitor, the solicitor will be considered to be acting for that party until the provisions of this Part have been complied with.

(Part 6 contains provisions about the address for service)

42.2   CHANGE OF SOLICITOR — DUTY TO GIVE NOTICE
(1) This rule applies where—
   (a) a party for whom a solicitor is acting wants to change his solicitor;
   (b) a party, after having conducted the claim in person, appoints a solicitor to act on his behalf (except where the solicitor is appointed only to act as an advocate for a hearing); or
   (c) a party, after having conducted the claim by a solicitor, intends to act in person.

(2) Where this rule applies, the party or his solicitor (where one is acting) must—
   (a) file notice of the change; and
   (b) serve notice of the change on every other party and, where paragraph (1)(a) or (c) applies, on the former solicitor.

(3) The notice must state the party's new address for service.

(4) The notice filed at court must state that notice has been served as required by paragraph (2)(b).

(5) Subject to paragraph (6), where a party has changed his solicitor or intends to act in person, the former solicitor will be considered to be the party's solicitor unless and until—
   (a) notice is served in accordance with paragraph (1); or
   (b) the court makes an order under rule 42.3 and the order is served as required by paragraph (3) of that rule.

(6) Where the certificate of an assisted person within the meaning of the Civil Legal Aid (General) Regulations 1989 is revoked or discharged—
   (a) the solicitor who acted for the assisted person shall cease to be the solicitor acting in the case as soon as his retainer is determined under regulation 83 of those Regulations; and
   (b) if the assisted person wishes to continue—
      (i) where he appoints a solicitor to act on his behalf paragraph (2) will apply as if he had previously conducted the claim in person; and
      (ii) where he wants to act in person he must give an address for service.

(Rule 6.5 deals with a party's address for service)

42.3   ORDER THAT A SOLICITOR HAS CEASED TO ACT
(1) A solicitor may apply for an order declaring that he has ceased to be the solicitor acting for a party.

(2) Where an application is made under this rule—
   (a) notice of the application must be given to the party for whom the solicitor is acting, unless the court directs otherwise; and
   (b) the application must be supported by evidence.

(3) Where the court makes an order that a solicitor has ceased to act—
   (a) a copy of the order must be served on every party to the proceedings; and

CPR PART 42 CHANGE OF SOLICITOR

(b) if it is served by a party or the solicitor, the party or the solicitor (as the case may be) must file a certificate of service.

42.4 REMOVAL OF SOLICITOR WHO HAS CEASED TO ACT ON APPLICATION OF ANOTHER PARTY

(1) Where—
  (a) a solicitor who has acted for a party—
    (i) has died;
    (ii) has become bankrupt;
    (iii) has ceased to practise; or
    (iv) cannot be found; and
  (b) the party has not given notice of a change of solicitor or notice of intention to act in person as required by rule 42.2(2),
any other party may apply for an order declaring that the solicitor has ceased to be the solicitor acting for the other party in the case.

(2) Where an application is made under this rule, notice of the application must be given to the party to whose solicitor the application relates unless the court directs otherwise.

(3) Where the court makes an order made under this rule—
  (a) a copy of the order must be served on every other party to the proceedings; and
  (b) where it is served by a party, that party must file a certificate of service.

PD 42 PRACTICE DIRECTION — CHANGE OF SOLICITOR

This practice direction supplements CPR Part 42

SOLICITOR ACTING FOR A PARTY

1.1 Rule 42.1 states that where the address for service of a party is the business address[1] of his solicitor, the solicitor will be considered to be acting for that party until the provisions of Part 42 have been complied with.

1.2 Subject to rule 42.2(6) (where the certificate of an assisted person within the meaning of the Civil Legal Aid (General) Regulations 1989 is revoked or discharged), where a party has changed his solicitor or intends to act in person, the former solicitor will be considered to be the party's solicitor unless or until:
 (1) a notice of the change is
  (a) filed with the court[2], and
  (b) served on every other party[3], or
 (2) the court makes an order under rule 42.3 and the order is served on every other party[4].
The notice should not be filed until every other party has been served.

1.3 A solicitor appointed to represent a party only as an advocate at a hearing will not be considered to be acting for that party within the meaning of Part 42.

NOTICE OF CHANGE OF SOLICITOR

2.1 Rule 42.2(1) sets out the circumstances following which a notice of the change must be filed and served.

2.2 A notice of the change giving the last known address of the former assisted person must also be filed and served on every party where, under rule 42.2(6):
 (1) the certificate of an assisted person within the meaning of the Civil Legal Aid (General) Regulations 1989 is revoked or discharged,
 (2) the solicitor who acted for the assisted person has ceased to act on determination of his retainer under regulation 83 of those Regulations, and
 (3) the assisted person wishes either to act in person or appoint another solicitor to act on his behalf.

2.3 In addition, where a party or solicitor changes his address for service, a notice of that change should be filed and served on every party.

2.4 A party who, having conducted a claim by a solicitor, intends to act in person must give in his notice an address for service that is within the jurisdiction[5].

2.5 Practice form N434 should be used to give notice of any change. The notice should be filed in the court office in which the claim is proceeding.

2.6 Where the claim is proceeding in the High Court the notice should be filed either in the appropriate District Registry or if the claim is proceeding in the Royal Courts of Justice, as follows:
 (1) a claim proceeding in the Queen's Bench Division — in the Action Department of the Central Office,
 (2) a claim proceeding in the Chancery Division — in Chancery Chambers,
 (3) a claim proceeding in the Crown Office — in the Crown Office,
 (4) a claim proceeding in the Admiralty and Commercial Registry — in the Admiralty and Commercial Registry, and
 (5) a claim proceeding in the Technology and Construction Court — in the Registry of the Technology and Construction Court.

---

[1] Rule 6.5 and the Practice Direction supplementing Part 6 contain information about the business address.
[2] Rule 42.2(2)(a)
[3] Rule 42.2(2)(b)
[4] Rule 42.2(5)
[5] See rule 6.5(3)

PD 42 PRACTICE DIRECTION — CHANGE OF SOLICITOR

2.7 Where the claim is the subject of an appeal to the Court of Appeal, the notice should also be filed in the Civil Appeals Office.

APPLICATION FOR AN ORDER THAT A SOLICITOR HAS CEASED TO ACT

3.1 A solicitor may apply under rule 42.3 for an order declaring that he has ceased to be the solicitor acting for a party.

3.2 The application should be made in accordance with Part 23[6] and must be supported by evidence[7]. Unless the court directs otherwise the application notice must be served on the party[8].

3.3 An order made under rule 42.3 must be served on every party and takes effect when it is served. Where the order is not served by the court, the person serving must file a certificate of service in practice form N215.

APPLICATION BY ANOTHER PARTY TO REMOVE A SOLICITOR

4.1 Rule 42.4 sets out circumstances in which any other party may apply for an order declaring that a solicitor has ceased to be the solicitor acting for another party in the proceedings.

4.2 The application should be made in accordance with Part 23 and must be supported by evidence. Unless the court directs otherwise the application notice must be served on the party to whose solicitor the application relates.

4.3 An order made under rule 42.4 must be served on every other party to the proceedings. Where the order is not served by the court, the person serving must file a certificate of service in practice form N215.

---

[6] See Part 23 and the Practice Direction which supplements it
[7] See Part 32 and the Practice Direction which supplements it for information about evidence
[8] Rule 42.3(2)

CPR PART 43 SCOPE OF COST RULES AND DEFINITIONS

CONTENTS OF THIS PART
Scope of this Part   Rule 43.1
Definitions and application   Rule 43.2
Meaning of summary assessment   Rule 43.3
Meaning of detailed assessment   Rule 43.4

43.1 SCOPE OF THIS PART

This Part contains definitions and interpretation of certain matters set out in the rules about costs contained in Parts 44 to 48.

(Part 44 contains general rules about costs; Part 45 deals with fixed costs; Part 46 deals with fast track trial costs; Part 47 deals with the detailed assessment of costs and related appeals and Part 48 deals with costs payable in special cases)

43.2 DEFINITIONS AND APPLICATION

(1) In Parts 44 to 48, unless the context otherwise requires—
    (a) 'costs' includes fees, charges, disbursements, expenses, remuneration, reimbursement allowed to a litigant in person under rule 48.6 and any fee or reward charged by a lay representative for acting on behalf of a party in proceedings allocated to the small claims track;
    (b) 'costs judge' means a taxing master of the Supreme Court;
    (c) 'costs officer' means—
        (i) a costs judge;
        (ii) a district judge; and
        (iii) an authorised court officer;
    (d) 'authorised court officer' means any officer of—
        (i) a county court;
        (ii) a district registry;
        (iii) the Principal Registry of the Family Division; or
        (iv) the Supreme Court Costs Office, whom the Lord Chancellor has authorised to assess costs.
    (e) 'fund' includes any estate or property held for the benefit of any person or class of person and any fund to which a trustee or personal representative is entitled in his capacity as such;
    (f) 'receiving party' means a party entitled to be paid costs;
    (g) 'paying party' means a party liable to pay costs;
    (h) 'assisted person' means an assisted person within the statutory provisions relating to legal aid; and
    (i) 'fixed costs' means the amounts which are to be allowed in respect of solicitors' charges in the circumstances set out in Part 45.
(2) The costs to which Parts 44 to 48 apply include—
    (a) the following costs where those costs may be assessed by the court—
        (i) costs of proceedings before an arbitrator or umpire;
        (ii) costs of proceedings before a tribunal or other statutory body; and
        (iii) costs payable by a client to his solicitor; and
    (b) costs which are payable by one party to another party under the terms of a contract, where the court makes an order for an assessment of those costs.

43.3 MEANING OF SUMMARY ASSESSMENT

'Summary assessment' means the procedure by which the court, when making an order about costs, orders payment of a sum of money instead of fixed costs or 'detailed assessment'.

43.4 MEANING OF DETAILED ASSESSMENT

'Detailed assessment' means the procedure by which the amount of costs is decided by a costs officer in accordance with Part 47.

PD COSTS PRACTICE DIRECTION ABOUT COSTS

Supplementing CPR Parts 43 to 48

INTRODUCTION

1. This Practice Direction [*] supplements Parts 43 to 48 of the Civil Procedure Rules. It applies to all proceedings to which those Parts apply.

2. Section III of the Directions Relating to Part 48 deals with transitional provisions affecting proceedings about costs which were pending before 26 April 1999.

3. Attention is drawn to the powers to make orders about costs conferred on the Supreme Court and any county court by Section 51 of the Supreme Court Act 1981.

4. In these Directions [*]:

'counsel' means a barrister or other person with a right of audience in relation to all proceedings in the High Court or in the County Courts in which he is instructed to act.

'solicitor' means a solicitor of the Supreme Court or other person with a right of audience in relation to all proceedings, who is conducting the claim or defence (as the case may be) on behalf of a party to proceedings and, where the context admits, includes a patent agent.

5. In respect of any document which is required by these Directions [*] to be signed by a party or his legal representative the Practice Direction supplementing Part 22 will apply as if the document in question was a statement of truth. (The Practice Direction supplementing Part 22 makes provision for cases in which a party is a child, a patient or a company or other corporation and cases in which a document is signed on behalf of a partnership.)

SCHEDULE OF COSTS FORMS [†]

1. *Statement of Costs (summary assessment)*
2. *Bill of Costs (detailed assessment)*
3. *Legal Aid Schedule of Costs*
4. *Certificates for inclusion in bills*
5. *Notice of Commencement of Assessment of Bill of Costs [Form N252]*
6. *Points of Dispute*
7. *Request for Default Costs Certificate [Form N254]*
8. *Request for a Detailed Assessment Hearing [Form N258]*
9. *Default Costs Certificate (County Court) [Form N255CC]*
10. *Default Costs Certificate (High Court) [Form N255HC]*
11. *Interim Costs Certificate [Form N257]*
12. *Final Costs Certificate (County Court) [Form N256CC]*
13. *Final Costs Certificate (High Court) [Form N256HC]*
14. *Notice of Amount Allowed on Provisional Assessment (Legal Aid only) [Form N253]*
15. Legal Aid Assessment Certificate
16. Notice of Appeal
17. Solicitors Act: order for delivery of bill
18. Solicitors Act: order for detailed assessment (client)
19. Solicitors Act: order for detailed assessment (solicitors)
20. Solicitors Act: breakdown of costs
21. Solicitors Act: request for a hearing date

[* Including PD 43, PD 44, PD 45, PD 46, PD 47 and PD 48, which are printed in this book after the Parts to which they relate.]

[† These forms are printed in appendix 3 to this book.]

PD 43 PRACTICE DIRECTION — SCOPE OF COSTS RULES AND DEFINITIONS

SECTION 1   MODEL FORMS FOR CLAIMS FOR COSTS

Rule 43.3   Meaning of summary assessment

1.1   Rule 43.3 defines summary assessment.

1.2   Form 1 of the Schedule of Costs Forms annexed to this Direction [see page 1317] is a model form of Statement of Costs to be used for summary assessments.

1.3   Further details about Statements of Costs are given in paragraph 4 of the Directions Relating to Part 44 (Procedure for assessing costs).

Rule 43.4   Meaning of detailed assessment

1.4   Rule 43.4 defines detailed assessment.

1.5   Form 2 of the Schedule of Costs Forms annexed to this Practice Direction [see page 1318] is a model form of bill of costs to be used for detailed assessments.

1.6   Further details about bills of costs are given in the next section of these Directions and in paragraph 2.7 of the Directions Relating to Part 47 (Procedure for detailed assessment of costs and default provisions).

1.7   Form 2 of the Schedule of Costs Forms [see page 1318] and the next section of this Practice Direction both refer to the ideal form of bills of costs. A party wishing to rely upon a bill which departs from the ideal form should include in the background information of the bill an explanation justifying the departure.

1.8   In any order of the court (whether made before or after 26 April 1999) the word 'taxation' will be taken to mean 'detailed assessment' and the words 'to be taxed' will be taken to mean 'to be decided by detailed assessment' unless in either case the context otherwise requires.

SECTION 2   FORM AND CONTENTS OF BILLS OF COSTS

2.1   A bill of costs may consist of such of the following sections as may be appropriate:

    (1)   title page;
    (2)   background information;
    (3)   items of costs claimed under the headings specified in paragraph 2.5;
    (4)   summary showing the total costs claimed on each page of the bill;
    (5)   schedules of time spent on non-routine attendances; and
    (6)   the certificates referred to in paragraph 2.14.

2.2   Where it is necessary or convenient to do so, a bill of costs may be divided into two or more parts, each part containing sections (2), (3) and (4) above. A division into parts will be necessary or convenient in the following circumstances:

(1)   Where the receiving party acted in person during the course of the proceedings (whether or not he also had a legal representative at that time) the bill should be divided into different parts so as to distinguish between:

    (a)   the costs claimed for work done by the legal representative; and
    (b)   the costs claimed for work done by the receiving party in person.

(2)   Where the receiving party was represented by different solicitors during the course of the proceedings, the bill should be divided into different parts so as to distinguish between the costs payable in respect of each solicitor.

(3)   Where the receiving party obtained legal aid in respect of all or part of the proceedings the bill should be divided into separate parts so as to distinguish between:

    (a)   costs claimed before legal aid was granted;
    (b)   costs claimed against the Legal Aid Board only; and
    (c)   any costs claimed after legal aid ceased.

(4)   Where value added tax (VAT) is claimed and there was a change in the rate of VAT during the course of the proceedings, the bill should be divided into separate parts so as to distinguish between:

PD 43 PRACTICE DIRECTION — SCOPE OF COSTS RULES AND DEFINITIONS

(a) costs claimed at the old rate of VAT; and
(b) costs claimed at the new rate of VAT.

(5) Where the bill covers costs payable under two or more orders under which there are different paying parties the bill should be divided into parts so as to deal separately with the costs payable by each paying party.

2.3 The title page of the bill of costs must set out:
(1) the full title of the proceedings;
(2) the name of the party whose bill it is and a description of the document showing the right to assessment (as to which see paragraph 4.5 of the Directions Relating to Part 47);
(3) if VAT is included as part of the claim for costs, the VAT number of the legal representative or other person in respect of whom VAT is claimed;
(4) details of all legal aid certificates and legal aid amendment certificates in respect of which claims for costs are included in the bill.

2.4 The background information included in the bill of costs should set out:
(1) a brief description of the proceedings up to the date of the notice of commencement;
(2) a statement of the status of the solicitor or solicitor's employee in respect of whom costs are claimed and (if those costs are calculated on the basis of hourly rates) the hourly rates claimed for each such person;
(3) a brief explanation of any agreement or arrangement between the receiving party and his solicitors which affects the costs claimed in the bill.

2.5 The bill of costs may consist of items under such of the following heads as may be appropriate:
(1) attendances on the court and counsel up to the date of the notice of commencement;
(2) attendances on and communications with the receiving party;
(3) attendances on and communications with witnesses including any expert witness;
(4) attendances to inspect any property or place for the purposes of the proceedings;
(5) searches and enquiries made at offices of public records, the Companies Registry and similar searches and enquiries;
(6) attendances on and communications with other persons;
(7) communications with the court and with counsel;
(8) work done in connection with arithmetical calculations of compensation and/or interest;
(9) work done on documents: preparing and considering documentation which was of and incidental to the proceedings, including time spent on pre-action protocols where appropriate and time spent collating documents;
(10) work done in connection with mediation, alternative dispute resolution and negotiations with a view to settlement if not already covered in the heads listed above;
(11) attendances on and communications with London and other agents and work done by them;
(12) other work done which was of or incidental to the proceedings and which is not already covered in the heads listed above.

2.6 In respect of each of the heads of costs:
(1) 'communications' means letters out and telephone calls;
(2) communications which are not routine communications must be set out in chronological order;
(3) routine communications should be set out as a single item at the end of each head.

2.7 Routine communications are letters out and telephone calls which by reason of their simplicity should not be regarded as letters of substance or telephone calls which properly amount to an attendance.

2.8 Each item claimed in the bill of costs must be consecutively numbered.

PD 43 PRACTICE DIRECTION — SCOPE OF COSTS RULES AND DEFINITIONS

2.9 In each part of the bill of costs which claims items under head (1) (attendances on court and counsel) a note should be made of:

(1) all relevant events, including events which do not constitute chargeable items;

(2) any orders for costs which the court made (whether or not a claim is made in respect of those costs in this bill of costs).

2.10 The numbered items of costs must be set out on paper divided into five columns, of which the last two columns should be left blank. The five columns should be headed as follows: Item, Amount claimed, VAT, Amount allowed, VAT.

2.11 In respect of heads (2) to (12) in paragraph 2.5 above, if the number of attendances and communications other than routine communications is five or more, the claim for the costs of those items in that section of the bill of costs should be for the total only and should refer to a schedule in which the full record of dates and details is set out. If the bill of costs contains more than one schedule each schedule should be numbered consecutively.

2.12 The bill of costs must not contain any claims in respect of costs or court fees which relate solely to the detailed assessment proceedings other than costs claimed for preparing and checking the bill.

2.13 The summary must show the total profit costs and disbursements claimed separately from the total VAT claimed. Where the bill of costs is divided into parts the summary must also give totals for each part. If each page of the bill gives a page total the summary must also set out the page totals for each page.

2.14 The bill of costs must contain such of the certificates, the texts of which are set out in Form 4 of the Schedule of Costs Forms annexed to this Practice Direction [see page 1333], as are appropriate.

2.15 The following provisions relate to work done by solicitors:

(1) Routine letters out and routine telephone calls will in general be allowed on a unit basis of 6 minutes each, the charge being calculated by reference to the appropriate hourly rate. The unit charge for letters out will include perusing and considering the relevant letters in and no separate charge should be made for incoming letters.

(2) E-mails received or sent by solicitors will not normally be allowed but the court may, in its discretion, allow an actual time charge for preparation of e-mails sent by solicitors which properly amount to attendances provided that the time taken has been recorded. The court may also, in its discretion, allow a sum in respect of e-mails sent to the client or others where it is satisfied that, had e-mails not been sent, the number of communications which it would have been reasonable to allow would have been substantially greater than the number actually claimed.

(3) Local travelling expenses incurred by solicitors will not be allowed. The definition of 'local' is a matter for the discretion of the court. While no absolute rule can be laid down, as a matter of guidance, 'local' will, in general, be taken to mean within a radius of 10 miles from the court dealing with the case at the relevant time.

(4) The cost of postage, couriers, outgoing telephone calls, fax and telex messages will in general not be allowed but the court may in its discretion allow such expenses in unusual circumstances or where the cost is unusually heavy.

(5) The cost of making copies of documents will not in general be allowed but the court may in its discretion make an allowance for copying in unusual circumstances or where the documents copied are unusually numerous in relation to the nature of the case. Where this discretion is invoked the number of copies made, their purpose and the costs claimed for them must be set out in the bill.

(6) Agency charges as between a principal solicitor and his agent will be dealt with on the principle that such charges, where appropriate, form part of the principal solicitor's charges. Where these charges relate to head (1) in paragraph 2.5 (attendances at court and on counsel) they should be included in their chronological order in that head. In other cases they should be included in head (11) (attendances on London and other agents).

Costs of preparing the bill
2.16 In head (12) in paragraph 2.5 (other work done) a claim may be made for the reasonable costs of preparing and checking the bill of costs.

SECTION 3 SPECIAL PROVISIONS RELATING TO VAT
3.1 This section deals with claims for value added tax (VAT) which are made in respect of costs being dealt with by way of summary assessment or detailed assessment.

VAT Registration Number
3.2 The number allocated by HM Customs and Excise to every person registered under the Value Added Tax Act 1983 (except a Government Department) must appear in a prominent place at the head of every statement, bill of costs, fee sheet, account or voucher on which VAT is being included as part of a claim for costs.

Entitlement to VAT on Costs
3.3 VAT should not be included in a claim for costs if the receiving party is able to recover the VAT as input tax. Where the receiving party is able to obtain credit from HM Customs and Excise for a proportion of the VAT as input tax, only that proportion which is not eligible for credit should be included in the claim for costs.
3.4 The receiving party has responsibility for ensuring that VAT is claimed only when the receiving party is unable to recover the VAT or a proportion thereof as input tax.
3.5 Where there is a dispute as to whether VAT is properly claimed the receiving party must provide a certificate signed by the solicitors or the auditors of the receiving party in the form in the Schedule of Certificates annexed to this Practice Direction [see page 1333]. Where the receiving party is a litigant in person who is claiming VAT, reference should be made by him to HM Customs and Excise and wherever possible a Statement to similar effect produced at the hearing at which the costs are assessed.
3.6 Where there is a dispute as to whether any service in respect of which a charge is proposed to be made in the bill is zero rated or exempt, reference should be made to HM Customs and Excise and wherever possible the view of HM Customs and Excise obtained and made known at the hearing at which the costs are assessed. Such application should be made by the receiving party. In the case of a bill from a solicitor to his own client such application should be made by the client.

Form of bill of costs where VAT rate changes
3.7 Where there is a change in the rate of VAT, suppliers of goods and services are entitled by ss. 88(1) and 88(2) of the VAT Act 1994 in most circumstances to elect whether the new or the old rate of VAT should apply to a supply where the basic and actual tax points span a period during which there has been a change in VAT rates.
3.8 It will be assumed, unless a contrary indication is given in writing, that an election to take advantage of the provisions mentioned in paragraph 3.7 above and to charge VAT at the lower rate has been made. In any case in which an election to charge at the lower rate is not made, such a decision must be justified to the court assessing the costs.

Apportionment
3.9 All bills of costs, fees and disbursements on which VAT is included must be divided into separate parts so as to show work done before, on and after the date or dates from which any change in the rate of VAT takes effect. Where, however, a lump sum charge is made for work which spans a period during which there has been a change in VAT rates, and paragraphs 3.7 and 3.8 above do not apply, reference should be made to paragraphs 8 and 9 of Appendix F of Customs' Notice 700 (or any revised edition of that notice), a copy of which should be in

PD 43 PRACTICE DIRECTION — SCOPE OF COSTS RULES AND DEFINITIONS

the possession of every registered trader. If necessary, the lump sum should be apportioned. The totals of profit costs and disbursements in each part must be carried separately to the summary.

3.10 Should there be a change in the rate between the conclusion of a detailed assessment and the issue of the final costs certificate, any interested party may apply for the detailed assessment to be varied so as to take account of any increase or reduction in the amount of tax payable. Once the final costs certificate has been issued, no variation under this paragraph will be permitted.

Disbursements

3.11 Petty (or general) disbursements such as postage, fares etc. which are normally treated as part of a solicitor's overheads and included in his profit costs should be charged with VAT even though they bear no tax when the solicitor incurs them. The cost of travel by public transport on a specific journey for a particular client where it forms part of the service rendered by a solicitor to his client and is charged in his bill of costs, attracts VAT.

3.12 Reference is made to the criteria set out in the VAT Guide (Customs and Excise Notice 700 — 1st August 1991 edition paragraph 83, or any revised edition of that Notice), as to expenses which are not subject to VAT. Charges for the cost of travel by public transport, postage, telephone calls and telegraphic transfers where these form part of the service rendered by the solicitor to his client are examples of charges which do not satisfy these criteria and are thus liable to VAT at the standard rate.

Legal Aid

3.13 VAT will be payable in respect of every supply made pursuant to a Legal Aid Certificate provided only that the person making the supply is a taxable person and that the assisted person is not resident outside the European Union. Where the assisted person is registered for VAT and the legal services paid for by the Legal Aid Board are in connection with the assisted person's business, the VAT on those services will be payable by the Legal Aid Board only.

3.14 In Legal Aid cases the legal aid summary must be drawn so as to show the total VAT on Counsel's fees as a separate item from the VAT on other disbursements and the VAT on profit costs.

Tax invoice

3.15 A bill of costs filed for detailed assessment is always retained by the Court. Accordingly if a solicitor waives his solicitor and client costs and accepts the costs certified by the court as payable by the unsuccessful party in settlement, it will be necessary for a short statement as to the amount of the certified costs and the VAT thereon to be prepared for use as the tax invoice.

Vouchers

3.16 Where receipted accounts for disbursements made by the solicitor or his client are retained as tax invoices a photostat copy of any such receipted account may be produced and will be accepted as sufficient evidence of payment when disbursements are vouched.

Certificates

3.17 In non legal aid cases the total VAT allowed will be shown in the final costs certificate as a separate item. In legal aid cases the VAT on Counsel's fees will be shown separately from the remaining VAT.

Litigants acting in person

3.18 Where a litigant acts in litigation on his own behalf he is not treated for the purposes of VAT as having supplied services and therefore no VAT is chargeable on that litigant's costs (even where, for example, that litigant is a solicitor or other legal representative).

3.19 Consequently in the circumstances described in the preceding paragraph, a bill of costs presented for agreement or assessment should not claim any VAT which will not be allowed on assessment.

Government Departments

3.20 On a detailed assessment between parties, where costs are being paid to a Government Department in respect of services rendered by its legal staff, VAT should not be added.

SECTION 4   ESTIMATES OF COSTS

4.1 This section sets out certain steps which parties must take in order to keep the other parties informed about their potential liability in respect of costs and in order to assist the court to decide what, if any, order to make about costs and about case management.

4.2 In this section an estimate of costs means an estimate of those costs already incurred and, if appropriate, to be incurred by the party who gives it which he intends, if he is successful in the case, to seek to recover from any other party under an order for costs.

4.3 The court may at any stage in a case order any party to file an estimate of costs and to serve copies of the estimate on all other parties. The court may direct that the estimate be prepared in such a way as to demonstrate the likely effects of giving or not giving a particular case management direction which the court is considering, for example a direction for a split trial or for the trial of a preliminary issue. The court may specify a time limit for filing and serving the estimate. However, if no time limit is specified the estimate should be filed and served within 28 days of the date of the order.

4.4 An estimate of costs should be substantially in the form of a Statement of Costs as illustrated in Form 1 of the Schedule of Costs Forms annexed to this Practice Direction [see page 1317].

4.5 (1) When a party to a claim which is outside the financial scope of the small claims track files an allocation questionnaire, he must also file an estimate of costs and serve a copy of it on every other party unless the court otherwise directs.

(2) When a party to a claim which is being dealt with on the fast track or the multi-track or under Part 8 files a listing questionnaire, he must also file an estimate of costs and serve a copy of it on every other party, unless the court otherwise directs.

(3) An estimate of costs filed with a listing questionnaire must be divided into parts to show the costs already incurred by the party separately from those which will be incurred by him if the case proceeds to trial.

(4) This paragraph does not apply to litigants in person.

CPR PART 44 GENERAL RULES ABOUT COSTS

CONTENTS OF THIS PART
Scope of this Part	Rule 44.1
Solicitor's duty to notify client	Rule 44.2
Court's discretion and circumstances to be taken into account when exercising its discretion as to costs	Rule 44.3
Basis of assessment	Rule 44.4
Factors to be taken into account in deciding the amount of costs	Rule 44.5
Fixed costs	Rule 44.6
Procedure for assessing costs	Rule 44.7
Time for complying with an order for costs	Rule 44.8
Costs on the small claims track and fast track	Rule 44.9
Limitation on amount court may allow where a claim allocated to the fast track settles before trial	Rule 44.10
Costs following allocation and re-allocation	Rule 44.11
Cases where costs orders deemed to have been made	Rule 44.12
Special situations	Rule 44.13
Court's powers in relation to misconduct	Rule 44.14

44.1 SCOPE OF THIS PART
This Part contains general rules about costs and entitlement to costs.
(The definitions contained in Part 43 are relevant to this Part)

44.2 SOLICITOR'S DUTY TO NOTIFY CLIENT
Where—
    (a) the court makes a costs order against a legally represented party; and
    (b) the party is not present when the order is made,
the party's solicitor must notify his client in writing of the costs order no later than 7 days after the solicitor receives notice of the order.

44.3 COURT'S DISCRETION AND CIRCUMSTANCES TO BE TAKEN INTO ACCOUNT WHEN EXERCISING ITS DISCRETION AS TO COSTS
    (1) The court has discretion as to—
        (a) whether costs are payable by one party to another;
        (b) the amount of those costs; and
        (c) when they are to be paid.
    (2) If the court decides to make an order about costs—
        (a) the general rule is that the unsuccessful party will be ordered to pay the costs of the successful party; but
        (b) the court may make a different order.
    (3) The general rule does not apply to the following proceedings—
        (a) proceedings in the Court of Appeal on an application or appeal made in connection with proceedings in the Family Division; or
        (b) proceedings in the Court of Appeal from a judgment, direction, decision or order given or made in probate proceedings or family proceedings.
    (4) In deciding what order (if any) to make about costs, the court must have regard to all the circumstances, including—
        (a) the conduct of all the parties;
        (b) whether a party has succeeded on part of his case, even if he has not been wholly successful; and
        (c) any payment into court or admissible offer to settle made by a party which is drawn to the court's attention (whether or not made in accordance with Part 36).
(Part 36 contains further provisions about how the court's discretion is to be exercised where a payment into court or an offer to settle is made under that Part)
    (5) The conduct of the parties includes—

(a) conduct before, as well as during, the proceedings and in particular the extent to which the parties followed any relevant pre-action protocol;
(b) whether it was reasonable for a party to raise, pursue or contest a particular allegation or issue;
(c) the manner in which a party has pursued or defended his case or a particular allegation or issue; and
(d) whether a claimant who has succeeded in his claim, in whole or in part, exaggerated his claim.

(6) The orders which the court may make under this rule include an order that a party must pay—
(a) a proportion of another party's costs;
(b) a stated amount in respect of another party's costs;
(c) costs from or until a certain date only;
(d) costs incurred before proceedings have begun;
(e) costs relating to particular steps taken in the proceedings;
(f) costs relating only to a distinct part of the proceedings; and
(g) interest on costs from or until a certain date, including a date before judgment.

(7) Where the court would otherwise consider making an order under paragraph (6)(f), it must instead, if practicable, make an order under paragraph (6)(a) or (c).

(8) Where the court has ordered a party to pay costs, it may order an amount to be paid on account before the costs are assessed.

(9) Where a party entitled to costs is also liable to pay costs the court may assess the costs which that party is liable to pay and either—
(a) set off the amount assessed against the amount the party is entitled to be paid and direct him to pay any balance; or
(b) delay the issue of a certificate for the costs to which the party is entitled until he has paid the amount which he is liable to pay.

44.4 BASIS OF ASSESSMENT

(1) Where the court is to assess the amount of costs (whether by summary or detailed assessment) it will assess those costs—
(a) on the standard basis; or
(b) on the indemnity basis,
but the court will not in either case allow costs which have been unreasonably incurred or are unreasonable in amount.
(Rule 48.3 sets out how the court decides the amount of costs payable under a contract)

(2) Where the amount of costs is to be assessed on the standard basis, the court will—
(a) only allow costs which are proportionate to the matters in issue; and
(b) resolve any doubt which it may have as to whether costs were reasonably incurred or reasonable and proportionate in amount in favour of the paying party.
(Factors which the court may take into account are set out in rule 44.5)

(3) Where the amount of costs is to be assessed on the indemnity basis, the court will resolve any doubt which it may have as to whether costs were reasonably incurred or were reasonable in amount in favour of the receiving party.

(4) Where—
(a) the court makes an order about costs without indicating the basis on which the costs are to be assessed; or
(b) the court makes an order for costs to be assessed on a basis other than the standard basis or the indemnity basis,
the costs will be assessed on the standard basis.

(5) This rule and Part 47 (detailed assessment of costs by a costs officer) do not apply to the extent that regulations made under the Legal Aid Act 1988 determine the amount payable.

(6) Where the amount of a solicitor's remuneration in respect of non-contentious business is regulated by any general orders made under the Solicitors Act

CPR PART 44   GENERAL RULES ABOUT COSTS

1974, the amount of the costs to be allowed in respect of any such business which falls to be assessed by the court will be decided in accordance with those general orders rather than this rule and rule 44.5.

44.5   FACTORS TO BE TAKEN INTO ACCOUNT IN DECIDING THE AMOUNT OF COSTS

(1) The court is to have regard to all the circumstances in deciding whether costs were—
    (a)   if it is assessing costs on the standard basis—
        (i)   proportionately and reasonably incurred; or
        (ii) were proportionate and reasonable in amount, or
    (b)   if it is assessing costs on the indemnity basis—
        (i)   unreasonably incurred; or
        (ii) unreasonable in amount.

(2) In particular the court must give effect to any orders which have already been made.

(3) The court must also have regard to—
    (a)   the conduct of all the parties, including in particular—
        (i)   conduct before, as well as during, the proceedings; and
        (ii) the efforts made, if any, before and during the proceedings in order to try to resolve the dispute;
    (b)   the amount or value of any money or property involved;
    (c)   the importance of the matter to all the parties;
    (d)   the particular complexity of the matter or the difficulty or novelty of the questions raised;
    (e)   the skill, effort, specialised knowledge and responsibility involved;
    (f)   the time spent on the case; and
    (g)   the place where and the circumstances in which work or any part of it was done.

(Rule 35.4(4) gives the court power to limit the amount that a party may recover with regard to the fees and expenses of an expert)

44.6   FIXED COSTS

A party may recover the fixed costs specified in Part 45 in accordance with that Part.

44.7   PROCEDURE FOR ASSESSING COSTS

Where the court orders a party to pay costs to another party (other than fixed costs) it may either—
    (a)   make a summary assessment of the costs; or
    (b)   order detailed assessment of the costs by a costs officer,
unless any rule, practice direction or other enactment provides otherwise.

(The costs practice direction sets out the factors which will affect the court's decision under this rule)

44.8   TIME FOR COMPLYING WITH AN ORDER FOR COSTS

A party must comply with an order for the payment of costs within 14 days of—
    (a)   the date of the judgment or order if it states the amount of those costs; or
    (b)   if the amount of those costs (or part of them) is decided later in accordance with Part 47, the date of the certificate which states the amount.

(Part 47 sets out the procedure for detailed assessment of costs)

44.9   COSTS ON THE SMALL CLAIMS TRACK AND FAST TRACK

(1) Part 27 (small claims) and Part 46 (fast track trial costs) contain special rules about—
    (a)   liability for costs;
    (b)   the amount of costs which the court may award; and
    (c)   the procedure for assessing costs.

(2) Once a claim is allocated to a particular track, those special rules shall apply to the period before, as well as after, allocation except where the court or a practice direction provides otherwise.

44.10 LIMITATION ON AMOUNT COURT MAY ALLOW WHERE A CLAIM ALLOCATED TO THE FAST TRACK SETTLES BEFORE TRIAL

(1) Where the court—
   (a) assesses costs in relation to a claim which—
      (i) has been allocated to the fast track; and
      (ii) settles before the start of the trial; and
   (b) is considering the amount of costs to be allowed in respect of a party's advocate for preparing for the trial,
it may not allow, in respect of those advocate's costs, an amount that exceeds the amount of fast track trial costs which would have been payable in relation to the claim had the trial taken place.

(2) When deciding the amount to be allowed in respect of the advocate's costs, the court shall have regard to—
   (a) when the claim was settled; and
   (b) when the court was notified that the claim had settled.

(3) In this rule, 'advocate' and 'fast track trial costs' have the meanings given to them by Part 46.

(Part 46 sets out the amount of fast track trial costs which may be awarded)

44.11 COSTS FOLLOWING ALLOCATION AND RE-ALLOCATION

(1) Any costs orders made before a claim is allocated will not be affected by allocation.

(2) Where—
   (a) a claim is allocated to a track; and
   (b) the court subsequently re-allocates that claim to a different track,
then unless the court orders otherwise, any special rules about costs applying—
      (i) to the first track, will apply to the claim up to the date of re-allocation; and
      (ii) to the second track, will apply from the date of re-allocation.

(Part 26 deals with the allocation and re-allocation of claims between tracks)

44.12 CASES WHERE COSTS ORDERS DEEMED TO HAVE BEEN MADE

(1) Where a right to costs arises under—
   (a) rule 3.7 (defendant's right to costs where claim struck out for non-payment of fees);
   (b) rule 36.13(1) (claimant's right to costs where he accepts defendant's Part 36 offer or Part 36 payment);
   (c) rule 36.14 (claimant's right to costs where defendant accepts the claimant's Part 36 offer); or
   (d) rule 38.6 (defendant's right to costs where claimant discontinues),
a costs order will be deemed to have been made on the standard basis.

(2) Interest payable pursuant to section 17 of the Judgments Act 1838 or section 74 of the County Courts Act 1984 on the costs deemed to have been ordered under paragraph (1) shall begin to run from the date on which the event which gave rise to the entitlement to costs occurred.

44.13 SPECIAL SITUATIONS

(1) Where the court makes an order which does not mention costs no party is entitled to costs in relation to that order.

(2) The court hearing an appeal may, unless it dismisses the appeal, make orders about the costs of the proceedings giving rise to the appeal as well as the costs of the appeal.

(3) Where proceedings are transferred from one court to another, the court to which they are transferred may deal with all the costs, including the costs before the transfer.

(4) Paragraph (3) is subject to any order of the court which ordered the transfer.

CPR PART 44   GENERAL RULES ABOUT COSTS

44.14   COURT'S POWERS IN RELATION TO MISCONDUCT
(1)   The court may make an order under this rule where—
   (a)   a party or his legal representative fails to conduct detailed assessment proceedings in accordance with Part 47 or any direction of the court; or
   (b)   it appears to the court that the conduct of a party or his legal representative, before or during the proceedings which gave rise to the assessment proceedings, was unreasonable or improper.
(2)   Where paragraph (1) applies, the court may—
   (a)   disallow all or part of the costs which are being assessed; or
   (b)   order the party at fault or his legal representative to pay costs which he has caused any other party to incur.
(3)   Where—
   (a)   the court makes an order under paragraph (2) against a legally represented party; and
   (b)   the party is not present when the order is made,
the party's solicitor must notify his client in writing of the order no later than 7 days after the solicitor receives notice of the order.

PD 44 PRACTICE DIRECTION — GENERAL RULES ABOUT COSTS

RULE 44.2 SOLICITOR'S DUTY TO NOTIFY CLIENT
1.1 For the purposes of rule 44.2 'client' includes a party for whom a solicitor is acting and any other person (for example an insurer or a trade union) who has instructed the solicitor to act or who is liable to pay his fees.
1.2 Where a solicitor notifies a client of an order under that rule, he must also explain why the order came to be made.
1.3 Although rule 44.2 does not specify any sanction for breach of the rule the court may, either in the order for costs itself or in a subsequent order, require the solicitor to produce to the court evidence showing that he took reasonable steps to comply with the rule.

RULE 44.3 COURT'S DISCRETION AND CIRCUMSTANCES TO BE TAKEN INTO ACCOUNT WHEN EXERCISING ITS DISCRETION AS TO COSTS
2.1 Attention is drawn to the factors set out in this rule which may lead the court to depart from the general rule stated in rule 44.3(2) and to make a different order about costs.
2.2 In a probate claim where a defendant has in his defence given notice that he requires the will to be proved in solemn form (see para 8.3 of the Contentious Probate Practice Direction Supplementing Part 49), the court will not make an order for costs against the defendant unless it appears that there was no reasonable ground for opposing the will. The term 'probate claim' is defined in para 1.2 of the Contentious Probate Practice Direction.
2.3 (1) The court may make an order about costs at any stage in a case.
(2) In particular the court may make an order about costs when it deals with any application, makes any order or holds any hearing and that order about costs may relate to the costs of that application, order or hearing.
2.4 There are certain costs orders which the court will commonly make in proceedings before trial. The following table sets out the general effect of these orders. The table is not an exhaustive list of the orders which the court may make.

Term	Effect
• Costs • Costs in any event	The party in whose favour the order is made is entitled to the costs in respect of the part of the proceedings to which the order relates, whatever other costs orders are made in the proceedings.
• Costs in the case • Costs in the application	The party in whose favour the court makes an order for costs at the end of the proceedings is entitled to his costs of the part of the proceedings to which the order relates.
• Costs reserved	The decision about costs is deferred to a later occasion, but if no later order is made the costs will be costs in the case.

PD 44 PRACTICE DIRECTION — GENERAL RULES ABOUT COSTS

Term	Effect
• Claimant's/Defendant's costs in the case/application.	If the party in whose favour the costs order is made is awarded costs at the end of the proceedings, that party is entitled to his costs of the part of the proceedings to which the order relates. If any other party is awarded costs at the end of the proceedings, the party in whose favour the costs order is made is not liable to pay the costs of any other party in respect of the part of the proceedings to which the order relates.
• Costs thrown away	Where, for example, a judgment or order is set aside, the party in whose favour the costs order is made is entitled to the costs which have been incurred as a consequence. This includes the costs of— (a) preparing for and attending any hearing at which the judgment or order which has been set aside was made; (b) preparing for and attending any hearing to set aside the judgment or order in question; (c) preparing for and attending any hearing at which the court orders the proceedings or the part in question to be adjourned; (d) any steps taken to enforce a judgment or order which has subsequently been set aside.
• Costs of and caused by	Where, for example, the court makes this order on an application to amend a statement of case, the party in whose favour the costs order is made is entitled to the costs of preparing for and attending the application and the costs of any consequential amendment to his own statement of case.
• Costs here and below	The party in whose favour the costs order is made is entitled not only to his costs in respect of the proceedings in which the court makes the order but also to his costs of the proceedings in any lower court. In the case of an appeal from a Divisional Court the party is not entitled to any costs incurred in any court below the Divisional Court.
• No order as to costs • Each party is to bear his own costs	Each party to pay his own costs of the part of the proceedings to which the order relates whatever costs order the court makes at the end of the proceedings.

2.5 Where, under rule 44.3(7), the court orders an amount to be paid before costs are assessed:
    (1) the order will state that amount, and
    (2) if no other date for payment is specified in the order rule 44.8 (Time for complying with an order for costs) will apply.

Fees of counsel
2.6 (1) This paragraph applies where the court orders the detailed assessment of the costs of a hearing at which one or more counsel appeared for a party.

(2) Where an order for costs states the opinion of the court as to whether or not the hearing was fit for representation by one or more counsel, a costs officer conducting a detailed assessment of costs to which that order relates will have regard to the opinion stated.

Fees payable to conveyancing counsel appointed by the court to assist it
2.7 (1) Where the court refers any matter to the conveyancing counsel of the court the fees payable to counsel in respect of the work done or to be done will be assessed by the court in accordance with Part 44.3.

(2) An appeal from a decision of the court in respect of the fees of such counsel will be dealt with under the general rules as to appeals unless the appeal is against the decision of a costs officer when the appeal will be dealt with in accordance with Part 47 Section 8. In either case the decision of the appellate court is final.

RULE 44.5 FACTORS TO BE TAKEN INTO ACCOUNT IN DECIDING THE AMOUNT OF COSTS
3.1 In applying the test of proportionality the court will have regard to rule 1.1(2)(c). The relationship between the total of the costs incurred and the financial value of the claim may not be a reliable guide. A fixed percentage cannot be applied in all cases to the value of the claim in order to ascertain whether or not the costs are proportionate.

3.2 In any proceedings there will be costs which will inevitably be incurred and which are necessary for the successful conduct of the case. Solicitors are not required to conduct litigation at rates which are uneconomic. Thus in a modest claim the proportion of costs is likely to be higher than in a large claim, and may even equal or possibly exceed the amount in dispute.

3.3 Where a trial takes place, the time taken by the court in dealing with a particular issue may not be an accurate guide to the amount of time properly spent by the legal or other representatives in preparation for the trial of that issue.

RULE 44.7 PROCEDURE FOR ASSESSING COSTS
4.1 Where the court does not order fixed costs (or no fixed costs are provided for) the amount of costs payable will be assessed by the court. This rule allows the court making an order about costs either:
    (a) to make a summary assessment of the amount of the costs, or
    (b) to order that the amount will be decided in accordance with Part 47 (a detailed assessment).

4.2 An order for costs, will be treated as an order for costs to be decided by a detailed assessment unless the order otherwise provides.

Summary assessment
4.3 (1) Whenever a court makes an order about costs which does not provide for fixed costs to be paid the court should consider whether to make a summary assessment of costs.

4.4 (1) The general rule is that the court will make a summary assessment of the costs:
    (a) at the conclusion of the trial of a case which has been dealt with on the fast track, in which case the order will deal with the costs of the whole claim, and
    (b) at the conclusion of any other hearing which has lasted less than one day, in which case the order will deal with the costs of the application or matter to which the hearing related;
unless there is good reason not to do so e.g. where the paying party shows substantial grounds for disputing the sum claimed for costs that cannot be dealt with summarily or there is insufficient time to carry out a summary assessment.

(2) The general rule in paragraph 1 does not apply to a mortgagee's costs incurred in mortgage possession proceedings or other proceedings relating to a

PD 44 PRACTICE DIRECTION — GENERAL RULES ABOUT COSTS

mortgage unless the mortgagee asks the court to make an order for his costs to be paid by another party. Instead, the principles explained by the Court of Appeal in *Gomba Holdings (UK) Ltd* v *Minories Finance Ltd (No. 2)* [1993] Ch 171 continue to apply. Section 1 of the Practice Direction relating to Part 48 also deals with a mortgagee's costs.

(3) The general rule is that no summary assessment of costs will be made if the court has ordered that the costs in question will be treated as costs in the case (as to which see paragraph 2.4 above).

(4) Where an application has been made and the parties to the application agree an order by consent without any party attending, the parties should agree a figure for costs to be inserted in the consent order or agree that there should be no order for costs. If the parties cannot agree the costs position attendance on the appointment will be necessary but unless good reason can be shown for the failure to deal with costs as set out above no costs will be allowed for that attendance.

4.5 (1) It is the duty of the parties and their legal representatives to assist the judge in making a summary assessment of costs in any case to which paragraph 4.4 above applies, in accordance with the following paragraphs.

(2) Each party who intends to claim costs must prepare a written statement of the costs he intends to claim showing separately in the form of a schedule:

    (a) the number of hours to be claimed,
    (b) the hourly rate to be claimed,
    (c) the grade of fee earner;
    (d) the amount and nature of any disbursement to be claimed, other than counsel's fee for appearing at the hearing,
    (e) the amount of solicitor's costs to be claimed for attending or appearing at the hearing,
    (f) the fees of counsel to be claimed in respect of the hearing, and
    (g) any Value Added Tax to be claimed on these amounts.

(3) The statement of costs must follow as closely as possible Form 1 of the Schedule of Costs Forms annexed to this practice direction [see page 1317] and must be signed by the party or his legal representative.

(4) The statement of costs must be filed at court and copies of it must be served on any party against whom an order for payment of those costs is intended to be sought. The statement of costs should be filed and the copies of it should be served as soon as possible and in any event not less than 24 hours before the date fixed for the hearing.

4.6 The failure by a party, without reasonable excuse, to comply with the foregoing paragraphs will be taken into account by the court in deciding what order to make about the costs of the claim, hearing or application, and about the costs of any further hearing or detailed assessment hearing that may be necessary as a result of that failure.

4.7 If the court makes a summary assessment of the costs the court will specify the amount payable as a single figure which will include:

    (a) all sums in respect of profit costs, disbursements and VAT which is allowed, and
    (b) the amount which is awarded under Part 46 (Fast Track Trial Costs).

4.8 The court awarding costs cannot make an order for a summary assessment of costs by a costs officer. If a summary assessment of costs is appropriate but the court awarding costs is unable to do so on the day, the court must give directions as to a further hearing.

4.9 (1) The court must not make a summary assessment of the costs of a receiving party who is an assisted person within the Legal Aid Act 1988.

(2) A summary assessment of costs payable by an assisted person is not by itself a determination of the assisted person's liability to pay those costs (as to which see Section 17 of the Legal Aid Act 1988). Accordingly the court may make a summary assessment of costs payable by an assisted person.

(3) The court may not make a summary assessment of the costs of a receiving party who is a child or patient within Part 21 unless the solicitor acting

PD 44 PRACTICE DIRECTION — GENERAL RULES ABOUT COSTS

for the child or patient has waived the right to further costs (see paragraph 1.2(c) of the Directions Relating to Part 48).

(4) The court may make a summary assessment of costs payable by a child or patient.

4.10 Paragraphs 4.4 and 4.5 do not apply where the parties have agreed the amount of costs.

Payments on account of costs

4.11 Whenever the court awards costs to be assessed by way of detailed assessment it should consider whether to exercise the power in rule 44.3(8) (Court's Discretion as to Costs) to order the paying party to pay such sum of money as it thinks just on account of those costs.

RULE 44.9 COSTS ON THE SMALL CLAIMS TRACK AND FAST TRACK

5.1 (1) Before a claim is allocated to one of those tracks the court is not restricted by any of the special rules that applies to it.

(2) Where a claim has been allocated to one of those tracks, the special rules which relate to that track will apply to work done before as well as after allocation save to the extent (if any) that an order for costs in respect of that work was made before allocation.

(3) (i) This paragraph applies where a claim issued for a sum in excess of the normal financial scope of the small claims track is allocated to that track only because an admission of part of the claim by the defendant reduces the amount in dispute to a sum within the normal scope of that track.
(See also paragraph 7.4 of the practice direction supplementing CPR Part 26)

(ii) On entering judgment for the admitted part before allocation of the balance of the claim the court may allow costs in respect of the proceedings down to that date.

RULE 44.11 COSTS FOLLOWING ALLOCATION AND RE-ALLOCATION

6.1 This paragraph applies where the court is about to make an order to re-allocate a claim from the small claims track to another track.

6.2 Before making the order to re-allocate the claim, the court must decide whether any party is to pay costs to any other party down to the date of the order to re-allocate in accordance with the rules about costs contained in Part 27 (The Small Claims Track).

6.3 If it decides to make such an order about costs, the court should make a summary assessment of those costs in accordance with that Part.

RULE 44.14 COURT'S POWERS IN RELATION TO MISCONDUCT

7.1 Before making an order under rule 44.14 the court must give the party or legal representative in question a reasonable opportunity to attend a hearing to give reasons why it should not make such an order.

7.2 Conduct before or during the proceedings which gave rise to the assessment which is unreasonable or improper includes steps which are calculated to prevent or inhibit the court from furthering the overriding objective.

7.3 Although rule 44.14(3) does not specify any sanction for breach of the obligation imposed by the rule the court may, either in the order under paragraph (2) or in a subsequent order, require the solicitor to produce to the court evidence that he took reasonable steps to comply with the obligation.

CPR PART 45 FIXED COSTS

CONTENTS OF THIS PART
Scope of this Part — Rule 45.1
Amount of fixed commencement costs — Rule 45.2
When defendant liable for fixed commencement costs — Rule 45.3
Costs on entry of judgment — Rule 45.4
Miscellaneous fixed costs — Rule 45.5

45.1 SCOPE OF THIS PART

(1) This Part sets out the amounts which, unless the court orders otherwise, are to be allowed in respect of solicitors' charges in the cases to which this Part applies.

(The definitions contained in Part 43 are relevant to this Part)

(2) This Part applies where—
 (a) the only claim is a claim for a specified sum of money and—
  (i) judgment in default is obtained under rule 12.4(1);
  (ii) judgment on admission is obtained under rule 14.4(3);
  (iii) judgment on admission on part of the claim is obtained under rule 14.5(6);
  (iv) summary judgment is given under Part 24;
  (v) the court has made an order to strike out$^{(GL)}$ a defence under rule 3.4(2)(a) as disclosing no reasonable grounds for defending the claim; or
  (vi) rule 45.3 applies; or
 (b) the only claim is a claim where the court gave a fixed date for the hearing when it issued the claim and judgment is given for the delivery of goods,
and in either case the value of the claim exceeds £25.

(The practice direction supplementing rule 7.9 sets out the types of case where a court may give a fixed date for a hearing when it issues a claim)

(3) The rules in this Part do not apply to the extent that regulations under the Legal Aid Act 1988 determine the amount of costs payable to legal representatives.

(4) Any appropriate court fee will be allowed in addition to the costs set out in this Part.

45.2 AMOUNT OF FIXED COMMENCEMENT COSTS

(1) The claim form may include a claim for fixed commencement costs.

(2) The amount of fixed commencement costs which the claim form may include shall be calculated by reference to the following table (Table 1).

(3) Additional costs may also be claimed in the circumstances specified in Table 3.

(4) The amount claimed, or the value of the goods claimed if specified, in the claim form is to be used for determining the band in the table that applies to the claim.

TABLE 1
FIXED COSTS ON COMMENCEMENT OF A CLAIM

Relevant band	Where the claim form is served by the court or by any method other than personal service by the claimant	Where • the claim form is served personally by the claimant; and • there is only one defendant	Where there is more than one defendant, for each additional defendant personally served at separate addresses by the claimant

Where— • the value of the claim exceeds £25 but does not exceed £500	£50	£60	£15
Where— • the value of the claim exceeds £500 but does not exceed £1,000	£70	£80	£15
Where— • the value of the claim exceeds £1,000 but does not exceed £5,000; or • the only claim is for delivery of goods and no value is specified or stated on the claim form	£80	£90	£15
Where— • the value of the claim exceeds £5,000	£100	£110	£15

45.3 WHEN DEFENDANT ONLY LIABLE FOR FIXED COMMENCEMENT COSTS

(1) Where—

(a) the only claim is for a specified sum of money; and

(b) the defendant pays the money claimed within 14 days after service of particulars of claim on him, together with the fixed commencement costs stated in the claim form,

the defendant is not liable for any further costs unless the court orders otherwise.

(2) Where—

(a) the claimant gives notice of acceptance of a payment into court in satisfaction of the whole claim;

(b) the only claim is for a specified sum of money; and

(c) the defendant made the payment into court within 14 days after service of the particulars of claim on him, together with the fixed costs stated in the claim form,

the defendant is not liable for any further costs unless the court orders otherwise.

45.4 COSTS ON ENTRY OF JUDGMENT

Where—

(a) the claimant has claimed fixed commencement costs under rule 45.2; and

(b) judgment is entered in the circumstances specified in the table in this rule (Table 2),

the amount to be included in the judgment in respect of the claimant's solicitor's charges is the aggregate of—

(i) the fixed commencement costs; and

(ii) the relevant amount shown in Table 2.

TABLE 2

FIXED COSTS ON ENTRY OF JUDGMENT

	Where the amount of the judgment exceeds £25 but does not exceed £5,000	Where the amount of the judgment exceeds £5,000
Where judgment in default of an acknowledgment of service is entered under rule 12.4(1) (entry of judgment by request on claim for money only)	£22	£30
Where judgment in default of a defence is entered under rule 12.4(1) (entry of judgment by request on claim for money only)	£25	£35
Where judgment is entered under rule 14.4 (judgment on admission), or rule 14.5 (judgment on admission of part of claim) and claimant accepts the defendant's proposal as to the manner of payment	£40	£55
Where judgment is entered under rule 14.4 (judgment on admission), or rule 14.5 (judgment on admission on part of claim) and court decides the date or times of payment	£55	£70
Where summary judgment is given under Part 24 or the court strikes out a defence under rule 3.4(2)(a), in either case, on application by a party	£175	£210
Where judgment is given on a claim for delivery of goods under a regulated agreement within the meaning of the Consumer Credit Act 1974 and no other entry in this table applies	£60	£85

45.5 MISCELLANEOUS FIXED COSTS

The table in this rule (Table 3) shows the amount to be allowed in respect of solicitor's charges in the. circumstances mentioned.

TABLE 3

MISCELLANEOUS FIXED COSTS

For service by a party of any document required to be served personally including preparing and copying a certificate of service for each individual served	£15
Where service by an alternative method is permitted by an order under rule 6.8 for each individual served	£25
Where a document is served out of the jurisdiction— (a) in Scotland, Northern Ireland, the Isle of Man or the Channel Islands; (b) in any other place	£65 £75

PD 45 PRACTICE DIRECTION — FIXED COSTS

FIXED COSTS IN SMALL CLAIMS

1.1 Under Rule 27.14 the costs which can be awarded to a claimant in a small claims track case include the fixed costs payable under Part 45 attributable to issuing the claim.

1.2 Those fixed costs shall be the sum of

(a) the fixed commencement costs calculated in accordance with Table 1 of Rule 45.2 and;

(b) the appropriate court fee or fees paid by the claimant.

FIXED COSTS ON THE ISSUE OF A DEFAULT COSTS CERTIFICATE

2.1 Unless paragraph 2.2 applies or unless the court orders otherwise, the fixed costs to be included in a default costs certificate are £80 plus a sum equal to any appropriate court fee payable on the issue of the certificate.

2.2 The fixed costs included in a certificate must not exceed the maximum sum specified for costs and court fee in the notice of commencement.

CPR PART 46 FAST TRACK TRIAL COSTS

CONTENTS OF THIS PART
Scope of this Part   Rule 46.1
Amount of fast track trial costs   Rule 46.2
Power to award more or less than the amount of fast track trial costs   Rule 46.3
Fast track trial costs where there is more than one claimant or defendant   Rule 46.4

46.1 SCOPE OF THIS PART
(1) This Part deals with the amount of costs which the court may award as the costs of an advocate for preparing for and appearing at the trial of a claim in the fast track (referred to in this rule as 'fast track trial costs').

(2) For the purposes of this Part—
(a) 'advocate' means a person exercising a right of audience as a representative of, or on behalf of, a party;
(b) 'fast track trial costs' means the costs of a party's advocate for preparing for and appearing at the trial, but does not include—
  (i) any other disbursements; or
  (ii) any value added tax payable on the fees of a party's advocate; and
(c) 'trial' includes a hearing where the court decides an amount of money or the value of goods following a judgment under Part 12 (default judgment) or Part 14 (admissions) but does not include—
  (i) the hearing of an application for summary judgment under Part 24; or
  (ii) the court's approval of a settlement or other compromise under rule 21.10.

(Part 21 deals with claims made by or on behalf of, or against, children and patients)

46.2 AMOUNT OF FAST TRACK TRIAL COSTS
(1) The following table shows the amount of fast track trial costs which the court may award (whether by summary or detailed assessment).

VALUE OF THE CLAIM	AMOUNT OF FAST TRACK TRIAL COSTS WHICH THE COURT MAY AWARD
Up to £3,000	£350
More than £3,000 but not more than £10,000	£500
More than £10,000	£750

(2) The court may not award more or less than the amount shown in the table except where—
(a) it decides not to award any fast track trial costs; or
(b) rule 46.3 applies,
but the court may apportion the amount awarded between the parties to reflect their respective degrees of success on the issues at trial.

(3) Where the only claim is for the payment of money—
(a) for the purpose of quantifying fast track trial costs awarded to a claimant, the value of the claim is the total amount of the judgment excluding—
  (i) interest and costs; and
  (ii) any reduction made for contributory negligence.
(b) for the purpose of the quantifying fast track trial costs awarded to a defendant, the value of the claim is—
  (i) the amount specified in the claim form (excluding interest and costs);
  (ii) if no amount is specified, the maximum amount which the claimant reasonably expected to recover according to the statement of value included in the claim form under rule 16.3; or

(iii) more than £10,000, if the claim form states that the claimant cannot reasonably say how much he expects to recover.

(4) Where the claim is only for a remedy other than the payment of money the value of the claim is deemed to be more than £3,000 but not more than £10,000, unless the court orders otherwise.

(5) Where the claim includes both a claim for the payment of money and for a remedy other than the payment of money, the value of the claim is deemed to be the higher of—

    (a) the value of the money claim decided in accordance with paragraph (3); or

    (b) the deemed value of the other remedy decided in accordance with paragraph (4),

unless the court orders otherwise.

(6) Where—

    (a) a defendant has made a counterclaim against the claimant;
    (b) the counterclaim has a higher value than the claim; and
    (c) the claimant succeeds at trial both on his claim and the counterclaim,

for the purpose of quantifying fast track trial costs awarded to the claimant, the value of the claim is the value of the defendant's counterclaim calculated in accordance with this rule.

(Rule 20.4 sets out how a defendant may make a counterclaim)

46.3 POWER TO AWARD MORE OR LESS THAN THE AMOUNT OF FAST TRACK TRIAL COSTS

(1) This rule sets out when a court may award—

    (a) an additional amount to the amount of fast track trial costs shown in the table in rule 46.2(1); and
    (b) less than those amounts.

(2) If—

    (a) in addition to the advocate, a party's legal representative attends the trial;
    (b) the court considers that it was necessary for a legal representative to attend to assist the advocate; and
    (c) the court awards fast track trial costs to that party,

the court may award an additional £250 in respect of the legal representative's attendance at the trial.

(Legal representative is defined in rule 2.3)

(3) If the court considers that it is necessary to direct a separate trial of an issue then the court may award an additional amount in respect of the separate trial but that amount is limited in accordance with paragraph (4) of this rule.

(4) The additional amount the court may award under paragraph 3 must not exceed two-thirds of the amount payable for that claim, subject to a minimum award of £350.

(5) Where the party to whom fast track trial costs are to be awarded is a litigant in person, the court will award—

    (a) if the litigant in person can prove financial loss, two-thirds of the amount that would otherwise be awarded; or
    (b) if the litigant in person fails to prove financial loss, an amount in respect of the time spent reasonably doing the work at the rate specified in the costs practice direction.

(6) Where a defendant has made a counterclaim against the claimant, and—

    (a) the claimant has succeeded on his claim; and
    (b) the defendant has succeeded on his counterclaim,

the court will quantify the amount of the award of fast track trial costs to which—

    (i) but for the counterclaim, the claimant would be entitled for succeeding on his claim; and
    (ii) but for the claim, the defendant would be entitled for succeeding on his counterclaim,

and make one award of the difference, if any, to the party entitled to the higher award of costs.

(7) Where the court considers that the party to whom fast track trial costs are to be awarded has behaved unreasonably or improperly during the trial, it may award that party an amount less than would otherwise be payable for that claim, as it considers appropriate.

(8) Where the court considers that the party who is to pay the fast track trial costs has behaved improperly during the trial the court may award such additional amount to the other party as it considers appropriate.

46.4 FAST TRACK TRIAL COSTS WHERE THERE IS MORE THAN ONE CLAIMANT OR DEFENDANT

(1) Where the same advocate is acting for more than one party—

(a) the court may make only one award in respect of fast track trial costs payable to that advocate; and

(b) the parties for whom the advocate is acting are jointly entitled to any fast track trial costs awarded by the court.

(2) Where—

(a) the same advocate is acting for more than one claimant; and

(b) each claimant has a separate claim against the defendant,

the value of the claim, for the purpose of quantifying the award in respect of fast track trial costs is to be ascertained in accordance with paragraph (3).

(3) The value of the claim in the circumstances mentioned in paragraph (2) is—

(a) where the only claim of each claimant is for the payment of money—

(i) if the award of fast track trial costs is in favour of the claimants, the total amount of the judgment made in favour of all the claimants jointly represented; or

(ii) if the award is in favour of the defendant, the total amount claimed by the claimants,

and in either case, quantified in accordance with rule 46.2(3);

(b) where the only claim of each claimant is for a remedy other than the payment of money, deemed to be more than £3,000 but not more than £10,000; and

(c) where claims of the claimants include both a claim for the payment of money and for a remedy other than the payment of money, deemed to be—

(i) more than £3,000 but not more than £10,000; or

(ii) if greater, the value of the money claims calculated in accordance with sub-paragraph (a) above.

(4) Where—

(a) there is more than one defendant; and

(b) any or all of the defendants are separately represented,

the court may award fast track trial costs to each party who is separately represented.

(5) Where—

(a) there is more than one claimant; and

(b) a single defendant,

the court may make only one award to the defendant of fast track trial costs, for which the claimants are jointly and severally liable[GL].

(6) For the purpose of quantifying the fast track trial costs awarded to the single defendant under paragraph (5), the value of the claim is to be calculated in accordance with paragraph (3) of this rule.

PD46 PRACTICE DIRECTION — FAST TRACK TRIAL COSTS

RULE 46.1 SCOPE OF PART 46

1.1 Part 46 applies to the costs of an advocate for preparing for and appearing at the trial of a claim in the fast track.

1.2 It applies only where, at the date of the trial, the claim is allocated to the fast track. It does not apply in any other case, irrespective of the financial value of the claim.

1.3 In particular it does not apply to:

(a) the hearing of a claim which is allocated to the small claims track with the consent of the parties given under rule 26.7(3); or

(b) a disposal hearing at which an amount to be paid under a judgment or order is decided by the court (see paragraph 12.8 of the Practice Direction which supplements Part 26 (Case Management — Preliminary Stage).

Cases which settle before trial

1.4 Attention is drawn to rule 44.10 (limitation on amount court may award where a claim allocated to the fast track settles before trial).

CPR PART 47 PROCEDURE FOR DETAILED ASSESSMENT OF COSTS AND DEFAULT PROVISIONS

CONTENTS OF THIS PART

I GENERAL RULES ABOUT DETAILED ASSESSMENT
Time when detailed assessment may be carried out — Rule 47.1
No stay of detailed assessment where there is an appeal — Rule 47.2
Powers of an authorised court officer — Rule 47.3
Venue for detailed assessment proceedings — Rule 47.4

II COSTS PAYABLE BY ONE PARTY TO ANOTHER — COMMENCEMENT OF DETAILED ASSESSMENT PROCEEDINGS
Application of this section — Rule 47.5
Commencement of detailed assessment proceedings — Rule 47.6
Period for commencing detailed assessment proceedings — Rule 47.7
Sanction for delay in commencing detailed assessment proceedings — Rule 47.8
Points of dispute and consequence of not serving — Rule 47.9
Procedure where costs are agreed — Rule 47.10

III COSTS PAYABLE BY ONE PARTY TO ANOTHER — DEFAULT PROVISIONS
Default costs certificate — Rule 47.11
Setting aside default costs certificate — Rule 47.12

IV COSTS PAYABLE BY ONE PARTY TO ANOTHER — PROCEDURE WHERE POINTS OF DISPUTE ARE SERVED
Optional reply — Rule 47.13
Detailed assessment hearing — Rule 47.14

V INTERIM COSTS CERTIFICATE AND FINAL COSTS CERTIFICATE
Power to issue an interim certificate — Rule 47.15
Final costs certificate — Rule 47.16

VI DETAILED ASSESSMENT PROCEDURE FOR COSTS OF AN ASSISTED PERSON WHERE COSTS ARE PAYABLE OUT OF THE LEGAL AID FUND
Detailed assessment procedure for costs of an assisted person where costs are payable out of the legal aid fund — Rule 47.17

VII COSTS OF DETAILED ASSESSMENT PROCEEDINGS
Liability for costs of detailed assessment proceedings — Rule 47.18
Offers to settle without prejudice save as to costs of the detailed assessment proceedings — Rule 47.19

VIII APPEAL AGAINST DECISIONS IN DETAILED ASSESSMENT PROCEEDINGS
Right to appeal — Rule 47.20
Preliminary requirements for bringing an appeal — Rule 47.21
Court to hear appeal — Rule 47.22
Duty to seek reasons — Rule 47.23
Obtaining the court's permission to appeal — Rule 47.24
Appeal procedure — Rule 47.25
Powers of the court on appeal — Rule 47.26

(The definitions contained in Part 43 are relevant to this Part)

CPR PART 47 PROCEDURE FOR DETAILED ASSESSMENT OF COSTS ETC.

I GENERAL RULES ABOUT DETAILED ASSESSMENT

47.1 TIME WHEN DETAILED ASSESSMENT MAY BE CARRIED OUT

The general rule is that the costs of any proceedings or any part of the proceedings are not to be assessed by the detailed procedure until the conclusion of the proceedings but the court may order them to be assessed immediately.

(The costs practice direction gives further guidance about when proceedings are concluded for the purpose of this rule)

47.2 NO STAY OF DETAILED ASSESSMENT WHERE THERE IS AN APPEAL

Detailed assessment is not stayed pending an appeal unless the court so orders.

47.3 POWERS OF AN AUTHORISED COURT OFFICER

(1) An authorised court officer has all the powers of the court when making a detailed assessment, except—
   (a) power to make a wasted costs order as defined in rule 48.7;
   (b) power to make an order under—
      (i) rule 44.14 (powers in relation to misconduct);
      (ii) rule 47.8 (sanction for delay in commencing detailed assessment proceedings);
      (iii) paragraph (2) (objection to detailed assessment by authorised court officer); and
   (c) power to make a detailed assessment of costs payable to a solicitor by his client, unless the costs are being assessed under rule 48.5 (costs where money is payable to a child or patient).

(2) Where a party objects to the detailed assessment of costs being made by an authorised court officer, the court may order it to be made by a costs judge or a district judge.

(The costs practice direction sets out the relevant procedure)

47.4 VENUE FOR DETAILED ASSESSMENT PROCEEDINGS

(1) All applications and requests in detailed assessment proceedings must be made to or filed at the appropriate office.

(The costs practice direction sets out the meaning of 'appropriate office' in any particular case)

(2) The court may direct that the appropriate office is to be the Supreme Court Costs Office.

(3) A county court may direct that another county court is to be the appropriate office.

(4) A direction under paragraph (3) may be made without proceedings being transferred to that court.

(Rule 30.2 makes provision for any county court to transfer the proceedings to another county court for detailed assessment of costs)

II COSTS PAYABLE BY ONE PARTY TO ANOTHER — COMMENCEMENT OF DETAILED ASSESSMENT PROCEEDINGS

47.5 APPLICATION OF THIS SECTION

This section of Part 47 applies where a costs officer is to make a detailed assessment of costs which are payable by one party to another.

47.6 COMMENCEMENT OF DETAILED ASSESSMENT PROCEEDINGS

(1) Detailed assessment proceedings are commenced by the receiving party serving on the paying party—
   (a) notice of commencement in the relevant practice form; and
   (b) a copy of the bill of costs.

(Rule 47.7 sets out the period for commencing detailed assessment proceedings)

(2) The receiving party must also serve a copy of the notice of commencement and the bill on any other relevant persons specified in the costs practice direction.

(3) A person on whom a copy of the notice of commencement is served under paragraph (2) is a party to the detailed assessment proceedings (in addition to the paying party and the receiving party).

(The costs practice direction deals with—
- other documents which the party must file when he requests detailed assessment;
- the court's powers where it considers that a hearing may be necessary;
- the form of a bill; and
- the length of notice which will be given if a hearing date is fixed)

47.7 PERIOD FOR COMMENCING DETAILED ASSESSMENT PROCEEDINGS

The following table shows the period for commencing detailed assessment proceedings.

SOURCE OF RIGHT TO DETAILED ASSESSMENT	TIME BY WHICH DETAILED ASSESSMENT PROCEEDINGS MUST BE COMMENCED
Judgment, direction, order, award or other determination	3 months after the date of the judgment etc. Where detailed assessment is stayed pending an appeal, 3 months after the date of the order lifting the stay
Discontinuance under Part 38	3 months after the date of service of notice of discontinuance under rule 38.3; or 3 months after the date of the dismissal of application to set the notice of discontinuance aside under rule 38.4
Acceptance of an offer to settle or a payment into court under Part 36	3 months after the date when the right to costs arose

47.8 SANCTION FOR DELAY IN COMMENCING DETAILED ASSESSMENT PROCEEDINGS

(1) Where the receiving party fails to commence detailed assessment proceedings within the period specified—
   (a) in rule 47.7; or
   (b) by any direction of the court,
the paying party may apply for an order requiring the receiving party to commence detailed assessment proceedings within such time as the court may specify.

(2) On an application under paragraph (1), the court may direct that, unless the receiving party commences detailed assessment proceedings within the time specified by the court, all or part of the costs to which the receiving party would otherwise be entitled will be disallowed.

(3) If—
   (a) the paying party has not made an application in accordance with paragraph (1); and
   (b) the receiving party commences the proceedings later than the period specified in rule 47.7,
the court may disallow all or part of the interest otherwise payable to the receiving party under—
   (i) section 17 of the Judgments Act 1838; or
   (ii) section 74 of the County Courts Act 1984,
but must not impose any other sanction except in accordance with rule 44.14 (powers in relation to misconduct).

(4) Where the costs to be assessed in a detailed assessment are payable out of the Legal Aid Fund, this rule applies as if the receiving party were the solicitor to whom the costs are payable and the paying party were the Legal Aid Board.

CPR PART 47 PROCEDURE FOR DETAILED ASSESSMENT OF COSTS ETC.

47.9 POINTS OF DISPUTE AND CONSEQUENCE OF NOT SERVING

(1) The paying party and any other party to the detailed assessment proceedings may dispute any item in the bill of costs by serving points of dispute on—
    (a) the receiving party; and
    (b) every other party to the detailed assessment proceedings.

(2) The period for serving points of dispute is 21 days after the date of service of the notice of commencement.

(3) If a party serves points of dispute after the period set out in paragraph (2), he may not be heard further in the detailed assessment proceedings unless the court gives permission.

(The costs practice direction sets out requirements about the form of points of dispute)

(4) The receiving party may file a request for a default costs certificate if—
    (a) the period set out in rule 47.9(2) for serving points of dispute has expired; and
    (b) he has not been served with any points of dispute.

(5) If any party (including the paying party) serves points of dispute before the issue of a default costs certificate the court may not issue the default costs certificate.

(Section IV of this Part sets out the procedure to be followed after points of dispute have been filed)

47.10 PROCEDURE WHERE COSTS ARE AGREED

(1) If the paying party and the receiving party agree the amount of costs, either party may apply for a costs certificate (either interim or final) in the amount agreed.

(Rule 47.15 and rule 47.16 contain further provisions about interim and final costs certificates respectively)

(2) An application for a certificate under paragraph (1) must be made—
    (a) where the right to detailed assessment arises from a judgment or court order—
        (i) to the court where the judgment or order was given or made, if the proceedings have not been transferred since then; or
        (ii) to the court to which the proceedings have been transferred; and
    (b) in any other case, to the court which would be the venue for detailed assessment proceedings under rule 47.4.

III COSTS PAYABLE BY ONE PARTY TO ANOTHER — DEFAULT PROVISIONS

47.11 DEFAULT COSTS CERTIFICATE

(1) Where the receiving party is permitted by rule 47.9 to obtain a default costs certificate, he does so by filing a request in the relevant practice form.

(The costs practice direction deals with the procedure by which the receiving party may obtain a default costs certificate)

(2) A default costs certificate will include an order to pay the costs to which it relates.

(3) Where a receiving party obtains a default costs certificate, the costs payable to him for the commencement of detailed assessment proceedings shall be the sum set out in the costs practice direction.

47.12 SETTING ASIDE DEFAULT COSTS CERTIFICATE

(1) The court must set aside a default costs certificate if the receiving party was not entitled to it.

(2) In any other case, the court may set aside or vary a default costs certificate if it appears to the court that there is some good reason why the detailed assessment proceedings should continue.

(3) Where—
    (a) the receiving party has purported to serve the notice of commencement on the paying party;
    (b) a default costs certificate has been issued; and

CPR PART 47 PROCEDURE FOR DETAILED ASSESSMENT OF COSTS ETC.

(c) the receiving party subsequently discovers that the notice of commencement did not reach the paying party at least 21 days before the default costs certificate was issued,
the receiving party must—
    (i)   file a request for the default costs certificate to be set aside; or
    (ii) apply to the court for directions.

(4) Where paragraph (3) applies, the receiving party may take no further step in—
    (a) the detailed assessment proceedings; or
    (b) the enforcement of the default costs certificate,
until the certificate has been set aside or the court has given directions.

(The costs practice direction contains further details about the procedure for setting aside a default costs certificate and the matters which the court must take into account)

IV COSTS PAYABLE BY ONE PARTY TO ANOTHER — PROCEDURE WHERE POINTS OF DISPUTE ARE SERVED

47.13 OPTIONAL REPLY

(1) Where any party to the detailed assessment proceedings serves points of dispute, the receiving party may serve a reply on the other parties to the assessment proceedings.

(2) He may do so within 21 days after service on him of the points of dispute to which his reply relates.

47.14 DETAILED ASSESSMENT HEARING

(1) Where points of dispute are served in accordance with this Part, the receiving party must file a request for a detailed assessment hearing.

(2) He must file the request within 3 months of the expiry of the period for commencing detailed assessment proceedings as specified—
    (a) in rule 47.7; or
    (b) by any direction of the court.

(3) Where the receiving party fails to file a request in accordance with paragraph (2), the paying party may apply for an order requiring the receiving party to file the request within such time as the court may specify.

(4) On an application under paragraph (3), the court may direct that, unless the receiving party requests a detailed assessment hearing within the time specified by the court, all or part of the costs to which the receiving party would otherwise be entitled will be disallowed.

(5) If—
    (a) the paying party has not made an application in accordance with paragraph (3); and
    (b) the receiving party files a request for a detailed assessment hearing later than the period specified in paragraph (2),
the court may disallow all or part of the interest otherwise payable to the receiving party under—
    (i)   section 17 of the Judgments Act 1838; or
    (ii) section 74 of the County Courts Act 1984,
but must not impose any other sanction except in accordance with rule 44.14 (powers in relation to misconduct).

(6) No person other than—
    (a) the receiving party;
    (b) the paying party; and
    (c) any party who has served points of dispute under rule 47.9,
may be heard at the detailed assessment hearing unless the court gives permission.

(7) Only items specified in the points of dispute may be raised at the hearing, unless the court gives permission.

(The costs practice direction specifies other documents which must be filed with the request for hearing and the length of notice which the court will give when it fixes a hearing date.)

CPR PART 47 PROCEDURE FOR DETAILED ASSESSMENT OF COSTS ETC.

V INTERIM COSTS CERTIFICATE AND FINAL COSTS CERTIFICATE

47.15 POWER TO ISSUE AN INTERIM CERTIFICATE
(1) The court may at any time after the receiving party has filed a request for a detailed assessment hearing—
    (a) issue an interim costs certificate for such sum as it considers appropriate;
    (b) amend or cancel an interim certificate.
(2) An interim certificate will include an order to pay the costs to which it relates, unless the court orders otherwise.
(3) The court may order the costs certified in an interim certificate to be paid into court.

47.16 FINAL COSTS CERTIFICATE
(1) In this rule a completed bill means a bill calculated to show the amount due following the detailed assessment of the costs.
(2) The period for filing the completed bill is 14 days after the end of the detailed assessment hearing.
(3) When a completed bill is filed the court will issue a final costs certificate and serve it on the parties to the detailed assessment proceedings.
(4) Paragraph (3) is subject to any order made by the court that a certificate is not to be issued until other costs have been paid.
(5) A final costs certificate will include an order to pay the costs to which it relates, unless the court orders otherwise.
(The costs practice direction deals with the form of a final costs certificate)

VI DETAILED ASSESSMENT PROCEDURE FOR COSTS OF AN ASSISTED PERSON WHERE COSTS ARE PAYABLE OUT OF THE LEGAL AID FUND

47.17 DETAILED ASSESSMENT PROCEDURE FOR COSTS OF AN ASSISTED PERSON WHERE COSTS ARE PAYABLE OUT OF THE LEGAL AID FUND
(1) Where the court is to assess costs of an assisted person which are payable out of the legal aid fund, the assisted person's solicitor may commence detailed assessment proceedings by filing a request in the relevant practice form.
(2) A request under paragraph (1) must be filed within 3 months after the date when the right to detailed assessment arose.
(3) The solicitor must also serve a copy of the request for detailed assessment on the assisted person, if notice of the assisted person's interest has been given to the court in accordance with legal aid regulations.
(4) Where the solicitor has certified that the assisted person wishes to attend an assessment hearing, the court will, on receipt of the request for assessment, fix a date for the assessment hearing.
(5) Where paragraph (3) does not apply, the court will, on receipt of the request for assessment provisionally assess the costs without the attendance of the solicitor, unless it considers that a hearing is necessary.
(6) After the court has provisionally assessed the bill, it will return the bill to the solicitor.
(7) The court will fix a date for an assessment hearing if the solicitor informs the court, within 14 days after he receives the provisionally assessed bill, that he wants the court to hold such a hearing.

VII COSTS OF DETAILED ASSESSMENT PROCEEDINGS

47.18 LIABILITY FOR COSTS OF DETAILED ASSESSMENT PROCEEDINGS
(1) The receiving party is entitled to his costs of the detailed assessment proceedings except where—
    (a) the provisions of any Act, any of these Rules or any relevant practice direction provide otherwise; or

(b) the court makes some other order in relation to all or part of the costs of the detailed assessment proceedings.

(2) In deciding whether to make some other order, the court must have regard to all the circumstances, including—

(a) the conduct of all the parties;
(b) the amount, if any, by which the bill of costs has been reduced; and
(c) whether it was reasonable for a party to claim the costs of a particular item or to dispute that item.

47.19 OFFERS TO SETTLE WITHOUT PREJUDICE SAVE AS TO COSTS OF THE DETAILED ASSESSMENT PROCEEDINGS

(1) Where—

(a) a party (whether the paying party or the receiving party) makes a written offer to settle the costs of the proceedings which gave rise to the assessment proceedings; and
(b) the offer is expressed to be without prejudice$^{(GL)}$ save as to the costs of the detailed assessment proceedings,

the court will take the offer into account in deciding who should pay the costs of those proceedings.

(2) The fact of the offer must not be communicated to the costs officer until the question of costs of the detailed assessment proceedings falls to be decided.

(The costs practice direction provides that rule 47.19 does not apply where the receiving party is an assisted person)

VIII APPEAL AGAINST DECISIONS IN DETAILED ASSESSMENT PROCEEDINGS

47.20 RIGHT TO APPEAL

(1) Any party to detailed assessment proceedings may appeal against any decision of the court in those proceedings, subject to the requirements of rule 47.21.

(2) For the purposes of this Section, an assisted person is not a party to the detailed assessment proceedings.

47.21 PRELIMINARY REQUIREMENTS FOR BRINGING AN APPEAL

(1) A party may not appeal against a decision in detailed assessment proceedings until he has—

(a) sought written reasons for the decision in accordance with rule 47.23; and
(b) obtained the court's permission where necessary in accordance with rule 47.24,

unless the court orders otherwise.

(2) Where a party has complied with the requirements under paragraph (1) he may file a notice of appeal in accordance with rule 47.25.

47.22 COURT TO HEAR APPEAL

(1) Where an appeal is made against a decision of an authorised court officer the appeal is—

(a) if the detailed assessment proceedings were in the High Court, to a costs judge or a district judge of that court; or
(b) if they were in a county court, to a district judge.

(2) Where an appeal is made to a costs judge or a district judge against a decision of an authorised court officer, a further appeal lies—

(a) if the detailed assessment proceedings were in the High Court, to a judge of that court; or
(b) if they were in a county court, to a circuit judge.

(3) Where an appeal against a decision of a costs judge or a district judge hearing the detailed assessment is made the appeal lies—

(a) if the detailed assessment proceedings were in the High Court, to a judge of that court; or
(b) if they were in a county court, to a circuit judge.

47.23 DUTY TO SEEK REASONS

(1) A party may seek reasons for a decision in detailed assessment proceedings by filing a request with the court that gave the decision.

(2) Where the party seeking reasons is the receiving party, he must file his request for reasons when he files the completed bill of costs.

(Rule 47.16 deals with completed bills of costs)

(3) Where the party seeking reasons is the paying party, he must file his request for reasons within 7 days after the end of the detailed assessment hearing.

47.24 OBTAINING THE COURT'S PERMISSION TO APPEAL

(1) Permission is not required to appeal against—
    (a) a decision of an authorised court officer; or
    (b) a decision of a costs judge or a district judge to impose a sanction on a legal representative under—
        (i) rule 44.14 (powers in relation to misconduct); or
        (ii) rule 48.7 (wasted costs order).

(2) Subject to paragraph (1)(b), permission is required to appeal against a decision of a costs judge or a district judge.

(3) Permission to appeal may be given by—
    (a) the costs judge or district judge who made the decision in question; or
    (b) a High Court judge or a circuit judge, as the case may be.

(4) A party may seek permission to appeal—
    (a) within 14 days after receiving written reasons under rule 47.23; or
    (b) if the court directs that reasons do not need to be obtained, within 7 days after the date of the direction.

47.25 APPEAL PROCEDURE

(1) A party who has a right to appeal may do so by filing a notice of appeal.

(2) Where the appeal is against a decision of an authorised court officer, he must file the notice—
    (a) within 14 days after service of the court officer's reasons on him; or
    (b) if the court has directed that reasons need not be obtained, within 7 days after the date of the direction.

(3) Where the appeal is against a decision of a costs judge or a district judge, he must file the notice within 14 days after the date of the court's decision to give permission to appeal.

(4) On receipt of a notice of appeal, the court will—
    (a) serve a copy of the notice on the other parties to the detailed assessment proceedings; and
    (b) give notice of the appeal hearing to those parties.

47.26 POWERS OF THE COURT ON APPEAL

(1) On an appeal from an authorised court officer the court will—
    (a) re-hear the proceedings which gave rise to the decision appealed against; and
    (b) make any order and give such directions as it considers appropriate.

(2) On an appeal from a costs judge or district judge, if the court is satisfied that the appeal should be allowed, it may make any order and give such directions as it considers appropriate.

(3) If on an appeal the court exercises the power to appoint assessors conferred—
    (a) by section 70 of the Supreme Court Act 1981; or
    (b) by section 63 of the County Courts Act 1984,
it must appoint at least two assessors.

(Rule 35.15 contains further provisions about the appointment of assessors)

(4) One assessor must be a district judge or costs judge and one must be a practising barrister or solicitor.

PD 47 PRACTICE DIRECTION — PROCEDURE FOR DETAILED ASSESSMENT OF COSTS AND DEFAULT PROVISIONS

SECTION I GENERAL RULES ABOUT DETAILED ASSESSMENT

Rule 47.1 Time when assessment may be carried out
1.1 (1) For the purposes of this rule, proceedings are concluded when the court has finally determined the matters in issue in the claim, whether or not there is an appeal.
 (2) For the purposes of this rule, the making of an award of provisional damages under Part 41 will be treated as a final determination of the matters in issue.
 (3) (a) A party who is served with a notice of commencement (see paragraph 2.3 below) may apply to a costs judge or a district judge to determine whether the party who served it is entitled to commence detailed assessment proceedings.
  (b) On hearing such an application the orders which the court may make include: an order allowing the detailed assessment proceedings to continue, or an order setting aside the notice of commencement.
 (4) A costs judge or a district judge may make an order allowing detailed assessment proceedings to be commenced where there is no realistic prospect of the claim continuing.

Rule 47.2 No stay of detailed assessment where there is an appeal
1.2 (1) Rule 47.2 provides that detailed assessment is not stayed pending an appeal unless the court so orders.
 (2) An application to stay the detailed assessment of costs pending an appeal may be made to the court whose order is being appealed or to the court who will hear the appeal.

Rule 47.3 Powers of an authorised court officer
1.3 (1) The court officers authorised by the Lord Chancellor to assess costs in the Supreme Court Costs Office and the Principal Registry of the Family Division are authorised to deal with claims for costs not exceeding £17,500 (excluding VAT) in the case of senior executive officers and £35,000 (excluding VAT) in the case of principal officers.
 (2) Where the receiving party, paying party and any other party to the detailed assessment proceedings who has served points of dispute are agreed that the assessment should not be made by an authorised court officer, the receiving party should so inform the court when requesting a hearing date. The court will then list the hearing before a costs judge or a district judge.
 (3) In any other case a party who objects to the assessment being made by an authorised court officer must make an application to the costs judge or district judge under Part 23 (General Rules about Applications for Court Orders) setting out the reasons for the objection and if sufficient reason is shown the court will direct that the bill be assessed by a costs judge or district judge.

Rule 47.4 Venue for detailed assessment proceedings
1.4 For the purposes of rule 47.4(1) the 'appropriate office' means
 (1) the district registry or county court in which the case was being dealt with when the judgment or order was made or the event occurred which gave rise to the right to assessment, or to which it has subsequently been transferred; or
 (2) the Principal Registry of the Family Division if the costs in question are the costs of any proceedings which were being dealt with in that registry when the judgment or order was made or when the event occurred which gave rise to the right to assessment, or which have subsequently been transferred to that registry; or

(3) in all other cases, the Supreme Court Costs Office.

1.5 (1) A direction under rule 47.4(2) or (3) specifying a particular court, registry or office as the appropriate office may be given on application or on the court's own initiative.

(2) Before making such a direction on its own initiative the court will give the parties the opportunity to make representations.

(3) Unless the Supreme Court Costs Office is the appropriate office for the purposes of Rule 47.4(1) an order directing that an assessment is to take place at the Supreme Court Costs Office will be made only if it is appropriate to do so having regard to the size of the bill of costs, the difficulty of the issues involved, the likely length of the hearing, the cost to the parties and any other relevant matter.

SECTION II — COSTS PAYABLE BY ONE PARTY TO ANOTHER — COMMENCEMENT OF DETAILED ASSESSMENT PROCEEDINGS

Rule 47.6 Commencement of detailed assessment proceedings

2.1 Form 2 of the Schedule of Costs Forms annexed to this Practice Direction [see page 1318] is a model form bill of costs for detailed assessment. Further information about bills of costs is set out in Sections 2 and 3 of the Direction relating to Part 43.

2.2 The receiving party must serve on the paying party and all other relevant persons the following documents:

(1) a notice of commencement,

(2) a copy of the bill of costs,

(3) copies of the fee notes of counsel and of any expert in respect of fees claimed in the bill,

(4) written evidence as to any other disbursement which is claimed and which exceeds £250,

(5) a statement giving the name and address for service of any person upon whom the receiving party intends to serve the notice of commencement.

2.3 (1) The notice of commencement must be in Form 5 of the Schedule of Costs Forms annexed to this Practice Direction [i.e., form N252].

(2) Before it is served it must be completed to show as separate items—

(a) the total amount of the bill of costs as drawn,

(b) the additional amounts which will be payable by way of fixed costs and court fees if a default costs certificate is obtained.

(3) The fixed costs payable in respect of solicitors' charges on the issue of a default costs certificate are £80.

2.4 (1) This paragraph applies where the notice of commencement is to be served outside England and Wales.

(2) The date to be inserted in the notice of commencement for the paying party to send points of dispute is a date (not less than 21 days from the date of service of the notice) which must be calculated by reference to the Practice Direction supplementing RSC Order 11 as if the notice were a claim form and as if the date to be inserted was the date for the filing of a defence.

2.5 (1) For the purposes of Rule 47.6(2) a 'relevant person' means:

(a) any person who has taken part in the proceedings which gave rise to the assessment and who is directly liable under an order for costs made against him,

(b) any person who has given to the receiving party notice in writing that he has a financial interest in the outcome of the assessment and wishes to be a party accordingly,

(c) any other person whom the court orders to be treated as such.

(2) Where a party is unsure whether a person is or is not a relevant person, that party may apply to the appropriate office for directions.

(3) The court will generally not make an order that the person in respect of whom the application is made will be treated as a relevant person, unless within a specified time he applies to the court to be joined as a party to the assessment proceedings in accordance with Part 19 (Addition and Substitution of Parties).

PD 47 PRACTICE DIRECTION — PROCEDURE FOR DETAILED ASSESSMENT ETC.

2.6 (1) This paragraph applies in cases in which the bill of costs is capable of being copied onto a computer disk.

(2) If, before the detailed assessment hearing, a paying party requests a disk copy of a bill to which this paragraph applies, the receiving party must supply him with a copy free of charge not more than 7 days after the date on which he received the request.

Rule 47.7 Period for commencing detailed assessment proceedings

2.7 The parties may agree under Rule 2.11 (Time limits may be varied by parties) to extend or shorten the time specified by Rule 47.7 for commencing the detailed assessment proceedings .

2.8 A party may apply to the appropriate office for an order under Rule 3.1(2)(a) to extend or shorten that time.

2.9 Attention is drawn to rule 47.6(1). The detailed assessment proceedings are commenced by service of the documents referred to.

2.10 Permission to commence assessment proceedings out of time is not required.

Rule 47.8 Sanction for delay in commencing detailed assessment proceedings

2.11 (1) An application for an order under rule 47.8 must be made in writing and be issued in the appropriate office.

(2) The application notice must be served at least 7 days before the hearing.

Rule 47.9 Points of dispute and consequences of not serving

2.12 The parties may agree under rule 2.11 (Time limits may be varied by parties) to extend or shorten the time specified by rule 47.9 for service of points of dispute. A party may apply to the appropriate office for an order under rule 3.1(2)(a) to extend or shorten that time.

2.13 Points of dispute should be short and to the point and should follow as closely as possible Form 6 of the Schedule of Costs Forms annexed to this Practice Direction [see page 1335].

2.14 Points of dispute must:
  (1) identify each item in the bill of costs which is disputed,
  (2) in each case state concisely the nature and grounds of dispute,
  (3) where practicable suggest a figure to be allowed for each item in respect of which a reduction is sought, and
  (4) be signed by the party serving them or his solicitor.

2.15 (1) The normal period for serving points of dispute is 21 days after the date of service of the notice of commencement.

(2) Where a notice of commencement is served on a party outside England and Wales the period within which that party should serve points of dispute is to be calculated by reference to the Practice Direction supplementing RSC Order 11 as if the notice of commencement was a claim form and as if the period for serving points of dispute were the period for filing a defence.

2.16 A party who serves points of dispute on the receiving party must at the same time serve a copy on every other party to the detailed assessment proceedings, whose name and address for service appears on the statement served by the receiving party in accordance with paragraph 2.2(5) above.

2.17 (1) This paragraph applies in cases in which Points of Dispute care capable of being copied onto a computer disk.

(2) If, within 14 days of the receipt of the Points of Dispute, the receiving party requests a disk copy of them, the paying party must supply him with a copy free of charge not more than 7 days after the date on which he received the request.

Rule 47.10 Procedure where costs are agreed

2.18 Where the parties have agreed terms as to the issue of a costs certificate (either interim or final) they should apply under Rule 40.6 (Consent judgments and orders) for an order that a certificate be issued in terms set out in the application. Such an application may be dealt with by a court officer, who may issue the certificate.

2.19 Where the receiving party claims that the paying party has agreed to pay costs but that he will neither pay those costs nor join in a consent application under paragraph 2.18, the receiving party may apply under Part 23 (General Rules about Applications for Court Orders) for certificate either interim or final to be issued.

2.20 An application under paragraph 2.18 must be supported by evidence and will be heard by a costs judge or a district judge. The respondent to the application must file and serve any evidence he relies on at least two days before the hearing date.

2.21 Nothing in rule 47.10 prevents parties who seek a judgment or order by consent from including in the draft a term that a party shall pay to another party a specified sum in respect of costs.

2.22 (1) The receiving party may discontinue the detailed assessment proceedings in accordance with Part 38 (Discontinuance).

(2) Where the receiving party discontinues the detailed assessment proceedings before a detailed assessment hearing has been requested, the paying party may apply to the appropriate office for an order about the costs of the detailed assessment proceedings.

(3) Where a detailed assessment hearing has been requested the receiving party may not discontinue unless the court gives permission.

(4) A bill of costs may be withdrawn by consent whether or not a detailed assessment hearing has been requested.

SECTION III — COSTS PAYABLE BY ONE PARTY TO ANOTHER — DEFAULT PROVISIONS

Rule 47.11 Default costs certificate

3.1 A request for the issue of a default costs certificate must be made in Form 7 of the Schedule of Costs Forms annexed to this Practice Direction [i.e., form N254] and must be signed by the receiving party or his solicitor.

3.2 The request must be filed at the appropriate office.

3.3 A default costs certificate will be in Form 9 or Form 10 of the Schedule of Costs Forms annexed to this Practice Direction [i.e., form N255CC or N255HC].

3.4 Attention is drawn to Rules 40.3 (Drawing up and Filing of Judgments and Orders) and 40.4 (Service of Judgments and Orders) which apply to the preparation and service of a default costs certificate. The receiving party will be treated as having permission to draw up a default costs certificate by virtue of this Practice Direction.

3.5 The issue of a default costs certificate does not prohibit, govern or affect any detailed assessment of the same costs which is made pursuant to the Legal Aid Act 1988.

3.6 An application for an order staying enforcement of a default costs certificate may be made either:

(1) to a costs judge or district judge of the court office which issued the certificate; or

(2) to the court (if different) which has general jurisdiction to enforce the certificate.

3.7 Proceedings for enforcement of default costs certificates may not be issued in the Supreme Court Costs Office.

Rule 47.12 Setting aside default costs certificate

3.8 (1) A court officer may set aside a default costs certificate at the request of the receiving party under Rule 47.12(3).

(2) A costs judge or a district judge will make any other order or give any directions under this rule.

3.9 (1) An application for an order under Rule 47.12(2) to set aside or vary a default costs certificate must be supported by evidence.

(2) In deciding whether to set aside or vary a certificate under Rule 47.12(2) the matters to which the court must have regard include whether the party seeking the order made the application promptly.

(3) As a general rule a default costs certificate will be set aside under Rule 47.12(2) only if the applicant shows a good reason for the court to do so and if he files with his application a draft of the points of dispute he proposes to serve if his application is granted.

3.10 (1) Attention is drawn to Rule 3.1(3) (which enables the court when making an order to make it subject to conditions) and to Rule 44.3(8) (which enables the court to order a party whom it has ordered to pay costs to pay an amount on account before the costs are assessed).

(2) A costs judge or a district judge may exercise the power of the court to make an order under Rule 44.3(8) although he did not make the order about costs which led to the issue of the default costs certificate.

3.11 If a default costs certificate is set aside the court will give directions for the management of the detailed assessment proceedings.

SECTION IV — COSTS PAYABLE BY ONE PARTY TO ANOTHER — PROCEDURE WHERE POINTS OF DISPUTE ARE SERVED

Rule 47.13 Optional reply

4.1 Where the receiving party wishes to serve a reply he must also serve a copy on every party to the detailed assessment proceedings. The time for doing so is within 21 days after service of the points of dispute.

Rule 47.14 Detailed assessment hearing

4.2 The time for requesting a detailed assessment hearing is within 3 months of the expiry of the period for commencing detailed assessment proceedings.

4.3 The request for a detailed assessment hearing must be in form 8 of the Schedule of Costs Forms annexed to this Practice Direction [i.e., form N258]. The request must be accompanied by:

(a) a copy of the notice of commencement of detailed assessment proceedings;

(b) a copy of the bill of costs;

(c) the document giving the right to detailed assessment (see paragraph 4.5 below);

(d) a copy of the points of dispute, annotated as necessary in order to show which items have been agreed and their value and to show which items remain in dispute;

(e) as many copies of the points of dispute so annotated as there are personswho have served points of dispute;

(f) a copy of any replies served;

(g) a copy of all orders made by the court relating to the costs which are to be assessed;

(h) copies of the fee notes and other written evidence as served on the paying party in accordance with paragraph 2.2 above;

(i) where there is a dispute as to the receiving party's liability to pay costs to the solicitors who acted for the receiving party, any letter or other written information provided by the solicitor to his client explaining how the solicitor's charges are to be calculated;

(j) a statement signed by the receiving party or his solicitor giving the name, address for service, reference and telephone number and fax number, if any, of:

(i) the receiving party;

(ii) the paying party;

(iii) any other person who has served points of dispute or who has given notice to the receiving party under paragraph 2.5 above;

and giving an estimate of the length of time the detailed assessment hearing will take;

(k) where the application for a detailed assessment hearing is made by a party other than the receiving party, such of the documents set out in this paragraph as are in the possession of that party;

(l) where the court is to assess the costs of an assisted person:

PD 47 PRACTICE DIRECTION — PROCEDURE FOR DETAILED ASSESSMENT ETC.

(i) the legal aid certificate, any amendment certificates, any authorities and any certificates of discharge or revocation of legal aid;

(ii) a certificate, in Form 4(2) of the Schedule of Costs Forms annexed to this Practice Direction [see page 1333];

(iii) if the assisted person has a financial interest in the detailed assessment hearing and wishes to attend, the postal address of that person to which the court will send notice of any hearing;

(iv) if the rates payable out of the legal aid fund are prescribed rates, a schedule to the bill of costs setting out all the items in the bill which are claimed against other parties calculated at the legal aid prescribed rates with or without any claim for enhancement: (further information as to this schedule is set out in Section IX (Legal aid costs at prescribed rates) below);

(v) A copy of any default costs certificate in respect of costs claimed in the bill of costs.

4.4 (1) This paragraph applies to any document described in paragraph 4.3(i) above which the receiving party has filed in the appropriate office. The document must be the latest relevant version and in any event have been filed not more than 2 years before filing the request for a detailed assessment hearing.

(2) In respect of any documents to which this paragraph applies, the receiving party may, instead of filing a copy of it, specify in the request for a detailed assessment hearing the case number under which a copy of the document was previously filed.

4.5 'The document giving the right to detailed assessment' means such one or more of the following documents as are appropriate to the detailed assessment proceedings:

(a) a copy of the judgment or order of the court giving the right to detailed assessment;

(b) a copy of the notice served under rule 3.7 (sanctions for non-payment of certain fees) where a claim is struck out under that rule;

(c) a copy of the notice of acceptance where an offer to settle is accepted under Part 36 (Offers to settle and payments into court);

(d) a copy of the notice of discontinuance in a case which is discontinued under Part 38 (Discontinuance);

(e) a copy of the award made on an arbitration under any Act or pursuant to an agreement, where no court has made an order for the enforcement of the award;

(f) a copy of the order, award or determination of a statutorily constituted tribunal or body;

(g) in a case under the Sheriffs Act 1887, the sheriff's bill of fees and charges, unless a court order giving the right to detailed assessment has been made;

(h) a notice of revocation or discharge under Regulation 82 of the Civil Legal Aid (General) Regulations 1989.

4.6 On receipt of the request for a detailed assessment hearing the court will fix a date for the hearing, or, if the costs officer so decides, will give directions or fix a date for a preliminary appointment.

4.7 (1) The court will give at least 14 days' notice of the time and place of the detailed assessment hearing to every person named in the statement referred to in paragraph 4.3(j) above.

(2) The court will when giving notice, give each person who has served points of dispute a copy of the points of dispute annotated by the receiving party in compliance with paragraph 4.3(d) above.

(3) Attention is drawn to rule 47.15(5) and (6): apart from the receiving party, only those who have served points of dispute may be heard on the detailed assessment unless the court gives permission, and only items specified in the points of dispute may be raised unless the court gives permission.

4.8 (1) If the receiving party does not file a request for a detailed assessment hearing within the prescribed time, the paying party may apply to the court to fix a time within which the receiving party must do so. The sanction, for failure to request a detailed assessment hearing within the time specified by the court, is that all or part of the costs may be disallowed (see rule 47.8(3) and (4)).

(2) Where the receiving party requests a detailed assessment hearing after the time specified in the rules but before the paying party has made an application to the court to specify a time, the only sanction which the court may impose is to disallow all or part of the interest which would otherwise be payable for the period of delay, unless the court exercises its powers under Rule 47.4 (court's powers in relation to misconduct).

4.9 If either party wishes to make an application in the detailed assessment proceedings the provisions of Part 23 (General Rules about Applications for Court Orders) apply.

4.10 (1) This paragraph deals with the procedure to be adopted where a date has been given by the court for a detailed assessment hearing and:

(a) the detailed assessment proceedings are settled, or

(b) a party to the detailed assessment proceedings wishes to apply to vary the date which the court has fixed, or

(c) the parties to the detailed assessment proceedings agree about changes they wish to make to any direction given for the management of the detailed assessment proceedings.

(2) If detailed assessment proceedings are settled, the receiving party must give notice of that fact to the court immediately, preferably by fax.

(3) A party who wishes to apply to vary a direction must do so in accordance with Part 23 (General Rules about Applications for Court Orders).

(4) If the parties agree about changes they wish to make to any direction given for the management of the detailed assessment proceedings:

(a) they must apply to the court for an order by consent; and

(b) they must file a draft of the directions sought and an agreed statement of the reasons why the variation is sought; and

(c) the court may make an order in the agreed terms or in other terms without a hearing, but it may direct that a hearing is to be listed.

4.11 (1) If a party wishes to vary his bill of costs, points of dispute or a reply, an amended or supplementary document must be filed with the court and copies of it must be served on all other relevant parties.

(2) Permission is not required to vary a bill of costs, points of dispute or a reply but the court may disallow the variation or permit it only upon conditions, including conditions as to the payment of any costs caused or wasted by the variation.

4.12 Unless the court directs otherwise the receiving party must file with the court the papers in support of the bill not less than 7 days before the date for the detailed assessment hearing and not more than 14 days before that date.

4.13 The papers to be filed in support of the bill and the order in which they are to be arranged, are as follows:

(i) instructions and briefs to counsel arranged in chronological order together with all advices, opinions and drafts received in response to such instructions;

(ii) reports and opinions of medical and other experts arranged in chronological order;

(iii) correspondence files and attendance notes;

(iv) any other relevant papers;

(v) in detailed assessment proceedings to which rule 48.9 (Conditional Fees) applies, a copy of the conditional fee agreements;

(vi) in detailed assessment proceedings in proceedings which commenced before 26 April 1999, a full set of any relevant pleadings which have been served by the parties but not filed at court.

4.14 Once the detailed assessment hearing has ended it is the responsibility of the legal representative appearing for the receiving party or, as the case may be, the receiving party in person to remove the papers filed in support of the bill.

SECTION V INTERIM COSTS CERTIFICATE AND FINAL COSTS CERTIFICATE

Rule 47.15 Power to issue an interim certificate

5.1 (1) A party wishing to apply for an interim certificate may do so by making an application in accordance with Part 23 (General Rules about Applications for Court Orders).

(2) Attention is drawn to the fact that the court's power to issue an interim certificate arises only after the receiving party has filed a request for a detailed assessment hearing.

Rule 47.16 Final costs certificate

5.2 At the detailed assessment hearing the court will indicate any disallowance or reduction in the sums claimed in the bill of costs by making an appropriate note on the bill.

5.3 Where the bill of costs is in the form illustrated in Form 2 of the Schedule of Costs Forms annexed to this Practice Direction [see page 1318], the receiving party must, in order to complete the bill after the detailed assessment hearing, enter in the fourth and fifth columns of the bill, the correct figures agreed or allowed in respect of each item and must re-calculate the summary of the bill appropriately.

5.4 The completed bill of costs must be filed with the court no later than 14 days after the detailed assessment hearing.

5.5 At the same time as filing the completed bill of costs, the party whose bill it is must also produce receipted fee notes and receipted accounts in respect of all disbursements except those covered by a certificate in Form 4(4) in the Schedule of Costs Forms annexed to this Practice Direction [see page 1334].

5.6 No final costs certificate will be issued until all relevant court fees payable on the assessment of costs have been paid.

5.7 If the receiving party fails to file a completed bill in accordance with rule 47.16 the paying party may make an application under Part 23 (General Rules about Applications for Court Orders) seeking an appropriate order under rule 3.1 (The Court's general powers of management).

5.8 A final costs certificate will show:

(a) the amount of any costs which have been agreed between the parties or which have been allowed on detailed assessment;

(b) where applicable the amount agreed or allowed in respect of VAT on the costs agreed or allowed.

This provision is subject to any contrary provision made by the statutory provisions relating to legal aid.

5.9 A final costs certificate will include disbursements in respect of the fees of counsel only if receipted fee notes or accounts in respect of those disbursements have been produced to the court and only to the extent indicated by those receipts.

5.10 Where the certificate relates to costs payable between parties a separate certificate will be issued for each party entitled to costs.

5.11 Model forms of an interim costs certificate (Form 11) and final costs certificates (Forms 12 and 13) are included in the Schedule of Costs Forms annexed to this Practice Direction [these are forms N257, N256CC and N256HC].

5.12 An application for an order staying enforcement of an interim costs certificate of final costs certificate may be made either:

(1) to a costs judge or district judge of the court office which issued the certificate; or

(2) to the court (if different) which has general jurisdiction to enforce the certificate

5.13 Proceedings for enforcement of interim costs certificates or final costs certificates may not be issued in the Supreme Court Costs Office.

SECTION VI DETAILED ASSESSMENT PROCEDURE FOR COSTS OF AN ASSISTED PERSON PAYABLE OUT OF THE LEGAL AID FUND

Rule 47.17 Detailed assessment procedure where costs are payable out of the Legal Aid Fund

6.1 The provisions of this section apply where the court is to assess costs which are payable only out of the legal aid fund. Sections IV and IX apply in cases involving costs by another person as well as costs payable only out of the legal aid fund.

6.2 The time for requesting a detailed assessment of legal aid costs is within 3 months after the date when the right to detailed assessment arose.

6.3 The request for a detailed assessment of legal aid costs must be in form 8 of the Schedule of Costs forms annexed to this Practice Direction [i.e., form N258]. The request must be accompanied by:

(a) a copy of the bill of costs;
(b) the document giving the right to detailed assessment (for further information as to this document, see paragraph 4.5 above);
(c) a copy of all orders made by the court relating to the costs which are to be assessed;
(d) copies of any fee notes of counsel and any expert in respect of fees claimed in the bill;
(e) written evidence as to any other disbursement which is claimed and which exceeds £250;
(f) the legal aid certificates, any amendment certificates, any authorities and any certificates of discharge or revocation of legal aid;
(g) the relevant papers in support of the bill as described in paragraph 4.13, above;
(h) a statement signed by the solicitor giving his name, address for service reference, telephone number and fax number if any and, if the assisted person has a financial interest in the detailed assessment and wishes to attend, giving the postal address of that person, to which the court will send notice of any hearing.

6.4 Rule 47.17 provides that the court will hold a detailed assessment hearing if the assisted person has a financial interest in the detailed assessment and wishes to attend. The court may also hold a detailed assessment hearing in any other case, instead of provisionally assessing a bill of costs, where it considers that a hearing is necessary. Before deciding whether a hearing is necessary under this rule, the court may require the solicitor, whose bill it is, to provide further information relating to the bill.

6.5 Where the court has provisionally assessed a bill of costs, it will send to the solicitor a notice in Form 14 in the Schedule of Costs Forms annexed to this Practice Direction [i.e., form N253] of the amount of costs which the court proposes to allow together with the bill itself.

6.6 The court will fix a date for a detailed assessment hearing if the solicitor informs the court within 14 days after he receives the notice of amount allowed on provisional assessment that he wants the court to hold such a hearing.

6.7 The court will give at least 14 days' notice of the time and place of the detailed assessment hearing to the solicitor and, if the assisted person has a financial interest in the detailed assessment and wishes to attend, to the assisted person.

6.8 If the solicitor whose bill it is, or any other party wishes to make an application in the detailed assessment proceedings, the provisions of Part 23 (General Rules about Applications for Court Orders) apply.

SECTION VII COSTS OF DETAILED ASSESSMENT PROCEEDINGS

Rule 47.18 Liability for costs of detailed assessment proceedings

7.1 As a general rule the court will assess the receiving party's costs of the detailed assessment proceedings and add them to the bill of costs.

7.2 If the costs of the detailed assessment proceedings are awarded to the paying party, the court will either assess those costs by summary assessment or make an order for them to be decided by detailed assessment.

7.3 Attention is drawn to the fact that in deciding what order to make about the costs of detailed assessment proceedings the court must have regard to the conduct of all parties, the amount by which the bill of costs has been reduced and whether it was reasonable for a party to claim the costs of a particular item or to dispute that item.

Rule 47.19 Offers to settle without prejudice save as to the costs of the detailed assessment proceedings

7.4 Rule 47.19 allows the court to take into account offers to settle, without prejudice save as to the costs of detailed assessment proceedings, when deciding who is liable for the costs of those proceedings. The rule does not specify a time within which such an offer should be made. An offer made by the paying party should usually be made within 14 days after service of the notice of commencement on that party. If the offer is made by the receiving party it should normally be made within 14 days after the service of points of dispute by the paying party. Offers made after these periods are likely to be given less weight by the court in deciding what order as to costs to make unless there is good reason for the offer being made at a later time.

7.5 Where an offer to settle is accepted, an application may be made for a certificate in agreed terms, or the bill of costs may be withdrawn, in accordance with Rule 47.10 (Procedure where costs are agreed).

7.6 Where the receiving party is an assisted person, an offer to settle without prejudice save as to the costs of the detailed assessment proceedings will not have the consequences specified under rule 47.19 unless the court so orders.

SECTION VIII APPEAL AGAINST DECISIONS IN DETAILED ASSESSMENT PROCEEDINGS

Rule 47.23 Duty to seek reasons

8.1 A party wishing to appeal must request written reasons for the decision in accordance in Rule 47.24 and obtain the court's permission in accordance with Rule 47.25 unless the court orders otherwise. The request must be made in writing and filed at the end of the detailed assessment hearing or subsequently in accordance with Rule 47.24(2) and (3). A request for reasons made by one party will be treated as a request made by all parties.

8.2 Attention is drawn to the time limits for requesting written reasons. In the case of the receiving party this is 14 days after the detailed assessment hearing (i.e. when the completed bill of costs is filed). In the case of the paying party it is within 7 days after the detailed assessment hearing.

8.3 A request for written reasons must clearly identify the particular parts of the decision for which reasons are requested.

8.4 Before it gives reasons the court may require the party seeking reasons to file a note of the decision in question and the reasons which the court gave for it at the hearing.

8.5 Where a party seeks requests written reasons the court may refuse the request. Such a refusal will usually be made only where the reasons underlying the decision are sufficiently recorded on the bill itself or in a note of the hearing which has been approved by the court.

8.6 The court will usually direct that written reasons are not necessary where the decision to be appealed against was a case management decision rather than a decision on the substance of the assessment proceedings.

8.7 A case management decision is one which does not decide the merits of the assessment proceedings. Examples are a decision to allow or refuse an extension of time, to adjourn proceedings or to add a party to the proceedings.

8.8 Where the court exercises any of its general case management powers under Part 3 the decision will generally be a case management decision.

8.9 Where written reasons are given the court will serve a copy of them on every party to the detailed assessment proceedings.

PD 47 PRACTICE DIRECTION — PROCEDURE FOR DETAILED ASSESSMENT ETC.

Rule 47.24 Obtaining the court's permission to appeal

8.10 A party may request permission to appeal by letter delivered to the court and copied to the other parties. The letter must correctly set out the title of the action and the court reference. It must also set out the basis upon which permission is sought.

8.11 As a general rule the court will not rule upon a request for permission to appeal without first providing written reasons for the decision to which the request relates or without first dispensing with the need for written reasons.

8.12 Attention is drawn to the time limits for seeking permission to appeal i.e. 14 days after receiving written reasons; or, if the court directs that no written reasons are required, within 7 days after service of that direction.

8.13 The time limit for appeal will be calculated without taking into account the day upon which the letter requesting permission was delivered to the court, the day upon which the party wishing to appeal received the court's reply to that letter or any day in between those days. (See Rule 2.8 (Time).)

8.14 In considering an application for permission to appeal the court will take into account:

(1) whether the ground of appeal has a reasonable prospect of success;

(2) whether the costs of the appeal are likely to be disproportionate; this factor is particularly relevant where the appeal is as to quantum only;

(3) if the appeal is against a case management decision, whether an appeal at that stage in the proceedings is appropriate.

Rule 47.25 Appeal procedure

8.15 The time for filing notice of appeal is set out at Rule 47.25. Attention is drawn to the fact that permission is not required to appeal against the decision of an authorised court officer or in respect of a decision of a Costs Judge or District Judge against a legal representative in relation to misconduct or in respect of wasted costs.

8.16 A notice of appeal against the decision of a Costs Officer must be in Form 16 of the Schedule of Costs Forms annexed to this Practice Direction [see page 1338]. The Notice must set out the grounds of appeal.

8.17 (1) If it is necessary to obtain the court's permission to appeal and the Costs Officer refuses to give permission, the party wishing to appeal must, before filing a notice of appeal, apply to the High Court Judge or Circuit Judge, as the case may be, on notice requesting permission.

(2) A copy of that notice must be served on all other parties who may be affected by the appeal.

(3) If the Judge who deals with the application grants permission to appeal the order made will extend the time for appealing.

(4) The extended period will be as stated in the order, or, if no period is stated will be the period up to 7 days after the date of the Judge's decision to give permission to appeal.

8.18 Where a decision of a costs judge or district judge on an appeal from an authorised court officer is taken on further appeal to a High Court judge or a circuit judge, the appellant must, before the hearing of the further appeal, file a note of the decision given by the costs judge or district judge. The note filed must be agreed (if possible) with the other parties to the appeal and must be approved by the costs judge or district judge.

SECTION IX LEGAL AID COSTS AT PRESCRIBED RATES

9.1 This section applies to a bill of costs of an assisted person which is payable by another person where the costs which can be claimed out of the legal aid fund are restricted to legal aid prescribed rates (with or without enhancement).

9.2 Where this section applies, the solicitor of the assisted person must file a legal aid schedule in accordance with Paragraph 4.3(1) above. The schedule should follow as closely as possible Form 3 of the Schedule of Costs Forms annexed to this Practice Direction [see page 1327].

9.3   The schedule must set out by reference to the item numbers in the bill of costs, all the costs claimed as payable by another person, but the arithmetic in the schedule should claim those items at prescribed rates only (with or without any claim for enhancement).

9.4   Where there has been a change in the prescribed rates during the period covered by the bill of costs, the schedule (as opposed to the bill) should be divided into separate parts, so as to deal separately with each change of rate. The schedule must also be divided so as to correspond with any divisions in the bill of costs.

9.5   Costs which are claimed as payable only out of the legal aid fund should be set out in a separate part or parts of the schedule.

9.6   The detailed assessment of the legal aid schedule will take place immediately after the detailed assessment of the bill of costs.

9.7   Attention is drawn to the possibility that, on occasions, the court may decide to conduct the detailed assessment of the legal aid schedule separately from any detailed assessment of the bill of costs. This will occur, for example, where a default costs certificate is obtained as between the parties but that certificate is not set aside at the time of the detailed assessment pursuant to the Legal Aid Act 1988.

CPR PART 48 COSTS — SPECIAL CASES

CONTENTS OF THIS PART
I COSTS PAYABLE BY OR TO PARTICULAR PERSONS
Pre-commencement disclosure and orders for disclosure against a
person who is not a party . . . Rule 48.1
Costs orders in favour of or against non-parties . . . Rule 48.2
Amount of costs where costs are payable pursuant to a contract . . . Rule 48.3
Limitations on court's power to award costs in favour of trustee or
personal representative . . . Rule 48.4
Costs where money is payable by or to a child or patient . . . Rule 48.5
Litigants in person . . . Rule 48.6

II COSTS RELATING TO SOLICITORS AND OTHER LEGAL
REPRESENTATIVES
Personal liability of legal representative for costs — wasted costs orders Rule 48.7
Basis of detailed assessment of solicitor and client costs . . . Rule 48.8
Conditional fees . . . Rule 48.9
Assessment procedure . . . Rule 48.10
(The definitions contained in Part 43 are relevant to this Part)

I COSTS PAYABLE BY OR TO PARTICULAR PERSONS

48.1 PRE-COMMENCEMENT DISCLOSURE AND ORDERS FOR DISCLOSURE AGAINST A PERSON WHO IS NOT A PARTY

(1) This paragraph applies where a person applies—
  (a) for an order under—
    (i) section 33 of the Supreme Court Act 1981; or
    (ii) section 52 of the County Courts Act 1984,
(which give the court powers exercisable before commencement of proceedings); or
  (b) for an order under—
    (i) section 34 of the Supreme Court Act 1981; or
    (ii) section 53 of the County Courts Act 1984, (which give the court power to make an order against a non-party for disclosure of documents, inspection of property etc.).

(2) The general rule is that the court will award the person against whom the order is sought his costs—
  (a) of the application; and
  (b) of complying with any order made on the application.

(3) The court may however make a different order, having regard to all the circumstances, including—
  (a) the extent to which it was reasonable for the person against whom the order was sought to oppose the application; and
  (b) whether the parties to the application have complied with any relevant pre-action protocol.

48.2 COSTS ORDERS IN FAVOUR OF OR AGAINST NON-PARTIES

(1) Where the court is considering whether to exercise its power under section 51 of the Supreme Court Act 1981(10) (costs are in the discretion of the court) to make a costs order in favour of or against a person who is not a party to proceedings—
  (a) that person must be added as a party to the proceedings for the purposes of costs only; and
  (b) he must be given a reasonable opportunity to attend a hearing at which the court will consider the matter further.

(2) This rule does not apply—
  (a) where the court is considering whether to—

(i) make an order against the Legal Aid Board;
(ii) make a wasted costs order (as defined in 48.7); and
(b) in proceedings to which rule 48.1 applies (pre-commencement disclosure and orders for disclosure against a person who is not a party).

48.3 AMOUNT OF COSTS WHERE COSTS ARE PAYABLE PURSUANT TO A CONTRACT

(1) Where the court assesses (whether by the summary or detailed procedure) costs which are payable by the paying party to the receiving party under the terms of a contract, the costs payable under those terms are, unless the contract expressly provides otherwise, to be presumed to be costs which—
(a) have been reasonably incurred; and
(b) are reasonable in amount,
and the court will assess them accordingly.
(The costs practice direction sets out circumstances where the court may order otherwise)
(2) This rule does not apply where the contract is between a solicitor and his client.

48.4 LIMITATIONS ON COURT'S POWER TO AWARD COSTS IN FAVOUR OF TRUSTEE OR PERSONAL REPRESENTATIVE

(1) This rule applies where—
(a) a person is or has been a party to any proceedings in the capacity of trustee or personal representative; and
(b) rule 48.3 does not apply.
(2) The general rule is that where he is entitled to be paid his costs of the proceedings out of any fund held by him as trustee or personal representative, those costs shall be assessed on the indemnity basis.
(3) The court may order otherwise if a trustee or personal representative has acted for a benefit other than that of the fund.

48.5 COSTS WHERE MONEY IS PAYABLE BY OR TO A CHILD OR PATIENT

(1) This rule applies to any proceedings where a party is a child or patient and—
(a) money is ordered or agreed to be paid to, or for the benefit of, that party; or
(b) money is ordered to be paid by him or on his behalf.
('Child' and 'patient' are defined in rule 2.3)
(2) The general rule is that—
(a) the court must order a detailed assessment of the costs payable by any party who is a child or patient to his solicitor; and
(b) on an assessment under paragraph (a), the court must also assess any costs payable to that party in the proceedings, unless the court has issued a default costs certificate in relation to those costs under rule 47.11.
(3) The court need not order detailed assessment of costs in the circumstances set out in the costs practice direction.
(4) Where—
(a) a claimant is a child or patient; and
(b) a detailed assessment has taken place under paragraph (2)(a),
the only amount payable by the child or patient to his solicitor is the amount which the court certifies as payable.
(This rule applies to a counterclaim by or on behalf of a child or patient by virtue of rule 20.3)

48.6 LITIGANTS IN PERSON

(1) This rule applies where the court orders (whether by summary assessment or detailed assessment) that the costs of a litigant in person are to be paid by any other person.

(2) The costs allowed under this rule must not exceed, except in the case of a disbursement, two-thirds of the amount which would have been allowed if the litigant in person had been represented by a legal representative.

(3) Costs allowed to the litigant in person shall be—

(a) such costs which would have been allowed if the work had been done or the disbursements made by a legal representative on the litigant in person's behalf;

(b) the payments reasonably made by him for legal services relating to the conduct of the proceedings; and

(c) the costs of obtaining expert assistance in connection with assessing the claim for costs.

(The costs practice direction deals with who may be an expert for the purpose of paragraph (2)(c))

(4) Subject to paragraph (2), the amount of costs to be allowed to the litigant in person for any item of work to which the costs relate shall, if he fails to prove financial loss, be an amount in respect of the time spent reasonably doing the work at the rate specified in the costs practice direction.

(5) A litigant who is allowed costs for attending at court to conduct his case is not entitled to a witness allowance in respect of such attendance in addition to those costs.

(6) For the purposes of this rule, a litigant in person includes—

(a) a company or other corporation which is acting without a legal representative; and

(b) a barrister, solicitor, solicitor's employee or other authorised litigator (as defined in the Courts and Legal Services Act 1990) who is acting for himself.

II COSTS RELATING TO SOLICITORS AND OTHER LEGAL REPRESENTATIVES

48.7 PERSONAL LIABILITY OF LEGAL REPRESENTATIVE FOR COSTS — WASTED COSTS ORDERS

(1) This rule applies where the court is considering whether to make an order under section 51(6) of the Supreme Court Act 1981 (court's power to disallow or (as the case may be) order a legal representative to meet, 'wasted costs').

(2) The court must give the legal representative a reasonable opportunity to attend a hearing to give reasons why it should not make such an order.

(3) For the purposes of this rule, the court may direct that privileged[GL] documents are to be disclosed to the court and, if the court so directs, to the other party to the application for an order.

(4) When the court makes a wasted costs order, it must specify the amount to be disallowed or paid.

(5) The court may direct that notice must be given to the legal representative's client, in such manner as the court may direct—

(a) of any proceedings under this rule; or

(b) of any order made under it against his legal representative.

(6) Before making a wasted costs order, the court may direct a costs judge or a district judge to inquire into the matter and report to the court.

(7) The court may refer the question of wasted costs to a costs judge or a district judge, instead of making a wasted costs order.

48.8 BASIS OF DETAILED ASSESSMENT OF SOLICITOR AND CLIENT COSTS

(1) This rule applies to every assessment of a solicitor's bill to his client except—

(a) a bill which is to be paid out of the legal aid fund under the Legal Aid Act 1988; or

(b) where the solicitor and his client have entered into a conditional fee agreement as defined by section 58 of the Courts and Legal Services Act 1990.

(1A) Section 74(3) of the Solicitors Act 1974 applies unless the solicitor and client have entered into a written agreement which expressly permits payment to the solicitor of an amount of costs greater than that which the client could have recovered from another party to the proceedings.

(2) Subject to paragraph (1A), costs are to be assessed on the indemnity basis but are to be presumed—
    (a) to have been reasonably incurred if they were incurred with the express or implied approval of the client;
    (b) to be reasonable in amount if their amount was expressly or impliedly approved by the client;
    (c) to have been unreasonably incurred if—
        (i) they are of an unusual nature or amount; and
        (ii) the solicitor did not tell his client that as a result he might not recover all of them from the other party.

48.9 CONDITIONAL FEES

(1) This rule applies to every assessment (whether by the summary or detailed procedure) of a solicitor's bill to his client where the solicitor and the client have entered into a conditional fee agreement as defined in section 58 of the Courts and Legal Services Act 1990.

(2) In this rule—
'the base costs' means the costs other than a percentage increase;
'percentage increase' means a percentage increase pursuant to a conditional fee agreement entered into between the solicitor and his client or between counsel and the solicitor, or counsel and the client; and
'costs' includes all fees, charges, disbursements and other expenses charged by the solicitor or counsel under the conditional fee agreement in question.

(3) On an assessment to which this rule applies, the client may apply for assessment of the base costs or of a percentage increase or of both.

(4) Where the client applies for assessment of the base costs, the base costs are to be assessed in accordance with rule 48.8(2) as if the solicitor and his client had not entered into a conditional fee agreement.

(5) Where the client applies for assessment of a percentage increase, the court may reduce the percentage increase where it considers it to be disproportionate having regard to all relevant factors as they reasonably appeared to the solicitor or counsel when the conditional fee agreement was entered into.

(6) The court will not vary a percentage increase where the client is a child or patient, except in accordance with paragraph (5).
(The costs practice direction specifies some of the relevant factors)

48.10 ASSESSMENT PROCEDURE

(1) This rule sets out the procedure to be followed where the court has made an order under Part III of the Solicitors Act 1974 for the assessment of costs payable to a solicitor by his client.

(2) The solicitor must serve a breakdown of costs within 28 days of the order for costs to be assessed.

(3) The client must serve points of dispute within 14 days after service on him of the breakdown of costs.

(4) If the solicitor wishes to serve a reply, he must do so within 14 days of service on him of the points of dispute.

(5) Either party may file a request for a hearing date—
    (a) after points of dispute have been served; but
    (b) no later than 3 months after the date of the order for the costs to be assessed.

(6) This procedure applies subject to any contrary order made by the court.

PD 48 PRACTICE DIRECTION — COSTS — SPECIAL CASES

SECTION I COSTS PAYABLE BY OR TO PARTICULAR PERSONS

Rule 48.3 Amount of costs where costs are payable under a contract
1.1 The principles set out in *Gomba Holdings (UK) Ltd v Minories Finance Ltd (No. 2)* [1993] Ch 171 continue to apply to a mortgagee's costs.
1.2 Rule 48.3 only applies if the court is assessing costs payable under a contract. It does not:
 (1) require the court to make an assessment of such costs; or
 (2) require a mortgagee to apply for an order for those costs that he has a contractual right to recover out of the mortgage funds.
1.3 Where the court is assessing costs payable under a contract, the court may make an order that all or part of the costs payable under the contract shall be disallowed if the court is satisfied by the paying party that costs have been unreasonably incurred or are unreasonable in amount.

Rule 48.5 Costs where money is payable by or to a child or patient
1.2 The circumstances in which the court need not order the assessment of costs under rule 48.6(2) are as follows:
 (a) where there is no need to do so to protect the interests of the child or patient or his estate;
 (b) where another party has agreed to pay a specified sum in respect of the costs of the child or patient and the solicitor acting for the child or patient has waived the right to claim further costs;
 (c) where the court has decided the costs payable to the child or patient by way of summary assessment and the solicitor acting for the child or patient has waived the right to claim further costs;
 (d) where an insurer or other person is liable to discharge the costs which the child or patient would otherwise be liable to pay to his solicitor and the court is satisfied that the insurer or other person is financially able to discharge those costs.

Rule 48.6 Litigants in person
1.3 In order to qualify as an expert for the purpose of Rule 48.6(3)(c) (expert assistance in connection with assessing the claim for costs), the person in question must be a:
 (1) barrister,
 (2) solicitor,
 (4) Fellow of the Institute of Legal Executives,
 (4) Fellow of the Association of Law Costs Draftsmen,
 (5) law costs draftsman who is a member of the Academy of Experts,
 (6) law costs draftsman who is a member of the Expert Witness Institute.
1.4 Where a litigant in person wishes to prove that he has suffered financial loss he should produce to the court any written evidence he relies on to support that claim, and serve a copy of that evidence on any party against whom he seeks costs at least 24 hours before the hearing at which the question may be decided.
1.5 Where a litigant in person commences detailed assessment proceedings under rule 47.6 he should serve copies of that written evidence with the notice of commencement.
1.6 The amount which may be allowed to a litigant in person under rule 46.3(5)(b) and rule 48.6(4) is £9.25 per hour.
1.7 Attention is drawn to rule 48.6(6)(b). A solicitor who, instead of acting for himself, is represented in the proceedings by his firm or by himself in his firm name, is not, for the purpose of the Civil Procedure Rules, a litigant in person.

PD 48 PRACTICE DIRECTION — COSTS — SPECIAL CASES

SECTION II COSTS RELATING TO SOLICITORS AND OTHER LEGAL REPRESENTATIVES

Rule 48.7 Personal liability of legal representative for costs — wasted costs orders

2.1 Rule 48.7 deals with wasted costs orders against legal representatives. Such orders can be made at any stage in the proceedings up to and including the proceedings relating to the detailed assessment of costs. In general, applications for wasted costs are best left until after the end of the trial.

2.2 The court may make a wasted costs order against a legal representative on an application under Part 23 or of its own initiative.

2.3 A party who wishes to apply for a wasted costs order must first give to the legal representative against whom the order is sought notice in writing:

(a) of what the legal representative is alleged to have done or failed to do, and

(b) the costs that he may be ordered to pay or which are sought against him.

The notice must be given at least 3 days before the hearing.

2.4 It is appropriate for the court to make a wasted costs order against a legal representative only if:

(a) he has acted improperly, unreasonably or negligently,

(b) his conduct has caused another party to incur unnecessary costs, and

(c) it is just in all the circumstances to order him to compensate that party for the whole or part of those costs.

2.5 The court will give directions about the procedure that will be followed in each case in order to ensure that the issues are dealt with in a way that is fair and as simple and summary as the circumstances permit.

2.6 As a general rule the court will consider whether to make a wasted costs order in two stages:

(a) in the first stage, the court must be satisfied:

(i) that it has before it evidence or other material which, if unanswered, would be likely to lead to a wasted costs order being made, and

(ii) the wasted costs proceedings are justified notwithstanding the likely costs involved.

(b) At the second stage (even if the court is satisfied under (a) above) the court will consider, after giving the legal representative an opportunity to put forward his case, whether it is appropriate to make a wasted costs order in accordance with paragraph 2.4 above.

2.7 Attention is drawn to Rule 48.7(3) which gives the court power to direct that privileged documents be disclosed to the court and, if appropriate, to the other party to the application for the wasted costs order.

2.8 A wasted costs order is an order that the legal representative pay a specified sum in respect of costs to another party or that costs relating to a specified sum or items of work be disallowed.

Rule 48.8 Basis of detailed assessment of solicitor and client costs

2.9 A client and his solicitor may agree whatever terms they consider appropriate about the payment of the solicitor's charges for his services. If however, the costs are of an unusual nature (either in amount or in the type of costs incurred) those costs will be presumed to have been unreasonably incurred unless the solicitor satisfies the court that he informed the client that they were unusual and, where the costs relate to litigation, that he informed the client they might not be allowed on an assessment of costs between the parties. That information must have been given to the client before the costs were incurred.

2.10 (1) Costs as between a solicitor and client are assessed on the indemnity basis, as defined by Rule 44.4; proportionality is therefore not relevant.

(2) Attention is drawn to the presumptions set out in rule 48.8(2). These presumptions may be rebutted by evidence to the contrary.

2.11 Rule 48.10 and paragraphs 2.16 to 2.36 of this Practice Direction deal with the procedure to be followed for obtaining the assessment of a solicitor's bill pursuant to an order under Part III of the Solicitors Act 1974.

PD 48 PRACTICE DIRECTION — COSTS — SPECIAL CASES

2.12 If a party fails to comply with the requirements of rule 48.10 concerning the service of a breakdown of costs or points of dispute, any other party may apply to the court in which the detailed assessment hearing should take place for an order requiring compliance with rule 48.10. If the court makes such an order, it may:

(a) make it subject to conditions including a condition to pay a sum of money into court; and

(b) specify the consequences of failure to comply with the order or a condition.

Rule 48.9 Conditional Fees

2.13 (1) A client who has entered into a conditional fee agreement with a solicitor may apply for assessment of the base costs (which is carried out in accordance with Rule 48.8(2) as if there were no conditional fee agreement) or for assessment of the percentage increase (success fee) or both.

(2) Where the court is to assess the percentage increase, proportionality is relevant and the court will have regard to all the relevant factors as they appeared to the solicitor or counsel when the conditional fee agreement was entered into.

2.14 Where the client applies to the court to reduce the percentage increase which the solicitor has charged the client under the conditional fee agreement, the client must set out in writing in his application:

(a) the reasons why the percentage increase should be reduced; and

(b) what the percentage increase should be.

2.15 The factors relevant to assessing the percentage increase include:

(a) the risk that the circumstances in which the fees or expenses would be payable might not occur;

(b) the disadvantages relating to the absence of payment on account;

(c) whether the amount which might be payable under the conditional fee agreement is limited to a certain proportion of any damages recovered by the client;

(d) whether there is a conditional fee agreement between the solicitor and counsel;

(e) the solicitor's liability for any disbursements.

2.16 When the court is considering the factors to be taken into account, it will have regard to the circumstances as they reasonably appeared to the solicitor or counsel when the conditional fee agreement was entered into or at the time of any variation of the agreement.

Rule 48.10 Assessment procedure

2.17 Paragraphs 2.18 to 2.36 apply to orders made under Part III of the Solicitors Act 1974 for the assessment of costs.

2.18 The procedure for obtaining an order under Part III of the Solicitors Act 1974 is by the alternative procedure for claims under Part 8. The provisions of RSC Order 106 appear, appropriately amended, in the Schedule to Part 50 (Application of the Schedules).

2.19 Model forms of order which the court may make are set out in Forms 17, 18 and 19 of the Schedule of Costs Forms annexed to this Practice Direction [see pages 1339–41].

2.20 Attention is drawn to the time limits within which the required steps must be taken: i.e. the solicitor must serve a breakdown of costs within 28 days of the order for costs to be assessed, the client must serve points of dispute within 14 days after service on him of the breakdown; and any reply must be served within 14 days of service of the points of dispute.

2.21 The breakdown of costs referred to in Rule 48.10 is a document which contains the following information:

(a) details of the work done under each of the bills sent for assessment; and

(b) in applications under Section 70 of the Solicitors Act 1974, an account showing money received by the solicitor to the credit of the client and sums paid out of that money on behalf of the client but not payments out which were made in satisfaction of the bill or of any items which are claimed in the bill.

2.22 Form 20 of the Schedule of Costs Forms annexed to this Practice Direction is a model form of breakdown of costs [see page 1342]. A party who is required to serve a breakdown of costs must also serve:

(1) copies of the fee notes of counsel and of any expert in respect of fees claimed in the breakdown, and

(2) written evidence as to any other disbursement which is claimed in the breakdown and which exceeds £250.

2.23 The provisions relating to default costs certificates (Rule 47.11) do not apply to cases to which Rule 48.10 applies.

2.24 Points of dispute should as far as practicable be in the form complying with paragraphs 2.12 and 2.13 of the Directions relating to Part 47.

2.25 The time for requesting a detailed assessment hearing is within 3 months after the date of the order of the costs to be assessed.

2.26 The form of request for a hearing date must be in Form 21 of the Schedule of Costs Forms annexed to this Practice Direction [see page 1343]. The request must be accompanied by copies of:

(a) the order sending the bill or bills for assessment;
(b) the bill or bills sent for assessment;
(c) the solicitor's breakdown of costs and any invoices or accounts served with that breakdown;
(d) a copy of the points of dispute, annotated as necessary in order to show which items have been agreed and their value and to show which items remain in dispute;
(e) as many copies of the points of dispute so annotated as there are other parties to the proceedings to whom the court should give details of the assessment hearing requested;
(f) a copy of any replies served;
(g) a statement signed by the party filing the request or his legal representative giving the names and addresses for service of all parties to the proceedings.

2.27 The request must include an estimate of the length of time the detailed assessment hearing will take.

2.28 On receipt of the request for a detailed assessment hearing the court will fix a date for the hearing or if the Costs Judge or District Judge so decides, will give directions or fix a date for a preliminary appointment.

2.29 (1) The court will give at least 14 days' notice of the time and place of the detailed assessment hearing to every person named in the statement referred to in paragraph 2.26(g) above.

(2) The court will when giving notice, give all parties other than the party who requested the hearing a copy of the points of dispute annotated by the party requesting the hearing in compliance with paragraph 2.26(e) above.

(3) Attention is drawn to rule 47.14(6) and (7): apart from the solicitor whose bill it is, only those parties who have served points of dispute may be heard on the detailed assessment unless the court gives permission, and only items specified in the points of dispute may be raised unless the court gives permission.

2.30 (1) If a party wishes to vary his breakdown of costs, points of dispute or reply, an amended or supplementary document must be filed with the court and copies of it must be served on all other relevant parties.

(2) Permission is not required to vary a breakdown of costs, points of dispute or a reply but the court may disallow the variation or permit it only upon conditions, including conditions as to the payment of any costs caused or wasted by the variation.

2.31 Unless the court directs otherwise the solicitor must file with the court the papers in support of the bill not less than 7 days before the date for the detailed assessment hearing and not more than 14 days before that date.

2.32 Once the detailed assessment hearing has ended it is the responsibility of the legal representative appearing for the solicitor or, as the case may be, the solicitor in person to remove the papers filed in support of the bill.

2.33 (1) Attention is drawn to rule 47.15 (power to issue an interim certificate).

(2) If, in the course of a detailed assessment hearing of a solicitor's bill to his client, it appears to the Costs Judge or District Judge that in any event the solicitor will be liable in connection with that bill to pay money to the client, he may issue an interim certificate specifying an amount which in his opinion is payable by the solicitor to his client. Such a certificate will include an order to pay the sum it certifies unless the court orders otherwise.

2.34 (1) Attention is drawn to rule 47.16 which requires the solicitor to file a completed bill within 14 days after the end of the detailed assessment hearing. The court may dispense with the requirement to file a completed bill. If it does so the time for a request by the solicitor for written reasons under rule 47.23 is 7 days after the date of the order dispensing with the requirement for a completed bill.

(2) After the detailed assessment hearing is concluded the court will:
    (a) complete the court copy of the bill so as to show the amount allowed,
    (b) determine the result of the cash account, and
    (c) award the costs of the detailed assessment hearing in accordance with Section 70(8) of the Solicitors Act 1974, and
    (d) issue a final costs certificate showing the amount due following the detailed assessment hearing.

2.35 A final costs certificate will include an order to pay the sum it certifies unless the court orders otherwise.

2.36 Attention is drawn to Section VIII of Part 47 (appeal against decisions in detailed assessment proceedings).

SECTION III TRANSITIONAL ARRANGEMENTS

3.1 (1) This section deals with the application of the Civil Procedure Rules ('CPR') to taxation proceedings commenced before 26th April 1999.

(2) In this section 'the previous rules' means the Rules of the Supreme Court ('RSC') or County Court Rules ('CCR'), as appropriate.

General scheme of transitional arrangements concerning costs proceedings

3.2 (1) Paragraph 18 of the Practice Direction which supplements Part 51 (Transitional Arrangements) provides that the CPR govern any assessments of costs which take place on or after 26th April 1999 and states a presumption to be applied in respect of costs for work undertaken before 26th April 1999.

(2) The following paragraphs provide four further transitional arrangements:
    (a) to provide an additional presumption to be applied when assessing costs which were awarded by an order made in a County Court before 26th April 1999 which allowed costs 'on Scale 1' to be determined in accordance with CCR Appendix A, or 'on the lower scale' to be determined in accordance with CCR Appendix C;
    (b) to preserve the effect of CCR Appendix B Part III paragraph 2;
    (c) to clarify the approach to be taken where a bill of costs was provisionally taxed before 26th April 1999 and the receiving party is unwilling to accept the result of the provisional taxation;
    (d) to preserve the right to carry in objections or apply for a reconsideration in all taxation proceedings commenced before 26th April 1999.

Scale 1 or lower scale costs

3.3 Where an order was made in county court proceedings before 26th April 1999 under which the costs were allowed on Scale 1 or the lower scale, the general presumption is that no costs will be allowed under that order which would not have been allowed in a taxation before 26th April 1999.

Fixed costs on the lower scale

3.4 The amount to be allowed as fixed costs for making or opposing an application for a rehearing to set aside a judgment given before 26th April 1999 where the costs are on lower scale is £11.25.

Bills provisionally taxed before 26th April 1999

3.5 In respect of bills of costs provisionally taxed before 26th April 1999:

(1) The previous rules apply on the question who can request a hearing and the time limits for doing so; and

(2) The CPR govern any subsequent hearing in that case.

Bills taxed before 26th April 1999

3.6 Where a bill of costs was taxed before 26th April 1999, the previous rules govern the steps which can be taken to challenge that taxation.

Other taxation proceedings

3.7 (1) This paragraph applies to taxation proceedings which were commenced before 26th April 1999, were assigned for taxation to a Taxing Master or District Judge, and which were still pending on 26th April 1999.

(2) Any assessment of costs that takes place in cases to which this paragraph applies which is conducted on or after 26th April 1999, will be conducted in accordance with the CPR.

(3) In addition to the possibility of appeal under rules 47.20 to 47.26 any party to a detailed assessment who is dissatisfied with any decision on a detailed assessment made by a costs judge or district judge may apply to that costs judge or district judge for a review of the decision. The review shall, for procedural purposes, be treated as if it were an appeal from an authorised court officer.

(4) The right of review provided by paragraph (3) above, will not apply in cases in which, at least 28 days before the date of the assessment hearing, all parties were served with notice that the rights of appeal in respect of that hearing would be governed only by Part 47 Section VIII (Appeal against Decisions in Detailed Assessment Proceedings).

(5) An order for the service of notice under sub-paragraph (4) above may be made on the application of any party to the detailed assessment proceedings or may be made by the court of its own initiative.

CPR PART 49 SPECIALIST PROCEEDINGS

49—(1) These Rules shall apply to the proceedings listed in paragraph (2) subject to the provisions of the relevant practice direction which applies to those proceedings.

(2) The proceedings referred to in paragraph (1) are—
- (a) admiralty proceedings;
- (b) arbitration proceedings;
- (c) commercial and mercantile actions;
- (d) Patents Court business (as defined by the relevant practice direction) and proceedings under—
   - (i) the Copyright, Designs and Patents Act 1988;
   - (ii) the Trade Marks Act 1994; and
   - (iii) the Olympic Symbol etc Protection Act 1995 and Olympics Association Right (Infringement Proceedings) Regulations 1995;
- (e) Technology and Construction Court Business (as defined by the relevant practice direction);
- (f) proceedings under the Companies Act 1985 and the Companies Act 1989; and
- (g) contentious probate proceedings.

PD 49 PRACTICE DIRECTION — CONTENTIOUS PROBATE PROCEEDINGS

This practice direction supplements CPR Part 49 and replaces RSC Order 76 and CCR Order 41

GENERAL

1.1 This Practice Direction applies to contentious probate proceedings and to applications for the rectification of a will both in the High Court and in the county court.

(For the rules and procedure relating to non-contentious probate proceedings, see the Non-Contentious Probate Rules 1987 as amended. The Non-Contentious Probate Rules deal, among other things, with the procedure for entering a caveat, for warning-off a caveat and for entering an appearance to a warning. If an application for the rectification of a will is not contentious, the application may be made to the Family Division: see Non-Contentious Probate Rules 1987, rule 55.)

(For the jurisdiction of a county court in respect of contentious probate proceedings and proceedings for the rectification of a will, see s.32 County Courts Act 1984.)

1.2 In this Practice Direction:

(i) 'probate claim' means a claim in respect of any contentious matter arising in connection with an application for the grant or revocation of probate or letters of administration and includes a claim for an order pronouncing for or against the validity of an alleged will, 'claim form' means a claim form by which a probate claim is begun and 'probate proceedings' means the proceedings in which a probate claim is brought.

(ii) 'relevant office' means:

(a) in the case of High Court proceedings in a Chancery district registry, that registry,

(b) in the case of any other High Court proceedings, Chancery Chambers at the Royal Courts of Justice, Strand, London, WC2A 2LL; and

(c) in the case of county court proceedings, the office of the county court in question.

(iii) 'testamentary script' means a will or draft thereof, written instructions for a will made by or at the request, or under the instructions, of the testator and any document purporting to be evidence of the contents, or to be a copy, of a will which is alleged to have been lost or destroyed.

COMMENCEMENT OF PROCEEDINGS

2.1 If a probate claim is to be commenced in the High Court, the claim form must be issued out of Chancery Chambers or one of the Chancery district registries.

(There are Chancery district registries at Birmingham, Bristol, Cardiff, Leeds, Liverpool, Manchester, Newcastle upon Tyne and Preston).

2.2 (i) If a claim form is wrongly issued out of a district registry other than a Chancery district registry, an application for the transfer of the claim to the Royal Courts of Justice or to a Chancery district registry should be made forthwith.

(ii) The court may, in a case to which paragraph 2.2(i) applies, order the transfer on its own initiative.

2.3 On the issue of a claim form the relevant office will send a notice to Leeds District Probate Registry, Coronet House, Queen Street, Leeds, LS1 2BA, DX 26451 Leeds (Park Square), Telephone 0113 243 1505, requesting that all testamentary scripts and other relevant documents in any probate registry be sent to the relevant office.

2.4 A claim form must, before it is issued, contain a statement of the nature of the interest of the claimant and of the defendant in the estate of the deceased to which the claim relates.

2.5 Every person who may be affected by a probate claim, either as a beneficiary under a will in issue or on an intestacy, and who is not joined as a party to the probate claim, should be given notice of the proceedings. It may in some cases be appropriate for a representation order to be sought under RSC Order 15, rule 13 (Schedule 1 to the CPR) or CCR Order 5, rule 6 (Schedule 2 to the CPR).

2.6 The court may direct that notice of the probate claim be served on any such person as is mentioned in paragraph 2.5 and, for that purpose, rule 13A of RSC Order 15 (Schedule 1 to the CPR) applies to probate claims in the county court as well as to probate claims in the High Court.

2.7 Every person who is entitled, or claims to be entitled, to administer the estate of a deceased person under an unrevoked grant of probate or letters of administration must be made a party to any probate claim seeking revocation of a grant.

2.8 The commencement of a probate claim will, unless a court otherwise directs, prevent any grant of probate or letters of administration being made until the probate claim has been disposed of (see rule 45 of the Non-Contentious Probate Rules 1987: but see also s. 117, Supreme Court Act, 1981 and paragraph 14 below).

LODGMENT OF GRANT IN ACTION FOR REVOCATION

3.1 Where, on the issue of a claim form seeking revocation of a grant of probate or letters of administration, the probate or letters of administration, as the case may be, have not been lodged in court, then:

(a) if a person to whom the grant was made is a claimant, he must lodge the probate or letters of administration in the relevant office within 7 days after the issue of the claim form;

(b) if a defendant to the action has the probate or letters of administration in his possession or under his control, he must lodge it or them in the relevant office within 14 days after the service of the claim form on him.

In this paragraph 'court' includes the principal registry of the Family Division or a district probate registry.

3.2 Any person who fails to comply with paragraph 3.1 may, on the application of any party to the probate claim, or by the court on its own initiative, be ordered to lodge the probate or letters of administration in the relevant office within a specified time.

3.3 Any person against whom an order is made under paragraph 3.2 shall not be entitled to take any step in the probate proceedings without the permission of the court until he has complied with the order.

ACKNOWLEDGMENT OF SERVICE

4. A defendant on whom a claim form is served must, subject to CPR rule 10.3(2), file an acknowledgment of service within 14 days after service of the claim form on him.

TESTAMENTARY SCRIPTS

5.1 Unless the court otherwise directs, the claimant and every defendant who has acknowledged service of the claim form must by affidavit or witness statement:

(a) describe any testamentary script of the deceased person, whose estate is the subject of the action, of which he has any knowledge or, if such be the case, state that he knows of no such script, and

(b) if any such script of which he has knowledge is not in his possession or under his control, give the name and address of the person in whose possession or under whose control it is or, if such be the case, state that he does not know the name or address of that person.

5.2 Any affidavit or witness statement required by paragraph 5.1 must be filed, and any testamentary script referred to therein which is in the possession or under the control of the deponent must be lodged in the relevant office within 14 days after the acknowledgment of service by a defendant to the claim or, if no defendant acknowledges service and the court does not otherwise direct, before an order is made for the trial of the claim.

PD 49 PRACTICE DIRECTION — CONTENTIOUS PROBATE PROCEEDINGS

5.3 Where any testamentary script required by paragraph 5.2 to be lodged in the relevant office or any part thereof is written in pencil, then, unless the court otherwise directs, a facsimile copy of that script, or of the page or pages thereof containing the part written in pencil, must also be lodged in the relevant office and the words which appear in pencil in the original must be underlined in red ink in the copy.

5.4 Except with the permission of the court, a party to a probate claim shall not be allowed to inspect an affidavit or witness statement filed under paragraph 5.2 or any testamentary script lodged under paragraph 5.3 unless and until an affidavit or witness statement sworn or made by him containing the information referred to in paragraph 5.1 has been filed.

5.5 Copies of testamentary scripts lodged under paragraph 5.2 should be filed with the originals. The testamentary scripts will remain in the relevant office until the probate claim has been disposed of.

5.6 It is important that testamentary scripts should not be marked in any way; nor should they be stapled or folded.

5.7 (i) Any party desiring to have any testamentary script subjected to examination by an expert should make an application in accordance with CPR Part 23.

(ii) The application notice or the written evidence in support should explain the nature and purpose of the examination and the points to which the examination should be directed.

(iii) The court may order such an examination on its own initiative.

FAILURE TO ACKNOWLEDGE SERVICE

6.1 A default judgment cannot be obtained on a probate claim and CPR rule 10.2 and Part 12 do not apply to probate claims.

6.2 Where any of several defendants to a probate claim fails to acknowledge service of the claim form, the claimant may, after the time for acknowledging service has expired and upon filing an affidavit or witness statement proving due service of the claim form on that defendant proceed with the probate claim as if that defendant had acknowledged service.

6.3 Where the defendant, or all the defendants, to a probate claim, fails or fail to acknowledge service of the claim form then, unless on the application of the claimant the Court orders the claim to be discontinued, the claimant may after the time for acknowledging service has expired apply to the court for an order for trial of the claim.

6.4 Before applying for an order under paragraph 6.3 the claimant must file an affidavit or witness statement proving due service of the claim form on the defendant or defendants and, if no particulars of claim were contained in or served with the claim form, he must file particulars of claim in the relevant office.

6.5 Where the court makes an order under paragraph 6.3, it may direct the claim to be tried on written evidence. (see also paragraph 10.3 below).

(For rules about written evidence, see Part 32 and the Practice Direction supplementing that Part).

SERVICE OF PARTICULARS OF CLAIM AND DEFENCE

7.1 The claimant in a probate claim must, unless the court gives permission to the contrary or particulars of claim were contained in or served with the claim form, serve particulars of claim on every defendant who acknowledges service of the claim form and must do so before the expiration of 28 days after acknowledgment of service by that defendant or of 8 days after the filing by that defendant of an affidavit or witness statement under paragraph 5.1, whichever is the later.

7.2 If particulars of claim were contained in or served with the claim form or are served before the claimant has complied with paragraphs 5.1 and 5.2 above, the time for filing a defence shall, subject to CPR 15.4(2), be 28 days after the affidavit or witness statement required by paragraph 5.1 has been filed and the testamentary scripts have been lodged.

DEFENCE AND COUNTERCLAIM

8.1 A defendant to a probate claim who alleges that he has any claim or is entitled to any remedy relating to the grant of probate of the will, or letters of administration of the estate, of the deceased person must add to his defence a counterclaim in respect of that matter.

8.2 If the claimant fails to serve particulars of claim, any such defendant may, with the permission of the Court, serve a counterclaim and the probate proceedings shall then continue as if the counterclaim were the particulars of claim and the counterclaiming defendant were the claimant.

8.3 A defendant may in his defence give notice that he will raise no positive case but will insist on the will being proved in solemn form of law and, for that purpose, will cross-examine the witnesses who attested the will.

(Attention is drawn to paragraph 2.2 of the Costs Practice Direction Relating to CPR Part 44 and supplementing CPR 44.3).

CONTENTS OF STATEMENTS OF CASE

9.1 Where the claimant in a probate claim disputes the interest of a defendant, he must state in his particulars of claim that he denies the interest of that defendant.

9.2 In a probate claim in which the interest by virtue of which a party claims to be entitled to a grant of letters of administration is disputed, the party disputing that interest must show in his statement of case that if the allegations he makes in it are proved he would be entitled to an interest in the estate.

9.3 Any party who wants to contend that at the time when a will, the subject of the probate claim, was alleged to have been executed the testator did not know and approve of its contents must specify in his statement of case the nature of the case on which he intends to rely, and no allegation in support of that contention which would be relevant in support of any of the following other contentions, that is to say:

(a) that the will was not duly executed,

(b) that at the time of the execution of the will the testator was not of sound mind, memory and understanding, and

(c) that the execution of the will was obtained by undue influence or fraud,

shall be made by that party unless that other contention also is made in his statement of case.

DEFAULT OF PLEADINGS

10.1 A default judgment cannot be obtained on a probate claim (see paragraph 6.1 above).

10.2 Where any party to a probate claim fails to serve on any other party a pleading which he is required by the CPR or this Practice Direction to serve on that other party, then, unless the court orders the claim to be discontinued or dismissed, that other party may, after the expiration of the period fixed by the CPR or this Practice Direction for service of the pleading in question, apply to the court for an order for trial of the probate claim; and if an order is made the court may direct the probate claim to be tried on written evidence.

10.3 If a trial is ordered under paragraph 10.2 (or under paragraph 6.2), the hearing may lead to an order pronouncing for the will in solemn form.

SUMMARY JUDGMENT

11. Where an order pronouncing for a will in solemn form is sought on an application for summary judgment, the evidence in support of the application must include an affidavit or a witness statement proving due execution of the will. (CPR Part 24 and the practice direction supplementing Part 24 deal with summary judgment applications).

DISCONTINUANCE AND DISMISSAL

12.1 CPR Part 38 does not apply to a probate claim.

12.2 At any stage of probate proceedings the court may, on the application of the claimant, or of any party to the probate claim who has acknowledged service of the claim form, order the claim to be discontinued or dismissed on such terms as to costs or otherwise as it thinks just, and may further order that a grant of probate of the will, or letters of administration of the estate, of the deceased person, as the case may be, which is the subject of the claim, be made to the person entitled thereto.

12.3 An application for an order under this rule may be made by application notice in accordance with CPR Part 23.

12.4 An order for the discontinuance or dismissal of a probate claim under paragraph 11.2 will normally lead to a grant of probate or of letters of administration in common form.

COMPROMISE OF ACTION

13.1 Where, whether before or after the service of the defence in a probate claim, the parties to the claim agree to a compromise, the Court may order the trial of the claim on written evidence.

(For a form of order which is also applicable to discontinuance and which may be adapted as appropriate, see Practice Form No. CH38).

13.2 Section 49 of the Administration of Justice Act 1985 permits a probate claim to be compromised without a trial if every 'relevant beneficiary' has consented to the proposed order.

13.3 Applications under section 49 may be heard by a master or district judge and should be supported by affidavit or witness statement identifying the 'relevant beneficiaries' and exhibiting their respective consents. Affidavits or witness statements of testamentary scripts (see paragraph 5 above) will still be necessary.

APPLICATION FOR ORDER TO BRING IN WILL, ETC.

14.1 Any application in a probate claim for an order under section 122 of the Supreme Court Act 1981 shall be for an order requiring a person to bring a will or other testamentary paper into the relevant office or to attend in court for examination.

14.2 An application under paragraph 13.1 shall be made by application notice in accordance with CPR Part 23. The application notice must be served on the person against whom the order is sought.

14.3 Any application in a probate claim for the issue of a witness summons under section 123 of the Act shall be for the issue of a witness summons requiring a person to bring into the relevant office a will or other testamentary paper.

14.4 An application under paragraph 13.3 may be made without notice and must be supported by an affidavit or witness statement setting out the grounds of the application.

14.5 An application under section 122 or 123 of the 1981 Act should be made to a master or district judge.

14.6 Any person against whom a witness summons is issued under section 123 of the 1981 Act and who denies that the will or other testamentary paper referred to in the witness summons is in his possession or under his control may file an affidavit or witness statement to that effect.

14.7 Section 32 of the County Courts Act 1984 enables orders under section 122 and 123 of the 1981 Act to be made in county court proceedings.

ADMINISTRATION PENDING THE DETERMINATION OF A PROBATE CLAIM

15.1 An application under section 117 of the Supreme Court Act 1981 for an order for the grant of administration may be made by application notice in the probate proceedings in question.

15.2 Where an order for a grant of administration is made under the said section 117, RSC Order 30 (Receivers) rules 2, 4 and 6 and (subject to subsection (3) of the said section) rule 3 (Schedule 1 to the CPR), shall apply as if the administrator were a receiver appointed by the court; and every application relating to the conduct of the administration shall be made by application notice in the probate proceedings in question.

15.3 An order under section 117 may be made by a master or district judge.

15.4 If an order is made under section 117 an application for the grant of letters of administration should be made at the principal probate registry of the Family Division.

15.5 The appointment of an administrator to whom letters of administration are granted following an order under section 117 will cease automatically when a final order in the probate proceedings is made but will continue pending any appeal.

PROBATE COUNTERCLAIM IN OTHER PROCEEDINGS

16.1 In these paragraphs 'probate counterclaim' means a counterclaim by which the defendant makes a probate claim in any proceedings other than probate proceedings.

16.2 Subject to the following paragraphs, this Practice Direction shall apply with the necessary modifications to a probate counterclaim as it applies to a probate claim begun by a probate claim form.

16.3 A probate counterclaim must contain a statement of the nature of the interest of the defendant and of the claimant in the estate of the deceased to which the counterclaim relates.

16.4 Unless within seven days after the service of a probate counterclaim in High Court proceedings an application is made for an order under CPR 3.2(e) or 3.4 for the probate counterclaim to be struck out or dealt with in separate proceedings and the application is granted, the court shall, if necessary on its own initiative, order the transfer of the proceedings to the Chancery Division (if it is not already assigned to that Division) and to either the Royal Courts of Justice or a Chancery district registry (if it is not already proceeding in one of those places).

16.5 If an order is made that a probate counterclaim be dealt with in separate proceedings, the order shall (if the proceedings are in the High Court) order the transfer of the probate counterclaim as required under paragraph 15.4.

RECTIFICATION OF WILLS

17.1 Where an application is made for the rectification of a will and the grant has not been lodged in court, paragraph 5 of this Practice Direction shall apply, with the necessary modifications, as if the proceedings were probate proceedings.

17.2 A copy of every order made for the rectification of a will shall be sent to the principal registry of the Family Division for filing, and a memorandum of the order shall be endorsed on, or permanently annexed to, the grant under which the estate is administered.

PD 49B PRACTICE DIRECTION — APPLICATIONS UNDER THE COMPANIES ACT 1985 AND THE INSURANCE COMPANIES ACT 1982

This practice direction supplements CPR Part 49 and replaces, with modifications, RSC Order 102 and CCR Order 49 rule 3

GENERAL
1. (1) In this practice direction:
'the Act' means the Companies Act 1985:
'the companies court registrar' means any officer of the High Court who is a registrar within the meaning of any rules for the time being in force relating to the winding-up of companies;
the court' includes the companies court registrar;
'the ICA' means the Insurance Companies Act 1982;
'the Rules' means the Civil Procedure Rules 1998.

(2) Applications under the Act may be made in the county court if the county court would have jurisdiction to wind up the company in question (see the definition of 'the court' in section 744 of the Act). A company can be wound up in the county court if its paid-up capital is not more than £120,000 (s. 117(2) Insolvency Act 1986).

(3) Every claim form or petition by which an application under the Act or the ICA is begun and all affidavits, witness statements, notices and other documents in those proceedings must be entitled in the matter of the company in question and in the matter of the Act, or the ICA as the case may be.

COMMENCEMENT OF PROCEEDINGS
2. (1) Except in the case of the applications mentioned in sub-paragraph (4) below, every application under the Act, whether made in the High Court or in the county court, must be made by the issue of a claim form and the use of the procedure set out in CPR Part 8, subject to any modification of that procedure under this practice direction or any other practice direction relating to applications under the Act.

(2) Notice of an application under section 721 of the Act need not be given to the respondent and the claim form need not be served on him.

(3) A claim form issued under this paragraph must, in the High Court, be issued out of the office of the companies court registrar or a chancery district registry or, in the county court, out of a county court office.

(4) This paragraph does not apply to applications under sections 459 or 460 of the Act or to applications under the ICA or to any of the applications specified in paragraph 4(1) of this practice direction.
3. All High Court applications under the Act shall be assigned to the Chancery Division.

APPLICATIONS MADE BY PETITION
4. (1) The following applications under the Act in addition to applications under sections 459 and 460 of the Act and applications under the ICA must be made by petition, namely, applications:

(a) under section 5 to cancel the alteration of a company's objects,

(b) under section 17 to cancel the alteration of a condition contained in a company's memorandum,

(c) under section 130 to confirm a reduction of the share premium account of a company,

(d) under section 136 to confirm a reduction of the share capital of a company,

(e) under section 127 to cancel any variation or abrogation of the rights attached to any class of shares in a company,

(f) under section 425 to sanction a compromise or arrangement between a company and its creditors or any class of them or between a company and its members or any class of them,

(g) under section 653 for an order restoring the name of a company to the register, where the application is made in conjunction with an application for the winding up of the company,

(h) under section 690 to cancel the alteration of the form of a company's constitution,

(i) under section 727 for relief from liability of an officer of a company or a person employed by a company as auditor,

(j) under section 54(1) to cancel a special resolution to which that section applies,

(k) under sections 157(2) or 176(1) to cancel a special resolution to which either of those sections applies, and

(l) under section 170 in relation to the reduction of capital redemption reserve.

(2) Paragraphs 5 to 14 of this practice direction apply to the applications specified in sub-paragraph (1).

5. (1) After the presentation of a petition by which any application mentioned in paragraph 4 is made, the petitioner, except where his application is one of those mentioned in sub-paragraph (2), must apply for directions by filing an application notice.

(2) The exceptions referred to in sub-paragraph (1) are:

(a) an application under section 425 of the Act to sanction a compromise or arrangement unless there is included in the petition for such sanction an application for an order under section 427 of the Act,

(b) an application under section 653 of the Act for an order restoring the name of a company to the register,

(c) an application under section 54(1) of the Act for an order cancelling a special resolution to which that section applies, and

(d) an application under section 157(2) or 176(1) of the Act for an order cancelling a special resolution to which those sections apply.

(3) At the directions hearing the court may by order give such directions for the hearing of the application as it thinks fit including, in particular, directions for the publication of notices and the making of any inquiry.

(4) Where the application made by the petition is to confirm a reduction of the share capital, the share premium account, or the capital redemption reserve, of a company the Court may give directions:

(a) for an inquiry to be made as to the debts of, and claims against, the company or as to any class or classes of such debts or claims,

(b) as to the proceedings to be taken for settling the list of creditors entitled to object to the reduction and fixing the date by reference to which the list is to be made,

and the power of the court under section 136(6) of the Act to direct that section 136(3) to (5) thereof shall not apply as regards any class of creditors may be exercised at any directions hearing.

REDUCTION OF CAPITAL AND SCHEMES OF ARRANGEMENT

6. (1) The consent of a creditor to such reduction as is mentioned in paragraph 5(4) may be proved in such manner as the Court thinks sufficient.

(2) The evidence in support of a petition to confirm a reduction of capital need not show as regards any issue of shares made since 1900 for a consideration other than cash that the statutory requirements as to registration were complied with. It is sufficient to state in the petition the extent to which any issued shares (other than shares issued otherwise than for cash before 1901) are or are deemed to be paid up.

(3) The existing practice will remain unaltered in respect of issues of shares otherwise than for cash made before 1901 whilst s. 25 of the Companies Act 1867 remained in operation.

7. (1) This paragraph applies to:

(a) schemes of arrangement under sections 425 to 427A of the Companies Act 1985, whether made with creditors or members,
(b) schemes for the transfer of the whole or part of the long-term business of an insurance company to which schedule 2C to the ICA applies, and
(c) reductions of capital, share premium account or capital redemption reserve.
References in this and subsequent paragraphs to 'schemes' are to schemes failing within (a) or (b) above, and references to 'reductions' are to reductions failing within (c) above.

(2) Petitions to sanction schemes will be heard by the Companies Court Judge.

(3) Petitions to confirm reductions will be heard by the Companies Court Registrar unless otherwise ordered. The Registrar will hear petitions to confirm reductions in open court on a Wednesday each week after completion of the list of winding up petitions.

SCHEMES AND REDUCTIONS IN THE LONG VACATION
8. (1) The following requirements must be satisfied for a hearing to be fixed to sanction a scheme and/or confirm a reduction in the Long Vacation:
(a) The application is one in which for financial, commercial or economic reasons a hearing before the end of the Long Vacation is desirable. This category will include cases of mergers and takeovers which arise in the summer and are likely to be affected by market fluctuations.
(b) The application is one which could not with reasonable diligence have been made and prosecuted in time to be heard before the Long Vacation begins.

(2) An informal application in chambers, to the Court Manager, accompanied by an advocate's certificate that requirements (a) and (b) are satisfied, must be made as soon as possible so that a suitable timetable may be settled, including a date for hearing.

(3) In the case of reductions to be heard by the Registrar, certain applications which do not fall within the above categories will be heard provided (i) that there is an urgent need for a hearing or (ii) that there is sufficient time available after the Registrar has disposed of the urgent applications.

(4) Applications to the Registrar in chambers for orders convening meetings to consider schemes and for directions on reduction applications will continue to be heard during the Long Vacation. Provided notice is given to the court before the Long Vacation begins, a timetable will be fixed which will enable any necessary documents to be settled in chambers and enable the Registrar to hear the application.

(5) The Vacation Judge will be available to hear petitions to sanction schemes and any petitions to confirm reductions which require to be heard by a judge on one Wednesday in August and two Wednesdays in September on dates to be arranged and subsequently notified in the Long Vacation Notice which is printed in the Daily Cause List.

(6) The Vacation Judge may also hear petitions to sanction schemes or confirm reductions on other days if he thinks fit.

9. (1) Attention is drawn to the undesirability of asking as a matter of course for a winding up order as an alternative to an order under s. 459 Companies Act 1985. The petition should not ask for a winding up order unless that is the relief which the petitioner prefers or it is thought that it may be the only relief to which the petitioner is entitled.

(2) Whenever a winding up order is asked for in a contributory's petition, the petition must state whether the petitioner consents or objects to an order under s. 127 of the Act in the standard form. If he objects, the written evidence in support must contain a short statement of his reasons.

(3) If the petitioner objects to a s. 127 order in the standard form but consents to such an order in a modified form, the petition must set out the form of order to which he consents, and the written evidence in support must contain a short statement of his reasons for seeking the modification.

(4) If the petition contains a statement that the petitioner consents to a s. 127 order, whether in the standard or a modified form, but the petitioner changes his

PD 49B PRACTICE DIRECTION — COMPANIES ACT 1985 ETC.

mind before the first hearing of the petition, he must notify the respondents and may apply on notice to a Judge for an order directing that no s. 127 order or a modified order only (as the case may be) shall be made by the Registrar, but validating dispositions made without notice of the order made by the Judge.

(5) If the petition contains a statement that the petitioner consents to a s. 127 order, whether in the standard or a modified form, the Registrar shall without further enquiry make an order in such form at the first hearing unless an order to the contrary has been made by the Judge in the meantime.

(6) If the petition contains a statement that the petitioner objects to a s. 127 order in the standard form, the company may apply (in the case of urgency, without notice) to the Judge for an order.

(7) Section 127 Order — Standard Form:

(Title etc.)

ORDER that notwithstanding the presentation of the said Petition

(1) payments made into or out of the bank accounts of the Company in the ordinary course of the business of the Company and

(2) dispositions of the property of the Company made in the ordinary course of its business for proper value between the date of presentation of the Petition and the date of judgment on the Petition or further order in the meantime shall not be void by virtue of the provisions of section 127 of the Insolvency Act 1986 in the event of an Order for the winding up of the Company being made on the said Petition Provided that (the relevant bank) shall be under no obligation to verify for itself whether any transaction through the company's bank accounts is in the ordinary course of business, or that it represents full market value for the relevant transaction.

This form of Order may be departed from where the circumstances of the case require.

CASE MANAGEMENT

10. Every application under the Act shall be allocated to the multi-track and the CPR relating to allocation questionnaires and track allocation will not apply.

SERVICE

11. Service of documents in proceedings in the High Court to which this practice direction applies will be the responsibility of the parties and will not be undertaken by the court. Subject to that CPR Part 6 applies.

FILING OF DOCUMENTS

12. (1) Where an application to which this practice direction relates is proceeding in any Chancery district registry, all affidavits and witness statements made in connection with the application must be filed in that registry.

(2) Where an application to which this practice direction relates is proceeding in any county court, all affidavits and witness statements made in connection with the application must be filed in the office of that county court.

DRAWING UP OF ORDERS

13. The court will draw up all orders with the following exceptions:

(a) orders by the Registrar on the application of the Official Receiver or for which the Treasury Solicitor is responsible under the existing practice,

(b) orders by the court in relation to reductions or schemes.

PD 49C PRACTICE DIRECTION — TECHNOLOGY AND CONSTRUCTION COURT

This practice direction supplements CPR Part 49 and replaces, with modifications, Order 36 of the Rules of the Supreme Court

GENERAL

1.1 This practice direction applies to cases allocated to the Technology and Construction Court ('the TCC').

1.2 A TCC claim is a claim which involves issues or questions which are technically complex or for which a trial by a judge of the TCC is for any other reason desirable.

1.3 TCC claims may be dealt with either in the High Court or, subject to paragraph 2.3 below, in a county court but cases allocated to the TCC will, unless and until a judge of the TCC otherwise directs, be dealt with by a judge of the TCC.

1.4 A judge will be appointed to be the judge in charge of the TCC (currently Mr Justice Dyson).

COMMENCEMENT OF PROCEEDINGS

2.1 Before the issue of a claim form relating to a TCC claim, the claim form, whether to be issued in the High Court or in a county court, should, if it is intended that the case be allocated to the TCC, be marked in the top right hand corner 'Technology and Construction Court'. The case will then be allocated to the TCC. The words 'Technology and Construction Court' should follow the reference to 'The ____ County Court' or 'The High Court, Queen's Bench Division', as the case may be.

2.2 The TCC is a specialist list for the purposes of CPR Part 30 (Transfer) but no order for the transfer of proceedings from or to the TCC shall be made unless the parties have either:

(1) had an opportunity of being heard on the issue, or
(2) consented to the order.

2.3 A claim form marked as mentioned in paragraph 2.1 may not be issued in a county court office other than:

(1) a County Court office where there is also a High Court District Registry; or
(2) the office of the Central London County Court.

2.4 Where a claim form marked as mentioned in paragraph 2.1 is issued in the Royal Courts of Justice, the case will be assigned to a named TCC judge (the 'assigned judge') who will have the primary responsibility for the case management of that case. All documents relating to that case should be marked, under the words 'Technology and Construction Court' in the title, with the name of the assigned judge.

APPLICATIONS

3.1 Where a claim form is to be marked as mentioned in paragraph 2.1, any application before issue of the claim form should be made to a judge of the TCC.

3.2 If an application is made before the issue of the claim form, the written evidence in support of the application must state, in addition to any other necessary matters, that the claimant intends to mark the claim form in accordance with paragraph 2.1.

3.3 Any application in a case which has been allocated to the TCC must be made to a judge of the TCC.

3.4 Where there is an assigned judge of a TCC case, any application in that case should be made to the assigned judge but, if the judge in charge of the TCC so authorises or if the assigned judge is not available, may be made to another judge of the TCC.

3.5 If an application is urgent and no TCC judge is available to deal with it, the application may be made to any judge who, if the case were not allocated to the TCC, would be authorised to deal with the application.

CASE MANAGEMENT

4.1 Every claim allocated to the TCC will be allocated to the multi-track and the CPR relating to track allocation will not apply.

4.2 Where a claim has been allocated to the TCC either on issue (i.e. in every case in which the claim form has been marked 'Technology and Construction Court') or by transfer to the TCC, an application for directions (including an application for a fixed date of hearing) must be made by the claimant within 14 days of the filing by the defendant of an acknowledgement of service or of a defence (whichever is the earlier) or, as the case may be, within 14 days of the date of the order of transfer.

4.3 If the claimant does not make an application in accordance with paragraph 4.2:

(1) any other party may do so or may apply for the claim of the claimant in default to be struck out or dismissed; or

(2) a TCC judge may on his own initiative fix a directions hearing.

4.4 The provisions of CPR Part 29 and the practice direction supplementing that Part apply to the case management of TCC cases except where inconsistent with this or any other TCC practice direction. But reference in those provisions to a listing questionnaire shall be read as references to a pre-trial review questionnaire and paragraphs 8 and 9 of the practice direction do not apply. Attention is drawn, in particular, to the following provisions of CPR Part 29 and the supplementing practice direction:

CPR Part 29
rule 29.3(2) (attendance of legal representatives)
rule 29.4 (agreed proposals)
rule 29.5 (variation of case management timetable)
rule 29.6 (pre-trial review (listing) questionnaire)

Practice Direction supplementing CPR Part 29
paragraphs 3.4 to 3.9 (general provisions)
paragraphs 5.1 to 5.8 (case management conferences)
paragraphs 6.1 to 6.5 (variation of directions)
paragraphs 7.1 to 7.4 (failure to comply with case management directions)
paragraphs 10,1 to 10.6 (the trial)

CASE MANAGEMENT CONFERENCE

5.1 The first case management conference will take place at the directions hearing referred to in paragraphs 4.2 and 4.3 above.

5.2 When the court notifies the parties of the time and date of the hearing of the first case management conference it will also send them a case management questionnaire and a case management directions form. These documents will be in the forms annexed to this practice direction, and marked respectively Appendix 1 and 2.

5.3 The parties shall complete, exchange and return both forms by no later than 4pm two days before the date on which the case management conference is to take place. The parties are encouraged to try to agree directions by reference to the case management directions form.

5.4 If a party fails to exchange or return the forms by the date specified, the court may make an order which leads to the claim or defence being struck out, or impose such other sanction as it sees fit, or may hold a case management conference without the forms.

5.5 At the first case management conference, the court will usually fix the date for trial of the case and of any preliminary issue that it orders to be tried. It will also give case management directions. The directions will usually include the fixing of a date for a pre-trial review.

5.6 Whenever possible, the trial of a case will be heard by the assigned judge of that case.

PRE-TRIAL REVIEW

6.1 When the court fixes the date for a pre-trial review it will also provide the parties with a pre-trial review questionnaire and a pre-trial review directions form. These documents will be in the forms annexed to this practice direction marked respectively as Appendix 3 and 4.

6.2 The parties shall complete, exchange and return both forms no later than 4pm two days before the date on which the pre-trial review is to take place. The parties are encouraged to try to agree directions by reference to the pre-trial review directions form.

6.3 If a party fails to exchange or return the pre-trial review questionnaire or pre-trial review directions form by the date specified, the court may make an order which leads to the claim or defence and any counterclaim being struck out, or it may impose such other sanction as it sees fit, or it may hold a pre-trial review without the forms.

6.4 At the pre-trial review, the court will give such directions for the conduct of the trial as it sees fit.

THE CIVIL PROCEDURE RULES

7.1 The Civil Procedure Rules and the practice directions supplementing them apply to TCC cases subject to the provisions of this practice direction and any other TCC practice direction.

PD 49C PRACTICE DIRECTION — TECHNOLOGY AND CONSTRUCTION COURT

APPENDIX 1

First Case Management Conference Questionnaire

In the County Court/ High Court
Queens's Bench Division
Technology and Construction Court

Claim No.

Last date for filing with court office

To

Please read the notes on page five before completing the questionnaire.

Please note the date by which it must be returned and the name of the court it should be returned to since this may be different from the court where proceedings were issued.

If you have settled this case (or if you settle it on a future date) and do not need to have it heard or tried, you must let the court know immediately.

A Settlement

Do you wish there to be a stay to attempt to settle the case by negotiations or by any other form of alternative dispute resolution? ☐ Yes ☐ No

If yes, at what stage and for how long?
If no, please give reasons.

B Transfer

If you think your case is suitable for a transfer to another court or track, say which:

Court: Chancery Division/Queen's Bench Division/another TCC Court/Commercial Court/County Court
Track: Small claims/fast track

Please give brief reasons for your choice:

C Pre-Action protocols

Have you complied with any pre-action protocol applicable to your claim? ☐ None applicable to this claim ☐ Yes ☐ No

If Yes, please say which protocol:

If No, please explain to what extent and for what reason it has not been complied with:

D Applications

If you have not already sent the court an application for summary judgment, do you intend to do so? ☐ Yes ☐ No

If you have not already issued a claim in the case against someone not yet a party, do you intend to apply for the court's permission to do so? ☐ Yes ☐ No

Have you any other applications to make? ☐ Yes ☐ No

In any such case, if Yes, please give details:

E Witnesses of fact

So far as you know at this stage, what witnesses of fact do you intend to call at the hearing?

Witness name	Witness to which facts

PD 49C   PRACTICE DIRECTION — TECHNOLOGY AND CONSTRUCTION COURT

F Experts' evidence

Do you wish to use expert evidence at the hearing? ☐ Yes ☐ No

Have you already copied any experts' report(s) to the other party(ies)? ☐ None obtained as yet ☐ Yes ☐ No

Please list the experts whose evidence you think you will use:

Expert's Name	Field of expertise (eg. architect, mechanical engineer)

Will you and the other party use the same expert(s)? ☐ Yes ☐ No

If No, please explain why not:

Should any, and if so what, inspections, samples, experiments or calculations by experts be directed? ☐ Yes ☐ No

Do you want your expert(s) to give evidence orally at the hearing or trial? ☐ Yes ☐ No

If Yes, give the reasons why you think oral evidence is necessary:

G Location of trial

Is there any reason why your case needs to be heard at a particular court? ☐ Yes ☐ No

If Yes, give reasons (eg. particular facilities required, convenience of witnesses, etc.)

and specify the court:

PD 49C PRACTICE DIRECTION — TECHNOLOGY AND CONSTRUCTION COURT

H Representation and estimate of hearing/trial time

Do you expect to be represented by a solicitor or counsel at the hearing/trial?	☐ No ☐ Solicitor ☐ Counsel
How long do you estimate it will take to put your case to the court at the hearing/trial?	days hours minutes
How long do you estimate for the whole of the trial, excluding judgment?	days hours minutes

If there are days when you, your representative, expert or an essential witness will not be able to attend court, give details:

Name	Dates not available

I Costs (only relates to costs incurred by legal representatives)

What is your estimate of your costs incurred to date, excluding disbursements, VAT and court fees?	£
What do you estimate your overall costs are likely to be, excluding disbursements, VAT and court fees?	£

J Other Information

Have you attached documents you wish the judge to take into account when considering what directions to make?	☐ Yes ☐ No
Have they been served on the other parties?	☐ Yes ☐ No
If Yes, say when	
Have the other parties agreed their content?	☐ Yes ☐ No
Have you attached a list of the directions you think appropriate for the management of your case on the case management directions form?	☐ Yes ☐ No
Are they agreed with the other parties?	☐ Yes ☐ No

Are there any other facts which might affect the timetable the court will set? If so, please state

Signed   Date
[Counsel][Solicitor][for the][Claimant][Defendant]

PD 49C PRACTICE DIRECTION — TECHNOLOGY AND CONSTRUCTION COURT

Notes for completing this Questionnaire

- If the case is not settled, a judge must give directions for its management. To help the judge give the most just and cost-effective directions, you must now complete the attached questionnaire.
- If you fail to return the questionnaire by the date given, the judge may make an order which leads to your claim or defence being struck out, or hold a case management conference without it. If there is a case management conference the judge may order any party who has not filed their questionnaire to pay, immediately, the costs of that hearing.
- If you wish to make an application, for example, for special directions, for summary judgment on the grounds that the other party has no reasonable chance of success in their claim or defence, or for permission to add another party to the claim, you should send it and any required fee with the completed questionnaire. If a hearing is fixed for your application, it may also be used as a case management conference.
- Any other documents you wish the judge to take into account should be filed with the questionnaire. But you must confirm that the documents have been sent to the other party, or parties, saying when they would have received them and whether they agreed their contents.
- Use a separate sheet if you need more space for your answers marking clearly which section the information refers to. Write the case number on it, sign and date it and attach it securely to the questionnaire.
- The letters below refer to the sections of the questionnaire and tell you what information is needed.

A Settlement
If you think that you and the other party may be able to negotiate a settlement you should tick the 'Yes' box. The court may order a stay, whether or not all the other parties to the case agree. Where a stay is granted it will be for an initial period which the judge will specify.

B Transfer

C Pre-action protocols
For certain kinds of claim, there are protocols which set out what ought to be done before court proceedings are issued. As at April 1999 there are protocols for clinical negligence and personal injury claims.

D Applications
If you intend to apply for summary judgment or for permission to add another party to the claim or make any application you should, if you have not already done so, file an application with your completed questionnaire.

E Witnesses of fact
Remember to include yourself, if you will be giving evidence; but not experts, who should be included in section E.

F Experts' evidence
Oral or written expert evidence will only be allowed at the trial with the court's permission. The judge will decide what permission it seems appropriate to give.

G Location of trial

H Representation and estimate of hearing time

APPENDIX 2
TECHNOLOGY AND CONSTRUCTION COURT
CASE MANAGEMENT CONFERENCE DIRECTIONS FORM

CLAIM 199   TCC No   . ORDER ON CASE MANAGEMENT CONFERENCE HELD   1999

( ) Trial: Week beginning   . Estimated length   days. [Directions, if appropriate, for separate trials of issues or for parties to serve and file proposals for such directions]

( ) This claim to be [consolidated] [managed and tried] with 19   TCC No   . [This] [19   TCC No   ] to be lead claim. [All directions in lead claim to apply to both claims unless otherwise directed.]

( ) Permission to amend [see below].

( ) Defence and any counterclaim to be served by   am/pm on   1999/20   .

( ) Reply to defence, if desired, and defence to any counterclaim, to be served by   am/pm on   1999/20   .

( ) Disclosure of documents by   am/pm on   1999/20   . [Standard disclosure dispensed with/limited/varied as follows:

].
( ) Claimant/defendant to serve a Scott Schedule [of defects and damages] [under paragraph   of the particulars of claim/defence] by   am/pm on   1999/20   . Column headings to be as follows: [see below].

( ) Defendant/claimant to respond to the Scott Schedule by   am/pm on   1999/20   . [Directions, if appropriate, for control of evidence of fact under rule 32.1]

( ) [No expert evidence without further order] [Permission for expert evidence on the following terms: (see below)].

( ) [Inspections to be made/samples to be obtained/experiments to be conducted/ calculations to be carried out as follows:

].
Experts in like fields to hold discussions in accordance with rule 35.12 by   am/pm on 1999/20   on [all the issues arising in their common fields] [the following issues:

Statements under rule 35.12(3) to be prepared and filed by   am/pm on   1999/20   .

( ) The parties are to consult with each other and the court with a view to arranging service and (where required) filing of statements of case, witness statements, experts' reports, disclosure lists and other documents in computer readable form as well as in hard copy. Format for court disks:

( ) [Time under paragraphs   above not to be extended without permission.]

( )

( ) Pre-trial Review: Time allowed: . Parties to complete, file and serve pre-trial questionnaire, after consultation, by   am/pm on   1999/20   .

( ) Liberty to restore. Costs in cause.

Permission to amend

The [Part 20] claimant/defendant to have permission to [re-]amend the [Part 20] particulars of claim/defence [and counterclaim]/reply to defence [and defence to counterclaim] in accordance with the draft initialled by the Judge. Re-service [to be effected by   am/pm on   1999/20   ] [deemed to have been effected today]. The [Part 20] defendant/claimant to have permission to [re-]amend the defence/reply to defence [and defence to counterclaim] by   am/pm on 1999/20   , limited to amendments consequential upon the amendment for which permission is first given above. The [Part 20] claimant/defendant to pay in any event the costs of and consequential upon that amendment, or thrown away thereby [and of this application].

Scott Schedule

Column headings: 1. Serial number.
2.
3.
4.
5.
6.
7.
8.
9.
10.
11.
12.

Expert Evidence

Party (or state 'Joint')	Field	Name	Date for exchange	Whether leave for oral evidence

Reports to be exchanged [and filed] by   am/pm on the dates specified.

PD 49C PRACTICE DIRECTION — TECHNOLOGY AND CONSTRUCTION COURT

APPENDIX 3

Pre-trial review Questionnaire

In the County Court/High Court
Queen's Bench Division
Technology and Construction Court
Claim No.
Last date for filing with court office

To

- The judge will use the information which you and the other party(ies) provide to conduct a pre-trial review.
- If you do not complete and return the questionnaire the judge may
  - make an order which leads to your statement of case (claim or defence) being struck out
  - conduct the pre-trial review without it. You may be ordered to pay (immediately) the other parties' costs of attending.

A Directions complied with

1. Have you complied with all the previous directions given by the court? ☐ Yes ☐ No
2. If no, please explain which directions are outstanding and why.

Directions outstanding	Reasons directions outstanding

3. Are any further directions required to prepare the case for trial? ☐ Yes ☐ No

If no, go to Section B

4. If yes, please explain directions required and give reasons.

Directions required	Reasons required

PD 49C PRACTICE DIRECTION — TECHNOLOGY AND CONSTRUCTION COURT

B Experts

1. Has the court already given permission for you to use written expert evidence? ☐ Yes ☐ No
   If no, go to Section C

2. If yes, please give name and field of expertise.

Name of expert	Whether joint expert *(please tick, if appropriate)*	Field of expertise

3. Have the experts held discussions as directed? ☐ Yes ☐ No
4. Have they filed statements as directed following those discussions? ☐ Yes ☐ No
5. Have the expert(s') report(s) been served and filed as ordered? ☐ Yes ☐ No
6. Has the court already given permission for the expert(s) to give oral evidence at the trial? *(If yes, go to section C)* ☐ Yes ☐ No
7. If no, are you seeking that permission? ☐ Yes ☐ No
   If no, go to section C

8. If yes, give your reasons for seeking permission.

9. If yes, what are the names, addresses and fields of expertise of your experts?

Expert 1	Expert 2	Expert 3	Expert 4

10. Please give details of any dates within the trial period when your expert(s) will not be available.

Name of expert	Dates not available

PD 49C PRACTICE DIRECTION — TECHNOLOGY AND CONSTRUCTION COURT

C Other witnesses

(If you are not calling other witnesses, go to section D)

1. How many other witnesses (including yourself) will be giving evidence on your behalf at the trial? *(do not include experts – see section B above)*

(Give number)

2. What are the names and addresses of your witnesses?

Witness 1	Witness 2	Witness 3	Witness 4

3. Please give details of any dates within the trial period when you or your witnesses will not be available?

Name of witness	Dates not available

4. Are any of the witness statements agreed? ☐ Yes ☐ No
(If no go to question C6)

5. If yes, give the name of the witness and the date of his or her statement

Name of witness	Date of statement

6. Do you or any of your witnesses need any special facilities? ☐ Yes ☐ No
(If no go to question C8)

7. If yes, what are they?

8. Will any of your witnesses be provided with an interpreter? ☐ Yes ☐ No
(If no go to section D)

9. If yes, say what type of interpreter e.g. language (stating which), deaf/blind etc.

PD 49C PRACTICE DIRECTION — TECHNOLOGY AND CONSTRUCTION COURT

D Legal representation

1. Who will be presenting your case at the hearing or trial? ☐ You ☐ Solicitor ☐ Counsel

2. Please give details of any dates within the trial period when the person presenting your case will not be available.

Name	Dates not available

E Other matters

1. How long do you estimate the whole of the trial will take, excluding judgment?

Minutes	Hours	Days

2. What is the estimated number of pages of evidence to be included in the trial bundle?

(please give number)

3. Please provide a case summary and proposals (agreed if possible) for directions to be given, by reference to the pre-trial review directions form.

Signed

Claimant/defendant or Counsel/Solicitor for the claimant/defendant

Date

APPENDIX 4
TECHNOLOGY AND CONSTRUCTION COURT
PRE-TRIAL REVIEW DIRECTIONS FORM

( ) [Directions in relation to orders not yet complied with]

( ) Trial bundle to include [all admissible disclosed documents required by either party] [documents in the following categories only:

Claimant/defendant to serve proposed index of trial bundle by   am/pm on   1999/20   .

Defendant/claimant to respond by   am/pm on   1999/20   . Trial bundle to be agreed by   am/pm on   1999/20 and filed by   am/pm on   1999/20 with any witness statements and experts' reports not already filed.

( ) Claimant/defendant to open trial and to serve and file chronology, cast list and note of opening by   am/pm on   1999/20   [Defendant/claimant to make an opening response and to serve and file a note of it by   am/pm on   1999/20   .]

( ) Disks (if obtainable) of statements of case, witness statements, experts' reports, trial bundle and opening notes, so far as not already filed, to be filed in   format by am/pm on   1999/20   .

( ) [Adjourned hearing of pre-trial review, if required]

( ) Costs in cause.

PD 49D   PRACTICE DIRECTION — COMMERCIAL COURT

This practice direction supplements CPR Part 49 and replaces, with modifications, Order 72 of the Rules of the Supreme Court

GENERAL
1.1   This practice direction applies to commercial claims in the Commercial Court of the Queen's Bench Division.
1.2   (1)   In this practice direction 'commercial claim' includes any case arising out of trade and commerce in general, including any case relating to:
    (i)   a business document or contract,
    (ii)   the export or import of goods,
    (iii)   the carriage of goods by land, sea, air or pipeline,
    (iv)   the exploitation of oil and gas reserves,
    (v)   insurance and re-insurance,
    (vi)   banking and financial services,
    (vii)   the operation of markets and exchanges,
    (viii)   business agency, and
    (ix)   arbitration
and 'commercial proceedings' has a corresponding meaning.
    (2)   'Judge' means Judge of the Commercial Court.
1.3   The rules relating to arbitration are set out in the Arbitration Practice Direction that supplements CPR Part 49.
1.4   The Civil Procedure Rules (the 'CPR') apply to commercial proceedings in the Commercial Court subject to the provisions of this practice direction and any Commercial Court practice direction.

THE COMMERCIAL LIST
2.1   There shall be a list called 'the commercial list' in which commercial claims in the Queen's Bench Division may be entered for trial in the Commercial Court, and one of the Commercial Court judges shall be in charge of that list.
2.2   All proceedings in the Commercial Court, including all pre-trial applications and any appeal from any judgment, order or decision of a master or district judge prior to the transfer of any case to the commercial list, shall be heard or otherwise dealt with by a Judge, except that:
    (i)   if an application is urgent and no Judge is available to deal with it, the application may be made to some other judge of the Queen's Bench Division authorised to hear applications in the Commercial Court; and
    (ii)   unless a Judge otherwise orders, all proceedings for the enforcement of any judgment or order for the payment of money given or made in the Commercial Court shall be referred to a master of the Queen's Bench Division.
2.3   The commercial list is a specialist list for the purposes of the CPR (see e.g. Rules 16.3(5) and 30.5 of the CPR).

ENTRY OF CASE IN COMMERCIAL LIST
3.1   The claim form by which a commercial claim intended to be entered in the commercial list is begun should be issued out of the Admiralty and Commercial Registry at the Royal Courts of Justice.
3.2   The claim form should, before it is issued, be marked with the words 'Queen's Bench Division, Commercial Court' and on the issue of the claim form out of the said Registry the case will be entered in the commercial list.
3.3   Where a claim form is to be marked as mentioned in paragraph 3.2, any application before issue of the claim form should be made to a Judge.
3.4   If an application is made before issue of the claim form, the written evidence in support of the application must state, in addition to any other necessary

matters, that the claimant intends to mark the claim form in accordance with paragraph 3.2.

3.5 If the Judge hearing an application made before the issue of the claim form is of the opinion that the case in question should not be entered in the commercial list, he may adjourn the application to be heard by a master or by a judge of the Queen's Bench Division who is not a judge of the Commercial Court.

4.1 At any stage of the proceedings of commercial proceedings not entered in the commercial list any party:

(1) may apply to a Judge for an order transferring the proceedings to the commercial list; or

(2) may apply to the court where the proceedings are being dealt with for an order that they be transferred to the commercial list.

4.2 On an application under paragraph 4.1(2) the court may not itself make the order for transfer, but, if it considers the proceedings might be suitable to be entered in the commercial list, may adjourn the application for hearing by a Judge.

4.3 Where the Judge orders commercial proceedings to be transferred to the commercial list he may also order the proceedings to be transferred to the Royal Courts of Justice and at the same time may give directions for the management of the case.

4.4 A Judge may, on his own initiative, (but not unless the parties have had an opportunity of being heard or have consented) or on the application of any party, order proceedings in the commercial list to be removed from that list.

4.5 Where a commercial claim has been entered in the commercial list by virtue of paragraph 3.2, an application by a defendant, including a Part 20 defendant, to remove it from that list must be made within 7 days after the defendant has filed an acknowledgment of service or a defence, whichever is the later.

DISPENSING WITH PARTICULARS OF CLAIM OR DEFENCE

5. The Judge may at any time, before or after the issue of the claim form, order that proceedings in the commercial list be tried without the filing or service of particulars of claim or of a defence or of any other statement of case.

DIRECTIONS AND CASE MANAGEMENT

6.1 All proceedings in the commercial list will be allocated to the multi-track and the CPR relating to allocation questionnaires and track allocation will not apply.

6.2 (1) If proceedings are transferred to the commercial list following an application under paragraph 4, then, unless the Judge who made the order for transfer gave directions for the management of the case, an application to a Judge for such directions shall be made within 14 days of the date of the order of transfer.

(2) If the claimant does not make an application in accordance with paragraph 6.2(1), any other party may do so, or may apply for the claim of the claimant in default to be struck out or dismissed.

SHIP'S PAPERS

7.1 Where in proceedings in the commercial list relating to a marine insurance policy an application for specific disclosure under Rule 31.12 of the CPR is made by the insurer, the Judge, if it appears to him to be necessary or expedient to do so, may make an order in such form as he thinks fit for the production of the documents specified in the order.

7.2 An order under this rule may be made at any stage of the proceedings and on such terms, if any, as to staying the proceedings or otherwise, as the Judge thinks fit.

ADMIRALTY AND COMMERCIAL REGISTRY

8.1 All administrative acts which under the Civil Procedure Rules or any Practice Direction are to be carried out by the Court office shall in relation to cases in the commercial list be carried out by or through the Admiralty and Commercial Registry.

PD 49D   PRACTICE DIRECTION — COMMERCIAL COURT

8.2   All documents which under the Civil Procedure Rules are to be filed with the Court office shall in cases in the commercial list be filed with the Admiralty and Commercial Registry.

8.3   All claim forms, arbitration forms (see the Arbitration practice direction supplementing CPR Part 49) issued in and other documents filed with the Admiralty and Commercial Registry are (if they need to be served) to be served by the parties, not by the Admiralty and Commercial Registry.

THE COMMERCIAL COURT GUIDE

9.1   The first edition of the Guide to Commercial Court Practice was published in 1986. The most recent edition has been the Fourth Edition published in 1997.

9.2   With the approval of the Judges of the Commercial Court a Fifth Edition has been prepared and adopted by the Commercial Court Committee. The Fifth Edition (now entitled 'The Commercial Court Guide') is designed to be introduced at the same time as the new Civil Procedure Rules and the practice directions that supplement them.

9.3   The Fifth Edition incorporates and adapts into one text provisions of the Fourth Edition and of the many Practice Directions and Statements appended to it. The revision also incorporates a number of new provisions.

9.4   The combined result is intended to be a Guide that will, in the specialist context of commercial cases, serve the 'overriding objective' defined in CPR Part 1. The Guide will be kept under review by the Judges of the Commercial Court and by the Commercial Court Committee.

9.5   The practice of the Commercial Court set out in this revised edition should be followed from 26 April 1999, subject to the provisions of this or any other Commercial Court practice direction and to any order that may be made in an individual case.

10.   This practice direction supersedes all previous practice directions and Practice Statements in the Commercial Court.

PD 49E PRACTICE DIRECTION — PATENTS ETC.

This practice direction supplements CPR Part 49 and replaces, with modifications, RSC Order 104, Order 100 and Order 93, rule 24 and CCR Order 48A and Order 49 rule 4A

GENERAL
1.1 This practice direction applies to the business of the Patents Court and proceedings under the Copyright, Designs and Patents Act 1988, the Trade Marks Acts 1938 and 1994 and the Olympic Symbol etc. Protection Act 1995 and Olympic Association Right (Infringement Proceedings) Regulations 1995.
1.2 The Civil Procedure Rules apply to Patents Court business and proceedings under the Copyright, Designs and Patents Act 1988, the Trade Marks Acts 1938 and 1994 and the Olympic Symbol etc Protection Act 1995 and Olympic Association Right (infringement Proceedings) Regulations 1995 subject to the provisions of this and any other Patents Court practice direction.
1.3 Definitions
In this Practice Direction:
'the 1949 Act' means the Patents Act 1949;
'the 1977 Act' means the Patents Act 1977;
'the Comptroller' means the Comptroller-General of Patents, Designs and Trade Marks;
'the Court,' means the Patents Court;
'existing patent' means a patent mentioned in section 127(2)(a) or (c) of the 1977 Act;
'the journal' means the journal published pursuant to rules made under section 123 (6) of the 1977 Act;
'1977 Act patent' means a patent under the 1977 Act;
'patent' means an existing patent or a 1977 Act patent and includes any application for a patent, supplementary protection certificate granted pursuant to the Patents (Supplementary Protection Certificates) Rules 1997, the Patents (Supplementary Protection Certificate for Medicinal Products) Regulations 1992 and the Patents (Supplementary Protection Certificate for Plant Protection Products) Regulations 1996.
'Patents Court' includes the Patents Court of the High Court and the Patents County Court.
'Patents Court business' includes:
    (a)   any claim under the Patents Acts 1949 to 1961 and 1977;
    (b)   any claim under the Registered Designs Acts 1949 to 1961;
    (c)   any claim under the Defence Contracts Act 1958, and
    (d)   all proceedings for the determination of a question or the making of a declaration relating to a patent (or an application for a patent) under the inherent jurisdiction of the High Court.
'the CPR' means the Civil Procedure Rules.

ALLOCATION OF PATENTS COURT BUSINESS
2.1 Patents Court business may be dealt with either in the High Court or the Patents county court.
2.2 Before the issue of a claim form relating to Patents Court business, the claim form, whether it is to be issued in the High Court or the county court, should be marked in the top right hand corner 'Patents Court' and the claim will then be allocated to the Patents Court.
2.3 The Patents Court is a specialist list for the purposes of Part 30 of the CPR but no order for the transfer of proceedings to or from the Patents Court shall be made unless the parties have either:
    (a)   had an opportunity of being heard on the issue, or

PD 49E PRACTICE DIRECTION — PATENTS ETC.

(b) consented to the order.

2.4 Every claim in the Patents Court will be allocated to the Multi-track and the CPR relating to allocation questionnaires and track allocation will not apply.

2.5 (1) Where a claim has been allocated to the Patents Court either on issue (ie. in every case in which the claim form has been marked Patents Court) or by transfer to the Patents Court, an application for directions (including an application for a fixed date of hearing) shall be made by the claimant within 14 days of the filing by the defendant of an acknowledgement of service or of a defence (whichever is the earlier) or, as the case may be, within 14 days of the date of the order of transfer.

(2) If the claimant does not make an application in accordance with paragraph 2.5, any other party may do so or may apply for the claim of the claimant in default to be struck out or dismissed.

(3) Any application under this paragraph must be made to a judge of the Patents Court unless a judge of the Patents Court otherwise directs.

(4) On the hearing of the application for directions under paragraph 2.5(1) the judge shall give directions for any further directions hearing and direct the time by which the hearing of any further application for directions is to take place.

2.6 Except where inconsistent with the provisions of this Practice Direction, CPR Part 29 and the Multi-track Practice Direction apply to Patents Court business.

2.7 This practice direction shall apply with any necessary modifications to proceedings in respect of Registered Designs.

SERVICE OF DOCUMENTS

3.1 This rule applies to the service of any document on a party until such time as that party has provided an address for service in accordance with CPR rule 6.5.

3.2 Subject to sub-paragraph (3) below, for the purposes of any proceedings relating to a patent or a registered design (including proceedings for revocation, declaration as to non-infringement or groundless threats of infringement proceedings or any other proceedings of a kind mentioned in this Practice Direction) where any document is served in the manner authorised by CPR Part 6 at an address for service given in the register kept under section 32 of the 1977 Act or, as the case may be, section 17 of the Registered Designs Act 1949:

(1) service shall be deemed to have been effected on the registered proprietor of the patent or registered design on the date on which the document was served at the said address;

(2) the party on whom service is deemed to have been effected under subparagraph (a) shall be treated, for the purposes of any provision of these rules which specifies a time-limit for responding to the document so served (whether by filing or serving an admission, filing a defence, acknowledging service, or otherwise), as having been served on the seventh day after the date on which the document was served at the said address.

3.3 Nothing in paragraph 3.2 shall prevent service being effected on the proprietor in accordance with the provisions of Part 6 of the CPR.

APPLICATION IN PROCEEDINGS BEFORE THE COURT FOR
PERMISSION TO AMEND A PATENT SPECIFICATION UNDER S. 30 OF
THE 1949 ACT OR S.75 OF THE 1977 ACT

4.1 A patentee or the proprietor of a patent intending to apply in proceedings before the Court under section 30 of the 1949 Act or under section 75 of the 1977 Act for permission to amend his specification must give notice of his intention to the Comptroller accompanied by a copy of an advertisement:

(1) identifying the proceedings pending before the Court in which it is intended to apply for such permission;

(2) giving particulars of the amendment sought;

(3) stating the applicant's address for service within the United Kingdom;

(4) stating that a Statement of Reasons is available from that address; and

(5) stating that any person intending to oppose the amendment must within 28 days after the appearance of the advertisement give written notice of his

intention to the applicant; such notice to be accompanied by a Statement of Opposition
and the Comptroller shall insert the advertisement once in the journal. A person who gives notice in accordance with the advertisement shall be entitled to be heard on the application subject to any direction of the Court as to costs.

4.2 The applicant must at the same time as giving notice to the Comptroller serve a copy of the Statement of Reasons together with a copy of the patent as proposed to be amended on all parties to the proceedings.

4.3 The Statement of Reasons referred to in paragraph 4.1(4) shall contain full particulars of the amendment sought, of the reasons therefor and of the reasons why the applicant contends that in the exercise of discretion the amendment should be allowed. In particular the Statement should contain

(1) A statement whether the amendment is by way of deletion of claims or rewriting of claims.

(2) Insofar as it involve re-writing claims, details as to why the proposed amendment is in accordance with the statutory requirements of an amendment.

(3) Insofar as the amendment is sought to distinguish (more clearly) over prior art, an indication of the prior art.

4.4 The Statement of Opposition shall contain full particulars of all grounds of opposition to the application to amend.

4.5 As soon as may be after the expiration of 35 days from the appearance of the advertisement the applicant must make his application under the said section 30 or 75, as the case may be, by an application notice in the proceedings before the Court; and the application notice, together with a copy of the specification certified by the Comptroller and showing in coloured ink the amendment sought, must be served on the Comptroller, the parties to the proceedings and any person who has given notice of his intention to oppose the amendment.

4.6 Not less than two days before the date fixed for the hearing of the application, the applicant, the Comptroller, the parties to the proceedings and any other opponent should serve on all other parties and on the Court a Statement of Directions being the directions which that party seeks for the further conduct of the proceedings. Any of the foregoing not serving a Statement of Directions shall take no further part in the proceedings without permission of the Court and shall not be liable for the costs thereof.

4.7 On the hearing of the amendment application the Court shall give such directions for its further conduct as it thinks necessary or expedient and, in particular, directions:

(1) determining whether the application shall be heard forthwith or with the other proceedings relating to the patent in question or separately and, if separately, fixing the date of hearing thereof;

(2) as to whether any evidence is necessary, and, if so, as to the manner in which the that evidence shall be given and, if written evidence is to be given, fixing the times within which the affidavits or witness statements must be filed;

(3) as to whether any disclosure is necessary, and, if so, as to the extent of disclosure and the manner and time within which the same is to be given.

4.8 Where the Court allows a specification to be amended, the applicant must forthwith file with the Comptroller an office copy of the order made in the Court and, if so required by the Court or Comptroller, leave at the Patent Office a new specification and drawings as amended, prepared in compliance with the 1949 or 1977 Act, whichever is applicable, and the rules made under those Acts respectively.

4.9 The Comptroller shall cause a copy of the order to be inserted at least once in the journal.

APPLICATION FOR REVOCATION

5.1 An application under section 72 of the 1977 Act for the revocation of a patent shall be commenced by the issue of a claim form. This direction does not apply to an application made in existing proceedings. An application in existing proceedings shall be made by way of a counterclaim or other Part 20 claim (as defined in CPR rule 20.2(1)).

CLAIM FOR INFRINGEMENT

6.1 The claimant in a claim for infringement must serve with his claim form particulars of the infringement relied on, showing which of the claims in the specification of the patent are alleged to be infringed and giving at least one instance of each type of infringement alleged.

6.2 If a defendant in such a claim alleges, as a defence to the claim, that at the time of the infringement there was in force a contract or licence relating to the patent made by or with the consent of the claimant and containing a condition or term void by virtue of section 44 of the 1977 Act, he must serve on the claimant particulars of the date of, and parties to, each such contract or licence and particulars of each such condition or term.

OBJECTIONS TO VALIDITY

7.1 A person who presents a claim for the revocation of a patent must serve with his claim form particulars of the objections to the validity of the patent on which he relies.

7.2 A party to a claim concerning a patent who either challenges the validity of the patent or applies by counterclaim or other Part 20 claim for revocation of the patent must serve his defence, counterclaim or other Part 20 claim (as the case may be), together with particulars of the objections to the validity of the patent on which he relies, within 42 days after service upon him of the claim form.

7.3 Particulars given pursuant to paragraph 7.1 or 7.2 must state every ground on which the validity of the patent is challenged and must include such particulars as will clearly define every issue (including any challenge to any claimed priority date) which it is intended to raise.

7.4 If the grounds stated in the particulars of objections include want of novelty or want of any inventive step, the particulars must state the manner, time and place of every prior publication or user relied upon and, if prior user is alleged, must:

(1) specify the name of every person alleged to have made such user,

(2) state whether such user is alleged to have continued until the priority date of the claim in question or of the invention, as may be appropriate, and, if not, the earliest and latest date on which such user is alleged to have taken place,

(3) contain a description accompanied by drawings, if necessary, sufficient to identify such user, and

(4) if such user relates to machinery or apparatus, state whether the machinery or apparatus is in existence and where it can be inspected.

7.5 If either (a) in the case of an existing patent one of the grounds stated in the particulars of objections is that the invention, so far as claimed in any claim of the complete specification, is not useful, or, (b) in the case of a patent one of the grounds stated in the particulars of objections is that the specification of the patent does not disclose the invention clearly enough and completely enough for the invention to be performed and it is intended, in connection with either of such grounds, to rely on the fact that an example of the invention which is the subject of any claim cannot be made to work, either at all or as described in the specification, the particulars must state that fact and identify each such claim and must include particulars of each such example, specifying the respects in which it is alleged that it does not work or does not work as described.

7.6 In any proceedings relating to a patent in which the validity of the patent has been put in issue on the ground of obviousness a party who wishes to rely on the commercial success of the patent must state in his pleadings the grounds upon which he so relies.

ADMISSIONS

8.1 Where a party desires any other party to admit any facts, he shall, within 21 days after service of a reply or after the expiration of the period fixed for the service thereof, serve on that other party a notice requiring him to admit for the purpose of the claim the facts specified in the notice.

8.2 A party upon whom a notice under paragraph 8.1 is served shall within 21 days after service thereof serve upon the party making the request a notice stating in respect of each fact specified in the notice whether or not he admits it.

DISCLOSURE AND INSPECTION

9.1 CPR Part 31 shall apply in a claim for infringement of a patent or a declaration of non-infringement of a patent or any proceedings where the validity of a patent is in issue.

9.2 Standard disclosure does not require the disclosure of documents in the following exempt classes:

(1) documents relating to the infringement of a patent by a product or process if, before serving a list of documents, the party against whom the allegation of infringement is made has served on the other parties full particulars of the product or process alleged to infringe, including if necessary drawings or other illustrations;

(2) documents relating to any ground on which the validity of a patent is put in issue, except documents which came into existence within the period beginning two years before the earliest claimed priority date and ending two years after that date; and

(3) documents relating to the issue of commercial success.

9.3 Where the issue of commercial success arises in any proceedings specified in paragraph 9.1, the patentee shall, within such time limit as the Court may direct, serve a schedule containing the following details:

(1) where the commercial success relates to an article or product:

(a) an identification of the article or product (for example by product code number) which the patentee asserts has been made in accordance with the claims of the patent;

(b) a summary by convenient periods of sales of any such article or product;

(c) a summary for the equivalent periods of sales, if any, of any equivalent prior article or product marketed before the article or product mentioned in sub-paragraph (a); and

(d) a summary by convenient periods of any expenditure on advertising and promotion which supported the marketing of the articles or products mentioned in sub-paragraphs (a) and (c),

(2) where the commercial success relates to the use of a process:

(a) an identification of the process the patentee asserts has been used in accordance with the claims of the patent;

(b) a summary by convenient periods of the revenues received from the use of such process;

(c) a summary for the equivalent periods of the revenues, if any, received from the use of any equivalent prior art process; and

(d) a summary by convenient periods of any expenditure which supported the use of the process mentioned in sub-paragraphs (a) and (c).

EXPERIMENTS

10.1 Where a party desires to establish any fact by experimental proof he must, at least 21 days before the service of the application notice for directions under paragraph 10.3 or within such other time as the Court may direct at a hearing for further directions pursuant to paragraph 2.5(4), serve on the other party a notice stating the facts which he desires to establish and giving full particulars of the experiments proposed to establish them.

10.2 A party upon whom a notice under paragraph 10.1 is served shall, within 21 days after service thereof, serve upon the other party a notice stating in respect of each fact whether or not he admits it.

10.3 Where any fact which a party desires to establish by experimental proof is not admitted he shall apply to the Court for directions in respect of such experiments.

APPLICATION FOR FURTHER DIRECTIONS

11.1 (1) The parties must comply with any directions given by the judge pursuant to paragraph 2.5(4) in respect of any hearing for further directions.

(2) If the claimant does not serve an application notice for further directions in accordance with this paragraph, the defendant may do so.

(3) The application notice must be accompanied by minutes of the order proposed, and such other documents as will be necessary for the hearing of the application.

11.2 At a further directions hearing under this paragraph the judge may give such directions relating to:

(1) the service of further pleadings or of further information pursuant to Part 18 of the CPR;

(2) disclosure and inspection of documents;

(3) requests for or the making of admissions pursuant to paragraphs 8.1 and 8.2 above and Part 14 of the CPR;

(4) the obtaining of written evidence relating to matters requiring expert knowledge, and for the filing of affidavits or witness statements and the service of copies thereof on the other parties,

(5) the holding of a meeting of such experts as the judge may specify, for the purpose of producing a joint report on the state of the relevant art;

(6) the exchanging of experts' reports, in respect of those matters on which they are not agreed;

(7) the making of experiments, tests, inspections or reports;

(8) the determination, as a preliminary issue, of any question that may arise (including any questions as to the construction of the specification or other documents)

and otherwise as the judge thinks necessary or expedient for the purpose of giving effect to the overriding objective. Where evidence is directed to be given by affidavit or witness statement, the witnesses must attend at the trial for cross-examination unless, with the concurrence of the Court, the parties otherwise agree.

11.3 On the hearing of an application under this paragraph the judge shall consider, if necessary of his own initiative, whether:

(a) the parties' advisers should be required to meet for the purpose of agreeing which documents will be required at the trial and of paginating such documents;

(b) an independent scientific adviser should be appointed to assist the Court, whether as an assessor under CPR rule 35.15 or otherwise.

RESTRICTIONS ON ADMISSION OF EVIDENCE

12.1 Except with the permission of the judge hearing any claim or other proceedings relating to a patent, no evidence shall be admissible in proof of any alleged infringement, or of any objection to the validity, of the patent, if the infringement or objection was not raised in the particulars of infringements or objections, as the case may be.

12.2 In any claim or other proceedings relating to a patent, evidence which is not in accordance with a statement contained in particulars of objections to the validity of the patent shall not be admissible in support of such an objection unless the judge hearing the proceeding allows the evidence to be admitted.

12.3 If any machinery or apparatus alleged to have been used before the priority date mentioned in paragraph 7.4(2) is in existence at the date of service of the particulars of objections, no evidence of its user before that date shall be admissible unless it is proved that the party relying on such user offered, where the machinery or apparatus is in his possession, inspection of it to the other parties to the proceedings or, where it is not, used all reasonable endeavours to obtain inspection of it for those parties.

DETERMINATION OF QUESTION OR APPLICATION WHERE COMPTROLLER DECLINES TO DEAL WITH IT

13 Where the Comptroller:

(1) declines to deal with a question under section 8 (7), 12 (2), 37 (8) or 61 (5) of the 1977 Act;

(2) declines to deal with an application under section 40 (5) of that Act, or

(3) certifies under section 72 (7)(b) of that Act that the question whether a patent should be revoked is one which would more properly be determined by the court,

any person entitled to do so may, within 28 days after the Comptroller's decision apply to the Court to determine the question or application.

APPLICATION BY EMPLOYEE FOR COMPENSATION UNDER SECTION 40 OF THE 1977 ACT

14.1 An application by an employee for compensation under section 40 (1) or (2) of the 1977 Act shall be begun by the issue of a claim form within the period which begins when the relevant patent is granted and which expires one year after it has ceased to have effect.

Provided that, where a patent has ceased to have effect by reason of a failure to pay any renewal fee within the period prescribed for the payment thereof and an application for restoration is made to the Comptroller under section 28 of the said Act, the said period shall:

(1) if restoration is ordered, continue as if the patent had remained continuously in effect, or

(2) if restoration is refused, be treated as expiring one year after the patent ceased to have effect or six months after the refusal, whichever is the later.

14.2 Either at the hearing of an application for directions under paragraph 2.5(1) or at a hearing of an application for further directions under paragraphs 11.1–11.3, the Court must give directions as to the manner in which the evidence (including any accounts of expenditure and receipts relating to the claim) shall be given at the hearing of the claim and, if written evidence is to be given, specify the period within which witness statements or affidavits must be filed.

14.3 The Court must also give directions as to the provision by the defendant to the claimant, or a person deputed by him for the purpose, of reasonable facilities for inspecting and taking extracts from the books of account by which the defendant proposes to verify the accounts mentioned in paragraph 14.2 or from which those accounts have been derived.

PROCEDURE FOR THE DETERMINATION OF CERTAIN DISPUTES

15.1 The following proceedings must be begun by the issue of a claim form, that is to say:

(1) proceedings for the determination of any dispute referred to the court under—

(a) section 48 of the 1949 Act or section 58 of the 1977 Act;
(b) paragraph 3 of Schedule 1 to the Registered Designs Act 1949;
(c) section 4 of the Defence Contracts Act 1958; or
(d) section 252 of the Copyright, Designs and Patent Act 1988;

(2) any application under section 45(3) of the 1977 Act.

APPEALS FROM THE COMPTROLLER

16.1 In this paragraph 'the Court' means the Patents Court of the High Court.

16.2 An appeal to the Court from a decision of the Comptroller in any case in which a right of appeal is given by the 1949 or 1977 Act must be brought by issuing a Notice of Appeal. The parties are, in this paragraph, referred to as 'appellant' and 'respondent' respectively.

16.3 The Notice of Appeal shall be issued:

(1) in the case of a decision on a matter of procedure, within 14 days after the date of the decision; and

(2) in any other case, within six weeks after the date of the decision.

16.4 The Comptroller may determine whether any decision is on a matter of procedure and any such determination shall itself be a decision on a matter of procedure.

16.5 Except with permission of the Court, no appeal shall be entertained unless the Notice of Appeal has been issued within the period specified in paragraph 16.3 or within such further time as the Comptroller may allow upon request made to him prior to the expiry of that period.

16.6 The Notice of Appeal may be given in respect of the whole or any specific part of the decision of the Comptroller and must specify the grounds of the appeal and the relief which the appellant seeks.

16.7 Except with the permission of the Court the appellant shall not be entitled on the hearing of the appeal to rely on any ground of appeal or to apply for any relief not specified in the Notice of Appeal.

16.8 The appellant shall, within 21 days of issuing the Notice of Appeal, serve a copy thereof on the Comptroller and any other party to the proceedings before the Comptroller.

16.9 After receiving the Notice of Appeal the Comptroller shall lodge with the Clerk or other person in charge of the Patents Court list all papers relating to the matter which is subject of the appeal.

16.10 A respondent who, not having appealed from the decision of the Comptroller, desires to contend on the appeal that the decision should be varied, either in any event or in the event of the appeal being allowed in whole or in part, must give notice to that effect, specifying the grounds of that contention and the relief which he seeks from the Court.

16.11 A respondent who desires to contend on the appeal that the decision of the Comptroller should be affirmed on grounds other than those set out in the decision must give notice to that effect, specifying the grounds of that contention.

16.12 A respondent's notice shall be served on the Comptroller and on the appellant and every other party to the proceedings before the Comptroller within 14 days after service of the Notice of Appeal by the respondent, or within such further time as the Court may direct.

16.13 A party by whom a respondent's notice is given must within 5 days after service of the notice on the appellant, furnish 2 copies of the notice to the Clerk or other person in charge of the Patents List

16.14 The Clerk or other person in charge of the Patents list shall give to the Comptroller and to the appellant and every other party to the proceedings before the Comptroller not less than seven days' notice of the date appointed for the hearing of the appeal, unless the Court directs shorter notice to be given.

16.15 An appeal shall be by way of rehearing and the evidence used on appeal shall be the same as that used before the Comptroller and, except with the permission of the Court, no further evidence shall be given.

16.16 Any notice given in proceedings under this rule may be signed by or served on any patent agent, or member of the Bar of England and Wales not in actual practice, who is acting for the person giving the notice or, as the case may be, the person on whom the notice is to be served, as if the patent agent or member of the Bar were a solicitor.

16.17 The Notice of Appeal shall be in the form annexed hereto or in such other form as may be approved by the Court.

COMMUNICATION OF INFORMATION TO THE EUROPEAN PATENT OFFICE

17.1 The Court may authorise the communication to the European Patent Office or the competent authority of any country which is a party to the European Patent Convention of any such information in the files of the court as the Court thinks fit.

17.2 Before complying with a request for the disclosure of information under paragraph 17.1 the Court shall afford to any party appearing to be affected by the request the opportunity of making representations, in writing or otherwise, on the question whether the information should be disclosed.

CLAIM FOR RECTIFICATION OF REGISTER OF PATENTS OR DESIGNS

18.1 Where a claim is made for the rectification of the register of patents, the claimant shall at the same time as serving the other party serve a copy of the claim form and the accompanying documents on the Comptroller, who shall be entitled to appear and to be heard on the application.

OTHER INTELLECTUAL PROPERTY MATTERS INCLUDED IN THIS PRACTICE DIRECTION

A. COPYRIGHT MATTERS

ADDITIONAL DAMAGES UNDER SECTION 97(2) OF THE COPYRIGHT, DESIGNS AND PATENTS ACT 1988.

19.1 Where a claimant seeks to recover additional damages under section 97(2) of the Copyright, Designs and Patents Act 1988, he must so state in his claim form and the particulars of claim must set out the grounds relied upon in support.

APPLICATIONS FOR DELIVERY UP AND FORFEITURE UNDER SECTIONS 99, 114, 195, 204, 230 OR 231 OF THE COPYRIGHT, DESIGNS AND PATENTS ACT 1988

20.1 An application under Sections 99, 114, 195, 204, 230 or 231 of the Copyright, Designs and Patents Act 1988 ('CDPA') shall be made by the issue of a claim form or, if made in existing proceedings, an application notice in those proceedings.

20.2 Where such an application. is made the applicant shall serve the claim form or application notice on all persons having an interest in the goods, material or articles within the meaning of sections 114, 204 or 231 of the CDPA insofar as such persons are reasonably ascertainable.

B. TRADEMARK MATTERS

DEFINITIONS

21.1 In this section of this practice direction:
'the 1938 Act' means the Trade Marks Act 1938 as amended by the Trade Marks (Amendment) Act 1984 and the Patents, Designs and Marks Act 1986;
'the 1994 Act' means the Trade Marks Act 1994;
'the Olympic Symbol Act' means the Olympic Symbol etc. (Protection) Act 1995;
'the Olympic Symbol Regulations' means the Olympic Association Right (Infringement Proceedings) Regulations 1995;
'the Registrar' means the Comptroller-General of Patents, Designs and Trade Marks;
'the register' means the register of trade marks maintained by the Registrar pursuant to section 63 of the 1994 Act;
'appointed person' means a person appointed by the Lord Chancellor to hear and decide appeals under the 1994 Act.

ASSIGNMENT TO THE CHANCERY DIVISION

22.1 Proceedings in the High Court under the 1938 Act, the 1994 Act or the Olympic Symbol Act and Regulations shall be dealt with in the Chancery Division.

APPEALS AND APPLICATIONS UNDER THE 1938 ACT, THE 1994 ACT AND THE OLYMPIC SYMBOL ACT AND THE OLYMPIC SYMBOL REGULATIONS

23.1 Every appeal to the High Court under the 1938 Act or the 1994 Act shall be heard and determined by a single judge.

23.2 Such appeals shall be brought by a Notice of Appeal in such form as may be approved by the court.

23.3 The Notice of Appeal must be issued within 28 days of the decision appealed from.

23.4 Within 21 days of issue the Notice of Appeal must be served on the Registrar and any Respondents and lodged with the Clerk or other person in charge of the Chancery List.

23.5 Every other application to the High Court under the said Acts and the Olympic Symbol Regulations must be begun by the issue of a claim form under CPR Part 8 or, if made in existing proceedings, an application notice in those proceedings.

23.6 Notices of Appeal, claim forms or application notices by which any such application is begun must be served on the Registrar.

23.7 Where:

(1) the Registrar refers to the High Court an application made to him under the 1938 Act or the 1994 Act;

(2) the Board of Trade under the 1938 Act or an appointed person under section 76 of the 1994 Act refers to that Court an appeal,

then unless within one month after receiving notification of the decision to refer, the applicant or the appellant, as the case may be, makes to that Court the application or appeal referred, he shall be deemed to have abandoned it.

23.8 The period prescribed above in relation to an appeal to which paragraph 23.1 applies or the period prescribed by paragraph 23.7 in relation to an application or appeal to which that paragraph applies, may be extended by the Registrar on the application of any party interested and may be so extended although the application is not made until after the expiration of that period, but the foregoing provision shall not be taken to affect the power of the Court to extend that period.

23.9 Where under subsection (6) of section 17 or subsection (9) of section 18 of the 1938 Act an appellant becomes entitled and intends to withdraw the application which is the subject-matter of the appeal, he must give notice of his intention to the Registrar and to any other party to the appeal within one month after the Court has given permission under the said subsection (6) or the said subsection (9), as the case may be, for further grounds of objection to be taken.

23.10 Where an application is made under section 19 of the 1994 Act or under regulation 5 of the Olympic Symbol Regulations the applicant shall serve the claim form or application notice on all persons having an interest in the goods, material or articles within the meaning of section 19 of the 1994 Act or Regulation 5 of the Olympic Symbol Regulations as the case may be insofar as such persons are reasonably ascertainable.

PROCEEDINGS FOR INFRINGEMENT OF REGISTERED TRADE MARK; VALIDITY OF REGISTRATION DISPUTED OR REVOCATION OR RECTIFICATION SOUGHT

24.1 Where in any proceedings a claim is made for relief for infringement of the rights conferred on the proprietor of a registered trade mark by section 9 of the 1994 Act, the party against whom the claim is made may in his defence put in issue the validity of the registration of that trade mark or may apply by counterclaim or other Part 20 claim for an order for revocation of the registration or for a declaration of invalidity of the registration or for rectification of the register, or may do any or all of those things.

24.2 A party to any such proceedings who in his pleading (whether a defence or counterclaim or other Part 20 claim) disputes the validity of the registration of a registered trade mark or seeks a declaration of invalidity or an order for revocation of the registration, or rectification of the register, must serve with his pleading particulars of the objections to the validity of the registration or of any grounds for revocation or rectification, on which he relies.

24.3 A party to any such proceedings who applies for an order for revocation of the registration or for a declaration of invalidity of the registration or for rectification of the register must serve on the Registrar a copy of his counterclaim or other Part 20 claim together with a copy of the particulars mentioned in paragraph 24.2 and the Registrar shall be entitled to take such part in the proceedings as he may think fit but need not serve a defence or other statement of case unless ordered to do so by the Court.

SERVICE OF DOCUMENTS

25.1 This rule applies to the service of any document on a party until such time as that party has provided an address for service in accordance CPR rule 6.5.

25.2 Subject to paragraph 25.3 for the purposes of any proceedings relating to a registered trade mark (including proceedings for revocation, declaration of invalidity or non-infringement or groundless threats of infringement proceedings or any other proceedings under the 1938 Act or the 1994 Act), where any document is served in the manner authorised by Part 6 of the CPR at an address for service given in the register kept under section 63 of the 1994 Act—

(1) service shall be deemed to have been effected on the registered proprietor of the trade mark on the date on which the document was served at the said address;

(2) the party on whom service is deemed to have been effected under sub-paragraph (1), shall be treated, for the purposes of any provision which specifies a time-limit for responding to the document so served (whether by acknowledging service, giving notice of intention to defend or otherwise), as having been served on the seventh day after the date on which the document was served at the said address.

25.3 Nothing in paragraph 25.2 shall prevent service being effected on the proprietor in accordance with the provisions of CPR Part 6.

SERVICE OF ORDERS ON THE REGISTRAR

Where an order is made by the Court in any case under the 1938 Act or the 1994 Act, the person in whose favour the order is made (if there is more than one, such one of them as the Court shall direct) shall serve an office copy of the order on the Registrar.

PD 49E   PRACTICE DIRECTION — PATENTS ETC.

IN THE HIGH COURT OF JUSTICE CHANCERY DIVISION PATENTS COURT

NOTICE OF APPEAL

(a) Here insert the nature of the application or proceedings, the name of the Patentee or Applicant the number of the Patent or Application for Letters Patent followed by the name of the Opponent (if any)
(b) Patent Agent or Applicant in person
(c) Here insert name(s) and full address(es) of Appellant(s)
(d) Here insert 'the decision "or" that part of the decision' as the case may be
(e) Here insert 'Comptroller General' or 'Officer acting for the Comptroller General' as the case may be
(f) Summarise the decision appealed against
(g) Here set out the grounds of appeal
(h) Here set out the relief which the Appellant seeks
(i) To be signed by the Appellant personally or by his duly authorised representative
(j) To be addressed to the other side and to their authorised representative and to the Comptroller-General at the Patent Office.

IN THE MATTER(a)

(e.g. of an Application by ....
and
an Opposition by ....

TAKE NOTICE that the HIGH COURT OF JUSTICE, CHANCERY DIVISION, PATENTS COURT, will be moved before a Judge of the Patents Court at a time to be set by the Patents Court not less than twenty-four days after service of this notice, or so soon thereafter as Counsel(b) can be heard by Counsel(b), on behalf of(c)

....
by the way of appeal from(d) ....
of the(e) ....
dated the ....day of .... 19 ....
whereby he(f) ....
....
....
....

The grounds of appeal are as follows:—(g)

I/WE ask the Patents Court to grant the relief set out below:—(h)

DATE ....
SIGNATURE ....(i)
ADDRESS ....
....
....
TO ....(j)
....

NOTE: Two copies of this Notice of Appeal must be sent to the Chancery Chambers (Room 307), Thomas More Building, Royal Courts of Justice, Strand, London WC2A 2LL. They must be accompanied with the remittance for the prescribed fee. The remittance must if sent by post be paid by Bankers Draft or **postal order made payable to H.M. Paymaster General and crossed.** A copy of the notice must be sent to the Comptroller-General at the Patent Office, Room GR15, Concept House, Cardiff Road, Gwent NP10 1RH and to any party entitled to appear before the Patents Court within the period prescribed by paragraph 16 of the **Patents Practice Direction**

PD 49F   PRACTICE DIRECTION — ADMIRALTY

This practice direction supplements CPR Part 49 and replaces, with modifications, Order 75 of the Rules of the Supreme Court

GENERAL

1.1   This practice direction applies to all Admiralty proceedings.

1.2   The provisions of the Civil Procedure Rules and the Practice Directions that supplement them apply to Admiralty proceedings subject to the provisions of this practice direction, any other Admiralty practice direction and, where applicable, the Commercial Court Guide (see paragraph 16 below).

1.3   'Admiralty proceedings' means proceedings in the Admiralty Court of the Queen's Bench Division of the High Court of Justice and in any other court exercising Admiralty jurisdiction.

1.4   In this Practice Direction:
   (a)   'the Admiralty Court' includes:
      (i)   the Admiralty Court of the Queen's Bench Division of the High Court of Justice; and
      (ii)   any other court exercising Admiralty jurisdiction.
   (b)   'claim *in rem*' means an Admiralty claim *in rem*;
   (c)   'claim *in personam*' means an Admiralty claim *in personam*;
   (d)   a 'collision claim' means a claim failing within section 20(3)(b) of the Supreme Court Act 1981, namely any action to enforce a claim for damage, loss of life or personal injury arising out of:
      (i)   a collision between ships; or
      (ii)   the carrying out or omission to carry out any manoeuvre in the case of one or more of two or more ships; or
      (iii)   non-compliance, on the part of one or more of two or more ships, with the collision regulations;
   (e)   a 'salvage claim' includes any claim in the nature of salvage, any claim for special compensation under Article 14 of Schedule 11 to the Merchant Shipping Act 1995, any claim for the apportionment of salvage and any claim arising out of or connected with any contract for salvage services;
   (f)   'caveat against arrest' means a caveat entered in the caveat book under paragraph 6.3(1);
   (g)   'caveat against release' means a caveat entered in the caveat book under paragraph 6.5(2);
   (h)   'caveat book' means the book kept in the Admiralty and Commercial Registry in which caveats under this practice direction are entered;
   (i)   'limitation claim' means a claim by shipowners of other persons under the Merchant Shipping Act 1995 for the limitation of the amount of their liability in connection with a ship or other property;
   (j)   'Marshal' means the Admiralty Marshal;
   (k)   'ship' includes any description of vessel used in navigation.
   (l)   'The Admiralty Registrar' means the Queen's Bench master with responsibility for Admiralty proceedings;
   (m)   '*in rem* claim form' means a claim form [by] which an *in rem* claim is brought.
   (n)   Any references to the Merchant Shipping Act 1995 include any re-enactment thereof.
   (o)   'the CPR' means the Civil Procedure Rules.

1.5   The following claims must be commenced in the Admiralty Court.
   (a)   Any claim *in rem*;
   (b)   Any collision claim;
   (c)   Any limitation claim;
   (d)   Any application to the court under the Merchant Shipping Act 1995;

(e) Any salvage claim.

1.6 Any other claim within the admiralty jurisdiction of the High Court may be commenced either in the Admiralty Court or in the Commercial Court.

1.7 Any claim may be transferred to the Admiralty Court with the consent of the Admiralty Court.

1.8 A claim within paragraph 1.5 wrongly commenced in any other court will be transferred automatically to the Admiralty Court.

1.9 A claim form by which a claim within paragraphs 1.5 or 1.6 is begun may be issued out of the Admiralty and Commercial Court Registry or the registry of any Admiralty Court.

1.10 If a claim form referred to in paragraph 1.9 is issued out of a registry other than the Admiralty and Commercial Registry that other registry will immediately after issue send a copy of the claim by facsimile to the Admiralty and Commercial Registry, and will also send the original file to the Admiralty and Commercial Registry.

1.11 Subject to paragraph 1.13, the Admiralty Registrar shall, after the issue of a claim form referred to in paragraph 1.9 issue a direction in writing stating:

(a) whether the claim should remain in the Admiralty Court or should be transferred to another court; and

(b) if the claim is to remain in the Admiralty Court, whether it should be in the Admiralty Judge's list or should be placed in the Admiralty Registrar's list for trial in London or elsewhere.

In issuing these directions the Admiralty Registrar will have regard to the nature of the issues in dispute and the criteria set out in Rule CPR rule 26.8 insofar as they are applicable.

1.12 Where the Admiralty Registrar directs that the claim should be placed in the Judge's list, case management directions will be given and any case management conference or pre-trial review will be heard by the Admiralty Judge.

1.13 All matters concerning the arrest, detention, sale of property and the determination of priorities in a claim *in rem*, all proceedings concerning the ownership or the mortgage of a vessel registered under the Merchant Shipping Act 1995, all proceedings in a limitation claim and proceedings against the International Oil Pollution Compensation Fund under s.175 of the Merchant Shipping Act 1995 shall be dealt with only by the Admiralty Court of the High Court.

1.14 All Admiralty proceedings will be allocated to the multi-track and the CPR relating to allocation questionnaires and track allocation will not apply.

CLAIMS *IN REM*

2.1 (1) A claim *in rem* is begun by issuing an *in rem* claim form in Admiralty Form No. ADM1.

(2) Subject to paragraph 4, the particulars of an *in rem* claim must

(a) be contained in or served with the *in rem* claim form; or

(b) be served on the Defendant by the Claimant within 75 days after service of the *in rem* claim form.

(3) The Claimant to a claim *in rem* may be named or may be described, but if not named in the *in rem* claim form shall upon the request of any other party, identify himself by name.

(4) The Defendant must be described in the claim form.

(5) An acknowledgment of service must be filed in every *in rem* claim. The period for filing the acknowledgment of service is 14 days after service of the claim form irrespective of whether the claim form contains particulars of claim. The acknowledgment must be in Admiralty Form No. ADM2. The person who acknowledges service must identify himself by name therein.

(6) The period within which an *in rem* claim form must be served is, subject to CPR rule 7.6, 12 months from the date of issue.

2.2 Service of an *in rem* claim form must be made in one of the following ways:

(a) Upon the property against which the claim *in rem* is brought by fixing the *in rem* claim form, or a copy of it, on the outside of the property proceeded against in a position which may reasonably be expected to be seen.

Where the property is freight, service may be made either on the cargo in respect of which the freight was earned or on the ship upon which that cargo was carried.

(b) If the property to be served is in the custody of a person who will not permit access to it, by leaving a copy of the *in rem* claim form with that person.

(c) Where the property has been sold by the Marshal, by filing the *in rem* claim form in the Admiralty and Commercial Registry.

(d) Where there is a caveat against arrest, on the person named in the caveat as being authorised to accept service.

(e) On any solicitor who has authority to accept service.

(f) On such person and in such manner as is stated to constitute effective service in any agreement providing for service of the proceedings;

(g) In any other manner directed under CPR rule 6.8 provided that the *res* or part thereof is within the jurisdiction of the Court; or

(h) In such other manner as may be provided by rule or by practice directions.

2.3 In cases where the property is to be arrested, or in cases where the property is already under arrest in current proceedings, the Marshal will effect service of the *in rem* claim form if the Claimant requests the Court to do so. In all other cases Admiralty *in rem* claim forms are to be served by the claimant, not the Registry.

2.4 Where an *in rem* claim form has been issued, any person who wishes to defend the claim may file an acknowledgment of service notwithstanding that the *in rem* claim form has not been served.

2.5 Except as otherwise provided in this practice direction, after acknowledgment of service has been filed, the procedure relating to the claim shall be the procedure applicable to a claim *in personam*, but the claim also continues to be a claim *in rem*.

2.6 Where the defendants are described and not named on the claim form, for example as 'The Owners of the Ship X', any acknowledgment of service in addition to stating the description appearing on the claim form shall also state the full names of the persons acknowledging service and the nature of their ownership. In the event of there being insufficient space on the acknowledgment of service form itself, such additional information shall appear on a separate document to accompany and be lodged with the acknowledgment of service form.

2.7 A Defendant who files an acknowledgment of service to an *in rem* claim form does not by doing so lose any right that he may have to dispute the Court's jurisdiction (see CPR10.13(b) and Part 11).

CLAIMS *IN PERSONAM*

3.1 (1) A claim form by which a claim *in personam* is brought (an *in personam* claim form in Admiralty Form ADM1A) may be served within the jurisdiction as provided in CPR Part 6 and, except in the case of a collision claim, may be served out of the jurisdiction as provided RSC Order 11 (Schedule 1 to the CPR).

(2) An *in personam* claim form may also be served out of the Jurisdiction where:

(a) the Defendant has agreed to submit the claim to the jurisdiction of the court; or

(b) the claim is in the nature of salvage and any part of the services took place within the jurisdiction; or

(c) the claim is to enforce a claim under sections 153 and/or 154 and/or 175 of the Merchant Shipping Act 1995 and the Court grants permission to serve the claim out of the jurisdiction.

(3) *In personam* claim forms are to be served by the claimants, not by the Registry.

3.2 (1) An *in personam* claim form may seek judgment on liability alone and request that the amount of the claim be referred to the Admiralty Registrar, or be dealt with as the Admiralty Registrar may direct.

(2) The Claimant in a claim *in personam* may be named or may be described in the claim form, but if not named, shall, upon the request of any other party, identity himself by name.

(3) The Defendant in a claim *in personam* must be named in the claim form.

(4) Subject to paragraph 4, the particulars of an *in personam* claim must
   (a) be contained in or served with the claim form; or
   (b) be served on the Defendant by the Claimant within 75 days after service of the claim form.

(5) The person who files a defence must identify himself by name in the defence.

3.3 An acknowledgment of service must be filed in every *in personam* claim. Subject to paragraph B7.4 of the Commercial Court Guide, the period for filing the acknowledgment of service is 14 days after service of the claim form irrespective of whether the claim form contains particulars of claim.

SPECIAL PROVISIONS RELATING TO COLLISION CLAIMS

4.1 (1) A collision claim is begun by issuing a claim form. The claim form need not contain or be followed by particulars of claim and CPR rule 7.4 will not apply.

(2) An acknowledgment of service must be filed in every collision claim.

4.2 (1) In any collision claim each party shall, within 2 months after the filing by the Defendant of the acknowledgment of service or, in the event that the Defendant makes an application under CPR Part 11 (disputing the jurisdiction or the exercise by the court of its jurisdiction), within 2 months of the determination of the Defendant's application, file in the Registry a completed Admiralty Form No. ADM3 ('a Preliminary Act').

(2) A Preliminary Act shall contain:
   (a) in Part One of the Form, answers to the questions set out in that Part; and
   (b) in Part Two of the Form, a statement:
      (i) that the information in Part One is incorporated in Part Two;
      (ii) of any other facts and matters upon which the party filing the Preliminary Act relies;
      (iii) of all allegations of negligence or other fault which the party filing the Preliminary Act makes;
      (iv) of the relief or remedy which the party filing the Preliminary Act claims.

(3) Each party must verify his Preliminary Act by a statement of truth.

(4) Upon filing their Preliminary Act each party must give notice that he has done so to each other party. Within 14 days after the last Preliminary Act is filed each party must serve on every other party a copy of his Preliminary Act.

(5) After each party has filed his Preliminary Act, the claim shall proceed as any other Admiralty claim.

4.3 In any collision claim an application under CPR Part 11 disputing the Court's jurisdiction must be made within 2 months of the filing of the acknowledgment of service.

4.4 A claim form in a collision claim may not be served out of the jurisdiction unless the case fails within section 22(2)(a) to (c) of the Supreme Court Act 1981 or the Defendant has submitted to or agreed to submit to the Jurisdiction of the court.

4.5 Where, in a collision claim *in rem*, ('the original claim'):
   (a) (i) a Part 20 claim; or
      (ii) a cross-claim *in rem*
arising out of the same collision or occurrence is made; and
   (b) (i) the party bringing the original claim has caused the arrest of a ship or has obtained security in order to prevent such arrest; and
      (ii) the party bringing the Part 20 claim or cross-claim is unable to arrest a ship or otherwise to obtain security,
then the party bringing the Part 20 claim or cross claim may apply to the Admiralty Court to stay the original claim until sufficient security is given to satisfy any judgment that may be given in favour of that party.

4.6 In collision claims the skeleton argument of each party should be accompanied by a plot or plots of that party's case or alternative cases as to the navigation of vessels during and leading to the collision. All plots must contain a sufficient indication of the assumptions used in the preparation of the plot.

4.7 Where the authenticity of any document or entry in any document is challenged or where it will be suggested at trial that a document or entry in a document was not made at the time or by the person stated or is in any other way challenged in a manner which may require a witness to be produced at trial to support the document or entry in the document, such challenge must be raised in good time in advance of the trial to enable any such witness to be produced. In addition, the skeleton argument should make it plain what challenges to documents or entries in documents will be made.

PROCEEDINGS AGAINST OR CONCERNING THE INTERNATIONAL OIL POLLUTION COMPENSATION FUND*

5.1 For the purposes of section 177 of the Merchant Shipping Act 1995 and the corresponding provision of Schedule 4 to the Act, any party to proceedings against an owner or guarantor in respect of liability under section 153 and/or section 154 of the said Act or the corresponding provisions of Schedule 4 to the Act may give the Fund notice of the proceedings by serving a notice in writing on the Fund together with a copy of the claim form and copies of the statements of case (if any) served in the proceedings.

5.2 The court will, on application by the Fund made without notice, grant permission to the Fund to intervene in any proceedings to which paragraph 5.1 applies, whether notice of the proceedings has been served on the Fund or not.

5.3 Where a judgment is given against the Fund in any proceedings under section 175 of the Merchant Shipping Act 1995 or the corresponding provision of Schedule 4 to the Act, the Admiralty Registrar will arrange for a stamped copy of the judgment to be sent to the Fund by post.

5.4 Notice by the Fund to the Admiralty Registrar of the matters set out in section 176(3)(b) of the Merchant Shipping Act 1995 and the corresponding section of Schedule 4 to the Act shall be in writing sent by post to, or delivered at, the Registry.

ARREST, RELEASE, INTERVENERS ETC.

6.1 Except as provided in this Practice Direction, the Claimant in a claim *in rem* and a judgment creditor in a claim *in rem* is entitled to have the property proceeded against arrested by the Admiralty Court by filing an application to arrest in Admiralty Form No. ADM4 (which shall also contain an undertaking) accompanied by a declaration in Admiralty Form No. ADM5 upon which the Admiralty Court will issue an arrest warrant.

6.2 (1) An application for arrest may be made by filing the application notice in the Admiralty and Commercial Registry or the registry of any Admiralty Court.

(2) When the relevant registry is closed an application for arrest shall be dealt with in such manner (if any) as may be provided in Admiralty practice directions.

(3) Any party making an application for arrest must (i) request a search to be made in the caveat book before the warrant is issued in order to ascertain whether there is a caveat in force with respect to that property and (ii) file a declaration in Admiralty Form No. ADM5 containing the particulars required in paragraph 6.2(4). However the Admiralty Court may, if it thinks fit, give permission for the issue of the arrest warrant notwithstanding that the declaration does not contain all those particulars.

(4) The declaration required by paragraph 6.2(3) must state:

(a) in every case:

(i) the nature of the claim or counterclaim and that it has not been satisfied and if it arises in connection with a ship, the name of that ship; and

(ii) the nature of the property to be arrested and, if the property is a ship, the name of the ship and her port of registry; and

(iii) the amount of the security sought, if any.

(b) in the case of a claim against a ship by virtue of section 21(4) of the Supreme Court Act 1981:

---

* See Chapter IV, Merchant Shipping Act 1995.

PD 49F PRACTICE DIRECTION — ADMIRALTY

(i) the name of the person who would be liable on the claim if it were commenced *in personam* ('the relevant person'); and

(ii) that the relevant person was when the cause of action arose the owner or charterer of, or in possession or in control of, the ship in connection with which the claim arose, specifying which; and

(iii) that at the time when the claim form was issued the relevant person was either the beneficial owner of all the shares in the ship in respect of which the warrant is required or (where appropriate) the charterer of it under a charter by demise, as the case may be; and

(c) in the cases set out in paragraphs 6.2(6) and 6.2(7) that the relevant notice has been sent or served, as appropriate; and

(d) in the case of a claim in respect of liability incurred under section 153 of the Merchant Shipping Act 1995, the facts relied on as establishing that the Court is not prevented from entertaining the claim by reason of section 166(2) of that Act; and must be sworn as an affidavit.

(5) No registry other than the Admiralty and Commercial Registry will issue an arrest warrant and where an application for arrest is made to any registry other than the Admiralty and Commercial Registry that registry will use its best endeavours to cause the application form and declaration and a copy of the form to be transmitted immediately to the Admiralty and Commercial Registry for consideration of the application and, if appropriate, the issue of the warrant. Thereafter the arrest shall be administered by the Marshal and all applications in respect thereof and in respect of the property under arrest other than an order for sale before judgment shall be made to and considered by the Admiralty Registrar himself or as he may direct.

(6) A warrant of arrest may not be issued as of right in the case of property in respect of which the beneficial ownership, as a result of a sale or disposal by any court exercising Admiralty jurisdiction, has changed since the claim form was issued.

(7) No warrant of arrest will be issued against a ship owned by a State where, by any convention or treaty, the United Kingdom has undertaken to minimise the possibility of arrest of ships of that State until notice in Admiralty Form No. ADM6 has been served on a consular officer at the consular office of that State in London or the port at which it is intended to cause the ship to be arrested and a copy of the notice is exhibited to the declaration filed under paragraph 6.2(3).

6.3 (1) Any person may file in the Admiralty and Commercial Registry a notice requesting a caveat against arrest in Admiralty Form No. ADM7, undertaking to file an acknowledgment of service and to give sufficient security to satisfy the claim with interest and costs. Upon filing the notice of request a caveat shall be entered in the caveat book. The record of such caveats shall be open for inspection as provided in the Admiralty practice directions. Caveats shall be valid for a period of 12 months but may be renewed for a similar period or periods. The entry of a caveat against arrest shall not be treated as a submission to the jurisdiction of the English Court.

(2) Where a Claimant in a limitation claim has constituted a limitation fund in accordance with Article 11 of the Convention on Limitation of Liability for Maritime Claims 1976 and desires to prevent the arrest of property for a claim which may be or has been made against the fund, he must file in the Admiralty and Commercial Registry a notice requesting a caveat, in Admiralty Form No. ADM8, signed by him or his solicitor:

(a) stating that a limitation fund in respect of the damage arising from the relevant incident has been constituted; and

(b) undertaking to acknowledge service of the claim form by which any claim may be begun against the property described in the notice;

and on the filing of the notice a caveat against the issue of a warrant to arrest the property described in the notice shall be entered in the caveat book.

(3) Property may be arrested notwithstanding that a caveat against arrest has been filed, but in such a case the Admiralty Court may if it considers that it is

appropriate to do so, order that the arrest be discharged and that the party procuring the arrest do pay compensation to the owner of or other persons interested in the property arrested.

6.4 (1) The arrest of property may only be effected by the Marshal or his substitute.

(2) Arrest is effected by service on the property of an arrest warrant in Admiralty Form No. ADM9 in the manner set out in paragraph 2.2(a) or, where it is not reasonably practicable to serve the warrant, by service of a notice of the issue of the warrant in that manner upon the property or by giving notice to those in charge of the property.

(3) Property under arrest may not be moved without an order of the Admiralty Court and the property may be immobilised or otherwise prevented from sailing in such manner as the Marshal or his substitute may decide is appropriate.

(4) Upon arrest, standard directions will be issued by the Admiralty Registrar in Admiralty Form No. ADM10.

6.5 (1) Where property is under arrest an *in rem* claim form may be served upon it and, in addition, it may be arrested by any other person claiming to have an *in rem* claim against it.

(2) Any person claiming to have an *in rem* right against any property under arrest who wishes to be given notice of any application to the court in respect of that property or its proceeds of sale may file in the Admiralty and Commercial Registry a notice requesting a caveat against release in Admiralty Form No. ADM11. Upon the filing of the notice of request, a caveat shall be entered in the caveat book. The record of such caveats shall be open for inspection as provided in the Admiralty practice directions.

6.6 (1) Property will be released from arrest if:

(a) it is sold by the Admiralty Court; or

(b) the Admiralty Court orders release upon application made by any party; or

(c) the arresting party and all caveators, if any, file in the Registry a request for release in Admiralty Form No. ADM12, or

(d) any party files in the Registry a request for release in Admiralty Form No. ADM12 (which shall also contain an undertaking) together with a consent to the release of the arresting party and all caveators, if any.

(2) Any application for release made when the Registry is closed shall be made in any manner as may be provided in Admiralty practice directions.

6.7 (1) Where the release of any property under arrest is delayed by the entry of a caveat under this rule, any person having an interest in the property may apply to the Admiralty Court for an order requiring the person who procured the entry of the caveat to pay damages to the applicant in respect of losses suffered by the applicant by reason of the delay and the Court may make such an order unless it is satisfied that the person procuring the entry of the caveat had a good and sufficient reason for doing so and for maintaining the caveat.

(2) Where an *in rem* claim form has been issued and security sought, any person who has filed an acknowledgment of service may apply to the Admiralty Court for an order specifying the amount and form of security to be provided.

(3) Where in relation to a claim *in rem* security has been provided to obtain the release of property under arrest or to prevent the arrest of property the Admiralty Court may at any stage:

(a) order that the amount of security be reduced, and may stay the claim pending compliance with such order;

(b) order that the Claimant be permitted to arrest or re-arrest the property proceeded against for the purposes of obtaining further security, provided that the total security provided shall not exceed the value of the property at the time of the original arrest or at the time security was first given if the property was not arrested.

6.8 Any person interested in property under arrest or in the proceeds of sale of property sold by the Admiralty Court or whose interests are affected by any order sought or made may be made a party to any claim in rem against the property or proceeds of sale where the Court considers it would be just and convenient and upon such terms as the Court may think fit.

6.9 Any application to the Admiralty Court concerning the sale of the property under arrest or the proceeds of sale of property sold by the Court shall be heard in public and the application notice served on all parties to the claim and caveators against the property or the proceeds of sale.

6.10 (1) Where a ship is not under arrest but cargo on board her is, and those interested in the ship wish to discharge the cargo which is under arrest, they may, without intervening in the action, request the Marshal to take the appropriate steps. If the Marshal considers the request reasonable and if the applicant gives an undertaking in writing satisfactory to the Marshal to pay on demand the fees of the Marshal and all expenses to be incurred by him or on his behalf in taking the desired steps, the Marshal will apply to the court for the appropriate order.

(2) Where those interested are unable or unwilling to arrange for such an undertaking to be given they may intervene in the action in which the cargo is under arrest and apply to the Admiralty Registrar for an order for discharge of the cargo and for directions as to the fees and expenses of the Marshal in and about the discharge and storage of the cargo pursuant to such order.

6.11 Where a ship is under arrest but cargo on board her is not, and those interested in the cargo wish to secure its discharge, one or other of the procedures outlined in paragraph 6.10(1) and 6.10(2) may be followed.

DEFAULT

7.1 If no acknowledgment of service and/or defence to a claim *in rem* (other than one to which paragraph 4 applies) is filed within the time required by this practice direction a Claimant may apply for judgment in default by filing an application in Admiralty Form No. ADM13, a certificate proving proper service of the claim form and evidence proving the claim to the satisfaction of the Admiralty Court. Where the claim form has been served by the Court it shall be presumed to have been properly served unless it is proved not to have been.

7.2 In the case of a claim to which paragraph 4 applies, where any party fails to file a Preliminary Act within the time specified any other party who has filed a Preliminary Act may apply for judgment in default:

(a) In a claim *in rem*, by filing an application in Admiralty Form No. ADM13, a certificate proving proper service of the claim form and evidence proving the claim to the satisfaction of the Admiralty Court. Where the claim form has been served by the Court it shall be presumed to have been properly served unless it is proved not to have been.

(b) in a claim *in personam*, in accordance with the rules in CPR Part 12 so far as applicable.

7.3 In the case of any other claim *in personam*, the rules as to judgment in default in CPR Part 12 will apply so far as applicable.

7.4 The Admiralty Court may, on such terms as it thinks just, set aside or vary any judgment entered in pursuance of paragraphs 7.1 or 7.2.

7.5 Where a claim form has been served upon a party at whose instance a caveat against arrest was issued the Claimant may, after filing evidence to the satisfaction of the Admiralty Court verifying the facts on which the claim is based, apply to the Court for judgment in default provided that:

(a) the sum claimed in the claim form does not exceed the amount specified in the undertaking given by that party or his solicitor to procure the entry of the caveat, and

(b) that party or his solicitor does not within 14 days after service of the claim form fulfil the undertaking given by him as aforesaid.

SALE BY THE COURT, PRIORITIES AND PAYMENT OUT

8.1 (1) An order for the survey, appraisement, or sale of a ship may be made in a claim *in rem* at any stage of the proceedings on the application of any party.

(2) An order for sale before judgment may only be made by the Admiralty Judge.

(3) Unless the Admiralty Court otherwise orders, an order for sale will be in Admiralty Form No. ADM14.

(4) In giving directions for sale the Admiralty Court may fix a time within which notice of claims against the proceeds of sale must be filed, and the time and manner in which notice of that time must be advertised.

8.2 (1) Any party with a judgment against the property or proceeds of sale may at any time after the time referred to in paragraph 8.1(4) apply to the Admiralty Court for the determination of priorities. The application notice must be served on all persons who have filed a claim against the property.

(2) Unless otherwise ordered by the Admiralty Judge, a determination of priorities may only be made by the Admiralty Judge.

8.3 Payment out of the proceeds of sale will be made only to judgment creditors and in accordance with the determination of priorities or as the Admiralty Court may otherwise order.

8.4 (1) When proceeds of sale are paid into court by the Marshal and such payment is in a foreign currency, the funds will be placed on one day call interest bearing account unless otherwise ordered by the court.

(2) An application to place foreign currency on longer term deposit unless made at the same time as the application for sale, or other prior application, may be made to the Admiralty Registrar. Notice of the placement of foreign currency in an interest bearing account shall be given to all parties interested in the fund by the party at whose instance the foreign currency is invested.

(3) Any interested party who wishes to object to the mode of investment of foreign currency paid into court may apply to the Admiralty Registrar for directions.

LIMITATION CLAIMS

9.1 (1) Limitation may be relied upon by way of defence to any claim.

(2) A limitation claim may be brought by counterclaim with the permission of the Admiralty Court.

(3) A limitation claim is begun by the issue of a claim form in Admiralty Form No. ADM15 ('a limitation claim form'). The limitation claim form must be accompanied by a declaration:

(a) proving the facts upon which the Claimant relies;

(b) stating the names and addresses (if known) of all persons who to the knowledge of the Claimant have claims against him in respect of the occurrence to which the claim relates, other than named defendants;

and sworn as an affidavit.

(4) The Claimant and at least one of the Defendants must be named in the limitation claim form, but all other Defendants may be described.

(5) The limitation claim form must be served on all named Defendants.

(6) The limitation claim form may not be served out of the jurisdiction unless:

(a) the case fails within section 22(2)(a) to (c) of the Supreme Court Act 1981;

(b) the Defendant has submitted to or agreed to submit to the jurisdiction of the court; or

(c) the Admiralty Court has jurisdiction over the claim under any applicable Convention.

(7) Every Defendant upon whom a limitation claim form is served must either:

(a) within 28 days of service file a defence to the limitation claim in Admiralty Form No. ADM16A or file a notice in Admiralty Form No. ADM16 that he admits the right of the claimant to limit liability; or

(b) if he wishes to dispute the jurisdiction of the court or to argue that the court should not exercise its jurisdiction file within 14 days of service or, if the limitation claim form is served out of the jurisdiction, within the time specified in RSC Order 11 rule 1A (Schedule 1 to the CPR), an acknowledgment of service in Admiralty Form No. ADM16B.

PD 49F PRACTICE DIRECTION — ADMIRALTY

(8) In the event that the Defendant files an acknowledgment of service pursuant to paragraph 9.1(7)(b) he will be treated as having accepted that the court has jurisdiction to hear the limitation claim unless he makes an application under CPR Part 11 within 14 days of filing his acknowledgment of service.

9.2 (1) Where one or more named Defendants admits the right to limit, the Claimant may file in the registry an application for a restricted limitation decree in Admiralty Form No. ADM17 and the Court will issue a decree in Admiralty Form No. ADM18 limiting liability only against such named Defendants as have admitted the Claimant's right to limit liability.

(2) A restricted limitation decree may be obtained against any named Defendant failing to file a defence within the time specified for doing so.

(3) A restricted decree need not be advertised, but a copy must be served on the Defendants to whom it applies.

(4) Where the right to limit is not admitted or the Claimant seeks a general limitation decree in Admiralty Form No. ADM19, he must within 7 days of the date of the filing of the defence of the named Defendant last served or the expiry of the time for doing so, apply for an appointment before the Admiralty Registrar for a case management conference at which directions will be given for the further conduct of the proceedings.

9.3 (1) When a limitation decree is granted the Admiralty Court:

(a) may order that any proceedings relating to any claim arising out of the occurrence be stayed;

(b) may order the Claimant to establish a limitation fund if one has not been established or make such other arrangements for payment of claims against which liability is limited as the Court considers appropriate;

(c) may, if the decree is a restricted limitation decree, distribute the limitation fund;

(d) shall, if the decree is a general limitation decree, give directions as to advertisement of the decree and fix a time within which notice of claims against the fund must be filed or an application made to set aside the decree.

(2) When the Admiralty Court grants a general limitation decree the Claimant must:

(a) advertise it in such manner and within such time as the Court shall direct;

(b) file in the registry a declaration that the decree has been advertised in accordance with (a) and copies of the advertisements.

9.4 Any person other than a named Defendant may apply to the Admiralty Registrar within the time fixed in the decree to have a general limitation decree set aside. Any such application must be supported by a declaration proving that the person has a good faith claim against the Claimant arising out of the occurrence and sufficient grounds for contending that the Claimant is not entitled to the decree obtained, either in the amount of limitation or at all.

9.5 (1) A limitation fund may be established before or after a limitation claim has been commenced.

(2) If a limitation claim is not commenced within 75 days of the date the fund was established, the fund will lapse and all monies in court, including any interest accrued therein, will be repaid to the person making the payment into court. The lapsing of a limitation fund shall not prevent the establishment of a new fund.

9.6 (1) The Claimant may constitute a limitation fund by paying into court the sterling equivalent of the number of special drawing rights to which he claims to be entitled to limit his liability under the Merchant Shipping Act 1995 together with interest thereon from the date of the occurrence giving rise to his liability to the date of payment into court.

(2) Where the Claimant does not know the sterling equivalent of the said number of special drawing rights on the date of payment into court he may calculate the same on the basis of the latest available published sterling equivalent of a special drawing right as fixed by the International Monetary Fund, and in the

event of the sterling equivalent of a special drawing right on the date of payment into court under paragraph (1) being different from that used for calculating the amount of that payment into court the Claimant may—

    (a) make up any deficiency by making a further payment into court which, if made within 14 days after the payment into court under paragraph (1), shall be treated, except for the purposes of the rules relating to the accrual of interest on money paid into court, as if it has been made on the date of that payment into court, or

    (b) apply to the Admiralty Court for payment out of any excess amount (together with any interest accrued thereon) paid into court under paragraph (1).

    (3) An application under paragraph 9.6(2)(b) may be made without notice to any party and must be supported by evidence to the satisfaction of the Court proving the sterling equivalent of the appropriate number of special drawing rights on the date of payment into court.

    (4) On making any payment into court under this rule, the Claimant shall give notice thereof in writing to every named Defendant, specifying the date of payment in, the amount paid in, the amount of interest included therein, the rate of such interest, and the period to which it relates.

The Claimant shall also give notice in writing to every Defendant of any excess amount (and any interest thereon) paid out to him under paragraph 9.6(2)(b).

    (5) Money paid into court under this paragraph shall not be paid out except under an order of the court.

  9.7 (1) A claim against the fund must be in Admiralty Form No. ADM20.

    (2) No later than the time fixed in the decree for filing claims, each of the Defendants must file and serve his statement of case on the limiting party and on all other Defendants. The statement of case must contain the particulars of the Defendant's claim. Any Defendant unable to do so must file a declaration in Admiralty Form No. ADM21 stating the reason for his inability. The declaration must be sworn as an affidavit.

    (3) Within 7 days of the time for filing claims or declarations, the Admiralty Registrar will fix a date for a case management conference at which directions will be given for the further conduct of the proceedings.

REFERENCES TO THE ADMIRALTY REGISTRAR

  10. (1) The Admiralty Court may at any stage in the claim refer any question or issue for determination by the Admiralty Registrar (a 'reference').

    (2) Unless otherwise ordered, where a reference has been ordered:

    (a) The Claimant must file and serve particulars of claim on all other parties within 14 days of the date of the order.

    (b) Any party opposing the claim must file a defence to the claim within 14 days of service of the particulars of claim upon him.

    (3) Within 7 days of the filing of the defence, the Claimant must apply for an appointment before the Admiralty Registrar for a case management conference at which directions will be given for the further conduct of the proceedings.

    (4) Any decision of the Admiralty Registrar on the hearing of the reference may be appealed to the Admiralty Judge, by Notice in Admiralty Form No. ADM25 filed within 75 days of the decision on the reference appealed against.

INSPECTION OF SHIP ETC.

  11 The Admiralty Court may, on the application of any interested persons or on its own initiative, make an order for the inspection by any person of any ship or other property, whether real or personal, the inspection of which may be necessary or desirable for the purpose of obtaining full information or evidence in connection with any issue in a claim or proposed claim whether *in rem* or *in personam*.

AGREEMENT OF SOLICITORS TO BE MADE AN ORDER OF THE COURT

  12 Subject to any restrictions contained in other Rules, any agreement in writing between the solicitors of the parties to any Admiralty claim dated and

signed by those solicitors may, if the Admiralty Registrar thinks it reasonable, be filed in the Admiralty and Commercial Registry and the agreement shall then become an order of the Admiralty Court.

UNDERTAKINGS

13 (1) Where in this practice direction any undertaking to the Marshal is required it shall be given in writing and to his satisfaction or in accordance with such other arrangements as he may require.

(2) Where any party is dissatisfied with a direction given by the Marshal in this respect he may apply to the Admiralty Registrar for a ruling.

STAY OF PROCEEDINGS

14 Where the Admiralty Court orders a stay of any claim *in rem*, any property under arrest in the action shall remain under arrest and any security representing the *res* shall remain in force unless the Court otherwise orders.

PROVISIONS FOR THE APPOINTMENT OF EXAMINERS IN ADMIRALTY ETC.

15 (1) The Admiralty Court may make an order with the consent of the parties for a deposition to be taken as if before an examiner but without the examiner actually being appointed or being present.

(2) Where an order is made under paragraph 15(1) provision may be made for any consequential matters, but in the absence of such provision the following provisions shall apply:

(a) the party whose witness is to be examined shall provide a shorthand writer to take down the evidence of the witness;

(b) any representative, being counsel or solicitor, of either of the parties shall have authority to administer the oath to the witness;

(c) the shorthand writer need not be sworn but shall certify in writing as correct a transcript of his notes of the evidence and deliver it to the solicitor for the party whose witness was examined, and that solicitor must file it in the Registry;

(d) unless the parties otherwise agree or the court otherwise orders, the transcript or a copy of it, shall be made available to the persons who acted as advocates at the examination before it is filed, and if any of those persons is of the opinion that the transcript does not accurately record the evidence he shall make a certificate specifying the corrections which in his opinion should be made and that certificate must be filed with the transcript.

(3) In a collision claim no order shall be made under CPR Part 34 authorising the examination of a witness before the Preliminary Acts have been filed, unless the Admiralty Court considers that there are special reasons for doing so.

(4) The Lord Chief Justice may appoint such number of barristers or solicitors as he thinks fit to act as examiners of the Admiralty Court in connection with Admiralty claims, and may revoke any such appointment.

THE COMMERCIAL COURT GUIDE

16.1 The practice of the Commercial Court set out in the Commercial Court Guide should, except where inapplicable, be followed in Admiralty proceedings subject to the provisions of this or any other Admiralty practice direction and to any order that may be made in an individual case.

16.2 Part D of the Commercial Court Guide shall be modified as follows:

(a) D3 shall not apply;

(b) In the Admiralty Court the Case Management Information Sheet should be in the form of Appendix 6 to the Commercial Court Guide but also include the following additional question:

(20) a. Do any of the issues contained in the List of Issues involve questions of navigation or other particular matters of an essentially Admiralty nature which require the trial to be before the Admiralty Judge or is there any other reason why you consider trial before the Admiralty Judge to be necessary?

b. Are you prepared to have the case tried before a deputy nominated by the Admiralty Judge who has experience of such questions or matters?

c. Do you consider that the court should sit with nautical or other Assessors? Are you intending to ask that the court sit with one or more Assessors who is not a Trinity Master? If so please state the reasons for such application.

16.3 One significant area of difference between practice in the Commercial Court and practice in the Admiralty Court is that in the Admiralty Court many interlocutory applications are normally heard by the Admiralty Registrar and this practice will continue, save as specifically mentioned elsewhere in this practice direction.

USE OF FAX WHEN REGISTRY IS CLOSED

17.1 When the Registry is closed (and only when it is closed) an Admiralty claim form may be issued on the following designated fax machine: 0171-936 6667 and only on that machine.

17.2 The procedure to be followed is set out in paragraph B3.11 and Appendix 3 of the Commercial Court Guide.

17.3 (1) When the Registry is closed (and only when it is closed) a notice requesting a caveat against release may be filed on the following designated fax machine: 0171-936 6056 and only on that machine. This machine is manned 24 hours a day by court security staff (telephone 0171-936 6000). The notice requesting the caveat should be transmitted with a note in the following form for ease of identification by security staff:

'CAVEAT AGAINST RELEASE

Please find notice requesting caveat against release of the . . . (name ship/ identify cargo) . . . for filing in the Admiralty Court and Commercial Registry.'

(2) The notice must be in Admiralty Form No. ADM11 and signed by a solicitor acting on behalf of the intending caveator.

17.4 (1) Subject to the provisions of paragraph 17.4(3) below, the filing of the notice takes place when the fax is recorded as having been received.

(2) When the Registry is next open to the public, the filing solicitor or his agent shall attend and deliver to the Registry the document which was transmitted by fax together with the transmission report. Upon satisfying himself that the document delivered fully accords with the document received by the Registry, the court office shall stamp the document delivered with the time and date at which the notice was received, enter the same in the caveat book and retain the same with the faxed copy.

(3) Unless otherwise ordered by the court, the stamped notice shall be conclusive proof that the notice was filed at the time and on the date stated.

(4) If the filing solicitor does not comply with the foregoing procedure, or if the notice is not stamped, the notice shall be deemed never to have been filed.

USE OF POSTAL FACILITIES IN THE REGISTRY

18.1 Applications together with the requisite documents may be posted to:
The Admiralty and Commercial Registry
Room E200
Royal Courts of Justice
Strand
London
WC2A 2LL

18.2 In addition to the classes of business for which the use of postal facilities is permitted by the CPR or the Commercial Court Guide, the filing of the following classes of documents shall also be permitted in Admiralty matters:

(1) Requests for notices of caveats
(2) Preliminary Acts
(3) Claims in References
(4) Agreements between solicitors under paragraph 12 of this practice direction.

18.3 Documents sent by post for filing must be accompanied by two copies of a list of the documents sent and an envelope properly addressed to the sender.

PD 49F PRACTICE DIRECTION — ADMIRALTY

18.4 On receipt of the documents in the Registry, the court officer will, if the circumstances are such that had the documents been presented personally they would have been filed, cause them to be filed and will, by post, notify the sender that this has been done. If the documents would not have been accepted if presented personally the court officer will not file them but will retain them in the Registry for collection by the sender and will, by post, so inform the sender.

18.5 When documents received through the post are filed by the court officer they will be sealed and entered as filed on the date on which they were received in the Registry.

DRAWING UP OF ORDERS

19 All orders made in Admiralty proceedings will be drawn up by the parties unless otherwise ordered by the court.

ASSESSORS

20.1 The usual practice in the Admiralty Court is to sit with Assessors when hearing collision claims or other cases involving issues of navigation or seamanship and the parties will not normally be permitted to call expert witnesses on matters of navigation or seamanship where the court sits with Assessors. The Assessors will usually be Trinity Masters. Parties should indicate at the Case Management Conference whether they consider that the case is suitable for Assessors and whether Assessors other than Trinity Masters would be appropriate.

20.2 Provision is made in CPR 35.15 for Assessors' remuneration. The usual practice is for the court to seek an undertaking from the claimant (or appellant) to pay the remuneration on demand after the case has concluded.

PD 49F PRACTICE DIRECTION — ADMIRALTY

Claim Form
(Admiralty claim in rem)

In the High Court of Justice
Queen's Bench Division
Admiralty Court

Claim No.	
Issue date	

SEAL

Admiralty claim in rem against

of the Port of

Claimant

Defendant(s)

Brief details of claim

The Admiralty Registry within the Royal Courts of Justice, Strand, London WC2A 2LC is open between 10am and 4.30pm Monday to Friday. District Registries with Admiralty jurisdiction are open between 10am and 4pm.
Please address all correspondence to the admiralty registry and quote the claim number.

ADM1 Claim form (Admiralty action in rem) (4.99)

Printed on behalf of The Court Service

PD 49F   PRACTICE DIRECTION — ADMIRALTY

	Claim No.	

Particulars of Claim (attached)(to follow)

Statement of Truth
*(I believe)(The Claimant believes) that the facts stated in these particulars of claim are true.
* I am duly authorised by the claimant to sign this statement

Full name _____

Name of claimant's solicitor's firm _____

signed _____ position or office held _____
*(Claimant)(Litigation friend)(Claimant's solicitor) (if signing on behalf of firm or company)
*delete as appropriate

Claimant's or claimant's solicitor's address to which documents or payments should be sent if different from overleaf including (if appropriate) details of DX, fax or e-mail.

PD 49F PRACTICE DIRECTION — ADMIRALTY

Notes for Claimant on completing an IN REM claim form

Further information may be obtained from the Admiralty & Commercial Registry, room E200 Royal Courts of Justice, London, WC2A 2LL. Tel. 0171 936 6112 Fax. 0171 936 6245.

Please read all these guidance notes before you begin completing the claim form. The notes follow the order in which information is required on the form.

You may only issue an IN REM claim form in the Admiralty Court of the High Court (The High Court means either a District Registry attached to a County Court or the Royal Courts of Justice in London).

Staff can help you fill in the claim form and give information about the procedure once it has been issued. But they cannot give legal advice. If you need legal advice, for example, about the likely success of your claim or the evidence you need to prove it, you should contact a solicitor or a Citizens Advice Bureau.

If you are filling in the claim form by hand, please use black ink and write in block capitals.

Copy the completed claim form and the defendant's notes for guidance so that you have one copy for yourself, one copy for the court and one copy for each Defendant. **You will need an additional copy of the claim form if you are seeking to arrest a vessel.** Send or take the forms to the court office with the appropriate fee. The court will tell you how much this is.

N.B. The time for filing an Acknowledgment of Service in an IN REM claim is within 14 days of service of the CLAIM FORM irrespective of whether or not the PARTICULARS OF CLAIM are served with it. The CLAIM FORM must therefore be served with the forms on which the defendant may reply to your claim.

Notes on completing the claim form

Heading

You should add to the heading the name of the court in which you are issuing:

either 'Royal Courts of Justice' or

'.................................... District Registry'

(inserting name of the District Registry)

Ship and port details

You should supply the name of the vessel or vessels you are proceeding against and the **Port of Registry** (**not** the Port where the vessel may be berthed). If you do not know the Port of Registry you should insert 'port of registry unknown'. If you are proceeding in addition or separately against other property, e.g. cargo, you should describe it.

Claimant details

As the person issuing the claim, you are called the 'claimant'. The person you are suing is called the 'defendant'. Claimants who are under 18 years old (unless otherwise permitted by the court), or patients within the meaning of the Mental Health Act 1983, must have a litigation friend to issue and conduct court proceedings on their behalf. Court staff will tell you more about what you need to do if this applies to you.

The Claimant in an in rem claim, whether or not an individual, may be named or described. If not named, you must provide a name upon the request of any other party. If described rather than named you must still give an address. See below as to the appropriate address.

Descriptions that may be used are 'The owners of the ship 'X' or 'The owners of cargo lately laden on board the vessel 'Y'. Court staff can advise you of other acceptable descriptions.

You must provide the following information about yourself according to the capacity in which you are suing. When suing as:-

an individual by name:
All known forenames and surname, (whether Mr, Mrs, Miss, Ms or Other e.g. Dr) and residential address (including postcode and telephone number) in England and Wales.

an individual by name who is under 18 write '(a child by Mr John Smith his litigation friend)' after the child's name

a patient within the meaning of the mental Health Act 1983
write "(by Mr John Smith his litigation friend)" after the patient's name

as an individual trading under another name
you must add the words "trading as" and the trading name e.g. "Mr John Smith trading as Smith's Groceries"

in a representative capacity
you must say what that capacity is e.g. "Mr John Smith as the representative of Mrs Mary Smith (deceased)

in the name of a club or other unincorporated association
add the words "suing on behalf of" followed by the name of the club or other unincorporated association.

a firm
Enter the name of the firm followed by the words "a firm" e.g. "Bandbox - a firm" and an address for service which is either a partner's residential address or the principal or last known place of business.

ADM1B Notes for claimant IN REM (4.99)   *Printed on behalf The Court Service*

PD 49F PRACTICE DIRECTION — ADMIRALTY

a corporation (other than a company)
Enter the full name of the corporation and the address which is either its principal office or any other place where the corporation carries on activities and which has a real connection with the claim

a company registered in England and Wales:
Enter the name of the company and an address which is either the company's registered office or any place of business that has a real, or the most, connection with the claim.

an overseas company (defined by s744 of the Companies Act 1985):
Enter the name of the company and either the address registered under s691 of the Act or the address of the place of business having a real or the most, connection with the claim

Defendant details

The defendant **must** be described and not named.

'The owners and/or demise charterers of the ship 'Z', unless it is known that the ship either is, or is not, under demise charter when the claim can be issued simply against 'the owners of the ship 'Z' or 'the demise charterers of the ship 'Z'

In ownership and/or possession actions, the defendant may be described as 'all other persons claiming ownership and/or possession of the ship 'A'.

When action is taken against cargo and/or freight the defendant may be described as 'owners of cargo now or lately laden on board the ship 'X' together with the freight earned thereon.

The defendant in an action against the proceeds of a Judicial sale by the Admiralty Marshal should be described as 'the owners of the proceeds of sale of the vessel 'Y'

Permutations of the above can be used as appropriate. The Court staff will advise you as necessary.

Brief details of claim

Note: the facts and full details about your claim should be set out in the 'particulars of claim' (see note under 'Particulars of Claim').

You must set out under **this** heading:

- a concise statement of the nature of your claim in rem
- the remedy you are seeking
- if your claim is for money, the amount you are claiming
- the amount of any interest you are claiming

If your claim is in foreign currency you should endorse the claim form with a certificate as to the sterling equivalent. Court staff will inform you of the appropriate certificate.

Particulars of claim

You may include your particulars of claim on the claim form in the space provided or in a separate document which you should head 'Particulars of Claim'. It should include the names and/or descriptions of the parties, the court, the claim number and your address for service and also contain a statement of truth. You should keep a copy for yourself, provide one for the court and one for each defendant.

Separate particulars of claim can either be served

- with the claim form **or**
- within 75 days after the date on which the claim form was served, provided that the service of the particulars of claim is not later than 12 months from the date of issue of the claim form.

Note: If the particulars of claim are not contained or served with the claim form you must include the following statement " Particulars of claim will follow if an acknowledgment of service is filed indicating an intention to defend the claim."

Your particulars of claim must include

- a concise statement of the facts on which you rely
- a statement (if applicable) to the effect that you are seeking aggravated damages or exemplary damages
- details of any interest which you are claiming
- any other matters required for your type of claim as set out in the relevant practice directions

Note: You are not required to complete and serve particulars of claim if your claim is in respect of a collision between ships.

Address for documents

Insert in this box the address at which you wish to receive documents and/or payments, if different from the address you have already given under the heading 'Claimant' The address must be in England or Wales. If you are willing to accept service by DX, fax or e-mail, add details

Statement of truth

This must be signed by you, by your solicitor or your litigation friend, as appropriate.

Where the claimant is a registered company or a corporation the claim must be signed by either the director, treasurer, secretary, chief executive, manager or other officer of the company or (in the case of a corporation) the mayor, chairman, president or town clerk.

PD 49F   PRACTICE DIRECTION — ADMIRALTY

Notes for defendant on replying to an in REM claim form

Please read these notes carefully - they may help you decide what to do about this claim. Further information can be obtained from the Admiralty & Commercial Registry, Royal Courts of Justice, Strand, London, WC2A 2LL.

You must file an acknowledgment of service within 14 days of the date of service of the Claim Form on your property (or a Solicitor acting on your behalf) irrespective of whether or not particulars of claim are served with it

If you do not file an acknowledgment of service, judgment may be given against you and if the property described on the claim form is under arrest of this court, it may be sold by order of the court.

You may either:

- pay the amount claimed
- provide security for the claim in a form acceptable to the Claimant
- admit that you owe all or part of the claim and ask for time to pay or
- dispute the claim.

The notes below tell you what to do.

The response pack, which should accompany the claim form, will tell you which forms to use for your reply.

Court staff can help you complete the forms of reply and tell you about court procedures. But they cannot give legal advice. If you need legal advice, for example about the likely success of disputing the claim, you should contact a solicitor or a Citizens Advice Bureau immediately.

Costs and Interest: Additional costs and interest may be added to the amount claimed on the front of the claim form if judgment is given against you.

Once your completed acknowledgment of service is received by the court, the claimant will send you the particulars of claim, unless previously sent to you.

Your response and what happens next

How to pay

Do not bring any payments to the court - they will not be accepted.

When making payments to the claimant, quote the claimant's reference (if any) and the claim number.

Make sure that you keep records and can account for any payments made. Proof may be required if there is any disagreement. It is not safe to send cash unless you use registered post.

Admitting the Claim

Claim for specified amount

If you admit all the claim, take or send the money, including any interest and costs, to the claimant at the address given for payment on the claim form within 14 days of receipt of the particulars of claim.

If you admit all the claim and you are asking for time to pay, complete Form N9A and send it to the claimant at the address given for payment on the claim form, within 14 days of receipt of the particulars of claim. The claimant will decide whether to accept your proposal for payment. If it is accepted, the claimant may request a judge to give judgment against you and you will be sent an order to pay. If your offer is not accepted, the judge will decide how you should pay or, if your vessel is under arrest, may order that your vessel be sold in order to satisfy the judgment.

If you admit only part of the claim, complete Form N9A and Form N9B (see "Disputing the Claim" overleaf) send them to the court within 14 days of receipt of the particulars of claim. At the same time send copies of the completed Forms N9A and N9B to the claimant who will decide whether to accept your part admission. If it is accepted, the claimant may request a judge to give judgment against you and the court will send you an order to pay or, if your vessel is under arrest, order that your vessel be sold in order to satisfy the judgment. If your part admission is not accepted, the case will proceed as a defended claim.

Claim for unspecified amount

If you admit liability for the whole claim but do not make an offer to satisfy the claim, complete Form N9C and send it to the court within 14 days of receipt of the particulars of claim. At the same time send a copy of the completed Form N9C to the claimant within the same period. The claimant may request a Judge to give judgment against you for an amount to be decided by the court, and costs. If your vessel is under arrest, the Judge may at the same time order that your vessel be sold.

If you admit liability for the claim and offer an amount of money to satisfy the claim, of receipt of the particulars of claim. At the same time send a copy of the completed Form N9C to the claimant. The claimant must indicate within 14 days if the offer is acceptable

PD 49F   PRACTICE DIRECTION — ADMIRALTY

and send you a copy. If a reply is not received, the claim will be stayed. If the amount you have offered is **accepted**, the claimant may request a Judge to give judgment against you for that amount.

If you have requested time to pay which is not accepted by the claimant, the rate of payment will be decided by the court, or, if your vessel is under arrest the court may order the vessel to be sold by the court

If your offer in satisfaction is not accepted.

The claimant may apply to the court for judgment against you for an amount to be decided by the court, and costs.

If your vessel is under arrest, order that your vessel be sold. You and the claimant will be sent a copy of the court's order.

Disputing the claim

If you are being sued as an individual for a specified amount of money and you dispute the claim, the claim may be transferred to your home court i.e. the one nearest your home or your solicitor's business address if different from the court where the claim was issued.

If you need longer than 14 days to prepare your defence or to contest the court's jurisdiction to try the claim, completion of the acknowledgment of service form will allow you 28 days from the date of service of the particulars of claim to serve your defence or make an application to contest the court's jurisdiction. The court will tell the claimant that your acknowledgment of service has been received.

If the case proceeds as a defended claim, the action will be allocated to the multi-track and the claimant will apply for a date to be fixed for a Case Management Conference before a Judge. You and the claimant will be required to file a completed case management information sheet at least 7 days before the Conference.

Further details are available from the Admiralty & Commercial Registry.

If your vessel is under the arrest of the court and you are disputing the claim you may nevertheless obtain the release of the vessel if you are able to offer security for the claim in a form acceptable by the claimant.

Claim for specified amount

If you wish to dispute the full amount claimed or wish to claim against the claimant (a counterclaim), complete Form N9B and send it to the court within 14 days of receipt of the particulars of claim. Send a copy of the completed Form N9B to the claimant within the same period.

If you admit part of the claim, complete the defence Form N9B and the Admission Form N9A and send them to the court within 14 days of receipt of the particulars of claim. At the same time send copies of the completed Forms N9B and N9A to the claimant within the same period.

If you dispute the claim because you have already paid it, complete Form N9B and send it to the court within 14 days of receipt of the particulars of claim. At the same time send a copy of the completed Form N9B to the claimant within the same period. The claimant will decide whether to proceed with the claim or withdraw it and notify the court and you within 28 days. If the claimant wishes to proceed, the case will proceed as a defended claim.

Claim for unspecified amount/non-money claims

If you dispute the claim or wish to claim against the claimant (counterclaim), complete Form N9D and send it to the court within 14 days of receipt of the particulars of claim. At the same time send a copy of the completed Form N9D to the claimant.

Personal injuries claims:

If the claim is for personal injuries and the claimant has attached a medical report to the particulars of claim, in your defence you should state whether you:

    agree with the report **or**

    dispute all or part of the report **and** give

    your reasons for doing so **or**

    neither agree nor dispute the report **or**

    have no knowledge of the report

Where you have obtained your own medical report, you should attach it to your defence.

If the claim is for personal injuries and the claimant has attached a schedule of past and future expenses and losses, in your defence you must state which of the items you:

    agree **or**

    dispute **and** supply alternative figures where appropriate **or**

    neither agree nor dispute or have no knowledge of

Statement of truth

This must be signed by you, by your solicitor or your litigation friend, as appropriate.

Where the defendant is **a registered company or a corporation** the response must be signed by either the director, treasurer, secretary, chief executive, manager or other officer of the company **or** (in the case of a corporation) the mayor, chairman, president or town clerk.

PD 49F   PRACTICE DIRECTION — ADMIRALTY

Response Pack
Admiralty claim in rem

You should read the 'notes for defendant' attached to the claim form which will tell you when and where to send the forms

Included in this pack are:
- **either Admission Form N9A**
  (if the claim is for a specified amount) or
  Admission Form N9C
  (if the claim is for an unspecified amount or is not a claim for money)
- **either Defence and Counterclaim Form N9B** (if the claim is for a specified amount) or **Defence and Counterclaim Form N9D** (if the claim is for an unspecified amount or is not a claim for money)
- **Acknowledgment of service** (see below)

You are required to complete an Acknowledgment of Service form within 14 days from service of the Claim Form on you whether or not Particulars of claim are served with the Claim Form.

Complete

If you admit the claim or the amount claimed and/or you want time to pay	the admission form
If you admit part of the claim	the admission form and the defence form
If you dispute the whole claim or wish to make a claim (a counterclaim) against the claimant	the defence form
If you need longer than 14 days to prepare your defence or to contest the court's jurisdiction to try the claim, completion of the acknowledgment of service form will allow you 28 days from service of particulars of claim to do so	the acknowledgment of service
If you do nothing, the claimant may ask a judge to give judgment against you and, if your vessel is under arrest, also request that your vessel be sold	

Acknowledgment of Service
Admiralty claim in rem

Description of defendant(s) :-

In the High Court of Justice
Queen's Bench Division
Admiralty Court

Claim No.	
Claimant(s) (including ref.)	
Defendant(s)	

Full name of person described above:-

Nature of ownership of property

The court office at

is open between 10am and 4.30pm Monday to Friday. Please address forms or letters to the Court Manager and quote the claim number.
ADM2 Acknowledgment of Service (4.99)   *Printed on behalf of The Court Service*

PD 49F   PRACTICE DIRECTION — ADMIRALTY

Address to which documents about this claim should be sent (including reference if appropriate)

		if applicable
	fax no.	
	DX no.	
Tel. no. Postcode	e-mail	

If you do not file an acknowledgment of service within 14 days of the claim form on you, whether or not particulars of claim are served with it, judgment may be given against you.

Tick the appropriate box

1. I intend to defend all of this claim ☐

2. I intend to defend part of this claim ☐

3. I intend to contest jurisdiction ☐

If you file an acknowledgment of service but do not file a defence within 28 days of the date of service of the particulars of claim, judgment may be given against you.

If you do not file an application within 28 days of the date of service of the particulars of claim it will be assumed that you accept the court's jurisdiction and judgment may be given against you.

Signed		**Position or office held** (if signing on behalf of firm or company)		**Date**	
	(Defendant)(Defendant's Solicitor) (Litigation friend)				

PD 49F PRACTICE DIRECTION — ADMIRALTY

Warrant of Arrest

In the High Court of Justice
Queen's Bench Division
Admiralty Court

Claim No.

Admiralty action in rem against:

Claimant(s)

Defendant(s)

ELIZABETH THE SECOND, by the Grace of God, of the United Kingdom of Great Britain and Northern Ireland and of Our other realms and territories Queen, Head of the Commonwealth, Defender of the Faith:

To the Admiralty Marshal of Our High Court of Justice, and to all singular his substitutes, Greeting. We hereby command you to arrest the ship

of the port of   and to keep same under arrest until you should receive further orders from Us.

WITNESS   , Lord High Chancellor of Great Britain, the   day of

The Claimant's claim is for [copy from Claim Form]

Taken out by

Solicitors for the

ADM9 Warrant of arrest (4.99)   Printed on behalf of The Court Service

Certificate as to Service

On the   day of

the within-named ship

lying at

was arrested by virtue of

for a short time on*

of the said ship, and on taking off the process, by leaving a copy thereof fixed in its place.

Signed: Date

*State on
which part of
the outside of
the ship's
superstructure

PD 49F   PRACTICE DIRECTION — ADMIRALTY

Claim Form (Admiralty limitation claim)	In the High Court of Justice Queen's Bench Division Admiralty Court
	Claim No.
	Issue date

Claimant(s)

SEAL

Defendant(s)

Details of limitation claim *(see also overleaf)*

Named defendant's name and address

The Admiralty Registry within the Royal Courts of Justice, Strand, London WC2A 2LC is open between 10am and 4.30pm Monday to Friday. District Registries with Admiralty jurisdiction are open between 10am and 4pm.
Please address all correspondence to the admiralty registry and quote the claim number.

ADM15 Claim form Admiralty limitation claim(4.99)   *Printed on behalf of The Court Service*

PD 49F   PRACTICE DIRECTION — ADMIRALTY

	Claim No.	

Details of limitation claim *(continued)*

Full name _____

Name of claimant's solicitor's firm _____

signed _____ position or office held _____

*(Claimant)(Litigation friend)(Claimant's solicitor) (if signing on behalf of firm or company)

*delete as appropriate

Claimant's or claimant's solicitor's address to which documents or payments should be sent if different from overleaf including (if appropriate) details of DX, fax or e-mail.

PD 49F   PRACTICE DIRECTION — ADMIRALTY

Notes for claimant on completing a claim form in an admiralty limitation claim

Further information may be obtained from the Admiralty and Commercial Registry, room E200 Royal Courts of Justice, London, WC2A 2LL. Tel. 0171 936 6112   Fax. 0171 936 6245.

Please read all these guidance notes before you begin completing the claim form. The notes generally follow the order in which information is required on the form.

You may only issue an Admiralty Limitation Claim Form in the Admiralty Court of the High Court (The High Court means either a District Registry (attached to a County Court) or the Royal Courts of Justice in London.)

Staff can help you fill in the claim form and give information about the procedure once it has been issued. But they cannot give legal advice. If you need legal advice, for example about the likely success of your claim or the evidence you need to prove it, you should contact a solicitor or a Citizens Advice Bureau.

If you are filling in the claim form by hand, please use black ink and write in block capitals.

You should file a sworn declaration at the court with your completed claim form:
- proving the facts you rely on in your claim; and
- stating the names and addresses (if known) of all persons who to your knowledge have claims against you in respect of the occurrence to which the claim relates (other than named defendants)

Copy the completed claim form, the defendant's notes for guidance and your sworn declaration so that you have one copy for yourself, one for the court and one for each 'named' defendant (see defendant details below). Send or take the forms to the court office with the appropriate fee. The court will tell you how much this is.

Each named defendant must be served with copies of the claim form, notes for guidance, your declaration and a response pack (ADM Form Nos 15, 15A, 15B, 16 and 16A).

Notes on completing the claim form

Heading

You should add to the heading the name of the court in which you are issuing:

either   'Royal Courts of Justice' or

'.................................. District Registry'

(inserting name of the District Registry)

Defendant details

At least one of the defendants in a limitation claim **must** be named.

All other defendants may be described e.g. "and all other persons claiming or being entitled to claim damages by reason of, or rising out of the collision between the ship "Alpha" and the ship "Omega" which occurred in the English Channel on or about the 6th October, 1999"

Claimant and named defendant details

The Claimant must be named not described.

As the person issuing the claim, you are called the "claimant"; the person you are suing is called the "defendant". Claimants who are under 18 years old (unless otherwise permitted by the court) and patients within the meaning of the Mental Health Act 1983 must have a litigation friend to issue and conduct court proceedings on their behalf. Court staff will tell you more about what you need to do if this applies to you.

You must provide the following information about yourself **and** the named defendants according to the capacity in which you are suing and in which the defendant is being sued.

When suing or being sued as :-

an individual: All known forenames and surname, (whether Mr, Mrs, Miss, Ms or Other e.g. Dr) and residential address **(including** postcode and telephone no. and any fax or e-mail number) in England and Wales. Where the defendant is a proprietor of a business, a partner in a firm or an individual sued in the name of a club or other unincorporated association, the address for service should be the usual or last known place of residence **or** principal place of business of the company, firm or club or other unincorporated association.

Where the individual is: under 18 write "(a child by Mr. John Smith his litigation friend)" after the child's name.

If the child is conducting proceedings on their own behalf write "(a child)" after the child's name.

a patient within the meaning of the Mental Health Act 1983 write "(by Mr. John Smith his litigation friend)" after the patient's name.

trading under another name you must add the words "trading as" and the trading name e.g. Mr. John Smith trading as Smith's Groceries".

suing or being sued in a representative capacity you must say what that capacity is e.g. "Mr. John Smith as the representative of Mrs Mary Smith (deceased).

suing or being sued in the name of a club or other unincorporated association add the words "suing/sued on behalf of" followed by the name of the club or other unincorporated association.

ADM15A Notes for Defendant(4.99)   *Printed on behalf of The Court Service*

792

PD 49F   PRACTICE DIRECTION — ADMIRALTY

a firm enter the name of the firm followed by the words "a firm" e.g. "Bandbox - a firm" and an address for service which is either a partner's residential address or the principal or last known place of business.

a corporation (other than a company) enter the full name of the corporation and the address which is either its principal office **or** any other place where the corporation carries on activities and which has a real connection with the claim.

a company registered in England and Wales enter the name of the company and an address which is either the company's registered office **or** any place of business that has a real, or the most, connection with the claim.

an overseas company (defined by s744 of the Companies Act 1985) enter the name of the company and either the address registered under s691 of the Act **or** the address of the place of business having a real, or the most, connection with the claim.

Details of claim

Under this heading you must set out:

- a brief description of the incident for which you are claiming to have your liability limited, including the date and place of the incident

- that your claim is limited to the provisions of the Merchant Shipping Act 1995

- that you are seeking all necessary and proper directions for the purposes of ascertaining and distributing the amount of your liability between the parties who are entitled to receive it.

Named defendant's name and address

Enter in this box the full name and address of the named defendant(s) to be served with the claim form (ie. one claim form for each defendant)

An Admiralty Limitation Claim form may NOT be served outside of England & Wales unless:

(a) the case falls within section 22(2)(a) to (c) of the Supreme Court Act 1981; or

(b) the defendant has submitted to or agreed to submit to the jurisdiction of the Admiralty Court; or

(c) the Admiralty Court has jurisdiction over such claim under any applicable Convention

Address for documents

Insert in this box the address at which you wish to receive documents, if different from the address you have already given under the heading "Claimant". The address you give must be either that of your solicitors or your residential or business address and must be in England and Wales. If you live or carry on business outside of England and Wales, you can give some other address within England and Wales. If you are willing to accept service by DX, fax or e-mail, add details.

793

PD 49F PRACTICE DIRECTION — ADMIRALTY

Notes for defendant (admiralty limitation claim)

Please read these notes carefully - they will help you decide what to do about this claim.

Further information may be obtained from the Admiralty and Commercial Registry, Room E200, Royal Courts of Justice, Strand, London WC2A 2LL. Tel: 0171 936 6112. Fax: 0171 936 6245.

You have only a limited time to reply to this claim - the notes below tell you what to do.

You may either:

- dispute the court's jurisdiction or contend that the court should not exercise it
- admit the claimant's right to limit liability
- dispute the claim

The response pack, which should accompany the claim form, will tell you which forms to use for your reply

If you **do not** respond in any way the court may grant the claimant a Limitation Decree in your absence

Court staff can tell you about procedures but they cannot give legal advice. If you need legal advice, you should contact a solicitor or Citizens Advice Bureau immediately.

Responding to this claim

Time for responding

You have from the date the claim form was served on you: 14 days to file an acknowledgment of service disputing the court's jurisdiction
or
28 days to file a completed defence or admission of the claimant's right to limit liability

(or, if the claim form was served outside of England and Wales, within the time specified by RSC Order 11 r.1A.)

If the claim form was:
- sent by post, the date of service is taken as the second day after posting (see date of postmark on the envelope)
- delivered or left at your address, the date of service will be the day after it was delivered.
- handed to you personally, the date of service will be the day it was given to you.

Completing the acknowledgment of service

You should tick either
- Box A - if you dispute the court's jurisdiction **or**
- Box B - if you contend that the court should not exercise its jurisdiction

and complete all the other details on the form.

You should send the completed form to the court and at the same time send a copy to the claimant.
You should file also an application at the court within 14 days of filing of your acknowledgment of service. The court will arrange a hearing date for the application.

If you do not file the application you will be treated as having accepted that the court has jurisdiction to hear the claim.

Completing the admission

You should complete admission form ADM16 and send it to the court and at the same time send a copy to the claimant. The claimant may file an application for the court to issue a restricted limitation decree limiting liability against any of the named defendants in the claim form who have filed an admission.

Completing the defence

You should file defence form ADM16A at the court and at the same time send a copy to the claimant. Within 7 days of filing of your defence (or filing of defence of other named defendants or expiry of the time for doing so) the claimant must apply for an appointment before the Admiralty Registrar for a case management conference. The court will give directions at this appointment for the future conduct of the case.

Statement of truth

This must be signed by you, by your solicitor or your litigation friend, as appropriate

If you do nothing

The claimant may apply for a limitation decree against you.

ADM15B Notes for Defendant(4.99)   *Printed on behalf of The Court Service*

PD 49F   PRACTICE DIRECTION — ADMIRALTY

Notice of admission of right of claimant to limit liability

In the **High Court of Justice
Queen's Bench Division
Admiralty Court**

Claimant(s)

Claim No.

Defendant(s)

TAKE NOTICE THAT pursuant to Part Y, rule 8.1(7) Admiralty Proceedings, the following defendant(s) *(name them)*

admit the right of the claimant in this action to limit their liability in accordance with the provisions of *(give details of the relevant Act)*

Signed

Date

ADM16 Notice of admission of right of claimant to limit liability (4.99)   *Printed on behalf of The Court Service*

PD 49F   PRACTICE DIRECTION — ADMIRALTY

Defence to admiralty limitation claim	**In the** High Court of Justice Queen's Bench Division Admiralty Court
Claimant(s)	**Claim No.**
Defendant(s)	

You have a limited number of days to file and serve this form. See notes for guidance attached to the claim form.

Signed
(To be signed by you or by your solicitor or litigation friend)

*(I believe)(The defendant believes) that the facts stated in this form are true. *I am duly authorised by the defendant to sign this statement

*delete as appropriate

Position or office held
(if signing on behalf of firm or company)

Date

Give an address to which notices about this case can be sent to you

Postcode

Tel. no.

if applicable

fax no.

DX no.

e-mail

ADM16A Defence to admiralty limitation claim (4.99)

Printed on behalf of The Court Service

PD 49F   PRACTICE DIRECTION — ADMIRALTY

Response Pack
(Admiralty Limitation claim)

You should read the 'notes for defendant' attached to the claim form which will tell you when and where to send the forms.

Included in this pack are:

Admission Form	Defence Form	Acknowledgment of service
ADM16	ADM16A	*(see below)*

Complete

If you wish to dispute the court's jurisdiction or argue that the court should not exercise its jurisdiction	the acknowledgment of service
If you admit the right of the claimant to limit liability	the admission form
If you dispute the claim	the defence form
If you do nothing, the claimant may apply for a restricted limitation decree against you	

Acknowledgment of Service
(Admiralty limitation claim)

Defendant's full name if different from the name given on the claim form

In the	High Court of Justice Queen's Bench Division Admiralty Court
Claim No.	
Claimant (including ref.)	
Defendant	

Address to which documents about this claim should be sent (including reference if appropriate)

if applicable

fax no.

DX no.

Tel. no.   Postcode

e-mail

Tick the appropriate box

A   I intend to dispute jurisdiction   ☐

B   I intend to argue that the court should not exercise its jurisdiction   ☐

You should file an application at the court within 14 days of service of this acknowledgment of service or you will be treated as having accepted the court's jurisdiction.

Signed
(Defendant)(Defendant's solicitor) (Litigation friend)

Position or office held
(if signing on behalf of firm or company)

Date

The Admiralty Registry within the Royal Courts of Justice, Strand, London WC2A 2LC is open between 10am and 4.30pm Monday to Friday. District Registries with Admiralty jurisdiction are open between 10am and 4pm.
Please address all correspondence to the admiralty registry and quote the claim number.

ADM16B Response Pack (4.99)   *Printed on behalf of The Court Service*

PD 49G PRACTICE DIRECTION — ARBITRATIONS

This practice direction supplements CPR Part 49 and replaces, with modifications, Order 73 of the Rules of the Supreme Court

PART I

THE OVERRIDING OBJECTIVE

1. This Part of this practice direction is founded on the general principles in section 1 of the Arbitration Act and shall be construed accordingly.

MEANING OF ARBITRATION APPLICATION

2.1 Subject to paragraph 22.2, 'arbitration application' means the following:
(1) an application to the court under the Arbitration Act;
(2) proceedings to determine:
  (a) whether there is a valid arbitration agreement;
  (b) whether an arbitration tribunal is properly constituted;
  (c) what matters have been submitted to arbitration in accordance with an arbitration agreement;
(3) proceedings to declare that an award made by an arbitral tribunal is not binding on a party;
(4) any other application affecting arbitration proceedings (whether instituted or anticipated) or to construe or affecting an arbitration agreement.

2.2 In this Part, an arbitration application does not include proceedings to enforce an award:
(1) to which Part III applies; or
(2) by a claim on the award.

INTERPRETATION

3. In this Part:
'applicant' means the party making an arbitration application and references to respondent shall be construed accordingly;
'the Arbitration Act' means the Arbitration Act 1996 and any expressions used in this Part and in Part I of the Arbitration Act have the same meanings in this Part as they have in that Part of the Arbitration Act.
'arbitration claim form' means the arbitration claim form by the issue of which an arbitration application is begun.

FORM AND CONTENT OF ARBITRATION CLAIM FORM

4.1 An arbitration claim form must be in the practice form No. 8A
4.2 Every arbitration claim form must:
(1) include a concise statement of
  (a) the remedy claimed, and
  (b) (where appropriate) the questions on which the applicant seeks the determination or direction of the Court;
(2) give details of any arbitration award that is challenged by the applicant, showing the grounds for any such challenge;
(3) where the applicant claims an order for costs, identify the respondent against whom the claim is made,
(4) (where appropriate) specify the section of the Arbitration Act under which the application is brought; and
(5) show that any statutory requirements have been satisfied including those set out, by way of example, in the Table below.

PD 49G PRACTICE DIRECTION — ARBITRATIONS

Application made	Statutory requirements
section 9 (stay of legal proceedings)	see section 9 (3)
section 12 (extensions of time for beginning arbitral proceedings)	see section 12 (2)
section 18 (failure of appointment procedure)	see section 18 (2)
section 21 (umpires)	see section 21 (5)
section 24 (removal of arbitrators)	see section 24 (2)
section 32 (preliminary point of jurisdiction)	see section 32 (3)
section 42 (enforcement of peremptory orders)	see section 42 (3)
section 44 (powers in support of arbitral proceedings)	see section 44 (4), (5)
section 45 (preliminary point of law)	see section 45 (3)
section 50 (extension of time for making award)	see section 50 (2)
section 56 (power to withhold award)	see section 56 (4)
sections 67, 68 (challenging the award)	see section 70 (2), (3)
section 69 (appeal on point of law)	see sections 69 (2), (4), 70(2), (3)
section 77 (service of documents)	see section 77(3)

4.3 The arbitration claim form must also state:

(1) whether it is made on notice or without notice and, if made on notice, must give the names and addresses of the persons on whom it is to be served, stating their role in the arbitration and whether they are made respondents to the application;

(2) whether (having regard to paragraph 15) the application will be heard by a judge sitting in public or in private; and

(3) the date and time when the application will be heard or that such date has not yet been fixed.

4.4 Every arbitration claim form shall be indorsed with the applicant's address for service in accordance with CPR Rule 6.5(2)

ISSUE OF ARBITRATION CLAIM FORM

5.1 These paragraphs (5.1 to 5.7) are is to be read with the provisions of the High Court and County Courts (Allocation of Arbitration Proceedings) Order 1996 which allocates proceedings under the Arbitration Act to the High Court and the county courts and specifies proceedings which may be commenced or taken only in the High Court or in a county court.

5.2 These paragraphs (5.1 to 5.7) do not apply to applications under section 9 of the Arbitration Act to stay legal proceedings.

5.3 Subject to paragraphs 5.1 and 5.2 above, an arbitration claim form by which proceedings are commenced may be issued:

(1) out of the Admiralty and Commercial Registry in the Royal Courts of Justice, in which case the arbitration application will be entered into the commercial list;

(2) out of a district registry where a Mercantile Court has been established, in which case the arbitration application will be entered into the list of that Mercantile Court; or

(3) out of the office of the Central London County Court, in which case the arbitration application will be entered into the Business List of that court.

(Attention is drawn to the provisions relating to the commencement of proceedings contained in the Commercial Court Practice Direction and the Mercantile Court and Business Lists Practice Direction which supplement CPR Part 49).

5.4 Except where an arbitration claim form is issued out of the Admiralty and Commercial Registry, the Judge in charge of the list into which the arbitration application has been entered shall:

(1) as soon as practicable after the issue of the arbitration claim form, and

(2) in consultation with the Judge in charge of the commercial list,

consider whether the application should be transferred to the Commercial Court or to any another list.

5.5 Where an arbitration claim form is issued out of the Admiralty and Commercial Registry, the Judge in charge of the commercial list may at any time after the issue of the arbitration claim form transfer the application to another list, court or Division of the High Court to which he has power to transfer proceedings.

5.6 In considering whether to transfer an arbitration application, the Judges referred to in paragraphs 5.4 and 5.5 shall have regard to the criteria specified in article 5(4) of the High Court and County Courts (Allocation of Arbitration Proceedings) Order 1996 and the application shall be transferred if those Judges so decide.

5.7 In this practice direction 'Judge in charge of the list' means:

  (a) In relation to the commercial list, a judge of the Commercial Court;

  (b) in relation to the list of a Mercantile Court, a Circuit mercantile judge of that court; and

  (c) in relation to the Business List in the Central London County Court, a Circuit Judge authorised to deal with cases in that list,

but nothing in this paragraph shall be construed as preventing the powers of a judge of the Commercial Court from being exercised by any judge of the High Court.

STAY OF LEGAL PROCEEDINGS

6.1 An application notice by which an application under section 9 of the Arbitration Act to stay legal proceedings is made shall be served:

  (1) in accordance with CPR Rule 6.5 on the party bringing the relevant legal proceedings and on any other party to those proceedings who has given an address for service; and

  (2) on any party to those legal proceedings who has not given an address for service, by sending to him (whether or not he is within the jurisdiction) at his last known address or at a place where it is likely to come to his attention, a copy of the application notice for his information.

6.2 Where a question arises as to whether an arbitration agreement has been concluded or as to whether the dispute which is the subject-matter of the proceedings falls within the terms of such an agreement, the Court may determine that question or give directions for its determination, in which case it may order the proceedings to be stayed pending the determination of that question.

SERVICE OF ARBITRATION CLAIM FORM

7.1 Subject to paragraphs 7.2 and 7.4 below and to paragraphs 6.1 and 8.1 to 8.4, an arbitration claim form shall be served in accordance with CPR Part 6.

7.2 Where the Court is satisfied on an application made without notice that

  (1) arbitral proceedings are taking place, or an arbitration award has been made, within the jurisdiction; and

  (2) an arbitration application is being made in connection with those arbitral proceedings or being brought to challenge the award or to appeal on a question of law arising out of the award; and

  (3) the respondent to the arbitration application (not being an individual residing or carrying on business within the jurisdiction or a body corporate having a registered office or a place of business within the jurisdiction)

    (a) is or was represented in the arbitral proceedings by a solicitor or other agent within the jurisdiction who was authorised to receive service of any notice or other document served for the purposes of those proceedings; and

    (b) has not (at the time when the arbitration application is made) determined the authority of that solicitor or agent,

the Court may authorise service of the arbitration claim form to be effected on the solicitor or agent instead of the respondent.

7.3 An order made under paragraph 7.2 must limit a time within which the respondent must acknowledge service and a copy of the order and of the arbitration claim form must be sent by post to the respondent at his address out of the jurisdiction.

7.4 Where an applicant has made an arbitration application (the first arbitration application) and a subsequent arbitration application arising out of the same arbitration or arbitration agreement is made by a party to the first arbitration application (other than the applicant), that party's arbitration claim form may be served in accordance with CPR rule 6.5 or may be served on the applicant at his address for service given in his arbitration claim form, and on any other party to the first arbitration application at the address for service given in that party's acknowledgement of service in the first arbitration application, and on any further arbitration application the same provisions as to service will apply.

7.5 For the purposes of service, an arbitration claim form is valid in the first instance:

(1) where service is to be effected out of the jurisdiction, for such period as the Court may fix;

(2) In any other case, for one month, beginning with the date of its issue.

SERVICE OUT OF THE JURISDICTION

8.1 The Court may give permission to serve an arbitration claim form out of the jurisdiction if the arbitration application falls into one of the categories mentioned in the following table and satisfies the conditions specified.

Nature of application	Conditions to be satisfied
1. The applicant seeks to challenge, or to appeal to the Court on a question of law arising out of, an arbitration award.	Award must have been made in England & Wales. Section 53 of the Arbitration Act shall apply for determining the place where award is treated as made.
2. The application is for an order under section 44 of the Arbitration Act (Court powers exercisable in support of arbitral proceedings). Where the application is for an interim remedy in support of arbitral proceedings which are taking (or will take) place outside England and Wales, the Court may give permission for service out of the jurisdiction notwithstanding that no other remedy is sought.	None.
3. The applicant seeks some other remedy or requires a question to be determined by the court, affecting an arbitration (whether pending or anticipated), an arbitration agreement or an arbitration award.	The seat of the arbitration is or will be in England & Wales or the conditions in Section 2(4) of the Arbitration Act are satisfied.

8.2 An application for the grant of permission under paragraph 8.1 must be supported by an affidavit or witness statement:

(1) stating, or, if the grounds were set out in the application notice, confirming the grounds on which the application is made; and

(2) showing in what place or country the person to be served is, or probably may be found, and no such permission shall be granted unless it shall be made sufficiently to appear to the Court that the case is a proper one for service out of the jurisdiction under this paragraph.

8.3 RSC Order 11, rules 5 to 8 (Schedule 1 to the CPR) shall apply to the service of an arbitration claim form under this paragraph as they apply to the service of other claim forms.

8.4 Any order made on an arbitration application may be served out of the jurisdiction with the permission of the court.

EVIDENCE IN SUPPORT OF ARBITRATION APPLICATION

9.1 The applicant shall file an affidavit or witness statement in support of the arbitration application which sets out the evidence on which he intends to rely and a copy of every affidavit or witness statement so filed must be served with the arbitration claim form.

9.2 Where an arbitration application is made with the written agreement of all the other parties to the arbitral proceedings or with the permission of the arbitral tribunal, the affidavit or witness statement in support must

(1) give details of the agreement or, as the case may be, permission; and

(2) exhibit copies of any document which evidences that agreement or permission.

REQUIREMENTS AS TO NOTICE

10.1 Where the Arbitration Act requires that an application to the Court is to be made upon notice to other parties notice shall be given by making those parties respondents to the application and serving on them the arbitration claim form and any affidavit or witness statement in support.

10.2 Where an arbitration application is made under section 24, 28 or 56 of the Arbitration Act, the arbitrators or, in the case of an application under section 24, the arbitrator concerned shall be made respondents to the application and notice shall be given by serving on them the arbitration claim form and any affidavit or witness statement in support.

10.3 In cases where paragraph 10.2 does not apply, an applicant shall be taken as having complied with any requirement to give notice to the arbitrator if he sends a copy of the arbitration claim form to the arbitrator for his information at his last known address with a copy of any affidavit or witness statement in support.

10.4 This paragraph does not apply to applications under section 9 of the Arbitration Act to stay legal proceedings.

ACKNOWLEDGMENT OF SERVICE

11.1 Service of an arbitration claim form may be acknowledged by completing an acknowledgment of service in Form No. N15A in accordance with CPR Rule 8.3.

11.2 A respondent who:

(1) fails to acknowledge service within the time limited for so doing; or

(2) having indicated on his acknowledgment of service that he does not intend to contest the arbitration application, then wishes to do so, shall not be entitled to contest the application without the permission of the Court.

11.3 The Court will not give notice of the date on which an arbitration application will be heard to a respondent who has failed to acknowledge service.

11.4 The failure of a respondent to give notice of intention to contest the arbitration application or to acknowledge service shall not affect the applicant's duty to satisfy the Court that the order applied for should be made.

11.5 This paragraph does not apply to:

(1) applications under section 9 of the Arbitration Act to stay legal proceedings; or

(2) subsequent arbitration applications.

ACKNOWLEDGMENT OF SERVICE, ETC., BY ARBITRATOR

12.1 An arbitrator who is sent a copy of an arbitration claim form for his information may make

(1) a request (without notice to any party) to be made a respondent; or

(2) representations to the Court under this rule,

and, where an arbitrator is ordered to be made a respondent, he shall acknowledge service within 14 days of the making of that order.

12.2 An arbitrator who wishes to make representations to the Court under this rule may file an affidavit or witness statement or make representations in writing to the Court.

12.3 The arbitrator shall as soon as is practicable send a copy of any document filed or made under paragraph 12.2 to all the parties to the arbitration application.

12.4 Nothing in this paragraph shall require the Court to admit a document filed or made under sub-paragraph (2) and the weight to be given to any such document shall be a matter for the Court.

AUTOMATIC DIRECTIONS

13.1 Unless the Court otherwise directs, the following directions shall take effect automatically.

13.2 A respondent who wishes to put evidence before the Court in response to any affidavit or witness statement filed in support of an arbitration application shall serve his affidavit or witness statement on the applicant before the expiration of 21 days after the time limited for acknowledging service or, in a case where a respondent is not required to file an acknowledgment of service, within 21 days after service of the arbitration claim form.

13.3 An applicant who wishes to put evidence before the court in response to an affidavit or witness statement filed under paragraph 13.2 shall serve his affidavit or witness statement on the respondent within 7 days after service of the respondent's evidence.

13.4 Where a date has not been fixed for the hearing of the arbitration application, the applicant shall, and the respondent may, not later than 14 days after the expiration of the time limit specified in paragraph 13.2, apply to the Court for such a date to be fixed.

13.5 Agreed indexed and paginated bundles of all the evidence and other documents to be used at the hearing shall be prepared by the applicant (with the co-operation of the respondent).

13.6 Not later than 5 clear days before the hearing date estimates for the length of the hearing shall be lodged with the Court together with a complete set of the documents to be used.

13.7 Not later than 2 days before the hearing date the applicant shall lodge with the Court:

(1) a chronology of the relevant events cross-referenced to the bundle of documents;

(2) (where necessary) a list of the persons involved;

(3) a skeleton argument which lists succinctly:

    (a) the issues which arise for decision,

    (b) the grounds of relief (or opposing relief) to be relied upon,

    (c) the submissions of fact to be made with the references to the evidence, and

    (d) the submissions of law with references to the relevant authorities,

and shall send copies to the respondent.

13.8 Not later than the day before the hearing date the respondent shall lodge with the Court a skeleton argument which lists succinctly:

(1) the issues which arise for decision,

(2) the grounds of relief (or opposing relief) to be relied upon,

(3) the submissions of fact to be made with the references to the evidence, and

(4) the submissions of law with references to the relevant authorities, and shall send a copy to the applicant.

DIRECTIONS BY THE COURT

14.1 The rules of the CPR relating to allocation questionnaires and track allocation do not apply to arbitration applications, and the Court may give such directions as to the conduct of the arbitration application as it thinks best adapted to secure the just, expeditious and economical disposal thereof.

14.2 Where the Court considers that there is or may be a dispute as to fact and that the just, expeditious and economical disposal of the application can best be secured by hearing the application on oral evidence or mainly on oral evidence, it may, if it thinks fit, order that no further evidence shall be filed and that the application shall be heard on oral evidence or partly on oral evidence and partly on written evidence, with or without cross-examination of any of the witnesses, as it may direct.

14.3 The Court may give directions as to the filing of evidence and as to the attendance of witnesses for cross-examination and any other directions which it could give in proceedings begun by claim form.

14.4 If the applicant makes default in complying with these provisions or with any order or direction of the Court as to the conduct of the application, or if the Court is satisfied that the applicant is not prosecuting the application with due despatch, the Court may order the application to be dismissed or may make such other order as may be just.

14.5 If the respondent fails to comply with these provisions or with any order or direction given by the Court in relation to the evidence to be relied on, or the submission to be made by that respondent, the Court may, if it thinks fit, hear and determine the application without having regard to that evidence or those submissions.

14.6 Unless the Court orders otherwise, affidavits and witness statements may contain hearsay.

HEARING OF APPLICATIONS: PUBLIC OR PRIVATE

15.1 The Court may order that any arbitration application be heard either in public or in private.

15.2 Subject to any order made under paragraph 15.1 and paragraph 15.3, all arbitration applications shall be heard in private.

15.3 Subject to any order made under paragraph 15.1, the determination of a preliminary point of law under section 45 of the Arbitration Act, or an appeal under section 69 on a question of law arising out of an award shall be heard in public.

15.4 Paragraph 15.3 shall not apply to:

(1) the preliminary question whether the Court is satisfied of the matters set out in section 45(2)(b); or

(2) an application for permission to appeal under section 69(2)(b).

SECURING THE ATTENDANCE OF WITNESSES

16.1 A party to arbitral proceedings being conducted in England and Wales who wishes to rely on section 43 of the Arbitration Act to secure the attendance of a witness may apply for a witness summons in accordance with Part 34 of the CPR to the Admiralty and Commercial Registry or, if the attendance of the witness is required within the district of a district registry, at that registry at the option of the party.

16.2 A witness summons shall not be issued until the applicant files an affidavit or witness statement which shows that the application is made with the permission of the tribunal or the agreement of the other parties.

SECURING FOR COSTS

17.1 Subject to section 70(6) of the Arbitration Act, the Court may order any applicant (including an applicant who has been granted permission to appeal) to provide security for costs of any arbitration application.

POWERS EXERCISABLE IN SUPPORT OF ARBITRAL PROCEEDINGS

18.1 Where the case is one of urgency, an application for an order under section 44 of the Arbitration Act (Court powers exercisable in support of arbitral proceedings) may be made without notice on affidavit or witness statement (before the issue of an arbitration claim form) and the affidavit or witness statement shall (in addition to dealing with the matters required to be dealt with by paragraphs 9.1 & 9.2) state the reasons:

(1) why the application is made without notice; and

(2) (where the application is made without the permission of the arbitral tribunal or the agreement of the other parties to the arbitral proceedings) why it was not practicable to obtain that permission or agreement; and

(3) why the witness believes that the condition in section 44 (5) is satisfied.

18.2 Where the case is not one of urgency, an application for an order under section 44 of the Arbitration Act shall be made on notice and the affidavit or witness statement in support shall (in addition to dealing with the matters required to be dealt with by paragraph 9 and paragraph 18.1(3) above) state that the application is made with the permission of the tribunal or the written agreement of the other parties to the arbitral proceedings.

18.3 Where an application for an order under section 44 of the Arbitration Act is made before the issue of an arbitration claim form, any order made by the Court may be granted on terms providing for the issue of an arbitration claim form and such other terms, if any, as the court thinks fit.

APPLICATIONS UNDER SECTIONS 32 AND 45 OF THE ARBITRATION ACT

19.1 This paragraph applies to the following arbitration applications:

(1) applications for the determination of a question as to the substantive jurisdiction of the arbitral tribunal under section 32 of the Arbitration Act; and

(2) applications for the determination of a preliminary point of law under section 45 of the Arbitration Act.

19.2 Where an application is made without the agreement in writing of all the other parties to the arbitral proceedings but with the permission of the arbitral tribunal, the affidavits or witness statements filed by the parties shall set out any evidence relied on by the parties in support of their contention that the Court should, or should not, consider the application.

19.3 As soon as practicable after the written evidence is filed, the Court shall decide whether or not it should consider the application and, unless the Court otherwise directs, shall so decide without a hearing.

APPLICATIONS FOR PERMISSION TO APPEAL

20.1 Where the applicant seeks permission to appeal to the Court on a question of law arising out of an arbitration award, the arbitration claim form shall identify the question of law and state the grounds on which the applicant alleges that permission should be granted.

20.2 The affidavit or witness statement in support of the application shall set out any evidence relied on by the applicant for the purpose of satisfying the Court of the matters mentioned in section 69 (3) of the Arbitration Act and for satisfying the Court that permission should be granted.

20.3 The affidavit or witness statement filed by the respondent to the application shall:

(1) state the grounds on which the respondent opposes the grant of permission;

(2) set out any evidence relied on by him relating to the matters mentioned in section 69 (3) of the Arbitration Act, and

(3) specify whether the respondent wishes to contend that the award should be upheld for reasons not expressed (or not fully expressed) in the award and, if so, state those reasons.

20.4 As soon as practicable after the filing of the affidavits and witness statements, the Court shall determine the application for permission in accordance with section 69 (5) of the Arbitration Act.

20.5 Where permission is granted, a date shall be fixed for the hearing of the appeal.

EXTENSION OF TIME: APPLICATIONS UNDER SECTION 12

21.1 An application for an order under section 12 of the Arbitration Act may include as an alternative an application for a declaration that such an order is not needed.

TIME LIMIT FOR CHALLENGES TO OR APPEALS FROM AWARDS

22.1 An applicant shall not be taken as having complied with the time limit of 28 days referred to in section 70 (3) of the Arbitration Act unless the arbitration claim form has been issued, and all the affidavits or witness statements in support have been filed, by the expiry of that time limit.

22.2 An applicant who wishes:

(1) to challenge an award under section 67 or 68 of the Arbitration Act; or

(2) to appeal under section 69 on a question o f law arising out of an award,

may, where the time limit of 28 days has not yet expired, apply without notice on affidavit or witness statement for an order extending that time limit.

PD 49G PRACTICE DIRECTION — ARBITRATIONS

22.3 In any case where an applicant seeks to challenge an award under section 67 or 68 of the Arbitration Act or to appeal under section 69 after the time limit of 28 days has already expired, the following provisions shall apply:

(1) the applicant must state in his arbitration claim form the grounds why an order extending time should be made and his affidavit or witness statement in support shall set out the evidence on which he relies;

(2) a respondent who wishes to oppose the making of an order extending time shall file an affidavit or witness statement within 7 days after service of the applicant's evidence, and

(3) the Court shall decide whether or not to extend time without a hearing unless it appears to the Court that a hearing is required, and, where the Court makes an order extending the time limit, the respondent shall file his affidavit or witness statement in response to the arbitration application 21 days after the making of the order.

PART II

APPLICATION OF THIS PART

23.1 This Part of this practice direction applies to any application to the Court to which the old law applies and, in this rule, 'the old law' means the enactments specified in section 107 of the Arbitration Act 1996 as they stood before their amendment or repeal by that Act.

23.2 This Part does not apply to proceedings to enforce an award:
(1) to which Part III of this practice direction applies; or
(2) by a claim based on the award.

23.3 Reference should be made to the other provisions of the CPR (except Parts I and III of this Part) for the procedure for any application not expressly provided for in this Part.

MATTERS FOR A JUDGE IN COURT

24.1 Every application to the Court:
(1) to remit an award under section 22 of the Arbitration Act 1950 ; or
(2) to remove an arbitrator or umpire under section 23(1) of that Act; or
(3) to set aside an award under section 23(2) of that Act, or
(4) to determine, under section 2(1) of the Arbitration Act 1979, any question of law arising in the course of a reference,
must be made by the issue of an arbitration claim form under CPR rule 8.6 (a Part 8 claim form).

24.2 Any appeal to the High Court under section 1(2) of the Arbitration Act 1979 shall be made by the issue of a Part 8 claim form.

24.3 An application for a declaration that an award made by an arbitrator or umpire is not binding on a party to the award on the ground that it was made without jurisdiction may be made by the issue of a Part 8 claim form, but the foregoing provision shall not be taken as affecting the judge's power to refuse to make such a declaration in proceedings begun otherwise.

MATTERS FOR JUDGE IN CHAMBERS OR MASTER

25.1 Subject to the foregoing provisions of this Order and the provisions of this rule, the jurisdiction of the High Court or a judge thereof under the Arbitration Act 1950 and the jurisdiction of the High Court under the Arbitration Act 1975 and the Arbitration Act 1979 may be exercised by a judge in chambers, a master or the Admiralty Registrar.

25.2 Any application
(1) for permission to appeal under section 1(2) of the Arbitration Act 1979, or
(2) under section 1(5) of that Act (including any application for permission), or
(3) under section 5 of that Act,
shall be made to a judge in chambers.

25.3 Any application to which this rule applies shall, where there are existing court proceedings be made by the issue of an application notice in those proceedings, and in any other case a Part 8 claim form.

25.4 Where an application is made under section 1(5) of the Arbitration Act 1979 (including any application for permission), the Part 8 claim form or the application notice as the case may be, must be served on the arbitrator or umpire and on any other party to the reference.

APPLICATIONS IN DISTRICT REGISTRIES

26.1 An application under section 12(4) of the Arbitration Act 1950 for an order that a witness summons shall issue to compel the attendance before an arbitrator or umpire of a witness may, if the attendance of the witness is required within the district of a district registry, be made at that registry, instead of at the Admiralty and Commercial Registry, at the option of the applicant.

TIME LIMITS AND OTHER SPECIAL PROVISIONS AS TO APPEALS AND APPLICATIONS UNDER THE ARBITRATION ACTS

27.1 An application to the Court:
 (1) to remit an award under section 22 of the Arbitration Act 1950; or
 (2) to set aside an award under section 23(2) of that Act or otherwise, or
 (3) to direct an arbitrator or umpire to state the reasons for an award under section 1(5) of the Arbitration Act 1979,
must be made, and the Part 8 claim form or application notice, as the case may be, must be served, within 21 days after the award has been made and published to the parties.

27.2 In the case of an appeal to the Court under section 1(2) of the Arbitration Act 1979, the application for permission to appeal, where permission is required, and the Part 8 claim form must be served and the appeal entered, within 21 days after the award has been made and published to the parties. Provided that, where reasons material to the appeal are given on a date subsequent to the publication of the award, the period of 21 days shall run from the date on which the reasons are given.

27.3 An application, under section 2(1) of the Arbitration Act 1979, to determine any question of law arising in the course of a reference, must be made, and the Part 8 claim form served, within 14 days after the arbitrator or umpire has consented to the application being made, or the other parties have so consented.

27.4 For the purpose of paragraph 27.3 the consent must be given in writing.

27.5 In the case of every appeal or application to which this paragraph applies, the Part 8 claim form or the application notice, as the case may be, must state the grounds of the appeal or application and, where the appeal or application is founded on evidence by affidavit or witness statement, or is made with the consent of the arbitrator or umpire or of the other parties, a copy of every affidavit or witness statement intended to be used, or, as the case may be, of every consent given in writing, must be served with the Part 8 claim form or application notice.

27.6 Without prejudice to sub-paragraph (5), in an appeal under section 1(2) of the Arbitration Act 1979 the statement of the grounds of the appeal shall specify the relevant parts of the award and reasons, or the relevant parts thereof, shall be lodged with the court and served with the Part 8 claim form.

27.7 In an application for permission to appeal under section 1(2) of the Arbitration Act 1979, any affidavit or witness statement verifying the facts in support of a contention that the question of law concerns a term of a contract or an event which is not a one-off term or event must be filed with the court and served with the Part 8 claim form.

27.8 Any affidavit or witness statement in reply to written evidence under subparagraph (7) shall be filed with the court and served on the applicant not less than two clear days before the hearing of the application.

27.9 A respondent to an application for permission to appeal under section 1(2) of the Arbitration Act 1979 who desires to contend that the award should be upheld on grounds not expressed or fully expressed in the award and reasons shall not less than two clear days before the hearing of the application file with the court and serve on the applicant a notice specifying the grounds of his contention.

APPLICATIONS AND APPEALS TO BE HEARD BY COMMERCIAL JUDGES

28.1 Any matter which is required, by paragraph 24 or 25, to be heard by a judge, shall be heard by a judge of the Commercial Court unless any such judge otherwise directs.

28.2 Nothing in the foregoing sub-paragraph shall be construed as preventing the powers of a judge of the Commercial Court from being exercised by any judge of the High Court.

SERVICE OUT OF THE JURISDICTION

29.1 Subject to paragraph 29.2,
(1) any Part 8 claim form whereby an application under the Arbitration Act 1950 or the Arbitration Act 1979, is made, or
(2) any order made on such an application,
may be served out of the jurisdiction with the permission of the Court provided that the arbitration to which the application relates is governed by English law or has been, is being or is to be held within the jurisdiction.

29.2 A Part 8 claim form whereby permission to enforce an award is sought may be served out of the jurisdiction with the permission of the Court whether or not the arbitration is governed by English law.

29.3 An application for the grant of permission under this paragraph must be supported by an affidavit or witness statement stating the grounds on which the application is made and showing in what place or country the person to be served is, or probably may be found; and no such permission shall be granted unless it shall be made to appear to the Court that the case is a proper one for service out of the jurisdiction under this paragraph.

29.4 RSC Order 11, rules 5 to 8, (Schedule 1 to the CPR) shall apply in relation to any such Part 8 claim form or order as is referred to in sub-paragraph (1) as they apply in relation to any other claim form.

PART III

APPLICATION OF THIS PART

30.1 This Part of this practice direction applies to all enforcement proceedings (other than by an action or claim on the award) regardless of when they are commenced and when the arbitral proceedings took place.

ENFORCEMENT OF AWARDS

31.1 This rule applies to applications to enforce awards which are brought in the High Court and such an application may be made in the Royal Courts of Justice or in any district registry.

31.2 An application for permission under:
(1) section 66 of the Arbitration Act 1996;
(2) section 101 of the Arbitration Act 1996;
(3) section 26 of the Arbitration Act 1950; or
(4) section 3(1)(a) of the Arbitration Act 1975;
to enforce an award in the same manner as a judgment or order may be made without notice by use of the practice form referred to in paragraph 4.1.

31.3 The Court hearing an application under paragraph 31.2 may direct that the form (in this Part of this practice direction called 'the enforcement form') is to be served on such parties to the arbitration as it may specify and the enforcement form may with the permission of the court be served out of the jurisdiction irrespective of where the award is, or is treated as, made.

31.4 Where a direction is given under paragraph 31.3, paragraphs 11.1 to 11.5 and 13.1 to 17.1 shall apply with the necessary modifications as they apply to applications under Part I of this practice direction.

31.5 Where the applicant applies to enforce an agreed award within the meaning of section 51(2) of the Arbitration Act 1996, the enforcement form must state that the award is an agreed award and any order made by the Court shall also contain such a statement.

31.6 An application for permission must be supported by affidavit or witness statement:
  (1) exhibiting
    (a) where the application is made under section 66 of the Arbitration Act 1996 or under section 26 of the Arbitration Act 1950, the arbitration agreement and the original award or, in either case, a copy thereof;
    (b) where the application is under section 101 of the Arbitration Act 1996, the documents required to be produced by section 102 of that Act;
    (c) where the application is under section 3(1)(a) of the Arbitration Act 1975, the documents required to be produced by section 4 of that Act;
  (2) stating the name and the usual or last known place of residence or business of the applicant and of the person against whom it is sought to enforce the award respectively,
  (3) stating, as the case may require, either that the award has not been complied with or the extent to which it has not been complied with at the date of the application.

31.7 An order giving permission must be drawn up by or on behalf of the applicant and must be served on the respondent by delivering a copy to him personally or by sending a copy to him at his usual or last known place of residence or business or in such other manner as the Court may direct.

31.8 The order may be served out of the jurisdiction without permission, and RSC Order 11, rules 5 to 8, (Schedule 1 to the CPR) shall apply in relation to such an order as they apply in relation to a claim form.

31.9 Within 14 days after service of the order or, if the order is to be served out of the jurisdiction, within such other period as the Court may fix, the respondent may apply to set aside the order and the award shall not be enforced until after the expiration of that period or, if the respondent applies within that period to set aside the order, until after the application is finally disposed of.

31.10 The copy of the order served on the respondent shall state the effect of paragraph 31.9.

31.11 In relation to a body corporate paragraphs 31.1–31.10 shall have effect as if for any reference to the place of residence or business of the applicant or the respondent there were substituted a reference to the registered or principal address of the body corporate.

Nothing in paragraphs 31.1–31.10 shall affect any enactment which provides for the manner in which a document may be served on a body corporate.

INTEREST ON AWARDS

32.1 Where an applicant seeks to enforce an award of interest, the whole or any part of which relates to a period after the date of the award, he shall file a certificate giving the following particulars:
  (1) whether simple or compound interest was awarded;
  (2) the date from which interest was awarded;
  (3) whether rests were provided for, specifying them;
  (4) the rate of interest awarded, and
  (5) a calculation showing the total amount claimed up to the date of the certificate and any sum which will become due thereafter on a per diem basis.

32.2 The certificate under paragraph 32.1 must be filed whenever the amount of interest has to be quantified for the purpose of obtaining a judgment or order under section 66 of the Arbitration Act (enforcement of the award) or for the purpose of enforcing such a judgment or order by one of the means mentioned in RSC Order 45, rule 1 (Schedule 1 to the CPR).

REGISTRATION IN HIGH COURT OF FOREIGN AWARDS

33.1 Where an award is made in proceedings on an arbitration in any part of Her Majesty's dominions or other territory to which Part I of the Foreign Judgments (Reciprocal Enforcement) Act 1933 extends, being a part to which Part II of the Administration of Justice Act 1920 extended immediately before the said Part I was extended thereto, then, if the award has, in pursuance of the law in force in the place where it was made, become enforceable in the same manner as a judgment given by a court in that place, RSC Order 71 (Schedule 1 to the CPR) shall apply in relation to the award as it applies in relation to a judgment given by that court, subject, however, to the following modifications:

(1) for references to the country of the original court there shall be substituted references to the place where the award was made; and

(2) the affidavit required by rule 3 of the said Order must state (in addition to the other matters required by that rule) that to the best of the information or belief of the deponent the award has, in pursuance of the law in force in the place where it was made, become enforceable in the same manner as a judgment given by a court in that place.

REGISTRATION OF AWARDS UNDER THE ARBITRATION (INTERNATIONAL INVESTMENT DISPUTES) ACT 1966

34.1 In paragraphs 34.1–34.7 and in any provision of this practice direction as applied by this paragraph:

'the Act of 1966' means the Arbitration (International Investment Disputes) Act 1966;

'award' means an award rendered pursuant to the Convention;

'the Convention' means the Convention referred to in section 1(1) of the Act of 1966;

'Judgment creditor' and 'judgment debtor' mean respectively the person seeking recognition or enforcement of an award and the other party to the award.

34.2 Subject to the provisions of paragraphs 34.1–34.7, the following provisions of RSC Order 71, namely, rules 1, 3(1) (except sub-paragraphs (c)(iv) and (d) thereof), 7 (except paragraph (3)(c)and (d)) thereof), and 10(3) shall apply with the necessary modifications in relation to an award as they apply in relation to a judgment to which Part II of the Foreign Judgments (Reciprocal Enforcement) Act 1933 applies.

34.3 An application to have an award registered in the High Court under section 1 of the Act of 1966 shall be made by claim form under CPR rule 8.6.

34.4 The witness statement or affidavit required by Order 71, rule 3, in support of an application for registration shall:

(1) in lieu of exhibiting the judgment or a copy thereof, exhibit a copy of the award certified pursuant to the Convention; and

(2) in addition to stating the matters mentioned in paragraph 3(1)(c)(i) and (ii) of the said rule 3, state whether at the date of the application the enforcement of the award has been stayed (provisionally or otherwise) pursuant to the Convention and whether any, and if so what, application has been made pursuant to the Convention, which, if granted, might result in a stay of the enforcement of the award.

34.5 There shall be kept in the Admiralty and Commercial Registry under the direction of the Senior Master a register of the awards ordered to be registered under the Act of 1966 and particulars shall be entered in the register of any execution issued on such an award.

34.6 Where it appears to the court on granting permission to register an award or an application made by the judgment debtor after an award has been registered:

(1) that the enforcement of the award has been stayed (whether provisionally or otherwise) pursuant to the Convention; or

(2) that an application has been made pursuant to the Convention, which, if granted, might result in a stay of the enforcement of the award,

the Court shall, or in the case referred to in sub-paragraph (2) may, stay execution of the award for such time as it considers appropriate in the circumstances.

34.7 An application by the judgment debtor under paragraph 34.6 shall be made by application notice and supported by affidavit.

PD 49H   PRACTICE DIRECTION — MERCANTILE COURTS AND BUSINESS LISTS

This practice direction supplements Part 49 of the CPR and replaces, with modifications, Order 48C of the County Court Rules 1981 and the practice directions establishing Mercantile Courts in Manchester, Liverpool, Birmingham, Bristol, Leeds and Newcastle-upon-Tyne. The Lord Chancellor has given his approval to a mercantile court being established in Cardiff. This practice direction complements the Commercial Court Practice Direction, also supplemental to Part 49.

GENERAL
  1.1 In this practice direction:
   (1) 'mercantile claim' means a claim relating to a commercial or business transaction and includes (but is not limited to) any claim relating to:
      (i) a business document or contract;
      (ii) the export or import of goods or the sale of goods;
      (iii) the carriage of goods by land, sea, air or pipeline;
      (iv) the exploitation of oil and gas reserves;
      (v) insurance and re-insurance;
      (vi) banking and financial services;
      (vii) the operation of markets and exchanges;
      (viii) business agency;
      (ix) the customs and practices of particular trades, businesses or commercial organisations;
      (x) commercial fraud;
      (xi) professional negligence in a commercial context;
      (xii) arbitration applications (paragraph 6 below)
   but does not include:
      (i) any claim concerning the sale of goods by or against an individual consumer; or
      (ii) any claim to which CPR Part 49 (other than rule 49(2)(c)) applies.
   and 'mercantile proceedings' has a corresponding meaning.
   (2) 'Mercantile Court' means one of the Mercantile Courts established to deal with mercantile claims in the High Court but does not include the Commercial Court of the Queen's Bench Division.
   (3) 'Authorised county court' means the Central London County Court and any other county court authorised by the Lord Chancellor to operate a Business list for the purposes of dealing with mercantile proceedings.
   (4) 'Mercantile judge' means, in relation to proceedings in the High Court, a judge, or a person authorised to sit as a judge, of a Mercantile Court and, in relation to proceedings in a county court, the judge or judges authorised to deal with cases in the Business list of an authorised county court.
  1.2 Mercantile proceedings may be dealt with in the High Court subject to the restrictions on claims that can be commenced in the High Court (see CPR rule 16.3(5) and paragraph 2.1 to 2.4 of the Practice Direction that supplements CPR Part 7), or may be dealt with in an authorised county court.
  1.3 The Civil Procedure Rules (the CPR) and the practice directions supplementing them apply to mercantile claims subject to the provisions of this practice direction.
  1.4 For the purposes of the CPR the list of a Mercantile Court and the Business list of an authorised county court is a specialist list (see eg. CPR rules 2.3(2) and 16.3(5)(d)).

COMMENCEMENT OF PROCEEDINGS:

High Court
  2.1 A mercantile claim intended to be entered in the commercial list of the Commercial Court Queen's Bench Division should be begun by a claim form

issued out of the Admiralty and Commercial Registry at the Royal Courts of Justice. (For further information reference should be made to the Commercial Court Practice Direction supplemental to CPR Part 49 and to the Commercial Court Guide).

2.2 (1) If a claimant wants a mercantile claim to be entered in the list of a Mercantile Court the claim should be begun by a claim form issued out of the district registry of the Mercantile Court in question and marked with the words 'Queen's Bench Division, ____ District Registry, Mercantile Court'.

(2) On the issue out of the said registry of a claim form so marked, the claim will be entered in the list of that Mercantile Court.

(3) Where a claim form is to be marked as mentioned in sub-paragraph (2), any application before the issue of the claim form should be made to a judge of that Mercantile Court.

(4) If an application is made before the issue of the claim form, the written evidence in support of the application must state, in addition to any other necessary matters, that the claimant intends to mark the claim form in accordance with sub-paragraph (1).

(5) If the mercantile judge hearing an application made before the issue of the claim form is of opinion that the claim should not be entered in the list of the Mercantile Court in question, he may adjourn the application to be heard by another judge or hear the application and direct that when the claim form is issued the claim should not be entered in that list.

County Court

2.3 (1) If a claimant wants a mercantile claim to be entered in the Business list of an authorised county court, the mercantile claim should be begun by a claim form issued out of the office of the county court in question and should be marked '____ County Court, Business list'.

(2) A claim form should not be issued and marked as mentioned in subparagraph (1) unless the mercantile claim has some connection with the Circuit in which the county court office is situated, for example, because:

(i) the balance of convenience points to having the mercantile claim tried in that county court, or

(ii) the commercial or business transaction in question took place within the Circuit in which the county court is situated or one of the parties resides or carries on business within that Circuit.

(3) Where the value of a mercantile claim does not exceed £15,000, a mercantile claim may not be issued and marked as mentioned in sub-paragraph (1) except with the permission of a mercantile Judge of the county court in question.

(4) A mercantile claim issued and marked as mentioned in sub-paragraph (1) will be entered in the Business list of the county court in question.

(5) Where a claim form is to be issued and marked as mentioned in sub-paragraph (1), any application before the issue of the claim form should be made to a mercantile judge of the county court in question.

(6) If an application is made before the issue of the claim form the written evidence in support of the application must state, in addition to any other necessary matters, that the claimant intends to issue and mark the claim form in accordance with sub-paragraph (1).

(7) If the mercantile judge hearing an application made before the issue of the claim form is of opinion that the claim should not be entered in the Business list of the county court in question, he may adjourn the application to be heard by another judge or hear the application and direct that when the claim form is issued the claim should not be entered in the Business list.

TRANSFER

3.1 Where mercantile proceedings are entered in the list of a Mercantile Court or in the Business list of an authorised county court, the provisions of CPR rule 26.2 (automatic transfer) do not apply.

3.2 At any stage in the course of mercantile proceedings not entered in the list of a Mercantile Court or the Business list of an authorised county court, any party

PD 49H PRACTICE DIRECTION — MERCANTILE COURTS AND BUSINESS LISTS

may apply for an order transferring the case to a Mercantile Court or to the Business list of an authorised county court.

3.3 An application under paragraph 3.2:

(1) may be made to a mercantile judge of the court to which it is proposed the case should be transferred; or

(2) may be made to the court where the mercantile proceedings are being dealt with.

3.4 The court where the mercantile proceedings are being dealt with may not itself make an order for transfer but, if it considers the case might be suitable to be dealt with by a Mercantile Court or in the Business list of an authorised county court, it may

(1) on an application under paragraph 3.3(2) adjourn the application for hearing by a mercantile judge of the court to which it is proposed the case should be transferred; or

(2) on its own initiative refer the case to a mercantile judge of that court for a decision as to whether an order for transfer should be made.

3.5 Where all parties consent to the transfer, an application for transfer should be made by letter addressed to the listing officer of the Mercantile Court or the authorised county court, as the case may be, enclosing the written consents of the other parties and the claim form and statements of case. The letter should state why the case is suitable for the Mercantile Court or, as the case may be, for the Business list of the authorised county court.

3.6 Where a mercantile judge orders mercantile proceedings to be transferred to the list of a Mercantile Court, or to the Business list of an authorised county court, he may at the same time give directions for the management of the case.

3.7 A mercantile judge may, on his own initiative (but not unless the parties have had an opportunity of making submissions), or on the application of any party, order a case in the list of a Mercantile Court or in the Business list of an authorised county court to be removed from that list and may at the same time give case management directions.

3.8 Where a case is in the list of a Mercantile Court by virtue of paragraph 2.2(2) or in a Business list by virtue of paragraph 2.3(4), an application by a defendant, including a Part 20 defendant, to remove it from that list must be made within 7 days after the defendant has filed an acknowledgement of service or a defence, whichever is the later.

3.9 Where proceedings in the Business list of an authorised county court are removed from that list, the mercantile judge may at the same time:

(1) make an order allocating the proceedings to a track in accordance with CPR Part 26; or

(2) give directions for the purposes of allocation; and

(3) give case management directions.

DISPENSING WITH PARTICULARS OF CLAIM OR DEFENCE

4. A mercantile judge may at any time, before or after the issue of the claim form, order that a case in the list of a Mercantile Court or in the Business list of an authorised county court be tried without the filing or service of particulars of claim or of a defence or of any other statement of case, but if such an order is made without any other party having had an opportunity to be heard that party may apply for it to be revoked.

DIRECTIONS AND CASE MANAGEMENT

5.1 All cases in the list of a Mercantile Court or in the Business list of an authorised county court will be allocated to the multi-track. Subject to paragraph 3.9, the CPR rules relating to allocation questionnaires and to track allocation will not apply to them. They will be subject to case management by the court.

5.2 (1) If mercantile proceedings are transferred to a Mercantile Court or a Business list under paragraph 3 then, unless the mercantile judge who made the order for transfer gave directions for the management of the case, an application to a mercantile judge for such directions shall be made within 14 days of the date of the order of transfer.

(2) If the claimant does not make an application in accordance with subparagraph (1), any other party may do so or may apply for the claim of the claimant in default to be struck out.

5.3 (1) Subject to sub-paragraphs (2) and (3), Interim applications in and trials of proceedings in a Mercantile Court or the Business list of an authorised county court shall be dealt with or heard, as the case may be, by a mercantile judge of the court in question;

(2) When an interim application needs to be dealt with urgently and a mercantile judge of the court in question is not available, the application may be dealt with by another judge, including a district judge.

(3) When the hearing of an application would involve the mercantile judge becoming aware of any matter which might embarrass him as the potential trial judge and there is no other mercantile judge of the court in question available to hear the application, the application may be heard by another judge, including a district judge.

(4) Matters concerning the enforcement of any judgment given in proceedings in a Mercantile Court or in the Business list of an authorised county court may be, and ordinarily will be, dealt with by a district judge.

(5) Subject to any express provision in a statute, rule or practice direction, sub-paragraphs (2), (3) and (4) above do not apply to applications for injunctions, freezing orders, search orders, committal or sequestration of assets.

(6) Nothing in this paragraph shall be construed as preventing the powers of a mercantile judge from being exercised by any judge of the High Court.

5.4 Paragraph 5 of the Practice Direction — The Multi-Track — supplementing CPR Part 29 applies to case management conferences in proceedings in a Mercantile Court or in the Business list of an authorised county court.

5.5 It is intended that a Mercantile Courts and Business Lists Guide will be prepared after consultation with the judges of the Mercantile Courts, the judges of the Central London County Court Business List and their respective Users Committees, and that the Guide will set out any special procedures to apply to the conduct of proceedings in Mercantile Courts and the Business lists of authorised county courts. In the meantime the practice set out in any 'approved Guide' (see paragraph 5.6 below) should be followed subject to the provisions of this or any other Mercantile Courts and Business Lists practice direction and to any order that may be made in an individual case.

5.6 (1) In relation to mercantile proceedings in any Mercantile Court or in the Business List of the Central London County Court, an 'approved Guide' is a Guide that has been approved by the Head of Civil Justice for the purpose of mercantile proceedings in that court or in that list.

(2) In relation to any Mercantile Court or Business list in respect of which there is for the time being no 'approved Guide', Section D of the Commercial Court Guide, 5th Edition, relating to Case Management in the Commercial Court, shall be treated as the 'approved Guide' for the purpose of mercantile proceedings in that court or in that list.

ARBITRATION APPLICATIONS AND PROCEEDINGS

6.1 An arbitration application (as defined in paragraph 2 of the Arbitration Practice Direction supplemental to CPR Part 49) and proceedings to enforce an award under section 26 of the Arbitration Act 1950 or under sections 66 or 101(2) of the Arbitration Act 1996, shall be treated as mercantile claims for the purposes of this practice direction and may be included in the mercantile list of a Mercantile Court or the Business list of an authorised county court.

6.2 A mercantile judge may also deal with any other application under the Arbitration Act 1979 which may be commenced in or transferred to the mercantile list of a Mercantile Court or the Business list of an authorised county court.

6.3 The provisions of the Arbitration Practice Direction supplemental to CPR Part 49 apply to such applications and proceedings.

REPEAL OF PREVIOUS LOCAL DIRECTIONS OR GUIDES

7. This practice direction supersedes as from 26 April 1999 any local practice directions or Guides applicable to mercantile proceedings in any Mercantile Court or in the Business List of the Central London County Court.

CPR PART 50 APPLICATION OF THE SCHEDULES

50—(1) The Schedules to these Rules set out, with modifications, certain provisions previously contained in the Rules of the Supreme Court 1965 and the County Court Rules 1981.

(2) These Rules apply in relation to the proceedings to which the Schedules apply subject to the provisions in the Schedules and the relevant practice directions.

(3) A provision previously contained in the Rules of the Supreme Court 1965—
    (a) is headed 'RSC';
    (b) is numbered with the Order and rule numbers it bore as part of the RSC; and
    (c) unless otherwise stated in the Schedules or the relevant practice direction, applies only to proceedings in the High Court.

(4) A provision previously contained in the County Court Rules 1981—
    (a) is headed 'CCR';
    (b) is numbered with the Order and rule numbers it bore as part of the CCR; and
    (c) unless otherwise stated in the Schedules or the relevant practice direction, applies only to proceedings in the county court.

(5) A reference in a Schedule to a rule by number alone is a reference to the rule so numbered in the Order in which the reference occurs.

(6) A reference in a Schedule to a rule by number prefixed by 'CPR' is a reference to the rule with that number in these Rules.

(7) In the Schedules, unless otherwise stated, 'the Act' means—
    (a) in a provision headed 'RSC', the Supreme Court Act 1981; and
    (b) in a provision headed 'CCR', the County Courts Act 1984.

CPR PART 51 TRANSITIONAL ARRANGEMENTS

51 A practice direction shall make provision for the extent to which these Rules shall apply to proceedings issued before 26 April 1999.

PD 51 PRACTICE DIRECTION — TRANSITIONAL ARRANGEMENTS

This practice direction supplements CPR Part 51.

CONTENTS OF THIS PRACTICE DIRECTION

1 (1) This Practice Direction deals with the application of the Civil Procedure Rules ('CPR') to proceedings issued before 26 April 1999 ('existing proceedings').

(2) In this Practice Direction 'the previous rules' means, as appropriate the Rules of the Supreme Court 1965 ('RSC') or County Court Rules 1981 ('CCR') in force immediately before 26 April 1999.

GENERAL SCHEME OF TRANSITIONAL ARRANGEMENTS

2 The general scheme is:

(a) to apply the previous rules to undefended cases, allowing them to progress to their disposal, but

(b) to apply the CPR to defended cases so far as is practicable.

WHERE THE PREVIOUS RULES WILL NORMALLY APPLY

General principle

3 Where an initiating step has been taken in a case before 26 April 1999, in particular one that uses forms or other documentation required by the previous rules, the case will proceed in the first instance under the previous rules. Any step which a party must take in response to something done by another party in accordance with the previous rules must also be in accordance with those rules.

Responding to old process

4 A party who is served with an old type of originating process (writ, summons etc.) on or after 26 April 1999 is required to respond in accordance with the previous rules and the instructions on any forms received with the originating process.

Filing and service of pleadings where old process served

5 Where a case has been begun by an old type of originating process (whether served before or after 26 April 1999), filing and service of pleadings will continue according to the previous rules.

AUTOMATIC DIRECTIONS/DISCOVERY

High court

6 (1) Where the timetable for automatic directions under RSC Order 25, rule 8 or automatic discovery under RSC Order 24 has begun to apply to proceedings before 26 April 1999, those directions will continue to have effect on or after 26 April 1999.

County Court

(2) Where automatic directions under CCR Order 17, rule 11 have begun to apply to existing proceedings before 26 April 1999 or the court has sent out notice that automatic directions under CCR Order 17, rule 11 (Form N.450) will apply (even if the timetable will not begin until 26 April 1999 or after), those directions will continue to have effect on or after 26 April 1999.

(3) However CCR Order 17, rule 11(9) will not apply and therefore proceedings will not be struck out where there has been no request for a hearing to be fixed within 15 months of the date when pleadings were deemed to close. (But see paragraph 19.)

High Court and County Court

(4) However, if the case comes before the court on or after 26 April 1999, the new rules may apply. (See paragraph 15.)

PD 51   PRACTICE DIRECTION — TRANSITIONAL ARRANGEMENTS

Default judgment

7   (1)   If a party wishes default judgment to be entered in existing proceedings, he must do so in accordance with the previous rules.

(2)   Where default judgment has been entered and there are outstanding issues to be resolved (e.g. damages to be assessed), the court officer may refer the proceedings to the judge, so that case management decisions about the proceedings and the conduct of the hearing can be made in accordance with the practice set out in paragraph 15.

(3)   If a party needs to apply for permission to enter default judgment, he must make that application under CPR Part 23 (general rules about applications for court orders).

(4)   An application to set aside judgment entered in default must be made under CPR Part 23 (general rules about applications for court orders) and CPR Part 13 (setting aside or varying default judgment) will apply to the proceedings as it would apply to default judgment entered under the CPR.

(5)   CPR rule 15.11 (claims stayed if it is not defended or admitted) applies to these proceedings.

Judgment on admission in the county court

8   (1)   If a party to existing proceedings in the county court wishes to request judgment to be entered on an admission, he must do so in accordance with the previous rules.

(2)   Where judgment has been entered and there are outstanding issues to be resolved (e.g. damages to be assessed), the court officer may refer the proceedings to the judge, so that case management decisions about the proceedings and the conduct of the hearing can be made in accordance with the practice set out in paragraph 15.

(3)   If a party needs to apply for permission to enter judgment, he must make that application under CPR Part 23 (general rules about applications for court orders).

Order inconsistent with CPR

9   Where a court order has been made before 26 April 1999, that order must still be complied with on or after 26 April 1999.

Steps taken before 26 April 1999

10   (1)   Where a party has taken any step in the proceedings in accordance with the previous rules that step will remain valid on or after 26 April 1999.

(2)   A party will not normally be required to take any action that would amount to taking that step again under the CPR. For example if discovery has been given, a party will not normally be required to provide disclosure under CPR Part 31.

WHERE THE CPR WILL NORMALLY APPLY

General principle

11   Where a new step is to be taken in any existing proceedings on or after 26 April 1999, it is to be taken under the CPR.

Part 1 (overriding objective) to apply

12   Part 1 (overriding objective) will apply to all existing proceedings from 26 April 1999 onwards.

Originating process

13   (1)   Only claim forms under the CPR will be issued by the court on or after 26 April 1999.

(2)   If a request to issue an old type of originating process (writ, summons etc.) is received at the court on or after 26 April 1999 it will be returned unissued.

(3)   An application made on or after 26 April 1999 to extend the validity of originating process issued before 26 April 1999 must be made in accordance with CPR Part 23 (general rules about applications for court orders), but the court will decide whether to allow the application in accordance with the previous law.

PD 51 PRACTICE DIRECTION — TRANSITIONAL ARRANGEMENTS

Application to the court

14 (1) Any application to the court made on or after 26 April 1999 must be made in accordance with CPR Part 23 (general rules about applications for court orders).

(2) Any other relevant CPR will apply to the substance of the application, unless this practice direction provides otherwise. (See paragraphs 13(3) (application to extend the validity of originating process) and 18(2) (costs)).

(3) For example, a party wishing to apply for summary judgment must do so having regard to the test in CPR Part 24. A party wishing to apply for an interim remedy must do so under CPR Part 25 etc.

(4) Any other CPR will apply as necessary. For example, CPR Part 4 will apply as to forms and CPR Part 6 will apply to service of documents.

(5) If the pleadings have not been filed at court, the applicant must file all pleadings served when he files his application notice.

First time before a judge on or after 26 April 1999

15 (1) When proceedings come before a judge (whether at a hearing or on paper) for the first time on or after 26 April 1999, he may direct how the CPR are to apply to the proceedings and may disapply certain provisions of the CPR. He may also give case management directions (which may include allocating the proceedings to a case management track).

(2) The general presumption will be that the CPR will apply to the proceedings from then on unless the judge directs or this practice direction provides otherwise. (See paragraphs 13(3) (application to extend the validity of originating process) and 18(2) (costs).)

(3) If an application has been issued before 26 April 1999 and the hearing of the application has been set for a date on or after 26 April 1999, the general presumption is that the application will be decided having regard to the CPR. (For example an application for summary judgment issued before 26 April 1999, with a hearing date set for 1 May 1999, will be decided having regard to the test in CPR Part 24 (summary Judgment).)

(4) When the first occasion on which existing proceedings are before a judge on or after 26 April 1999 is a trial or hearing of a substantive issue, the general presumption is that the trial or hearing will be conducted having regard to the CPR.

Where pleadings deemed to close on or after 26 April 1999

16 (1) This paragraph applies to existing proceedings where pleadings are deemed to close on or after 26 April 1999. However, this paragraph does not apply to those county court proceedings where notice that automatic directions apply (Form N.450) has been sent (in which case the automatic directions will apply — see paragraph 6).

(2) CPR Part 26 (case management — preliminary stage) applies to these proceedings.

(3) If a defence is filed at court on or after 26 April 1999, the court will serve an allocation questionnaire where CPR rule 26.3 would apply, unless it dispenses with the need for one.

(4) If pleadings have not been filed at court (this will normally be the case in the Queen's Bench Division) the claimant must file copies of all the pleadings served within 14 days of the date that pleadings are deemed to close.

(5) Unless it dispenses with the need for one, the court will then serve an allocation questionnaire.

(6) In the previous rules pleadings are deemed to close:
    (a) High court—
        (i) 14 days after service of any reply, or
        (ii) if there is no reply, 14 days after service of the defence to counter-claim, or
        (iii) if there is no reply or defence to counterclaim, 14 days after the service of the defence.

PD 51 PRACTICE DIRECTION — TRANSITIONAL ARRANGEMENTS

(b) County court—

14 days after the delivery of a defence or, where a counterclaim is served with the defence, 28 days after the delivery of the defence.

(7) Where there are 2 or more defendants the court will normally wait until the claimant has filed copies of all the pleadings before serving an allocation questionnaire. However, the court may (in cases where there is a delay) serve allocation questionnaires despite the fact that pleadings have not closed in respect of any other defendant.

(8) The court will then allocate the proceedings in accordance with CPR rule 26.5.

(9) The CPR will then apply generally to the proceedings.

Agreement to apply the CPR

17 The parties may agree in writing that the CPR will apply to any proceedings from the date of the agreement. When they do so:

(a) all those who are parties at that time must agree,
(b) the CPR must apply in their entirety,
(c) the agreement is irrevocable,
(d) the claimant must file a copy of the agreement at court.

Costs

18 (1) Any assessment of costs that takes place on or after 26 April 1999 will be in accordance with CPR Parts 43 to 48.

(2) However, the general presumption is that no costs for work undertaken before 26 April 1999 will be disallowed if those costs would have been allowed in a costs taxation before 26 April 1999.

(3) The decision as to whether to allow costs for work undertaken on or after 26 April will generally be taken in accordance with CPR Parts 43 to 48.

(The costs practice direction contains more information on the operation of the transitional arrangements in relation to costs.)

Existing proceedings after one year

19 (1) If any existing proceedings have not come before a judge, at a hearing or on paper, between 26 April 1999 and 25 April 2000, those proceedings shall be stayed.

(2) Any party to those proceedings may apply for the stay to be lifted.

(3) Proceedings of the following types will not be stayed as a result of this provision:

(a) where the case has been given a fixed trial date which is after 25 April 2000,
(b) personal injury cases where there is no issue on liability but the proceedings have been adjourned by court order to determine the prognosis,
(c) where the court is dealing with the continuing administration of an estate or a trust or a receivership,
(d) applications relating to funds in court.

GLOSSARY

SCOPE
This glossary is a guide to the meaning of certain legal expressions as used in these Rules, but it does not give the expressions any meaning in the Rules which they do not otherwise have in the law.

EXPRESSION	MEANING
Affidavit	A written, sworn statement of evidence.
Alternative dispute resolution	Collective description of methods of resolving disputes otherwise than through the normal trial process.
Base rate	The interest rate set by the Bank of England which is used as the basis for other banks' rates.
Contribution	A right of someone to recover from a third person all or part of the amount which he himself is liable to pay.
Counterclaim	A claim brought by a defendant in response to the claimant's claim, which is included in the same proceedings as the claimant's claim.
Cross-examination (and see 'evidence in chief')	Questioning of a witness by a party other than the party who called the witness.
Damages	A sum of money awarded by the court as compensation to the claimant.
• aggravated damages	Additional damages which the court may award as compensation for the defendant's objectionable behaviour.
• exemplary damages	Damages which go beyond compensating for actual loss and are awarded to show the court's disapproval of the defendant's behaviour.
Defence of tender before claim	A defence that, before the claimant started proceedings, the defendant unconditionally offered to the claimant the amount due or, if no specified amount is claimed, an amount sufficient to satisfy the claim.
Evidence in chief (and see 'cross-examination')	The evidence given by a witness for the party who called him.
Indemnity	A right of someone to recover from a third party the whole amount which he himself is liable to pay.
Injunction	A court order prohibiting a person from doing something or requiring a person to do something.
Joint liability (and see 'several liability')	Parties who are jointly liable share a single liability and each party can be held liable for the whole of it.
Limitation period	The period within which a person who has a right to claim against another person must start court proceedings to establish that right. The expiry of the period may be a defence to the claim.
List	Cases are allocated to different lists depending on the subject matter of the case. The lists are

GLOSSARY

	used for administrative purposes and may also have their own procedures and judges.
Official copy	A copy of an official document, supplied and marked as such by the office which issued the original.
Practice form	Form to be used for a particular purpose in proceedings, the form and purpose being specified by a practice direction.
Pre-action protocol	Statements of understanding between legal practitioners and others about pre-action practice and which are approved by a relevant practice direction.
Privilege	The right of a party to refuse to disclose a document or produce a document or to refuse to answer questions on the ground of some special interest recognised by law.
Seal	A seal is a mark which the court puts on a document to indicate that the document has been issued by the court.
Service	Steps required by rules of court to bring documents used in court proceedings to a person's attention.
Set aside	Cancelling a judgment or order or a step taken by a party in the proceedings.
Several liability (and see 'joint liability')	A person who is severally liable with others may remain liable for the whole claim even where judgment has been obtained against the others.
Stay	A stay imposes a halt on proceedings, apart from taking any steps allowed by the Rules or the terms of the stay. Proceedings can be continued if a stay is lifted.
Strike out	Striking out means the court ordering written material to be deleted so that it may no longer be relied upon.
Without prejudice	Negotiations with a view to a settlement are usually conducted 'without prejudice', which means that the circumstances in which the content of those negotiations may be revealed to the court are very restricted.

CPR SCHEDULE 1

RSC ORDER 10
SERVICE OF ORIGINATING PROCESS: GENERAL PROVISIONS

Rule 4 SERVICE OF CLAIM FORM IN CERTAIN ACTIONS FOR POSSESSION OF LAND
Where a claim form contains a claim for the possession of land, the court may—
    (a) if satisfied on an application without notice being served on any other party that no person appears to be in possession of the land and that service cannot be otherwise effected on any defendant, authorise service on that defendant to be effected by affixing a copy of the claim form to some conspicuous part of the land;
    (b) if satisfied on such an application that no person appears to be in possession of the land and that service could not otherwise have been effected on any defendant, order that service already effected by affixing a copy of the claim form to some conspicuous part of the land shall be treated as good service on that defendant.

RSC ORDER 11
SERVICE OF PROCESS, ETC., OUT OF THE JURISDICTION

Rule 1 PRINCIPAL CASES IN WHICH SERVICE OF CLAIM FORM OUT OF JURISDICTION IS PERMISSIBLE
    (1) Provided that the claim form is not a claim form to which paragraph (2) of this rule applies, a claim form may be served out of the jurisdiction with the permission of the court if—
    (a) a remedy is sought against a person domiciled within the jurisdiction;
    (b) an injunction is sought ordering the defendant to do or refrain from doing anything within the jurisdiction (whether or not damages are also claimed in respect of a failure to do or the doing of that thing);
    (c) the claim is brought against a person duly served within or out of the jurisdiction and a person out of the jurisdiction is a necessary or proper party thereto;
    (d) the claim is brought to enforce, rescind, dissolve, annul or otherwise affect a contract, or to recover damages or obtain any other remedy in respect of the breach of a contract, being (in either case) a contract which—
        (i) was made within the jurisdiction; or
        (ii) was made by or through an agent trading or residing within the jurisdiction on behalf of a principal trading or residing out of the jurisdiction; or
        (iii) is by its terms, or by implication, governed by English law, or
        (iv) contains a term to the effect that the High Court shall have jurisdiction to hear and determine any claim in respect of the contract;
    (e) the claim is brought in respect of a breach committed within the jurisdiction of a contract made within or out of the jurisdiction, and irrespective of the fact, if such be the case, that the breach was preceded or accompanied by a breach committed out of the jurisdiction that rendered impossible the performance of so much of the contract as ought to have been performed within the jurisdiction;
    (f) the claim is founded on a tort and the damage was sustained, or resulted from an act committed, within the jurisdiction;
    (g) the whole subject-matter of the proceedings is land situate within the jurisdiction (with or without rents or profits) or the perpetuation of testimony relating to land so situate;
    (h) the claim is brought to construe, rectify, set aside or enforce an act, deed, will, contract, obligation or liability affecting land situate within the jurisdiction;

(i) the claim is made for a debt secured on immovable property or is made to assert, declare or determine proprietary or possessory rights, or rights of security, in or over movable property, or to obtain authority to dispose of movable property, situate within the jurisdiction;

(j) the claim is brought to execute the trusts of a written instrument being trusts that ought to be executed according to English law and of which the person to be served with the claim form is a trustee, or for any remedy which might be obtained in any such action;

(k) the claim is made for the administration of the estate of a person who died domiciled within the jurisdiction or for any remedy which might be obtained in any such action;

(l) the claim is brought in a probate action;

(m) the claim is brought to enforce any judgment or arbitral award;

(n) the claim is brought against a defendant not domiciled in Scotland or Northern Ireland in respect of a claim by the Commissioners of Inland Revenue for or in relation to any of the duties or taxes which have been, or are for the time being, placed under their care and management;

(o) the claim is brought under the Nuclear Installations Act 1965 or in respect of contributions under the Social Security Contributions and Benefits Act 1992;

(p) the claim is made for a sum to which the Directive of the Council of the European Communities dated 15 March 1976 No. 76/308/EEC applies, and service is to be effected in a country which is a member State of the European Economic Community;

(q) the claim is made under the Drug Trafficking Offences Act 1994;

(r) the claim is made under the Financial Services Act 1986 or the Banking Act 1987;

(s) the claim is made under Part VI of the Criminal Justice Act 1988;

(t) the claim is brought for money had and received or for an account or other remedy against the defendant as constructive trustee, and the defendant's alleged liability arises out of acts committed, whether by him or otherwise, within the jurisdiction;

(u) the claim is made under the Immigration (Carriers' Liability) Act 1987.

(2) A claim form may be served out of the jurisdiction on a defendant without the permission of the court provided that each claim against that defendant is either—

(a) a claim which by virtue of the Civil Jurisdiction and Judgments Act 1982 the court has power to hear and determine, made in proceedings to which the following conditions apply—

(i) no proceedings between the parties concerning the same cause of action are pending in the courts of any other part of the United Kingdom or of any other Convention territory; and

(ii) either the defendant is domiciled in any part of the United Kingdom or in any other Convention territory, or the proceedings begun by the claim form are proceedings to which Article 16 of Schedule 1, 3C or 4 refers, or the defendant is a party to an agreement conferring jurisdiction to which Article 17 of Schedule 1, 3C or 4 to that Act applies; or

(b) a claim which by virtue of any other enactment the High Court has power to hear and determine notwithstanding that the person against whom the claim is made is not within the jurisdiction of the Court or that the wrongful act, neglect or default giving rise to the claim did not take place within its jurisdiction.

(4) For the purposes of this rule, and of rule 9 of this order, domicile is to be determined in accordance with the provisions of sections 41 to 46 of the Civil Jurisdiction and Judgments Act 1982 and 'Convention territory' means the territory or territories of any Contracting State, as defined by section 1(3) of that Act, to which, as defined in section 1(1) of that Act, the Brussels or the Lugano Convention apply.

Rule 1A THE PERIOD FOR FILING AN ACKNOWLEDGMENT OF SERVICE OR FILING OR SERVING AN ADMISSION WHERE THE CLAIM FORM IS SERVED UNDER RULE 1(2)

(1) This rule sets out the period for filing an acknowledgment of service under CPR Part 10 or filing or serving an admission under CPR Part 14 where a claim form has been served out of the jurisdiction under rule 1(2).

(2) If the claim form is to be served under rule 1(2)(a) in Scotland, Northern Ireland or in the European territory of another contracting state the period is—

(a) Where the defendant is served with a claim form which states that particulars of claim are to follow, 21 days after the service of the particulars of claim; and

(b) in any other case, 21 days after service of the claim form.

(3) If the claim form is to be served under rule 1(2)(a) in any other territory of a Contracting State the period is—

(a) where the defendant is served with a claim form which states that particulars of claim are to follow, 31 days after the service of the particulars of claim; and

(b) in any other case, 31 days after service of the claim form.

(4) If the claim form is to be served under—

(a) rule 1(2)(a) in a country not referred to in paragraphs (2) or (3); or

(b) rule 1(2)(b),

the period is set out in the relevant practice direction.

Rule 1B THE PERIOD FOR FILING A DEFENCE WHERE THE CLAIM FORM IS SERVED UNDER RULE 1(2)

(1) This rule sets out the period for filing a defence under CPR Part 15 where a claim form has been served out of the jurisdiction under rule 1(2).

(2) If the claim form is to be served under rule 1(2)(a) in Scotland, Northern Ireland or in the European territory of another contracting state the period is—

(a) 21 days after service of the particulars of claim; or

(b) if the defendant files an acknowledgment of service under CPR Part 10, 35 days after service of the particulars of claim.

(3) If the claim form is to be served under rule 1(2)(a) in any other territory of a Contracting State the period is—

(a) 31 days after service of the particulars of claim; or

(b) if the defendant files an acknowledgment of service under CPR Part 10, 45 days after service of the particulars of claim.

(4) If the claim form is to be served under—

(a) rule 1(2)(a) in a country not referred to in paragraphs (2) or (3); or

(b) rule 1(2)(b),

the period is set out in the relevant practice direction.

Rule 4 APPLICATION FOR, AND GRANT OF, PERMISSION TO SERVE CLAIM FORM OUT OF JURISDICTION

(1) An application for the grant of permission under rule 1(1) must be supported by written evidence stating—

(a) the grounds on which the application is made;

(b) that in the belief of the witness the claimant has a good cause of action;

(c) in what place or country the defendant is, or probably may be found; and

(d) where the application is made under rule 1(1)(c), the grounds for the belief of the witness that there is between the claimant and the person on whom a claim form has been served a real issue which the claimant may reasonably ask the court to try.

(2) No such permission shall be granted unless it shall be made sufficiently to appear to the court that the case is a proper one for service out of the jurisdiction under this order.

(3) Where the application is for the grant of permission under rule 1 to serve a claim form in Scotland or Northern Ireland, if it appears to the court that there may be a concurrent remedy there, the court, in deciding whether to grant

permission shall have regard to the comparative cost and convenience of proceeding there or in England, and (where that is relevant) to the powers and jurisdiction of the sheriff court in Scotland or the county courts or courts of summary jurisdiction in Northern Ireland.

(4) An order granting under rule 1 permission to serve a claim form, out of the jurisdiction must specify the periods within which the defendant may—
  (a) file an acknowledgment of service in accordance with CPR Part 10;
  (b) file or serve an admission in accordance with CPR Part 14; and
  (c) file a defence in accordance with CPR Part 15.

Rule 5 SERVICE OF CLAIM FORM ABROAD: GENERAL

(1) Subject to paragraphs (2) to (8) of this rule—
  (a) a claim form must be served personally on each defendant by the claimant or his agent;
  (b) where a defendant's solicitor indorses on the claim form a statement that he accepts service of the claim form on behalf of that defendant, the claim form shall be deemed to have been duly served on that defendant and to have been so served on the date on which the indorsement was made;
  (c) where a claim form is not duly served on a defendant but he acknowledges service of it, the claim form shall be deemed, unless the contrary is shown, to have been duly served on him and to have been so served on the date on which he acknowledges service;
  (d) CPR rule 6.8 (service by an alternative method) shall apply in relation to the claim form.

(2) Nothing in this rule or in any order or direction of the court made by virtue of it shall authorise or require the doing of anything in a country in which service is to be effected which is contrary to the law of that country.

(3) A claim form which is to be served out of the jurisdiction—
  (a) need not be served personally on the person required to be served so long as it is served on him in accordance with the law of the country in which service is effected; and
  (b) need not be served by the claimant or his agent if it is served by a method provided for by rule 6 or rule 7.

(5) An official certificate stating that a claim form as regards which rule 6 has been complied with has been served on a person personally or in accordance with the law of the country in which service was effected, on a specified date, being a certificate—
  (a) by a British consular authority in that country;
  (b) by the government or judicial authorities of that country; or
  (c) by any other authority designated in respect of that country under the Hague Convention,
shall be evidence of the facts so stated.

(6) An official certificate by the Secretary of State stating that a claim form has been duly served on a specified date in accordance with a request made under rule 7 shall be evidence of that fact.

(7) A document purporting to be such a certificate as is mentioned in paragraph (5) or (6) shall, until the contrary is proved, be deemed to be such a certificate.

(8) In this rule and rule 6 'the Hague Convention' means the Convention on the service abroad of judicial and extra-judicial documents in civil or commercial matters signed at the Hague on 15 November, 1965.

Rule 6 SERVICE OF CLAIM FORM ABROAD THROUGH FOREIGN GOVERNMENTS, JUDICIAL AUTHORITIES AND BRITISH CONSULS

(1) Save where a claim form is to be served pursuant to paragraph (2A) this rule does not apply to service in—
  (a) Scotland, Northern Ireland, the Isle of Man or the Channel Islands;
  (b) any independent Commonwealth country;
  (c) any associated state;

(d) any colony;
(e) the Republic of Ireland.

(2) Where in accordance with these rules a claim form is to be served on a defendant in any country with respect to which there subsists a Civil Procedure Convention (other than the Hague Convention) providing for service in that country of process of the High Court, the claim form may be served—
(a) through the judicial authorities of that country; or
(b) through a British consular authority in that country (subject to any provision of the convention as to the nationality of persons who may be so served).

(2A) Where in accordance with these rules a claim form is to be served on a defendant in any country which is a party to the Hague Convention, the claim form may be served—
(a) through the authority designated under the Convention in respect of that country; or
(b) if the law of that country permits—
(i) through the judicial authorities of that country, or
(ii) through a British consular authority in that country.

(3) Where in accordance with these rules a claim form is to be served on a defendant in any country with respect to which there does not subsist a Civil Procedure Convention providing for service in that country of process of the High Court, the claim form may be served—
(a) through the government of that country, where that government is willing to effect service; or
(b) through a British consular authority in that country, except where service through such an authority is contrary to the law of that country.

(4) A person who wishes to serve a claim form by a method specified in paragraph (2), (2A) or (3) must file in the Central Office of the Supreme Court a request for service of the claim form by that method, together with a copy of the claim form and an additional copy thereof for each person to be served.

(5) Every copy of a claim form filed under paragraph (4) must be accompanied by a translation of the claim form in the official language of the country in which service is to be effected or, if there is more than one official language of that country, in any one of those languages which is appropriate to the place in that country where service is to be effected: provided that this paragraph shall not apply in relation to a copy of a claim form which is to be served in a country the official language of which is, or the official languages of which include, English, or is to be served in any country by a British consular authority on a British subject, unless the service is to be effected under paragraph (2) and the Civil Procedure Convention with respect to that country expressly requires the copy to be accompanied by a translation.

(6) Every translation lodged under paragraph (5) must be certified by the person making it to be a correct translation; and the certificate must contain a statement of that person's full name, of his address and of his qualifications for making the translation.

(7) Documents duly filed under paragraph (4) shall be sent by the Senior Master to the Parliamentary Under-Secretary of State to the Foreign Office with a request that he arrange the claim form to be served by the method indicated in the request lodged under paragraph (4) or, where alternative methods are so indicated, by such one of those methods as is most convenient.

Rule 7 SERVICE OF CLAIM FORM IN CERTAIN ACTIONS UNDER CERTAIN ACTS

(1) Subject to paragraph (4) where a person to whom permission has been granted under rule 1 to serve a claim form on a State, as defined in section 14 of the State Immunity Act 1978, wishes to have the claim form served on that State, he must file in the Central Office—
(a) a request for service to be arranged by the Secretary of State; and
(b) a copy of the claim form; and

(c) except where the official language of the State is, or the official languages of the State include, English, a translation of the claim form in the official language or one of the official languages of that State.

(2) Rule 6(6) shall apply in relation to a translation filed under paragraph (1) of this rule as it applies in relation to a translation filed under paragraph (5) of that rule.

(3) Documents duly filed under this rule shall be sent by the Senior Master to the Secretary of State with a request that the Secretary of State arrange for the claim form to be served.

(4) Where section 12(6) of the State Immunity Act 1978 applies and the State has agreed to a method of service other than that provided by the preceding paragraphs, the claim form may be served either by the method agreed or in accordance with the preceding paragraphs of this rule.

Rule 8 UNDERTAKING TO PAY EXPENSES OF SERVICE BY SECRETARY OF STATE

Every request lodged under rule 6(4) or rule 7 must contain an undertaking by the person making the request to be responsible personally for all expenses incurred by the Secretary of State in respect of the service requested and, on receiving due notification of the amount of those expenses, to pay that amount to the Finance Officer of the office of the Secretary of State and to produce a receipt for the payment to the proper officer of the High Court.

Rule 8A APPLICATIONS FOR AN INTERIM REMEDY UNDER SECTION 25(1) OF THE CIVIL JURISDICTION AND JUDGMENTS ACT 1982

(1) A claim form for an interim remedy under section 25(1) of the Civil Jurisdiction and Judgments Act 1982 (as extended by Order in Council made under section 25(3)) may be served out of the jurisdiction with the permission of the court.

(2) An application for the grant of permission under paragraph (1) must be supported by written evidence stating—

(a) the grounds on which the application is made;
(b) that in the belief of the witness the claimant has a good claim to an interim remedy;
(c) in what place or country the defendant is, or probably may be, found.

(3) The following provisions of this order shall apply, with the necessary modifications, where service is to be effected under this rule as they apply where service is effected under rule 1—

Rule 1A (period for acknowledging service or filing or serving admission)
Rule 1B (period for filing defence);
Rule 4 (2), (3) and (4) (grant of permission);
Rule 5 (service of claim form abroad: general);
Rule 6 (service of claim form abroad through foreign governments, etc.); and
Rule 8 (undertaking to pay expenses of service).

Rule 9 SERVICE OF PETITION AND ORDER ETC.

(1) Rule 1 of this order shall apply to the service out of the jurisdiction of a petition or an application notice issued before proceedings have started as it applies to service of a claim form.

(4) Any application notice issued or order made in any proceedings may be served out of the jurisdiction with the permission of the court but permission shall not be required for such service in any proceedings in which the claim form may by these rules or under any Act be served out of the jurisdiction without permission.

(5) Rule 4 (1), (2) and (3) shall, so far as applicable, apply in relation to an application for the grant of permission under this rule as they apply in relation to an application for the grant of permission under rule 1.

(7) Rules 5, 6 and 8 shall apply in relation to any document for the service of which out of the jurisdiction permission has been granted under this rule as they apply in relation to a claim form.

CPR SCHEDULE 1

Rule 9A SERVICE OF PART 20 CLAIM FORM
(1) This rule applies to any Part 20 claim, except—
  (a) a counterclaim; and
  (b) a claim for a contribution or indemnity made in accordance with CPR rule 20.6.
(2) Permission may be granted to serve a Part 20 claim form on any necessary or proper party to the proceedings brought against the defendants in accordance with rule 1(1)(c).

Rule 10 ORDER TO APPLY TO COUNTY COURT
This order applies to proceedings in any county court in addition to proceedings in the High Court.

RSC ORDER 15
CAUSES OF ACTION, COUNTERCLAIMS AND PARTIES

Rule 6A PROCEEDINGS AGAINST ESTATES
(1) Where any person against whom a claim would have lain has died but the cause of action survives, the claim may, if no grant of probate or administration has been made, be brought against the estate of the deceased.
(2) Without prejudice to the generality of paragraph (1), a claim brought against 'the personal representatives of A.B. deceased' shall be treated, for the purposes of that paragraph, as having been brought against his estate.
(3) A claim purporting to have been commenced against a person shall be treated, if he was dead at its commencement, as having been commenced against his estate in accordance with paragraph (1), whether or not a grant of probate or administration was made before its commencement.
(4) In any such claim as is referred to in paragraph (1) or (3)—
  (a) the claimant shall, during the period of validity for service of the claim form, apply to the court for an order appointing a person to represent the deceased's estate for the purpose of the proceedings or, if a grant of probate or administration has been made for an order that the personal representative of the deceased be made a party to the proceedings, and in either case for an order that the proceedings be carried on against the person appointed or, as the case may be, against the personal representative, as if he had been substituted for the estate;
  (b) the court may, at any stage of the proceedings and on such terms as it thinks just and either of its own motion or on application, make any such order as is mentioned in paragraph (a) and allow such amendments (if any) to be made and make such other order as the court thinks necessary in order to ensure that all matters in dispute in the proceedings may be effectually and completely determined and adjudicated upon.
(5) Before making an order under paragraph (4) the court may require notice to be given to any insurer of the deceased who has an interest in the proceedings and to such (if any) of the persons having an interest in the estate as it thinks fit.
(5A) Where an order is made under paragraph (4) appointing the Official Solicitor to represent the deceased's estate, the appointment shall be limited to his accepting service of the claim form by which the proceedings were begun unless, either on making such an order or on a subsequent application, the court, with the consent of the Official Solicitor, directs that the appointment shall extend to taking further steps in the proceedings.
(6) Where an order is made under paragraph (4), rules 7(4) and 8(3) and (4) shall apply as if the order had been made under rule 7 on the application of the claimant.
(7) Where no grant of probate or administration has been made, any judgment or order given or made in the proceedings shall bind the estate to the same extent as it would have been bound if a grant had been made and a personal representative of the deceased had been a party to the proceedings.

Rule 7 CHANGE OF PARTIES BY REASON OF DEATH, ETC.

(1) Where a party to a claim dies or becomes bankrupt but the cause of action survives, the claim shall not abate by reason of the death or bankruptcy.

Rule 9 FAILURE TO PROCEED AFTER DEATH OF PARTY

(1) If after the death of a claimant or defendant in any claim the cause of action survives, but no order under rule 7 is made substituting as claimant any person in whom the cause of claim vests or, as the case may be, the personal representatives of the deceased defendant, the defendant or, as the case may be, those representatives may apply to the court for an order that unless the claim is proceeded with within such time as may be specified in the order the claim shall be struck out as against the claimant or defendant, as the case may be, who has died; but where it is the claimant who has died, the court shall not make an order under this rule unless satisfied that due notice of the application has been given to the personal representatives (if any) of the deceased claimant and to any other interested persons who, in the opinion of the court, should be notified.

Rule 11 RELATOR ACTIONS

Before the name of any person is used in any claim as a relator, that person must give a written authorisation so to use his name to his solicitor and the authorisation must be filed in the Central Office of the Supreme Court or Chancery Chambers, or, if the claim form is to issue out of a district registry, in that registry.

Rule 12 REPRESENTATIVE PROCEEDINGS

(1) Where numerous persons have the same interest in any proceedings, not being such proceedings as are mentioned in rule 13, the proceedings may be begun, and, unless the court otherwise orders, continued, by or against any one or more of them as representing all or as representing all except one or more of them.

(2) At any stage of proceedings under this rule the court may, on the application of the claimant, and on such terms, if any, as it thinks fit, appoint any one or more of the defendants or other persons as representing whom the defendants are sued to represent all, or all except one or more, of those persons in the proceedings; and where, in exercise of the power conferred by this paragraph, the court appoints a person not named as a defendant, it shall make an order adding that person as a defendant.

(3) A judgment or order given in proceedings under this rule shall be binding on all the persons as representing whom the claimants sue or, as the case may be, the defendants are sued, but shall not be enforced against any person not a party to the proceedings except with the permission of the court.

(4) An application for the grant of permission under paragraph (3) must be made in accordance with CPR Part 23 (general rules about applications for court orders) and the application notice must be served personally on the person against whom it is sought to enforce the judgment or order.

(5) Notwithstanding that a judgment or order to which any such application relates is binding on the person against whom the application is made, that person may dispute liability to have the judgment or order enforced against him on the ground that by reason of facts and matters particular to his case he is entitled to be exempted from such liability.

(6) The court hearing an application for the grant of permission under paragraph (3) may order the question whether the judgment or order is enforceable against the person against whom the application is made to be tried and determined in any manner in which any issue or question in claim may be tried and determined.

Rule 12A DERIVATIVE CLAIMS

(1) This rule applies to every claim by one or more shareholders of a company where the cause of action is vested in the company and relief is accordingly sought on its behalf (referred to in this rule as a 'derivative claim').

(2) Where a defendant in a derivative claim has responded to the particulars of claim, the claimant must apply to the court for permission to continue the claim.

(3) The application must be supported by a witness statement or affidavit verifying the facts on which the claim and the entitlement to sue on behalf of the company are based.

(4) Unless the court otherwise orders, the application must be issued within 21 days after the relevant date, and must be served, together with the witness statement or affidavit in support and any exhibits to the witness statement or affidavit, not less than 10 clear days before the return day on all defendants who have responded to the particulars of claim; any defendant so served may show cause against the application by witness statement or affidavit or otherwise.

(5) In paragraph (4), 'the relevant date' means the later of—
   (a) the date of service of the particulars of claim; and
   (b) the date when the defendant responded to the particulars of claim (provided that, where there is more than one defendant, that date shall be the earliest date when any of them respond).

(6) Nothing in this rule shall prevent the claimant from applying for interim relief pending the determination of an application for permission to continue the claim.

(7) In a derivative claim, CPR rule 15.4 (period for filing a defence) shall not have effect unless the Court grants permission to continue the claim and, in that case, shall have effect as if it required the defendant to serve a defence within 14 days after the order giving permission to continue, or within such other period as the court may specify.

(8) On the hearing of the application under paragraph (2), the court may—
   (a) grant permission to continue the claim, for such period and upon such terms as the court may think fit;
   (b) subject to paragraph (11), dismiss the claim;
   (c) adjourn the application and give such directions as to joinder of parties, the filing of further evidence, disclosure, cross examination of witnesses and otherwise as it may consider expedient.

(9) If the claimant does not apply for permission to continue the claim as required by paragraph (2) within the time laid down in paragraph (4), any defendant who has responded to the particulars of claim may apply for an order to dismiss the proceedings or any claim made in them by way of derivative claim.

(10) On the hearing of such an application for dismissal, the court may—
   (a) subject to paragraph (11), dismiss the claim.
   (b) if the claimant so requests, grant the claimant (on such terms as to costs or otherwise as the court may think fit) an extension of time to apply for permission to continue the claim; or
   (c) make such other order as may in the circumstances be appropriate.

(11) Where only part of the relief claimed is sought on behalf of the company, the court may dismiss the claim for that part of the relief under paragraphs (8) and (10), without prejudice to the claimant's right to continue the claim as to the remainder of the relief and CPR rule 15.4 (period for filing a defence) shall apply as modified by paragraph (7).

(12) If there is a material change in circumstances after the Court has given permission to the claimant to continue the claim in pursuance of an application under paragraph (2), any defendant who has responded to the particulars of claim may make an application supported by witness statement or affidavit requiring the claimant to show cause why the court should not dismiss the proceedings or any claim made in them by way of derivative claim. On such application the court shall have the same powers as it would have had upon an application under paragraph (2).

(13) The claimant may include in an application under paragraph (2) an application for an indemnity out of the assets of the company in respect of costs incurred or to be incurred in the claim and the Court may grant such indemnity upon such terms as may in the circumstances be appropriate.

(14) So far as possible, any application under paragraph (13) and any application by the claimant under CPR Part 24 shall be made so as to be heard at the same time as the application under paragraph (2).

CPR SCHEDULE 1

Rule 13 REPRESENTATION OF INTERESTED PERSONS WHO CANNOT BE ASCERTAINED, ETC.

(1) In any proceedings concerning—
   (a) the estate of a deceased person; or
   (b) property subject to a trust; or
   (c) the construction of a written instrument, including a statute,

the court, if satisfied that it is expedient so to do, and that one or more of the conditions specified in paragraph (2) are satisfied, may appoint one or more persons to represent any person (including an unborn person) or class who is or may be interested (whether presently or for any future, contingent or unascertained interest) in or affected by the proceedings.

(2) The conditions for the exercise of the power conferred by paragraph (1) are as follows—
   (a) that the person, the class or some member of the class, cannot be ascertained or cannot readily be ascertained;
   (b) that the person, class or some member of the class, though ascertained, cannot be found;
   (c) that, though the person or the class and the members thereof can be ascertained and found, it appears to the court expedient (regard being had to all the circumstances, including the amount at stake and the degree of difficulty of the point to be determined) to exercise the power for the purposes of saving expense.

(3) Where, in any proceedings to which paragraph (1) applies, the court exercises the power conferred by that paragraph, a judgment or order of the court given or made when the person or persons appointed in exercise of that power are before the court shall be binding on the person or class represented by the person or persons so appointed.

(4) Where, in any such proceedings, a compromise is proposed and some of the persons who are interested in, or who may be affected by, the compromise are not parties to the proceedings (including unborn or unascertained persons) but—
   (a) there is some other person in the same interest before the court who assents to the compromise or on whose behalf the court sanctions the compromise, or
   (b) the absent persons are represented by a person appointed under paragraph (1) who so assents,

the court, if satisfied that the compromise will be for the benefit of the absent persons and that it is expedient to exercise this power, may approve the compromise and order that it shall be binding on the absent persons, and they shall be bound accordingly except where the order has been obtained by fraud or non-disclosure of material facts.

Rule 13A NOTICE OF CLAIM TO NON-PARTIES

(1) At any stage in a claim to which this rule applies, the court may, on the application of any party or of its own motion, direct that notice of the claim be served on any person who is not a party thereto but who will or may be affected by any judgment given therein.

(2) An application under this rule may be made without notice being served on any other party and shall be supported by a witness statement or affidavit stating the grounds of the application.

(3) Every notice of a claim under this rule shall be in Form No. 52 in the relevant practice direction and shall be issued out of the appropriate office, and the copy to be served shall be a sealed copy accompanied by a copy of the claim form and of all other statements of case served in the claim and by a form of acknowledgment of service with such modifications as may be appropriate.

(4) A person may, within 14 days of service on him of a notice under this rule, acknowledge service of the claim form and shall thereupon become a party to the claim, but in default of such acknowledgment and subject to paragraph (5) he shall be bound by any judgment given in the claim as if he was a party thereto.

(5) If at any time after service of such notice on any person the claim form is amended so as substantially to alter the relief claimed, the court may direct that

the judgment shall not bind such person unless a further notice together with a copy of the amended claim form is issued and served upon him under this rule.
   (6) This rule applies to any claim relating to—
      (a) the estate of a deceased person; or
      (b) property subject to a trust.
   (7) CPR rule 7.2(2) shall apply in relation to a notice of a claim under this rule as if the notice were a claim form and the person by whom the notice is issued were the claimant.

Rule 14 REPRESENTATION OF BENEFICIARIES BY TRUSTEES, ETC.

   (1) Any proceedings, including proceedings to enforce a security by foreclosure or otherwise, may be brought by or against trustees, executors or administrators in their capacity as such without joining any of the persons having a beneficial interest in the trust or estate, as the case may be; and any judgment or order given or made in those proceedings shall be binding on those persons unless the court in the same or other proceedings otherwise orders on the ground that the trustees, executors or administrators, as the case may be, could not or did not in fact represent the interests of those persons in the first-mentioned proceedings.
   (2) Paragraph (1) is without prejudice to the power of the court to order any person having such an interest as aforesaid to be made a party to the proceedings or to make an order under rule 13.

Rule 15 REPRESENTATION OF DECEASED PERSON INTERESTED IN PROCEEDINGS

   (1) Where in any proceedings it appears to the court that a deceased person was interested in the matter in question in the proceedings and that he has no personal representative, the court may, on the application of any party to the proceedings, proceed in the absence of a person representing the estate of the deceased person or may by order appoint a person to represent that estate for the purposes of the proceedings; and any such order, and any judgment or order subsequently given or made in the proceedings, shall bind the estate of the deceased person to the same extent as it would have been bound had a personal representative of that person been a party to the proceedings.
   (2) Before making an order under this rule, the court may require notice of the application for the order to be given to such (if any) of the persons having an interest in the estate as it thinks fit.

Rule 16 DECLARATORY JUDGMENT

No claim or other proceeding shall be open to objection on the ground that a merely declaratory judgment or order is sought thereby, and the court may make binding declarations of right whether or not any consequential relief is or could be claimed.

Rule 17 CONDUCT OF PROCEEDINGS

The court may give the conduct of any claim, inquiry or other proceeding to such person as it thinks fit.

RSC ORDER 17
INTERPLEADER

Rule 1 ENTITLEMENT TO RELIEF BY WAY OF INTERPLEADER

   (1) Where—
      (a) a person is under a liability in respect of a debt or in respect of any money, goods or chattels and he is, or expects to be, sued for or in respect of that debt or money or those goods or chattels by two or more persons making adverse claims thereto; or
      (b) claim is made to any money, goods or chattels taken or intended to be taken by a sheriff in execution under any process, or to the proceeds or value of any such goods or chattels, by a person other than the person against whom the process is issued,

the person under liability as mentioned in sub-paragraph (a) or (subject to rule 2) the sheriff, may apply to the court for relief by way of interpleader.

(2) References in this Order to a sheriff shall be construed as including references to any other officer charged with the execution of process by or under the authority of the High Court.

Rule 2 CLAIM TO GOODS, ETC., TAKEN IN EXECUTION

(1) Any person making a claim to or in respect of any money, goods or chattels taken or intended to be taken in execution under process of the court, or to the proceeds or value of any such goods or chattels, must give notice of his claim to the sheriff charged with the execution of the process and must include in his notice a statement of his address, and that address shall be his address for service.

(2) On receipt of a claim made under this rule the sheriff must forthwith give notice thereof to the execution creditor and the execution creditor must, within seven days after receiving the notice, give notice to the sheriff informing him whether he admits or disputes the claim. An execution creditor who gives notice in accordance with this paragraph admitting a claim shall only be liable to the sheriff for any fees and expenses incurred by the sheriff before receipt of that notice.

(3) Where—
 (a) the sheriff receives a notice from an execution creditor under paragraph (2) disputing a claim, or the execution creditor fails, within the period mentioned in that paragraph, to give the required notice; and
 (b) the claim made under this rule is not withdrawn,
the sheriff may apply to the court for relief under this order.

(4) A sheriff who receives a notice from an execution creditor under paragraph (2) admitting a claim made under this rule shall withdraw from possession of the money, goods or chattels claimed and may apply to the court for relief under this order of the following kind, that is to say, an order restraining the bringing of a claim against him for or in respect of his having taken possession of that money or those goods or chattels.

Rule 2A CLAIM IN RESPECT OF GOODS PROTECTED FROM SEIZURE

(1) Where a judgment debtor whose goods have been seized, or are intended to be seized, by a sheriff under a writ of execution claims that such goods are not liable to execution by virtue of section 138(3A) of the Act, he must within 5 days of the seizure give notice in writing to the sheriff identifying all those goods in respect of which he makes such a claim and the grounds of such claim in respect of each item.

(2) Upon receipt of a notice of claim under paragraph (1), the sheriff must forthwith give notice thereof to the execution creditor and to any person who has made a claim to, or in respect of, the goods under rule 2(1) and the execution creditor and any person who has made claim must, within 7 days of receipt of such notice, inform the sheriff in writing whether he admits or disputes the judgment debtor's claim in respect of each item.

(3) The sheriff shall withdraw from possession of any goods in respect of which the judgment debtor's claim is admitted or if the execution creditor or any person claiming under rule 2(1) fails to notify him in accordance with paragraph (2) and the sheriff shall so inform the parties in writing.

(4) Where the sheriff receives notice from—
 (a) the execution creditor; or
 (b) any such person to whom notice was given under paragraph (2),
that the claim or any part thereof is disputed, he must forthwith seek the directions of the court and may include therein an application for an order restraining the bringing of any claim against him for, or in respect of, his having seized any of those goods or his having failed so to do.

(5) The sheriff's application for directions under paragraph (4) shall be made by an application in accordance with CPR Part 23 and, on the hearing of the application, the court may—
 (a) determine the judgment debtor's claim summarily; or

(b) give such directions for the determination of any issue raised by such claim as may be just.

(6) A Master and a district judge of a district registry shall have power to make an order of the kind referred to in paragraph (4) and the reference to Master shall be construed in accordance with rule 4.

Rule 3 MODE OF APPLICATION

(1) An application for relief under this order must be made by claim form unless made in an existing claim, in which case it must be made by accordance with CPR Part 23.

(2) Where the applicant is a sheriff who has withdrawn from possession of money, goods or chattels taken in execution and who is applying for relief under rule 2(4) the claim form must be served on any person who made a claim under that rule to or in respect of that money or those goods or chattels, and that person may attend the hearing of the application.

(4) Subject to paragraph (5) a claim form or application notice under this rule must be supported by evidence that the applicant—

(a) claims no interest in the subject-matter in dispute other than for charges or costs;

(b) does not collude with any of the claimants to that subject-matter; and

(c) is willing to pay or transfer that subject-matter into court or to dispose of it as the court may direct.

(5) Where the applicant is a sheriff, he shall not provide such evidence as is referred to in paragraph (4) unless directed by the court to do so.

(6) Any person who makes a claim under rule 2 and who is served with a claim form under this rule shall within 14 days serve on the execution creditor and the sheriff a witness statement or affidavit specifying any money and describing any goods and chattels claimed and setting out the grounds upon which such claim is based.

(7) Where the applicant is a sheriff a claim form under this rule must give notice of the requirement in paragraph (6).

Rule 4 TO WHOM SHERIFF MAY APPLY FOR RELIEF

An application to the court for relief under this order may, if the applicant is a sheriff, be made—

(a) where the claim in question is proceeding in the Royal Courts of Justice, to a Master or, if the execution to which the application relates has been or is to be levied in the district of a District Registry, either to a Master or to the district judge of that Registry;

(b) where the claim in question is proceeding in a District Registry, to the district judge of that Registry or, if such execution has been or is to be levied in the district of some other District Registry or outside the district of any District Registry, either to the said district judge or to the district judge of that other registry or to a Master as the case may be.

Where the claim in question is proceeding in the Admiralty Court or the Family Division, references in this rule to a Master shall be construed as references to the Admiralty Registrar or to a Registrar of that Division.

Rule 5 POWERS OF COURT HEARING CLAIM

(1) Where on the hearing of a claim under this order all the persons by whom adverse claims to the subject-matter in dispute (hereafter in this Order referred to as 'the interpleader claimants') appear, the court may order—

(a) that any interpleader claimant be made a defendant in any claim pending with respect to the subject-matter in dispute in substitution for or in addition to the applicant for relief under this order; or

(b) that an issue between the interpleader claimants be stated and tried and may direct which of the interpleader claimants is to be claimant and which defendant.

(2) Where—

(a) the applicant under this order is a sheriff; or

(b) all the interpleader claimants consent or any of them so requests; or

(c) the question at issue between the interpleader claimants is a question of law and the facts are not in dispute,

the court may summarily determine the question at issue between the interpleader claimants and make an order accordingly on such terms as may be just.

(3) Where an interpleader claimant, having been duly served with a claim form under this order, does not appear at the hearing or, having appeared, fails or refuses to comply with an order made in the proceedings, the court may make an order declaring the interpleader claimant, and all persons claiming under him, for ever barred from prosecuting his claim against the applicant for such relief and all persons claiming under him, but such an order shall not affect the rights of the interpleader claimants as between themselves.

Rule 6 POWER TO ORDER SALE OF GOODS TAKEN IN EXECUTION
Where an application for relief under this order is made by a sheriff who has taken possession of any goods or chattels in execution under any process, and an interpleader claimant alleges that he is entitled, under a bill of sale or otherwise. to the goods or chattels by way of security for debt, the court may order those goods or chattels or any part thereof to be sold and may direct that the proceeds of sale be applied in such manner and on such terms as may be just and as may be specified in the order.

Rule 7 POWER TO STAY PROCEEDINGS
Where a defendant to a claim applies for relief under this Order in the claim, the court may by order stay all further proceedings in the claim.

Rule 8 OTHER POWERS
(1) Subject to the foregoing rules of this Order, the court may in or for the purposes of any interpleader proceedings make such order as to costs or any other matter as it thinks just.

(2) Where the interpleader claimant fails to appear at the hearing, the Court may direct that the sheriff's and execution creditor's costs shall be assessed by a master or, where the hearing was heard in a district registry, by a district judge of that registry and the following CPR rules shall apply—
    (a) 44.4 (basis of assessment);
    (b) 44.5 (factors to be taken into account in deciding the amount of costs);
    (c) 48.4 (limitations on court's power to award costs in favour of trustee or personal representative); and
    (d) 48.6 (litigants in person).

(3) Where the claim in question is proceeding in the Admirality Court or the Family Division, references in this rule to a Master shall be construed as references to the Admiralty Registrar or to a Registrar of that Division.

Rule 9 ONE ORDER IN SEVERAL PROCEEDINGS
Where the Court considers it necessary or expedient to make an order in any interpleader proceedings in several proceedings pending in several Divisions, or before different judges of the same Division, the court may make such an order; and the order shall be entitled in all those causes or matters and shall be binding on all the parties to them.

Rule 10 DISCLOSURE
CPR Parts 31 and 18 shall, with the necessary modifications, apply in relation to an interpleader issue as they apply in relation to any other proceedings.

Rule 11 TRIAL OF INTERPLEADER ISSUE
(1) CPR Part 39 shall, with the necessary modifications, apply to the trial of an interpleader issue as it applies to the trial of a claim.

(2) The court by whom an interpleader issue is tried may give such judgment or make such order as finally to dispose of all questions arising in the interpleader proceedings.

CPR SCHEDULE 1

RSC ORDER 23
SECURITY FOR COSTS

Rule A1 ORDER TO APPLY TO HIGH COURT AND COUNTY COURT
This order applies to proceedings both in the High Court and the county court.

Rule 1 SECURITY FOR COSTS OF PROCEEDINGS, ETC.
(1) Where, on the application of a defendant, it appears to the court—
    (a) that the claimant is ordinarily resident out of the jurisdiction; or
    (b) that the claimant (not being a claimant who is suing in a representative capacity) is a nominal claimant who is suing for the benefit of some other person and that there is reason to believe that he will be unable to pay the costs of the defendant if ordered to do so; or
    (c) subject to paragraph (2) that the claimant's address is not stated in the claim form or other originating process or is incorrectly stated therein; or
    (d) that the claimant has changed his address during the course of the proceedings with a view to evading the consequences of the litigation,
then if, having regard to all the circumstances of the case, the court thinks it just to do so, it may order the claimant to give such security for the defendant's costs of the proceedings as it thinks just.
(2) The court shall not require a claimant to give security by reason only of paragraph (1)(c) if he satisfies the court that the failure to state his address or the mis-statement thereof was made innocently and without intention to deceive.
(3) The references in the foregoing paragraphs to a claimant and a defendant shall be construed as references to the person (howsoever described on the record) who is in the position of claimant or defendant, as the case may be, in the proceeding in question, including a proceeding on a counterclaim.

Rule 2 MANNER OF GIVING SECURITY
Where an order is made requiring any party to give security for costs, the security shall be given in such manner, at such time, and on such terms (if any) as the court may direct.

Rule 3 SAVING FOR ENACTMENTS
This order is without prejudice to the provisions of any enactment which empowers the court to require security to be given for the costs of any proceedings.

RSC ORDER 30
RECEIVERS

Rule A1 ORDER TO APPLY TO HIGH COURT AND COUNTY COURT
This order applies to proceedings both in the High Court and the county court.

Rule 1 APPLICATION FOR RECEIVER AND INJUNCTION
(1) An application for the appointment of a receiver made in existing proceedings must be made in accordance with CPR Part 23 and the practice direction supplementing that Part.
(2) An application for an injunction ancillary or incidental to an order appointing a receiver may be joined with the application for such order.
(3) The relevant practice direction will apply to an application for the immediate grant of such an injunction.

Rule 2 GIVING OF SECURITY BY RECEIVER
(1) A judgment or order directing the appointment of a receiver may include such directions as the court thinks fit as to the giving of security by the person appointed.
(2) Where by virtue of any judgment or order appointing a person named therein to be receiver a person is required to give security in accordance with this rule he must give security approved by the court duly to account for what he receives as receiver and to deal with it as the court directs.

(3) Unless the court otherwise directs, the security shall be by guarantee.

(4) The guarantee must be filed in the office or registry of the court in which the claim is proceeding and it shall be kept as of record until duly vacated.

Rule 3 REMUNERATION OF RECEIVER

(1) A person appointed receiver shall be allowed such proper remuneration, if any, as may be authorised by the court.

(2) The court may direct that such remuneration shall be—

(a) fixed by reference to such scales or rates of professional charges as it thinks fit; or

(b) assessed by a costs judge or a district judge.

(3) Where remuneration is assessed by a costs judge or district judge following a direction under paragraph 2(b), CPR rules 44.4(1) and (2) and 44.5(1) will apply as though the remuneration were costs directed to be assessed on the standard basis.

(4) An appeal shall lie from the assessment in accordance with section 8 of CPR Part 47 (CPR rules 47.21 to 47.27).

Rule 4 SERVICE OF ORDER AND NOTICE

A copy of the judgment or order appointing a receiver shall be served by the party having conduct of the proceedings on the receiver and all other parties to the proceedings in which the receiver has been appointed.

Rule 5 RECEIVER'S ACCOUNTS

(1) A receiver shall submit such accounts to such parties at such intervals or on such dates as the court may direct.

(2) Any party to whom a receiver is required to submit accounts may, on giving reasonable notice to the receiver, inspect, either personally or by an agent, the books and other papers relating to such accounts.

(3) Any party who is dissatisfied with the accounts of the receiver may give notice specifying the item or items to which objection is taken and requiring the receiver within not less than 14 days to file his accounts with the court and a copy of such notice shall be filed in the office or registry of the court dealing with the proceedings.

(4) Following an examination by or on behalf of the court of an item or items in an account to which objection is taken the result of such examination must be certified by a Master, the Admiralty Registrar, a district judge of the Family Division or a district judge, as the case may be, and an order may thereupon be made as to the incidence of any costs or expenses incurred.

Rule 6 PAYMENT INTO COURT BY RECEIVER

The court may fix the amounts and frequency of payments into court to be made by a receiver.

Rule 7 DEFAULT BY RECEIVER

(1) Where a receiver fails to attend for the examination of any account of his, or fails to submit any account, provide access to any books or papers or do any other thing which he is required to submit, provide or do, he and any or all of the parties to the cause or matter in which he was appointed may be required to attend the court to show cause for the failure, and the court may give such directions as it thinks proper including, if necessary, directions for the discharge of the receiver and the appointment of another and the payment of costs.

(2) Without prejudice to paragraph (1) where a receiver fails to attend for the examination of any account of his or fails to submit any account or fails to pay into court on the date fixed by the court any sum required to be so paid, the court may disallow any remuneration claimed by the receiver and may, where he has failed to pay any such sum into court, charge him with interest at the rate currently payable in respect of judgment debts in the High Court on that sum while in his possession as receiver.

Rule 8 DIRECTIONS TO RECEIVERS

A receiver may at any time request the court to give him directions and such request shall state in writing the matters with regard to which directions are required.

RSC ORDER 31
SALES, ETC. OF LAND BY ORDER OF COURT: CONVEYANCING COUNSEL OF THE COURT

Rule A1 ORDER TO APPLY TO HIGH COURT AND COUNTY COURT

This order applies to proceedings both in the High Court and the county court.

I. SALES, ETC. OF LAND BY ORDER OF COURT

Rule 1 POWER TO ORDER SALE OF LAND

Where in any proceedings relating to any land it appears necessary or expedient for the purposes of the proceedings that the land or any part thereof should be sold, the court may order that land or part to be sold, and any party bound by the order and in possession of that land or part, or in receipt of the rents and profits thereof, may be compelled to deliver up such possession or receipt to the purchaser or to such other person as the court may direct.

In this order 'land' includes any interest in, or right over, land.

Rule 2 MANNER OF CARRYING OUT SALE

(1) Where an order is made directing any land to be sold, the court may permit the party or person having the conduct of the sale to sell the land in such manner as he thinks fit, or may direct that the land be sold in such manner as the court may either by the order or subsequently direct for the best price that can be obtained, and all proper parties shall join in the sale and conveyance as the court shall direct.

(2) The court may give such directions as it thinks fit for the purpose of effecting the sale, including, without prejudice to the generality of the foregoing words, directions—

    (a) appointing the party or person who is to have the conduct of the sale;

    (b) fixing the manner of sale, whether by contract conditional on the approval of the court, private treaty, public auction, tender or some other manner;

    (c) fixing a reserve or minimum price;

    (d) requiring payment of the purchase money into court or to trustees or other persons;

    (e) for settling the particulars and conditions of sale;

    (f) for obtaining evidence of the value of the property;

    (g) fixing the security (if any) to be given by the auctioneer, if the sale is to be by public auction, and the remuneration to be allowed him;

    (h) requiring an abstract of the title to be referred to conveyancing counsel of the court or some other conveyancing counsel for his opinion thereon and to settle the particulars and conditions of sale.

Rule 3 CERTIFYING RESULT OF SALE

(1) If either the court has directed payment of the purchase money into court or the court so directs, the result of a sale by order of the court must be certified—

    (a) in the case of a sale by public auction, by the auctioneer who conducted the sale; and

    (b) in any other case, by the solicitor of the party or person having the conduct of the sale,

and the court may require the certificate to be verified by the witness statement or affidavit of the auctioneer or solicitor, as the case may be.

(2) The solicitor of the party or person having the conduct of the sale must file the certificate and any witness statement or affidavit in the office of the court dealing with the proceedings.

Rule 4 MORTGAGE, EXCHANGE OR PARTITION UNDER ORDER OF THE COURT

Rules 2 and 3 shall, so far as applicable and with the necessary modifications, apply in relation to the mortgage, exchange or partition of any land under an order of the court as they apply in relation to the sale of any land under such an order.

II. CONVEYANCING COUNSEL OF THE COURT

Rule 5 REFERENCE OF MATTERS TO CONVEYANCING COUNSEL OF COURT

The court may refer to the conveyancing counsel of the court—

  (a) any matter relating to the investigation of the title to any property with a view to an investment of money in the purchase or on mortgage thereof, or with a view to the sale thereof;

  (b) any matter relating to the settlement of a draft of a conveyance, mortgage, settlement or other instrument; and

  (c) any other matter it thinks fit, and may act upon his opinion in the matter referred.

Rule 6 OBJECTION TO CONVEYANCING COUNSEL'S OPINION

Any party may object to the opinion given by any conveyancing counsel on a reference under rule 5, and if he does so the point in dispute shall be determined by the judge.

Rule 8 OBTAINING COUNSEL'S OPINION ON REFERENCE

The order referring any matter to conveyancing counsel of the court shall be recorded in the books of the court and a copy of such order shall be sent by the court to counsel and shall constitute sufficient authority for him to proceed with the reference.

RSC ORDER 44
PROCEEDINGS UNDER JUDGMENTS AND ORDERS: CHANCERY DIVISION

Rule 1 APPLICATION TO ORDERS

In this order references to a judgment include references to an order.

Rule 2 SERVICE OF NOTICE OF JUDGMENT ON PERSON NOT A PARTY

  (1) Where in a claim for—
    (a) the administration of the estate of a deceased person; or
    (b) the execution of a trust; or
    (c) the sale of any property,
the court gives a judgment or makes a direction which affects persons not parties to the claim, the court may when giving the judgment or at any stage of the proceedings under the judgment direct notice of the judgment to be served on any such person and any person so served shall, subject to paragraph (4), be bound by the judgment as if he had originally been a party to the claim.

  (2) If it appears that it is not practicable to serve notice of a judgment on a person directed to be served the court may dispense with service and may also order that such person be bound by the judgment.

  (3) Every notice of a judgment for service under this rule must be indorsed with a memorandum in Form No. 52A in the relevant practice direction and accompanied by a form of acknowledgment of service with such modifications as may be appropriate and the copy of the notice to be served shall be a sealed copy.

  (4) A person served with notice of a judgment may, within one month after service of the notice on him, and after acknowledging service apply to the court to discharge, vary or add to the judgment.

  (5) A person served with notice of a judgment may, after acknowledging service of the notice, attend the proceedings under the judgment.

  (6) CPR Part 10 except for CPR rule 10.2 shall apply in relation to the acknowledgment of service of a notice of judgment as if the judgment were a claim

form, the person by whom the notice is served were the claimant and the person on whom it is served were a defendant.

Rule 3 DIRECTIONS BY THE COURT

(1) Where a judgment given in a proceedings in the Chancery Division contains directions which make it necessary to proceed in private under the judgment the court may, when giving the judgment or at any time during proceedings under the judgment, give further directions for the conduct of those proceedings, including, in particular, directions with respect to—

    (a) the manner in which any account or inquiry is to be prosecuted;

    (b) the evidence to be adduced in support thereof;

    (c) the preparation and service on the parties to be bound thereby of the draft of any deed or other instrument which is directed by the judgment to be settled by the court and the service of any objections to the draft;

    (d) the parties required to attend all or any part of the proceedings;

    (e) the representation by the same solicitors of parties who constitute a class and by different solicitors of parties who ought to be separately represented; and

    (f) the time within which each proceeding is to be taken, and may fix a day or days for the further attendance of the parties.

(2) The court may revoke or vary any directions given under this rule.

Rule 4 APPLICATION OF RULES 5 TO 8

Rules 5 to 8 apply—

    (a) where in proceedings for the administration under the direction of the court of the estate of a deceased person the judgment directs any account of debts or other liabilities of the deceased's estate to be taken or any inquiry for next of kin or other ascertained claimants to be made; and

    (b) where in proceedings for the execution under the direction of the court of a trust the judgment directs any such inquiry to be made,

and those rules shall, with the necessary modifications, apply where in any other proceedings the judgment directs an account of debts or other liabilities to be taken or any inquiry to be made.

Rule 5 ADVERTISEMENTS FOR CREDITORS AND OTHER CLAIMANTS

The court may, when giving a judgment or at any stage of proceedings under a judgment, give directions for the issue of advertisements for creditors or other claimants and may fix the time within which creditors and claimants may respond.

Rule 6 EXAMINATION OF CLAIMS

(1) Where an account of debts or other liabilities of the estate of a deceased person has been directed, such party as the court may direct must—

    (a) examine the claims of persons claiming to be creditors of the estate;

    (b) determine, so far as he is able, to which of such claims the estate is liable; and

    (c) at least seven clear days before the time appointed for adjudicating on claims, make a witness statement or affidavit stating his findings and his reasons for them and listing all the other debts of the deceased which are or may still be due.

(2) Where an inquiry for next of kin or other unascertained claimants has been directed, such party as the court may direct must—

    (a) examine the claims;

    (b) determine, so far as he is able, which of them are valid; and

    (c) at least seven clear days before the time appointed for adjudicating on claims, make a witness statement or affidavit stating his findings and his reasons for them.

(3) If the personal representatives or trustees concerned are not the parties directed by the court to examine claims, they must join with the party directed to examine them in making the witness statement or affidavit required by this rule.

CPR SCHEDULE 1

Rule 7 ADJUDICATION ON CLAIMS
For the purpose of adjudicating on claims the court may—
    (a)   direct any claim to be investigated in such manner as it thinks fit;
    (b)   require any claimant to attend and prove his claim or to furnish further particulars or evidence of it; or
    (c)   allow any claim after or without proof thereof.

Rule 8 NOTICE OF ADJUDICATION
The court shall give directions that there be served on every creditor whose claim or any part thereof has been allowed or disallowed, and who did not attend when the claim was disposed of, a notice informing him of that fact.

Rule 9 INTEREST ON DEBTS
(1) Where an account of the debts of a deceased person is directed by any judgment, then, unless the deceased's estate is insolvent or the court otherwise orders, interest shall be allowed—
    (a)   on any such debt as carries interest, at the rate it carries; and
    (b)   on any other debt, from the date of the judgment at the rate payable on judgment debts at that date.

(2) A creditor who has established his debt in proceedings under the judgment and whose debt does not carry interest shall be entitled to interest on his debt in accordance with paragraph (1)(b) out of any assets which may remain after satisfying the costs of the proceedings, the debts which have been established and the interest on such of those debts as by law carry interest.

(3) For the purpose of this rule 'debt' includes funeral, testamentary or administration expenses and, in relation to expenses incurred after the judgment, for the reference in paragraph (1)(b) to the date of the judgment there shall be substituted a reference to the date when the expenses became payable.

Rule 10 INTEREST ON LEGACIES
Where an account of legacies is directed by any judgment, then, subject to any directions contained in the will or codicil in question and to any order made by the court, interest shall be allowed on each legacy at the rate of 6 per cent. per annum beginning at the expiration of one year after the testator's death.

Rule 11 MASTER'S ORDER
(1) The result of proceedings before a Master under a judgment shall be stated in the form of an order.

(2) Subject to any direction of the Master under paragraph (3) or otherwise an order under this rule shall have effect as a final order disposing of the proceedings in which it is made.

(3) An order under this rule shall contain such directions as the Master thinks fit as to the further consideration of the proceedings in which it is made.

(4) Every order made under this rule shall have immediate binding effect on the parties to the proceedings in which it is made and copies of the order shall be served on such of the parties as the Master may direct.

Rule 12 APPEAL AGAINST MASTER'S ORDER
Subject to Order 58, rule 2, rule 1 of that order shall apply to an order made pursuant to rule 11 above, save that—
    (a)   except where paragraph (e) below applies, the notice referred to in Order 58, rule 1(2) shall state the grounds of the appeal, and must be issued within 14 days after the order is made;
    [(b)   *revoked*]
    (c)   no fresh evidence (other than evidence as to matters which have occurred after the date of the Master's order) shall be admitted except on special grounds;
    (d)   the judge hearing the appeal shall have the same power to draw inferences of fact as. has the Court of Appeal under Order 59, rule 10(3);
    (e)   if the order is to be acted on by the Accountant-General or is an order passing a receiver's account, notice of appeal must be issued not later than two

clear days after the making of the order and, where the order is to be acted on by the Accountant-General, a copy of it must be served on the Accountant-General as soon as practicable after it is made.

RSC ORDER 45
ENFORCEMENT OF JUDGMENTS AND ORDERS: GENERAL

Rule 1 ENFORCEMENT OF JUDGMENT, ETC., FOR PAYMENT OF MONEY

(1) Subject to the provisions of these rules, a judgment or order for the payment of money, not being a judgment or order for the payment of money into court, may be enforced by one or more of the following means, that is to say—

    (a) writ of fieri facias;
    (b) garnishee proceedings;
    (c) a charging order;
    (d) the appointment of a receiver;
    (e) in a case in which rule 5 applies, an order of committal;
    (f) in such a case, writ of sequestration.

(2) Subject to the provisions of these rules, a judgment or order for the payment of money into court may be enforced by one or more of the following means, that is to say—

    (a) the appointment of a receiver;
    (b) in a case in which rule 5 applies, an order of committal;
    (c) in such a case, writ of sequestration.

(3) Paragraphs (1) and (2) are without prejudice to any other remedy available to enforce such a judgment or order as is therein mentioned or to the power of a court under the Debtors Acts 1869 and 1878, to commit to prison a person who makes default in paying money adjudged or ordered to be paid by him, or to the right of a person prosecuting a judgment or order for the payment of money to a person to apply under section 105(1) of the County Courts Act 1984, to have the judgment or order enforced in a county court, or to the enactments relating to bankruptcy or the winding up of companies.

(4) In this order references to any writ shall be construed as including references to any further writ in aid of the first mentioned writ.

Rule 2 NOTICE OF SEIZURE

When first executing a writ of fieri facias, the Sheriff or his officer shall deliver to the debtor or leave at each place where execution is levied a notice in Form No. 55 in the relevant Practice Direction informing the debtor of the execution.

Rule 3 ENFORCEMENT OF JUDGMENT FOR POSSESSION OF LAND

(1) Subject to the provisions of these rules, a judgment or order for the giving of possession of land may be enforced by one or more of the following means, that is to say—

    (a) writ of possession;
    (b) in a case in which rule 5 applies, an order of committal;
    (c) in such a case, writ of sequestration.

(2) A writ of possession to enforce a judgment or order for the giving of possession of any land shall not be issued without the permission of the court except where the judgment or order was given or made in mortgage proceedings to which Order 88 applies.

(3) Such permission shall not be granted unless it is shown—

    (a) that every person in actual possession of the whole or any part of the land has received such notice of the proceedings as appears to the court sufficient to enable him to apply to the court for any relief to which he may be entitled; and

    (b) if the operation of the judgment or order is suspended by subsection (2) of section 16 of the Landlord and Tenant Act, 1954, that the applicant has not received notice in writing from the tenant that he desires that the provisions of paragraphs (a) and (b) of that subsection shall have effect.

(4) A writ of possession may include provision for enforcing the payment of any money adjudged or ordered to be paid by the judgment or order which is to be enforced by the writ.

Rule 4 ENFORCEMENT OF JUDGMENT FOR DELIVERY OF GOODS

(1) Subject to the provisions of these rules, a judgment or order for the delivery of any goods which does not give a person against whom the judgment is given or order made the alternative of paying the assessed value of the goods may be enforced by one or more of the following means, that is to say—

    (a) writ of delivery to recover the goods without alternative provision for recovery of the assessed value thereof (hereafter in this rule referred to as a 'writ of specific delivery');

    (b) in a case in which rule 5 applies, an order of committal;

    (c) in such a case, writ of sequestration.

(2) Subject to the provisions of these rules, a judgment or order for the delivery of any goods or payment of their assessed value may be enforced by one or more of the following means, that is to say—

    (a) writ of delivery to recover the goods or their assessed value;

    (b) by order of the court, writ of specific delivery;

    (c) in a case in which rule 5 applies, writ of sequestration.

An application for an order under sub-paragraph (b) shall be made in accordance with CPR Part 23, which must be served on the defendant against whom the judgment or order sought to be enforced was given or made.

(3) A writ of specific delivery, and a writ of delivery to recover any goods or their assessed value, may include provision for enforcing the payment of any money adjudged or ordered to be paid by the judgment or order which is to be enforced by the writ.

(4) A judgment or order for the payment of the assessed value of any goods may be enforced by the same means as any other judgment or order for the payment of money.

Rule 5 ENFORCEMENT OF JUDGMENT TO DO OR ABSTAIN FROM DOING ANY ACT

(1) Where—

    (a) a person required by a judgment or order to do an act within a time specified in the judgment or order refuses or neglects to do it within that time or, as the case may be, within that time as extended or abridged under a court order or CPR rule 2.11; or

    (b) a person disobeys a judgment or order requiring him to abstain from doing an act,

then, subject to the provisions of these rules, the judgment or order may be enforced by one or more of the following means, that is to say—

    (i) with the permission of the court, a writ of sequestration against the property of that person;

    (ii) where that person is a body corporate, with the permission of the court, a writ of sequestration against the property of any director or other officer of the body;

    (iii) subject to the provisions of the Debtors Act 1869 and 1878, an order of committal against that person or, where that person is a body corporate, against any such officer.

(2) Where a judgment or order requires a person to do an act within a time therein specified and an order is subsequently made under rule 6 requiring the act to be done within some other time, references in paragraph (1) of this rule to a judgment or order shall be construed as references to the order made under rule 6.

(3) Where under any judgment or order requiring the delivery of any goods the person liable to execution has the alternative of paying the assessed value of the goods, the judgment or order shall not be enforceable by order of committal under paragraph (1), but the court may, on the application of the person entitled to enforce the judgment or order, make an order requiring the first mentioned person to deliver the goods to the applicant within a time specified in the order, and that order may be so enforced.

CPR SCHEDULE 1

Rule 6 JUDGMENT, ETC. REQUIRING ACT TO BE DONE: ORDER FIXING TIME FOR DOING IT

(1) Notwithstanding that a judgment or order requiring a person to do an act specifies a time within which the act is to be done, the court shall have power to make an order requiring the act to be done within another time, being such time after service of that order, or such other time, as may be specified therein.

(2) Where a judgment or order requiring a person to do an act does not specify a time within which the act is to be done, the court shall have power subsequently to make an order requiring the act to be done within such time after service of that order, or such other time, as may be specified therein.

(3) An application for an order under this rule must be made in accordance with CPR Part 23 and the application notice must, be served on the person required to do the act in question.

Rule 7 SERVICE OF COPY OF JUDGMENT, ETC., PREREQUISITE TO ENFORCEMENT UNDER RULE 5

(1) In this rule references to an order shall be construed as including references to a judgment.

(2) Subject to paragraphs (6) and (7) of this rule, an order shall not be enforced under rule 5 unless—

(a) a copy of the order has been served personally on the person required to do or abstain from doing the act in question; and

(b) in the case of an order requiring a person to do an act, the copy has been so served before the expiration of the time within which he was required to do the act.

(3) Subject as aforesaid, an order requiring a body corporate to do or abstain from doing an act shall not be enforced as mentioned in rule 5(1)(b)(ii) or (iii) unless—

(a) a copy of the order has also been served personally on the officer against whose property permission is sought to issue a writ of sequestration or against whom an order of committal is sought; and

(b) in the case of an order requiring the body corporate to do an act, the copy has been so served before the expiration of the time within which the body was required to do the act.

(4) There must be prominently displayed on the front of the copy of an order served under this rule a warning to the person on whom the copy is served that disobedience to the order would be a contempt of court punishable by imprisonment, or (in the case of an order requiring a body corporate to do or abstain from doing an act) punishable by sequestration of the assets of the body corporate and by imprisonment of any individual responsible.

(5) With the copy of an order required to be served under this rule, being an order requiring a person to do an act, there must also be served a copy of any order or agreement under CPR rule 2.11 extending or abridging the time for doing the act and, where the first-mentioned order was made under rule 5(3) or 6 of this order, a copy of the previous order requiring the act to be done.

(6) An order requiring a person to abstain from doing an act may be enforced under rule 5 notwithstanding that service of a copy of the order has not been effected in accordance with this rule if the court is satisfied that pending such service, the person against whom or against whose property is sought to enforce the order has had notice thereof either—

(a) by being present when the order was made; or

(b) by being notified of the terms of the order, whether by telephone, telegram or otherwise.

(7) The court may dispense with service of a copy of an order under this rule if it thinks it just to do so.

Rule 8 COURT MAY ORDER ACT TO BE DONE AT EXPENSE OF DISOBEDIENT PARTY

If an order of mandamus, a mandatory order, an injunction or a judgment or order for the specific performance of a contract is not complied with, then, without prejudice to its powers under section 39 of the Act and its powers to punish the disobedient party for contempt, the court may direct that the act required to be done may, so far as practicable, be done by the party by whom the order or judgment was obtained or some other person appointed by the court, at the cost of the disobedient party, and upon the act being done the expenses incurred may be ascertained in such manner as the court may direct and execution may issue against the disobedient party for the amount so ascertained and for costs.

Rule 9 EXECUTION BY OR AGAINST PERSON NOT BEING A PARTY

(1) Any person, not being a party to proceedings, who obtains any order or in whose favour any order is made, shall be entitled to enforce obedience to the order by the same process as if he were a party.

(2) Any person, not being a party to proceedings, against whom obedience to any judgment or order may be enforced, shall be liable to the same process for enforcing obedience to the judgment or order as if he were a party.

Rule 10 CONDITIONAL JUDGMENT: WAIVER

A party entitled under any judgment or order to any relief subject to the fulfilment of any condition who fails to fulfil that condition is deemed to have abandoned the benefit of the judgment or order, and, unless the court otherwise directs, any other person interested may take any proceedings which either are warranted by the judgment or order or might have been taken if the judgment or order had not been given or made.

Rule 11 MATTERS OCCURRING AFTER JUDGMENT: STAY OF EXECUTION, ETC.

Without prejudice to Order 47, rule 1, a party against whom a judgment has been given or an order made may apply to the court for a stay of execution of the judgment or order or other relief on the ground of matters which have occurred since the date of the judgment or order, and the court may by order grant such relief, and on such terms, as it thinks just.

Rule 12 FORMS OF WRITS

(1) A writ of fieri facias must be in such of the Forms Nos. 53 to 63 in the relevant practice direction as is appropriate in the particular case.

(2) A writ of delivery must be in Form No. 64 or 65 in the relevant practice direction, whichever is appropriate.

(3) A writ of possession must be in Form No. 66 or 66A in the relevant practice direction, whichever is appropriate.

(4) A writ of sequestration must be in Form No. 67 in the relevant practice direction.

Rule 13 ENFORCEMENT OF JUDGMENTS AND ORDERS FOR RECOVERY OF MONEY, ETC.

(1) Rule 1(1) of this order, with the omission of sub-paragraphs (e) and (f) thereof, and Orders 46 to 51 shall apply in relation to a judgment or order for the recovery of money as they apply in relation to a judgment or order for the payment of money.

(2) Rule 3 of this order, with the omission of paragraphs (1)(b) and (c) thereof, and Order 47, rule 3(2) shall apply in relation to a judgment or order for the recovery of possession of land as they apply in relation to a judgment or order for the giving or delivery of possession of land.

(3) Rule 4 of this order, with the omission of paragraph 1(b) and (c) and (2)(c) thereof, and Order 47, rule 3(2) shall apply in relation to a judgment or order that a person do have a return of any goods and to a judgment or order that a person do have a return of any goods or do recover the assessed value thereof as they apply in relation to a judgment or order for the delivery of any goods and a judgment or order for the delivery of any goods or payment of the assessed value thereof respectively.

Rule 14 ENFORCEMENT OF DECISIONS OF VALUE ADDED TAX TRIBUNALS

(1) An application under section 29 of the Finance Act 1985 for registration of a decision of a Value Added Tax Tribunal on an appeal under section 83 of the Value Added Tax Act 1994 shall be made by a request in writing to the head clerk of the Crown Office—

(a) exhibiting the decision or a duly authenticated copy thereof;

(b) stating, so far as is known to the witness, the name and occupation and the usual or last known address or place of business of the person against whom it is sought to enforce the decision; and

(c) stating, to the best of the information and belief of the witness, the amount which as a result of the decision is, or is recoverable as, tax from such person at the date of the application and the amount then remaining unpaid of any costs awarded to the Commissioners of Customs and Excise by the decision.

(2) Notice of the registration of a decision must be served on the person against whom it is sought to enforce the decision by delivering it to him personally or by sending it to him at his usual or last known address or place of business or in such manner as the court may direct.

(3) There shall be kept in the Central Office under the direction of the Senior Master a register of the decisions registered under section 29 of the Finance Act 1985, and there shall be included in the register particulars of any execution issued on a decision so registered.

RSC ORDER 46
WRITS OF EXECUTION: GENERAL

Rule 1 DEFINITION

In this order, unless the context otherwise requires, 'writ of execution' includes a writ of fieri facias, a writ of possession, a writ of delivery, a writ of sequestration and any further writ in aid of any of the aforementioned writs.

Rule 2 WHEN PERMISSION TO ISSUE ANY WRIT OF EXECUTION IS NECESSARY

(1) A writ of execution to enforce a judgment or order may not issue without the permission of the court in the following cases, that is to say—

(a) where 6 years or more have elapsed since the date of the judgment or order;

(b) where any change has taken place, whether by death or otherwise, in the parties entitled or liable to execution under the judgment or order;

(c) where the judgment or order is against the assets of a deceased person coming to the hands of his executors or administrators after the date of the judgment or order, and it is sought to issue execution against such assets;

(d) where under the judgment or order any person is entitled to a remedy subject to the fulfilment of any condition which it is alleged has been fulfilled;

(e) where any goods sought to be seized under a writ of execution are in the hands of a receiver appointed by the court or a sequestrator.

(2) Paragraph (1) is without prejudice to section 2 of the Reserve and Auxiliary Forces (Protection of Civil Interests) Act 1951, or any other enactment or rule by virtue of which a person is required to obtain the permission of the court for the issue of a writ of execution or to proceed to execution on or otherwise to the enforcement of a judgment or order.

(3) Where the court grants permission, whether under this rule or otherwise, for the issue of a writ of execution and the writ is not issued within one year after the date of the order granting such permission, the order shall cease to have effect, without prejudice, however, to the making of a fresh order.

Rule 3 PERMISSION REQUIRED FOR ISSUE OF WRIT IN AID OF OTHER WRIT

A writ of execution in aid of any other writ of execution shall not issue without the permission of the court.

Rule 4 APPLICATION FOR PERMISSION TO ISSUE WRIT

(1) An application for permission to issue a writ of execution may be made in accordance with CPR Part 23 but the application notice need not be served on the respondent unless the court directs.

(2) Such an application must be supported by a witness statement or affidavit—

(a) identifying the judgment or order to which the application relates and, if the judgment or order is for the payment of money, stating the amount originally due thereunder and the amount due thereunder at the date the application notice is filed;

(b) stating, where the case falls within rule 2(1)(a), the reasons for the delay in enforcing the judgment or order;

(c) stating, where the case falls within rule 2(1)(b), the change which has taken place in the parties entitled or liable to execution since the date of the judgment or order;

(d) stating, where the case falls within rule 2(1)(c) or (d), that a demand to satisfy the judgment or order was made on the person liable to satisfy it and that he has refused or failed to do so;

(e) giving such other information as is necessary to satisfy the court that the applicant is entitled to proceed to execution on the judgment or order in question and that the person against whom it is sought to issue execution is liable to execution on it.

(3) The court hearing such application may grant permission in accordance with the application or may order that any issue or question, a decision on which is necessary to determine the rights of the parties, be tried in any manner in which any question of fact or law arising in proceedings may be tried and, in either case, may impose such terms as to costs or otherwise as it thinks just.

Rule 5 APPLICATION FOR PERMISSION TO ISSUE WRIT OF SEQUESTRATION

(1) Notwithstanding anything in rules 2 and 4, an application for permission to issue a writ of sequestration must be made in accordance with CPR Part 23 and be heard by a judge.

(2) Subject to paragraph (3), the application notice, stating the grounds of the application and accompanied by a copy of the witness statement or affidavit in support of the application, must be served personally on the person against whose property it is sought to issue the writ.

(3) The court may dispense with service of the application notice under this rule if it thinks it just to do so.

(4) The judge hearing an application for permission to issue a writ of sequestration may sit in private in any case in which, if the application were for an order of committal, he would be entitled to do so by virtue of Order 52, rule 6 but, except in such a case, the application shall be heard in public.

Rule 6 ISSUE OF WRIT OF EXECUTION

(1) Issue of a writ of execution takes place on its being sealed by a court officer of the appropriate office.

(2) Before such a writ is issued, a praecipe for its issue must be filed.

(3) The praecipe must be signed by or on behalf of the solicitor of the person entitled to execution or, if that person is acting in person, by him.

(4) No such writ shall be sealed unless at the time of the tender thereof for sealing—

(a) the person tendering it produces—

(i) the judgment or order on which the writ is to issue, or an office copy thereof,

(ii) where the writ may not issue without the permission of the court, the order granting such permission or evidence of the granting of it;

(iii) where judgment on failure to acknowledge service has been entered against a State, as defined in section 14 of the State Immunity Act 1978, evidence that the State has been served in accordance with CPR rule 40.10 and that the judgment has taken effect; and

(b) the court officer authorised to seal it is satisfied that the period, if any, specified in the judgment or order for the payment of any money or the doing of any other act thereunder has expired.

(5) Every writ of execution shall bear the date of the day on which it is issued.

(6) In this rule 'the appropriate office' means—

(a) where the proceedings in which execution is to issue are in a District Registry, that Registry;

(b) where the proceedings are in the Principal Registry of the Family Division, that Registry;

(c) where the proceedings are Admiralty proceedings or commercial proceedings which are not in a District Registry, the Admiralty and Commercial Registry;

(ca) where the proceedings are in the Chancery Division, Chancery Chambers;

(d) in any other case, the Central Office of the Supreme Court.

Rule 8 DURATION AND RENEWAL OF WRIT OF EXECUTION

(1) For the purpose of execution, a writ of execution is valid in the first instance for 12 months beginning with the date of its issue.

(2) Where a writ has not been wholly executed the court may by order extend the validity of the writ from time to time for a period of 12 months at any one time beginning with the day on which the order is made, if an application for extension is made to the court before the day next following that on which the writ would otherwise expire or such later day, if any, as the court may allow.

(3) Before a writ the validity of which had been extended under paragraph (2) is executed either the writ must be sealed with the seal of the office out of which it was issued showing the date on which the order extending its validity was made or the applicant for the order must serve a notice (in Form No. 71 in the relevant practice direction) sealed as aforesaid, on the sheriff to whom the writ is directed informing him of the making of the order and the date thereof.

(4) The priority of a writ, the validity of which has been extended under this rule, shall be determined by reference to the date on which it was originally delivered to the sheriff.

(5) The production of a writ of execution, or of such a notice as is mentioned in paragraph (3) purporting in either case to be sealed as mentioned in that paragraph, shall be evidence that the validity of that writ, or, as the case may be, of the writ referred to in that notice, has been extended under paragraph (2).

(6) If, during the validity of a writ of execution, an interpleader summons is issued in relation to an execution under that writ, the validity of the writ shall be extended until the expiry of 12 months from the conclusion of the interpleader proceedings.

Rule 9 RETURN TO WRIT OF EXECUTION

(1) Any party at whose instance or against whom a writ of execution was issued may serve a notice on the sheriff to whom the writ was directed requiring him, within such time as may be specified in the notice, to indorse on the writ a statement of the manner in which he has executed it and to send to that party a copy of the statement.

(2) If a sheriff on whom such a notice is served fails to comply with it the party by whom it was served may apply to the court for an order directing the sheriff to comply with the notice.

RSC ORDER 47
WRITS OF FIERI FACIAS

Rule 1 POWER TO STAY EXECUTION BY WRIT OF FIERI FACIAS

(1) Where a judgment is given or an order made for the payment by any person of money, and the court is satisfied, on an application made at the time of the judgment or order, or at any time thereafter, by the judgment debtor or other party liable to execution—

(a) that there are special circumstances which render it inexpedient to enforce the judgment or order; or

(b) that the applicant is unable from any cause to pay the money,

then, notwithstanding anything in rule 2 or 3, the court may by order stay the execution of the judgment or order by writ of fieri facias either absolutely or for such period and subject to such conditions as the court thinks fit.

(2) An application under this rule, if not made at the time the judgment is given or order made, must be made in accordance with CPR Part 23 and may be so made notwithstanding that the party liable to execution did not acknowledge service of the claim form or serve a defence or take any previous part in the proceedings.

(3) The grounds on which an application under this rule is made must be set out in the application notice and be supported by a witness statement or affidavit made by or on behalf of the applicant substantiating the said grounds and, in particular, where such application is made on the grounds of the applicant's inability to pay, disclosing his income, the nature and value of any property of his and the amount of any other liabilities of his.

(4) The application notice and a copy of the supporting witness statement or affidavit must, not less than 4 clear days before the hearing, be served on the party entitled to enforce the judgment or order.

(5) An order staying execution under this rule may be varied or revoked by a subsequent order.

Rule 2 TWO OR MORE WRITS OF FIERI FACIAS

(1) A party entitled to enforce a judgment or order by writ of fieri facias may issue two or more such writs, directed to the sheriffs of different counties, at either the same time or different times, to enforce that judgment or order, but no more shall be levied under all those writs together than is authorised to be levied under one of them.

(2) Where a party issues two or more writs of fieri facias directed to the sheriffs of different counties to enforce the same judgment or order he must inform each sheriff of the issue of the other writ or writs.

Rule 3 SEPARATE WRITS TO ENFORCE PAYMENT OF COSTS, ETC.

(1) Where only the payment of money, together with costs to be assessed in accordance with CPR Part 47 (detailed costs assessment), is adjudged or ordered, then, if when the money becomes payable under the judgment or order the costs have not been assessed, the party entitled to enforce that judgment or order may issue a writ of fieri facias to enforce payment of the sum (other than for costs) adjudged or ordered and, not less than 8 days after the issue of that writ, he may issue a second writ to enforce payment of the assessed costs.

(2) A party entitled to enforce a judgment or order for the delivery of possession of any property (other than money) may, if he so elects, issue a separate writ of fieri facias to enforce payment of any damages or costs awarded to him by that judgment or order.

Rule 4 NO EXPENSES OF EXECUTION IN CERTAIN CASES

Where a judgment or order is for less than £600 and does not entitle the claimant to costs against the person against whom the writ of fieri facias to enforce the judgment or order is issued, the writ may not authorise the sheriff to whom it is directed to levy any fees, poundage or other costs of execution.

Rule 5 WRIT OF FIERI FACIAS DE BONIS ECCLESIASTICIS, ETC.

(1) Where it appears upon the return of any writ of fieri facias that the person against whom the writ was issued has no goods or chattels in the county of the sheriffs to whom the writ was directed but that he is the incumbent of a benefice named in the return, then, after the writ and return have been filed, the party by whom the writ of fieri facias was issued may issue a writ of fieri facias de bonis ecclesiasticis or a writ of sequestrari de bonis ecclesiasticis directed to the bishop of the diocese within which that benefice is.

CPR SCHEDULE 1

(2) Any such writ must be delivered to the bishop to be executed by him.

(3) Only such fees for the execution of any such writ shall be taken by or allowed to the bishop or any diocesan officer as are for the time being authorised by or under any enactment, including any measure of the General Synod.

Rule 6 ORDER FOR SALE OTHERWISE THAN BY AUCTION

(1) An order of the court under section 145 of the Bankruptcy Act 1883, that a sale under an execution may be made otherwise than by public auction may be made on the application of the person at whose instance the writ of execution under which the sale is to be made was issued or the person against whom that writ was issued (in this rule referred to as 'the judgment debtor') or the sheriff to whom it was issued.

(2) Such an application must be made in accordance with CPR Part 23 and the application notice must contain a short statement of the grounds of the application.

(3) Where the applicant for an order under this rule is not the sheriff, the sheriff must, on the demand of the applicant, send to the applicant a list containing the name and address of every person at whose instance any other writ of execution against the goods of the judgment debtor was issued and delivered to the sheriff (in this rule referred to as 'the sheriff's list'); and where the sheriff is the applicant, he must prepare such a list.

(4) Not less than 4 clear days before the hearing the applicant must serve the application notice on each of the other persons by whom the application might have been made and on every person named in the sheriff's list.

(5) Service of the application notice on a person named in the sheriff's list is notice to him for the purpose of section 12 of the Bankruptcy Act 1890 (which provides that the court shall not consider an application for permission to sell privately goods taken in execution until notice directed by rules of court has been given to any other execution creditor).

(6) The applicant must produce the sheriff's list to the court on the hearing of the application.

(7) Every person on whom the application notice was served may attend and be heard on the hearing of the application.

RSC ORDER 48
EXAMINATION OF JUDGMENT DEBTOR, ETC.

Rule 1 ORDER FOR EXAMINATION OF JUDGMENT DEBTOR

(1) Where a person has obtained a judgment or order for the payment by some other person (hereinafter referred to as 'the judgment debtor') of money, the court may, on an application made without notice being served on any other party by the person entitled to enforce the judgment or order, order the judgment debtor or, if the judgment debtor is a body corporate, an officer thereof, to attend before such Master, Registrar, district judge or nominated officer as the court may appoint and be orally examined on the questions—

(a) whether any and, if so, what debts are owing to the judgment debtor; and

(b) whether the judgment debtor has any and, if so, what other property or means of satisfying the judgment or order;

and the court may also order the judgment debtor or officer to produce any books or documents in the possession of the judgment debtor relevant to the questions aforesaid at the time and place appointed for the examination.

In this paragraph 'district judge' includes the district judge of a district registry or county court, and where the court appoints such a district judge without specifying him personally, the examination may, if he thinks fit, be conducted on his behalf by a nominated officer of that registry or county court.

(2) An order under this rule must be served personally on the judgment debtor and on any officer of a body corporate ordered to attend for examination.

(3) Any difficulty arising in the course of an examination under this rule before a nominated officer, including any dispute with respect to the obligation of the

person being examined to answer any question put to him, may be referred to the Senior Master or Practice Master (or, in the case of an examination at the Principal Registry of the Family Division, a district registry or a county court, a district judge of that registry, district registry or county court respectively) and he may determine it or give such directions for determining it as he thinks fit.

(4) In this rule 'nominated officer' in relation to an examination which is to take place at the Central Office of the Supreme Court, the Principal Registry of the Family Division, a district registry or a county court means such of the officers of that office, registry or county court as may be nominated for the purposes of this rule by the Senior Master, the Senior District judge of the Family Division or the district judge of that district registry or county court respectively.

Rule 2 EXAMINATION OF PARTY LIABLE TO SATISFY OTHER JUDGMENT

Where any difficulty arises in or in connection with the enforcement of any judgment or order, other than such a judgment or order as is mentioned in rule 1, the court may make an order under that rule for the attendance of the party liable to satisfy the judgment or order and for his examination on such questions as may be specified in the order, and that rule shall apply accordingly with the necessary modifications.

Rule 3 EXAMINER TO MAKE RECORD OF DEBTOR'S STATEMENT

The officer conducting the examination shall take down, or cause to be taken down, in writing the statement made by the judgment debtor or other person at the examination, read it to him and ask him to sign it; and if he refuses the officer shall sign the statement.

RSC ORDER 49
GARNISHEE PROCEEDINGS

Rule 1 ATTACHMENT OF DEBT DUE TO JUDGMENT DEBTOR

(1) Where a person (in this order referred to as 'the judgment creditor') has obtained a judgment or order for the payment by some other person (in this order referred to as 'the judgment debtor') of a sum of money amounting in value to at least £50, not being a judgment or order for the payment of money into court, and any other person within the jurisdiction (in this order referred to as 'the garnishee') is indebted to the judgment debtor, the court may, subject to the provisions of this order and of any enactment, order the garnishee to pay the judgment creditor the amount of any debt due or accruing due to the judgment debtor from the garnishee, or so much thereof as is sufficient to satisfy that judgment or order and the costs of the garnishee proceedings.

(2) An order under this rule shall in the first instance be an order to show cause, specifying the time and place for further consideration of the matter, and in the meantime attaching such debt as is mentioned in paragraph (1) or so much thereof as may be specified in the order, to answer the judgment or order mentioned in that paragraph and the costs of the garnishee proceedings.

(3) Among the conditions mentioned in section 40 of the Supreme Court Act 1981 (which enables any sum standing to the credit of a person in certain types of account to be attached notwithstanding that certain conditions applicable to the account in question have not been satisfied) there shall be included any condition that a receipt for money deposited in the account must be produced before any money is withdrawn.

(4) An order under this rule shall not require a payment which would reduce below £1 the amount standing in the name of the judgment debtor in an account with a building society or a credit union.

Rule 2 APPLICATION FOR ORDER

(1) An application for an order under rule 1 must be made in accordance with CPR Part 23 but the application notice need not be served on the judgment debtor.

(2) An application must be supported by a witness statement or affidavit—
 (a) stating the name and last known address of the judgment debtor;

(b) identifying the judgment or order to be enforced and stating the amount of such judgment or order and the amount remaining unpaid under it at the time of the application;

(c) stating that to the best of the information or belief of the witness the garnishee (naming him) is within the jurisdiction and is indebted to the judgment debtor and stating the sources of the witness's information or the grounds for his belief; and

(d) stating, where the garnishee is a deposit-taking institution having more than one place of business, the name and address of the branch at which the judgment debtor's account is believed to be held and the number of that account or, if it be the case, that all or part of this information is not known to the witness.

Rule 3 SERVICE AND EFFECT OF ORDER TO SHOW CAUSE

(1) Unless the court otherwise directs, an order under rule 1 to show cause must be served—

(a) on the garnishee personally, at least 15 days before the time appointed thereby for the further consideration of the matter; and

(b) on the judgment debtor, at least 7 days after the order has been served on the garnishee and at least 7 days before the time appointed by the order for the further consideration of the matter.

(2) Such an order shall bind in the hands of the garnishee as from the service of the order on him any debt specified in the order or so much thereof as may be so specified.

Rule 4 NO APPEARANCE OR DISPUTE OF LIABILITY BY GARNISHEE

(1) Where on the further consideration of the matter the garnishee does not attend or does not dispute the debt due or claimed to be due from him to the judgment debtor, the court may make an order absolute under rule 1 against the garnishee.

(2) An order absolute under rule 1 against the garnishee may be enforced in the same manner as any other order for the payment of money.

Rule 5 DISPUTE OF LIABILITY BY GARNISHEE

Where on the further consideration of the matter the garnishee disputes liability to pay the debt due or claimed to be due from him to the judgment debtor, the court may summarily determine the question at issue or order that any question necessary for determining the liability of the garnishee be tried in any manner in which any question or issue in proceedings may be tried, without, if it orders trial before a Master, the need for any consent by the parties.

Rule 6 CLAIMS OF THIRD PERSONS

(1) If in garnishee proceedings it is brought to the notice of the court that some other person than the judgment debtor is or claims to be entitled to the debt sought to be attached or has or claims to have a charge or lien upon it, the court may order that person to attend before the court and state the nature of his claim with particulars thereof.

(2) After hearing any person who attends before the court in compliance with an order under paragraph (1) the court may summarily determine the questions at issue between the claimants or make such other order as it thinks just, including an order that any question or issue necessary for determining the validity of the claim of such other person as is mentioned in paragraph (1) be tried in such manner as is mentioned in rule 5.

Rule 8 DISCHARGE OF GARNISHEE

Any payment made by a garnishee in compliance with an order absolute under this order, and any execution levied against him in pursuance of such an order, shall be a valid discharge of his liability to the judgment debtor to the extent of the amount paid or levied notwithstanding that the garnishee proceedings are subsequently set aside or the judgment or order from which they arose reversed.

Rule 9 MONEY IN COURT

(1) Where money is standing to the credit of the judgment debtor in court, the judgment creditor shall not be entitled to take garnishee proceedings in respect of that money but may apply to the court in accordance with CPR Part 23 for an order that the money or so much thereof as is sufficient to satisfy the judgment or order sought to be enforced and the costs of the application be paid to the judgment creditor.

(2) On filing an application notice under this rule the applicant must produce the application notice at the office of the Accountant General and leave a copy at that office, and the money to which the application relates shall not be paid out of court until after the determination of the application. If the application is dismissed, the applicant must give notice of that fact to the Accountant General.

(3) Unless the court otherwise directs, the application notice must be served on the judgment debtor at least 7 days before the hearing.

(4) Subject to Order 75, rule 24, the court hearing an application under this rule may make such order with respect to the money in court as it thinks just.

Rule 10 COSTS

The costs of any application for an order under rule 1 or 9, and of any proceedings arising therefrom or incidental thereto, shall, unless the Court otherwise directs, be retained by the judgment creditor out of the money recovered by him under the order and in priority to the judgment debt.

RSC ORDER 50
CHARGING ORDERS, STOP ORDERS, ETC.

Rule 1 ORDER IMPOSING A CHARGE ON A BENEFICIAL INTEREST

(1) The power to make a charging order under section 1 of the Charging Orders Act 1979 (referred to in this order as 'the Act') shall be exercisable by the court.

(2) An application by a judgment creditor for a charging order in respect of a judgment debtor's beneficial interest must be in accordance with CPR Part 23, but the application notice need not be served on the judgment debtor, and any order made on such an application shall in the first instance be an order, made in Form No. 75 in the relevant Practice Direction, to show cause, specifying the time and place for further consideration of the matter and imposing the charge in any event until that time.

(3) The application shall be supported by a witness statement or affidavit—

(a) identifying the judgment or order to be enforced and stating the amount unpaid at the date of the application;

(b) stating the name of the judgment debtor and of any creditor of his whom the applicant can identify;

(c) giving full particulars of the subject-matter of the intended charge, including, in the case of securities other than securities in court, the full title of the securities, their amount and the name in which they stand and, in the case of funds in court, the number of the account; and

(d) verifying that the interest to be charged is owned beneficially by the judgment debtor.

(4) Unless the court otherwise directs, a witness statement or affidavit for the purposes of this rule may contain statements of information or belief with the sources and grounds thereof.

(5) An application may be made for a single charging order in respect of more than one judgment or order against the debtor.

Rule 2 SERVICE OF NOTICE OF ORDER TO SHOW CAUSE

(1) On the making of an order to show cause, notice of the order shall, unless the court otherwise directs, be served as follows—

(a) a copy of the order, together with a copy of the witness statement or affidavit in support, shall be served on the judgment debtor;

(b) where the order relates to securities other than securities in court, copies of the order shall also be served—

(i) in the case of government stock for which the Bank of England keeps the Register, on the Bank of England;

(ii) in the case of government stock to which (i) does not apply, on the keeper of the register;

(iii) in the case of stock of any body incorporated within England and Wales, on that body, or, where the register is kept by the Bank of England, on the Bank of England;

(iv) in the case of stock of any body incorporated outside England and Wales or of any state or territory outside the United Kingdom, being stock registered in a register kept in England and Wales, on the keeper of the register;

(v) in the case of units of any unit trust in respect of which a register of the unit holders is kept in England and Wales, on the keeper of the register;

(c) where the order relates to a fund in court, a copy of the order shall be served on the Accountant-General at the Court Funds Office; and

(d) where the order relates to an interest under a trust, copies of the order shall be served on such of the trustees as the court may direct.

(2) Without prejudice to the provisions of paragraph (1), the court may, on making the order to show cause, direct the service of copies of the order, and of the witness statement or affidavit in support, on any other creditor of the judgment debtor or on any other interested person as may be appropriate in the circumstances.

(3) Documents to be served under this rule must be served at least seven days before the time appointed for the further consideration of the matter.

Rule 3 ORDER MADE ON FURTHER CONSIDERATIONS

(1) On the further consideration of the matter the court shall either make the order absolute, with or without modifications, or discharge it.

(2) Where the order is made absolute, it shall be made in Form No. 76 in the relevant practice direction, and where it is discharged, the provisions of rule 7, regarding the service of copies of the order of discharge, shall apply.

Rule 4 ORDER IMPOSING A CHARGE ON AN INTEREST HELD BY A TRUSTEE

(1) Save as provided by this rule, the provisions of rules 1, 2 and 3 shall apply to an order charging an interest held by a trustee as they apply to an order charging the judgment debtor's beneficial interest.

(2) Instead of verifying the judgment debtor's beneficial ownership of the interest to be charged, the witness statement or affidavit required by rule 1(3) shall state the ground on which the application is based and shall verify the material facts.

(3) On making the order to show cause, the court shall give directions for copies of the order, and of the witness statement or affidavit in support, to be served on such of the trustees and beneficiaries, if any, as may be appropriate.

(4) Rules 5, 6 and 7 shall apply to an order charging an interest held by a trustee as they apply to an order charging the judgment debtor's beneficial interest, except that, where the order is made under subsection (ii) or (iii) of section 2(1)(b) of the Act references in those rules to 'the judgment debtor' shall be references to the trustee.

(5) Forms No. 75 and 76 in the relevant practice direction shall be modified so as to indicate that the interest to be charged is held by the debtor as trustee or, as the case may be, that it is held by a trustee (to be named in the order) on trust for the debtor beneficially.

Rule 5 EFFECT OF ORDER IN RELATION TO SECURITIES OUT OF COURT

(1) No disposition by the judgment debtor of his interest in any securities to which an order to show cause relates made after the making of that order shall, so long as that order remains in force, be valid as against the judgment creditor.

(2) Until such order is discharged or made absolute, the Bank of England (or other person or body served in accordance with rule 2(1)(b)), shall not permit any transfer of any of the securities specified in the order, or pay any dividend, interest or redemption payment in relation thereto, except with the authority of the court, and, if it does so, shall be liable to pay the judgment creditor the value of the securities transferred or, as the case may be, the amount of the payment made or, if that value or amount is more than sufficient to satisfy the judgment or order to which such order relates, so much thereof as is sufficient to satisfy it.

(3) If the court makes the order absolute, a copy of the order, including a stop notice as provided in Form No. 76 in the relevant Practice Direction, shall be served on the Bank of England, or on such other person or body specified in rule 2(1)(b) as may be appropriate and, save as provided in rule 7(5), rules 11 to 14 shall apply to such a notice as they apply to a stop notice made and served under rule 11.

(4) This rule does not apply to orders in respect of securities in court.

Rule 6 EFFECT OF ORDER IN RELATION TO FUNDS IN COURT
(1) Where an order to show cause has been made in relation to funds in court (including securities in court) and a copy thereof has been served on the Accountant General in accordance with rule 2, no disposition by the judgment debtor of any interest to which the order relates, made after the making of that order, shall, so long as the order remains in force, be valid as against the judgment creditor.

(2) If the court makes the order absolute, a copy of the order shall be served on the Accountant General at the Court Funds Office.

Rule 7 DISCHARGE, ETC., OF CHARGING ORDER
(1) Subject to paragraph (2), on the application of the judgment debtor or any other person interested in the subject matter of the charge, the court may, at any time, whether before or after the order is made absolute, discharge or vary the order on such terms (if any) as to costs or otherwise as it thinks just.

(2) Where an application is made for the discharge of a charging order in respect of the judgment debtor's land on the ground that the judgment debt has been satisfied, the applicant shall state in his application, and the court shall specify in its order, the title number of the land in the case of registered land, and the entry number of any relevant land charge in the case of unregistered land.

(3) The application notice seeking the discharge or variation of the order shall be served on such interested parties as the court may direct.

(4) Where an order is made for the discharge or variation of a charging order in respect of funds in court, a copy thereof shall be served on the Accountant General at the Court Funds Office.

(5) Where an order is made for the discharge or variation of a charging order in respect of securities other than securities in court, a copy thereof shall be served on the Bank of England or on such other person or body specified in rule 2(1)(b) as may be appropriate, and the service thereof shall discharge, or, as the case may be, vary, any stop notice in respect of such securities which may be in force pursuant to the original order.

Rule 9 JURISDICTION OF MASTER, ETC. TO GRANT INJUNCTION
A Master and the Admiralty Registrar and a district judge of the Family Division shall have power to grant an injunction if, and only so far as, it is ancillary or incidental to an order under rule 1, 3 or 4 and an application for an injunction under this rule may be joined with the application for the order under rule 1, 3 or 4 to which it relates.

Rule 9A ENFORCEMENT OF CHARGING ORDER BY SALE
(1) Proceedings for the enforcement of a charging order by sale of the property charged must be begun by a claim form issued out of Chancery Chambers or out of one of the Chancery District Registries.

(2) The provisions of Order 88 shall apply to all such proceedings.

CPR SCHEDULE 1

Rule 10 FUNDS IN COURT: STOP ORDER

(1) The court, on the application of any person—

(a) who has a mortgage or charge on the interest of any person in funds in court; or

(b) to whom that interest has been assigned; or

(c) who is a judgment creditor of the person entitled to that interest,

may make an order prohibiting the transfer, sale, delivery out, payment or other dealing with such funds, or any part thereof, or the income thereon, without notice to the applicant.

(2) An application for an order under this rule must, if there are existing proceedings, be made in accordance with CPR Part 23 by filing an application notice relating to the funds in Court, or, if there are no such proceedings, by a claim.

(3) The application notice or claim form must be served on every person whose interest may be affected by the order applied for and on the Accountant-General but shall not be served on any other person.

(4) Without prejudice to the court's powers and discretion as to costs, the court may order the applicant for an order under this rule to pay the costs of any party to the proceedings relating to the funds in question, or of any person interested in those funds, occasioned by the application.

Rule 11 SECURITIES NOT IN COURT: STOP NOTICE

(1) Any person claiming to be beneficially entitled to an interest in any securities of the kinds set out in section 2(2)(b) of the Act, other than securities in court, who wishes to be notified of any proposed transfer or payment of those securities may avail himself of the provisions of this rule.

(2) A person claiming to be so entitled must file in Chancery Chambers or in a District Registry—

(a) a witness statement or affidavit identifying the securities in question and describing his interest therein by reference to the document under which it arises; and

(b) a notice in Form No. 80 in the relevant practice direction (a stop notice) signed by the witness who made the witness statement or affidavit, and annexed to it, addressed to the Bank of England or, as the case may be, the body, state, territory or unit trust concerned,

and must serve an office copy of the witness statement or affidavit, and a copy of the notice sealed with the seal of Chancery Chambers or the District Registry, on the Bank or other person or body, as provided in rule 2(1)(b).

(3) There must be indorsed on the witness statement or affidavit filed under this rule a note stating the address to which any such notice as is referred to in rule 12 is to be sent and, subject to paragraph (4), that address shall for the purpose of that rule be the address for service of the person on whose behalf the witness statement or affidavit is filed.

(4) A person on whose behalf a witness statement or affidavit under this rule is filed may change his address for service for the purpose of rule 12 by serving on the Bank of England, or other person or body, a notice to that effect, and, as from the date of service of such a notice the address stated therein shall for the purpose of that rule be the address for service of that person.

Rule 12 EFFECT OF STOP NOTICE

Where a stop notice has been served in accordance with rule 11, then, so long as the stop notice is in force, the Bank of England or other person or body on which it is served shall not register a transfer of the securities or take any other step restrained by the stop notice until 14 days after sending notice thereof, by ordinary first class post, to the person on whose behalf the stop notice was filed, but shall not by reason only of that notice refuse to register a transfer, or to take any other step, after the expiry of that period.

Rule 13 AMENDMENT OF STOP NOTICE

If any securities are incorrectly described in a stop notice which has been filed and of which a sealed copy has been served in accordance with rule 11, an amended stop notice may be filed and served in accordance with the same procedure and shall take effect as a stop notice on the day on which the sealed copy of the amended notice is served.

Rule 14 WITHDRAWAL ETC. OF STOP NOTICE

(1) The person on whose behalf a stop notice was filed may withdraw it by serving a request for its withdrawal on the Bank of England or other person or body on whom the notice was served.

(2) Such request must be signed by the person on whose behalf the notice was filed and his signature must be witnessed by a practising solicitor.

(3) The court, on the application of any person claiming to be beneficially entitled to an interest in the securities to which a stop notice relates, may by order discharge the notice.

(4) An application for an order under paragraph (3) must be made in the Chancery Division by a claim form, and the claim form must be served on the person on whose behalf a stop notice was filed.

Rule 15 ORDER PROHIBITING TRANSFER, ETC. OF SECURITIES

(1) The court, on the application of any person claiming to be beneficially entitled to an interest in any securities of the kinds set out in section 2(2)(b) of the Act may by order prohibit the Bank of England or other person or body concerned from registering any transfer of the securities or taking any other step to which section 5(5) of the Act applies. The order shall specify the securities to which the prohibition relates, the name in which they stand and the steps which may not be taken, and shall state whether the prohibition applies to the securities only or to the dividends or interest as well.

(2) An application for an order under this rule must be made by claim form or if made in existing proceedings, in accordance with CPR Part 23 in the Chancery Division.

(3) The court, on the application of any person claiming to be entitled to an interest in any securities to which an order under this rule relates, may vary or discharge the order on such terms (if any) as to costs or otherwise as it thinks fit.

RSC ORDER 51
RECEIVERS: EQUITABLE EXECUTION

Rule 1 APPOINTMENT OF RECEIVER BY WAY OF EQUITABLE EXECUTION

Where an application is made for the appointment of a receiver by way of equitable execution, the court in determining whether it is just or convenient that the appointment should be made shall have regard to the amount claimed by the judgment creditor, to the amount likely to be obtained by the receiver and to the probable costs of his appointment and may direct an inquiry on any of these matters or any other matter before making the appointment.

Rule 2 MASTERS ETC. MAY APPOINT RECEIVER

A Master and the Admiralty Registrar and a district judge of the Family Division shall have power to make an order for the appointment of a receiver by way of equitable execution and to grant an injunction if, and only so far as, the injunction is ancillary or incidental to such an order.

Rule 3 APPLICATION OF RULES AS TO APPOINTMENT OF RECEIVER, ETC.

An application for the appointment of a receiver by way of equitable execution may be made in accordance with Order 30, rule 1, and rules 2 to 6 of that order shall apply in relation to a receiver appointed by way of equitable execution as they apply in relation to a receiver appointed for any other purpose.

CPR SCHEDULE 1

RSC ORDER 52
COMMITTAL

Rule 1 COMMITTAL FOR CONTEMPT OF COURT

(1) The power of the High Court or Court of Appeal to punish for contempt of court may be exercised by an order of committal.

(2) Where contempt of court—
  (a) is committed in connection with—
    (i) any proceedings before a Divisional Court of the Queen's Bench Division; or
    (ii) criminal proceedings, except where the contempt is committed in the face of the court or consists of disobedience to an order of the court or a breach of an undertaking to the court; or
    (iii) proceedings in an inferior court; or
  (b) is committed otherwise than in connection with any proceedings, then, subject to paragraph (4), an order of committal may be made only by a Divisional Court of the Queen's Bench Division.
This paragraph shall not apply in relation to contempt of the Court of Appeal.

(3) Where contempt of court is committed in connection with any proceedings in the High Court, then, subject to paragraph (2), an order of committal may be made by a single judge of the Queen's Bench Division except where the proceedings were assigned or subsequently transferred to some other Division, in which case the order may be made only by a single judge of that other Division.

The reference in this paragraph to a single judge of the Queen's Bench Division shall, in relation to proceedings in any court the judge or judges of which are, when exercising the jurisdiction of that court, deemed by virtue of any enactment to constitute a court of the High Court, be construed as a reference to a judge of that court.

(4) Where by virtue of any enactment the High Court has power to punish or take steps for the punishment of any person charged with having done anything in relation to a court, tribunal or person which would, if it had been done in relation to the High Court, have been a contempt of that court, an order of committal may be made by a single judge of the Queen's Bench Division.

Rule 2 APPLICATION TO DIVISIONAL COURT

(1) No application to a Divisional Court for an order of committal against any person may be made unless permission to make such an application has been granted in accordance with this rule.

(2) An application for such permission must be made without notice to a Divisional Court, except in vacation when it may be made to a judge in chambers and must be supported by a statement setting out the name and description of the applicant, the name, description and address of the person sought to be committed and the grounds on which his committal is sought, and by an affidavit, to be filed before the application is made, verifying the facts relied on.

(3) The applicant must give notice of the application for permission not later than the preceding day to the Crown Office and must at the same time lodge in that office copies of the statement and affidavit.

(4) Where an application for permission under this rule is refused by a judge in chambers, the applicant may make a fresh application for such permission to a Divisional Court.

(5) An application made to a Divisional Court by virtue of paragraph (4) must be made within 8 days after the judge's refusal to give permission or, if a Divisional Court does not sit within that period, on the first day on which it sits thereafter.

Rule 3 APPLICATION FOR ORDER AFTER LEAVE TO APPLY GRANTED

(1) When permission has been granted under rule 2 to apply for an order of committal, the application for the order must be made to a Divisional Court and, unless the court or judge granting permission has otherwise directed, there must

be at least 14 clear days between the service of the claim form and the day named therein for the hearing.

(2) Unless within 14 days after such permission was granted, the claim form is issued the permission shall lapse.

(3) Subject to paragraph 4, the claim form, accompanied by a copy of the statement and affidavit in support of the application for permission, must be served personally on the person sought to be committed.

(4) Without prejudice to the powers of the court or judge under Part 6 of the CPR, the court or judge may dispense with service under this rule if it or he thinks it just to do so.

Rule 4 APPLICATION TO COURT OTHER THAN DIVISIONAL COURT

(1) Where an application for an order of committal may be made to a court other than a Divisional Court, the application must be made by claim form or application notice and be supported by an affidavit.

(2) Subject to paragraph (3) the claim form or application notice, stating the grounds of the application and accompanied by a copy of the affidavit in support of the application, must be served personally on the person sought to be committed.

(3) Without prejudice to its powers under Part 6 of the CPR, the court may dispense with service under this rule if it thinks it just to do so.

(4) This rule does not apply to committal applications which under rules 1(2) and 3(1) should be made to a Divisional Court but which, in vacation, have been properly made to a single judge in accordance with RSC Order 64, rule 4.

Rule 5 SAVING FOR POWER TO COMMIT WITHOUT APPLICATION FOR PURPOSE

Nothing in the foregoing provisions of this order shall be taken as affecting the power of the High Court or Court of Appeal to make an order of committal of its own initiative against a person guilty of contempt of court.

Rule 6 PROVISIONS AS TO HEARING

(1) Subject to paragraph (2), the court hearing an application for an order of committal may sit in private in the following cases, that is to say—

(a) where the application arises out of proceedings relating to the wardship or adoption of an infant or wholly or mainly to the guardianship, custody, maintenance or upbringing of an infant, or rights of access to an infant;

(b) where the application arises out of proceedings relating to a person suffering or appearing to be suffering from mental disorder within the meaning of the Mental Health Act 1983;

(c) where the application arises out of proceedings in which a secret process, discovery or invention was in issue;

(d) where it appears to the court that in the interests of the administration of justice or for reasons of national security the application should be heard in private;

but, except as aforesaid, the application shall be heard in public.

(2) If the court hearing an application in private by virtue of paragraph (1) decides to make an order of committal against the person sought to be committed, it shall in public state—

(a) the name of that person;

(b) in general terms the nature of the contempt of court in respect of which the order of committal is being made; and

(c) the length of the period for which he is being committed.

(3) Except with the permission of the court hearing an application for an order of committal, no grounds shall be relied upon at the hearing except the grounds set out in the statement under rule 2 or, as the case may be, in the claim form or application notice under rule 4.

(4) If on the hearing of the application the person sought to be committed expresses a wish to give oral evidence on his own behalf, he shall be entitled to do so.

CPR SCHEDULE 1

Rule 7 POWER TO SUSPEND EXECUTION OF COMMITTAL ORDER

(1) The court by whom an order of committal is made may by order direct that the execution of the order of committal shall be suspended for such period or on such terms or conditions as it may specify.

(2) Where execution of an order of committal is suspended by an order under paragraph (1), the applicant for the order of committal must, unless the court otherwise directs, serve on the person against whom it was made a notice informing him of the making and terms of the order under that paragraph.

Rule 8 DISCHARGE OF PERSON COMMITTED

(1) The court may, on the application of any person committed to prison for any contempt of court, discharge him.

(2) Where a person has been committed for failing to comply with a judgment or order requiring him to deliver any thing to some other person or to deposit it in court or elsewhere, and a writ of sequestration has also been issued to enforce that judgment or order, then, if the thing is in the custody or power of the person committed, the commissioners appointed by the writ of sequestration may take possession of it as if it were the property of that person and, without prejudice to the generality of paragraph (1), the court may discharge the person committed and may give such directions for dealing with the thing taken by the commissioners as it thinks fit.

(RSC Order 46, rule 5 contains rules relating to writs of sequestration)

Rule 9 SAVING FOR OTHER POWERS

Nothing in the foregoing provisions of this order shall be taken as affecting the power of the court to make an order requiring a person guilty of contempt of court, or a person punishable by virtue of any enactment in like manner as if he had been guilty of contempt of the High Court, to pay a fine or to give security for his good behaviour, and those provisions, so far as applicable, and with the necessary modifications, shall apply in relation to an application for such an order as they apply in relation to an application for an order of committal.

RSC ORDER 53
APPLICATIONS FOR JUDICIAL REVIEW

Rule 1 CASES APPROPRIATE FOR APPLICATION FOR JUDICIAL REVIEW

(1) An application for—

(a) an order of mandamus, prohibition or certiorari; or

(b) an injunction under section 30 of the Act restraining a person from acting in any office in which he is not entitled to act,

shall be made by way of an application for judicial review in accordance with the provisions of this order.

(2) An application for a declaration or an injunction (not being an injunction mentioned in paragraph (1)(b)) may be made by way of an application for judicial review, and on such an application the court may grant the declaration or injunction claimed if it considers that, having regard to—

(a) the nature of the matters in respect of which a remedy may be granted by way of an order of mandamus, prohibition or certiorari;

(b) the nature of the persons and bodies against whom a remedy may be granted by way of such an order; and

(c) all the circumstances of the case, it would be just and convenient for the declaration or injunction to be granted on an application for judicial review.

Rule 2 JOINDER OF CLAIMS FOR RELIEF

On an application for judicial review any remedy mentioned in rule 1(1) or (2) may be claimed as an alternative or in addition to any other remedy so mentioned if it arises out of or relates to or is connected with the same matter.

Rule 3 GRANT OF LEAVE TO APPLY FOR JUDICIAL REVIEW

(1) No application for judicial review shall be made unless the permission of the court has been obtained in accordance with this rule.

(2) An application for permission must be made to a judge by filing in the Crown Office—
- (a) an application notice in Form No. 86A containing a statement of—
    - (i) the name and description of the applicant;
    - (ii) the relief sought and the grounds upon which it is sought;
    - (iii) the name and address of the applicant's solicitors (if any); and
    - (iv) the applicant's address for service; and
- (b) written evidence verifying the facts relied on.

(2A) The documents referred to in paragraphs (2)(a) and (b) need not be served on any other person.

(3) The judge may determine the application without a hearing, unless a hearing is requested in the notice of application; in any case, the Crown Office shall serve a copy of the judge's order on the applicant.

(4) Where the application for permission is refused by the judge, or is granted on terms, the applicant may renew it by applying—
- (a) in any criminal cause or matter, to a Divisional Court of the Queen's Bench Division;
- (b) in any other case, to a single judge or, if the court so directs, to a Divisional Court of the Queen's Bench Division:

Provided that no application for permission may be renewed in any non-criminal cause or matter in which the judge has refused permission under paragraph (3) after a hearing.

(5) In order to renew his application for permission the applicant must, within 10 days of being served with notice of the judge's refusal, lodge in the Crown Office notice of his intention in Form No. 86B.

(6) The court hearing an application for permission may allow the applicant's statement to be amended, whether by specifying different or additional grounds or relief or otherwise, on such terms, if any, as it thinks fit.

(7) The court shall not grant permission unless it considers that the applicant has a sufficient interest in the matter to which the application relates.

(8) Where permission is sought to apply for an order of certiorari to remove for the purpose of its being quashed any judgment, order, conviction or other proceeding which is subject to appeal and a time is limited for the bringing of the appeal, the court may adjourn the application for permission until the appeal is determined or the time for appealing has expired.

(9) If the court grants permission, it may impose such terms as to costs and as to giving security as it thinks fit.

(10) Where permission to apply for judicial review is granted, then—
- (a) if the relief sought is an order of prohibition or certiorari and the court so directs, the grant shall operate as a stay of the proceedings to which the application relates until the determination of the application or until the court otherwise orders;
- (b) if any other relief is sought, the court may at any time grant in the proceedings interim remedies in accordance with CPR Part 25.

Rule 4 DELAY IN APPLYING FOR RELIEF

(1) An application for permission to apply for judicial review shall be made promptly and in any event within three months from the date when grounds for the application first arose unless the court considers that there is good reason for extending the period within which the application shall be made.

(2) Where an order of certiorari is sought in respect of any judgment, order, conviction or other proceeding, the date when grounds for the application first arose shall be taken to be the date of that judgment, order, conviction or proceeding.

(3) Paragraph (1) is without prejudice to any statutory provision which has the effect of limiting the time within which an application for judicial review may be made.

Rule 5 MODE OF APPLYING FOR JUDICIAL REVIEW

(1) In any criminal cause or matter, where permission has been granted to make an application for judicial review, the application shall be made to a Divisional Court of the Queen's Bench Division.

(2) In any other such cause or matter, the application shall be made to a judge unless the court directs that it shall be made to a Divisional Court of the Queen's Bench Division.

(2A) An application for judicial review shall be made by a claim form.

(3) The claim form must be served on all persons directly affected and where it relates to any proceedings in or before a court and the object of the application is either to compel the court or an officer of the court to do any act in relation to the proceedings or to quash them or any order made therein, the claim form must also be served on the Clerk or Registrar of the court and, where any objection to the conduct of the judge is to be made, on the judge.

(4) Unless the court granting permission has otherwise directed, there must be at least 10 days between the service of the claim form and the hearing.

(5) The application must be entered for hearing within 14 days after the grant of permission.

(6) Written evidence giving the names and addresses of, and the places and dates of service on, all persons who have been served with the claim form must be filed before the application is entered for hearing and, if any person who ought to be served under this rule has not been served, the written evidence must state that fact and the reason for it; and shall be before the court on the hearing of the application

(7) If on the hearing of the application the court is of opinion that any person who ought, whether under this rule or otherwise, to have been served has not been served, the court may adjourn the hearing on such terms (if any) as it may direct in order that the claim form may be served on that person.

Rule 6 STATEMENTS AND EVIDENCE

(1) Copies of the statement in support of an application for permission under rule 3 must be served with the claim form and, subject to paragraph (2), no grounds shall be relied upon or any remedy sought at the hearing except the grounds and remedies set out in the statement.

(2) The court may on hearing of the application for judicial review allow the applicant to amend his statement, whether by specifying different or additional grounds or otherwise, on such terms, if any, as it thinks fit and may allow further written evidence to be relied on by him

(3) Where the applicant intends to ask to be allowed to amend his statement or to rely on further written evidence he shall give notice of his intention and of any proposed amendment to every other party.

(4) Any respondent who intends to use written evidence at the hearing shall file it in the Crown Office and give notice thereof to the applicant as soon as practicable and in any event, unless the Court otherwise directs, within 56 days after service upon him of the documents required to be served by paragraph (1).

(5) Each party to the application must supply to every other party on demand and on payment of the proper charges copies of any written evidence which he proposes to rely on at the hearing, including, in the case of the applicant, the written evidence in support of the application for permission under rule 3.

Rule 7 CLAIM FOR DAMAGES

(1) On an application for judicial review the court may, subject to paragraph (2) award damages to the applicant if—

(a) he has included in the statement in support of his application for permission under rule 3 a claim for damages arising from any matter to which the application relates; and

(b) the court is satisfied that, if the claim had been made in proceedings for damages begun by the applicant at the time of making his application for judicial review, he could have been awarded damages.

(2) CPR Part 16 shall apply to a statement relating to a claim for damages as it applies to a statement of case.

Rule 8 APPLICATION FOR DISCLOSURE, FURTHER INFORMATION, CROSS-EXAMINATION, ETC.

(1) Unless the court otherwise directs, any interlocutory application in proceedings on an application for judicial review may be made to any judge or a Master of the Queen's Bench Division, notwithstanding that the application for judicial review has been made to and is to be heard by a Divisional Court.

In this paragraph 'interlocutory application' includes an application for an order under CPR Part 31 or CPR Part 18 or for an order for permission to cross-examine any person who has given written evidence or for an order dismissing the proceedings by consent of the parties.

(2) In relation to an order made by a Master pursuant to paragraph (1) Order 58, rule 1, shall, where the application for judicial review is to be heard by a Divisional Court, have effect as if a reference to that court were substituted for the reference to a judge in Chambers.

(3) This rule is without prejudice to any statutory provision or rule of law restricting the making of an order against the Crown.

Rule 9 HEARING OF APPLICATION FOR JUDICIAL REVIEW

(1) On the hearing of any application for judicial review under rule 5, any person who desires to be heard in opposition to the application, and appears to the court to be a proper person to be heard, shall be heard, notwithstanding that he has not been served with the claim form.

(2) Where the remedy sought is or includes an order of certiorari to remove any proceedings for the purpose of quashing them, the applicant may not question the validity of any order, warrant, commitment, conviction, inquisition or record unless before the hearing of the application he has filed in the Crown Office a copy thereof verified by witness statement or affidavit or accounts for his failure to do so to the satisfaction of the court hearing the application.

(3) Where an order of certiorari is made in any such case as is referred to in paragraph (2) the order shall, subject to paragraph (4) direct that the proceedings shall be quashed forthwith on their removal into the Queen's Bench Division.

(4) Where an order of certiorari is sought and the court is satisfied that there are grounds for quashing the decision to which the application relates, the court may, in addition to quashing it, remit the matter to the court, tribunal or authority concerned with a direction to reconsider it and reach a decision in accordance with the findings of the court.

(5) Where the remedy sought is a declaration, an injunction or damages and the court considers that it should not be granted on an application for judicial review but might have been granted if it had been sought in a claim begun by the applicant at the time of making his application for judicial review, the court may, instead of refusing the application, order the judicial review proceedings to continue as proceedings brought under CPR Part 7 and if it does so may give any directions it considers appropriate.

Rule 10 SAVING FOR PERSON ACTING IN OBEDIENCE TO MANDAMUS

No action or proceeding shall be begun or prosecuted against any person in respect of anything done in obedience to an order of mandamus.

Rule 11 PROCEEDINGS FOR DISQUALIFICATION OF MEMBER OF LOCAL AUTHORITY

(1) Proceedings under section 92 of the Local Government Act 1972 must be begun by the issue of a claim form and brought before a Divisional Court of the Queen's Bench Division.

(1A) Unless otherwise directed, there must be at least 10 days between the service of the claim form and the hearing.

(2) The claim form must set out the name and description of the applicant, the remedy sought and the grounds on which it is sought, and must be supported by written evidence verifying the facts relied on.

(3) Copies of any written evidence must be filed in the Crown Office before the proceedings are entered for hearing and must be supplied to any other party on demand and on payment of the proper charges.

(4) The provisions of rules 5, 6 and 9(1) as to the persons on whom the claim form is to be served and as to the hearing shall apply, with the necessary modifications, to proceedings under the said section 92 as they apply to an application for judicial review.

Rule 12 CONSOLIDATION OF APPLICATIONS

Where there is more than one application pending under section 30 of the Act, or section 92 of the Local Government Act 1972, against several persons in respect of the same office, and on the same grounds, the court may order the applications to be consolidated.

Rule 13 APPEAL FROM JUDGE'S ORDER

No appeal shall lie from an order made under paragraph (3) of rule 3 on an application for leave which may be renewed under paragraph (4) of that rule.

Rule 14 MEANING OF 'COURT'

In relation to the hearing by a judge of an application for leave under rule 3 or of an application for judicial review, any reference in this order to 'the Court' shall, unless the context otherwise requires, be construed as a reference to the judge.

RSC ORDER 54
APPLICATIONS FOR WRIT OF HABEAS CORPUS

Rule 1 APPLICATION FOR WRIT OF HABEAS CORPUS AD SUBJICIENDUM

(1) Subject to rule 11, an application for a writ of habeas corpus ad subjiciendum shall be made to a judge in court, except that—

　　(a) it shall be made to a Divisional Court of the Queen's Bench Division if the court so directs;

　　(b) it may be made to a judge otherwise than in court at any time when no judge is sitting in court; and

　　(c) any application on behalf of a child must be made in the first instance to a judge otherwise than in court.

(2) An application for such writ may be made without notice being served on any other party and, subject to paragraph (3) must be supported by a witness statement or affidavit by the person restrained showing that it is made at his instance and setting out the nature of the restraint.

(3) Where the person restrained is unable for any reason to make the witness statement or affidavit required by paragraph (2) the witness statement or affidavit may be made by some other person on his behalf and that witness statement or affidavit must state that the person restrained is unable to make the witness statement or affidavit himself and for what reason.

Rule 2 POWER OF COURT TO WHOM APPLICATION MADE WITHOUT NOTICE BEING SERVED ON ANY OTHER PARTY

(1) The court or judge to whom an application under rule 1 is made without notice being served on any other party may make an order forthwith for the writ to issue, or may—

　　(a) where the application is made to a judge otherwise than in court, direct the issue of a claim form seeking the writ, or that an application therefor be made by claim form to a Divisional Court or to a judge in court;

　　(b) where the application is made to a judge in court, adjourn the application so that notice thereof may be given, or direct that an application be made by claim form to a Divisional Court;

　　(c) where the application is made to a Divisional Court, adjourn the application so that notice thereof may be given.

(2) The claim form must be served on the person against whom the issue of the writ is sought and on such other persons as the court or judge may direct, and,

unless the court or judge otherwise directs, there must be at least 8 clear days between the service of the claim form and the date named therein for the hearing of the application.

Rule 3 COPIES OF WITNESS STATEMENTS OR AFFIDAVITS TO BE SUPPLIED

Every party to an application under rule 1 must supply to every other party on demand and on payment of the proper charges copies of the witness statements or affidavits which he proposes to use at the hearing of the application.

Rule 4 POWER TO ORDER RELEASE OF PERSON RESTRAINED

(1) Without prejudice to rule 2(1), the court or judge hearing an application for a writ of habeas corpus ad subjiciendum may in its or his discretion order that the person restrained be released, and such order shall be a sufficient warrant to any governor of a prison, constable or other person for the release of the person under restraint.

(2) Where such an application in criminal proceedings is heard by a judge and the judge does not order the release of the person restrained, he shall direct that the application be made by claim form to a Divisional Court of the Queen's Bench Division.

Rule 5 DIRECTIONS AS TO RETURN TO WRIT

Where a writ of habeas corpus ad subjiciendum is ordered to issue, the court or judge by whom the order is made shall give directions as to the court or judge before whom, and the date on which, the writ is returnable.

Rule 6 SERVICE OF WRIT AND NOTICE

(1) Subject to paragraphs (2) and (3), a writ of habeas corpus ad subjiciendum must be served personally on the person to whom it is directed.

(2) If it is not possible to serve such writ personally, or if it is directed to a governor of a prison or other public official, it must be served by leaving it with a servant or agent of the person to whom the writ is directed at the place where the person restrained is confined or restrained.

(3) If the writ is directed to more than one person, the writ must be served in manner provided by this rule on the person first named in the writ, and copies must be served on each of the other persons in the same manner as the writ.

(4) There must be served with the writ a notice (in Form No. 90 in the relevant practice direction) stating the court or judge before whom and the date on which the person restrained is to be brought and that in default of obedience proceedings for committal of the party disobeying will be taken.

Rule 7 RETURN TO THE WRIT

(1) The return to a writ of habeas corpus ad subjiciendum must be indorsed on or annexed to the writ and must state all the causes of the detainer of the person restrained.

(2) The return may be amended, or another return substituted therefor, by permission of the court or judge before whom the writ is returnable.

Rule 8 PROCEDURE AT HEARING OF WRIT

When a return to a writ of habeas corpus ad subjiciendum is made, the return shall first be read, and motion then made for discharging or remanding the person restrained or amending or quashing the return, and where that person is brought up in accordance with the writ, his counsel shall be heard first, then the counsel for the Crown, and then one counsel for the person restrained in reply.

Rule 9 BRINGING UP PRISONER TO GIVE EVIDENCE, ETC.

(1) An application for a writ of habeas corpus ad testificandum or of habeas corpus ad respondendum must be made on witness statement or affidavit to a judge.

(2) An application for an order to bring up a prisoner, otherwise than by writ of habeas corpus, to give evidence in any proceedings, civil or criminal, before any court, tribunal or justice, must be made on witness statement or affidavit to a judge.

Rule 10 FORM OF WRIT
A writ of habeas corpus must be in Form No. 89, 91 or 92 in the relevant practice direction, whichever is appropriate.

Rule 11 APPLICATIONS RELATIVE TO THE CUSTODY, ETC., OF CHILD
An application by a parent or guardian of a child for a writ of habeas corpus ad subjiciendum relative to the custody, care or control of the child must be made in the Family Division, and this order shall accordingly apply to such applications with the appropriate modifications.

RSC ORDER 55
APPEALS TO HIGH COURT FROM COURT, TRIBUNAL OR PERSON: GENERAL

Rule 1 APPLICATION
(1) Subject to paragraphs (2), (3) and (4), this order shall apply to every appeal which by or under any enactment lies to the High Court from any court, tribunal or person.

(2) This order shall not apply to an appeal by case stated or to any appeal to which the arbitration practice direction applies.

(3) The following rules of this order shall not apply to an appeal from a county court to a single judge under section 375 of the Insolvency Act 1986, but subject to the Insolvency Rules 1986, as amended, Order 59 shall, with the necessary modifications, apply to such an appeal as it applies to an appeal from a county court to the Court of Appeal.

(4) The following rules of this order shall, in relation to an appeal to which this order applies, have effect subject to any provision made in relation to that appeal by any other provision of these rules or by or under any enactment.

(5) In this order references to a tribunal shall be construed as references to any tribunal constituted by or under any enactment other than any of the ordinary courts of law.

Rule 2 COURT TO HEAR APPEAL
Except where it is otherwise provided by these rules or by or under any enactment, an appeal to which this order applies shall be assigned to the Queen's Bench Division and shall be heard and determined—

(a) where the decision of the High Court on the appeal is final, by a Divisional Court, and

(b) in any other case, by a single judge.

Rule 3 BRINGING OF APPEAL
(1) An appeal to which this order applies shall be by way of rehearing and must be brought by notice of appeal.

(2) Every notice by which such an appeal is brought must state the grounds of the appeal and, if the appeal is against a judgment, order or other decision of a court, must state whether the appeal is against the whole or a part of that decision and, if against a part only, must specify the part.

(3) The bringing of such an appeal shall not operate as a stay of proceedings on the judgment, determination or other decisions against which the appeal is brought unless the court by which the appeal is to be heard or the court, tribunal or person by which or by whom the decision was given so orders.

Rule 4 SERVICE OF NOTICE OF APPEAL AND ENTRY OF APPEAL
(1) The persons to be served with the notice of appeal are the following—

(a) if the appeal is against a judgment, order or other decision of a court, the registrar or clerk of the court and any party to the proceedings in which the decision was given who is directly affected by the appeal;

(b) if the appeal is against an order, determination, award or other decision of a tribunal, Minister of the Crown, government department or other person, the chairman of the tribunal, Minister, government department or person, as the case

CPR SCHEDULE 1

may be, and every party to the proceedings (other than the appellant) in which the decision appealed against was given.

(2) The notice must be served, and the appeal entered, within 28 days after the date of the judgment, order, determination or other decision against which the appeal is brought.

(3) In the case of an appeal against a judgment, order or decision of a court, the period specified in paragraph (2) shall be calculated from the date of the judgment or order or the date on which the decision was given.

(4) In the case of an appeal against an order, determination, award or other decision of a tribunal, Minister, government department or other person, the period specified in paragraph (2) shall be calculated from the date on which notice of the decision, or, in a case where a statement of the reasons for a decision was given later than such notice, on which such a statement was given to the appellant by the person who made the decision or by a person authorised in that behalf to do so.

Rule 5 DATE OF HEARING OF APPEAL
Unless the court having jurisdiction to determine the appeal otherwise directs, an appeal to which this order applies shall not be heard sooner than 21 days after service of notice of the motion by which the appeal is brought.

Rule 6 AMENDMENT OF GROUNDS OF APPEAL, ETC.
(1) The notice by which an appeal to which this order applies is brought may be amended by the appellant, without permission, by supplementary notice served not less than 7 days before the day appointed for the hearing of the appeal, on each of the persons on whom the notice to be amended was served.

(2) Within 2 days after service of a supplementary notice under paragraph (1) the appellant must file two copies of the notice in the office in which the appeal is entered.

(3) Except with the permission of the court hearing any such appeal, no grounds other than those stated in the notice by which the appeal is brought or any supplementary notice under paragraph (1) may be relied upon by the appellant at the hearing; but that court may amend the grounds so stated or make any other order, on such terms as it thinks just, to ensure the determination on the merits of the real question in controversy between the parties.

Rule 6A INTERLOCUTORY APPLICATIONS
(1) Unless the court otherwise directs, any interlocutory application in proceedings to which this order applies may be made to any judge or a Master of the Queen's Bench Division or, as the case may be, any judge or a district judge of the Family Division, notwithstanding that the appeal is to be heard by a Divisional Court.

In this paragraph 'interlocutory application' includes an application for the extension of time for the service of the notice of appeal or the entry of the appeal or for the amendment of the notice of appeal.

(2) In relation to an order made by a Master or district judge pursuant to paragraph (1), Order 58, rule 1 shall, where the appeal is to be heard by a Divisional Court, have effect as if a reference to that court were substituted for the reference to a judge.

(3) This rule is without prejudice to any statutory provision or rule of law restricting the making of an order against the Crown.

Rule 7 POWERS OF COURT HEARING APPEAL
(1) In addition to the power conferred by rule 6(3) the court hearing an appeal to which this order applies shall have the powers conferred by the following provisions of this rule.

(2) The court shall have power to receive further evidence on questions of fact, and the evidence may be given in such manner as the court may direct either by oral examination in court, by witness statement or affidavit, by deposition taken before an examiner or in some other manner.

CPR SCHEDULE 1

(3) The court shall have power to draw any inferences of fact which might have been drawn in the proceedings out of which the appeal arose.

(4) It shall be the duty of the appellant to apply to the judge or other person presiding at the proceedings in which the decision appealed against was given for a signed copy of any note made by him of the proceedings and to furnish that copy for the use of the court; and in default of production of such a note, or if such note is incomplete, in addition to such note, the court may hear and determine the appeal on any other evidence or statement of what occurred in those proceedings as appears to the court to be sufficient.

Except where the court otherwise directs, a witness statement or affidavit or note by a person present at the proceedings shall not be used in evidence under this paragraph unless it was previously submitted to the person presiding at the proceedings for his comments.

(5) The court may give any judgment or decision or make any order which ought to have been given or made by the court, tribunal or person and make such further or other order as the case may require or may remit the matter with the opinion of the court for rehearing and determination by it or him.

(6) The court may, in special circumstances, order that such security shall be given for the costs of the appeal as may be just.

(7) The court shall not be bound to allow the appeal on the ground merely of misdirection, or of the improper admission or rejection of evidence, unless in the opinion of the court substantial wrong or miscarriage has been thereby occasioned.

Rule 8 RIGHT OF MINISTER, ETC., TO APPEAR AND BE HEARD

Where an appeal to which this order applies is against an order, determination or other decision of a Minister of the Crown or government department, the Minister or department, as the case may be, shall be entitled to appear and be heard in the proceedings on the appeal.

RSC ORDER 56
APPEALS, ETC., TO HIGH COURT BY CASE STATED: GENERAL

Rule 1 APPEALS FROM THE CROWN COURT BY CASE STATED

(1) Except where they relate to affiliation proceedings or to care proceedings under the Children and Young Persons Act 1969 all appeals from the Crown Court by case stated shall be heard and determined—

    (a) in any criminal proceedings, by a Divisional Court of the Queen's Bench Division;

    (b) in any other proceedings, by a single judge, or if the court so directs, by a Divisional Court of the Queen's Bench Division.

(3) An appeal from the Crown Court by case stated shall not be entered for hearing unless and until the case and a copy of the judgment, order or decision in respect of which the case has been stated and, if that judgment, order or decision was given or made on an appeal to the Crown Court, a copy of the judgment, order or decision appealed from, have been filed in the Crown Office.

(4) No such appeal shall be entered after the expiration of 10 days from the receipt by the appellant of the case unless the delay is accounted for to the satisfaction of the Divisional Court.

Notice of intention to apply for an extension of time for entry of the appeal must be served on the respondent at least 2 clear days before the day named in the notice for the hearing of the application.

(5) Where any such appeal has not been entered by reason of a default in complying with the provisions of this rule, the Crown Court may proceed as if no case had been stated.

Rule 4 NOTICE OF ENTRY OF APPEAL

Within 4 days after an appeal from the Crown Court by case stated is entered for hearing, the appellant must serve notice of the entry of the appeal on the respondent.

Rule 4A APPEALS RELATING TO AFFILIATION PROCEEDINGS AND CARE PROCEEDINGS

Appeals from the Crown Court by case stated which relate to affiliation proceedings or to care proceedings under the Children and Young Persons Act 1969 shall be heard and determined by a single judge, or if the court so directs, a Divisional Court of the Family Division, and the foregoing provisions of this order shall accordingly apply to such appeals with the substitution of references to the principal registry of the Family Division for references to the Crown Office and such other modifications as may be appropriate.

Rule 5 APPEAL FROM MAGISTRATES' COURT BY CASE STATED

(1) Except as provided by paragraph (2) all appeals from a Magistrates' Court by case stated shall be heard and determined—

(a) in any criminal proceedings, by a Divisional Court of the Queen's Bench Division;

(b) in any other proceedings, by a single judge or, if the court so directs, by a Divisional Court of the Queen's Bench Division.

(2) An appeal by way of case stated against an order or determination of a Magistrates' Court shall be heard and determined by a single judge or, if the court so directs, a Divisional Court of the Family Division if the order or determination appealed against was made or given in family proceedings.

Rule 6 CASE STATED BY MAGISTRATES' COURT: FILING CASE, ETC.

(1) Where a case has been stated by a magistrates' court the appellant must—

(a) within 10 days after receiving the case, file it in the Crown Office or, if the appeal falls to be heard by a Divisional Court of the Family Division, the principal registry of the Family Division; and

(b) within 4 days after filing the case as aforesaid serve on the respondent a notice of the entry of appeal together with a copy of the case.

(2) Unless the court having jurisdiction to determine the appeal otherwise directs, the appeal shall not be heard sooner than 8 clear days after service of notice of the entry of the appeal.

Rule 7 CASE STATED BY MINISTERS, TRIBUNAL, ETC.

(1) The jurisdiction of the High Court under any enactment to hear and determine a case stated by a Minister of the Crown, government department, tribunal or other person, or a question of law referred to that court by such a Minister or department or a tribunal or other person by way of case stated, shall be exercised by a single judge of the Queen's Bench Division, except where it is otherwise provided by these rules or by or under any enactment.

(2) The jurisdiction of the High Court under any enactment to hear and determine an application for an order directing such a Minister or department or a tribunal or other person to state a case for determination by the High Court, or to refer a question of law to that court by way of case stated, shall be exercised by the court or judge having jurisdiction to hear and determine that case or question except where by some other provision of these rules or by or under any enactment it is otherwise provided.

(3) This rule and rules 8 to 12 of this order shall apply to proceedings for the determination of such a case, question or application and, in relation to any such proceedings, shall have effect subject to any provision made in relation to those proceedings by any other provision of these rules or by or under any enactment.

(4) In this order references to a tribunal shall be construed as references to any tribunal constituted by or under any enactment other than any of the ordinary courts of law.

(5) In the following rules references to a Minister shall be construed as including references to a government department, and in those rules and this rule 'case' includes a special case.

Rule 8 APPLICATION FOR ORDER TO STATE A CASE

(1) An application to the court for an order directing a Minister, tribunal or other person to state a case for determination by the court or to refer a question

of law to the court by way of case stated must be made by claim form; and the persons to be served with the claim form are the Minister, secretary of the tribunal or other person, as the case may be, and every party (other than the applicant) to the proceedings to which the application relates.

(2) The claim form must state the grounds of the application, the question of law on which it is sought to have the case stated and any reasons given by the Minister, tribunal or other person for his or its refusal to state a case.

(3) The claim must be entered for hearing, and the claim form served, within 14 days after receipt by the applicant of notice of the refusal of his request to state a case.

Rule 9 SIGNING AND SERVICE OF CASE

(1) A case stated by a tribunal must be signed by the chairman or president of the tribunal, and a case stated by any other person must be signed by him or by a person authorised in that behalf to do so.

(2) The case must be served on the party at whose request, or as a result of whose application to the court, the case was stated; and if a Minister, tribunal, arbitrator or other person is entitled by virtue of any enactment to state a case, or to refer a question of law by way of case stated, for determination by the High Court without request being made by any party to the proceedings before that person, the case must be served on such party to those proceedings as the Minister, tribunal, arbitrator or other person, as the case may be, thinks appropriate.

(3) When a case is served on any party under paragraph (2) notice must be given to every other party to the proceedings in question that the case has been served on the party named, and on the date specified, in the notice.

Rule 10 PROCEEDINGS FOR DETERMINATION OF CASE

(1) Proceedings for the determination by the High Court of a case stated, or a question of law referred by way of case stated, by a Minister, tribunal, arbitrator or other person must be begun by claim form by the person on whom the case was served in accordance with rule 9(2) or, where the case is stated without a request being made, by the Minister, secretary of the tribunal, arbitrator or other person by whom the case is stated.

(2) The applicant shall serve the claim form under paragraph (1), together with a copy of the case, on—

(a) the Minister, secretary of the tribunal, arbitrator or other person by whom the case was stated, unless that Minister, tribunal, arbitrator or other person is the applicant;

(b) every party (other than the applicant) to the proceedings in which the question of law to which the case relates arose; and

(c) any other person (other than the applicant) served with the case under rule 9(2).

(3) The claim form must set out the applicant's contentions on the question of law to which the case stated relates.

(4) The claim must be entered for hearing, and the claim form served, within 14 days after the case stated was served on the applicant.

(5) If the applicant fails to enter the claim within the period specified in paragraph (4) then, after obtaining a copy of the case from the Minister, tribunal, arbitrator or other person by whom the case was stated, any other party to the proceedings in which the question of law to which the case relates arose may, within 14 days after the expiration of the period so specified, begin proceedings for the determination of the case, and paragraphs (1) to (4) shall have effect accordingly with the necessary modifications.

The references in this paragraph to the period specified in paragraph (4) shall be construed as including references to that period as extended by any order of the court.

(6) The documents required to be filed in accordance with Order 57, rule 2, before entry of the claim include a copy of the case stated.

(7) Unless the court having jurisdiction to determine the case otherwise directs, the claim shall not be heard sooner than 7 days after service of the claim form.

CPR SCHEDULE 1

Rule 11 AMENDMENT OF CASE
The court hearing a case stated by a Minister, tribunal, arbitrator or other person may amend the case or order it to be returned to that person for amendment, and may draw inferences of fact from the facts stated in the case.

Rule 12 RIGHT OF MINISTER TO APPEAR AND BE HEARD
In proceedings for the determination of a case stated, or of a question of law referred by way of case stated, the Minister, chairman or president of the tribunal, arbitrator or other person by whom the case was stated shall be entitled to appear and be heard.

Rule 12A EXTRADITION
 (1) Rules 5 and 6 of this order shall apply to appeals by case stated under—
  (a) section 7 of the Criminal Justice Act 1988; and
  (b) section 7A of the Fugitive Offenders Act 1967,
as they apply to appeals by case stated from a Magistrates' Court and references in those rules to appellant and respondent shall be construed as references to the requesting state and the person whose surrender is sought respectively.

 (2) An application for an order under either of the sections mentioned in paragraph (1) or under section 2A of the Backing of Warrants (Republic of Ireland) Act 1965 requiring a court to state a case shall be made in accordance with rule 8 of this order the references in that rule to a tribunal and the secretary of a tribunal being construed for this purpose as references to the court and the clerk of the court respectively.

Rule 13 INTERLOCUTORY APPLICATIONS
 (1) Unless the court otherwise directs, any interlocutory application in proceedings to which this order applies may be made to any judge or a Master of the Queen's Bench Division or, as the case may be, any judge or a district judge of the Family Division, notwithstanding that the appeal has been brought by case stated and is to be heard by a Divisional Court.
In this paragraph 'interlocutory application' includes an application for an order extending the time for entry of the appeal or for service of notice of entry of the appeal.

 (2) In relation to an order made by a Master or district judge pursuant to paragraph (1), Order 58, rule 1 shall, where the application is to be heard by a Divisional Court, have effect as if a reference to that court were substituted for the reference to a judge.

 (3) This rule is without prejudice to any statutory provision or rule of law restricting the making of an order against the Crown.

RSC ORDER 57
DIVISIONAL COURT PROCEEDINGS, ETC.: SUPPLEMENTARY PROVISIONS

Rule 1 APPLICATION
 (1) Subject to paragraph (2) this order shall apply to—
  (a) any proceedings before a Divisional Court;
  (b) any proceedings before a single judge under Order 52, rule 2, Order 53, Order 54, Order 64, rule 4, or Order 79;
  (c) any proceedings before a single judge, being proceedings which consist of or relate to an appeal to the High Court from any court, tribunal or person including an appeal by case stated and the reference of a question of law by way of case stated.

 (2) The following rules of this order shall not apply to an appeal from a county court to a single judge under section 375 of the Insolvency Act 1986.

Rule 2 ENTRY OF CLAIMS
 (1) Every claim in proceedings to which this order applies must be entered for hearing in the appropriate office; and entry shall be made when a copy of the claim

form, and any other documents required to be lodged before entry, have been filed in that office.

(2) The party entering the claim for hearing must file in the appropriate office copies of the proceedings for the use of the judges.

(3) Except where it relates to proceedings in the Admiralty Court every claim entered for hearing by a Divisional Court of the Queen's Bench Division shall be entered in the Divisional Court list.

(4) In this rule 'the appropriate office' means—

(a) in relation to proceedings in the Queen's Bench Division (including the Admiralty Court) the Crown Office or the Admiralty and Commercial Registry, as the circumstances of the case require;

(b) in relation to proceedings in the Chancery Division, Chancery Chambers;

(c) in relation to proceedings in the Family Division, the principal registry of the Family Division.

Rule 3 ISSUE, ETC., OF CLAIM FORM

A claim form by which any proceedings to which this order applies are begun must be issued—

(a) in the case of proceedings in the Family Division, out of the principal registry of the Family Division; and

(b) in the case of any other proceedings, out of the Crown Office, Chancery Chambers or the Admiralty and Commercial Registry, as the circumstances of the case require.

Rule 4 FILING OF WITNESS STATEMENTS OR AFFIDAVITS AND DRAWING UP OF ORDERS

(1) Every witness statement or affidavit used in proceedings to which this order applies must be filed in the Crown Office, Chancery Chambers or the Admiralty and Commercial Registry, as the circumstances of the case require.

(2) Every order made in proceedings to which this order applies in the Queen's Bench Division shall be drawn up in the Crown Office or the Admiralty and Commercial Registry, as the circumstances of the case require, and a copy of any order made by a judge sitting in private in any such proceedings must be filed in that office.

Rule 5 ISSUE OF WRITS

Every writ issued in proceedings to which this Order applies must be prepared by the party seeking to issue it and—

(a) shall be issued out of the Crown Office, Chancery Chambers or the principal registry of the Family Division, as the circumstances of the case require; and

(b) must, together with the return to it and a copy of any order made on it, be filed in the Crown Office, Chancery Chambers or the principal registry of the Family Division, as the circumstances of the case require.

Rule 6 CUSTODY OF RECORDS

The master of the Crown Office or the Admiralty and Commercial Registry, as the circumstances of the case require shall have the custody of the records of or relating to proceedings in the Queen's Bench Division to which this Order applies.

RSC ORDER 58
APPEALS FROM MASTERS, REGISTRARS, REFEREES AND JUDGES

Rule 1 APPEALS FROM CERTAIN DECISIONS OF MASTERS, ETC. TO JUDGE SITTING IN PRIVATE

(1) Except as provided by rule 2, an appeal shall lie to a judge from any judgment, order or decision of a Master, the Admiralty Registrar or a district judge of the Family Division.

(2) The appeal shall be brought by serving on every other party to the proceedings in which the judgment, order or decision was given or made a notice of appeal.

(3) Unless the court otherwise orders, the notice must be issued within 5 days after the judgment, order or decision appealed against was given or made and must be served within five days after issue and an appeal to which this rule applies shall not be heard sooner than two clear days after such service.

(3A) When it issues the notice of appeal, the court will fix a date for the hearing.

(4) Except so far as the court may otherwise direct, an appeal under this rule shall not operate as a stay of the proceedings in which the appeal is brought.

Rule 2 APPEALS FROM CERTAIN DECISIONS OF MASTERS, ETC., TO COURT OF APPEAL

(1) An appeal shall lie to the Court of Appeal from any judgment, order or decision of a Master given or made at trial—

(a) on the hearing or determination of any cause, matter, question or issue tried before him; or

(b) on an assessment of damages or of the value of goods, or an assessment of interest,

and where a judgment, order or decision of a kind referred to in paragraph (b) includes or involves a determination of any other matter, an appeal shall lie to the Court of Appeal in relation to such other matter.

(An appeal from the decision of a Master made other than at trial shall be made to the judge in accordance with rule 1.)

Rule 3 APPEALS FROM DISTRICT JUDGES

(1) An appeal shall lie from any judgment, order or decision of a district judge in any proceedings in any Division in the same circumstances and, except as provided by paragraph (2) subject to the same conditions as if the judgment, order or decision were given or made by a Master or Registrar in those proceedings in that Division, and the provisions of these rules with respect to appeals shall apply accordingly.

(2) In relation to an appeal from a judgment, order or decision of a district judge, rule 1 shall have effect subject to the modification that for the first reference therein to 5 days and the reference therein to 2 clear days there shall be substituted references to 7 days and 3 clear days respectively.

Rule 4 APPEALS FROM JUDGE OF THE TECHNOLOGY AND CONSTRUCTION COURT

Subject to section 18 of the Act (which shall apply in relation to a decision of a judge of the Technology and Construction Court as if he were a judge of the High Court), an appeal shall lie to the Court of Appeal from a decision of a judge of the Technology and Construction Court as if he were a judge of the High Court.

RSC ORDER 59
APPEALS TO THE COURT OF APPEAL

Rule 1 APPLICATION OF ORDER TO APPEALS

This order applies, subject to the provisions of these Rules with respect to particular appeals, to every appeal to the Court of Appeal (including so far as it is applicable thereto, any appeal to that court from a judge of the Technology and Construction Court, master or other officer of the Supreme Court or from any tribunal from which an appeal lies to that court under or by virtue of any enactment) not being an appeal for which other provision is made by these Rules, and references to 'the court below' apply to any court, tribunal or person from which such an appeal lies.

Rule 1B CLASSES OF CASE WHERE PERMISSION TO APPEAL IS REQUIRED

(1) Permission is required for every appeal except an appeal against—

(a) the making of a committal order;
(b) a refusal to grant habeas corpus; or
(c) an order made under section 25 of the Children Act 1989 (secure accommodation orders).

(2) A respondent who wishes to serve a respondent's notice to which rule 6(1)(a) applies must first obtain permission to cross-appeal unless the case is one to which sub-paragraphs (a), (b) or (c) of paragraph (1) applies.

(3) Permission to appeal or cross-appeal to the Court of Appeal may be given by the court below or by the Court of Appeal.

Rule 2 APPLICATION OF ORDER TO APPLICATIONS FOR NEW TRIAL

This order (except so much of rule 3(1) as provides that an appeal shall be by way of rehearing and except rule 11(1)) applies to an application to the Court of Appeal for a new trial or to set aside a verdict, finding or judgment after trial with or without a jury, as it applies to an appeal to that court, and references in this order to an appeal and to an appellant shall be construed accordingly.

Rule 2A INTERPRETATION

In this order 'a single judge' means a single judge of the Court of Appeal and 'the registrar' means the registrar of civil appeals.

GENERAL PROVISIONS AS TO APPEALS

Rule 2B WHO MAY EXERCISE THE POWERS OF THE COURT OF APPEAL

Subject to section 58(1) of the Act the functions of the Court of Appeal may be performed by—
(a) that court;
(b) a single judge; or
(c) the registrar

Rule 2C VARIATION OF TIME

Any date set by the court or this order for doing any act may not be varied by the parties.
(CPR Rule 2.11 allows the parties to vary a date by written agreement except where these Rules provide otherwise or the court orders otherwise.)

Rule 3 NOTICE OF APPEAL

(1) An appeal to the Court of Appeal shall be by way of rehearing and must be brought by notice of appeal.

(2) Notice of appeal may be given either in respect of the whole or in respect of any specified part of the judgment or order of the court below; and every such notice must specify the grounds of the appeal and the precise form of the order which the appellant proposes to ask the Court of Appeal to make.

(3) Except with the permission of the Court of Appeal, a single judge or the registrar, the appellant shall not be entitled on the hearing of an appeal to rely on any grounds of appeal, or to apply for any relief, not specified in the notice of appeal.

(4) Every notice of appeal must specify the list of appeals to which the appellant proposes that the appeal should be assigned.

(5) A notice of appeal must be served on all parties to the proceedings in the court below who are directly affected by the appeal; and, subject to rule 8, it shall not be necessary to serve the notice on parties not so affected.

(6) No notice of appeal shall be given by a respondent in a case to which rule 6(1) relates.

Rule 4 TIME FOR APPEALING

(1) Except as otherwise provided by this order, every notice of appeal must be served under rule 3(5) not later than 4 weeks after the date on which the judgment or order of the court below was sealed or otherwise perfected.

(2) In the case of an appeal from a decision in respect of which a certificate has been granted under section 12 of the Administration of Justice Act 1969 the period

referred to in paragraph (1) shall be calculated from the end of the time during which, in accordance with section 13(5) of that Act, no appeal lies to the Court of Appeal.

(3) Where permission to appeal is granted by the Court of Appeal or the court below upon an application made within the time limited for serving notice of appeal under paragraph (1), a notice of appeal may, instead of being served within that time, be served within 7 days after the date when permission is granted.

Rule 5 SETTING DOWN APPEAL

(1) Within 7 days after the later of (i) the date on which service of the notice of appeal was effected, or (ii) the date on which the judgment or order of the court below was sealed or otherwise perfected, the appellant must set down his appeal by filing with the court—

    (a) a copy of the said judgment or order; and

    (b) two copies of the notice of appeal, one of which shall be indorsed with the amount of the fee paid, and the other indorsed with a certificate of the date of service of the notice.

(2) Upon the said documents being so filed, the court shall enter the appeal in the records of the court and assign it to the appropriate list of appeals.

(3) The appropriate list of appeals for the purpose of paragraph (2) shall be decided by the registrar, without prejudice, however, to any decision of the Court of Appeal on the question whether the judgment or order appealed against is interlocutory or final.

(4) Within 4 days of receipt of notification from the office of the registrar that the appeal has been entered in the records of the court, the appellant must give notice to that effect to all parties on whom the notice of appeal was served, specifying the Court of Appeal reference allocated to that appeal.

Rule 6 RESPONDENT'S NOTICE

(1) A respondent who, having been served with a notice of appeal, desires—

    (a) to contend on the appeal that the decision of the court below should be varied, either in any event or in the event of the appeal being allowed in whole or in part; or

    (b) to contend that the decision of the court below should be affirmed on grounds other than those relied upon by that court;

must give notice to that effect, specifying the grounds of his contention and, in a case to which paragraph (a) relates, the precise form of the order which he proposes to ask the court to make.

(2) Except with the permission of the Court of Appeal or a single judge or the registrar, a respondent shall not be entitled on the hearing of the appeal to apply for any remedy not specified in a notice under paragraph (1) or to rely, in support of any contention, upon any ground which has not been specified in such a notice or relied upon by the court below.

(3) Any notice given by a respondent under this rule (in this order referred to as a 'respondent's notice') must be served on the appellant, and on all parties to the proceedings in the court below who are directly affected by the contentions of the respondent, and must be served within 21 days after the service of the notice of appeal on the respondent.

(4) A party by whom a respondent's notice is given must, within 4 days after the later of (i) the date on which the service of the respondent's notice was effected or (ii) the date on which he was notified under rule 5(4) that the appeal had been entered in the records of the court, file with the court two copies of the respondent's notice, one of which shall be indorsed with the amount of the fee paid, and the other indorsed with a certificate of the date of service of such respondent's notice.

Rule 7 AMENDMENT OF NOTICE OF APPEAL AND RESPONDENT'S NOTICE

(1) A notice of appeal or respondent's notice may be amended—

    (a) with the permission of the Court of Appeal, a single judge or the registrar, at any time;

(b) without such permission, by supplementary notice served, before the date on which the appeal first appears in the Document List referred to in rule 9(1) on each of the parties on whom the notice to be amended was served.

(2) A party by whom a supplementary notice is served under this rule must, within 2 days after service of the notice, file two copies of the notice at the court.

Rule 8 DIRECTIONS OF THE COURT AS TO SERVICE

(1) The Court of Appeal or a single judge or the registrar may in any case direct that a notice of appeal or respondent's notice be served on any party to the proceedings in the court below on whom it has not been served, or on any person not party to those proceedings.

(2) Where a direction is given under paragraph (1) the hearing of the appeal may be postponed or adjourned for such period and on such terms as may be just and such judgment may be given and such order made on the appeal as might have been given or made if the persons served in pursuance of the direction had originally been parties.

Rule 9 DOCUMENTS TO BE FILED BY APPELLANT

Not more than 14 days after an appeal or application first appears in a list to be called 'the Document List' the appellant must file documents with the court in accordance with the relevant practice direction.

Rule 10 GENERAL POWERS OF THE COURT

(1) In relation to an appeal the Court of Appeal shall have all the powers and duties of the court below.

(2) The Court of Appeal shall have power to receive further evidence on questions of fact, either by oral examination in court, by witness statement or affidavit, or by deposition taken before an examiner, but, in the case of an appeal from a judgment after trial or hearing of any proceedings on the merits, no such further evidence (other than evidence as to matters which have occurred after the date of the trial or hearing) shall be admitted except on special grounds.

(3) The Court of Appeal shall have power to draw inferences of fact and to give any judgment and make any order which ought to have been given or made, and to make such further or other order as the case may require.

(4) The powers of the Court of Appeal under the foregoing provisions of this rule may be exercised notwithstanding that no notice of appeal or respondent's notice has been given in respect of any particular part of the decision of the court below or by any particular party to the proceedings in that court, or that any ground for allowing the appeal or for affirming or varying the decision of that court is not specified in such a notice; and the Court of Appeal may make any order, on such terms as the court thinks just, to ensure the determination on the merits of the real question in controversy between the parties.

(5) The Court of Appeal may, in special circumstances, order that such security shall be given for the costs of an appeal as may be just.

(6) The powers of the Court of Appeal in respect of an appeal shall not be restricted by reason of any interlocutory order from which there has been no appeal.

(7) Documents impounded by order of the Court of Appeal shall not be delivered out of the custody of that court except in compliance with an order of that court:

Provided that where a Law Officer or the Director of Public Prosecutions makes a written request in that behalf, documents so impounded shall be delivered into his custody.

(8) Documents impounded by order of the Court of Appeal, while in the custody of that court, shall not be inspected except by a person authorised to do so by an order of that court.

(9) In any proceedings incidental to any cause or matter pending before the Court of Appeal, the powers conferred by this rule on the court shall be exercisable in relation to—

(a) the grant, variation, discharge or enforcement of an injunction, or an undertaking given in lieu of an injunction; and

(b) the grant or lifting of a stay of execution or proceedings,
only by the court or a single judge

Rule 11 POWERS OF THE COURT AS TO NEW TRIALS

(1) On the hearing of any appeal the Court of Appeal may, if it thinks fit, make any such order as could be made in pursuance of an application for a new trial or to set aside a verdict, finding or judgment of the court below.

(2) The Court of Appeal shall not be bound to order a new trial on the ground of misdirection, or of the improper admission or rejection of evidence, or because the verdict of the jury was not taken upon a question which the judge at the trial was not asked to leave to them, unless in the opinion of the Court of Appeal some substantial wrong or miscarriage has been thereby occasioned.

(3) A new trial may be ordered on any question without interfering with the finding or decision on any other question; and if it appears to the Court of Appeal that any such wrong or miscarriage as is mentioned in paragraph (2) affects part only of the matter in controversy, or one or some only of the parties, the court may order a new trial as to that part only, or as to that party or those parties only, and give final judgment as to the remainder.

(4) In any case where the Court of Appeal has power to order a new trial on the ground that damages awarded by a jury are excessive or inadequate, the court may, instead of ordering a new trial, substitute for the sum awarded by the jury such sum as appears to the court to be proper; but except as aforesaid the Court of Appeal shall not have power to reduce or increase the damages awarded by a jury.

Rule 12 EVIDENCE ON APPEAL

Where any question of fact is involved in an appeal, the evidence taken in the court below bearing on the question shall, subject to any direction of the Court of Appeal, or a single judge or the registrar, be brought before that Court as follows—

(a) in the case of evidence taken by affidavit or witness statement, by the production of a true copy of such affidavit or witness statement;

(b) in the case of evidence given orally, by a copy of so much of the transcript of the official shorthand note as is relevant or by a copy of the judge's note, where he has intimated that in the event of an appeal his note will be sufficient, or by such other means as the Court of Appeal, or a single judge or the registrar, may direct.

Rule 12A NON-DISCLOSURE OF PAYMENT INTO COURT

(1) Where—

(a) any question on an appeal in a claim for a debt, damages or salvage relates to liability for the debt, damages or salvage or to the amount thereof; and

(b) money was paid into court under CPR Part 36 or CPR rule 37.3 in the proceedings in the court below before judgment,

neither the fact of the payment nor the amount thereof shall be stated in the notice of appeal or the respondent's notice or in any supplementary notice or be communicated to the Court of Appeal until all such questions have been decided.

This rule shall not apply in the case of an appeal as to costs only or an appeal in a claim to which a defence of tender before claim was made.

(2) To comply with this rule the appellant must cause to be omitted from the copies of the documents filed by him under rule 9 every part thereof which states that money was paid into court in the proceedings in that court before judgment.

Rule 13 STAY OF EXECUTION, ETC.

(1) Except so far as the court below or the Court of Appeal or a single judge may otherwise direct—

(a) an appeal shall not operate as a stay of execution or of proceedings under the decision of the court below;

(b) no intermediate act or proceeding shall be invalidated by an appeal.

(2) On an appeal from the High Court, interest for such time as execution has been delayed by the appeal shall be allowed unless the Court of Appeal otherwise orders.

Rule 14 APPLICATIONS TO COURT OF APPEAL

(1) Unless otherwise directed, every application to the Court of Appeal, a single judge or the registrar must be made by application notice in accordance with CPR Part 23.

(2) An application to the Court of Appeal for permission to appeal shall—

(a) include, where necessary, any application to extend the time for appealing; and

(b) be made in writing without notice being served on any other party setting out the reasons why permission should be granted and, if the time for appealing has expired, the reasons why the application was not made within that time unless the court otherwise directs,

and the court may grant or refuse the application or direct that the application be renewed at a hearing either with or without notice being served on any other party.

(2A) If an application under paragraph (2) is refused otherwise than after a hearing, the applicant shall be entitled, within 7 days after he has been given notice of the refusal, to renew his application; and such renewed application shall be heard without notice being served on any other party unless the court otherwise directs.

(2B) If an application under paragraph (2) is granted otherwise than after a hearing with notice, notice of the order shall be served on the party or parties affected by the appeal and any such party shall be entitled, within 7 days after service of the notice, to apply with notice to have the grant of permission reconsidered unless the court otherwise directs.

(3) Where an application without notice being served on any other party has been refused by the court below, an application for a similar purpose may be made to the Court of Appeal without notice being served on any other party within 7 days after the date of the refusal.

(4) Wherever under these rules an application may be made either to the court below or to the Court of Appeal, it shall not be made in the first instance to the Court of Appeal, except where there are special circumstances which make it impossible or impracticable to apply to the court below or unless the court otherwise directs.

(5) Where an application is made to the Court of Appeal with regard to arbitration proceedings before a judge-arbitrator or judge-umpire, which would, in the case of an ordinary arbitrator or umpire, be made to the High Court, the provisions of the Arbitration Practice Direction relating to such applications shall apply as appropriate.

(6) Where an application is made to the Court of Appeal under section 1(5) of the Arbitration Act 1979 (including any application for permission) notice thereof must be served on the judge-arbitrator or judge-umpire and on any other party to the reference.

(9) The registrar may refer to a single judge any matter which he thinks should properly be decided by a single judge, and, following such reference, the judge may either dispose of the matter or refer it back to the registrar with such direction as the single judge thinks fit.

(10) A single judge may refer to the Court of Appeal any matter which he thinks should properly be decided by that court, and, following such reference, that court may either dispose of the matter or refer it back to a single judge or the registrar, with such directions as that court thinks fit.

(11) An appeal shall lie to a single judge from any determination made by the registrar and shall be brought by way of fresh application made within 10 days of the determination appealed against.

(12) An appeal shall lie to the Court of Appeal from any determination by a single judge, not being the determination of an application for permission to appeal, and shall be brought by way of fresh application made within 10 days of the determination appealed against.

Provided that an appeal shall not lie to the Court of Appeal without the permission of that court in respect of a determination of the registrar which has been reviewed by a single judge.

CPR SCHEDULE 1

Rule 15 EXTENSION OF TIME
(1) The period for serving notice of appeal under rule 4 or for making application without notice being served on any other party under rule 14(3) may be extended or abridged by the court below on application made before the expiration of that period.

SPECIAL PROVISIONS AS TO PARTICULAR APPEALS

Rule 16 APPEAL AGAINST DECREE NISI
(1) The following provisions of this rule shall apply to any appeal to the Court of Appeal in a matrimonial cause against a decree nisi of divorce or nullity of marriage.

(2) The period of 4 weeks specified in rule 4 shall be calculated from the date on which the decree was pronounced and rule 15 shall not apply in relation to that period.

(2A) The notice of appeal shall be served on the appropriate district judge as well as on the party or parties required to be served under rule 3.

(3) The appellant must, within the period mentioned in paragraph (2) and after service of the notice of appeal, file with the court a copy of that decree and two copies of the notice of appeal (one of which shall be indorsed with the amount of the fee paid and the other indorsed with a certificate of the date of service of the notice); and the appeal shall not be competent unless this paragraph has been complied with.

(4) For the purposes of rule 5 the leaving of the said copies shall be sufficient for the setting down of the appeal and rule 5(1) shall not apply.

(5) A party who intends to apply without notice being served on any other party to the Court of Appeal to extend the period referred to in paragraphs (2) and (3) must give notice of his intention to the appropriate district judge before the application is made; and where any order is made by the Court of Appeal extending the said period, it shall be the duty of the registrar of civil appeals forthwith to give notice of the making of the order and of the terms thereof to the appropriate district judge.

(6) In this rule 'the appropriate district judge' means—

   (a) in relation to a cause pending in a county court, the district judge of that court;

   (b) in relation to a cause proceeding in the principal registry of the Family Division, the senior district judge of that Division; and

   (c) in relation to a cause proceeding in a district registry, the district judge of that registry.

Rule 17 APPEAL AGAINST ORDER FOR REVOCATION OF PATENT
(1) The following provisions of this rule shall apply to any appeal to the Court of Appeal from an order for the revocation of a patent.

(2) The notice of appeal must be served on the Comptroller-General of Patents, Designs and Trade Marks (in this rule referred to as 'the Comptroller') as well as on the party or parties required to be served under rule 3.

(3) If, at any time before the appeal comes on for hearing, the respondent decides not to appear on the appeal or not to oppose it, he must forthwith serve notice of his decision on the Comptroller and the appellant, and any such notice served on the Comptroller must be accompanied by a copy of the petition or of the statements of case in the claim and the written evidence filed therein.

(4) The Comptroller must, within 14 days after receiving notice of the respondent's decision, serve on the appellant a notice stating whether or not he intends to appear on the appeal.

(5) The Comptroller may appear and be heard in opposition to the appeal—

   (a) in any case where he has given notice under paragraph (4) of his intention to appear; and

   (b) in any other case (including, in particular, a case where the respondent withdraws his opposition to the appeal during the hearing) if the Court of Appeal so directs or allows.

(6) The Court of Appeal may make such orders for the postponement or adjournment of the hearing of the appeal as may appear to the court necessary for the purpose of giving effect to the foregoing provisions of this rule.

Rule 18 APPEAL FROM PATENTS COURT ON APPEAL FROM COMPTROLLER

In the case of an appeal to the Court of Appeal from a decision of the Patents Court on an appeal from a decision of the Comptroller-General of Patents, Designs and Trade Marks the notice of appeal must be served on the Comptroller-General as well as on the party or parties required to be served under rule 3.

Rule 19 APPEAL FROM COUNTY COURT

(1) The following provisions of this rule shall apply to any appeal to the Court of Appeal from a county court other than an appeal against a decree nisi of divorce or nullity of marriage.

(2) The appellant must, within the time specified in rule 4, serve the notice of appeal on the district judge of the county court as well as on the party or parties required to be served under rule 3.

(3) In relation to the appeal rule 4(1) and rule 5(1) shall have effect as if for the words 'the date on which the judgment or order of the court below was sealed or otherwise perfected' there were substituted the words 'the date on which the court below gave its decision.'

(5) Rule 13(1)(a) shall not apply, but the appeal shall not operate as a stay of execution or of proceedings in the county court unless the judge of that court or the Court of Appeal so orders or unless, within 10 days after the date of the judgment or order appealed against, the appellant deposits a sum fixed by the judge not exceeding the amount of the money or the value of the property affected by the judgment or order, or gives such security for the said sum as the judge may direct.

(6) In the case of an appeal to the Court of Appeal from the decision of a county court on the hearing of an appeal from a registration officer under section 56 of the Representation of the People Act 1983, notice of the decision of the Court of Appeal shall be given by the registrar of civil appeals to the registration officer, specifying every alteration to be made in pursuance of the decision in the register or list concerned, and a copy of every such notice shall be sent to the district judge of the county court.

(7) In relation to any proceedings in the principal registry of the Family Division which by virtue of any statutory provision are treated as pending in a county court, paragraphs (1) to (5) shall have effect with the necessary modifications as if the principal registry were a county court.

Rule 20 APPEALS IN CASES OF CONTEMPT OF COURT

(1) In the case of an appeal to the Court of Appeal under section 13 of the Administration of Justice Act 1960, the notice of appeal must be served on the court from whose order or decision the appeal is brought as well as on the party or parties required to be served under rule 3.

This paragraph shall not apply in relation to an appeal to which rule 19 applies.

(2) Where, in the case of an appeal under the said section 13 to the Court of Appeal or to the House of Lords from the Court of Appeal, the appellant is in custody, the Court of Appeal may order his release on his giving security (whether by recognisance, with or without sureties, or otherwise and for such reasonable sum as that court may fix) for his appearance within 10 days after the judgment of the Court of Appeal or, as the case may be, of the House of Lords on the appeal shall have been given, before the court from whose order or decision the appeal is brought unless the order or decision is reversed by that judgment.

(3) An application for the release of a person under paragraph (2) pending an appeal to the Court of Appeal or House of Lords under the said section 13 must be made in accordance with CPR Part 23, and the application notice must, at least 24 hours before the day named therein for the hearing, be served on the court from whose order or decision the appeal is brought and on all parties to the proceedings in that court who are directly affected by the appeal.

(4) Order 79, rule 9(6), (6A), (6B) and (8) shall apply in relation to the grant of bail under this rule by the Court of Appeal in a case of criminal contempt of court as they apply in relation to the grant of bail in criminal proceedings by the High Court, but with the substitution for references to a judge of references to the Court of Appeal and for references to the defendant of references to the appellant.

(5) When granting bail under this rule in a case of civil contempt of court, the Court of Appeal may order that the recognisance or other security to be given by the appellant or the recognisance of any surety shall be given before any person authorised by virtue of section 119(1) of the Magistrates' Courts Act 1980 to take a recognisance where a magistrates' court having power to take it has, instead of taking it, fixed the amount in which the principal and his sureties, if any, are to be bound. An order by the Court of Appeal granting bail as aforesaid must be in Form 98 in the relevant practice direction with the necessary adaptations.

(6) Where in pursuance of an order of the Court of Appeal under paragraph (5) of this rule a recognisance is entered into or other security given before any person, it shall be the duty of that person to cause the recognisance of the appellant or any surety or, as the case may be, a statement of the other security given, to be transmitted forthwith to the clerk of the court which committed the appellant; and a copy of such recognisance or statement shall at the same time be sent to the governor or keeper of the prison or other place of detention in which the appellant is detained, unless the recognisance or security was given before such governor or keeper.

(8) The powers conferred on the Court of Appeal by paragraphs (2), (4), (5) and (6) of this rule may be exercised by a single judge.

Rule 21 APPEALS FROM SOCIAL SECURITY COMMISSIONERS

(1) This rule shall apply to any appeal to the Court of Appeal under section 14 of the Social Security Act 1980 (appeal from the decision of a Commissioner on a question of law, with the permission of the Commissioner or of the Court of Appeal).

(2) The notice of appeal must be served within 6 weeks from the date on which notice of the Commissioner's grant or refusal of permission was given in writing to the appellant and must be served on the Secretary of State and any person appointed by him to proceed with a claim as well as on the party or parties required to be served under rule 3.

(3) The provisions of rule 4(3) apply to this rule, with the substitution for the reference in rule 4(3) to paragraph (1) of a reference to paragraph (2).

Rule 22 APPEALS FROM VALUE ADDED TAX TRIBUNALS

(1) An application to the Court of Appeal for permission to appeal from a value added tax tribunal direct to that court under section 26 of the Finance Act 1985 shall be made within 28 days from the date on which the tribunal certifies that its decision involves a point of law relating wholly or mainly to the construction of an enactment or of a statutory instrument, or of any of the Community Treaties or any Community Instrument, which has been fully argued before it and fully considered by it.

(2) Such an application shall be made by the parties jointly by filing a copy of the decision, endorsed with the certificate of the tribunal and a statement of the grounds of the application, with the court, and shall be determined by a single judge of the Court of Appeal, who may do so without a hearing.

(3) In the case of all applications, the court shall notify the parties of the determination of the single judge, and—

(a) where permission to appeal to the Court of Appeal is granted, the appellant shall within 14 days after such notification serve the notice of appeal on the chairman of the tribunal as well as on the party or parties required to be served by rule 3;

(b) where permission to appeal to the Court of Appeal is refused, the period specified in Order 55, rule 4(2) for appealing to the High Court shall be calculated from the date of notification of the refusal.

Rule 23 DISMISSAL OF PATIENT'S APPEAL BY CONSENT

Where the receiver or other person authorised under Part VII of the Mental Health Act 1983 to conduct legal proceedings in the name of the patient or on his behalf has also been authorised by the Court of Protection under its seal to consent to the dismissal of an appeal to the Court of Appeal by that patient, the appeal may be dismissed by consent without a hearing.

Rule 24 APPEALS FROM IMMIGRATION APPEALS TRIBUNAL

(1) This rule shall apply to any appeal to the Court of Appeal under section 9 of the Asylum and Immigration Appeals Act 1993 (appeal on a question of law from a final determination of an Immigration Appeals Tribunal, with the permission of the Immigration Appeals Tribunal or the Court of Appeal).

(2) Rule 4(1) shall have effect as if for the words 'the date on which the judgment or order of the court below was sealed or otherwise perfected' there were substituted the words 'the date of the tribunal's written decision to grant or refuse permission to appeal'.

(3) The notice of appeal must be served on the other party or parties to the proceedings before the tribunal, and on the chairman.

(5) Rule 13 shall not apply.

Rule 25 APPEALS FROM SPECIAL COMMISSIONERS

(1) An application to the Court of Appeal for permission to appeal from the Special Commissioners direct to that court under section 56A of the Taxes Management Act 1970 shall be made within 28 days from the date on which the Special Commissioners certify that their decision involves a point of law relating wholly or mainly to the construction of an enactment which was fully argued before them and fully considered by them.

(2) Such an application shall be made by the parties jointly filing a copy of the decision, endorsed with the certificate of the Special Commissioners, and a statement of the grounds of the application with the court. The application shall be determined by a single judge of the Court of Appeal, who may make his determination without a hearing.

(3) The court shall notify the parties of the determination of the single judge, and—

(a) where permission to appeal to the Court of Appeal is granted, the applicant shall within 14 days after such notification serve the notice of appeal on the Clerk to the Special Commissioners as well as on all parties directly affected by the proceedings before the Special Commissioners;

(b) where permission to appeal to the Court of Appeal is refused, the period specified in Order 55, rule 4(2) for appealing to the High Court shall be calculated from the date of notification of the refusal.

RSC ORDER 60
APPEALS TO COURT OF APPEAL FROM THE RESTRICTIVE PRACTICES COURT

Rule 1 APPEAL TO BE BROUGHT BY NOTICE OF APPEAL

An appeal to the Court of Appeal from the Restrictive Practices Court under the Restrictive Practices Court Act 1976 must be brought by notice of appeal, and the notice of appeal must state any question of law and, in the case of proceedings under Part III of the Fair Trading Act 1973, any question of fact on which the appeal is brought together in each case with the appellant's contentions thereon.

Rule 2 SERVICE OF NOTICE OF APPEAL

(1) Within 28 days after the appellant receives a copy of the judgment constituting the case stated by the Restrictive Practices Court or within 28 days of the date on which permission to appeal to the Court of Appeal was granted, he must serve the notice of appeal and a copy of the judgment on every other party to the proceedings before that court and must serve the notice of appeal on that court.

(2) Where the appellant applies to the said court for the court's judgment to be amplified or amended—
(a) he shall be deemed for the purpose of paragraph (1) to have received a copy of the judgment on the date on which he receives a copy of the order made on his application; and
(b) the judgment constituting the case stated shall be the judgment with such amplifications or amendments, if any, as may be specified in that order.

Rule 3 ENTRY, ETC. OF APPEAL
(1) Within 7 days after service of the notice of appeal, the appellant must file the judgment constituting the case and two copies of the notice with the Court of Appeal and Order 59, rule 5 shall apply subject to any necessary modifications.
(2) The office of the Court of Appeal shall notify the Restrictive Practices Court of the decision of the Court of Appeal on the appeal and of any directions given by the Court of Appeal thereon.

Rule 4 POWERS OF COURT OF APPEAL
The Court of Appeal shall have power to draw inferences of fact from the facts set forth in the judgment of the Restrictive Practices Court constituting the case.

RSC ORDER 61
APPEALS FROM TRIBUNALS TO COURT OF APPEAL BY CASE STATED

Rule 1 STATEMENT OF CASE BY LANDS TRIBUNAL
(1) The time within which a person aggrieved by a decision of the Lands Tribunal as being erroneous in point of law may under section 3(4) of the Lands Tribunal Act 1949, or any other enactment require the tribunal to state a case for the decision of the Court of Appeal shall be 4 weeks from the date of the decision, and the application for the statement of the case must be made to the registrar of the tribunal in writing.
(2) A case stated by the tribunal must state the facts on which the decision was based and the decision of the tribunal and must be signed by the member or members of the tribunal by whom it was given.
(3) The case must be stated as soon as may be after the application therefor is made and must be sent by post to the applicant.
(4) Where the decision of the Lands Tribunal in respect of which a case is stated states all the relevant facts found by the Tribunal and indicates the questions of law on which the decision of the Court of Appeal is sought, a copy of the decision signed by the person who presided at the hearing shall be annexed to the case, and the facts so found and the questions of law to be decided shall be sufficiently stated in the case by referring to the statement thereof in the decision.

Rule 2 STATEMENT OF CASE BY OTHER TRIBUNALS
(1) Where any tribunal is empowered or may be required to state a case on a question of law for determination by the Court of Appeal, any party to the proceedings who is aggrieved by the tribunal's refusal to state a case may apply to the Court of Appeal or a single judge of that court for an order requiring the tribunal to state a case.
(2) An application under this rule must be made in accordance with CPR Part 23 and the application notice, stating in general terms the grounds of the application, together with the question of law on which it is desired that a case shall be stated and any reasons given by the tribunal for its refusal, must within 28 days after the refusal, be served on the clerk or registrar of the tribunal and on every other party to the proceedings before the tribunal.
(3) Within 7 days after service of the application notice, the applicant must file two copies of the application notice with the Court of Appeal.
(4) Where a tribunal is ordered under this rule to state a case, the tribunal must, within such period as may be specified in the order, state a case, stating the

facts on which the decision of the tribunal was based and the decision, sign it and cause it to be sent by post to the applicant.

(5) Rule 1(4) shall apply in relation to a case stated by a tribunal other than the Lands Tribunal as it applies in relation to a case stated by that tribunal.

(6) In this rule, references to a tribunal other than the Lands Tribunal include references to a judge of the Commercial Court acting as an arbitrator or umpire under section 4 of the Administration of Justice Act 1970.

Rule 3 PROCEEDINGS ON CASE STATED

(A1) An application for permission to appeal to the Court of Appeal from any tribunal to which this order applies may be combined with an application to the tribunal to state a case.

(A2) An application for permission to appeal may not be made to the Court of Appeal until the tribunal has stated a case.

(1) The party at whose instance a case has been stated by any tribunal to which this order applies must, within 21 days after the date on which permission to appeal to the Court of Appeal was granted—

(a) serve on every other party to the proceedings before the tribunal a copy of the case, together with a notice of appeal setting out his contentions on the question of law; and

(b) serve a copy of the notice on the clerk or registrar of the tribunal.

(2) Within 7 days after service of the notice of appeal, the said party must file the case, and two copies of the notice with the Court of Appeal and Order 59, rule 5 shall apply subject to any necessary modifications.

(3) Where any enactment under which the case is stated provides that a Minister or government department shall have a right to be heard in the proceedings on the case, a copy of the case and of the notice of appeal served under paragraph (1) must be served on that Minister or department.

(4) On the hearing of the case, the Court of Appeal may amend the case or order it to be sent back to the tribunal for amendment.

(5) Order 59 shall, so far as applicable, apply, in relation to a case stated by a tribunal to which this order applies.

(6) The office of the Court of Appeal shall notify the clerk or registrar of the tribunal of the decision of the Court of Appeal on the case and of any directions given by that court thereon.

RSC ORDER 62
COSTS

APPENDIX 3

FIXED COSTS
The scale of costs set out in this Appendix shall apply in the cases to which the Appendix refers.

PART II — COSTS ON JUDGMENT WITHOUT TRIAL FOR POSSESSION OF LAND

1—(1) Where the claim is for the possession of land, and the claimant obtains judgment—

(a) under CPR Part 12 (default judgment); or
(c) under CPR Part 24 (summary judgment)

for possession of the land and costs, then, subject to sub-paragraph (2), there shall be allowed the costs prescribed by paragraph 2 of this Part of this Appendix.

(2) Where the claimant is also entitled under the judgment to damages to be assessed, or where the plaintiff claims any remedy of the nature specified in Order 88, rule 1 (mortgage claims), this Part of this Appendix shall not apply.

CPR SCHEDULE 1

2   The costs to be allowed under this Part of this Appendix shall be £143.75, together with any court fee, and additional costs where appropriate set out the Table below.

ADDITIONAL COSTS

B. *Additional costs*

Amount to be allowed	£
(1) Where there is more than one defendant, in respect of each additional defendant served	£13.75
(2) Where service by an alternative method is ordered and effected, in respect of each defendant served	£53.25
(3) Where service out of the jurisdiction is ordered and effected, in the case of service—	
(a) in Scotland, Northern Ireland, the Isle of Man or the Channel Islands	£68.25
(b) in any other place out of the jurisdiction	£77.00
(4) In the case of default judgment under CPR Part 12 or summary judgment under CPR Part 24 the claimant makes an affidavit of service for the purpose of a judgment where the defendant failed to respond to the claim form (the allowance to include the search fee)	£20.50
(5) In the case of summary judgment under CPR Part 24 where an affidavit of service of the Part 23 application is required	£20.50
(6) In the case of summary judgment under CPR Part 24 for each adjournment of the application	£20.50

PART III — Miscellaneous

This Part shows the amount to be allowed in respect of enforcement costs.

2   Where a certificate in respect of money provisions contained in a judgment is registered in the High Court in the Register of United Kingdom judgments under Schedule 6 to the Civil Jurisdiction and Judgments Act 1982, there shall be allowed—

Costs of registration	£39.00

2A   Where costs are allowed under the following paragraphs of this Part, the appropriate court fees shall be allowed in addition.

3   Where, upon the application of any person who has obtained a judgment or order against a debtor for the recovery or payment of money, a garnishee order is made under Order 49, rule 1, against a garnishee attaching debts due or accruing due from the debtor, the following costs shall be allowed—

(a) to the garnishee to be deducted by him from any debt due by him as aforesaid before payment to the applicant	£23.00

(b) to the applicant, to be retained, unless the court otherwise orders, out of the money recovered by him under the garnishee order and in priority to the amount of the debt owing to him under the judgment or order—
   (i) Basic costs

If the amount recovered by the applicant from the garnishee is—	
less than £150	one half of the amount recovered
not less than £150	£98.50
(ii) Additional costs	
Where the garnishee fails to attend the hearing of the application and an affidavit of service is required	£18.00

CPR SCHEDULE 1

4 Where a charging order is granted and made absolute there shall be allowed—

Basic costs	£110.00
Additional costs where an affidavit of service is required together with such reasonable disbursements in respect of search fees and the registration of the order as the court may allow.	£18.00

5 Where leave is given under Order 45, rule 3, to enforce a judgment or order for the giving of possession of land by writ of possession, if the costs are allowed on the judgment or order there shall be allowed the following costs, which shall be added to the judgment or order—

Basic costs	£42.50
Where notice of the proceedings has been given to more than one person, in respect of each additional person	£2.75

6 Where a writ of execution within the meaning of Order 46, rule 1, is issued against any party, there shall be allowed—

Costs of issuing execution	£51.75

RSC ORDER 64
SITTINGS, VACATIONS AND OFFICE HOURS

Rule 4 DIVISIONAL COURT BUSINESS DURING VACATION
Proceedings which require to be immediately or promptly heard and which by virtue of the following provisions must be brought in a Divisional Court may, in vacation, be brought before a single judge:
  (a) Order 52, rules 1(2) and 3(1);
  (b) Order 53, rules 3(4)(a) and 5(1);
  (c) Order 55, rule 2(a);
  (d) Order 56, rule 1(1)(a).

RSC ORDER 69
SERVICE OF FOREIGN PROCESS

Rule 1 DEFINITIONS
In this Order—
  'a convention country' means a foreign country in relation to which there subsists a civil procedure convention providing for service in that country of process of the High Court, and includes a country which is a party to the Convention on the Service Abroad of Judicial and Extra-judicial Documents in Civil or Commercial Matters signed at the Hague on 15 November 1965;
  'officer of the county court' means any clerk or bailiff in the service of a county court;
  'process' includes a citation;
  'process server' means the process server appointed under rule 4 or his authorised agent.

Rule 2 APPLICATIONS
This order applies to the service on a person in England or Wales of any process in connection with civil or commercial proceedings in a foreign court or tribunal where the Senior Master receives a written request for service—
  (a) from Her Majesty's Principal Secretary of State for Foreign and Commonwealth Affairs, with a recommendation by him that service should be effected; or
  (b) where the foreign court or tribunal is in a convention country, from a consular or other authority of that country.

Rule 3 SERVICE OF PROCESS
  (1) The request shall be accompanied by a translation thereof in English, two copies of the process and, unless the foreign court or tribunal certifies that the

person to be served understands the language of the process, two copies of a translation thereof.

(2) Subject to paragraphs (3) and (5) and to any enactment providing for the manner of service of documents on corporate bodies, the process shall be served by the process server's leaving a copy of the process and a copy of the translation or certificate, as the case may be, with the person to be served.

(3) The provisions of CPR rule 6.2(1)(c) and CPR rule 6.7 regarding service by leaving at a place specified in CPR rule 6.5, shall apply to the service of foreign process as they apply to the service of claim form, except that service may be proved by a witness statement or affidavit or by a certificate or report in such form as the Senior Master may direct.

(4) The process server shall send to the Senior Master a copy of the process and a witness statement or affidavit, certificate or report proving due service of process or stating the reason why service could not be effected, as the case may be, and shall, if the court so directs, specify the costs incurred in effecting or attempting to effect service.

(5) CPR rule 6.8 (service by an alternative method) shall apply to the service of foreign process as it applies to the service of claim forms, except that the Senior Master may make an order for alternative service of foreign process on the basis of the process server's witness statement or affidavit, certificate or report, without an application being made to him in that behalf.

(6) The Senior Master shall send a certificate, together with a copy of the process, to the consular or other authority or the Secretary of State, as the case may be, stating—

(i) when and how service was effected or the reason why service could not be effected, as the case may be;

(ii) where appropriate, the amount certified by the costs judge to be the costs of effecting or attempting to effect service.

(7) The certificate under paragraph (6) shall be sealed with the seal of the Supreme Court for use out of the jurisdiction.

Rule 4 APPOINTMENT OF PROCESS SERVER
The Lord Chancellor may appoint a process server for the purposes of this order.

RSC ORDER 70
OBTAINING EVIDENCE FOR FOREIGN COURTS, ETC.

Rule 1 INTERPRETATION AND EXERCISE OF JURISDICTION
(1) In this Order 'the Act of 1975' means the Evidence (Proceedings in Other Jurisdictions) Act 1975 and expressions used in this order which are used in that Act shall have the same meaning as in that Act.

(2) The power of the High Court to make an order under section 2 of the Act of 1975 may be exercised by a Master of the Queen's Bench Division.

Rule 2 APPLICATION FOR ORDER
(1) Subject to paragraph (3) and rule 3 an application for an order under the Act of 1975 must be made without notice being served on any other party and must be supported by witness statement or affidavit.

(2) There shall be exhibited to the witness statement or affidavit the request in pursuance of which the application is made, and if the request is not in the English language, a translation thereof in that language.

(3) Where on an application under section 1 of the Act of 1975 as applied by section 92 of the Patents Act 1977 an order is made for the examination of witnesses the court may allow an officer of the European Patent Office to attend the examination and examine the witnesses or request the court or the examiner before whom the examination takes place to put specified questions to them.

Rule 3 APPLICATION BY TREASURY SOLICITOR IN CERTAIN CASES
Where a request—

(a) is received by the Secretary of State and sent by him to the Senior Master with an intimation that effect should be given to the request without requiring an application for that purpose to be made by the agent in England of any party to the matter pending or contemplated before the foreign court or tribunal; or

(b) is received by the Senior Master in pursuance of a Civil Procedure Convention providing for the taking of the evidence of any person in England or Wales for the assistance of a court or tribunal in the foreign country, and no person is named in the document as the person who will make the necessary application on behalf of such party,

the Senior Master shall send the document to the Treasury Solicitor and the Treasury Solicitor may, with the consent of the Treasury, make an application for an order under the Act of 1975, and take such other steps as may be necessary, to give effect to the request.

Rule 4 PERSON TO TAKE AND MANNER OF TAKING EXAMINATION

(1) Any order made in pursuance of this order for the examination of a witness may order the examination to be taken before any fit and proper person nominated by the person applying for the order or before an examiner of the court or before such other qualified person as to the court seems fit.

(2) Subject to rule 6 and to any special directions contained in any order made in pursuance of this Order for the examination of any witness, the examination shall be taken in manner provided by CPR rules 34.9 and 34.10 and an order may be made under CPR rule 34.14, for payment of the fees and expenses due to the examiner, and those rules shall apply accordingly with any necessary modifications.

Rule 5 DEALING WITH DEPOSITION

Unless any order made in pursuance of this order for the examination of any witness otherwise directs, the examiner before whom the examination was taken must send the deposition of that witness to the Senior Master, and the Senior Master shall—

(a) give a certificate sealed with the seal of the Supreme Court for use out of the jurisdiction identifying the documents annexed thereto, that is to say, the request, the order of the court for examination and the deposition taken in pursuance of the order; and

(b) send the certificate with the documents annexed thereto to the Secretary of State, or, where the request was sent to the Senior Master by some other person in accordance with a Civil Procedure Convention to that other person, for transmission to the court or tribunal out of the jurisdiction requesting the examination.

Rule 6 CLAIM TO PRIVILEGE

(1) The provisions of this rule shall have effect where a claim by a witness to be exempt from giving any evidence on the ground specified in section 3(1)(b) of the Act of 1975 is not supported or conceded as mentioned in subsection (2) of that section.

(2) The examiner may, if he thinks fit, require the witness to give the evidence to which the claim relates and, if the examiner does not do so, the court may do so, on the application without notice being served on any other party of the person who obtained the order under section 2.

(3) If such evidence is taken—

(a) it must be contained in a document separate from the remainder of the deposition of the witness;

(b) the examiner shall send to the Senior Master with the deposition a statement signed by the examiner setting out the claim and the ground on which it was made;

(c) on receipt of the statement the Senior Master shall, notwithstanding anything in rule 5, retain the document containing the part of the witness's evidence to which the claim relates and shall send the statement and a request to determine the claim to the foreign court or tribunal with the documents mentioned in rule 5;

(d) if the claim is rejected by the foreign court or tribunal, the Senior Master shall send to that court or tribunal the document containing that part of the witness's evidence to which the claim relates, but if the claim is upheld he shall send the document to the witness, and shall in either case notify the witness and the person who obtained the order under section 2 of the court or tribunal's determination.

RSC ORDER 71
RECIPROCAL ENFORCEMENT OF JUDGMENTS AND ENFORCEMENT OF EUROPEAN COMMUNITY JUDGMENTS AND RECOMMENDATIONS ETC. UNDER THE MERCHANT SHIPPING (LINER CONFERENCES) ACT 1982

I. Reciprocal Enforcement: the Administration of Justice Act 1920 and the Foreign Judgments (Reciprocal Enforcement) Act 1933

Rule 1 POWERS UNDER RELEVANT ACTS EXERCISABLE BY JUDGE OR MASTER
The powers conferred on the High Court by Part II of the Administration of justice Act 1920 (in this Part of this Order referred to as the 'Act of 1920') or Part I of the Foreign Judgments (Reciprocal Enforcement) Act 1933 (in this Part of this order referred to as the 'Act of 1933') may be exercised by a judge and a Master of the Queen's Bench Division.

Rule 2 APPLICATION FOR REGISTRATION
 (1) An application—
  (a) under section 9 of the Act of 1920, in respect of a judgment obtained in a superior court in any part of Her Majesty's dominions or other territory to which Part II of that Act applies; or
  (b) under section 2 of the Act of 1933, in respect of a judgment to which Part I of that Act applies,
to have the judgment registered in the High Court may be made without notice being served on any other party, but the court hearing the application may direct that a claim form be filed and served.

Rule 3 EVIDENCE IN SUPPORT OF APPLICATION
 (1) An application for registration must be supported by a witness statement or affidavit—
  (a) exhibiting the judgment or a verified or certified or otherwise duly authenticated copy thereof, and where the judgment is not in the English language, a translation thereof in that language certified by a notary public or authenticated by witness statement or affidavit;
  (b) stating the name, trade or business and the usual or last known place of abode or business of the judgment creditor and the judgment debtor respectively, so far as known to the witness;
  (c) stating to the best of the information or belief of the witness—
   (i) that the judgment creditor is entitled to enforce the judgment;
   (ii) as the case may require, either that at the date of the application the judgment has not been satisfied, or the amount in respect of which it remains unsatisfied;
   (iii) where the application is made under the Act of 1920, that the judgment does not fall within any of the cases in which a judgment may not be ordered to be registered under section 9 of that Act;
   (iv) where the application is made under the Act of 1933, that at the date of the application the judgment can be enforced by execution in the country of the original court and that, if it were registered, the registration would not be, or be liable to be, set aside under section 4 of that Act.
  (d) specifying, where the application is made under the Act of 1933, the amount of the interest, if any, which under the law of the country of the original court has become due under the judgment up to the time of registration;
  (e) verifying that the judgment is not a judgment to which section 5 of the Protection of Trading Interests Act 1980 applies.

(2) Where a judgment sought to be registered under the Act of 1933 is in respect of different matters, and some, but not all, of the provisions of the judgment are such that if those provisions had been contained in separate judgments, those judgments could properly have been registered, the witness statement or affidavit must state the provisions in respect of which it is sought to register the judgment.

(3) In the case of an application under the Act of 1933, the witness statement or affidavit must be accompanied by such other evidence with respect to the enforceability of the judgment by execution in the country of the original court, and of the law of that country under which any interest has become due under the judgment, as may be required having regard to the provisions of the Order in Council extending that Act to that country.

Rule 4 SECURITY FOR COSTS

Save as otherwise provided by any relevant Order in Council, the court may order the judgment creditor to give security for the costs of the application for registration and of any proceedings which may be brought to set aside the registration.

Rule 5 ORDER FOR REGISTRATION

(1) An order giving permission to register a judgment must be drawn up by, or on behalf of, the judgment creditor.

(2) Except where the order is made by claim form, no such order need be served on the judgment debtor.

(3) Every such order shall state the period within which an application may be made to set aside the registration and shall contain a notification that execution on the judgment will not issue until after the expiration of that period.

(4) The court may, on an application made at any time while it remains competent for any party to apply to have the registration set aside, extend the period (either as originally fixed or as subsequently extended) within which an application to have the registration set aside may be made.

Rule 6 REGISTER OF JUDGMENTS

(1) There shall be kept in the Central Office of the Supreme Court under the direction of the Senior Master a register of the judgments ordered to be registered under the Act of 1920 and a register of the judgments ordered to be registered under the Act of 1933.

(2) There shall be included in each such register particulars of any execution issued on a judgment ordered to be so registered.

Rule 7 NOTICE OF REGISTRATION

(1) Notice of the registration of a judgment must be served on the judgment debtor by delivering it to him personally or by sending it to him at his usual or last known place of abode or business or in such other manner as the court may direct.

(2) Permission is not required to serve such a notice out of the jurisdiction, and Order 11, rules 5, 6 and 8, shall apply in relation to such a notice as they apply in relation to a claim form.

(3) The notice of registration must state—
  (a) full particulars of the judgment registered and the order for registration,
  (b) the name and address of the judgment creditor or of his solicitor or agent on whom, and at which, any application notice or other document issued by the judgment debtor may be served,
  (c) the right of the judgment debtor to apply to have the registration set aside, and
  (d) the period within which an application to set aside the registration may be made.

Rule 9 APPLICATION TO SET ASIDE REGISTRATION

(1) An application to set aside the registration of a judgment must be made in accordance with CPR Part 23 and be supported by witness statement or affidavit.

(2) The court hearing such application may order any issue between the judgment creditor and the judgment debtor to be tried in any manner in which an issue in a claim may be ordered to be tried.

(3) Where the court hearing an application to set aside the registration of a judgment registered under the Act of 1920 is satisfied that the judgment falls within any of the cases in which a judgment may not be ordered to be registered under section 9 of that Act or that it is not just or convenient that the judgment should be enforced in England or Wales or that there is some other sufficient reason for setting aside the registration, it may order the registration of the judgment to be set aside on such terms as it thinks fit.

Rule 10 ISSUE OF EXECUTION

(1) Execution shall not issue on a judgment registered under the Act of 1920 or the Act of 1933 until after the expiration of the period which, in accordance with rule 5(3) is specified in the order for registration as the period within which an application may be made to set aside the registration or, if that period has been extended by the court, until after the expiration of that period as so extended.

(2) If an application is made to set aside the registration of a judgment, execution on the judgment shall not issue until after such application is finally determined.

(3) Any party wishing to issue execution on a judgment registered under the Act of 1920 or the Act of 1933 must produce to the court officer a witness statement or affidavit of service of the notice of registration of the judgment and any order made by the court in relation to the judgment.

Rule 11 DETERMINATION OF CERTAIN QUESTIONS

If, in any case under the Act of 1933, any question arises whether a foreign judgment can be enforced by execution in the country of the original court, or what interest is payable under a foreign judgment under the law of the original court, that question shall be determined in accordance with the provisions in that behalf contained in the Order in Council extending Part I of that Act to that country.

Rule 12 RULES TO HAVE EFFECT SUBJECT TO ORDERS IN COUNCIL

The foregoing rules shall, in relation to any judgment registered or sought to be registered under the Act of 1933, have effect subject to any such provisions contained in the Order in Council extending Part I of that Act to the country of the original court as are declared by the order to be necessary for giving effect to the agreement made between Her Majesty and that country in relation to matters with respect to which there is power to make those rules.

Rule 13 CERTIFIED COPY OF HIGH COURT JUDGMENT

(1) An application under section 10 of the Act of 1920 or section 10 of the Act of 1933 for a certified copy of a judgment entered in the High Court must be made without notice being served on any other party on witness statement or affidavit to a master or, in the case of a judgment given in proceedings in the Family Division, to a district judge of that Division.

(2) A witness statement or affidavit by which an application under section 10 of the Act of 1920 is made must give particulars of the judgment, show that the judgment creditor wishes to secure the enforcement of the judgment in a part (stating which) of Her Majesty's dominions outside the United Kingdom to which Part II of that Act extends and state the name, trade or business and the usual or last known place of abode of the judgment creditor and the judgment debtor respectively, so far as known to the witness.

(3) A witness statement or affidavit by which an application under section 10 of the Act of 1933 is made must—

(a) give particulars of the proceedings in which the judgment was obtained;

(b) have annexed to it a copy of the claim form by which the proceedings were begun, the evidence of service thereof on the defendant, copies of the statements of case or pleadings, if any, and a statement of the grounds on which the judgment was based;

(c) state whether the defendant did or did not object to the jurisdiction, and, if so, on what grounds;

(d) show that the judgment is not subject to any stay of execution;

(e) state that the time for appealing has expired or, as the case may be, the date on which it will expire and in either case whether notice of appeal against the judgment has been entered; and

(f) state the rate at which the judgment carries interest.

(4) The certified copy of the judgment shall be an office copy sealed with the seal of the Supreme Court and indorsed with a certificate signed by a Master or, where appropriate, a district judge or a registrar certifying that the copy is a true copy of a judgment obtained in the High Court of England and that it is issued in accordance with section 10 of the Act of 1920 or section 10 of the Act of 1933, as the case may be.

(5) Where the application is made under section 10 of the Act of 1933 there shall also be issued a certificate (signed by a Master or, where appropriate, a district judge or a registrar and sealed with the seal of the Supreme Court) having annexed to it a copy of the claim form or other process by which the proceedings were begun, and stating—

(a) the manner in which the claim form was served on the defendant or that the defendant acknowledged service thereof;

(b) what objections, if any, were made to the jurisdiction;

(c) what statements of case, if any, were served;

(d) the grounds on which the judgment was based;

(e) that the time for appealing has expired or, as the case may be, the date on which it will expire;

(f) whether notice of appeal against the judgment has been entered; and

(g) such other particulars as it may be necessary to give to the court in the foreign country in which it is sought to obtain execution of the judgment,

and a certificate (signed and sealed as aforesaid) stating the rate at which the judgment carries interest.

II. Enforcement of European Community Judgments

Rule 15 INTERPRETATION

In this Part of this order 'the Order in Council' means the European Communities (Enforcement of Community Judgments) Order 1972, and expressions used in the Order in Council shall, unless the context otherwise requires, have the same meanings as in that order.

Rule 16 FUNCTIONS UNDER ORDER IN COUNCIL EXERCISABLE BY JUDGE OR MASTER

The functions assigned to the High Court by the Order in Council may be exercised by a judge and a Master of the Queen's Bench Division.

Rule 17 APPLICATION FOR REGISTRATION OF COMMUNITY JUDGMENT, ETC.

An application for the registration in the High Court of a Community judgment or Euratom inspection order may be made without notice being served on any other party.

Rule 18 EVIDENCE IN SUPPORT OF APPLICATION

(1) An application for registration must be supported by a witness statement or affidavit exhibiting—

(a) the Community judgment and the order for its enforcement or, as the case may be, the Euratom inspection order or, in either case, a duly authenticated copy thereof; and

(b) where the Community judgment or Euratom inspection order is not in the English language, a translation into English certified by a notary public or authenticated by witness statement or affidavit.

(2) Where the application is for registration of a Community judgment under which a sum of money is payable, the witness statement or affidavit shall also state—

(a) the name and occupation and the usual or last known place of abode or business of the judgment debtor, so far as known to the witness; and

(b) to the best of the witness's information and belief that at the date of the application the European Court has not suspended enforcement of the judgment and that the judgment is unsatisfied or, as the case may be, the amount in respect of which it remains unsatisfied.

Rule 19 REGISTER OF JUDGMENTS AND ORDERS

(1) There shall be kept in the Central Office of the Supreme Court under the direction of the Senior Master a register of the Community judgments and Euratom inspection orders registered under the Order in Council.

(2) There shall be included in the register particulars of any execution issued on a judgment so registered.

Rule 20 NOTICE OF REGISTRATION

(1) Upon registering a Community judgment or Euratom inspection order, the court shall forthwith send notice of the registration to every person against whom the judgment was given or the order was made.

(2) The notice of registration shall have annexed to it a copy of the registered Community judgment and the order for its enforcement or, as the case may be, a copy of the Euratom inspection order, and shall state the name and address of the person on whose application the judgment or order was registered or of his solicitor or agent on whom process may be served.

(3) Where the notice relates to a Community judgment under which a sum of money is payable, it shall also state that the judgment debtor may apply within 28 days of the date of the notice, or thereafter with the permission of the court, for the variation or cancellation of the registration on the ground that the judgment had been partly or wholly satisfied at the date of registration.

Rule 21 ISSUE OF EXECUTION

Execution shall not issue without the permission of the Court on a Community judgment under which a sum of money is payable until the expiration of 28 days after the date of notice of registration of the judgment or, as the case may be, until any application made within that period for the variation or cancellation of the registration has been determined.

Rule 22 APPLICATION TO VARY OR CANCEL REGISTRATION

An application for the variation or cancellation of the registration of a Community judgment on the ground that the judgment had been wholly or partly satisfied at the date of registration shall be made by claim form supported by witness statement or affidavit.

Rule 23 APPLICATION FOR REGISTRATION OF SUSPENSION ORDER

An application for the registration in the High Court of an order of the European Court that enforcement of a registered Community judgment be suspended may be made without notice being served on any other party by lodging a copy of the order in the Central Office of the Supreme Court.

Rule 24 APPLICATION FOR ENFORCEMENT OF EURATOM INSPECTION ORDER

An application for an order under Article 6 of the Order in Council for the purpose of ensuring that effect is given to a Euratom inspection order may, in case of urgency, be made without notice being served on any other party on witness statement or affidavit but, except as aforesaid, shall be made by claim form.

III. Reciprocal Enforcement: the Civil Jurisdiction and Judgments Act 1982

Rule 25 INTERPRETATION

(1) In this Part of this Order—

'the Act of 1982' means the Civil Jurisdiction and Judgments Act 1982:
'Convention territory' means the territory or territories of any Contracting State, as defined by section 1(3) of the Act of 1982, to which the Brussels Convention or the Lugano Convention as defined in section 1(1) of the Act of 1982 apply;
'judgment' is to be construed in accordance with the definition of 'judgment' in section 50 of the Act of 1982;
'money provision' means a provision for the payment of one or more sums of money;
'non-money provision' means a provision for any relief or remedy not requiring payment of a sum of money;
'protective measures' means the protective measures referred to in Art 39 of Schedule 1 or of Schedule 3C to the Act of 1982.

(2) For the purposes of this Part of this Order domicile is to be determined in accordance with the provisions of sections 41 to 46 of the Act of 1982.

Rule 26 ASSIGNMENT OF BUSINESS AND EXERCISE OF POWERS
Any application to the High Court under the Act of 1982 shall be assigned to the Queen's Bench Division.

Rule 27 APPLICATION FOR REGISTRATION
An application for registration of a judgment under section 4 of the Act of 1982 shall be made without notice being served on any other party.

Rule 28 EVIDENCE IN SUPPORT OF APPLICATION
(1) An application for registration under section 4 of the Act of 1982 must be supported by a witness statement or affidavit—
    (a) exhibiting—
        (i) the judgment or a verified or certified or otherwise duly authenticated copy thereof together with such other document or documents as may be requisite to show that, according to the law of the State in which it has been given, the judgment is enforceable and has been served;
        (ii) in the case of a judgment given in default, the original or a certified true copy of the document which establishes that the party in default was served with the document instituting the proceedings or with an equivalent document;
        (iii) where it is the case, a document showing that the party making the application is in receipt of legal aid in the State in which the judgment was given;
        (iv) where the judgment or document is not in the English language, a translation thereof into English certified by a notary public or a person qualified for the purpose in one of the Contracting States or authenticated by witness statement or affidavit;
    (b) stating—
        (i) whether the judgment provides for the payment of a sum or sums of money;
        (ii) whether interest is recoverable on the judgment or part thereof in accordance with the law of the State in which the judgment was given, and if such be the case, the rate of interest, the date from which interest is recoverable, and the date on which interest ceases to accrue;
    (c) giving an address within the jurisdiction of the court for service of process on the party making the application and stating, so far as is known to the witness, the name and the usual or last known address or place of business of the person against whom judgment was given;
    (d) stating to the best of the information or belief of the witness—
        (i) the grounds on which the right to enforce the judgment is vested in the party making the application;
        (ii) as the case may require, either that at the date of the application the judgment has not been satisfied, or the part or amount in respect of which it remains unsatisfied.

(2) Where the party making the application does not produce the documents referred to in paragraphs (1)(a)(ii) and (iii) of this rule, the Court may—
    (a) fix a time within which the documents are to be produced; or
    (b) accept equivalent documents; or
    (c) dispense with production of the documents.

Rule 29 SECURITY FOR COSTS

Notwithstanding the provisions of Order 23, a party making an application for registration under section 4 of the Act of 1982 shall not be required solely on the ground that he is not domiciled or resident within the jurisdiction, to give security for costs of the application.

Rule 30 ORDER FOR REGISTRATION

(1) An order giving permission to register a judgment under section 4 of the Act of 1982 must be drawn up by or on behalf of the party making the application for registration.

(2) Every such order shall state the period within which an appeal may be made against the order for registration and shall contain a notification that execution on the judgment will not issue until after the expiration of that period.

(3) The notification referred to in paragraph (2) shall not prevent any application for protective measures pending final determination of any issue relating to enforcement of the judgment.

Rule 31 REGISTER OF JUDGMENTS REGISTERED UNDER S. 4 OF THE ACT OF 1982

There shall be kept in the Central Office of the Supreme Court under the direction of the Senior Master a register of the judgments ordered to be registered under section 4 of the Act of 1982.

Rule 32 NOTICE OF REGISTRATION

(1) Notice of the registration of a judgment must be served on the person against whom judgment was given by delivering it to him personally or by sending it to him at his usual or last known address or place of business or in such other manner as the court may direct.

(2) Permission is not required to serve such a notice out of the jurisdiction and Order 11, rules 5, 6 and 8 shall apply in relation to such a notice as they apply in relation to a claim form.

(3) The notice of registration must state—
    (a) full particulars of the judgment registered and the order for registration;
    (b) the name of the party making the application and his address for service within the jurisdiction;
    (c) the right of the person against whom judgment was given to appeal against the order for registration; and
    (d) the period within which an appeal against the order for registration may be made.

Rule 33 APPEALS

(1) An appeal under article 37 or article 40 of Schedule 1 or 3C to the Act of 1982 must be made to a judge by application in accordance with CPR Part 23.

(2) A claim form in an appeal to which this rule applies must be served—
    (a) in the case of an appeal under the said article 37 of Schedule 1 or 3C, within one month of service of notice of registration of the judgment, or two months of service of such notice where that notice was served on a party not domiciled within the jurisdiction;
    (b) in the case of an appeal under the said article 40 of Schedule 1 or 3C, within one month of the determination of the application under rule 27.

(3) If the party against whom judgment was given is not domiciled in a Convention territory and an application is made within two months of service of

notice of registration, the court may extend the period within which an appeal may be made against the order for registration.

Rule 34 ISSUE OF EXECUTION

(1) Execution shall not issue on a judgment registered under section 4 of the Act of 1982 until after the expiration of the period specified in accordance with rule 30(2) or, if that period has been extended by the Court, until after the expiration of the period so extended.

(2) If an appeal is made under rule 33(1), execution on the judgment shall not issue until after such appeal is determined.

(3) Any party wishing to issue execution on a judgment registered under section 4 of the Act of 1982 must produce to the court officer a witness statement or affidavit of service of the notice of registration of the judgment and of any order made by the court in relation to the judgment.

(4) Nothing in this rule shall prevent the court from granting protective measures pending final determination of any issue relating to enforcement of the judgment.

Rule 35 APPLICATION FOR RECOGNITION

(1) Registration of the judgment under these rules shall serve for the purposes of the second paragraph of Article 26 of Schedule 1 or 3C to the Act of 1982 as a decision that the judgment is recognised.

(2) Where it is sought to apply for recognition of a judgment, the foregoing rules of this Order shall apply to such application as they apply to an application for registration under section 4 of the Act, with the exception that the applicant shall not be required to produce a document or documents which establish that according to the law of the State in which it has been given the judgment is enforceable and has been served, or the document referred to in rule 28 (1)(a)(iii).

Rule 36 ENFORCEMENT OF HIGH COURT JUDGMENTS IN OTHER CONTRACTING STATES

(1) An application under section 12 of the Act of 1982 for a certified copy of a judgment entered in the High Court must be made without notice being served on any other party on witness statement or affidavit to the court.

(2) A witness statement or affidavit by which an application under section 12 of the Act of 1982 is made must—

    (a) give particulars of the proceedings in which the judgment was obtained;

    (b) have annexed to it a copy of the claim form, by which the proceedings were begun, the evidence of service thereof on the defendant, copies of the statements of case, if any, and a statement of the grounds on which the judgment was based together, where appropriate, with any document under which the applicant is entitled to legal aid or assistance by way of representation for the purposes of the proceedings;

    (c) state whether the defendant did or did not object to the jurisdiction, and, if so, on what grounds;

    (d) show that the judgment has been served in accordance with CPR Part 6 and CPR rule 40.4 and is not subject to any stay of execution;

    (e) state that the time for appealing has expired, or, as the case may be, the date on which it will expire and in either case whether notice of appeal against the judgment has been given; and

    (f) state—

        (i) whether the judgment provides for the payment of a sum or sums of money;

        (ii) whether interest is recoverable on the judgment or part thereof and if such be the case, the rate of interest, the date from which interest is recoverable, and the date on which interest ceases to accrue.

(3) The certified copy of the judgment shall be an office copy sealed with the seal of the Supreme Court and there shall be issued with the copy of the judgment a certificate in Form 110, signed by a High Court judge, the Admiralty Registrar, a Master or a district judge and sealed with the seal of the Supreme Court, having annexed to it a copy of the claim form by which the proceedings were begun.

Rule 37 ENFORCEMENT OF UNITED KINGDOM JUDGMENTS IN OTHER PARTS OF THE UNITED KINGDOM: MONEY PROVISIONS

(1) An application for registration in the High Court of a certificate in respect of any money provisions contained in a judgment given in another part of the United Kingdom to which section 18 of the Act of 1982 applies may be made by producing at the Central Office of the Supreme Court, within six months from the date of its issue, a certificate in the appropriate form prescribed under that Act together with a copy thereof certified by the applicant's solicitor to be a true copy.

(2) A certificate under paragraph (1) must be filed in the Central Office of the Supreme Court and the certified copy thereof, sealed by an officer of the office in which the certificate is filed, shall be returned to the applicant's solicitor.

(3) A certificate in respect of any money provisions contained in a judgment of the High Court to which section 18 of the Act of 1982 applies may be obtained by producing the form of certificate prescribed in Form 111 at the office in which the judgment is entered, together with a witness statement or affidavit made by the party entitled to enforce the judgment—

(a) giving particulars of the judgment, stating the sum or aggregate of the sums (including any costs or expenses) payable and unsatisfied under the money provisions contained in the judgment, the rate of interest, if any, payable thereon and the date or time from which any such interest began to accrue;

(b) verifying that the time for appealing against the judgment has expired, or that any appeal brought has been finally disposed of and that enforcement of the judgment is not stayed or suspended; and

(c) stating to the best of the information or belief of the witness the usual or last known address of the party entitled to enforce the judgment and of the party liable to execution on it.

Rule 38 ENFORCEMENT OF UNITED KINGDOM JUDGMENTS IN OTHER PARTS OF THE UNITED KINGDOM: NON-MONEY PROVISIONS

(1) An application for registration in the High Court of a judgment which contains non-money provisions, being a judgment given in another part of the United Kingdom to which section 18 of the Act of 1982 applies, may be made without notice being served on any other party, but the court hearing the application may direct a claim form to be filed and served to which rule 2 shall apply.

(2) An application under paragraph (1) must be accompanied by a certified copy of the judgment issued under Schedule 7 to the Act of 1982 and a certificate in the appropriate form prescribed for the purposes of paragraph 4(1)(b) of that Schedule issued not more than six months before the date of application.

(3) Rules 30 and 32 of this order shall apply to judgments registered under Schedule 7 to the Act of 1982 as they apply to judgments registered under section 4 of that Act.

(4) Paragraphs (1) and (2) of rule 9 shall apply to applications to set aside registration of a judgment under Schedule 7 to the Act of 1982 as they apply to judgments registered under the Administration of Justice Act 1920 and the Foreign Judgments (Reciprocal Enforcement) Act 1933.

(5) A certified copy of a judgment of the High Court to which section 18 of the Act of 1982 applies and which contains any non-money provision may be obtained by an application on witness statement or affidavit to the Court.

(5A) An application referred to in paragraph (5) need not be served on any other party.

(6) The requirements in paragraph (3) of rule 37 shall apply with the necessary modifications to a witness statement or affidavit made in an application under paragraph (5) of this rule.

(7) A certified copy of a judgment shall be an office copy sealed with the seal of the Supreme Court to which shall be annexed a certificate in Form 112.

Rule 39 REGISTER OF UNITED KINGDOM JUDGMENTS
There shall be kept in the Central Office of the Supreme Court under the direction of the Senior Master a register of the certificates in respect of judgments and of the judgments ordered to be registered in the Central Office of the Supreme Court under Schedule 6, or, as the case may be, Schedule 7 to the Act.

Rule 39A AUTHENTIC INSTRUMENTS AND COURT SETTLEMENTS
Rules 27 to 35 inclusive (except rule 28(1)(a)(ii)) shall apply to—
   (1)   an authentic instrument to which either article 50 of Schedule 1 to the Act of 1982 or article 50 of Schedule 3C to the Act applies; and
   (2)   a settlement to which either article 51 of Schedule 1 to the Act of 1982 or article 51 of Schedule 3C to that Act applies,
as they apply to a judgment subject to any necessary modifications.

IV.   Enforcement of Recommendations etc. under the Merchant Shipping (Liner Conferences) Act 1982

Rule 40 EXERCISE OF POWERS
The powers conferred on the High Court under the Merchant Shipping (Liner Conferences) Act 1982 (in this Part of this order referred to as 'the Act of 1982') may be exercised by a Commercial Judge.

Rule 41 APPLICATION FOR REGISTRATION
An application under section 9 of the Act of 1982 for the registration of a recommendation, determination or award, shall be made by claim form.

Rule 42 EVIDENCE IN SUPPORT OF APPLICATION
   (1)   An application under section 9 of the Act of 1982 for the registration of a recommendation must be supported by a witness statement or affidavit—
      (a)   exhibiting a verified or certified or otherwise duly authenticated copy of the recommendation and the reasons therefor and of the record of settlement;
      (b)   where the recommendation and reasons or the record of settlement is not in the English language, a translation thereof into English certified by a notary public or authenticated by witness statement or affidavit;
      (c)   exhibiting copies of the acceptance of the recommendation by the parties upon whom it is binding, where the acceptance was in writing, or otherwise verifying the acceptance;
      (d)   giving particulars of the failure to implement the recommendation; and
      (e)   verifying that none of the grounds which would render the recommendation unenforceable under section 9(2) of the Act of 1982 is applicable.
   (2)   An application under section 9 of the Act of 1982 for the registration of a determination or award as to costs must be supported by a witness statement or affidavit—
      (a)   exhibiting a verified or certified or otherwise duly authenticated copy of the recommendation or other document containing the pronouncement on costs; and
      (b)   stating that such costs have not been paid.

Rule 43 ORDER FOR REGISTRATION
   (1)   An order giving permission to register a recommendation, determination or award under section 9 of the Act of 1982 must be drawn up by or on behalf of the party making the application for registration.
   (2)   Such an order shall contain a provision that the reasonable costs of registration be taxed.

Rule 44 REGISTER OF RECOMMENDATIONS ETC.
   (1)   There shall be kept in the Admiralty and Commercial Registry under the direction of the Senior Master a register of the recommendations, determinations and awards ordered to be registered under section 9 of the Act of 1982.
   (2)   There shall be included in such register particulars of the enforcement of a recommendation, determination or award so registered.

CPR SCHEDULE 1

RSC ORDER 74
APPLICATIONS AND APPEALS UNDER THE MERCHANT SHIPPING ACT 1995

Rule 1 ASSIGNMENT OF PROCEEDINGS

(1) Subject to paragraph (2), proceedings by which any application is made to the High Court under the Merchant Shipping Act 1995 shall be assigned to the Queen's Bench Division and taken by the Admiralty Court.

Rule 2 APPEALS AND RE-HEARINGS

(1) An appeal to the High Court under section 28 of the Pilotage Act 1913 against a decision of a county court judge or a magistrate shall be heard and determined by a Divisional Court of the Queen's Bench Division constituted as far as practicable of Admiralty Judges.

(2) Subject to the provisions of this rule, Orders 55 and 57 shall apply in relation to an appeal to the High Court under the Merchant Shipping Act 1995 and for this purpose a re-hearing and an application under section 61 of the Merchant Shipping Act 1995 shall be treated as an appeal.

(3) In the case of an appeal to which paragraph (2) applies, the documents required to be filed before entry for the purposes of Order 57, rule 2(1) shall include the report, if any, to the Secretary of State containing the decision from which the appeal is brought.

(4) Where a re-hearing by the High Court is ordered under sections 64 or 269 of the Merchant Shipping Act 1995, the Secretary of State shall cause such reasonable notice to be given to the parties whom he considers to be affected by the re-hearing as the circumstances of the case may, in his opinion, permit.

RSC ORDER 77
PROCEEDINGS BY AND AGAINST THE CROWN

Rule 1 APPLICATION AND INTERPRETATION

(1) These rules apply to civil proceedings to which the Crown is a party subject to the following rules of this order.

(2) In this order—
'civil proceedings by the Crown', 'civil proceedings against the Crown' and 'civil proceedings by or against the Crown' have the same respective meanings as in Part II of the Crown Proceedings Act 1947, and do not include any of the proceedings specified in section 23(3) of that Act;
'civil proceedings to which the Crown is a party' has the same meaning as it has for the purposes of Part IV of the Crown Proceedings Act 1947, by virtue of section 38(4) of that Act;
'order against the Crown' means any order (including an order for costs) made in any civil proceedings by or against the Crown or in any proceedings on the Crown side of the Queen's Bench Division, or in connection with any arbitration to which the Crown is a party, in favour of any person against the Crown or against a government department or against an officer of the Crown as such;
'order' includes a judgment, decree, rule, award or declaration.

Rule 2 TRANSFER OF PROCEEDINGS

(1) Subject to paragraph (2) in civil proceedings by or against the Crown no order shall be made under CPR Part 30, for the transfer of the proceedings, or of any application therein, from the Royal Courts of Justice to a district registry, except with the consent of the Crown.

(2) In any civil proceedings against the Crown begun by the issue of a claim form out of a district registry the Crown may acknowledge service of the claim form either in the district registry or, at the option of the Crown, in the appropriate office of the Supreme Court at the Royal Courts of Justice, and where service is acknowledged in an office of the Supreme Court at the Royal Courts of Justice the

claim shall thereafter proceed in the Royal Courts of Justice and no order shall be made under CPR Part 30 for the transfer of any proceedings before the trial from the Royal Courts of Justice to a district registry.

Rule 3 PARTICULARS TO BE INCLUDED IN CLAIM FORM

(1) In the case of a claim form which begins civil proceedings against the Crown the contents of the claim form required by CPR rule 16.2 shall include a statement of the circumstances in which the Crown's liability is alleged to have arisen and as to the government department and officers of the Crown concerned.

(2) If in civil proceedings against the Crown a defendant considers that the claim form does not contain a sufficient statement as required by this rule, he may, before the expiration of the time limited for acknowledging service of the claim form, apply to the claimant by notice for a further and better statement containing such information as may be specified in the notice.

(3) Where a defendant gives a notice under this rule, the time limited for acknowledging service of the claim form shall not expire until 4 days after the defendant has notified the claimant in writing that the defendant is satisfied with the statement supplied in compliance with the notice or 4 days after the court has, on the application of the claimant in accordance with CPR Part 23, decided that no further information as to the matters referred to in paragraph (1) is reasonably required.

(3A) An application notice under paragraph (3) shall be served on the defendant not less than 7 days before the hearing.

Rule 4 SERVICE ON THE CROWN

(1) Order 11 and any other provision of these rules relating to service out of the jurisdiction shall not apply in relation to the service of any process by which civil proceedings against the Crown are begun.

(2) Personal service of any document required to be served on the Crown for the purpose of or in connection with any civil proceedings is not requisite; but where the proceedings are by or against the Crown service on the Crown must be effected—

   (a) by leaving the document at the office of the person who is in accordance with section 18 of the Crown Proceedings Act 1947, to be served, or of any agent whom that person has nominated for the purpose, but in either case with a member of the staff of that person or agent; or

   (b) by posting it in a prepaid envelope addressed to the person who is to be served as aforesaid or to any such agent as aforesaid.

(3) Any document (other than a claim form) service of which is effected under paragraph 2(a) between 12 noon on a Saturday and midnight on the following day or after 4 in the afternoon on any other weekday shall, for the purpose of computing any period of time after service of that document, be deemed to have been served on the Monday following that Saturday or on the day following that other weekday, as the case may be.

(4) Where by virtue of these rules any document is required to be served on any person but is not required to be served personally and at the time when service is to be effected that person is in default as to acknowledgment of service or has no address for service, the document need not be served on that person unless the court otherwise directs or any of these rules otherwise provides.

(5) (a) No process shall be served or executed within the jurisdiction on a Sunday except, in case of urgency, with the permission of the court.

   (b) For the purposes of this rule 'process' includes a claim form, judgment, application or other notice, order, petition, or warrant.

Rule 6 COUNTERCLAIM AND SET-OFF

(1) A person may not in any proceedings by the Crown make any counterclaim or claim a set-off in his statement of case if the proceedings are for the recovery of, or the counterclaim or set-off arises out of a right or claim to repayment in respect of, any taxes, duties or penalties.

(2) No counterclaim may be made, or set-off claimed in its statements of case, without the permission of the court, by the Crown in proceedings against the Crown, or by any person in proceedings by the Crown—
    (a) if the Crown is sued or sues in the name of a Government department and the subject-matter of the counterclaim or set-off does not relate to that department; or
    (b) if the Crown is sued or sues in the name of the Attorney-General.
(3) Any application for permission under this rule must be made in accordance with CPR Part 23.

Rule 7 SUMMARY JUDGMENT
(1) No application shall be made against the Crown—
    (a) under CPR Part 24 in any proceedings against the Crown;
    (b) for summary judgment on a counterclaim under CPR Part 24 in any proceedings by the Crown.
(2) Where an application is made by the Crown under CPR Part 24 the affidavit or witness statement required in support of the application must be made by—
    (a) the solicitor acting for the Crown; or
    (b) an officer duly authorised by the solicitor so acting or by the department concerned;
and the witness statement or affidavit shall be sufficient if it states that in the belief of the witness the applicant is entitled to the relief claimed and there is no defence to the claim or part of a claim to which the application relates or no defence except as to the amount of any damages claimed.

Rule 8 SUMMARY APPLICATIONS TO THE COURT IN CERTAIN REVENUE MATTERS
(1) This rule applies to applications under section 14 of the Crown Proceedings Act 1947.
(2) An application to which this rule applies shall be made by claim form.
(3) The person from whom any account or information or payment is claimed or by whom any books are required to be produced must be made a defendant to the application.
(4) A claim form under this rule—
    (a) must be entitled in the matter or matters out of which the need for the application arises and in the matter of the Crown Proceedings Act 1947; and
    (b) must refer to the enactment under which the account or information or payment or the production of books is claimed and, where information is claimed, must show (by appropriate questions or otherwise) what information is required.
(5) Upon any application to which this rule applies a witness statement or affidavit by a duly authorised officer of the Government department concerned setting out the state of facts upon which the application is based and stating that he has reason to think that those facts exist shall be evidence of those facts; and if evidence is filed disputing any of those facts, further evidence may be filed, and the court may either decide the matter upon the witness statements or affidavits (after any cross-examination that may have been ordered) or may direct that it be decided by oral evidence in court.
(6) An order in favour of the Crown on an application to which this rule applies shall, unless the court otherwise determines, name a time within which each of its terms is to be complied with.
(8) Nothing in this rule shall, in relation to any case in which the only remedy claimed by the Crown is the payment of money, be construed as requiring the Crown to proceed by way of an application to which this rule applies or as preventing the Crown from availing itself of any other procedure which is open to it under these rules.

Rule 8A JOINDER OF COMMISSIONERS OF INLAND REVENUE
Nothing in CPR rule 19.3 shall be construed as enabling the Commissioners of Inland Revenue to be added as a party to any proceedings except with their consent signified in writing or in such manner as may be authorised.

Rule 9 JUDGMENT IN DEFAULT

(1) Except with the permission of the court, no judgment in default under CPR Part 12 shall be entered against the Crown in civil proceedings against the Crown.

(2) Except with the permission of the court, a defendant shall not enter default judgment against the Crown as a third party.

(3) An application for permission under this rule may be made by an application in accordance with CPR Part 23 and the application notice must be served not less than 7 days before the return day.

Rule 10 THIRD PARTY NOTICES

(1) A Part 20 claim for service on the Crown, where the Crown is not already a party shall not be issued without the permission of the court, and the application for the grant of such permission must be made by application in accordance with CPR Part 23, and the application notice must be served on the claimant and the Crown.

(2) Permission to issue such a claim for service on the Crown shall not be granted unless the court is satisfied that the Crown is in possession of all such information as it reasonably requires as to the circumstances in which it is alleged that the liability of the Crown has arisen and as to the departments and officers of the Crown concerned.

Rule 11 INTERPLEADER: APPLICATION FOR ORDER AGAINST CROWN

No order shall be made against the Crown under Order 17, rule 5(3) except by application, notice of which must be served not less than 7 days before the return day.

Rule 12 DISCLOSURE AND FURTHER INFORMATION

(3) Where in any proceedings an order of the court directs that a list of documents made in answer to an order for disclosure against the Crown shall be verified by witness statement or affidavit, the witness statement or affidavit shall be made by such officer of the Crown as the court may direct.

(4) Where in any proceedings an order is made under the said section 28 for further information to be provided by the Crown, the court shall direct by what officer of the Crown the further information is to be provided.

Rule 13 PLACE OF TRIAL

(1) Civil proceedings by or against the Crown shall not, except with the consent of the Crown, be directed to be tried elsewhere than at the Royal Courts of Justice.

(2) Nothing in any of these rules shall prejudice the right of the Crown to demand a local venue for the trial of any proceedings in which the Attorney-General has waived his right to a trial at bar.

Rule 14 EVIDENCE

(1) Civil proceedings against the Crown may be instituted to perpetuate any testimony in any case in which the Crown is alleged to have an interest or estate in the honour, title, dignity or office or property in question.

(2) For the avoidance of doubt it is hereby declared that any powers exercisable by the court in regard to the taking of evidence are exercisable in proceedings by or against the Crown as they are exercisable in proceedings between subjects.

Rule 15 EXECUTION AND SATISFACTION OF ORDERS

(1) Nothing in Orders 45 to 52 shall apply in respect of any order against the Crown.

(2) An application under the proviso to subsection (1) of section 25 of the Crown Proceedings Act 1947, for a direction that a separate certificate shall be issued under that subsection with respect to the costs (if any) ordered to be paid to the applicant, may be made to the court without notice being served on any other party.

(3) Any such certificate must be in Form No. 95 or 96 in the relevant practice direction, whichever is appropriate.

Rule 16 ATTACHMENT OF DEBTS, ETC.

(1) No order—
   (a) for the attachment of debts under Order 49; or
   (b) for the appointment of a sequestrator under Order 45; or
   (c) for the appointment of a receiver under Order 30 or 51,

shall be made or have effect in respect of any money due or accruing due, or alleged to be due or accruing due, from the Crown.

(1A) No application shall be made under paragraph (2) unless the order of the court to be enforced is for a sum of money amounting in value to at least £50.

(2) Every application to the court for an order under section 27(1) of the Crown Proceedings Act 1947 restraining any person from receiving money payable to him by the Crown and directing payment of the money to the applicant or some other person must be made by claim form and, unless the court otherwise directs, served—
   (a) on the Crown at least 15 days before the return day; and
   (b) on the person to be restrained or his solicitor at least 7 days after the claim form has been served on the Crown and at least 7 days before the return day.

(2A) An application under paragraph (2) must be supported by a witness statement or affidavit—
   (a) setting out the facts giving rise to the application;
   (b) stating the name and last known address of the person to be restrained;
   (c) identifying the order to be enforced and stating the amount of such order and the amount remaining unpaid under it at the time of the application; and
   (d) identifying the particular debt from the Crown in respect of which the application is made.

(2B) Where the debt from the Crown in respect of which the application is made is money payable by the Crown to a person on account of a deposit in the National Savings Bank, the witness statement or affidavit must state the name and address of the branch of the Post Office at which the account is believed to be held and the number of that account or, if it be the case, that all or part of this information is not known to the witness.

(2C) A Master, the Admiralty Registrar and a district judge of the Family Division shall have power to hear an application under paragraph (2).

(3) Order 49, rules 5 and 6, shall apply in relation to such an application as is mentioned in paragraph (2) for an order restraining a person from receiving money payable to him by the Crown as those rules apply to an application under Order 49, rule 1, for an order for the attachment of a debt owing to any person from a garnishee, except that the court shall not have power to order execution to issue against the Crown.

Rule 17 PROCEEDINGS RELATING TO POSTAL PACKETS

(1) An application by any person under section 30(5) of the Post Office Act 1969, for permission to bring proceedings in the name of the sender or addressee of a postal packet or his personal representatives must be made by claim form in the Queen's Bench Division.

(2) The Crown and the person in whose name the applicant seeks to bring proceedings must be made defendants to a claim under this rule.

Rule 18 APPLICATIONS UNDER SECTIONS 17 AND 29 OF CROWN PROCEEDINGS ACT

(1) Every application to the Court under section 17(4) of the Crown Proceedings Act 1947, must be made by claim form.

(2) An application such as is referred to in section 29(2) of the Crown Proceedings Act 1947, may be made to the court at any time before trial in accordance with CPR Part 23, or may be made at the trial of the proceedings.

CPR SCHEDULE 1

RSC ORDER 79
CRIMINAL PROCEEDINGS

Rule 8 ESTREAT OF RECOGNIZANCES

(1) No recognizance acknowledged in or removed into the Queen's Bench Division shall be estreated without the order of a judge.

(2) Every application to estreat a recognizance in the Queen's Bench Division must be made by claim form and will be heard by a judge and must be supported by a witness statement or affidavit showing in what manner the breach has been committed and proving that the claim form was duly served.

(2A) When it issues the claim form the court will fix a date for the hearing of the application.

(3) A claim form under this rule must be served at least 2 clear days before the day named therein for the hearing.

(4) On the hearing of the application the judge may, and if requested by any party shall, direct any issue of fact in dispute to be tried by a jury.

(5) If it appears to the judge that a default has been made in performing the conditions of the recognizance, the judge may order the recognizance to be estreated.

Rule 9 BAIL

(1) Subject to the provisions of this rule, every application to the High Court in respect of bail in any criminal proceeding—

(a) where the defendant is in custody, must be made by claim form to a judge to show cause why the defendant should not be granted bail;

(b) where the defendant has been admitted to bail, must be made by claim form to a judge to show cause why the variation in the arrangements for bail proposed by the applicant should not be made.

(2) Subject to paragraph (5), the claim form (in Form No. 97 or 97A in the relevant practice direction) must, at least 24 hours before the day named therein for the hearing, be served—

(a) where the application was made by the defendant, on the prosecutor and on the Director of Public Prosecutions, if the prosecution is being carried on by him;

(b) where the application was made by the prosecutor or a constable under section 3(8) of the Bail Act 1976, on the defendant.

(3) Subject to paragraph (5), every application must be supported by witness statement or affidavit.

(4) Where a defendant in custody who desires to apply for bail is unable through lack of means to instruct a solicitor, he may give notice in writing to the court stating his desire to apply for bail and requesting that the Official Solicitor shall act for him in the application, and the court may assign the Official Solicitor to act for the applicant accordingly.

(5) Where the Official Solicitor has been so assigned the court may dispense with the requirements of paragraphs (1) to (3) and deal with the application in a summary manner.

(6) Where the court grants the defendant bail, the order must be in Form No. 98 in the relevant practice direction and a copy of the order shall be transmitted forthwith—

(a) where the proceedings in respect of the defendant have been transferred to the Crown Court for trial or where the defendant has been committed to the Crown Court to be sentenced or otherwise dealt with, to the appropriate officer of the Crown Court;

(b) in any other case, to the clerk of the court which committed the defendant.

(6A) The recognizance of any surety required as a condition of bail granted as aforesaid may, where the defendant is in a prison or other place of detention, be entered into before the governor or keeper of the prison or place as well as before the persons specified in section 8(4) of the Bail Act 1976.

(6B) Where under section 3(5) or (6) of the Bail Act 1976 the court imposes a requirement to be complied with before a person's release on bail, it may give directions as to the manner in which and the person or persons before whom the requirement may be complied with.

(7) A person who in pursuance of an order for the grant of bail made by the court under this rule proposes to enter into a recognizance or give security must, unless the court otherwise directs, give notice (in Form No. 100 in the relevant practice direction) to the prosecutor at least 24 hours before he enters into the recognizance or complies with the requirements as aforesaid.

(8) Where in pursuance of such an order as aforesaid a recognizance is entered into or requirement complied with before any person, it shall be the duty of that person to cause the recognizance or, as the case may be, a statement of the requirement complied with to be transmitted forthwith—

(a) where the proceedings in respect of the defendant have been transferred to the Crown Court for trial or where the defendant has been committed to the Crown Court to be sentenced or otherwise dealt with, to the appropriate officer of the Crown Court;

(b) in any other case, to the clerk of the court which committed the defendant, and a copy of such recognizance or statement shall at the same time be sent to the governor or keeper of the prison or other place of detention in which the defendant is detained, unless the recognizance was entered into or the requirement complied with before such governor or keeper.

(10) An order varying the arrangements under which the defendant has been granted bail shall be in Form 98A in the relevant practice direction and a copy of the order shall be transmitted forthwith—

(a) where the proceedings in respect of the defendant have been transferred to the Crown Court for trial or where the defendant has been committed to the Crown Court to be sentenced or otherwise dealt with, to the appropriate officer of the Crown Court;

(b) in any other case, to the clerk of the court which committed the defendant.

(11) Where in pursuance of an order of the High Court or the Crown Court a person is released on bail in any criminal proceeding pending the determination of an appeal to the High Court or House of Lords or an application for an order of certiorari, then, upon the abandonment of the appeal or application, or upon the decision of the High Court or House of Lords being given, any justice (being a justice acting for the same petty sessions area as the magistrates' court by which that person was convicted or sentenced) may issue process for enforcing the decision in respect of which such appeal or application was brought or, as the case may be, the decision of the High Court or House of Lords.

(12) If an applicant to the High Court in any criminal proceedings is refused bail, the applicant shall not be entitled to make a fresh application for bail to any other judge or to a Divisional Court.

(13) The record required by section 5 of the Bail Act 1976 to be made by the High Court shall be made by including in the file relating to the case in question a copy of the relevant order of the Court and shall contain the particulars set out in Form No. 98 or 98A in the relevant practice direction, whichever is appropriate, except that in the case of a decision to withhold bail the record shall be made by inserting a statement of the decision on the court's copy of the relevant claim form and including it in the file relating to the case in question.

(14) In the case of a person whose return or surrender is sought under the Extradition Act 1989, this rule shall apply as if references to the defendant were references to that person and references to the prosecutor were references to the state seeking the return or surrender of that person.

RSC ORDER 81
PARTNERS

Rule 1 CLAIMS BY AND AGAINST FIRMS WITHIN JURISDICTION
Subject to the provisions of any enactment, any two or more persons claiming to be entitled, or alleged to be liable, as partners in respect of a cause of action and

carrying on business within the jurisdiction may sue, or be sued, in the name of the firm (if any) of which they were partners at the time when the cause of action accrued.

Rule 2 DISCLOSURE OF PARTNERS' NAMES

(1) Any defendant to a claim brought by partners in the name of a firm may serve on the claimants or their solicitor a notice requiring them or him forthwith to furnish the defendant with a written statement of the names and places of residence of all the persons who were partners in the firm at the time when the cause of action accrued; and if the notice is not complied with the court may order the claimants or their solicitor to furnish the defendant with such a statement and to verify it on oath or otherwise as may be specified in the order, or may order that further proceedings in the claim be stayed on such terms as the court may direct.

(2) When the names of the partners have been declared in compliance with a notice or order given or made under paragraph (1) the proceedings shall continue in the name of the firm but with the same consequences as would have ensued if the persons whose names have been so declared had been named as claimants in the claim form.

(3) Paragraph (1) shall have effect in relation to a claim brought against partners in the name of a firm as it has effect in relation to a claim brought by partners in the name of a firm but with the substitution, for references to the defendant and the claimants, of references to the claimant and the defendants respectively, and with the omission of the words 'or may order' to the end.

Rule 4 ACKNOWLEDGMENT OF SERVICE IN A CLAIM AGAINST FIRM

(1) Where persons are sued as partners in the name of their firm, service may not be acknowledged in the name of the firm but only by the partners thereof in their own names, but the claim shall nevertheless continue in the name of the firm.

(2) Where in a claim against a firm the claim form by which the claim is begun is served on a person as a partner, that person, if he denies that he was a partner or liable as such at any material time, may acknowledge service of the claim form and state in his acknowledgment that he does so as a person served as a partner in the defendant firm but who denies that he was a partner at any material time.

An acknowledgment of service given in accordance with this paragraph shall, unless and until it is set aside, be treated as an acknowledgment by the defendant firm.

(3) Where an acknowledgment of service has been given by a defendant in accordance with paragraph (2) then—

(a) the claimant may either apply to the court to set it aside on the ground that the defendant was a partner or liable as such at a material time or may leave that question to be determined at a later stage of the proceedings;

(b) the defendant may either apply to the court to set aside the service of the claim form on him on the ground that he was not a partner or liable as such at a material time or may at the proper time serve a defence on the claimant denying in respect of the claimant's claim either his liability as a partner or the liability of the defendant firm or both.

(4) The court may at any stage of the proceedings in a claim in which a defendant has acknowledged service in accordance with paragraph (2) on the application of the claimant or of that defendant, order that any question as to the liability of that defendant or as to the liability of the defendant firm be tried in such manner and at such time as the court directs.

Rule 5 ENFORCING JUDGMENT OR ORDER AGAINST FIRM

(1) Where a judgment is given or order made against a firm, execution to enforce the judgment or order may, subject to rule 6, issue against any property of the firm within the jurisdiction.

(2) Where a judgment is given or order made against a firm, execution to enforce the judgment or order may, subject to rule 6 and to the next following paragraph, issue against any person who—

(a) acknowledged service of the claim form as a partner; or

(b) having been served as a partner with the claim form, failed to acknowledge service of it; or
(c) admitted in his statement of case that he is a partner; or
(d) was adjudged to be a partner.

(3) Execution to enforce a judgment or order given or made against a firm may not issue against a member of the firm who was out of the jurisdiction when the claim form was issued unless he—
(a) acknowledged service of the claim form as a partner; or
(b) was served within the jurisdiction with the claim form as a partner; or
(c) was, with the permission of the court given under Order 11, served out of the jurisdiction with the claim form, as a partner,
and, except as provided by paragraph (1) and by the foregoing provisions of this paragraph, a judgment or order given or made against a firm shall not render liable, release or otherwise affect a member of the firm who was out of the jurisdiction when the claim form was issued.

(4) Where a party who has obtained a judgment or order against a firm claims that a person is liable to satisfy the judgment or order as being a member of the firm, and the foregoing provisions of this rule do not apply in relation to that person, that party may apply to the court for permission to issue execution against that person, the application to be made in accordance with CPR Part 23 and the application notice must be served personally on that person.

(5) Where the person against whom an application under paragraph (4) is made does not dispute his liability, the court hearing the application may, subject to paragraph (3) give permission to issue execution against that person, and, where that person disputes his liability, the court may order that the liability of that person be tried and determined in any manner in which any issue or question in a claim may be tried and determined.

Rule 6 ENFORCING JUDGMENT OR ORDER IN ACTIONS BETWEEN PARTNERS, ETC.

(1) Execution to enforce a judgment or order given or made in—
(a) a claim by or against a firm in the name of the firm against or by a member of the firm; or
(b) a claim by a firm in the name of the firm against a firm in the name of the firm where those firms have one or more members in common,
shall not issue except with the permission of the court.

(2) The court hearing an application under this rule may give such directions, including directions as to the taking of accounts and the making of inquiries, as may be just.

Rule 7 ATTACHMENT OF DEBTS OWED BY FIRM

(1) An order may be made under Order 49, rule 1, in relation to debts due or accruing due from a firm carrying on business within the jurisdiction notwithstanding that one or more members of the firm is resident out of the jurisdiction.

(2) An order to show cause under the said rule 1 relating to such debts as aforesaid must be served on a member of the firm within the jurisdiction or on some other person having the control or management of the partnership business.

(3) Where an order made under the said rule 1 requires a firm to appear before the court, an appearance by a member of the firm constitutes a sufficient compliance with the order.

Rule 9 APPLICATION TO PERSON CARRYING ON BUSINESS IN ANOTHER NAME

An individual carrying on business within the jurisdiction in a name or style other than his own name, may whether or not he is within the jurisdiction be sued in that name or style as if it were the name of a firm, and rules 2 to 8 shall, so far as applicable, apply as if he were a partner and the name in which he carries on business were the name of his firm.

CPR SCHEDULE 1

Rule 10 APPLICATIONS FOR ORDERS CHARGING PARTNER'S INTEREST IN PARTNERSHIP PROPERTY, ETC.

(1) Every application to the court by a judgment creditor of a partner for an order under section 23 of the Partnership Act 1890 (which authorises the High Court or a judge thereof to make certain orders on the application of a judgment creditor of a partner, including an order charging the partner's interest in the partnership property) and every application to the court by a partner of the judgment debtor made in consequence of the first mentioned application must be made in accordance with CPR Part 23.

(2) A Master or the Admiralty Registrar or a district judge may exercise the powers conferred on a judge by the said section 23.

(3) Every application notice issued by a judgment creditor under this rule, and every order made on such an application, must be served on the judgment debtor and on such of his partners as are within the jurisdiction or, if the partnership is a cost book company, on the judgment debtor and the purser of the company.

(4) Every application notice issued by a partner of a judgment debtor under this rule, and every order made on such an application, must be served—

   (a) on the judgment creditor; and
   (b) on the judgment debtor; and
   (c) on such of the other partners of the judgment debtor as do not join in the application and are within the jurisdiction or, if the partnership is a cost book company, on the purser of the company.

(5) An application notice or order served in accordance with this rule on the purser of a cost book company or, in the case of a partnership not being such a company, on some only of the partners thereof, shall be deemed to have been served on that company or on all the partners of that partnership, as the case may be.

RSC ORDER 82
DEFAMATION CLAIMS

Rule 1 APPLICATION
These rules apply to claims for libel or slander subject to the following rules of this order.

Rule 2 INDORSEMENT OF CLAIM IN LIBEL CLAIM
Before a claim form in a claim for libel is issued it must be indorsed with a statement giving sufficient particulars of the publications in respect of which the claim is brought to enable them to be identified.

Rule 3 OBLIGATION TO GIVE PARTICULARS

(1) Where in a claim for libel or slander the claimant alleges that the words or matters complained of were used in a defamatory sense other than their ordinary meaning, he must give particulars of the facts and matters on which he relies in support of such sense.

(2) Where in a claim for libel or slander the defendant alleges that, in so far as the words complained of consist of statements of fact, they are true in substance and in fact, and in so far as they consist of expressions of opinion, they are fair comment on a matter of public interest, or states in his statement of case to the like effect, he must give particulars stating which of the words complained of he alleges are statements of fact and of the facts and matters he relies on in support of the allegation that the words are true.

(2A) Subject to paragraph (2B), where the defendant makes an allegation as described in paragraph (2), the claimant shall serve a reply specifically admitting or denying any such allegation raised by the defendant and specifying any fact or matter upon which he relies in opposition to the defendant's allegations.

(2B) No reply shall be required under paragraph (2A) where all the facts or matters on which the claimant intends to rely in opposition to the defendant's allegations as described in paragraph (2) are already particularised elsewhere in the statements of case.

(3) Where in a claim for libel or slander the claimant alleges that the defendant maliciously published the words or matters complained of, he need not in his particulars of claim give particulars of the facts on which he relies in support of the allegation of malice, but if the defendant states in his statement of case that any of those words or matters are fair comment on a matter of public interest or were published upon a privileged occasion and the claimant intends to allege that the defendant was actuated by express malice, he must serve a reply giving particulars of the fact and matters from which the malice is to be inferred.

(3A) The claimant must give full particulars in the particulars of claim of the facts and matters on which he relies in support of his claim for damages, including details of any conduct by the defendant which it is alleged has increased the loss suffered and of any loss which is peculiar to the claimant's own circumstances.

(4) This rule shall apply in relation to a counterclaim for libel or slander as if the party making the counterclaim were the claimant and the party against whom it is made the defendant.

Rule 3A RULING ON MEANING

(1) At any time after the service of the particulars of claim either party may apply to the court for an order determining whether or not the words complained of are capable of bearing a particular meaning or meanings attributed to them in the statements of case.

(2) If it appears to the court on the hearing of an application under paragraph (1) that none of the words complained of are capable of bearing the meaning or meanings attributed to them in the statements of case, it may dismiss the claim or make such other order or give such judgment in the proceedings as may be just.

(3) Subject to paragraph (4), each party to the proceedings may make only one application under paragraph (1).

(4) Where a party has made an application under paragraph (1) and the respondent to that application subsequently amends his statements of case to allege a new meaning, the court may allow the other party to make a further application under paragraph (1) in relation to that new meaning.

(5) This rule shall apply in relation to a counterclaim for libel or slander as if the party making the counterclaim were the claimant and the party against whom it is made the defendant, and as if the counterclaim were the. statement of claim.

Rule 4 PROVISIONS AS TO PAYMENT INTO COURT

(1) Where in a claim for libel or slander against several defendants sued jointly the claimant, in accordance with CPR rule 36.11(1) accepts money paid into court by any of those defendants in satisfaction of his cause of action against that defendant, then, notwithstanding anything in CPR rule 36.17, the claim shall be stayed as against that defendant only, but—

(a) the sum recoverable under any judgment given in the claimant's favour against any other defendant in the claim by way of damages shall not exceed the amount (if any) by which the amount of the damages exceeds the amount paid into court by the defendant as against whom the claim has been stayed; and

(b) the claimant shall not be entitled to his costs of the claim against the other defendant after the date of the payment into court unless either the amount of the damages awarded to him is greater than the amount paid into court and accepted by him or the court is of opinion that there was reasonable ground for him to proceed with the claim against the other defendant.

(2) Where in a claim for libel a party in his statement of case relies on the defence for which section 2 of the Libel Act 1843, provides, CPR rule 36.19 shall not apply in relation to that statement of case.

Rule 5 STATEMENT IN OPEN COURT

(1) Where a party wishes to accept money paid into court in satisfaction of a cause of action for libel or slander, malicious prosecution or false imprisonment, that party may before or after accepting the money apply to the court in accordance with CPR Part 23 for permission to make a statement in terms approved by the court.

(2) Where a party to a claim for libel or slander, malicious prosecution or false imprisonment which is settled before trial desires to make a statement referred to in paragraph (1), an application must be made to the court for an order that the claim be set down for trial, and before the date fixed for the trial the statement must be submitted for the approval of the court before whom it is to be made.

(3) The court may approve a statement under paragraph (1) or (2) which refers not only to a cause of action mentioned in those paragraphs but also to any other cause of action joined thereto.

Rule 6 FURTHER INFORMATION NOT ALLOWED IN CERTAIN CASES
In a claim for libel or slander where the defendant states in his statement of case that the words or matters complained of are fair comment on a matter of public interest or were published on a privileged occasion, no further information as to the defendant's sources of information or grounds of belief shall be allowed.

Rule 8 FULFILMENT OF OFFER OF AMENDS UNDER SECTION 4 OF THE DEFAMATION ACT 1952
(1) An application to the court under section 4 of the Defamation Act 1952, to determine any question as to the steps to be taken in fulfilment of an offer of amends made under that section must, unless the application is made in the course of proceedings for libel or slander in respect of the publication to which the offer relates, be made in private in the Queen's Bench Division, but only a judge may determine such question.

(2) Such an application is to be made by a claim form.

RSC ORDER 85
ADMINISTRATION AND SIMILAR ACTIONS

Rule 1 INTERPRETATION
In this order 'administration claim' means a claim for the administration under the direction of the court of the estate of a deceased person or for the execution under the direction of the court of a trust.

Rule 2 DETERMINATION OF QUESTIONS, ETC., WITHOUT ADMINISTRATION
(1) A claim may be issued for the determination of any question or for any remedy which could be determined or granted, as the case may be, in an administration claim and a claim need not be made for the administration or execution under the direction of the court of the estate or trust in connection with which the question arises or the remedy is sought.

(2) Without prejudice to the generality of paragraph (1), a claim may be brought for the determination of any of the following questions—

(a) any question arising in the administration of the estate of a deceased person or in the execution of a trust;

(b) any question as to the composition of any class of persons having a claim against the estate of a deceased person or a beneficial interest in the estate of such a person or in any property subject to a trust;

(c) any question as to the rights or interests of a person claiming to be a creditor of the estate of a deceased person or to be entitled under a will or on the intestacy of a deceased person or to be beneficially entitled under a trust.

(3) Without prejudice to the generality of paragraph (1), a claim may be brought for any of the following remedies—

(a) an order requiring an executor, administrator or trustee to furnish and, if necessary, verify accounts;

(b) an order requiring the payment into court of money held by a person in his capacity as executor, administrator or trustee;

(c) an order directing a person to do or abstain from doing a particular act in his capacity as executor, administrator or trustee;

(d) an order approving any sale, purchase, compromise or other transaction by a person in his capacity as executor, administrator or trustee;

(e) an order directing any act to be done in the administration of the estate of a deceased person or in the execution of a trust which the court could order to be done if the estate or trust were being administered or executed, as the case may be, under the direction of the court.

Rule 3 PARTIES

(1) All the executors or administrators of the estate or trustees of the trust, as the case may be, to which an administration claim or such a claim as is referred to in rule 2 relates must be parties to the proceedings, and where the proceedings are made by executors, administrators or trustees, any of them who does not consent to being joined as a claimant must be made a defendant.

(2) Notwithstanding anything in CPR Rule 19.2 and without prejudice to the powers of the court under that CPR Part, all the persons having a beneficial interest in or claim against the estate or having a beneficial interest under the trust, as the case may be, to which such a claim as is mentioned in paragraph (1) relates need not be parties to the proceedings; but the claimant may make such of those persons, whether all or anyone or more of them, parties as, having regard to the nature of the remedy claimed in the proceedings, he thinks fit.

(3) Where, in proceedings under a judgment or order given or made in a claim for the administration under the direction of the court of the estate of a deceased person, a claim in respect of a debt or other liability is made against the estate by a person not a party to the proceedings, no party other than the executors or administrators of the estate shall be entitled to appear in any proceedings relating to that claim without the permission of the court, and the court may direct or allow any other party to appear either in addition to, or in substitution for, the executors or administrators on such terms as to costs or otherwise as it thinks fit.

Rule 5 JUDGMENTS AND ORDERS IN ADMINISTRATION CLAIMS

(1) A judgment or order for the administration or execution under the direction of the court of an estate or trust need not be given or made unless in the opinion of the court the questions at issue between the parties cannot properly be determined otherwise than under such a judgment or order.

(2) Where an administration claim is brought by a creditor of the estate of a deceased person or by a person claiming to be entitled under a will or on the intestacy of a deceased person or to be beneficially entitled under a trust, and the claimant alleges that no or insufficient accounts have been furnished by the executors, administrators or trustees, as the case may be, then, without prejudice to its other powers, the court may—

(a) order that proceedings be stayed for a period specified in the order and that the executors, administrators or trustees, as the case may be, shall within that period furnish the claimant with proper accounts;

(b) if necessary to prevent proceedings by other creditors or by other persons claiming to be entitled as aforesaid, give judgment or make an order for the administration of the estate to which the claim relates and include therein an order that no proceedings are to be taken under the judgment or order, or under any particular account or inquiry directed, without the permission of the judge in person.

Rule 6 CONDUCT OF SALE OF TRUST PROPERTY

Where in an administration claim an order is made for the sale of any property vested in executors, administrators or trustees, those executors, administrators or trustees, as the case may be, shall have the conduct of the sale unless the court otherwise directs.

RSC ORDER 87
DEBENTURE HOLDERS' CLAIMS: RECEIVER'S REGISTER

Rule 1 RECEIVER'S REGISTER

Every receiver appointed by the court in proceedings to enforce registered debentures or registered debenture stock shall, if so directed by the court, keep a register of transfers of, and other transmissions of title to, such debentures or stock (in this order referred to as 'the receiver's register').

CPR SCHEDULE 1

Rule 2 REGISTRATION OF TRANSFERS, ETC.

(1) Where a receiver is required by rule 1 to keep a receiver's register, then, on the application made in accordance with CPR Part 23 of any person entitled to any debentures or debenture stock by virtue of any transfer or other transmission of title, and on production of such evidence of identity and title as the receiver may reasonably require, the receiver shall, subject to the following provisions of this rule, register the transfer or other transmission of title in that register.

(2) Before registering a transfer the receiver must, unless the due execution of the transfer is proved by witness statement or affidavit, send by post to the registered holder of the debentures or debenture stock transferred at his registered address a notice stating—

(a) that an application for the registration of the transfer has been made; and

(b) that the transfer will be registered unless within the period specified in the notice the holder informs the receiver that he objects to the registration,

and no transfer shall be registered until the period so specified has elapsed. The period to be specified in the notice shall in no case be less than 7 days after a reply from the registered holder would in the ordinary course of post reach the receiver if the holder had replied to the notice on the day following the day when in the ordinary course of post the notice would have been delivered at the place to which it was addressed.

(3) On registering a transfer or other transmission of title under this rule the receiver must indorse a memorandum thereof on the debenture or certificate of debenture stock, as the case may be, transferred or transmitted, containing a reference to the proceedings and to the order appointing him receiver.

Rule 3 APPLICATION FOR RECTIFICATION OF RECEIVER'S REGISTER

(1) Any person aggrieved by any thing done or omission made by a receiver under rule 2 may apply in accordance with CPR Part 23 to the court for rectification of the receiver's register, the application to be made in the proceedings in which the receiver was appointed.

(2) The copy of the application notice shall in the first instance be served only on the claimant or other party having the conduct of the proceedings but the court may direct a copy of the application notice to be served on any other person appearing to be interested.

(3) The court hearing an application under this rule may decide any question relating to the title of any person who is party to the application to have his name entered in or omitted from the receiver's register and generally may decide any question necessary or expedient to be decided for the rectification of that register.

Rule 4 RECEIVER'S REGISTER EVIDENCE OF TRANSFERS, ETC.

Any entry made in the receiver's register, if verified by a witness statement or affidavit made by the receiver or by such other person as the court may direct, shall in all proceedings in which the receiver was appointed be evidence of the transfer or transmission of title to which the entry relates and, in particular, shall be accepted as evidence thereof for the purpose of any distribution of assets, notwithstanding that the transfer or transmission has taken place after the making of a certificate in the proceedings certifying the holders of the debentures or debenture stock certificates.

Rule 5 PROOF OF TITLE OF HOLDER OF BEARER DEBENTURE, ETC.

(1) This rule applies in relation to proceedings to enforce bearer debentures or to enforce debenture stock in respect of which the company has issued debenture stock bearer certificates.

(2) Notwithstanding that judgment has been given in the proceedings and that a certificate has been made therein certifying the holders of such debentures or certificates as are referred to in paragraph (1), the title of any person claiming to be such a holder shall (in the absence of notice of any defect in the title) be sufficiently proved by the production of the debenture or debenture stock certificate, as the case may be, together with a certificate of identification signed by the person producing the debenture or certificate identifying the debenture or certifi-

cate produced and certifying the person (giving his name and address) who is the holder thereof.

(3) Where such a debenture or certificate as is referred to in paragraph (1) is produced in Chancery Chambers, the solicitor of the claimant in the proceedings must cause to be indorsed thereon a notice stating—

(a) that the person whose name and address is specified in the notice (being the person named as the holder of the debenture or certificate in the certificate of identification produced under paragraph (2)) has been recorded in Chancery Chambers as the holder of the debenture or debenture stock certificate, as the case may be; and

(b) that that person will, on producing the debenture or debenture stock certificate, as the case may be, be entitled to receive payment of any dividend in respect of that debenture or stock unless before payment a new holder proves his title in accordance with paragraph (2); and

(c) that if a new holder neglects to prove his title as aforesaid he may incur additional delay, trouble and expense in obtaining payment.

(4) The solicitor of the claimant in the proceedings must preserve any certificates of identification produced under paragraph (2) and must keep a record of the debentures and debenture stock certificates so produced and of the names and addresses of the persons producing them and of the holders thereof, and, if the court requires it, must verify the record by witness statement or affidavit.

Rule 6 REQUIREMENTS IN CONNECTION WITH PAYMENTS

(1) Where in proceedings to enforce any debentures or debenture stock an order is made for payment in respect of the debentures or stock, the Accountant General shall not make a payment in respect of any such debenture or stock unless either there is produced to him the certificate for which paragraph (2) provides or the court has in the case in question for special reason dispensed with the need for the certificate and directed payment to be made without it.

(2) For the purpose of obtaining any such payment the debenture or debenture stock certificate must be produced to the solicitor of the claimant in the proceedings or to such other person as the court may direct, and that solicitor or other person must indorse thereon a memorandum of payment and must make and sign a certificate certifying that the statement set out in the certificate has been indorsed on the debenture or debenture stock certificate, as the case may be, and send the certificate to the Accountant General.

RSC ORDER 88
MORTGAGE CLAIMS

Rule 1 APPLICATION AND INTERPRETATION

(1) This order applies to any claim by a mortgagee or mortgagor or by any person having the right to foreclose or redeem any mortgage, being a claim in which there is a claim for any of the following remedies, namely—

(a) payment of moneys secured by the mortgage;
(b) sale of the mortgaged property;
(c) foreclosure;
(d) delivery of possession (whether before or after foreclosure or without foreclosure) to the mortgagee by the mortgagor or by any other person who is or is alleged to be in possession of the property;
(e) redemption;
(f) reconveyance of the property or its release from the security;
(g) delivery of possession by the mortgagee.

(2) In this order 'mortgage' includes a legal and an equitable mortgage and a legal and an equitable charge, and references to a mortgagor, a mortgagee and mortgaged property shall be construed accordingly.

(3) A claim to which this order applies is referred to in this order as a mortgage claim.

(4) These rules apply to mortgage claims subject to the following provisions of this order.

Rule 2 ASSIGNMENT OF CERTAIN ACTIONS TO CHANCERY DIVISION
Without prejudice to section 61(1) of the Act (which provides for the assignment to the Chancery Division of proceedings for the purposes, among others, of the redemption or foreclosure of mortgages and the sale and distribution of the proceeds of property subject to any lien or charge) any claim in which there is a claim for—
  (a) payment of moneys secured by a mortgage of any real or leasehold property; or
  (b) delivery of possession (whether before or after foreclosure) to the mortgagee of any such property by the mortgagor or by any other person who is or is alleged to be in possession of the property, shall be assigned to the Chancery Division.

Rule 3 COMMENCEMENT OF CLAIM
  (1) A claim form by which a mortgage claim is begun may not be issued out of a district registry, which is not a Chancery district registry, unless the mortgaged property is situated in the district of the registry.
  (3) The claim form by which a mortgage claim is begun shall be indorsed with or contain a statement showing—
  (a) where the mortgaged property is situated; and
  (b) if the claimant claims possession of the mortgaged property and it is situated outside Greater London, whether the property consists of or includes a dwelling house, and a certificate that the claim is not one to which section 141 of the Consumer Credit Act 1974 applies.

Rule 4 CLAIM FOR POSSESSION: FAILURE BY A DEFENDANT TO ACKNOWLEDGE SERVICE
  (1) Where in a mortgage claim in the Chancery Division being a claim in which the claimant is the mortgagee and claims delivery of possession or payment of moneys secured by the mortgage or both, any defendant fails to acknowledge service of the claim form, the following provisions of this rule shall apply, and references in those provisions to the defendant shall be construed as references to any such defendant.
  (2) Not less than 4 clear days before the day fixed for the first hearing of the claim the claimant must serve on the defendant a copy of the notice of appointment for the hearing and a copy of the witness statement or affidavit in support of the claim.
  (4) Where the hearing is adjourned, then, subject to any directions given by the court, the claimant must serve notice of the appointment for the adjourned hearing, together with a copy of any further witness statement or affidavit intended to be used at that hearing, on the defendant not less than 2 clear days before the day fixed for the hearing.
  (5) Service under paragraph (2) or (4) and the manner in which it was effected, may be proved by a certificate signed by the claimant, if he sues in person, and otherwise by his solicitor.
  The certificate may be indorsed on the witness statement or affidavit in support of the claim or, as the case may be, on any further witness statement or affidavit intended to be used at an adjourned hearing.
  (6) A copy of any exhibit to a witness statement or affidavit need not accompany the copy of the witness statement or affidavit served under paragraph (2) or (4).

Rule 5 CLAIM IN CHANCERY DIVISION FOR POSSESSION OR PAYMENT: EVIDENCE
  (1) The witness statement or affidavit in support of the claim (other than a claim to which rule 5A applies) to which this rule applies is begun must comply with the following provisions of this rule.

CPR SCHEDULE 1

This rule applies to a mortgage claim in the Chancery Division in which the claimant is the mortgagee and claims delivery of possession or payment of moneys secured by the mortgage or both.

(2) The witness statement or affidavit must exhibit a true copy of the mortgage and the original mortgage or, in the case of a registered charge, the charge certificate must be produced at the hearing of the claim.

(2A) Unless the court otherwise directs the witness statement or affidavit may contain statements of information or belief with the sources and grounds thereof.

(3) Where the claimant claims delivery of possession the witness statement or affidavit must show the circumstances under which the right to possession arises and, except where the court in any case or class of case otherwise directs, the state of the account between the mortgagor and mortgagee with particulars of—

    (a) the amount of the advance;
    (b) the amount of the periodic payments required to be made;
    (c) the amount of any interest or instalments in arrear at the date of issue of the claim form and at the date of the witness statement or affidavit; and
    (d) the amount remaining due under the mortgage.

(4) Where the claimant claims delivery of possession the witness statement or affidavit must—

    (a) give particulars of every person who to the best of the claimant's knowledge is in possession of the mortgaged property; and
    (b) state, in the case of a dwelling house, whether—
        (i) a land charge of Class F has been registered, or a notice or caution registered under section 2(7) of the Matrimonial Homes Act 1967 or a notice registered under section 2(8) of the Matrimonial Homes Act 1983 has been entered, and, if so, on whose behalf; and
        (ii) he has served notice of the proceedings on the person on whose behalf the land charge is registered or the notice or caution entered.

(5) If the mortgage creates a tenancy other than a tenancy at will between the mortgagor and mortgagee, the witness statement or affidavit must show how and when the tenancy was determined and if by service of notice when the notice was duly served.

(6) Where the claimant claims payment of money secured by the mortgage the witness statement or affidavit must show how the claim is calculated including—

    (a) the amount of the advance and the amount and dates of any periodic repayments and any interest claimed;
    (b) the amount which would have to be paid (after taking into account any adjustment for early settlement) in order to redeem the mortgage at the date of commencement of the proceedings and at a stated date not more than 14 days after the date of commencement of the proceedings, specifying the amount of the solicitor's costs and administrative charges which would be payable;
    (c) the dates between which a particular rate of interest applied, the number of days in that period, and the capital on which the interest was calculated.

(7) Where the claimant's claim includes a claim for interest to judgment, the witness statement or affidavit must state the amount of a day's interest.

Rule 5A CLAIM FOR THE ENFORCEMENT OF CHARGING ORDER BY SALE

(1) This rule applies to a mortgage claim in the Chancery Division to enforce a charging order by sale of the property charged.

(2) The witness statement or affidavit in support of the claim must—

    (a) identify the charging order sought to be enforced and the subject matter of the charge;
    (b) specify the amount in respect of which the charge was imposed and the balance outstanding at the date of the witness statement or affidavit;
    (c) verify, so far as known, the debtor's title to the property charged;
    (d) identify any prior incumbrancer on the property charged stating, so far as is known, the names and addresses of the incumbrancers and the amounts owing to them;

(e) set out the claimant's proposals as to the manner of sale of the property charged together with estimates of the gross price which would be obtained on a sale in that manner and of the costs of such a sale; and

(f) where the property charged consists of land in respect of which the claimant claims delivery of possession—

(i) give particulars of every person who to the best of the claimant's knowledge is in possession of the property charged or any part of it; and

(ii) state, in the case of a dwelling house, whether a land charge of Class F has been registered, or a notice or caution pursuant to section 2(7) of the Matrimonial Homes Act 1967, or a notice pursuant to section 2(8) of the Matrimonial Homes Act 1983 has been entered and, if so, on whose behalf, and whether he has served notice of the proceedings on the person on whose behalf the land charge is registered or the notice or caution entered.

Rule 7 FORECLOSURE IN REDEMPTION CLAIM

Where foreclosure has taken place by reason of the failure of the claimant in a mortgage claim for redemption to redeem, the defendant in whose favour the foreclosure has taken place may apply in accordance with CPR Part 23 for an order for delivery to him of possession of the mortgaged property, and the court may make such order thereon as it thinks fit.

RSC ORDER 91
REVENUE PROCEEDINGS

Rule 1 ASSIGNMENT TO CHANCERY DIVISION, ETC.

The following proceedings, namely—

(a) any case stated for the opinion of the High Court under—

(i) section 13 of the Stamp Act 1891 or

(ii) section 705A of the Income and Corporation Taxes Act 1988; or

(iii) regulation 22 of the General Commissioners (jurisdiction and Procedure) Regulations 1994;

(b) any appeal to the High Court under—

(i) section 53, 56A or 100C(4) of the Taxes Management Act 1970; or

(ii) section 222(3), 225, 249(3) or 251 of the Inheritance Tax Act 1984; or

(iii) regulation 8(3) or 10 of the Stamp Duty Reserve Tax Regulations 1986;

(c) any application for permission to appeal under the said section 222(3) or the said regulation 8(3); and

(d) proceedings to which the provisions of section 56A of the Taxes Management Act 1970 apply under any enactment or regulation,

shall be assigned to the Chancery Division and heard and determined by a single judge.

Rule 2 APPEAL UNDER SECTION 222 OF THE INHERITANCE TAX ACT 1984

(1) Order 55 shall not apply in relation to an appeal to the High Court under section 222(3) of the Inheritance Tax Act 1984 or regulation 8(3) of the Stamp Duty Reserve Tax Regulations 1986.

(2) Such an appeal must be brought by a notice of appeal which must—

(a) state the date on which the Commissioners of Inland Revenue (in this rule referred to as the 'Board') gave notice to the appellant under section 221 of the said Act or regulation 6 of the said Regulations of the determination which is the subject of the appeal;

(b) state the date on which the appellant gave to the Board notice of appeal under section 222(1) of the said Act, or regulation 8(1) of the said Regulations and, if the notice was not given within the time limited, whether the Board or the Special Commissioners have given consent to the appeal being brought out of time, and, if they have, the date on which it was given; and

(c) either state that the appellant and the Board have agreed that the appeal may be to the High Court or contain an application for permission to appeal to the High Court.

(3) At the time of issuing the notice of appeal the appellant shall file in Chancery Chambers—

(a) two copies of the notice referred to in paragraph (2)(a);

(b) two copies of the notice of appeal (under section 222(1) of the said Act, or regulation 8(1) of the said Regulations) referred to in paragraph (2)(b); and

(c) where the notice of appeal contains an application for permission to appeal, a witness statement or affidavit setting out the grounds on which it is alleged that the matters to be decided on the appeal are likely to be substantially confined to questions of law.

(4) The notice of appeal must be issued and served on the Board within 30 days of the date on which the appellant gave to the Board notice of appeal under section 222(1) of the said Act or regulation 8(1) of the said Regulations or, if the Board or the Special Commissioners have given consent to the appeal being brought out of time, within 30 days of the date on which such consent was given.

(5) The notice of appeal, must specify a date of hearing being not less than 40 days from the issue of the notice of appeal.

(6) Where the notice of appeal contains an application for permission to appeal to the High Court, a copy of the witness statement or affidavit lodged pursuant to paragraph (3)(c) shall be served on the Board with the notice of appeal and the Board may, within 30 days after service, file in the judge's chambers a witness statement or affidavit in answer and a copy of any such witness statement or affidavit shall be served by the Board on the appellant.

(7) Except with the permission of the court, the appellant shall not be entitled on the hearing of an appeal to rely on any grounds of appeal not specified in the notice referred to in paragraph (2)(b).

Rule 3 SETTING DOWN CASE STATED UNDER TAXES MANAGEMENT ACT 1970

(1) At any time after a case stated under section 705A of the Income and Corporation Taxes Act 1988 or regulation 22 of the General Commissioners (Jurisdiction and Procedure) Regulations 1994 has been filed in Chancery Chambers either party may set down the case for hearing.

(2) On setting down the case the party who sets it down must give notice to the other party that he has done so.

Rule 4 CASE STATED: NOTICE TO BE GIVEN OF CERTAIN MATTERS

Not less than 10 days before the hearing of such a case as is mentioned in rule 1(a) either party must give notice to the other of any point which he intends to take at the hearing and which might take the other party by surprise and leave at Chancery Chambers two copies of the notice for the use of the court.

Rule 5 APPEALS UNDER SECTION 53 AND 100C(4) OF THE TAXES MANAGEMENT ACT 1970

(1) The notice of appeal by which an appeal under section 53 or 100C(4) of the Taxes Management Act 1970 or section 249(3) or 251 of the Inheritance Tax Act 1984 is brought must be issued out of Chancery Chambers.

(2) Order 55, rule 3(2), shall apply in relation to the notice of appeal as if the decision, award or determination appealed against were the decision of a court.

(3) The persons to be served with the notice are the General or Special Commissioners against whose decision, award or determination the appeal is brought and—

(a) in the case of an appeal brought under section 100C(4) of the Taxes Management Act 1970 or section 249(3) of the Inheritance Tax Act 1984 by any party other than the defendant in the proceedings before the Commissioners, that defendant;

(b) in any other case, the Commissioners of Inland Revenue.

(4) Order 55, rules 4(2) and 5, shall apply in relation to any such appeal as if for the period of 28 days and 21 days therein specified there were substituted a period of 30 days and 35 days respectively.

(5) Within 30 days after the service on them of the notice by which any such appeal is brought, the General or Special Commissioners, as the case may be, must file in Chancery Chambers two copies of a note of their findings and of the reasons for their decision, award or determination and must serve a copy of the note on every other party to the appeal.

(6) Any document required or authorised to be served on the General or Special Commissioners in proceedings to which this rule relates may be served by delivering or sending it to their clerk.

(7) Order 57 shall not apply to proceedings to which this rule applies.

Rule 5A APPEALS UNDER SECTION 56A OF THE TAXES MANAGEMENT ACT 1970, SECTION 225 OF THE INHERITANCE TAX ACT 1984 AND REGULATION 10 OF THE STAMP DUTY RESERVE TAX REGULATIONS 1986

(1) This rule applies to appeals under section 56A of the Taxes Management Act 1970, section 225 of the Inheritance Tax Act 1984 and regulation 10 of the Stamp Duty Reserve Tax Regulations 1986.

(2) The notice of appeal by which such an appeal is brought must be issued out of Chancery Chambers.

(3) Order 55, rule 3(2) shall apply in relation to the notice of appeal as if the decision or determination appealed against were the decision of a court.

(4) Order 55, rule 4(2) shall apply in relation to such an appeal as if for the period of 28 days specified in that rule there were substituted a period of 56 days, except where the appeal is made following the refusal of the Special Commissioners to issue a certificate under section 56A(2)(b) of the Taxes Management Act 1970 or the refusal of permission to appeal to the Court of Appeal under section 56A(2)(c) of that Act.

(5) Where the appeal is made following the refusal of the Special Commissioners to issue a certificate under section 56A(2)(b) of the Taxes Management Act 1970, the period of 28 days specified in Order 55, rule 4(2) shall be calculated from the date of the release of the decision of the Special Commissioners containing the refusal.

(6) Where the appeal is made following the refusal of permission to appeal to the Court of Appeal under section 56A(2)(c) of the Taxes Management Act 1970, the period of 28 days specified in Order 55, rule 4(2) shall be calculated from the date when permission is refused.

(7) Order 57 shall not apply to proceedings to which this rule applies.

Rule 6 APPEALS FROM VALUE ADDED TAX TRIBUNALS

(1) A party to proceedings before a value added tax tribunal who is dissatisfied in point of law with a decision of the tribunal may appeal under section 11(1) of the Tribunals and Inquiries Act 1992 to the High Court and Order 94, rule 9 shall not apply in relation to such an appeal.

(2) Such an appeal shall be heard and determined by a single judge of the Chancery Division.

(3) Order 55, rule 4(2) shall apply in relation to any such appeal as if for the period of 28 days specified in that rule there were substituted a period of 56 days, except where the appeal is made following the refusal of the Value Added Tax Tribunal to grant a certificate under article 2(b) of the Value Added Tax Tribunal Appeals Order 1986.

(3A) Where the tribunal has refused to grant a certificate under article 2(b) of the Value Added Tax Tribunal Appeals Order 1986, the 28-day period mentioned in Order 55, rule 4(2) shall be calculated from the date of the release of the decision of the tribunal containing the refusal.

(4) This rule is without prejudice to the right of the parties to appeal direct to the Court of Appeal in accordance with Order 59, rule 22.

RSC ORDER 92
LODGMENT, INVESTMENT, ETC., OF FUNDS IN COURT: CHANCERY DIVISION

Rule 1 PAYMENT INTO COURT BY LIFE ASSURANCE COMPANY

(1) A company wishing to make a payment into court under the Life Assurance Companies (Payment into Court) Act, 1896 (hereinafter referred to as 'the Act of 1896') must file a witness statement or affidavit, made by its secretary or other authorised officer, setting out—

    (a) a short description of the policy in question and a statement of the persons entitled thereunder with their names and addresses so far as known to the company;

    (b) a short statement of the notices received by the company claiming an interest in or title to the money assured, or withdrawing any such claim, with the dates of receipt thereof and the names and addresses of the persons by whom they were given;

    (c) a statement that, in the opinion of the board of directors of the company, no sufficient discharge can be obtained otherwise than by payment into court under the Act of 1896;

    (d) the submission by the company to pay into court such further sum, if any, as the court may direct and to pay any costs ordered by the court to be paid by the company;

    (e) an undertaking by the company forthwith to send to the Accountant-General any notice of claim received by the company after the making of the witness statement or affidavit with a letter referring to the title of the witness statement or affidavit; and

    (f) an address where the company may be served with any application, claim form, court order, or notice of any proceedings, relating to the money paid into court.

(2) The company shall not deduct from the money payable by them under the policy any costs of or incidental to the payment into court.

(3) No payment shall be made into court under the Act of 1896 where any proceedings to which the company is a party are pending in relation to the policy or moneys thereby assured except with the leave of the court to be obtained by an application made in accordance with CPR Part 23.

(4) Unless the court otherwise directs, a CPR Part 23 application by which a claim with respect to money paid into court under the Act of 1896 is made shall not, except where the application includes an application for payment of a further sum of costs by the company who made the payment, be served on that company, but it must be served on every person who appears by the witness statement or affidavit on which the payment into court was made to be entitled to, or interested in, the money in court or to have a claim upon it or who has given a notice of claim which has been sent to the Accountant-General in accordance with the undertaking referred to in rule 1(1)(e).

Rule 2 PAYMENT INTO COURT UNDER TRUSTEE ACT 1925

(1) Subject to paragraph (2) any trustee wishing to make a payment into court under section 63 of the Trustee Act 1925, must make and file a witness statement or affidavit setting out—

    (a) a short description of the trust and of the instrument creating it or, as the case may be, of the circumstances in which the trust arose;

    (b) the names of the persons interested in or entitled to the money or securities to be paid into court with their addresses so far as known to him;

    (c) his submission to answer all such inquiries relating to the application of such money or securities as the court may make or direct; and

    (d) an address where he may be served with any application notice or order, or notice of any proceedings, relating to the money or securities paid into court.

(2) Where the money or securities represents a legacy, or residue or any share thereof, to which a child or a person resident outside the United Kingdom is

absolutely entitled, no witness statement or affidavit need be filed under paragraph (1) and the money or securities may be paid into court in the manner prescribed by the Supreme Court Funds Rules for the time being in force.

Rule 3A PAYMENTS INTO COURT UNDER SECTION 26 OF THE BANKING ACT 1987

Where the Bank of England, having sold shares in pursuance of an order under section 26 of the Banking Act 1987, pays the proceeds of sale, less the costs of the sale, into court, it shall cause a witness statement or affidavit to be made and filed setting out the names and, so far as known, the addresses of the persons beneficially entitled to the proceeds of sale and shall file a copy of the order.

Rule 4 NOTICE OF LODGMENT

Any person who has lodged money or securities in court in accordance with rule 1, 2, or 3A must forthwith send notice of the lodgment to every person appearing from the witness statement or affidavit on which the lodgment was made to be entitled to, or to have an interest in, the money or securities lodged.

Rule 5 APPLICATIONS WITH RESPECT TO FUNDS IN COURT

(1) Where an application to the High Court—

(a) for the payment or transfer to any person of any funds in court standing to the credit of any cause or matter or for the transfer of any such funds to a separate account or for the payment to any person of any dividend of or interest on any securities or money comprised in such funds;

(b) for the investment, or change of investment, of any funds in court;

(c) for payment of the dividends of or interest on any funds in court representing or comprising money or securities lodged in court under any enactment; or

(d) for the payment or transfer out of court of any such funds as are mentioned in sub-paragraph (c),

is made in the Chancery Division the application may be disposed of by the court sitting in private.

(2) Subject to paragraph (3), any such application made in the Chancery Division must be made by the issue of a claim form, unless the application is made in pending proceedings or an application for the same purpose has previously been made by such a claim form.

(3) Where an application under paragraph 1(d) is required to be made by a claim form, then, if the funds to which the application relates do not exceed £15,000 in value, and subject to paragraph (4), the application may be made to the Chief Master, or to such master as he may designate, and the master may dispose of the application or may direct it to be made by a claim form. Unless otherwise directed, an application under this paragraph shall be made by witness statement or affidavit, and need not be served on any other person.

(4) Where the application to which paragraph (3) applies relates to funds lodged in court in a Chancery district registry, the application may be made to, and the power conferred by paragraph (3) on a master may be exercised by, the district judge of that registry.

(5) This rule does not apply to any application for an order under CPR Part 36 and CPR Part 37.

RSC ORDER 93
APPLICATIONS AND APPEALS TO HIGH COURT UNDER VARIOUS ACTS: CHANCERY DIVISION

Rule 1 NOTICE OF PETITION UNDER SECTION 55 OF THE NATIONAL DEBT ACT 1870

Where a petition is presented under section 55 of the National Debt Act 1870, the petitioner must, before the petition is heard, apply to a judge of the Chancery Division for directions with respect to giving notice of the claim to which the petition relates, and the judge may direct that notice thereof be given by advertisement or in such other manner as he may direct or may dispense with the giving of such notice.

Rule 2 APPLICATION UNDER THE PUBLIC TRUSTEE ACT 1906
Without prejudice to sections 10(2) and 13(7) of the Public Trustee Act, 1906, the jurisdiction of the High Court under that Act shall be exercised by a judge of the Chancery Division sitting in private.

Rule 4 PROCEEDINGS UNDER THE TRUSTEE ACT 1925
All proceedings brought in the High Court under the Trustee Act 1925, shall be assigned to the Chancery Division.

Rule 5 APPLICATION UNDER SECTION 2(3) OF THE PUBLIC ORDER ACT 1936
(1) Proceedings by which an application is made to the High Court under section 2(3) of the Public Order Act 1936, shall be assigned to the Chancery Division.
(2) Such an application shall be made by claim form and the persons to be made defendants to the claim shall be such persons as the Attorney-General may determine.
(3) In the absence of other sufficient representation the court may appoint the Official Solicitor to represent any interests which in the opinion of the court ought to be represented on any inquiry directed by the court under the said section 2(3).

Rule 6 APPLICATION UNDER THE VARIATION OF TRUSTS ACT 1958
(1) Proceedings by which an application is made to the High Court under section 1 of the Variation of Trusts Act 1958, shall be assigned to the Chancery Division.
(2) Such an application shall be made by claim form and in addition to any other persons who are necessary and proper defendants to the claim, the settlor and any other person who provided property for the purposes of the trusts to which the application relates must, if still alive and not the claimant, be made a defendant unless the court for some special reason otherwise directs.

Rule 9 RIGHT OF APPEAL UNDER THE LAW OF PROPERTY ACT
An appeal shall lie to the High Court against a decision of the Minister of Agriculture, Fisheries and Food under paragraph 16 of Schedule 15 to the Law of Property Act 1922.

Rule 10 DETERMINATION OF APPEAL OR CASE STATED UNDER VARIOUS ACTS
(1) An appeal to the High Court against an order of a county court made under the Land Registration Act 1925 shall be heard and determined by a Divisional Court of the Chancery Division.
(2) Subject to paragraph (1) any appeal to the High Court, and any case stated or question referred for the opinion of that court, under any of the following enactments, that is to say—
- (c) paragraph 16 of Schedule 15 to the Law of Property Act 1922;
- (d) the Industrial Assurance Act 1923;
- (f) the Land Registration Act 1925;
- (g) section 205(4) of the Water Resources Act 1991;
- (j) section 38 (3) of the Clergy Pensions Measure 1961;
- (m) the Industrial and Provident Societies Act 1965;
- (n) section 173 of the Pension Schemes Act 1993;
- (o) section 151 of the Pension Schemes Act 1993.

shall be heard and determined by a single judge of the Chancery Division.
(3) No appeal shall lie from the decision of the court on an appeal under any of the enactments mentioned in paragraph (2)(c), (f) or (o) except with the permission of the court or the Court of Appeal.

Rule 11 APPEAL UNDER SECTION 17 OF THE INDUSTRIAL ASSURANCE ACT 1923

(1) An application to the judge for permission to appeal to the High Court against a direction of the Commissioner under section 17(3) of the Industrial Assurance Act 1923 must be made within 21 days after the date of the Commissioner's refusal or direction.

(2) An application for the grant of such permission must be made without notice being served on any other party by a witness statement or affidavit stating the material facts, the effect of the Commissioner's refusal or direction, the grounds on which the application is made and that the witness is advised and believes that the applicant has good grounds for appealing.

(3) No order under this rule granting permission to appeal shall be drawn up but the court officer shall indorse on the notice of appeal by which the appeal is brought a note signed by him stating that permission to appeal was granted by the court and the date on which it was granted. A copy of such note shall appear on any copy of such notice served on a respondent to the appeal.

(4) Order 55, rule 4(2) shall not apply in relation to an appeal with respect to which permission has been granted under this rule, but the notice of appeal by which the appeal is brought must be served, and the appeal entered, within 28 days after permission to appeal was granted.

Rule 12 APPEALS, ETC., AFFECTING INDUSTRIAL AND PROVIDENT SOCIETIES, ETC.

(1) At any stage of the proceedings on an appeal under—
   (a) the Friendly Societies Act 1896 or the Friendly Societies Act 1974;
   (c) the Industrial Assurance Act 1923; or
   (e) the Industrial and Provident Societies Act 1965,
the court may direct that the notice of appeal by which the appeal is brought be served on any person or may direct that notice be given by advertisement or otherwise of the bringing of the appeal, the nature thereof and the time when it will or is likely to be heard or may give such other directions as it thinks proper for enabling any person interested in the society, trade union, alleged trade union or industrial assurance company concerned or in the subject-matter of the appeal to appear and be heard on the appeal.

(2) An application for directions under paragraph (1) may be made by either party to the appeal in accordance with CPR Part 23 returnable at Chancery Chambers.

Rule 15 APPLICATION UNDER SECTION 19 OR 27 OF THE LEASEHOLD REFORM ACT 1967

Proceedings by which an application is made to the High Court under section 19 or 27 of the Leasehold Reform Act 1967 shall be assigned to the Chancery Division.

Rule 16 PROCEEDINGS UNDER THE COMMONS REGISTRATION ACT 1965

(1) Proceedings in the High Court under section 14 or 18 of the Commons Registration Act 1965 shall be assigned to the Chancery Division.

(2) The time within which a person aggrieved by the decision of a Commons Commissioner may require the Commissioner to state a case for the opinion of the High Court pursuant to the said section 18 shall be six weeks from the date on which notice of the decision was sent to the person aggrieved.

(3) An appeal by way of case stated under the said section 18 shall be heard and determined by a single judge.

Rule 17 PROCEEDINGS UNDER SECTION 21 OR 25 OF THE LAW OF PROPERTY ACT 1969

Proceedings in the High Court under section 21 or 25 of the Law of Property Act 1969 shall be assigned to the Chancery Division.

Rule 18 PROCEEDINGS UNDER SECTION 86 OF THE CIVIL AVIATION ACT 1982

(1) Proceedings in the High Court for the amendment of any register of aircraft mortgages kept pursuant to an Order in Council made under section 86 of the Civil Aviation Act 1982 shall be assigned to the Chancery Division.

(2) Such proceedings shall be brought by claim form and every person, other than the claimant, appearing in the register as mortgagee or mortgagor of the aircraft in question shall be made a defendant to the claim.

(3) A copy of the claim form shall also be sent to the Civil Aviation Authority and the Authority shall be entitled to be heard in the proceedings.

Rule 19 PROCEEDINGS UNDER SECTION 85 (7) OF THE FAIR TRADING ACT 1973 AND THE CONTROL OF MISLEADING ADVERTISEMENTS REGULATIONS 1988

(1) Proceedings to which this rule applies shall be assigned to the Chancery Division and may be begun by claim form.

(2) This rule applies to any application to the High Court for an order under section 85(7) of the Fair Trading Act 1973, or under any provision to which that section applies or under the Control of Misleading Advertisements Regulations 1988.

Rule 20 PROCEEDINGS UNDER SECTION 50 OF THE ADMINISTRATION OF JUSTICE ACT 1985

(1) Proceedings by which an application is made to the High Court under section 50 of the Administration of Justice Act 1985 for an order appointing a substituted personal representative or terminating the appointment of an existing personal representative shall be assigned to the Chancery Division.

(2) An application under the said section 50 shall be made by claim form or, if it is made in existing proceedings, by an application in accordance with CPR Part 23.

(3) All the existing personal representatives and, subject to any direction of the court, such of the persons having a beneficial interest in the estate as the claimant thinks fit, must be made parties to the application.

(4) Such an application must be supported by:

(a) a sealed or certified copy of the grant of probate or letters of administration; and

(b) a witness statement or affidavit containing the grounds of the application and the following particulars so far as the claimant can gain information with regard to them—

(i) short particulars of the property comprised in the estate, with an approximate estimate of its income, and capital value;

(ii) short particulars of the liabilities of the estate;

(iii) particulars of the persons who are in possession of the documents relating to the estate;

(iv) the names of the beneficiaries and short particulars of their respective interests; and

(v) the name, address and occupation of any proposed substituted personal representative;

(c) where the application is for the appointment of a substituted personal representative—

(i) a signed or (in the case of the Public Trustee or a corporation) sealed consent to act; and

(ii) a witness statement or affidavit as to the fitness of the proposed substituted personal representative, if an individual, to act.

(5) On the hearing of an application under the said section 50 the personal representative shall produce to the Court the grant of representation to the deceased's estate and, if an order is made under the said section, the grant (together with a sealed copy of the order) shall be sent to and remain in the custody of the Principal Registry of the Family Division until a memorandum of the order has been endorsed on or permanently annexed to the grant.

CPR SCHEDULE 1

Rule 21 PROCEEDINGS UNDER SECTION 48 OF THE ADMINISTRATION OF JUSTICE ACT 1985
Proceedings by which an application is made to the High Court under section 48 of the Administration of Justice Act 1985 shall be assigned to the Chancery Division and shall be begun by claim form but the claim need not be served on any other party.

Rule 22 PROCEEDINGS UNDER THE FINANCIAL SERVICES ACT, 1986

(1) In this rule 'the Act' means the Financial Services Act 1986 and a section referred to by number means the section so numbered in that Act.

(2) Proceedings in the High Court under the Act (other than application for mandamus) and actions for damages for breach of a statutory duty imposed by the Act shall be assigned to the Chancery Division.

(3) Such proceedings and actions shall be begun by claim form except for applications by petition by the Secretary of State or a designated agency under section 72.

(4) No order shall be made under sections 6, 61, 71, 91, 104, 131, 184 or paragraph 22 of Schedule 11 against any person unless he is a party to the relevant proceedings.

Where there is a question of the construction of any of the rules or regulations referred to in section 61(1)(a) of the Act, the Secretary of State, designated agency, or any person referred to in section 61(1)(a)(iv) may make representations to the court.

Rule 23 PROCEEDINGS UNDER THE BANKING ACT 1987

(1) In this rule 'the Act' means the Banking Act 1987 and a section referred to by number means the section so numbered in the Act.

(2) Proceedings in the High Court under the following sections of the Act shall be assigned to the Chancery Division and shall be begun—

   (a)   as to applications under section 26(3), 71(3) and (5) and 77(3) and (5), by claim form;
   (b)   as to appeals under section 31(1), by notice of appeal;
   (c)   as to applications under sections 48(1), 49(1) and 93(1) and (2), by claim form.

(3) No order shall be made under section 48(1) against any person unless he is a party to the proceedings.

(4) Where an application has been made under section 71(3) or (5) or section 77(3) or (5) the Bank of England shall within 28 days after service on it of copies of the claimant's witness statement or affidavit evidence cause a witness statement or affidavit to be made, filed and served on the claimant setting out the reasons for its objection to the claimant's name.

RSC ORDER 94
APPLICATIONS AND APPEALS TO HIGH COURT UNDER VARIOUS ACTS: QUEEN'S BENCH DIVISION

Rule 1 JURISDICTION OF HIGH COURT TO QUASH CERTAIN ORDERS, SCHEMES, ETC.

(1) Where by virtue of any enactment the High Court has jurisdiction, on the application of any person, to quash or prohibit any order, scheme, certificate or plan, any amendment or approval of a plan, any decision of a Minister or government department or any action on the part of a Minister or government department, the jurisdiction shall be exercisable by a single judge of the Queen's Bench Division.

(2) The application must be made by claim form which must state the grounds of the application.

Rule 2 FILING AND SERVICE OF CLAIM FORM

(1) A claim form under rule 1 must be filed at the Crown Office, and served, within the time limited by the relevant enactment for making the application.

(2) Subject to paragraph (4) the claim form must be served on the appropriate Minister or government department, and—

    (a) if the application relates to a compulsory purchase order made by an authority other than the appropriate Minister or government department, or to a clearance order under the Housing Act 1985, on the authority by whom the order was made;

    (b) if the application relates to a scheme or order to which Schedule 2 to the Highways Act 1980, applies made by an authority other than the Secretary of State, on that authority;

    (c) if the application relates to a structure plan, local plan or other development plan within the meaning of the Town and Country Planning Act 1990, on the local planning authority who prepared the plan;

    (d) if the application relates to any decision or order, or any action on the part of a Minister of the Crown to which section 21 of the Land Compensation Act 1961, or section 288 of the Town and Country Planning Act 1990, applies, on the authority directly concerned with such decision, order or action or, if that authority is the applicant, on every person who would, if he were aggrieved by the decision, order or action, be entitled to apply to the High Court under the said section 21 or the said section 245, as the case may be;

    (e) if the application relates to a scheme to which Schedule 32 to the Local Government, Planning and Land Act 1980 applies, on the body which adopted the scheme.

(3) In paragraph (2) 'the appropriate Minister or government department' means the Minister of the Crown or government department by whom the order, scheme, certificate, plan, amendment, approval or decision in question was or may be made, authorised, confirmed, approved or given or on whose part the action in question was or may be taken.

(4) Where the application relates to an order made under the Road Traffic Regulation Act 1984, the claim form must be served—

    (a) if the order was made by a Minister of the Crown, on that Minister;

    (b) if the order was made by a local authority with the consent, or in pursuance of a direction, of a Minister of the Crown, on that authority and also on that Minister;

    (c) in any other case, on the local authority by whom the order was made.

Rule 3 FILING OF WITNESS STATEMENT OR AFFIDAVITS, ETC.

(1) Evidence at the hearing of an application under rule 1 shall be by witness statement or affidavit.

(2) Any witness statement or affidavit in support of the application must be filed by the applicant in the Crown Office within 14 days after service of the claim form and the applicant must, at the time of filing, serve a copy of the witness statement or affidavit and of any exhibit thereto on the respondent.

(3) Any witness statement or affidavit in opposition to the application must be filed by the respondent in the Crown Office within 21 days after the service on him under paragraph (2) of the applicant's witness statement or affidavit and the respondent must, at the time of filing, serve a copy of his witness statement or affidavit and of any exhibit thereto on the applicant.

(4) When filing a witness statement or affidavit under this rule a party must leave a copy thereof and of any exhibit thereto at the Crown Office for the use of the court.

(5) Unless the court otherwise orders, an application under rule 1 shall not be heard earlier than 14 days after the time for filing a witness statement or affidavit by the respondent has expired.

Rule 4 RECTIFICATION OF REGISTER OF DEEDS OF ARRANGEMENT

(1) Every application to the Court under section 7 of the Deeds of Arrangement Act 1914, for an order—

    (a) that any omission to register a deed of arrangement within the time prescribed by that Act be rectified by extending the time for such registration; or

(b) that any omission or mis-statement of the name, residence or description of any person be rectified by the insertion in the register of his true name, residence or description,

must be made by witness statement or affidavit without notice being served on any other party to a master of the Queen's Bench Division.

(2) The witness statement or affidavit must set out particulars of the deed of arrangement and of the omission or mis-statement in question and must state the grounds on which the application is made.

Rule 5 EXERCISE OF JURISDICTION UNDER REPRESENTATION OF THE PEOPLE ACTS

(1) Proceedings in the High Court under the Representation of the People Acts shall be assigned to the Queen's Bench Division.

(2) Subject to paragraphs (3) and (4) the jurisdiction of the High Court under the said Acts in matters relating to parliamentary and local government elections shall be exercised by a Divisional Court.

(3) Paragraph (2) shall not be construed as taking away from a single judge or a Master any jurisdiction under the said Acts which, but for that paragraph, would be exercisable by a single judge or, as the case may be, by a Master.

(4) Where the jurisdiction of the High Court under the said Acts is by a provision of any of those Acts made exercisable in matters relating to parliamentary elections by a single judge, that jurisdiction in matters relating to local government elections shall also be exercisable by a single judge.

Rule 6 APPEAL TO HIGH COURT WHERE COURT'S DECISION IS FINAL

(1) This rule applies to an appeal to the High Court under any of the following enactments, namely—

(a) section 22 of the Architects Act 1997;
(b) sections 82(3) and 83(2) of the Medicines Act 1968;
(d) section 12 of the Nurses, Midwives & Health Visitors Act 1997;
(e) section 10 of the Pharmacy Act 1954.

(2) Every appeal to which this rule applies must be supported by witness statement or affidavit and, if the court so directs, by evidence given orally.

(4) Order 55, rule 4(2) shall apply in relation to an appeal under the enactments mentioned in paragraph (1)(c) and (h) as if for the period of 28 days therein specified there were substituted a period of 21 days.

(5) In the case of an appeal under an enactment specified in column (1) of the following table, the persons to be made respondents are the persons specified in relation to that enactment in column (2) of that table and the person to be served with notice of appeal is the person so specified in column (3) thereof.

(1) Enactment	(2) Respondents	(3) Person to be served
Architects Act 1997, s.22	The Architects' Registration Council of the United Kingdom	The registrar of the Council
Medicines Act 1968, s.82(3) and s.83(2)	The Pharmaceutical Society of Great Britain	The registrar of the Society
Nurses, Midwives and Health Visitors Act, 1997 s. 12	The United Kingdom Central Council for Nursing Midwifery and Health Visiting	The registrar of the Council
Pharmacy Act, 1954, s. 10	The Pharmaceutical Society of Great Britain	The registrar of the Society

Rule 7 REFERENCE OF QUESTION OF LAW BY AGRICULTURAL LAND TRIBUNAL

(1) Any question of law referred to the High Court by an Agricultural Land Tribunal under section 6 of the Agriculture (Miscellaneous Provisions) Act 1954, shall be referred by way of case stated by the tribunal.

(2) The claim form by which an application is made to the court for an order under the said section 6 directing such a tribunal to refer a question of law to the court, and the claim form by which an application is made to the court to determine a question of law so referred, must, where the proceedings before the tribunal arose on an application under section 11 of the Agricultural Holdings Act 1986 be served on the authority having power to enforce the statutory requirement specified in the application as well as on every other party to those proceedings and on the secretary of the tribunal.

(3) Where in accordance with the provisions of this rule a claim form is served on the authority mentioned in paragraph (2) that authority shall be entitled to appear and be heard in the proceedings.

Rule 8 TRIBUNALS AND INQUIRIES ACT 1992: APPEAL FROM TRIBUNAL

(1) A person who was a party to proceedings before any such tribunal as is mentioned in section 11(1) of the Tribunals and Inquiries Act 1992 and is dissatisfied in point of law with the decision of the tribunal may appeal to the High Court.

(2) Order 55, rule 4(1)(b) shall apply in relation to such an appeal as if for the reference to the chairman of a tribunal there were substituted—

(a) in the case of a tribunal which has no chairman or member who acts as a chairman, a reference to the member or members of the tribunal; and

(b) in the case of any such tribunal as is specified in paragraph 16 of Schedule 1 to the said Act of 1992, a reference to the secretary of the tribunal.

(3) Where such an appeal is against the decision of—

(a) the tribunal constituted under section 46 of the National Health Service Act 1977 or

(b) a tribunal established under section 1 of the Industrial Tribunals Act 1996, Order 55, rule 4(2) shall apply in relation to the appeal as if for the period of 28 days therein specified there were substituted, in the case of the tribunal mentioned in sub-paragraph (a) a period of 14 days and, in the case of a tribunal mentioned in sub-paragraph (b) a period of 42 days.

Rule 9 TRIBUNALS AND INQUIRIES ACT 1992: CASE STATED BY TRIBUNAL

(1) Any such tribunal as is mentioned in section 11(1) of the Tribunals and Inquiries Act 1992 may, of its own initiative or at the request of any party to proceedings before it, state in the course of proceedings before it in the form of a special case for the decision of the High Court any question of law arising in the proceedings.

(2) Any party to proceedings before any such tribunal who is aggrieved by the tribunal's refusal to state such a case may apply to the High Court for an order directing the tribunal to do so.

(3) A case stated by any such tribunal which has no chairman or member who acts as a chairman must be signed by the member or members of the tribunal.

Rule 10 TRIBUNALS AND INQUIRIES ACT 1971: APPEAL FROM MINISTER OF TRANSPORT

(1) A person who is dissatisfied on a point of law with a decision of the Secretary of State on such an appeal as is mentioned in section 13(5) of the Tribunals and Inquiries Act 1971, and had, or if aggrieved would have had, a right to appeal to that Secretary of State, whether or not he exercised that right, may appeal to the High Court.

(2) The persons to be served with the notice of appeal by which such an appeal is brought are the Secretary of State and every person who had, or if aggrieved would have had, a right to appeal to the Secretary of State.

(3) The court hearing the appeal may remit the matter to the Secretary of State to the extent necessary to enable him to provide the court with such further information in connection with the matter as the court may direct.

(4) If the court is of the opinion that the decision appealed against was erroneous on a point of law, it shall not set aside or vary that decision but shall

remit the matter to the Minister with the opinion of the court for rehearing and determination by him.

(5) Order 55, rule 7(5) shall not apply in relation to the appeal.

Rule 10A CONSUMER CREDIT ACT 1974: APPEAL FROM SECRETARY OF STATE

(1) A person who is dissatisfied in point of law with a decision of the Secretary of State on an appeal under section 41 of the Consumer Credit Act 1974 from a determination of the Director General of Fair Trading and had a right to appeal to the Secretary of State, whether or not he exercised that right, may appeal to the High Court.

(2) The persons to be served with the notice of appeal by which such an appeal is brought are the Secretary of State and, where the appeal is by a licensee under a group licence against compulsory variation, suspension or revocation of that licence, the original applicant, if any; but the court may in any case direct that the notice of appeal be served on any other person.

(3) The court hearing the appeal may remit the matter to the Secretary of State to the extent necessary to enable him to provide the court with such further information in connection with the matter as the court may direct.

(4) If the court is of the opinion that the decision appealed against was erroneous in point of law, it shall not set aside or vary that decision but shall remit the matter to the Secretary of State with the opinion of the court for hearing and determination by him.

(5) Order 55, rule 7(5) shall not apply in relation to the appeal.

Rule 11 CASE STATED BY MENTAL HEALTH REVIEW TRIBUNAL

(1) In this rule 'the Act' means the Mental Health Act 1983.

(2) The reference in paragraph (3) to a party to proceedings before a Mental Health Review Tribunal, and the references in Order 56, rules 8(1), 9(2) and 10 to a party to proceedings shall be construed as references to—

   (a) the person who initiated the proceedings; and

   (b) any person to whom, in accordance with rules made under section 78 of the Act, the tribunal sent notice of the application or reference or a request instead of notice of reference.

(3) A party to proceedings before a Mental Health Review Tribunal shall not be entitled to apply to the High Court for an order under section 78(8) of the Act directing the tribunal to state a case for determination by the court unless—

   (a) within 21 days after the decision of the tribunal was communicated to him in accordance with rules made under section 78 of the Act he made a written request to the tribunal to state a case, and

   (b) either the tribunal failed to comply with the last-mentioned request within 21 days after it was made or the tribunal refused to comply with it.

(4) The period for issuing the claim form by which an application to the court for such an order as is mentioned in paragraph (3) is made, and for service of the claim form shall be—

   (a) where the tribunal refused the applicant's request to state a case, 14 days after receipt by the applicant of notice of the refusal of his request;

   (b) where the tribunal failed to comply with that request within the period mentioned in paragraph (3)(b) 14 days after the expiration of that period.

(5) A Mental Health Review Tribunal by whom a case is stated shall be entitled to appear and be heard in the proceedings for the determination of the case.

(6) If the court is of opinion that any decision of such a tribunal on the question of law raised by the case was erroneous, the court may give any direction which the tribunal ought to have given under Part V of the Act.

Rule 12 APPLICATIONS FOR PERMISSION UNDER SECTION 289(6) OF THE TOWN AND COUNTRY PLANNING ACT 1990 AND SECTION 65(5) OF THE PLANNING (LISTED BUILDINGS AND CONSERVATION AREAS) ACT 1990

(1) An application for permission to appeal to the High Court under section 289 of the Town and Country Planning Act 1990 or section 65 of the Planning

(Listed Buildings and Conservation Areas) Act 1990 shall be made within 28 days after the date on which notice of the decision was given to the applicant.

(2) An application shall—
    (a) include, where necessary, any application to extend the time for applying;
    (b) be in writing setting out the reasons why permission should be granted, and if the time for applying has expired, the reasons why the application was not made within that time;
    (c) be made by filing it in the Crown Office together with the decision, a draft claim form, and a witness statement or affidavit verifying any facts relied on;
    (d) before being filed under sub-paragraph (c), be served together with the draft claim form and a copy of the witness statement or affidavit to be filed with the application, upon the persons who are referred to in rule 13(5); and
    (e) be accompanied by a witness statement or affidavit giving the names and addresses of, and the places and dates of service on, all persons who have been served with the application and, if any person who ought to be served has not been served, the witness statement or affidavit must state that fact and the reason for it.

(3) An application shall be heard—
    (a) by a single judge;
    (b) unless the court otherwise orders, not less than 21 days after it was filed at the Crown Office.

Any person served with the application shall be entitled to appear and be heard.

(4) If on the hearing of an application the court is of opinion that any person who ought to have been served has not been served, the court may adjourn the hearing on such terms (if any) as it may direct in order that the application may be served on that person.

(5) If the court grants permission—
    (a) it may impose such terms as to costs and as to giving security as it thinks fit;
    (b) it may give directions; and
    (c) the claim form by which the appeal is to be brought shall be served and filed within 7 days of the grant.

(6) Any respondent who intends to use a witness statement or affidavit at the hearing shall file it in the Crown Office and serve a copy thereof on the applicant as soon as is practicable and in any event, unless the court otherwise allows, at least 2 days before the hearing.

The court may allow the applicant to use a further witness statement or affidavit.

Rule 13 PROCEEDINGS UNDER SECTIONS 289 AND 290 OF THE TOWN AND COUNTRY PLANNING ACT 1990 AND UNDER SECTION 65 OF THE PLANNING (LISTED BUILDINGS AND CONSERVATION AREAS) ACT 1990

(1) In this rule a reference to 'section 65' is a reference to section 65 of the Planning (Listed Buildings and Conservation Areas) Act 1990, but, save as aforesaid, a reference to a section by number is a reference to the section so numbered in the Town and Country Planning Act 1990.

(2) An appeal shall lie to the High Court on a point of law against a decision of the Secretary of State under subsection (1) or (2) of section 289 or under subsection (1) of section 65 at the instance of any person or authority entitled to appeal under any of those subsections respectively.

(3) In the case of a decision to which section 290 applies, the person who made the application to which the decision relates, or the local planning authority, if dissatisfied with the decision in point of law, may appeal against the decision to the High Court.

(4) Any appeal under section 289(1) or (2), section 65(1) or section 290, and any case stated under section 289(3) or section 65(2), shall be heard and determined by a single judge unless the court directs that the matter shall be heard and determined by a Divisional Court.

(5) The persons to be served with the claim form by which an appeal to the High Court is brought by virtue of section 289(1) or (2), section 65(1) or section 290 are—

(a) the Secretary of State;
(b) the local planning authority who served the notice or gave the decision, as the case may be, or, where the appeal is brought by that authority, the appellant or applicant in the proceedings in which the decision appealed against was given;
(c) in the case of an appeal brought by virtue of section 289(1) or section 65(1), any other person having an interest in the land to which the notice relates, and;
(d) in the case of an appeal brought by virtue of section 289(2), any other person on whom the notice to which those proceedings related was served.

(6) The court hearing any such appeal may remit the matter to the Secretary of State to the extent necessary to enable him to provide the court with such further information in connection with the matter as the court may direct.

(7) Where the court is of opinion that the decision appealed against was erroneous in point of law, it shall not set aside or vary that decision but shall remit the matter to the Secretary of State with the opinion of the court for re-hearing and determination by him.

(8) Order 55, rule 7(5) shall not apply in relation to any such appeal.

(9) The court may give directions as to the exercise, until an appeal brought by virtue of section 289(1) is finally concluded and any rehearing and determination by the Secretary of State has taken place, of the power to serve, and institute proceedings (including criminal proceedings) concerning—
(a) a stop notice under section 183; and
(b) a breach of condition notice under section 187A.

Rule 14 APPLICATIONS UNDER SECTION 13 OF THE CORONERS ACT 1988

(1) Any application under section 13 of the Coroners Act 1988 shall be heard and determined by a Divisional Court.

(2) The application must be made by claim form and the claim form must state the grounds of the application and, unless the application is made by the Attorney-General, shall be accompanied by his fiat.

(3) The claim form must be filed in the Crown Office and served upon all persons directly affected by the application within six weeks after the grant of the fiat.

Rule 15 APPLICATIONS UNDER SECTION 42 OF THE SUPREME COURT ACT 1981

(1) Every application to the High Court by the Attorney-General under section 42 of the Supreme Court Act 1981 shall be heard and determined by a Divisional Court.

(2) The application must be made by claim form which, together with a witness statement or affidavit in support, shall be filed in the Crown Office and served on the person against whom the order is sought.

Rule 16 PROCEEDINGS UNDER THE PROTECTION FROM HARASSMENT ACT 1997

(1) In this rule, 'the Act' means the Protection from Harassment Act 1997.

(2) This rule shall apply to injunctions granted on or after 1st September 1998 and injunctions granted before that date shall be treated as if this rule had not come into force.

(3) Proceedings in the High Court under section 3 of the Act shall be assigned to the Queen's Bench Division.

(4) An application for the issue of a warrant for the arrest of the defendant under section 3(3) of the Act shall—
(a) state that it is an application for the issue of a warrant for the arrest of the defendant;
(b) set out the grounds for making the application and be supported by an affidavit or evidence on oath;
(c) state whether the claimant has informed the police of the defendant's conduct as described in sub-paragraph (b); and

(d) state whether, to the claimant's knowledge, criminal proceedings are being pursued.
(5) The Court before whom a person is brought following his arrest may—
(a) determine whether the facts, and the circumstances which led to the arrest, amounted to disobedience of the injunction, or
(b) adjourn the proceedings and, where such an order is made, the arrested person shall be released and—
(i) may be dealt with within 14 days of the day on which he was arrested; and
(ii) be given not less than 2 days' notice of the adjourned hearing.
(6) This rule applies to proceedings under section 3 of the Act in a county court with the following modifications—
(a) Such proceedings in a county court shall be begun—
(i) in the court for the district in which the claimant resides or carries on business; or
(ii) in the court for the district in which the defendant resides or carries on business.
(b) Where a county court—
(i) grants an injunction under section 3 of the Act; or
(ii) issues a warrant for the arrest of the defendant,
the injunction or warrant shall be issued in the appropriate prescribed form.

RSC ORDER 95
BILLS OF SALE ACTS 1878 AND 1882 AND THE INDUSTRIAL AND PROVIDENT SOCIETIES ACT 1967

Rule 1 RECTIFICATION OF REGISTER

(1) Every application to the court under section 14 of the Bills of Sale Act 1878, for an order—
(a) that any omission to register a bill of sale or a witness statement or affidavit of renewal thereof within the time prescribed by that Act be rectified by extending the time for such registration; or
(b) that any omission or mis-statement of the name, residence or occupation of any person be rectified by the insertion in the register of his true name, residence or occupation,
must be made by witness statement or affidavit to a Master of the Queen's Bench Division, and a copy of the witness statement or affidavit need not be served on any other person.
(2) Every application for such an order as is described in paragraph (1) shall be supported by a witness statement or affidavit setting out particulars of the bill of sale and of the omission or mis-statement in question and stating the grounds on which the application is made.

Rule 2 ENTRY OF SATISFACTION

(1) Every application under section 15 of the Bills of Sale Act 1878, to a Master of the Queen's Bench Division for an order that a memorandum of satisfaction be written on a registered copy of a bill of sale must be made by claim form.
(1A) If a consent to the satisfaction signed by the person entitled to the benefit of the bill of sale can be obtained, the claim form and the documents set out in paragraph (2) must not be served on any other person.
(2) Where paragraph (1A) applies, the claim form must be supported by—
(a) particulars of the consent referred to in that paragraph; and
(b) a witness statement or affidavit by a witness who attested the consent verifying the signature on it.
(3) Where paragraph (1A) does not apply, the claim form must be served on the person entitled to the benefit of the bill of sale and must be supported by evidence that the debt (if any) for which the bill of sale was made has been satisfied or discharged.

CPR SCHEDULE 1

Rule 3 RESTRAINING REMOVAL ON SALE OF GOODS SEIZED
An application to the court under the proviso to section 7 of the Bills of Sale Act (1878) Amendment Act 1882 must be made by the issue of a claim form.

Rule 4 SEARCH OF REGISTER
Any Master of the Queen's Bench Division shall, on a request in writing giving sufficient particulars, and on payment of the prescribed fee, cause a search to be made in the register of bills of sale and issue a certificate of the result of the search.

Rule 5 APPLICATION UNDER SECTION 1(5) OF THE INDUSTRIAL AND PROVIDENT SOCIETIES ACT 1967
Every application to the court under section 1(5) of the Industrial and Provident Societies Act 1967 for an order—
    (a) that the period for making an application for recording a charge be extended; or
    (b) that any omission from or mis-statement in such an application be rectified,
must be made to a Master of the Queen's Bench Division by witness statement or affidavit setting out particulars of the charge and of the omission or mis-statement in question and stating the grounds of the application, and need not be served on any other person.

Rule 6 ASSIGNMENT OF BOOK DEBTS
    (1) There shall continue to be kept in the Central Office, under the supervision of the registrar, a register of assignments of book debts.
    (2) Every application for registration of an assignment of a book debt under section 344 of the Insolvency Act 1986 shall be made by producing at the Filing and Record Department of the Central Office—
        (a) a true copy of the assignment, and of every schedule thereto; and
        (b) a witness statement or affidavit verifying the date and the time, and the due execution of the assignment in the presence of the witness, and setting out the particulars of the assignment and the parties thereto.
    (3) On an application being made in accordance with the preceding paragraph, the documents there referred to shall be filed, and the particulars of the assignment, and of the parties to it, shall be entered in the register.
    (4) In this rule, 'the registrar' has the meaning given in section 13 of the Bills of Sale Act 1878.

RSC ORDER 96
THE MINES (WORKING FACILITIES AND SUPPORT) ACT 1966, ETC.

Rule 1 ASSIGNMENT TO CHANCERY DIVISION
Any proceedings in which the jurisdiction conferred on the High Court by section 1 of the Railway and Canal Commission (Abolition) Act 1949 is invoked shall be assigned to the Chancery Division and be begun by claim form which need not be served on any other party.

Rule 2 REFERENCE BY SECRETARY OF STATE OF CERTAIN APPLICATIONS
Where under any provision of the Mines (Working Facilities and Support) Act 1966, the Secretary of State refers any application to the High Court, he shall—
    (a) file the reference, signed by him or by an officer authorised by him for the purpose, in Chancery Chambers, together with all documents and plans deposited with him by the applicant; and
    (b) within 3 days after doing so give notice to the applicant of the filing of the reference.

Rule 3 ISSUE OF CLAIM FORM
Within 10 days after receipt of the notice mentioned in rule 2(b) the applicant must issue a claim form which need not be served on any other party which must state

CPR SCHEDULE 1

the application of the applicant under the said Act of 1966 and any other relief sought.

Rule 4 APPOINTMENT FOR DIRECTIONS

(1) Within 7 days after issue of the claim form the applicant, having applied at Chancery Chambers for the name of the Master assigned to hear the claim, must take an appointment before that Master for the hearing of the claim and must forthwith serve notice of the appointment on the Secretary of State.

(2) Not less than 2 clear days before the day appointed for the first hearing of the claim, the applicant must leave at Chancery Chambers—

(a) a witness statement or affidavit of facts in support of the claim, giving particulars of all persons known to the applicant to be interested in or affected by the application; and

(b) a draft of any proposed advertisement or notice of the application.

(3) On the appointment the master shall—

(a) fix a time within which any notice of objection under rule 5 must be given;

(b) fix a date for the further hearing of the claim; and

(c) direct what, if any, advertisements and notices of the application and of the date fixed for the further hearing of the claim are to be inserted and given, and what persons, if any, are to be served with a copy of the application and of any other document in the proceedings.

(4) Any such advertisement or notice must include a statement of the effect of rule 5.

Rule 5 OBJECTIONS TO APPLICATION

(1) Any person wishing to oppose the application must, within the time fixed by the Master under rule 4 (3), serve on the applicant a notice of objection stating—

(a) his name and address and the name and address of his solicitor, if any;

(b) the grounds of his objection and any alternative methods of effecting the objects of the application which he alleges may be used; and

(c) the facts on which he relies.

(2) Any notice required to be served on a person who has given notice of objection (hereafter in this order referred to as 'the objector') may be served by delivering it or sending it by prepaid post—

(a) where the name and address of a solicitor is stated in the notice of objection, to the solicitor at that address; and

(b) in any other case, to the objector at his address stated in the notice of objection.

(3) An objector shall be entitled to appear in person or by a solicitor or counsel at the further hearing of the claim and to take such part in the proceedings as the Master or judge thinks fit; but if he does not so appear his notice of objection shall be of no effect and he shall not be entitled to take any part in the proceedings unless the Master or judge otherwise orders.

Rule 6 LIST OF OBJECTORS

Not less than 2 clear days before the day fixed for the further hearing of the claim, the applicant must leave at Chancery Chambers any notices of objection served on the applicant together with a list arranged in 3 columns stating—

(a) in column 1, the names and addresses of the objectors;

(b) in column 2, the names and addresses of their respective solicitors, if any; and

(c) in column 3, short summaries of their respective grounds of objection.

Rule 7 DIRECTIONS ON FURTHER HEARING

At the further hearing of the claim the Master shall—

(a) give directions as to the procedure to be followed before the claim is set down for hearing, including, if he thinks fit, a direction—

(i) that further particulars be given of any of the grounds or facts relied on in support of or in opposition to the application made by the claim;

(ii) that the applicant may serve a reply to any notice of objection;
(iii) that any particular fact be proved by witness statement or affidavit;
(iv) that statements of case or points of claim or defence be served; and
(b) adjourn the claim for hearing before the judge in such manner as he shall think best adapted to secure the just, expeditious and economical disposal of the proceedings.

Rule 8 OTHER APPLICATIONS
Rules 2 to 7 shall, so far as applicable and with the necessary adaptations, apply in relation to any other application to the High Court falling within rule 1 as they apply in relation to an application under the Mines (Working Facilities and Support) Act 1966.

RSC ORDER 97
THE LANDLORD AND TENANT ACTS 1927, 1954 AND 1987

Rule 1 INTERPRETATION
(1) In this order, 'the act of 1927' means the Landlord and Tenant Act 1927, 'the Act of 1954' means the Landlord and Tenant Act 1954 and 'the Act of 1987' means the Landlord and Tenant Act 1987.
(2) In relation to any proceedings under Part II of the Act of 1954, any reference in this order to a landlord shall, if the interest of the landlord in question is subject to a mortgage and the mortgagee is in possession or a receiver appointed by the mortgagee or by the court is in receipt of the rents and profits, be construed as a reference to the mortgagee.

Rule 2 ASSIGNMENT OF PROCEEDINGS TO CHANCERY DIVISION, ETC.
All proceedings in the High Court under Part I of the Act of 1927 or Part II of the Act of 1954 or the Act of 1987 shall be assigned to the Chancery Division and, subject to rules 9A and 12, be begun by claim form.

Rule 3 ISSUE, ETC., OF CLAIM FORM
(1) Any claim or application under Part I of the Act of 1927 or Part II of the Act of 1954 or the Act of 1987 may be issued out of the district registry for the district in which the premises to which the claim or application relates are situated instead of Chancery Chambers.
(3) The court will set a day for the hearing of such a claim which shall be a day which will allow an interval of at least 14 days between the date of service of the claim form and the day so fixed.

Rule 4 CLAIM FOR COMPENSATION IN RESPECT OF IMPROVEMENT
(1) A claim under section 1 of the Act of 1927 for compensation in respect of any improvement, and a claim by a mesne landlord under section 8 of that Act, must be a written claim, signed by the claimant or his solicitor or agent, containing—
(a) a statement of the name and address of the claimant and of the landlord against whom the claim is made;
(b) a description of the holding in respect of which the claim is made and of the trade or business carried on there;
(c) a concise statement of the nature of the claim;
(d) particulars of the improvement, including the date when it was completed and the cost thereof, and
(e) a statement of the amount claimed.
(2) Where any document relating to any proposed improvement, or to any claim, is sent to or served on a mesne landlord in pursuance of Part I of the Act of 1927, he must forthwith serve on his immediate superior landlord a copy of the document, together with a notice in writing stating the date on which he received the document, and if the last-mentioned landlord is himself a mesne landlord he must accordingly comply with this paragraph.

Rule 5 PROCEEDINGS UNDER PART I OF THE ACT OF 1927

(1) The claim form by which any claim or application under Part I of the Act of 1927 is made must state—

(a) the nature of the claim or application or the matter to be determined;

(b) the holding in respect of which the claim or application is made and the trade or business carried on there;

(c) particulars of the improvement or proposed improvement to which the claim or application relates; and

(d) if the claim is for payment of compensation, the amount claimed.

(2) The claimant's immediate landlord shall be made a defendant.

(3) No witness statement or affidavit shall be filed in the first instance in support of or in answer to any such claim form.

(4) Any certificate of the court under section 3 of the Act of 1927 that an improvement is a proper improvement or has been duly executed shall be embodied in an order.

Rule 6 APPLICATION FOR NEW TENANCY UNDER SECTION 24 OF THE ACT OF 1954

(1) The claim form by which an application under section 24 of the Act of 1954 for a new tenancy is made must state—

(a) the premises to which the application relates and where a business is carried on there, the nature of such business;

(b) particulars of the claimant's current tenancy of the premises and of every notice or request given or made in respect of that tenancy under section 25 or 26 of that Act; and

(c) the claimant's proposals as to the terms of the new tenancy applied for including, in particular, terms as to the duration thereof and as to the rent payable thereunder.

(2) The person who, in relation to the claimant's current tenancy, is the landlord as defined by section 44 of the Act of 1954 shall be made a defendant.

(3) A claim form under this rule must be served within 2 months after the date of issue whether served within or out of the jurisdiction and CPR rules 7.5(2) and 7.5(3) will not apply.

Rule 6A APPLICATION TO AUTHORISE AGREEMENT

(1) An application under section 38(4) of the Act of 1954 for the authorisation of an agreement shall be made without notice being served on any other party by claim form and may be heard and determined in private.

(2) Notwithstanding that the application must be made jointly by the landlord or proposed landlord and the tenant or proposed tenant and the claim form is accordingly issued by one solicitor on behalf of both of them, they may appear and be heard at any hearing by separate solicitors or counsel or, in the case of an individual applicant, in person; and where at any stage of the proceedings it appears to the court that one of the applicants is not but ought to be separately represented, the court may adjourn the proceedings until he is.

Rule 7 EVIDENCE ON APPLICATION UNDER SECTION 24 OF THE ACT OF 1954

(1) Not less than 14 days before the day fixed for the first hearing in an application under section 24 of the Act of 1954 for a new tenancy the claimant must file a witness statement or affidavit verifying the statements of fact made in the claim form.

(2) Not less than 4 days before the day fixed for the first hearing the defendant must file a witness statement or affidavit stating—

(a) whether he opposes the grant of a new tenancy and, if he does, on what grounds;

(b) whether, if a new tenancy is granted, he objects to any of the claimant's proposals as to the terms thereof and, if he does, the terms to which he objects and the terms he proposes insofar as they differ from the terms proposed by the claimant;

(c) whether he is a tenant under a lease having less than 14 years unexpired at the date of the termination of the claimant's current tenancy, and, if he is, the name and address of his immediate landlord.

Rule 8 PARTIES TO CERTAIN PROCEEDINGS

(1) Any person affected by any proceedings under rule 5, 6, 14, 15, 16 or 17 may apply to be made a party to the proceedings and the court may give such directions on the application as appear necessary.

(2) An application under paragraph (1) must in the first instance be made without notice being given to any other party but the court may require notice thereof to be given to the parties to the proceedings before making any order.

(3) The foregoing provisions are without prejudice to the power of the court, either with or without an application by any party, to order notice of the proceedings to be given to any person or any person to be made a party to the proceedings, but nothing in this rule shall be construed as requiring the court to make any such order and, if it appears that any person though he is affected by the proceedings is not sufficiently affected for it to be necessary for him to be made a party to the proceedings or given notice thereof, the court may refuse to make him a party or, as the case may be, to require him to be given notice of the proceedings.

Rule 9 ORDER DISMISSING APPLICATION UNDER SECTION 24 WHICH IS SUCCESSFULLY OPPOSED

Where the court hearing an application under section 24 of the Act of 1954 is precluded by section 31 of that Act from making an order for the grant of a new tenancy by reason of any of the grounds specified in section 30(1) of that Act, the order dismissing the application shall state all the grounds by reason of which the court is so precluded.

Rule 9A APPLICATION TO DETERMINE INTERIM RENT

(1) An application under section 24A of the Act of 1954 to determine an interim rent shall—

(a) if the tenant has begun proceedings for a new tenancy under section 24 of the Act, be made by an application in accordance with CPR Part 23 in those proceedings; and

(b) in any other case, be made by claim form.

Rule 10 OTHER APPLICATIONS UNDER PART II OF THE ACT OF 1954

(1) An application for an order under section 31(2)(b) of the Act of 1954 and, unless made at the hearing of the application under section 24 thereof, an application for a certificate under section 37(4) of that Act may be made without notice being served on any other party.

(2) The mesne landlord to whose consent an application for the determination of any question arising under paragraph 4(3) of Schedule 6 to the Act of 1954 relates shall be made a defendant to the claim.

Rule 11 TRANSFER OF PROCEEDINGS FROM COUNTY COURT

(2) Any proceedings under Part I of the Act of 1927 or Part II of the Act of 1954 that have been transferred from a county court shall proceed in the High Court as if they had been begun by claim form issued out of Chancery Chambers, and within 7 days after receipt of notification of the transfer the claimant must apply in the High Court for the appointment of a day and time for the attendance of the parties before the court.

(3) If the claimant fails to apply for an appointment within the period prescribed by paragraph (2) the defendant may do so.

Rule 12 APPLICATION FOR RELIEF UNDER SECTION 16, ETC., OF THE ACT OF 1954

In any such proceedings as are mentioned in section 16(1) of the Act of 1954, paragraph 9(1) of Schedule 5 to that Act or paragraph 10(1) of that Schedule, an application for relief under that section or paragraph, as the case may be, may be made—

(a) in the applicant's statement of case; or
(b) in accordance with CPR Part 23 at any time before the trial; or
(c) at the trial.

Rule 13 EVIDENCE OF RATEABLE VALUE

Where any dispute as to the rateable value of any holding has been referred under section 37(5) of the Act of 1954 to the Commissioners of Inland Revenue for decision by a valuation officer, any document purporting to be a statement by the valuation officer of his decision shall be admissible as evidence of the matters contained in it.

Rule 14 APPLICATION UNDER SECTION 19 OF THE ACT OF 1987

A copy of the notice served under section 19(2)(a) of the Act of 1987 shall be appended to the claim form issued under section 19(1) thereof, and an additional copy of the notice shall be filed.

Rule 16 APPLICATION FOR ACQUISITION ORDER UNDER SECTION 29 OF THE ACT OF 1987

(1) An application for an acquisition order under section 29 of the Act of 1987 shall—

(a) identify the premises to which the application relates and give such details of them as are necessary to show that section 25 of the Act of 1987 applies thereto;

(b) give such details of the applicants as are necessary to show that they constitute the requisite majority of qualifying tenants;

(c) state the name and address of the applicants and of the landlord of the premises, or, where the landlord cannot be found or his identity ascertained, the steps taken to find him or ascertain his identity;

(d) state the name and address of the person nominated by the applicants for the purposes of Part III of the Act of 1987;

(e) state the name and address of every person known to the applicants who is likely to be affected by the application, including, but not limited to, the other tenants of flats contained in the premises (whether or not they could have made an application), any mortgagee or superior landlord of the landlord, and any tenant's association; and

(f) state the grounds of the application,

and a copy of the notice served on the landlord under section 27 of the Act of 1987 shall be appended to the claim form, unless the requirement to serve such a notice has been dispensed with, and an additional copy of the notice shall be filed.

(2) The defendants to an application for an acquisition order under section 29 of the Act of 1987 shall be the landlord of the premises and the nominated person, where he is not an applicant.

(3) A copy of the claim form shall be served on each of the persons named by the applicant under paragraph (1)(e), together with a notice stating that he may apply under rule 8 to be made a party to the proceedings.

(4) Where the nominated person pays money into court in accordance with an order under section 33(1) of the Act of 1987, he shall file a copy of the certificate of the surveyor selected under section 33(2)(a) thereof.

Rule 17 APPLICATION FOR ORDER UNDER SECTION 38 OR SECTION 40 OF THE ACT OF 1987

(1) An application for an order under section 38 or section 40 of the Act of 1987 shall state—

(a) the name and address of the applicant and of the other current parties to the lease or leases to which the application relates;

(b) the date of and parties to the lease or leases, the premises demised thereby, the relevant terms thereof and the variation sought;

(c) the name and address of every person who the applicant knows or has reason to believe is likely to be affected by the variation, including, but not limited to, the other tenants of flats contained in the premises of which the demised premises form a part, any mortgagee or superior landlord of the landlord, any mortgagee of the applicant, and any tenants' association; and

    (d)   the grounds of the application.

(2) The other current parties to the lease or leases shall be made defendants to the application.

(3) A copy of the application shall be served by the applicant on each of the persons named by the applicant under paragraph (1)(c) and by the defendant on any other person who he knows or has reason to believe is likely to be affected by the variation, together, in each case, with a notice stating that the person may apply under rule 8 to be made a party to the proceedings.

(4) Any application under section 36 of the Act of 1987 shall be contained in the defendant's witness statement or affidavit, and paragraphs (1) to (3) shall apply to such an application as if the defendant were an applicant.

Rule 18 SERVICE OF NOTICES IN PROCEEDINGS UNDER THE ACT OF 1987

Where a notice is to be served in or before proceedings under the Act of 1987, it shall be served in accordance with section 54 and, in the case of service on a landlord, it shall be served at the address furnished under section 48(1).

Rule 19 TENANTS' ASSOCIATIONS

In rules 15, 16 and 17 a reference to a tenants' association is a reference to a recognised tenants' association within the meaning of section 29 of the Landlord and Tenant Act 1985 which represents tenants of the flats of which the demised premises form a part.

RSC ORDER 98
LOCAL GOVERNMENT FINANCE ACT 1982, PART III

Rule 1 INTERPRETATION

In this order 'the Act' means the Local Government Finance Act 1982 and a section referred to by number means the section so numbered in that Act.

Rule 2 APPLICATION BY AUDITOR FOR DECLARATION

(1) Any application for a declaration under section 19(1) of the Act that an item of account is contrary to law shall be made by claim form.

(2) The claim form shall be served on the body to whose accounts the application relates and on any person against whom an order is sought under section 19(2).

(3) Not later than 7 days after filing the claim form in the Crown Office in accordance with Order 57, rule 2, the applicant shall file in that office a witness statement or affidavit stating the facts on which he intends to rely at the hearing of the application.

(4) The claim shall be entered for hearing within 6 weeks after the claim form has been filed in the Crown Office but, unless the court otherwise directs, the application shall not be heard sooner than 28 days after service of the claim form.

Rule 3 APPEAL AGAINST DECISION OF AUDITOR

(1) A claim form by which an appeal is brought under section 19(4) or section 20(3) against the decision of an auditor shall be served on—

    (a)   the auditor who for the time being has responsibility for the audit of the accounts of the body in relation to whom the appeal relates;

    (b)   that body; and

    (c)   in the case of an appeal against a decision not to certify under section 20(1) that a sum or amount is due from another person, that person.

(2) Order 55, rules 4(2) and 5, shall apply to the appeal with the modification that the period of 28 days mentioned in the said rule 4(2) shall be calculated from the day on which the appellant received the auditor's statement of the reasons for his decision pursuant to a requirement under section 19(4) or section 20(2).

CPR SCHEDULE 1

(3) Not later than seven days after filing the claim form in the Crown Office in accordance with Order 57, rule 2, the appellant must file in that office a witness statement or affidavit stating—
 (a) the reasons stated by the auditor for his decision;
 (b) the date on which he received the auditor's statement;
 (c) the facts on which he intends to rely at the hearing of the appeal;
 (d) in the case of a decision not to apply for a declaration, such facts within the appellant's knowledge as will enable the court to consider whether to exercise the powers conferred on it by section 19(2).

Rule 4 GENERAL PROVISIONS
(1) Any proceedings in which the jurisdiction conferred on the High Court by section 19 or section 20 of the Act is invoked shall be assigned to the Queen's Bench Division and be heard by a single judge, unless the court directs that the matter shall be heard by a Divisional Court; and the court may, at any stage direct that any officer or member of the body to whose accounts the application of appeal relates be joined as a respondent.
(2) Except insofar as the court directs that the evidence on any such application or appeal shall be given orally, it shall be given by witness statement or affidavit.
(3) The applicant or appellant must forthwith after filing any witness statement or affidavit under rule 2(3) or 3(3) serve a copy thereof on every respondent and any person intending to oppose the application or appeal must, not less than 4 days before the hearing, serve on the applicant or appellant a copy of any witness statement or affidavit filed by him in opposition.
(4) Except by permission of the court, no witness statement or affidavit may be used at the hearing unless a copy thereof was served in accordance with paragraph (3).

RSC ORDER 99
INHERITANCE (PROVISION FOR FAMILY AND DEPENDANTS) ACT 1975

Rule A1 ORDER TO APPLY TO HIGH COURT AND COUNTY COURT
This order applies to proceedings both in the High Court and the county court.

Rule 1 INTERPRETATION
In this order 'the Act' means the Inheritance (Provision for Family and Dependants) Act 1975 and a section referred to by number means the section so numbered in that Act.

Rule 2 ASSIGNMENT TO CHANCERY OR FAMILY DIVISION IF PROCEEDINGS IN HIGH COURT
Proceedings in the High Court under the Act may be assigned to the Chancery Division or to the Family Division.

Rule 3 APPLICATION FOR FINANCIAL PROVISION
(1) An application under section 1 is made by the issue of a claim form.
(3) There shall be filed with the court a witness statement or affidavit by the applicant in support of the claim, exhibiting an official copy of the grant of representation to the deceased's estate and of every testamentary document admitted to proof, and a copy of the witness statement or affidavit shall be served on every defendant with the claim form.

Rule 4 POWERS OF COURT AS TO PARTIES
(1) The court may at any stage of proceedings under the Act direct that any person be added as a party to the proceedings or that notice of the proceedings be served on any person.
(2) Order 15, rule 13 shall apply to proceedings under the Act as it applies to the proceedings mentioned in paragraph (1) of that rule.

CPR SCHEDULE 1

Rule 5 WITNESS STATEMENT OR AFFIDAVIT IN ANSWER

(1) A defendant to an application under section 1 who is a personal representative of the deceased shall and any other defendant may, within 21 days after service of the claim form on him, inclusive of the day of service, file with the court a witness statement or affidavit in answer to the application.

(2) The witness statement or affidavit filed by a personal representative pursuant to paragraph (1) shall state to the best of the witness's ability—

(a) full particulars of the value of the deceased's net estate, as defined by section 25(1);

(b) the person or classes of persons beneficially interested in the estate, giving the names and (in the case of those who are not already parties) the addresses of all living beneficiaries, and the value of their interests so far as ascertained;

(c) if such be the case, that any living beneficiary (naming him) is a child or patient within the meaning of CPR rule 21.1(2); and

(d) any facts known to the witness which might affect the exercise of the court's powers under the Act.

(3) Every defendant who lodges a witness statement or affidavit shall at the same time serve a copy on the claimant and on every other defendant who is not represented by the same solicitor.

Rule 6 SEPARATE REPRESENTATION

Where an application under section 1 is made jointly by two or more applicants and the claim form is accordingly issued by one solicitor on behalf of all of them, they may, if they have conflicting interests, appear on any hearing of the claim by separate solicitors or counsel or in person, and where at any stage of the proceedings it appears to the court that one of the applicants is not but ought to be separately represented, the court may adjourn the proceedings until he is.

Rule 7 ENDORSEMENT OF MEMORANDUM ON GRANT

On the hearing of an application under section 1 the personal representative shall produce to the court the grant of representation to the deceased's estate and, if an order is made under the Act, the grant shall remain in the custody of the court until a memorandum of the order has been endorsed on or permanently annexed to the grant in accordance with section 19(3).

Rule 9 SUBSEQUENT APPLICATIONS IN PROCEEDINGS UNDER SECTION 1

Where an order has been made on an application under section 1, any subsequent application under the Act, whether made by a party to the proceedings or by any other person, shall be made by the issue of an application notice in accordance with CPR Part 23.

Rule 10 DRAWING UP AND SERVICE OF ORDERS

The provisions of the Family Proceedings Rules relating to the drawing up and service of orders shall apply to proceedings in the Family Division under this order as if they were proceedings under those rules.

In this rule 'Family Proceedings Rules' means rules made under section 40 of the Matrimonial and Family Proceedings Act 1984.

RSC ORDER 101
THE PENSIONS APPEAL TRIBUNALS ACT 1943

Rule 1 ASSIGNMENT TO QUEEN'S BENCH DIVISION

Proceedings in the High Court under the Pensions Appeal Tribunals Act 1943, shall be assigned to the Queen's Bench Division.

Rule 2 CONSTRUCTION OF REFERENCE TO JUDGE

In this order references to the judge shall be construed as references to the judge nominated by the Lord Chancellor under section 6(2) of the Pensions Appeal Tribunals Act 1943.

CPR SCHEDULE 1

Rule 3 APPLICATION FOR PERMISSION TO APPEAL

(1) An application to the judge for permission to appeal against the decision of a Pensions Appeal Tribunal may not be made unless an application for such permission was made to the tribunal and was refused and must be made within 28 days after the date of the tribunal's refusal.

(2) The application to the judge, which may be made without notice being served on any other party must be made by filing in the Crown Office a written statement of—

(a) the name and description of the applicant;
(b) the point of law as respects which the applicant alleges that the tribunal's decision was erroneous; and
(c) the date of the tribunal's decision refusing permission to appeal.

(3) If the application is made with the consent of the other party to the proceedings before the tribunal, that fact shall be included in the statement.

(4) On the making of the application the court officer shall request the chairman of the tribunal to give the judge a written statement of the reasons for the tribunal's decision to refuse permission to appeal, and within 7 days after receiving the request the chairman shall give the judge such a statement.

(5) The judge may determine the application without a hearing or may direct that the application be set down for hearing in private.

(6) Where the application is determined without a hearing, a copy of the judge's order shall be sent from the Crown Office to the applicant and to the other party to the proceedings before the tribunal; and where the application is to be set down for hearing, notice of the day and time fixed for the hearing shall be sent from that office to the applicant.

Rule 4 APPEAL

(1) Without prejudice to Order 55, rule 3(2), the notice of appeal by which an appeal against the decision of a Pensions Appeal Tribunal is brought must state the question of law on which the appeal is brought, the date on which permission to appeal was granted and whether such permission was granted by the judge or the tribunal.

(2) Order 55, rules 3(3) and 4(2), shall not apply in relation to such an appeal, but the notice must be served and the appeal entered within 28 days after permission to appeal was granted.

(3) Within 28 days after service of the notice of appeal on him, the chairman of the tribunal must state a case setting out the facts on which the decision appealed against was based and must file the case in the Crown Office and serve a copy thereof on the appellant and on the respondent.

(4) Order 55, rule 5, shall apply in relation to such an appeal as if for the period of 21 days therein mentioned there were substituted a period of 6 weeks.

(5) At the hearing of the appeal the judge may order the case to be returned to the chairman for amendment.

(6) Order 55, rule 7(2), shall not apply in relation to the appeal.

(7) A copy of the judge's order on the appeal must be sent by the court officer to the appellant, the respondent and the chairman of the tribunal.

RSC ORDER 106
PROCEEDINGS RELATING TO SOLICITORS: THE SOLICITORS ACT, 1974

Rule 1 INTERPRETATION

(1) In this order—
'the Act' means the Solicitors Act 1974 and a section referred to by number means the section so numbered in that Act;
'appeal' means an appeal to the High Court against an order made by the tribunal on an application or complaint under the Act.

(2) Expressions used in this order which are used in the Act have the same meanings in this order as in the Act.

CPR SCHEDULE 1

Rule 2 JURISDICTION UNDER PART III OF ACT

(2) The jurisdiction of the High Court under Part III of the Act may be exercised by—
 (a) A judge;
 (b) A master, a taxing master or a district judge of the Family Division; or
 (c) A district judge if the costs are for contentious business done in proceedings in the district registry of which he is the district judge or for non contentious business.

Rule 3 POWER TO ORDER SOLICITOR TO DELIVER CASH ACCOUNT, ETC.

(1) Where the relationship of solicitor and client exists or has existed the court may, on the application of the client or his personal representatives, make an order for—
 (a) the delivery by the solicitor of a cash account;
 (b) the payment or delivery up by the solicitor of money or securities;
 (c) the delivery to the claimant of a list of the moneys or securities which the solicitor has in his possession or control on behalf of the claimant;
 (d) the payment into or lodging in court of any such moneys or securities.

(2) An application for an order under this rule must be made by the issue of a claim form, or if in proceedings by an application in accordance with CPR Part 23.

(3) If the defendant alleges that he has a claim for costs, the court may make such order for detailed assessment in accordance with CPR Part 47 and payment, or securing the payment, thereof and the protection of the defendant's lien, if any, as the court thinks fit.

Rule 5A CERTIFICATE TO BE SUBMITTED WITH SOLICITOR'S APPLICATION FOR DETAILED ASSESSMENT

A solicitor who applies for an order under the Act for the detailed assessment in accordance with CPR Part 47 of his bill of costs shall lodge with his application a certificate that all the relevant requirements of the Act have been satisfied.

Rule 6 APPLICATIONS UNDER SCHEDULE 1 TO ACT

(1) Proceedings in the High Court under Schedule 1 to the Act shall be assigned to the Chancery Division.

(2) The claim form by which an application for an order under the said Schedule is made must be entitled in the matter of a solicitor, or a deceased solicitor, as the case may be (without naming him) and in the matter of the Act.

(3) Where an order has been made under paragraph 9(4), 9(5) or 10 of the said Schedule an application for an order under paragraph 9(8) or 9(10) may be made in accordance with CPR Part 23 in the proceedings in which the first mentioned order was made.

Rule 7 DEFENDANTS TO APPLICATIONS UNDER SCHEDULE 1 TO ACT

The defendant to a claim by which an application for an order under Schedule 1 to the Act is made shall be—
 (a) if the application is for an order under paragraph 5 thereof, the solicitor or, as the case may be, every member of the firm, on whose behalf the money in respect of which the order is sought is held;
 (b) if the application is for an order under paragraph 6(4) or 9(8) thereof, the Law Society;
 (c) if the application is for an order under paragraph 8, 9(4) or 9(5) thereof, the person against whom the order is sought;
 (d) if the application is for an order under paragraph 9(10) thereof, the person from whom the Law Society obtained possession of the documents by virtue of paragraph 9 or 10;
 (e) if the application is for an order under paragraph 10 thereof for the re-direction of postal packets addressed to a solicitor or his firm, the solicitor or, as the case may be, every member of the firm;

(f) if the application is for an order under paragraph 11 thereof, the solicitor or personal representative in substitution for whom the appointment of a new trustee is sought and, if he is a co-trustee, the other trustee or trustees.

Rule 8 INTERIM ORDER RESTRICTING PAYMENT OUT OF BANKING ACCOUNT

At any time after the issue of a claim form by which an application for an order under paragraph 5 of Schedule 1 to the Act is made, the court may, on the application of the claimant made without notice in accordance with CPR Part 23 make an interim order under that paragraph to have effect until the hearing of the application and include therein a further order requiring the defendant to show cause at the hearing why an order under that paragraph should not be made.

Rule 9 ADDING PARTIES, ETC.

The court may, at any stage of proceedings under Schedule 1 to the Act, order any person to be added as a party to the proceedings or to be given notice thereof.

Rule 10 SERVICE OF DOCUMENTS

(1) Any document required to be served on the Law Society in proceedings under this order shall be served by sending it by prepaid post to the secretary of the Law Society.

(2) Subject to paragraph (1) a claim form by which an application under Schedule 1 to the Act is made, an order under paragraph 5 of that Schedule or rule 8 and any other document not required to be served personally which is to be served on a defendant to proceedings under the said Schedule shall, unless the court otherwise directs, be deemed to be properly served by sending it by prepaid post to the defendant at his last known address.

Rule 11 CONSTITUTION OF DIVISIONAL COURT TO HEAR APPEALS

Every appeal shall be heard by a Divisional Court of the Queen's Bench Division consisting, unless the Lord Chief Justice otherwise directs, of not less than three judges.

Rule 12 TITLE, SERVICE, ETC., OF NOTICE OF APPEAL

(1) The notice of appeal by which an appeal is brought must be entitled in the matter of a solicitor, or, as the case may be, a solicitor's clerk, without naming him, and in the matter of the Act.

(2) Unless the court otherwise orders, the persons to be served with such notice are every party to the proceedings before the tribunal and the Law Society.

(3) Order 55, rule 4(2) shall apply in relation to the appeal as if for the period of 28 days therein specified there were substituted a period of 14 days.

(4) Order 55, rule 4(4) shall not apply and the said period of 14 days shall begin with the day on which a statement of the tribunal's findings was filed pursuant to section 48(1).

Rule 13 LAW SOCIETY TO PRODUCE CERTAIN DOCUMENTS

(1) Within 7 days after being served with the notice of appeal the Law Society must lodge in the Crown Office three copies of each of the following documents—

(a) the order appealed against, together with the statement of the tribunal's findings required by section 48(1) of the Act;

(b) any document lodged by a party with the tribunal which is relevant to a matter in issue on the appeal; and

(c) the transcript of the shorthand note, or, as the case may be, the note taken by the chairman of the tribunal of the evidence in the proceedings before the tribunal.

(2) At the hearing of the appeal the court shall direct by whom the costs incurred in complying with paragraph (1) are to be borne and may order them to be paid to the Law Society by one of the parties notwithstanding that the Society does not appear at the hearing.

Rule 14 RESTRICTION ON REQUIRING SECURITY FOR COSTS
No person other than an appellant who was the applicant in the proceedings before the tribunal, shall be ordered to give security for the costs of an appeal.

Rule 15 DISCIPLINARY COMMITTEE'S OPINION MAY BE REQUIRED
The court may direct the tribunal to furnish the court with a written statement of their opinion on the case which is the subject-matter of an appeal or on any question arising therein, and where such a direction is given, the clerk to the tribunal must as soon as may be lodge three copies of such statement in the Crown Office and at the same time send a copy to each of the parties to the appeal.

Rule 16 PERSONS ENTITLED TO BE HEARD ON APPEAL
A person who has not been served with the notice of appeal but who desires to be heard in opposition to the appeal shall, if he appears to the court to be a proper person to be so heard, be entitled to be so heard.

Rule 17 DISCONTINUANCE OF APPEAL
(1) An appellant may at any time discontinue his appeal by serving notice of discontinuance on the clerk to the tribunal and every other party to the appeal and, if the appeal has been entered, by lodging a copy of the notice in the Crown Office.

(2) Where an appeal has been discontinued in accordance with paragraph (1) it shall be treated as having been dismissed with an order for payment by the appellant of the costs of and incidental to the appeal, including any costs incurred by the Law Society in complying with rule 13(1).

RSC ORDER 108
PROCEEDINGS RELATING TO CHARITIES: THE CHARITIES ACT 1993

Rule 1 INTERPRETATION
In this order—
'the Act' means the Charities Act 1993;
'certificate' means a certificate that a case is a proper one for an appeal;
'charity proceedings' means proceedings in the High Court under the court's jurisdiction with respect to charities or under the court's jurisdiction with respect to trusts in relation to the administration of a trust for charitable purposes;
'the Commissioners' means the Charity Commissioners for England and Wales.

Rule 2 ASSIGNMENT TO CHANCERY DIVISION
Charity proceedings and proceedings brought in the High Court by virtue of the Act shall be assigned to the Chancery Division.

Rule 3 APPLICATION FOR PERMISSION TO APPEAL OR TO TAKE CHARITY PROCEEDINGS
(1) An application shall not be made under section 16(13) of the Act for permission to appeal against an order of the Commissioners unless the applicant has requested the Commissioners to grant a certificate and they have refused to do so.

(2) An application under section 33(5) of the Act for permission to start charity proceedings must be made within 21 days after the refusal by the Commissioners of an order authorising proceedings.

(3) The application must be made by lodging in Chancery Chambers a statement showing—
(a) the name, address and description of the applicant;
(b) particulars of the order against which it is desired to appeal or of the proceedings which it is desired to take;
(c) the date of the Commissioners' refusal to grant a certificate or an order authorising the taking of proceedings;
(d) the grounds on which the applicant alleges that it is a proper case for an appeal or for taking proceedings.

(4) The application may be made without notice in the first instance and if it is made with the consent of any other party to the proposed appeal or proposed proceedings that fact shall be mentioned in the statement.

(5) If the judge on considering the application so directs, the Commissioners shall furnish him with a written statement of their reasons for refusing a certificate or, as the case may be, an order authorising the taking of proceedings, and a copy of any such statement shall be sent from Chancery Chambers to the applicant.

(6) Unless, after considering the applicant's statement and the statement (if any) of the Commissioners, the judge decides to give the permission applied for without a hearing, the application shall be set down for hearing, and the hearing may be in private if the judge so directs.

(7) Where the application is determined without a hearing, a copy of the judge's order shall be sent from Chancery Chambers to the applicant and the Commissioners; and where the application is to be set down for hearing, notice of the day and time fixed for the hearing shall be sent from that office to the applicant.

Rule 4 APPLICATION FOR ENFORCEMENT OF ORDER OR DIRECTION OF COMMISSIONERS
Order 52, rule 1(4), shall apply in relation to an application under section 88 of the Act as if for the reference in that rule to a single judge of the Queen's Bench Division there was substituted a reference to a single judge of the Chancery Division.

Rule 5 APPEAL AGAINST ORDER, ETC., OF COMMISSIONERS
(1) An appeal against an order or decision of the Commissioners shall be heard and determined by a single judge.

(2) Such an appeal must be brought by a notice of appeal to which the Attorney-General, unless he is the appellant, shall be made a defendant in addition to any other person who is a proper defendant thereto.

(3) A notice of appeal under this rule must state the grounds of the appeal and, except with the permission of the judge hearing the appeal, the appellant shall not be entitled to rely on any ground not so stated.

Rule 6 SERVICE ON COMMISSIONERS
Any document required or authorised to be served on the Commissioners in proceedings to which this order relates must be served on the Treasury Solicitor in accordance with Order 77, rule 4(2).

RSC ORDER 109
THE ADMINISTRATION OF JUSTICE ACT 1960

Rule 1 APPLICATIONS UNDER ACT
(1) Any of the following applications, that is to say—

(a) an application under section 2 of the Administration of Justice Act 1960, or under that section as applied by section 13 of that Act, to extend the time within which an application may be made to a Divisional Court for permission to appeal to the House of Lords under section 1 of that Act, or section 13 thereof, from an order or decision of that court, and

(b) an application by a defendant under section 9(3) of that Act to a Divisional Court for permission to be present on the hearing of any proceedings preliminary or incidental to an appeal to the House of Lords under section 1 of that Act from a decision of that court

must be made to a Divisional Court except in vacation when it may be made to a judge.

(2) Any such application to a Divisional Court, if not made in the proceedings before the Divisional Court from whose order or decision the appeal in question is brought, must be made by the issue of a claim form.

(3) Any such application to a judge must, in the case of such an application as is referred to in paragraph (1)(a) be made by the issue of a claim form and, in the case of such an application as is referred to in paragraph (1)(b) need not be served on any other person unless, in the latter case, the judge otherwise directs.

(4) No application notice or copy of the claim form (as the case may be) by which such an application as is referred to in paragraph (1)(b) is made, need be given to any party affected thereby unless the Divisional Court otherwise directs.

(5) Where any application to which this rule applies is made in vacation to a single judge and the judge refuses the application, the applicant shall be entitled to have the application determined by a Divisional Court.

Rule 2 APPEALS UNDER SECTION 13 OF ACT

(1) An appeal to a Divisional Court of the High Court under section 13 of the Administration of Justice Act 1960, shall be heard and determined by a Divisional Court of the Queen's Bench Division.

(3) Order 55, rules 4(2) and 5, shall not apply in relation to an appeal to a Divisional Court under the said section 13.

(4) Unless the court gives permission, there shall be not more than 4 clear days between the date on which the order or decision appealed against was made and the day named in the notice of appeal for the hearing of the appeal.

(5) The notice must be served, and the appeal entered, not less than one clear day before the day named in the notice for the hearing of the appeal.

Rule 3 RELEASE OF APPELLANT ON BAIL

(1) Where, in the case of an appeal under section 13 of the Administration of justice Act 1960, to a Divisional Court or to the House of Lords from a Divisional Court, the appellant is in custody, the High Court may order his release on his giving security (whether by recognizance, with or without sureties, or otherwise and for such reasonable sum as the court may fix) for his appearance, within 10 days after the judgment of the Divisional Court or, as the case may be, of the House of Lords, on the appeal before the court from whose order or decision the appeal is brought unless the order or decision is reversed by that judgment.

(2) Order 79, rule 9(1) to (6) and (8) shall apply in relation to an application to the High Court for bail pending an appeal under the said section 13 to which this rule applies, and to the admission of a person to bail in pursuance of an order made on the application, as they apply in relation to an application to that court for bail in criminal proceedings, and to the admission of a person to bail in pursuance of an order made on the application, but with the substitution, for references to the defendant, of references to the appellant, and, for references to the prosecutor, of references to the court officer of the court from whose order or decision the appeal is brought and to the parties to the proceedings in that court who are directly affected by the appeal.

RSC ORDER 110
ENVIRONMENTAL CONTROL PROCEEDINGS

Rule 1 INJUNCTIONS TO PREVENT ENVIRONMENTAL HARM

(1) An injunction under—

    (a) section 187B or 214A of the Town and Country Planning Act 1990;

    (b) section 44A of the Planning (Listed Buildings and Conservation Areas) Act 1990; or

    (c) section 26AA of the Planning (Hazardous Substances) Act 1990

may be granted against a person whose identity is unknown to the applicant; and in the following provisions of this rule such an injunction against such a person is referred to as 'an injunction under paragraph (1)' and the person against whom it is sought is referred to as 'the defendant'.

(2) An applicant for an injunction under paragraph (1) shall, in the claim form, describe the defendant by reference to—

    (a) a photograph,

    (b) a thing belonging to or in the possession of the defendant, or

    (c) any other evidence,

with sufficient particularity to enable service to be effected.

(3) An applicant for an injunction under paragraph (1) shall file in support of the application evidence by witness statement or affidavit—

CPR SCHEDULE 1

(a) verifying that he was unable to ascertain, within the time reasonably available to him, the defendant's identity,

(b) setting out the action taken to ascertain the defendant's identity, and

(c) verifying the means by which the defendant has been described in the application and that the description is the best that the applicant is able to provide.

(4) Paragraph (2) is without prejudice to the power of the Court to make an order for service by an alternative method or dispensing with service.

RSC ORDER 111
THE SOCIAL SECURITY ADMINISTRATION ACT 1992

Rule 1 JUDGE BY WHOM APPEALS AND REFERENCES TO BE HEARD
Any appeal to the High Court against a decision of the Secretary of State on a question of law under the Social Security Administration Act 1992, and any question of law referred to the High Court by the Secretary of State under the Act, shall be heard and determined by a single judge of the Queen's Bench Division.

Rule 2 APPEAL: PRELIMINARY STATEMENT OF FACTS BY SECRETARY OF STATE
Any person who by virtue of section 18 or 58(8) of the Social Security Administration Act 1992 is entitled and wishes to appeal against a decision of the Secretary of State on a question of law must within the prescribed period or within such further time as the Secretary of State may allow serve on the Secretary of State a notice of appeal requiring him to state a case setting out the facts on which his decision was based and his decision.

If within 28 days after receipt of notice of the decision a request is made to the Secretary of State in accordance with regulations made under the Act to furnish a statement of the grounds of the decision, the prescribed period for the purpose of this rule shall be 28 days after receipt of that statement, and if no such request is made within 28 days after receipt of notice of the decision the prescribed period for that purpose shall be 28 days after receipt of that notice.

Rule 3 SPECIAL PROVISIONS AS TO APPEALS
Order 55 shall not apply in relation to an appeal under the said section 18 or 58(8) but Order 56, rules 9 to 12, shall apply in relation to the case stated by the Secretary of State for the purpose of any such appeal as they apply in relation to any other case stated by a Minister except that Order 56, rule 10(4) and (7) as so applied, shall have effect as if for the period of 14 days and 7 days therein specified there were substituted a period of 28 days.

Rule 4 REFERENCE OF QUESTION OF LAW
(1) Where under the said section 18 or 58(8) the Secretary of State refers to the High Court for decision any question of law, he must state that question together with the facts relating thereto in a case.

(2) Order 56, rules 9(1), 10(1), 11 and 12, shall apply in relation to a case stated under paragraph (1) of this rule as they apply in relation to any other case stated by a Secretary of State.

(3) The notice of appeal by which proceedings for the determination of the question of law stated in the case are begun, together with a copy of the case, must be served by the Secretary of State on every person as between whom and the Secretary of State the question has arisen.

(4) Unless the court having jurisdiction to determine the question of law otherwise directs, the appeal or reference shall not be heard sooner than 28 days after service of notice of appeal.

Rule 5 POWERS OF COURT HEARING APPEAL OR REFERENCE
(1) Without prejudice to Order 56, rule 11, as applied by rules 3 and 4 of this order, the court hearing an appeal or reference under the said section 18 or 58(8) may order the case stated by the Secretary of State to be returned to the Secretary of State for him to hear further evidence.

(2) The court hearing such an appeal or reference shall determine all questions arising thereon, and in the case of any such appeal may reverse, affirm or amend the decision appealed against or make such other order as it thinks fit.

RSC ORDER 112
APPLICATIONS FOR USE OF BLOOD TESTS IN DETERMINING PATERNITY

Rule 1 INTERPRETATION
In this order—
'the Act' means Part III of the Family Law Reform Act 1969;
'blood samples' and 'blood tests' have the meanings assigned to them by section 25 of the Act;
'direction' means a direction for the use of blood tests under section 20(1) of the Act;
'the court officer' means the officer of the court who draws up a direction.

Rule 2 APPLICATION FOR DIRECTION
(1) Except with the permission of the court, an application in any proceedings for a direction shall be in accordance with CPR Part 23 and a copy of the application notice shall be served on every party to the proceedings (other than the applicant) and to any other person from whom the direction involves the taking of blood samples.
(3) Any notice required by this rule to be served on a person who is not a party to the proceedings shall be served on him personally.

Rule 3 APPLICATIONS INVOLVING CHILDREN UNDER 16 AND PATIENTS
Where an application is made for a direction in respect of a person who is either—
    (a) under 16; or
    (b) suffering from a mental disorder within the meaning of the Mental Health Act 1983 and incapable of understanding the nature and purpose of blood tests,
the application notice shall state the name and address of the person having the care and control of the person under disability and shall be served on him instead of on the person under disability.

Rule 4 ADDITION AS A PARTY OF PERSON TO BE TESTED
Where an application is made for a direction involving the taking of blood samples from a person who is not a party to the proceedings in which the application is made, the court may at any time direct that person to be made a party to the proceedings.

Rule 5 SERVICE OF DIRECTION AND ADJOURNMENT OF PROCEEDINGS
Where the court gives a direction in any proceedings, the court officer shall send a copy to every party to the proceedings and to every other person from whom the direction involves the taking of blood samples and, unless otherwise ordered, further consideration of the proceedings shall be adjourned until the court receives a report pursuant to the direction.

Rule 6 SERVICE OF COPY REPORT
On receipt by the court of a report made pursuant to a direction, the proper officer shall send a copy to every party to the proceedings and to every other person from whom the direction involved the taking of blood samples.

RSC ORDER 113
SUMMARY PROCEEDINGS FOR POSSESSION OF LAND

Rule 1 PROCEEDINGS TO BE BROUGHT BY CLAIM FORM
(1) Where a person claims possession of land which he alleges is occupied solely by a person or persons (not being a tenant or tenants holding over after the

termination of the tenancy) who entered into or remained in occupation without his licence or consent or that of any predecessor in title of his, the proceedings shall be brought by claim form in accordance with the provisions of this order.

(2) Where proceedings of the type referred to in paragraph (1) are brought, the court will fix a day for the hearing when it issues the claim form.

Rule 1A JURISDICTION OF MASTERS

Proceedings under this order may be heard and determined by a Master, who may refer them to a judge if he thinks they should properly be decided by the judge.

Rule 2 FORMS OF CLAIM FORM

(1) The claim form shall be as set out in the relevant practice direction and no acknowledgment of service of it shall be required.

(2) The claim form shall be endorsed with or contain a statement showing whether possession is claimed in respect of residential premises or in respect of other land.

Rule 3 WITNESS STATEMENT OR AFFIDAVIT IN SUPPORT

The claimant shall file in support of the claim form a witness statement or affidavit stating—

    (a) his interest in the land;

    (b) the circumstances in which the land has been occupied without licence or consent and in which his claim to possession arises; and

    (c) that he does not know the name of any person occupying the land who is not named in the claim form;

and, unless the court directs, any such witness statement or affidavit may contain statements of information or belief with the sources and grounds thereof.

Rule 4 SERVICE OF CLAIM FORM

(1) Where any person in occupation of the land is named in the claim form, the claim form together with a copy of the witness statement or affidavit in support shall be served on him—

    (a) personally; or

    (b) by leaving a copy of the claim form and of the witness statement or affidavit or sending them to him, at the premises; or

    (c) in such other manner as the court may direct.

(2) Where any person not named as a defendant is in occupation of the land, the claim form shall be served (whether or not it is also required to be served in accordance with paragraph (1)), unless the court otherwise directs, by—

    (a) affixing a copy of the claim form and a copy of the witness statement or affidavit to the main door or other conspicuous part of the premises and, if practicable, inserting through the letter-box at the premises a copy of the claim form and a copy of the witness statement or affidavit enclosed in a sealed transparent envelope addressed to 'the occupiers'; or

    (b) placing stakes in the ground at conspicuous parts of the occupied land, to each of which shall be affixed a sealed transparent envelope addressed to 'the occupiers' and containing a copy of the claim form and a copy of the witness statement or affidavit.

(2A) Every copy of a claim form for service under paragraph (1) or (2) shall be sealed with the seal of the Office of the Supreme Court out of which the claim form was issued.

Rule 5 APPLICATION BY OCCUPIER TO BE MADE A PARTY

Any person not named as a defendant who is in occupation of the land and wishes to be heard on the question whether an order for possession should be made may apply at any stage of the proceedings to be joined as a defendant.

Rule 6 ORDER FOR POSSESSION

(1) A final order for possession in proceedings under this order shall, except in case of emergency and by permission of the court, not be made—

    (a) in the case of residential premises, less than five clear days after the date of service; and

CPR SCHEDULE 1

(b) in the case of other land, less than two clear days after the date of service.

(2) An order for possession in proceedings under this order shall be in Form No. 42A.

(3) Nothing in this order shall prevent the court from ordering possession to be given on a specified date, in the exercise of any power which could have been exercised if possession had been sought otherwise than in accordance with this Order.

Rule 7 WRIT OF POSSESSION

(1) Order 45, rule 3(2) shall not apply in relation to an order for possession under this order but no writ of possession to enforce such an order shall be issued after the expiry of three months from the date of the order without the permission of the court.

An application for permission may be made without notice being served on any other party unless the court otherwise directs.

(2) The writ of possession shall be in Form No. 66A.

Rule 8 SETTING ASIDE ORDER

The court may, on such terms as it thinks just, set aside or vary any order made in proceedings under this order.

RSC ORDER 114
REFERENCES TO THE EUROPEAN COURT

Rule 1 INTERPRETATION

In this order—

'the court' means the court by which an order is made and includes the Court of Appeal;

'the European Court' means the Court of Justice of the European Communities; and

'order' means an order referring a question to the European Court for a preliminary ruling under article 177 of the Treaty establishing the European Community, article 150 of the Treaty establishing the European Atomic Energy Community or article 41 of the Treaty establishing the European Coal and Steel Community or for a ruling on the interpretation of any of the Brussels Conventions (within the meaning of section 1(1) of the Civil Jurisdiction and Judgments Act 1982) or any of the instruments referred to in section 1 of the Contracts (Applicable Law) Act 1990.

Rule 2 MAKING OF ORDER

(1) An order may be made by the court of its own initiative at any stage in proceedings, or on application by a party before or at the trial or hearing thereof.

(2) Where an application is made before the trial or hearing, it shall be made in accordance with CPR Part 23.

(3) In the High Court no order shall be made except by a judge in person.

Rule 3 SCHEDULE TO ORDER TO SET OUT REQUEST FOR RULING

An order shall set out in a schedule the request for the preliminary ruling of the European Court, and the court may give directions as to the manner and form in which the schedule is to be prepared.

Rule 4 STAY OF PROCEEDINGS PENDING RULING

The proceedings in which an order is made shall, unless the court otherwise orders, be stayed until the European Court has given a preliminary ruling on the question referred to it.

Rule 5 TRANSMISSION OF ORDER TO THE EUROPEAN COURT

When an order has been made, the Senior Master shall send a copy thereof to the Registrar of the European Court; but in the case of an order made by the High Court, he shall not do so, unless the court otherwise orders, until the time for appealing against the order has expired or, if an appeal is entered within that time, until the appeal has been determined or otherwise disposed of.

Rule 6 APPEALS FROM ORDERS MADE BY HIGH COURT
On an appeal to the Court of Appeal from an order made by the High Court the period within which a notice of appeal must be served under Order 59, rule 4(1) shall be 14 days.

RSC ORDER 115
CONFISCATION AND FORFEITURE IN CONNECTION WITH CRIMINAL PROCEEDINGS

I. Drug Trafficking Act 1994 and Criminal Justice (International Co-operation) Act 1990

Rule 1 INTERPRETATION
(1) In this Part of this order, 'The Act' means the Drug Trafficking Act 1994 and a section referred to by number means the section so numbered in the Act.

(2) Expressions used in this Part of this order which are used in the Act have the same meanings in this Part of this order as in the Act and include any extended meaning given by the Criminal Justice (Confiscation) (Northern Ireland) Order 1990.

Rule 2 ASSIGNMENT OF PROCEEDINGS
Subject to rule 12, the jurisdiction of the High Court under the Act shall be exercised by a judge of the Chancery Division or of the Queen's Bench Division.

Rule 2A TITLE OF PROCEEDINGS
An application made in accordance with CPR Part 23, or a claim form issued in relation to proceedings under this Part of this order shall be entitled in the matter of the defendant, naming him, and in the matter of the Act, and all subsequent documents in the matter shall be so entitled.

Rule 2B APPLICATION FOR CONFISCATION ORDER
(1) An application by the prosecutor for a confiscation order under section 19 shall be made in accordance with CPR Part 23 where there have been proceedings against the defendant in the High Court, and shall otherwise be made by the issue of a claim form.

(2) The application shall be supported by a witness statement or affidavit giving full particulars of the following matters—
  (a) the grounds for believing that the defendant has died or absconded;
  (b) the date or approximate date on which the defendant died or absconded;
  (c) where the application is made under section 19(2), the offence or offences of which the defendant was convicted, and the date and place of conviction;
  (d) where the application is made under section 19(4), the proceedings which have been initiated against the defendant (including particulars of the offence and the date and place of institution of those proceedings); and
  (e) where the defendant is alleged to have absconded, the steps taken to contact him.

(3) The prosecutor's statement under section 11 shall be exhibited to the witness statement or affidavit and shall include the following particulars—
  (a) the name of the defendant;
  (b) the name of the person by whom the statement is given;
  (c) such information known to the prosecutor as is relevant to the determination whether the defendant has benefited from drug trafficking and to the assessment of the value of his proceeds of drug trafficking.

(4) Unless the court otherwise orders, a witness statement or affidavit under paragraph (2) may contain statements of information and belief, with their sources and grounds.

(5) The application and the witness statement or affidavit in support shall be served not less than 7 days before the date fixed for the hearing of the application on—

(a) the defendant (or on the personal representatives of a deceased defendant);
(b) any person who the prosecutor reasonably believes is likely to be affected by the making of a confiscation order; and
(c) the receiver, where one has been appointed in the matter.

Rule 3 APPLICATION FOR RESTRAINT ORDER OR CHARGING ORDER

(1) An application for a restraint order under section 26 or for a charging order under section 27 (to either of which may be joined an application for the appointment of a receiver) may be made by the prosecutor by the issue of a claim form notice of which need not be served on any other party.

(2) An application under paragraph (1) shall be supported by a witness statement or affidavit, which shall—
(a) give the grounds for the application; and
(b) to the best of the witness's ability, give full particulars of the realisable property in respect of which the order is sought and specify the person or persons holding such property.

(3) Unless the court otherwise directs, a witness statement or affidavit under paragraph (2) may contain statements of information or belief with the sources and grounds thereof.

Rule 4 RESTRAINT ORDER AND CHARGING ORDER

(1) A restraint order may be made subject to conditions and exceptions, including but not limited to conditions relating to the indemnifying of third parties against expenses incurred in complying with the order, and exceptions relating to living expenses and legal expenses of the defendant, but the prosecutor shall not be required to give an undertaking to abide by any order as to damages sustained by the defendant as a result of the restraint order.

(2) Unless the court otherwise directs, a restraint order made where notice of it has not been served on any person shall have effect until a day which shall be fixed for the hearing where all parties may attend on the application and a charging order shall be an order to show cause, imposing the charge until such day.

(3) Where a restraint order is made the prosecutor shall serve copies of the order and of the witness statement or affidavit in support on the defendant and on all other named persons restrained by the order and shall notify all other persons or bodies affected by the order of its terms.

(4) Where a charging order is made the prosecutor shall serve copies of the order and of the witness statement or affidavit in support on the defendant and, where the property to which the order relates is held by another person, on that person and shall serve a copy of the order on such of the persons or bodies specified in Order 50, rule 2(1)(b) to (d) as shall be appropriate.

Rule 5 DISCHARGE OR VARIATION OF ORDER

(1) Any person or body on whom a restraint order or a charging order is served or who is notified of such an order may make an application in accordance with CPR Part 23 to discharge or vary the order.

(2) The application notice and any witness statement or affidavit in support shall be lodged with the court and served on the prosecutor and, where he is not the applicant, on the defendant, not less than two clear days before the date fixed for the hearing of the application.

(3) Upon the court being notified that proceedings for the offences have been concluded or that the amount, payment of which is secured by a charging order has been paid into court, any restraint order or charging order, as the case may be, shall be discharged.

(4) The court may also discharge a restraint order or a charging order upon receiving notice from the prosecutor that it is no longer appropriate for the restraint order or the charging order to remain in place.

Rule 6 FURTHER APPLICATION BY PROSECUTOR

(1) Where a restraint order or a charging order has been made the prosecutor may apply by an application in accordance with CPR Part 23 with notice or, where

the case is one of urgency or the giving of notice would cause a reasonable apprehension of dissipation of assets, without notice—
    (a) to vary such order; or
    (b) for a restraint order or a charging order in respect of other realisable property; or
    (c) for the appointment of a receiver.
(2) An application under paragraph (1) shall be supported by a witness statement or affidavit which, where the application is for a restraint order or a charging order, shall to the best of the witness's ability give full particulars of the realisable property in respect of which the order is sought and specify the person or persons holding such property.
(3) The application and witness statement or affidavit in support shall be lodged with the court and served on the defendant and, where one has been appointed in the matter, on the receiver, not less than two clear days before the date fixed for the hearing of the application.
(4) Rule 4(3) and (4) shall apply to the service of restraint orders and charging orders respectively made under this rule on persons other than the defendant.

Rule 7 REALISATION OF PROPERTY
(1) An application by the prosecutor under section 29 shall, where there have been proceedings against the defendant in the High Court, be made by an application in accordance with CPR Part 23 and shall otherwise be made by the issue of a claim form
(2) The application notice or claim form, as the case may be, shall be served with the evidence in support not less than 7 days before the date fixed for the hearing of the application or claim on—
    (a) the defendant;
    (b) any person holding any interest in the realisable property to which the application relates; and
    (c) the receiver, where one has been appointed in the matter.
(3) The application shall be supported by a witness statement or affidavit, which shall, to the best of the witness's ability, give full particulars of the realisable property to which it relates and specify the person or persons holding such property, and a copy of the confiscation order, of any certificate issued by the Crown Court under section 5(2) and of any charging order made in the matter shall be exhibited to such witness statement or affidavit.
(4) The Court may, on an application under section 29—
    (a) exercise the power conferred by section 30(2) to direct the making of payments by a receiver;
    (b) give directions in respect of the property interests to which the application relates; and
    (c) make declarations in respect of those interests.

Rule 8 RECEIVERS
(1) Subject to the provisions of this rule, the provisions of Order 30, rules 2 to 8 shall apply where a receiver is appointed in pursuance of a charging order or under sections 26 or 29.
(2) Where the receiver proposed to be appointed has been appointed receiver in other proceedings under the Act, it shall not be necessary for a witness statement or affidavit of fitness to be sworn or for the receiver to give security, unless the court otherwise orders.
(3) Where a receiver has fully paid the amount payable under the confiscation order and any sums remain in his hands, he shall make an application to the court for directions in accordance with CPR Part 23, as to the distribution of such sums.
(4) An application under paragraph (3) shall be served with any evidence in support not less than 7 days before the date fixed for the hearing of the application on—
    (a) the defendant; and
    (b) any other person who held property realised by the receiver.

(5) A receiver may apply for an order to discharge him from his office by making an application in accordance with CPR Part 23, which shall be served, together with any evidence in support, on all persons affected by his appointment not less than 7 days before the day fixed for the hearing of the application.

Rule 9 CERTIFICATE OF INADEQUACY

(1) The defendant or a receiver appointed under section 26 or 29 or in pursuance of a charging order may apply in accordance with CPR Part 23 for a certificate under section 17(1).

(2) An application under paragraph (1) shall be served with any supporting evidence not less than 7 days before the date fixed for the hearing of the application on the prosecutor and, as the case may be, on either the defendant or the receiver (where one has been appointed).

Rule 9A CERTIFICATE UNDER SECTION 16

An application under section 16(2) (increase in realisable property) shall be served with any supporting evidence not less than 7 days before the date fixed for the hearing of the application on the defendant and, as the case may be, on either the prosecutor or (where one has been appointed in the matter) on the receiver.

Rule 10 COMPENSATION

An application for an order under section 18 shall be made in accordance with CPR Part 23, which shall be served, with any supporting evidence, on the person alleged to be in default and on the relevant authority under section 18(5) not less than 7 days before the date fixed for the hearing of the application.

Rule 11 DISCLOSURE OF INFORMATION

(1) An application by the prosecutor under section 59 shall be made in accordance with CPR Part 23 and the application notice shall state the nature of the order sought and whether material sought to be disclosed is to be disclosed to a receiver appointed under section 26 or 29 or in pursuance of a charging order or to a person mentioned in section 59(8).

(2) The application notice and witness statement or affidavit in support shall be served on the authorised Government Department in accordance with Order 77, rule 4 not less than 7 days before the date fixed for the hearing of the application.

(3) The witness statement or affidavit in support of an application under paragraph (1) shall state the grounds for believing that the conditions in section 59(4) and, if appropriate, section 59(7) are fulfilled.

Rule 11A COMPENSATION FOR, DISCHARGE AND VARIATION OF CONFISCATION ORDER

(1) An application under section 21, 22 or 23 shall be made in accordance with CPR Part 23 which, together with any evidence in support, shall be lodged with the court and served on the prosecutor not less than 7 days before the day fixed for the hearing of the application.

(2) Notice shall also be served on any receiver appointed in pursuance of a charging order or under section 26 or 29.

(3) An application for an order under section 22 shall be supported by a witness statement or affidavit giving details of—
    (a) the confiscation order made under section 19(4);
    (b) the acquittal of the defendant;
    (c) the realisable property held by the defendant; and
    (d) the loss suffered by the applicant as a result of the confiscation order.

(4) An application for an order under section 23 shall be supported by a witness statement or affidavit giving details of—
    (a) the confiscation order made under section 19(4);
    (b) the date on which the defendant ceased to be an absconder;
    (c) the date on which proceedings against the defendant were instituted and a summary of the steps taken in the proceedings since then; and

(d) any indication given by the prosecutor that he does not intend to proceed against the defendant.

(5) An application made under section 21 shall be supported by a witness statement or affidavit giving details of—
    (a) the confiscation order made under section 19(4);
    (b) the circumstances in which the defendant ceased to be an absconder; and
    (c) the amounts referred to in section 21(2).

(6) Where an application is made for an order under section 23(3) or 24(2)(b), the witness statement or affidavit shall also include—
    (a) details of the realisable property to which the application relates; and
    (b) details of the loss suffered by the applicant as a result of the confiscation order.

(7) Unless the court otherwise orders, a witness statement or affidavit under paragraphs (3) to (6) may contain statements of information and belief, with the sources and grounds thereof.

Rule 12 EXERCISE OF POWERS UNDER SECTIONS 37 AND 40

The powers conferred on the High Court by sections 37 and 40 may be exercised by a judge or a Master of the Queen's Bench Division.

Rule 13 APPLICATION FOR REGISTRATION

An application for registration of an order specified in an Order in Council made under section 37 or of an external confiscation order under section 40(1) must be made in accordance with CPR Part 23, and may be made without notice.

Rule 14 EVIDENCE IN SUPPORT OF APPLICATION UNDER SECTION 37

An application for registration of an order specified in an Order in Council made under section 37 must be made in accordance with CPR Part 23, and be supported by a witness statement or affidavit—
    (i) exhibiting the order or a certified copy thereof; and
    (ii) stating, to the best of the witness's knowledge, particulars of what property the person against whom the order was made holds in England and Wales, giving the source of the witness's knowledge.

Rule 15 EVIDENCE IN SUPPORT OF APPLICATION UNDER SECTION 40(1)

(1) An application for registration of an external confiscation order must be made in accordance with CPR Part 23, and be supported by a witness statement or affidavit—
    (a) exhibiting the order or a verified or certified or otherwise duly authenticated copy thereof and, where the order is not in the English language, a translation thereof into English certified by a notary public or authenticated by witness statement or affidavit; and
    (b) stating—
        (i) that the order is in force and is not subject to appeal;
        (ii) where the person against whom the order was made did not appear in the proceedings, that he received notice thereof in sufficient time to enable him to defend them;
        (iii) in the case of money, either that at the date of the application the sum payable under the order has not been paid or the amount which remains unpaid, as may be appropriate, or, in the case of other property, the property which has not been recovered; and
        (iv) to the best of the witness's knowledge, particulars of what property the person against whom the order was made holds in England and Wales, giving the source of the witness's knowledge.

(2) Unless the court otherwise directs, a witness statement or affidavit for the purposes of this rule may contain statements of information or belief with the sources and grounds thereof.

Rule 16 REGISTER OF ORDERS

(1) There shall be kept in the Central Office under the direction of the Master of the Crown Office a register of the orders registered under the Act.

(2) There shall be included in such register particulars of any variation or setting aside of a registration and of any execution issued on a registered order.

Rule 17 NOTICE OF REGISTRATION
(1) Notice of the registration of an order must be served on the person against whom it was obtained by delivering it to him personally or by sending it to him at his usual or last known address or place of business or in such other manner as the court may direct.
(2) Service of such a notice out of the jurisdiction is permissible without leave, and Order 11, rules 5, 6 and 8 shall apply in relation to such a notice as they apply in relation to a claim form.

Rule 18 APPLICATION TO VARY OR SET ASIDE REGISTRATION
An application made in accordance with CPR Part 23 by the person against whom an order was made to vary or set aside the registration of an order must be made to a judge and be supported by witness statement or affidavit.

Rule 19 ENFORCEMENT OF ORDER
(2) If an application is made under rule 18, an order shall not be enforced until after such application is determined.

Rule 20 VARIATION, SATISFACTION AND DISCHARGE OF REGISTERED ORDER
Upon the court being notified by the applicant for registration that an order which has been registered has been varied, satisfied or discharged, particulars of the variation, satisfaction or discharge, as the case may be, shall be entered in the register.

Rule 21 RULES TO HAVE EFFECT SUBJECT TO ORDERS IN COUNCIL
Rules 12 to 20 shall have effect subject to the provisions of the Order in Council made under section 37 or, as the case may be, of the Order in Council made under section 39.

Rule 21A CRIMINAL JUSTICE (INTERNATIONAL CO-OPERATION) ACT 1990: EXTERNAL FORFEITURE ORDERS
The provisions of this Part of this order shall, with such modifications as are necessary and subject to the provisions of any Order in Council made under section 9 of the Criminal Justice (International Co-operation) Act 1990, apply to proceedings for the registration and enforcement of external forfeiture orders as they apply to such proceedings in relation to external confiscation orders.

For the purposes of this rule, an external forfeiture order is an order made by a court in a country or territory outside the United Kingdom which is enforceable in the United Kingdom by virtue of any such Order in Council.

II. Part VI of the Criminal Justice Act 1988

Rule 22 INTERPRETATION
(1) In this Part of this order, 'the 1988 Act' means the Criminal Justice Act 1988 and a section referred to by number means the section so numbered in that Act.
(2) Expressions which are used in this Part of this order which are used in the 1988 Act have the same meanings in this Part of this order as in the 1988 Act and include any extended meaning given by the Criminal Justice (Confiscation) (Northern Ireland) Order 1990.

Rule 23 APPLICATION OF PART I OF ORDER 115
Part I of Order 115 (except rule 11) shall apply for the purposes of proceedings under Part VI of the 1988 Act with the necessary modifications and, in particular—
(a) references to drug trafficking offences and to drug trafficking shall be construed as references to offences to which Part VI of the 1988 Act applies and to committing such an offence;
(b) references to the Drug Trafficking Act 1994 shall be construed as references to the 1988 Act and references to sections 5(2), 26, 27, 29, 30(2), 17(1),

18, 18(5), 39 and 40 of the 1994 Act shall be construed as references to sections 73(6), 77, 78, 80, 81, 81(1), 83(1), 89, 89(5), 96 and 97 of the 1988 Act respectively;

    (c) rule 3(2) shall have effect as if the following sub-paragraphs were substituted for sub-paragraphs (a) and (b)—

        '(a) state, as the case may be, either that proceedings have been instituted against the defendant for an offence to which Part VI of the 1988 Act applies (giving particulars of the offence) and that they have not been concluded or that, whether by the laying of an information or otherwise, a person is to be charged with such an offence;

        (b) state, as the case may be, either that a confiscation order has been made or the grounds for believing that such an order may be made;'

    (d) rule 7(3) shall have effect as if the words 'certificate issued by a magistrates' court or the Crown Court' were substituted for the words 'certificate issued by the Crown Court';

    (e) rule 8 shall have effect as if the following paragraph were added at the end—

        '(6) Where a receiver applies in accordance with CPR Part 23 for the variation of a confiscation order, the application notice shall be served, with any supporting evidence, on the defendant and any other person who may be affected by the making of an order under section 83 of the 1988 Act, not less than 7 days before the date fixed for the hearing of the application.';

    (f) rule 11 shall apply with the necessary modifications where an application is made under section 93J of the 1988 Act for disclosure of information held by government departments.

III: Prevention of Terrorism (Temporary Provisions) Act 1989

Rule 24 INTERPRETATION

In this Part of this order—

    (a) 'the Act' means the Prevention of Terrorism (Temporary Provisions) Act 1989;

    (b) 'Schedule 4' means Schedule 4 to the Act; and

    (c) expressions used have the same meanings as they have in Part III of, and Schedule 4 to, the Act.

Rule 25 ASSIGNMENT OF PROCEEDINGS

(1) Subject to paragraph (2), the jurisdiction of the High Court under the Act shall be exercised by a judge of the Queen's Bench Division or of the Chancery Division sitting in private.

(2) The jurisdiction conferred on the High Court by paragraph 9 of Schedule 4 may also be exercised by a Master of the Queen's Bench Division.

Rule 26 APPLICATION FOR RESTRAINT ORDER

(1) An application for a restraint order under paragraphs 3 and 4 of Schedule 4 may be made by the prosecutor by a claim form, which need not be served on any person.

(2) An application under paragraph (1) shall be supported by a witness statement or affidavit, which shall—

    (a) state, as the case may be, either that proceedings have been instituted against a person for an offence under Part III of the Act and that they have not been concluded or that, whether by the laying of an information or otherwise, a person is to be charged with such an offence; and, in either case, give particulars of the offence;

    (b) state, as the case may be, that a forfeiture order has been made in the proceedings or the grounds for believing that such an order may be made;

    (c) to the best of the witness's ability, give full particulars of the property in respect of which the order is sought and specify the person or persons holding such property and any other persons having an interest in it;

    (d) where proceedings have not been instituted, verify that the prosecutor is to have the conduct of the proposed proceedings;

(e) where proceedings have not been instituted, indicate when it is intended that they should be instituted.

(3) A claim form under paragraph (1) shall be entitled in the matter of the defendant, naming him, and in the matter of the Act, and all subsequent documents in the matter shall be so entitled.

(4) Unless the court otherwise directs, a witness statement or affidavit under paragraph (2) may contain statements of information or belief with the sources and grounds thereof.

Rule 27 RESTRAINT ORDER

(1) A restraint order may be made subject to conditions and exceptions, including but not limited to conditions relating to the indemnifying of third parties against expenses incurred in complying with the order, and exceptions relating to living expenses and legal expenses of the defendant; but the prosecutor shall not be required to give an undertaking to abide by any order as to damages sustained by the defendant as a result of the restraint order.

(2) Unless the court otherwise directs, a restraint order made without notice of it being served on any person shall have effect until a day which shall be fixed for the hearing where all parties may attend on the application.

(3) Where a restraint order is made the prosecutor shall serve copies of the order and of the witness statement or affidavit in support on the defendant and on all other persons affected by the order.

Rule 28 DISCHARGE OR VARIATION OF ORDER

(1) Subject to paragraph (2), an application to discharge or vary a restraint order shall be made in accordance with CPR Part 23.

(2) Where the case is one of urgency, an application under this rule by the prosecutor may be made without notice.

(3) The application and any witness statement or affidavit in support shall be lodged with the court and, where the application is made in accordance with CPR Part 23 the application notice shall be served on the following persons (other than the applicant)—

    (a) the prosecutor;
    (b) the defendant; and
    (c) all other persons restrained or otherwise affected by the order;

not less than two clear days before the date fixed for the hearing of the application.

(4) Where a restraint order has been made and has not been discharged, the prosecutor shall notify the court when proceedings for the offence have been concluded, and the court shall thereupon discharge the restraint order.

(5) Where an order is made discharging or varying a restraint order, the applicant shall serve copies of the order of discharge or variation on all persons restrained by the earlier order and shall notify all other persons affected of the terms of the order of discharge or variation.

Rule 29 COMPENSATION

An application for an order under paragraph 7 of Schedule 4 shall be made in accordance with CPR Part 23, and the application notice, shall be served, with any supporting evidence, on the person alleged to be in default and on the relevant authority under paragraph 7(5) not less than 7 days before the date fixed for the hearing of the application.

Rule 30 APPLICATION FOR REGISTRATION

An application for registration of a Scottish order, a Northern Ireland order or an Islands order must be made in accordance with CPR Part 23 and may be made without notice.

Rule 31 EVIDENCE IN SUPPORT OF APPLICATION

(1) An application for registration of any such order as is mentioned in rule 30 must be supported by a witness statement or affidavit—

    (a) exhibiting the order or a certified copy thereof; and

(b) which shall, to the best of the witness's ability, give particulars of such property in respect of which the order was made as is in England and Wales, and specify the person or persons holding such property.

(2) Unless the court otherwise directs, a witness statement or affidavit for the purposes of this rule may contain statements of information or belief with the sources and grounds thereof.

Rule 32 REGISTER OF ORDERS

(1) There shall be kept in the Central Office under the direction of the Master of the Crown Office a register of the orders registered under the Act.

(2) There shall be included in such register particulars of any variation or setting aside of a registration, and of any execution issued on a registered order.

Rule 33 NOTICE OF REGISTRATION

(1) Notice of the registration of an order must be served on the person or persons holding the property referred to in rule 3 1 (1)(b) and any other persons appearing to have an interest in that property.

(2) Service of such a notice out of the jurisdiction is permissible without leave, and Order 11, rules 5, 6 and 8 shall apply in relation to such a notice as they apply in relation to a claim form.

Rule 34 APPLICATION TO VARY OR SET ASIDE REGISTRATION

An application to vary or set aside the registration of an order must be made to a judge in accordance with CPR Part 23 and be supported by a witness statement or affidavit.

This rule does not apply to a variation or cancellation under rule 36.

Rule 35 ENFORCEMENT OF ORDER

(2) If an application is made under rule 34, an order shall not be enforced until after such application is determined.

(3) This rule does not apply to the taking of steps under paragraph 5 or 6 of Schedule 4, as applied by paragraph 9(6) of that Schedule.

Rule 36 VARIATION AND CANCELLATION OF REGISTRATION

If effect has been given (whether in England or Wales or elsewhere) to a Scottish, Northern Ireland or Islands order, or if the order has been varied or discharged by the court by which it was made, the applicant for registration shall inform the court and—

(a) if such effect has been given in respect of all the money or other property to which the order applies, or if the order has been discharged by the court by which it was made, registration of the order shall be cancelled;

(b) if such effect has been given in respect of only part of the money or other property, or if the order has been varied by the court by which it was made, registration of the order shall be varied accordingly.

RSC ORDER 116
THE CRIMINAL PROCEDURE AND INVESTIGATIONS ACT 1996

Rule 1 APPLICATION

This Order shall apply in relation to acquittals in respect of offences alleged to be committed on or after 15th April 1997.

Rule 2 INTERPRETATION

In this Order, unless the context otherwise requires—

'the Act' means the Criminal Procedure and Investigations Act 1996;

'acquitted person' means a person whose acquittal of an offence is the subject of a certification under section 54(2) of the Act, and 'acquittal' means the acquittal of that person of that offence;

'magistrates' court' has the same meaning as in section 148 of the Magistrates' Courts Act 1980;

'prosecutor' means the individual or body which acted as prosecutor in the proceedings which led to the acquittal;

'record of court proceedings' means—
    (a) (where the proceedings took place in the Crown Court) a transcript of the evidence, or
    (b) a note of the evidence made by the justices' clerk,
in the proceedings which led to the conviction for the administration of justice offence referred to in section 54(1)(b) of the Act or, as the case may be, the proceedings which led to the acquittal;
    'single judge' means a judge of the Queen's Bench Division;
    'witness' means a witness whose evidence is contained in a witness statement or affidavit filed under rule 5, 7, 8 or 9.

Rule 3 ASSIGNMENT OF PROCEEDINGS
The jurisdiction of the High Court under section 54(3) of the Act shall be exercised by a single judge.

Rule 4 TIME LIMIT FOR MAKING APPLICATION
An application under section 54(3) of the Act shall be made not later than 28 days after—
    (a) the expiry of the period allowed for appealing (whether by case stated or otherwise), or making an application for leave to appeal, against the conviction referred to in section 54(1)(b) of the Act; or
    (b) where notice of appeal or application for leave to appeal against the conviction is given, the determination of the appeal or application for leave to appeal and, for this purpose, 'determination' includes abandonment (within the meaning of rule 10 of the Criminal Appeal Rules 1968 or, as the case may be, rule 11 of the Crown Court Rules 1982).

Rule 5 APPLICATION
(1) An application under section 54(3) of the Act shall be made by claim form which shall be issued out of the Crown Office by the prosecutor.
(2) The application shall be accompanied by—
    (a) a witness statement or affidavit which deals with the conditions in section 55(1), (2) and (4) of the Act and which exhibits any relevant documents (which may include a copy of any record of court proceedings);
    (b) a copy of the certification under section 54(2) of the Act.

Rule 6 NOTICE TO THE ACQUITTED PERSON
(1) The prosecutor shall, within 4 days of the issue of the application, serve written notice on the acquitted person that the application has been issued.
(2) The notice given under paragraph (1) shall—
    (a) specify the date on which the application was issued;
    (b) be accompanied by a copy of the application and of the documents which accompanied it;
    (c) inform the acquitted person that—
        (i) the result of the application may be the making of an order by the High Court quashing the acquittal, and
        (ii) if he wishes to respond to the application, he must, within 28 days of the date of service on him of the notice, file in the Crown Office any witness statement or affidavit on which he intends to rely.

Rule 7 WITNESS STATEMENT OR AFFIDAVIT OF SERVICE ON AN ACQUITTED PERSON
The prosecutor shall, as soon as practicable after service of the notice under rule 6, file at the Crown Office a witness statement or affidavit of service which exhibits a copy of the notice.

Rule 8 RESPONSE OF ACQUITTED PERSON
(1) If the acquitted person wishes to respond to the application, he shall, within 28 days of service on him of notice under rule 6, file in the Crown Office a witness statement or affidavit which—

(a) deals with the conditions in section 55(1), (2) and (4) of the Act; and
(b) exhibits any relevant documents (which may include a copy of any record of court proceedings).
(2) The acquitted person shall, within 4 days of the filing of the documents mentioned in paragraph (1), serve copies of them on the prosecutor.

Rule 9 EVIDENCE

(1) A witness statement or affidavit filed under rule 5, 7, 8 or this rule may contain statements of information or belief with the sources and grounds thereof.
(2) The prosecutor may, not later than 10 days after expiry of the period allowed under rule 8(1), apply for an order granting permission to file further evidence without notice being served on any other party.
(3) If the single judge grants permission, the order shall specify a period within which further evidence or records are to be filed, and the Crown Office shall serve a copy of the order on the prosecutor and on the acquitted person.
(4) The prosecutor shall, within 4 days of filing further evidence in the Crown Office, serve a copy of that evidence on the acquitted person.

Rule 10 DETERMINATION OF THE APPLICATION

(1) Subject to paragraph (3), the single judge shall determine whether or not to make an order under section 54(3) of the Act on the basis of the written material provided under rules 5, 7, 8 and 9 in the absence of the prosecutor, the acquitted person, or of any witness.
(2) The determination shall not be made, and any hearing under paragraph (3) shall not take place, before the expiry of—
(a) 10 days after the expiry of the period allowed under rule 8(1), or
(b) 10 days after the expiry of the period allowed by any order made under rule 9(3).
(3) The single judge may, of his own initative or on the application of the prosecutor or acquitted person, order a hearing of the application if he thinks fit.
(4) An application under paragraph (3) shall state whether a hearing is desired in order for a deponent for the other party to attend and be cross-examined, and, if so, the reasons for wishing the witness to attend.
(5) An application under paragraph (3) shall be made no later than 7 days after the expiry of the period allowed—
(a) under rule 8(1), or
(b) by any order made under rule 9(3).
(6) Where a hearing is ordered, the single judge may, of his own initiative or on the application of the prosecutor or acquitted person, order a witness to attend in order to be cross-examined.
(7) The prosecutor or the acquitted person, as the case may be, shall within 4 days after filing the application under paragraph (3), serve a copy of it on the other party, and file in the Crown Office a witness statement or affidavit of service.
(8) A party served under paragraph (7) shall, within 5 days of service, file any representations he wishes to make as to whether or not a hearing should be ordered.
(9) Subject to paragraph (10) below—
(a) the single judge shall not determine an application for a hearing under paragraph (3) unless—
(i) a witness statement or affidavit of service has been filed as required by paragraph (7), and
(ii) the period for filing representations allowed under paragraph (8) has elapsed, or
(iii) representations have been filed under paragraph (8).
(b) The requirements imposed by sub-paragraph (a)(i) and (iii) are satisfied even though the witness statement or affidavit of service or, as the case may be, the representations are filed outside the time limits allowed.
(10) Where after an application for a hearing has been made—
(a) no witness statement or affidavit or service has been filed, and

(b) no representations under paragraph (8) have been received after the expiry of 7 days from the filing of the application,
the single judge may reject the application.

(11) Where after a hearing is ordered, either the prosecutor or the acquitted person desires a witness for the other party to attend the hearing in order to be cross-examined, he must apply for an order under paragraph (5) giving his reasons without notice being served on any other party.

(12) The Crown Office shall serve notice on the prosecutor and the acquitted person of any order made under the foregoing paragraphs of this rule and, where a hearing is ordered, the notice shall—

(a) set out the date, time and place of the hearing, and
(b) give details of any witness ordered to attend for cross-examination.

(13) A hearing ordered under paragraph (3) above shall be in public unless the single judge otherwise directs.

(14) The Crown Office shall serve notice of any order made under section 54(3) of the Act quashing the acquittal or of a decision not to make such an order on the prosecutor, the acquitted person and—

(a) where the court before which the acquittal or conviction occurred was a magistrates' court, on the justices' clerk;

(b) where the court before which the acquittal or conviction occurred was the Crown Court, on the appropriate officer of the Crown Court sitting at the place where the acquittal or conviction occurred.

PD RSC ORD. 11 PRACTICE DIRECTION — SERVICE OUT OF THE JURISDICTION

This practice direction supplements RSC Order 11 (Schedule 1 to the CPR)

MATTERS TO BE INCLUDED IN CLAIM FORMS

1.1 CPR Part 7 provides that when particulars of claim are served on a defendant they must be accompanied by:
(a) a form for defending the claim;
(b) a form for admitting the claim; and
(c) a form for acknowledging service.

1.2 In addition, the particulars of claim must be accompanied by the complete Response Pack. The Response Pack must clearly state the appropriate period for responding to the claim form, as specified in this Practice Direction, and accordingly both Form N9 and Form N1C and other relevant forms must be amended.

1.3 Where the claim form is to be served in a place or country listed in the table below in accordance with paragraph 6.4, the particulars of claim, if not included in it, must accompany the claim form.

1.4 Where a claim form is served out of the jurisdiction without permission under Schedule 1, RSC O.11 r. 1(2), it must include a certificate that the court has power under the Civil Jurisdiction and Judgments Act 1982 to hear the claim, and that no proceedings involving the same issues are pending between the parties in the courts of any part of the United Kingdom or any other Convention territory as specified in RSC O.11, r. 1(2)(a)(i).

1.5 The usual form of words of the certificate will be:

'We certify that the High Court of England and Wales has power under the Civil Jurisdiction and Judgments Act 1982 to hear this claim and that no proceedings are pending between the parties in Scotland, Northern Ireland or another Convention territory of any contracting state as defined by section 1(3) of the Act.'

1.6 The usual form of words of the certificate where the proceedings begun by the claim form are proccedings to which Article 16 of Schedule 1, 3C or 4 to that Act refers will be:

'We certify that the High Court of England and Wales has power under the Civil Jurisdiction and Judgments Act 1982, the claim having as its object rights in rem in immovable property or tenancies in immovable property (or otherwise in accordance with the provisions of Article 16 of Schedule 1, 3C or 4 to that Act) to which Article 16 of Schedule 1, 3C or 4 to that Act applies, to hear the claim and that no proceedings are pending between the parties in Scotland, Northern Ireland or another Convention territory of any contracting state as defined by Section 1(3) of the Act.'

1.7 The usual form of words of the certificate where the defendant is a party to an agreement conferring jurisdiction to which Article 17 of Schedule 1, 3C or 4 to that Act applies will be:

'We certify that the High Court of England and Wales has power under the Civil Jurisdiction and Judgments Act 1982, the defendant being a party to an agreement conferring jurisdiction to which Article 17 of Schedule 1, 3C or 4 to that Act applies, to hear the claim and that no proceedings are pending between the parties in Scotland, Northern Ireland or another Convention territory of any contracting state as defined by Section 1(3) of the Act.'

1.8 If a certificate under paragraph 1.4 is omitted, the issued claim form will be marked, 'Not for service out of the jurisdiction.'

DOCUMENTS TO BE FILED

2.1 The claimant must file the following documents for each person to be served:

(1) a request for service of the claim form by one of the methods under O. 11, rr. 5 and 6 or for service:
   (a) under any order for service by an alternative method,
   (b) in accordance with the law of the country in which service is to be effected,
   (c) in a country which is a party to the Hague Convention of 1965 on the Service Abroad of Judicial and Extrajudicial Documents in Civil and Commercial Matters[1] in accordance with the provisions of that Convention,
   (d) in a country in respect of which there subsists a civil procedure convention (other than the Hague Convention) in accordance with the provisions of such a convention,
(2) a sealed original of the claim form and accompanying documents,
(3) a duplicate copy of the claim form and accompanying documents,
(4) copies of the particulars of claim (see paragraph 1.3 above),
(5) the response pack amended as necessary (see paragraph 1.2 above),
(6) any translation required under RSC Order 11 rule 6(5) and paragraph 3.3, in duplicate;
and
(7) a statement by the person making any translation that it is a correct translation, as required by RSC Order 11, rule 6(6), in duplicate.

2.2 (1) Care should be taken to ensure that the method of service requested under paragraph 2.1(1) is a method recognised in the country in which service is to be effected.
  (2) Service in the countries listed in RSC O. 11, r. 6(1) should be effected by the claimant or his agent direct.

2.3 The request for service must include an undertaking under RSC Order 11, rule 8 by the person making the request:
  (1) to be responsible for all expenses incurred by the Foreign and Commonwealth Office, and
  (2) to pay those expenses to the Foreign and Commonwealth Office on being informed of the amount.

2.4 RSC Order 11 rule 7(1) sets out the documents to be filed where a claimant wishes to serve the claim form on a State. The additional documents listed in paragraph 2.1 must also be filed in such cases.

2.5 Where the claimant files the documents specified, he must obtain a sealed copy and an ordinary copy and take them to the Foreign Process Office.

2.6 In certain countries the documents filed will require legalisation. The Foreign Process Office (Rm. E219, The Royal Courts of Justice) will advise as to particular cases.

TRANSLATIONS

3.1 RSC Order 11 rule 6(5) provides that, except in certain specified instances (see paragraph 3.4 below), every copy of the claim form filed under RSC Order 11 rule 6 (service through judicial authorities, foreign governments and British Consular authorities) or RSC Order 11 rule 7 (service of claim form on a State), must be accompanied by a translation of the claim form.

3.2 RSC O. 11 r. 6(5) and (6) apply to particulars of claim where they are not included in the claim form.

3.3 Where a translation of the claim form is required under RSC O. 11 r. 6(5), the claimant must also file a translation of the forms in the Response Pack.

3.4 Unless made necessary by the particular circumstances of the case, translations are not required where the claim form is to be served:
  (1) in a country where English is an official language (Rule 6(5));
  (2) by a British consular authority on a British subject, unless a Civil Procedure Convention expressly requires a translation (Rule 6(5));
  (3) on a State in which English is an official language (Rule 7(1)(c)).
(It should be noted that English is not an official language in the Province of Quebec.)

---

[1] November 15, 1965; TS50 (1969); Cmnd. 3986

SERVICE WITH THE PERMISSION OF THE COURT UNDER CERTAIN ACTS

4.1 RSC Order 11, rule 1 provides that a claim form may be served out of the jurisdiction with the court's permission if the claim is made under certain specified enactments.

4.2 These are:

(1) claims under the Nuclear Installations Act 1965[2],

(2) claims in respect of contributions under the Social Security Contributions and Benefits Act 1992[3],

(3) claims for a sum to which the Directive of the Council of the European Communities dated 15 March 1976 No. 76/308/EEC applies, where service is to be effected in a member state of the European Economic Community,

(4) claims under the Drug Trafficking Offences Act 1994[4],

(5) claims under the Financial Services Act 1986[5],

(6) claims under the Banking Act 1987[6],

(7) claims under Part VI of the Criminal Justice Act 1988[7], and

(8) claims under the Immigration (Carriers' Liability) Act 1987[8].

SERVICE OF OTHER DOCUMENTS:

5.1 RSC Order 11, r. 1(2) (service without the court's permission) and RSC Order 11, rule 1(1) (service with the court's permission) apply to service out of the jurisdiction of a petition, application notice or order as they apply to service of a claim form.

5.2 Applications to which this paragraph applies include applications made under CPR Rule 23.2(4) before a claim has been started; for example

(1) applications made under CPR Rule 25.4(1)(b) for order for disclosure, inspection etc, before a claim has been made, or

(2) orders for disclosure under CPR Rule 31.16 before proceedings have started.

5.3 RSC Order 11, rule 4 applies where appropriate to an application for permission to serve documents under this paragraph.

5.4 RSC Order 11, rules 5–9 apply to any document for which permission has been granted under this paragraph as they apply to a claim form.

5.5 Paragraphs 6, 7 and 8 of this Practice Direction apply as appropriate to response to service of any other document as they apply to response to service of a claim form.

PERIOD FOR RESPONDING TO A CLAIM FORM

6.1 Where the permission of the court is required, under RSC Order 11, rule 4, for a claim form to be served out of the jurisdiction, Rule 4(4) requires the order granting permission to specify the period within which the defendant may respond to the claim form.

6.2 RSC Order 11, rule 1A sets out period for filing an acknowledgment of service or filing or serving an admission where a claim form has been served out of the jurisdiction without permission under rule 1(2).

6.3 RSC Order 11, rule 1B sets out the period for filing a defence where a claim form has been served out of the jurisdiction without permission under Rule 1(2).

6.4 The table below specifies the periods for responding to a claim form which has been served out of the jurisdiction without permission—

(1) Under RSC Order 11, rule 1(2) in a country not covered by rule 1A(2)or (3); or

---

[2] 1965 c.57
[3] 1992 c.4
[4] 1994 c.37
[5] 1986 c.60
[6] 1987 c.22
[7] 1988 c.33
[8] 1987 c.24

(2) Under rule 1(2)(a).

6.5 Where an order grants permission to serve a claim form out of the jurisdiction under RSC Order 11, rule 1(1), the periods within which the defendant may:

(1) file an acknowledgment of service in accordance with CPR Part 10,
(2) file or serve an admission in accordance with CPR Part 14, and
(3) file a defence in accordance with CPR Part 15,

which, in accordance with RSC Order 11, rule 4(4), are required to be specified in the order will be calculated having regard to the table below.

PERIOD FOR FILING ACKNOWLEDGMENT OF SERVICE OR FILING OR SERVING AN ADMISSION

7.1 This paragraph sets out the period for filing an acknowledgment of service under CPR Part 10 or filing or serving an admission under CPR Part 14 where a claim form has been served in a place or country listed in the table.

7.2 The period for filing an acknowledgment of service or filing or serving an admission is the number of days listed in the table after service of the claim form.

7.3 For example, where a defendant has been served with a claim form in the Bahamas, the period for acknowledging service or admitting the claim is 22 days after service.

PERIOD FOR FILING A DEFENCE

8.1 This paragraph sets out the period for filing a defence under CPR Part 15 where a claim form has been served in a place or country listed in the table.

8.2 The period for filing a defence is (1) the number of days listed in the table after service of the claim form, or (2) where the defendant has filed an acknowledgment of service, the number of days listed in the table plus an additional 14 days after service of the claim form.

8.3 For example, where a defendant has been served with a claim form in Gibraltar and has acknowledged service, the period for filing a defence is 45 days after service of the claim form.

ADDRESS FOR SERVICE

9. CPR rule 6.5(2) provides that a party must give an address for service within the jurisdiction.

SERVICE OF APPLICATION NOTICE

10.1 Where an application notice or order needs to be served out of the jurisdiction, the period for responding to service is 7 days less than the number of days listed in the table.

10.2 When applying for a date for a hearing adequate time must be allowed for service of the response to the application notice or order.

FURTHER INFORMATION

11.1 For further information concerning service out of the jurisdiction contact the Foreign Process Office (Rm. E219, The Royal Courts of Justice).

TABLE

Place or country	number of days
Abu Dhabi	22
Afghanistan	23
Albania	25
Algeria	22
Angola	22
Anguilla	31
Antigua	23
Antilles (Netherlands)	31
Argentina	22
Armenia	21

PD RSC ORD. 11 PRACTICE DIRECTION — SERVICE OUT OF THE JURISDICTION

Place or country	number of days
Ascension	31
Australia	25
Austria	21
Azores	23
Bahamas	22
Bahrain	22
Balearic Islands	21
Bangladesh	23
Barbados	23
Belarus	21
Belgium	21
Belize	23
Benin	25
Bermuda	31
Bhutan	28
Bolivia	23
Bosnia-Hercegovina	21
Botswana	23
Brazil	22
Brunei	25
Bulgaria	23
Burkina Faso	23
Burma	23
Burundi	22
Cameroon	22
Canada	22
Canary Islands	22
Cape Verde Islands	25
Caroline Islands	31
Cayman Islands	31
Central African Republic	25
Chad	25
Chile	22
China	24
Christmas Island	27
Cocos (Keeling) Islands	41
Colombia	22
Comoros	23
Congo (People's Republic)	25
Corsica	21
Costa Rica	23
Croatia	21
Cuba	24
Cyprus	31
Cyrenaica (see Libya)	21
Czech Republic	21
Denmark	21
Djibouti	22
Dominica	23
Dominican Republic	23
Dubai	22
Ecuador	22
Egypt (Arab Republic)	22
El Salvador (Republic of)	25
Equatorial Guinea	23
Estonia	21
Ethiopia	22

PD RSC ORD. 11 PRACTICE DIRECTION — SERVICE OUT OF THE JURISDICTION

Place or country	number of days
Falkland Islands and Dependencies	31
Faroe Islands	31
Fiji	23
Finland	24
France	21
French Guiana	31
French Polynesia	31
French West Indies	31
Gabon	25
Gambia	22
Georgia	21
Germany	21
Ghana	22
Gibraltar	31
Greece	21
Greenland	31
Grenada	24
Guatemala	24
Guernsey	18
Guyana	22
Haiti	23
Holland (Netherlands)	21
Honduras	24
Hong Kong	31
Hungary	22
Iceland	22
India	23
Indonesia	22
Iran	22
Iraq	22
Ireland (Republic of)	21
Ireland (Northern)	21
Isle of Man	18
Israel	22
Italy	21
Ivory Coast	22
Jamaica	22
Japan	23
Jersey	18
Jordan	23
Kampuchea	38
Kazakhstan	21
Kenya	22
Kirgizstan	21
Korea (North)	28
Korea (South)	24
Kuwait	22
Laos	30
Latvia	21
Lebanon	22
Lesotho	23
Liberia	22
Libya	21
Liechtenstein	21
Lithuania	21
Luxembourg	21
Macau	31

PD RSC ORD. 11   PRACTICE DIRECTION — SERVICE OUT OF THE JURISDICTION

Place or country	number of days
Macedonia	21
Madagascar	23
Madeira	31
Malawi	23
Malaya	24
Maldive Islands	26
Mali	25
Malta	21
Mariana Islands	26
Marshall Islands	32
Mauritania	23
Mauritius	22
Mexico	23
Moldova	21
Monaco	21
Montserrat	31
Morocco	22
Mozambique	23
Nauru Island	36
Nepal	23
Netherlands	21
Nevis	24
New Caledonia	31
New Hebrides (now Vanuatu)	29
New Zealand	26
New Zealand Island Territories	50
Nicaragua	24
Niger (Republic of)	25
Nigeria	22
Norfolk Island	31
Norway	21
Oman (Sultanate of)	22
Pakistan	23
Panama (Republic of)	26
Papua New Guinea	26
Paraguay	22
Peru	22
Philippines	23
Pitcairn Island	31
Poland	21
Portugal	21
Portuguese Timor	31
Puerto Rico	23
Qatar	23
Reunion	31
Romania	22
Russia	21
Rwanda	23
Sabah	23
St. Helena	31
St. Kitts–Nevis	24
St. Lucia	24
St. Pierre and Miquelon	31
St. Vincent and the Grenadines	24
Samoa (U.S.A. Territory) (See also Western Samoa)	30
Sarawak	28
Saudi Arabia	24

Place or country	number of days
Scotland	21
Senegal	22
Seychelles	22
Sharjah	24
Sierra Leone	22
Singapore	22
Slovakia	21
Slovenia	21
Society Islands (French Polynesia)	31
Solomon Islands	29
Somali Democratic Republic	22
South Africa (Republic of)	22
South Georgia (Falkland Island Dependencies)	31
South Orkneys	21
South Shetlands	21
Spain	21
Spanish Territories of North Africa	31
Sri Lanka	23
Sudan	22
Suriname	22
Swaziland	22
Sweden	21
Switzerland	21
Syria	23
Taiwan	23
Tajikistan	21
Tanzania	22
Thailand	23
Tibet	34
Tobago	23
Togo	22
Tonga	30
Tortola	31
Trinidad & Tobago	23
Tristan da Cunha	31
Tunisia	22
Turkey	21
Turkmenistan	21
Turks & Caicos Islands	31
Uganda	22
Ukraine	21
United States of America	22
Uruguay	22
Uzbekistan	21
Vanuatu	29
Vatican City State	21
Venezuela	22
Vietnam	28
Virgin Islands — British (Tortola)	31
Virgin Islands — U.S.A	24
Wake Island	25
Western Samoa	34
Yemen (Republic of)	30
Yugoslavia (except for Bosnia-Hercegovina, Croatia, Macedonia and Slovenia)	21
Zaire	25
Zambia	23
Zimbabwe	22

PD RSC ORD. 31 PRACTICE DIRECTION — SALE, ETC. OF LAND BY ORDER OF COURT: CONVEYANCING COUNSEL OF THE COURT

This practice direction supplements RSC Order 31 (Schedule 1 to the CPR)

SALES, ETC. OF LAND BY ORDER OF COURT

1. It should be noted that Order 31 now applies not only to proceedings in the High Court but also to county court proceedings.

2. An application under rule 1 of Order 31 should be made by issuing an application notice in the proceedings in question.
(Part 23 and the practice direction that supplements Part 23 contain rules about applications.)

3. If the land to be sold is subject to any incumbrance, the court may, on an application under section 50 of the Law of Property Act 1925, direct that a sum sufficient to provide for the incumbrance and for further costs and expenses be paid into court. The land may then be sold free from the incumbrance (s. 50(2) ibid.).

4. Any application under section 50 should, if made in existing proceedings, be made in accordance with CPR Part 23.

MANNER OF CARRYING OUT SALE

5. Where a sale has been directed by the court, any party who wishes to bid should, before the sale, apply to the court for permission to do so. If all parties are given permission to bid, the conduct of the sale may be given to an independent person, usually a solicitor.

CONVEYANCING COUNSEL TO THE COURT

6. Not only the High Court but also a county court may refer a matter to conveyancing counsel of the court under Order 31 rule 5.

7.1 Notice of every reference under Order 31 rule 5 should be given to the Chief Chancery Master.

7.2 Unless the reference was to a particular conveyancing counsel, matters referred to conveyancing counsel of the court will be distributed among them in rotation in accordance with arrangements made by the Chief Chancery Master.

7.3 The proper officer of the court that has referred the matter must supply the conveyancing counsel to whom the matter has been allocated with a copy of the order of the court referring the matter and all other necessary documents.

7.4 The fees of conveyancing counsel will be fixed by a costs judge, subject to an appeal to the judge whose decision will be final (see the Costs Practice Direction relating to Part 44, paragraph 2.7).

PD RSC ORD. 52 PRACTICE DIRECTION — COMMITTAL APPLICATIONS

This practice direction is supplemental to RSC Order 52 (Schedule 1 to the CPR) and CCR Order 29 (Schedule 2 to the CPR)

GENERAL

1.1 This practice direction applies to any application for an order for committal of a person to prison for contempt of court (a 'committal application').

1.2 Where the alleged contempt of court consists of or is based upon disobedience to an order made in a county court or breach of an undertaking given to a county court or consists of an act done in the course of proceedings in a county court, or where in any other way the alleged contempt is contempt of a county court, the committal application may be made in the county court in question.

1.3 In every other case, a committal application must be made in the High Court.

COMMENCEMENT OF COMMITTAL PROCEEDINGS

2.1 A committal application must, subject to paragraph 2.2, be commenced by the issue of a claim form. The Part 8 claim form must be used (see paragraph 2.5).

2.2 (1) If the committal application is made in existing proceedings:

(a) it may be commenced by the filing of an application notice in those proceedings, and

(b) the application notice must state that the application is made in existing proceedings and its title and reference number must correspond with those of the existing proceedings.

(c) in this paragraph 'existing proceedings' means proceedings in respect of which a final judgment has not yet been given.

2.3 If the committal application is one which cannot be made without permission, the claim form or application notice, as the case may be, may not be issued or filed until the requisite permission has been granted.

2.4 If the permission of the court is needed in order to make a committal application:

(1) the permission must be applied for by filing an application notice (see CPR rule 23.2(4));

(2) the application notice need not be served on the respondent;

(3) the date on which and the name of the judge by whom the requisite permission was granted must be stated on the claim form or application notice by which the committal application is commenced;

(4) the permission may only be granted by a judge who, under paragraph 11, would have power to hear the committal application if permission were granted; and

(5) CPR rules 23.9 and 23.10 do not apply.

2.5 If the committal application is commenced by the issue of a claim form, CPR Part 8 shall, subject to the provisions of this practice direction, apply as though references to 'claimant' were references to the person making the committal application and references to 'defendant' were references to the person against whom the committal application is made (in this practice direction referred to as 'the respondent') but:

(1) the claim form together with copies of all written evidence in support must, unless the court otherwise directs, be served personally on the respondent,

(2) the claim form must set out in full the grounds on which the committal application is made and should identify, separately and numerically, each alleged act of contempt,

(3) an amendment to the claim form can be made with the permission of the court but not otherwise, and

(4) CPR rule 8.4 does not apply.

2.6 If a committal application is commenced by the filing of an application notice, CPR Part 23 shall, subject to the provisions of this practice direction, apply, but:

(1) the application notice together with copies of all written evidence in support must, unless the court otherwise directs, be served personally on the respondent,

(2) the application notice must set out in full the grounds on which the committal application is made and should identify, separately and numerically, each alleged act of contempt,

(3) an amendment to the application notice can be made with the permission of the court but not otherwise, and

(4) the court may not dispose of the committal application without a hearing.

WRITTEN EVIDENCE

3.1 Written evidence in support of or in opposition to a committal application must be given by affidavit.

3.2 Written evidence served in support of or in opposition to a committal application must, unless the court otherwise directs, be filed.

3.3 A respondent, notwithstanding that he has not filed or served any written evidence, may give oral evidence at the hearing if he expresses a wish to do so. If he does so, he may be cross-examined.

3.4 A respondent may, with the permission of the court, call a witness to give oral evidence at the hearing notwithstanding that the witness has not sworn an affidavit.

CASE MANAGEMENT AND DATE OF HEARING

4.1 The applicant for the committal order must, when lodging the claim form or application notice with the court for issuing or filing, as the case may be, obtain from the court a date for the hearing of the committal application.

4.2 Unless the court otherwise directs, the hearing date of a committal application shall be not less than 14 clear days after service of the claim form or of the application notice, as the case may be, on the respondent. The hearing date must be specified in the claim form or application notice or in a Notice of Hearing or Application attached to and served with the claim form or application notice.

4.3 The court may, however, at any time give case management directions, including directions for the service of written evidence by the respondent and written evidence in reply by the applicant, or may convene and hold a directions hearing.

4.4 The court may on the hearing date:

(1) give case management directions with a view to a hearing of the committal application on a future date, or

(2) if the committal application is ready to be heard, proceed forthwith to hear it.

STRIKING OUT

5. The court may, on application by the respondent or on its own initiative, strike out a committal application if it appears to the court:

(1) that the committal application and the evidence served in support of it disclose no reasonable ground for alleging that the respondent is guilty of a contempt of court,

(2) that the committal application is an abuse of the court's process or, if made in existing proceedings, is otherwise likely to obstruct the just disposal of those proceedings, or

(3) that there has been a failure to comply with a rule, practice direction or court order.

MISCELLANEOUS

6. CPR rules 35.7 (court's power to direct that evidence is to be given by a single joint expert), 35.8 (Instructions to single joint expert) and 35.9 (Power of

court to direct a party to provide information) do not apply to committal applications.

7. An order under CPR rule 18.1 (Order for a party to give additional information) may not be made against a respondent to a committal application.

8. A committal application may not be discontinued without the permission of the court.

9. A committal application should normally be heard in public (see CPR rule 39.2), but if it is heard in private and the court finds the respondent guilty of contempt of court, the judge shall state in public:

(1) the name of the respondent,

(2) in general terms the nature of the contempt or contempts found proved, and

(3) the penalty (if any) imposed.

10. Any procedural defect in the commencement or conduct by the applicant of a committal application may be waived by the court if satisfied that no injustice has been caused to the respondent by the defect.

11. Except where under an enactment a Master or district judge has power to make a committal order[1], a committal order can only be made:

(1) in High Court proceedings, by a High Court Judge or a person authorised to act as such,[2]

(2) in county court proceedings by a Circuit Judge or a person authorised to act or capable by virtue of his office of acting as such[3].

---

[1] e.g. ss. 14 and 118, County Courts Act 1984.
[2] see s. 9(1), Supreme Court Act 1981.
[3] see s. 5(3), County Courts Act 1984.

PD RSC ORD. 53 PRACTICE DIRECTION — SCHEDULE 1, ORDER 53 (APPLICATION FOR JUDICIAL REVIEW)

This practice direction supplements CPR Part 50, and Schedule 1 to the CPR

TERMINOLOGY

1.1 In this practice direction:
  (1) 'Order 53' means those provisions contained in Schedule 1, RSC Order 53, which were previously contained in the Rules of the Supreme Court (1965);
  (2) a reference to a rule or Part prefixed with CPR is a reference to a rule or Part contained in the CPR rules; and
  (3) a reference to a rule number alone is a reference to the rule so numbered in Order 53.

SCOPE

2.1 This practice direction supplements Order 53 (which sets out the procedure for applying for judicial review) by providing further detail about the application.

2.2 This practice direction must be read together with Order 53.

2.3 It also lists at paragraph 8 other practice directions which governed procedure relating to Order 53 before 26 April 1999 and which will continue to do so.

CLAIM FORM

3.1 Rule 5(2A) specifies that an application for judicial review must be made by claim form. The claim form to be used is Form 86, modified in accordance with the guidance contained in the Forms practice direction.

3.2 The claimant must also use a modified Form 86 where he is making an application under rule 11(1) (Proceedings for disqualification of a member of a local authority).

APPLICATION FOR JUDICIAL REVIEW

4.1 In order to comply with the requirement in rule 6(1) (copy of the statement in support of the application for permission to be served), Form 86A must be attached to Form 86 (the claim form) and served with it.

MEANING OF WRITTEN EVIDENCE

5.1 The written evidence required by:
  (1) rule 5.6 (written evidence to be filed before the application is entered for hearing);
  (2) rule 6 (statements and evidence); and
  (3) rule 11 (proceedings for disqualification of member of a local authority, may be either an affidavit or a witness statement.)
(CPR rule 32.16 provides for the form of an affidavit, CPR rule 32.8 provides for the form of a witness statement, and CPR rule 22.1 requires a witness statement to be verified by a statement of truth).

SERVICE

6.1 The Crown Office will prepare and serve all orders of the court.
(CPR rule 6.3 provides that the court will normally serve a document which it has issued or prepared).

6.2 All other documents (and copies) must be prepared and served by the parties.

CASES ENTERED IN THE CROWN OFFICE LIST

7.1 When an application is entered in accordance with rule 5(5):
  (a) for judicial review; or

(b) under rule 11(1) (Proceedings for disqualification of member of local authority),
the application must be entered in the Crown Office List in accordance with Practice Direction (Crown Office List) [1987] 1 WLR 232, [1987] 1 All ER 368. (In Schedule 1, RSC Order 57 rule 2 provides for the entry of claims in the appropriate office and for the filing of copy documents for the use of the court)

PRACTICE DIRECTIONS ETC., WHICH APPLY TO PROCEEDINGS UNDER ORDER 53

8. The Practice Directions, Statements and Practice Notes set out in Table 1 continue to apply to proceedings under Order 53 on and after 26 April 1999.

Table 1

Practice Direction etc.	Content
Practice Note [1983] 2 All ER 1020	Urgent matters outside London — consultation of Crown Office and continuation in London; Delay in applying for permission to apply for judicial review
Practice Note (Crown Office List) [1987] 1 All ER 1184	Need for accuracy in time estimates
Practice Direction (Crown Office List) [1987] 1 WLR 232, [1987] 1 All ER 368.	Parts of the List.
Practice Note [1991] 1 All ER 1055	Permission to apply for judicial review and time allowed for such applications
Practice Direction (Crown Office List: Preparation for hearings) [1994] 4 All ER 671, [1994] 1 WLR 1551 (18th November 1994).	Preparation for hearings; Documentation; Time limits; Skeleton arguments: amendment of grounds.
Practice Direction (Crown Office List: Consent Orders) [1997] 1 WLR 825	Consent orders
Practice Note [1997] 1 All ER 128 (6th December 1997)	Permission to apply for judicial review — Documents to be lodged; — relevant legislative provisions and statutory instruments
Practice Statement (Supreme Court: Judgments) [1998] 1 WLR 825, [1998] 2 All ER 638.	Judgments

PD RSC ORD. 54 PRACTICE DIRECTION — SCHEDULE 1, ORDER 54 (APPLICATION FOR WRIT OF HABEAS CORPUS)

This practice direction supplements CPR Part 50, and Schedule 1 to the CPR

TERMINOLOGY
1.1 In this practice direction:
(1) 'Order 54' means those provisions contained in Schedule 1, RSC Order 54 which were previously contained in the Rules of the Supreme Court (1965);
(2) a reference to a rule or Part prefixed with CPR is a reference to a rule or Part contained in the CPR rules; and
(3) a reference to a rule number alone is a reference to the rule so numbered in Order 54.

SCOPE
2.1 This practice direction supplements Order 54 (which sets out how to apply for a writ of habeas corpus) by providing further detail about the application.
2.2 This practice direction must be read together with Order 54.
2.3 It also lists at paragraph 7 other practice directions which governed procedure relating to Order 54 before 26 April 1999 and which will continue to do so.

FORM TO BE USED WHERE COURT DIRECTS CLAIM FORM TO BE USED
3.1 Where the court directs that an application be made by claim form, under:
(1) rule 2, (on hearing application under rule 1); or
(2) rule 4(2) (application in criminal proceedings ordered to be made to Divisional Court of the Queen's Bench Division),
the claimant must use Form 87 modified in accordance with the guidance set out in the Forms practice direction.

FORM TO BE USED FOR NOTICE OF ADJOURNED APPLICATION DIRECTED BY COURT
4.1 Where the court directs under rule 2(1)(c) that an application made under rule 1 is adjourned to allow for service of notice of the application, such notice must be given in modified Form 88.

SERVICE
5.1 The party seeking the writ must serve:
(1) the claim form in accordance with rule 2(2); and
(2) the writ of habeas corpus ad subjiciendum and notice in Form 90, as modified, in accordance with rule 6.
(CPR rule 6.3 provides that the court will normally serve a document which it has issued or prepared).

THE CROWN OFFICE LIST
6.1 When the court directs that an application is to be made by claim form under:
(1) rule 2(1) (powers of court to whom application made under rule 1); or
(2) rule 4(2) (power of court in where application made in criminal proceedings)
the application must be entered in the Crown Office List in accordance with Practice Direction (Crown Office List) [1987] 1 WLR 232, [1987] 1 All ER 368. (In Schedule 1, RSC Order 57 rule 2 provides for the entry of claims in the appropriate office and for the filing of copy documents for the use of the court)

PRACTICE DIRECTIONS ETC., WHICH APPLY TO ORDER 54

7.1 On and after 26 April 1999, the Practice Directions, Statements and Practice Notes set out in Table 1 continue to apply to proceedings under Order 54.

Table 1

Practice Direction etc.	Content
Practice Note [1983] 2 All ER 1020	Urgent matters outside London — consultation of Crown Office and continuation in London;
Practice Note (Crown Office List) [1987] 1 All ER 1184	Need for accuracy in time estimates
Practice Direction (Crown Office List) [1987] 1 WLR 232, [1987] 1 All ER 368.	Parts of the List.
Practice Direction (Crown Office List: Preparation for hearings) [1994] 4 All ER 671, [1994] 1 WLR 1551 (18th November 1994).	Preparation for hearings; Documentation; Time limits; Skeleton arguments: amendment of grounds.
Practice Direction (Crown Office List: Consent Orders) [1997] 1 WLR 825	Consent orders
Practice Statement (Supreme Court: Judgments) [1998] 1 WLR 825, [1998] 2 All ER 638.	Judgments

PD RSC ORD. 58 PRACTICE DIRECTION — APPEALS FROM MASTERS ETC.

This practice direction supplements RSC Order 58, rule 2

1.1 RSC Order 58, rule 2 (Schedule 1 to the Civil Procedure Rules) provides for an appeal from certain decisions of Masters or District Judges (High Court) to the Court of Appeal. This provision is not intended to alter the route of appeal from a decision of a Master or District Judge.

1.2 Where, before 26 April 1999, an appeal would have lain from a decision of a Master or District Judge to a judge under RSC Order 58, rule 1, it shall continue to do so under the Civil Procedure Rules.

1.3 RSC Order 58, rule 2(1)(a) provides that an appeal lies to the Court of Appeal from a decision of a Master or District Judge made 'at trial, . . . on the hearing or determination of any cause, matter, question or issue tried before him'. This provision only applies where the parties have given their consent for the Master or District Judge to try a case which has been allocated to the multi-track under Part 26 (see paragraph 4.1 of PD 2B).

CPR SCHEDULE 2

CCR ORDER 1
CITATION, APPLICATION AND INTERPRETATION

Rule 6 APPLICATION OF RSC TO COUNTY COURT PROCEEDINGS
Where by virtue of these rules or section 76 of the Act or otherwise any provision of the RSC is applied in relation to proceedings in a county court, that provision shall have effect with the necessary modifications and in particular—

    (b) any reference in that provision to a Master, district judge of the Principal Registry of the Family Division, the Admiralty registrar, or a district judge or taxing officer shall be construed as a reference to the district judge of the county court; and

    (d) any reference in that provision to an office of the Supreme Court having the conduct of the business of a division or court or a district registry shall be construed as a reference to the county court office.

CCR ORDER 3
COMMENCEMENT OF PROCEEDINGS

Rule 6 APPEALS TO COUNTY COURT

(1) Where by or under any Act an appeal lies to a county court from any order, decision or award of any tribunal or person, then, subject to any special provision made by or under the Act, the provisions of this rule shall apply.

(2) The appellant shall, within 21 days after the date of the order, decision or award, file—

    (a) a request for the entry of the appeal, stating the names and addresses of the persons intended to be served (in this rule called 'respondents') and the appellant's address for service, together with as many copies of the request as there are respondents; and

    (b) a copy of the order, decision or award appealed against.

(3) Where the provision under which the appeal lies requires the appellant to give to the other parties notice in writing of his intention to appeal and of the grounds of his appeal, the appellant shall file a copy of such notice with the request, and in any other case he shall include in his request a statement of the grounds of the appeal.

(4) On the filing of the documents mentioned in paragraphs (2) and (3) the court officer shall—

    (a) enter the appeal in the records of the court and fix the return day;

    (b) prepare a notice to each respondent of the day on which the appeal will be heard and annex each copy of the request for the entry of the appeal to a copy of the notice; and

    (c) deliver a notice of issue to the appellant.

(5) The return day shall be a day fixed for the hearing of the appeal by the judge (or, if the district judge has jurisdiction to hear the appeal, by the district judge) or, if the court so directs, a day fixed for a pre-trial review.

(6) The notice of the day of hearing shall be served—

    (a) by the appellant delivering the notice to the respondent personally; or

    (b) by the court sending it by first-class post to the respondent—

        (i) at his address for service; or

        (ii) where CPR rule 6.5(5) applies at the place of service specified in that rule.

(7) Unless the appellant otherwise requests, service shall be effected in accordance with paragraph (6)(b).

(8) Where a notice is served in accordance with paragraph (6)(b) the date of service shall, unless the contrary is shown, be deemed to be the seventh day after the date on which the notice was sent to the respondent.

(9) Where—
(a) a notice has been sent by post in accordance with paragraph (6)(b) to the respondent's address for service; and
(b) the notice has been returned to the court office undelivered,
the court shall send notice of non-service to the appellant pursuant to CPR Rule 6.11 together with a notice informing him that he may request bailiff service at that address.

(10) If the appellant requests bailiff service under paragraph (9), it shall be effected by a bailiff of the court—
(a) inserting the notice, enclosed in an envelope addressed to the respondent, through the letter-box at the respondent's address for service;
(b) delivering the notice to some person, apparently not less than 16 years old, at the respondent's address for service; or
(c) delivering the notice to the respondent personally.

(11) Service of a notice shall be effected not less than 21 days before the hearing, but service may be effected at any time before the hearing on the appellant satisfying the court by witness statement or affidavit that the respondent is about to remove from his address for service.

CCR ORDER 4
VENUE FOR BRINGING PROCEEDINGS

Rule 3 PROCEEDINGS RELATING TO LAND
Proceedings—
(a) for the recovery of land;
(b) for the foreclosure or redemption of any mortgage or, subject to Order 31, rule 4, for enforcing any charge or lien on land; or
(c) for the recovery of moneys secured by a mortgage or charge on land, may be commenced only in the court for the district in which the land or any part of the land is situated.

CCR ORDER 5
CAUSES OF ACTION AND PARTIES

Rule 5 REPRESENTATIVE PROCEEDINGS
(1) Where numerous persons have the same interest in any proceedings, not being such proceedings as are mentioned in rule 6, the proceedings may be begun and, unless the court otherwise orders, continued, by or against any one or more of them as representing all or all except one or more of them.

(2) At any stage of proceedings under this rule the court may—
(a) on the application of a claimant who is suing in a representative capacity, appoint him to represent all, or all except one or more, of the persons on whose behalf he sues;
(b) on the application of the claimant or of a defendant who is sued in a representative capacity, appoint any one or more of the defendants or other persons on whose behalf the defendants are sued to represent all, or all except one or more, of those persons.
Where in the exercise of the power conferred by sub-paragraph (b) the court appoints a person not named as a defendant, it shall make an order under CPR rule 19.1 adding that person as a defendant.

(3) An application under paragraph (2)—
(a) if made under sub-paragraph (a), may be made without notice being served on any other party;
(b) if made under sub-paragraph (b), shall be made on notice—
(i) where the applicant is the claimant, to the person sought to be appointed; or
(ii) where the applicant is a defendant, to the claimant and to any person, other than the applicant, sought to be appointed;
and in each case the notice shall state the facts on which the applicant relies and the names and addresses or, where appropriate a collective description, of the persons to be represented.

(4) Where an order is made granting an application under paragraph (2)(b), the court shall send notice of the order to the person to whom notice of the application was given and shall notify other persons affected by the order in such manner as the court may direct.

(5) A judgment or order given or made in proceedings under this rule shall be binding on all persons on whose behalf the claimant sues or, as the case may be, the defendant is sued but shall not be enforced against any person not a party to the proceedings except with the permission of the court.

(6) An application for permission under paragraph (5) shall be made on notice to the person against whom it is sought to enforce the judgment or order and, notwithstanding that the judgment or order is binding on him, he may dispute liability to have it enforced against him on the ground that by reason of facts and matters particular to his case he is entitled to be exempted from such liability.

Rule 6 REPRESENTATION OF PERSON OR CLASS

(1) In any proceedings concerning—
   (a) the estate of a deceased person;
   (b) property subject to a trust; or
   (c) the construction of a written statement, including a statute,

the court may appoint one or more persons to represent any person (including an unborn person) or class who is or may be interested in or affected by the proceedings, if the person. the class or some member of the class cannot readily be ascertained or cannot be found or if it otherwise appears to the court expedient to exercise this power for the purpose of saving expense.

(2) A judgment or order given or made when a person or persons appointed under paragraph (1) is or are before the court shall be binding on the person or class so represented.

(3) Where. in proceedings to which paragraph (1) applies, a compromise is proposed and some of the persons who are interested in or who may be affected by the compromise (including unborn or unascertained persons) are not parties to the proceedings but—
   (a) there is some person in the same interest before the court who assents to the compromise or on whose behalf the court sanctions the compromise; or
   (b) the absent persons are represented by a person appointed under paragraph (1) who so assents,

the court, if satisfied that the compromise will be for the benefit of the absent persons and that it is expedient to exercise this power, may approve the compromise and order that it shall be binding on the absent persons, and they shall be bound accordingly except where the order has been obtained by fraud or non-disclosure of material facts.

Rule 7 REPRESENTATION OF ESTATE WHERE NO PERSONAL REPRESENTATIVE

(1) Where in any proceedings it appears to the court that a deceased person who was interested in the matter in question in the proceedings has no personal representative, the court may, on the application of any party to the proceedings—
   (a) proceed in the absence of a person representing the estate of the deceased person; or
   (b) by order appoint a person to represent the estate for the purpose of the proceedings.

(2) Any such order, and any judgment or order subsequently given or made in the proceedings, shall bind the estate of the deceased person to the same extent as if a personal representative of that person had been a party to the proceedings.

(3) Before making an order under this rule, the court may require notice of the application for the order to be given to such of the persons having an interest in the estate as it thinks fit.

Rule 8 PROCEEDINGS AGAINST ESTATES

(1) Where any person against whom a claim would have laid has died but the cause of action survives, the claim may, if no grant of probate or administration has been made, be brought against the estate of the deceased.

(2) Without prejudice to the generality of paragraph (1), a claim brought against 'the personal representatives of A.B. deceased' shall be treated, for the purposes of that paragraph, as having been brought against his estate.

(3) A claim purporting to have been commenced against a person shall be treated, if he was dead at its commencement, as having been commenced against his estate in accordance with paragraph (1),
whether or not a grant of probate or administration was made before its commencement.

(4) In any such claim as is referred to in paragraph (1) or (3)—

(a) the claimant shall, where the court fixed a date for the hearing when it issued the claim, on or before that date, or, in any other case within the time allowed for service of the claim form, apply to the court for an order appointing a person to represent the deceased's estate for the purpose of the proceedings or, if a grant of probate or administration has been made, for an order that the personal representative of the deceased be made a party to the proceedings, and in either case for an order that the proceedings be carried on against the person so appointed or, as the case may be, against the personal representative, as if he had been substituted for the estate;

(b) the court may, at any stage of the proceedings and on such terms as it thinks just and either of its own motion or on application, make any such order as is mentioned in sub-paragraph (a) and allow such amendments (if any) to be made and make such other order as the court thinks necessary in order to ensure that all matters in dispute in the proceedings may be effectually and completely determined and adjudicated upon.

(5) Before making an order under paragraph (4) the court may require notice to be given to any insurer of the deceased who has an interest in the proceedings and to such (if any) of the persons having an interest in the estate as it thinks fit.

(6) Where an order is made under paragraph (4), the person against whom the proceedings are to be carried on shall be served with a copy of the order, together with a copy of the application notice if any.

(7) Where no grant of probate or administration has been made, any judgment or order given or made in the proceedings shall bind the estate to the same extent as it would have been bound if a grant had been made and a personal representative of the deceased had been a party to the proceedings.

Rule 9 PARTNERS MAY SUE AND BE SUED IN FIRM NAME

(1) Subject to the provisions of any enactment, any two or more persons claiming to be entitled, or alleged to be liable, as partners in respect of a cause of action and carrying on business within England or Wales may sue or be sued in the name of the firm of which they were partners when the cause of action arose.

(2) Where partners sue or are sued in the name of the firm, the partners shall, on demand made in writing by any other party, forthwith deliver to the party making the demand and file a statement of the names and places of residence of all the persons who were partners in the firm when the cause of action arose.

(3) If the partners fail to comply with such a demand, the court, on application by any other party, may order the partners to furnish him with such a statement and to verify it on oath and may direct that in default—

(a) if the partners are claimants, the proceedings be stayed on such terms as the court thinks fit; or

(b) if the partners are defendants, they be debarred from defending the claim.

(4) When the names and places of residence of the partners have been stated in compliance with a demand or order under this rule, the proceedings shall continue in the name of the firm.

Rule 10 DEFENDANT CARRYING ON BUSINESS IN ANOTHER NAME

(1) A person carrying on business in England or Wales in a name other than his own name may, whether or not he is within the jurisdiction, be sued—

(a) in his own name, followed by the words 'trading as A.B.', or

(b) in his business name, followed by the words '(a trading name)'.

(2) Where a person is sued in his business name in accordance with paragraph (1)(b), the provisions of these rules relating to claims against firms shall, subject to the provisions of any enactment, apply as if he were a partner and the name in which he carried on business were the name of his firm.

Rule 12 FAILURE TO PROCEED AFTER DEATH OF PARTY

(1) If, after the death of a claimant or defendant in any claim or matter, the cause of action survives but no order is made substituting any person in whom the cause of action vests or, as the case may be, the personal representatives of the deceased defendant, the defendant or, as the case may be, those representatives may apply to the court for an order that unless the claim is proceeded with within such time as may be specified in the order the claim shall be struck out as against the claimant or defendant who has died; but where it is the claimant who has died, the court shall not make an order unless satisfied that notice of the application has been given to the personal representatives (if any) of the deceased claimant and to any other interested person who the court considers should be notified.

(2) Where a counterclaim is made by a defendant to any claim this rule shall apply in relation to the counterclaim as if the counterclaim were separate claim and as if the defendant making a counterclaim were claimant and the person against whom it is made a defendant.

Rule 13 CLAIM TO MONEY IN COURT WHERE CHANGE IN PARTIES AFTER JUDGMENT

(1) Where any change had taken place after judgment, by death, assignment or otherwise, in the parties to any claim and there is money standing in court to the credit of the claim, any person claiming to be entitled to the money may give to the court notice of his claim, accompanied by a witness statement or affidavit verifying the facts stated in the notice.

(2) The district judge may, if satisfied as to the entitlement of the person giving notice, cause the money to be paid to him or may refer the claim to the judge and may require the claimant to give notice of the claim to any other person.

(3) It shall not be necessary for notice to be given under this rule where the person claiming to be entitled to the money in court has obtained permission under Order 26, rule 5, to issue a warrant of execution.

Rule 14 BANKRUPTCY OF CLAIMANT

Rules 11 and 13 shall not apply to any case for which provision is made by section 49 of the Act.

CCR ORDER 6
PARTICULARS OF CLAIM

Rule 3 RECOVERY OF LAND

(1) In a claim for recovery of land the particulars of claim shall—
 (a) identify the land sought to be recovered;
 (b) state whether the land consists of or includes a dwelling-house;
 (c) give details about the agreement or tenancy, if any, under which the land is held, stating when it commenced and the amount of money payable by way of rent or licence fee;
 (d) in a case to which section 138 of the Act applies (forfeiture for non-payment of rent), state the daily rate at which the rent in arrear is to be calculated; and
 (e) state the ground on which possession is claimed, whether statutory or otherwise.

(2) In proceedings for forfeiture where the claimant knows of any person entitled to claim relief against forfeiture as underlessee (including a mortgagee) under section 146(4) of the Law of Property Act 1925 or under section 138(9C) of the County Courts Act 1984, the particulars of claim shall give the name and address of that person and the claimant shall file a copy of the particulars of claim for service on him.

(3) Where possession of land which consists of or includes a dwelling house is claimed because of non-payment of rent, the particulars of claim shall be in the prescribed form and shall also—
    (a) state the amount due at the commencement of the proceedings;
    (b) give—
        (i) (whether by means of a schedule or otherwise) particulars of all the payments which have been missed altogether; and
        (ii) where a history of late or under-payments is relied upon, sufficient details to establish the claimant's case;
    (c) state any previous steps which the claimant has taken to recover arrears of rent and, in the case of court proceedings, state—
        (i) the dates when proceedings were commenced and concluded; and
        (ii) the dates and terms of any orders made;
    (d) give such relevant information as is known by the claimant about the defendant's circumstances and, in particular, whether (and, if so, what) payments on his behalf are made direct to the claimant by or under the Social Security Contributions and Benefits Act 1992; and
    (e) if the claimant intends as part of his case to rely on his own financial or other circumstances, give details of all relevant facts or matters.

Rule 5 MORTGAGE CLAIM

(1) Where a claimant claims as mortgagee payment of moneys secured by a mortgage of real or leasehold property or possession of such property, the particulars of claim shall contain the information required under this rule and, as the case may be, by rule 5A.

(2) Where there is more than one loan secured by the mortgage, the information required under the following paragraphs of this rule and under rule 5A shall be provided in respect of each loan agreement.

(3) The particulars shall state the date of the mortgage and identify the land sought to be recovered.

(4) Where possession of the property is claimed, the particulars of claim shall state whether or not the property consists of or includes a dwelling-house within the meaning of section 21 of the Act.

(5) The particulars shall state whether or not the loan which is secured by the mortgage is a regulated consumer credit agreement and, if so, specify the date on which any notice required by section 76 or section 87 of the Consumer Credit Act 1974 was given.

(6) The particulars shall show the state of account between the claimant and the defendant by including—
    (a) the amount of the advance and of any periodic repayment and any payment of interest required to be made;
    (b) the amount which would have to be paid (after taking into account any adjustment for early settlement) in order to redeem the mortgage at a stated date not more than 14 days after the commencement of proceedings specifying the amount of solicitor's costs and administrative charges which would be payable;
    (c) where the loan which is secured by the mortgage is a regulated consumer credit agreement, the total amount outstanding under the terms of the mortgage;
    (d) the rate of interest payable—
        (i) at the commencement of the mortgage;
        (ii) immediately before any arrears referred to in sub-paragraph (e) accrued; and
        (iii) where it differs from that provided under (ii) above, at the commencement of the proceedings; and
    (e) the amount of any interest or instalments in arrear at the commencement of the proceedings.

(7) The particulars of claim shall state any previous steps which the claimant has taken to recover the moneys secured by the mortgage or the mortgaged property and, in the case of court proceedings, state—
    (a) the dates when proceedings were commenced and concluded; and

(b) the dates and terms of any orders made.

(8) In this rule 'mortgage' includes a legal or equitable mortgage and a legal or equitable charge, and references to the mortgaged property and mortgagee shall be construed accordingly.

Rule 5A MORTGAGE CLAIM — DWELLING-HOUSE

(1) This rule applies where a claimant claims as mortgagee possession of land which consists of or includes a dwelling-house and in such a case the particulars of claim shall be in the prescribed form.

(2) Where the claimant's claim is brought because of failure to make the periodic payments due, the particulars of claim shall—

(a) give details (whether by means of a schedule or otherwise) of all the payments which have been missed altogether;

(b) where a history of late or under-payments is relied upon, provide sufficient details to establish the claimant's case;

(c) give details of any other payments required to be made as a term of the mortgage (such as for insurance premiums, legal costs, default interest, penalties, administrative or other charges) together with any other sums claimed stating the nature and amount of each such charge, whether any payment is in arrear and whether or not it is included in the amount of any periodic payment;

(d) give such relevant information as is known by the claimant about the defendant's circumstances and, in particular, whether (and, if so, what) payments on his behalf are made direct to the claimant by or under the Social Security Contributions and Benefits Act 1992.

(3) In a claim to which this rule applies, the claimant shall state in his particulars of claim whether there is any person on whom notice of the claim is required to be served in accordance with section 8(3) of the Matrimonial Homes Act 1983 and, if so, he shall state the name and address of that person and shall file a copy of the particulars of claim for service on that person.

(4) In this rule 'mortgage' has the same meaning as in rule 5(8).

Rule 6 HIRE-PURCHASE

(1) Where a claimant claims the delivery of goods let under a hire-purchase agreement or a conditional sale agreement to a person other than a body corporate, he shall in his particulars state in the order following—

(a) the date of the agreement and the parties to it with the number of the agreement or sufficient particulars to enable the debtor to identify the agreement;

(b) where the claimant was not one of the original parties to the agreement, the means by which the rights and duties of the creditor under the agreement passed to him;

(c) whether the agreement is a regulated agreement and, if it is not a regulated agreement, the reason why;

(d) the place where the agreement was signed by the debtor (if known);

(e) the goods claimed;

(f) the total price of the goods;

(g) the paid-up sum;

(h) the unpaid balance of the total price;

(i) whether a default notice or a notice under section 76(1) or section 98(1) of the Consumer Credit Act 1974 has been served on the debtor, and if it has, the date on which and the manner in which it was so served;

(j) the date when the right to demand delivery of the goods accrued;

(k) the amount (if any) claimed as an alternative to the delivery of the goods; and

(l) the amount (if any) claimed in addition to the delivery of the goods or any claim under sub-paragraph (k), stating the cause of action in respect of which each such claim is made.

(2) Where a claimant's claim arises out of a hire-purchase agreement or a conditional sale agreement but is not for the delivery of goods, he shall in his particulars state in the order following—

(a) the date of the agreement and the parties to it with the number of the agreement or sufficient particulars to enable the debtor to identify the agreement;
(b) where the claimant was not one of the original parties to the agreement, the means by which the rights and duties of the creditor under the agreement passed to him;
(c) whether the agreement is a regulated agreement and, if it is not a regulated agreement, the reason why;
(d) the place where the agreement was signed by the debtor (if known);
(e) the goods let under the agreement;
(f) the amount of the total price;
(g) the paid-up sum;
(h) the amount (if any) claimed as being due and unpaid in respect of any instalment or instalments of the total price; and
(i) the nature and amount of any other claim and the circumstances in which it arises.
(3) Expressions used in this rule which are defined by the Consumer Credit Act 1974 have the same meanings in this rule as they have in that Act.

CCR ORDER 7
SERVICE OF DOCUMENTS

Rule 15 RECOVERY OF LAND
(1) Where, in the case of a claim form for the recovery of land which is to be served by bailiff, the court is of the opinion that it is impracticable to serve the claim form in accordance with any of the foregoing provisions of CPR Part 6, the claim form may be served in a manner authorised by this rule.
(2) The claim form may be served on any person on the premises who is the husband or wife of the defendant or on any person who has or appears to have the authority of the defendant—
(a) to reside or carry on business in the premises or to manage them on behalf of the defendant or to receive any rents or profits of the premises or to pay any outgoings in respect of the premises; or
(b) to safeguard or deal with the premises or with the furniture or other goods on the premises, and service on any such person shall be effected in the manner required for service of the notice of the day of hearing in accordance with Order 3, rule 6.
(3) Paragraph (2) shall apply to a man and woman who are living with each other in the same household as husband and wife as it applies to the parties to a marriage.
(4) Where the premises are vacant or are occupied only by virtue of the presence of furniture or other goods, the claim form may be served by affixing it to some conspicuous part of the premises.
(5) Unless the court otherwise orders, service of a claim form in accordance with this rule shall be good service on the defendant, but if a claim for the recovery of money is joined with the claim for recovery of land, the court shall order the claim form to be marked 'not served' with respect to the money claim unless in special circumstances the court thinks it just to hear and determine both claims.

Rule 15A MORTGAGE POSSESSION CLAIMS
(1) After the issue of the claim form in a mortgage possession claim the claimant shall not less than 14 days before the hearing send to the address of the property sought to be recovered a notice addressed to the occupiers which—
(a) states that possession proceedings have been commenced in respect of the property;
(b) shows the name and address of the claimant, of the defendant and of the court which issued the claim form; and
(c) gives details of the case number and of the hearing date.
(2) The claimant shall either—
(a) not less than 14 days before the hearing, file a certificate stating that a notice has been sent in accordance with paragraph (1); or

(b) exhibit the notice to any witness statement or affidavit used at the hearing.

(3) In this rule 'mortgage possession claim' means a claim in which the claimant claims as mortgagee possession of land which consists of or includes a dwelling-house and 'mortgage' has the same meaning as in Order 6, rule 5(8).

CCR ORDER 13
APPLICATIONS AND ORDERS IN THE COURSE OF PROCEEDINGS

Rule 1 GENERAL PROVISIONS

(10) An appeal shall lie to a judge from any order made by a district judge on in the course of proceedings.

(11) An appeal under paragraph (10) shall be made on notice, which shall be filed and served on the opposite party within 5 days after the order appealed from or such further time as the judge may allow.

CCR ORDER 16
TRANSFER OF PROCEEDINGS

Rule 7 INTERPLEADER PROCEEDINGS UNDER EXECUTION

(1) This rule applies to interpleader proceedings under an execution which are ordered to be transferred from the High Court.

(2) Notice of the hearings or pre-trial review of the proceedings shall be given by the court officer to the sheriff as well as to every other party to the proceedings.

(3) The interpleader claimant shall, within 8 days of the receipt by him of the notice referred to in paragraph (2), file in triplicate particulars of any goods alleged to be his property and the grounds of his interpleader claim and the court officer shall send a copy to the execution creditor and to the sheriff, but the judge may hear the proceedings or, as the case may be, the district judge may proceed with the pre-trial review, if he thinks fit, notwithstanding that the particulars have not been filed.

(4) Subject to any directions in the order of the High Court, damages may be claimed against the execution creditor in the same manner as in interpleader proceedings commenced in a county court.

(5) On any day fixed for the pre-trial review of the proceedings or for the hearing of any application by the sheriff or other party for directions the court may order the sheriff—

(a) to postpone the sale of the goods seized;

(b) to remain in possession of such goods until the hearing of the proceedings; or

(c) to hand over possession of such goods to the district judge,

and, where a direction is given under sub-paragraph (c), the district judge shall be allowed reasonable charges for keeping possession of the goods, not exceeding those which might be allowed to the sheriff, and, if the district judge is directed to sell the goods, such charges for the sale as would be allowed under an execution issued by the county court.

(6) No order made in the proceedings shall prejudice or affect the rights of the sheriff to any proper charges and the judge may make such order with respect to them as may be just.

(7) The charges referred to in paragraphs (5) and (6) shall ultimately be borne in such manner as the judge shall direct.

(8) The order made at the hearing of the proceedings shall direct how any money in the hands of the sheriff is to be disposed of.

CCR ORDER 19
REFERENCE TO EUROPEAN COURT

Rule 15 MAKING AND TRANSMISSION OF ORDER

(1) In this rule 'the European Court' means the Court of justice of the European Communities and 'order' means an order referring a question to the European Court for a preliminary ruling under article 177 of the Treaty establishing the European Economic Community, article 150 of the Treaty establishing the

European Atomic Energy Community or article 41 of the Treaty establishing the European Coal and Steel Community.

(2) An order may be made by the judge before or at the trial or hearing of any claim and either of his own initiative or on the application of any party.

(3) An order shall set out in a schedule the request for the preliminary ruling of the European Court, and the judge may give directions as to the manner and form in which the schedule is to be prepared.

(4) The proceedings in which an order is made shall, unless the judge otherwise orders, be stayed until the European Court has given a preliminary ruling on the question referred to it.

(5) When an order has been made, the court officer shall send a copy thereof to the Senior Master for transmission to the Registrar of the European Court; but, unless the judge otherwise orders, the copy shall not be sent to the Senior Master until the time for appealing to the Court of Appeal against the order has expired or, if an appeal is entered within that time, until the appeal has been determined or otherwise disposed of.

(6) Nothing in these rules shall authorise the district judge to make an order.

CCR ORDER 22
JUDGMENTS AND ORDERS

Rule 8 CERTIFICATE OF JUDGMENT

(1) Any person who wishes to have a certificate of any judgment or order given or made in a claim shall make a request in writing to the court stating—

    (a) if he is a party to the claim whether the certificate—

        (i) is required for the purpose of taking proceedings on the judgment or order in another court;

        (ii) is required for the purpose of enforcing the judgment or order in the High Court; or

        (iii) is for the purpose of evidence only;

    (b) if he is not a party to the claim, the purpose for which the certificate is required, the capacity in which he asks for it and any other facts showing that the certificate may properly be granted.

(1A) Where the certificate is required for the purpose of enforcing the judgment or order in the High Court, the applicant shall also either—

    (a) state that it is intended to enforce the judgment or order by execution against goods; or

    (b) confirm that an application has been made for an order under section 42 of the Act (transfer to High Court by order of a county court) and attach a copy of the application to the request for a certificate.

(2) Where the request is made by a person who is not a party to the claim, the request shall be referred to the district judge, who may, if he thinks fit, refer it to the judge.

(3) Without prejudice to paragraph (2), for the purposes of section 12(2) of the Act a certificate under this rule may be signed by the court manager or any other officer of the court acting on his behalf.

Rule 10 VARIATION OF PAYMENT

(1) Where a judgment or order has been given or made for the payment of money, the person entitled to the benefit of the judgment or order or, as the case may be, the person liable to make the payment (in this rule referred to as 'the judgment creditor' and 'the debtor' respectively) may apply in accordance with the provisions of this rule for a variation in the date or rate of payment.

(2) The judgment creditor may apply in writing, without notice being served on any other party, for an order that the money, if payable in one sum, be paid at a later date than that by which it is due or by instalments or, if the money is already payable by instalments, that it be paid by the same or smaller instalments, and the court officer may make an order accordingly unless no payment has been made under the judgment or order for 6 years before the date of the application in which case he shall refer the application to the district judge.

(3) The judgment creditor may apply to the district judge on notice for an order that the money, if payable in one sum, be paid at an earlier date than that by which it is due or, if the money is payable by instalments, that it be paid in one sum or by larger instalments, and any such application shall be made in writing stating the proposed terms and the grounds on which it is made.

(4) Where an application is made under paragraph (3)—
   (a) the proceedings shall be automatically transferred to the debtor's home court if the judgment or order was not given or made in that court; and
   (b) the court officer shall fix a day for the hearing of the application before the district judge and give to the judgment creditor and the debtor not less than 8 days' notice of the day so fixed,
and at the hearing the district judge may make such order as seems just.

(5) The debtor may apply for an order that the money, if payable in one sum, be paid at a later date than that by which it is due or by instalments or, if the money is already payable by instalments, that it be paid by smaller instalments, and any such application shall be in the appropriate form stating the proposed terms, the grounds on which it is made and including a signed statement of the debtor's means.

(6) Where an application is made under paragraph (5), the court officer shall—
   (a) send the judgment creditor a copy of the debtor's application (and statement of means); and
   (b) require the judgment creditor to notify the court in writing, within 14 days of service of notification upon him, giving his reasons for any objection he may have to the granting of the application.

(7) If the judgment creditor does not notify the court of any objection within the time stated, the court officer shall make an order in the terms applied for.

(8) Upon receipt of a notice from the judgment creditor under paragraph (6), the court officer may determine the date and rate of payment and make an order accordingly.

(9) Any party affected by an order made under paragraph (8) may, within 14 days of service of the order on him and giving his reasons, apply on notice for the order to be re-considered and, where such an application is made—
   (a) the proceedings shall be automatically transferred to the debtor's home court if the judgment or order was not given or made in that court; and
   (b) the court officer shall fix a day for the hearing of the application before the district judge and give to the judgment creditor and the debtor not less than 8 days' notice of the day so fixed.

(10) On hearing an application under paragraph (9), the district judge may confirm the order or set it aside and make such new order as he thinks fit and the order so made shall be entered in the records of the court.

(11) Any order made under any of the foregoing paragraphs may be varied from time to time by a subsequent order made under any of those paragraphs.

Rule 11 SET-OFF OF CROSS-JUDGMENTS

(1) An application under section 72 of the Act for permission to set off any sums, including costs, payable under several judgments or orders each of which was obtained in a county court shall be made in accordance with this rule.

(2) Where the judgments or orders have been obtained in the same county court, the application may be made to that court on the day when the last judgment or order is obtained, if both parties are present, and in any other case shall be made on notice.

(3) Where the judgments or orders have been obtained in different county courts, the application may be made to either of them on notice, and notice shall be given to the other court.

(4) The district judge of the court to which the application is made and the district judge of any other court to which notice is given under paragraph (3) shall forthwith stay execution on any judgment or order in his court to which the application relates and any money paid into court under the judgment or order shall be retained until the application has been disposed of.

(5) The application may be heard and determined by the court and any order giving permission shall direct how any money paid into court is to be dealt with.

(6) Where the judgments or orders have been obtained in different courts, the court in which an order giving permission is made shall send a copy of the order to the other court, which shall deal with any money paid into that court in accordance with the order.

(7) The court officer or, as the case may be, each of the court officers affected shall enter satisfaction in the records of his court for any sums ordered to be set off, and execution or other process for the enforcement of any judgment or order not wholly satisfied shall issue only for the balance remaining payable.

(8) Where an order is made by the High Court giving permission to set off sums payable under several judgments and orders obtained respectively in the High Court and a county court, the court officer of the county court shall, on receipt of a copy of the order, proceed in accordance with paragraph (7).

Rule 13 ORDER OF APPELLATE COURT

Where the Court of Appeal or High Court has heard and determined an appeal from a county court, the party entitled to the benefit of the order of the Court of Appeal or High Court shall deposit the order or an office copy thereof in the office of the county court.

CCR ORDER 24
SUMMARY PROCEEDINGS FOR THE RECOVERY OF LAND

Part I — Land

Rule 1 PROCEEDINGS TO BE BY CLAIM FORM

(1) Where a person claims possession of land which he alleges is occupied solely by a person or persons (not being a tenant or tenants holding over after the termination of the tenancy) who entered into or remained in occupation without his licence or consent or that of any predecessor in title of his, the proceedings may be brought by claim form in accordance with the provisions of this order.

(2) Where proceedings of the type referred to in paragraph (1) are brought, the court will fix a day for the hearing when it issues the claim form.

Rule 2 WITNESS STATEMENT OR AFFIDAVIT IN SUPPORT

(1) The applicant shall file in support of the claim form a witness statement or affidavit stating—
   (a) his interest in the land;
   (b) the circumstances in which the land has been occupied without licence or consent and in which his claim to possession arises; and
   (c) that he does not know the name of any person occupying the land who is not named in the claim form.

(2) Where the applicant considers that service in accordance with rule 3(2)(b) may be necessary, he shall provide, together with the claim form, sufficient stakes and sealable transparent envelopes for such service.

Rule 3 SERVICE OF CLAIM FORM

(1) Where any person in occupation of the land is named in the claim form, the application shall be served on him—
   (a) by delivering to him personally a copy of the claim form, together with the notice of the return day and a copy of the witness statement or affidavit in support;
   (b) by an officer of the court leaving the documents mentioned in sub-paragraph (a), or sending them to him, at the premises;
   (c) in accordance with CPR rule 6.4(2); or
   (d) in such other manner as the court may direct.

(2) Where any person not named as a respondent is in occupation of the land, the claim form shall be served (whether or not it is also required to be served in accordance with paragraph (1)), unless the court otherwise directs, by—

(a) affixing a copy of each of the documents mentioned in paragraph (1)(a) to the main door or other conspicuous part of the premises and, if practicable, inserting through the letterbox at the premises a copy of those documents enclosed in a sealed transparent envelope addressed to 'the occupiers'; or

(b) placing stakes in the ground at conspicuous parts of the occupied land, to each of which shall be affixed a sealed transparent envelope addressed to 'the occupiers' and containing a copy of each of the documents mentioned in paragraph (1)(a).

Rule 4 APPLICATION BY OCCUPIER TO BE MADE A PARTY

A person not named as a respondent who is in occupation of the land and wishes to be heard on the question whether an order for possession should be made may apply at any stage of the proceedings to be joined as respondent, and the notice of the return day shall contain a notice to that effect.

Rule 5 HEARING OF CLAIM

(1) Except in case of urgency and by permission of the court, the day fixed for the hearing of the claim—

(a) in the case of residential premises, shall not be less than 5 days after the day of service; and

(b) in the case of other land, shall not be less than 2 days after the day of service.

(3) An order for possession in proceedings under this Order shall be to the effect that the applicant do recover possession of the land mentioned in the claim form.

(4) Nothing in this Order shall prevent the court from ordering possession to be given on a specified date in the exercise of any power which could have been exercised if possession had been sought otherwise than in accordance with this Order.

Rule 6 WARRANT OF POSSESSION

(1) Subject to paragraphs (2) and (3), a warrant of possession to enforce an order for possession under this Order may be issued at any time after the making of the order and subject to the provisions of Order 26, rule 17, a warrant of restitution may be issued in aid of the warrant of possession.

(2) No warrant of possession shall be issued after the expiry of 3 months from the date of the Order without the permission of the court, and an application for such permission may be made without notice being served on any other party unless the court otherwise directs.

(3) Nothing in this rule shall authorise the issue of a warrant of possession before the date on which possession is ordered to be given.

Rule 7 SETTING ASIDE ORDER

The judge or district judge may, on such terms as he thinks just, set aside or vary any order made in proceedings under this Order.

Part II — Interim Possession Orders

Rule 8 DEFINITIONS AND INTERPRETATION

(1) In this Part of this Order—

(a) 'applicant' means a person who applies for an interim possession order;

(b) 'premises' means premises within the meaning of section 12 of the Criminal Law Act 1977; and

(c) 'respondent' means a person against whom an application for an interim possession order is made, whether or not that person is named in the application or order.

(2) Where a rule in this Part of this order requires an act to be done within a specified number of hours, CPR rule 2.8(4) shall not apply to the calculation of the period of time within which the act must be done.

Rule 9 CONDITIONS FOR INTERIM POSSESSION ORDER APPLICATION

In proceedings for possession under Part I of this Order, an application may be made for an interim possession order where the following conditions are satisfied—

(a) the only claim made in the proceedings is for the recovery of premises;
(b) the claim is made by a person who—
  (i) has an immediate right to possession of the premises; and
  (ii) has had such a right throughout the period of unlawful occupation complained of;
(c) the claim is made against a person (not being a tenant holding over after the termination of the tenancy) who entered the premises without the applicant's consent and has not subsequently been granted such consent, but no application for an interim possession order may be made against a person who entered the premises with the consent of the person who, at the time of entry, had an immediate right to possession of the premises; and
(d) the claim is made within 28 days of the date on which the applicant first knew, or ought reasonably to have known, that the respondent, or any of the respondents, was in occupation.

Rule 10 ISSUE OF THE APPLICATIONS

(1) In proceedings in which an application for an interim possession order is made, unless otherwise provided, rules 2 to 7 shall not apply.
(2) The applicant shall file—
  (a) a claim form;
  (b) a witness statement or affidavit in support; and
  (c) an application notice,
each of which shall be in the appropriate prescribed form, together with sufficient copies for service on the respondent.
(3) The witness statement or affidavit shall be sworn by the applicant personally or, where the application for an interim possession order is made by a body corporate, shall be sworn by an officer of the body corporate duly authorised to swear the witness statement or affidavit on its behalf.
(4) On the filing of the documents mentioned in paragraph (2), the court shall—
  (a) issue the claim form and the application for an interim possession order;
  (b) fix an appointment for the application to be considered; and
  (c) insert the time of that appointment in the application notice filed under paragraph (2) and in the copy to be served on the respondent.
(5) The time fixed for consideration of the application for an interim possession order shall be as soon as possible after the documents have been filed, but not less than 3 days after the date on which the application for an interim possession order is issued.

Rule 11 SERVICE OF THE NOTICE OF APPLICATION

(1) Within 24 hours of the issue of the application for an interim possession order, the applicant shall serve the following documents on the respondent, namely—
  (a) the application notice; and
  (b) the prescribed form of respondent's witness statement or affidavit, which shall be attached to the application notice.
(2) The applicant shall serve the documents mentioned in paragraph (1) by fixing a copy of them to the main door or other conspicuous part of the premises and, if practicable, inserting through the letter-box at the premises a copy of the documents in a sealed, transparent envelope addressed to 'the occupiers'.
(3) Additionally (but not alternatively), the applicant may place stakes in the ground at conspicuous parts of the premises to each of which shall be fixed a sealed transparent envelope addressed to 'the occupiers' and containing a copy of the documents.
(4) At or before the time fixed for consideration of the application for an interim possession order, the applicant shall file a witness statement or affidavit of service in the prescribed form in relation to the documents mentioned in paragraph (1).

(5) At any time before the time fixed for consideration of the application for an interim possession order the respondent may file a witness statement or affidavit in the prescribed form in response to the application.

Rule 12 CONSIDERATION OF THE APPLICATION

(1) If the respondent has filed a witness statement or affidavit in accordance with rule 11(5), he may attend before the court when the application for an interim possession order is considered to answer such questions on his witness statement or affidavit or on the applicant's witness statement or affidavit as the court may put to him.

(2) The parties' witness statements or affidavits shall be read in evidence and no oral evidence shall be adduced except in response to questions put by the court.

(3) If the court so directs, an application for an interim possession order may be dealt with in private and in the absence of one or both of the parties.

(4) In deciding whether to grant an interim possession order the court shall have regard to whether the applicant has given or is prepared to give undertakings in support of his application—

(a) to reinstate the respondent if, after an interim possession order has been made, the court holds that the applicant was not entitled to the order;

(b) to pay damages if, after an interim possession order has been made, the court holds that the applicant was not entitled to the order;

(c) not to damage the premises pending final determination of the possession proceedings;

(d) not to grant a right of occupation to any other person pending final determination of the possession proceedings; and

(e) not to damage or dispose of any of the respondent's possessions pending final determination of the possession proceedings.

(5) The court shall make an interim possession order if—

(a) the applicant has filed a witness statement or affidavit of service of the notice of application; and

(b) the court is satisfied that—

(i) the conditions specified in rule 9 are met; and

(ii) any undertakings given by the applicant as a condition of making the order are adequate.

(6) An interim possession order shall be in a prescribed form and shall be to the effect that the respondent vacate the premises specified in the claim form within 24 hours of service of the order.

(7) On the making of an interim possession order, the court shall fix a return date for the hearing of the claim which shall be not less than 7 days after the date on which the interim possession order is made.

(8) Where an interim possession order is made, the court officer shall submit a draft of the order as soon as possible to the judge or district judge by whom it was made for approval, and when the draft order has been approved the court shall insert in the order the time limit for service under rule 13(1).

(9) Where the court does not make an interim possession order—

(a) the court officer shall fix a return date for the hearing of the claim;

(b) the court may give directions for the further conduct of the matter; and

(c) subject to such directions, the matter shall proceed in accordance with Part I of this Order.

(10) When it has considered the application for an interim possession order, the court shall give a copy of the respondent's witness statement or affidavit (if any) to the applicant, if the applicant requests such a copy.

(11) The court shall serve any directions made under paragraph (9) on the parties and at the same time shall serve on the respondent a copy of the claim form and witness statement or affidavit in support.

Rule 13 SERVICE AND ENFORCEMENT OF THE INTERIM POSSESSION ORDER

(1) An interim possession order must be served within 48 hours of the judge or district judge's approving the draft order under rule 12(8).

(2) The applicant shall serve copies of the claim form, the applicant's witness statement or affidavit and the interim possession order in accordance with rule 11(2) and (3) or in such other manner as the court may direct.

(3) Order 26, rule 17 (enforcement of warrant of possession) shall not apply to the enforcement of an interim possession order.

(4) If an interim possession order is not served within the time limit specified by this rule or by any order extending or abridging time, the applicant may apply to the court for directions for the application for possession to continue under Part I of this Order as if it had not included a claim for an interim possession order.

Rule 14 MATTERS ARISING AFTER MAKING OF AN INTERIM POSSESSION ORDER

(1) Before the return date the applicant shall file a witness statement or affidavit of service in the prescribed form in relation to the documents specified in rule 13(2), and no final order for possession may be made unless such a witness statement or affidavit has been filed.

(2) The interim possession order shall expire on the return date.

(3) On the return date the court may make such order as appears appropriate and may in particular—
   (a) make a final order for possession;
   (b) dismiss the claim for possession;
   (c) give directions for the application for possession to continue under Part I of this order as if it had not included a claim for an interim possession order.

(4) An order may be made on the return date in the absence of one or both of the parties.

(5) If the court holds that the applicant was not entitled to an interim possession order, the respondent may apply for relief pursuant to any undertakings given by the applicant.

(6) Unless it otherwise directs, the court shall serve a copy of any order or directions made under this rule on the parties.

(7) Unless the court otherwise directs, service on the respondent under paragraph (6) shall be in accordance with rule 11(2) and (3).

(8) Rule 6 (warrant of possession) shall apply to the enforcement of a final order for possession made under this rule.

Rule 15 APPLICATION TO SET ASIDE AN INTERIM POSSESSION ORDER

(1) If the respondent has vacated the premises, he may apply on grounds of urgency for the interim possession order to be set aside before the return date.

(2) An application under this rule shall be supported by a witness statement or affidavit.

(3) On receipt of an application to set aside, the judge or district judge shall give directions as to—
   (a) the date for the hearing; and
   (b) the period of notice, if any, to be given to the applicant and the mode of service of any such notice.

(4) No application to set aside an interim possession order may be made under CPR Part 39.3.

(5) Where no notice is required under paragraph (3)(b), the only matter to be dealt with at the hearing shall be whether the interim possession order should be set aside (and the consequent application of any undertaking given under rule 12(4)(a)) and all other matters shall be dealt with on the return date.

(6) The court shall serve on the applicant a copy of any order made under paragraph (5) and, where no notice is required under paragraph (3)(b), the court shall at the same time serve a copy of the respondent's application to set aside and the witness statement or affidavit in support.

(7) Where notice is required under paragraph (3)(b), the court may treat the application as an application to bring forward the return date, in which case rule 14(2) to (8) shall apply accordingly.

CCR ORDER 25
ENFORCEMENT OF JUDGMENTS AND ORDERS: GENERAL

Rule 1 JUDGMENT CREDITOR AND DEBTOR

In this order and Orders 26 to 29 judgment creditor' means the person who has obtained or is entitled to enforce a judgment or order and 'debtor' means the person against whom it was given or made.

Rule 2 TRANSFER OF PROCEEDINGS FOR ENFORCEMENT

(1) Where, with a view to enforcing a judgment or order obtained by him in a county court, a judgment creditor desires to apply for—
  (a) the oral examination of the debtor;
  (b) a charging order under section 1 of the Charging Orders Act 1979;
  (c) an attachment of earnings order; or
  (d) the issue of a judgment summons,

and the application is required by any provision of these rules to be made to another county court, the judgment creditor shall make a request in writing to the court officer of the court in which the judgment or order was obtained for the transfer of the proceedings to the other court.

(2) On receipt of a request under paragraph (1), the court officer shall make an order transferring the proceedings to the other court and shall—
  (a) make an entry of the transfer in the records in his court; and
  (b) send to the court to which the proceedings have been transferred a certificate of the judgment or order stating the purpose for which it has been issued, and, if requested by that officer, all the documents in his custody relating to the proceedings.

(3) When the proceedings have been transferred to the other court—
  (a) that court shall give notice of the transfer to the judgment creditor and the debtor;
  (b) any payment which, by or under these rules or the Court Funds Rules 1987, is authorised or required to be made into court shall be made into that court; and
  (c) subject to sub-paragraph (d), any subsequent steps in the proceedings shall be taken in that court, but
  (d) any application or appeal under Order 37 shall be made to the court in which the judgment or order was obtained.

(4) If the judgment creditor desires to make a subsequent application for any of the remedies mentioned in paragraph (1)(a) to (d) and the application is required to be made to another court, he may make a request under paragraph (1) to the court to which the proceedings have been transferred and paragraphs (2) and (3) shall apply with the necessary modifications.

Rule 3 ORAL EXAMINATION OF DEBTOR

(1) Where a person has obtained a judgment or order in a county court for the payment of money or where an order has been made under rule 12 of this Order, the appropriate court may, on an application made by the judgment creditor without notice being served on any other party, order the debtor or, if the debtor is a body corporate, an officer thereof to attend before the court officer and be orally examined as to the debtor's means of satisfying the judgment or order, and may also order the person to be examined to produce at the time and place appointed for the examination any books or documents in his possession relevant to the debtor's means.

(1A) An application under paragraph (1) shall certify the amount of money remaining due under the judgment, order or award (as that word is defined by rule 12(1) of this Order).

(2) The appropriate court for the purposes of paragraph (1) shall be the court for the district in which the person to be examined (or, if there are more such persons than one, any of them) resides or carries on business.

(3) The order shall be served in the manner required for service of the notice of the day of hearing in accordance with Order 3, rule 6 except that Order 3, rule 6(11) will not apply.

CPR SCHEDULE 2

(4) If the person to be examined fails to attend at the time and place fixed for the examination, the court may adjourn the examination and make a further order for his attendance and any such order shall direct that any payments made thereafter shall be paid into court and not direct to the judgment creditor.

(5) Nothing in Order 29, rule 1(2) to (7) shall apply to an order made under paragraph (4), but Order 27, rules 7B and 8, shall apply, with the necessary modifications, as they apply to orders made under section 23(1) of the Attachment of Earnings Act 1971 except that for a period of 5 days specified in paragraph (1) of Order 27, rule 8 there shall be substituted a period of 10 days.

(5A) Where an examination has been adjourned, the judgment creditor, if requested to do so by the person to be examined not less than 7 days before the day fixed for the adjourned examination shall pay to him a sum reasonably sufficient to cover his expenses in travelling to and from the court unless such a sum was paid to him at the time of service of the order for oral examination.

(5B) The judgment creditor shall, not more than 4 days before the day fixed for the adjourned examination, file a certificate stating either that no request has been made under paragraph (5A) or that a sum has been paid in accordance with such a request.

(5C) Where the person to be examined has made a request under paragraph (5A), he shall not be committed to prison under Order 29, rule 1(1) for having failed to attend at the time and place fixed for the adjourned examination unless the judgment creditor has paid to him a sum reasonably sufficient to cover the travelling expenses before the day fixed for the adjourned examination.

(6) CPR rule 34.8 (evidence by deposition) shall apply with the necessary modifications, to an examination under this rule as it applies to an examination under that Part save that CPR rule 34.8(6)(b) shall not apply.

(7) Nothing in this rule shall be construed as preventing the court, before deciding whether to make an order under paragraph (1), from giving the person to be examined an opportunity of making a statement in writing or a witness statement or affidavit as to the debtor's means.

Rule 4 EXAMINATION OF DEBTOR UNDER JUDGMENT NOT FOR MONEY

Where any difficulty arises in or in connection with the enforcement of any judgment or order for some relief other than the payment of money, the court may make an order under rule 3 for the attendance of the debtor and for his examination on such questions as may be specified in the order, and that rule shall apply accordingly with the necessary modifications.

Rule 5 PROVISION OF INFORMATION

(1) The requests and applications mentioned in paragraph (2) are—
    (a) a request for a warrant of execution, delivery or possession;
    (b) a request for a judgment summons or warrant of committal;
    (c) an application for a garnishee order under Order 30, rule 1; and
    (d) an application for a charging order.

(2) Where the judgment creditor has filed any request or application referred to in paragraph (1) or is seeking to enforce a judgment or order by making an application under rule 3 or under Order 27 or 32, he shall forthwith notify the court of any payment received from the debtor in respect of the judgment to be enforced after the date of the application and before—
    (a) the final return to the warrant of execution, delivery or possession; or
    (b) in any other case, the date fixed for the hearing of the application.

(3) Without prejudice to rule 8(9), where the judgment creditor applies to re-issue enforcement proceedings, he shall file a request in that behalf certifying the amount of money remaining due under the judgment or order and that the whole or part of any instalment due remains unpaid and stating why re-issue is necessary.

Rule 5A INTEREST ON JUDGMENT DEBTS

Where the judgment creditor claims interest pursuant to the County Courts (Interest on Judgment Debts) Order 1991 and takes proceedings to enforce

payment under the relevant judgment (within the meaning of article 4(1) of that Order), any request or application for enforcement made in those proceedings shall be accompanied by two copies of a certificate giving details of—
  (a) the amount of interest claimed and the sum on which it is claimed;
  (b) the dates from and to which interest has accrued; and
  (c) the rate of interest which has been applied and, where more than one rate of interest has been applied, the relevant dates and rates.

Rule 6 DESCRIPTION OF PARTIES
Where the name or address of the judgment creditor or the debtor as given in the request for the issue of a warrant of execution or delivery, judgment summons or warrant of committal differs from his name or address in the judgment or order sought to be enforced and the judgment creditor satisfies the court officer that the name or address as given in the request is applicable to the person concerned, the judgment creditor or the debtor, as the case may be, shall be described in the warrant or judgment summons as 'C.D. of [name and address as given in the request] suing [or sued] as A.D. of [name and address in the judgment or order]'.

Rule 7 RECORDING AND GIVING INFORMATION AS TO WARRANTS AND ORDERS
  (1) Subject to paragraph (1A), every district judge by whom a warrant or order is issued or received for execution shall from time to time state in the records of his court what has been done in the execution of the warrant or order.
  (1A) Where a warrant of execution issued by a court ('the home court') is sent to another court for execution ('the foreign court'), paragraph (1) shall not apply to the district judge of the home court, but when such a warrant is returned to the home court under paragraph (7), the court officer of the home court shall state in the records of his court what has been done in the execution of the warrant or order.
  (2) If the warrant or order has not been executed within one month from the date of its issue or receipt by him, the court officer of the court responsible for its execution shall, at the end of that month and every subsequent month during which the warrant remains outstanding, send notice of the reason for non-execution to the judgment creditor and, if the warrant or order was received from another court, to that court.
  (3) The district judge responsible for executing a warrant or order shall give such information respecting it as may reasonably be required by the judgment creditor and, if the warrant or order was received by him from another court, by the district judge of that court.
  (4) Where money is received in pursuance of a warrant of execution or committal sent by one court to another court, the foreign court shall, subject to paragraph (5) and to section 346 of Insolvency Act 1986 and section 326 of the Companies Act 1948 send the money to the judgment creditor in the manner prescribed by the Court Funds Rules 1987 and, where the money is received in pursuance of a warrant of committal, make a return to the home court.
  (5) Where interpleader proceedings are pending, the court shall not proceed in accordance with paragraph (4) until the interpleader proceedings are determined and the district judge shall then make a return showing how the money is to be disposed of and, if any money is payable to the judgment creditor, the court shall proceed in accordance with paragraph (4).
  (6) Where a warrant of committal has been received from another court, the foreign court shall, on the execution of the warrant, send notice thereof to the home court.
  (7) Mere a warrant of execution has been received from another court, either—
    (a) on the execution of the warrant; or
    (b) if the warrant is not executed—
      (i) on the making of a final return to the warrant; or
      (ii) on suspension of the warrant under rule 8 (suspension of judgment or execution) or Order 26, rule 10 (withdrawal and suspension of warrant at creditor's request),
the foreign court shall return the warrant to the home court.

Rule 8 SUSPENSION OF JUDGMENT OR EXECUTION

(1) The power of the court to suspend or stay a judgment or order or to stay execution of any warrant may be exercised by the district judge or, in the case of the power to stay execution of a warrant of execution and in accordance with the provisions of this rule, by the court officer.

(2) An application by the debtor to stay execution of a warrant of execution shall be in the appropriate form stating the proposed terms, the grounds on which it is made and including a signed statement of the debtor's means.

(3) Where the debtor makes an application under paragraph (2), the court shall—

(a) send the judgment creditor a copy of the debtor's application (and statement of means); and

(b) require the creditor to notify the court in writing, within 14 days of service of notification upon him, giving his reasons for any objection he may have to the granting of the application.

(4) If the judgment creditor does not notify the court of any objection within the time stated, the court officer may make an order suspending the warrant on terms of payment.

(5) Upon receipt of a notice by the judgment creditor under paragraph (3)(b), the court officer may, if the judgment creditor objects only to the terms offered, determine the date and rate of payment and make an order suspending the warrant on terms of payment.

(6) Any party affected by an order made under paragraph (5) may, within 14 days of service of the order on him and giving his reasons, apply on notice for the order to be reconsidered and the court shall fix a day for the hearing of the application before the district judge and give to the judgment creditor and the debtor not less than 8 days' notice of the day so fixed.

(7) On hearing an application under paragraph (6), the district judge may confirm the order or set it aside and make such new order as he thinks fit and the order so made shall be entered in the records of the court.

(8) Where the judgment creditor states in his notice under paragraph (3)(b) that he wishes the bailiff to proceed to execute the warrant, the court shall fix a day for a hearing before the district judge of the debtor's application and give to the judgment creditor and to the debtor not less than 2 days' notice of the day so fixed.

(9) Subject to any directions given by the district judge, where a warrant of execution has been suspended, it may be re-issued on the judgment creditor's filing a request pursuant to rule 5(3) showing that any condition subject to which the warrant was suspended has not been complied with.

(10) Where an order is made by the district judge suspending a warrant of execution, the debtor may be ordered to pay the costs of the warrant and any fees or expenses incurred before its suspension and the order may authorise the sale of a sufficient portion of any goods seized to cover such costs, fees and expenses and the expenses of sale.

Rule 9 ENFORCEMENT OF JUDGMENT OR ORDER AGAINST FIRM

(1) Subject to paragraph (2), a judgment or order against a firm may be enforced against—

(a) any property of the firm;

(b) any person who admitted in the proceedings that he was a partner or was adjudged to be a partner;

(c) any person who was served as a partner with the claim form if—

(i) judgment was entered under CPR Part 12, in default of defence or under CPR Part 14 on admission; or

(iii) the person so served did not appear at the trial or hearing of the proceedings.

(2) A judgment or order may not be enforced under paragraph (1) against a member of the firm who was out of England and Wales when the claim form was issued unless he—

(a) was served within England and Wales with the claim form as a partner; or

(b) was, with the permission of the court under RSC Order 11, rule 1 served out of England and Wales with the claim form as a partner,
and, except as provided by paragraph (1)(a) and by the foregoing provisions of this paragraph, a judgment or order obtained against a firm shall not render liable, release or otherwise affect a member of the firm who was out of England and Wales when the claim form was issued.

(3) A judgment creditor who claims to be entitled to enforce a judgment or order against any other person as a partner may apply to the court for permission to do so by filing an application notice in accordance with CPR Part 23.

(4) An application notice under paragraph (3) shall be served on the alleged partner, not less than three days before the hearing of the application, in the manner required for service of the notice of the day of hearing in accordance with Order 3, rule 6 and on the hearing of the application, if the alleged partner does not dispute his liability, the court may, subject to paragraph (2), give permission to enforce the judgment or order against him and, if he disputes liability, the court may order that the question of his liability be tried and determined in such a manner as the court thinks fit.

(5) The foregoing provisions of this rule shall not apply where it is desired to enforce in a county court a judgment or order of the High Court, or a judgment, order, decree or award of any court or arbitrator which is or has become enforceable as if it were a judgment or order of the High Court, and in any such case the provisions of the RSC relating to the enforcement of a judgment or order against a firm shall apply.

Rule 10 ENFORCING JUDGMENT BETWEEN A FIRM AND ITS MEMBERS

(1) Execution to enforce a judgment or order given or made in—

(a) proceedings by or against a firm, in the name of the firm against or by a member of the firm; or

(b) proceedings by a firm in the name of the firm against a firm in the name of the firm where those firms have one or more members in common,
shall not issue without the permission of the court.

(2) On an application for permission the court may give such directions, including directions as to the taking of accounts and the making of inquiries, as may be just.

Rule 11 ENFORCEMENT OF HIGH COURT JUDGMENT

(1) A judgment creditor who desires to enforce a judgment or order of the High Court, or a judgment, order, decree or award of any court or arbitrator which is or has become enforceable as if it were a judgment or order of the High Court, shall file in the appropriate court (with such documents as are required to be filed for the purpose of enforcing a judgment or order of a county court)—

(a) an office copy of the judgment or order or, in the case of a judgment, order, decree or award of a court other than the High Court or an arbitrator, such evidence of the judgment, order, decree or award and of its enforceability as a judgment of the High Court as the district judge may require;

(b) a certificate verifying the amount due under the judgment, order, decree or award;

(c) where a writ of execution has been issued to enforce it, a copy of the sheriff's return to the writ; and

(d) a copy of the order to transfer the proceedings to the county court.

(2) in this rule the 'appropriate court' means the county court in which the relevant enforcement proceedings might, by virtue of these rules, be brought if the judgment or order had been obtained in proceedings commenced in a county court.

Provided that if under these rules the court in which the relevant enforcement proceedings might be brought is identified by reference to the court in which the judgment or order has been obtained the appropriate court shall be the court for the district in which the debtor resides or carries on business.

(3) The provisions of this rule are without prejudice to Order 26, rule 2.

Rule 12 ENFORCEMENT OF AWARD OF TRIBUNAL

(1) This rule applies where any enactment (other than these rules) provides that if a county court so orders, a sum of money is recoverable as if payable under an order of a county court, and in this rule an application for such an order is referred to as an application to enforce an award and 'award' means the award, order, agreement or decision which it is sought to enforce.

(2) Unless these rules otherwise provide, an application to enforce an award shall be made without notice by—

(a) certifying the amount remaining due to the applicant; and

(b) producing either the original or a copy of the award and by filing a copy.

(3) Unless otherwise provided, the application shall be made to the court for the district in which the person against whom the award was made resides or carries on business or, where that person does not reside or carry on business within England and Wales, to the court for the district in which the applicant resides or carries on business.

(4) The order may be made by the court officer.

Rule 13 TRANSFER TO HIGH COURT FOR ENFORCEMENT

(1) Where the judgment creditor makes a request for a certificate of judgment under Order 22, rule 8(1) for the purpose of enforcing the judgment or order in the High Court by execution against goods, the grant of a certificate by the court shall take effect as an order to transfer the proceedings to the High Court and the transfer shall have effect on the grant of that certificate.

(2) On the transfer of proceedings in accordance with paragraph (1), the court shall give notice to the debtor that the proceedings have been transferred and shall make an entry of that fact in the records of his court.

(3) In a case where a request for a certificate of judgment is made under Order 22, rule 8(1) for the purpose of enforcing a judgment or order in the High Court and—

(a) an application for a variation in the date or rate of payment of money due under a judgment or order;

(b) an application under either CPR rule 39.3(3) or CPR rule 13.4;

(c) a request for an administration order; or

(d) an application for a stay of execution under section 88 of the Act,

is pending, the request for the certificate shall not be dealt with until those proceedings are determined.

CCR ORDER 26
WARRANTS OF EXECUTION, DELIVERY AND POSSESSION

Rule 1 APPLICATION FOR WARRANT OF EXECUTION

(1) A judgment creditor desiring a warrant of execution to be issued shall file a request in that behalf certifying—

(a) the amount remaining due under the judgment or order; and

(b) where the order made is for payment of a sum of money by instalments—

(i) that the whole or part of any instalment due remains unpaid; and

(ii) the amount for which the warrant is to be issued.

(1A) The court officer shall discharge the functions—

(a) under section 85(2) of the Act of issuing a warrant of execution;

(b) under section 85(3) of the Act of entering in the record mentioned in that subsection and on the warrant the precise time of the making of the application to issue the warrant, and

(c) under section 103(1) of the Act of sending the warrant of execution to another county court.

(2) Where the court has made an order for payment of a sum of money by instalments and default has been made in payment of such an instalment, a warrant of execution may be issued for the whole of the said sum of money and costs then remaining unpaid or, subject to paragraph (3), for such part as the judgment creditor may request, not being in the latter case less than £50 or the amount of one monthly instalment or, as the case may be, 4 weekly instalments, whichever is the greater.

(3) In any case to which paragraph (2) applies no warrant shall be issued unless at the time when it is issued—
(a) the whole or part of an instalment which has already become due remains unpaid; and
(b) any warrant previously issued for part of the said sum of money and costs has expired or has been satisfied or abandoned.
(4) Where a warrant is issued for the whole or part of the said sum of money and costs, the court officer shall, unless the district judge responsible for execution of the warrant directs otherwise, send a warning notice to the person against whom the warrant is issued and, where such a notice is sent, the warrant shall not be levied until 7 days thereafter.
(5) Where judgment is given or an order made for payment otherwise than by instalments of a sum of money and costs to be assessed in accordance with CPR Part 47 (detailed assessment procedure) and default is made in payment of the sum of money before the costs have been assessed, a warrant of execution may issue for recovery of the sum of money and a separate warrant may issue subsequently for the recovery of the costs if default is made in payment of them.

Rule 2 EXECUTION OF HIGH COURT JUDGMENT
(1) Where it is desired to enforce by warrant of execution a judgment or order of the High Court, or a judgment, order, decree or award which is or has become enforceable as if it were a judgment of the High Court, the request referred to in rule 1(1) may be filed in any court in the district of which execution is to be levied.
(2) Subject to Order 25, rule 9(5), any restriction imposed by these rules on the issue of execution shall apply as if the judgment, order, decree or award were a judgment or order of the county court, but permission to issue execution shall not be required if permission has already been given by the High Court.
(3) Notice of the issue of the warrant shall be sent by the county court to the High Court.

Rule 3 EXECUTION AGAINST FARMER
If after the issue of a warrant of execution the district judge for the district in which the warrant is to be executed has reason to believe that the debtor is a farmer, the execution creditor shall, if so required by the district judge, furnish him with an official certificate, dated not more than three days beforehand, of the result of a search at the Land Registry as to the existence of any charge registered against the debtor under the Agricultural Credits Act 1928.

Rule 4 CONCURRENT WARRANTS
Two or more warrants of execution may be issued concurrently for execution in different districts, but—
(a) no more shall be levied under all the warrants together than is authorised to be levied under one of them; and
(b) the costs of more than one such warrant shall not be allowed against the debtor except by order of the court.

Rule 5 PERMISSION TO ISSUE CERTAIN WARRANTS
(1) A warrant of execution shall not issue without the permission of the court where—
(a) six years or more have elapsed since the date of the judgment or order;
(b) any change has taken place, whether by death or otherwise in the parties entitled to enforce the judgment or order or liable to have it enforced against them;
(c) the judgment or order is against the assets of a deceased person coming into the hands of his executors or administrators after the date of the judgment or order and it is sought to issue execution against such assets; or
(d) any goods to be seized under a warrant of execution are in the hands of a receiver appointed by a court.
(2) An application for permission shall be supported by a witness statement or affidavit establishing the applicant's right to relief and may be made without notice

being served on any other party in the first instance but the court may direct the application notice to be served on such persons as it thinks fit.

(3) Where, by reason of one and the same event, a person seeks permission under paragraph (1)(b) to enforce more judgments or orders than one, he may make one application only, specifying in a schedule all the judgments or orders in respect of which it is made, and if the application notice is directed to be served on any person, it need set out only such part of the application as affects him.

(4) Paragraph (1) is without prejudice to any enactment, rule or direction by virtue of which a person is required to obtain the permission of the court for the issue of a warrant or to proceed to execution or otherwise to the enforcement of a judgment or order.

Rule 6 DURATION AND RENEWAL OF WARRANT

(1) A warrant of execution shall, for the purpose of execution, be valid in the first instance for 12 months beginning with the date of its issue, but if not wholly executed, it may be renewed from time to time, by order of the court, for a period of 12 months at any one time, beginning with the day next following that on which it would otherwise expire, if an application for renewal is made before that day or such later day (if any) as the court may allow.

(2) A note of any such renewal shall be indorsed on the warrant and it shall be entitled to priority according to the time of its original issue or, where appropriate, its receipt by the district judge responsible for its execution.

Rule 7 NOTICE ON LEVY

Any bailiff upon levying execution shall deliver to the debtor or leave at the place where execution is levied a notice of the warrant.

Rule 8 BANKRUPTCY OR WINDING UP OF DEBTOR

(1) Where the district judge responsible for the execution of a warrant is required by any provision of the Insolvency Act 1986 or any other enactment relating to insolvency to retain the proceeds of sale of goods sold under the warrant or money paid in order to avoid a sale, the court shall, as soon as practicable after the sale or the receipt of the money, send notice to the execution creditor and, if the warrant issued out of another court, to that court.

(2) Where the district judge responsible for the execution of a warrant—
  (a) receives notice that a bankruptcy order has been made against the debtor or, if the debtor is a company, that a provisional liquidator has been appointed or that an order has been made or a resolution passed for the winding up of the company; and
  (b) withdraws from possession of goods seized or pays over to the official receiver or trustee in bankruptcy or, if the debtor is a company, to the liquidator the proceeds of sale of goods sold under the warrant or money paid in order to avoid a sale or seized or received in part satisfaction of the warrant,
the court shall send notice to the execution creditor and, if the warrant issued out of another court, to that court.

(3) Where the court officer of a court to which a warrant issued out of another court has been sent for execution receives any such notice as is referred to in paragraph (2)(a) after he has sent to the home court any money seized or received in part satisfaction of the warrant, he shall forward the notice to that court.

Rule 10 WITHDRAWAL AND SUSPENSION OF WARRANT AT CREDITOR'S REQUEST

(1) Where an execution creditor requests the district judge responsible for executing a warrant to withdraw from possession, he shall, subject to the following paragraphs of this rule, be treated as having abandoned the execution, and the court shall mark the warrant as withdrawn by request of the execution creditor.

(2) Where the request is made in consequence of a claim having been made under Order 33, rule 1, to goods seized under the warrant, the execution shall be treated as being abandoned in respect only of the goods claimed.

(3) If the district judge responsible for executing a warrant is requested by the execution creditor to suspend it in pursuance of an arrangement between him and

the debtor, the court shall mark the warrant as suspended by request of the execution creditor and the execution creditor may subsequently apply to the district judge holding the warrant for it to be re-issued and, if he does so, the application shall be deemed for the purpose of section 85(3) of the Act to be an application to issue the warrant.

(4) Nothing in this rule shall prejudice any right of the execution creditor to apply for the issue of a fresh warrant or shall authorise the re-issue of a warrant which has been withdrawn or has expired or has been superseded by the issue of a fresh warrant.

Rule 11 SUSPENSION OF PART WARRANT

Where a warrant issued for part of a sum of money and costs payable under a judgment or order is suspended on payment of instalments, the judgment or order shall, unless the court otherwise directs, be treated as suspended on those terms as respects the whole of the sum of money and costs then remaining unpaid.

Rule 12 INVENTORY AND NOTICE WHERE GOODS REMOVED

(1) Where goods seized in execution are removed, the court shall forthwith deliver or send to the debtor a sufficient inventory of the goods removed and shall, not less than 4 days before the time fixed for the sale, give him notice of the time and place at which the goods will be sold.

(2) The inventory and notice shall be given to the debtor by delivering them to him personally or by sending them to him by post at his place of residence or, if his place of residence is not known, by leaving them for him, or sending them to him by post, at the place from which the goods were removed.

Rule 13 ACCOUNT OF SALE

Where goods are sold under an execution, the court shall furnish the debtor with a detailed account in writing of the sale and of the application of the proceeds.

Rule 14 NOTIFICATION TO FOREIGN COURT OF PAYMENT MADE

Where, after a warrant has been sent to a foreign court for execution but before a final return has been made to the warrant, the home court is notified of a payment made in respect of the sum for which the warrant is issued, the home court shall send notice of the payment to the foreign court.

Rule 15 ORDER FOR PRIVATE SALE

(1) Subject to paragraph (6), an order of the court under section 97 of the Act that a sale under an execution may be made otherwise than by public auction may be made on the application of the execution creditor or the debtor or the district judge responsible for the execution of the warrant.

(2) Where he is not the applicant for an order under this rule, the district judge responsible for the execution of the warrant shall, on the demand of the applicant, furnish him with a list containing the name and address of every execution creditor under any other warrant or writ of execution against the goods of the debtor of which the district judge has notice, and where the district judge is the applicant, he shall prepare such a list.

(3) Not less than 4 days before the day fixed for the hearing of the application, the applicant shall give notice of the application to each of the other persons by whom the application might have been made and to every person named in the list referred to in paragraph (2).

(4) The applicant shall produce the list to the court on the hearing of the application.

(5) Every person to whom notice of the application was given may attend and be heard on the hearing of the application.

(6) Where the district judge responsible for the execution of the warrant is the district judge by whom it was issued and he has no notice of any other warrant or writ of execution against the goods of the debtor, an order under this rule may be made by the court of its own motion with the consent of the execution creditor and the debtor or after giving them an opportunity of being heard.

CPR SCHEDULE 2

Rule 16 WARRANT OF DELIVERY

(1) Except where an Act or rule provides otherwise, a judgment or order for the delivery of any goods shall be enforceable by warrant of delivery in accordance with this rule.

(2) If the judgment or order does not give the person against whom it was given or made the alternative of paying the value of the goods, it may be enforced by a warrant of specific delivery, that is to say, a warrant to recover the goods without alternative provision for recovery of their value.

(3) If the judgment or order is for the delivery of the goods or payment of their value, it may be enforced by a warrant of delivery to recover the goods or their value.

(4) Where a warrant of delivery is issued, the judgment creditor shall be entitled, by the same or a separate warrant, to execution against the debtor's goods for any money payable under the judgment or order which is to be enforced by the warrant of delivery.

(4A) Where a judgment or order is given or made for the delivery of goods or payment of their value and a warrant is issued to recover the goods or their value, money paid into court under the warrant shall be appropriated first to any sum of money and costs awarded.

(5) The foregoing provisions of this Order, so far as applicable, shall have effect, with the necessary modifications, in relation to warrants of delivery as they have effect in relation to warrants of execution.

Rule 17 WARRANT OF POSSESSION

(1) A judgment or order for the recovery of land shall be enforceable by warrant of possession.

(2) Without prejudice to paragraph (3A), the person desiring a warrant of possession to be issued shall file a request in that behalf certifying that the land has not been vacated in accordance with the judgment or order for the recovery of the said land.

(3) Where a warrant of possession is issued, the judgment creditor shall be entitled, by the same or a separate warrant, to execution against the debtor's goods for any money payable under the judgment or order which is to be enforced by the warrant of possession.

(3A) In a case to which paragraph (3) applies or where an order for possession has been suspended on terms as to payment of a sum of money by instalments, the judgment creditor shall in his request certify—

    (a) the amount of money remaining due under the judgment or order; and

    (b) that the whole or part of any instalment due remains unpaid.

(4) A warrant of restitution may be issued, with the permission of the court, in aid of any warrant of possession.

(5) An application for permission under paragraph (4) may be made without notice being served on any other party and shall be, supported by evidence of wrongful re-entry into possession following the execution of the warrant of possession and of such further facts as would, in the High Court, enable the judgment creditor to have a writ of restitution issued.

(6) Rules 5 and 6 shall apply, with the necessary modifications, in relation to a warrant of possession and any further warrant in aid of such a warrant as they apply in relation to a warrant of execution.

Rule 18 SAVING FOR ENFORCEMENT BY COMMITTAL

Nothing in rule 16 or 17 shall prejudice any power to enforce a judgment or order for the delivery of goods or the recovery of land by an order of committal.

CCR ORDER 27
ATTACHMENT OF EARNINGS

Part I — General

Rule 1 INTERPRETATION

(1) In this order—

CPR SCHEDULE 2

'the Act of 1971' means the Attachment of Earnings Act 1971 and, unless the context otherwise requires, expressions used in that Act have the same meanings as in that Act.

Rule 2 INDEX OF ORDERS

(1) The court officer of every court shall keep a nominal index of the debtors residing within the district of his court in respect of whom there are in force attachment of earnings orders which have been made by that court or of which the court officer has received notice from another court.

(2) Where a debtor in respect of whom a court has made an attachment of earnings order resides within the district of another court, the court officer of the first-mentioned court shall send a copy of the order to the court officer of the other court for entry in his index.

(3) The court officer shall, on the request of any person having a judgment or order against a person believed to be residing within the district of the court, cause a search to be made in the index of the court and issue a certificate of the result of the search.

Rule 3 APPROPRIATE COURT

(1) Subject to paragraphs (2) and (3), an application for an attachment of earnings order may be made to the court for the district in which the debtor resides.

(2) If the debtor does not reside within England or Wales, or the creditor does not know where he resides, the application may be made to the court in which, or for the district in which, the judgment or order sought to be enforced was obtained.

(3) Where the creditor applies for attachment of earnings orders in respect of two or more debtors jointly liable under a judgment or order, the application may be made to the court for the district in which any of the debtors resides, so however that if the judgment or order was given or made by any such court, the application shall be made to that court.

Rule 4 MODE OF APPLYING

(1) A judgment creditor who desires to apply for an attachment of earnings order shall file his application certifying the amount of money remaining due under the judgment or order and that the whole or part of any instalment due remains unpaid and, where it is sought to enforce an order of a magistrates' court—
    (a) a certified copy of the order; and
    (b) a witness statement or affidavit verifying the amount due under the order or, if payments under the order are required to be made to the clerk to the magistrates' court, a certificate by that clerk to the same effect.

(2) On the filing of the documents mentioned in paragraph (1) the court officer shall, where the order to be enforced is a maintenance order, fix a day for the hearing of the application.

Rule 5 SERVICE AND REPLY

(1) Notice of the application together with a form of reply in the appropriate form, shall be served on the debtor in the manner required for service of the notice of the day of hearing in accordance with Order 3, rule 6 except that Order 3, rule 6(11) shall not apply.

(2) The debtor shall, within 8 days after service on him of the documents mentioned in paragraph (1), file a reply in the form provided, and the instruction to that effect in the notice to the debtor shall constitute a requirement imposed by virtue of section 14(4) of the Act of 1971:

Provided that no proceedings shall be taken for an offence alleged to have been committed under section 23(2)(c) or (f) of the Act of 1971 in relation to the requirement unless the said documents have been served on the debtor personally or the court is satisfied that they came to his knowledge in sufficient time for him to comply with the requirement.

(2A) Nothing in paragraph (2) shall require a defendant to file a reply if, within the period of time mentioned in that paragraph, he pays to the judgment creditor the money remaining due under the judgment or order and, where such payment is made, the judgment creditor shall so inform the court officer.

(3) On receipt of a reply the court officer shall send a copy to the applicant.

Rule 6 NOTICE TO EMPLOYER
Without prejudice to the powers conferred by section 14(1) of the Act of 1971, the court officer may, at any stage of the proceedings, send to any person appearing to have the debtor in his employment a notice requesting him to give to the court, within such period as may be specified in the notice, a statement of the debtor's earnings and anticipated earnings with such particulars as may be so specified.

Rule 7 ATTACHMENT OF EARNINGS ORDER
(1) On receipt of the debtor's reply, the court officer may, if he has sufficient information to do so, make an attachment of earnings order and a copy of the order shall be sent to the parties and to the debtor's employer.
(2) Where an order is made under paragraph (1), the judgment creditor or the debtor may, within 14 days of service of the order on him and giving his reasons, apply on notice for the order to be re-considered and the court officer shall fix a day for the hearing of the application and give to the judgment creditor and the debtor not less than 2 days' notice of the day so fixed.
(3) On hearing an application under paragraph (2), the district judge may confirm the order or set it aside and make such new order as he thinks fit and the order so made shall be entered in the records of the court.
(4) Where an order is not made under paragraph (1), the court officer shall refer the application to the district judge who shall, if he considers that he has sufficient information to do so without the attendance of the parties, determine the application.
(5) Where the district judge does not determine the application under paragraph (4), he shall direct that a day be fixed for the hearing of the application whereupon the court officer shall fix such a day and give to the judgment creditor and the debtor not less than 8 days' notice of the day so fixed.
(6) Where an order is made under paragraph (4), the judgment creditor or the debtor may, within 14 days of service of the order on him and giving his reasons, apply on notice for the order to be re-considered; and the court officer shall fix a day for the hearing of the application and give to the judgment creditor and the debtor not less than 2 days' notice of the day so fixed.
(7) On hearing an application under paragraph (6), the district judge may confirm the order or set it aside and make such new order as he thinks fit and the order so made shall be entered in the records of the court.
(8) If the creditor does not appear at the hearing of the application under paragraph (5) but—
　(a) the court has received a witness statement or affidavit of evidence from him; or
　(b) the creditor requests the court in writing to proceed in his absence,
the court may proceed to hear the application and to make an order thereon.
(9) An attachment of earnings order may be made to secure the payment of a judgment debt if the debt is—
　(a) of not less than £50; or
　(b) for the amount remaining payable under a judgment for a sum of not less than £50.

Rule 7A FAILURE BY DEBTOR
(1) If the debtor has failed to comply with rule 5(2) or to make payment to the judgment creditor, the court officer may issue an order under section 14(1) of the Act of 1971 which shall—
　(a) be indorsed with or incorporate a notice warning the debtor of the consequences of disobedience to the order;
　(b) be served on the debtor personally; and
　(c) direct that any payments made thereafter shall be paid into the court and not direct to the judgment creditor.
(2) Without prejudice to rule 16, if the person served with an order made pursuant to paragraph (1) fails to obey it or to file a statement of his means or to

make payment, the court officer shall issue a notice calling on that person to show good reason why he should not be imprisoned and any such notice shall be served on the debtor personally not less than 5 days before the hearing.

(3) Order 29, rule 1 shall apply, with the necessary modifications and with the substitution of references to the district judge for references to the judge, where a notice is issued under paragraph (2) or (4) of that rule.

(4) In this rule 'statement of means' means a statement given under section 14(1) of the Act of 1971.

Rule 7B SUSPENDED COMMITTAL ORDER

(1) If the debtor fails to attend at an adjourned hearing of an application for an attachment of earnings order and a committal order is made, the judge or district judge may direct that the committal order shall be suspended so long as the debtor attends at the time and place specified in the committal order and paragraphs (2), (4) and (5) of Order 28, rule 7 shall apply, with the necessary modifications, where such a direction is given as they apply where a direction is given under paragraph (1) of that rule.

(2) Where a committal order is suspended under paragraph (1) and the debtor fails to attend at the time and place specified under paragraph (1), a certificate to that effect given by the court officer shall be sufficient authority for the issue of a warrant of committal.

Rule 8 FAILURE BY DEBTOR — MAINTENANCE ORDERS

(1) An order made under section 23(1) of the Act of 1971 for the attendance of the debtor at an adjourned hearing of an application for an attachment of earnings order to secure payments under a maintenance order shall—

(a) be served on the debtor personally not less than 5 days before the day fixed for the adjourned hearing; and

(b) direct that any payments made thereafter shall be paid into the court and not direct to the judgment creditor.

(2) An application by a debtor for the revocation of an order committing him to prison and, if he is already in custody, for his discharge under subsection (7) of the said section 23 shall be made to the judge or district judge in writing without notice to any other party showing the reasons for the debtor's failure to attend the court or his refusal to be sworn or to give evidence, as the case may be, and containing an undertaking by the debtor to attend the court or to be sworn or to give evidence when next ordered or required to do so.

(3) The application shall, if the debtor has already been lodged in prison, be attested by the governor of the prison (or any other officer of the prison not below the rank of principal officer) and in any other case be made on witness statement or affidavit.

(4) Before dealing with the application the judge or district judge may, if he thinks fit, cause notice to be given to the judgment creditor that the application has been made and of a day and hour when he may attend and be heard.

Rule 9 COSTS

(1) Where costs are allowed to the judgment creditor on an application for an attachment of earnings order, there may be allowed—

(a) a charge of a solicitor for attending the hearing and, if the court so directs, for serving the application;

(b) if the court certifies that the case is fit for counsel, a fee to counsel; and

(c) the court fee on the issue of the application.

(2) For the purpose of paragraph (1)(a) a solicitor who has prepared on behalf of the judgment creditor a witness statement or affidavit or request under rule 7(8) shall be treated as having attended the hearing.

(3) The costs may be fixed and allowed without detailed assessment under CPR Part 47.

Rule 10 CONTENTS AND SERVICE OF ORDER

(1) An attachment of earnings order shall contain such of the following particulars relating to the debtor as are known to the court, namely—

(a) his full name and address;
(b) his place of work; and
(c) the nature of his work and his works number, if any, and those particulars shall be the prescribed particulars for the purposes of section 6(3) of the Act of 1971.

(2) An attachment of earnings order and any order varying or discharging such an order shall be served on the debtor and on the person to whom the order is directed, and CPR Part 6 and CPR rules 40.4 and 40.5 shall apply with the further modification that where the order is directed to a corporation which has requested the court that any communication relating to the debtor or to the class of persons to whom he belongs shall be directed to the corporation at a particular address, service may, if the district judge thinks fit, be effected on the corporation at that address.

(3) Where an attachment of earnings order is made to enforce a judgment or order of the High Court or a magistrates' court, a copy of the attachment of earnings order and of any order discharging it shall be sent by the court officer of the county court to the court officer of the High Court, or, as the case may be, the clerk of the magistrates' court.

Rule 11 APPLICATION TO DETERMINE WHETHER PARTICULAR PAYMENTS ARE EARNINGS

An application to the court under section 16 of the Act of 1971 to determine whether payments to the debtor of a particular class or description are earnings for the purpose of an attachment of earnings order may be made to the district judge in writing and the court officer shall thereupon fix a date and time for the hearing of the application by the court and give notice thereof to the persons mentioned in the said section 16(2)(a), (b) and (c).

Rule 12 NOTICE OF CESSER

Where an attachment of earnings order ceases to have effect under section 8(4) of the Act of 1971, the court officer of the court in which the matter is proceeding shall give notice of the cesser to the person to whom the order was directed.

Rule 13 VARIATION AND DISCHARGE BY COURT OF OWN MOTION

(1) Subject to paragraph (9), the powers conferred by section 9(1) of the Act of 1971 may be exercised by the court of its own motion in the circumstances mentioned in the following paragraphs.

(2) Where it appears to the court that a person served with an attachment of earnings order directed to him has not the debtor in his employment, the court may discharge the order.

(3) Where an attachment of earnings order which has lapsed under section 9(4) of the Act of 1971 is again directed to a person who appears to the court to have the debtor in his employment, the court may make such consequential variations in the order as it thinks fit.

(4) Where, after making an attachment of earnings order, the court makes or is notified of the making of another such order in respect of the same debtor which is not to secure the payment of a judgment debt or payments under an administration order, the court may discharge or vary the first-mentioned order having regard to the priority accorded to the other order by paragraph 8 of Schedule 3 to the Act of 1971.

(5) Where, after making an attachment of earnings order, the court makes an order under section 4(1)(b) of the Act of 1971 or makes an administration order, the court may discharge the attachment of earnings order or, if it exercises the power conferred by section 5(3) of the said Act, may vary the order in such manner as it thinks fit.

(6) On making a consolidated attachment of earnings order the court may discharge any earlier attachment of earnings order made to secure the payment of a judgment debt by the same debtor.

(7) Where it appears to the court that a bankruptcy order has been made against a person in respect of whom an attachment of earnings order is in force to

secure the payment of a judgment debt, the court may discharge the attachment of earnings order.

(8) Where an attachment of earnings order has been made to secure the payment of a judgment debt and the court grants permission to issue execution for the recovery of the debt, the court may discharge the order.

(9) Before varying or discharging an attachment of earnings order of its own motion under any of the foregoing paragraphs of this rule, the court shall, unless it thinks it unnecessary in the circumstances to do so, give the debtor and the person on whose application the order was made an opportunity of being heard on the question whether the order should be varied or discharged, and for that purpose the court officer may give them notice of a date, time and place at which the question will be considered.

Rule 14 TRANSFER OF ATTACHMENT ORDER

(1) Where the court by which the question of making a consolidated attachment order falls to be considered is not the court by which any attachment of earnings order has been made to secure the payment of a judgment debt by the debtor, the district judge of the last-mentioned court shall, at the request of the district judge of the first-mentioned court, transfer to that court the matter in which the attachment of earnings order was made.

(2) Without prejudice to paragraph (1), if in the opinion of the judge or district judge of any court by which an attachment of earnings order has been made, the matter could more conveniently proceed in some other court, whether by reason of the debtor having become resident in the district of that court or otherwise, he may order the matter to be transferred to that court.

(3) The court to which proceedings arising out of an attachment of earnings are transferred under this rule shall have the same jurisdiction in relation to the order as if it has been made by that court.

Rule 15 EXERCISE OF POWER TO OBTAIN STATEMENT OF EARNINGS ETC.

(1) An order under section 14(1) of the Act of 1971 shall be indorsed with or incorporate a notice warning the person to whom it is directed of the consequences of disobedience to the order and shall be served on him personally.

(2) Order 34, rule 2, shall apply, with the necessary modifications, in relation to any penalty for failure to comply with an order under the said section 14(1) or, subject to the proviso to rule 5(2), any penalty for failure to comply with a requirement mentioned in that rule, as it applies in relation to a fine under section 55 of the County Courts Act 1984.

Rule 16 OFFENCES

(1) Where it is alleged that a person has committed any offence mentioned in section 23(2)(a), (b), (d), (e) or (f) of the Act of 1971 in relation to proceedings in, or to an attachment of earnings order made by, a county court, the district judge shall, unless it is decided to proceed against the alleged offender summarily, issue a summons calling upon him to show cause why he should not be punished for the alleged offence.

The summons shall be served on the alleged offender personally not less than 14 days before the return day.

(2) Order 34, rules 3 and 4, shall apply, with the necessary modifications, to proceedings for an offence under section 23(2) of the Act of 1971 as they apply to proceedings for offences under the County Courts Act 1984.

Rule 17 MAINTENANCE ORDERS

(1) The foregoing rules of this Order shall apply in relation to maintenance payments as they apply in relation to a judgment debt, subject to the following paragraphs.

(2) An application for an attachment of earnings order to secure payments under a maintenance order made by a county court shall be made to that county court.

(3) Any application under section 32 of the Matrimonial Causes Act 1973 for permission to enforce the payment of arrears which became due more than 12 months before the application for an attachment of earnings order shall be made in that application.

(3A) Notice of the application together with a form of reply in the appropriate form shall be served in the manner required for service of the notice of the day of hearing in accordance with Order 3, rule 6.

(3B) Rule 5(2A) shall not apply.

(4) An application by the debtor for an attachment of earnings order to secure payments under a maintenance order may be made on the making of the maintenance order or an order varying the maintenance order, and rules 4 and 5 shall not apply.

(5) Rule 7 shall have effect as if for paragraphs (1) to (8) there were substituted the following paragraph—

'(1) An application for an attachment of earnings order may be heard and determined by the district judge, who shall hear the application in private.'

(6) Rule 9 shall apply as if for the reference to the amount payable under the relevant adjudication there were substituted a reference to the arrears due under the related maintenance order.

(7) Where an attachment of earnings order made by the High Court designates the court officer of a county court as the collecting officer, that officer shall, on receipt of a certified copy of the order from the court officer of the High Court, send to the person to whom the order is directed a notice as to the mode of payment.

(8) Where an attachment of earnings order made by a county court to secure payments under a maintenance order ceases to have effect and—

(a) the related maintenance order was made by that court; or

(b) the related maintenance order was an order of the High Court and—

(i) the court officer of the county court has received notice of the cessation from the court officer of the High Court; or

(ii) a committal order has been made in the county court for the enforcement of the related maintenance order,

the court officer of the county court shall give notice of the cessation to the person to whom the attachment of earnings order was directed.

(9) Where an attachment of earnings order has been made by a county court to secure payments under a maintenance order, notice under section 10(2) of the Act of 1971 to the debtor and to the person to whom the district judge is required to pay sums received under the order shall be in the form provided for that purpose, and if the debtor wishes to request the court to discharge the attachment of earnings order or to vary it otherwise than by making the appropriate variation, he shall apply to the court, within 14 days after the date of the notice, for the remedy desired.

(10) Rule 13 shall have effect as if for paragraphs (4) to (7) there were substituted the following paragraph—

'(4) Where it appears to the court by which an attachment of earnings order has been made that the related maintenance order has ceased to have effect, whether by virtue of the terms of the maintenance order or under section 28 of the Matrimonial Causes Act 1973 or otherwise, the court may discharge or vary the attachment of earnings order.'

Part II — Consolidated Attachment of Earnings Orders

Rule 18 CASES IN WHICH CONSOLIDATED ORDER MAY BE MADE

Subject to the provisions of rules 19 to 21, the court may make a consolidated attachment order where—

(a) two or more attachment of earnings orders are in force to secure the payment of judgment debts by the same debtor; or

(b) on an application for an attachment of earnings order to secure the payment of a judgment debt, or for a consolidated attachment order to secure the payment of two or more judgment debts, it appears to the court that an attachment of earnings order is already in force to secure the payment of a judgment debt by the same debtor.

Rule 19 APPLICATION FOR CONSOLIDATED ORDER

(1) An application for a consolidated attachment order may be made—
　(a) by the debtor in respect of whom the order is sought; or
　(b) by any person who has obtained or is entitled to apply for an attachment of earnings order to secure the payment of a judgment debt by that debtor.

(2) An application under paragraph (1) may be made in the proceedings in which any attachment of earnings order (other than a priority order) is in force and rules 3, 4 and 5 of this order shall not apply.

(3) Where the judgment which it is sought to enforce was not given by the court which made the attachment of earnings order, the judgment shall be automatically transferred to the court which made the attachment of earnings order.

(3A) An application under paragraph (1)(b) shall certify the amount of money remaining due under the judgment or order and that the whole or part of any instalment due remains unpaid.

(3B) Where an application for a consolidated attachment of earnings order is made, the court officer shall—
　(a) notify any party who may be affected by the application of its terms; and
　(b) require him to notify the court in writing, within 14 days of service of notification upon him, giving his reasons for any objection he may have to the granting of the application.

(3C) If notice of any objection is not given within the time stated, the court officer shall make a consolidated attachment of earnings order.

(3D) If any party objects to the making of a consolidated attachment of earnings order, the court officer shall refer the application to the district judge who may grant the application after considering the objection made and the reasons given.

(3E) In the foregoing paragraphs of this rule, a party affected by the application means—
　(a) where the application is made by the debtor, the creditor in the proceedings in which the application is made and any other creditor who has obtained an attachment of earnings order which is in force to secure the payment of a judgment debt by the debtor;
　(b) where the application is made by the judgment creditor, the debtor and every person who, to the knowledge of the applicant, has obtained an attachment of earnings order which is in force to secure the payment of a judgment debt by the debtor.

(4) A person to whom two or more attachment of earnings orders are directed to secure the payment of judgment debts by the same debtor may request the court in writing to make a consolidated attachment order to secure the payment of those debts, and on receipt of such a request paragraphs (3B) to (3E) shall apply, with the necessary modifications, as if the request were an application by the judgment creditor.

Rule 20 MAKING OF CONSOLIDATED ORDER BY COURT OF ITS OWN MOTION

Where an application is made for an attachment of earnings order to secure the payment of a judgment debt by a debtor in respect of whom an attachment of earnings order is already in force to secure the payment of another judgment debt and no application is made for a consolidated attachment order, the court officer may make such an order of his own motion after giving all persons concerned an opportunity of submitting written objections.

Rule 21 EXTENSION OF CONSOLIDATED ORDER

(1) Where a consolidated attachment order is in force to secure the payment of two or more judgment debts, any creditor to whom another judgment debt is

owed by the same judgment debtor may apply to the court by which the order was made for it to be extended so as to secure the payment of that debt as well as the first-mentioned debts and, if the application is granted, the court may either vary the order accordingly or may discharge it and make a new consolidated attachment order to secure payment of all the aforesaid judgment debts.

(2) An application under this rule shall be treated for the purposes of rules 19 and 20 as an application for a consolidated attachment order.

Rule 22 PAYMENTS UNDER CONSOLIDATED ORDER
Instead of complying with section 13 of the Act of 1971, a court officer who receives payments made to him in compliance with a consolidated attachment order shall, after deducting such court fees, if any, in respect of proceedings for or arising out of the order as are deductible from those payments, deal with the sums paid as he would if they had been paid by the debtor to satisfy the relevant adjudications in proportion to the amounts payable thereunder, and for that purpose dividends may from time to time be declared and distributed among the creditors entitled thereto.

CCR ORDER 28
JUDGMENT SUMMONSES

Rule 1 APPLICATION FOR JUDGMENT SUMMONS
(1) An application for the issue of a judgment summons may be made to the court for the district in which the debtor resides or carries on business or, if the summons is to issue against two or more persons jointly liable under the judgment or order sought to be enforced, in the court for the district in which any of the debtors resides or carries on business.

(2) The judgment creditor shall make his application by filing a request in that behalf certifying the amount of money remaining due under the judgment or order, the amount in respect of which the judgment summons is to issue and that the whole or part of any instalment due remains unpaid.

Rule 2 MODE OF SERVICE
(1) Subject to paragraph (2), a judgment summons shall be served personally on every debtor against whom it is issued.

(2) Where the judgment creditor or his solicitor gives a certificate for postal service in respect of a debtor residing or carrying on business within the district of the court, the judgment summons shall, unless the district judge otherwise directs, be served on that debtor by an officer of the court sending it to him by first-class post at the address stated in the request for the judgment summons and, unless the contrary is shown, the date of service shall be deemed to be the seventh day after the date on which the judgment summons was sent to the debtor.

(3) Where a judgment summons has been served on a debtor in accordance with paragraph (2), no order of commitment shall be made against him unless—
    (a) he appears at the hearing; or
    (b) the judge is satisfied that the summons came to his knowledge in sufficient time for him to appear at the hearing.

(4) Where a judgment summons is served personally, there may, if the judgment creditor so desires, be paid to the debtor at the time of service a sum reasonably sufficient to cover his expenses in travelling to and from the court.

Rule 3 TIME FOR SERVICE
(1) A judgment summons shall be served not less than 14 days before the day fixed for the hearing.

(2) A notice of non-service shall be sent pursuant to CPR rule 6.11 in respect of a judgment summons which has been sent by post under rule 2(2) and has been returned to the court office undelivered.

(3) CPR rules 7.5 and 7.6 shall apply, with the necessary modifications, to a judgment summons as they apply to a claim form.

CPR SCHEDULE 2

Rule 4 ENFORCEMENT OF DEBTOR'S ATTENDANCE

(1) Order 27, rules 7, 11 and 8, shall apply, with the necessary modifications, to an order made under section 110(1) of the Act for the attendance of the debtor at an adjourned hearing of a judgment summons as they apply to an order made under section 23(1) of the Attachment of Earnings Act 1971 for the attendance of the debtor at an adjourned hearing of an application for an attachment of earnings order.

(2) At the time of service of the order there shall be paid or tendered to the debtor a sum reasonably sufficient to cover his expenses in travelling to and from the court, unless such a sum was paid to him at the time of service of the judgment summons.

Rule 5 EVIDENCE BY WITNESS STATEMENT OR AFFIDAVIT

Where the judgment creditor does not reside or carry on business within the district of the court from which the judgment summons issued, evidence by witness statement or affidavit shall be admissible on his behalf without any notice having been given, unless the judge otherwise directs.

Rule 7 SUSPENSION OF COMMITTAL ORDER

(1) If on the hearing of a judgment summons a committal order is made, the judge may direct execution of the order to be suspended to enable the debtor to pay the amount due.

(2) A note of any direction given under paragraph (1) shall be entered in the records of the court and notice of the suspended committal order shall be sent to the debtor.

(3) Where a judgment summons is issued in respect of one or more but not all of the instalments payable under a judgment or order for payment by instalments and a committal order is made and suspended under paragraph (1), the judgment or order shall, unless the judge otherwise orders, be suspended for so long as the, execution of the committal order is suspended.

(4) Where execution of a committal order is suspended under paragraph (1) and the debtor subsequently desires to apply for a further suspension, the debtor shall attend at or write to the court office and apply for the suspension he desires, stating the reasons for his inability to comply with the terms of the original suspension, and the court shall fix a day for the hearing of the application by the judge and give at least 3 days' notice thereof to the judgment creditor and the debtor.

(5) The district judge may suspend execution of the committal order pending the hearing of an application under paragraph (4).

Rule 8 NEW ORDER ON JUDGMENT SUMMONS

(1) Where on the hearing of a judgment summons, the judge makes a new order for payment of the amount of the judgment debt remaining unpaid, there shall be included in the amount payable under the order for the purpose of any enforcement proceedings, otherwise than by judgment summons, any amount in respect of which a committal order has already been made and the debtor imprisoned.

(2) No judgment summons under the new order shall include any amount in respect of which the debtor was imprisoned before the new order was made, and any amount subsequently paid shall be appropriated in the first instance to the amount due under the new order.

Rule 9 NOTIFICATION OF ORDER ON JUDGMENT OF HIGH COURT

(1) Notice of the result of the hearing of a judgment summons on a judgment or order of the High Court shall be sent by the county court to the High Court.

(2) If a committal order or a new order for payment is made on the hearing, the office copy of the judgment or order filed under Order 25, rule 11, shall be deemed to be a judgment or order of the court in which the judgment summons is heard, and if the judgment creditor subsequently desires to issue a judgment summons in another county court, Order 25, rule 2, shall apply with the necessary modifications.

Rule 10 COSTS ON JUDGMENT SUMMONS

(1) No costs shall be allowed to the judgment creditor on the hearing of a judgment summons unless—

(a) a committal order is made; or

(b) the sum in respect of which the judgment summons was issued is paid before the hearing.

(2) Where costs are allowed to the judgment creditor,

(a) there may be allowed—

(i) a charge of the judgment creditor's solicitor for attending the hearing and, if the judge so directs, for serving the judgment summons;

(ii) a fee to counsel if the court certifies that the case is fit for counsel;

(iii) any travelling expenses paid to the debtor, and

(iv) the court fee on the issue of the judgment summons.,

(b) the costs may be fixed and allowed without detailed assessment under CPR Part 47;

(3) For the purposes of paragraph (2)(a)(i) a solicitor who has prepared on behalf of the judgment creditor a witness statement or affidavit under rule 5 shall be treated as having attended the hearing.

Rule 11 ISSUE OF WARRANT OF COMMITTAL

(1) A judgment creditor desiring a warrant to be issued pursuant to a committal order shall file a request in that behalf.

(2) Where two or more debtors are to be committed in respect of the same judgment or order, a separate warrant of committal shall be issued for each of them.

(3) Where a warrant of committal is sent to a foreign court for execution, that court shall indorse on it a notice as to the effect of section 122(3) of the Act addressed to the governor of the prison of that court.

Rule 12 NOTIFICATION TO FOREIGN COURT OF PART PAYMENT BEFORE DEBTOR LODGED IN PRISON

Where, after a warrant of committal has been sent to a foreign court for execution but before the debtor is lodged in prison, the home court is notified that an amount which is less than the sum on payment of which the debtor is to be discharged has been paid, the home court shall send notice of the payment to the foreign court.

Rule 13 PAYMENT AFTER DEBTOR LODGED IN PRISON

(1) Where, after the debtor has been lodged in prison under a warrant of committal, payment is made of the sum on payment of which the debtor is to be discharged, then—

(a) if the payment is made to the court responsible for the execution of the warrant, the court officer shall make and sign a certificate of payment and send it by post or otherwise to the gaoler;

(b) if the payment is made to the court which issued the warrant of committal after the warrant has been sent to a foreign court for execution, the home court shall send notice of the payment to the foreign court, and the court officer at the foreign court shall make and sign a certificate of payment and send it by post or otherwise to the gaoler;

(c) if the payment is made to the gaoler, he shall sign a certificate of payment and send the amount to the court which made the committal order.

(2) Where, after the debtor has been lodged in prison under a warrant of committal, payment is made of an amount less than the sum on payment of which the debtor is to be discharged, then subject to paragraph (3), paragraph (1)(a) and (b) shall apply with the substitution of references to a notice of payment for the references to a certificate of payment and paragraph (1)(c) shall apply with the omission of the requirement to make and sign a certificate of payment.

(3) Where, after the making of a payment to which paragraph (2) relates, the balance of the sum on payment of which the debtor is to be discharged is paid, paragraph (1) shall apply without the modifications mentioned in paragraph (2).

Rule 14 DISCHARGE OF DEBTOR OTHERWISE THAN ON PAYMENT

(1) Where the judgment creditor lodges with the district judge a request that a debtor lodged in prison under a warrant of committal may be discharged from custody, the district judge shall make an order for the discharge of the debtor in respect of the warrant of committal and the court shall send the gaoler a certificate of discharge.

(2) Where a debtor who has been lodged in prison under a warrant of committal desires to apply for his discharge under section 121 of the Act, the application shall be made to the judge in writing and without notice showing the reasons why the debtor alleges that he is unable to pay the sum in respect of which he has been committed and ought to be discharged and stating any offer which he desires to make as to the terms on which his discharge is to be ordered, and Order 27, rule 8(3) and (4), shall apply, with the necessary modifications, as it applies to an application by a debtor for his discharge from custody under section 23(7) of the Attachment of Earnings Act 1971.

(3) If in a case to which paragraph (2) relates the debtor is ordered to be discharged from custody on terms which include liability to re-arrest if the terms are not complied with, the judge may, on the application of the judgment creditor if the terms are not complied with, order the debtor to be re-arrested and imprisoned for such part of the term of imprisonment as remained unserved at the time of discharge.

(4) Where an order is made under paragraph (3), a duplicate warrant of committal shall be issued, indorsed with a certificate signed by the court officer as to the order of the judge.

CCR ORDER 29
COMMITTAL FOR BREACH OF ORDER OR UNDERTAKING

Rule 1 ENFORCEMENT OF JUDGMENT TO DO OR ABSTAIN FROM DOING ANY ACT

(1) Where a person required by a judgment or order to do an act refuses or neglects to do it within the time fixed by the judgment or order or any subsequent order, or where a person disobeys a judgment or order requiring him to abstain from doing an act, then, subject to the Debtors Acts 1869 and 1878 and to the provisions of these rules, the judgment or order may be enforced, by order of the judge, by a committal order against that person or, if that person is a body corporate, against any director or other officer of the body.

(2) Subject to paragraphs (6) and (7), a judgment or order shall not be enforced under paragraph (1) unless—

(a) a copy of the judgment or order has been served personally on the person required to do or abstain from doing the act in question and also, where that person is a body corporate, on the director or other officer of the body against whom a committal order is sought; and

(b) in the case of a judgment or order requiring a person to do an act, the copy has been so served before the expiration of the time within which he was required to do the act and was accompanied by a copy of any order, made between the date of the judgment or order and the date of service, fixing that time.

(3) Where a judgment or order enforceable by committal order under paragraph (1) has been given or made, the court officer shall, if the judgment or order is in the nature of an injunction, at the time when the judgment or order is drawn up, and in any other case on the request of the judgment creditor, issue a copy of the judgment or order, indorsed with or incorporating a notice as to the consequences of disobedience, for service in accordance with paragraph (2).

(4) If the person served with the judgment or order fails to obey it, the judgment creditor may issue a claim form or, as the case may be, an application notice seeking the committal for contempt of court of that person and subject to paragraph (7), the claim form or application notice shall be served on him personally.

(4A) The claim form or application notice (as the case may be) shall—

(a) identify the provisions of the injunction or undertaking which it is alleged have been disobeyed or broken;

(b) list the ways in which it is alleged that the in unction has been disobeyed or the undertaking has been broken;

(c) be supported by an affidavit stating the grounds on which the application is made, and unless service is dispensed with under paragraph (7), a copy of the affidavit shall be served with the claim form or application notice.

(5) If a committal order is made, the order shall be for the issue of a warrant of committal and, unless the judge otherwise orders—

(a) a copy of the order shall be served on the person to be committed either before or at the time of the execution of the warrant; or

(b) where the warrant has been signed by the judge, the order for issue of the warrant may be served on the person to be committed at any time within 36 hours after the execution of the warrant.

(6) A judgment or order requiring a person to abstain from doing an act may be enforced under paragraph (1) notwithstanding that service of a copy of the judgment or order has not been effected in accordance with paragraph (2) if the judge is satisfied that, pending such service, the person against whom it is sought to enforce the judgment or order has had notice thereof either—

(a) by being present when the judgment or order was given or made; or

(b) by being notified of the terms of the judgment or order whether by telephone, telegram or otherwise.

(7) Without prejudice to its powers under Part 6 of the CPR, the court may dispense with service of a copy of a judgment or order under paragraph (2) or a claim form or application notice under paragraph (4) if the court thinks it just to do so.

(8) Where service of the claim form or application notice has been dispensed with under paragraph (7) and a committal order is made in the absence of the respondent, the judge may on his own initiative fix a date and time when the person to be committed is to be brought before him or before the court.

Rule 1A UNDERTAKING GIVEN BY PARTY

Rule 1 (except paragraph (6)) shall apply to undertakings as it applies to orders with the necessary modifications and as if—

(a) for paragraph (2) of that rule there were substituted the following—

'(2) A copy of the document recording the undertaking shall be delivered by the court officer to the party giving the undertaking—

(a) by handing a copy of the document to him before he leaves the court building; or

(b) where his place of residence is known, by posting a copy to him at his place of residence; or

(c) through his solicitor,

and, where delivery cannot be effected in this way, the court officer shall deliver a copy of the document to the party for whose benefit the undertaking is given and that party shall cause it to be served personally as soon as is practicable'.

(b) in paragraph (7), the words from 'a copy of' to 'paragraph (2) or' were omitted.

Rule 2 SOLICITOR'S UNDERTAKING

(1) An undertaking given by a solicitor in relation to any proceeding in a county court may be enforced, by order of the judge of that court, by committal order against the solicitor.

(2) Where it appears to the judge that a solicitor has failed to carry out any such undertaking, he may of his own initiative direct the court officer to issue a notice calling on the solicitor to show cause why he should not be committed to prison.

(3) Where any party to the proceedings desires to have the undertaking enforced by committal order, the court officer shall, on the application of the party

CPR SCHEDULE 2

supported by an affidavit setting out the facts on which the application is based, issue such a notice as is referred to in paragraph (2).

Rule 3 DISCHARGE OF PERSON IN CUSTODY

(1) Where a person in custody under a warrant or order, other than a warrant of committal to which Order 27, rule 8, or Order 28, rule 4 or 14, relates, desires to apply to the court for his discharge, he shall make his application in writing attested by the governor of the prison (or any other officer of the prison not below the rank of principal officer) showing that he has purged or is desirous of purging his contempt and shall, not less than one day before the application is made, serve notice of it on the party, if any, at whose instance the warrant or order was issued.

(2) If the committal order—

    (a) does not direct that any application for discharge shall be made to a judge; or

    (b) was made by the district judge under section 118 of the Act,

any application for discharge may be made to the district judge.

(3) Nothing in paragraph (1) shall apply to an application made by the Official Solicitor in his official capacity for the discharge of a person in custody.

CCR ORDER 30
GARNISHEE PROCEEDINGS

Rule 1 ATTACHMENT OF DEBT DUE TO JUDGMENT DEBTOR

(1) Where a person (in this Order called 'the judgment creditor') has obtained in a county court a judgment or order for the payment of a sum of money amounting in value to at least £50 by some other person ('the judgment debtor') and any person within England and Wales ('the garnishee') is indebted to the judgment debtor, that court may, subject to the provisions of this Order and of any enactment, order the garnishee to pay the judgment creditor the amount of any debt due or accruing due from the garnishee to the judgment debtor or so much thereof as is sufficient to satisfy the judgment or order against the judgment debtor and the costs of the garnishee proceedings.

(2) An order under this rule shall in the first instance be an order to show cause, specifying the place and time for the further consideration of the matter (in this Order called 'the return day') and in the meantime attaching the debt due or accruing due from the garnishee or so much of it as is sufficient for the purpose aforesaid.

(3) Among the conditions mentioned in section 108(3) of the Act (which enables any sum standing to the credit of a person in certain types of account to be attached notwithstanding that certain conditions applicable to the account in question have not been satisfied) there shall be included any condition that a receipt for money deposited in the account must be produced before any money is withdrawn.

(5) An order under this rule shall not require a payment which would reduce below £1 the amount standing in the name of the judgment debtor in an account with a building society or a credit union.

Rule 2 APPLICATION FOR ORDER

An application for an order under rule 1 may be made without notice being served on any other party by filing a witness statement or affidavit—

    (a) stating the name and last known address of the judgment debtor;

    (b) identifying the judgment or order to be enforced and stating the amount of such judgment or order;

    (c) stating that, to the best of the information or belief of the witness, the garnishee (giving his name and address) is indebted to the judgment debtor;

    (d) where the garnishee is a deposit-taking institution having more than one place of business, giving the name and address of the branch at which the judgment debtor's account is believed to be held and the number of that account or, if it be the case, that all or part of this information is unknown to the witness; and

    (e) certifying the amount of money remaining due under the judgment or order and that the whole or part of any instalment due remains unpaid.

CPR SCHEDULE 2

Rule 3 PREPARATION, SERVICE AND EFFECT OF ORDER TO SHOW CAUSE

(1) An order under rule 1 to show cause shall be drawn up by the court with sufficient copies for service under this rule.

(2) Unless otherwise directed, a copy of the order shall be served—

(a) on the garnishee in the manner required for the notice of the day of hearing in accordance with Order 3, rule 6 at least 15 days before the return day;

(b) on the judgment debtor in accordance with CPR Part 6 at least 7 days after a copy has been served on the garnishee and at least 7 days before the return day,

and as from such service on the garnishee the order shall bind in his hands any debt due or accruing due from the garnishee to the judgment debtor, or so much thereof as is sufficient to satisfy the judgment or order obtained by the judgment creditor against the judgment debtor, and the costs entered on the order to show cause.

Rule 5 NOTICE BY DEPOSIT-TAKING INSTITUTION DENYING INDEBTEDNESS

Where the garnishee being a deposit-taking institution alleges that it does not hold any money to the credit of the judgment debtor, the garnishee may, at any time before the return day, give notice to that effect to the court and to the judgment creditor and thereupon, subject to rule 8 the proceedings against the garnishee shall be stayed.

Rule 7 ORDER WHERE NO NOTICE GIVEN ETC.

(1) Where the garnishee—

(a) does not give notice under rule 5; and

(b) does not on the return day appear or dispute the debt due or claimed to be due from him to the judgment debtor,

then, if the judgment debtor does not appear or show cause to the contrary, the court may, if it thinks fit, make an order absolute under rule 1 against the garnishee.

(2) An order absolute under rule 1 may be enforced in the same manner as any other order for the payment of money.

Rule 8 DIRECTIONS WHERE DISPUTE AS TO NOTICE UNDER RULE 5

Where the garnishee in a notice given under rule 5 makes an allegation which the judgment creditor disputes, the court shall on the return day give directions for the determination of the question at issue.

Rule 9 DETERMINATION OF LIABILITY IN OTHER CASES

Where in a case in which no notice has been given under rule 5 the garnishee on the return day disputes liability to pay the debt due or claimed to be due from him to the judgment debtor, the court may summarily determine the question at issue or order that any question necessary for determining the liability of the garnishee be tried in any manner in which any question or issue in proceedings may be tried.

Rule 10 TRANSFER OF PROCEEDINGS

A garnishee who does not reside or carry on business within the district of the court in which the garnishee proceedings have been commenced and who desires to dispute liability for the debt due or claimed to be due from him to the judgment debtor may apply without notice being served on any other party in writing to that court for an order transferring the proceedings in which the judgment or order sought to be enforced was obtained to the court for the district in which the garnishee resides or carries on business, and the court applied to may, if it thinks fit, grant the application after considering any representations which it may give the judgment creditor and the judgment debtor an opportunity of making.

Rule 11 DISCHARGE OF GARNISHEE

Any payment made by a garnishee in compliance with an order absolute in garnishee proceedings, and any execution levied against him in pursuance of such an order, shall be a valid discharge of his liability to the judgment debtor to the extent of the amount paid or levied (otherwise than in respect of any costs ordered to be paid by the garnishee personally), notwithstanding that the garnishee proceedings are subsequently set aside or the judgment or order from which they arise is reversed.

Rule 12 MONEY IN COURT

(1) Where money is standing to the credit of the judgment debtor in any county court, the judgment creditor shall not be entitled to take garnishee proceedings in respect of the money but may apply to the court on notice for an order that the money or so much of it as is sufficient to satisfy the judgment or order sought to be enforced and the costs of the application be paid to the judgment creditor.

(2) On receipt of notice of an application under paragraph (1) the court officer shall retain the money in court until the application has been determined.

(3) The court hearing an application under paragraph (1) may make such order with respect to the money in court as it thinks just.

Rule 13 COSTS OF JUDGMENT CREDITOR

Any costs allowed to the judgment creditor on an application for an order under rule 1 or 12 which in the former case are not ordered to be paid by the garnishee personally shall, unless the court otherwise directs be retained by the judgment creditor out of the money recovered by him under the order in priority to the amount due under the judgment or order obtained by him against the judgment debtor.

Rule 14 ATTACHMENT OF DEBT OWED BY FIRM

(1) An order may be made under rule 1 in relation to a debt due or accruing due from a firm carrying on business within England and Wales, notwithstanding that one or more members of the firm may be resident out of England and Wales.

(2) An order to show cause under rule 1 relating to such a debt shall be served on a member of the firm within England and Wales or on some other person having the control or management of the partnership business.

Rule 15 POWERS OF DISTRICT JUDGE

The powers conferred on the court by any provision of this Order may be exercised by the judge or district judge.

CCR ORDER 31
CHARGING ORDERS

Rule 1 APPLICATION FOR CHARGING ORDER

(1) An application to a county court for a charging order under section 1 of the Charging Orders Act 1979 may be made—

(a) if the order is sought in respect of a fund in court, to the court where the money is lodged;

(b) subject to (a), if the judgment or order sought to be enforced is that of a county court, to the court in which the judgment or order was obtained or, if the proceedings have been transferred to another court under CPR rule 30.2(1)(b)(ii) or Order 25, rule 2, the court to which it has been transferred.

(c) subject to (a) and (b), to the court for the district in which the debtor resides or carries on business or, if there is no such district, to the court for the district in which the judgment creditor resides or carries on business.

(1A) An application for a charging order under paragraph 11 of Schedule 4 to the Local Government Finance Act 1992 shall be made to the court for the district in which the relevant dwelling (within the meaning of section 3 of that Act) is situated.

(2) The application may be made without notice being served on any other party by filing a witness statement or affidavit—

(a) stating the name and address of the debtor and, if known, of every creditor of his whom the applicant can identify;

(aa) certifying the amount of money remaining due under the judgment or order and that the whole or part of any instalment due remains unpaid;
(b) identifying the subject matter of the intended charge;
(c) either verifying the debtor's beneficial ownership of the asset to be charged or, where the asset is held by one or more trustees (including where the asset is land which is jointly owned) and the applicant relies on paragraph (b) of section 2(1) of the said Act of 1979, stating on which of the three grounds appearing in that paragraph the application is based and verifying the material facts;
(d) stating, in the case of securities other than securities in court, the name and address of the person or body to be served for the purpose of protecting the intended charge;
(e) stating, where the subject matter is an interest under a trust, or held by a trustee, the names and addresses of such trustees and beneficiaries as are known to the applicant.

Where the judgment or order to be enforced is a judgment or order of the High Court or a judgment, order, decree or award of a court or arbitrator which is or has become enforceable as if it were a judgment or order of the High Court, the applicant shall file with his witness statement or affidavit the documents mentioned in Order 25, rule 11(a) and (c), and the witness statement or affidavit shall verify the amount unpaid at the date of the application.

(3) Subject to paragraph (1), an application may be made for a single charging order in respect of more than one judgment or order against a debtor.

(4) Upon the filing of the witness statement or affidavit mentioned in paragraph (2), the application shall be entered in the records of the court, and if, in the opinion of the district judge, a sufficient case for such an order is made in the witness statement or affidavit, the district judge shall make a charging order nisi fixing a day for the further consideration of the matter by the court.

(5) A copy of the order shall be sent by the court officer to the judgment creditor and, where funds in court are to be charged, shall be served by the court officer on the Accountant-General at the Court Funds Office.

(6) Copies of the order and of the witness statement or affidavit shall be served by the judgment creditor on—
(a) the debtor;
(b) the other creditors named in the witness statement or affidavit (unless the district judge otherwise directs); and
(c) where a trust is involved, on any trustee holding the asset to be charged, where the applicant relies on paragraph (b) of section 2(1) of the said Act of 1979 and on such other trustees and beneficiaries as the district judge may direct.

(7) Where an interest in securities not in court is to be charged, copies of the order nisi shall be served by the judgment creditor on the person or body required to be served in like circumstances by RSC Order 50, rule 2(1)(b).

(8) The documents required by the foregoing paragraphs to be served shall be served in accordance with CPR Part 6 not less than 7 days before the day fixed for the further consideration of the matter.

(9) Upon further consideration of the matter service required under paragraph (6) or (7) shall be proved by witness statement or affidavit.

Rule 2 ORDER ON FURTHER CONSIDERATION OF APPLICATION FOR CHARGING ORDER

(1) On the day fixed under rule 1(4) for the further consideration of the matter, the court shall either make the order absolute, with or without modifications, or discharge it.

(2) If an order absolute is made, a copy shall be served by the court officer, in accordance with CPR Part 6 on each of the following persons, namely—
(a) the debtor;
(b) the applicant for the order;
(c) where funds in court are charged, the Accountant-General at the Court Funds Office; and

(d) unless otherwise directed, any person or body on whom a copy of the order nisi was served pursuant to rule 1(7).

(3) Every copy of an order served on a person or body under paragraph (2)(d) shall contain a stop notice.

Rule 3 EFFECT OF CHARGING ORDER ETC.

(1) Where a charging order nisi or a charging order absolute has been made and served in accordance with rule 1 or 2, it shall have the same effect as an order made and served in like circumstances under RSC Order 50.

(2) The court may vary or discharge a charging order in the like circumstances and in accordance with the same procedure, with the necessary modifications, as a like order made by the High Court.

(3) The powers of the court under rule 2 or the last preceding paragraph, except the power to vary an order made by the judge, may be exercised by the district judge.

Rule 4 ENFORCEMENT OF CHARGING ORDER BY SALE

(1) Proceedings in a county court for the enforcement of a charging order by sale of the property charged shall be commenced by a claim form, which shall be filed in the appropriate court, together with a witness statement or affidavit and a copy thereof—

(a) identifying the charging order sought to be enforced and the subject matter of the charge;

(b) specifying the amount in respect of which the charge was imposed and the balance outstanding at the date of the application;

(c) verifying, so far as known, the debtor's title to the property charged;

(d) identifying any prior incumbrances on the property charged, with, so far as known, the names and addresses of the incumbrancers and the amounts owing to them; and

(e) giving an estimate of the price which would be obtained on sale of the property.

(2) The appropriate court shall be—

(a) if the charging order was made by a county court, that court;

(b) in any other case, the court for the district in which the debtor resides or carries on business or, if there is no such district, the court for the district in which the judgment creditor resides or carries on business.

(3) A copy of the witness statement or affidavit filed under paragraph (1) shall be served on the respondent with a copy of the claim form and a notice to each respondent of the date of the hearing.

(4) The proceedings may be heard and determined by a district judge.

(5) The net proceeds of sale, after discharging any prior incumbrances and deducting the amount referred to in paragraph (1)(b) and the costs of the sale, shall be paid into court.

CCR ORDER 33
INTERPLEADER PROCEEDINGS

Part I — Under Execution

Rule 1 NOTICE OF CLAIM

(A1) In this Part of this order 'the interpleader claimant' means any person making a claim to or in respect of goods seized in execution or the proceeds or value thereof and 'the interpleader claim' means that claim.

(1) The interpleader claimant shall deliver to the bailiff holding the warrant of execution, or file in the office of the court for the district in which the goods were seized, notice of his claim stating—

(a) the grounds of the interpleader claim or, in the case of a claim for rent, the particulars required by section 102(2) of the Act; and

(b) the interpleader claimant's full name and address.

(2) On receipt of an interpleader claim made under this rule, the court shall—

(a) send notice thereof to the execution creditor; and
(b) except where the interpleader claim is to the proceeds or value of the goods, send to the interpleader claimant a notice requiring him to make a deposit or give security in accordance with section 100 of the Act.

Rule 2 REPLY TO INTERPLEADER CLAIM

(1) Within 4 days after receiving notice of an interpleader claim under rule 1(2) the execution creditor shall give notice to the court informing him whether he admits or disputes the interpleader claim or requests the district judge to withdraw from possession of the goods or money claimed.

(2) If, within the period aforesaid, the execution creditor gives notice to the court admitting the interpleader claim or requesting the district judge to withdraw from possession of the goods or money claimed, the execution creditor shall not be liable to the district judge for any fees or expenses incurred after receipt of the notice.

Rule 3 ORDER PROTECTING DISTRICT JUDGE

Where the execution creditor gives the court such a notice as is mentioned in rule 2(2), the district judge shall withdraw from possession of the goods or money claimed and may apply to the judge, on notice to the interpleader claimant, for an order restraining the bringing of a claim against the district judge for or in respect of his having taken possession of the goods or money and on the hearing of the application the judge may make such order as may be just.

Rule 4 ISSUE OF INTERPLEADER PROCEEDINGS

(1) Where the execution creditor gives notice under rule 2(1) disputing an interpleader claim made under rule 1 or fails, within the period mentioned in rule 2(1), to give the notice required by that rule, the district judge shall, unless the interpleader claim is withdrawn, issue an interpleader notice to the execution creditor and the interpleader claimant.

(2) On the issue of an interpleader notice under paragraph (1) the court officer shall enter the proceedings in the records of the court, fix a day for the hearing by the judge and prepare sufficient copies of the notice for service under this rule.

(3) Subject to paragraph (4) the notice shall be served on the execution creditor and the interpleader claimant in the manner required for service of the notice of the day of hearing in accordance with Order 3, rule 6.

(4) Service shall be effected not less than 14 days before the return day.

Rule 5 CLAIM FOR DAMAGES

Where in interpleader proceedings under an execution the interpleader claimant claims from the execution creditor or the district judge, or the execution creditor claims from the district judge, damages arising or capable of arising out of the execution—

(a) the party claiming damages shall, within 8 days after service of the notice on him under rule 4(3), give notice of this claim to the court and to any other party against whom the claim is made, stating the amount and the grounds of the claim; and

(b) the party from whom damages are claimed may pay money into court in satisfaction of the claim as if the interpleader proceedings were a claim brought in accordance with CPR Part 7 by the person making the claim.

Part II Otherwise than under Execution

Rule 6 APPLICATION FOR RELIEF

(1) Where a person (in this Part of this order called 'the applicant') is under a liability in respect of a debt or any money or goods and he is, or expects to be, sued for or in respect of the debt, money or goods by two or more persons making adverse claims thereto ('the interpleader claimants'), he may apply to the court, in accordance with these rules, for relief by way of interpleader.

(2) The application shall be made to the court in which the claim is pending against the applicant or, if no claim is pending against him, to the court in which he might be sued.

(3) The application shall be made by filing a witness statement or affidavit showing that—
(a) the applicant claims no interest in the subject-matter in dispute other than for charges or costs;
(b) the applicant does not collude with any of the interpleader claimants; and
(c) the applicant is willing to pay or transfer the subject-matter into court or to dispose of it as the court may direct,
together with as many copies of the witness statement or affidavit as there are interpleader claimants.

Rule 7 RELIEF IN PENDING CLAIM
Where the applicant is a defendant in a pending claim—
(a) the witness statement or affidavit and copies required by rule 6(3) shall be filed within 14 days after service on him of the claim form;
(b) the return day of the application shall be a day fixed for the pre-trial review of the claim including the interpleader proceedings and, if a day has already been fixed for the pre-trial review or hearing of the claim, the court shall, if necessary, postpone it;
(c) the interpleader claimant, the applicant and the claimant in the claim shall be given notice of the application, which shall be prepared by the court together with sufficient copies for service;
(d) the notice to the interpleader claimant shall be served on him, together with a copy of the witness statement or affidavit filed under rule 6(3) and of the claim form and particulars of claim in the claim, not less than 21 days before the return day in the same manner as an interpleader notice in accordance with rule 4(3);
(e) the notices to the applicant and the claimant shall be sent to them by the court and the notice to the claimant shall be accompanied by a copy of the said witness statement or affidavit.

Rule 8 RELIEF OTHERWISE THAN IN PENDING CLAIM
Where the applicant is not a defendant in a pending claim—
(a) the court shall enter the proceedings in the records of the court;
(b) the court shall fix a day for the pre-trial review or, if the court so directs, a day for the hearing of the proceedings and shall prepare and issue an interpleader notice, together with sufficient copies for service;
(c) the notice together with a copy of the witness statement or affidavit filed under rule 6(3), shall be served on each of the claimants not less than 21 days before the return day in the same manner as an interpleader notice to be served under rule 4(3); and
(d) the court shall deliver or send a notice of issue to the applicant.

Rule 9 PAYMENT INTO COURT ETC.
Before or after the court officer proceeds under rule 7 or 8 the district judge may direct the applicant to bring the subject-matter of the proceedings into court, or to dispose of it in such manner as the district judge thinks fit, to abide the order of the court.

Rule 10 REPLY BY INTERPLEADER CLAIMANT
(1) An interpleader claimant shall, within 14 days after service on him of the notice under rule 7(c) or the interpleader notice under rule 8(c), file—
(a) a notice that he makes no interpleader claim; or
(b) particulars stating the grounds of his interpleader claim to the subject-matter,
together in either case with sufficient copies for service under paragraph (2).
(2) The court shall send to each of the other parties a copy of any notice or particulars filed under paragraph (1).
(3) The court may, if it thinks fit, hear the proceedings although no notice or particulars have been filed.

Rule 11 ORDER BARRING INTERPLEADER CLAIM ETC.
(1) Where an interpleader claimant does not appear on any day fixed for a pre-trial review or the hearing of interpleader proceedings, or fails or refuses to comply with an order made in the proceedings, the court may make an order barring his interpleader claim.
(2) If, where the applicant is a defendant in a pending claim, the claimant does not appear on any day fixed for a pre-trial review or the hearing of the interpleader proceedings, the claim including the interpleader proceedings may be struck out.
(3) In any other case where a day is fixed for the hearing of interpleader proceedings, the court shall hear and determine the proceedings and give judgment finally determining the rights and claims of the parties.
(4) Where the court makes an order barring the interpleader claim of an interpleader claimant, the order shall declare the interpleader claimant, and all persons claiming under him, forever barred from prosecuting his interpleader claim against the applicant and all persons claiming under him, but unless the interpleader claimant has filed a notice under rule 10 that he makes no interpleader claim, such an order shall not affect the rights of the interpleader claimants as between themselves.

CCR ORDER 34
PENAL AND DISCIPLINARY PROVISIONS

Rule 1 ISSUE AND SERVICE OF SUMMONS FOR OFFENCE UNDER SECTION 14, 92 OR 124 OF THE ACT
Where—
    (a) it is alleged that any person has committed an offence under section 14 or 92 of the Act by assaulting an officer of the court while in the execution of his duty, or by rescuing or attempting to rescue any goods seized in execution, and the alleged offender has not been taken into custody and brought before the judge; or
    (b) a complaint is made against an officer of the court under section 124 of the Act for having lost the opportunity of levying execution,
the court officer shall issue a summons, which shall be served on the alleged offender personally not less than 8 days before the return day appointed in the summons.

Rule 1A COMMITTAL UNDER SECTION 14, 92 OR 118 OF THE ACT
Rule 1(5) of Order 29 shall apply, with the necessary modifications, where an order is made under section 14, 92 or 118 of the Act committing a person to prison.

Rule 2 NOTICE TO SHOW CAUSE BEFORE OR AFTER FINE UNDER SECTION 55 OF THE ACT
Before or after imposing a fine on any person under section 55 of the Act for disobeying a witness summons or refusing to be sworn or give evidence, the judge may direct the court officer to give to that person notice that if he has any cause to show why a fine should not be or should not have been imposed on him, he may show cause in person or by witness statement or affidavit or otherwise on a day named in the notice, and the judge after considering the cause shown may make such order as he thinks fit.

Rule 3 NON-PAYMENT OF FINE
(1) If a fine is not paid in accordance with the order imposing it, the court officer shall forthwith report the matter to the judge.
(2) Where by an order imposing a fine, the amount of the fine is directed to be paid by instalments and default is made in the payment of any instalment, the same proceedings may be taken as if default had been made in payment of the whole of the fine.
(3) If the judge makes an order for payment of a fine to be enforced by warrant of execution, the order shall be treated as an application made to the district judge for the issue of the warrant at the time when the order was received by him.

Rule 4 REPAYMENT OF FINE
If, after a fine has been paid, the person on whom it was imposed shows cause sufficient to satisfy the judge that, if it had been shown at an earlier date, he would not have imposed a fine or would have imposed a smaller fine or would not have ordered payment to be enforced, the judge may order the fine or any part thereof to be repaid.

CCR ORDER 35
ENFORCEMENT OF COUNTY COURT JUDGMENTS OUTSIDE ENGLAND AND WALES

Part I — Enforcement outside United Kingdom

Rule 1 INTERPRETATION OF PART I
In this Part of this order 'the Act of 1933' means the Foreign Judgments (Reciprocal Enforcement) Act 1933, 'the Act of 1982' means the Civil Jurisdiction and Judgments Act 1982 and expressions which are defined in those Acts have the same meaning in this Part of this order as they have in those Acts.

Rule 2 APPLICATION UNDER SECTION 10 OF THE ACT OF 1933 FOR CERTIFIED COPY OF COUNTY COURT JUDGMENT
　(1)　An application under section 10 of the Act of 1933 for a certified copy of a judgment of a county court may be made by filing a witness statement or affidavit, made by a solicitor of the party entitled to enforce the judgment, or by the party himself, if he is acting in person.
　(2)　A witness statement or affidavit by which an application under section 10 of the Act of 1933 is made must—
　　　(a)　give particulars of the proceedings in which the judgment was obtained;
　　　(b)　have annexed to it evidence of service on the defendant of the claim form or other process by which the proceedings were begun (where service was effected otherwise than through the court), copies of the statements of case, if any, and a statement of the grounds on which the judgment was based;
　　　(c)　state whether the defendant did or did not object to the jurisdiction, and, if so, on what grounds;
　　　(d)　show that the judgment is not subject to any stay of execution;
　　　(e)　state that the time for appealing or applying for a re-hearing has expired, or, as the case may be, the date on which it will expire and in either case whether notice of appeal against the judgment has been given or an application for a re-hearing has been made; and
　　　(f)　state whether interest is recoverable on the judgment or part thereof and, if so, the rate and period in respect of which it is recoverable.
　(3)　The certified copy of the judgment shall be a sealed copy indorsed with a certificate signed by the district judge certifying that the copy is a true copy of a judgment obtained in the county court and that it is issued in accordance with section 10 of the Act of 1933.
　(4)　There shall also be issued a sealed certificate signed by the district judge and having annexed to it a copy of the claim form or other process by which the proceedings were begun and stating—
　　　(a)　the manner in which the claim form or other process was served on the defendant or that the defendant has delivered to the court an admission, defence or counterclaim;
　　　(b)　what objections, if any, were made to the jurisdiction;
　　　(c)　what statements of case, if any, were filed;
　　　(d)　the grounds on which the judgment was based;
　　　(e)　that the time for appealing or applying for a re-hearing has expired or, as the case may be, the date on which it will expire;
　　　(f)　whether notice of appeal against the judgment has been given or an application for a re-hearing has been made;
　　　(g)　whether interest is recoverable on the judgment or part thereof and, if such be the case, the rate of interest, the date from which interest is recoverable, and the date on which interest ceases to accrue; and

CPR SCHEDULE 2

(h) such other particulars as it may be necessary to give the court in the foreign country in which it is sought to obtain execution of the judgment.

Rule 3 APPLICATION UNDER SECTION 12 OF THE ACT OF 1982 FOR CERTIFIED COPY OF COUNTY COURT JUDGMENT

(1) An application under section 12 of the Act of 1982 for a certified copy of a judgment of a county court may be made by filing a witness statement or affidavit made by a solicitor of the party entitled to enforce the judgment, or by the party himself, if he is acting in person.

(2) A witness statement or affidavit by which an application under section 12 of the Act of 1982 is made must—

 (a) give particulars of the proceedings in which the judgment was obtained;

 (b) have annexed to it evidence of service on the defendant of the claim form or other process by which the proceedings were begun (where service was effected otherwise than through the court), copies of the statements of case, if any, and a statement of the grounds on which the judgment was based together with, where appropriate, any document under which the applicant is entitled to legal aid or assistance by way of representation for the purposes of the proceedings;

 (c) state whether the defendant did or did not object to the jurisdiction and, if so, on what grounds;

 (d) show that the judgment has been served in accordance with CPR Part 6 and CPR rule 40.4 and is not subject to any stay of execution;

 (e) state that the time for appealing or applying for a re-hearing has expired, or, as the case may be, the date on which it will expire and in either case whether notice of appeal against the judgment has been given or an application for a re-hearing has been made; and

 (f) state—

  (i) whether the judgment provides for the payment of a sum or sums of money;

  (ii) whether interest is recoverable on the judgment or part thereof and, if such be the case, the rate of interest, the date from which interest is recoverable, and the date on which interest ceases to accrue.

(3) The certified copy of the judgment shall be a sealed copy and there shall be issued with the copy of the judgment a sealed certificate signed by the district judge and having annexed to it a copy of the claim form or other process by which the proceedings were begun.

Part II — Enforcement in other Parts of the United Kingdom

Rule 4 INTERPRETATION OF PART II

In this Part of this Order—

'the Act of 1982' means the Civil Jurisdiction and Judgments Act 1982,

'money provision' means a provision in any judgment to which section 18 of the Act of 1982 applies for the payment of one or more sums of money,

'non-money provision' means a provision in any judgment to which section 18 of the Act of 1982 applies for any relief or remedy not requiring payment of a sum of money.

Rule 5 APPLICATION FOR CERTIFICATE OF MONEY PROVISION

(1) A certificate in respect of any money provision contained in a judgment of the county court may be obtained by filing a witness statement or affidavit made by the solicitor of the party entitled to enforce the judgment, or by the party himself if he is acting in person, together with a form of certificate.

(2) A witness statement or affidavit by which an application under paragraph (1) is made must—

 (a) give particulars of the judgment, stating the rate of payment, if any, specified under the money provisions contained in the judgment, the sum or aggregate of sums (including any costs or expenses) remaining unsatisfied, the rate of interest, if any, applicable and the date or time from which any such interest began to accrue;

(b) verify that the time for appealing against the judgment or for applying for a re-hearing has expired, or that any appeal or re-hearing has been finally disposed of and that enforcement of the judgment is not stayed or suspended; and

(c) state to the best of the information or belief of the witness the usual or last known address of the party entitled to enforce the judgment and of the party liable to execution on it.

(3) The court officer shall enter on the certificate—
  (a) the number of the proceedings;
  (b) the amount remaining due under the judgment;
  (c) the rate of interest payable on the judgment debt, and the date or time from which any such interest began to accrue;
  (d) a note of the costs, if any, allowed for obtaining the certificate; and
  (e) the date on which the certificate is issued.

Rule 6 APPLICATION FOR CERTIFIED COPY OF JUDGMENT CONTAINING NON-MONEY PROVISION

(1) A certified copy of a judgment of a county court which contains any non-money provision may be obtained by filing a witness statement or affidavit made by the solicitor of the party entitled to enforce the judgment, or by the party himself, if he is acting in person.

(2) The requirements in paragraph (2) of rule 5 shall apply with the necessary modifications to a witness statement or affidavit made in an application under paragraph (1) of this rule.

(3) The certified copy of a judgment shall be a sealed copy to which shall be annexed a certificate signed by the court officer and stating that the conditions specified in paragraph (3)(a) and (b) of Schedule 7 to the Act of 1982 are satisfied in relation to the judgment.

CCR ORDER 37
REHEARING, SETTING ASIDE AND APPEAL FROM DISTRICT JUDGE

Rule 1 REHEARING

(1) In any proceedings tried without a jury the judge shall have power on application to order a rehearing where no error of the court at the hearing is alleged.

(2) Unless the court otherwise orders, any application under paragraph (1) shall be made to the judge by whom the proceedings were tried.

(3) A rehearing may be ordered on any question without interfering with the finding or decision on any other question.

(4) Where the proceedings were tried by the district judge, the powers conferred on the judge by paragraphs (1) and (3) shall be exercisable by the district judge and paragraph (2) shall not apply.

(5) Any application for a rehearing under this rule shall be made on notice stating the grounds of the application and the notice shall be served on the opposite party not more than 14 days after the day of the trial and not less than 7 days before the day fixed for the hearing of the application.

(6) On receipt of the notice, the court officer shall, unless the court otherwise orders, retain any money in court until the application has been heard.

Rule 6 APPEAL FROM DISTRICT JUDGE

(1) Any party affected by a judgment or final order of the district judge may, except where he has consented to the terms of the order, appeal from the judgment or order to the judge, who may, upon such terms as he thinks fit—
  (a) set aside or vary the judgment or order or any part of it;
  (b) give any other judgment or make any other order in substitution for the judgment or order appealed from;
  (c) remit the claim or any question in the claim to the district judge for rehearing or further consideration; or
  (d) order a new trial to take place before himself or another judge of the court on a day to be fixed.

CPR SCHEDULE 2

(2) The appeal shall be made on notice, which shall state the grounds of the appeal and be served within 14 days after the day on which judgment or order appealed from was given or made.

Rule 8 IMPOSITION OF TERMS AND STAY OF EXECUTION

(1) An application to the judge or district judge under any of the foregoing rules may be granted on such terms as he thinks reasonable.

(2) Notice of any such application shall not of itself operate as a stay of execution on the judgment or order to which it relates but the court may order a stay of execution pending the hearing of the application or any rehearing or new trial ordered on the application.

(3) If a judgment or order is set aside under any of the foregoing rules, any execution issued on the judgment or order shall cease to have effect unless the court otherwise orders.

CCR ORDER 38
COSTS

Rule 18 FIXED COSTS

(1) Appendix B shall effect for the purpose of showing the total amount which, in the several cases to which Appendix B applies, shall be allowed to the solicitor for the claimant as fixed costs without assessment (whether by the summary or the detailed procedure), unless the court otherwise orders.

(2) In a claim to which Appendix B or CPR Part 45 does not apply no amount shall be entered on the claim form for the charges of the claimant's solicitor, but the words 'to be assessed' shall be inserted.

APPENDIX B

Part I — Claims for the recovery of property, applications to enforce an award

DIRECTIONS

1 The Tables in this Part of this Appendix show the amount to be entered on the claim form or application in respect of solicitors' charges—

(c) in a claim for the recovery of property, including land, with or without a claim for a sum of money (other than a claim to which CPR Part 45 applies), for the purpose of Part II of this Appendix or of fixing the amount which the plaintiff may receive in respect of solicitors' charges without assessment whether by the detailed or summary procedure in the event of the defendant giving up possession and paying the amount claimed, if any, and costs;

(e) in proceedings for the enforcement of a tribunal or other award, for the purposes only of Order 25, rule 12.

2 In addition to the amount entered in accordance with the relevant Table the appropriate court fees shall be entered on the application.

3 In the Tables the expression 'claim' means—

(a) the sum of money claimed; or

(b) in relation to a claim for the recovery of land (with or without a claim for a sum of money), a sum exceeding £600 but not exceeding £2,000;

(c) in relation to a claim for the recovery of property other than money or land, the value of the property claimed or in the case of goods supplied under a hire purchase agreement, the unpaid balance of the total price.

4 The Tables do not apply where the application or the claim form is to be served out of England and Wales or where service by an alternative method is ordered.

TABLES OF FIXED COSTS

Table I
Where claim exceeds £25 but does not exceed £250

Amount of charges	£
(a) Where service is not by solicitor	30.75
(b) Where service is by solicitor	35.00

Table II
Where claim exceeds £250 but does not exceed £600

Amount of charges	£
(a) Where service is not by solicitor	41.00
(b) Where service is by solicitor	48.50

Table III
Where claim exceeds £600 but does not exceed £2,000

Amount of charges	£
(a) Where service is not by solicitor	69.50
(b) Where service is by solicitor	77.00

Table IV
Where claim exceeds £2,000

Amount of charges	£
(a) Where service is not by solicitor	75.50
(b) Where service is by solicitor	82.00

Part II — Judgments

DIRECTIONS

Where an amount in respect of solicitors' charges has been entered on the claim form under Part I of this Appendix and judgment is given in the circumstances mentioned in paragraphs (d) in column 1 of the following Table, the amount to be included in the judgment in respect of the solicitors' charges shall, be the amount entered on the application or the claim form together with the amount shown in column 2 of the Table under the sum of money by reference to which the amount entered on the application or the claim form was fixed. Where judgment is given for a sum less than the amount claimed or for the delivery of goods of which the value or the balance of the total price is a sum less than the amount claimed, the foregoing paragraph shall, unless the court otherwise directs, have effect as if the amount entered on the application or the claim form had been fixed by reference to that sum.

CPR SCHEDULE 2

FIXED COSTS ON JUDGMENTS

Column 1	Column 2 Sum of money		
	A exceeding £25 but not exceeding £600 £	B exceeding £600 but not exceeding £3,000 £	C exceeding £3,000 £
(d) Where judgment is given in a fixed date action for— (i) delivery of goods where goods are not subject to a regulated agreement; or (ii) possession of land suspended on payment of arrears of rent, whether claimed or not, in addition to current rent, and the defendant has neither delivered a defence, admission or counterclaim, nor otherwise denied liability	38.50	57.25	70.75

(Delivery of goods claims subject to a regulated agreement are dealt with by CPR Part 45)

Part III — Miscellaneous Proceedings

The following Table shows the amount to be allowed in respect of solicitors' charges in the circumstances mentioned. The appropriate court fee shall be allowed in addition.

Amount to be allowed	£
3 For filing a request for the issue of a warrant of execution for a sum exceeding £25	£2.25
4 For service of any document required to be served personally (other than an application for an attachment of earnings order or a judgment summons unless allowed under Order 27, rule 9(1)(a), or Order 28, rule 10(2)(a)(i)), including copy and preparation of certificate of service	£8.50
5 For service by an alternative method, including attendances, making appointments to serve claim forms, preparing and attending to swear and file affidavits and to obtain order, and the fees paid for oaths	£25.00
6 For each attendance on the hearing of an application for an attachment of earnings order of a judgment summons where costs are allowed under Order 27, rule 9, or Order 28, rule 10	£8.50
7 For the costs of the judgment creditor when allowed in garnishee proceedings or an application under Order 30, rule 12 (a) where the money recovered is less than £70.00	one half of the amount recovered
(b) where the money recovered is not less than £70.00	£46.50
8 For the costs of the judgment creditor when allowed on an application for a charging order	£71.00
9 For obtaining a certificate of judgment where costs allowed under Order 35, rule 5(3)(d)	£8.00

CPR SCHEDULE 2

10 Where an order for possession is made under rule 6 or rule 6A of Order 49 without the attendance of the claimant, for preparing and filing the application, the documents attached to the application and the request for possession   £79.50

11 On examination of a witness under CCR Order 25, rule 3 where any responsible representative of the solicitor attends, for each half-hour or part thereof   £15.00

CCR ORDER 39
ADMINISTRATION ORDERS

Rule 1 EXERCISE OF POWERS BY DISTRICT JUDGE

Any powers conferred on the court by Part VI of the Act, section 4 of the Attachment of Earnings Act 1971 or this Order may be exercised by the district judge or, in the circumstances mentioned in this Order, by the court officer.

Rule 2 REQUEST AND LIST OF CREDITORS

(1) A debtor who desires to obtain an administration order under Part VI of the Act shall file a request in that behalf in the court for the district in which he resides or carries on business.

(2) Where on his examination under Order 25, rule 3, or otherwise, a debtor furnishes to the court on oath a list of his creditors and the amounts which he owes to them respectively and sufficient particulars of his resources and needs, the court may proceed as if the debtor had filed a request under paragraph (1).

(3) Where a debtor is ordered to furnish a list under section 4(1)(b) of the said Act of 1971, then, unless otherwise directed, the list shall be filed within 14 days after the making of the order.

Rule 3 VERIFICATION ON OATH

The statements in the request mentioned in rule 2(1) and the list mentioned in rule 2(3) shall be verified by the debtor on oath.

Rule 5 ORDERS MADE BY THE COURT OFFICER

(1) The question whether an administration order should be made, and the terms of such an order, may be decided by the court officer in accordance with the provisions of this rule.

(2) On the filing of a request or list under rule 2, the court officer may, if he considers that the debtor's means are sufficient to discharge in full and within a reasonable period the total amount of the debts included in the list, determine the amount and frequency of the payments to be made under such an order ('the proposed rate') and—

(a) notify the debtor of the proposed rate requiring him to give written reasons for any objection he may have to the proposed rate within 14 days of service of notification upon him;

(b) send to each creditor mentioned in the list provided by the debtor a copy of the debtor's request or of the list together with the proposed rate;

(c) require any such creditor to give written reasons for any objection he may have to the making of an administration order within 14 days of service of the documents mentioned in sub-paragraph (b) upon him.

Objections under sub-paragraph (c) may be to the making of an order, to the proposed rate or to the inclusion of a particular debt in the order.

(3) Where no objection under paragraph (2)(a) or (c) is received within the time stated, the court officer may make an administration order providing for payment in full of the total amount of the debts included in the list.

(4) Where the debtor or a creditor notifies the court of any objection within the time stated, the court officer shall fix a day for a hearing at which the district judge will decide whether an administration order should be made and the court officer shall give not less than 14 days' notice of the day so fixed to the debtor and to each creditor mentioned in the list provided by the debtor.

(5) Where the court officer is unable to fix a rate under paragraph (2) (whether because he considers that the debtor's means are insufficient or otherwise), he shall refer the request to the district judge.

(6) Where the district judge considers that he is able to do so without the attendance of the parties, he may fix the proposed rate providing for payment of the debts included in the list in full or to such extent and within such a period as appears practicable in the circumstances of the case.

(7) Where the proposed rate is fixed under paragraph (6), paragraphs (2) to (4) shall apply with the necessary modifications as if the rate had been fixed by the court officer.

(8) Where the district judge does not fix the proposed rate under paragraph (6), he shall direct the court officer to fix a day for a hearing at which the district judge will decide whether an administration order should be made and the court officer shall give not less than 14 days' notice of the day so fixed to the debtor and to each creditor mentioned in the list provided by the debtor.

(9) Where an administration order is made under paragraph (3), the court officer may exercise the power of the court under section 5 of the Attachment of Earnings Act 1971 to make an attachment of earnings order to secure the payments required by the administration order.

Rule 6 NOTICE OF OBJECTION BY CREDITOR

(1) Any creditor to whom notice has been given under rule 5(8) and who objects to any debt included in the list furnished by the debtor shall, not less than 7 days before the day of hearing, give notice of his objection, stating the grounds thereof, to the court officer, to the debtor and to the creditor to whose debt he objects.

(2) Except with the permission of the court, no creditor may object to a debt unless he has given notice of his objection under paragraph (1).

Rule 7 PROCEDURE ON DAY OF HEARING

On the day of the hearing—

    (a) any creditor, whether or not he is mentioned in the list furnished by the debtor, may attend and prove his debt or, subject to rule 6, object to any debt included in that list;

    (b) every debt included in that list shall be taken to be proved unless it is objected to by a creditor or disallowed by the court or required by the court to be supported by evidence;

    (c) any creditor whose debt is required by the court to be supported by evidence shall prove his debt;

    (d) the court may adjourn proof of any debt and, if it does so, may either adjourn consideration of the question whether an administration order should be made or proceed to determine the question, in which case, if an administration order is made, the debt, when proved, shall be added to the debts scheduled to the order;

    (e) any creditor whose debt is admitted or proved, and, with the permission of the court, any creditor the proof of whose debt has been adjourned, shall be entitled to be heard and to adduce evidence on the question whether an administration order should be made and, if so, in what terms.

Rule 8 DIRECTION FOR ORDER TO BE SUBJECT TO REVIEW

(1) The court may, on making an administration order or at any subsequent time, direct that the order shall be subject to review at such time or at such intervals as the court may specify.

(2) Where the court has directed that an administration order shall be subject to review, the court officer shall give to the debtor and to every creditor who appeared when the order was made not less than 7 days' notice of any day appointed for such a review.

(3) Nothing in this rule shall require the court officer to fix a day for a review under rule 13A.

Rule 9 SERVICE OF ORDER

Where an administration order is made, the court officer shall send a copy to—
    (a)   the debtor;
    (b)   every creditor whose name was included in the list furnished by the debtor;
    (c)   any other creditor who has proved his debt; and
    (d)   every other court in which, to the knowledge of the district judge, judgment has been obtained against the debtor or proceedings are pending in respect of any debt scheduled to the order.

Rule 10 SUBSEQUENT OBJECTION BY CREDITOR

(1) After an administration order has been made, a creditor who has not received notice under rule 5 and who wishes to object to a debt scheduled to the order, or to the manner in which payment is directed to be made by instalments, shall give notice to the court officer of his objection and of the grounds thereof.

(2) On receipt of such notice the court shall consider the objection and may—
    (a)   allow it;
    (b)   dismiss it; or
    (c)   adjourn it for hearing on notice being given to such persons and on such terms as to security for costs or otherwise as the court thinks fit.

(3) Without prejudice to the generality of paragraph (2), the court may dismiss an objection if it is not satisfied that the creditor gave notice of it within a reasonable time of his becoming aware of the administration order.

Rule 11 SUBSEQUENT PROOF BY CREDITOR

(1) Any creditor whose debt is not scheduled to an administration order, and any person who after the date of the order became a creditor of the debtor, shall, if he wishes to prove his debt, send particulars of his claim to the court officer, who shall give notice of it to the debtor and to every creditor whose debt is so scheduled.

(2) If neither the debtor nor any creditor gives notice to the court officer, within 7 days after receipt of notice under paragraph (1), that he objects to the claim, then, unless it is required by the court to be supported by evidence, the claim shall be taken to be proved.

(3) If the debtor or a creditor gives notice of objection within the said period of 7 days or the court requires the claim to be supported by evidence, the court officer shall fix a day for consideration of the claim and give notice of it to the debtor, the creditor by whom the claim was made and the creditor, if any, making the objection, and on the hearing the court may either disallow the claim or allow it in whole or in part.

(4) If a claim is taken to be proved under paragraph (2) or allowed under paragraph (3), the debt shall be added to the schedule to the order and a copy of the order shall then be sent to the creditor by whom the claim was made.

Rule 12 PERMISSION TO PRESENT BANKRUPTCY PETITION

An application by a creditor under section 112(4) of the Act for permission to present or join in a bankruptcy petition shall be made on notice to the debtor in accordance with CPR Part 23, but the court may, if it thinks fit, order that notice be given to any other creditor whose debt is scheduled to the administration order.

Rule 13 CONDUCT OF ORDER

(1) The court manager or such other officer of the court as the court making an administration order shall from time to time appoint shall have the conduct of the order and shall take all proper steps to enforce the order (including exercising the power of the court under section 5 of the Attachment of Earnings Act 1971 to make an attachment of earnings order to secure payments required by the administration order) or to bring to the attention of the court any matter which may make it desirable to review the order.

(2) Without prejudice to section 115 of the Act, any creditor whose debt is scheduled to the order may, with the permission of the court, take proceedings to enforce the order.

(3) The debtor or, with the permission of the court, any such creditor may apply to the court to review the order.

(4) When on a matter being brought to its attention under paragraph (1) the court so directs or the debtor or a creditor applies for the review of an administration order, rule 8(2) shall apply as if the order were subject to review under that rule.

(5) Nothing in this rule shall require the court officer to fix a day for a review under rule 13A.

Rule 13A REVIEW BY COURT OFFICER IN DEFAULT OF PAYMENT

(1) Where it appears that the debtor is failing to make payments in accordance with the order, the court officer shall (either of his own initiative or on the application of a creditor whose debt is scheduled to the administration order) send a notice to the debtor—
   (a) informing him of the amounts which are outstanding; and
   (b) requiring him (within 14 days of service of the notice upon him) to—
      (i) make the payments as required by the order; or
      (ii) explain his reasons for failing to make the payments; and
      (iii) make a proposal for payment of the amounts outstanding; or
      (iv) make a request to vary the order.

(2) If the debtor does not comply with paragraph (1)(b) within the time stated, the court officer shall revoke the administration order.

(3) The court officer shall refer a notice given by a debtor under paragraph (1)(b)(ii), (iii) or (iv) to the district judge who may—
   (a) without requiring the attendance of the parties—
      (i) revoke the administration order or vary it so as to provide for payment of the debts included in the order in full or to such extent and within such a period as appears practicable in the circumstances of the case; or
      (ii) suspend the operation of the administration order for such time and on such terms as he thinks fit; or
   (b) require the court officer to fix a day for the review of the administration order and to give to the debtor and to every creditor whose debt is scheduled to the administration order not less than 8 days' notice of the day so fixed.

(4) Any party affected by an order made under paragraph (2) or (3)(a) may, within 14 days of service of the order on him and giving his reasons, apply on notice for the district judge to consider the matter afresh and the court officer shall fix a day for the hearing of the application before the district judge and give to the debtor and to every creditor whose debt is scheduled to the administration order not less than 8 days' notice of the day so fixed.

(5) On hearing an application under paragraph (4), the district judge may confirm the order or set it aside and make such new order as he thinks fit and the order so made shall be entered in the records of the court.

Rule 14 REVIEW OF ORDER

(1) On the review of an administration order the court may—
   (a) if satisfied that the debtor is unable from any cause to pay any instalment due under the order, suspend the operation of the order for such time and on such terms as it thinks fit;
   (b) if satisfied that there has been a material change in any relevant circumstances since the order was made, vary any provision of the order made by virtue of section 112(6) of the Act;
   (c) if satisfied that the debtor has failed without reasonable cause to comply with any provision of the order or that it is otherwise just and expedient to do so, revoke the order, either forthwith or on failure to comply with any condition specified by the court; or
   (d) make an attachment of earnings order to secure the payments required by the administration order or vary or discharge any such attachment of earnings order already made.

(2) The court officer shall send a copy of any order varying or revoking an administration order to the debtor, to every creditor whose debt is scheduled to

the administration order and, if the administration order is revoked, to any other court to which a copy of the administration order was sent pursuant to rule 9.

Rule 16 DISCHARGE OF ATTACHMENT OF EARNINGS ORDER
On the revocation of an administration order any attachment of earnings order made to secure the payments required by the administration order shall be discharged.

Rule 17 DECLARATION OF DIVIDENDS
(1) The officer having the conduct of an administration order shall from time to time declare dividends and distribute them among the creditors entitled to them.

(2) When a dividend is declared, notice shall be sent by the officer to each of the creditors.

Rule 18 CREDITORS TO RANK EQUALLY
All creditors scheduled under section 113(d) of the Act before an administration order is superseded under section 117(2) of the Act shall rank equally in proportion to the amount of their debts subject to the priority given by the said paragraph (d) to those scheduled as having been creditors before the date of the order, but no payment made to any creditor by way of dividend or otherwise shall be disturbed by reason of any subsequent proof by any creditor under the said paragraph (d).

Rule 19 CHANGE OF DEBTOR'S ADDRESS
(1) A debtor who changes his residence shall forthwith inform the court of his new address.

(2) Mere the debtor becomes resident in the district of another court, the court in which the administration order is being conducted may transfer the proceedings to that other court.

CCR ORDER 42
PROCEEDINGS BY AND AGAINST THE CROWN

Rule 1 APPLICATION AND INTERPRETATION
(1) These rules apply to any proceedings, so far as they are civil proceedings to which the Crown is a party, subject to the following rules of this order.

(2) Except where the context otherwise requires, references in these rules to a claim for the recovery of land or other property shall be construed as including references to proceedings against the Crown for an order declaring that the claimant is entitled as against the Crown to the land or property or to the possession of it.

(3) In this order—
'the Act of 1947' means the Crown Proceedings Act 1947;
'civil proceedings by the Crown' and 'civil proceedings against the Crown' and 'civil proceedings by or against the Crown' have the same respective meanings as in Part II of the Act of 1947 and do not include any of the proceedings specified in section 23(3) of that Act;
'civil proceedings to which the Crown is a party' has the same meaning as it has for the purposes of Part IV of the Act of 1947 by virtue of section 38(4) of that Act.

Rule 4 PARTICULARS OF CLAIM IN CLAIM AGAINST THE CROWN
The particulars of claim shall, in the case of civil proceedings against the Crown, include a statement of the circumstances in which the Crown's liability is said to have arisen and as to the government department and officers of the Crown concerned.

Rule 5 SUBSEQUENT PROCEDURE IN CLAIM
(1) If in a claim against the Crown the defendant considers that the particulars of claim do not contain a sufficient statement as required by rule 4, he may, before the time for delivering a defence has expired, file two copies of a demand for further information as specified in the demand and thereupon the court officer shall serve one copy on the claimant.

(2) Where the defendant files a demand under paragraph (1), the time for delivering a defence shall not expire until 4 days after the defendant has given notice to the court and the claimant that the defendant is satisfied with the information supplied in compliance with the demand or 4 days after the court has, on the application of the claimant of which not less than 7 days' notice has been given to the defendant, decided that no further information as to the matters referred to in rule 4 is reasonably required.

(3) Except with the permission of the court, no default judgment shall be entered under CPR Part 12 in a claim against the Crown.

(4) An application for permission under paragraph (3) shall be made on not less than 7 days' notice to the defendant.

(5) No application against the Crown shall be made under CPR Part 24 (summary judgment).

Rule 6 SUBSEQUENT PROCEDURE IN FIXED DATE CLAIM

(1) In the case of a fixed date claim against the Crown, on the filing of the claim form the court shall—

(a) enter a plaint in the records of the court and deliver to the claimant a notice of issue omitting any reference to a return day;

(b) serve on the defendant a copy of the particulars of claim if they are filed with the claim form and the notice of issue and of the effect of paragraphs (3) and (5).

(2) Upon the service of the notice mentioned in paragraph (1)(b) all further proceedings in the claim shall be stayed except as provided in this rule.

(3) If the defendant considers that the particulars of claim do not contain a sufficient statement as required by rule 4, he may, within 21 days after service on him of the particulars of claim, file in the court office two copies of a demand for further information as specified in the demand and thereupon the court shall serve one copy on the claimant.

(4) If within the said period the defendant does not file two copies of such a demand, then, subject to paragraph (5), the stay of proceedings provided for by paragraph (2) shall cease to have effect at the end of that period.

(5) If within the said period the defendant files a statement that no such demand will be made, the stay of proceedings provided for by paragraph (2) shall cease to have effect forthwith.

(6) If within the said period the defendant files two copies of such a demand, the stay of proceedings provided for by paragraph (2) shall cease to have effect when the defendant gives notice to the court and the claimant that the defendant is satisfied with the information supplied in compliance with the demand or when the court decides, on the application of the claimant of which not less than 7 days' notice has been given to the defendant, that no further information as to the matters referred to in rule 4, is reasonably required.

(7) When the stay of proceedings provided for by paragraph (2) ceases to have effect, the court shall fix a return day and give notice of it to the claimant and shall proceed to issue the claim form.

Rule 7 SERVICE ON THE CROWN

(1) RSC Order 11 and any other provision of these rules relating to service of process out of England and Wales shall apply in relation to civil proceedings by the Crown but shall not apply in relation to civil proceedings against the Crown.

(2) Personal service of any document which is to be served on the Crown for the purpose of or in connection with civil proceedings by or

(3) Any such document may be served on the Crown—

(a) by leaving the document at the office of the person to be served in accordance with section 18 of the Act of 1947, or any agent whom he has nominated for the purpose, but in either case with a member of the staff of that person or agent; or

(b) by posting it in a prepaid envelope addressed to the person to be served in accordance with the said section 18 or to any such agent as aforesaid.

Rule 8 SPECIAL PROVISIONS REGARDING ORDERS MADE BY THE COURT OF ITS OWN INITIATIVE AGAINST THE CROWN

(2) No order shall be made against the Crown by the court of its own initiative—

    (a) (i) requiring the Crown to file or serve any statement of case or give any particulars which the court thinks necessary for defining the issues in the proceedings; and

        (ii) at the same or any subsequent time directing that the claim be dismissed or the defendant be debarred from defending altogether or that anything in any statement of case of which particulars have been ordered be struck out unless the order is obeyed;

    (b) ordering one or more questions or issues to be tried before the others; or

    (c) at a hearing other than the trial.

Rule 9 COUNTERCLAIM IN PROCEEDINGS BY OR AGAINST THE CROWN

(1) In proceedings by the Crown for the recovery of taxes, duties or penalties the defendant shall not be entitled to avail himself of any set-off or counterclaim and accordingly the claim form to be served on the defendant and the forms for defending the claim, admitting the claim and acknowledging service, to accompany the claim form shall omit any reference to a counterclaim.

(2) In proceedings of any other nature by the Crown the defendant shall not be entitled to avail himself of any set-off or counterclaim arising out of a right or claim to repayment in respect of any taxes, duties or penalties.

(3) In any proceedings by the Crown the defendant shall not be entitled, and in any proceedings against the Crown the Crown shall not be entitled, without the permission of the court to be obtained on application of which not less than 7 days' notice has been given to the claimant, to make any counterclaim or claim in his statements of case to be entitled to any set-off if—

    (a) the Crown sues or is sued in the name of a Government department and the subject-matter of the set-off or counterclaim does not relate to that department; or

    (b) the Crown sues or is sued in the name of the Attorney-General.

Rule 10 ADJUSTMENT OF LIABILITY UNDER JUDGMENT FOR TAXES

Where the Crown has obtained a judgment for taxes but subsequently the tax liability is reduced, whether by reason of an appeal against an assessment or otherwise, and the Crown has given notice of the reduction to the court and to the debtor, the sum remaining unsatisfied under the judgment shall be reduced accordingly, but the amount of the reduction shall not rank as a payment under the judgment.

Rule 11 PART 20 CLAIM AGAINST THE CROWN WHERE THE CROWN IS NOT ALREADY A PARTY

(1) A Part 20 claim for service on the Crown where the Crown is not already a party shall not be issued without the permission of the court to be obtained on application in accordance with CPR Part 23.

(1A) An application notice under paragraph (1) must be served on the Crown and the claimant at least 7 days before the hearing.

(2) Permission shall not be granted under paragraph (1) unless the court is satisfied that the Crown is in possession of all such information as it reasonably requires as to the circumstances in which it is alleged that the liability of the Crown has arisen and as to the departments and officers of the Crown concerned.

Rule 12 DISCLOSURE AGAINST THE CROWN

(2) Where in any proceedings an order of the court directs that a list of documents made in answer to an order for disclosure against the Crown shall be verified by witness statement or affidavit, the witness statement or affidavit shall be made by such officer of the Crown as the court may direct.

(3) The court may direct which officer of the Crown shall make the disclosure statement required by CPR rule 31.10(5).

Rule 13 EXECUTION AND SATISFACTION OF ORDERS AGAINST THE CROWN

(1) Nothing in Orders 25 to 31 or RSC Order 30 (in so far as it applies to proceedings in the county court) shall apply in respect of any order against the Crown.

(2) A certificate issued under section 25(1) of the Act of 1947 shall be in the form used under Order 22, rule 8, with such variations as the circumstances of the case may require.

Rule 14 ATTACHMENT OF DEBTS ETC.

(1) No order for the attachment of a debt under Order 30 or for the appointment of a receiver under RSC Order 30 shall be made or have effect in respect of any money due or accruing due, or alleged to be due or accruing due, from the Crown.

(2) Where such an order could have been obtained in a county court if the money had been due or accruing due from a subject, an application may be made to that county court in accordance with CPR Part 23 for an order under section 27 of the Act of 1947 restraining the person to whom the money is payable by the Crown from receiving the money and directing payment to the applicant or to the receiver.

(3) The application shall be supported by a witness statement or affidavit setting out the facts giving rise to it and in particular identifying the particular debt from the Crown in respect of which it is made.

(4) Notice of the application together with a copy of the witness statement or affidavit shall be served on the Crown and, unless the court otherwise directs, on the person to be restrained or his solicitor at least 7 days before the day fixed for the hearing.

(5) Order 30, rules 7 to 9, shall apply, with the necessary modifications, in relation to an application under the said section 27 as they apply in relation to an application for an order under Order 30, rule 1, except that the court shall not have power to issue execution against the Crown.

CCR ORDER 43
THE LANDLORD AND TENANT ACTS 1927, 1954, 1985 AND 1987

Rule 1 INTERPRETATION

(1) In this order 'the Act of 1927' means the Landlord and Tenant Act 1927, 'the Act of 1954' means the Landlord and Tenant Act 1954, 'the Act of 1985' means the Landlord and Tenant Act 1985 and 'the Act of 1987' means the Landlord and Tenant Act 1987.

(2) In relation to any proceedings under the Act of 1954 any reference in this Order to a landlord shall, if the interest of the landlord in question is subject to a mortgage and the mortgagee is in possession or a receiver appointed by the mortgagee or by the court is in receipt of the rents and profits, be construed as a reference to the mortgagee.

Rule 2 COMMENCEMENT OF PROCEEDINGS AND ANSWER

(1) Proceedings in a county court under the Act of 1927 or of 1954, or of 1985 or of 1987 shall be commenced by claim form and the respondent shall file an answer.

(2) The court shall fix a return day which, unless it otherwise directs, shall be a day fixed for the case management hearing of the proceedings.

Rule 3 CLAIM FOR COMPENSATION IN RESPECT OF IMPROVEMENT

(1) A claim under section 1 of the Act of 1927 for compensation in respect of any improvement, or a claim by a mesne landlord under section 8(1) of that Act, shall be in writing, signed by the claimant, his solicitor or agent, and shall contain—
　(a) a statement of the name and address of the claimant and of the landlord against whom the claim is made;
　(b) a description of the holding in respect of which the claim arises and of the trade or business carried on there;

(c) a concise statement of the nature of the claim;
(d) particulars of the improvement including the date when it was completed and the cost of it; and
(e) a statement of the amount claimed.

(2) Where any document relating to any proposed improvement, or to any claim, is sent to or served on a mesne landlord in pursuance of Part I of the Act of 1927, he shall forthwith serve on his immediate landlord a copy of the document, together with a notice in writing stating the date when the document was received by the mesne landlord, and if the immediate landlord is himself a mesne landlord, he shall, forthwith on receipt of the documents aforesaid, serve on his immediate landlord a similar copy and notice and so on from landlord to landlord.

(3) Any document required to be served under paragraph (2) shall be served in the manner prescribed by section 23 of the Act of 1927.

Rule 4 PROCEEDINGS UNDER PART I OF THE ACT OF 1927

(1) Subject to paragraph (2), the claim form by which proceedings under Part I of the Act of 1927 are commenced shall state—
(a) the nature of the claim or application or matter to be determined;
(b) the holding in respect of which the claim or application is made, its rateable value and the trade or business carried on there;
(c) particulars of the improvement or proposed improvement to which the claim or application relates; and
(d) if the claim is for payment of compensation, the amount claimed.

(2) In any case to which rule 3(1) relates the particulars required by paragraph (1) may, so far as they are contained in a claim made in accordance with that rule, be given by appending a copy of the claim to the claim form.

(3) The applicant's immediate landlord shall be made respondent to the application.

(4) Any certificate of the court under section 3 of the Act of 1927 that an improvement is a proper improvement or has been duly executed shall be embodied in an order.

Rule 5 PROCEEDINGS UNDER PART I OF THE ACT OF 1954

(1) A respondent to an application under section 7 of the Act of 1954 who resists any of the applicant's proposals as to the terms of a statutory tenancy shall state in his answer the terms which he proposes in their place.

(2) The particulars in an application under section 13 of the Act of 1954 for the recovery of possession shall state, in addition to the matters set out in Order 6, rule 3—
(a) the date and terms of the lease under which the tenant holds or has held the property;
(b) the date of service upon the tenant of the landlord's notice to resume possession and the date of termination specified in the notice;
(c) where the tenant has notified the landlord that he is not willing to give up possession, the date of the notification; and
(d) where the claimant is not both the freeholder of the property comprised in the tenancy and the immediate landlord of the defendant, details of the interest constituting him the landlord for the purpose of proceedings under Part I of the Act of 1954.

(3) Where an order has been made under paragraph 1 of the Second Schedule to the Act of 1954 for the reduction of rent of any premises on the ground of failure by the landlord to do initial repairs, and it is subsequently agreed between the landlord and the tenant that the repairs to which the order relates have been carried out, the landlord shall file a copy of the agreement, and a note thereof shall be entered in the records of the court.

(4) Where the court makes an order for the recovery of possession of the property in proceedings to which paragraph 9 of the Fifth Schedule to the Act of 1954 applies, the claimant shall, if the occupying tenant is not a party to the

proceedings, forthwith notify him of the terms of the order and inform him of his rights to obtain relief under subparagraph (2) of that paragraph.

(5) If a copy of a notice under section 16(2) of the Act of 1954 or paragraph 9(2) or 10(2) of the Fifth Schedule to that Act is lodged in court, a note of the lodgment shall be entered in the records of the court.

Rule 6 APPLICATION FOR NEW TENANCY UNDER SECTION 24 OF THE ACT OF 1954

(1) An application under section 24 of the Act of 1954 for a new tenancy shall state—

(a) the premises to which the application relates, their rateable value and the business carried on there;

(b) particulars of the applicant's current tenancy of the premises and of every notice or request given or made in respect of that tenancy under section 25 or 26 of that Act;

(c) the applicant's proposals as to the terms of the new tenancy applied for, including, in particular, terms as to the duration thereof and as to the rent payable thereunder;

(d) the name and address of any person other than the respondent who, to the knowledge of the applicant, has an interest in reversion in the premises expectant (whether immediately or in not more than 14 years) on the termination of the applicant's current tenancy; and

(c) the name and address of any person having an interest in the premises other than a freehold interest or tenancy who, to the knowledge of the applicant, is likely to be affected by the grant of a new tenancy.

(2) The person who, in relation to the applicant's current tenancy, is the landlord as defined by section 44 of the Act of 1954 shall be made respondent to the application.

(3) A claim form under this rule must be served within 2 months after the date of issue whether served within or out of the jurisdiction and CPR rule 7.5(2) and 7.5(3) will not apply.

Rule 7 ANSWER TO APPLICATION FOR NEW TENANCY UNDER SECTION 24 OF THE ACT OF 1954

Every answer by a respondent to an application to which rule 6 relates shall state—

(a) whether or not the respondent opposes the grant of a new tenancy and, if so, on what grounds;

(b) whether or not, if a new tenancy is granted, the respondent objects to any of the terms proposed by the applicant and, if so, the terms to which he objects and the terms which he proposes in so far as they differ from those proposed by the applicant;

(c) whether the respondent is a tenant under a lease having less than 14 years unexpired at the date of the termination of the applicant's current tenancy and, if he is, the name and address of any person who, to the knowledge of the respondent, has an interest in reversion in the premises expectant (whether immediately or in not more than 14 years from the said date) on the termination of the respondent's tenancy;

(d) the name and address of any person having an interest in the premises other than a freehold interest or tenancy who is likely to be affected by the grant of a new tenancy; and

(e) if the applicant's current tenancy is one to which section 32(2) of the Act of 1954 applies, whether the respondent requires that any new tenancy ordered to be granted shall be a tenancy of the whole of the property comprised in the applicant's current tenancy.

Rule 8 ORDER DISMISSING APPLICATION UNDER SECTION 24 WHICH IS SUCCESSFULLY OPPOSED

Where the court hearing an application under section 24 of the Act of 1954 is precluded by section 31 of that Act from ordering the grant of a new tenancy by reason of any of the grounds specified in section 30(1) of that Act, the order dismissing the application shall state all the grounds by reason of which the court is so precluded.

Rule 9 OTHER APPLICATIONS UNDER PART II OF THE ACT OF 1954
An application for an order under section 31(2)(b) of the Act of 1954 and, unless made at the hearing of the application under section 24, an application for a certificate under section 37(4) of that Act may be made to the district judge without notice being served on any other party.

Rule 10 SERVICE OF ORDER IN PROCEEDINGS UNDER PART II OF THE ACT OF 1954
A copy of any order made on an application to which rule 6 or 9 relates shall be sent by the court to every party to the proceedings.

Rule 11 PROOF OF DETERMINATION OF RATEABLE VALUE
Where pursuant to section 37(5) of the Act of 1954 any dispute as to the rateable value of any premises has been referred to the Commissioners of Inland Revenue for decision by a valuation officer, whether for the purpose of section 37(2) or of section 63 of that Act, any document purporting to be a notification by the valuation officer of his decision shall be admissible in any proceedings in a county court as evidence of the matters contained therein.

Rule 13 PROVISIONS AS TO ASSESSORS
(1) This rule applies to proceedings under Part I of the Act of 1927 or Part I or II of the Act of 1954, where an assessor is summoned by the judge under section 63(1) of the County Courts Act 1984, as extended by section 63 of the Act of 1954.

(3) Any report made by the assessor pursuant to paragraph (a) of section 63(6) of the Act of 1954 shall be filed by the assessor, together with a copy for each party to the proceedings, and thereupon the court shall send a copy to each party and shall, if the further consideration of the proceedings has not been adjourned to a day named, fix a day for further consideration and give notice thereof to all parties.

Rule 15 DISTRICT JUDGE'S JURISDICTION
(1) If on the day fixed for the hearing of an application under section 7 or section 24 of the Act of 1954 the district judge is satisfied that—

(a) the parties to the application have agreed, in the case of an application under section 7, on the matters specified in subsection (2) of that section, or, in the case of an application under section 24, on the subject, period and terms of the new tenancy;

(b) the owner of any reversionary interest in the property consents thereto; and

(c) there are no other persons with interests in the property who are likely to be affected,

the district judge shall have power to make an order giving effect to the agreement.

(2) An application under section 38(4) of the Act of 1954 for the authorisation of an agreement may be heard and determined by the district judge and may be dealt with in private.

Rule 16 APPLICATION UNDER SECTION 12(2) OF THE ACT OF 1985
An application under section 12(2) of the Act of 1985 for an order authorising the inclusion in a lease of provisions excluding or modifying the provisions of section 11 of that Act may be heard and determined by the district judge and may, if the court thinks fit, be dealt with in private.

Rule 16A TRANSFER TO LEASEHOLD VALUATION TRIBUNAL
Where a question arising in proceedings is ordered to be transferred to a leasehold valuation tribunal for determination under section 31C of the Landlord and Tenant Act 1985 the court shall—

(a) send notice of the transfer to all parties to the proceedings; and

(b) send to the leasehold valuation tribunal copies certified by the district judge of all entries in the records of the court relating to the question, together with the order of transfer and all documents filed in the proceedings which relate to the question.

Rule 17 APPLICATION UNDER SECTION 19 OF THE ACT OF 1987

A copy of the notice served under section 19(2)(a) of the Act of 1987 shall be appended to the claim form seeking an order under section 19(1) thereof, and an additional copy of the notice shall be filed.

Rule 19 APPLICATION FOR ACQUISITION ORDER UNDER SECTION 29 OF THE ACT OF 1987

(1) An application for an acquisition order under section 29 of the Act of 1987 shall—

(a) identify the premises to which the application relates and give such details of them as are necessary to show that section 25 of the Act of 1987 applies to them;

(b) give such details of the applicants as are necessary to show that they constitute the requisite majority of qualifying tenants;

(c) state the names and addresses of the applicants and of the landlord of the premises, or, where the landlord cannot be found or his identity ascertained, the steps taken to find him or ascertain his identity;

(d) state the name and address of the person nominated by the applicants for the purposes of Part III of the Act of 1987;

(e) state the name and address of every person known to the applicants who is likely to be affected by the application, including, but not limited to, the other tenants of flats contained in the premises (whether or not they could have made an application), any mortgagee or superior landlord of the landlord, and any tenants' association; and

(f) state the grounds of the application,

and a copy of the notice served on the landlord under section 27 of the Act of 1987 shall be appended to the claim form unless the requirement to serve such a notice has been dispensed with, and an additional copy of the notice shall be filed.

(2) The respondents to an application for an acquisition order under section 29 of the Act of 1987 shall be the landlord of the premises and the nominated person, where he is not an applicant.

(3) A copy of the application shall be served on each of the persons named by the applicant under paragraph (1)(e), together with a notice stating that he may apply under rule 14 to be made a party to the proceedings.

(4) Where the nominated person pays money into court in accordance with an order under section 33(1) of the Act of 1987, he shall file a copy of the certificate of the surveyor selected under section 33(2)(a) thereof.

Rule 20 APPLICATION FOR ORDER UNDER SECTION 38 OR SECTION 40 OF THE ACT OF 1987

(1) An application for an order under section 38 or section 40 of the Act of 1987 shall state—

(a) the name and address of the applicant and of the other current parties to the lease or leases to which the application relates;

(b) the date of the lease or leases, the premises demised thereby, the relevant terms thereof and the variation sought;

(c) the name and address of every person who the applicant knows or has reason to believe is likely to be affected by the variation, including, but not limited to, the other tenants of flats contained in the premises of which the demised premises form a part, any previous parties to the lease, any mortgagee or superior landlord of the landlord, any mortgagee of the applicant, and any tenants' association; and

(d) the grounds of the application.

(2) The other current parties to the lease or leases shall be made respondents to the application.

(3) A copy of the application shall be served by the applicant on each of the persons named by the applicant under paragraph (1)(c) and by the respondent on

any other person who he knows or has reason to believe is likely to be affected by the variation, together, in each case, with a notice stating that the person may apply to be made a party to the proceedings.

(4) An application under section 36 of the Act of 1987 shall be contained in the respondent's answer, and paragraphs (1) to (3) shall apply to such an application as if the respondent were the applicant.

Rule 21 SERVICE OF DOCUMENTS IN PROCEEDINGS UNDER THE ACT OF 1987

(1) Where a claim form or answer is to be served in proceedings under the Act of 1987 it shall be served by the applicant or, as the case may be, by the respondent.

(2) Where a notice is to be served in or before proceedings under the Act of 1987, it shall be served in accordance with section 54 and, in the case of service on a landlord, it shall be served at the address furnished under section 48(1).

Rule 22 TENANTS' ASSOCIATIONS

In rules 18, 19 and 20 a reference to a tenants' association is a reference to a recognised tenants' association within the meaning of section 29 of the Act of 1985 which represents tenants of the flats of which the demised premises form a part.

CCR ORDER 44
THE AGRICULTURAL HOLDINGS ACT 1986

Rule 1 ORDER TO ARBITRATOR TO STATE CASE

(1) An application under paragraph 26 of Schedule 11 to the Agricultural Holdings Act 1986 for an order directing an arbitrator to state, in the form of a special case for the opinion of the court, a question of law arising in the course of the arbitration shall include a concise statement of the question of law.

(2) The arbitrator shall not be made a respondent to the application, but if the judge grants the application, a copy of the order shall be served on the arbitrator.

Rule 2 SPECIAL CASE STATED BY ARBITRATOR

(1) Where, pursuant to the said paragraph 26, an arbitrator states, in the form of a special case for the opinion of the court, any question of law arising in the course of the arbitration, the case shall contain a statement of such facts and reference to such documents as may be necessary to enable the judge to decide the question of law.

(2) The case shall be signed by the arbitrator and shall be lodged in the court office by the arbitrator or any party to the arbitration, together with a copy for the use of the judge.

(3) The court officer shall fix a day for the hearing of the special case and give notice thereof to the parties.

(4) On the hearing the judge shall be at liberty to draw any inferences of fact from the case and the documents referred to therein.

(5) The judge may remit the case to the arbitrator for restatement or further statement.

(6) A copy of the order made by the judge on the hearing shall be served on the parties to the arbitration and on the arbitrator.

Rule 3 REMOVAL OF ARBITRATOR OR SETTING ASIDE AWARD

(1) An application under paragraph 27 of Schedule 11 to the said Act of 1986 for the removal of an arbitrator on the ground of his misconduct or for an order setting aside an award on the ground that the arbitrator has misconducted himself or that an arbitration or award has been improperly procured or that there is an error of law on the face of the award shall be made within 21 days after the date of the award.

(2) The arbitrator and all parties to the arbitration, other than the applicant, shall be made respondents.

Rule 4 ENFORCEMENT OF ORDER IMPOSING PENALTY

(1) When taking any proceedings for the enforcement in a county court of an order under section 27 of the Agricultural Holdings Act 1986, the party in whose favour the order was made shall file—

CPR SCHEDULE 2

(a) a certified copy of the order; and

(b) a certificate specifying the amount due under the order and stating whether any previous proceedings have been taken for its enforcement and, if so, the nature of the proceedings and their result.

(2) Where it is desired to enforce the order by warrant of execution, the proceedings may be taken in any court in the district of which execution is to be levied.

CCR ORDER 45
THE REPRESENTATION OF THE PEOPLE ACT 1983

Rule 1 APPLICATION FOR DETAILED ASSESSMENT OF RETURNING OFFICER'S ACCOUNT

(1) An application by the Secretary of State under section 30 of the Representation of the People Act 1983 for the detailed assessment of a returning officer's account shall be made by claim form and on issuing the claim form the court will fix a day for the hearing which shall be a day for proceeding with the detailed assessment if the application is granted.

(2) Where on the application the returning officer desires to apply to the court to examine any claim made against him in respect of matters charged in the account, the application shall be made in writing and filed, together with a copy thereof, within 7 days after service on the returning officer of the copy of the application for detailed assessment.

(3) On the filing of an application under paragraph (2) the court officer shall fix a day for the hearing and give notice thereof to the returning officer, and a copy of the application and of the notice shall be served on the claimant in the manner required for service of the notice of the day of hearing in accordance with Order 3, rule 6.

(4) The examination and detailed assessment may, if the court thinks fit, take place on the same day, but the examination shall be determined before the detailed assessment is concluded.

(5) The application for detailed assessment and any application under paragraph (2) may be heard and determined by the district judge and a copy of the order made on the application shall be served on the Secretary of State and the returning officer and, in the case of an application under paragraph (2), on the claimant.

Rule 2 APPEAL FROM DECISION OF REGISTRATION OFFICER

(1) Where notice of appeal from a decision of a registration officer is given pursuant to regulations made under section 53 of the said Act of 1983 the registration officer shall, within 7 days after receipt of the notice by him, forward the notice by post to the court in which the appeal is required to be brought, together with the statement mentioned in those regulations.

(2) The appeal shall be brought in the court for the district in which the qualifying premises are situated.

In this paragraph 'qualifying premises' means the premises in respect of which—

(a) the person whose right to be registered in the register of electors is in question on the appeal is entered on the electors' list or is registered or claims to be entitled to be registered; or

(b) the person whose right to vote by proxy or by post is in question on the appeal is or will be registered in the register of electors; or

(c) the elector whose proxy's right to vote by post is in question on the appeal is or will be registered in the register of electors,

as the case may be.

(3) The respondents to the appeal shall be the registration officer and the party (if any) in whose favour the decision of the registration officer was given.

(4) On the hearing of the appeal—

(a) the statement forwarded to the court by the registration officer and any document containing information furnished to the court by the registration officer pursuant to the regulations mentioned in paragraph (1) shall be admissible as evidence of the facts stated therein; and

(b) the judge shall have power to draw all inferences of fact which might have been drawn by the registration officer and to give any decision and make any order which ought to have been given or made by the registration officer.

(5) A respondent to an appeal other than the registration officer shall not be liable for or entitled to costs, unless he appears before the court in support of the decision of the registration officer.

Rule 3 SELECTED APPEALS

(1) Where two or more appeals to which rule 2 relates involve the same point of law, the judge may direct that one appeal shall be heard in the first instance as a test case and thereupon the court shall send a notice of the direction to the parties to the selected appeal and the parties to the other appeals.

(2) If within 7 days after service of such notice on him any party to an appeal other than the selected appeal gives notice to the court that he desires the appeal to which he is a party to be heard—

(a) the appeal shall be heard after the selected appeal is disposed of;
(b) the court shall give the parties to the appeal notice of the day on which it will be heard;
(c) the party giving notice under this paragraph shall not be entitled to receive any costs occasioned by the separate hearing of the appeal to which he is a party, unless the judge otherwise orders.

(3) If no notice is given under paragraph (2) within the time limited—

(a) the decision on the selected appeal shall bind the parties to each other appeal without prejudice to their right to appeal to the Court of Appeal;
(b) an order similar to the order in the selected appeal shall be made in each other appeal without further hearing;
(c) the party to each other appeal who is in the same interest as the unsuccessful party to the selected appeal shall be liable for the costs of the selected appeal in the same manner and to the same extent as the unsuccessful party to that appeal and an order directing him to pay such costs may be made and enforced accordingly.

CCR ORDER 46
THE LEGITIMACY ACT 1976

Rule 1 MANNER OF APPLICATION

(1) An application to a county court under section 45(2) of the Matrimonial Causes Act 1973 for a declaration of legitimation by virtue of the Legitimacy Act 1976 shall be made by claim form stating—

(a) the grounds on which the applicant relies;
(b) the date and place of birth of the applicant and the maiden name of his mother and, if it be the case, that the applicant is known by a name other than that which appears in the certificate of his birth; and
(c) particulars of every person whose interest may be affected by the proceedings and his relationship, if any, to the applicant, including any person other than the applicant's father to whom his mother was married at the date of his birth.

(2) The application may be filed in the court for the district in which the applicant resides or the marriage leading to the legitimation was celebrated, or if neither the residence of the applicant nor the place of the marriage is in England or Wales, then in the Westminster County Court.

(3) The applicant shall file with the claim form—

(a) a witness statement or affidavit by him (or, if he is a child, by his litigation friend) verifying the application; and
(b) any birth, death or marriage certificate intended to be relied on at the hearing.

Rule 2 PRELIMINARY CONSIDERATION AND SERVICE

(1) On the filing of the documents mentioned in rule 1, the court officer shall fix a day for a case management hearing and give notice thereof to the Attorney-General.

(2) It shall not be necessary to serve the application on the Attorney-General otherwise than by delivering a copy of it to him in accordance with section 45(6) of the Matrimonial Causes Act 1973.

(3) At the case management hearing the court shall give directions as to the persons, if any, other than the Attorney-General, who are to be made respondents to the application.

(4) Where in the opinion of the court it is impracticable to serve a respondent other than the Attorney-General in accordance with the rules relating to service or it is otherwise necessary or expedient to dispense with service of the claim form on any such respondent, the court may make an order dispensing with service on him.

Rule 3 ANSWER

(1) The Attorney-General may file an answer to the application within 14 days after directions have been given at the case management hearing.

(2) Any other respondent who wishes to oppose the application or to dispute any of the facts alleged in it shall, within 14 days after service of the application on him, file an answer to the application.

(3) A respondent who files an answer shall file with it as many copies as there are other parties to the proceedings and the court shall send one of the copies to each of those parties.

CCR ORDER 47
DOMESTIC AND MATRIMONIAL PROCEEDINGS

Rule 5 FAMILY LAW REFORM ACT 1969

(1) In this rule—
'blood samples' and 'blood tests' have the meanings assigned to them by section 25 of the Family Law Reform Act 1969; and
'direction' means a direction for the use of blood tests under section 20(1) of that Act.

(2) Except with the permission of the court, an application in any proceedings for a direction shall be made on notice to every party to the proceedings (other than the applicant) and to any other person from whom the direction involves the taking of blood samples.

(3) Where an application is made for a direction involving the taking of blood samples from a person who is not a party to the proceedings in which the application is made, the application notice shall be served on him personally and the court may at any time direct him to be made a party to the proceedings.

(4) Where an application is made for a direction in respect of a person (in this paragraph referred to as a person under disability) who is either—
    (a) under 16; or
    (b) suffering from mental disorder within the meaning of the Mental Health Act 1983 and incapable of understanding the nature and purpose of blood tests,
the notice of application shall state the name and address of the person having the care and control of the person under disability and shall be served on him instead of on the person under disability.

(5) Where the court gives a direction in any proceedings, the court officer shall send a copy to every party to the proceedings and to every other person from whom the direction involves the taking of blood samples, and, unless otherwise ordered, the proceedings shall stand adjourned until the court receives a report pursuant to the direction.

(6) On receipt by the court of a report made pursuant to a direction, the court officer shall send a copy to every party to the proceedings and to every other person from whom the direction involved the taking of blood samples.

CCR ORDER 48B
ENFORCEMENT OF PARKING PENALTIES UNDER THE ROAD TRAFFIC ACT 1991

Rule 1 APPLICATION AND INTERPRETATION

(1) This Order applies for the recovery of—

CPR SCHEDULE 2

(a) increased penalty charges provided for in parking charge certificates issued under paragraph 6 of Schedule 6 to the 1991 Act; and

(b) amounts payable by a person other than an authority under an adjudication of a parking adjudicator pursuant to section 73 of the 1991 Act.

(2) In this Order, unless the context otherwise requires—

'authority' means the local authority which served the charge certificate;

'order' means an order made under paragraph 7 of Schedule 6 to the 1991 Act or, as the case may be, under section 73 of that Act;

'the Order' means the Enforcement of Road Traffic Debts Order 1993 made under section 78 of the 1991 Act as it applies to a local authority;

'relevant period' means the period of 21 days allowed for serving a statutory declaration by paragraph 8(1) of Schedule 6 to the 1991 Act or, where a longer period has been allowed pursuant to paragraph 8(4) of the said Schedule, that period;

'respondent' means the person on whom the charge certificate was served or, as the case may be, the person (other than an authority) by whom the amount due under an adjudication of a parking adjudicator is payable;

'specified debts' means the Part II debts specified in article 2 of the order;

'statutory declaration' means a declaration in the appropriate form which complies with paragraph 8(2) of Schedule 6 to the 1991 Act; and

'the 1991 Act' means the Road Traffic Act 1991.

(3) Unless the context otherwise requires, expressions which are used in the 1991 Act have the same meaning in this order as they have in that Act.

(4) The references in paragraph (2) to a local authority mean—

(a) in England, a London authority, a county or district council or the Council of the Isles of Scilly; and

(b) in Wales, a county or county borough council.

Rule 1A ESTABLISHMENT OF THE PARKING ENFORCEMENT CENTRE

(1) There shall be a parking enforcement centre ('the Centre') situated at such place or places as the Lord Chancellor may determine and having such functions relating to proceedings under this Order and other related matters as he may direct.

(2) For any purpose connected with the exercise of the Centre's functions—

(a) the Centre shall be deemed to be part of the office of the court whose name appears on the documents to which the functions relate or in whose name the documents are issued;

(b) any officer of the Centre shall, in exercising its functions, be deemed to act as a court officer of that court,

and these rules shall have effect accordingly.

Rule 2 REQUESTS FOR ORDERS

(1) An authority which wishes to take proceedings under this Order shall give notice to the court officer and, where the court officer so allows, requests for orders may be made, and such orders may be enforced, in accordance with the following provisions of this Order.

(2) An authority shall file a request for an order in the appropriate form scheduling the increased penalty charges in respect of which an order is sought.

(3) The authority shall in the request or in another manner approved by the court officer—

(a) certify—

(i) that 14 days have elapsed since service of the charge certificate; .

(ii) the amount due under the charge certificate and the date on which the charge certificate was served; and

(iii) that the amount due remains unpaid;

(b) give the charge certificate number;

(c) specify (whether by reference to the appropriate code or otherwise) the grounds stated in the notice to owner on which the parking attendant who issued the penalty charge notice believed that a penalty charge was payable with respect to the vehicle;

(d) state—
  (i) the name and address of the respondent and, where known, his title;
  (ii) the registration number of the vehicle concerned;
  (iii) (whether by reference to the appropriate charge certificate's number or otherwise) the authority's address for service;
  (iv) the court fee.

(4) If satisfied that the request is in order, the court officer shall order that the increased charge (together with the court fee) may be recovered as if it were payable under a county court order by sealing the request and returning it to the authority.

(5) When the court officer so orders and on receipt of the sealed request, the authority may draw up the order and shall annex to any such order a form of statutory declaration for the respondent's use.

(6) Within 14 days of receipt of the sealed request, the authority shall serve the order (and the form of statutory declaration) on the respondent by—
  (a) delivering the order to the respondent personally; or
  (b) sending it by first-class post to the respondent at the address given in the request.

(6A) Where an order is served in accordance with paragraph (6)(b), the date of service shall, unless the contrary is shown, be deemed to be the seventh day after the date on which the order was sent to the respondent.

(6B) Subject to paragraphs (6C) and (6D), where partners are served in the name of their firm, service of an order shall be good service on all the partners, whether any of them is out of England and Wales or not, if the order is—
  (a) delivered to a partner personally; or
  (b) served by a court officer sending it by first class post to the firm at the address stated in the request.

(6C) Where the partnership has to the knowledge of the authority been dissolved before the service of the order, the order shall be served upon every person within the jurisdiction sought to be made liable.

(6D) Unless the authority, or its solicitor, otherwise requests, service on the partnership shall be effected in accordance with paragraph (6B)(b).

(6E) Where an order is served in accordance with paragraph (6B)(b) the date of service shall, unless the contrary is shown, be deemed to be the seventh day after the date on which the order was sent to the respondent.

(6F) Service on a corporation may be effected by serving it on the mayor, chairman or president of the body or the chief executive, clerk, secretary, treasurer or other similar officer thereof.

(6G) Service of an order on a company registered in England and Wales may be effected by serving it at the registered office or at any place of business of the company which has some real connection with an issue in the proceedings.

(6H) Where an order has been served under paragraph (6G) other than at the registered office, and after a request for a warrant of execution has been sealed, it appears to the court officer that the order did not come to the attention of the appropriate person within the company in due time, the court may, on application under CPR Part 23 or of its own initiative, set aside the warrant, and may give such directions as it considers appropriate.

(7) Where an authority requests an order in respect of amounts payable by a person other than an authority under an adjudication of a parking adjudicator pursuant to section 73 of the 1991 Act, paragraphs (2) and (3) shall apply with the necessary modifications and in addition the authority shall—
  (a) state the date on which the adjudication was made;
  (b) provide details of the order made on the adjudication; and
  (c) certify the amount awarded by way of costs and that the amount remains unpaid.

Rule 3 DOCUMENTS

(1) Where by or under this order any document is required to be filed, that requirement shall be deemed to be satisfied if the information which would be

contained in the document is delivered in computer-readable form but nothing in this paragraph shall be taken as enabling an authority to commence proceedings without supplying a written request in the appropriate form under rule 2(2).

(2) For the purposes of paragraph (1), information which would be contained in a document relating to one case may be combined with information of the same nature relating to another case.

(3) Where by or under this order or by virtue of any order a document which contains information is required to be produced, that requirement shall be deemed to be satisfied if a copy of the document is produced from the computer records kept for storing such information.

Rule 4 FUNCTIONS OF COURT OFFICER

(1) The functions of the district judge under paragraph 8(4) and (5)(d) of Schedule 6 to the 1991 Act (longer period for service of the statutory declaration and notice of effect of statutory declaration) may be exercised by the court officer.

(2) Where pursuant to paragraph 8(4) of Schedule 6 to the 1991 Act a longer period is allowed for service of the statutory declaration, the court officer shall notify the authority and the respondent accordingly.

Rule 5 ENFORCEMENT OF ORDERS

(1) Subject to the Order and to this rule, the following provisions of Orders 25 to 27, 30 and 31 of these Rules shall apply for the enforcement of specified debts—

Order 25, rules 1, 2 (except paragraph (3)(b), (c) and (d)), 3, 5 (except paragraph (1)(a) and (b)) and 9;

Order 26, rule 5;

Order 27, rules 1 to 7, 7A, 9 to 16 and 18 to 22;

Order 30, rules 1 to 3, 5 and 7 to 15;

Order 31, rules 1 to 4.

(2) CPR rule 30.2(1)(b)(ii) (court may order transfer of proceedings to enforce judgment or order to another county court if proceedings could be more conveniently or fairly taken there) applies to proceedings under this order.

(3) An authority desiring to issue a warrant of execution shall file a request in that behalf in the appropriate form or in another manner approved by the court officer—

(a) certifying the amount remaining due under the order;

(b) specifying the date of service of the order on the respondent; and

(c) certifying that the relevant period has elapsed.

(4) The court shall seal the request and return it to the authority which shall, within 7 days of the sealing of the request, prepare the warrant in the appropriate form.

(5) No payment under a warrant shall be made to the court.

(6) A warrant shall, for the purpose of execution, be valid for 12 months beginning with the date of its issue and nothing in this rule or in Order 26 shall authorise an authority to renew a warrant.

(7) Where an order is deemed to have been revoked under paragraph 8(5) of Schedule 6 to the 1991 Act—

(a) the court shall serve a copy of the statutory declaration on the authority;

(b) any execution issued on the order shall cease to have effect; and

(c) on receipt of the court officer's notice under paragraph 8(5)(d) of Schedule 6, the authority shall forthwith inform any bailiff instructed to levy execution of the withdrawal of the warrant.

(8) In addition to the requirements of that rule, any application by an authority under Order 25, rule 2, shall—

(a) where the authority has not attempted to enforce by execution, give the reasons why no such attempt was made;

(b) certify that there has been no relevant return to the warrant of execution;

(c) specify the date of service of the order on the respondent; and

(d) certify that the relevant period has elapsed.

(9) An application under Order 30, rule 2 and (unless provided pursuant to an application under Order 25, rule 2) any application by an authority under Order

25, rule 3, Order 27, rule 4(1) or Order 31, rule 1(2) shall, in addition to the requirements of those rules—
   (a) where the authority has not attempted to enforce by execution, give the reasons why no such attempt was made;
   (b) certify that there has been no relevant return to the warrant of execution;
   (c) specify the date of service of the order on the respondent; and
   (d) certify that the relevant period has elapsed.
(10) In paragraphs (8) and (9) 'no relevant return to the warrant' means that—
   (a) the bailiff has been unable to seize goods because he has been denied access to the premises occupied by the respondent or because the goods have been removed from those premises;
   (b) any goods seized under the warrant of execution are insufficient to satisfy the specified debt and the cost of execution; or
   (c) the goods are insufficient to cover the cost of their removal and sale.
(11) If the court officer allows, an authority may combine information relating to one charge certificate with information concerning the same respondent in another charge certificate in any request made, or any application brought, under one of the provisions mentioned in paragraph (8) or (9) above.

CCR ORDER 48D
ENFORCEMENT OF FIXED PENALTIES UNDER THE ROAD TRAFFIC (VEHICLE EMISSIONS) (FIXED PENALTY) REGULATIONS 1997

RULE 1 APPLICATION AND INTERPRETATION
(1) This Order applies for the recovery of fixed penalties as defined in regulations 2(1)(b) and 9 of the 1997 Regulations.
(2) In this Order, unless the context otherwise requires—
   'authority' means a participating authority as defined in regulation 2(1)(f) of the 1997 Regulations;
   'order' means an order made under regulation 10(1) of the 1997 Regulations;
   'the Order' means the Enforcement of Road Traffic Debts Order 1993;
   'respondent' means the person on whom the fixed penalty notice was served;
   'specified debts' means the Part II debts specified in article 2(1)(a) of the Order;
   'the 1997 Regulations' means the Road Traffic (Vehicle Emissions) (Fixed Penalty) Regulations 1997.
(3) Unless the context otherwise requires, expressions which are used in the 1997 Regulations have the same meaning in this Order as they have in those Regulations.

RULE 2 THE PARKING ENFORCEMENT CENTRE
The parking enforcement centre established in rule 1A of Order 48B shall have such functions relating to proceedings under this Order and other related matters as the Lord Chancellor may direct.

RULE 3 REQUESTS FOR ORDERS AND WARRANTS OF EXECUTION
(1) An authority which wishes to take proceedings under this Order shall give notice to the court officer and, where the court officer so allows, a combined request for an order and a warrant of execution may be made, and such an order may be enforced and a warrant executed in accordance with the following provisions of this Order.
(2) An authority shall file a combined request for an order and a warrant of execution in the appropriate form or in another manner approved by the court officer scheduling the fixed penalties in respect of which an order and warrant of execution are sought.
(3) The authority shall in the request or in another manner approved by the court officer—
   (a) certify—

(i) that 56 days have elapsed since the issue of the fixed penalty notice,
(ii) the amount due under the fixed penalty notice and the date on which it was issued, and
(iii) that the amount due remains unpaid;
(b) give the number of the fixed penalty notice;
(c) specify (whether by reference to the appropriate code or otherwise) the grounds stated in the fixed penalty notice and in regulation 2(1)(d) of the 1997 Regulations on which the authorised person who issued the fixed penalty notice believed that a fixed penalty was payable with respect to that vehicle;
(d) state—
(i) the name and address of the respondent and where known, his title;
(ii) the registration number of the vehicle concerned;
(iii) (whether by reference to the appropriate fixed penalty notice number or otherwise) the authority's address for service;
(iv) the court fee.
(4) If satisfied that the combined request is in order, the court officer shall order that the fixed penalty (together with the court fee) may be recovered as if it were payable under a county court order by sealing the request and returning it to the authority.
(5) When the court officer so orders and on receipt of the sealed request, the authority shall, within 7 days of the sealing of the request, prepare the warrant in the appropriate form.

RULE 4 DOCUMENTS
(1) Rule 3 of Order 48B shall apply to this Order with the modification referred to in paragraph (2).
(2) The reference to rule 2(2) in rule 3(1) of Order 48B shall be a reference to rule 3(2) of this Order.

RULE 5 ENFORCEMENT OF ORDERS
(1) Rule 5 of Order 48B shall apply to this Order with the modifications referred to in paragraphs (2), (3) and (4).
(2) Paragraphs (3), (4) and (7) of rule 5 shall not apply.
(3) Sub-paragraphs (c) and (d) of rule 5(9) shall not apply.
(4) In paragraph (11) of rule 5, the references to the words 'charge certificate' shall be references to the words 'fixed penalty notice'.
(5) Where a fixed penalty notice is withdrawn under regulation 12 of the 1997 Regulations—
(a) any order made or warrant issued in respect of that fixed penalty notice is deemed to be revoked;
(b) any execution issued onthe order shall cease to have effect, and
(c) the authority shall forthwith inform any bailiff instructed to levy execution of the withdrawal of the warrant.

CCR ORDER 49
MISCELLANEOUS STATUTES

Rule 1 ACCESS TO NEIGHBOURING LAND ACT 1992
(1) In this rule, 'the 1992 Act' means the Access to Neighbouring Land Act 1992, a section referred to by number means the section so numbered in the 1992 Act and expressions which are defined in the 1992 Act have the same meaning in this rule as they have in that Act.
(2) An application for an access order under section 1 of the 1992 Act shall be made by the issue of a claim form which shall be filed in the court for the district in which the dominant land is situated.
(3) The application shall—
(a) identify the dominant land and the servient land and state whether the dominant land is or includes residential land;

(b) specify the works alleged to be necessary for the preservation of the whole or a part of the dominant land;
(c) state why entry upon the servient land is required and specify the area to which access is required by reference, if possible, to a plan annexed to the application;
(d) give the name of the person who will be carrying out the works if it is known at the time of the application;
(e) state the proposed date on which, or the dates between which, the works are to be started and their approximate duration; and
(f) state what (if any) provision has been made by way of insurance in the event of possible injury to persons or damage to property arising out of the proposed works.
(4) The respondents shall be the owner and the occupier of the servient land and any respondent who wishes to be heard on the application shall file an answer within 14 days after the date of service of the application on him.
(5) Order 24, rule 3 shall apply with the necessary modifications to service of the claim form under this rule.
(6) The court may direct that a copy of the claim form shall be served on any person who may be affected by the proposed entry and any such person may, within 14 days after service of the claim form on him, apply to be made a respondent to the application.
(7) The application may be heard and determined by the district judge.

Rule 1A ADMINISTRATION OF JUSTICE ACT 1970

Any claim by a mortgagee for possession of a dwelling-house, being a claim to which section 36 of the Administration of Justice Act 1970 applies, shall be dealt with by the court sitting in private unless the court otherwise directs.

Rule 2 CHANCEL REPAIRS ACT 1932

(1) A notice to repair under section 2 of the Chancel Repairs Act 1932 shall—
(a) identify the responsible authority by whom it is given and the chancel alleged to be in need of repair;
(b) state the repairs alleged to be necessary and the grounds on which the person to whom the notice is addressed is alleged to be liable to repair the chancel; and
(c) call upon that person to put the chancel in proper repair, and shall be served in accordance with paragraph 1A.
(1A) The notice may be served—
(a) where no solicitor is acting for the person to be served, by delivering it to him personally, or by delivering it at, or sending it by first-class post to his address for service or, if he has no address for service by—
(i) delivering it at his residence or by sending it by first-class post to his last known residence; or
(ii) in the case of a proprietor of a business, delivering it at his place of business or sending it by first class post to his last known place of business.
(b) Where a solicitor is acting for the person to be served—
(i) by delivering it at, or sending it by first-class post to the solicitor's address for service; or
(ii) where the solicitor's address for service includes a numbered box at a document exchange, by leaving it at that document exchange or at a document exchange which transmits documents daily to that document exchange.
(c) For the purpose of this rule first class post means prepaid post or post in respect of which prepayment is not required.
(d) Any document which is left at a document exchange shall be deemed served on the second day after the day on which it was left, unless the contrary is shown.
(e) In determining for the purposes of this rule—
(i) whether a document exchange transmits documents daily to another document exchange; and

(ii) the second day after the day on which a document was left at a document exchange,

any day on which the court office is closed shall be excluded.

(2) Proceedings to recover the sum required to put a chancel in proper repair shall be started by a claim form.

(3) An application for the permission of the court under the proviso to subsection (2) of the said section 2 may be made in accordance with CPR Part 23.

(4) If the court is satisfied that the defendant has a defence to the claim on the merits, the court may, on an application made by the defendant in accordance with CPR Part 23 order the claimant to give security for the defendant's costs.

(5) Where judgment is given for the payment of a sum of money in respect of repairs not yet executed, the court may order that the money be paid into court and dealt with in such manner as the court may direct for the purpose of ensuring that the money is spent in executing the repairs, but nothing in this paragraph shall prejudice a solicitor's lien for costs.

Rule 4 CONSUMER CREDIT ACT 1974

(1) In this rule 'the Act' means the Consumer Credit Act 1974, a section referred to by number means the section so numbered in the Act and expressions which are defined in the Act have the same meaning in this rule as they have in the Act.

(2) This rule only applies to claims relating to land.

(Claims under the Act relating to money only shall be started by a claim form issued in accordance with CPR Part 7, and claims relating to recovery of goods shall be made in accordance with the procedure set out in the CPR Consumer Credit Act practice direction)

(3) Where in any claim relating to a regulated agreement the debtor or any surety has not been served with the claim form, the court may, on the claimant's application made in accordance with CPR Part 23 without notice, at or before the hearing of the claim, dispense with the requirement in section 141(5) that the debtor or surety, as the case may be, shall be made a party to the proceedings.

(4) Where a claim relating to a regulated agreement is brought by a person to whom a former creditor's rights and duties under the agreement have been passed by assignment or by operation of law, the requirement in section 141(5) that all parties to the agreement shall be made parties to the claim shall not apply to the former creditor unless the court so directs.

(5) An application under section 129(1)(b) may be made by a claim form and the claim form—

(a) shall be filed in the court for the district in which the applicant resides or carries on business; and

(b) shall state—

(i) the date of the agreement and the parties to it with the number of the agreement or sufficient particulars to enable the respondent to identify the agreement and details of any sureties;

(ii) if the respondent was not one of the original parties to the agreement, the name of the original party to the agreement;

(iii) the names and addresses of the persons intended to be served with the application;

(iv) the place where the agreement was signed by the applicant;

(v) details of the notice served by the respondent giving rise to the application;

(vi) the total unpaid balance admitted to be due under the agreement and the amount of any arrears (if known) together with the amount and frequency of the payments specified by the agreement;

(vii) the applicant's proposals as to payment of any arrears and of future instalments together with details of his means;

(viii) where the application relates to a breach of the agreement other than the non-payment of money, the applicant's proposals for remedying it.

(6) Any application under section 131 may be heard and determined by the judge or by the district judge.

(9) An application for an enforcement order may be made—
   (a) by a claim form asking for permission to enforce the agreement in respect of which the order is sought; or
   (b) if, apart from the need to obtain an enforcement order, the creditor is entitled to payment of the money or possession of land to which the agreement relates, by a claim to recover the money or land.

(10) A claim form under paragraph (9)(a) and the particulars of claim in a claim brought pursuant to paragraph (9)(b) shall state the circumstances rendering an enforcement order necessary.

(11) Paragraph (9) shall apply to an order under section 86(2), 92(2) or 126 as it applies to an enforcement order, so however that in the case of an order under section 86(2) the personal representatives of the deceased debtor or hirer shall be made parties to the proceedings in which the order is sought, or, if no grant of representation has been made to his estate, the applicant shall, forthwith after commencing the proceedings, apply to the court for directions as to what persons, if any, shall be made parties to the proceedings as being affected or likely to be affected by the enforcement of the agreement.

(14) An application to a county court under section 139(1)(a) for a credit agreement to be reopened shall be made by a claim form.

(15) Where in any such proceedings in a county court as are mentioned in section 139(1)(b) or (c), the debtor or a surety desires to have a credit agreement reopened, he shall, within 14 days after the service of the claim form on him, give notice to that effect to the court and to every other party to the proceedings and thereafter the debtor or surety, as the case may be, shall be treated as having delivered a defence or answer.

Rule 4A APPLICATIONS UNDER SECTION 114, 204 AND 231 OF THE COPYRIGHT, DESIGNS AND PATENTS ACT 1988

The CPR Patents Courts practice direction shall apply with the necessary modifications to proceedings brought under sections 114(1), 204(1) and 231(1) of the Copyright, Designs and Patents Act 1988.

Rule 5 FAIR TRADING ACT 1973

(1) In this rule a section referred to by number means the section so numbered in the Fair Trading Act 1973 and 'the Director' means the Director General of Fair Trading.

(2) Proceedings in a county court under section 35, 38 or 40 shall be started by a claim form.

(3) The respondent shall file an answer.

(4) Where in any proceedings under section 35 or 38 the Director intends to apply for a direction under section 40(2) that any order made against a body corporate (in this rule referred to as the 'respondent body') which is a member of a group of interconnected bodies corporate shall be binding on all members of the group, he shall file notice of his intention together with as many copies of the claim form and of the notice as are required for the purposes of paragraph (5).

(5) A copy of any notice under paragraph (4) shall be served on the respondent body and a copy of the notice together with a copy of the claim form and a notice of the return day shall be served on each of the bodies corporate specified in the notice under paragraph (4).

(6) The respondent body may at any time serve on the Director a notice containing particulars of any interconnected body corporate not mentioned in a notice under paragraph (4).

(7) With a view to deciding whether or in respect of which bodies notice should be given under paragraph (4) the Director may serve on the respondent body a notice requiring that body to give to him within 14 days after service of the notice particulars of any interconnected bodies corporate belonging to the same group as the respondent body and a copy of any such notice shall be filed.

(8) An application under section 40(3) shall be made on notice to the respondent body and every interconnected body belonging to the same group.

Rule 6 HOUSING ACT 1988: ASSURED TENANCIES

(1) In this rule

'the 1988 Act' means the Housing Act 1988;

'dwelling-house' has the same meaning as in Part I of the 1988 Act;

a Ground referred to by number means the Ground so numbered in Schedule 2 to the 1988 Act;

'the requisite notice' means such a notice as is mentioned in any of those Grounds; and

'the relevant date' means the beginning of the tenancy.

(2) This rule applies to proceedings brought by a landlord to recover possession of a dwelling-house which has been let on an assured tenancy in a case where all the conditions mentioned in paragraph (3) below are satisfied.

(3) The conditions referred to in paragraph (2) are these—

   (a) The tenancy and any agreement for the tenancy were entered into on or after 15 January 1989.

   (b) The proceedings are brought—
      (i) on Ground 1 (landlord occupation);
      (ii) on Ground 3 (former holiday occupation);
      (iii) on Ground 4 (former student letting); or
      (iv) on Ground 5 (occupation by a minister of religion).

   (c) The only purpose of the proceedings is to recover possession of the dwelling-house and no other claim is made in the proceedings (such as for arrears of rent).

   (d) The tenancy is an assured tenancy within the meaning of the 1988 Act (and consequently is not a protected, statutory or housing association tenancy under the Rent Act 1977), and—
      (i) is the subject of a written agreement; or
      (ii) is on the same terms (though not necessarily as to rent) as a tenancy which was the subject of a written agreement and arises by virtue of section 5 of the 1988 Act; or
      (iii) relates to the same or substantially the same premises which were let to the same tenant and is on the same terms (though not necessarily as to rent or duration) as a tenancy which was the subject of a written agreement.

Where the tenancy in relation to which the proceedings are brought arises by virtue of section 5 of the 1988 Act but follows a tenancy which was the subject of an oral agreement, the condition mentioned in sub-paragraph (d)(ii) or (iii) above is not satisfied.

   (e) The proceedings are brought against the tenant to whom the requisite notice was given.

   (f) The tenant was given the requisite notice, not later than the relevant date.

   (g) The tenant was given notice in accordance with section 8 of the 1988 Act that proceedings for possession would be brought.

(4) Where the conditions mentioned in paragraph (3) of this rule are satisfied, the landlord may bring possession proceedings under this rule instead of making a claim in accordance with Order 6, rule 3 (claim for recovery of land by claim form).

(5) The application must be made in the prescribed form, and a copy of the application, with a copy for each defendant, must be filed in the court for the district in which the dwelling-house is situated.

(6) The application shall include the following information and statements—

   (a) a statement identifying the dwelling-house which is the subject matter of the proceedings;

   (b) a statement identifying the nature of the tenancy, namely—
      (i) whether it is the subject of a written agreement; or
      (ii) whether the tenancy arises by virtue of section 5 of the 1988 Act; or
      (iii) where it is the subject of an oral agreement whether the tenancy is periodic or for a fixed term and, if for a fixed term, the length of the term and the date of termination;

(c) a statement that the dwelling-house (or another dwelling-house) was not let to the tenant by the landlord (or any of his predecessors) before 15 January 1989;
(d) the date on which and the method by which the requisite notice was given to the tenant;
(e) a statement identifying the Ground on which possession is claimed giving sufficient particulars to substantiate the claimant's claim to be entitled to possession on that Ground;
(f) a statement that a notice was served on the tenant in accordance with section 8 of the 1988 Act—
    (i) specifying the date on which and the method by which the notice was served; and
    (ii) confirming that the period of notice required by section 8 of the 1988 Act has been given; and
(g) the amount of rent which is currently payable.

(7) Copies of the following documents shall be attached to the application—
    (i) the first written tenancy agreement and the current (or most recent) written tenancy agreement;
    (ii) the requisite notice (referred to in paragraph (6)(d) above); and
    (iii) the notice served in accordance with section 8 of the 1988 Act, together with any other documents necessary to prove the claim.

(8) The statements made in the application and any documents attached to the application shall be verified by the claimant on oath.

(9) Service of the application and of the attachments shall be effected by an officer of the court sending them by first-class post to the defendant at the address stated in the application and paragraphs (8) and (9) of Order 3, rule 6 (commencement of proceedings) and Order 7, rule 15 (service of claim form for recovery of land) shall apply as they apply where service is effected under those rules.

(10) A defendant who wishes to oppose the claimant's application must, within 14 days after the service of the application on him, complete and deliver at the court office the form of reply which was attached to the application.

(11) On receipt of the defendant's reply the court shall—
(a) send a copy of it to the claimant;
(b) refer the reply and the claimant's application to the judge, and where a reply is received after the period mentioned in paragraph (10) but before a request is filed in accordance with paragraph (12) the reply shall be referred without delay to the judge.

(12) Where the period mentioned in paragraph (10) has expired without the defendant filing a reply, the claimant may file a written request for an order for possession and the court shall without delay refer the claimant's application to the judge.

(13) After considering the application and the defendant's reply (if any), the judge shall either—
(a) make an order for possession under paragraph (15); or
(b) fix a day for a hearing under paragraph (14) and give directions regarding the steps to be taken before and at the hearing.

(14) The court shall fix a day for the hearing of the application where the judge is not satisfied as to any of the following—
(a) that the requisite notice was given before the relevant date;
(b) that a notice was served in accordance with section 8 of the 1988 Act and that the time limits specified in the 1988 Act have been complied with;
(c) that service of the application was duly effected; or
(d) that the claimant has established that he is entitled to recover possession under the Ground relied on against the defendant.

(15) Except where paragraph (14) applies, the judge shall without delay make an order for possession without requiring the attendance of the parties.

(16) Where a hearing is fixed under paragraph (14)—
(a) the court shall give to all parties not less than 14 days' notice of the day fixed;

(b) the judge may give such directions regarding the steps to be taken before and at the hearing as may appear to him to be necessary or desirable.

(17) The court may, on application made on notice in accordance with CPR Part 23 within 14 days of service of the order or of its own initiative, set aside, vary or confirm any order made under paragraph (15).

(18) A district judge shall have power to hear and determine an application to which this rule applies and references in this rule to the judge shall include references to the district judge.

Rule 6A HOUSING ACT 1988: ASSURED SHORTHOLD TENANCIES

(1) In this rule, 'the 1988 Act' means the Housing Act 1988 and 'dwelling-house' has the same meaning as in Part I of the 1988 Act.

(2) This rule applies to proceedings brought by a landlord under section 21 of the 1988 Act to recover possession of a dwelling-house let on an assured shorthold tenancy on the expiry or termination of that tenancy in a case where all the conditions mentioned in paragraph (3) below (or, as the case may be, paragraph (9)) are satisfied.

(3) The conditions referred to in paragraph (2) are these—

(a) The tenancy and any agreement for the tenancy were entered into on or after 15 January 1989.

(b) The only purpose of the proceedings is to recover possession of the dwelling-house and no other claim is made in the proceedings (such as for arrears of rent).

(c) The tenancy—

(i) was an assured shorthold tenancy and not a protected, statutory or housing association tenancy under the Rent Act 1977;

(ii) did not immediately follow an assured tenancy which was not an assured shorthold tenancy;

(iii) fulfilled the conditions provided by section 19A or section 20(1)(a) to (c) of the 1988 Act; and

(iv) was the subject of a written agreement.

(d) Where the tenancy and any agreement for the tenancy were entered into before 28 February 1997, a notice in writing was served on the tenant in accordance with section 20(2) of the 1988 Act and the proceedings are brought against the tenant on whom that notice was served.

(e) A notice in accordance with section 21(1)(b) of the 1988 Act was given to the tenant in writing.

(4) Where the conditions mentioned in paragraph (3) or paragraph (9) of this rule are satisfied, the landlord may bring possession proceedings under this rule instead of making a claim in accordance with Order 6, rule 3 (claim for recovery of land by claim form).

(5) The application must be made in the prescribed form and a copy of the application, with a copy for each defendant, shall be filed in the court for the district in which the dwelling-house is situated.

(6) The application shall include the following information and statements—

(a) A statement identifying the dwelling-house which is the subject matter of the proceedings.

(b) A statement that the dwelling-house (or another dwelling-house) was not let to the tenant by the landlord (or any of his predecessors) before 15 January 1989.

(c) A statement that possession is claimed on the expiry of an assured shorthold tenancy under section 21 of the 1988 Act giving sufficient particulars to substantiate the claimant's claim to be entitled to possession.

(d) Where the tenancy and any agreement for the tenancy were entered into before 28 February 1997, a statement that a written notice was served on the tenant in accordance with section 20(2) of the 1988 Act.

(e) A statement that a notice in writing was given to the tenant in accordance with section 21(1) of the 1988 Act specifying the date on which, and the method by which, the notice was given.

CPR SCHEDULE 2

(f) In a case where the original fixed term tenancy has expired, a statement that no other assured tenancy is in existence other than an assured shorthold periodic tenancy (whether statutory or not).

(g) A statement confirming that there is no power under the tenancy agreement for the landlord to determine the tenancy (within the meaning given for the purposes of Part I of the 1988 Act by section 45(4) of the 1988 Act) at a time earlier than 6 months from the beginning of the tenancy.

(h) A statement that no notice under section 20(5) of the 1988 Act has been served.

(7) Copies of the following documents shall be attached to the application—

(i) the first written tenancy agreement and the current (or most recent) written tenancy agreement;

(ii) where the tenancy and any agreement for the tenancy were entered into before 28 February 1997 the written notice served in accordance with section 20(2) of the 1988 Act; and

(iii) the notice in writing given in accordance with section 21 of the 1988 Act,

together with any other documents necessary to prove the claim.

(8) The statements made in the application and any documents attached to the application shall be verified by the claimant on oath.

(9) Where on the coming to an end of an assured shorthold tenancy (including a tenancy which was an assured shorthold but ceased to be assured before it came to an end) a new assured shorthold tenancy of the same or substantially the same premises (in this paragraph referred to as 'the premises') comes into being under which the landlord and the tenant are the same as at the coming to an end of the earlier tenancy, then the provisions of this rule apply to that tenancy but with the following conditions instead of those in paragraph (3)—

(a) The tenancy and any agreement for the tenancy were entered into on or after 15 January 1989.

(b) The only purpose of the proceedings is to recover possession of the dwelling-house and no other claim is made in the proceedings (such as for arrears of rent).

(c) The tenancy in relation to which the proceedings are brought—

(i) is an assured shorthold tenancy within the meaning of section 20 of the 1988 Act and consequently is not a protected, statutory or housing association tenancy under the Rent Act 1977;

(ii) did not immediately follow an assured tenancy which was not an assured shorthold tenancy; and—

(aa) is the subject of a written agreement; or

(ab) is on the same terms (though not necessarily as to rent) as a tenancy which was the subject of a written agreement and arises by virtue of section 5 of the 1988 Act; or

(ac) relates to the same or substantially the same premises which were let to the same tenant and is on the same terms (though not necessarily as to rent or duration) as a tenancy which was the subject of a written agreement.

Where the tenancy in relation to which the proceedings are brought arises by virtue of section 5 of the 1988 Act but follows a tenancy which was the subject of an oral agreement, the conditions mentioned in sub-paragraph (c)(ii)(ab) or (ac) above is not satisfied.

(d) Where the agreement and any agreement for the tenancy were entered into before 28 February 1997, a written notice was served in accordance with section 20(2) of the 1988 Act on the tenant in relation to the first assured shorthold tenancy of the premises and the proceedings are brought against the tenant on whom that notice was served.

(e) A notice in writing was given to the tenant in accordance with section 21(4) of the 1988 Act.

(10) In a case to which paragraph (9) applies, the application shall include the following information and statements—

(a) A statement identifying the dwelling-house which is the subject matter of the proceedings.

(b) A statement identifying the nature of the tenancy, namely—
  (i) whether it is the subject of a written agreement;
  (ii) whether the tenancy arises by virtue of section 5 of the 1988 Act; or
  (iii) where it is the subject of an oral agreement, that the tenancy is periodic or for a fixed term, and if for a fixed term, the length of the term and the date of termination.

(c) A statement that the dwelling-house (or another dwelling-house) was not let to the tenant by the landlord (or any of his predecessors) before 15 January 1989.

(d) A statement that possession is claimed under section 21 of the 1988 Act giving sufficient particulars to substantiate the claimant's claim to be entitled to possession.

(e) Where the tenancy and any agreement for the tenancy were entered into before 28 February 1997, a statement that a written notice was served in accordance with section 20(2) of the 1988 Act in relation to the first assured shorthold tenancy of the premises on the tenant against whom the proceedings are brought.

(f) A statement that a notice in writing was given to the tenant in accordance with section 21(4) of the 1988 Act specifying the date on which, and the method by which, the notice was given.

(g) In a case where the tenancy is a fixed term tenancy which has expired, a statement that no other assured tenancy is in existence other than an assured shorthold periodic tenancy (whether statutory or not).

(h) A statement confirming that there was no power under the tenancy agreement for the landlord to determine (within the meaning given for the purposes of Part I of the 1988 Act by section 45(4) of the 1988 Act) the first assured shorthold tenancy of the premises to the tenant against whom the proceedings are brought at a time earlier than 6 months from the beginning of the tenancy.

(i) A statement that no notice under section 20(5) of the 1988 Act has been served.

(j) The amount of rent which is currently payable.

(11) Service of the application and of the attachments shall be effected by an officer of the court sending them by first-class post to the defendant at the address stated in the application and paragraphs (8) and (9) of Order 3, rule 6 (commencement of proceedings) and Order 7, rule 15 (service of claim form for recovery of land) shall apply as they apply where service is effected under those rules.

(12) A defendant who wishes to oppose the claimant's application must, within 14 days after the service of the application on him, complete and deliver at the court office the form of reply which was attached to the application.

(13) On receipt of the defendant's reply the court shall—
  (a) send a copy of it to the claimant;
  (b) refer the reply and the claimant's application to the judge and where a reply is received after the period mentioned in paragraph (12) but before a request is filed in accordance with paragraph (14) the reply shall be referred without delay to the judge.

(14) Where the period mentioned in paragraph (12) has expired without the defendant filing a reply, the claimant may file a written request for an order for possession and the court shall without delay refer any such request to the judge.

(15) After considering the application and the defendant's reply (if any), the judge shall either—
  (a) make an order for possession under paragraph (17); or
  (b) fix a day for a hearing under paragraph (16) and give directions regarding the steps to be taken before and at the hearing.

(16) The court shall fix a day for the hearing of the application where the judge is not satisfied as to any of the following—

(a) where the tenancy and any agreement for the tenancy were entered into before 28 February 1997 that a written notice was served in accordance with section 20 of the 1988 Act;
(b) that a written notice was given in accordance with section 21 of the 1988 Act;
(c) that service of the application was duly effected; or
(d) that the claimant has established that he is entitled to recover possession under section 21 of the 1988 Act against the defendant.
(17) Except where paragraph (16) applies, the judge shall without delay make an order for possession without requiring the attendance of the parties.
(18) Where a hearing is fixed under paragraph (16)—
(a) the court shall give to all parties not less than 14 days' notice of the day so fixed;
(b) the judge may give such directions regarding the steps to be taken before and at the hearing as may appear to him to be necessary or desirable.
(19) The court may, on application made on notice in accordance with CPR Part 23 within 14 days of service of the order or of its own initiative, set aside, vary or confirm any order made under paragraph (17).
(20) A district judge shall have power to hear and determine an application to which this rule applies and references in this rule to the judge shall include references to the district judge.

Rule 6B HOUSING ACT 1996: INJUNCTIONS AND POWERS OF ARREST
(1) An application for an injunction under section 152 of the Housing Act 1996 may be made by a claim in the appropriate prescribed form and shall be commenced in the court for the district in which the respondent resides or the conduct complained of occurred.
(2) Every application shall—
(a) state the terms of the injunction applied for; and
(b) be supported by a witness statement or affidavit in which the grounds on which the application is made are set out.
(3) Every application made on notice must be served, together with a copy of the witness statement or affidavit, by the applicant on the respondent personally not less than 2 days before the date on which the application will be heard.
(4) Where an application is made without giving notice, the witness statement or affidavit in support shall explain why notice was not given and the application and witness statement or affidavit shall be served (with a copy of any order made by the court), on the respondent personally without delay.
(5) Unless otherwise directed, every application made on notice shall be heard in public.
(6) Where in exercise of the powers conferred by section 152(6) or 153(1) of the Housing Act 1996, a power of arrest is attached to any provision of an injunction ('a relevant provision')—
(a) each relevant provision shall be set out in a separate clause of the injunction and no such clause shall refer to any form of conduct which would not entitle a constable to arrest the respondent under paragraph (a), (b) or (c) of section 152(1) or under paragraph (a), (b) or (c) of section 153(5) of the Housing Act 1996; and
(b) the applicant shall deliver a copy of the relevant provisions to the police officer for the time being in charge of any police station for the area where the conduct occurred.
(7) Where an order is made varying or discharging any relevant provision of an injunction to which a power of arrest has been attached, the court shall—
(a) immediately inform the police officer for the time being in charge of the police station to which a copy of the relevant provisions was delivered under paragraph (6); and
(b) deliver a copy of the order to any police officer so informed.
(8) The judge before whom a person is brought following his arrest may adjourn the proceedings and, where such an order is made, the arrested person shall be released and—

(a) be dealt with (whether by the same or another judge) within 14 days of the day on which he was arrested; and

(b) be given not less than 2 days' notice of the adjourned hearing.

Nothing in this paragraph shall prevent the issue of a notice under Order 29 rule 1(4) if the arrested person is not dealt with within the period mentioned in sub-paragraph (a).

(9) In relation to a person who is in custody under such an order and warrant of a county court, Order 29, rule 3, shall have effect as if the order and warrant were issued at the instance of the person who made the application.

(10) Order 29, rule 1 shall apply where an application is made to commit a person—

(a) for breach of an injunction granted; or

(b) arrested under a power of arrest attached to an injunction under Chapter III of Part V of the Housing Act 1996,

as if references in that rule to the judge included references to a district judge.

(11) In paragraph (8) 'arrest' means the arrest of a person pursuant to a power of arrest which, in exercise of the powers conferred by section 152(6) or 153(1) of the Housing Act 1996, has been attached to an injunction.

(12) The jurisdiction of the court under sections 152 to 157 of the Housing Act 1996 may be exercised by a district judge.

Rule 7 INJUNCTIONS TO PREVENT ENVIRONMENTAL HARM: TOWN AND COUNTRY PLANNING ACT 1990 ETC.

(1) An injunction under—

(a) section 187B or 214A of the Town and Country Planning Act 1990;

(b) section 44A of the Planning (Listed Buildings and Conservation Areas) Act 1990; or

(c) section 26AA of the Planning (Hazardous Substances) Act 1990,

may be granted against a person whose identity is unknown to the applicant; and in the following provisions of this rule such an injunction against such a person is referred to as 'an injunction under paragraph (1)', and the person against whom it is sought is referred to as 'the respondent'.

(2) An applicant for an injunction under paragraph (1) shall describe the respondent by reference to—

(a) a photograph;

(b) a thing belonging to or in the possession of the respondent; or

(c) any other evidence,

with sufficient particularity to enable service to be effected, and the form of the claim form used shall be modified accordingly.

(3) An applicant for an injunction under paragraph (1) shall file evidence by witness statement or affidavit—

(a) verifying that he was unable to ascertain, within the time reasonably available to him, the respondent's identity;

(b) setting out the action taken to ascertain the respondent's identity; and

(c) verifying the means by which the respondent has been described in the claim form and that the description is the best that the applicant is able to provide.

(4) Paragraph (2) is without prejudice to the power of the court to make an order in accordance with CPR Part 6 for service by an alternative method or dispensing with service.

Rule 8 LEASEHOLD REFORM ACT 1967

(1) In this rule a section referred to by number means the section so numbered in the Leasehold Reform Act 1967 and 'Schedule 2' means Schedule 2 to that Act.

(2) Where a tenant of a house and premises desires to pay money into court pursuant to section 11(4) or section 13(1) or (3)—

(a) he shall file in the office of the appropriate court a witness statement or affidavit stating—

(i) the reasons for the payment into court;

(ii) the house and premises to which the payment relates and the name and address of the landlord; and

(iii) so far as they are known to the tenant, the name and address of every person who is or may be interested in or entitled to the money;

(b) on the filing of the witness statement or affidavit the tenant shall pay the money into court and the court officer shall enter the matter in the records of the court and send notice of the payment to the landlord and to every person whose name and address are given in the witness statement or affidavit pursuant to sub-paragraph (a)(iii);

(c) any subsequent payment into court by the landlord pursuant to section 11(4) shall be made to the credit of the same account as the payment into court by the tenant and sub-paragraphs (a) and (b) shall apply as if for the references to the tenant and the landlord there were substituted references to the landlord and the tenant respectively;

(d) the appropriate court for the purposes of sub-paragraph (a) shall be the court for the district in which the property is situated or, if the payment into court is made by reason of a notice under section 13(3), any other county court specified in the notice.

(3) Where the proceedings on an application are ordered to be transferred to a leasehold valuation tribunal under section 21(3), the court shall—

(a) send notice of the transfer to all parties to the application; and

(b) send to the leasehold valuation tribunal copies certified by the district judge of all entries in the records of the court relating to the application, together with the order of transfer and all documents filed in the proceedings.

(4) Where an application is made under section 17 or 18 for an order for possession of a house and premises the respondent shall—

(a) forthwith after being served with the application, serve on every person in occupation of the property or part of it under an immediate or derivative sub-tenancy, a notice informing him of the proceedings and of his right under paragraph 3(4) of Schedule 2 to appear and be heard in the proceedings with the permission of the court; and

(b) within 14 days after being served with the application, file an answer stating the grounds, if any, on which he intends to oppose the application and giving particulars of every such sub-tenancy.

Rule 9 LEASEHOLD REFORM, HOUSING AND URBAN DEVELOPMENT ACT 1993

(1) In this rule—

(a) 'the 1993 Act' means the Leasehold Reform, Housing and Urban Development Act 1993;

(b) a section or Schedule referred to by number means the section or Schedule so numbered in the 1993 Act; and

(c) expressions used in this rule have the same meaning as they have in the 1993 Act.

(2) Where an application is made under section 23(1) by a person other than the reversioner—

(a) on the issue of the application, the applicant shall send a copy of the application to the reversioner;

(b) the applicant shall promptly inform the reversioner either—

(i) of the court's decision; or

(ii) that the application has been withdrawn.

(3) Where an application is made under section 26(1) or (2) or section 50(1) or (2) it shall be made by the issue of a claim form which must not be served on any other person to the district judge, who may grant or refuse it or give directions for its future conduct, including the addition as respondents of such persons as appear to have an interest in it.

(4) Where an application is made under section 26(3), it shall be made by the issue of a claim form and—

(a) the applicants shall serve notice of the application on any person who they know or have reason to believe is a relevant landlord, giving particulars of the application and the return date and informing that person of his right to be joined as a party to the proceedings;

(b) the landlord whom it is sought to appoint as the reversioner shall be a respondent to the application, and shall file an answer;

(c) a person on whom notice is served under sub-paragraph (a) shall be added as a respondent to the proceedings when he gives notice in writing to the court of his wish to be added as party, and the court shall notify all other parties of the addition.

(5) Where a person wishes to pay money into court under section 27(3), section 51(3) or paragraph 4 of Schedule 8, rule 8(2) shall apply as it applies to payments into court made under the Leasehold Reform Act 1967, subject to the following modifications—

(a) references in rule 8 to the payment of money into court by a tenant shall be construed as references to the person or persons making a payment into court under the 1993 Act;

(b) the reference in rule 8(2)(a)(ii) to 'house and premises' shall be construed as a reference to the interest or interests in the premises to which the payment into court relates, or, where the payment into court is made under section 51(3), to the flat to which it relates;

(c) the witness statement or affidavit filed by the tenant under rule 8(2)(a) shall include details of any vesting order; and

(d) the appropriate court for the purposes of that sub-paragraph shall be—

(i) where a vesting order has been made, the court which made the vesting order; or

(ii) where no such order has been made, the court in whose district the premises are situated.

(6) Where an order is made under section 91(4), rule 8(3) (transfer to leasehold valuation tribunal) shall apply as it applies on the making of an order under section 21(3) of the Leasehold Reform Act 1967.

(7) Where a relevant landlord acts independently under Schedule 1, paragraph 7, he shall be entitled to require any party to proceedings under the 1993 Act (as described in paragraph 7(1)(b) of Schedule 1) to supply him, on payment of the reasonable costs of copying, with copies of all documents which that party has served on the other parties to the proceedings.

Rule 10 LOCAL GOVERNMENT FINANCE ACT 1982

(1) In this rule a section referred to by number means the section so numbered in the Local Government Finance Act 1982.

(2) Proceedings in a county court under section 19 or section 20 shall be commenced in the court for the district in which the principal office of the body to whose accounts the application relates (in this rule referred to as 'the body concerned') is situated.

(3) A claim form for a declaration under section 19(1) shall state the facts on which the applicant intends to rely at the hearing of the application and the respondents to the application shall be the body concerned and any person against whom an order is sought under section 19(2).

(4) An appeal under section 19(4) or section 20(3) against a decision of an auditor shall be brought within 28 days of the receipt by the appellant of the auditor's statement of the reasons for his decision.

(5) The notice of appeal to which paragraph (4) relates shall state—

(a) the reasons stated by the auditor for his decision;

(b) the date on which the appellant received the auditor's statement;

(c) the facts on which the appellant intends to rely at the hearing of the appeal; and

(d) in the case of a decision not to apply for a declaration, such facts within the appellant's knowledge as will enable the court to consider whether to exercise the powers conferred on it by section 19(2).

(6) The respondents to the appeal shall be—

(i) the auditor who for the time being has responsibility for the audit of the accounts of the body concerned;

(ii) the body concerned; and

(iii) in the case of an appeal against a decision not to certify under section 20(1) that a sum or amount is due from any person, that person.

(7) The court may at any stage of an application or appeal under section 19 or section 20 direct that any officer or member of the body concerned be added to the proceedings as a respondent.

Rule 11 LOCAL GOVERNMENT (MISCELLANEOUS PROVISIONS) ACT 1976

A person who appeals against a notice under section 21, 23 or 35 of the Local Government (Miscellaneous Provisions) Act 1976 shall state in his notice of appeal the grounds of the appeal and where one of those grounds is that it would have been fairer to serve the notice on another person or, as the case may be, that it would be reasonable for the whole or part of the expenses to which the notice relates to be paid by some other person, that person shall be made a respondent to the appeal, unless the court on the application of the appellant made without notice, otherwise directs.

Rule 12 MENTAL HEALTH ACT 1983

(1) In this rule—

a section referred to by number means the section so numbered in the Mental Health Act 1983 and 'Part II' means Part II of that Act;

'place of residence' means, in relation to a patient who is receiving treatment as an in-patient in a hospital or other institution, that hospital or institution;

'hospital authority' means the managers of a hospital as defined in section 145(1).

(2) An application to a county court under Part II shall be made by a claim form filed in the court for the district in which the patients' place of residence is situated or, in the case of an application made under section 30 for the discharge or variation of an order made under section 29, in that court or in the court which made the order.

(3) Where an application is made under section 29 for an order that the functions of the nearest relative of the patient shall be exercisable by some other person—

(a) the nearest relative shall be made a respondent to the application unless the application is made on the grounds set out in subsection (3)(a) of the said section or the court otherwise orders; and

(b) the court may order that any other person, not being the patient, shall be made a respondent.

(4) On the hearing of the application the court may accept as evidence of the facts stated therein any report made by a medical practitioner and any report made in the course of his official duties by—

(a) a probation officer; or

(b) an officer of a local authority or of a voluntary organisation exercising statutory functions on behalf of a local authority; or

(c) an officer of a hospital authority,

provided that the respondent shall be told the substance of any part of the report bearing on his fitness or conduct which the judge considers to be material for the fair determination of the application.

(5) Unless otherwise ordered, an application under Part II shall be heard and determined by the court sitting in private.

(6) For the purpose of determining the application the judge may interview the patient either in the presence of or separately from the parties and either at the court or elsewhere, or may direct the district judge to interview the patient and report to the judge in writing.

Rule 13 MOBILE HOMES ACT 1983

(1) An application—

(a) under section 1 or 2 of the Mobile Homes Act 1983; or

(b) pursuant to paragraph 4, 5 or 6 of Part I of Schedule 1 to that Act; or

(c) with respect to any question arising under paragraph 8(1) or 9 of the same Part of that Schedule,

shall be made by a claim form and the respondent shall file an answer.

(2) Any application to which paragraph 1(b) applies may include an application for an order enforcing the rights mentioned in section 3(1)(b) of the Caravan Sites Act 1968.

Rule 15 POST OFFICE ACT 1969

(1) An application under section 30(5) of the Post Office Act 1969 for permission to bring proceedings in the name of the sender or addressee of a postal packet or his personal representatives shall be made by a claim form.

(2) The respondents to the application shall be the Post Office and the person in whose name the applicant seeks to bring proceedings.

Rule 16 RENTCHARGES ACT 1977

Where for the purposes of section 9 of the Rentcharges Act 1977 the sum required to redeem a rentcharge is to be paid into the county court, it shall be paid into the court for the district in which the land affected by the rentcharge or any part thereof is situated.

Rule 17 SEX DISCRIMINATION ACT 1975 AND RACE RELATIONS ACT 1976

(1) In this rule—

(a) 'the Act of 1975' and 'the Act of 1976' mean respectively the Sex Discrimination Act 1975 and the Race Relations Act 1976;

(b) in relation to proceedings under either of those Acts expressions which are used in the Act concerned have the same meanings in this rule as they have in that Act;

(c) in relation to proceedings under the Act of 1976 'court' means a designated county court and 'district' means the district assigned to such a court for the purposes of that Act.

(2) A claimant who brings a claim under section 66 of the Act of 1975 or section 57 of the Act of 1976 shall forthwith give notice to the Commission of the commencement of the proceedings and file a copy of the notice.

(3) CPR Rule 35.15 shall have effect in relation to an assessor who is to be appointed in proceedings under section 66(1) of the Act of 1975.

(4) Proceedings under section 66, 71 or 72 of the Act of 1975 or section 57, 62 or 63 of the Act of 1976 may be commenced—

(a) in the court for the district in which the defendant resides or carries on business; or

(b) in the court for the district in which the act or any of the acts in respect of which the proceedings are brought took place.

(5) An appeal under section 68 of the Act of 1975 or section 59 of the Act of 1976 against a requirement of a non-discrimination notice shall be brought in the court for the district in which the acts to which the requirement relates were done.

(6) Where the claimant in any claim alleging discrimination has questioned the defendant under section 74 of the Act of 1975 or section 66 of the Act of 1976—

(a) either party may make an application to the court in accordance with CPR Part 23 to determine whether the question or any reply is admissible under that section; and

(b) CPR Rule 3.4 shall apply to the question and any answer as it applies to any statement of case.

(7) Where in any claim the Commission claim a charge for expenses incurred by them in providing the claimant with assistance under section 75 of the Act of 1975 or section 66 of the Act of 1976—

(a) the Commission shall, within 14 days after the determination of the claim, give notice of the claim to the court and the claimant and thereafter no money paid into court for the benefit of the claimant, so far as it relates to any costs or expenses, shall be paid out except in pursuance of an order of the court; and

(b) the court may order the expenses incurred by the Commission to be assessed whether by the summary or detailed procedure as if they were costs payable by the claimant to his own solicitor for work done in connection with the proceedings.

CPR SCHEDULE 2

(8) Where an application is made for the removal or modification of any term of a contract to which section 77(2) of the Act of 1975 or section 72(2) of the Act of 1976 applies, all persons affected shall be made respondents to the application, unless in any particular case the court otherwise directs, and the proceedings may be commenced—
  (a) in the court for the district in which the respondent or any of the respondents resides or carries on business; or
  (b) in the court for the district in which the contract was made.

Rule 18A TELECOMMUNICATIONS ACT 1984

CPR Rule 35.15 applies to proceedings under paragraph 5 of Schedule 2 to the Telecommunications Act 1984.

Rule 18B APPLICATIONS UNDER SECTION 19 OF THE TRADE MARKS ACT 1994

The CPR Patents Court Practice direction shall apply with the necessary modifications to proceedings brought under section 19 of the Trade Marks Act 1994 in a county court.

Rule 19 TRADE UNION AND LABOUR RELATIONS CONSOLIDATION ACT 1992

(1) Where a complainant desires to have an order of the Certification Officer under section 82 of the Trade Union and Labour Relations Consolidation Act 1992 recorded in the county court, he shall produce the order and a copy thereof to the court for the district in which he resides or the head or main office of the trade union is situate.

(2) The order shall be recorded by filing it, and the copy shall be sealed and dated and returned to the complainant.

(3) The sealed copy shall be treated as if it were the notice of issue in a claim begun by the complainant.

(4) The costs, if any, allowed for recording the order shall be recoverable as if they were payable under the order.

(5) The order shall not be enforced until proof is given to the satisfaction of the court that the order has not been obeyed and, if the order is for payment of money, of the amount remaining unpaid.

Rule 20 TRUSTEE ACT 1925, SECTION 63

(1) Any person wishing to make a payment into court under section 63 of the Trustee Act 1925 shall make and file in the office of the appropriate court a witness statement or an affidavit setting out—
  (a) a brief description of the trust and of the instrument creating it or, as the case may be, of the circumstances in which the trust arose;
  (b) so far as known to him, the names and addresses of the persons interested in or entitled to the money or securities to be paid into court;
  (c) his submission to answer all such inquiries relating to the application of such money or securities as the court may make or direct;
  (d) his place of residence; and
  (e) an address where he may be served with any notice or application relating to such money or securities.

(2) The appropriate court for the purposes of paragraph (1) shall be the court for the district in which the person or any of the persons making the payment into court resides.

(3) The costs incurred in the payment into court shall be assessed by the detailed procedure and the amount of the assessed costs may be retained by the person making the payment into court.

(4) The district judge may require, in addition to the witness statement or affidavit, such evidence as he thinks proper with regard to the matter in respect of which the payment into court is made.

(5) On the making of the payment into court the court shall send notice thereof to each person mentioned in the witness statement or affidavit pursuant to paragraph (1)(b).

(6) An application for the investment or payment out of court of any money or securities paid into court under paragraph (1) may be made without notice but on the hearing of the application the court may require notice to be served on such person as it thinks fit and fix a day for the further hearing.

(7) No witness statement or affidavit in support of the application shall be necessary in the first instance but the court may direct evidence to be adduced in such manner as it thinks fit.

(8) The application may be heard and determined by the district judge.

(9) Paragraphs (6) to (8) are without prejudice to any provision of the County Court Funds Rules enabling or requiring the court to transfer money from a deposit to an investment account of its own motion.

PRACTICE DIRECTION FOR THE COURT OF APPEAL (CIVIL DIVISION)

1. INTRODUCTION

1.1. Jurisdiction of the Court of Appeal
   1.1.1. The Court of Appeal is a superior court of record. It exercises all the jurisdiction conferred on it by the Supreme Court Act 1981. In any appeal to the Civil Division of the Court of Appeal, and in relation to the amendment, execution and enforcement of any judgment or order made on such appeal, it has the same authority and jurisdiction as the court or tribunal from which the appeal is brought. When rules of court permit, any incidental jurisdiction in any proceedings pending before the Civil Division of the Court of Appeal, not involving the determination of an appeal, may be exercised, with or without a hearing, by a single judge of that Court, or by the master.

1.2. Consolidated Practice Directions
   1.2.1. This is a consolidation, with some amendments, of all the principal Practice Directions which apply to proceedings in the Court of Appeal (see the list at Annex A). It covers the process of instituting proceedings, documentation including skeleton arguments, the requirement for permission to appeal, judgments, case management and Alternative Dispute Resolution. It also deals with particular aspects of the current practice of the Court of Appeal, for example, the making of references to the European Court of Justice under Article 177 of the EC Treaty. It should be noted that permission to appeal is now required in the vast majority of cases. This consolidated Practice Direction applies equally to appeals to the Court in family cases. Further or amended directions may be issued once the new Civil Procedure Rules, governing the work of the Court of Appeal, have been made.

1.3. The Civil Appeals Office
   1.3.1. The administrative work of the Civil Appeals Office is conducted under the direction of the Head of the Civil Appeals Office. When acting in a judicial capacity he is known as master. In this Practice Direction the term master is used with that specific meaning. Provision is also made for the appointment of deputy masters.

1.4. Litigants in person
   1.4.1. All of this Practice Direction may be of relevance to litigants in person but the key points of which they need to be aware will be found at section 8.

2. PERMISSION TO APPEAL

2.1. When is permission required?
   2.1.1. Most appeals require the permission of the court below (the court which made the decision which is challenged) or of the Court of Appeal to bring an appeal.
   2.1.2. Since 1 January 1999, permission has been required for all appeals except appeals against:
      (a)   committal orders;
      (b)   refusals to grant habeas corpus; and
      (c)   secure accommodation orders made pursuant to section 25 of the Children Act 1989.
(see RSC Order 59 r. 1B(1)(a)–(c))
   2.1.3. The experience of the Court of Appeal is that many appeals and applications for permission to appeal are made which are quite hopeless. They demonstrate basic misconceptions as to the purpose of the civil appeal system and the different roles played by appellate courts and courts below. The court below

has a crucial role in determining applications for permission to appeal. This guidance indicates how applicants, and courts, should approach the matter.

2.2. *From which court should permission to appeal be sought?*

2.2.1. The court which has just reached a decision is often in the best position to judge whether there should be an appeal. It should not leave the decision to the Court of Appeal. Courts below can help to minimise the delay and expense which an appeal involves. Where the parties are present for delivery of the judgment, it should be routine for the judge below to ask whether either party wants permission to appeal and to deal with the matter then and there. However, if the court below is in doubt whether an appeal would have a realistic prospect of success or involves a point of general principle, the safe course is to refuse permission to appeal. It is always open to the Court of Appeal to grant it.

2.2.2. The advantages which flow from permission being considered by the court of first instance are lost if the application cannot be listed before the judge who made the decision which is the subject of the application. Where it is not possible for the application for permission to be listed before the same judge, or where undue delay would be caused by so listing it, the Court of Appeal will be sympathetic to applicants who claim that it was impracticable for them to make their application to the court below and will not require such an application to be made.

2.3. *Oral or paper hearings*

2.3.1. Many applications to the Court of Appeal for permission to appeal are considered in the first instance by a single Lord Justice on paper, but in some cases the Court directs that the application should proceed straight to an oral hearing. Usually, only applications for permission where the applicant is legally represented are dealt with on paper. However, some applications from litigants in person may be deemed suitable to be dealt with in the same way. Following a notification that the Lord Justice is minded to refuse permission to appeal and in the absence of a request for an oral hearing being received within 14 days, the application will be determined in open court without further reference to the applicant.

2.3.2. Whether the application is dealt with on paper or at a hearing the applicant should not burden the Court with documents which are not relevant to the application. The letter from the Civil Appeals Office acknowledging entry of the application in the records of the Court sets out the Court's requirements concerning application bundles.

2.4. *Applications for permission listed for oral hearing*

2.4.1. If the single Lord Justice, on consideration of the papers, grants permission or directs an oral hearing of the application, directions may be given on paper as to (1) the maximum time to be allowed to each party for oral argument on the appeal or the oral hearing of the application for permission, as the case may be; (2) the filing and service of skeleton arguments; and (3) other directions for the progress of the case.

2.4.2. Where an application for permission to appeal is listed for oral hearing, whether initially or after a decision on paper, the following directions will apply.

2.4.3. In all cases where the application is listed for an oral hearing at which the Court has directed that other parties are to have the opportunity to attend, the applicant's solicitors (or the applicant, if acting in person) must, on receipt of notification from the Civil Appeals Office that such a hearing has been directed, immediately supply the respondent's solicitors (or the respondent, if in person) with a copy of the application bundle (including a copy of the transcript or note of judgment) in exactly the same form as the bundles filed for the use of the Court of Appeal. For the purposes only of providing the copy of the application bundle to the respondent's side photocopies of transcripts of judgment and, where relevant, evidence, may be used. The costs of provision of that bundle shall be borne by the applicant initially, but will form part of the costs of the application.

2.5. *Time allowed for oral hearings*

2.5.1. In the absence of specific directions, the Court of Appeal will expect oral argument in support of applications for permission to appeal, or renewed applications for permission to apply for judicial review, to be confined to a maximum of 20 minutes.

2.6. Skeleton arguments for applications for permission to appeal

2.6.1. In order to assist the Court of Appeal to deal efficiently with applications for permission to appeal, all represented applicants for permission must provide a skeleton argument and applicants in person are strongly encouraged to do so. Three copies of the skeleton argument must accompany the bundle of documents which the applicant's solicitors lodge with the Civil Appeals Office for the application. (These copies should be filed with, but not bound in, the bundle.) Where dates are of significance in relation to the proposed appeal, a chronology should be filed and served with the applicant's skeleton argument.

2.6.2. If the application is listed for oral hearing at which the Court has directed that other parties are to have the opportunity to attend, the respondent's skeleton argument must be filed and served within 14 days of receipt of the applicant's bundle. Where an application for permission to appeal is listed for hearing, with the appeal to follow if permission is granted, the timetable for skeleton arguments will be the same as in the case of an appeal, and the amount of time allowed for oral argument will depend on the time estimate for the appeal.

2.7. Renewed applications for permission to apply for judicial review

2.7.1. The applicant's advocate (and where any respondent will be represented at the Court of Appeal hearing, that party's advocate) must file four copies of their skeleton arguments with the Civil Appeals Office with the application bundles.

2.7.2. This applies only to renewed applications for permission to apply for judicial review. Where permission to apply has been granted and the substantive application for judicial review has been dealt with in the High Court, any application to the Court of Appeal for permission to appeal against that decision will be governed by the general provisions for such applications.

2.8. The general test for permission

2.8.1. There is no limit on the number of appeals the Court of Appeal is prepared to hear. It is therefore not relevant to consider whether the Court of Appeal might prefer to select for itself which appeals it would like to hear. The general rule applied by the Court of Appeal, and thus the relevant basis for first instance courts deciding whether to grant permission, is that permission will be given unless an appeal would have no real prospect of success. A fanciful prospect is insufficient. Permission may also be given in exceptional circumstances even though the case has no real prospect of success if there is an issue which, in the public interest, should be examined by the Court of Appeal. Examples are where a case raises questions of great public interest or questions of general policy, or where authority binding on the Court of Appeal may call for reconsideration. The approach will differ depending on the category and subject matter of the decision and the reason for seeking permission to appeal, as will be indicated below. However, if the issue to be raised on the appeal is of general importance that will be a factor in favour of granting permission. On the other hand, if the issues are not generally important and the costs of an appeal will far exceed what is at stake, that will be a factor which weighs against the grant of permission to appeal.

2.9. A point of law

2.9.1. Permission should not be granted unless the judge considers that there is a realistic prospect of the Court of Appeal coming to a different conclusion on a point of law which will materially affect the outcome of the case. An appeal on the grounds that there is no evidence to support a finding is an appeal on a point of law, but it is insufficient to show that there was little evidence.

2.10. A question of fact

2.10.1. The Court of Appeal will rarely interfere with a decision based on the judge's evaluation of oral evidence as to the primary facts or if an appeal would involve examining the fine detail of the judge's factual investigation. Permission is more likely to be appropriate where what is being challenged is the inference which the judge has drawn from the primary facts, or where the judge has not received any particular benefit from having actually seen the witnesses, and it is properly arguable that materially different inferences should be drawn from the evidence. In such a case the judge, if he grants permission, should expressly indicate that this is the basis on which permission is given.

2.10.2. If a case is one which has involved considering many witnesses and/or documents, it will be especially important that the trial court considers whether to grant permission and, where it refuses permission, gives its reasons for doing so. This is because in a case of this sort the Court of Appeal is less able to assess whether an appeal is appropriate.

2.11. Questions of discretion

2.11.1. The Court of Appeal does not interfere with the exercise of discretion by a judge unless satisfied the judge was wrong. The burden on an appellant is a heavy one (many family cases do not qualify for permission for this reason). It will be rare, therefore, for a trial judge to give permission on a pure question of discretion. He may do so if the case raises a point of general principle on which the opinion of a higher court is required.

2.12. Appeals from interlocutory orders

2.12.1. An interlocutory order is an order which does not entirely determine the proceedings. Where the application is for permission to appeal from an interlocutory order, additional considerations arise:

(a) the point may not be of sufficient significance to justify the costs of an appeal;

(b) the procedural consequences of an appeal (e.g. loss of the trial date) may outweigh the significance of the interlocutory issue;

(c) it may be more convenient to determine the point at or after the trial.

2.12.2. In all cases under (a) permission to appeal should be refused. In the case of (b) and (c) it will be necessary to consider whether to refuse permission or adjourn the application until after trial so as to preserve the appellant's right to appeal.

2.13. Limited and conditional permission

2.13.1. Permission may be limited to one or more points. It may also be conditional, e.g. on some special order for costs. If a court grants permission on one or more issues only, it should expressly refuse permission on other issues. The reason for this is that the other issues can then only be raised with the permission of the Court of Appeal.

2.13.2. If an appellant wishes to raise additional issues for which there is no permission to appeal, written notice of this must be given to all other parties and the Court of Appeal within 28 days of permission being granted, or 28 days prior to the hearing, if this is earlier. Unless there are special reasons for making an application earlier, to avoid additional expense the application to raise an additional issue should be dealt with at the outset of the appeal and all parties should normally be prepared to argue the additional issues at that hearing. If, however, a respondent considers the additional issues will have a significant effect on the preparation necessary for, or the length of, the hearing, he may inform the appellant within 14 days of receiving the notice that he requires an application to be made prior to the hearing. An application should then be made in writing within 14 days accompanied, if necessary, by short written submissions, which should be served on the respondent. The respondent may deliver short written submissions within a further 14 days. The court will, where practicable, give its decision as to whether the additional issues can be argued prior to the hearing of the appeal.

2.14. Reasons

2.14.1. When permission is refused by the court below, the Court gives short reasons which are primarily intended to inform the applicant why permission is refused. Where permission is granted, reasons may be given which are intended to identify for the benefit of the parties and the Court hearing the appeal why it was thought right to give permission. There may be only one issue that the judge or judges giving permission considered it was necessary to draw to the attention of the parties and the Court hearing the appeal. It is a misconception to assume that, because only one aspect of the proposed appeal was mentioned in any reasons which were given, permission was granted under a misapprehension that there were not other issues to be determined on any appeal unless the reasons make this clear.

2.14.2. When the Lord Justice is minded to refuse permission to appeal, his or her reasons for doing so will be sent to the applicant's solicitors (or the applicant, if in person). A letter will accompany the Lord Justice's comments informing the applicant of the right to seek an oral hearing. (An example of the letter that will be sent is at Annex B to this Practice Direction.) The Lord Justice will direct whether the oral hearing should be before one or two Lords Justices.

2.15. The Form

2.15.1. At Annex C to this Practice Direction is a generic example of the form which the judge should complete when he grants or refuses permission to appeal, giving his reasons. The reasons for the decision need only be brief, e.g. difficult point of law or pure question of fact. All parties will, on request, be given a copy of the form. It is the applicant's responsibility to annex the form to his notice of application where he has been refused permission, or to his notice of appeal where he has been granted permission.

2.16. Directions

2.16.1. When an application for permission to appeal is referred to the single Lord Justice on the papers alone and the Lord Justice decides to grant permission, the Lord Justice may give directions for the subsequent progress of the appeal.

2.17. Legally aided applicants

2.17.1. In any case where the applicant is legally aided and the single Lord Justice is minded to refuse permission to appeal on paper, the applicant's solicitor must send to the relevant legal aid office a copy of the single Lord Justice's comments (together with any reasons he/she gave for refusing permission) as soon as it has been received from the Civil Appeals Office. The court will require confirmation that this has been done in any case where an application for permission to appeal is renewed before the full court on legal aid.

2.18. Applications to set aside grant of permission to appeal to the Court of Appeal

2.18.1. There is a heavy onus on a respondent who seeks to set aside permission. Before making such an application, the respondent must bear in mind that the fact that the appeal has no real prospect of success does not necessarily mean that permission should not have been given. The applicant will be required to establish that there was no good reason for giving permission, which may not be the same thing. In addition, it should be borne in mind, prior to making such an application, that this court is likely to be very unsympathetic to it being made if it will in effect involve the parties in exactly the same expense as determining the appeal itself, and will not necessarily save the time of the Court but risk the Court having to have two hearings when only one would be necessary had there been no application to set aside.

2.19. More than one level of appeal

2.19.1. Where there has already been one unsuccessful appeal to a court (not a tribunal) against the decision being challenged, for example from a District Judge to a Circuit Judge or from a Master to a High Court Judge, and the application is for permission for a further appeal to the Court of Appeal, a more restrictive approach to the test for permission to appeal should be adopted. Permission should be granted only if the case raises a point of principle or practice or the case is one which for some other compelling reason should be considered by the Court of Appeal.

PRACTICE DIRECTION FOR THE COURT OF APPEAL (CIVIL DIVISION)

3. SKELETON ARGUMENTS

3.1. Introduction

3.1.1. Skeleton arguments are, as their name implies, a very abbreviated note of the argument and in no way usurp any part of the function of oral argument in court. They are an aide-mémoire for convenience of reference before and during the hearing.

3.2. When are they required?

3.2.1. Skeleton arguments are compulsory in the case of all appeals (and full-court applications) to the Civil Division of the Court of Appeal, and in the case of all applications for permission to appeal (heard by a single judge), except (i) in cases which are heard as a matter of great urgency and (ii) any individual case where the court otherwise directs. Litigants in person are strongly encouraged to provide skeleton arguments.

3.3. The necessity for skeleton arguments

3.3.1. Before the appeal is called on, the judges will normally have read the notice of appeal, any respondent's notice and the judgment appealed from. The purpose of this pre-reading is not to form any view of the merits of the appeal, but to familiarise themselves with the issues and scope of the dispute and thereby avoid the necessity for a lengthy, or often any, opening of the appeal.

3.3.2. This process is assisted by the provision of skeleton arguments, which are much more informative than a notice of appeal or a respondent's notice, being fuller. During the hearing of the appeal itself, skeleton arguments enable much time to be saved because they reduce or obviate the need for the judges to take a longhand note, sometimes at dictation speed, of the submissions and authorities and other documents referred to. Furthermore, in some circumstances a skeleton argument can do double duty not only as a note for the judges but also as a note from which counsel can argue the appeal. It cannot be over-emphasised that skeleton arguments are not formal documents. They are simply a tool to be used in the interests of greater efficiency.

3.4. Form and content

3.4.1. To facilitate filing of skeleton arguments in the Civil Appeals Office, advocates must ensure:

(a) that their names are typed at the end of their skeleton arguments; and

(b) that the correct Court of Appeal reference number is shown on the front page. Where a skeleton argument covers two or more appeals, or applications, which are due to be heard together the reference numbers for all of them must be given.

3.4.2. The skeleton arguments should contain a numbered list of the points which the advocate proposes to argue, stated in no more than one or two sentences, the object being to identify each point, not to argue it or to elaborate on it. Each listed point should be followed by full references to the material to which the advocate will refer in support of it, i.e. the relevant pages or passages in authorities, bundles of documents, witness statements, transcripts and the judgment under appeal. It should also contain anything which the advocate would expect to be taken down by the court during the hearing, such as propositions of law, chronologies of events, lists of dramatis personae and, where necessary, glossaries of terms. If more convenient, these can of course be annexed to the skeleton argument rather than being included in it. Both the court and the opposing advocate can then work on the material without writing it down, thus saving considerable time and labour.

3.5. Length

3.5.1. The purpose of a skeleton argument is to identify and summarise the points, not to argue them fully on paper. A skeleton argument should therefore be as succinct as possible. In the case of a normal length appeal against a final order (i.e. an appeal in the range of one to two days), skeleton arguments should not

PRACTICE DIRECTION FOR THE COURT OF APPEAL (CIVIL DIVISION)

normally exceed 10 pages in the case of an appeal on law and 15 pages in the case of an appeal on fact.

3.5.2. In the case of points of law, the skeleton argument should state the point and cite the principal authority or authorities in support, with references to the particular page(s) where the principle concerned is enunciated. In the case of questions of fact, it should state briefly the basis on which it is contended that the Court of Appeal can interfere with the finding of fact concerned, with cross-references to the passages in the transcript or notes of evidence which bear on the point.

3.6. Chronologies

3.6.1. The court wishes to emphasise the importance of advocates for the appellant preparing a written chronology of events relevant to the appeal. If practicable the chronology should be agreed with the respondent(s). This should be a separate document in order that it can readily be consulted in conjunction with other papers. The appellant's advocate's skeleton argument must be accompanied by the written chronology of events relevant to the appeal cross-referenced to the core bundle or appeal bundle.

3.7. Respondent's skeleton argument

3.7.1. In the case of respondents who wish only to contend that the judgment of the court below is correct for the reasons given, the respondent's advocate can send in a letter to that effect in place of a skeleton argument. Where, however, the respondent is going to rely on any authority or refer to any evidence which is not dealt with in the judgment of the court below, a respondent's skeleton argument must be filed. The respondent's advocate must always file a skeleton argument in any case where there is a respondent's notice.

3.8. Skeleton arguments and litigants in person

3.8.1. In the interests of avoiding placing undue burdens on them litigants in person are not obliged to file skeleton arguments in support of their appeals and applications, but are strongly encouraged to do so. Where the litigant in person does decide to put in a skeleton argument he/she must;

(a) file four copies of it with the Civil Appeals Office within the time limit which would apply if an advocate were acting; and

(b) provide the respondent's advocate with a copy of it no later than the date on which the copies are filed with the Civil Appeals Office.

3.9. Timetable for skeleton arguments

3.9.1. If any advocate does not have instructions or all necessary papers sufficiently far in advance to be able to complete and file the skeleton argument on time, he/she should write to the master immediately.

3.10. Applications for extensions of time to file skeleton arguments

3.10.1. Applications for extensions of time must be made by the advocate personally (not by his or her clerk, or instructing solicitor). Such applications should be made by letter or fax setting out the reasons why the prescribed timetable could not be complied with and what further time is required. Such letters should be filed with, or posted to, the Case Section Support and Documents Room (Room E307, Royal Courts of Justice, Strand, London WC2A 2LL); the fax number is 0171-936 6810. That office will then pass the letter or fax to the master or the relevant Lord Justice.

3.11. Skeleton arguments and time limits

3.11.1. The court expects the time limits to be strictly adhered to and extensions of time will only be granted if it is satisfied that there are good reasons for doing so.

3.12. Skeleton arguments and the Short Warned List

3.12.1. In the case of appeals and applications assigned to the Short Warned List, applications for extensions of time for filing skeleton arguments will normally be dealt with by the master and the letter or fax should therefore be addressed to him. Requests for cases to be removed from the Short Warned List and given a fixture will not automatically relieve advocates from the obligation to file skeleton arguments. In most instances, before deciding whether the case should be taken out of the Short Warned List, the master or supervising Lord Justice will need to see the skeleton arguments in order to assist him to determine whether the case is one which satisfies the test for being given a fixture or second fixture. Where skeleton arguments are required for that purpose, the Civil Appeals Listing Office will inform the advocates concerned.

3.13. Skeleton arguments for appeals and full court applications
3.13.1. Where permission to appeal is granted by the Court of Appeal, the appellant (and any respondent who has filed a skeleton argument in response to the permission application) may use the same skeleton arguments for the purposes of the appeal (subject to making any minor amendments which they consider necessary, such as changes to page references), or they may prepare fresh skeleton arguments for the purposes of the appeal.
3.13.2. The appellant's solicitors must include with the appeal bundle, or the bundle for any full court application, four copies of their skeleton argument. (These copies should be filed with, but not bound in, the bundle.) The appellant's solicitors must also include a copy of that skeleton argument with the set of bundles served on the respondent. Appellants are reminded of the obligation to serve a set of bundles on the respondent at the same time as the appeal bundles are filed with the Civil Appeals Office.
3.13.3. The respondent's solicitors must file with the Civil Appeals Office four copies of their skeleton argument within 21 days of the date on which the appellant's bundle was served on them or, if earlier, not later than 14 days before the appeal hearing. No supplemental or revised skeleton arguments may be filed without the permission of the Court. Permission will only be granted if there are good reasons for doing so.

3.14. Application or appeals in linked or similar cases
3.14.1. Where advocates are aware that an application or appeal in which they are instructed is linked with another case, or raises issues similar to or connected with, those raised in other applications and appeals, they should inform the master, by letter, as soon as practicable.

4. CASE MANAGEMENT

4.1. Supervising Lords Justices
4.1.1. A group of supervising Lords Justices maintain oversight of groups of appeals. This involves them in specific case management as well as keeping abreast of developments in their areas of litigation. They will welcome general information from the professional bodies and specialist associations about difficulties or initiatives of which the Court of Appeal should be aware. The membership of the team will change from time to time. The names of the current supervising Lords Justices and their areas of responsibility are set out in Annex D.

4.2. Case management
4.2.1. When it appears to the court that it would for any reason be advantageous to do so, the Court will invite the parties' advocates and any party acting in person to attend a directions hearing held in advance of the main hearing. Such directions hearings may be conducted by the full Court, a single Lord Justice or the master.
4.2.2. Supervising Lords Justices will give directions concerning the progress and future conduct of appeals on their own initiative wherever they think fit, and most requests from parties for expedition or for other directions to be given will be referred to the relevant supervising Lord Justice.
4.2.3. So far as possible, directions will be given on paper, in the interests of saving costs. In those cases where a hearing is necessary, it will be conducted before the supervising Lord Justice in private (unless otherwise directed) and therefore

both solicitors and counsel will have a right of audience. It will rarely be necessary for more than one counsel, or, where counsel has not been briefed, for more than one solicitor to attend on behalf of any particular party.

4.2.4. Directions hearings will not be allowed to develop into satellite litigation. They are intended to be a speedy and informal means of arriving at practical solutions to unresolved problems relating to the preparation for and future conduct of the appeal. Attempts at 'point scoring' will not be tolerated. The supervising Lord Justice will have read in advance the judgment under appeal, the notice of appeal and any respondent's notice, together with any correspondence or other documents which raise or define the issues to be decided at the directions hearing. Advocates should therefore proceed straightaway to make their points about those issues briefly and without any opening or preamble. The costs of such directions hearings will be in the discretion of the Court in the usual way. Although a shorthand note of the hearing will be taken, a detailed or lengthy judgment will not normally be given.

4.2.5. To ensure that all requests for directions are centrally monitored and correctly allocated, all requests for directions or rulings (whether relating to listing or any other matters) should be made to the Civil Appeals Listing Office. Those seeking directions or rulings must not approach the supervising Lord Justice either directly, or via his or her clerk.

4.2.6. If directions are requested or needed close to the hearing date, the matter will normally be referred to the presiding Lord Justice of the court in which the appeal is due to be heard. He or she will then make the necessary directions as a single Lord Justice or refer the matter to the full court.

4.2.7. The management of the list will continue to be dealt with by the listing officer under the oversight of the master. Subject to any direction given in any individual case by the full Court or by a Lord Justice, the master and deputy masters will continue to exercise their powers to give directions.

4.2.8. The Court may at any time give directions whether in individual cases or through information leaflets in relation to the documents to be produced. It may also give directions as to the manner in which documents are to be presented and as to other matters incidental to the conduct of the appeal, as appear best adapted to secure the just, expeditious and economical disposal of the appeal.

4.2.9. Directions regarding documentation may be given without a hearing. The master may at any time issue a notice requiring the parties to an appeal or application to attend before him. Any party given notice of an appeal or application may apply at any time for an appointment before the master.

5. RECEIVING AND PROCESSING APPEALS AND APPLICATIONS

5.1. The principal features of the system

5.1.1. In the case of notices of appeal and applications which are filed by personal attendance at the Civil Appeals Office Registry, the staff on the counter will not carry out any check on whether permission to appeal is required or whether there is any other jurisdictional bar to the appeal or application being accepted. The counter staff will carry out a preliminary check on the following:

(a) whether the relevant time limits have been complied with;

(b) whether a copy of the order being appealed has been filed;

(c) in the case of applications (other than in time applications for permission to appeal), whether the statement of truth in the application notice has been signed and whether a witness statement or an affidavit in support of the application is included with the papers; and

(d) whether the correct court fee has been paid.

5.1.2. If the person dealing with the matter at the counter considers that the appeal is out of time, or that any of the other requirements listed above have not been complied with, he/she will inform the solicitor, or solicitor's clerk, of this and will not take the papers in. If the solicitor who has the conduct of the case considers that all relevant time limits and other formalities have been complied with, that solicitor (not the clerk) should telephone the Civil Appeals Office or send a letter or fax, and the matter will be referred to the master.

5.1.3. If the member of the staff at the counter considers that the time limits and other formalities have been complied with, he/she will accept the papers; but they will then be referred to an office lawyer and, if necessary, the master. If it is considered that, for any reason, the appeal or application has not been validly instituted or is one which the Court has no jurisdiction to entertain, the appellant's/applicant's solicitor (or the appellant/applicant if in person) will be informed of this, normally by letter or telephone. Any query concerning the office lawyer's decision will be referred to the master.

5.1.4. It follows from the arrangements set out above that the fact that the staff in the Civil Appeals Office have accepted the notice of appeal or application concerned must not be taken to be an indication, still less a guarantee, that the appeal or application is validly instituted or is one which the court has jurisdiction to entertain.

5.1.5. Appeals and applications filed by post will be similarly dealt with. The staff in the registry will carry out the preliminary check on time limits and formalities, and then the papers will be referred for legal scrutiny.

5.1.6. If, after the preliminary check, the appeal or application is considered to be in order, it will be set down (i.e. entered in the records of the Court of Appeal) and given a reference number. The appellant's/applicant's solicitors (or the appellant/applicant if in person) will then be informed by a letter from the Civil Appeals Office that the appeal/application has been set down; that letter will give the appeal/application reference number (which should be quoted when writing or telephoning) and will specify what further steps must be complied with by the appellant's/applicant's side and within what timetable. When an appeal is set down the appellant must inform the respondent of the reference number and the timetable.

5.1.7. It is important to emphasise that these procedures for vetting appeals and applications are intended to assist the court in the management of its case load and to ensure, so far as possible, that invalid appeals or applications are not accepted. They do not, however, relieve any party (whether represented or acting in person) of the obligation to comply with the requirements of all of the relevant rules and directions and that party's solicitor, or the party himself/herself, as the case may be, will remain solely responsible for all consequences, including the costs, of any failure to comply with any relevant requirement.

5.1.8. It is unwise for solicitors, or litigants in person, to leave it until the last day, or even close to the last day, of the period concerned before posting or bringing the requisite documents to the Civil Appeals Office.

5.2. Notice of appeal

5.2.1. Except for appeals and decisions of the Social Security Commissioners on questions of law and appeals from certain tribunals (see RSC Order 59 rule 21 and Order 61), there is a single time limit for serving the notice of appeal of four weeks from the date on which the judgment or order of the court below was sealed or otherwise perfected, unless this limit is abridged or extended by order of the court below, the master, a Lord Justice or the Court of Appeal (see RSC Order 59 r. 4(1)). Such applications are ordinarily heard by the master.

5.3. Contents of Notice of Appeal

5.3.1. A notice of appeal which complies fully with RSC Order 59 rule 3 will both define and confine the area of controversy on the hearing of the appeal, thus saving both time and expense to the parties.

5.3.2. The notice of appeal must contain a certificate stating which track the case is currently allocated to in the Court below.

5.3.3. There is no form of notice of appeal fixed by statute or the rules. If a notice of appeal does not contain the following suggested statement or certificate, it will not for that reason alone be invalid. However the following suggestions are recommended in order to save the parties time, trouble and expense.

(a) On setting down an appeal to the Court of Appeal one copy of the notice of appeal should be endorsed with a certificate of the solicitors for the appellant

PRACTICE DIRECTION FOR THE COURT OF APPEAL (CIVIL DIVISION)

(or the appellant himself if in person) stating the date or dates on which notice of appeal was served on the party or parties named as respondents and on the county court or tribunal as appropriate. The officer receiving the notice of appeal should satisfy himself that it was served in due time on the respondents and on the appropriate court or tribunal where required and must refuse to set the appeal down if it appears that the notice was served out of time. The copy of the notice of appeal containing the certificate as to service shall be in the custody of the officer in attendance on the Court of Appeal when the appeal comes on to be heard.

(b) Notices of appeal should contain, after the signature by the solicitor for the appellant, a statement as follows:

'No notice as to the date on which this appeal will be in the list for hearing will be given: it is the duty of solicitors to keep themselves informed as to the state of the lists. A respondent intending to appear in person should inform the Civil Appeals Office Registry, Royal Courts of Justice, WC2A 2LL, of that fact and give his address; if he does so he will be notified to the address given of the date when the appeal is expected to be heard.' The form of the notice of appeal will be found at Annex E.

5.4. The list of appeals

5.4.1. RSC Order 59 rule 3(4) requires the notice of appeal to specify the list of appeals in which the appellant proposes that the appeal shall be set down. There are final and interlocutory lists as described in Annex F.

5.5. Setting down the appeal

5.5.1. Order 59 rule 5 requires the appellant to 'set down' the appeal within seven days after the later of (i) the date on which service of the notice of appeal was effected, or (ii) the date on which the judgment or order of the court below was sealed or otherwise perfected. The time limit is important and will be strictly enforced. 'Setting down' means filing the notice of appeal with the court, accompanied by the documents specified in RSC O. 59 r. 5(1). Any application to extend time for setting down must be made to the master.

5.6. Respondent's Notice

5.6.1. RSC O. 59 r. 6 makes provision for the service of a respondents' notice within 21 days after the service of the notice of appeal and its subsequent filing. The content of any such notice is as important as that of the notice of appeal and for the same reason, it defines and confines the scope of the argument on the appeal, enables the members of the Court to inform themselves in advance of the hearing of what the appeal is about and so saves both time and expense. Again the time limit is important and will be strictly enforced, any application for an extension of time must be made to the master unless the appeal is before the Court itself at the time when the application is made.

5.7. Amendment of notice of appeal and respondent's notice

5.7.1. It can happen that, on reflection, it is thought desirable to amend such notices. Rule 7 allows this to be done without leave at any time before the appeal first appears in the documents list. An application for permission to amend should be made to the master on notice to all other parties, unless the appeal is already before the Court for some other purpose.

5.8. Appearance of appeal or application in the documents list

5.8.1. Once an appeal or application appears in the document list, the appellant has fourteen days in which to file the various documents specified at paragraph 7.2. and 7.3. A notice of appeal and respondent's notice may be amended as of right before the case enters the documents list, but thereafter only with permission.

5.9. Constitution of Courts

5.9.1. Section 54(4) of the Supreme Court Act 1981 and the Court of Appeal (Civil Division) Order 1982, S1 1982/543, have authorised the constitution of Courts consisting of two judges instead of three in certain specified circumstances, mainly appeals from interlocutory decisions, which includes most family and divorce matters, and appeals from the county courts. It will sometimes happen that, whilst an appeal is of such a nature that there is jurisdiction for a two-judge Court to hear it, issues of complexity or general importance arise such that a three-judge Court is desirable. Should this appear to the master to be the case, he will list the appeal for hearing by a three-judge Court. In addition the parties that this is the case may apply to the master for a special listing before a three-judge Court, but should not adopt this course unless there are compelling reasons for so doing.

5.10. Documents needed for filing an application

5.10.1. Upon filing an application, the following documents are to be filed in duplicate in addition to the relevant court fee:
   (a) the application notice;
   (b) the order under appeal;
   (c) in the case of an application for permission to appeal, the order of the court below refusing such permission and any written reasons given;
   (d) any witness statement or affidavit in support of the application. In the case of an application for permission to appeal, the statement of truth must be signed or a witness statement or affidavit be filed only if the application is made after the expiry of the time limit or if a stay of execution or other remedy is requested;
   (e) in the case of an application for permission to appeal, the draft notice of appeal or document stating the grounds of the proposed appeal.

5.10.2 The application notice must contain a certificate stating which track the case is currently allocated to in the Court below.

5.10.3. The forms of notice of application are at Annex G.

5.11. Internal appeals and referrals

5.11.1. The master has power to refer matters to a single judge and the single judge power to refer matters to the Court of Appeal. The judicial decision of the master may be appealed to a single Lord Justice and the determination of the single Lord Justice may be appealed to the full Court of Appeal. However, in respect of a determination by the master, there is no right of appeal to the Court of Appeal without the leave of that Court if the master's determination has been reviewed by the single Lord Justice.

5.12. Time estimates

5.12.1. In all cases where there are solicitors acting for the appellant they must file with the Civil Appeals Office within 14 days after an appeal has been entered in the records of the Court, an estimate of the length of the appeal hearing (exclusive of judgment). That time estimate must be on the form sent to the solicitors with the letter from the Civil Appeals Office acknowledging that the appeal has been entered in the records of the Court. The procedure is as follows:
   (a) Form must be duly completed and signed by the appellant's advocate.
   (b) Within that 14 day time limit the original of that completed form must be sent or delivered to the Civil Appeals Office and a photocopy must be sent to the respondent's advocate, either directly or through the respondent's solicitors.
   (c) The respondent's advocate must consider the appellant's estimate as soon as it has been received and notify the Civil Appeals Office within 14 days (by filing the photocopy of the form with the respondent's section of it completed and signed) if his/her own estimate differs from that of the appellant's advocate. In the absence of such notification the respondent's advocate will be deemed to have accepted the estimate from the appellant's side.

5.12.2. Where the court directs that an application for permission to appeal shall be listed for hearing with the appeal to follow if permission is granted and the court has not specified what length of time is to be allowed for oral argument, the appellant's advocate must provide a certified time estimate of the length of the hearing on the assumption that permission will be granted and the court will hear argument on the appeal. The procedure is the same as in paragraph 5.12.1., except that (1) the time-limit will be 14 days after the date of the direction that the

PRACTICE DIRECTION FOR THE COURT OF APPEAL (CIVIL DIVISION)

application be listed with appeal to follow, and (2) the estimate need not be on any special form.

5.12.3. A copy of the certified estimate must be placed and kept with each advocate's papers. Each time the advocate for any party is asked to give any advice or to deal with anything in connection with the appeal he/she must check whether the estimate is still correct. The fact that a time estimate has been filed in the case does not prevent the Court from allocating its own time estimate.

5.13. Revised estimates

5.13.1. If, for any other reason, the original estimate requires revision, the Civil Appeals Office should be informed immediately in writing by the advocate concerned.

5.14. Appeal bundles

5.14.1. On filing the appeal bundles with the Civil Appeals Office, the appellant's solicitors must supply the respondent's solicitors (or the respondent, if in person) with a set of the appeal bundles in exactly the same form as the bundles filed for the use of the Court of Appeal. The costs of provision of bundles for the respondent shall be borne by the appellant initially, but will form part of the costs of the appeal.

5.14.2. Appellants will not, however, be required to furnish respondents with transcripts of judgment and evidence. The appellant's solicitors (or the appellant, if in person) must notify the respondent's solicitors (or the respondent, if in person) of what transcripts have been provided for the court so that they can order transcripts for their own use and also make representations if they consider that further transcripts will be required.

Respondents must order and pay for transcripts for the use of their solicitors and advocates (see Section 7 Documentation).

6. LISTING AND HEAR-BY DATES

6.1. Introduction

6.1.1. Listing is carried out for the whole of the Court of Appeal rather than for individual courts. In order to ensure, so far as possible, that cases are heard in their proper place in the list, each appeal is given a target date (known as its 'hear-by date'). Because some types of appeal are inherently more urgent than others (for instance, family cases) different hear-by dates are set for different species of appeals; a list of the current hear-by dates is annexed to this practice direction at Annex H. The aim is that appeals should be listed so that they are heard neither significantly earlier, nor significantly later, than their respective hear-by dates. In the interests of flexibility the listing officer has a discretion to fix the hearing date within a reasonable band on either side of the hear-by date. That system will not always apply to appeals assigned to the Short Warned List; such cases may be put into the list considerably earlier than their hear-by dates and may not be called on for hearing until some time thereafter.

6.1.2. In relation to applications for permission to appeal or renewed applications for permission to apply for judicial review it will not be possible, save in exceptional circumstances, to list such cases to suit advocates availability.

6.1.3. Appeals will only be expedited so as to be heard well in advance of their hearby dates, or deferred significantly thereafter, if there is a judicial direction to that effect. Requests for expedition should be made to the master, initially by letter: see paragraph 6.6. below. Informal requests for listing significantly before the hear-by date may be made to the Listing Officer.

6.2. Fixtures

6.2.1. A 'fixture' means a hearing date fixed in advance: it means that the hearing is fixed to begin on a specified date or on the next following sitting day at the option of the court. Appeals (other than (a) those assigned to the Short Warned List, (b) those given second fixtures; and (c) cases where special listing directions have been given) will be given fixtures. If it does not prove to be possible for the court concerned to take the appeal on the specified date or on the following sitting day, and the Listing Office is unable to transfer the appeal to another court, the hearing date will have to be rearranged.

6.3. Second fixtures

6.3.1. Some appeals are designated by the court as 'second fixtures.' A second fixture is a hearing date arranged in advance on the express basis that the list is fully booked for the period in question and therefore the case will be heard only if a suitable gap occurs in the list. Any second fixture for which space does not become available will be given a first fixture on the earliest convenient date.

6.4. The Short Warned List

6.4.1. Cases assigned to the Short Warned List are put 'on call' from a specified date and will then be called on for hearing as and when gaps occur in the Court of Appeal list. Short Warned List cases are not called in chronological order of setting down or assignment to that list; which case will be called on will depend upon the length of the gap, the subject-matter of the case and the constitution of the court. Because the number of last-minute settlements in the Court of Appeal varies enormously, it is not possible to predict when any particular Short Warned List case will be called on for hearing.

6.5. Short Warned List (procedure)

6.5.1. The system applicable to cases assigned to the Short Warned List is as follows.

(a) The parties' solicitors are notified by letter from the Civil Appeals Office that the case has been assigned to the Short Warned List.

(b) It is the duty of the solicitors to all parties (whether appellants, or respondents) on receipt of that letter from the Civil Appeals Office to inform their advocates forthwith of the fact that the case has been assigned to the Short Warned List.

(c) The Listing Office will notify counsel's clerks by telephone of the date from which the case will be 'on call' and it will remain in the Short Warned List liable to be called on either on half a day's notice or (if the master has so directed, on 48 hours' notice). The listing officers will put Short Warned List cases 'on call' in such numbers and from such dates as the state of the list requires.

(d) It is the duty of solicitors to inform their lay clients when a case has been assigned to the Short Warned List and what the consequences of that will be. It is important that this is done so that the clients are not taken by surprise if, as is quite likely, they have to be represented at the Court of Appeal hearing by a different advocate. The supervising Lord Justice or the master will consider applications to remove appeals from the Short Warned List and give them a fixture or second fixture provided that the application is made at the correct time and on valid grounds. Any such application must be made as soon as the solicitors have been notified that the appeal has been assigned to that list (i.e. immediately on receipt of the letter referred to in paragraph (a) above). It is far too late to do so when, or after, the case has been put 'on call'.

6.5.2. It is not a valid ground for taking a case out of the Short Warned List that the parties' advocates of first choice may not be available to represent them at the appeal hearing. A case assigned to the Short Warned List will only be taken out of that list and given a fixture or second fixture if it is, viewed objectively, one which cannot be properly presented save by a particular advocate.

6.5.3. It follows that if any party's advocate of first choice is, for whatever reason, not available to appear on the date for which a Short Warned List case is called on, then a substitute advocate must be instructed immediately. Time should not be spent asking that the case should not be called on for that particular date because the advocate is unavailable.

6.5.4. Between 75 per cent and 80 per cent, of cases are given fixtures. The master is charged with the duty of selecting the minority of cases which, in his view, can reasonably be expected to be mastered by an advocate other than the one originally instructed on half a day's notice or, in the case of those so designated, on 48 hours' notice. These are then assigned to the Short Warned List and the assignment notified to the parties.

6.5.5. The supervising Lord Justice or the master will always consider applications to remove appeals from the Short Warned List on the grounds that they are not of the appropriate character. However, such applications must be made as soon as the parties are notified that the appeal has been assigned to that list. It is far too late to do so when, or after, notification is given that such an appeal is on call.

6.5.6. Once an appeal is 'called on for hearing' it becomes the immediate personal professional duty of the advocate instructed in the appeal to take all practicable measures with a view to ensuring that his lay client is represented at the hearing by the advocate who is fully instructed and able to argue the appeal.

6.5.7. The court has power under section 51 of the Supreme Court Act 1981, as substituted by section 4 of the Courts and Legal Services Act 1990, to order the advocate who has failed in his duty to pay any 'wasted costs'. Further or alternatively the court has power to refer counsel's conduct either personally or vicariously by his clerk, to the Bar Council for consideration of whether disciplinary proceedings should be taken.

6.6. Expedition

6.6.1. In the interests of saving costs the supervising Lord Justice or master decide as many requests for expedition as possible on paper without a hearing. Requests for expedition should initially be made to the master by letter (or, if time is short, by fax) setting out succinctly and in short compass the grounds on which expedition is sought, and, if it is granted, how soon the appeal needs to be heard. At the same time a copy of that letter (or fax) must be sent to the other party's solicitors so that they know at the earliest possible stage that an expedited hearing is being sought, and why.

6.6.2. Subject to the qualification referred to below, the letter to the master requesting expedition should be accompanied by a transcript or note of the judgment being appealed, draft grounds of appeal, and a realistic advocate's time estimate of the anticipated length of the appeal. Where, however, a very early hearing is needed (i.e. a hearing within days), the letter requesting expedition should be sent to the master (with copy to the other side) without waiting for the transcript or note of judgment and the draft grounds of appeal, so that the court has the maximum possible notice that such a high degree of expedition is sought.

6.6.3. Because of the 'immense pressures on its lists the Court of Appeal is no longer able to expedite as many cases as in the past. Attention is drawn to the current practice of the court as summarised in *Unilever plc v Chefaro Proprietaries Ltd* [1995] 1 WLR 243 and paragraph 6.7.

6.7. Orders for expedited hearing of an appeal

6.7.1. There is a time lag between the date an appeal is set down and the date it is heard. The court has in general been sparing in its grant of applications for expedition, and has imposed a high threshold which a party must cross before its application for an expedited hearing will be granted. Where that threshold is crossed and an expedited hearing is ordered, the court will in fixing the date for that hearing give weight not to the wishes of the parties to that appeal but to the interests of other parties adversely affected by the order. It will do its utmost, for example, to avoid cancelling a fixture that has already been cancelled on a previous occasion. The greater the expedition ordered, the less regard can usually be had to the parties' preferences concerning dates.

6.7.2. Expedition will not normally be granted unless the party seeking it is willing, if necessary, to change advocate. In an appropriate case the respondent may also have to change advocate; this possible adverse consequence will cause the court to lean against the making of an order save in a clear case. In granting an application for expedition, the court may seek to mitigate the disruption caused to other parties by giving procedural directions not currently given in the ordinary run of cases with a view to ensuring that the appeal is heard in the minimum time necessary to achieve a just result.

6.7.3. The following guidance must be flexibly applied according to the facts of the particular application for expedition. However, some appeals are so urgent that justice can only be done if the appeal is heard immediately or within days. This category includes:

(a) appeals against committal orders, particularly if the adverse finding is challenged or the sentence is short;

(b) cases in which children are likely to suffer extraordinary prejudice (that is prejudice beyond that almost inevitably consequent on involvement in proceedings) if a decision is delayed;

(c) cases under the 1980 Hague Convention on the Civil Aspects of Child Abduction (Cmnd 8281);

(d) asylum appeals concerning return to third countries, where the right to return may be jeopardised by delay;

(e) cases in which the execution of a possession order is imminent and which appear to have some merit;

(f) cases in which a decision is about to be taken or implemented which will be irrevocable or confer rights on third parties;

(g) cases in which the publication of allegedly unlawful material is imminent;

(h) appeals against judicial decisions made in the course of continuing proceedings.

6.7.4. In all these cases, not least (e), the court will expect the parties involved to approach it as soon as they learn of the order which it is sought to challenge. When the approach is left until the eleventh hour, or the necessary materials are not provided, it may well prove impracticable to arrange a hearing.

6.7.5. The court recognises the need to try to arrange expedited hearings where it appears that, without such expedition,

(a) a party may lose its livelihood, business or home or suffer irreparable loss or extraordinary hardship;

(b) the appeal will become futile;

(c) the resolution of numerous cases turning on the outcome of a case under appeal, will be unreasonably delayed, or the orderly management of class or multi-party litigation in a lower court will be disrupted;

(d) widespread divergences of practice are likely to continue, with the prospect of multiple appeals until the correct practice is laid down;

(e) there would be serious detriment to good public administration or to the interests of members of the public not concerned in the instant appeal.

6.7.6. When these criteria are not satisfied, the court will not ordinarily grant an expedited hearing of appeals on preliminary issues, or substantial interlocutory appeals (even where this means the loss of a trial date), or appeals concerning the construction of a standard document.

7. DOCUMENTATION

7.1. Directions of the Court of Appeal concerning bundles of documents for the purposes of appeals and full court applications

7.1.1. It is the duty of those acting for appellants to ensure that the bundles of documents filed for the use of the court comply with the relevant rules and directions. It is also their duty to file the bundles within the time limit prescribed by RSC O. 59, r. 9(1). Neglect of these duties may lead to the appeal or application being dismissed. For that reason, attention is drawn, in particular, to the following requirements.

7.2. Documents for applications

7.2.1. In general, the following are required:

(a) The document used to institute the application to the Court of Appeal.

(b) The notice of appeal or draft notice of appeal.

(c) The Order of the court below being appealed.

(d) Any order of the court below which refused permission to appeal and the form giving reasons.

PRACTICE DIRECTION FOR THE COURT OF APPEAL (CIVIL DIVISION)

(e) Any affidavit or witness statement lodged with the Civil Appeals Office in support of the application.

(f) Transcripts or notes of judgment (explained in more detail under appeals heading) save that in the case of applications for permission to appeal, in the absence of a transcript, the note of judgment does not need to be approved by the judge.

(g) Claim form, statements of case.

(h) Any application notice (or case management documentation) relevant to the subject of the appeal.

(i) If the order or judgment arose from an appeal from or setting aside of another judge's order (e.g. from District Judge to Circuit Judge), the first order, the reasons given and the application notice used to appeal from that order.

(j) Relevant affidavits, witness statements, summaries, experts' reports and exhibits.

(k) Such other documents as the Court may direct.

7.3. Documents for appeals

7.3.1. In general, the following are required:

(a) The notice of appeal.

(b) Any respondent's notice.

(c) Any supplementary notice served under rule 7.

(d) The judgment or order of the court/tribunal below.

(e) The document by which the proceedings in the court below were begun (for civil courts, usually a claim form).

(f) Any application notice which led to the order which is the subject of the appeal.

(g) The statements of case (pleadings) if any, and in Admiralty cases, the preliminary acts, if any.

(h) The approved transcript of the judge's reasons for giving the judgment or making the order of the court/tribunal below. If that is not available, the advocates' note of the judge's reasons approved, wherever possible, by the judge.

(i) The parts of the transcript of evidence given in the court below which are relevant to any question at issue on the appeal. In the absence of an approved transcript, the relevant parts of the judge's note of the evidence.

(j) If the order or judgment arose from an appeal from or setting aside of another judge's order (e.g. from District Judge to Circuit Judge), the first order, the reasons given and the application notice used to appeal from that order.

(k) The relevant affidavits, witness statements summaries, experts' reports, exhibits or parts of exhibits, as were in evidence in the court below.

(l) Any order, whether of the Court of Appeal or court below, granting permission to appeal and, in the case of the court below, the form giving reasons.

(m) Where permission to appeal was granted by the Court of Appeal at an oral hearing, the transcript of that decision.

7.4. Applications and appeals

7.4.1. Appellants/applicants are notified of the number of judges (including in Admiralty cases, assessors) due to hear their case. The appellant/applicant must provide sufficient copies and bundles for each judge.

7.5. Transcripts

7.5.1. All transcripts lodged (whether of evidence or of the judgment) must be official copies provided by the shorthandwriters or transcribers. Appellants are not permitted to file photocopies which they have had taken.

7.5.2. Where proceedings in any court have been officially recorded in shorthand, by stenographic machine, or on tape, official transcripts of the judgment, and, where relevant, the evidence, must be filed with the Court of Appeal, and, unless the court otherwise directs, notes of judgment or evidence will not be accepted. Normally the court will only accept notes in place of transcripts where the case requires such an urgent hearing that there is not time to obtain them.

7.5.3. Where, however, either in any division of the High Court or in a county court, the judge handed down his/her judgment, photocopies of the text of that

PRACTICE DIRECTION FOR THE COURT OF APPEAL (CIVIL DIVISION)

handed-down judgment (signed by the judge) can be lodged for the purposes of an appeal to the Court of Appeal in place of official transcripts of the judgment.

7.6. Transcripts of Court of Appeal judgments

7.6.1. Court of Appeal (Civil Division) transcripts are held in the Supreme Court Library. Parties requiring copies of them can obtain them from the shorthand writers or transcribers on payment of the usual charges. Advocates who propose to refer to such transcripts should satisfy themselves that arrangements are being made for copies to be available to the Court and to other advocates concerned.

7.7. Notes of judgment

7.7.1. In cases where the judge's judgment was not officially recorded and was not handed-down, the advocate or the solicitor who appeared for the appellant in the court below must prepare a note of the judge's judgment, agree it (if possible) with the advocate or solicitor who appeared for the respondent, and submit it to the judge for approval. If the parties' advocates (or solicitors) are not able to reach agreement about the note speedily, they should submit their rival notes of judgment to the judge, stating that they are unable to agree a note. In the case of an application for permission to appeal the applicant's advocate's note of judgment does not have to be approved by either the respondent's advocate or judge.

7.7.2. Where the note of judgment has not been received back from the judge by the time the bundles are ready to be filed, copies of the unapproved note of judgment should be filed with the bundles; the approved note of judgment should then be substituted as soon as it is to hand. In those cases where the appellant is appealing in person, advocates or solicitors for the respondent must make available their notes of judgment without charge, whether or not the appellant has made any note of the reasoned judgment.

7.8. County court notes of evidence

7.8.1. In county court cases, where the evidence was not officially recorded, a typed copy of the judge's notes of evidence must be obtained from the county court concerned and a photocopy of those notes must be included in each bundle. Directives have been sent to county courts asking them to arrange for the notes of evidence to be transcribed as soon as the notice of appeal has been served on the county court (unless the evidence was tape recorded). The notes should then be ready for despatch to the appellant's solicitors (or the appellant, if in person) as soon as they formally request them and make provision for the copying charges.

7.9. Transcripts at public expense

7.9.1. An appellant or respondent acting in person will not be required to pay for a transcript where a certificate is given under this paragraph. Otherwise, the appellant or respondent will pay for any transcript required for the Court of Appeal in the first instance. The Court may in certain circumstances certify that it is proper for the cost of a transcript to be borne by public funds. These circumstances are where it is satisfied that an appellant (or respondent) is in such poor financial circumstances that the cost of a transcript would be an excessive burden on him, and, in the case of a transcript of evidence, also that there is reasonable ground for the appeal.

7.9.2. Where the Court is of opinion that it is necessary to see a transcript of proceedings and judgment (with or without a transcript of the evidence) relating to an appellant whose financial circumstances are as described above, it may certify that transcripts or all or any part of the proceedings and judgment may properly be supplied for the use of the Court at the expense of public funds. The Court for these purposes includes both the judge (of whatever level) whose decision is under appeal, and the Court of Appeal, a single judge of the Court of Appeal or the master. An appellant for these purposes includes a person who is seeking permission to appeal to the Court of Appeal.

7.10. Core bundles

7.10.1. In cases where the appellant seeks to place before the court bundles of documents comprising more than 100 pages, (exclusive of the judgment appealed against) the appellant's solicitors must prepare and file with the court the requisite number of copies of a core bundle containing the documents central to the appeal.

7.10.2. In all cases where the appellant or applicant is represented only core bundles are to be filed without any trial or other bundles. Core bundles must contain only those documents which the Lords Justices will need to pre-read or to which it will be necessary to refer at the hearing, either in support of, or in opposition to, the appeal or application. As soon as the appeal or application has been filed, the appellant's or applicant's solicitors must give careful consideration (with the advice of their advocate where appropriate) to the necessary content of the core bundles. If they are in any doubt concerning the documents which the other side will need, they must consult the respondent's solicitors at an early stage.

7.11. Time for filing core bundles
7.11.1. No later than the date stated in the letter from the Civil Appeals Office acknowledging entry of the case in the court's records, the appellant's solicitors must file with the Civil Appeals Office Case Section Support and Documents Room the number of sets of core bundles specified in that letter. No other bundles are to be filed.

7.11.2. One set of the full trial bundles should be brought to the Court of Appeal hearing, but not filed in advance.

7.12. Contents of core bundles
7.12.1. Each core bundle must always include the notice of appeal, the order appealed against, any other relevant orders made in the court below, the respondent's notice (if any) and the note of judgment and notes of evidence (if relevant). If it is a case where there are transcripts of the judgment/evidence, then those should not be bound in the core bundle, but kept separate, see below. In addition, the core bundle should include such of the documents put in evidence in the court below as are central to the appeal.

7.13. Core bundles and litigants in person
7.13.1. For information helpful to litigants in person see paragraph 8.2.

7.14. Pagination
7.14.1. Bundles must be paginated. At present, many bundles are numbered merely by document. This is incorrect. Each page must be numbered individually and consecutively, starting with page 1 at the top of the bundle and working continuously through to the end.

7.15. Index
7.15.1. There must be an index at the front of the bundle listing the documents and giving the page references for each. In the case of documents such as letters, invoices, bank statements etc., they can be shown in the index by a general description; it is not necessary to list every letter, invoice etc. separately. But if a letter or other such document is particularly important to the case, then it should be listed separately in the index so that attention is drawn to it. In particular in the case of appeals and applications in judicial review proceedings, the letter or other document which constitutes the decision sought to be reviewed must be separately itemised in the index (whether or not it forms part of the exhibit to an affidavit). Where each set of bundles consists of more than one file or bundle, an index covering all of them should be placed at the beginning of Bundle A; there should not be separate indexes for each physical bundle comprised in the set.

7.16. Binding of bundles
7.16.1. All the documents (with the exception of transcripts) must be bound together in some form (e.g. lever arch files, ring-binders, plastic binders, or laced through holes in the top left-hand corner).

7.17. Legibility
7.17.1. All documents must be legible. In particular, care must be taken to ensure that the edges of pages are not cut off by the photocopying machine or

rendered illegible by the binding. If it proves impossible to produce adequate copies of individual documents, or if manuscript documents are illegible, typewritten copies of the relevant pages should also be interleaved at the appropriate place in the bundle.

7.18. Applications for permission to adduce further evidence
7.18.1 Where (as is often the case) the court has directed that an application for permission to adduce further evidence is to be listed for hearing at the same time as the appeal, separate bundles must nevertheless be filed in respect of that application so that the further evidence can readily be distinguished from the evidence which was before the court below.

7.19. Time limits for filing documents
7.19.1. Time limits must be complied with and will be strictly enforced except where there are good grounds for granting an extension.

7.20. Responsibility of the solicitor on the record
7.20.1. The solicitor in charge of the case must personally satisfy himself/ herself, and is responsible as an officer of the court for ensuring that the documentation is in order before it is delivered to the court. London agents too have a responsibility; they should be prepared to answer any questions which may arise as to the sufficiency of the documentation.

7.21. Affidavits
See Practice Direction to CPR Part 32.

8. LITIGANTS IN PERSON (LITIGANTS WITHOUT LAWYERS)

8.1. Applications for permission to appeal and appeals by litigants in person
8.1.1. So that the Court of Appeal can check whether it has jurisdiction to hear an application for permission to appeal, or a full appeal, litigants in person should take or send to the Civil Appeal Office:
  (a) a copy of the order or decision by the court against which he or she seeks to appeal; and
  (b) details of his or her name, address and telephone number.
8.1.2. If the application or appeal is one where the Court of Appeal has jurisdiction, the Civil Appeals Office will provide the litigant with notes for guidance on how to proceed.
8.1.3. If the application or appeal is not one where the Court of Appeal has jurisdiction, the Civil Appeals Office will write to the litigant to explain the reasons why.
8.1.4. It is emphasised that the administrative and legal staff in the Civil Appeals Office will need time to deal with these matters. Litigants are therefore advised to make sure that they communicate with the Civil Appeals Office as soon as possible after the order or decision by the court against which they wish to appeal has been given, and *well* before the expiry of the time limit for serving notice of appeal. The provision of this information at short notice can be made only in urgent circumstances. A case will not be regarded as urgent merely because a party has left it too close to the expiry of the time limit before taking the necessary steps to make the application or file an appeal. A case will be treated as urgent only if a direction to the effect is made by the Court.

8.2. Appeal and application bundles
8.2.1. Information about how to prepare for applications or appeals by preparing sets or a set (bundles) of documents for the use of the Court of Appeal can be found in two leaflets, one for applications and one for appeals. The Civil Appeals Office will send a copy of the relevant leaflet to the litigant with the letter confirming the matter has entered the records of the Court of Appeal.
8.2.2. It is then the responsibility of the litigant to comply with the requirements set out in the leaflet. In particular, litigants should refer to the checklist in the leaflet, which highlights the key requirements. When the litigant is sure that his or her bundles of documents comply with the requirements in the leaflet, he or she should sign the checklist and return it to the Civil Appeals Office with the bundles.

8.2.3. In certain circumstances, the Court may require fewer documents than are required for formal bundles for an application. Except in cases which are so urgent that there is no time to do so, the Civil Appeals Office will write to litigants to tell them whether limited documentation or full bundles are required.

8.2.4. Paragraphs 7.5. and 7.9. gives details about obtaining transcripts of judgment for incorporation in the bundles. Litigants who require help with the preparation of their bundles can obtain this from the Citizens' Advice Bureau in the Royal Courts of Justice. In appropriate cases (for example, where for whatever reason the litigant is unable to prepare his or her own bundles) the Citizens' Advice Bureau may arrange for the bundles to be prepared for the litigant free of charge.

8.3. Skeleton arguments

8.3.1. Skeleton arguments are short written statements of the arguments in support of an application or appeal. Litigants in person are not obliged to send to the court skeleton arguments in support of their applications and appeals, but are strongly encouraged to do so. If they do, they should try to comply with the directions given in the section entitled 'skeleton arguments' (section 3). Many litigants in person find that setting out the arguments which they wish to raise in court in advance can be of great assistance when, at a hearing, the Court asks the them to explain what their case is about.

8.3.2. A litigant who wishes to prepare a skeleton argument can obtain advice on how to do this from the Citizens' Advice Bureau in the Royal Courts of Justice. In appropriate cases the Citizens' Advice Bureau will prepare the skeleton argument for the litigant free of charge.

9. RESERVED JUDGMENTS OF THE COURT OF APPEAL

9.1. Availability of handed down judgments in advance of the hearing

9.1.1. Unless the court otherwise orders — for example, if a judgment contains price-sensitive information — copies of the written judgment will now be made available in these cases to the parties' legal advisers at about 4 pm on the second working day before judgment is due to be pronounced on condition that the contents are not communicated to the parties themselves until one hour before the listed time for pronouncement of judgment. Delivery to legal advisers is made primarily to enable them to consider the judgment and decide what consequential orders they should seek. The condition is imposed to prevent the outcome of the case being publicly reported before judgment is given, since the judgment is confidential until then. Some judges may decide to allow the parties' legal advisers to communicate the contents of the judgment to their clients two hours before the listed time, in order that they may be able to submit minutes of the proposed order, agreed by their clients, to the judge before the judge comes into court, and it will be open to judges to permit more information about the result of a case to be communicated on a confidential basis to the client at an earlier stage if good reason is shown for making such a direction.

9.1.2. If, for any reason, a party's legal advisers have special grounds for seeking a relaxation of the usual condition restricting disclosure to the party itself, a request for relaxation of the condition may be made informally through the judge's clerk (or through the associate, if the judge has no clerk). A copy of the written judgment will be made available to any party who is not legally represented at the same time as to legal advisers. It must be treated as confidential until judgment is given.

9.1.3. Every page of every judgment which is made available in this way will be marked 'Unapproved judgment: No permission is granted to copy or use in court'. These words will carry the authority of the judge, and will mean what they say.

9.1.4. The time at which copies of the judgment are being made available to the parties' legal advisers has been brought forward in order to enable them to submit any written suggestions to the judge about typing errors, wrong references and other minor corrections of that kind in good time, so that, if the judge thinks fit, the judgment can be corrected before it is handed down formally in court. The parties' legal advisers are therefore being requested to submit a written list of corrections of this kind to the judge's clerk (or to the associate, if the judge has no clerk) by 12 noon on the day before judgment is handed down. If it is not possible to comply with this deadline, any later corrections approved by the judge will be included in the final text which the official shorthand writer (or the judge's clerk, in courts which lack an official shorthand writer) will incorporate into the approved official text of the judgment as soon as practicable. In divisions of the court which have two or more judges, the list should be submitted in each case to the judge who is to deliver the judgment in question. Lawyers are not being asked to carry out proof-reading for the judiciary, but a significant cause of the present delays is the fact that minor corrections of this type are being mentioned to the judge for the first time in court, when there is no time to make any necessary corrections to the text.

9.2. *Availability of approved versions of handed down judgments*
9.2.1. This course will make it very much easier for the judge to make any necessary corrections and to hand down the judgment formally as the approved judgment of the court without any need for the delay involved in requiring the court shorthand writer, in courts which have an official shorthand writer, to resubmit the judgment to the judge for approval. It will always be open to the judge to direct the shorthand writer at the time of the hearing in court to include in the text of the judgment any last minute corrections which are mentioned for the first time in court, or which it has proved impracticable to incorporate in the judgments handed down. In such an event the judge will make it clear whether the shorthand writer can publish the judgment, as corrected, as the approved judgment of the court without any further reference to the judge, or whether it should be resubmitted to the judge for approval. It will be open to judges, if they wish, to decline to approve their judgments at the time they are delivered, in which case the existing practice of submitting the judgment for their approval will continue.

9.3. *Handing down judgment in court: availability of uncorrected copies*
9.3.1. When the court hands down its written judgment, it will pronounce judgment in open court. Copies of the written judgment will then be made available to accredited representatives of the media, and to accredited law reporters who are willing to comply with the restrictions on copying, who identify themselves as such. In cases of particular interest to the media, it is helpful if requests for copies can be intimated to the judge's clerk, or the presiding Lord Justice's clerk, in advance of judgment, so that the likely demand for copies can be accurately estimated. Because there will usually be insufficient time for the judge's clerk to prepare the necessary number of copies of the corrected judgment in advance, in most cases these uncorrected copies will similarly bear the warning 'Unapproved Judgment: No permission is granted to copy or use in court.' The purpose of these arrangements is to place no barrier in the way of accredited representatives of the media who wish to report the judgments of the court immediately in the usual way, or to accredited law reporters who wish to prepare a summary or digest of the judgment or to read it for the purpose of deciding whether to obtain an approved version for reporting purposes. Its purpose is to put a stop to the dissemination of unapproved, uncorrected, judgments for other purposes, while seeking to ensure that everyone who is interested in the judgment (other than the immediate parties) may be able to buy a copy of the approved judgment in most cases much more quickly than is possible at present.
9.3.2. If any member of the public (other than a party to the case) or any law reporter who is not willing to comply with the restrictions on copying, wishes to read the written judgment of the court on the occasion when it is handed down, a copy will be made available for him or her to read and note in court on request made to the associate or to the clerk to the judge or the presiding Lord Justice. The copy must not be removed from the court and must be handed back after reading. The object is to ensure that such a person is in no worse a position than if the judgment had been read aloud in full.

9.4. *Availability of approved judgments*
9.4.1. In courts without an official shorthand writer, the approved judgment should contain on its frontispiece the rubric 'Judgment: Approved by the court for

handing down (subject to editorial corrections)', and every page of a judgment which is handed down in this form will be marked in a similar manner. There will be no embargo on copying a judgment handed down in this form, so long as its status is made clear, and at present no charge will be made for permission to copy it. In future, all judgments delivered at the Royal Courts of Justice will be published in a common format. For cases decided in the two divisions of the Court of Appeal and in the Crown Office List, copies of the approved judgment can be ordered from the official shorthand writers, on payment of the appropriate fee. In the other courts in the Royal Courts of Justice, copies of the approved judgment can be ordered from the Mechanical Recording Department, on payment of the fee prescribed for copy documents. Disks containing the judgment will also be available from the official shorthandwriters, and the Mechanical Recording Department, where relevant, on payment of an appropriate charge. It is hoped that in most cases copies of the approved judgment will be available from these sources on the same day as the judgment is handed down: they should no longer be sought from judges' clerks.

9.5. Restrictions on disclosure or reporting
9.5.1. Anyone who is supplied with a copy of the handed-down judgment, or who reads it in court, will be bound by any direction which the court may have given in a child case under section 39 of the Children and Young Persons Act 1933, or any other form of restriction on disclosure, or reporting, of information in the judgment.

9.6. Availability of approved versions of extempore judgments
9.6.1. Delays have also been experienced in the publication of approved versions of judgments which were not reserved, whether they are produced by the official shorthand writers or by contractors transcribing the tapes which have been mechanically recorded.

9.6.2. Sometimes the delay is caused in courts without an official shorthand writer because a transcript is bespoken by one of the parties a long time after the judgment was delivered. If a transcribed copy of such a judgment is to be required, in connection with an appeal, for example, it should be ordered as soon as practicable after judgment was delivered.

9.6.3. Delays are also sometimes caused in these cases because judgments are delivered to a judge for approval without supplying the judge with copies of the material quoted in the judgment. In future no judge should be invited to approve any such transcript unless the transcriber has been provided by the party ordering the transcript with copies of all the material from which the judge has quoted. If the transcript is ordered by a person who is not a party to the case (such as a law reporter), that person should make arrangements with one of the parties to ensure that the transcriber (and the judge) will have access to all the material quoted in the judgment.

9.6.4. From time to time delays are also caused because judges have been slow in returning approved transcripts to the transcribers. Judges should endeavour to return approved transcripts to the transcribers within two weeks of their being delivered to them for approval. If anyone encounters serious delay on this account, the relevant Head of Division should be informed.

9.6.5. Where a reserved written judgment has not been reported, reference must still be made in court to the approved official transcript (if this is available) and not to the approved transcript which is handed down, since this may have been subject to late revision after the text was prepared for handing down.

9.7. Advocates' fees and notes of judgments
9.7.1. Advocates' brief (or, where appropriate, refresher) fee includes
   (a) remuneration for taking a note of the judgment of the court;
   (b) having the note transcribed accurately;
   (c) submitting the note to the judge for approval where appropriate;
   (d) revising it if so requested by the judge, and
   (e) providing any copies required for the Court of Appeal, instructing solicitors and lay client.

9.7.2. Accordingly, save in exceptional circumstances, there can be no justification for charging any additional fee for such work.

9.7.3. When required to attend on a later day to take a judgment not delivered at the end of the hearing, the advocate will, subject to the rules of the court, ordinarily be entitled to a further fee for such attendance. This note does not affect that entitlement.

10. MISCELLANEOUS DIRECTIONS

10.1. Citation of authority

10.1.1. When authority is cited, whether in written or oral submissions, the following practice should in general be followed.

10.1.2. If a case is reported in the official Law Reports published by the Incorporated Council of Law Reporting for England and Wales that report should be cited. These are the most authoritative reports; they contain a summary of argument; and they are the most readily available. If a case is not (or not yet) reported in the official Law Reports but is reported in the Weekly Law Reports or the All England Law Reports that report should be cited. If a case is not reported in any of these series of reports, a report in any of the specialist series of reports may be cited. Such reports may not be readily available: photostat copies of the leading authorities or the relevant parts of such authorities should be annexed to written submissions; and it is helpful if photostat copies of the frequently used series are made available in court. It is recognised that occasions arise when one report is fuller than another, or when there are discrepancies between reports. On such occasions, the practice outlined above need not be followed. It is always helpful if alternative references are given.

10.1.3. Where a reserved written judgment has not been reported, reference should be made to the official transcript (if this is available) and not the handed-down text of the judgment. If the judgment under appeal has been reported before the hearing and counsel wish to argue from the published report rather than from the official transcript, the court should be provided with photocopies of the report for the use of the judges in order that they may be able to annotate it as the argument proceeds.

10.1.4. Advocates are reminded that lists of authorities, including textbooks, to which they wish to refer should be delivered to the Head Usher's office not later than 5.30 p.m. on the working day before the day when the hearing of the application or appeal is due to commence. Advocates should also seek confirmation that an adequate number of copies are available for the use of the court and, if this is not the case, should themselves provide an appropriate number of photocopies.

10.1.5. Where, as is often the case, one or other party chooses to provide photocopies of the principal authorities (including textbook extracts and academic articles) relied on, the benefit to the court is greatly enhanced if (i) a list of those authorities, and the photocopies, are lodged with the skeleton argument so that they can be used by the members of the court when preparing for the hearing; (ii) counsel liaise with each other so as to ensure, so far as possible, that the authorities provided are not duplicated. The photocopies need only include, for each law report, the headnote and the pages containing the particular passages relied on and, for each textbook and article, the title pages and the pages containing the particular passages relied on.

10.1.6. Permission to cite unreported cases will not usually be granted unless advocates are able to assure the court that the transcript in question contains a relevant statement of legal principle not found in reported authority and that the authority is not cited because of the phraseology used or as an illustration of the application of an established legal principle.

10.2. Hansard extracts

Application

10.2.1. This Direction concerns both final and interlocutory hearings in which any party intends to refer to the reports of parliamentary proceedings as reported in the official reports of parliamentary proceedings as reported in the official reports of either House of Parliament, *Hansard*. No other report of parliamentary proceedings is to be cited.

Documents to be served

10.2.2. Any party intending to refer to any extract from *Hansard* in support of any such argument as was permitted by the decisions in *Pepper* v *Hart* [1993] AC 593, [1992] 3 WLR 1032, and *Pickstone* v *Freemans plc* [1989] AC 66, [1988] 3 CMLR 221, HL, or otherwise, must unless the judge otherwise directs, serve upon all other parties and the court copies of any such extract together with a brief summary of the argument intended to be based upon such report.

Time for service

10.2.3. Unless the judge otherwise directs, service upon other parties to the proceedings and the court of the extract and summary of arguments referred to above is to be effected not less than five clear working days before the first day of the hearing. That applies whether or not there is a fixed date. Solicitors must keep themselves informed as to the state of the lists where no fixed date had been given.

Methods of service

10.2.4. A service on the court is to be effected by sending to the Court of Appeal, Civil Division, three copies to the Civil Appeals Office, Case Support Section, Room E307, Royal Courts of Justice, Strand, London WC2A 2LL.

Failure to serve

10.2.5. If any party fails to comply with this Practice Direction the court might make such order, relating to costs and otherwise, as is in all the circumstances appropriate.

10.3.1. Judicial review, renewal of application for permission to apply

10.3.2. A refusal in a non-criminal cause or matter by a Divisional Court of the Queen's Bench Division or by a single judge for permission to apply for judicial review is renewable to the Court of Appeal within 7 days of the decision.

10.3.3. If, following a refusal by the Divisional Court or a single judge, the Court of Appeal grants permission to apply for judicial review, the substantive application should be made to the Divisional Court unless the Court of Appeal otherwise orders. The Court of Appeal will not normally so order unless the court below is bound by authority or for some other reason an appeal to the Court of Appeal is inevitable.

10.3.4. Where the Court of Appeal grants a renewed application for permission to apply for judicial review, except where the Court of Appeal reserves the application to itself, the application should be set down in the Crown Office list to be heard by a single judge, unless a judge nominated to try cases in that list directs that the application is to be heard by a Divisional Court of the Queen's Bench Division.

10.4. Dismissal of appeals/applications by consent

10.4.1. Where an appellant is of full legal capacity and does not desire to prosecute an appeal, he may present a request signed by his solicitor stating that he is of full legal capacity and asking to have the appeal dismissed, in which case (subject to the request being initialled by a judge of the court or by the master) the appeal will be dismissed and struck out of the list, and an order will, if necessary, be drawn up directing payment of the costs by the appellant, such costs to be assessed in case the parties differ. Where the parties are of full legal capacity and a settlement has been reached disposing of the appeal, they may present a request signed by the solicitors for all parties to the appeal, stating that they are of full legal capacity, including the terms of settlement and asking that the appeal be dismissed by consent, in which case (subject to the request being initialled by a judge of the court or by the master) the appeal will be dismissed and struck out of the list and an order will, if necessary, be drawn up.

10.4.2. If the appellant desires to have the appeal dismissed without costs, his request must be accompanied by a consent signed by the respondents' solicitors stating that the respondents are of full legal capacity and consent to the dismissal of the appeal without costs, in which case (subject to the request being initialled by a judge of the court or by the master) the appeal will be dismissed and struck out of the list.

10.4.3. Where any party has no solicitor on the record, any such request or consent must be signed by him personally. All other applications as to the dismissal of an appeal and all applications for an order by consent reversing or varying the order under appeal will be placed in the list and dealt with in court.

10.4.4. Forms of request appear at Annex I.

10.5. Allowing appeals or applications by consent

10.5.1. In cases where parties who are of full legal capacity seek an order to allow the appeal by consent, a copy of the proposed consent order signed by the parties' solicitors (and stating that the parties are of full legal capacity), together with a document setting out the relevant history of the proceedings and the matters relied on as justifying the proposed order, should be sent to the master who will refer them to a Lord Justice for consideration. He or she will either make the order or direct that it should be referred to two Lords Justices for hearing in open court.

10.6. Structured settlements and consent orders involving a party under a disability

10.6.1. The following guidance applies in respect of settlements which require the court's approval.

10.6.2. The types of case concerned are: (1) consent orders relating to appeals and applications where one of the parties is a child or a patient; and (2) structured settlements which are agreed upon at the Court of Appeal stage.

10.7. Procedure

10.7.1. The following procedure should be adopted:

(a) In cases where a consent order needs approval because one of the parties is a child a copy of the proposed order signed by the parties' solicitors should be sent to the master, together with an opinion from the advocate acting on behalf of the child. If on consideration of the documents the court considers that the consent order should be approved, the matter will be listed, but without any party being represented, and the order will be made in open court (see *Hadfield* v *Knowles* [1996] 1 WLR 1003).

(b) Where a party is a patient and the case is not covered by RSC, O. 59, r. 23, the same procedure will be adopted, but the documents filed should also include any relevant reports prepared for the Court of Protection and a document evidencing formal approval by that court where required.

(c) The same procedure should be followed in the case of a structured settlement which has been negotiated in a case which is under appeal and the documents filed should include those which would be required in the case of a structured settlement dealt with at first instance.

10.7.2. If, in any of those categories of case, the court requires further documents before deciding whether to approve the order or settlement, the master or a member of his staff will notify the solicitors of what is required. In future the court will only list any such case for mention at a hearing to be attended by the parties' advocates if the court considers that there are problems about the proposed order or settlement which cannot be satisfactorily resolved in any other way or that, for some other special reason, such a hearing is necessary or desirable.

10.8. Sittings of Court of Appeal in vacation

10.8.1. The Court of Appeal will sit in vacation on such days as the Master of the Rolls may direct and may hear such appeals or applications as the court may direct. Details of the number of courts sitting in August and September will be published each year, normally before Easter.

PRACTICE DIRECTION FOR THE COURT OF APPEAL (CIVIL DIVISION)

10.9. Solicitor's rights of audience

10.9.1. In addition to the cases in which solicitors already have rights of audience in the Supreme Court, and without prejudice to the discretion of a judge to allow a solicitor to represent his client in open court in an emergency, a solicitor may appear in the Supreme Court in formal or unopposed proceedings, that is to say those proceedings where (a) by reason of agreement between the parties there is unlikely to be any argument and (b) the court will not be called on to exercise a discretion.

10.9.2. A solicitor may also represent his client in the Supreme Court when judgment is delivered in open court following a hearing in private at which that solicitor conducted the case for his client.

10.10. Admiralty appeals: assessors

10.10.1. The relevant practice direction has not been consolidated and will be found at [1965] 1 WLR 853.

10.11. Use of unofficial tape recorders in court

10.11.1. Section 9 of the Contempt of Court Act 1981 contains provisions governing the unofficial use of tape recorders in court. The relevant practice direction has not been consolidated but will be found at [1981] 1 WLR 1526.

11. ALTERNATIVE DISPUTE RESOLUTION (ADR)

11.1.1 A pro bono scheme commenced in 1997. The scheme has to take into account the fact that cases which have already been tried at first instance raise different issues, so far as ADR is concerned, to cases which have yet to be tried.

11.1.2. The scheme has recently been refined. Now in appropriate cases, as soon as an appeal [is] set down with the Civil Appeals Office, a letter of invitation to consider ADR, signed by the Master of the Rolls, is sent to the parties' solicitors. The letter encloses an explanatory leaflet and a response form. A member of staff is available to answer queries, provide general information and help with specific cases.

11.1.3. The supervising Lords Justices responsible for particular categories of work are vigilant in their case management for those cases that appear suitable for referral to ADR. Recently a very substantial commercial appeal was compromised as result of a referral by the supervising Lord Justice. Equally, presiding Lords Justices are able to propose a referral to ADR at the determination of appeals which otherwise will lead to a re-hearing or the issue of further proceedings.

11.1.4. Legal aid covers the costs of ADR for an assisted party.

11.1.5. Further information is available from the Civil Appeals Office, Royal Courts of Justice, Strand, London, WC2A 2LL (tel. 0171 936 6486).

12. SUPPLY OF DOCUMENTS FROM CIVIL APPEALS OFFICE FILES

12.1.1 The Civil Procedure Rules CPR rule 5.4 makes general provision for the supply of documents from court records. This note sets out the practice of the Court of Appeal (Civil Division). Requests must usually be made in writing.

12.1.2. The person making the request should,
  (a) cite the Court of Appeal reference number;
  (b) explain what efforts have been made to obtain the document from another party to the appeal and state what reasons have been given by that other party for refusing to supply a copy;
  (c) enclose the prescribed fee.

12.1.3. The master may, in the first instance, determine a request without a hearing. He may also, instead of giving permission or supplying the document, give directions regarding the supply of the document by another person. He may also refer the application to a Lord Justice or the court.

12.1.4. Requests to see skeleton arguments may alternatively be made orally to the associate in at the time of the hearing in open court.

12.1.5. Below, guidance is set out in tabular form:

PRACTICE DIRECTION FOR THE COURT OF APPEAL (CIVIL DIVISION)

INFORMATION	CAN THE INFORMATION BE RELEASED?
Listing of case	Yes, but only after 1500 hrs the day before the hearing when the information is made public. Otherwise leave of the court is required. The Court list comprises the name and number of the case. Apply to the Listing Office.
From which court the appeal came	Yes. Apply to the case section.
Notice of appeal	At the discretion of the court. In general the Court will grant requests to see notices of appeal which have been served on the respondent, and respondent's notices after they have been served on the appellant. Notices of appeal relating to cases involving children will not normally be disclosed nor other notices of appeal which assert confidentiality or the existence of a reporting restriction.
Skeleton arguments	Yes, available in court from Court clerk. Representatives of the media or members of the public can read the skeleton arguments in the courtroom, but may not take copies away. Skeleton arguments cannot be read without the permission of the Court in any cases involving minor children or any other cases where the Court has imposed a reporting restriction.
Files, bundles and computer records	Documents on the Court file (other than skeleton arguments, see above) cannot be shown to anyone without the leave of the Court.
Court orders given or made in open court	Yes. Refer to Associates.
Judgment	Yes. Refer to official shorthand writers or Supreme Court Library.

13. HEARINGS IN PRIVATE

13.1. Hearings in private

13.1.1. Exceptional circumstances will have to be shown before the court will be prepared to hear an application or appeal in private. Where the advocate forms the view that it is necessary, in the interests of justice, that a preliminary application or an appeal should be heard in private, he or she should approach the master indicating his or her view. The reasons should be put into writing, signed by the advocate and handed to the master. In so doing, it should be understood that the advocate is expressing his personal professional view and is not making a submission on behalf of his client. This will enable the court to make a preliminary decision as to whether the application should initially be made in private or in open court. This procedure will avoid the problem which arises where the very reasons which justify a hearing in private must themselves be put forward in private if they are to be put forward at all.

14. REFERENCES TO THE EUROPEAN COURT OF JUSTICE

14.1. References to the European Court of Justice by the Court of Appeal and the High Court under Article 177 of the EC Treaty

14.1.1. Before making a reference to the European Court of Justice under Article 77 of the EC Treaty the Court of Appeal should pay close attention to (a) the terms of that Article, (b) Order 114 of the Rules of the Supreme Court and (c) Practice Form 109. Close attention should also be paid to the Guidance of the European Court of Justice on References by National Courts for Preliminary Rulings: this is set out in paragraph 14.2. below.

14.1.2. It is the responsibility of the Court of Appeal, not the parties, to settle the terms of the reference. This should identify as clearly, succinctly and simply as the nature of the case permits the question to which the British court seeks an answer. It is very desirable that language should be used which lends itself readily to translation.

14.1.3. The referring court should, in a single document scheduled to the order:

(a) identify the parties and summarise the nature and history of the proceedings;

(b) summarise the salient facts, indicating whether these are proved or admitted or assumed;

(c) make reference to the rules of national law (substantive and procedural) relevant to the dispute;

(d) summarise the contentions of the parties so far as relevant;

(e) explain why a ruling of the European Court is sought, identifying the EC provisions whose effect is in issue;

(f) formulate, without avoidable complexity, the question(s) to which an answer is requested.

14.1.4. Where the document is in the form of a judgment, as will often be convenient, passages which are not relevant to the reference should be omitted from the text scheduled to the order. Incorporation of appendices, annexes or enclosures as part of the document should be avoided, unless the relevant passages lend themselves readily to translation and are clearly identified.

14.1.5. The referring court should ensure that the order of reference, when finalised, is promptly passed to the Senior Master of the Queen's Bench Division so that it may be transmitted to Luxembourg without avoidable delay. The title of the referring court should be Court of Appeal (Civil Division) (England & Wales).

14.2. Guidance of the European Court of Justice on References by National Courts for Preliminary Rulings

14.2.1. The development of the Community legal order is largely the result of cooperation between the Court of Justice of the European Communities and national courts and tribunals through the preliminary procedure under Article 177 E.C. and the corresponding provisions of the ECSC and Euratom treaties. In order to make this co-operation more effective, and so enable the Court of Justice better to meet the requirements of national courts by providing helpful answers to preliminary questions, this Note for Guidance is addressed to all interested parties, in particular to all national courts and tribunals. It must be emphasised that the Note is for guidance only and has no binding or interpretative effect in relation to the provisions governing the preliminary ruling procedure. It merely contains practical information which, in the light of experience in applying preliminary ruling procedure, may help to prevent the kind of difficulties which the Court has sometimes encountered.

14.2.2. Any court or tribunal of a Member State may ask the Court of Justice to interpret a rule of Community law, whether contained in the Treaties or in acts of secondary law, if it considers that this is necessary for it to give judgment in a case pending before it.

14.2.3. Courts or tribunals against whose decisions there is no judicial remedy under national law must refer questions of interpretation arising before them to the

PRACTICE DIRECTION FOR THE COURT OF APPEAL (CIVIL DIVISION)

Court of Justice, unless the Court has already ruled on the point or unless the correct application of the rule of Community law is obvious.

14.2.4. The Court of Justice has jurisdiction to rule on the validity of acts of the Community institutions. National courts or tribunals may reject a plea challenging the validity of such an act. But where a national court (even one whose decision is still subject to appeal) intends to question the validity of a Community act, it must refer that question to the Court of Justice.

14.2.5. Where, however, a national court or tribunal has serious doubts about the validity of a Community act on which a national measure is based, it may, in exceptional cases, temporarily suspend application of the latter measure or grant other interim relief with respect to it. It must then refer the question of validity to the Court of Justice, stating the reasons for which it considers that the Community act is not valid.

14.2.6. Questions referred for a preliminary ruling must be limited to the interpretation or validity of a provision of Community law, since the Court of Justice does not have jurisdiction to interpret national law or assess its validity. It is for the referring court or tribunal to apply the relevant rule of Community law in the specific case pending before it.

14.2.7. The order of the national court or tribunal referring a question to the Court of Justice for a preliminary ruling may be in any form allowed by national procedural law. Reference of a question or questions to the Court of Justice generally involves stay of the national proceedings until the Court has given its ruling, but the decision to stay proceedings is one which it is for the national court alone to take in accordance with its own national law.

14.2.8. The order of reference containing the question or questions referred to the Court will have to be translated by the Court's translators into the other official languages of the Community. Questions concerning the interpretation or validity of Community law are frequently of general interest and the Member States and Community institutions are entitled to submit observations. It is therefore desirable that the reference should be drafted as clearly and precisely as possible.

14.2.9. The order for reference should contain a statement of reasons which is succinct but sufficiently complete to give the Court, and those to whom it must be notified (the Member States, the Commission and in certain cases the Council and the European Parliament), a clear understanding of the factual and legal context of the main proceedings.

14.2.10. In particular, it should include:
– a statement of the facts which are essential to a full understanding of the legal significance of the main proceedings;
– an exposition of the national law which may be applicable;
– a statement of the reasons which have prompted the national court to refer the question or questions to the Court of Justice; and
– where appropriate, a summary of the arguments of the parties.

14.2.11. The aim should be to put the Court of Justice in a position to give the national court an answer which will be of assistance to it.

14.2.12. The order for reference should also be accompanied by copies of any documents needed for a proper understanding of the case, especially the text of the applicable national provisions. However, as the case-file or documents annexed to the order for reference are not always translated in full into the other official languages of the Community, the national court should ensure that the order for reference itself includes all the relevant information.

14.2.13. A national court or tribunal may refer a question to the Court of Justice as soon as it finds that a ruling on the point or points of interpretation or validity is necessary to enable it to give judgment. It must be stressed, however, that it is not for the Court of Justice to decide issues of fact or to resolve disputes as to the interpretation or application of rules of national law. It is therefore desirable that a decision to refer should not be taken until the national proceedings have reached a stage where the national court is able to define, if only as a working hypothesis, the factual and legal context of the question; on any view, the

PRACTICE DIRECTION FOR THE COURT OF APPEAL (CIVIL DIVISION)

administration of justice is likely to be best served if the reference is not made until both sides have been heard.

14.2.14. The order for reference and the relevant documents should be sent by the national court directly to the Court of Justice, by registered post, addressed to:
The Registry
Court of Justice of the European Communities
L-2925, Luxembourg
Telephone (352) 43031

14.2.15. The Court Registry will remain in contact with the national court until judgment is given, and will send copies of the various documents (written observations, Report for the Hearing, Opinion of the Advocate General). The Court will also send its judgment to the national court. The Court would appreciate being informed about the application of its judgment in the national proceedings and being sent a copy of the national court's final decision.

14.2.16. Proceedings for a preliminary ruling before the Court of Justice are free of charge. The Court does not rule on costs.

ANNEX A

INDIVIDUAL PRACTICE DIRECTIONS FOR COURT OF APPEAL (CIVIL DIVISION)

(in chronological order)

1. [1926] WN 308 statutory orders private or local Acts should be supplied to the Court
2. Practice Direction [1938] WN 89
3. Practice Direction (CA: Dismissal of Appeal) [1983] 1 WLR 85
4. Practice Direction; Contents of Notice of Appeal [1953] 2 All ER 1510, [1953] 1 WLR 1503, 30/11/53 [In the text issued by the Lord Chancellor's Department there is no item 5.]
6. Practice Note; Application for Judicial Review substantive hearings [1956] 1 WLR 430
7. Transcripts of Court of Appeal Judgments [1978] 1 WLR 600, 24/2/78
8. Use of unofficial tape recorders in court [1981] 3 All ER 848, 19/11/81
9. Practice Note [1982] 3 All ER 376, CA practice and procedure
10. (Practice Direction: Judicial Review: Appeals) Lane LCJ, Donaldson MR [1982] 1 WLR 1375, 2/11/82
11. Practice Direction: Judicial Review: Appeals [1990] 1 All ER 128
12. Practice Note; Hearing of *Anton Piller* appeals in camera [1982] 3 All ER 924, 5/11/82
13. Practice Note: Skeleton arguments [1983] 2 All ER 34, 12/4/83
14. Practice Note: Affidavits, exhibits and documents [1983] 3 All ER 33, 21/7/83
15. Practice Note: Estimate of length of hearing [1983] 3 All ER 544, 28/10/83
16. Practice Direction (Court of Appeal: Applications to a single Judge) [1985] 1 WLR 739
17. Practice Note: Skeleton arguments [1985] 3 All ER 384, 17/10/85
18. Practice Direction: Solicitor's rights of Audience [1986] 2 All ER 226, 9/5/86
19. Practice Note: Appeal where judgment under appeal has been reported [1987] 1 All ER 928, 13/3/87
20. September sittings in CA (CA sittings in the Long Vacation) [1987] 1 All ER 1067
21. Mode of Address of Lady Justice Butler-Sloss, *Palmer* v *Palmer* (1988) *The Times*, 15 June 1988
22. Practice Note: Short Warned List [1989] 1 All ER 891, 1/3/89
23. Practice Direction (QBD Service of Documents) [1985]
24. (Practice Statement: Fee note for Judgment) (1989) *The Times*, 12 May 1989
25. Practice Direction: Receiving and processing appeals and applications [1990] 3 All ER 981, 24/10/90

26. PD (Appeals: Short Warned Lists; counsel's duty where appointments clash) (No.2) [1992] 1 WLR 485
27. Counsel's fee notes of judgments PN [1994] 1 All ER 96, 13/12/93
28. Reserved judgments PN [1995] 3 All ER 247, 22/6/95
29. PD (Citation of Authority) 23 June 1995, [1995] 1 WLR 1096
30. 26 July 1995 Bingham MR [1995] 1 WLR 1188. Practice Statement (CA: procedural changes) WB 59/9/36
31. Bingham MR on CA Procedure (Previous consolidation)
32. Citation of authorities PN [1996] 3 All ER 382
33. Practice Note sub nom. *Hadfield* v *Knowles* [1996] 1 WLR 1003 (structured settlements and consent orders involving party under disability), 16/5/96
34. 12 May 1997, [1997] 1 WLR 1013, CA: Amended Procedure WB 59/9/66
35. Orders for expedited hearings, *Unilever plc* v *Chefaro Proprietaries Ltd* [1995] 1 WLR 243
36. Practice Registrar (unreported PN) 5/97
37. 5 November 1997, [1997] 1 WLR 1535 (CA procedure changes) (Skeleton Arguments and procedural changes) WB 59/9/35
38. 7 November 1997 modifies PD on skeletons
39. (Practice Note) [1997] 1 WLR 1538 on grounds for leave to Appp1084 WB 59/14/19
40. Practice Statement (Supreme Court; judgments) 22/4/98, [1998] 1 WLR 825 Bingham LCJ
41. Practice Statement (Supreme Court: judgments) (No. 2) 2/12/98, *The Times*, 2 December 1998
42. Hear-by dates; revised table of dates 10/11/98
43. 11/98 Lord Woolf MR's PD on leave to appeal to CA.
44. Guidance on applications to the European Court of Justice under Article 177 EC 1/99.

ANNEX B

Dear

Re:

The application for permission to appeal in this case has been assigned to a Lord Justice (a judge of the Court of Appeal), who has considered the papers filed in support of the application. On the basis of the information provided, the Lord Justice is minded to refuse the application for the reasons attached to this letter.

You have the right to seek an oral hearing of the application. The advocate or party appearing at an oral hearing would need to be prepared to deal with the reasons attached to this letter and to answer any further questions that may be asked about the application. The assigned Lord Justice has directed that any oral hearing shall be before a single Lord Justice/two Lords Justices.

Wherever possible the assigned Lord Justice will conduct the oral hearing, either sitting alone or with another Lord Justice as the case may be. The oral hearing will be conducted in public in open court, unless the Court directs otherwise.

If you wish to have an oral hearing, you must notify this Office in writing within 14 days of receiving this letter. In cases where a hearing before two Lords Justices has been directed a second set of the application bundle(s) must be lodged with that notification. If the Office has not received such notification within the 14 day time limit, the application will be dealt with on the basis of the information already submitted and without any further participation by you. It will be dealt with in open court, and you will be sent an order giving the Court's decision.

Where an applicant is legally aided, and the single Lord Justice is minded to refuse the application on the papers, the applicant's solicitor must send to the relevant Legal Aid Office a copy of this letter and its attachment as soon as they have been received. The Court will require confirmation that this has been done in any case

PRACTICE DIRECTION FOR THE COURT OF APPEAL (CIVIL DIVISION)

where an application for permission to appeal proceeds to an oral hearing before the Court on legal aid.

Unrepresented litigants are advised that help with their application may be available from the Citizens' Advice Bureau at the Royal Courts of Justice.

Yours faithfully,

Listing Office

Enc.

ANNEX C

IN THE COURT APPLICATION FOR PERMISSION TO APPEAL TO THE COURT OF APPEAL (CIVIL DIVISION)

Title of proceedings   Claim

                                                            CA Ref

Heard/tried before (insert name of Judge):   Court no.

Nature of hearing:

Date of hearing/judgment

Results of hearing (attach copy of order):

Claimant/Defendant's application for permission to appeal*   Allowed/
                                                              Refused*

Reasons for decision (*to be completed by the Judge*):

Judge's signature:

Note to the Applicant:

When completed, this form should be filed in the Civil Appeals Office on a renewed application for permission to appeal or when setting down an appeal.

* Delete as appropriate

ANNEX D

Current supervising Lords Justices

Butler-Sloss LJ and Thorpe LJ	Family appeals
Morritt LJ and Chadwick LJ	Appeals from the Chancery Division
Pill LJ	Appeals from the Lands Tribunal and cases involving issues relating to planning, highways, footpaths or the Countryside Act 1968
Aldous LJ	Patent appeals
Schiemann LJ	Public law appeals (including appeals from the Immigration Appeal Tribunal) and cases involving European Community law
Brooke LJ and Mantell LJ	Appeals from the county courts (other than family cases)
May LJ	Appeals from the Queen's Bench Division and appeals relating to civil procedure rules
Clarke LJ	Appeals from the Commercial court
Mummery LJ	Appeals from tribunals (other than the Immigration Appeal Tribunal and the Lands Tribunal)

PRACTICE DIRECTION FOR THE COURT OF APPEAL (CIVIL DIVISION)

ANNEX E

NOTICE OF APPEAL

IN THE COURT OF APPEAL   Lower Court reference (Claim No.)

ON APPEAL FROM THE
[HIGH COURT OF JUSTICE
(CHANCERY or QUEEN'S BENCH or FAMILY) DIVISION
[DIVISIONAL COURT]] [or]
_____COUNTY COURT

BETWEEN:
_____Claimant
                                                  (Plaintiff)/Petitioner
and
_____ Defendant/Respondent

TAKE NOTICE that the _____ will apply to the Court of Appeal to appeal from the judgment/order of the Honourable Mr/Mrs Justice/His/Her Honour Judge _____ made on the_____ day of _____ 19_____. By that order the Judge ordered that
_____
_____

The [Claimant](Plaintiff)[Defendant] proposes to ask the Court of Appeal FOR AN ORDER that the judgment/order be set aside [and that judgment be entered in the above-mentioned claim for the
_____
_____
_____

or alternatively that a new trial may be ordered] AND FOR AN ORDER that the _____ be ordered (adjudged) to pay to the _____ his/her costs of this appeal and the costs of the proceedings in the court below

AND FURTHER TAKE NOTICE that the grounds of this appeal are that
1 _____
2 _____

AND FURTHER TAKE NOTICE that the above named _____ proposes that this appeal be assigned to the [(Chancery or Queen's Bench or Family) Division or County Courts] Final/Interlocutory List

I CERTIFY THAT THIS CLAIM IS CURRENTLY ALLOCATED TO THE SMALL CLAIMS/FAST/MULTI-TRACK IN THE _____COURT.

DATED this _____ day of _____ 19

            (SIGNED) _____
            (Address) _____
                      _____
                      _____
                      _____
            (Telephone No.) _____
            (Reference No.) _____

TO the above named
and to Messrs _____ his/her Solicitors

PRACTICE DIRECTION FOR THE COURT OF APPEAL (CIVIL DIVISION)

(Address) _____
_____
_____
_____

(Solicitor's Reference) _____

[and to the District Judge of _____ the County Court]

No notice as to the date on which this appeal will be in the list for hearing will be given: it is the duty of solicitors to keep themselves informed as to the state of the lists. A Respondent intending to appear in person should inform the Civil Appeals Office, Room E330, Royal Courts of Justice, Strand, London WC2A 2LL, of that fact and give his address; if he does so he will be notified to the address given of the date when the appeal is expected to be heard.

I certify that a true copy of this notice was served on the _____'s solicitors on the _____ day of _____ 19_____ [and that a true copy of this notice was served on (upon) the District Judge of the _____ County Court on the _____ day of 19_____]

(Signed)

IN THE COURT OF APPEAL

ON APPEAL FROM THE
[HIGH COURT OF JUSTICE
(CHANCERY or QUEEN's BENCH or FAMILY)
DIVISION
[DIVISIONAL COURT] [or]
_____ COUNTY COURT

Claimant
(Plaintiff)/Petitioner

v.

Defendant/Respondent

——————————————
Notice of Appeal
——————————————

(Address) _____
_____
_____
_____

(Telephone No.) _____

ANNEX F
LIST OF COURT LISTS
County Courts:
Final List; Interlocutory List;
Final List (Admiralty); Interlocutory List (Admiralty);
Final List (Family); Interlocutory List (Family)

Chancery Division:
Final List; Interlocutory List;
Final List (Bankruptcy); Interlocutory List (Bankruptcy);
Final List (Patents); Interlocutory List (Patents);
Final List (Revenue); Interlocutory List (Revenue)

Employment Appeal Tribunal:
Final List; Interlocutory List

Family Division:
Final List; Interlocutory List

PRACTICE DIRECTION FOR THE COURT OF APPEAL (CIVIL DIVISION)

Queen's Bench Division:
Final List; Interlocutory List;
Final List (Admiralty); Interlocutory List (Admiralty);
Final List (Commercial); Interlocutory List (Commercial);
Final List (Crown Office and Divisional Court);
   Interlocutory List (Crown Office and Divisional Court)

Appeal Tribunals:
Final List (Lands Tribunal); Interlocutory List (Lands Tribunal);
Final List (other tribunals); Interlocutory List (other tribunals);
Final List (Social Security Commissioners);
   Interlocutory List, (Social Security Commissioners)
Final List (Immigration Appeal Tribunal)

ANNEX G (1)

APPLICATION NOTICE

IN THE COURT OF APPEAL   Lower Court reference (Claim No.)
ON APPEAL FROM THE
[HIGH COURT OF JUSTICE
(CHANCERY or QUEEN'S BENCH or FAMILY) DIVISION
[DIVISIONAL COURT]] [or]
_____COUNTY COURT

BETWEEN:
_____Claimant
                                                            (Plaintiff)/Petitioner
and
_____ Defendant/Respondent

Section A
[Complete this section in all cases]

TAKE NOTICE that the Claimant (Plaintiff)/Defendant (in person) will apply to the Court of Appeal for an order that _____
_____
_____

AND FOR AN ORDER that *(set out costs order applied for)* _____

AND FURTHER TAKE NOTICE that the application will be heard at the Royal Courts of Justice, Strand, London WC2A 2LL on a date and at a time to be notified by the Civil Appeals Office

Section B

I(We) wish to rely on the following evidence in support of this application *(here set out the reasons why the application should be granted)* _____
_____
_____
_____
_____
_____
_____

PRACTICE DIRECTION FOR THE COURT OF APPEAL (CIVIL DIVISION)

STATEMENT OF TRUTH

*(I believe) (The applicant believes) that the facts stated above are true
* *delete as appropriate*

Signed _____
(Applicant)('s Solicitor)
('s litigation friend)
Date

Position or
office held _____

(if signing on behalf of firm or company)

Section C
[*Complete this section in all cases*]

I CERTIFY THAT THIS CLAIM IS CURRENTLY ALLOCATED TO THE SMALL CLAIMS/FAST/MULTI-TRACK IN THE _____ COURT.

DATED this _____ day of _____ 19____

(SIGNED) _____

(Address) _____
_____

(Telephone No.) _____
(Reference No.) _____

TO: Messrs _____
Solicitors for the Claimant (Plaintiff)/Defendant/Petitioner/Respondent whose address for service is:

(Address) _____
_____
_____

(Solicitor's Reference) _____

ANNEX G (2)

APPLICATION NOTICE FOR PERMISSION TO APPEAL (AND A STAY OF EXECUTION)

IN THE COURT OF APPEAL   Lower Court reference (Claim No.)

ON APPEAL FROM THE
[HIGH COURT OF JUSTICE
(CHANCERY or QUEEN'S BENCH or FAMILY) DIVISION
[DIVISIONAL COURT]] [or]
_____COUNTY COURT

BETWEEN:
_____Claimant
(Plaintiff)/Petitioner
and
_____ Defendant/Respondent

Section A
[*Complete this section in all cases*]

_____ TAKE NOTICE that the Claimant (Plaintiff)/Defendant/Petitioner/Respondent (in person) will apply to the Court of Appeal for an order that he/she be granted permission to appeal from the order of _____

PRACTICE DIRECTION FOR THE COURT OF APPEAL (CIVIL DIVISION)

dated _____ 19____ (and that, if permission is granted, execution of the said order should be stayed pending the hearing of the Claimant's (Plaintiff's)/Defendant's/Petitioner's/Respondent's appeal).

AND FURTHER TAKE NOTICE that the grounds of the proposed appeal are as set out in the draft Notice of Appeal attached

Section B

[*To be completed only in cases where the application for permission to appeal is being made after the time for appealing has expired or where a stay of execution is applied for*]

I (We) wish to rely on the following evidence in support of this application (*here set out the reasons why the application was not made before the expiry of the time for appealing and/or why a stay of execution should be granted*)

_____
_____
_____
_____
_____
_____
_____

STATEMENT OF TRUTH

*(I believe) (The applicant believes) that the facts stated above are true
* delete as appropriate

Signed _____
(Applicant)('s Solicitor)
('s litigation friend)
Date

Position or office held _____

(if signing on behalf of firm or company)

Section C
[*Complete this section in all cases*]

I CERTIFY THAT THIS CLAIM IS CURRENTLY ALLOCATED TO THE SMALL CLAIMS/FAST/MULTI-TRACK IN THE _____ COURT.

DATED this _____ day of _____ 19____

(SIGNED) _____

(Address) _____
_____

(Telephone No.) _____
(Reference No.) _____

TO: Messrs _____

Solicitors for the Claimant (Plaintiff)/Defendant/Petitioner/Respondent whose address for service is:

(Address) _____
_____
_____

(Solicitor's Reference) _____

(Solicitor's Reference) _____

PRACTICE DIRECTION FOR THE COURT OF APPEAL (CIVIL DIVISION)

ANNEX H

HEAR-BY DATES

The current Hear-by Dates are set out in the table below. They apply to all cases entered in the Court's records on or after 1 December 1998.

	TYPE OF CASE	HEAR-BY DATE
Family	Child cases	3 months
	Financial and other	6 months
Crown Office Cases and Immigration appeals	Immigration Appeals Crown Office Interlocutory	3 months
	Other Crown Office final orders	9 months
High Court	Order 14	3 months
	Other interlocutory orders*	5 months
	Bankruptcy and Directors' Disqualification cases	5 months
	Limitation as a preliminary issue in personal injury cases	5 months
	All other preliminary issues	8 months
	Personal injury final orders	12 months
	Other final orders	15 months
County Court	Interlocutory orders	4 months
	Possession	4 months
	All preliminary issues	4 months
	Personal injury final orders	8 months
	Other final orders	12 months
Tribunals (other than immigration appeals)		12 months

* Includes appeals confined to RSC Order 14A. For appeals referring to Order 14A and another issue, the Hear-by Date will be determined by the other issue.

It should be noted that expedition continues to be available in accordance with *Unilever plc v Chefaro Proprietaries Ltd* [1995] 1 WLR 246 (Practice Note). In addition, from 16 November 1998 very serious or distressing personal injury cases will be treated as being in the category of urgent appeals set out in that Practice Note.

ANNEX I (1)

REQUEST FOR DISMISSAL OF AN APPEAL

PLEASE NOTE: SECTION A IS TO BE COMPLETED WHERE THERE IS NO RESPONDENT'S NOTICE AND THE APPEAL IS BEING DISMISSED

PRACTICE DIRECTION FOR THE COURT OF APPEAL (CIVIL DIVISION)

WITH COSTS; IN THAT CASE, ONLY THE APPELLANT'S SOLICITOR (OR THE APPELLANT, IF ACTING IN PERSON) NEED SIGN.

IN ALL OTHER CASES SECTION B MUST BE COMPLETED AND IT MUST BE SIGNED BY THE SOLICITORS FOR ALL PARTIES (AND BY ANY PARTY ACTING IN PERSON).

IN THE COURT OF APPEAL   Appeal No.

ON APPEAL FROM

BETWEEN:

Claimant
(Plaintiff)/Appellant
Petitioner/Respondent

and

Defendant/Appellant
Respondent/Respondent

Section A

WE, the solicitors* for the above-named Appellant, who is of full legal capacity, REQUEST the dismissal of the appeal in the above matter with costs.

DATED this   day of   19

(Signed) _____
*(Solicitor for Appellant)

Section B

WE, the solicitors* for the above-named Respondent and Appellant, who are of full legal capacity, REQUEST the dismissal of the appeal [and respondent's notice]† in the above matter with no order as to costs [or specify other costs order required].

DATED this   day of   19

(Signed) _____
*(Solicitor for Appellant)
(Signed) _____
*(Solicitor for Respondent)

* If any party is acting in person, please modify the wording as appropriate.
† Delete where not applicable.

ANNEX I (2)

GENERAL FORM OF REQUEST FOR DISMISSAL OF AN APPLICATION

PLEASE NOTE: SECTION A IS TO BE COMPLETED WHERE THE APPLICATION IS BEING DISMISSED WITH COSTS; IN THAT CASE, ONLY THE APPLICANT'S SOLICITOR (OR THE APPLICANT, IF ACTING IN PERSON) NEED SIGN.

IN ALL OTHER CASES SECTION B MUST BE COMPLETED AND IT MUST BE SIGNED BY THE SOLICITORS FOR ALL PARTIES (AND BY ANY PARTY ACTING IN PERSON).

IN THE COURT OF APPEAL   Application No.

ON APPEAL FROM

BETWEEN:

Claimant

PRACTICE DIRECTION FOR THE COURT OF APPEAL (CIVIL DIVISION)

(Plaintiff)/Appellant
Petitioner/Respondent

and

Defendant/Applicant
Respondent/Respondent

Section A

WE, the solicitors* for the above-named Appellant, who is of full legal capacity, REQUEST the dismissal of the appeal in the above matter with costs.

DATED this   day of   19

(Signed) _____
*(Solicitor for Applicant)

Section B

WE, the solicitors* for the above-named Respondent and Appellant, who are of full legal capacity, REQUEST the dismissal the application in the above matter with no order as to costs [*or specify other costs order required*].

DATED this   day of   19

(Signed) _____
*(Solicitor for Applicant)

(Signed) _____
*(Solicitor for Respondent)

* If any party is acting in person, please modify the wording as appropriate.

ANNEX I (3)

REQUEST FOR A DISMISSAL OF AN APPLICATION WHICH HAS NOT BEEN SERVED ON ANY OTHER PARTY

THIS FORM IS FOR USE ONLY FOR AN APPLICATION WHICH HAS *NOT* BEEN SERVED ON ANY OTHER PARTY

IN THE COURT OF APPEAL   Application No.

ON APPEAL FROM

BETWEEN:

Claimant
(Plaintiff)/Applicant
Petitioner/Respondent

and

Defendant/Applicant

WE, the solicitors* for the above-named Applicant, who is of full legal capacity,

(1) CERTIFY that the application in the above matter has not been served on any other party and

(2) REQUEST the dismissal of the said application with no order for costs.

DATED this   day of   19

(Signed) _____
*(Solicitor for Applicant)

* If any party is acting in person, please modify the wording as appropriate.

PRACTICE DIRECTION — INSOLVENCY PROCEEDINGS

PART ONE

1. GENERAL
   1.1 In this Practice Direction:
   (1) 'The ACT' means the Insolvency Act 1986;
   (2) 'The Insolvency Rules' means the rules for the time being in force and made under s. 411 and s. 412 of the Act in relation to insolvency proceedings;
   (3) 'CPR' means the Civil Procedure Rules and 'CPR' followed by a Part or rule by number means the Part or rule with that number in those Rules;
   (4) 'RSC' followed by an Order by number means the Order with that number set out in Schedule 1 to the CPR;
   (5) 'Insolvency proceedings' means any proceedings under the Act, the Insolvency Rules, the Administration of Insolvent Estates of Deceased Persons Order 1986 (SI 1986 No. 1999), the Insolvent Partnerships Order 1986 (SI 1986 No. 2124) or the Insolvent Partnerships Order 1994 (SI 1994 No. 2421).
   1.2 This Practice Direction shall come into effect on 26th April 1999 and shall replace all previous Practice Notes and Practice Directions relating to insolvency proceedings.
   1.3 Except where the Insolvency Rules otherwise provide, service of documents in insolvency proceedings in the High Court will be the responsibility of the parties and will not be undertaken by the court.
   1.4 Where CPR Part 2.4 provides for the court to perform any act, that act may be performed by a Registrar in Bankruptcy for the purpose of insolvency proceedings in the High Court.
   1.5 A writ of execution to enforce any order made in insolvency proceedings in the High Court may be issued on the authority of a Registrar.

PART TWO COMPANIES

2. ADVERTISEMENT OF WINDING-UP PETITION
   2.1 Insolvency Rule 4.11(2)(b) is mandatory, and designed to ensure that the class remedy of winding up by the court is made available to all creditors, and is not used as a means of putting pressure on the company to pay the petitioner's debt. Failure to comply with the rule, without good reason accepted by the court, may lead to the summary dismissal of the petition on the return date (Insolvency Rule 4.11(5)). If the court, in its discretion, grants an adjournment, this will be on condition that the petition is advertised in due time for the adjourned hearing. No further adjournment for the purpose of advertisement will normally be granted.
   2.2 Copies of every advertisement published in connection with a winding-up petition must be lodged with the Court as soon as possible after publication and in any event not later than the day specified in Insolvency Rule 4.14 of the Insolvency Rules 1986. This direction applies even if the advertisement is defective in any way (e.g. is published at a date not in accordance with the Insolvency Rules, or omits or misprints some important words) or if the petitioner decides not to pursue the petition (e.g. on receiving payment).

3. CERTIFICATE OF COMPLIANCE — TIME FOR FILING
   3.1 In the High Court in order to assist practitioners and the Court the time laid down by Insolvency Rule 4.14 of the Insolvency Rules 1986, for filing a certificate of compliance and a copy of the advertisement, is hereby extended to not later than 4.30 p.m. on the Friday preceding the day on which the petition is to be heard. Applications to file the certificate and the copy advertisement after 4.30 p.m. on the Friday will only be allowed if some good reason is shown for the delay.

4. ERRORS IN PETITIONS

4.1 Applications for leave to amend errors in petitions which are discovered subsequent to a winding-up order being made should be made to the Court Manager in the High Court and to the District Judge in the county court.

4.2 Where the error is an error in the name of the company, the Court Manager in the High Court and the District Judge in the county court may make any necessary amendments to ensure that the winding-up order is drawn with the correct name of the company inserted. If there is any doubt, e.g. where there might be another company in existence which could be confused with the company to be wound up, the Court Manager will refer the application to the Registrar and the District Judge may refer it to the Judge.

4.3 Where an error is an error in the registered office of the company and any director or member of the company claims that the company was unaware of the petition by reason of it having been served at the wrong registered office, it will be open to them to apply to rescind the winding-up order in the usual way.

4.4 Where it is discovered that the company had been struck off the Register of Companies prior to the winding-up order being made, the matter must be restored to the list before the order is entered to enable an order for the restoration of the name to be made as well as the order to wind up.

5. DISTRIBUTION OF BUSINESS

5.1 The following applications shall be made direct to the Judge and, unless otherwise ordered, shall be heard in public:

(1) Applications to commit any person to prison for contempt;

(2) Applications for urgent interim relief (e.g. applications pursuant to s. 127 of the Act prior to any winding-up order being made);

(3) Applications to restrain the presentation or advertisement of a petition to wind up; or

(4) Applications for the appointment of a provisional liquidator;

(5) Petitions for administration orders or an interim order upon such a Petition;

(6) Applications after an administration order has been made pursuant to s. 14(3) of the Act (for directions) or s. 18(3) of the Act (to vary or discharge the order);

(7) Petitions to discharge administration orders and to wind up;

(8) Applications pursuant to s. 5(3) of the Act (to stay a winding up or discharge an administration order or for directions) where a voluntary arrangement has been approved;

(9) Appeals from a decision made by a County Court or by a Registrar of the High Court.

5.2 Subject to paragraph 5.4 below all other applications shall be made to the Registrar or the District Judge in the first instance who may give any necessary directions and may, in the exercise of his discretion, either hear and determine it himself or refer it to the Judge.

5.3 The following matters will also be heard in public:

(1) Petitions to wind up;

(2) Public examinations;

(3) All matters and applications heard by the Judge, except those referred by the Registrar or the District Judge to be heard in private or so directed by the Judge to be heard.

5.4 In accordance with directions given by the Lord Chancellor the Registrar has authorised certain applications in the High Court to be dealt with by the Court Manager of the Companies Court, pursuant to Insolvency Rule 13.2(2). The applications are:

(1) To extend or abridge time prescribed by the Insolvency Rules in connection with winding up (Insolvency Rules 4.3 and 12.9);

(2) For substituted service of winding-up petitions (Insolvency Rule 4.8(6));

(3) To withdraw petitions (Insolvency Rule 4.15);

(4) For the substitution of a petitioner (Insolvency Rule 4.19);

(5) By the Official Receiver for limited disclosure of a statement of affairs (Insolvency Rule 4.35);

(6) By the Official Receiver for relief from duties imposed upon him by the rules (Insolvency Rule 4.47);

(7) By the Official Receiver for permission to give notice of a meeting by advertisement only (Insolvency Rule 4.59);

(8) To transfer proceedings from the High Court to a County Court (Insolvency Rule 7.11);

(9) For permission to amend any originating application.

[N.B. In District Registries all such applications must be made to the District Judge.]

6. DRAWING UP OF ORDERS

6.1 The Court will draw up all orders except orders on the application of the Official Receiver or for which the Treasury Solicitor is responsible under the existing practice.

7. RESCISSION OF A WINDING-UP ORDER

7.1 Any application for the rescission of a winding-up order shall be made within seven days after the date on which the order was made (Insolvency Rule 7.47(4)). Notice of any such application must be given to the Official Receiver.

7.2 Applications will only be entertained if made (a) by a creditor, or (b) by a contributory, or (c) by the company jointly with a creditor or with a contributory. The application must be supported by written evidence of assets and liabilities.

7.3 In the case of an unsuccessful application the costs of the petitioning creditor, the supporting creditors and of the Official Receiver will normally be ordered to be paid by the creditor or the contributory making or joining in the application. The reason for this is that if the costs of an unsuccessful application are made payable by the company, they fall unfairly on the general body of creditors.

7.4 Cases in which the making of the winding-up order has not been opposed may, if the application is made promptly, be dealt with on a statement by the applicant's legal representative of the circumstances; but apart from such cases, the court will normally require any application to be supported by written evidence.

7.5 There is no need to issue a form of application (Form 7.2) as the petition is restored before the Court.

8. RESTRAINT OF PRESENTATION OF A WINDING-UP PETITION

8.1 An application to restrain presentation of a winding-up petition must be made to the Judge by the issue of an Originating Application (Form 7.1).

PART THREE PERSONAL INSOLVENCY — BANKRUPTCY

9. DISTRIBUTION OF BUSINESS

9.1 The following applications shall be made direct to the Judge and unless otherwise ordered shall be heard in public:

(1) Applications for the committal of any person to prison for contempt;

(2) Application for injunctions or for the modification or discharge of injunctions;

(3) Applications for interlocutory relief or directions after the matter has been referred to the Judge.

9.2 All other applications shall be made to the Registrar or the District Judge in the first instance. He shall give any necessary directions and may, if the application is within his jurisdiction to determine, in his discretion either hear and determine it himself or refer it to the Judge.

9.3 The following matters shall be heard in public:

(1) The public examination of debtors;

(2) Opposed applications for discharge or for the suspension or lifting of the suspension of discharge;

(3) Opposed applications for permission to be a director;

(4) In any case where the petition was presented or the receiving order or order for adjudication was made before the appointed day, those matters and applications specified in Rule 8 of the Bankruptcy Rules 1952;

(5) All matters and applications heard by the Judge, except matters and applications referred by the Registrar or the District Judge to be heard by the Judge in private or directed by the Judge to be so heard.

9.4 All petitions presented will be listed under the name of the debtor.

9.5 In accordance with Directions given by the Lord Chancellor the Registrar has authorised certain applications in the High Court to be dealt with by the Court Manager of the Bankruptcy Court pursuant to Insolvency Rule 13.2(2). The applications are:

(1) by petitioning creditors: to extend time for hearing petitions (s. 376 of the Act).

(2) by the Official Receiver:

(a) To transfer proceedings from the High Court to a County Court (Insolvency Rule 7.13);

(b) to amend the full title of the proceedings (Insolvency Rules 6.35 and 6.47).

[NB In District Registries all such applications must be made to the District Judge]

10. SERVICE ABROAD OF STATUTORY DEMAND

10.1 A statutory demand is not a document issued by the Court. Leave to serve out of the jurisdiction is not, therefore, required.

10.2 Insolvency Rule 6.3(2) ('Requirements as to service') applies to service of the statutory demand whether outside or within the jurisdiction.

10.3 A creditor wishing to serve a statutory demand outside the jurisdiction in a foreign country with which a civil procedure convention has been made (including the Hague Convention) may and, if the assistance of a British Consul is desired, must adopt the procedure prescribed by RSC Order 11 Rule 6. In the case of any doubt whether the country is a 'convention country', enquiries should be made of the Queen's Bench Masters' Secretary Department, Room E216, Royal Courts of Justice.

10.4 In all other cases, service of the demand must be effected by private arrangement in accordance with Insolvency Rule 6.3(2) and local foreign law.

10.5 When a statutory demand is to be served out of the jurisdiction, the time limits of 21 days and 18 days respectively referred to in the demand must be amended. For this purpose reference should be made to the table set out in the practice direction supplementing RSC Order 11 in Schedule 1 to the CPR.

10.6 A creditor should amend the statutory demand as follows:

(1) For any reference to 18 days there must be substituted the appropriate number of days set out in the table plus 4 days, and

(2) for any reference to 21 days must be substituted the appropriate number of days in the table plus 7 days.

Attention is drawn to the fact that in all forms of the statutory demand the figure 18 and the figure 21 occurs in more than one place.

11. SUBSTITUTED SERVICE

STATUTORY DEMANDS

11.1 The creditor is under an obligation to do all that is reasonable to bring the statutory demand to the debtor's attention and, if practicable, to cause personal service to be effected. Where it is not possible to effect prompt personal service, service may be effected by other means such as first class post or by insertion through a letter box.

11.2 Advertisement can only be used as a means of substituted service where:

(1) The demand is based on a judgment or order of any Court;

(2) The debtor has absconded or is keeping out of the way with a view to avoiding service and,

(3) There is no real prospect of the sum due being recovered by execution or other process.

PRACTICE DIRECTION — INSOLVENCY PROCEEDINGS

As there is no statutory form of advertisement, the Court will accept an advertisement in the following form:

STATUTORY DEMAND

(Debt for liquidated sum payable immediately following a judgment or order of the Court)

_____

To (Block letters)

of

TAKE NOTICE that a statutory demand has been issued by:

Name of Creditor:

Address:

The creditor demands payment of £   the amount now due on a judgment
or order of the (High Court of Justice   Division)(............. County
Court) dated the   day of 199   .

The statutory demand is an important document and it is deemed to have been served on you on the date of the first appearance of this advertisement. You must deal with this demand within 21 days of the service upon you or you could be made bankrupt and your property and goods taken away from you. If you are in any doubt as to your position, you should seek advice immediately from a solicitor or your nearest Citizens' Advice Bureau. The statutory demand can be obtained or is available for inspection and collection from:

Name:

Address:

(Solicitor for) the Creditor

Tel. No.   Reference:

<u>You have only 21 days from the date of the first appearance of this advertisement before the creditor may present a Bankruptcy Petition. You have only 18 days from that date within which to apply to the Court to set aside the demand.</u>

  11.3 In all cases where substituted service is effected, the creditor must have taken all those steps which would justify the Court making an order for substituted service of a petition. The steps to be taken to obtain an order for substituted service of a petition are set out below. Failure to comply with these requirements may result in the Court declining to file the petition: Insolvency Rule 6.11(9).

PETITIONS
  11.4 In most cases, evidence of the following steps will suffice to justify an order for substituted service:
    (1) One personal call at the residence and place of business of the debtor where both are known or at either of such places as is known. Where it is known that the debtor has more than one residential or business address, personal calls should be made at all the addresses.
    (2) Should the creditor fail to effect service, a first class prepaid letter should be written to the debtor referring to the call(s), the purpose of the same and the failure to meet with the debtor, adding that a further call will be made for the same purpose on the   day of 19   at   hours at   (place). At least two business days notice should be given of the appointment and copies of the letter sent to all known addresses of the debtor. The appointment letter should also state that
        (a) in the event of the time and place not being convenient, the debtor is to name some other time and place reasonably convenient for the purpose;

(b) (Statutory Demands) if the debtor fails to keep the appointment the creditor proposes to serve the debtor by [advertisement] [post] [insertion through a letter box] or as the case may be, and that, in the event of a bankruptcy petition being presented, the Court will be asked to treat such service as service of the demand on the debtor;

(c) (Petitions) if the debtor fails to keep the appointment, application will be made to the Court for an order for substituted service either by advertisement, or in such other manner as the Court may think fit.

(3) In attending any appointment made by letter, inquiry should be made as to whether the debtor has received all letters left for him. If the debtor is away, inquiry should also be made as to whether or not letters are being forwarded to an address within the jurisdiction (England and Wales) or elsewhere.

(4) If the debtor is represented by a Solicitor, an attempt should be made to arrange an appointment for personal service through such Solicitor. The Insolvency Rules enable a Solicitor to accept service of a statutory demand on behalf of his client but there is no similar provision in respect of service of a bankruptcy petition.

(5) The written evidence filed pursuant to Insolvency Rule 6.11 should deal with all the above matters including all relevant facts as to the debtor's whereabouts and whether the appointment letter(s) have been returned.

11.5 Where the Court makes an order for service by first class ordinary post, the order will normally provide that service be deemed to be effected on the seventh day after posting. The same method of calculating service may be applied to calculating the date of service of a statutory demand.

12. SETTING ASIDE A STATUTORY DEMAND

12.1 The application (Form 6.4) and written evidence in support (Form 6.5) exhibiting a copy of the statutory demand must be filed in Court within 18 days of service of the statutory demand on the debtor. Where service is effected by advertisement in a newspaper the period of 18 days is calculated from the date of the first appearance of the advertisement. Three copies of each document must be lodged with the application to enable the Court to serve notice of the hearing date on the applicant, the creditor and the person named in Part B of the statutory demand.

12.2 Where, to avoid expense, copies of the documents are not lodged with the application in the High Court, any order of the Registrar fixing a venue is conditional upon copies of the documents being lodged on the next business day after the Registrar's order otherwise the application will be deemed to have been dismissed.

12.3 Where the statutory demand is based on a judgment or order, the Court will not at this stage go behind the judgment or order and inquire into the validity of the debt nor, as a general rule, will it adjourn the application to await the result of an application to set aside the judgment or order.

12.4 Where the debtor (a) claims to have a counterclaim, set off or cross demand (whether or not he could have raised it in the action in which the judgment or order was obtained) which equals or exceeds the amount of the debt or debts specified in the statutory demand or (b) disputes the debt (not being a debt subject to a judgment or order) the Court will normally set aside the statutory demand if, in its opinion, on the evidence there is a genuine triable issue.

12.5 A debtor who wishes to apply to set aside a statutory demand after the expiration of 18 days from the date of service of the statutory demand must apply for an extension of time within which to apply. If the applicant wishes to apply for an injunction to restrain presentation of a petition the application must be made to the Judge. Paragraphs 1 and 2 of Form 6.5 (Affidavit in Support of Application to set Aside Statutory Demand) should be used in support of the application for an extension of time with the following additional paragraphs:

'3. That to the best of my knowledge and belief the creditor(s) named in the demand has/have not presented a petition against me.

4. That the reasons for my failure to apply to set aside the demand within 18 days after service are as follows: . . .'

If application is made to restrain presentation of a bankruptcy petition the following additional paragraph should be added:

'5. Unless restrained by injunction the creditor(s) may present a bankruptcy petition against me.'

13. PROOF OF SERVICE OF A STATUTORY DEMAND

13.1 Insolvency Rule 6.11(3) provides that, if the Statutory Demand has been served personally, the written evidence must be provided by the person who effected that service. Insolvency Rule 6.11(4) provides that, if service of the demand (however effected) has been acknowledged in writing, the evidence of service must be provided by the creditor or by a person acting on his behalf. Insolvency Rule 6.11(5) provides that, if neither paragraphs (3) or (4) apply, the written evidence must be provided by a person having direct knowledge of the means adopted for serving the demand.

13.2 Form 6.11 (Evidence of personal service of the statutory demand): this form should only be used where the demand has been served personally and acknowledged in writing (see Insolvency Rule 6.11(4)). If the demand has not been acknowledged in writing, the written evidence should be provided by the Process Server and Paragraphs 2 and 3 (part of Form 6.11) should be omitted (see Insolvency Rule 6.11(3)).

13.3 Form 6.12 (Evidence of Substituted Service of the Statutory Demand): this form can be used whether or not service of the demand has been acknowledged in writing. Paragraphs 4 and 5 (part) provide for the alternatives. Practitioners are reminded, however, that the appropriate person to provide the written evidence may not be the same in both cases. If the demand has been acknowledged in writing, the appropriate person is the creditor or a person acting on his behalf. If the demand has not been acknowledged, that person must be someone having direct knowledge of the means adopted for serving the demand.

Practitioners may find it more convenient to allow process servers to carry out the necessary investigation whilst reserving to themselves the service of the demand. In these circumstances Paragraph 1 should be deleted and the following paragraph substituted:

'1. Attempts have been made to serve the demand, full details of which are set out in the accompanying affidavit of . . .'.

13.4 'Written evidence' means an affidavit or a witness statement.

14. EXTENSION OF HEARING DATE OF PETITION

14.1 Late applications for extension of hearing dates under Insolvency Rule 6.28, and failure to attend on the listed hearing of a petition, will be dealt with as follows:

(1) If an application is submitted less than two clear working days before the hearing date (for example, later than Monday for Thursday, or Wednesday for Monday) the costs of the application will not be allowed under Insolvency Rule 6.28(3).

(2) If the petition has not been served and no extension has been granted by the time fixed for the hearing of the petition, and if no one attends for the hearing, the petition will be re-listed for hearing about 21 days later. The Court will notify the petitioning creditor's solicitors (or the petitioning creditor in person), and any known supporting or opposing creditors or their solicitors, of the new date and times. Written evidence should then be filed on behalf of the petitioning creditor explaining fully the reasons for the failure to apply for an extension or to appear at the hearing, and (if appropriate) giving reasons why the petition should not be dismissed.

(3) On the re-listed hearing the Court may dismiss the petition if not satisfied it should be adjourned or a further extension granted.

14.2 All applications for extension should include a statement of the date fixed for the hearing of the petition.

14.3 The petitioning creditor should attend (by solicitors or in person) on or before the hearing date to ascertain whether the application has reached the file and been dealt with. It should not be assumed that an extension will be granted.

15. BANKRUPTCY PETITION

To help in the completion of the form of a creditor's bankruptcy petition, attention is drawn to the following points:

15.1 The petition does not require dating, signing or witnessing.

15.2 In the title it is only necessary to recite the debtor's name e.g. Re John William Smith or Re J W Smith (Male). Any alias or trading name will appear in the body of the petition. This also applies to all other statutory forms other than those which require the 'full title'.

15.3 Where the petition is based on a statutory demand, only the debt claimed in the demand may be included in the petition.

15.4 In completing Paragraph 2 of the petition, attention is drawn to Insolvency Rule 6.8(1)(a) to (c), particularly where the 'aggregate sum' is made up of a number of debts.

15.5 Date of service of the statutory demand (paragraph 4 of the petition):

(1) In the case of personal service, the date of service as set out in the affidavit of service should be recited and whether service is effected *before/after* 1700 hours on Monday to Friday or at any time on a Saturday or a Sunday: see CPR Part 6.7(2) and (3).

(2) In the case of substituted service (otherwise than by advertisement), the date alleged in the affidavit of service should be recited: see '11. Substituted Service' above.

(3) In the strictly limited case of service by advertisement under Insolvency Rule 6.3, the date to be alleged is the date of the advertisement's appearance or, as the case may be, its first appearance: see Insolvency Rules 6.3(3) and 6.11(8).

15.6 There is no need to include in the petition details of the person authorised to present it.

15.7 Certificates at the end of the petition:

(1) The period of search for prior petitions has been reduced to eighteen months.

(2) Where a statutory demand is based wholly or in part on a County Court judgment, the following certificate is to be added:

'I/We certify that on the   day of   19   I/We attended on the County Court and was/were informed by an officer of the Court that no money had been paid into Court in the action or matter

           v   Claim No   pursuant to the statutory demand.'

This certificate will not be required when the demand also requires payment of a separate debt, not based on a County Court judgment, the amount of which exceeds the bankruptcy level (at present £750).

15.8 Deposit on petition: the deposit will be taken by the Court and forwarded to the Official Receiver. In the High Court, the petition fee and deposit should be handed to the Supreme Court Accounts Office, Fee Stamping Room, who will record the receipt and will impress two entries on the original petition, one in respect of the Court fee and the other in respect of the deposit. In the County Court, the petition fee and deposit should be handed to the duly authorised officer of the Court's staff who will record its receipt.

In all cases cheque(s) for the whole amount should be made payable to 'HM Paymaster General'.

15.9 On the hearing of a petition for a bankruptcy order, in order to satisfy the Court that the debt on which the petition is founded has not been paid or secured or compounded the Court will normally accept as sufficient a certificate signed by the person representing the petitioning creditor in the following form:

'I certify that I have/my firm has made enquiries of the petitioning creditor(s) within the last business day prior to the hearing/adjourned hearing and to the best of my knowledge and belief the debt on which the petition is founded is still due and owing and has not been paid or secured or compounded save as to .... Signed .... Dated ....

For convenience in the High Court this certificate will be incorporated in the attendance slip, which will be filed after the hearing. A fresh certificate will be required on each adjourned hearing.

16. ORDERS WITHOUT ATTENDANCE

16.1 In suitable cases the Court will normally be prepared to make orders under Part VIII of the Act (Individual Voluntary Arrangements), without the attendance of either party, provided there is no bankruptcy order in existence and (so far as is known) no pending petition. The orders are:

(1) A fourteen day interim order with the application adjourned 14 days for consideration of the nominee's report, where the papers are in order, and the nominee's signed consent to act includes a waiver of notice of the application or a consent by the nominee to the making of an interim order without attendance.

(2) A standard order on consideration of the nominee's report, extending the interim order to a date 7 weeks after the date of the proposed meeting, directing the meeting to be summoned and adjourning to a date about 3 weeks after the meeting. Such an Order may be made without attendance if the nominee's report has been delivered to the Court and complies with Section 256(1) of the Act and Insolvency Rule 5.10(2) and (3) and proposes a date for the meeting not less than 14 days from that on which the nominee's report is filed in Court under Insolvency Rule 5.10 nor more than 28 days from that on which that report is considered by the Court under Insolvency Rule 5.12.

(3) A 'concertina' Order, combining orders as under (1) and (2) above. Such an order may be made without attendance if the initial application for an interim order is accompanied by a report of the nominee and the conditions set out in (1) and (2) above are satisfied.

(4) A final order on consideration of the Chairman's report. Such an order may be made without attendance if the Chairman's report has been filed and complies with Insolvency Rule 5.22(1). The order will record the effect of the Chairman's report and may discharge the interim order.

16.2 Provided that the conditions as under 16.1(2) and (4) above are satisfied and that the appropriate report has been lodged with the Court in due time the parties need not attend or be represented on the adjourned hearing for consideration of the Nominee's report or of the Chairman's report (as the case may be) unless they are notified by the Court that attendance is required. Sealed copies of the order made (in all four cases as above) will be posted by the Court to the applicant or his Solicitor and to the Nominee.

16.3 In suitable cases the Court may also make consent orders without attendance by the parties. The written consent of the parties will be required. Examples of such orders are as follows:

(1) On applications to set aside a statutory demand, orders:

(a) dismissing the application, with or without an order for costs as may be agreed (permission will be given to present a petition on or after the seventh day after the date of the order, unless a different date is agreed);

(b) setting aside the demand, with or without an order for costs as may be agreed; or

(c) giving permission to withdraw the application with or without an order for costs as may be agreed.

(2) On petitions: where there is a list of supporting or opposing creditors in Form 6.21, or a statement signed by or on behalf of the petitioning creditor that no notices have been received from supporting or opposing creditors, orders:

(a) dismissing the petition, with or without an order for costs as may be agreed, or

(b) if the petition has not been served, giving permission to withdraw the petition (with no order for costs).

(3) On other applications, orders:

(a) for sale of property, possession of property, disposal of proceeds of sale

(b) giving interim directions

(c) dismissing the application, with or without an order for costs as may be agreed

(d) giving permission to withdraw the application, with or without an order for costs as may be agreed.

PRACTICE DIRECTION — INSOLVENCY PROCEEDINGS

If, (as may often be the case with orders under sub-paragraphs (3)(a) or (b) above) an adjournment is required, whether generally with liberty to restore or to a fixed date, the order by consent may include an order for the adjournment. If adjournment to a date is requested, a time estimate should be given and the Court will fix the first available date and time on or after the date requested.

16.4 The above lists should not be regarded as exhaustive, nor should it be assumed that an order will be made without attendance as requested.

16.5 The procedure outlined above is designed to save time and costs but is not intended to discourage attendance.

16.6 Applications for consent orders without attendance should be lodged at least two clear working days (and preferably longer) before any fixed hearing date.

16.7 Whenever a document is lodged or a letter sent, the correct case number, code (if any) and year (for example 123/SD/99 or 234/99) should be quoted. A note should also be given of the date and time of the next hearing (if any).

16.8 Attention is drawn to Paragraph 4.4(3) of the Practice Direction relating to CPR Part 44.

PART 4 APPEALS

17. APPEALS

17.1 An appeal from a decision made in a County Court by a Circuit or District Judge or in the High Court by a Registrar in Bankruptcy lies without leave to a Single Judge of the High Court ('Single Judge'): Section 375(2) of the Act and Insolvency Rule 7.48(2).

17.2 Such appeals are set down and heard as follows:

(1) An appeal from the decision of the Registrar in Bankruptcy shall, or from any decision made in any County Court may, be set down and heard in London by a High Court Judge of the Chancery Division or by a person authorised to sit in that capacity.

(2) An appeal from a decision made in a County Court exercising jurisdiction over an area within the Northern and North Eastern Circuits may be set down in Manchester for hearing in Leeds, Liverpool, Manchester, Preston or Newcastle upon Tyne by a High Court Judge of the Chancery Division or a person authorised to sit in that capacity.

(3) An appeal from a decision made in the County Court exercising jurisdiction over an area within the Birmingham, Bristol or Cardiff Chancery District Registries may be set down in the Registry appropriate to the area in which the decision was made for hearing in Birmingham, Bristol or Cardiff by a High Court Judge or a person authorised to sit in that capacity.

17.3 The procedure and practice of the Supreme Court relating to appeals to the Court of Appeal (RSC Order 59) apply to appeals in insolvency proceedings: Insolvency Rule 7.49(1).

17.4 In relation to any appeal under s. 375(2) of the Act to a Single Judge of the Chancery Division of the High Court any reference to the Court of Appeal in the CPR is replaced by reference to that Judge and any reference to the Registrar of Civil Appeals is replaced by a reference to a Bankruptcy Registrar who deals with insolvency appeals referred to below as the Registrar of Bankruptcy Appeals: Insolvency Rule 7.49(2).

17.5 The following applications shall be made to the Single Judge:
 (1) for injunctions pending a substantive hearing of the appeal;
 (2) by way of appeal from the Registrar of Bankruptcy Appeals;
 (3) for expedition or vacation of the hearing date of an appeal;
 (4) for permission to issue a witness summons on an appeal;
 (5) any application that may be dealt with or referred to the Single Judge by the Registrar of Bankruptcy Appeals.

17.6 The following applications may be made to a Bankruptcy Registrar who deals with Insolvency Proceedings (the Registrar of Bankruptcy Appeals):
 (a) for extension of time for serving a notice of appeal;
 (b) for extension of time for setting down a notice of appeal;

PRACTICE DIRECTION — INSOLVENCY PROCEEDINGS

(c) for extension of time for serving a respondent's notice;
(d) for permission to amend a notice of appeal or a respondent's notice;
(e) for security for costs of an appeal;
(f) for permission to adduce further evidence on appeal;
(g) for service of a notice of appeal or respondent's notice by substituted service.

17.7 A form of notice of appeal appropriate to Insolvency Appeals to the Single Judge is set out in *Atkin's Court Forms*, Volume 7, or may be obtained in London from the Fees Room, The Royal Courts of Justice or from the addresses set out in Paragraph 17.9(5) below.

17.8 Applications to the Registrar of Bankruptcy Appeals may be made on Bankruptcy Application Form 7.2 which may be obtained from the Fees Room, The Royal Courts of Justice, or from the addresses set out in Paragraph 17.9(5) below, and should be lodged at the address set out in Paragraph 17.9(5)(a) below.

17.9 The following practice applies to all appeals to a Single Judge of the High Court whether set down in London, or set down at one of the other venues referred to in Paragraph 17.2 above:

(1) a notice of appeal must be served not later than 28 days, such time to run:

(a) in the case of an appeal from an order made in the County Court from the date the order is made (RSC Order 59 rules 4 and 19);

(b) in the case of an appeal from an order made by a Registrar in Bankruptcy from the date on which the order is sealed or otherwise perfected (RSC Order 59 rule 4(1)).

(2) notice of appeal must be served on all parties to the proceedings below who are directly affected by the appeal. This will include the Circuit or the District Judge of the appropriate County Court and where a bankruptcy order has been made the Official Receiver.

(3) notice of appeal must be served by the appellant or by the legal representative of the appellant and may be effected by the following methods:

(a) by leaving the document at the proper address of the person to be served;
(b) by post;
(c) through a document exchange;
(d) if both appellant and respondent are represented by solicitors by fax or by other electronic method together with a hard copy posted to the party concerned on the same day as the fax or other electronic method is sent;
(e) by substituted service with leave of the Court.

(4) after service the appellant must set down the notice of appeal within seven days of the later of (i) the date on which service of the notice of appeal was effected or (ii) the date on which the judgment or order of the Court below was sealed or otherwise perfected, by lodging the documents listed below:

(a) two copies of the notice of appeal, one of which must be endorsed with a certificate of the date and method of service and stamped with the appropriate fee,
(b) a copy of the order under appeal, and
(c) the estimate of time for the hearing.

(5) the above documents may be lodged personally or by post at the address of the appropriate venue listed below:

(a) If the appeal is to be set down and heard in London the documents must be lodged at Room 110, Thomas More Building, The Royal Courts of Justice, Strand, London WC2A 2LL.

(b) If the appeal is to be set down in Manchester the documents must be lodged at the Chancery Section, Courts of Justice, Crown Square, Manchester M3 3FL.

(c) If the appeal is to be set down in Birmingham, the documents must be lodged at the Registry of the Chancery Division of the High Court, 33 Bull Street, Birmingham B4 6DS

PRACTICE DIRECTION — INSOLVENCY PROCEEDINGS

(d) If the appeal is to be set down in Bristol the documents must be lodged at the District Registry of the Chancery Division of the High Court, Third Floor, Greyfriars, Lewins Mead, Bristol BS1 2NR.

(e) If the appeal is to be set down in Cardiff the documents must be lodged at the District Registry in the Chancery Division of the High Court, First Floor, 2 Park Street, Cardiff CF1 1MR.

(6) If the documents are correct and in order the Court at which the documents are lodged will fix a hearing date and will also fix the place of hearing. That Court will send letters to all the parties to the appeal informing them of the date and place of hearing and indicating the time estimate given by the appellant. The parties will be invited to notify the Court of any alternative or revised time estimates. In the absence of any such notification the estimate of the appellant will be taken as agreed. The Court will also send to the appellant a document setting out the Courts requirement concerning the form and content of the bundle of documents for the use of the Single Judge. Such bundle of documents must be lodged by the appellant at the address of the appropriate venue as set out in subparagraph 17.9(5) above not later than 7 days before the date fixed for the hearing. Failure to do so may result in the appeal being dismissed by the Judge.

(7) Skeleton arguments, accompanied by a written chronology of events relevant to the appeal, should be lodged at the address of the appropriate venue as set out in sub-paragraph 17.9(5) above, at least two clear days before the date fixed for the hearing. Failure to lodge may result in an adverse costs order by the Single Judge on the hearing of the appeal.

(8) A notice of appeal and a respondent's notice may be amended:

(a) With the permission of the Registrar of Bankruptcy Appeals or of the Single Judge at any time;

(b) Without permission by supplementary notice served:

(1) in the case of a notice of appeal not later than five days after setting down the notice of appeal, and

(2) in the case of a respondent's notice not later than five days after setting down the respondent's notice.

After service two copies of the amended notice must be lodged at the address of the appropriate venue as set out in sub-paragraph 17.9(5) above, one copy endorsed with the date on which service was effected and stamped with the appropriate fee.

(9) Where an appellant does not wish to continue with the appeal or where the appeal has been settled, the appeal may be dismissed by consent on paper without a hearing. An order to that effect signed by each party or letters of consent from each party must be lodged not later than 24 hours before the date fixed for the hearing of the appeal at the address of the appropriate venue as set out in sub-paragraph 17.9(5) above and will be dealt with by the Single Judge.

17.10 An appeal from a decision made by the Single Judge lies to the Court of Appeal with the leave of that Judge or of the Court of Appeal (see Insolvency Rule 7.48(2)). Application for such leave to appeal should be made to the Single Judge at the conclusion of his judgment on the appeal. If a party fails to apply at that time he may apply to the Single Judge for permission. Such application together with draft intended grounds of appeal must be lodged at the address of the appropriate venue as set out in sub-paragraph 17.9(5) above within 28 days of the sealing of the Order made on the appeal. The application will first be considered by the Single Judge who heard the appeal who may refuse leave or give such directions as the Single Judge thinks fit for the disposal of the application. Any application made after the 28 day period has expired must be made direct to the Court of Appeal.

PRACTICE DIRECTION — DIRECTORS DISQUALIFICATION PROCEEDINGS

PART ONE

1. APPLICATION AND INTERPRETATION

1.1 In this practice direction:

(1) 'the Act' means the Company Directors Disqualification Act 1986;

(2) 'the Disqualification Rules' means the rules for the time being in force made under section 411 of the Insolvency Act 1986 in relation to disqualification proceedings[1];

(3) 'the Insolvency Rules' means the rules for the time being in force made under sections 411 and 412 of the Insolvency Act 1986 in relation to insolvency proceedings;

(4) 'CPR' means the Civil Procedure Rules 1998 and 'CPR' followed by 'Part' or 'Rule' and a number means the part or Rule with that number in those Rules;

(5) 'disqualification proceedings' has the meaning set out in paragraph 1.3 below;

(6) 'a disqualification application' is an application under the Act for the making of a disqualification order;

(7) 'registrar' means any judge of the High Court or the county court who is a registrar within the meaning of the Insolvency Rules;

(8) 'companies court registrar' means any judge of the High Court sitting in the Royal Courts of Justice in London who is a registrar within the meaning of the Insolvency Rules.

1.2 This practice direction shall come into effect on 26 April 1999 and shall replace all previous practice directions relating to disqualification proceedings.

1.3 This practice direction applies to the following proceedings ('disqualification proceedings'):

(1) disqualification applications made:

(a) under section 2(2)(a) of the Act (after the person's conviction of an indictable offence in connection with the affairs of a company);

(b) under section 3 of the Act (on the ground of persistent breaches of provisions of companies legislation);

(c) under section 4 of the Act (on the ground of fraud etc);

(d) by the Secretary of State or the official receiver under section 7(1) of the Act (on the ground of the person's unfitness to be concerned in the management of a company); or

(e) by the Secretary of State under section 8 of the Act (following a report made by inspectors or 'in consequence of information or documents obtained);

(2) any application made under section 7(2) or 7(4) of the Act; and

(3) any application made under sections 12(2) or 17 of the Act and any application for permission to act notwithstanding a disqualification order which was made under any statutory predecessor of the Act;

(4) any application for a court order made under CPR Part 23 in the course of any of the proceedings set out in sub-paragraphs (1) to (3) above.

2. MULTI-TRACK

2.1 All disqualification proceedings are allocated to the multi-track. The CPR relating to allocation questionnaires and track allocation shall not apply.

3. RIGHTS OF AUDIENCE

3.1 Official receivers and deputy official receivers have right of audience in any proceedings to which this Practice Direction applies, including cases where a

---

[1] The current rules are the Insolvent Companies (Disqualification of Unfit Directors) Proceedings Rules 1987.

disqualification application is made by the Secretary of State or by the official receiver at his direction, and whether made in the High Court or a county court[2].

PART TWO DISQUALIFICATION APPLICATIONS

4. COMMENCEMENT

4.1 A disqualification application must be commenced by a claim form issued:

(1) in the High Court out of the office of the companies court registrar or a chancery district registry; and

(2) in the county court, out of a county court office.

Sections 2(2)(a), 3(4), 4(2), 6(3) and 8(3) of the Act identify the courts which have jurisdiction to deal with disqualification applications.

4.2 Disqualification applications shall be made by the issue of a claim form in the form annexed hereto and the use of the procedure set out in CPR Part 8[3], subject to any modification of that procedure under this practice direction and (where the application is made under sections 7 or 8 of the Act) the Disqualification Rules[4]. CPR rule 8.1(3) (power of the Court to order the application to continue as if the claimant had not used the Part 8 Procedure) shall not apply.

4.3 When the claim form is issued, the claimant will be given a date for the first hearing of the disqualification application. This date is to be not less than eight weeks from the date of issue of the claim form[5]. The first hearing will be before a registrar.

5. HEADINGS

5.1 Every claim form by which an application under the Act is begun and all affidavits, notices and other documents in the proceedings must be entitled in the matter of the company or companies in question and in the matter of the Act. In the case of any disqualification application under section 7 of the Act it is not necessary to mention in the heading any company other than that referred to in section 6(1)(a).

6. THE CLAIM FORM

6.1 CPR Rule 8.2 does not apply. The claim form must state:

(1) that CPR Part 8 (as modified by this practice direction) applies, and (if the application is made under sections 7 or 8 of the Act) that the application is made in accordance with the Disqualification Rules[6];

(2) that the claimant seeks a disqualification order, and the section of the Act pursuant to which the disqualification application is made;

(3) the period for which, in accordance with the Act, the court has power to impose a disqualification period.

The periods are as follows:

(a) where the application is under section 2 of the Act, for a period of up to 15 years;

(b) where the application is under section 3 of the Act, for a period of up to 5 years;

(c) where the application is under section 4 of the Act, for a period of up to 15 years;

(d) where the application is under section 5 of the Act, for a period of up to 5 years;

---

[2] Rule 10 of the Insolvent Companies (Disqualification of Unfit Directors) Proceedings Rules 1987.

[3] Rule 2(2) of the Insolvent Companies (Disqualification of Unfit Directors) Proceedings Rules 1987 as amended.

[4] For convenience, relevant references to the Insolvency Companies (Disqualification of Unfit Directors) Proceedings Rules 1987, which apply to disqualification applications under sections 7 and 8 of the Act (see rule 1(3)(a) and (b)) are set out in footnotes to this Practice Direction.

[5] Rule 7(1) of the Insolvent Companies (Disqualification of Unfit Directors) Proceedings Rules 1987.

[6] Rule 4(a) of the Insolvent Companies (Disqualification of Unfit Directors) Proceedings Rules 1987.

(e) where the application is under section 7 of the Act, for a period of not less than 2, and up to 15, years[7];

(f) where the application is under section 8 of the Act, for a period of up to 15 years[8].

(4) in cases where the application is made under sections 7 or 8 of the Act, that on the first hearing of the application, the court may hear and determine it summarily, without further or other notice to the defendant, and that, if the application is so determined, the court may impose a period of disqualification of up to 5 years but that if at the hearing of the application the court, on the evidence then before it, is minded to impose, in the case of any defendant, disqualification for any period longer than 5 years, it will not make a disqualification order on that occasion but will adjourn the application to be heard (with further evidence, if any) at a later date that will be notified to the defendant[9];

(5) that any evidence which the defendant wishes the court to take into consideration must be filed in court in accordance with the time limits set out in paragraph 9 below (which time limits shall be set out in the notes to the Claim Form)[10].

7. SERVICE OF THE CLAIM FORM

7.1 Service of claim forms in disqualification proceedings will be the responsibility of the parties and will not be undertaken by the court.

7.2 The claim form shall be served by the claimant on the defendant. It may be served by sending it by first class post to his last known address; and the date of service shall, unless the contrary is shown, be deemed to be the 7th day following that on which the claim form was posted[11]. CPR r. 6.7(1) shall be modified accordingly. Otherwise CPR Part 6 applies.

7.3 Where any claim form or order of the court or other document is required under any disqualification proceedings to be served on any person who is not in England and Wales, the court may order service on him to be effected within such time and in such manner as it thinks fit, may require such proof of service as it thinks fit[12], and may give such directions as to acknowledgment of service as it thinks fit.

7.4 The claim form served on the defendant shall be accompanied by an acknowledgment of service.

8. ACKNOWLEDGMENT OF SERVICE

8.1 The form of acknowledgment of service is annexed to this practice direction. CPR rules 8.3(2) and 8.3(3)(a) do not apply to disqualification applications.

8.2 The form of acknowledgment of service shall state that the defendant should indicate[13]:

(1) whether he contests the application on the grounds that, in the case of any particular company:

(a) he was not a director or shadow director of that company at a time when conduct of his, or of other persons, in relation to that company is in question; or

---

[7] Rule 4(b)(i) of the Insolvent Companies (Disqualification of Unfit Directors) Proceedings Rules 1987.
[8] Rule 4(b)(ii) of the Insolvent Companies (Disqualification of Unfit Directors) Proceedings Rules 1987.
[9] Rule 4(c) and (d) of the Insolvent Companies (Disqualification of Unfit Directors) Proceedings Rules 1987.
[10] Rule 4(e) of the Insolvent Companies (Disqualification of Unfit Directors) Proceedings Rules 1987.
[11] Rule 5(1) of the Insolvent Companies (Disqualification of Unfit Directors) Proceedings Rules 1987.
[12] Rule 5(2) of the Insolvent Companies (Disqualification of Unfit Directors) Proceedings Rules 1987.
[13] Rule 5(4) of the Insolvent Companies (Disqualification of Unfit Directors) Proceedings Rules 1987.

(b) his conduct as director or shadow director of that company was not as alleged in support of the application for a disqualification order;

(2) whether, in the case of any conduct of his, he disputes the allegation that such conduct makes him unfit to be concerned in the management of a company; and

(3) whether he, while not resisting the application for a disqualification order, intends to adduce mitigating factors with a view to reducing the period of disqualification.

8.3 The defendant shall:

(1) (subject to paragraph 7.2 above) file an acknowledgment of service in the prescribed form not more than 14 days after service of the claim form; and

(2) serve the acknowledgment of service on the claimant and any other party.

8.4 Where the defendant has failed to file an acknowledgment of service and the time period for doing so has expired, the defendant may attend the hearing of the application but may not take part in the hearing unless the court gives permission.

9. EVIDENCE

9.1 Evidence in disqualification applications shall be by affidavit, except where the official receiver is a party, in which case his evidence may be in the form of a written report (with or without affidavits by other persons) which shall be treated as if it had been verified by affidavit by him and shall be prima facie evidence of any matter contained in it[14].

9.2 In the affidavits or (as the case may be) the official receiver's report in support of the application, there shall be included a statement of the matters by reference to which it is alleged that a disqualification order should be made against the defendant[15].

9.3 When the claim form is issued:

(1) the affidavit or report in support of the disqualification application must be filed in court;

(2) exhibits must be lodged with the court where they shall be retained until the conclusion of the proceedings; and

(3) copies of the affidavit/ report and exhibits shall be served with the claim form on the defendant[16].

9.4 The defendant shall, within 28 days from the date of service of the claim form[17]:

(1) file in court any affidavit evidence in opposition to the disqualification application that he or she wishes the court to take into consideration; and

(2) lodge the exhibits with the court where they shall be retained until the conclusion of the proceedings; and

(3) at the same time, serve upon the claimant a copy of the affidavits and exhibits.

9.5 In cases where there is more than one defendant, each defendant is required to serve his evidence on the other defendants unless the court otherwise orders.

9.6 The claimant shall, within 14 days from receiving the copy of the defendant's evidence[18]:

---

[14] Rule 3(2) of the Insolvent Companies (Disqualification of Unfit Directors) Proceedings Rules 1987. Section 441 of the Companies Act 1985 makes provision for the admissibility in legal proceedings of a certified copy of a report of inspectors appointed under Part XIV of the Companies Act 1985.

[15] Rule 3(3) of the Insolvent Companies (Disqualification of Unfit Directors) Proceedings Rules 1987.

[16] Rule 3(1) of the Insolvent Companies (Disqualification of Unfit Directors) Proceedings Rules 1987.

[17] Rule 6(1) of the Insolvent Companies (Disqualification of Unfit Directors) Proceedings Rules 1987.

[18] Rule 6(2) of the Insolvent Companies (Disqualification of Unfit Directors) Proceedings Rules 1987.

(1) file in court any further affidavit or report in reply he wishes the court to take into consideration; and

(2) lodge the exhibits with the court where they shall be retained until the conclusion of the proceedings; and

(3) at the same time serve a copy of the affidavits/reports and exhibits upon the defendant.

9.7 Prior to the first hearing of the disqualification application, the time for serving evidence may be extended by written agreement between the parties. After the first hearing, the extension of time for serving evidence is governed by CPR rules 2.11 and 29.5.

9.8 So far as is possible all evidence should be filed before the first hearing of the disqualification application.

10. THE FIRST HEARING OF THE DISQUALIFICATION APPLICATION

10.1 The date fixed for the hearing of the disqualification application shall be not less than 8 weeks from the date of issue of the claim form.[19]

10.2 The hearing shall in the first instance be before the registrar[20].

10.3 The registrar shall either determine the case on the date fixed or give directions and adjourn it[21].

10.4 All interim directions should insofar as possible be sought at the first hearing of the disqualification application so that the disqualification application can be determined at the earliest possible date. The parties should take all such steps as they respectively can to avoid successive directions hearings.

10.5 In the case of disqualification applications made under sections 7 or 8 of the Act, the registrar shall adjourn the case for further consideration if:

(1) he forms the provisional opinion that a disqualification order ought to be made, and that a period of disqualification longer than 5 years is appropriate[22], or

(2) he is of opinion that questions of law or fact arise which are not suitable for summary determination[23].

10.6 If the registrar adjourns the application for further consideration he shall:

(1) direct whether the application is to be heard by a registrar or by a judge[24]. This direction may at any time be varied by the court either on application or of its own initiative. If the court varies the direction in the absence of any of the parties, notice will be given to the parties;

(2) consider whether or not to adjourn the application to a judge so that the judge can give further directions;

(3) consider whether or not to make any direction with regard to fixing the trial date or a trial window;

(4) state the reasons for the adjournment[25].

11. CASE MANAGEMENT

11.1 On the first or any subsequent hearing of the disqualification application, the registrar may also give directions as to the following matters:

(1) the filing in court and the service of further evidence (if any) by the parties[26];

---

[19] Rule 7(1) of the Insolvent Companies (Disqualification of Unfit Directors) Proceedings Rules 1987.
[20] Rule 7(2) of the Insolvent Companies (Disqualification of Unfit Directors) Proceedings Rules 1987.
[21] Rule 7(3) of the Insolvent Companies (Disqualification of Unfit Directors) Proceedings Rules 1987.
[22] Rule 7(4)(a) of the Insolvent Companies (Disqualification of Unfit Directors) Proceedings Rules 1987.
[23] Rule 7(4)(b) of the Insolvent Companies (Disqualification of Unfit Directors) Proceedings Rules 1987.
[24] Rule 7(5)(a) of the Insolvent Companies (Disqualification of Unfit Directors) Proceedings Rules 1987.
[25] Rule 7(5)(b) of the Insolvent Companies (Disqualification of Unfit Directors) Proceedings Rules 1987.
[26] Rule 7(5)(c)(ii) of the Insolvent Companies (Disqualification of Unfit Directors) Proceedings Rules 1987.

PRACTICE DIRECTION — DIRECTORS DISQUALIFICATION PROCEEDINGS

(2) the timetable for the steps to be taken between the giving of directions and the hearing of the application;

(3) such other matters as the registrar thinks necessary or expedient with a view to an expeditious disposal of the application or the management of it generally[27];

(4) the time and place of the adjourned hearing[28]; and

(5) the manner in which and the time within which notice of the adjournment and the reasons for it are to be given to the parties[29].

11.2 Where a case is adjourned other than to a judge, it may be heard by the registrar who originally dealt with the case or by another registrar[30].

11.3 If the companies court registrar adjourns the application to a judge to give further directions, the application will usually be listed before the companies court judge in a Monday morning list.

11.4 If the companies court registrar adjourns the application to a judge, all directions having been complied with and the evidence being complete, the application will be referred to the Listing Office and any practice direction relating to listing shall apply accordingly.

11.5 In all disqualification applications, the Court may direct a pre-trial review ('PTR'), a case management conference or listing questionnaires (in the form annexed to this practice direction) and will fix a trial date or trial period in accordance with the provisions of CPR Part 29 ('The Multi-Track') as modified by any relevant practice direction made thereunder.

11.6 In contested disqualification applications, the registrar may, at a hearing of the claim, direct:

(1) that a PTR be fixed for a date approximately six weeks after the close of evidence;

(2) that each party complete a listing questionnaire and return it to the court not later than two clear working days before the hearing of the PTR.

11.7 At the hearing of the PTR, the registrar may give any further directions as appropriate and, where the application is to be heard in the Royal Courts of Justice in London, unless the trial date has already been fixed, will direct Counsel's clerks to attend Room TM 4.09 to obtain an appointment to fix a trial date within 5 days from the hearing of the PTR. The parties may not by agreement extend the period for attendance to fix a trial date. In the event of non-compliance, the court will fix a date for trial and give notice of the date to the parties.

11.8 In all cases, the parties must inform the court immediately of any material change to the information provided in a listing questionnaire.

12. THE TRIAL

12.1 Trial bundles containing copies of:

(1) the claim form;

(2) the acknowledgment of service;

(3) all evidence filed by or on behalf of each of the parties to the proceedings, together with the exhibits thereto;

(4) all relevant correspondence; and

(5) such other documents as the parties consider necessary;

shall be lodged with the court.

12.2 Skeleton arguments should be prepared by all the parties in all but the simplest cases whether the case is to be heard by a registrar or a judge. They should comply with all relevant guidelines.

12.3 The advocate for the claimant should also in all but the simplest cases provide: (a) a chronology; (b) a dramatis personae; (c) in respect of each

---

[27] Rule 7(5)(c)(iii) of the Insolvent Companies (Disqualification of Unfit Directors) Proceedings Rules 1987.

[28] Rule 7(5)(c)(iv) of the Insolvent Companies (Disqualification of Unfit Directors) Proceedings Rules 1987.

[29] Rule 7(5)(c)(i) of the Insolvent Companies (Disqualification of Unfit Directors) Proceedings Rules 1987.

[30] Rule 7(6) of the Insolvent Companies (Disqualification of Unfit Directors) Proceedings Rules 1987.

defendant, a list of references to the relevant evidence.

12.4 The documents mentioned in paragraph 12.1–12.3 above must be delivered to the court in accordance with any order of the court and/or any relevant practice direction.

   (1) If the case is to be heard by a judge sitting in the Royal Courts of Justice, London, but the name of the judge is not known, or the judge is a deputy judge, these documents must be delivered to the Clerk of the Lists. If the name of the judge (other than a deputy judge) is known, these documents must be delivered to the judge's clerk;

   (2) If the case is to be heard by a companies court registrar, these documents must be delivered to Room 409, Thomas More Building, Royal Courts of Justice. Copies must be provided to the other party so far as possible when they are delivered to the court;

   (3) If the case is to be heard in the Chancery district registries in Birmingham, Bristol, Cardiff, Leeds, Liverpool, Manchester or Newcastle, the addresses for delivery are set out in Annex 1;

   (4) If the case is to be heard in a county court, the documents should be delivered to the relevant county court office.

12.5 Copies of documents delivered to the court must, so far as possible, be provided to each of the other parties to the claim.

12.6 The provisions in paragraphs 12.1 to 12.5 above are subject to any order of the court making different provision.

13. SUMMARY PROCEDURE

13.1 If the parties decide to invite the court to deal with the application under the procedure adopted in *Re Carecraft Construction Co. Ltd* [1994] 1 WLR 172, they should inform the court immediately and obtain a date for the hearing of the application.

13.2 Whenever the *Carecraft* procedure is adopted, the claimant must:

   (1) except where the court otherwise directs, submit a written statement containing in respect of each defendant any material facts which (for the purposes of the application) are either agreed or not opposed (by either party); and

   (2) specify in writing the period of disqualification which the parties accept that the agreed or unopposed facts justify or the band of years (e.g. 4 to 6 years) or bracket (i.e. 2 to 5 years; 6 to 10 years; 11 to 15 years) into which they will submit the case falls.

13.3 Paragraph 12.4 of the above applies to the documents mentioned in paragraph 13.2 above unless the court otherwise directs.

13.4 Unless the Court otherwise orders, a hearing under the *Carecraft* procedure will be held in private.

13.5 If the Court is minded to make a disqualification order having heard the parties' representations, it will usually give judgment and make the disqualification order in public. Unless the Court otherwise orders, the written statement referred to in paragraph 13.2 shall be annexed to the disqualification order.

13.6 If the Court refuses to make the disqualification order under the *Carecraft* procedure, the Court shall give further directions for the hearing of the application.

14. MAKING AND SETTING ASIDE OF DISQUALIFICATION ORDER

14.1 The court may make a disqualification order against the defendant, whether or not the latter appears, and whether or not he has completed and returned the acknowledgment of service of the claim form, or filed evidence[31].

14.2 Any disqualification order made in the absence of the defendant may be set aside or varied by the court on such terms as it thinks just[32].

---

[31] Rule 8(1) of the Insolvent Companies (Disqualification of Unfit Directors) Proceedings Rules 1987.
[32] Rule 8(2) of the Insolvent Companies (Disqualification of Unfit Directors) Proceedings Rules 1987.

PRACTICE DIRECTION — DIRECTORS DISQUALIFICATION PROCEEDINGS

15. SERVICE OF DISQUALIFICATION ORDERS
15.1 Service of disqualification orders will be the responsibility of the claimant.

16. COMMENCEMENT OF DISQUALIFICATION ORDER
16.1 Unless the court otherwise orders, a disqualification order takes effect at the beginning of the 21st day after the day on which the order is made[33].

PART THREE APPLICATIONS UNDER SECTIONS 7(2) AND 7(4) OF THE ACT

17. APPLICATIONS FOR PERMISSION TO MAKE A DISQUALIFICATION APPLICATION AFTER THE END OF THE PERIOD OF 2 YEARS SPECIFIED IN SECTION 7(2) OF THE ACT
17.1 Such applications shall be made by Application Notice under CPR Part 23, and the Part 23 Practice Direction shall apply save as modified below.

18. APPLICATIONS FOR EXTRA INFORMATION MADE UNDER SECTION 7(4) OF THE ACT
18.1 Such applications may be made:
(1) by Practice Form N.208 under CPR Part 8; or
(2) by Application Notice in existing disqualification claim proceedings.

19. PROVISIONS APPLICABLE TO APPLICATIONS UNDER SECTIONS 7(2) AND 7(4) OF THE ACT
19.1 Headings: Every claim form and notice by which such an application is begun and all affidavits, notices and other documents in relation thereto must be entitled in the matter of the company or companies in question and in the matter of the Act.
19.2 Service:
(1) Service of application notices seeking orders under section 7(2) or 7(4) of the Act will be the responsibility of the applicant and will not be undertaken by the court.
(2) Where any application notice or order of the court or other document is required in any application under section 7(2) or section 7(4) of the Act to be served on any person who is not in England and Wales, the court may order service on him to be effected within such time and in such manner as it thinks fit, may require such proof of service as it thinks fit, and may make such directions as to acknowledgment of service as it thinks fit.

PART FOUR APPLICATIONS FOR PERMISSION TO ACT

20. COMMENCING AN APPLICATION FOR PERMISSION TO ACT
20.1 This practice direction governs applications for permission made under:
(1) section 1(1) and section 17 of the Act;
(2) section 12 of the Act; and
(3) any application for permission made under any disqualification order which was made under any statutory predecessor of the Act.
20.2 Sections 12 and 17(2) of the Act identify the courts which have jurisdiction to deal with applications for permission to act. Subject to these sections, such applications may be made:
(1) by Practice Form N.208 under CPR Part 8; or
(2) by application notice in an existing disqualification application.

21. HEADINGS
21.1 Every claim form or application notice by which an application for permission to act is begun, and all affidavits, notices and other documents in the application must be entitled in the matter of the company or companies in question and in the matter of the Act.

---

[33] Rule 9 of the Insolvent Companies (Disqualification of Unfit Directors) Proceedings Rules 1987.

22. EVIDENCE

22.1 Evidence in support of an application for permission to act shall be by affidavit.

23. SERVICE

23.1 In all cases, the claim form or application notice (as appropriate), together with the evidence in support thereof, must be served on the Secretary of State.

PART FIVE APPLICATIONS

24. FORM OF APPLICATION

24.1 CPR Part 23 and the Part 23 practice direction (General Rules about Applications for Court Orders) shall apply in relation to applications governed by this practice direction (see paragraph 1.3(4) above) save as modified below.

25. HEADINGS

25.1 Every notice and all affidavits in relation thereto must be entitled in the same manner as the Claim Form in the proceedings in which the application is made.

26. SERVICE

26.1 Service of application notices in disqualification proceedings will be the responsibility of the parties and will not be undertaken by the court.

26.2 Where any application notice or order of the court or other document is required in any application to be served on any person who is not in England and Wales, the court may order service on him to be effected within such time and in such manner as it thinks fit, and may also require such proof of service as it thinks fit.

PART SIX DISQUALIFICATION PROCEEDINGS OTHER THAN IN THE ROYAL COURTS OF JUSTICE

27.1 Where a disqualification application is made by a claim form issued other than in the Royal Courts of Justice this practice direction shall apply with the following modifications

(1) Upon the issue of the claim form the court shall endorse it with the date and time for the first hearing before a district judge. The powers exercisable by a registrar under this practice direction shall be exercised by a district judge.

(2) If the district judge (either at the first hearing or at any adjourned hearing before him) directs that the disqualification claim is to be heard by a High Court judge or by an authorised circuit judge he will direct that the case be entered forthwith in the list for hearing by that judge and the court will allocate (i) a date for the hearing of the trial by that judge and (ii) unless the district judge directs otherwise a date for the hearing of a P.T.R. by the trial judge.

ANNEX 1

Birmingham: The Chancery Listing Officer, The District Registry of the Chancery Division of the High Court, 33 Bull Street, Birmingham B4 6DS.

Bristol: The Chancery Listing Officer, The District Registry of the Chancery Division of the High Court, 3rd Floor, Greyfriars, Lewins Mead, Bristol BS1 2NR.

Cardiff: The Chancery Listing Officer, The District Registry of the Chancery Division of the High Court, 1st Floor, 2 Park Street, Cardiff CF1 1NR.

Leeds: The Chancery Listing Officer, The District Registry of the Chancery Division of the High Court, Leeds Combined Court Centre, The Court House, 1 Oxford Row, Leeds LS1 3BG.

Liverpool and Manchester: The Chancery Listing Officer, The District Registry of the Chancery Division of the High Court, Manchester Courts of Justice, Crown Square, Manchester M60 9DJ.

Newcastle: The Chancery Listing Officer, The District Registry of the Chancery Division of the High Court, The Law Courts, Quayside, Newcastle upon Tyne NE1 3LA.

PRACTICE DIRECTION — DIRECTORS DISQUALIFICATION PROCEEDINGS

Claim Form (CPR Part 8)

DISQUALIFICATION PROCEEDINGS

In the

Claim No.

IN THE MATTER OF [INSERT NAME OF COMPANY: SEE THE PRACTICE DIRECTION]

AND IN THE MATTER OF COMPANY DIRECTORS DISQUALIFICATION ACT 1986

Claimant

Defendant(s)

SEAL

Name(s) and address(es) of Defendant(s)

£

Court fee	
Solicitors costs	
Issue date	

The court office at

is open between 10 am and 4 pm Monday to Friday. When corresponding with the court, please address forms or letters to the Court Manager and quote the case number.

Claim form (CPR Part 8)

PRACTICE DIRECTION — DIRECTORS DISQUALIFICATION PROCEEDINGS

	Claim No.	

Details of claim

LET the Defendant(s) attend before the Registrar/District Judge] on

Date ....
Time .... hours
Place ....

On the hearing of an application by [ ], the Claimant, for a disqualification order under section [ ] of the Company Directors Disqualification Act 1986 that:

The grounds upon which the Claimant seeks a Disqualification Order are [*set out below/summarised in the [affadavit/report] of [ ] [sworn/dated] [DATE] a true copy of which is served herewith.]

* delete as appropriate

NOTE: IF YOU DO NOT ATTEND, THE COURT MAY MAKE SUCH ORDER AS IT THINKS FIT

ENDORSEMENT

1. CPR Part 8 as modified by the Practice Direction relating to disqualification proceedings applies to this claim.

[2. This claim is made in accordance with the Insolvent Companies (Disqualification of Unfit Directors) Rules 1987 (SI 1987/2023).]

3. The court has power to impose a disqualification period as follows:-

    where the application is under section 2 of the Company Directors Disqualification Act, for a period of up to 15 years;

    where the application is under section 3 of the Company Directors Disqualification Act, for a period of up to 5 years;

    where the application is under section 4 of the Company Directors Disqualification Act, for a period of up to 15 years;

    where the application is under section 5 of the Company Directors Disqualification Act, for a period of up to 5 years;

    where the application is under section 7 of the Company Directors Disqualification Act, for a period of not less than 2, and up to 15, years;

PRACTICE DIRECTION — DIRECTORS DISQUALIFICATION PROCEEDINGS

where the application is under section 8 of the Company Directors Disqualification Act, for a period of up to 15 years.

[4. On the first hearing of the claim, the court may hear and determine the claim summarily, without further or other notice to you, and, if it is so determined, the court may impose a disqualification for a period of up to 5 years.]

[5. If at the hearing of the application the court, on the evidence then before it, is minded to impose, in the case of any Defendant, disqualification for any period longer than 5 years, it will not make a disqualification order on the first hearing but will adjourn the application to be heard (with further evidence, if any) at a later date that will be notified to the Defendant. At the second hearing, the court may impose a disqualification period of more than 5 years without any further reference to you.]

6. Your attention is drawn to the possibility of resolving the claim pursuant to the summary procedure adopted in *Re Carecraft Construction Co. Ltd* [1994] 1 WLR 172 (as clarified by the decision of the Court of Appeal in *Secretary of State v Rogers* [1996] 1 WLR 1569).

Statement of Truth
*(I believe)(The Claimant believes) that the facts stated in this claim form are true.
* I am duly authorised by the claimant to sign this statement

Full name of the claimant _____

Name of claimant's solicitor's firm _____

Signed _____ position or office held _____

*(Claimant)(Litigation friend)(Claimant's solicitor)   (if signing on behalf of firm or company)
*delete as appropriate

Claimant's or claimant's solicitor's address to which documents should be sent if different from overleaf. If you are prepared to accept service by DX, fax or e-mail, please add details.

Notes for claimant on completing a Part 8 claim form

- Please read all of these guidance notes before you begin completing the claim form. The notes follow the order in which information is required on the form.
- Court staff can help you fill in the claim form and give information about procedure once it has been issued. But they cannot give legal advice. If you need legal advice, for example, about the likely success of your claim or the evidence you need to prove it, you should contact a solicitor or a Citizens Advice Bureau.
- If you are filling in the claim form by hand, please use black ink and write in block capitals.
- You must file any evidence to support your claim either in or with the claim form in the form of an affidavit or affirmation.
- Copy the completed claim form, the defendant's notes for guidance and your written evidence so that you have one copy for yourself, one copy for the court and one copy for each defendant. Send or take the forms and evidence to the court office with the appropriate fee. The court will tell you how much this is.

Notes on completing the claim form

Heading
You must fill in the heading of the form to indicate whether you want the claim to be issued in a county court or in the High Court (The High Court means either a District Registry (attached to a county court) or the Royal Courts of Justice in London).

Use whichever of the following is appropriate:
'In the..........................county court'
(inserting the name of the court)

or

'In the High Court of Justice Chancery Division
and ....District Registry'
(inserting the name of the District Registry)

or

'In the High Court of Justice Chancery Division, Companies Court
Royal Courts of Justice'

Claimant and defendant details
As the person issuing the claim, you are called the 'claimant'; the person you are suing is called the 'defendant'. You must provide the following information about yourself **and** the defendant according to the capacity in which you are suing and in which the defendant is being sued. When suing or being sued as:-

an individual:
All known forenames and surname, (whether Mr, Mrs, Miss, Ms or Other e.g. Dr) and residential address (**including** postcode and telephone and any fax or e-mail number) in England and Wales. Where the defendant is a proprietor of a business, a partner in a firm or an individual sued in the name of a club or other unincorporated association, the address for service should be the usual or last known place of residence or principal place of business of the company, firm or club or other unincorporated association.

PRACTICE DIRECTION — DIRECTORS DISQUALIFICATION PROCEEDINGS

Where the individual is:

a firm:

Enter the name of the firm followed by the words 'a firm' e.g. 'Bandbox - a firm' and an address for service which is either a partner's residential address or the principal or last known place of business.

a corporation (other than a company):

Enter the full name of the corporation and the address which is either its principal office or any other place where the corporation carries on activities and which has a real connection with the claim.

a company registered in England and Wales:

Enter the name of the company and an address which is either the company's registered office or any place of business that has a real, or the most, connection with the claim e.g. the shop where the goods were bought.

an overseas company (defined by s744 of the Companies Act 1985):
Enter the name of the company and either the address registered under s69 1 of the Act or the address of the place of business having a real, or the most, connection with the claim.

Defendant's name and address
Enter in this box the full name and address of the defendant to be served with the claim form (ie. one claim form for each defendant). If the defendant is to be served outside England and Wales, you may need to obtain the court's permission.

Address for documents
Insert in this box the address at which you wish to receive documents, if different from the address you have already given under the heading 'Claimant'. The address you give must be either that of your solicitors or your residential or business address and must be in England or Wales. If you live or carry on business outside of England and Wales, you can give some other address within England and Wales.

Endorsement
If the claim is not brought under section 7 or section 8 of the Company Directors Disqualification Act 1986, paragraphs 2, 4 and 5 of the endorsement should be deleted.

Statement of truth
This must be signed by you, by your solicitor or your litigation friend, as appropriate.

Where the claimant is a registered company or a corporation the claim must be signed by either the director, treasurer, secretary, chief executive, manager or other officer of the company or (in the case of a corporation) the mayor, chairman, president or town clerk.

PRACTICE DIRECTION — DIRECTORS DISQUALIFICATION PROCEEDINGS

Notes for defendant
(Part 8 Claim Form: Disqualification Proceedings)

Please read these notes carefully - they will help you to decide what to do about this claim.

- You have 14 days from the date on which you were served with the claim form (see below) in which to respond to the claim by completing and returning the acknowledgment of service enclosed with this claim form.
- If you **do not return** the acknowledgment of service, you will be allowed to attend any hearing of this claim but you will not be allowed to take part in the hearing unless the court gives you permission to do so.

Court staff can tell you about procedures but they cannot give legal advice. If you need legal advice, you should contact a solicitor or Citizens Advice Bureau immediately

Responding to this claim

Time for responding
The completed acknowledgment of service must be returned to the court office within 14 days of the date on which the claim form was served on you. If the claim form was
- sent by post, the 14 days begins 7 days from the date of the postmark on the envelope.
- delivered or left at your address, the 14 days begins the day after it was delivered.
- handed to you personally, the 14 days begins on the day it was given to you.

Completing the acknowledgment of service
You should complete section A, B, or C as appropriate **and all** of section D.

Section A - contesting the claim
If you wish to contest the remedy sought by the claimant in the claim form, you should complete section A.

Section B – mitigation
If you do not wish to resist the claim for a disqualification order, but would like to adduce mitigating circumstances with a view to justifying only a short period of disqualification, you should complete section B.

Section C - disputing the court's jurisdiction
You should indicate your intention by completing section C and filing an application disputing the court's jurisdiction within 14 days of filing of your acknowledgment of service at the court. The court will arrange a hearing date for the application and tell you and the claimant when and where to attend.

Written evidence
Any evidence which you wish to be taken into consideration by the Court must be filed in Court within 28 days from the date of service of the claim form upon you. The evidence must be in the form of an affidavit.

Serving other parties
At the same time as you file your affidavit evidence with the court, you must also send copies of both the form and any written evidence to the Claimant named on the claim form.

What happens next
The date of the first hearing of the claim is set out under "Details of Claim" above.

Statement of truth
This must be signed by you, by your solicitor or your litigation friend, as appropriate.
Where the claimant is a registered company or a corporation the claim must be signed by either the director, treasurer, secretary, chief executive, manager or other officer of the company or (in the case of a corporation) the mayor, chairman, president or town clerk.

Acknowledgment of Service (Part 8)

DISQUALIFICATION PROCEEDINGS

In the	
Claim No.	
Claimant (including ref)	
Defendant	

You should read the 'notes for defendant' attached to the claim form which will tell you when and where to send this form.

State the full name of the Defendant by whom or on whose behalf the service of the claim form is being acknowledged

If you wish to contest the claim — complete section A

If you do not wish to dispute the claim — complete section B

If the claim form was served outside England and Wales and you wish to dispute the court's jurisdiction — complete section C

A

TICK ALL APPROPRIATE BOXES

☐ I intend to contest the claim on the grounds that:-

☐ I was not a director or shadow director _____ of please insert the name of each of the companies concerned) at a time when my conduct, or the conduct of other presons, is in question

☐ My conduct as a director or shadow director was not as alleged in support of the application for a disqualification order

☐ I dispute the allegation that my conduct makes me unfit to be concerned in the management of a company

B

TICK ALL APPROPRIATE BOXES

☐ I do not wish to resist the claim for a disqualification order.

☐ I would like to adduce mitigating circumstances with a view to reducing the period of disqualification.

PRACTICE DIRECTION — DIRECTORS DISQUALIFICATION PROCEEDINGS

	Claim No.	

C

TICK ALL APPROPRIATE BOXES

☐   The claim form was served outside England or Wales, and I intend to dispute jurisdiction

(you should file your application within 14 days of the date on which you file this acknowledgment of service with the court)

D

Signed

(To be signed by you or by your solicitor or litigation friend)

Statement of Truth

*(I believe)(The Claimant believes) that the facts stated in this claim form are true.
*I am duly authorised by the defendant to sign this statement

Full name of the defendant _____

Name of defendant's solicitor _____

Signed _____

Position or office held (if signing on behalf of a company) _____

*(Defendant)(Litigation friend)(Defendant's solicitor)

* *Delete as appropriate*

Date

Give an address to which notices about this case can be sent to you

		if applicable
	fax no.	
	DX no.	
Postcode	E-mail	
Tel No.		

1141

Listing questionnaire

DISQUALIFICATION PROCEEEDINGS

To

In the

Claim No	
Last date for filing with the court	

Name of Company	
Name of Claimant	
Name of Defendant	
Name of Solicitor	
Name of Counsel	

- The court will use the information which you and the other party(ies) provide to decide whether to hold a pre-trial review, to fix a date for trial, to confirm the estimated length of trial and to set a timetable for the trial itself.

- If you do not complete and return the questionnaire the procedural judge may

    - make an order which leads to your evidence being struck out.

    - decide to hold a listing hearing. You may be ordered to pay (immediately) the other parties' costs of attending.

    - If there is sufficient information, list the case for trial and give any appropriate directions.

A Directions complied with

1. Have you complied with all the previous directions given by the court? ☐ Yes ☐ No

2. If no please explain which directions are outstanding and why

Directions outstanding	Reasons directions outstanding

3. Are any further directions required to prepare the case for trial? ☐ Yes ☐ No

4. If yes, please explain directions required and give reasons

Directions required	Reasons directions required

B Experts

1. Has the court already given permission for you to use written expert evidence? ☐ Yes ☐ No *(if no go to section B6)*

2. If yes please give name and field of expertise.

Name of expert	Whether joint expert	Field of expertise

3. Have the expert(s') report(s) been agreed with the other parties? ☐ Yes ☐ No

4. Have the experts met to discuss their reports? ☐ Yes ☐ No

5. Has the court already given permission for the expert(s) to give oral evidence at the trial? ☐ Yes ☐ No *(if yes go to Q7)*

6. If no are you seeking that permission? ☐ Yes ☐ No *(if no go to Section C)*

7. If yes, give your reasons for seeking permission.

8. If yes what are the names, addresses and fields of expertise of your experts?

Expert 1	Expert 2	Expert 3	Expert 4

9. Please give details of any dates within the trial period when your expert(s) will not be available.

Name of expert	Dates not available

C Other witnesses

(If you are not calling other witnesses go to section D)

1. **How many other witnesses (including yourself) will be giving evidence on your behalf at the trial** *(do not inlcude experts see section B above)*

   (Give number)

2. **What are the names and adresses of your witnesses?**

Witness 1	Witness 2	Witness 3	Witness 4

3. **Please give details of any dates within the trial period when you or your witnesses will not be available?**

Name of witness	Dates not available

4. **Are any of the affidavits agreed?** ☐ Yes ☐ No

   (if no go to question C6)

5. **If yes, give the name of the witness and the date of his or her affidavit.**

Name of witness	Date of Affidavit

6. **Do you or any of the witnesses need any special facilities?** ☐ Yes ☐ No

   (if no go to question C8)

7. **If yes, what are they?**

PRACTICE DIRECTION — DIRECTORS DISQUALIFICATION PROCEEDINGS

8. Will any of your witnesses be provided with an interpreter? ☐ Yes ☐ No

(if no go to section D)

9. If yes, say what type of interpreter e.g. language (stating which), deaf/blind etc.?

D Legal Representation

1. Who will be representing your case at the hearing or trial? ☐ You ☐ Solicitor ☐ Counsel

2. Please give details of any dates within the trial period when the person presenting your case will not be available

Name	Dates not available

E Summary disposal under the Carecraft procedure

1. Have you discussed with the other parties named on the claim form the possibility of resolving this case under the procedure adopted in <u>RE Carecraft Construction Co. Ltd</u> [1994] 1 WLR 172 ("a Carecraft application"). <u>If not this should be discussed as soon as possible and in any event prior to the hearing of any pre-trial review.</u>   ☐ Yes ☐ No

2. Please state whether the case should be listed for a Carecraft disposal or for full trial at a time and date to be fixed.

☐ Carecraft
☐ Full Trial

3. If such a Carecraft Application is to be made, the agreed written statement of facts must be submitted by the claimant as set out in the Practice Direction relating to disqualification proceedings and delivered to the Court not later than 2 working days before the date upon which it is intended to make the application and in any event as soon as possible.

PRACTICE DIRECTION — DIRECTORS DISQUALIFICATION PROCEEDINGS

F Other matters

1. **How long do you estimate the trial will take, including cross-examination and closing arguments?**

Minutes	Hours	Days

If your estimate alters, a fresh estimate of the length of the trial, signed by the advocates for all parties, must be delivered to the appropriate court as soon as practicable. It is the responsbility of the Solicitors for each party to see that this is done.

2. **What is the estimated number of pages of evidence to be included in the trial bundle?**

(please give number)

Signed

Claimant/defendant or Counsel/Solicitor for the claimant/defendant

Dated

PRACTICE DIRECTION RELATING TO THE USE OF THE WELSH LANGUAGE IN CASES IN THE CIVIL COURTS IN WALES

The purpose of this practice direction is to reflect the principle of the Welsh Language Act 1993 that in the administration of justice in Wales, the English and Welsh languages should be treated on the basis of equality.

1. GENERAL
    1.1 This practice direction applies to civil proceedings in courts in Wales.
    1.2 The existing practice of conducting a hearing entirely in the Welsh language on an ad hoc basis and without notice will continue to apply when all parties and witnesses directly involved at the time consent to the proceedings being so conducted.
    1.3 In every case in which it is possible that the Welsh language may be used by any party or witness [or in any document which may be placed before the court], the parties or their legal representatives must inform the court of that fact so that appropriate arrangements can be made for the management and listing of the case.
    1.4 If costs are incurred as a result of a party failing to comply with this direction, a costs Order may be made against him or his legal representative.
    1.5 Where a case is tried with a jury, the law does not permit the selection of jurors in a manner which enables the court to discover whether a juror does or does not speak Welsh or to secure a jury whose members are bilingual to try a case in which the Welsh language may be used.

2. THE ALLOCATION QUESTIONNAIRE
    2.1 In any proceedings in which a party is required to complete an allocation questionnaire, he must include details relating to the possible use of Welsh i.e. details of any person wishing to give oral evidence in Welsh and of any documents in Welsh (e.g. documents to be disclosed under Part 31 or witness statements) which that party expects to use.
    2.2 A party must include the details mentioned in paragraph 2.1 in the allocation questionnaire even if he has already informed the court of the possible use of Welsh in accordance with the provisions of section 1 above.

3. CASE MANAGEMENT
    3.1 At any interlocutory hearing, the court will take the opportunity to consider whether it should give case management directions. To assist the court, a party or his legal representative should draw the court's attention to the possibility of Welsh being used in the proceedings, even where he has already done so in compliance with other provisions of this direction.
    3.2 In any case where a party is required to complete a listing questionnaire and has already intimated the intention to use Welsh, he should confirm the intended use of Welsh in the listing questionnaire and provide any details which have not been set out in the allocation questionnaire.

4. LISTING BY THE COURT
    4.1 The diary manager, in consultation with the Designated Civil Judge, will ensure that a case in which the Welsh language is to be used is listed:
        (a) wherever practicable before a Welsh speaking judge; and
        (b) where translation facilities are needed, at a court with simultaneous translation facilities.

5. INTERPRETERS
    5.1 Whenever an interpreter is needed to translate evidence from English to Welsh or from Welsh to English, the Court Manager in whose court the case is to

be heard will take steps to secure the attendance of an interpreter whose name is included in the list of approved court interpreters.

6. WITNESSES AND JURORS

6.1 When each witness is called, the court officer administering the oath or affirmation will inform the witness that he or she may be sworn or may affirm in Welsh or English as he or she wishes.

6.2 Where a case is tried with a jury, the court officer swearing in the jury will inform the jurors in open court that each juror may take the oath or may affirm in Welsh or English as he or she wishes.

7. ROLE OF THE LIAISON JUDGE

7.1 If any question or difficulty arises concerning the implementation of this practice direction, contact should in the first place be made with the Liaison Judge for the Welsh language.

CYFARWYDDIADAU YMARFER AR DDEFNYDDIO'R IAITH GYMRAEG MEWN ACHOSION YN Y LLYSOEDD SIFIL YNG NGHYMRU

Diben y cyfarwyddiadau ymarfer hyn yw adlewyrchu egwyddor Deddf yr Iaith Gymraeg 1993 sef y dylid trin y Gymraeg a'r Saesneg yn gyfartal wrth weinyddu cyfiawnder yng Nghymru.

1. CYFFREDINOL

1.1 Mae'r cyfarwyddiadau ymarfer hyn yn berthnasol i achosion sifil mewn llysoedd yng Nghymru.

1.2 Bydd yr ymarfer presennol o gynnal gwrandawiad yn gyfan gwbl yn y Gymraeg ar sail *ad hoc* a heb rybudd yn parhau'n ddilys pan fo pob parti a phob tyst sy'n ymwneud yn uniongyrchol â'r achos ar y pryd yn cytuno iddo gael ei gynnal felly.

1.3 Ym mhob achos lle y bydd tyst neu barti o bosibl am ddefnyddio'r Gymraeg [neu lle o bosibl y defnyddir y Gymraeg mewn unrhyw ddogfen a gyflwynir gerbron y llys], cyfrifoldeb y parti neu ei gynrychiolwyr cyfreithiol yw hysbysu'r llys o hyn fel y gellir gwneud trefniadau priodol ar gyfer trin a rhestru'r achos.

1.4 Os achosir costau yn sgil methu â chydymffurfio â'r Cyfarwyddiadau hyn, gellir codi gorchymyn costau yn erbyn y parti neu ei gynrychiolydd cyfreithiol.

1.5 Pan fydd achos yn cael ei brofi gyda rheithgor, nid yw'r gyfraith yn caniatáu dethol rheithgor mewn modd sy'n galluogi'r Llys i ganfod a yw Rheithiwr yn siarad Cymraeg ai peidio nac i sicrhau Rheithgor y mae ei aelodau yn ddwyieithog i wrando achos lle o bosibl y defnyddir y Gymraeg.

2. YR HOLIADUR DYRANNU

2.1 Mewn unrhyw achos lle y mae gofyn i barti lenwi holiadur dyrannu, rhaid iddo gynnwys manylion ynghylch defnydd posibl o'r Gymraeg, h.y. manylion unrhyw berson a ddymunai roi tystiolaeth lafar yn y Gymraeg ac unrhyw ddogfennau yn y Gymraeg (e.e. dogfennau i'w datgelu o dan Ran 31 neu ddatganiadau tystion) y mae'r parti hwnnw'n disgwyl eu defnyddio.

2.2 Rhaid i barti gynnwys y manylion a nodir ym mharagraff 2.1 yn yr holiadur dyrannu, hyd yn oed os yw ef eisoes wedi hysbysu'r llys am ddefnydd posibl o'r Gymraeg yn unol â gofynion adran 1 uchod.

3. RHEOLI ACHOSION

3.1 Mewn unrhyw wrandawiad yng nghwrs achos bydd y llys yn manteisio ar y cyfle i ystyried a ddylai roi cyfarwyddiadau rheoli achos. I gynorthwyo'r llys, dylai parti neu ei gynrychiolydd cyfreithiol dynnu sylw'r llys at y posibilrwydd y gallai'r Gymraeg gael ei defnyddio yn yr achos, hyd yn oed os yw ef eisoes wedi gwneud hynny wrth gydymffurfio â gofynion eraill y cyfarwyddiadau hyn.

3.2 Mewn unrhyw achos pan fydd gofyn i barti lenwi holiadur rhestru a'r parti hwnnw eisoes wedi nodi ei fwriad i ddefnyddio'r Gymraeg, dylai gadarnhau ei fwriad i ddefnyddio'r Gymraeg yn yr holiadur rhestru, a rhoi unrhyw fanylion na chafodd eu nodi yn yr holiadur dyrannu.

4. RHESTRU GAN Y LLYS

4.1 Bydd rheolwr y dyddiadur, mewn ymgynghoriad â'r Barnwr Sifil Dynodedig, yn sicrhau y bydd achos lle y defnyddir y Gymraeg yn cael ei restru:

    (a) pryd bynnag y bydd hynny'n ymarferol bosibl, gerbron barnwr Cymraeg ei iaith; a

    (b) lle y bo angen cyfleusterau cyfieithu, mewn llys gyda chyfleusterau cyfieithu ar y pryd.

5. CYFIEITHWYR

5.1 Pryd bynnag y bydd angen cyfieithydd i gyfieithu tysiolaeth o'r Saesneg i'r Gymraeg neu o'r Gymraeg i'r Saesneg, bydd Rheolwr y Llys lle y cynhelir yr achos yn sicrhau y trefnir i gyfieithydd, y mae ei enw ar restr y llys o gyfieithwyr cymeradwy, fod yn bresennol.

6. TYSTION A RHEITHWYR

6.1 Wrth i bob tyst gael ei alw, bydd y swyddog llys sy'n gweinyddu'r llw neu'r cadarnhad yn hysbysu'r tyst y gall ef dyngu llw neu gadarnhau yn y Gymraeg neu yn y Saesneg yn ôl ei ddymuniad.

6.2 Pan gaiff achos ei brofi gan reithgor, bydd y swyddog llys sy'n gweinyddu llwon y rheithwyr yn hysbysu'r rheithwyr mewn llys agored y caiff pob rheithiwr dyngu llw neu gadarnhau yn y Gymraeg neu yn y Saesneg yn ôl ei ddymuniad.

7. RÔL Y BWRNWR CYSWLLT

7.1 Os cyfyd unrhyw gwestiwn neu broblem ynghylch gweithredu'r cyfarwyddiadau uchod, dylid yn y lle cyntaf gysylltu â'r Barnwr Cyswllt dros faterion y Gymraeg ar y Gylchdaith.

PRACTICE DIRECTION — DEVOLUTION ISSUES (AND CROWN OFFICE APPLICATIONS IN WALES)

This Practice Direction is divided into 4 parts:

Part I   Introduction
Part II   Directions applicable to all proceedings
Part III Directions applicable to specific proceedings (paragraphs 14.2 and 14.3 deal with Crown Office applications in Wales)
Part IV   Appeals

PART 1 INTRODUCTION

DEFINITIONS

1. In this Practice Direction:
'the Assembly' means the National Assembly for Wales or Cynulliad Cenedlaethol Cymru
'the GWA' means the Government of Wales Act 1998
'the NIA' means the Northern Ireland Act 1998
'the SA' means the Scotland Act 1998
'the Acts' mean the GWA, the NIA and the SA
'the Judicial Committee' means the Judicial Committee of the Privy Council
'the CPR' means the Civil Procedure Rules 1998
'the FPR' means the Family Proceedings Rules 1991
'the FPC' means the Family Proceedings Courts (Children Act 1989) Rules 1991
'devolution issue' has the same meaning as in paragraph 1, schedule 8 to the GWA; paragraph 1, schedule 10 to the NIA; and paragraph 1, schedule 6 of the SA
'devolution issue notice' means a notice that a devolution issue has arisen in proceedings.

SCOPE

2.1 This Practice Direction supplements the provisions dealing with devolution issues in the Acts. It deals specifically with the position if a devolution issue arises under the GWA. If a devolution issue arises under the NIA or the SA the procedure laid down in this Practice Direction should be adapted as required.

2.2 This Practice Direction also deals with Crown Office applications in Wales (see paragraphs 14.2 and 14.3).

THE DEVOLUTION LEGISLATION

3.1 Schedule 8 to the GWA contains provisions dealing with devolution issues arising out of the GWA; schedule 10 to the NIA contains provisions dealing with devolution issues arising out of the NIA; and schedule 6 to the SA contains provisions dealing with devolution issues arising out of the SA.

3.2 Broadly a devolution issue will involve a question whether a devolved body has acted or proposes to act within its powers (which includes not acting incompatibly with Convention rights[1] and Community law[2]) or has failed to

---

[1] The rights and fundamental freedoms set out in: (a) Articles 2 to 12 and 14 of the European Convention on Human Rights ('ECHR'), (b) Articles 1 to 3 of the First Protocol (agreed at Paris on 20th March 1952), and (c) Articles 1 and 2 of the Sixth Protocol (agreed at Strasbourg on 11th May 1994), as read with Articles 16 and 18 of the ECHR (Section 1 Human Rights Act 1998; s. 107(1) and (5) GWA; sections 6(2); 24(1) and 98(1) NIA; sections 29(2); 57(2) and 126(1) SA).

[2] All the rights, powers, liabilities, obligations and restrictions from time to time created or arising by or under the Community Treaties; and all the remedies and procedures from time to time provided for by or under the Community Treaties (sections 106(7) and 155(1), GWA; sections 6(2); 24(1) and 98(1), NIA; sections 29(2); 57(2) and 126(9) SA).

comply with a duty imposed on it. Reference should be made to the Acts where 'devolution issue' is defined.

3.3 (1) If a devolution issue under the GWA arises in proceedings, the court must order notice of it to be given to the Attorney General and the Assembly if they are not already a party. They have a right to take part as a party in the proceedings so far as they relate to a devolution issue, if they are not already a party (paragraph 5, schedule 8 to the GWA.) If they do take part, they may require the court to refer the devolution issue to the Judicial Committee (paragraph 30, schedule 8 to the GWA)[3].

(2) There are similar provisions in the NIA and the SA although the persons to be notified are different (paragraphs 13, 14, and 33, schedule 10 to the NIA; paragraphs 16, 17 and 33, schedule 6 to the SA).

3.4 Under all the Acts the court may refer a devolution issue to another court as follows:

(1) A magistrates' court may refer a devolution issue arising in civil or summary proceedings to the High Court (paragraphs 6 and 9, schedule 8 to the GWA; paragraphs 15 and 18, schedule 10 to the NIA; and paragraphs 18 and 21, schedule 6 to the SA).

(2) The Crown Court may refer a devolution issue arising in summary proceedings to the High Court and a devolution issue arising in proceedings on indictment to the Court of Appeal (paragraph 9, schedule 8 to the GWA; paragraph 18, schedule 10 to the NIA; paragraph 21, schedule 6 to the SA).

(3) A county court, the High Court (unless the devolution issue has been referred to the High Court)[4], and the Crown Court[5] may refer a devolution issue arising in civil proceedings to the Court of Appeal (paragraph 7, schedule 8 to the GWA; paragraph 16, schedule 10 to the NIA; paragraph 19, schedule 6 to the SA).

(4) A tribunal from which there is no appeal must, and any other tribunal may, refer a devolution issue to the Court of Appeal (paragraph 8, schedule 8 to the GWA; paragraph 17, schedule 10 to the NIA; paragraph 20, schedule 6 to the SA).

(5) The Court of Appeal may refer a devolution issue to the Judicial Committee, unless the devolution issue was referred to it by another court (paragraph 10, schedule 8 to the GWA; paragraph 19, schedule 10 to the NIA; paragraph 22, schedule 6 to the SA).

(6) An appeal against the determination of a devolution issue by the High Court or the Court of Appeal on a reference lies to the Judicial Committee with the leave of the court concerned, or, failing such leave, with special leave of the Judicial Committee (paragraph 11, schedule 8 to the GWA; paragraph 20, schedule 10 to the NIA; paragraph 23, schedule 6 to the SA).

3.5 A court may take into account additional expense which the court considers that a party has incurred as a result of the participation of the Attorney General or the Assembly in deciding any question as to costs (paragraph 35, schedule 8 to the GWA).

---

[3] If the Attorney General or the Assembly had become a party to the original proceedings but did not exercise their right to require the devolution issue to be referred to the Judicial Committee and the court decided the case, they would have the same rights of appeal as parties. These would not allow them to appeal a decision made in proceedings on indictment, although the Attorney General has a power under section 36 of the Criminal Justice Act 1972 to refer a point of law to the Court of Appeal where the defendant has been acquitted in a trial on indictment.
Paragraph 31, schedule 8 to the GWA, allows the Attorney General and Assembly to refer to the Judicial Committee any devolution issue which is not the subject of proceedings. This power could possibly be used if a court reached a decision where they had not been parties and so had no rights of appeal but such a reference could not affect the decision of the court.

[4] If an appeal by way of case stated in criminal proceedings goes to the Divisional Court there appears to be no power for the Divisional Court to refer a devolution issue to the Court of Appeal.

[5] eg in appeals from a magistrates' court in a licensing matter.

PART II DIRECTIONS APPLICABLE TO ALL PROCEEDINGS

SCOPE

4. Paragraphs 5 to 13 apply to proceedings in England and Wales in the magistrates' courts, the county courts, the Crown Court, the High Court and the Court of Appeal (Civil and Criminal Division). Paragraph 10 also applies to the form and procedure for a reference to the Court of Appeal by a tribunal.

RAISING THE QUESTION AS TO WHETHER A DEVOLUTION ISSUE ARISES

5.1 Where a party to any form of proceedings wishes to raise an issue which may be a devolution issue whether as a claim (or part of a claim) to enforce or establish a legal right or to seek a remedy or as a defence (or part of a defence), the provisions of this Practice Direction apply in addition to the rules of procedure applicable to the proceedings in which the issue arises.

5.2 A court may, of its own volition, require the question of whether a devolution issue arises to be considered, if the materials put before the court indicate such an issue may arise, even if the parties have not used the term 'devolution issue'.

DETERMINATION BY A COURT OF WHETHER A DEVOLUTION ISSUE ARISES

6.1 The court may give such directions as it considers appropriate to obtain clarification or additional information to establish whether a devolution issue arises.

6.2 In determining whether a devolution issue arises the court, notwithstanding the contention of a party to the proceedings, may decide that a devolution issue shall *not* be taken to arise if the contention appears to the court to be frivolous or vexatious (paragraph 2 of schedule 8 to the GWA).

6.3 If the court determines that a devolution issue arises it must state what that devolution issue is clearly and concisely.

NOTICE OF DEVOLUTION ISSUE TO THE ATTORNEY GENERAL AND THE ASSEMBLY

7.1 If a court determines that a devolution issue arises in the proceedings, it must order a devolution issue notice substantially in the form numbered 'DI 1' in Annex 1 to be given to the Attorney General and the Assembly unless they are already a party to the proceedings (paragraph 5(1), schedule 8 to the GWA).

7.2 A court receiving a reference does not have to serve a devolution issue notice unless it determines that a devolution issue that was not identified by the court making the reference has arisen. In that case the court receiving the reference must serve a devolution issue notice which must:

    (1) state what devolution issue has been referred to it;

    (2) state what further devolution issue has arisen; and

    (3) identify the referring court.

7.3 If the devolution issue has arisen in criminal proceedings, the devolution issue notice must state:

    (1) whether the proceedings have been adjourned;

    (2) whether the defendant is remanded in custody; and

    (3) if the defendant has been remanded in custody and his trial has not commenced, when the custody time limit expires[6].

7.4 If the devolution issue arises in an appeal, the devolution issue notice must:

    (1) state that the devolution issue arises in an appeal;

    (2) identify the court whose decision is being appealed; and

    (3) state whether the devolution issue is raised for the first time on appeal; or, if it is not, state that the devolution issue was raised in the court whose decision is being appealed, what decision was reached by that court, and the date of the previous notice to the Attorney General and the Assembly.

---

[6] Custody time limits are imposed by the Prosecution of Offences (Custody Time Limits) Regulations 1987 as amended.

7.5 The devolution issue notice will specify a date which will be 14 days, or such longer period as the court may direct (see below), after the date of the devolution issue notice as the date by which the Attorney General or the Assembly must notify the court that he or it wishes to take part as a party to the proceedings, so far as they relate to a devolution issue.

7.6 The court may, in exceptional circumstances, specify a date longer than 14 days after the date of the devolution issue notice as the date by which the Attorney General and the Assembly must notify the court that he or it wishes to take part as a party to the proceedings. The court may do this before the notice is given, or before or after the expiry of the period given in the notice.

7.7 (1) On the date of the devolution issue notice,

(a) the devolution issue notice for the Attorney General must be faxed to him by the court[7]; and

(b) the devolution issue notice for the Assembly must be faxed by the court to the Counsel General for the Assembly.

(2) On the same day as a fax is sent a copy of the devolution issue notice must be sent by the court by first class post to the Attorney General and the Counsel General for the Assembly.

7.8 The court may, on such terms as it considers appropriate, order such additional documents to be served (eg in civil proceedings, the claim form) or additional information to be supplied with the devolution issue notice.

7.9 (1) When a court orders a devolution issue notice to be given the court may make such further orders as it thinks fit in relation to any adjournment, stay, continuance of the proceedings, or interim measures, during the period within which the Attorney General and the Assembly have to notify the court if they intend to take part as a party to the proceedings.

(2) Before ordering an adjournment in criminal proceedings, the court will consider all material circumstances, including whether it would involve delay that might extend beyond the custody time limits if the defendant is remanded in custody and his trial has not commenced.

7.10 If neither the Attorney General nor the Assembly notify the court within the specified time that he or it wishes to take part as a party to the proceedings:

(1) the proceedings should immediately continue on expiry of the period within which they had to notify the court; and

(2) the court has no duty to inform them of the outcome of the proceedings apart from the duty to notify them if the court decides to refer the devolution issue to another court (see paragraph 10.3(5)).[8]

ADDING THE ATTORNEY GENERAL OR THE ASSEMBLY TO THE PROCEEDINGS AND THEIR RIGHT TO REQUIRE REFERRAL OF A DEVOLUTION ISSUE TO THE JUDICIAL COMMITTEE

8.1 If the Attorney General or the Assembly wishes to take part as a party to the proceedings so far as they relate to a devolution issue, he or it must send to the court and the other parties (and to each other if only one of them has become a party) a notice substantially in the form numbered 'DI 2' shown in Annex 1 within the time specified in the devolution issue notice.

8.2 On receipt of this form the court may give such consequential directions as it considers necessary.

8.3 If the Attorney General or the Assembly is a party to the proceedings, and either of them wishes to require the court to refer the devolution issue to the Judicial Committee, he or it must as soon as practicable send to the court and the other parties (and to each other if only one of them has become a party) a notice substantially in the form numbered 'DI 3' shown in Annex 1.

---

[7] See Annex 2 for information about fax numbers and addresses.

[8] If there is an appeal, the appeal court will serve a devolution issue notice on the Attorney General and the Assembly (see paragraph 7.4).

DETERMINATION BY THE COURT OF WHETHER OR NOT TO MAKE A REFERENCE OF A DEVOLUTION ISSUE IF THE ATTORNEY GENERAL OR THE ASSEMBLY DO NOT REQUIRE A REFERENCE

9.1 If the court is not required to refer the devolution issue to the Judicial Committee, the court will decide whether it should refer the devolution issue to the relevant court as specified in paragraph 3.4.

9.2 Before deciding whether to make a reference the court may hold a directions hearing or give written directions as to the making of submissions on the question of whether to make a reference.

9.3 The court may make a decision on the basis of written submissions if its procedures permit this and it wishes to do so, or the court may have a hearing before making a decision.

9.4 In exercising its discretion as to whether to make a reference, the court will have regard to all relevant circumstances and in particular to:

 (1) the importance of the devolution issue to the public in general;

 (2) the importance of the devolution issue to the original parties to the proceedings;

 (3) whether a decision on the reference of the devolution issue will be decisive of the matters in dispute between the parties;

 (4) whether all the relevant findings of fact have been made (a devolution issue will not, unless there are exceptional circumstances, be suitable for a reference if it has to be referred on the basis of assumed facts);

 (5) the delay that a reference would entail particularly in cases involving children and criminal cases (including whether the reference is likely to involve delay that would extend beyond the expiry of the custody time limits if the defendant is remanded in custody and his trial has not commenced); and

 (6) additional costs that a reference might involve[9].

9.5 The court should state its reasons for making or declining to make a reference.

9.6 If the court decides not to refer the case, it will give directions for the future conduct of the action, which will include directions as to the participation of the Attorney General and the Assembly if they are parties.

FORM AND PROCEDURE FOR REFERENCES

10.1 If the court or tribunal is required by the Attorney General or the Assembly (in relation to any proceedings before the court to which he or it is a party) to refer the devolution issue to the Judicial Committee:

 (1) the court or tribunal will make the reference as soon as practicable after receiving the notice from the Attorney General or the Assembly substantially in the form numbered 'DI 3' shown in Annex 1, and follow the procedure for references in the Judicial Committee (Devolution Issues) Rules Order 1999; and

 (2) the court or tribunal may order the parties, or any of them, to draft the reference.

10.2 If the Court of Appeal decides to refer the devolution issue to the Judicial Committee:

 (1) It will follow the procedure in the Judicial Committee (Devolution Issues) Rules Order 1999; and

 (2) the court may order the parties, or any of them, to draft the reference.

10.3 If any other court or tribunal decides, or if a tribunal is required, to refer the devolution issue to another court:

 (1) the reference must be substantially in the form numbered 'DI 4' shown in Annex 1 and must set out the following:

  (a) the question referred;

---

[9] In criminal cases section 16 of the Prosecution of Offences Act 1985 does not enable a court receiving a reference to make a defendant's costs order. If the defendant is subsequently acquitted by the court who made the reference that court can make a defendant's costs order. However it would not cover the costs of the reference as 'proceedings' is defined in section 21 as including proceedings in any court below but makes no mention of proceedings on a reference.

PRACTICE DIRECTION — DEVOLUTION ISSUES

(b) the addresses of the parties, except in the case of family proceedings, for which see paragraphs 15.2–4;
    (c) a concise statement of the background of the matter including:
        (i) the facts of the case, including any relevant findings of fact by the referring court or lower courts; and
        (ii) the main issues in the case and the contentions of the parties with regard to them;
    (d) the relevant law, including the relevant provisions of the GWA;
    (e) the reasons why an answer to the question is considered necessary for the purpose of disposing of the proceedings;
  (2) all judgments already given in the proceedings will be annexed to the reference;
  (3) the court may order the parties, or any of them, to draft the reference;
  (4) the court or tribunal will transmit the reference to:
    (a) the Civil Appeals Office Registry if the reference is to the Court of Appeal from a county court, the High Court or the Crown Court in civil proceedings, or from a tribunal;
    (b) the Registrar of Criminal Appeals if the reference is to the Court of Appeal from the Crown Court in proceedings on indictment; and
    (c) the Crown Office if the reference is to the High Court from a magistrates' court in civil or summary proceedings or from the Crown Court in summary proceedings[10].
If the reference is transmitted to Cardiff an additional copy of the reference must be filed so that it can be retained by the Cardiff Office. The original reference will be forwarded to the Crown Office in London.
  (5) at the same time as the reference is transmitted to the court receiving the reference a copy of the reference will be sent by first class post to:
    (a) the parties;
    (b) the Attorney General if he is not already a party; and
    (c) the Assembly if it is not already a party;
  (6) each person on whom a copy of the reference is served must within 21 days notify the court to which the reference is transmitted and the other persons on whom the reference is served whether they wish to be heard on the reference;
  (7) the court receiving the reference (either the Court of Appeal or the High Court) will give directions for the conduct of the reference, including the lodging of cases or skeleton arguments; and transmit a copy of the determination on the reference to the referring court; and
  (8) if there has been an appeal to the Judicial Committee against a decision of the High Court or the Court of Appeal on a reference, and a copy of the Judicial Committee's decision on that appeal has been sent to the High Court or Court of Appeal (as the case may be), that court will send a copy to the court which referred the devolution issue to it.
10.4 When a court receives notification of the decision on a reference, it will determine how to proceed with the remainder of the case.

POWER OF THE COURT TO DEAL WITH PENDING PROCEEDINGS IF A REFERENCE IS MADE (WHETHER BY THE ATTORNEY GENERAL, THE ASSEMBLY OR THE COURT)

11. If a reference is made the court will adjourn or stay the proceedings in which the devolution issue arose, unless it otherwise orders; and will make such further orders as it thinks fit in relation to any adjournment or stay.

THE WELSH LANGUAGE

12.1 If any party wishes to put forward a contention in relation to a devolution

---

[10] See Annex 2 for the relevant addresses. It shows The Law Courts, Cathays Park, Cardiff CF10 3PG and the Royal Courts of Justice, Strand, London WC2A 2LL as alternative addresses for transmitting documents to the Crown Office. If the order is transmitted to Cardiff, the additional copy will be forwarded by the Cardiff Office to the Crown Office in London.

PRACTICE DIRECTION — DEVOLUTION ISSUES

issue that involves comparison of the Welsh and English texts of any Assembly subordinate legislation, that party must give notice to the court as soon as possible.

12.2 Upon receipt of the notification, the court will consider the appropriate means of determining the issue, including, if necessary, the appointment of a Welsh speaking judicial assessor to assist the court.

12.3 Parties to any proceedings in which the Welsh language may be used must also comply with the Practice Direction of 16th October 1998 (relating to proceedings in the Crown Court) and the Practice Direction of 26th April 1999 (relating to civil proceedings). These Practice Directions apply, as appropriate, to proceedings involving a devolution issue in which the Welsh language may be used.

CROWN PROCEEDINGS ACT 1947 (SECTION 19)

13. Where the court has determined that a devolution issue arises, the Attorney General will give any necessary consent to:

  (1) the proceedings being transferred to The Law Courts, Cathays Park, Cardiff CF10 3PG, or to such other district registry as shall (exceptionally) be directed by the court; and

  (2) to the trial taking place at Cardiff or at such other trial location as shall (exceptionally) be directed by the court.

PART III DIRECTIONS APPLICABLE TO SPECIFIC PROCEEDINGS

JUDICIAL REVIEW PROCEEDINGS; CROWN OFFICE APPLICATIONS IN WALES

14.1 RSC Order 53, schedule 1 to the CPR contains the procedure to be followed in applications for judicial review.

14.2 Notwithstanding Queen's Bench Practice Direction 23 and prescribed forms 86A and 86B[11] facilities will be available for applications for judicial review to be lodged at The Law Courts, Cathays Park, Cardiff CF10 3PG if the relief sought or the grounds of the application involve either or both of the following:

  (1) a devolution issue arising out of the GWA;

  (2) an issue concerning the Welsh Assembly, the Welsh executive, or any Welsh public body (including a Welsh local authority) even if it does not involve a devolution issue.

Such applications may continue to be lodged at the Crown Office in London, if the applicant prefers to do that.

14.3 If applications are lodged at Cardiff an additional copy of the application must be filed so that it can be retained by the Cardiff Office. The original application will be forwarded to the Crown Office in London.

14.4 If a party intends to raise a devolution issue, the application notice must (in addition to the matters listed in RSC Order 53, rule 3(2)(a)):

  (1) specify that the applicant wishes to raise a devolution issue and identify the relevant provisions of the GWA; and

  (2) contain a summary of the facts and circumstances and points of law on the basis of which it is alleged that a devolution issue arises in sufficient detail to enable the court to determine whether a devolution issue arises.

FAMILY PROCEEDINGS IN THE MAGISTRATES' COURTS, THE COUNTY COURTS AND THE HIGH COURT

15.1 In any proceedings in which any question with respect to the upbringing of a child arises, the court shall have regard to the general principle that any delay in determining the question is likely to prejudice the welfare of the child[12].

---

[11] Queen's Bench Practice Direction 23 2C(2) provides that wherever practicable proceedings should be commenced in London, although applications can be made outside London in cases of urgency. Prescribed forms 86A and 86B give the address for delivery of the forms as the Crown Office, Royal Courts of Justice, Strand, London WC2A 2LL. It is hoped that these forms will be amended to give The Law Courts, Cathays Park, Cardiff CF10 3PG as an alternative address for the Crown Office.

[12] Section 1(2), Children Act 1989.

PRACTICE DIRECTION — DEVOLUTION ISSUES

15.2 If the FPR apply, the court will comply with rule 10.21[13].
15.3 If Part IV of the FPR applies, the court will comply with rule 4.23[14].
15.4 If the FPC apply, the court will comply with Rules 23 and 33A[15].
15.5 If the proceedings are listed in column (1) of Appendix 3 to the FPR or Schedule 2 to the FPC, a copy of any notice to be given to the parties must also be given to the persons set out in column (iv) of Appendix 3 or Schedule 2 as the case may be.
15.6 A party wishing to raise a devolution issue must, wherever possible, raise it (giving full particulars of the provisions relied on) in the application or answer or at the first directions hearing where appropriate.
15.7 If a party has not raised a devolution issue as above, the party must seek the permission of the court to raise it at a later stage.
15.8 Where a court has referred the devolution issue to another court and has received notification of the decision on the reference, the matter should so far as is practicable be placed before the same judge or magistrates who dealt with the case before the reference.

CIVIL PROCEEDINGS IN THE COUNTY COURTS AND THE HIGH COURT

16.1 A party wishing to raise a devolution issue must specify in the claim form, or if he is a defendant, in the defence (or written evidence filed with the acknowledgement of service in a Part 8 claim) that the claim raises a devolution issue and the relevant provisions of the GWA.
16.2 The particulars of claim or defence if the devolution issue is raised by the defendant (or written evidence filed with the acknowledgement of service in a Part 8 claim) must contain the facts and circumstances and points of law on the basis of which it is alleged that a devolution issue arises in sufficient detail to enable the court to determine whether a devolution issue arises in the proceedings.
16.3 Whether or not the allocation rules apply, if a question is raised during the proceedings that might be a devolution issue, then a directions hearing must

---

[13] Rule 10.21 states: (1) Subject to rule 2.3 [of the FPR] nothing in these rules shall be construed as requiring any party to reveal the address of their private residence (or that of any child) save by order of the court. (2) Where a party declines to reveal an address in reliance upon paragraph (1) above, he shall give notice of that address to the court in Form C8 and that address shall not be revealed to any person save by order of the court.

[14] Rule 4.23 states: (1) Notwithstanding any rule of court to the contrary, no document, other than a record of an order, held by the court and relating to proceedings to which [Part IV] applies shall be disclosed, other than to— (a) a party, (b) the legal representative of a party, (c) the guardian ad litem, (d) the Legal Aid Board, or (e) a welfare officer, without the leave of the judge or the district judge. (2) Nothing in this rule shall prevent the notification by the court or the proper officer of a direction under section 37(1) to the authority concerned. (3) Nothing in this rule shall prevent the disclosure of a document prepared by a guardian ad litem for the purpose of— (a) enabling a person to perform functions required by regulations made under section 41(7); (b) assisting a guardian ad litem or a reporting officer (within the meaning of section 65(1)(b) of the Adoption Act 1976) who is appointed under any enactment to perform his functions.

[15] Rule 23 states: (1) No document, other than a record of an order, held by the court and relating to relevant proceedings shall be disclosed, other than to— (a) a party, (b) the legal representative of a party, (c) the guardian ad litem, (d) the Legal Aid Board, or (e) a welfare officer, without leave of the justices' clerk or the court. (2) Nothing in this rule shall prevent the notification by the court or the justices' clerk of a direction under section 37(1) to the authority concerned. (3) Nothing in this rule shall prevent the disclosure of a document prepared by a guardian ad litem for the purpose of— (a) enabling a person to perform functions required by regulations made under section 41(7); (b) assisting a guardian ad litem or a reporting officer (within the meaning of section 65(1)(b) of the Adoption Act 1976) who is appointed under any enactment to perform his functions.
Rule 33A states: (1) Nothing in these Rules shall be construed as requiring any party to reveal the address of their private residence (or that of any child) except by order of the court. (2) Where a party declines to reveal an address in reliance upon paragraph (1) he shall give notice of that address to the court in Form C8 and that address shall not be revealed to any person except by order of the court.

take place and the matter must be referred to a circuit judge (in county court actions) or a High Court judge (in High Court actions) for determination as to whether a devolution issue arises and for further directions.

16.4 If a party fails to specify in the appropriate document that a devolution issue arises but that party subsequently wishes to raise a devolution issue, that party must seek the permission of the court.

16.5 Where any party has specified that a devolution issue arises, no default judgment can be obtained.

CRIMINAL PROCEEDINGS IN THE CROWN COURT

17. If the defendant wishes to raise a devolution issue he should do so at the Plea and Directions Hearing.

CRIMINAL AND CIVIL PROCEEDINGS IN THE MAGISTRATES' COURTS

18.1 (1) Where a defendant, who has been charged or has had an information laid against him in respect of a criminal offence and has entered a plea of 'Not Guilty', wishes to raise a devolution issue he should, wherever possible, give full particulars of the provisions relied on by notice in writing.

(2) Where a party to a complaint, or applicant for a licence wishes to raise a devolution issue he should, wherever possible, give full particulars of the provisions relied on by notice in writing.

(3) Such notice should be given to the prosecution (and other party if any) and the court as soon as practicable after the 'Not Guilty" plea is entered or the complaint or application is made as the case may be.

18.2 Where proceedings are to be committed or transferred to the Crown Court by the magistrates, the question as to whether a devolution issue arises shall be a matter for the Crown Court.

PART IV APPEALS

APPEALS TO THE COURT OF APPEAL (CIVIL AND CRIMINAL DIVISION)

19.1 This paragraph applies if a devolution issue is raised in any appeal to either the Civil or the Criminal Division of the Court of Appeal.

19.2 The devolution issue may already have been raised in the court whose decision is being appealed. The devolution issue may, however, be raised for the first time on appeal.

19.3 Where an application for permission to appeal is made, or an appeal is brought where permission is not needed, the appellant must specify in the application notice (or the notice of appeal or notice of motion as the case may be):

(1) that the appeal raises a devolution issue and the relevant provisions of the GWA;

(2) the facts and circumstances and points of law on the basis of which it is alleged that a devolution issue arises in sufficient detail to enable the court to determine whether a devolution issue arises; and

(3) whether the devolution issue was considered in the court below, and, if so, provide details of the decision.

19.4 An appellant may not seek to raise a devolution issue without the permission of the court after he has filed an application notice; or a notice of appeal or notice of motion (if no application notice).

19.5 Where permission to appeal is sought and a party to the appeal wishes to raise a devolution issue which was not raised in the lower court, the court will determine if a devolution issue arises before deciding whether to grant leave to appeal.

APPEALS TO THE CROWN COURT

20. A notice of appeal from a decision of the magistrates' courts to the Crown Court must specify whether the devolution issue was considered in the court below and if so, provide details of the decision. If it was not so considered, the notice should specify:

(1) that the appeal raises a devolution issue and the relevant provisions of the GWA; and

(2) the facts and circumstances and points of law on the basis of which it is alleged that a devolution issue arises in sufficient detail to enable the court to determine whether a devolution issue arises.

ANNEX 1

DI 1
DEVOLUTION ISSUES

NOTICE OF DEVOLUTION ISSUE TO ATTORNEY GENERAL AND THE NATIONAL ASSEMBLY FOR WALES

[NAME OF CASE]

Take notice that the above mentioned case has raised a devolution issue as defined by Schedule 8 to the Government of Wales Act 1998. Details of the devolution issue are given in the attached schedule.

This notice meets the notification requirements under paragraph 5(1) of Schedule 8 to the Government of Wales Act 1998. You may take part as a party to these proceedings, so far as they relate to a devolution issue (paragraph 5(2) of Schedule 8). If you want to do this you must notify the court by completing the attached form, and returning it to the court at [address] by [date].

DATED

To: The Attorney General
The National Assembly for Wales
Other parties (where appropriate)

DI 2
DEVOLUTION ISSUES

NOTICE OF INTENTION OF ATTORNEY GENERAL OR THE NATIONAL ASSEMBLY FOR WALES TO BECOME PARTY TO PROCEEDINGS, SO FAR AS THEY RELATE TO A DEVOLUTION ISSUE, UNDER PARAGRAPH 5(2) SCHEDULE 8 TO THE GOVERNMENT OF WALES ACT 1998

In the [name of court]

[case name]

Take notice that the [Attorney General] [the National Assembly for Wales] intends to take part as a party to proceedings so far as they relate to a devolution issue as permitted by paragraph 5(2) of Schedule 8 to the Government of Wales Act 1998 in relation to the devolution issue raised by [ ], of which notice was received by the [Attorney General] [Assembly] on [ ].

[The [ ] also gives notice that it [requires the matter to be referred to] [is still considering whether to require the matter to be referred to] the Judicial Committee of the Privy Council under paragraph 30 of Schedule 8 to the Government of Wales Act 1998.]

[DATE]

On behalf of the [Attorney General]
[National Assembly for Wales]

To: The clerk of the court at [ ]
The parties to the case
[Attorney General] [National Assembly for Wales]

DI 3
DEVOLUTION ISSUES

NOTICE BY ATTORNEY GENERAL OR NATIONAL ASSEMBLY FOR WALES THAT THEY REQUIRE DEVOLUTION ISSUE TO BE REFERRED TO THE JUDICIAL COMMITTEE OF THE PRIVY COUNCIL

In the [court]

[case name]

PRACTICE DIRECTION — DEVOLUTION ISSUES

The [Attorney General] [National Assembly for Wales] gives notice that the devolution issue, which has been raised in the above case and to which [he] [it] is a party, must be referred to the Judicial Committee of the Privy Council under paragraph 30 of Schedule 8 to the Government of Wales Act 1998.

[DATE]

On behalf of the [Attorney General]
[National] Assembly for Wales]

To: The clerk of the court at [ ]
The parties to the case
[Attorney General] [National Assembly for Wales]

DI 4
DEVOLUTION ISSUES

REFERENCE BY THE COURT OR TRIBUNAL OF DEVOLUTION ISSUE TO [HIGH COURT] [COURT OF APPEAL] [JUDICIAL COMMITTEE OF THE PRIVY COUNCIL]

In the [court]

[case name]

It is ordered that the devolution issue(s) set out in the schedule be referred to the [High Court] [Court of Appeal] [Judicial Committee of the Privy Council] for determination in accordance with paragraph [ ] of Schedule 8 to the Government of Wales Act 1998.

It is further ordered that the proceedings be stayed until the [High Court] [Court of Appeal] [Judicial Committee of the Privy Council] determine the devolution issue[s] or until further order.

DATED

Judge/clerk to the magistrates' court
Chairman of the Tribunal
[Address]

SKELETON REFERENCE TO BE ATTACHED TO FORM DI 4

In the [court]

[case name]

    (a) [The question referred.]
    (b) [The addresses of the parties]
    (c) [A concise statement of the background to the matters including—
        (i) The facts of the case including any relevant findings of fact by the referring court or lower courts; and
        (ii) The main issues in the case and the contentions of the parties with regard to them;]
    (d) [the relevant law including the relevant provisions of the Government of Wales Act 1998]
    (e) [the reasons why an answer to the question is considered necessary for the purpose of disposing of the proceedings.]

[All judgments already given in the proceedings are annexed to this reference.]

ANNEX 2 ADDRESSES

1. Notices to the National Assembly for Wales (Cynulliad Cenedlaethol Cymru) must be sent to the Counsel General to the National Assembly for Wales, Crown Buildings, Cathays Park, Cardiff CF99 1NA. Fax number: (01222) 826798.

PRACTICE DIRECTION — DEVOLUTION ISSUES

2. Notices to the Attorney General must be sent to the Attorney General's Chambers, 9 Buckingham Gate, London SW1E 6JP. Fax number 0171 271 2433.

3. References to the Crown Office under paragraph 9.3(1)c of the Practice Direction may be sent to the Crown Office, Royal Courts of Justice, Strand, London WC2A 2LL; or the Law Courts, Cathays Park, Cardiff CF10 3PG (2 copies).

EXPLANATORY NOTE

4. The addresses and fax numbers above are the best information available. However it is possible that these (particularly the fax numbers and address for Notices to the Assembly) may change. It would therefore be advisable to confirm the numbers before sending information.

CYFARWYDDYD YMARFER — MATERION YN YMWNEUD Â DATGANOLI (A CHEISIADAU SWYDDFA'R GORON YNG NGHYMRU)

Rhennir y cyfarwyddyd ymarfer hwn yn 4 rhan:
Rhan I   Cyflwyniad
Rhan II Cyfarwyddiadau perthnasol i bob achos
Rhan III Cyfarwyddiadau perthnasol i achosion penodol (mae paragraffau 14.2 ac 14.3 yn delio â cheisiadau Swyddfa'r Goron yng Nghymru)
Rhan IV Apeliadau

RHAN I CYFLWYNIAD

DIFFINIADAU

1. Yn y Cyfarwyddyd Ymarfer hwn:
golyga 'y Cynulliad' Gynulliad Cenedlaethol Cymru
golyga 'DLC' Ddeddf Llywodraeth Cymru 1998
golyga 'DGI' Ddeddf Gogledd Iwerddon 1998
golyga 'DA' Ddeddf yr Alban 1998
golyga 'y Deddfau' DLC, DGI a DA
golyga 'y Pwyllgor Barnwrol' Bwyllgor Barnwrol y Cyfrin-Gyngor
golyga 'RTS' Reolau Trefn Sifil 1998
golyga 'RAT' Reolau Achosion Teulu 1991
golyga 'LAT' Reolau 1991 (Deddf Plant 1989) Llysoedd Achosion Teulu
golyga 'RGL' Reolau Y Goruchel Lys
mae gan 'mater datganoli' yr un ystyr ag ym mharagraff 1, atodlen 8 DLG; paragraff 1, atodlen 10 DGI; a pharagraff 1, atodlen 6 DA
golyga 'rhybudd mater datganoli' rybudd bod mater datganoli wedi codi yn yr achos

YSTOD

2.1 Mae'r Cyfarwyddyd Ymarfer hwn yn ategu'r darpariaethau sy'n delio â materion datganoli yn y Deddfau. Mae'n delio'n benodol â'r sefyllfa os yw mater datganoli'n codi o dan DLC. Os yw mater datganoli'n codi o dan DGI neu DA dylid addasu'r drefn a osodir yn y Cyfarwyddyd Ymarfer hwn fel y bo'r angen.

2.2 Mae'r Cyfarwyddyd Ymarfer hwn hefyd yn delio â cheisiadau Swyddfa'r Goron yng Nghymru (gweler paragraffau 14.2 ac 14.3).

DEDDFWRIAETH DATGANOLI

3.1 Mae atodlen 8 DLC yn cynnwys darpariaethau'n delio â materion datganoli sy'n deillio o DLC; mae atodlen 10 DGI yn cynnwys darpariaethau'n delio â materion datganoli'n deillio o DGI; ac mae atodlen 6 DA yn cynnwys darpariaethau'n delio â materion datganoli'n deillio o DA.

3.2 Yn gyffredinol bydd mater datganoli'n ymwneud ag a yw corff datganoledig wedi gweithredu neu'n bwriadu gweithredu o fewn ei bwerau (sy'n cynnwys peidio â gweithredu'n anghydnaws â hawliau Confensiwn[1] a deddf Cymuned[2]) neu wedi

---

[1] Nodir hawliau a rhyddid sylfaenol yn: (a) Erthyglau 2 i 12 ac 14 Confensiwn Ewropeaidd ar Hawliau Dynol ('CEHD'), (b) Erthyglau 1 i 3 o'r Protocol Cyntaf (cytunwyd ym Mharis 20 Mawrth 1952), ac (c) Erthyglau 1 a 2 y Chweched Protocol (cytunwyd yn Strasbourg 11 Mai 1994), fel y'u darllenir gydag Erthyglau 16 ac 18 CEHD (Adran 1 Deddf Hawliau Dynol 1998; a. 107(1) a (5) DLC; adrannau 6(2); 24(1) a 98(1) DGI; adrannau 29(2); 57(2) a 126(1) DA).

[2] Yr holl hawliau, pwerau, rhwymedigaethau, goblygiadau a chyfyngiadau a grewyd neu sy'n deillio o bryd i'w gilydd gan neu o dan Gytundebau Cymuned; a'r holl rwymediau a threfniadaethau a ddarparwyd o bryd i'w gilydd ar gyfer, gan neu o dan Gytundebau Cymuned (adrannau 106(7) a 155(1), DLC; adrannau 6(2); 24(1) a 98(1), DGI; adrannau 29(2); 57(2) a 126(9) DA).

methu â chydymffurfio â dyletswydd a osodwyd arno. Dylid cyfeirio at y Deddfau lle caiff 'mater datganoli' ei ddiffinio.

3.3 (1) Os yw mater datganoli o dan DLC yn codi yn yr achos, rhaid i'r llys orchymyn bod rhybudd o hyn yn cael ei roi i'r Twrnai Cyffredinol ac i'r Cynulliad os nad ydynt eisoes yn barti. Mae ganddynt hawl i gymryd rhan fel parti yn yr achos i'r graddau y maent yn berthnasol i fater datganoli, os nad ydynt eisoes yn barti (paragraff 5, atodlen 8 i DLC). Os ydynt yn cymryd rhan, gallant fynnu bod y llys yn cyfeirio'r mater datganoli 1'r Pwyllgor Barnwrol (paragraff 30, atodlen 8 DLC)[3].

(2) Ceir darpariaethau tebyg yn DGI a DA er bod y bobl i'w hysbysu'n wahanol (paragraffau 13, 14, a 33, atodlen 10 DGI; paragraffau 16, 17 a 33, atodlen 6 DA).

3.4 O dan yr holl Ddeddfau gall y llys gyfeirio mater datganoli i lys arall fel a ganlyn:

(1) Gall llys ynadon gyfeirio mater datganoli'n codi o achos sifil neu ddiannod i'r Uchel Lys (paragraffau 6 a 9, atodlen 8 DLC; paragraffau 15 ac 18, atodlen 10 DGI; a pharagraffau 18 a 21, atodlen 6 DA).

(2) Gall Llys y Goron gyfeirio mater datganoli'n codi mewn achos diannod i'r Uchel Lys a mater datganoli'n codi mewn achosion ar dditiad i'r Llys Apêl (paragraff 9, atodlen 8 DLC; paragraff 18, atodlen 10 DGI, paragraff 21, atodlen 6 DA).

(3) Gall llys sirol, yr Uchel Lys (oni bal bod y mater datganoli wedi ei gyfeirio i'r Uchel Lys)[4], a Llys y Goron[5] gyfeirio mater datganoli'n codi o achos sifil i'r Llys Apêl (paragraff 7, atodlen 8 DLC; paragraff 16, atodlen 10 DGI, paragraff 19, atodlen 6 DA).

(4) Rhaid i dribiwnlys lle nad oes apêl, a gall unrhyw dribiwnlys arall, gyfeirio mater datganoli i'r Llys Apêl (paragraff 8, atodlen 8 DLC; paragraff 17, atodlen 10 DGI; paragraff 20, atodlen 6 DA).

(5) Gall y Llys Apêl gyfeirio mater datganoli i'r Pwyllgor Barnwrol, oni bai bod y mater datganoli wedi ei gyfeirio iddo gan lys arall (paragraff 10, atodlen 8 DLC; paragraff 19, atodlen 10 DGI; paragraff 22, atodlen 6 DA).

(6) Y Pwyllgor Barnwrol sydd 1 ddelio ag apêl yn erbyn cyfeirio penderfyniad ar fater datganoli i'r Uchel Lys neu Lys Apêl, gyda chaniatâd y llys perthnasol, neu o fethu â chael caniatâd o'r fath, gyda chaniatâd arbennig y Pwyllgor Barnwrol (paragraff 11, atodlen 8 DLC; paragraff 20, atodlen 10 DGI; paragraff 23, atodlen 6 DA).

3.5 Gall llys gymryd i ystyriaeth dreuliau ychwanegol y mae'r llys yn tybio bod parti wedi eu talu wrth i'r Twrnai Cyffredinol neu'r Cynulliad gymryd rhan wrth benderfynu unrhyw gwestiwn ar gostau (paragraff 35, atodlen 8 DLC).

RHAN II CYFARWYDDIADAU PERTHNASOL I BOB ACHOS

YSTOD

4. Mae paragraffau 5 i 13 yn berthnasol i achosion yng Nghymru a Lloegr mewn llysoedd ynadon, llysoedd sirol, Llys y Goron, yr Uchel Lys a'r Llys Apêl (Adran Sifil a Throseddol). Mae paragraff 10 hefyd yn berthnasol i ffurf a threfn cyfeirio i Lys Apêl gan dribiwnlys.

---

[3] Pe bai'r Twrnai Cyffredinol neu'r Cynulliad wedi dod yn barti i'r achos gwreiddiol ond heb ymarfer eu hawl i fynnu bod y mater datganoli'n cael ei gyfeirio i'r Pwyllgor Barnwroi a'r llys wedi penderfynu'r achos, byddai ganddynt yr un hawl apêl â phartïon. Ni fyddai'r rhain yn caniatáu apêl iddynt ar benderfyniad a wnaed mewn achos ar dditiad, er bod gan y Twrnai Cyffredinol bŵer o dan adran 36 Deddf Cyfiawnder Troseddol 1972 i gyfeirio pwynt o gyfraith i'r Llys Apêl lle bo'r diffynnydd wedi ei ryddhau mewn prawf ar dditiad.

Mae paragraff 31, atodlen 8 DLC, yn caniatáu i'r Twrnai Cyffredinol ac i'r Cynulliad gyfeirio i'r Pwyllgor Barnwrol unrhyw fater datganoli nad yw'n destun achos. Gellid defnyddio'r pŵer hwn pe bai llys yn penderfynu a hwythau heb fod yn bartïon ac felly heb hawl apêl ond ni allai cyfeirio o'r fath effeithio penderfyniad y llys.

[4] Os yw apêl mewn ffurfachos datganedig mewn achos troseddol yn mynd i Lys Adrannol ymddengys nad oes pŵer gan y Llys Adrannol i gyfeirio mater datganoli i'r Llys Apêl.

[5] e.e. mewn apeliadau o lys ynadon ar fater trwyddedu

CODI CWESTIWN A YW MATER DATGANOLI'N CODI

5.1 Lle y mae parti i unrhyw ffurf o achos am godi mater a all fod yn fater datganoli, boed fel cais (neu ran o gais) i orfodi neu i sefydlu hawl gyfreithiol neu i geisio rhwymedi neu fel amddiffyniad (neu ran o amddiffyniad), bydd darpariaethau'r Cyfarwyddyd Ymarfer hwn yn berthnasol yn ogystal â'r rheolau trefn sy'n berthnasol i'r achos y cwyd y mater ohono.

5.2 Gall llys, o'i ewyllys ei hun, fynnu bod ystyriaeth yn cael el roi i'r cwestiwn a yw mater datganoli'n codi, os ywr defnyddiau a osodwyd gerbron y llys yn nodi y gall mater o'r fath godi, hyd yn oed os nad yw'r partïon wedi defnyddio'r term 'mater datganoli'.

PENDERFYNIAD GAN LYS A YW MATER DATGANOLI'N CODI

6.1 Gall y llys rol cyfarwyddiadau y cred eu bod yn addas i gaei eglurhad neu wybodaeth ychwanegol i bennu a yw mater datganoli'n codi.

6.2 Wrth bennu a yw mater datganoli'n codi, gall y llys, beth bynnag fo haeriad parti i'r llys, benderfynu *nad* yw mater datganoli'n codi os yw'r haeriad yn ymddangos i'r llys yn wamal neu'n flinderus (paragraff 2, atodlen 8 DLC).

6.3 Os yw'r llys yn penderfynu bod mater datganoli'n codi rhaid iddo ddatgan yn glir ac yn gryno beth yw'r mater datganoli.

RHYBUDD O FATER DATGANOLI I'R TWRNAI CYFFREDINOL AC I'R CYNULLIAD

7.1 Os yw llys yn penderfynu bod mater datganoli'n codi yn yr achos, rhaid iddo orchymyn rhybudd mater datganoli o ran sylwedd yn ffurflen rhif 'DI 1' yn Atodiad 1 i'w rhoi i'r Twrnai Cyffredinol ac i'r Cynulliad oni bai eu bod eisoes yn barti i'r achos (paragraff 5(1), atodlen 8 DLC).

7.2 Nid oes rhaid i lys sy'n derbyn y cyfeirio gyhoeddi rhybudd mater datganoli oni bai ei fod yn penderfynu fod mater datganoli wedi codi na chafodd el nodi gan y llys sy'n gwneud y cyfeirio. Yn yr achos hwnnw rhaid i'r llys sy'n derbyn y cyfeirio gyhoeddi rhybudd mater datganoli. Rhaid i'r rhybudd hwn:

(1) nodi pa fater neu faterion datganoli sydd wedi cael ei gyfeirio neu eu cyfeirio iddo;

(2) nodi pa fater neu faterion datganoli pellach sydd wedi codi; a

(3) nodi'r llys sy'n cyfeirio.

7.3 Os yw'r mater datganoli wedi codi mewn achos troseddol, rhaid i'r rhybudd mater datganoli nodi:

(1) a yw'r achos wedi cael ei ohirio;

(2) a yw'r diffynnydd wedi ei gadw yn y ddalfa; ac

(3) os yw'r diffynnydd wedi ei gadw yn y ddalfa ac os nad yw ei brawf wedi dechrau, pryd y bydd terfyn amser cadw yn y ddalfa'n dod i ben.[6]

7.4 Os yw'r mater datganoli'n codi mewn apêl, rhaid i'r rhybudd mater datganoli:

(1) nodi bod y mater datganoli'n codi mewn apêl;

(2) nodi'r llys yr apelir yn erbyn ei benderfyniad; a

(3) nodi a godir y mater dataganoli ei godi am y tro cyntaf ar apêl; neu os na chodir, nodi bod y mater datganoli wedi el godi yn y llys y mae apêl yn erbyn ei benderfyniad, pa benderfyniad a wnaed yn y llys hwnnw, a dyddiad y rhybudd blaenorol i'r Twrnai Cyffredinol ac i'r Cynulliad.

7.5 Bydd y rhybudd mater datganoli'n pennu dyddiad a fydd yn 14 diwrnod, neu'n gyfnod hwy yn ôl cyfarwyddyd y llys (gweler isod), ar ôl dyddiad y rhybudd mater datganoli, fel y dyddiad y bydd rhaid i'r Twrnai Cyffredinol neu'r Cynulliad roi gwybod i'r llys a ydyw am gymryd rhan fel parti i'r achos, o ran ei berthynas i fater datganoli.

7.6 Gall y llys, mewn amgylchiadau eithriadol, nodi dyddiad hwy na 14 diwrnod ar ôl dyddiad y rhybudd mater datganoli fel y dyddiad y bydd rhaid i'r Twrnai Cyffredinol neu'r Cynulliad rol gwybod i'r llys a ydyw am gymryd rhan fel parti i'r achos. Gall y llys wneud hyn cyn rhoi'r rhybudd, neu cyn neu ar ôl diwedd y cyfnod a roddir yn y rhybudd.

---

[6] Caiff terfynau amser cadw yn y ddalfa eu gosod gan Reoliadau Erlyn Troseddau (Terfynau Amser yn y Ddalfa) 1987 fel y'u gwellwyd.

PRACTICE DIRECTION — DEVOLUTION ISSUES (WELSH TEXT)

7.7 (1) Ar ddyddiad y rhybudd mater datganoli
(a) Rhaid i'r rhybudd mater datganoli i'r Twrnai Cyffredinol gael ei ffacsio ato gan y llys[7]; a
(b) Rhaid i'r rhybudd mater datganoli i'r Cynulliad gael ei ffacsio gan y llys at Gwnsel Cyffredinol y Cynulliad;
(2) Yr un dydd ag yr anfonir ffacs rhaid anfon copi o'r rhybudd mater datganoli gan y llys gyda phost dosbarth cyntaf at y Twrnai Cyffredinol ac at Gwnsel Cyffredinol y Cynulliad.

7.8 Gall y llys, ar delerau yr ystyria'n addas, orchymyn bod dogfennau ychwanegol yn cael eu cyflwyno (ee mewn achos sifil, y ffurflen hawlio) neu bod gwybodaeth ychwanegol yn cael ei darparu gyda'r rhybudd mater datganoli.

7.9 (1) Pan fo llys yn gorchymyn bod rhybudd mater datganoli'n cael ei roi gall y llys wneud gorchmynion pellach fel y gwêl yn dda mewn perthynas â gohirio, atal neu barhau'r achos, neu fesurau dros dro, yn ystod y cyfnod y mae rhaid i'r Twrnai Cyffredinol a'r Cynulliad roi gwybod i'r llys a ydynt yn bwriadu cymryd rhan fel parti i'r achos.
(2) Cyn gorchymyn gohiriad mewn achos troseddol, bydd y llys yn ystyried yr holl amgylchiadau perthnasol, gan gynnwys a fyddai'n golygu gohirio a allai estyn y tu hwnt i derfynau amser cadw yn y ddalfa os yw'r diffynnydd wedi ei gadw yn y ddalfa ac os nad yw ei brawf wedi dechrau.

7.10 Os nad yw'r Twrnai Cyffredinol na'r Cynulliad yn rhoi gwybod i'r llys o fewn yr amser penodedig ei fod am gymryd rhan fel parti i'r achos:
(1) dylai'r achos fynd yn ei flaen ar unwaith ar ddiwedd y cyfnod yr oedd ganddynt i rol gwybod i'r ilys; a
(2) nid oes dyletswydd ar y llys i rol gwybod iddynt o ganlyniad yr achos ac eithrio'r ddyletswydd i roi gwybod iddynt a yw'r llys yn penderfynu cyfeirio'r mater datganoli i lys arall (gweler paragraff 10.3 (5)).[8]

YCHWANEGU'R TWRNAI CYFFREDINOL NEU'R CYNULLIAD AT YR ACHOS A'U HAWL I FYNNU CYFEIRIO MATER DATGANOLI I'R PWYLLGOR BARNWROL

8.1 Os yw'r Twrnai Cyffredinol neu'r Cynulliad am gymryd rhan fel parti i'r achos cyhyd ag y bo'n ymwneud â mater datganoli, rhaid iddo anfon i'r llys ac at y partïon eraill (ac at ei gilydd os un ohonynt yn unig sydd wedi dod yn barti) rybudd o ran sylwedd yn y ffurflen a rifwyd 'DI 2' a ddangosir yn Atodiad 1 o fewn yr amser a nodir yn y rhybudd mater datganoli.

8.2 Wrth dderbyn y ffurflen hon gall y llys roi cyfarwyddiadau dilynol fel y gwêl yn angenrheidiol.

8.3 Os yw'r Twrnai Cyffredinol neu'r Cynulliad yn barti i'r achos, ac os yw'r naill neu'r llall ohonynt am fynnu bod y llys yn cyfeirio'r mater datganoli i Bwyllgor Barnwrol, rhaid iddo cyn gynted ag y bo'n ymarferol anfon rhybudd o ran sylwedd yn y ffurflen a rifwyd 'DI 3' yn Atodiad 1 i'r llys ac at y partïon eraill (ac at ei gilydd os un ohonynt yn unig sydd wedi dod yn barti).

PENDERFYNIAD GAN Y LLYS AR GYFEIRIO MATER DATGANOLI AI PEIDIO OS NAD YW'R TWRNAI CYFFREDINOL NEU'R CYNULLIAD YN MYNNU CYFEIRIO

9.1 Os nad oes gofyn i'r llys gyfeirio'r mater datganoli i'r Pwyllgor Barnwrol, bydd y llys yn penderfynu a ddylai gyfeirio'r mater datganoli i'r llys perthnasol fel y nodir ym mharagraff 3.4.

9.2 Cyn penderfynu a ddylid cyfeirlo, gall y llys gynnal gwrandawiad cyfarwyddo neu roi cyfarwyddiadau ysgrifenedig ar wneud argymhellion ynglŷn â chyfeirio neu beidio.

9.3 Gall y llys benderfynu ar sail argymhellion ysgrifenedig os yw ei drefniadaeth yn caniatâu hyn ac os yw'n dymuno gwneud hyn, neu gall y llys gynnal gwrandawiad cyn penderfynu.

---

[7] Gweler Atodiad 2 am wybodaeth am rifau ffacs a chyfeiriadau.
[8] Os oes apêl, bydd y llys apêl yn cyflwyno rhybudd mater datganoli i'r Twrnai Cyffredinol ac i'r Cynulliad (gweler paragraff 7.4).

PRACTICE DIRECTION — DEVOLUTION ISSUES (WELSH TEXT)

9.4 Wrth ddefnyddio'i ddisgresiwn a ydyw am gyfeirio, bydd y llys yn ystyried yr holl amgylchiadau perthnasol ac yn enwedig:
   (1) pwysigrwydd y mater datganoli i'r cyhoedd yn gyffredinol;
   (2) pwysigrwydd y mater datganoli i bartïon gwreiddiol yr achos;
   (3) a fyddai penderfyniad ar gyfeirio'r mater datganoli yn dyngedfennol yn y materion o anghydfod rhwng y partïon;
   (4) a yw holl ganfyddiadau perthnasol ffeithiau wedi eu gwneud (nt fydd mater datganoli, oni bai bod mgylchiadau eithriadol, yn addas i'w gyfeirio os oes rhaid iddo gael el gyfeirio ar sail ffeithiau tybiedig);
   (5) y gohirio y byddai cyfeirio'n ei olygu yn enwedig mewn achosion sy'n cynnwys plant ac achosion troseddol (gan gynnwys a yw'r cyfeirio'n debyg o olygu gohirio a fyddai'n estyn y tu hwnt i ddiwedd y terfynau amser ar gadw yn y ddalfa os yw'r diffynnydd wedi ei gadw yn y ddalfa ac os nad yw ei brawf wedi dechrau); a
   (6) costau ychwanegol y gallai cyfeirio eu golygu.[9]

9.5 Dylai'r llys nodi ei resymau dros wneud neu wrthod cyfeirio.

9.6 Os yw'r llys yn penderfynu peidio â chyfeirio'r achos, bydd yn rhoi cyfarwyddiadau ar gyfer trin yr achos yn y dyfodol, a fydd yn cynnwys cyfarwyddiadau ar y rhan a gymer y Twrnai Cyffredinol a'r Cynulliad os ydynt yn bartïon.

FFURFLEN A THREFN CYFEIRIO

10.1 Os yw'r Twrnai Cyffredinol neu'r Cynulliad yn hawlio bod y llys neu'r tribiwnlys (mewn perthynas ag unrhyw achos gerbron y llys y mae'n barti iddo) yn cyfeirio'r mater datganoli l'r Pwyllgor Barnwrol:
   (1) bydd y llys neu'r triblwnlys yn gwneud y cyfeirio cyn gynted ag y bo'n ymarferol ar ôl derbyn y rhybudd oddi wrth y Twrnai Cyffredinol neu'r Cynulliad o ran sylwedd yn y ffurflen a rifwyd 'DI 3' a ddangosir yn Atodiad 1, ac yn dilyn y drefn ar gyfer cyfeirio yng Ngorchymyn Rheolau'r Pwyllgor Barnwrol (Materion Datganoli) 1999; a
   (2) gall y llys neu'r tribiwnlys orchymyn y partïon, neu unrhyw un ohonynt, i lunio'r cyfeirio.

10.2 Os yw'r Llys Apêl yn penderfynu cyfeirio'r mater datganoli i'r Pwyllgor Barnwrol:
   (1) bydd yn dilyn y drefn yng Ngorchymyn Rheolau'r Pwyllgor Barnwrol (Materion Datganoli) 1999; a
   (2) gall y llys orchymyn y partïon, neu unrhyw un ohonynt, i lunio'r cyfeirio.

10.3 Os yw unrhyw lys neu dribiwnlys arall yn penderfynu cyfeirio'r mater datganoli i unrhyw lys arall, neu os mynnir bod tribiwnlys yn gwneud hynny:
   (1) rhaid i'r cyfeirio fod o ran sylwedd yn y ffurflen a rifwyd 'DI 4' a ddangosir yn Atodiad i a rhaid iddo nodi'r canlynol:
      (a) y cwestewn a gyfeirir;
      (b) cyfeiriadau'r partïon, ac eithrio mewn achosion teulu, gweler paragraffau 15.2–4;
      (c) datganiad cryno o gefndir y mater gan gynnwys:
         (i) ffeithiau'r achos, gan gynnwys unrhyw ganfyddiadau ffeithiol perthnasol gan y llys cyfeirio neu'r llysoedd is; a
         (ii) y prif bynciau yn yr achos a haeriadau'r partïon ynglŷn â hwy;
      (ch) y gyfraith berthnasol, gan gynnwys darpariaethau perthnasol DLC;
      (d) y rhesymau pam caiff ateb i'r cwestiwn ei ystyried yn angenrheidiol er mwyn gwaredu'r achos;
   (2) bydd pob dyfarniad a roddwyd eisoes yn yr achos yn cael ei atodi i'r cyfeirio;
   (3) gall y llys orchymyn y partïon, neu unrhyw un ohonynt, i lunio'r cyfeirio;
   (4) bydd y llys neu'r tribiwnlys yn trosglwyddo'r cyfeirio.i:

---

[9] Mewn achosion troseddol nid yw adran 16 Deddf Erlyn Troseddau 1985 yn galluogi llys sy'n derbyn cyfeirio i wneud gorchymyn costau diffynydd. Os yw'r diffynnydd wedi hyn yn cael ei ryddhau gan y llys sydd wedi gwneud y cyfeirio, gall y llys hwnnw wneud gorchymyn costau diffynydd. Serch hynny ni fyddai'n ymwneud â chostau'r cyfeirio gan fod 'achos' sy'n cael ei ddiffinio yn adran 21 yn cynnwys achos mewn unrhyw lys llai ond nid yw'n sôn am achos ar ôl cyfeirio.

PRACTICE DIRECTION — DEVOLUTION ISSUES (WELSH TEXT)

　　　　(a) Cofrestrfa'r Swyddfa Apeliadau Cyhoeddus os yw'r cyfeirio i'r Llys Apêl oddi wrth Lys Sirol, yr Uchel Lys neu Lys y Goron mewn achos sifil, neu oddl wrth dribiwnlys;
　　　　(b) Cofrestrydd Apeliadau Troseddol os yw'r cyfeirio i'r Llys Apêl oddi wrth Lys y Goron mewn achos ar dditiad; a
　　　　(c) Swyddfa'r Goron os ywr cyfeirio i'r Uchel Lys o lys ynadon mewn achos sifil neu ddiannod neu oddi wrth Lys y Goron mewn achos diannod.[10]
Os caiff y gorchymyn el drosglwyddo i Gaerdydd rhaid ffeilio copi ychwanegol o'r gorchymyn fel y gellir ei gadw gan Swyddfa Caerdydd. Caiff y cyfeirio gwreiddioi ei anfon i Swyddfa'r Goron yn Llundain.
　　　(5) yr un pryd ag y caiff y cyfeirio ei drosglwyddo i'r llys sy'n derbyn y cyfeirio anfonir copi o'r cyfeirio gyda'r post dosbarth cyntaf at:
　　　　(a) y partïon;
　　　　(b) y Twrnai Cyffredinol os nad yw ef eisoes yn barti; a
　　　　(c) y Cynulliad os nad yw eisoes yn barti;
　　　(6) rhaid i bob un y cyflwynir copi o'r trosglwyddo iddo roi gwybod i'r llys y trosglwyddir y cyfeirio iddo ac i eraill y cyflwynir y cyfeirio iddynt o fewn 21 dydd a ydynt am gael eu clywed ar y cyfeirio;
　　　(7) bydd y llys sy'n derbyn y cyfeirio (naill ai'r Llys Apêl neu'r Uchel Lys) yn rhoi cyfarwyddiadau ar sut y trafodir y cyfeirio, gan gynnwys cyflwyro argymhellion neu ddadleuon sgerbwd; a throsglwyddo copi o'r penderfyniad ar y cyfeirio i'r llys cyfeirio; a
　　　(8) os ceir apêl i'r Pwyllgor Barnwrol yn erbyn penderfyniad Uchel Llys neu Lys Apêl ar gyfeirio, ac os oes copi o benderfyniad y Pwyllgor Barnwrol ar yr apêl wedi ei anfon i'r Uchel Lys neu i'r Llys Apêl (fel y bo'n briodol), bydd y llys yn anfon copi i'r llys a gyfeiriodd y mater datganoli iddo.
　10.4　Pan fo llys yn derbyn hysbysiad o benderfyniad ar gyfeirlo, bydd yn penderfynu ar sut i fwrw ymlaen â gweddill yr achos.

PŴER LLYS I DDELIO AG ACHOS YN YR ARFAETH OS GWNEIR CYFEIRIO (NAILL AI GAN Y TWRNAI CYFFREDINOL, Y CYNULLIAD NEU'R LLYS)
　11.　Os gwneir cyfeirlo bydd y llys yn gohirio neu'n atal yr achos lle y cododd y mater datganoli, oni bai ei fod yn gorchymyn fel arall; a bydd yn gwneud gorchmynion pellach fel y gwêl yn dda mewn perthynas ag unrhyw ohirio neu atal.

YR IAITH GYMIRAEG
　12.1　Os yw unrhyw barti'n dymuno cynnig haeriad ynglŷn â mater datganoli sy'n cynnwys cymharu testunau Cymraeg a Saesneg unrhyw ddeddfwriaeth eiladd o eiddo'r Cynulliad, rhaid i'r parti hwnnw roi rhybudd i'r llys cyn gynted ag y bo modd.
　12.2　Wrth dderbyn yr hysbysiad, bydd y llys yn ystyried y dull priodol o benderfynu'r mater, gan gynnwys, os oes angen, benodi asesydd barnwrol Cymraeg i gynorthwyo'r llys.
　12.3　Rhaid i bartïon i unrhyw achos lle y caiff y Gymraeg o bosib ei defnyddio hefyd gydymffurfio â Chyfarwyddyd Ymarfer 16 Hydref 1998 (yn ymwneud ag achosion yn Llys y Goron) a Chyfarwyddyd Ymarfer 26 Ebrill 1999 (yn ymwneud ag achosion sifil). Mae'r Cyfarwyddiadau Ymarfer hyn yn gyrnwys, fel y bo'n addas, i achosion yn ymwneud ä mater datganoli lle y bydd y Gymraeg o bosib yn cael el defnyddio.

DEDDF ACHOSION Y GORON 1947 (ADRAN 19)
　13.　Lle y mae llys wedi penderfynu bod achos datganoli'n codi, bydd y Twrnai Cyffredinol yn rhoi unrhyw gydsyniad angenrheidiol i:

---

[10] Gweler Atodiad 2 am gyfeiriadau perthnasol. Dengys Lysoedd Cyfraith, Parc Cathays, Caerdydd CF10 3PG a Llysoedd Barn Brenhinol, Strand, Llundain WC2A 21LL fel cyfeiriadau eraill am drosglwyddo dogfennau i Swyddfa'r Goron. Os caiff y gorchymyn ei drosglwyddo i Gaerdydd, caiff y gwreiddiol ei anfon gan Swyddfa Caerdydd i Swyddfa'r Goron yn Llundain.

PRACTICE DIRECTION — DEVOLUTION ISSUES (WELSH TEXT)

(1) drosglwyddo'r achos i Ganolfan Llys y Goron yn y Llysoedd Barn, Parc Cathays, Caerdydd CF10 3PG, neu i gofrestrfa ranbarthol arall a gaiff (yn eithriadol) ei chyfarwyddo gan y llys; a

(2) gynnal yr achos yng Nghaerdydd neu mewn lleoliad prawf arall a gaiff (yn eithriadol) ei chyfarwyddo gan y llys.

RHAN III CYFARWYDDIADAU PERTHNASOL I ACHOSION PENODOL

ACHOSION ADOLYGIAD BARNWROL; CEISIADAU SWYDDFA'R GORON YNG NGHYMRU

14.1 Mae Gorchymyn RGL 53, atodlen 1 RTS yn cynnwys y drefn i'w dilyn mewn ceisiadau am adolygiad barnwrol.

14.2 Er gwaethaf Cyfarwyddyd Ymarfer 23 Mainc y Frenhines a ffurflenni penodedig 86A ac 86B[11] bydd cyfleusterau ar gael i geisladau am arolwg barnwrol gael eu rhoi i'r Llysoedd Barn, Parc Cathays, Caerdydd, CF10 3PG os yw'r rhyddhad a geisir neu os yw sail y cais yn ymwneud â'r naill neu'r llall neu â'r ddau o'r canlynol:

(1) mater datganoli'n codi o DLC;

(2) mater yn ymwneud A Chynulliad Cymru, y gweinyddiad Cymreig, neu unrhyw gorff cyhoeddus Cymreig (gan gyrinwys awdurdod addysg lleol) hyd yn oed os nad yw'n ymwneud â mater datganoli.

Gellir parhau i roi ceisiadau o'r fath i Swyddfa'r Goron yn Llundain, os yw'r ceisydd yn dymuno hynny.

14.3 Os caiff ceisiadau eu rhoddi yng Nghaerdydd rhaid ffeilio copi ychwanegol o'r cais fel y gellir ei gadw gan y Swyddfa yng Nghaerdydd. Caiff y cais gwreiddiol ei anfon ymlaen i Swyddfa'r Goron yn Llundain.

14.4 Os yw parti'n bwriadu codi mater datganoli, rhaid i'r rhybudd cais (yn ogystal â'r materion a restrir yng Ngorchymyn 53 RGL, rheol 3(2)(a)):

(1) nodi bod y ceisydd yn dymuno codi mater datganoli ac enwi darpariaethau perthnasol DLC; a

(2) cynnwys crynodeb o'r ffeithiau a'r amgylchiadau a'r pwyntiau cyfraith yr honnir ar eu sail bod mater datganoli'n, codi, gan wneud hynny'n ddigon manwl i alluogi'r llys i benderfynu a yw mater datganoli'n codi.

ACHOSION TEULU MEWN LLYSOEDD YNADON, Y LLYSOEDD SIROL A'R UCHEL LYS

15.1 Mewn unrhyw achos lle y mae unrhyw gwestiwn yin codi ynglŷn â chodi plentyn, bydd y llys yn rhoi sylw i'r egwyddor gyffredinol fod unrhyw oedi wrth benderfynu'r mater yin debyg o niweidio lles y plentyn.[12]

15.2 Os yw'r RAT yin berthnasol, bydd y llys yn cydymffurfio â rheol 10.21.[13]

---

[11] Mae Cyfarwyddyd Ymarfer 23 2C(2) Mainc y Frenhines yn darparu lle bynnag y bo'n ymarferol y dylid cychwyn achosion yn Llundain, er y gellir gwneud ceisiadau y tu allan i Llundain mewn achosion brys. Mae ffurflenni penodedig 86A ac 86B yn nodi mai Swyddfa'r Goron, Llysoedd Barn Brenhinol Strand, Llundain, WC2A 21LL yw'r cyfeiriad i anfon ffurflenni iddo. Gobeithir y bydd y ffurflenni hyn yn cael eu newid i roi'r Llysoedd Barn, Parc Cathays, Caerdydd, CF10 3PG yn gyfeiriad arall ar gyfer Swyddfa'r Goron.

[12] Adran 1(2), Deddf Plant 1989.

[13] Noda Rheol 10.21: (1) Yn amodoi i reol 2.3 [RAT] nid oes dim yn y rheolau hyn i gael ei ddeall mewn modd a fyddai'n hawlio bod unrhyw barti'n datgelu cyfeiriad ei drigfan breifat (neu un unrhyw blentyn) ac eithno trwy orchymyn y llys. (2) Lle y bo parti'n gwrthod datgelu cyfeiriad wrth ddibynnu ar baragraff (1) uchod, bydd yn rhoi rhybudd o'r cyfeiriad hwnnw i'r llys yn Ffurflen C8 ac ni chaiff y cyfeiriad hwnnw ei ddatgelu i unrhyw un heblaw trwy orchymyn y llys.

15.3 Os yw Rhan IV RAT yn berthnasol, bydd y llys yn cydymffurfio â rheol 4.23.[14]

15.4 Os yw LAT yn berthnasol, bydd y llys yn cydymffurfio â Rheolau 23 a 33A.[15]

15.5 Os caiff yr achos ei restru yng ngholofn (i) Atodiad 3 RAT neu Atodlen 2 LAT, rhaid i gopi o unrhyw rybudd a roddir i'r partïon gael ei roi hefyd i'r rhai a nodir yng ngholofn (iv) Atodiad 3 neu Atodlen 2 fel y bo'n addas.

15.6 Rhaid i barti sy'n dymuno codi mater datganoli, lle y bo modd, ei godi (gan roi manylion llawn y darpariaethau y dibynnir arnynt) yn y cais neu ateb neu yn y gwrandawiad cyfarwyddiadau cyntaf lle y bo'n addas.

15.7 Os nad yw parti wedi codi mater datganoli fel uchod, rhaid i'r parti geisio caniatâd y llys i godi'r mater yn ddiweddarach.

15.8 Lle y mae llys wedi cyfeirio mater datganoli i lys arall ac wedi derbyn rhybudd o'r penderfyniad ar y cyfeirio, dylai'r mater cyhydag y bo modd gael ei roi gerbron yr un barnwr neu'r un ynadon a ddeliodd â'r achos cyn y cyfeirio.

ACHOSION SIFIL YN Y LLYSOEDD SIROL A'R UCHEL LYS

16.1 Rhaid i barti sydd am godi mater datganoli nodi yn y ffurflen gais, neu os ef yw'r diffynnydd, yn yr amddiffyniad (neu dystiolaeth ysgrifenedig wedi ei ffeilio gyda'r gydnabyddiaeth cyflwyniad mewn cais Rhan 8) fod y cais yn codi mater datganoli a darpariaethau perthnasol DLC.

16.2 Rhaid i'r manylion cais neu amddiffyniad os yw'r mater datganoli yn cael ei godi gan y diffynnydd (neu dystiolaeth ysgrifenedig a ffeiliwyd gyda'r gydnabyddiaeth cyflwyniad mewn cais Rhan 8) gynnwys yn ddigon manwl y ffeithiau a'r amgylchiadau a'r pwyntiau cyfraith yr honnir ar eu sail bod mater datganoli'n codi i alluogi'r llys i benderfynu a yw mater datganoli'n codi yn yr achos.

16.3 Os yw'r rheolau dyrannu'n berthnasol ai peidio, os caiff cwestiwn ei godi yn ystod yr achos a allai fod yn fater datganoli, yna rhaid i wrandawiad cyfarwyddiadau gael ei gynnal a rhaid i'r mater gael ei gyfeirio i farnwr cylchdaith (mewn achosion llys sirol) neu i farnwr Uchel Lys (mewn achosion Uchel Lys) i benderfynu a oes mater datganoli'n codi ac i gael cyfarwyddiadau pellach.

16.4 Os yw parti'n methu â nodi yn y ddogfen briodol bod mater datganoli'n codi, ond os yw'r parti hwnnw wedi hynny'n dymuno codi mater datganoli, rhaid i'r parti hwnnw geisio caniatâd y llys.

---

[14] Noda Rheol 4.23: (1) Er gwaethaf unrhyw reol llys i'r gwrthwyneb, ni chaiff unrhyw ddogfen, ac eithrio cofnod o orchymyn, a ddelir gan y llys ac sy'n ymwneud ag achos y mae [Rhan IV] yn berthnasol iddo, ei datgelu, ac eithrio i— (a) barti, (b) cynrychiolydd cyfreithiol parti (c) gwarcheidwad ad litem, (ch) y Bwrdd Cymorth Cyfreithiol, neu (d) swyddog lles, heb ganiatâd y barnwr neu'r barnwr rhanbarthol. (2) Ni fydd dim yn y rheol hon yn rhwystro rhoi rhybudd i'r awdurdod perthnasol gan y llys neu swyddog addas o dan gyfarwyddyd adran 37(1). (3) Ni fydd dim yn y rheol hon yn rhwystro datgelu dogfen a baratowyd gan warcheidwad ad litem ar gyfer dibenion— (a) galluogi person i gyflawni swyddogaethau a fynnir gan reoliadau a wnaed o dan adran 41(7); (b) cynorthwyo gwarcheidwad ad litem neu swyddog hysbysu (o fewn ystyr adran 65(1)(b) Deddf Mabwysiadu 1976) a benodir o dan unrhyw ddeddfiad i gyflawni ei swyddogaethau.

[15] Noda Rheol 23: (1) Ni chaiff unrhyw ddogfen, ac eithrio cofnod o orchymyn, a ddelir gan y llys ac sy'n ymwneud ag achosion perthnasol ei datgelu, heblaw i— (a) parti, (b) cynrychiolydd cyfreithiol parti, (c) y gwarcheidwad ad litem, (ch) y Bwrdd Cymorth Cyfreithiol, neu (d) swyddog lles, heb ganiatâd clerc yr ustusiaid neu'r llys. (2) Ni fydd dim yn y rheol hon yn atal y llys neu glerc yr ustusiaid rhag rhoi gwybod am gyfarwyddyd o dan adran 37(1) i'r awdurdod perthnasol. (3) Ni fydd dim yn y rheol hon yn rhwystro datgelu dogfen a baratowyd gan warcheidwad ad litem ar gyfer dibenion— (a) galluogi person i gyflawni swyddogaethau a fynnir gan reoliadau a wnaed o dan adran 41(7); (b) cynorthwyo gwarcheidwad ad litem neu swyddog hysbysu (o fewn ystyr adran 65(1)(b) Deddf Mabwysiadu 1976) a benodir o dan unrhyw ddeddfiad i gyflawni ei swyddogaethau.
Noda Rheol 33A (1) Nid oes dim yn y rheolau hyn i gael ei ddeall mewn modd a fyddai'n hawlio bod unrhyw barti'n datgelu cyfeiriad ei drigfan breifat (neu un unrhyw blentyn) ac eithrio trwy orchymyn y llys. (2) Lle y bo parti'n gwrthod datgelu cyfeiriad wrth ddibynnu ar baragraff (1) uchod, bydd yn rhoi rhybudd o'r cyfeiriad hwnnw i'r llys yn Ffurflen C8 ac ni chaiff y cyfeiriad hwnnw ei ddatgelu i unrhyw un ac eithrio trwy orchymyn y llys.

16.5 Lle y bo unrhyw barti wedi nodi bod mater datganoli'n codi, ni ellir cael dyfarniad trwy ddiffyg.

ACHOSION TROSEDDOL YN LLYS Y GORON

17 Os yw'r diffynnydd am godi mater datganoli dylai ef wneud hynny yn y Gwrandawiad Ple a Chyfarwyddiadau.

ACHOSION TROSEDDOL A SIFIL YN LLYSOEDD YR YNADON

18.1 (1) Lle y bo diffynnydd, sydd wedi ei gyhuddo neu sydd wedi cael gwybodaeth wedi ei gosod yn ei erbyn ef ynglŷn â thramgwydd droseddol ac sydd wedi nodi ple 'Dieuog', am godi mater datganoli, dylai, lle y bo modd, roi manylion llawn y darpariaethau y dibynnir arnynt trwy roi rhybudd ysgrifenedig.

(2) Lle y mae parti i gwyn, neu geisydd am drwydded am godi mater datganoli dylai, lle y bo modd, roi manylion llawn y darpariaethau y dibynnir arnynt trwy roi rhybudd ysgrifenedig.

(3) Dylid rhoi'r rhybudd hwn i'r erlyniad (ac i unrhyw barti arall os oes un) ac i'r llys cyn gynted ag sy'n ymarferol ar ôl cyflwyno ple 'Dieuog' neu ar ôl gwneud y gwyn neu'r cais fel y bo'n addas.

18.2 Lle y caiff achos ei draddodi neu el drosglwyddo i Lys y Goron gan yr ynadon, Llys y Goron sydd i benderfynu a oes mater datganoli'n codi.

RHAN IV APELIADAU

APELIADAU I'R LLYS APÊL (ADRAN SIFIL A THROSEDDOL)

19.1 Mae'r paragraff hwn yn berthnasol os yw mater datganoli'n codi mewn unrhyw apêl i Adran Sifil neu Adran Droseddol y Llys Apêl.

19.2 Mae'n bosibl bod y mater datganoli eisoes wedi codi yn y llys yr apelir yn erbyn ei benderfyniad. Gall y mater datganoli, serch hynny, godi am y tro cyntaf wrth apelio.

19.3 Lle y gwneir cais am ganiatâd i apelio, neu lle gwneir apêl pan nad oes angen caniatâd, rhaid i'r apelydd nodi yn y rhybudd cais (neu'r rhybudd apêl neu rybudd cynnig fel y bo'n addas):

(1) fod yr apêl yn codi mater datganoli a darpariaethau perthnasol DLC;

(2) yn ddigon manwI y ffeithiau a'r amgylchiadau a'r pwyntiau cyfraith yr honnir ar eu sail bod mater datganoli'n codi i alluogi'r llys i benderfynu a yw mater datganoli'n codi yn yr achos; a

(3) a ystyriwyd y mater datganoli yn y llys is, ac os felly, roi manylion y penderfyniad.

19.4 Ni chaiff apelydd geisio codi mater datganoli heb ganiatâd y llys ar ôl iddo ffeilio rhybudd cals; neu rybudd apêl neu rybudd cynnig (os nad oes rhybudd cais).

19.5 Lle y ceisir caniatâd i apelio a lle y mae parti i'r apêl am godi mater datganoli na chodwyd yn y llys is, bydd y llys yn penderfynu a oes mater datganoli'n codi cyn penderfynu rhoi caniatâd i apelio.

APELIADAU I LYS Y GORON

20 Rhaid i rybudd apello o benderfynlad llys yr ynadon i Lys y Goron nodi a ystyriwyd y mater datganoli yn y llys is, ac os felly, roi manylion y penderfyniad. Os nad ystyriwyd hyn, dylai'r rhybudd nodi:

(1) fod yr apêl yn codi mater datganoli a darpariaethau perthnasol DLC; a

(2) yn ddigon manwl y ffeithiau a'r amgylchiadau a'r pwyntiau cyfraith yr honnir ar eu sail bod mater datganoli'n codi i alluogi'r llys i benderfynu a yw mater datganoli'n codi yn yr achos.

ATODIAD 1

DI 1
MATERION DATGANOLI

RHYBUDD MATER DATGANOLI I'R TWRNAI CYFFREDINOL AC I GYNULLIAD CENEDLAETHOL CYMRU

[ENW'R ACHOS]

Bydded hysbys fod yr achos a grybwyllir uchod wedi codi mater datganoli fel y'i diffiniwyd gan Atodien 8 Deddf Llywodraeth Cymru 1998. Rhoddir manylion y mater datganoli yn yr atodlen a atodir.

Mae'r rhybudd hwn yn diwallu gofynion rhybuddio o dan baragraff 5(1) Atodlen 8 Deddf Llywodraeth Cymru 1998. Gellwch gymryd rhan fel parti i'r achos hwn, cyhyd ag y bo'n ymwneud â mater datganoli (paragraff 5(2) Atodlen 8). Os ydych am wneud hyn rhaid i chi roi gwybod i'r llys trwy gwblhau'r ffurflen atodedig, a'i dychwelyd i'r llys yn [cyfeiriad] erbyn [dyddiad].

DYDDIAD

At: Y Twrnai Cyffredinol
Cynulliad Cendlaethol Cymru
Partïon eraill (lle y bo'n addas)

D1 2
MATERION DATGANOLI

RHYBUDD O FWRIAD Y TWRNAI CYFFREDINOL NEU GYNULLIAD CENEDLAETHOL CYMRU I DDOD YN BARTI I ACHOS, CYHYD AG Y BO'N BERTHNASOL I FATER DATGANOLI, O DAN BARAGRAFF 5(2) ATODLEN 8 DEDDF LLYWODRAETH CYMRU 1998

Yn [enw'r llys]

[enw'r achos]

Bydded hysbys fod y [Twrnai Cyffredinol] [Cynulliad Cenedlaethol Cymru] yn bwriadu cymryd rhan fel parti i'r achos, cyhyd ag y bo'n ymwneud â mater datganoli fel a ganiateir gan baragraff 5(2) Atodlen 8 Deddf Llywodraeth Cymru 1998 mewn perthynas â'r mater datganoli a godwyd gan [ ], y derbyniwyd rhybudd ohono gan y [Twrnai Cyffredinol] [Cynulliad] ar [ ].

[Mae'r [ ] hefyd yn ei gwneud yn hysbys ei fod [yn mynnu bod y mater yn cael ei gyfeirio i] [yn dal i ystyried a ddylai fynnu bod y mater yn cael ei gyfeirio i] Bwyllgor Barnwrol y Cyfrin Gyngor o dan baragraff 30 Atodlen 8 Deddf Llywodraeth Cymru 1998.]

[DYDDIAD]

Ar ran y [Twrnai Cyffredinol] [Cynulliad
Cenedlaethol Cymru]
At: Glerc y llys yn [ ]
Y partïon i'r achos
[Twrnai Cyffredinol [[Cynulliad Cendlaethol Cymru]

DI 3
MATERION DATGANOLI

RHYBUDD GAN Y TWRNAI CYFFREDINOL NEU GYNULLIAD CENEDLAETHOL CYMRU EU BOD YN MYNNU BOD Y MATER DATGANOLI'N CAEL EI GYFEIRIO I BWYLLGOR BARNWROL Y CYFRIN GYNGOR

Yn y [Ilys]

[enw'r achos]

Mae'r [Twrnai Cyffredinol] [Cynulliad Cenedlaethol Cymru] yn ei gwneud yn hysbys fod rhaid cyfeirio'r mater datganoli, a godwyd yn yr achos uchod y mae'n barti iddo, gael el gyfeirio i Bwyllgor Barnwrol y Cyfrin Gyngor o dan baragraff 30 Atodlen 8 Deddf Llywodraeth Cymru 1998.

[DYDDIAD]

Ar ran y [Twrnai Cyffredinol] [Cynulliad
Cenedlaethol Cymru]

PRACTICE DIRECTION — DEVOLUTION ISSUES (WELSH TEXT)

At: Glerc y llys yn [ ]
Y partïon ir achos
[Twrnai Cyffredinol [[Cynuillad Cendlaethol Cymru]

DI 4
MATERION DATGANOLI

CYFEIRIO MATER DATGANOLI GAN Y LLYS NEU DRIBIWNLYS I [UCHEL LYS] [LYS APÊL] [BWYLLGOR BARNWROL Y CYFRIN GYNGOR]

Yn y [llys]

[enw'r achos]

Gorchmynnir cyfeirio'r mater(ion) datganoli a nodir yn yr atodlen [i'r Uchel Lys] [i'r Llys Apêl] [i Bwyllgor Barnwrol y Cyfrin Gyngor] i'w benderfynu yn unol â pharagraff [ ] Atodlen 8 Deddf Llywodraeth Cymru 1998.

Gorchmynnir ymhellach fod yr achos yn cael ei ohirio nes bod [yr Uchel Lys] [y Llys Apêl] [Pwyllgor Barnwrol y Cyfrin Gyngor] yn penderfynu ar y mater[ion] datganoli neu nes gorchymyn pellach.

DYDDIAD

Barnwr/clerc y ilys ynadon
Cadeirydd y Tribiwnlys
[Cyfeiriad]

CYFEIRIO SGERBWD I'W ATODI WRTH FFURFLEN DI 4

Yn y [llys]

[enw'r achos]

(a) [Y cwestiwn a gyfeiriwyd.]
(b) [Cyfeiriadau'r partïon]
(c) [Datganiad cryno o gefndir y materion gan gynnwys—
  (i) Ffeithiau'r achos gan gynnwys unrhyw ganfyddiadau o ffaith gan y llys cyfeirio neu lysoedd is; a
  (ii) Y prif bynciau yn yr achos a haeriadau'r partïon ynglŷn â hwy;]
(ch) [Y ddeddf berthnasol gan gynnwys darpariaethau perthnasol Deddf Llywodraeth Cymru 1998]
(d) [Y rhesymau pam ystyrir bod ateb i'r cwestiwn yin angenrheidiol ar gyfer dibenion gwaredu'r achos.]

[Caiff yr holl ddyfarniadau a roddwyd eisoes yn yr achos eu hatodi wrth y cyfeirio hwn.]

ATODIAD 2 CYFEIRIADAU

1. Rhaid i hysbysiadau i Gynulliad Cenedlaethol Cymru gael eu hanfon at Gwnsel Cyffredinol Cynulliad Cenedlaethol Cymru, Adeiladau'r Goron, Parc Cathays, Caerdydd. Rhif ffacs 01222 826798.

2. Rhaid anfon hysbysiadau at y Twrnai Cyffredinol i Siambrau'r Twrnai Cyffredinol, 9 Buckingham Gate, Llundain, SW1E 6JP. Rhif ffacs 0171 271 2433.

3. Gellir anfon cyfeirio i Swyddfa'r Goron o dan baragraff 9.3(1)c y Cyfarwyddyd Ymarfer i Swyddfa'r Goron, Llysoedd Barn Brenhinol Strand, Llundain WC2A 2LL; neu i'r Llysoedd Barn, Parc Cathays, Caerdydd, CF10 3PG (2 gopi).

NODYN EGLURHAOL

4. Y cyfeiriadau a'r rhifau ffacs uchod yw'r wybodaeth orau sydd ar gael, serch hynny y mae'n bosibl i'r rhain (yn enwedig y rhifau ffacs a'r cyfeiriad am Hysbysiadau i'r Cynulliad) newid, a byddai felly'n ddoeth cadarnhau'r rhifau cyn anfon gwybodaeth.

CHANCERY DIVISION PRACTICE DIRECTIONS

These Chancery Division Practice Directions (CDPDs) govern the practice to be followed in the Chancery Division. Apart from CDPD 5, Listing, they do not apply to the Bankruptcy Court, the Companies Court or the Patents Court which have their own Practice Directions. They apply to claims in District Registries save where inappropriate or where local directions apply.

These directions come into force on 26 April 1999. They replace the Directions printed in Part 2B of Volume 2 of the Supreme Court Practice.

CONTENTS

CDPD 1 Appeals
CDPD 2 Hearings by Chancery Judges out of London
CDPD 3 Judge's Applications
CDPD 4 Landlord and Tenant
CDPD 5 Listing
CDPD 6 Masters
CDPD 7 Mortgages and Possession Orders
CDPD 8 Orders
CDPD 9 Probate
CDPD 10 Sale
CDPD 11 Title to proceedings
CDPD 12 Trusts
Appendix 1 Queen's Bench Masters Practice Directions
Appendix 2 Administration of Chancery Chambers and Companies and Bankruptcy Courts
Appendix 3 Written Evidence Lodgement Form

CDPD 1 APPEALS

A Contempt of court: appeals from Chancery Division
Notices of appeal which by RSC, ord. 59, r. 20(1), are required to be served on 'the proper officer of the Court from whose order or decision the appeal is brought' may be served on the Chief Master of the Chancery Division and such service may be effected by leaving a copy of the notice of appeal with the Clerk of the Lists in Room W.16, Royal Courts of Justice, Strand, London WC2A 2LL.

B Dismissal by consent
In connection with cases stated on appeal from the Income Tax Commissioners and all appeals from Chancery Masters the Chancery Division adopts the practice of the Court of Appeal for the dismissal of appeals by consent as set out in the notes in RSC, ord. 59, r. 1(15). A document signed by solicitors for all parties must be lodged with the Chancery Listing Office (Room W.15), Royal Courts of Justice, Strand, London WC2A 2LL, requesting dismissal of the appeal. The appeal can be dismissed without any hearing by an order made in the name of the Vice Chancellor. Any orders with directions as to costs will be drawn by the Chancery Associates.

C Masters
(i) A litigant who is dissatisfied with a decision of a Master has a right of appeal from the Master to a Judge in chambers under RSC, ord. 58, r. 1. The appeal is brought by a notice of appeal and this is issued out of Room W.15. It is not necessary to state the grounds of appeal. The Appellant opens the appeal, but, even if the appeal is against only part of the Master's order, the whole of the summons is treated as being before the Judge, who will make such order on it as he thinks fit.

(ii) The following documents must be lodged within 5 days after the judgment order or decision appealed against: (a) Two copies of the notice of appeal Form PF110, containing the following information: (i) the name of the Master against whose decision the appeal is brought (ii) the terms of the order appealed against and the date of the order (iii) the relief sought on the appeal (iv) the name and address of the party issuing the notice of appeal, and the name and address of each party to whom the notice of appeal is addressed, together with their respective telephone numbers and references and (v) if the appeal is out of time and the Master has refused an extension, a request to the Judge to extend the time. (b) A cheque, or postal order or money order, crossed and made payable to H.M. Paymaster General for the fee of £100. In the case of a litigant in person, cash, a postal order or bankers' draft must be sent. (N.B.: The documents may be lodged by post.)

(iii) An appeal will be treated as having been made at the date and time of the actual receipt of the requisite documents at Chancery Chambers. No acknowledgment will be sent unless this is requested and a stamped addressed envelope is sent for this purpose.

For Listing of Appeals from Masters see CDPD 5.

CDPD 2 HEARINGS BY CHANCERY JUDGES OUT OF LONDON

A

The places at which Chancery Courts normally sit out of London are Birmingham, Bristol, Cardiff, Leeds, Liverpool, Manchester, Newcastle upon Tyne and Preston. Each of these places has a Chancery District Registry.

There are two Chancery Judges who have been appointed to supervise the arrangements for the hearing of Chancery cases out of London. Mr Justice Jacob is currently the Chancery Supervising Judge for Birmingham, Bristol and Cardiff and is concerned with Chancery hearings on the Western, Wales and Chester, and Midland and Oxford Circuits. Mr Justice Blackburne, as Vice Chancellor of the County Palatine of Lancaster, is concerned with Chancery hearings for the Northern and North Eastern Circuits. Both High Court Judges regularly take substantial Chancery matters for hearing outside London. Mr Justice Blackburne sits regularly in Manchester, Liverpool, Leeds and Newcastle and (as business may require) in Preston. If appropriate he will also sit at other court centres on the two circuits (e.g. Carlisle, Durham, Lancaster and Sheffield).

There are Specialist Circuit Judges who have the authority to exercise the powers of a Judge of the Chancery Division and who normally sit out of London. They exercise a general Chancery jurisdiction, subject to exceptions. Those exceptions are proceedings directly concerning revenue; proceedings before the Patents Court constituted as part of the Chancery Division under s. 96 of the Patents Act 1977.

Arrangements can be made for other Judges of the Chancery Division (or a deputy High Court Judge) to hear cases at one of the above principal court centres, either where the case is proceeding in the District Registry but pressure on local judicial manpower calls for outside assistance, or where the case is proceeding in the Central Registry but circumstances make it appropriate that the case be tried at an out of London court centre.

Currently the Circuit Judges who sit regularly in Chancery out of London are:
His Honour Judge Weeks QC (Bristol)
His Honour Judge Boggis QC (Birmingham)
His Honour Judge Moseley QC (Cardiff)
His Honour Judge Howarth (Manchester and Liverpool)
His Honour Judge Maddocks (Manchester and Liverpool)
His Honour Judge Behrens (Leeds and Newcastle)

Judge Howarth and Judge Maddocks also hear Preston cases but take them in either Manchester or Liverpool. Judge Cooke and Judge Gilliland QC (who normally sits in Salford hearing Technology and Construction cases) also assist in the disposal of Chancery business on the Northern and North Eastern Circuits.

In addition certain other Circuit Judges are authorised to take Chancery cases on the same basis.

CHANCERY DIVISION PRACTICE DIRECTIONS

B Trials

(i) If a Chancery case is proceeding in any District Registry other than a Chancery District Registry, the case should normally be transferred to the appropriate Chancery District Registry upon the first occasion the case comes before the court.

(ii) The venue of a Chancery trial out of London will normally be one of the centres mentioned above. However in many circumstances (e.g. because of the number or age of local witnesses, the need for a site visit, or travel problems) arrangements can be made for the Chancery Court to sit elsewhere.

(iii) In cases of exceptional difficulty or importance the trial may be by a High Court Judge. Arrangements can also be made in exceptional circumstances for a High Court Judge to deal with any of the matters excepted from the jurisdiction of an authorised Circuit Judge. Such a Judge may be one of the Chancery Judges other than Jacob or Blackburne JJ.

(iv) Where it is desired that a hearing be outside one of the normal Chancery Centres, or be taken by a High Court Judge, inquiries should normally in the first instance be made to the Listing Officer for the area concerned. If the need arises, inquiries can also be made to clerk to Mr Justice Jacob (phone 0171 936 6771, fax 0171 936 6650) or the clerk to Mr Justice Blackburne (phone 0171 936 6512, fax 0171 936 7379). If no relevant clerk is available, inquiries should be made to the clerk in charge of the Chancery Lists in London.

C Applications

(a) Subject to the following paragraphs any application should normally be made to a District Judge (unless it relates to a matter which a District Judge does not have power to hear).

(b) If the application relates to a matter which may significantly affect the conduct of the trial (e.g. relates to significant new evidence) and is made within 3 months before the date fixed for trial, the application should normally be made to a High Court Judge or Circuit Judge.

(c) A District Judge may of his or her own motion (for instance because of the complexity of the matter or the need for specialist attention) direct that an application be referred to High Court or Circuit Judge.

(d) At any time if the parties agree that the matter is appropriate to be heard by a Judge (High Court or Circuit), the parties may jointly apply in writing to the District Judge for the application to be referred directly to a High Court or Circuit Judge. They will be informed of the result of their application by post or by telephone. If it is successful, details of availability and a time estimate must be lodged with the relevant Listing Officer who will fix a date for the hearing. If it is unsuccessful, oral application may be made to the District Judge.

D Application days before a Judge

Normally one day a week is reserved for the hearing of applications and short appeals, including all interim matters. All matters will be called into Court at the commencement of the day in order to work out a running order. Matters will be heard without the court going into private session unless good reason is shown. Rights of audience are unaffected.

Applications days are: Monday in Birmingham, Thursday in Bristol and Friday in Cardiff. In Manchester and Liverpool application days are on either Tuesday or Thursday of each week. In Leeds and Newcastle applications are heard on average fortnightly.

E Applications out of hours and telephone applications

These are governed by the general rules, save that in the case of applications out of hours, the party applying should contact the relevant court office, the main relevant telephone numbers being:

Birmingham (Midland and Oxford Circuit):
West Side: 01399–618079
East Side: 01399–618078
Bristol: 01399–618088

CHANCERY DIVISION PRACTICE DIRECTIONS

Cardiff: 01399–618086
Manchester and Liverpool: 01399–618080
Leeds and Newcastle: 01399–618082
In case of difficulty, contact the Royal Courts of Justice on 0171–936–6260.

F Agreed interim orders
Normally a hearing will not be necessary. The procedure is as in the general rules.

A Judge is unlikely to agree to more than two consent adjournments of an interim application. Applications to vacate a trial date will require substantial justification and a hearing, normally before the Trial Judge.

G Contacting the Court
The following are the Court addresses, telephone and fax numbers:
   Birmingham. The Priory Courts, 33 Bull Street, Birmingham B4 6DW. Telephone: 0121–681–3033. Fax: 0121–681–3121.
   Bristol: The Law Courts, Small Street, Bristol BS1 1DA. Telephone: 0117–976–3098. Fax: 0117–976–3074.
   Cardiff: The Civil Justice Centre, 2 Park Street, Cardiff CF1 1ET. Telephone: 01222–376402. Fax: 01222–376470.
   Leeds: The Court House, 1 Oxford Row, Leeds LS1 3BG. Telephone: 0113–283–0040. Fax: 0113–244–8507.
   Liverpool: Queen Elizabeth II Law Courts, Derby Square, Liverpool L2 1XA Telephone: 0151–473–7373. Fax: 0151–227–2806.
   Manchester: The Courts of Justice, Crown Square, Manchester M3 3FL. Telephone: 0161–954–1800. Fax: 0161–832–5179.
   Newcastle: The Law Courts, Quayside, Newcastle upon Tyne NE1 3LB. Telephone: 0191–201–2000. Fax: 0191–201–2001.
   Preston: The Law Courts, Openshaw Place, Ringway, Preston PR1 2LL. Telephone: 01772–832–300. Fax: 01772–832–476.
In some centres resources do not permit the listing telephone numbers to be attended personally at all times. In cases of urgency, solicitors, counsel and counsel's clerks may come into the Chancery Court and leave messages with the member of staff sitting in Court.

H Local listing arrangements
Listing arrangements may vary at different centres, depending on availability of Judges and courtrooms. The current details are as follows:

Birmingham: shared and early listing
   1 *The shared list*
The shared list is primarily for use by the three specialised lists of the Birmingham District Registry — those operated by the Chancery, Mercantile and Technology and Construction Courts.

The shared list is in addition to the normal lists of those Courts and allows better use to be made of judicial time. Given the settlement rate of trials in the three divisions, two additional cases, the fourth and fifth fixtures, will be listed at any one time, in addition to the three cases listed before the three specialist courts. Those two additional cases will be taken by any of the Section 9 Judges who become available. Cases are only entered into the shared list if there is a very strong expectation that they will be heard on the day fixed.

In order, therefore, for a case to enter the shared list it must be suitable for hearing before any of the Section 9 specialist Judges.

Suitability for listing a case in the shared list may be suggested by the District Judge at directions stage, or by the parties when setting the case down. It is likely that fourth and fifth fixtures will be allocated an earlier trial date than a case which has to be heard by the appropriate specialist Judge.

The final decision to list a case in the shared list will lie with Judge Boggis QC for Chancery cases, Judge Lee QC or Judge Gibbs QC for Mercantile cases, and Judge Alton for Technology and Construction cases.

CHANCERY DIVISION PRACTICE DIRECTIONS

2 Early listing
Where a case with a time estimate of 2 days or less is unable to be listed within the following three-month period, the case will be listed in the usual way with as early a date as possible, but a note will be made of the case and put on the file. If due to settlement or adjournment of other cases, an earlier date becomes available, the parties will be informed that an earlier date has become available, and they will be given the opportunity to have their case brought forward to that earlier date.

Judge Boggis QC will make the decision at setting-down stage as to whether a case may be marked for the possibility of earlier hearing; suitable cases will be those which are to be argued on law alone and applications by order.

If a case is listed in this way, the notice of hearing will inform the parties accordingly.

Bristol: reserve listing
In order to make available earlier hearing dates than would otherwise be possible, a reserve list is operated for Chancery cases listed to be heard in the Bristol District Registry. Cases in the reserve list are given a fixed date, usually as a second fixture. A second fixture will only be given when there is a very strong expectation of the case being heard on that date. Other Judges are called upon in the event of both first and second fixtures being effective.

Cardiff: reserve listing
Judge Moseley QC sits both as a Chancery Judge and a Judge of the Technology and Construction Court. His list contains both categories of case. All cases are allocated a fixed starting date but some are first and some second fixtures. Other Judges are called upon in the event of both first and second fixtures being effective. A Mercantile Judge for Wales is due to be appointed shortly. His or her arrival may lead to a revision of present listing arrangements. Any discussions concerning listing should be with the Chancery Listing Clerk in Cardiff.

Manchester, Liverpool and Preston
1 The shared list
When sitting at the same court centre (as is usually the case) Judge Howarth and Judge Maddocks will assist each other in the disposal of their respective daily lists. If necessary and they are available at the relevant court centre, Judge Kershaw QC and Judge Hegarty QC (who are the local Mercantile Judges) will assist in the disposal of business.

2 Second fixtures
To maximise the use of court resources, second (and sometimes third) fixtures are listed on each Judge's daily list. Parties to such fixtures are notified not later than 3.30 p.m. on the working day preceding the day for which the case is listed (and frequently considerably before then) if the second (or, as appropriate, third) fixture will be in the list for trial.

Leeds and Newcastle
1 The shared list
When sitting at the same time in Leeds or Newcastle Judge Behrens and Judge McGonigal (the principal Mercantile Judge on the North Eastern Circuit) will assist each other in the disposal of their respective daily lists.

2 Second fixtures
The same practice is adopted as is operated in Manchester and Liverpool.

CDPD 3 JUDGE'S APPLICATIONS

'Judge's Applications' means applications for interim remedies or other urgent applications made to a Judge.

All applications which are within the jurisdiction of the Master should be made to the Master and not the Judge unless there is a sufficient degree of urgency or other good reason which justifies making the application to the Judge.

CHANCERY DIVISION PRACTICE DIRECTIONS

A Application days
Every weekday (except the last day of each sittings) will be an application day.

B Applications Judge
(i) A Judge ('the applications Judge') will be assigned to hear Judge's applications on each application day.
(ii) If the volume of applications requires it any other Judge available to assist with applications will hear such Judge's applications as the applications Judge directs.
(iii) An application notice of a Judge's application, other than in the Patents Court, need not state the name of the Judge to whom the application will be made. It is sufficient to state 'the Chancery Applications Judge' or, in the case of an application in the Companies Court, 'the Companies Judge'. The names of those Judges appear in the Daily Cause List and also in the Chancery Division term list.

C Adjournment of Judge's Applications
(i) If all parties to an application agree to do so it can be adjourned for not more than 14 days by counsel or solicitors attending before the Chancery Listing Officer (Room W.15) at any time before 4 p.m. on the day before the hearing of the application and producing a consent or consents signed by counsel or solicitors representing all parties agreeing to the adjournment. A litigant in person who is a party must attend before the Chancery Listing Officer as well as signing a consent.
(ii) Not more than three successive adjournments may be made and no adjournment shall be made to the last two applications days of any sitting.
(iii) The above procedure applies to Judge's applications which the parties agree should be adjourned to be heard as applications by order. In addition to the consents required under (i), above, an agreed timetable for the filing of any evidence must be produced to the Chancery Listing Officer. Any application arising from the default of a party in abiding by the timetable and any application by the parties to extend the timetable must be made in court.
(iv) Undertakings previously given to the court may be continued unchanged over the duration of any adjournment. Adjournments on which an undertaking is to be varied or a new undertaking given must be dealt with in court.

D Order of hearing
The Judge hearing Judge's applications will continue to exercise his discretion as to the order in which he hears them, so that he may, for instance, give priority to any application that he considers to be sufficiently urgent, as may be the case with some applications made without notice. Subject to this:
(a) applications affecting the liberty of the subject will continue to take priority over all applications;
(b) ineffective applications that is to say matters which are to be adjourned or have been settled;
(c) all other applications listed, unlisted and made without notice will be heard in the order determined by the applications Judge;
(d) applications likely to last more than two hours will normally be made applications by order unless the state of work permits the Judge to deal with them as they arise;
(e) when another Judge is available to assist with applications, the applications Judge may transfer to him such applications as he considers appropriate, irrespective of priority;
(f) any application which at the end of the day is part heard will normally head the listed Judge's applications for the next court day, followed by any listed applications that have not been reached;
(g) the Judge will usually give effect to any variation in this order of priority which is agreed by all who are affected.

CDPD 4 LANDLORD AND TENANT

Grant of a new business tenancy — claim form
(i) Where the parties are in negotiation on the grant of a new tenancy and neither side wishes to press on with the proceedings the tenant may request the

Court not immediately to set a day for the hearing upon issue or service of the Claim Form but to await a request from either party that a hearing date be set. Either party may at any time thereafter request a hearing to be fixed.

(ii) It is of the greatest importance that the landlord should be informed promptly of the issue of the Claim Form, which must be served strictly within two calendar months from the date of issue. It is not to be assumed that the time will necessarily be extended if this requirement is not complied with.

(iii) If the landlord wishes the Court to determine an interim rent under s. 24A of the Landlord and Tenant Act 1954, but is content that the determination should await the determination of the application for a new lease, and in reliance on the procedure specified above the tenant's Claim Form has not been brought on for hearing, he may likewise make an application for the determination of the interim rent which states the hearing as being for a day to be fixed instead of for a date and time. Such an application must be served promptly, and it may be brought on for hearing by either party on a date to be fixed by the Court on not less than three days' notice to the opposing party.

CDPD 5 LISTING

A General
  (i) The Lists
There are three main lists in the Chancery Division: the Trial List, the General List and the Interim Hearings List. (There is also a Patents List which is controlled separately by the Judge in charge of the Patents List.)

The Trial List is for all trials to be heard with witnesses.

The Interim Hearings List is for interim applications including appeals from Masters.

The General List is for other matters, including revenue, bankruptcy and pensions appeals, Part 8 proceedings, applications for judgment and all companies matters.

In the Royal Courts of Justice the fixing of trial dates and windows in the multi-track is regulated by a Practice Direction issued by the Vice Chancellor [see page 1192].

  (ii) Responsibility for listing
The Clerk of the Lists (Room W.15, Royal Courts of Justice) is in general responsible for listing. All applications relating to listing should in the first instance be made to him. Any party dissatisfied with any decision of the Clerk of the Lists may, on one clear day's notice to all other parties, apply to the Judge in charge of the list. Any such application should be made within seven days of the decision of the Clerk of the Lists and be arranged through the Chancery Listing Officer.

  (iii) General and Interim Hearings Lists
  The Warned Lists
On each Friday of term and on such other days as may be appropriate, the Clerk of the Lists will publish a Warned List, showing the matters in the General and Interim Hearings Lists that are liable to be heard in the following week. Any matter for which no date has been fixed is liable to appear in the list for hearing with no warning save that given by the next day's cause list posted each afternoon outside Room W.15. The parties may by consent 'offer' a case for a designated date following entry into the Warned List in accordance with the local directions notice issued by the Clerk of the Lists.

  (iv) Estimates of duration
    (a) If the estimated length of the trial is varied, or the case settled, withdrawn or discontinued, the solicitors for the parties must forthwith inform the Clerk of the Lists in writing. If the case is settled but the parties wish the Master to make a consent order, the solicitor must notify the Clerk of the Lists in writing, whereupon he will take the case out of the list and notify the Master. The Master may then make the consent order.

    (b) Seven days before the date for trial, the claimant's solicitors must inform the Clerk of the Lists whether there is any variation in the estimate of duration, and in particular whether the case is likely to be disposed of in some summary way.

CHANCERY DIVISION PRACTICE DIRECTIONS

If the claimant is in person, this must be done by the solicitor for the first-named defendant who has instructed a solicitor. If a summary disposal is likely, the solicitor must keep the Clerk of the Lists informed of any developments as soon as they occur.

(v) *General*
   (a) Unassigned cases

    I In addition to those cases listed to be heard by individual Judges, the Daily Cause List for each day may list one or more cases from any of the three main Lists to be heard on that day but not assigned to a particular Judge ('an unassigned case'). If on any day the case assigned to a particular Judge proves to be ineffective, he will hear an unassigned case. It is hoped that the great majority of unassigned cases will be heard on the day that they are listed but this cannot be absolutely guaranteed. It is not the practice to list cases as unassigned unless the parties consent and there are no witnesses.

    II Solicitors and counsel engaged in cases listed as unassigned should communicate with the Chancery Listing Officer who will notify them as soon as possible which Judge is to hear the case.

   (b) Appeals from Masters

Appeals from Masters will appear in the Interim Hearings List. Such appeals (stamped with the appropriate fee) must be lodged in Room W.15. On being notified that the case has been listed the solicitors should forthwith inform the Chancery Listing Officer whether they intend to instruct counsel and, if so, the names of counsel.

B *Listing of particular business*
  (i) *Bankruptcy*
    (a) Bankruptcy appeals

Notice of appeal from the decision of a Registrar or of a county court should be lodged in Room TM1.10. The appeal will be entered in the General List, usually with a fixed date. The date of hearing will be fixed by the Chancery Listing Officer in the usual manner.

    (b) Bankruptcy applications

All originating and ordinary applications to the Judge should be lodged with the Deputy Court Manager in Bankruptcy. Urgent applications without notice for (i) the committal of any person to prison for contempt, or (ii) injunctions or the modification or discharge of injunctions will be passed directly to the clerk of the Chancery Applications Judge for hearing by that Judge. All applications on notice for (i) and (ii) above, and applications referred to the Judge by the Registrar, will be listed by the Chancery Listing Officer. Applications estimated not to exceed two hours will be heard by the Applications Judge. The Listing Officer shall give at least three clear days notice of the hearing to the applicant and any respondents who attend before the Registrar. Applications over two hours will be heard on a fixed or floating date by such Judges as are available.

  (ii) *Companies Court*

Applications and petitions adjourned by the Registrar and applications which are presently heard by the Companies Judge on each Monday of a term will be listed by the Chancery Clerk of the Lists. Any such applications and petitions which are estimated to exceed two hours will be liable to be stood over to a date to be fixed by the Chancery Clerk of the Lists. All such matters will be placed in the General List.

  (iii) *Applications adjourned to the Judge*

Applications adjourned by the Master to the Judge will be added to the Interim Hearings List.

  (iv) *Judge's applications*
    (a) General listing of Judge's applications

    I The Chancery Listing Office is responsible for the listing of Judge's applications.

    II A Judge's application will only be listed if (1) two copies of the Claim Form and (2) two copies of the application notice (one stamped with the appropriate fee) are lodged at the Chancery Listing Office, Room W.15 Royal

Courts of Justice, before 12 noon on the day before the date for which notice of the application has been given or on the preceding Friday if the date for which notice has been given is a Monday.

(b) Adjourning Judge's applications

I In court

When a Judge's application is adjourned in court, the Associate in attendance will notify the Chancery Listing Office of the day to which it has been adjourned and the office will list the application for that day.

II Out of court

If a Judge's application is by consent adjourned, the Chancery Listing Office will list the application for the day to which it has been adjourned.

(For jurisdiction of Chancery Listing Officer to adjourn Judge's applications see CDPD 3.)

(c) Judge's applications without notice

I If it is desired to have an urgent hearing of a Judge's application listed, two copies of the order sought should be lodged as well as an application notice. If the application is to be made in private, it will be listed as 'Application without notice' without naming the parties. Where, for example, publicity would defeat the object of hearing, if the application were heard in public, the Judge may hear the application in private (see CPR rule 39.2). Where an application is very urgent and the Applications Judge is unable to hear it promptly, it may be heard by any Judge who is available, though the request for this must be made to the Clerk to the Applications Judge, or, in default, to the Chancery Listing Officer.

II Urgent Judge's applications without notice

A party wishing to apply urgently to a Judge for remedies without notice to the respondent must notify the clerk to the Applications Judge by telephone.

(d) Applications by order

If a Judge directs that an application is to be an application by order (as will usually be done if the hearing is likely to exceed two hours), the solicitors or the clerks to counsel concerned should apply to the Chancery Listing Officer for a fixed or floating date for the hearing. Before so applying there must be lodged with the Clerk of the Lists a certificate signed by the advocate stating the estimated length of the hearing of the application. Applications by order may be entered in the Interim Hearings List and, if not fixed by arrangement with the Chancery Listing Officer, will be liable to be listed for hearing in accordance with the timetable fixed by the Judge.

(e) Short service of Judge's applications

Permission to serve short notice of a Judge's application may be obtained on application without notice to the Applications Judge. Such permission cannot be given by a Master.

(v) Revenue appeals

Appeals will be entered in the General List, usually with fixed dates, and will be heard by such Judges as are available. The dates for hearing shall be settled in the usual way on application to the Chancery Listing Officer. Where it would assist counsel and solicitors with their other commitments, the Chancery Listing Officer, if requested, will endeavour to fix two or more revenue appeals so that they will come on consecutively.

(vi) Short applications

An application for judgment in default made to a Judge (because the Master has no jurisdiction) should be made to the Applications Judge.

(vii) Summary judgment

Where an application for summary judgment includes an application for an injunction, it usually has to be made to a Judge because in most cases the Master cannot grant an injunction save in terms agreed by the parties. In such cases the application should be made returnable before the Judge in the General List instead of the Master. The return date to be inserted in the application notice should be a Monday at least 14 clear days after the application notice has been served. The application notice should be issued in the Chancery Listing Office (Room W.15) when there must be lodged two copies of the application notice, and the witness statements or affidavits in support with the exhibits. On the return date the application will normally be adjourned to a date to be fixed if the hearing, whether opposed or unopposed, is likely to take longer than 30 minutes. The adjourned date will be fixed in the usual way through the Chancery Listing Officer, and a certificate signed by an advocate as to the estimated length of the hearing must be lodged with the Chancery Listing Officer.

(viii) Variation of trusts: application to a Judge

Applications under the Variation of Trusts Act 1958 for hearing by a Judge may be listed for hearing in the General List without any direction by a Master on the lodgment (in Room W.15) of a certificate signed by advocates for all the parties, stating: (i) that the evidence is complete and has been filed; (ii) that the application is ready for hearing, and (iii) the estimated length of the hearing. The hearing will be in private unless there is a contentious issue (see CPR rule 39.2(f) and the PD supplementing CPR Part 39 para. 1.5(11)).

CDPD 6 MASTERS

Arrangement of business

(i) Assignment of cases

Cases are assigned to Masters in accordance with the last digit of the claim number as follows:

0 and 1 Master Bragge
2 and 3 Master Bowman
4 and 5 Master Bowles
6 and 7 Chief Master Winegarten
8 and 9 Master Moncaster

(ii) Oral applications without notice to the Masters

   (a) Masters are normally available to hear oral applications without notice at 2.15 p.m. on working days. Notice should be given to the Master's Clerk in Room TM7.09 or by telephone on 0171-936-7391 or by fax on 0171-936-7422 by 4.30 p.m. on the previous day, except in cases of real emergency when notice may be given at any time, so that the file will be before the Master.

   (b) If the assigned Master is not available on any particular day, the applicant will be informed and (except in cases of emergency), asked to come when the assigned Master is next available. Applications will only be heard by another Master in cases of emergency or when the assigned Master is on vacation.

CDPD 7 MORTGAGES AND POSSESSION ORDERS

A Mortgages

   (i) RSC, ord. 88, r. 5(2), requires that in mortgage claims a copy of the mortgage must be exhibited to the witness statement or affidavit in support of the claim, and the original mortgage or charge certificate must be produced at the hearing.

   (ii) Most building society mortgages now incorporate standard mortgage conditions, and in such cases a copy of the relevant conditions must also be exhibited.

   (iii) Some standard forms of building society mortgage are now so abbreviated that they give no particulars of the amount of the advance, the term of the loan, the rate of interest or the amount of the instalments, but all these matters are defined in the mortgage conditions by reference to the offer letter. Where the offer letter is thus in effect incorporated into the mortgage by reference, that also should be exhibited to the witness statement or affidavit.

   (iv) Many bank mortgages, although expressed in the usual bank 'all monies' form, are also qualified by an offer letter or other side letter, providing for repayment of the advance by instalments. In *Governor and Company of the Bank of Scotland* v *Grimes* [1985] QB 1179, it was held that in such cases the mortgage may be treated as an instalment mortgage for the purposes of Administration of Justice Act 1970, s. 36 and Administration of Justice Act 1973, s. 8. In these cases also the relevant letter should be exhibited to the witness statement or affidavit in support.

B *Suspended possession orders*

(i) A suspended possession order is an order under which a person is entitled to a remedy subject to the fulfilment of a condition for the purposes of RSC, ord. 46, r. 2(1)(d), so that ord. 46, r. 4, accordingly applies. Permission to issue execution should not be given without notice and it follows that the Court must therefore direct an application for such permission to be made upon notice (r. 4(1)).

(ii) Suspended orders are made frequently in mortgagees' possession claims by virtue of s. 36 of the Administration of Justice Act 1970 and in such claims the defendant is often in default of acknowledging service of the claim form.

(iii) Where a defendant has not acknowledged service no special directions as to service are needed but a claimant requiring permission to issue execution on a suspended possession order when there has been a default of acknowledging service must send a copy of the application notice and of the witness statement or affidavit in support of the application to each defendant in default at his last known address, so as to reach him not less than three clear days before the hearing, and will lodge with the Masters' clerk, at least one clear day before the hearing, the witness statement or affidavit in support of the application endorsed with a certificate by the claimant's solicitor in the form following or as near thereto as may be appropriate:

'I certify that on —— day the —— day of 19 —— a copy of the application notice herein dated 19 —— together with a true copy of the within document was sent by pre-paid letter post addressed to the defendant at his last known address being [insert address].

Claimant's Solicitor.'

No further proof of service should normally be required in default cases.

(iv) The same principles apply and the same practice will be followed where leave to issue execution is required because six years or more have elapsed since the date of an unsuspended possession order or because there has been a change in the party liable to execution. (See RSC, ord. 46, r. 2.)

(v) Applications for permission to issue execution because of a change of the party entitled to execution or to issue a writ of restitution may be dealt with without notice.

CDPD 8 ORDERS

A *Drafting of orders*

(i) *Orders made by Masters*

Orders made by Masters will be drawn up by the court, and unless the court has any questions a sealed order will be sent to each party.

(ii) *Orders made by Judges*

(a) Agreed statements of the terms of order

Where a Judge directs that a statement of the terms of the order be agreed and signed by counsel, the agreed statement may either be handed to the Associate in court or else lodged in Room TM3.07. In each case the claim number should be shown. Agreed statements will normally be adopted as the order of the Court.

(b) Drafting by the Court

The Court will draw up the order unless it directs or permits a party to draw it up or directs that an agreed statement of its terms be filed or that no order need be drawn up. Unless the Court has any questions it will seal and serve the order without reference to the parties. If the order is unusually complicated it may be necessary to submit a draft to the parties.

If the order is to be drawn up by a party two engrossments of the order proposed should be lodged at or posted to:

CHANCERY DIVISION PRACTICE DIRECTIONS

Order and Accounts Section
Room TM3.07 Thomas More Building
Royal Courts of Justice
Strand
London WC2A 2LL

(c) Orders on application

When the Court directs that an agreed statement of the terms of an order (formerly called 'minutes of order') be filed, the statement, signed by counsel or solicitors who attended the hearing should be lodged in Room TM3.07. The agreed statement will normally be adopted as the order of the Court.

(iii) Forms of order

Recitals will be kept to a minimum, and the body of the order will be confined to setting out the decision of the Court and the directions required to give effect to it. If upon receipt of an order any party is of the opinion that it is not drawn in such a way as to give effect to the decision of the court, prompt notice must be given to the Order and Accounts Section in Room TM3.07 and to all other parties setting out the reasons for dissatisfaction. If the differences cannot be resolved the objecting party may apply on notice for the order to be amended.

(iv) Copies of orders

Copies of orders may be obtained from Room TM3.07 upon payment of the appropriate fee.

B Consent orders

(i) Consent orders under the Inheritance (Provision for Family and Dependants) Act 1975

Every final order embodying terms of compromise made in proceedings in the Chancery Division under the 1975 Act shall contain a direction that a memorandum of the order shall be endorsed on or permanently annexed to the probate or letters of administration and a copy of the order shall be sent to the Principal Registry of the Family Division with the relevant grant of probate or letters of administration for endorsement, notwithstanding that any particular order may not, strictly speaking, be an order under the 1975 Act.

(ii) Consents by parties not attending the hearing

(a) Where the respondent to a Judge's application does not appear either by counsel or solicitors or in person, the applicant sometimes asks the Court to make a consent order, relying on a letter of consent from the respondent or his solicitors, or sometimes on a draft statement of agreed terms of order signed by the respondent's solicitors.

(b) If the remedy sought by the applicant falls wholly within the remedy or remedies claimed in the application notice, no difficulty normally arises, for the Court is able to grant the remedy even if there is no effective consent by the respondent.

(c) Where, however, the order sought goes outside the remedy or remedies claimed in the application notice, or even in the claim form, or when undertakings are proffered by the respondent, the practice has varied and it has become desirable to establish a simple and uniform procedure and so save costs. Subject always to the discretion of the Court, no order will normally be made in such cases unless a consent signed by or on behalf of the respondent is put before the Court in accordance with the following provisions: (1) Where there are solicitors on the record for the respondent, the Court will normally accept as sufficient a written consent signed by those solicitors on their headed notepaper. (2) Where there are solicitors for the respondent but they are not on the record, the court will normally accept as sufficient a written consent signed by those solicitors on their headed notepaper only if in the consent (or in some other document) the solicitors certify that they have fully explained to the respondent the effect of the order and that the respondent appeared to have understood the explanation. (3) Where there is a written consent signed by a respondent who is acting in person, the Court will normally not accept it as being sufficient unless the Court is satisfied that the respondent understands the effect of the order, either by reason of the circumstances (e.g. that the respondent is himself a barrister or solicitor) or by means of other material (e.g. that the respondent's consent is given in reply to a letter to him which sufficiently explained the effect of the order in simple language). (4) Where the respondent offers any undertaking to the Court (a) the letter or other document offering the undertaking must be signed by the respondent personally, (b) solicitors must certify on their headed notepaper that the signature is the signature of the respondent and (c) the solicitor must similarly certify, if the case falls within sub-para. (2) or sub-para. (3) above, that they have explained to the respondent the consequences of giving the undertaking and that the respondent appeared to understand the explanation.

(d) This procedure will apply generally to all applications in the Chancery Division, and it will apply whether the order is sought by a claimant or a defendant or by the applicant or the respondent.

(iii) Tomlin order

Where proceedings are to be stayed on agreed terms to be scheduled to the order, the draft order should be drawn so as to read as follows: 'And the Claimant and the Defendant having agreed to the terms set forth in the schedule hereto, it is ordered that all further proceedings in this claim be stayed, except for the purpose of carrying such terms into effect. Liberty to apply as to carrying such terms into effect.' This form of order is called a 'Tomlin order'.

CDPD 9 PROBATE

A Verification of original will or codicil

(i) When the Court orders trial of a contentious probate claim on written evidence under paragraph 10 or 13 of the Contentious Probate Proceedings Practice Direction or when an application for summary judgment is made it is necessary for an attesting witness to sign a witness statement or swear an affidavit of due execution of any will or codicil sought to be admitted to probate. The will or codicil is at that stage in the Court's possession and cannot be handed out of court for use as an exhibit to the witness statement or affidavit so that the attesting witness has to attend at the Royal Courts of Justice.

(ii) Where an attesting witness is unable to visit the Royal Courts of Justice in order to sign his witness statement or swear his affidavit in the presence of an officer of the court the solicitor concerned may request from the Chancery Registry, Room TM7.09, Thomas More Building, Royal Courts of Justice, Strand, London WC2A 2LL a photographic copy of the will or codicil in question. This will be certified as authentic by the Court and may be exhibited to the witness statement or affidavit of due execution in lieu of the original. The witness statement or affidavit must in that case state that the exhibited document is an authenticated copy of the document signed in the witness's presence.

B Transmission of scripts in cases tried outside London

When a probate claim is listed for trial outside London the solicitor for the party responsible for preparing the court bundle must write to the Chancery Registry, Room TM7.09, Thomas More Building, Royal Courts of Justice, Strand, London WC2A 2LL and request that the scripts be forwarded to the appropriate District Registry.

C Lodgment of scripts

When a party lodges an original script in Court he should at the same time lodge a copy thereof. If a script is not lodged by a party, e.g. when it is forwarded by the Family Division to the Chancery Division, the party relying on it should lodge a copy thereof in Chancery Chambers before the first hearing at which the script has to be considered. Photographic copies are preferred but typed copies are acceptable.

CDPD 10 SALE

Estate agents' and auctioneers' charges

(i) The charges of estate agents and auctioneers selling freehold or leasehold property pursuant to orders of the Chancery Division will normally be considered reasonable by the Court if they do not exceed the rate of commission which that agent would normally charge on a sole agency basis, and they do not exceed $2\frac{1}{2}$ per cent of the sale price, exclusive of value added tax.

(ii) These charges are to include all commission, valuations, expenses and other disbursements, including making affidavits, the cost of advertising and all other work except surveys. The allowance for a survey will be at the Court's discretion.

(iii) If (a) an agent's charges do not fall within the limits set out in para. (i) or (b) there is a sale of any investment property, business property or farm property or (c) a property is sold in lots or by valuation, an application must be made to the Court to authorise the fee to be charged.

CDPD 11 TITLE TO PROCEEDINGS

The general rule is that the title should contain only the parties to the proceedings, but there is one exception: where the proceedings relate to the administration of an estate or a probate claim they should be entitled 'In the estate of AB deceased'.

If proceedings are under an Act of Parliament, the Act need not be mentioned in the title but should be referred to in the body of the claim form.

CDPD 12 TRUSTS

A Application under s. 48 of the Administration of Justice Act 1985

(i) Applications under s. 48 of the Administration of Justice Act 1985 and RSC, ord. 93, r. 21, should be made by Part 8 Claim Form (N208). The claim need not be served on any other party. It should be supported by a witness statement or affidavit to which are exhibited: (a) copies of all relevant documents, (b) instructions to a person with a 10-year High Court qualification within the meaning of the Courts and Legal Services Act 1990 ('the qualified person'), (c) the qualified person's opinion, (d) draft terms of the desired order.

(ii) The witness statement or affidavit (or exhibits thereto) should state: (a) the names of all persons who are, or may be, affected by the order sought, (b) all surrounding circumstances admissible and relevant in construing the document, (c) the date of qualification of the qualified person and his experience in the construction of trust documents, (d) the approximate value of the fund or property in question, (e) whether it is known to the applicant that a dispute exists and, if so, details of such dispute.

(iii) When the file is placed before the Master he will consider whether the evidence is complete and if it is send the file to the Judge.

(iv) The Judge will consider the papers and, if necessary, direct service of notices under RSC, ord. 15, r. 13A, or request such further information as he may desire. If the Judge is satisfied that the order sought is appropriate, the order will be made and sent to the claimant.

(v) If following service of notices under ord. 15, r. 13A, any acknowledgment of service is received, the claimant must apply to the Master (on notice to the parties who have so acknowledged service) for directions. If the claimant desires to pursue the application to the court, in the ordinary case the Master will direct that the case proceeds as a Part 8 claim.

(vi) If on the hearing of the claim the Judge is of the opinion that any party who entered an acknowledgment of service has no reasonably tenable argument contrary to the qualified person's opinion, in the exercise of his discretion he may order such party to pay any costs thrown away, or part thereof.

B Disability of trustee

(i) There must be medical evidence showing incapacity to act as a trustee at the date of issue of the claim form and that the incapacity is continuing at the date of signing the witness statement or swearing the affidavit. The witness statement or affidavit should also show incapacity to execute transfers, where a vesting order of stocks and shares is asked for.

(ii) The trustee under disability should be made a defendant to the claim but need not be served unless he is sole trustee or has a beneficial interest.

C Funds

Lodgment under s. 63 of the Trustee Act 1925

(i) Lodgment into the High Court of amounts of cash or securities of less than £500.00 under s. 63 of the Trustee Act 1925, and r. 14(1) of the Court Funds Rules 1987, will not be accepted by the Accountant-General unless the Chief Master (or Vacation Master) so signifies in writing.

(ii) The Accountant-General will refer the applicant to the Chief Master (or Vacation Master) who will consider whether there is a more economical method of preserving the fund than lodging it in the High Court or, failing that, may suggest that the money be lodged in a county court (which has power to accept sums of up to £30,000 lodged under s. 63 of the Trustee Act 1925).

(iii) If the Chief Master (or the Vacation Master) decides that a particular lodgment should be made in the High Court, he will so signify on the back of the request (in respect of applications under r. 14(1)(ii)(a)) or the office copy schedule to the affidavit (in respect of applications under r. 14(1)(ii)(b)).

D Original Documents

At the hearing of any case where a will is to be construed, the probate of the will must be in court at the opening of the case. When the construction of a document other than a will is to be considered, the original document must be similarly available. The court should not be asked to construe any document by reference to a mere copy.

E Property in Scotland

In applications for vesting orders under the Trustee Act 1925 any investments or property situate in Scotland should be set out in a separate schedule to the claim form, and the claim form should ask that the trustees may be at liberty to apply for a vesting order in Scotland in respect thereto.

The form of the order to be made in such cases will (with any necessary variation) be as follows:

> It is ordered that the —— as Trustees be at liberty to take all steps that may be necessary to obtain a vesting order in Scotland relating to the securities specified in the schedule herein.

F Variation of trusts

(i) Application to Judge

See Practice Direction CDPD 5.B(viii).

(ii) Counsel's opinion

(a) Where any children or unborn beneficiaries will be affected by an arrangement under the Variation of Trusts Act 1958, evidence must normally be before the Court which shows that their litigation friends or the trustees support the arrangements as being in the interests of the children or unborn beneficiaries, and exhibits a case to counsel and counsel's written opinion to this effect. In complicated cases a written opinion is usually essential to the understanding of the litigation friends and the trustees, and to the consideration by the court of the merits and fiscal consequences of the arrangement.

(b) Where the interests of two or more children, or two or more of the children and unborn beneficiaries, are similar, a single written case to counsel and opinion will suffice; and no case to counsel and written opinion is required in respect of those who fall within the proviso to s. 1(1) of the Act (Discretionary interests under protective trusts). Further, in proper cases the requirement of a case to counsel and a written opinion may at any stage be dispensed with by the Master or the Judge.

(iii) Stamp duty

(a) An undertaking by solicitors with regard to stamping is not required to be included in an order under the Variation of Trusts Act 1958 whether made by a Judge or Master.

(b) The Commissioners of Inland Revenue consider that the stamp duty position of duplicate orders is as follows:

(i) Orders confined to the lifting of protective trusts. These orders are not liable for duty at all and should not be presented to a stamp office.

(ii) Orders affecting voluntary dispositions *inter vivos*. These orders may be certified under the Stamp Duty (Exempt Instruments) Regulations 1987 (SI 1987 No. 516), as within category L in the schedule to those regulations, in which case they should not be presented to a stamp office. Without such a certificate they attract 50p duty under the head 'Conveyance or transfer of any kind not hereinbefore described'.

(iii) Orders outside categories (i) and (ii) above that contain declarations of the trust, i.e. that effect no disposition of trust property. These orders attract 50p fixed duty under the head 'Declaration of trust'. They may be presented for stamping at any stamp office in the usual way, or sent for adjudication if preferred.

G Estates of deceased Lloyd's names

(i) Personal representatives who wish to apply to the Court for permission to distribute the estate of a deceased Lloyd's name following the decision of Lindsay J in *Re Yorke* [1997] 4 All ER 907, may, until further notice and if appropriate in the particular estate, adopt the following procedure.

(ii) The procedure will be appropriate where:

(a) all liabilities of the estate in respect of syndicates of which the name was a member have been reinsured (whether directly or indirectly) into the Equitas group and

(b) the only reason for delaying distribution of the estate is the possibility of personal liability to Lloyd's creditors.

(iii) In these circumstances personal representatives may apply by a Part 8 Claim Form (Form N208) headed 'In the Matter of the Estate of [ ] deceased (a Lloyd's estate) and In the Matter of the Practice Direction dated 21 November 1997' for leave to distribute the estate on the footing that no or no further provision need be made for Lloyd's creditors. The Claim Form need not be served on any other party.

(iv) The Claim should be supported by a witness statement or an affidavit substantially in the form in the Chancery Masters' Practice Forms adapted as necessary to the particular circumstances and accompanied by draft minutes of the desired order substantially in the form in the Chancery Masters' Practice Forms. It should be supported by a Statement of Costs in the form specified in the Costs Practice Direction for the summary assessment of costs, or the signed consent of the residuary beneficiaries to the amount of costs claimed by the personal representatives.

(v) The application will be considered in the first instance by the Master who, if satisfied that the papers are in order and that the relief sought should be granted, may make the order without requiring the attendance of the applicants and send it to them. If not so satisfied, the Master may give directions for the further disposal of the application, including the joinder of contingent creditors as defendants.

(vi) The procedure described in this Practice Direction at present applies only to estates whose liabilities have been reinsured into Equitas. Extensions to the procedure to deal with other cases may be considered in due course.

APPENDIX 1 QUEEN'S BENCH MASTERS PRACTICE DIRECTIONS
[This appendix has not yet been published.]

APPENDIX 2 ADMINISTRATION OF CHANCERY CHAMBERS AND COMPANIES AND BANKRUPTCY COURT
This Appendix is set out at Appendix 6 to the Chancery Guide.

APPENDIX 3 WRITTEN EVIDENCE LODGMENT FORM

CHANCERY CHAMBERS

TO FILING SECTION — ROOM TM3.07
CLAIM NO:
SHORT TITLE:

Herewith Affidavit or witness statement of ....
/or if other document specify ....
filed in respect of:

		TICK
1.	Application before Judge on	
2.	Application before Master on	
3.	Charging Order	
4.	Garnishee Order	
5.	Permission to issue [claim for] possession	
6.	Service by alternative method	
7.	Service out of Jurisdiction	
8.	Evidence	
9.	Oral examination of debtor	
10.	To enable a Master's order to be drawn	
11.	Other (Specify)	

Signed:

Solicitors for Claimant/Defendant

Other (please specify)

Telephone No:

Ref

PRACTICE DIRECTION, CHANCERY AND QUEEN'S BENCH DIVISIONS EXCLUDING THE ADMIRALTY AND COMMERCIAL COURTS, AND THE TECHNOLOGY AND CONSTRUCTION COURT — THE FIXING OF TRIAL DATES AND WINDOWS IN THE MULTI-TRACK)

GENERAL

The Royal Courts of Justice presents unique problems in terms of fixing trial dates. The number of Judges and Masters involved and their geographical location in tandem with the offices awaiting the installation of a fully integrated IT Support System scheduled for the summer of 2000 has caused, for the time being at least, a different approach to the fixing of trials in the Chancery and Queen's Bench Divisions. Moreover, the requirements of Judges to go on Circuit, sit in the Criminal Division of the Court of Appeal, deal with cases in the Crown Office and other lists make it difficult to fix dates for trials before particular Judges. Accordingly, the following will only apply to the Listing Offices in those Divisions in the Royal Courts of Justice.

PROCEDURE

1. At as early an interim stage as practicable, the Court will give directions with a view to fixing the trial date or the week within which the trial is to begin (the trial window).

2. For that purpose the Court may:
    (a) direct that the trial do not begin earlier than a specified date calculated to provide enough time for the parties to complete any necessary preparations for trial; and/or
    (b) direct that the trial date be within a specified period; and/or
    (c) specify the trial date or window.

3. If directions under (2)(a) or (2)(b) are given the Court will direct the parties to attend upon the Listing Officer at such time as may be specified in order to fix the trial date or trial window.

4. The claimant must, unless some other party agrees to do so, take out an appointment with the Listing Officer within 7 days of obtaining the direction in paragraph (3) above and give notice of the appointment to all other parties. If an appointment is not taken out within the 7 days, the Listing Office will appoint a date for a listing hearing and give notice of the date to all parties.

5. At the listing hearing the Listing Officer will take account, in so far as it is practical to do so of any difficulties the parties may have as to availability of counsel, experts and witnesses. The Listing Officer will, nevertheless, try to ensure the speedy disposal of the trial by arranging a firm trial date as soon as possible within the trial period or, as the case may, after the 'not before' date directed by the court under (2)(a) above. (If a case summary has been prepared (see the Multi-Track Practice Direction, paras 5.6 and 5.7) the claimant must produce a copy at the listing hearing together with a copy of the particulars of claim and any Orders relevant to the fixing of the trial date.)

6. The Listing Officer will notify the Masters' Support staff of any trial date or trial window given. In accordance with rule 29.2(3) notice will also be given to all the parties.

7. A party who wishes to appeal a date or window allocated by the Listing Officer must, within 7 days of the allocation, make an application to the Judge nominated by each Division to hear such applications. The application notice should be filed in the Listing Office and served, giving one clear day's notice, on the other parties.

Issued by direction of the Vice Chancellor.

APPENDIX 2
PRE-ACTION PROTOCOLS

CONTENTS

Practice Direction — Protocols	1194
Pre-action Protocol for Personal Injury Claims	1196
Pre-action Protocol for the Resolution of Clinical Disputes	1206

PRACTICE DIRECTION — PROTOCOLS

GENERAL

1.1 This Practice Direction applies to the pre-action protocols which have been approved by the Head of Civil Justice.

1.2 The pre-action protocols which have been approved are specified in the Schedule to this Practice Direction. Other pre-action protocols may subsequently be added.

1.3 Pre-action protocols outline the steps parties should take to seek information from and to provide information to each other about a prospective legal claim.

1.4 The objectives of pre-action protocols are—

(1) to encourage the exchange of early and full information about the prospective legal claim,

(2) to enable parties to avoid litigation by agreeing a settlement of the claim before the commencement of proceedings,

(3) to support the efficient management of proceedings where litigation cannot be avoided.

COMPLIANCE WITH PROTOCOLS

2.1 The Civil Procedure Rules enable the court to take into account compliance or non-compliance with an applicable protocol when giving directions for the management of proceedings (see CPR rules 3.1(4) and (5) and 3.9(e)) and when making orders for costs (see CPR rule 44.3(5)(a)).

2.2 The court will expect all parties to have complied in substance with the terms of an approved protocol.

2.3 If, in the opinion of the court, non-compliance has led to the commencement of proceedings which might otherwise not have needed to be commenced, or has led to costs being incurred in the proceedings that might otherwise not have been incurred, the orders the court may make include—

(1) an order that the party at fault pay the costs of the proceedings, or part of those costs, of the other party or parties;

(2) an order that the party at fault pay those costs on an indemnity basis;

(3) if the party at fault is a claimant in whose favour an order for the payment of damages or some specified sum is subsequently made, an order depriving that party of interest on such sum and in respect of such period as may be specified, and/or awarding interest at a lower rate than that at which interest would otherwise have been awarded;

(4) if the party at fault is a defendant and an order for the payment of damages or some specified sum is subsequently made in favour of the claimant, an order awarding interest on such sum and in respect of such period as may be specified at a higher rate, not exceeding 10% above base rate (cf. CPR rule 36.21(2)), than the rate at which interest would otherwise have been awarded.

2.4 The court will exercise its powers under paragraphs 2.1 and 2.3 with the object of placing the innocent party in no worse a position than he would have been in if the protocol had been complied with.

3.1 A claimant may be found to have failed to comply with a protocol by, for example—

(a) not having provided sufficient information to the defendant, or

(b) not having followed the procedure required by the protocol to be followed (e.g. not having followed the medical expert instruction procedure set out in the Personal Injury Protocol).

3.2 A defendant may be found to have failed to comply with a protocol by, for example—

(a) not making a preliminary response to the letter of claim within the time fixed for that purpose by the relevant protocol (21 days under the Personal Injury Protocol, 14 days under the Clinical Negligence Protocol),

(b) not making a full response within the time fixed for that purpose by the relevant protocol (3 months of the letter of claim under the Clinical Negligence Protocol, 3 months from the date of acknowledgment of the letter of claim under the Personal Injury Protocol),

(c) not disclosing documents required to be disclosed by the relevant protocol.

PRE-ACTION BEHAVIOUR IN OTHER CASES

4. In cases not covered by any approved protocol, the court will expect the parties, in accordance with the overriding objective and the matters referred to in CPR 1.1(2)(a), (b) and (c), to act reasonably in exchanging information and documents relevant to the claim and generally in trying to avoid the necessity for the start of proceedings.

COMMENCEMENT

5.1 Compliance or non-compliance, as the case may be, with the protocols specified in the Schedule will be taken into account by the court in dealing with any proceedings commenced after 26 April 1999 but will not be taken into account by the court in dealing with proceedings started before that date.

5.2 Where, in respect of proceedings commenced after 26 April 1999, the parties have by work done before that date substantially achieved the object designed to be achieved by steps to be taken under a protocol, the parties need not take those steps and their failure to do so will not be treated, for the purposes of paragraphs 2 and 3, as non-compliance.

5.3 Where, in respect of proceedings commenced after 26 April 1999, the parties have not had time since the publication of the protocols in January 1999 to comply with the applicable provisions, their failure to have done so will not be treated, for the purposes of paragraphs 2 and 3, as non-compliance.

5.4 As and when an additional protocol is approved, a Practice Direction will specify the date after which compliance or non-compliance with that protocol will be taken into account by the court.

SCHEDULE

1. Personal Injury Protocol.

2. Clinical Negligence Protocol.

PRE-ACTION PROTOCOL FOR PERSONAL INJURY CLAIMS

CONTENTS

1	Introduction	1196
2	Notes of guidance	1196
3	The protocol	1198
Annex A	Letter of claim	1200
Annex B	Standard disclosure lists. Fast track disclosure	1201
Annex C	Letter of instruction to medical expert	1204

1 INTRODUCTION

1.1 Lord Woolf in his final Access to Justice Report of July 1996 recommended the development of pre-action protocols:

'To build on and increase the benefits of early but well informed settlement which genuinely satisfy both parties to dispute.'

1.2 The aims of pre-action protocols are:
- more pre-action contact between the parties
- better and earlier exchange of information
- better pre-action investigation by both sides
- to put the parties in a position where they may be able to settle cases fairly and early without litigation
- to enable proceedings to run to the court's timetable and efficiently, if litigation does become necessary.

1.3 The concept of protocols is relevant to a range of initiatives for good litigation and pre-litigation practice, especially:
- predictability in the time needed for steps pre-proceedings
- standardisation of relevant information, including documents to be disclosed.

1.4 The Courts will be able to treat the standards set in protocols as the normal reasonable approach to pre-action conduct. If proceedings are issued, it will be for the court to decide whether non-compliance with a protocol should merit adverse consequences. Guidance on the court's likely approach will be given from time to time in practice directions.

1.5 If the court has to consider the question of compliance after proceedings have begun, it will not be concerned with minor infringements, e.g. failure by a short period to provide relevant information. One minor breach will not exempt the 'innocent' party from following the protocol. The court will look at the effect of non-compliance on the other party when deciding whether to impose sanctions.

2 NOTES OF GUIDANCE

2.1 The protocol has been kept deliberately simple to promote ease of use and general acceptability. The notes of guidance which follow relate particularly to issues which arose during the piloting of the protocol.

SCOPE OF THE PROTOCOL

2.2 This protocol is intended to apply to all claims which include a claim for personal injury and to the entirety of those claims: not only to the personal injury element of a claim which also includes, for instance, property damage.

2.3 This protocol is primarily designed for those road traffic, tripping and slipping and accident at work cases which include an element of personal injury with a value of less than £15,000 which are likely to be allocated to the fast track. This is because time will be of the essence, after proceedings are issued, especially

PRE-ACTION PROTOCOL FOR PERSONAL INJURY CLAIMS

for the defendant, if a case is to be ready for trial within 30 weeks of allocation. Also, proportionality of work and costs to the value of what is in dispute is particularly important in lower value claims. For some claims within the value 'scope' of the fast track some flexibility in the timescale of the protocol may be necessary; see also paragraph 3.8.

2.4 However, the 'cards on the table' approach advocated by the protocol is equally appropriate to some higher value claims. The spirit, if not the letter of the protocol, should still be followed for multi-track type claims. In accordance with the sense of the civil justice reforms, the court will expect to see the spirit of reasonable pre-action behaviour applied in all cases, regardless of the existence of a specific protocol.

2.5 The timetable and the arrangements for disclosing documents and obtaining expert evidence may need to be varied to suit the circumstances of the case. Where one or both parties consider the detail of the protocol is not appropriate to the case, and proceedings are subsequently issued, the court will expect an explanation as to why the protocol has not been followed, or has been varied.

EARLY NOTIFICATION

2.6 The claimant's legal representative may wish to notify the defendant and/or his insurer as soon as they know a claim is likely to be made, but before they are able to send a detailed letter of claim, particularly for instance, when the defendant has no or limited knowledge of the incident giving rise to the claim or where the claimant is incurring significant expenditure as a result of the accident which he hopes the defendant might pay for, in whole or in part. If the claimant's representative chooses to do this, it will not start the timetable for responding.

THE LETTER OF CLAIM

2.7 The specimen letter of claim at Annex A will usually be sent to the individual defendant. In practice, he/she may have no personal financial interest in the financial outcome of the claim/dispute because he/she is insured. Court imposed sanctions for non-compliance with the protocol may be ineffective against an insured. This is why the protocol emphasises the importance of passing the letter of claim to the insurer and the possibility that the insurance cover might be affected. If an insurer receives the letter of claim only after some delay by the insured, it would not be unreasonable for the insurer to ask the claimant for additional time to respond.

REASONS FOR EARLY ISSUE

2.8 The protocol recommends that a defendant be given three months to investigate and respond to a claim before proceedings are issued. This may not always be possible, particularly where a claimant only consults a solicitor close to the end of any relevant limitation period. In these circumstances, the claimant's solicitor should give as much notice of the intention to issue proceedings as is practicable and the parties should consider whether the court might be invited to extend time for service of the claimant's supporting documents and for service of any defence, or alternatively, to stay the proceedings while the recommended steps in the protocol are followed.

STATUS OF LETTERS OF CLAIM AND RESPONSE

2.9 Letters of claim and response are not intended to have the same status as a statement of case in proceedings. Matters may come to light as a result of investigation after the letter of claim has been sent, or after the defendant has responded, particularly if disclosure of documents takes place outside the recommended three-month period. These circumstances could mean that the 'pleaded' case of one or both parties is presented slightly differently than in the letter of claim and response. It would not be consistent with the spirit of the protocol for a party to 'take a point' on this in the proceedings, provided that there was no obvious intention by the party who changed their position to mislead the other party.

DISCLOSURE OF DOCUMENTS

2.10 The aim of the early disclosure of documents by the defendant is not to encourage 'fishing expeditions' by the claimant, but to promote an early exchange of relevant information to help in clarifying or resolving issues in dispute. The claimant's solicitor can assist by identifying in the letter of claim or in a subsequent letter the particular categories of documents which they consider are relevant.

EXPERTS

2.11 The protocol encourages joint selection of, and access to, experts. Most frequently this will apply to the medical expert, but on occasions also to liability experts, e.g. engineers. The protocol promotes the practice of the claimant obtaining a medical report, disclosing it to the defendant who then asks questions and/or agrees it and does not obtain his own report. But it maintains the flexibility for each party to obtain their own expert's report, if necessary after proceedings have commenced, with the leave of the court. It would also be for the court to decide whether the costs of more than one expert's report should be recoverable.

2.12 Some solicitors choose to obtain medical reports through medical agencies, rather than directly from a specific doctor or hospital. The defendant's prior consent to the action should be sought and, if the defendant so requests, the agency should be asked to provide in advance the names of the doctor(s) whom they are considering instructing.

NEGOTIATIONS/SETTLEMENT

2.13 Parties and their legal representatives are encouraged to enter into discussions and/or negotiations prior to starting proceedings. The protocol does not specify when or how this might be done but parties should bear in mind that the courts increasingly take the view that litigation should be a last resort, and that claims should not be issued prematurely when a settlement is in reasonable prospect.

STOCKTAKE

2.14 Where a claim is not resolved when the protocol has been followed, the parties might wish to carry out a 'stocktake' of the issues in dispute, and the evidence that the court is likely to need to decide those issues, before proceedings are started. Where the defendant is insured and the pre-action steps have been conducted by the insurer, the insurer would normally be expected to nominate solicitors to act in the proceedings and the claimant's solicitor is recommended to invite the insurer to nominate solicitors to act in the proceedings and do so 7–14 days before the intended issue date.

3 THE PROTOCOL

LETTER OF CLAIM

3.1 The claimant shall send to the proposed defendant two copies of a letter of claim, immediately sufficient information is available to substantiate a realistic claim and before issues of quantum are addressed in detail. One copy of the letter is for the defendants, the second for passing on to his insurers.

3.2 The letter shall contain a **clear summary of the facts** on which the claim is based together with an indication of the **nature of any injuries** suffered and of **any financial loss incurred**. In cases of road traffic accidents, the letter should provide the name and address of the hospital where treatment has been obtained and the claimant's hospital reference number.

3.3 Solicitors are recommended to use a **standard format** for such a letter — an example is at Annex A: this can be amended to suit the particular case.

3.4 The letter should ask for **details of the insurer** and that a copy should be sent by the proposed defendant to the insurer where appropriate. If the insurer is known, a copy shall be sent directly to the insurer. Details of the claimant's National Insurance number and date of birth should be supplied to the defendant's insurer once the defendant has responded to the letter of claim and confirmed the identity of the insurer. This information should not be supplied in the letter of claim.

3.5 **Sufficient information** should be given in order to enable the defendant's insurer/solicitor to commence investigations and at least put a broad valuation on the 'risk'.

3.6 The **defendant should reply within 21 calendar days** of the date of posting of the letter identifying the insurer (if any). If there has been no reply by the defendant or insurer within 21 days, the claimant will be entitled to issue proceedings.

3.7 The **defendant**('s insurers) will have a **maximum of three months** from the date of acknowledgment of the claim **to investigate**. No later than the end of that period the defendant (insurer) shall reply, stating whether liability is denied and, if so, giving reasons for their denial of liability.

3.8 Where the accident occurred outside England and Wales and/or where the defendant is outside the jurisdiction, the time periods of 21 days and three months may reasonably be extended up to 42 days and six months.

3.9 Where **liability is admitted**, the presumption is that the defendant will be bound by this admission for all claims with a total value of up to £15,000.

DOCUMENTS

3.10 If the **defendant denies liability**, he should enclose with the letter of reply, **documents** in his possession which are **material to the issues** between the parties, and which would be likely to be ordered to be disclosed by the court, either on an application for pre-action disclosure, or on disclosure during proceedings.

3.11 Attached at Annex B are **specimen**, but non-exhaustive, **lists** of documents likely to be material in different types of claim. Where the claimant's investigation of the case is well advanced, the letter of claim could indicate which classes of documents are considered relevant for early disclosure. Alternatively these could be identified at a later stage.

3.12 Where the defendant admits primary liability, but alleges contributory negligence by the claimant, the defendant should give reasons supporting those allegations and disclose those documents from Annex B which are relevant to the issues in dispute. The claimant should respond to the allegations of contributory negligence before proceedings are issued.

SPECIAL DAMAGES

3.13 The claimant will send to the defendant as soon as practicable a Schedule of Special Damages with supporting documents, particularly where the defendant has admitted liability.

EXPERTS

3.14 Before any party instructs an expert he should give the other party a list of the **name**(s) of **one or more experts** in the relevant speciality whom he considers are suitable to instruct.

3.15 Where a medical expert is to be instructed the claimant's solicitor will organise access to relevant medical records — see specimen letter of instruction at Annex C.

3.16 **Within 14 days** the other party may indicate **an objection** to one or more of the named experts. The first party should then instruct a mutually acceptable expert.

3.17 If the second party objects to all the listed experts, the parties may then instruct **experts of their own choice**. It would be for the court to decide subsequently, if proceedings are issued, whether either party had acted unreasonably.

3.18 If the **second party does not object to an expert nominated**, he shall not be entitled to rely on his own expert evidence within that particular speciality unless:
 (a) the first party agrees,
 (b) the court so directs, or
 (c) the first party's expert report has been amended and the first party is not prepared to disclose the original report.

3.19 **Either party may send to an agreed expert written questions** on the report, relevant to the issues, via the first party's solicitors. The expert should send answers to the questions separately and directly to each party.

PRE-ACTION PROTOCOL FOR PERSONAL INJURY CLAIMS

3.20 The cost of a report from an agreed expert will usually be paid by the instructing first party: the costs of the expert replying to questions will usually be borne by the party which asks the questions.

3.21 Where the defendant admits liability in whole or in part, before proceedings are issued, any medical report obtained by agreement under this protocol should be disclosed to the other party. The claimant should delay issuing proceedings for 21 days from disclosure of the report, to enable the parties to consider whether the claim is capable of settlement. The Civil Procedure Rules Part 36 permit claimants and defendants to make offers to settle pre-proceedings.

ANNEX A LETTER OF CLAIM

To
Defendant

Dear Sirs

Re: Claimant's full name
Claimant's full address
Claimant's Clock or Works Number
Claimant's Employer (*name and address*)

We are instructed by the above named to claim damages in connection with *an accident at work/road traffic accident/tripping accident* on   day of   (*year*) at (*place of accident which must be sufficiently detailed to establish location*)

Please confirm the identity of your insurers. Please note that the insurers will need to see this letter as soon as possible and it may affect your insurance cover and/or the conduct of any subsequent legal proceedings if you do not send this letter to them.

The circumstances of the accident are:—
(*brief outline*)

The reason why we are alleging fault is:
(*simple explanation e.g. defective machine, broken ground*)

A description of our clients' injuries is as follows:—
(*brief outline*)

(*In cases of road traffic accidents*)
Our client (*state hospital reference number*) received treatment for the injuries at (*name and address of hospital*).

He is employed as (*occupation*) and has had the following time off work (*dates of absence*). His approximate weekly income is (*insert if known*).

If you are our client's employers, please provide us with the usual earnings details which will enable us to calculate his financial loss.

We are obtaining a police report and will let you have a copy of the same upon your undertaking to meet half the fee.

We have also sent a letter of claim to (*name and address*) and a copy of that letter is attached. We understand their insurers are (*name, address and claims number if known*).

At this stage of our enquiries we would expect the documents contained in parts (*insert appropriate parts of standard disclosure list*) to be relevant to this action.

A copy of this letter is attached for you to send to your insurers. Finally we expect an acknowledgment of this letter within 21 days by yourselves or your insurers.

Yours faithfully

PRE-ACTION PROTOCOL FOR PERSONAL INJURY CLAIMS

ANNEX B   STANDARD DISCLOSURE LISTS
FAST TRACK DISCLOSURE

RTA CASES

SECTION A
In all cases where liability is at issue—
  (i)   Documents identifying nature, extent and location of damage to defendant's vehicle where there is any dispute about point of impact.
  (ii) MOT certificate where relevant.
  (iii) Maintenance records where vehicle defect is alleged or it is alleged by defendant that there was an unforeseen defect which caused or contributed to the accident.

SECTION B
Accident involving commercial vehicle as potential defendant—
  (i)   Tachograph charts or entry from individual control book.
  (ii) Maintenance and repair records required for operators' licence where vehicle defect is alleged or it is alleged by defendants that there was an unforeseen defect which caused or contributed to the accident.

SECTION C
Cases against local authorities where highway design defect is alleged—
  (i)   Documents produced to comply with Section 39 of the Road Traffic Act 1988 in respect of the duty designed to promote road safety to include studies into road accidents in the relevant area and documents relating to measures recommended to prevent accidents in the relevant area.

HIGHWAY TRIPPING CLAIMS

Documents from Highway Authority for a period of 12 months prior to the accident—
  (i)   Records of inspection for the relevant stretch of highway.
  (ii) Maintenance records including records of independent contractors working in relevant area.
  (iii) Records of the minutes of Highway Authority meetings where maintenance or repair policy has been discussed or decided.
  (iv) Records of complaints about the state of highways.
  (v)   Records of other accidents which have occurred on the relevant stretch of highway.

WORKPLACE CLAIMS

  (i)   Accident book entry.
  (ii)   First aider report.
  (iii) Surgery record.
  (iv)   Foreman/supervisor accident report.
  (v)   Safety representatives accident report.
  (vi)   RIDDOR report to HSE.
  (vii) Other communications between defendants and HSE.
  (viii) Minutes of Health and Safety Committee meeting(s) where accident/matter considered.
  (ix)   Report to DSS.
  (x)   Documents listed above relative to any previous accident/matter identified by the claimant and relied upon as proof of negligence.
  (xi)   Earnings information where defendant is employer.

Documents produced to comply with requirements of the Management of Health and Safety at Work Regulations 1992—
  (i)   Pre-accident Risk Assessment required by Regulation 3.
  (ii) Post-accident Re-Assessment required by Regulation 3.
  (iii) Accident Investigation Report prepared in implementing the requirements of Regulations 4, 6 and 9.

(iv) Health Surveillance Records in appropriate cases required by Regulation 5.
(v) Information provided to employees under Regulation 8.
(vi) Documents relating to the employees health and safety training required by Regulation 11.

WORKPLACE CLAIMS — DISCLOSURE WHERE SPECIFIC REGULATIONS APPLY

SECTION A — WORKPLACE (HEALTH SAFETY AND WELFARE) REGULATIONS 1992
(i) Repair and maintenance records required by Regulation 5.
(ii) Housekeeping records to comply with the requirements of Regulation 9.
(iii) Hazard warning signs or notices to comply with Regulation 17 (Traffic Routes).

SECTION B — PROVISION AND USE OF WORK EQUIPMENT REGULATIONS 1992
(i) Manufacturers' specifications and instructions in respect of relevant work equipment establishing its suitability to comply with Regulation 5.
(ii) Maintenance log/maintenance records required to comply with Regulation 6.
(iii) Documents providing information and instructions to employees to comply with Regulation 8.
(iv) Documents provided to the employee in respect of training for use to comply with Regulation 9.
(v) Any notice, sign or document relied upon as a defence to alleged breaches of Regulations 14 to 18 dealing with controls and control systems.
(vi) Instruction/training documents issued to comply with the requirements of Regulation 22 insofar as it deals with maintenance operations where the machinery is not shut down.
(vii) Copies of markings required to comply with Regulation 23.
(viii) Copies of warnings required to comply with Regulation 24.

SECTION C — PERSONAL PROTECTIVE EQUIPMENT AT WORK REGULATIONS 1992
(i) Documents relating to the assessment of the Personal Protective Equipment to comply with Regulation 6.
(ii) Documents relating to the maintenance and replacement of Personal Protective Equipment to comply with Regulation 7.
(iii) Record of maintenance procedures for Personal Protective Equipment to comply with Regulation 7.
(iv) Records of tests and examinations of Personal Protective Equipment to comply with Regulation 7.
(v) Documents providing information, instruction and training in relation to the Personal Protective Equipment to comply with Regulation 9.
(vi) Instructions for use of Personal Protective Equipment to include the manufacturers' instructions to comply with Regulation 10.

SECTION D — MANUAL HANDLING OPERATIONS REGULATIONS 1992
(i) Manual Handling Risk Assessment carried out to comply with the requirements of Regulation 4(1)(b)(i).
(ii) Re-assessment carried out post-accident to comply with requirements of Regulation 4(1)(b)(i).
(iii) Documents showing the information provided to the employee to give general indications related to the load and precise indications on the weight of the load and the heaviest side of the load if the centre of gravity was not positioned centrally to comply with Regulation 4(1)(b)(iii).
(iv) Documents relating to training in respect of manual handling operations and training records.

PRE-ACTION PROTOCOL FOR PERSONAL INJURY CLAIMS

SECTION E — HEALTH AND SAFETY (DISPLAY SCREEN EQUIPMENT) REGULATIONS 1992

(i) Analysis of work stations to assess and reduce risks carried out to comply with the requirements of Regulation 2.

(ii) Re-assessment of analysis of work stations to assess and reduce risks following development of symptoms by the claimant.

(iii) Documents detailing the provision of training including training records to comply with the requirements of Regulation 6.

(iv) Documents providing information to employees to comply with the requirements of Regulation 7.

SECTION F — CONTROL OF SUBSTANCES HAZARDOUS TO HEALTH REGULATIONS 1988

(i) Risk assessment carried out to comply with the requirements of Regulation 6.

(ii) Reviewed risk assessment carried out to comply with the requirements of Regulation 6.

(iii) Copy labels from containers used for storage handling and disposal of carcinogenics to comply with the requirements of Regulation 7(2A)(h).

(iv) Warning signs identifying designation of areas and installations which may be contaminated by carcinogenics to comply with the requirements of Regulation 7(2A)(h).

(v) Documents relating to the assessment of the Personal Protective Equipment to comply with Regulation 7(3A).

(vi) Documents relating to the maintenance and replacement of Personal Protective Equipment to comply with Regulation 7(3A).

(vii) Record of maintenance procedures for Personal Protective Equipment to comply with Regulation 7(3A).

(viii) Records of tests and examinations of Personal Protective Equipment to comply with Regulation 7(3A).

(ix) Documents providing information, instruction and training in relation to the Personal Protective Equipment to comply with Regulation 7(3A).

(x) Instructions for use of Personal Protective Equipment to include the manufacturers' instructions to comply with Regulation 7(3A).

(xi) Air monitoring records for substances assigned a maximum exposure limit or occupational exposure standard to comply with the requirements of Regulation 7.

(xii) Maintenance examination and test of control measures records to comply with Regulation 9.

(xiii) Monitoring records to comply with the requirements of Regulation 10.

(xiv) Health surveillance records to comply with the requirements of Regulation 11.

(xv) Documents detailing information, instruction and training including training records for employees to comply with the requirements of Regulation 12.

(xvi) Labels and Health and Safety data sheets supplied to the employers to comply with the CHIP Regulations.

SECTION G — CONSTRUCTION (DESIGN AND MANAGEMENT) REGULATIONS 1994

(i) Notification of a project form (HSE F10) to comply with the requirements of Regulation 7.

(ii) Health and Safety Plan to comply with requirements of Regulation 15.

(iii) Health and Safety file to comply with the requirements of Regulations 12 and 14.

(iv) Information and training records provided to comply with the requirements of Regulation 17.

(v) Records of advice from and views of persons at work to comply with the requirements of Regulation 18.

SECTION H — PRESSURE SYSTEMS AND TRANSPORTABLE GAS CONTAINERS REGULATIONS 1989

(i) Information and specimen markings provided to comply with the requirements of Regulation 5.

(ii) Written statements specifying the safe operating limits of a system to comply with the requirements of Regulation 7.

(iii) Copy of the written scheme of examination required to comply with the requirements of Regulation 8.

(iv) Examination records required to comply with the requirements of Regulation 9.

(v) Instructions provided for the use of operator to comply with Regulation 11.

(vi) Records kept to comply with the requirements of Regulation 13.

(vii) Records kept to comply with the requirements of Regulation 22.

SECTION I — LIFTING PLANT AND EQUIPMENT (RECORDS OF TEST AND EXAMINATION ETC.) REGULATIONS 1992

(i) Record kept to comply with the requirements of Regulation 6.

SECTION J — THE NOISE AT WORK REGULATIONS 1989

(i) Any risk assessment records required to comply with the requirements of Regulations 4 and 5.

(ii) Manufacturers' literature in respect of all ear protection made available to claimant to comply with the requirements of Regulation 8.

(iii) All documents provided to the employee for the provision of information to comply with Regulation 11.

SECTION K — CONSTRUCTION (HEAD PROTECTION) REGULATIONS 1989

(i) Pre-accident assessment of head protection required to comply with Regulation 3(4).

(ii) Post-accident re-assessment required to comply with Regulation 3(5).

SECTION L — THE CONSTRUCTION (GENERAL PROVISIONS) REGULATIONS 1961

(i) Report prepared following inspections and examinations of excavations etc. to comply with the requirements of Regulation 9.

(ii) Report prepared following inspections and examinations of work in cofferdams and caissons to comply with the requirements of Regulations 17 and 18.

N.B. Further Standard Discovery lists will be required prior to full implementation.

ANNEX C   LETTER OF INSTRUCTION TO MEDICAL EXPERT

Dear Sir,

Re: (*Name and Address*)
D.O.B. —
Telephone No. —
Date of Accident —

We are acting for the above named in connection with injuries received in an accident which occurred on the above date. The main injuries appear to have been **(main injuries)**.

We should be obliged if you would examine our Client and let us have a full and detailed report dealing with any relevant pre-accident medical history, the injuries sustained, treatment received and present condition, dealing in particular with the capacity for work and giving a prognosis.

It is central to our assessment of the extent of our Client's injuries to establish the extent and duration of any continuing disability. Accordingly, in the prognosis section we would ask you to specifically comment on any areas of continuing complaint or disability or impact on daily living. If there is such continuing disability you should comment upon the level of suffering or inconvenience caused and, if you are able, give your view as to when or if the complaint or disability is likely to resolve.

Please send our Client an appointment direct for this purpose. Should you be able to offer a cancellation appointment please contact our Client direct. We confirm we will be responsible for your reasonable fees.

We are obtaining the notes and records from our Client's GP and Hospitals attended and will forward them to you when they are to hand/or please request the GP and Hospital records direct and advise that any invoice for the provision of these records should be forwarded to us.

In order to comply with Court Rules we would be grateful if you would insert above your signature a statement that the contents are true to the best of your knowledge and belief.

In order to avoid further correspondence we can confirm that on the evidence we have there is no reason to suspect we may be pursuing a claim against the hospital or its staff.

We look forward to receiving your report within _____ weeks. If you will not be able to prepare your report within this period please telephone us upon receipt of these instructions.

When acknowledging these instructions it would assist if you could give an estimate as to the likely time scale for the provision of your report and also an indication as to your fee.

Yours faithfully

PRE-ACTION PROTOCOL FOR THE RESOLUTION OF CLINICAL DISPUTES
Clinical Disputes Forum

CONTENTS

Executive summary		1206
1	Why this protocol?	1206
2	The aims of the protocol	1208
3	The protocol	1209
4	Experts	1212
5	Alternative approaches to settling disputes	1212
Annex A	Illustrative flowchart	1213
Annex B	Medical negligence and personal injury claims: a protocol for obtaining hospital medical records	1214
Annex C	Templates for letters of claim and response	1219
Annex D	Lord Woolf's recommendations	1221
Annex E	How to contact the Forum	1221

EXECUTIVE SUMMARY

1. The Clinical Disputes Forum is a multi-disciplinary body which was formed in 1997, as a result of Lord Woolf's 'Access to Justice' inquiry. One of the aims of the Forum is to find less adversarial and more cost-effective ways of resolving disputes about healthcare and medical treatment. The names and addresses of the Chairman and Secretary of the Forum can be found at Annex E.

2. This protocol is the Forum's first major initiative. It has been drawn up carefully, including extensive consultations with most of the key stakeholders in the medico-legal system.

3. The protocol—
- encourages a climate of openness when something has 'gone wrong' with a patient's treatment or the patient is dissatisfied with that treatment and/or the outcome. This reflects the new and developing requirements for clinical governance within healthcare;
- provides **general guidance** on how this more open culture might be achieved when disputes arise;
- recommends a **timed sequence** of steps for patients and healthcare providers, and their advisers, to follow when a dispute arises. This should facilitate and speed up exchanging relevant information and increase the prospects that disputes can be resolved without resort to legal action.

4. This protocol has been prepared by a working party of the Clinical Disputes Forum. It has the support of the Lord Chancellor's Department, the Department of Health and NHS Executive, the Law Society, the Legal Aid Board and many other key organisations.

1 WHY THIS PROTOCOL?

MISTRUST IN HEALTHCARE DISPUTES

1.1 The number of complaints and claims against hospitals, GPs, dentists and private healthcare providers is growing as patients become more prepared to question the treatment they are given, to seek explanations of what happened, and to seek appropriate redress. Patients may require further treatment, an apology, assurances about future action, or compensation. These trends are unlikely to change. The Patients' Charter encourages patients to have high expectations, and a revised NHS Complaints Procedure was implemented in 1996. The civil justice reforms and new Rules of Court should make litigation quicker, more user friendly and less expensive.

PRE-ACTION PROTOCOL FOR THE RESOLUTION OF CLINICAL DISPUTES

1.2 It is clearly in the interests of patients, healthcare professionals and providers that patients' concerns, complaints and claims arising from their treatment are resolved as quickly, efficiently and professionally as possible. A climate of mistrust and lack of openness can seriously damage the patient/clinician relationship, unnecessarily prolong disputes (especially litigation), and reduce the resources available for treating patients. It may also cause additional work for, and lower the morale of, healthcare professionals.

1.3 At present there is often mistrust by both sides. This can mean that patients fail to raise their concerns with the healthcare provider as early as possible. Sometimes patients may pursue a complaint or claim which has little merit, due to a lack of sufficient information and understanding. It can also mean that patients become reluctant, once advice has been taken on a potential claim, to disclose sufficient information to enable the provider to investigate that claim efficiently and, where appropriate, resolve it.

1.4 On the side of the healthcare provider this mistrust can be shown in a reluctance to be honest with patients, a failure to provide prompt clear explanations, especially of adverse outcomes (whether or not there may have been negligence) and a tendency to 'close ranks' once a claim is made.

WHAT NEEDS TO CHANGE

1.5 If that mistrust is to be removed, and a more co-operative culture is to develop—
- healthcare professionals and providers need to adopt a constructive approach to complaints and claims. They should accept that concerned patients are entitled to an explanation and an apology, if warranted, and to appropriate redress in the event of negligence. An overly defensive approach is not in the long-term interest of their main goal: patient care;
- patients should recognise that unintended and/or unfortunate consequences of medical treatment can only be rectified if they are brought to the attention of the healthcare provider as soon as possible.

1.6 A protocol which sets out 'ground rules' for the handling of disputes at their early stages should, if it is to be subscribed to, and followed—
- encourage greater openness between the parties;
- encourage parties to find the most appropriate way of resolving the particular dispute;
- reduce delay and costs;
- reduce the need for litigation.

WHY THIS PROTOCOL NOW?

1.7 Lord Woolf in his Access to Justice Report in July 1996, concluded that major causes of costs and delay in medical negligence litigation occur at the pre-action stage. He recommended that patients and their advisers, and healthcare providers, should work more closely together to try to resolve disputes co-operatively, rather than proceed to litigation. He specifically recommended a pre-action protocol for medical negligence cases.

1.8 A fuller summary of Lord Woolf's recommendations is at Annex D.

WHERE THE PROTOCOL FITS IN

1.9 Protocols serve the needs of litigation and pre-litigation practice, especially—
- predictability in the time needed for steps pre-proceedings;
- standardisation of relevant information, including records and documents to be disclosed.

1.10 Building upon Lord Woolf's recommendations, the Lord Chancellor's Department is now promoting the adoption of protocols in specific areas, including medical negligence.

1.11 It is recognised that contexts differ significantly. For example: patients tend to have an ongoing relationship with a GP, more so than with a hospital; clinical staff in the National Health Service are often employees, while those in the private sector may be contractors; providing records quickly may be relatively easy for GPs and dentists, but can be a complicated procedure in a large multi-department hospital. The protocol which follows is intended to be sufficiently broadly based, and flexible, to apply to all aspects of the health service: primary and secondary; public and private sectors.

ENFORCEMENT OF THE PROTOCOL AND SANCTIONS

1.12 The civil justice reforms will be implemented in April 1999. One new set of Court Rules and procedures is replacing the existing rules for both the High Court and county courts. This and the personal injury protocol are being published with the Rules, practice directions and key court forms. The courts will be able to treat the standards set in protocols as the normal reasonable approach to pre-action conduct.

1.13 If proceedings are issued it will be for the court to decide whether non-compliance with a protocol should merit sanctions. Guidance on the court's likely approach will be given from time to time in practice directions.

1.14 If the court has to consider the question of compliance after proceedings have begun it will not be concerned with minor infringements, e.g. failure by a short period to provide relevant information. One minor breach will not entitle the 'innocent' party to abandon following the protocol. The court will look at the effect of non-compliance on the other party when deciding whether to impose sanctions.

2 THE AIMS OF THE PROTOCOL

2.1 The *general* aims of the protocol are—
- to maintain/restore the patient/healthcare provider relationship;
- to resolve as many disputes as possible without litigation.

2.2 The *specific* objectives are—

OPENNESS
- to encourage early communication of the perceived problem between patients and healthcare providers;
- to encourage patients to voice any concerns or dissatisfaction with their treatment as soon as practicable;
- to encourage healthcare providers to develop systems of early reporting and investigation for serious adverse treatment outcomes and to provide full and prompt explanations to dissatisfied patients;
- to ensure that sufficient information is disclosed by both parties to enable each to understand the other's perspective and case, and to encourage early resolution.

TIMELINESS
- to provide an early opportunity for healthcare providers to identify cases where an investigation is required and to carry out that investigation promptly;
- to encourage primary and private healthcare providers to involve their defence organisations or insurers at an early stage;
- to ensure that all relevant medical records are provided to patients or their appointed representatives on request, to a realistic timetable by any healthcare provider;
- to ensure that relevant records which are not in healthcare providers' possession are made available to them by patients and their advisers at an appropriate stage;
- where a resolution is not achievable to lay the ground to enable litigation to proceed on a reasonable timetable, at a reasonable and proportionate cost and to limit the matters in contention;
- to discourage the prolonged pursuit of unmeritorious claims and the prolonged defence of meritorious claims.

AWARENESS OF OPTIONS
- to ensure that patients and healthcare providers are made aware of the available options to pursue and resolve disputes and what each might involve.

2.3 This protocol does not attempt to be prescriptive about a number of related clinical governance issues which will have a bearing on healthcare providers' ability to meet the standards within the protocol. Good clinical governance requires the following to be considered—

(a) **Clinical risk management:** the protocol does not provide any detailed guidance to healthcare providers on clinical risk management or the adoption of risk management systems and procedures. This must be a matter for the NHS Executive, the National Health Service Litigation Authority, individual trusts and providers, including GPs, dentists and the private sector. However, effective co-ordinated, focused clinical risk management strategies and procedures can help in managing risk and in the early identification and investigation of adverse outcomes.

(b) **Adverse outcome reporting:** the protocol does not provide any detailed guidance on which adverse outcomes should trigger an investigation. However, healthcare providers should have in place procedures for such investigations, including recording of statements of key witnesses. These procedures should also cover when and how to inform patients that an adverse outcome has occurred.

(c) **The professional's duty to report:** the protocol does not recommend changes to the codes of conduct of professionals in healthcare, or attempt to impose a specific duty on those professionals to report known adverse outcomes or untoward incidents. Lord Woolf in his final report suggested that the professional bodies might consider this. The General Medical Council is preparing guidance to doctors about their duty to report adverse incidents and to co-operate with inquiries.

3 THE PROTOCOL

3.1 This protocol is not a comprehensive code governing all the steps in clinical disputes. Rather it attempts to set out **a code of good practice** which parties should follow when litigation might be a possibility.

3.2 The **commitments** section of the protocol summarises the guiding principles which healthcare providers and patients and their advisers are invited to endorse when dealing with patient dissatisfaction with treatment and its outcome, and with potential complaints and claims.

3.3 The **steps** section sets out in a more prescriptive form, a recommended sequence of actions to be followed if litigation is a prospect.

GOOD PRACTICE COMMITMENTS

3.4 **Healthcare providers** should—

(i) ensure that **key staff**, including claims and litigation managers, are appropriately trained and have some knowledge of healthcare law, and of complaints procedures and civil litigation practice and procedure;

(ii) develop an approach to **clinical governance** that ensures that clinical practice is delivered to commonly accepted standards and that this is routinely monitored through a system of clinical audit and clinical risk management (particularly adverse outcome investigation);

(iii) set up **adverse outcome reporting systems** in all specialties to record and investigate unexpected serious adverse outcomes as soon as possible. Such systems can enable evidence to be gathered quickly, which makes it easier to provide an accurate explanation of what happened and to defend or settle any subsequent claims;

(iv) use the results of **adverse incidents and complaints positively** as a guide to how to improve services to patients in the future;

(v) ensure **that patients receive clear and comprehensible information** in an accessible form about how to raise their concerns or complaints;

(vi) establish **efficient and effective systems of recording and storing patient records**, notes, diagnostic reports and X-rays, and to retain these in accordance with Department of Health guidance (currently for a minimum of eight years in the case of adults, and all obstetric and paediatric notes for children until they reach the age of 25);

(vii) **advise patients** of a serious adverse outcome and provide on request to the patient or the patient's representative an oral or written explanation of what happened, information on further steps open to the patient, including where appropriate an offer of future treatment to rectify the problem, an apology, changes in procedure which will benefit patients and/or compensation.

3.5 **Patients and their advisers** should—

(i) **report any concerns and dissatisfaction** to the healthcare provider as soon as is reasonable to enable that provider to offer clinical advice where possible, to advise the patient if anything has gone wrong and take appropriate action;

(ii) consider the **full range of options** available following an adverse outcome with which a patient is dissatisfied, including a request for an explanation, a meeting, a complaint, and other appropriate dispute resolution methods (including mediation) and negotiation, not only litigation;

(iii) **inform the healthcare provider when the patient is satisfied** that the matter has been concluded: legal advisers should notify the provider when they are no longer acting for the patient, particularly if proceedings have not started.

PROTOCOL STEPS

3.6 The steps of this protocol which follow have been kept deliberately simple. An illustration of the likely sequence of events in a number of healthcare situations is at Annex A.

OBTAINING THE HEALTH RECORDS

3.7 Any request for records by the **patient** or their adviser should—

- **provide sufficient information** to alert the healthcare provider where an adverse outcome has been serious or had serious consequences;
- be as **specific as possible** about the records which are required.

3.8 Requests for copies of the patient's clinical records should be made using the Law Society and Department of Health approved **standard forms** (enclosed at Annex B), adapted as necessary.

3.9 The copy records should be provided **within 40 days** of the request and for a cost not exceeding the charges permissible under the Access to Health Records Act 1990 (currently a maximum of £10 plus photocopying and postage).

3.10 In the rare circumstances that the healthcare provider is in difficulty in complying with the request within 40 days, the **problem should be explained** quickly and details given of what is being done to resolve it.

3.11 It will not be practicable for healthcare providers to investigate in detail each case when records are requested. But healthcare providers should **adopt a policy on which cases will be investigated** (see paragraph 3.5 on clinical governance and adverse outcome reporting).

3.12 If the healthcare provider fails to provide the health records within 40 days, the patient or their adviser can then apply to the court for an **order for pre-action disclosure**. The new Civil Procedure Rules should make pre-action applications to the court easier. The court will also have the power to impose costs sanctions for unreasonable delay in providing records.

3.13 If either the patient or the healthcare provider considers **additional health records are required from a third party**, in the first instance these should be requested by or through the patient. Third party healthcare providers are expected to co-operate. The Civil Procedure Rules will enable patients and healthcare providers to apply to the court for pre-action disclosure by third parties.

LETTER OF CLAIM

3.14 Annex C1 to this protocol provides **a template for the recommended contents of a letter of claim:** the level of detail will need to be varied to suit the particular circumstances.

3.15 If, following the receipt and analysis of the records, and the receipt of any further advice (including from experts if necessary — see Section 4), the patient/

adviser decides that there are grounds for a claim, they should then send, as soon as practicable, to the healthcare provider/potential defendant, a **letter of claim**.

3.16 This letter should contain a **clear summary of the facts** on which the claim is based, including the alleged adverse outcome, and the **main allegations of negligence**. It should also describe the **patient's injuries**, and present condition and prognosis. The **financial loss** incurred by the plaintiff should be outlined with an indication of the heads of damage to be claimed and the scale of the loss, unless this is impracticable.

3.17 In more complex cases a **chronology** of the relevant events should be provided, particularly if the patient has been treated by a number of different healthcare providers.

3.18 The letter of claim **should refer to any relevant documents**, including health records, and if possible enclose copies of any of those which will not already be in the potential defendant's possession, e.g. any relevant general practitioner records if the plaintiff's claim is against a hospital.

3.19 **Sufficient information** must be given to enable the healthcare provider defendant to **commence investigations** and to put an initial valuation on the claim.

3.20 Letters of claim are **not** intended to have the same formal status as a **pleading**, nor should any sanctions necessarily apply if the letter of claim and any subsequent statement of claim in the proceedings differ.

3.21 **Proceedings should not be issued until after three months from the letter of claim**, unless there is a limitation problem and/or the patient's position needs to be protected by early issue.

3.22 The patient or their adviser may want to make an **offer to settle** the claim at this early stage by putting forward an amount of compensation which would be satisfactory (possibly including any costs incurred to date). If an offer to settle is made, generally this should be supported by a medical report which deals with the injuries, condition and prognosis, and by a schedule of loss and supporting documentation. The level of detail necessary will depend on the value of the claim. Medical reports may not be necessary where there is no significant continuing injury, and a detailed schedule may not be necessary in a low value case. The Civil Procedure Rules are expected to set out the legal and procedural requirements for making offers to settle.

THE RESPONSE

3.23 Attached at Annex C2 is a template for the suggested contents of the **letter of response**.

3.24 The healthcare provider should **acknowledge** the letter of claim **within 14 days of receipt** and should identify who will be dealing with the matter.

3.25 The healthcare provider should, **within three months** of the letter of claim, provide a **reasoned answer**—
- if the **claim is admitted** the healthcare provider should say so in clear terms;
- if only **part of the claim is admitted** the healthcare provider should make clear which issues of breach of duty and/or causation are admitted and which are denied and why;
- if it is intended that any **admissions will be binding**;
- if the claim is denied, this should include specific comments on the allegations of negligence, and if a synopsis or chronology of relevant events has been provided and is disputed, the healthcare provider's version of those events;
- where additional documents are relied upon, e.g. an internal protocol, copies should be provided.

3.26 If the patient has made an offer to settle, the healthcare provider should **respond to that offer** in the response letter, preferably with reasons. The provider may make its own offer to settle at this stage, either as a counter-offer to the patient's, or of its own accord, but should accompany any offer by any supporting medical evidence, and/or by any other evidence in relation to the value of the claim which is in the healthcare provider's possession.

3.27 If the parties reach agreement on liability, but time is needed to resolve the value of the claim, they should aim to agree a reasonable period.

4 EXPERTS

4.1 In clinical negligence disputes **expert opinions** may be needed—
- on breach of duty and causation;
- on the patient's condition and prognosis;
- to assist in valuing aspects of the claim.

4.2 The civil justice reforms and the new **Civil Procedure Rules** will encourage economy in the use of experts and a **less adversarial expert culture**. It is recognised that in clinical negligence disputes, the parties and their advisers will require flexibility in their approach to expert evidence. Decisions on whether experts might be instructed jointly, and on whether reports might be disclosed sequentially or by exchange, should rest with the parties and their advisers. Sharing expert evidence may be appropriate on issues relating to the value of the claim. However, this protocol does not attempt to be prescriptive on issues in relation to expert evidence.

4.3 Obtaining expert evidence will often be an expensive step and may take time, especially in specialised areas of medicine where there are limited numbers of suitable experts. Patients and healthcare providers, and their advisers, will therefore need to consider carefully how best to obtain any necessary expert help quickly and cost-effectively. Assistance with locating a suitable expert is available from a number of sources.

5 ALTERNATIVE APPROACHES TO SETTLING DISPUTES

5.1 It would not be practicable for this protocol to address in any detail how a patient or their adviser, or healthcare provider, might decide which method to adopt to resolve the particular problem. But the courts increasingly expect parties to try to settle their differences by agreement before issuing proceedings.

5.2 Most disputes are resolved by **discussion and negotiation**. Parties should bear in mind that carefully planned face-to-face meetings may be particularly helpful in exploring further treatment for the patient, in reaching understandings about what happened, and on both parties' positions, in narrowing the issues in dispute and, if the timing is right, in helping to settle the whole matter.

5.3 Summarised below are some other alternatives for resolving disputes—
- The revised **NHS Complaints Procedure**, which was implemented in April 1996, is designed to provide patients with an explanation of what happened and an apology if appropriate. It is not designed to provide compensation for cases of negligence. However, patients might choose to use the procedure if their only, or main, goal is to obtain an explanation, or to obtain more information to help them decide what other action might be appropriate.
- **Mediation** may be appropriate in some cases: this is a form of facilitated negotiation assisted by an independent neutral party. It is expected that the new Civil Procedure Rules will give the court the power to stay proceedings for one month for settlement discussions or mediation.
- Other methods of resolving disputes include **arbitration, determination by an expert, and early neutral evaluation** by a medical or legal expert. The Lord Chancellor's Department has produced a booklet on **'Resolving Disputes Without Going to Court'**, LCD 1995, which lists a number of organisations that provide alternative dispute resolution services.

PRE-ACTION PROTOCOL FOR THE RESOLUTION OF CLINICAL DISPUTES

ANNEX A   ILLUSTRATIVE FLOWCHART

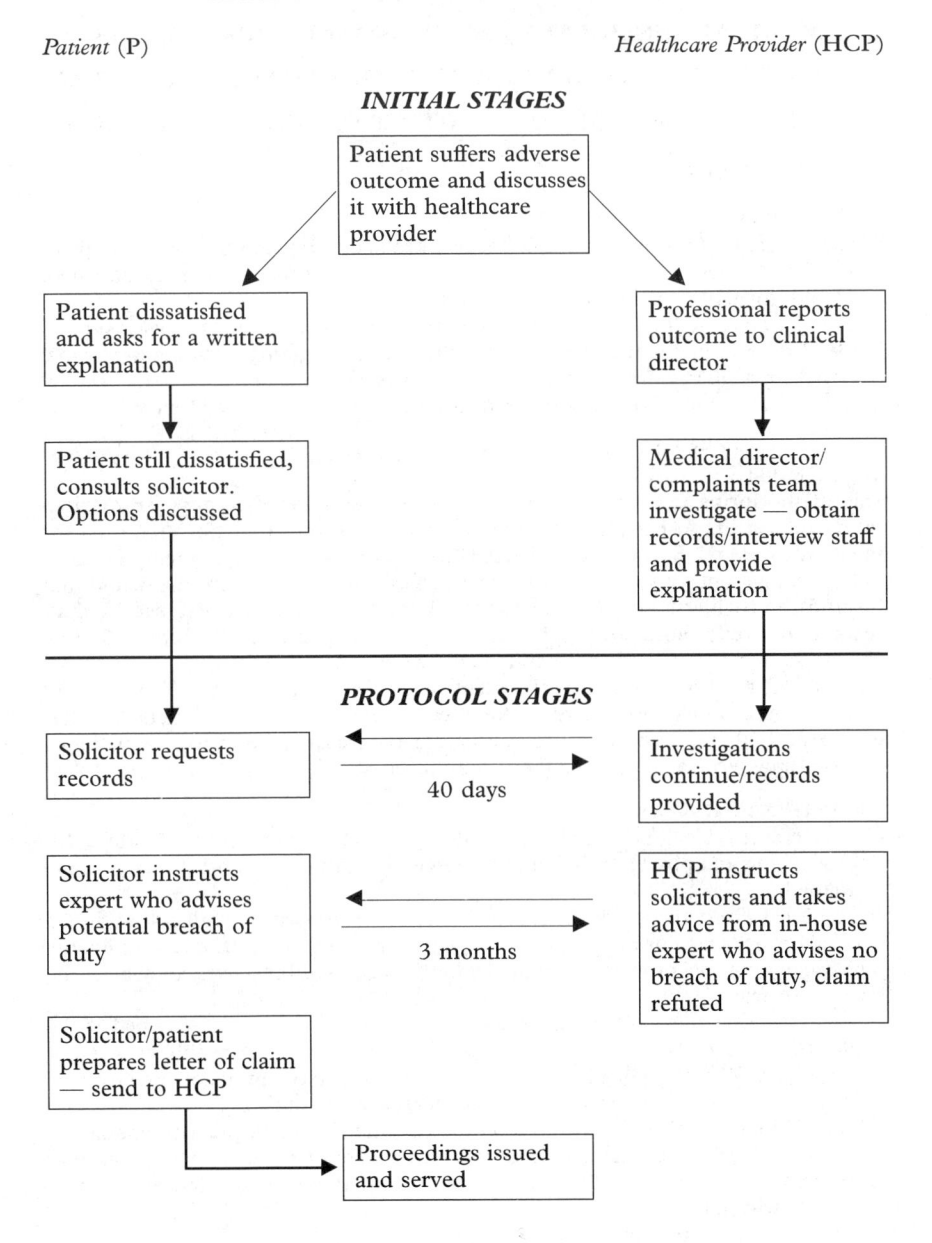

Patient (P)   *Healthcare Provider* (HCP)

INITIAL STAGES

Patient suffers adverse outcome and discusses it with healthcare provider

- Patient dissatisfied and asks for a written explanation
- Patient still dissatisfied, consults solicitor. Options discussed

- Professional reports outcome to clinical director
- Medical director/complaints team investigate — obtain records/interview staff and provide explanation

PROTOCOL STAGES

Patient side		Healthcare Provider side
Solicitor requests records	← 40 days →	Investigations continue/records provided
Solicitor instructs expert who advises potential breach of duty	← 3 months →	HCP instructs solicitors and takes advice from in-house expert who advises no breach of duty, claim refuted
Solicitor/patient prepares letter of claim — send to HCP		

Proceedings issued and served

PRE-ACTION PROTOCOL FOR THE RESOLUTION OF CLINICAL DISPUTES

ANNEX B

MEDICAL NEGLIGENCE AND PERSONAL INJURY CLAIMS

A PROTOCOL FOR OBTAINING HOSPITAL MEDICAL RECORDS

APPLICATION ON BEHALF OF A PATIENT FOR HOSPITAL MEDICAL RECORDS FOR USE WHEN COURT PROCEEDINGS ARE CONTEMPLATED

PURPOSE OF THE FORMS

This application form and response forms have been prepared by a working party of the Law Society's Civil Litigation Committee and approved by the Department of Health for use in NHS and Trust hospitals.

The purpose of the forms is to standardise and streamline the disclosure of medical records to a patient's solicitors, who are investigating pursuing a personal injury claim against a third party, or a medical negligence claim against the hospital to which the application is addressed and/or other hospitals or general practitioners.

USE OF THE FORMS

Use of the forms is entirely voluntary and does not prejudice any party's right under the Access to Health Records Act 1990, the Data Protection Act 1984, or ss 33 and 34 of the Supreme Court Act 1981. However, it is Department of Health policy that patients be permitted to see what has been written about them, and that healthcare providers should make arrangements to allow patients to see all their records, not only those covered by the Access to Health Records Act 1990. The aim of the forms is to save time and costs for all concerned for the benefit of the patient and the hospital and in the interests of justice. Use of the forms should make it unnecessary in most cases for there to be exchanges of letters or other enquiries. If there is any unusual matter not covered by the form, the patient's solicitor may write a separate letter at the outset.

CHARGES FOR RECORDS

The Access to Health Records Act 1990 prescribes a maximum fee of £10. Photocopying and postage costs can be charged in addition. No other charges may be made.

The NHS Executive guidance makes it clear to healthcare providers that 'it is a perfectly proper use' of the 1990 Act to request records in that framework for the purpose of potential or actual litigation, whether against a third party or against the hospital or trust.

The 1990 Act does not permit differential rates of charges to be levied if the application is made by the patient, or by a solicitor on his or her behalf, or whether the response to the application is made by the healthcare provider directly (the medical records manager or a claims manager) or by a solicitor.

The NHS Executive guidance recommends that the same practice should be followed with regard to charges when the records are provided under a voluntary agreement as under the 1990 Act, except that in those circumstances the £10 access fee will not be appropriate.

The NHS Executive also advises—

- that the cost of photocopying may include 'the cost of staff time in making copies' and the costs of running the copier (but not costs of locating and sifting records);
- that the common practice of setting a standard rate for an application or charging an administration fee is not acceptable because there will be cases when this fails to comply with the 1990 Act.

RECORDS: WHAT MIGHT BE INCLUDED

X-rays and test results form part of the patient's records. Additional charges for copying X-rays are permissible. If there are large numbers of X-rays, the records officer should check with the patient/solicitor before arranging copying.

Reports on an 'adverse incident' and reports on the patient made for risk management and audit purposes may form part of the records and be disclosable: the exception will be any specific record or report made solely or mainly in connection with an actual or potential claim.

RECORDS: QUALITY STANDARDS

When copying records healthcare providers should ensure—
1. All documents are legible, and complete, if necessary by photocopying at less than 100% size.
2. Documents larger than A4 in the original, e.g. ITU charts, should be reproduced in A3, or reduced to A4 where this retains readability.
3. Documents are only copied on one side of paper, unless the original is two sided.
4. Documents should not be unnecessarily shuffled or bound and holes should not be made in the copied papers.

ENQUIRIES/FURTHER INFORMATION

Any enquiries about the forms should be made initially to the solicitors making the request. Comments on the use and content of the forms should be made to the Secretary, Civil Litigation Committee, The Law Society, 113 Chancery Lane, London WC2A 1PL, telephone 0171 320 5739, or to the NHS Management Executive, Quarry House, Quarry Hill, Leeds LS2 7UE.

The Law Society

May 1998

PRE-ACTION PROTOCOL FOR THE RESOLUTION OF CLINICAL DISPUTES

APPLICATION ON BEHALF OF A PATIENT FOR HOSPITAL MEDICAL RECORDS FOR USE WHEN COURT PROCEEDINGS ARE CONTEMPLATED

This should be completed as fully as possible

Insert Hospital Name and Address

TO: Medical Records Officer
Hospital

1(a)	Full name of patient (including previous surnames)	
(b)	Address now	
(c)	Address at start of treatment	
(d)	Date of birth (and death, if applicable)	
(e)	Hospital ref. no if available	
(f)	N.I. number, if available	
2	This application is made because the patient is considering	
	(a) a claim against your hospital as detailed in para 7 overleaf	YES/NO
	(b) pursuing an action against someone else	YES/NO
3	Department(s) where treatment was received	
4	Name(s) of consultant(s) at your hospital in charge of the treatment	
5	Whether treatment at your hospital was private or NHS, wholly or in part	
6	A description of the treatment received, with approximate dates	
7	If the answer to Q2(a) is 'Yes' details of	
	(a) the likely nature of the claim	
	(b) grounds for the claim	
	(c) approximate dates of the events involved	
8	If the answer to Q2(b) is 'Yes' insert	
	(a) the names of the proposed defendants	

	(b) whether legal proceedings yet begun	YES/NO
	(c) if appropriate, details of the claim and action number	
9	We confirm we will pay reasonable copying charges	
10	We request prior details of	
	(a) photocopying and administration charges for medical records	YES/NO
	(b) number of and cost of copying X-ray and scan films	YES/NO
11	Any other relevant information, particular requirements, or any particular documents *not* required (e.g. copies of computerised records)	
	Signature of Solicitor	
	Name	
	Address	
	Ref.	
	Telephone Number	
	Fax number	

Please print name beneath each signature.
Signature by child over 12 but under
18 years also requires signature by parent

Signature of patient

Signature of parent or next friend
if appropriate

Signature of personal representative
where patient has died

PRE-ACTION PROTOCOL FOR THE RESOLUTION OF CLINICAL DISPUTES

FIRST RESPONSE TO APPLICATION FOR HOSPITAL RECORDS

	NAME OF PATIENT Our ref Your ref	
1	Date of receipt of patient's application	
2	We intend that copy medical records will be dispatched within 6 weeks of that date	YES/NO
3	We require pre-payment of photocopying charges	YES/NO
4	If estimate of photocopying charges requested or pre-payment required the amount will be	£ / notified to you
5	The cost of X-ray and scan films will be	£ / notified to you
6	If there is any problem, we shall write to you within those 6 weeks	YES/NO
7	Any other information	
	Please address further correspondence to	
	Signed	
	Direct telephone number	
	Direct fax number	
	Dated	

PRE-ACTION PROTOCOL FOR THE RESOLUTION OF CLINICAL DISPUTES

SECOND RESPONSE ENCLOSING PATIENT'S HOSPITAL MEDICAL RECORDS

Address Our Ref.
  Your Ref.

1	NAME OF PATIENT: We confirm that the enclosed copy medical records are all those within the control of the hospital, relevant to the application which you have made to the best of our knowledge and belief, subject to paras 2–5 below	YES/NO
2	Details of any other documents which have not yet been located	
3	Date by when it is expected that these will be supplied	
4	Details of any records which we are not producing	
5	The reasons for not doing so	
6	An invoice for copying and administration charges is attached	YES/NO
	Signed	
	Date	

ANNEX C   TEMPLATES FOR LETTERS OF CLAIM AND RESPONSE

C1 LETTER OF CLAIM

Essential Contents

1. **Client's name, address, date of birth, etc.**
2. **Dates of allegedly negligent treatment**
3. **Events giving rise to the claim:**

- an outline of what happened, including details of other relevant treatments to the client by other healthcare providers.

4. **Allegation of negligence and causal link with injuries:**

- an outline of the allegations or a more detailed list in a complex case;
- an outline of the causal link between allegations and the injuries complained of.

PRE-ACTION PROTOCOL FOR THE RESOLUTION OF CLINICAL DISPUTES

5. **The Client's injuries, condition and future prognosis**
6. **Request for clinical records (if not previously provided)**

- use the Law Society form if appropriate or adapt;
- specify the records require;
- if other records are held by other providers, and may be relevant, say so;
- state what investigations have been carried out to date, e.g. information from client and witnesses, any complaint and the outcome, if any clinical records have been seen or experts advice obtained.

7. **The likely value of the claim**

- an outline of the main heads of damage, or, in straightforward cases, the details of loss.

Optional information

What investigations have been carried out

An offer to settle without supporting evidence

Suggestions for obtaining expert evidence

Suggestions for meetings, negotiations, discussion or mediation

Possible enclosures

Chronology

Clinical records request form and client's authorisation

Expert report(s)

Schedules of loss and supporting evidence

C2 LETTER OF RESPONSE

Essential Contents

1. Provide **requested records** and invoice for copying:

- explain if records are incomplete or extensive records are held and ask for further instructions;
- request additional records from third parties.

2. **Comments on events and/or chronology:**

- if events are disputed or the healthcare provider has further information or documents on which they wish to rely, these should be provided, e.g. internal protocol;
- details of any further information needed from the patient or a third party should be provided.

3. **If breach of duty and causation are accepted:**

- suggestions might be made for resolving the claim and/or requests for further information;
- a response should be made to any offer to settle.

4. **If breach of duty and/or causation are denied:**

- a bare denial will not be sufficient. If the healthcare provider has other explanations for what happened, these should be given at least in outline;
- suggestions might be made for the next steps, e.g. further investigations, obtaining expert evidence, meetings/ negotiations or mediation, or an invitation to issue proceedings.

Optional Matters

An offer to settle if the patient has not made one, or a counter offer to the patient's with supporting evidence

Possible enclosures:

Clinical records

Annotated chronology

Expert reports

ANNEX D LORD WOOLF'S RECOMMENDATIONS

1. Lord Woolf in his Access to Justice Report in July 1996, following a detailed review of the problems of medical negligence claims, identified that one of the major sources of **costs and delay** is **at the pre-litigation** stage because—
    (a) Inadequate incident reporting and record keeping in hospitals, and mobility of staff, make it difficult to establish facts, often several years after the event.
    (b) Claimants must incur the cost of an expert in order to establish whether they have a viable claim.
    (c) There is often a long delay before a claim is made.
    (d) Defendants do not have sufficient resources to carry out a full investigation of every incident, and do not consider it worthwhile to start an investigation as soon as they receive a request for records, because many cases do not proceed beyond that stage.
    (e) Patients often give the defendant little or no notice of a firm intention to pursue a claim. Consequently, many incidents are not investigated by the defendants until after proceedings have started.
    (f) Doctors and other clinical staff are traditionally reluctant to admit negligence or apologise to, or negotiate with, claimants for fear of damage to their professional reputations or career prospects.
2. Lord Woolf acknowledged that under the present arrangements **healthcare providers**, faced with possible medical negligence claims, have a number of **practical problems** to contend with—
    (a) Difficulties of finding patients' records and tracing former staff, which can be exacerbated by late notification and by the health care provider's own failure to identify adverse incidents.
    (b) The healthcare provider may have only treated the patient for a limited time or for a specific complaint: the patient's previous history may be relevant but the records may be in the possession of one of several other healthcare providers.
    (c) The large number of potential claims which do not proceed beyond the stage of a request for medical records, or an explanation; and that it is difficult for healthcare providers to investigate fully every case whenever a patient asks to see the records.

ANNEX E HOW TO CONTACT THE FORUM

The Clinical Disputes Forum

Chairman

Dr Alastair Scotland
Director of Medical Education
Chelsea and Westminster Hospital
369 Fulham Road
London
SW1 9NH   Telephone: 0181 746 8000

Secretary

Sarah Leigh
c/o Margaret Dangoor
3 Clydesdale Gardens
Richmond
Surrey
TW10 5EG   Telephone: 0181 408 1012

APPENDIX 3
FORMS

The Court Service is responsible for the forms to be used with the Civil Procedure Rules. This appendix reproduces the forms as they were established on 1 August 1999.

In this version of the forms the statement of the opening hours of 'the court office' gives county court office hours. The office hours of the Royal Courts of Justice are different (see PD 2).

For this appendix the forms have been reduced to approximately 70 per cent of their actual size.

CONTENTS

N1 Claim Form (CPR Part 7)	1225
N1A Notes for claimant	1227
N1C Notes for defendant	1229
N1 (FD) Notes for defendant (Consumer Credit Act claim)	1231
N9 Response pack	1232
N9A Admission (specified amount)	1233
N9B Defence and counterclaim (specified amount)	1235
N9C Admission (unspecified amount, non-money and return of goods claims)	1237
N9D Defence and counterclaim (unspecified amount, non-money and return of goods claims)	1239
N10 Notice that acknowledgment of service has been filed	1241
N20 Witness summons	1242
N21 Order for examination of deponent (before the hearing)	1244
N150 Allocation questionnaire	1246
N152 Notice that a defence/counterclaim has been filed	1251
N153 Notice of allocation or listing hearing	1252
N154 Notice of allocation to the fast track	1253
N155 Notice of allocation to the multi-track	1254
N156 Request for further information (allocation)	1255
N157 Notice of allocation to the small claims track	1256
N158 Notice of allocation to the small claims track (preliminary hearing)	1257
N159 Notice of allocation to the small claims track (no hearing)	1258
N160 Notice of allocation to the small claims track (with parties' consent)	1259
N170 Listing questionnaire	1260
N173 Notice to pay fee	1264
N205A Notice of issue (specified amount)	1265
N205B Notice of issue (unspecified amount)	1267
N205C Notice of issue (non-money claim)	1268
N208 Claim form (CPR Part 8)	1269
N208A Notes for claimant (CPR Part 8)	1271
N208C Notes for defendant (CPR Part 8)	1273
N209 Notice of issue (Part 8 claim)	1274
N210 Acknowledgment of service (Part 8 claim)	1275
N211 Claim form (additional claims — CPR Part 20)	1277
N211A Notes for claimant (Part 20 claim form)	1279
N211C Notes for defendant (Part 20 claim form)	1281
N212 Notice of issue (Part 20 claim)	1282
N213 Acknowledgment of service (Part 20 claim)	1283

APPENDIX 3 FORMS

N215 Certificate of service	1284
N218 Notice of service on partner	1286
N225 Request for judgment and reply to admission (specified amount)	1287
N225A Notice of part admission (specified amount)	1288
N226 Notice of admission (unspecified amount)	1289
N227 Request for judgment by default (amount to be decided by the court)	1290
N228 Notice of admission — return of goods (hire-purchase or conditional sale)	1291
N235 Certificate of suitability of litigation friend	1292
N236 Notice of defence that amount claimed has been paid	1294
N242A Notice of payment into court (in settlement)	1295
N243 Notice of acceptance and request for payment	1297
N244 Application notice	1298
N252 Notice of commencement of assessment of bill of costs	1300
N253 Notice of amount allowed on provisional assessment (legal aid only)	1301
N254 Request for a default costs certificate	1302
N255CC Default costs certificate (county court)	1303
N255HC Default costs certificate (High Court)	1304
N256CC Final costs certificate (county court)	1305
N256HC Final costs certificate (High Court)	1306
N257 Interim costs certificate	1307
N258 Request for detailed assessment hearing	1308
N265 List of documents: standard disclosure	1309
N266 Notice to admit facts	1311
N268 Notice to prove documents at trial	1312
N279 Notice of discontinuance	1313
N292 Order on settlement on behalf of child or patient	1314
N294 Claimant's application for a variation order	1315
N434 Notice of change of solicitor	1316
Schedule of costs forms: form 1 Statement of costs (summary assessment)	1317
Schedule of costs forms: form 2 Bill of costs (detailed assessment)	1318
Schedule of costs forms: form 3 Legal aid schedule of costs	1327
Schedule of costs forms: form 4 Certificates for inclusion in bills	1333
Schedule of costs forms: form 6 Points of dispute	1335
Schedule of costs forms: form 15 Legal aid assessment certificate	1337
Schedule of costs forms: form 16 Notice of appeal	1338
Schedule of costs forms: form 17 Solicitors Act: order for delivery of bill	1339
Schedule of costs forms: form 18 Order on client's application for detailed assessment of solicitor's bill	1340
Schedule of costs forms: form 19 Order on solicitor's application for assessment under the Solicitors Act 1974 Part III	1341
Schedule of costs forms: form 20 Solicitors Act: breakdown of costs	1342
Schedule of costs forms: form 21 Request for detailed assessment hearing pursuant to an order under Part III of the Solicitors Act 1974	1343

APPENDIX 3   FORMS

| **Claim Form** | In the |
| | Claim No. |

Claimant

SEAL

Defendant(s)

Brief details of claim

Value

Defendant's name and address

£

Amount claimed	
Court fee	
Solicitor's costs	
Total amount	
Issue date	

The court office at
is open between 10 am and 4 pm Monday to Friday. When corresponding with the court, please address forms or letters to the Court Manager and quote the claim number.

N1 Claim form (CPR Part 7) (4.99)   *Printed on behalf of The Court Service*

APPENDIX 3   FORMS

| | Claim No. | |

Particulars of Claim (attached)(to follow)

Statement of Truth
*(I believe)(The Claimant believes) that the facts stated in these particulars of claim are true.
* I am duly authorised by the claimant to sign this statement

Full name _____

Name of claimant's solicitor's firm _____

signed _____ position or office held _____
*(Claimant)(Litigation friend)(Claimant's solicitor) (if signing on behalf of firm or company)
*delete as appropriate

Claimant's or claimant's solicitor's address to which documents or payments should be sent if different from overleaf including (if appropriate) details of DX, fax or e-mail.

APPENDIX 3   FORMS

Notes for claimant on completing a claim form
Further information may be obtained from the court in a series of free leaflets.

- Please read all of these guidance notes before you begin completing the claim form. The notes follow the order in which information is required on the form.
- Court staff can help you fill in the claim form and give information about procedure once it has been issued. But they cannot give legal advice. If you need legal advice, for example, about the likely success of your claim or the evidence you need to prove it, you should contact a solicitor or a Citizens Advice Bureau.
- If you are filling in the claim form by hand, please use black ink and write in block capitals.
- Copy the completed claim form and the defendant's notes for guidance so that you have one copy for yourself, one copy for the court and one copy for each defendant. Send or take the forms to the court office with the appropriate fee. The court will tell you how much this is.

Notes on completing the claim form

Heading

You must fill in the heading of the form to indicate whether you want the claim to be issued in a county court or in the High Court (The High Court means either a District Registry (attached to a county court) or the Royal Courts of Justice in London). There are restrictions on claims which may be issued in the High Court (see 'Value' overleaf).

Use whichever of the following is appropriate:

'In the ....County Court'
(inserting the name of the court)

or

'In the High Court of Justice........................Division'
(inserting e.g. 'Queen's Bench' or 'Chancery' as appropriate)
'..............................District Registry'
(inserting the name of the District Registry)

or

'In the High Court of Justice........................Division,
(inserting eg. 'Queen's Bench' or 'Chancery' as appropriate)
Royal Courts of Justice'

Claimant and defendant details

As the person issuing the claim, you are called the 'claimant'; the person you are suing is called the 'defendant'. Claimants who are under 18 years old (unless otherwise permitted by the court) and patients within the meaning of the Mental Health Act 1983, must have a litigation friend to issue and conduct court proceedings on their behalf. Court staff will tell you more about what you need to do if this applies to you.

You must provide the following information about yourself **and** the defendant according to the capacity in which you are suing and in which the defendant is being sued. When suing or being sued as:-

an individual:

All known forenames and surname, whether Mr, Mrs, Miss, Ms or Other (e.g. Dr) and residential address (**including** postcode and telephone number) in England and Wales. Where the defendant is a proprietor of a business, a partner in a firm or an individual sued in the name of a club or other unincorporated association, the address for service should be the usual or last known place of residence **or** principal place of business of the company, firm or club or other unincorporated association.

Where the individual is:

under 18 write '(a child by Mr Joe Bloggs his litigation friend)' after the child's name. If the child is conducting proceedings on their own behalf write '(a child)' after the child's name.

a patient within the meaning of the Mental Health Act 1983 write '(by Mr Joe Bloggs his litigation friend)' after the patient's name.

trading under another name

you must add the words 'trading as' and the trading name e.g. 'Mr John Smith trading as Smith's Groceries'

suing or being sued in a representative capacity

you must say what that capacity is e.g. 'Mr Joe Bloggs as the representative of Mrs Sharon Bloggs (deceased)'.

suing or being sued in the name of a club or other unincorporated association

add the words 'suing/sued on behalf of' followed by the name of the club or other unincorporated association.

a firm

enter the name of the firm followed by the words 'a firm', e.g. 'Bandbox - a firm' and an address for service which is either a partner's residential address or the principal or last known place of business.

a corporation (other than a company)

enter the full name of the corporation and the address which is either its principal office **or** any other place where the corporation carries on activities and which has a real connection with the claim.

a company registered in England and Wales

enter the name of the company and an address which is either the company's registered office **or** any place of business that has a real, or the most, connection with the claim e.g. the shop where the goods were bought.

an overseas company (defined by s744 of the Companies Act 1985)

enter the name of the company and either the address registered under s691 of the Act **or** the address of the place of business having a real, or the most, connection with the claim.

N1A Notes for claimant (4.99)   *Printed on behalf The Court Service*

Brief details of claim

Note: The facts and full details about your claim and whether or not you are claiming interest, should be set out in the 'particulars of claim' *(see note under 'Particulars of Claim')*.

You must set out under **this** heading:
- a concise statement of the nature of your claim
- the remedy you are seeking e.g. payment of money; an order for return of goods or their value; an order to prevent a person doing an act; damages for personal injuries.

Value

If you are claiming a **fixed amount of money** (a 'specified amount') write the amount in the box at the bottom right-hand corner of the claim form against 'amount claimed'.

If you are <u>not</u> claiming a fixed amount of money (an 'unspecified amount') under 'Value' write "I expect to recover" followed by whichever of the following applies to your claim:
- "not more than £5,000" **or**
- "more than £5,000 but not more than £15,000" **or**
- "more than £15,000"

If you are **not able** to put a value on your claim, write "I cannot say how much I expect to recover".

Personal injuries

If your claim is for 'not more than £5,000' and includes a claim for personal injuries, you must also write "My claim includes a claim for personal injuries and the amount I expect to recover as damages for pain, suffering and loss of amenity is" followed by either:
- "not more than £1,000" **or**
- "more than £1,000"

Housing disrepair

If your claim is for 'not more than £5,000' and includes a claim for housing disrepair relating to residential premises, you must also write "My claim includes a claim against my landlord for housing disrepair relating to residential premises. The cost of the repairs or other work is estimated to be" followed by either:
- "not more than £1,000" **or**
- "more than £1,000"

If within this claim, you are making a claim for other damages, you must also write:

"I expect to recover as damages" followed by either:
- "not more than £1,000" **or**
- "more than £1,000"

Issuing in the High Court

You may only issue in the High Court if one of the following statements applies to your claim:-

"By law, my claim must be issued in the High Court. The Act which provides this is ....(specify Act)"

or

"I expect to recover more than £15,000"

or

"My claim includes a claim for personal injuries and the value of the claim is £50,000 or more"

or

"My claim needs to be in a specialist High Court list, namely................................(state which list)".

If one of the statements does apply and you wish to, or must by law, issue your claim in the High Court, write the words "I wish my claim to issue in the High Court because" followed by the relevant statement e.g. "I wish my claim to issue in the High Court because my claim includes a claim for personal injuries and the value of my claim is £50,000 or more."

Defendant's name and address

Enter in this box the full names and address of the defendant receiving the claim form (i.e. one claim form for each defendant). If the defendant is to be served outside England and Wales, you may need to obtain the court's permission.

Particulars of claim

You may include your particulars of claim on the claim form in the space provided or in a separate document which you should head 'Particulars of Claim'. It should include the names of the parties, the court, the claim number and your address for service and also contain a statement of truth. You should keep a copy for yourself, provide one for the court and one for each defendant. Separate particulars of claim can either be served
- with the claim form **or**
- within 14 days after the date on which the claim form was served.

If your particulars of claim are served separately from the claim form, they must be served with the forms on which the defendant may reply to your claim.

Your particulars of claim must include
- a concise statement of the facts on which you rely
- a statement (if applicable) to the effect that you are seeking aggravated damages or exemplary damages
- details of any interest which you are claiming
- any other matters required for your type of claim as set out in the relevant practice direction

Address for documents

Insert in this box the address at which you wish to receive documents and/or payments, if different from the address you have already given under the heading 'Claimant'. The address must be in England or Wales. If you are willing to accept service by DX, fax or e-mail, add details.

Statement of truth

This must be signed by you, by your solicitor or your litigation friend, as appropriate.

Where the claimant is a registered company or a corporation the claim must be signed by either the director, treasurer, secretary, chief executive, manager or other officer of the company or (in the case of a corporation) the mayor, chairman, president or town clerk.

APPENDIX 3   FORMS

Notes for defendant on replying to the claim form

**Please read these notes carefully - they will help you decide what to do about this claim.
Further information may be obtained from the court in a series of free leaflets**

- If this claim form was received with the particulars of claim completed or attached, you must reply within 14 days of the date it was served on you. If the words 'particulars of claim to follow' are written in the particulars of claim box, you should not reply until after you are served with the particulars of claim (which should be no more than 14 days after you received the claim form). If the claim was sent by post, the date of service is taken as the second day after posting (see post mark). If the claim form was delivered or left at your address, the date of service will be the day after it was delivered.
- You may either
    - pay the amount claimed
    - admit that you owe all or part of the claim and ask for time to pay or
    - dispute the claim
- If you do not reply, judgment may be entered against you.
- The notes below tell you what to do.
- The response pack will tell you which forms to use for your reply. (The pack will accompany the particulars of claim if they are served after the claim form).
- Court staff can help you complete the forms of reply and tell you about court procedures. But they cannot give legal advice. If you need legal advice, for example about the likely success of disputing the claim, you should contact a solicitor or a Citizens Advice Bureau immediately.

Registration of Judgments: If the claim results in a judgment being made against you in a **county court**, your name and address may be entered in the Register of County Court Judgments. This may make it difficult for you to obtain credit.
Costs and Interest: Additional costs and interest may be added to the amount claimed on the front of the claim form if judgment is entered against you. In a county court, if judgment is for £5,000 or more, or is in respect of a debt which attracts contractual or statutory interest for late payment, the claimant may be entitled to further interest.

Your response and what happens next

How to pay

Do not bring any payments to the court - they will not be accepted.

When making payments to the claimant, quote the claimant's reference (if any) and the claim number.

Make sure that you keep records and can account for any payments made. Proof may be required if there is any disagreement. It is not safe to send cash unless you use registered post.

Admitting the Claim

Claim for specified amount

If you admit all the claim, take or send the money, including any interest and costs, to the claimant at the address given for payment on the claim form, within 14 days.

If you admit all the claim and you are asking for time to pay, complete Form N9A and send it to the claimant at the address given for payment on the claim form, within 14 days. The claimant will decide whether to accept your proposal for payment. If it is accepted, the claimant may request the court to enter judgment against you and you will be sent an order to pay. If your offer is not accepted, the court will decide how you should pay.

If you admit only part of the claim, complete Form N9A and Form N9B (see 'Disputing the Claim' overleaf) and send them to the court within 14 days. The claimant will decide whether to accept your part admission.

If it is accepted, the claimant may request the court to enter judgment against you and the court will send you an order to pay. If your part admission is not accepted, the case will proceed as a defended claim.

Claim for unspecified amount

If you admit liability for the whole claim but do not make an offer to satisfy the claim, complete Form N9C and send it to the court within 14 days. A copy will be sent to the claimant who may request the court to enter judgment against you for an amount to be decided by the court, and costs. The court will enter judgment and refer the court file to a judge for directions for management of the case. You and the claimant will be sent a copy of the court's order.

If you admit liability for the claim and offer an amount of money to satisfy the claim, complete Form N9C and send it to the court within 14 days. The claimant will be sent a copy and asked if the offer is acceptable. The claimant must reply to the court within 14 days and send you a copy. If a reply is not received, the claim will be stayed. If the amount you have offered is **accepted -**

- the claimant may request the court to enter judgment against you for that amount.
- if you have requested time to pay which is not accepted by the claimant, the rate of payment will be decided by the court.

N1C Notes for defendants (4.99)   *Printed on behalf of The Court Service*

If your offer in satisfaction is **not accepted** -
- the claimant may request the court to enter judgment against you for an amount to be decided by the court, and costs; and
- the court will enter judgment and refer the court file to a judge for directions for management of the case. You and the claimant will be sent a copy of the court's order.

Disputing the claim

If you are being sued as an individual for a specified amount of money and you dispute the claim, the claim may be transferred to your home court i.e. the one nearest your home or your solicitor's practice if different from the court where the claim was issued.

If you need longer than 14 days to prepare your defence or to contest the court's jurisdiction to try the claim, complete the Acknowledgment of Service form and send it to the court within 14 days. This will allow you 28 days from the date of service of the particulars of claim to file your defence or make an application to contest the court's jurisdiction. The court will tell the claimant that your Acknowledgment of Service has been received.

If the case proceeds as a defended claim, you and the claimant will be sent an Allocation Questionnaire. You will be told the date by which it must be returned to the court. The information you give on the form will help a judge decide whether your case should be dealt with in the small claims track, fast track or multi-track. After a judge has considered the completed questionnaires, you will be sent a notice of allocation setting out the judge's decision. The notice will tell you the track to which the claim has been allocated and what you have to do to prepare for the hearing or trial. **Leaflets telling you more about the tracks are available from the court office.**

Claim for specified amount

If you wish to dispute the full amount claimed or wish to claim against the claimant (a counterclaim), complete Form N9B and send it to the court within 14 days.

If you admit part of the claim, complete the Defence Form N9B <u>and</u> the Admission Form N9A and send them both to the court within 14 days. The claimant will decide whether to accept your part admission in satisfaction of the claim (see under 'Admitting the Claim - specified amount'). If the claimant does not accept the amount you have admitted, the case will proceed as a defended claim.

If you dispute the claim because you have already paid it, complete Form N9B and send it to the court within 14 days. The claimant will have to decide whether to proceed with the claim or withdraw it and notify the court and you within 28 days. If the claimant wishes to proceed, the case will proceed as a defended claim.

Claim for unspecified amount/return of goods/non-money claims

If you dispute the claim or wish to claim against the claimant (counterclaim), complete Form N9D and send it to the court within 14 days.

Personal injuries claims:

If the claim is for personal injuries and the claimant has attached a medical report to the particulars of claim, in your defence you should state whether you:
- agree with the report **or**
- dispute all or part of the report **and** give your reasons for doing so **or**
- neither agree nor dispute the report **or** have no knowledge of the report

Where you have obtained your own medical report, you should attach it to your defence.

If the claim is for personal injuries and the claimant has attached a schedule of past and future expenses and losses, in your defence you must state which of the items you:
- agree **or**
- dispute **and** supply alternative figures where appropriate **or**
- neither agree nor dispute or have no knowledge of

Address where notices can be sent

This must be either your solicitor's address, your own residential or business address in England and Wales or (if you live elsewhere) some other address within England and Wales.

Statement of truth

This must be signed by you, by your solicitor or your litigation friend, as appropriate.

Where the defendant is **a registered company or a corporation** the response must be signed by either the director, treasurer, secretary, chief executive, manager or other officer of the company **or** (in the case of a corporation) the mayor, chairman, president or town clerk.

1230

APPENDIX 3   FORMS

Notes for defendant on replying to the claim form (Consumer Credit Act claim)

Please read these notes carefully - they will help you decide what to do about this claim. You will have received a notice of hearing telling you when and where to come to court with the claim form. A leaflet is available from the court office about what happens when you come to a court hearing.

- You must reply to the claim form within 14 days of the date it was served on you. If the claim form was
    - sent by post, the date of service is taken as the second day after posting (see post mark)
    - delivered or left at your address, the date of service will be the day after it was delivered
    - handed to you personally, the date of service will be the day it was given to you
- You may either
    - pay the amount claimed
    - admit liability for the claim and offer to make payments to keep the goods
    - dispute the claim
- If you do not reply or attend the hearing, judgment may be entered against you.
- The notes below tell you what to do.
- Court staff can help you complete the forms of reply and tell you about court procedure. But they cannot give legal advice. If you need legal advice, for example about the likely success of disputing the claim, you should contact a solicitor or a Citizens Advice Bureau immediately.

Registration of Judgments: If the claim results in a judgment being made against you in a **county court**, your name and address may be entered in the Register of County Court Judgments. This may make it difficult for you to obtain credit.
Costs and Interest: Additional costs and interest may be added to the amount claimed on the front of the claim form if judgment is entered against you. In a county court, if judgment is for £5,000 or more, or is in respect of a debt which attracts contractual or statutory interest for late payment, the claimant may be entitled to further interest.

Your response and what happens next

How to pay

Do not bring any payments to the court - they will not be accepted.

When making payments to the claimant, quote the claimant's reference (if any) and the claim number.

Make sure that you keep records and can account for any payments made. Proof may be required if there is any disagreement. It is not safe to send cash unless you use registered post.

Admitting the Claim

If you admit liability for the claim and offer to make payments in order to keep the goods. Complete Form N9C and send it to the court within 14 days. **Remember** to keep a copy for yourself. The court will send a copy of your admission to the claimant and ask if your offer is acceptable.

If the claimant **accepts your offer** and asks the court to enter judgment before the date of the hearing, you will be sent a copy of the judgment and need not come to the hearing. If you do not hear from the court it is in your interests to attend the hearing.

If your offer is **not accepted**, you should attend the hearing. The court will treat your admission as evidence so remember to bring a copy of your admission with you to the hearing.

Disputing the claim

If you dispute the claim or wish to claim against the claimant (counterclaim), complete Form N9D and send it to the court within 14 days. **Remember** to keep a copy for yourself and to bring it with you to the hearing. The court will send a copy of your defence to the claimant. At the hearing the court may make a final order or judgment in the claim. If the court agrees that you have a valid defence (or counterclaim), it will tell you and the claimant what to do to prepare for a future hearing. If you send your defence to the court after the 14 days has expired, and you want to rely on it at the hearing, the court may take your failure to file it on time into account when deciding what order to make in respect of costs.

Statement of truth

This must be signed by you, by your solicitor or your litigation friend, as appropriate.

Where the defendant is **a registered company or a corporation** the response must be signed by either the director, treasurer, secretary, chief executive, manager or other officer of the company **or** (in the case of a corporation) the mayor, chairman, president or town clerk.

N1(FD)(Consumer Credit Act claim) (4.99)   *Printed on behalf of The Court*

APPENDIX 3   FORMS

Response Pack

You should read the 'notes for defendant' attached to the claim form which will tell you when and where to send the forms.

Included in this pack are:
- either **Admission Form N9A** (if the claim is for a specified amount) or **Admission Form N9C** (if the claim is for an unspecified amount or is not a claim for money)
- either **Defence and Counterclaim Form N9B** (if the claim is for a specified amount) or **Defence and Counterclaim Form N9D** (if the claim is for an unspecified amount or is not a claim for money)
- **Acknowledgment of service** (see below)

Complete

If you admit the claim or the amount claimed and/or you want time to pay	the admission form
If you admit part of the claim	the admission form and the defence form
If you dispute the whole claim or wish to make a claim (a counterclaim) against the claimant	the defence form
If you need 28 days (rather than 14) from the date of service to prepare your defence, or wish to contest the court's jurisdiction	the acknowledgment of service
If you do nothing, judgment may be entered against you	

Acknowledgment of Service

Defendant's full name if different from the name given on the claim form

In the	
Claim No.	
Claimant (including ref.)	
Defendant	

Address to which documents about this claim should be sent (including reference if appropriate)

	if applicable
fax no.	
DX no.	
e-mail	

Tel. no.   Postcode

Tick the appropriate box

1. I intend to defend all of this claim ☐
2. I intend to defend part of this claim ☐
3. I intend to contest jurisdiction ☐

If you file an acknowledgment of service but do not file a defence within 28 days of the date of service of the claim form, or particulars of claim if served separately, judgment may be entered against you.

If you do not file an application within 28 days of the date of service of the claim form, or particulars of claim if served separately, it will be assumed that you accept the court's jurisdiction and judgment may be entered against you.

Signed _____

(Defendant)(Defendant's Solicitor) (Litigation friend)

Position or office held
(if signing on behalf of firm or company)

Date

The court office at
is open between 10 am and 4 pm Monday to Friday. When corresponding with the court, please address forms or letters to the Court Manager and quote the claim number.

N9 Response Pack (4.99)   Printed on behalf of The Court Service

Admission (specified amount)

- You have a limited number of days to complete and return this form
- Before completing this form, please read the notes for guidance attached to the claim form

When to fill in this form
- Only fill in this form if you are admitting all or some of the claim **and** you are asking for time to pay

How to fill in this form
- Tick the correct boxes and give as much information as you can. **Then sign and date the form.** If necessary provide details on a separate sheet, add the claim number and attach it to this form.
- Make your offer of payment in box 11 on the back of this form. **If you make no offer the claimant will decide how much and when you should pay.**
- If you are not an individual, you should ensure that you provide sufficient details about the assets and liabilities of your firm, company or corporation to support any offer of payment made in box 11.
- You can get help to complete this form at **any** county court office or Citizens Advice Bureau.

Where to send this form
- **If you admit the claim in full**
  Send the completed form to the address shown on the claim form as one to which documents should be sent.
- **If you admit only part of the claim**
  Send the form **to the court** at the address given on the claim form, together with the defence form (N9B).

How much of the claim do you admit?
- [ ] I admit the full amount claimed as shown on the claim form **or**
- [ ] I admit the amount of £ _____

In the
Claim No.	
Claimant (including ref.)	
Defendant	

1 Personal details
Surname _____
Forename _____
- [ ] Mr   [ ] Mrs   [ ] Miss   [ ] Ms
- [ ] Married   [ ] Single   [ ] Other (specify) _____
Age _____
Address _____
Postcode _____
Tel. no. _____

2 Dependants *(people you look after financially)*
Number of children in each age group
under 11 ___   11-15 ___   16-17 ___   18 & over ___
Other dependants *(give details)* _____

3 Employment
- [ ] **I am employed as a** _____
  My employer is _____
  Jobs other than main job *(give details)* _____
- [ ] **I am self employed as a** _____
  Annual turnover is .... £ _____
  - [ ] **I am not** in arrears with my national insurance contributions, income tax and VAT
  - [ ] **I am** in arrears and I owe.......... £ _____
  Give details of:
  (a) contracts and other work in hand _____
  (b) any sums due for work done _____
- [ ] I have been unemployed for ___ years ___ months
- [ ] I am a pensioner

4 Bank account and savings
- [ ] I have a bank account
  - [ ] The account is in credit by........ £ _____
  - [ ] The account is overdrawn by.... £ _____
- [ ] I have a savings or building society account
  The amount in the account is.......... £ _____

5 Residence
I live in [ ] my own house   [ ] lodgings
          [ ] my jointly owned house   [ ] council accommodation
          [ ] rented accommodation

N9A Form of admission and statement of means to accompany Form N1 (4.99)   *Printed on behalf of The Court Service*

APPENDIX 3   FORMS

6 Income

My usual take home pay *(including overtime, commission, bonuses etc)*	£	per
Income support	£	per
Child benefit(s)	£	per
Other state benefit(s)	£	per
My pension(s)	£	per
Others living in my home give me	£	per
Other income *(give details below)*		
	£	per
	£	per
	£	per
Total income	**£**	**per**

7 Expenses

(Do not include any payments made by other members of the household out of their own income)

I have regular expenses as follows:

Mortgate *(including second mortgage)*	£	per
Rent	£	per
Council tax	£	per
Gas	£	per
Electricity	£	per
Water charges	£	per
TV rental and licence	£	per
HP repayments	£	per
Mail order	£	per
Housekeeping, food, school meals	£	per
Travelling expenses	£	per
Children's clothing	£	per
Maintenance payments	£	per
Others *(not court orders or credit debts listed in boxes 9 and 10)*		
	£	per
	£	per
	£	per
Total expenses	**£**	**per**

8 Priority debts

(This section is for arrears only. Do not include regular expenses listed in box 7.)

Rent arrears	£	per
Mortgage arrears	£	per
Council tax/Community Charge arrears	£	per
Water charges arrears	£	per
Fuel debts: Gas	£	per
Electricity	£	per
Other	£	per
Maintenance arrears	£	per
Others *(give details below)*		
	£	per
	£	per
Total priority debts	**£**	**per**

9 Court orders

Court	Claim No.	£	per

Total court order instalments	**£**	**per**

Of the payments above, I am behind with payments to *(please list)*

10 Credit debts

Loans and credit card debts *(please list)*

	£	per
	£	per
	£	per

Of the payments above, I am behind with payments to *(please list)*

11 Offer of payment

☐ I can pay the amount admitted on

or

☐ I can pay by monthly instalments of £

If you cannot pay immediately, please give brief reasons below

12 Declaration

I declare that the details I have given above are true to the best of my knowledge

Signed

Date

Position or office held
(if signing on behalf of firm or company)

APPENDIX 3   FORMS

Defence and Counterclaim (specified amount)

- Fill in this form if you wish to dispute all or part of the claim and/or make a claim against the claimant (counterclaim).
- You have a limited number of days to complete and return this form to the court.
- Before completing this form, please read the notes for guidance attached to the claim form.
- Please ensure that all boxes at the top right of this form are completed. You can obtain the correct names and number from the claim form. The court cannot trace your case without this information.

How to fill in this form
- Complete sections 1 and 2. Tick the correct boxes and give the other detail asked for.
- Set out your defence in section 3. If necessary continue on a separate piece of paper making sure that the claim number is clearly shown on it. In your defence you must state which allegations in the particulars of claim you deny and your reasons for doing so. **If you fail to deny an allegation it may be taken that you admit it.**
- If you dispute only some of the allegations you must
  - specify which you admit and which you deny; and
  - give your own version of events if different from the claimant's.

In the

Claim No.

Claimant (including ref.)

Defendant

- If you wish to make a claim against the claimant (a counterclaim) complete section 4.
- Complete and sign section 5 before sending this form to the court. Keep a copy of the claim form and this form.

Legal Aid
- You may be entitled to legal aid. Ask about the legal aid scheme at any county court office, Citizens Advice Bureau, legal advice centre or firm of solicitors displaying the legal aid sign.

1. How much of the claim do you dispute?

☐ I dispute the full amount claimed as shown on the claim form

or

☐ I admit the amount of £ _____

If you dispute only part of the claim you must **either**:
- pay the amount admitted to the person named at the address for payment on the claim form (see How to Pay in the notes on the back of, or attached to, the claim form). Then send this defence to the court

or
- complete the admission form **and** this defence form and send them to the court.

☐ I paid the amount admitted on (*date*) _____
or
☐ I enclose the completed form of admission
(*go to section 2*)

2. Do you dispute this claim because you have already paid it? *Tick whichever applies*

☐ **No** (*go to section 3*)

☐ **Yes** I paid £ _____ to the claimant

on _____ (*before the claim form was issued*)

Give details of where and how you paid it in the box below (*then go to section 5*)

3. Defence

N9B Defence and Counterclaim (specified amount)(4.99) *Printed on behalf of The Court Service*

APPENDIX 3 FORMS

Defence (continued)

Claim No.

4. If you wish to make a claim against the claimant (a counterclaim)

If your claim is for a specific sum of money, how much are you claiming? £

- To start your counterclaim, you will have to pay a fee. Court staff will tell you how much you have to pay
- You may not be able to make a counterclaim where the claimant is the Crown (e.g. a Government Department). Ask at your local county court office for further information.

My claim is for (*please specify nature of claim*)

What are your reasons for making the counterclaim?
If you need to continue on a separate sheet put the claim number in the top right hand corner

5. Signed
(To be signed by you or by your solicitor or litigation friend)

*(I believe)(The defendant believes) that the facts stated in this form are true. *I am duly authorised by the defendant to sign this statement

delete as appropriate

Position or office held (if signing on behalf of firm or company)

Date

Give an address to which notices about this case can be sent

Postcode
Tel. no.

if applicable
fax no.
DX no.
e-mail

Admission (unspecified amount, non-money and return of goods claims)

- Before completing this form please read the notes for guidance attached to the claim form. If necessary provide details on a separate sheet, add the claim number and attach it to this form.
- If you are not an individual, you should ensure that you provide sufficient details about the assets and liabilities of your firm, company or corporation to support any offer of payment made.

In the	
Claim No.	
Claimant (including ref.)	
Defendant	

In non-money claims only
☐ I admit liability for the whole claim
(Complete section 12)

In return of goods cases only
Are the goods still in your possession?
☐ Yes   ☐ No

Section A Response to claim *(tick one box only)*

☐ I admit liability for the whole claim but want the court to decide the amount I should pay / value of the goods

OR

☐ I admit liability for the claim and offer to
pay [   ] in satisfaction of the claim
(Complete sections B and 12)

Section B How are you going to pay the amount you have admitted? *(tick one box only)*

☐ I offer to pay on *(date)* [   ]

OR

☐ I cannot pay the amount immediately because *(state reason)*
[   ]

AND
I offer to pay by instalments of £ [   ]
per (week)(month)
starting *(date)* [   ]

1 Personal details

Surname [   ]
Forename [   ]

☐ Mr .   ☐ Mrs   ☐ Miss   ☐ Ms
☐ Married ☐ Single ☐ Other *(specify)* [   ]

Age [   ]

Address [   ]
Postcode [   ]
Tel. no. [   ]

2 Dependants *(people you look after financially)*

Number of children in each age group

under 11 [ ]   11-15 [ ]   16-17 [ ]   18 & over [ ]

Other dependants [   ]
(give details)

3 Employment

☐ I am employed as a [   ]
My employer is [   ]
Jobs other than main job *(give details)* [   ]

☐ I am self employed as a [   ]
Annual turnover is.................. £ [   ]

☐ **I am not** in arrears with my national insurance contributions, income tax and VAT

☐ **I am** in arrears and I owe.......... £ [   ]

Give details of:
(a) contracts and other work in hand [   ]
(b) any sums due for work done [   ]

☐ I have been unemployed for [ ] years [ ] months

☐ I am a pensioner

4 Bank account and savings

☐ I have a bank account
  ☐ The account is in credit by........ £ [   ]
  ☐ The account is overdrawn by.... £ [   ]

☐ I have a savings or building society account
  The amount in the account is.......... £ [   ]

5 Residence

I live in
☐ my own property   ☐ lodgings
☐ jointly owned house   ☐ rented property
☐ council accommodation

N9C Admission (unspecified amount and non-money claims) (4.99)

APPENDIX 3 FORMS

6 Income

My usual take home pay *(including overtime, commission, bonuses etc)*	£	per
Income support	£	per
Child benefit(s)	£	per
Other state benefit(s)	£	per
My pension(s)	£	per
Others living in my home give me	£	per
Other income *(give details below)*		
	£	per
	£	per
	£	per
Total income	£	per

7 Expenses

(Do not include any payments made by other members of the household out of their own income)

I have regular expenses as follows:

Mortgage *(including second mortgage)*	£	per
Rent	£	per
Council Tax	£	per
Gas	£	per
Electricity	£	per
Water charges	£	per
TV rental and licence	£	per
HP repayments	£	per
Mail order	£	per
Housekeeping, food, school meals	£	per
Travelling expenses	£	per
Children's clothing	£	per
Maintenance payments	£	per
Others *(not court orders or credit debts listed in boxes 9 and 10)*		
	£	per
	£	per
	£	per
Total expenses	£	per

8 Priority debts

(This section is for arrears only. Do not include regular expenses listed in box 7.)

Rent arrears	£	per
Mortgage arrears	£	per
Council tax/Community Charge arrears	£	per
Water charges arrears	£	per
Fuel debts: Gas	£	per
Electricity	£	per
Other	£	per
Maintenance arrears	£	per
Others *(give details below)*		
	£	per
	£	per
Total priority debts	£	per

9 Court orders

Court	Claim No.	£	per

Total court order instalments	£	per

Of the payments above, I am behind with payments to *(please list)*

10 Credit debts

Loans and credit card debts *(please list)*

	£	per
	£	per
	£	per

Of the payments above, I am behind with payments to *(please list)*

11 Declaration

I declare that the details I have given above are true to the best of my knowledge

Signed

Date

Position or office held *(if signing on behalf of firm or company)*

Defence and Counterclaim
(unspecified amount, non-money and return of goods claims)

In the

Claim No.

Claimant (including ref.)

Defendant

- Fill in this form if you wish to dispute all or part of the claim and/or make a claim against the claimant (counterclaim)
- You have a limited number of days to complete and return this form to the court.
- Before completing this form, please read the notes for guidance attached to the claim form.
- Please ensure that all the boxes at the top right of this form are completed. You can obtain the correct names and number from the claim form. The court cannot trace your case without this information.

How to fill in this form
- Set out your defence in section 1. If necessary continue on a separate piece of paper making sure that the claim number is clearly shown on it. In your defence you must state which allegations in the particulars of claim you deny and your reasons for doing so. **If you fail to deny an allegation it may be taken that you admit it.**
- If you dispute only some of the allegations you must
  - specify which you admit and which you deny; and
  - give your own version of events if different from the claimant's.
- If the claim is for money and you dispute the claimant's statement of value, you must say why and if possible give your own statement of value.
- If you wish to make a claim against the claimant (a counterclaim) complete section 2.
- Complete and sign section 3 before returning this form.

Where to send this form
- send or take this form immediately to the court at the address given on the claim form.
- Keep a copy of the claim form and the defence form.

Legal Aid
- You may be entitled to legal aid. Ask about the legal aid scheme at any county court office, Citizens Advice Bureau, legal advice centre or firm of solicitors displaying the legal aid sign.

1. Defence

N9D Defence and Counterclaim (unspecified amount and non-money claims) (4.99)   *Printed on behalf of The Court Service*

APPENDIX 3   FORMS

Defence (continued)   Claim No.

2. If you wish to make a claim against the claimant (a counterclaim)

If your claim is for a specific sum of money, how much are you claiming? £

- To start your counterclaim, you will have to pay a fee. Court staff will tell you how much you have to pay.
- You may not be able to make a counterclaim where the claimant is the Crown (e.g. a Government Department). Ask at your local county court office for further information.

My claim is for *(please specify)*

What are your reasons for making the counterclaim?
If you need to continue on a separate sheet put the claim number in the top right hand corner

3. Signed
(To be signed by you or by your solicitor or litigation friend)

*(I believe)(The defendant believes) that the facts stated in this form are true. *I am duly authorised by the defendant to sign this statement

*delete as appropriate

Position or office held
(if signing on behalf of firm or company)

Date

Give an address to which notices about this case can be sent

Postcode

Tel. no.

if applicable

fax no.

DX no.

e-mail

1240

Notice that Acknowledgment of Service has been filed

To the [Claimant]['s Solicitor]

In the	
Claim No.	
Claimant (including ref)	
Defendant (including ref)	
Date	

The defendant filed an Acknowledgment of Service on

The defendant responded to the claim indicating an intention to [defend all of the claim.][defend part of the claim.][contest the court's jurisdiction.]

The defendant has 28 days from the date of service of the claim form with particulars of claim, or of the particulars of claim, to file [a defence.][an application to contest the court's jurisdiction.]

[The defendant's name has been corrected to read .]

[The defendant has given the following address for service of documents:]

[The acknowledgment was filed by the solicitors acting for the defendant who have given the following name and address for service of documents: .]

The court office at
is open between 10 am and 4 pm Monday to Friday. When corresponding with the court, please address forms or letters to the Court Manager and quote the claim number
N10 Notice that Acknowledgment of Service has been Filed

APPENDIX 3   FORMS

Witness Summons

In the	
Claim No.	
Claimant (including ref)	
Defendant (including ref)	
Issued on	

To

You are summoned to attend at *(court address)*

            (am)(pm) on   of   at

(and each following day of the hearing until the court tells you that you are no longer required.)

☐ to give evidence in respect of the above claim

☐ to produce the following document(s) *(give details)*

The sum of £   is paid or offered to you with this summons. This is to cover your travelling expenses to and from court and includes an amount by way of compensation for loss of time.

This summons was issued on the application of the claimant (defendant) or the claimant's (defendant's) solicitor whose name, address and reference number is:

Do not ignore this summons

If you were offered money for travel expenses and compensation for loss of time, at the time it was served on you, and you
- fail to attend or produce documents as required by the summons; or
- refuse to take an oath or affirm for the purpose of answering questions about your evidence or the documents you have been asked to produce

you may be liable to a fine or imprisonment and may in addition be ordered to pay any costs resulting from your failure to attend or refusal to take an oath or affirm.

The court office at
is open between 10 am and 4 pm Monday to Friday. When corresponding with the court, please address forms or letters to the Court Manager and quote the claim number.

N20 Witness Summons (4.99)   *Printed on behalf of The Court Service*

APPENDIX 3   FORMS

Certificate of service

Claim No.

I certify that the order of which this is a true copy, was served by posting to _____

(the witness) on _____ at the address stated on the summons in accordance with the request of the applicant or his solicitor.

I enclosed a P.O. for £ _____ for the witness's expenses and compensation for loss of time.

Signed _____
Officer of the Court

APPENDIX 3   FORMS

Order for Examination of Deponent
(before the hearing)

In the	
Claim No.	
Claimant (including ref)	
Defendant (including ref)	
Date	

To

Upon the application of the [claimant][defendant],[Master][District Judge] has **ordered you to attend**

at   [am][pm] on   of

at

to be examined on oath.

[and] to produce the following document(s)]

[£   to cover your travelling expenses to and from the place of examination and compensation for your loss of time is attached]

[Sum to be offered or handed to deponent £   for travelling expenses to and from the place of examination (and compensation for loss of time)]

Do not ignore this order
If you were offered money for travel expenses and compensation for loss of time at the time it was served on you and you
- fail to attend or produce documents as required by the order: or
- refuse to take an oath or affirm for the purpose of the examination or to answer any lawful question or produce any document at the examination

you may be liable to fine and may in addition be ordered to pay any costs resulting from your failure to attend or refusal to take an oath or affirm.

The court office at
is open between 10 am and 4 pm Monday to Friday. When corresponding with the court, please address forms or letters to the Court Manager and quote the claim number.
N21 Order for Examination of Deponent (before the hearing)

Certificate of service

Claim No.

I certify that the order of which this is a true copy, was served by posting to _____

(the deponent) on _____ at the address stated in the order.

I enclosed a P.O. for £ ____ for the deponent's expenses and compensation for loss of time.

Signed _____
Officer of the Court

APPENDIX 3   FORMS

Allocation Questionnaire	In the
	Claim No.
	Last date for filing with court office

To

SEAL

Please read the notes on page five before completing the questionnaire.

Please note the date by which it must be returned and the name of the court it should be returned to since this may be different from the court where proceedings were issued.

If you have settled this case (or if you settle it on a future date) and do not need to have it heard or tried, you must let the court know immediately.

A Settlement

Do you wish there to be a one month stay to attempt to settle the case?   ☐ Yes   ☐ No

B Track

Which track do you consider is most suitable for your case? *(Tick one box)*   ☐ small claims   ☐ fast track   ☐ multi-track

If you think your case is suitable for a specialist list, say which:

If you have indicated a track which would not be the normal track for the case, please give brief reasons for your choice:

N150 Allocation Questionnaire (6.99)   *Printed on behalf of The Court Service*

APPENDIX 3   FORMS

C Pre-Action protocols

Have you complied with any pre-action protocol applicable to your claim?

☐ None applicable to this claim   ☐ Yes   ☐ No

If Yes, please say which protocol:

If No, please explain to what extent and for what reason it has not been complied with:

D Applications

If you have not already sent the court an application for summary judgment, do you intend to do so?   ☐ Yes   ☐ No

If you have not already issued a claim in the case against someone not yet a party, do you intend to apply for the court's permission to do so?   ☐ Yes   ☐ No

In either case, if Yes, please give details:

E Witnesses of fact

So far as you know at this stage, what witnesses of fact do you intend to call at the hearing?

Witness name	Witness to which facts

APPENDIX 3   FORMS

F Experts' evidence

Do you wish to use expert evidence at the hearing? ☐ Yes ☐ No

Have you already copied any experts' report(s) to the other party(ies)? ☐ None obtained as yet ☐ Yes ☐ No

Please list the experts whose evidence you think you will use:

Expert's Name	Field of expertise (eg. orthopaedic surgeon, mechanical engineer)

Will you and the other party use the same expert(s)? ☐ Yes ☐ No

If No, please explain why not:

Do you want your expert(s) to give evidence orally at the hearing or trial? ☐ Yes ☐ No

If Yes, give the reasons why you think oral evidence is necessary:

G Location of trial

Is there any reason why your case needs to be heard at a particular court? ☐ Yes ☐ No

If Yes, give reasons (eg. particular facilities required, convenience of witnesses, etc.)

and specify the court:

APPENDIX 3   FORMS

H Representation and estimate of hearing/trial time

Do you expect to be represented by a solicitor or counsel at the hearing/trial? ☐ No ☐ Solicitor ☐ Counsel

How long do you estimate it will take to put your case to the court at the hearing/trial?   days   hours   minutes

If there are days when you, your representative, expert or an essential witness will not be able to attend court, give details:

Name	Dates not available

I Costs (only relates to costs incurred by legal representatives)

What is your estimate of costs incurred to date? £

What do you estimate the overall costs are likely to be? £

J Other Information

Have you attached documents you wish the judge to take into account when allocating the case? ☐ Yes ☐ No

Have they been served on the other parties? ☐ Yes ☐ No

If Yes, say when

Have the other parties agreed their content? ☐ Yes ☐ No

Have you attached a list of the directions you think appropriate for the management of your case? ☐ Yes ☐ No

Are they agreed with the other parties? ☐ Yes ☐ No

Are there any other facts which might affect the timetable the court will set? If so, please state

Signed _____   Date _____

[Counsel][Solicitor][for the][Claimant][Defendant]

APPENDIX 3 FORMS

Notes for completing an Allocation Questionnaire

- If the case is not settled, a judge must allocate it to an appropriate case management track. To help the judge choose the most just and cost-effective track, you must now complete the attached questionnaire.
- If you fail to return the allocation questionnaire by the date given, the judge may make an order which leads to your claim or defence being struck out, or hold an allocation hearing. If there is an allocation hearing the judge may order any party who has not filed their questionnaire to pay, immediately, the costs of that hearing.
- If you wish to make an application, for example, for summary judgment on the grounds that the other party has no reasonable chance of success in their claim or defence, or for permission to add another party to the claim, you should send it and any required fee with the completed allocation questionnaire. If a hearing is fixed for your application, it may also be used as an allocation hearing.
- Any other documents you wish the judge to take into account should be filed with the questionnaire. But you must confirm that the documents have been sent to the other party, or parties, saying when they would have received them and whether they agreed their contents.
- Use a separate sheet if you need more space for your answers marking clearly which section the information refers to. Write the case number on it, sign and date it and attach it securely to the questionnaire.
- The letters below refer to the sections of the questionnaire and tell you what information is needed.

A Settlement
If you think that you and the other party may be able to negotiate a settlement you should tick the 'Yes' box. The court may order a stay, whether or not all the other parties to the case agree. You should still complete the rest of the questionnaire even if you are requesting a stay. Where a stay is granted it will be for an initial period of one month.

B Track
The basic guide by which cases are normally allocated to a track depends on the money value of the claim, although other factors such as the complexity of the case will also be considered:

Small Claims track	Claims valued at £5,000 or less unless they include a claim for personal injuries worth over £1,000; or a claim for housing disrepair where the costs of the repairs or other work is more than £1,000 and any other claim for damages is more than £1,000
Fast track	Claims valued at more than £5,000 but not more than £15,000
Multi-track	Claims over £15,000

A leaflet available from the court office explains these limits in greater detail.

C Pre-action protocols
For certain kinds of claim, there are protocols which set out what ought to be done before court proceedings are issued. As at April 1999 there are protocols for clinical negligence and personal injury claims.

D Applications
If you intend to apply for summary judgment or for permission to add another party to the claim or make any other application you should, if you have not already done so, file the application with your completed allocation questionnaire.

E Witnesses of fact
Remember to include yourself, if you will be giving evidence; but not experts, who should be included in section F.

F Experts' evidence
Oral or written expert evidence will only be allowed at the trial with the court's permission. The judge will decide what permission it seems appropriate to give when the case is allocated to track.

G Location of trial
High Court cases are usually heard at the Royal Courts of Justice or certain Civil Trial Centres. Other multi-track cases are heard at the Civil Trial Centre for the court where they are proceeding. Fast track cases are usually heard either at the court in which they are proceeding or its Civil Trial Centre. The court office will tell you which is the Civil Trial Centre for any particular county court. Small claim cases are usually heard at the court in which they are proceeding.

H Representation and estimate of hearing time
If the case is allocated to the fast track, no more than one day will be allowed for the trial of the whole case.

I Costs
Estimates should be given using Form 1 which can be found in the Schedule of Costs Forms set out in the Civil Procedure Rules. The form should be attached to and returned with your completed questionnaire.

Notice that a [Defence] [Counterclaim] has been filed

To [Claimant][Defendant] ['s Solicitor]

In the	
Claim No.	
Claimant including ref.	
Defendant including ref.	
Date	

[The defendant has filed a [defence][counterclaim], [a copy][copies] of which [is][are] enclosed with this notice. An allocation questionnaire is also enclosed which contains notes for guidance on how to complete it.]

[You have already been sent [a copy of a defence][copies of defences] received from [one][   ] of the defendants in this claim. The time for all the defendants to file their defences has now elapsed and I am enclosing an allocation questionnaire for you to complete.[No further defences have been received.][A copy][Copies] of the final [defence][counterclaim] received [is][are] also enclosed.]]

You must complete the allocation questionnaire on or before [   ] and return it to the court office at [   ]

[If you intend to defend the counterclaim, you must file a copy of your defence with your completed allocation questionnaire. Your defence must contain a statement of truth.]

The court office at
is open between 10 am and 4 pm Monday to Friday. When corresponding with the court, please address forms or letters to the Court Manager and quote the claim number.
N152 Notice that a [Defence] [Counterclaim] has been filed

Notice of Allocation or Listing Hearing

To [Claimant][Defendant][s' Solicitor]

In the	
Claim No.	
Claimant (including ref.)	
Defendant (including ref.)	
Date	

Seal

[Master][District Judge]   has considered the statements of case and allocation [listing] questionnaires filed in this claim [counterclaim] and decided that a hearing is necessary before a final decision about [allocation][listing] can be made.

[Reasons for the hearing are as follows:-

                                                                                                                              ]

The [Master][District Judge] orders you to attend at   [am][pm] on the   of

at

[The [Master][District Judge] directs the [claimant][defendant] to provide the following [further] information and send copies to the court and the other parties by .... :-   ]

Note: If you fail to attend the hearing, the court may order you to pay the costs of the other party, or parties, that do attend. Failure to pay those costs within the time stated may lead to your statement of case being struck out.

The court office at

is open between 10 am and 4 pm Monday to Friday. Address all communications to the Court Manager quoting the claim number.

N153 Notice of Allocation or Listing Hearing

APPENDIX 3   FORMS

Notice of Allocation to the Fast Track	In the	
	Claim No.	
To [Claimant][Defendant]['s Solicitor]	**Claimant** (including ref)	
	Defendant (including ref)	
	Date	

(Seal)

[Master][District Judge]   has considered the statements of case and allocation questionnaires filed, and allocated the [claim] [counterclaim] to **the fast track**.

The trial of this [claim] [counterclaim] will take place during the period commencing   of and ending on   of   at a venue to be notified.

The [Master][District Judge] orders that you and the other parties prepare for the trial as follows:-

[The reason[s] the judge has given for allocation to this track [is][are] that   .]

Notes:

- You and the other party, or parties, may agree to extend the time periods given in the directions above provided this **does not** affect the date given for returning the listing questionnaire or the date of the trial or trial period.

- If you do not comply with these directions, any other party to the claim will be entitled to apply to the court for an order that your statement of case (claim or defence) be struck out.
- Leaflets explaining more about what happens when your case is allocated to the fast track are available from the court office.

The court office at
is open between 10 am and 4 pm Monday to Friday. Address all communications to the Court Manager quoting the claim number.

N154 Notice of Allocation to the Fast Track

Notice of Allocation to the Multi-track

In the

Claim No.	
Claimant (including ref)	
Defendant (including ref)	
Date	

To [Claimant][Defendant]['s Solicitor]

Seal

[Master][District Judge]   has considered the statements of case and allocation questionnaires filed and allocated the claim [counterclaim] to **the multi-track**.

The [Master][District Judge] has ordered that:-

[The claim is being transferred to the [Civil Trial Centre at   County Court]
[Division of the Royal Courts of Justice] where all future applications, correspondence and so on will be dealt with]

[The reason[s] the judge has given for allocation to this track [is][are] that   .]

Notes:

- You and the other party, or parties, may agree to extend the time periods given in the directions above provided this **does not** affect the date given for any case management conference, for returning the listing questionnaire, for any pre trial review or the date of the trial or trial period.

- If you do not comply with these directions, any other party to the claim will be entitled to apply to the court for an order that your statement of case (claim or defence) be struck out.
- Leaflets explaining more about what happens when your case is allocated to the Multi-track are available from the court office.

The court office at

is open between 10 am and 4 pm Monday to Friday. Address all communications to the Court Manager quoting the claim number.
N155 Notice of Allocation to Multi-track

APPENDIX 3   FORMS

Order for Further Information (allocation)

In the	
Claim No.	
Claimant (including ref.)	
Defendant (including ref.)	
Date	

To [Claimant][Defendant]['s Solicitor]

(Seal)

[Master][District Judge]   has considered the statements of case and allocation questionnaires filed and requires further information before making a final decision about allocation.

The [Master][District Judge] orders the [claimant][defendant] to provide information about:-

This information and any accompanying documents should be delivered to the court and copied to the other parties on or before[   ]

Note: Where an allocation hearing is necessary because a party does not provide the information ordered above, the court may order that party to pay the costs of any other party attending the hearing.

The court office at

is open between 10 am and 4 pm Monday to Friday. Address all communications to the Court Manager quoting the claim number.

N156 Request for Further Information (allocation)

APPENDIX 3   FORMS

Notice of Allocation to the Small Claims Track

In the

County Court

Claim No.	
Claimant (including ref)	
Defendant (including ref)	
Date	

To Claimant][Defendant]['s Solicitor]

Seal

District Judge   has considered the statements of case and allocation questionnaires filed and allocated the claim [counterclaim] to **the small claims track**.

The hearing of this claim [counterclaim] will take place at   [am][pm]on the   of
at

The judge has estimated that the hearing of this claim [counterclaim] should take no longer than [mins][hours]. This is the total time for you, the other party [parties] and any witnesses to put your evidence and for the judge to reach a decision. To help prepare the claim [counterclaim] for hearing, the judge has ordered that you comply with the following directions:-

[The reason[s] the judge has given for allocation to this track [is][are] that   .]

Notes
- If you cannot, or choose not to, attend the hearing, you must write and tell the court **at least 7 days before the date of the hearing**. The district judge will hear the case in your absence, but will take account of your statement of case and any other documents you have filed.

- If you do not attend the hearing and do not give notice that you will not attend, the district judge may strike out your claim, defence or counter claim. If the claimant attends but the defendant does not, the district judge may make a decision based on the evidence of the claimant only.
- Leaflets explaining more about what you should do and what happens when your case is allocated to the small claims track are available from the court office.

The court office at

is open between 10 am and 4 pm Monday to Friday. Address all communications to the Court Manager quoting the claim number.
N157 Notice of Allocation to the Small Claims Track

APPENDIX 3   FORMS

Notice of Allocation to the Small Claims Track
(preliminary hearing)

To [Claimant][Defendant]['s Solicitor]

In the	
Claim No.	
Claimant (including ref.)	
Defendant (including ref.)	
Date	

Seal

District Judge .... has considered the statements of case and allocation questionnaires filed and allocated the claim [counterclaim] to the **small claims track**.

Before the claim [counterclaim] is listed for hearing, the judge has ordered that a preliminary hearing should take place [because] :-

[special directions are needed in this claim [counterclaim] to prepare for the final hearing which the judge would prefer to explain to you in person.]

[to consider whether the [claim][counterclaim] can be disposed of because the [claimant][defendant] has no real prospect of success at a final hearing.]

The preliminary hearing will take place at   [am][pm] on the   of

at

[The reason[s] the judge has given for allocation to this track [is][are] that   .]

Notes
- If you do not attend the hearing the court may make an order in your absence.
- If it is practical to do so and you and the other parties agree, the judge may decide to treat the preliminary hearing as a final hearing.
- Leaflets explaining more about what you should do and what happens when your case is allocated to the small claims track are available from the court office.

The court office at

is open between 10 am and 4 pm Monday to Friday. Address all communications to the Court Manager quoting the claim number.

N158 Notice of Allocation to the Small Claims Track (preliminary hearing)

APPENDIX 3 FORMS

Notice of Allocation to the Small Claims Track
(no hearing)

To [Claimant][Defendant]['s Solicitor]

In the	
	County Court
Claim No.	
Claimant (including ref)	
Defendant (including ref)	
Date	

Seal

District Judge   has considered the statements of case and allocation questionnaires filed and allocated the claim [counterclaim] to the **small claims track**.

The judge proposes to deal with the claim [counterclaim] without a hearing, that is, on the papers alone but can only do this if all parties agree.

Please tell the court whether or not you agree to your case being dealt with in this way by completing the lower half of this form and returning a copy to the court on or before _____. You must at the same time send a copy of it to all other parties.

> Leaflets explaining more about what you should do and what happens when your case is allocated to the Small Claims Track are available from the court office.

Reply to the court
Tick A or B and C

A ☐ I agree that the claim [counterclaim] should be dealt with on the papers alone.

or

B ☐ I do not agree that the claim [counterclaim] should be dealt with on the papers alone.

and

C ☐ I have sent a copy of this completed form to the other party.

In the	
	County Court
Claim No.	
Claimant (including ref)	
Defendant (including ref)	

Signed _____   Position or office held _____
(Claimant)(Defendant)('s Solicitor)('s litigation friend)   (if signing on behalf of firm or company)

Date _____

The court office at
is open between 10 am and 4 pm Monday to Friday. Address all communications to the Court Manager quoting the claim number.
N159 Notice of Allocation to the Small Claims Track (no hearing)

APPENDIX 3   FORMS

Notice of Allocation to the Small Claims Track
(with parties' consent)

To [Claimant][Defendant]['s Solicitors]

In the	**County Court**
Claim No.	
Claimant (including ref)	
Defendant (including ref)	
Date	

Seal

District Judge   has considered the statements of case and allocation questionnaires filed and, with the consent of the parties, allocated the claim [counterclaim] to **the small claims track**.

The hearing of the claim [counterclaim] will take place at   [am][pm] on the   of   at

The judge has estimated that the hearing of this claim [counterclaim] should take no longer than   mins/hours and has ordered that you must comply with the following directions which will tell you what to do to prepare for the trial:

Notes

- If you cannot, or choose not to, attend the hearing, you must write and tell the court at **least 7 days before the date of the hearing** The district judge will hear the case in your absence, but will take account of your statement of case and any other documents you have filed.
- As you have consented to your claim [counterclaim] being heard in the small claims track, any costs allowed to the successful party will be limited to the maximum sum which can be awarded in the fast track.
- If you do not attend the hearing and do not give notice that you will not attend, the district judge may strike out your claim, defence or counterclaim. If the claimant attends but the defendant does not, the district judge may make a decision based on the evidence of the claimant only.
- Leaflets telling you more about the small claims track are available from the court office.

The court office at

is open between 10 am and 4 pm Monday to Friday. When corresponding with the court, please address forms or letters to the Court Manager and quote the claim number

N160 Notice of Allocation to the Small Claims Track (with parties' consent)

APPENDIX 3 FORMS

Listing Questionnaire

In the

Claim No.

Last date for filing with court office

To

- The court will use the information which you and the other party(ies) provide to fix a date for trial (or to confirm the date and time if one has already been fixed), to confirm the estimated length of trial and to set a timetable for the trial itself. In multi-track cases the court will also decide whether to hold a pre-trial review.
- If you do not complete and return the questionnaire the procedural judge may
    - make an order which leads to your statement of case (claim or defence) being struck out.
    - decide to hold a listing hearing. You may be ordered to pay (immediately) the other parties' costs of attending.
    - if there is sufficient information, list the case for trial and give any appropriate directions.
    - separate estimates of costs incurred to date and those which will be incurred if the case proceeds to trial should be given using Form 1 in the Schedule of Costs Forms set out in the Civil Procedure Rules. This form should be attached to and returned with your completed questionnaire. (This relates only to costs incurred by legal representatives).

A Directions complied with

1. Have you complied with all the previous directions given by the court?   ☐ Yes   ☐ No
2. If no, please explain which directions are outstanding and why.

Directions outstanding	Reasons directions outstanding

3. Are any further directions required to prepare the case for trial?   ☐ Yes   ☐ No

If no, go to Section B

4. If yes, please explain directions required and give reasons.

Directions required	Reasons required

N170 Listing Questionnnaire (6.99)   *Printed on behalf of The Court Service*

1260

B Experts

1. Has the court already given permission for you to use written expert evidence?   ☐ Yes   ☐ No
   (If no, go to Section B6)

2. If yes, please give name and field of expertise.

Name of expert	Whether joint expert *(please tick, if appropriate)*	Field of expertise

3. Have the expert(s') report(s) been agreed with the other parties?   ☐ Yes   ☐ No

4. Have the experts met to discuss their reports?   ☐ Yes   ☐ No

5. Has the court already given permission for the expert(s) to give oral evidence at the trial?   ☐ Yes   ☐ No
   (If yes go to Q8)

6. If no are you seeking that permission?   ☐ Yes   ☐ No
   (If yes go to section Q7)   *(If no go to section C)*

7. Give your reasons for seeking permission.

8. What are the names, addresses and fields of expertise of your experts?

Expert 1	Expert 2	Expert 3	Expert 4

9. Please give details of any dates within the trial period when your expert(s) will not be available.

Name of expert	Dates not available

APPENDIX 3   FORMS

C Other witnesses
(If you are not calling other witnesses, go to section D)

1. How many other witnesses (including yourself) will be giving evidence on your behalf at the trial? *(do not include experts - see section B above)*

(Give number)

2. What are the names and addresses of your witnesses?

Witness 1	Witness 2	Witness 3	Witness 4

3. Please give details of any dates within the trial period when you or your witnesses will not be available?

Name of witness	Dates not available

4. Are any of the witness statements agreed?   ☐ Yes   ☐ No
(If no go to question 6)

5. If yes, give the name of the witness and the date of his or her statement

Name of witness	Date of statement

6. Do you or any of your witnesses need any special facilities?   ☐ Yes   ☐ No
(If no go to question 8)

7. If yes, what are they?

8. Will any of your witnesses be provided with an interpreter?   ☐ Yes   ☐ No
(If no go to section D)

9. If yes, say what type of interpreter e.g. language (stating which), deaf/blind etc.

APPENDIX 3   FORMS

D Legal representation

1. Who will be presenting your case at the hearing or trial? ☐ You   ☐ Solicitor   ☐ Counsel

2. Please give details of any dates within the trial period when the person presenting your case will not be available.

Name	Dates not available

E Other matters

1. How long do you estimate the trial will take, including cross-examination and closing arguments?

Minutes	Hours	Days

If your case is allocated to the fast track the maximum time allowed for the whole case will be no more than one day.

2. What is the estimated number of pages of evidence to be included in the trial bundle?

(please give number)

Fast track cases only

3. The court will normally give you 3 weeks notice in the fast track of the date fixed for a fast track trial unless, in exceptional circumstances, the court directs that shorter notice will be given. Would you be prepared to accept shorter notice of the date fixed for trial?   ☐ Yes   ☐ No

Signed _____

Claimant/defendant or Counsel/Solicitor for the claimant/defendant

Date _____

APPENDIX 3   FORMS

Notice to Pay Fee	In the	
	Claim No.	
To the [Claimant][Defendant] ['s Solicitor]	Claimant including ref.	
	Defendant including ref.	
	Date	

[On the [   ] the court received your [allocation] [listing] questionnaire.

Either a fee of £   or an application for a fee exemption or remission should have accompanied the questionnaire. Neither was enclosed.]

[Your [claim] [counterclaim] was [allocated to the] [fast track] [multi-track] [listed for trial] on [   ]. A fee of £   was payable unless you had made an application for a fee exemption on remission. Neither have been received.]

If by [   ] you have not paid the fee or applied for a fee exemption or remission, your [claim] [counterclaim] will be struck out and you will be liable for the costs which the [claimant][defendant] has incurred.

Note:

If your [claim][counterclaim] is struck out, you may apply to the court for it to be reinstated. An order reinstating your [claim][counterclaim] will only have effect if within two days of the order you:-
- pay the fee; or
- send the court evidence of your exemption from payment or remission of the fee

The court office at
is open between 10 am and 4 pm Monday to Friday. When corresponding with the court, please address forms or letters to the Court Manager and quote the claim number.
N173 Notice to Pay Fee

APPENDIX 3   FORMS

Notice of Issue
(specified amount)

To the Claimant ['s Solicitor]

Your claim was issued on [   ].
The court sent it to the defendant by first class post on [   ]
and it will be deemed to be served on [   ].
The defendant has until [   ] to reply.

The defendant may

- **Pay** you your total claim.
- **File an acknowledgment of service.** This will allow the defendant 28 days from the date of service of your particulars of claim to file a defence or contest the court's jurisdiction.
- **Dispute the whole claim.** The court will send you a copy of the defence.
- **Admit that all the money is owed.** The defendant will send you a completed admission form and you may ask the court to enter judgment using the request below.

For further information please turn over

In the	
The court office at	
is open between 10 am & 4 pm Monday to Friday Tel:	
Claim No.	
Claimant (including ref.)	
Defendant(s)	
Issue fee	£

- **Admit that only part of your claim is owed.** The court will send you a copy of the reply form and you will have to decide what to do next.
- **Not reply at all.** You may ask the court to enter judgment using the request below.

Note: If the claim is disputed and the defendant is an individual, the claim may be transferred to either the defendant's local court or, if he or she is represented, the one nearest the business address of the solicitor.

Request for Judgment

- Tick and complete either A or B. Remember to sign and date the form. Your signature certifies that the information you have given is correct.
- If the defendant has given an address on the form of admission to which correspondence should be sent, which is different from the address shown on the claim form, you must tell the court.
- Complete all the judgment details at C.

A ☐ The defendant has not filed an admission or defence to my claim or an application to contest the court's jurisdiction.

Decide how and when you want the defendant to pay. You can ask for the judgment to be paid by instalments or in one payment.

B ☐ The defendant admits that all the money is owed

Tick only **one** box below and return the completed slip to the court.

☐ **I accept the defendant's proposal for payment**
Say how the defendant intends to pay. The court will send the defendant an order to pay. You will also be sent a copy.

☐ **The defendant has not made any proposal for payment**
Say how you want the defendant to pay. You can ask for the judgment to be paid by instalments or in one payment. The court will send the defendant an order to pay. You will also be sent a copy.

☐ **I do NOT accept the defendant's proposal for payment**
Say how you want the defendant to pay. Give your reasons for objecting to the defendant's offer of payment in Part D overleaf. Return this slip to the court **with the defendant's admission** (or a copy). The court will fix a rate of payment and send the defendant an order to pay. You will also be sent a copy.

I certify that the information given is correct

Signed .... Date ....
(Claimant)(Claimant's Solicitor)(Litigation friend)

N205A Notice of Issue (specified amount) and request for judgment

In the	
Claim No.	
Claimant (including ref.)	
Defendant(s) (including ref.)	

C   Judgment details

I would like the defendant to be ordered to pay

☐ (immediately)
☐ (by instalments of £   per month)
☐ (in full **by**   )

Amount of claim as stated in claim form (including interest at date of issue)	
Interest since date of claim (if any) .... Period from................to	
Rate ....%	
Court fees shown on claim	
Solicitor's costs (if any) on issuing claim	
Sub Total	
Solicitor's costs (if any) on entering judgment	
Sub Total	
Deduct amount (if any) paid since issue	
Amount payable by defendant	

1265

APPENDIX 3 FORMS

Notes for Guidance

- The claim form must be served on the defendant within 4 months of the date of issue (6 months if you are serving outside England or Wales). You may be able to apply to extend the time for serving the claim form but the application must generally be made before the 4-month or 6-month period expires.

- If the defendant does not file an admission, defence or counterclaim; or if the defendant admits the whole claim with or without an offer of payment, you may ask for judgment. If you do not request judgment within 6 months of the end of the period for filing a defence, your claim will be stayed. This means that the only action you can take is to apply to a judge for an order lifting the stay.

- You should keep a record of any payments you receive from the defendant. If there is a hearing or you wish to take steps to enforce the judgment, you will need to satisfy the court about the balance outstanding. You should give the defendant a receipt and payment in cash should always be acknowledged. You should tell the defendant how much he owes if he asks.

- **You must inform the court IMMEDIATELY if you receive any payment before a hearing date or after you have sent a request for enforcement to the court.**

- Further information in leaflet form can be obtained free of charge from the court.

Part D

Objections to the defendant's proposal for payment   **Claim Number** [   ]

APPENDIX 3   FORMS

Notice of Issue
(unspecified amount)

To the Claimant['s Solicitor]

Your claim was issued on [   ].
The court sent it to the defendant by first class post on [   ]
and it will be deemed to be served on [   ].
The defendant has until [   ] to reply.

The defendant may either

- **Pay an amount into court to satisfy your claim.** This is called a 'payment in satisfaction'. The court will notify you of the payment and you will have to decide whether to accept the amount offered.
- **Offer to pay you an amount to satisfy your claim and/or ask for time to pay.** The court will send you a copy of the defendant's reply and you will have to decide what you want to do.
- **Admit liability for your claim but not offer an amount in satisfaction.** The court will send you a copy of the defendants's reply and you will be able to request judgment for amount to be decided by the court and costs.

In the	
The court office at	
is open between 10 am & 4 pm Monday to Friday Tel:	
Claim No.	
Claimant (including ref.)	
Defendant(s)	
Issue fee	£

- **File an acknowledgment of service.** This will allow the defendant 28 days from the date of service of your particulars of claim to file a defence or contest the court's jurisdiction. The court will send you a notice that an acknowledgment has been filed.
- **Dispute your claim.** The court will send you a copy of the defence and tell you what to do next.
- **Not reply at all.** You may ask the court to enter judgment for an amount to be decided by the court by completing the tear off portion on this form. A hearing will be arranged to determine the amount the defendant should pay you. **If you do not request judgment within 6 months of the date for filing a defence, your claim will be stayed. This means that the only action open to you would be to apply to a judge for an order lifting the stay.**

✂ --

Request for Judgment

Notes:

- The court will notify both you and the defendant of any steps you should take to prepare for the hearing at which the court will decide what amount you are entitled to.
- You should notify the court immediately if your claim is settled or you decide that you do not wish to proceed.

In the	
Claim No.	
Claimant (including ref)	
Defendant(s)	

To the court

The defendant has **not** filed an admission or defence to my claim, or an application to contest the court's jurisdiction and the time for doing so has expired.

I request that judgment be entered for an amount including costs, to be decided by the court.

Signed _____   Date _____

(Claimant)(Claimant's solicitor)(Litigation friend)

N205B Notice of Issue (unspecified amount) and request for judgment

APPENDIX 3   FORMS

Notice of Issue
(non-money claim)

In the	
Claim No.	
Claimant (including ref.)	
Defendant(s)	
Issue fee	£

To the Claimant ['s Solicitor]

Your claim was issued on [   ].

[The court sent it to the defendant by the first class post on [   ] and it will be deemed served on [   ]. The defendant has until [   ] to reply.]

[The claim form [which includes particulars of claim] is returned to you, with the relevant response forms for you to serve them on the defendant[s].]

Notes for guidance

- The claim form and the particulars of claim, if served separately, must be served on the defendant within 4 months of the date of issue (6 months if you are serving outside England and Wales). You may be able to apply to extend the time for serving the claim form but the application must generally be made before the 4-month or 6-month period expires.

- You must inform the court immediately if your claim is settled or discontinued.

The defendant may

- **admit the truth of the whole or any part of your claim.** The court will send you a copy of the defendant's admission and tell you what to do next.

- **file an acknowledgment of service.** This will allow the defendant 28 days from the date of service of your particulars of claim to file a defence or contest the court's jurisdiction.

- **dispute the whole claim.** The court will send you a copy of the defence.

- **not reply at all.** You may make an application to the court for judgment. A fee may be payable.

The court office at
is open between 10 am and 4 pm Monday to Friday. When corresponding with the court, please address forms or letters to the Court Manager and quote the claim number.
N205C Notice of Issue (non-money claim)

APPENDIX 3 FORMS

Claim Form
(CPR Part 8)

In the

Claim No.

Claimant

SEAL

Defendant(s)

Details of claim (see also overleaf)

Defendant's name and address

£

Court fee	
Solicitor's costs	
Issue date	

The court office at

is open between 10 am and 4 pm Monday to Friday. When corresponding with the court, please address forms or letters to the Court Manager and quote the claim number.

N208 Claim form (CPR Part 8)(4.99)

Printed on behalf of The Court Service

APPENDIX 3   FORMS

| | Claim No. | |

Details of claim (continued)

Statement of Truth
*(I believe)(The Claimant believes) that the facts stated in these particulars of claim are true.
* I am duly authorised by the claimant to sign this statement

Full name _____

Name of claimant's solicitor's firm _____

signed_____ position or office held_____
*(Claimant)(Litigation friend)(Claimant's solicitor) (if signing on behalf of firm or company)
*delete as appropriate

Claimant's or claimant's solicitor's address to which documents should be sent if different from overleaf. If you are prepared to accept service by DX, fax or e-mail, please add details.

APPENDIX 3 FORMS

Notes for claimant on completing a Part 8 claim form

- Please read all of these guidance notes before you begin completing the claim form. The notes follow the order in which information is required on the form.
- Court staff can help you fill in the claim form and give information about procedure once it has been issued. But they cannot give legal advice. If you need legal advice, for example, about the likely success of your claim or the evidence you need to prove it, you should contact a solicitor or a Citizens' Advice Bureau.
- If you are filling in the claim form by hand, please use black ink and write in block capitals.
- You must file any written evidence to support your claim either in or with the claim form. Your written evidence must be verified by a statement of truth.
- Copy the completed claim form, the defendant's notes for guidance and your written evidence so that you have one copy for yourself, one copy for the court and one copy for each defendant. Send or take the forms and evidence to the court office with the appropriate fee. The court will tell you how much this is.

Notes on completing the claim form

Heading

You must fill in the heading of the form to indicate whether you want the claim to be issued in a county court or in the High Court (The High Court means either a District Registry (attached to a county court) or the Royal Courts of Justice in London).

Use whichever of the following is appropriate:

'In the .... County Court'
(inserting the name of the court)

or

'In the High Court of Justice .... Division'
(inserting eg. 'Queen's Bench' or 'Chancery' as appropriate)
'.............................. District Registry'
(inserting the name of the District Registry)

or

'In the High Court of Justice .... Division,
(inserting eg. 'Queen's Bench' or 'Chancery' as appropriate)
Royal Courts of Justice'

Claimant and defendant details

As the person issuing the claim, you are called the 'claimant'; the person you are suing is called the 'defendant'. Claimants who are under 18 years old (unless otherwise permitted by the court) and patients within the meaning of the Mental Health Act 1983 must have a litigation friend to issue and conduct court proceedings on their behalf. Court staff will tell you more about what you need to do if this applies to you.

You must provide the following information about yourself **and** the defendant according to the capacity in which you are suing and in which the defendant is being sued. When suing or being sued as:-

an individual:

All known forenames and surname, whether Mr, Mrs, Miss, Ms or Other (e.g. Dr) and residential address **(including** postcode and telephone and any fax or e-mail number) in England and Wales. Where the defendant is a proprietor of a business, a partner in a firm or an individual sued in the name of a club or other unincorporated association, the address for service should be the usual or last known place of residence **or** principal place of business of the company, firm or club or other unincorporated association.

Where the individual is:

under 18 write '(a child by Mr Joe Bloggs his litigation friend)' after the child's name.

a patient within the meaning of the Mental Health Act 1983 write '(by Mr Joe Bloggs his litigation friend)' after the patient's name

trading under another name

you must add the words 'trading as' and the trading name e.g. 'Mr John Smith trading as Smith's Groceries'

suing or being sued in a representative capacity

you must say what that capacity is e.g. 'Mr Joe Bloggs as the representative of Mrs Sharon Bloggs (deceased)'.

suing or being sued in the name of a club or other unincorporated association

add the words 'suing/sued on behalf of' followed by the name of the club or other unincorporated association.

a firm

enter the name of the firm followed by the words 'a firm' e.g. 'Bandbox - a firm' and an address for service which is either a partner's residential address or the principal or last known place of business.

a corporation (other than a company)

enter the full name of the corporation and the address which is either its principal office **or** any other place where the corporation carries on activities and which has a real connection with the claim.

a company registered in England and Wales

enter the name of the company and an address which is either the company's registered office **or** any place of business that has a real, or the most, connection with the claim e.g. the shop where the goods were bought.

an overseas company (defined by s744 of the Companies Act 1985)

enter the name of the company and either the address registered under s691 of the Act **or** the address of the place of business having a real, or the most, connection with the claim.

N208A Notes for Claimant (CPR Part 8)(4.99)   *Printed on behalf of The Court Service*

Details of claim

Under this heading you must set out either
- the question(s) you wish the court to decide; **or**
- the remedy you are seeking and the legal basis for your claim; **and**
- if your claim is being made under a specific CPR Part or practice direction, you must state which.

Defendant's name and address

Enter in this box the full name and address of the defendant to be served with the claim form (i.e. one claim form for each defendant). If the defendant is to be served outside England and Wales, you may need to obtain the court's permission.

Address for documents

Insert in this box the address at which you wish to receive documents, if different from the address you have already given under the heading 'Claimant'. The address you give must be either that of your solicitors or your residential or business address and must be in England or Wales. If you live or carry on business outside of England and Wales, you can give some other address within England and Wales.

Statement of truth

This must be signed by you, by your solicitor or your litigation friend, as appropriate.

Where the claimant is a registered company or a corporation the claim must be signed by either the director, treasurer, secretary, chief executive, manager or other officer of the company or (in the case of a corporation) the mayor, chairman, president or town clerk.

APPENDIX 3   FORMS

Notes for defendant (Part 8 claim form)

Please read these notes carefully - they will help you to decide what to do about this claim.

- You have 14 days from the date on which you were served with the claim form (see below) in which to respond to the claim by completing and returning the acknowledgment of service enclosed with this claim form.
- If you **do not return** the acknowledgment of service, you will be allowed to attend any hearing of this claim but you will **not** be allowed to take part in the hearing unless the court gives you permission to do so.

Court staff can tell you about procedures but they cannot give legal advice. If you need legal advice, you should contact a solicitor or Citizens Advice Bureau immediately

Responding to this claim

Time for responding

The completed acknowledgment of service must be returned to the court office within 14 days of the date on which the claim form was served on you. If the claim form was

- sent by post, the 14 days begins 2 days from the date of the postmark on the envelope.
- delivered or left at your address, the 14 days begins the day after it was delivered.
- handed to you personally, the 14 days begins on the day it was given to you.

Completing the acknowledgment of service

You should complete section A, B, **or** C as appropriate **and all** of section D.

Section A - contesting the claim

If you wish to contest the remedy sought by the claimant in the claim form, you should complete section A. If you seek a remedy different from that sought by the claimant, you should give full details in the space provided.

Section B - disputing the court's jurisdiction

You should indicate your intention by completing section B and filing an application disputing the court's jurisdiction within 14 days of filing your acknowledgment of service at the court. The court will arrange a hearing date for the application and tell you and the claimant when and where to attend.

Section C - objecting to use of procedure

If you believe that the claimant should not have issued the claim under Part 8 because:

- there **is** a substantial dispute of fact involved and
- you do not agree that the rule or practice direction stated does provide for the claimant to use this procedure

you should complete section C setting out your reasons in the space provided.

Written evidence

If you wish to file written evidence in reply to the claimant's written evidence, you must send it to the court with your acknowledgment of service. Your written evidence must be verified by a statement of truth or the court may disallow it.

Serving other parties

At the same time as you file your completed acknowledgment of service (and any written evidence) with the court, you must also send copies of both the form and any written evidence to any other party named on the claim form.

What happens next

The claimant may, within 14 days of receiving any written evidence from you, file further evidence in reply. On receipt of your acknowledgment of service and any evidence from the claimant in reply, the court file will be referred to the judge for directions for the disposal of the claim. The court will contact you and tell you what to do next.

Note: The court may already have given directions or arranged a hearing. If so, you will have received a copy with the claim form. You should comply with any directions and attend any hearing in addition to completing, filing and serving your acknowledgment of service.

Statement of truth

This must be signed by you, by your solicitor or your litigation friend, as appropriate.

Where the claimant is a registered company or a corporation the claim must be signed by either the director, treasurer, secretary, chief executive, manager or other officer of the company or (in the case of a corporation) the mayor, chairman, president or town clerk.

N208C Notes for defendant (CPR Part 8) (4.99)   Printed on behalf of the Court Service

APPENDIX 3   FORMS

Notice of Issue
(Part 8 claim)

To the Claimant ['s Solicitor]

In the	
Claim No.	
Claimant (including ref.)	
Defendant(s)	
Issue fee	£

Your claim was issued under Part 8 of the CPR on [   ].

The court sent it with a copy of your witness statement(s) to the defendant by the first class post on [   ] and it will be deemed served on [   ]. The defendant has until [   ] to reply.

[As you requested the claim form is returned to you, with copy[ies] of your witness statement(s) for you to serve on the defendant[s]].

Notes for guidance

Service of the claim form
- The claim form must be served on the defendant within 4 months of the date of issue (6 months if you are serving outside England & Wales). You may apply for an order extending the time for serving the claim form but the application must generally be made before the 4-month or 6-month period expires.

Replying to the claim form
- the defendant must file an acknowledgment of service with the court together with any written evidence to be relied on within 14 days of service of the claim form. At the same time, the defendant must send copies to you and all other parties.
- if the defendant files written evidence, you will have 14 days from receiving it in which to file any further evidence in reply. You must at the same time send copies to all other parties to the claim.

The defendant may
- contest your claim and seek a remedy different from that sought by yourself
- object to your using this procedure and set out his reasons for doing so
- dispute the court's jurisdiction

What happens next
- the court file will be referred to a judge for directions for the disposal of the claim 14 days after the expiry of the time for filing the acknowledgment of service
- the file will not be referred if the court has already arranged a hearing date or given directions

Failure to reply
- if an acknowledgment of service is not filed, the defendant may attend any hearing in the claim but may not take part at the hearing unless the court gives permission.

You must inform the court immediately if your claim is settled or discontinued.

The court office at
is open between 10 am and 4 pm Monday to Friday. When corresponding with the court, please address forms or letters to the Court Manager and quote the claim number.

N209 Notice of Issue (CPR Part 8) (4.99)   *Printed on behalf of The Court Service*

1274

Acknowledgment of Service
(Part 8 claim)

In the	
Claim No.	
Claimant (including ref)	
Defendant	

You should read the 'notes for defendant' attached to the claim form which will tell you when and where to send this form.

If you wish to contest the claim	complete section **A**
If you wish to dispute the court's jurisdiction	complete section **B**
If you believe the claimant should not have used this procedure	complete section **C**

A

☐ I intend to contest this claim

  And (if applicable) I also seek the following different remedy to that claimed by the claimant:

B

☐ I intend to dispute jurisdiction
  (you should file your application within 14 days of the date on which you file this acknowledgment of service with the court)

The court office at
is open between 10 am and 4 pm Monday to Friday. When corresponding with the court, please address forms or letters to the Court Manager and quote the claim number.

N210 Acknowledgment of Service (CPR Part 8) (4.99) — Printed on behalf of The Court Service

APPENDIX 3 FORMS

| | Claim No. | |

C

☐ I object to the claimant issuing under this procedure

And my reasons for objecting are:

D

Signed
(To be signed by you or by your solicitor or litigation friend)

*(I believe)(The defendant believes) that the facts stated in this form are true. *I am duly authorised by the defendant to sign this statement

delete as appropriate

Position or office held
(if signing on behalf of firm or company)

Date

Give an address to which notices about this case can be sent

Postcode

Tel. no.

if applicable

fax no.

DX no.

e-mail

1276

APPENDIX 3   FORMS

Claim Form
(Additional claims - CPR Part 20)

In the

Claim No.

Claimant(s)

Defendant(s)

Part 20 Claimant(s)

Part 20 Defendant(s)

Brief details of claim

Value

SEAL

Defendant's name and address

	£
Amount claimed	
Court fee	
Solicitor's costs	
Total amount	
Issue date	

The court office at

is open between 10 am and 4 pm Monday to Friday. When corresponding with the court, please address forms or letters to the Court Manager and quote the claim number.

N211 Claim Form (CPR Part 20)(4.99)   *Printed on behalf of The Court Service*

APPENDIX 3   FORMS

	Claim No.

Particulars of Claim (attached)

Statement of Truth
*(I believe)(The Part 20 Claimant believes) that the facts stated in these particulars of claim are true.
* I am duly authorised by the Part 20 claimant to sign this statement

Full name _____

Name of Part 20 claimant's solicitor's firm _____

signed _____ position or office held _____
*(Part 20 Claimant)('s solicitor)(Litigation friend) (if signing on behalf of firm or company)
*delete as appropriate

Part 20 Claimant ('s solicitor's) address to which documents or payments should be sent if different from overleaf. If you are prepared to accept service by DX, fax or e-mail, please add details.

APPENDIX 3   FORMS

Notes for Part 20 claimant on completing a Part 20 claim form

- Please read all of these guidance notes before you begin completing the claim form. The notes follow the order in which information is required on the form. Unless you issue your Part 20 claim before or at the same time as filing your defence to the main claim, (in other words the claim being brought against you as defendant) you will first need to obtain the court's permission to do so.
- Court staff can help you fill in the claim form and give information about procedure once it has been issued. But they cannot give legal advice. If you need legal advice, for example about the likely success of your claim or the evidence you need to prove it, you should contact a solicitor or a Citizens Advice Bureau.
- If you are filling in the claim form by hand, please use black ink and write in block capitals.
- When you have completed the claim form, copy the claim form and the defendant's notes for guidance so that you have one copy for yourself, one copy for the court, one copy for the Part 20 defendant and a copy for each of the other parties to the main claim. Send or take the forms to the court office with the appropriate fee, the court will tell you how much this is.
- Unless the court has ordered otherwise, the Part 20 defendant should be served with the claim form within 14 days of your defence being filed, together with copies of all the statements of case filed in the main claim. The parties to the main claim must also at the same time be served with copies of the Part 20 claim form and particulars of claim, if these are separate from the claim.
- The defendant is added as a party to the main claim once served with the Part 20 claim form

Notes on completing the claim form

Heading

The name of the court and the claim number will be the same as on the claim form in the main claim. You should copy those details on to your Part 20 claim form.

Claimant and defendant details

You should copy the claimant and defendant details from the main claim in to the claimant and defendant boxes. You should enter your name in to the Part 20 claimant box and the name of the person you are claiming against in to the Part 20 defendant box. Claimants who are under 18 years old (unless otherwise permitted by the court), and patients within the meaning of the Mental Health Act 1983 must have a litigation friend to issue and conduct court proceedings on their behalf. Court staff will tell you more about what you need to do if this applies to you.

You must provide the following information about yourself **and** the Part 20 defendant according to the capacity in which you are suing and in which the defendant is being sued.
When suing or being sued as:-

an individual:

All known forenames and surname, whether Mr, Mrs, Miss, Ms or Other (e.g. Dr) and residential address (**including** postcode, telephone and any fax or e-mail number) in England and Wales. Where the defendant is a proprietor of a business, a partner in a firm or an individual sued in the name of a club or other unincorporated association, the address for service should be the usual or last known place of residence **or** principal place of business of the company, firm or club or other unincorporated association.

Where the individual is:

under 18 write '(a child by Mr Joe Bloggs his litigation friend)' after the child's name.

a patient within the meaning of the Mental Health Act 1983 write '(by Mr Joe Bloggs his litigation friend)' after the patient's name

trading under another name

you must also add the words 'trading as' and the trading name e.g. 'Mr John Smith trading as Smith's Groceries'.

suing or being sued in a representative capacity

you must say what that capacity is e.g. 'Mr Joe Bloggs as the representative of Mrs Sharon Bloggs (deceased)'.

suing or being sued in the name of a club or other unincorporated association

add the words 'suing/sued on behalf of' followed by the name of the club or other unincorporated association.

a firm

enter the name of the firm followed by the words 'a firm' e.g. 'Bandbox - a firm' and an address for service which is either a partner's residential address or the principal or last known place of business.

a corporation (other than a company)

enter the full name of the corporation and the address which is either its principal office **or** any other place where the corporation carries on activities and which has a real connection with the claim.

a company registered in England and Wales

enter the name of the company and an address which is either the company's registered office **or** any place of business that has a real, or the most, connection with the claim e.g. the shop where the goods were bought.

an overseas company (defined by s744 of the Companies Act 1985)

enter the name of the company and either the address registered under s691 of the Act **or** the address of the place of business having a real, or the most, connection with the claim.

N211A Notes for claimant (CPR Part 20) (4.99)   *Printed on behalf of The Court Service*

APPENDIX 3   FORMS

Brief details of claim

Note: The facts and full details about your claim and whether or not you are claiming interest, should be set out in the 'particulars of claim' *(see note under 'Particulars of Claim').*
You must set out under **this** heading:
- a concise statement of the nature of your claim
- the remedy you are seeking

Value

Note:-
If you are issuing your Part 20 claim in the High Court, you do not have to give a statement of value.

If you are issuing in the county court and claiming a fixed amount of money (a 'specified amount') write the amount in the box at the bottom right-hand corner of the claim form against 'amount claimed'.

If you are not claiming a fixed amount of money (an 'unspecified amount') under 'Value' write "I expect to recover" followed by whichever of the following applies to your claim:
- "not more than £5,000" **or**
- "more than £5,000 but not more than £15,000"**or**
- "more than £15,000"

If your claim is for 'not more than £5,000' and includes a claim for **personal injuries**, you must also write "My claim includes a claim for personal injuries and the amount I expect to recover as damages for pain, suffering and loss of amenity is" followed by either:
- "not more than £1,000" **or**
- "more than £1,000"

If your claim is for 'not more than £5,000' and includes a claim for **housing disrepair** relating to residential premises, you must also write "My claim includes a claim against my landlord for housing disrepair relating to residential premises. The costs of the repairs and other work is estimated to be" followed by either:
- "not more than £1,000" **or**
- "more than £1,000"

"I expect to recover as damages in respect of repairs and other work" followed by either:
- "not more than £1,000" **or**
- "more than £1,000"

If you are not able to put a value on your claim, write "I cannot say how much I expect to recover".

Defendant's name and address

Enter in this box the full names and address of the Part 20 defendant receiving the claim form (i.e. one claim form for each Part 20 defendant) If the defendant is to be served outside of England and Wales, you may need to obtain the court's permission.

Particulars of claim

You may include your particulars of claim on the claim form in the space provided or in a separate document which you should head 'Particulars of Claim'. It should include the names of the parties, the court, the claim number and your address for service and also contain a statement of truth. You should keep a copy for yourself, provide one for the court, one for each defendant and one for all other parties in the main claim. Separate particulars of claim **must** be served with the claim form. You should also attach copies of all statements of case already served in the main claim for service on the defendant.

Your particulars of claim must include
- a concise statement of the facts on which you rely
- a statement (if applicable) to the effect that you are seeking aggravated damages or exemplary damages
- details of any interest which you are claiming
- any other matters required for your type of claim as set out in the relevant practice direction

Address for documents

Insert in this box the address at which you wish to receive documents and/or payments, if different from the address you have already given under the heading 'Claimant'. The address you give must be either that of your solicitors or your residential or business address and must be in England or Wales. If you live or carry on business outside England and Wales, you can give some other address within England and Wales.

Statement of truth

This must be signed by you, by your solicitor or your litigation friend, as appropriate.
Where the claimant is a registered company or a corporation the claim must be signed by either the director, treasurer, secretary, chief executive, manager or other officer of the company or (in the case of a corporation) the mayor, chairman, president or town clerk.

APPENDIX 3   FORMS

Notes for defendant on replying to the Part 20 claim form

Please read these notes carefully - they will help you decide what to do about this claim.

- You must reply to this claim form within 14 days of the date it was served on you. If the claim was
  - sent by post, the date of service is taken as the second day after posting (see post mark).
  - delivered or left at your address, the date of service will be the day after it was delivered.
  - handed to you personally, the 14 days begins on the day it was given to you.
- You may either
  - pay the amount claimed
  - admit the truth of all or part of the claim or
  - dispute the claim
- If you do not reply, the court will consider that you have admitted the claim and judgment may be entered against you.
- The notes below tell you what to do and which forms to use for your reply.
- Court staff can help you complete the forms of reply and tell you about court procedures. But they cannot give legal advice. If you need legal advice, for example about the likely success of disputing the claim, you should contact a solicitor or a Citizens Advice Bureau immediately.

Registration of Judgments: If the claim results in a judgment being made against you in a **county court**, your name and address may be entered in the Register of County Court Judgments. This may make it difficult for you to obtain credit.
Costs and Interest: Additional costs and interest may be added to the amount claimed on the front of the claim form if judgment is entered against you. In a county court, if judgment is for £5,000 or more, or is in respect of a debt which attracts contractual or statutory interest for late payment, the claimant may be entitled to further interest.

Your response and what happens next

How to pay
Do not bring any payments to the court - they will not be accepted.

When making payments to the claimant, quote the claimant's reference (if any) and the claim number.

Make sure that you keep records and can account for any payments made. Proof may be required if there is any disagreement. It is not safe to send cash unless you use registered post.

Admitting the Claim
Claim for a specified amount
Complete Form N9A and send it to the claimant at the address given for payment on the claim form within 14 days. You should at the same time send a copy to all the other parties to the main claim (in other words the claim where the Part 20 claimant is the defendant).
Claim for an unspecified amount
Complete Form N9C and send it to the court within 14 days. A copy will be sent to the claimant.
What happens next
The claimant may apply to the court for judgment to be entered on your admission. The court will arrange a hearing and tell you and the claimant where and when to attend.

Disputing the claim
Complete the form of defence (either N9B if the claim is for a specified amount or N9D if the claim is for an unspecified amount) and return it to the court within 14 days. On receipt of your defence, the court will arrange a hearing and tell you and the claimant when and where to attend. At the hearing the judge will usually give directions as to the future case management of the claim but may make any other order, e.g. striking out all or part of a statement of case.

If you need longer than 14 days to prepare your defence, complete the acknowledgment of service Form N212 and return it to the court. This will allow you 28 days from the date of service of the claim form to file your defence.

Contesting the court's jurisdiction
Complete the acknowledgment of service Form N212 and return it to the court within 14 days. You should make an application to the court within 28 days of service of the claim. An application form (N244) can be obtained from the court and a fee may be payable.

If you do nothing
If you do nothing or you send an acknowledgment of service to the court but fail to send your defence, you will be considered to have admitted the claim and be bound by any judgment or decision made in the main claim where it relates to this claim against you.

Statement of truth
This must be signed by you, by your solicitor or your litigation friend, as appropriate.

Where the defendant is **a registered company or a corporation** the response must be signed by either the director, treasurer, secretary, chief executive, manager or other officer of the company **or** (in the case of a corporation) the mayor, chairman, president or town clerk.

N211C Notes for defendant (CPR Part 20) (4.99)   *Printed on behalf of The Court*

APPENDIX 3   FORMS

Notice of Issue
(Part 20 claim)

In the	
Claim No.	
Claimant (including ref.)	
Defendant(s) (including ref.)	
Part 20 Claimant (including ref.)	
Part 20 Defendant(s)	
Issue fee	£

To the Claimant ['s Solicitor]

Your Part 20 claim was issued on [   ].

The court sent it and accompanying papers to the defendant by the first class post on [   ] and it will be deemed served on [   ]. The defendant has until [   ] to reply.

[As you requested the claim form [which includes particulars of claim] is returned to you, [with the relevant response forms] for you to serve them on the defendants[s]. You must also serve copies of any statements of case already filed in the main claim.]

Notes for guidance

Service
- The claim form must be served on the Part 20 defendant within 14 days of filing your defence to the main claim unless the court has directed otherwise.

Entering default judgment
- you will need the court's permission to enter judgment in default if you have **not** satisfied any default judgment against you in the main claim **or** you wish to obtain judgment for any remedy other than a contribution or an indemnity

The defendant may
- **admit the truth of the whole or any part of your claim.** You may apply to the court for judgment to be entered on the admission.
- **dispute all or part of your claim.** The court will arrange a hearing and tell you and the other parties to the claim when and where to attend. At the hearing the judge will usually give directions about the future case management of the claim but may make any other order considered appropriate, e.g. striking out all or part of a statement of case.
- **not reply at all.** The defendant will be considered to have admitted your claim and be bound by any judgment or decision made in the main claim where it relates to this claim.

You must inform the court immediately if your claim is settled or discontinued.

The court office at
is open between 10 am and 4 pm Monday to Friday. When corresponding with the court, please address forms or letters to the Court Manager and quote the claim number.
N212 Notice of Issue (CPR Part 20 claim)   *Printed on behalf of The Court Service*

APPENDIX 3 FORMS

Acknowledgment of Service (Part 20 claim)	In the	
Defendant's full name if different from the name given on the claim form	Claim No.	
	Claimant (including ref.)	
	Defendant(s) (including ref.)	
	Part 20 Claimant (including ref.)	
	Part 20 Defendant(s)	

Address to which documents about this claim should be sent (including reference if appropriate)

		if applicable
	fax no.	
	DX no.	
Tel. no. Postcode	e-mail	

Tick the appropriate box

1. I intend to defend all of this claim ☐
2. I intend to defend part of this claim ☐
3. I intend to contest jurisdiction ☐

If you file an acknowledgment of service but do not file a defence within 28 days of the date of service of the claim form, you will be considered to have admitted the claim and will be bound by any judgment entered against the Part 20 claimant in the main claim.

If you do not file an application within 28 days of the date of service of the claim form it will be assumed that you accept the court's jurisdiction and judgment may be entered against you.

Signed _____
(Defendant)(Defendant's Solicitor)
(Litigation friend)

Position or office held _____
(if signing on behalf of firm or company)

Date _____

The court office at
is open between 10 am and 4 pm Monday to Friday. When corresponding with the court, please address forms or letters to the Court Manager and quote the claim number.

N213 Acknowledgment of Service (CPR Part 20) (4.99)   *Printed on behalf of The Court Service*

APPENDIX 3   FORMS

Certificate of Service	**In the**	
	Claim No.	
	Claimant	
	Defendant	

On the .... *(insert date)*

the .... *(insert title or description of documents served)*

a copy of which is attached to this notice was served on *(insert name of person served, including position i.e. partner, director if appropriate)*

....

Tick as appropriate

☐ by first class post   ☐ by Document Exchange

☐ by delivering to or leaving   ☐ by handing it to or leaving it with [ ]

☐ by fax machine (..................time sent)
(you may want to enclose a copy of the transmission sheet)

☐ by e-mail

☐ by other means *(please specify)* [ ]

at *(insert address where service effected, include fax or DX number or e-mail address)*

[ ]

being the defendant's:

☐ residence   ☐ registered office

☐ place of business   ☐ other *(please specify)* ....

The date of service is therefore deemed to be .... *(insert date - see over for guidance)*

I confirm that at the time of signing this Certificate the document has not been returned to me as undelivered.

Signed ....
         (Claimant)(Defendant)('s Solicitor)('s Litigation friend)

Position or office held ....
(if signing on behalf of firm or company)

Date ....

N215 Certificate of Service (4.99)   *Printed on behalf on The Court Service*

APPENDIX 3 FORMS

Notes for guidance
Please note that these notes are only a guide and are not exhaustive
If you are in doubt you should refer to Part 6 of the rules

Where to serve

Nature of party to be served	Place of service
Individual	• usual or last known residence
Proprietor of business	• usual or last known residence; or • place of business or last known place of business
Individual who is suing or being sued in the name of a firm	• usual or last known residence; or • principal or last known place of business of the firm
Corporation (incorporated in England and Wales) other than a company	• principal office of the corporation; or • any place of within the jurisdiction where the corporation carries on its activities and which has a real connection with the claim
Company registered in England and Wales	• principal office of the company or corporation; or • any place of business of the company within the jurisdiction which has a real connection with the claim

Personal Service A document is served personally on an individual by leaving it with that individual. A document is served personally on a company or other corporation by leaving it with a person holding a senior position within the company or corporation. In the case of a partnership, you must leave it with either a partner or a person having control or management at the principal place of business. Where a solicitor is authorised to accept service on behalf of a party, service must be effected on the solicitor, unless otherwise ordered.

Deemed Service Part 6.7(1). A document which is served in accordance with these rules or any relevant practice direction shall be deemed to be served on the day shown in the following table.

Method of service	Deemed day of service
First class post	The second day after it was posted
Document exchange	The second day after it was left at the document exchange
Delivering the document to or leaving it at a permitted address	The day after it was delivered to or left at the permitted address
Fax	If it is transmitted on a business day before 4pm., on that day, or otherwise on the business day after the day on which it was transmitted.
Other electronic method	The second day after the day on which it was transmitted.

- If a document (other than a claim form) is served after 5 p.m. on a business day, or at any time on a Saturday, Sunday or a bank holiday, the document shall, for the purpose of calculating any period of time after service of the document, be treated as having been served on the next business day.

- In this context "business day" means any day except Saturday, Sunday or a bank holiday; and "bank holiday" includes Christmas Day and Good Friday.

Service of documents on children and patients - The rules relating to service on children and patients are contained in Part 6.6 of the rules.

Claim Forms - The general rules about service are subject to the special rules about service of claim forms contained in rules 6.12 to 6.16.

Note
In the column headed 'Place of service', the second point against 'Corporation . . .' should read: 'any place of business within the jurisdiction . . .'.

APPENDIX 3   FORMS

Notice of Service on Partner

In the	
Claim No.	
Claimant (including ref.)	
Defendant	

The (claim form) (particulars of claim) served with this notice (is) (are) served on you

(tick only one box)

☐ as a partner of the business

☐ as a person having control or management of the partnership business

☐ as both a partner and as a person having control or management of the partnership business

named in the claim form (particulars of claim).

Signed _____   **Date** _____
   Claimant ('s solicitor)

N218 Notice of Service on Partner (4.99)   *Printed on behalf of The Court Service*

APPENDIX 3   FORMS

Request for Judgment and reply to Admission (specified amount)

In the	
Claim No.	
Claimant (including ref)	
Defendant (including ref)	

- Tick box A or B. If you tick box B you must complete the details in that part and in part C. Make sure that all the case details are given. Remember to sign and date the form. Your signature certifies that the information you have given is correct.
- If the defendant has given an address on the form of admission to which correspondence should be sent, which is different from the address shown on the claim form, you must tell the court.
- Return the completed form to the court.

A ☐ **The defendant has not filed an admission or defence to my claim**

Complete all the judgment details at C. Decide how and when you want the defendant to pay. You can ask for the judgment to be paid by instalments or in one payment.

B ☐ **The defendant admits that all the money is owed**

Tick only **one** box below and complete all the judgment details at C.

☐ **I accept the defendant's proposal for payment**

Say how the defendant intends to pay. The court will send the defendant an order to pay. You will also be sent a copy.

☐ **The defendant has not made any proposal for payment**

Say how you want the defendant to pay. You can ask for the judgment to be paid by instalments or in one payment. The court will send the defendant an order to pay. You will also be sent a copy.

☐ **I do NOT accept the defendant's proposal for payment**

Say how you want the defendant to pay. Give your reasons for objecting to the defendant's offer of payment in the space opposite. (Continue on the back of this form if necessary.) Send this form to the court **with defendant's admission N9A**. The court will fix a rate of payment and send the defendant an order to pay. You will also be sent a copy.

C Judgment details

I would like the judgment to be paid

☐ (immediately)

☐ (by instalments of £ _____ per month)

☐ (in full by _____)

Amount of claim as admitted (including interest at date of issue) ....

Interest since date of claim (if any) ....

Period from .... to ....

Rate .... %

Court fees shown on claim

Solicitor's costs (if any) on issuing claim

Sub Total

Solicitor's costs (if any) on entering judgment

Sub Total

Deduct amount (if any) paid since issue

Amount payable by defendant

I certify that the information given is correct

Signed _____ **Position or office held** _____

(Claimant)(Claimant's Solicitor)(Litigation friend)   (if signing on behalf of firm or company)

Date _____

The court office at

is open between 10 am and 4 pm Monday to Friday. When corresponding with the court, please address forms and letters to the Court Manager and quote the Claim number.

N225 Request for Judgment and reply to Admission (specified amount) (4.99)   *Printed on behalf of The Court Service*

Notice of Part Admission (specified amount)

To the Claimant['s Solicitor]

In the	
Claim No.	
Claimant (including ref)	
Defendant (including ref)	
Date	

The defendant has partly admitted your claim (see the attached forms N9A and N9B).

- **Please tell the court what you wish to do by completing the lower half of this form and returning it to the court on or before [ ]** At the same time you must send a copy to the defendant. If you do not return this form to the court by the date shown, your claim will be stayed. No further action will be taken by the court until the form is received.
- You must tick box A or B. If you tick box B you must also complete the details in that part and part C.
- Remember to sign and date the notice.

A ☐ **I DO NOT accept the defendant's part admission**

If you tick this box the claim will proceed as a defended claim. If the defendant is an individual and lives in, or the defendant's solicitor's business is in, another court's area, the claim may be transferred to that court. You and the defendant will be sent an allocation questionnaire and the date by which it must be returned to the court. The information you give will help a judge decide whether your case should be dealt with in the small claims, fast or multi-track. Leaflets telling you more about the tracks are available from the court office. You will be sent a notice of allocation setting out the judge's decision.

B ☐ **I ACCEPT the amount admitted by the defendant in satisfaction of my claim**

Tick only **one** box and follow the instructions given.

☐ **I accept the defendant's proposal for payment**
Complete all the judgment details at C. The court will enter judgment in accordance with the offer and will send the defendant an order to pay. You will also be sent a copy.

☐ **The defendant has not made any proposal for payment**
Complete all the judgment details at C. Say how you want the defendant to pay. You can ask for the judgment to be paid by instalments or in one payment. The court will send the defendant an order to pay. You will also be sent a copy.

☐ **I do NOT accept the defendant's proposal for payment**
Complete all the judgment details at C and say how you want the defendant to pay. Give your reasons for objecting to the defendant's offer of payment in the space opposite. (Continue on the back of this form if necessary.) The court will fix a rate of payment and send the defendant an order to pay. You will also be sent a copy.

C Judgment details

I would like the judgment to be paid

☐ (immediately)
☐ (by instalments of £   per month)
☐ (in full by   )

Amount of claim as admitted	
Court fees entered on claim	
Solicitor's costs (if any) on issuing claim	
Sub Total	
Solicitor's costs (if any) on entering judgment	
Sub Total	
Deduct amount (if any) paid since issue	
Amount payable by defendant	

I certify that the information given is correct

Signed .... Dated ....

N225A Notice of Part Admission (specified amount)

APPENDIX 3   FORMS

Notice of Admission
(unspecified amount)

To the Claimant['s Solicitor]

In the	
Claim No.	
Claimant (including ref)	
Defendant (including ref)	
Date	

Important notes for claimant

- Enclosed with this notice is a copy of the defendant's admission of your claim (Form N9C).
- You must tick either A or C **or** complete B and D and return the form to the court **on or before** [   ]. At the same time you must send a copy to the defendant. If you do not return the form by this date, your claim will be stayed. No further action will be taken by the court until the form is received.
- Remember to sign and date the notice.

A ☐ **I DO NOT accept the amount offered by the defendant in satisfaction of my claim. I wish judgment to be entered for an amount to be decided by the court.**

The court will enter judgment and refer the court file to a judge for directions for management of the case. You and the defendant will be sent a copy of the court's order.

B ☐ **I ACCEPT the amount admitted by the defendant in satisfaction of my claim**

Tick only **one** box and follow the instructions given.

☐ **I accept the defendant's proposal for payment**

Complete all the judgment details at D. The court will enter judgment in accordance with the offer and will send the defendant an order to pay. You will also be sent a copy.

☐ **I do NOT accept the defendant's proposal for payment**

Complete all the judgment details at D and say how you want the defendant to pay. Give your reasons for objecting to the defendant's offer of payment in the space opposite. (Continue on the back of this form if necessary.) The court will fix a rate of payment and send the defendant an order to pay. You will also be sent a copy.

C ☐ **The defendant has admitted liability but has not made any proposal for payment**

The court will enter judgment and refer the court file to a judge for directions for management of the case. You and the defendant will be sent a copy of the court's order.

D   Judgment details

If you are not accepting the defendant's proposal for payment, say how you would like judgment to be paid.

I would like the judgment to be paid

☐ (immediately)

☐ (by instalments of £   per month)

☐ (in full by   )

Enter amounts as shown   £

Amount of offer ....

Court fees entered on claim ....

Solicitor's costs (if any) on issuing claim

Solicitor's costs (if any) on entering judgment

                                                Sub Total

Deduct amount (if any) paid since issue

                        Balance payable by defendant

I certify that the information given is correct

Signed ....   Date ....

N226 Notice of Admission (unspecified amount)

APPENDIX 3 FORMS

Request for Judgment by Default
(amount to be decided by the court)

In the	
Claim No.	
Claimant (including ref)	
Defendant	

To the court

The defendant has not filed [an acknowledgment of service][a defence] to my claim and the time for doing so has expired.

I request judgment to be entered against the defendant for an amount to be decided by the court and costs.

Signed _____

(Claimant)(Claimant's Solicitor)(Litigation friend)

Position or office held _____
(if signing on behalf of firm or company)

Date _____

Note: The court will enter judgment and refer the court file to a judge who will give directions for the management of the case including its allocation to track.

The Court Manager

The court office at
is open between 10 am and 4 pm Monday to Friday. When corresponding with the court, please address forms or letters to the Court Manager and quote the claim number.

N227 Request for Judgment by Default (amount to be decided by the court)(4.99) Printed on behalf of The Court Service

Notice of Admission – Return of Goods
(hire-purchase or conditional sale)

To the Claimant['s solicitor]

In the	
Claim No.	
Claimant (including ref)	
Defendant (including ref)	
Date	

Enclosed with this notice is a copy of the defendant's admission of your claim
- Tick and complete either A or B and make sure that the judgment details at C are completed.
- Remember to sign and date the form. Your signature certifies that the information you have given is correct.
- Return the form to the court within 14 days.

A ☐ I DO NOT accept the amount admitted by the defendant in satisfaction of my claim

You should attend court on the day fixed for the hearing. If you do not attend, an order may be made in your absence.

B ☐ I ACCEPT the amount admitted by the defendant in satisfaction of my claim

Tick only **one** box below and follow the instructions given.

☐ **I accept the defendant's proposal for payment**
Complete all the judgment details at C. The court will make an order under sections 133 and 135 of the Consumer Credit Act 1974 for the return of the goods, suspended in accordance with the offer.
You will not have to attend court on the day fixed for the hearing.

☐ **The defendant has not made any proposal for payment**
Complete all the judgment details at C. Say how you want the defendant to pay. You can ask for the judgment to be paid by instalments or in one payment. The court will send the defendant an order to pay. You will also be sent a copy.

☐ **I do NOT accept the defendant's proposal for payment**
Complete all the judgment details at C and say how you want the defendant to pay. Give your reasons for objecting to the defendant's offer of payment in the space opposite. (Continue on the back of this form if necessary.) The court will fix a rate of payment and send the defendant an order to pay. You will also be sent a copy.

C Judgement details

If you are not accepting the defendant's offer, say how you would like the judgement to be paid.

I would like the judgment to be paid

☐ (immediately)

☐ (by instalments of £ .... per month)

☐ (in full by ....)

List goods to be returned ....

Enter amounts as shown
Amount of the unpaid balance of total price as stated in the claim .... £

Deduct amount (if any) paid since issue ....

Balance of total price

Court fees entered on claim ....

Solicitor's costs (if any) on issuing claim ....

Solicitors's costs (if any) on entering judgment ....

Total of fees and solicitor's costs

I certify that the information given is correct

Signed .... Date ....

N228 Notice of Admission – Return of Goods (hire-purchase or conditional sale agreement)

Certificate of Suitability of Litigation Friend

If you are acting
- **for a child**, you must serve a copy of the completed form on a parent or guardian of the child, or if there is no parent or guardian, the carer or the person with whom the child lives
- **for a patient**, you must serve a copy of the completed form on the person authorised under Part VII of the Mental Health Act 1983 or, if no person is authorised, the carer or person with whom the patient lives unless you **are** that person. You must also complete a certificate of service (obtainable from the court office)

You should send the completed form to the court with the claim form (if acting for the claimant) or when you take the first step on the defendant's behalf in the claim together with the certificate of service (if applicable)

In the	
Claim No.	
Claimant (including ref.)	
Defendant (including ref.)	

You do not need to complete this form if you do have an authorisation under Part VII of the Mental Health Act 1983 to conduct legal proceedings on the person's behalf.

I consent to act as litigation friend for (claimant)(defendant)

I believe that the above named person is a

☐ child   ☐ patient *(give your reasons overleaf and attach a copy of any medical evidence in support)*

I am able to conduct proceedings on behalf of the above named person competently and fairly and I have no interests adverse to those of the above named person.

*delete if you are acting for the defendant

'I undertake to pay any costs which the above named claimant may be ordered to pay in these proceedings subject to any right I may have to be repaid from the assets of the claimant.

Please write your name in capital letters

☐ Mr   ☐ Mrs   ☐ Miss   Surname ....
☐ Ms   ☐ Other _____   Forenames ....

Address to which documents in this case are to be sent.

I certify that the information given in this form is correct

Signed .... Date ....

The court office at
is open between 10 am and 4 pm Monday to Friday. When corresponding with the court, please address forms or letters to the Court Manager and quote the claim number.
N235 Certificate of Suitability of Litigation Friend (4.99)   *Printed on behalf of The Court Service*

APPENDIX 3   FORMS

| | Claim No. | |

My reasons for believing that the (claimant)(defendant) is a patient are:-

APPENDIX 3   FORMS

Notice of Defence that Amount claimed has been paid	**In the**	
	Claim No.	
To the Claimant ['s Solicitor]	**Claimant** (including ref.)	
	Defendant (including ref.)	

The defendant says that the amount you are claiming has been paid (see attached Form N9B).

Please tell the court what you wish to do by completing the lower half of this form and returning it to the court on or before [   ]. You must send a copy of the completed form to the defendant as well as to the court.

- If you disagree with the defendant and wish to proceed with your claim, the court will contact you and tell you what to do next. If the defendant is an individual and lives in, or the defendant's solicitor's business is in, another court's area, the claim may be transferred to that court.
- If you do not return this form to the court by the date shown, your claim will be stayed. The only action which you will be able to take will be to apply to a judge for an order lifting the stay. A fee is payable on the application.

Claimant's reply	**In the**	
	Claim No.	
To the court	**Claimant** (including ref.)	
I have read Form N9B and	**Defendant** (including ref.)	
please tick 1 or 2 and 3		

1. ☐ I wish to proceed with the claim

    or

2. ☐ I do not wish to proceed with the claim.

    and

3. ☐ I have sent a copy of this completed form to the defendant.

Signed		Position or office held	
	(Claimant)(Claimant's Solicitor)(Litigation friend)	(if signing on behalf of firm or company)	
Date			

The court office at
is open between 10 am and 4 pm Monday to Friday. Address all communication to the Court Manager quoting the claim number
N236 Notice of Defence that Amount Claimed has been Paid - Claimant's Reply

APPENDIX 3   FORMS

Notice of Payment into court (in settlement - Part 36)	**In the**

Claim No.	
Claimant (including ref)	
Defendant (including ref)	

To the Claimant ('s Solicitor)

Take notice the defendant _____ has paid £ _____ (a further amount of £ _____) into court in settlement of
(tick as appropriate)

☐ the whole of your claim
☐ part of your claim *(give details below)*
☐ a certain issue or issues in your claim *(give details below)*

The (part) (issue or issues) to which it relates is(are):*(give details)*

☐ It is in addition to the amount of £_____ already paid into court on
☐ It is not inclusive of interest and an additional amount of £ _____ is offered for interest *(give details of the rate(s) and period(s) for which the amount of interest is offered.)*

☐ It takes into account all(part) of the following counterclaim:*(give details of the party and the part of the counterclaim to which the payment relates)*

☐ It takes into account the interim payment(s) made in the following amount(s) on the following date(s): *(give details)*

Note: This notice will need to be modified where an offer of provisional damages is made (CPR Part 36.7) and/or where it is made in relation to a mixed (money and non-money) claim in settlement of the whole claim (CPR Part 36.4).

242A Notice of payment into court (in settlement) (4.99)   The Court Service Publications Unit

APPENDIX 3 FORMS

For cases where the Social Security (Recovery of Benefits) Act 1997 applies

The gross amount of the compensation payment is £ _____

The defendant has reduced this sum by £ _____ in accordance with section 8 of and Schedule 2 to the Social Security (Recovery of Benefits) Act 1997, which was calculated as follows:

Type of Benefit	Amount

The amount paid into court is the net amount after deduction of the amount of benefit.

Signed _____
Defendant('s solicitor)

Position held _____
(If signing on behalf of a firm or company)

Date _____

242A Notice of payment into court (in settlement) (4.99)　　　　The Court Service Publications Unit

APPENDIX 3   FORMS

Notice of acceptance of payment into court (Part 36)

In the	
Claim No.	
Claimant (including ref.)	
Defendant (including ref.)	

Note: to the claimant
If you wish to accept the payment made into court without needing the court's permission you should:
- send this completed notice to the defendant not more than 21 days after you received this notice
- and at the same time send a copy to the court

Delete as appropriate I accept the payment into court in settlement of (the whole of)(part of)*(certain issue(s) in)* my claim set out in the notice of payment into court received on   *(insert date)*

I declare that:-

☐ it is not more than 21 days since I received the notice of payment into court
or
☐ it is more than 21 days since I received the notice and I have agreed the following costs provisions with the other party(ies) *(give details below)*
or
☐ the defendant's payment was made less than 21 days before the start of the trial and I have agreed the following costs provisions with the other party(ies) *(give details below)*

And I request payment of the money held in court to be made to

claimant's (solicitor's) full name and address (and ref)

name and address of bank   sort code

title of account   account number

Signed   Position held
                                                            (If signing on behalf of a firm
Claimant('s Solicitor)   or company)

Date

N243 Notice of acceptance and request for payment (4.99)   The Court Service Publications Unit

APPENDIX 3 FORMS

Application Notice

- You must complete Parts A **and** B, **and** Part C if applicable
- Send any relevant fee and the completed application to the court with any draft order, witness statement or other evidence; and sufficient copies of these for service on each respondent

You should provide this information for listing the application
1. Do you wish to have your application dealt with at a hearing?
Yes ☐ No ☐ If Yes, please complete 2
2. Time estimate_____ (hours)_____ (mins)
Is this agreed by all parties? Yes ☐ No ☐
Level of judge _____
3. Parties to be served: _____

In the	
Claim no.	
Warrant no. (If applicable)	
Claimant (including ref.)	
Defendant(s) (including ref.)	
Date	

Part A

1. Enter your full name, or name of solicitor

   I (We)[1] _____ (on behalf of)(the claimant)(the defendant)

2. State clearly what order you are seeking and if possible attach a draft

   intend to apply for an order (a draft of which is attached) that[2]

   because[3]

3. Briefly set out why you are seeking the order. Include the material facts on which you rely, identifying any rule or statutory provision

Part B

I (We) wish to rely on: *tick one box*

the attached (witness statement)(affidavit) ☐   my statement of case ☐

evidence in Part C overleaf in support of my application ☐

4. If you are not already a party to the proceedings, you must provide an address for service of documents

Signed _____   Position or office held _____
(Applicant)('s Solicitor)('s litigation friend)   (if signing on behalf of firm or company)

Address to which documents about this claim should be sent (including reference if appropriate)[4]

		if applicable
	fax no.	
	DX no.	
Tel. no. _____ Postcode _____	e-mail	

The court office at
is open from 10am to 4pm Monday to Friday. When corresponding with the court please address forms or letters to the Court Manager and quote the claim number.

N244 Application Notice (4.99)   *Printed on behalf of The Court Service*

APPENDIX 3   FORMS

Part C	Claim No.

I (We) wish to rely on the following evidence in support of this application:

Statement of Truth

*(I believe)(The applicant believes) that the facts stated in this application are true
* *delete as appropriate*

Signed _____

(Applicant)('s Solicitor)('s litigation friend)

Position or office held _____
(if signing on behalf of firm or company)

Date _____

APPENDIX 3   FORMS

Notice of Commencement of Assessment of Bill of Costs

In the	
Claim No.	
Claimant (include Ref.)	
Defendant (include Ref.)	

To the claimant(defendant)

Following an .... *(insert name of document eg. order, judgement)* dated .... (copy attached) I have prepared my Bill of Costs for assessment. The Bill totals £ .... If you choose to dispute this bill and your objections are not upheld at the assessment hearing, the full amount payable (including the assessment fee) will be £ .... together with interest *(see note below)* I shall also seek the costs of the assessment hearing

You must send me any points of dispute by .... *(insert date 21 days from the date of service of the certificate).*

Your points of dispute must include

- details of the items in the bill of costs which are disputed
- concise details of the nature and grounds of the dispute for each item and, if you seek a reduction in those items, suggest, where practicable, a reduced figure

You must also serve copies of your points of dispute on all other parties to the assessment identified below.

I certify that I have also served the following (persons)(person) with a copy of this certificate and my Bill of Costs

If I have not received your points of dispute by the above date, I will ask the court to issue a default costs certificate for the full amount of my bill (see above) plus fixed costs and court fee as specified in the Costs Practice Direction and the Civil Courts Fees Order.

Signed .... Date ....
(Claimant)(Defendant)('s Solicitor)

Note: Interest may be added to all High Court judgments and certain county court judgments under the Judgments Act 1838, the County Courts Act 1984 and the Late Payment of Commercial Debts (Interest) Act 1998.

The court office at
is open between 10 am and 4 pm Monday to Friday. When corresponding with the court, please address forms or letters to the Court Manager and quote the claim number.

N252 Notice of Commencement of Assessment of Bill of Costs (4.99)   *Printed on behalf of The Court Service*

APPENDIX 3 FORMS

Notice of Amount allowed on Provisional Assessment
(Legal Aid only)

To [Claimant][Defendant]['s Solicitor]

In the	
Claim No.	
Claimant (including ref)	
Defendant (including ref)	
Date	

Take notice that the [claimant's][defendant's] bill of costs in this action has been provisionally assessed and is returned with this notice

If you wish to be heard on the assessment, you must, within 14 days of the receipt of this notice inform the court in writing and return the bill of costs to the court. A date for assessment will then be fixed.

If you (and counsel, if any) accept the provisional assessment as final, please return the bill together with the balance of the assessment fee.

The court office at

is open between 10 am and 4 pm Monday to Friday. Address all communications to the Court Manager quoting the claim number.
N253 Notice of Amount allowed on Provisional Assessment

Request for a Default Costs Certificate

In the	
Claim No.	
Claimant (include Ref.)	
Defendant (include Ref.)	

I certify that the attached Notice of Commencement was served on the paying party ....

(and give details of any other party served with the notice)

on .... *(insert date)*

I also certify that I have not received any points of dispute and that the time for receiving them has now elapsed.

I now request the court to issue a certificate for the amount of the bill of costs plus such fixed costs and court fees as are appropriate in this case.

Signed .... Date ....
(Claimant)(Defendant)('s Solicitor)

The court office at
is open between 10 am and 4 pm Monday to Friday. When corresponding with the court, please address forms or letters to the Court Manager and quote the claim number.

N254 Request for a Default Costs Certificate (4.99) — *Printed on behalf of The Court Service*

APPENDIX 3   FORMS

Default Costs Certificate

In the	
	County Court
Claim No.	
Claimant (inlcuding ref)	
Defendant (inlcuding ref)	
Date	

To [Claimant][Defendant]['s Solicitor]

As you have not raised any points of dispute on the [defendant's][claimant's] bill of costs, the costs of the claim have been allowed and the total sum of £   is now payable.

You must pay this amount to the [defendant][claimant] [within 14 days from the date of this order] [on or before [   ]]

The date from which any entitlement to interest under this certficate commences is [date]

Take Notice

To the defendant (claimant)
If you do not pay in accordance with this order your goods may be removed and sold or other enforcement proceedings may be taken against you. If your circumstances change and you cannot pay, ask at the court office about what you can do

Further interest may be added if judgment has been given for £5,000 or more or is in respect of a debt which attracts contractual or statutory interest for late payment.

Address for Payment

This judgment has been registered on the Register of County Court Judgments. This may make it difficult for you to get credit. **If you pay in full within one month** you can ask the court to cancel the entry on the Register. You will need to give proof of payment. You can (for a fee) also obtain a Certificate of Cancellation from the court. If you pay the debt in full after one month you can ask the court to mark the entry on the Register as satisfied and (for a fee) obtain a Certificate of Satisfaction to prove that the debt has been paid.

How to Pay

- PAYMENT(S) MUST BE MADE to the person named at the address for payment quoting their reference and the court case number.
- **DO NOT bring or send payments to the court. THEY WILL NOT BE ACCEPTED.**
- You should allow at least 4 days for your payment to reach the claimant (defendant) or his representative.
- Make sure that you keep records and can account for all payments made. Proof may be required if there is any disagreement. It is not safe to send cash unless you use registered post.
- A leaflet giving further advice about payment can be obtained from the court.
- If you need more information you should contact the claimant (defendant) or his representative.

The court office at
is open between 10 am and 4 pm Monday to Friday. Address all communications to the Court Manager quoting the claim number
N255CC Default costs certificate

APPENDIX 3   FORMS

Default Costs Certificate

In the High Court of Justice	
Division District Registry	
Claim No.	
Claimant (inlcuding ref)	
Defendant (inlcuding ref)	
Date	

To [Claimant][Defendant]['s Solicitor]

As you have not raised any points of dispute on the [defendant's][claimant's] bill of costs, the costs of the claim have been allowed and the total sum of £   is now payable.

You must pay this amount to the [defendant][claimant] [within 14 days from the date of this order] [on or before [   ]]

The date from which any entitlement to interest under this certficate commences is [date]

――――― Take Notice ―――――

To the defendant (claimant)

If you do not pay in accordance with this order your goods may be removed and sold or other enforcement proceedings may be taken against you. If your circumstances change and you cannot pay, ask at the court office about what you can do

――――― Address for Payment ―――――   ――――― How to Pay ―――――

- PAYMENT(S) MUST BE MADE to the person named at the address for payment quoting their reference and the court case number.
- DO NOT bring or send payments to the court. THEY WILL NOT BE ACCEPTED.
- You should allow at least 4 days for your payment to reach the claimant (defendant) or his representative.
- Make sure that you keep records and can account for all payments made. Proof may be required if there is any disagreement. It is not safe to send cash unless you use registered post.
- A leaflet giving further advice about payment can be obtained from the court.
- If you need more information you should contact the claimant (defendant) or his representative.

The court office at
is open between 10 am and 4 pm Monday to Friday. Address all communications to the Court Manager quoting the claim number
N255HC Default costs certificate

APPENDIX 3   FORMS

Final Costs Certificate

In the

County Court

Claim No.	
Claimant (including ref)	
Defendant (including ref)	
Date	

To [Claimant][Defendant]['s Solicitor]

Upon the [claimant][defendant] filing a completed bill of costs in this claim

District Judge [   ] has assessed the total costs as £   [including £   for the costs of the detailed assessment]

[And £   already having been paid under the interim costs certificate issued on [   ]]

You must pay [the balance of] £   to the [claimant][defendant] [within 14 days from the date of this order] [on or before[   ]]

The date from which any entitlement to interest under this certficate commences is [date]

――――― **Take Notice** ―――――

To the defendant (claimant)

If you do not pay in accordance with this order your goods may be removed and sold or other enforcement proceedings may be taken against you. If your circumstances change and you cannot pay, ask at the court office about what you can do

Further interest may be added if judgment has been given for £5,000 or more or is in respect of a debt which attracts contractual or statutory interest for late payment.

――――― **Address for Payment** ―――――

This judgment has been registered on the Register of County Court Judgments. This may make it difficult for you to get credit. **If you pay in full within one month** you can ask the court to cancel the entry on the Register. You will need to give proof of payment. You can (for a fee) also obtain a Certificate of Cancellation from the court. If you pay the debt in full after one month you can ask the court to mark the entry on the Register as satisfied and (for a fee) obtain a Certificate of Satisfaction to prove that the debt has been paid.

――――― **How to Pay** ―――――

- **PAYMENT(S) MUST BE MADE** to the person named at the address for payment quoting their reference and the court case number.
- **DO NOT bring or send payments to the court. THEY WILL NOT BE ACCEPTED.**
- You should allow <u>at least</u> 4 days for your payment to reach the claimant (defendant) or his representative.
- Make sure that you keep records and can account for all payments made. Proof may be required if there is any disagreement. It is not safe to send cash unless you use registered post.
- A leaflet giving further advice about payment can be obtained from the court.
- If you need more information you should contact the claimant (defendant) or his representative.

The court office at
is open between 10 am and 4 pm Monday to Friday. Address all communications to the Court Manager quoting the claim number

N256CC Final Costs Certificate

APPENDIX 3   FORMS

Final Costs Certificate

In the High Court of Justice	
	Division
	District Registry
Claim No.	
Claimant (including ref)	
Defendant (including ref)	
Date	

To [Claimant][Defendant]['s Solicitor]

Upon the [claimant][defendant] filing a completed bill of costs in this claim

Master [   ] has assessed the total costs as £   [including £   for the costs of the detailed assessment]

[And £   already having been paid under the interim costs certificate issued on [   ]]

You must pay [the balance of] £   to the [claimant][defendant] [within 14 days from the date of this order] [on or before[   ]]

The date from which any entitlement to interest under this certficate commences is [date]

──────── Take Notice ────────

To the defendant (claimant)

If you do not pay in accordance with this order your goods may be removed and sold or other enforcement proceedings may be taken against you. If your circumstances change and you cannot pay, ask at the court office about what you can do

──── Address for Payment ────

──── How to Pay ────

- PAYMENT(S) MUST BE MADE to the person named at the address for payment quoting their reference and the court case number.
- DO NOT bring or send payments to the court. THEY WILL NOT BE ACCEPTED.
- You should allow <u>at least</u> 4 days for your payment to reach the claimant (defendant) or his representative.
- Make sure that you keep records and can account for all payments made. Proof may be required if there is any disagreement. It is not safe to send cash unless you use registered post.
- A leaflet giving further advice about payment can be obtained from the court.
- If you need more information you should contact the claimant (defendant) or his representative.

The court office at
is open between 10 am and 4 pm Monday to Friday. Address all communications to the Court Manager quoting the claim number
N256HC Final Costs Certificate

APPENDIX 3   FORMS

Interim costs certificate

In the

Claim No.	
Claimant (including ref)	
Defendant (including ref)	
Date	

To [Claimant][Defendant]['s Solicitor]

Upon application by the [claimant][defendant] for [a detailed assessment hearing] [the issue of an interim costs certificate by agreement].

[Master][District Judge][   ] has ordered that you must pay £   to the [claimant][defendant] [within 14 days from the date of this order][on or before [   ]] [into court to await the issue of a final costs certificate].

──── **Take Notice** ────

To the defendant (claimant)

If you do not pay in accordance with this order your goods may be removed and sold or other enforcement proceedings may be taken against you. If your circumstances change and you cannot pay, ask at the court office about what you can do

──── **Address for Payment** ────

──── **How to Pay** ────

- PAYMENT(S) MUST BE MADE to the person named at the address for payment quoting their reference and the court case number.
- DO NOT bring or send payments to the court. THEY WILL NOT BE ACCEPTED.
- You should allow at least 4 days for your payment to reach the claimant (defendant) or his representative.
- Make sure that you keep records and can account for all payments made. Proof may be required if there is any disagreement. It is not safe to send cash unless you use registered post.
- A leaflet giving further advice about payment can be obtained from the court.
- If you need more information you should contact the claimant (defendant) or his representative.

The court office at
is open between 10 am and 4 pm Monday to Friday. Address all communications to the Court Manager quoting the claim number

N257 Interim Costs Certificate

APPENDIX 3   FORMS

Request for Detailed Assessment Hearing	In the	
	Claim No.	
	Claimant (include Ref.)	
	Defendant (include Ref.)	

I certify that the attached Notice of Commencement was served on the paying party

(and give details of any other party served with the notice)

on   *(insert date)*

I now ask the court to arrange an assessment hearing (provisionally assess the bill - legal aid case only)

I enclose copies of *(tick as appropriate)*

- ☐ Bill of Costs
- ☐ the paying party's points of dispute annotated as necessary in order to show which items have been agreed and their value and to show which items remain in dispute and their value;
- ☐ points in reply (if any)
- ☐ a copy of the authority for the assessment;
- ☐ a copy of all the orders made by the court relating to the costs of the proceedings which are to be assessed;
- ☐ any fee notes of counsel and receipts or accounts for other disbursements relating to items in dispute;
- ☐ [where solicitors' costs are disputed] the client care letter delivered to the receiving party or the solicitor's retainer.
- ☐ all civil legal aid certificate and amendments to them; notice of discharge or revocation and specific legal aid authorities;

I believe the hearing with take   *(give estimate of time court should allow).*

I certify that the assisted person wishes to attend the assessment hearing *(delete if not applicable).*

I enclose my fee of £

Signed .... Date ....

(Claimant)(Defendant)('s Solicitor)

The court office at

is open between 10 am and 4 pm Monday to Friday. When corresponding with the court, please address forms or letters to the Court Manager and quote the claim number.

N258 Request for Detailed Assessment Hearing (4.99)   *Printed on behalf of The Court Service*

APPENDIX 3   FORMS

List of Documents:
Standard Disclosure

Notes:
- The rules relating to standard disclosure are contained in Part 31 of the Civil Procedure Rules.
- Documents to be included under standard disclosure are contained in Rule 31.6
- A document has or will have been in your control if you have or have had possession, or a right of possession, of it **or** a right to inspect or take copies of it.

In the	
Claim No.	
Claimant (including ref)	
Defendant (including ref)	
Date	

Disclosure Statement

I state that I have carried out a reasonable and proportionate search to locate all the documents which I am required to disclose under the order made by the court on   [19   ][20   ].

(I did not search for documents -

1. pre-dating..

2. located elsewhere than...
   ....

3. in categories other than..
   ....)

I certify that I understand the duty of disclosure and to the best of my knowledge I have carried out that duty. I further certify that the list of documents set out in or attached to this form, is a complete list of all documents which are or have been in my control and which I am obliged under the order to disclose.

I understand that I must inform the court and the other parties immediately if any further document required to be disclosed by Rule 31.6 comes into my control at any time before the conclusion of the case.

(I have not permitted inspection of documents within the category or class of documents (as set out below) required to be disclosed under Rule 31(6)(b)or (c) on the grounds that to do so would be disproportionate to the issues in the case.)

Signed _____   **Date** _____

(Claimant)(Defendant)('s litigation friend)

Position or office held
(if signing on behalf of firm or company) Please state why you are the appropriate person to make the disclosure statement.

continued overleaf

N265 List of Documents: Standard Disclosure (4.99)   *Printed on behalf of The Court Service*

APPENDIX 3   FORMS

List and number here, in a convenient order, the documents (or bundles of documents if of the same nature, e.g. invoices) in your control, which you do not object to being inspected. Give a short description of each document or bundle so that it can be identified, and say if it is kept elsewhere i.e. with a bank or solicitor	I have control of the documents numbered and listed here. I do not object to you inspecting them/producing copies.
List and number here, as above, the documents in your control which you object to being inspected. (Rule 31.19)	I have control of the documents numbered and listed here, but I object to you inspecting them:
Say what your objections are	I object to you inspecting these documents because:
List and number here, the documents you once had in your control, but which you no longer have. For each document listed, say when it was last in your control and where it is now.	I have had the documents numbered and listed below, but they are no longer in my control.

Notice to admit facts

In the	
Claim No.	
Claimant (include Ref.)	
Defendant (include Ref.)	

I (We) give notice that you are requested to admit the following facts or part of case in this claim:

I (We) confirm that any admission of fact(s) or part of case will only be used in this claim.

Signed _____
(Claimant)(Defendant)('s solicitor)

Position or office held _____
(If signing on behalf of firm or company)

Date _____

Admission of facts

I (We) admit the facts or part of case (set out above)(in the attached schedule) for the purposes of this claim only and on the basis that the admission will not be used on any other occasion or by any other person.

Signed _____
(Claimant)(Defendant)('s solicitor)

Position or office held _____
(If signing on behalf of firm or company)

Date _____

The court office at
is open between 10 am and 4 pm Monday to Friday. Address all communication to the Court Manager quoting the claim number
N266 Notice to admit facts (4.99)

Notice to prove documents at trial

In the	
Claim No.	
Claimant (include Ref.)	
Defendant (include Ref.)	

I (We) give notice that you are requested to prove the following documents disclosed under CPR Part 31 in this claim at the trial:

Signed _____
(Claimant)(Defendant)('s solicitor)

Position or office held _____
(If signing on behalf of firm or company)

Date _____

The court office at
is open between 10 am and 4 pm Monday to Friday. Address all communication to the Court Manager quoting the claim number

N268 Notice to prove documents at trial (4.99)

APPENDIX 3   FORMS

Notice of Discontinuance

In the	
Claim No.	
Claimant (including ref.)	
Defendant (including ref.)	

Note: Where another party must consent to the proceedings being discontinued, a copy of their consent must be attached to, and served with, this form.

To the court

The claimant (defendant)

(tick only one box)

☐   discontinues all of this (claim) (counterclaim)

☐   discontinues that part of this claim (counterclaim) relating to: *(specify which part)*

against the (defendant) (following defendants) (claimant) (following claimants)

(.. *(enter name of Judge)* granted permission for the claimant to discontinue (all) (part) of this (claim)(counterclaim) by order dated ....)

I certify that I have served a copy of this notice on every other party to the proceedings

Signed _____   **Position or office held** _____

(Claimant)(Defendant)('s solicitor)(Litigation friend)   *(if signing on behalf of firm or company)*

Date _____

The court office at

is open between 10 am and 4 pm Monday to Friday. When corresponding with the court, please address forms or letters to the Court Manager and quote the claim number.

N279 Notice of Discontinuance(4.99)   *Printed on behalf of The Court Service*

APPENDIX 3 FORMS

Order on settlement on behalf of child or patient

In the	
Claim No.	
Claimant (including ref)	
Defendant (including ref)	

To the [Claimant][Defendant]['s solicitor]

An application was made on [date] by [counsel][solicitors] for the claimant [and was attended by [counsel][solicitors] for the defendant].

[Master][District Judge]   approved the following terms of settlement and made them an Order of the Court.

BY CONSENT IT IS ORDERED that:-

The claimant may accept the sum of [£ ....] in satisfaction of the claim[s].

(where the claim is in respect of a Fatal Accident)
[The said sum of [£   ] is apportioned as follows:-
   a) under the Law Reform (Miscellaneous Provisions) Act 1934 the sum of [£.................]
   b) under the Fatal Accidents Act 1976;
     (i) [£ ....] to the personal claim of the claimant.
     (ii)[£ ....] to the personal claim of the child dependant[s]
     [.....................][.....................]]

[The defendant pay the sum of [£ ....] to the claimant's [solicitors] [litigation friend] on or before [................].]

The defendant pay the [further] sum of [£............] into the [office of this court] [Court Funds Office] on or before [......................] [subject to a first charge under section 16(6) of the Legal Aid Act 1988] to be invested and accumulated in the Special Investment Account pending further order.

[The claimant's solicitor apply to the court for further investment directions on or before [................].]

(where the claimant is a Patient)

[The claimant's solicitor to apply to the Court of Protection for the appointment of a receiver on or before [....................] and upon such appointment being made the sum of [£] [subject to a first charge under section 16(6) of the Legal Aid Act 1988] together with any interest accrued on that sum from the date of this order to be carried over to the Court of Protection to the credit of the claimant there to be dealt with as the Court of Protection thinks fit.]

[Any accrued up to the date of this order on any money in court paid in by or on behalf of the defendant be paid out to the defendant's solicitors.]

The defendant pay the claimant's costs be assessed with permission to request assessment to be dispensed with [and the claimant's solicitor waiving any claim to further costs].

[The claimant's costs be [assessed] in accordance with Regulation 107 of the Civil Legal Aid (General) Regulations 1989.]

Upon payment of the sum(s) and costs referrred to above, the defendant be discharged from further liability in respect of all claims made by the claimant against him in these proceedings.

All further proceedings be stayed except that either party has permission to apply to the court for the purpose of carrying this order into effect.

The court office at
is open between 10 am and 4 pm Monday to Friday. When corresponding with the court, please address forms or letters to the Court Manager and quote the claim

N292 Order on settlement on behalf of child or patient

Claimant's Application for a Variation Order (without hearing)

Defendant's address

In the	
Claim No.	
Claimant (including ref.)	
Defendant (including ref.)	

(seal)

I apply to the court for an order that the amount due and unpaid under the judgment or order in this claim be paid by instalments of £ .... for every month/week because

(give your reason for making this application in the box below)

Signed .... **Date** ....
Claimant('s solicitor)('s litigation friend)

Judgment details

Date of judgment or order

How payment was ordered

Outstanding debt
including any interest where judgment was entered for £5,000 or more, or is in respect of a debt which attracts contractual or statutory interest for late payment

AMOUNT REMAINING DUE* £

The court office at
is open between 10 am and 4 pm Monday to Friday. Address all communications to the Court Manager quoting the claim number.
N294 Claimant's Application for a Variation Order Our Ref. 499 (3/12)

Notice of Change of Solicitor

Note: You should tick either box A **or** B as appropriate **and** box C. Complete details as necessary.

In the	
Claim No.	
Claimant (including ref.)	
Defendant	

I (We) give notice that

A ☐ my solicitor *(insert name and address)*
has ceased to act for me and I shall now be acting in person.

B ☐ we *(insert name of solicitor)*
have been instructed to act on behalf of the claimant (defendant) in this claim
(in place of *(insert name and address of previous solicitors)*
....)

C ☐ I (we) have served notice of this change on every party to claim (and on the former solicitor).

Address to which documents about this claim should be sent (including any reference)

	if applicable
	fax no.
	DX no.
Postcode	e-mail

Signed _____ **Position or office held** _____

(Claimant)(Defendant)('s Solicitor)(Litigation friend)   If signing on behalf of firm or company

Date _____

The court office at
is open between 10 am and 4 pm Monday to Friday. When corresponding with the court, please address forms or letters to the Court Manager and quote the claim number.

N434 Notice of Change of Solicitor (4.99)   *Printed on behalf of The Court Service*

APPENDIX 3 FORMS

SCHEDULE OF COSTS FORMS: FORM 1

Statement of Costs
(summary assessment)

COURT   CASE REFERENCE
JUDGE/MASTER
CASE TITLE

    [Party]'s Statement of Costs for the hearing on [date]

Description of fee earners*
(1) [name] [grade] [hourly rate claimed]
(2) [name] [grade] [hourly rate claimed]

Attendances on [Party]
[number] hours at £   £

Attendances on opponents
[number] hours at £   £

Attendances on others
(1) [number] hours at £   £
(2) [number] hours at £   £

Work done on documents
[number] hours at £   £

Attendance at hearing
[number] hours at £   £
[number] hours travel and waiting at £   £

Counsel's fees [name] [year of call]
Fee for [advice/conference/documents]   £
Fee for hearing   £

Other expenses
[court fees]   £
Others [give brief description]   £_____

TOTAL   £
Amount of VAT claimed
   on solicitors' and counsel's fees   £
   on other expenses   £

GRAND TOTAL   £_____

The costs estimated above do not exceed the costs which the [party] is liable to pay in respect of the work which this estimate covers.

Dated   Signed
                                   Name of firm of solicitors
                                   [partner] for the [party]

* 4 grades of fee earner are suggested: (1) partners and solicitors with over 4 years PQE (2) solicitors with up to 4 years PQE and senior legal executives (3) legal executives and senior para-legals (4) trainee solicitors and junior para-legals. In respect of each fee earner communications should be treated as attendances and routine communications should be claimed at one tenth of the hourly rate.

APPENDIX 3   FORMS

SCHEDULE OF COSTS FORMS: FORM 2

Bill of Costs (detailed assessment)

IN THE HIGH COURT OF JUSTICE   1997-B-9999
QUEEN'S BENCH DIVISION
BRIGHTON DISTRICT REGISTRY

BETWEEN   AB   Claimant
                               - and -
                                 CD   Defendant

CLAIMANT'S BILL OF COSTS TO BE ASSESSED PURSUANT TO THE ORDER DATED 26 FEBRUARY 1999 AND IN ACCORDANCE WITH REGULATION 107A OF THE CIVIL LEGAL AID (GENERAL) REGULATIONS 1989

Legal Aid Certificate No. 01.01.96.32552X issued on 9 September 1997.

VAT NO. 23 3 4404 90

In these proceedings the claimant sought compensation for personal injuries and other losses suffered in a road accident which occurred on Wednesday 1 January 1997 near the junction between Bolingbroke Lane and Regency Road, Brighton, East Sussex. The claimant had been travelling as a front seat passenger in a car driven by the defendant. The claimant suffered severe injuries when, because of the defendant's negligence, the car left the road and collided with a brick wall.

The defendant was later convicted of various offences arising out of the accident including careless driving and driving under the influence of drink or drugs.

In the civil action the defendant alleged that immediately before the car journey began the claimant had known that the defendant was under the influence of alcohol and therefore consented to the risk of injury or was contributorily negligent as to it. It was also alleged that, immediately before the accident occurred, the claimant wrongfully took control of the steering wheel so causing the accident to occur.

The claimant first instructed solicitors, E F & Co, in this matter in July 1997. The writ was issued in October 1997 and in February 1998 the claimant successfully applied for an interim payment. in July 1998 the proceedings were listed for a two day trial commencing 25 February 1999. At that trial the defendant was found liable but the compensation payable was reduced by 25% in order to take account of contributory negligence by the claimant. The claimant was awarded a total of £78,256.83 plus £1,207.16 interest plus costs.

The proceedings were conducted on behalf of the claimant by an assistant solicitor, admitted November 1996. The bill is divided into four parts.

Part 1   Costs payable by the defendant
This covers the period from 8 July 1997 to 8 September 1997 which was financed under the Legal Aid Green Form scheme. In this part the solicitor's time is charged at £120 per hour, letters out and telephone calls at £12 each and travel and waiting at £60 per hour. However, the claim for costs is limited to the sum payable under the Green Form scheme, £95 plus VAT of £16.62.

Part 2   Costs payable by the defendant
This part covers the period from 9 September 1997 to 19 May 1998 which was financed under the legal aid scheme. In this part the solicitor's time has been charged as in Part 1.

Part 3 Costs payable only out of the legal aid fund
This part covers the same period as Part 2. In this part the solicitor's time is charged at the prescribed hourly rates plus enhancement of 50% (having regard to the exceptional competence skill and expertise with which the work was done and the degree of responsibility accepted by the solicitor).

Preparation: £74.00
Attending counsel in conference or at court: £36.40
Travelling and waiting: £32.70
Routine letters out: £7.40
Routine telephone calls: £4.10

Part 4 Costs payable by the defendant
This part covers the period from 19 May 1998 to the present time. Once the claimant had become financially ineligible for legal aid, E F & Co agreed to continue acting for him on payment of disbursements and profit costs for E F & Co at the following hourly rates.
Assistant solicitor: £120.00
Costs draftsman: £90.00
Trainee solicitor: £60.00

APPENDIX 3　FORMS

Item		Amount Claimed	VAT	Amount Allowed	VAT
Part 1: COSTS PAYABLE BY THE DEFENDANT					
Attendances on claimant					
(1) 8th July 1997 — First instructions — 0.75 hours	90.00	*	*		
(2) Routine letters out — 3	36.00				
Attendances on witnesses of fact					
(3) Routine letters out — 2	24.00	*	*		
Attendances on the Defendant					
(4) 8th July 1997 — Timed letter sent — 0.5 hours	60.00	*	*		
(Total claim for Part 1 is limited to £95 plus VAT of £16.62)*					
To Summary		95.00	16.62		
PART 2: COSTS PAYABLE BY THE DEFENDANT					
Attendances on court and counsel					
9th September 1997 — legal aid certificate issued					
11th September 1997 — Conference with counsel Engaged 2.5 hours	300.00				
Travel & waiting 2.25 hours	135.00				
(5) Total solicitor's fee for conference		435.00	76.12		
(6) Counsel's fee for conference		250.00	43.75		
7th October 1997 — Issue of writ					
(7) Writ fee		500.00			
21st October 1997 — Writ and Statement of Claim served					
25th November 1997 — Time for service of defence extended by agreement to 15th January 1998					

APPENDIX 3 FORMS

Item	Amount Claimed	VAT	Amount Allowed	VAT
25th November 1997 — Summons for interim payment issued				
(8) Court fee for summons	50.00			
28th November 1998 — Affidavit of AB sworn				
(9) Paid oath fee	14.00			
15th January 1998 — Defence served				
16th January 1998 — Instructions to Counsel to advise on evidence and settle 2 witness statements				
29th January 1998 — Advice on evidence received				
(10) Counsel's fee for advice on evidence (Miss GH)	400.00	70.00		
(11) Counsel's fee for settling 2 witness statements	120.00	21.00		
6th February 1998: Claimant's application for an interim payment (interim payment of £10,873.67) ordered with claimant's costs in the case: certificate for counsel				
Engaged 0.33 hours	40.00			
Travel & waiting 2.00 hours	120.00			
(12) Total solicitor's fee for attending	160.00	28.00		
(13) Counsel's brief fee (Miss GH)	120.00	21.00		
20th March 1998: Exchange of witness statements				
15th April 1998: Payment into court of £25,126.33 — in addition to the interim payment and a further payment to the Compensation Recovery Unit				
20th April 1998: Telephone conference with counsel				
Engaged 0.5 hours	60.00			
(14) Total solicitor's fee for conference	60.00	10.50		
(15) Counsel's fee for conference (Miss GH)	216.00	37.80		

APPENDIX 3 FORMS

Item	Amount Claimed	VAT	Amount Allowed	VAT
Attendances on claimant Timed attendances in person and by telephone — see Schedule 1 (16) Total fees for Schedule 1 — 6.5 hours (17) Routine letters out and telephone calls — 18 (10 + 8)	 780.00 216.00	 136.50 37.80		
Attendances on witnesses of fact Timed attendances in person, by letter out and by telephone — see Schedule 2 (18) Total fees for Schedule 2 — 3.9 hours (19) Paid travelling on 9th October 1997	 468.00 22.96	 81.90 4.01		
Attendances on medical expert (Dr. IJ) (20) 11th September 1997 — long letter out — 0.33 hours (21) 30th January 1998 — long letter out — 0.25 hours (22) 23rd April 1998 — telephone call — 0.2 hours (23) Routine letters out and telephone calls — 6 (24) Dr IJ's fee for report	40.00 30.00 24.00 72.00 350.00	7.00 5.25 4.20 12.60 		
Attendances on solicitors for defendant (25) Routine letters out and telephone calls — 12 and 4	192.00	33.60		
Routine attendances on court (26) Routine letters out to court — 6	72.00	12.60		
Routine attendances on counsel (27) Routine letters out and telephone calls to counsel — 11 (7 + 4)	132.00	23.10		
Work done on arithmetic (28) 18th September 1997: 1 hour (29) 3rd November 1997: 0.75 hours (30) 23rd February 1998: 0.5 hours	120.00 90.00 60.00	21.00 15.75 10.50		

APPENDIX 3   FORMS

Item		Amount Claimed	VAT	Amount Allowed	VAT
Work done on documents Timed items: see Schedule 3 (31) Total fees for Schedule 3 — 39 hours		4680.00	819.00		
Work done on negotiations 23rd March 1998: meeting at offices of solicitors for defence Engaged 1.5 hours Travel & waiting 1.25 hours (32) Total solicitor's fee for meeting	180.00 75.00	255.00	44.63		
To Summary		9928.96	1577.61		
PART 3: COSTS PAYABLE ONLY OUT OF THE LEGAL AID FUND					
Claimant (33) 11th September 1997 telephone call Engaged 0.25 hours Enhancement 50%	18.50 <u>9.25</u>	27.75	4.85		
(34) 18th April 1998: telephone call Engaged 0.1 hours Enhancement 50%	4.10 2.05	6.15	1.08		
Legal Aid Board (35) 12th May 1998: report on case Engaged 0.5 hours Enhancement 50%	37.00 <u>18.50</u>	55.50	9.71		
(36) Routine letters out and telephone calls Letters out 2 Telephone calls 4 Enhancement 50%	14.80 16.40 <u>15.60</u>	46.80	8.19		

Item	Amount Claimed	VAT	Amount Allowed	VAT
Other work done				
(37) Preparing and checking bill — (part: 2 hours)	200.00	35.00		
To Summary	336.20	58.83		
PART 4: COSTS PAYABLE BY THE DEFENDANT				
Attendance on court and counsel				
19th May 1998: Discharge of legal aid certificate				
16th July 1998: Set down for trial (date fixed, 2 days -starting 25th February 1999)				
(38) 4th December 1998: Setting down fee	150.00			
25th February 1999: attending first day of trial: adjourned part heard				
Engaged in court: 5 hours — 600.00				
Engaged in conference: 0.75 hours — 90.00				
Travel & waiting: 1.5 hours — 90.00				
(39) Total solicitor's fee for attending	780.00	136.50		
(40) Counsel's brief fee (Miss GH)	1750.00	306.25		
(41) Fee of expert witness (Dr. IJ)	850.00			
(42) Expenses of witnesses of fact	84.00			
26th February 1999: attending second day of trial when judgment was given for the claimant in the sum of £78,256.83 plus £1207.16 interest plus costs				
Engaged in court: 3 hours — 360.00				
Engaged in conference: 1.5 hours — 180.00				
Travel and waiting: 1.5 hours — 90.00				
(43) Total solicitor's fee for attending	630.00	110.25		
(44) Counsel's fee for second day (Miss GH)	650.00	113.75		

APPENDIX 3 FORMS

Item	Amount Claimed	VAT	Amount Allowed	VAT
Claimant				
(45) 20th May 1998: telephone call 0.2 hours	24.00	4.20		
(46) 20th February 1999: telephone call 0.33 hours	40.00	7.00		
(47) 22nd February 1999: telephone call 0.25 hours	30.00	5.25		
(48) Routine letters out and telephone calls — 8 (4 + 4)	96.00	16.80		
Witnesses of fact				
(49) Routine letters out and telephone calls — 6 (4 + 2)	72.00	12.60		
Medical expert (Dr. IJ)				
(50) Routine letters out and telephone calls — 4 (2 + 2)	48.00	8.40		
Solicitors for defendant				
(51) 19th February 1998: telephone call — 0.25 hours	30.00	5.25		
(52) Routine letters out and telephone calls — 8 (6 + 2)	90.00	15.75		
Communications with the court				
(53) Routine letters out and telephone calls — 3 (2 + 1)	36.00	6.30		
Communications with counsel				
(54) Routine letters out and telephone calls — 8 (4 + 4)	96.00	16.80		
Work done on documents				
(55) Timed and estimated items: see Schedule 4	1200.00	210.00		
4 hours at £120	480.00			
12 hours at £60	720.00			

Item	Amount Claimed	VAT	Amount Allowed	VAT
Other work done				
Preparing and checking bill				
Engaged: assistant solicitor — 1 hour	120.00			
Engaged: costs draftsman — 6 hours	480.00			
(56) Total fees for preparing and checking bill	600.00	105.00		
To Summary	7256.00	1080.10		
Summary				
Costs Payable by the Defendant				
Part 1	95.00	16.62		
Part 2	9928.96	1577.61		
Part 4	7256.00	1080.10		
Total Costs payable by the Defendant	17279.96	2674.33		
Costs Payable out of the Legal Aid Fund				
Part 3	336.20	58.83		
Total costs payable out of the Legal Aid Fund	336.20	58.83		
Grand Totals				
Costs payable by the Defendant	17279.96	2674.33		
Costs payable out of the Legal Aid Fund	336.20	58.83		
Grand Total	17616.16	2733.16		

APPENDIX 3   FORMS

SCHEDULE OF COSTS FORMS: FORM 3

Legal Aid Schedule of Costs

IN THE HIGH COURT OF JUSTICE   1997-B-9999
QUEEN'S BENCH DIVISION
BRIGHTON DISTRICT REGISTRY

BETWEEN   AB   Claimant
                            - and -
                              CD   Defendant

CLAIMANT'S BILL OF COSTS: LEGAL AID SCHEDULE

APPENDIX 3 FORMS

Item	Amount Claimed	VAT	Amount Allowed	VAT
PART 2: COSTS PAYABLE BY THE DEFENDANT				
(5) Solicitor's fee for conference	164.58	28.80		
(6) Counsel's fee	250.00	43.75		
(7) Writ fee	500.00			
(8) Summons fee	50.00			
(9) Oath fee	14.00			
(10) Counsel's fee	400.00	70.00		
(11) Counsel's fee	120.00	21.00		
(12) Solicitor's fee for hearing	77.52	13.57		
(13) Counsel's fee	120.00	21.00		
(14) Solicitor's fee for conference	18.20	3.18		
(15) Counsel's fee	216.00	37.80		
(16) Timed attendances on claimant 6.5 hours £481.00 Enhancement £240.50	721.50	126.27		
(17) Routine attendances on claimant Letters out 10 £74.00 Telephone calls 8 £32.80	106.80	18.69		

1328

APPENDIX 3   FORMS

Item		Amount Claimed	VAT	Amount Allowed	VAT
(18) Timed attendances on witnesses of fact	3.9 hours £288.60 Enhancement 50% £144.30	432.90	75.76		
(19) Paid travelling		22.96	4.01		
(20) Timed attendance on medical expert	0.33 hours £24.64 Enhancement 50% £12.32	36.96	6.47		
(21) Timed attendance on medical expert	0.25 hours £19.50 Enhancement 50% £9.25	27.75	4.85		
(22) Timed attendance on medical expert	0.2 hours £14.80 Enhancement 50% 7.40	22.20	3.88		
(23) Routine attendances on medical expert	Letters out 4 £29.60 Telephone calls 2 £8.20	37.80	6.62		
(24) Medical expert's fee		350.00			
(25) Routine attendances on solicitors for defendant	Letters out 12 £88.80 Telephone calls 4 £16.40	105.20	18.41		
(26) Routine attendances on court	Letters out 6 £44.40	44.40	7.77		

APPENDIX 3 FORMS

Item		Amount Claimed	VAT	Amount Allowed	VAT
(27) Routine attendances on counsel	Letters out 7 £51.80 Telephone calls 4 £16.40	68.20	11.94		
(28) Work done on arithmetic	1 hour 74.00 Enhancement 50% £37.00	111.00	19.42		
(29) Work done on arithmetic	0.75 hours £55.50 Enhancement 50% £27.75	83.25	14.57		
(30) Work done on arithmetic	0.5 hours £37.00 Enhancement 50% £18.50	55.50	9.71		
(31) Work done on documents	39 hours £2,886.00 Enhancement 50% £1,443.00	4,329.00	757.58		
TOTALS FOR PART 2		8,485.72	1,325.00		
PART 4: COSTS PAYABLE BY THE DEFENDANT					
(38) Court fee		150.00			
(39) Solicitor's fee for hearing	5.75 hours £209.30 Travel & waiting £41.05	258.35	45.21		
(40) Counsel's fee		1,750.00	306.25		

APPENDIX 3 FORMS

Item	Amount Claimed	VAT	Amount Allowed	VAT
(41) Expert's fee	850.00			
(42) Witnesses' expenses	84.00			
(43) Solicitor's fee for hearing 4.5 hours £163.80 Travel and waiting £49.05	212.85	37.25		
(44) Counsel's fee	650.00	113.75		
(45) Timed attendance on claimant 0.2 hours £14.80 Enhancement 50% £7.40	22.20	3.88		
(46) Timed attendance on claimant 0.33 hours £24.64 Enhancement 50% £12.32	36.96	6.47		
(47) Timed attendance on claimant 0.25 hours £18.50 Enhancement 50% £9.25	27.75	4.85		
(48) Routine attendances on claimant Letters out 4 £29.60 Telephones 4 £16.40	46.00	8.05		
(49) Routine attendances on witnesses Letters out 4 £29.60 Telephones 2 £8.20	37.80	6.62		

APPENDIX 3   FORMS

Item		Amount Claimed	VAT	Amount Allowed	VAT
(50) Routine attendances on medical expert	Letters out 2 £14.80 Telephones 2 £8.20	23.00	4.02		
(51) Timed attendance on solicitors for defendant Enhancement 50% £9.25	0.25 hours £18.50	27.75	4.86		
(52) Routine attendances on solicitors for defendant	Letters out 6 £44.40 Telephones 2 £8.20	52.60	9.21		
(53) Routine attendances on court	Letters out 2 £14.80 Telephones 1 £4.10	18.90	3.31		
(54) Routine attendances on counsel	Letters out 4 £29.60 Telephones 4 £16.40	46.00			
(55) Work done on documents	16 hours £1,184.00 Enhancement 50% £592.00	1,776.00	310.80		
(56) Preparing and checking bill		600.00	105.00		
TOTALS FOR PART 4		6,670.16	977.58		
GRAND TOTALS FOR PARTS 2 AND 4		15,155.88	2,302.06		

APPENDIX 3   FORMS

SCHEDULE OF COSTS FORMS: FORM 4

Certificates for inclusion in bills

- An appropriate certificate under heading (1) is required in all cases. The appropriate certificate under (2) is required in all cases in which the receiving party is an assisted person. Certificates (3), (4) and (5) are optional. Certificate (5) may be included in the bill, or, if the dispute as to VAT recoverability arises after service of the bill, may be filed and served as a supplementary document amending the bill under paragraph 4.11 of the Directions Relating to Part 47.
- All certificates must be signed by the receiving party or by his solicitor. Where the bill claims costs in respect of work done by more than one form of solicitors a certificate in the form of the final paragraph of certificate (1), appropriately completed, should be signed on behalf of each firm of solicitors.

(1) GENERAL CERTIFICATE AS TO INTEREST, PAYMENTS AND ACCURACY

I certify that:

☐ No rulings have been made in this case which affects my entitlement (if any) to interest on costs.

or

☐ The only rulings made in this case as to interest on costs are as follows: [give brief details as to the date of each ruling, the name of the Judge who made it and the text of the ruling]

and

☐ No payments have been made by any paying party on account of costs included in this bill of costs.

or

☐ The following payments have been made on account of costs included in this bill of costs:
[give brief details of the amounts, the dates of payment and the name of the person by or on whose behalf they were paid]

and (where costs are claimed for work done by a solicitor)

☐ This bill is both accurate and complete and that in relation to each and every item included in Part(s) . . . of the bill the costs claimed herein do not exceed the costs which the receiving party/parties is/are required to pay me/my firm.

(2) CERTIFICATE AS TO INTEREST OF ASSISTED PERSON PURSUANT TO REGULATION 119 OF THE CIVIL LEGAL AID (GENERAL) REGULATIONS 1989

I certify that the assisted person has no financial interest in the detailed assessment.

or

I certify that a copy of this bill has been sent to the assisted person pursuant to Regulation 119 of the Civil Legal Aid General Regulations 1989 with an explanation of his/her interest in the detailed assessment and the steps which can be taken to safeguard that interest in the assessment. He/she has/has not requested that the costs officer be informed of his/her interest and has/has not requested that notice of the detailed assessment hearing be sent to him/her.

(3) CONSENT TO THE SIGNING OF THE CERTIFICATE WITHIN 21 DAYS OF DETAILED ASSESSMENT PURSUANT TO REGULATIONS 112 AND 121 OF THE CIVIL LEGAL AID (GENERAL) REGULATIONS 1989

I certify that notice of the fees reduced or disallowed on detailed assessment has been given in writing to counsel on [date].

or

I certify that: there having been no reduction or disallowance of counsel's fees it is not necessary to give notice to counsel.

I/we consent to the signing forthwith of the costs officer's certificate.

(4) CERTIFICATE IN RESPECT OF DISBURSEMENTS NOT EXCEEDING £500

I hereby certify that all disbursements listed in this bill which individually do not exceed £500 (other than those relating to counsel's fees) have been duly discharged.

(5) CERTIFICATE AS TO RECOVERY OF VAT

With reference to the pending assessment of the [claimant's/defendant's] costs and disbursements herein which are payable by the [claimant/defendant] we the undersigned [solicitors to] [auditors of] the [claimant/defendant] hereby certify that the [claimant/defendant] on the basis of its last completed VAT return [would/would not be entitled to recover/would be entitled to recover only ____ per cent of the] Value Added Tax on such costs and disbursements, as input tax pursuant to Section 14 of the Value Added Tax Act 1983.

APPENDIX 3   FORMS

SCHEDULE OF COSTS FORMS: FORM 6

Points of Dispute

IN THE HIGH COURT OF JUSTICE   1997-B-9999

QUEEN'S BENCH DIVISION
BRIGHTON DISTRICT REGISTRY

BETWEEN   AB   Claimant

- and -

CD   Defendant

POINTS OF DISPUTE SERVED BY THE DEFENDANT

Item	Dispute	Claimant's Comments
General point	Hourly rates claimed for the solicitor and trainee are excessive. Reduce to £100 and £50 respectively plus VAT. These items should be recalculated at the reduced rates.	
(5)	The duration of the conference is excessive. Reduce to one hour i.e. £212.50 at reduced rates.	
(11)	The total fees for items (10) and (11) are excessive. Reduce item (11) to £50.	
(12)	Allow at reduced rates only.	
(14)	Telephone conference not justified. Disallow.	
(15)	Telephone conference not justified. Disallow	
(16)	6.5 hours is excessive. Reduce to 3 hours i.e. £300 at reduced rates.	
(17)(18)(20)(21)(22)(23)(25)(26)	Allow at reduced rates only.	
(27)	The claim for routine attendances on counsel is excessive. Reduce to 6 units i.e. £60 at reduced rates.	
(28)(29)(30)	Allow at reduced rates only	

APPENDIX 3 FORMS

Item	Dispute	Claimant's Comments
(31)	The total claim for documents in this part is excessive. A reasonable allowance in respect of documents concerning court and counsel is 8 hours, for documents concerning witnesses and the expert witness, 6.5 hours for other documents, 5.5 hours. Reduce to 20 hours i.e. £2,000 at reduced rates.	
(32)(39)(43)(45)	Allow at reduced rates only	
(46)	Telephone call not justified. Disallow.	
(47)	Telephone call not justified. Disallow.	
(48)(49)(50)(51)(52)(53)	Allowed at reduced rates only.	
(54)	The claim for routine attendances on counsel is excessive. Reduce to 4 units i.e. £40 at reduced rates.	
(55)	Allow at reduced rates only.	
(56)	The time claimed is excessive. Reduce solicitor's time to 0.5 hours i.e. to £50 at reduced rates and reduce the costs draftsman's time to three hours i.e. £240 (£290 in total).	

Served on [date] by [name] [solicitors for] the Defendant.

APPENDIX 3   FORMS

SCHEDULE OF COSTS FORMS: FORM 15

Legal Aid Assessment Certificate

In the	
Claim No.	
Legal Aid Certificate No.	
Solicitors Ref.	

Claimant

Defendant

The costs in this matter have been assessed as set out in boxes A, B and C below and are claimed from the Legal Aid Fund.

The costs are those of the   ☐ Claimant   ☐ Defendant   ☐ Other

They were taxed in the   ☐ High Court   ☐ County Court (please tick appropriate boxes)

Total pre-certificate costs, which are not being claimed, were   £ _____
(Include disbursements, profit costs and VAT)

Dated .... **Signed** ....

A. Costs payable by another party as allowed or as in legal aid schedule if appropriate
(Do not include any pre-certificate costs, or the costs of assessment)

B. Legal aid only costs
(Do not include the costs of assessment)

Profit Costs	
VAT	
Counsel's Fees	
VAT	
Disbursements	
VAT (Where appropriate)	
Total	£

Profit Costs	
VAT	
Counsel's Fees	
VAT	
Disbursements	
VAT (Where appropriate)	
Total	£

C. Costs of assessment
(Allowed in respect of A and B above)

C. Total claimed
(Add totals A, B and C)

For Part A	
VAT	
Court Fee (where appropriate)	
For Part B	
VAT	
Court fee (Where appropriate)	
Total	£

Total part A	
Total part B	
Total part C	
Total	£

Sealed by the court on ....

APPENDIX 3   FORMS

SCHEDULE OF COSTS FORMS: FORM 16

Notice of Appeal

In the	
Claim No.	
Claimant (including ref)	
Defendant (including ref)	
Date	

[The party wishes] [I wish] to appeal against [some of] the decision(s) made by the costs officer at the hearing on [date] concerning the detailed assessment of [the party's] bill of costs. The grounds of appeal are:

[Each ground must be numbered. Grounds which relate to decisions on items in the bill of costs must also state the number of the item, a short description of the item, the amount claimed and the amount allowed. Some illustrations are given below.]

Ground 1
Decision to refuse permission to amend the Points of Dispute.
   [Here state the grounds upon which the appellant intends to rely]

Ground 2
Bill item 6, counsel's fee, £250 plus VAT claimed £250 plus VAT allowed.
   [Here state the grounds upon which the appellant intends to rely]

Ground 3
Bill item 28, attendances on expert witnesses, £480 plus VAT claimed, £420 plus VAT allowed.
   [Here state the grounds upon which the appellant intends to rely]

I now enclose copies of (*tick as appropriate*)

☐ The Costs Certificate or other order being appealed

☐ Costs Officer's written reasons (or order dispensing with written reasons)

☐ Bill of Costs

☐ Points of Dispute lodged with request for detailed assessment hearing

☐ Points in Reply (if any)

☐ The authority for the detailed assessment

To [*Costs Officer whose decision is being appealed*] and to [*the intended respondents to the appeal*]

Signed _____   Date _____
   [Party] [Party's Solicitor]

APPENDIX 3   FORMS

SCHEDULE OF COSTS FORMS: FORM 17

Solicitors Act: order for delivery of bill

DATED the [DATE]

IN THE HIGH COURT OF JUSTICE [Claim No.]

[DIVISION]

[JUDGE TYPE] [JUDGE NAME]

BETWEEN:

[CLAIMANT]

Claimant

-and-

[DEFENDANT]

Defendant

UPON THE APPLICATION OF THE [PARTY]

[the parties and their representatives who attended]

AND UPON HEARING

AND UPON READING the documents on the Court File

IT IS ORDERED THAT

(1) The [PARTY] must within [NUMBER OF DAYS] deliver to the [PARTY], or to his solicitor, a bill of costs in all causes and matters in which he has been concerned for the [PARTY]

(2) The [PARTY] must give credit in that bill for all money received by him from or on account of the [PARTY]

APPENDIX 3   FORMS

SCHEDULE OF COSTS FORMS: FORM 18

**Order on Client's Application
for Detailed Assessment
of Solicitor's Bill**

DATED the [DATE]

IN THE HIGH COURT OF JUSTICE   [Claim No.]

[DIVISION]

[JUDGE TYPE] [JUDGE NAME]

BETWEEN:

[CLAIMANT]

Claimant

-and-

[DEFENDANT]

Defendant

UPON THE APPLICATION OF THE [PARTY]

[the parties and their representatives who attended]

AND UPON HEARING

AND UPON READING the documents on the Court File

IT IS ORDERED THAT

(1) A detailed assessment must be made of the bill dated [   ] delivered to the claimant by the defendant.

(2) On making the detailed assessment, the court must also assess the costs of these proceedings and certify what is due to or from either party in respect of the bill and the costs of these proceedings.

(3) Until these proceedings are concluded the defendant must not commence or continue any proceedings against the claimant in respect of the bill mentioned above.

(4) Upon payment by the claimant of any sum certified as due to the defendant in these proceedings the defendant must deliver to the claimant all the documentation in the defendant's possession or control which belong to the claimant.

SCHEDULE OF COSTS FORMS: FORM 19

**Order on Solicitor's Application
for Assessment under the
Solicitors Act 1974 Part III**

Upon hearing . . . upon reading . . .

IT IS ORDERED THAT

(1) A detailed assessment must be made of the bill dated [   ] delivered to the defendant by the claimant.

(2) If the defendant attends the detailed assessment the court making that assessment must also assess the costs of these proceedings and certify what is due to or from either party in respect of the bill and the costs of these proceedings.

(3) Until these proceedings are concluded the claimant must not commence or continue any proceedings against the defendant in respect of the bill mentioned above.

(4) Upon payment by the defendant of any sum certified as due to the claimant in these proceedings the claimant must deliver to the defendant all the documentation in the claimant's possession or control which belong to the defendant.

APPENDIX 3 FORMS

SCHEDULE OF COSTS FORMS: FORM 20

Solicitors Act: Breakdown of Costs

IN THE HIGH COURT OF JUSTICE   Claim No.

QUEEN'S BENCH DIVISION

SUPREME COURT COSTS OFFICE

BETWEEN

EF

Claimant

-and-

GH & Co.

Defendants

BREAKDOWN OF DEFENDANT'S BILL OF COSTS DATED 26 FEBRUARY 1999 TO BE ASSESSED PURSUANT TO THE ORDER DATED 27 APRIL 1999

The claimant instructed the defendants in connection with a summons for careless or inconsiderate driving which had been served upon him. By letter dated 21 October 1998 the defendants wrote to the claimant setting out their terms of business including the hourly rates of fee earners who would act on his instructions. On 23 October 1998 the claimant dated and signed a copy of that letter and returned it to the defendants so indicating his acceptance of the terms set out.

The proceedings were of the highest importance to the claimant who feared losing his licence and who wished to defend any civil proceedings that might be taken against him as a result of the prosecution. The defendants entered into correspondence with the CPS and eventually obtained their witness statements and invited them to consent to an adjournment because of the absence overseas of an important witness for the claimant (Mr LM). Eventually the defendants successfully applied to the court for an adjournment, and also applied for and obtained a witness summons. At the trial the claimant was found guilty and was fined £300 and 4 points were endorsed on his driving licence.

Proceedings were conducted by an assistant solicitor admitted in 1990 whose time is charged at an agreed rate of £150 per hour with routine letters out and telephone calls at an agreed rate of £15 each. At the trial a trainee attended with counsel. The trainee's time is charged at an agreed rate of £75 per hour.

Cash account for client: EF

Received	£	Paid	£
From client on account generally: 22 October 1998	1,500.00	Refund to client: 26 February 1999	385.00
From client on account generally: 12 February 1998	1,000.00	Balancing item	2,115.00
	2,500.00		2,500.00

Balance due to client EF: £2,115

SCHEDULE OF COSTS FORMS: FORM 21

Request for Detailed Assessment Hearing Pursuant to an Order under Part III of the Solicitors Act 1974

In the	
Claim No.	
Claimant (including ref.)	
Defendant (including ref.)	

I certify that the [*party*] has served a breakdown of costs in this case and the [*party*] has served points of dispute thereon.

I now ask the court to arrange an assessment hearing. The names, addresses and references of the parties upon whom the court should give notice of the hearing are as follows:

I enclose copies of (*tick as appropriate*)

- [ ] the order made under Part III of the Solicitors Act 1974 in this case
- [ ] Bills of Costs to be assessed
- [ ] breakdown of costs
- [ ] any fee notes of counsel and receipts or accounts for other disbursements served with the breakdown of costs
- [ ] the [party's] points of dispute plus copies to be sent to the other parties to these proceedings details of whom are given above
- [ ] points in reply (if any)

I believe the hearing will take .... (give estimate of time court should allow).

I enclose my fee of £ ....

Signed .... Date ....
    (Claimant)(Defendant)(Solicitor)

APPENDIX 4
CIVIL PROCEDURE ACT 1997

1997 CHAPTER 12

An Act to amend the law about civil procedure in England and Wales; and for connected purposes. [27th February 1997]

BE IT ENACTED by the Queen's most Excellent Majesty, by and with the advice and consent of the Lords Spiritual and Temporal, and Commons, in this present Parliament assembled, and by the authority of the same, as follows:—

Rules and directions

1. Civil Procedure Rules

(1) There are to be rules of court (to be called 'Civil Procedure Rules') governing the practice and procedure to be followed in—
   (a) the civil division of the Court of Appeal,
   (b) the High Court, and
   (c) county courts.

(2) Schedule 1 (which makes further provision about the extent of the power to make Civil Procedure Rules) is to have effect.

(3) The power to make Civil Procedure Rules is to be exercised with a view to securing that the civil justice system is accessible, fair and efficient.

2. Rule Committee

(1) Civil Procedure Rules are to be made by a committee known as the Civil Procedure Rule Committee, which is to consist of—
   (a) the Master of the Rolls,
   (b) the Vice-Chancellor, and
   (c) the persons currently appointed by the Lord Chancellor under subsection (2).

(2) The Lord Chancellor must appoint—
   (a) one judge of the Supreme Court,
   (b) one Circuit judge,
   (c) one district judge,
   (d) one person who is a Master referred to in Part II of Schedule 2 to the Supreme Court Act 1981,
   (e) three persons who have a Supreme Court qualification (within the meaning of section 71 of the Courts and Legal Services Act 1990), including at least one with particular experience of practice in county courts,
   (f) three persons who have been granted by an authorised body, under Part II of that Act, the right to conduct litigation in relation to all proceedings in the Supreme Court, including at least one with particular experience of practice in county courts,
   (g) one person with experience in and knowledge of consumer affairs, and
   (h) one person with experience in and knowledge of the lay advice sector.

(3) Before appointing a judge of the Supreme Court under subsection (2)(a), the Lord Chancellor must consult the Lord Chief Justice.

(4) Before appointing a person under paragraph (e) or (f) of subsection (2), the Lord Chancellor must consult any body which—
   (a) has members. who are eligible for appointment under that paragraph, and
   (b) is an authorised body for the purposes of section 27 or 28 of the Courts and Legal Services Act 1990.

(5) The Lord Chancellor may reimburse the members of the Civil Procedure Rule Committee their travelling and out-of-pocket expenses.

(6) The Civil Procedure Rule Committee must, before making or amending Civil Procedure Rules—
   (a) consult such persons as they consider appropriate, and
   (b) meet (unless it is inexpedient to do so).
(7) The Civil Procedure Rule Committee must, when making Civil Procedure Rules, try to make rules which are both simple and simply expressed.
(8) Rules made by the Civil Procedure Rule Committee must be signed by at least eight members of the Committee and be submitted to the Lord Chancellor, who may allow or disallow them.

3. Section 2: supplementary
(1) Rules made and allowed under section 2 are to—
   (a) come into force on such day as the Lord Chancellor may direct, and
   (b) be contained in a statutory instrument to which the Statutory Instruments Act 1946 is to apply as if it contained rules made by a Minister of the Crown.
(2) A statutory instrument containing Civil Procedure Rules shall be subject to annulment in pursuance of a resolution of either House of Parliament.

4. Power to make consequential amendments
(1) The Lord Chancellor may by order amend, repeal or revoke any enactment to the extent he considers necessary or desirable in consequence of—
   (a) section 1 or 2, or
   (b) Civil Procedure Rules.
(2) The Lord Chancellor may by order amend, repeal or revoke any enactment passed or made before the commencement of this section to the extent he considers necessary or desirable in order to facilitate the making of Civil Procedure Rules.
(3) Any power to make an order under this section is exercisable by statutory instrument.
(4) A statutory instrument containing an order under subsection (1) shall be subject to annulment in pursuance of a resolution of either House of Parliament.
(5) No order may be made under subsection (2) unless a draft of it has been laid before and approved by resolution of each House of Parliament.

5. Practice directions
(1) Practice directions may provide for any matter which, by virtue of paragraph 3 of Schedule 1, may be provided for by Civil Procedure Rules.
(2) After section 74 of the County Courts Act 1984 there is inserted—

'*Practice directions*

74A. Practice directions
(1) Directions as to the practice and procedure of county courts may be made by the Lord Chancellor.
(2) Directions as to the practice and procedure of county courts may not be made by any other person without the approval of the Lord Chancellor.
(3) The power of the Lord Chancellor to make directions under subsection (1) includes power—
   (a) to vary or revoke directions made by him or any other person, and
   (b) to make different provision for different cases or different areas, including different provision—
      (i) for a specific court, or
      (ii) for specific proceedings, or a specific jurisdiction,
specified in the directions.
(4) References in this section to the Lord Chancellor include any person authorised by him to act on his behalf.'

Civil Justice Council

6. Civil Justice Council
(1) The Lord Chancellor is to establish and maintain an advisory body, to be known as the Civil Justice Council.

(2) The Council must include—
  (a) members of the judiciary,
  (b) members of the legal professions,
  (c) civil servants concerned with the administration of the courts,
  (d) persons with experience in and knowledge of consumer affairs,
  (e) persons with experience in and knowledge of the lay advice sector, and
  (f) persons able to represent the interests of particular kinds of litigants (for example, businesses or employees).

(3) The functions of the Council are to include—
  (a) keeping the civil justice system under review,
  (b) considering how to make the civil justice system more accessible, fair and efficient,
  (c) advising the Lord Chancellor and the judiciary on the development of the civil justice system,
  (d) referring proposals for changes in the civil justice system to the Lord Chancellor and the Civil Procedure Rule Committee, and
  (e) making proposals for research.

(4) The Lord Chancellor may reimburse the members of the Council their travelling and out-of-pocket expenses.

Court orders

7. Power of courts to make orders for preserving evidence, etc

(1) The court may make an order under this section for the purpose of securing, in the case of any existing or proposed proceedings in the court—
  (a) the preservation of evidence which is or may be relevant, or
  (b) the preservation of property which is or may be the subject-matter of the proceedings or as to which any question arises or may arise in the proceedings.

(2) A person who is, or appears to the court likely to be, a party to proceedings in the court may make an application for such an order.

(3) Such an order may direct any person to permit any person described in the order, or secure that any person so described is permitted—
  (a) to enter premises in England and Wales, and
  (b) while on the premises, to take in accordance with the terms of the order any of the following steps.

(4) Those steps are—
  (a) to carry out a search for or inspection of anything described in the order, and
  (b) to make or obtain a copy, photograph, sample or other record of anything so described.

(5) The order may also direct the person concerned—
  (a) to provide any person described in the order, or secure that any person so described is provided, with any information or article described in the order, and
  (b) to allow any person described in the order, or secure that any person so described is allowed, to retain for safe keeping anything described in the order.

(6) An order under this section is to have effect subject to such conditions as are specified in the order.

(7) This section does not affect any right of a person to refuse to do anything on the ground that to do so might tend to expose him or his spouse to proceedings for an offence or for the recovery of a penalty.

(8) In this section—
  'court' means the High Court, and
  'premises' includes any vehicle;
and an order under this section may describe anything generally, whether by reference to a class or otherwise.

8. Disclosure etc. of documents before action begun

(1) The Lord Chancellor may by order amend the provisions of section 33(2) of the Supreme Court Act 1981, or section 52(2) of the County Courts Act 1984 (power of court to order disclosure etc. of documents where claim may be made in respect of personal injury or death), so as to extend the provisions—

APPENDIX 4 CIVIL PROCEDURE ACT 1997

    (a) to circumstances where other claims may be made, or
    (b) generally.
  (2) The power to make an order under this section is exercisable by statutory instrument which shall be subject to annulment in pursuance of a resolution of either House of Parliament.

General

9. Interpretation
  (1) A court the practice and procedure of which is governed by Civil Procedure Rules is referred to in this Act as being 'within the scope' of the rules; and references to a court outside the scope of the rules are to be read accordingly.
  (2) In this Act—
    'enactment' includes an enactment contained in subordinate legislation (within the meaning of the Interpretation Act 1978), and
    'practice directions' means directions as to the practice and procedure of any court within the scope of Civil Procedure Rules.

10. Minor and consequential amendments
Schedule 2 (which makes minor and consequential amendments) is to have effect.

11. Short title, commencement and extent
  (1) This Act may be cited as the Civil Procedure Act 1997.
  (2) Sections 1 to 10 are to come into force on such day as the Lord Chancellor may by order made by statutory instrument appoint, and different days may be appointed for different purposes.
  (3) This Act extends to England and Wales only.

Note
Section 11 came into force on royal assent (27 February 1997). Apart from some provisions of sch. 2 which are listed in the note at the end of that schedule, all other provisions of the Act were brought into force on 27 April 1997 by the Civil Procedure Act 1997 (Commencement No. 1) Order 1997 (SI 1997/841).

Section 1

SCHEDULES

SCHEDULE 1

CIVIL PROCEDURE RULES

Matters dealt with by the former rules

1. Among the matters which Civil Procedure Rules may be made about are any matters which were governed by the former Rules of the Supreme Court or the former county court rules (that is, the Rules of the Supreme Court (Revision) 1965 and the County Court Rules 1981).

Exercise of jurisdiction

2. Civil Procedure Rules may provide for the exercise of the jurisdiction of any court within the scope of the rules by officers or other staff of the court.

Removal of proceedings

3.—(1) Civil Procedure Rules may provide for the removal of proceedings at any stage—
    (a) within the High Court (for example, between different divisions or different district registries), or
    (b) between county courts.
  (2) In sub-paragraph (1)—
    (a) 'provide for the removal of proceedings' means—
      (i) provide for transfer of proceedings, or
      (ii) provide for any jurisdiction in any proceedings to be exercised (whether concurrently or not) elsewhere within the High Court or, as the case may be, by another county court without the proceedings being transferred, and

APPENDIX 4 CIVIL PROCEDURE ACT 1997

(b) 'proceedings' includes any part of proceedings.

Evidence

4. Civil Procedure Rules may modify the rules of evidence as they apply to proceedings in any court within the scope of the rules.

Application of other rules

5.—(1) Civil Procedure Rules may apply any rules of court which relate to a court which is outside the scope of Civil Procedure Rules.

(2) Any rules of court, not made by the Civil Procedure Rule Committee, which apply to proceedings of a particular kind in a court within the scope of Civil Procedure Rules may be applied by Civil Procedure Rules to other proceedings in such a court.

(3) In this paragraph 'rules of court' includes any provision governing the practice and procedure of a court which is made by or under an enactment.

(4) Where Civil Procedure Rules may be made by applying other rules, the other rules may be applied—
 (a) to any extent,
 (b) with or without modification, and
 (c) as amended from time to time.

Practice directions

6. Civil Procedure Rules may, instead of providing for any matter, refer to provision made or to be made about that matter by directions.

Different provision for different cases etc.

7. The power to make Civil Procedure Rules includes power to make different provision for different cases or different areas, including different provision—
 (a) for a specific court or specific division of a court, or
 (b) for specific proceedings, or a specific jurisdiction, specified in the rules.

Section 10 SCHEDULE 2

MINOR AND CONSEQUENTIAL AMENDMENTS

Supreme Court Act 1981 (c. 54)

1.—(1) The Supreme Court Act 1981 is amended as follows.

(2) In section 18 (restrictions on appeals), in subsections (1A) and (1B)(a), for 'Rules of the Supreme Court' there is substituted 'rules of court'.

(3) In section 68 (exercise of High Court jurisdiction otherwise than by judges)—
 (a) in subsection (1), paragraph (c) and the word 'or' immediately preceding it are omitted,
 (b) in subsection (2)—
  (i) paragraph (a) is omitted, and
  (ii) in paragraph (b), for 'any such person' there is substituted 'a special referee',
 (c) in subsection (3), for the words from 'any' onwards there is substituted 'a special referee or any officer or other staff of the court', and
 (d) in subsection (4)—
  (i) after 'decision of' there is inserted '(a)', and
  (ii) after 'subsection (1)' there is inserted—
  'or
 (b) any officer or other staff of the court'.

(4) In section 84 (power to make rules of court)—
 (a) in subsection (1), for 'Supreme Court' there is substituted 'Crown Court and the criminal division of the Court of Appeal',

APPENDIX 4   CIVIL PROCEDURE ACT 1997

    (b) subsection (4) is omitted,
    (c) for subsections (5) and (6) there is substituted—
      '(5) Special rules may apply—
        (a) any rules made under this section, or
        (b) Civil Procedure Rules,
to proceedings to which the special rules apply.
      (5A) Rules made under this section may apply—
        (a) any special rules, or
        (b) Civil Procedure Rules,
to proceedings to which rules made under this section apply.
      (6) Where rules may be applied under subsection (5) or (5A), they may be applied—
        (a) to any extent,
        (b) with or without modification, and
        (c) as amended from time to time.', and
    (d) in subsection (9), for 'Supreme Court Rule Committee' there is substituted 'Civil Procedure Rule Committee'.
  (5) Section 85 (Supreme Court Rule Committee) is omitted.
  (6) In section 87 (particular matters for which rules of court may provide)—
    (a) subsections (1) and (2) are omitted, and
    (b) in subsection (3), for 'Supreme Court' there is substituted 'Crown Court or the criminal division of the Court of Appeal'.
  (7) In section 151 (interpretation)—
    (a) in subsection (3), after the second 'rules of court' there is inserted 'in relation to the Supreme Court' and for 'Supreme Court Rule Committee' there is substituted 'Civil Procedure Rule Committee', and
    (b) in subsection (4), the definition of 'Rules of the Supreme Court' is omitted.

County Courts Act 1984 (c. 28)

2.—(1) The County Courts Act 1984 is amended as follows.
  (2) For 'county court rules', wherever occurring, there is substituted 'rules of court'.
  (3) For 'rule committee', wherever occurring, there is substituted 'Civil Procedure Rule Committee'.
  (4) In section 1 (county courts to be held for districts), in subsection (1), for the words from 'throughout' to 'the district' there is substituted 'each court'.
  (5) In section 3 (places and times of sittings of courts), subsection (3) is omitted.
  (6) Section 75 (county court rules) is omitted.
  (7) In section 77(1), for 'the rules of the Supreme Court' there is substituted 'Civil Procedure Rules'.
  (8) In section 81(2), for 'any rules of the Supreme Court' there is substituted 'Civil Procedure Rules'.
  (9) In section 147(1), the definitions of 'county court rules' and 'the rule committee' are omitted.

Matrimonial and Family Proceedings Act 1984 (c. 42)

3. In section 40 of the Matrimonial and Family Proceedings Act 1984 (family proceedings rules)—
    (a) after subsection (3) there is inserted—
      '(3A) Rules made under this section may make different provision for different cases or different areas, including different provision—
        (a) for a specific court, or
        (b) for specific proceedings, or a specific jurisdiction,
specified in the rules.', and
    (b) in subsection (4), the words from the first 'in' to 'and may' are omitted.

APPENDIX 4   CIVIL PROCEDURE ACT 1997

Courts and Legal Services Act 1990 (c. 41)

4. In section 120 of the Courts and Legal Services Act 1990 (regulations and orders), in subsection (4), '1(1)' is omitted.

Note

The Civil Procedure Act 1997 (Commencement No. 1) Order 1997 (SI 1997/841) made the following provisions about the commencement of sch. 2:

Paragraphs 1(1), (2) and (4)(c), 2(1), (2), (4) and (5), and 4 were brought into force on 27 April 1997. Paragraph 3(a) was brought into force on 14 March 1997.

The remaining sub-paragraphs were brought into force on 26 April 1999 by the Civil Procedure Act 1997 (Commencement No. 2) Order 1999 (SI 1999/1009).

APPENDIX 5
FEES ORDERS

CONTENTS

Supreme Court Fees Order 1999 (SI 1999/687)	1352
Non-contentious Probate Fees Order 1999 (SI 1999/688)	1360
County Court Fees Order 1999 (SI 1999/689)	1363
Family Proceedings Fees Order 1999 (SI 1999/690)	1375

SUPREME COURT FEES ORDER 1999
(SI 1999/687)

The Lord Chancellor, in exercise of the powers conferred on him by section 130 of the Supreme Court Act 1981, sections 414 and 415 of the Insolvency Act 1986, and section 128 of the Finance Act 1990, with the concurrence of the Lord Chief Justice, the Master of the Rolls, the President of the Family Division, the Vice-Chancellor and the Treasury under section 130(2) of the Supreme Court Act 1981, and with the sanction of the Treasury under sections 414(1) and 415(1) of the Insolvency Act 1986, makes the following Order:

1. Citation and commencement
This Order may be cited as the Supreme Court Fees Order 1999 and shall come into force on 26th April 1999.

2. Interpretation
In this Order, unless the context otherwise requires—
    (a) a fee referred to by number means the fee so numbered in Schedule 1 to this Order;
    (b) 'the CPR' means the Civil Procedure Rules 1998; and
    (c) expressions also used in the CPR have the same meaning as in those Rules.

3. Fees to be taken
The fees set out in column 2 of Schedule 1 to this Order shall be taken in the Supreme Court in respect of the items described in column 1 in accordance with and subject to the directions specified in column 1.

4. The provisions of this Order shall not apply to—
    (a) non-contentious probate business;
    (b) proceedings in the Court of Protection, except in so far as any fee prescribed in section 1 of Schedule 1 is applicable;
    (c) the enrolment of documents;
    (d) criminal proceedings (except proceedings on the Crown side of the Queen's Bench Division to which the fees contained in Schedule 1 are applicable);
    (e) proceedings by sheriffs, under-sheriffs, deputy-sheriffs or other officers of the sheriff; and
    (f) family proceedings.

5. Exemptions, reductions and remissions
(1) No fee shall be payable under this Order by a party who, at the time when a fee would otherwise become payable—
    (a) is in receipt of any qualifying benefit, and
    (b) is not in receipt of representation under Part IV of the Legal Aid Act 1988 for the purposes of the proceedings.
(2) The following are qualifying benefits for the purposes of paragraph (1)(a) above—
    (a) income support;
    (b) family credit and disability working allowance under Part VII of the Social Security Contributions and Benefits Act 1992; and
    (c) income-based jobseeker's allowance under the Jobseekers Act 1995.

6. Where it appears to the Lord Chancellor that the payment of any fee prescribed by this Order would, owing to the exceptional circumstances of the particular case, involve undue financial hardship, he may reduce or remit the fee in that case.

APPENDIX 5   FEES ORDERS

7. Where by any convention entered into by Her Majesty with any foreign power it is provided that no fee shall be required to be paid in respect of any proceedings, the fees specified in this Order shall not be taken in respect of those proceedings.

8. Revocations

The Orders specified in Schedule 2 shall be revoked, except as to any fee or other sum due or payable under those Orders before the commencement of this Order.

Dated 5th March 1999   *Irvine of Lairg*, C.

We concur,

Bingham of Cornhill, C.J.,
Woolf, M.R.,
Stephen Brown, P.,
Richard Scott, V.-C.

Dated 2nd March 1999

We concur,

Clive J. C. Betts
Bob Ainsworth
Two of the Lords Commissioners
of Her Majesty's Treasury

Dated 8th March 1999

SCHEDULE 1
FEES TO BE TAKEN

Column 1 Number and description of fee	Column 2 Amount of fee
Section 1. Fees payable in the High Court only **1. Commencement of proceedings**	
1.1 On the commencement of originating proceedings (including originating proceedings issued after leave to issue is granted) to recover a sum of money, where the sum claimed: (a) does not exceed £50,000 (b) exceeds £50,000 or is not limited	 £300 £400
1.2 On the commencement of originating proceedings for any other remedy or relief (including originating proceedings issued after leave to issue is granted)	£120
Fees 1.1 and 1.2 Recovery of land or goods Where a claim for money is additional or alternative to a claim for recovery of land or goods, only fee 1.2 shall be payable.	
Fees 1.1 and 1.2 Claims other than recovery of land or goods Where a claim for money is additional to a non money claim (other than a claim for recovery of land or goods) then fee 1.1 shall be payable in addition to fee 1.2. Where a claim for money is alternative to a non money claim (other than a claim for recovery of land or goods), only fee 1.1 shall be payable.	
Fees 1.1 and 1.2 Generally Where more than one non money claim is made in the same proceedings, fee 1.2 shall be payable once only, in addition to any fee which may be payable under fee 1.1.	
Fees 1.1 and 1.2 shall not be payable where fee 1.5(b) or fee 6 apply.	

APPENDIX 5 FEES ORDERS

Column 1 Number and description of fee	Column 2 Amount of fee
Fees 1.1 and 1.2 Amendment of claim or counterclaim Where the claim or counterclaim is amended, and the fee paid before amendment is less than that which would have been payable if the document, as amended, had been so drawn in the first instance, the party amending the document shall pay the difference.	
1.3 On the filing of proceedings against a party or parties not named in the originating proceedings	£30
Fee 1.3 shall be payable by a defendant who adds or substitutes a party or parties to the proceedings or by a claimant who adds or substitutes a defendant or defendants.	
1.4 On the filing of a counterclaim	The same fee as if the relief or remedy sought were the subject of separate proceedings
1.5 (a) On an application for leave to issue originating proceedings	£30
(b) On an application for an order under Part III of the Solicitors Act 1974 for the assessment of costs payable to a solicitor by his client	£30
2. General Fees 2.1 On the claimant filing an allocation questionnaire; or • where the court dispenses with the need for an allocation questionnaire, within 14 days of the date of despatch of the notice of allocation to track; or • where the CPR or a Practice Direction provide for automatic allocation or provide that the rules on allocation shall not apply, within 28 days of the filing of the defence (or the filing of the last defence if there is more than one defendant), or within 28 days of the expiry of the time permitted for filing all defences if sooner	£80
Fee 2.1 shall be payable by the claimant except where the action is proceeding on the counterclaim alone, when it shall be payable by the defendant— • on the defendant filing an allocation questionnaire; or • where the court dispenses with the need for an allocation questionnaire, within 14 days of the date of despatch of the notice of allocation to track; or • where the CPR or a Practice Direction provide for automatic allocation or provide that the rules on allocation shall not apply, within 28 days of the filing of the defence to the counterclaim (or the filing of the last defence to the counterclaim if there is more than one party entitled to file a defence to a counterclaim), or within 28 days of the expiry of the time permitted for filing all defences to the counterclaim if sooner	

APPENDIX 5 FEES ORDERS

Column 1 Number and description of fee	*Column 2* Amount of fee
2.2 On the claimant filing a listing questionnaire; or • where the court fixes the trial date or trial week without the need for a listing questionnaire, within 14 days of the date of despatch of the notice (or the date when oral notice is given if no written notice is given) of the trial week or the trial date if no trial week is fixed Fee 2.2 shall be payable by the claimant except where the action is proceeding on the counterclaim alone, when it shall be payable by the defendant— • on the defendant filing a listing questionnaire; or • where the court fixes the trial date or trial week without the need for a listing questionnaire, within 14 days of the date of despatch of the notice (or the date when oral notice is given if no written notice is given) of the trial week or the trial date if no trial week is fixed Where the court receives notice in writing— • before the trial date has been fixed or, • where a trial date has been fixed, at least 7 days before the trial date, from the party who paid fee 2.2 that the case is settled or discontinued, fee 2.2 shall be refunded. *Fees 2.1 and 2.2 Generally* Fees 2.1 and 2.2 shall be payable once only in the same proceedings. Fees 2.1 and 2.2 shall be payable as appropriate where the court allocates a case to a track for a trial of the assessment of damages. Fee 2.1 shall not be payable where the procedure in Part 8 of the CPR is used.	£400
2.3 Where no other fee is specified, on filing a notice of appeal (including an appeal against an allocation decision), or a case stated or a special case for the opinion of the High Court pursuant to statute, or a notice of cross appeal, or a respondent's notice of appeal	£100
2.4 On an application on notice where no other fee is specified	£50
2.5 On an application by consent or without notice for a judgment or order where no other fee is specified For the purpose of fee 2.5 a request for a judgment or order on admission or in default shall not constitute an application and no fee shall be payable.	£25
2.6 On an application for a summons or order for a witness to attend court to be examined on oath, other than an application for which fee 3.2 is payable	£30
2.7 On an application to vary a judgment or suspend enforcement (where more than one remedy is sought in the same application only one fee shall be payable)	£25

APPENDIX 5 FEES ORDERS

Column 1 Number and description of fee	Column 2 Amount of fee
3. Enforcement 3.1 On sealing a writ of execution/possession/delivery	£20
Where the recovery of a sum of money is sought in addition to a writ of possession and delivery, no further fee is payable.	
3.2 On an application to question a judgment debtor or other person on oath in connection with enforcement of a judgment	£40
3.3 On an application for a garnishee order nisi or a charging order nisi, or the appointment of a receiver by way of equitable execution	£50
Fee 3.3 shall be payable in respect of each party against whom the order is sought.	
3.4 On an application for a judgment summons	£80
3.5 On a request or application to register a judgment or order, or for leave to enforce an arbitration award, or for a certified copy of a judgment or order for use abroad	£30
4. Miscellaneous proceedings or matters	
Bills of Sale 4.1 On filing any document under the Bills of Sale Acts 1878 and 1882	£10
Searches 4.2 For an official certificate of the result of a search for each name, in any register or index held by the court; or in the Court Funds Office, for an official certificate of the result of a search of unclaimed balances for a specified period of up to 50 years	£5
4.3 On a search in person of the bankruptcy and companies records, including inspection, for each 15 minutes or part of 15 minutes	£5

Judge sitting as arbitrator
4.4 On the appointment of—
    (a) a judge of the Commercial Court as an arbitrator or umpire under section 93 of the Arbitration Act 1996; or
    (b) a judge of the Technology and Construction Court as an arbitrator or umpire under section 93 of the Arbitration Act 1996
	£1,800
	
	£1,400

4.5 For every day or part of a day (after the first day) of the hearing before—
    (a) a judge of the Commercial Court; or
    (b) a judge of the Technology and Construction Court, so appointed as arbitrator or umpire
	
	£1,800
	£1,400

Where fee 4.5 has been paid on the appointment of a judge of the Commercial Court or a judge of the Technology and Construction Court as an arbitrator or umpire but the arbitration does not proceed to a hearing or an award, the fee shall be refunded.	

APPENDIX 5   FEES ORDERS

Column 1 Number and description of fee	Column 2 Amount of fee
5. Fees payable in Admiralty Matters In the Admiralty Registrar and Marshal's Office—	
5.1 On the issue of a warrant for the arrest of a ship or goods	£100
5.2 On the sale of a ship or goods— subject to a minimum fee of £200, 　(a)　for every £100 or fraction of £100 of the price up to £100,000 　(b)　for every £100 or fraction of £100 of the price exceeding £100,000	£1 50p
Where there is sufficient proceeds of sale in court, fee 5.2 shall be taken by transfer from the proceeds of sale in court.	
5.3 On entering a reference for hearing by the Registrar	£50
6. Companies Act 1985 and Insolvency Act 1986 6.1 On entering a bankruptcy petition: 　(a)　if presented by a debtor or the personal representative of a deceased debtor 　(b)　if presented by a creditor or other person	 £120 £150
6.2 On entering a petition for an administration order	£100
6.3 On entering any other petition	£150
One fee only is payable where more than one petition is presented in relation to a partnership.	
6.4 (a)　On a request for a certificate of discharge from bankruptcy 　(b)　and after the first certificate for each copy	£50 £1
Requests and applications with no fee No fee is payable on a request or on an application to the Court by the Official Receiver when applying only in the capacity of Official Receiver to the case (and not as trustee or liquidator), or on an application to set aside a statutory demand.	
Section 2. Fees payable in both the High Court and in the Court of Appeal	
7. Copy Documents 7.1 On a request for a copy of any document (including a faxed copy where requested) or for examining a plain copy and marking it as an office copy: 　(a)　per page for the first five pages of each document 　(b)　per page for subsequent pages	 £1 25p
Fee 7.1 is payable whether or not the copy is issued as an office copy.	
7.2 Where copies of any document are made available on a computer disk or in other electronic form, for each such copy	£3

APPENDIX 5 FEES ORDERS

Column 1 Number and description of fee	Column 2 Amount of fee
8. Affidavits 8.1 On taking an affidavit or an affirmation or attestation upon honour in lieu of an affidavit or a declaration except for the purpose of receipt of dividends from the Accountant General and for a declaration by a shorthand writer appointed in insolvency proceedings —for each person making any of the above	£5
8.2 For each exhibit referred to in an affidavit, affirmation, attestation or declaration for which fee 8.1 is payable	£2
Section 3. Fees payable in the Court of Appeal only	
9. Fees payable in appeals to the Court of Appeal 9.1 On filing a notice of appeal	£200
9.2 On filing a respondent's notice	£100
9.3 On filing any application notice	£100
Section 4. Fees payable on the determination of costs	
10. Determination of costs Transitional Provision Where a bill of costs or a request for detailed assessment or a request for a detailed assessment hearing is filed pursuant to an order made by the court before the coming into operation of this Order, or an application is made to review a taxing officer's decision made before the coming into operation of this Order, the fees payable shall be those which applied immediately before this Order came into force.	
10.1 On the filing of a request for detailed assessment where the party filing the request is legally aided and no other party is ordered to pay the costs of the proceedings	£120
10.2 On the filing of a request for a detailed assessment hearing in any case where fee 10.1 does not apply; or on the filing of a request for a hearing date for the assessment of costs payable to a solicitor by his client pursuant to an order under Part III of the Solicitors Act 1974	£160
10.3 On an application for the issue of a default costs certificate	£40
10.4 On an appeal against a decision made in detailed assessment proceedings or on an application to set aside a default costs certificate	£50
10.5 On applying for the court's approval of a Legal Aid Assessment Certificate	£20
Fee 10.5 is payable at the time of applying for the court's approval and is recoverable only against the Legal Aid Fund.	

APPENDIX 5 FEES ORDERS

SCHEDULE 2
ORDERS REVOKED

Title	Reference
The Supreme Court Fees Order 1980	S.I. 1980/821
The Supreme Court Fees (Amendment) Order 1980	S.I. 1980/1060
The Supreme Court Fees (Amendment) Order 1982	S.I. 1982/1707
The Supreme Court Fees (Amendment) Order 1983	S.I. 1983/1680
The Supreme Court Fees (Amendment) Order 1986	S.I. 1986/637
The Supreme Court Fees (Amendment No. 2) Order 1986	S.I. 1986/2144
The Supreme Court Fees (Amendment) Order 1988	S.I. 1988/510
The Supreme Court Fees (Amendment) Order 1990	S.I. 1990/1460
The Supreme Court Fees (Amendment) Order 1993	S.I. 1993/3191
The Supreme Court Fees (Amendment) Order 1995	S.I. 1995/2629
The Supreme Court Fees (Amendment) Order 1996	S.I. 1996/3191
The Supreme Court Fees (Amendment) Order 1997	S.I. 1997/2672

NON-CONTENTIOUS PROBATE FEES ORDER 1999
(SI 1999/688)

The Lord Chancellor, in exercise of the powers conferred on him by section 130 of the Supreme Court Act 1981, with the concurrence of the Lord Chief Justice, the Master of the Rolls, the President of the Family Division, the Vice-Chancellor and the Treasury under section 130(2) of the Supreme Court Act 1981, makes the following Order:

1. Citation and commencement
This Order may be cited as the Non-Contentious Probate Fees Order 1999 and shall come into force on 26th April 1999.

2. Interpretation
In this Order, unless the context otherwise requires—
　(a) a fee referred to by number means the fee so numbered in Schedule 1 to this Order;
　(b) 'assessed value' means the value of the net real and personal estate (excluding settled land if any) passing under the grant as shown—
　　(i) in the Inland Revenue affidavit (for a death occurring before 13th March 1975), or
　　(ii) in the Inland Revenue account (for a death occurring on or after 13th March 1975), or
　　(iii) in a case in which, in accordance with arrangements made between the President of the Family Division and the Commissioners of Inland Revenue, or regulations made under section 256(1)(a) of the Inheritance Tax Act 1984 and from time to time in force, no such affidavit or account is required to be delivered, in the oath which is sworn to lead to the grant,
and in the case of an application to reseal a grant means the value, as so shown, passing under the grant upon its being resealed;
　(c) 'authorised place of deposit' means any place in which, by virtue of a direction given under section 124 of the Supreme Court Act 1981 original wills and other documents under the control of the High Court (either in the principal registry or in any district registry) are deposited and preserved;
　(d) 'grant' means a grant of probate or letters of administration;
　(e) 'district registry' includes the probate registry of Wales, any district probate registry and any sub-registry attached to it;
　(f) 'the principal registry' means the Principal Registry of the Family Division and any sub-registry attached to it.

3. Fees to be taken
The fees set out in column 2 of Schedule 1 to this Order shall be taken in the principal registry and in each district registry in respect of the items described in column 1 in accordance with and subject to any directions specified in column 1.

4. Exclusion of certain death gratuities
In determining the value of any personal estate for the purposes of this Order there shall be excluded the value of a death gratuity payable under section 17(2) of the Judicial Pensions Act 1981 or section 4(3) of the Judicial Pensions and Retirement Act 1993, or payable to the personal representatives of a deceased civil servant by virtue of a scheme made under section 1 of the Superannuation Act 1972.

5. Exemptions, reductions and remissions
　(1) Where it appears to the Lord Chancellor that the payment of any fee prescribed by this Order would, owing to the exceptional circumstances of the particular case, involve undue hardship, he may reduce or remit the fee in that case.

APPENDIX 5 FEES ORDERS

(2) Where by any convention entered into by Her Majesty with any foreign power it is provided that no fee shall be required to be paid in respect of any proceedings, the fees specified in this Order shall not be taken in respect of those proceedings.

(3) Where any application for a grant is withdrawn before the issue of a grant, a registrar may reduce or remit a fee.

(4) Fee 7 shall not be taken where a search is made for research or similar purposes by permission of the President of the Family Division for a document over 100 years old filed in the principal registry or a district registry or another authorised place of deposit.

6. Revocations

The Orders specified in Schedule 2 shall be revoked, except as to any fee or other sum due or payable under those Orders before the commencement of this Order.

Dated 5th March 1999   *Irvine of Lairg*, C.

We concur,

Bingham of Cornhill, C.J.,
Woolf, M.R.,
Stephen Brown, P.,
Dated 2nd March 1999   *Richard Stott*, V.-C

We concur,

Clive J. C. Betts
Bob Ainsworth
Two of the Lords Commissioners
Dated 8th March 1999   *of Her Majesty's Treasury*

SCHEDULE 1
FEES TO BE TAKEN

Column 1 Number and description of fee	Column 2 Amount of fee
1. Application for a grant On an application for a grant (or for resealing a grant) other than on an application to which fee 3 applies, where the value of the estate exceeds £5,000	£50
2. Personal application fee Where the application under fee 1 is made by a personal applicant (not being an application to which fee 3 applies) fee 2 is payable in addition to fee 1, where the value of the estate exceeds £5,000	£80
3. Special applications For a duplicate or second or subsequent grant (including one following a revoked grant) in respect of the same deceased person, other than a grant preceded only by a grant limited to settled land, to trust property, or to part of the estate	£15
4. Caveats For the entry or the extension of a caveat	£15
5. Search On an application for a standing search to be carried out in an estate, for each period of six months including the issue of a copy grant and will, if any (irrespective of the number of pages)	£5

APPENDIX 5 FEES ORDERS

Column 1 Number and description of fee	Column 2 Amount of fee
6. Deposit of wills On depositing a will for safe custody in the principal registry or a district registry	£15
7. Inspection On inspection of any will or other document retained by the registry (in the presence of an officer of the registry)	£15

8. Copy documents
On a request for a copy of any document whether or not provided as a certified copy:
  (a) for the first copy
  (b) for every subsequent copy of the same document if supplied at the same time
  (c) where copies of any document are made available on a computer disk or in other electronic form, for each such copy
  (d) where a search of the index is required, in addition to fee 8(a), (b) or (c) as appropriate, for each period of 4 years searched after the first 4 years
	
	£5
	£1
	
	£3
	
	£3

9. Oaths Except on a personal application for a grant for administering an oath,	
9.1 for each deponent to each affidavit	£5
9.2 for marking each exhibit	£2
10. Determination of costs For determining costs	The same fees as are payable from time to time for determining costs under the Supreme Court Fees Order 1999 (the relevant fees are set out in fee 3 in Schedule 1 to that Order)
11. Settling documents For perusing and settling citations, advertisements, oaths, affidavits, or other documents, for each document settled	£10

SCHEDULE 2
ORDERS REVOKED

Title	S.I. number
The Non-Contentious Probate Fees Order 1981	S.I. 1981/861
The Non-Contentious Probate Fees (Amendment) Order 1981	S.I. 1981/1103
The Non-Contentious Probate Fees (Amendment) Order 1986	S.I. 1986/705
The Non-Contentious Probate Fees (Amendment) (No. 2) Order 1986	S.I. 1986/2185
The Non-Contentious Probate Fees (Amendment) Order 1987	S.I. 1987/1176
The Non-Contentious Probate Fees (Amendment) Order 1989	S.I. 1989/1140

COUNTY COURT FEES ORDER 1999
(SI 1999/689)

The Lord Chancellor, in exercise of the powers conferred on him by section 128 of the County Courts Act 1984, sections 414 and 415 of the Insolvency Act 1986 and section 128 of the Finance Act 1990, with the concurrence of the Treasury under section 128(1) of the County Courts Act 1984, and with the sanction of the Treasury under sections 414(1) and 415(1) of the Insolvency Act 1986, makes the following Order:

1. Citation and commencement
This Order maybe cited as the County Court Fees Order 1999 and shall come into force on 26th April 1999.

2. Interpretation
In this Order, unless the context otherwise requires—
    (a) a fee referred to by number means the fee so numbered in Schedule 1 to this Order;
    (b) 'CCBC' means County Court Bulk Centre;
    (c) 'the CPR' means the Civil Procedure Rules 1998;
    (d) expressions also used in the CPR have the same meaning as in those Rules; and
    (e) 'CPC' means Claim Production Centre.

3. Fees to be taken
The fees set out in column 2 of Schedule 1 to this Order shall be taken in county courts in respect of the items described in column 1 in accordance with and subject to the directions specified in column 1.

4. The provisions of this Order shall not apply to family proceedings.

5. Exemptions, reductions and remissions
(1) No fee shall be payable under this Order by a party who, at the time when a fee would otherwise become payable—
    (a) is in receipt of any qualifying benefit, and
    (b) is not in receipt of representation under Part IV of the Legal Aid Act 1988 for the purposes of the proceedings.
(2) The following are qualifying benefits for the purposes of paragraph (1)(a) above—
    (a) income support;
    (b) family credit and disability working allowance under Part VII of the Social Security Contributions and Benefits Act 1992; and
    (c) income-based jobseeker's allowance under the Jobseekers Act 1995.
(3) Paragraph (1) shall not apply to fee 4.8 (fee payable on a consolidated attachment of earnings order or an administration order).

6. Where it appears to the Lord Chancellor that the payment of any fee prescribed by this Order would, owing to the exceptional circumstances of the particular case, involve undue financial hardship, he may reduce or remit the fee in that case.

7. Where by any convention entered into by Her Majesty with any foreign power it is provided that no fee shall be required to be paid in respect of any proceedings, the fees specified in this Order shall not be taken in respect of those proceedings.

8. Revocations
The Orders specified in Schedule 2 shall be revoked, except as to any fee or other sum due or payable under those Orders before the commencement of this Order.

APPENDIX 5 FEES ORDERS

Dated 5th March 1999   *Irvine of Lairg*, C.

We concur,

Clive J. C. Betts
Bob Ainsworth
Two of the Lords Commissioners
of Her Majesty's Treasury

Dated 8th March 1999

SCHEDULE 1
FEES TO BE TAKEN

Column 1 Number & description of fee	*Column 2* Amount of fee
1. Commencement of proceedings	
1.1 On the commencement of originating proceedings (including originating proceedings issued after leave to issue is granted) to recover a sum of money, except in CPC cases, where the sum claimed:	(a) does not exceed £200 .... £20 (b) exceeds £200 but not £300 .... £30 (c) exceeds £300 but not £400 .... £40 (d) exceeds £400 but not £500 .... £50 (e) exceeds £500 but not £1,000 .... £70 (f) exceeds £1,000 but not £5,000 .. £100 (g) exceeds £5,000 but not £15,000 .. £200 (h) exceeds £15,000 but not £50,000 £300 (i) exceeds £50,000 or not limited £400
1.2 On the commencement of originating proceedings to recover a sum of money in CPC cases, where the sum claimed:	(a) does not exceed £200 .... £15 (b) exceeds £200 but not £300 .... £25 (c) exceeds £300 but not £400 .... £35 (d) exceeds £400 but not £500 .... £45 (e) exceeds £500 but not £1,000 .... £65 (f) exceeds £1,000 but not £5,000 .... £95 (g) exceeds £5,000 but not £15,000 .. £195 (h) exceeds £15,000 but not £50,000 £295 (i) exceeds £50,000 or not limited £395
1.3 On the commencement of originating proceedings for any other remedy or relief (including originating proceedings issued after leave to issue is granted)	£120
Fees 1.1 and 1.3 Recovery of land or goods Where a claim for money is additional or alternative to a claim for recovery of land or goods, only fee 1.3 shall be payable.	

APPENDIX 5 FEES ORDERS

Column 1 Number & description of fee	*Column 2* Amount of fee
Fees 1.1 and 1.3 Claims other than recovery of land or goods Where a claim for money is additional to a non money claim (other than a claim for recovery of land or goods) then fee 1.1 shall be payable in addition to fee 1.3. Where a claim for money is alternative to a non money claim (other than a claim for recovery of land or goods) then fee 1.1 or fee 1.3 shall be payable, whichever is the greater.	
Fees 1.1 and 1.3 Generally Where more than one non money claim is made in the same proceedings, fee 1.3 shall be payable once only, in addition to any fee which may be payable under fee 1.1.	
Fees 1.1 and 1.3 shall not be payable where fee 1.6(b) or fee 8 apply.	
Fees 1.1 and 1.3 Amendment of claim or counterclaim Where the claim or counterclaim is amended, and the fee paid before amendment is less than that which would have been payable if the document, as amended, had been so drawn in the first instance, the party amending the document shall pay the difference.	
1.4 On the filing of proceedings against a party or parties not named in the originating proceedings	£30
Fee 1.4 shall be payable by a defendant who adds or substitutes a party or parties to the proceedings or by a claimant who adds or substitutes a defendant or defendants.	
1.5 On the filing of a counterclaim	The same fee as if the relief or remedy sought were the subject of separate proceedings

APPENDIX 5 FEES ORDERS

Column 1 Number & description of fee	*Column 2* Amount of fee
1.6(a) On an application for leave to issue originating proceedings	£30
(b) On an application for an order under Part III of the Solicitors Act 1974 for the assessment of costs payable to a solicitor by his client	£30
2. General Fees 2.1 On the claimant filing an allocation questionnaire; or • where the court dispenses with the need for an allocation questionnaire, within 14 days of the date of despatch of the notice of allocation to track; or • where the CPR or a Practice Direction provide for automatic allocation or provide that the rules on allocation shall not apply, within 28 days of the filing of the defence (or the filing of the last defence is there is more than one defendant), or within 28 days of the expiry of the time permitted for filing all defences if sooner Fee 2.1 shall be payable by the claimant except where the action is proceeding on the counterclaim alone, when it shall be payable by the defendant— • on the defendant filing an allocation questionnaire; or • where the court dispenses with the need for an allocation questionnaire, within 14 days of the date of despatch of the notice of allocation to track; or	£80

1366

Column 1 Number & description of fee	Column 2 Amount of fee
• where the CPR or a Practice Direction provide for automatic allocation or provide that the rules on allocation shall not apply, within 28 days of the filing of the defence to the counterclaim (or the filing of the last defence to the counterclaim if there is more than one party entitled to file a defence to a counterclaim), or within 28 days of the expiry of the time permitted for filing all defences to the counterclaim if sooner	
2.2 On the claimant filing a listing questionnaire; or • where the court fixes the trial date or trial week without the need for a listing questionnaire, within 14 days of the date of despatch of the notice (or the date when oral notice is given if no written notice is given) of the trial week or the trial date if no trial week is fixed: (a) if the case is on the multi-track (b) in any other case	 £300 £200
Fee 2.2 shall be payable by the claimant except where the action is proceeding on the counterclaim alone, when it shall be payable by the defendant— • on the defendant filing a listing questionnaire; or	

APPENDIX 5 FEES ORDERS

Column 1 Number & description of fee	Column 2 Amount of fee
• where the court fixes the trial date or trial week without the need for a listing questionnaire, within 14 days of the date of despatch of the notice (or the date when oral notice is given if no written notice is given) of the trial week or the trial date if no trial week is fixed Where the court receives notice in writing— • before the trial date has been fixed or, • where a trial date has been fixed, at least 7 days before the trial date, from the party who paid fee 2.2 that the case is settled or discontinued, fee 2.2 shall be refunded. *Fees 2.1 and 2.2 Generally* Fees 2.1 and 2.2 shall be payable once only in the same proceedings. Fees 2.1 and 2.2 shall be payable as appropriate where the court allocates a case to a track for a trial of the assessment of damages. Fee 2.1 shall not be payable where the procedure in Part 8 of the CPR is used. Fee 2.2 shall not be payable in respect of a small claims hearing.	
2.3 On filing notice of appeal including an appeal against an allocation decision where no other fee is specified	£100
2.4 On an application on notice other than an application to fix the rate of payment before judgment where no other fee is specified	£50

APPENDIX 5   FEES ORDERS

Column 1 Number & description of fee	*Column 2* Amount of fee
2.5 On an application by consent or without notice for a judgment or order where no other fee is specified For the purpose of fee 2.5 a request for a judgment or order on admission or in default shall not constitute an application and no fee shall be payable.	£25
2.6 On an application for a summons or order for a witness to attend court to be examined on oath, other than an application for which fee 4.3 is payable	£30
2.7 On an application to vary a judgment or suspend enforcement (where more than one remedy is sought in the same application only one fee shall be payable)	£25
3. Determination of costs Transitional provision Where a bill of costs or a request for detailed assessment or a request for a detailed assessment hearing is filed pursuant to an order made by the court before the coming into operation of this Order, or an application is made to the judge to review a taxation made before the coming into operation of this Order, the fees payable shall be those which applied immediately before this Order came into force.	
3.1 On the filing of a request for detailed assessment where the party filing the request is legally aided and no other party is ordered to pay the costs of the proceedings	£80

1369

APPENDIX 5   FEES ORDERS

Column 1 Number & description of fee	Column 2 Amount of fee
3.2 On the filing of a request for a detailed assessment hearing in any case where fee 3.1 does not apply; or on the filing of a request for a hearing date for the assessment of costs payable to a solicitor by his client pursuant to an order under Part III of the Solicitors Act 1974 Where there is a combined party and party and legal aid determination of costs, fee 3.2 shall be attributed proportionately to the party and party and legal aid portions of the bill on the basis of the amount allowed.	£120
3.3 On an application for the issue of a default costs certificate	£40
3.4 On an appeal against a decision made in detailed assessment proceedings or on an application to set aside a default costs certificate	£50
3.5 On applying for the court's approval of a Legal Aid Assessment Certificate Fee 3.5 is payable at the time of applying for approval and is recoverable only against the Legal Aid Fund.	£20
4. Enforcement 4.1 On an application for or in relation to enforcement of a judgment or order of a county court or through a county court:	
in cases other than CCBC cases, by the issue of a warrant of execution against goods except a warrant to enforce payment of a fine; in CCBC cases, by the issue of a warrant of execution against goods except a warrant to enforce payment of a fine	(a) Where the amount for which the warrant issues does not exceed £125 .... £25 (b) Where the amount for which the warrant issues exceeds £125 .... £45 (c) Where the amount for which the warrant issues does not exceed £125 .... £20 (d) Where the amount for which the warrant issues exceeds £125 .... £40

APPENDIX 5   FEES ORDERS

Column 1 Number & description of fee	Column 2 Amount of fee
4.2 On a request for a further attempt at execution of a warrant at a new address following a notice of the reason for non-execution (except a further attempt following suspension and CCBC cases)	£20
4.3 On an application to question a judgment debtor or other person on oath in connection with enforcement of a judgment	£40
4.4 On an application for a garnishee order nisi or a charging order nisi, or the appointment of a receiver by way of equitable execution	£50
Fee 4.4 shall be payable in respect of each party against whom the order is sought.	
4.5 On an application for a judgment summons	£80
4.6 On the issue of a warrant of possession or a warrant of delivery	£80
Where the recovery of a sum of money is sought in addition, no further fee is payable.	
4.7 On an application for an attachment of earnings order (other than a consolidated attachment of earnings order) to secure payment of a judgment debt	£50
Fee 4.7 is payable for each defendant against whom an order is sought. Fee 4.7 is not payable where the attachment of earnings order is made on the hearing of a judgment summons.	
4.8 On a consolidated attachment of earnings order or on an administration order	for every £1 or part of a £1 of the money paid into court in respect of debts due to creditors. 10p

APPENDIX 5 FEES ORDERS

Column 1 Number & description of fee	Column 2 Amount of fee
Fee 4.8 shall be calculated on any money paid into court under any order at the rate in force at the time when the order was made (or, where the order has been amended, at the time of the last amendment before the date of payment).	
4.9 On the application for the recovery of a tribunal award	£30
4.10 On a request for an order to recover an increased penalty charge provided for in a parking charge certificate issued under paragraph 6 of Schedule 6 to the Road Traffic Act 1991 or on a request for an order to recover amounts payable by a person other than a London authority under an adjudication of a parking adjudicator pursuant to section 73 of the Road Traffic Act 1991; on a request to issue a warrant of execution to enforce such an order Fee 4.10 is payable on a request for an order but no further fee is payable on a request to issue a warrant of execution.	£5
5. Sale 5.1 For removing or taking steps to remove goods to a place of deposit	The reasonable expenses incurred
Fee 5.1 is to include the reasonable expenses of feeding and caring for any animals.	
5.2 For advertising a sale by public auction pursuant to section 97 of the County Courts Act 1984	The reasonable expenses incurred
5.3 For the appraisement of goods	5p in the £1 or part of a £1 of the appraised value

APPENDIX 5 FEES ORDERS

Column 1 Number & description of fee	Column 2 Amount of fee
5.4 For the sale of goods (including advertisements, catalogues, sale and commission and delivery of goods)	15p in the £1 or part of a £1 on the amount realised by the sale or such other sum as the district judge may consider to be justified in the circumstances
5.5 Where no sale takes place by reason of an execution being withdrawn, satisfied or stopped	(a) 10p in the £1 or part of a £1 on the value of the goods seized, the value to be the appraised value where the goods have been appraised or such other sum as the district judge may consider to be justified in the circumstances; and in addition (b) any sum payable under fee 5.1, 5.2 or 5.3
6. Copy documents 6.1 On a request for a copy of any document (including a faxed copy where requested) or for examining a plain copy and marking it as an office copy; (a) per page for the first five pages of each document (b) per page for subsequent pages	 £1 25p
Fee 6.1 is payable whether or not the copy is issued as an office copy.	
6.2 Where copies of any document are made available on a computer disk or in other electronic form, for each such copy	£3
7. Registry of County Court Judgments 7.1 On a request for the issue of a certificate of satisfaction	 £10
8. Companies Act 1985 and Insolvency Act 1986 8.1 On entering a bankruptcy petition: (a) if presented by a debtor or the personal representative of a deceased debtor (b) if presented by a creditor or other person	 £120 £150
8.2 On entering a petition for an administration order	£100
8.3 On entering any other petition	£150

APPENDIX 5 FEES ORDERS

Column 1 Number & description of fee	Column 2 Amount of fee
One fee only is payable where more than one petition is presented in relation to a partnership.	
8.4(a) On a request for a certificate of discharge from bankruptcy	£50
(b) and after the first certificate, for each copy	£1
Requests and applications with no fee No fee is payable on a request or on an application to the court by the Official Receiver when applying only in the capacity of Official Receiver to the case (and not as trustee or liquidator), or on an application to set aside a statutory demand.	

SCHEDULE 2
ORDERS REVOKED

Title	*Reference*
The County Court Fees Order 1982	S.I. 1982/1706
The County Court Fees (Amendment) Order 1983	S.I. 1983/1681
The County Court Fees (Amendment) Order 1985	S.I. 1985/574
The County Court Fees (Amendment No. 2) Order 1985	S.I. 1985/1834
The County Court Fees (Amendment) Order 1986	S.I. 1986/633
The County Court Fees (Amendment No. 2) Order 1986	S.I. 1986/2143
The County Court Fees (Amendment) Order 1988	S.I. 1988/509
The County Court Fees (Amendment) Order 1992	S.I. 1992/2762
The County Court Fees (Amendment) Order 1994	S.I. 1994/1936
The County Court Fees (Amendment) Order 1995	S.I. 1995/2627
The County Court Fees (Amendment) Order 1996	S.I. 1996/3189
The County Court Fees (Amendment) Order 1997	S.I. 1997/787
The County Court Fees (Amendment) (No. 2) Order 1997	S.I. 1997/2670

FAMILY PROCEEDINGS FEES ORDER 1999
(SI 1999/690)

The Lord Chancellor, in exercise. of the powers conferred on him by section 41 of the Matrimonial and Family Proceedings Act 1984 and section 415 of the Insolvency Act 1986, with the concurrence of the Treasury under section 41 of the Matrimonial and Family Proceedings Act 1984, and with the sanction of the Treasury under section 415(1) of the Insolvency Act 1986, makes the following Order:

1. Citation and commencement
This Order may be cited as the Family Proceedings Fees Order 1999 and shall come into force on 26th April 1999.

2. Interpretation
In this Order, unless the context otherwise requires—
   (a) a fee referred to by number means the fee so numbered in Schedule 1 to this Order;
   (b) a rule or form referred to by number alone means the rule or form so numbered in the Family Proceedings Rules 1991; and
   (c) expressions also used in the Family Proceedings Rules 1991 have the same meaning as in those Rules.

3. Fees to be taken
The fees set out in column 2 of Schedule 1 to this Order shall be taken in family proceedings in the High Court or in a county court in respect of the items described in column 1 in accordance with and subject to the directions specified in column 1.

4. Exemptions, reductions and remissions
   (1) No fee shall be payable under this Order by a party who, at the time when a fee would otherwise become payable—
   (a) is in receipt of legal advice and assistance under Part III of the Legal Aid Act 1988 in connection with the matter to which the proceedings relate, or
   (b) is in receipt of any qualifying benefit and is not in receipt of representation under Part IV of the Legal Aid Act 1988 for the purposes of the proceedings, or
   (c) is not a beneficiary of a trust fund in court of a value of more than £50,000 and is—
      (i) under the age of eighteen, or
      (ii) a person for whose financial relief an order under paragraph 2 of Schedule 1 to the Children Act 1989 is in force or is being applied for.
   (2) The following are qualifying benefits for the purposes of paragraph (1)(b) above—
   (a) income support;
   (b) family credit and disability working allowance under Part VII of the Social Security Contributions and Benefits Act 1992; and
   (c) income-based jobseeker's allowance under the Jobseekers Act 1995.

5. Where it appears to the Lord Chancellor that the payment of any fee prescribed by this Order would, owing to the exceptional circumstances of the particular case, involve undue hardship, he may reduce or remit the fee in that case.

6. Where by any convention entered into by Her Majesty with any foreign power it is provided that no fee shall be required to be paid in respect of any proceedings, the fees specified in this Order shall not be taken in respect of those proceedings.

APPENDIX 5   FEES ORDERS

7. Revocations
The Orders specified in Schedule 2 shall be revoked, except as to any fee or other sum due or payable under those Orders before the commencement of this Order.

Dated 5th March 1999   *Irvine of Lairg*, C.

We concur,

Clive J. C. Betts
Bob Ainsworth
Two of the Lords Commissioners of
Dated 8th March 1999   Her Majesty's Treasury

SCHEDULE 1
FEES TO BE TAKEN

Column 1 Number and description of fee	Column 2 Amount of fee
Section 1. Fees to be taken in the High Court and in the county courts	
Commencement of proceedings 1.1 On filing originating proceedings where no other fee is specified	£120
1.2 On presenting any petition, other than a second petition with leave granted under rule 2.6(4)	£150
1.3 On applying for either a non-molestation order or an occupation order under Part IV of the Family Law Act 1996, or on applying simultaneously for both a non-molestation order and an occupation order	£40
1.4 On amending a petition or presenting a second or subsequent petition with leave granted under rule 2.6(4)	£50
1.5 On filing an answer to a petition or a cross-petition	£100
1.6 On an application for an order under Part III of the Solicitors Act 1974 for the assessment of costs payable to a solicitor by his client	£30
2. Proceedings under the Children Act 1989 On filing an application or requesting leave under the following provisions of the Children Act 1989—	
2.1 Parental responsibility, guardians, section 8 orders etc. (a) section 4(1)(a), or (3), 5(1), 10(1) or (2) (b) section 6(7), or 13(1)	£80 £80
2.2 Financial provision for children (a) paragraph 1(1), 2(1), 6(5) or 14(1) of Schedule 1 (b) paragraph 1(4), 2(5), 5(6), 6(7), 6(8), 8(2), 10(2), or 11 of Schedule 1	£80 £80
2.3 Secure accommodation (a) Section 25	£80
2.4 Care, supervision, etc. (a) section 31 For the purposes of fee 2.4(a) a care order does not include an interim care order, and a supervision order does not include an interim supervision order.	£80

APPENDIX 5 FEES ORDERS

Column 1 Number & description of fee	Column 2 Amount of fee
(b)　section 33(7), 38(8)(b), 39(1), (2), (3) or (4), paragraph 6 of Schedule 3 or paragraph 11(3) of Schedule 14	£80
2.5　Contact with child in care 　(a)　section 34(2), (3), (4) or (9);	£80
2.6　Placement abroad 　(a)　paragraph 19(1) of Schedule 2	£80
2.7　Education supervision 　(a)　section 36(1) 　(b)　paragraph 15(2) or 17(1) of Schedule 3	£80 £80
2.8　Child assessment order 　(a)　section 43(1)	£80
2.9　Emergency protection 　(a)　section 43(12) 　(b)　section 44, 45, 46 or 48	£80 £80
2.10　Recovery of children 　(a)　section 50	£80
2.11　Miscellaneous 　(a)　section 102	£80
2.12　Appeals 　(a)　On commencing an appeal under section 94 of, or paragraph 23(11) of Schedule 2 to, the Children Act 1989	£80
2.13　Interim care/supervision orders 　(a)　On an application for an interim care order or an interim supervision order to be made under section 38(1) of the Children Act 1989 where an application for a care order or an application for a supervision order has already been made, and at least one interim care order or at least one interim supervision order has been made in the proceedings	£30
Fee 2 In the notes to fee 2 'numbered fee' means each of the following fees: 2.1(a); 2.1(b); 2.2(a); 2.2(b); 2.3(a); 2.4(a); 2.4(b); 2.5(a); 2.6(a); 2.7(a); 2.7(b); 2.8(a); 2.9(a); 2.9(b); 2.10(a); 2.11(a); 2.12(a) and 2.13(a).	
Where an application is made or filed, or (as the case may be) leave is sought or an appeal commenced, under or relating to provisions of the Children Act 1989 which are listed in two or more different numbered fees, each of those fees shall be payable.	
Where an application is made or filed, or (as the case may be) leave is sought or an appeal commenced under or relating to two or more provisions of the Children Act 1989 which are listed in the same numbered fee, that fee shall be payable only once.	
Where the same application is made or filed, or (as the case may be) leave is sought or an appeal commenced, in respect of two or more children at the same time, only one fee shall be payable in respect of each numbered fee.	

APPENDIX 5 FEES ORDERS

Column 1 Number & description of fee	Column 2 Amount of fee
3. Adoption and wardship applications 3.1 On commencing proceedings under the Adoption Act 1976 other than under section 21 of that Act	£120
3.2 On commencing proceedings under section 21 of the Adoption Act 1976	£120
3.3 On applying for the exercise by the High Court of its inherent jurisdiction with respect to children	£120
4. Applications in proceedings 4.1 On an application for an order without notice or by consent (including an application to make a decree nisi absolute) except where separately listed in this schedule	£30
4.2 On a request for directions for trial (other than in uncontested divorce proceedings, in which no fee is chargeable) except where separately listed in this schedule	£30
4.3 On an application on notice except where separately listed in this schedule	£60
5. Appeal from a district judge 5.1 On filing a notice of appeal from a district judge to a judge	£80
6. Searches 6.1 On making a search in the central index of decrees absolute kept at the Principal Registry of the Family Division for any specified period of ten calendar years or, if no such period is specified, for the ten most recent years, and, if appropriate, providing a certificate of decree absolute	£20
6.2 On making a search in the central index of parental responsibility agreements kept at the Principal Registry of the Family Division in accordance with regulations made under section 4(2) of the Children Act 1989 and, if appropriate, providing a copy of an agreement	£20
6.3 On making a search in the index of decrees absolute kept at any divorce county court or district registry for any specified period of ten calendar years or, if no period is specified, for the ten most recent years, and if appropriate, providing a certificate of decree absolute	£5

7. Copy documents
7.1 On a request for a copy of any document (including a faxed copy where requested) or for examining a plain copy and marking it as an office copy:
  (a) per page for the first five pages of each document
  (b) per page for subsequent pages
	
	£1
	25p

7.2 Where copies of any document are made available on a computer disk or in other electronic form, for each such copy	£3

APPENDIX 5 FEES ORDERS

Column 1 Number & description of fee	Column 2 Amount of fee
8. Determination of costs Transitional Provision Where a bill of costs (or a request for detailed assessment or a request for a detailed assessment hearing as the case may be) is filed pursuant to an order made by the court before the coming into operation of this Order the fees payable shall be those which applied immediately before the coming into force of this Order.	
8.1 On the filing of a bill of costs for taxation (or a request for detailed assessment or a request for a detailed assessment hearing as the case may be); or on the filing of a request for a hearing date for the assessment of costs payable to a solicitor by his client pursuant to an order under Part III of the Solicitors Act 1974	£80
Where there is a combined party and party and legal aid determination of costs, fee 8.1 shall be attributed proportionately to the party and party and legal aid portions of the bill on the basis of the amount allowed.	
8.2 On a request for a review of taxation or an appeal against taxation (or an appeal against a decision made in detailed assessment proceedings as the case may be)	£50
8.3 On applying for the court's approval of a Legal Aid Taxation Certificate or (as the case may be) of a Legal Aid Assessment Certificate	£20
Fee 8.3 is payable at the time of applying for approval and is recoverable only against the Legal Aid Fund.	
9. Registration of maintenance orders On an application for a maintenance order to be— 9.1 registered under the Maintenance Orders Act 1950 or the Maintenance Orders Act 1958	£30
9.2 sent abroad for enforcement under the Maintenance Orders (Reciprocal Enforcement) Act 1972	£30

10. Insolvency Act 1986
On entering a bankruptcy petition:
   (a) if presented by a debtor or the personal representative of a deceased debtor
   (b) if presented by a creditor or other person
	£120
	
	£150

10.2 On entering any other petition	£150
One fee only is payable where more than one petition is presented in relation to a partnership.	
10.3(a) On a request for a certificate for discharge from bankruptcy (b) and after the first certificate for each copy	£50 £1
Requests and applications with no fee No fee is payable on a request or on an application to the Court by the Official Receiver when applying only in the capacity of Official Receiver to the case (and not as trustee or liquidator), or on an application to set aside a statutory demand.	

APPENDIX 5   FEES ORDERS

Column 1 Number & description of fee	Column 2 Amount of fee
Section 2. Fees to be taken in the county courts only	

11. Service
11.1   On a request for service by bailiff, of any document except:
   (a)   an order for a debtor to attend the adjourned hearing of a judgment summons;
   (b)   an interpleader summons under an execution
   (c)   an order made under section 23 of the Attachment of Earnings Act 1971 (enforcement provisions); or
   (d)   an order for a debtor to attend an adjourned oral examination of his means
	£10

12. Enforcement in the county courts 12.1 On an application for or in relation to enforcement of a judgment or order of a county court or through a county court, by the issue of a warrant of execution against goods except a warrant to enforce payment of a fine	(a) Where the amount for which the warrant issues does not exceed £125.....£25 (b) Where the amount for which the warrant issues exceeds £125.....£45
12.2 On a request for a further attempt at execution of a warrant at a new address following a notice of the reason for non-execution (except a further attempt following suspension)	£20
12.3 On an application to question a judgment debtor or other person on oath in connection with enforcement of a judgment	£40
12.4 On an application for a garnishee order nisi or a charging order nisi, or the appointment of a receiver by way of equitable execution	£50
Fee 12.4 shall he payable in respect of each party against whom the order is sought.	
12.5 On an application for a judgment summons	£80
12.6 On the issue of a warrant of possession or a warrant of delivery	£80
Where the recovery of a sum of money is sought in addition, no further fee is payable.	
12.7 On an application for an attachment of earnings order (other than a consolidated attachment of earnings order) to secure money due under an order made in family proceedings	£50
Fee 12.7 is payable for each defendant against whom an order is sought.	
Fee 12.7 is not payable where the attachment of earnings order is made on the hearing of a judgment summons.	

APPENDIX 5   FEES ORDERS

Column 1 Number & description of fee	Column 2 Amount of fee
13. Sale 13.1 For removing or taking steps to remove goods to a place of deposit	The reasonable expenses incurred
Fee 13.1 is to include the reasonable expenses of feeding and caring for animals.	
13.2 For advertising a sale by public auction pursuant to section 97 of the County Courts Act 1984	The reasonable expenses incurred
13.3 For the appraisement of goods	5p in the £1 or part of a £1 of the appraised value
13.4 For the sale of goods (including advertisements, catalogues, sale and commission and delivery of goods)	15p in the £1 or part of a £1 on the amount realised by the sale or such other sum as the district judge may consider to be justified in the circumstances
13.5 Where no sale takes place by reason of an execution being withdrawn, satisfied or stopped	(a) 10p in the £1 or part of a £1 on the value of the goods seized, the value to be the appraised value where the goods have been appraised or such other sum as the district judge may consider to be justified in the circumstances; and in addition (b) any sum payable under fee 13.1, 13.2 or 13.3.
Section 3. Fees to be taken in the High Court only **14. Enforcement in the High Court** 14.1 On sealing a writ of execution/possession/delivery	£20
Where the recovery of a sum of money is sought in addition to a writ of possession and delivery, no further fee is payable.	

APPENDIX 5 FEES ORDERS

Column 1 Number & description of fee	Column 2 Amount of fee
14.2 On an application to question a judgment debtor or other person on oath in connection with enforcement of a judgment	£40
14.3 On an application for a garnishee order nisi or a charging order nisi, or the appointment of a receiver by way of equitable execution	£50
Fee 14.3 shall be payable in respect of each party against whom the order is sought.	
14.4 On an application for a judgment summons	£80
14.5 On a request or application to register a judgment or order; or for leave to enforce an arbitration award; or for a certified copy of a judgment or order for use abroad	£30
15. Affidavits 15.1 On taking an affidavit or an affirmation or attestation upon honour in lieu of an affidavit or a declaration; and	£5
15.2 for each exhibit referred to and required to be marked	£2

SCHEDULE 2
ORDERS REVOKED

Title	Reference
The Family Proceedings Fees Order 1991	S.I. 1991/2114
The Family Proceedings Fees (Amendment) Order 1995	S.I. 1995/2628
The Family Proceedings Fees (Amendment) Order 1996	S.I. 1996/3190
The Family Proceedings Fees (Amendment) Order 1997	S.I. 1997/788
The Family Proceedings Fees (Amendment) (No. 2) Order 1997	S.I. 1997/1080
The Family Proceedings Fees (Amendment) (No. 3) Order 1997	S.I. 1997/1899
The Family Proceedings Fees (Amendment) (No. 4) Order 1997	S.I. 1997/2671

INDEX

Abandoning, discontinuance
  compared 288–9
Access to Justice with Conditional Fees
  (1998) 33, 42–3
Accident Line Scheme 33, 38
Acknowledgment of service 86
  amendment 79
  content 79
  defence 100
  judgment in default *see* Default
    judgment
  N210 86, 1275–6
  Part 8 procedure 86, 1275–6
  requirement for 78
  signature 79
  time for filing 78–9
  withdrawal 79
Action *see* Claim
'Active management' *see* Case
  management
Administrative responsibility 5
see also Case management
Admissions 101, 110
  general rule 76
  money claim 76–8
    offers to settle 78
    part claim, specified sum 77–8
    unspecified sum 78
    whole claim, specified sum 77
  notice to admit facts 241–2
  notice to admit or produce
    documents 242
  transitional provisions 15
Adultery particulars 95
Adversarial culture 12
Affidavits 21, 129, 239
  alterations 133
  binding 133
  body of 132
  commencement 132
  corner markings 132
  defective 134
  examples 130–1
  exhibits 132–3, 134
  failure to comply with practice
    direction 134
  filing 133
  form 130–4, 241
  heading 132
  jurat 133
  made outside jurisdiction 241
  margin reference 132
  printing 133

Affidavits – *continued*
  search orders 154–5
  voluminous 134
Agreed bundles 296
Allocation
  costs before 308–9
  courts 53–4
  see also Track allocation
Alternative dispute resolution 4, 10
  interim injunctions 158
Anton Piller orders *see* Search orders
Appeals
  against costs assessment 319–20
  case stated 24
    to Court of Appeal 330–1
    to High Court 330
  costs after 309
  county court
    from county court judges 324–5
    from district judges 324
    rehearings 324
  Divisional Court proceedings 330
  European Court reference 28, 331
  High Court
    final order 327
    from district judges 325
    from High Court judges 325–7
    from masters 325
    interim orders 325–7
    restrictions 325–7
  judicial review 329–30
  leave *see* permission
  notice 24
  permission 323
    exempt appeals 327
    limited 328
    refusal reasons 328
    skeleton arguments 328
    test 327–8
  re-enacted 29
  skeleton arguments
    appeal applications 329
    leave applications 328
  small claims
    notice 188
    procedure 189
    rights 188
  terminological changes 323–4
  to Court of Appeal
    case stated 330–1
    document list 329
    from county court 324–5
    from High Court 325–7

1383

Appeals – *continued*
   from Restrictive Practices
      Court 330
   from tribunals 330–1
   permission 327–8
   respondent's notice 329
   skeleton arguments 329
   time for appealing 327
   to High Court
      case stated 330
      from tribunals 330
   tribunals
      to Court of Appeal 330–1
      to High Court 330
   variation of directions 332
Applications
   in chambers *see* private
   interim *see* Interim applications
   judicial review 28
   notices 22
   private 22
   summary judgment *see* Summary
      judgment
   without notice 22, 123–4
      public hearing or secrecy 124
Appropriate office 314–15
Arrest warrants 28
Assessment of costs 312–13
   appeals against decisions 319–20
   appropriate office 314–15
   bill of costs 315–16, 1318–26
   commencement of proceedings
      315
   costs of assessment 318–19
   disputed points 316–17
      default costs certificate 317,
         1303–4
      reply 317
   final costs certificate 319,
      1305–6
   hearing 317–18
   hearing request form 1308
   interim costs certificate 319, 1307
   misconduct of assessment 320
   solicitor and own client procedure
      318
   Solicitors Act 1974 Part III 318
   summary 202, 312
   time limits 319
Assessment of damages
   case management 169–70
   costs in small claims 190
   directions 170
   disposal hearings 170
   hearing 170
Assessors
   appointment 261–2
   remuneration 262

Association of Personal Injury
   Lawyers 45
Barristers
   case management conference 6–7
   overriding objectives and 10
   role 9
   uplift 36
Bill of costs 315–16, 1318–26
Binding of affidavits 133
Brussels Convention viii

Calderbank letters 264, 319
   see also Part 36 offers
Capping
   conditional fees 37
   fast track costs 311
Case law 19–20
   old 20–1
Case management 4, 8
   conference *see* Case management
      conference
   costs and 303–4
   damage assessment cases 169–70
      directions 170
      disposal hearings 170
      hearing 170
   interim orders 120–1, 134
   late application to call witnesses
      237
   multi-track 6, 204, 205–6
   orders on court initiative 120–1,
      128
   overriding objective and 160
   Part 20 claim 110–11
   procedural judges 160, 161
   sanctions
      avoidance of 175
      court approach 174–5
      default of due compliance 173
      form of order with 175–6
      non-compliance
         with directions 173–4
         with order imposing sanction
            176
         with pre-action protocols
            176–7
      relief 176
      striking out 173
   stay for settlement 168–9
   subsequent 170–2
   timetables *see* Timetables
   track allocation *see* Track allocation
Case management conference
   attendance 210
   barrister and solicitor at 6–7
   business 210
   directions 211–12
   interim applications at 123

INDEX

Case management conference – *continued*
  lay client 7
  listing 210
  multi-track 209–12
  reasons for calling 209
Case stated appeals 24
  to Court of Appeal 330–1
  to High Court 330
Case summary
  fast track 201–2
  multi-track 211, 295
Certificates
  costs
    default 317
    final 319
    interim 319
  disclosure compliance 7
  London Certificate 89
  recoverable benefit 274
  of service 69–70, 1284–5
Champerty 39
Chancery proceedings 27, 54
'Cheque rule' 21, 144
Children 58, 61–4
  conditional fees 39
  costs 63
  investment of funds 63–4
  private hearing 297
  proceedings without litigation friend 62
  service on 63, 73
  see also Litigation friend
Civil Procedure Act 1997, text 1344–50
Civil Procedure Rules 1998
  agreement to apply 17
  drafting deficiencies 23
  glossary 822–3
  interpretation 18–21
    case law 19–21
    purposive 18–19
  originating process 23–5
  preserved rules 25–9
  procedural code 18, 20
  re-enacted provisions 21–30
    general application 25–9
    proceedings pursuant to statute 29–30
  scope 13–14
  text 333–1070
  transitional provisions *see* Transitional provisions
Claim
  action 90
  defending *see* Defence
  foreign currency 92–3
  form *see* Claim form

Claim – *continued*
  particulars *see* Particulars of claim
Claim form 21, 24
  brief details of claim 91
  claim for money 91
  content 90–3
  counterclaims *see* Part 20 claim
  heading 90
  issue 65
  listing of all forms 1223–1343
  N1 65, 90–3, 1225
  N208 65, 98
    example 1269–70
    see also Part 8 claim
Part 8 claim 24, 64
  acknowledgment of service 86, 1275–6
  directions 85, 86–7
  failing to file acknowledgment 86
  multi-track allocation 86
  N208 65, 98, 1269–70
  oral evidence 85
  subsequent procedure 86–7
  track allocation 162
  when used 85–6
  written evidence 85
Part 20 claim 24, 90, 1277–83
  by defendant 107–12
  by third party 108
  case management 110–11
  content 105–6, 109–10
  contribution claim 110, 112
  default judgment 84, 110, 111–12
  defence
    content 107
    requirements 107
  filing 108–9
  general requirements 105
  indemnity claim 110, 112
  permission of court 105
    consideration 109
    not required 108
    required 108–9
  procedure 105, 110–11
  service 110
  particulars *see* Particulars of claim
  rationalisation 88–9
  remedy sought 91
  service *see* Service
  standard procedure 64
  statement of case *see* Statements of case
  statement of truth 93
  statement of value 91–3
  summons 25, 90

INDEX

Claimant 57
  joint 58
  service effected by 75–6
Client
  case management conference 7
  conduct and costs 7
  cooperation requirement 7
  disclosure compliance certificate 7
  involvement in process 7–8
  overriding objectives and 7–8
  pre-trial review 7
Clinical disputes protocols 4, 45, 1206–22
Club, as party 58
Companies
  overseas 72
  parties 58, 61
  service on 70, 71, 72, 73
Compromise 288
Conditional fees 12, 31–43, 303, 320–1
  Access to Justice 33, 42–3
  agreement
    assessment of costs 35–8
    content 35
  assessment
    agreement costs 35–8
    level 33
    percentage increase 36–8
    success fee 36–8
  calculation 32
  cap 37
  certainty 34
  children 39
  context 32–4
  disbursements 37
  enhanced fee 36
  experts 40
  extension to other areas 33, 41–2
  fast track 39–40
  interim costs 38–9
  lightning factor 37
  multi-track 41
  offers to settle 41
  overriding objectives and 32
  patients 39
  personal injuries 32, 33
  plain English agreement 33
  pre-action protocols 40
  proportionality 34, 38, 39
  ready reckoner 37
  risk assessment 37
  specified proceedings 32
  success fee 32
    assessment 36–8
  transparency 34
  uplift 36
  see also Costs

Conditional Fees - A Survival Guide (Napier and Bawdon) 33, 37
Conduct of parties, costs and 7, 46–7
Confidentiality 11
Consent orders
  administrative 125–6
  approved 126
  drawing up 126
Contribution, Part 20 claim 11, 110
Conveyancing counsel 29
Cooperation
  client requirement 7
  culture 12
  experts 252
  interim injunctions 158
  pre-action disclosure duty 227
Copies 222, 225
Costs 302–22
  after discontinuance 290
  appropriate office 314–15
  assessment 312–13
    appeals against decisions 319–20
    appropriate office 314–15
    bill of costs 315–16, 1318–26
    commencement of proceedings 315
    costs of assessment 318–19
    disputed points 316–17
      default costs certificate 317, 1303–4
      reply 317
    final costs certificate 319, 1305–6
    hearing 317–18
    hearing request form 1308
    interim costs certificate 319, 1307
    misconduct of assessment 320
    solicitor and own client procedure 318
    Solicitors Act 1974 Part III 318
    summary 202, 312
    time limits 319
  base 35–6
  basic 35–6
  bill of 315–16, 1318–26
  case management and 303–4
  certificates
    default 317, 1303–4
    final 319, 1305–6
    interim 319, 1307
  children and patients 63
  conditional fee agreements *see* Conditional fees
  conduct of parties 7, 46–7
  disclosure

INDEX

Costs – *continued*
  non-party 228
  pre-action 227
  discretion of court 304–5, 313
  estimates required 303
  fast track 203, 303, 310–12
    capping 311
    degree of certainty 310
    settlement before trial 312
    solicitor attending with counsel 311–12
    split trials 312
    summary assessment 202
  fixed 29, 40
  front loading 12
  general principles 304–5
  indemnity basis 314
  interim
    conditional fees 38–9
    summary determination 126–7
  interim costs certificate 319, 1307
  interim injunctions 34, 157–8
  litigants in person 321
  litigation friend 63
  offers to settle 280, 281–2, 319
  options 32
  orders *see* Costs orders
  Part 36 offer 281–2
  pre-action protocols and 304–5
  predictability 303
  quantification
    choice of basis 314
    discretion 313
    indemnity basis 314
    standard basis 313–14
    see also assessment
  reforms 5
  rights to
    discontinuance 310
    offers to settle 309–10
    payments into court 309–10
  schedule of costs forms 1317–43
  security for 27
  small claims 303
    after allocation 189
    assessment of damages and disposals 190
    before allocation 189
    exceptional cases 190
    reallocation from 190
    unreasonable behaviour 190
  standard basis 313–14
  Supreme Court Costs Office 314
  Supreme Court Taxing Office 314
  transitional provisions 17–18
  transparency 34
  unreasonable failure and allocation of 7

Costs – *continued*
  wasted costs order 320, 321–2
  see also Conditional fees
Costs officer 312
Costs orders
  after appeal 309
  costs after transfer 308
  costs in any event 306
  costs in the application 306
  costs before track allocation 308–9
  costs in the case 306
  costs of and caused by 306
  costs here and below 307
  costs reserved 306
  costs thrown away 306
  disclosure and 308
  fixed costs on judgments 307–8
  interim 305–7
    detailed assessment 307
    meanings 306–7
    summary assessment 307
  no order 307
  non-parties 308, 310
  notifying client 309
  range 305
  reallocation from small claims 309
  wasted costs order 320, 321–2
Counterclaim *see* Part 20 claim
County court 23, 53
  application of RSC to proceedings 25
  claims prohibited in 53–4
  Crown proceedings 27
  judgment on admissions 15
  originating processes 23–4
  register of judgments 300
  transfer between 56
  see also Appeals
Court of Appeal
  case law 19–21
  see also Appeals
Courts
  allocation of business 53–4
  case management role 8
  Chancery business 27, 54
  county court *see* County court
  defendant's home court 55, 179
  High Court *see* High Court
  jurisdiction 53
    disputing 84
  leave *see* permission
  London certificate 89
  orders on court initiative 128
  payment *see* Payment into court
  permission *see* Permission of court
  pre-issue applications 147
  procedural judges 160, 161

INDEX

Courts – *continued*
  Queen's Bench Division 54
  reforms 5
  Restrictive Practices Court 330
  Royal Courts of Justice 89
  service effected by 69, 75
  transfer 161–2
    on application 55–7
    automatic 55
    between county courts 56
    costs 308
    procedure 57
    specifying court 57
    within High Court 56–7
  trial location 298
  unified rules 23
  wrong court 57
  see also Appeals
Credibility, absent witness 245
Cross-examination 234
  experts 256, 259
  on hearsay 245
  order for 239–40
  witnesses 239, 298
Crown
  service on 74
  summary judgment against 142
Crown proceedings 27
Culture, adversarial and cooperative 12

Damages
  aggravated 94
  assessment
    case management 169–70
    costs in small claims 190
    directions 170
    hearings 170
  exemplary 94
  further deterioration 300
  provisional 94
    judgment for 299–300
Date for trial
  confirmation on listing 202
  fast track 196–7, 202
  fixing 196–7, 212
  multi-track 197, 212
Declarations 135
Defamation claims
  defence 103
  particulars 95
Default judgment
  acknowledgment of service 79, 111
  applications
    compulsory 81–2
    CPR Part 23 82
    two or more defendants 82

Default judgment – *continued*
  conditions for entering 80
  mechanisms for entering 79–80
  N205A 81, 1265–6
  N225B 81, 1267
  N227 81, 1290
  N255 81, 1303
  Part 20 claim 84, 110, 111–12
  request for 80–1
    specified sum claim 80, 81
    unspecified sum claim 81
  setting aside
    duty of claimant 83
    entered wrongly 83
    not entered wrongly 83
    Part 23 procedure 84
    principles 82–3
    procedure 84
  transitional provisions 15
Defence
  acknowledgment of service 100
  address for service 102
  admission 101
  contents 101–3
  defamation claim 103
  denial 101
  limitation period 103
  money claimed had be paid 107
  period for filing 100–1
  personal injury claim 102–3
  reply to
    content 106
    requirements 106
  representative capacity 102
  requirement for 99–100
  service 100
    extension of time 101
  set-off 103
  statement of case 99
  statement of truth 99
  stay of claim 101
  summary judgment application filed before 142
  tender 103
  to counterclaim 107
Defendant
  home court 55, 179
  Part 20 claim 107–12
Delay
  filing allocation questionnaires 163
  interim injunctions 158–9
  pre-action 44
  see also Timetables
Delivery up of goods 135
Deponents 21, 249
  see also Depositions

INDEX

Depositions
  examination
    conduct 250
    order for 249–50
    out of jurisdiction 251
  examiner
    appointment 251
    fees and expenses 251
  use
    at hearing 250
    subsequent 250–1
Directions
  agreed 198, 254
    pre-trial review 214
  appealing variation of 332
  disclosure 193–4
    multi-track 209
  expert evidence 194–6, 254
    expert's right to ask for 261
    fees 257–8
    information provision 258
    multi-track 209
  fast track 193–8, 254
    agreed 198
    expert evidence 254
    varying timetable 198–9
  fixing date for trial 196–7
  further information requests 196
  further statements of case 196
  multi-track 207–9, 211–12, 254
    agreed 208–9, 214, 254
    on allocation 207–9
    avoiding hearing for 208–9
    disclosure 209
    evidence 209
    expert evidence 254
    given at other hearings 214–15
    inadequate information 207–8
    informed decisions 207
    objections to 215–16
    pre-trial review 214
    unusual 211–12
    usual 211
  non-compliance sanctions 173–4
  Part 8 procedure 85, 86–7
  pre-action injunctions 148–9
  pre-trial review 214
  small claims
    further 183
    special 183
    standard 182–3
  trial bundles 295
  unusual 211–12
  usual 211
  witness statements 194
Disbursements 37
Disclosure 217–32
  agreement 224

Disclosure – *continued*
  compliance certificate 7
  confidentiality 11
  continuing duty 224
  copies 222, 225
  costs
    non-party 228, 308
    orders 308
    pre-action 227
  dealing justly 218
  documents
    control of party 219, 222
    copies 222, 225
    list 222–3
    meaning 221–2
    statements of case 225
    subsequent use 231–2
  expert evidence 259
    failure to disclose 261
  extent of search 7
  failure to disclose 231
    expert evidence 261
  fast track 192, 193–4
  list of documents 222–3
  multi-track 209
  N265 222–3, 225, 1309–10
  non-party
    application 228
    costs 228, 308
    form of order 228
    objections 228–9
    other powers to order 229
  overriding objective 218
  pre-action 135, 136
    cooperation duty 227
    costs 227
    'fishing expeditions' 226
    form of order 227
    objections to 228–9
    other powers to order 229
    protocols 47
    test for grant 226–7
  pre-commencement costs 308
  principles 219
  privilege 230, 231
  procedure
    N265 222–3, 225, 1309–10
    standard disclosure 222–4, 1309–10
  proportionality 218, 219, 230–1
  public interest immunity 229–30
  solicitors' duties 221
  specific 224–5
  standard 219, 1309–10
    disproportionate inspection 220, 221
    limitation of 221
    procedure 222–4

INDEX

Disclosure – *continued*
    reasonable search 220
    requirements 219–20
    statement 223–4
        signature on 224
    subsequent use of documents 231–2
    uncontrolled discovery 218
    withholding 229–31
    see also Inspection
Discontinuance
    abandonment compared 288–9
    compromise 288
    consent 289
    costs 310
    costs after 290
    effect 290
    notice 288, 289, 290, 1313
    permission to discontinue 289
    procedure 289–90
    setting aside notice 290
    subsequent proceedings 290
    unless orders 288
    what may be discontinued 289
Divisional Court, vacation business 28
Documents
    disclosure
        control of party 219, 222
        copies 222, 225
        list 222–3
        meaning 221–2
        statements of case 225
    notice to admit or produce 242
    production appointment 248
    trial bundles 295–6
    witness summons to produce 247–8

Emergency actions
    applications without notice 123–4
    pre-issue applications 146, 147, 148
Enforcement, re-enacted 28–9
Estreatment of recognisances 28
European Court reference 28, 331
Evidence
    affidavits *see* Affidavits
    consent of trustee 242
    court's power to control 233–4
    cross-examination 234, 239–40, 256, 259, 298
    deposition *see* Depositions
    documents
        notice to admit or produce 242
        production appointment 248
        trial bundles 295–6

Evidence – *continued*
        witness summons to produce 247–8
    electronic communication 234–5
    exhibits 132–3, 134, 298
    expert *see* Expert evidence
    facts in statement of case 129
    foreign law 242
    hearsay *see* Hearsay
    in-chief 235
    interim applications 128–34, 239, 240
    interim injunctions 150–3
    models 245–6
    N244 applications 129–30
    non-verbal 245–6
    notice to admit facts 241–2
    notice to admit or produce documents 242
    oral 234, 239
    Part 8 procedure 85, 86, 87
    photographs 245–6
    plans 245–6
    pre-issue applications 147
    proceedings other than trial 239–40
    recording 186
    restriction of witness numbers 234
    statements of case as 240
    summary judgment 143
    use at trial 298
    video link 234–5
    weight 130
    witnesses *see* Witness statements; Witness summons; Witnesses
    written 234
Ex parte applications 123–4
    see also Applications, without notice
Exhibits 132–3, 134, 298
Expert evidence 246
    agreed statement 195
    court's restriction on use 253
    directions
        fast track 192, 194–6, 201, 254
        information provision 258
        multi-track 209, 254
    disclosure 259
        failure to disclose 261
    fast track 192
    report content 258–9
        instructions 258
    statement of truth 258
    use by other parties 259
    written instructions 253
    written reports 255
Experts
    assessors 261–2
    conditional fees 40

INDEX

Experts – *continued*
  cooperative approach 252
  cross-examination 256, 259
  directions
    fees 257–8
    right to ask for 261
  discussions 260
  duties 253
  fees 40, 254, 257–8
  identification 253–4
  instructions 257–8
  meetings 253
  personal injuries pre-action protocol 48–9
  questions to 195–6, 255–6
  single joint 254–5, 256–8
    instructions 257–8
  training 253
  without prejudice meetings 195, 254, 260

Fast track 161
  allocation decision 170, 172
  allocation rules 166–7
  case summary 201–2
  conditional fees 39–40
  costs 5, 203, 303, 310–12
    capping 311
    degree of certainty 310
    settlement before trial 312
    solicitor attending with counsel 311–12
    split trials 312
    summary assessment 202
  date for trial
    confirmation on listing 202
    fixing 196–7
  directions 193–8, 254
    agreed 198
    expert evidence 254
    varying timetable 198–9
    see also individual directions eg disclosure
  disclosure 192, 193–4
  expert evidence 192, 194–6, 201, 254
  financial control 6
  further information requests 196
  further statements of case 196
  interlocutory applications 192
  listing 199–202, 292–3
    case summary 201–2
    costs summary assessment 202
    date confirmation 202
    expert directions 201
    timetable 201
    trial bundles 201
  listing questionnaires 199–201

Fast track – *continued*
  filing directions 196, 199–201
  preparation before claim 192–3
  timetable 191–2, 197–8, 201
  trial 202
  trial bundles 201, 295
  witness statements 194
Fatal accidents, particulars of claim 95
Fees *see* Conditional fees; Costs
Filing 69
  affidavits 133
  defence 100–1
  Part 20 claim 108–9
  request 25
'Fishing expeditions' 226
Fixed costs 29, 40
Foreign currency claim 92–3
Foreign law, evidence 242
Forfeiture, summary judgment 143
Forms
  samples 1223–1343
  see also individual forms eg N208
Forum non conveniens 22
Freezing injunctions 135, 181
  applications without notice 124
  court for application 121
  definition 153
  examples 153
  secrecy 153
  status of judge 146
Funding 32
Further and better particulars *see* Further information
Further information
  principle 112
  proportionality 113
  request
    content 113
    directions 196
    form 113
    making 112–13
  response
    content 114–15
    form 114–15
    no or insufficient 114
    objections to responding 115
    ordered by court 114
    restrictions on use 116
Further statements of case 196

Glossary 822–3

Habeas corpus 28
Hearings
  by telephone 127, 148
  costs assessment 317–18

INDEX

Hearings – *continued*
  course of proceedings applications 151–2
  damages assessment 170
  dispensing with 147
  interim applications
    by telephone 127
    court 127–8
    disposal without 126
    non-attendance 128
  open court 297
  pre-action injunctions 148
  pre-issue applications 147, 148
  private 297
  public 185
  small claims 292
    conduct of 184–8
    evidence recording 186
    giving reasons 186
    method of proceeding 185–6
    non-attendance of parties 186–7
    proceeding without 184
    public 185
    representation 185
  summary judgment 144
  see also Trial
Hearsay 237, 238
  cross-examination 245
  definition 243
  notice of intention to rely 243–4
    not required 244–5
  weight assessment 244
  witness absent 244, 245
High Court
  Chancery business 27, 54
  claims which must be in 53–4
  originating processes 23
  Queen's Bench Division 54
  transfers within 56–7
  see also Appeals
Hire-purchase claims 95

Indemnity
  costs basis 314
  Part 20 claim 110, 112
Information
  further *see* Further information
  inadequate 207–8
Injunctions
  court for application 121
  Mareva see Freezing injunctions
Inspection 218, 219
  copying 225
  disproportionate 220, 221, 230–1
  documents in statements of case 225
  inadvertent disclosure 231

Inspection – *continued*
  non-verbal evidence 246
  pre-action 135, 136
  privilege 230, 231
  public interest immunity 229–30
  specific 224–5
  witness statements 240–1
Insurance
  Accident Line Scheme 33, 38
  after the event policy 32–3
  legal expense 32
  premium paid by unsuccessful party 43
Insurers 31
Intellectual property cases 14, 155
Interim applications
  with allocation questionnaire 123
  case management conference 123
  choice of court 121
  consent orders
    administrative 125–6
    approved 126
    drawing up 126
  costs 34, 126–7
  dispensing with notice 147
  disposal without hearing 126
  documentation 124–5
  evidence 128–34, 239, 240
  ex parte 123–4
  hearing
    by telephone 127
    court 127–8
    dispensing with 147
    non-attendance 128
    without 126
  N244 124, 147, 1275–6
    evidence in support 129–30
  obligation to apply early 123
  orders on court initiative 128
  payments 137
  pre-action remedies 121, 122
  service 125
  timing 121–3
  with notice 124–8
  without notice 22, 123–4
    public hearing or secrecy 124
Interim costs
  conditional fees 38–9
  detailed assessment 307
  meanings 306–7
  orders 305–7
  summary assessment 307
Interim injunctions
  alternative dispute resolution 158
  cooperation 158
  costs 157–8
  course of proceedings applications 150–2

INDEX

Interim injunctions – *continued*
  evidence in support 150–1
  hearing 151–2
  procedure 150–1
  service 150
  service of order 152
  time 150
  urgency 151
  criteria for obtaining 155–9
  delays 158–9
  evidence in support 152–3
  freezing injunctions 135, 181
    applications without notice 124
    court for application 121
    definition 153
    examples 153
    secrecy 153
    status of judge 146
  hearing 151–2
  pre-action injunctions, service 148–9
  pre-issue applications 146–9
    court 147
    desirability 146
    directions 148–9
    evidence 147
    hearing 147, 148
    N244 147
    notice 147
    procedure 147–8
    secrecy requirement 147
    service 147
    urgency 146, 147, 148
  proportionality 157–8
  search orders 135, 181
    affidavit evidence 154–5
    court for application 121
    definition 153
    format 154
    procedures 154
    report on 155
    status of judge 146
  status of judge 146
Interim orders 120–1, 135–6
  case management and 134
  county court appeals 324
  date for compliance 136
  drawing up 134
  High Court appeals 325–7
  initiative of court 120–1
  powers to grant 146
  time of order 145
Interim payments 135
  adjustment 139
  amount 139
  definition 136
  grounds 137–8
  multiple defendants

Interim payments – *continued*
  non-personal injuries 138–9
  personal injuries 139
  multi-track 137
  non-disclosure 139
  personal injury claims 138, 139
  procedure 137
  small claims 136–7
  standard of proof 138
  time for applying 137
Interim remedies *see* Interim injunctions; Interim orders
Interlocutory applications *see* Application, notices; Interim applications
Interlocutory orders *see* Interim orders
International aspects 29
Interpleader notice 24, 27
Interpretation 18–21
  case law 19–21
  purposive 18–19
Interrogatories *see* Further information
Issue identification 6, 7

Joinder of parties 58–9
Judges
  deployment 5
  non-disclosure of offers to settle 279
  procedural 160, 161
  responsibility 5
  see also Appeals
Judgments
  on admissions 15
  appeals 300
  counterclaims 299
  county court register 300
  default *see* Default judgment
  detention of goods 299
  drawing up 299–300
  error correction 300
  interest on debts 301
  interim payments 299
  provisional damages 299–300
  recording 299
  re-enacted 28
  summary *see* Summary judgment
Judicial review 28, 329–30
Jurisdiction 53
  disputing 84
  service outside 22, 25–6, 74
Jury trial 297

Ladd v *Marshall* rule 22
Landlord and tenant 181
Law Society, Accident Line Scheme 33, 38

INDEX

Leave of court 22
  see also Appeals, permission
Legal aid 32, 286
  withdrawal 33
Legal expense insurance 32, 33, 38
Lightning factor 37
Limitation period 103
  addition of parties after 60
  defence 103
  pre-action protocols 49
  service 74–5
  statement of case amendment after 118
Listing
  case summary 201–2
  costs summary assessment 202
  date confirmation 202
  expert directions 201
  fast track 199–202, 292–3
  hearings 213
  multi-track 293
  settlement notification 293
  timetable 201
  trial bundles 201, 295–6
  urgent applications 293
Listing officers 293
Listing questionnaires
  exchange 213
  failure to file 213
  fast track 196, 199–201
  fees 213
  filing directions 196, 199–201
  listing hearings 213
  multi-track 212–13, 1260–3
  N170 212, 1260–3
  purpose 213
Litigants in person 321
Litigation friend 58, 61–3
  appointment 62
  liability for costs 63
  persons able to be 61–2
  proceedings without 62
  service of documents 63
  termination of appointment 62–3
London certificate 89
Lugano Convention viii, 22

Maintenance 39
Mareva injunctions *see* Freezing injunctions
Masters 325
Medical litigation, pre-action protocols 4, 45, 1196–1222
Models 245–6
Mortgage actions
  particulars of claim 95
  service 74

Multi-track 161
  allocation 55
    decision 170, 172
    directions on 207–9
    rules 167
  case management 6, 204, 205–6
    conference *see* case management conferences
    see also timetable
  case management conferences 209–12
    attendance 210
    business 210
    directions 211–12
    lay client 7
    listing 210
  case summary 211, 295
  conditional fees 12, 41
  date for trial 197, 212
  directions 207–9, 211–12, 254
    agreed 208–9, 214, 254
    on allocation 207–9
    avoiding hearing for 208–9
    disclosure 209
    evidence 209
    expert evidence 254
    given at other hearings 214–15
    hearing for 208–9
    inadequate information 207–8
    informed decisions 207
    objections to 215–16
    pre-trial review 214
    unusual 211–12
    usual 211
  disclosure 209
  expert evidence 254
  hearing
    for directions 208–9
    see also Trial
  inadequate information 207–8
  interim payments 137
  listing 293
  listing questionnaires
    exchange 213
    failure to file 213
    fees 213
    listing hearings 213
    N170 212, 1260–3
    purpose 213
  N156 207, 1255
  N170 212, 1260–3
  Part 8 procedure 86
  pre-trial review 213–14, 292, 293, 294
    attendance 214
    directions 214
    notice 214
  timetable

INDEX

Multi-track – *continued*
  non-compliance 216
  variation by agreement 215
  variation by court 215
  variation 'key dates' 215

N1 65, 90–3
  content 90–3
  example 1225–6
N156 207, 1255
N170 212, 1260–3
N205A 81, 1265–6
N205B 81, 1267
N208 65, 98, 1269–70
N210 86, 1275–6
N227 81, 1290
N244 1298–9
  applications 124
  evidence in support 129–30
  pre-issue applications 147
N255 81, 1303–4
N265 222–3, 225, 1309–10
N279 288, 289, 290, 1313
Non-attendance
  at trial 300
  interim application hearing 128
  setting aside judgment for 187–8
  small claims hearing 186–7
  witness 238, 244, 245
Non-parties
  costs orders 308, 310
  disclosure
    application 228
    form of order 228
    objections 228–9
    other powers to order 229
Non-verbal evidence 245–6
  inspection 246
Notice of appeal 24
Notice to admit facts 241–2
Notice to admit or produce
  documents 242

Offers to settle 263–84
  Calderbank offer 264, 319
  conditional fees 41
  costs 280, 309–10, 319
  court intervention
    clarification 281
    costs order 280
    order to pay money out of court 280
    orders 281
    permission 280
    withdrawal or reduction 281
  non-disclosure 279
  Part 36 offers 264–5
    acceptance

Offers to settle – *continued*
    consequences 269
    defendant's offer 269–71
    effects 270–1
    multiple defendants 271
    notice 269
    permission 269
  clarification 281
  costs consequences 281–2
  defendant's 267–71
    acceptance 269–71
    claimant 268
    notice 268–9
    reference to interim payment 268
    rejection 271
    withdrawal 269
  permission 280
  unacceptable offer 282–4
  Part 36 payment 264–5
    defendant's 271–5
    permission 280
    unacceptable payment 282–4
  payment into court 264–5
    withdrawal or reduction 281
  see also Part 36 payment
  pre-action 265–6
    accepted after issue 266
    accepted before issue 267
    contents 266
    formal 265–6
    informal 265
    not accepted 266–7
    without prejudice 265
  procedure 33
  without prejudice 267
Open court hearing 297
Orders
  on court initiative 128
  re-enacted 28
  summary judgment 144
  see also individual orders eg Freezing injunctions; Search orders
Originating processes 23–5
  application 23, 24
  by witness statement 24
  case stated 24
  county courts 23–4
  filing a request 25
  High Court 23
  Insolvency Rules 24
  interpleader notice 24
  motion 23
  notice of appeal 24
  petition 23
  summons 23, 25
  writ 23

INDEX

Originating processes – *continued*
  see also Claim form; Part 8 procedure
Overriding objective 5–6
  advice to clients 11
  barrister 10
  case management *see* Case management
  clients 7–8
  conditional fees *see* Conditional fees
  confidentiality 11
  dealing justly 3, 218
  disclosure *see* Disclosure
  proportionality *see* Proportionality
  solicitor and 10
Overseas companies 72

Part 8 claim 24, 64
  acknowledgment of service 86
  directions 85, 86–7
  failing to file acknowledgment 86
  form contents 98
  multi-track allocation 86
  N208 65, 1269–70
  oral evidence 85
  subsequent procedure 86–7
  track allocation 162
  when used 85–6
  written evidence 85
Part 20 claim 24, 90, 108
  by defendant 107–12
  by third party 108
  case management 110–11
  content 105–6, 109–10
  contribution claim 110, 112
  default judgment 84, 110, 111–12
  defence
    content 107
    requirement 107
  filing 108–9
  general requirements 105
  indemnity claim 110, 112
  permission of court 105
    consideration 109
    not required 108
    required 108–9
  procedure 105, 110–11
  service 110
Part 36 offers 264–5
  acceptance
    consequences 269
    defendant's offer 269–71
    effects 270–1
    multiple defendants 271
    notice 269
    permission 269
  clarification 281
  costs consequences 281–2

Part 36 offers – *continued*
  defendant's 267–71
    acceptance 269–71
    claimant 268
    notice 268–9
    reference to interim payment 268
    rejection 271
    withdrawal 269
  permission 280
  unacceptable offer 282–4
Part 36 payment 264–5
  defendant's 271–5
  permission 280
  unacceptable payment 282–4
Particulars of claim 65
  adultery 95
  content 93–4
  damages 94
  documents 95
  points of law 95–6
  requirement 93
  responding to 76
  special requirements 95
  witnesses 95
Parties
  addition
    after limitation period 60
    application 59
    consequential directions 60
    hearing 60
    order 60
    permission of court 59
    principles 59
    procedure 59–60
    transfer of interest or liability 60
  children and patients 58, 61–4
    costs 63
    investment of funds 63–4
    proceedings without litigation friend 62
    service on 63, 73
    see also litigation friend
  clubs 58
  companies 58, 61
  conduct and costs 7, 46–7
  description 57–8
  documents in control of 219, 222
  joinder 58–9
  litigation friend 58, 61–3
    appointment 62
    liability for costs 63
    persons able to be 61–2
    proceedings without 62
    service of documents 63
    termination of appointment 62–3
  mistake in name 118

INDEX

Parties – *continued*
  names 58, 118
  partnerships 26, 58, 61
  patients *see* children and patients;
    litigation friend
  personal representatives 58, 64
  service of documents 69
  sole traders 26–7
  substitution
    application 59
    consequential directions 60
    hearing 60
    order 60
    principles 59
    procedure 59–60
    transfer of interest or liability 60
  unincorporated organisations 58
Partnerships
  parties 26, 58, 61
  service on 71, 72
  statement of truth signature 96
Paternity claim 95
Patients 58, 61–4
  conditional fees 39
  costs 63
  investment of funds 63–4
  proceedings without litigation
    friend 62
  service on 63, 73
  see also Litigation friend
Payments, interim *see* Interim
  payments
Payments into court 264
  costs rights 309–10
  Part 36 offer
    acceptance, claimant's 276–7
    claimant's
      acceptance 276–7
      failure to beat 278–9
      notice 276
    penalties on defendant 275–6
    rejection 277
    defendant's 278
    failure to beat 278–9
  Part 36 payment 264–5
    acceptance
      after defence of tender 275
      combined payment and offer
        275
      defendant's 274–5
      multiple defendants 275
      permission 274–5
    defendant's
      acceptance 274–5
      making payment 272–4
      material to be filed 272
      mixed claims 272
      notice 273–4

Payments into court – *continued*
      recoverable benefit certificate
        274
      service 274
      social security deduction 273
    failure to beat 277
  withdrawal or reduction 281
Permission of court 22
  addition of parties 59
  Part 20 claim 105
    consideration 109
    not required 108
    required 108–9
Personal injuries
  conditional fees 32, 33
  defence 102–3
  interim payments 138, 139
  particulars of claim 4, 95
  pre-action protocol 45, 47–9
    experts 48–9
    limitation period 49
    small claims 49
    text 1196–1205
Personal representatives
  defence 102
  parties 58, 64
Petitions 23, 24
Photographs 245–6
Plaintiff *see* Claimant
Plans 245–6
Pleadings *see* Statements of case
Pre-action disclosure 47, 135, 136
  cooperation duty 227
  costs 227
  'fishing expeditions' 226
  form of order 227
  objections 228–9
  other powers to order 229
  test for grant 226–7
Pre-action protocols
  clinical disputes 4, 45, 1206–22
  conditional fees 40
  co-operation 46
  costs 46–7, 304–5
  disclosure 47
  experts 48–9
  failure to comply 45–7
  future protocols 49–50
  joint experts 254–5
  limitation period 49
  non-compliance sanctions 176–7
  Part 36 offers 265–6
  personal injuries 45, 47–9,
    1196–1205
  practice direction 1194–5
  purpose 44
  sanctions 45–6
  small claims 49

INDEX

Pre-action protocols – *continued*
   transitional provisions 49
Pre-action remedies 121, 122
Preparation days 292
Pre-trial hearings, witness attendance 240
Pre-trial review 123, 292, 293, 294
   attendance 214
   directions 214
   lay client 7
   multi-track 213–14
   notice 214
   statement of issues 294–5
The Price of Success - Lawyers, Clients and Conditional Fees (Yarrow) 33
Printing of affidavits 133
Private applications 22
Private hearing 297
Private privilege 230
Privilege 230
   inadvertent disclosure 231
   public interest immunity 229–30
Procedural judges 160, 161
Property forfeiture 143
Proportionality 161
   conditional fees 34, 38, 39
   disclosure 218, 219, 230–1
   further information requests 113
   importance of case 3
   interim injunctions 157–8
Protocols *see* Pre-action protocols
Public interest immunity 229–30

Quantification of costs
   assessment 312–13
     appeals against decisions 319–20
     appropriate office 314–15
     bill of costs 315–16, 1318–26
     commencement of proceedings 315
     costs of assessment 318–19
     detailed 312–13
     discretion 313
     disputed points 316–17
       default costs certificate 317, 1303–4
       reply 317
     final costs certificate 319, 1305–6
     hearing 317–18
     hearing request form 1308
     interim costs certificate 319, 1307
     misconduct of assessment 320
     solicitor and own client procedure 318

Quantification of costs – *continued*
     Solicitors Act 1974 Part III 318
     summary 312
     time limits 319
   basis
     choice 314
     indemnity 314
     standard 313–14
Queen's Bench Division 54
Questionnaires
   allocation *see* Track allocation
   listing *see* Listing questionnaires

Ready reckoner 37
Real prospect of success test 141, 143–4, 180
Reasonable prospect of success test 20
Recognisances 28
Recovery of goods 95
Recovery of land 135–6
   particulars of claim 95
   service 74
Reforms
   complexity reduction 4–5
   costs 5
   court structure 5
   judge deployment 5
   judicial and administrative responsibility 5
   litigation avoidance 4
   outline 2–3
   principles underlying 3–5
   tactical considerations 11–12
   timescale reduction 5
   see also Overriding objective
Reply to defence
   contents 106
   general requirements 106
   procedural requirements 106
Representation, small claims hearing 185
Request, filing 25
Rescission 143
Responsibility
   administrative 5
     see also Case management
   judicial 5
Restrictive Practices Court 330
Risk assessment, conditional fees 37
Royal Courts of Justice 160
   London certificate 89
   track allocation 167–8

Sanctions
   false statements 239
   see also Case management

INDEX

Search
  costs 220
  reasonable 220
  see also Disclosure
Search orders 135, 181
  court for application 121
  status of judge 146
Secrecy
  freezing injunctions 124, 153
  pre-issue applications 147
Security for costs 27
Service 25
  acknowledgment 65, 86
    amendment 79
    content 79
    defence 100
    judgment in default *see* Default judgment
    N210 86, 1275–6
    Part 8 procedure 86, 1275–6
    requirement for 78
    signature 79
    time for filing 78–9
    withdrawal 79
  address in defence 102
  alternative method 73–4
  applications 125
  by claimant 75–6
  by courts 69, 75
  by party 69
  certificate of 69–70, 1284–5
  children 63, 73
  claim form 65–75
    late *see* extension of time application
  companies 70, 71, 72, 73
  computing time 74–5
  course of proceedings applications 150
  Crown 74
  dates 73
  deemed dates 73
  defective 74
  defence 100
    address for 102
    extension of time 101
  dispensing with 74
  document exchange 69, 70, 71–2
  e-mail 68, 72
  extension of time application
    after expiry 67–8
    'good reason' 67
    grounds 67
    procedure 66–7
  fax 68, 70, 71–2
  filing 69
  HM Forces 70
  leaving at place specified 70

Service – *continued*
  mortgage possession actions 74
  outside jurisdiction 22, 25–6, 74
  Part 8 claim 86
  Part 20 claim 110
  Part 36 payment notice 274
  partnerships 71, 72
  patients 63, 73
  personal 69, 70
  persons able to serve 68–9
  place of service 70–1
  postal 69, 70–1
  pre-action injunctions 148–9
  pre-issue applications 147
  recovery of land proceedings 74
  response pack 65
  solicitor's address 285
  substituted 73–4
  time limits 74–5
  US Air Force 70
  witness statements 235
    failure to serve 236–7
  witness summaries 236–7
  witness summons 249
Set-offs
  defence 103
  summary judgment 21
Setting aside judgment
  duty of claimant 83
  entered wrongly 83
  new hearing date 188
  non-attendance 187–8
  not entered wrongly 83
  Part 23 procedure 84
  principles 82–3
  procedure 84
Settlement
  encouragement 12
  notifying listing officer 293
  offers *see* Offers to settle
  stays for purpose of 10–11
Signature
  acknowledgment of service 79
  disclosure statement 224
  statement of truth 96, 97
Single joint expert 254–5, 256–8
Sir Lindsay Parkinson and Co. Ltd v *Triplan Ltd*, principles 22
Skeleton arguments
  appeal applications 329
  leave to appeal applications 328
  trial time limits and 299
Slippage 101
Small claims 161
  allocation decision 170, 172
  allocation rules 165–6
  appeals
    notice 188

INDEX

Small claims – *continued*
   procedure 189
   rights 188
  costs 303
   after allocation 189
   assessment of damages and
     disposals 190
   before allocation 189
   exceptional cases 190
   reallocation from small
     claims 190
   unreasonable behaviour 190
  directions
   further 183
   special 183
   standard 182–3
  distinctive features 181
  evidence recording 186
  exception 181
  fixed final hearing date
   special directions 183
   standard directions 182–3
  hearing 292
   conduct of 184–8
   evidence recording 186
   giving reasons 186
   method of proceeding 185–6
   non-attendance of parties
     186–7
   proceeding without 184
   public 185
   representation 185
  interim payments 136–7
  interim remedy 146
  issues 180–1
  jurisdiction 179–80
  landlord and tenant 181
  non-attendance
   notice 186–7
   rehearing 187–8
   setting aside judgment 187–8
  pre-action protocols 49
  procedure after allocation 182–4
  reallocation costs 309
  rehearing 187–8
  remedies 181
  restriction on Rules application
    181–2
  specified amount of money 179
  stay for settlement 179–80
  summary judgment 180
  venue 179
Sole traders 26–7
Solicitors
  advice to clients 11
  bankruptcy 287
  case management conference 6–7
  change of representative 285–7

Solicitors – *continued*
  notice of change 286
  presumed continuation 286
  coming off the record 286–7
  confidentiality 11
  death 287
  legal aid 286
  misconduct for time wasting
    10–11
  on claim form 285
  overriding objectives and 10
  presumed continuation 286
  removal on application of another
    party 287
  requirements 8
  retainers 285
  rights of audience 7
  role 9
  service address 285
  statements of truth 10, 96, 97
  withdrawal 286–7
Specific performance 143
Split trials 312
Standard basis, costs 313–14
Starting proceedings *see* Claim form;
    Originating proceedings
Statement of issues 294–5
Statement of truth 7, 89, 93
  authorisation to sign 10
  defence verification 99
  expert evidence 258
  failure to provide 98
  false 96–8
  format 96
  legal adviser and 96, 97
  liability 96–8
  partnership 96
  requirements 96
  signature on 96, 97
  solicitor signing 10, 96, 97
  statements of case 7
  status 97
Statement of value 91–3
  computation of value 92
  foreign currency 92–3
Statements, witness *see* Witness
    statements
Statements of case 27, 88
  abuse of process 140
  amendments
   after limitation period expired
    118
   format 117
   mistaken name of party 118
   permission not required 116
   permission required 116–17
  defence *see* Defence
  dispensing with 93

INDEX

Statements of case – *continued*
  evidential value 98, 129, 240
  failure to verify 98
  further 196
  London certificate 89
  simplification of terminology 89–90
  statement of truth *see* Statement of truth
  striking out all or part 140
  subsequent 106–7
Stay of claim, no defence 101
Stay for settlement 10–11
  allocation questionnaires 179–80
  case management 168–9
Striking out 140–1
  abuse of process 140
  court sanction 173
  no reasonable cause of action 140
Substituted service 73–4
Success fee 32
  see also Conditional fees
Summary judgment
  application filed before defence 142
  application procedure 142–3
  court's initiative 141
  Crown 142
  defendant and 141
  directions for hearing 144
  evidence 143
  excluded proceedings 142
  forfeiture 143
  function 141
  notice 143
  orders available 144
  real prospect of success test 141, 143–4, 180
  rescission 143
  set-offs 21
  specific performance 143
  split orders 144
  time for application 141–2
Summary possession proceedings 27
Summons *see* Claim form
Supreme Court Costs Office 314
Supreme Court Taxing Office 314

Tape-recordings 186
Telephone hearings 127, 148
Tender 103
Third party proceedings *see* Part 20 claim
Time limits
  service 74–5
  see also Limitation period
Timetables 4, 293–4
  fast track 191–2, 197–8, 201

Timetables – *continued*
  multi-track 215, 216
  non-compliance 6, 216
  objective 294
  sanctions for default 6
  setting 293–4
    in advance 292
  variation
    by agreement 215
    by court 215
    'key dates' 215
Tomlin order 126
Track allocation
  changing tracks 168
  costs before 308–9
  discretionary factors 167
  fast track 166–7, 170, 172
  further information 164
  hearing 164
  multi-track 167, 170, 172
  no monetary value claims 167
  notice of allocation 168
  questionnaires 162–4, 179
    additional information 163
    delay in filing 163
    failure to file 164
    stay for settlement 169, 179–80
  reallocation from small claims 309
  routes 170, 171
  Royal Court of Justice trial 167–8
  rules 164–8
  small claims 165–6, 170, 172
  time of decision 162
Transfer of court 161–2
  application 55–7
  automatic 55
  between county courts 56
  costs 308
  procedure 57
  specifying court 57
  within High Court 56–7
Transitional provisions 14–18
  agreeing to apply CPR 17
  applying new rules 17
  before 26 April 1999
    claims issued but not served 15
    claims where pleadings not closed 15
    directions or discovery commenced by not completed 16
    orders made in existing proceedings 16
    costs 17–18
    default judgments 15
  on or after 26 April 1999
    applications in existing proceedings 16–17

INDEX

Transitional provisions – *continued*
  issuing and renewing proceedings 16
  pre-action protocols 49
Transparency 34
Trial 291–301
  by jury 297
  conduct of 298–9
  date
    confirmation on listing 202
    fast track 196–7, 202
    fixing 196–7, 212
    multi-track 197, 212
  disposal without oral hearing 296
  evidence 298
  exhibits 298
  fast track 201, 295
  judgments
    appeals 300
    counterclaims 299
    county court register 300
    detention of goods 299
    drawing up 299–300
    error correction 300
    interest on debts 301
    interim payments 299
    provisional damages 299–300
    recording 299
  listing
    fast track 292–3
    multi-track 293
    settlement before trial 293
  listing officers 293
  listing questionnaire 293
  location 298
  non-attendance 300
  open court 297
  preparation days 292
  private 297
  split 312
  statement of issues 294–5
  timetables 293–4
    objective 294
    setting 293–4
    setting in advance 292
  witness presence 237, 238, 244, 245
  witness statements 237–9, 298
  written preparation 292
Trial bundles
  agreed 296
  binding 296
  content 295–6
  directions 295
  fast track 201, 295
  lodging 295
Tribunals, appeals from
  to Court of Appeal 330–1
  to High Court 330
Trustee consent 242

Unincorporated organisations 58
Unless orders 288
Urgency
  interim injunctions 151
  pre-issue applications 146, 147, 148

Vacation business 28
Venue 25

Warrants for arrest 28
Wasted costs order 320, 321–2
Without prejudice meetings, experts 195, 254, 260
Without prejudice offers 265, 267
Witness statements 21, 129
  admissibility 238
  cross-examination on 239
  evidence outside 238
  false statements 239
  fast track 194
  form 235–6
  hearsay evidence 237, 238
  inspection 240–1
  originating processes 24
  service 235
    failure to serve 236–7
  use
    at trial 237–9, 298
    by another party 238–9
    for other purposes 240–1
Witness summaries 236
  service 236–7
Witness summons
  in aid of inferior court or tribunal 248–9
  compensation and expenses in 249
  definition 247
  issue 28, 248
  production appointment 248
  production of documents 247–8
  service 249
  time for serving 249
  variation 248
Witnesses 21
  absence 237, 238, 244, 245
  compensation for loss of time 249
  credibility 245
  cross-examination 239, 298
  expert *see* Expert evidence: Experts
  in particulars of claim 95
  late application to call 237
  name and address 236
  pre-trial hearing attendance 240
  restriction on numbers 234
  travel expenses 249
  unavailable 238
Writ 90
  see also Claim form

Blackstone's Civil Practice 2000

In January 2000 Blackstone Press will publish the first edition of *Blackstone's Civil Practice*. This new annual civil work will incorporate all developments in civil law since 26 April 1999. *Blackstone's Civil Practice* follows the successful formula laid down in *Blackstone's Criminal Practice* in providing an annual text that is easy-to-use, portable, authoritative, and at a price that all practitioners can afford.

This voucher entitles you to a **£20 discount** from your purchase of the 2000 edition of *Blackstone's Civil Practice*. Simply complete the details below, tear out the page and send it in with your order to claim the discount.

£20 discount for Blackstone's Civil Practice 2000

Name ....

Address ....

....

Post Code ....

Telephone Number...

For more information please contact customer services on (020) 8740 2277 or fax us on (020) 8743 2292

Blackstone Press Ltd., Aldine Place, London W12 8AA
Visit our website: www.blackstonepress.com